Microsoft® Office 365™

OFFICE 2016

INTRODUCTORY

Microsoft® Office 365™

OFFICE 2016

INTRODUCTORY

Steven M. Freund
Corinne L. Hoisington
Mary Z. Last
Philip J. Pratt
Susan L. Sebok
Misty E. Vermaat

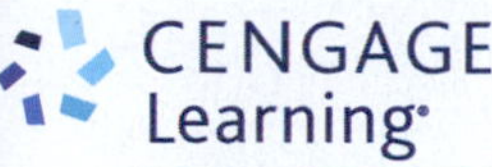

SHELLY CASHMAN SERIES®

Australia • Brazil • Japan • Korea • Mexico • Singapore • Spain • United Kingdom • United States

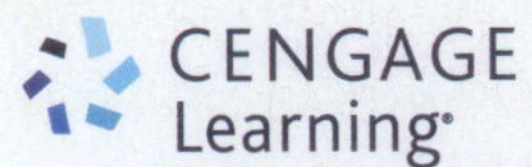

Microsoft® Office 2016: Introductory
Steven M. Freund, Corinne L. Hoisington, Mary Z. Last, Philip J. Pratt, Susan L. Sebok, Misty E. Vermaat

SVP, GM Skills & Global Product Management: Dawn Gerrain

Product Director: Kathleen McMahon

Senior Product Team Manager: Lauren Murphy

Associate Product Managers: William Guiliani, Melissa Stehler

Senior Director, Development: Marah Bellegarde

Product Development Manager: Leigh Hefferon

Managing Content Developer: Emma F. Newsom

Developmental Editors: Amanda Brodkin, Deb Kaufmann, Lyn Markowicz, Lisa Ruffolo, Karen Stevens

Product Assistant: Erica Chapman

Manuscript Quality Assurance: Jeffrey Schwartz, John Freitas, Serge Palladino, Susan Pedicini, Danielle Shaw, Susan Whalen

Senior Production Director: Wendy Troeger

Production Director: Patty Stephan

Senior Content Project Manager: Matthew Hutchinson

Manufacturing Planner: Julio Esperas

Designer: Diana Graham

Text Designer: Joel Sadagursky

Cover Template Designer: Diana Graham

Cover image(s): karawan/Shutterstock.com; Mrs. Opossum/Shutterstock.com

Compositor: Lumina Datamatics, Inc.

Vice President, Marketing: Brian Joyner

Marketing Director: Michele McTighe

Marketing Manager: Stephanie Albracht

The material in this book was written using Microsoft Office 2016 and was Quality Assurance tested before the publication date. As Microsoft continually updates Office 2016 and Office 365, your software experience may vary slightly from what is seen in the printed text.

Mac users: If you're working through this product using a Mac, some of the steps may vary. Additional information for Mac users is included with the data files for this product.

Library of Congress Control Number: 2015958650

ISBN: 978-1-305-87001-7

ISBN: 978-1-305-87004-8 (spiralbound)

ISBN: 978-1-305-87003-1 (casebound)

Cengage Learning
20 Channel Center Street
Boston, MA 02210
USA

Cengage Learning is a leading provider of customized learning solutions with employees residing in nearly 40 different countries and sales in more than 125 countries around the world. Find your local representative at **www.cengage.com.**

Cengage Learning products are represented in Canada by Nelson Education, Ltd.

To learn more about Cengage Learning, visit **www.cengage.com**

Purchase any of our products at your local college store or at our preferred online store **www.cengagebrain.com**

Printed in the United States of America
Print Number: 01 Print Year: 2017

Microsoft® Office 365™
OFFICE 2016

INTRODUCTORY

Contents

Productivity Apps for School and Work

Microsoft Office 2016 and Windows 10

Office 2016 and Windows 10: Essential Concepts and Skills

Microsoft **Word 2016**

MODULE ONE

Creating, Formatting, and Editing a Word Document with a Picture

MODULE TWO

Creating a Research Paper with References and Sources

MODULE THREE

Creating a Business Letter with a Letterhead and Table

Microsoft PowerPoint 2016

MODULE ONE

Creating and Editing a Presentation with Pictures

MODULE TWO

Enhancing a Presentation with Pictures, Shapes, and WordArt

MODULE THREE

Reusing a Presentation and Adding Media and Animation

Microsoft **Excel 2016**

MODULE ONE

Creating a Worksheet and a Chart

MODULE TWO

Formulas, Functions, and Formatting

MODULE THREE

Working with Large Worksheets, Charting, and What-If Analysis

Microsoft Access 2016

MODULE ONE

Databases and Database Objects: An Introduction

MODULE TWO

Querying a Database

MODULE THREE

Maintaining a Database

Microsoft Outlook 2016

MODULE ONE

Managing Email Messages with Outlook

MODULE TWO
Managing Calendars with Outlook

Microsoft® Office 365™
OFFICE 2016

INTRODUCTORY

Productivity Apps for School and Work

OneNote
Sway
Office Mix
Edge

Corinne Hoisington

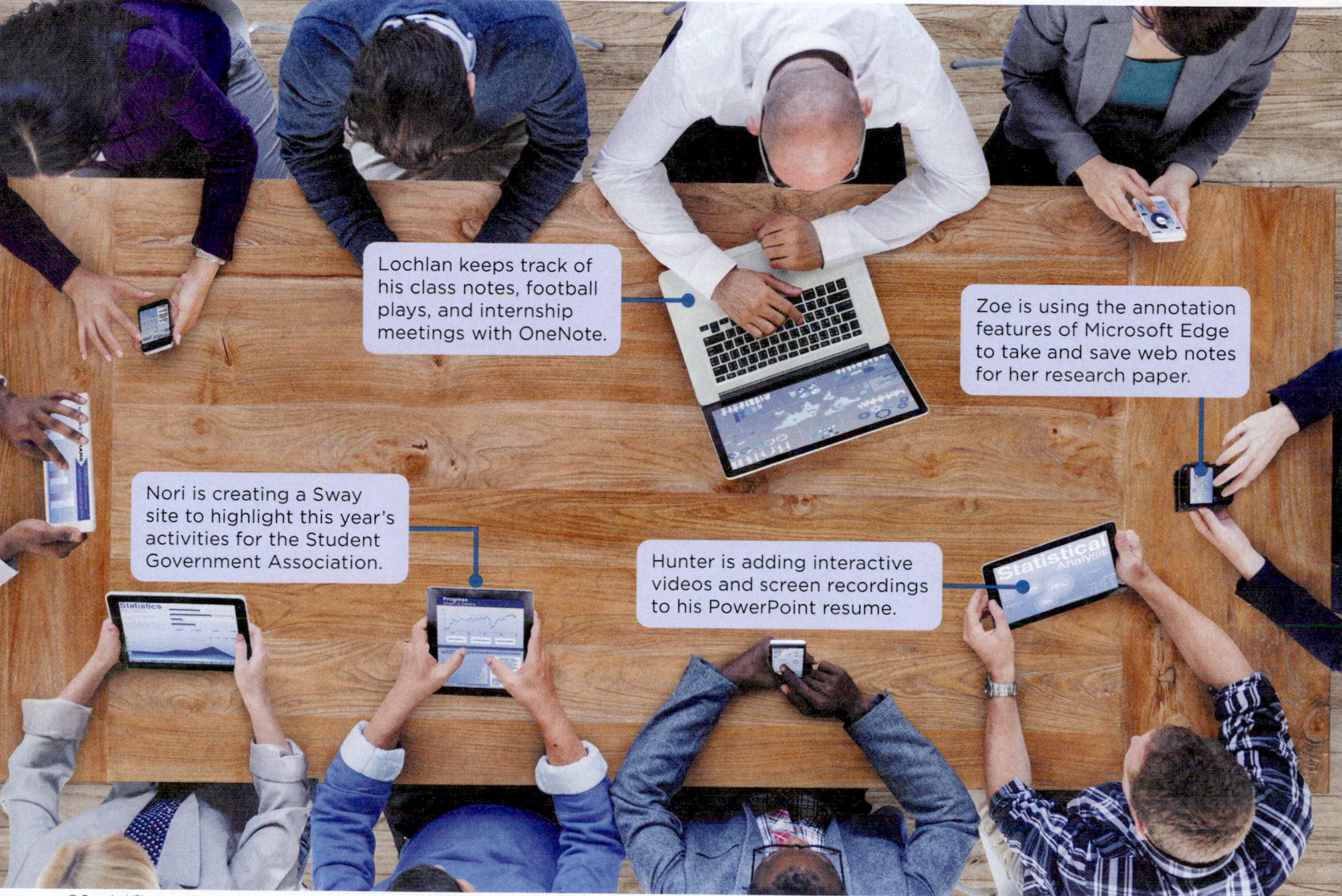

Lochlan keeps track of his class notes, football plays, and internship meetings with OneNote.
Zoe is using the annotation features of Microsoft Edge to take and save web notes for her research paper.
Nori is creating a Sway site to highlight this year's activities for the Student Government Association.
Hunter is adding interactive videos and screen recordings to his PowerPoint resume.
Statistical Analysis
Statistics
Progress

Being computer literate no longer means mastery of only Word, Excel, PowerPoint, Outlook, and Access. To become technology power users, Hunter, Nori, Zoe, and Lochlan are exploring Microsoft OneNote, Sway, Mix, and Edge in Office 2016 and Windows 10.

In this Module

Learn to use productivity apps!
Links to companion **Sways**, featuring **videos** with hands-on instructions, are located on www.cengagebrain.com.

Introduction to OneNote 2016

Bottom Line

- OneNote is a note-taking app for your academic and professional life.
- Use OneNote to get organized by gathering your ideas, sketches, webpages, photos, videos, and notes in one place.

notebook | section tab | To Do tag | screen clipping | note | template | Microsoft OneNote Mobile app | sync | drawing canvas | inked handwriting | Ink to Text

As you glance around any classroom, you invariably see paper notebooks and notepads on each desk. Because deciphering and sharing handwritten notes can be a challenge, Microsoft OneNote 2016 replaces physical notebooks, binders, and paper notes with a searchable, digital notebook. OneNote captures your ideas and schoolwork on any device so you can stay organized, share notes, and work with others on projects. Whether you are a student taking class notes as shown in **Figure 1** or an employee taking notes in company meetings, OneNote is the one place to keep notes for all of your projects.

Figure 1: OneNote 2016 notebook

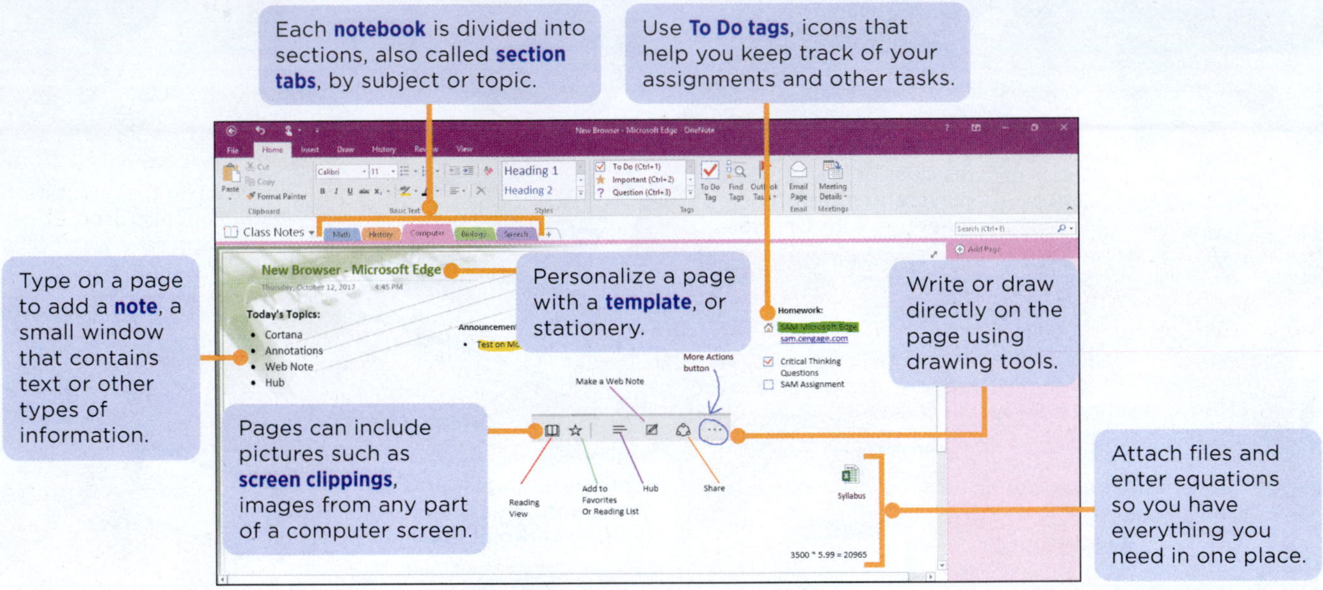

Each **notebook** is divided into sections, also called **section tabs**, by subject or topic.

Use **To Do tags**, icons that help you keep track of your assignments and other tasks.

Type on a page to add a **note**, a small window that contains text or other types of information.

Personalize a page with a **template**, or stationery.

Write or draw directly on the page using drawing tools.

Pages can include pictures such as **screen clippings**, images from any part of a computer screen.

Attach files and enter equations so you have everything you need in one place.

Creating a OneNote Notebook

OneNote is divided into sections similar to those in a spiral-bound notebook. Each OneNote notebook contains sections, pages, and other notebooks. You can use OneNote for school, business, and personal projects. Store information for each type of project in different notebooks to keep your tasks separate, or use any other organization that suits you. OneNote is flexible enough to adapt to the way you want to work.

When you create a notebook, it contains a blank page with a plain white background by default, though you can use templates, or stationery, to apply designs in categories such as Academic, Business, Decorative, and Planners. Start typing or use the buttons on the Insert tab to insert notes, which are small resizable windows that can contain text, equations, tables, on-screen writing, images, audio and video recordings, to-do lists, file attachments, and file printouts. Add as many notes as you need to each page.

Learn to use OneNote!

Links to companion **Sways**, featuring **videos** with hands-on instructions, are located on www.cengagebrain.com.

Syncing a Notebook to the Cloud

OneNote saves your notes every time you make a change in a notebook. To make sure you can access your notebooks with a laptop, tablet, or smartphone wherever you are, OneNote uses cloud-based storage, such as OneDrive or SharePoint. **Microsoft OneNote Mobile app**, a lightweight version of OneNote 2016 shown in **Figure 2**, is available for free in the Windows Store, Google Play for Android devices, and the AppStore for iOS devices.

If you have a Microsoft account, OneNote saves your notes on OneDrive automatically for all your mobile devices and computers, which is called **syncing**. For example, you can use OneNote to take notes on your laptop during class, and then open OneNote on your phone to study later. To use a notebook stored on your computer with your OneNote Mobile app, move the notebook to OneDrive. You can quickly share notebook content with other people using OneDrive.

Figure 2: Microsoft OneNote Mobile app

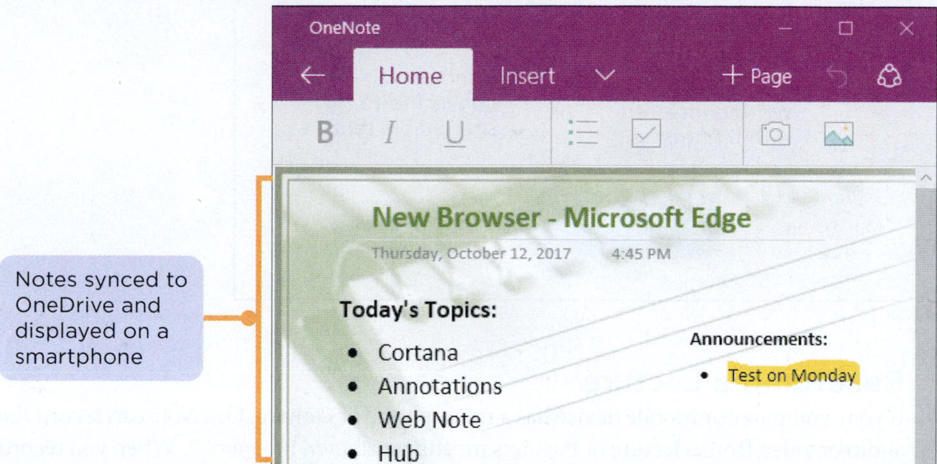

Taking Notes

Use OneNote pages to organize your notes by class and topic or lecture. Beyond simple typed notes, OneNote stores drawings, converts handwriting to searchable text and mathematical sketches to equations, and records audio and video.

OneNote includes drawing tools that let you sketch freehand drawings such as biological cell diagrams and financial supply-and-demand charts. As shown in **Figure 3**, the Draw tab on the ribbon provides these drawing tools along with shapes so you can insert diagrams and other illustrations to represent your ideas. When you draw on a page, OneNote creates a **drawing canvas**, which is a container for shapes and lines.

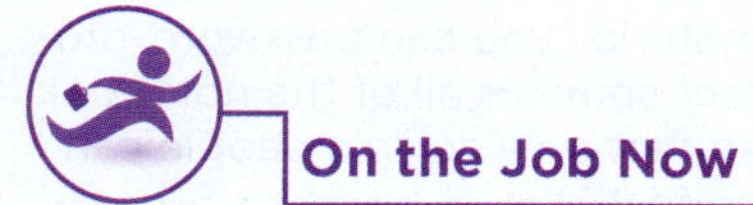

On the Job Now

OneNote is ideal for taking notes during meetings, whether you are recording minutes, documenting a discussion, sketching product diagrams, or listing follow-up items. Use a meeting template to add pages with content appropriate for meetings.

Figure 3: Tools on the Draw tab

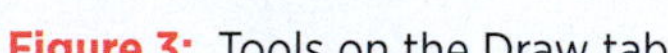

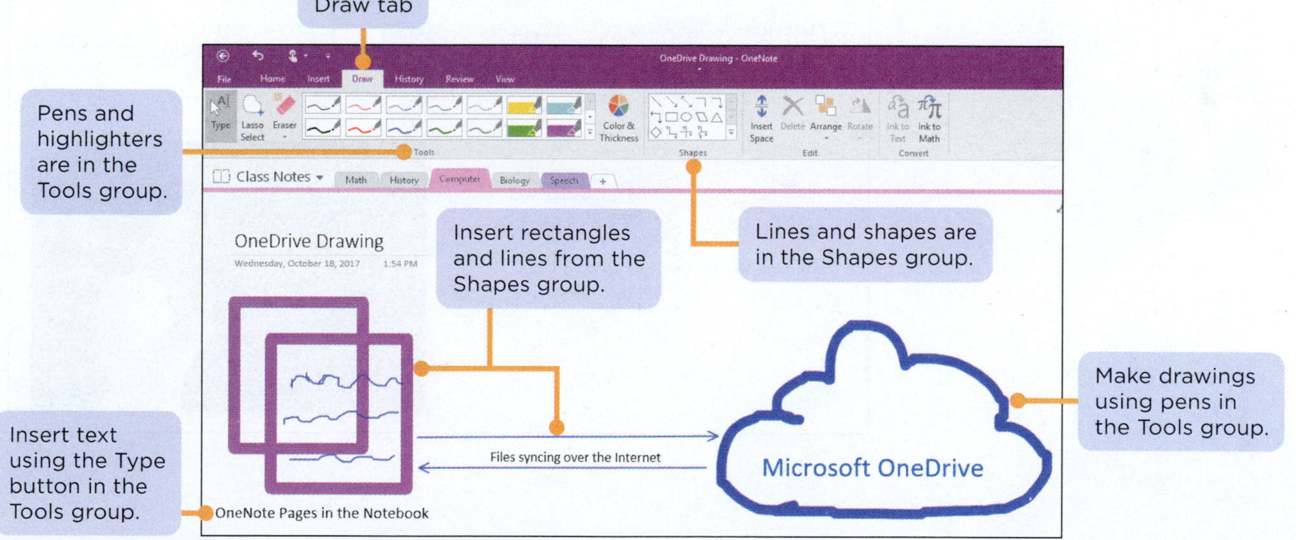

Converting Handwriting to Text

When you use a pen tool to write on a notebook page, the text you enter is called **inked handwriting**. OneNote can convert inked handwriting to typed text when you use the **Ink to Text** button in the Convert group on the Draw tab, as shown in **Figure 4**. After OneNote converts the handwriting to text, you can use the Search box to find terms in the converted text or any other note in your notebooks.

Figure 4: Converting handwriting to text

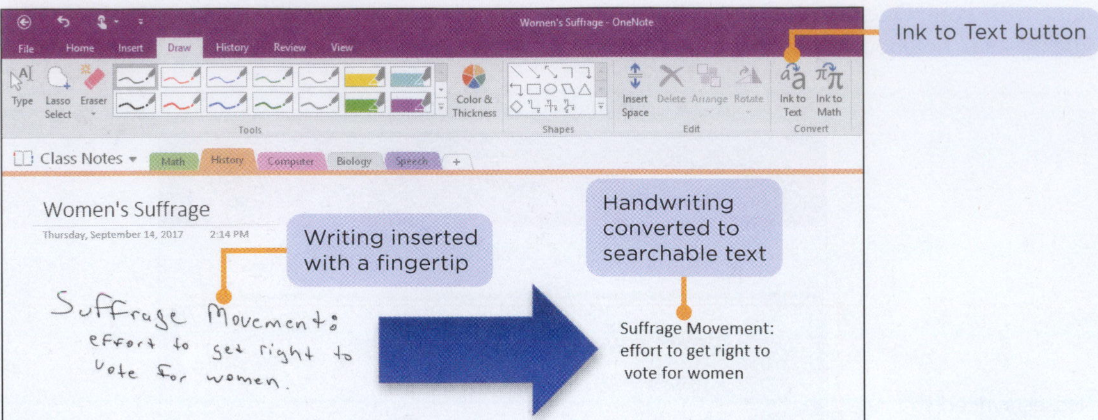

On the Job Now

Use OneNote as a place to brainstorm ongoing work projects. If a notebook contains sensitive material, you can password-protect some or all of the notebook so that only certain people can open it.

Recording a Lecture

If your computer or mobile device has a microphone or camera, OneNote can record the audio or video from a lecture or business meeting as shown in **Figure 5**. When you record a lecture (with your instructor's permission), you can follow along, take regular notes at your own pace, and review the video recording later. You can control the start, pause, and stop motions of the recording when you play back the recording of your notes.

Figure 5: Video inserted in a notebook

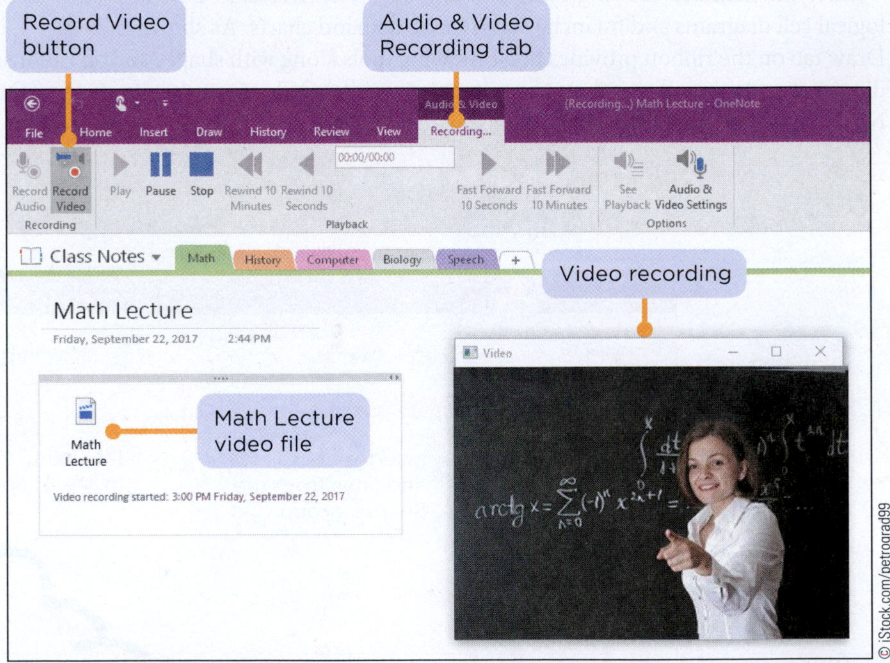

© iStock.com/petrograd99

Try This Now

> **Learn to use OneNote!**
> Links to companion **Sways**, featuring **videos** with hands-on instructions, are located on www.cengagebrain.com.

1: Taking Notes for a Week

As a student, you can get organized by using OneNote to take detailed notes in your classes. Perform the following tasks:

a. Create a new OneNote notebook on your Microsoft OneDrive account (the default location for new notebooks). Name the notebook with your first name followed by "Notes," as in **Caleb Notes**.
b. Create four section tabs, each with a different class name.
c. Take detailed notes in those classes for one week. Be sure to include notes, drawings, and other types of content.
d. Sync your notes with your OneDrive. Submit your assignment in the format specified by your instructor.

2: Using OneNote to Organize a Research Paper

You have a research paper due on the topic of three habits of successful students. Use OneNote to organize your research. Perform the following tasks:

a. Create a new OneNote notebook on your Microsoft OneDrive account. Name the notebook **Success Research**.
b. Create three section tabs with the following names:
   - **Take Detailed Notes**
   - **Be Respectful in Class**
   - **Come to Class Prepared**
c. On the web, research the topics and find three sources for each section. Copy a sentence from each source and paste the sentence into the appropriate section. When you paste the sentence, OneNote inserts it in a note with a link to the source.
d. Sync your notes with your OneDrive. Submit your assignment in the format specified by your instructor.

3: Planning Your Career

Note: This activity requires a webcam or built-in video camera on any type of device.

Consider an occupation that interests you. Using OneNote, examine the responsibilities, education requirements, potential salary, and employment outlook of a specific career. Perform the following tasks:

a. Create a new OneNote notebook on your Microsoft OneDrive account. Name the notebook with your first name followed by a career title, such as **Kara - App Developer**.
b. Create four section tabs with the names **Responsibilities, Education Requirements, Median Salary**, and **Employment Outlook**.
c. Research the responsibilities of your career path. Using OneNote, record a short video (approximately 30 seconds) of yourself explaining the responsibilities of your career path. Place the video in the Responsibilities section.
d. On the web, research the educational requirements for your career path and find two appropriate sources. Copy a paragraph from each source and paste them into the appropriate section. When you paste a paragraph, OneNote inserts it in a note with a link to the source.
e. Research the median salary for a single year for this career. Create a mathematical equation in the Median Salary section that multiplies the amount of the median salary times 20 years to calculate how much you will possibly earn.
f. For the Employment Outlook section, research the outlook for your career path. Take at least four notes about what you find when researching the topic.
g. Sync your notes with your OneDrive. Submit your assignment in the format specified by your instructor.

Introduction to Sway

Sway site | responsive design | Storyline | card | Creative Commons license | animation emphasis effects | Docs.com

Bottom Line

- Drag photos, videos, and files from your computer and content from Facebook and Twitter directly to your Sway presentation.
- Run Sway in a web browser or as an app on your smartphone, and save presentations as webpages.

Expressing your ideas in a presentation typically means creating PowerPoint slides or a Word document. Microsoft Sway gives you another way to engage an audience. Sway is a free Microsoft tool available at Sway.com or as an app in Office 365. Using Sway, you can combine text, images, videos, and social media in a website called a **Sway site** that you can share and display on any device. To get started, you create a digital story on a web-based canvas without borders, slides, cells, or page breaks. A Sway site organizes the text, images, and video into a **responsive design**, which means your content adapts perfectly to any screen size as shown in **Figure 6**. You store a Sway site in the cloud on OneDrive using a free Microsoft account.

Figure 6: Sway site with responsive design

Learn to use Sway!

Links to companion **Sways**, featuring **videos** with hands-on instructions, are located on www.cengagebrain.com.

Creating a Sway Presentation

You can use Sway to build a digital flyer, a club newsletter, a vacation blog, an informational site, a digital art portfolio, or a new product rollout. After you select your topic and sign into Sway with your Microsoft account, a **Storyline** opens, providing tools and a work area for composing your digital story. See **Figure 7**. Each story can include text, images, and videos. You create a Sway by adding text and media content into a Storyline section, or **card**. To add pictures, videos, or documents, select a card in the left pane and then select the Insert Content button. The first card in a Sway presentation contains a title and background image.

Figure 7: Creating a Sway site

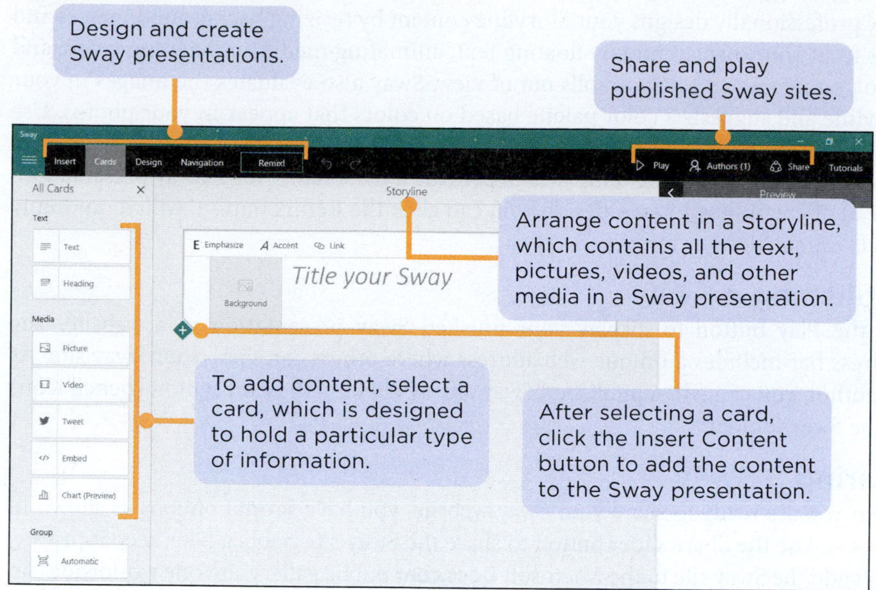
Design and create Sway presentations.
Share and play published Sway sites.
Arrange content in a Storyline, which contains all the text, pictures, videos, and other media in a Sway presentation.
To add content, select a card, which is designed to hold a particular type of information.
After selecting a card, click the Insert Content button to add the content to the Sway presentation.
Title your Sway

Adding Content to Build a Story

As you work, Sway searches the Internet to help you find relevant images, videos, tweets, and other content from online sources such as Bing, YouTube, Twitter, and Facebook. You can drag content from the search results right into the Storyline. In addition, you can upload your own images and videos directly in the presentation. For example, if you are creating a Sway presentation about the market for commercial drones, Sway suggests content to incorporate into the presentation by displaying it in the left pane as search results. The search results include drone images tagged with a **Creative Commons license** at online sources as shown in Figure 8. A Creative Commons license is a public copyright license that allows the free distribution of an otherwise copyrighted work. In addition, you can specify the source of the media. For example, you can add your own Facebook or OneNote pictures and videos in Sway without leaving the app.

On the Job Now

If you have a Microsoft Word document containing an outline of your business content, drag the outline into Sway to create a card for each topic.

Figure 8: Images in Sway search results

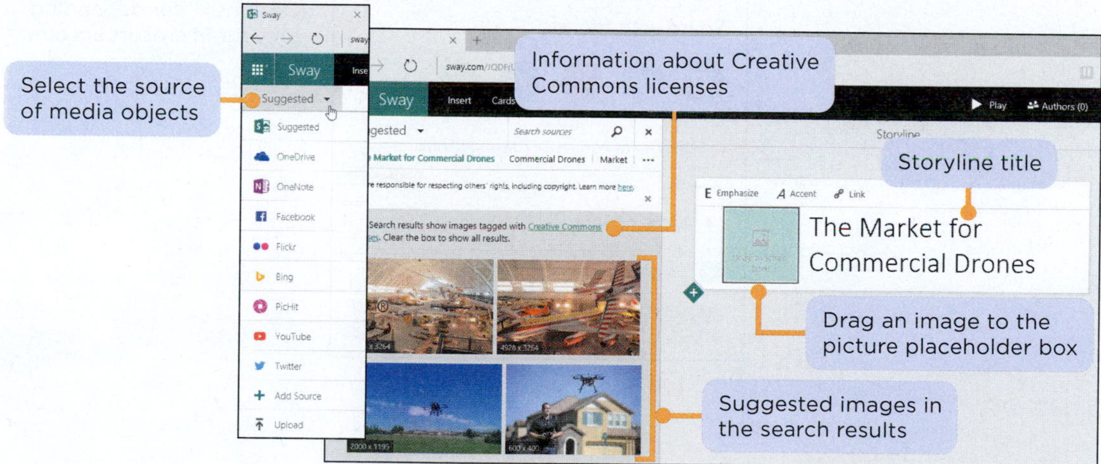
Select the source of media objects
Information about Creative Commons licenses
Storyline title
The Market for Commercial Drones
Drag an image to the picture placeholder box
Suggested images in the search results

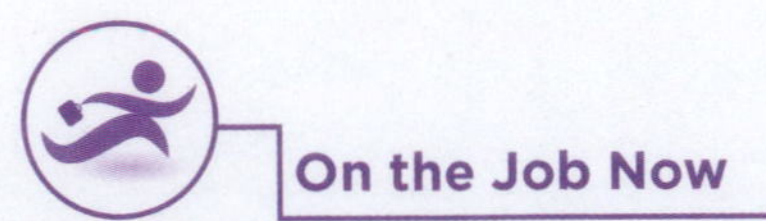

If your project team wants to collaborate on a Sway presentation, click the Authors button on the navigation bar to invite others to edit the presentation.

Designing a Sway

Sway professionally designs your Storyline content by resizing background images and fonts to fit your display, and by floating text, animating media, embedding video, and removing images as a page scrolls out of view. Sway also evaluates the images in your Storyline and suggests a color palette based on colors that appear in your photos. Use the Design button to display tools including color palettes, font choices, **animation emphasis effects**, and style templates to provide a personality for a Sway presentation. Instead of creating your own design, you can click the Remix button, which randomly selects unique designs for your Sway site.

Publishing a Sway

Use the Play button to display your finished Sway presentation as a website. The Address bar includes a unique web address where others can view your Sway site. As the author, you can edit a published Sway site by clicking the Edit button (pencil icon) on the Sway toolbar.

Sharing a Sway

When you are ready to share your Sway website, you have several options as shown in **Figure 9**. Use the Share slider button to share the Sway site publically or keep it private. If you add the Sway site to the Microsoft **Docs.com** public gallery, anyone worldwide can use Bing, Google, or other search engines to find, view, and share your Sway site. You can also share your Sway site using Facebook, Twitter, Google+, Yammer, and other social media sites. Link your presentation to any webpage or email the link to your audience. Sway can also generate a code for embedding the link within another webpage.

Figure 9: Sharing a Sway site

Share button
Play
Authors (1)
Share
Share
Just me
Drag the slider button to Just me to keep the Sway site private
Share with the world
Post the Sway site on Docs.com
Docs.com - Your public gallery
Share with friends
Options differ depending on your Microsoft account
Send friends a link to the Sway site
https://sway.com/JQDFrUaxmg4lEbbk
More options
Viewers can duplicate this Sway
Stop sharing

Try This Now

Learn to use Sway!

Links to companion **Sways**, featuring **videos** with hands-on instructions, are located on www.cengagebrain.com.

1: Creating a Sway Resume

Sway is a digital storytelling app. Create a Sway resume to share the skills, job experiences, and achievements you have that match the requirements of a future job interest. Perform the following tasks:

a. Create a new presentation in Sway to use as a digital resume. Title the Sway Storyline with your full name and then select a background image.
b. Create three separate sections titled **Academic Background, Work Experience**, and **Skills**, and insert text, a picture, and a paragraph or bulleted points in each section. Be sure to include your own picture.
c. Add a fourth section that includes a video about your school that you find online.
d. Customize the design of your presentation.
e. Submit your assignment link in the format specified by your instructor.

2: Creating an Online Sway Newsletter

Newsletters are designed to capture the attention of their target audience. Using Sway, create a newsletter for a club, organization, or your favorite music group. Perform the following tasks:

a. Create a new presentation in Sway to use as a digital newsletter for a club, organization, or your favorite music group. Provide a title for the Sway Storyline and select an appropriate background image.
b. Select three separate sections with appropriate titles, such as Upcoming Events. In each section, insert text, a picture, and a paragraph or bulleted points.
c. Add a fourth section that includes a video about your selected topic.
d. Customize the design of your presentation.
e. Submit your assignment link in the format specified by your instructor.

3: Creating and Sharing a Technology Presentation

To place a Sway presentation in the hands of your entire audience, you can share a link to the Sway presentation. Create a Sway presentation on a new technology and share it with your class. Perform the following tasks:

a. Create a new presentation in Sway about a cutting-edge technology topic. Provide a title for the Sway Storyline and select a background image.
b. Create four separate sections about your topic, and include text, a picture, and a paragraph in each section.
c. Add a fifth section that includes a video about your topic.
d. Customize the design of your presentation.
e. Share the link to your Sway with your classmates and submit your assignment link in the format specified by your instructor.

Bottom Line

- Office Mix is a free PowerPoint add-in from Microsoft that adds features to PowerPoint.
- The Mix tab on the PowerPoint ribbon provides tools for creating screen recordings, videos, interactive quizzes, and live webpages.

Introduction to Office Mix

add-in | clip | slide recording | Slide Notes | screen recording | free-response quiz

To enliven business meetings and lectures, Microsoft adds a new dimension to presentations with a powerful toolset called Office Mix, a free add-in for PowerPoint. (An **add-in** is software that works with an installed app to extend its features.) Using Office Mix, you can record yourself on video, capture still and moving images on your desktop, and insert interactive elements such as quizzes and live webpages directly into PowerPoint slides. When you post the finished presentation to OneDrive, Office Mix provides a link you can share with friends and colleagues. Anyone with an Internet connection and a web browser can watch a published Office Mix presentation, such as the one in **Figure 10**, on a computer or mobile device.

Figure 10: Office Mix presentation

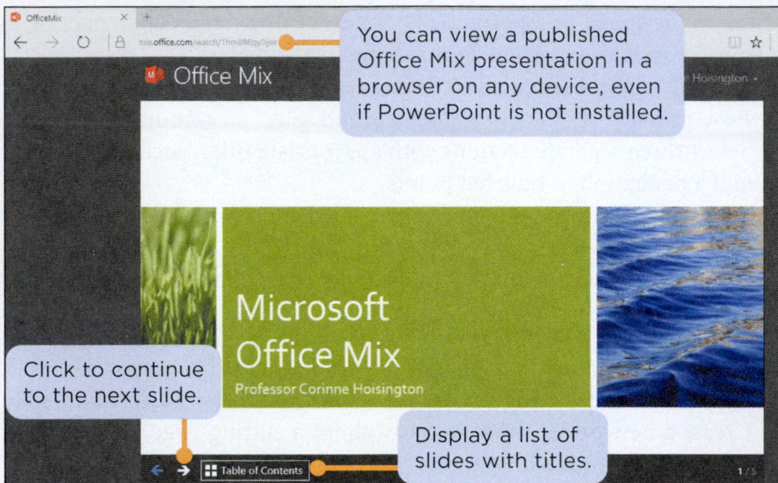

Learn to use Office Mix!
Links to companion **Sways**, featuring **videos** with hands-on instructions, are located on www.cengagebrain.com.

Adding Office Mix to PowerPoint

To get started, you create an Office Mix account at the website mix.office.com using an email address or a Facebook or Google account. Next, you download and install the Office Mix add-in (see **Figure 11**). Office Mix appears as a new tab named Mix on the PowerPoint ribbon in versions of Office 2013 and Office 2016 running on personal computers (PCs).

Figure 11: Getting started with Office Mix

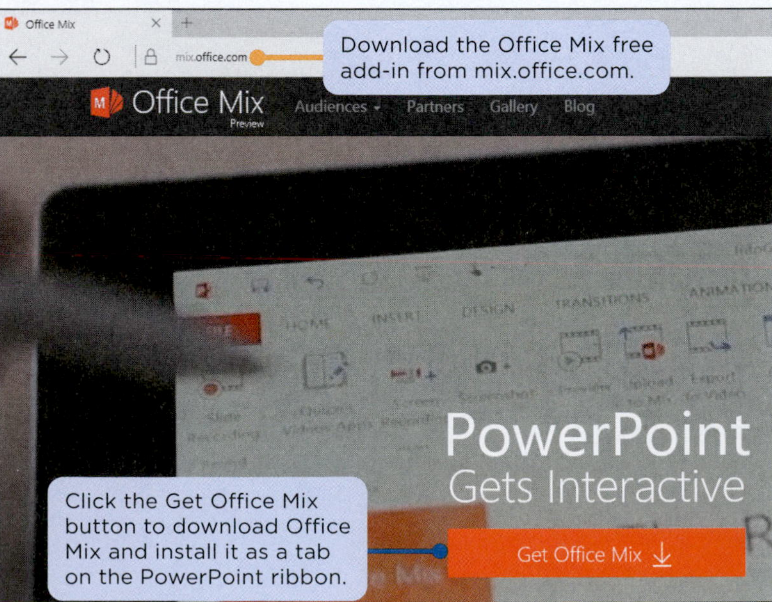

Capturing Video Clips

A **clip** is a short segment of audio, such as music, or video. After finishing the content on a PowerPoint slide, you can use Office Mix to add a video clip to animate or illustrate the content. Office Mix creates video clips in two ways: by recording live action on a webcam and by capturing screen images and movements. If your computer has a webcam, you can record yourself and annotate the slide to create a **slide recording** as shown in **Figure 12**.

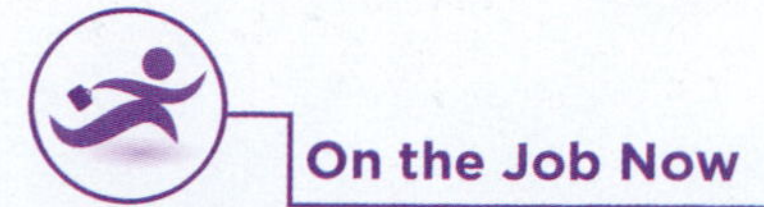

On the Job Now

Companies are using Office Mix to train employees about new products, to explain benefit packages to new workers, and to educate interns about office procedures.

Figure 12: Making a slide recording

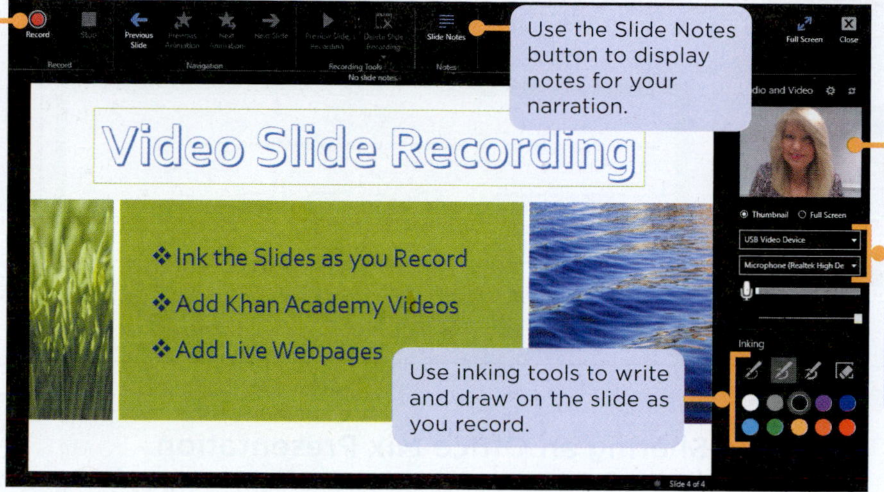

Record your voice; also record video if your computer has a camera.
Use the Slide Notes button to display notes for your narration.
For best results, look directly at your webcam while recording video.
Choose a video and audio device to record images and sound.
Use inking tools to write and draw on the slide as you record.
Video Slide Recording
Ink the Slides as you Record
Add Khan Academy Videos
Add Live Webpages

When you are making a slide recording, you can record your spoken narration at the same time. The **Slide Notes** feature works like a teleprompter to help you focus on your presentation content instead of memorizing your narration. Use the Inking tools to make annotations or add highlighting using different pen types and colors. After finishing a recording, edit the video in PowerPoint to trim the length or set playback options.

The second way to create a video is to capture on-screen images and actions with or without a voiceover. This method is ideal if you want to show how to use your favorite website or demonstrate an app such as OneNote. To share your screen with an audience, select the part of the screen you want to show in the video. Office Mix captures everything that happens in that area to create a **screen recording**, as shown in **Figure 13**. Office Mix inserts the screen recording as a video in the slide.

On the Job Now

To make your video recordings accessible to people with hearing impairments, use the Office Mix closed-captioning tools. You can also use closed captions to supplement audio that is difficult to understand and to provide an aid for those learning to read.

Figure 13: Making a screen recording

Record the action on the screen within the red dashed outline.
Record audio while capturing your on-screen actions.
Select Area button
Watched Mixes
Uploaded Mixes

Inserting Quizzes, Live Webpages, and Apps

To enhance and assess audience understanding, make your slides interactive by adding quizzes, live webpages, and apps. Quizzes give immediate feedback to the user as shown in **Figure 14**. Office Mix supports several quiz formats, including a **free-response quiz** similar to a short answer quiz, and true/false, multiple-choice, and multiple-response formats.

Figure 14: Creating an interactive quiz

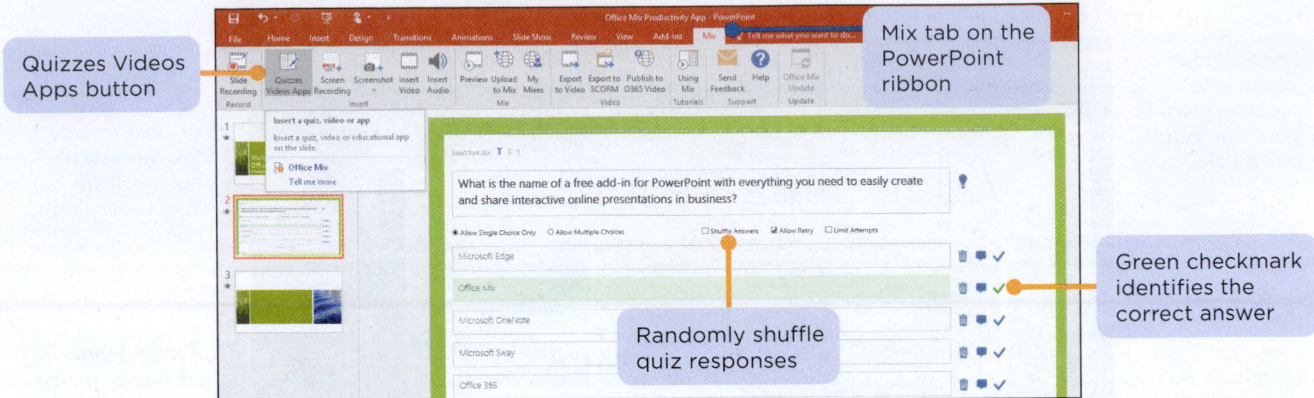

Sharing an Office Mix Presentation

When you complete your work with Office Mix, upload the presentation to your personal Office Mix dashboard as shown in **Figure 15**. Users of PCs, Macs, iOS devices, and Android devices can access and play Office Mix presentations. The Office Mix dashboard displays built-in analytics that include the quiz results and how much time viewers spent on each slide. You can play completed Office Mix presentations online or download them as movies.

Figure 15: Sharing an Office Mix presentation

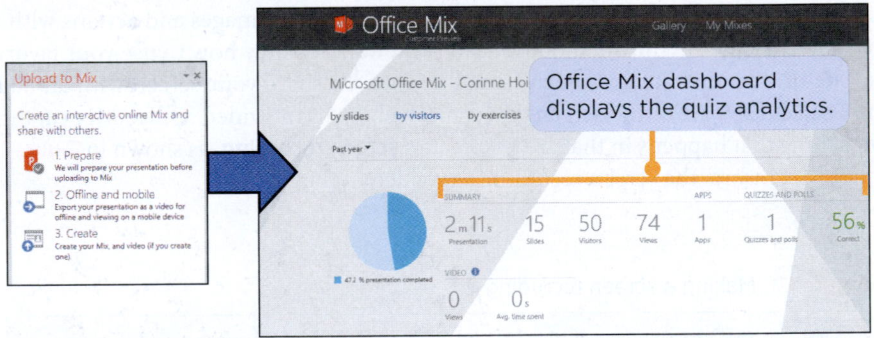

Try This Now

> **Learn to use Office Mix!**
> Links to companion **Sways**, featuring **videos** with hands-on instructions, are located on www.cengagebrain.com.

1: Creating an Office Mix Tutorial for OneNote

Note: This activity requires a microphone on your computer.

Office Mix makes it easy to record screens and their contents. Create PowerPoint slides with an Office Mix screen recording to show OneNote 2016 features. Perform the following tasks:

a. Create a PowerPoint presentation with the Ion Boardroom template. Create an opening slide with the title **My Favorite OneNote Features** and enter your name in the subtitle.
b. Create three additional slides, each titled with a new feature of OneNote. Open OneNote and use the Mix tab in PowerPoint to capture three separate screen recordings that teach your favorite features.
c. Add a fifth slide that quizzes the user with a multiple-choice question about OneNote and includes four responses. Be sure to insert a checkmark indicating the correct response.
d. Upload the completed presentation to your Office Mix dashboard and share the link with your instructor.
e. Submit your assignment link in the format specified by your instructor.

2: Teaching Augmented Reality with Office Mix

Note: This activity requires a webcam or built-in video camera on your computer.

A local elementary school has asked you to teach augmented reality to its students using Office Mix. Perform the following tasks:

a. Research augmented reality using your favorite online search tools.
b. Create a PowerPoint presentation with the Frame template. Create an opening slide with the title **Augmented Reality** and enter your name in the subtitle.
c. Create a slide with four bullets summarizing your research of augmented reality. Create a 20-second slide recording of yourself providing a quick overview of augmented reality.
d. Create another slide with a 30-second screen recording of a video about augmented reality from a site such as YouTube or another video-sharing site.
e. Add a final slide that quizzes the user with a true/false question about augmented reality. Be sure to insert a checkmark indicating the correct response.
f. Upload the completed presentation to your Office Mix dashboard and share the link with your instructor.
g. Submit your assignment link in the format specified by your instructor.

3: Marketing a Travel Destination with Office Mix

Note: This activity requires a webcam or built-in video camera on your computer.

To convince your audience to travel to a particular city, create a slide presentation marketing any city in the world using a slide recording, screen recording, and a quiz. Perform the following tasks:

a. Create a PowerPoint presentation with any template. Create an opening slide with the title of the city you are marketing as a travel destination and your name in the subtitle.
b. Create a slide with four bullets about the featured city. Create a 30-second slide recording of yourself explaining why this city is the perfect vacation destination.
c. Create another slide with a 20-second screen recording of a travel video about the city from a site such as YouTube or another video-sharing site.
d. Add a final slide that quizzes the user with a multiple-choice question about the featured city with five responses. Be sure to include a checkmark indicating the correct response.
e. Upload the completed presentation to your Office Mix dashboard and share your link with your instructor.
f. Submit your assignment link in the format specified by your instructor.

Introduction to Microsoft Edge

Reading view | Hub | Cortana | Web Note | Inking | sandbox

Microsoft Edge is the default web browser developed for the Windows 10 operating system as a replacement for Internet Explorer. Unlike its predecessor, Edge lets you write on webpages, read webpages without advertisements and other distractions, and search for information using a virtual personal assistant. The Edge interface is clean and basic, as shown in **Figure 16**, meaning you can pay more attention to the webpage content.

Bottom Line

- Microsoft Edge is the name of the new web browser built into Windows 10.
- Microsoft Edge allows you to search the web faster, take web notes, read webpages without distractions, and get instant assistance from Cortana.

Figure 16: Microsoft Edge tools

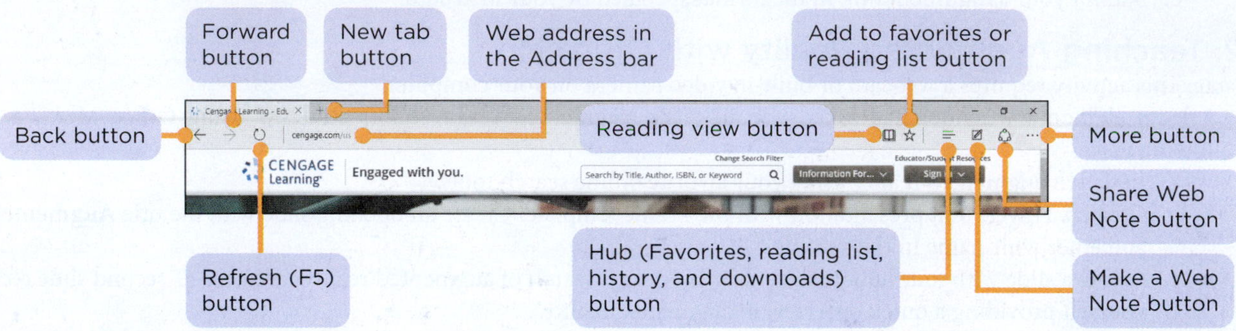

Learn to use Edge!
Links to companion **Sways**, featuring **videos** with hands-on instructions, are located on www.cengagebrain.com.

Browsing the Web with Microsoft Edge

One of the fastest browsers available, Edge allows you to type search text directly in the Address bar. As you view the resulting webpage, you can switch to **Reading view**, which is available for most news and research sites, to eliminate distracting advertisements. For example, if you are catching up on technology news online, the webpage might be difficult to read due to a busy layout cluttered with ads. Switch to Reading view to refresh the page and remove the original page formatting, ads, and menu sidebars to read the article distraction-free.

Consider the **Hub** in Microsoft Edge as providing one-stop access to all the things you collect on the web, such as your favorite websites, reading list, surfing history, and downloaded files.

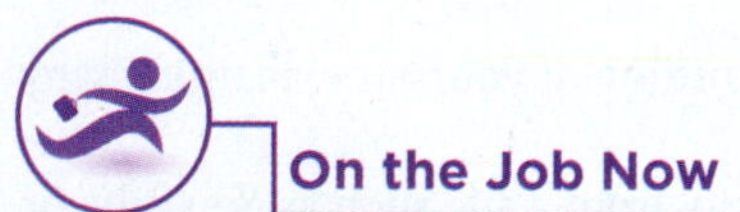

On the Job Now

Businesses started adopting Internet Explorer more than 20 years ago simply to view webpages. Today, Microsoft Edge has a different purpose: to promote interaction with the web and share its contents with colleagues.

Locating Information with Cortana

Cortana, the Windows 10 virtual assistant, plays an important role in Microsoft Edge. After you turn on Cortana, it appears as an animated circle in the Address bar when you might need assistance, as shown in the restaurant website in **Figure 17**. When you click the Cortana icon, a pane slides in from the right of the browser window to display detailed information about the restaurant, including maps and reviews. Cortana can also assist you in defining words, finding the weather, suggesting coupons for shopping, updating stock market information, and calculating math.

Figure 17: Cortana providing restaurant information

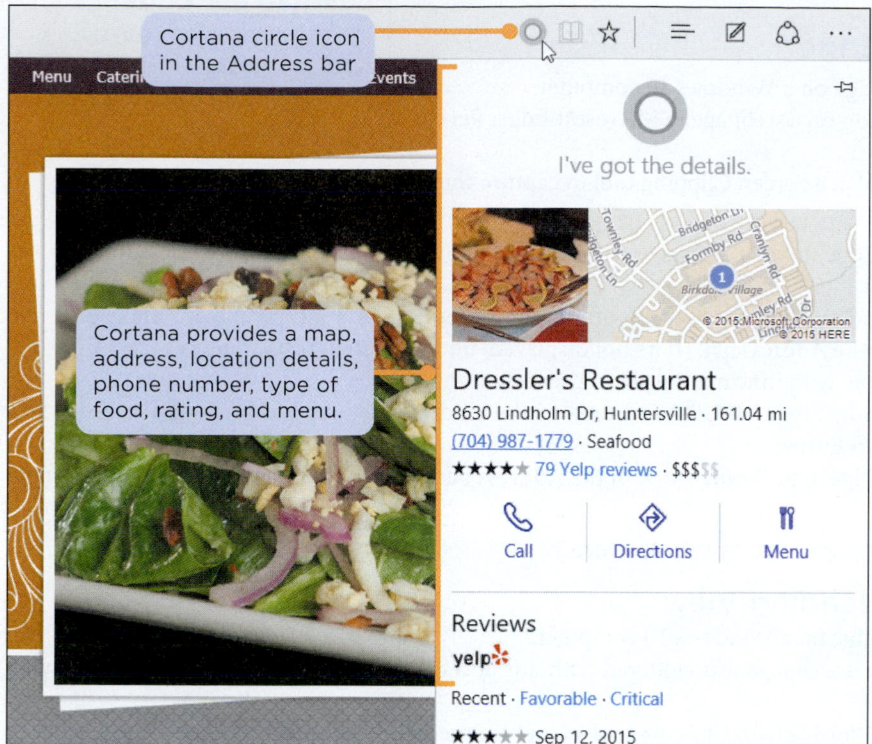

Annotating Webpages

One of the most impressive Microsoft Edge features are the **Web Note** tools, which you use to write on a webpage or to highlight text. When you click the Make a Web Note button, an **Inking** toolbar appears, as shown in **Figure 18**, that provides writing and drawing tools. These tools include an eraser, a pen, and a highlighter with different colors. You can also insert a typed note and copy a screen image (called a screen clipping). You can draw with a pointing device, fingertip, or stylus using different pen colors. Whether you add notes to a recipe, annotate sources for a research paper, or select a product while shopping online, the Web Note tools can enhance your productivity. After you complete your notes, click the Save button to save the annotations to OneNote, your Favorites list, or your Reading list. You can share the inked page with others using the Share Web Note button.

To enhance security, Microsoft Edge runs in a partial sandbox, an arrangement that prevents attackers from gaining control of your computer. Browsing within the **sandbox** protects computer resources and information from hackers.

Figure 18: Web Note tools in Microsoft Edge

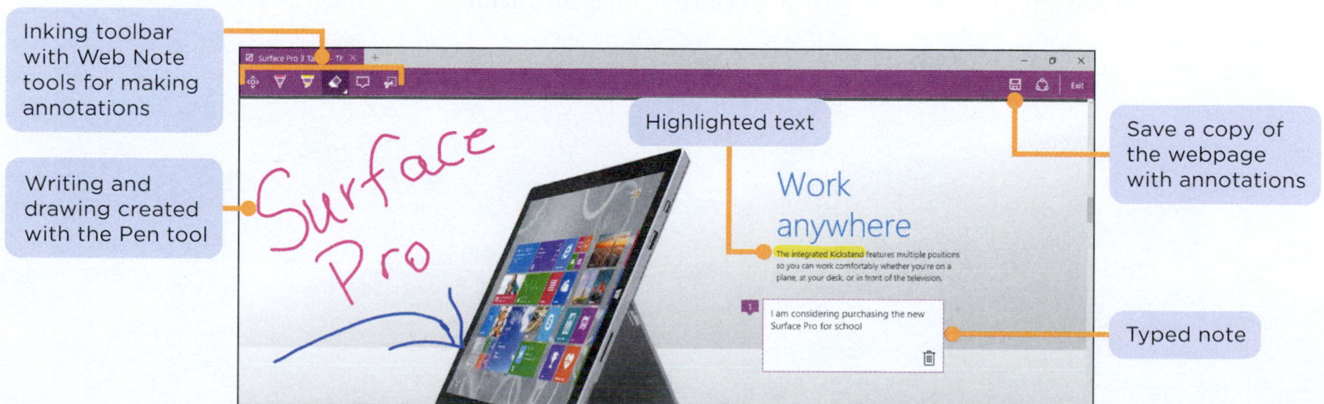

Try This Now

> **Learn to use Edge!**
> Links to companion **Sways**, featuring **videos** with hands-on instructions, are located on www.cengagebrain.com.

1: Using Cortana in Microsoft Edge

Note: This activity requires using Microsoft Edge on a Windows 10 computer.

Cortana can assist you in finding information on a webpage in Microsoft Edge. Perform the following tasks:

a. Create a Word document using the Word Screen Clipping tool to capture the following screenshots.
   - Screenshot A—Using Microsoft Edge, open a webpage with a technology news article. Right-click a term in the article and ask Cortana to define it.
   - Screenshot B—Using Microsoft Edge, open the website of a fancy restaurant in a city near you. Make sure the Cortana circle icon is displayed in the Address bar. (If it's not displayed, find a different restaurant website.) Click the Cortana circle icon to display a pane with information about the restaurant.
   - Screenshot C—Using Microsoft Edge, type **10 USD to Euros** in the Address bar without pressing the Enter key. Cortana converts the U.S. dollars to Euros.
   - Screenshot D—Using Microsoft Edge, type **Apple stock** in the Address bar without pressing the Enter key. Cortana displays the current stock quote.

b. Submit your assignment in the format specified by your instructor.

2: Viewing Online News with Reading View

Note: This activity requires using Microsoft Edge on a Windows 10 computer.

Reading view in Microsoft Edge can make a webpage less cluttered with ads and other distractions. Perform the following tasks:

a. Create a Word document using the Word Screen Clipping tool to capture the following screenshots.
   - Screenshot A—Using Microsoft Edge, open the website **mashable.com**. Open a technology article. Click the Reading view button to display an ad-free page that uses only basic text formatting.
   - Screenshot B—Using Microsoft Edge, open the website **bbc.com**. Open any news article. Click the Reading view button to display an ad-free page that uses only basic text formatting.
   - Screenshot C—Make three types of annotations (Pen, Highlighter, and Add a typed note) on the BBC article page displayed in Reading view.

b. Submit your assignment in the format specified by your instructor.

3: Inking with Microsoft Edge

Note: This activity requires using Microsoft Edge on a Windows 10 computer.

Microsoft Edge provides many annotation options to record your ideas. Perform the following tasks:

a. Open the website **wolframalpha.com** in the Microsoft Edge browser. Wolfram Alpha is a well-respected academic search engine. Type **US$100 1965 dollars in 2015** in the Wolfram Alpha search text box and press the Enter key.

b. Click the Make a Web Note button to display the Web Note tools. Using the Pen tool, draw a circle around the result on the webpage. Save the page to OneNote.

c. In the Wolfram Alpha search text box, type the name of the city closest to where you live and press the Enter key. Using the Highlighter tool, highlight at least three interesting results. Add a note and then type a sentence about what you learned about this city. Save the page to OneNote. Share your OneNote notebook with your instructor.

d. Submit your assignment link in the format specified by your instructor.

Office 2016 and Windows 10: Essential Concepts and Skills

Objectives

You will have mastered the material in this module when you can:

- Use a touch screen
- Perform basic mouse operations
- Start Windows and sign in to an account
- Identify the objects on the Windows 10 desktop
- Identify the apps in and versions of Microsoft Office 2016
- Run an app
- Identify the components of the Microsoft Office ribbon
- Create folders
- Save files
- Change screen resolution
- Perform basic tasks in Microsoft Office apps
- Manage files
- Use Microsoft Office Help and Windows Help

This introductory module covers features and functions common to Office 2016 apps, as well as the basics of Windows 10.

Roadmap

In this module, you will learn how to perform basic tasks in Windows and the Office apps. The following roadmap identifies general activities you will perform as you progress through this module:

1. SIGN IN to an account
2. USE WINDOWS
3. USE Office APPS
4. FILE and Folder MANAGEMENT
5. SWITCH between APPS

6. SAVE and Manage FILES
7. CHANGE SCREEN RESOLUTION
8. EXIT Office APPS
9. USE ADDITIONAL Office APPS
10. USE Office and Windows HELP

At the beginning of the step instructions throughout each module, you will see an abbreviated form of this roadmap. The abbreviated roadmap uses colors to indicate module progress: gray means the module is beyond that activity, blue means the task being shown is covered in that activity, and black means that activity is yet to be covered. For example, the following abbreviated roadmap indicates the module would be showing a task in the USE APPS activity.

1 SIGN IN | 2 USE WINDOWS | 3 USE APPS | 4 FILE MANAGEMENT | 5 SWITCH APPS | 6 SAVE FILES
7 CHANGE SCREEN RESOLUTION | 8 EXIT APPS | 9 USE ADDITIONAL APPS | 10 USE HELP

Use the abbreviated roadmap as a progress guide while you read or step through the instructions in this module.

Introduction to the Windows 10 Operating System

Windows 10 is the newest version of Microsoft Windows, which is a popular and widely used operating system (Figure 1). An **operating system** (**OS**) is a set of programs that coordinate all the activities among computer or mobile device hardware.

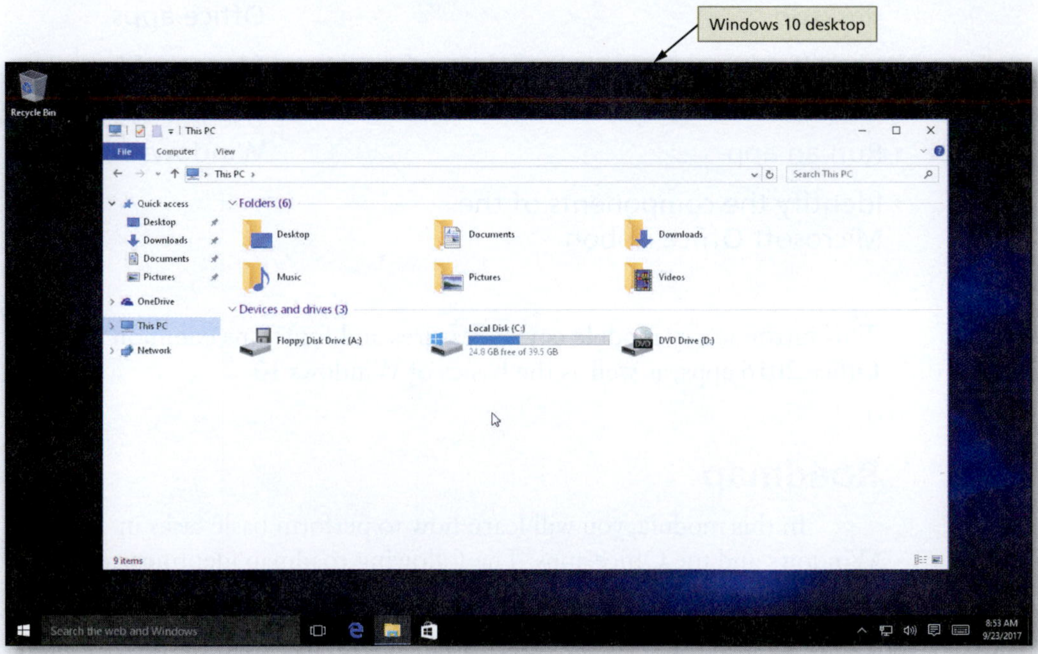

Figure 1

The Windows operating system simplifies the process of working with documents and apps by organizing the manner in which you interact with the computer. Windows is used to run apps. An application, or **app**, consists of programs designed to make users more productive and/or assist them with personal tasks, such as word processing or browsing the web.

Using a Touch Screen and a Mouse

Windows users who have computers or devices with touch screen capability can interact with the screen using gestures. A **gesture** is a motion you make on a touch screen with the tip of one or more fingers or your hand. Touch screens are convenient because they do not require a separate device for input. Table 1 presents common ways to interact with a touch screen.

If you are using your finger on a touch screen and are having difficulty completing the steps in this module, consider using a stylus. Many people find it easier to be precise with a stylus than with a finger. In addition, with a stylus you see the pointer. If you still are having trouble completing the steps with a stylus, try using a mouse.

Table 1 Touch Screen Gestures

Motion	Description	Common Uses	Equivalent Mouse Operation
Tap	Quickly touch and release one finger one time.	Activate a link (built-in connection). Press a button. Run a program or an app.	Click
Double-tap	Quickly touch and release one finger two times.	Run a program or an app. Zoom in (show a smaller area on the screen, so that contents appear larger) at the location of the double-tap.	Double-click
Press and hold	Press and hold one finger to cause an action to occur, or until an action occurs.	Display a shortcut menu (immediate access to allowable actions). Activate a mode enabling you to move an item with one finger to a new location.	Right-click
Drag, or slide	Press and hold one finger on an object and then move the finger to the new location.	Move an item around the screen. Scroll.	Drag
Swipe	Press and hold one finger and then move the finger horizontally or vertically on the screen.	Select an object. Swipe from edge to display a bar such as the Action Center, Apps bar, and Navigation bar (all discussed later).	Drag
Stretch	Move two fingers apart.	Zoom in (show a smaller area on the screen, so that contents appear larger).	None
Pinch	Move two fingers together.	Zoom out (show a larger area on the screen, so that contents appear smaller).	None

CONSIDER THIS

Will your screen look different if you are using a touch screen?
The Windows and Microsoft Office interface varies slightly if you are using a touch screen. For this reason, you might notice that your screen looks slightly different from the screens in the module.

Windows users who do not have touch screen capabilities typically work with a mouse that has at least two buttons. For a right-handed user, the left button usually is

BTW
Pointer
If you are using a touch screen, the pointer may not appear on the screen as you perform touch gestures. The pointer will reappear when you begin using the mouse.

the primary mouse button, and the right mouse button is the secondary mouse button. Left-handed people, however, can reverse the function of these buttons.

Table 2 explains how to perform a variety of mouse operations. Some apps also use keys in combination with the mouse to perform certain actions. For example, when you hold down the CTRL key while rolling the mouse wheel, text on the screen may become larger or smaller based on the direction you roll the wheel. The function of the mouse buttons and the wheel varies depending on the app.

Table 2 Mouse Operations

Operation	Mouse Action	Example*	Equivalent Touch Gesture
Point	Move the mouse until the pointer on the desktop is positioned on the item of choice.	Position the pointer on the screen.	None
Click	Press and release the primary mouse button, which usually is the left mouse button.	Select or deselect items on the screen or run an app or app feature.	Tap
Right-click	Press and release the secondary mouse button, which usually is the right mouse button.	Display a shortcut menu.	Press and hold
Double-click	Quickly press and release the primary mouse button twice without moving the mouse.	Run an app or app feature.	Double-tap
Triple-click	Quickly press and release the primary mouse button three times without moving the mouse.	Select a paragraph.	Triple-tap
Drag	Point to an item, hold down the primary mouse button, move the item to the desired location on the screen, and then release the mouse button.	Move an object from one location to another or draw pictures.	Drag or slide
Right-drag	Point to an item, hold down the right mouse button, move the item to the desired location on the screen, and then release the right mouse button.	Display a shortcut menu after moving an object from one location to another.	Press and hold, then drag
Rotate wheel	Roll the wheel forward or backward.	Scroll vertically (up and down).	Swipe
Free-spin wheel	Whirl the wheel forward or backward so that it spins freely on its own.	Scroll through many pages in seconds.	Swipe
Press wheel	Press the wheel button while moving the mouse.	Scroll continuously.	None
Tilt wheel	Press the wheel toward the right or left.	Scroll horizontally (left and right).	None
Press thumb button	Press the button on the side of the mouse with your thumb.	Move forward or backward through webpages and/or control media, games, etc.	None

*Note: The examples presented in this column are discussed as they are demonstrated in this chapter.

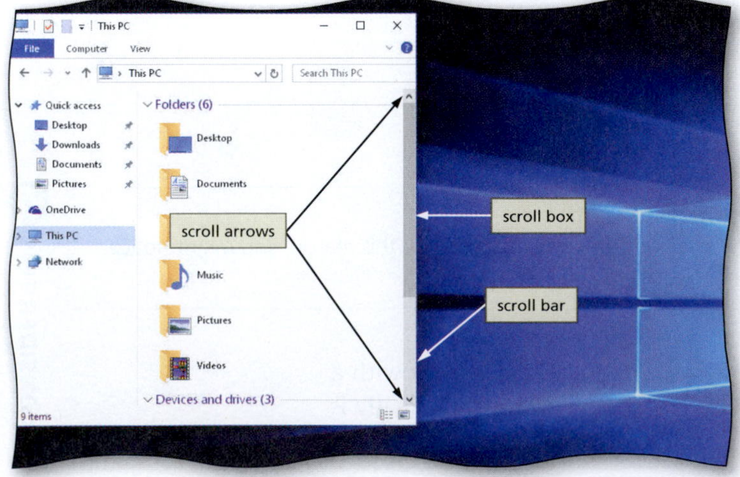

Figure 2

Scrolling

A **scroll bar** is a horizontal or vertical bar that appears when the contents of an area may not be visible completely on the screen (Figure 2). A scroll bar contains **scroll arrows** and a **scroll box** that enable you to view areas that currently cannot be seen on the screen. Clicking the up and down scroll arrows moves the screen content up or down one line. You also can click above or below the scroll box to move up or down a section, or drag the scroll box up or down to move to a specific location.

Keyboard Shortcuts

In many cases, you can use the keyboard instead of the mouse to accomplish a task. To perform tasks using the keyboard, you press one or more keyboard keys, sometimes identified as a **keyboard shortcut**. Some keyboard shortcuts consist of a single key, such as the F1 key. For example, to obtain help in many apps, you can press the F1 key. Other keyboard shortcuts consist of multiple keys, in which case a plus sign separates the key names, such as CTRL+ESC. This notation means to press and hold down the first key listed, press one or more additional keys, and then release all keys. For example, to display the Start menu, press CTRL+ESC, that is, hold down the CTRL key, press the ESC key, and then release both keys.

BTW
Minimize Wrist Injury
Computer users frequently switch between the keyboard and the mouse during a word processing session; such switching strains the wrist. To help prevent wrist injury, minimize switching. For instance, if your fingers already are on the keyboard, use keyboard keys to scroll. If your hand already is on the mouse, use the mouse to scroll. If your hand is on the touch screen, use touch gestures to scroll.

Starting Windows

It is not unusual for multiple people to use the same computer in a work, educational, recreational, or home setting. Windows enables each user to establish a **user account**, which identifies to Windows the resources, such as apps and storage locations, a user can access when working with the computer.

Each user account has a user name and may have a password and an icon, as well. A **user name** is a unique combination of letters or numbers that identifies a specific user to Windows. A **password** is a private combination of letters, numbers, and special characters associated with the user name that allows access to a user's account resources. An icon is a small image that represents an object; thus, a **user icon** is a picture associated with a user name.

When you turn on a computer, Windows starts and displays a **lock screen** consisting of the time and date (Figure 3). To unlock the screen, click the lock screen. Depending on your computer's settings, Windows may or may not display a sign-in screen that shows the user names and user icons for users who have accounts on the computer. This **sign-in screen** enables you to sign in to your user account and makes the computer available for use. Clicking the user icon begins the process of signing in, also called logging on, to your user account.

Figure 3

At the bottom of the sign-in screen is the 'Connect to Internet' button, 'Ease of access' button, and a Shut down button. Clicking the 'Connect to Internet' button displays a list of each network connection and its status. You also can connect to or disconnect from a network. Clicking the 'Ease of access' button displays the Ease of access menu, which provides tools to optimize a computer to accommodate the needs of the mobility, hearing, and vision impaired users. Clicking the Shut down button displays a menu containing commands related to putting the computer or mobile device in a low-power state, shutting it down, and restarting the computer or mobile device. The commands available on your computer or mobile device may differ.

- The Sleep command saves your work, turns off the computer fans and hard drive, and places the computer in a lower-power state. To wake the computer from sleep mode, press the power button or lift a laptop's cover, and sign in to your account.
- The Shut down command exits running apps, shuts down Windows, and then turns off the computer.
- The Restart command exits running apps, shuts down Windows, and then restarts Windows.

To Sign In to an Account

1 SIGN IN | **2** USE WINDOWS | **3** USE APPS | **4** FILE MANAGEMENT | **5** SWITCH APPS | **6** SAVE FILES
7 CHANGE SCREEN RESOLUTION | **8** EXIT APPS | **9** USE ADDITIONAL APPS | **10** USE HELP

The following steps, which use SCSeries as the user name, sign in to an account based on a typical Windows installation. ***Why?*** *After starting Windows, you might be required to sign in to an account to access the computer or mobile device's resources.* You may need to ask your instructor how to sign in to your account.

- Click the lock screen (shown in Figure 3) to display a sign-in screen.
- Click the user icon (for SCSeries, in this case) on the sign-in screen, which depending on settings, either will display a second sign-in screen that contains a Password text box (Figure 4) or will display the Windows desktop (Figure 5).

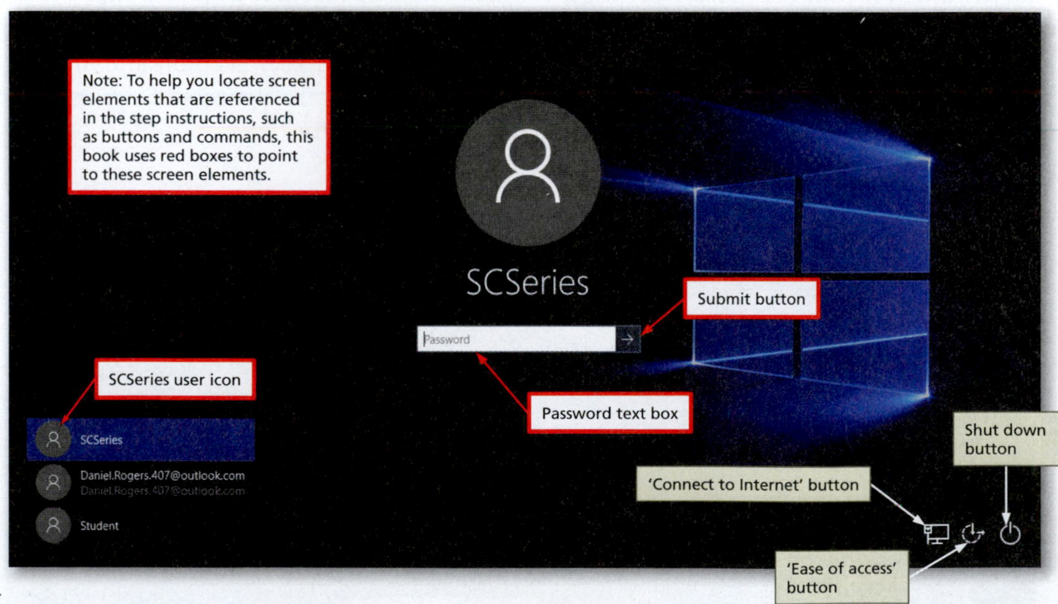

Figure 4

Q&A Why do I not see a user icon?
Your computer may require you to type a user name instead of clicking an icon.

What is a text box?
A text box is a rectangular box in which you type text.

Why does my screen not show a Password text box?
Your account does not require a password.

- If Windows displays a sign-in screen with a Password text box, type your password in the text box.

2

- Click the Submit button (shown in Figure 4) to sign in to your account and display the Windows desktop (Figure 5).

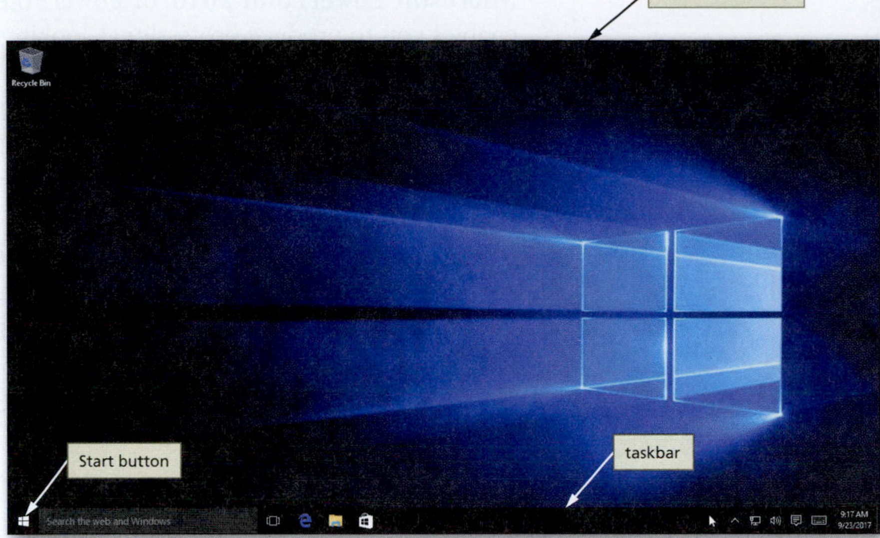

Figure 5

Q&A

Why does my desktop look different from the one in Figure 5?
The Windows desktop is customizable, and your school or employer may have modified the desktop to meet its needs. Also, your screen resolution, which affects the size of the elements on the screen, may differ from the screen resolution used in this book. Later in this module, you learn how to change screen resolution.

How do I type if my tablet has no keyboard?
You can use your fingers to press keys on a keyboard that appears on the screen, called an on-screen keyboard, or you can purchase a separate physical keyboard that attaches to or wirelessly communicates with the tablet.

The Windows Desktop

The Windows 10 desktop (Figure 5) and the objects on the desktop emulate a work area in an office. Think of the Windows desktop as an electronic version of the top of your desk. You can perform tasks such as placing objects on the desktop, moving the objects around the desktop, and removing items from the desktop.

When you run an app in Windows 10, it appears on the desktop. Some icons also may be displayed on the desktop. For instance, the icon for the **Recycle Bin**, the location of files that have been deleted, appears on the desktop by default. A **file** is a named unit of storage. Files can contain text, images, audio, and video. You can customize your desktop so that icons representing programs and files you use often appear on your desktop.

Introduction to Microsoft Office 2016

Microsoft Office 2016 is the newest version of Microsoft Office, offering features that provide users with better functionality and easier ways to work with the various files they create. This version of Office also is designed to work more optimally on mobile devices and online.

Microsoft Office 2016 Apps

Microsoft Office 2016 includes a wide variety of apps, such as Word, PowerPoint, Excel, Access, Outlook, Publisher, and OneNote:

- **Microsoft Word 2016**, or Word, is a full-featured word processing app that allows you to create professional-looking documents and revise them easily.

- **Microsoft PowerPoint 2016**, or PowerPoint, is a complete presentation app that enables you to produce professional-looking presentations and then deliver them to an audience.
- **Microsoft Excel 2016**, or Excel, is a powerful spreadsheet app that allows you to organize data, complete calculations, make decisions, graph data, develop professional-looking reports, publish organized data to the web, and access real-time data from websites.
- **Microsoft Access 2016**, or Access, is a database management system that enables you to create a database; add, change, and delete data in the database; ask questions concerning the data in the database; and create forms and reports using the data in the database.
- **Microsoft Outlook 2016**, or Outlook, is a communications and scheduling app that allows you to manage email accounts, calendars, contacts, and access to other Internet content.
- **Microsoft Publisher 2016**, or Publisher, is a desktop publishing app that helps you create professional-quality publications and marketing materials that can be shared easily.
- **Microsoft OneNote 2016**, or OneNote, is a note taking app that allows you to store and share information in notebooks with other people.

Microsoft Office 2016 Suites

A **suite** is a collection of individual apps available together as a unit. Microsoft offers a variety of Office suites, including a stand-alone desktop app, Microsoft Office 365, and Microsoft Office Online. **Microsoft Office 365**, or Office 365, provides plans that allow organizations to use Office in a mobile setting while also being able to communicate and share files, depending upon the type of plan selected by the organization. **Microsoft Office Online** includes apps that allow you to edit and share files on the web using the familiar Office interface.

During the Office 365 installation, you select a plan, and depending on your plan, you receive different apps and services. Office Online apps do not require a local installation and can be accessed through OneDrive and your browser. **OneDrive** is a cloud storage service that provides storage and other services, such as Office Online, to computer users.

CONSIDER THIS

How do you sign up for a OneDrive account?

- Use your browser to navigate to onedrive.live.com.
- Create a Microsoft account by clicking the Sign up button and then entering your information to create the account.
- Sign in to OneDrive using your new account or use it in Office to save your files on OneDrive.

Apps in a suite, such as Microsoft Office, typically use a similar interface and share features. Once you are comfortable working with the elements and the interface and performing tasks in one app, the similarity can help you apply the knowledge and skills you have learned to another app(s) in the suite. For example, the process for saving a file in Word is the same in PowerPoint, Excel, and some of the other Office apps. While briefly showing how to use several Office apps, this module illustrates some of the common functions across the apps and identifies the characteristics unique to these apps.

Running and Using an App

To use an app, you must instruct the operating system to run the app. Windows provides many different ways to run an app, one of which is presented in this section (other ways to run an app are presented throughout this module). After an app is running, you can use it to perform a variety of tasks. The following pages use Word to discuss some elements of the Office interface and to perform tasks that are common to other Office apps.

Word

Word is a full-featured word processing app that allows you to create many types of personal and business documents, including flyers, letters, memos, resumes, reports, fax cover sheets, mailing labels, and newsletters. Word also provides tools that enable you to create webpages and save these webpages directly on a web server. Word has many features designed to simplify the production of documents and add visual appeal. Using Word, you easily can change the shape, size, and color of text. You also can include borders, shading, tables, images, pictures, charts, and web addresses in documents.

To Run an App Using the Start Menu and Create a Blank Document

1 SIGN IN | 2 USE WINDOWS | 3 USE APPS | 4 FILE MANAGEMENT | 5 SWITCH APPS | 6 SAVE FILES
7 CHANGE SCREEN RESOLUTION | 8 EXIT APPS | 9 USE ADDITIONAL APPS | 10 USE HELP

Across the bottom of the Windows 10 desktop is the taskbar. The taskbar contains the **Start button**, which you use to access apps, files, folders, and settings. A **folder** is a named location on a storage medium that usually contains related documents.

Clicking the Start button displays the Start menu. The **Start menu** allows you to access programs, folders, and files on the computer or mobile device and contains commands that allow you to start programs, store and search for documents, customize the computer or mobile device, and sign out of a user account or shut down the computer or mobile device. A **menu** is a list of related items, including folders, programs, and commands. Each **command** on a menu performs a specific action, such as saving a file or obtaining help. ***Why?*** *When you install an app, for example, the app's name will be added to the All apps list on the Start menu.*

The following steps, which assume Windows is running, use the Start menu to run an Office app and create a blank document based on a typical installation. You may need to ask your instructor how to run an Office app on your computer. Although the steps illustrate running the Word app, the steps to run any Office app are similar.

1

- Click the Start button on the Windows 10 taskbar to display the Start menu (Figure 6).

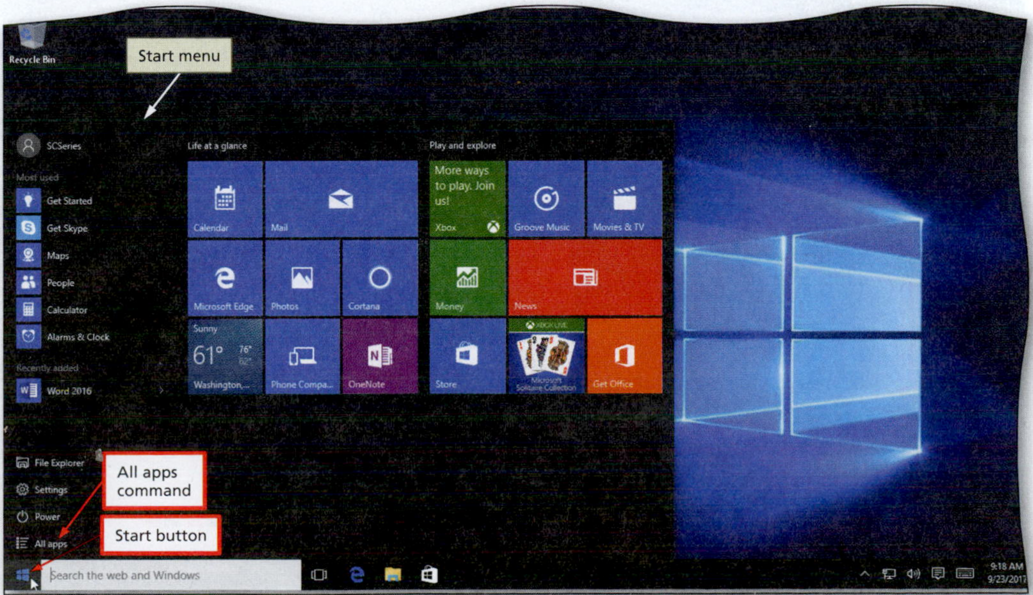

Figure 6

- Click All apps at the bottom of the left pane of the Start menu to display a list of apps installed on the computer or mobile device. If necessary, scroll to display the app you wish to run (Figure 7).

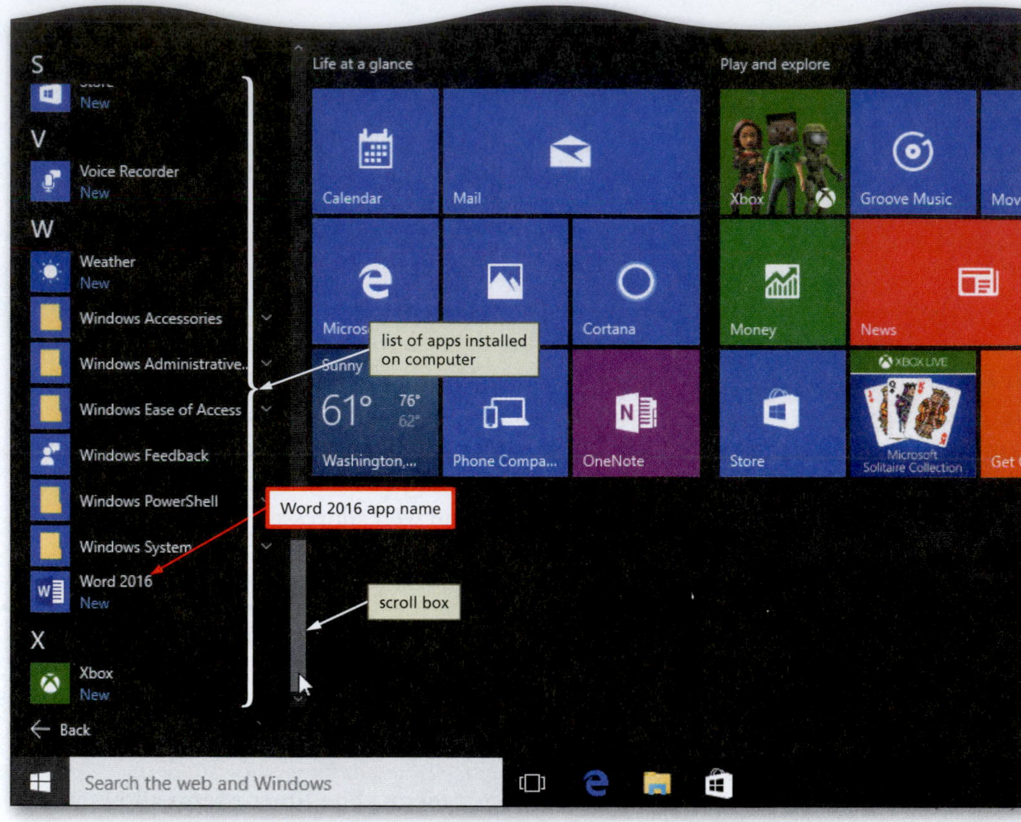

Figure 7

3

- If the app you wish to run is located in a folder, click or scroll to and then click the folder in the All apps list to display a list of the folder's contents.
- Click, or scroll to and then click, the program name (Microsoft Word 2016, in this case) in the list to run the selected program (Figure 8).

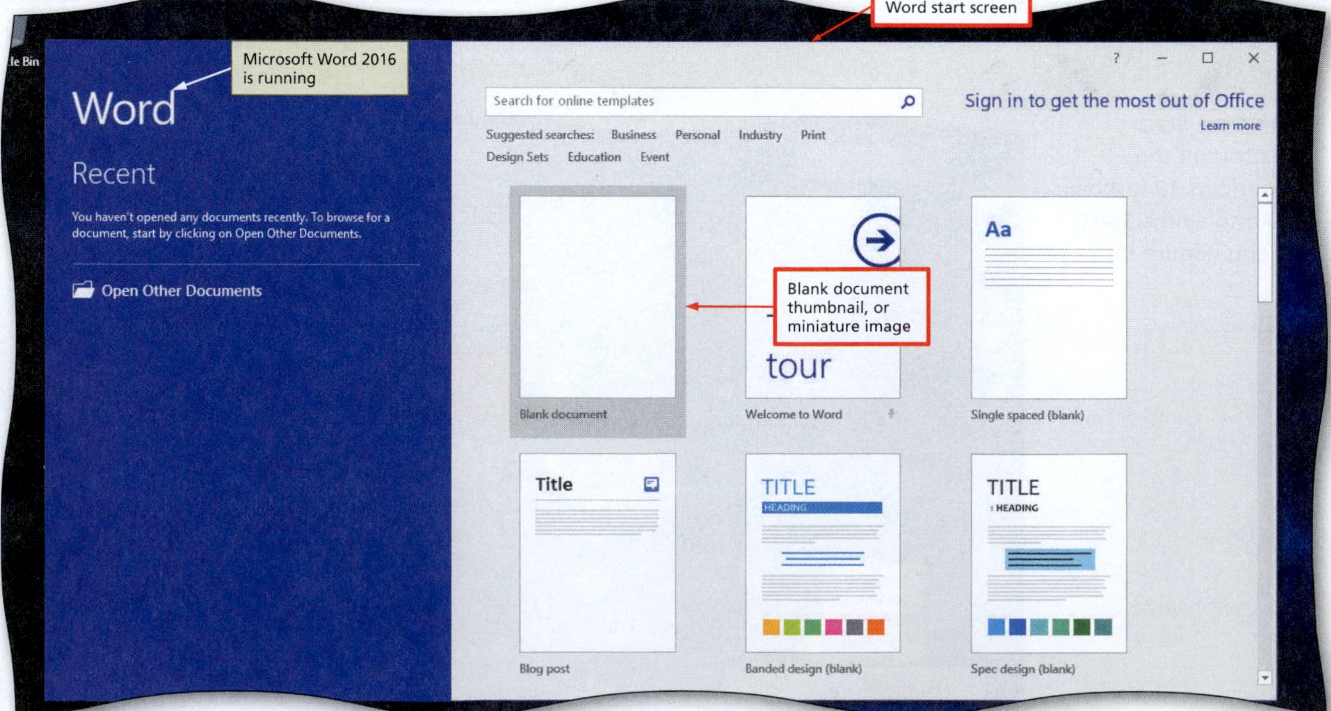

Figure 8

4

- Click the Blank document thumbnail on the Word start screen to create a blank Word document in the Word window (Figure 9).

Q&A What happens when you run an app?
Some apps provide a means for you to create a blank document, as shown in Figure 8; others immediately display a blank document in an app window, such as the Word window shown in Figure 9. A **window** is a rectangular area that displays data and information. The top of a window has a **title bar**, which is a horizontal space that contains the window's name.

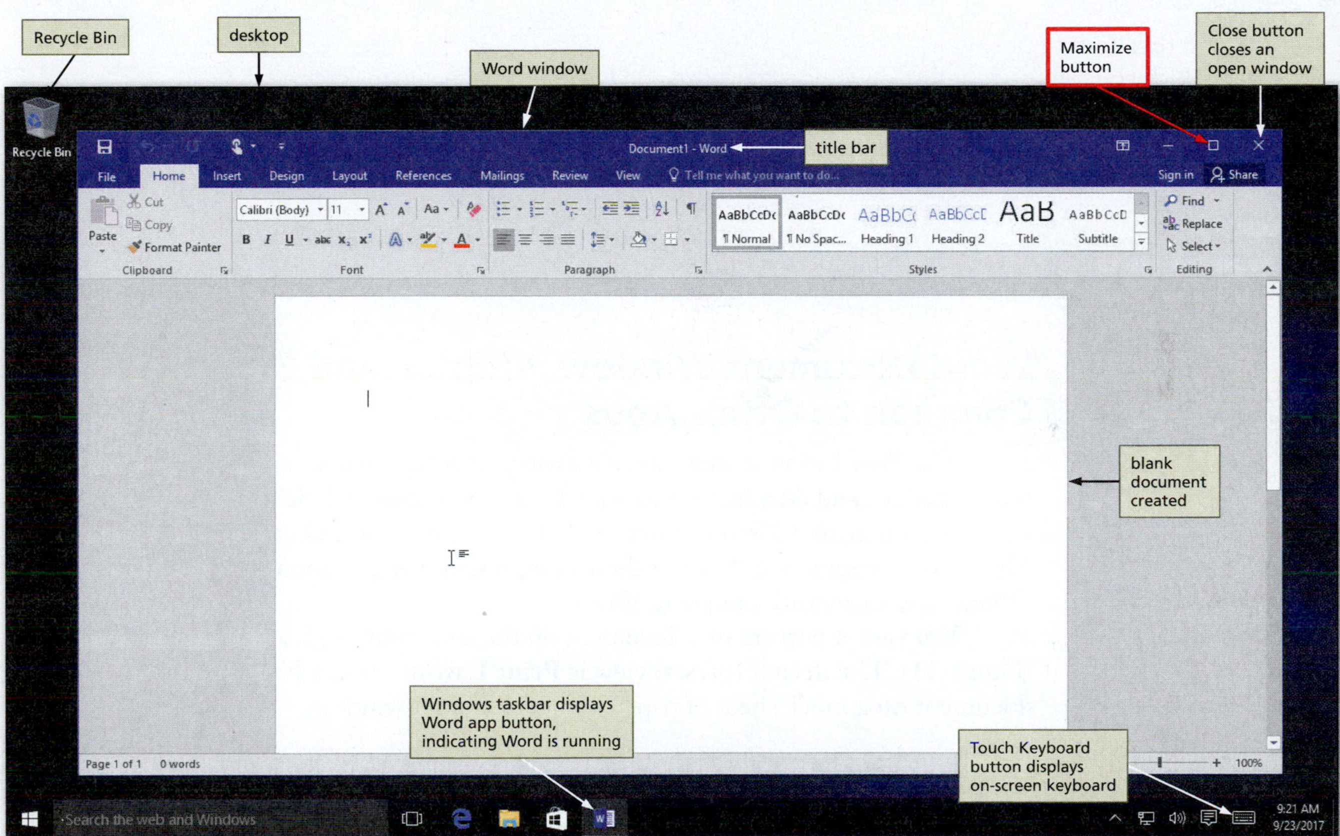

Figure 9

Other Ways

1. Type app name in search box, click app name in results list
2. Double-click file created in app you want to run

To Maximize a Window

1 SIGN IN | 2 USE WINDOWS | 3 USE APPS | 4 FILE MANAGEMENT | 5 SWITCH APPS | 6 SAVE FILES
7 CHANGE SCREEN RESOLUTION | 8 EXIT APPS | 9 USE ADDITIONAL APPS | 10 USE HELP

Sometimes content is not visible completely in a window. One method of displaying the entire contents of a window is to **maximize** it, or enlarge the window so that it fills the entire screen. The following step maximizes the Word window; however, any Office app's window can be maximized using this step. ***Why?*** *A maximized window provides the most space available for using the app.*

- If the app window is not maximized already, click the Maximize button (shown in Figure 9) next to the Close button on the window's title bar (the Word window title bar, in this case) to maximize the window (Figure 10).

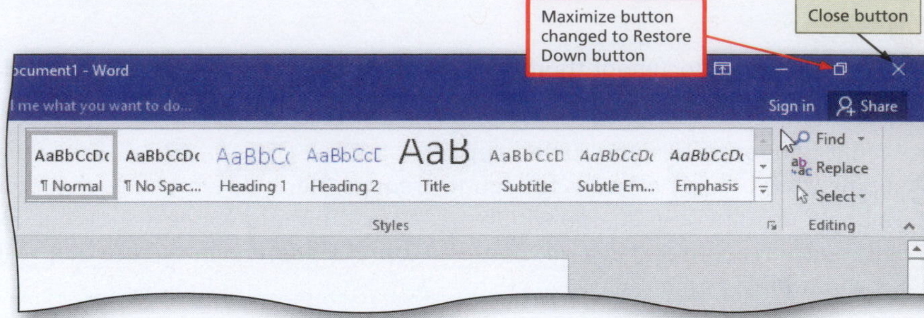

Figure 10

Q&A

What happened to the Maximize button?

It changed to a Restore Down button, which you can use to return a window to its size and location before you maximized it.

How do I know whether a window is maximized?

A window is maximized if it fills the entire display area and the Restore Down button is displayed on the title bar.

Other Ways

1. Double-click title bar
2. Drag title bar to top of screen

BTW

Touch Keyboard

To display the on-screen touch keyboard, click the Touch Keyboard button on the Windows taskbar. When finished using the touch keyboard, click the X button on the touch keyboard to close the keyboard.

Word Document Window, Ribbon, and Elements Common to Office Apps

The Word window consists of a variety of components to make your work more efficient and documents more professional. These include the document window, ribbon, Tell Me box, mini toolbar, shortcut menus, Quick Access Toolbar, and Microsoft Account area. Most of these components are common to other Microsoft Office apps; others are unique to Word.

You view a portion of a document on the screen through a **document window** (Figure 11). The default (preset) view is **Print Layout view**, which shows the document on a mock sheet of paper in the document window.

Scroll Bars You use a scroll bar to display different portions of a document in the document window. At the right edge of the document window is a vertical scroll bar. If a document is too wide to fit in the document window, a horizontal scroll bar also appears at the bottom of the document window. On a scroll bar, the position of the scroll box reflects the location of the portion of the document that is displayed in the document window.

Status Bar The **status bar**, located at the bottom of the document window above the Windows taskbar, presents information about the document, the progress of current tasks, and the status of certain commands and keys; it also provides controls for viewing the document. As you type text or perform certain tasks, various indicators and buttons may appear on the status bar.

The left side of the status bar in Figure 11 shows the current page followed by the total number of pages in the document, the number of words in the document, and an icon to check spelling and grammar. The right side of the status bar includes buttons and controls you can use to change the view of a document and adjust the size of the displayed document.

Ribbon The ribbon, located near the top of the window below the title bar, is the control center in Word and other Office apps (Figure 12). The ribbon provides easy, central access to the tasks you perform while creating a document. The ribbon consists

VISIT NATIONAL MONUMENTS
CONTACT YOUR TRA
FOR ADDITIONAL
AND SPECIAL R
(555) 555-22
stored document
Word window
document window
number of pages in document
current page
number of words in document
'Spelling and Grammar Check' icon
status bar
Print Layout button is selected when you first install Word
adjusts size of displayed document

Figure 11

Home tab
arrow
main tabs
Tell Me box
in-ribbon gallery
button
ribbon
gallery scroll arrows
More button
groups
scroll bar
status bar

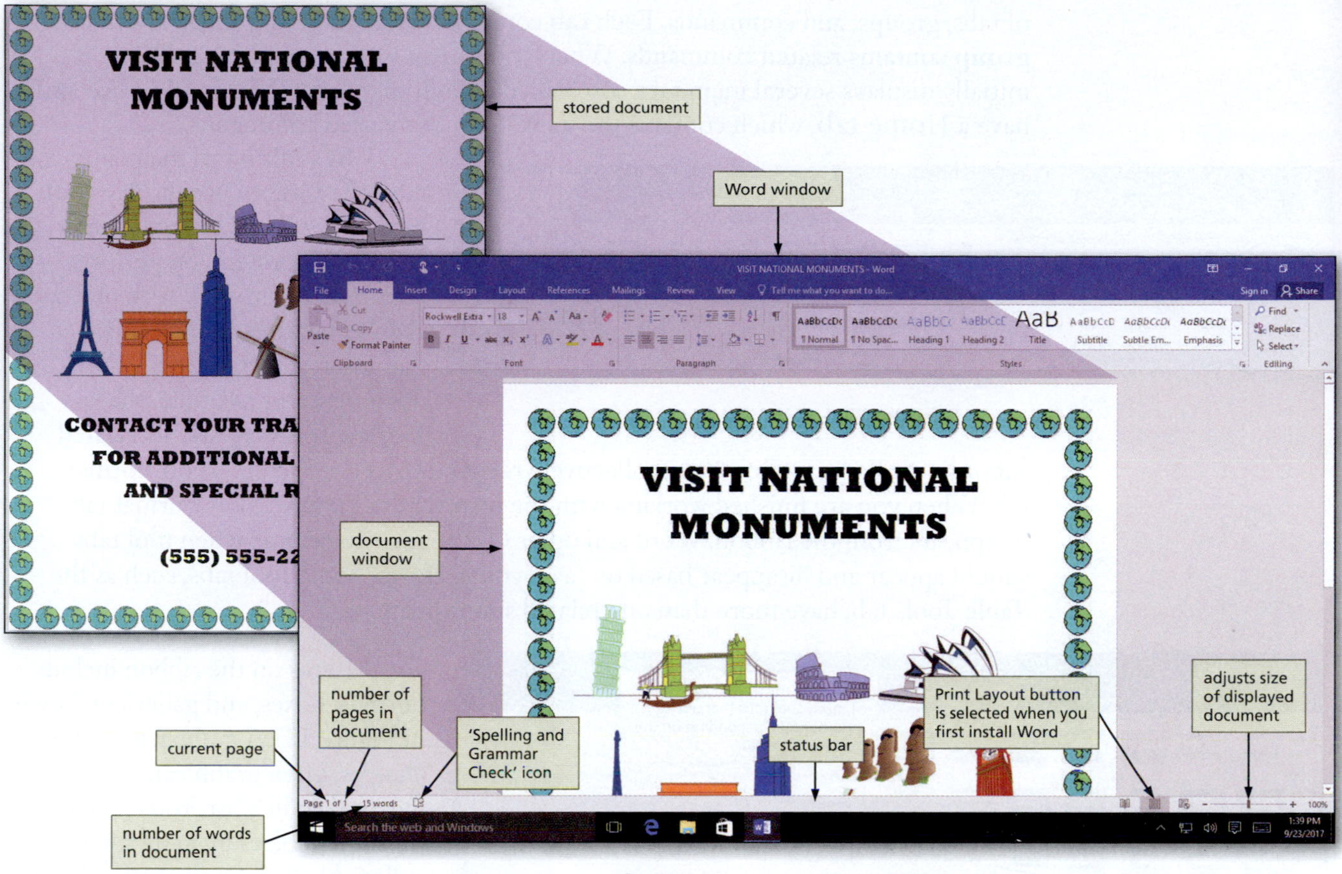

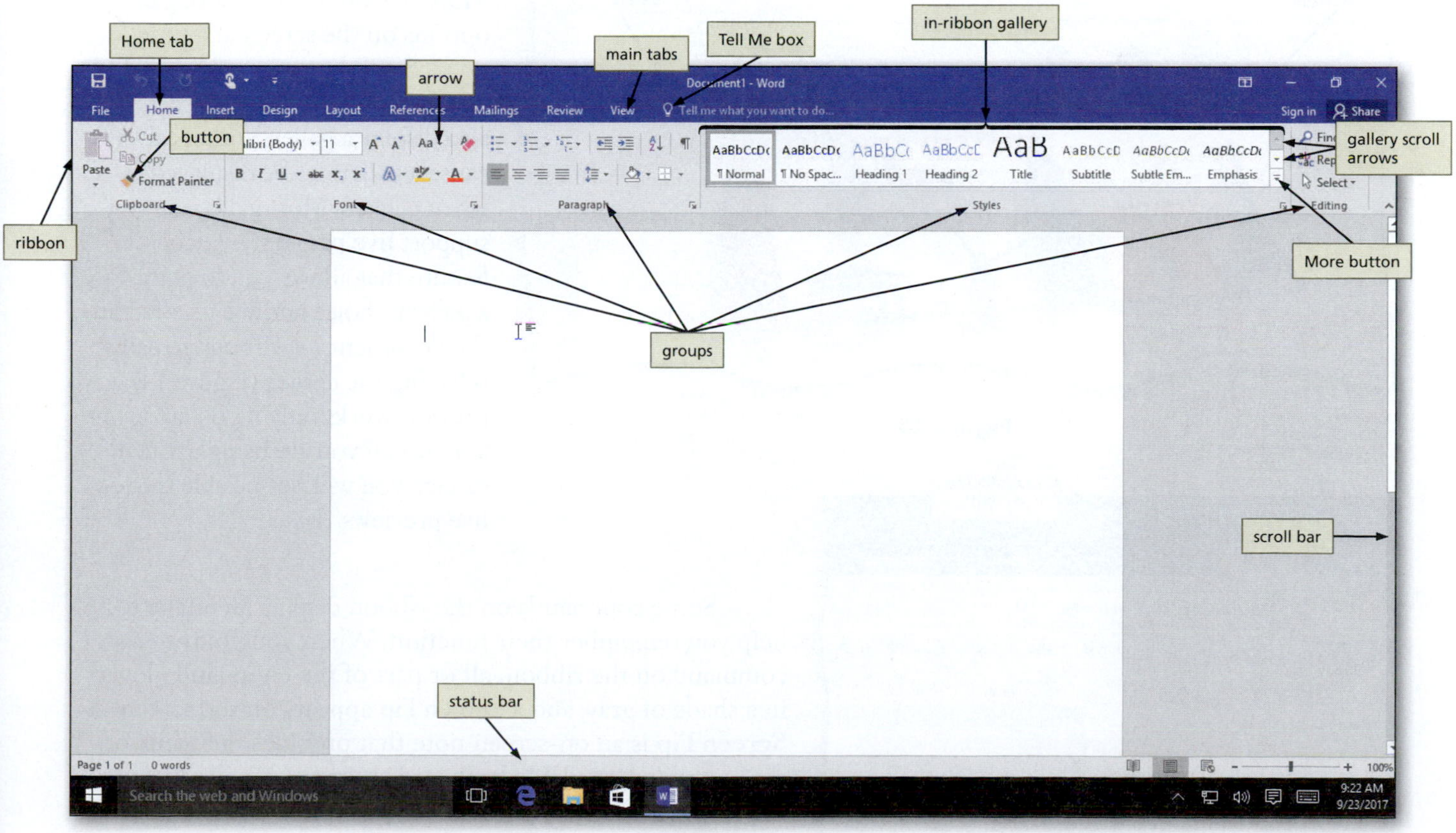

Figure 12

of tabs, groups, and commands. Each **tab** contains a collection of groups, and each **group** contains related commands. When you run an Office app, such as Word, it initially displays several main tabs, also called default or top-level tabs. All Office apps have a Home tab, which contains the more frequently used commands.

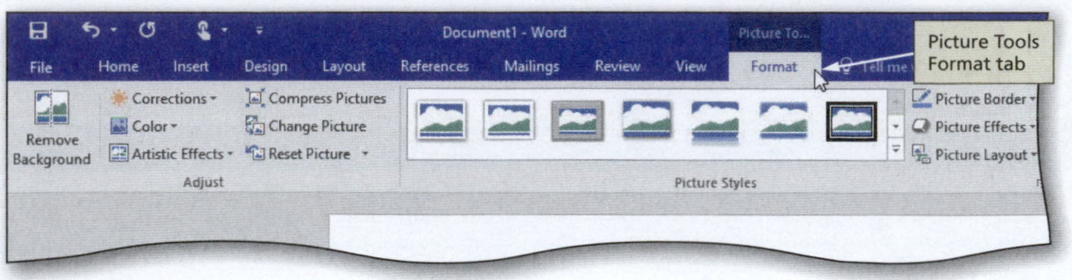

Figure 13

In addition to the main tabs, the Office apps display **tool tabs**, also called contextual tabs (Figure 13), when you perform certain tasks or work with objects such as pictures or tables. If you insert a picture in a Word document, for example, the Picture Tools tab and its related subordinate Format tab appear, collectively referred to as the Picture Tools Format tab. When you are finished working with the picture, the Picture Tools Format tab disappears from the ribbon. Word and other Office apps determine when tool tabs should appear and disappear based on tasks you perform. Some tool tabs, such as the Table Tools tab, have more than one related subordinate tab.

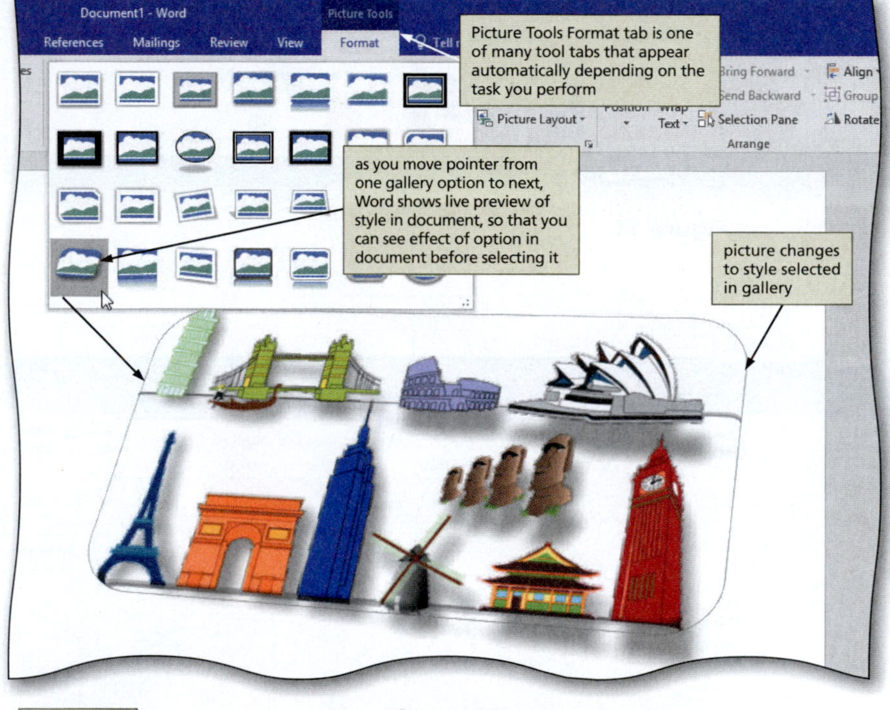

Figure 14

Items on the ribbon include buttons, boxes, and galleries (shown in Figure 12). A **gallery** is a set of choices, often graphical, arranged in a grid or in a list. You can scroll through choices in an in-ribbon gallery by clicking the gallery's scroll arrows. Or, you can click a gallery's More button to view more gallery options on the screen at a time.

Some buttons and boxes have arrows that, when clicked, also display a gallery; others always cause a gallery to be displayed when clicked. Most galleries support **live preview**, which is a feature that allows you to point to a gallery choice and see its effect in the document — without actually selecting the choice (Figure 14). Live preview works only if you are using a mouse; if you are using a touch screen, you will not be able to view live previews.

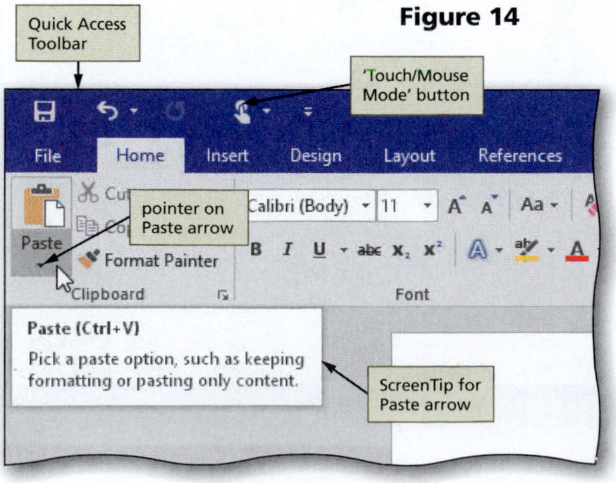

Quick Access Toolbar

'Touch/Mouse Mode' button

pointer on Paste arrow

Paste (Ctrl+V)

Pick a paste option, such as keeping formatting or pasting only content.

ScreenTip for Paste arrow

Figure 15

Some commands on the ribbon display an image to help you remember their function. When you point to a command on the ribbon, all or part of the command glows in a shade of gray, and a ScreenTip appears on the screen. A **ScreenTip** is an on-screen note that provides the name of the command, available keyboard shortcut(s), a description of the command, and sometimes instructions for how to obtain help about the command (Figure 15).

Some groups on the ribbon have a small arrow in the lower-right corner, called a **Dialog Box Launcher**, that when clicked, displays a dialog box or a task pane with additional options for the group (Figure 16). When presented with a dialog box, you make selections and must close the dialog box before returning to the document. A **task pane**, in contrast to a dialog box, is a window that can remain open and visible while you work in the document.

BTW

Touch Mode

The Office and Windows interfaces may vary if you are using touch mode. For this reason, you might notice that the function or appearance of your touch screen differs slightly from this module's presentation.

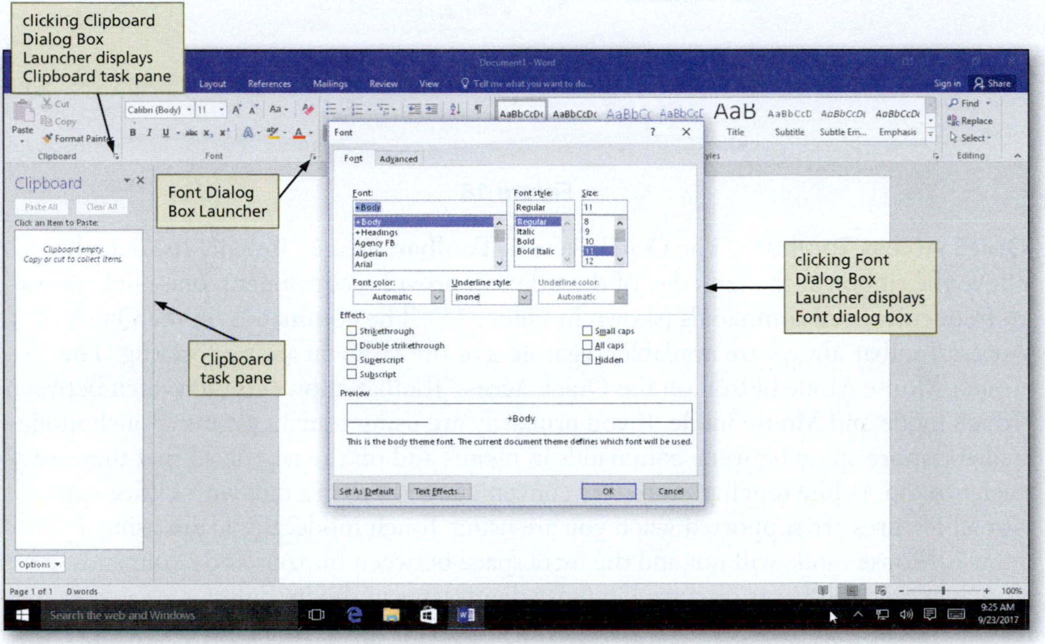

Figure 16

Tell Me Box The **Tell Me box**, which appears to the right of the tabs on the ribbon, is a type of search box that helps you to perform specific tasks in an Office app (Figure 17). As you type in the Tell Me box, the word-wheeling feature displays search results that are refined as you type. For example, if you want to center text in a document, you can type "center" in the Tell Me box and then select the appropriate command. The Tell Me box also lists the last five commands accessed from the box.

Mini Toolbar The **mini toolbar**, which appears automatically based on tasks you perform, contains commands related to changing the appearance of text in a document (Figure 18). If you do not use the mini toolbar, it disappears from the screen. The buttons, arrows, and boxes on the mini toolbar vary, depending on whether you are using Touch mode versus Mouse mode. If you right-click an item in the document window, Word displays both the mini toolbar and a shortcut menu, which is discussed in a later section in this module.

All commands on the mini toolbar also exist on the ribbon. The purpose of the mini toolbar is to minimize hand or mouse movement.

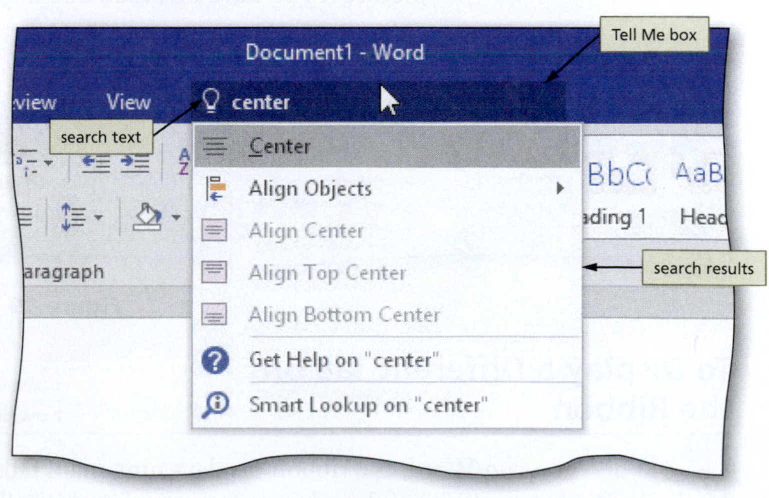

Figure 17

BTW
Turning Off the Mini Toolbar
If you do not want the mini toolbar to appear, click File on the ribbon to open the Backstage view, click the Options tab in the Backstage view, if necessary, click General (Options dialog box), remove the check mark from the 'Show Mini Toolbar on selection' check box, and then click the OK button.

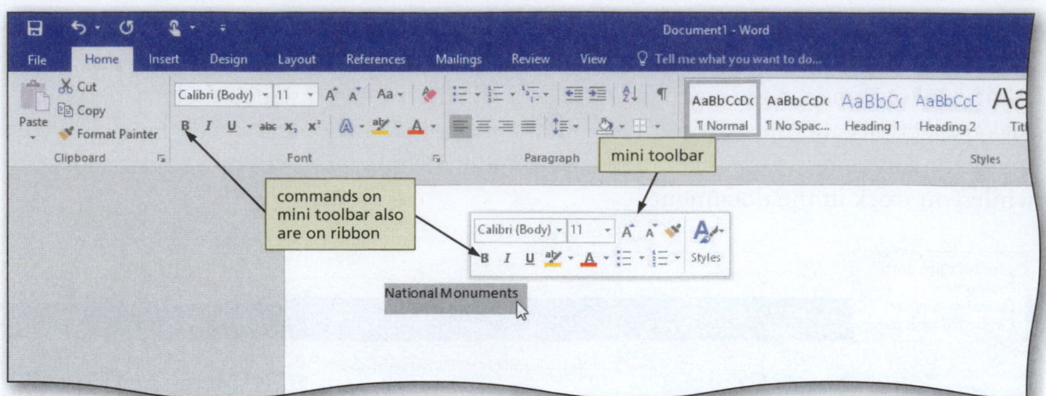

Figure 18

Quick Access Toolbar The **Quick Access Toolbar**, located initially (by default) above the ribbon at the left edge of the title bar, provides convenient, one-click access to frequently used commands (shown in Figure 15). The commands on the Quick Access Toolbar always are available, regardless of the task you are performing. The Touch/Mouse Mode button on the Quick Access Toolbar allows you to switch between Touch mode and Mouse mode. If you primarily are using touch gestures, Touch mode will add more space between commands in menus and on the ribbon so that they are easier to tap. While touch gestures are convenient ways to interact with Office apps, not all features are supported when you are using Touch mode. If you are using a mouse, Mouse mode will not add the extra space between buttons and commands. The Quick Access Toolbar is discussed in more depth later in the module.

KeyTips If you prefer using the keyboard instead of the mouse, you can press the ALT key on the keyboard to display **KeyTips**, or keyboard code icons, for certain commands (Figure 19). To select a command using the keyboard, press the letter or number displayed in the KeyTip, which may cause additional KeyTips related to the selected command to appear. To remove KeyTips from the screen, press the ALT key or the ESC key until all KeyTips disappear, or click anywhere in the app window.

Microsoft Account Area In this area, you can use the Sign in link to sign in to your Microsoft account. Once signed in, you will see your account information, as well as a picture if you have included one in your Microsoft account.

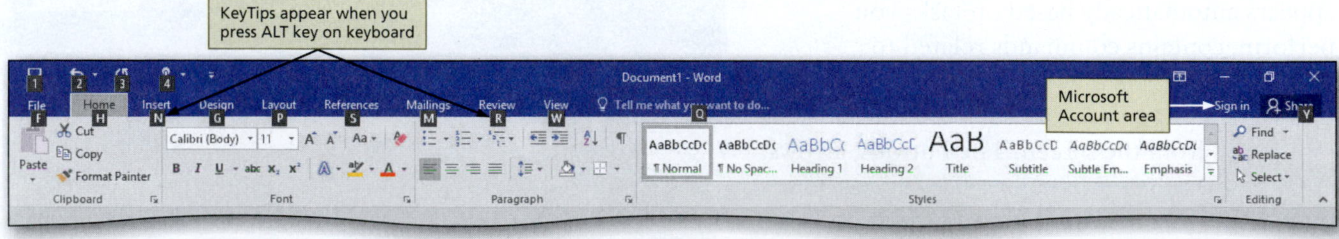

Figure 19

To Display a Different Tab on the Ribbon

1 SIGN IN | 2 USE WINDOWS | **3 USE APPS** | 4 FILE MANAGEMENT | 5 SWITCH APPS | 6 SAVE FILES
7 CHANGE SCREEN RESOLUTION | 8 EXIT APPS | 9 USE ADDITIONAL APPS | 10 USE HELP

When you run Word, the ribbon displays nine main tabs: File, Home, Insert, Design, Layout, References, Mailings, Review, and View. The tab currently displayed is called the **active tab**.

The following step displays the Insert tab, that is, makes it the active tab. ***Why?*** *When working with an Office app, you may need to switch tabs to access other options for working with a document.*

1

- Click Insert on the ribbon to display the Insert tab (Figure 20).

Experiment

- Click the other tabs on the ribbon to view their contents. When you are finished, click Insert on the ribbon to redisplay the Insert tab.

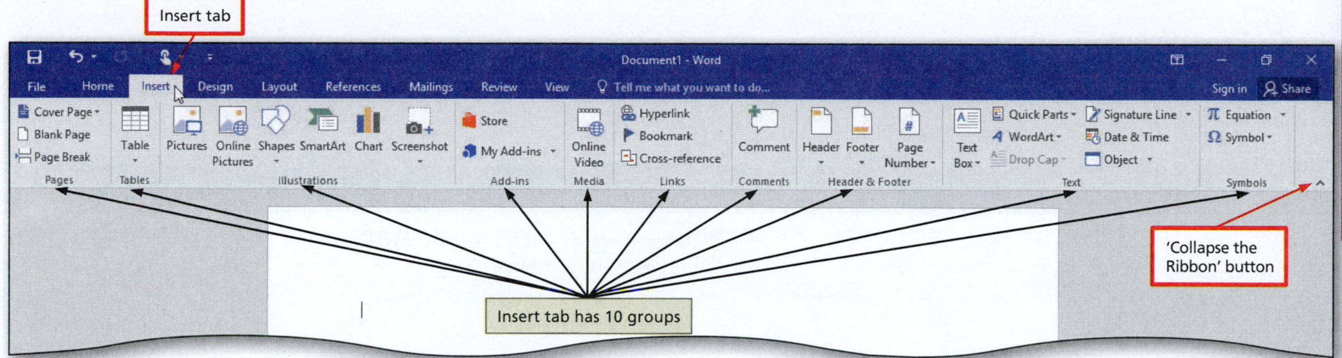

Figure 20

Other Ways

1. Press ALT, press letter corresponding to tab to display
2. Press ALT, press LEFT ARROW or RIGHT ARROW until desired tab is displayed

To Collapse and Expand the Ribbon and Use Full Screen Mode

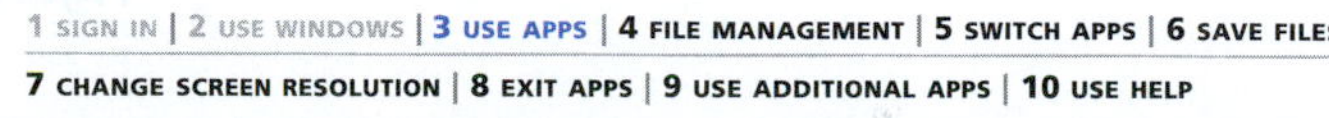

To display more of a document or other item in the window of an Office app, some users prefer to collapse the ribbon, which hides the groups on the ribbon and displays only the main tabs, or to use **Full Screen mode**, which hides all the commands and just displays the document. Each time you run an Office app, the ribbon appears the same way it did the last time you used that Office app. The modules in this book, however, begin with the ribbon appearing as it did at the initial installation of the software.

The following steps collapse, expand, and restore the ribbon in an Office app and then switch to Full Screen mode. ***Why?*** *If you need more space on the screen to work with your document, you may consider collapsing the ribbon or switching to Full Screen mode to gain additional workspace.*

1

- Click the 'Collapse the Ribbon' button on the ribbon (shown in Figure 20) to collapse the ribbon (Figure 21).

Q&A What happened to the 'Collapse the Ribbon' button?
The 'Pin the ribbon' button replaces the 'Collapse the Ribbon' button when the ribbon is collapsed. You will see the 'Pin the ribbon' button only when you expand a ribbon by clicking a tab.

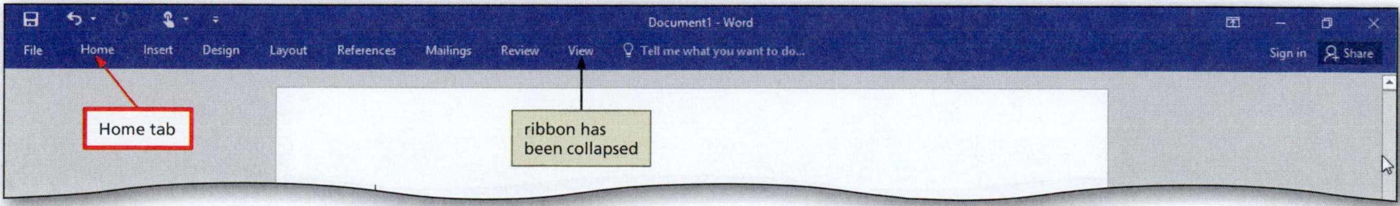

Figure 21

2

- Click Home on the ribbon to expand the Home tab (Figure 22).

Q&A Why would I click the Home tab?
If you want to use a command on a collapsed ribbon, click the main tab to display the groups for that tab. After you select a command on the ribbon and resume working in the document, the groups will be collapsed once again. If you decide not to use a command on the ribbon, you can collapse the groups by clicking the same main tab or clicking in the app window.

Experiment

- Click Home on the ribbon to collapse the groups again. Click Home on the ribbon to expand the Home tab.

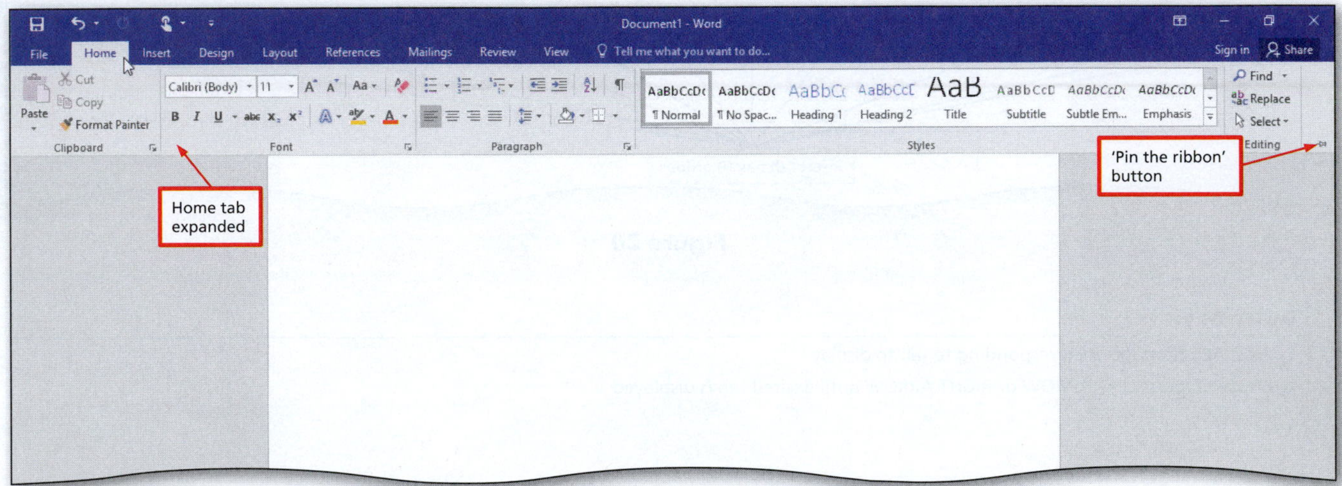

Figure 22

3

- Click the 'Pin the ribbon' button on the expanded Home tab to restore the ribbon.
- Click the 'Ribbon Display Options' button to display the Ribbon Display Options menu (Figure 23).

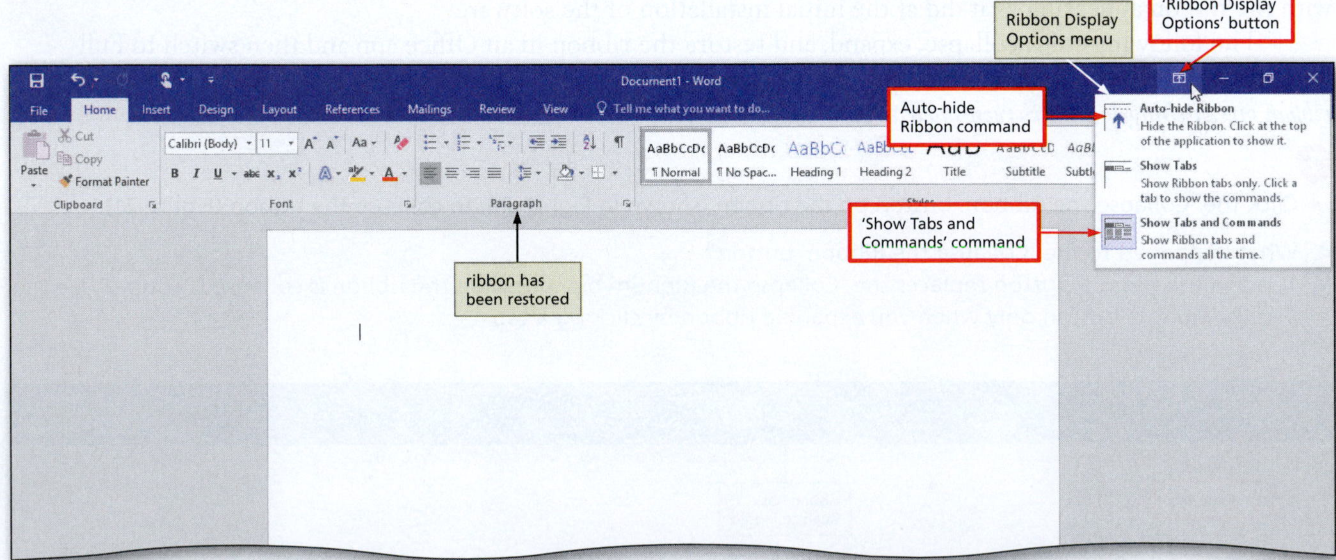

Figure 23

4

- Click Auto-hide Ribbon to hide all the commands from the screen (Figure 24).
- Click the ellipsis to temporarily display the ribbon.
- Click the 'Ribbon Display Options' button to display the Ribbon Display Options menu (shown in Figure 23).
- Click 'Show Tabs and Commands' to exit Full Screen mode.

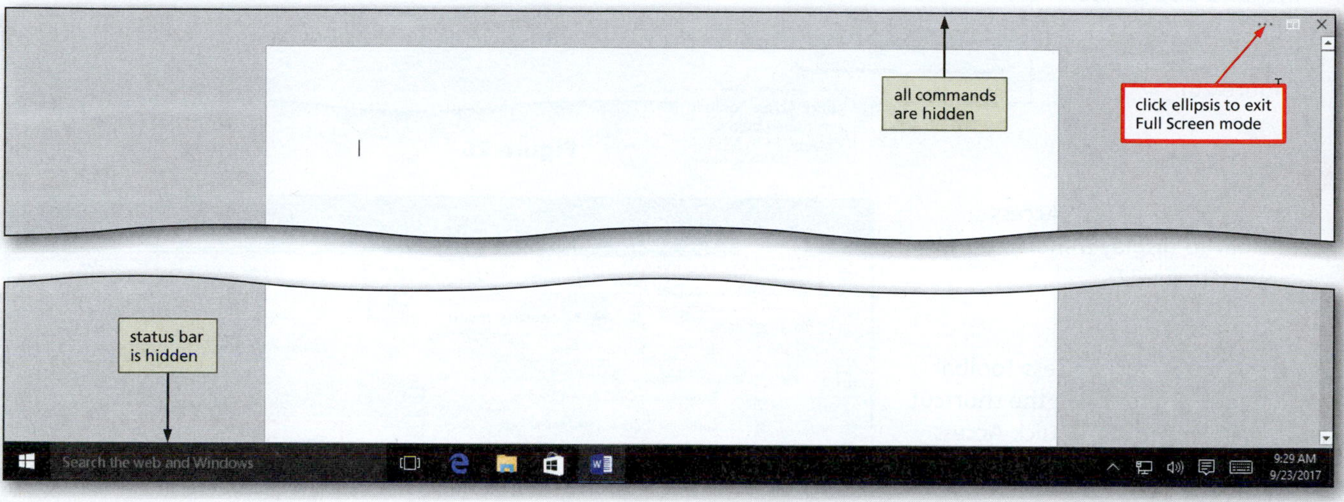

Figure 24

Other Ways

1. Double-click a main tab on the ribbon
2. Press CTRL+F1

To Use a Shortcut Menu to Relocate the Quick Access Toolbar

1 SIGN IN | 2 USE WINDOWS | **3 USE APPS** | **4 FILE MANAGEMENT** | **5 SWITCH APPS** | **6 SAVE FILES**
7 CHANGE SCREEN RESOLUTION | **8 EXIT APPS** | **9 USE ADDITIONAL APPS** | **10 USE HELP**

When you right-click certain areas of the Word and other Office app windows, a shortcut menu will appear. A **shortcut menu** is a list of frequently used commands that relate to an object. ***Why?*** *You can use shortcut menus to access common commands quickly.* When you right-click the status bar, for example, a shortcut menu appears with commands related to the status bar. When you right-click the Quick Access Toolbar, a shortcut menu appears with commands related to the Quick Access Toolbar. The following steps use a shortcut menu to move the Quick Access Toolbar, which by default is located on the title bar.

1

- Right-click the Quick Access Toolbar to display a shortcut menu that presents a list of commands related to the Quick Access Toolbar (Figure 25).

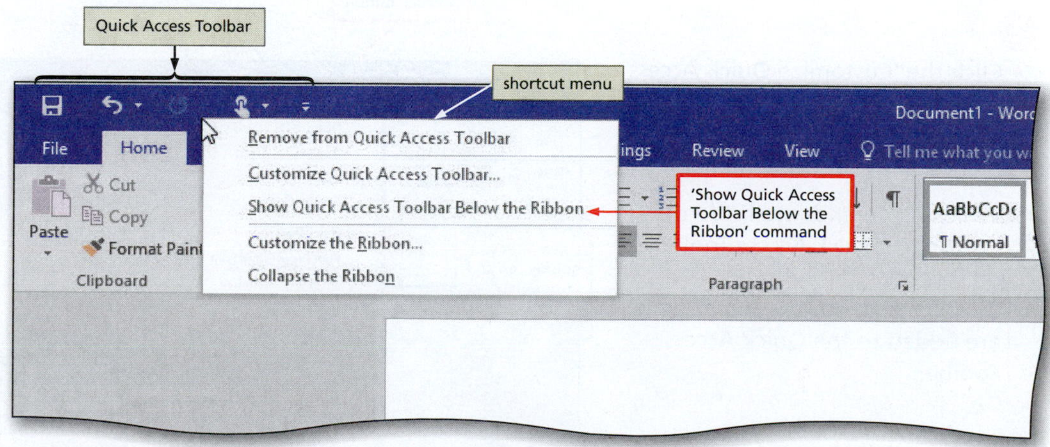

Figure 25

- Click 'Show Quick Access Toolbar Below the Ribbon' on the shortcut menu to display the Quick Access Toolbar below the ribbon (Figure 26).

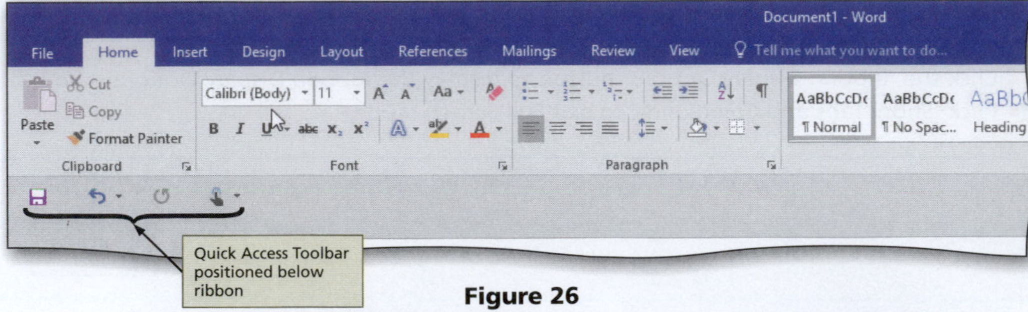

Figure 26

- Right-click the Quick Access Toolbar to display a shortcut menu (Figure 27).

- Click 'Show Quick Access Toolbar Above the Ribbon' on the shortcut menu to return the Quick Access Toolbar to its original position (shown in Figure 25).

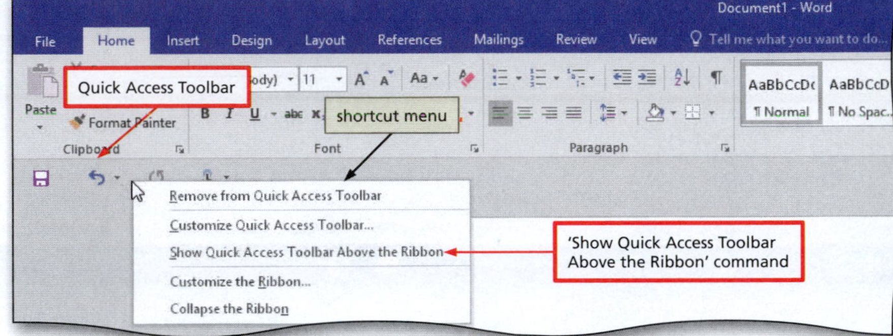

Figure 27

Other Ways

1. Click 'Customize Quick Access Toolbar' button on Quick Access Toolbar, click 'Show Below the Ribbon' or 'Show Above the Ribbon'

To Customize the Quick Access Toolbar

1 SIGN IN | 2 USE WINDOWS | 3 USE APPS | 4 FILE MANAGEMENT | 5 SWITCH APPS | 6 SAVE FILES
7 CHANGE SCREEN RESOLUTION | 8 EXIT APPS | 9 USE ADDITIONAL APPS | 10 USE HELP

The Quick Access Toolbar provides easy access to some of the more frequently used commands in the Office apps. By default, the Quick Access Toolbar contains buttons for the Save, Undo, and Redo commands. If your computer or mobile device has a touch screen, the Quick Access Toolbar also might display the Touch/Mouse Mode button. You can customize the Quick Access Toolbar by changing its location in the window, as shown in the previous steps, and by adding more buttons to reflect commands you would like to access easily. The following steps add the Quick Print button to the Quick Access Toolbar. ***Why?** Adding the Quick Print button to the Quick Access Toolbar speeds up the process of printing.*

- Click the 'Customize Quick Access Toolbar' button to display the Customize Quick Access Toolbar menu (Figure 28).

Q&A Which commands are listed on the Customize Quick Access Toolbar menu?
It lists commands that commonly are added to the Quick Access Toolbar.

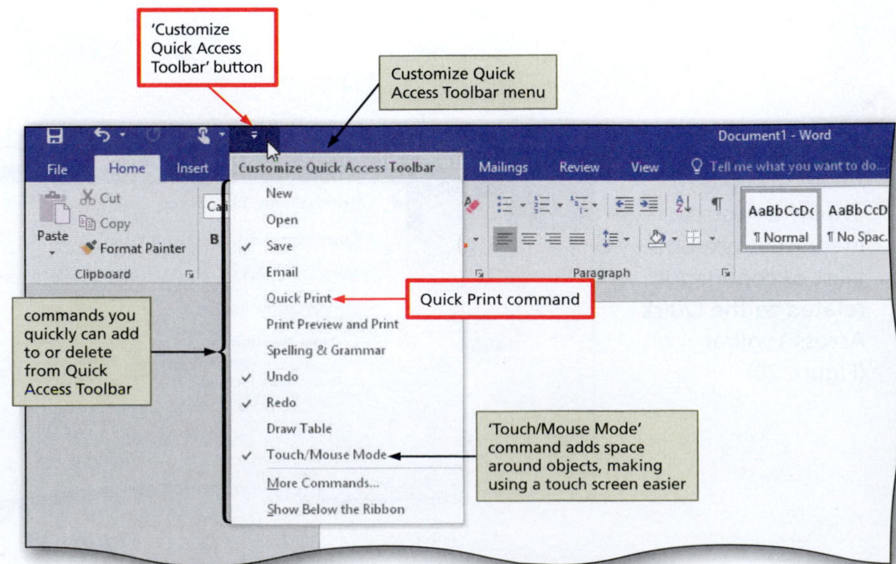

Figure 28

2

- Click Quick Print on the Customize Quick Access Toolbar menu to add the Quick Print button to the Quick Access Toolbar (Figure 29).

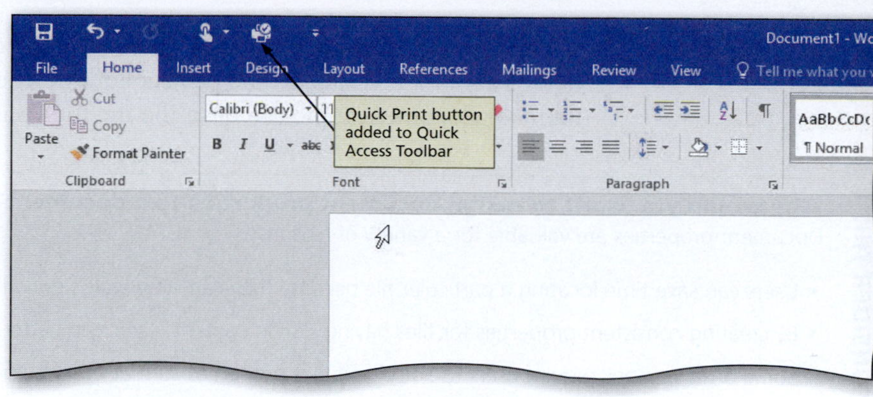

Figure 29

Q&A How would I remove a button from the Quick Access Toolbar?
You would right-click the button you wish to remove and then click 'Remove from Quick Access Toolbar' on the shortcut menu or click the 'Customize Quick Access Toolbar' button on the Quick Access Toolbar and then click the button name in the Customize Quick Access Toolbar menu to remove the check mark.

To Enter Text in a Document

1 SIGN IN | 2 USE WINDOWS | 3 USE APPS | 4 FILE MANAGEMENT | 5 SWITCH APPS | 6 SAVE FILES
7 CHANGE SCREEN RESOLUTION | 8 EXIT APPS | 9 USE ADDITIONAL APPS | 10 USE HELP

The first step in creating a document is to enter its text by typing on the keyboard. By default, Word positions text at the left margin as you type. The following steps type this first line of a flyer. ***Why?*** *To begin creating a flyer, for example, you type the headline in the document window.*

1

- Type `VISIT NATIONAL MONUMENTS` as the text (Figure 30).

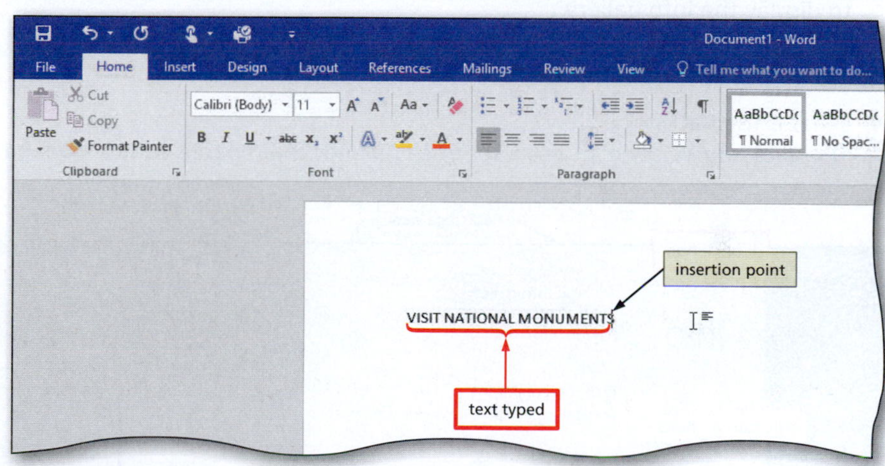

Figure 30

Q&A What is the blinking vertical bar to the right of the text?
The blinking bar is the insertion point, which indicates where text, graphics, and other items will be inserted in the document. As you type, the insertion point moves to the right, and when you reach the end of a line, it moves down to the beginning of the next line.

What if I make an error while typing?
You can press the BACKSPACE key until you have deleted the text in error and then retype the text correctly.

2

- Press the ENTER key to move the insertion point to the beginning of the next line (Figure 31).

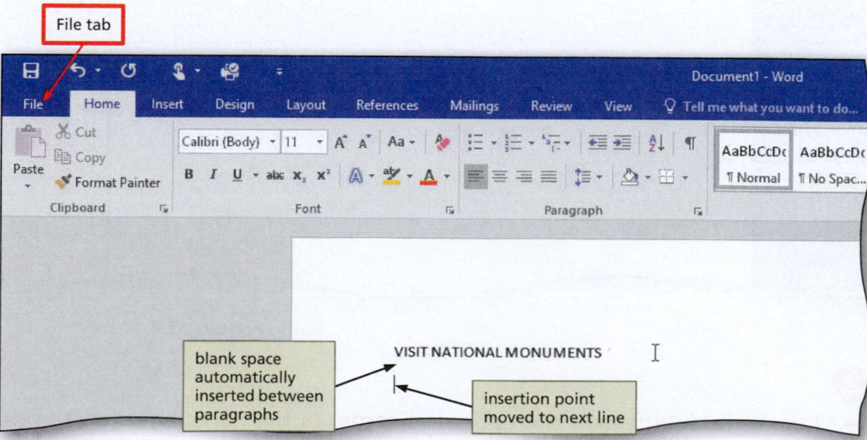

Figure 31

Q&A Why did blank space appear between the entered text and the insertion point?
Each time you press the ENTER key, Word creates a new paragraph and inserts blank space between the two paragraphs. Depending on your settings, Office may or may not insert a blank space between the two paragraphs.

Document Properties

You can organize and identify your files by using **document properties**, which are the details about a file, such as the project author, title, and subject. For example, a class name or document topic can describe the file's purpose or content.

CONSIDER THIS

Why would you want to assign document properties to a document?

Document properties are valuable for a variety of reasons:

- Users can save time locating a particular file because they can view a file's document properties without opening the file.
- By creating consistent properties for files having similar content, users can better organize their files.
- Some organizations require users to add document properties so that other employees can view details about these files.

To Change Document Properties

You can change the document properties while working with the file in an Office app. When you save the file, the Office app (Word, in this case) will save the document properties with the file. The following steps change document properties. ***Why?*** *Adding document properties will help you identify characteristics of the file without opening it.*

1

- Click File on the ribbon to open the Backstage view and then, if necessary, click the Info tab in the Backstage view to display the Info gallery.
- Click to the right of the Comments property in the Properties list, and type `CIS 101 Assignment` in the text box (Figure 32).

Q&A What is the Backstage view?
The **Backstage view** contains a set of commands that enable you to manage documents and provides data about the documents.

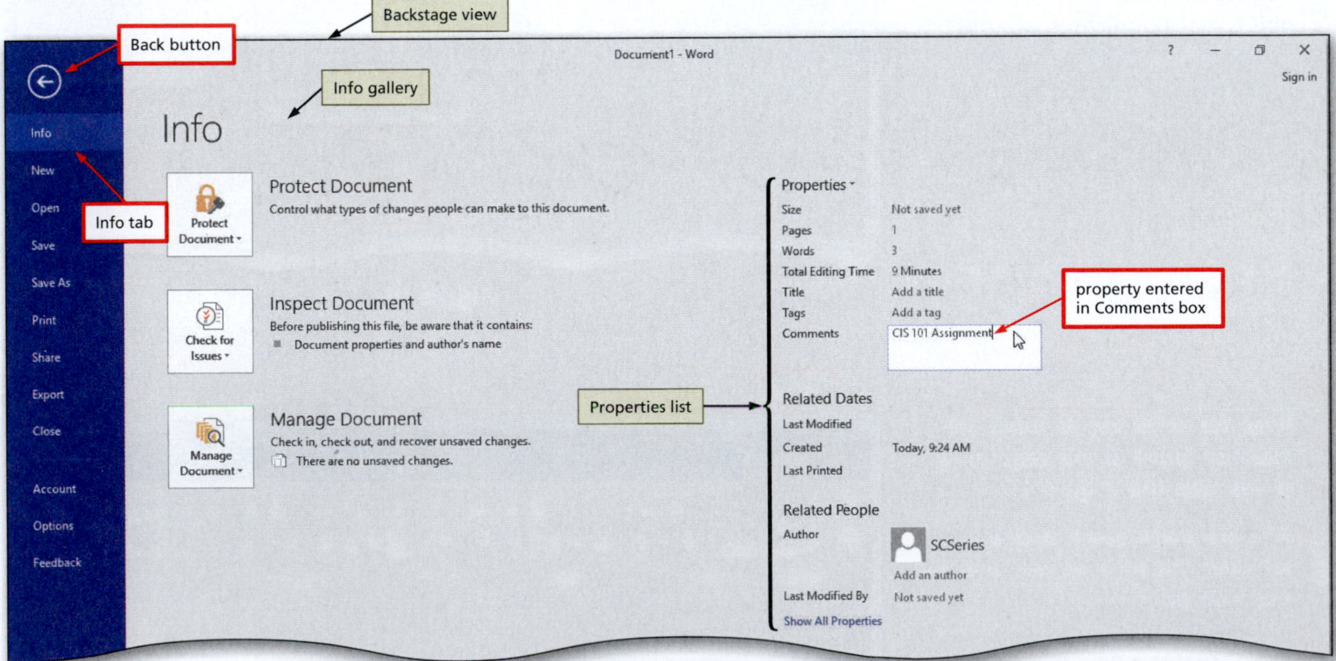

Figure 32

2

- Click the Back button in the upper-left corner of the Backstage view to return to the document window.

Printing, Saving, and Organizing Files

While you are creating a document, the computer or mobile device stores it in memory. When you save a document, the computer or mobile device places it on a storage medium, such as a hard disk, solid state drive (SSD), USB flash drive, or optical disc. The storage medium can be permanent in your computer, may be portable where you remove it from your computer, or may be on a web server you access through a network or the Internet.

A saved document is referred to as a file. A **file name** is the name assigned to a file when it is saved. When saving files, you should organize them so that you easily can find them later. Windows provides tools to help you organize files.

BTW

File Type

Depending on your Windows settings, the file type .docx may be displayed immediately to the right of the file name after you save the file. The file type .docx is a Word 2016 document.

Printing a Document

After creating a document, you may want to print it. Printing a document enables you to distribute it to others in a form that can be read or viewed but typically not edited.

CONSIDER THIS

What is the best method for distributing a document?

The traditional method of distributing a document uses a printer to produce a hard copy. A **hard copy** or **printout** is information that exists on a physical medium, such as paper. Hard copies can be useful for the following reasons:

- Some people prefer proofreading a hard copy of a document rather than viewing it on the screen to check for errors and readability.
- Hard copies can serve as a backup reference if your storage medium is lost or becomes corrupted and you need to recreate the document.

Instead of distributing a hard copy of a document, users can distribute the document as an electronic image that mirrors the original document's appearance. The electronic image of the document can be sent as an email attachment, posted on a website, or copied to a portable storage medium, such as a USB flash drive. Two popular electronic image formats, sometimes called fixed formats, are PDF by Adobe Systems and XPS by Microsoft. In Word, you can create electronic image files through the Save As dialog box and the Export, Share, and Print tabs in the Backstage view. Electronic images of documents, such as PDF and XPS, can be useful for the following reasons:

- Users can view electronic images of documents without the software that created the original document (e.g., Word). For example, to view a PDF file you use a program called Adobe Reader, which can be downloaded free from Adobe's website.
- Sending electronic documents saves paper and printer supplies. Society encourages users to contribute to **green computing**, which involves reducing the electricity consumed and environmental waste generated when using computers, mobile devices, and related technologies.

To Print a Document

1 SIGN IN | 2 USE WINDOWS | 3 USE APPS | 4 FILE MANAGEMENT | 5 SWITCH APPS | 6 SAVE FILES
7 CHANGE SCREEN RESOLUTION | 8 EXIT APPS | 9 USE ADDITIONAL APPS | 10 USE HELP

With the document opened, you may want to print it. ***Why?*** *Because you want to see how the text will appear on paper, you want to print a hard copy on a printer.* The following steps print a hard copy of the contents of the document.

- Click File on the ribbon to open the Backstage view.
- Click the Print tab in the Backstage view to display the Print gallery (Figure 33).

Q&A

How can I print multiple copies of my document?
Increase the number in the Copies box in the Print gallery.

What if I decide not to print the document at this time?
Click the Back button in the upper-left corner of the Backstage view to return to the document window.

2

- Verify that the selected printer will print a hard copy of the document. If necessary, click the Printer Status button to display a list of available printer options and then click the desired printer to change the currently selected printer.

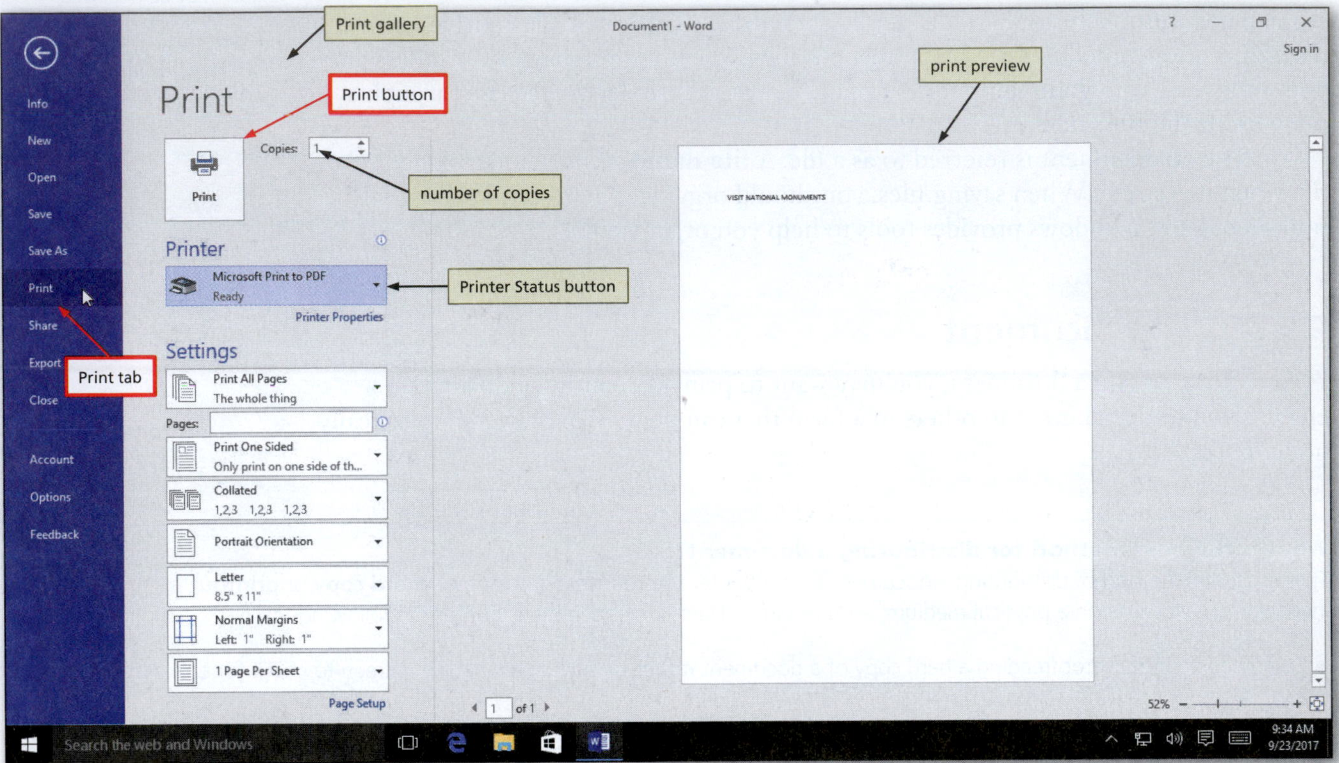

Figure 33

3

- Click the Print button in the Print gallery to print the document on the currently selected printer.
- When the printer stops, retrieve the hard copy (Figure 34).

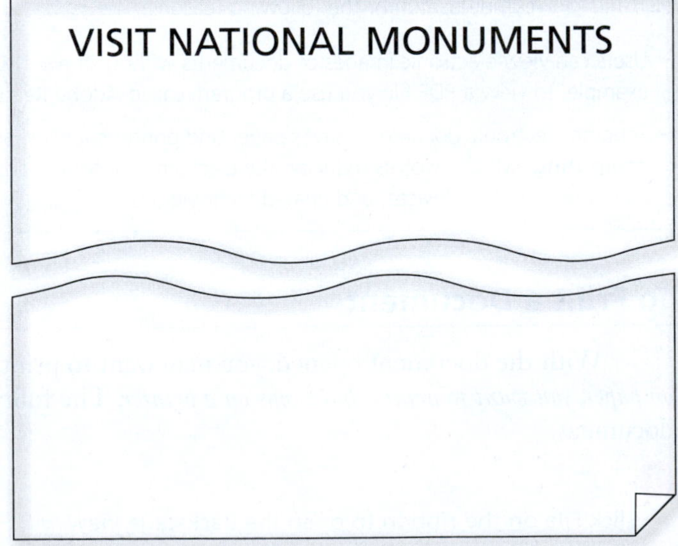

Figure 34

Q&A What if I want to print an electronic image of a document instead of a hard copy?
You would click the Printer Status button in the Print gallery and then select the desired electronic image option, such as Microsoft XPS Document Writer, which would create an XPS file.

Other Ways

1. Press CTRL+P

Organizing Files and Folders

A file contains data. This data can range from a research paper to an accounting spreadsheet to an electronic math quiz. You should organize and store files in folders to avoid misplacing a file and to help you find a file quickly.

If you are taking an introductory computer class (CIS 101, for example), you may want to design a series of folders for the different subjects covered in the class. To accomplish this, you can arrange the folders in a hierarchy for the class, as shown in Figure 35.

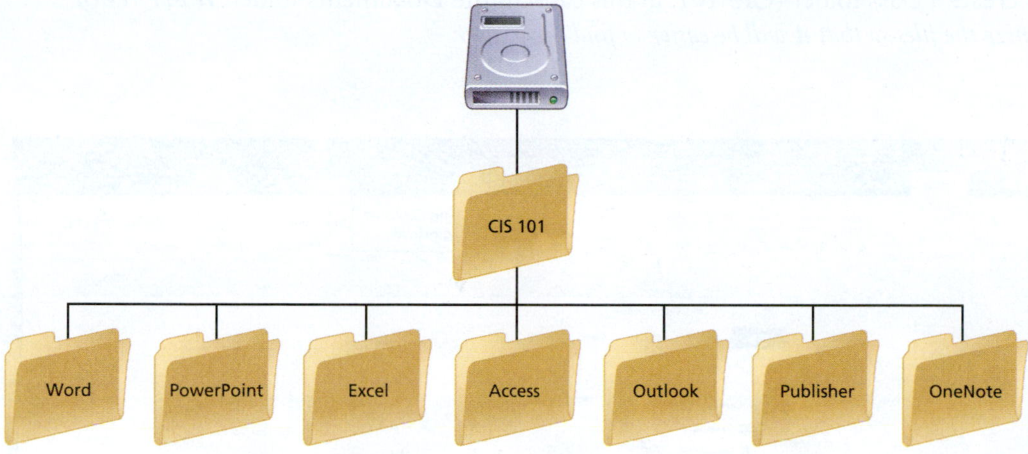

Figure 35

The hierarchy contains three levels. The first level contains the storage medium, such as a hard drive. The second level contains the class folder (CIS 101, in this case), and the third level contains seven folders, one each for a different Office app that will be covered in the class (Word, PowerPoint, Excel, Access, Outlook, Publisher, and OneNote).

When the hierarchy in Figure 35 is created, the storage medium is said to contain the CIS 101 folder, and the CIS 101 folder is said to contain the separate Office folders (i.e., Word, PowerPoint, Excel, etc.). In addition, this hierarchy easily can be expanded to include folders from other classes taken during additional semesters.

The vertical and horizontal lines in Figure 35 form a pathway that allows you to navigate to a drive or folder on a computer or network. A **path** consists of a drive letter (preceded by a drive name when necessary) and colon, to identify the storage device, and one or more folder names. A hard disk typically has a drive letter of C. Each drive or folder in the hierarchy has a corresponding path.

By default, Windows saves documents in the Documents folder, music in the Music folder, photos in the Pictures folder, videos in the Videos folder, and downloads in the Downloads folder.

The following pages illustrate the steps to organize the folders for this class and save a file in one of those folders:

1. Create the folder identifying your class.
2. Create the Word folder in the folder identifying your class.
3. Create the remaining folders in the folder identifying your class (one each for PowerPoint, Excel, Access, Outlook, Publisher, and OneNote).
4. Save a file in the Word folder.
5. Verify the location of the saved file.

To Create a Folder

When you create a folder, such as the CIS 101 folder shown in Figure 35, you must name the folder. A folder name should describe the folder and its contents. A folder name can contain spaces and any uppercase or lowercase characters, except a backslash (\), slash (/), colon (:), asterisk (*), question mark (?), quotation marks ("), less than symbol (<), greater than symbol (>), or vertical bar (|). Folder names cannot be CON, AUX, COM1, COM2, COM3, COM4, LPT1, LPT2, LPT3, PRN, or NUL. The same rules for naming folders also apply to naming files.

The following steps create a class folder (CIS 101, in this case) in the Documents folder. ***Why?*** *When storing files, you should organize the files so that it will be easier to find them later.*

1

- Click the File Explorer button on the taskbar to run the File Explorer.
- If necessary, double-click This PC in the navigation pane to expand the contents of your computer.
- Click the Documents folder in the navigation pane to display the contents of the Documents folder in the file list (Figure 36).

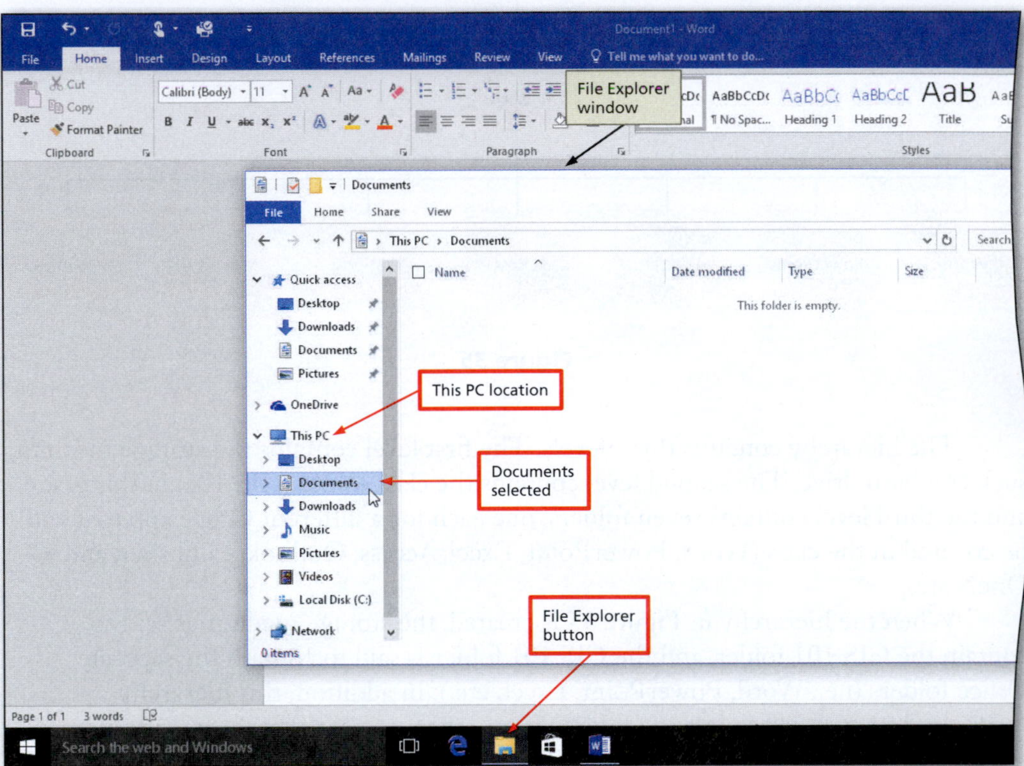

Figure 36

2

- Click the New folder button on the Quick Access Toolbar to create a new folder with the name, New folder, selected in a text box (Figure 37).

Q&A Why is the folder icon displayed differently on my computer or mobile device?
Windows might be configured to display contents differently on your computer or mobile device.

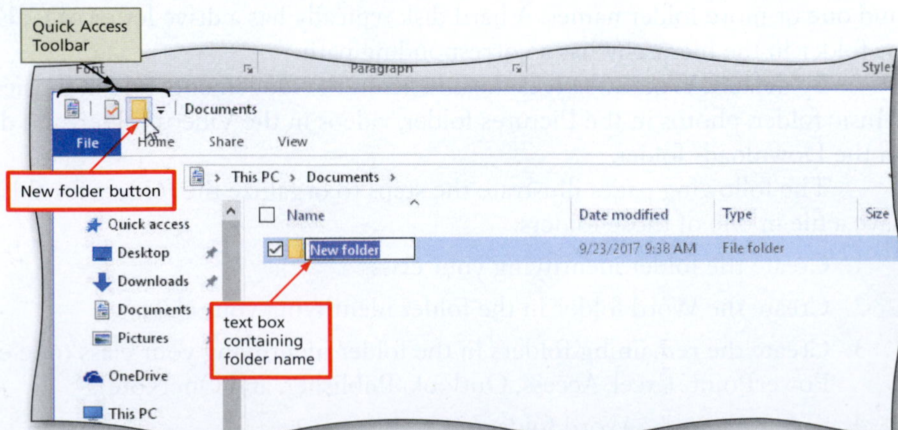

Figure 37

- Type `CIS 101` (or your class code) in the text box as the new folder name.
- If requested by your instructor, add your last name to the end of the folder name.
- Press the ENTER key to change the folder name from New folder to a folder name identifying your class (Figure 38).

Q&A What happens when I press the ENTER key?
The class folder (CIS 101, in this case) is displayed in the file list, which contains the folder name, date modified, type, and size.

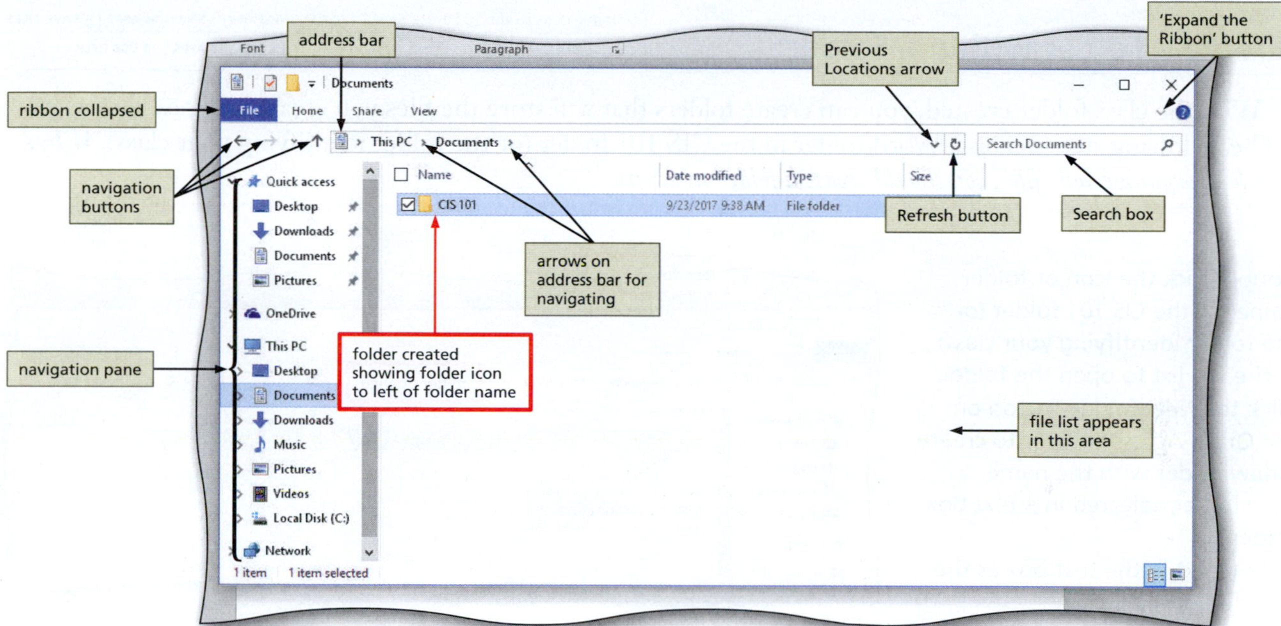

Figure 38

Other Ways

1. Press CTRL+SHIFT+N
2. Click the New folder button (Home tab | New group)

Folder Windows

The File Explorer window (shown in Figure 38) is called a folder window. Recall that a folder is a specific named location on a storage medium that contains related files. Most users rely on **folder windows** for finding, viewing, and managing information on their computers. Folder windows have common design elements, including the following (shown in Figure 38).

- The **address bar** provides quick navigation options. The arrows on the address bar allow you to visit different locations on the computer or mobile device.
- The buttons to the left of the address bar allow you to navigate the contents of the navigation pane and view recent pages.
- The **Previous Locations arrow** displays the locations you have visited.
- The **Refresh button** on the right side of the address bar refreshes the contents of the folder list.
- The **Search box** contains the dimmed words, Search Documents. You can type a term in the search box for a list of files, folders, shortcuts, and elements containing that term within the location you are searching.

- The **ribbon** contains four tabs used to accomplish various tasks on the computer related to organizing and managing the contents of the open window. This ribbon works similarly to the ribbon in the Office apps.
- The **navigation pane** on the left contains the Quick access area, the OneDrive area, the This PC area, and the Network area.
- The **Quick Access area** shows locations you access frequently. By default, this list contains links only to your Desktop, Downloads, Documents, and Pictures.

To Create a Folder within a Folder

With the class folder created, you can create folders that will store the files you create using each Office app. The following step creates a Word folder in the CIS 101 folder (or the folder identifying your class). ***Why?*** *To be able to organize your files, you should create a folder structure.*

1

- Double-click the icon or folder name for the CIS 101 folder (or the folder identifying your class) in the file list to open the folder.
- Click the New folder button on the Quick Access Toolbar to create a new folder with the name, New folder, selected in a text box folder.
- Type `Word` in the text box as the new folder name.
- Press the ENTER key to rename the folder (Figure 39).

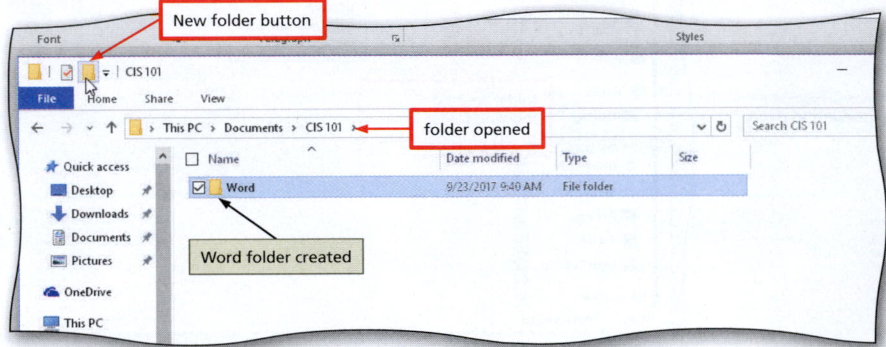

Figure 39

Other Ways

1. Press CTRL+SHIFT+N
2. Click the New folder button (Home tab | New group)

To Create the Remaining Folders

The following steps create the remaining folders in the folder identifying your class (in this case, CIS 101).

1 Click the New folder button on the Quick Access Toolbar to create a new folder with the name, New folder, selected in a text box.

2 Type `PowerPoint` in the text box as the new folder name.

3 Press the ENTER key to rename the folder.

4 Repeat Steps 1 through 3 to create each of the remaining folders, using Excel, Access, Outlook, Publisher, and OneNote as the folder names (Figure 40).

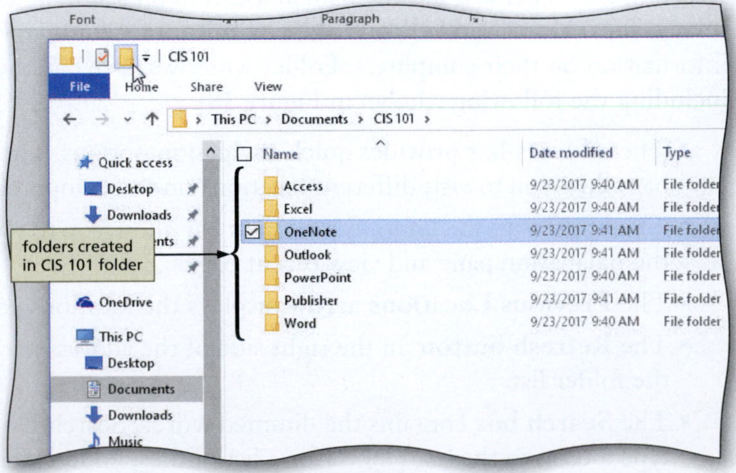

Figure 40

To Expand a Folder, Scroll through Folder Contents, and Collapse a Folder

Folder windows display the hierarchy of items and the contents of drives and folders in the file list. You might want to expand a folder in the navigation pane to view its contents, scroll through its contents, and collapse it when you are finished viewing its contents. ***Why?*** *When a folder is expanded, you can see all the folders it contains. By contrast, a collapsed folder hides the folders it contains.* The following steps expand, scroll through, and then collapse the folder identifying your class (CIS 101, in this case).

1

- Double-click the Documents folder in the This PC area of the navigation pane, which expands the folder to display its contents and displays a black arrow to the left of the Documents folder icon (Figure 41).

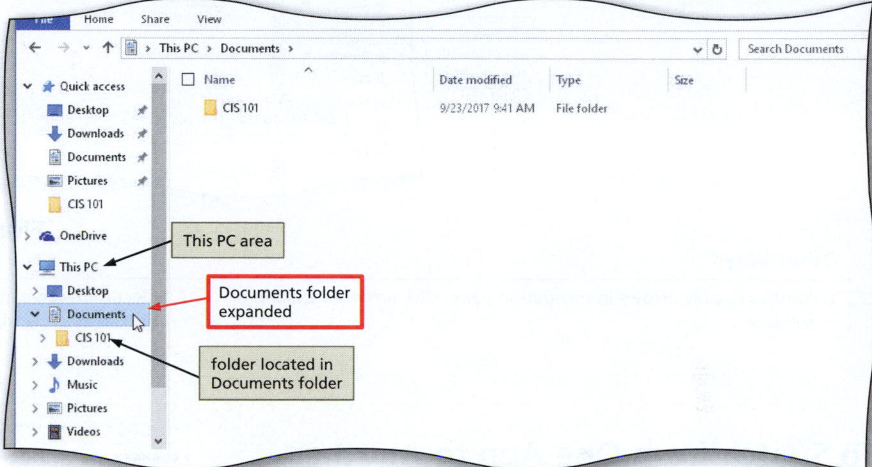

Figure 41

2

- Double-click the CIS 101 folder, which expands the folder to display its contents and displays a black arrow to the left of the folder icon (Figure 42).

- Drag the scroll box down or click the down scroll arrow on the vertical scroll bar to display additional folders at the bottom of the navigation pane. Drag the scroll box up or click the scroll bar above the scroll box to move the scroll box to the top of the navigation pane. Drag the scroll box down the scroll bar until the scroll box is halfway down the scroll bar.

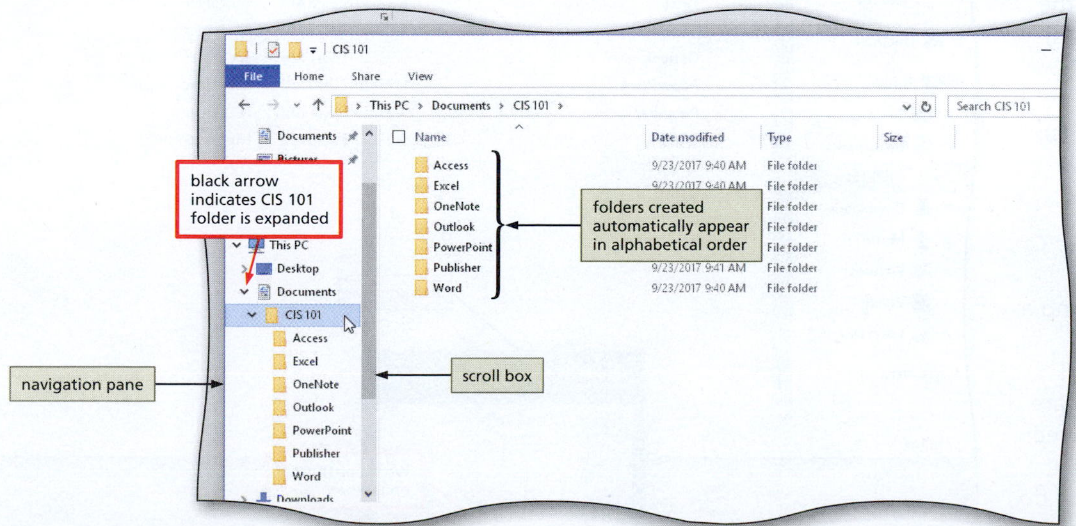

Figure 42

3

- Double-click the folder identifying your class (CIS 101, in this case) to collapse the folder (Figure 43).

Q&A Why are some folders indented below others?
A folder contains the indented folders below it.

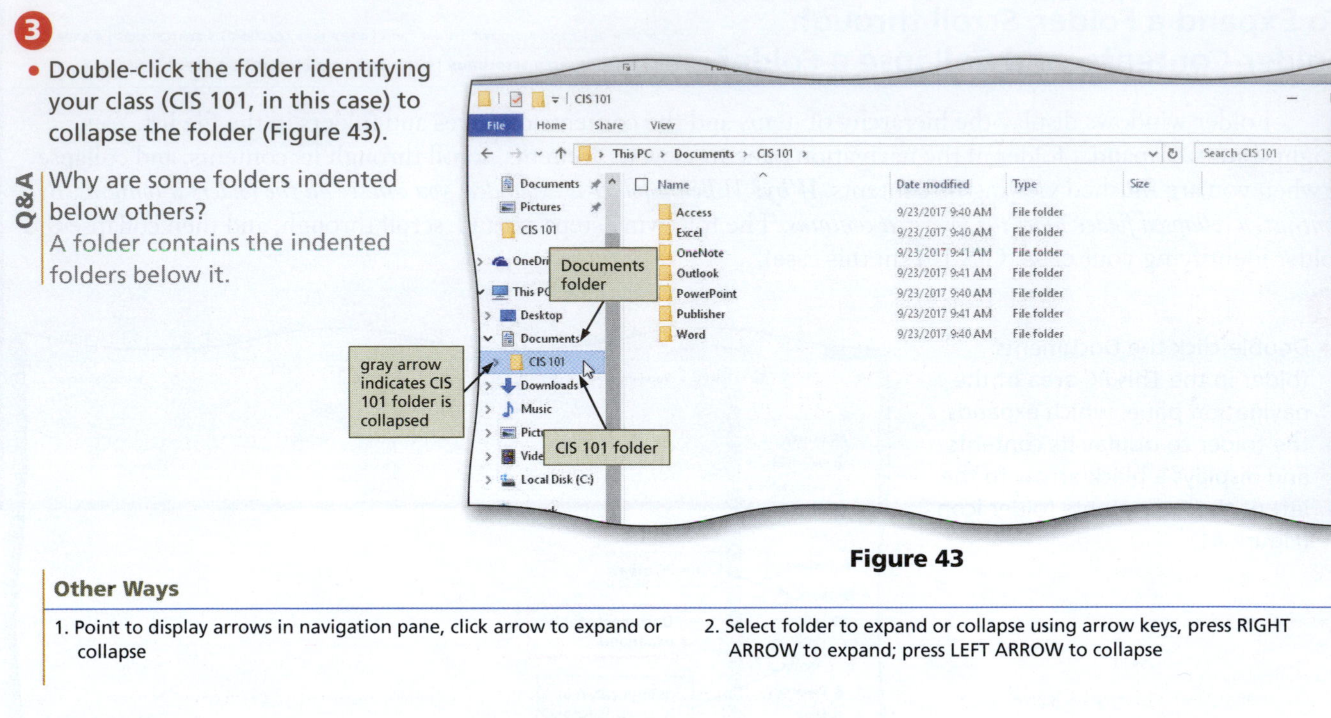

Figure 43

Other Ways

1. Point to display arrows in navigation pane, click arrow to expand or collapse
2. Select folder to expand or collapse using arrow keys, press RIGHT ARROW to expand; press LEFT ARROW to collapse

To Switch from One App to Another

1 SIGN IN | 2 USE WINDOWS | 3 USE APPS | 4 FILE MANAGEMENT | **5 SWITCH APPS** | 6 SAVE FILES
7 CHANGE SCREEN RESOLUTION | 8 EXIT APPS | 9 USE ADDITIONAL APPS | 10 USE HELP

The next step is to save the Word file containing the headline you typed earlier. Word, however, currently is not the active window. You can use the button on the taskbar and live preview to switch to Word and then save the document in the Word document window.

Why? *By clicking the appropriate app button on the taskbar, you can switch to the open app you want to use.* The steps below switch to the Word window; however, the steps are the same for any active Office app currently displayed as a button on the taskbar.

1

- Point to the Word app button on the taskbar to see a live preview of the open document(s) or the window title(s) of the open document(s), depending on your computer's configuration (Figure 44).

Q&A What if I am using a touch screen?
Live preview will not work if you are using a touch screen. If you are using a touch screen and do not have a mouse, proceed to Step 2.

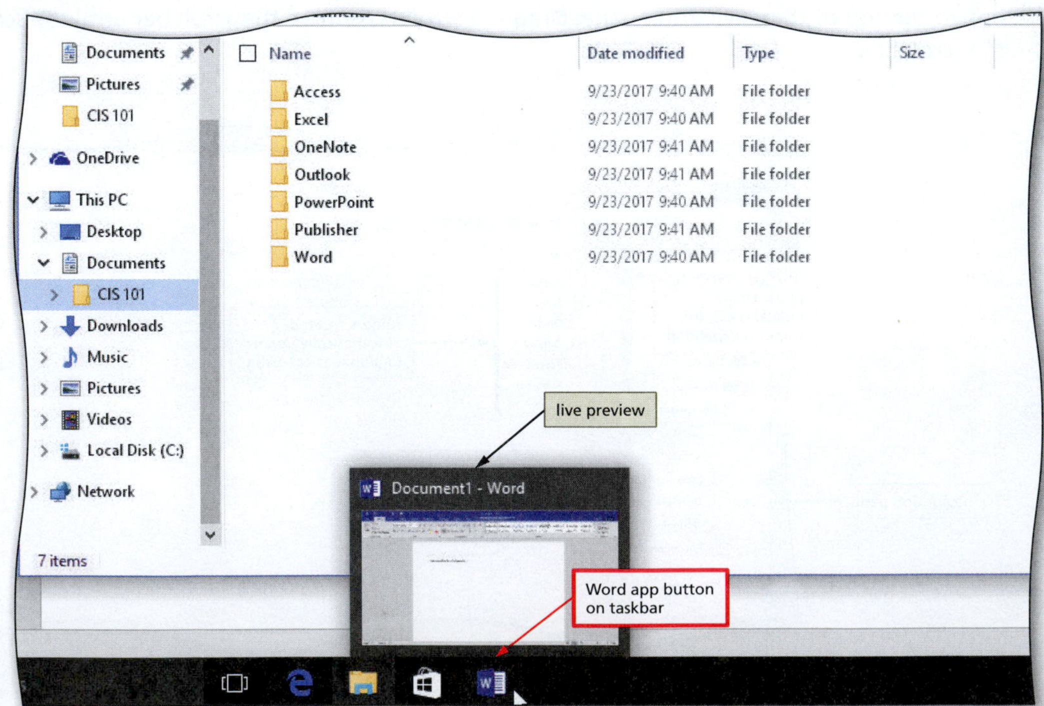

Figure 44

2

- Click the button or the live preview to make the app associated with the app button the active window (Figure 45).

Q&A What if multiple documents are open in an app?
Click the desired live preview to switch to the window you want to use.

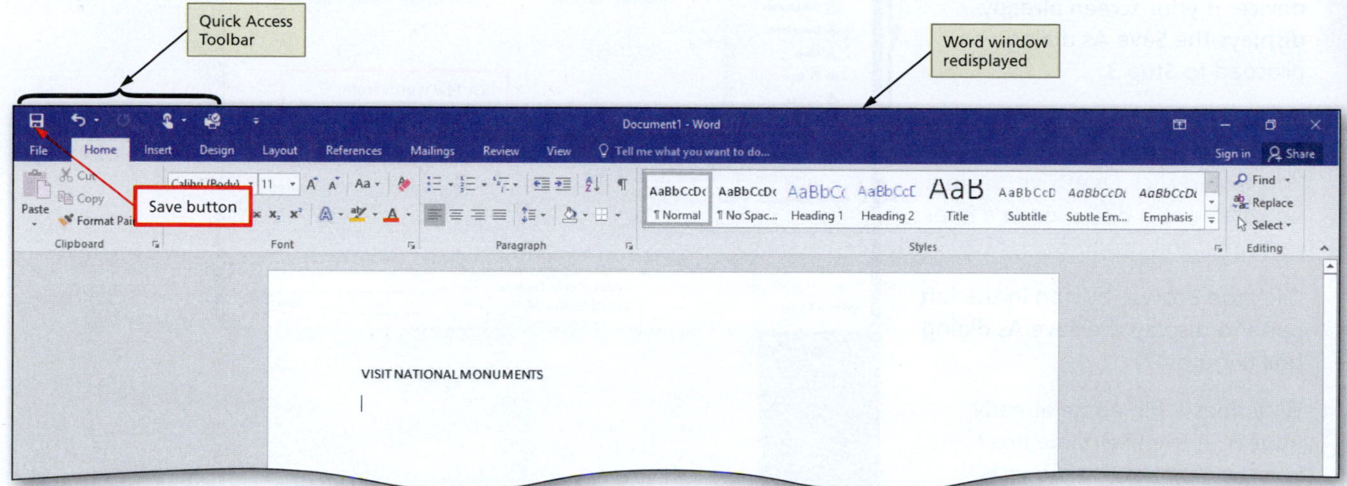

Figure 45

Other Ways

1. Press ALT+TAB until app you wish to display is selected

To Save a File in a Folder

1 SIGN IN | 2 USE WINDOWS | 3 USE APPS | 4 FILE MANAGEMENT | 5 SWITCH APPS | 6 SAVE FILES
7 CHANGE SCREEN RESOLUTION | 8 EXIT APPS | 9 USE ADDITIONAL APPS | 10 USE HELP

With the folders for storing your files created, you can save the Word document. ***Why?** Without saving a file, you may lose all the work you have done and will be unable to reuse or share it with others later.* The following steps save a file in the Word folder contained in your class folder (CIS 101, in this case) using the file name, National Monuments.

1

- Click the Save button (shown in Figure 45) on the Quick Access Toolbar, which depending on settings, will display either the Save As gallery in the Backstage view (Figure 46) or the Save As dialog box (Figure 47).

Q&A What if the Save As gallery is not displayed in the Backstage view?
Click the Save As tab to display the Save As gallery.

How do I close the Backstage view?
Click the Back button in the upper-left corner of the Backstage view to return to the app window.

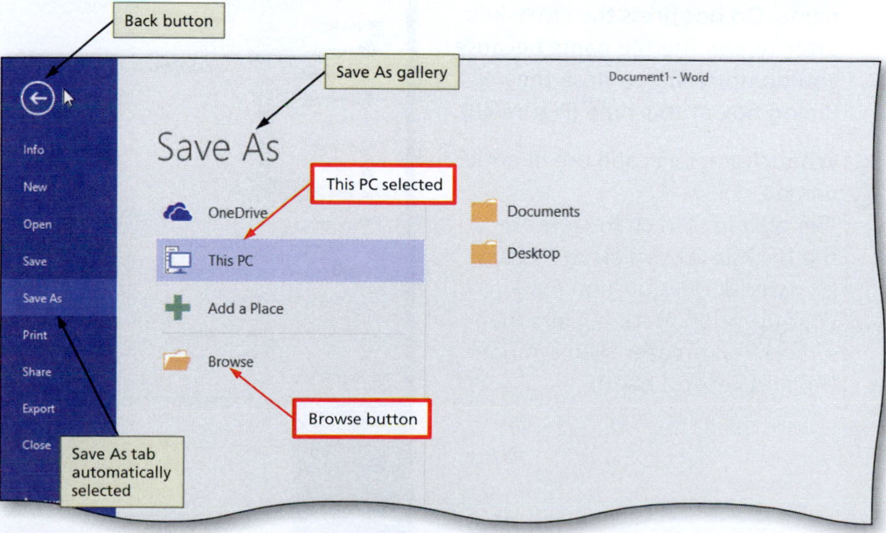

Figure 46

2

- If your screen displays the Backstage view, click This PC, if necessary, to display options in the right pane related to saving on your computer or mobile device; if your screen already displays the Save As dialog box, proceed to Step 3.

Q&A What if I wanted to save on OneDrive instead?
You would click OneDrive. Saving on OneDrive is discussed in a later section in this module.

- Click the Browse button in the left pane to display the Save As dialog box (Figure 47).

Q&A Why does a file name already appear in the File name box?
Word automatically suggests a file name the first time you save a document. The file name normally consists of the first few words contained in the document. Because the suggested file name is selected, you do not need to delete it; as soon as you begin typing, the new file name replaces the selected text.

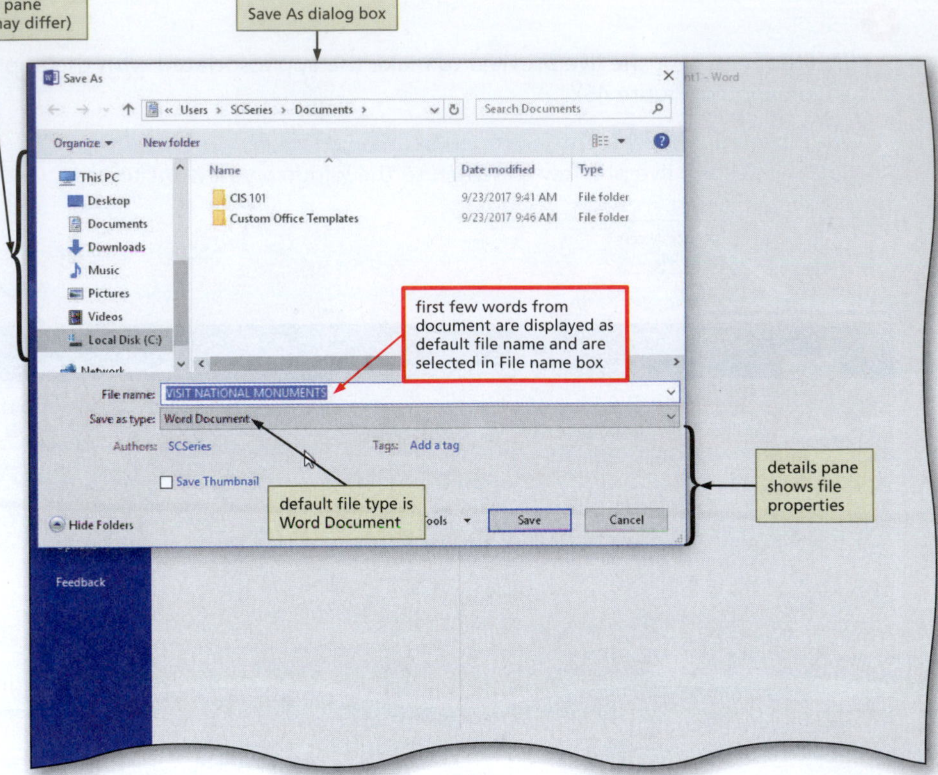

Figure 47

3

- Type **`National Monuments`** in the File name box (Save As dialog box) to change the file name. Do not press the ENTER key after typing the file name because you do not want to close the dialog box at this time (Figure 48).

Q&A What characters can I use in a file name?
The only invalid characters are the backslash (\), slash (/), colon (:), asterisk (*), question mark (?), quotation mark ("), less than symbol (<), greater than symbol (>), and vertical bar (|).

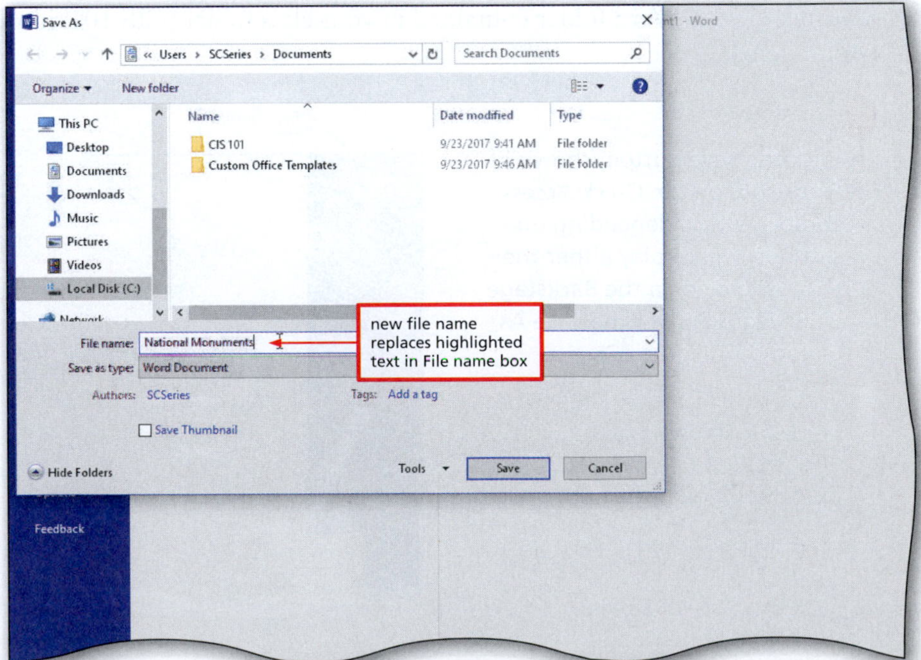

Figure 48

- Navigate to the desired save location (in this case, the Word folder in the CIS 101 folder [or your class folder] in the Documents folder) by performing the tasks in Steps 4a and 4b.

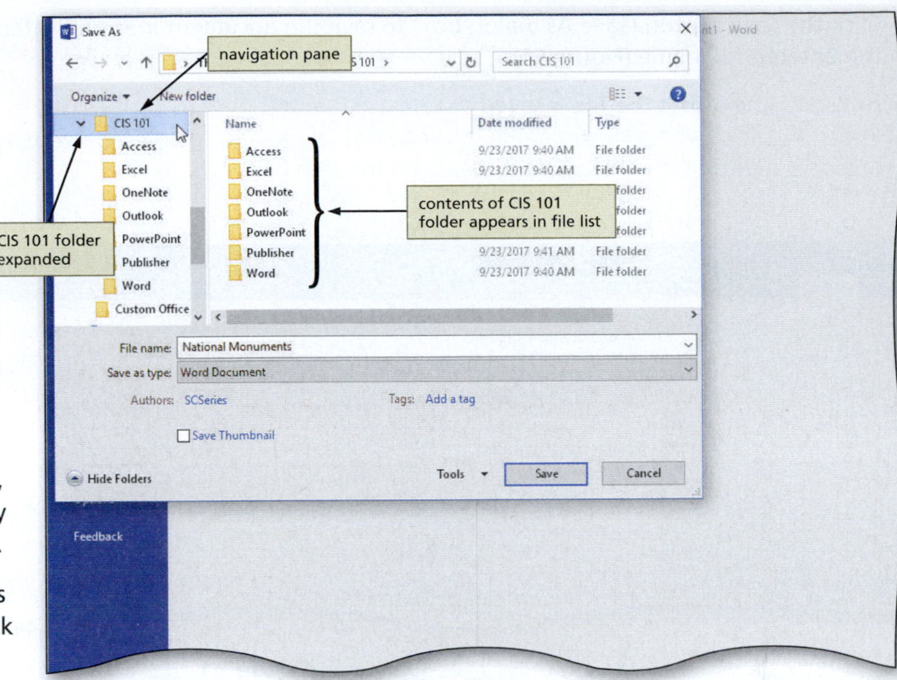

Figure 49

- If the Documents folder is not displayed in the navigation pane, drag the scroll bar in the navigation pane until Documents appears.
- If the Documents folder is not expanded in the navigation pane, double-click Documents to display its folders in the navigation pane.
- If your class folder (CIS 101, in this case) is not expanded, double-click the CIS 101 folder to select the folder and display its contents in the navigation pane (Figure 49).

Q&A What if I do not want to save in a folder?
Although storing files in folders is an effective technique for organizing files, some users prefer not to store files in folders. If you prefer not to save this file in a folder, select the storage device on which you wish to save the file and then proceed to Step 5.

4b

- Click the Word folder in the navigation pane to select it as the new save location and display its contents in the file list (Figure 50).

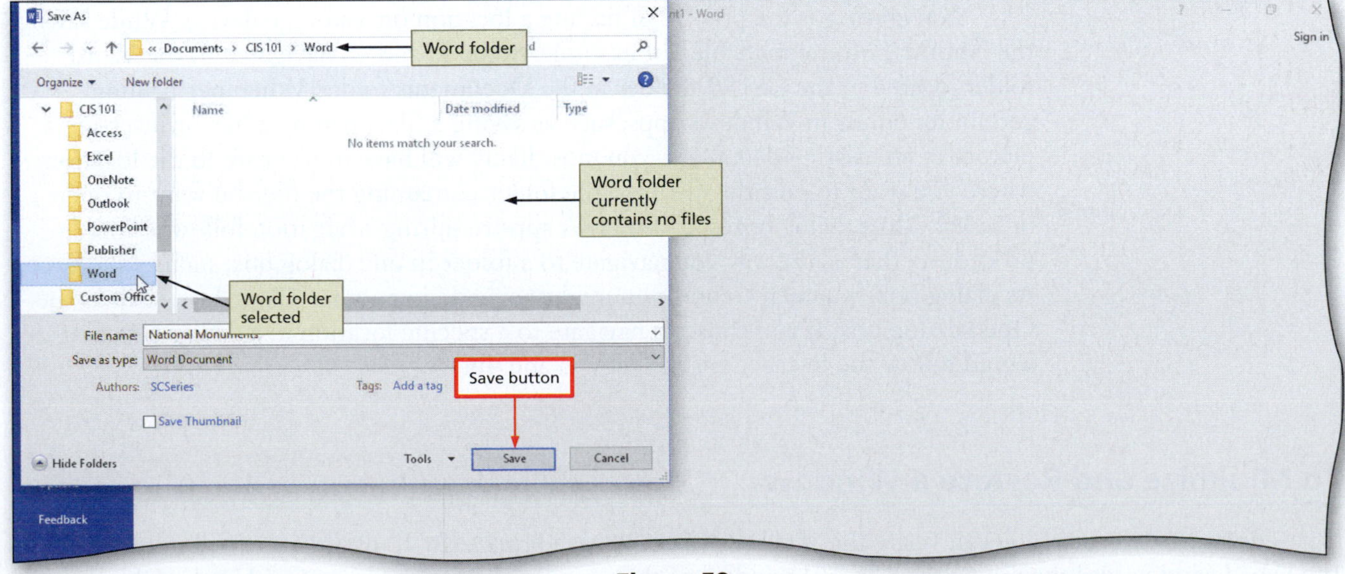

Figure 50

- Click the Save button (Save As dialog box) to save the document in the selected folder in the selected location with the entered file name (Figure 51).

Q&A | How do I know that the file is saved?
While an Office app is saving a file, it briefly displays a message on the status bar indicating the amount of the file saved. In addition, the file name appears on the title bar.

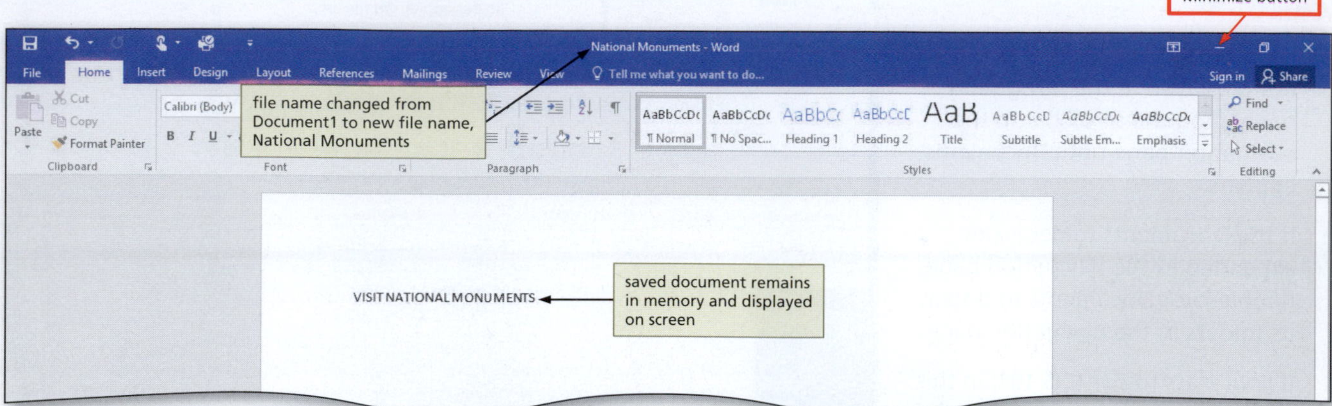

Figure 51

Other Ways

1. Click File on ribbon, click Save As in Backstage view, click This PC, click Browse button, type file name (Save As dialog box), navigate to desired save location, click Save button
2. Press F12, type file name (Save As dialog box), navigate to desired save location, click Save button

CONSIDER THIS

How often should you save a document?

It is important to save a document frequently for the following reasons:

- The document in memory might be lost if the computer is turned off or you lose electrical power while an app is running.
- If you run out of time before completing a project, you may finish it at a future time without starting over.

Navigating in Dialog Boxes

Navigating is the process of finding a location on a storage device. While saving the National Monuments file, for example, Steps 4a and 4b navigated to the Word folder located in the CIS 101 folder in the Documents folder. When performing certain functions in Windows apps, such as saving a file, opening a file, or inserting a picture in an existing document, you most likely will have to navigate to the location where you want to save the file or to the folder containing the file you want to open or insert. Most dialog boxes in Windows apps requiring navigation follow a similar procedure; that is, the way you navigate to a folder in one dialog box, such as the Save As dialog box, is similar to how you might navigate in another dialog box, such as the Open dialog box. If you chose to navigate to a specific location in a dialog box, you would follow the instructions in Steps 4a and 4b.

To Minimize and Restore a Window

1 SIGN IN | **2 USE WINDOWS** | 3 USE APPS | 4 FILE MANAGEMENT | 5 SWITCH APPS | 6 SAVE FILES
7 CHANGE SCREEN RESOLUTION | 8 EXIT APPS | 9 USE ADDITIONAL APPS | 10 USE HELP

Before continuing, you can verify that the Word file was saved properly. To do this, you will minimize the Word window and then open the CIS 101 window so that you can verify the file is stored in the CIS 101 folder on the hard drive. A **minimized window** is an open window that is hidden from view but can be displayed quickly by clicking the window's button on the taskbar.

In the following example, Word is used to illustrate minimizing and restoring windows; however, you would follow the same steps regardless of the Office app you are using. ***Why?*** *Before closing an app, you should make sure your file saved correctly so that you can find it later.*

The following steps minimize the Word window, verify that the file is saved, and then restore the minimized window.

1

- Click the Minimize button on the app's title bar (shown in Figure 51) to minimize the window (Figure 52).

Q&A Is the minimized window still available?

The minimized window, Word in this case, remains available but no longer is the active window. It is minimized as a button on the taskbar.

- If the File Explorer window is not open on the screen, click the File Explorer button on the taskbar to make the File Explorer window the active window.

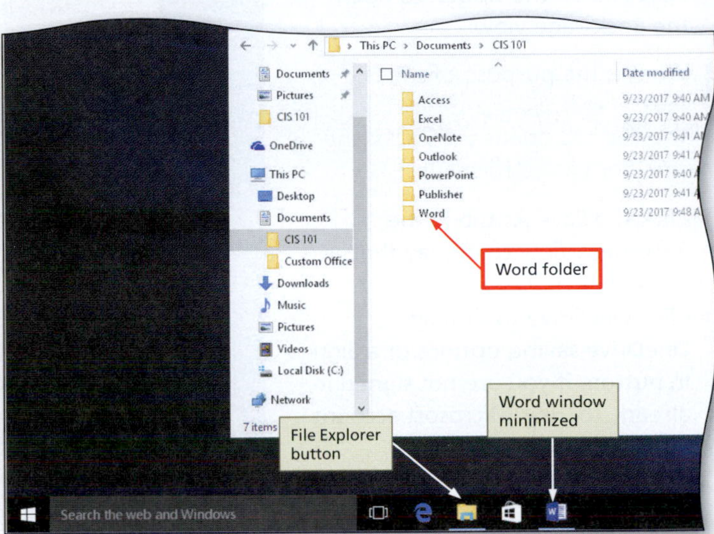

Figure 52

2

- Double-click the Word folder in the file list to select the folder and display its contents (Figure 53).

Q&A Why does the File Explorer button on the taskbar change?

A selected app button indicates that the app is active on the screen. When the button is not selected, the app is running but not active.

3

- After viewing the contents of the selected folder, click the Word button on the taskbar to restore the minimized window (as shown in Figure 51).

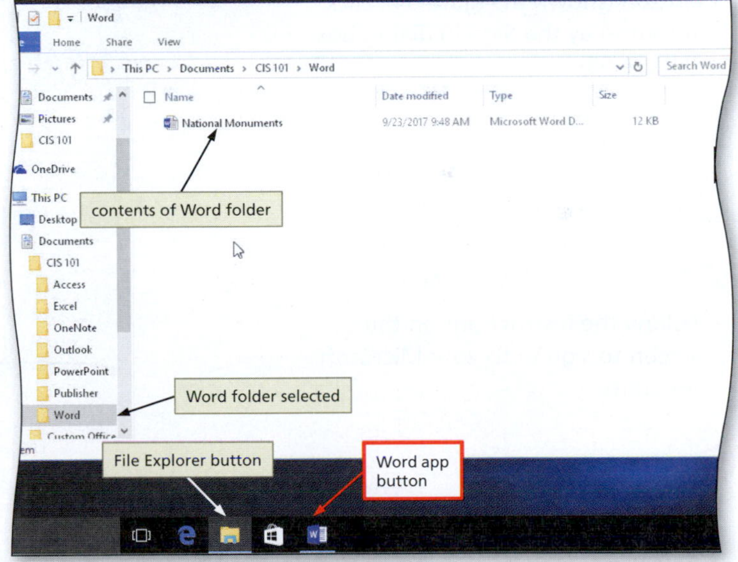

Figure 53

Other Ways

1. Right-click title bar, click Minimize on shortcut menu, click taskbar button in taskbar button area
2. Press WINDOWS+M, press WINDOWS+SHIFT+M
3. Click Word app button on taskbar to minimize window. Click Word app button again to restore window.

1 SIGN IN | 2 USE WINDOWS | 3 USE APPS | 4 FILE MANAGEMENT | 5 SWITCH APPS | **6 SAVE FILES**
7 CHANGE SCREEN RESOLUTION | 8 EXIT APPS | 9 USE ADDITIONAL APPS | 10 USE HELP

To Save a File on OneDrive

One of the features of Office is the capability to save files on OneDrive so that you can use the files on multiple computers or mobile devices without having to use an external storage device, such as a USB flash drive. Storing files on OneDrive also enables you to share files more efficiently with others, such as when using Office Online and Office 365.

In the following example, Word is used to save a file on OneDrive. ***Why?*** *Storing files on OneDrive provides more portability options than are available from storing files in the Documents folder.*

You can save files directly on OneDrive from within an Office app. The following steps save the current Word file on OneDrive. These steps require you have a Microsoft account and an Internet connection.

- Click File on the ribbon to open the Backstage view.

Q&A What is the purpose of the File tab?
The File tab opens the Backstage view for each Office app.

- Click the Save As tab in the Backstage view to display the Save As gallery.
- Click OneDrive to display OneDrive saving options or a Sign In button, if you are not signed in already to your Microsoft account (Figure 54).

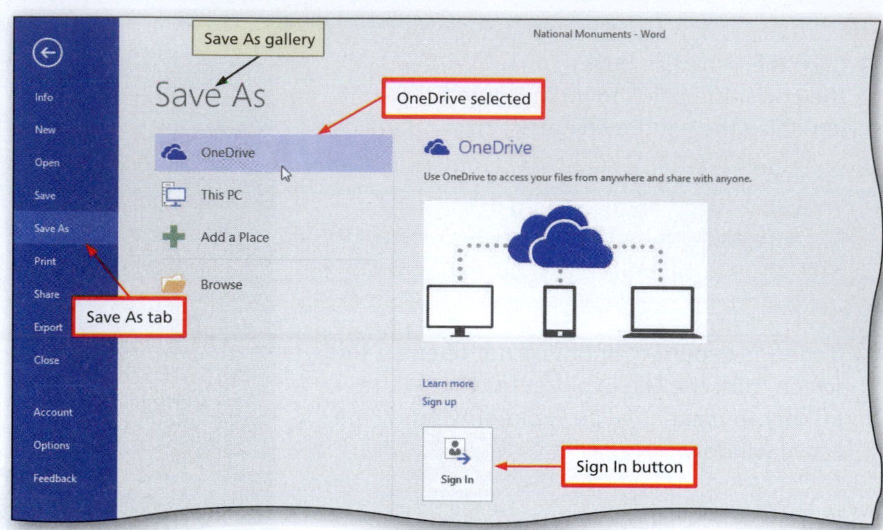

Figure 54

- If your screen displays a Sign In button (shown in Figure 54), click it to display the Sign in dialog box (Figure 55).

Q&A What if the Sign In button does not appear?
If you already are signed into your Microsoft account, the Sign In button will not be displayed. In this case, proceed to Step 3.

- Follow the instructions on the screen to sign in to your Microsoft account.

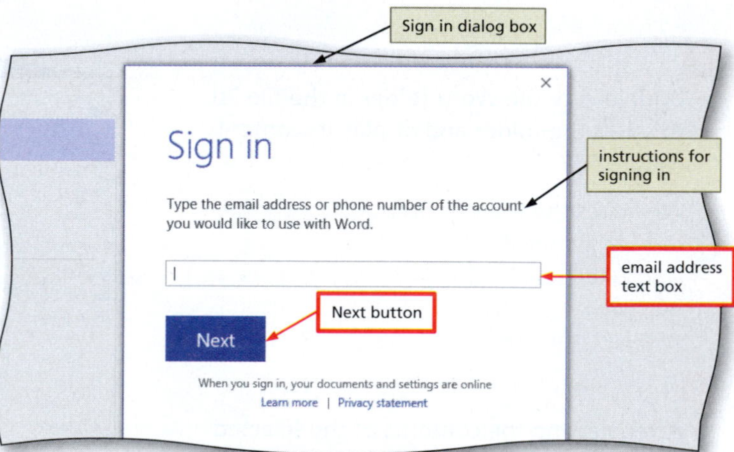

Figure 55

- If necessary, click OneDrive in the left pane.
- In the Backstage view, click the Documents folder in the right pane to display the Save As dialog box (Figure 56).

- Click the Save button (Save As dialog box) to save the file on OneDrive.

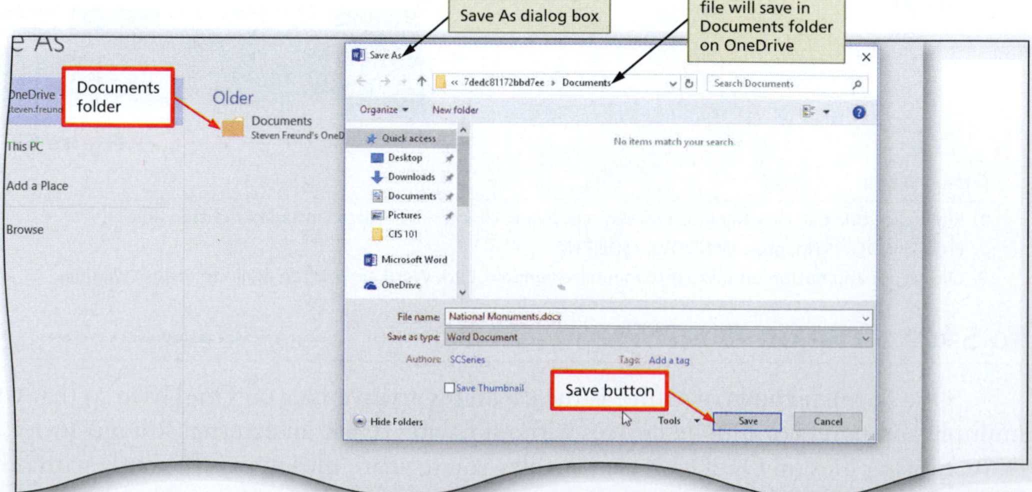

Figure 56

To Sign Out of a Microsoft Account

If you are using a public computer or otherwise wish to sign out of your Microsoft account, you should sign out of the account from the Accounts gallery in the Backstage view. Signing out of the account is the safest way to make sure that nobody else can access online files or settings stored in your Microsoft account. ***Why?*** *For security reasons, you should sign out of your Microsoft account when you are finished using a public or shared computer. Staying signed in to your Microsoft account might enable others to access your files.*

The following steps sign out of a Microsoft account from Word. You would use the same steps in any Office app. If you do not wish to sign out of your Microsoft account, read these steps without performing them.

1. Click File on the ribbon to open the Backstage view.
2. Click the Account tab to display the Account gallery (Figure 57).
3. Click the Sign out link, which displays the Remove Account dialog box. If a Can't remove Windows accounts dialog box appears instead of the Remove Account dialog box, click the OK button and skip the remaining steps.

Q&A Why does a Can't remove Windows accounts dialog box appear?
If you signed in to Windows using your Microsoft account, then you also must sign out from Windows, rather than signing out from within Word. When you are finished using Windows, be sure to sign out at that time.

4. Click the Yes button (Remove Account dialog box) to sign out of your Microsoft account on this computer.

Q&A Should I sign out of Windows after removing my Microsoft account?
When you are finished using the computer, you should sign out of Windows for maximum security.

5. Click the Back button in the upper-left corner of the Backstage view to return to the document.

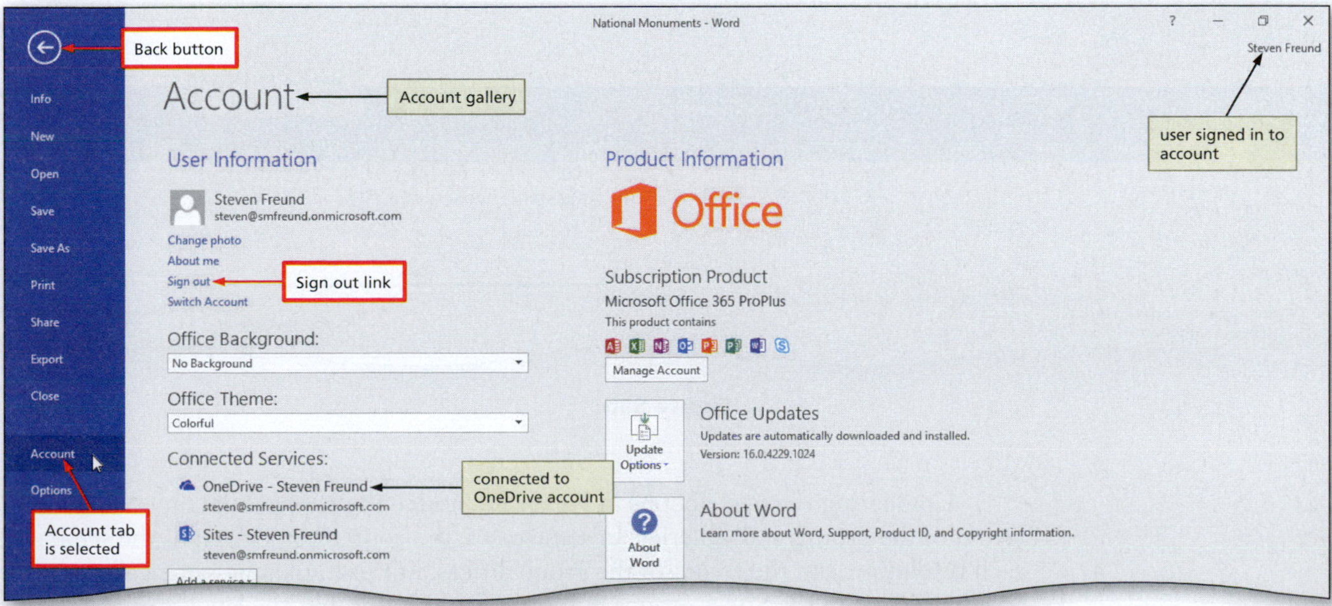

Figure 57

Screen Resolution

Screen resolution indicates the number of pixels (dots) that the computer uses to display the letters, numbers, graphics, and background you see on the screen. When you increase the screen resolution, Windows displays more information on the screen, but the information decreases in size. The reverse also is true: as you decrease the screen resolution, Windows displays less information on the screen, but the information increases in size.

Screen resolution usually is stated as the product of two numbers, such as 1366 × 768 (pronounced "thirteen sixty-six by seven sixty-eight"). A 1366 × 768 screen resolution results in a display of 1366 distinct pixels on each of 768 lines, or about 1,050,624 pixels. Changing the screen resolution affects how the ribbon appears in Office apps and some Windows dialog boxes. Figure 58 shows the Word ribbon at screen resolutions of 1366 × 768 and 1024 × 768. All of the same commands are available regardless of screen resolution. The app (Word, in this case), however, makes changes to the groups and the buttons within the groups to accommodate the various screen resolutions. The result is that certain commands may need to be accessed differently depending on the resolution chosen. A command that is visible on the ribbon and available by clicking a button at one resolution may not be visible and may need to be accessed using its Dialog Box Launcher at a different resolution.

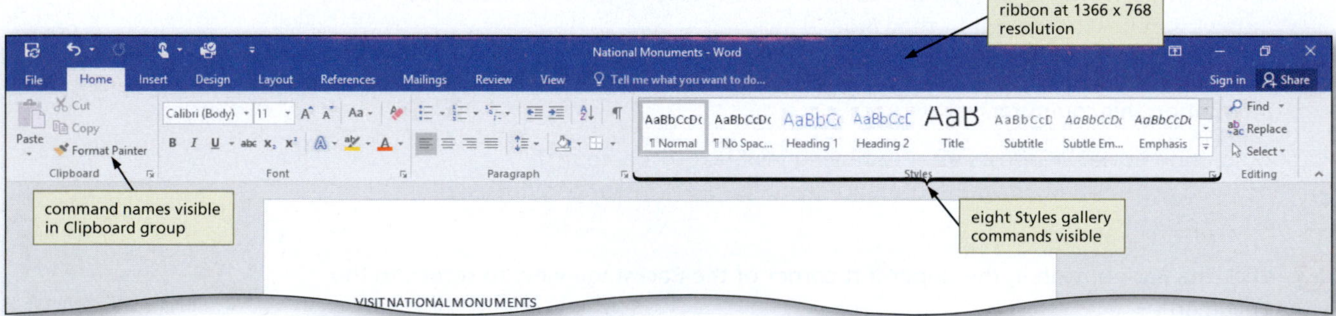

Figure 58a

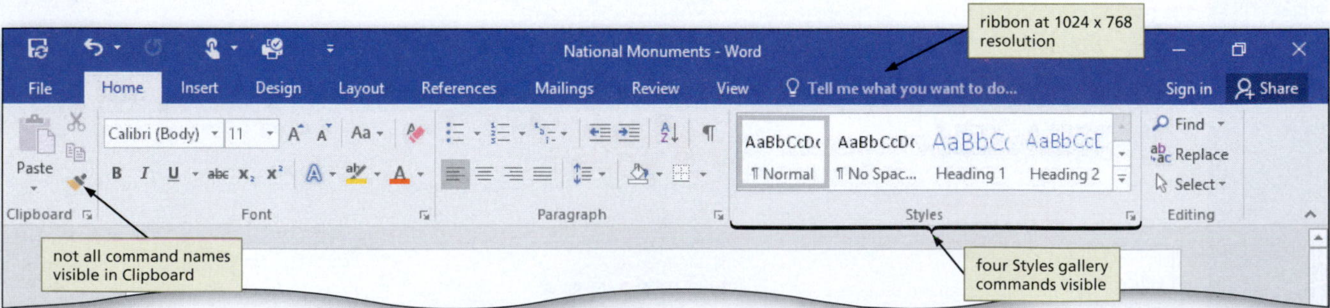

Figure 58b

Comparing the two ribbons in Figure 58, notice the changes in content and layout of the groups and galleries. In some cases, the content of a group is the same in each resolution, but the layout of the group differs. For example, the same gallery and buttons appear in the Styles groups in the two resolutions, but the layouts differ. In other cases, the content and layout are the same across the resolution, but the level of detail differs with the resolution.

To Change the Screen Resolution

If you are using a computer to step through the modules in this book and you want your screen to match the figures, you may need to change your screen's resolution. ***Why?*** *The figures in this book use a screen resolution of 1366 × 768.* The following steps change the screen resolution to 1366 × 768. Your computer already may be set to 1366 × 768. Keep in mind that many computer labs prevent users from changing the screen resolution; in that case, read the following steps for illustration purposes.

1

- Click the Show desktop button, which is located at the far-right edge of the taskbar, to display the Windows desktop.
- Right-click an empty area on the Windows desktop to display a shortcut menu that contains a list of commands related to the desktop (Figure 59).

Q&A Why does my shortcut menu display different commands?
Depending on your computer's hardware and configuration, different commands might appear on the shortcut menu.

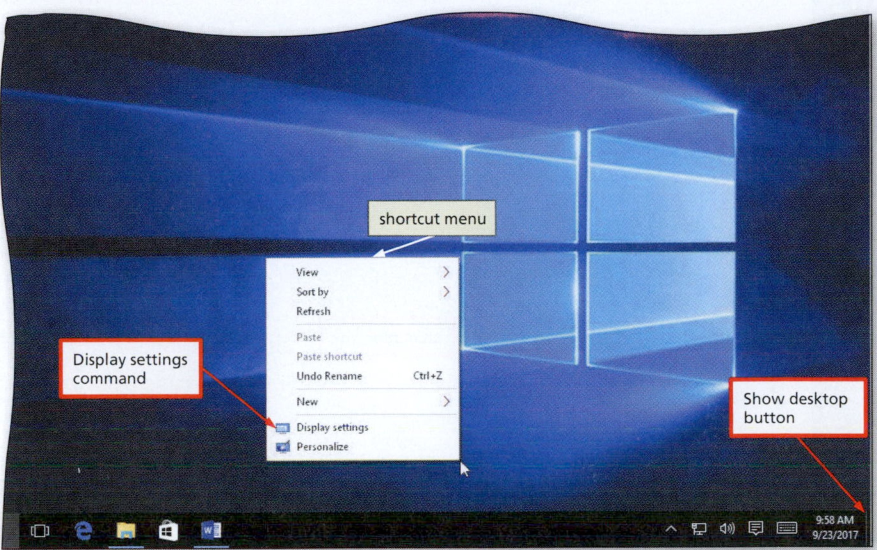

Figure 59

2

- Click Display settings on the shortcut menu to open the Settings app window. If necessary, scroll to display the 'Advanced display settings' link (Figure 60).

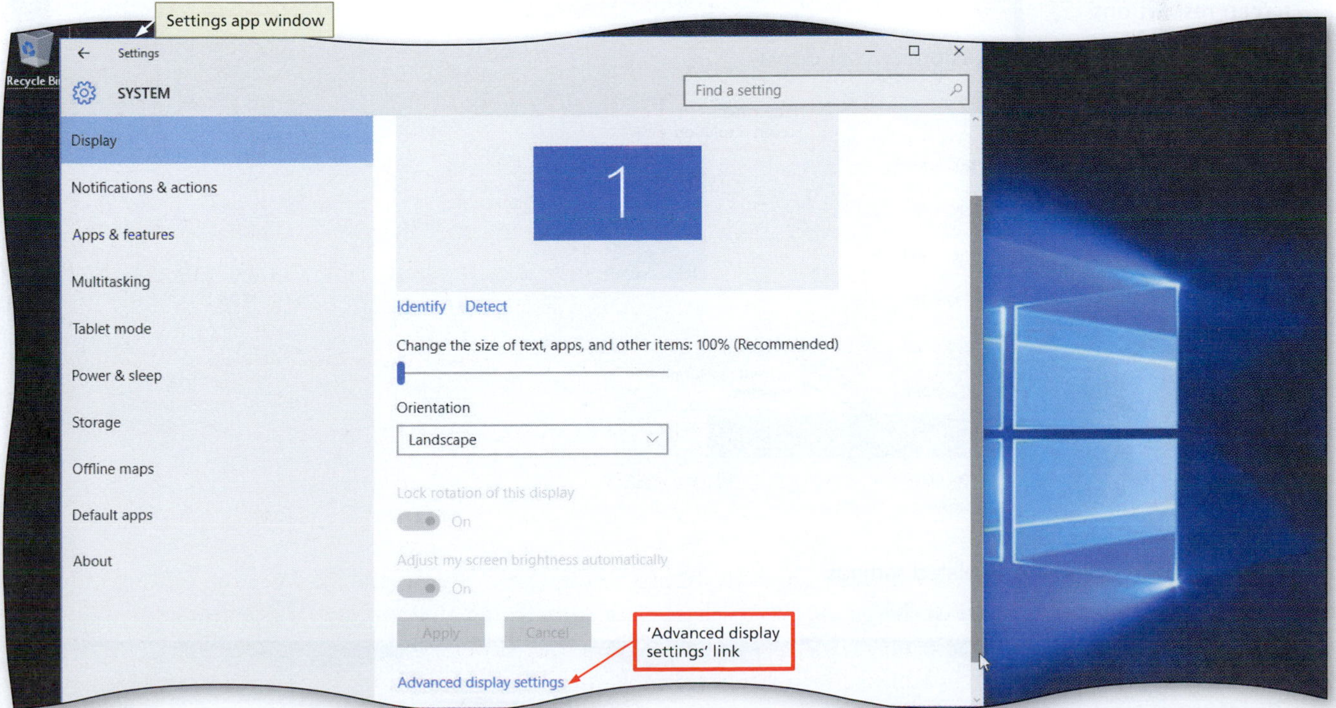

Figure 60

- Click 'Advanced display settings' in the Settings window to display the advanced display settings.
- If necessary, scroll to display the Resolution box (Figure 61).

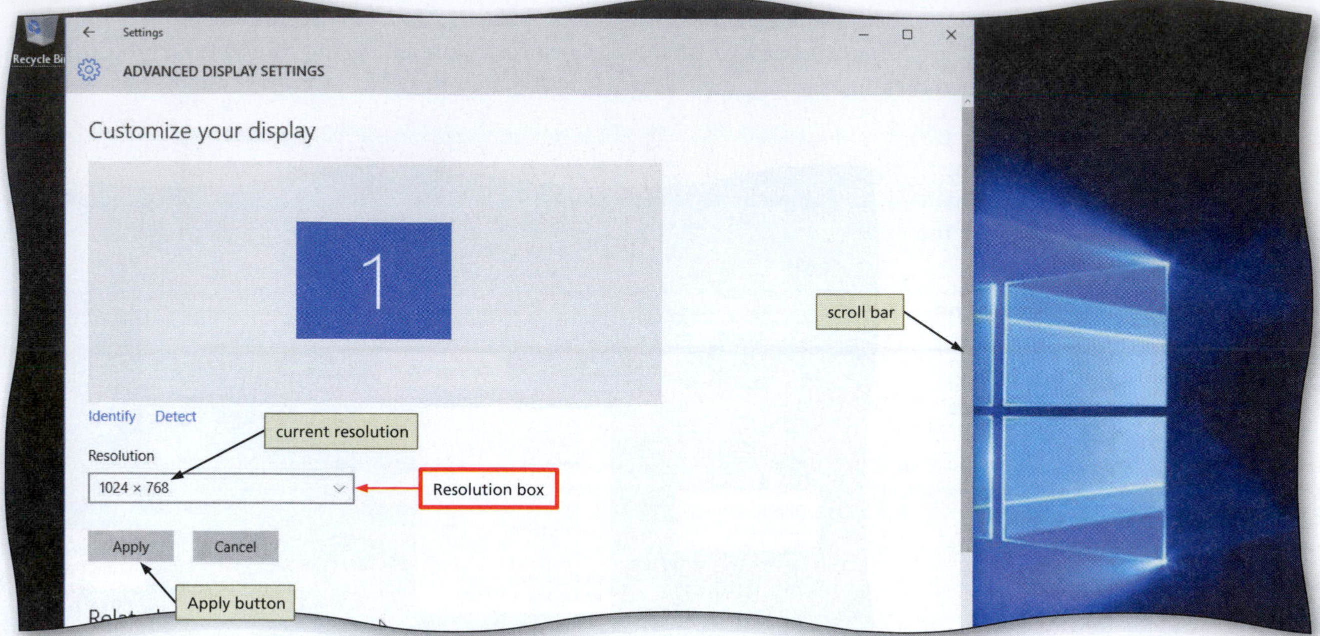

Figure 61

- Click the Resolution box to display a list of available screen resolutions (Figure 62).
- If necessary, scroll to and then click 1366 × 768 to select the screen resolution.

Q&A What if my computer does not support the 1366 × 768 resolution?
Some computers do not support the 1366 × 768 resolution. In this case, select a resolution that is close to the 1366 × 768 resolution.

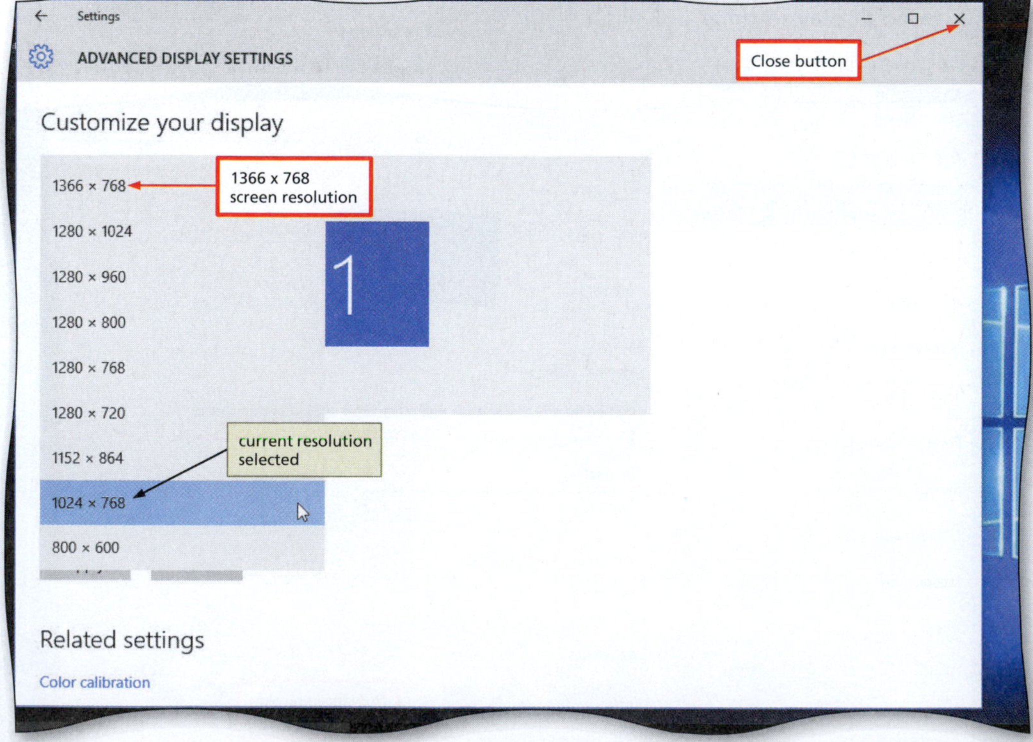

Figure 62

- Click the Apply button (Advanced Display Settings window) (shown in Figure 61) to change the screen resolution and display a confirmation message (Figure 63).
- Click the Keep changes button to accept the new screen resolution.
- Click the Close button (shown in Figure 62) to close the Settings app window.

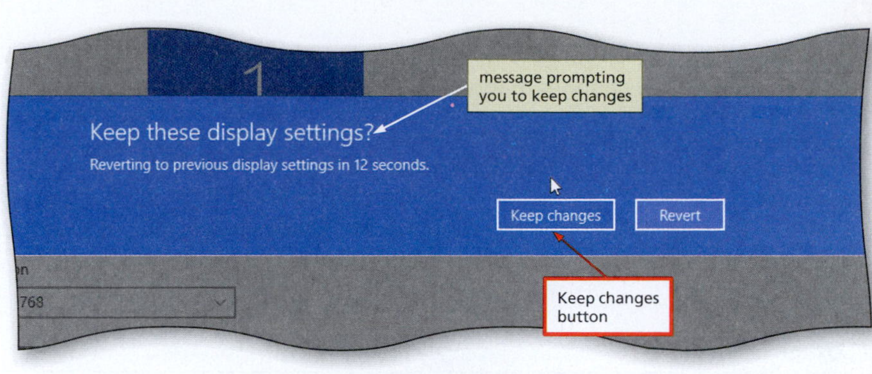

Figure 63

Other Ways

1. Click Start button, click Settings, click System, click Display, click 'Advanced display settings,' select desired resolution in Resolution box, click Apply button, click Keep changes button
2. Type `screen resolution` in search box, click 'Change the screen resolution,' select desired resolution in Resolution box, click Apply, click Keep changes

To Exit an Office App with One Document Open

When you exit an Office app, such as Word, if you have made changes to a file since the last time the file was saved, the Office app displays a dialog box asking if you want to save the changes you made to the file before it closes the app window. ***Why?*** *The dialog box contains three buttons with these resulting actions: the Save button saves the changes and then exits the Office app, the Don't Save button exits the Office app without saving changes, and the Cancel button closes the dialog box and redisplays the file without saving the changes.*

If no changes have been made to an open document since the last time the file was saved, the Office app will close the window without displaying a dialog box.

The following steps exit an Office app. In the following example, Word is used to illustrate exiting an Office app; however, you would follow the same steps regardless of the Office app you were using.

- If necessary, click the Word app button on the taskbar to display the Word window on the desktop (Figure 64).

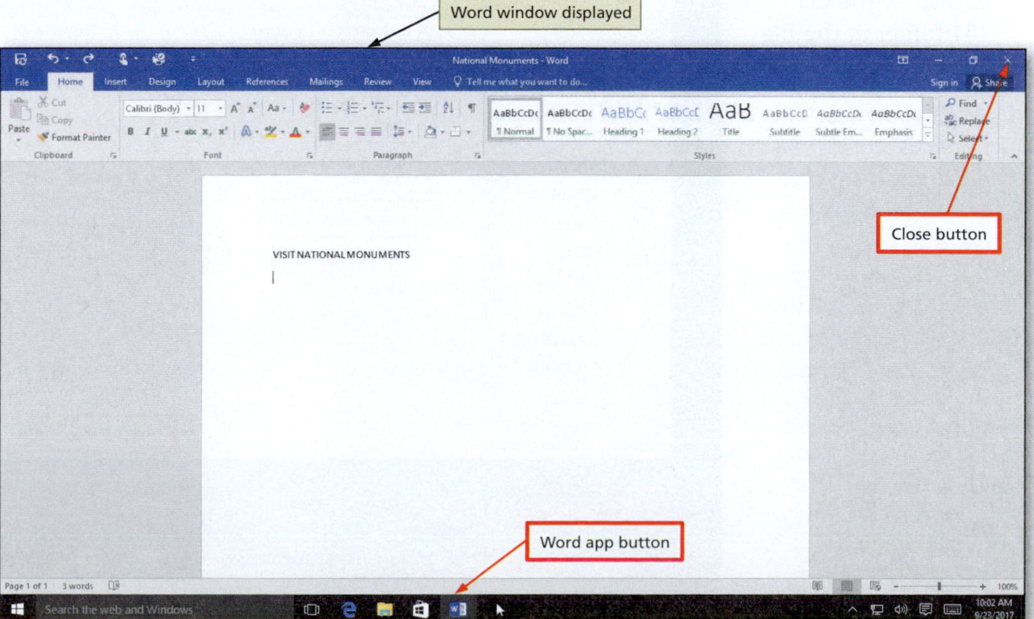

Figure 64

- Click the Close button to close the document and exit Word. If a Microsoft Word dialog box appears, click the Save button to save any changes made to the document since the last save.

Q&A What if I have more than one document open in an Office app?
You could click the Close button for each open document. When you click the last open document's Close button, you also exit the Office app. As an alternative that is more efficient, you could right-click the app button on the taskbar and then click 'Close all windows' on the shortcut menu, or press ALT+F4 to close all open documents and exit the Office app.

Other Ways

1. Right-click the Office app button on Windows taskbar, click Close window on shortcut menu
2. Press ALT+F4

To Copy a Folder to OneDrive

To back up your files or easily make them available on another computer or mobile device, you can copy them to OneDrive. The following steps copy your CIS 101 folder to OneDrive. If you do not have access to a OneDrive account, read the following steps without performing them. ***Why?*** *It often is good practice to have a backup of your files so that they are available in case something happens to your original copies.*

1

- Click the File Explorer button on the taskbar to make the folder window the active window.
- Click Documents in the This PC area of the navigation pane to display the CIS 101 folder in the file list.

Q&A What if my CIS 101 folder is stored in a different location?
Use the navigation pane to navigate to the location of your CIS 101 folder. The CIS 101 folder should be displayed in the file list once you have located it.

- Click the CIS 101 folder in the file list to select it (Figure 65).

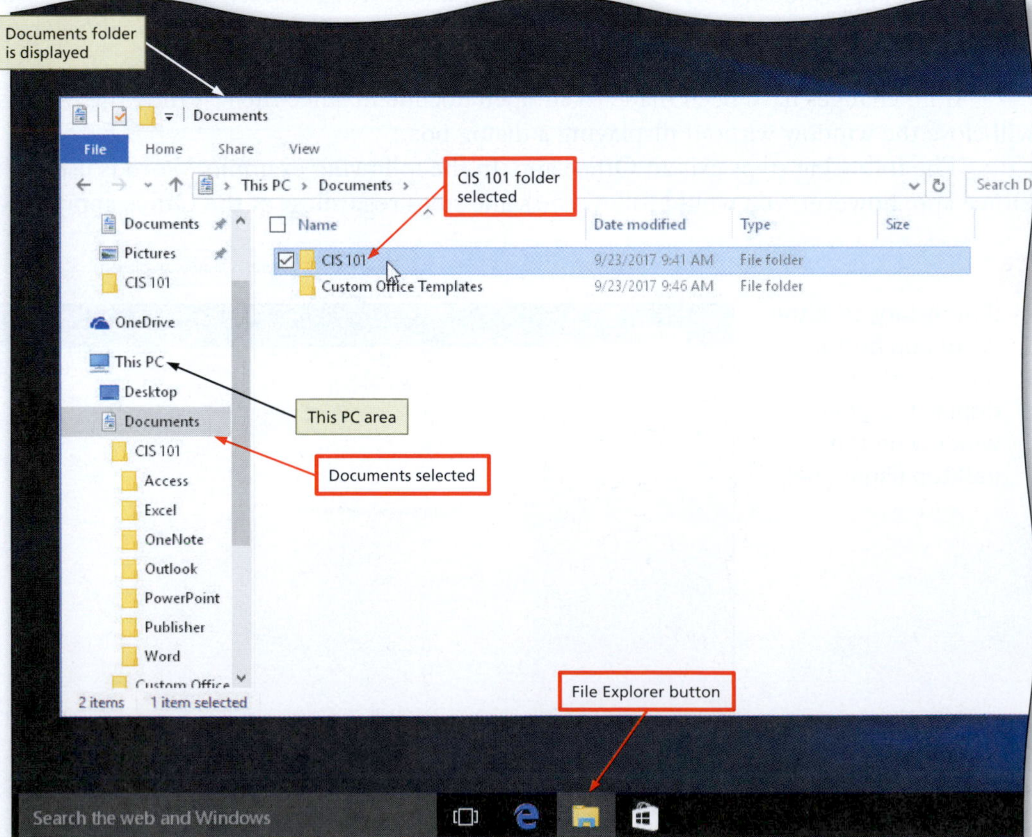

Figure 65

2

- Click Home on the ribbon to display the Home tab.
- Click the Copy to button (Home tab | Organize group) to display the Copy to menu (Figure 66).

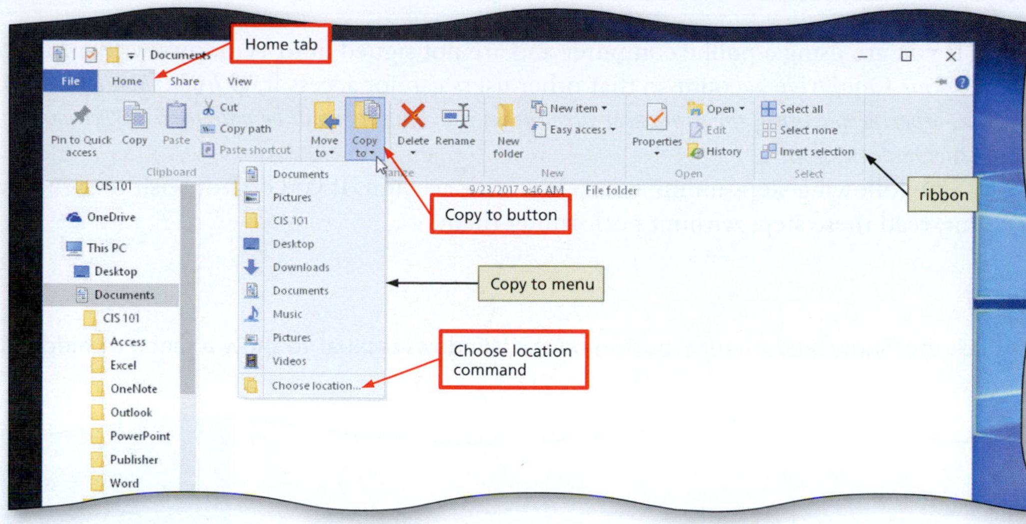

Figure 66

3

- Click Choose location on the Copy to menu to display the Copy Items dialog box.
- Click OneDrive (Copy Items dialog box) to select it (Figure 67).

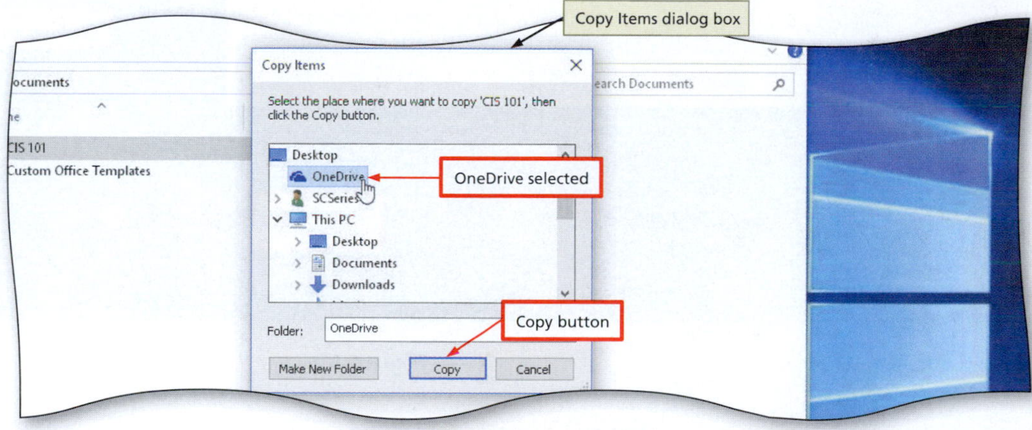

Figure 67

4

- Click the Copy button (Copy Items dialog box) to copy the selected folder to OneDrive.
- Click OneDrive in the navigation pane to verify the CIS 101 folder displays in the file list (Figure 68).

Why does a Microsoft OneDrive dialog box display when I click OneDrive in the navigation pane?

If you are not currently signed in to Windows using a Microsoft account, you will manually need to sign in to a Microsoft account to save files to OneDrive. Follow the instructions on the screen to sign in to your Microsoft account.

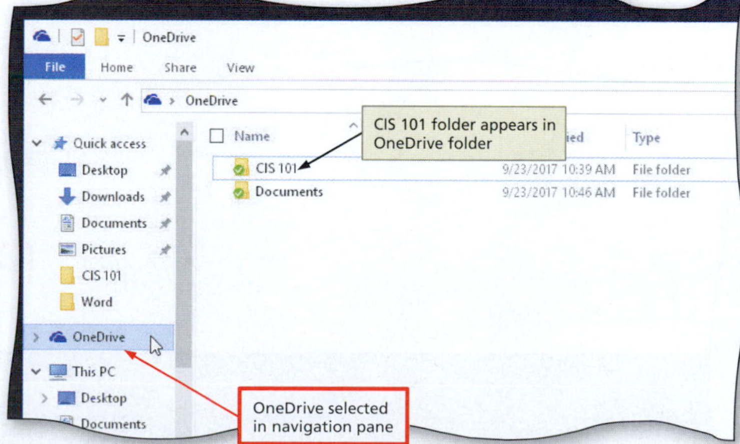

Figure 68

Other Ways

1. In File Explorer, select folder to copy, click Copy button (Home tab | Clipboard group), display contents of OneDrive in file list, click Paste button (Home tab | Clipboard group)
2. In File Explorer, select folder to copy, press CTRL+C, display contents of OneDrive in file list, press CTRL+V
3. Drag folder to copy to OneDrive in navigation pane

To Unlink a OneDrive Account

If you are using a public computer and are not signed in to Windows with a Microsoft account, you should unlink your OneDrive account so that other users cannot access it. ***Why?*** *If you do not unlink your OneDrive account, other people using the same user account on the computer will be able to view, remove, and add to files stored in your OneDrive account.*

The following steps unlink your OneDrive account. If you do not wish to sign out of your Microsoft account, read these steps without performing them.

1

- Click the 'Show hidden icons' button on the Windows taskbar to show a menu of hidden icons (Figure 69).

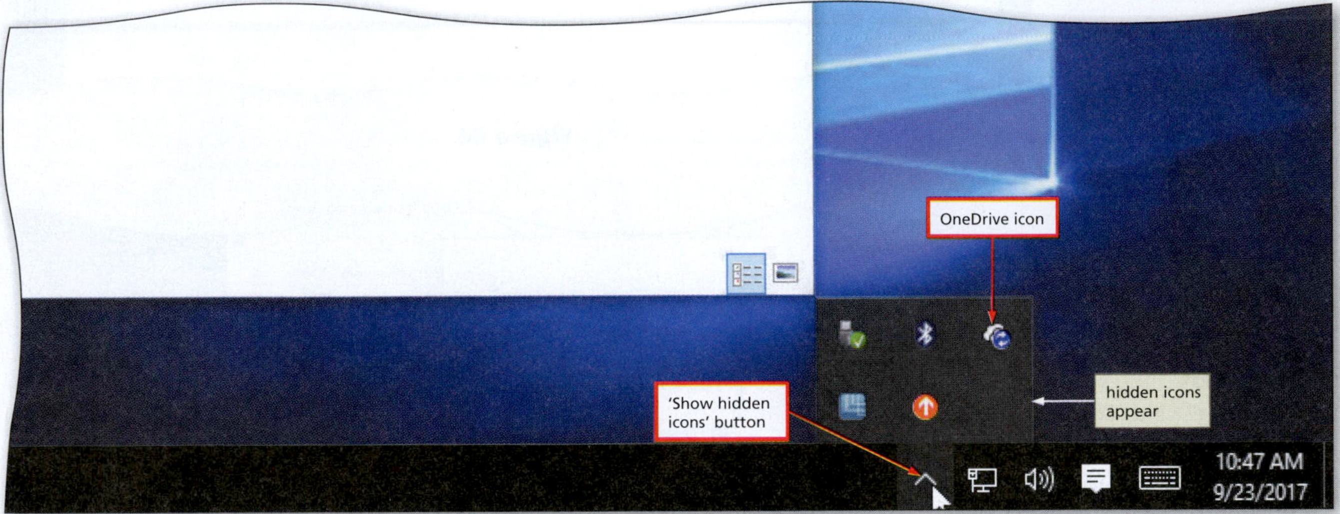

Figure 69

2

- Right click the OneDrive icon (shown in Figure 69) to display a shortcut menu (Figure 70).

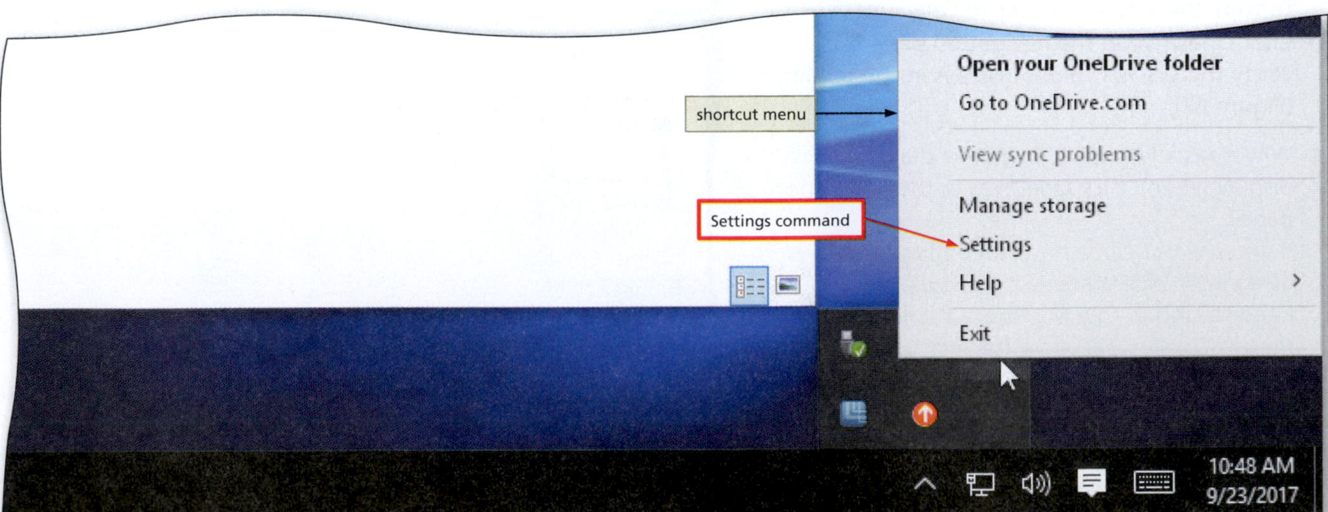

Figure 70

3

- Click Settings on the shortcut menu to display the Microsoft OneDrive dialog box (Figure 71).

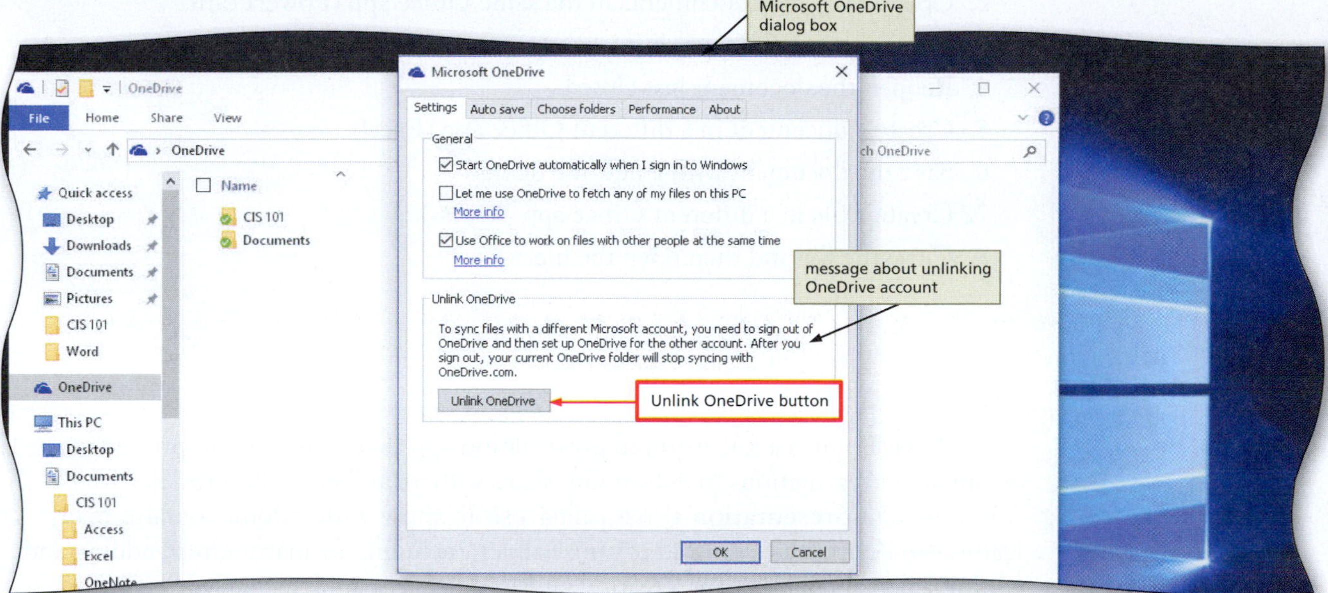

Figure 71

4

- If necessary, click the Settings tab.
- Click the Unlink OneDrive button (Microsoft OneDrive dialog box) to unlink the OneDrive account (Figure 72).
- When the Microsoft OneDrive dialog box appears with a Welcome to OneDrive message, click the Close button.
- Minimize the File Explorer window.

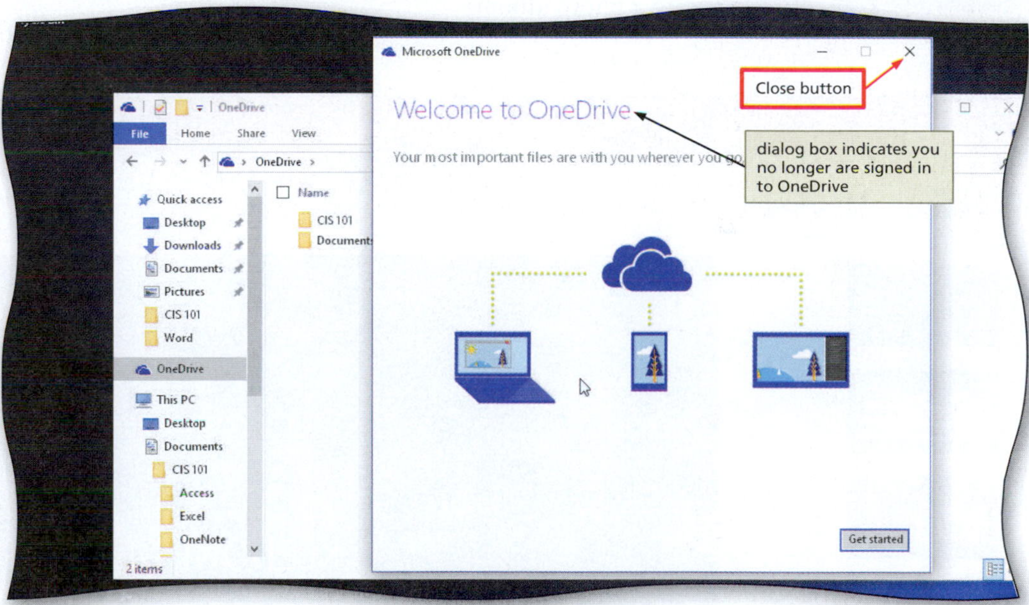

Figure 72

Break Point: If you wish to take a break, this is a good place to do so. To resume at a later time, continue to follow the steps from this location forward.

Additional Microsoft Office Apps

The previous section used Word to illustrate common features of Office and some basic elements unique to Word. The following sections present elements unique to PowerPoint, Excel, and Access, as well as illustrate additional common features of Office.

In the following pages, you will learn how to do the following:

1. Run an Office app (PowerPoint) using the search box.
2. Create two small documents in the same Office app (PowerPoint).
3. Close one of the documents.
4. Reopen the document just closed.
5. Create a document in a different Office app (Excel).
6. Save the document with a new file name.
7. Create a file in a different Office app (Access).
8. Close the file and then open the file.

PowerPoint

PowerPoint is a full-featured presentation app that allows you to produce compelling presentations to deliver and share with an audience (Figure 73). A PowerPoint **presentation** also is called a **slide show**. PowerPoint contains many features to design, develop, and organize slides, including formatting text, adding and editing video and audio clips, creating tables and charts, applying artistic effects to pictures, animating graphics, and collaborating with friends and colleagues. You then can turn your presentation into a video, broadcast your slide show on the web, or create a photo album.

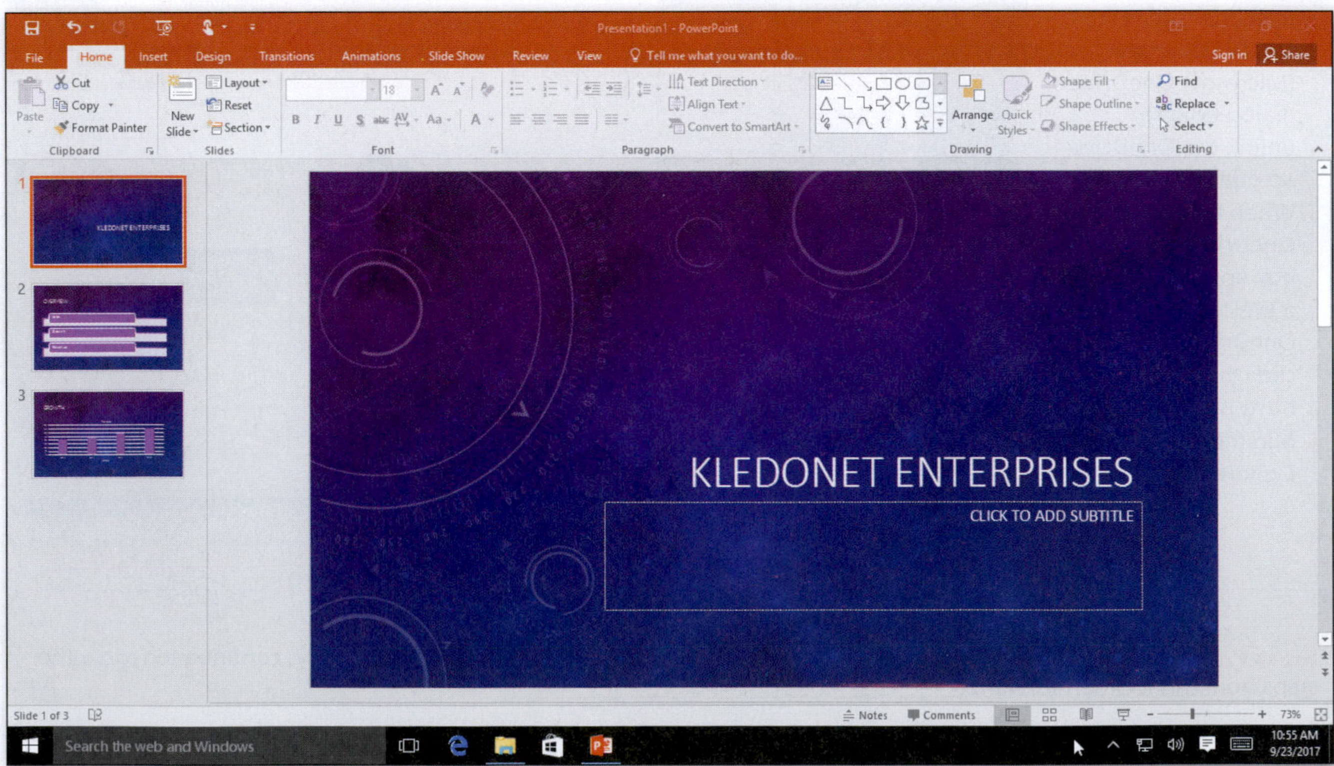

Figure 73

To Run an App Using the Search Box

The following steps, which assume Windows is running, use the search box to run the PowerPoint app based on a typical installation; however, you would follow similar steps to run any Office app. ***Why?** Some people prefer to use the search box to locate and run an app, as opposed to searching through a list of all apps on the Start menu.* You may need to ask your instructor how to run apps for your computer.

1

- Type `PowerPoint 2016` as the search text in the search box and watch the search results appear in the search results (Figure 74).

Q&A Do I need to type the complete app name or use correct capitalization?
No, you need to type just enough characters of the app name for it to appear in the search results. For example, you may be able to type PowerPoint or powerpoint, instead of PowerPoint 2016.

2

- Click the app name, PowerPoint 2016 in this case, in the search results to run PowerPoint (Figure 75).

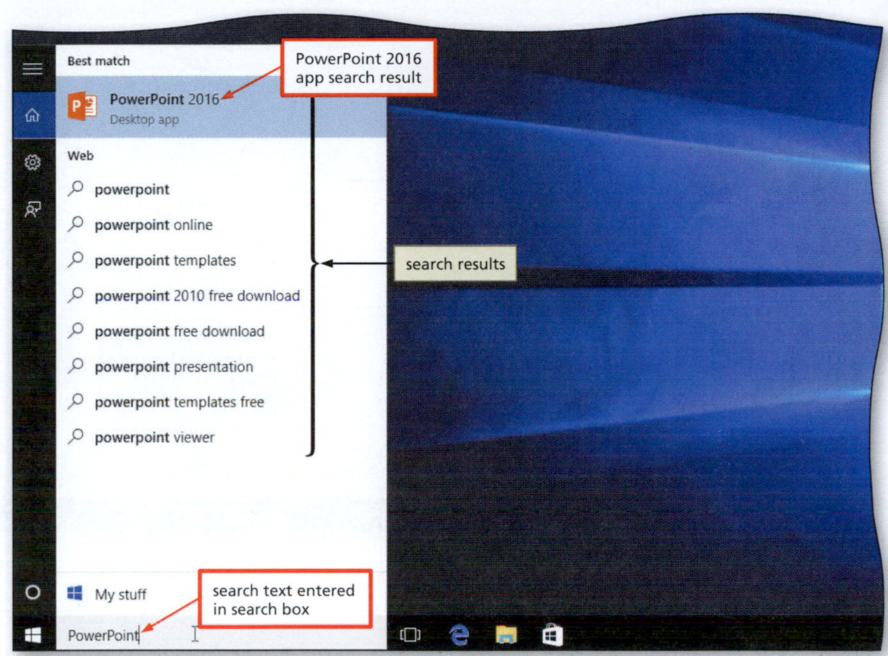

Figure 74

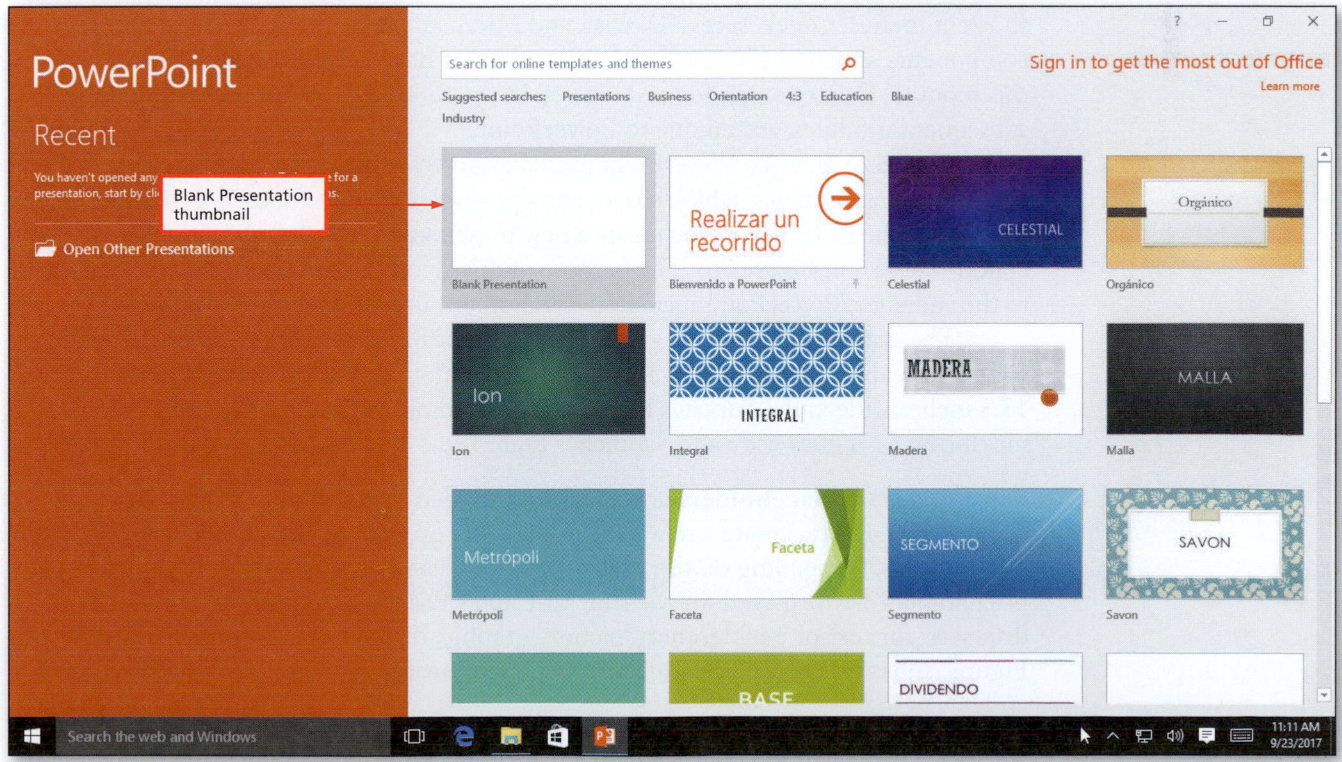

Figure 75

3

- Click the Blank Presentation thumbnail to create a blank presentation and display it in the PowerPoint window.
- If the app window is not maximized, click the Maximize button on its title bar to maximize the window (Figure 76).

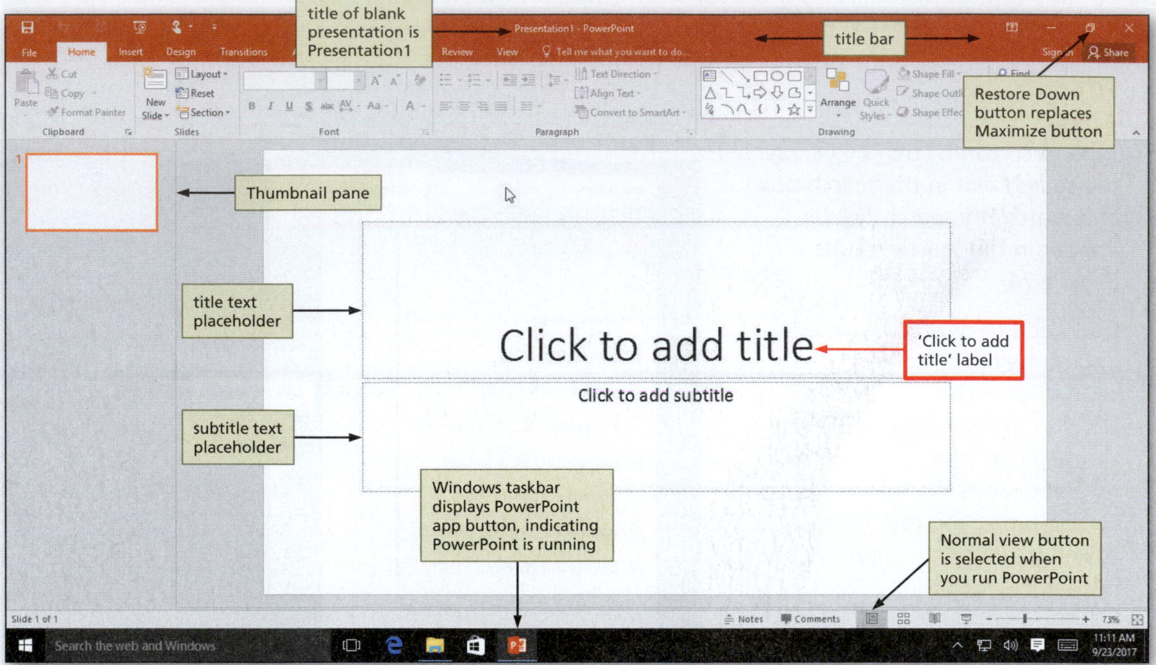

Figure 76

The PowerPoint Window and Ribbon

The PowerPoint window consists of a variety of components to make your work more efficient and documents more professional: the window, ribbon, mini toolbar, shortcut menus, Quick Access Toolbar, and Microsoft Account area. Many of these components are common to other Office apps and have been discussed earlier in this module. Other components, discussed in the following paragraphs and later in subsequent modules, are unique to PowerPoint.

The basic unit of a PowerPoint presentation is a **slide**. A slide may contain text and objects, such as graphics, tables, charts, and drawings. **Layouts** are used to position this content on the slide. When you create a new presentation, the default **Title Slide** layout appears (shown in Figure 76). The purpose of this layout is to introduce the presentation to the audience. PowerPoint includes several other built-in standard layouts.

The default slide layouts are set up in **landscape orientation**, where the slide width is greater than its height. In landscape orientation, the slide size is preset to 13.3 inches wide and 7.5 inches high when printed on a standard sheet of paper measuring 11 inches wide and 8.5 inches high.

Placeholders **Placeholders** are boxes with dashed or solid borders that are displayed when you create a new slide. All layouts except the Blank slide layout contain placeholders. Depending on the particular slide layout selected, title and subtitle placeholders are displayed for the slide title and subtitle; a content placeholder is displayed for text or a table, chart, picture, graphic, or movie. The title slide in Figure 76 has two text placeholders for the main heading, or title, and the subtitle.

Ribbon The ribbon in PowerPoint is similar to the one in Word and the other Microsoft Office apps. When you run PowerPoint, the ribbon displays nine main tabs: File, Home, Insert, Design, Transitions, Animations, Slide Show, Review, and View.

To Enter Content in a Title Slide

With the exception of a blank slide, PowerPoint assumes every new slide has a title. Many of PowerPoint's layouts have both a title text placeholder and at least one content placeholder. To make creating a presentation easier, any text you type after a new slide appears becomes title text in the title text placeholder. As you begin typing text in the title text placeholder, the title text also is displayed in the Slide 1 thumbnail in the Thumbnail pane. The title for this presentation is Mara's Marbles. The following step enters a presentation title on the title slide. ***Why?*** *In general, every presentation should have a title to describe what the presentation will be covering.*

1

- Click the 'Click to add title' label located inside the title text placeholder (shown in Figure 76) to select the placeholder.
- Type **Mara's Marbles** in the title text placeholder. Do not press the ENTER key because you do not want to create a new line of text (Figure 77).

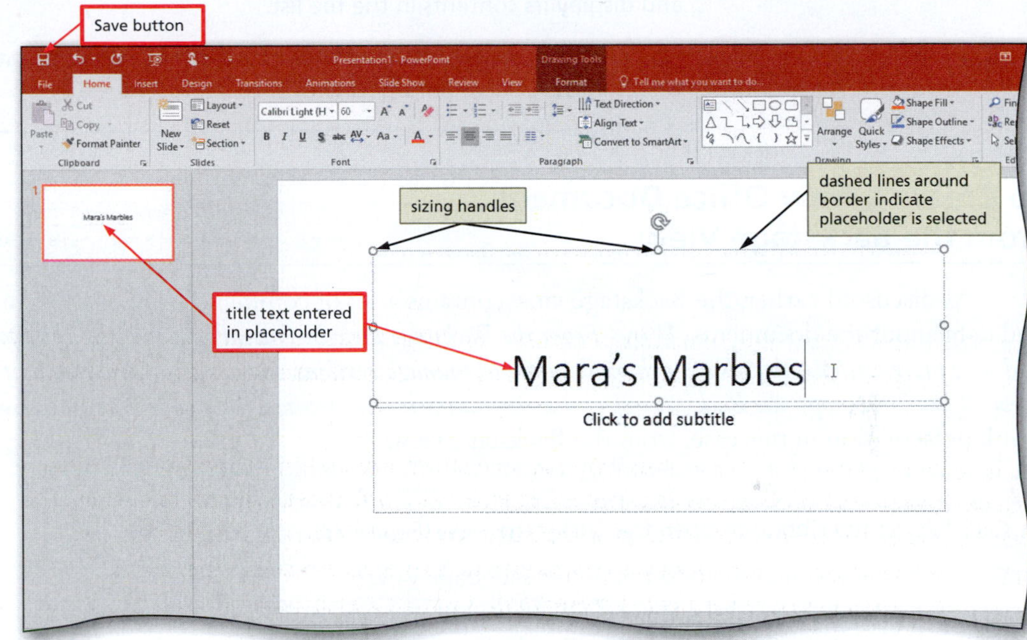

Figure 77

To Save a File in a Folder

The following steps save the presentation in the PowerPoint folder in the class folder (CIS 101, in this case) in the Documents folder using the file name, Mara's Marbles.

1 Click the Save button on the Quick Access Toolbar (shown in Figure 77), which depending on settings will display either the Save As gallery in the Backstage view or the Save As dialog box.

2 If your screen displays the Backstage view, click This PC, if necessary, to display options in the right pane related to saving on your computer; if your screen already displays the Save As dialog box, proceed to Step 4.

3 Click the Browse button in the left pane to display the Save As dialog box.

4 If necessary, type **Mara's Marbles** in the File name box (Save As dialog box) to change the file name. Do not press the ENTER key after typing the file name because you do not want to close the dialog box at this time.

5 Navigate to the desired save location (in this case, the PowerPoint folder in the CIS 101 folder [or your class folder] in the Documents folder). For specific instructions, perform the tasks in Steps 5a through 5e.

5a If the Documents folder is not displayed in the navigation pane, slide to scroll or drag the scroll bar in the navigation pane until Documents appears.

5b If the Documents folder is not expanded in the navigation pane, double-click Documents to display its folders in the navigation pane.

5c If the Documents folder is not expanded in the navigation pane, double-click Documents to display its folders in the navigation pane.

5d If your class folder (CIS 101, in this case) is not expanded, double-click the CIS 101 folder to select the folder and display its contents in the navigation pane.

5e Click the PowerPoint folder in the navigation pane to select it as the new save location and display its contents in the file list.

6 Click the Save button (Save As dialog box) to save the presentation in the selected folder in the selected location with the entered file name.

To Create a New Office Document from the Backstage View

1 SIGN IN | 2 USE WINDOWS | 3 USE APPS | 4 FILE MANAGEMENT | 5 SWITCH APPS | 6 SAVE FILES
7 CHANGE SCREEN RESOLUTION | 8 EXIT APPS | 9 USE ADDITIONAL APPS | 10 USE HELP

As discussed earlier, the Backstage view contains a set of commands that enable you to manage documents and data about the documents. ***Why?*** *From the Backstage view in PowerPoint, for example, you can create, open, print, and save presentations. You also can share documents, manage versions, set permissions, and modify document properties. In other Office 2016 apps, the Backstage view may contain features specific to those apps.* The following steps create a file, a blank presentation in this case, from the Backstage view.

1

- Click File on the ribbon to open the Backstage view (Figure 78).

Q&A What is the purpose of the Info tab in the Backstage view?
The Info tab, which is selected by default when you click File on the ribbon, allows you to protect your document, inspect your document, and manage versions of your document as well as view all the file properties, such as when the file was created.

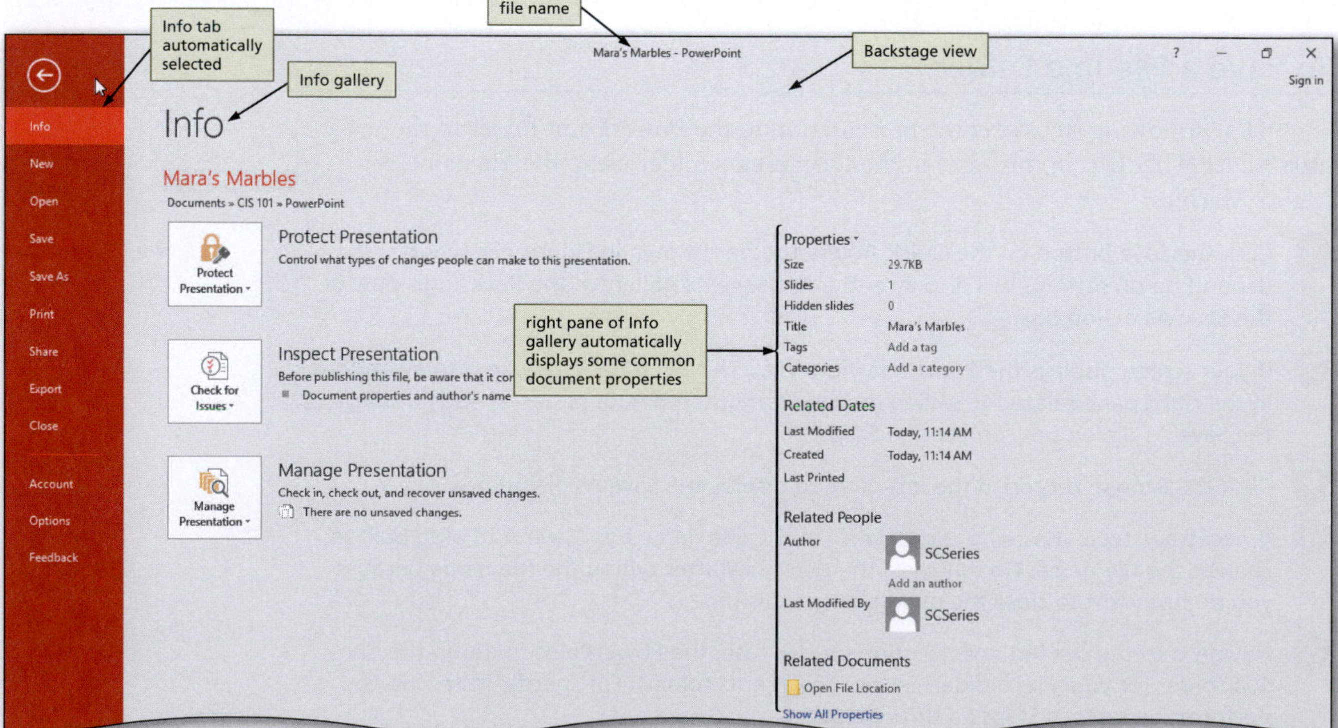

Figure 78

2

- Click the New tab in the Backstage view to display the New gallery (Figure 79).

Q&A Can I create documents through the Backstage view in other Office apps?
Yes. If the Office app has a New tab in the Backstage view, the New gallery displays various options for creating a new file.

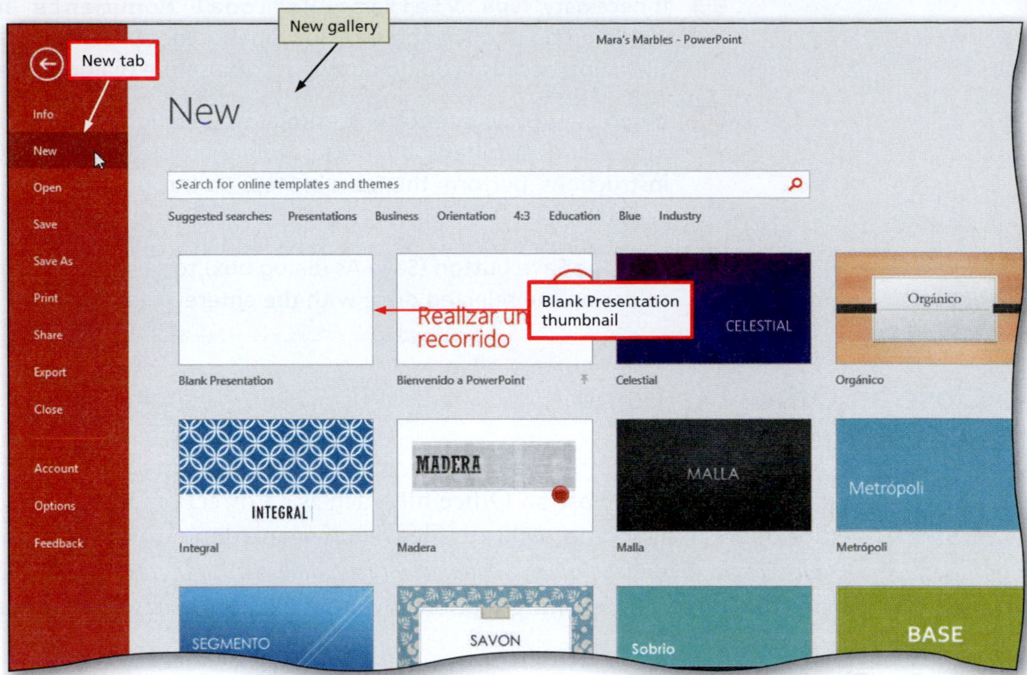

Figure 79

3

- Click the Blank Presentation thumbnail in the New gallery to create a new presentation.

Other Ways

1. Press CTRL + N

To Enter Content in a Title Slide of a Second PowerPoint Presentation

The presentation title for this presentation is Visiting National Monuments. The following steps enter a presentation title on the title slide.

1. Click the title text placeholder to select it.
2. Type `Visiting National Monuments` in the title text placeholder. Do not press the ENTER key.

To Save a File in a Folder

The following steps save the second presentation in the PowerPoint folder in the class folder (CIS 101, in this case) in the Documents folder using the file name, Visiting National Monuments.

1. Click the Save button on the Quick Access Toolbar, which depending on settings will display either the Save As gallery in the Backstage view or the Save As dialog box.
2. If your screen displays the Backstage view, click This PC, if necessary, to display options in the right pane related to saving on your computer; if your screen already displays the Save As dialog box, proceed to Step 4.
3. Click the Browse button in the left pane to display the Save As dialog box.

4. If necessary, type **`Visiting National Monuments`** in the File name box (Save As dialog box) to change the file name. Do not press the ENTER key after typing the file name because you do not want to close the dialog box at this time.

5. If necessary, navigate to the desired save location (in this case, the PowerPoint folder in the CIS 101 folder [or your class folder] in the Documents folder). For specific instructions, perform the tasks in Steps 5a through 5e in the previous section titled To Save a File in a Folder.

6. Click the Save button (Save As dialog box) to save the presentation in the selected folder on the selected drive with the entered file name.

To Close an Office File Using the Backstage View

1 SIGN IN | 2 USE WINDOWS | 3 USE APPS | 4 FILE MANAGEMENT | 5 SWITCH APPS | 6 SAVE FILES
7 CHANGE SCREEN RESOLUTION | 8 EXIT APPS | 9 USE ADDITIONAL APPS | 10 USE HELP

Sometimes, you may want to close an Office file, such as a PowerPoint presentation, entirely and start over with a new file. You also may want to close a file when you are done working with it. ***Why?*** *You should close a file when you are done working with it so that you do not make inadvertent changes to it.* The following steps close the current active Office file, that is, the Visiting National Monuments presentation, without exiting the active app (PowerPoint, in this case).

1

- Click File on the ribbon to open the Backstage view (Figure 80).

2

- Click Close in the Backstage view to close the open file (Visiting National Monuments, in this case) without exiting the active app.

Q&A What if the Office app displays a dialog box about saving?
Click the Save button if you want to save the changes, click the Don't Save button if you want to ignore the changes since the last time you saved, and click the Cancel button if you do not want to close the document.

Can I use the Backstage view to close an open file in other Office apps, such as Word and Excel?
Yes.

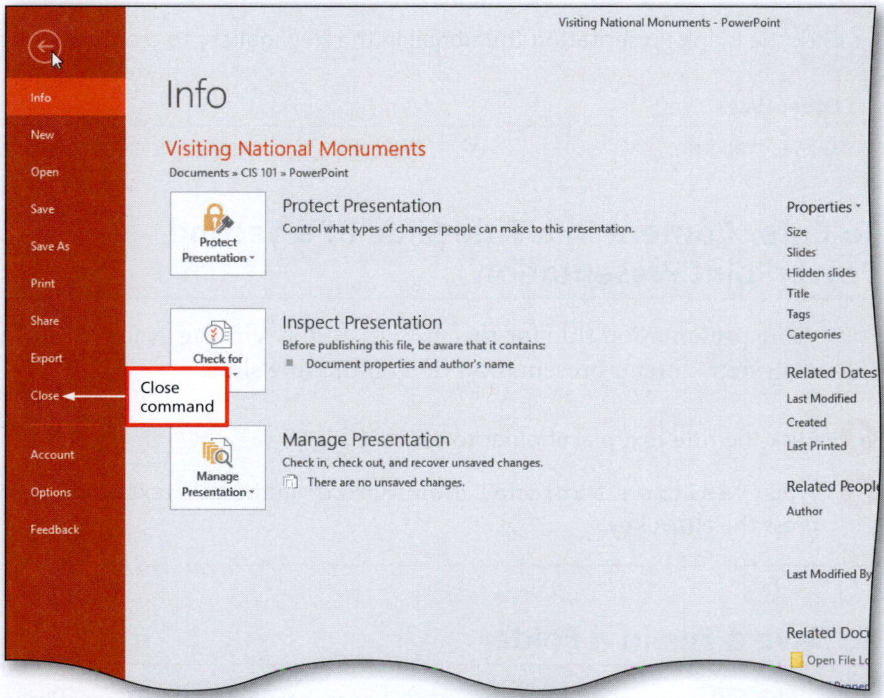

Figure 80

Other Ways

1. Press CTRL+F4

To Open a Recent Office File Using the Backstage View

1 SIGN IN | 2 USE WINDOWS | 3 USE APPS | 4 FILE MANAGEMENT | 5 SWITCH APPS | 6 SAVE FILES
7 CHANGE SCREEN RESOLUTION | 8 EXIT APPS | 9 USE ADDITIONAL APPS | 10 USE HELP

You sometimes need to open a file that you recently modified. ***Why?*** *You may have more changes to make, such as adding more content or correcting errors.* The Backstage view allows you to access recent files easily. The following steps reopen the Visiting National Monuments file just closed.

1

- Click File on the ribbon to open the Backstage view.
- Click the Open tab in the Backstage view to display the Open gallery (Figure 81).

2

- Click the desired file name in the Recent list, Visiting National Monuments in this case, to open the file.

Q&A Can I use the Backstage view to open a recent file in other Office apps, such as Word and Excel?
Yes, as long as the file name appears in the list of recent files.

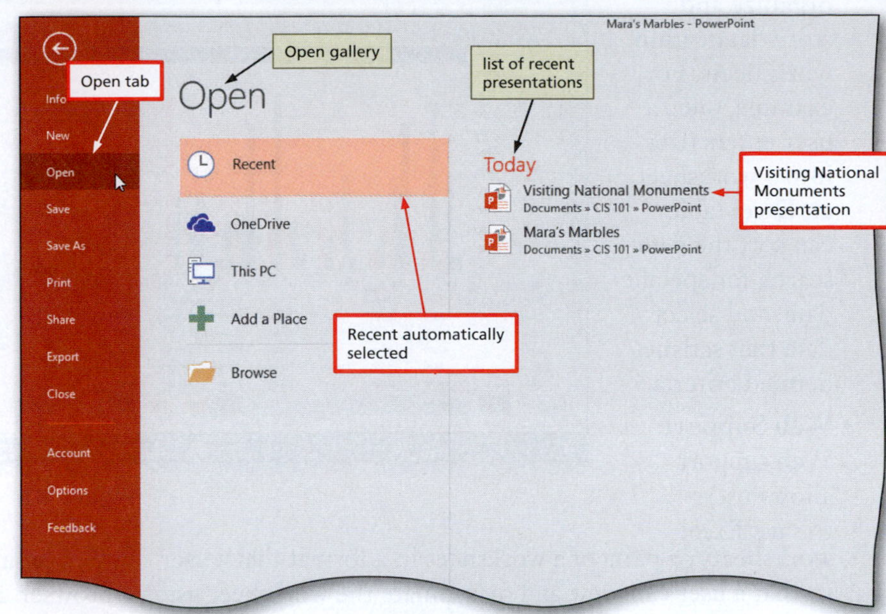

Figure 81

Other Ways

1. Click File on ribbon, click Open in Backstage view, click This PC, click Browse button, navigate to file (Open dialog box), click Open button

To Exit an Office App

You are finished using PowerPoint. Thus, you should exit this Office app. The following steps exit PowerPoint.

1 If you have one Office document open, click the Close button on the right side of the title bar to close the document and exit the Office app; or if you have multiple Office documents open, right-click the app button on the taskbar and then click 'Close all windows' on the shortcut menu, or press ALT+F4 to close all open documents and exit the Office app.

Q&A If I am using a touch screen, could I press and hold the Close button until all windows close and the app exits?
Yes.

2 If a dialog box appears, click the Save button to save any changes made to the document since the last save.

Excel

Excel is a powerful spreadsheet app that allows users to organize data, complete calculations, make decisions, graph data, develop professional-looking reports (Figure 82), publish organized data to the web, and access real-time data from websites. The four major parts of Excel are:

- **Workbooks and Worksheets:** A **workbook** is like a notebook. Inside the workbook are sheets, each of which is called a **worksheet**. Thus, a workbook is a collection of worksheets. Worksheets allow users to enter, calculate, manipulate, and analyze data, such as numbers and text. The terms worksheet and spreadsheet are interchangeable.
- **Charts:** Excel can draw a variety of charts, such as column charts and pie charts.

- **Tables:** Tables organize and store data within worksheets. For example, once a user enters data into a worksheet, an Excel table can sort the data, search for specific data, and select data that satisfies defined criteria.
- **Web Support:** Web support allows users to save Excel worksheets or parts of a worksheet in a format that a user can view in a browser, so that a user can view and manipulate the worksheet using a browser. Excel web support also provides access to real-time data, such as stock quotes, using web queries.

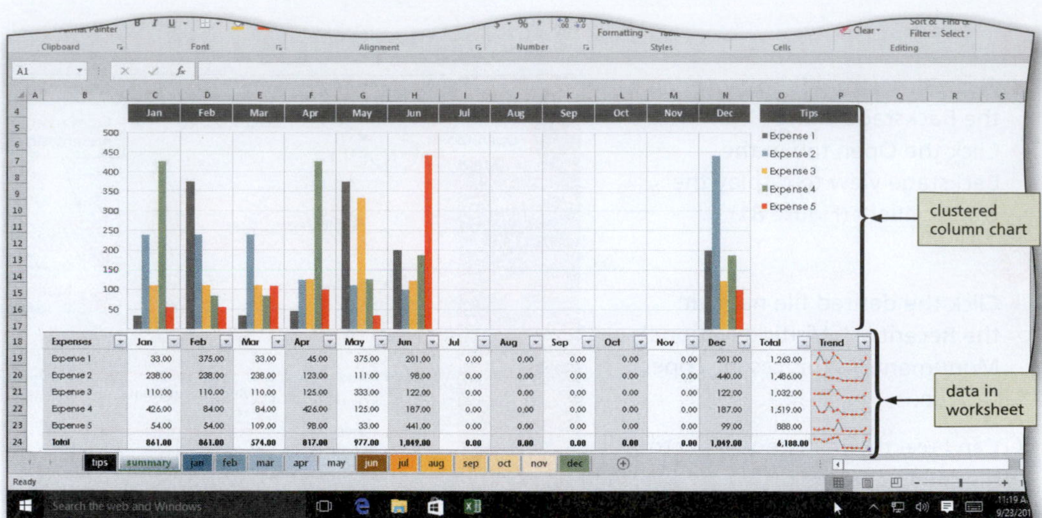

Figure 82

To Create a New Blank Office Document from File Explorer

1 SIGN IN | 2 USE WINDOWS | 3 USE APPS | 4 FILE MANAGEMENT | 5 SWITCH APPS | 6 SAVE FILES
7 CHANGE SCREEN RESOLUTION | 8 EXIT APPS | 9 USE ADDITIONAL APPS | 10 USE HELP

File Explorer provides a means to create a blank Office document without running an Office app. The following steps use File Explorer to create a blank Excel document. ***Why?*** *Sometimes you might need to create a blank document and then return to it later for editing.*

- If necessary, click the File Explorer button on the taskbar to make the folder window the active window.
- If necessary, double-click the Documents folder in the navigation pane to expand the Documents folder.
- If necessary, double-click your class folder (CIS 101, in this case) in the navigation pane to expand the folder.
- Click the Excel folder in the navigation pane to display its contents in the file list.
- With the Excel folder selected, right-click an open area in the file list to display a shortcut menu.
- Point to New on the shortcut menu to display the New submenu (Figure 83).

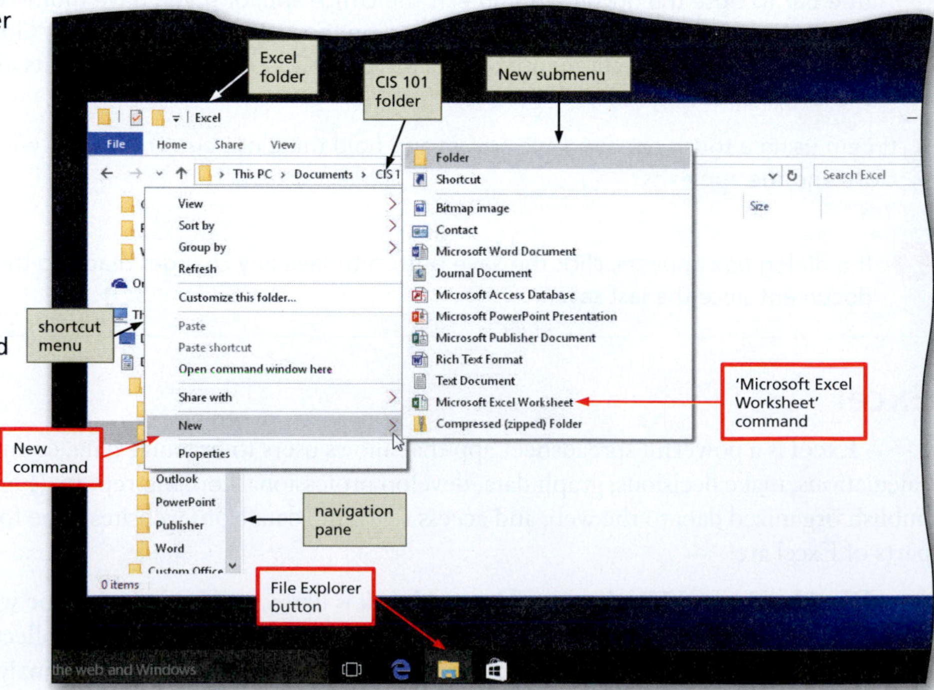

Figure 83

- Click 'Microsoft Excel Worksheet' on the New submenu to display an icon and text box for a new file in the current folder window with the file name, New Microsoft Excel Worksheet, selected (Figure 84).

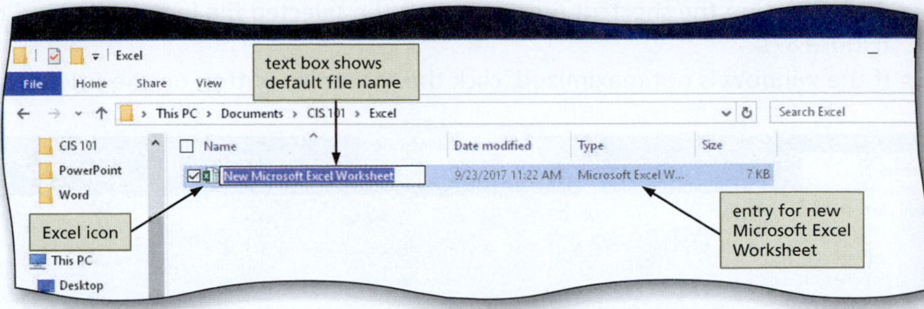

Figure 84

- Type `Silver Sky Hardware` in the text box and then press the ENTER key to assign a new file name to the new file in the current folder (Figure 85).

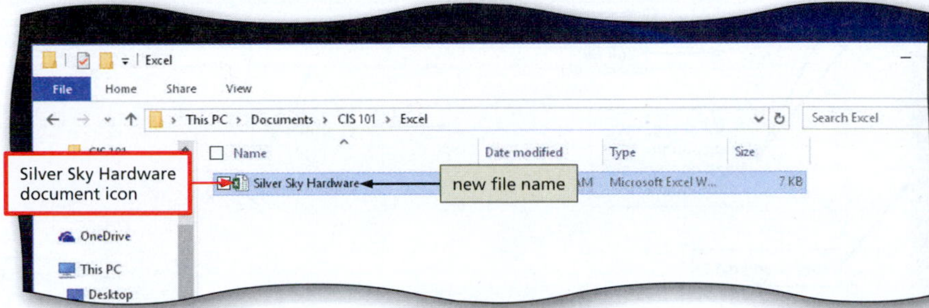

Figure 85

To Run an App from File Explorer and Open a File

1 SIGN IN | 2 USE WINDOWS | 3 USE APPS | 4 FILE MANAGEMENT | 5 SWITCH APPS | 6 SAVE FILES
7 CHANGE SCREEN RESOLUTION | 8 EXIT APPS | **9 USE ADDITIONAL APPS** | **10 USE HELP**

Previously, you learned how to run an Office app using the Start menu and the search box. The following steps, which assume Windows is running, use File Explorer to run the Excel app based on a typical installation. ***Why?*** *Another way to run an Office app is to open an existing file from File Explorer, which causes the app in which the file was created to run and then open the selected file.* You may need to ask your instructor how to run Office apps for your computer.

- If necessary, display the file to open in the folder window in File Explorer (shown in Figure 85).
- Right-click the file icon or file name (Silver Sky Hardware, in this case) to display a shortcut menu (Figure 86).

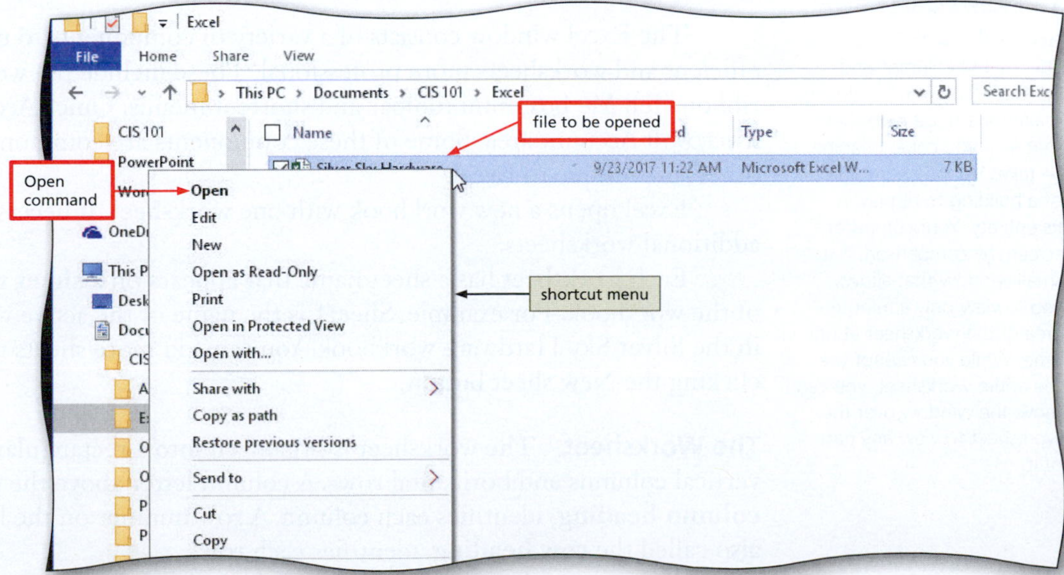

Figure 86

2

- Click Open on the shortcut menu to open the selected file in the app used to create the file, Excel in this case (Figure 87).
- If the window is not maximized, click the Maximize button on the title bar to maximize the window.

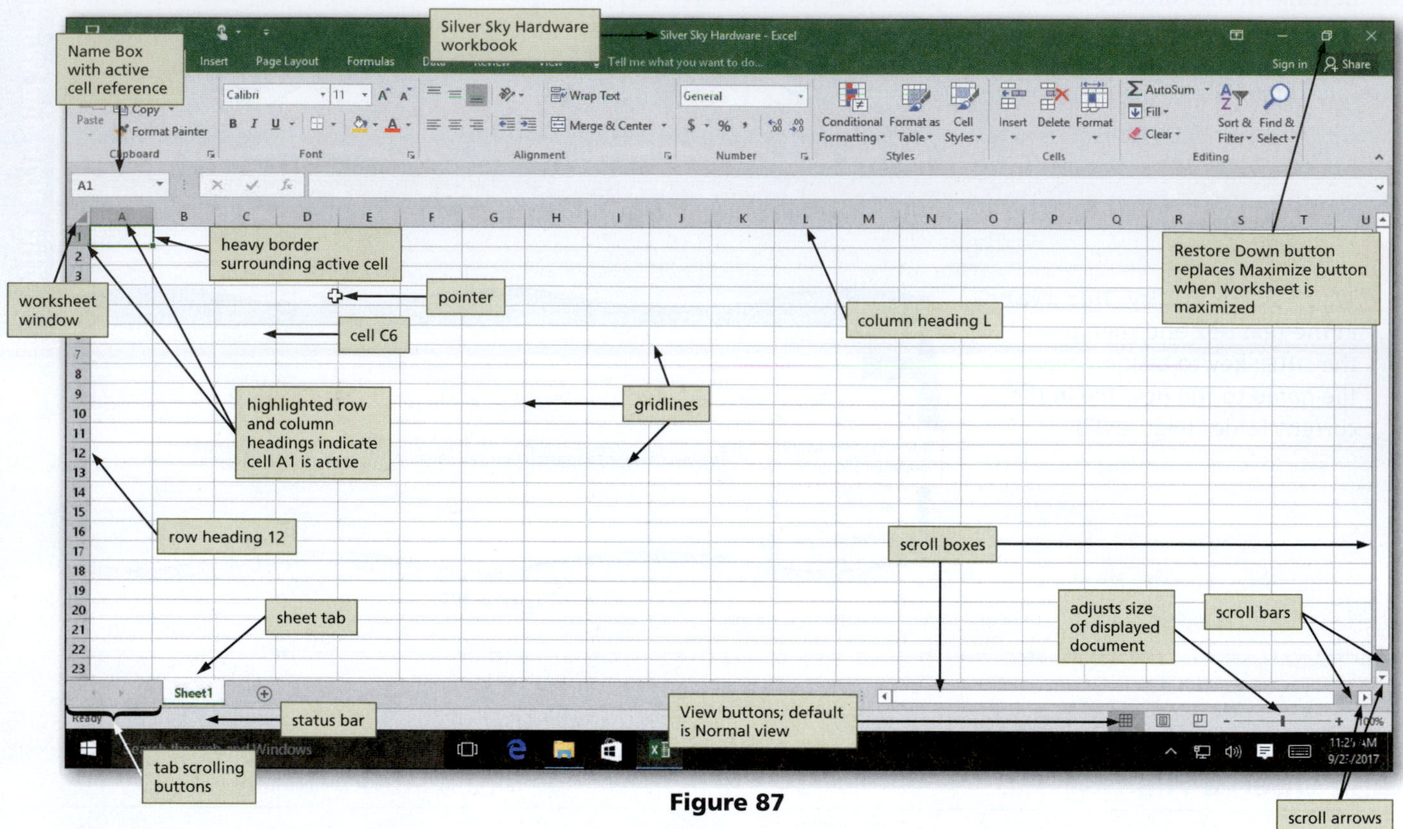

Figure 87

Q&A Instead of using File Explorer, can I run Excel using the same method shown previously for Word and PowerPoint?
Yes, you can use any method of running an Office app to run Excel.

BTW
The Worksheet Size and Window
The 16,384 columns and 1,048,576 rows in Excel make for a huge worksheet that — if you could imagine — takes up the entire side of a building to display in its entirety. Your computer screen, by comparison, is a small window that allows you to view only a minute area of the worksheet at one time. While you cannot see the entire worksheet, you can move the window over the worksheet to view any part of it.

Unique Features of Excel

The Excel window consists of a variety of components to make your work more efficient and worksheets more professional. These include the worksheet window, ribbon, Tell Me box, mini toolbar and shortcut menus, Quick Access Toolbar, and Microsoft Account area. Some of these components are common to other Office apps; others are unique to Excel.

Excel opens a new workbook with one worksheet. If necessary, you can add additional worksheets.

Each worksheet has a sheet name that appears on a **sheet tab** at the bottom of the workbook. For example, Sheet1 is the name of the active worksheet displayed in the Silver Sky Hardware workbook. You can add more sheets to the workbook by clicking the New sheet button.

The Worksheet The worksheet is organized into a rectangular grid containing vertical columns and horizontal rows. A column letter above the grid, also called the **column heading**, identifies each column. A row number on the left side of the grid, also called the **row heading**, identifies each row.

The intersection of each column and row is a cell. A **cell** is the basic unit of a worksheet into which you enter data. Each worksheet in a workbook has 16,384 columns and 1,048,576 rows for a total of 17,179,869,184 cells. Only a small fraction of the active worksheet appears on the screen at one time.

A cell is referred to by its unique address, or **cell reference**, which is the coordinates of the intersection of a column and a row. To identify a cell, specify the column letter first, followed by the row number. For example, cell reference C6 refers to the cell located at the intersection of column C and row 6 (Figure 87).

One cell on the worksheet, designated the **active cell**, is the one into which you can enter data. The active cell in Figure 87 is A1. The active cell is identified in three ways. First, a heavy border surrounds the cell; second, the active cell reference shows immediately above column A in the Name box; and third, the column heading A and row heading 1 are highlighted so that it is easy to see which cell is active (Figure 87).

The horizontal and vertical lines on the worksheet itself are called **gridlines**. Gridlines make it easier to see and identify each cell in the worksheet. If desired, you can turn the gridlines off so that they do not show on the worksheet. While learning Excel, gridlines help you to understand the structure of the worksheet.

The pointer in Figure 87 has the shape of a block plus sign. The pointer appears as a block plus sign whenever it is located in a cell on the worksheet. Another common shape of the pointer is the block arrow. The pointer turns into the block arrow when you move it outside the worksheet or when you drag cell contents between rows or columns.

BTW

Customizing the Ribbon

In addition to customizing the Quick Access Toolbar, you can add items to and remove items from the ribbon. To customize the ribbon, click File on the ribbon to open the Backstage view, click the Options tab in the Backstage view, and then click Customize Ribbon in the left pane of the Options dialog box. More information about customizing the ribbon is presented in a later module.

Ribbon When you run Excel, the ribbon displays eight main tabs: File, Home, Insert, Page Layout, Formulas, Data, Review, and View. The Formulas and Data tabs are specific to Excel. The Formulas tab allows you to work with Excel formulas, and the Data tab allows you to work with data processing features such as importing and sorting data.

Formula Bar As you type, Excel displays the entry in the **formula bar**, which appears below the ribbon (Figure 88). You can make the formula bar larger by dragging the sizing handle at the bottom of the formula bar or clicking the expand button to the right of the formula bar. Excel also displays the active cell reference in the **Name box** on the left side of the formula bar.

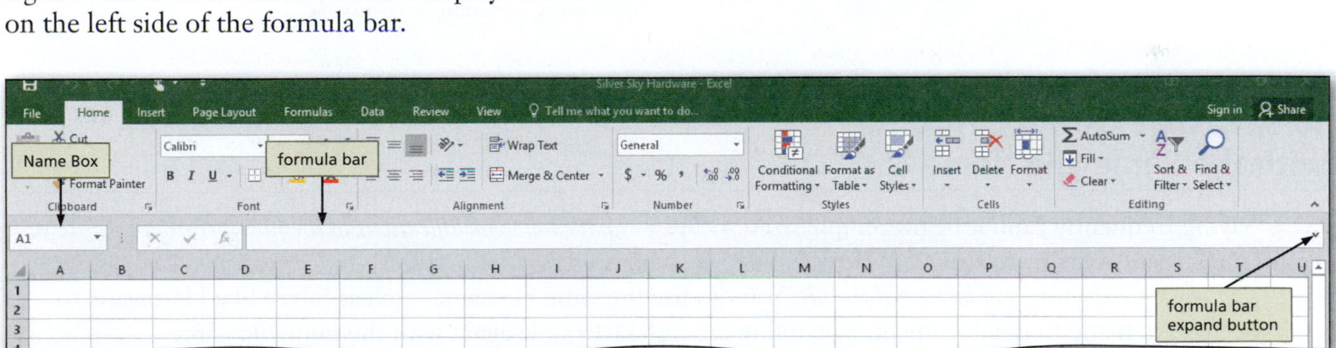

Figure 88

To Enter a Worksheet Title

1 SIGN IN | 2 USE WINDOWS | 3 USE APPS | 4 FILE MANAGEMENT | 5 SWITCH APPS | 6 SAVE FILES
7 CHANGE SCREEN RESOLUTION | 8 EXIT APPS | 9 USE ADDITIONAL APPS | 10 USE HELP

To enter data into a cell, you first must select it. The easiest way to select a cell (make it active) is to use the mouse to move the block plus sign pointer to the cell and then click. An alternative method is to use the arrow keys that are located just to the right of the typewriter keys on the keyboard. An arrow key selects the cell adjacent to the active cell in the direction of the arrow on the key.

In Excel, any set of characters containing a letter, hyphen (as in a telephone number), or space is considered text. **Text** is used to place titles, such as worksheet titles, column titles, and row titles, on the worksheet. The following steps enter the worksheet title in cell A1. ***Why?*** *A title informs others as to the contents of the worksheet, such as information regarding a company.*

- If it is not already the active cell, click cell A1 to make it the active cell.
- Type `Silver Sky Hardware` in cell A1 (Figure 89).

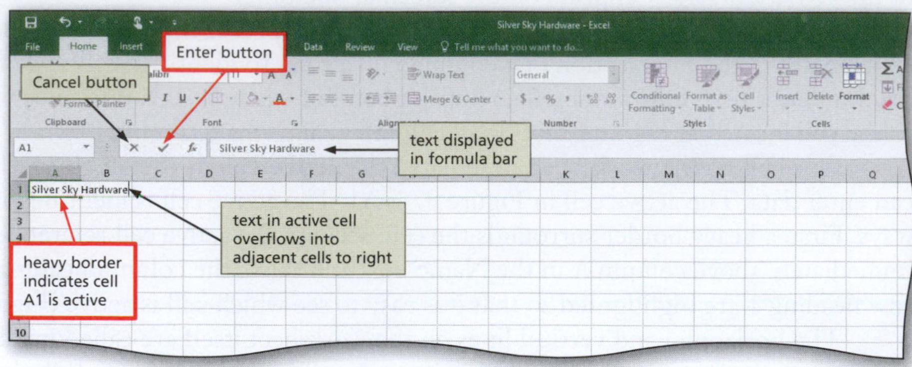

Figure 89

- Click the Enter button to complete the entry and enter the worksheet title in cell A1 (Figure 90).

Q&A Why do some commands on the ribbon appear dimmed?
Excel dims the commands that are unavailable for use at the current time.

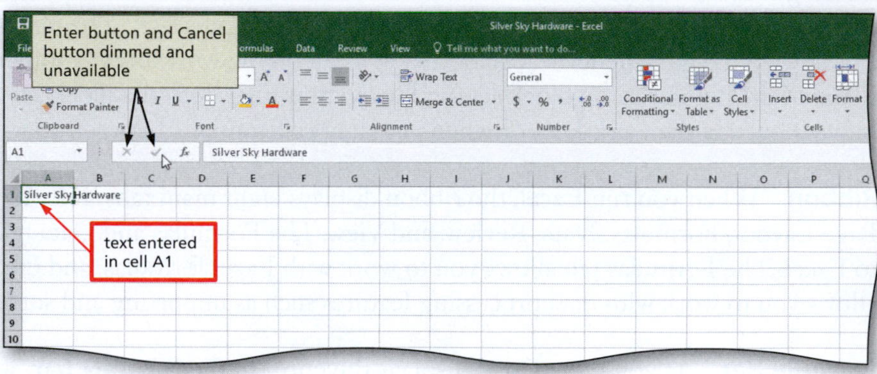

Figure 90

Other Ways

1. To complete entry, click any cell other than active cell
2. To complete entry, press ENTER, HOME, PAGE UP, PAGE DOWN, END, UP ARROW, DOWN ARROW, LEFT ARROW, or RIGHT ARROW

To Save an Existing Office File with the Same File Name

Saving frequently cannot be overemphasized. ***Why?*** *You have made modifications to the file (spreadsheet) since you created it. Thus, you should save again. Similarly, you should continue saving files frequently so that you do not lose the changes you have made since the time you last saved the file.* You can use the same file name, such as Silver Sky Hardware, to save the changes made to the document. The following step saves a file again with the same file name.

- Click the Save button on the Quick Access Toolbar to overwrite the previously saved file (Silver Sky Hardware, in this case) in the Excel folder (Figure 91).

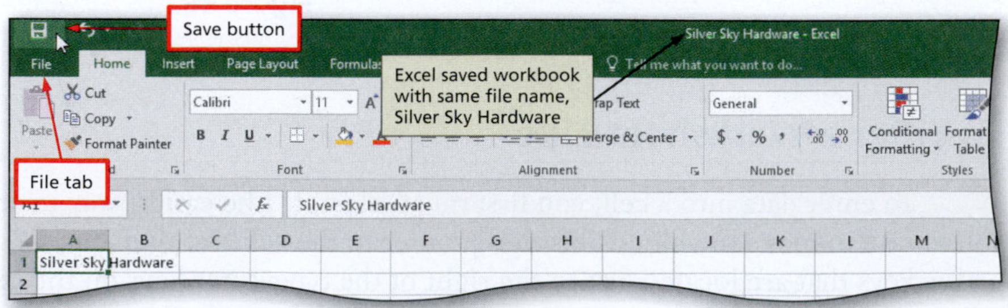

Figure 91

Other Ways

1. Press CTRL+S
2. Press SHIFT+F12

To Save a File with a New File Name

You might want to save a file with a different file name or to a different location. For example, you might start a homework assignment with a data file and then save it with a final file name for submission to your instructor, saving it to a location designated by your instructor. The following steps save a file with a different file name.

1. Click the File tab to open the Backstage view.
2. Click the Save As tab to display the Save As gallery.
3. If necessary, click This PC to display options in the right pane related to saving on your computer.
4. Click the Browse button in the left pane to display the Save As dialog box.
5. Type `Silver Sky Hardware Sales Summary` in the File name box (Save As dialog box) to change the file name. Do not press the ENTER key after typing the file name because you do not want to close the dialog box at this time.
6. If necessary, navigate to the desired save location (in this case, the Excel folder in the CIS 101 folder [or your class folder] in the Documents folder). For specific instructions, perform the tasks in Steps 5a through 5e in the previous section titled To Save a File in a Folder, replacing the PowerPoint folder with the Excel folder.
7. Click the Save button (Save As dialog box) to save the worksheet in the selected folder on the selected drive with the entered file name.

To Exit an Office App

You are finished using Excel. The following steps exit Excel.

1. If you have one Office document open, click the Close button on the right side of the title bar to close the document and exit the Office app; or if you have multiple Office documents open, right-click the app button on the taskbar and then click 'Close all windows' on the shortcut menu, or press ALT+F4 to close all open documents and exit the Office app.
2. If a dialog box appears, click the Save button to save any changes made to the file since the last save.

Access

The term **database** describes a collection of data organized in a manner that allows access, retrieval, and use of that data. **Access** is a database management system. A **database management system** is software that allows you to use a computer to create a database; add, change, and delete data in the database; create queries that allow you to ask questions concerning the data in the database; and create forms and reports using the data in the database.

To Run an App

The following steps, which assume Windows is running, run the Access app based on a typical installation. You may need to ask your instructor how to run apps for your computer.

1. Type `Access 2016` as the search text in the search box and watch the search results appear in the search results.
2. Click the app name, Access 2016 in this case, in the search results to run Access.
3. If the window is not maximized, click the Maximize button on its title bar to maximize the window (Figure 92).

Q&A Do I have to run Access using these steps?

No. You can use any previously discussed method of running an Office app to run Access.

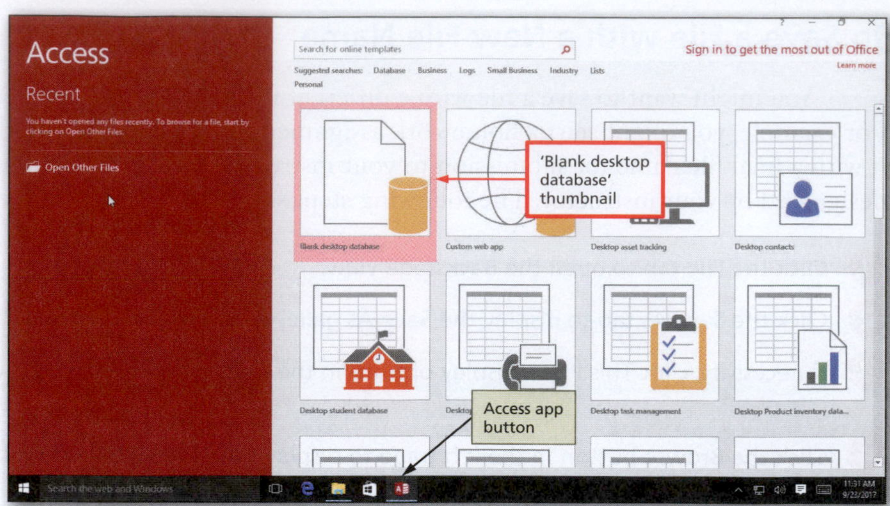

Figure 92

Unique Elements in Access

You work on objects such as tables, forms, and reports in the **Access work area**. Figure 93 shows a work area with multiple objects open. **Object tabs** for the open objects appear at the top of the work area. You select an open object by clicking its tab. In the figure, the Customer List table is the selected object. To the left of the work area is the Navigation Pane, which contains a list of all the objects in the database. You use this pane to open an object. You also can customize the way objects are displayed in the Navigation Pane.

Because the Navigation Pane can take up space in the window, you may not have as much open space for working as you would with Word or Excel. You can use the 'Shutter Bar Open/Close Button' to minimize the Navigation Pane when you are not using it, which allows more space to work with tables, forms, reports, and other database elements.

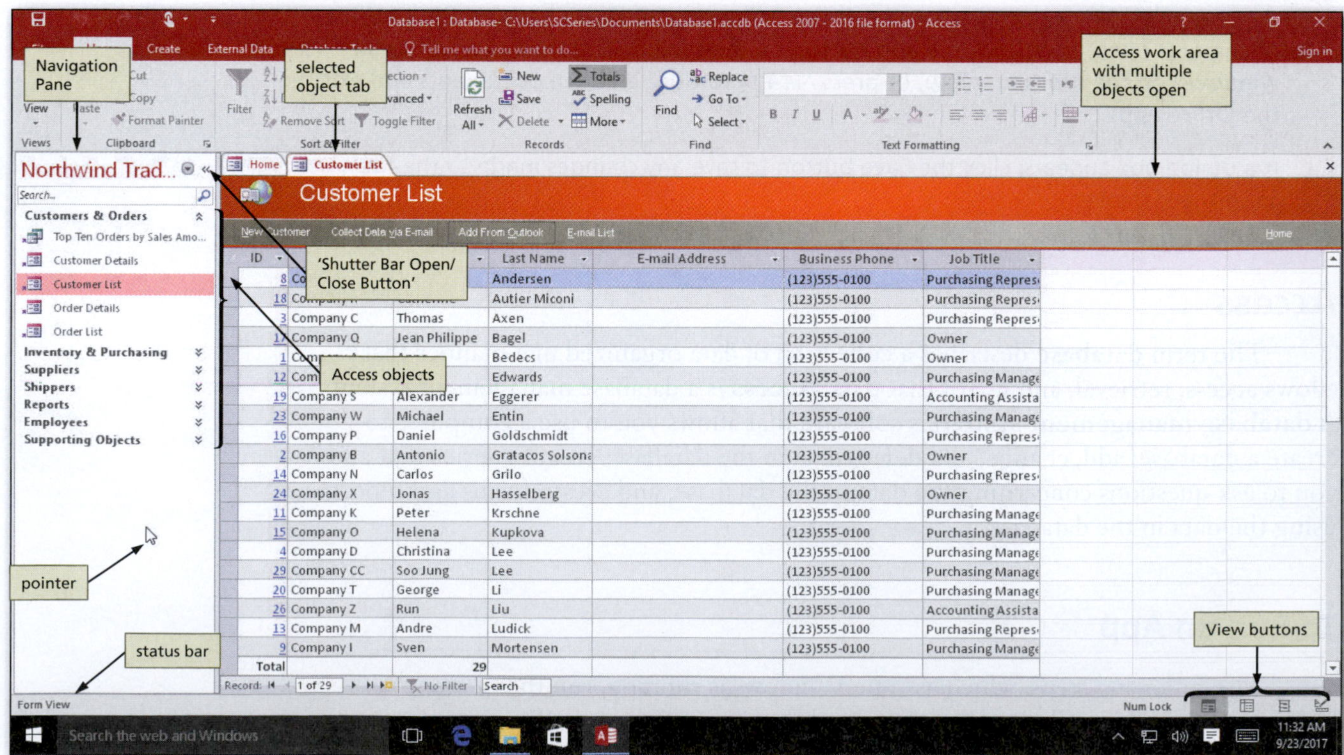

Figure 93

Ribbon When you run Access, the ribbon displays five main tabs: File, Home, Create, External Data, and Database Tools. Access has unique groupings such as Sort & Filter and Records that are designed specifically for working with databases. Many of the formatting options are reserved for the tool tabs that appear when you are working with forms and reports.

To Create an Access Database

1 SIGN IN | 2 USE WINDOWS | 3 USE APPS | 4 FILE MANAGEMENT | 5 SWITCH APPS | 6 SAVE FILES
7 CHANGE SCREEN RESOLUTION | 8 EXIT APPS | 9 USE ADDITIONAL APPS | 10 USE HELP

Unlike the other Office apps, Access saves a database when you first create it. When working in Access, you will add data to an Access database. As you add data to a database, Access automatically saves your changes rather than waiting until you manually save the database or exit Access. Recall that in Word and Excel, you entered the data first and then saved it.

Because Access automatically saves the database as you add and change data, you do not always have to click the Save button on the Quick Access Toolbar. Instead, the Save button in Access is used for saving the objects (including tables, queries, forms, reports, and other database objects) a database contains. You can use either the 'Blank desktop database' option or a template to create a new database. If you already know the organization of your database, you would use the 'Blank desktop database' option. If not, you can use a template. Templates can guide you by suggesting some commonly used database organizations.

The following steps use the 'Blank desktop database' option to create a database named Rimitoein Electronics in the Access folder in the class folder (CIS 101, in this case) in the Documents folder. ***Why?*** *You have decided to use Microsoft Access to maintain large amounts of data.*

1

- Click the 'Blank desktop database' thumbnail (shown in Figure 92) to select the database type.
- Type **Rimitoein Electronics** in the File Name text box (Blank desktop database dialog box) to enter the new file name. Do not press the ENTER key after typing the file name because you do not want to create the database at this time (Figure 94).

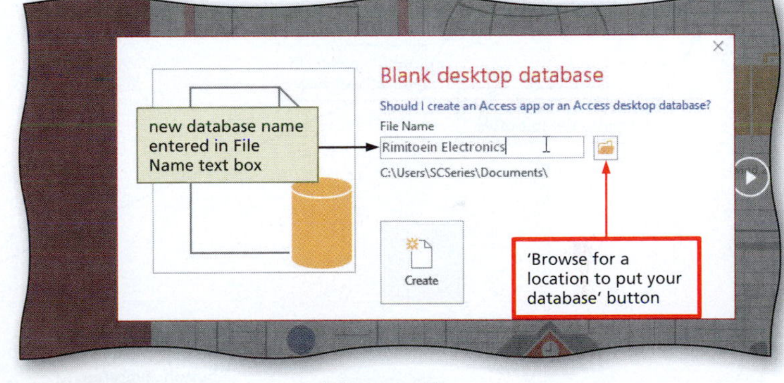

Figure 94

2

- Click the 'Browse for a location to put your database' button to display the File New Database dialog box.
- Navigate to the location for the database, that is, the Documents folder, then to the folder identifying your class (CIS 101, in this case), and then to the Access folder (Figure 95). For specific instructions, perform the tasks in Steps 5a through 5e in the previous section titled To Save a File in a Folder, replacing the PowerPoint folder with the Access folder.

Q&A Why does the 'Save as type' box say Microsoft Access 2007-2016 Databases?

Microsoft Access database formats change with some new versions of Microsoft Access. The most recent format is the Microsoft Access 2007-2016 Databases format, which was released with Access 2007.

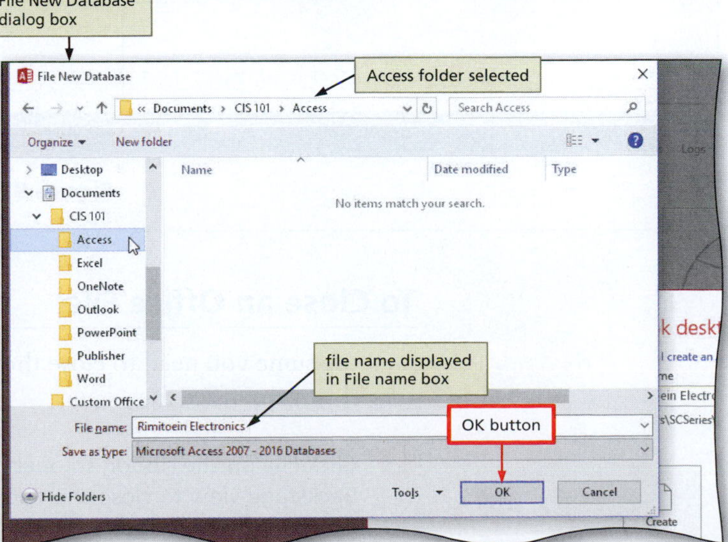

Figure 95

- Click the OK button (File New Database dialog box) to select the Access folder as the location for the database and close the dialog box (Figure 96).

4

- Click the Create button (Blank desktop database dialog box) to create the database on the selected drive in the selected folder with the file name, Rimitoein Electronics (Figure 97).

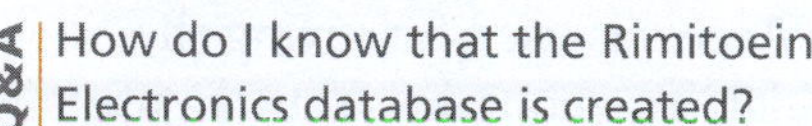

Q&A How do I know that the Rimitoein Electronics database is created?
The file name of the database appears on the title bar.

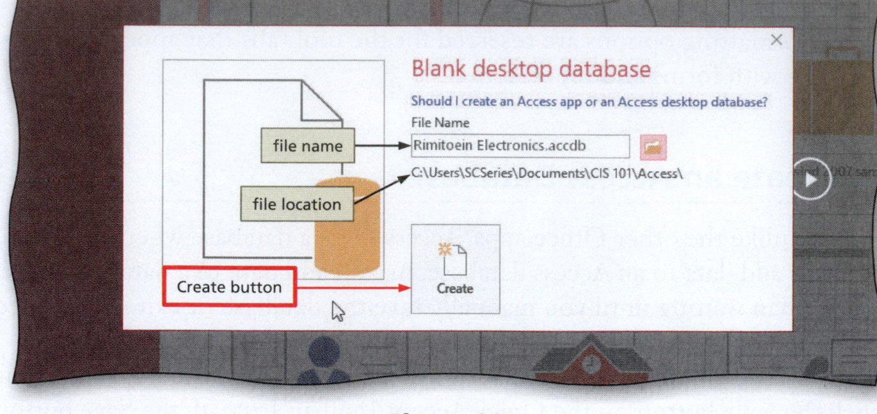

Figure 96

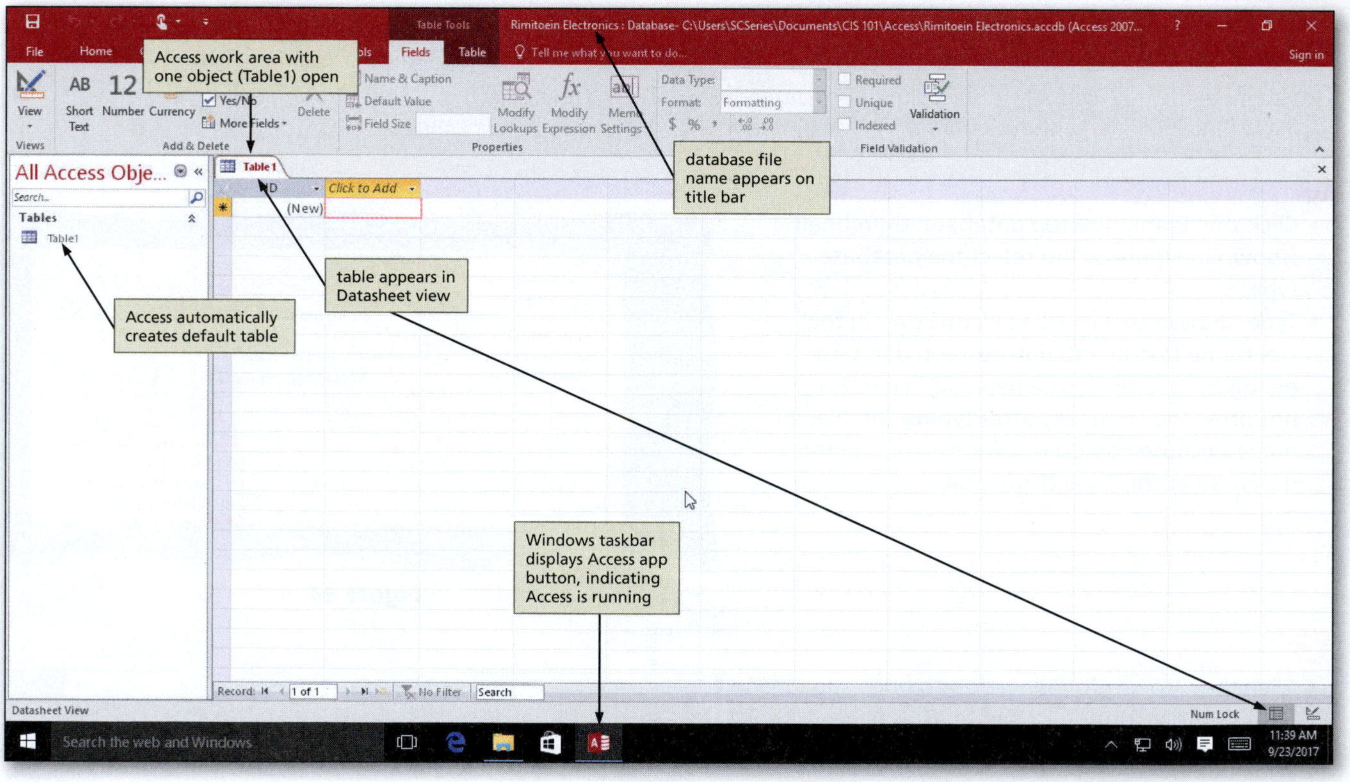

Access work area with one object (Table1) open

database file name appears on title bar

table appears in Datasheet view

Access automatically creates default table

Windows taskbar displays Access app button, indicating Access is running

Figure 97

To Close an Office File

Assume you need to close the Access database and return to it later. The following step closes an Office file.

1 Click File on the ribbon to open the Backstage view and then click Close in the Backstage view to close the open file (Rimitoein Electronics, in this case) without exiting the active app.

Q&A Why is Access still on the screen?
When you close a database, the app remains running.

To Open an Existing Office File

Assume you wish to continue working on an existing file, that is, a file you previously saved. Earlier in this module, you learned how to open a recently used file through the Backstage view. The following step opens a database, specifically the Rimitoein Electronics database, that recently was saved. ***Why?*** *Because the file has been created already, you just need to reopen it.*

- Click File on the ribbon to open the Backstage view and then click Open in the Backstage view to display the Open gallery in the Backstage view.
- Click This PC to display recent folders accessed on your computer.
- Click the Browse button to display the Open dialog box.
- If necessary, navigate to the location of the file to open.
- Click the file to open, Rimitoein Electronics in this case, to select the file (Figure 98).
- Click the Open button (Open dialog box) to open the file. If necessary, click the Enable Content button.

Q&A Why did the Security Warning appear?
The Security Warning appears when you open an Office file that might contain harmful content. The files you create in this module are not harmful, but you should be cautious when opening files from other people.

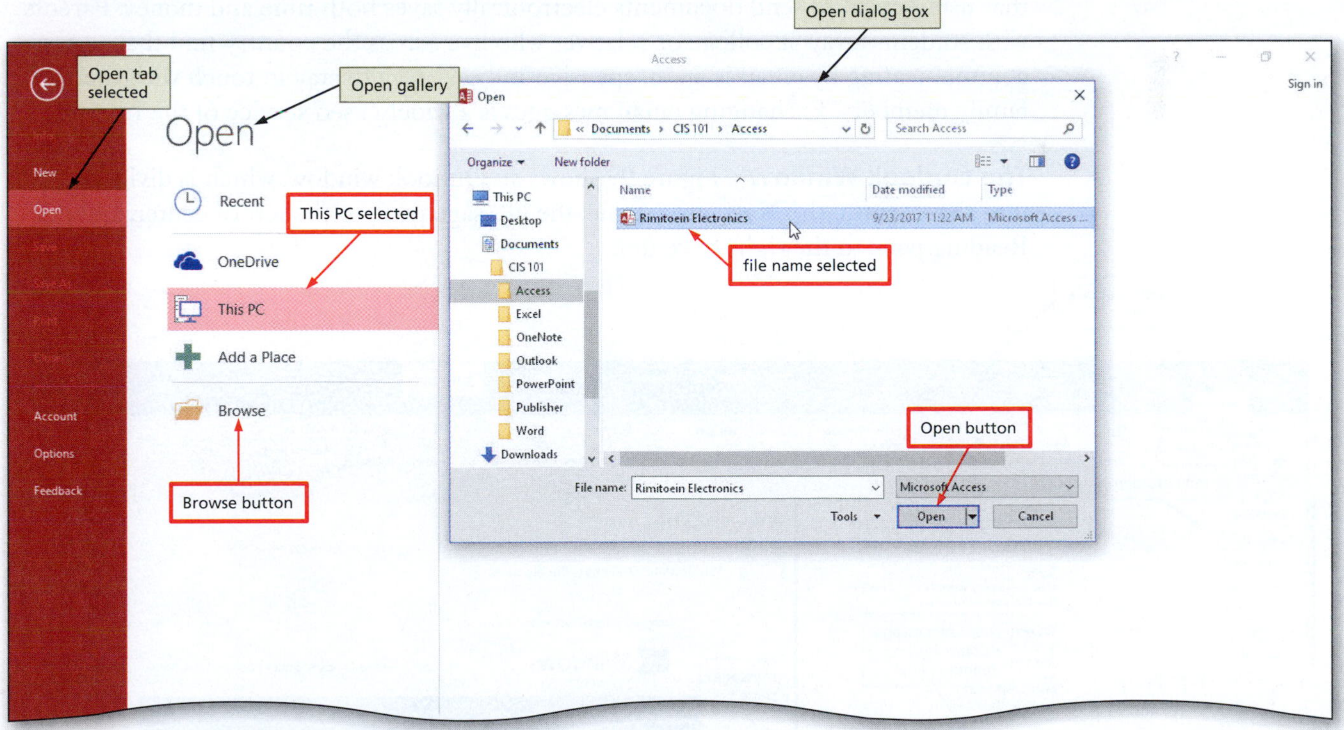

Figure 98

Other Ways

1. Press CTRL+O
2. Navigate to file in File Explorer window, double-click file name

To Exit an Office App

You are finished using Access. The following step exits Access.

1 Click the Close button on the right side of the title bar to close the file and exit the Office app.

Other Office Apps

In addition to the Office apps discussed thus far, three other apps are useful when collaborating and communicating with others: Outlook, Publisher, and OneNote.

Outlook

Outlook is a powerful communications and scheduling app that helps you communicate with others, keep track of contacts, and organize your calendar. Apps such as Outlook provide a way for individuals and workgroups to organize, find, view, and share information easily. Outlook allows you to send and receive email messages and provides a means to organize contacts. Users can track email messages, meetings, and notes related to a particular contact. Outlook's Calendar, People, Tasks, and Notes components aid in this organization. Contact information readily is available from the Outlook Calendar, Mail, People, and Task components by accessing the Search Contacts feature.

Email is the transmission of messages and files over a computer network. Email has become an important means of exchanging information and files between business associates, classmates and instructors, friends, and family. Businesses find that using email to send documents electronically saves both time and money. Parents with students away at college or relatives who live across the country find that communicating by email is an inexpensive and easy way to stay in touch with their family members. Exchanging email messages is a widely used service of the Internet.

The Outlook Window Figure 99 shows an Outlook window, which is divided into three panes: the Navigation pane, the message pane to the left of center, and the Reading pane to the right of center.

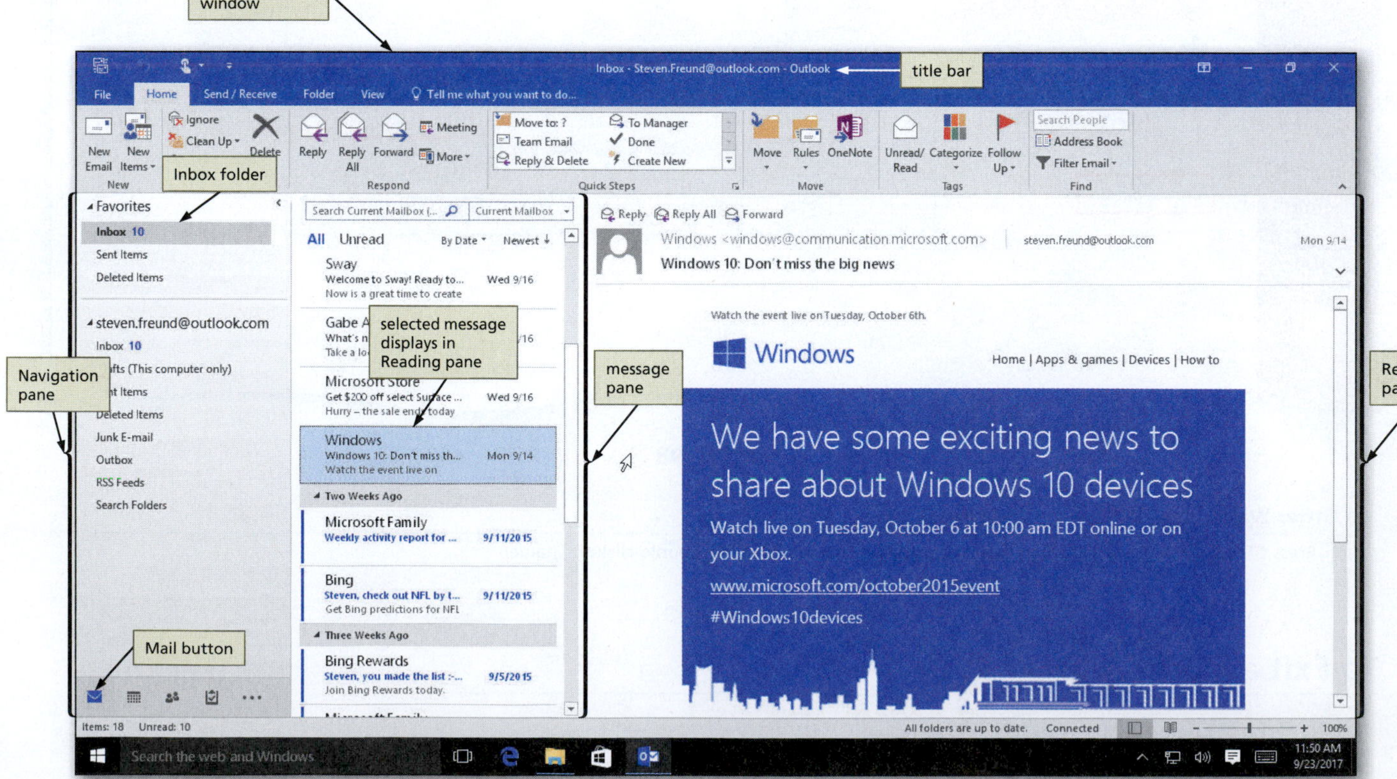

Figure 99

When an email message is open in Outlook, it is displayed in a Message window (Figure 100). When you open a message, the Message tab on the ribbon appears, which contains the more frequently used commands.

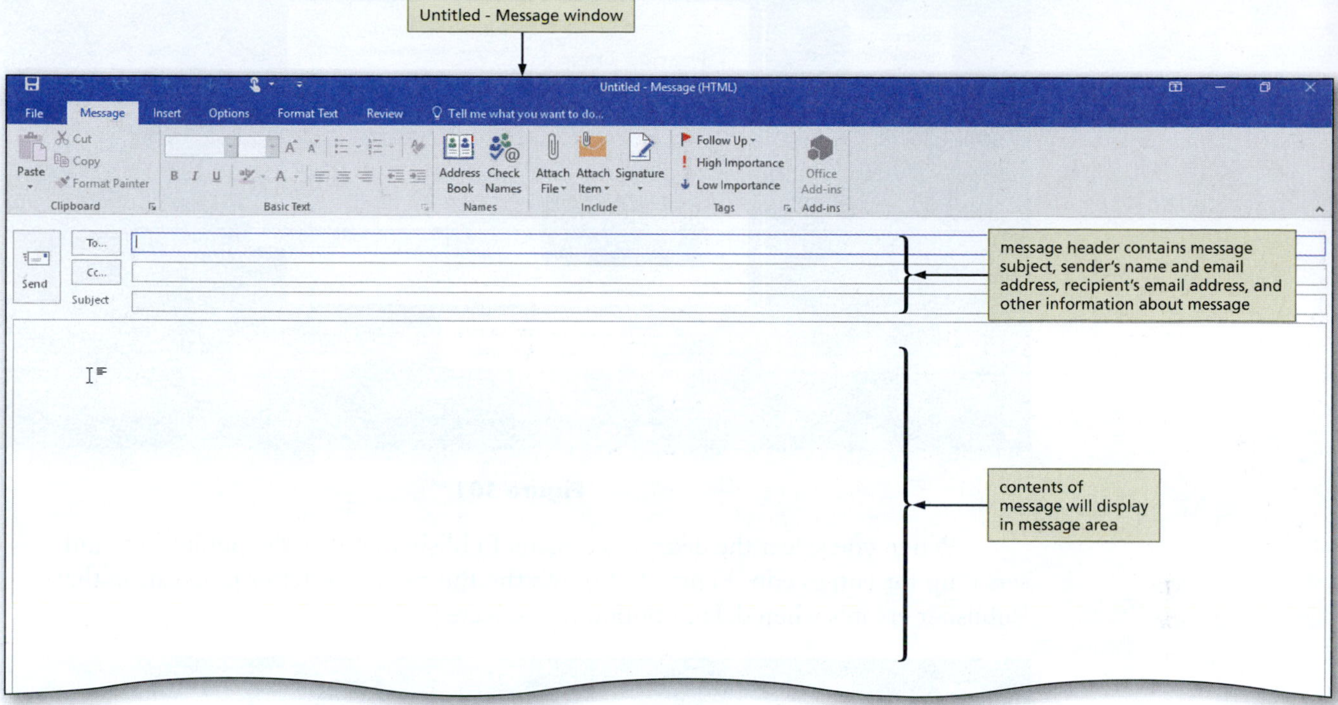

Figure 100

Publisher

Publisher is a powerful desktop publishing (DTP) app that assists you in designing and producing professional-quality documents that combine text, graphics, illustrations, and photos. DTP software provides additional tools beyond those typically found in word processing apps, including design templates, graphic manipulation tools, color schemes or libraries, advanced layout and printing tools, and web components. For large jobs, businesses use DTP software to design publications that are camera ready, which means the files are suitable for outside commercial printing. In addition, DTP software can be used to create webpages and interactive web forms.

Publisher is used by people who regularly produce high-quality color publications, such as newsletters, brochures, flyers, logos, signs, catalogs, cards, and business forms. Publisher has many features designed to simplify production and make publications visually appealing. Using Publisher, you easily can change the shape, size, and color of text and graphics. You can include many kinds of graphical objects, including mastheads, borders, tables, images, pictures, charts, and web objects in publications, as well as integrate spreadsheets and databases.

BTW

Running Publisher

When you first run Publisher, the New templates gallery usually is displayed in the Backstage view. If it is not displayed, click File on the ribbon, click the Options tab in the Backstage view, click General (Publisher Options dialog box), and then click 'Show the New template gallery when starting Publisher' to select the check box in the right pane.

The Publisher Window Publisher initially displays a list of publication types. **Publication types** are typical publications used by desktop publishers. The more popular types are displayed in the center of the window.

Once you select a publication type, a dialog box is displayed to allow you to create the publication (Figure 101). Some templates are installed with Publisher, and others are available online. In Figure 101, the Business newsletter publication dialog box is displayed.

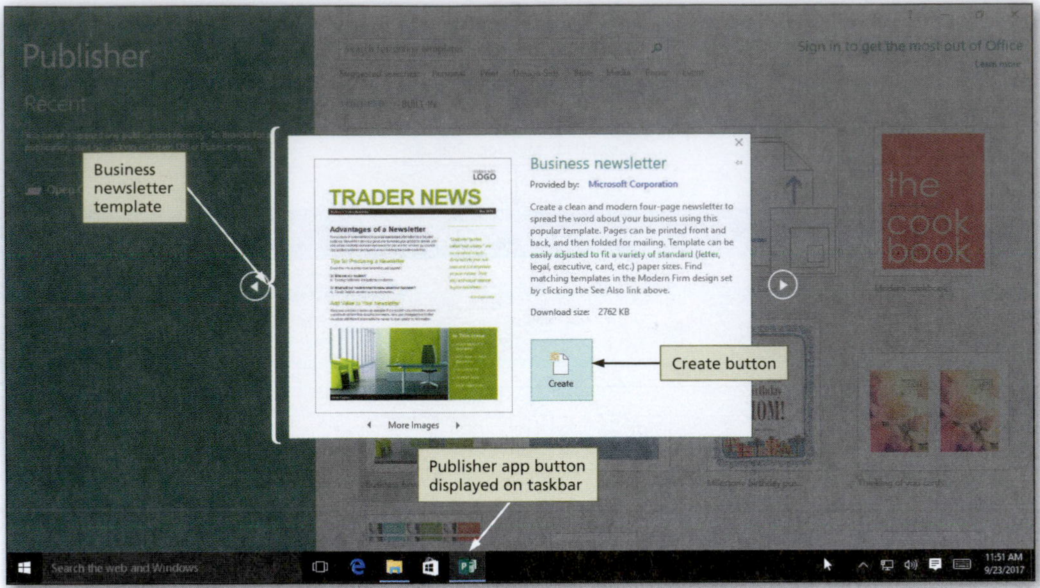

Figure 101

When you select the desired template, Publisher creates the publication and sets it up for you to edit. Figure 102 shows the Business newsletter publication that Publisher creates when default options are selected.

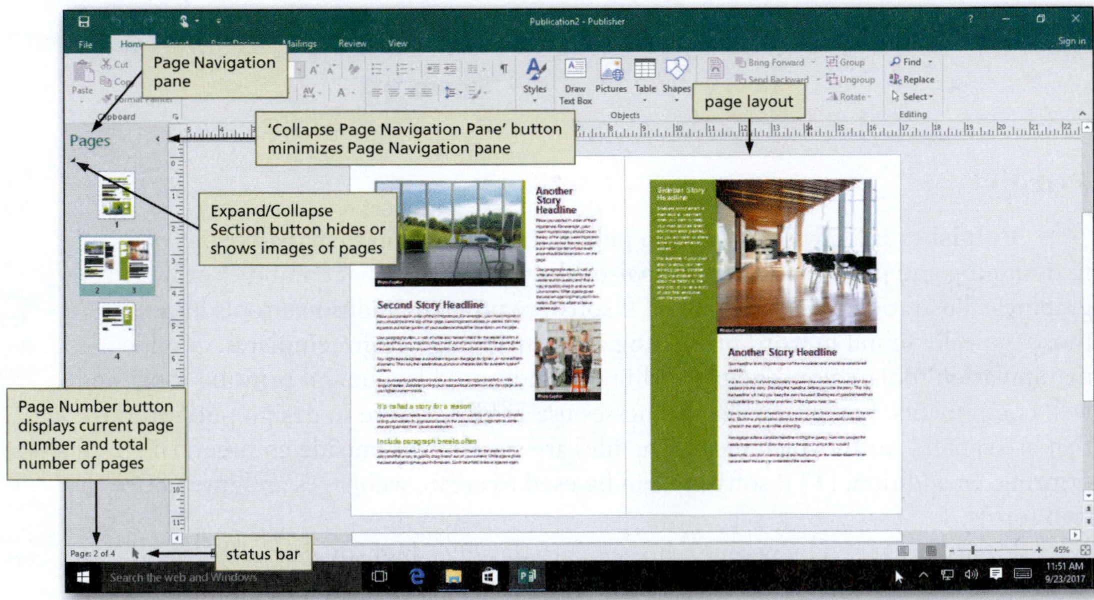

Figure 102

OneNote

OneNote is a note taking app that assists you in entering, saving, organizing, searching, and using notes. It enables you to create pages, which are organized in sections, just as in a physical notebook. In OneNote, you can type notes anywhere on a page and then easily move the notes around on the page. You can create lists and outlines, use handwriting to enter notes, and create drawings. If you use a tablet to add handwritten notes to a document, OneNote can convert the handwriting to text. It also can perform searches on the handwritten entries. Pictures and data from other apps easily are incorporated in your notes.

In addition to typing and handwriting, you can take audio notes. For example, you could record conversations during a meeting or lecture. As you record, you can take additional notes. When you play back the audio notes, you can synchronize the additional notes you took; that is, OneNote will show you during playback the exact points at which you added the notes. A variety of note flags, which are symbols that call your attention to notes on a page, enable you to flag notes as being important. You then can use the Note Flags summary to view the flagged notes, which can be sorted in a variety of ways.

OneNote includes tools to assist you with organizing a notebook and navigating its contents. It also includes a search feature, making it easy to find the specific notes in which you are interested. For short notes that you always want to have available readily, you can use Side Notes, which are used much like the sticky notes that you might use in a physical notebook.

OneNote Window All activity in OneNote takes place in the **notebook** (Figure 103). Like a physical notebook, the OneNote notebook consists of notes that are placed on **pages**. The pages are grouped into **sections**, which can be further grouped into **folders**. (No folders are shown in the notebook in the figure.) You can use the Search box to search for specific text in your notes.

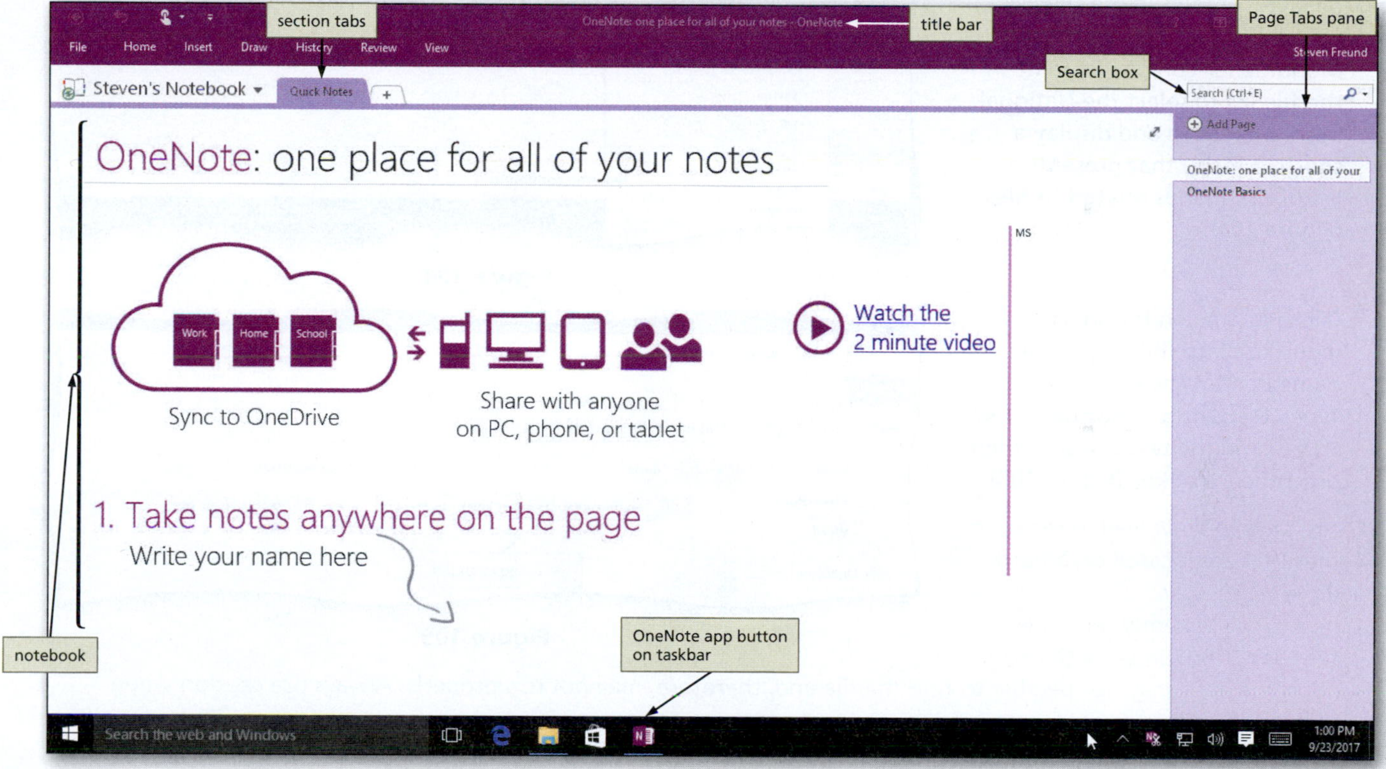

Figure 103

You can add pages to the notebook using the Add Page button in the Page Tabs pane. If page tabs are displayed, you can switch to a page by clicking its tab. Figure 103 shows the Quick Notes page being displayed for the notebook.

Break Point: If you wish to take a break, this is a good place to do so. To resume at a later time, continue to follow the steps from this location forward.

Renaming, Moving, and Deleting Files

Earlier in this module, you learned how to organize files in folders, which is part of a process known as **file management**. The following sections cover additional file management topics including renaming, moving, and deleting files.

To Rename a File

1 SIGN IN | 2 USE WINDOWS | 3 USE APPS | 4 FILE MANAGEMENT | 5 SWITCH APPS | 6 SAVE FILES
7 CHANGE SCREEN RESOLUTION | 8 EXIT APPS | 9 USE ADDITIONAL APPS | 10 USE HELP

In some circumstances, you may want to change the name of, or rename, a file or a folder. ***Why?*** *You may want to distinguish a file in one folder or drive from a copy of a similar file, or you may decide to rename a file to better identify its contents.* The following steps change the name of the National Monuments file in the Word folder to National Monuments Flyer.

- If necessary, click the File Explorer button on the taskbar to make the folder window the active window.
- Navigate to the location of the file to be renamed (in this case, the Word folder in the CIS 101 [or your class folder] folder in the Documents folder) to display the file(s) it contains in the file list.
- Right-click the National Monuments icon or file name in the file list to select the National Monuments file and display a shortcut menu that presents a list of commands related to files (Figure 104).

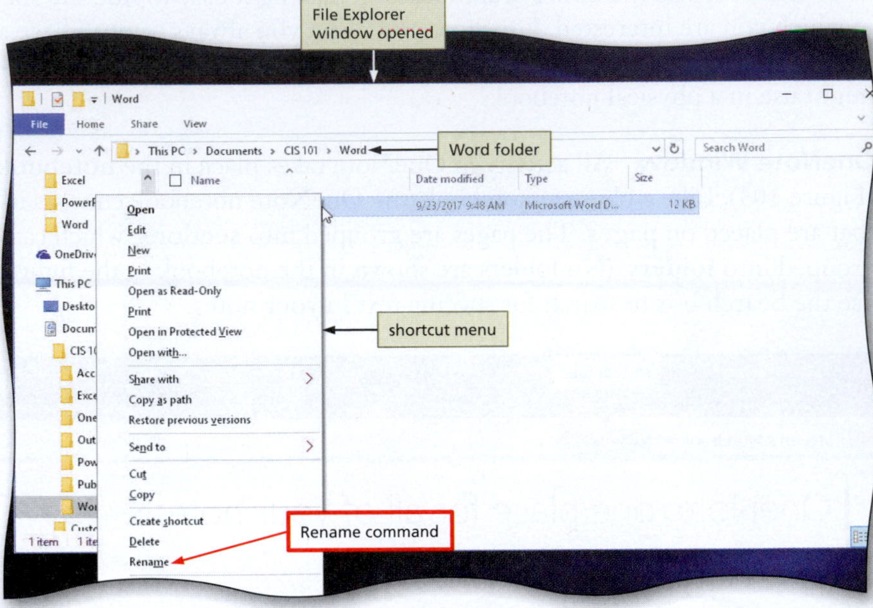

Figure 104

- Click Rename on the shortcut menu to place the current file name in a text box.
- Type **National Monuments Flyer** in the text box and then press the ENTER key (Figure 105).

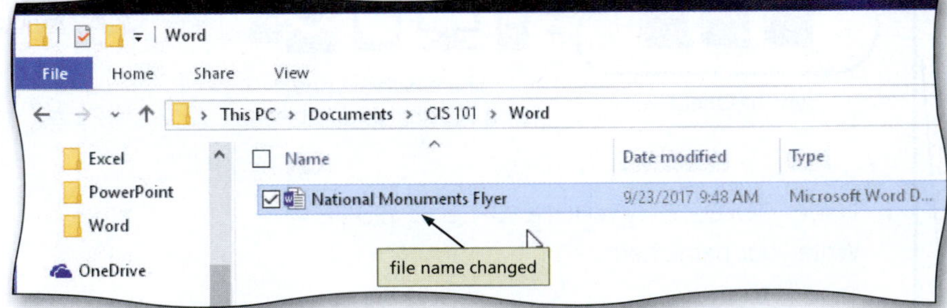

Figure 105

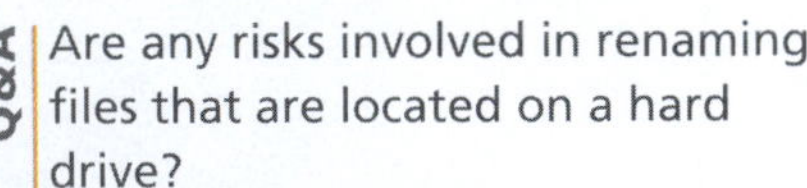

Q&A Are any risks involved in renaming files that are located on a hard drive?

If you inadvertently rename a file that is associated with certain apps, the apps may not be able to find the file and, therefore, may not run properly. Always use caution when renaming files.

Can I rename a file when it is open?

No, a file must be closed to change the file name.

Other Ways

1. Select file, press F2, type new file name, press ENTER 2. Select file, click Rename (Home tab | Organize group), type new file name, press ENTER

To Move a File

1 SIGN IN | 2 USE WINDOWS | 3 USE APPS | 4 FILE MANAGEMENT | 5 SWITCH APPS | 6 SAVE FILES
7 CHANGE SCREEN RESOLUTION | 8 EXIT APPS | 9 USE ADDITIONAL APPS | 10 USE HELP

Why? *At some time, you may want to move a file from one folder, called the source folder, to another, called the destination folder.* When you move a file, it no longer appears in the original folder. If the destination and the source folders are on the same media, you can move a file by dragging it. If the folders are on different media, then you will need to right-drag the file, and then click Move here on the shortcut menu. The following step moves the Silver Sky Hardware Sales Summary file from the Excel folder to the OneNote folder.

- In File Explorer, navigate to the location of the file to be moved (in this case, the Excel folder in the CIS 101 folder [or your class folder] in the Documents folder).
- Click the Excel folder in the navigation pane to display the files it contains in the right pane (Figure 106).
- Drag the Silver Sky Hardware Sales Summary file in the right pane to the OneNote folder in the navigation pane.

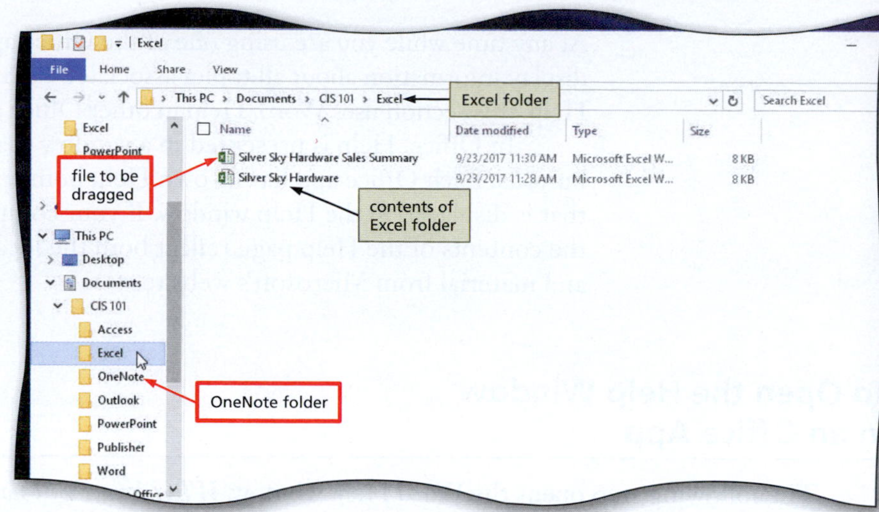

Figure 106

Other Ways

1. Right-click file to move, click Cut on shortcut menu, right-click destination folder, click Paste on shortcut menu
2. Select file to move, press CTRL+X, select destination folder, press CTRL+V

To Delete a File

1 SIGN IN | 2 USE WINDOWS | 3 USE APPS | **4 FILE MANAGEMENT** | 5 SWITCH APPS | 6 SAVE FILES
7 CHANGE SCREEN RESOLUTION | 8 EXIT APPS | 9 USE ADDITIONAL APPS | **10 USE HELP**

A final task you may want to perform is to delete a file. Exercise extreme caution when deleting a file or files. When you delete a file from a hard drive, the deleted file is stored in the Recycle Bin where you can recover it until you empty the Recycle Bin. If you delete a file from removable media, such as a USB flash drive, the file is deleted permanently. The next steps delete the Visiting National Monuments file from the PowerPoint folder. ***Why?*** *When a file no longer is needed, you can delete it to conserve space on your storage location.*

- In File Explorer, navigate to the location of the file to be deleted (in this case, the PowerPoint folder in the CIS 101 folder [or your class folder] in the Documents folder).
- Click the Visiting National Monuments icon or file name in the right pane to select the file.
- Right-click the selected file to display a shortcut menu (Figure 107).

- Click Delete on the shortcut menu to delete the file.
- If a dialog box appears, click the Yes button to delete the file.

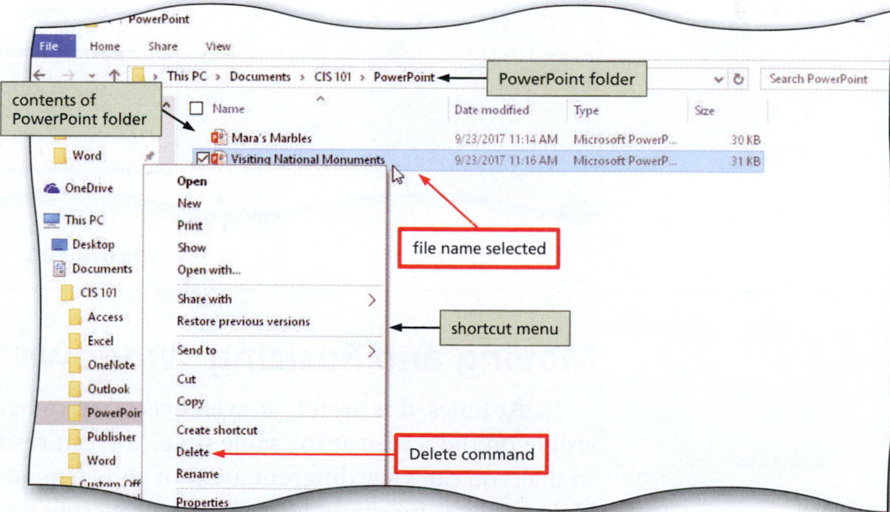

Figure 107

Q&A Can I use this same technique to delete a folder?

Yes. Right-click the folder and then click Delete on the shortcut menu. When you delete a folder, all of the files and folders contained in the folder you are deleting, together with any files and folders on lower hierarchical levels, are deleted as well. For example, if you delete the CIS 101 folder, you will delete all folders and files inside the CIS 101 folder.

Other Ways

1. Select file, press DELETE

Microsoft Office and Windows Help

At any time while you are using one of the Office apps, you can use Office Help to display information about all topics associated with the app. To illustrate the use of Office Help, this section uses Word. Help in other Office apps operates in a similar fashion.

In Office, Help is presented in a window that has browser-style navigation buttons. Each Office app has its own Help home page, which is the starting Help page that is displayed in the Help window. If your computer is connected to the Internet, the contents of the Help page reflect both the local help files installed on the computer and material from Microsoft's website.

To Open the Help Window in an Office App

1 SIGN IN | 2 USE WINDOWS | 3 USE APPS | 4 FILE MANAGEMENT | 5 SWITCH APPS | 6 SAVE FILES
7 CHANGE SCREEN RESOLUTION | 8 EXIT APPS | 9 USE ADDITIONAL APPS | **10 USE HELP**

The following step opens the Word Help window. ***Why?*** *You might not understand how certain commands or operations work in Word, so you can obtain the necessary information using help.*

- Run an Office app, in this case Word.
- Click the Blank document thumbnail to display a blank document.
- Press F1 to open the app's Help window (Figure 108).

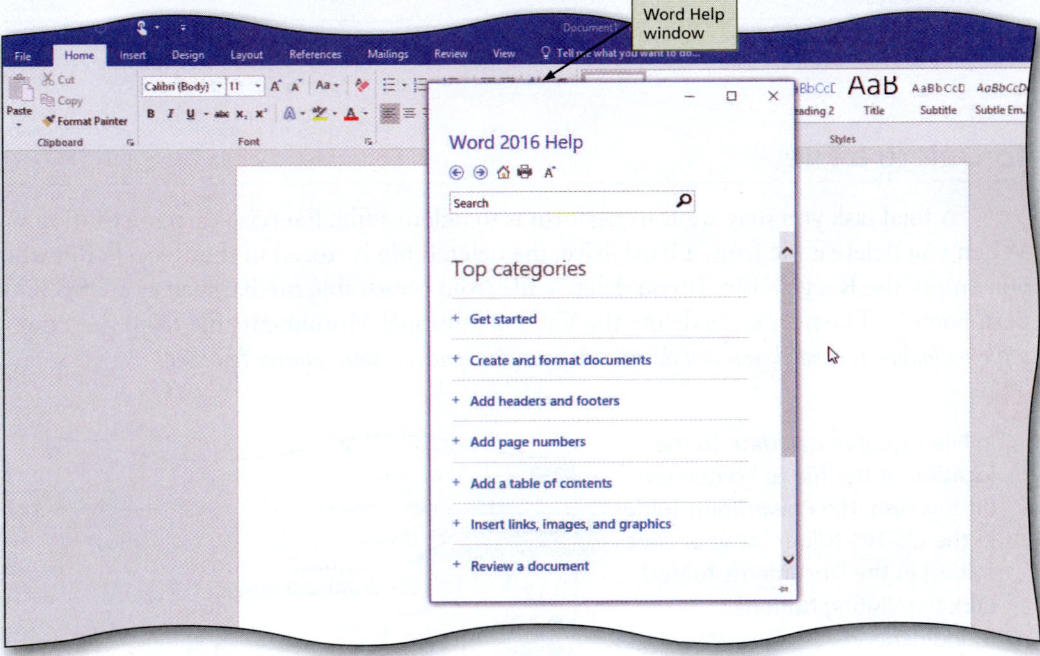

Figure 108

Moving and Resizing Windows

At times, it is useful, or even necessary, to have more than one window open and visible on the screen at the same time. You can resize and move these open windows so that you can view different areas of and elements in the window. In the case of the Help window, for example, it could be covering document text in the Word window that you need to see.

To Move a Window by Dragging

1 SIGN IN | **2 USE WINDOWS** | 3 USE APPS | 4 FILE MANAGEMENT | 5 SWITCH APPS | 6 SAVE FILES
7 CHANGE SCREEN RESOLUTION | 8 EXIT APPS | 9 USE ADDITIONAL APPS | 10 USE HELP

You can move any open window that is not maximized to another location on the desktop by dragging the title bar of the window. ***Why?*** *You might want to have a better view of what is behind the window or just want to move the window so that you can see it better.* The following step drags the Word Help window to the upper-left corner of the desktop.

- Drag the window title bar (the Word Help window title bar, in this case) so that the window moves to the upper-left corner of the desktop, as shown in Figure 109.

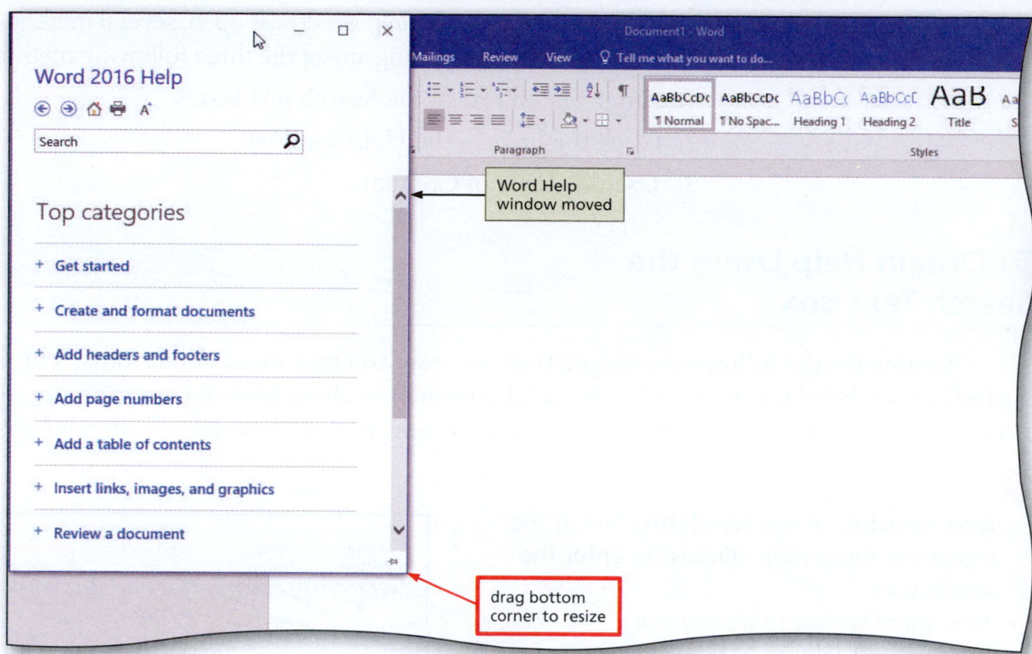

Figure 109

To Resize a Window by Dragging

1 SIGN IN | **2 USE WINDOWS** | 3 USE APPS | 4 FILE MANAGEMENT | 5 SWITCH APPS | 6 SAVE FILES
7 CHANGE SCREEN RESOLUTION | 8 EXIT APPS | 9 USE ADDITIONAL APPS | 10 USE HELP

A method used to change the size of the window is to drag the window borders. The following step changes the size of the Word Help window by dragging its borders. ***Why?*** *Sometimes, information is not visible completely in a window, and you want to increase the size of the window.*

- If you are using a mouse, point to the lower-right corner of the window (the Word Help window, in this case) until the pointer changes to a two-headed arrow.
- Drag the bottom border downward to display more of the active window (Figure 110).

Q&A Can I drag other borders on the window to enlarge or shrink the window?
Yes, you can drag the left, right, and top borders and any window corner to resize a window.

Q&A Will Windows remember the new size of the window after I close it?
Yes. When you reopen the window, Windows will display it at the same size it was when you closed it.

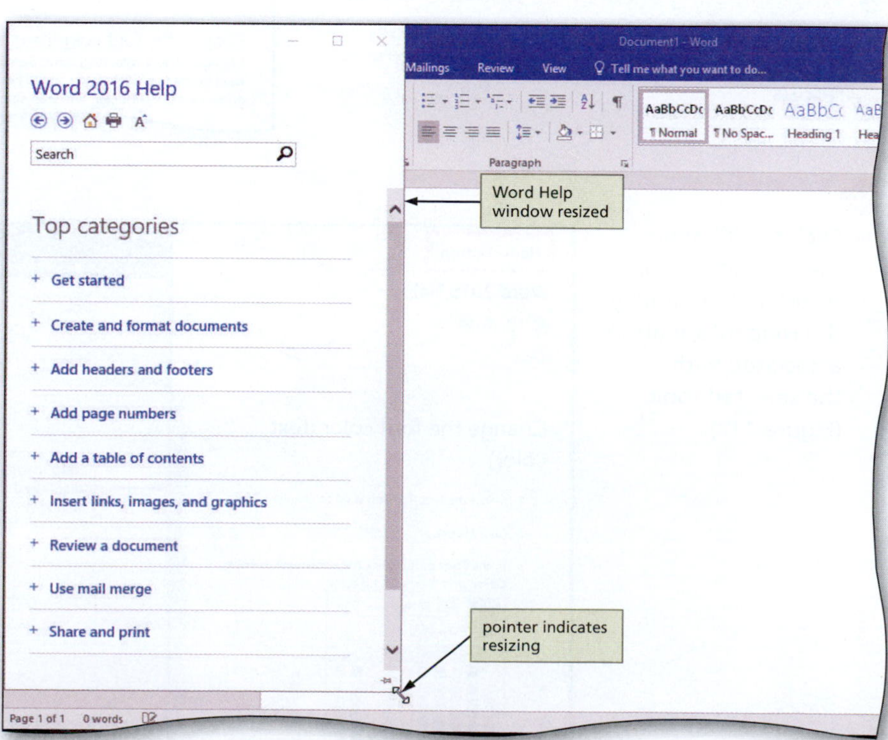

Figure 110

Using Office Help

Once an Office app's Help window is open, several methods exist for navigating Help. You can search for help by using any of the three following methods from the Help window:

1. Enter search text in the Search text box.
2. Click the links in the Help window.
3. Use the Table of Contents.

To Obtain Help Using the Search Text Box

1 SIGN IN | 2 USE WINDOWS | 3 USE APPS | 4 FILE MANAGEMENT | 5 SWITCH APPS | 6 SAVE FILES
7 CHANGE SCREEN RESOLUTION | 8 EXIT APPS | 9 USE ADDITIONAL APPS | **10 USE HELP**

Assume for the following example that you want to know more about fonts. The following steps use the 'Search online help' text box to obtain useful information about fonts by entering the word, fonts, as search text. ***Why?*** *You may not know the exact help topic you are looking to find, so using keywords can help narrow your search.*

- Type **fonts** in the Search text box at the top of the Word Help window to enter the search text.
- Press the ENTER key to display the search results (Figure 111).

Q&A Why do my search results differ?
If you do not have an Internet connection, your results will reflect only the content of the Help files on your computer. When searching for help online, results also can change as material is added, deleted, and updated on the online Help webpages maintained by Microsoft.

Q&A Why were my search results not very helpful?
When initiating a search, be sure to check the spelling of the search text; also, keep your search specific to return the most accurate results.

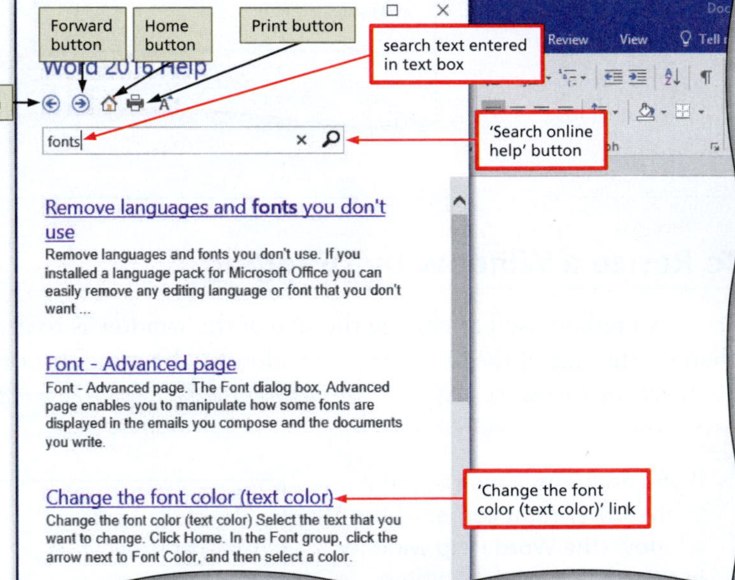

Figure 111

- Click the 'Change the font color (text color)' link to display the Help information associated with the selected topic (Figure 112).

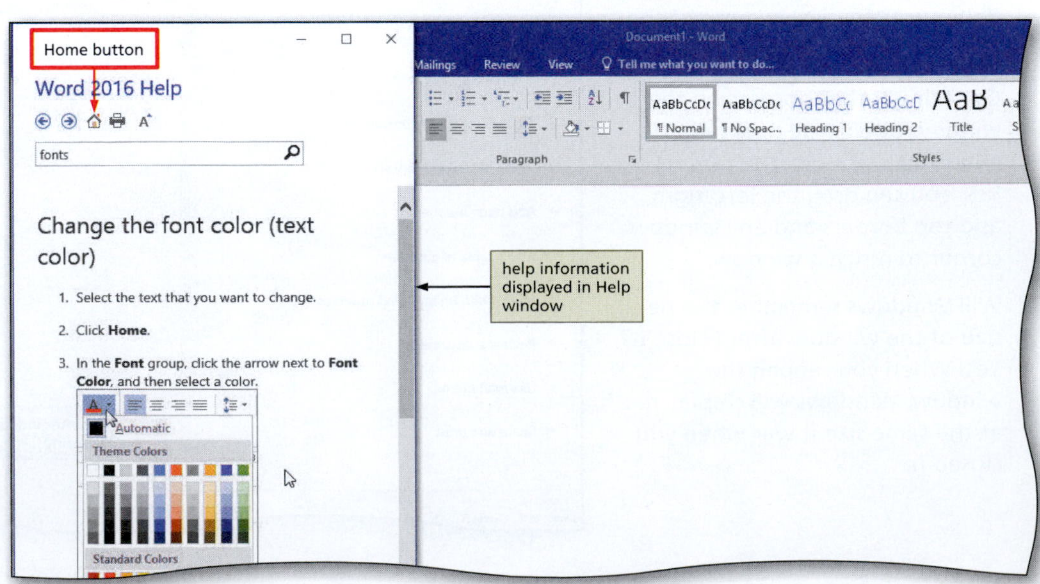

Figure 112

3

- Click the Home button in the Help window to clear the search results and redisplay the Help home page (Figure 113).
- Click the Close button in the Word 2016 Help window to close the window.

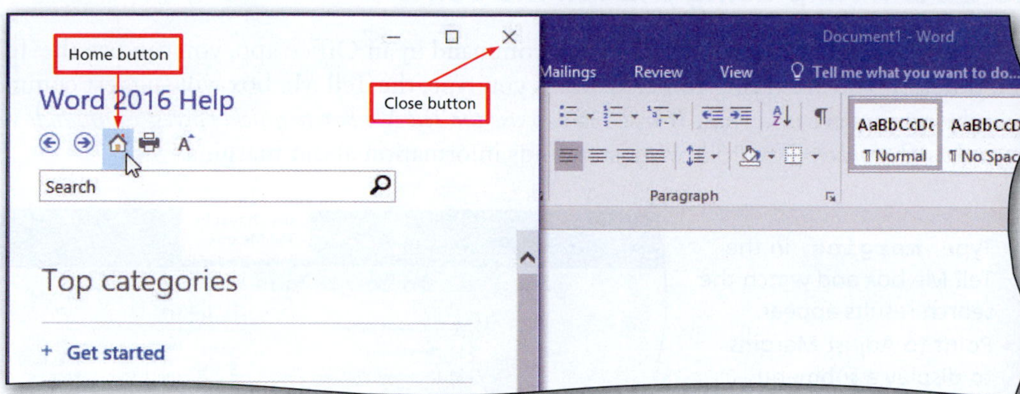

Figure 113

Obtaining Help while Working in an Office App

Help in the Office apps provides you with the ability to obtain help directly, without opening the Help window and initiating a search. For example, you may be unsure about how a particular command works, or you may be presented with a dialog box that you are not sure how to use.

Figure 114 shows one option for obtaining help while working in an Office app. If you want to learn more about a command, point to its button and wait for the ScreenTip to appear. If the Help icon and 'Tell me more' link appear in the ScreenTip, click the 'Tell me more' link or press the F1 key while pointing to the button to open the Help window associated with that command.

Figure 115 shows a dialog box that contains a Help button. Clicking the Help button or pressing the F1 key while the dialog box is displayed opens a Help window. The Help window contains help about that dialog box, if available. If no help file is available for that particular dialog box, then the main Help window opens.

As mentioned previously, the Tell Me box is available in most Office apps and can perform a variety of functions. One of these functions is to provide easy access to commands by typing a description of the command.

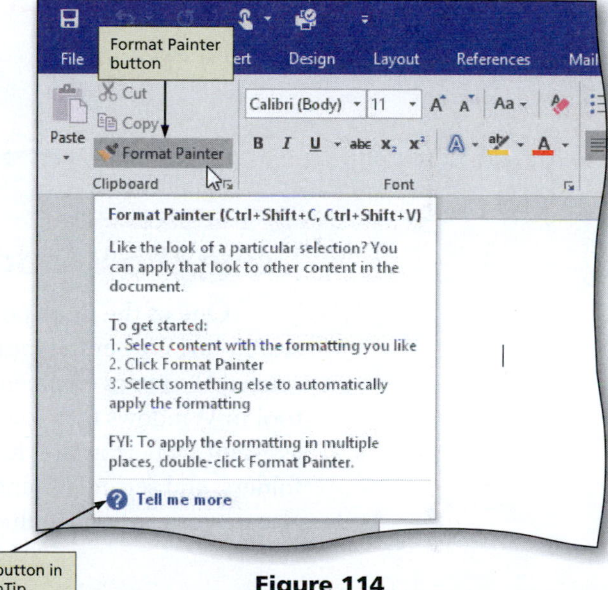

Figure 114

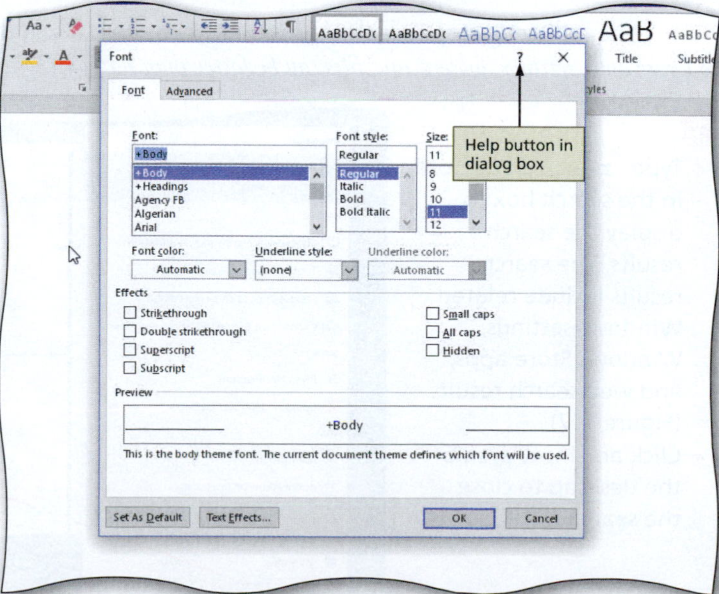

Figure 115

To Obtain Help Using the Tell Me Box

If you are having trouble finding a command in an Office app, you can use the Tell Me box to search for the function you are trying to perform. As you type, the Tell Me box will suggest commands that match the search text you are entering. ***Why?*** *You can use the Tell Me box to quickly access commands you otherwise may be unable to find on the ribbon.* The following step finds information about margins.

- Type **`margins`** in the Tell Me box and watch the search results appear.
- Point to Adjust Margins to display a submenu displaying the various margin settings (Figure 116).
- Click an empty area of the document window to close the search results.

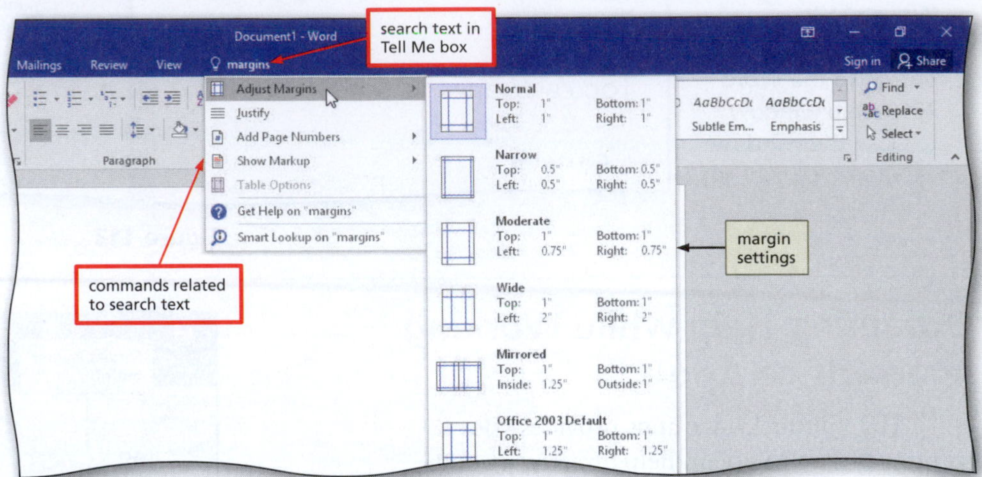

Figure 116

2

- Exit Microsoft Word.

Using the Windows Search Box

One of the more powerful Windows features is the Windows search box. The search box is a central location from where you can type search text and quickly access related Windows commands or web search results. In addition, **Cortana** is a new search tool in Windows that you can access using the search box. It can act as a personal assistant by performing functions such as providing ideas; searching for apps, files, and folders; and setting reminders. In addition to typing search text in the search box, you also can use your computer or mobile device's microphone to give verbal commands.

To Use the Windows Search Box

The following step uses the Windows search box to search for a Windows command. ***Why?*** *Using the search box to locate apps, settings, folders, and files can be faster than navigating windows and dialog boxes to search for the desired content.*

- Type **`notification`** in the search box to display the search results. The search results include related Windows settings, Windows Store apps, and web search results (Figure 117).
- Click an empty area of the desktop to close the search results.

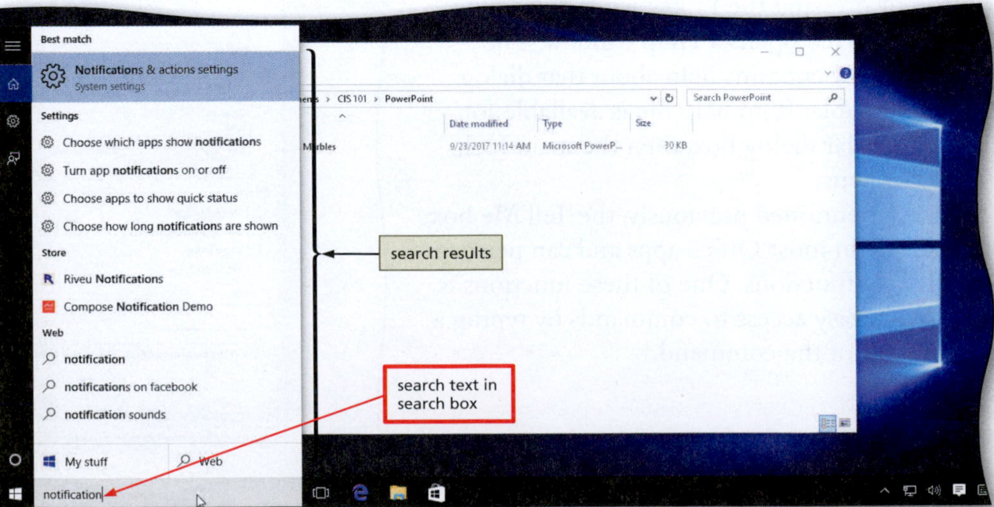

Figure 117

Summary

In this module, you learned how to use the Windows interface, several touch screen and mouse operations, file and folder management, some basic features of some Microsoft Office apps (including Word, PowerPoint, Excel, and Access), and discovered the common elements that exist among these different Office apps. You also were introduced to additional Office apps, including Outlook, Publisher, and OneNote. Topics covered included signing in, using Windows, using apps, file management, switching between apps, saving files, changing screen resolution, exiting apps, using additional apps, and using help.

CONSIDER THIS: PLAN AHEAD

What guidelines should you follow to plan your projects?

The process of communicating specific information is a learned, rational skill. Computers and software, especially Microsoft Office 2016, can help you develop ideas and present detailed information to a particular audience and minimize much of the laborious work of drafting and revising projects. No matter what method you use to plan a project, it is beneficial to follow some specific guidelines from the onset to arrive at a final product that is informative, relevant, and effective. Use some aspects of these guidelines every time you undertake a project, and others as needed in specific instances.

1. Determine the project's purpose.
   a) Clearly define why you are undertaking this assignment.
   b) Begin to draft ideas of how best to communicate information by handwriting ideas on paper; composing directly on a laptop, tablet, or mobile device; or developing a strategy that fits your particular thinking and writing style.
2. Analyze your audience.
   a) Learn about the people who will read, analyze, or view your work.
   b) Determine their interests and needs so that you can present the information they need to know and omit the information they already possess.
   c) Form a mental picture of these people or find photos of people who fit this profile so that you can develop a project with the audience in mind.
3. Gather possible content.
   a) Locate existing information that may reside in spreadsheets, databases, or other files.
   b) Conduct a web search to find relevant websites.
   c) Read pamphlets, magazine and newspaper articles, and books to gain insights of how others have approached your topic.
   d) Conduct personal interviews to obtain perspectives not available by any other means.
   e) Consider video and audio clips as potential sources for material that might complement or support the factual data you uncover.
4. Determine what content to present to your audience.
   a) Write three or four major ideas you want an audience member to remember after reading or viewing your project.
   b) Envision your project's endpoint, the key fact you wish to emphasize, so that all project elements lead to this final element.
   c) Determine relevant time factors, such as the length of time to develop the project, how long readers will spend reviewing your project, or the amount of time allocated for your speaking engagement.
   d) Decide whether a graph, photo, or artistic element can express or enhance a particular concept.
   e) Be mindful of the order in which you plan to present the content, and place the most important material at the top or bottom of the page, because readers and audience members generally remember the first and last pieces of information they see and hear.

CONSIDER THIS

How should you submit solutions to questions in the assignments identified with a symbol?

Every assignment in this book contains one or more questions with a symbol. These questions require you to think beyond the assigned file. Present your solutions to the question in the format required by your instructor. Possible formats may include one or more of these options: write the answer; create a document that contains the answer; present your answer to the class; discuss your answer in a group; record the answer as audio or video using a webcam, smartphone, or portable media player; or post answers on a blog, wiki, or website.

Apply Your Knowledge

Reinforce the skills and apply the concepts you learned in this module.

Creating a Folder and a Document

Instructions: You will create a PowerPoint Assignments folder and then create a PowerPoint presentation and save it in the folder.

Perform the following tasks:

1. Open the File Explorer window and then double-click to open the Documents folder.
2. Click the New folder button on the Quick Access Toolbar to display a new folder icon and text box for the folder name.
3. Type **`PowerPoint Assignments`** in the text box to name the folder. Press the ENTER key to create the folder in the Documents folder.
4. Run PowerPoint and create a new blank presentation.
5. Enter **`Technology Update`** in the title text placeholder (Figure 118).
6. Click the Save button on the Quick Access Toolbar. Navigate to the PowerPoint folder in the Documents folder and then save the document using the file name, Apply 1 Presentation.
7. If your Quick Access Toolbar does not show the Quick Print button, add the Quick Print button to the Quick Access Toolbar. Print the presentation using the Quick Print button on the Quick Access Toolbar. When you are finished printing, remove the Quick Print button from the Quick Access Toolbar.
8. Submit the printout to your instructor.
9. Exit PowerPoint.
10. What other commands might you find useful to include on the Quick Access Toolbar?

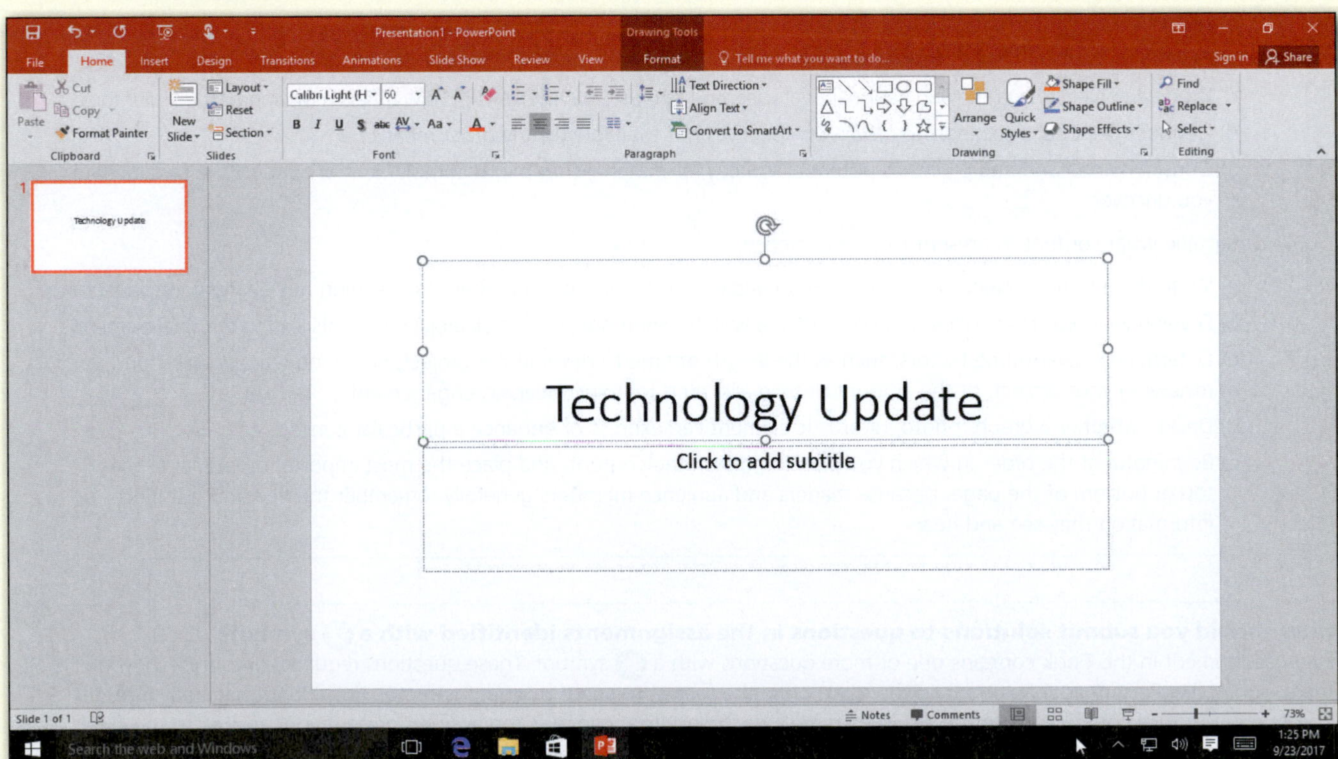

Figure 118

Extend Your Knowledge

Extend the skills you learned in this module and experiment with new skills. You will use Help to complete the assignment.

Using Help

Instructions: Use Office Help to perform the following tasks.

Perform the following tasks:

1. Run Word.
2. Click the Microsoft Word Help button to open the Word Help window (Figure 119).
3. Search Word Help to answer the following questions.
   a. What are the steps to create a hanging indent?
   b. What is mail merge?
4. With the Word app still running, run PowerPoint.
5. Click the Microsoft PowerPoint Help button on the title bar to open the PowerPoint Help window.
6. Search PowerPoint Help to answer the following questions.
   a. How can you create a Venn diagram?
   b. How do you add slide numbers to each slide?
7. Exit PowerPoint.
8. Run Excel.
9. Click the Microsoft Excel Help button to open the Excel Help window.
10. Search Excel Help to answer the following questions.
    a. What different types of charts are available in Excel?
    b. What is Flash Fill?
11. Exit Excel.
12. Run Access.
13. Click the Microsoft Access Help button to open the Access Help window.
14. Search Access Help to answer the following questions.
    a. What is a query?
    b. What are data types?
15. Exit Access.
16. Type the answers from your searches in a new blank Word document. Save the document with a new file name and then submit it in the format specified by your instructor.
17. Exit Word.
18. What search text did you use to perform the searches above? Did it take multiple attempts to search and locate the exact information for which you were searching?

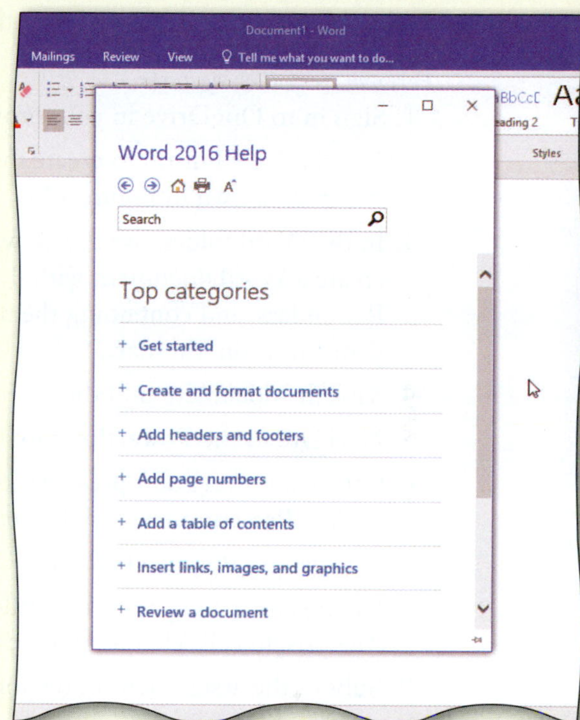

Figure 119

Expand Your World

Creating Office Online Documents

Create a solution that uses cloud or web technologies by learning and investigating on your own from general guidance.

Instructions: Create the folders shown in Figure 120. Then, using the respective Office Online app, create a small file to save in each folder (i.e., create a Word document to save in the Word folder, a PowerPoint presentation to save in the PowerPoint folder, and so on).

Perform the following tasks:

1. Sign in to OneDrive in your browser.
2. Use the New button to create the folder structure shown in Figure 120.
3. In the Word folder, use the New button to create a Word document with the file name, Reminders, and containing the text, Lunch with Lucas on Tuesday.
4. Save the document and then exit the app.

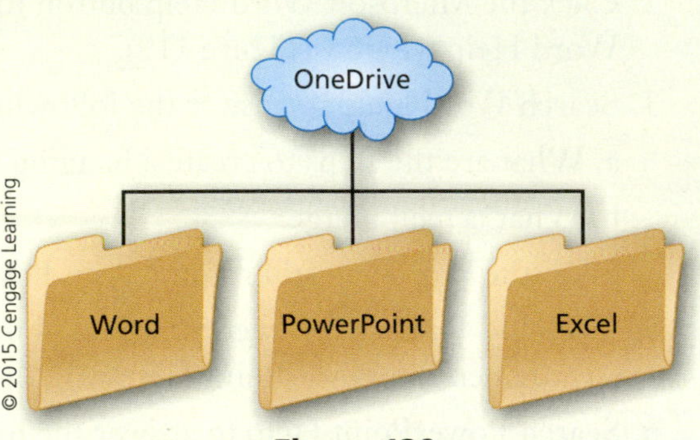

Figure 120

5. Navigate to the PowerPoint folder.
6. Create a PowerPoint presentation called Widget Sales with one slide containing the title text, Online Presentation, and then exit the app.
7. Navigate to the Excel folder.
8. Create an Excel spreadsheet called Widget Sales Analysis containing the text, Sales Cost Analysis, in cell A1, and then exit the app.
9. Submit the assignment in the format specified by your instructor.
10. Based on your current knowledge of OneDrive, do you think you will use it? What about the Office Online apps?

In the Labs

Design, create, modify, and/or use files following the guidelines, concepts, and skills presented in this module. Labs 1 and 2, which increase in difficulty, require you to create solutions based on what you learned in the module; Lab 3 requires you to apply your creative thinking and problem-solving skills to design and implement a solution.

Lab 1: Creating Folders for a Bookstore

Problem: Your friend works for a local bookstore. He would like to organize his files in relation to the types of books available in the store. He has seven main categories: fiction, biography, children, humor, social science, nonfiction, and medical. You are to create a folder structure similar to Figure 121.

Perform the following tasks:

1. Click the File Explorer button on the taskbar and display the contents of the Documents folder.
2. In the Documents folder, create the main folder and name it Book Categories.
3. Navigate to the Book Categories folder.

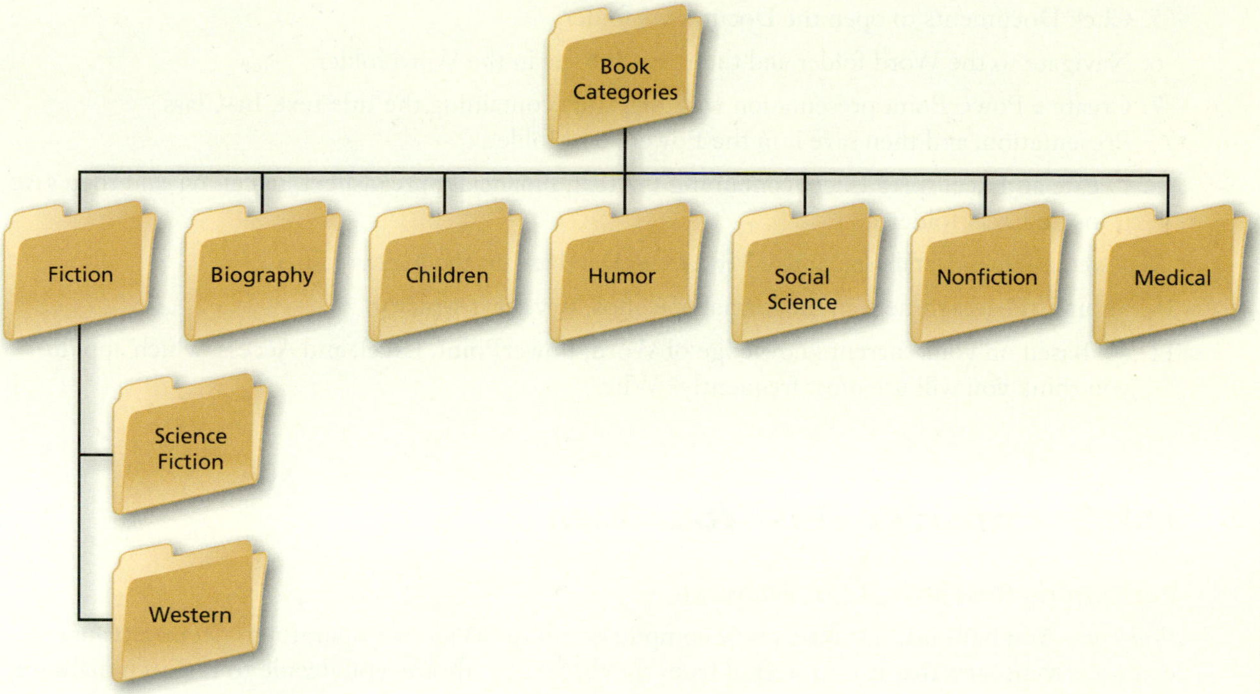

Book Categories
Fiction
Biography
Children
Humor
Social Science
Nonfiction
Medical
Science Fiction
Western

Figure 121

4. Within the Book Categories folder, create a folder for each of the following: Fiction, Biography, Children, Humor, Social Science, Nonfiction, and Medical.
5. Within the Fiction folder, create two additional folders, one for Science Fiction and the second for Western.
6. Submit the assignment in the format specified by your instructor.
7. Think about how you use your computer for various tasks (consider personal, professional, and academic reasons). What folders do you think will be required on your computer to store the files you save?

Lab 2: Creating Office Documents and Saving Them in Appropriate Folders

Problem: You are taking a class that requires you to create a Word, PowerPoint, Excel, and Access file. You will save these files to folders named for four different Office apps (Figure 122).

Perform the following tasks:

1. Create the folders shown in Figure 122.
2. Create a Word document containing the text, Week 1 Notes.
3. In the Backstage view, click Save As and then click This PC.
4. Click the Browse button to display the Save As dialog box.

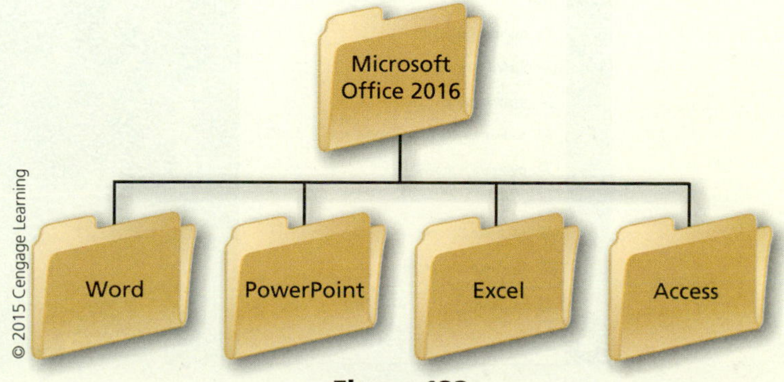

Figure 122

5. Click Documents to open the Documents folder.
6. Navigate to the Word folder and then save the file in the Word folder.
7. Create a PowerPoint presentation with one slide containing the title text, In-Class Presentation, and then save it in the PowerPoint folder.
8. Create an Excel spreadsheet containing the text, Financial Spreadsheet, in cell A1 and then save it in the Excel folder.
9. Save an Access database named, My Movie Database, in the Access folder.
10. Submit the assignment in the format specified by your instructor.
11. Based on your current knowledge of Word, PowerPoint, Excel, and Access, which app do you think you will use most frequently? Why?

Lab 3: Consider This: Your Turn

Performing Research about Malware

Problem: You have just installed a new computer with the Windows operating system. Because you want to be sure that it is protected from the threat of malware, you decide to research malware, malware protection, and removing malware.

Part 1: Research the following three topics: malware, malware protection, and removing malware. Use the concepts and techniques presented in this module to use the search box to find information regarding these topics. Create a Word document that contains steps to properly safeguard a computer from malware, ways to prevent malware, as well as the different ways to remove malware or a virus should your computer become infected. Submit your assignment in the format specified by your instructor.

Part 2: You made several decisions while searching for this assignment. What decisions did you make? What was the rationale behind these decisions? How did you locate the required information about malware?

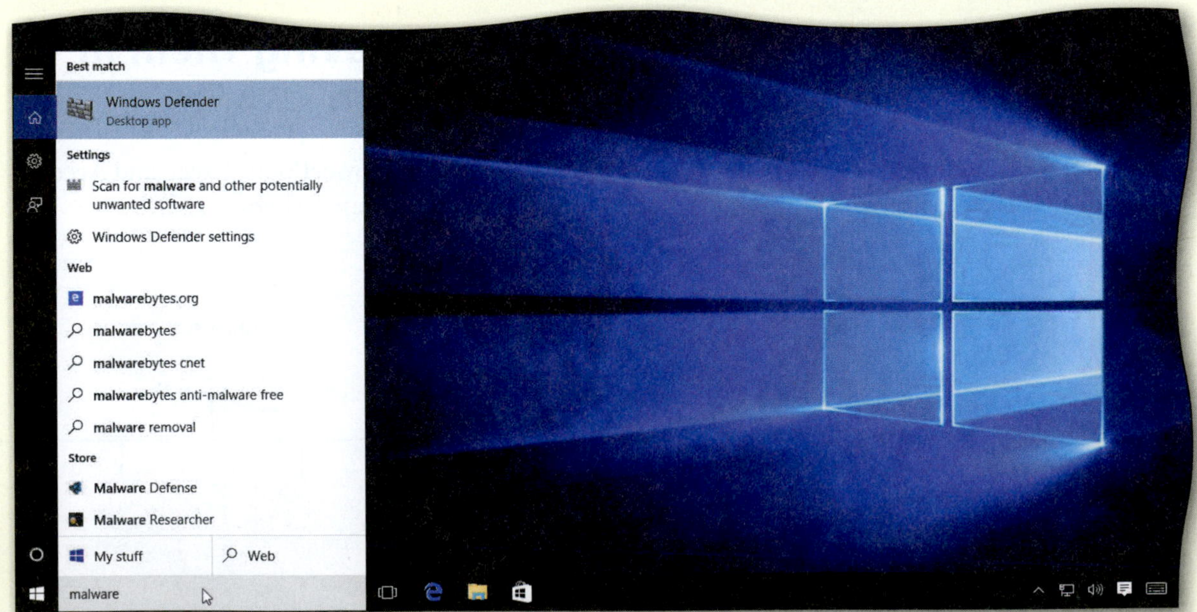

Figure 123

1 Creating, Formatting, and Editing a Word Document with a Picture

Objectives

You will have mastered the material in this module when you can:

- Enter text in a Word document
- Check spelling as you type
- Format paragraphs
- Format text
- Undo and redo commands or actions
- Change theme colors
- Insert digital pictures in a Word document
- Resize pictures
- Format pictures
- Add a page border
- Adjust spacing
- Correct errors and revise a document

Introduction

To advertise a sale, promote a business, publicize an event, or convey a message to the community, you may want to create a flyer and hand it out in person or post it in a public location. Libraries, schools, community organizations, grocery stores, coffee shops, and other places often provide bulletin boards or windows for flyers. You also see flyers posted on webpages, on social media, or in email messages.

Flyers announce personal items for sale or rent (car, boat, apartment); events, such as garage or block sales; services being offered (animal care, housecleaning, lessons, tours); membership, sponsorship, or donation requests (club, community organization, charity); and other messages, such as a lost or found pet.

Project — Flyer with a Picture

Individuals and businesses create flyers to gain public attention. Flyers, which usually are a single page in length, are an inexpensive means of reaching the community. Many flyers, however, go unnoticed because they are designed poorly.

The project in this module follows general guidelines and uses Word to create the flyer shown in Figure 1–1. This colorful, eye-catching flyer announces surfing lessons. The picture of the surfer riding a wave, taken with a digital camera, entices passersby or viewers to stop and look at the flyer. The headline on the flyer is large and colorful to draw attention into the text. The body copy below the picture briefly describes what is included in the lessons, along with a bulleted list that concisely highlights important information. The signature line of the flyer calls attention to the contact phone number. The word, expert, and the signature line are in a different color so that they stand apart from the rest of the text on the flyer. Finally, the graphical page border nicely frames and complements the contents of the flyer.

page border
SURF'S UP!
headline
digital picture of surfer
Learn to surf or improve your form and skills on the waves through expert instruction from our award-winning surf school.
• Private or group lessons
• Reef shoes and surfboard rental included
• Photo and video packages available
body copy
bulleted list
To sign up for a lesson, call 555-SURF!
signature line

Figure 1–1

In this module, you will learn how to create the flyer shown in Figure 1–1. The following roadmap identifies general activities you will perform as you progress through this module:

1. ENTER TEXT in a new document.
2. FORMAT the TEXT in the flyer.
3. INSERT a PICTURE, called Surfer, in the flyer.
4. FORMAT the PICTURE in the flyer.
5. ENHANCE the PAGE with a border and spacing.
6. CORRECT errors AND REVISE text in the flyer.

To Run Word and Specify Settings

If you are using a computer to step through the project in this module and you want your screens to match the figures in this book, you should change your screen's resolution to 1366 × 768. For information about how to change a computer's resolution, refer to the Office and Windows module at the beginning of this book.

1. Run Word and create a blank document in the Word window.
2. If the Word window is not maximized, click the Maximize button on its title bar to maximize the window.
3. If the Print Layout button on the status bar is not selected (shown in Figure 1–2), click it so that your screen is in Print Layout view.

Q&A What is Print Layout view?
The default (preset) view in Word is **Print Layout view**, which shows the document on a mock sheet of paper in the document window.

4. If Normal (Home tab | Styles group) is not selected in the Styles gallery (shown in Figure 1–2), click it so that your document uses the Normal style.

Q&A What is the Normal style?
When you create a document, Word formats the text using a particular style. The default style in Word is called the **Normal style**, which is discussed later in this book.

What if rulers appear on my screen?
Click View on the ribbon to display the View tab and then remove the check mark from the View Ruler check box (View tab | Show group).

For an introduction to Office and instructions about how to perform basic tasks in Office apps, read the Office and Windows module at the beginning of this book, where you can learn how to run an application, use the ribbon, save a file, open a file, print a file, exit an application, use Help, and much more.

For an introduction to Windows and instructions about how to perform basic Windows tasks, read the Office and Windows module at the beginning of this book, where you can learn how to resize windows, change screen resolution, create folders, move and rename files, use Windows Help, and much more.

Entering Text

The first step in creating a document is to enter its text. With the projects in this book, you enter text by typing on the keyboard. By default, Word positions text you type at the left margin. In a later section of this module, you will learn how to format, or change the appearance of, the entered text.

BTW
The Word Window
The modules in this book begin with the Word window appearing as it did at the initial installation of the software. Your Word window may look different depending on your screen resolution and other Word settings.

1 ENTER TEXT | 2 FORMAT TEXT | 3 INSERT PICTURE
4 FORMAT PICTURE | 5 ENHANCE PAGE | 6 CORRECT & REVISE

To Type Text

To begin creating the flyer in this module, type the headline in the document window. ***Why?** The headline is the first line of text in the Surf Flyer.* The following steps type the first line of text in the document.

- Type **Surf's Up!** as the headline (Figure 1–2).

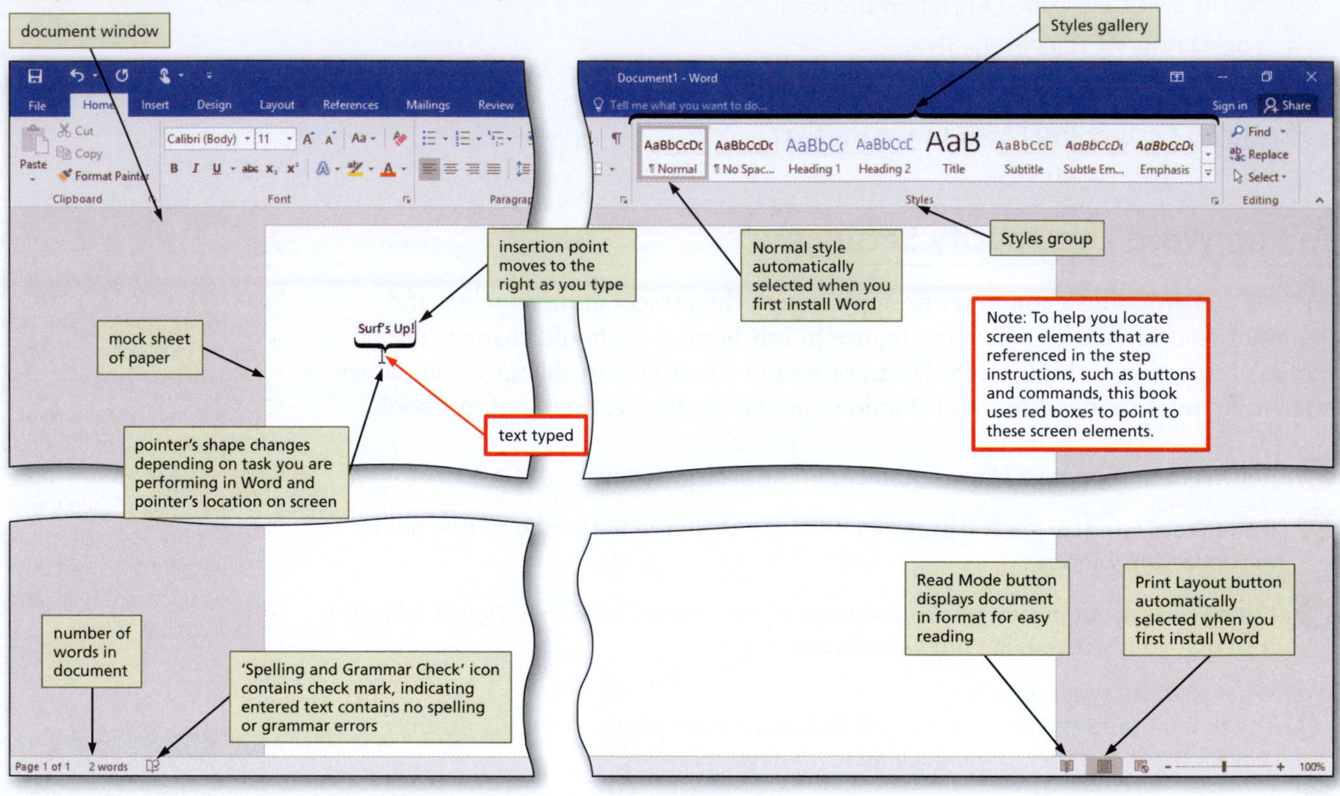

Figure 1–2

Q&A What if I make an error while typing?
You can press the BACKSPACE key until you have deleted the text in error and then retype the text correctly.

What is the purpose of the 'Spelling and Grammar Check' icon on the status bar?
The **'Spelling and Grammar Check' icon** displays either a check mark to indicate the entered text contains no spelling or grammar errors, or an X to indicate that it found potential errors. Word flags potential errors in the document with a red, green, or blue wavy underline. Later in this module, you will learn how to fix flagged errors.

- Press the ENTER key to move the insertion point to the beginning of the next line (Figure 1–3).

Q&A Why did blank space appear between the headline and the insertion point?
Each time you press the ENTER key, Word creates a new paragraph and inserts blank space between the two paragraphs. Later in this module, you will learn how to increase and decrease the spacing between paragraphs.

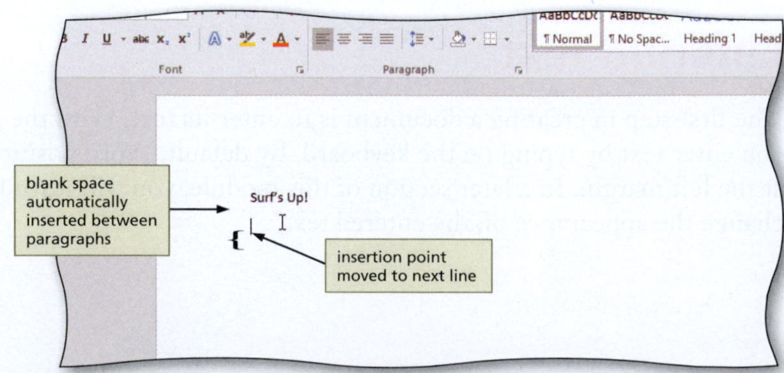

Figure 1–3

CONSIDER THIS

How do you use the touch keyboard with a touch screen?

To display the on-screen touch keyboard, tap the Touch Keyboard button on the Windows taskbar as shown in the Office and Windows module at the beginning of this book. When finished using the touch keyboard, tap the X button on the touch keyboard to close the keyboard.

To Display Formatting Marks

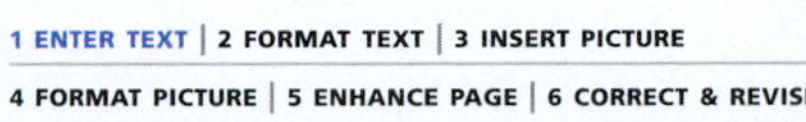

You may find it helpful to display formatting marks while working in a document. ***Why?*** *Formatting marks indicate where in a document you pressed the* ENTER *key,* SPACEBAR, *and other nonprinting characters.* A **formatting mark** is a character that Word displays on the screen but is not visible on a printed document. For example, the paragraph mark (¶) is a formatting mark that indicates where you pressed the ENTER key. A raised dot (·) shows where you pressed the SPACEBAR. Formatting marks are discussed as they appear on the screen.

Depending on settings made during previous Word sessions, your Word screen already may display formatting marks (Figure 1–4). The following step displays formatting marks, if they do not show already on the screen.

1

- If the Home tab is not the active tab, click Home on the ribbon to display the Home tab.
- If it is not selected already, click the 'Show/Hide ¶' button (Home tab | Paragraph group) to display formatting marks on the screen (Figure 1–4).

Q&A What if I do not want formatting marks to show on the screen?

You can hide them by clicking the 'Show/Hide ¶' button (Home tab | Paragraph group) again. It is recommended that you display formatting marks so that you visually can identify when you press the ENTER key, SPACEBAR, and other keys associated with nonprinting characters. Most of the document windows presented in this book, therefore, show formatting marks.

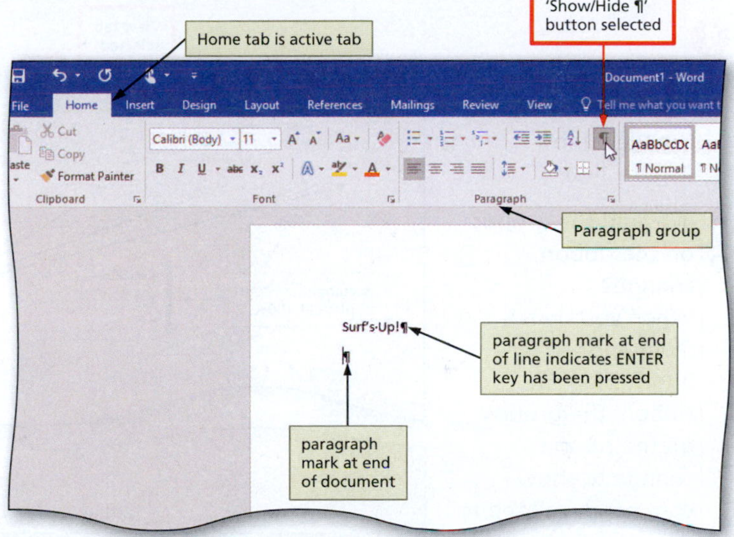

Figure 1–4

Other Ways

1. Press CTRL+SHIFT+*

To Insert a Blank Line

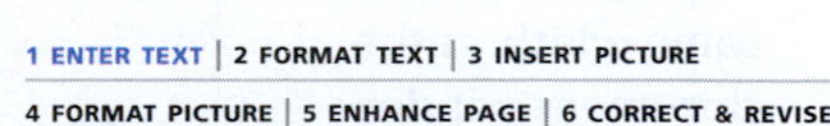

In the flyer, the digital picture of the surfer appears between the headline and body copy. You will not insert this picture, however, until after you enter and format all text. ***Why?*** *Although you can format text and insert pictures in any order, for illustration purposes, this module formats all text first before inserting the picture. Thus, you leave a blank line in the document as a placeholder for the picture.*

To enter a blank line in a document, press the ENTER key without typing any text on the line. The following step inserts one blank line below the headline.

- Press the ENTER key to insert a blank line in the document (Figure 1–5).

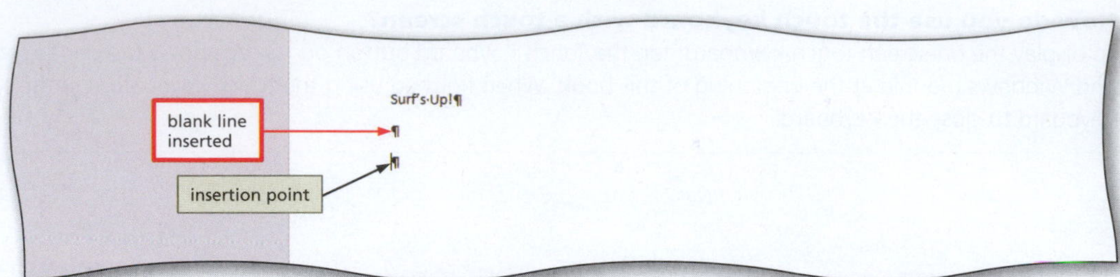

Figure 1–5

To Zoom Page Width

1 ENTER TEXT | 2 FORMAT TEXT | 3 INSERT PICTURE
4 FORMAT PICTURE | 5 ENHANCE PAGE | 6 CORRECT & REVISE

The next step in creating this flyer is to enlarge the contents that appear on the screen. ***Why?*** *You would like the text on the screen to be larger so that it is easier to read.* The document currently displays at 100% (shown in Figure 1–6). With Word, you can zoom page width, which zooms (enlarges or shrinks) the mock sheet of paper on the screen so that it is the width of the Word window. The following steps zoom page width.

- Click View on the ribbon to display the View tab (Figure 1–6).

Q&A Why did the groups on the ribbon change?
When you switch from one tab to another on the ribbon, the groups on the ribbon change to show commands related to the selected tab.

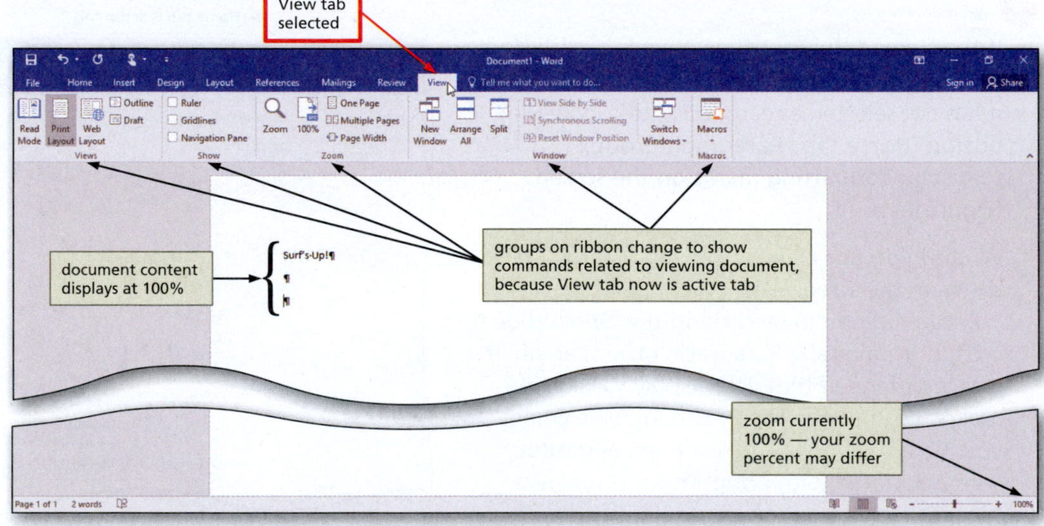

Figure 1–6

- Click the Page Width button (View tab | Zoom group) to display the page the same width as the document window (Figure 1–7).

Q&A If I change the zoom, will the document print differently?
Changing the zoom has no effect on the printed document.

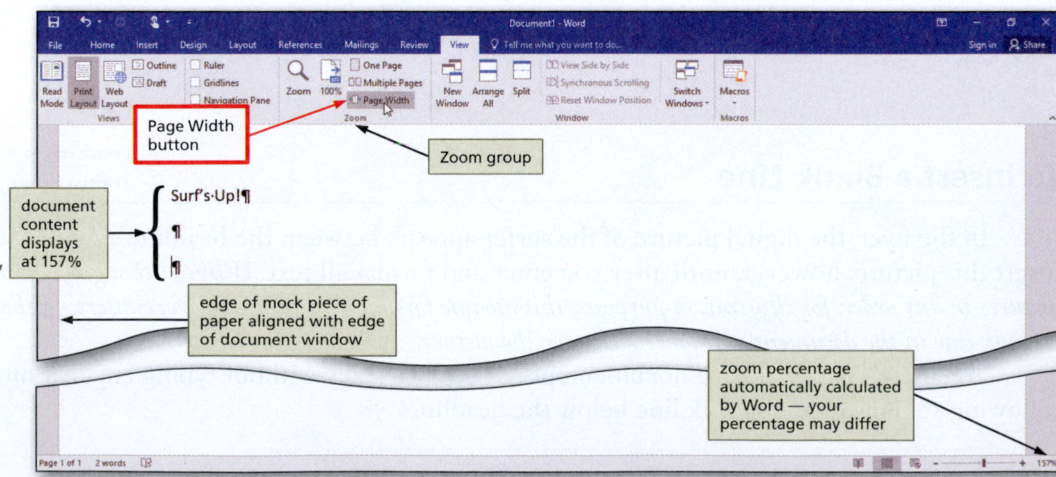

Figure 1–7

Q&A What are the other predefined zoom options?
Through the View tab | Zoom group or the Zoom dialog box (Zoom button in Zoom group), you can zoom to one page (an entire single page appears in the document window), many pages (multiple pages appear at once in the document window), page width, text width, and a variety of set percentages. Whereas page width zoom places the edges of the page at the edges of the document window, text width zoom places the document contents at the edges of the document window.

Other Ways

1. Click Zoom button (View tab | Zoom group), click Page width (Zoom dialog box), click OK button

Wordwrap

Wordwrap allows you to type words in a paragraph continually without pressing the ENTER key at the end of each line. As you type, if a word extends beyond the right margin, Word also automatically positions that word on the next line along with the insertion point.

Word creates a new paragraph each time you press the ENTER key. Thus, as you type text in the document window, do not press the ENTER key when the insertion point reaches the right margin. Instead, press the ENTER key only in these circumstances:

1. To insert a blank line(s) in a document (as shown in previous steps)
2. To begin a new paragraph
3. To terminate a short line of text and advance to the next line
4. To respond to questions or prompts in Word dialog boxes, task panes, and other on-screen objects

BTW
Zooming
If text is too small for you to read on the screen, you can zoom the document by dragging the Zoom slider on the status bar or by clicking the Zoom Out or Zoom In buttons on the status bar. Changing the zoom has no effect on the printed document.

1 ENTER TEXT | 2 FORMAT TEXT | 3 INSERT PICTURE
4 FORMAT PICTURE | 5 ENHANCE PAGE | 6 CORRECT & REVISE

To Wordwrap Text as You Type

The next step in creating the flyer is to type the body copy. ***Why?*** *In many flyers, the body copy text appears below the headline.* The following steps illustrate how the body copy text wordwraps as you enter it in the document, which means you will not have to press the ENTER key at the end of the line.

1

- Type the first sentence of the body copy: `Learn to surf or improve your form and skills on the waves through expert instruction from our award-winning surf school.`

Q&A Why does my document wrap on different words?
The printer connected to a computer is one factor that can control where wordwrap occurs for each line in a document. Thus, it is possible that the same document could wordwrap differently if printed on different printers.

2

- Press the ENTER key to position the insertion point on the next line in the document (Figure 1–8).

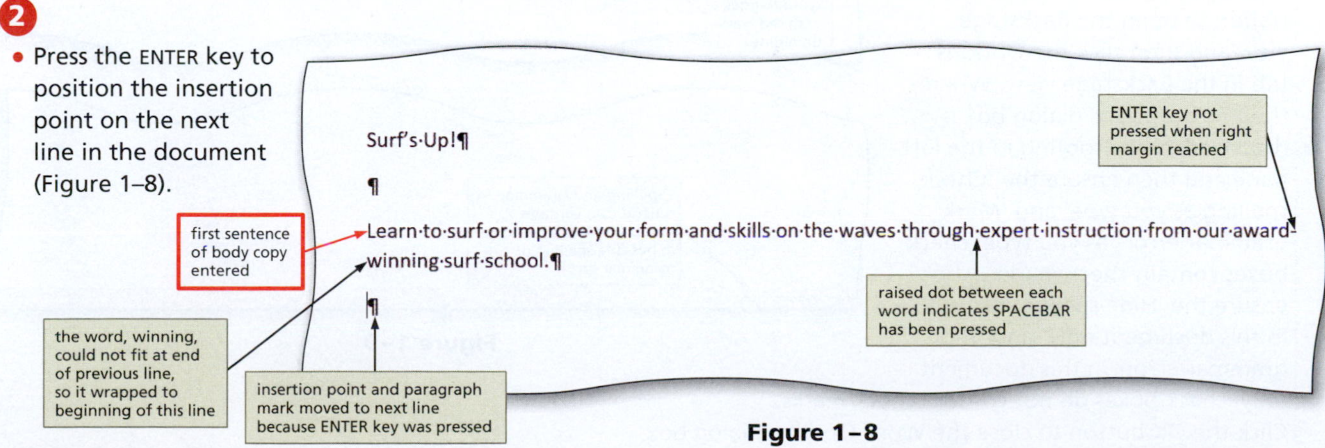
Surf's·Up!¶
¶
Learn·to·surf·or·improve·your·form·and·skills·on·the·waves·through·expert·instruction·from·our·award-
winning·surf·school.¶
¶
ENTER key not pressed when right margin reached
first sentence of body copy entered
raised dot between each word indicates SPACEBAR has been pressed
the word, winning, could not fit at end of previous line, so it wrapped to beginning of this line
insertion point and paragraph mark moved to next line because ENTER key was pressed

Figure 1–8

Spelling and Grammar Check

As you type text in a document, Word checks your typing for possible spelling and grammar errors. If all of the words you have typed are in Word's dictionary and your grammar is correct, as mentioned earlier, the Spelling and Grammar Check icon on the status bar displays a check mark. Otherwise, the icon shows an X. In this case, Word flags the potential error(s) in the document window with a red, green, or blue wavy underline.

- A red wavy underline means the flagged text is not in Word's dictionary (because it is a proper name or misspelled).
- A green wavy underline indicates the text may be incorrect grammatically.
- A blue wavy underline indicates the text may contain a contextual spelling error, such as the misuse of homophones (words that are pronounced the same but that have different spellings or meanings, such as one and won).

Although you can check the entire document for spelling and grammar errors at once, you also can check flagged errors as they appear on the screen.

A flagged word is not necessarily misspelled. For example, many names, abbreviations, and specialized terms are not in Word's main dictionary. In these cases, you can instruct Word to ignore the flagged word. As you type, Word also detects duplicate words while checking for spelling errors. For example, if your document contains the phrase, to the the store, Word places a red wavy underline below the second occurrence of the word, the.

BTW
Automatic Spelling Correction
As you type, Word automatically corrects some misspelled words. For example, if you type recieve, Word automatically corrects the misspelling and displays the word, receive, when you press the SPACEBAR or type a punctuation mark. To see a complete list of automatically corrected words, click File on the ribbon to open the Backstage view, click the Options tab in the Backstage view, click Proofing in the left pane (Word Options dialog box), click the AutoCorrect Options button, and then scroll through the list near the bottom of the dialog box.

To Check Spelling and Grammar as You Type

1 ENTER TEXT | 2 FORMAT TEXT | 3 INSERT PICTURE
4 FORMAT PICTURE | 5 ENHANCE PAGE | 6 CORRECT & REVISE

In the following steps, the word, group, has been misspelled intentionally as goup. ***Why?*** *These steps illustrate Word's check spelling as you type feature. If you are completing this project on a computer, your flyer may contain different or no misspelled words, depending on the accuracy of your typing.*

- Type **Private or goup** and then press the SPACEBAR, so that a red wavy line appears below the misspelled word (Figure 1–9).

Q&A What if Word does not flag my spelling and grammar errors with wavy underlines?
To verify that the check spelling and grammar as you type features are enabled, click File on the ribbon to open the Backstage view and then click the Options tab in the Backstage view. When the Word Options dialog box is displayed, click Proofing in the left pane and then ensure the 'Check spelling as you type' and 'Mark grammar errors as you type' check boxes contain check marks. Also ensure the 'Hide spelling errors in this document only' and 'Hide grammar errors in this document only' check boxes do not contain check marks. Click the OK button to close the Word Options dialog box.

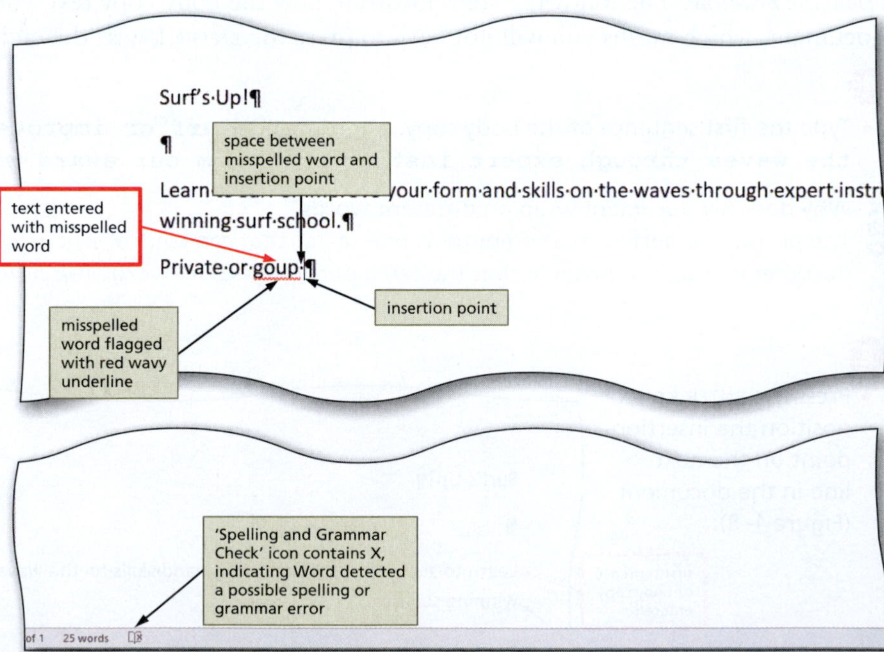

Figure 1–9

- Right-click the flagged word (goup, in this case) to display a shortcut menu that presents a list of suggested spelling corrections for the flagged word (Figure 1–10).

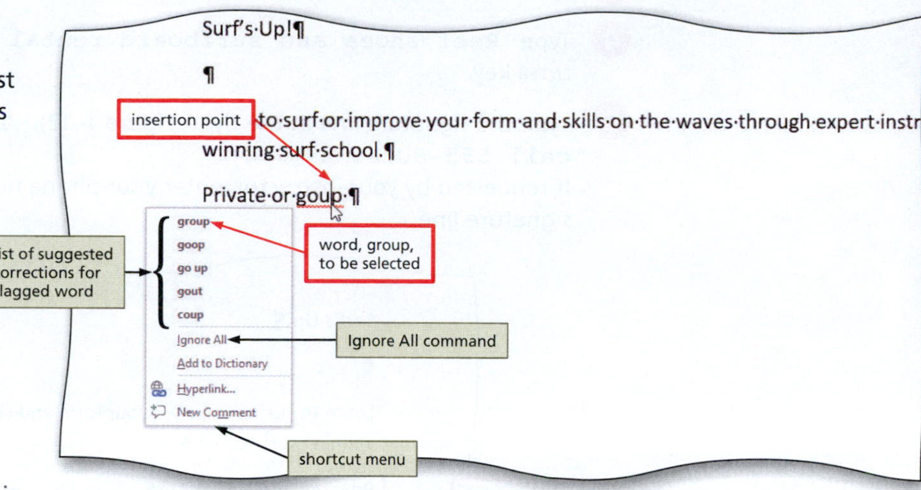

Figure 1–10

Q&A

What if, when I right-click the misspelled word, my desired correction is not in the list on the shortcut menu?
You can click outside the shortcut menu to close the shortcut menu and then retype the correct word.

What if a flagged word actually is, for example, a proper name and spelled correctly?
Right-click it and then click Ignore All on the shortcut menu to instruct Word not to flag future occurrences of the same word in this document.

3

- Click group on the shortcut menu to replace the misspelled word in the document with a correctly spelled word (Figure 1–11).

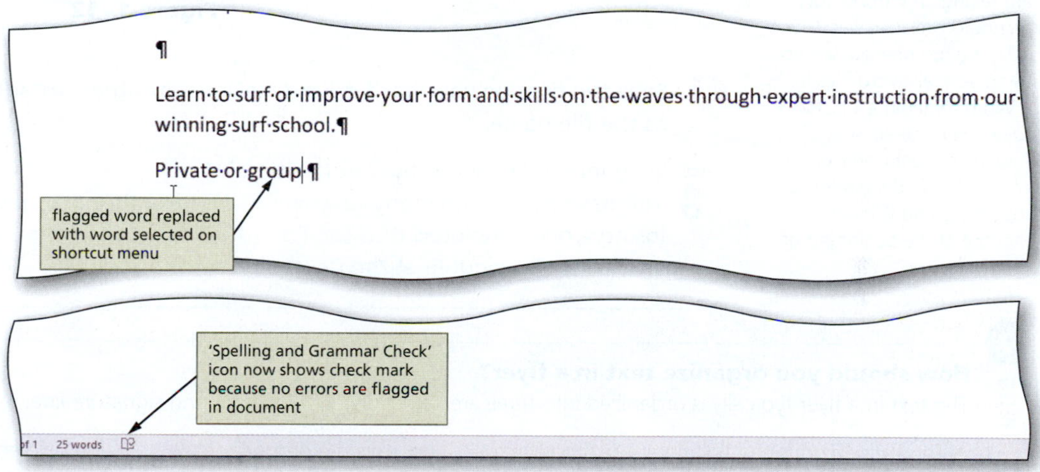

Figure 1–11

Other Ways

1. Click 'Spelling and Grammar Check' icon on status bar, click desired word in Spelling pane, click Change button, click OK button

To Enter More Text

In the flyer, the text yet to be entered includes the remainder of the body copy, which will be formatted as a bulleted list, and the signature line. The following steps enter the remainder of text in the flyer.

1. Press the END key to move the insertion point to the end of the current line.
2. Type `lessons` and then press the ENTER key.

3. Type **Photo and video packages available** and then press the ENTER key.

4. Type **Reef shoes and surfboard rental included** and then press the ENTER key.

5. Type the signature line in the flyer (Figure 1–12): **To sign up for a lesson, call 555-SURF!**
If requested by your instructor, enter your phone number instead of 555-SURF in the signature line.

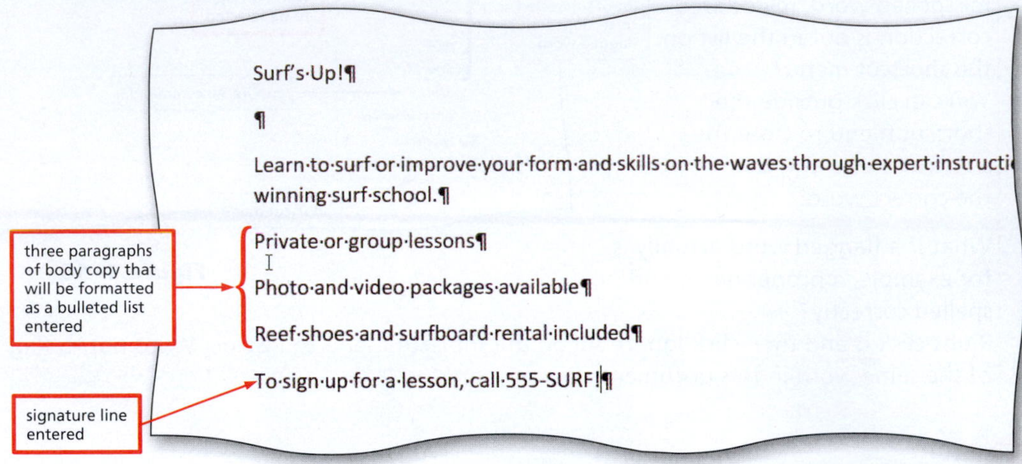
Surf's·Up!¶
¶
Learn·to·surf·or·improve·your·form·and·skills·on·the·waves·through·expert·instructi
winning·surf·school.¶
three paragraphs of body copy that will be formatted as a bulleted list entered
Private·or·group·lessons¶
Photo·and·video·packages·available¶
Reef·shoes·and·surfboard·rental·included¶
signature line entered
To·sign·up·for·a·lesson,·call·555-SURF!¶

Figure 1–12

6. Save the flyer on your hard drive, OneDrive, or other storage location using Surf Flyer as the file name.

Q&A Why should I save the flyer at this time?
You have performed many tasks while creating this flyer and do not want to risk losing work completed thus far. For information about how to save, refer to the Office and Windows module at the beginning of this book.

BTW
Organizing Files and Folders
You should organize and store files in folders so that you easily can find the files later. For example, if you are taking an introductory technology class called CIS 101, a good practice would be to save all Word files in a Word folder in a CIS 101 folder. For a discussion of folders and detailed examples of creating folders, refer to the Office and Windows module at the beginning of this book.

CONSIDER THIS

How should you organize text in a flyer?
The text in a flyer typically is organized into three areas: headline, body copy, and signature line.

- The **headline** is the first line of text on the flyer. It conveys the product or service being offered (such as a car for sale, lessons, or sightseeing tours) or the benefit that will be gained (such as a convenience, better performance, greater security, higher earnings, or more comfort), or it can contain a message (such as a lost or found pet).
- The **body copy** consists of text between the headline and the signature line. This text highlights the key points of the message in as few words as possible. It should be easy to read and follow. While emphasizing the positive, the body copy must be realistic, truthful, and believable.
- The **signature line**, which is the last line of text on the flyer, contains contact information or identifies a call to action.

Navigating a Document

You view only a portion of a document on the screen through the document window. At some point when you type text or insert graphics, Word probably will **scroll** the top or bottom portion of the document off the screen. Although you cannot see the text and graphics once they scroll off the screen, they remain in the document.

You can use touch gestures, the keyboard, or a mouse to scroll to a different location in a document and/or move the insertion point around a document. If you are using a touch screen, simply use your finger to slide the document up or down to display a different location in the document and then tap to move the insertion point to a new location. When you use the keyboard, the insertion point automatically moves when you press the desired keys. For example, the previous steps used the END key to move the insertion point to the end of the current line. Table 1–1 outlines various techniques to navigate a document using the keyboard.

Table 1–1 Moving the Insertion Point with the Keyboard

Insertion Point Direction	Key(s) to Press	Insertion Point Direction	Key(s) to Press
Left one character	LEFT ARROW	Up one paragraph	CTRL+UP ARROW
Right one character	RIGHT ARROW	Down one paragraph	CTRL+DOWN ARROW
Left one word	CTRL+LEFT ARROW	Up one screen	PAGE UP
Right one word	CTRL+RIGHT ARROW	Down one screen	PAGE DOWN
Up one line	UP ARROW	To top of document window	ALT+CTRL+PAGE UP
Down one line	DOWN ARROW	To bottom of document window	ALT+CTRL+PAGE DOWN
To end of line	END	To beginning of document	CTRL+HOME
To beginning of line	HOME	To end of document	CTRL+END

With the mouse, you can use the scroll arrows or the scroll box on the scroll bar to display a different portion of the document in the document window and then click the mouse to move the insertion point to that location. Table 1–2 explains various techniques for using the scroll bar to scroll vertically with the mouse.

Table 1–2 Using the Scroll Bar to Scroll Vertically with the Mouse

Scroll Direction	Mouse Action	Scroll Direction	Mouse Action
Up	Drag the scroll box upward.	Down one screen	Click anywhere below the scroll box on the vertical scroll bar.
Down	Drag the scroll box downward.	Up one line	Click the scroll arrow at the top of the vertical scroll bar.
Up one screen	Click anywhere above the scroll box on the vertical scroll bar.	Down one line	Click the scroll arrow at the bottom of the vertical scroll bar.

Formatting Paragraphs and Characters

With the text for the flyer entered, the next step is to **format**, or change the appearance of, its text. A paragraph encompasses the text from the first character in the paragraph up to and including its paragraph mark (¶). **Paragraph formatting** is the process of changing the appearance of a paragraph. For example, you can center or add bullets to a paragraph. Characters include letters, numbers, punctuation marks, and symbols. **Character formatting** is the process of changing the way characters appear on the screen and in print. You use character formatting to emphasize certain words and improve readability of a document. For example, you can color, italicize, or underline characters. Often, you apply both paragraph and character formatting to the same text. For example, you may center a paragraph (paragraph formatting) and underline some of the characters in the same paragraph (character formatting).

Although you can format paragraphs and characters before you type, many Word users enter text first and then format the existing text. Figure 1–13a shows the flyer in this module before formatting its paragraphs and characters. Figure 1–13b shows the flyer after formatting. As you can see from the two figures, a document that is formatted is easier to read and looks more professional. The following sections discuss how to format the flyer so that it looks like Figure 1–13b.

BTW
Minimize Wrist Injury
Computer users frequently switch among the keyboard, the mouse, and touch gestures during a word processing session; such switching strains the wrist. To help prevent wrist injury, minimize switching. For instance, if your hand already is on the mouse, use the mouse to scroll. If your fingers already are on the keyboard, use keyboard keys to scroll. If your fingertips already are on the screen, use your finger to slide the document to a new location.

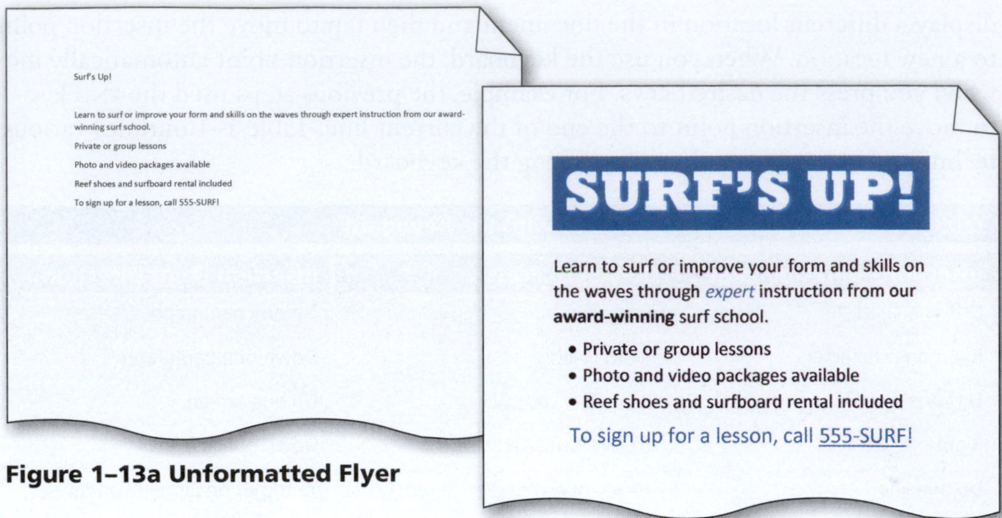
Surf's Up!
Learn to surf or improve your form and skills on the waves through expert instruction from our award-winning surf school.
Private or group lessons
Photo and video packages available
Reef shoes and surfboard rental included
To sign up for a lesson, call 555-SURF!
SURF'S UP!
Learn to surf or improve your form and skills on the waves through expert instruction from our award-winning surf school.
• Private or group lessons
• Photo and video packages available
• Reef shoes and surfboard rental included
To sign up for a lesson, call 555-SURF!

Figure 1–13a Unformatted Flyer

Figure 1–13b Formatted Flyer

Figure 1–13

BTW

Character Widths

Many word processing documents use variable character fonts, where some characters are wider than others; for example, the letter w is wider than the letter i.

Font, Font Sizes, and Themes

Characters that appear on the screen are a specific shape and size. The **font**, or typeface, defines the appearance and shape of the letters, numbers, and special characters. In Word, the default font usually is Calibri (shown in Figure 1–14). You can leave characters in the default font or change them to a different font. **Font size** specifies the size of the characters and is determined by a measurement system called points. A single **point** is about 1/72 of one inch in height. The default font size in Word typically is 11 (Figure 1–14). Thus, a character with a font size of 11 is about 11/72 or a little less than 1/6 of one inch in height. You can increase or decrease the font size of characters in a document.

A document **theme** is a set of unified formats for fonts, colors, and graphics. Word includes a variety of document themes to assist you with coordinating these visual elements in a document. The default theme fonts are Calibri Light for headings and Calibri for body text. By changing the document theme, you quickly can give your document a new look. You also can define your own document themes.

CONSIDER THIS

How do I know which formats to use in a flyer?

In a flyer, consider the following formatting suggestions.

- **Increase the font size of characters.** Flyers usually are posted on a bulletin board or in a window. Thus, the font size should be as large as possible so that passersby easily can read the flyer. To give the headline more impact, its font size should be larger than the font size of the text in the body copy. If possible, make the font size of the signature line larger than the body copy but smaller than the headline.
- **Change the font of characters.** Use fonts that are easy to read. Try to use only two different fonts in a flyer; for example, use one for the headline and the other for all other text. Too many fonts can make the flyer visually confusing.
- **Change the paragraph alignment.** The default alignment for paragraphs in a document is **left-aligned**, that is, flush at the left margin of the document with uneven right edges. Consider changing the alignment of some of the paragraphs to add interest and variety to the flyer.
- **Highlight key paragraphs with bullets.** A bulleted paragraph is a paragraph that begins with a dot or other symbol. Use bulleted paragraphs to highlight important points in a flyer.
- **Emphasize important words.** To call attention to certain words or lines, you can underline them, italicize them, or bold them. Use these formats sparingly, however, because overuse will minimize their effect and make the flyer look too busy.
- **Use color.** Use colors that complement each other and convey the meaning of the flyer. Vary colors in terms of hue and brightness. Headline colors, for example, can be bold and bright. Signature lines should stand out more than body copy but less than headlines. Keep in mind that too many colors can detract from the flyer and make it difficult to read.

To Center a Paragraph

The headline in the flyer currently is left-aligned (shown in Figure 1–14). ***Why?*** *Word, by default, left-aligns text, unless you specifically change the alignment.* You want the headline to be **centered**, that is, positioned horizontally between the left and right margins on the page. Recall that Word considers a single short line of text, such as the one-word headline, a paragraph. Thus, you will center the paragraph containing the headline. The following steps center a paragraph.

1

- Click Home on the ribbon to display the Home tab.
- Click somewhere in the paragraph to be centered (in this case, the headline) to position the insertion point in the paragraph to be centered (Figure 1–14).

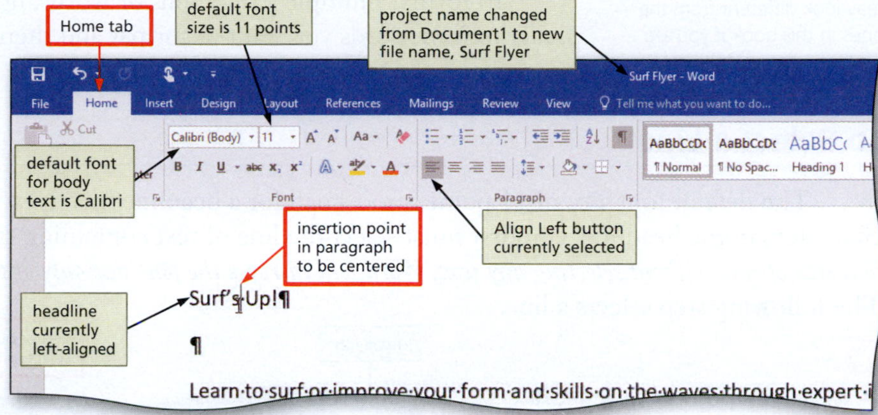

Figure 1–14

2

- Click the Center button (Home tab | Paragraph group) to center the paragraph containing the insertion point (Figure 1–15).

Q&A What if I want to return the paragraph to left-aligned?
You would click the Center button again or click the Align Left button (Home tab | Paragraph group).

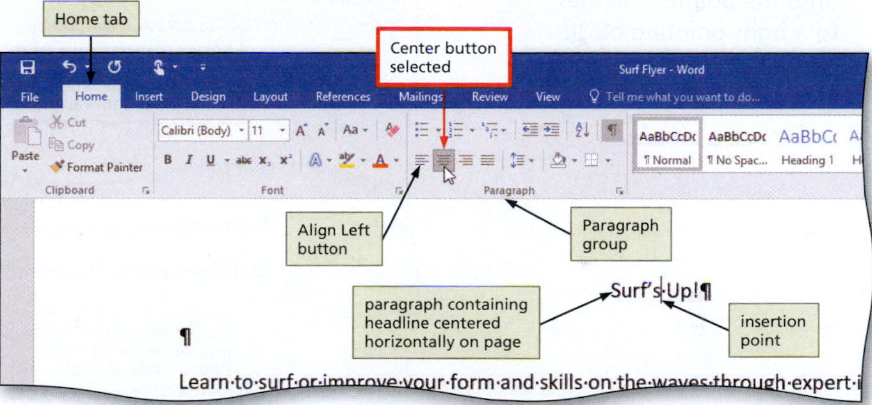

Figure 1–15

Other Ways

1. Right-click paragraph (or if using touch, tap 'Show Context Menu' button on mini toolbar), click Paragraph on shortcut menu, click Indents and Spacing tab (Paragraph dialog box), click Alignment arrow, click Centered, click OK button
2. Click Paragraph Settings Dialog Box Launcher (Home tab or Layout tab | Paragraph group), click Indents and Spacing tab (Paragraph dialog box), click Alignment arrow, click Centered, click OK button
3. Press CTRL+E

To Center Another Paragraph

In the flyer, the signature line is to be centered to match the paragraph alignment of the headline. The following steps center the signature line.

1 Click somewhere in the paragraph to be centered (in this case, the signature line) to position the insertion point in the paragraph to be formatted.

2 Click the Center button (Home tab | Paragraph group) to center the paragraph containing the insertion point (shown in Figure 1–16).

BTW
File Type
Depending on your Windows settings, the file type .docx may be displayed on the title bar immediately to the right of the file name after you save the file. The file type .docx identifies a Word 2016 document.

BTW

The Ribbon and Screen Resolution

Word may change how the groups and buttons within the groups appear on the ribbon, depending on the computer or mobile device's screen resolution. Thus, your ribbon may look different from the ones in this book if you are using a screen resolution other than 1366 × 768.

Formatting Single versus Multiple Paragraphs and Characters

As shown in the previous sections, to format a single paragraph, simply position the insertion point in the paragraph to make it the current paragraph and then format the paragraph. Similarly, to format a single word, position the insertion point in the word to make it the current word, and then format the word.

To format multiple paragraphs or words, however, you first must select the paragraphs or words you want to format and then format the selection.

To Select a Line

1 ENTER TEXT | **2 FORMAT TEXT** | **3 INSERT PICTURE**
4 FORMAT PICTURE | **5 ENHANCE PAGE** | **6 CORRECT & REVISE**

The default font size of 11 point is too small for a headline in a flyer. To increase the font size of the characters in the headline, you first must select the line of text containing the headline. ***Why?*** *If you increase the font size of text without selecting any text, Word will increase the font size only of the word containing the insertion point.* The following step selects a line.

- Move the pointer to the left of the line to be selected (in this case, the headline) until the pointer changes to a right-pointing block arrow (Figure 1–16).

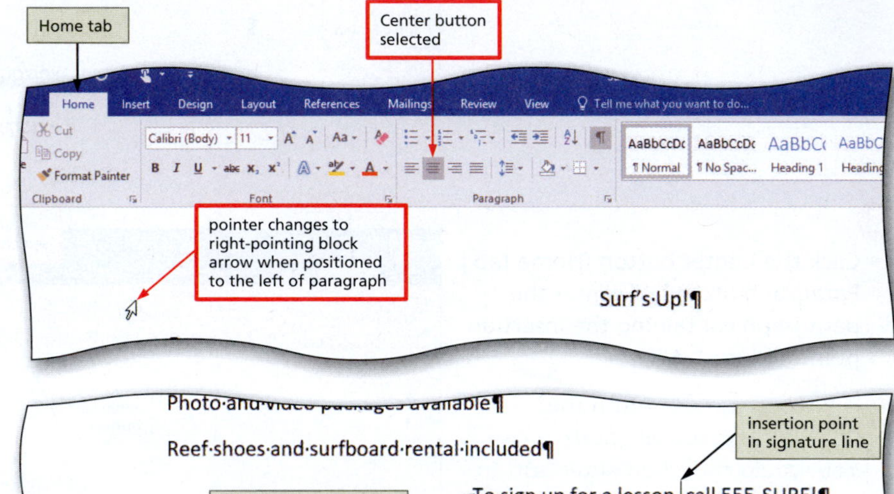

Figure 1–16

- While the pointer is a right-pointing block arrow, click the mouse button to select the entire line to the right of the pointer (Figure 1–17).

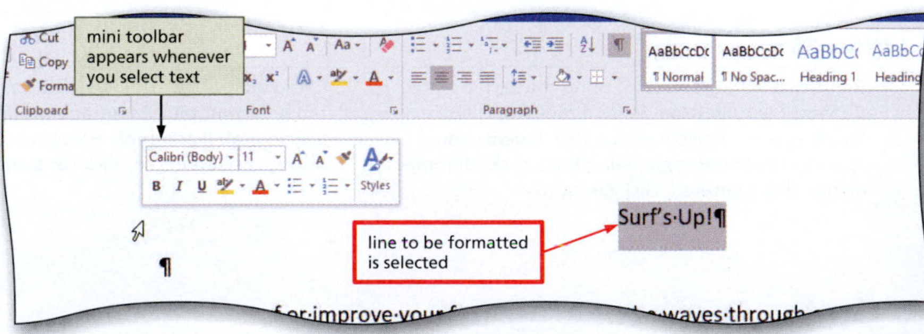

Figure 1–17

Q&A

What if I am using a touch screen?
You would double-tap to the left of the line to be selected to select the line.

Why is the selected text shaded gray?
If your screen normally displays dark letters on a light background, which is the default setting in Word, then selected text is displayed with a light shading color, such as gray, on the dark letters. Note that the selection that appears on the text does not print.

Other Ways

1. Drag pointer through line
2. With insertion point at beginning of desired line, press CRTL+SHIFT+DOWN ARROW

To Change the Font Size of Selected Text

The next step is to increase the font size of the characters in the selected headline. ***Why?*** *You would like the headline to be as large as possible and still fit on a single line, which in this case is 72 point.* The following steps increase the font size of the headline from 11 to 72 point.

1

- With the text selected, click the Font Size arrow (Home tab | Font group) to display the Font Size gallery (Figure 1–18).

Q&A

What is the Font Size arrow?
The Font Size arrow is the arrow to the right of the Font Size box, which is the text box that displays the current font size.

Why are the font sizes in my Font Size gallery different from those in Figure 1–18?
Font sizes may vary depending on the current font and your printer driver.

What happened to the mini toolbar?
The mini toolbar disappears if you do not use it. These steps use the Font Size arrow on the Home tab instead of the Font Size arrow on the mini toolbar.

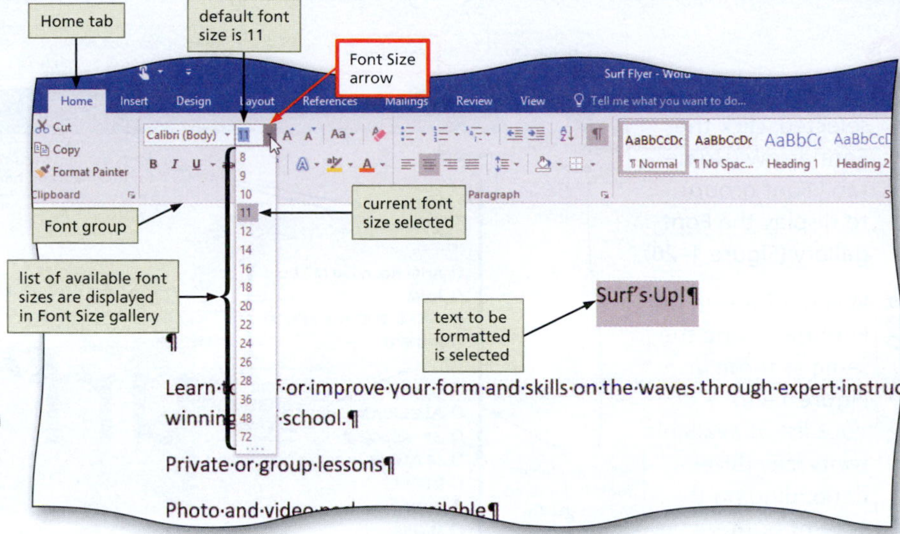

Figure 1–18

2

- Point to 72 in the Font Size gallery to display a live preview of the selected text at the selected point size (Figure 1–19).

Q&A

What is live preview?
Recall from the Office and Windows module at the beginning of this book that live preview is a feature that allows you to point to a gallery choice and see its effect in the document — without actually selecting the choice.

Can I use live preview on a touch screen?
Live preview is not available on a touch screen.

font size of selected text changes to 72 points, showing live preview of font size to which you are pointing in gallery

Surf's·Up!¶

pointer on 72

selection on text disappears temporarily while you use live preview

Figure 1–19

 **Experiment**

- Point to various font sizes in the Font Size gallery and watch the font size of the selected text change in the document window.

3

- Click 72 in the Font Size gallery to increase the font size of the selected text.

Other Ways

1. Click Font Size arrow on mini toolbar, click desired font size in Font Size gallery
2. Right-click selected text (or, if using touch, tap 'Show Context Menu' button on mini toolbar), click Font on shortcut menu, click Font tab (Font dialog box), select desired font size in Size list, click OK button
3. Click Font Dialog Box Launcher, (Home tab | Font group) click Font tab (Font dialog box), select desired font size in Size list, click OK button
4. Press CTRL+D, click Font tab (Font dialog box), select desired font size in Size list, click OK button

To Change the Font of Selected Text

The default theme font for headings is Calibri Light and for all other text, called body text in Word, is Calibri. Many other fonts are available, however, so that you can add variety to documents.

The following steps change the font of the headline from Calibri to Rockwell Extra Bold. ***Why?*** *To draw more attention to the headline, you change its font so that it differs from the font of other text in the flyer.*

1

- With the text selected, click the Font arrow (Home tab | Font group) to display the Font gallery (Figure 1–20).

Q&A Will the fonts in my Font gallery be the same as those in Figure 1–20?
Your list of available fonts may differ, depending on the type of printer you are using and other settings.

What if the text no longer is selected?
Follow the steps described earlier to select a line.

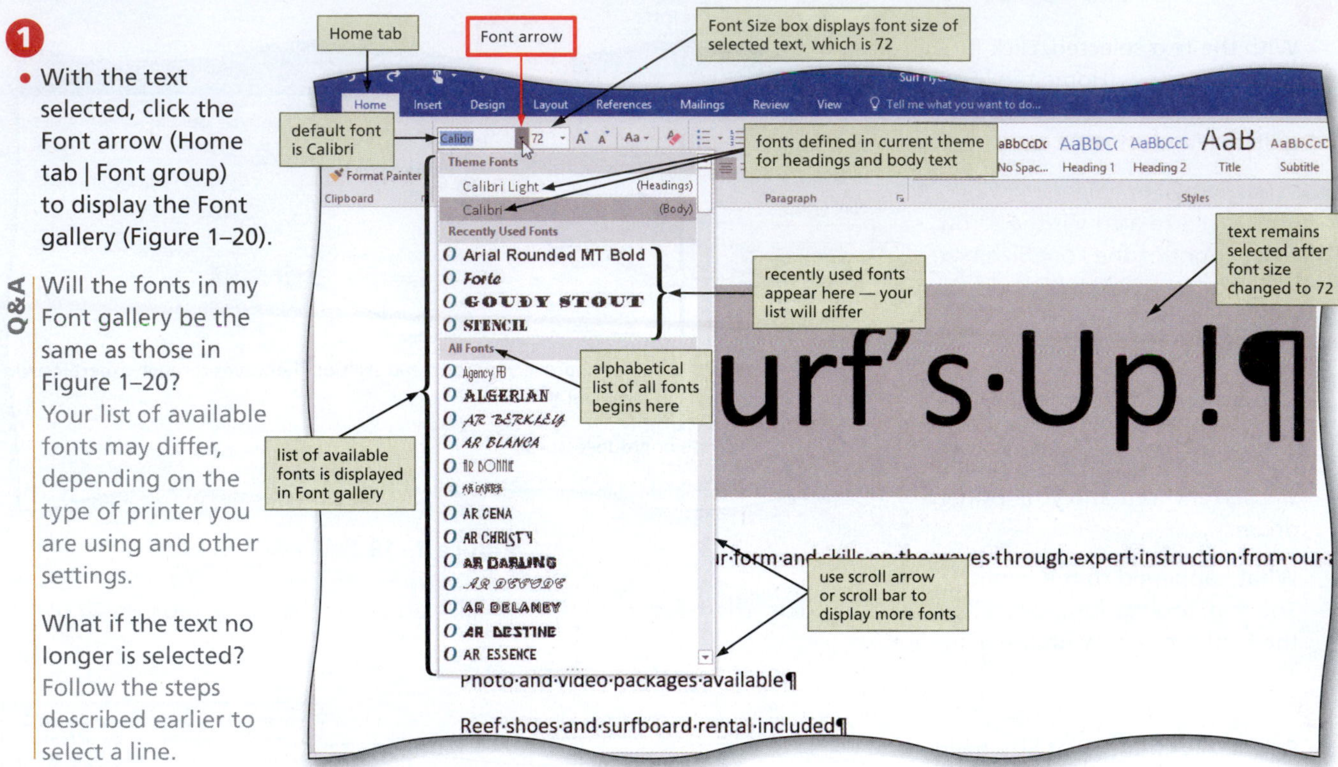

Figure 1–20

2

- If necessary, scroll through the Font gallery to display Rockwell Extra Bold (or a similar font).
- Point to 'Rockwell Extra Bold' (or a similar font) to display a live preview of the selected text in the selected font (Figure 1–21).

Experiment

- Point to various fonts in the Font gallery and watch the font of the selected text change in the document window.

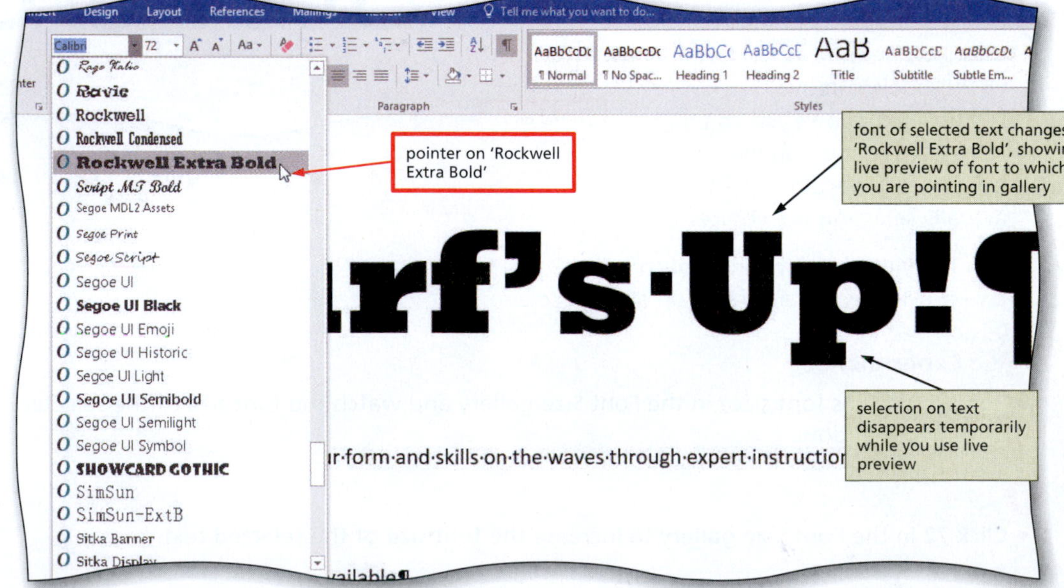

Figure 1–21

3

- Click 'Rockwell Extra Bold' (or a similar font) in the Font gallery to change the font of the selected text.

Q&A If the font I want to use appears in the Recently Used Fonts list in the Font gallery, could I click it there instead?
Yes.

Other Ways

1. Click Font arrow on mini toolbar, click desired font in Font gallery
2. Right-click selected text (or, if using touch, tap 'Show Context Menu' button on mini toolbar), click Font on shortcut menu, click Font tab (Font dialog box), select desired font in Font list, click OK button
3. Click Font Dialog Box Launcher (Home tab | Font group), click Font tab (Font dialog box), select desired font in Font list, click OK button
4. Press CTRL+D, click Font tab (Font dialog box), select desired font in Font list, click OK button

To Change the Case of Selected Text

The headline currently shows the first letter in each word capitalized, which sometimes is referred to as initial cap. The following steps change the headline to uppercase. ***Why?*** *To draw more attention to the headline, you would like the entire line of text to be capitalized, or in uppercase letters.*

1

- With the text selected, click the Change Case button (Home tab | Font group) to display the Change Case gallery (Figure 1–22).

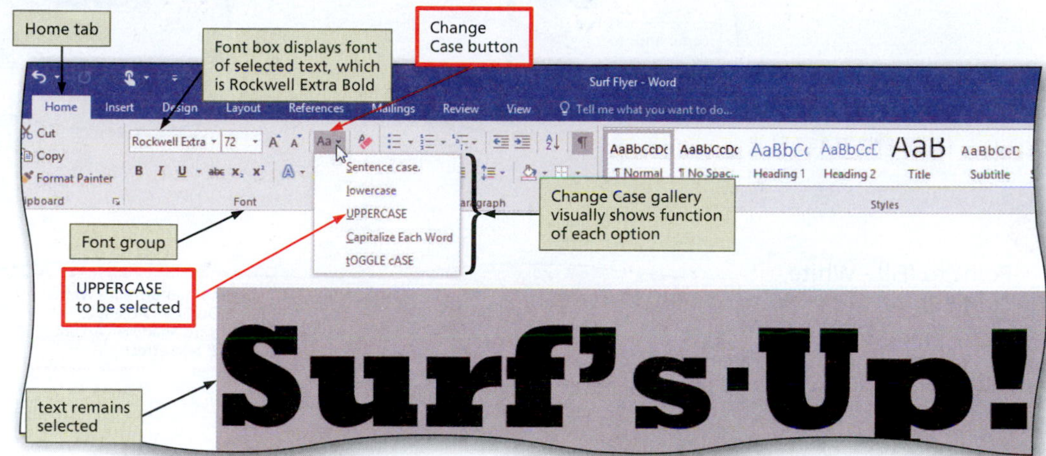

Figure 1–22

2

- Click UPPERCASE in the Change Case gallery to change the case of the selected text (Figure 1–23).

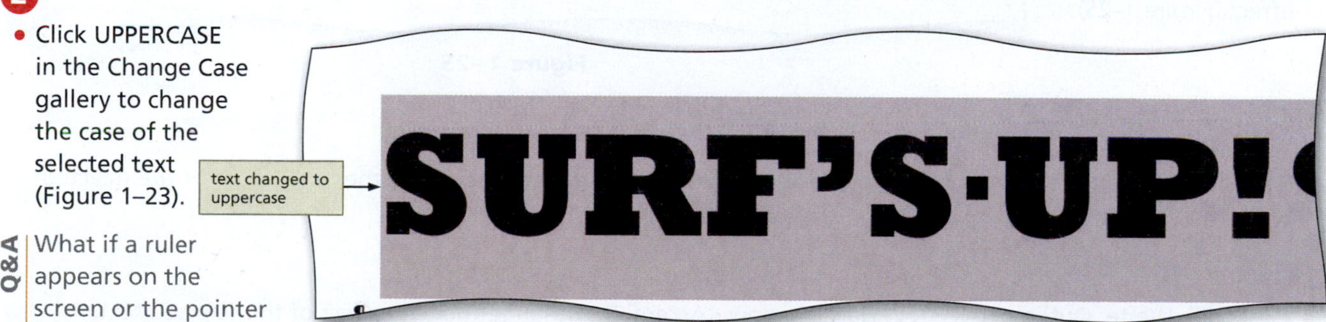

Figure 1–23

Q&A What if a ruler appears on the screen or the pointer shape changes?
If you are using a mouse, depending on the position of your pointer and locations you click on the screen, a ruler may appear automatically or the pointer's shape may change. Simply move the mouse and the ruler should disappear and/or the pointer shape will change.

Other Ways

1. Right-click selected text (or, if using touch, tap 'Show Context Menu' button on mini toolbar), click Font on shortcut menu, click Font tab (Font dialog box), select All caps in Effects area, click OK button
2. Click Font Dialog Box Launcher (Home tab | Font group), click Font tab (Font dialog box), select All caps in Effects area, click OK button
3. Press SHIFT+F3 repeatedly until text is desired case

To Apply a Text Effect to Selected Text

Word provides many text effects to add interest and variety to text. The following steps apply a text effect to the headline. ***Why?*** *You would like the text in the headline to be even more noticeable.*

1

- With the text selected, click the 'Text Effects and Typography' button (Home tab | Font group) to display the Text Effects and Typography gallery (Figure 1–24).

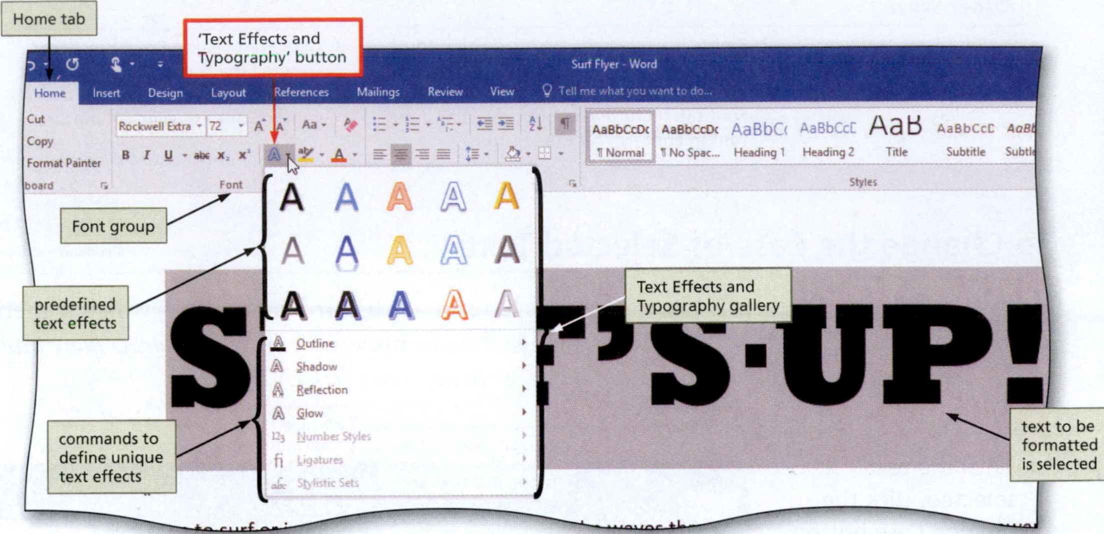

Figure 1–24

2

- Point to 'Fill - White, Outline - Accent 2, Hard Shadow - Accent 2' (fourth text effect in third row) to display a live preview of the selected text with the selected text effect (Figure 1–25).

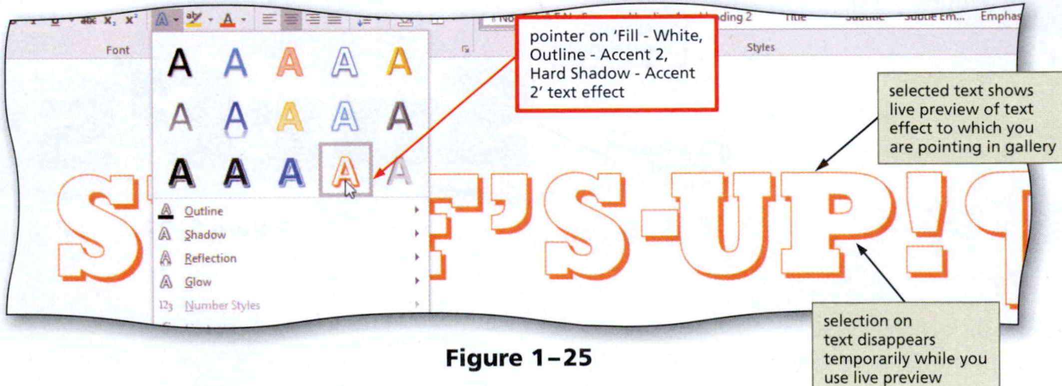

Figure 1–25

Experiment

- Point to various text effects in the Text Effects and Typography gallery and watch the text effects of the selected text change in the document window.

3

- Click 'Fill - White, Outline - Accent 2, Hard Shadow - Accent 2' to change the text effect of the selected text.

4

- Click anywhere in the document window to remove the selection from the selected text.

Other Ways

1. Right-click selected text (or, if using touch, tap 'Show Context Menu' button on mini toolbar), click Font on shortcut menu, click Font tab (Font dialog box), click Text Effects button, expand Text Fill or Text Outline section and then select the desired text effect(s) (Format Text Effects dialog box), click OK button, click OK button
2. Click Font Dialog Box Launcher (Home tab | Font group), click Font tab (Font dialog box), click Text Effects button, expand Text Fill or Text Outline section and then select desired text effect (Format Text Effects dialog box), click OK button, click OK button

To Shade a Paragraph

When you **shade** text, Word colors the rectangular area behind any text or graphics. If the text to shade is a paragraph, Word shades the area from the left margin to the right margin of the current paragraph. To shade a paragraph, place the insertion point in the paragraph. To shade any other text, you must first select the text to be shaded.

This flyer uses a shading color for the headline. ***Why?*** *To make the headline of the flyer more eye-catching, you shade it.* The following steps shade a paragraph.

1

- Click somewhere in the paragraph to be shaded (in this case, the headline) to position the insertion point in the paragraph to be formatted.
- Click the Shading arrow (Home tab | Paragraph group) to display the Shading gallery (Figure 1–26).

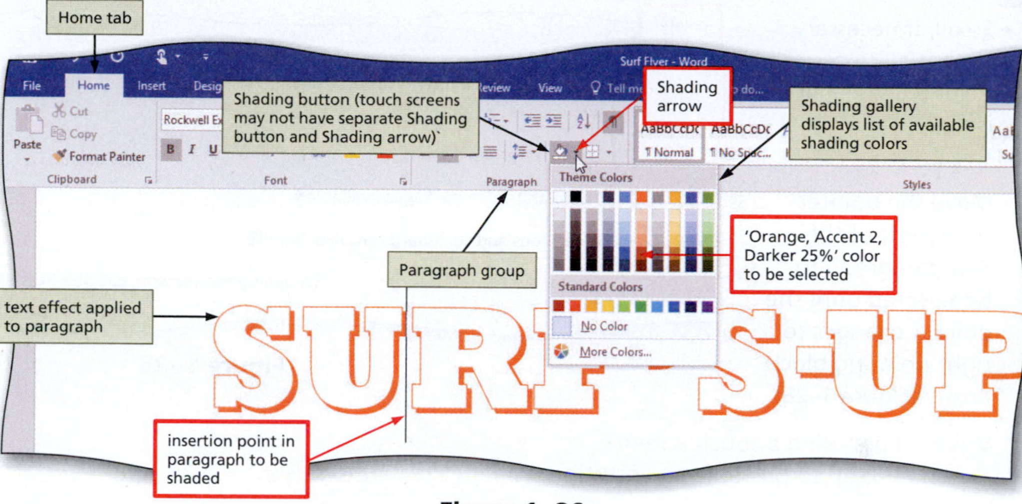

Figure 1–26

Q&A What if I click the Shading button by mistake?
Click the Shading arrow and proceed with Step 2. Note that if you are using a touch screen, you may not have a separate Shading button.

Why does my Shading gallery display different colors?
Your color scheme setting may display colors in a different order or may be different from Office, which is the default color scheme. To change the color scheme, click Design on the ribbon, click the Theme Colors button (Design tab | Document Formatting group), and then click Office in the Theme Colors gallery.

Experiment

- Point to various colors in the Shading gallery and watch the shading color of the current paragraph change.

2

- Click 'Orange, Accent 2, Darker 25%' (sixth color in fifth row) to shade the current paragraph (Figure 1–27).

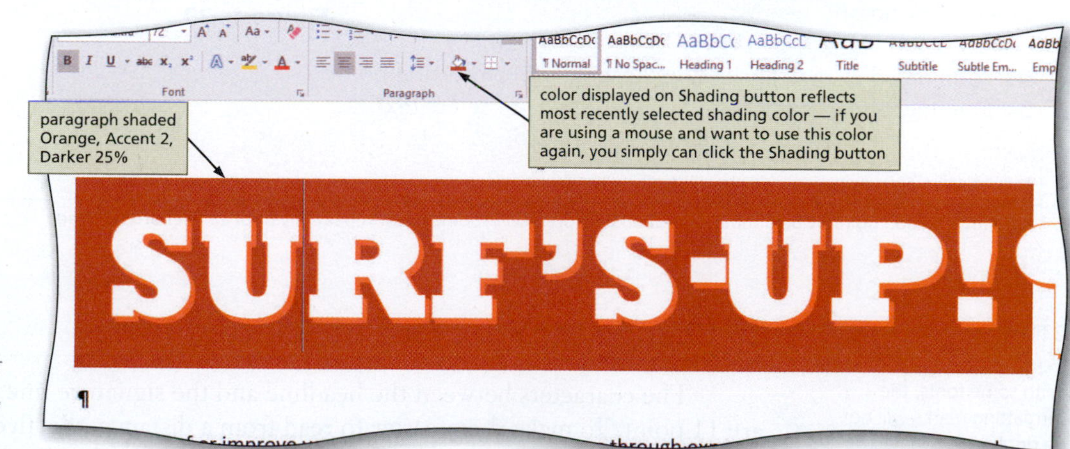

Figure 1–27

Q&A What if I apply a dark shading color to dark text?
When the font color of text is Automatic, the color usually is black. If you select a dark shading color, Word automatically may change the text color to white so that the shaded text is easier to read.

Other Ways

1. Click Borders arrow (Home tab | Paragraph group), click Borders and Shading, click Shading tab (Borders and Shading dialog box), click Fill arrow, select desired color, click OK button

To Select Multiple Lines

The next formatting step for the flyer is to increase the font size of the characters between the headline and the signature line. ***Why?*** *You want this text to be easier to read from a distance.*

To change the font size of the characters in multiple lines, you first must select all the lines to be formatted. The following steps select multiple lines.

- Scroll, if necessary, so that all text below the headline is displayed on the screen.
- Move the pointer to the left of the first paragraph to be selected until the pointer changes to a right-pointing block arrow (Figure 1–28).

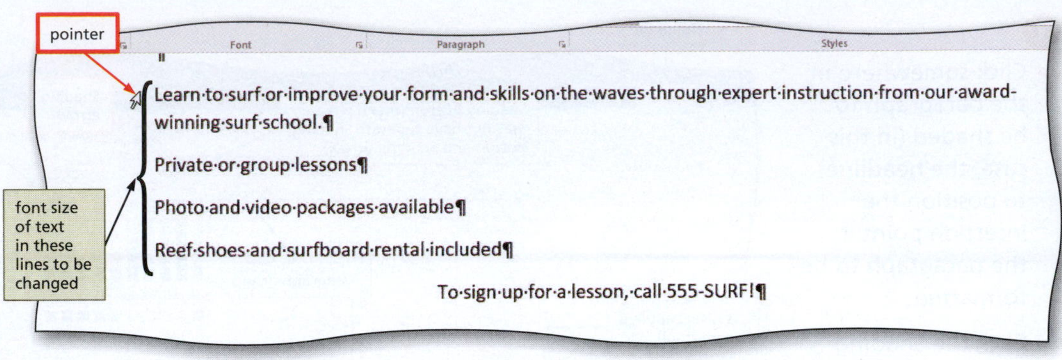
pointer
Font
Paragraph
Styles
Learn·to·surf·or·improve·your·form·and·skills·on·the·waves·through·expert·instruction·from·our·award-winning·surf·school.¶
Private·or·group·lessons¶
Photo·and·video·packages·available¶
Reef·shoes·and·surfboard·rental·included¶
To·sign·up·for·a·lesson,·call·555-SURF!¶
font size of text in these lines to be changed

Figure 1–28

Q&A What if I am using a touch screen?
You would tap to position the insertion point in the text to select.

- While the pointer is a right-pointing block arrow, drag downward to select all lines that will be formatted (Figure 1–29).

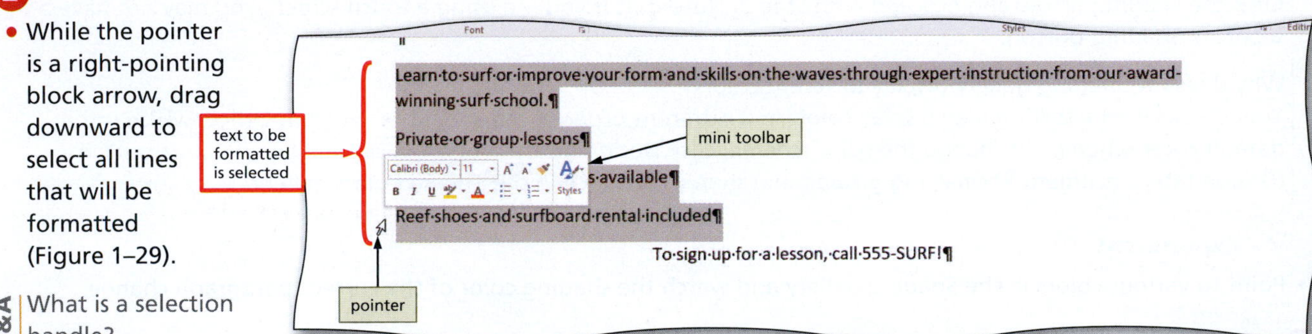
Font
Styles
Learn·to·surf·or·improve·your·form·and·skills·on·the·waves·through·expert·instruction·from·our·award-winning·surf·school.¶
Private·or·group·lessons¶
text to be formatted is selected
mini toolbar
Calibri (Body)
11
Styles
s·available¶
Reef·shoes·and·surfboard·rental·included¶
To·sign·up·for·a·lesson,·call·555-SURF!¶
pointer

Figure 1–29

Q&A What is a selection handle?
When working on a touch screen, a **selection handle** (small circle) appears below the insertion point. Using a fingertip, you drag a selection handle to select text.

Other Ways

1. With insertion point at beginning of desired line, press SHIFT+DOWN ARROW repeatedly until all lines are selected

BTW
Formatting Marks
With some fonts, the formatting marks will not be displayed properly on the screen. For example, the raised dot that signifies a blank space between words may be displayed behind a character instead of in the blank space, causing the characters to look incorrect.

To Change the Font Size of Selected Text

The characters between the headline and the signature line in the flyer currently are 11 point. To make them easier to read from a distance, this flyer uses a 24-point font size for these characters. The following steps change the font size of the selected text.

1. With the text selected, click the Font Size arrow (Home tab | Font group) to display the Font Size gallery.
2. Click 24 in the Font Size gallery to increase the font size of the selected text.

3 Click anywhere in the document window to remove the selection from the text.

4 If necessary, scroll so that you can see all the resized text on the screen (Figure 1–30).

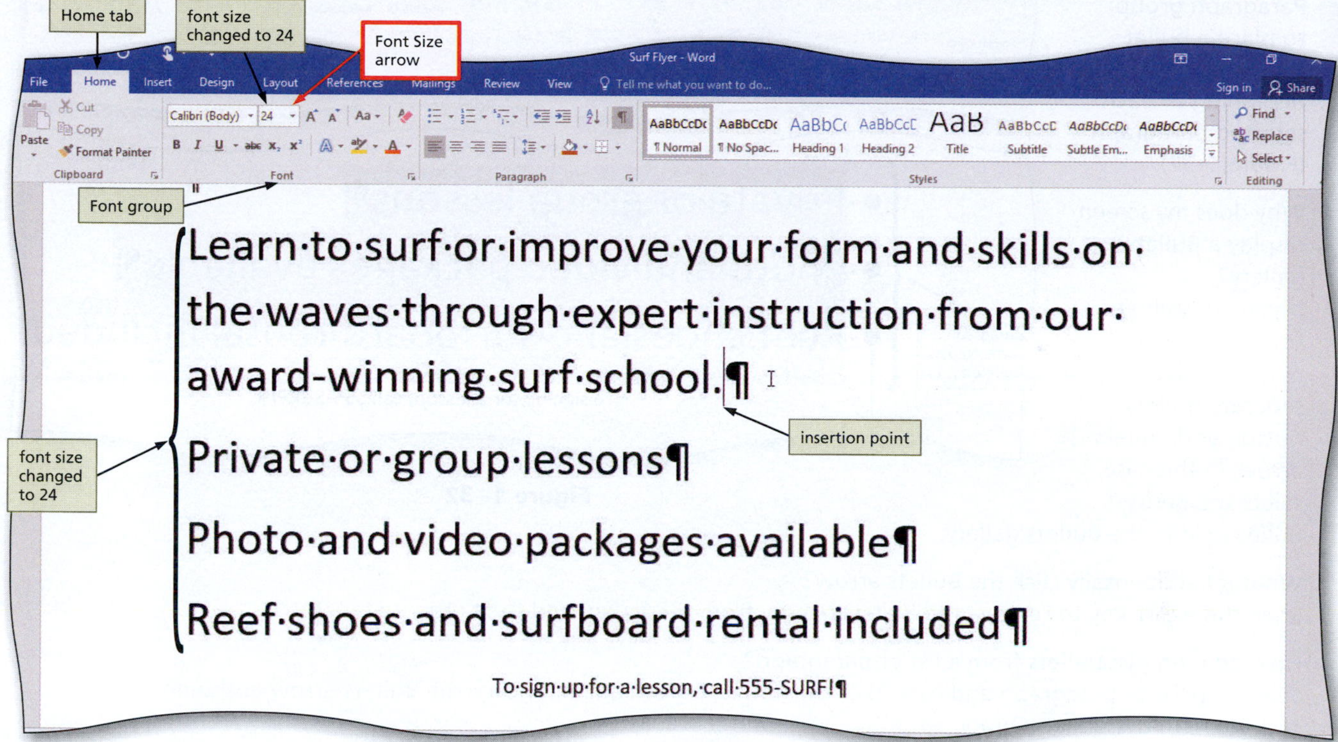

Home tab
font size changed to 24
Font Size arrow
Font group
Learn·to·surf·or·improve·your·form·and·skills·on· the·waves·through·expert·instruction·from·our· award-winning·surf·school.¶
insertion point
font size changed to 24
Private·or·group·lessons¶
Photo·and·video·packages·available¶
Reef·shoes·and·surfboard·rental·included¶
To·sign·up·for·a·lesson,·call·555-SURF!¶

Figure 1–30

To Bullet a List of Paragraphs

1 ENTER TEXT | 2 FORMAT TEXT | 3 INSERT PICTURE
4 FORMAT PICTURE | 5 ENHANCE PAGE | 6 CORRECT & REVISE

A **bulleted list** is a series of paragraphs, each beginning with a bullet character. The next step is to format the three paragraphs about the lessons that are above the signature line in the flyer as a bulleted list.

To format a list of paragraphs with bullets, you first must select all the lines in the paragraphs. ***Why?*** *If you do not select all paragraphs, Word will place a bullet only in the paragraph containing the insertion point.* The following steps bullet a list of paragraphs.

1

- Move the pointer to the left of the first paragraph to be selected until the pointer changes to a right-pointing block arrow.
- Drag downward until all paragraphs that will be formatted with a bullet character are selected (Figure 1–31).

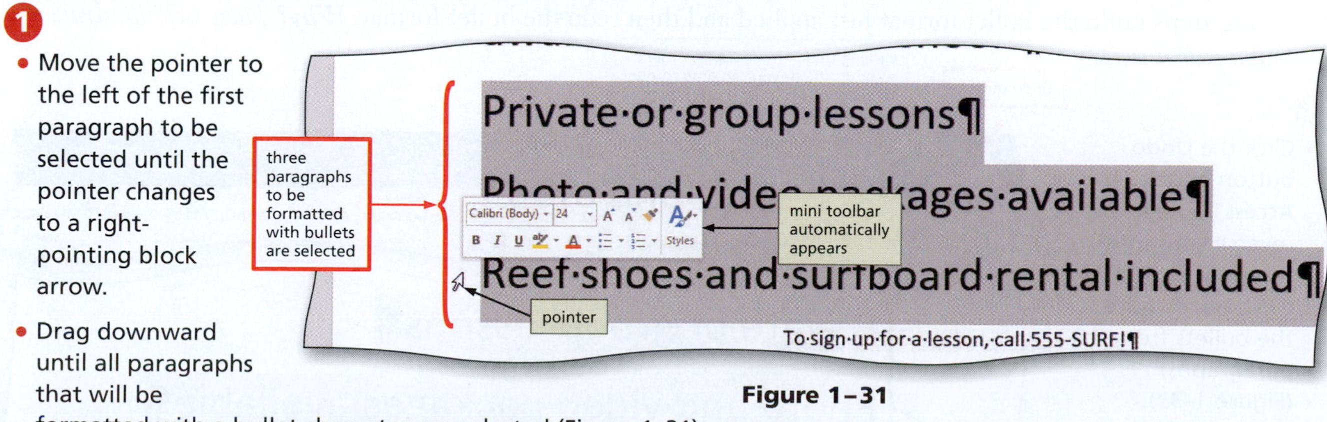

three paragraphs to be formatted with bullets are selected
Private·or·group·lessons¶
Photo·and·video·packages·available¶
mini toolbar automatically appears
Reef·shoes·and·surfboard·rental·included¶
pointer
To·sign·up·for·a·lesson,·call·555-SURF!¶

Figure 1–31

Q&A What if I am using a touch screen?

Tap to position the insertion point in the text to select and then drag the selection handle(s) as necessary to select the text that will be formatted.

2

- Click the Bullets button (Home tab | Paragraph group) to place a bullet character at the beginning of each selected paragraph (Figure 1–32).

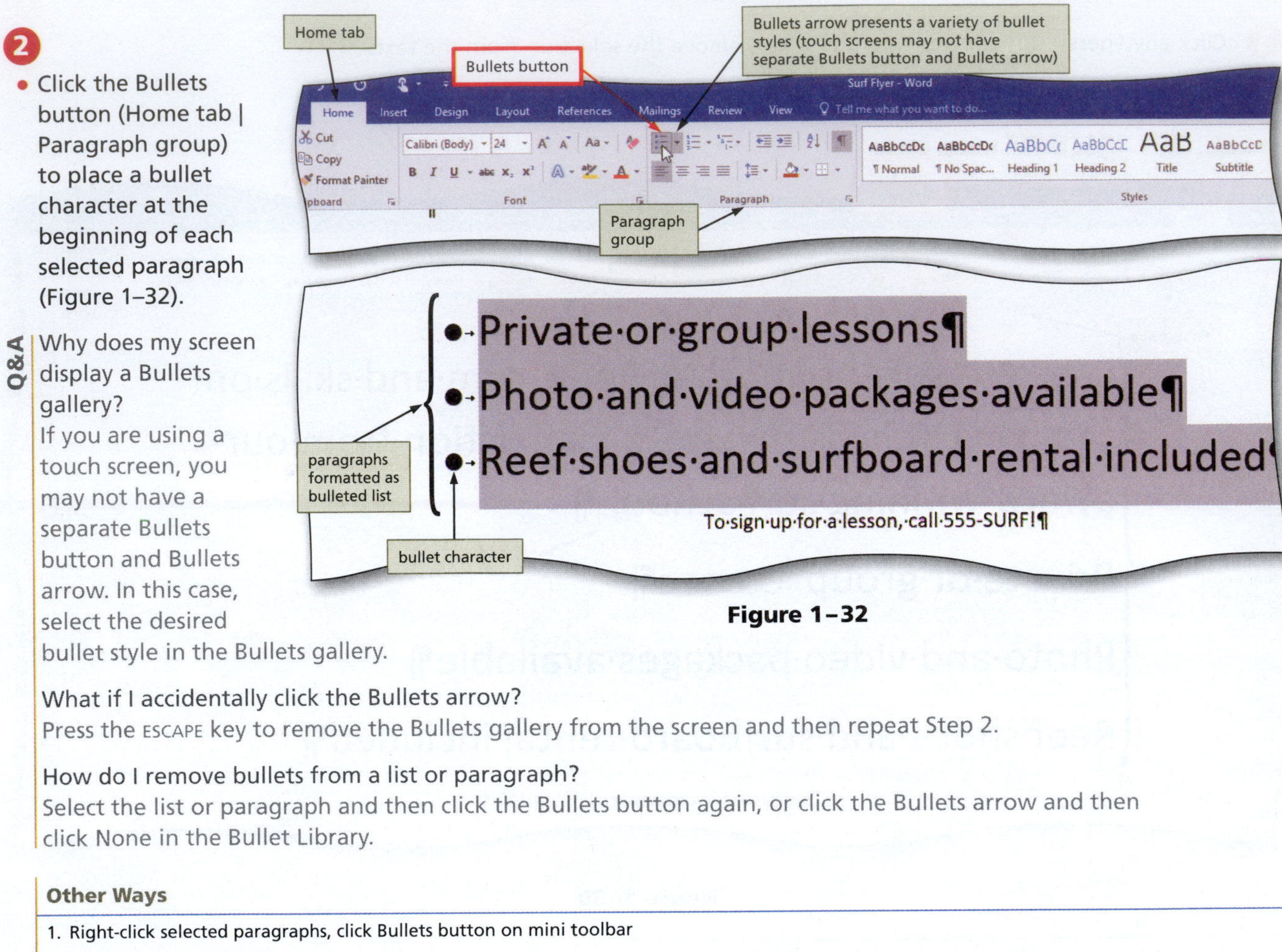

Figure 1–32

Q&A

Why does my screen display a Bullets gallery?
If you are using a touch screen, you may not have a separate Bullets button and Bullets arrow. In this case, select the desired bullet style in the Bullets gallery.

What if I accidentally click the Bullets arrow?
Press the ESCAPE key to remove the Bullets gallery from the screen and then repeat Step 2.

How do I remove bullets from a list or paragraph?
Select the list or paragraph and then click the Bullets button again, or click the Bullets arrow and then click None in the Bullet Library.

Other Ways

1. Right-click selected paragraphs, click Bullets button on mini toolbar

1 ENTER TEXT | **2 FORMAT TEXT** | 3 INSERT PICTURE
4 FORMAT PICTURE | 5 ENHANCE PAGE | 6 CORRECT & REVISE

To Undo and Redo an Action

Word provides a means of canceling your recent command(s) or action(s). For example, if you format text incorrectly, you can undo the format and try it again. When you point to the Undo button, Word displays the action you can undo as part of a ScreenTip.

If, after you undo an action, you decide you did not want to perform the undo, you can redo the undone action. Word does not allow you to undo or redo some actions, such as saving or printing a document. The following steps undo the bullet format just applied and then redo the bullet format. ***Why?** These steps illustrate the undo and redo actions.*

1

- Click the Undo button on the Quick Access Toolbar to reverse your most recent action (in this case, remove the bullets from the paragraphs) (Figure 1–33).

Undo button
clicking Undo arrow displays a series of prior actions you can drag through to undo (touch screens may not have separate Undo button and Undo arrow)
Redo button
Private·or·group·lessons¶
Photo·and·video·packages·available¶
Reef·shoes·and·surfboard·rental·included¶
bullet format undone

Figure 1–33

- Click the Redo button on the Quick Access Toolbar to reverse your most recent undo (in this case, place a bullet character on the paragraphs again) (shown in Figure 1–32).

Other Ways

1. Press CTRL+Z to undo; press CTRL+Y to redo

To Italicize Text

1 ENTER TEXT | 2 FORMAT TEXT | 3 INSERT PICTURE
4 FORMAT PICTURE | 5 ENHANCE PAGE | 6 CORRECT & REVISE

Italic text has a slanted appearance. The next step is to italicize the word, expert, in the flyer to further emphasize it. As with a single paragraph, if you want to format a single word, you do not need to select it. ***Why?*** *To format a single word, you simply position the insertion point somewhere in the word and apply the desired format.* The following step italicizes a word.

- Click somewhere in the word to be italicized (expert, in this case) to position the insertion point in the word to be formatted.
- Click the Italic button (Home tab | Font group) to italicize the word containing the insertion point (Figure 1–34).

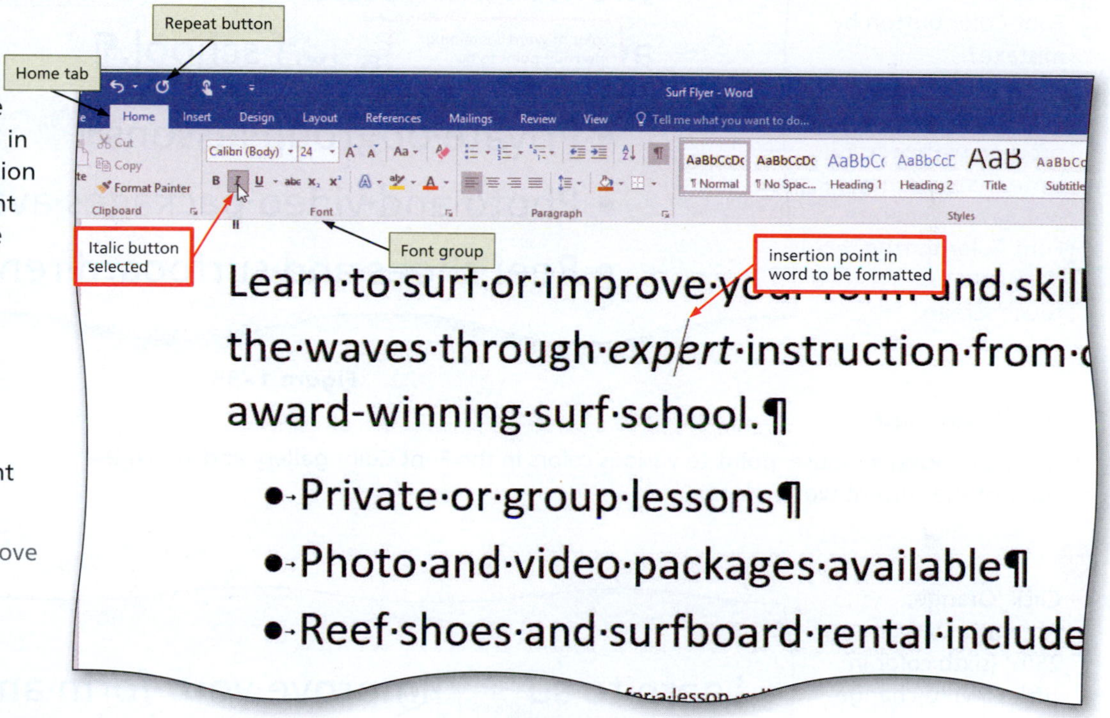

Figure 1–34

Q&A

How would I remove an italic format?
You would click the Italic button a second time, or you immediately could click the Undo button on the Quick Access Toolbar or press CTRL+Z.

How can I tell what formatting has been applied to text?
The selected buttons and boxes on the Home tab show formatting characteristics of the location of the insertion point. With the insertion point in the word, expert, the Home tab shows these formats: 24-point Calibri italic font.

Why did the appearance of the Redo button change?
It changed to a Repeat button. When it is a Repeat button, you can click it to repeat your last action. For example, you can select different text and then click the Repeat button to apply (repeat) the italic format to the selected text.

Other Ways

1. Click Italic button on mini toolbar
2. Right-click selected text (or, if using touch, tap 'Show Context Menu' button on mini toolbar), click Font on shortcut menu, click Font tab (Font dialog box), click Italic in Font style list, click OK button
3. Click Font Dialog Box Launcher (Home tab | Font group), click Font tab (Font dialog box), click Italic in Font style list, click OK button
4. Press CTRL+I

To Color Text

The following steps change the color of the word, expert. ***Why?** To emphasize the word even more, you change its color.*

1

- With the insertion point in the word to format, click the Font Color arrow (Home tab | Font group) to display the Font Color gallery (Figure 1–35).

Q&A What if I click the Font Color button by mistake?
Click the Font Color arrow and then proceed with Step 2. Note that you may not have a separate Font Color button if you are using a touch screen.

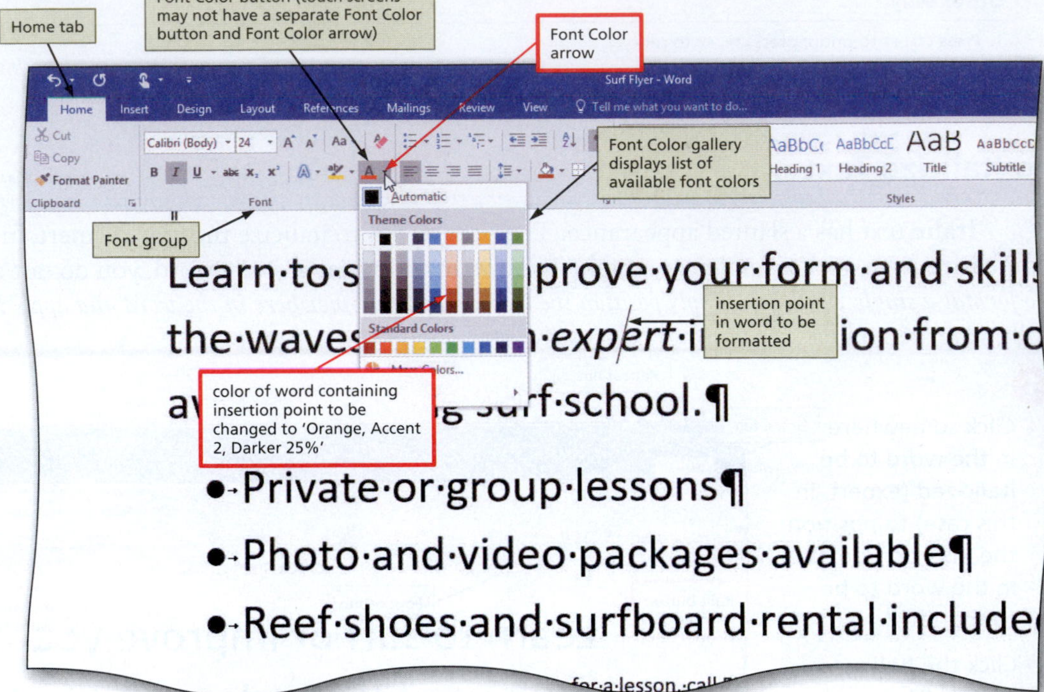

Figure 1–35

 **Experiment**

- If you are using a mouse, point to various colors in the Font Color gallery and watch the color of the current word change.

2

- Click 'Orange, Accent 2, Darker 25%' (sixth color in fifth row) to change the color of the text (Figure 1–36).

Q&A How would I change the text color back to black?
You would position the insertion point in the word or select the text, click the Font Color arrow (Home tab | Font group) again, and then click Automatic in the Font Color gallery.

Figure 1–36

Other Ways

1. Click Font Color arrow on mini toolbar, click desired color
2. Right-click selected text (or, if using touch, tap 'Show Context Menu' button on mini toolbar), click Font on shortcut menu, click Font tab (Font dialog box), click Font color arrow, click desired color, click OK button
3. Click Font Dialog Box Launcher (Home tab | Font group), click Font tab (Font dialog box), click Font color arrow, click desired color, click OK button

To Use the Mini Toolbar to Format Text

Recall from the Office and Windows module at the beginning of this book that the mini toolbar automatically appears based on certain tasks you perform. ***Why?*** *Word places commonly used buttons and boxes on the mini toolbar for your convenience. If you do not use the mini toolbar, it disappears from the screen.* All commands on the mini toolbar also exist on the ribbon.

The following steps use the mini toolbar to change the color and font size of text in the signature line of the flyer.

1

- Move the pointer to the left of the line to be selected until the pointer changes to a right-pointing block arrow and then click to select the line and display the mini toolbar (Figure 1–37).

Q&A What if I am using a touch screen? Double-tap to the left of the line to be selected to select the line and then tap the selection to display the mini toolbar. If you are using a touch screen, the buttons and boxes on the mini toolbar differ. For example, it contains a 'Show Context Menu' button at the far-right edge, which you tap to display a shortcut menu.

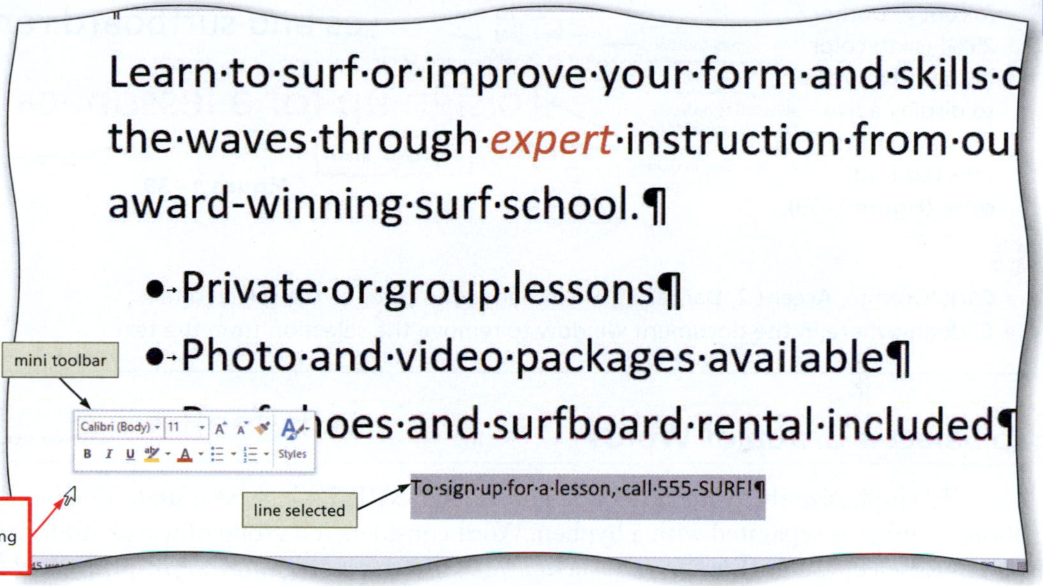

Figure 1–37

2

- Click the Font Size arrow on the mini toolbar to display the Font Size gallery.
- Point to 28 in the Font Size gallery to display a live preview of the selected font size (Figure 1–38).

3

- Click 28 in the Font Size gallery to increase the font size of the selected text.

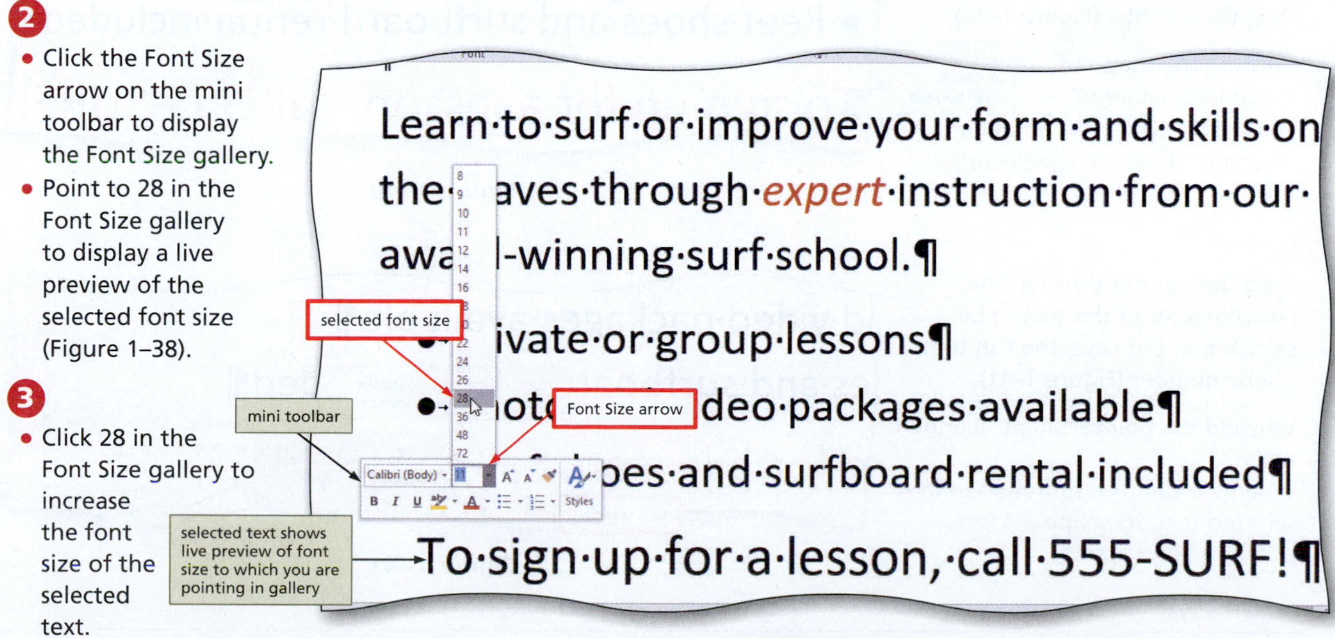
Learn·to·surf·or·improve·your·form·and·skills·on
the·waves·through·expert·instruction·from·our·
award-winning·surf·school.¶
selected font size
mini toolbar
Font Size arrow
selected text shows live preview of font size to which you are pointing in gallery
To·sign·up·for·a·lesson,·call·555-SURF!¶

Figure 1–38

- With the text still selected and the mini toolbar still displayed, click the Font Color arrow on the mini toolbar to display the Font Color gallery.
- Point to 'Orange, Accent 2, Darker 25%' (sixth color in the fifth row) to display a live preview of the selected font color (Figure 1–39).

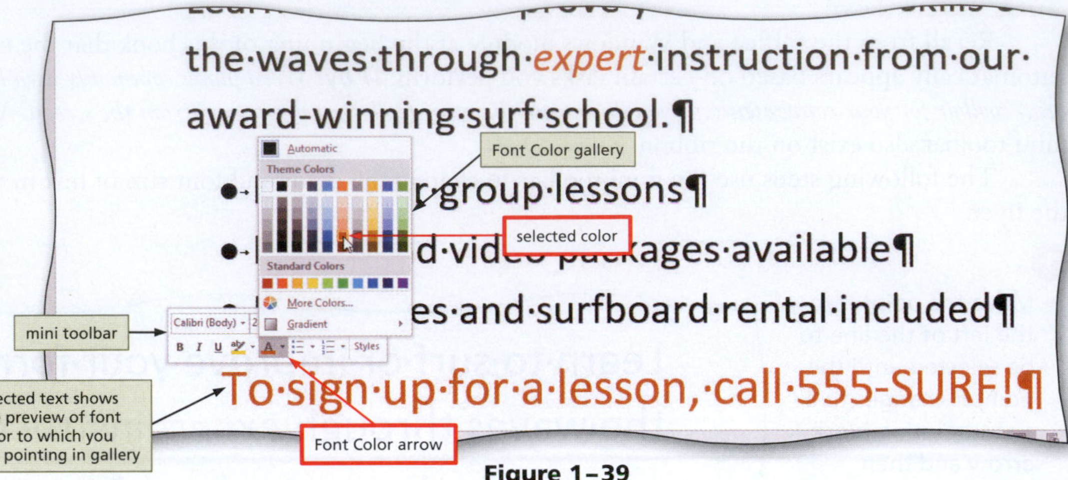

Figure 1–39

- Click 'Orange, Accent 2, Darker 25%' to change the color of the selected text.
- Click anywhere in the document window to remove the selection from the text.

To Select a Group of Words

1 ENTER TEXT | 2 FORMAT TEXT | 3 INSERT PICTURE
4 FORMAT PICTURE | 5 ENHANCE PAGE | 6 CORRECT & REVISE

To emphasize the contact phone number (555-SURF), this text is underlined in the flyer. Because the phone number is separated with a hyphen, Word considers it a group of words. To format a group of words, you first must select them. ***Why?*** *If you underline text without selecting any text first, Word will underline only the word containing the insertion point.* The following steps select a group of words.

- Position the pointer immediately to the left of the first character of the text to be selected, in this case, the 5 in 555 (Figure 1–40).

Q&A Why did the shape of the pointer change?
The pointer's shape is an I-beam when positioned in unselected text in the document window.

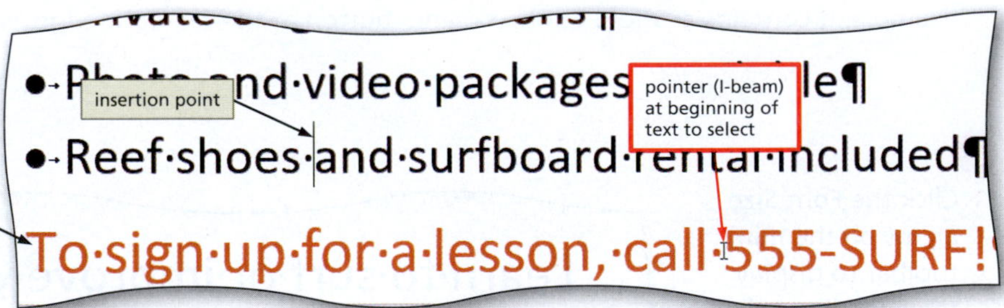

Figure 1–40

- Drag the pointer through the last character of the text to be selected, in this case, the F in the phone number (Figure 1–41).

Q&A Why did the pointer shape change again?
When the pointer is positioned in selected text, its shape is a left-pointing block arrow.

Figure 1–41

Other Ways

1. With insertion point at beginning of first word in group, press CTRL+SHIFT+RIGHT ARROW repeatedly until all words are selected

To Underline Text

Underlined text prints with an underscore (_) below each character. In the flyer, the contact phone number, 555-SURF, in the signature line is underlined. ***Why?*** *Underlines are used to emphasize or draw attention to specific text.* The following step formats selected text with an underline.

1

- With the text selected, click the Underline button (Home tab | Font group) to underline the selected text (Figure 1–42).

Q&A What if my screen displays an Underline gallery?
If you are using a touch screen, you may not have a separate Underline button and Underline arrow. In this case, select the desired underline style in the Underline gallery.

If a button exists on the mini toolbar, can I click that instead of using the ribbon?
Yes.

How would I remove an underline?
You would click the Underline button a second time, or you immediately could click the Undo button on the Quick Access Toolbar.

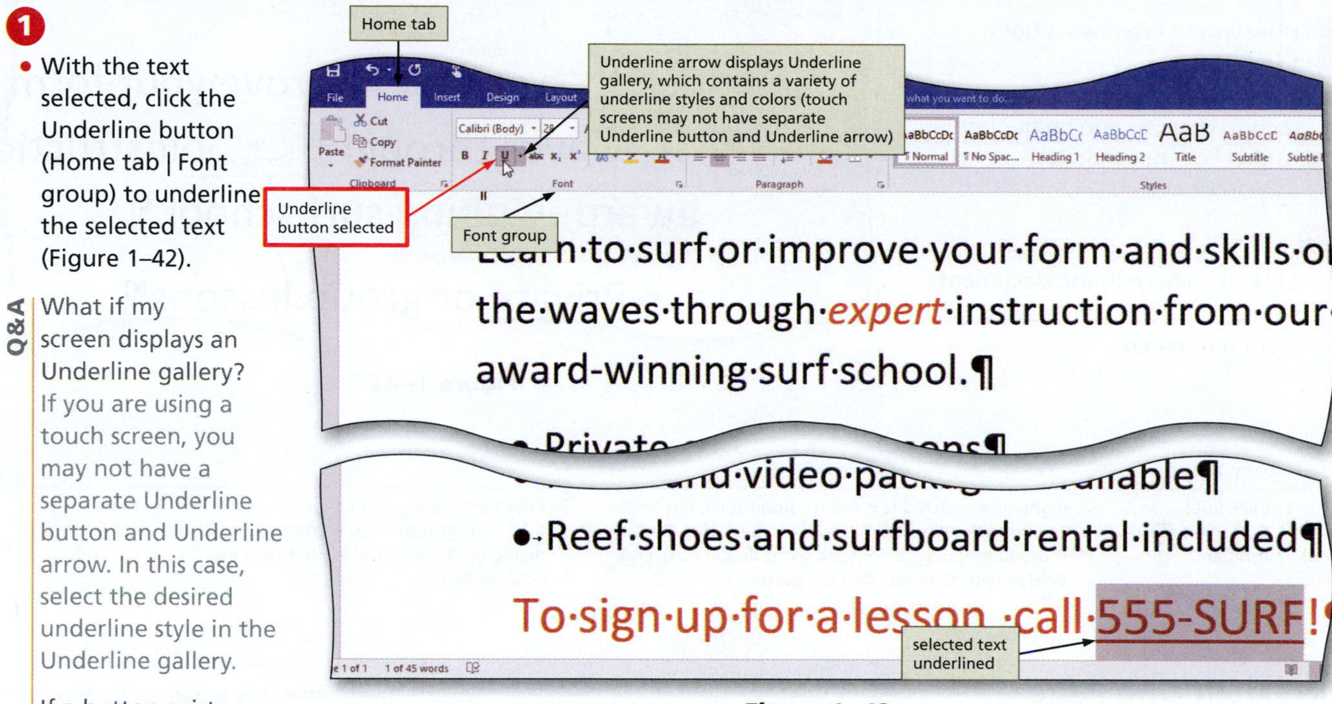

Figure 1–42

Other Ways

1. Click Underline button on mini toolbar
2. Right-click text (or, if using touch, tap 'Show Context Menu' button on mini toolbar), click Font on shortcut menu, click Font tab (Font dialog box), click Underline style box arrow, click desired underline style, click OK button
3. Click Font Dialog Box Launcher (Home tab | Font group), click Font tab (Font dialog box), click Underline style arrow, click desired underline style, click OK button
4. Press CTRL+U

To Bold Text

Bold characters appear somewhat thicker and darker than those that are not bold. The following steps format the text, award-winning, in bold characters. ***Why?*** *To further emphasize this text, it is bold in the flyer.* Recall that if you want to format a single word, you simply position the insertion point in the word and then format the word. To format text that consists of more than one word, as you have learned previously, you select the text first.

1

- Select the text to be formatted (the text, award-winning, in this case); that is, position the pointer immediately to the left of the first character of the text to be selected and then drag the pointer through the last character of the text to be selected.

What if I am using a touch screen?
Tap to position the insertion point in the text you want to select and then drag the selection handle(s) to select the text to be formatted.

- With the text selected, click the Bold button (Home tab | Font group) to bold the selected text (Figure 1–43).

Q&A How would I remove a bold format?
You would click the Bold button a second time, or you immediately could click the Undo button on the Quick Access Toolbar.

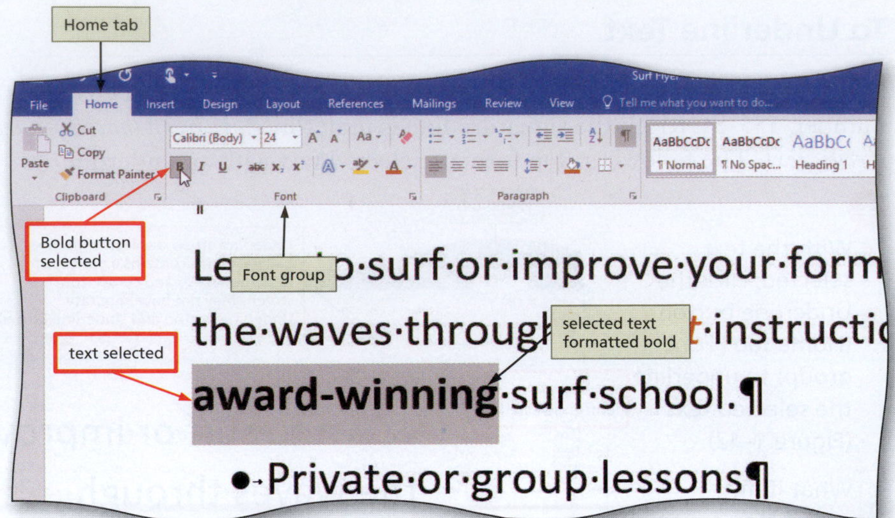
Home tab
Bold button selected
Font group
text selected
selected text formatted bold
Learn to surf or improve your form
the waves through expert instructi
award-winning surf school.¶
•Private or group lessons¶

Figure 1–43

- Click anywhere in the document window to remove the selection from the screen.

Other Ways

1. Click Bold button on mini toolbar
2. Right-click selected text (or, if using touch, tap 'Show Context Menu' button on mini toolbar), click Font on shortcut menu, click Font tab (Font dialog box), click Bold in Font style list, click OK button
3. Click Font Dialog Box Launcher (Home tab | Font group), click Font tab (Font dialog box), click Bold in Font style list, click OK button
4. Press CTRL+B

1 ENTER TEXT | **2 FORMAT TEXT** | 3 INSERT PICTURE
4 FORMAT PICTURE | 5 ENHANCE PAGE | 6 CORRECT & REVISE

To Zoom One Page

Earlier in this module, you changed the zoom to page width so that the text on the screen was larger and easier to read. In the next set of steps, you want to see the entire page (as a mock sheet of paper) on the screen at once. *Why? You want be able to see the effect of adjusting colors in the document as a whole.* The next step displays a single page in its entirety in the document window as large as possible.

1

- Click View on the ribbon to display the View tab.
- Click the One Page button (View tab | Zoom group) to display the entire page in the document window as large as possible (Figure 1–44).

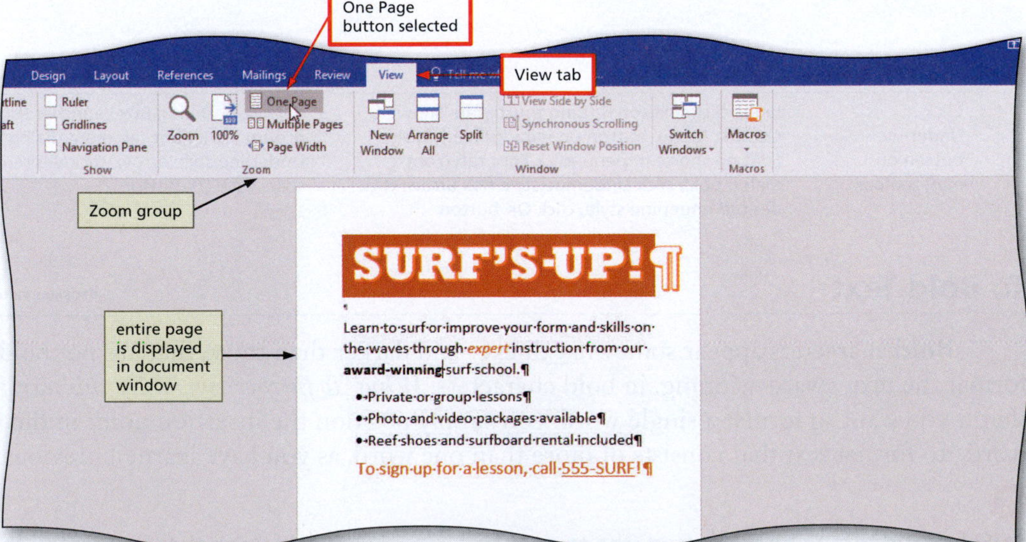
One Page button selected
View tab
Zoom group
entire page is displayed in document window
SURF'S UP!¶
Learn to surf or improve your form and skills on the waves through expert instruction from our award-winning surf school.¶
•Private or group lessons¶
•Photo and video packages available¶
•Reef shoes and surfboard rental included¶
To sign up for a lesson, call 555-SURF!¶

Figure 1–44

Other Ways

1. Click Zoom button (View tab | Zoom group), click Whole page (Zoom dialog box), click OK button

CONSIDER THIS

What colors should I choose when creating documents?
When choosing color, associate the meaning of the color with your message:

- Red expresses danger, power, or energy and often is associated with sports or physical exertion.
- Brown represents simplicity, honesty, and dependability.
- Orange denotes success, victory, creativity, and enthusiasm.
- Yellow suggests sunshine, happiness, hope, liveliness, and intelligence.
- Green symbolizes growth, healthiness, harmony, and healing and often is associated with safety or money.
- Blue indicates integrity, trust, importance, confidence, and stability.
- Purple represents wealth, power, comfort, extravagance, magic, mystery, and spirituality.
- White stands for purity, goodness, cleanliness, precision, and perfection.
- Black suggests authority, strength, elegance, power, and prestige.
- Gray conveys neutrality and, thus, often is found in backgrounds and other effects.

To Change Theme Colors

1 ENTER TEXT | 2 FORMAT TEXT | 3 INSERT PICTURE
4 FORMAT PICTURE | 5 ENHANCE PAGE | 6 CORRECT & REVISE

A **color scheme** in Word is a document theme that identifies complementary colors for text, background, accents, and links in a document. With more than 20 predefined color schemes, Word provides a simple way to coordinate colors in a document.

The default color scheme is called Office. In the flyer, you will change the color scheme. ***Why?*** *You want the colors in the flyer to represent integrity, trust, confidence, stability, healthiness, harmony, blooming, and safety, which are conveyed by shades of blues and greens. In Word, the Blue color scheme uses these colors.* The following steps change theme colors.

- Click Design on the ribbon to display the Design tab.
- Click the Theme Colors button (Design tab | Document Formatting group) to display the Theme Colors gallery.
- Point to Blue in the Theme Colors gallery to display a live preview of the selected theme color (Figure 1–45).

- Point to various color schemes in the Theme Colors gallery and watch the colors change in the document.

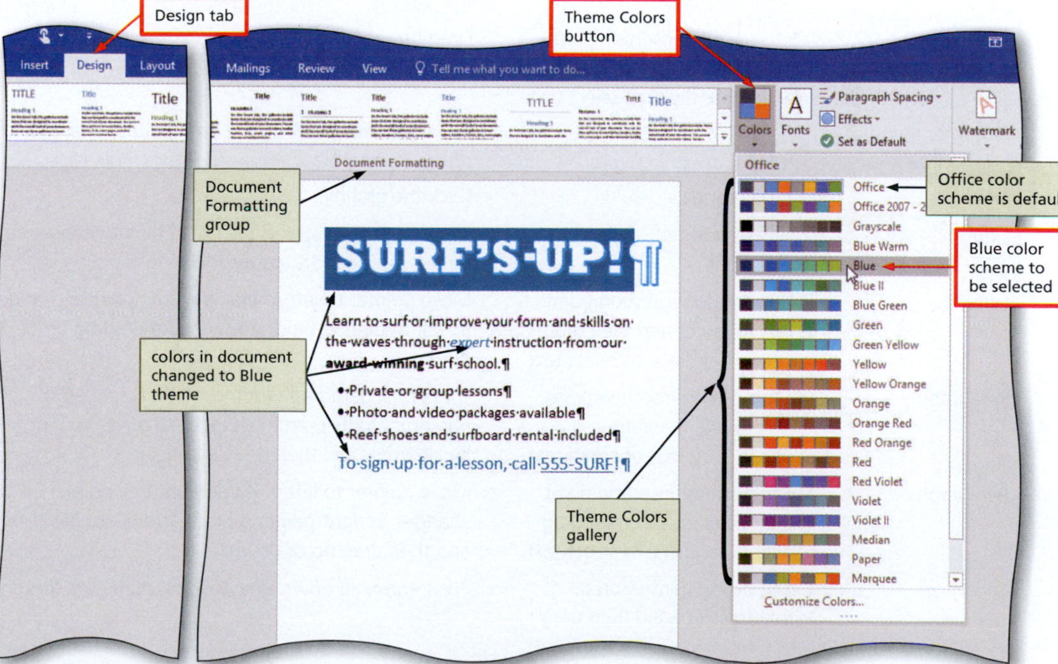

Figure 1–45

- Click Blue in the Theme Colors gallery to change the document theme colors.

Q&A What if I want to return to the original color scheme?
You would click the Theme Colors button again and then click Office in the Theme Colors gallery.

To Zoom Page Width

Because the document contents are small when displayed on one page, the next steps zoom page width again.

1. Click View on the ribbon to display the View tab.
2. Click the Page Width button (View tab | Zoom group) to display the page the same width as the document window (shown earlier in the module in Figure 1–7).
3. Save the flyer again on the same storage location with the same file name.

Q&A Why should I save the flyer again?
You have made several modifications to the flyer since you last saved it; thus, you should save it again.

BTW
Selecting Nonadjacent Items
In Word, you can use keyboard keys to select nonadjacent items, that is, items not next to each other. This is helpful when you are applying the same formatting to multiple items. To select nonadjacent items (text or graphics), select the first item, such as a word or paragraph, as usual; then, press and hold down the CTRL key. While holding down the CTRL key, select additional items.

Selecting Text

In many of the previous steps, you have selected text. Table 1–3 summarizes the techniques used to select various items.

Table 1–3 Techniques for Selecting Text

Item to Select	Touch	Mouse	Keyboard (where applicable)
Block of text	Tap to position insertion point in text to select and then drag selection handle(s) to select text.	Click at beginning of selection, scroll to end of selection, position pointer at end of selection, hold down SHIFT key, and then click; or drag through the text.	
Character(s)	Tap to position insertion point in text to select and then drag selection handle(s) to select text.	Drag through character(s).	SHIFT+RIGHT ARROW or SHIFT+LEFT ARROW
Document		Move pointer to left of text until pointer changes to right-pointing block arrow and then triple-click.	CTRL+A
Graphic	Tap the graphic.	Click the graphic.	
Line	Double-tap to left of line to be selected.	Move pointer to left of line until pointer changes to right-pointing block arrow and then click.	HOME, then SHIFT+END or END, then SHIFT+HOME
Lines	Tap to position insertion point in text to select and then drag selection handle(s) to select text.	Move pointer to left of first line until pointer changes to right-pointing block arrow and then drag up or down.	HOME, then SHIFT+DOWN ARROW or END, then SHIFT+UP ARROW
Paragraph	Tap to position insertion point in text to select and then drag selection handle(s) to select text.	Triple-click paragraph; or move pointer to left of paragraph until pointer changes to right-pointing block arrow and then double-click.	CTRL+SHIFT+DOWN ARROW or CTRL+SHIFT+UP ARROW
Paragraphs	Tap to position insertion point in text to select and then drag selection handle(s) to select text.	Move pointer to left of paragraph until pointer changes to right-pointing block arrow, double-click, and then drag up or down.	CTRL+SHIFT+DOWN ARROW or CTRL+SHIFT+UP ARROW repeatedly
Sentence	Tap to position insertion point in text to select and then drag selection handle(s) to select text.	Press and hold down CTRL key and then click sentence.	
Word	Double-tap word.	Double-click word.	CTRL+SHIFT+RIGHT ARROW or CTRL+SHIFT+LEFT ARROW
Words	Tap to position insertion point in text to select and then drag selection handle(s) to select text.	Drag through words.	CTRL+SHIFT+RIGHT ARROW or CTRL+SHIFT+LEFT ARROW repeatedly

Break Point: If you wish to take a break, this is a good place to do so. You can exit Word now. To resume at a later time, run Word, open the file called Surf Flyer, and continue following the steps from this location forward. For a detailed example of exiting Word, running Word, and opening a file, refer to the Office and Windows module at the beginning of the book.

Inserting and Formatting a Picture in a Word Document

With the text formatted in the flyer, the next step is to insert a digital picture in the flyer and format the picture. Flyers usually contain a graphical image(s), such as a picture, to attract the attention of passersby. In the following sections, you will perform these tasks:

1. Insert a digital picture into the flyer.
2. Reduce the size of the picture.
3. Change the look of the picture.

CONSIDER THIS

How do I locate a graphic file to use in a document?

To use a graphic in a Word document, the image must be stored digitally in a file. Files containing graphics are available from a variety of sources:

- The web has images available, some of which are free, while others require a fee.
- You can take a picture with a digital camera or smartphone and **download** it, which is the process of copying the digital picture from the camera or phone to your computer.
- With a scanner, you can convert a printed picture, drawing, or diagram to a digital file.

If you receive a picture from a source other than yourself, do not use the file until you are certain it does not contain a virus. A **virus** is a computer program that can damage files and programs on your computer. Use an antivirus program to verify that any files you use are virus free.

To Center Another Paragraph

In the flyer, the digital picture of a surfer should be centered on the blank line below the headline. The blank paragraph below the headline currently is left-aligned. The following steps center this paragraph.

1. Click Home on the ribbon to display the Home tab.
2. Click somewhere in the paragraph to be centered (in this case, the blank line below the headline) to position the insertion point in the paragraph to be formatted.
3. Click the Center button (Home tab | Paragraph group) to center the paragraph containing the insertion point (shown in Figure 1–46).

To Insert a Picture

1 ENTER TEXT | 2 FORMAT TEXT | **3 INSERT PICTURE**
4 FORMAT PICTURE | 5 ENHANCE PAGE | 6 CORRECT & REVISE

The next step in creating the flyer is to insert a digital picture of a surfer in the flyer on the blank line below the headline. The picture, which was taken with a digital camera, is available on the Data Files. Please contact your instructor for information about accessing Data Files.

The following steps insert a picture, which, in this example, is located in the Module 01 folder in the Data Files folder. ***Why?*** *It is good practice to organize and store files in folders so that you easily can find the files at a later date.*

1

- If necessary, position the insertion point at the location where you want to insert the picture (in this case, on the centered blank paragraph below the headline).
- Click Insert on the ribbon to display the Insert tab (Figure 1–46).

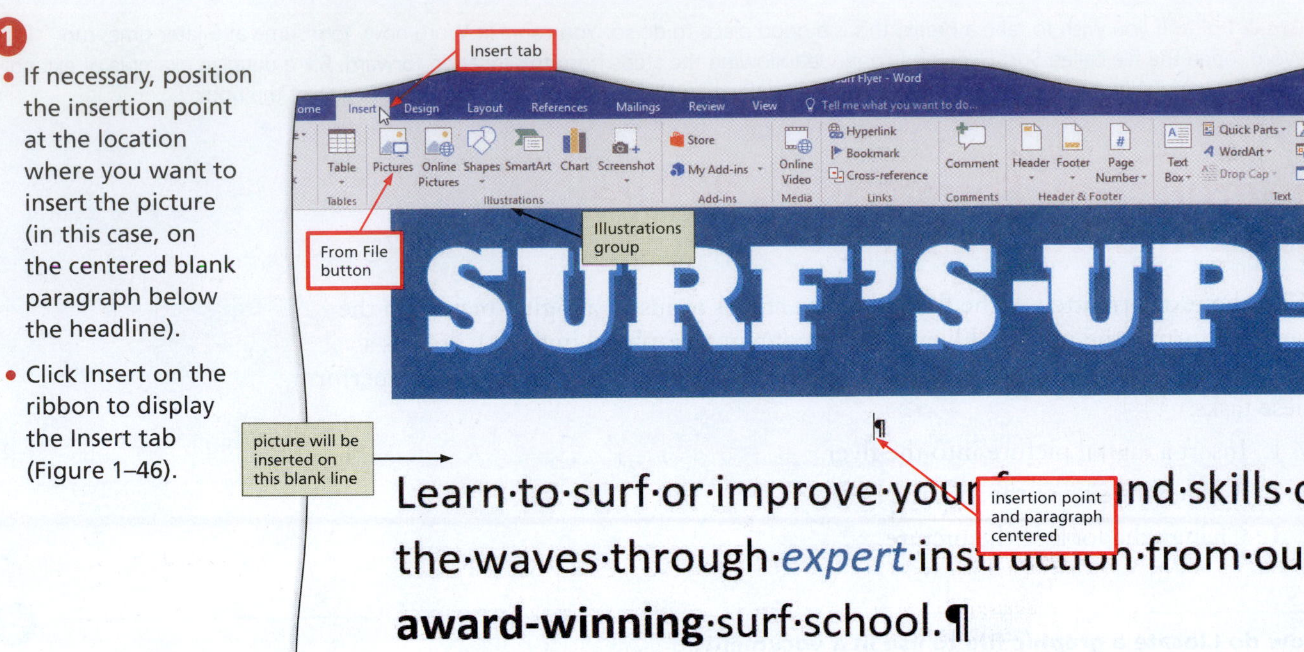

Figure 1–46

2

- Click the From File button (Insert tab | Illustrations group) (shown in Figure 1–46) to display the Insert Picture dialog box (shown in Figure 1–47).

3

- Navigate to the desired picture location (in this case, the Module 01 folder in the Data Files folder). For a detailed example of this procedure, refer to Steps 4a and 4b in the To Save a File in a Folder section in the Office and Windows module at the beginning of this book.
- Click Surfing to select the file (Figure 1–47).

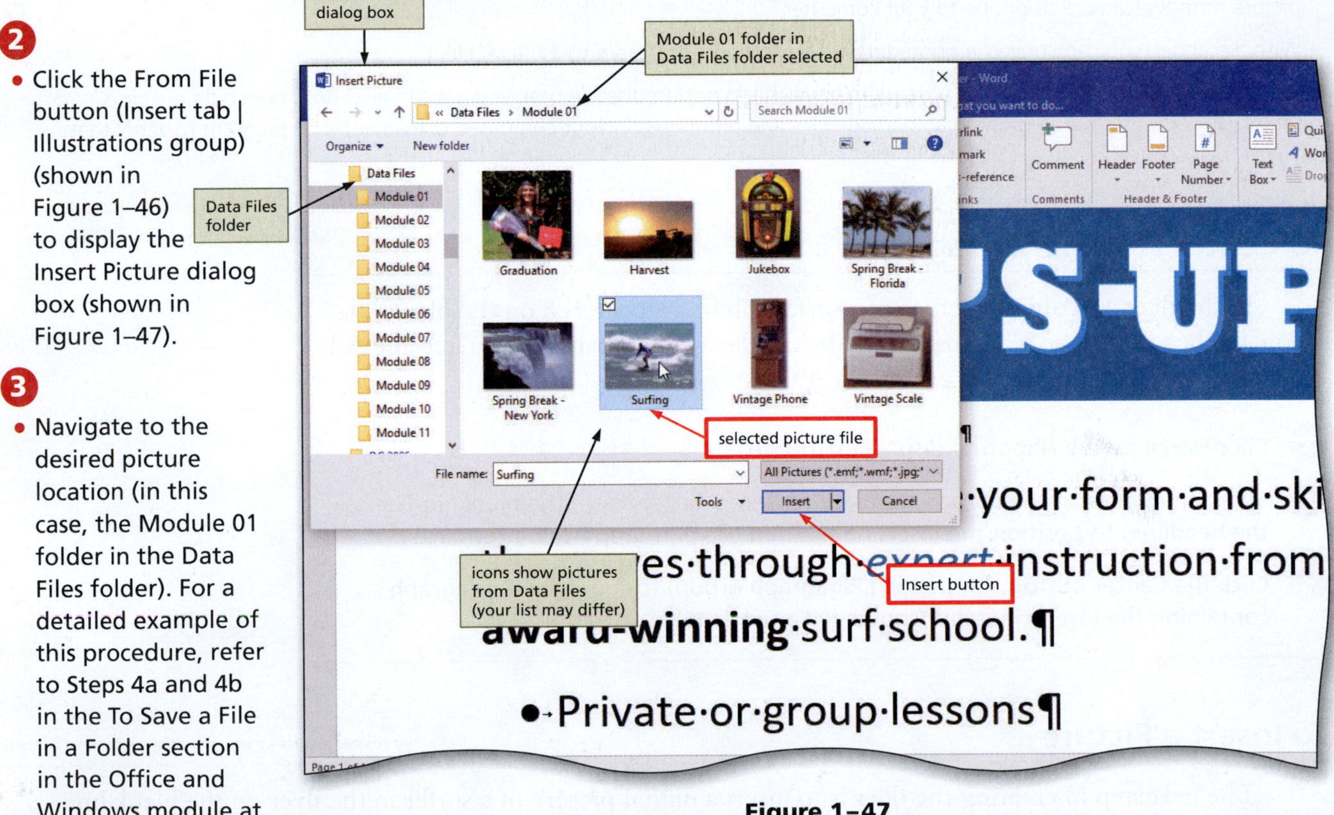

Figure 1–47

- Click the Insert button (Insert Picture dialog box) to insert the picture at the location of the insertion point in the document (Figure 1–48).

Q&A

What are the symbols around the picture?
A selected graphic appears surrounded by a **selection rectangle**, which has small squares and circles, called **sizing handles**, at each corner and middle location.

What is the purpose of the Layout Options button?
When you click the Layout Options button, Word provides options for changing how the graphic is positioned with text in the document.

Figure 1–48

CONSIDER THIS

How do you know where to position a graphic on a flyer?
The content, size, shape, position, and format of a graphic should capture the interest of passersby, enticing them to stop and read the flyer. Often, the graphic is the center of attention and visually the largest element on a flyer. If you use colors in the graphical image, be sure they are part of the document's color scheme.

To Zoom the Document

In the steps in the following sections, you will work with the picture just inserted. The next task is to adjust the zoom percentage. ***Why?*** *Currently, you can see only a small amount of text with the picture. Seeing more of the document at once helps you determine the appropriate size for the picture.* The following step zooms the document.

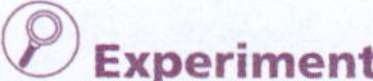

- Repeatedly click the Zoom Out and Zoom In buttons on the status bar and watch the size of the document change in the document window.

Q&A What if I am using a touch screen?
Repeatedly pinch (move two fingers together on the screen) and stretch (move two fingers apart on the screen) and watch the size of the document change in the document window.

- Click the Zoom Out or Zoom In button as many times as necessary until the Zoom button on the status bar displays 40% on its face (Figure 1–49).

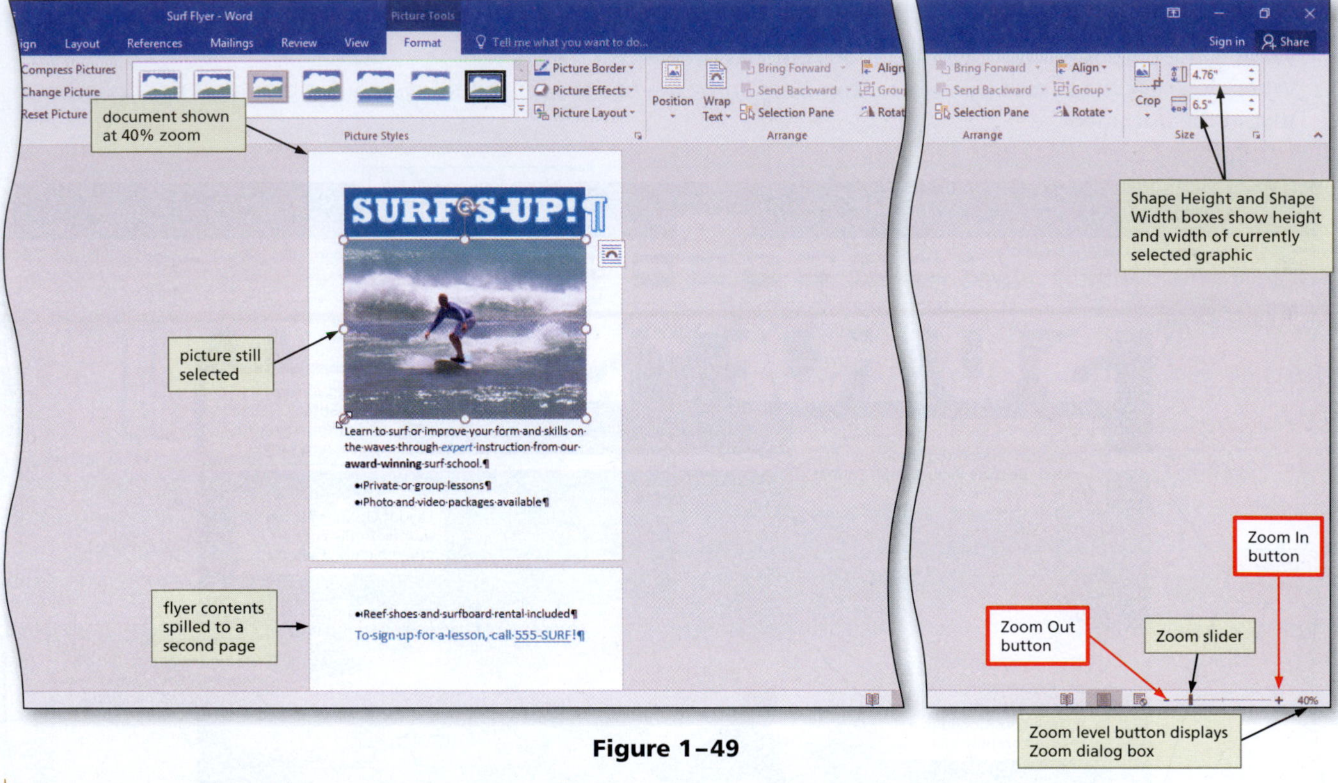

Figure 1–49

Other Ways

1. Drag Zoom slider on status bar
2. Click Zoom level button on status bar, select desired zoom percent or type (Zoom dialog box), click OK button
3. Click Zoom button (View tab | Zoom group), select desired zoom percent or type (Zoom dialog box), click OK button

To Resize a Graphic

1 ENTER TEXT | 2 FORMAT TEXT | 3 INSERT PICTURE
4 FORMAT PICTURE | 5 ENHANCE PAGE | 6 CORRECT & REVISE

Resizing includes both increasing and reducing the size of a graphic. The next step is to resize the picture so that it is smaller in the flyer. ***Why?*** *You want the graphic and all the text on the flyer to fit on a single sheet of paper.* The following steps resize a selected graphic.

1

- Be sure the graphic still is selected.

Q&A What if my graphic (picture) is not selected?
To select a graphic, click it.

- Point to the lower-left corner sizing handle on the picture so that the pointer shape changes to a two-headed arrow (Figure 1–50).

Figure 1–50

2

- Drag the sizing handle diagonally inward until the lower-left corner of the picture is positioned approximately as shown in Figure 1–51. Do not release the mouse button at this point.

What if I am using a touch screen?
Drag a corner of the graphic, without lifting your finger, until the graphic is the desired size.

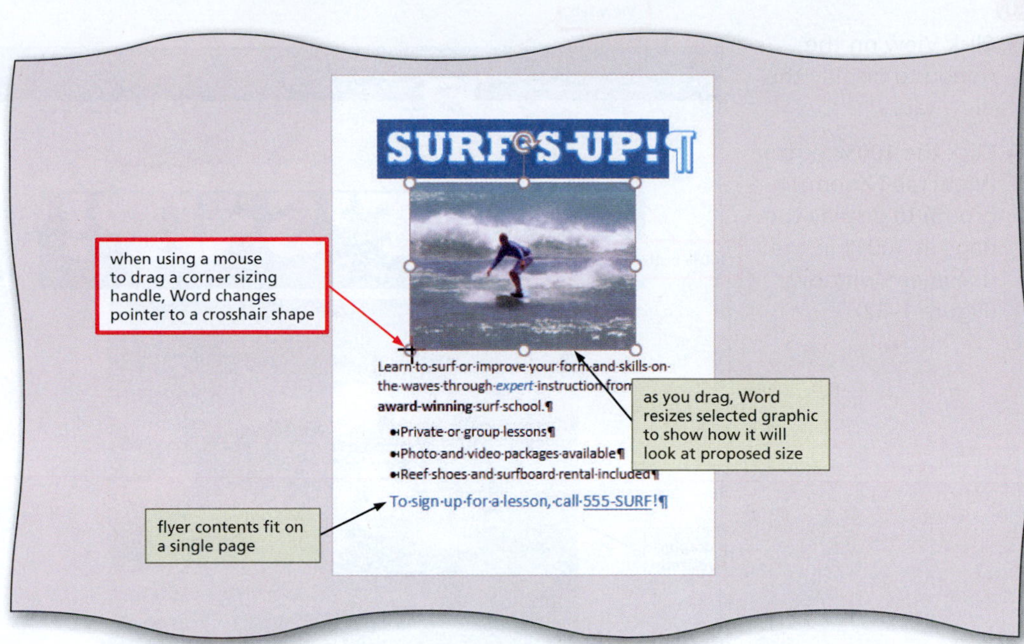
SURF'S UP!
when using a mouse to drag a corner sizing handle, Word changes pointer to a crosshair shape
as you drag, Word resizes selected graphic to show how it will look at proposed size
flyer contents fit on a single page
Learn to surf or improve your form and skills on the waves through expert instruction from award-winning surf school.
Private or group lessons
Photo and video packages available
Reef shoes and surfboard rental included
To sign up for a lesson, call 555-SURF!

Figure 1–51

3

- Release the mouse button to resize the graphic, which, in this case, should have a height of about 3.7" and a width of about 5.06".

Q&A

How can I see the height and width measurements?
Look in the Size group on the Picture Tools Format tab to see the height and width measurements of the currently selected graphic (shown in Figure 1–49).

What if the graphic is the wrong size?
Repeat Steps 1, 2, and 3, or enter the desired height and width values in the Shape Height and Shape Width boxes (Picture Tools Format tab | Size group).

What if I want to return a graphic to its original size and start again?
With the graphic selected, click the Size Dialog Box Launcher (Picture Tools Format tab | Size group), click the Size tab (Layout dialog box), click the Reset button, and then click the OK button.

Other Ways

1. Enter height and width of graphic in Shape Height and Shape Width boxes (Picture Tools Format tab | Size group)
2. Click Advanced Layout: Size Dialog Box Launcher (Picture Tools Format tab | Size group), click Size tab (Layout dialog box), enter desired height and width values in boxes, click OK button

To Zoom 100%

1 ENTER TEXT | 2 FORMAT TEXT | 3 INSERT PICTURE
4 FORMAT PICTURE | 5 ENHANCE PAGE | 6 CORRECT & REVISE

In the next series of steps, you will format the picture. Earlier in this module, you changed the zoom to 40% so that you could see more of the page while resizing the graphic. The following step zooms the screen to 100%. ***Why?*** *You want the contents of the image to be enlarged a bit, while still seeing some of the text in the document.*

- Click View on the ribbon to display the View tab.
- Click the 100% button (View tab | Zoom group) to display the page at 100% in the document window (Figure 1–52).

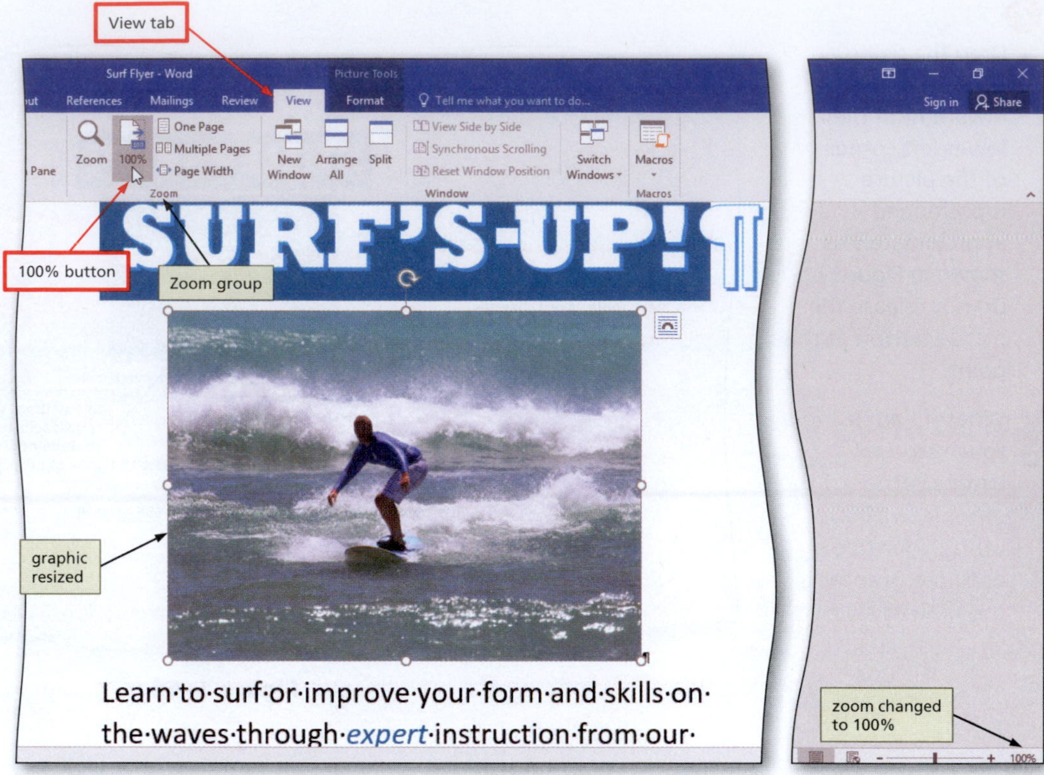

Figure 1–52

Other Ways

1. Click Zoom button (View tab | Zoom group), click 100% (Zoom dialog box), click OK button

To Apply a Picture Style

1 ENTER TEXT | 2 FORMAT TEXT | 3 INSERT PICTURE
4 FORMAT PICTURE | 5 ENHANCE PAGE | 6 CORRECT & REVISE

A **style** is a named group of formatting characteristics. Word provides more than 25 picture styles. ***Why?*** *Picture styles enable you easily to change a picture's look to a more visually appealing style, including a variety of shapes, angles, borders, and reflections.* The flyer in this module uses a style that applies an oval shape to the picture. The following steps apply a picture style to a picture.

1

- Ensure the graphic still is selected and then click Picture Tools Format on the ribbon to display the Picture Tools Format tab (Figure 1–53).

Q&A What if my graphic (picture) is not selected?

To select a graphic, click it.

What is the white circle attached to top of the selected graphic?

It is called a rotate handle. When you drag a graphic's **rotate handle,** the graphic moves in either a clockwise or counterclockwise direction.

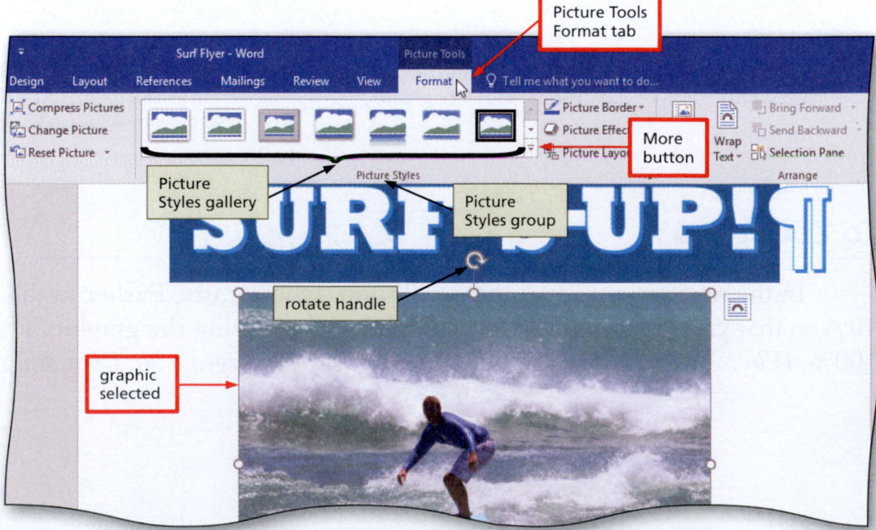

Figure 1–53

2

- Click the More button in the Picture Styles gallery (Picture Tools Format tab | Picture Styles group) (shown in Figure 1–53) to expand the gallery.
- Point to 'Soft Edge Oval' in the Picture Styles gallery to display a live preview of that style applied to the picture in the document (Figure 1–54).

Experiment

- Point to various picture styles in the Picture Styles gallery and watch the style of the picture change in the document window.

- Click 'Soft Edge Oval' in the Picture Styles gallery (sixth style in third row) to apply the style to the selected picture.

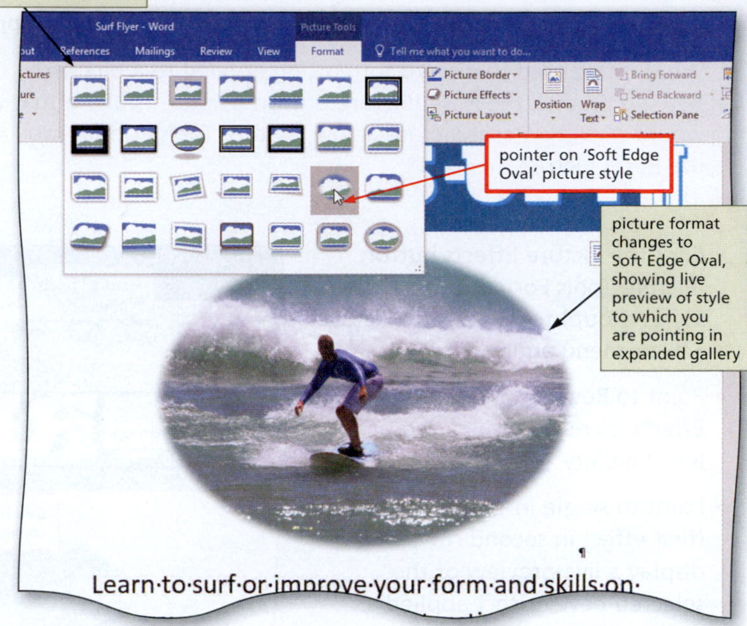

Figure 1–54

Other Ways

1. Right-click picture, click 'Picture Styles' on mini toolbar, select desired style

To Apply Picture Effects

1 ENTER TEXT | 2 FORMAT TEXT | 3 INSERT PICTURE
4 FORMAT PICTURE | 5 ENHANCE PAGE | 6 CORRECT & REVISE

Word provides a variety of picture effects, such as shadows, reflections, glow, soft edges, bevel, and 3-D rotation. The difference between the effects and the styles is that each effect has several options, providing you with more control over the exact look of the image.

In this flyer, the picture has a slight lime green glow effect and beveled edges. The following steps apply picture effects to the selected picture. ***Why?*** *Picture effects enable you to further customize a picture.*

- With the picture still selected, click the Picture Effects button (Picture Tools Format tab | Picture Styles group) to display the Picture Effects menu.
- Point to Glow on the Picture Effects menu to display the Glow gallery.
- Point to 'Lime, 5 pt glow, Accent color 6' in the Glow Variations area (rightmost glow in first row) to display a live preview of the selected glow effect applied to the picture in the document window (Figure 1–55).

Experiment

- If you are using a mouse, point to various glow effects in the Glow gallery and watch the picture change in the document window.

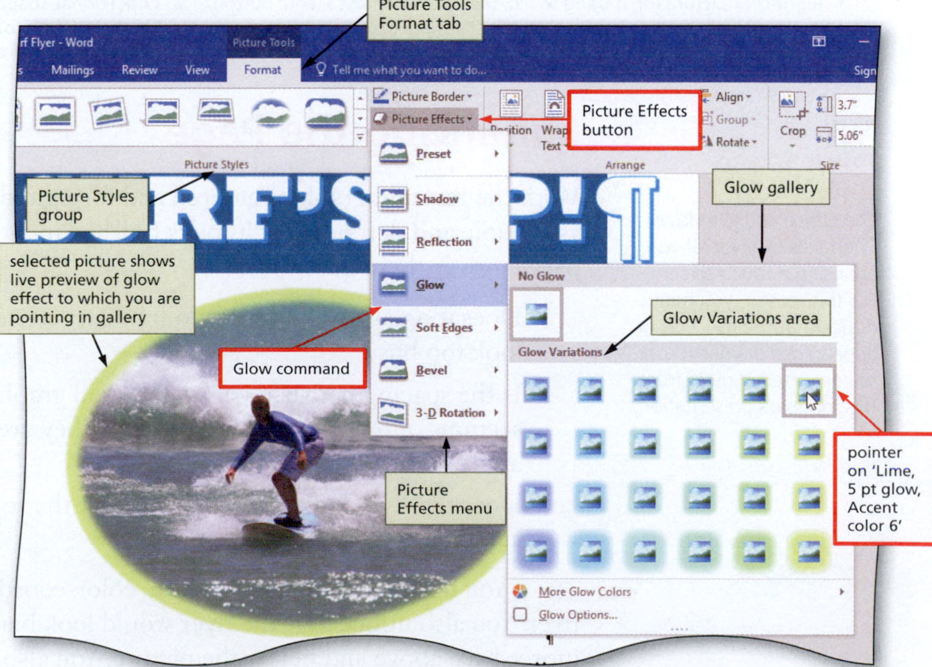

Figure 1–55

2

- Click 'Lime, 5 pt glow, Accent color 6' in the Glow gallery to apply the selected picture effect.

Q&A What if I wanted to discard formatting applied to a picture?
You would click the Reset Picture button (Picture Tools Format tab | Adjust group). To reset formatting and size, you would click the Reset Picture arrow (Picture Tools Format tab | Adjust group) and then click 'Reset Picture & Size' on the Reset Picture menu.

3

- Click the Picture Effects button (Picture Tools Format tab | Picture Styles group) to display the Picture Effects menu again.
- Point to Bevel on the Picture Effects menu to display the Bevel gallery.
- Point to Angle in the Bevel area (first effect in second row) to display a live preview of the selected bevel effect applied to the picture in the document window (Figure 1–56).

Experiment

- If you are using a mouse, point to various bevel effects in the Bevel gallery and watch the picture change in the document window.

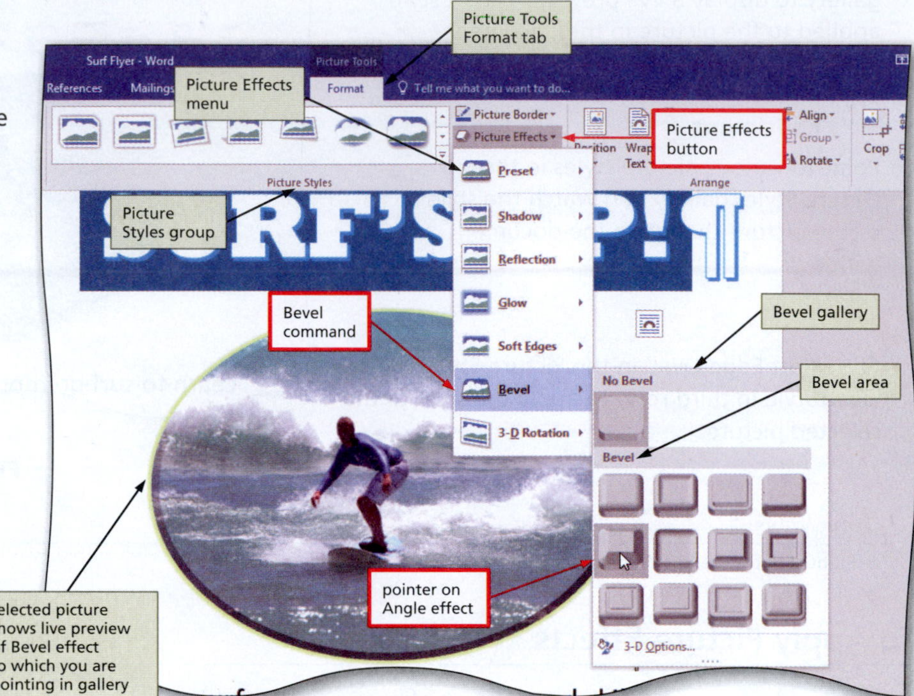

Figure 1–56

4

- Click Angle in the Bevel gallery to apply the selected picture effect.

Other Ways

1. Right-click picture (or, if using touch, tap 'Show Context Menu' button on mini toolbar), click Format Object or Format Picture on shortcut menu, click Effects button (Format Picture task pane), select desired options, click Close button
2. Click Format Shape Dialog Box Launcher (Picture Tools Format tab | Picture Styles group), click Effects button (Format Picture task pane), select desired options, click Close button

BTW
Touch Screen Differences
The Office and Windows interfaces may vary if you are using a touch screen. For this reason, you might notice that the function or appearance of your touch screen differs slightly from this module's presentation.

Enhancing the Page

With the text and graphics entered and formatted, the next step is to look at the page as a whole and determine if it looks finished in its current state. As you review the page, answer these questions:

- Does it need a page border to frame its contents, or would a page border make it look too busy?
- Is the spacing between paragraphs and graphics on the page adequate? Do any sections of text or graphics look as if they are positioned too closely to the items above or below them?
- Does the flyer have too much space at the top or bottom? Should the contents be centered vertically?

You determine that a graphical, color-coordinated border would enhance the flyer. You also notice that the flyer would look better proportioned if it had a little more space above and below the picture. You also want to ensure that the contents are centered vertically. The following sections make these enhancements to the flyer.

To Add a Page Border

In Word, you can add a border around the perimeter of an entire page. The flyer in this module has a lime border. ***Why?*** *This border color complements the color of the flyer contents.* The following steps add a page border.

1

- Click Design on the ribbon to display the Design tab.
- Click the 'Borders and Shading' button (Design tab | Page Background group) to display the Borders and Shading dialog box (Figure 1–57).

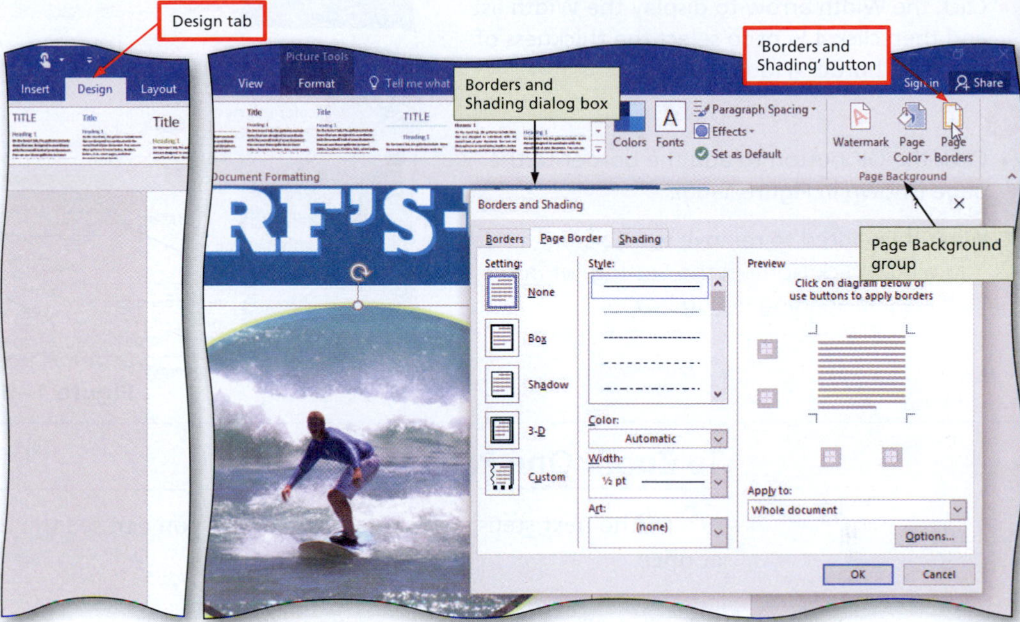

Figure 1–57

2

- Scroll to, if necessary, and then click the sixth border style in the Style list (Borders and Shading dialog box) to select the style.
- Click the Color arrow to display a Color palette (Figure 1–58).

Figure 1–58

- Click 'Lime, Accent 6, Lighter 40%' (rightmost color in fourth row) in the Color palette to select the color for the page border.
- Click the Width arrow to display the Width list and then click 4 ½ pt to select the thickness of the page border (Figure 1–59).

- Click the OK button to add the border to the page (shown in Figure 1–60).

Q&A What if I wanted to remove the border?
You would click None in the Setting list in the Borders and Shading dialog box.

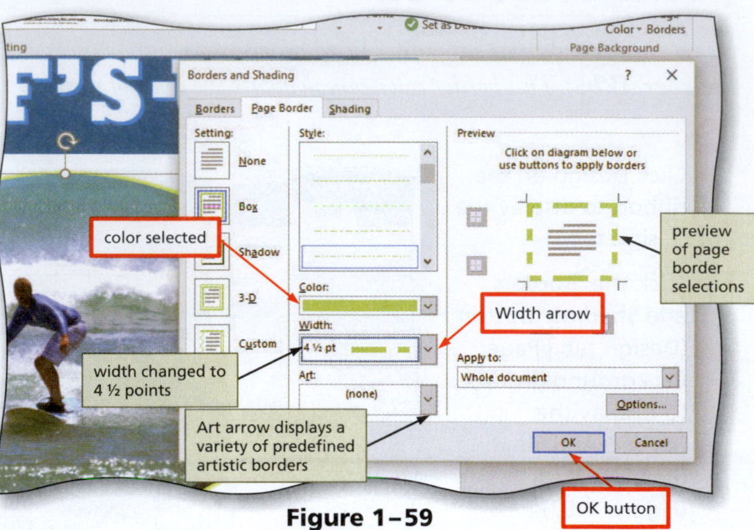

Figure 1–59

To Zoom One Page

The next steps zoom one page so that you can see the entire page on the screen at once.

1. Click View on the ribbon to display the View tab.
2. Click the One Page button (View tab | Zoom group) to display the entire page in the document window as large as possible.

To Change Spacing before and after Paragraphs

1 ENTER TEXT | 2 FORMAT TEXT | 3 INSERT PICTURE
4 FORMAT PICTURE | 5 ENHANCE PAGE | 6 CORRECT & REVISE

The default spacing above (before) a paragraph in Word is 0 points and below (after) is 8 points. In the flyer, you want to increase the spacing below the paragraph containing the headline and above the signature line. ***Why?*** *The flyer spacing will look more balanced with spacing increased above and below these paragraphs.* The following steps change the spacing above and below a paragraph.

- Position the insertion point in the paragraph to be adjusted, in this case, the paragraph containing the headline.

Q&A What happened to the Picture Tools Format tab?
When you click outside of a graphic or press a key to scroll through a document, Word deselects the graphic and removes the Picture Tools Format tab from the screen. That is, this tab appears only when a graphic is selected.

- Click Layout on the ribbon to display the Layout tab.
- Click the Spacing After up arrow (Layout tab | Paragraph group) so that 12 pt is displayed in the Spacing After box to increase the space below the current paragraph (Figure 1–60).

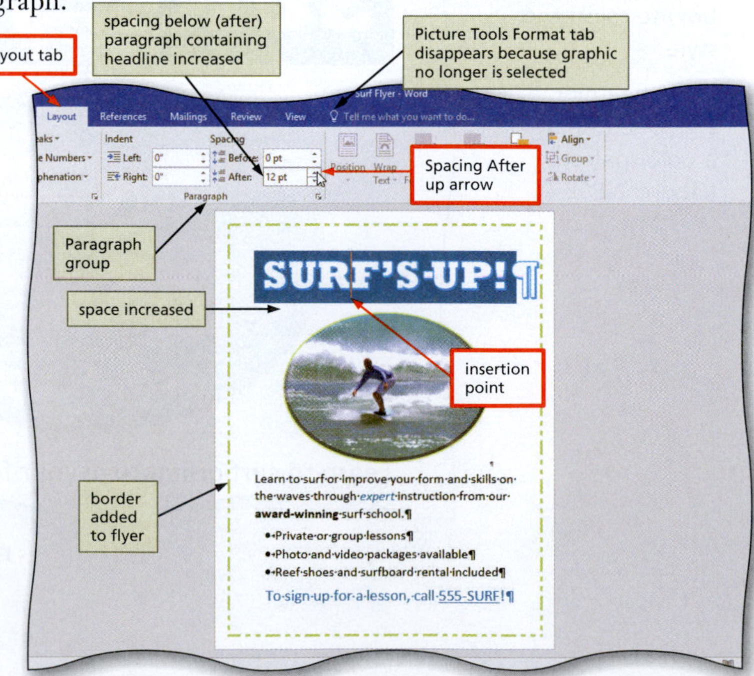

Figure 1–60

2

- Position the insertion point in the paragraph to be adjusted, in this case, the paragraph containing the signature line.
- Click the Spacing Before up arrow (Layout tab | Paragraph group) as many times as necessary so that 12 pt is displayed in the Spacing Before box to increase the space above the current paragraph (Figure 1–61).
- If the text flows to two pages, reduce the spacing above and below paragraphs as necessary.

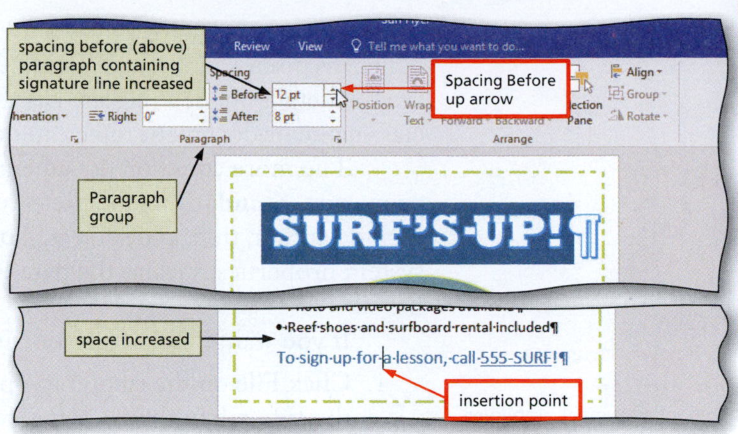

Figure 1–61

Other Ways

1. Right-click paragraph (or, if using touch, tap 'Show Context Menu' button on mini toolbar), click Paragraph on shortcut menu, click Indents and Spacing tab (Paragraph dialog box), enter spacing before and after values, click OK button
2. Click Paragraph Settings Dialog Box Launcher (Home tab or Layout tab | Paragraph group), click Indents and Spacing tab (Paragraph dialog box), enter spacing before and after values, click OK button

1 ENTER TEXT | 2 FORMAT TEXT | 3 INSERT PICTURE
4 FORMAT PICTURE | **5 ENHANCE PAGE** | **6 CORRECT & REVISE**

To Center Page Contents Vertically

In Word, you can center the page contents vertically. *Why? This places the same amount of space at the top and bottom of the page.* The following steps center page contents vertically.

1

- If necessary, click Layout on the ribbon to display the Layout tab.
- Click the Page Setup Dialog Box Launcher (Layout tab | Page Setup group) to display the Page Setup dialog box.
- Click the Layout tab (Page Setup dialog box) to display the Layout sheet (Figure 1–62).

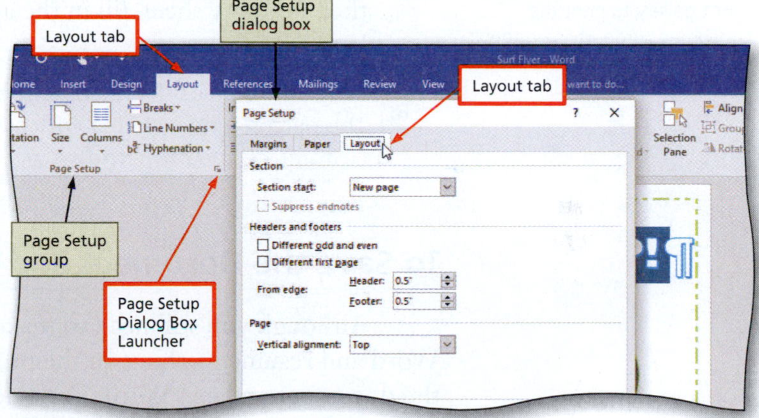

Figure 1–62

2

- Click the Vertical alignment arrow (Page Setup dialog box) to display the list of alignment options and then click Center in the list (Figure 1–63).

3

- Click the OK button to center the page contents vertically on the screen (shown in Figure 1–1 at the beginning of this module).

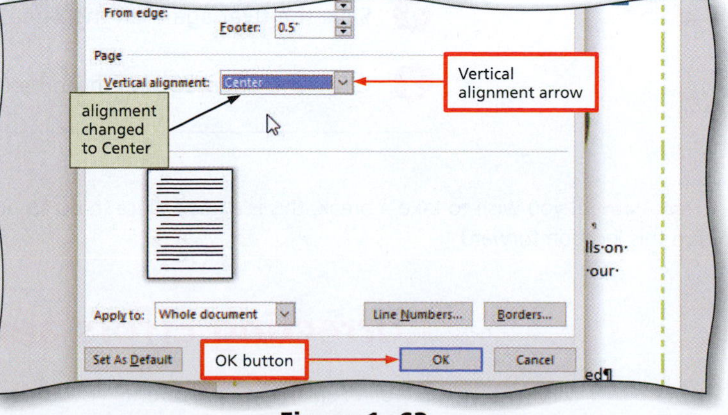

Figure 1–63

Q&A What if I wanted to change the alignment back?

You would select the Top vertical alignment from the Vertical alignment list in the Layout sheet (Page Setup dialog box).

To Change Document Properties

Word helps you organize and identify your files by using **document properties**, which, as discussed in the Office and Windows module at the beginning of this book, are the details about a file, such as the project author, title, and subject. For example, a class name or document topic can describe the file's purpose or content.

The more common document properties are standard and automatically updated properties. **Standard properties** are associated with all Microsoft Office files and include author, title, and subject. **Automatically updated properties** include file system properties, such as the date you create or change a file, and statistics, such as the file size.

BTW
Printing Document Properties
To print document properties, click File on the ribbon to open the Backstage view, click the Print tab in the Backstage view to display the Print gallery, click the first button in the Settings area to display a list of options specifying what you can print, click Document Info in the list to specify you want to print the document properties instead of the actual document, and then click the Print button in the Print gallery to print the document properties on the currently selected printer.

If you wanted to change document properties, you would follow these steps.

1. Click File on the ribbon to open the Backstage view and then, if necessary, click the Info tab in the Backstage view to display the Info gallery.
2. If the property you wish to change is displayed in the Properties list in the right pane of the Info gallery, try to click to the right of the property. If a text box appears to the right of the property, type the text for the property in the text box and then click the Back button in the upper-left corner of the Backstage view to return to the Word window. Skip the remaining steps.
3. If the property you wish to change is not displayed in the Properties list in the right pane of the Info gallery or you cannot change it in the Info gallery, click the Properties button in the right pane to display the Properties menu and then click Advanced Properties on the Properties menu to display the Properties dialog box. If necessary, click the Summary tab (Properties dialog box) to display the Summary sheet, fill in the appropriate text boxes, and then click the OK button.

Q&A
Why are some of the document properties in the dialog box already filled in?
The person who installed Office 2016 on your computer or network may have set or customized the properties.

To Save the Document and Exit Word

Although you still need to make some edits to this document, you want to exit Word and resume working on the project at a later time. Thus, the following steps save the document and exit Word. For a detailed example of the procedure summarized below, refer to the Office and Windows module at the beginning of this book.

1. Save the flyer again on the same storage location with the same file name.
2. Close the open document and exit Word.

Break Point: If you wish to take a break, this is a good place to do so. To resume at a later time, continue following the steps from this location forward.

Correcting Errors and Revising a Document

After creating a document, you may need to change it. For example, the document may contain an error, or new circumstances may require you to add text to the document.

Types of Changes Made to Documents

The types of changes made to documents normally fall into one of the three following categories: additions, deletions, or modifications.

Additions Additional words, sentences, or paragraphs may be required in a document. Additions occur when you omit text from a document and want to insert it later. For example, you may want to add your email address to the flyer.

Deletions Sometimes, text in a document is incorrect or no longer is needed. For example, you may discover that the lessons no longer include reef shoes. In this case, you would delete the words, reef shoes, from the flyer.

Modifications If an error is made in a document or changes take place that affect the document, you might have to revise a word(s) in the text. For example, the phone number may change.

To Run Word, Open a Document, and Specify Settings

Once you have created and saved a document, you may need to retrieve it from storage. For example, you might want to revise the document or distribute it. Earlier in this module you saved the flyer using the file name, Surf Flyer. The following steps run Word, open this document, and specify settings. For a detailed example of the procedures summarized below for running Word or opening a document, refer to the Office and Windows module.

1. Run Word.
2. Open the document named Surf Flyer from the Recent list or use the Open dialog box to navigate to the location of the file and then open it in the Word window.
3. If the Word window is not maximized, click the Maximize button on its title bar to maximize the window.
4. Click View on the ribbon to display the View tab and then click the 100% button (View tab | Zoom group) to display the page at 100% in the document window.

BTW

Word Help

At any time while using Word, you can find answers to questions and display information about various topics through Word Help. Used properly, this form of assistance can increase your productivity and reduce your frustrations by minimizing the time you spend learning how to use Word. For instructions about Word Help and exercises that will help you gain confidence in using it, read the Office and Windows module at the beginning of this book.

To Insert Text in an Existing Document

1 ENTER TEXT | 2 FORMAT TEXT | 3 INSERT PICTURE
4 FORMAT PICTURE | 5 ENHANCE PAGE | **6 CORRECT & REVISE**

Word inserts text to the left of the insertion point. The text to the right of the insertion point moves to the right and downward to fit the new text. The following steps insert the word, today, to the left of the word, or, in the flyer. ***Why?*** *These steps illustrate the process of inserting text.*

1

- Scroll through the document and then click to the left of the location of text to be inserted (in this case, the o in or) to position the insertion point where text should be inserted (Figure 1–64).

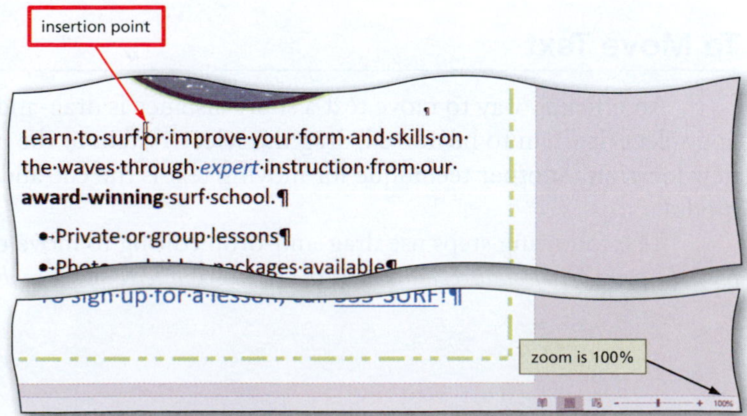
insertion point
Learn·to·surf·or·improve·your·form·and·skills·on·
the·waves·through·expert·instruction·from·our·
award-winning·surf·school.¶
•·Private·or·group·lessons¶
zoom is 100%

Figure 1–64

- Type today and then press the SPACEBAR to insert the word to the left of the insertion point (Figure 1–65).

Q&A Why did the text move to the right as I typed?
In Word, the default typing mode is **insert mode**, which means as you type a character, Word moves all the characters to the right of the typed character one position to the right.

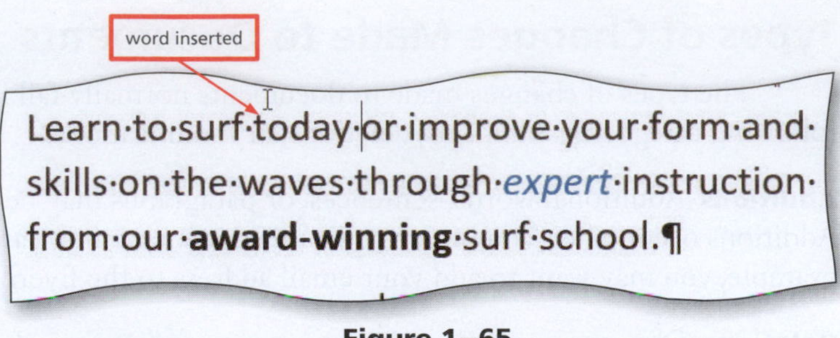
word inserted
Learn·to·surf·today·or·improve·your·form·and·
skills·on·the·waves·through·expert·instruction·
from·our·award-winning·surf·school.¶

Figure 1–65

To Delete Text

1 ENTER TEXT | 2 FORMAT TEXT | 3 INSERT PICTURE
4 FORMAT PICTURE | 5 ENHANCE PAGE | 6 CORRECT & REVISE

It is not unusual to type incorrect characters or words in a document. As discussed earlier in this module, you can click the Undo button on the Quick Access Toolbar to undo a command or action immediately — this includes typing. Word also provides other methods of correcting typing errors.

To delete an incorrect character in a document, simply click next to the incorrect character and then press the BACKSPACE key to erase to the left of the insertion point, or press the DELETE key to erase to the right of the insertion point.

To delete a word or phrase, you first must select the word or phrase. The following steps select the word, today, which was just added in the previous steps, and then delete the selection. ***Why?*** *These steps illustrate the process of selecting a word and then deleting selected text.*

- Double-click the word to be selected (in this case, today) to select the word (Figure 1–66).

2

- Press the DELETE key to delete the selected text.

Q&A What if I am using a touch screen?
Tap the selected text to display the mini toolbar and then tap the Cut button on the mini toolbar to delete the selected text.

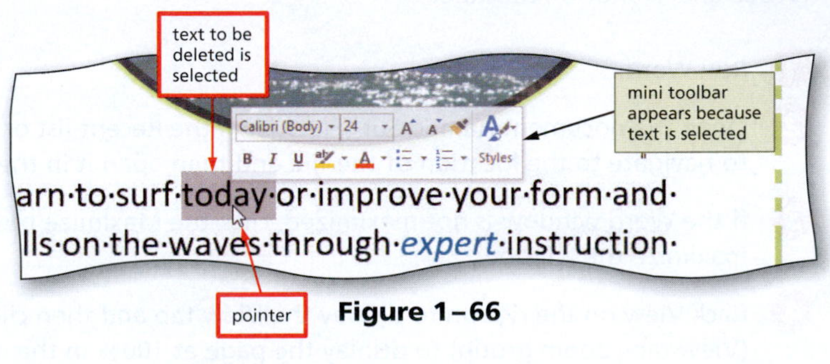
text to be deleted is selected
mini toolbar appears because text is selected
Calibri (Body)
24
Styles
arn·to·surf·today·or·improve·your·form·and·
lls·on·the·waves·through·expert·instruction·
pointer

Figure 1–66

Other Ways

1. Right-click selected item, click Cut on shortcut menu	2. Select item, press BACKSPACE to delete to left of insertion point or press DELETE to delete to right of insertion point	3. Select item, press CTRL+X

To Move Text

1 ENTER TEXT | 2 FORMAT TEXT | 3 INSERT PICTURE
4 FORMAT PICTURE | 5 ENHANCE PAGE | 6 CORRECT & REVISE

An efficient way to move text a short distance is drag-and-drop editing. With **drag-and-drop editing**, you select the item to be moved, drag the selected item to the new location, and then drop, or insert, it in the new location. Another technique for moving text is the cut-and-paste technique, which is discussed in the next module.

The following steps use drag-and-drop editing to move text. ***Why?*** *While proofreading the flyer, you realize that the body copy would read better if the last two bulleted paragraphs were reversed.*

- Position the pointer in the paragraph to be moved (in this case, the last bulleted item) and then triple-click to select the paragraph.
- With the pointer in the selected text, press and hold down the mouse button, which displays a small dotted box with the pointer (Figure 1–67).

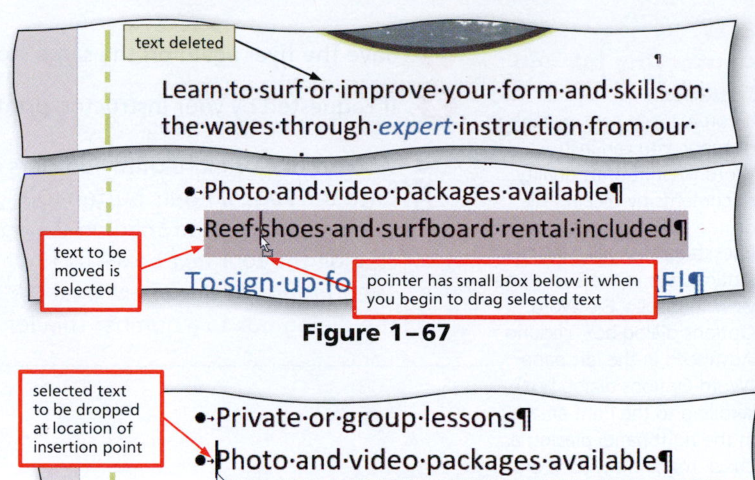

text deleted
Learn·to·surf·or·improve·your·form·and·skills·on·
the·waves·through·expert·instruction·from·our·
•·Photo·and·video·packages·available¶
•·Reef·shoes·and·surfboard·rental·included¶
text to be moved is selected
To·sign·up·fo
pointer has small box below it when you begin to drag selected text
selected text to be dropped at location of insertion point
•·Private·or·group·lessons¶
•·Photo·and·video·packages·available¶
•·Reef·shoes·and·surfboard·rental·included¶

Figure 1–67

- Drag the insertion point to the location where the selected text is to be moved, as shown in Figure 1–68.

Figure 1–68

- Release the mouse button to move the selected text to the location of the dotted insertion point (Figure 1–69).

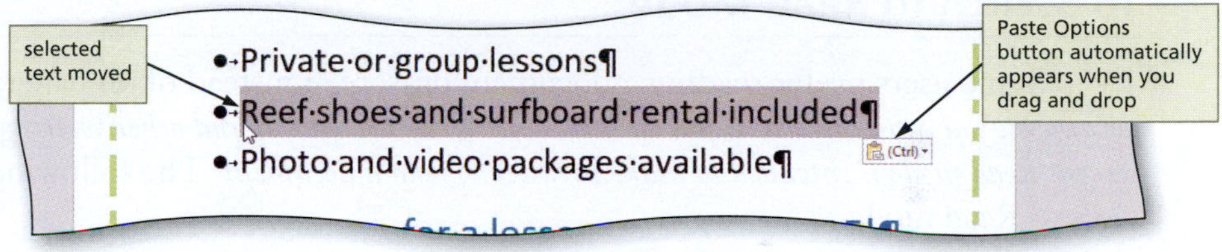

selected text moved
•·Private·or·group·lessons¶
•·Reef·shoes·and·surfboard·rental·included¶
•·Photo·and·video·packages·available¶
(Ctrl)
Paste Options button automatically appears when you drag and drop

Figure 1–69

Q&A What if I accidentally drag text to the wrong location?
Click the Undo button on the Quick Access Toolbar and try again.

Can I use drag-and-drop editing to move any selected item?
Yes, you can select words, sentences, phrases, and graphics and then use drag-and-drop editing to move them.

What is the purpose of the Paste Options button?
If you click the Paste Options button, a menu appears that allows you to change the format of the item that was moved. The next module discusses the Paste Options menu.

- Click anywhere in the document window to remove the selection from the bulleted item.

Q&A What if I am using a touch screen?
If you have a stylus, you can follow Steps 1 through 3 using the stylus. If you are using your finger, you will need to use the cut-and-paste technique: tap to position the insertion point in the text to be moved and then drag the selection handles as necessary to select the text that you want to move; tap the selection to display the mini toolbar and then tap the Cut button on the mini toolbar to remove the text; tap to position the insertion point at the location where you want to move the text; display the Home tab and then tap the Paste button on the Home tab to place the text at the location of the insertion point. The next module discusses this procedure in more depth.

Other Ways

1. Click Cut button (Home tab | Clipboard group), click where text or object is to be pasted, click Paste button (Home tab | Clipboard group)
2. Right-click selected text, click Cut on mini toolbar or shortcut menu, right-click where text or object is to be pasted, click Paste on mini toolbar or 'Keep Source Formatting' on shortcut menu
3. Press CTRL+X, position insertion point where text or object is to be pasted, press CTRL+V

To Save and Print the Document

It is a good practice to save a document before printing it, in the event you experience difficulties printing. The following steps save and print the document. For a detailed example of the procedure summarized next for saving and printing a document, refer to the Office and Windows module at the beginning of this book.

BTW
Conserving Ink and Toner
If you want to conserve ink or toner, you can instruct Word to print draft quality documents by clicking File on the ribbon to open the Backstage view, clicking the Options tab in the Backstage view to display the Word Options dialog box, clicking Advanced in the left pane (Word Options dialog box), scrolling to the Print area in the right pane, placing a check mark in the 'Use draft quality' check box, and then clicking the OK button. Then, use the Backstage view to print the document as usual.

1. Save the flyer again on the same storage location with the same file name.
2. If requested by your instructor, print the flyer.

Q&A What if one or more of my borders do not print?
Click the Page Borders button (Design tab | Page Background group), click the Options button (Borders and Shading dialog box), click the Measure from arrow and click Text, change the four text boxes to 15 pt, and then click the OK button in each dialog box. Try printing the document again. If the borders still do not print, adjust the boxes in the dialog box to a number smaller than 15 point.

To Switch to Read Mode

1 ENTER TEXT | 2 FORMAT TEXT | 3 INSERT PICTURE
4 FORMAT PICTURE | 5 ENHANCE PAGE | 6 CORRECT & REVISE

Some users prefer reading a document on-screen instead of on paper. ***Why?*** *If you are not composing a document, you can switch to* ***Read mode****, which hides the ribbon and other writing tools so that more content fits on the screen. Read mode is intended to make it easier to read a document.* The following step switches from Print Layout view to Read mode.

- Click the Read Mode button on the status bar to switch to Read mode (Figure 1–70).

- Click the arrows to advance forward and then move backward through the document.

Q&A Besides reading, what can I do in Read mode?
You can zoom, copy text, highlight text, search, add comments, and more.

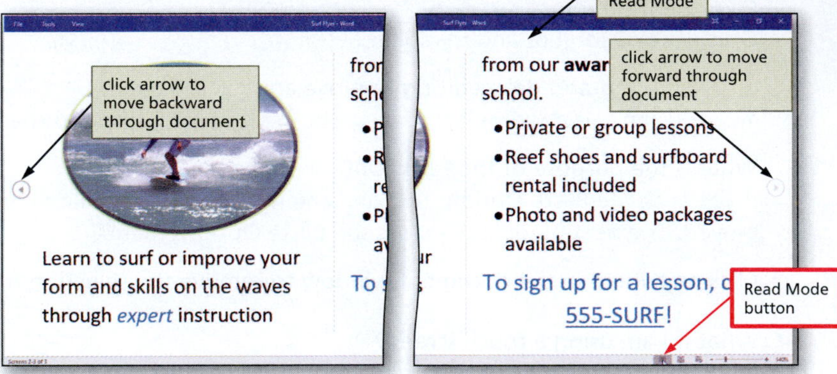
document appears in Read Mode
click arrow to move backward through document
click arrow to move forward through document
Learn to surf or improve your form and skills on the waves through expert instruction
from our awar
school.
•Private or group lessons
•Reef shoes and surfboard rental included
•Photo and video packages available
To sign up for a lesson, c
555-SURF!
Read Mode button
Figure 1–70

Other Ways
1. Click Read Mode button (View tab | Views group)

BTW
Distributing a Document
Instead of printing and distributing a hard copy of a document, you can distribute the document electronically. Options include sending the document via email; posting it on cloud storage (such as OneDrive) and sharing the file with others; posting it on social media, a blog, or other website; and sharing a link associated with an online location of the document. You also can create and share a PDF or XPS image of the document, so that users can view the file in Acrobat Reader or XPS Viewer instead of in Word.

To Switch to Print Layout View

1 ENTER TEXT | 2 FORMAT TEXT | 3 INSERT PICTURE
4 FORMAT PICTURE | 5 ENHANCE PAGE | 6 CORRECT & REVISE

The next steps switch back to Print Layout view. ***Why?*** *If you want to show the document on a mock sheet of paper in the document window, along with the ribbon and other writing tools, you should switch to Print Layout view.* The following step switches to Print Layout view.

1

- Click the Print Layout button on the status bar to switch to Print Layout view (Figure 1–71).
- Because the project now is complete, you can exit Word.

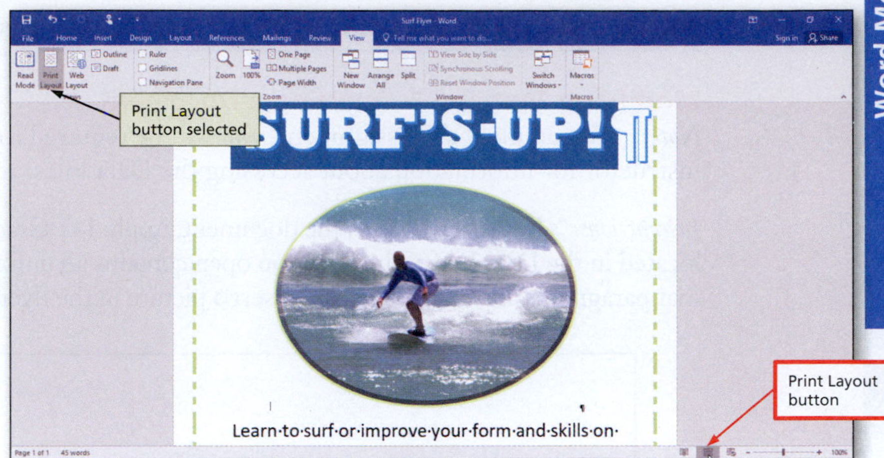

Figure 1–71

Other Ways

1. Click Print Layout button (View tab | Views group)
2. Click View on the ribbon, click Edit Document

Summary

In this module, you have learned how to enter text in a document, correct spelling errors as you type, format paragraphs and characters, insert and format a picture, add a page border, adjust paragraph and page spacing, and correct errors and revise a document.

CONSIDER THIS: PLAN AHEAD

What decisions will you need to make when creating your next flyer?

Use these guidelines as you complete the assignments in this module and create your own flyers outside of this class.

1. Choose the text for the headline, body copy, and signature line — using as few words as possible to make a point.
2. Format various elements of the text.
   a) Select appropriate font sizes for text in the headline, body copy, and signature line.
   b) Select appropriate fonts for text in the headline, body copy, and signature line.
   c) Adjust paragraph alignment, as appropriate.
   d) Highlight key paragraphs with bullets.
   e) Emphasize important words.
   f) Use color to convey meaning and add appeal.
3. Find an eye-catching graphic(s) that conveys the overall message and meaning of the flyer.
4. Establish where to position and how to format the graphical image(s) so that the image grabs the attention of passersby and draws them into reading the flyer.
5. Determine whether the flyer needs enhancements, such as a graphical, color-coordinated border, or spacing adjustments to improve readability or overall appearance.
6. Correct errors and revise the document as necessary.
   a) Post the flyer on a wall and make sure all text and images are legible from a distance.
   b) Ask someone else to read the flyer and give you suggestions for improvements.
7. Determine the best method for distributing the document, such as printing, sending via email, or posting on the web or social media.

Apply Your Knowledge

Reinforce the skills and apply the concepts you learned in this module.

Modifying Text and Formatting a Document

Note: To complete this assignment, you will be required to use the Data Files. Please contact your instructor for information about accessing the Data Files.

Instructions: Run Word. Open the document, Apply 1–1 Graduation Flyer Unformatted, which is located in the Data Files. The flyer you open contains an unformatted flyer. You are to modify text, format paragraphs and characters, and insert a picture in the flyer to create the flyer shown in Figure 1–72.

Figure 1–72

Perform the following tasks:

1. Correct each spelling (red wavy underline) and grammar (green and blue wavy underlines) error by right-clicking the flagged text and then clicking the appropriate correction on the shortcut menu.

2. Delete the word, degree, in the sentence below the headline.
3. Insert the word, need, between the words, or directions (so that it reads: Questions or need directions?), in the second to last line of the flyer.
4. Change the word, on, to the word, by, in the last line so that the text reads: Please RSVP by May 18.
5. If requested by your instructor, change the phone number in the flyer to your phone number.
6. Center the headline and the last two paragraphs of the flyer.
7. Select the third, fourth, and fifth paragraphs of text in the flyer and add bullets to the selected paragraphs.
8. Change the theme colors to the Blue II color scheme.
9. Change the font and font size of the headline to 48-point Arial Rounded MT Bold, or a similar font. Change the case of the word, Celebrate, in the headline to uppercase letters. Apply the text effect called Fill - Dark Green, Accent 1, Outline - Background 1, Hard Shadow - Accent 1 to the entire headline. Change the font color of the headline text to Dark Green, Accent 5, Darker 25%.
10. Change the font size of the sentence below the headline, the bulleted list, and the last line of flyer to 26 point.
11. Use the mini toolbar to change the font size of the sentence below the bulleted list to 18 point.
12. Switch the last two bulleted paragraphs. That is, select the '125 Park Court in Condor' bullet and move it so that it is the second bulleted paragraph.
13. Select the words, open house, in the paragraph below the headline and italicize these words. Undo this change and then redo the change.
14. Select the text, Saturday, May 27, in the first bulleted paragraph and bold this text. Change the font color of this same text to Dark Red.
15. Underline the word, and, in the third bulleted paragraph.
16. Bold the text, Please RSVP by May 18., in the last line of the flyer. Shade this same text Dark Green, Accent 5, Darker 50%. If the font color does not automatically change to a lighter color, change its color to White, Background 1.
17. Change the zoom so that the entire page is visible in the document window.
18. Insert the picture of the graduate centered on the blank line below the headline. The picture is called Graduation and is available on the Data Files. Resize the picture so that it is approximately 2.9" × 2.89". Apply the Simple Frame, Black picture style to the inserted picture.
19. Change the spacing before the first bulleted paragraph to 12 points and the spacing after the last bulleted paragraph to 24 points.
20. The entire flyer should fit on a single page. If it flows to two pages, resize the picture or decrease spacing before and after paragraphs until the entire flyer text fits on a single page.
21. Change the zoom to text width, then page width, then 100% and notice the differences.
22. If requested by your instructor, enter the text, Graduation Open House, as the keywords in the document properties. Change the other document properties, as specified by your instructor.
23. Click File on the ribbon and then click Save As. Save the document using the file name, Apply 1-1 Graduation Flyer Formatted.
24. Print the document. Switch to Read Mode and browse pages through the document. Switch to Print Layout view.
25. Submit the revised document, shown in Figure 1–72, in the format specified by your instructor.
26. Exit Word.
27. If this flyer were announcing a victory parade instead of a graduation, which color scheme would you apply and why?

Extend Your Knowledge

Extend the skills you learned in this module and experiment with new skills. You may need to use Help to complete the assignment.

Modifying Text and Picture Formats and Adding Page Borders

Note: To complete this assignment, you will be required to use the Data Files. Please contact your instructor for information about accessing the Data Files.

Figure 1–73

Instructions: Run Word. Open the document, Extend 1–1 Painting Lessons Flyer Draft, from the Data Files. You will enhance the look of the flyer shown in Figure 1–73. *Hint:* Remember, if you make a mistake while formatting the picture, you can reset it by using the Reset Picture button or Reset Picture arrow (Picture Tools Format tab | Adjust group).

Perform the following tasks:

1. Use Help to learn about the following: remove bullets, grow font, shrink font, art page borders, decorative underline(s), picture bullets, picture border shading, picture border color, shadow picture effects, and color saturation and tone.
2. Remove the bullet from the last paragraph of the flyer.
3. Select the text, Painting Lessons, and use the 'Increase Font Size' button (Home tab | Font group) to increase its font size.
4. Add an art page border to the flyer. If the border is not in color, add color to it if the border supports color.
5. Change the solid underline below the word, all, to a decorative underline. Change the color of the underline.
6. Change the style of the bullets to picture bullet(s). Adjust the hanging indent, if necessary, to align the text in the bulleted list.
7. Change the color of the picture border. Add a shadow picture effect to the picture.
8. Change the color saturation and color tone of the picture.
9. If requested by your instructor, change the name of the art studio (Bakersfield) to your last name.

10. Save the revised document with the file name, Extend 1–1 Painting Lessons Flyer Final, and then submit it in the format specified by your instructor.
11. In this assignment, you changed the bullets to picture bullets. Which bullet character did you select and why?

Expand Your World

Create a solution that uses cloud or web technologies by learning and investigating on your own from general guidance.

Using Word Online to Create a Flyer with a Picture

Note: To complete this assignment, you will be required to use the Data Files. Please contact your instructor for information about accessing the Data Files.

Instructions: You will use Word Online to prepare a flyer. The text for the unformatted flyer is shown in Figure 1–74. You will enter the text in Word Online and then use its tools to enhance the look of the flyer.

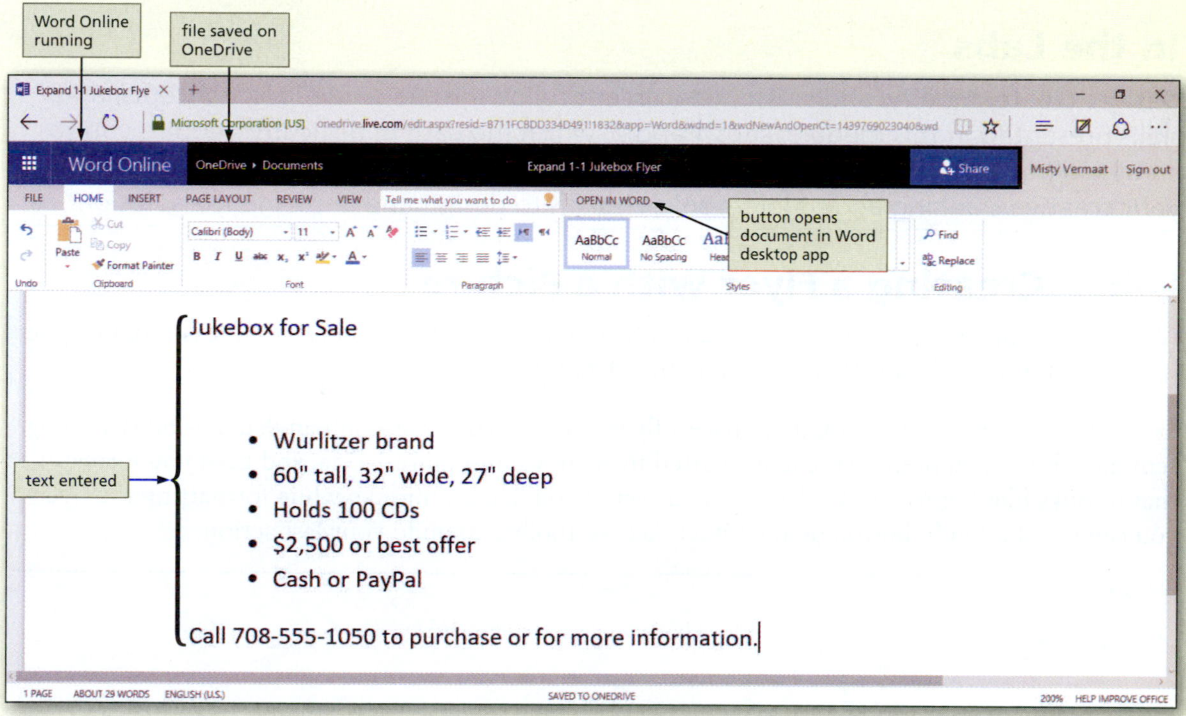

Figure 1–74

Perform the following tasks:

1. Run a browser. Search for the text, Word Online, using a search engine. Visit several websites to learn about Word Online. Navigate to the Office Online website. You will need to sign in to your OneDrive account.
2. Create a new blank Word document using Word Online. Name the document Expand 1–1 Jukebox Flyer.
3. Notice the differences between Word Online and the Word desktop app you used to create the project in this module.
4. Enter the text in the flyer, shown in Figure 1–74, checking spelling as you type.
5. Insert the picture called Jukebox, which is located in the Data Files.

Continued >

Expand Your World *continued*

6. Use the features available in Word Online, along with the concepts and techniques presented in this module, to format this flyer. Be sure to change the font and font size of text, center a paragraph(s), italicize text, color text, underline text, and apply a picture style. Resize the picture. Adjust spacing above and below paragraphs as necessary. The flyer should fit on a single page.
7. If requested by your instructor, replace the phone number in the flyer with your phone number.
8. Save the document again. Click the button to open the document in the Word desktop app. If necessary, sign in to your Microsoft account when prompted. Notice how the document appears in the Word desktop app.
9. Using either Word Online or the Word desktop app, submit the document in the format requested by your instructor. Exit Word Online. If necessary, sign out of your OneDrive account and your Microsoft account in Word.
10. What is Word Online? Which features that are covered in this module are not available in Word Online? Do you prefer using Word Online or the Word desktop app? Why?

In the Labs

Design, create, modify, and/or use a document following the guidelines, concepts, and skills presented in this module. Labs 1 and 2, which increase in difficulty, require you to create solutions based on what you learned in the module; Lab 3 requires you to apply your creative thinking and problem-solving skills to design and implement a solution.

Lab 1: Creating a Flyer with a Picture

Note: To complete this assignment, you will be required to use the Data Files. Please contact your instructor for information about accessing the Data Files.

Problem: Your boss asked you to prepare a flyer that advertises the company's commodity trading seminars. First, you prepare the unformatted flyer shown in Figure 1–75a, and then you format it so that it looks like Figure 1–75b. *Hint:* Remember, if you make a mistake while formatting the flyer, you can use the Undo button on the Quick Access Toolbar to undo your last action.

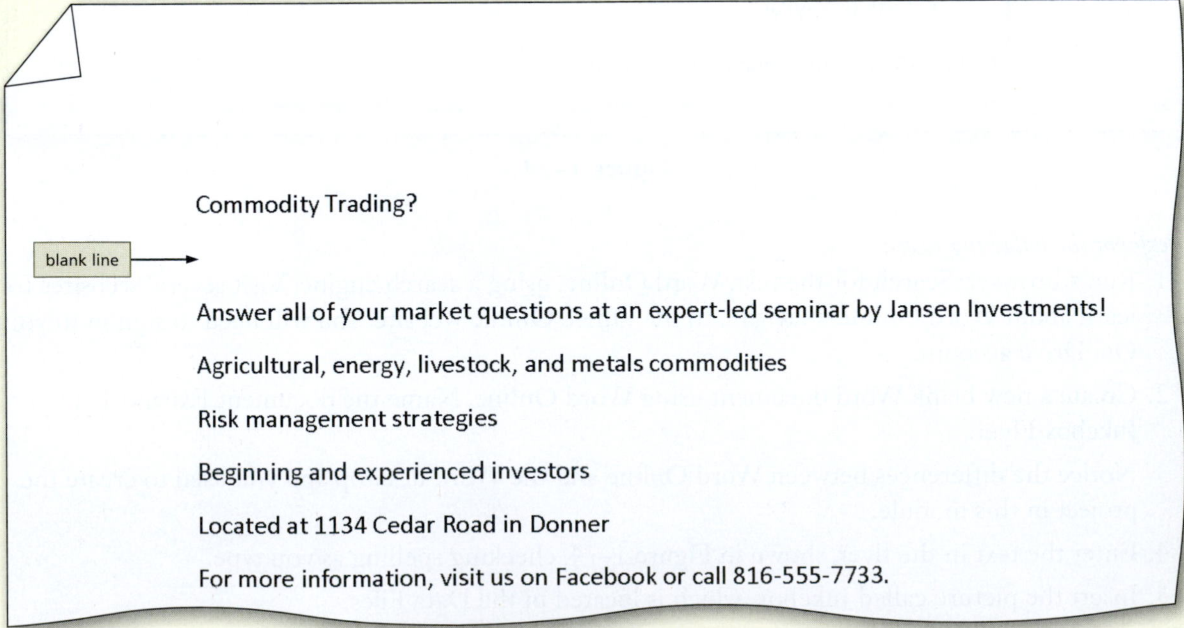

Commodity Trading?
blank line
Answer all of your market questions at an expert-led seminar by Jansen Investments!
Agricultural, energy, livestock, and metals commodities
Risk management strategies
Beginning and experienced investors
Located at 1134 Cedar Road in Donner
For more information, visit us on Facebook or call 816-555-7733.

Figure 1–75a Unformatted Text

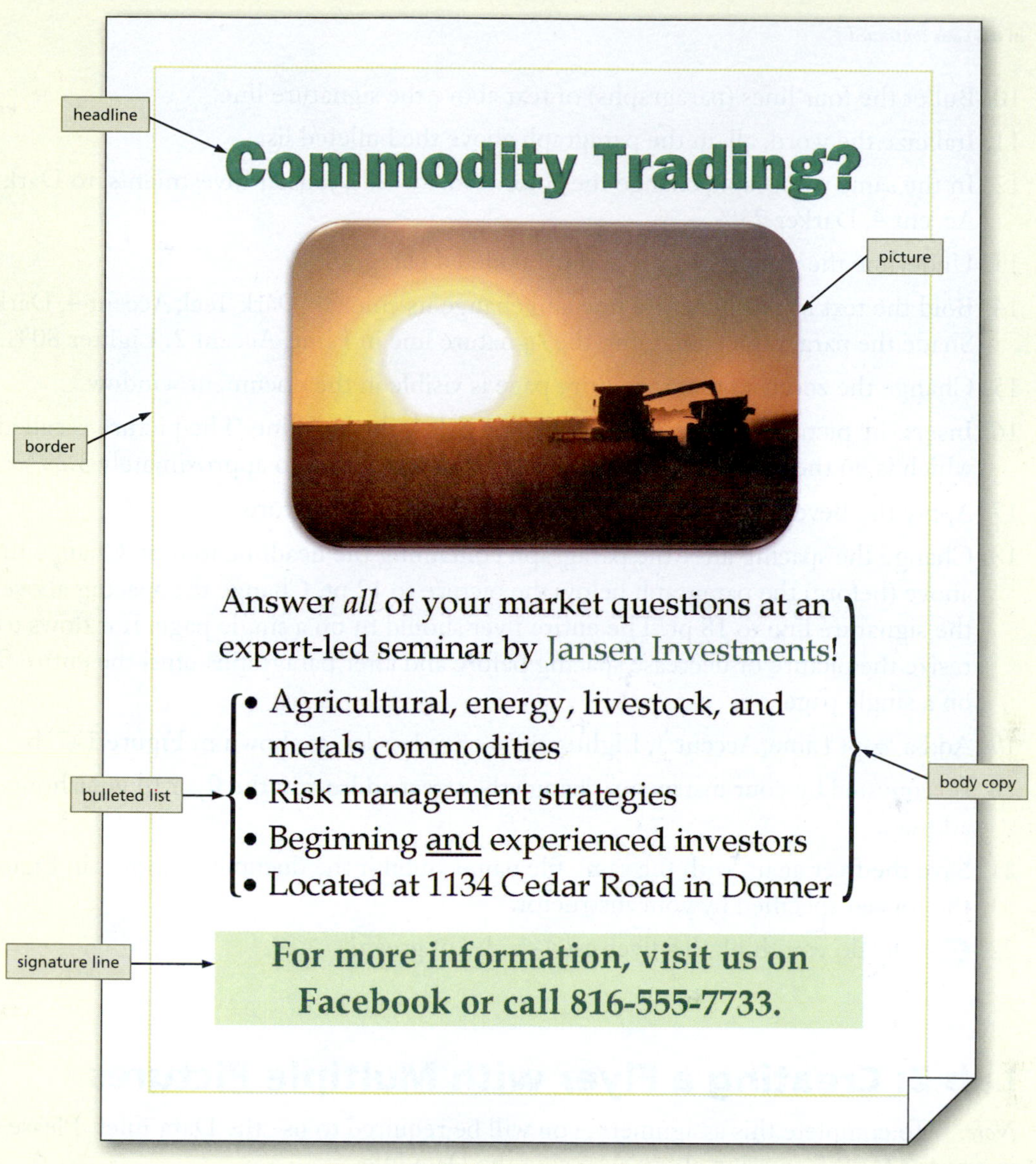

Figure 1–75b Formatted Document

Perform the following tasks:

1. Run Word. Display formatting marks on the screen.
2. Type the flyer text, unformatted, as shown in Figure 1–75a, inserting a blank line between the headline and the body copy. If Word flags any misspelled words as you type, check their spelling and correct them.
3. Save the document using the file name, Lab 1–1 Commodity Trading Flyer.
4. Center the headline and the signature line.
5. Change the theme colors to Green.
6. Change the font size of the headline to 48 point and the font to Franklin Gothic Heavy or a similar font. Apply the text effect called Fill - Dark Teal, Accent 4, Soft Bevel.
7. Change the font size of body copy between the headline and the signature line to 24 point.
8. Change the font size of the signature line to 26 point.
9. Change the font of the body copy and signature line to Book Antiqua.

Continued >

In the Labs *continued*

10. Bullet the four lines (paragraphs) of text above the signature line.
11. Italicize the word, all, in the paragraph above the bulleted list.
12. In the same paragraph, change the color of the words, Jansen Investments, to Dark Teal, Accent 4, Darker 25%.
13. Underline the word, and, in the third bulleted paragraph.
14. Bold the text in the signature line and change its color to Dark Teal, Accent 4, Darker 25%. Shade the paragraph containing the signature line in Lime, Accent 2, Lighter 80%.
15. Change the zoom so that the entire page is visible in the document window.
16. Insert the picture centered on a blank line below the headline. The picture is called Harvest, which is on the Data Files. Reduce the size of the picture to approximately 3.29" × 5.11".
17. Apply the Bevel Rectangle picture style to the inserted picture.
18. Change the spacing after the paragraph containing the headline to 0 pt. Change the spacing above (before) the paragraph below the picture to 12 pt. Change the spacing above (before) the signature line to 18 pt. The entire flyer should fit on a single page. If it flows to two pages, resize the picture or decrease spacing before and after paragraphs until the entire flyer text fits on a single page.
19. Add a ½-pt Lime, Accent 3, Lighter 40% page border, as shown in Figure 1–75b.
20. If requested by your instructor, change the street address in the flyer to your home street address.
21. Save the flyer again with the same file name. Submit the document, shown in Figure 1–75b, in the format specified by your instructor.
22. Why do you think this flyer used shades of green?

Lab 2: Creating a Flyer with Multiple Pictures

Note: To complete this assignment, you will be required to use the Data Files. Please contact your instructor for information about accessing the Data Files.

Problem: Your boss at Gingham Travel has asked you to prepare a flyer that promotes its business. You prepare the flyer shown in Figure 1–76. *Hint*: Remember, if you make a mistake while formatting the flyer, you can use the Undo button on the Quick Access Toolbar to undo your last action.

Perform the following tasks:

1. Run Word. Type the flyer text, unformatted. If Word flags any misspelled words as you type, check their spelling and correct them.
2. Save the document using the file name, Lab 1–2 Spring Break Flyer.
3. Change the theme colors to the Aspect color scheme.
4. Add bullets to the four paragraphs shown in the figure. Center all paragraphs, except the paragraphs containing the bulleted list.
5. Change the font size of both lines in the headline to 48 point. Change the font of the first line in the headline to Ravie, or a similar font, and the second line in the headline to Arial Rounded MT Bold, or a similar font. Apply this text effect to the first line in the headline: Fill - Dark Purple, Accent 1, Outline - Background 1, Hard Shadow - Accent 1. Shade the second line of the headline to the Dark Green, Accent 4 color, and change the font color to White, Background 1.

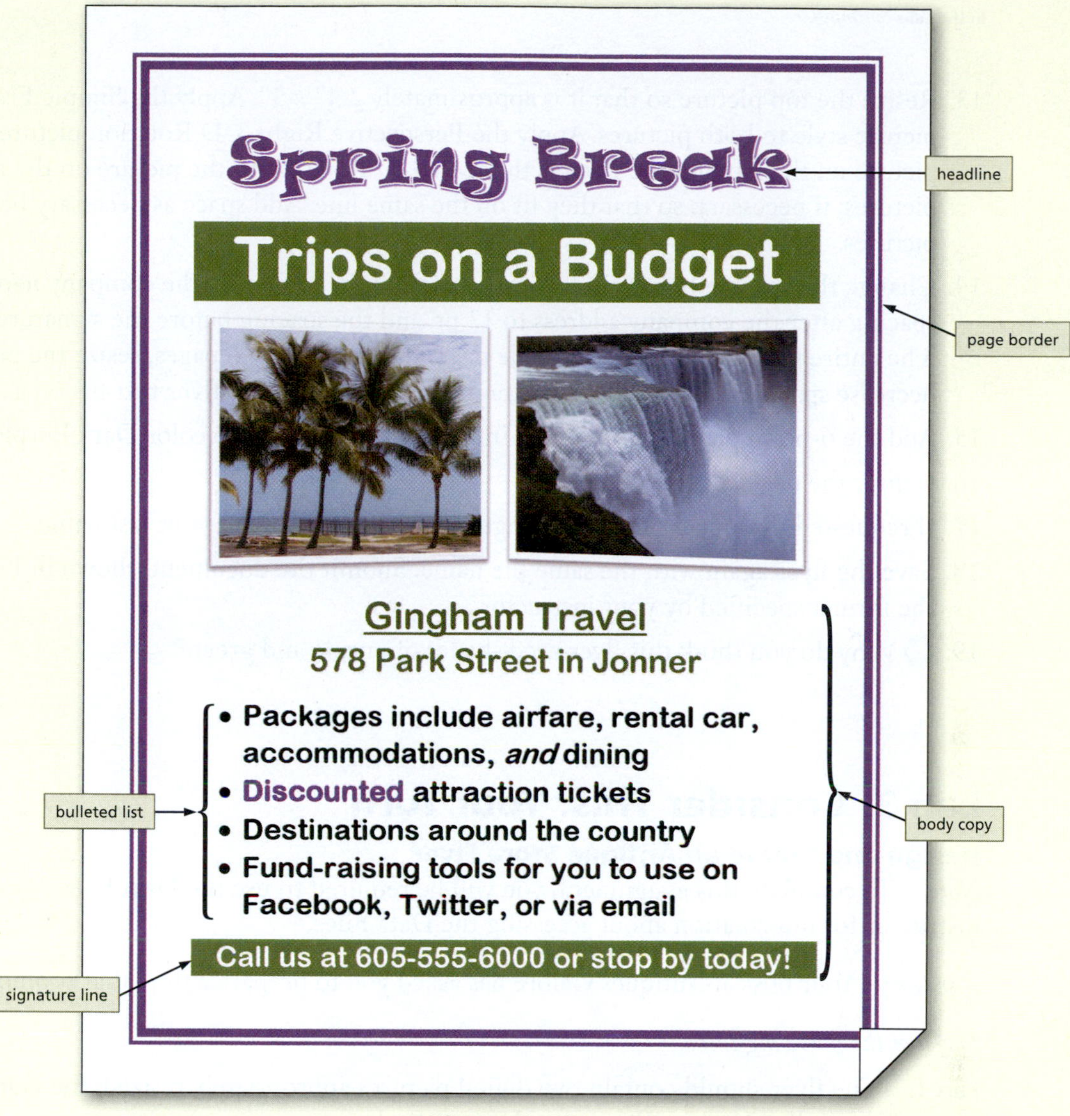

Figure 1–76

6. Change the font of all text below the headline to Arial Rounded MT Bold. Change the font size of the company name to 28 point, the company address to 24 point, and the bulleted list and signature line to 22 point.
7. Change the color of the company name and address to Dark Green, Accent 4, Darker 25%. Underline the company name.
8. Italicize the word, and, in the first bulleted paragraph.
9. Bold the word, Discounted, in the second bulleted paragraph. Change the color of this same word to Dark Purple, Accent 5.
10. Shade the signature line to the Dark Green, Accent 4 color, and change the font color to White, Background 1.
11. Change the zoom so that the entire page is visible in the document window.
12. Insert two pictures on the same blank line below the headline. The pictures are called Spring Break - Florida and Spring Break - New York, which are both in the Data Files.

Continued >

In the Labs *continued*

13. Resize the top picture so that it is approximately 2.4" × 3". Apply the Simple Frame, White picture style to both pictures. Apply the Perspective Right 3-D Rotation picture effect to the picture on the left and the Perspective Left 3-D Rotation to the picture on the right. Resize the pictures, if necessary, so that they fit on the same line. Add space as necessary between the two pictures.
14. Change the spacing before and after the paragraph containing the company name to 0 pt, the spacing after the company address to 12 pt, and the spacing before the signature line to 12 pt. The entire flyer should fit on a single page. If it flows to two pages, resize the pictures or decrease spacing before and after paragraphs until the entire flyer text fits on a single page.
15. Add the 6-point page border shown in Figure 1–76, using the color Dark Purple, Accent 5.
16. Center the page contents vertically.
17. If requested by your instructor, change the company name to your last name.
18. Save the flyer again with the same file name. Submit the document, shown in Figure 1–76, in the format specified by your instructor.
19. Why do you think this flyer used shades of purple and green?

Lab 3: Consider This: Your Turn

Design and Create an Antique Store Flyer

Note: To complete this assignment, you will be required to use the Data Files. Please contact your instructor for information about accessing the Data Files.

Problem: Your boss at Antiques Galore has asked you to prepare a flyer that promotes its business.

Perform the following tasks:

Part 1: The flyer should contain two digital pictures appropriately resized; the Data Files contains two pictures called Vintage Phone and Vintage Scale, or you can use your own digital pictures if they are appropriate for the topic of the flyer. The flyer should contain the headline, Antiques Galore, and this signature line: Questions? Call 312-555-2000 or find us on Facebook. The body copy consists of the following text, in any order: We sell all types of vintage items and also buy items individually or as an entire estate. Bring your items in for a free appraisal!; 1,200 square foot shop; Collectibles, costume jewelry, furniture, paintings, pottery, toys, and more!; Affordable items with new inventory daily; Located at 229 Center Street in Snow Hill; Open from 9:00 a.m. to 8:00 p.m. daily.

Use the concepts and techniques presented in this module to create and format this flyer. Be sure to check spelling and grammar. Submit your assignment and answers to the Part 2 critical thinking questions in the format specified by your instructor.

Part 2: You made several decisions while creating the flyer in this assignment: where to place text, how to format the text (i.e., font, font size, paragraph alignment, bulleted paragraphs, underlines, italics, bold, color, etc.), which graphics to use, where to position the graphics, how to format the graphics, and which page enhancements to add (i.e., borders and spacing). What was the rationale behind each of these decisions? When you proofread the document, what further revisions did you make and why? How would you recommend distributing this flyer?

2 Creating a Research Paper with References and Sources

Objectives

You will have mastered the material in this module when you can:

- Describe the MLA documentation style for research papers
- Modify a style
- Change line and paragraph spacing in a document
- Use a header to number pages of a document
- Apply formatting using keyboard shortcuts
- Modify paragraph indentation
- Insert and edit citations and their sources
- Add a footnote to a document
- Insert a manual page break
- Create a bibliographical list of sources
- Cut, copy, and paste text
- Find text and replace text
- Find a synonym
- Check spelling and grammar at once
- Look up information

Introduction

In both academic and business environments, you will be asked to write reports. Business reports range from proposals to cost justifications to five-year plans to research findings. Academic reports focus mostly on research findings.

A **research paper** is a document you can use to communicate the results of research findings. To write a research paper, you learn about a particular topic from a variety of sources (research), organize your ideas from the research results, and then present relevant facts and/or opinions that support the topic. Your final research paper combines properly credited outside information along with personal insights. Thus, no two research papers — even if they are about the same topic — will or should be the same.

Project — Research Paper

When preparing a research paper, you should follow a standard documentation style that defines the rules for creating the paper and crediting sources. A variety of documentation styles exists, depending on the nature of the research paper. Each style

BTW
APA Appendix
If you are required to create a research paper that uses APA style instead of MLA style, you can visit www.cengagebrain.com for the steps required to create this module's research paper. Alternately, you can utilize any number of APA guidelines available in print or online, or ask your instructor.

requires the same basic information; the differences in styles relate to requirements for presenting the information. For example, one documentation style uses the term, bibliography, for the list of sources, whereas another uses the term, references, and yet a third prefers the term, works cited. Two popular documentation styles for research papers are the **Modern Language Association of America** (**MLA**) and **American Psychological Association** (**APA**) styles. This module uses the MLA documentation style because it is used in a wide range of disciplines.

The project in this module follows research paper guidelines and uses Word to create the short research paper shown in Figure 2–1. This paper, which discusses using headphones and earbuds safely, follows the MLA documentation style. Each page contains a page number. The first two pages present the name and course information (student name, instructor name, course name, and paper due date), paper title, an introduction with a thesis statement, details that support the thesis, and a conclusion. This section of the paper also includes references to research sources and a footnote. The third page contains a detailed, alphabetical list of the sources referenced in the research paper. All pages include a header at the upper-right edge of the page.

In this module, you will learn how to create the research paper shown in Figure 2–1. The following roadmap identifies general activities you will perform as you progress through this module:

1. CHANGE the DOCUMENT SETTINGS.
2. CREATE the HEADER for each page of the research paper.
3. TYPE the RESEARCH PAPER text WITH CITATIONS.
4. CREATE an ALPHABETICAL WORKS CITED page.
5. PROOFREAD AND REVISE the RESEARCH PAPER.

MLA Documentation Style

The research paper in this project follows the guidelines presented by the MLA. To follow the MLA documentation style, use a 12-point Times New Roman or similar font. Double-space text on all pages of the paper using one-inch top, bottom, left, and right margins. Indent the first word of each paragraph one-half inch from the left margin. At the right margin of each page, place a page number one-half inch from the top margin. On each page, precede the page number with your last name.

The MLA documentation style does not require a title page. Instead, place your name and course information in a block at the left margin beginning one inch from the top of the page. Center the title one double-spaced line below your name and course information.

BTW
APA Documentation Style
In the APA style, a separate title page is required instead of placing name and course information on the paper's first page. Double-space all pages of the paper with one-inch top, bottom, left, and right margins. Indent the first word of each paragraph one-half inch from the left margin. In the upper-right margin of each page, including the title page, place a running head that consists of the page number preceded by a brief summary of the paper title.

In the text of the paper, place author references in parentheses with the page number(s) of the referenced information. The MLA documentation style uses in-text **parenthetical references** instead of noting each source at the bottom of the page or at the end of the paper. In the MLA documentation style, notes are used only for optional content or bibliographic notes.

If used, content notes elaborate on points discussed in the paper, and bibliographic notes direct the reader to evaluations of statements in a source or provide a means for identifying multiple sources. Use a superscript (raised number) both to signal that a note exists and to sequence the notes (shown in Figure 2–1). Position notes at the bottom of the page as footnotes or at the end of the paper as endnotes. Indent the first line of each note one-half inch from the left margin. Place one space following the superscripted number before beginning the note text. Double-space the note text (shown in Figure 2–1).

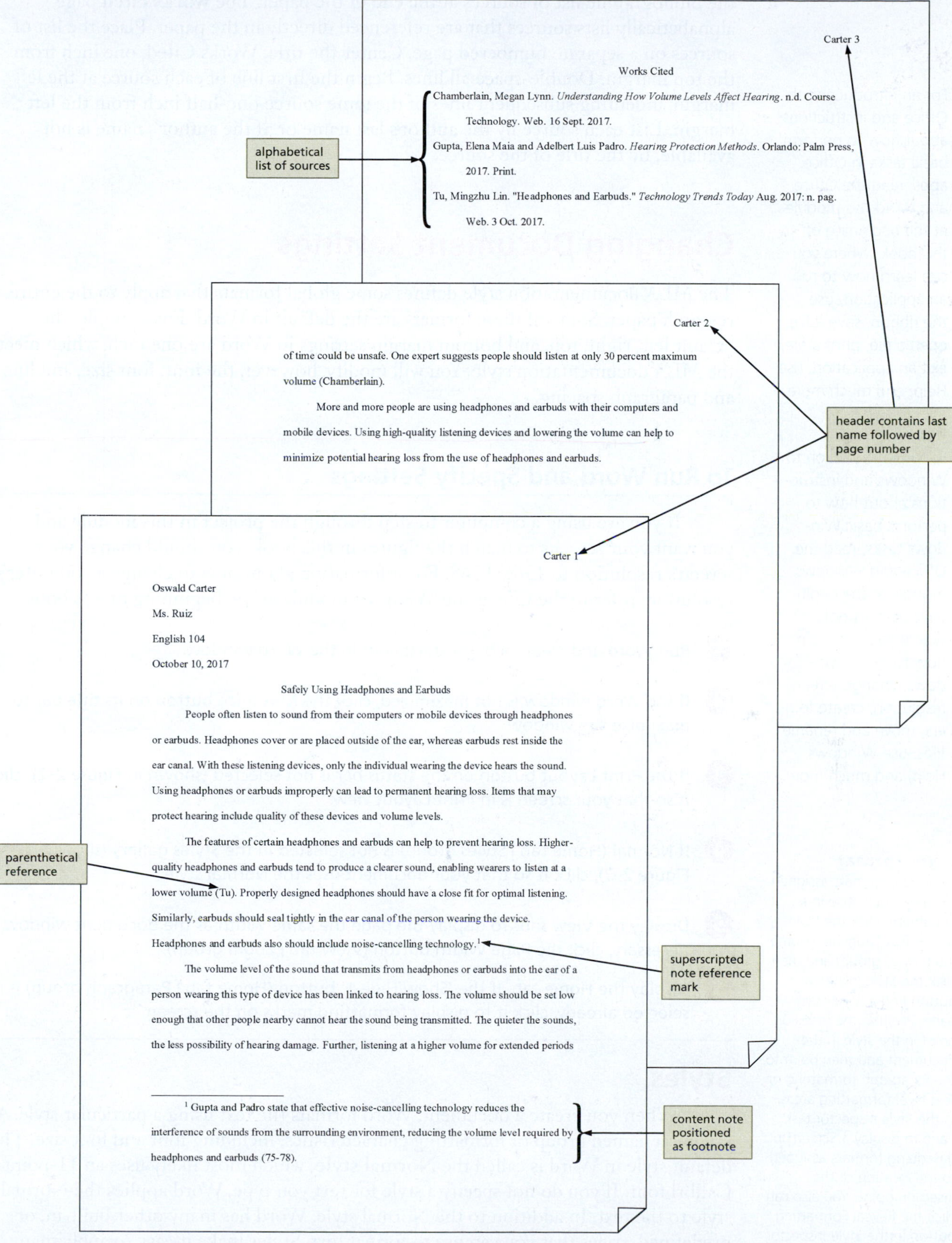
Carter 3
Works Cited
Chamberlain, Megan Lynn. *Understanding How Volume Levels Affect Hearing*. n.d. Course Technology. Web. 16 Sept. 2017.
Gupta, Elena Maia and Adelbert Luis Padro. *Hearing Protection Methods*. Orlando: Palm Press, 2017. Print.
Tu, Mingzhu Lin. "Headphones and Earbuds." *Technology Trends Today* Aug. 2017: n. pag. Web. 3 Oct. 2017.
alphabetical list of sources
Carter 2
of time could be unsafe. One expert suggests people should listen at only 30 percent maximum volume (Chamberlain).
More and more people are using headphones and earbuds with their computers and mobile devices. Using high-quality listening devices and lowering the volume can help to minimize potential hearing loss from the use of headphones and earbuds.
header contains last name followed by page number
Carter 1
Oswald Carter
Ms. Ruiz
English 104
October 10, 2017
Safely Using Headphones and Earbuds
People often listen to sound from their computers or mobile devices through headphones or earbuds. Headphones cover or are placed outside of the ear, whereas earbuds rest inside the ear canal. With these listening devices, only the individual wearing the device hears the sound. Using headphones or earbuds improperly can lead to permanent hearing loss. Items that may protect hearing include quality of these devices and volume levels.
The features of certain headphones and earbuds can help to prevent hearing loss. Higher-quality headphones and earbuds tend to produce a clearer sound, enabling wearers to listen at a lower volume (Tu). Properly designed headphones should have a close fit for optimal listening. Similarly, earbuds should seal tightly in the ear canal of the person wearing the device. Headphones and earbuds also should include noise-cancelling technology.[1]
The volume level of the sound that transmits from headphones or earbuds into the ear of a person wearing this type of device has been linked to hearing loss. The volume should be set low enough that other people nearby cannot hear the sound being transmitted. The quieter the sounds, the less possibility of hearing damage. Further, listening at a higher volume for extended periods
[1] Gupta and Padro state that effective noise-cancelling technology reduces the interference of sounds from the surrounding environment, reducing the volume level required by headphones and earbuds (75-78).
parenthetical reference
superscripted note reference mark
content note positioned as footnote

Figure 2–1

The MLA documentation style uses the term, works cited, to refer to the bibliographic list of sources at the end of the paper. The **works cited** page alphabetically lists sources that are referenced directly in the paper. Place the list of sources on a separate numbered page. Center the title, Works Cited, one inch from the top margin. Double-space all lines. Begin the first line of each source at the left margin, indenting subsequent lines of the same source one-half inch from the left margin. List each source by the author's last name or, if the author's name is not available, by the title of the source.

For an introduction to Office and instructions about how to perform basic tasks in Office apps, read the Office and Windows module at the beginning of this book, where you can learn how to run an application, use the ribbon, save a file, open a file, print a file, exit an application, use Help, and much more.

Changing Document Settings

The MLA documentation style defines some global formats that apply to the entire research paper. Some of these formats are the default in Word. For example, the default left, right, top, and bottom margin settings in Word are one inch, which meets the MLA documentation style. You will modify, however, the font, font size, and line and paragraph spacing.

For an introduction to Windows and instructions about how to perform basic Windows tasks, read the Office and Windows module at the beginning of this book, where you can learn how to resize windows, change screen resolution, create folders, move and rename files, use Windows Help, and much more.

To Run Word and Specify Settings

If you are using a computer to step through the project in this module and you want your screens to match the figures in this book, you should change your screen's resolution to 1366 × 768. For information about how to change a computer's resolution, refer to the Office and Windows module at the beginning of this book.

1. Run Word and create a blank document in the Word window.
2. If the Word window is not maximized, click the Maximize button on its title bar to maximize the window.
3. If the Print Layout button on the status bar is not selected (shown in Figure 2–2), click it so that your screen is in Print Layout view.
4. If Normal (Home tab | Styles group) is not selected in the Styles gallery (shown in Figure 2–2), click it so that your document uses the Normal style.
5. Display the View tab. To display the page the same width as the document window, if necessary, click the Page Width button (View tab | Zoom group).
6. Display the Home tab. If the 'Show/Hide ¶' button (Home tab | Paragraph group) is not selected already, click it to display formatting marks on the screen.

BTW

Style Formats

To see the formats assigned to a particular style in a document, click the Styles Dialog Box Launcher (Home tab | Styles group) and then click the Style Inspector button in the Styles task pane. Position the insertion point in the style in the document and then point to the Paragraph formatting or Text level formatting areas in the Style Inspector task pane to display a ScreenTip describing formats assigned to the location of the insertion point. You also can click the Reveal Formatting button in the Style Inspector task pane or press SHIFT+F1 to display the Reveal Formatting task pane.

Styles

When you create a document, Word formats the text using a particular style. A **style** is a named group of formatting characteristics, including font and font size. The default style in Word is called the **Normal style**, which most likely uses an 11-point Calibri font. If you do not specify a style for text you type, Word applies the Normal style to the text. In addition to the Normal style, Word has many other built-in, or predefined, styles that you can use to format text. Styles make it easy to apply many formats at once to text. You can modify existing styles and create your own styles. Styles are discussed as they are used in this book.

To Modify a Style

The MLA documentation style requires that all text in the research paper use a 12-point Times New Roman or similar font. If you change the font and font size using buttons on the ribbon, you will need to make the change many times during the course of creating the paper. ***Why?*** *Word formats various areas of a document based on the Normal style, which uses an 11-point Calibri font. For example, body text, headers, and bibliographies all display text based on the Normal style.*

Thus, instead of changing the font and font size for various document elements, a more efficient technique is to change the Normal style for this document to use a 12-point Times New Roman font. ***Why?*** *By changing the Normal style, you ensure that all text in the document will use the format required by the MLA.* The following steps change the Normal style.

1

- Right-click Normal in the Styles gallery (Home tab | Styles group) to display a shortcut menu related to styles (Figure 2–2).

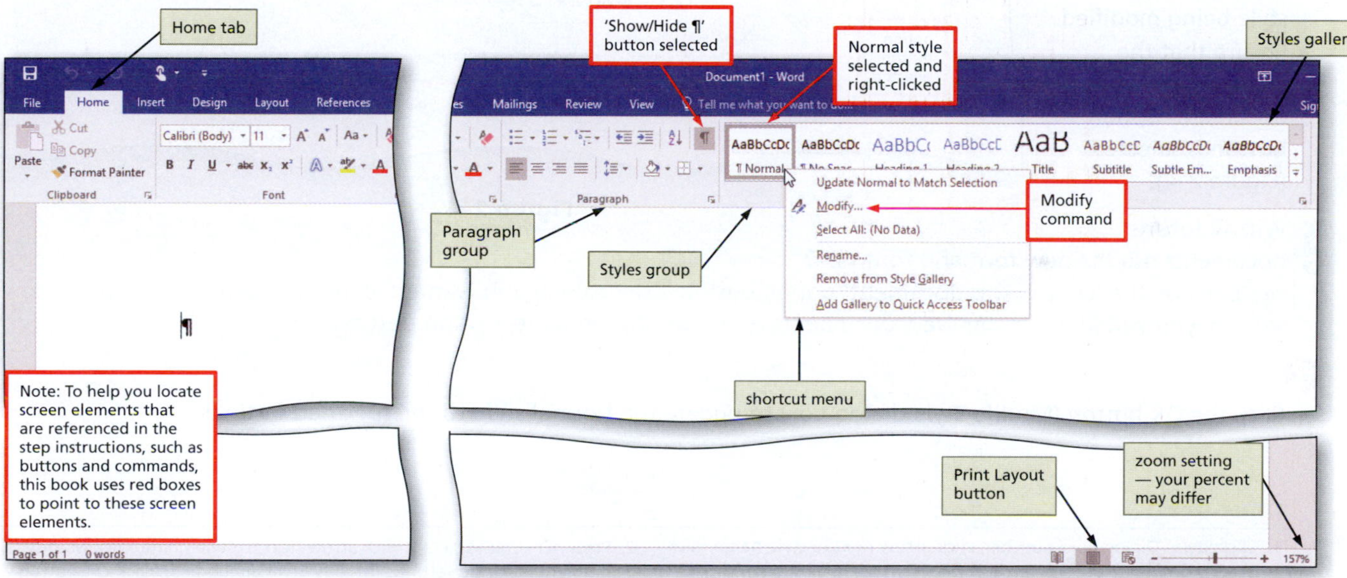

Figure 2–2

2

- Click Modify on the shortcut menu to display the Modify Style dialog box (Figure 2–3).

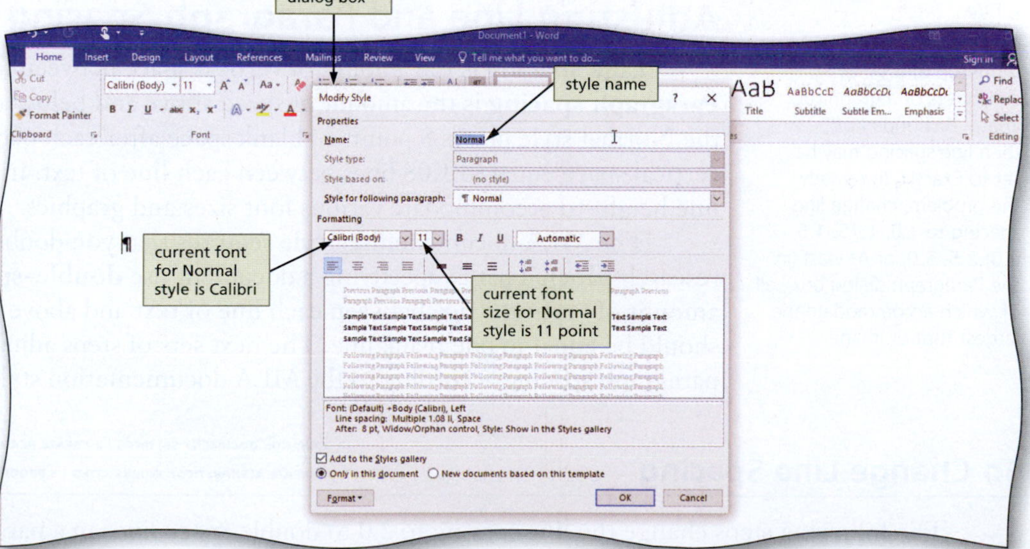

Figure 2–3

- Click the Font arrow (Modify Style dialog box) to display the Font list. Scroll to and then click Times New Roman in the list to change the font for the style being modified.
- Click the Font Size arrow (Modify Style dialog box) and then click 12 in the Font Size list to change the font size for the style being modified.
- Ensure that the 'Only in this document' option button is selected (Figure 2–4).

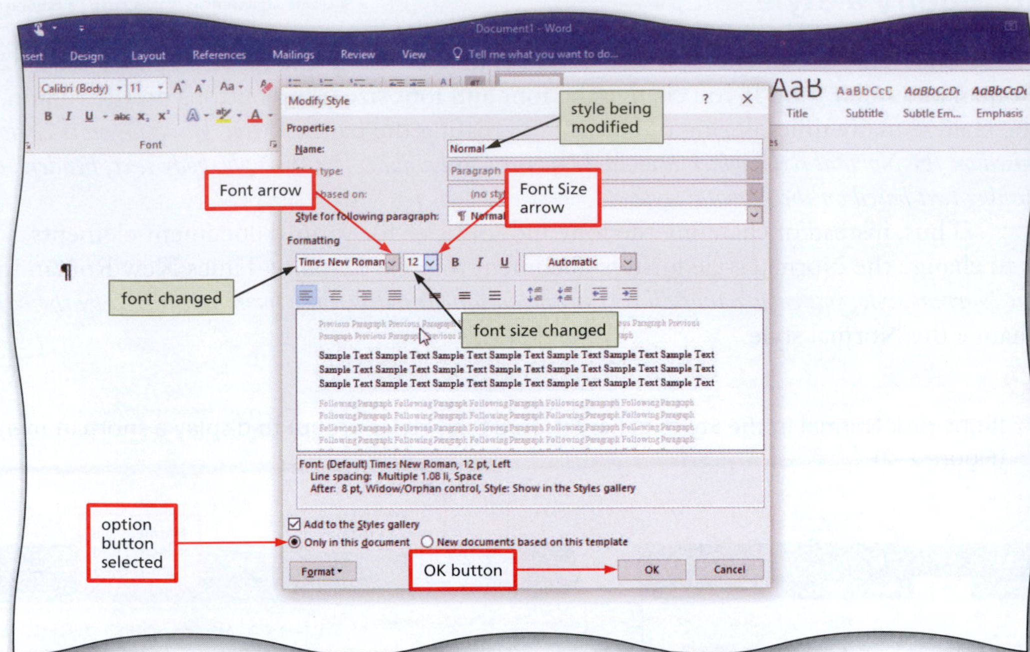

Figure 2–4

Q&A Will all future documents use the new font and font size?

No, because the 'Only in this document' option button is selected. If you wanted all future documents to use a new setting, you would select the 'New documents based on this template' option button.

- Click the OK button (Modify Style dialog box) to update the Normal style to the specified settings.

Other Ways

1. Click Styles Dialog Box Launcher, click arrow next to style name, click Modify on menu, change settings (Modify Style dialog box), click OK button
2. Press ALT+CTRL+SHIFT+S, click arrow next to style name, click Modify on menu, change settings (Modify Style dialog box), click OK button

BTW

Line Spacing

If the top of a set of characters or a graphical image is chopped off, then line spacing may be set to Exactly. To remedy the problem, change line spacing to 1.0, 1.15, 1.5, 2.0, 2.5, 3.0, or At least (in the Paragraph dialog box), all of which accommodate the largest font or image.

Adjusting Line and Paragraph Spacing

Line spacing is the amount of vertical space between lines of text in a paragraph. **Paragraph spacing** is the amount of space above and below a paragraph. By default, the Normal style places 8 points of blank space after each paragraph and inserts a vertical space equal to 1.08 lines between each line of text. It also automatically adjusts line height to accommodate various font sizes and graphics.

The MLA documentation style requires that you double-space the entire research paper. That is, specifying a document use **double-space** means that the amount of vertical space between each line of text and above and below paragraphs should be equal to one blank line. The next sets of steps adjust line spacing and paragraph spacing according to the MLA documentation style.

To Change Line Spacing

1 CHANGE DOCUMENT SETTINGS | 2 CREATE HEADER | 3 TYPE RESEARCH PAPER WITH CITATIONS
4 CREATE ALPHABETICAL WORKS CITED | 5 PROOFREAD & REVISE RESEARCH PAPER

The following steps change the line spacing to 2.0 to double-space lines in a paragraph. ***Why?*** *The lines of the research paper should be double-spaced, according to the MLA documentation style.*

1

- Click the 'Line and Paragraph Spacing' button (Home tab | Paragraph group) to display the Line and Paragraph Spacing gallery (Figure 2–5).

Q&A What do the numbers in the Line and Paragraph Spacing gallery represent?
The options 1.0, 2.0, and 3.0 set line spacing to single, double, and triple, respectively. Similarly, the 1.15, 1.5, and 2.5 options set line spacing to 1.15, 1.5, and 2.5 lines. All of these options adjust line spacing automatically to accommodate the largest font or graphic on a line.

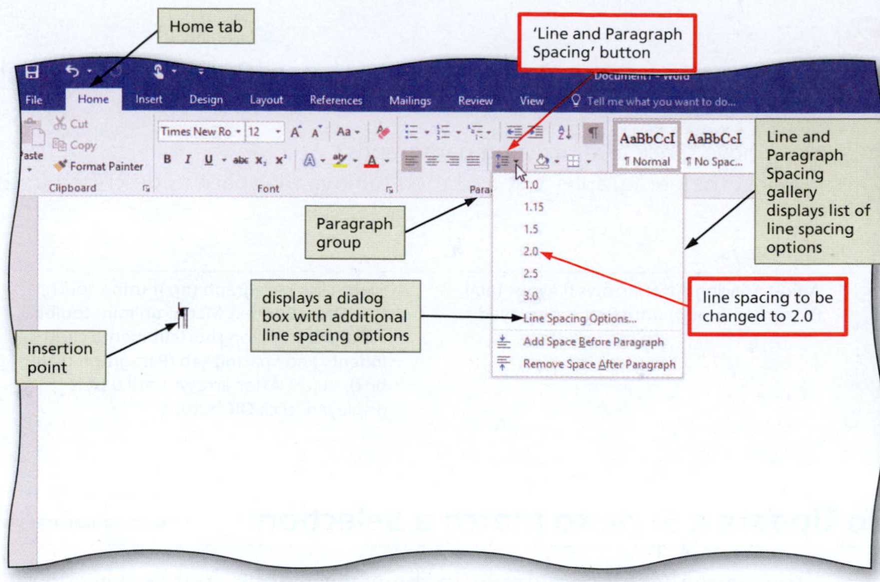

Figure 2–5

2

- Click 2.0 in the Line and Paragraph Spacing gallery to change the line spacing at the location of the insertion point.

Q&A Can I change the line spacing of existing text?
Yes. Select the text first and then change the line spacing as described in these steps.

Other Ways

1. Right-click paragraph (or, if using touch, tap 'Show Context Menu' on mini toolbar), click Paragraph on shortcut menu, or click Indents and Spacing tab (Paragraph dialog box), click Line spacing arrow, select desired spacing, click OK button
2. Click Paragraph Settings Dialog Box Launcher (Home tab or Layout tab | Paragraph group), click Indents and Spacing tab (Paragraph dialog box), click Line spacing arrow, select desired spacing, click OK button
3. Press CTRL+2 for double-spacing

To Remove Space after a Paragraph

1 CHANGE DOCUMENT SETTINGS | 2 CREATE HEADER | 3 TYPE RESEARCH PAPER WITH CITATIONS
4 CREATE ALPHABETICAL WORKS CITED | 5 PROOFREAD & REVISE RESEARCH PAPER

The following steps remove space after a paragraph. ***Why?*** *The research paper should not have additional blank space after each paragraph, according to the MLA documentation style.*

1

- Click the 'Line and Paragraph Spacing' button (Home tab | Paragraph group) to display the Line and Paragraph Spacing gallery (Figure 2–6).

Q&A Why does a check mark appear to the left of 2.0 in the gallery?
The check mark indicates the currently selected line spacing.

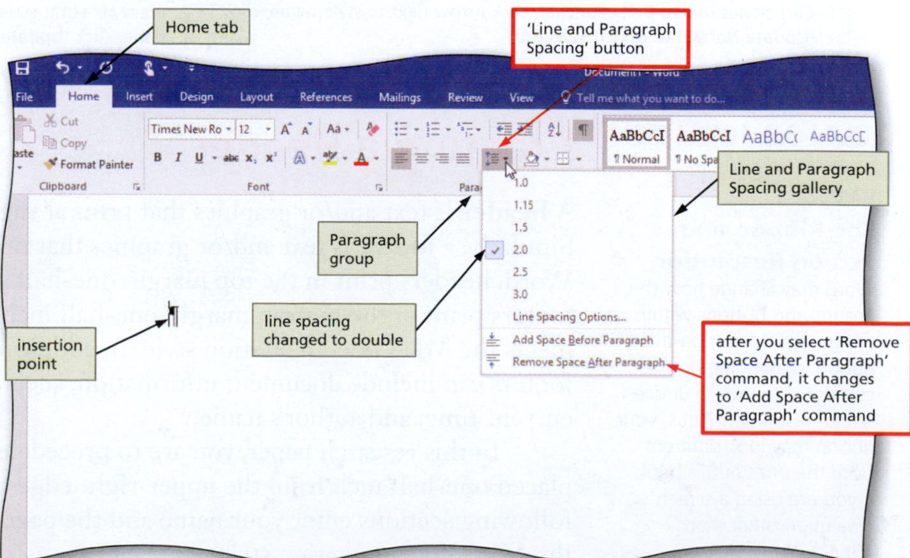

Figure 2–6

2

- Click 'Remove Space After Paragraph' in the Line and Paragraph Spacing gallery so that no blank space appears after paragraphs.

Q&A Can I remove space after existing paragraphs?
Yes. Select the paragraphs first and then remove the space as described in these steps.

Other Ways

1. Adjust Spacing After arrows (Layout tab | Paragraph group) until 0 pt is displayed
2. Right-click paragraph (or, if using touch, tap 'Show Context Menu' on mini toolbar), click Paragraph on shortcut menu, click Indents and Spacing tab (Paragraph dialog box), adjust After arrows until 0 pt is displayed, click OK button
3. Click Paragraph Settings Dialog Box Launcher (Home tab or Layout tab | Paragraph group), click Indents and Spacing tab (Paragraph dialog box), adjust After arrows until 0 pt is displayed, click OK button

To Update a Style to Match a Selection

1 CHANGE DOCUMENT SETTINGS | 2 CREATE HEADER | 3 TYPE RESEARCH PAPER WITH CITATIONS
4 CREATE ALPHABETICAL WORKS CITED | 5 PROOFREAD & REVISE RESEARCH PAPER

To ensure that all paragraphs in the paper will be double-spaced and do not have space after the paragraphs, you want the Normal style to include the line and paragraph spacing changes made in the previous two sets of steps. The following steps update the Normal style. ***Why?*** *You can update a style to reflect the settings of the location of the insertion point or selected text. Because no text has been typed in the research paper yet, you do not need to select text prior to updating the Normal style.*

1

- Right-click Normal in the Styles gallery (Home tab | Styles group) to display a shortcut menu (Figure 2–7).

2

- Click 'Update Normal to Match Selection' on the shortcut menu to update the selected (or current) style to reflect the settings at the location of the insertion point.

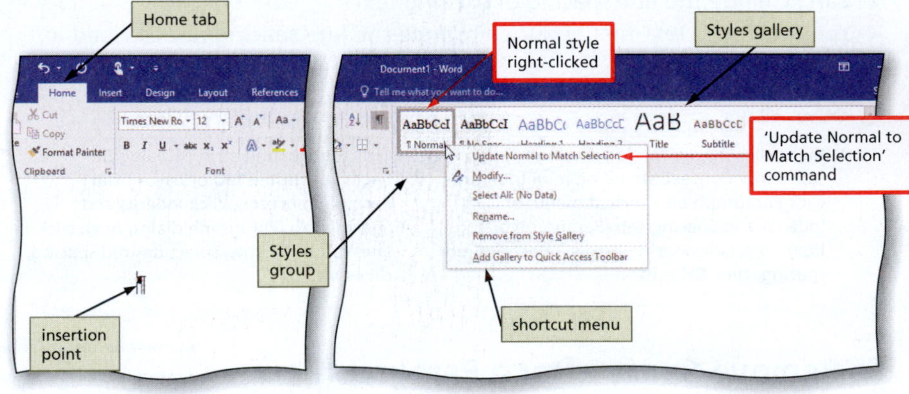

Figure 2–7

Other Ways

1. Click Styles Dialog Box Launcher, click arrow next to style name, click 'Update Normal to Match Selection'
2. Press ALT+CTRL+SHIFT+S, click arrow next to style name in Styles pane, click 'Update Normal to Match Selection'

Creating a Header

A **header** is text and/or graphics that print at the top of each page in a document. Similarly, a **footer** is text and/or graphics that print at the bottom of every page. In Word, headers print in the top margin one-half inch from the top of every page, and footers print in the bottom margin one-half inch from the bottom of each page, which meets the MLA documentation style. In addition to text and graphics, headers and footers can include document information, such as the page number, current date, current time, and author's name.

In this research paper, you are to precede the page number with your last name placed one-half inch from the upper-right edge of each page. The procedures in the following sections enter your name and the page number in the header, as specified by the MLA documentation style.

BTW
The Ribbon and Screen Resolution
Word may change how the groups and buttons within the groups appear on the ribbon, depending on the computer or mobile device's screen resolution. Thus, your ribbon may look different from the ones in this book if you are using a screen resolution other than 1366 x 768.

To Switch to the Header

The following steps switch from editing the document text to editing the header. ***Why?*** *To enter text in the header, you instruct Word to edit the header.*

- Click Insert on the ribbon to display the Insert tab.
- Click the 'Add a Header' button (Insert tab | Header & Footer group) to display the Add a Header gallery (Figure 2–8)

Experiment

- Click the down scroll arrow in the Add a Header gallery to see the available built-in headers.

Q&A

Can I use a built-in header for this research paper?
None of the built-in headers adheres to the MLA documentation style; thus, you should enter your own header content instead of using a built-in header for this research paper.

How would I remove a header from a document?
You would click Remove Header in the Add a Header gallery. Similarly, to remove a footer, you would click Remove Footer in the Add a Footer gallery.

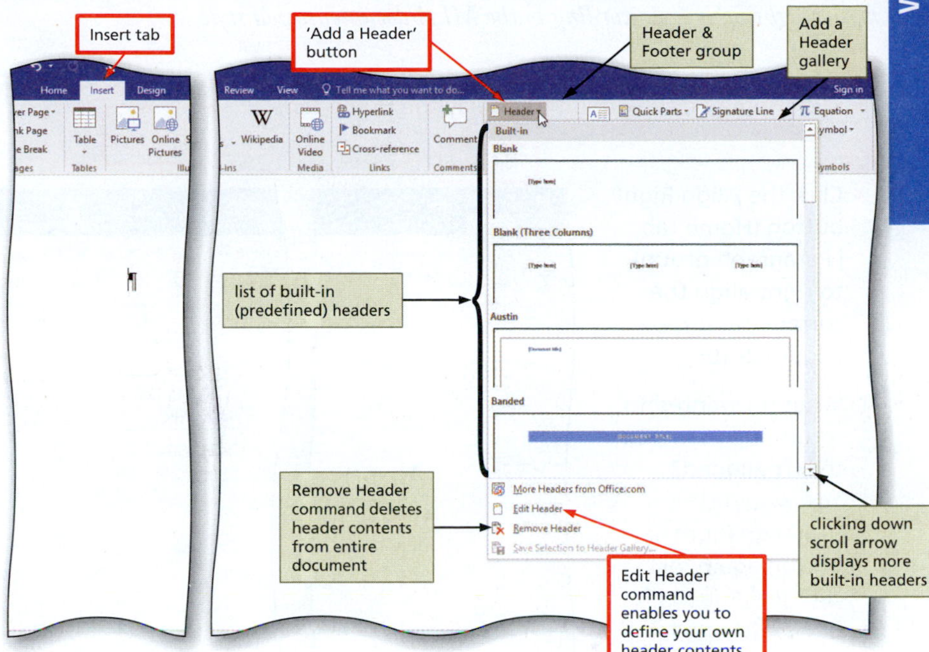

Figure 2–8

- Click Edit Header in the Add a Header gallery to switch from the document text to the header, which allows you to edit the contents of the header (Figure 2–9).

Q&A

How do I remove the Header & Footer Tools Design tab from the ribbon?
When you are finished editing the header, you will close it, which removes the Header & Footer Tools Design tab.

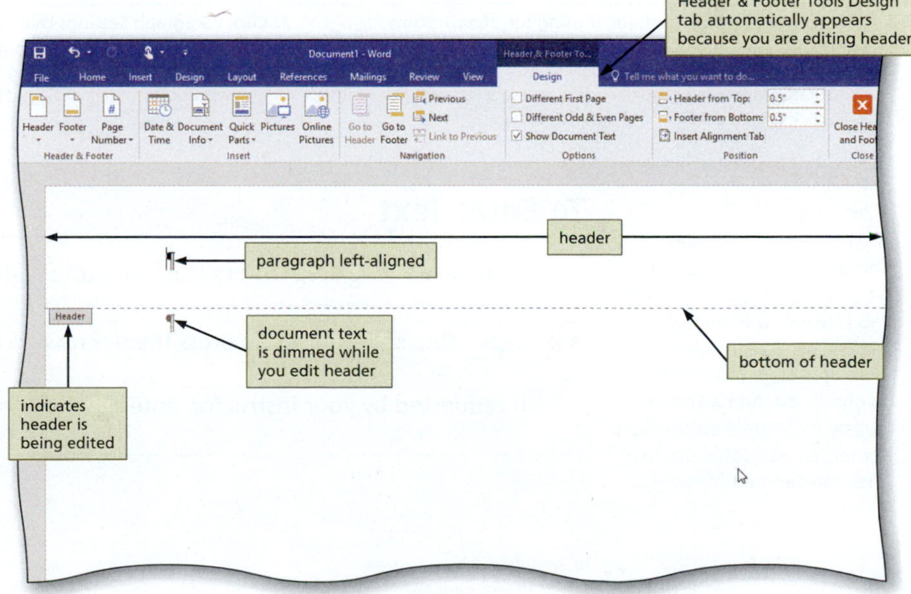

Figure 2–9

Other Ways

1. Double-click dimmed header
2. Right-click header in document, click Edit Header button that appears

To Right-Align a Paragraph

The paragraph in the header currently is left-aligned (shown in Figure 2–9). The following steps right-align this paragraph. ***Why?*** *Your last name and the page number should print* ***right-aligned****; that is, they should print at the right margin, according to the MLA documentation style.*

- Click Home on the ribbon to display the Home tab.

- Click the Align Right button (Home tab | Paragraph group) to right-align the current paragraph (Figure 2–10).

Q&A What if I wanted to return the paragraph to left-aligned?
You would click the Align Right button again, or click the Align Left button (Home tab | Paragraph group).

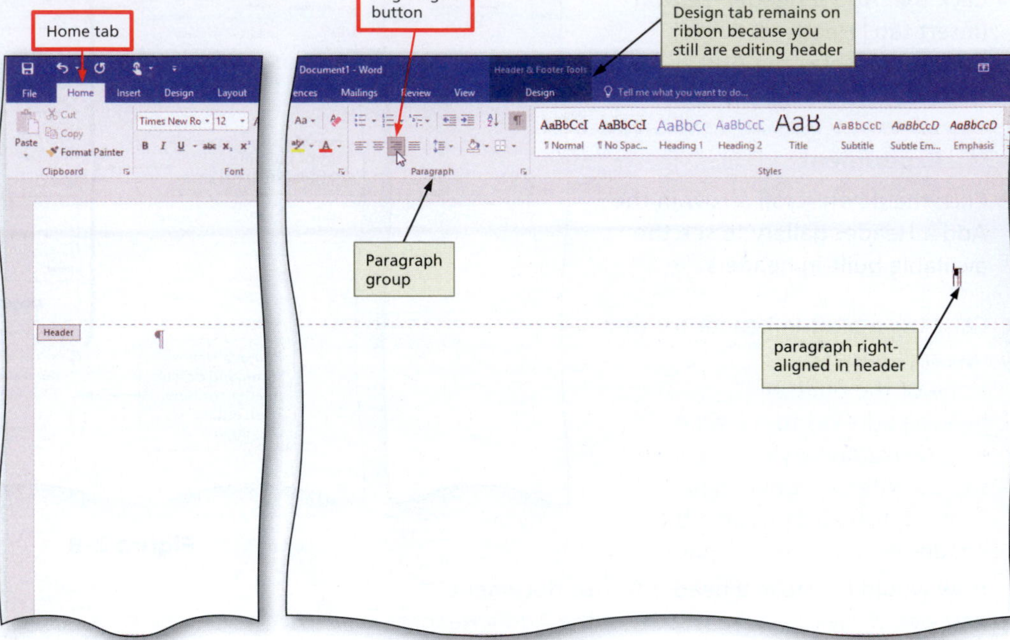

Figure 2–10

Other Ways

1. Right-click paragraph (or, if using touch, tap 'Show Context Menu' button on mini toolbar), click Paragraph on shortcut menu, click Indents and Spacing tab (Paragraph dialog box), click Alignment arrow, click Right, click OK button
2. Click Paragraph Settings Dialog Box Launcher (Home tab or Layout tab | Paragraph group), click Indents and Spacing tab (Paragraph dialog box), click Alignment arrow, click Right, click OK button
3. Press CTRL+R

BTW
Footers
If you wanted to create a footer, you would click the 'Add a Footer' button (Insert tab | Header & Footer group) and then select the desired built-in footer or click Edit Footer in the Add a Footer gallery to create a customized footer; or, you could double-click the dimmed footer.

To Enter Text

The following step enters the last name right-aligned in the header area.

1. Type `Carter` and then press the SPACEBAR to enter the last name in the header.

If requested by your instructor, enter your last name instead of Carter in the header.

To Insert a Page Number

The following steps insert a page number at the location of the insertion point. ***Why?*** *The MLA documentation style requires a page number following the last name in the header.*

1

- Click Header & Footer Tools Design on the ribbon to display the Header & Footer Tools Design tab.
- Click the 'Add Page Numbers' button (Header & Footer Tools Design tab | Header & Footer group) to display the Add Page Numbers menu.

Q&A Why does the button name in the step differ from the name on the face of the button in the figure?
The text that appears on the face of the button may vary, depending on screen resolution. The name that appears in the ScreenTip (when you point to the button), however, never changes. For this reason, this book uses the name that appears in the ScreenTip to identify buttons, boxes, and other on-screen elements.

- Point to Current Position on the Add Page Numbers menu to display the Current Position gallery (Figure 2–11).

Experiment

- Click the down scroll arrow in the Current Position gallery to see the available page number formats.

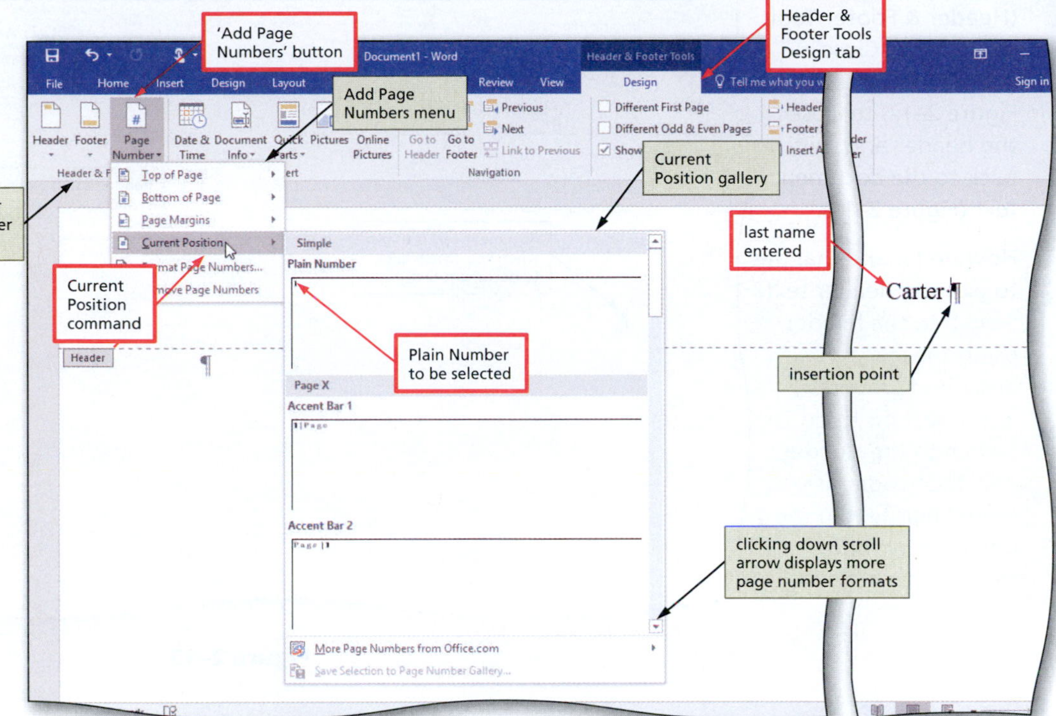

Figure 2–11

2

- If necessary, scroll to the top of the Current Position gallery.
- Click Plain Number in the Current Position gallery to insert an unformatted page number at the location of the insertion point (Figure 2–12).

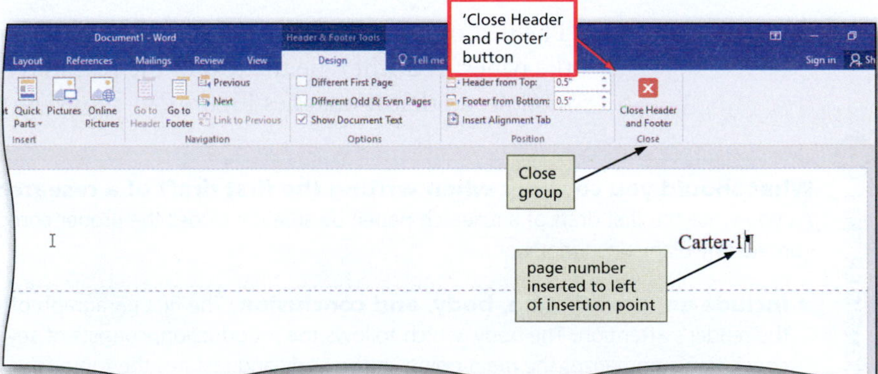

Figure 2–12

Other Ways

1. Click 'Add Page Numbers' button (Insert tab | Header & Footer group)
2. Click 'Explore Quick Parts' button (Insert tab | Text group or Header & Footer Tools Design tab | Insert group), click Field on Explore Quick Parts menu, select Page in Field names list (Field dialog box), select desired format in Format list, click OK button

To Close the Header

The next task is to switch back to the document text. ***Why?*** *You are finished entering text in the header.* The following step closes the header.

- Click the 'Close Header and Footer' button (Header & Footer Tools Design tab | Close group) (shown in Figure 2–12) to close the header and switch back to the document text (Figure 2–13).

Q&A How do I make changes to existing header text?
Switch to the header using the steps described previously in the section titled To Switch to the Header, edit the header as you would edit text in the document window, and then switch back to the document text.

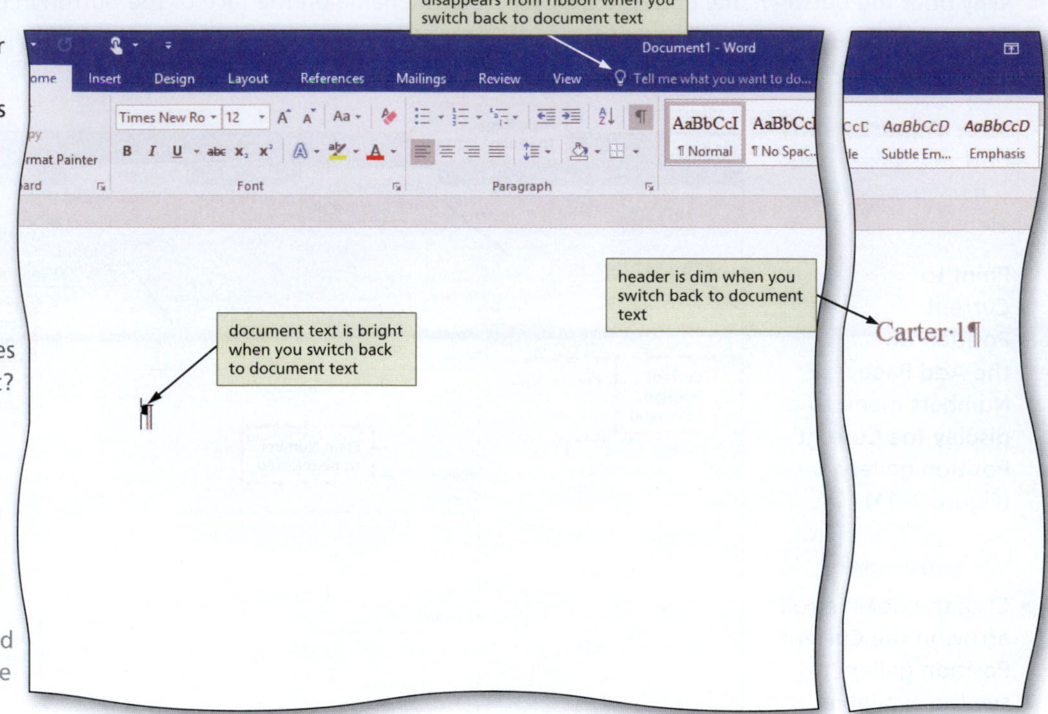

Figure 2–13

Other Ways

1. Double-click dimmed document text

Typing the Research Paper Text

The text of the research paper in this module encompasses the first two pages of the paper. You will type the text of the research paper and then modify it later in the module, so that it matches Figure 2–1 shown at the beginning of this module.

CONSIDER THIS

What should you consider when writing the first draft of a research paper?
As you write the first draft of a research paper, be sure it includes the proper components, uses credible sources, and does not contain any plagiarized material.

- **Include an introduction, body, and conclusion.** The first paragraph of the paper introduces the topic and captures the reader's attention. The body, which follows the introduction, consists of several paragraphs that support the topic. The conclusion summarizes the main points in the body and restates the topic.
- **Evaluate sources for authority, currency, and accuracy.** Be especially wary of information obtained on the web. Any person, company, or organization can publish a webpage on the Internet. When considering the source, consider the following:
  - Authority: Does a reputable institution or group support the source? Is the information presented without bias? Are the author's credentials listed and verifiable?
  - Currency: Is the information up to date? Are dates of sources listed? What is the last date revised or updated?
  - Accuracy: Is the information free of errors? Is it verifiable? Are the sources clearly identified?

- **Acknowledge all sources of information; do not plagiarize.** Sources of research include books, magazines, newspapers, and the Internet. As you record facts and ideas, list details about the source: title, author, place of publication, publisher, date of publication, etc. When taking notes, be careful not to **plagiarize**. That is, do not use someone else's work and claim it to be your own. If you copy information directly, place it in quotation marks and identify its source. Not only is plagiarism unethical, but it is considered an academic crime that can have severe punishments, such as failing a course or being expelled from school.

When you summarize, paraphrase (rewrite information in your own words), present facts, give statistics, quote exact words, or show a map, chart, or other graphic, you must acknowledge the source. Information that commonly is known or accessible to the audience constitutes common knowledge and does not need to be acknowledged. If, however, you question whether certain information is common knowledge, you should document it — just to be safe.

To Enter Name and Course Information

As discussed earlier in this module, the MLA documentation style does not require a separate title page for research papers. Instead, place your name and course information in a block at the top of the page, below the header, at the left margin. The following steps enter the name and course information in the research paper.

BTW
Date Formats
The MLA style prefers the day-month-year (10 October 2017) or month-day-year (October 10, 2017) format.

1. Type `Oswald Carter` as the student name and then press the ENTER key.
2. Type `Ms. Ruiz` as the instructor name and then press the ENTER key.
3. Type `English 104` as the course name and then press the ENTER key.
4. Type `October 10, 2017` as the paper's due date and then press the ENTER key (Figure 2–14).

If requested by your instructor, enter your name and course information instead of the information shown above.

Q&A Why did the word, October, appear on the screen as I began typing the month name?
Word has an AutoComplete feature, where it predicts some words or phrases as you are typing and displays its prediction in a ScreenTip. If the AutoComplete prediction is correct, you can press the ENTER key (or, if using touch, tap the ScreenTip) to instruct Word to finish your typing with the word or phrase that appears in the ScreenTip.

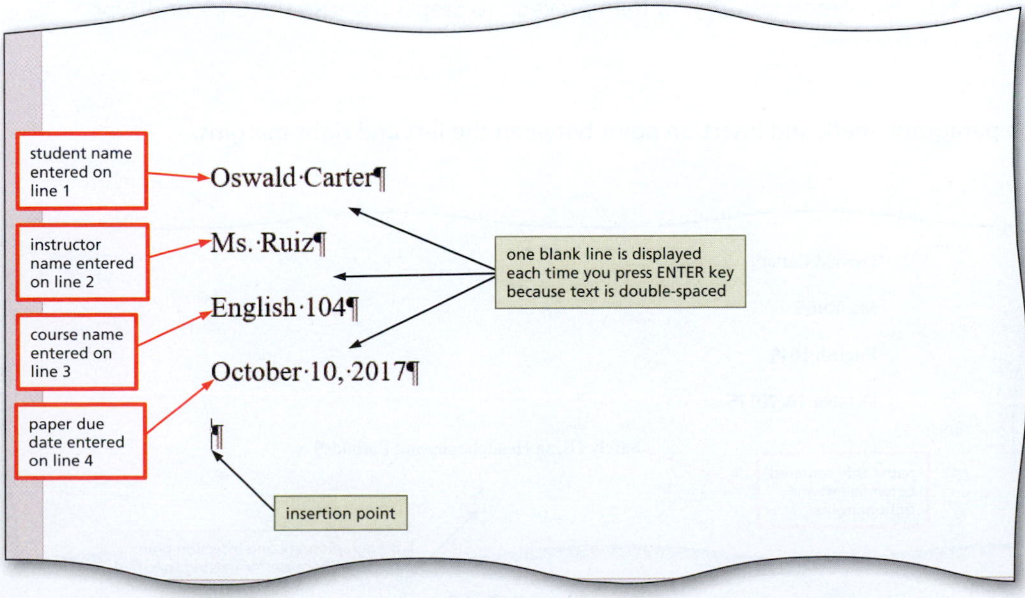

Figure 2–14

To Click and Type

The next task is to enter the title of the research paper centered between the page margins. In Module 1, you used the Center button (Home tab | Paragraph group) to center text and graphics. As an alternative, if you are using a mouse, you can use Word's Click and Type feature to format and enter text, graphics, and other items. ***Why?*** *With* ***Click and Type****, you can double-click a blank area of the document window and Word automatically formats the item you type or insert according to the location where you double-clicked.* The following steps use Click and Type to center and then type the title of the research paper.

Experiment

- Move the pointer around the document below the entered name and course information and observe the various icons that appear with the I-beam.
- Position the pointer in the center of the document at the approximate location for the research paper title until a center icon appears below the I-beam (Figure 2–15).

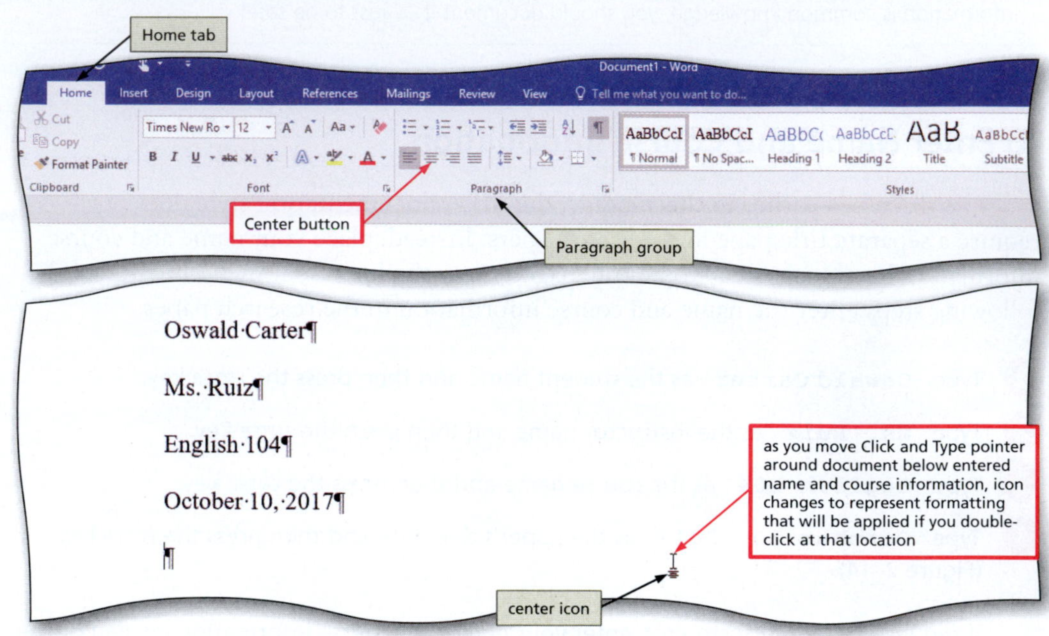

Figure 2–15

Q&A What are the other icons that appear in the Click and Type pointer?
A left-align icon appears to the right of the I-beam when the Click and Type pointer is in certain locations on the left side of the document window. A right-align icon appears to the left of the I-beam when the Click and Type pointer is in certain locations on the right side of the document window.

What if I am using a touch screen?
Tap the Center button (Home tab | Paragraph group) and then proceed to Step 3 because the Click and Type feature does not work with a touch screen.

- Double-click to center the paragraph mark and insertion point between the left and right margins.

- Type `Safely Using Headphones and Earbuds` as the paper title and then press the ENTER key to position the insertion point on the next line (Figure 2–16).

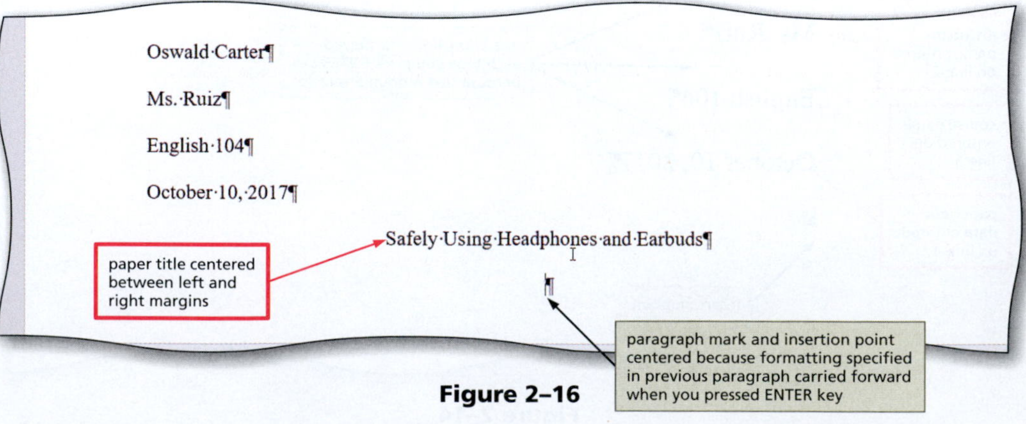

Figure 2–16

Keyboard Shortcuts

Word has many **keyboard shortcuts**, sometimes called shortcut keys or keyboard key combinations, for your convenience while typing. Table 2–1 lists the common keyboard shortcuts for formatting characters. Table 2–2 lists common keyboard shortcuts for formatting paragraphs.

Table 2–1 Keyboard Shortcuts for Formatting Characters

Character Formatting Task	Keyboard Shortcut
All capital letters	CTRL+SHIFT+A
Bold	CTRL+B
Case of letters	SHIFT+F3
Decrease font size	CTRL+SHIFT+<
Decrease font size 1 point	CTRL+[
Double-underline	CTRL+SHIFT+D
Increase font size	CTRL+SHIFT+>
Increase font size 1 point	CTRL+]
Italic	CTRL+I
Remove character formatting (plain text)	CTRL+SPACEBAR
Small uppercase letters	CTRL+SHIFT+K
Subscript	CTRL+EQUAL SIGN
Superscript	CTRL+SHIFT+PLUS SIGN
Underline	CTRL+U
Underline words, not spaces	CTRL+SHIFT+W

Table 2–2 Keyboard Shortcuts for Formatting Paragraphs

Paragraph Formatting	Keyboard Shortcut
1.5 line spacing	CTRL+5
Add/remove one line above paragraph	CTRL+0 (ZERO)
Center paragraph	CTRL+E
Decrease paragraph indent	CTRL+SHIFT+M
Double-space lines	CTRL+2
Hanging indent	CTRL+T
Increase paragraph indent	CTRL+M
Justify paragraph	CTRL+J
Left-align paragraph	CTRL+L
Remove hanging indent	CTRL+SHIFT+T
Remove paragraph formatting	CTRL+Q
Right-align paragraph	CTRL+R
Single-space lines	CTRL+1

To Format Text Using a Keyboard Shortcut

The paragraphs below the paper title should be left-aligned, instead of centered. Thus, the next step is to left-align the paragraph below the paper title. When your fingers already are on the keyboard, you may prefer using keyboard shortcuts to format text as you type it.

The following step left-aligns a paragraph using the keyboard shortcut CTRL+L. (Recall from Module 1 that a notation such as CTRL+L means to press the letter L on the keyboard while holding down the CTRL key.)

1. Press CTRL+L to left-align the current paragraph, that is, the paragraph containing the insertion point (shown in Figure 2–17).

Q&A Why would I use a keyboard shortcut instead of the ribbon to format text?
Switching between the mouse and the keyboard takes time. If your hands are already on the keyboard, use a keyboard shortcut. If your hand is on the mouse, use the ribbon.

2. Save the research paper on your hard drive, OneDrive, or other storage location using the file name, Headphones and Earbuds Paper.

Q&A Why should I save the research paper at this time?
You have performed many tasks while creating this flyer and do not want to risk losing work completed thus far.

BTW
Keyboard Shortcuts
To print a complete list of keyboard shortcuts in Word, press F1 to display the Word Help window, type `keyboard shortcuts` in the Search box in the Word Help window, press the ENTER key, click the Keyboard shortcuts for Microsoft Word link, click the Print button in the Help window, and then click the Print button in the Print dialog box.

To Display the Rulers

1 CHANGE DOCUMENT SETTINGS | 2 CREATE HEADER | 3 TYPE RESEARCH PAPER WITH CITATIONS
4 CREATE ALPHABETICAL WORKS CITED | 5 PROOFREAD & REVISE RESEARCH PAPER

According to the MLA documentation style, the first line of each paragraph in the research paper is to be indented one-half inch from the left margin. Although you can use a dialog box to indent paragraphs, Word provides a quicker way through the **horizontal ruler**. This ruler is displayed at the top edge of the document window just below the ribbon. Word also provides a **vertical ruler** that is displayed along the left edge of the Word window. The following step displays the rulers. ***Why?*** *You want to use the horizontal ruler to indent paragraphs.*

- If necessary, scroll the document so that the research paper title is at the top of the document window.
- Click View on the ribbon to display the View tab.
- If the rulers are not displayed, click the View Ruler check box (View tab | Show group) to place a check mark in the check box and display the horizontal and vertical rulers on the screen (Figure 2–17).

Q&A What tasks can I accomplish using the rulers?
You can use the rulers to indent paragraphs, set tab stops, change page margins, and adjust column widths.

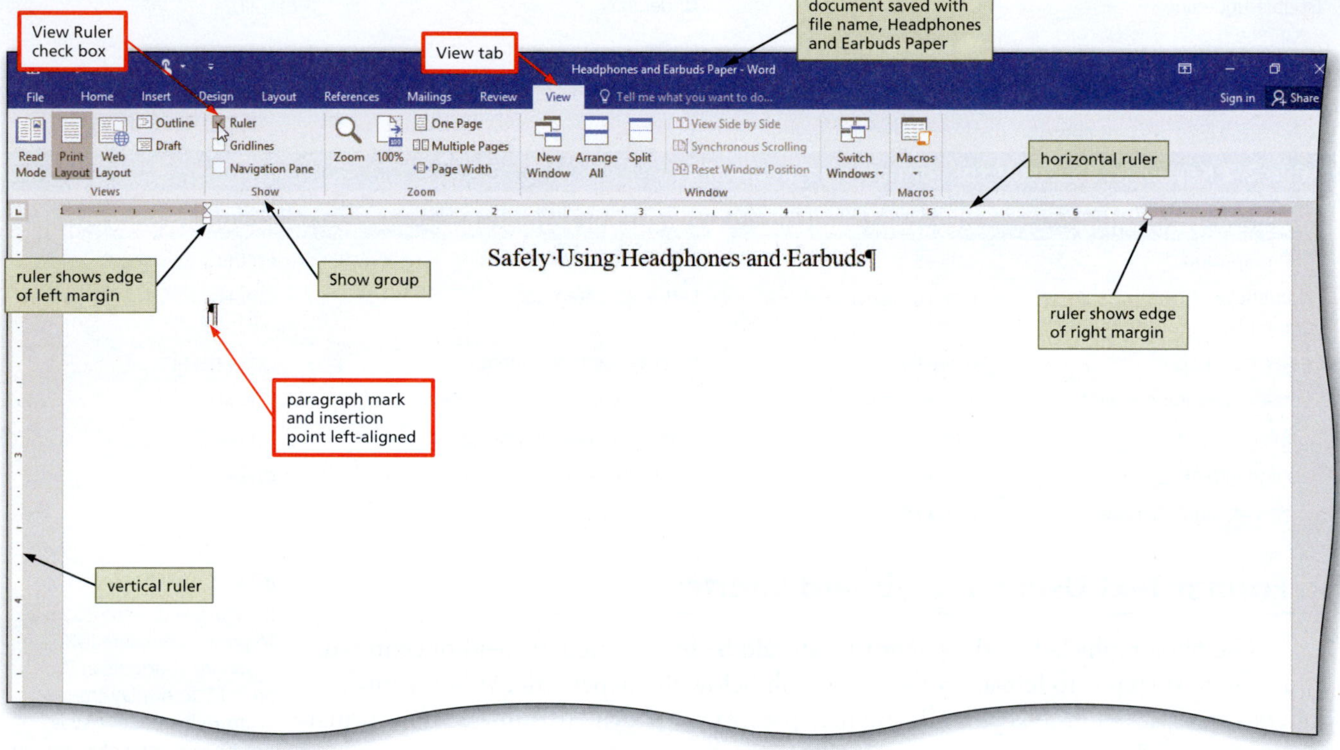

Figure 2–17

To First-Line Indent Paragraphs

1 CHANGE DOCUMENT SETTINGS | 2 CREATE HEADER | 3 TYPE RESEARCH PAPER WITH CITATIONS
4 CREATE ALPHABETICAL WORKS CITED | 5 PROOFREAD & REVISE RESEARCH PAPER

If you are using a mouse, you can use the horizontal ruler, usually simply called the **ruler**, to indent just the first line of a paragraph, which is called a **first-line indent**. The left margin on the ruler contains two triangles above a square. The **'First Line Indent' marker** is the top triangle at the 0" mark on the ruler (shown in Figure 2–18). The bottom triangle is discussed later in this module. The small square at the 0" mark is the Left Indent marker. The **Left Indent marker** allows you to change the entire left margin, whereas the 'First Line Indent' marker indents only the first line of the paragraph.

The following steps first-line indent paragraphs in the research paper. ***Why?*** *The first line of each paragraph in the research paper is to be indented one-half inch from the left margin, according to the MLA documentation style.*

1

- With the insertion point on the paragraph mark below the research paper title, point to the 'First Line Indent' marker on the ruler (Figure 2–18).

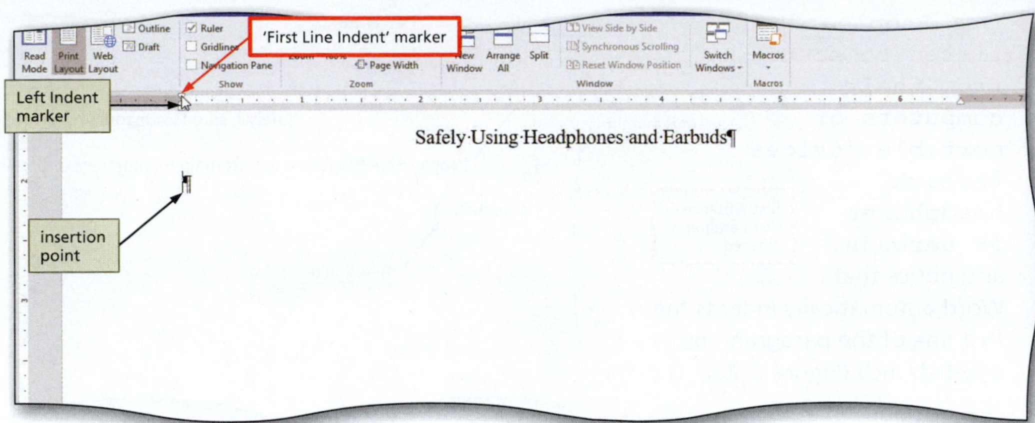

Figure 2–18

2

- Drag the 'First Line Indent' marker to the .5" mark on the ruler to display a vertical dotted line in the document window, which indicates the proposed indent location of the first line of the paragraph (Figure 2–19).

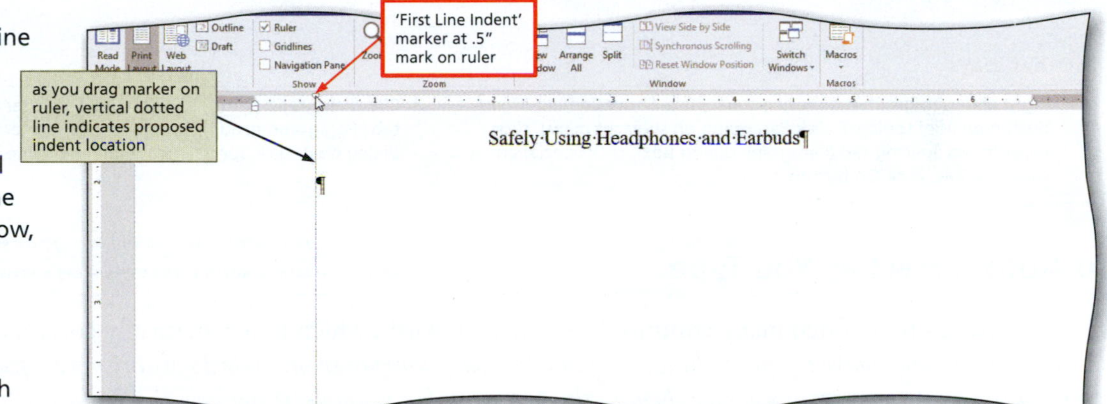

Figure 2–19

3

- Release the mouse button to place the 'First Line Indent' marker at the .5" mark on the ruler, or one-half inch from the left margin (Figure 2–20).

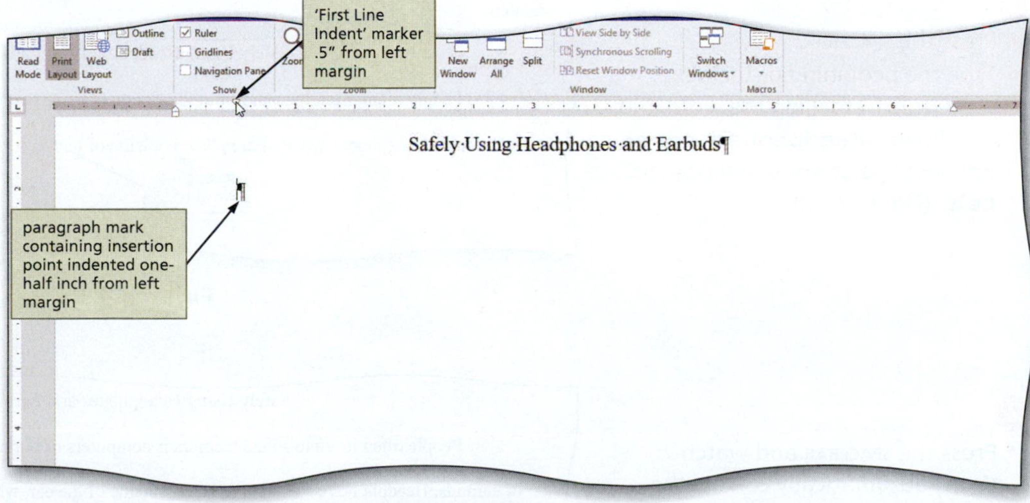

Figure 2–20

Q&A What if I am using a touch screen?

If you are using a touch screen, you cannot drag the 'First Line Indent' marker and must follow these steps instead: tap the Paragraph Settings Dialog Box Launcher (Home tab or Layout tab | Paragraph group) to display the Paragraph dialog box, tap the Indents and Spacing tab (Paragraph dialog box), tap the Special arrow, tap First line, and then tap the OK button.

- Type **`People often listen to sound from their computers or portable devices through headphones or earbuds.`** and notice that Word automatically indents the first line of the paragraph by one-half inch (Figure 2–21).

first line of paragraph indented one-half inch from left margin

first sentence in first paragraph entered

Safely·Using·Headphones·and·Earbuds¶

People·often·listen·to·sound·from·their·computers·or·portable·devices·through·headphones·or·earbuds.¶

insertion point

Figure 2–21

Q&A Will I have to set a first-line indent for each paragraph in the paper?
No. Each time you press the ENTER key, paragraph formatting in the previous paragraph carries forward to the next paragraph. Thus, once you set the first-line indent, its format carries forward automatically to each subsequent paragraph you type.

Other Ways

1. Right-click paragraph (or, if using touch, tap 'Show Context Menu' button on mini toolbar), click Paragraph on shortcut menu, click Indents and Spacing tab (Paragraph dialog box), click Special arrow, click First line, click OK button
2. Click Paragraph Settings Dialog Box Launcher (Home tab or Layout tab | Paragraph group), click Indents and Spacing tab (Paragraph dialog box), click Special arrow, click First line, click OK button

To AutoCorrect as You Type

1 CHANGE DOCUMENT SETTINGS | 2 CREATE HEADER | **3 TYPE RESEARCH PAPER WITH CITATIONS**
4 CREATE ALPHABETICAL WORKS CITED | 5 PROOFREAD & REVISE RESEARCH PAPER

Word has predefined many commonly misspelled words, which it automatically corrects for you. ***Why?*** *As you type, you may make typing, spelling, capitalization, or grammar errors. Word's* ***AutoCorrect*** *feature automatically corrects these kinds of errors as you type them in the document. For example, if you type the characters, ahve, Word automatically changes it to the correct spelling, have, when you press the* SPACEBAR *or a punctuation mark key, such as a period or comma.*

The following steps intentionally misspell the word, the, as teh to illustrate the AutoCorrect feature.

- Press the SPACEBAR.
- Type the beginning of the next sentence, misspelling the word, the, as follows: **`Headphones cover or are placed outside of teh`** (Figure 2–22).

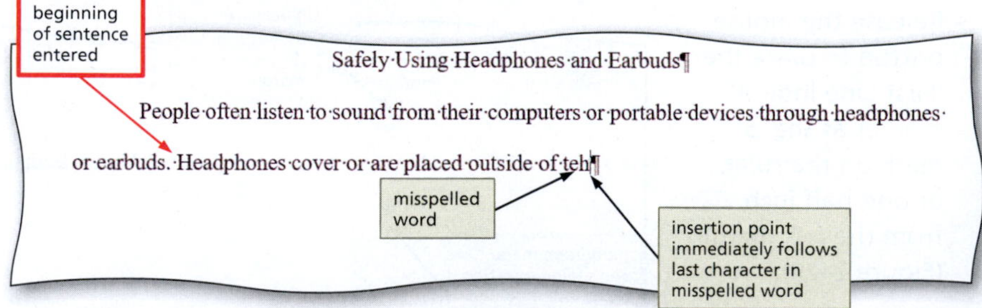

Figure 2–22

- Press the SPACEBAR and watch Word automatically correct the misspelled word.
- Type the rest of the sentence (Figure 2–23): **`ear, whereas earbuds rest inside the ear canal.`**

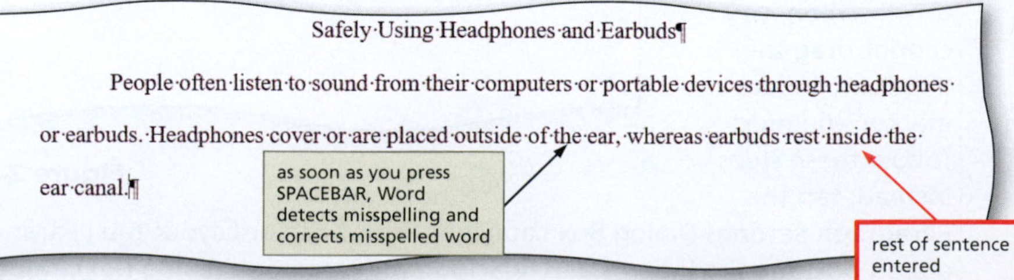

Figure 2–23

To Use the AutoCorrect Options Button

The following steps illustrate the AutoCorrect Options button and menu. ***Why?*** *If you are using a mouse, when you position the pointer on text that Word automatically corrected, a small blue box appears below the text. If you point to the small blue box, Word displays the AutoCorrect Options button. When you click the* ***AutoCorrect Options button****, Word displays a menu that allows you to undo a correction or change how Word handles future automatic corrections of this type.*

- Position the pointer in the text automatically corrected by Word (the word, the, in this case) to display a small blue box below the automatically corrected word (Figure 2–24).

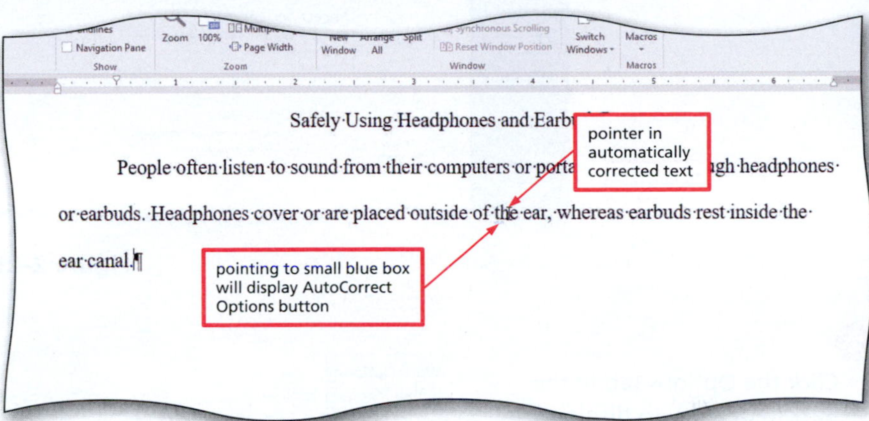

Figure 2–24

- Point to the small blue box to display the AutoCorrect Options button.
- Click the AutoCorrect Options button to display the AutoCorrect Options menu (Figure 2–25).
- Press the ESC key to remove the AutoCorrect Options menu from the screen.

Q&A Do I need to remove the AutoCorrect Options button from the screen?
No. When you move the pointer, the AutoCorrect Options button will disappear from the screen. If, for some reason, you wanted to remove the AutoCorrect Options button from the screen, you could press the ESC key a second time.

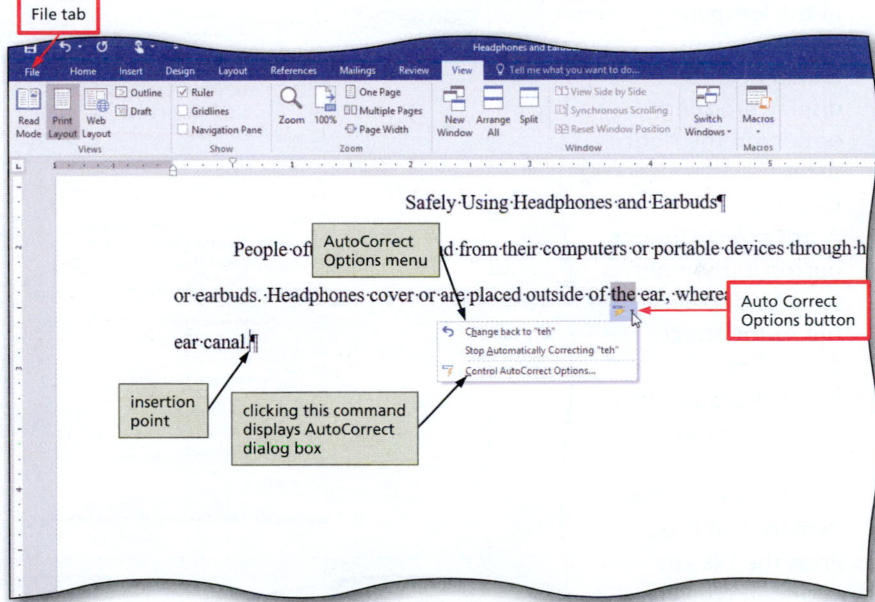

Figure 2–25

To Create an AutoCorrect Entry

The next steps create an AutoCorrect entry. ***Why?*** *In addition to the predefined list of AutoCorrect spelling, capitalization, and grammar errors, you can create your own AutoCorrect entries to add to the list. For example, if you tend to mistype the word computer as comptuer, you should create an AutoCorrect entry for it.*

1

- Click File on the ribbon (shown in Figure 2–25) to open the Backstage view (Figure 2–26).

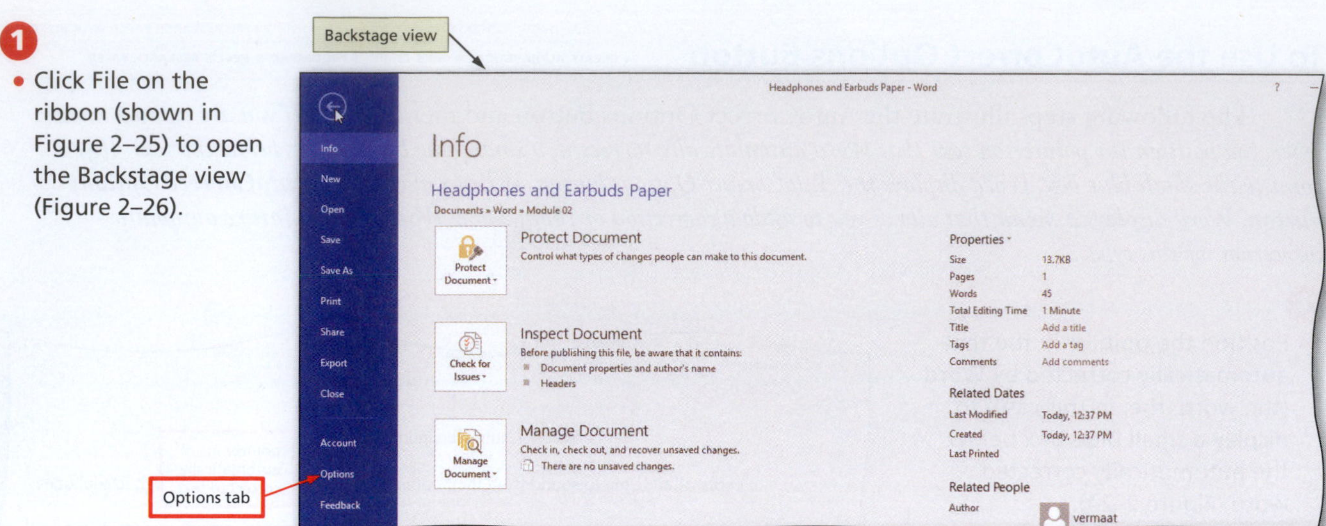

Figure 2–26

2

- Click the Options tab in the Backstage view to display the Word Options dialog box.
- Click Proofing in the left pane (Word Options dialog box) to display proofing options in the right pane.
- Click the AutoCorrect Options button in the right pane to display the AutoCorrect dialog box.
- When Word displays the AutoCorrect dialog box, type `comptuer` in the Replace text box.
- Press the TAB key and then type `computer` in the With text box (Figure 2–27).

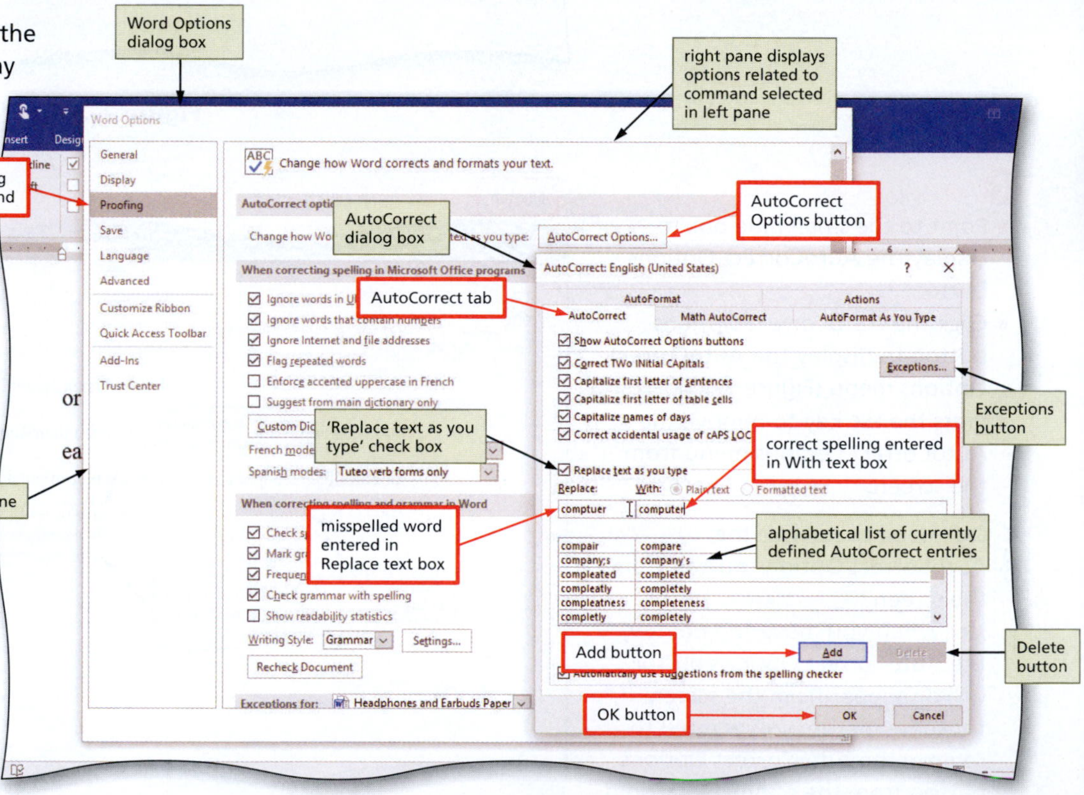

Figure 2–27

How would I delete an existing AutoCorrect entry?

You would select the entry to be deleted in the list of defined entries in the AutoCorrect dialog box and then click the Delete button (AutoCorrect dialog box).

3

- Click the Add button (AutoCorrect dialog box) to add the entry alphabetically to the list of words to correct automatically as you type. (If your dialog box displays a Replace button instead, click it and then click the Yes button in the Microsoft Word dialog box to replace the previously defined entry.)
- Click the OK button (AutoCorrect dialog box) to close the dialog box.
- Click the OK button (Word Options dialog box) to close the dialog box.

The AutoCorrect Dialog Box

In addition to creating AutoCorrect entries for words you commonly misspell or mistype, you can create entries for abbreviations, codes, and so on. For example, you could create an AutoCorrect entry for asap, indicating that Word should replace this text with the phrase, as soon as possible.

If, for some reason, you do not want Word to correct automatically as you type, you can turn off the Replace text as you type feature by clicking the Options tab in the Backstage view, clicking Proofing in the left pane (Word Options dialog box), clicking the AutoCorrect Options button in the right pane (shown in Figure 2–27), removing the check mark from the 'Replace text as you type' check box, and then clicking the OK button in each open dialog box.

The AutoCorrect sheet in the AutoCorrect dialog box (Figure 2–27) contains other check boxes that correct capitalization errors if the check boxes are selected:

- If you type two capital letters in a row, such as TH, Word makes the second letter lowercase, Th.
- If you begin a sentence with a lowercase letter, Word capitalizes the first letter of the sentence.
- If you type the name of a day in lowercase letters, such as tuesday, Word capitalizes the first letter in the name of the day, Tuesday.
- If you leave the CAPS LOCK key on and begin a new sentence, such as aFTER, Word corrects the typing, After, and turns off the CAPS LOCK key.

If you do not want Word to perform any of these corrections automatically, simply remove the check mark from the appropriate check box in the AutoCorrect dialog box.

Sometimes, you do not want Word to AutoCorrect a particular word or phrase. For example, you may use the code, WD., in your documents. Because Word automatically capitalizes the first letter of a sentence, the character you enter following the period will be capitalized (in the previous sentence, it would capitalize the letter i in the word, in). To allow the code, WD., to be entered into a document and still leave the AutoCorrect feature turned on, you would set an exception. To set an exception to an AutoCorrect rule, click the Options tab in the Backstage view, click Proofing in the left pane (Word Options dialog box), click the AutoCorrect Options button in the right pane, click the Exceptions button (Figure 2–27), click the appropriate tab in the AutoCorrect Exceptions dialog box, type the exception entry in the text box, click the Add button, click the Close button (AutoCorrect Exceptions dialog box), and then click the OK button in each of the remaining dialog boxes.

BTW

Automatic Corrections

If you do not want to keep a change made automatically by Word and you immediately notice the automatic correction, you can undo the change by clicking the Undo button on the Quick Access Toolbar or pressing CTRL+Z. You also can undo a correction through the AutoCorrect Options button (Word Options dialog box) (shown in Figure 2–27).

To Enter More Text

The next task is to continue typing text in the research paper up to the location of the in-text parenthetical reference. The following steps enter this text.

1. With the insertion point positioned at the end of the first paragraph in the paper, as shown in Figure 2–25, press the SPACEBAR and then type these three sentences, intentionally misspelling the word sound as sould: **`With these listening devices, only the individual wearing the device hears the sould. Using headphones or earbuds improperly can lead to permanent hearing loss. Items that may protect hearing include quality of these devices and volume levels.`**

Q&A

Why is the word, sound, misspelled?

Later in this module, you will use Word's check spelling and grammar at once feature to check the entire document for errors.

BTW

Spacing after Punctuation

Because word processing documents use variable character fonts, it often is difficult to determine in a printed document how many times someone has pressed the SPACEBAR between sentences. Thus, the rule is to press the SPACEBAR only once after periods, colons, and other punctuation marks.

2. Press the ENTER key to start a new paragraph.

3. Type `The features of certain headphones and earbuds can help to prevent hearing loss. Higher-quality headphones and earbuds tend to produce a clearer sound, enabling wearers to listen at a lower volume` and then press the SPACEBAR (Figure 2–28).

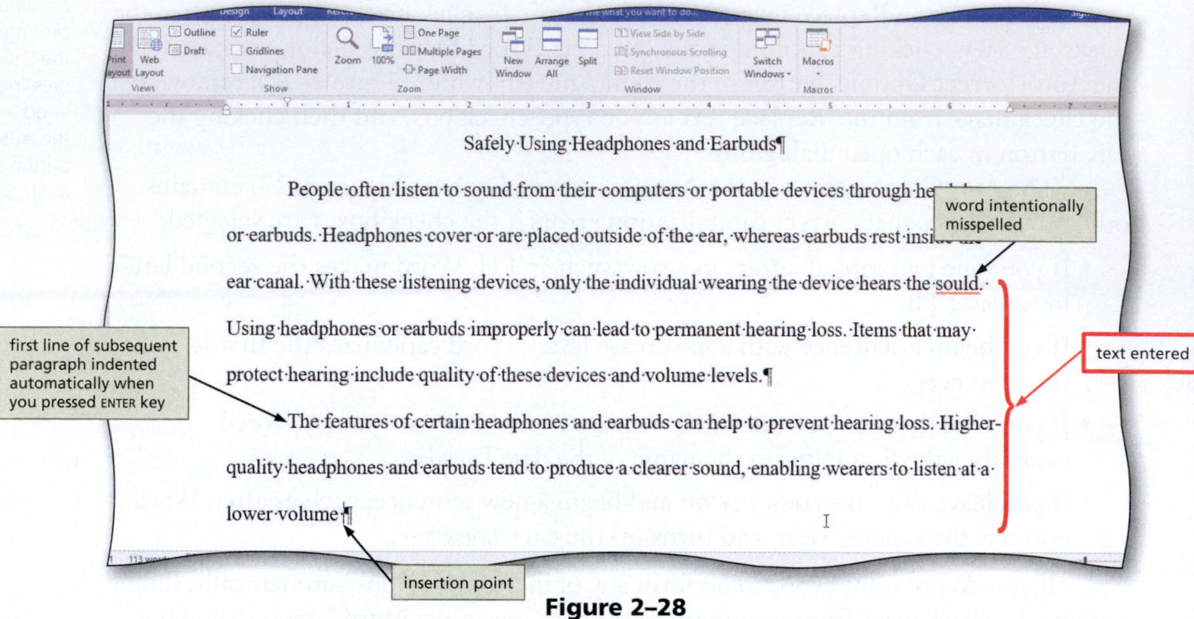

Figure 2–28

Citations

Both the MLA and APA guidelines suggest the use of in-text parenthetical references (placed at the end of a sentence), instead of footnoting each source of material in a paper. These parenthetical references, called citations in Word, guide the reader to the end of the paper for complete information about the source.

Word provides tools to assist you with inserting citations in a paper and later generating a list of sources from the citations. With a documentation style selected, Word automatically formats the citations and list of sources according to that style. The process for adding citations in Word is as follows:

1. Modify the documentation style, if necessary.
2. Insert a citation placeholder.
3. Enter the source information for the citation.

You can combine Steps 2 and 3, where you insert the citation placeholder and enter the source information at once. Or, you can insert the citation placeholder as you write and then enter the source information for the citation at a later time. While creating the research paper in this module, you will use both methods.

BTW
Word Help
At any time while using Word, you can find answers to questions and display information about various topics through Word Help. Used properly, this form of assistance can increase your productivity and reduce your frustrations by minimizing the time you spend learning how to use Word. For instructions about Word Help and exercises that will help you gain confidence in using it, read the Office and Windows module at the beginning of this book.

To Change the Bibliography Style

The first step in inserting a citation is to be sure the citations and sources will be formatted using the correct documentation style, called the bibliography style in Word. ***Why?** You want to ensure that Word is using the MLA documentation style for this paper.* The following steps change the specified documentation style.

- Click References on the ribbon to display the References tab.
- Click the Bibliography Style arrow (References tab | Citations & Bibliography group) to display the Bibliography Style gallery, which lists predefined documentation styles (Figure 2–29).

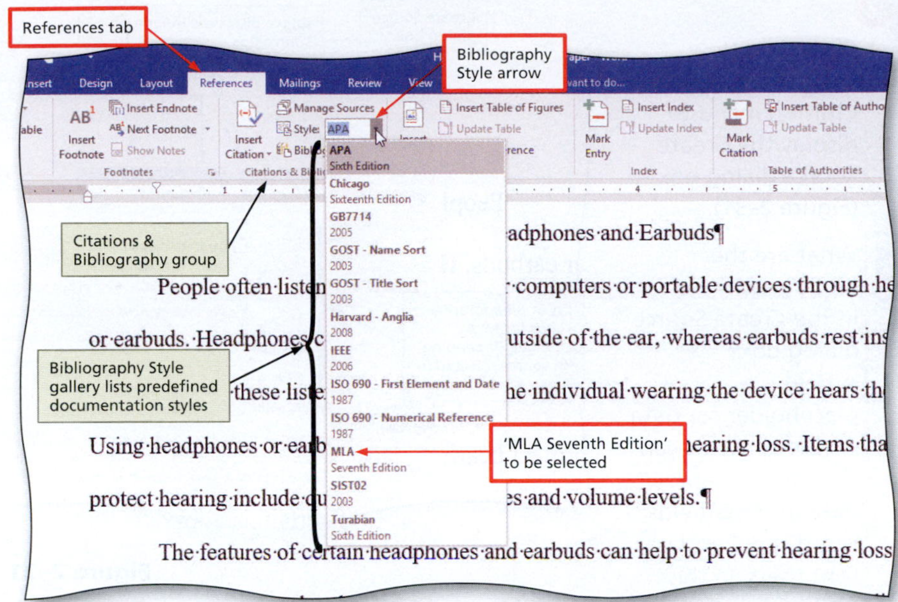

Figure 2–29

2

- Click 'MLA Seventh Edition' in the Bibliography Style gallery to change the documentation style to MLA.

Q&A What if I am using a different edition of a documentation style shown in the Bibliography Style gallery?
Select the closest one and then, if necessary, perform necessary edits before submitting the paper.

CONSIDER THIS

What details are required for sources?

During your research, be sure to record essential publication information about each of your sources. Following is a sample list of types of required information for the MLA documentation style.

- Book: full name of author(s), complete title of book, edition (if available), volume (if available), publication city, publisher name, publication year, and publication medium
- Magazine: full name of author(s), complete title of article, magazine title, issue number (if available), date of magazine, page numbers of article, publication medium, and date viewed (if medium is a website)
- Website: full name of author(s), title of website, website publisher or sponsor (if none, write N.p.), publication date (if none, write n.d.), publication medium, and date viewed

To Insert a Citation and Create Its Source

1 CHANGE DOCUMENT SETTINGS | 2 CREATE HEADER | **3 TYPE RESEARCH PAPER WITH CITATIONS**
4 CREATE ALPHABETICAL WORKS CITED | 5 PROOFREAD & REVISE RESEARCH PAPER

With the documentation style selected, the next task is to insert a citation at the location of the insertion point and enter the source information for the citation. You can accomplish these steps at once by instructing Word to add a new source. The following steps add a new source for a magazine (periodical) article on the web. ***Why?*** *The material preceding the insertion point was summarized from an online magazine article.*

- With the insertion point at the location for the citation (as shown in Figure 2–28), click the Insert Citation button (References tab | Citations & Bibliography group) to display the Insert Citation menu (Figure 2–30).

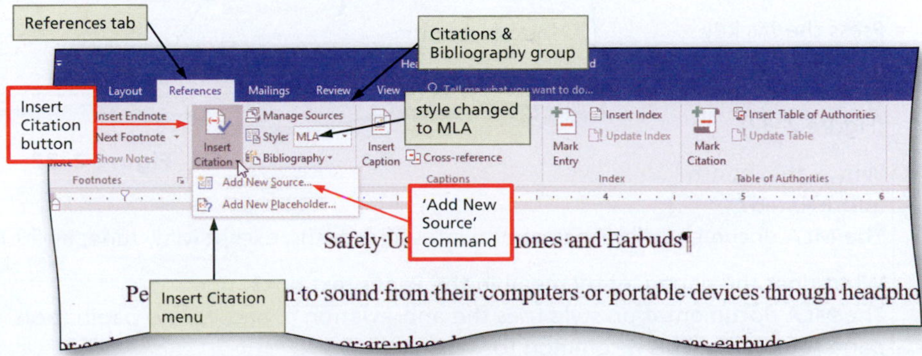

Figure 2–30

2

- Click 'Add New Source' on the Insert Citation menu to display the Create Source dialog box (Figure 2–31).

Q&A What are the Bibliography Fields in the Create Source dialog box?
A **field** is a placeholder for data whose contents can change. You enter data in some fields; Word supplies data for others. In this case, you enter the contents of the fields for a particular source, for example, the author name in the Author field.

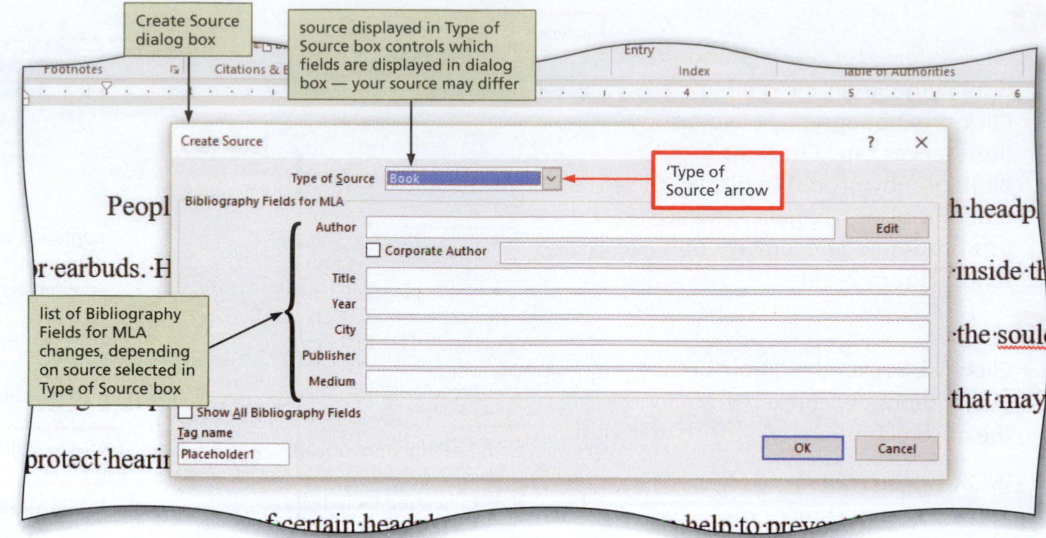

Figure 2–31

Experiment

- Click the 'Type of Source' arrow and then click one of the source types in the list, so that you can see how the list of fields changes to reflect the type of source you selected.

3

- If necessary, click the 'Type of Source' arrow (Create Source dialog box) and then click 'Article in a Periodical', so that the list shows fields required for a magazine (periodical).
- Click the Author text box. Type `Tu, Mingzhu Lin` as the author.
- Click the Title text box. Type `Headphones and Earbuds` as the article title.
- Press the TAB key and then type `Technology and Trends Today` as the periodical title.
- Press the TAB key and then type `2017` as the year.
- Press the TAB key and then type `Aug.` as the month.
- Press the TAB key twice and then type `n. pag.` as the number of pages.
- Press the TAB key and then type `Web` as the medium (Figure 2–32).

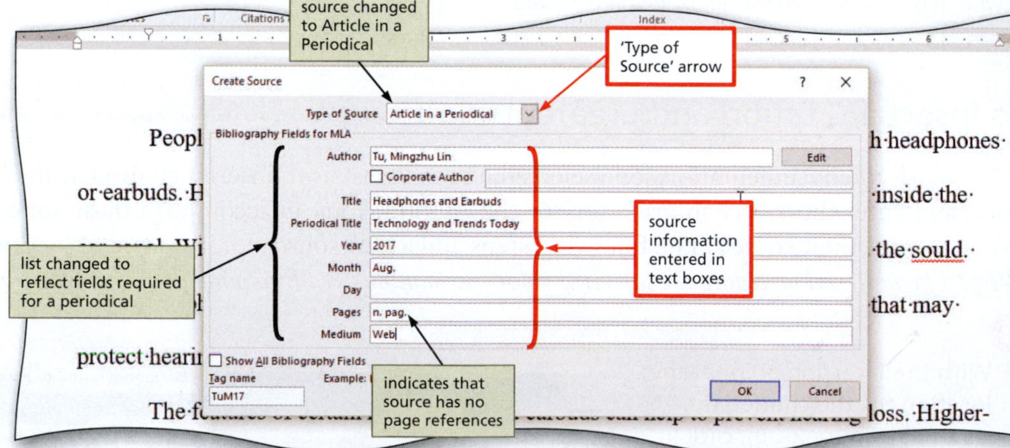

Figure 2–32

Q&A Why is the month abbreviated?
The MLA documentation style abbreviates all months, except May, June, and July, when they appear in a source.

What does the n. pag. entry mean in the Pages text box?
The MLA documentation style uses the abbreviation n. pag. for no pagination, which indicates the source has no page references. This is common for web sources.

4

- Place a check mark in the 'Show All Bibliography Fields' check box so that Word displays all fields available for the selected source, including the date viewed (accessed) fields.
- If necessary, scroll to the bottom of the Bibliography Fields list to display the date viewed (accessed) fields.
- Click the Year Accessed text box. Type `2017` as the year.
- Press the TAB key and then type `Oct.` as the month accessed.
- Press the TAB key and then type `3` as the day accessed (Figure 2–33).

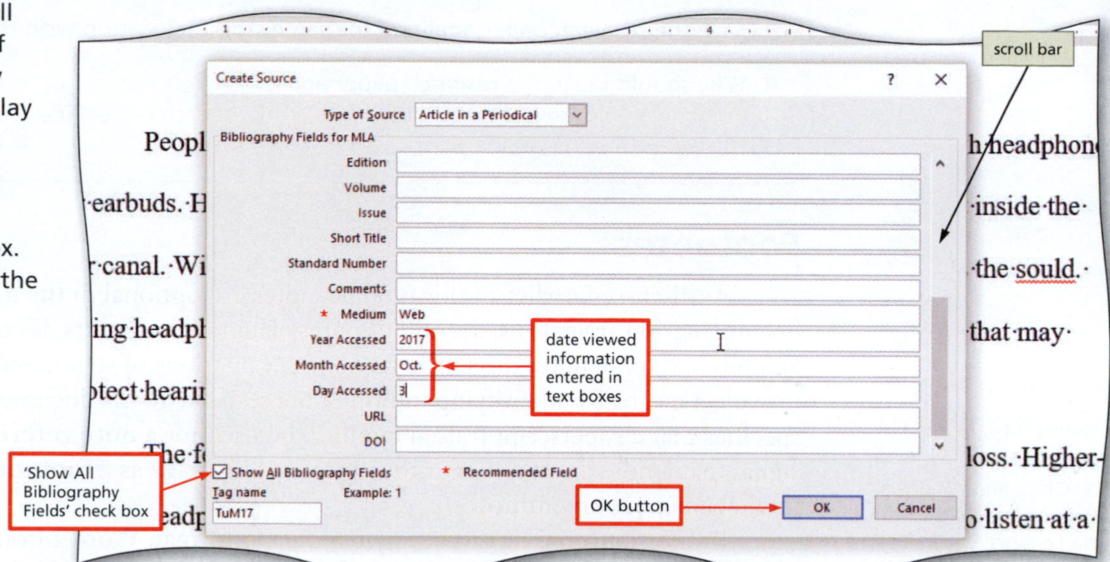

Figure 2–33

What if some of the text boxes disappear as I enter the fields?
With the 'Show All Bibliography Fields' check box selected, the dialog box may not be able to display all fields at the same time. In this case, some may scroll up off the screen.

5

- Click the OK button to close the dialog box, create the source, and insert the citation in the document at the location of the insertion point.
- Press the END key to move the insertion point to the end of the line, if necessary, which also deselects the citation.
- Press the PERIOD key to end the sentence (Figure 2–34).

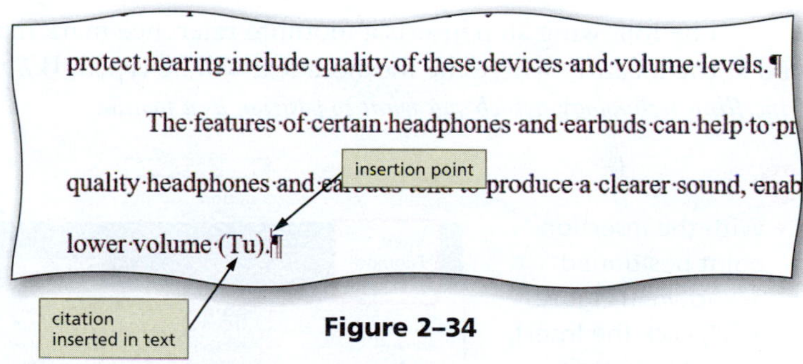

Figure 2–34

To Enter More Text

The next task is to continue typing text in the research paper up to the location of the footnote. The following steps enter this text.

1 Press the SPACEBAR.

2 Type the next sentences (Figure 2–35): **`Properly designed headphones`**

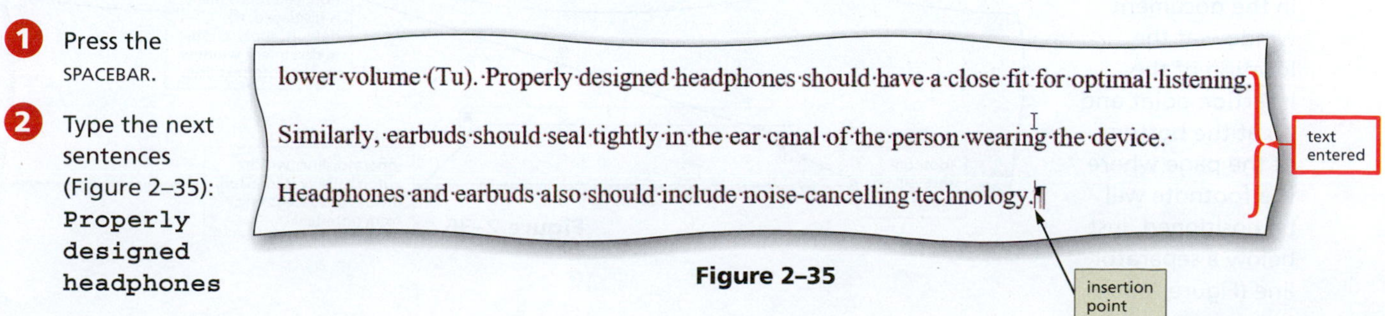

Figure 2–35

```
should have a close fit for optimal listening. Similarly,
earbuds should seal tightly in the ear canal of the person
wearing the device. Headphones and earbuds also should
include noise-cancelling technology.
```

3 Save the research paper again on the same storage location with the same file name.

Q&A Why should I save the research paper again?
You have made several modifications to the research paper since you last saved it; thus, you should save it again.

Footnotes

BTW
Touch Screen Differences
The Office and Windows interfaces may vary if you are using a touch screen. For this reason, you might notice that the function or appearance of your touch screen differs slightly from this module's presentation.

As discussed earlier in this module, notes are optional in the MLA documentation style. If used, content notes elaborate on points discussed in the paper, and bibliographic notes direct the reader to evaluations of statements in a source or provide a means for identifying multiple sources. The MLA documentation style specifies that a superscript (raised number) be used for a **note reference mark** to signal that a note exists either at the bottom of the page as a **footnote** or at the end of the document as an **endnote**.

In Word, **note text** can be any length and format. Word automatically numbers notes sequentially by placing a note reference mark both in the body of the document and to the left of the note text. If you insert, rearrange, or remove notes, Word renumbers any subsequent note reference marks according to their new sequence in the document.

To Insert a Footnote Reference Mark

1 CHANGE DOCUMENT SETTINGS | 2 CREATE HEADER | 3 TYPE RESEARCH PAPER WITH CITATIONS
4 CREATE ALPHABETICAL WORKS CITED | 5 PROOFREAD & REVISE RESEARCH PAPER

The following step inserts a footnote reference mark in the document at the location of the insertion point and at the location where the footnote text will be typed. *Why? You will insert a content note elaborating on noise-cancelling technology, which you want to position as a footnote.*

- With the insertion point positioned as shown in Figure 2–35, click the Insert Footnote button (References tab | Footnotes group) to display a note reference mark (a superscripted 1) in two places: (1) in the document window at the location of the insertion point and (2) at the bottom of the page where the footnote will be positioned, just below a separator line (Figure 2–36).

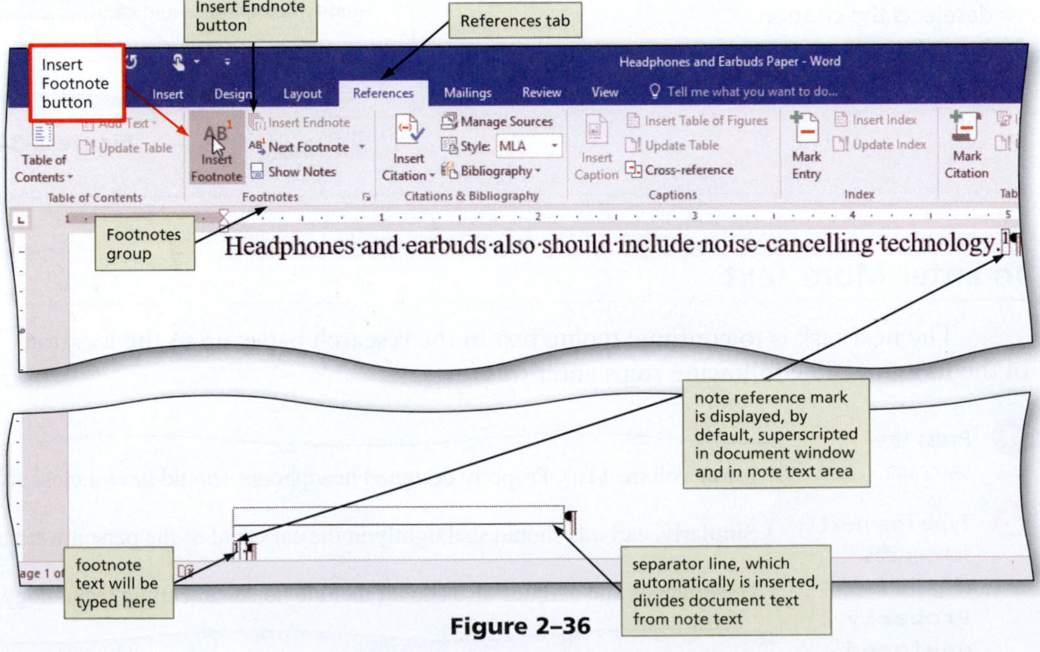

Figure 2–36

Q&A What if I wanted notes to be positioned as endnotes instead of as footnotes?
You would click the Insert Endnote button (References tab | Footnotes group), which places the separator line and the endnote text at the end of the document, instead of the bottom of the page containing the reference.

Other Ways

1. Press ALT+CTRL+F

To Enter Footnote Text

The following step types the footnote text to the right of the note reference mark below the separator line.

Type the footnote text up to the citation (shown in Figure 2–37): **Gupta and Padro state that effective noise-cancelling technology reduces the interference of sounds from the surrounding environment, reducing the volume level required by headphones and earbuds** and then press the SPACEBAR.

To Insert a Citation Placeholder

1 CHANGE DOCUMENT SETTINGS | 2 CREATE HEADER | 3 TYPE RESEARCH PAPER WITH CITATIONS
4 CREATE ALPHABETICAL WORKS CITED | 5 PROOFREAD & REVISE RESEARCH PAPER

Earlier in this module, you inserted a citation and its source at once. In Word, you also can insert a citation without entering the source information. ***Why?*** *Sometimes, you may not have the source information readily available and would prefer to enter it at a later time.*

The following steps insert a citation placeholder in the footnote, so that you can enter the source information later.

1

- With the insertion point positioned as shown in Figure 2–37, click the Insert Citation button (References tab | Citations & Bibliography group) to display the Insert Citation menu (Figure 2–37).

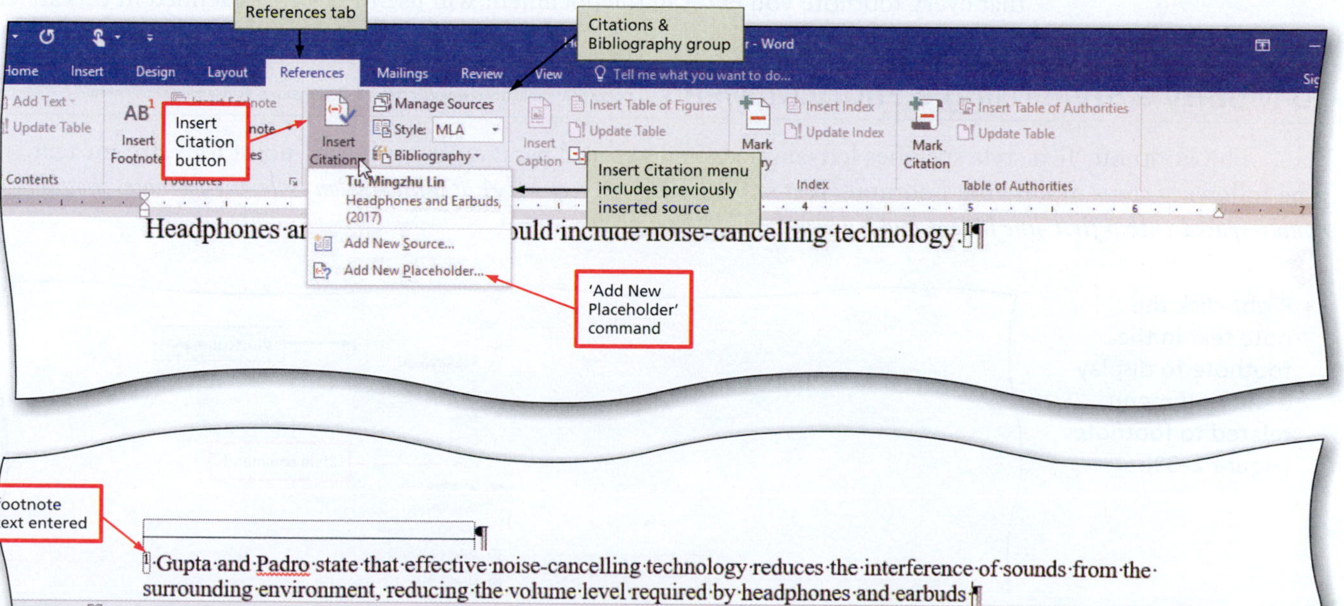

Figure 2–37

2

- Click 'Add New Placeholder' on the Insert Citation menu to display the Placeholder Name dialog box.
- Type `Gupta` as the tag name for the source (Figure 2–38).

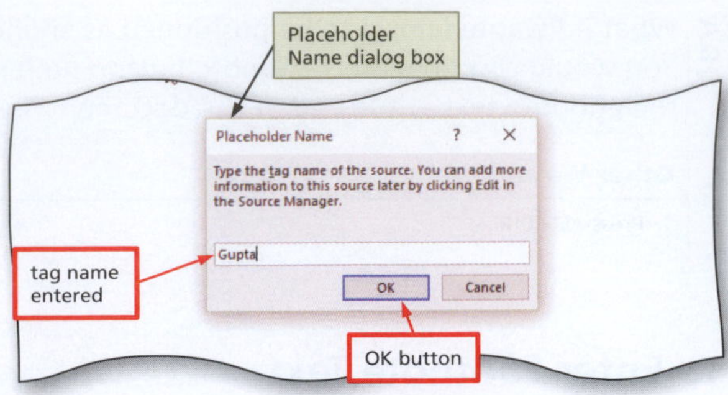

Figure 2–38

Q&A What is a tag name?
A tag name is an identifier that links a citation to a source. Word automatically creates a tag name when you enter a source. When you create a citation placeholder, enter a meaningful tag name, which will appear in the citation placeholder until you edit the source.

3

- Click the OK button (Placeholder Name dialog box) to close the dialog box and insert the entered tag name in the citation placeholder in the document (shown in Figure 2–39).
- Press the PERIOD key to end the sentence.

Q&A What if the citation is in the wrong location?
Click the citation to select it and then drag the citation tab (on the upper-left corner of the selected citation) to any location in the document.

Footnote Text Style

When you insert a footnote, Word formats it using the Footnote Text style, which does not adhere to the MLA documentation style. For example, notice in Figure 2–37 that the footnote text is single-spaced, left-aligned, and a smaller font size than the text in the research paper. According to the MLA documentation style, notes should be formatted like all other paragraphs in the paper.

You could change the paragraph formatting of the footnote text to first-line indent and double-spacing and then change the font size from 10 to 12 point. If you use this technique, however, you will need to change the format of the footnote text for each footnote you enter into the document.

A more efficient technique is to modify the format of the Footnote Text style so that every footnote you enter in the document will use the formats defined in this style.

To Modify a Style Using a Shortcut Menu

1 CHANGE DOCUMENT SETTINGS | 2 CREATE HEADER | 3 TYPE RESEARCH PAPER WITH CITATIONS
4 CREATE ALPHABETICAL WORKS CITED | 5 PROOFREAD & REVISE RESEARCH PAPER

The Footnote Text style specifies left-aligned single-spaced paragraphs with a 10-point font size for text. The following steps modify the Footnote Text style. ***Why?*** *To meet MLA documentation style, the footnotes should be double-spaced with a first-line indent and a 12-point font size for text.*

1

- Right-click the note text in the footnote to display a shortcut menu related to footnotes (Figure 2–39).

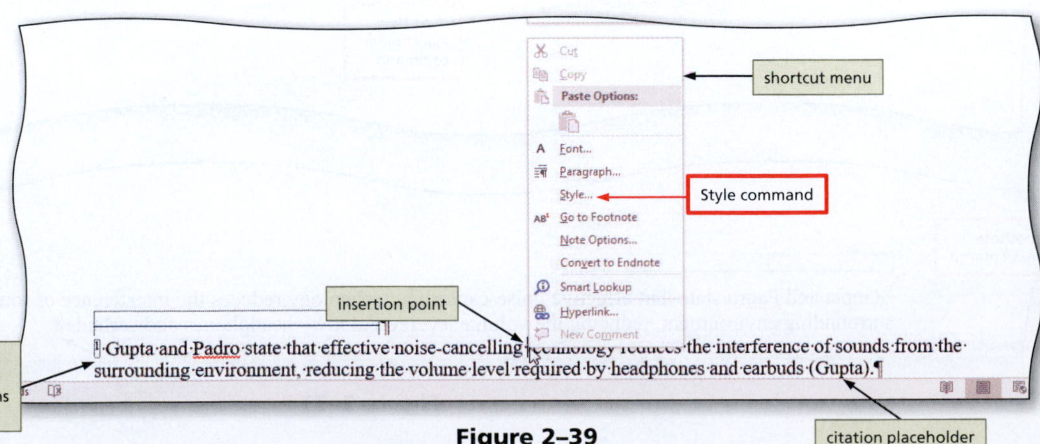

Figure 2–39

2

- Click Style on the shortcut menu to display the Style dialog box. If necessary, click the Category arrow, click All styles in the Category list, and then click Footnote Text in the Styles list to select the style to modify.
- Click the Modify button (Style dialog box) to display the Modify Style dialog box.
- Click the Font Size arrow (Modify Style dialog box) to display the Font Size list and then click 12 in the Font Size list to change the font size.
- Click the Double Space button to change the line spacing.
- Click the Format button to display the Format menu (Figure 2–40).

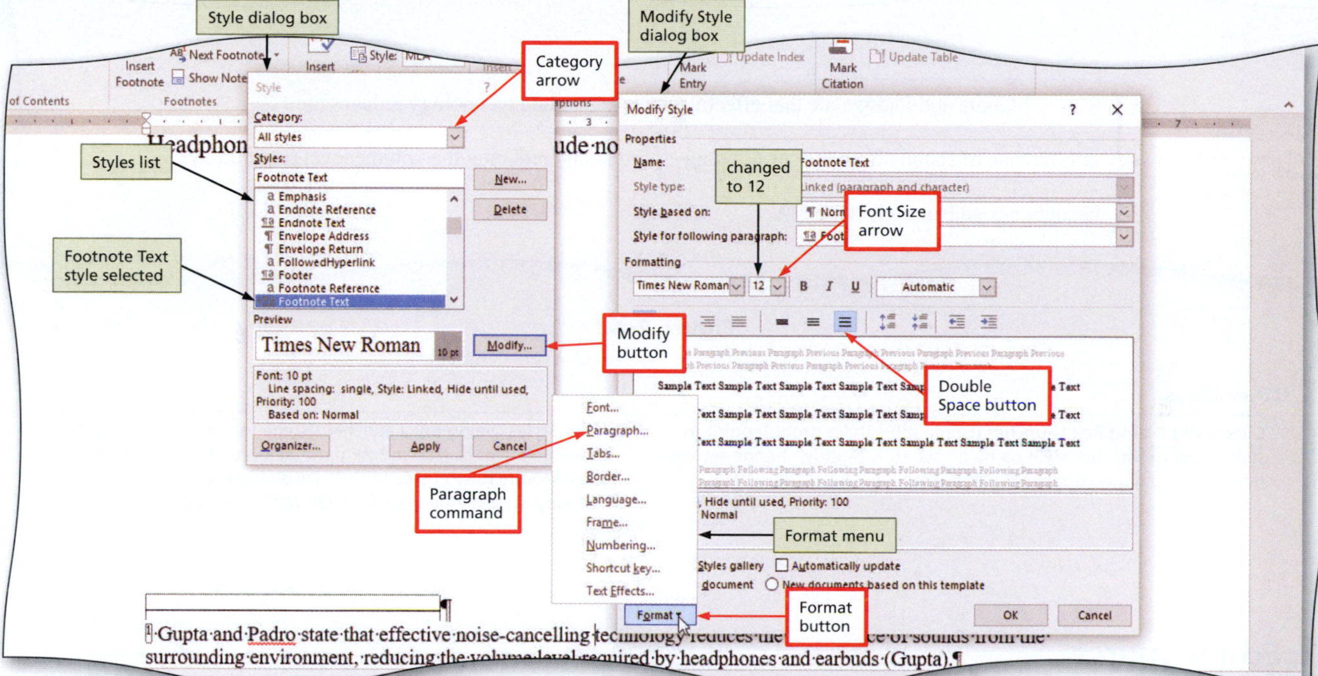

Figure 2–40

3

- Click Paragraph on the Format menu (Modify Style dialog box) to display the Paragraph dialog box.
- Click the Special arrow in the Indentation area (Paragraph dialog box) and then click First line (Figure 2–41).

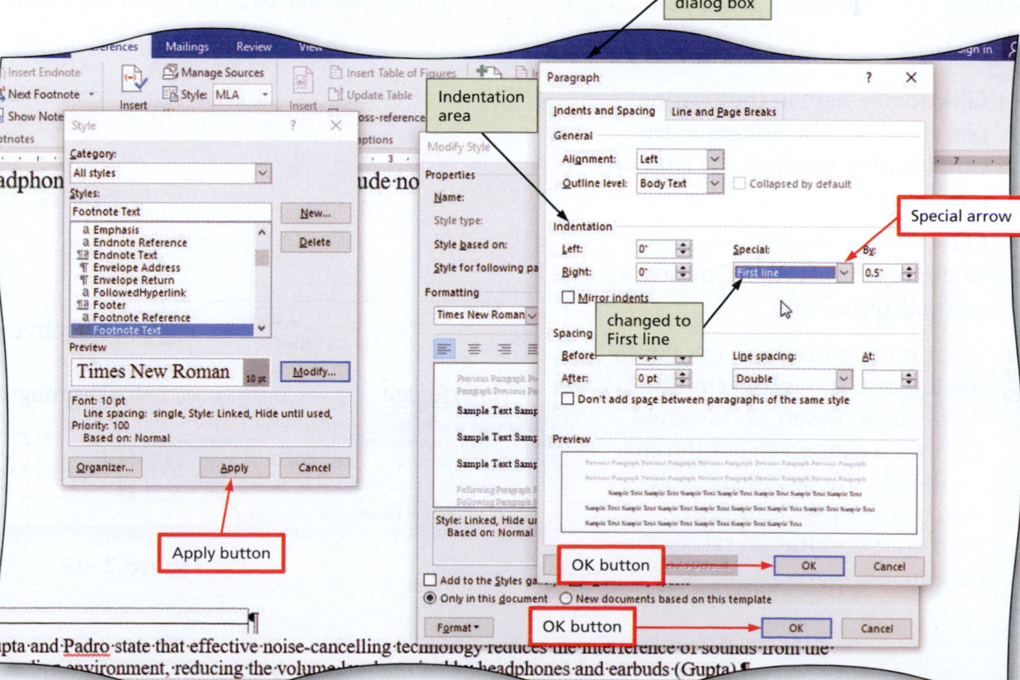

Figure 2–41

- Click the OK button (Paragraph dialog box) to close the dialog box.
- Click the OK button (Modify Style dialog box) to close the dialog box.
- Click the Apply button (Style dialog box) to apply the style changes to the footnote text (Figure 2–42).

Q&A Will all footnotes use this modified style?
Yes. Any future footnotes entered in the document will use a 12-point font with the paragraphs first-line indented and double-spaced.

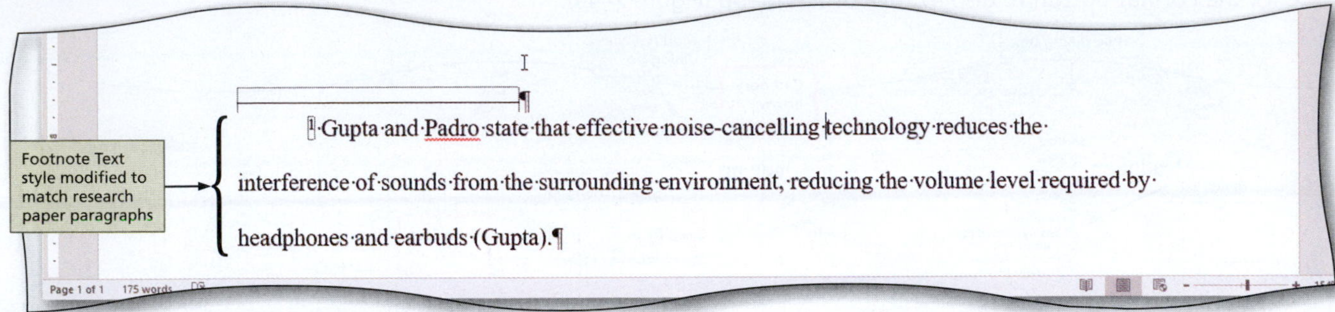

Figure 2–42

Other Ways

1. Click Styles Dialog Box Launcher (Home tab | Styles group), point to style name in list, click style name arrow, click Modify, change settings (Modify Style dialog box), click OK button
2. Click Styles Dialog Box Launcher (Home tab | Styles group), click Manage Styles button in task pane, select style name in list, click Modify button (Manage Styles dialog box), change settings (Modify Style dialog box), click OK button in each dialog box

To Edit a Source

1 CHANGE DOCUMENT SETTINGS | 2 CREATE HEADER | 3 TYPE RESEARCH PAPER WITH CITATIONS
4 CREATE ALPHABETICAL WORKS CITED | 5 PROOFREAD & REVISE RESEARCH PAPER

When you typed the footnote text for this research paper, you inserted a citation placeholder for the source. The following steps edit a source. ***Why?*** *Assume you now have the source information and are ready to enter it.*

- Click somewhere in the citation placeholder to be edited, in this case (Gupta), to select the citation placeholder.
- Click the Citation Options arrow to display the Citation Options menu (Figure 2–43).

Q&A What is the purpose of the tab to the left of the selected citation?
If, for some reason, you wanted to move a citation to a different location in the document, you would select the citation and then drag the citation tab to the desired location.

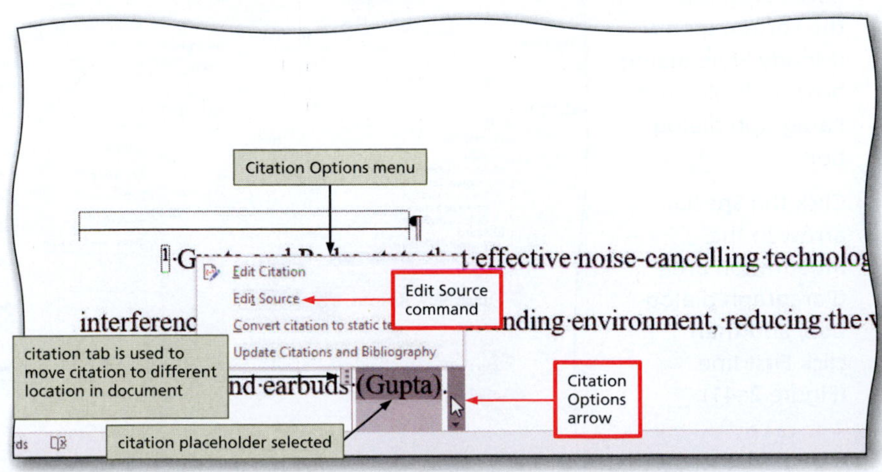

Figure 2–43

2

- Click Edit Source on the Citation Options menu to display the Edit Source dialog box.
- If necessary, click the 'Type of Source' arrow (Edit Source dialog box) and then click Book, so that the list shows fields required for a book.
- Because this source has two authors, click the Edit button to display the Edit Name dialog box, which assists you with entering multiple author names.
- Type **Gupta** as the first author's last name; press the TAB key and then type **Elena** as the first name; press the TAB key and then type **Maia** as the middle name (Figure 2–44).

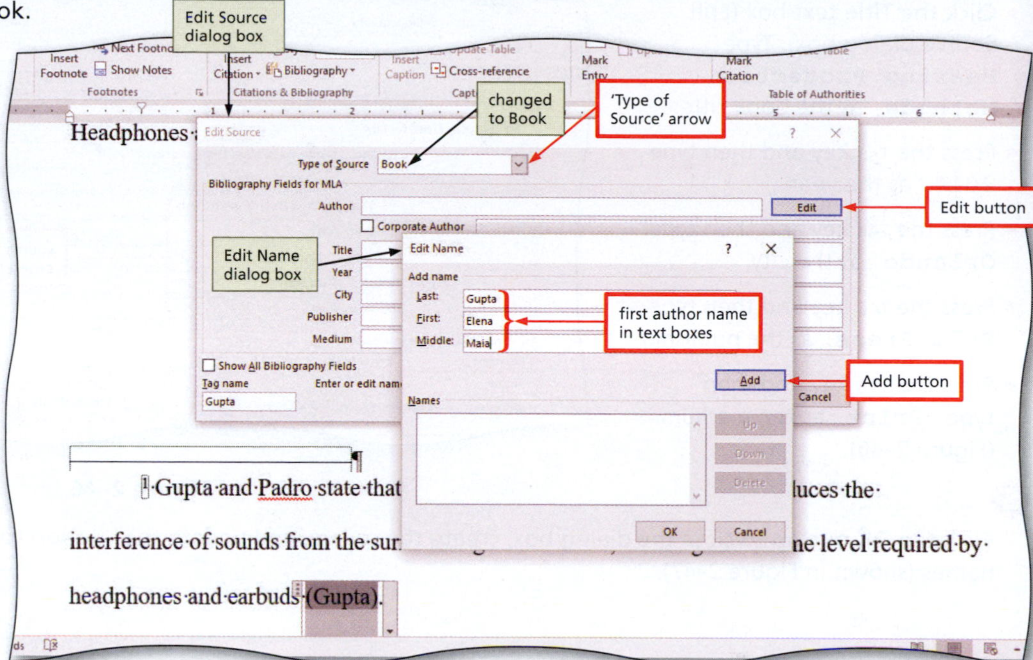

Figure 2–44

Q&A What if I already know how to punctuate the author entry properly?
You can enter the name directly in the Author box.

3

- Click the Add button (Edit Name dialog box) to add the first author name to the Names list.
- Type **Padro** as the second author's last name; press the TAB key and then type **Adelbert** as the first name; press the TAB key and then type **Luis** as the middle name.
- Click the Add button (Edit Name dialog box) to add the second author name to the Names list (Figure 2–45).

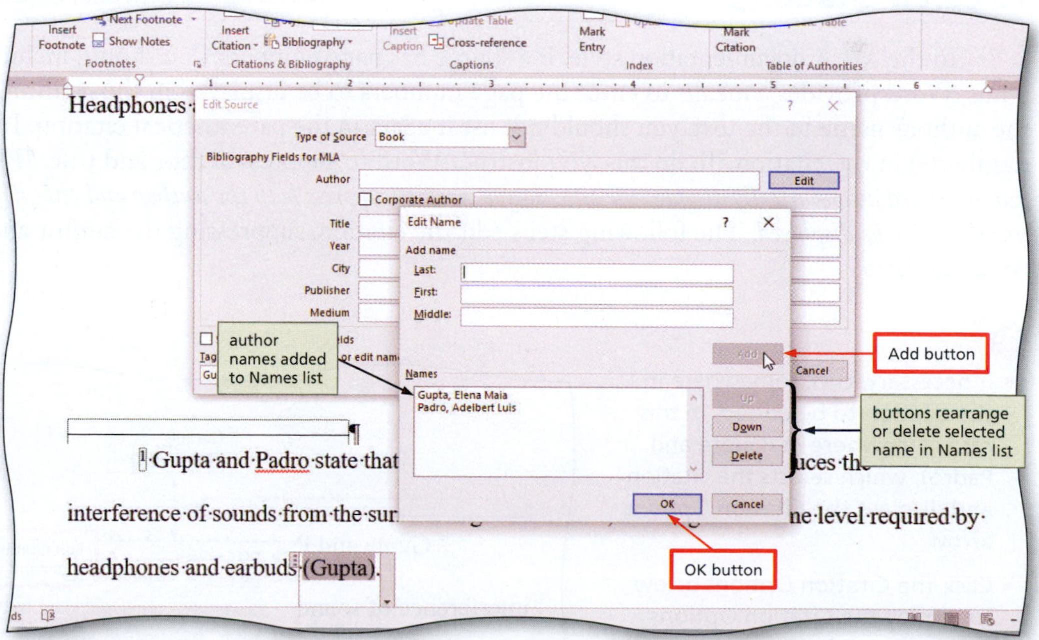

Figure 2–45

- Click the OK button (Edit Name dialog box) to add the author names that appear in the Names list to the Author box in the Edit Source dialog box.
- Click the Title text box (Edit Source dialog box). Type **Hearing Protection Methods** as the book title.
- Press the TAB key and then type **2017** as the year.
- Press the TAB key and then type **Orlando** as the city.
- Press the TAB key and then type **Palm Press** as the publisher.
- Press the TAB key and then type **Print** as the medium (Figure 2–46).

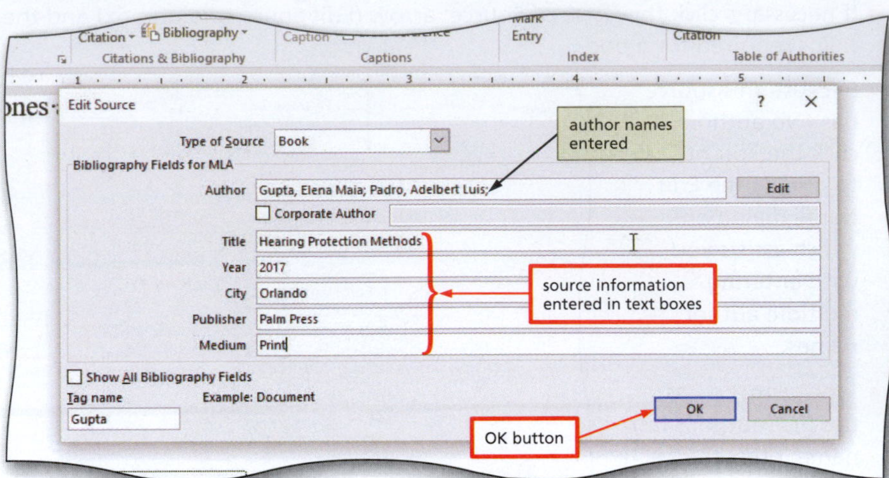

Figure 2–46

- Click the OK button to close the dialog box, create the source, and update the citation to display both author last names (shown in Figure 2–47).

Other Ways

1. Click Manage Sources button (References tab | Citations & Bibliography group), click placeholder source in Current List, click Edit button (Source Manager dialog box)

To Edit a Citation

1 CHANGE DOCUMENT SETTINGS | 2 CREATE HEADER | 3 TYPE RESEARCH PAPER WITH CITATIONS
4 CREATE ALPHABETICAL WORKS CITED | 5 PROOFREAD & REVISE RESEARCH PAPER

In the MLA documentation style, if a source has page numbers, you should include them in the citation. Thus, Word provides a means to enter the page numbers to be displayed in the citation. Also, if you reference the author's name in the text, you should not list it again in the parenthetical citation. Instead, just list the page number(s) in the citation. To do this, you instruct Word to suppress author and title. ***Why?*** *If you suppress the author, Word automatically displays the title, so you need to suppress both the author and title if you want just the page number(s) to be displayed.* The following steps edit the citation, suppressing the author and title but displaying the page numbers.

- If necessary, click somewhere in the citation to be edited, in this case somewhere in (Gupta and Padro), which selects the citation and displays the Citation Options arrow.
- Click the Citation Options arrow to display the Citation Options menu (Figure 2–47).

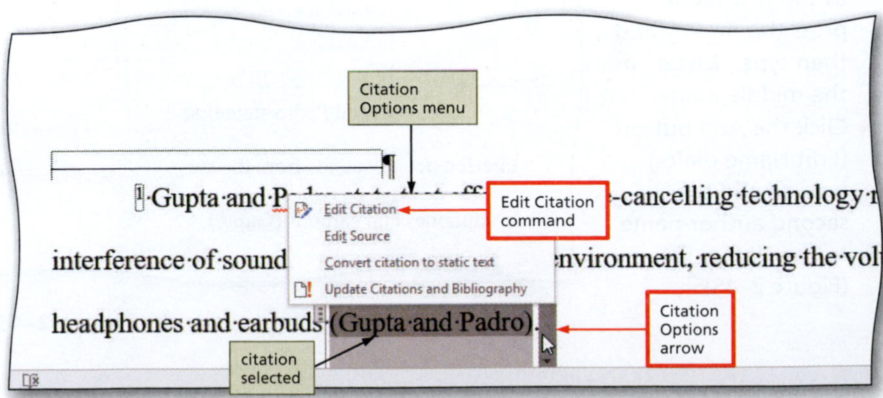

Figure 2–47

2

- Click Edit Citation on the Citation Options menu to display the Edit Citation dialog box.
- Type `75-78` in the Pages text box (Edit Citation dialog box).
- Click the Author check box to place a check mark in it.
- Click the Title check box to place a check mark in it (Figure 2–48).

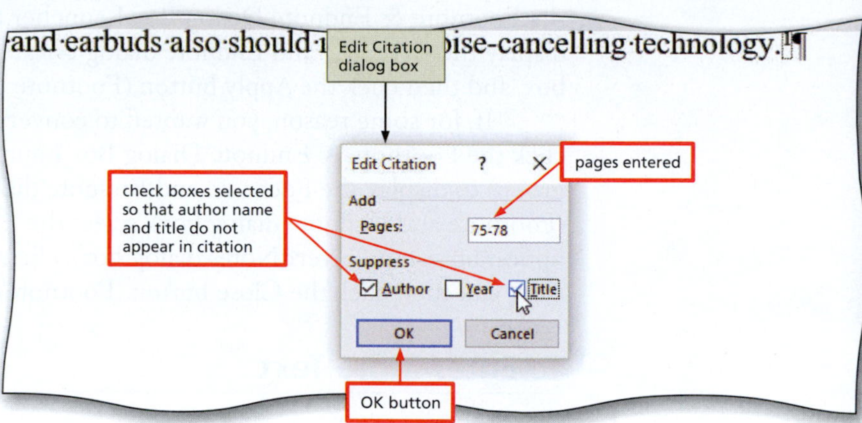

Figure 2–48

3

- Click the OK button to close the dialog box, remove the author names from the citation in the footnote, suppress the title from showing, and add page numbers to the citation.
- Press the END key to move the insertion point to the end of the line, which also deselects the citation (Figure 2–49).

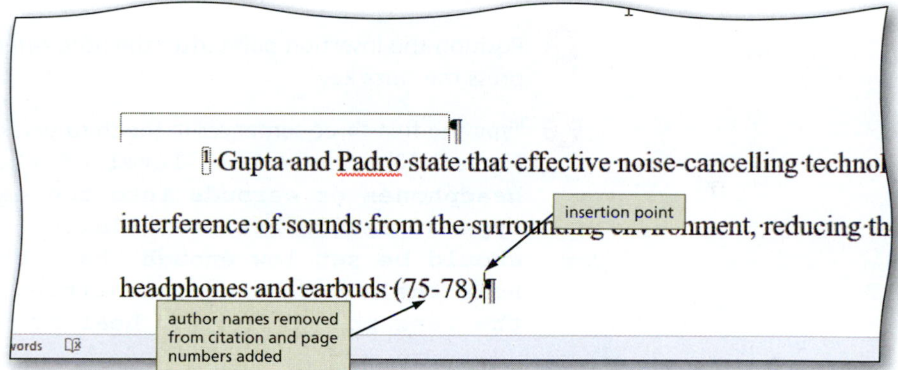

Figure 2–49

Working with Footnotes and Endnotes

You edit footnote text just as you edit any other text in the document. To delete or move a note reference mark, however, the insertion point must be in the document text (not in the footnote text).

To delete a note, select the note reference mark in the document text (not in the footnote text) by dragging through the note reference mark and then click the Cut button (Home tab | Clipboard group). Or, click immediately to the right of the note reference mark in the document text and then press the BACKSPACE key twice, or click immediately to the left of the note reference mark in the document text and then press the DELETE key twice.

To move a note to a different location in a document, select the note reference mark in the document text (not in the footnote text), click the Cut button (Home tab | Clipboard group), click the location where you want to move the note, and then click the Paste button (Home tab | Clipboard group). When you move or delete notes, Word automatically renumbers any remaining notes in the correct sequence.

If you are using a mouse and position the pointer on the note reference mark in the document text, the note text is displayed above the note reference mark as a ScreenTip. To remove the ScreenTip, move the pointer.

If, for some reason, you wanted to change the format of note reference marks in footnotes or endnotes (i.e., from 1, 2, 3 to A, B, C), you would click the Footnote & Endnote Dialog Box Launcher (References tab | Footnotes group) to display the Footnote and Endnote dialog box, click the Number format arrow (Footnote and Endnote dialog box), click the desired number format in the list, and then click the Apply button.

BTW

Footnote and Endnote Location

You can change the location of footnotes from the bottom of the page to the end of the text by clicking the Footnote & Endnote Dialog Box Launcher (References tab | Footnotes group), clicking the Footnotes arrow (Footnote and Endnote dialog box), and then clicking Below text. Similarly, clicking the Endnotes arrow (Footnote and Endnote dialog box) enables you to change the location of endnotes from the end of the document to the end of a section.

If, for some reason, you wanted to change a footnote number, you would click the Footnote & Endnote Dialog Box Launcher (References tab | Footnotes group) to display the Footnote and Endnote dialog box, enter the desired number in the Start at box, and then click the Apply button (Footnote and Endnote dialog box).

If, for some reason, you wanted to convert footnotes to endnotes, you would click the Footnote & Endnote Dialog Box Launcher (References tab | Footnotes group) to display the Footnote and Endnote dialog box, click the Convert button (Footnote and Endnote dialog box), select the 'Convert all footnotes to endnotes' option button (Convert Notes dialog box), click the OK button (Convert Notes dialog box), and then click the Close button (Footnote and Endnote dialog box).

To Enter More Text

The next task is to continue typing text in the body of the research paper. The following steps enter this text.

1. Position the insertion point after the note reference mark in the document and then press the ENTER key.

2. Type the first three sentences in the third paragraph of the research paper (shown in Figure 2–50): **The volume level of the sound that transmits from headphones or earbuds into the ear of a person wearing this type of device has been linked to hearing loss. The volume should be set low enough that other people nearby cannot hear the sound being transmitted. The quieter the sounds, the less possibility of hearing damage.**

To Count Words

1 CHANGE DOCUMENT SETTINGS | 2 CREATE HEADER | 3 TYPE RESEARCH PAPER WITH CITATIONS
4 CREATE ALPHABETICAL WORKS CITED | 5 PROOFREAD & REVISE RESEARCH PAPER

Often when you write papers, you are required to compose the papers with a minimum number of words. The minimum requirement for the research paper in this module is 275 words. You can look on the status bar and see the total number of words thus far in a document. For example, Figure 2–50 shows the research paper has 231 words, but you are not sure if that count includes the words in your footnote. The following steps display the Word Count dialog box. ***Why?** You want to verify that the footnote text is included in the count.*

1

- Click the Word Count indicator on the status bar to display the Word Count dialog box.
- If necessary, place a check mark in the 'Include textboxes, footnotes and endnotes' check box (Word Count dialog box) (Figure 2–50).

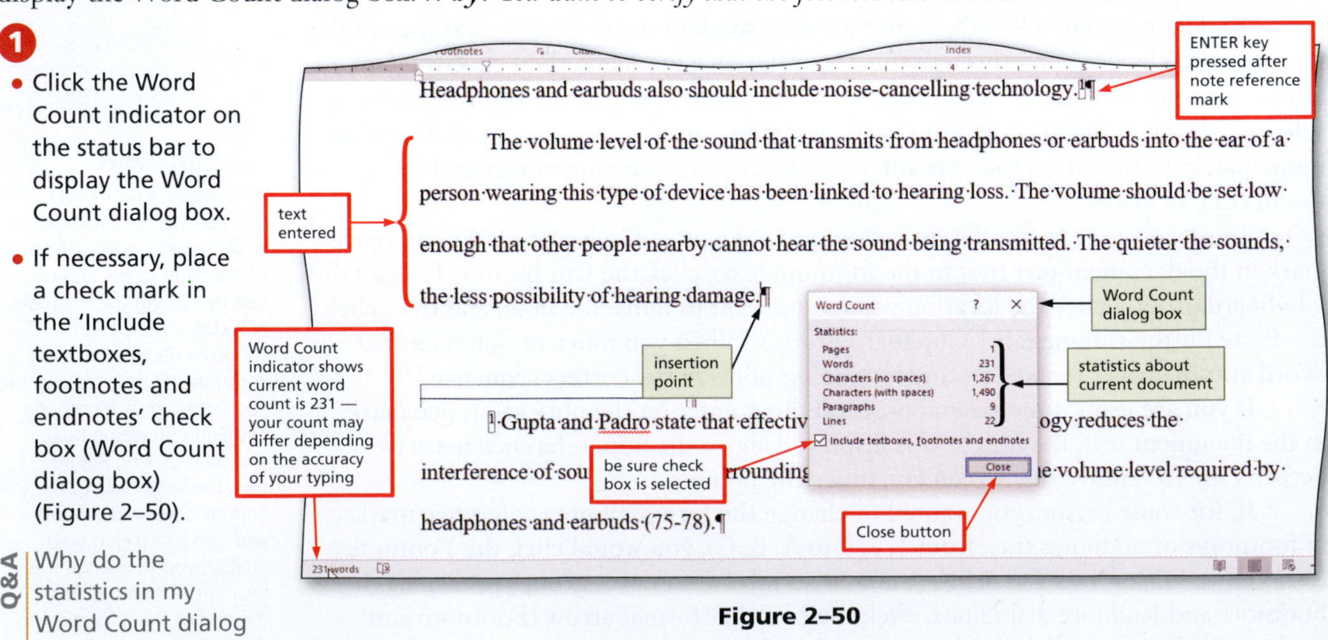

Figure 2–50

Q&A Why do the statistics in my Word Count dialog box differ from those in Figure 2–50?
Depending on the accuracy of your typing, your statistics may differ.

2

- Click the Close button (Word Count dialog box) to close the dialog box.

Q&A Can I display statistics for just a section of the document?
Yes. Select the section and then click the Word Count indicator on the status bar to display statistics about the selected text.

Other Ways

1. Click Word Count button (Review tab | Proofing group)
2. Press CTRL+SHIFT+G

Automatic Page Breaks

As you type documents that exceed one page, Word automatically inserts page breaks, called **automatic page breaks** or **soft page breaks**, when it determines the text has filled one page according to paper size, margin settings, line spacing, and other settings. If you add text, delete text, or modify text on a page, Word recalculates the location of automatic page breaks and adjusts them accordingly.

Word performs page recalculation between the keystrokes, that is, in between the pauses in your typing. Thus, Word refers to the automatic page break task as **background repagination**. An automatic page break will occur in the next set of steps.

To Enter More Text and Insert a Citation Placeholder

The next task is to type the remainder of the third paragraph in the body of the research paper. The following steps enter this text and a citation placeholder at the end of the paragraph.

1 With the insertion point positioned at the end of the third sentence in the third paragraph, as shown in Figure 2–50, press the SPACEBAR.

2 Type the rest of the third paragraph: `Further, listening at a higher volume for extended periods of time could be unsafe. One expert suggests people should listen at only 30 percent maximum` and then press the SPACEBAR.

Q&A Why does the text move from the second page to the first page as I am typing?
Word, by default, will not allow the first line of a paragraph to be by itself at the bottom of a page (an **orphan**) or the last line of a paragraph to be by itself at the top of a page (a **widow**). As you type, Word adjusts the placement of the paragraph to avoid orphans and widows.

3 Click the Insert Citation button (References tab | Citations & Bibliography group) to display the Insert Citation menu. Click 'Add New Placeholder' on the Insert Citation menu to display the Placeholder Name dialog box.

4 Type `Chamberlain` as the tag name for the source.

5 Click the OK button (Placeholder Name dialog box) to close the dialog box and insert the tag name in the citation placeholder (shown in Figure 2–51).

6 Press the PERIOD key to end the sentence.

BTW
Page Break Locations
As you type, your page break may occur at different locations depending on Word settings and the type of printer connected to the computer.

To Hide and Show White Space

With the page break and header, it is difficult to see the entire third paragraph at once on the screen. With the screen in Print Layout view, you can hide white space, which is the space that is displayed at the top and bottom of pages (including headers and footers) and also the space between pages. The following steps hide white space, if your screen displays it, and then shows white space. ***Why?*** *You want to see as much of the third paragraph as possible at once, which spans the bottom of the first page and the top of the second page.*

1

- Position the pointer in the document window in the space between pages so that the pointer changes to a 'Hide White Space' button (Figure 2–51).

Q&A What if I am using a touch screen?
Proceed to step 2.

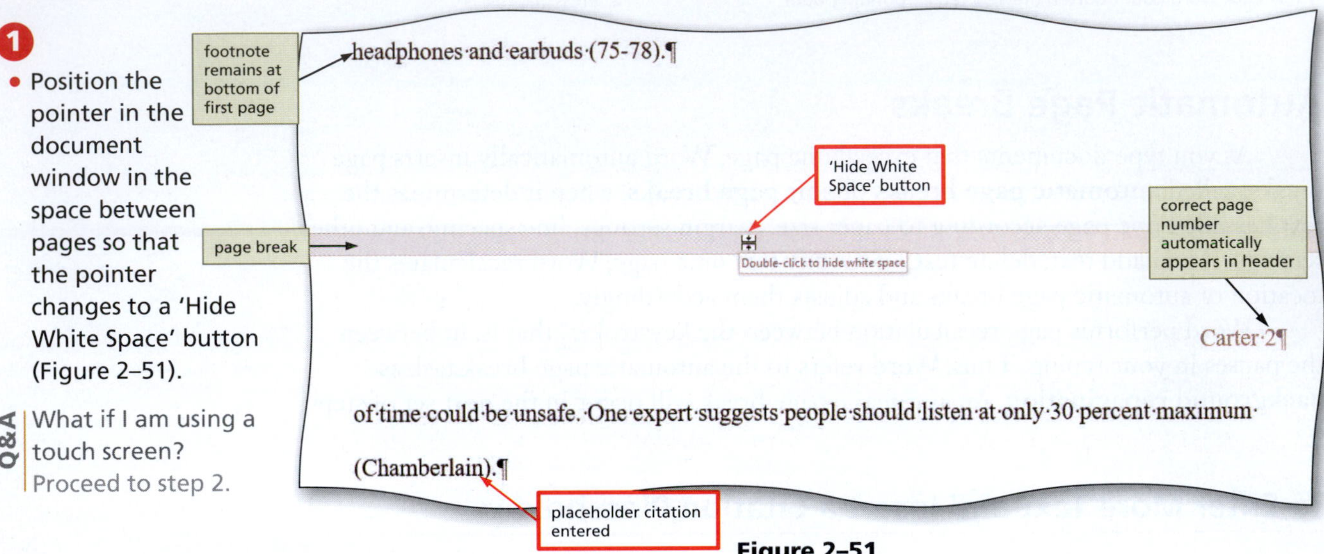

Figure 2–51

2

- Double-click while the pointer is a 'Hide White Space' button to hide white space.

Q&A What if I am using a touch screen?
Double-tap in the space between pages.

Does hiding white space have any effect on the printed document?
No.

3

- Position the pointer in the document window on the page break between pages so that the pointer changes to a 'Show White Space' button (Figure 2–52).

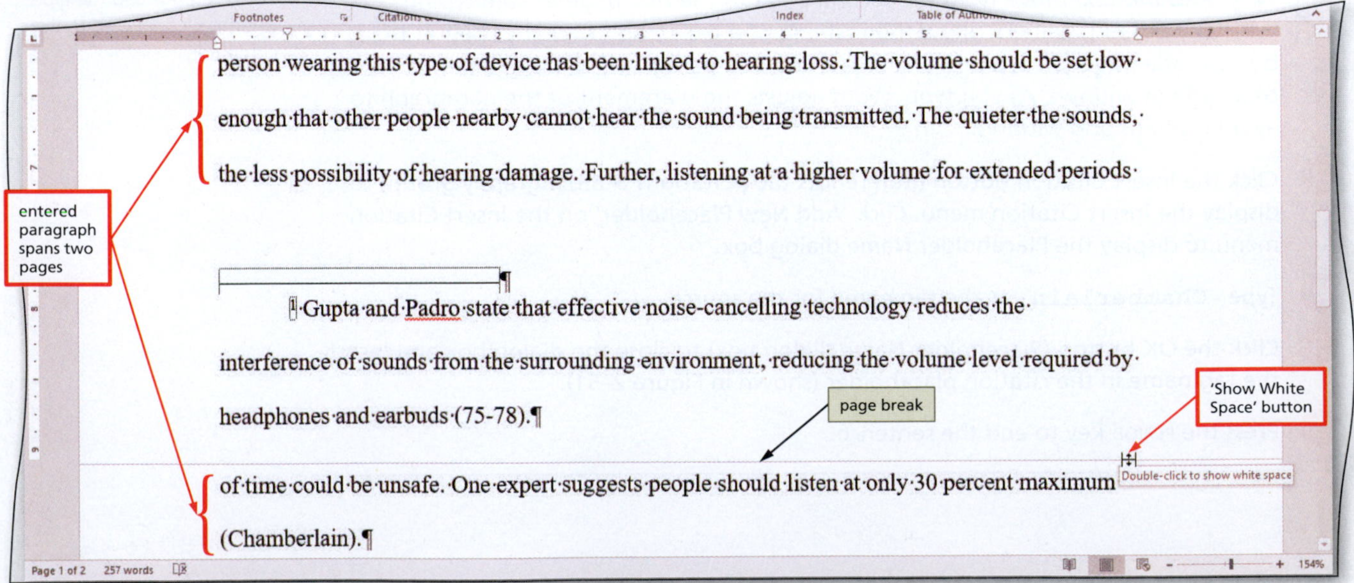

Figure 2–52

4

- Double-click while the pointer is a 'Show White Space' button to show white space.

Q&A What if I am using a touch screen?
Double-tap the page break.

Other Ways

1. Click File on ribbon, click Options tab in Backstage view, click Display in left pane (Word Options dialog box), remove or select check mark from 'Show white space between pages in Print Layout view' check box, click OK button

To Edit a Source

When you typed the third paragraph of the research paper, you inserted a citation placeholder, Chamberlain, for the source. You now have the source information, which is for a website, and are ready to enter it. The following steps edit the source for the Chamberlain citation placeholder.

1. Click somewhere in the citation placeholder to be edited, in this case (Chamberlain), to select the citation placeholder.
2. Click the Citation Options arrow to display the Citation Options menu.
3. Click Edit Source on the Citation Options menu to display the Edit Source dialog box.
4. If necessary, click the 'Type of Source' arrow (Edit Source dialog box); scroll to and then click Web site, so that the list shows fields required for a Web site.
5. Place a check mark in the 'Show All Bibliography Fields' check box to display more fields related to Web sites.
6. Click the Author text box. Type `Chamberlain, Megan Lynn` as the author.
7. Click the 'Name of Web Page' text box. Type `Understanding How Volume Levels Affect Hearing` as the webpage name.
8. Click the Production Company text box. Type `Course Technology` as the production company.
9. Click the Year Accessed text box. Type `2017` as the year accessed (Figure 2–53).

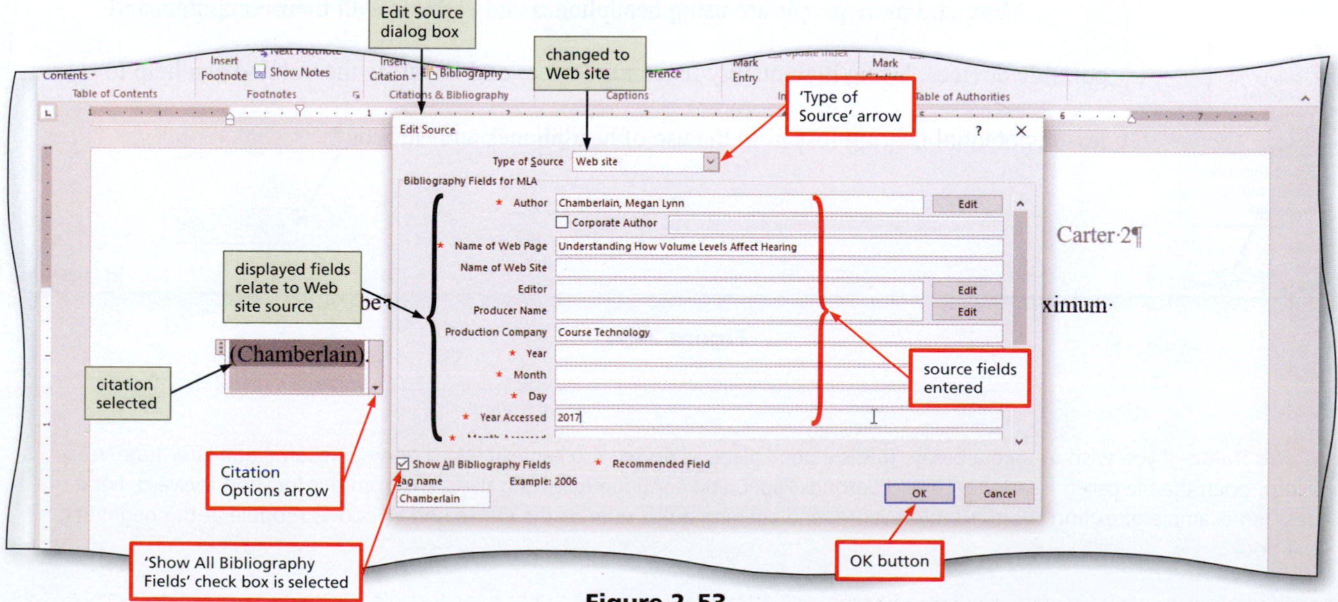

Figure 2–53

10. Press the TAB key and then type `Sept.` as the month accessed.
11. Press the TAB key and then type `16` as the day accessed.
12. Press the TAB key as many times as necessary to move the insertion point to the Medium text box and then type `Web` as the Medium.

Q&A Do I need to enter a web address (URL)?
The latest MLA documentation style update does not require the web address in the source.

13. Click the OK button to close the dialog box and create the source.

BTW
Organizing Files and Folders
You should organize and store files in folders so that you easily can find the files later. For example, if you are taking an introductory technology class called CIS 101, a good practice would be to save all Word files in a Word folder in a CIS 101 folder. For a discussion of folders and detailed examples of creating folders, refer to the Office and Windows module at the beginning of this book.

To Enter More Text

The next task is to type the last paragraph of text in the research paper. The following steps enter this text.

1. Press the END key to position the insertion point at the end of the third paragraph and then press the ENTER key.
2. Type the last paragraph of the research paper (Figure 2–54): **More and more people are using headphones and earbuds with their computers and portable devices. Using high-quality listening devices and lowering the volume can help to lessen potential hearing loss from the use of headphones and earbuds.**
3. Save the research paper again on the same storage location with the same file name.

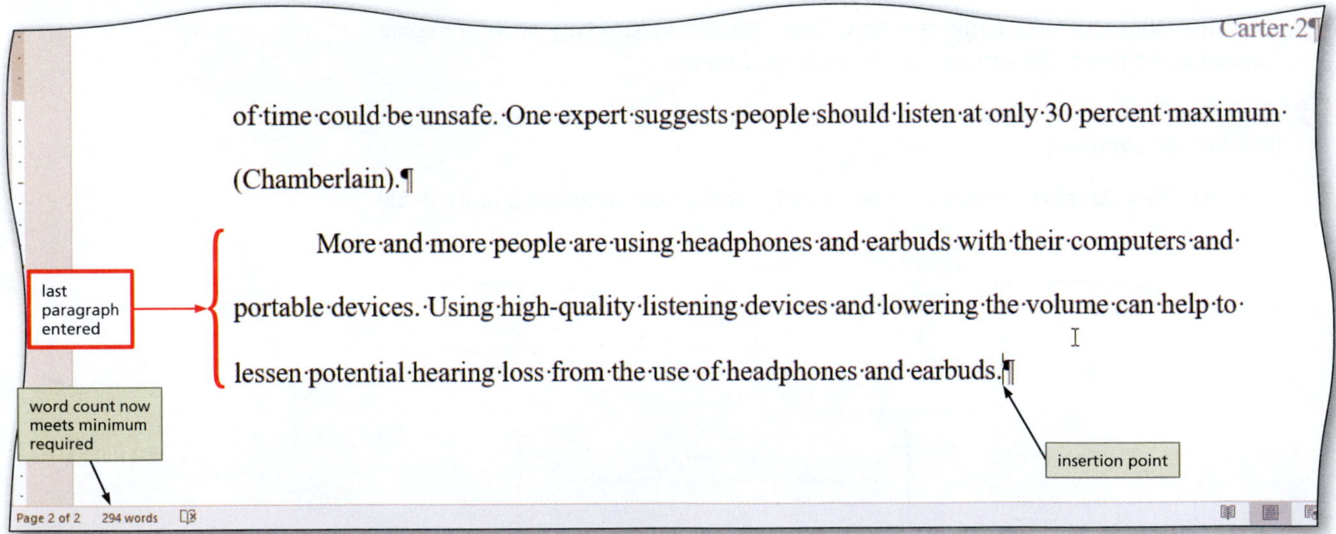

Figure 2–54

Break Point: If you wish to take a break, this is a good place to do so. You can exit Word now. To resume at a later time, run Word, open the file called Headphones and Earbuds Paper, and continue following the steps from this location forward. For a detailed example of exiting Word, running Word, and opening a file, refer to the Office and Windows module at the beginning of the book.

Creating an Alphabetical Works Cited Page

According to the MLA documentation style, the **works cited page** is a list of sources that are referenced directly in a research paper. You place the list on a separate numbered page with the title, Works Cited, centered one inch from the top margin. The works are to be alphabetized by the author's last name or, if the work has no author, by the work's title. The first line of each entry begins at the left margin. Indent subsequent lines of the same entry one-half inch from the left margin.

CONSIDER THIS

What is a bibliography?

A **bibliography** is an alphabetical list of sources referenced in a paper. Whereas the text of the research paper contains brief references to the source (the citations), the bibliography lists all publication information about the source. Documentation styles differ significantly in their guidelines for preparing a bibliography. Each style identifies formats for various sources, including books, magazines, pamphlets, newspapers, websites, television programs, paintings, maps, advertisements, letters, memos, and much more. You can find information about various styles and their guidelines in printed style guides and on the web.

To Page Break Manually

1 CHANGE DOCUMENT SETTINGS | 2 CREATE HEADER | 3 TYPE RESEARCH PAPER WITH CITATIONS
4 CREATE ALPHABETICAL WORKS CITED | 5 PROOFREAD & REVISE RESEARCH PAPER

The next step is to insert a manual page break following the body of the research paper. ***Why?*** *According to the MLA documentation style, the works cited are to be displayed on a separate numbered page.*

A **manual page break**, or **hard page break**, is one that you force into the document at a specific location. Word never moves or adjusts manual page breaks. Word, however, does adjust any automatic page breaks that follow a manual page break. Word inserts manual page breaks immediately above or to the left of the location of the insertion point. The following step inserts a manual page break after the text of the research paper.

- Verify that the insertion point is positioned at the end of the text of the research paper, as shown in Figure 2–54.
- Click Insert on the ribbon to display the Insert tab.
- Click the 'Insert a Page Break' button (Insert tab | Pages group) to insert a manual page break immediately to the left of the insertion point and position the insertion point immediately below the manual page break (Figure 2–55).

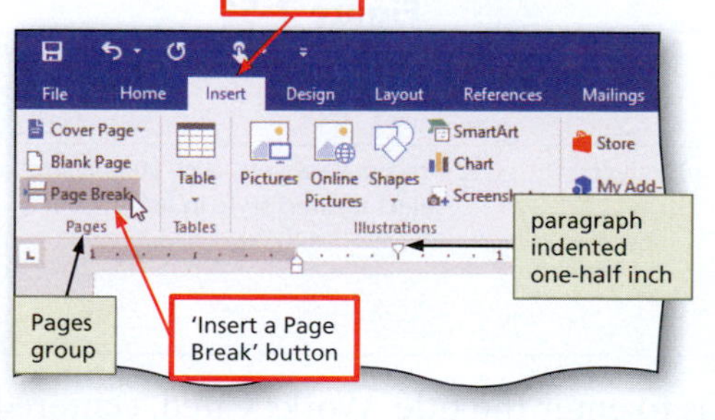

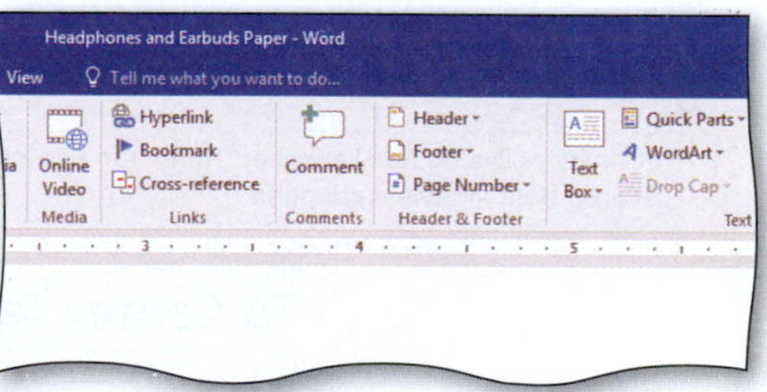

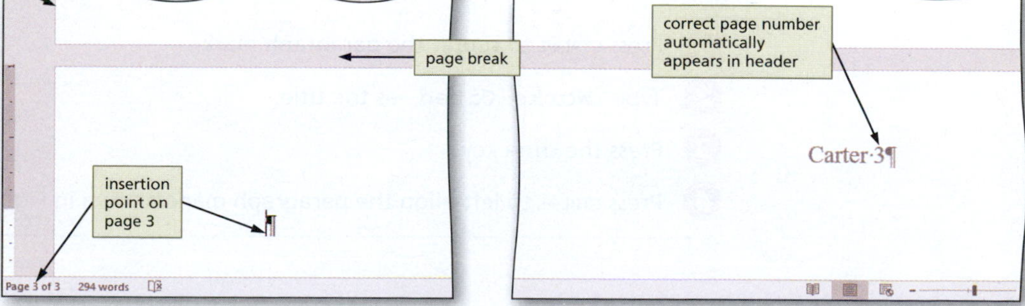

Figure 2–55

Other Ways

1. Press CTRL+ENTER

To Apply a Style

1 CHANGE DOCUMENT SETTINGS | 2 CREATE HEADER | 3 TYPE RESEARCH PAPER WITH CITATIONS
4 CREATE ALPHABETICAL WORKS CITED | 5 PROOFREAD & REVISE RESEARCH PAPER

The works cited title is to be centered between the margins of the paper. If you simply issue the Center command, the title will not be centered properly. ***Why?*** *It will be to the right of the center point because earlier you set the first-line indent for paragraphs to one-half inch.*

To properly center the title of the works cited page, you could drag the 'First Line Indent' marker back to the left margin before centering the paragraph, or you could apply the Normal style to the location of the insertion point. Recall that you modified the Normal style for this document to 12-point Times New Roman with double-spaced, left-aligned paragraphs that have no space after the paragraphs.

To apply a style to a paragraph, first position the insertion point in the paragraph and then apply the style. The following step applies the modified Normal style to the location of the insertion point.

- Click Home on the ribbon to display the Home tab.
- With the insertion point on the paragraph mark at the top of page 3 (as shown in Figure 2–55) even if Normal is selected, click Normal in the Styles gallery (Home tab | Styles group) to apply the Normal style to the paragraph containing the insertion point (Figure 2–56).

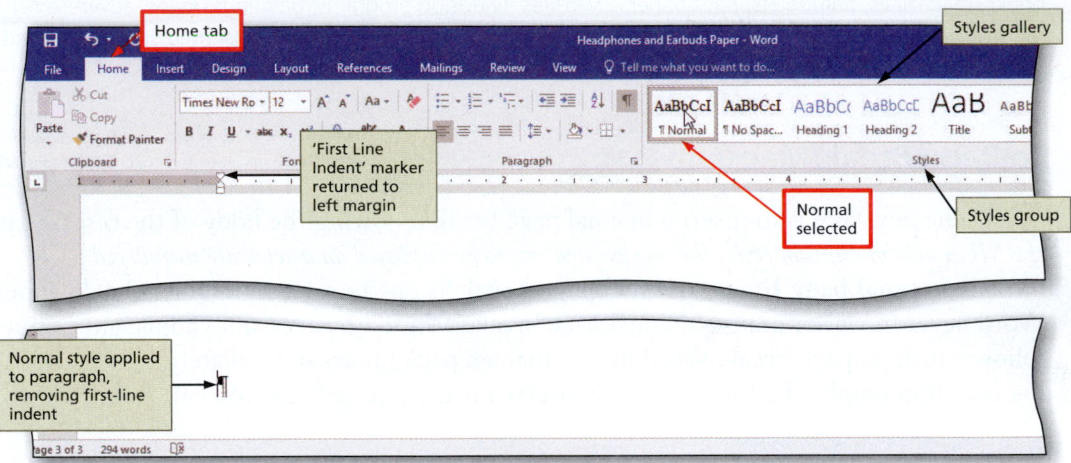

Figure 2–56

Other Ways

1. Click Styles Dialog Box Launcher (Home tab | Styles group), select desired style in Styles task pane
2. Press CTRL+SHIFT+S, click Style Name arrow in Apply Styles task pane, select desired style in list

To Center Text

The next task is to enter the title, Works Cited, centered between the margins of the paper. The following steps use a keyboard shortcut to format the title.

1. Press CTRL+E to center the paragraph mark.
2. Type `Works Cited` as the title.
3. Press the ENTER key.
4. Press CTRL+L to left-align the paragraph mark (shown in Figure 2–57).

To Create a Bibliographical List

1 CHANGE DOCUMENT SETTINGS | 2 CREATE HEADER | 3 TYPE RESEARCH PAPER WITH CITATIONS
4 CREATE ALPHABETICAL WORKS CITED | 5 PROOFREAD & REVISE RESEARCH PAPER

While typing the research paper, you created several citations and their sources. The next task is to use Word to format the list of sources and alphabetize them in a **bibliographical list**. ***Why?*** *Word can create a bibliographical list with each element of the source placed in its correct position with proper punctuation, according to the specified style, saving you time looking up style guidelines. For example, in this research paper, the book source will list, in* *this order, the author name(s), book title, publisher city, publishing company name, and publication year with the correct punctuation between each element according to the MLA documentation style.* The following steps create an MLA-styled bibliographical list from the sources previously entered.

1

- Click References on the ribbon to display the References tab.
- With the insertion point positioned as shown in Figure 2–57, click the Bibliography button (References tab | Citations & Bibliography group) to display the Bibliography gallery (Figure 2–57).

Q&A Will I select the Works Cited option from the Bibliography gallery?
No. The title it inserts is not formatted according to the MLA documentation style. Thus, you will use the Insert Bibliography command instead.

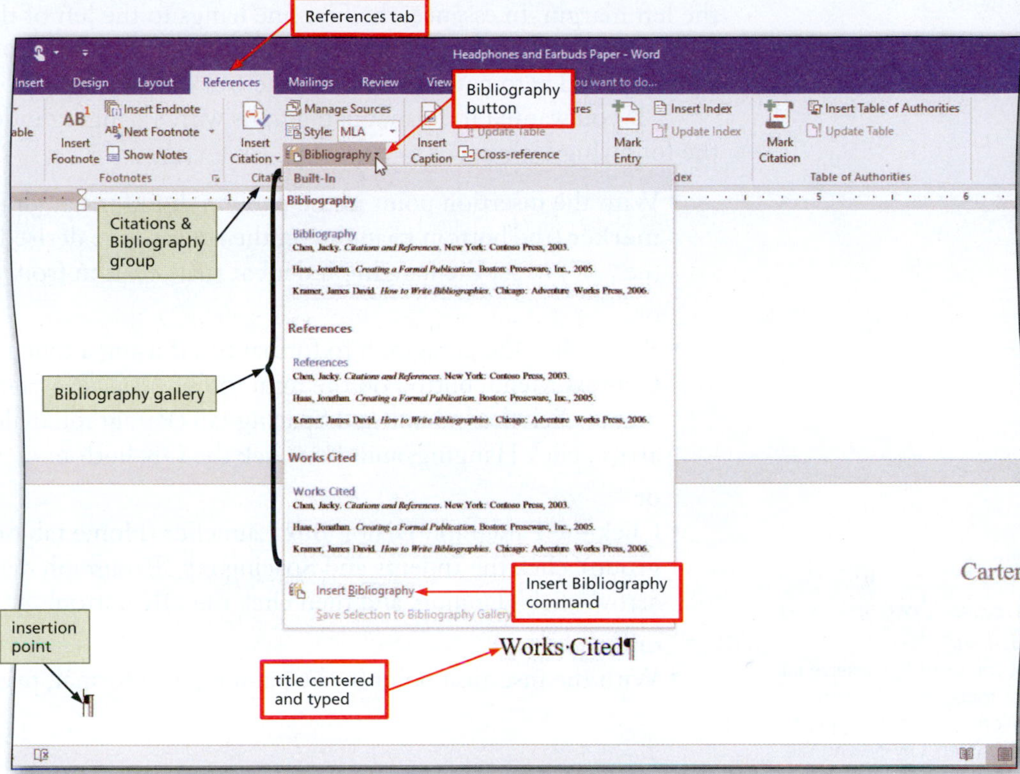

Figure 2–57

- Click Insert Bibliography in the Bibliography gallery to insert a list of sources at the location of the insertion point.
- If necessary, scroll to display the entire list of sources in the document window (Figure 2–58).

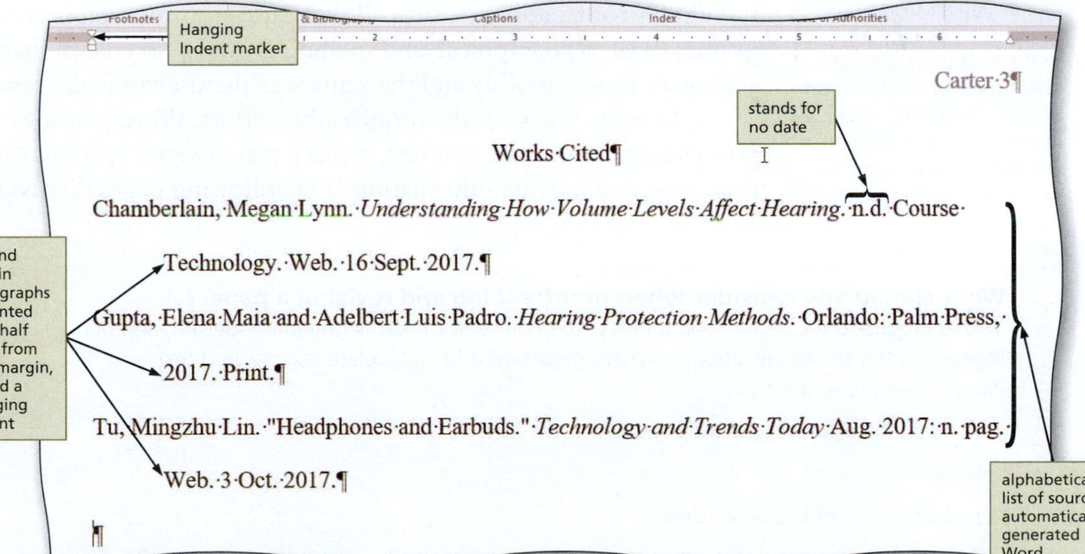

Figure 2–58

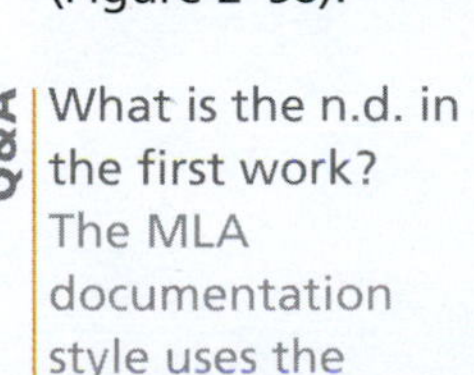

Q&A What is the n.d. in the first work?
The MLA documentation style uses the abbreviation n.d. for no date (for example, no date appears on the webpage).

- Save the research paper again on the same storage location with the same file name.

To Format Paragraphs with a Hanging Indent

Notice in Figure 2–58 that the first line of each source entry begins at the left margin, and subsequent lines in the same paragraph are indented one-half inch from the left margin. In essence, the first line hangs to the left of the rest of the paragraph; thus, this type of paragraph formatting is called a **hanging indent**. The Bibliography style in Word automatically formats the works cited paragraphs with a hanging indent.

If you wanted to format paragraphs with a hanging indent, you would use one of the following techniques.

- With the insertion point in the paragraph to format, drag the **Hanging Indent marker** (the bottom triangle) on the ruler to the desired mark on the ruler (i.e., .5") to set the hanging indent at that location from the left margin.

  or
- Right-click the paragraph to format (or, if using a touch screen, tap the 'Show Context Menu' button on the mini toolbar), click Paragraph on the shortcut menu, click the Indents and Spacing tab (Paragraph dialog box), click the Special arrow, click Hanging, and then click the OK button.

  or
- Click the Paragraph Dialog Box Launcher (Home tab or Layout tab | Paragraph group), click the Indents and Spacing tab (Paragraph dialog box), click the Special arrow, click Hanging, and then click the OK button.

  or
- With the insertion point in the paragraph to format, press CTRL+T.

BTW

Conserving Ink and Toner

If you want to conserve ink or toner, you can instruct Word to print draft quality documents by clicking File on the ribbon to open the Backstage view, clicking the Options tab in the Backstage view to display the Word Options dialog box, clicking Advanced in the left pane (Word Options dialog box), scrolling to the Print area in the right pane, placing a check mark in the 'Use draft quality' check box, and then clicking the OK button. Then, use the Backstage view to print the document as usual.

Proofreading and Revising the Research Paper

As discussed in Module 1, once you complete a document, you might find it necessary to make changes to it. Before submitting a paper to be graded, you should proofread it. While **proofreading**, ensure all the source information is correct and look for grammatical, typographical, and spelling errors. Also ensure that transitions between sentences flow smoothly and the sentences themselves make sense.

To assist you with the proofreading effort, Word provides several tools. You can go to a page, copy text, find text, replace text, insert a synonym, check spelling and grammar, and look up information. The following pages discuss these tools.

CONSIDER THIS

What should you consider when proofreading and revising a paper?

As you proofread the paper, look for ways to improve it. Check all grammar, spelling, and punctuation. Be sure the text is logical and transitions are smooth. Where necessary, add text, delete text, reword text, and move text to different locations. Ask yourself these questions:

- Does the title suggest the topic?
- Is the thesis clear?
- Is the purpose of the paper clear?
- Does the paper have an introduction, body, and conclusion?
- Does each paragraph in the body relate to the thesis?
- Is the conclusion effective?
- Are sources acknowledged correctly?

To Modify a Source

1 CHANGE DOCUMENT SETTINGS | 2 CREATE HEADER | 3 TYPE RESEARCH PAPER WITH CITATIONS
4 CREATE ALPHABETICAL WORKS CITED | **5 PROOFREAD & REVISE RESEARCH PAPER**

While proofreading the paper, you notice an error in the magazine title; specifically, the word, and, should be removed. If you modify the contents of any source, the list of sources automatically updates. ***Why?*** *Word automatically updates the contents of fields, and the bibliography is a field.* The following steps delete a word from the title of the magazine article.

- Click the Manage Sources button (References tab | Citations & Bibliography group) to display the Source Manager dialog box.
- Click the source you wish to edit in the Current List, in this case the article by Tu, to select the source.
- Click the Edit button (Source Manager dialog box) to display the Edit Source dialog box.
- In the Periodical Title text box, delete the word, and, from the title (Figure 2–59).

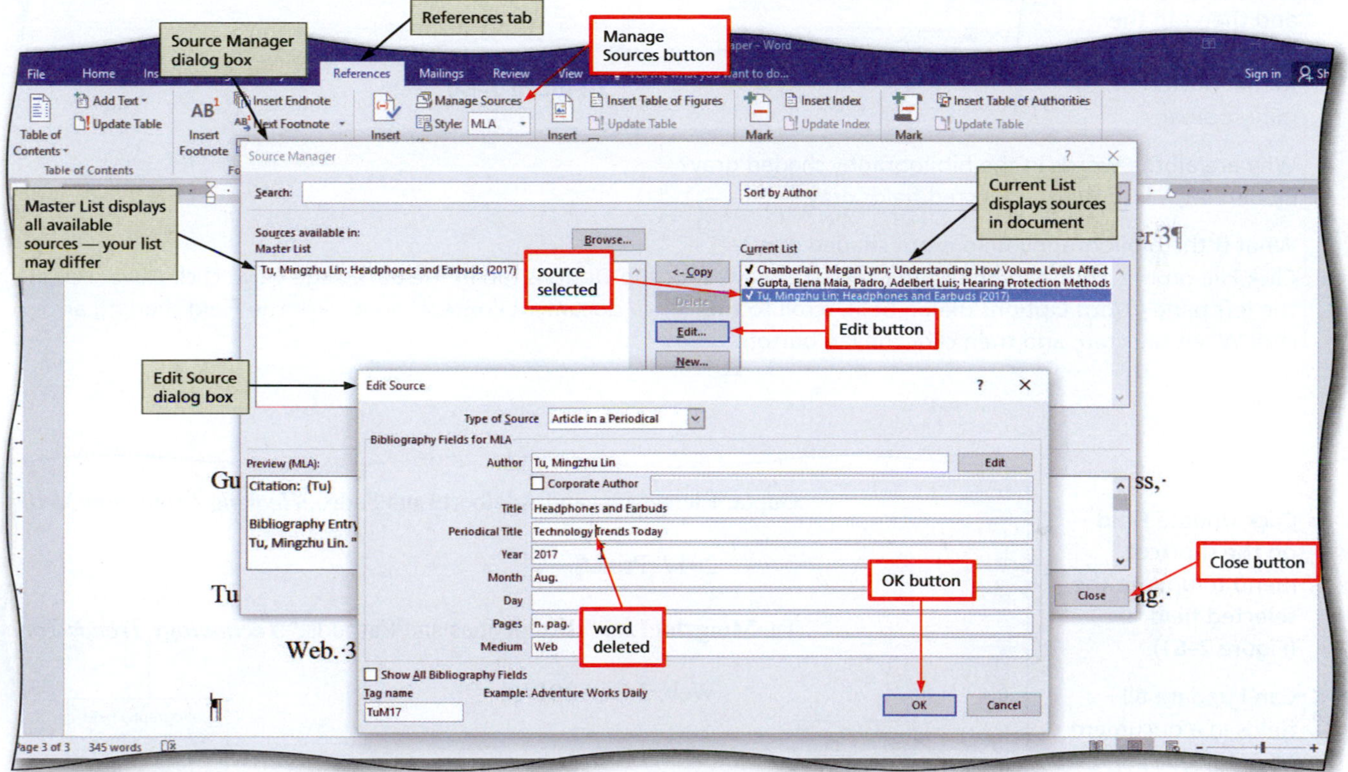

Figure 2–59

- Click the OK button (Edit Source dialog box) to close the dialog box.
- If a Microsoft Word dialog box appears, click its Yes button to update all occurrences of the source.
- Click the Close button (Source Manager dialog box) to update the list of sources and close the dialog box.

To Update a Field

1 CHANGE DOCUMENT SETTINGS | 2 CREATE HEADER | 3 TYPE RESEARCH PAPER WITH CITATIONS
4 CREATE ALPHABETICAL WORKS CITED | **5 PROOFREAD & REVISE RESEARCH PAPER**

Depending on settings, the bibliography field may not automatically reflect the edited magazine title. Thus, the following steps update the bibliography field. ***Why?*** *Because the bibliography is a field, you may need to instruct Word to update its contents.*

1

- Right-click anywhere in the bibliography text to display a shortcut menu related to fields (Figure 2–60).

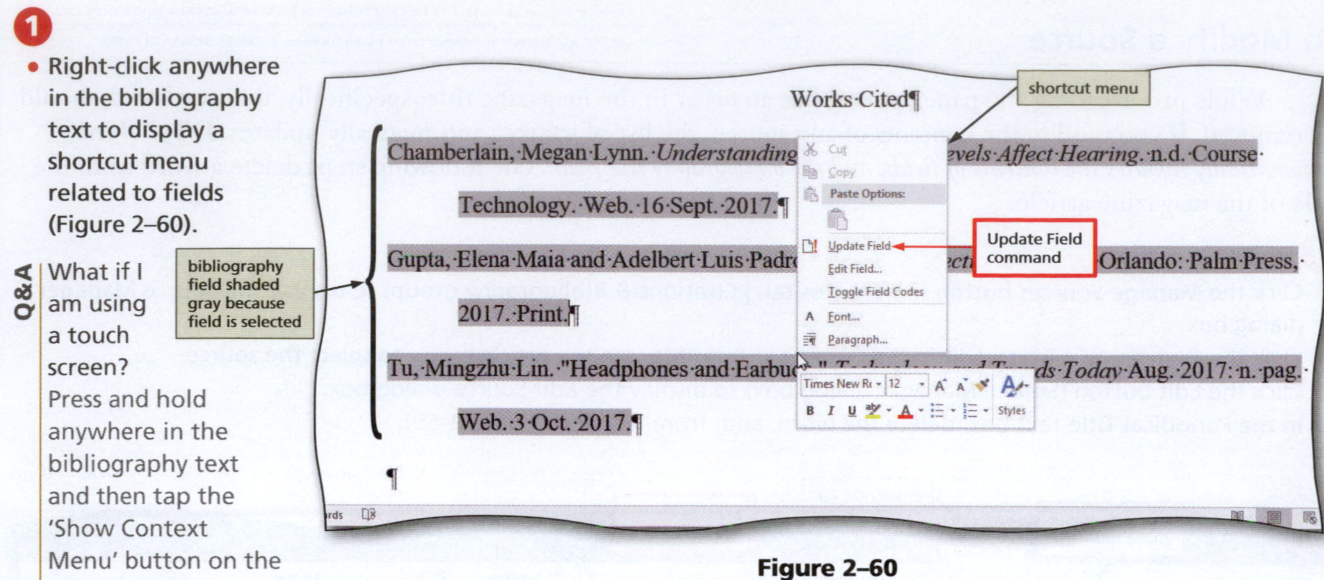

Figure 2–60

Q&A

What if I am using a touch screen?
Press and hold anywhere in the bibliography text and then tap the 'Show Context Menu' button on the mini toolbar.

Why are all the words in the bibliography shaded gray?
By default, Word shades selected fields gray.

What if the bibliography field is not shaded gray?
Click File on the ribbon to open the Backstage view, click the Options tab in the Backstage view, click Advanced in the left pane (Word Options dialog box), scroll to the 'Show document content' area, click the Field shading arrow, click When selected, and then click the OK button.

2

- Click Update Field on the shortcut menu to update the selected field (Figure 2–61).

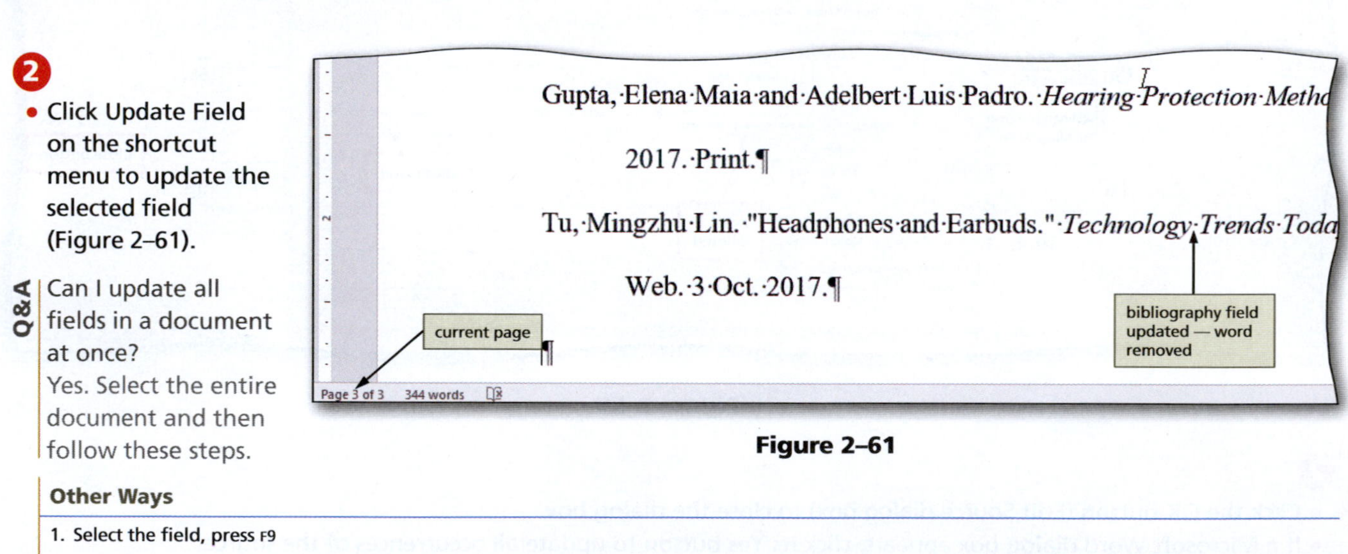

Figure 2–61

Q&A

Can I update all fields in a document at once?
Yes. Select the entire document and then follow these steps.

Other Ways

1. Select the field, press F9

To Convert a Field to Regular Text

If, for some reason, you wanted to convert a field, such as the bibliography field, to regular text, you would perform the following steps. Keep in mind, though, once you convert the field to regular text, it no longer is a field that can be updated.

1. Click somewhere in the field to select it, in this case, somewhere in the bibliography.
2. Press CTRL+SHIFT+F9 to convert the selected field to regular text.

To Go to a Page

The next task in revising the paper is to modify text on the second page of the document. ***Why?*** *You want to copy text from one location to another on the second page.* You could scroll to the desired location in the document, or you can use the Navigation Pane to browse through pages in a document. The following steps display the top of the second page in the document window and position the insertion point at the beginning of that page.

1

- Click View on the ribbon to display the View tab.
- Place a check mark in the 'Open the Navigation Pane' check box (View tab | Show group) to open the Navigation Pane on the left side of the Word window.
- If necessary, click the Pages tab in the Navigation Pane to display thumbnails of the pages in the document.
- Scroll to, if necessary, and then click the thumbnail of the second page to display the top of the selected page in the top of the document window (Figure 2–62).

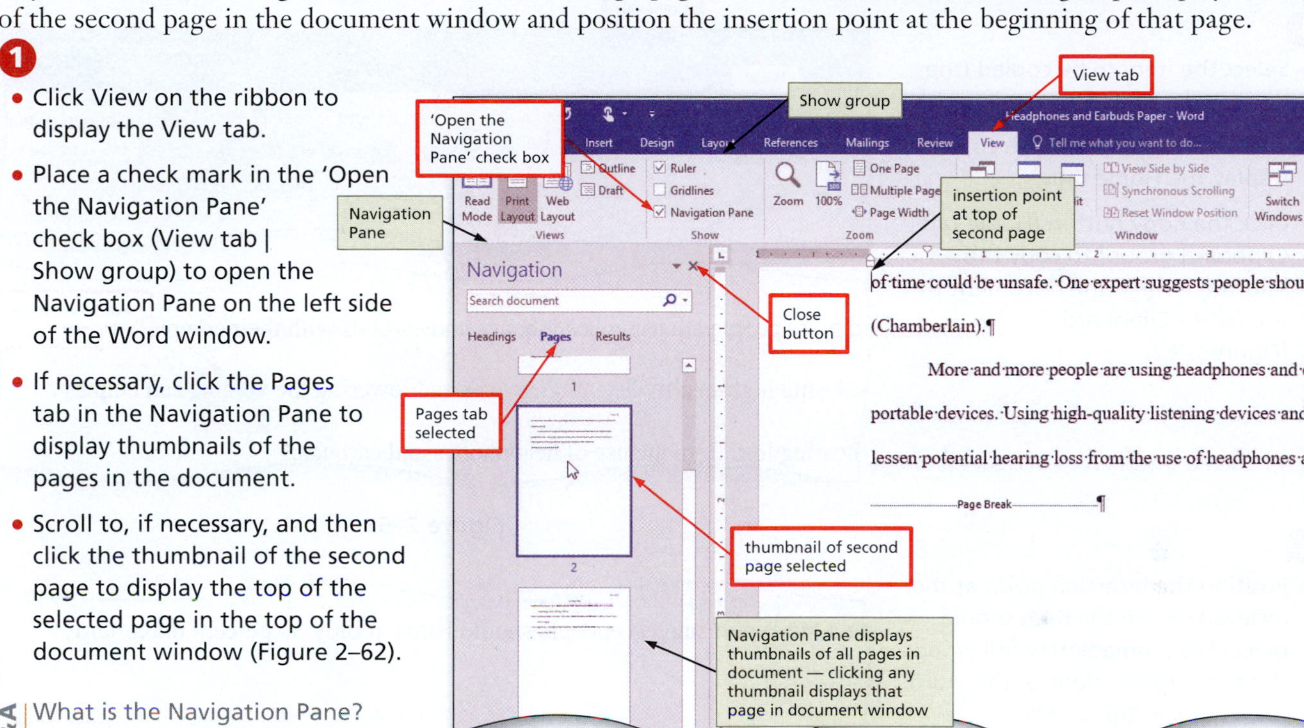

Figure 2–62

Q&A What is the Navigation Pane?
The Navigation Pane is a window that enables you to browse through headings in a document, browse through pages in a document, or search for text in a document.

2

- Click the Close button in the Navigation Pane to close the pane.

Other Ways

1. Click Find arrow (Home tab | Editing group), click Go To on Find menu, click Go To tab (Find and Replace dialog box), enter page number, click Go To button
2. Click Page Number indicator on status bar, click Pages tab in Navigation Pane, click thumbnail of desired page (Navigation Pane)
3. Press CTRL+G, enter page number (Find and Replace dialog box), click Go To button

Copying, Cutting, and Pasting

While proofreading the research paper, you decide it would read better if the word, volume, in the second sentence of the last paragraph also appeared after the word, maximum, in the last sentence of the previous paragraph. You could type the word at the desired location, but you decide to use the Office Clipboard. The **Office Clipboard** is a temporary storage area that holds up to 24 items (text or graphics) copied from any Office program. The Office Clipboard works with the copy, cut, and paste commands:

- **Copying** is the process of placing items on the Office Clipboard, leaving the item in the document.
- **Cutting** removes the item from the document before placing it on the Office Clipboard.
- **Pasting** is the process of copying an item from the Office Clipboard into the document at the location of the insertion point.

To Copy and Paste

In the research paper, you copy a word from one location to another. ***Why?*** *The sentence reads better with the word, volume, inserted after the word, maximum.* The following steps copy and paste a word.

- Select the item to be copied (the word, volume, in this case).
- Click Home on the ribbon to display the Home tab.
- Click the Copy button (Home tab | Clipboard group) to copy the selected item in the document to the Office Clipboard (Figure 2–63).

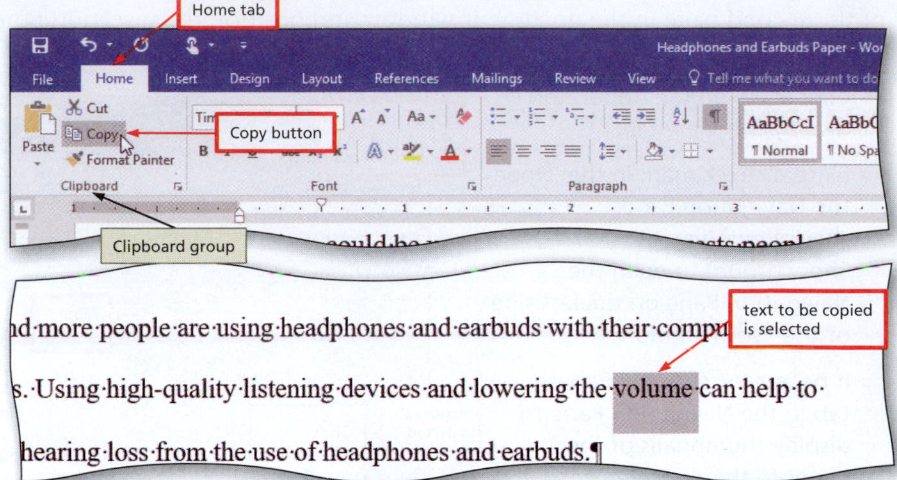

Figure 2–63

2

- Position the insertion point at the location where the item should be pasted (immediately following the space to the right of the word, maximum, in this case) (Figure 2–64).

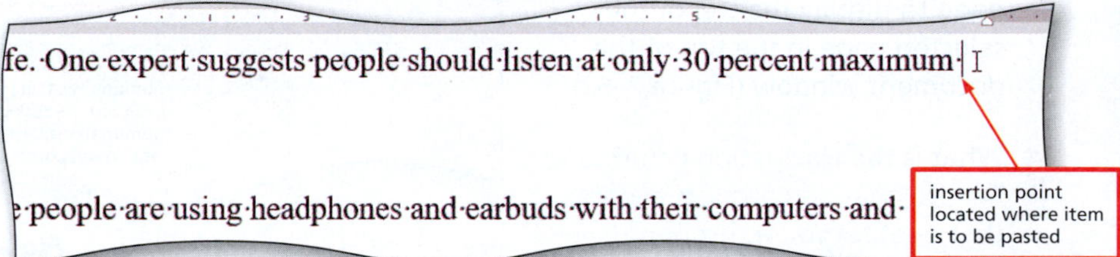

Figure 2–64

3

- Click the Paste button (Home tab | Clipboard group) to paste the copied item in the document at the location of the insertion point (Figure 2–65).

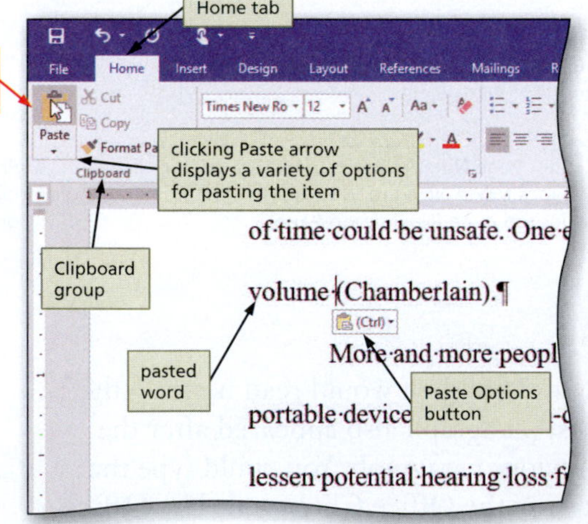

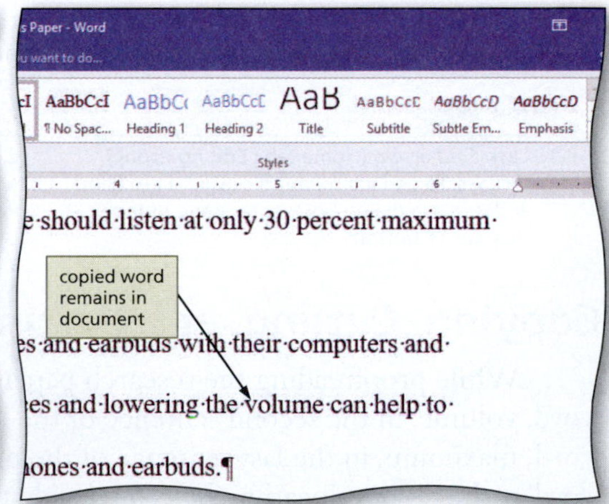

Figure 2–65

Q&A What if I click the Paste arrow by mistake?

Click the Paste arrow again to remove the Paste menu and repeat Step 3.

Other Ways

1. Click Copy on shortcut menu (or, if using touch, tap Copy on mini toolbar), right-click where item is to be pasted, click 'Keep Source Formatting' in Paste Options area on shortcut menu (or, if using touch, tap Paste on mini toolbar)
2. Select item, press CTRL+C, position insertion point at paste location, press CTRL+V

To Display the Paste Options Menu

1 CHANGE DOCUMENT SETTINGS | 2 CREATE HEADER | 3 TYPE RESEARCH PAPER WITH CITATIONS
4 CREATE ALPHABETICAL WORKS CITED | 5 PROOFREAD & REVISE RESEARCH PAPER

When you paste an item or move an item using drag-and-drop editing, which was discussed in the previous module, Word automatically displays a Paste Options button near the pasted or moved text (shown in Figure 2–65). ***Why?*** *The Paste Options button allows you to change the format of a pasted item. For example, you can instruct Word to format the pasted item the same way as where it was copied (the source) or format it the same way as where it is being pasted (the destination).* The following steps display the Paste Options menu.

1

- Click the Paste Options button to display the Paste Options menu (Figure 2–66).

Q&A What are the functions of the buttons on the Paste Options menu?
In general, the left button indicates the pasted item should look the same as it did in its original location (the source). The second button formats the pasted text to match the rest of the item where it was pasted (the destination). The third button removes all formatting from the pasted item. The 'Set Default Paste' command displays the Word Options dialog box. Keep in mind that the buttons shown on a Paste Options menu will vary, depending on the item being pasted.

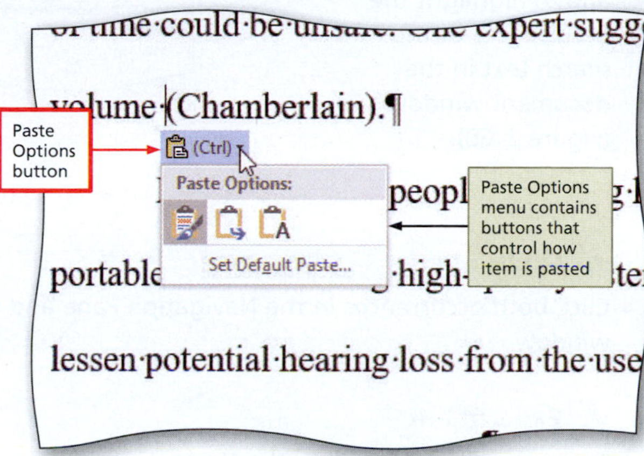

Figure 2–66

2

- Click anywhere to remove the Paste Options menu from the window.

Other Ways

1. CTRL or ESC (to remove the Paste Options menu)

To Find Text

1 CHANGE DOCUMENT SETTINGS | 2 CREATE HEADER | 3 TYPE RESEARCH PAPER WITH CITATIONS
4 CREATE ALPHABETICAL WORKS CITED | 5 PROOFREAD & REVISE RESEARCH PAPER

While proofreading the paper, you would like to locate all occurrences of the word, portable. ***Why?*** *You are contemplating changing occurrences of this word to the word, mobile.* The following steps find all occurrences of specific text in a document.

1

- Click the Find button (Home tab | Editing group) to display the Navigation Pane.

Q&A What if I am using a touch screen?
Tap the Find button (Home tab | Editing group) and then tap Find on the menu.

- If necessary, click the Results tab in the Navigation Pane, which displays a Search box where you can type text for which you want to search (Figure 2–67).

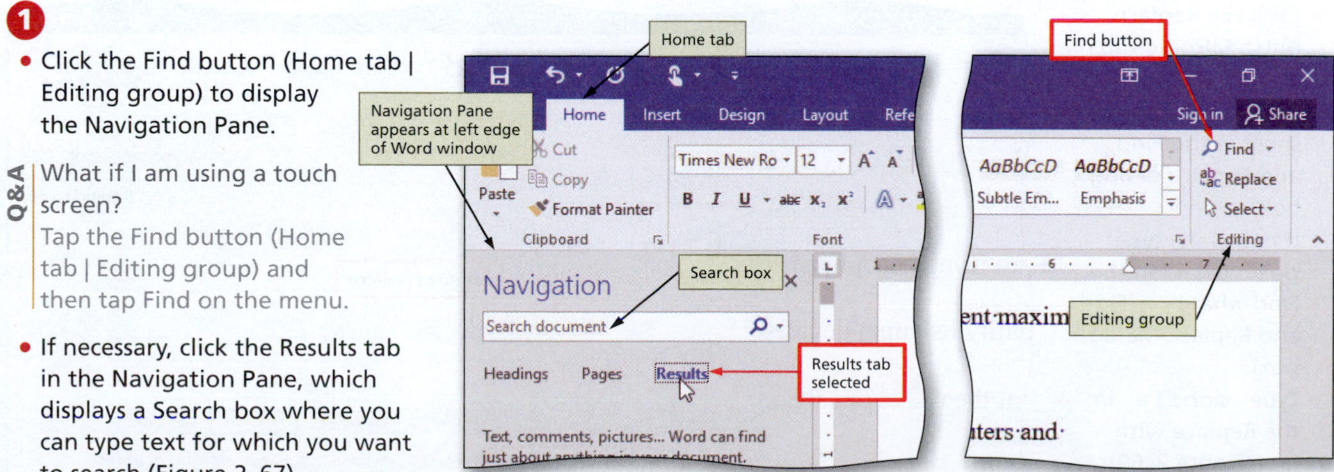

Figure 2–67

- Type **portable** in the Navigation Pane Search box to display all occurrences of the typed text, called the search text, in the Navigation Pane and to highlight the occurrences of the search text in the document window (Figure 2–68).

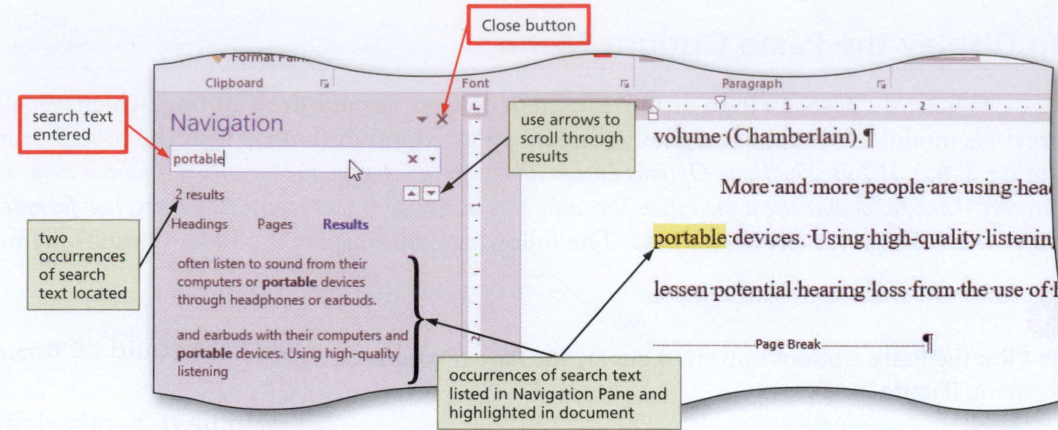

Figure 2–68

Experiment

- Click both occurrences in the Navigation Pane and watch Word display the associated text in the document window.

Experiment

- Type various search text in the Navigation Pane Search box, and watch Word both list matches in the Navigation Pane and highlight matches in the document window.
- Click the Close button in the Navigation Pane to close the pane.

Other Ways

1. Click Find arrow (Home tab | Editing group), click Find on Find menu, enter search text in Navigation Pane
2. Click Page Number indicator on status bar, enter search text in Navigation Pane
3. Press CTRL+F, enter search text in Navigation Pane

To Replace Text

1 CHANGE DOCUMENT SETTINGS | 2 CREATE HEADER | 3 TYPE RESEARCH PAPER WITH CITATIONS
4 CREATE ALPHABETICAL WORKS CITED | 5 PROOFREAD & REVISE RESEARCH PAPER

You decide to change all occurrences of the word, portable, to the word, mobile. ***Why?*** *The term, mobile devices, is more commonly used than portable devices.* Word's find and replace feature locates each occurrence of a word or phrase and then replaces it with text you specify. The following steps find and replace text.

- Click the Replace button (Home tab | Editing group) to display the Replace sheet in the Find and Replace dialog box.
- If necessary, type **portable** in the Find what box (Find and Replace dialog box).
- Type **mobile** in the Replace with box (Figure 2–69).

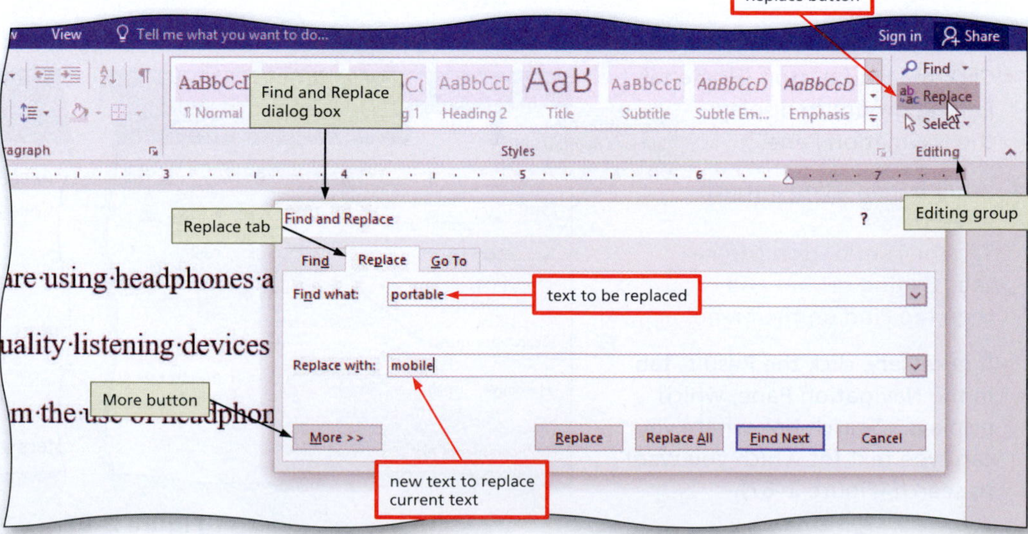

Figure 2–69

- Click the Replace All button to instruct Word to replace all occurrences of the Find what text with the Replace with text (Figure 2–70). If Word displays a dialog box asking if you want to continue searching from the beginning of the document, click the Yes button.

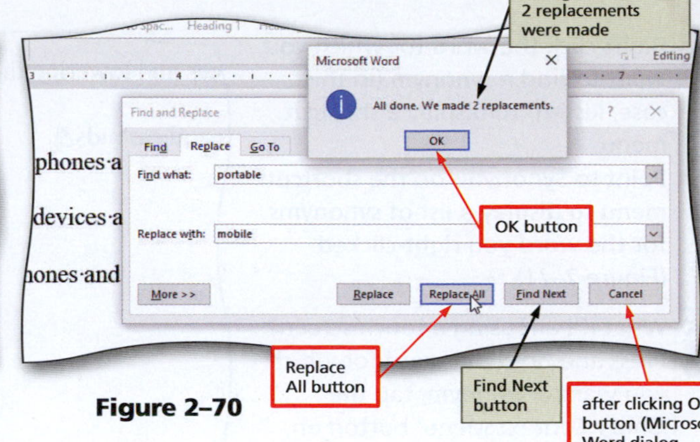

Figure 2–70

Q&A Does Word search the entire document?
If the insertion point is at the beginning of the document, Word searches the entire document; otherwise, Word may search from the location of the insertion point to the end of the document and then display a dialog box asking if you want to continue searching from the beginning. You also can search a section of text by selecting the text before clicking the Replace or Replace All button.

- Click the OK button (Microsoft Word dialog box) to close the dialog box.
- Click the Close button (Find and Replace dialog box) to close the dialog box.

Other Ways

1. Press CTRL+H

Find and Replace Dialog Box

The Replace All button (Find and Replace dialog box) replaces all occurrences of the Find what text with the Replace with text. In some cases, you may want to replace only certain occurrences of a word or phrase, not all of them. To instruct Word to confirm each change, click the Find Next button (Find and Replace dialog box) (shown in Figure 2–70), instead of the Replace All button. When Word locates an occurrence of the text, it pauses and waits for you to click either the Replace button or the Find Next button. Clicking the Replace button changes the text; clicking the Find Next button instructs Word to disregard the replacement and look for the next occurrence of the Find what text.

If you accidentally replace the wrong text, you can undo a replacement by clicking the Undo button on the Quick Access Toolbar. If you used the Replace All button, Word undoes all replacements. If you used the Replace button, Word undoes only the most recent replacement.

BTW
Finding Formatting
To search for formatting or a special character, click the More button in the Find and Replace dialog box (shown in Figure 2–69). To find formatting, use the Format button in the Find dialog box. To find a special character, use the Special button.

To Find and Insert a Synonym

In this project, you would like a synonym for the word, lessen, in the last paragraph of the research paper. ***Why?** When writing, you may discover that you used the same word in multiple locations or that a word you used was not quite appropriate, which is the case here.* In these instances, you will want to look up a **synonym**, or a word similar in meaning, to the duplicate or inappropriate word. A **thesaurus** is a book of synonyms. Word provides synonyms and a thesaurus for your convenience. The following steps find a suitable synonym.

- Right-click the word for which you want to find a synonym (in this case, lessen) to display a shortcut menu.
- Point to Synonyms on the shortcut menu to display a list of synonyms for the word you right-clicked (Figure 2–71).

Q&A What if I am using a touch screen?
Press and hold the word for which you want a synonym, tap the 'Show Context Menu' button on the mini toolbar, and then tap Synonyms on the shortcut menu.

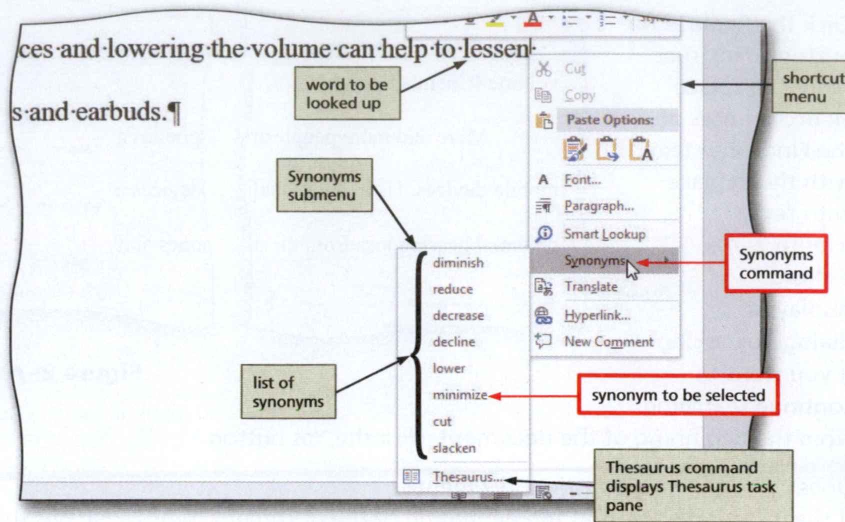

Figure 2–71

- Click the synonym you want (in this case, minimize) on the Synonyms submenu to replace the selected word in the document with the selected synonym (Figure 2–72).

Figure 2–72

Q&A What if the synonyms list on the shortcut menu does not display a suitable word?
You can display the thesaurus in the Thesaurus task pane by clicking Thesaurus on the Synonyms submenu. The Thesaurus task pane displays a complete thesaurus, in which you can look up synonyms for various meanings of a word. You also can look up an antonym, or word with an opposite meaning.

Other Ways

1. Click Thesaurus button (Review tab | Proofing group)
2. Press SHIFT+F7

To Check Spelling and Grammar at Once

1 CHANGE DOCUMENT SETTINGS | 2 CREATE HEADER | 3 TYPE RESEARCH PAPER WITH CITATIONS
4 CREATE ALPHABETICAL WORKS CITED | 5 PROOFREAD & REVISE RESEARCH PAPER

As discussed in Module 1, Word checks spelling and grammar as you type and places a wavy underline below possible spelling or grammar errors. Module 1 illustrated how to check these flagged words immediately. The next steps check spelling and grammar at once. ***Why?*** *Some users prefer to wait and check their entire document for spelling and grammar errors at once.*

Note: In the following steps, the word, sound, has been misspelled intentionally as sould to illustrate the use of Word's check spelling and grammar at once feature. If you are completing this project on a computer or mobile device, your research paper may contain different misspelled words, depending on the accuracy of your typing.

- Press CTRL+HOME because you want the spelling and grammar check to begin from the top of the document.
- Click Review on the ribbon to display the Review tab.

- Click the 'Spelling & Grammar' button (Review tab | Proofing group) to begin the spelling and grammar check at the location of the insertion point, which, in this case, is at the beginning of the document.
- Click the desired word in the list of suggestions in the Spelling task pane (sound, in this case) (Figure 2–73).

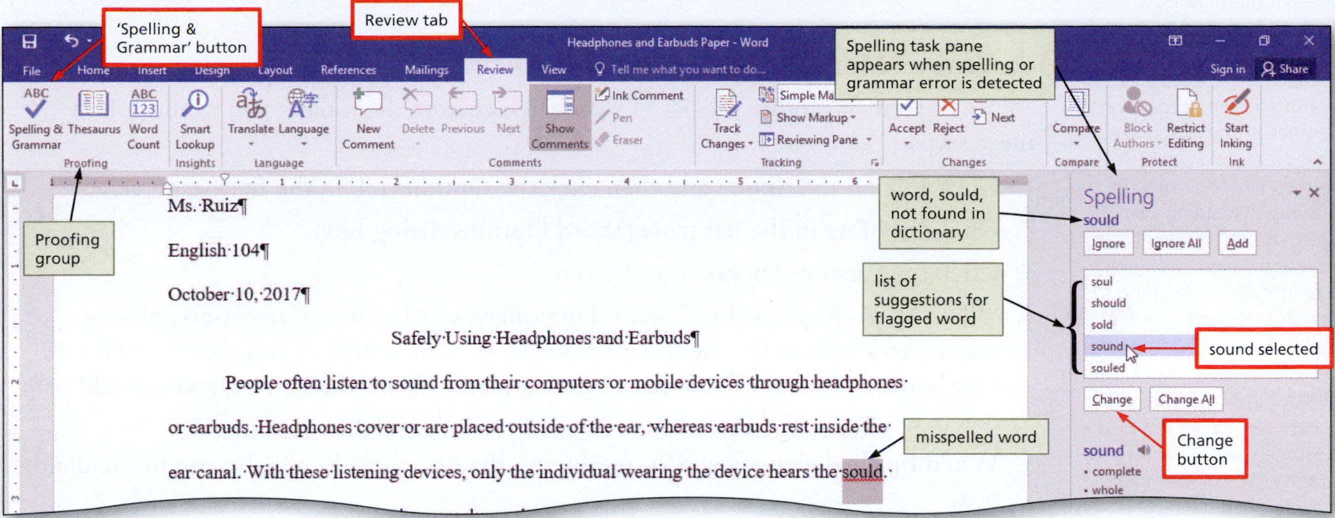

Figure 2–73

- With the word, sound, selected in the list of suggestions, click the Change button (Spelling task pane) to change the flagged word to the selected suggestion and then continue the spelling and grammar check until the next error is identified or the end of the document is reached (Figure 2–74).

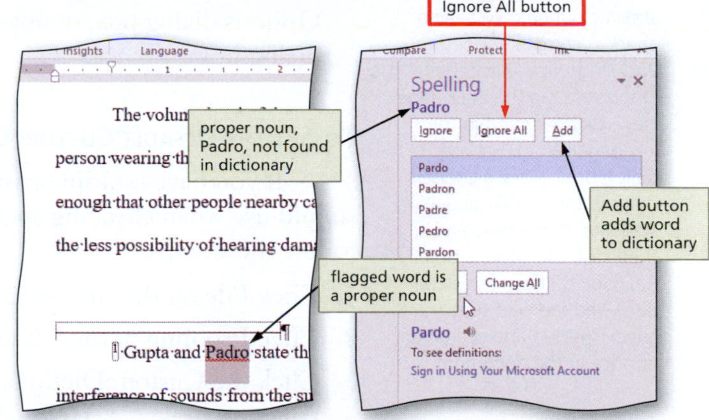

Figure 2–74

- Because the flagged word is a proper noun and spelled correctly, click the Ignore All button (Spelling task pane) to ignore this and future occurrences of the flagged proper noun and then continue the spelling and grammar check until the next error is identified or the end of the document is reached.

4

- When the spelling and grammar check is finished and Word displays a dialog box, click its OK button.

Q&A Can I check spelling of just a section of a document?
Yes, select the text before starting the spelling and grammar check.

Other Ways

1. Click 'Spelling and Grammar Check' icon on status bar
2. Press F7

The Main and Custom Dictionaries

As shown in the previous steps, Word may flag a proper noun as an error because the proper noun is not in its main dictionary. You may want to add some proper nouns that you use repeatedly, such as a company name or employee names, to Word's dictionary. To prevent Word from flagging proper nouns as errors, you can add the proper nouns to the custom dictionary. To add a correctly spelled word to the custom dictionary, click the Add button (Spelling task pane) or right-click the flagged word (or, if using touch, press and hold and then tap 'Show Context Menu' button on the mini toolbar) and then click 'Add to Dictionary' on the shortcut menu. Once you have added a word to the custom dictionary, Word no longer will flag it as an error.

BTW
Readability Statistics
You can instruct Word to display readability statistics when it has finished a spelling and grammar check on a document. Three readability statistics presented are the percent of passive sentences, the Flesch Reading Ease score, and the Flesch-Kincaid Grade Level score. The Flesch Reading Ease score uses a 100-point scale to rate the ease with which a reader can understand the text in a document. A higher score means the document is easier to understand. The Flesch-Kincaid Grade Level score rates the text in a document on a U.S. school grade level. For example, a score of 10.0 indicates a student in the tenth grade can understand the material. To show readability statistics when the spelling check is complete, open the Backstage view, click the Options tab in the Backstage view, click Proofing in the left pane (Word Options dialog box), place a check mark in the 'Show readability statistics' check box, and then click the OK button. Readability statistics will be displayed the next time you check spelling and grammar at once in the document.

To View or Modify Entries in a Custom Dictionary

To view or modify the list of words in a custom dictionary, you would follow these steps.

1. Click File on the ribbon and then click the Options tab in the Backstage view.
2. Click Proofing in the left pane (Word Options dialog box).
3. Click the Custom Dictionaries button.
4. When Word displays the Custom Dictionaries dialog box, if necessary, place a check mark next to the dictionary name to view or modify. Click the 'Edit Word List' button (Custom Dictionaries dialog box). (In this dialog box, you can add or delete entries to and from the selected custom dictionary.)
5. When finished viewing and/or modifying the list, click the OK button in the dialog box.
6. Click the OK button (Custom Dictionaries dialog box).
7. If the 'Suggest from main dictionary only' check box is selected in the Word Options dialog box, remove the check mark. Click the OK button (Word Options dialog box).

To Set the Default Custom Dictionary

If you have multiple custom dictionaries, you can specify which one Word should use when checking spelling. To set the default custom dictionary, you would follow these steps.

1. Click File on the ribbon and then click the Options tab in the Backstage view.
2. Click Proofing in the left pane (Word Options dialog box).
3. Click the Custom Dictionaries button.
4. When the Custom Dictionaries dialog box is displayed, place a check mark next to the desired dictionary name. Click the Change Default button (Custom Dictionaries dialog box).
5. Click the OK button (Custom Dictionaries dialog box).
6. If the 'Suggest from main dictionary only' check box is selected in the Word Options dialog box, remove the check mark. Click the OK button (Word Options dialog box).

To Look Up Information

1 CHANGE DOCUMENT SETTINGS | 2 CREATE HEADER | 3 TYPE RESEARCH PAPER WITH CITATIONS
4 CREATE ALPHABETICAL WORKS CITED | **5 PROOFREAD & REVISE RESEARCH PAPER**

If you are connected to the Internet, you can use the Insights task pane to search through various forms of reference information, including images, on the web and/or look up a definition of a word. The following steps use the Insights task pane to look up a definition of a word. ***Why?*** *Assume you want to see some images and know more about the word, headphones.*

- Position the insertion point in the word you want to look up (in this case, headphones).
- Click the Smart Lookup button (Review tab | Insights group) to open the Insights task pane (Figure 2–75).

Q&A Why does my Insights task pane look different?
Depending on your settings, your Insights task pane may appear different from the figure shown here.

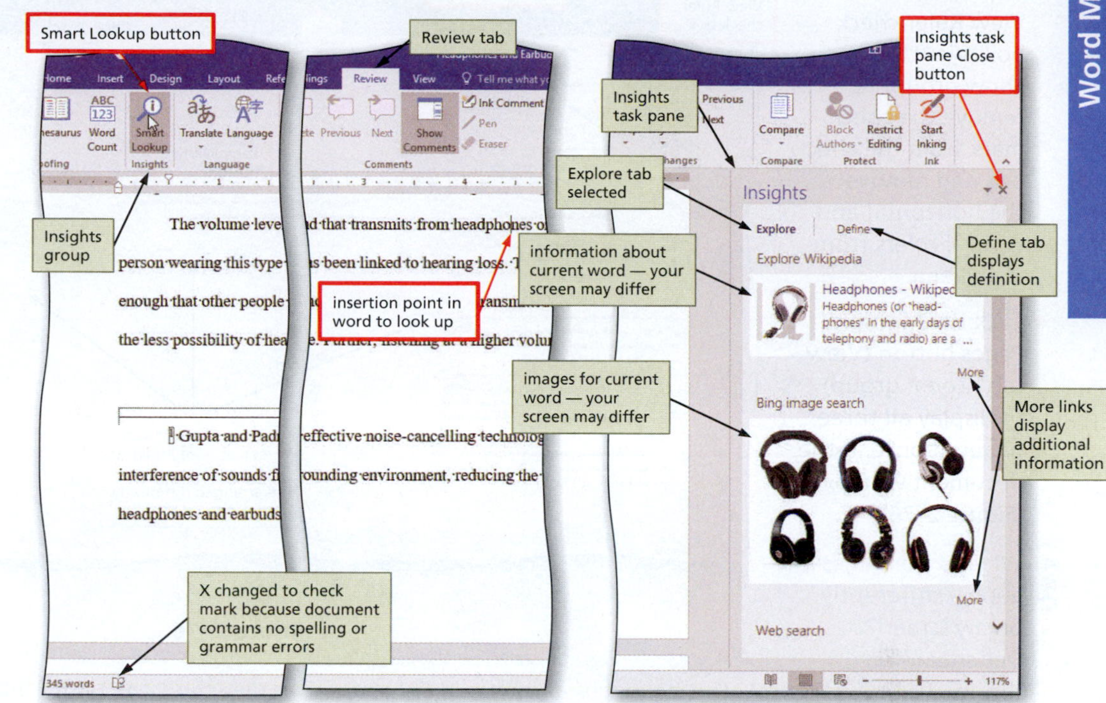

Figure 2–75

Experiment

- With the Explore tab selected in the Insights task pane, scroll through the information and images that appear in the Insights task pane. Click the Define tab in the Insights task pane to see a definition of the current word. Click the Explore tab to redisplay information from the web and images of the current word. Click one of the More links in the Insights task pane to view additional information. Click the Back button at the top of the Insights task pane to return to the previous display.

Q&A Can I copy information from the Insights task pane into my document?
Yes, you can use the Copy and Paste commands. When using Word to insert material from the Insights task pane or any other online reference, however, be careful not to plagiarize.

- Click the Close button in the Insights task pane.

Q&A Is the Research task pane from previous Word editions still available?
Yes. While holding down the ALT key, you can click the word you want to look up (such as headphones) to open the Research task pane and display a dictionary entry for the ALT+clicked word.

To Zoom Multiple Pages

1 CHANGE DOCUMENT SETTINGS | 2 CREATE HEADER | 3 TYPE RESEARCH PAPER WITH CITATIONS
4 CREATE ALPHABETICAL WORKS CITED | **5 PROOFREAD & REVISE RESEARCH PAPER**

The next steps display multiple pages in the document window at once. ***Why?*** *You want to be able to see all pages in the research paper on the screen at the same time. You also hide formatting marks and the rulers so that the display is easier to view.*

- Click Home on the ribbon to display the Home tab.
- If the 'Show/Hide ¶' button (Home tab | Paragraph group) is selected, click it to hide formatting marks.
- Click View on the ribbon to display the View tab.

- If the rulers are displayed, click the View Ruler check box (View tab | Show group) to remove the check mark from the check box and remove the horizontal and vertical rulers from the screen.
- Click the Multiple Pages button (View tab | Zoom group) to display all three pages at once in the document window (Figure 2–76).

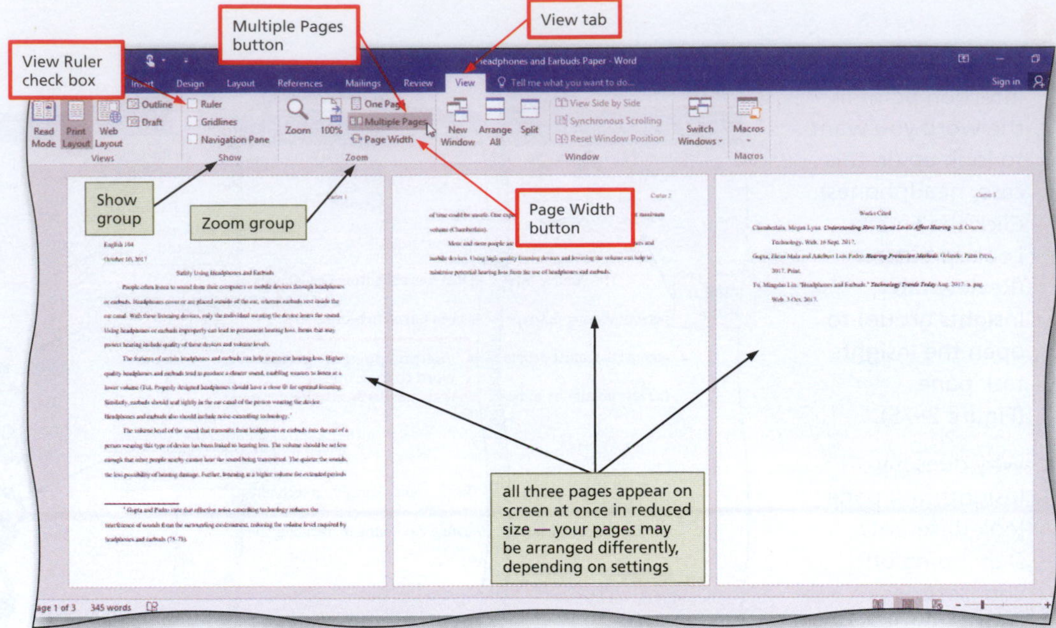

Figure 2–76

Q&A Why do the pages appear differently on my screen?
Depending on settings, Word may display all the pages as shown in Figure 2–76 or may show the pages differently.

2

- When finished, click the Page Width button (View tab | Zoom group) to return to the page width zoom.

To Change Read Mode Color

1 CHANGE DOCUMENT SETTINGS | 2 CREATE HEADER | 3 TYPE RESEARCH PAPER WITH CITATIONS
4 CREATE ALPHABETICAL WORKS CITED | 5 PROOFREAD & REVISE RESEARCH PAPER

You would like to read the entire research paper using Read mode but would like to change the background color of the Read mode screen. ***Why?*** *You prefer a different background color for reading on the screen.* The following steps change the color of the screen in Read mode.

1

- Click the Read Mode button on the status bar to switch to Read mode.
- Click the View tab to display the View menu.
- Point to Page Color on the View menu to display the Page Color submenu (Figure 2–77).

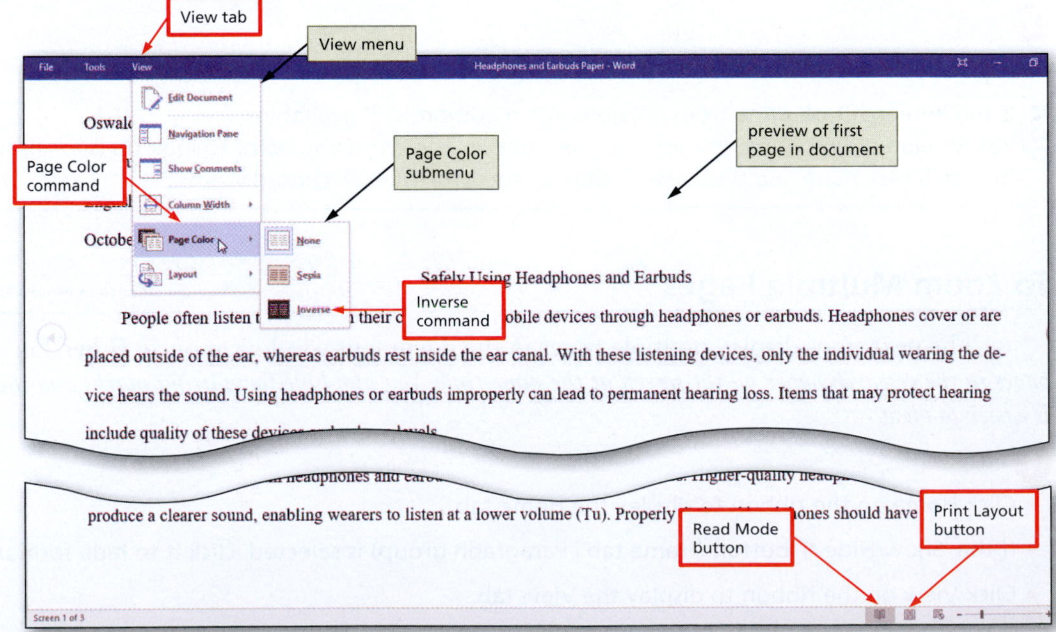

Figure 2–77

2

- Click Inverse on the Page Color submenu to change the color of the Read mode screen to inverse (Figure 2–78).

3

- When finished, click the Print Layout button (shown in Figure 2–77) on the status bar to return to Print Layout view.

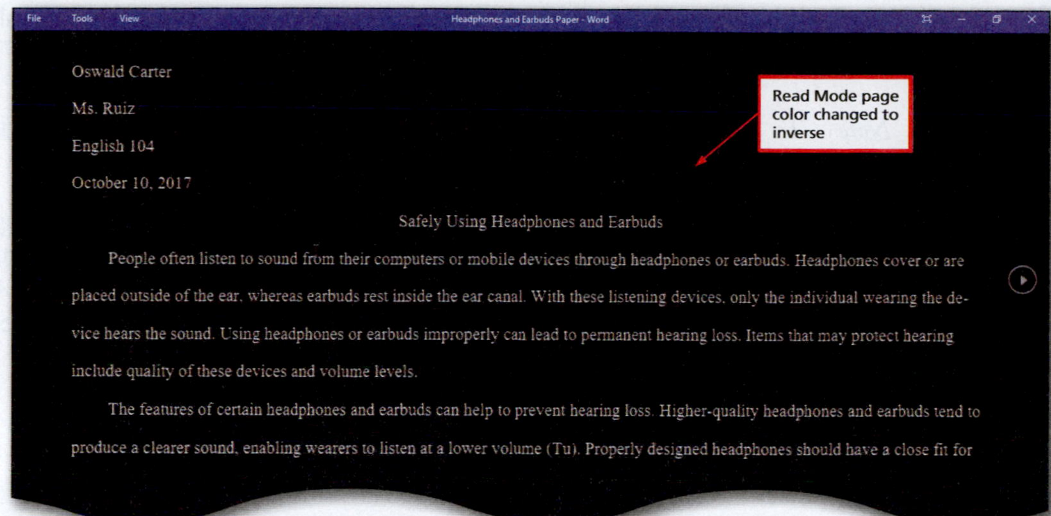

Figure 2–78

To Save and Print the Document and Exit Word

The following steps save and print the document and then exit Word. For a detailed example of the procedure summarized below, refer to the Office and Windows module at the beginning of this book.

1. Save the research paper again on the same storage location with the same file name.
2. If requested by your instructor, print the research paper.
3. Exit Word.

Summary

In this module, you have learned how to modify styles, adjust line and paragraph spacing, use headers to number pages, insert and edit citations and their sources, add footnotes, create a bibliographical list of sources, update a field, go to a page, copy and paste text, find and replace text, check spelling and grammar, and look up information.

CONSIDER THIS: PLAN AHEAD

What decisions will you need to make when creating your next research paper?

Use these guidelines as you complete the assignments in this module and create your own research papers outside of this class.

1. Select a topic.
   a) Spend time brainstorming ideas for a topic.
   b) Choose a topic you find interesting.
   c) For shorter papers, narrow the scope of the topic; for longer papers, broaden the scope.
   d) Identify a tentative thesis statement, which is a sentence describing the paper's subject matter.
2. Research the topic and take notes, being careful not to plagiarize.
3. Organize your notes into related concepts, identifying all main ideas and supporting details in an outline.
4. Write the first draft from the outline, referencing all sources of information and following the guidelines identified in the required documentation style.
5. Create the list of sources, using the formats specified in the required documentation style.
6. Proofread and revise the paper.

Apply Your Knowledge

Reinforce the skills and apply the concepts you learned in this module.

Revising Text and Paragraphs in a Document

Note: To complete this assignment, you will be required to use the Data Files. Please contact your instructor for information about accessing the Data Files.

Instructions: Run Word. Open the document, Apply 2-1 3-D Printers Paragraph Draft, which is located in the Data Files. The document you open contains a paragraph of text. You are to revise the document as follows: move a word, move another word and change the format of the moved word, change paragraph indentation, change line spacing, find all occurrences of a word, replace all occurrences of a word with another word, locate a synonym, and edit the header. The modified paragraph is shown in Figure 2–79.

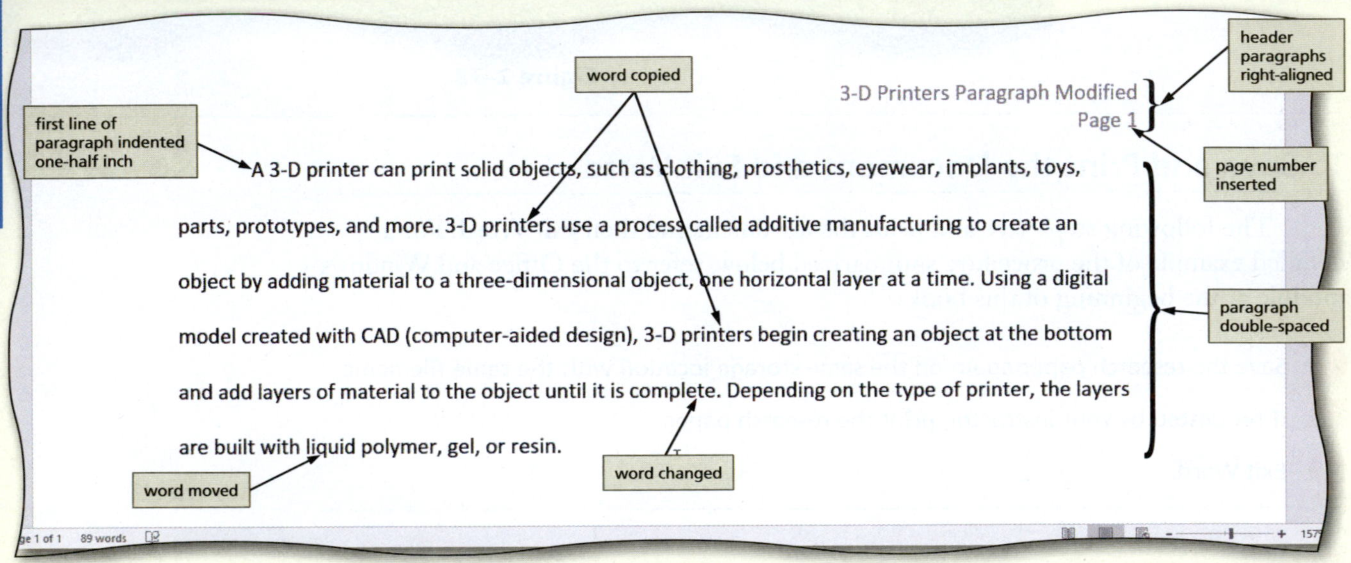

Figure 2–79

Perform the following tasks:

1. Copy the text, printers, from the second sentence and paste it in the third sentence after the underlined word, liquid.
2. Select the underlined word, liquid, in the third sentence. Use drag-and-drop editing to move the selected word, liquid, so that it is before the word, polymer, in the last sentence. (If you are using a touch screen, use the cut and paste commands to move the word.) Click the Paste Options button that displays to the right of the moved word, liquid. Remove the underline format from the moved word by clicking 'Keep Text Only' on the Paste Options menu.
3. Display the ruler, if necessary. Use the ruler to indent the first line of the paragraph one-half inch. (If you are using a touch screen, use the Paragraph dialog box.)
4. Change the line spacing of the paragraph to double.
5. Use the Navigation Pane to find all occurrences of the word, printer. How many are there?
6. Use the Find and Replace dialog box to replace all occurrences of the word, 3D, with the word, 3-D. How many replacements were made?
7. Use the Navigation Pane to find the word, finished. Use Word's thesaurus to change the word, finished, to the word, complete. What other words are in the list of synonyms?

8. Switch to the header so that you can edit it. In the first line of the header, change the word, Draft, to the word, Modified, so that it reads: 3-D Printers Paragraph Modified.
9. In the second line of the header, insert a page number (a plain number with no formatting) one space after the word, Page.
10. Change the alignment of both lines of text in the header from left-aligned to right-aligned. Switch back to the document text.
11. If requested by your instructor, enter your first and last name on a separate line below the page number in the header.
12. Click File on the ribbon and then click Save As. Save the document using the file name, Apply 2-1 3-D Printers Paragraph Modified.
13. Submit the modified document, shown in Figure 2–79, in the format specified by your instructor.
14. Use the Insights task pane to look up the word prosthetics. Click the Explore tab in the Insights task pane. Which web articles appeared? What images appeared? Click the Define tab in the Insights task pane. Which dictionary was used?
15. Answer the questions posed in #5, #6, #7, and #14. How would you find and replace a special character, such as a paragraph mark?

Extend Your Knowledge

Extend the skills you learned in this module and experiment with new skills. You may need to use Help to complete the assignment.

Working with References and Proofing Tools

Note: To complete this assignment, you will be required to use the Data Files. Please contact your instructor for information about accessing the Data Files.

Instructions: Run Word. Open the document, Extend 2-1 Databases Paper Draft, from the Data Files. You will add another footnote to the paper, convert the footnotes to endnotes, modify the Endnote Text style, change the format of the note reference marks, use Word's readability statistics, translate the document to another language (Figure 2–80), and convert the document from MLA to APA documentation style.

Perform the following tasks:

1. Use Help to learn more about footers, footnotes and endnotes, readability statistics, bibliography styles, AutoCorrect, and Word's translation features.
2. Delete the footer from the document.
3. Insert a second footnote at an appropriate place in the research paper. Use the following footnote text: A data warehouse is a huge database that stores and manages the data required to analyze past and current transactions.
4. Change the location of the footnotes from bottom of page to below text. How did the placement of the footnotes change?
5. Convert the footnotes to endnotes. Where are the endnotes positioned?
6. Modify the Endnote Text style to 12-point Times New Roman font, double-spaced text with a hanging-line indent.
7. Change the format of the note reference marks to capital letters (A, B, etc.).

Continued >

Extend Your Knowledge *continued*

8. Add an AutoCorrect entry that replaces the word, buziness, with the word, business. Type the following sentence as the first sentence in the last paragraph of the paper, misspelling the word, business, as buziness to test the AutoCorrect entry: `Organizations often use a database to manage buziness or other functions.` Delete the AutoCorrect entry that replaces buziness with the word, business.
9. Display the Word Count dialog box. How many words, characters without spaces, characters with spaces, paragraphs, and lines are in the document? Be sure to include footnote and endnote text in the statistics.
10. Check spelling of the document, displaying readability statistics. What are the Flesch-Kincaid Grade Level and the Flesch Reading Ease score? Modify the paper to increase the reading ease score. How did you modify the paper? What are the new statistics?
11. If requested by your instructor, change the student name at the top of the paper to your name, including the last name in the header.
12. Save the revised document with the file name, Extend 2-1 Databases Paper Modified, and then submit it in the format specified by your instructor.
13. If you have an Internet connection, translate the research paper into a language of your choice using the Translate button (Review tab | Language group), as shown in Figure 2–80. Submit the translated document in the format specified by your instructor. Use the Mini Translator to hear how to pronounce three words in your paper.
14. Select the entire document and then change the documentation style from MLA to APA. Save the APA version of the document with a new file name. Compare the APA version to the MLA version. If you have a hard copy of each and your instructor requests it, circle the differences between the two documents.
15. Answer the questions posed in #4, #5, #9, and #10. Where did you insert the second footnote and why?

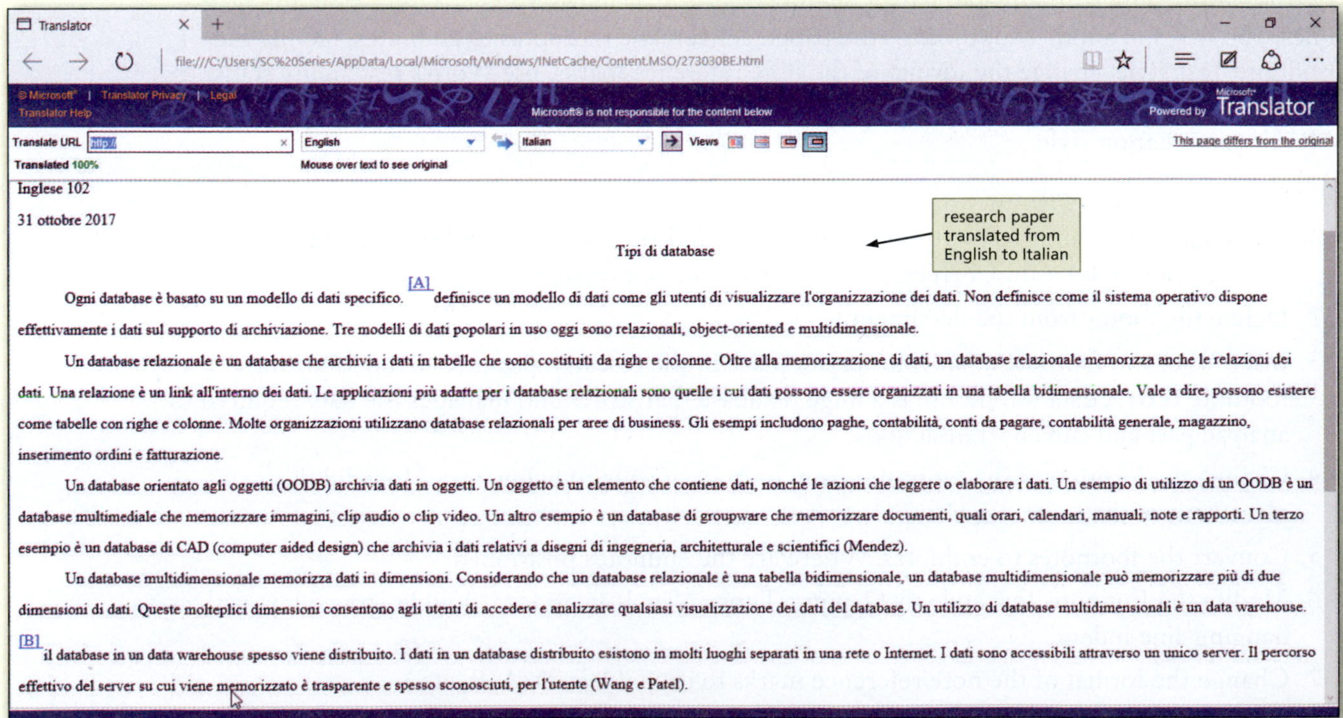

Figure 2–80

Expand Your World

Create a solution that uses cloud or web technologies by learning and investigating on your own from general guidance.

Using an Online Bibliography Tool to Create a List of Sources

Instructions: Assume you are using a computer or mobile device that does not have Word but has Internet access. To make use of time between classes, you use an online bibliography tool to create a list of sources that you can copy and paste into the Works Cited pages of a research paper that is due tomorrow.

Perform the following tasks:

1. Run a browser. Search for the text, online bibliography tool, using a search engine. Visit several of the online bibliography tools and determine which you would like to use to create a list of sources. Navigate to the desired online bibliography tool.
2. Use the online bibliography tool to enter list of sources shown below (Figure 2–81):

   Alverez, Juan and Tracy Marie Wilson. *Radon in the Home*. Chicago: Martin Publishing, 2017. Print.

   Buchalski, Leonard Adam. *Radon and Your Health*. Los Angeles: Coastal Works, 2017. Print.

   Johnson, Shantair Jada. "Radon Facts." *Environment Danger* Aug. 2017. Web. 31 Aug. 2017.

   Slobovnik, Vincent Alexander. *The Radon Guide*. Aug. 2017. Course Technology. Web. 18 Sept. 2017.

   Wakefield, Ginger Lynn and Bethany Olivia Ames. "Radon Removal Systems." *Living Well Today* Aug. 2017. Web. 3 Oct. 2017.

   Zhao, Shen Li. *Radon Testing Procedures*. Sept. 2017. Course Technology. Web. 8 Sept. 2017.
3. If requested by your instructor, replace the name in one of the sources above with your name.
4. Search for another source that discusses radon issues in the home. Add that source.
5. Copy and paste the list of sources into a Word document.
6. Save the document with the file name, Expand 2-1 Radon Issues Sources. Submit the document in the format specified by your instructor.
7. Which online bibliography tools did you evaluate? Which one did you select to use and why? Do you prefer using the online bibliography tool or Word to create sources? Why? What differences, if any, did you notice between the list of sources created with the online bibliography tool and the lists created when you use Word?

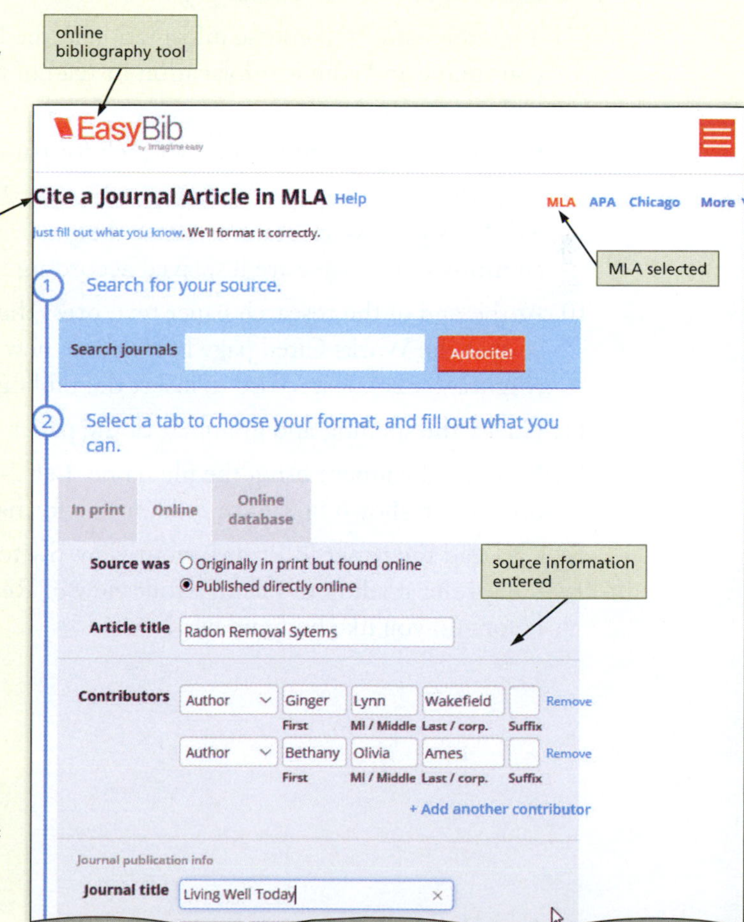

Figure 2–81

In the Labs

Design, create, modify, and/or use a document following the guidelines, concepts, and skills presented in this module. Labs 1 and 2, which increase in difficulty, require you to create solutions based on what you learned in the module; Lab 3 requires you to apply your creative thinking and problem-solving skills to design and implement a solution.

Lab 1: Preparing a Short Research Paper

Problem: You are a college student currently enrolled in an introductory English class. Your assignment is to prepare a short research paper (300–350 words) in any area of interest to you. The requirements are that the paper be presented according to the MLA documentation style and have three references. At least one of the three references must be from the web. You prepare the paper shown in Figure 2–82, which discusses wearable devices.

Perform the following tasks:

1. Run Word. If necessary, display formatting marks on the screen.
2. Modify the Normal style to the 12-point Times New Roman font.
3. Adjust line spacing to double.
4. Remove space below (after) paragraphs.
5. Update the Normal style to reflect the adjusted line and paragraph spacing.
6. Create a header to number pages.
7. Type the name and course information at the left margin. If requested by your instructor, use your name and course information instead of the information shown in Figure 2–82a. Center and type the title.
8. Set a first-line indent to one-half inch for paragraphs in the body of the research paper.
9. Type the research paper as shown in Figures 2–82a and 2–82b. Change the bibliography style to MLA. As you insert citations, enter their source information (shown in Figure 2–82c). Edit the citations so that they are displayed according to Figures 2–82a and 2–82b.
10. At the end of the research paper text, press the ENTER key and then insert a manual page break so that the Works Cited page begins on a new page. Enter and format the works cited title (Figure 2–82c). Use Word to insert the bibliographical list (bibliography).
11. Check the spelling and grammar of the paper at once.
12. Save the document using the file name, Lab 2–1 Wearable Devices Paper. Submit the document, shown in Figure 2–82, in the format specified by your instructor.
13. Read the paper in Print Layout view. Switch to Read mode and scroll through the pages. Do you prefer reading in Print Layout view or Read mode? Why? In Read mode, which of the page colors do you like best and why?

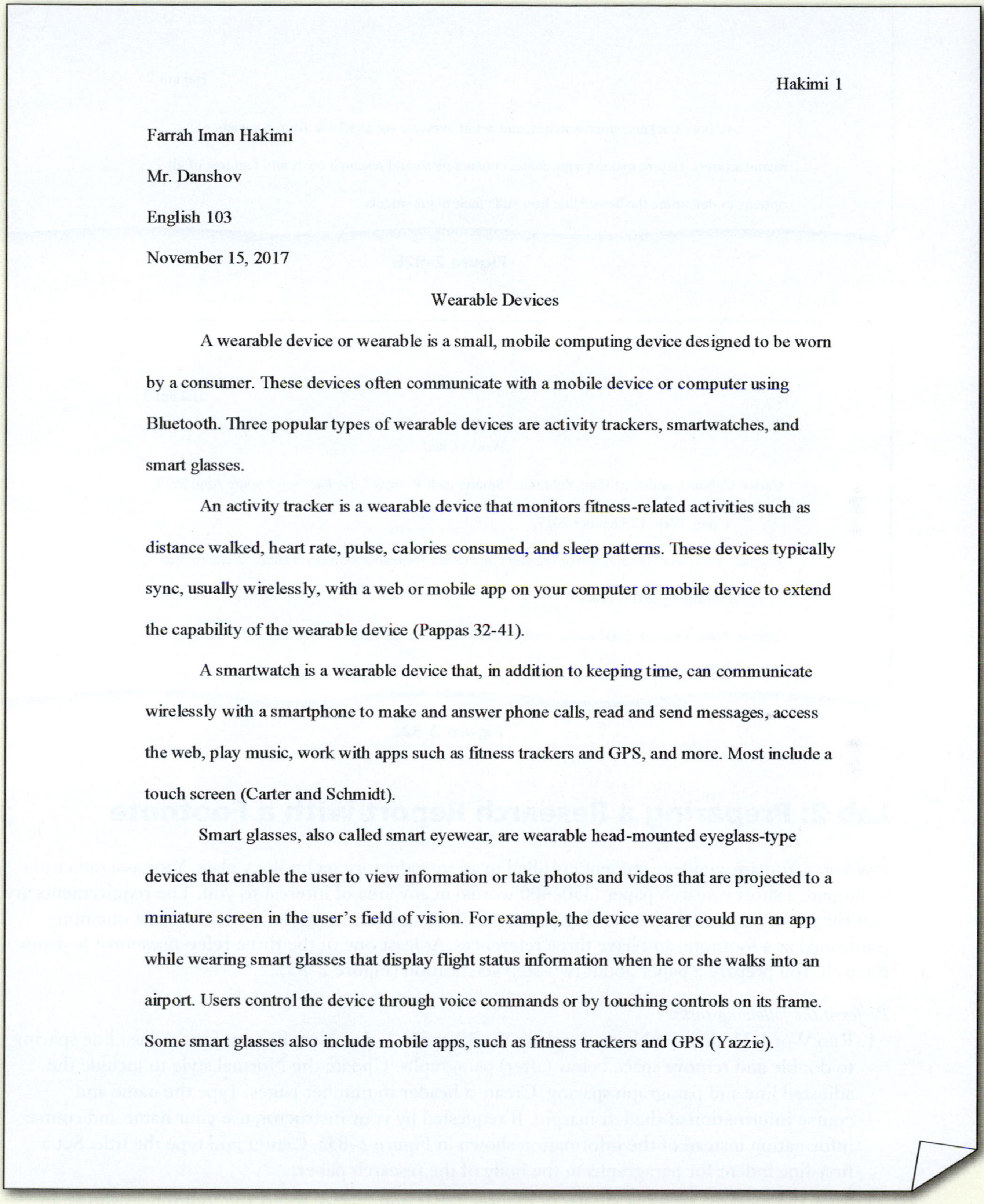

Hakimi 1

Farrah Iman Hakimi

Mr. Danshov

English 103

November 15, 2017

Wearable Devices

A wearable device or wearable is a small, mobile computing device designed to be worn by a consumer. These devices often communicate with a mobile device or computer using Bluetooth. Three popular types of wearable devices are activity trackers, smartwatches, and smart glasses.

An activity tracker is a wearable device that monitors fitness-related activities such as distance walked, heart rate, pulse, calories consumed, and sleep patterns. These devices typically sync, usually wirelessly, with a web or mobile app on your computer or mobile device to extend the capability of the wearable device (Pappas 32-41).

A smartwatch is a wearable device that, in addition to keeping time, can communicate wirelessly with a smartphone to make and answer phone calls, read and send messages, access the web, play music, work with apps such as fitness trackers and GPS, and more. Most include a touch screen (Carter and Schmidt).

Smart glasses, also called smart eyewear, are wearable head-mounted eyeglass-type devices that enable the user to view information or take photos and videos that are projected to a miniature screen in the user's field of vision. For example, the device wearer could run an app while wearing smart glasses that display flight status information when he or she walks into an airport. Users control the device through voice commands or by touching controls on its frame. Some smart glasses also include mobile apps, such as fitness trackers and GPS (Yazzie).

Figure 2–82a

Continued >

In the Labs *continued*

Hakimi 2

Activity trackers, smartwatches, and smart eyewear are available from a variety of manufacturers. Before making a purchase, consumers should research costs and features of all options to determine the device that best suits their requirements.

Figure 2–82b

Hakimi 3

Works Cited

Carter, Calvin J. and Karl Hans Schmidt. "Smartwatch Review." *Technology Trends* Aug. 2017: n. pag. Web. 12 October 2017.

Pappas, Anastasia Maria. *Activity Trackers and Other Wearable Devices*. Dallas: Western Star Publishing, 2017. Print.

Yazzie, Nina Tamaya. *Evaluating Today's Smart Glasses*. 25 Aug. 2017. Course Technology. Web. 25 Sept. 2017.

Figure 2–82c

Lab 2: Preparing a Research Report with a Footnote

Problem: You are a college student enrolled in an introductory technology class. Your assignment is to prepare a short research paper (350–400 words) in any area of interest to you. The requirements are that the paper be presented according to the MLA documentation style, contain at least one note positioned as a footnote, and have three references. At least one of the three references must be from the web. You prepare a paper about two-step verification (Figure 2–83).

Perform the following tasks:

1. Run Word. Modify the Normal style to the 12-point Times New Roman font. Adjust line spacing to double and remove space below (after) paragraphs. Update the Normal style to include the adjusted line and paragraph spacing. Create a header to number pages. Type the name and course information at the left margin. If requested by your instructor, use your name and course information instead of the information shown in Figure 2–83a. Center and type the title. Set a first-line indent for paragraphs in the body of the research paper.
2. Type the research paper as shown in Figures 2–83a and 2–83b. Insert the footnote as shown in Figure 2–83a. Change the Footnote Text style to the format specified in the MLA documentation

Wagner 1

Bryan Wagner

Dr. Rosenberg

Technology 104

October 27, 2017

Two-Step Verification

In an attempt to protect personal data and information from online thieves, many organizations, such as financial institutions or universities, that store sensitive or confidential items use a two-step verification process. With two-step verification, a computer or mobile device uses two separate methods, one after the next, to verify the identity of a user.

ATMs (automated teller machines) usually require a two-step verification. Users first insert their ATM card into the ATM (Step 1) and then enter a PIN, or personal identification number, (Step 2) to access their bank account. If someone steals these cards, the thief must enter the user's PIN to access the account (Tanaka).

Another use of two-step verification requires a mobile phone and a computer or mobile device.[1] When users sign in to an account on a computer or mobile device, they enter a user name and password (Step 1). Next, they are prompted to enter another authentication code (Step 2), which is sent as a text or voice message or via an app on a smartphone. This second code generally is valid for a set time, sometimes only for a few minutes or hours. If users do not sign in during this time limit, they must repeat the process and request another verification code

---

[1] According to Moore and O'Sullivan, users should register an alternate mobile phone number, landline phone number, email address, or other form of contact beyond a mobile phone number so that they still can access their accounts even if they lose their mobile phone (54).

Figure 2–83a

Wagner 2

(Marcy). Microsoft and Google commonly use two-step verification when users sign in to these websites (Moore and O'Sullivan).

Some organizations use two separate methods to verify the identity of users. These two-step verification procedures are designed to protect users' sensitive and confidential items from online thieves.

Figure 2–83b

Continued >

style. Change the bibliography style to MLA. As you insert citations, use the following source information, entering it according to the MLA style:

a. Type of Source: Article in a Periodical
   Author: Hana Kei Tanaka
   Article Title: Safeguards against Unauthorized Access and Use
   Periodical Title: Technology Today
   Year: 2017
   Month: Sept.
   Pages: no pages used
   Medium: Web
   Year Accessed: 2017
   Month Accessed: Oct.
   Day Accessed: 3

b. Type of Source: Web site
   Author: Fredrick Lee Marcy
   Name of webpage: Two-Step Verification
   Year/Month/Date: none given
   Production Company: Course Technology
   Medium: Web
   Year Accessed: 2017
   Month Accessed: Sept.
   Day Accessed: 18

c. Type of Source: Book
   Author: Aaron Bradley Moore and Brianna Clare O'Sullivan
   Title: Authentication Techniques
   Year: 2017
   City: Detroit
   Publisher: Great Lakes Press
   Medium: Print

3. At the end of the research paper text, press the ENTER key once and insert a manual page break so that the Works Cited page begins on a new page. Enter and format the works cited title. Use Word to insert the bibliographical list.
4. Check the spelling and grammar of the paper.
5. Save the document using the file name, Lab 2–2 Two-Step Verification Paper. Submit the document, shown in Figure 2–83, in the format specified by your instructor.
6. This paper uses web sources. What factors should you consider when selecting web sources?

Lab 3: Consider This: Your Turn

Create a Research Paper about Wireless Communications

Note: To complete this assignment, you will be required to use the Data Files. Please contact your instructor for information about accessing the Data Files.

Problem: As a student in an introductory computer class, your instructor has assigned a brief research paper that discusses wireless communications.

Perform the following tasks:

Part 1: The source for the text in your research paper is in a file called Lab 2–3 Consider This Your Turn Wireless Communications Notes, which is located in the Data Files. If your instructor requests, use the Insights task pane to obtain information from another source and include that information as a note positioned as a footnote in the paper, along with entering its corresponding source information as appropriate. Add an AutoCorrect entry to correct a word you commonly mistype. If necessary, set the default dictionary. Add one of the source last names to the dictionary.

Using the concepts and techniques presented in this module, organize the notes in the text in the file on the Data Files, rewording as necessary, and then create and format this research paper according to the MLA documentation style. Be sure to check spelling and grammar of the finished paper. Submit your assignment and answers to the critical thinking questions in the format specified by your instructor.

Part 2: You made several decisions while creating the research paper in this assignment: how to organize the notes, where to place citations, how to format sources, and which source on the web to use for the footnote text (if requested by your instructor). What was the rationale behind each of these decisions? When you proofread the document, what further revisions did you make and why?

3 Creating a Business Letter with a Letterhead and Table

Objectives

You will have mastered the material in this module when you can:

- Change margins
- Insert and format a shape
- Change text wrapping
- Insert an online picture and format it
- Insert a symbol
- Add a border to a paragraph
- Clear formatting
- Convert a hyperlink to regular text
- Apply a style
- Set and use tab stops
- Insert the current date
- Create, modify, and insert a building block
- Insert a Word table, enter data in the table, and format the table
- Address and print an envelope

Introduction

In a business environment, people use documents to communicate with others. Business documents can include letters, memos, newsletters, proposals, and resumes. An effective business document clearly and concisely conveys its message and has a professional, organized appearance. You can use your own creative skills to design and compose business documents. Using Word, for example, you can develop the content and decide on the location of each item in a business document.

Project — Business Letter with a Letterhead and Table

At some time, you more than likely will prepare a business letter. Contents of business letters include requests, inquiries, confirmations, acknowledgements, recommendations, notifications, responses, thank you letters, invitations, offers, referrals, complaints, and more.

The project in this module follows generally accepted guidelines for writing letters and uses Word to create the business letter shown in Figure 3–1. This business

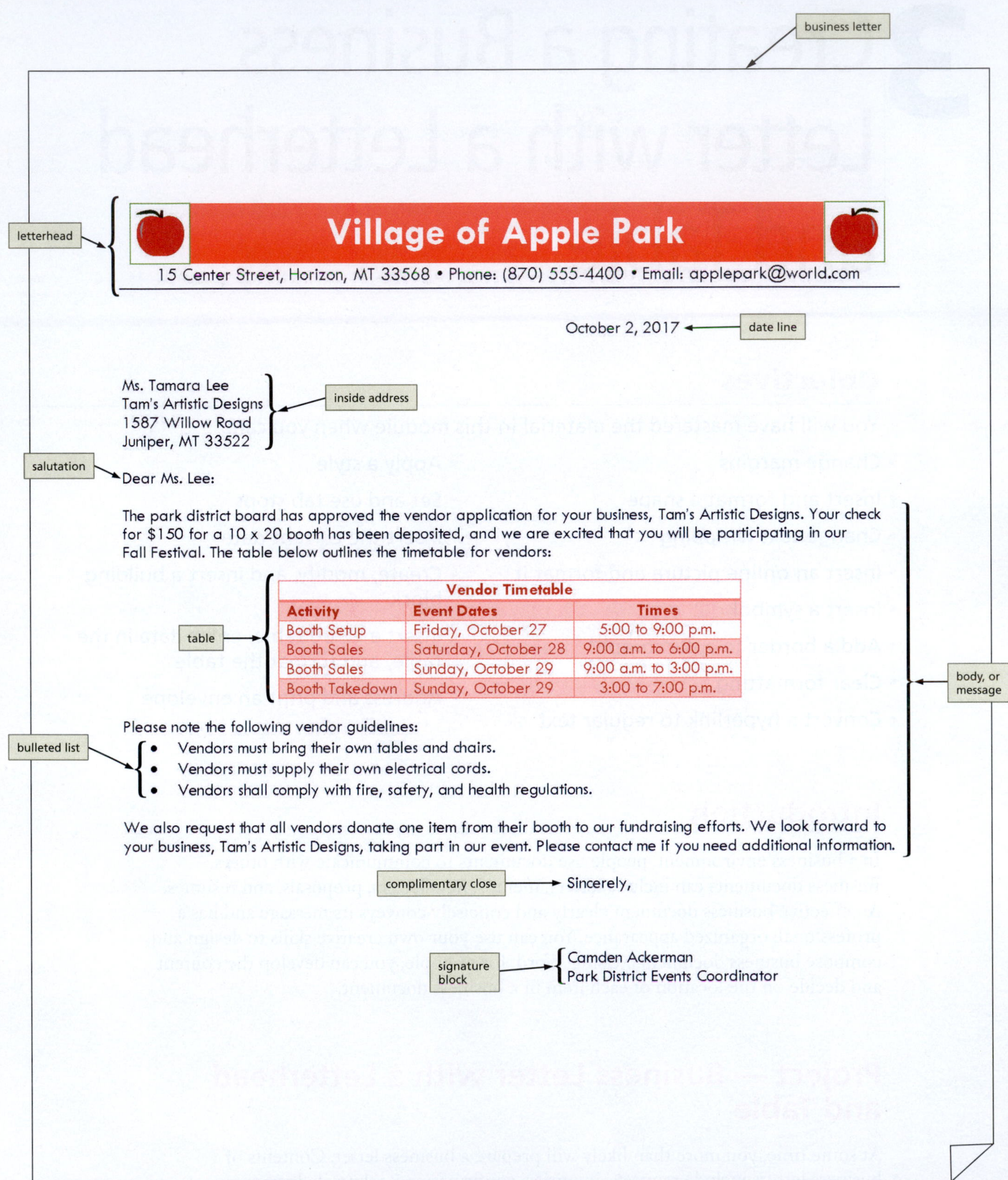
business letter

letterhead

Village of Apple Park

15 Center Street, Horizon, MT 33568 • Phone: (870) 555-4400 • Email: applepark@world.com

October 2, 2017

date line

Ms. Tamara Lee
Tam's Artistic Designs
1587 Willow Road
Juniper, MT 33522

inside address

salutation

Dear Ms. Lee:

body, or message

The park district board has approved the vendor application for your business, Tam's Artistic Designs. Your check for $150 for a 10 x 20 booth has been deposited, and we are excited that you will be participating in our Fall Festival. The table below outlines the timetable for vendors:

table

Vendor Timetable		
Activity	**Event Dates**	**Times**
Booth Setup	Friday, October 27	5:00 to 9:00 p.m.
Booth Sales	Saturday, October 28	9:00 a.m. to 6:00 p.m.
Booth Sales	Sunday, October 29	9:00 a.m. to 3:00 p.m.
Booth Takedown	Sunday, October 29	3:00 to 7:00 p.m.

Please note the following vendor guidelines:

bulleted list

- Vendors must bring their own tables and chairs.
- Vendors must supply their own electrical cords.
- Vendors shall comply with fire, safety, and health regulations.

We also request that all vendors donate one item from their booth to our fundraising efforts. We look forward to your business, Tam's Artistic Designs, taking part in our event. Please contact me if you need additional information.

complimentary close

Sincerely,

signature block

Camden Ackerman
Park District Events Coordinator

Figure 3–1

letter is a letter from the park district events coordinator at the Village of Apple Park that confirms a vendor application to participate in its community event. The letter includes a custom letterhead, as well as all essential business letter components: date line, inside address, salutation, body, complimentary close, and signature block. To easily present the vendor timetable during the event, the letter shows this information in a table. The vendor guidelines appear in a bulleted list.

In this module, you will learn how to create the letter shown in Figure 3–1. The following roadmap identifies general activities you will perform as you progress through this module:

1. CREATE AND FORMAT a LETTERHEAD WITH GRAPHICS.
2. SPECIFY the LETTER FORMATS according to business letter guidelines.
3. INSERT a TABLE in the letter.
4. FORMAT the TABLE in the letter.
5. INSERT a BULLETED LIST in the letter.
6. ADDRESS an ENVELOPE for the letter.

For an introduction to Windows and instructions about how to perform basic Windows tasks, read the Office and Windows module at the beginning of this book, where you can learn how to resize windows, change screen resolution, create folders, move and rename files, use Windows Help, and much more.

To Run Word and Change Word Settings

If you are using a computer to step through the project in this module and you want your screens to match the figures in this book, you should change your screen's resolution to 1366 × 768. For information about how to change a computer's resolution, refer to the Office and Windows module at the beginning of this book.

The following steps run Word, display formatting marks, and change the zoom to page width.

1. Run Word and create a blank document in the Word window. If necessary, maximize the Word window.
2. If the Print Layout button on the status bar is not selected (shown in Figure 3–2), click it so that your screen is in Print Layout view.
3. If the 'Show/Hide ¶' button (Home tab | Paragraph group) is not selected already, click it to display formatting marks on the screen.
4. To display the page the same width as the document window, if necessary, click the Page Width button (View tab | Zoom group).

For an introduction to Office and instructions about how to perform basic tasks in Office apps, read the Office and Windows module at the beginning of this book, where you can learn how to run an application, use the ribbon, save a file, open a file, print a file, exit an application, use Help, and much more.

To Change Margin Settings

1 CREATE & FORMAT LETTERHEAD WITH GRAPHICS | 2 SPECIFY LETTER FORMATS
3 INSERT TABLE | 4 FORMAT TABLE | 5 INSERT BULLETED LIST | 6 ADDRESS ENVELOPE

Word is preset to use standard 8.5-by-11-inch paper, with 1-inch top, bottom, left, and right margins. The business letter in this module uses .75-inch left and right margins and 1-inch top and bottom margins. ***Why?*** *You would like more text to fit from left to right on the page.*

When you change the default (preset) margin settings, the new margin settings affect every page in the document. If you wanted the margins to affect just a portion of the document, you would divide the document into sections (discussed in a later module), which enables you to specify different margin settings for each section. The following steps change margin settings.

1

- Display the Layout tab.
- Click the Adjust Margins button (Layout tab | Page Setup group) to display the Adjust Margins gallery (Figure 3–2).

2

- Click Moderate in the Adjust Margins gallery to change the margins to the specified settings.

Q&A What if the margin settings I want are not in the Adjust Margins gallery?
You can click Custom Margins in the Adjust Margins gallery and then enter your desired margin values in the top, bottom, left, and right boxes in the Page Setup dialog box.

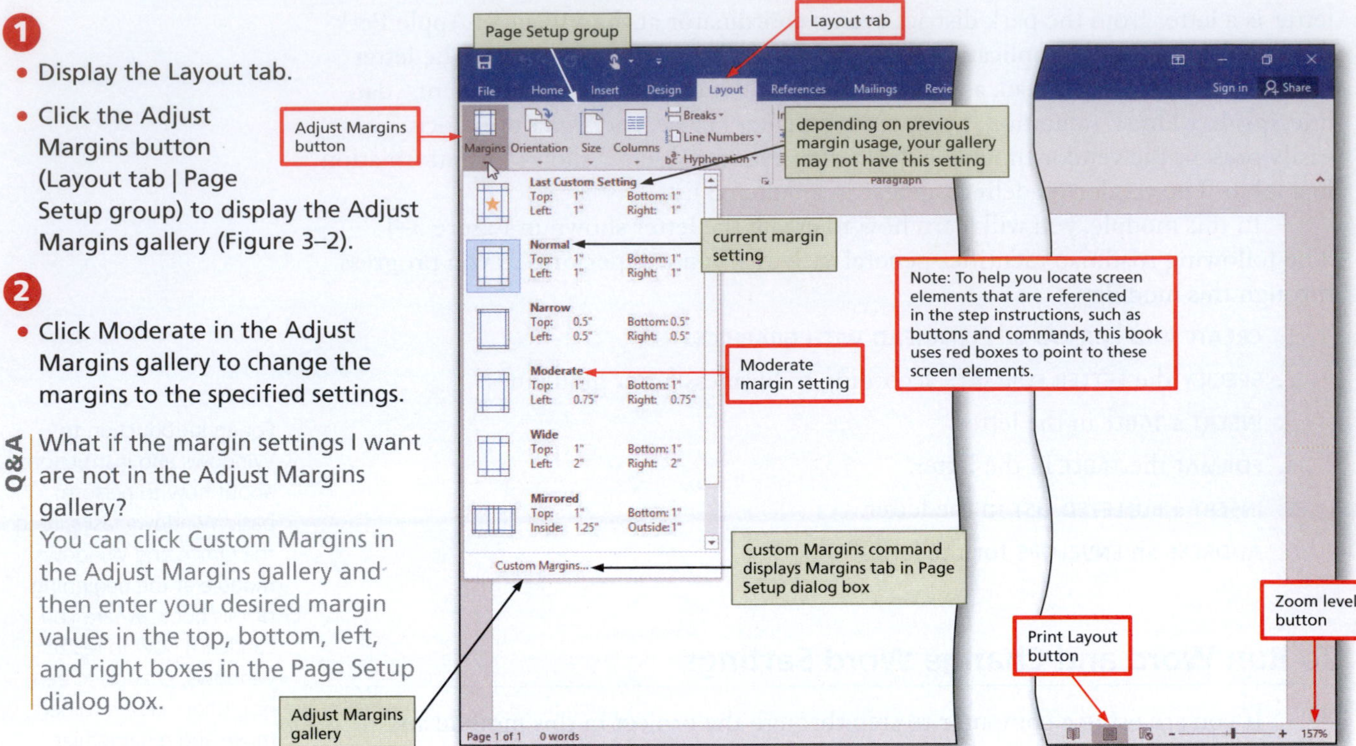

Figure 3–2

Other Ways

1. Position pointer on margin boundary on ruler; when pointer changes to two-headed arrow, drag margin boundary on ruler

Creating a Letterhead

The cost of preprinted letterhead can be high. An alternative is to create your own letterhead and save it in a file. When you want to create a letter at a later time, you can start by using the letterhead file. The following sections create a letterhead and then save it in a file for future use.

CONSIDER THIS

What is a letterhead?

A **letterhead** is the section of a letter that identifies an organization or individual. Often, the letterhead appears at the top of a letter. Although you can design and print a letterhead yourself, many businesses pay an outside firm to design and print their letterhead, usually on higher-quality paper. They then use the professionally preprinted paper for external business communications.

If you do not have preprinted letterhead paper, you can design a creative letterhead. It is important the letterhead appropriately represent the essence of the organization or individual (i.e., formal, technical, creative, etc.). That is, it should use text, graphics, formats, and colors that reflect the organization or individual. The letterhead should leave ample room for the contents of the letter.

When designing a letterhead, consider its contents, placement, and appearance.

- **Contents of letterhead.** A letterhead should contain these elements:
  - Complete legal name of the individual, group, or company
  - Complete mailing address: street address including building, room, suite number, or post office box, along with city, state, and postal code
  - Phone number(s) and fax number, if applicable
  - Email address

– Website address, if applicable

– Many letterheads also include a logo or other image; if an image is used, it should express the organization or individual's personality or goals

- **Placement of elements in the letterhead.** Many letterheads center their elements across the top of the page. Others align some or all of the elements with the left or right margins. Sometimes, the elements are split between the top and bottom of the page. For example, a name and logo may be at the top of the page with the address at the bottom of the page.
- **Appearance of letterhead elements.** Use fonts that are easy to read. Give the organization or individual name impact by making its font size larger than the rest of the text in the letterhead. For additional emphasis, consider formatting the name in bold, italic, or a different color. Choose colors that complement each other and convey the goals of the organization or individual.

When finished designing the letterhead, determine if a divider line would help to visually separate the letterhead from the remainder of the letter.

The letterhead for the letter in this module consists of the organization's name, appropriate graphics, postal address, phone number, and email address. The name and graphics are enclosed in a rectangular shape (shown in Figure 3–1), and the contact information is below the shape. You will follow these general steps to create the letterhead in this module:

1. Insert and format a shape.
2. Enter and format the organization name in the shape.
3. Insert, format, and position the images in the shape.
4. Enter the contact information below the shape.
5. Add a border below the contact information.

BTW
The Ribbon and Screen Resolution
Word may change how the groups and buttons within the groups appear on the ribbon, depending on the computer or mobile device's screen resolution. Thus, your ribbon may look different from the ones in this book if you are using a screen resolution other than 1366 x 768.

To Insert a Shape

1 CREATE & FORMAT LETTERHEAD WITH GRAPHICS | 2 SPECIFY LETTER FORMATS
3 INSERT TABLE | 4 FORMAT TABLE | 5 INSERT BULLETED LIST | 6 ADDRESS ENVELOPE

Word has a variety of predefined shapes, which are a type of drawing object, that you can insert in documents. A **drawing object** is a graphic that you create using Word. Examples of shape drawing objects include rectangles, circles, triangles, arrows, flowcharting symbols, stars, banners, and callouts. The following steps insert a rectangle shape in the letterhead. ***Why?*** *The organization's name is placed in a rectangle for emphasis and visual appeal.*

- Display the Insert tab.
- Click the 'Draw a Shape' button (Insert tab | Illustrations group) to display the Draw a Shape gallery (Figure 3–3).

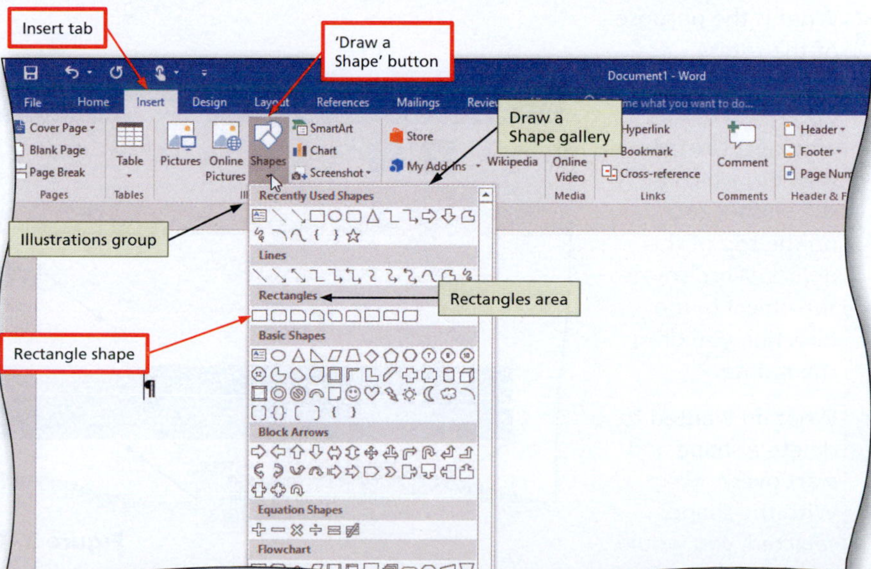

Figure 3–3

2

- Click the Rectangle shape in the Rectangles area in the Draw a Shape gallery, which removes the gallery.

Q&A What if I am using a touch screen?
The shape is inserted in the document window. Skip Steps 3 and 4, and proceed to Step 5.

- Position the pointer (a crosshair) in the approximate location for the upper-left corner of the desired shape (Figure 3–4).

Q&A What is the purpose of the crosshair pointer?
You drag the crosshair pointer from the upper-left corner to the lower-right corner to form the desired location and size of the shape.

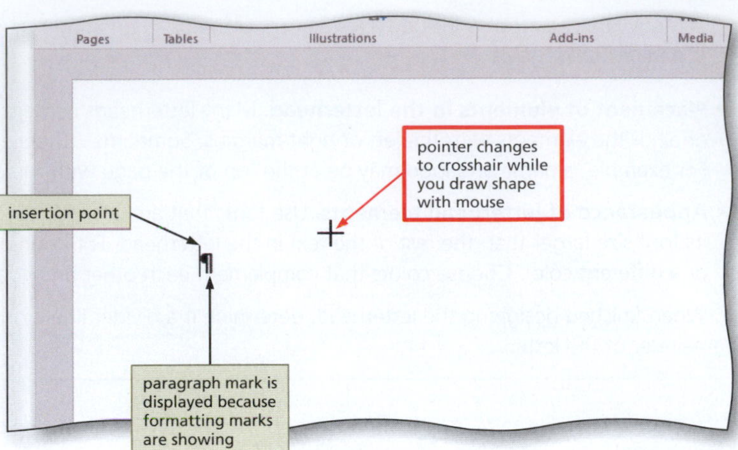

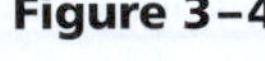

Figure 3–4

3

- Drag the mouse to the right and downward to form the boundaries of the shape, as shown in Figure 3–5. Do not release the mouse button.

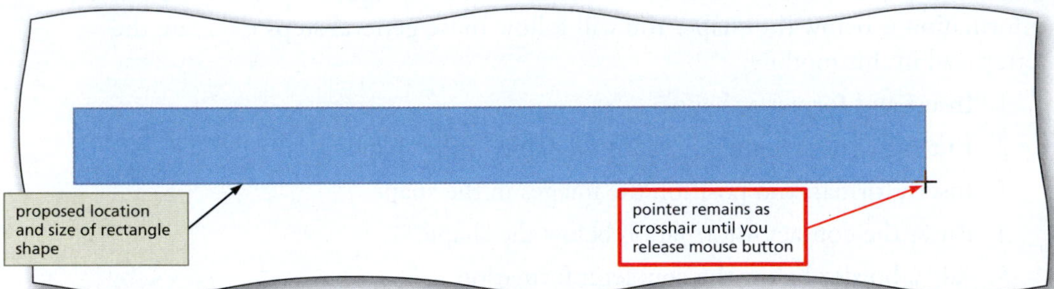

Figure 3–5

4

- Release the mouse button so that Word draws the shape according to your drawing in the document window.

5

- Verify your shape is the same approximate height and width as the one in this project by reviewing, and if necessary changing, the values in the Shape Height box and Shape Width boxes (Drawing Tools Format tab | Size group) to 0.53" and 5.7" by typing each value in the respective box and then pressing the ENTER key (Figure 3–6).

Q&A What is the purpose of the rotate handle?
When you drag an object's **rotate handle**, which is the white circle on the top of the object, Word rotates the object in the direction you drag the mouse.

What if I wanted to delete a shape and start over?
With the shape selected, you would press the DELETE key.

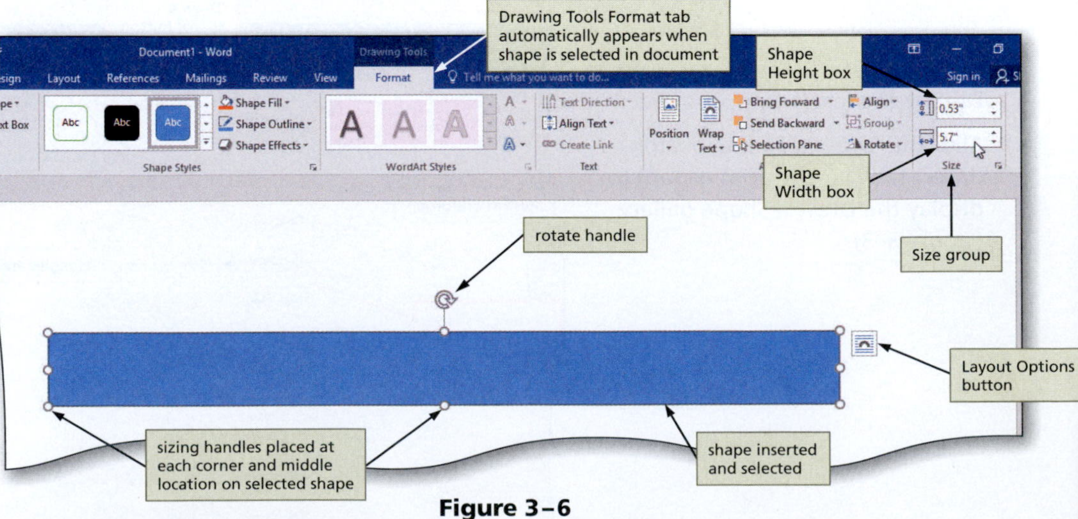

Figure 3–6

Floating versus Inline Objects

When you insert an object in a document, Word inserts it as either an inline object or a floating object. An **inline object** is an object that is part of a paragraph. With inline objects, you change the location of the object by setting paragraph options, such as centered, right-aligned, and so on. For example, when you inserted the picture of the surfer in Module 1, Word inserted it as an inline object. A **floating object**, by contrast, is an object that can be positioned at a specific location in a document or in a layer over or behind text in a document. The shape you just inserted is a floating object. You have more flexibility with floating objects because you can position a floating object anywhere on the page.

In addition to changing an object from inline to floating and vice versa, Word provides several floating options, which (along with inline) are called text wrapping options because they affect how text wraps with or around the object. Table 3–1 presents the various text wrapping options.

Table 3–1 Text Wrapping Options

Text Wrapping Option	Object Type	How It Works
In Line with Text	Inline	Object positioned according to paragraph formatting; for example, if paragraph is centered, object will be centered with any text in the paragraph.
Square	Floating	Text wraps around object, with text forming a box around the object.
Tight	Floating	Text wraps around object, with text forming to shape of the object.
Through	Floating	Object appears at beginning, middle, or end of text. Moving object changes location of text.
Top and Bottom	Floating	Object appears above or below text. Moving object changes location of text.
Behind Text	Floating	Object appears behind text.
In Front of Text	Floating	Object appears in front of text and may cover the text.

To Change an Object's Position

1 CREATE & FORMAT LETTERHEAD WITH GRAPHICS | 2 SPECIFY LETTER FORMATS
3 INSERT TABLE | 4 FORMAT TABLE | 5 INSERT BULLETED LIST | 6 ADDRESS ENVELOPE

You can specify an object's vertical position on a page (top, middle, bottom) and its horizontal position (left, center, right). The following steps change the position of an object, specifically, the rectangle shape. ***Why?*** *You want the shape to be centered at the top of the page in the letterhead.*

1

- With the shape still selected, click the Position Object button (Drawing Tools Format tab | Arrange group) to display the Position Object gallery (Figure 3–7).

Q&A What if the shape is not still selected?
Click the shape to select it.

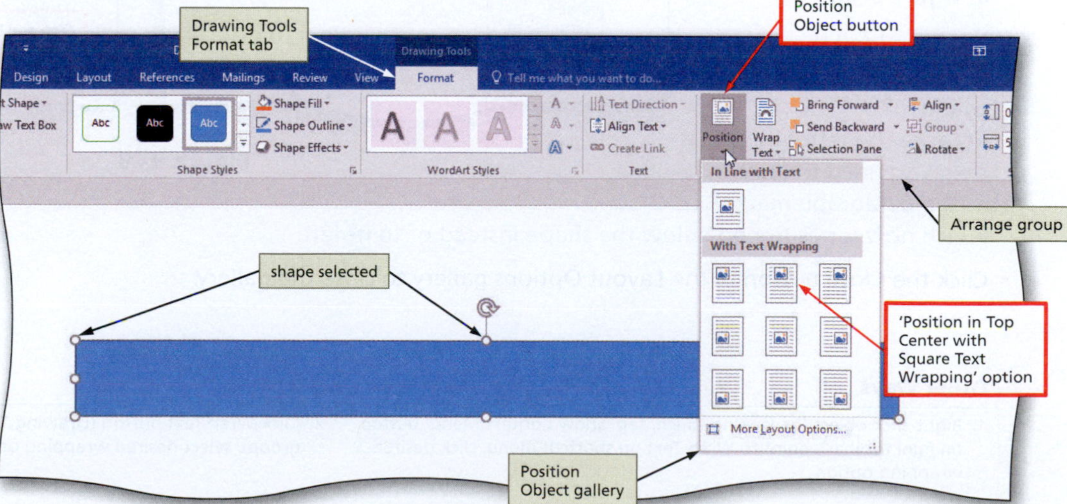

Figure 3–7

Experiment

- Point to various options in the Position Object gallery and watch the shape move to the selected position option.

2

- Click 'Position in Top Center with Square Text Wrapping' in the Position Object gallery so that the object does not cover the document and is centered at the top of the document.

Other Ways

1. Click Layout Options button attached to graphic (shown in Figure 3–8), click See more link in Layout Options gallery, click Horizontal Alignment arrow and select alignment (Layout dialog box), click Vertical Alignment arrow and select alignment, click OK button
2. Click Advanced Layout: Size Dialog Box Launcher (Drawing Tools Format tab | Size group), click Position tab (Layout dialog box), click Horizontal Alignment arrow and select alignment, click Vertical Alignment arrow and select alignment, click OK button

To Change an Object's Text Wrapping

When you insert a shape in a Word document, the default text wrapping is In Front of Text, which means the object will cover any text behind it. The previous steps, which changed the shape's position, changed the text wrapping to Square. In the letterhead, you want the shape's text wrapping to be Top and Bottom. ***Why?*** *You want the letterhead above the contents of the letter when you type it, instead of covering the contents of the letter.* The following steps change an object's text wrapping.

1

- With the shape still selected, click the Layout Options button attached to the graphic to display the Layout Options gallery (Figure 3–8).

2

- Click 'Top and Bottom' in the Layout Options gallery so that the object does not cover the document text (shown in Figure 3–9).

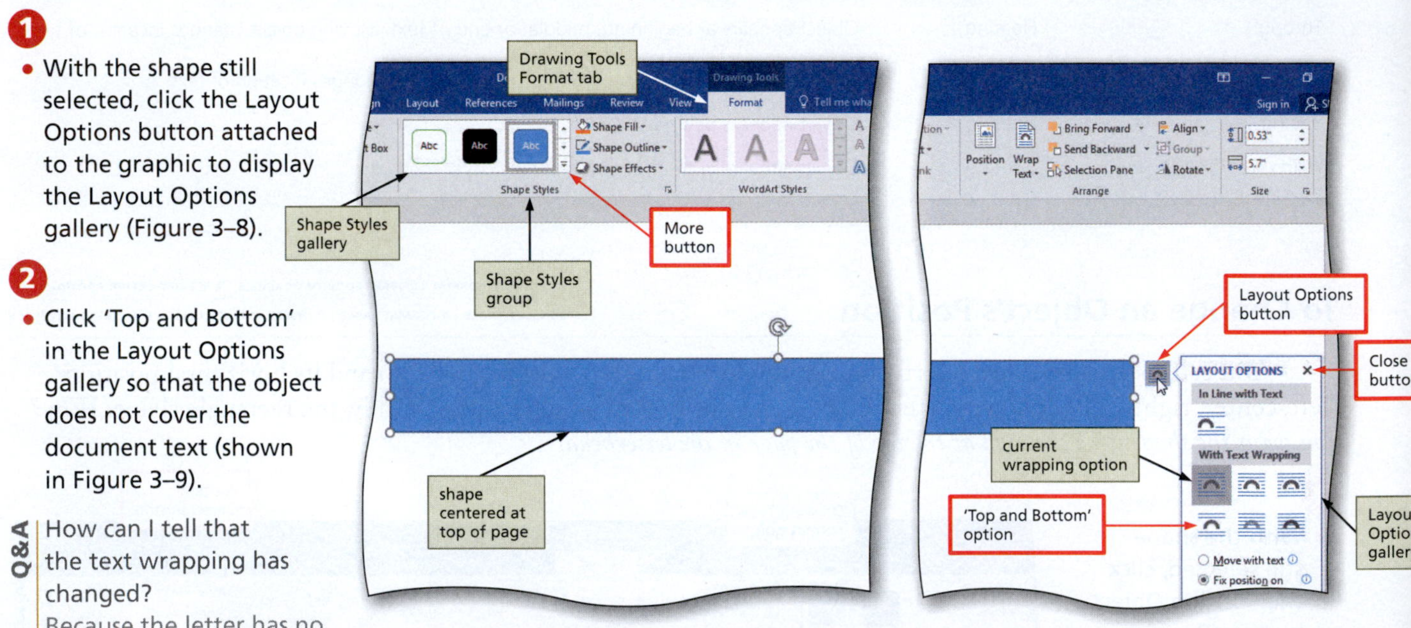

Figure 3–8

Q&A How can I tell that the text wrapping has changed?
Because the letter has no text, you need to look at the paragraph mark, which now is positioned below the shape instead of to its left.

- Click the Close button in the Layout Options gallery to close the gallery.

Other Ways

1. Right-click object (or, if using touch, tap 'Show Context Menu' button on mini toolbar), point to Wrap Text on shortcut menu, click desired wrapping option
2. Click Wrap Text button (Drawing Tools Format tab | Arrange group), select desired wrapping option

To Apply a Shape Style

1 CREATE & FORMAT LETTERHEAD WITH GRAPHICS | 2 SPECIFY LETTER FORMATS
3 INSERT TABLE | 4 FORMAT TABLE | 5 INSERT BULLETED LIST | 6 ADDRESS ENVELOPE

Why apply a shape style? *Word provides a Shape Styles gallery so that you easily can change the appearance of the shape.* The following steps apply a shape style to the rectangle shape.

1

- With the shape still selected, click the More button (shown in Figure 3–8) in the Shape Styles gallery (Drawing Tools Format tab | Shape Styles group) to expand the gallery.

Q&A What if the shape no longer is selected?
Click the shape to select it.

- Point to 'Moderate Effect - Gray-50%, Accent 3' (fourth effect in fifth row) in the Shape Styles gallery to display a live preview of that style applied to the shape in the document (Figure 3–9).

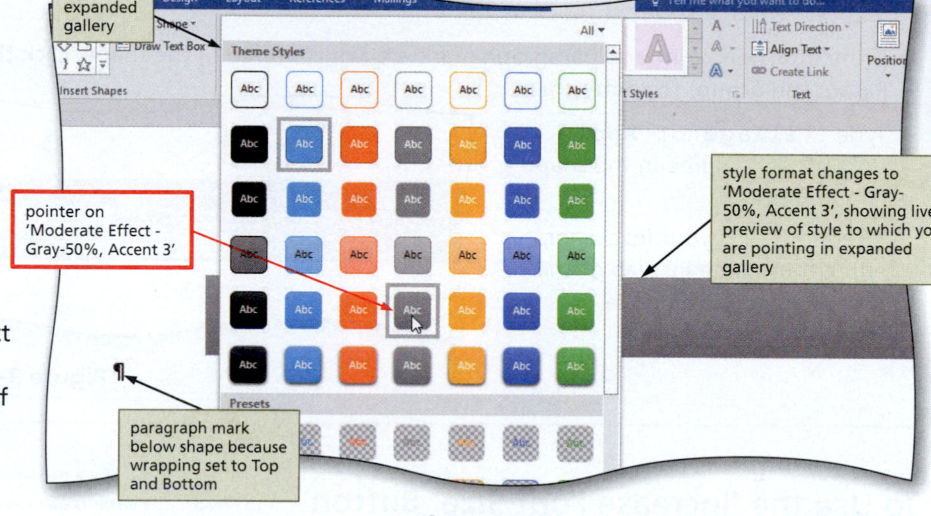

Figure 3–9

Experiment

- Point to various styles in the Shape Styles gallery and watch the style of the shape change in the document.

2

- Click 'Moderate Effect - Gray-50%, Accent 3' in the Shape Styles gallery to apply the selected style to the shape.

Other Ways

1. Right-click shape, click 'Shape Quick Styles' button on mini toolbar, select desired style
2. Click Format Shape Dialog Box Launcher (Drawing Tools Format tab | Shape Styles group), click 'Fill & Line' button (Format Shape task pane), expand Fill section, select desired colors, click Close button

To Add Text to a Shape

1 CREATE & FORMAT LETTERHEAD WITH GRAPHICS | 2 SPECIFY LETTER FORMATS
3 INSERT TABLE | 4 FORMAT TABLE | 5 INSERT BULLETED LIST | 6 ADDRESS ENVELOPE

The following steps add text (the organization name) to a shape. ***Why?*** *In the letterhead for this module, the name is in the shape. Similarly, an individual could put his or her name in a shape on a letterhead in order to create personalized letterhead.*

1

- Right-click the shape to display a mini toolbar and/or shortcut menu (Figure 3–10).

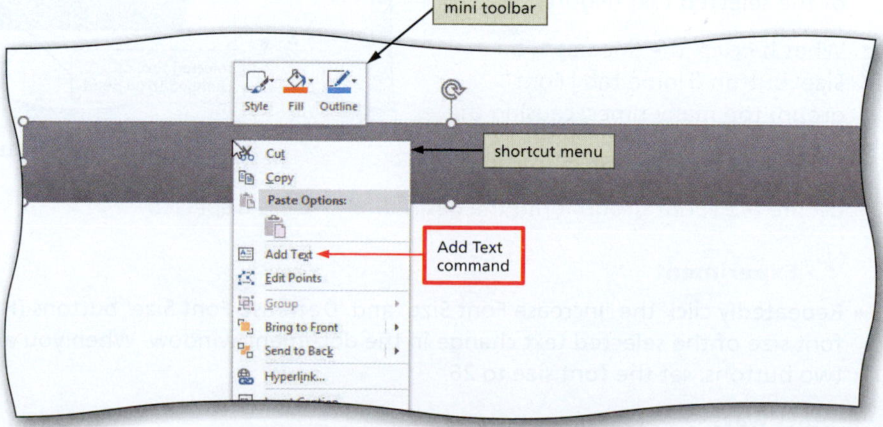

Figure 3–10

2

- Click Add Text on the shortcut menu to place an insertion point in the shape.

Q&A What if I am using a touch screen?
Tap the Edit Text button on the mini toolbar.

Why do the buttons on my mini toolbar differ?
If you are using a mouse in Mouse mode, the buttons on your mini toolbar will differ from those that appear when you use a touch screen in Touch mode.

- If the insertion point and paragraph mark are not centered in the shape, click the Center button (Home tab | Paragraph group) to center them.
- Type `Village of Apple Park` as the name in the shape (Figure 3–11).

If requested by your instructor, enter your name instead of the name shown in Figure 3–11.

Figure 3–11

To Use the 'Increase Font Size' Button

1 CREATE & FORMAT LETTERHEAD WITH GRAPHICS | 2 SPECIFY LETTER FORMATS
3 INSERT TABLE | 4 FORMAT TABLE | 5 INSERT BULLETED LIST | 6 ADDRESS ENVELOPE

In previous modules, you used the Font Size arrow (Home tab | Font group) to change the font size of text. Word also provides an 'Increase Font Size' button (Home tab | Font group), which increases the font size of selected text each time you click the button. The following steps use the 'Increase Font Size' button to increase the font size of the name in the shape to 26 point. ***Why?*** *You want the name to be as large as possible in the shape.*

1

- Drag through the text to be formatted (in this case, the name in the shape).

2

- If necessary, display the Home tab.
- Repeatedly click the 'Increase Font Size' button (Home tab | Font group) until the Font Size box displays 26 to increase the font size of the selected text (Figure 3–12).

Figure 3–12

Q&A What if I click the 'Increase Font Size' button (Home tab | Font group) too many times, causing the font size to be too big?
Click the 'Decrease Font Size' button (Home tab | Font group) until the desired font size is displayed.

Experiment

- Repeatedly click the 'Increase Font Size' and 'Decrease Font Size' buttons (Home tab | Font group) and watch the font size of the selected text change in the document window. When you are finished experimenting with these two buttons, set the font size to 26.

Other Ways

1. Press CTRL+SHIFT+>

To Bold Selected Text

To make the name stand out even more, bold it. The following steps bold the selected text.

1. With the text selected, click the Bold button (Home tab | Font group) to bold the selected text (shown in Figure 3–13).

2. Click anywhere in the text in the shape to remove the selection and place the insertion point in the shape.

To Change the Document Theme

1 CREATE & FORMAT LETTERHEAD WITH GRAPHICS | 2 SPECIFY LETTER FORMATS
3 INSERT TABLE | 4 FORMAT TABLE | 5 INSERT BULLETED LIST | 6 ADDRESS ENVELOPE

A **document theme** is a coordinated combination of colors, fonts, and effects. The current default document theme is Office, which uses Calibri and Calibri Light as its font and shades of grays and blues primarily. The following steps change the document theme to Circuit for the letter in this module. ***Why?*** *You want to use shades of reds and oranges in the letterhead because those colors are associated with energy, success, creativity, and enthusiasm.*

1

- Display the Design tab.
- Click the Themes button (Design tab | Document Formatting group) to display the Themes gallery.
- Point to Circuit in the Themes gallery to display a live preview of that theme applied to the document (Figure 3–13).

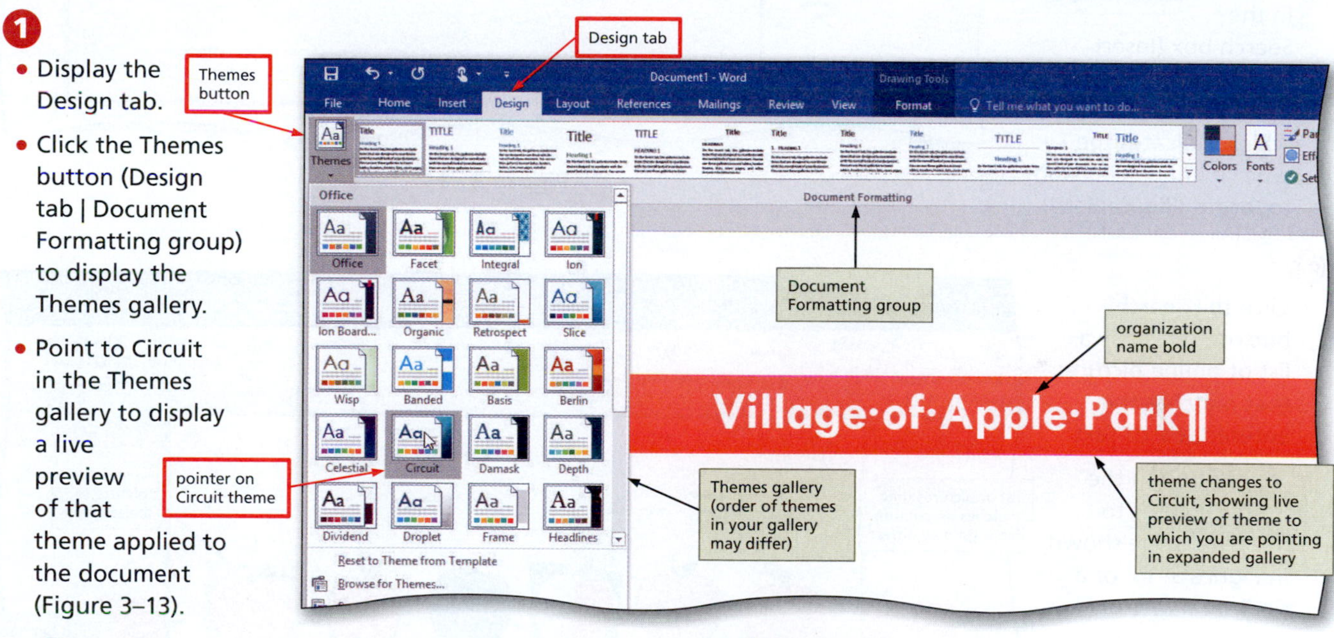

Figure 3–13

Experiment

- Point to various themes in the Themes gallery and watch the color scheme and font set change in the document window.

2

- Click Circuit in the Themes gallery to change the document theme.

To Insert an Online Picture

1 CREATE & FORMAT LETTERHEAD WITH GRAPHICS | 2 SPECIFY LETTER FORMATS
3 INSERT TABLE | 4 FORMAT TABLE | 5 INSERT BULLETED LIST | 6 ADDRESS ENVELOPE

Files containing graphics are available from a variety of sources. In the Module 1 flyer, you inserted a digital picture taken with a camera. In this project, you insert a picture from the web. Microsoft Office applications can access a collection of royalty-free photos and animations.

The letterhead in this project contains a picture of an apple (shown in Figure 3–1). ***Why?*** *Because the name of the organization is Village of Apple Park, an apple is an appropriate image for this letterhead.* The following steps insert an online picture in the document.

1

- If necessary, click the paragraph mark below the shape to position the insertion point where you want to insert the picture.
- Display the Insert tab.
- Click the Online Pictures button (Insert tab | Illustrations group) to display the Insert Pictures dialog box.
- Type **apple** in the Search box (Insert Pictures dialog box) to specify the search text, which indicates the type of image you want to locate (Figure 3–14).

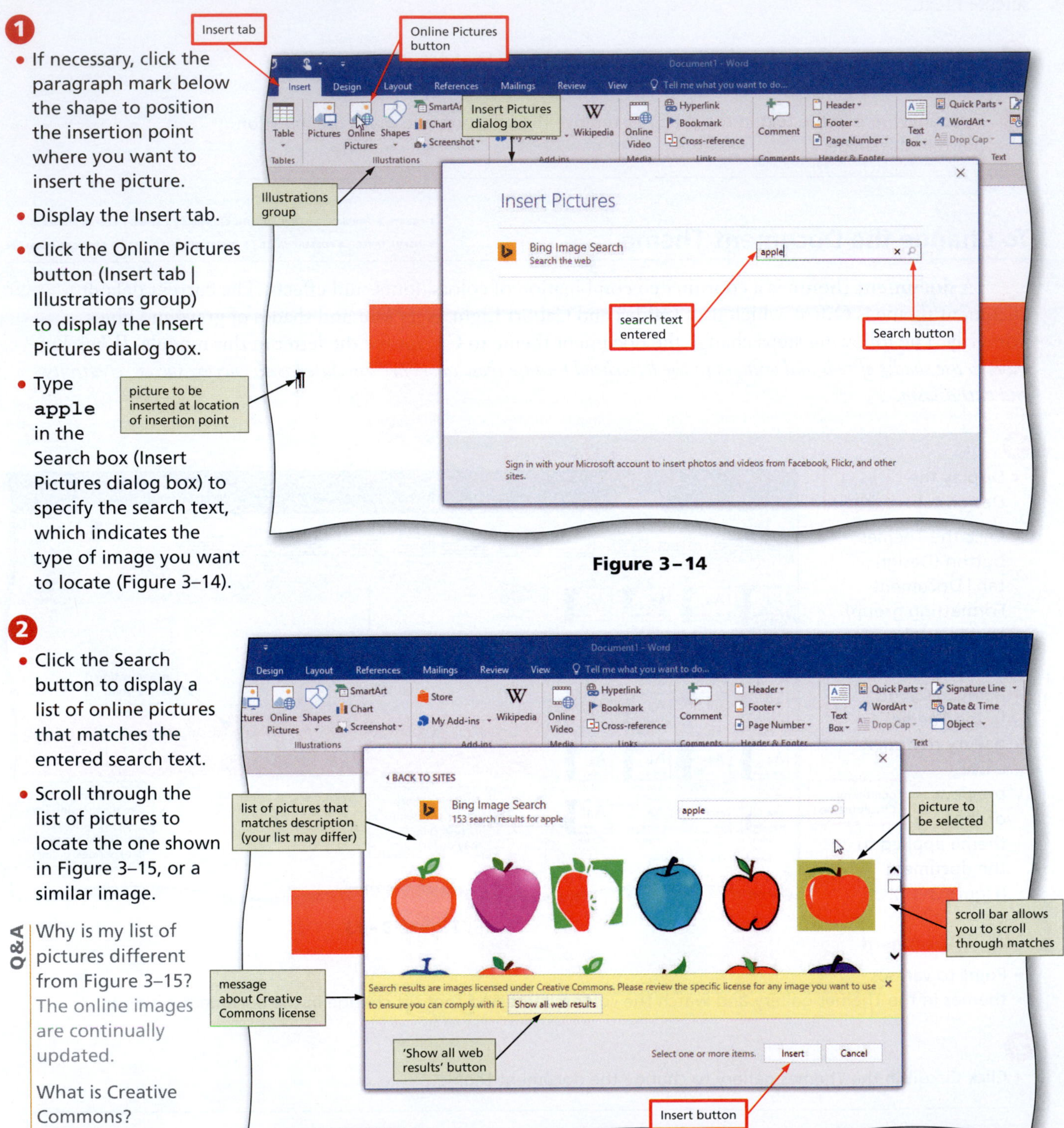

Figure 3–14

2

- Click the Search button to display a list of online pictures that matches the entered search text.
- Scroll through the list of pictures to locate the one shown in Figure 3–15, or a similar image.

Figure 3–15

Q&A

Why is my list of pictures different from Figure 3–15?

The online images are continually updated.

What is Creative Commons?

Creative Commons is a nonprofit organization that provides several standard licensing options that owners of creative works may specify when granting permission for others to use their digital content, such as the online pictures that appear in the Bing Image Search. Be sure to follow an image's guidelines when using it in a document.

Q&A What if I cannot locate the image in Figure 3–15, and I would like to use that exact image?

The image is located in the Data Files. You can click the Cancel button and then click the From File button (Insert tab | Illustrations group), navigate to the file called apple-02.wmf in the Data Files, and then click the Insert button (Insert Picture dialog box).

3

- If necessary, click the 'Show all web results' button to display more images that match the search text.
- Click the desired picture to select it.
- Click the Insert button to insert the selected image in the document at the location of the insertion point. If necessary, scroll to display the image (picture) in the document window (Figure 3–16).

Figure 3–16

To Resize a Graphic to a Percent of the Original Size

1 CREATE & FORMAT LETTERHEAD WITH GRAPHICS | 2 SPECIFY LETTER FORMATS
3 INSERT TABLE | 4 FORMAT TABLE | 5 INSERT BULLETED LIST | 6 ADDRESS ENVELOPE

Instead of dragging a sizing handle to change the graphic's size, as you learned in Module 1, you can specify that the graphic be resized to a percent of its original size. In this module, the graphic is resized to 8 percent of its original size. ***Why?*** *The original size of the picture is too large for the letterhead.* The following steps resize a graphic to a percent of the original.

1

- With the graphic still selected, click the Advanced Layout: Size Dialog Box Launcher (Picture Tools Format tab | Size group) to display the Size sheet in the Layout dialog box.

Q&A What if the graphic is not selected or the Picture Tools Format tab is not on the ribbon?

Click the graphic to select it or double-click the graphic to make the Picture Tools Format tab the active tab.

2

- In the Scale area (Layout dialog box), double-click the current value in the Height box to select it.
- Type 8 in the Height box and then press the TAB key to display the same percent value in the Width box (Figure 3–17).

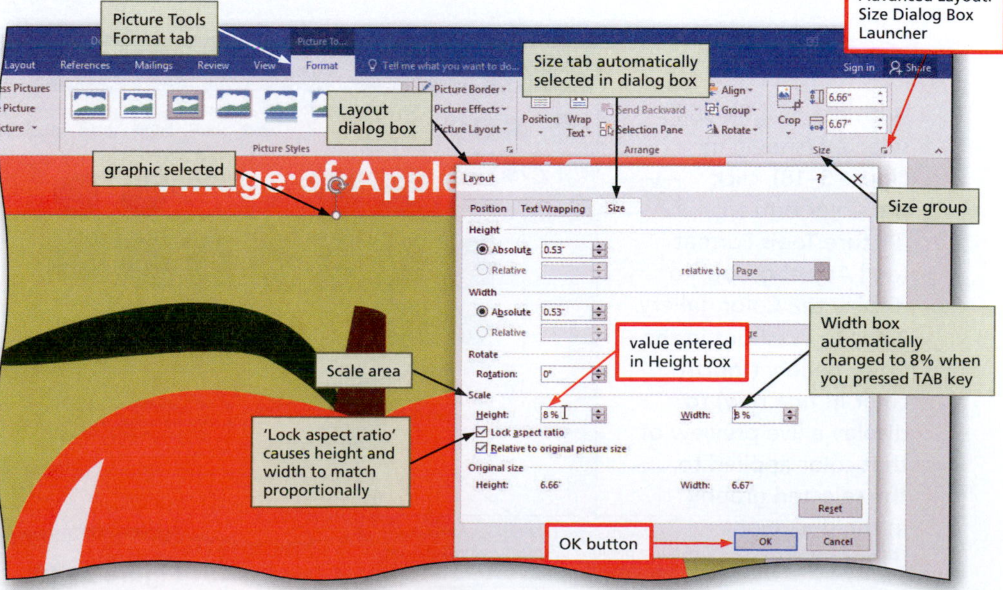

Figure 3–17

Q&A

Why did Word automatically fill in the value in the Width box?
When the 'Lock aspect ratio' check box (Layout dialog box) is selected, Word automatically maintains the size proportions of the graphic.

How do I know to use 8 percent for the resized graphic?
The larger graphic consumed too much room on the page. Try various percentages to determine the size that works best in the letterhead design.

3

- Click the OK button to close the dialog box and resize the selected graphic.
- If necessary, scroll to display the top of the document
- Verify that the Shape Height and Shape Width boxes (Picture Tools Format tab | Size group) display 0.53". If they do not, change their values to 0.53" (Figure 3–18).

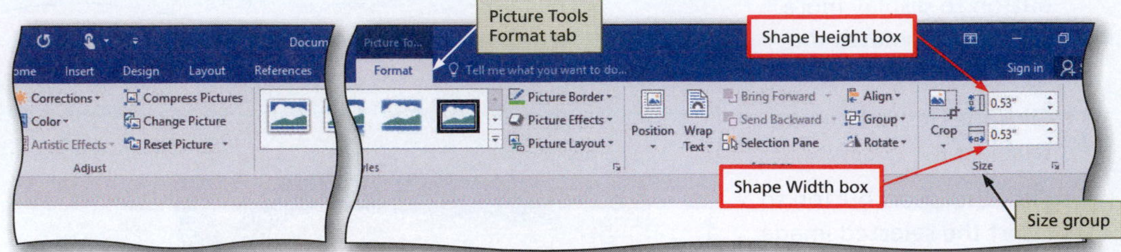

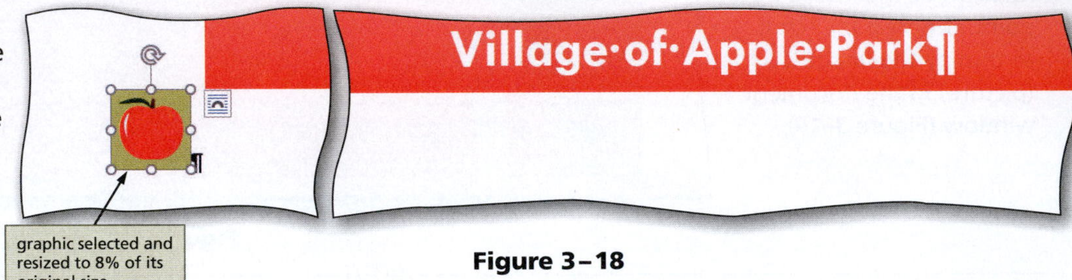

Figure 3–18

Other Ways

1. Click Layout Options button attached to graphic, click See more link in the Layout Options gallery, click Size tab (Layout dialog box), enter height and width values, click OK button
2. Right-click graphic, click 'Size and Position' on shortcut menu, enter height and width values (Layout dialog box), click OK button

To Change the Color of a Graphic

1 CREATE & FORMAT LETTERHEAD WITH GRAPHICS | 2 SPECIFY LETTER FORMATS
3 INSERT TABLE | 4 FORMAT TABLE | 5 INSERT BULLETED LIST | 6 ADDRESS ENVELOPE

In Word, you can change the color of a graphic. The apple image (graphic) currently is a bright red color. The following steps change the color of the graphic. ***Why?*** *Because the image in this project will be placed beside the rectangle shape, you prefer to use lighter colors.*

1

- With the graphic still selected (shown in Figure 3–18), click the Color button (Picture Tools Format tab | Adjust group) to display the Color gallery.
- Point to Washout in the Color gallery (fourth color in first row) to display a live preview of that color applied to the selected graphic in the document (Figure 3–19).

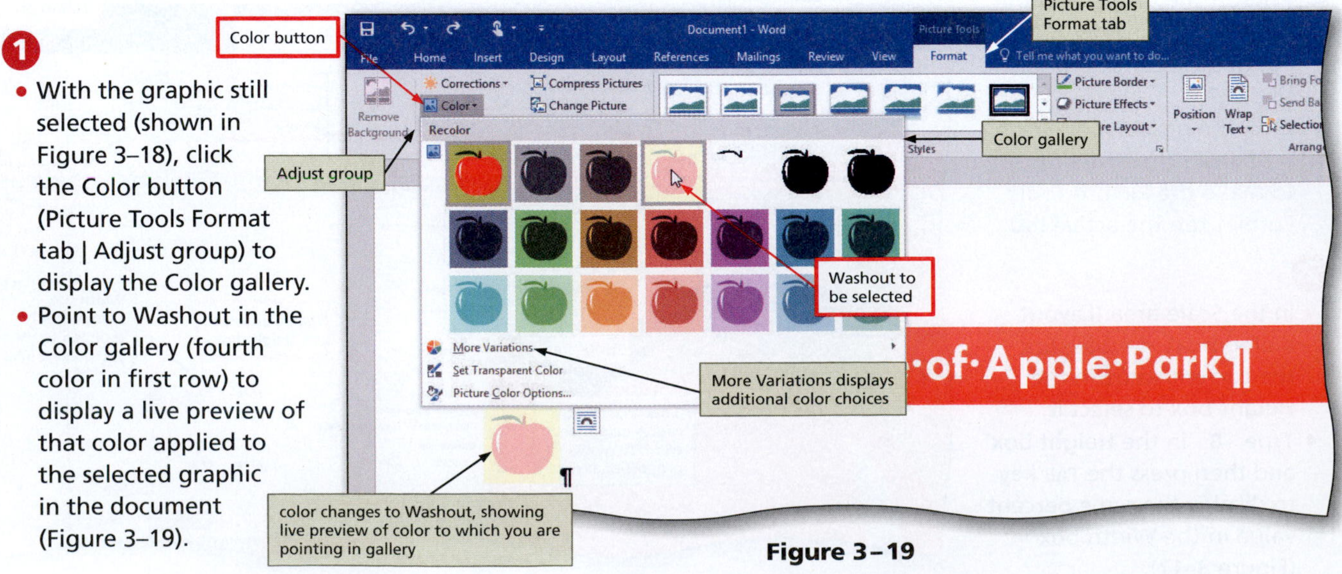

Figure 3–19

Experiment

- Point to various colors in the Color gallery and watch the color of the graphic change in the document.

2

- Click Washout in the Color gallery to change the color of the selected graphic.

Q&A How would I change a graphic back to its original colors?
With the graphic selected, you would click No Recolor, which is the upper-left color in the Color gallery.

Other Ways

1. Click Format Shape Dialog Box Launcher (Picture Tools Format tab | Picture Styles group), click Picture button (Format Picture task pane), expand Picture Color section, select desired options
2. Right-click graphic (or, if using touch, tap 'Show Context Menu' button on mini toolbar), click Format Picture on shortcut menu (or, if using touch, tap Format Object), click Picture button (Format Picture task pane), expand Picture Color section, select desired options

To Set a Transparent Color in a Graphic

1 CREATE & FORMAT LETTERHEAD WITH GRAPHICS | 2 SPECIFY LETTER FORMATS
3 INSERT TABLE | 4 FORMAT TABLE | 5 INSERT BULLETED LIST | 6 ADDRESS ENVELOPE

In Word, you can make one color in a graphic transparent; that is, you remove the color. You would make a color transparent if you wanted to remove part of a graphic or see text or colors behind a graphic. The following steps set the light green background around the apple in a transparent color. *Why? You prefer the light green color to be transparent.*

1

- With the graphic still selected, click the Color button (Picture Tools Format tab | Adjust group) to display the Color gallery (Figure 3–20).

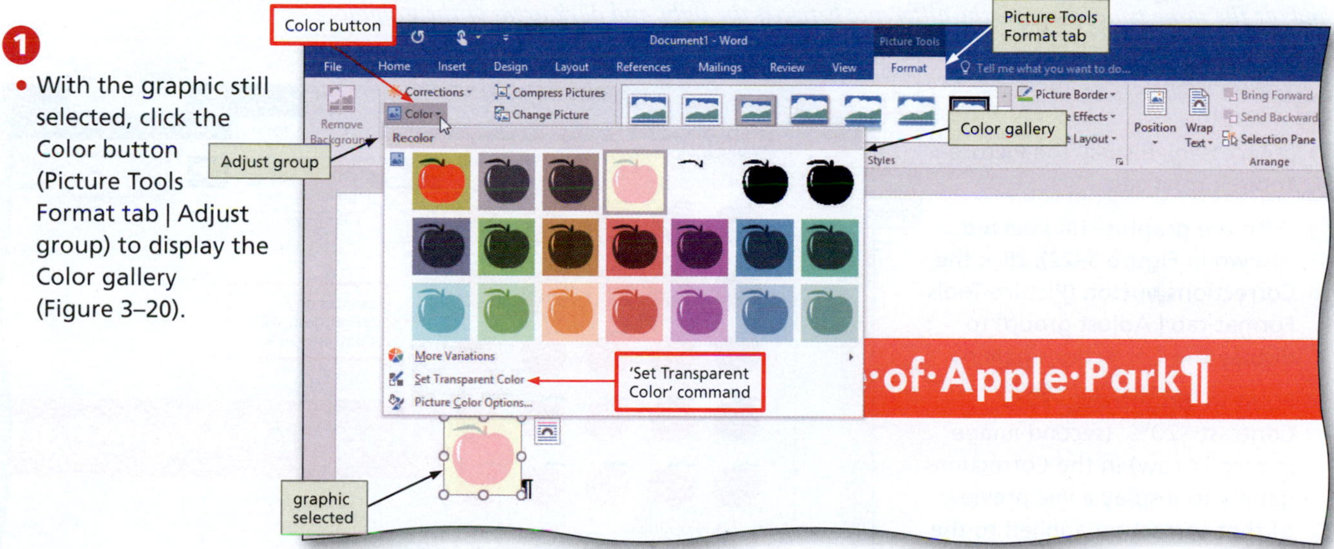

Figure 3–20

2

- Click 'Set Transparent Color' in the Color gallery to display a pen pointer in the document window.

Q&A What if I am using a touch screen?
You may need to use a stylus or mouse to perform these steps.

- Position the pen pointer in the graphic where you want to make the color transparent (Figure 3–21).

Q&A Can I make multiple colors in a graphic transparent?
No, you can make only one color transparent.

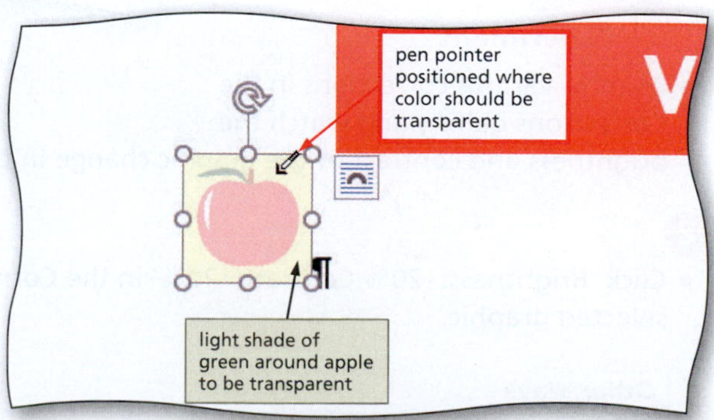

Figure 3–21

3

- Click the location in the graphic where you want the color to be transparent (Figure 3–22).

Q&A What if I make the wrong color transparent?
Click the Undo button on the Quick Access Toolbar, or press CTRL+Z, and then repeat these steps.

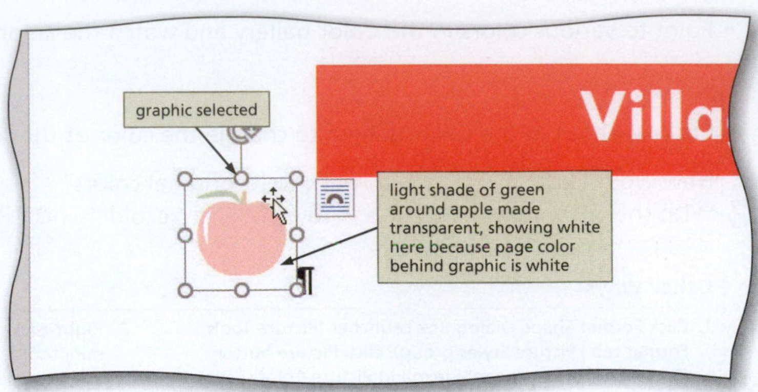

Figure 3–22

To Adjust the Brightness and Contrast of a Graphic

1 CREATE & FORMAT LETTERHEAD WITH GRAPHICS | 2 SPECIFY LETTER FORMATS
3 INSERT TABLE | 4 FORMAT TABLE | 5 INSERT BULLETED LIST | 6 ADDRESS ENVELOPE

In Word, you can adjust the brightness, or lightness, of a graphic and also the **contrast**, or the difference between the lightest and darkest areas of the graphic. The following steps decrease the brightness and contrast of the apple graphic, each by 20%. ***Why?*** *You want to darken the graphic slightly to increase its emphasis on the page and, at the same time, decrease the difference between the light and dark areas of the graphic.*

1

- If necessary, display the Picture Tools Format tab.
- With the graphic still selected (shown in Figure 3–22), click the Corrections button (Picture Tools Format tab | Adjust group) to display the Corrections gallery.
- Point to 'Brightness: -20% Contrast: -20%' (second image in second row) in the Corrections gallery to display a live preview of that correction applied to the graphic in the document (Figure 3–23).

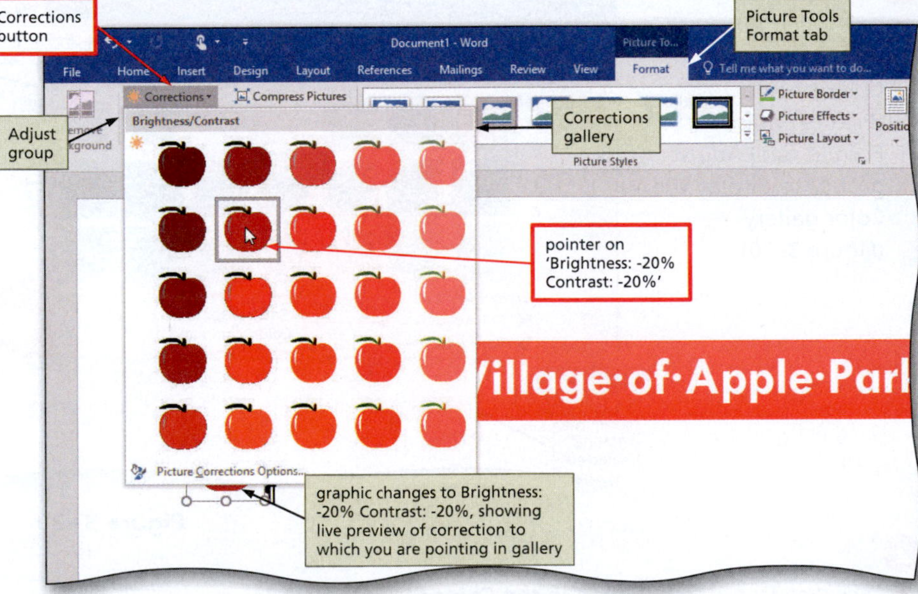

Figure 3–23

Experiment

- Point to various corrections in the Corrections gallery and watch the brightness and contrast of the graphic change in the document.

2

- Click 'Brightness: -20% Contrast: -20%' in the Corrections gallery to change the brightness and contrast of the selected graphic.

Other Ways

1. Click Format Shape Dialog Box Launcher (Picture Tools Format tab | Picture Styles group), click Picture button (Format Picture task pane), expand Picture Corrections section, select desired options
2. Right-click graphic (or, if using touch, tap 'Show Context Menu' button on mini toolbar), click Format Picture on shortcut menu (or, if using touch, tap Format Object on shortcut menu), click Picture button (Format Picture task pane), expand Picture Corrections section, select desired options

To Change the Border Color on a Graphic

The apple graphic currently has no border (outline). The following steps change the border color on the graphic. ***Why?*** *You would like the graphic to have a lime border so that it is in the same color family as the leaf on the apple.*

1

- Click the Picture Border arrow (Picture Tools Format tab | Picture Styles group) to display the Picture Border gallery.
- Point to 'Lime, Accent 1, Darker 25%' (fifth theme color in fifth row) in the Picture Border gallery to display a live preview of that border color around the picture (Figure 3–24).

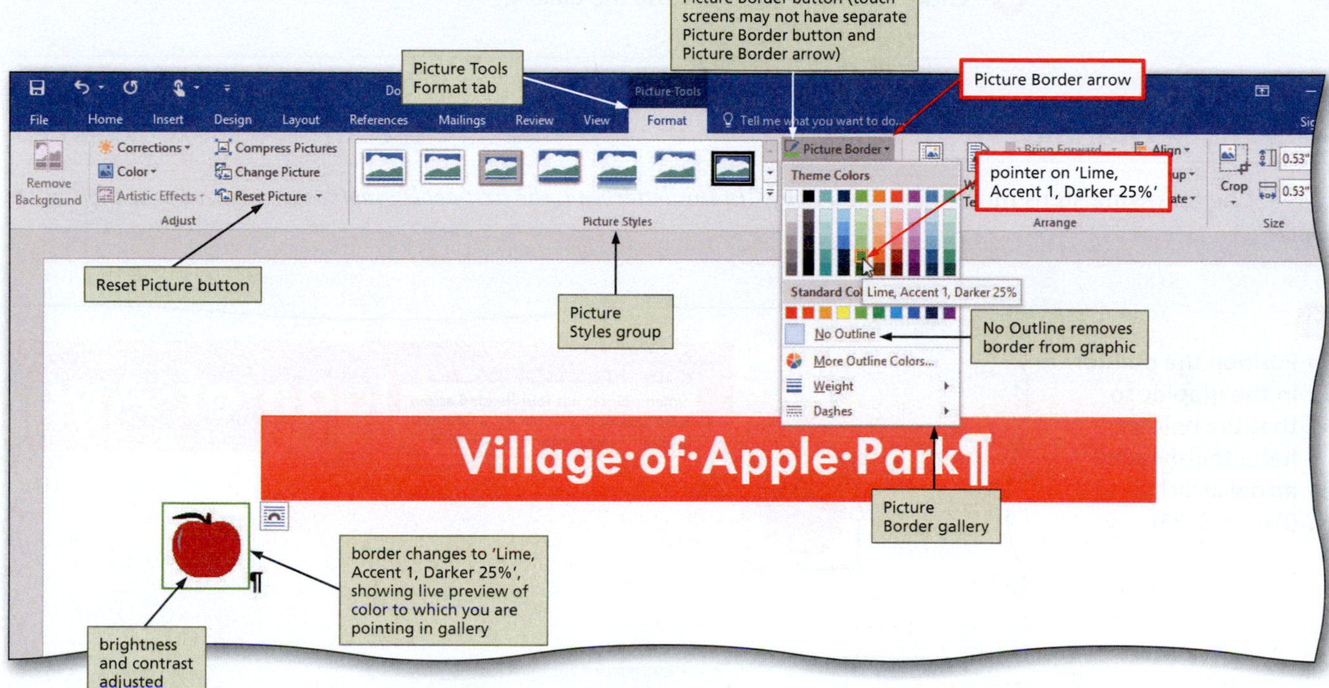

Figure 3–24

Q&A What if I click the Picture Border button by mistake?
Click the Picture Border arrow and proceed with Step 2.

Experiment

- Point to various colors in the Picture Border gallery and watch the border color on the graphic change in the document window.

2

- Click 'Lime, Accent 1, Darker 25%' in the Picture Border gallery to change the picture border color.

Q&A How would I remove a border from a graphic?
With the graphic selected, you would click No Outline in the Picture Border gallery.

Can I remove all formatting applied to a graphic and start over?
Yes. With the graphic selected, you would click the Reset Picture button (Picture Tools Format tab | Adjust group).

To Change an Object's Text Wrapping

The apple graphic is to be positioned to the left of the shape. By default, when you insert a picture, it is formatted as an inline graphic. Inline graphics cannot be moved to a precise location on a page. Recall that inline graphics are part of a paragraph and, thus, can be positioned according to paragraph formatting, such as centered or left-aligned. To move the graphic to the left of the shape, you format it as a

BTW
Touch Screen Differences
The Office and Windows interfaces may vary if you are using a touch screen. For this reason, you might notice that the function or appearance of your touch screen differs slightly from this module's presentation.

floating object with In Front of Text wrapping. The following steps change a graphic's text wrapping.

1. If necessary, click the graphic to select it.
2. Click the Layout Options button attached to the graphic to display the Layout Options gallery.
3. Click 'In Front of Text' in the Layout Options gallery so that you can position the object on top of any item in the document, in this case, on top of the rectangular shape.
4. Click the Close button to close the gallery.

1 CREATE & FORMAT LETTERHEAD WITH GRAPHICS | 2 SPECIFY LETTER FORMATS
3 INSERT TABLE | 4 FORMAT TABLE | 5 INSERT BULLETED LIST | 6 ADDRESS ENVELOPE

To Move a Graphic

The following steps move a graphic. ***Why?*** *In this letterhead, the first apple graphic is positioned to the left of the shape.*

- Position the pointer in the graphic so that the pointer has a four-headed arrow attached to it (Figure 3–25).

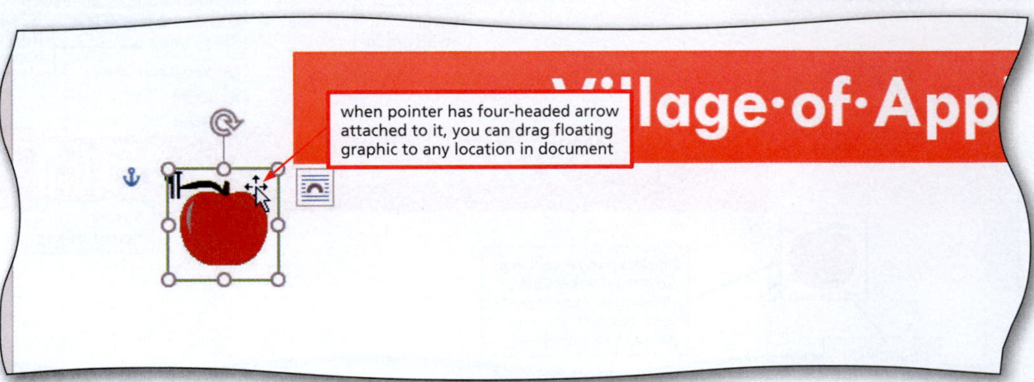
Village·of·App
when pointer has four-headed arrow attached to it, you can drag floating graphic to any location in document

Figure 3–25

- Drag the graphic to the left of the shape, as shown in Figure 3–26.

Q&A What if I moved the graphic to the wrong location?
Repeat these steps. You can drag a floating graphic to any location in a document.

Why do green lines appear on my screen as I drag a graphic?
You have alignment guides set, which help you line up graphics. To set alignment guides, click the Align Objects button (Picture Tools Format tab | Arrange group) and then click 'Use Alignment Guides'.

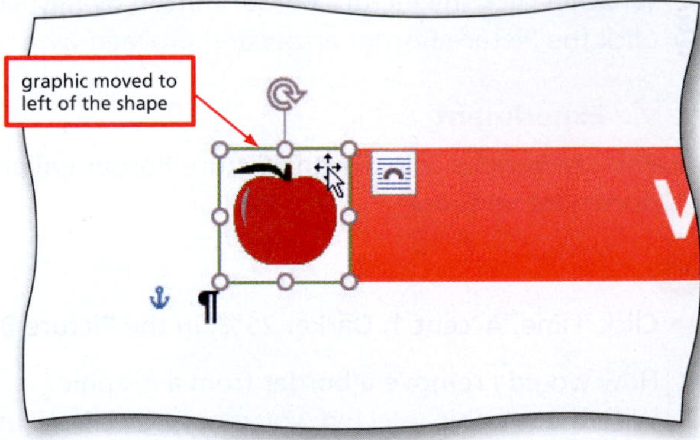
graphic moved to left of the shape
V

Figure 3–26

To Copy a Graphic

In this project, the same apple graphic is to be placed to the right of the shape. Instead of performing the same steps to insert and format a second identical apple graphic, you can copy the graphic to the Office Clipboard, paste the graphic from the Office Clipboard, and then move the graphic to the desired location.

You use the same steps to copy a graphic as you used in Module 2 to copy text. The following steps copy a graphic.

1. If necessary, click the graphic to select it.
2. Display the Home tab.
3. Click the Copy button, shown in Figure 3–27 (Home tab | Clipboard group), to copy the selected item to the Office Clipboard.

To Use Paste Options

1 CREATE & FORMAT LETTERHEAD WITH GRAPHICS | 2 SPECIFY LETTER FORMATS
3 INSERT TABLE | 4 FORMAT TABLE | 5 INSERT BULLETED LIST | 6 ADDRESS ENVELOPE

The following steps paste a graphic using the Paste Options gallery. ***Why?*** *Recall from Module 2 that you can specify the format of a pasted item using Paste Options.*

1

- Click the Paste arrow (Home tab | Clipboard group) to display the Paste gallery.

Q&A What if I accidentally click the Paste button?
Click the Paste Options button below the graphic pasted in the document to display a Paste Options gallery.

- Point to the 'Keep Source Formatting' button in the Paste gallery to display a live preview of that paste option (Figure 3–27).

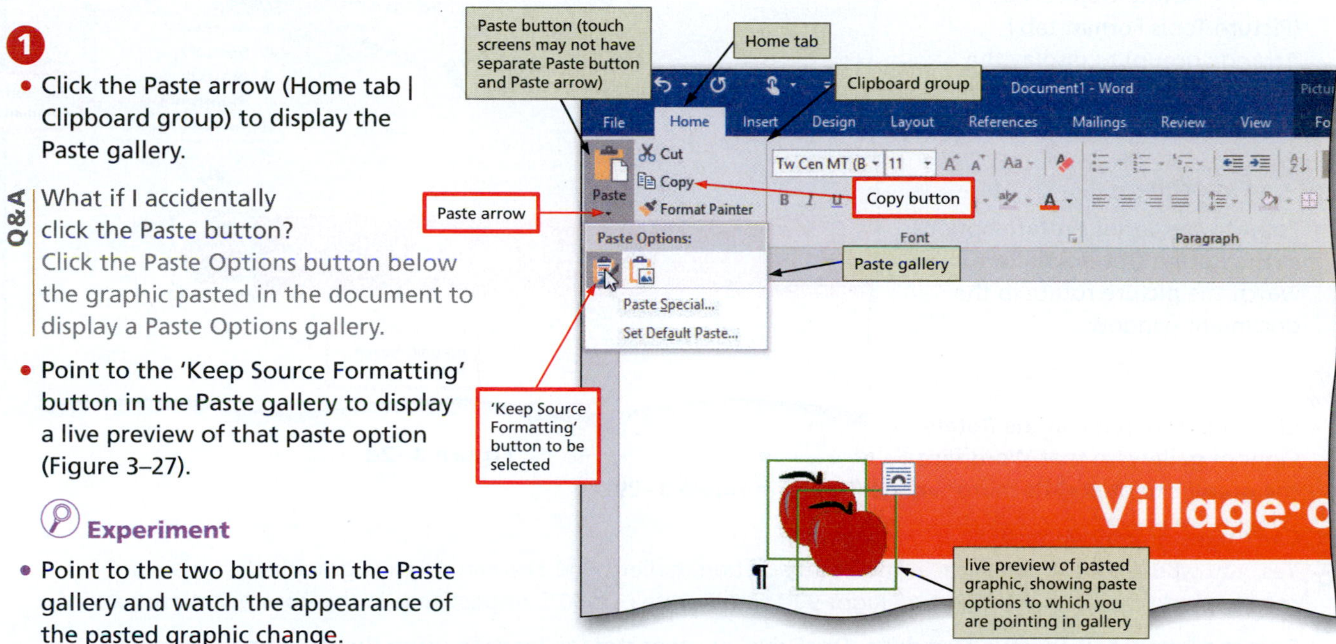

Figure 3–27

Experiment

- Point to the two buttons in the Paste gallery and watch the appearance of the pasted graphic change.

Q&A What do the buttons in the Paste gallery mean?
The 'Keep Source Formatting' button indicates the pasted graphic should have the same formats as it did in its original location. The Picture button removes some formatting from the graphic.

Why are these paste buttons different from the ones in Module 2?
The buttons that appear in the Paste gallery differ depending on the item you are pasting. Use live preview to see how the pasted object will look in the document.

2

- Click the 'Keep Source Formatting' button in the Paste gallery to paste the object using the same formatting as the original.

To Move a Graphic

The next step is to move the second apple graphic so that it is positioned to the right of the rectangle shape. The following steps move a graphic.

1. If you are using a mouse, position the pointer in the graphic so that the pointer has a four-headed arrow attached to it.
2. Drag the graphic to the location shown in Figure 3–28.

To Flip a Graphic

1 CREATE & FORMAT LETTERHEAD WITH GRAPHICS | 2 SPECIFY LETTER FORMATS
3 INSERT TABLE | 4 FORMAT TABLE | 5 INSERT BULLETED LIST | 6 ADDRESS ENVELOPE

The following steps flip a graphic horizontally. ***Why?*** *In this letterhead, you want the leaves on the apple graphics to point toward the edge of the paper.*

- If necessary, display the Picture Tools Format tab.
- With the graphic still selected, click the Rotate Objects button (Picture Tools Format tab | Arrange group) to display the Rotate Objects gallery (Figure 3–28).

Experiment

- Point to the various rotate options in the Rotate Options gallery and watch the picture rotate in the document window.

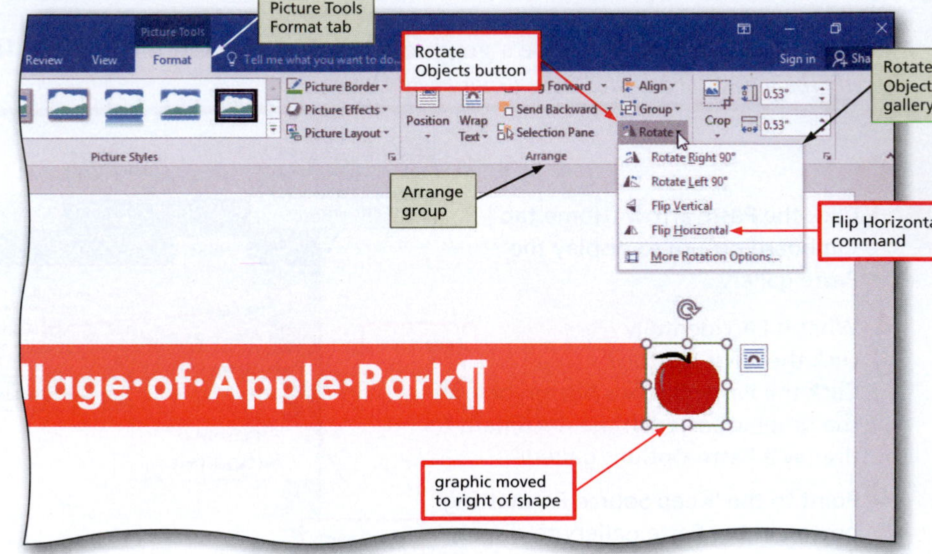

Figure 3–28

- Click Flip Horizontal in the Rotate Options gallery, so that Word flips the graphic to display its mirror image (shown in Figure 3–29).

Q&A Can I flip a graphic vertically?
Yes, you would click Flip Vertical in the Rotate Options gallery. You also can rotate a graphic clockwise or counterclockwise by clicking 'Rotate Right 90°' and 'Rotate Left 90°', respectively, in the Rotate Options gallery.

- Save the letterhead on your hard drive, OneDrive, or other storage location using the file name, Apple Park Letterhead.

Q&A Why should I save the letterhead at this time?
You have performed many tasks while creating this letterhead and do not want to risk losing work completed thus far.

To Format and Enter Text

The contact information for the letterhead in this project is located on the line below the shape containing the name. The following steps format and then enter the mailing address in the letterhead.

1. Position the insertion point on the line below the shape containing the name.
2. If necessary, display the Home tab. Click the Center button (Home tab | Paragraph group) to center the paragraph.
3. Click the 'Increase Font Size' button (Home tab | Font group) to increase the font size to 12 point.
4. Type `15 Center Street, Horizon, MT 33568` and then press the SPACEBAR (shown in Figure 3–29).

To Insert a Symbol from the Symbol Dialog Box

Word provides a method of inserting dots and other symbols, such as letters in the Greek alphabet and mathematical characters, that are not on the keyboard. The following steps insert a dot symbol, sometimes called a bullet symbol, in the letterhead. ***Why?*** *You want a visual separator between the mailing address and phone number in the letterhead and also between the phone number and email address.*

1

- If necessary, position the insertion point as shown in Figure 3–29.
- Display the Insert tab.
- Click the 'Insert a Symbol' button (Insert tab | Symbols group) to display the Insert a Symbol gallery (Figure 3–29).

Q&A What if the symbol I want to insert already appears in the Insert a Symbol gallery?
You can click any symbol shown in the Insert a Symbol gallery to insert it in the document.

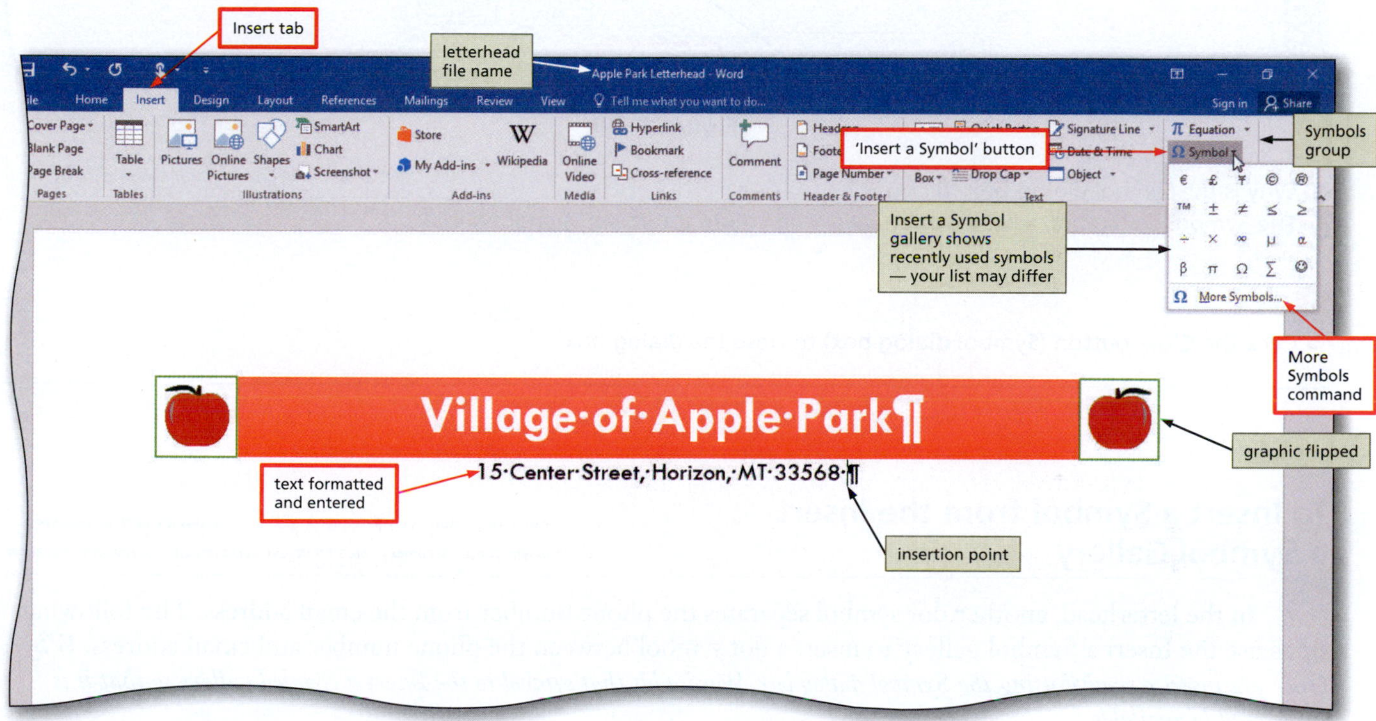

Figure 3–29

2

- Click More Symbols in the Insert a Symbol gallery to display the Symbol dialog box.
- If the font in the Font box is not (normal text), click the Font arrow (Symbol dialog box) and then scroll to and click (normal text) to select this font.
- If the subset in the Subset box is not General Punctuation, click the Subset arrow and then scroll and click General Punctuation to select this subset.
- In the list of symbols, if necessary, scroll to the dot symbol shown in Figure 3–30 and then click the symbol to select it.
- Click the Insert button (Symbol dialog box) to place the selected symbol in the document to the left of the insertion point (Figure 3–30).

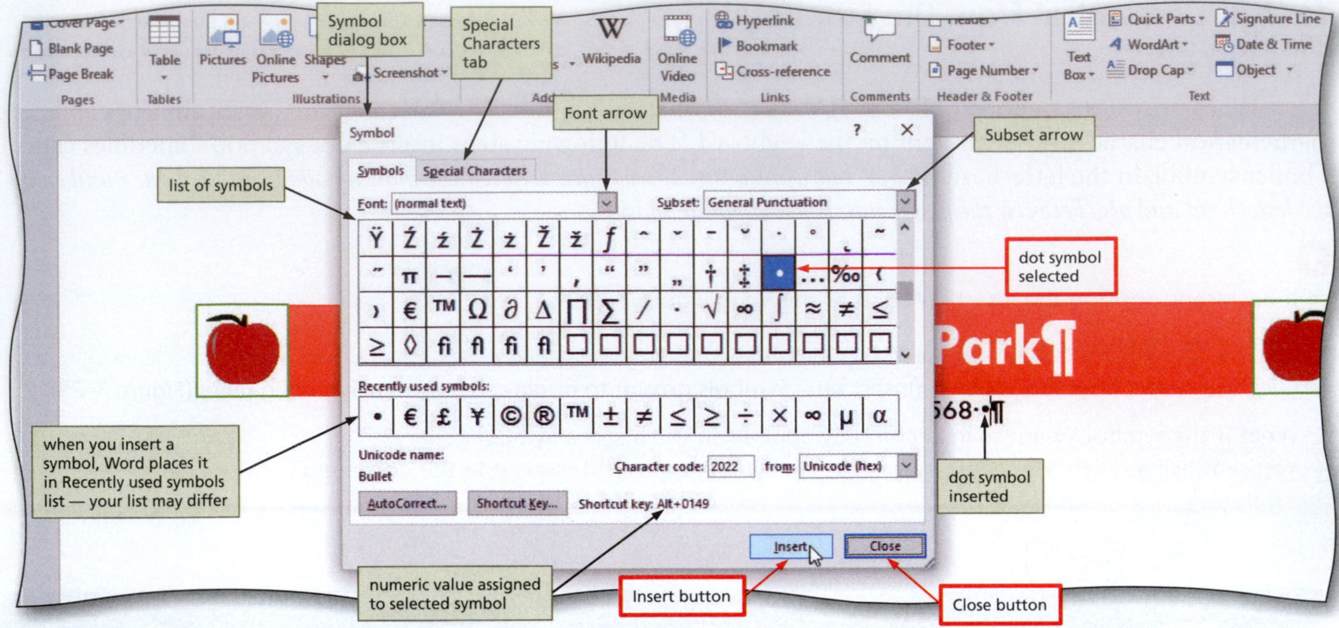

Figure 3–30

Q&A Why is the Symbol dialog box still open?
The Symbol dialog box remains open, allowing you to insert additional symbols.

3

- Click the Close button (Symbol dialog box) to close the dialog box.

To Insert a Symbol from the Insert a Symbol Gallery

1 CREATE & FORMAT LETTERHEAD WITH GRAPHICS | 2 SPECIFY LETTER FORMATS
3 INSERT TABLE | 4 FORMAT TABLE | 5 INSERT BULLETED LIST | 6 ADDRESS ENVELOPE

In the letterhead, another dot symbol separates the phone number from the email address. The following steps use the Insert a Symbol gallery to insert a dot symbol between the phone number and email address. ***Why?*** *Once you insert a symbol using the Symbol dialog box, Word adds that symbol to the Insert a Symbol gallery so that it is more readily available.*

1

- Press the SPACEBAR, type **Phone: (870) 555-4400** and then press the SPACEBAR.

2

- Click the 'Insert a Symbol' button (Insert tab | Symbols group) to display the Insert a Symbol gallery (Figure 3–31).

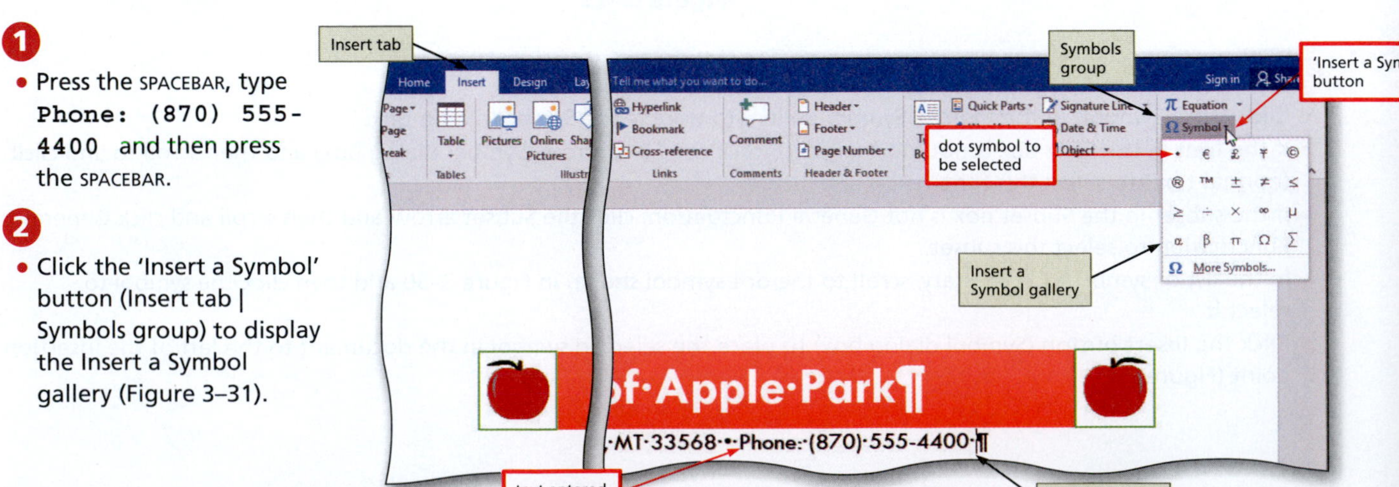

Figure 3–31

Why is the dot symbol now in the Insert a Symbol gallery?

When you insert a symbol from the Symbol dialog box, Word automatically adds the symbol to the Insert a Symbol gallery.

3

- Click the dot symbol in the Insert a Symbol gallery to insert the symbol at the location of the insertion point (shown in Figure 3–32).

To Enter Text

The following steps enter the email address in the letterhead.

1 Press the SPACEBAR.

2 Type **`Email: applepark@world.com`** to finish the text in the letterhead (Figure 3–32).

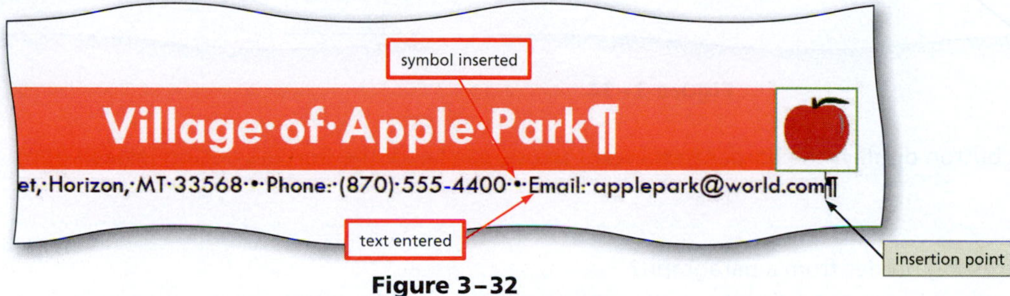

Figure 3–32

BTW

Inserting Special Characters

In addition to symbols, you can insert a variety of special characters, including dashes, hyphens, spaces, apostrophes, and quotation marks. Click the Special Characters tab in the Symbol dialog box (shown in Figure 3–30), click the desired character in the Character list, click the Insert button, and then click the Close button (Symbol dialog box).

To Bottom Border a Paragraph

1 CREATE & FORMAT LETTERHEAD WITH GRAPHICS | 2 SPECIFY LETTER FORMATS
3 INSERT TABLE | 4 FORMAT TABLE | 5 INSERT BULLETED LIST | 6 ADDRESS ENVELOPE

In Word, you can draw a solid line, called a **border**, at any edge of a paragraph. That is, borders may be added above or below a paragraph, to the left or right of a paragraph, or in any combination of these sides.

The letterhead in this project has a border that extends from the left margin to the right margin immediately below the mailing address, phone, and email address information. *Why? The horizontal line separates the letterhead from the rest of the letter.* The following steps add a bottom border to a paragraph.

1

- Display the Home tab.
- With the insertion point in the paragraph to border, click the Borders arrow (Home tab | Paragraph group) to display the Borders gallery (Figure 3–33).

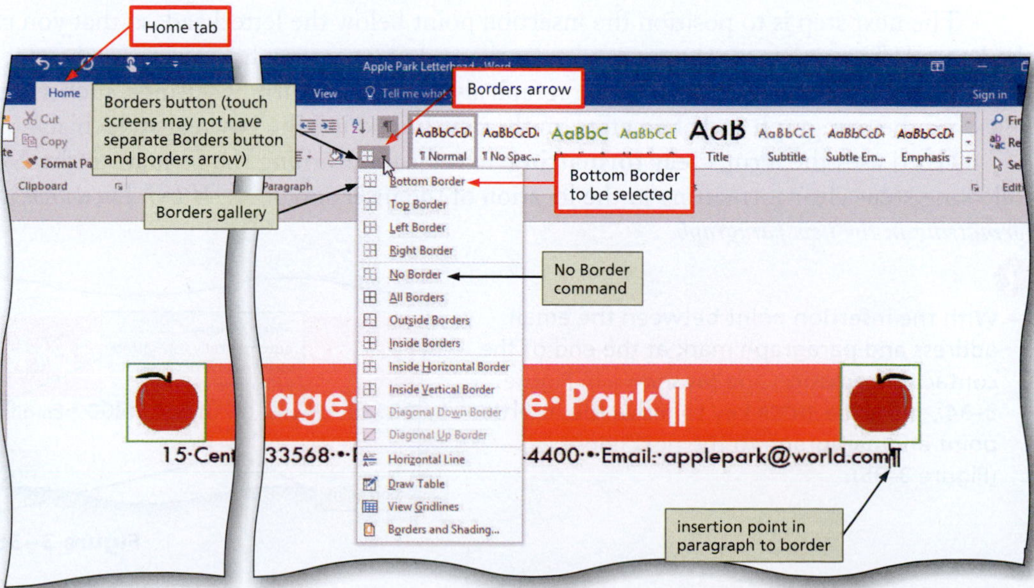

Figure 3–33

- Click Bottom Border in the Borders gallery to place a border below the paragraph containing the insertion point (Figure 3–34).

Figure 3–34

Q&A

If the face of the Borders button displays the border icon I want to use, can I click the Borders button instead of using the Borders arrow?
Yes.

How would I remove an existing border from a paragraph?
If, for some reason, you wanted to remove a border from a paragraph, you would position the insertion point in the paragraph, click the Borders arrow (Home tab | Paragraph group), and then click No Border in the Borders gallery.

Other Ways

1. Click 'Borders and Shading' button (Design tab | Page Background group), click Borders tab (Borders and Shading dialog box), select desired border options, click OK button

To Clear Formatting

1 CREATE & FORMAT LETTERHEAD WITH GRAPHICS | 2 SPECIFY LETTER FORMATS
3 INSERT TABLE | 4 FORMAT TABLE | 5 INSERT BULLETED LIST | 6 ADDRESS ENVELOPE

The next step is to position the insertion point below the letterhead, so that you can type the contents of the letter. When you press the ENTER key at the end of a paragraph containing a border, Word moves the border forward to the next paragraph. The paragraph also retains all current settings, such as the center format. Instead, you want the paragraph and characters on the new line to use the Normal style: black font with no border.

Word uses the term, **clear formatting**, to refer to returning the formats to the Normal style. The following steps clear formatting at the location of the insertion point. ***Why?*** *You do not want to retain the current formatting in the new paragraph.*

- With the insertion point between the email address and paragraph mark at the end of the contact information line (as shown in Figure 3–34), press the ENTER key to move the insertion point and paragraph to the next line (Figure 3–35).

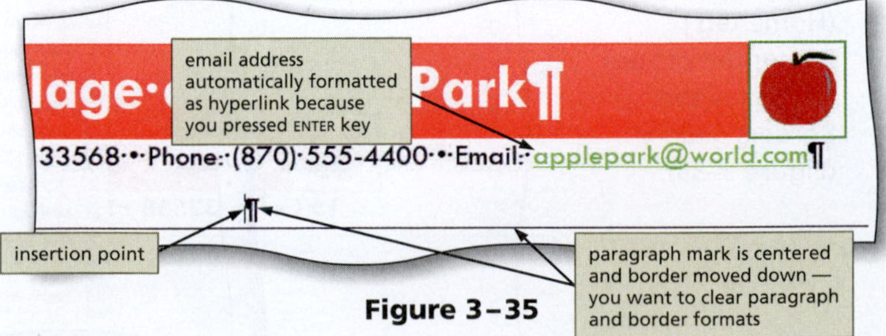

Figure 3–35

- Click the 'Clear All Formatting' button (Home tab | Font group) to apply the Normal style to the location of the insertion point (Figure 3–36).

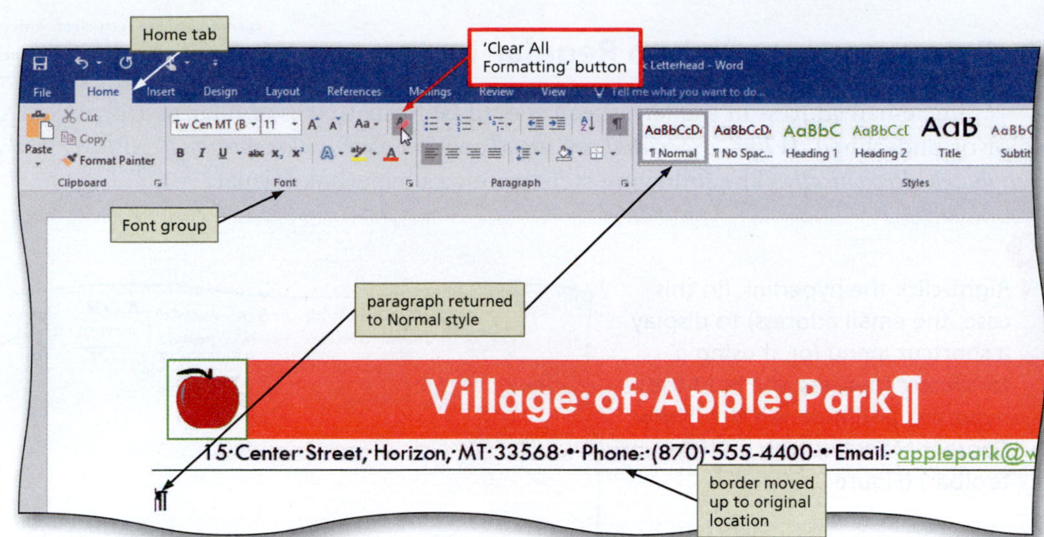

Figure 3–36

Other Ways

1. Click More button in Styles gallery (Home tab | Styles group), click Clear Formatting
2. Click Styles Dialog Box Launcher (Home tab | Styles group), click Clear All in Styles task pane
3. Select text, press CTRL+SPACEBAR, press CTRL+Q

AutoFormat As You Type

As you type text in a document, Word automatically formats some of it for you. For example, when you press the ENTER key or SPACEBAR after typing an email address or web address, Word automatically formats the address as a hyperlink, that is, in a different color and underlined. In Figure 3–35, for example, Word formatted the email address as a hyperlink because you pressed the ENTER key at the end of the line. Table 3–2 outlines commonly used AutoFormat As You Type options and their results.

Table 3–2 Commonly Used AutoFormat As You Type Options

Typed Text	AutoFormat As You Type Feature	Example
Quotation marks or apostrophes	Changes straight quotation marks or apostrophes to curly ones	"the" becomes “the”
Text, a space, one hyphen, one or no spaces, text, space	Changes the hyphen to an en dash	ages 20-45 becomes ages 20–45
Text, two hyphens, text, space	Changes the two hyphens to an em dash	Two types--yellow and red becomes Two types—yellow and red
Web or email address followed by SPACEBAR or ENTER key	Formats web or email address as a hyperlink	www.cengagebrain.com becomes www.cengagebrain.com
Number followed by a period, hyphen, right parenthesis, or greater than sign and then a space or tab followed by text	Creates a numbered list	1. Word 2. PowerPoint becomes 1. Word 2. PowerPoint
Asterisk, hyphen, or greater than sign and then a space or tab followed by text	Creates a bulleted list	* Home tab * Insert tab becomes • Home tab • Insert tab
Fraction and then a space or hyphen	Condenses the fraction entry so that it consumes one space instead of three	1/2 becomes ½
Ordinal and then a space or hyphen	Makes part of the ordinal a superscript	3rd becomes 3rd

To Convert a Hyperlink to Regular Text

The email address in the letterhead should be formatted as regular text; that is, it should not be a different color or underlined. ***Why?*** *Hyperlinks are useful only in online documents, and this letter will be printed instead of distributed electronically.* The following steps remove a hyperlink format.

1

- Right-click the hyperlink (in this case, the email address) to display a shortcut menu (or, if using a touch screen, press and hold the hyperlink and then tap the 'Show Context Menu' button on the mini toolbar) (Figure 3–37).

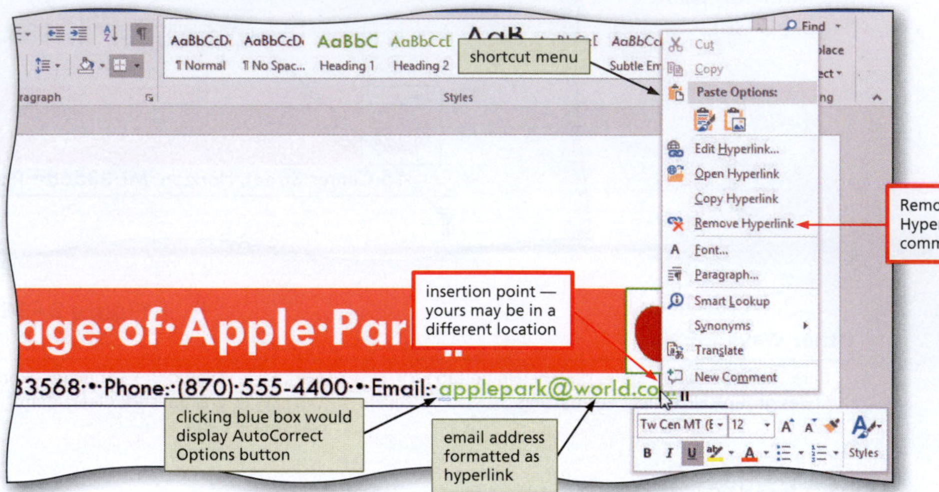

Figure 3–37

2

- Click Remove Hyperlink on the shortcut menu to remove the hyperlink format from the text.
- Position the insertion point on the paragraph mark below the border because you are finished with the letterhead (Figure 3–38).

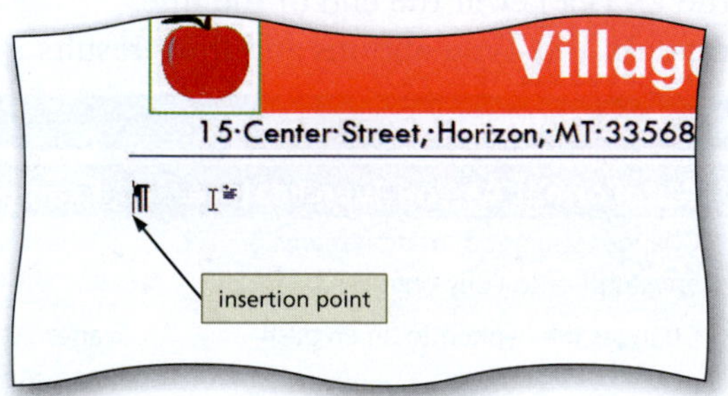

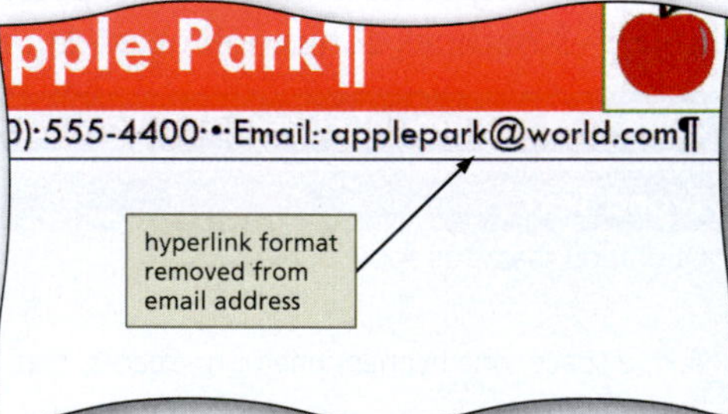

Figure 3–38

Q&A Could I have used the AutoCorrect Options button instead of the Remove Hyperlink command?
Yes. Alternatively, you could have pointed to the small blue box at the beginning of the hyperlink, clicked the AutoCorrect Options button, and then clicked Undo Hyperlink on the AutoCorrect Options menu.

- Save the letterhead again on the same storage location with the same file name.

Other Ways

1. With insertion point in hyperlink, click 'Add a Hyperlink' button (Insert tab | Links group), click Remove Link button

Break Point: If you wish to take a break, this is a good place to do so. You can exit Word now. To resume at a later time, run Word, open the file called Apple Park Letterhead, and continue following the steps from this location forward.

Creating a Business Letter

With the letterhead for the business letter complete, the next task is to create the remainder of the content in the letter. The following sections use Word to create a business letter that contains a table and a bulleted list.

CONSIDER THIS

What should you consider when writing a business letter?

A finished business letter should look like a symmetrically framed picture with evenly spaced margins, all balanced below an attractive letterhead. The letter should be well written, properly formatted, logically organized, and use visuals where appropriate. The content of a letter should contain proper grammar, correct spelling, logically constructed sentences, flowing paragraphs, and sound ideas.

Be sure to include all essential elements, use proper spacing and formats, and determine which letter style to use.

- **Include all essential letter elements.** All business letters contain the same basic elements, including the date line, inside address, message, and signature block (shown in Figure 3–1 at the beginning of this module). If a business letter does not use a letterhead, then the top of the letter should include return address information in a heading.
- **Use proper spacing and formats for the contents of the letter below the letterhead.** Use a font that is easy to read, in a size between 8 and 12 point. Add emphasis with bold, italic, and bullets where appropriate, and use tables to present numeric information. Paragraphs should be single-spaced, with double-spacing between paragraphs.
- **Determine which letter style to use.** You can follow many different styles when creating business letters. A letter style specifies guidelines for the alignment and spacing of elements in the business letter.

If possible, keep the length of a business letter to one page. Be sure to proofread the finished letter carefully.

To Save a Document with a New File Name

The current open file has the name Apple Park Letterhead, which is the name of the organization letterhead. Because you want the letterhead file to remain intact so that you can reuse it, you save the document with a new file name. The following step saves a document with a new file name. For a detailed example of the procedure summarized below, refer to the Office and Windows module at the beginning of this book.

Save the letter on your hard drive, OneDrive, or other storage location using a new file name, Lee Vendor Letter.

BTW
Organizing Files and Folders
You should organize and store files in folders so that you easily can find the files later. For example, if you are taking an introductory technology class called CIS 101, a good practice would be to save all Word files in a Word folder in a CIS 101 folder. For a discussion of folders and detailed examples of creating folders, refer to the Office and Windows module at the beginning of this book.

To Apply a Style

1 CREATE & FORMAT LETTERHEAD WITH GRAPHICS | **2 SPECIFY LETTER FORMATS**
3 INSERT TABLE | 4 FORMAT TABLE | 5 INSERT BULLETED LIST | 6 ADDRESS ENVELOPE

Recall that the Normal style in Word places 8 points of blank space after each paragraph and inserts a vertical space equal to 1.08 lines between each line of text. You will need to modify the spacing used for the paragraphs in the business letter. ***Why?*** *Business letters should use single spacing for paragraphs and double spacing between paragraphs.*

Word has many built-in, or predefined, styles that you can use to format text. The No Spacing style, for example, defines line spacing as single and does not insert any additional blank space between lines when you press the ENTER key. To apply a style to a paragraph, you first position the insertion point in the paragraph. The following step applies the No Spacing style to a paragraph.

1

- With the insertion point positioned in the paragraph to be formatted, click No Spacing in the Styles gallery (Home tab | Styles group) to apply the selected style to the current paragraph (Figure 3–39).

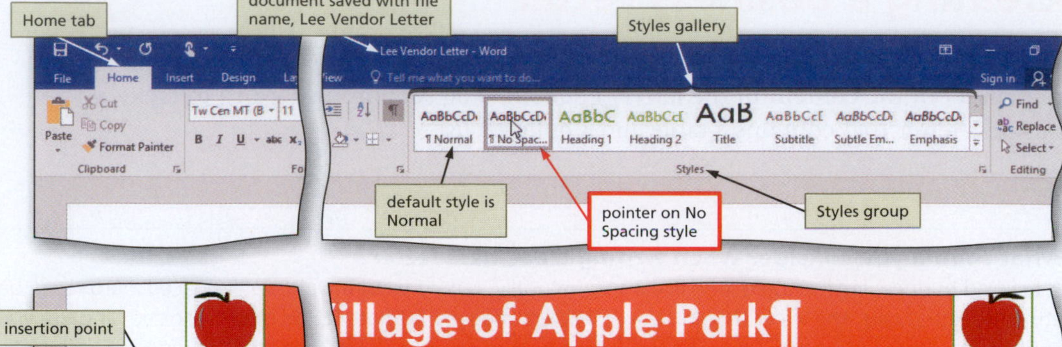

Figure 3–39

Q&A Will this style be used in the rest of the document?

Yes. The paragraph formatting, which includes the style, will carry forward to subsequent paragraphs each time you press the ENTER key.

Other Ways

1. Click Styles Dialog Box Launcher (Home tab | Styles group), click desired style in Styles task pane
2. Press CTRL+SHIFT+S, click Style Name arrow in Apply Styles task pane, click desired style in list

CONSIDER THIS

What elements should a business letter contain?

Be sure to include all essential business letter elements, properly spaced, in your letter:

- The **date line**, which consists of the month, day, and year, is positioned two to six lines below the letterhead.
- The **inside address**, placed three to eight lines below the date line, usually contains the addressee's courtesy title plus full name, job title, business affiliation, and full geographical address.
- The **salutation**, if present, begins two lines below the last line of the inside address. If you do not know the recipient's name, avoid using the salutation "To whom it may concern" — it is impersonal. Instead, use the recipient's title in the salutation, e.g., Dear Personnel Director. In a business letter, use a colon (:) at the end of the salutation; in a personal letter, use a comma.
- The body of the letter, the **message**, begins two lines below the salutation. Within the message, paragraphs are single-spaced with one blank line between paragraphs.
- Two lines below the last line of the message, the **complimentary close** is displayed. Capitalize only the first word in a complimentary close.
- Type the **signature block** at least four blank lines below the complimentary close, allowing room for the author to sign his or her name.

CONSIDER THIS

What are the common styles of business letters?

Three common business letter styles are the block, the modified block, and the modified semi-block. Each style specifies different alignments and indentations.

- In the block letter style, all components of the letter begin flush with the left margin.
- In the modified block letter style, the date, complimentary close, and signature block are positioned approximately one-half inch to the right of center or at the right margin. All other components of the letter begin flush with the left margin.
- In the modified semi-block letter style, the date, complimentary close, and signature block are centered, positioned approximately one-half inch to the right of center or at the right margin. The first line of each paragraph in the body of the letter is indented one-half to one inch from the left margin. All other components of the letter begin flush with the left margin.

The business letter in this project follows the modified block style.

Using Tab Stops to Align Text

A **tab stop** is a location on the horizontal ruler that tells Word where to position the insertion point when you press the TAB key on the keyboard. Word, by default, places a tab stop at every one-half inch mark on the ruler. You also can set your own custom tab stops. Tab settings are a paragraph format. Thus, each time you press the ENTER key, any custom tab stops are carried forward to the next paragraph.

To move the insertion point from one tab stop to another, press the TAB key on the keyboard. When you press the TAB key, a **tab character** formatting mark appears in the empty space between the tab stops.

When you set a custom tab stop, you specify how the text will align at a tab stop. The tab marker on the ruler reflects the alignment of the characters at the location of the tab stop. Table 3–3 shows types of tab stop alignments in Word and their corresponding tab markers.

Table 3–3 Types of Tab Stop Alignments

Tab Stop Alignment	Tab Marker	Result of Pressing TAB Key	Example
Left Tab	∟	Left-aligns text at the location of the tab stop	toolbar ruler
Center Tab	⊥	Centers text at the location of the tab stop	toolbar ruler
Right Tab	┘	Right-aligns text at the location of the tab stop	toolbar ruler
Decimal Tab	⊥.	Aligns text on decimal point at the location of the tab stop	45.72 223.75
Bar Tab	|	Aligns text at a bar character at the location of the tab stop	| toolbar | ruler

To Display the Ruler

One way to set custom tab stops is by using the horizontal ruler. Thus, the following steps display the ruler in the document window.

1. If the rulers are not showing, display the View tab.
2. Click the View Ruler check box (View tab | Show group) to place a check mark in the check box and display the horizontal and vertical rulers on the screen (shown in Figure 3–40).

To Set Custom Tab Stops

The first required element of the business letter is the date line, which in this letter is positioned two lines below the letterhead. The date line contains the month, day, and year, and begins four inches from the left margin. ***Why?*** *Business letter guidelines specify to begin the date line approximately one-half inch to the right of center. Thus, you should set a custom tab stop at the 4" mark on the ruler.* The following steps set a left-aligned tab stop.

- With the insertion point on the paragraph mark below the border (shown in Figure 3–39), press the ENTER key so that a blank line appears above the insertion point.
- If necessary, click the tab selector at the left edge of the horizontal ruler until it displays the type of tab you wish to use, which is the Left Tab icon in this case.
- Position the pointer on the 4″ mark on the ruler, which is the location of the desired custom tab stop (Figure 3–40).

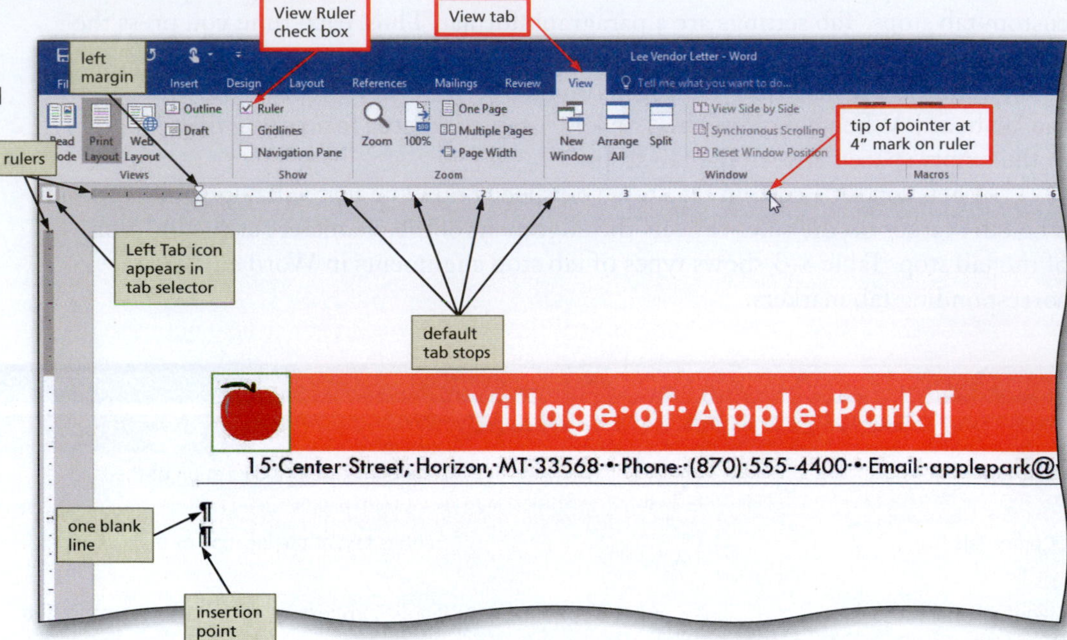

Figure 3–40

Q&A What is the purpose of the tab selector?
Before using the ruler to set a tab stop, ensure the correct tab stop icon appears in the tab selector. Each time you click the tab selector, its icon changes. The Left Tab icon is the default. For a list of the types of tab stops, see Table 3–3.

- Click the 4″ mark on the ruler to place a tab marker at that location (Figure 3–41).

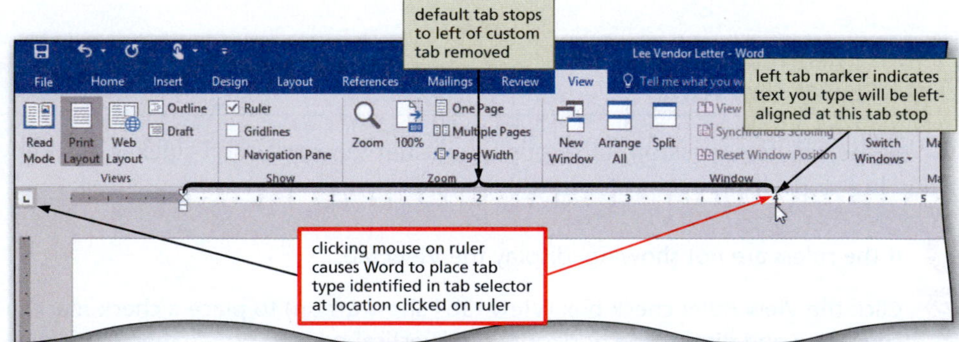

Figure 3–41

Q&A What if I click the wrong location on the ruler?
You can move a custom tab stop by dragging the tab marker to the desired location on the ruler. Or, you can remove an existing custom tab stop by pointing to the tab marker on the ruler and then dragging the tab marker down and out of the ruler.

What if I am using a touch screen?
Display the Home tab, tap the Paragraph Settings Dialog Box Launcher (Home tab | Paragraph group), tap the Tabs button (Paragraph dialog box), type 4 in the Tab stop position box (Tabs dialog box), tap the Set button, and then tap the OK button to set a custom tab stop and place a corresponding tab marker on the ruler.

Other Ways

1. Click Paragraph Dialog Box Launcher (Home tab or Layout tab | Paragraph group), click Tabs button (Paragraph dialog box), type tab stop position (Tabs dialog box), click Set button, click OK button

To Insert the Current Date in a Document

The next step is to enter the current date at the 4" tab stop in the document. ***Why?*** *The date in this letter will be positioned according to the guidelines for a modified block style letter.* In Word, you can insert a computer's system date in a document. The following steps insert the current date in the letter.

1

- Press the TAB key to position the insertion point at the location of the tab stop in the current paragraph.
- Display the Insert tab.
- Click the 'Insert Date and Time' button (Insert tab | Text group) to display the Date and Time dialog box.
- Select the desired format (Date and Time dialog box), in this case October 2, 2017.
- If the Update automatically check box is selected, click the check box to remove the check mark (Figure 3–42).

Q&A Why should the Update automatically check box not be selected?
In this project, the date at the top of the letter always should show today's date (for example, October 2, 2017). If, however, you wanted the date always to change to reflect the current computer date (for example, showing the date you open or print the letter), then you would place a check mark in this check box.

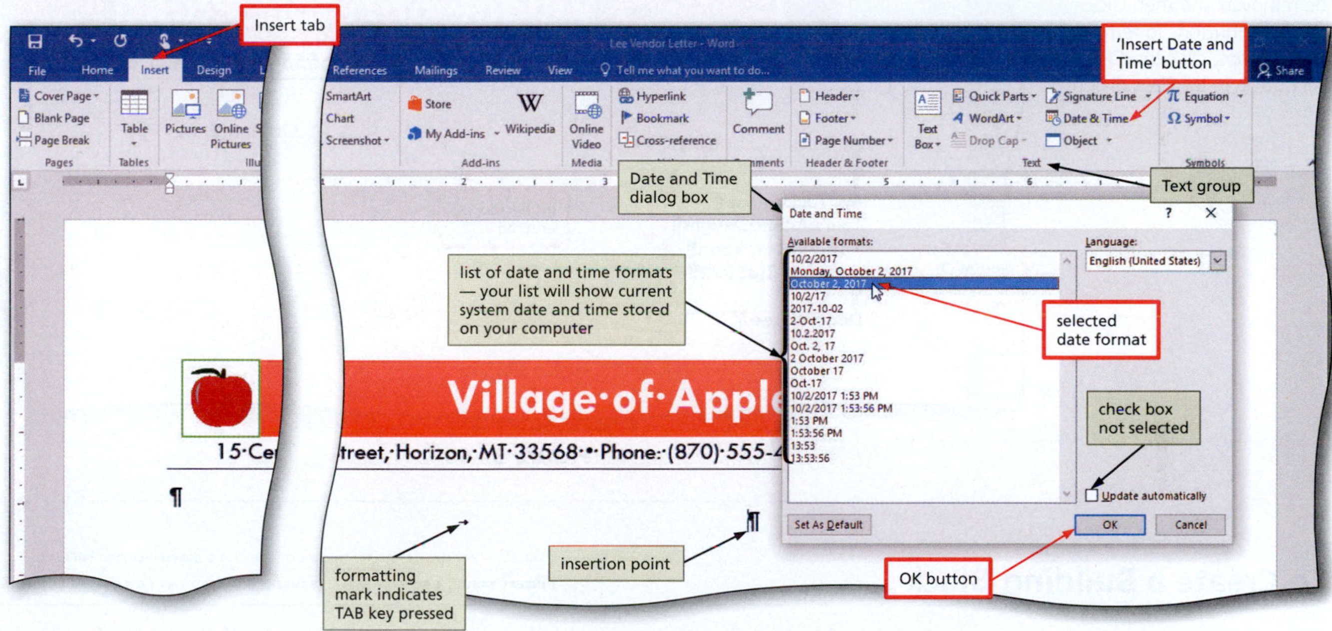

Figure 3–42

2

- Click the OK button to insert the current date at the location of the insertion point (Figure 3–43).

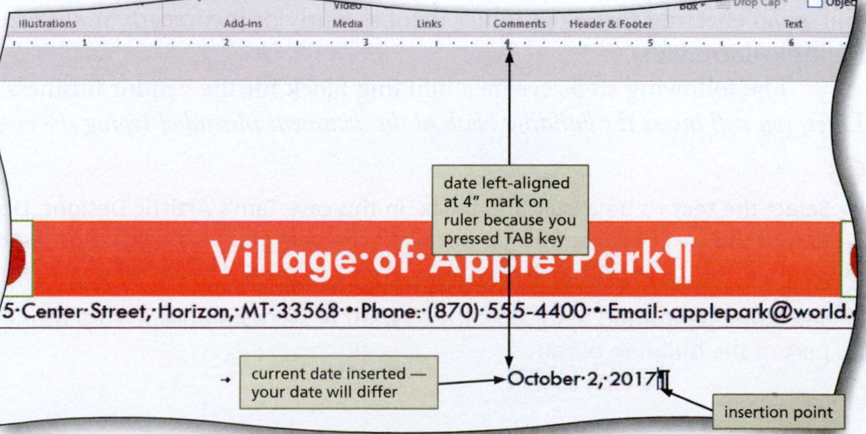

Figure 3–43

BTW

Tabs Dialog Box

You can use the Tabs dialog box to set, change the alignment of, and remove custom tab stops. To display the Tabs dialog box, click the Paragraph Settings Dialog Box Launcher (Home tab or Layout tab | Paragraph group) and then click the Tabs button (Paragraph dialog box). To set a custom tab stop, enter the desired tab position (Tabs dialog box) and then click the Set button. To change the alignment of a custom tab stop, click the tab stop position to be changed, click the new alignment, and then click the Set button. To remove an existing tab stop, click the tab stop position to be removed and then click the Clear button. To remove all tab stops, click the Clear All button in the Tabs dialog box.

To Enter the Inside Address and Salutation

The next step in composing the business letter is to type the inside address and salutation. The following steps enter this text.

1. With the insertion point at the end of the date (shown in Figure 3–43), press the ENTER key three times.
2. Type `Ms. Tamara Lee` and then press the ENTER key.
3. Type `Tam's Artistic Designs` and then press the ENTER key.
4. Type `1587 Willow Road` and then press the ENTER key.
5. Type `Juniper, MT 33522` and then press the ENTER key twice.
6. Type `Dear Ms. Lee:` to complete the inside address and salutation entries. Scroll up, if necessary (Figure 3–44).

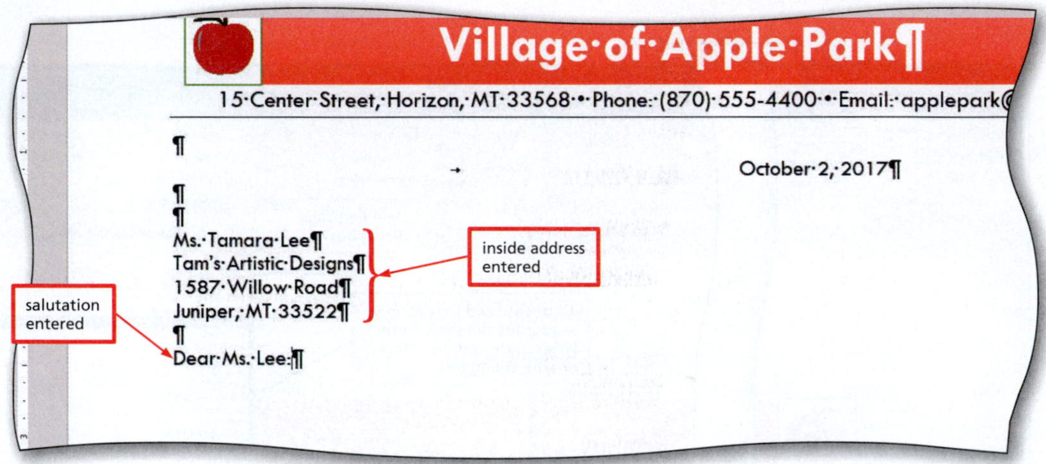

Figure 3–44

To Create a Building Block

1 CREATE & FORMAT LETTERHEAD WITH GRAPHICS | 2 SPECIFY LETTER FORMATS
3 INSERT TABLE | 4 FORMAT TABLE | 5 INSERT BULLETED LIST | 6 ADDRESS ENVELOPE

If you use the same text or graphic frequently, you can store the text or graphic as a **building block** and then insert the stored building block entry in the open document, as well as in future documents. That is, you can create the entry once as a building block and then insert the building block when you need it. In this way, you avoid entering text or graphics inconsistently or incorrectly in different locations throughout the same or multiple documents.

The following steps create a building block for the vendor business name, Tam's Artistic Designs. ***Why?*** *Later, you will insert the building block in the document instead of typing the vendor business name again.*

1

- Select the text to be a building block, in this case Tam's Artistic Designs. Do not select the paragraph mark at the end of the text because you do not want the paragraph to be part of the building block.

Q&A

Why is the paragraph mark not part of the building block?

Select the paragraph mark only if you want to store paragraph formatting, such as indentation and line spacing, as part of the building block.

- Click the 'Explore Quick Parts' button (Insert tab | Text group) to display the Explore Quick Parts gallery (Figure 3–45).

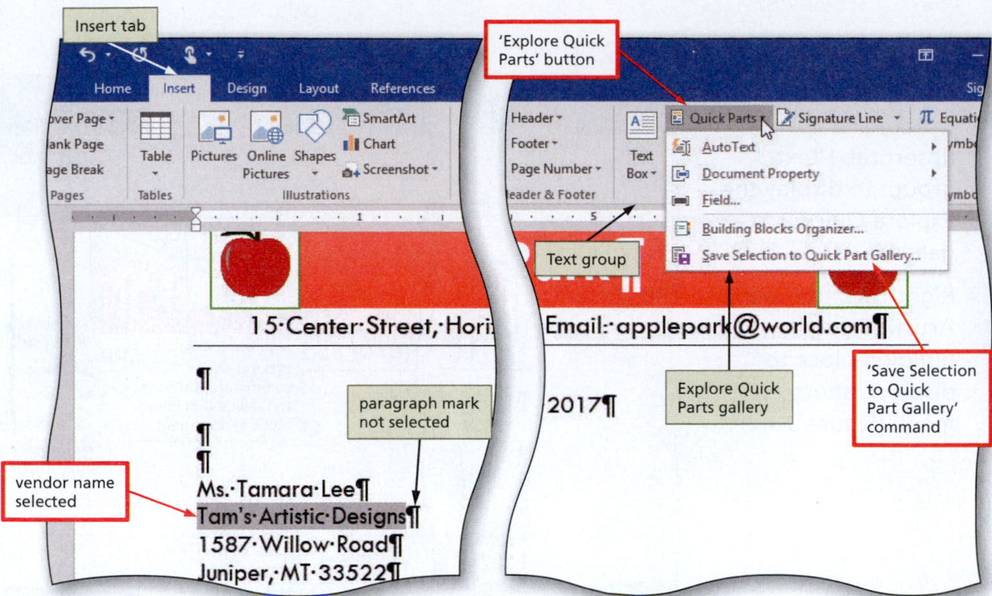

Figure 3–45

- Click 'Save Selection to Quick Part Gallery' in the Explore Quick Parts gallery to display the Create New Building Block dialog box.
- Type `tad` in the Name text box (Create New Building Block dialog box) to replace the proposed building block name (Tam's Artistic, in this case) with a shorter building block name (Figure 3–46).

- Click the OK button to store the building block entry and close the dialog box.
- If Word displays another dialog box, click the Yes button to save changes to the building blocks.

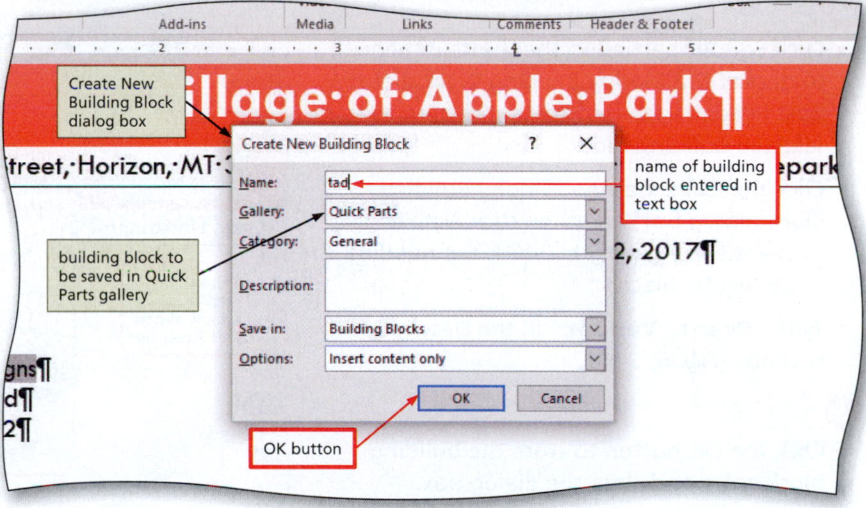

Figure 3–46

Q&A Will this building block be available in future documents?
When you exit Word, a dialog box may appear asking if you want to save changes to the building blocks. Click the Save button if you want to use the new building block in future documents.

To Modify a Building Block

1 CREATE & FORMAT LETTERHEAD WITH GRAPHICS | 2 SPECIFY LETTER FORMATS
3 INSERT TABLE | 4 FORMAT TABLE | 5 INSERT BULLETED LIST | 6 ADDRESS ENVELOPE

When you save a building block in the Explore Quick Parts gallery, the building block is displayed at the top of the Explore Quick Parts gallery. When you point to the building block in the Explore Quick Parts gallery, a ScreenTip displays the building block name. If you want to display more information when the user points to the building block, you can include a description in the ScreenTip.

The following steps modify a building block to include a description and change its category to AutoText. ***Why?*** *Because you want to reuse this text, you place it in the AutoText gallery, which also is accessible through the Explore Quick Parts gallery.*

- Click the 'Explore Quick Parts' button (Insert tab | Text group) to display the Explore Quick Parts gallery.
- Right-click the Tam's Artistic Design building block to display a shortcut menu (Figure 3–47).

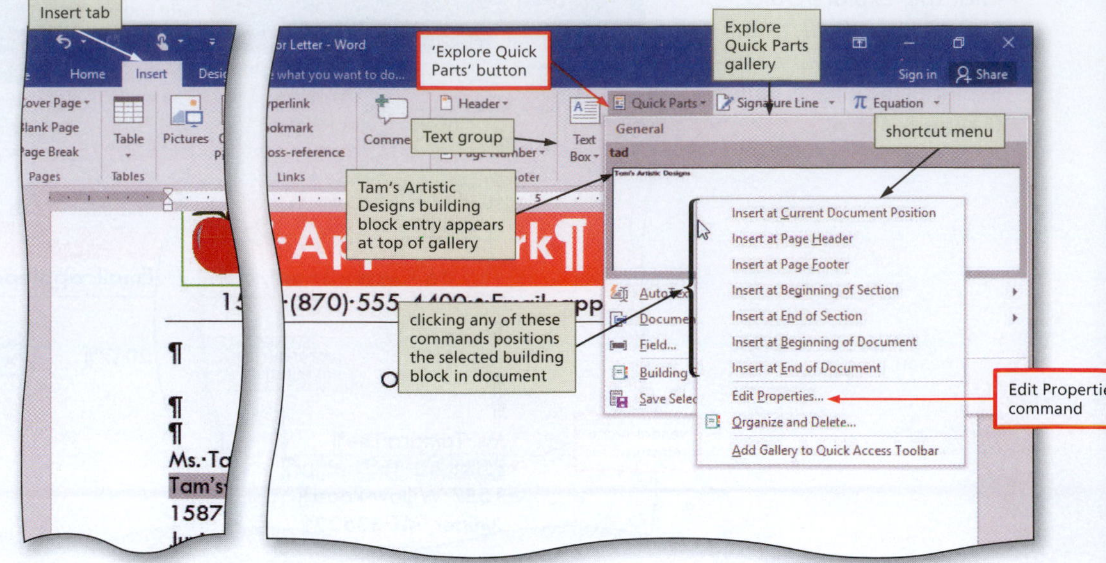

Figure 3–47

- Click Edit Properties on the shortcut menu to display the Modify Building Block dialog box, filled in with information related to the selected building block.
- Click the Gallery arrow (Modify Building Block dialog box) and then click AutoText to change the gallery in which the building block will be placed.
- Type **`Event Vendor`** in the Description text box (Figure 3–48).

- Click the OK button to store the building block entry and close the dialog box.
- Click the Yes button when asked if you want to redefine the building block entry.

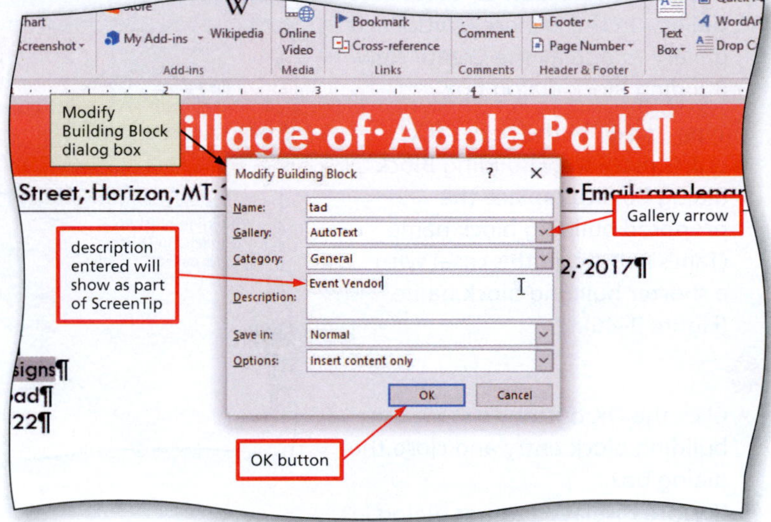

Figure 3–48

To Insert a Building Block

1 CREATE & FORMAT LETTERHEAD WITH GRAPHICS | 2 SPECIFY LETTER FORMATS
3 INSERT TABLE | 4 FORMAT TABLE | 5 INSERT BULLETED LIST | 6 ADDRESS ENVELOPE

The vendor business name, Tam's Artistic Designs, appears in the first sentence in the body of the letter. You will type the building block name, tad, and then instruct Word to replace this building block name with the stored building block entry, Tam's Artistic Designs. The following steps insert a building block. ***Why?*** *Instead of typing the name, you will insert the stored building block.*

- Click to the right of the colon in the salutation and then press the ENTER key twice to position the insertion point one blank line below the salutation.

- Type the beginning of the first sentence as follows, entering the building block name as shown: `The park district board has approved the vendor application for your business, tad` (Figure 3–49).

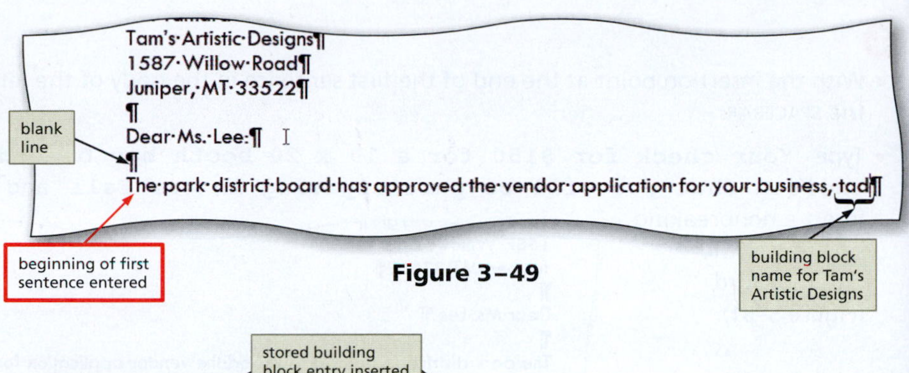

Figure 3–49

2

- Press the F3 key to instruct Word to replace the building block name (tad) with the stored building block entry (Tam's Artistic Designs).
- Press the PERIOD key (Figure 3–50).

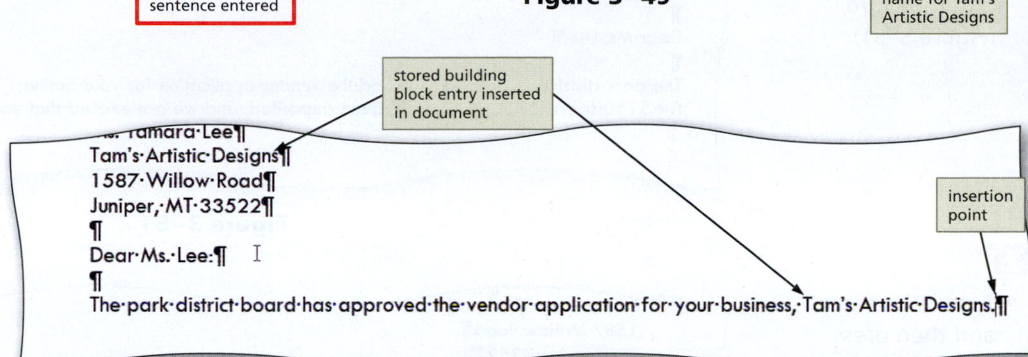

Figure 3–50

Other Ways

1. Click 'Explore Quick Parts' button (Insert tab | Text group), if necessary point to AutoText, select desired building block
2. Click 'Explore Quick Parts' button (Insert tab | Text group), click Building Blocks Organizer, select desired building block, click Insert button

Building Blocks versus AutoCorrect

In Module 2, you learned how to use the AutoCorrect feature, which enables you to insert and create AutoCorrect entries, similarly to how you created and inserted building blocks in this module. The difference between an AutoCorrect entry and a building block entry is that the AutoCorrect feature makes corrections for you automatically as soon as you press the SPACEBAR or type a punctuation mark, whereas you must instruct Word to insert a building block. That is, you enter the building block name and then press the F3 key, or click the Explore Quick Parts button and select the building block from one of the galleries or the Building Blocks Organizer.

To Insert a Nonbreaking Space

1 CREATE & FORMAT LETTERHEAD WITH GRAPHICS | 2 SPECIFY LETTER FORMATS
3 INSERT TABLE | 4 FORMAT TABLE | 5 INSERT BULLETED LIST | 6 ADDRESS ENVELOPE

Some compound words, such as proper nouns, dates, units of time and measure, abbreviations, and geographic destinations, should not be divided at the end of a line. These words either should fit as a unit at the end of a line or be wrapped together to the next line.

Word provides two special characters to assist with this task: the nonbreaking space and the nonbreaking hyphen. A **nonbreaking space** is a special space character that prevents two words from splitting if the first word falls at the end of a line. Similarly, a **nonbreaking hyphen** is a special type of hyphen that prevents two words separated by a hyphen from splitting at the end of a line.

The following steps insert a nonbreaking space between the two words, Fall Festival. ***Why?** You want these two words to appear on the same physical line.*

- With the insertion point at the end of the first sentence in the body of the letter (as shown in Figure 3–50), press the SPACEBAR.
- Type `Your check for $150 for a 10 x 20 booth has been deposited, and we are excited that you will be participating in our Fall` and then press CTRL+SHIFT+SPACEBAR to insert a nonbreaking space after the entered word (Figure 3–51).

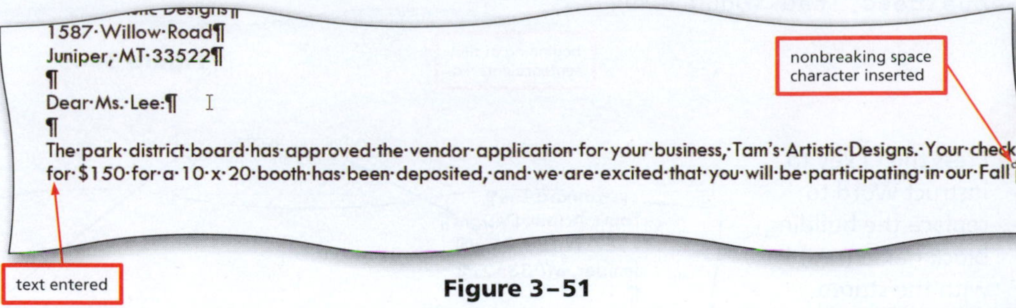

Figure 3–51

- Type `Festival` and then press PERIOD key (Figure 3–52).

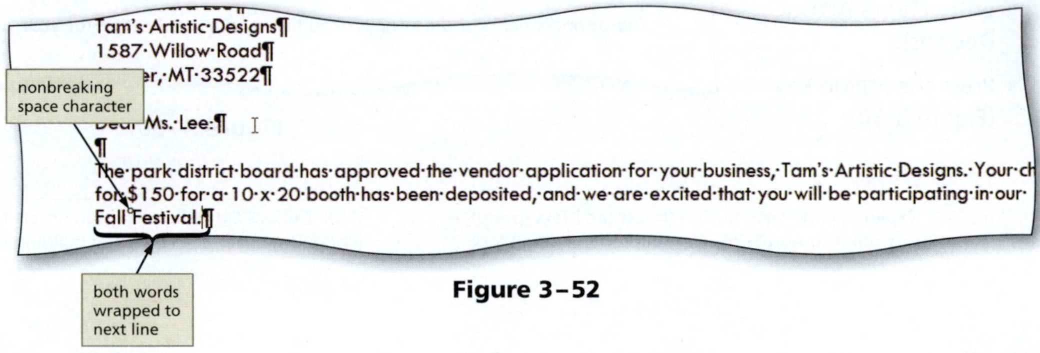

Figure 3–52

Other Ways

1. Click 'Insert a Symbol' button (Insert tab | Symbols group), click More Symbols, click Special Characters tab (Symbol dialog box), click Nonbreaking Space in Character list, click Insert button, click Close button

BTW
Nonbreaking Hyphen
If you wanted to insert a nonbreaking hyphen, you would press CTRL+SHIFT+HYPHEN.

To Enter Text

The next step in creating the letter is to enter the rest of the text in the first paragraph. The following steps enter this text.

1. Press the SPACEBAR.
2. Type this sentence: `The table below outlines the timetable for vendors:`
3. Press the ENTER key twice to place a blank line between paragraphs (shown in Figure 3–53).

Q&A Why does my document wrap on different words?
Differences in wordwrap may relate to the printer connected to your computer. Thus, it is possible that the same document could wordwrap differently if associated with a different printer.

4. Save the letterhead again on the same storage location with the same file name.

Break Point: If you wish to take a break, this is a good place to do so. You can exit Word now. To resume at a later time, run Word, open the file called Lee Vendor Letter, and continue following the steps from this location forward.

Tables

The next step in composing the business letter is to place a table listing the vendor timetable (shown in Figure 3–1). A Word **table** is a collection of rows and columns. The intersection of a row and a column is called a **cell**, and cells are filled with data.

The first step in creating a table is to insert an empty table in the document. When inserting a table, you must specify the total number of rows and columns required, which is called the **dimension** of the table. The table in this project has three columns. You often do not know the total number of rows in a table. Thus, many Word users create one row initially and then add more rows as needed. In Word, the first number in a dimension is the number of columns, and the second is the number of rows. For example, in Word, a 3 × 1 (pronounced "three by one") table consists of three columns and one row.

1 CREATE & FORMAT LETTERHEAD WITH GRAPHICS | 2 SPECIFY LETTER FORMATS
3 INSERT TABLE | 4 FORMAT TABLE | 5 INSERT BULLETED LIST | 6 ADDRESS ENVELOPE

To Insert an Empty Table

The next step is to insert an empty table in the letter. The following steps insert a table with three columns and one row at the location of the insertion point. ***Why?*** *The first column will identify the activity, the second will identify the event dates, and the third will identify the activity times. You will start with one row and add them as needed.*

1

- Scroll the document so that you will be able to see the table in the document window.
- Display the Insert tab.
- With the insertion point positioned as shown in Figure 3–53, click the 'Add a Table' button (Insert tab | Tables group) to display the Add a Table gallery (Figure 3–53).

Experiment

- Point to various cells on the grid to see a preview of various table dimensions in the document window.

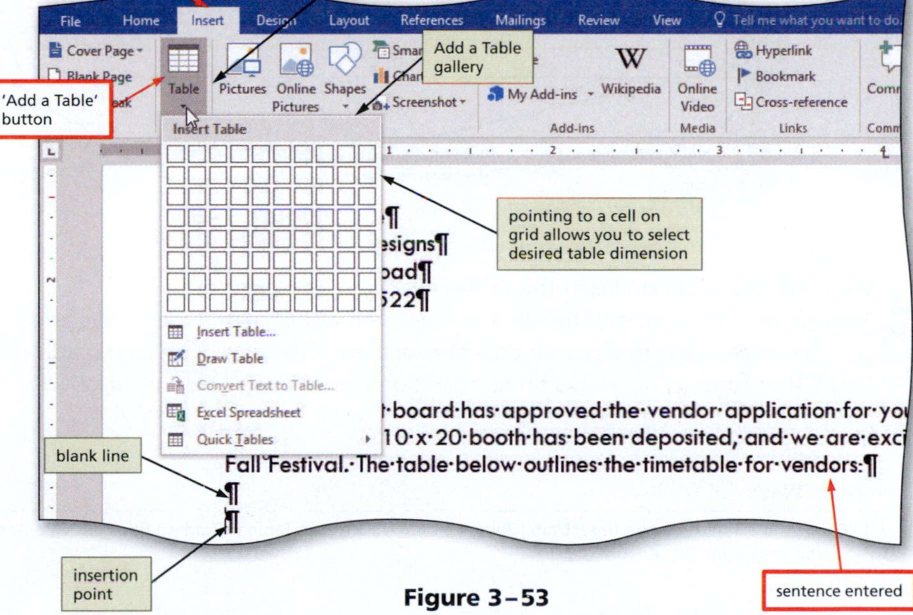

Figure 3–53

- Position the pointer on the cell in the first row and third column of the grid to preview the desired table dimension in the document (Figure 3–54).

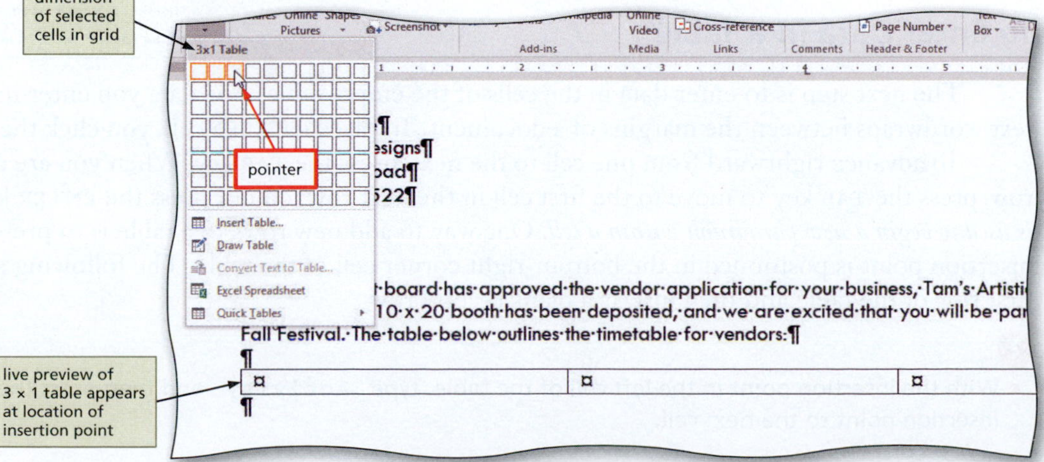

Figure 3–54

- Click the cell in the first row and third column of the grid to insert an empty table with one row and three columns in the document.
- If necessary, scroll the document so that the table is visible (Figure 3–55).

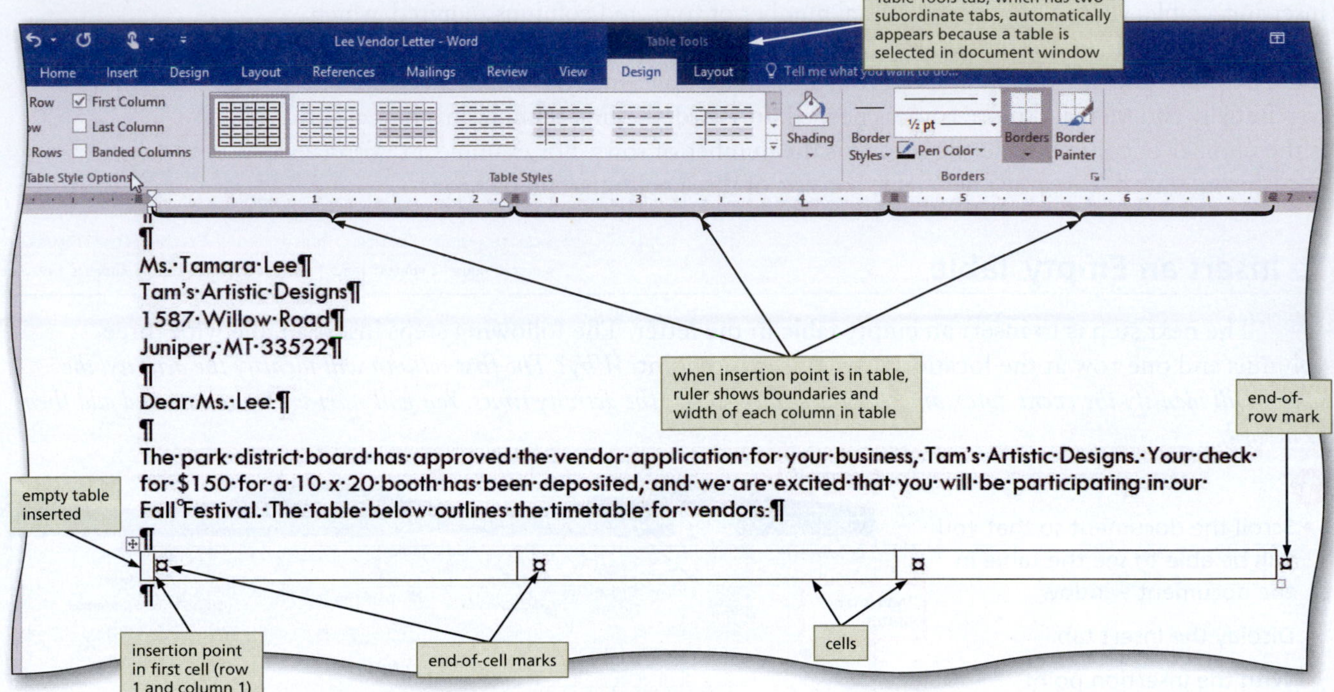

Figure 3–55

Q&A What are the small circles in the table cells?
Each table cell has an **end-of-cell mark**, which is a formatting mark that assists you with selecting and formatting cells. Similarly, each row has an **end-of-row mark**, which you can use to add columns to the right of a table. Recall that formatting marks do not print on a hard copy. The end-of-cell marks currently are left-aligned, that is, positioned at the left edge of each cell.

Other Ways

1. Click 'Add a Table' button (Insert tab | Tables group), click Insert Table in Add a Table gallery, enter number of columns and rows (Insert Table dialog box), click OK button

To Enter Data in a Table

1 CREATE & FORMAT LETTERHEAD WITH GRAPHICS | 2 SPECIFY LETTER FORMATS
3 INSERT TABLE | 4 FORMAT TABLE | 5 INSERT BULLETED LIST | 6 ADDRESS ENVELOPE

The next step is to enter data in the cells of the empty table. The data you enter in a cell wordwraps just as text wordwraps between the margins of a document. To place data in a cell, you click the cell and then type.

To advance rightward from one cell to the next, press the TAB key. When you are at the rightmost cell in a row, press the TAB key to move to the first cell in the next row; do not press the ENTER key. ***Why?** The ENTER key is used to begin a new paragraph within a cell.* One way to add new rows to a table is to press the TAB key when the insertion point is positioned in the bottom-right corner cell of the table. The following step enters data in the first row of the table and then inserts a blank second row.

- With the insertion point in the left cell of the table, type `Activity` and then press the TAB key to advance the insertion point to the next cell.

- Type **Event Dates** and then press the TAB key to advance the insertion point to the next cell.
- Type **Times** and then press the TAB key to add a second row at the end of the table and position the insertion point in the first column of the new row (Figure 3–56).

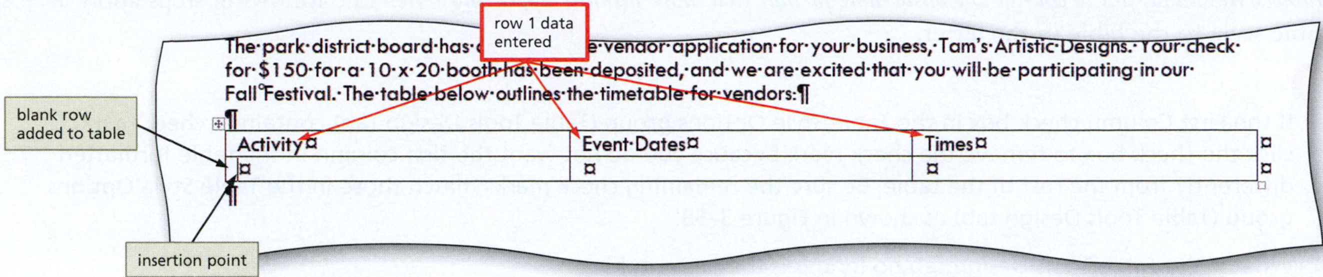

Figure 3–56

Q&A | How do I edit cell contents if I make a mistake?
Click in the cell and then correct the entry.

To Enter More Data in a Table

The following steps enter the remaining data in the table.

1. Type **Booth Setup** and then press the TAB key to advance the insertion point to the next cell. Type **Friday, October 27** and then press the TAB key to advance the insertion point to the next cell. Type **5:00 to 9:00 p.m.** and then press the TAB key to add a row at the end of the table and position the insertion point in the first column of the new row.
2. In the third row, type **Booth Sales** in the first column, **Saturday, October 28** in the second column, and **9:00 a.m. to 6:00 p.m.** in the third column. Press the TAB key to position the insertion point in the first column of a new row.
3. In the fourth row, type **Booth Sales** in the first column, **Sunday, October 29** in the second column, and **9:00 a.m. to 3:00 p.m.** in the third column. Press the TAB key.
4. In the fifth row, type **Booth Takedown** in the first column, **Sunday, October 29** in the second column, and **3:00 to 7:00 p.m.** in the third column (Figure 3–57).

BTW
Tables
For simple tables, such as the one just created, Word users often select the table dimension in the Add a Table gallery to create the table. For a more complex table, such as one with a varying number of columns per row, Word has a Draw Table feature that allows users to draw a table in the document using a pencil pointer. To use this feature, click the 'Add a Table' button (Insert tab | Tables group) and then click Draw Table on the Add a Table menu.

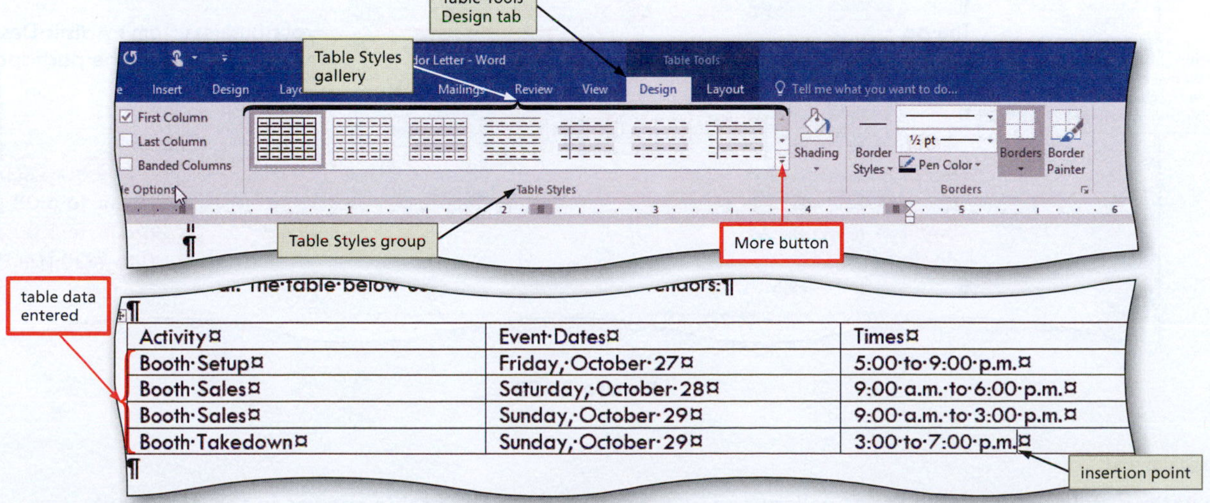

Figure 3–57

To Apply a Table Style

Word provides a gallery of more than 90 table styles, which include a variety of colors and shading. ***Why?*** *Table styles allow you to change the basic table format to a more visually appealing style.* The following steps apply a table style to the table in the letter.

- If the First Column check box in the Table Style Options group (Table Tools Design tab) contains a check mark, click the check box to remove the check mark because you do not want the first column in the table formatted differently from the rest of the table. Be sure the remaining check marks match those in the Table Style Options group (Table Tools Design tab) as shown in Figure 3–58.

Q&A

What if the Table Tools Design tab no longer is the active tab?
Click in the table and then display the Table Tools Design tab.

What do the options in the Table Style Options group mean?
When you apply table styles, if you want the top row of the table (header row), a row containing totals (total row), first column, or last column to be formatted differently, select those check boxes. If you want the rows or columns to alternate with colors, select Banded Rows or Banded Columns, respectively.

- With the insertion point in the table, click the More button in the Table Styles gallery (Table Tools Design tab | Table Styles group), shown in Figure 3–57, to expand the gallery.
- Scroll and then point to 'Grid Table 6 Colorful - Accent 3' in the Table Styles gallery to display a live preview of that style applied to the table in the document (Figure 3–58).

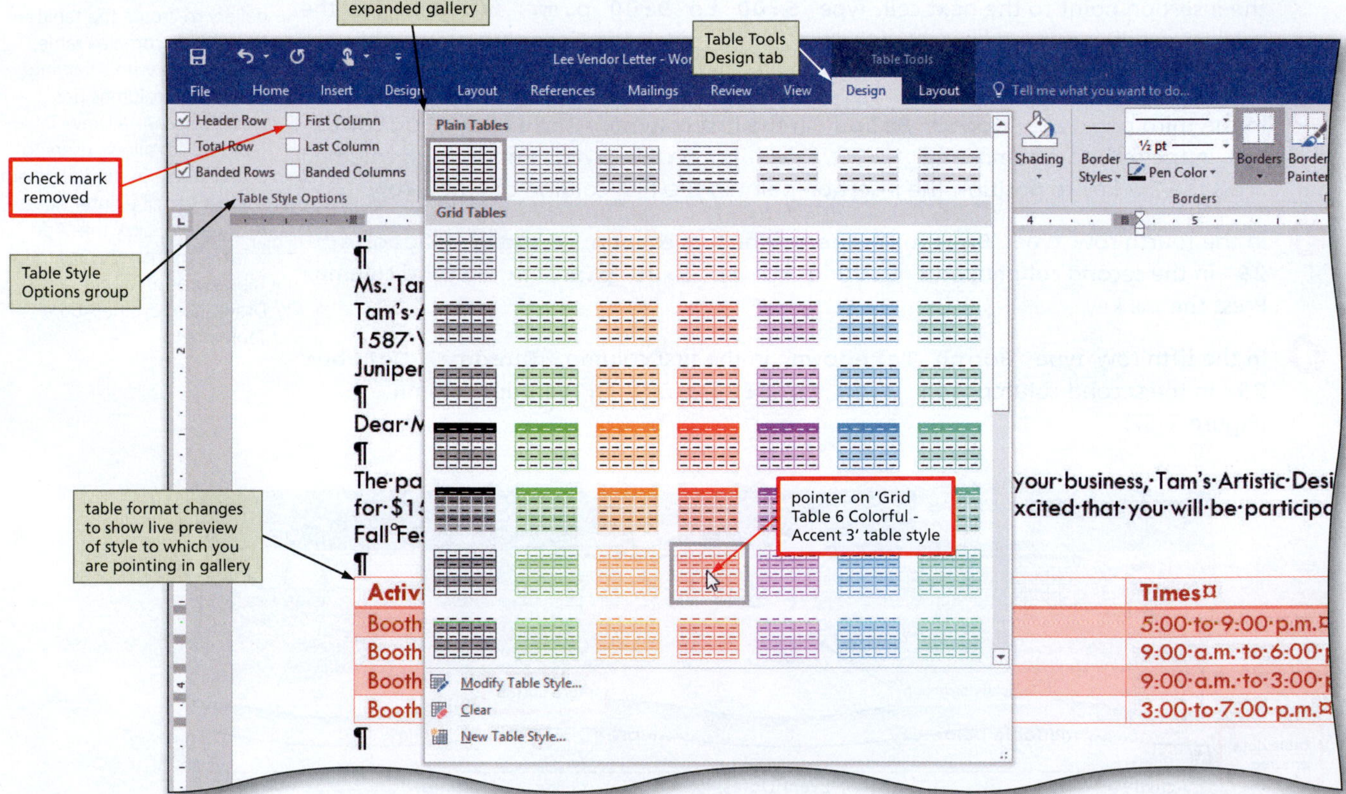

Figure 3–58

Experiment

- Point to various styles in the Table Styles gallery and watch the format of the table change in the document window.

- Click 'Grid Table 6 Colorful - Accent 3' in the Table Styles gallery to apply the selected style to the table. Scroll up, if necessary (Figure 3–59).

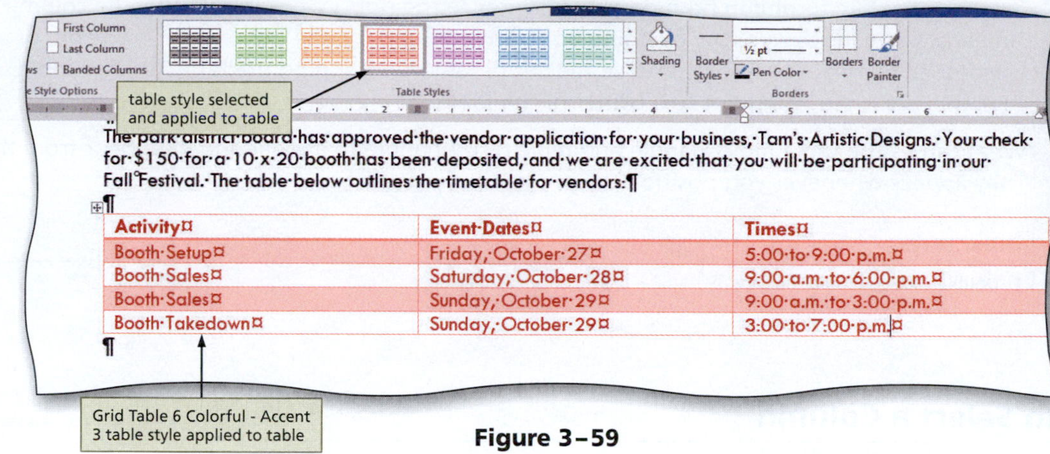

Figure 3–59

- Select and remove check marks from various check boxes in the Table Style Options group and watch the format of the table change in the document window. When finished experimenting, be sure the check marks match those shown in Figure 3–58.

To Resize Table Columns to Fit Table Contents

1 CREATE & FORMAT LETTERHEAD WITH GRAPHICS | 2 SPECIFY LETTER FORMATS
3 INSERT TABLE | 4 FORMAT TABLE | 5 INSERT BULLETED LIST | 6 ADDRESS ENVELOPE

The table in this project currently extends from the left margin to the right margin of the document. The following steps instruct Word to fit the width of the columns to the contents of the table automatically. ***Why?*** *You want each column to be only as wide as the longest entry in the table. That is, the first column must be wide enough to accommodate the words, Booth Takedown, and the second column should be only as wide as the words, Saturday, October 28, and so on.*

- With the insertion point in the table, display the Table Tools Layout tab.
- Click the AutoFit button (Table Tools Layout tab | Cell Size group) to display the AutoFit menu (Figure 3–60).

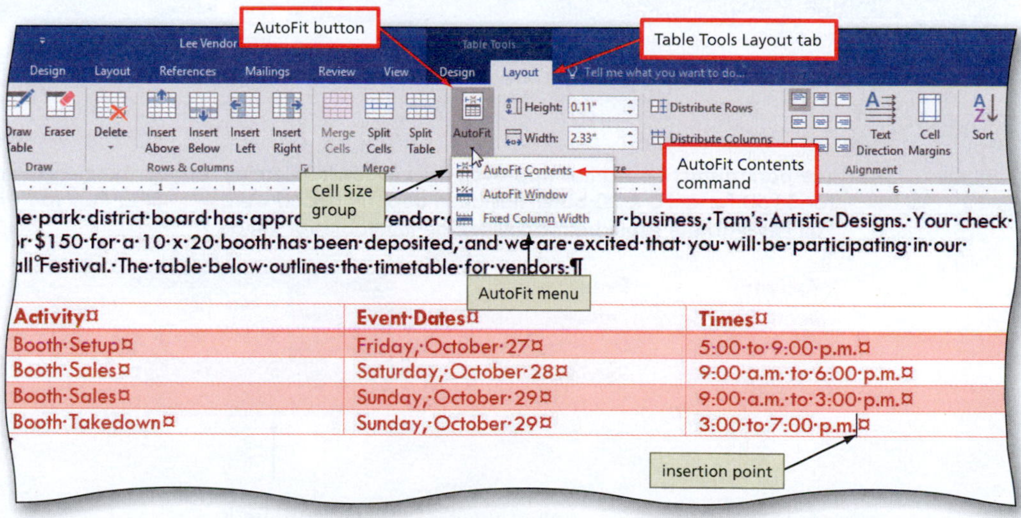

Figure 3–60

2

- Click AutoFit Contents on the AutoFit menu, so that Word automatically adjusts the widths of the columns based on the text in the table (Figure 3–61).

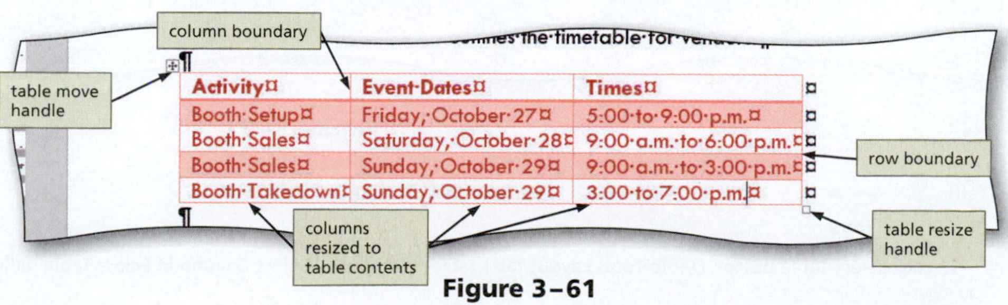

Figure 3–61

Q&A Can I resize columns manually?
Yes, you can drag a **column boundary**, the border to the right of a column, until the column is the desired width. Similarly, you can resize a row by dragging the **row boundary**, the border at the bottom of a row, until the row is the desired height. You also can resize the entire table by dragging the **table resize handle**, which is a small square that appears when you point to a corner of the table.

What causes the table move handle and table resize handle to appear and disappear from the table?
They appear whenever you position the pointer in the table.

Other Ways

1. Double-click column boundary

To Select a Column

1 CREATE & FORMAT LETTERHEAD WITH GRAPHICS | 2 SPECIFY LETTER FORMATS
3 INSERT TABLE | 4 FORMAT TABLE | 5 INSERT BULLETED LIST | 6 ADDRESS ENVELOPE

The next task is to change the alignment of the data in cells in the third column of the table. To do this, you first must select the column. ***Why?*** *If you want to format the contents of a single cell, simply position the insertion point in the cell. To format a series of cells, you first must select them.* The following step selects a column.

- Position the pointer at the boundary above the column to be selected, the third column in this case, so that the pointer changes to a downward pointing arrow and then click to select the column (Figure 3–62).

Q&A What if I am using a touch screen?
Position the insertion point in the third column, tap the Select Table button (Table Tools Layout tab | Table group), and then tap Select Column on the Select Table menu.

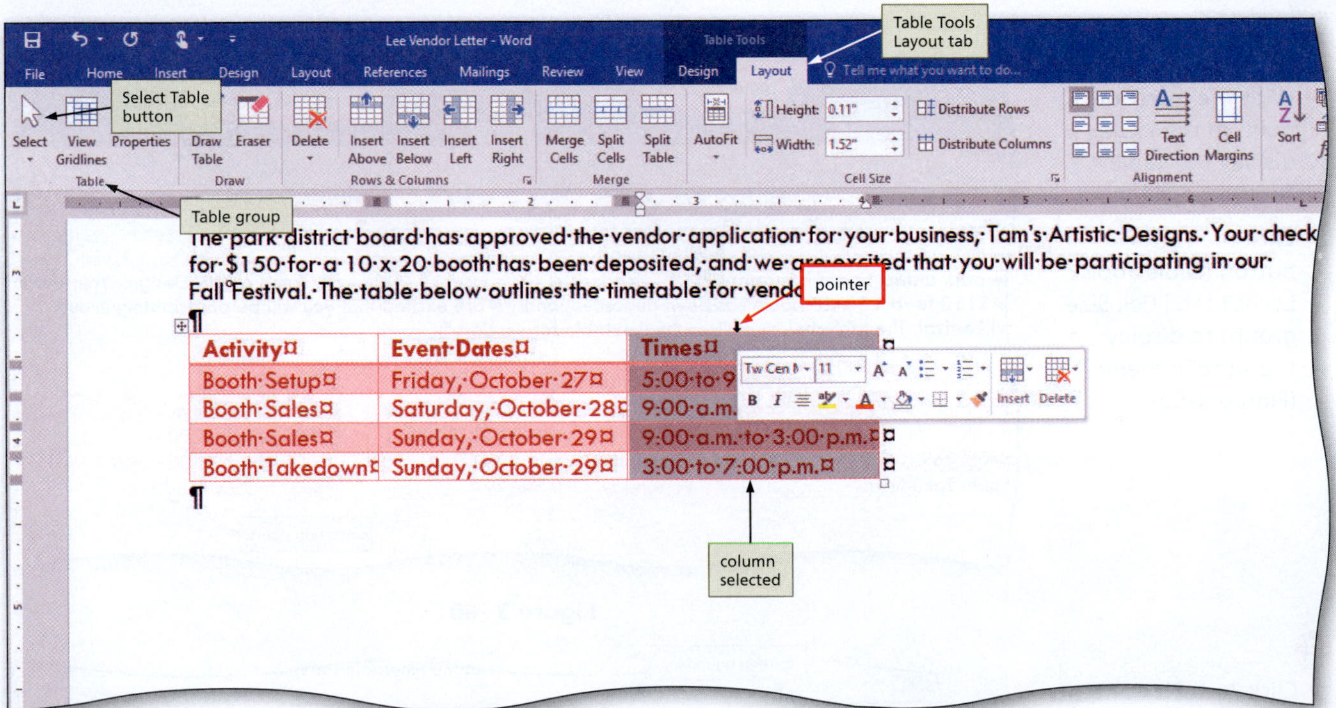

Figure 3–62

Other Ways

1. Click Select Table button (Table Tools Layout tab | Table group), click Select Column in Select Table gallery

Selecting Table Contents

When working with tables, you may need to select the contents of cells, rows, columns, or the entire table. Table 3–4 identifies ways to select various items in a table.

Table 3–4 Selecting Items in a Table

Item to Select	Action
Cell	Point to left edge of cell and then click when the pointer changes to a small solid upward angled pointing arrow. Or Position insertion point in cell, click Select Table button (Table Tools Layout tab | Table group), and then click Select Cell on the Select Table menu.
Column	Point to border at top of column and then click when the pointer changes to a small solid downward-pointing arrow. Or Position insertion point in column, click Select Table button (Table Tools Layout tab | Table group), and then click Select Column on the Select Table menu.
Row	Point to the left of the row and then click when pointer changes to a right-pointing block arrow. Or Position insertion point in row, click Select Table button (Table Tools Layout tab | Table group), and then click Select Row on the Select Table menu.
Multiple cells, rows, or columns adjacent to one another	Drag through cells, rows, or columns.
Multiple cells, rows, or columns not adjacent to one another	Select first cell, row, or column (as described above) and then hold down CTRL key while selecting next cell, row, or column.
Next cell	Press TAB key.
Previous cell	Press SHIFT+TAB
Table	Point somewhere in table and then click table move handle that appears in upper-left corner of table (shown in Figure 3-63). Or Position insertion point in table, click Select Table button (Table Tools Layout tab | Table group), and then click Select Table on the Select Table menu.

BTW

Word Help

At any time while using Word, you can find answers to questions and display information about various topics through Word Help. Used properly, this form of assistance can increase your productivity and reduce your frustrations by minimizing the time you spend learning how to use Word. For instructions about Word Help and exercises that will help you gain confidence in using it, read the Office and Windows module at the beginning of this book.

To Align Data in Cells

1 CREATE & FORMAT LETTERHEAD WITH GRAPHICS | 2 SPECIFY LETTER FORMATS
3 INSERT TABLE | **4 FORMAT TABLE** | 5 INSERT BULLETED LIST | 6 ADDRESS ENVELOPE

The next step is to change the alignment of the data in cells in the third column of the table. In addition to aligning text horizontally in a cell (left, center, or right), you can align it vertically within a cell (top, center, bottom). When the height of the cell is close to the same height as the text, however, differences in vertical alignment are not readily apparent, which is the case for this table. The following step centers data in cells. ***Why?*** *The column containing the times would look better if its contents are centered.*

1

- With the cells (column) selected, as shown in Figure 3–62, click the desired alignment, in this case the 'Align Top Center' button (Table Tools Layout tab | Alignment group) to center the contents of the selected cells (Figure 3–63).

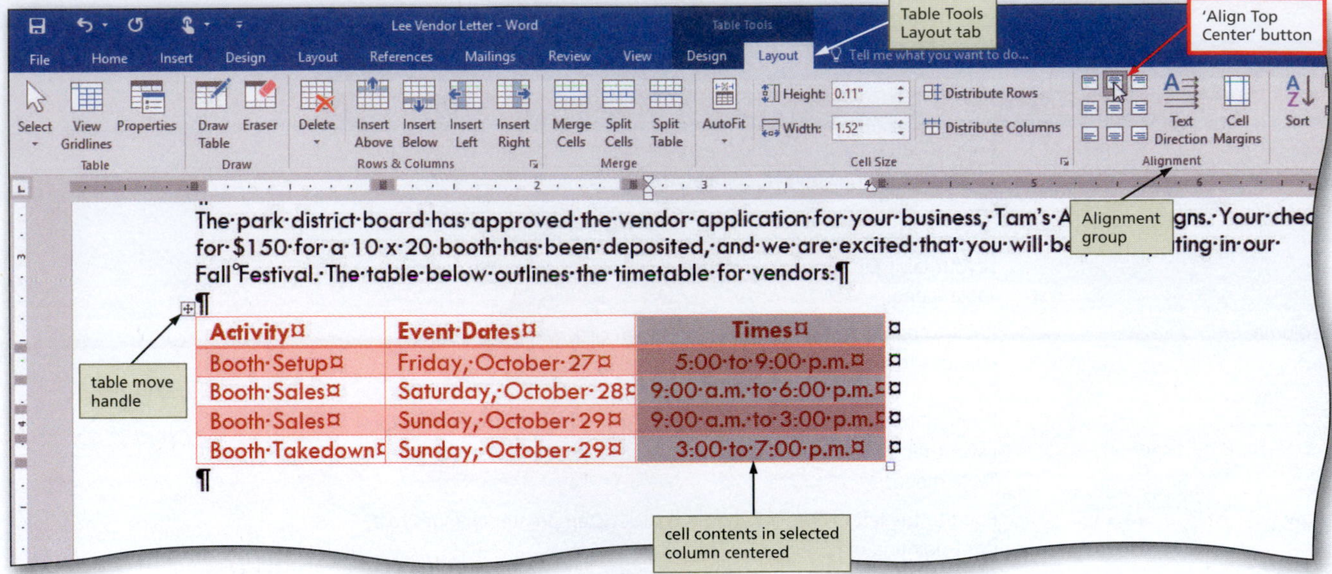

Figure 3–63

To Center a Table

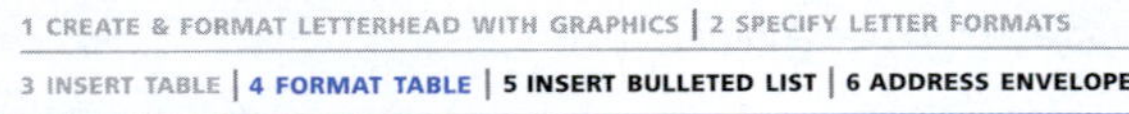

When you first create a table, it is left-aligned; that is, it is flush with the left margin. In this letter, the entire table should be centered between the margins of the page. To center a table, you first select the entire table. The following steps select and center a table using the mini toolbar. ***Why?*** *Recall that you can use buttons and boxes on the mini toolbar instead of those on the ribbon.*

1

- Position the pointer in the table so that the table move handle appears (shown in Figure 3–63).

Q&A What if the table move handle does not appear?
You also can select a table by clicking the Select Table button (Table Tools Layout tab | Table group) and then clicking Select Table on the menu.

2

- Click the table move handle to select the entire table (Figure 3–64).

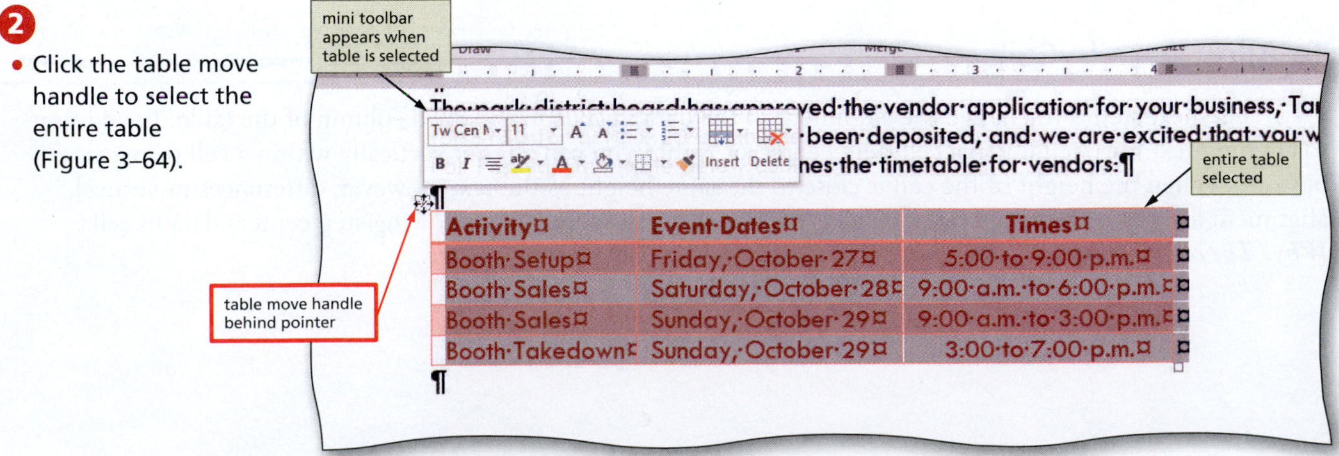

Figure 3–64

What if I am using a touch screen?
Tap the Select Table button (Table Tools Layout tab | Table group) and then tap Select Table on the Select Table menu to select the table.

3

- Click the Center button on the mini toolbar to center the selected table between the left and right page margins (Figure 3–65).

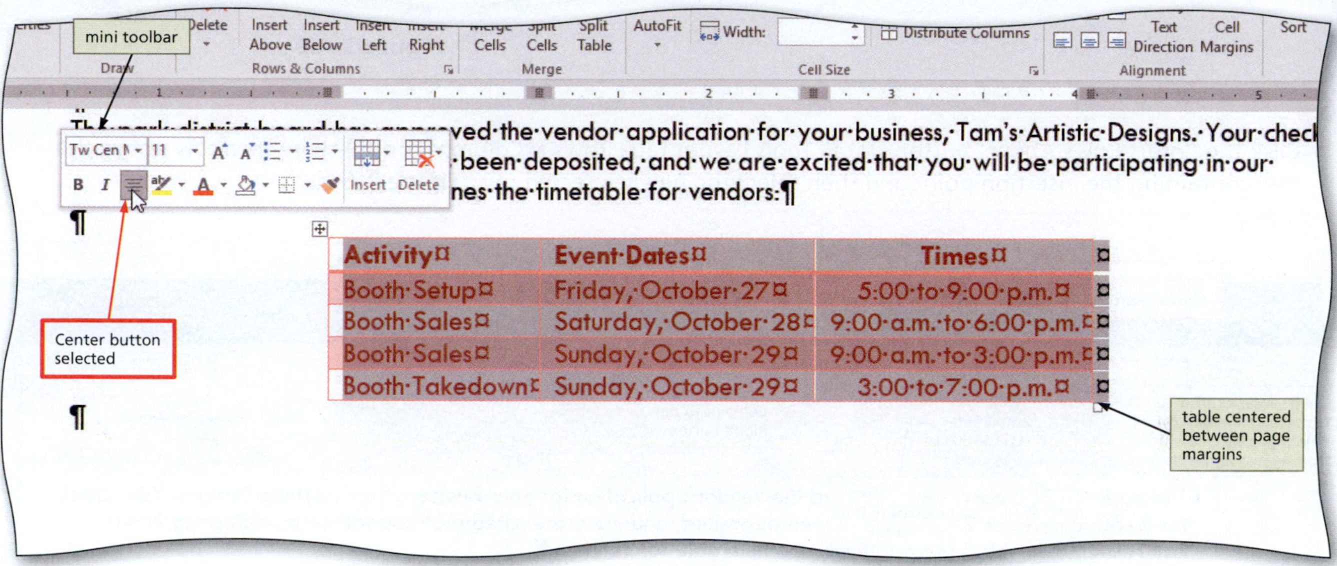

Figure 3–65

Q&A

Could I have clicked the Center button on the Home tab?
Yes. If the command you want to use is not on the currently displayed tab on the ribbon and it is available on the mini toolbar, use the mini toolbar instead of switching to a different tab. This technique minimizes mouse movement.

What if I am using a touch screen?
Display the Home tab and then tap the Center button (Home tab | Paragraph group) to center the table.

To Insert a Row in a Table

The next step is to insert a row at the top of the table. ***Why?*** *You want to place a title on the table.* As discussed earlier, you can insert a row at the end of a table by positioning the insertion point in the bottom-right corner cell and then pressing the TAB key. You cannot use the TAB key to insert a row at the beginning or middle of a table. Instead, you use the 'Insert Rows Above' or 'Insert Rows Below' command (Table Tools Layout tab | Rows & Columns group) or the Insert Control (shown in Figure 3–70). The following steps insert a row at the top of a table.

- Position the insertion point somewhere in the first row of the table because you want to insert a row above this row (Figure 3–66).

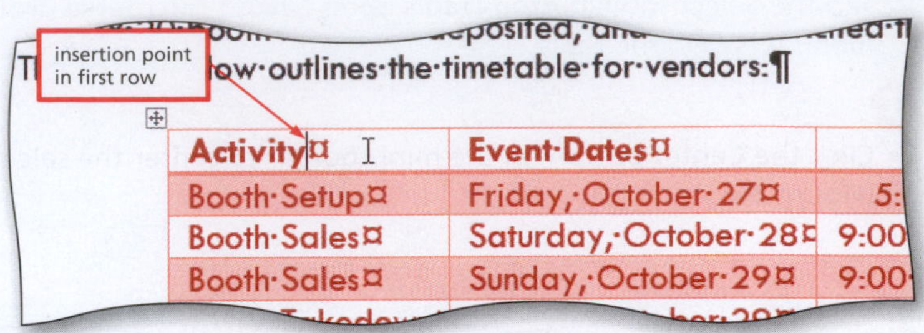

Figure 3–66

2

- Click the 'Insert Rows Above' button (Table Tools Layout tab | Rows & Columns group) to insert a row above the row containing the insertion point and then select the newly inserted row (Figure 3–67).

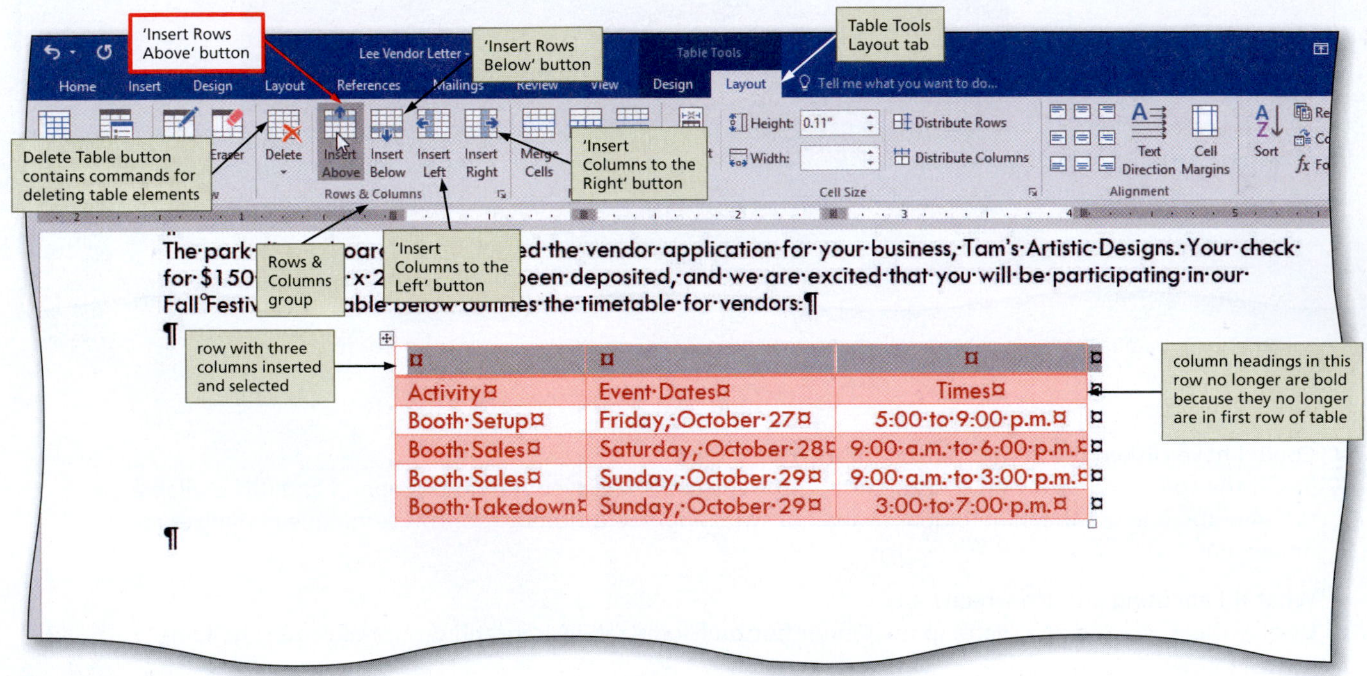

Figure 3–67

Q&A

Do I have to insert rows above the row containing the insertion point?
No. You can insert below the row containing the insertion point by clicking the 'Insert Rows Below' button (Table Tools Layout tab | Rows & Columns group).

Why did the colors in the second row change?
The table style specifies to format the header row differently, which is the first row.

Other Ways

1. Point to the left of the table and click the desired Insert Control
2. Right-click row, point to Insert on shortcut menu (or, if using touch, tap Insert Table button on mini toolbar), click desired option on Insert submenu

To Insert a Column in a Table

If you wanted to insert a column in a table, instead of inserting rows, you would perform the following steps.

1. Point above the table and then click the desired Insert Control.

or

1. Position the insertion point in the column to the left or right of where you want to insert the column.
2. Click the 'Insert Columns to the Left' button (Table Tools Layout tab | Rows & Columns group) to insert a column to the left of the current column, or click the 'Insert Columns to the Right' button (Table Tools Layout tab | Rows & Columns group) to insert a column to the right of the current column.

or

1. Right-click the table, point to Insert on the shortcut menu (or, if using touch, tap Insert Table button on the mini toolbar), and then click 'Insert Columns to the Left' or 'Insert Columns to the Right' on the Insert submenu (or, if using touch, tap Insert Left or Insert Right).

BTW

Resizing Table Columns and Rows

To change the width of a column or height of a row to an exact measurement, hold down the ALT key while dragging markers on the ruler. Or, enter values in the 'Table Column Width' or 'Table Row Height' boxes (Table Tools Layout tab | Cell Size group).

To Merge Cells

1 CREATE & FORMAT LETTERHEAD WITH GRAPHICS | 2 SPECIFY LETTER FORMATS
3 INSERT TABLE | 4 FORMAT TABLE | 5 INSERT BULLETED LIST | 6 ADDRESS ENVELOPE

The row just inserted has one cell for each column, in this case, three cells (shown in Figure 3–67). The top row of the table, however, is to be a single cell that spans all rows. ***Why?*** *The top row contains the table title, which should be centered above the columns of the table.* Thus, the following steps merge the three cells into a single cell.

- With the cells to merge selected (as shown in Figure 3–67), click the Merge Cells button (Table Tools Layout tab | Merge group) to merge the selected cells into a single cell (Figure 3–68).

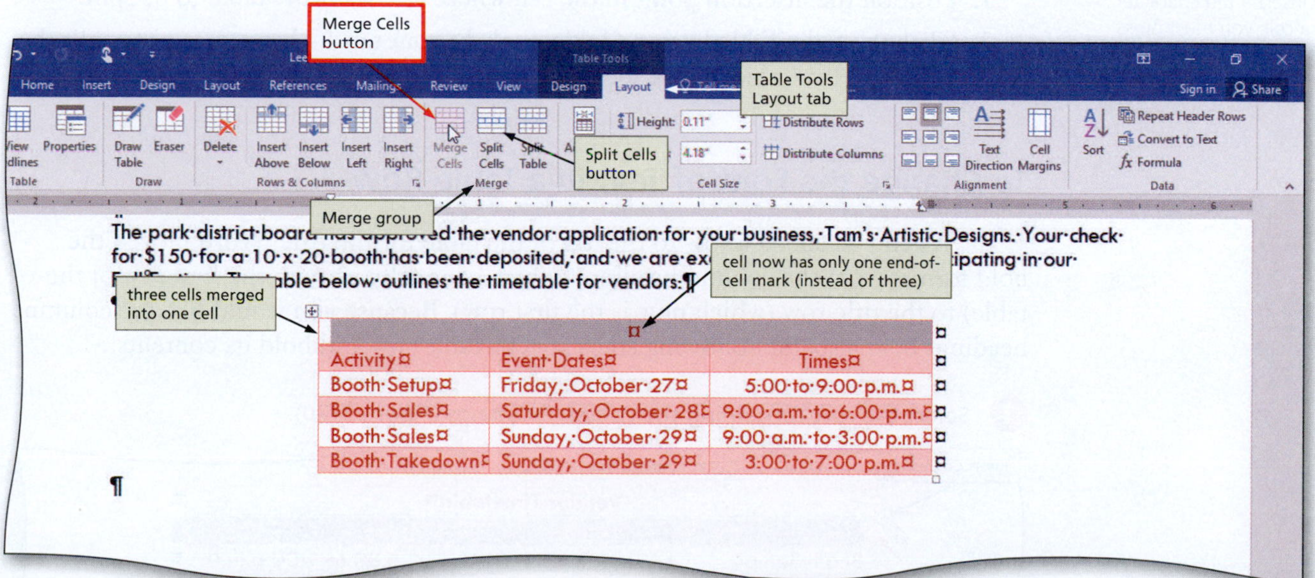

Figure 3–68

- Position the insertion point in the first row and then type **Vendor Timetable** as the table title (Figure 3–69).

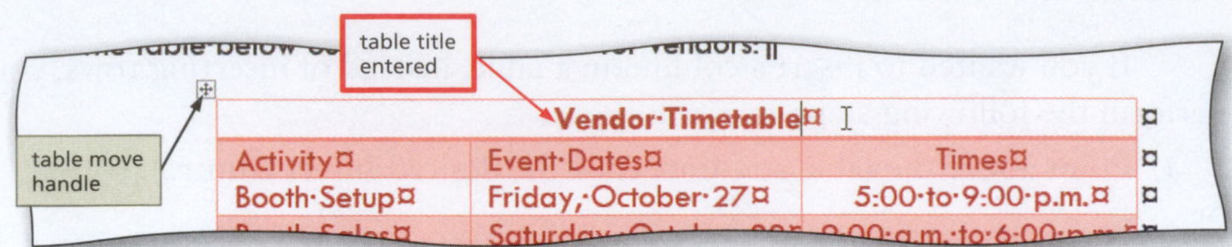

Figure 3–69

Other Ways

1. Right-click selected cells (or, if using touch, tap 'Show Context Menu' button on mini toolbar), click Merge Cells on shortcut menu

BTW

Moving Tables

If you wanted to move a table to a new location, you would point to the upper-left corner of the table until the table move handle appears (shown in Figure 3–69), point to the table move handle, and then drag it to move the entire table to a new location.

To Split Table Cells

Instead of merging multiple cells into a single cell, sometimes you want to split a single cell into multiple cells. If you wanted to split cells, you would perform the following steps.

1. Position the insertion point in the cell to split.
2. Click the Split Cells button (Table Tools Layout tab | Merge group) (or, if using touch, tap 'Show Context Menu' button on mini toolbar), or right-click the cell and then click Split Cells on the shortcut menu, to display the Split Cells dialog box.
3. Enter the number of columns and rows into which you want the cell split (Split Cells dialog box).
4. Click the OK button.

BTW

Tab Character in Tables

In a table, the TAB key advances the insertion point from one cell to the next. To insert a tab character in a cell, you must press CTRL+TAB.

To Split a Table

Instead of splitting table cells into multiple cells, sometimes you want to split a single table into multiple cells. If you wanted to split a table, you would perform the following steps.

1. Position the insertion point in the cell where you want the table to be split.
2. Click the Split Table button (Table Tools Layout tab | Merge group) to split the table into two tables at the location of the insertion point.

To Change the Font of Text in a Table Row

When you added a row to the top of the table for the title, Word moved the bold format from the column headings (which originally were in the first row of the table) to the title row (which now is the first row). Because you would like the columns headings bold also, the following steps select a table row and bold its contents.

1. Select the row containing the column headings (Figure 3–70).

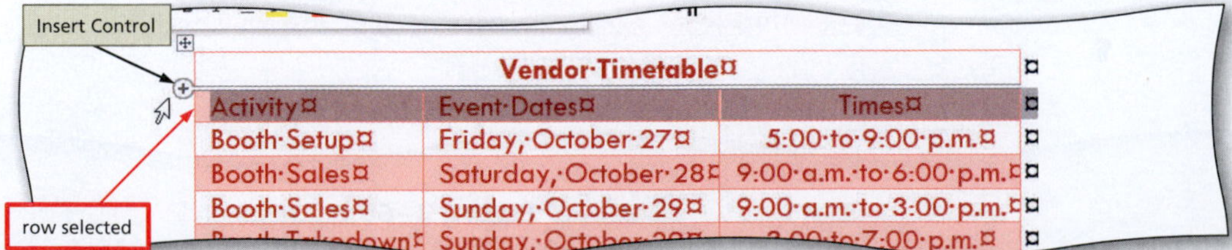

Figure 3–70

2 With the text selected, click the Bold button (Home tab | Font group) to bold the selected text.

Q&A What is the symbol that appeared to the left of the table?
When you select a row or column in a table, Word displays an Insert Control. You can click the **Insert Control** to add a row or column to the table at that location.

Deleting Table Data

If you want to delete row(s) or delete column(s) from a table, position the insertion point in the row(s) or column(s) to delete, click the Delete Table button (Table Tools Layout tab | Rows & Columns group), and then click Delete Rows or Delete Columns on the Delete Table menu. Or, select the row or column to delete, right-click the selection, and then click Delete Rows or Delete Columns on the mini toolbar or shortcut menu.

To delete the contents of a cell, select the cell contents and then press the DELETE or BACKSPACE key. You also can drag and drop or cut and paste the contents of cells. To delete an entire table, select the table, click the Delete Table button (Table Tools Layout tab | Rows & Columns group), and then click Delete Table on the Delete Table menu. To delete the contents of a table and leave an empty table, you would select the table and then press the DELETE key.

BTW
AutoFormat Options
Before you can use them, AutoFormat options must be enabled. To check if an AutoFormat option is enabled, click File on the ribbon to open the Backstage view, click the Options tab in the Backstage view, click Proofing in the left pane (Word Options dialog box), click the AutoCorrect Options button, click the AutoFormat As You Type tab, select the appropriate check boxes, and then click the OK button in each open dialog box.

To Add More Text

The table now is complete. The next step is to enter text below the table. The following steps enter text.

1 Position the insertion point on the paragraph mark below the table and then press the ENTER key.

2 Type `Please note the following vendor guidelines:` and then press the ENTER key (shown in Figure 3–71).

To Bullet a List as You Type

1 CREATE & FORMAT LETTERHEAD WITH GRAPHICS | 2 SPECIFY LETTER FORMATS
3 INSERT TABLE | 4 FORMAT TABLE | **5 INSERT BULLETED LIST** | 6 ADDRESS ENVELOPE

In Module 1, you learned how to apply bullets to existing paragraphs. If you know before you type that a list should be bulleted, you can use Word's AutoFormat As You Type feature to bullet the paragraphs as you type them (see Table 3–2 shown earlier in this module). ***Why?*** *The AutoFormat As You Type feature saves you time because it applies formats automatically.* The following steps add bullets to a list as you type.

1
- Press the ASTERISK key (*) as the first character on the line (Figure 3–71).

2
- Press the SPACEBAR to convert the asterisk to a bullet character.

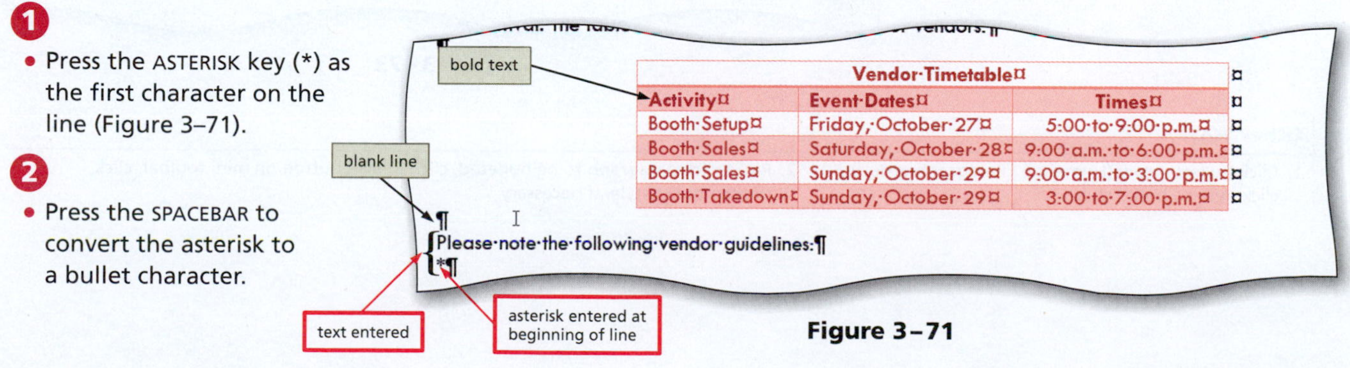

Figure 3–71

Q&A What if I did not want the asterisk converted to a bullet character?
You could undo the AutoFormat by clicking the Undo button; pressing CTRL+Z; clicking the AutoCorrect Options button that appears to the left of the bullet character as soon as you press the SPACEBAR and then clicking Undo Automatic Bullets on the AutoCorrect Options menu; or clicking the Bullets button (Home tab | Paragraph group).

3

- Type **`Vendors must bring their own tables and chairs.`** as the first bulleted item.
- Press the ENTER key to place another bullet character at the beginning of the next line (Figure 3–72).

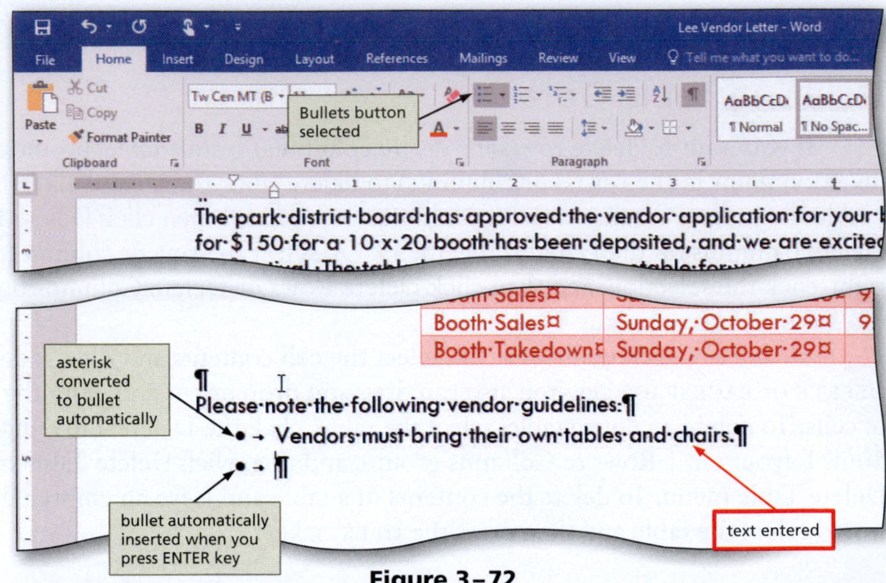

Figure 3–72

4

- Type **`Vendors must supply their own electrical cords.`** and then press the ENTER key.
- Type **`Vendors shall comply with fire, safety, and health regulations.`** and then press the ENTER key.
- Press the ENTER key to turn off automatic bullets as you type (Figure 3–73).

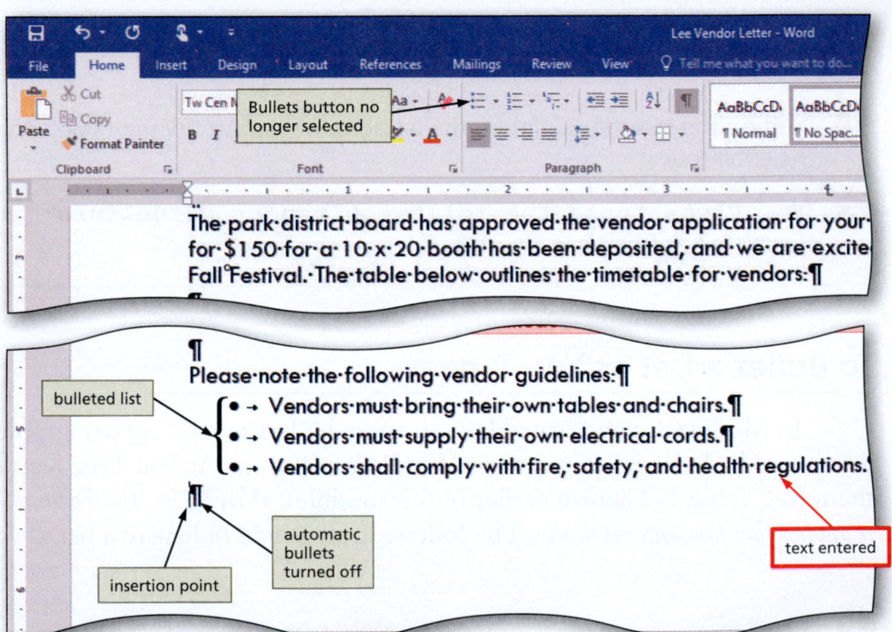

Figure 3–73

Q&A Why did automatic bullets stop?
When you press the ENTER key without entering any text after the automatic bullet character, Word turns off the automatic bullets feature.

Other Ways

1. Click Bullets arrow (Home tab | Paragraph group), click desired bullet style
2. Right-click paragraph to be bulleted, click Bullets button on mini toolbar, click desired bullet style, if necessary

To Enter More Text and then Save and Print the Letter

The following steps enter the remainder of text in the letter.

1. With the insertion point positioned on the paragraph below the bulleted list, press the ENTER key and then type the paragraph shown in Figure 3–74, making certain you use the building block name, tad, to insert the organization name.

2. Press the ENTER key twice. Press the TAB key to position the insertion point at the tab stop set at the 4" mark on the ruler. Type `Sincerely,` and then press the ENTER key four times.

3. Press the TAB key to position the insertion point at the tab stop set at the 4" mark on the ruler. Type `Camden Ackerman` and then press the ENTER key.

   If requested by your instructor, enter your name instead of the name stated above.

4. Press the TAB key to position the insertion point at the tab stop set at the 4" mark on the ruler. Type `Park District Events Coordinator` to finish the letter. Scroll up, if necessary (Figure 3–74).

5. Save the letter again on the same storage location with the same file name.

6. If requested by your instructor, print the letter.

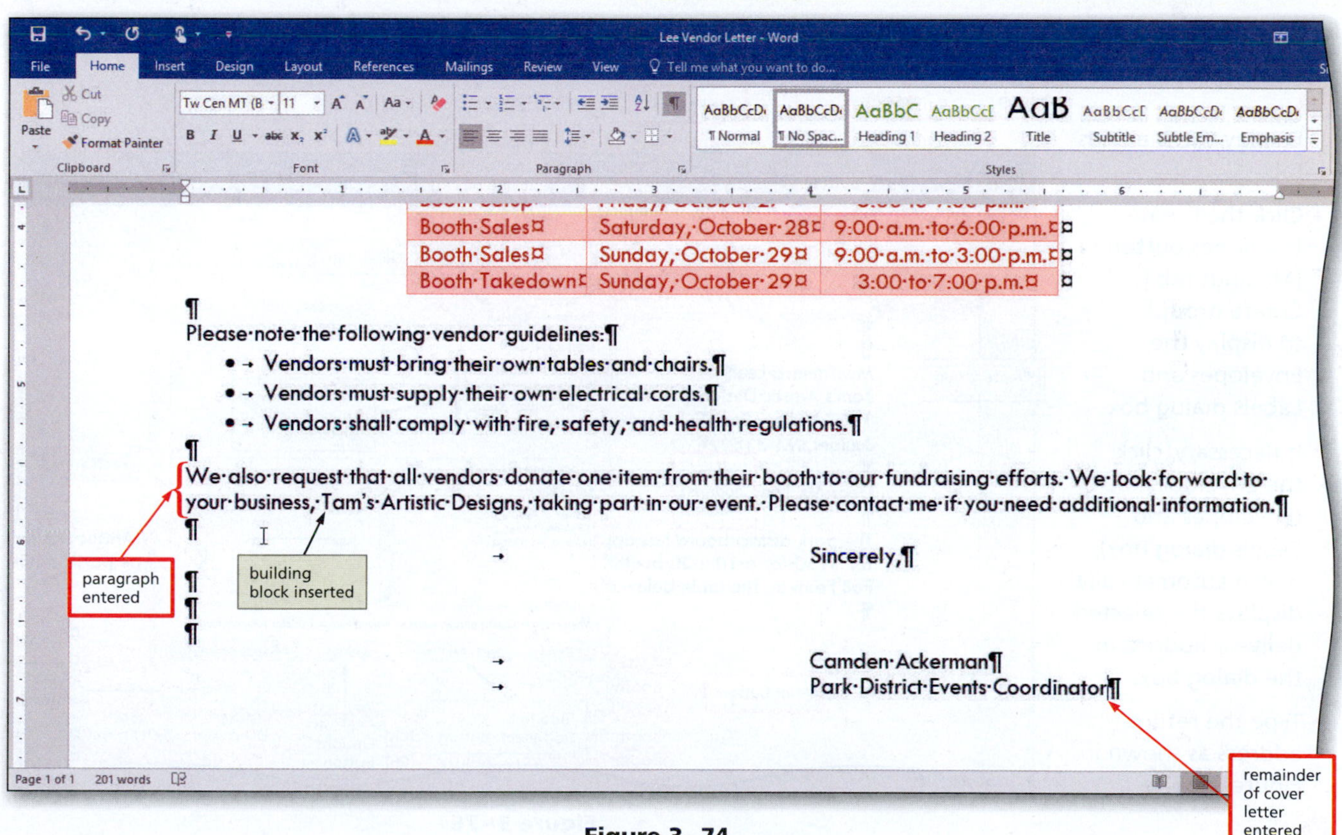

Figure 3–74

BTW

Conserving Ink and Toner

If you want to conserve ink or toner, you can instruct Word to print draft quality documents by clicking File on the ribbon to open the Backstage view, clicking the Options tab in the Backstage view to display the Word Options dialog box, clicking Advanced in the left pane (Word Options dialog box), scrolling to the Print area in the right pane, placing a check mark in the 'Use draft quality' check box, and then clicking the OK button. Then, use the Backstage view to print the document as usual.

Addressing and Printing Envelopes and Mailing Labels

With Word, you can print mailing address information on an envelope or on a mailing label. Computer-printed addresses look more professional than handwritten ones.

To Address and Print an Envelope

1 CREATE & FORMAT LETTERHEAD WITH GRAPHICS | 2 SPECIFY LETTER FORMATS
3 INSERT TABLE | 4 FORMAT TABLE | 5 INSERT BULLETED LIST | 6 ADDRESS ENVELOPE

The following steps address and print an envelope. If you are in a lab environment, check with your instructor before performing these steps. ***Why?** Some printers may not accommodate printing envelopes; others may stop printing until an envelope is inserted.*

1

- Scroll through the letter to display the inside address in the document window.
- Drag through the inside address to select it (Figure 3–75).

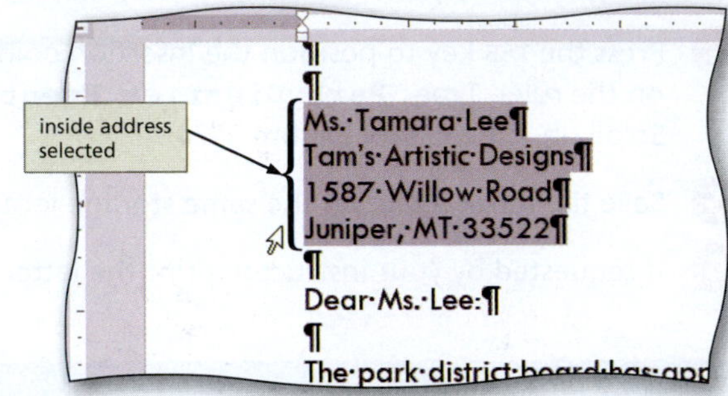

Figure 3–75

2

- Display the Mailings tab.
- Click the Create Envelopes button (Mailings tab | Create group) to display the Envelopes and Labels dialog box.
- If necessary, click the Envelopes tab (Envelopes and Labels dialog box), which automatically displays the selected delivery address in the dialog box.
- Type the return address as shown in Figure 3–76.

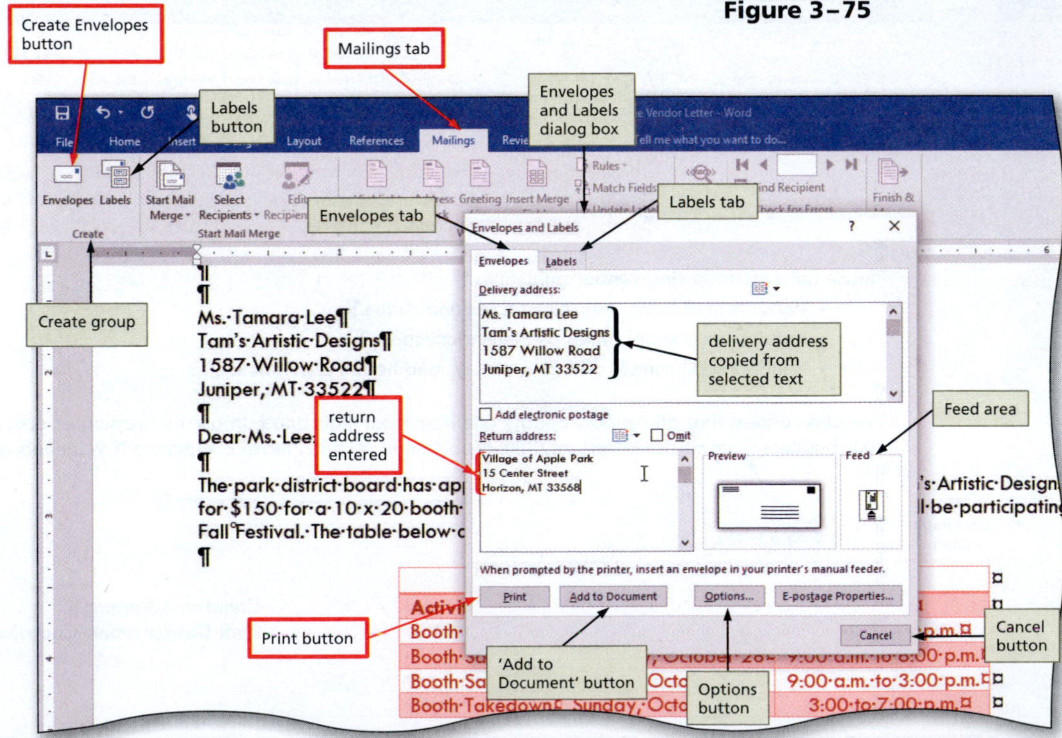

Figure 3–76

3

- Insert an envelope in your printer, as shown in the Feed area of the dialog box (your Feed area may be different depending on your printer).
- If your printer can print envelopes, click the Print button (Envelopes and Labels dialog box) to print the envelope; otherwise, click the Cancel button to close the dialog box.
- Because the project now is complete, you can exit Word.

Envelopes and Labels

Instead of printing the envelope immediately, you can add it to the document by clicking the 'Add to Document' button (Envelopes and Labels dialog box) (shown in Figure 3–76). To specify a different envelope or label type (identified by a number on the box of envelopes or labels), click the Options button (Envelopes and Labels dialog box) (shown in Figure 3–76).

Instead of printing an envelope, you can print a mailing label. To do this, click the Labels button (Mailings tab | Create group) (shown in Figure 3–76) and then type the delivery address in the Delivery address box. To print the same address on all labels on the page, select the 'Full page of the same label' option button in the Print area. Click the Print button (Envelopes and Labels dialog box) to print the label(s).

BTW

Distributing a Document

Instead of printing and distributing a hard copy of a document, you can distribute the document electronically. Options include sending the document via email; posting it on cloud storage (such as OneDrive) and sharing the file with others; posting it on social media, a blog, or other website; and sharing a link associated with an online location of the document. You also can create and share a PDF or XPS image of the document, so that users can view the file in Acrobat Reader or XPS Viewer instead of in Word.

Summary

In this module, you have learned how to use Word to change margins, insert and format a shape, change text wrapping, insert and format a picture, move and copy graphics, insert symbols, add a border, clear formatting, convert a hyperlink to regular text, set and use tab stops, insert the current date, create and insert building blocks, insert and format tables, and address and print envelopes and mailing labels.

CONSIDER THIS: PLAN AHEAD

What decisions will you need to make when creating your next business letter?

Use these guidelines as you complete the assignments in this module and create your own business letters outside of this class.

1. Create a letterhead.
   a) Ensure that the letterhead contains a complete legal name, mailing address, phone number, and if applicable, fax number, email address, web address, logo, or other image.
   b) Place elements in the letterhead in a visually appealing location.
   c) Format the letterhead with appropriate fonts, font sizes, font styles, and color.
2. Compose an effective business letter.
   a) Include a date line, inside address, message, and signature block.
   b) Use proper spacing and formats for letter contents.
   c) Follow the alignment and spacing guidelines based on the letter style used (i.e., block, modified block, or modified semi-block).
   d) Ensure the message is well written, properly formatted, and logically organized.

BTW

Saving a Template

As an alternative to saving the letterhead as a Word document, you could save it as a template. To do so, click File on the ribbon to open the Backstage view, click the Export tab to display the Export gallery, click 'Change File Type', click Template in the right pane, click the Save As button, enter the template file name (Save As dialog box), if necessary select the Templates folder, and then click the Save button in the dialog box. To use the template, tap or click File on the ribbon to open the Backstage view, click the New tab to display the New gallery, click the PERSONAL tab in the New gallery, and then click the template icon or file name.

Apply Your Knowledge

Reinforce the skills and apply the concepts you learned in this module.

Working with Tabs and a Table

Note: To complete this assignment, you will be required to use the Data Files. Please contact your instructor for information about accessing the Data Files.

Instructions: Run Word. Open the document called Apply 3–1 Fall Semester Schedule Draft located on the Data Files. The document is a Word table that you are to edit and format. The revised table is shown in Figure 3–77.

Fall Semester Schedule

Class/Activity	Monday	Tuesday	Wednesday	Thursday	Friday	Saturday
ENG 101	9:30-11:00 a.m.		9:30-11:00 a.m.			
COM 110		12:30-2:00 p.m.		12:30-2:00 p.m.		
MAT 120	1:00-2:00 p.m.		1:00-2:00 p.m.		1:00-2:00 p.m.	
CHM 102	3:30-5:00 p.m.		3:30-5:00 p.m.		3:00-5:00 p.m.	
MUS 152		9:30-11:00 a.m.		9:30-11:00 a.m.		
Yoga	6:00-7:00 p.m.			3:00-4:00 p.m.		8:00-9:00 a.m.
Work		4:00-8:00 p.m.			8:00-11:00 a.m.	1:00-4:00 p.m.

Figure 3–77

Perform the following tasks:

1. Change the document theme to Organic.
2. In the line containing the table title, Fall Semester Schedule, remove the tab stop at the 1" mark on the ruler.
3. Set a centered tab at the 3" mark on the ruler. Move the centered tab stop to the 3.5" mark on the ruler.
4. Bold the characters in the title. Use the 'Increase Font Size' button to increase their font size to 14. Change their color to Red, Accent 4, Darker 25%.
5. In the table, delete the row containing the HIS 107 class.
6. In the table, delete the Sunday column.

7. Insert a column between the Monday and Wednesday columns. Fill in the column as follows:

   Column Title – Tuesday

   COM 110 – 12:30-2:00 p.m.

   MUS 152 – 9:30-11:00 a.m.

   If the column heading, Tuesday, is not bold, apply the bold format to the text in this cell.
8. Insert a new row at the bottom of the table. In the first cell of the new row, enter the word, Work, in the cell. If this cell's contents are bold, remove the bold format. Fill in the cells in the remainder of the row as follows:

   Tuesday – 4:00-8:00 p.m.

   Friday – 8:00-11:00 a.m.

   Saturday – 1:00-4:00 p.m.
9. In the Table Style Options group (Table Tools Design tab), ensure that these check boxes have check marks: Header Row, Banded Rows, and First Column. The Total Row, Last Column, and Banded Columns check boxes should not have check marks.
10. Apply the Grid Table 5 Dark - Accent 4 style to the table.
11. Select the entire table. Click the 'Decrease Font Size' button once to decrease the font size of all characters in the table to 10 point.
12. Make all columns as wide as their contents (AutoFit Contents). Note that you may need to perform this step a couple of times to achieve the desired results.
13. Align center left all cells in the first column.
14. Align center the column headings containing the weekday names.
15. Align center right all cells containing times.
16. Center the table between the left and right margins of the page.
17. If requested by your instructor, enter your name on the line below the table.
18. Save the document using the file name, Apply 3–1 Fall Semester Schedule Modified, and submit the document (shown in Figure 3–77) in the format specified by your instructor.
19. If you wanted to add a row to the middle of the table, how would you add the row?

Extend Your Knowledge

Extend the skills you learned in this module and experiment with new skills. You may need to use Help to complete the assignment.

Working with Formulas, Graphics, Sorting, Picture Bullets, and Mailing Labels

Note: To complete this assignment, you will be required to use the Data Files. Please contact your instructor for information about accessing the Data Files.

Instructions: Run Word. Open the document called Extend 3–1 Donation Letter Draft located on the Data Files. You will use the Format Picture task pane, group objects, enter formulas in the table, change the table style, sort paragraphs, use picture bullets, move tabs, and print mailing labels.

Perform the following tasks:

1. Use Help to learn about grouping objects, entering formulas, sorting, picture bullets, and printing mailing labels.

Continued >

Extend Your Knowledge *continued*

2. Select the graphic of the globe in the hand, click the Format Shape Dialog Box Launcher (Picture Tools Format tab | Picture Styles group) to display the Format Picture task pane, and then click the Picture button in the task pane (Figure 3–78). Experiment with all the buttons in the task pane and modify the look of the graphic to your preferences.

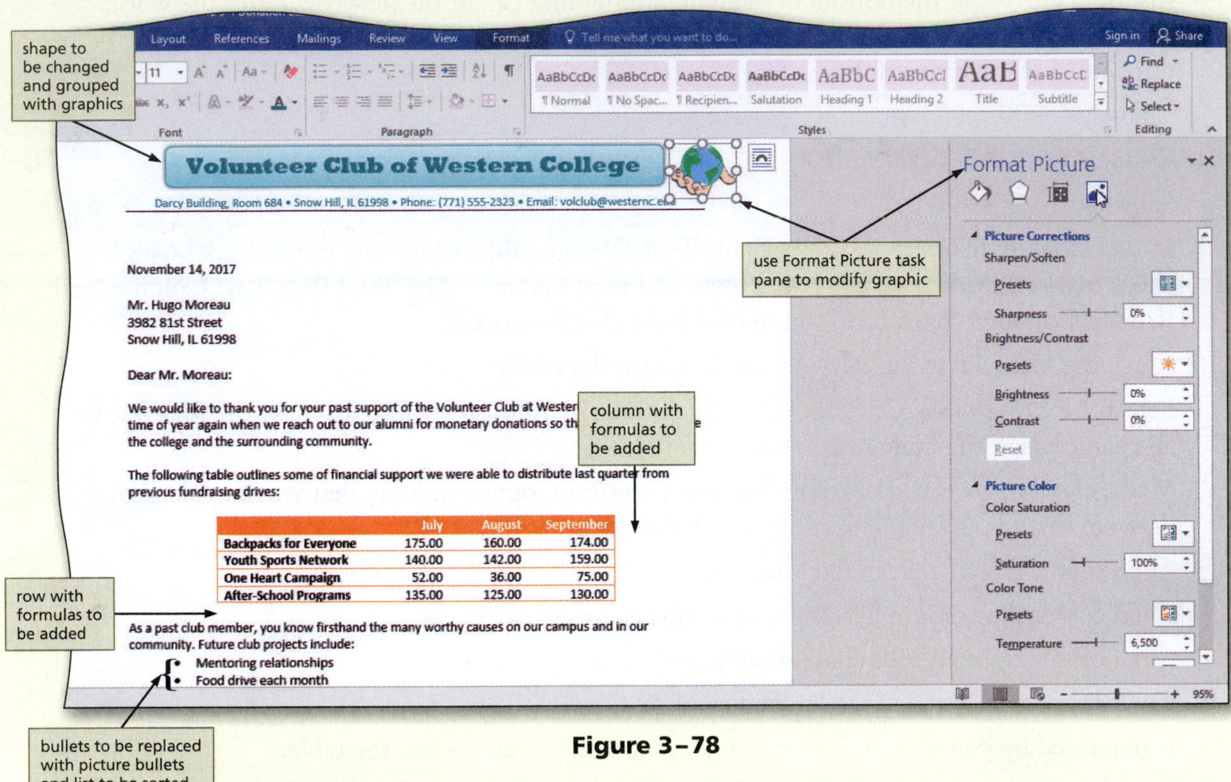

Figure 3–78

3. Select the shape around the Volunteer Club of Western College title and then use the Edit Shape button (Drawing Tools Format tab | Insert Shapes group) to change the shape to your preference. Position the globe in the hand graphic in the desired location to the right of the shape.
4. Copy and paste the modified globe in the hand graphic, flip it horizontally, and then position it on the opposite site of the shape. Group the two globe in hand graphics with the shape at the top of the letterhead. Change the text wrapping of the grouped shape to Top and Bottom.
5. Add a row to the bottom of the table. Insert the word, Total, in the first column of the new row. In the cell to contain the total for September, use the Formula dialog box to insert a formula that adds the cells in the column so that the total amount is displayed; in the dialog box, select a number format so that the total displays with dollar signs. *Hint:* Click the Formula button (Table Tools Format tab | Data group). Repeat this process for the August and July totals. Which formula did you use? Which number format?
6. Add a column to the right of the table. Insert the word, Total, as the column heading for the new column. Use the Formula dialog box to insert a formula that adds the cells each row so that the total amount is displayed. Use the same number format as you used in the previous step. Which formula did you use? What is the grand total for the quarter?

7. Position the insertion point in the table and one at a time, select and deselect each check box in the Table Style Options group. What are the functions of each check box: Header Row, Total Row, Banded Rows, First Column, Last Column, and Banded Columns? Select the check boxes you prefer for the table.
8. Sort the paragraphs in the bulleted list.
9. Change the bullets in the bulleted list to picture bullets.
10. Set a tab stop for the date line at the 4" mark on the ruler. Move the tab stops in the complimentary close and signature block from the 3.5" mark to the 4" mark on the ruler.
11. If requested by your instructor, change the name in the signature block to your name.
12. Save the revised document using the file name, Extend 3-1 Donation Letter Modified, and then submit it in the format specified by your instructor.
13. If requested by your instructor, print a single mailing label for the letter and then a full page of mailing labels, each containing the address shown in Figure 3–78.
14. Answer the questions posed in #5, #6, and #7. Why would you group objects? Which picture bullet did you use and why?

Expand Your World

Create a solution that uses cloud or web technologies by learning and investigating on your own from general guidance.

Using Google Docs to Upload and Edit Files

Notes:

- To complete this assignment, you will be required to use the Data Files. Please contact your instructor for information about accessing the Data Files.
- To complete this assignment, you will use a Google account, which you can create at no cost. If you do not have a Google account and do not want to create one, read this assignment without performing the instructions.

Instructions: You have created a letter in Word at your office and want to proofread and edit it at home. The problem is that you do not have Word at home. You do, however, have an Internet connection at home. Because you have a Google account, you upload your Word document to Google Drive so that you can view and edit it later from a computer that does not have Word installed.

Perform the following tasks:

1. In Word, open the document, Expand 3-1 Inquiry Letter in Word, from the Data Files. Look through the letter so that you are familiar with its contents and formats. If desired, print the letter so that you easily can compare it to the Google Docs converted file. Close the document.
2. Run a browser. Search for the text, google docs, using a search engine. Visit several websites to learn about Google Docs and Google Drive. Navigate to the Google website. Read about how to create files in Google Docs and upload files to Google Drive. If you do not have a Google account and you want to create one, follow the instructions to create an account. If you do not have a Google account and you do not want to create one, read the remaining instructions without performing them. If you have a Google account, sign in to your account.
3. If necessary, display Google Drive. Upload the file, Expand 3-1 Inquiry Letter in Word, to Google Drive.

Continued >

Expand Your World *continued*

4. Rename the file on Google Drive to Expand 3–1 Inquiry Letter in Google. Open the file in Google Docs (Figure 3–79). What differences do you see between the Word document and the Google Docs converted document?

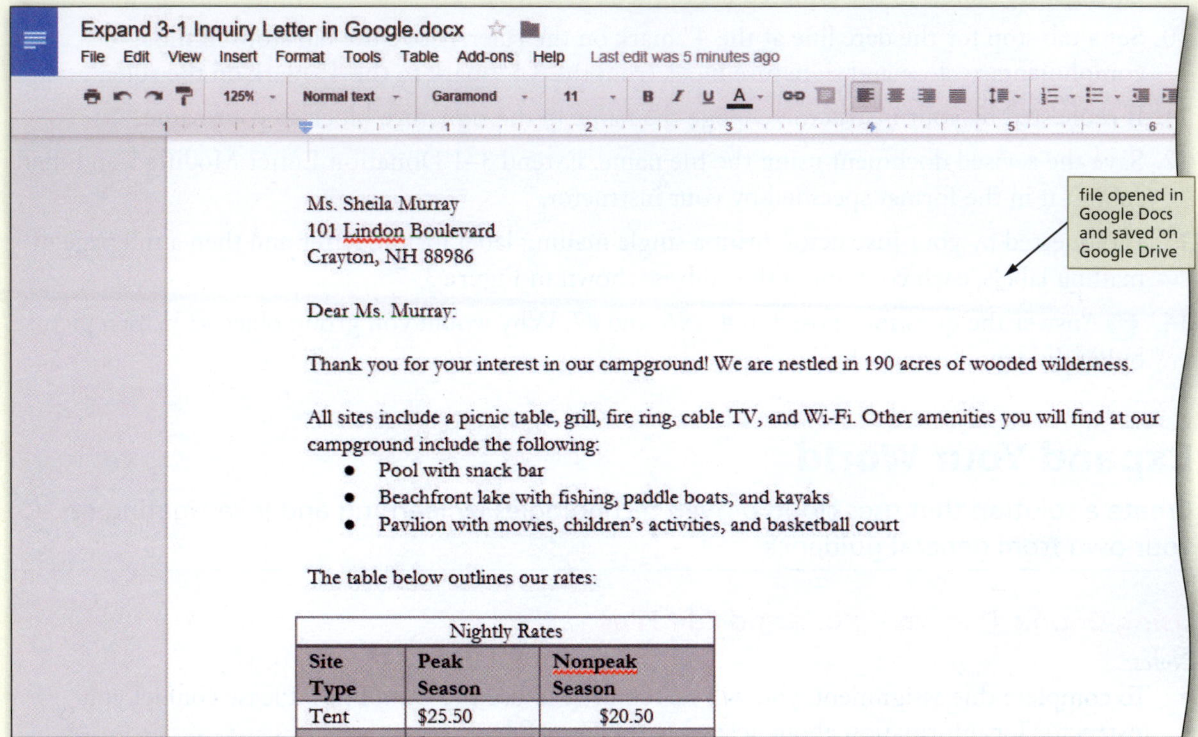

Figure 3–79

5. Fix the document in Google Docs so that it looks appealing, based on the concepts and techniques learned in this module. Add another item to the bulleted list: Fully-stocked camp store with attached laundry facilities. Add a row to the table: Pavilion, $20.00, $40.00. Insert a horizontal line below the line containing the mailing address.
6. If requested by your instructor, change the name in the signature block to your name.
7. Download the revised document to your local storage media, changing its format to Microsoft Word. Submit the document in the format requested by your instructor.
8. What is Google Drive? What is Google Docs? Answer the question posed in #4. Do you prefer using Google Docs or Word? Why?

In the Labs

Design, create, modify, and/or use a document following the guidelines, concepts, and skills presented in this module. Labs 1 and 2, which increase in difficulty, require you to create solutions based on what you learned in the module; Lab 3 requires you to apply your creative thinking and problem-solving skills to design and implement a solution.

Lab 1: Creating a Letter with a Letterhead

Problem: As a junior at your school, you are seeking a summer internship. One letter you prepare is shown in Figure 3–80.

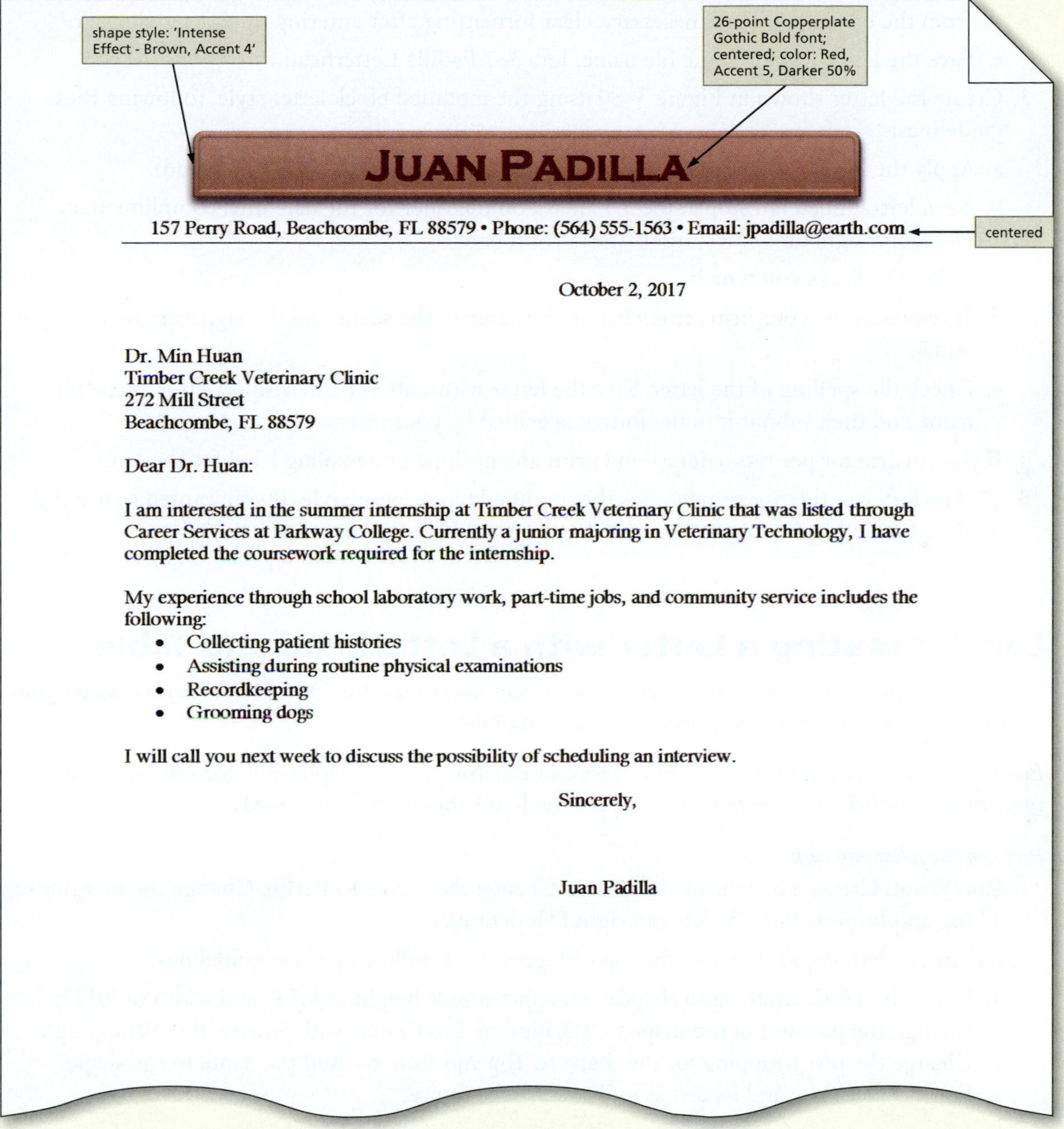

Figure 3–80

Perform the following tasks:

1. Run Word. Create a new blank document. Change the theme to Slate.
2. Create the letterhead shown at the top of Figure 3–80, following these guidelines:
   a. Insert the Rounded Same Side Corner Rectangle shape at an approximate height of 0.53" and width of 5.4". Change position of the shape to 'Position in Top Center with Square Text

Continued >

Wrapping'. Change the text wrapping for the shape to Top and Bottom. Add the student name, Juan Padilla, to the shape. Format the shape and its text as indicated in the figure.

b. Insert the dot symbols as shown in the contact information. Remove the hyperlink format from the email address. If necessary, clear formatting after entering the bottom border.

c. Save the letterhead with the file name, Lab 3–1 Padilla Letterhead.

3. Create the letter shown in Figure 3–80 using the modified block letter style, following these guidelines:

   a. Apply the No Spacing Quick Style to the document text (below the letterhead).

   b. Set a left-aligned tab stop at the 3.5" mark on the ruler for the date line, complimentary close, and signature block. Insert the current date.

   c. Bullet the list as you type it.

   d. If requested by your instructor, change the name in the shape and the signature block to your name.

   e. Check the spelling of the letter. Save the letter with Lab 3–1 Internship Letter as the file name and then submit it in the format specified by your instructor.

4. If your instructor permits, address and print an envelope or a mailing label for the letter.

5. The letter in this assignment uses the modified block letter style. If you wanted to use the modified semi-block letter style, what changes would you make to this letter?

Lab 2: Creating a Letter with a Letterhead and Table

Note: To complete this assignment, you may be required to use the Data Files. Please contact your instructor for information about accessing the Data Files.

Problem: As the community education class coordinator, you are responsible for sending class registration confirmation letters. You prepare the letter shown in Figure 3–81.

Perform the following tasks:

1. Run Word. Create a new blank document. Change the theme to Berlin. Change the margins to 1" top and bottom and .75" left and right (Moderate).

2. Create the letterhead shown at the top of Figure 3–81, following these guidelines:

   a. Insert the Horizontal Scroll shape at an approximate height of 0.74" and width of 6.32". Change the position of the shape to 'Position in Top Center with Square Text Wrapping'. Change the text wrapping for the shape to Top and Bottom. Add the name to the shape. Format the shape and its text as indicated in the figure.

   b. Insert a picture of a rose, similar to the one shown in the figure (the exact figure, if required, is located in the Data Files). Resize the picture, change its text wrapping to In Front of Text, and move it to the left on the shape. Change its color tone to Temperature: 4700K. Copy the picture and move the copy of the image to the right on the shape, as shown in the figure. Flip the copied image horizontally.

   c. Insert the small open diamond symbols as shown in the contact information. Remove the hyperlink format from the email address. If necessary, clear formatting after entering the bottom border.

   d. Save the letterhead with the file name, Lab 3–2 Rosewood Letterhead.

3. Create the letter shown in Figure 3–81, following these guidelines:
   a. Apply the No Spacing Quick Style to the document text (below the letterhead).
   b. Set a left-aligned tab stop at the 4" mark on the ruler for the date line, complimentary close, and signature block. Insert the current date.

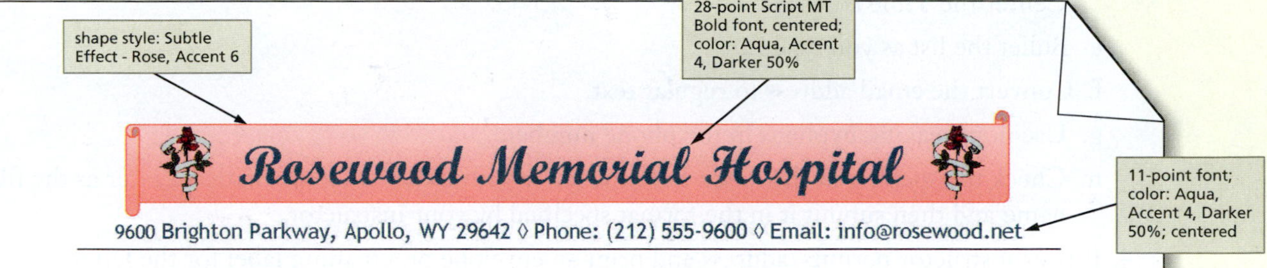

October 16, 2017

Ms. Natalia Zajak
88 Sycamore Street
Apollo, WY 29642

Dear Ms. Zajak:

Thank you for your interest in our community education classes. We look forward to seeing you! The table below confirms the classes in which you are registered during November:

November Class Registration Confirmation			
Class	**Date**	**Time**	**Location**
Diabetes Risk Assessment	November 6	5:00 to 6:00 p.m.	Suite 101
First Aid and CPR	November 11	9:00 a.m. to 3:00 p.m.	Suite 220
Healthy Cooking	November 14	4:00 to 5:00 p.m.	Suite 203
Basics of Meditation	November 17	11:00 a.m. to 12:30 p.m.	Suite 124

table style: Grid Table 5 Dark - Accent 4; table style options: Header Row and Banded Rows

bold text

Please note the following:

- Arrive 10 minutes early for all classes.
- No outside food or drink allowed in classrooms.
- Kindly give 48-hour cancellation notice.

If you have any questions, please contact me via email at jgreen@rosewood.net or phone at 212-555-9612.

Sincerely,

Jerome Green
Community Education Class Coordinator

Figure 3–81

Continued >

In the Labs *continued*

c. If requested by your instructor, change the name in the inside address and salutation to your name.

d. Insert and center the table. Format the table as specified in the figure. Make all columns as wide as their contents (AutoFit Contents). Left-align the Class, Date, and Location columns. Center the Time column.

e. Bullet the list as you type it.

f. Convert the email address to regular text.

g. Use nonbreaking hyphens in the phone number.

h. Check the spelling of the letter. Save the letter with Lab 3–2 Confirmation Letter as the file name and then submit it in the format specified by your instructor.

4. If your instructor permits, address and print an envelope or a mailing label for the letter.

5. What is the purpose of the nonbreaking hyphens in this letter? Why do you think the picture in this letter used a text wrapping of In Front of Text? If the table used banded columns instead of banded rows, how would its appearance change?

Lab 3: Consider This: Your Turn

Create a Letter to a Potential Employer

Note: To complete this assignment, you may be required to use the Data Files. Please contact your instructor for information about accessing the Data Files.

Problem: As an intern in the career development office at your school, your boss has asked you to prepare a sample letter to a potential employer. Students seeking employment will use this letter as a reference document when creating their own letters.

Perform the following tasks:

Part 1: Using your name, mailing address, phone number, and email address, create a letterhead for the letter. Once the letterhead is designed, write the letter to this potential employer: Ms. Latisha Adams, Personnel Director, Cedar Plank Hotels, 85 College Grove Lane, P.O. Box 582, Gartner, TX 74812.

The draft wording for the letter is as follows:

First paragraph:

I am responding to your advertisement in the Texas Post for the Assistant Manager position. I have the credentials you are seeking and believe I can be a valuable asset to Cedar Plank Hotels.

Second paragraph:

In May, I will be earning my bachelor's degree in Hospitality Management from Greenville College. My relevant coursework includes the following:

Below the second paragraph, insert the following table:

Restaurant management	18 hours
Nutrition	15 hours
Tourism management	12 hours
Hotel management	12 hours

Third paragraph:
In addition to my college coursework, I have the following experience:

Below the third paragraph, insert the following items as a bulleted list:
Assistant to school cafeteria director; Volunteer in Hope Mission kitchen; Developed website and Facebook page for local cafe.

Last paragraph:
I look forward to hearing from you to schedule an interview and to discuss my career opportunities at Cedar Plank Hotels.

The letter should contain a letterhead that uses a shape and picture(s); a table with an appropriate table title, column headings, and table style applied (unformatted table shown above); and a bulleted list (to present the experience). Insert nonbreaking spaces in the company name. Create a building block for the company name, edit the building block so that it has a ScreenTip, and insert the building block whenever you have to enter the company name.

Use the concepts and techniques presented in this module to create and format a letter according to a letter style, creating appropriate paragraph breaks and rewording the draft as necessary. The unformatted paragraphs in the letter are in a file called Lab 3–1 Letter Paragraphs, which is located on the Data Files. If you prefer, you can copy and paste this text into your letter instead of typing the paragraphs yourself. Use your name in the signature line in the letter. Be sure to check the spelling and grammar of the finished letter. Submit your assignment in the format specified by your instructor.

Part 2: You made several decisions while creating the letter in this assignment: where to position elements in the letterhead, how to format elements in the letterhead, which graphics to use in the letterhead, which theme to use in the letter, which font size to use for the letter text, which table style to use, and which letter style to use. What was the rationale behind each of these decisions?

1 Creating and Editing a Presentation with Pictures

Objectives

You will have mastered the material in this module when you can:

- Select and change a document theme and variant
- Create a title slide and a text slide with a multilevel bulleted list
- Add new slides and change slide layouts
- Insert pictures into slides with and without content placeholders
- Move and resize pictures
- Change font size and color
- Bold and italicize text
- Duplicate a slide
- Arrange slides
- Select slide transitions
- View a presentation in Slide Show view

Introduction

A PowerPoint **presentation**, also called a **slide show**, can help you deliver a dynamic, professional-looking message to an audience. PowerPoint allows you to produce slides to use in an academic, business, or other environment. The collection of slides in a presentation is called a **deck**, resembling a deck of cards that are stacked on top of each other. A common use of slide decks is to enhance an oral presentation. A speaker might desire to convey information, such as urging students to volunteer at a fund-raising event, explaining changes in employee compensation packages, or describing a new laboratory procedure. The PowerPoint slides should reinforce the speaker's message and help the audience retain the information presented. Custom slides can fit your specific needs and contain diagrams, charts, tables, pictures, shapes, video, sound, and animation effects to make your presentation more effective. An accompanying handout gives audience members reference notes and review material for your presentation.

Project — Presentation with a Bulleted List and Pictures

In this module's project, you will follow proper design guidelines and learn to use PowerPoint to create, save, and view the slides shown in Figures 1–1a through 1–1e. The objective is to produce a presentation, titled Tall Oaks, to promote three programs at the nature center. This slide show has a variety of pictures and visual elements to add interest and give facts about the events. Some of the text has formatting and color enhancements. Transitions help one slide flow gracefully into the next during a slide show.

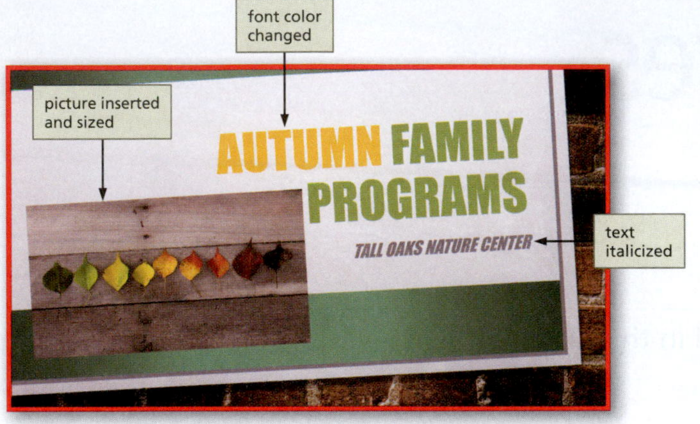

(a) Slide 1 (Title Slide with Picture)

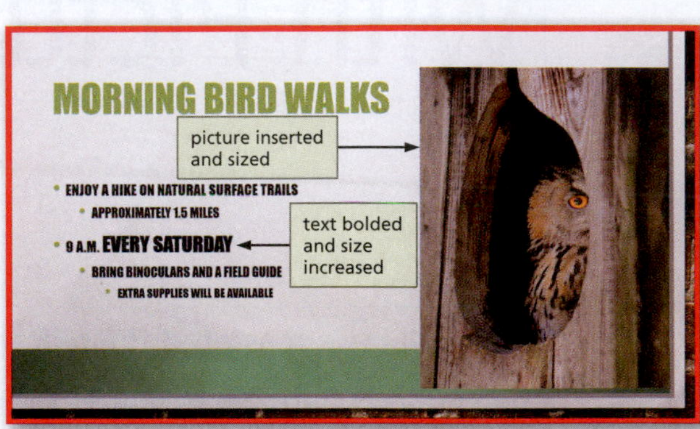

(b) Slide 2 (Multilevel Bulleted List with Picture)

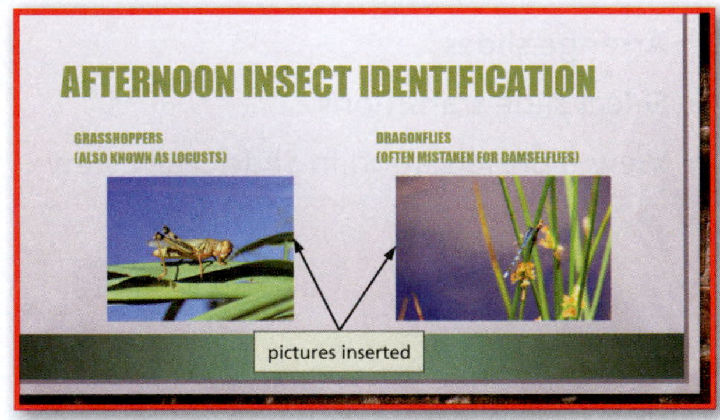

(c) Slide 3 (Comparison Layout and Pictures)

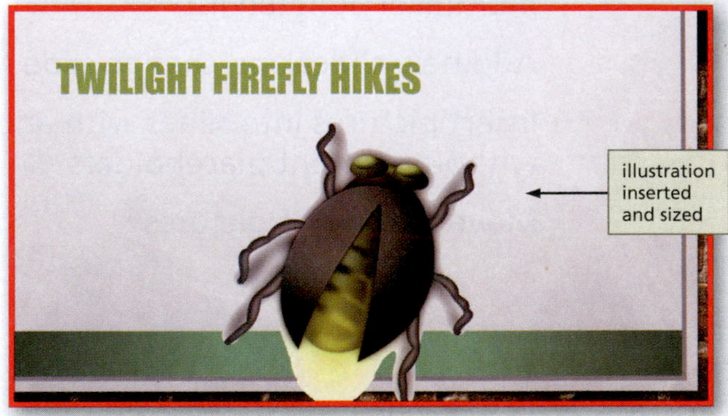

(d) Slide 4 (Title and Illustration)

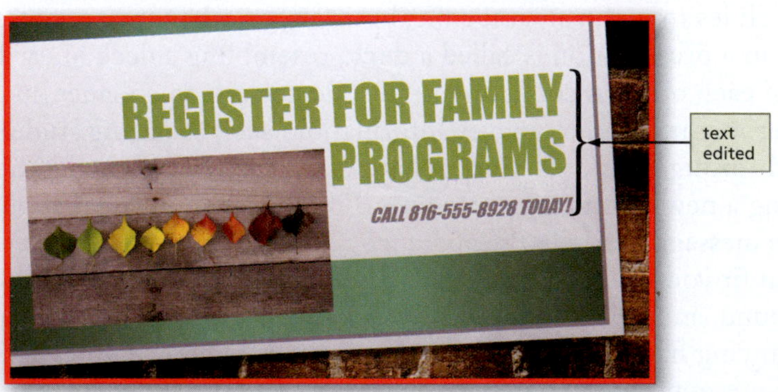

(e) Slide 5 (Closing Slide)

Figure 1–1

In this module, you will learn how to perform basic tasks using PowerPoint. The following roadmap identifies general activities you will perform as you progress through this module:

1. **INSERT** the four **PRESENTATION SLIDES**, using various layouts.
2. **ENTER** the **TEXT** for the slides.
3. **FORMAT** the **TEXT** on each slide.
4. **INSERT GRAPHICAL ELEMENTS**, including pictures.
5. **SIZE AND POSITION** the graphical elements.
6. **ENHANCE** the **SLIDE SHOW** by adding a closing slide and transition.
7. **DISPLAY** the **SLIDES**.

For an introduction to Office and instructions about how to perform basic tasks in Office apps, read the Office and Windows module at the beginning of this book, where you can learn how to run an application, use the ribbon, save a file, open a file, print a file, exit an application, use Help, and much more.

Choosing a Document Theme and Variant

You easily can give the slides in a presentation a professional and integrated appearance by using a theme. A document **theme** is a specific design with coordinating colors, fonts, and special effects such as shadows and reflections. Several themes are available when you run PowerPoint, each with a specific name. Using one of the formatted themes makes creating a professional-looking presentation easier and quicker than using the Blank Presentation template, where you would need to make all design decisions.

Each theme has a set of four alternate designs, called **variants**. Each variant has the same overall composition, but the colors, fonts, and design elements differ. Once you select a theme, you then can select a variation that best fits your overall design needs. If you later decide that another theme or variant would better fit the presentation's general theme, you can change these elements while you are developing slides.

For an introduction to Windows and instructions about how to perform basic Windows tasks, read the Office and Windows module at the beginning of this book, where you can learn how to resize windows, change screen resolution, create folders, move and rename files, use Windows Help, and much more.

To Choose a Document Theme and Variant

1 INSERT PRESENTATION SLIDES | 2 ENTER TEXT | 3 FORMAT TEXT | 4 INSERT GRAPHICAL ELEMENTS
5 SIZE & POSITION | 6 ENHANCE SLIDE SHOW | 7 DISPLAY SLIDES

When you begin creating a new PowerPoint presentation, you need to select a theme. You either can start with no design elements by using the Blank Presentation, or you can select one of the available professionally designed themes. The following steps apply the Berlin theme and then change the variant. ***Why?*** *The title slide will have text and a picture, so you want to select a theme, like Berlin, with an uncluttered background. The presentation discusses three events occurring at the nature center, and green is the color commonly associated with nature's forests and grasslands. The default Berlin theme is predominantly orange and black, but one of its variants is green and is an appropriate choice to relate to the nature concept.*

BTW

The PowerPoint Window

The modules in this book begin with the PowerPoint window appearing as it did at the initial installation of the software. Your PowerPoint window may look different depending on your screen resolution and other PowerPoint settings.

1

- Run PowerPoint and point to the Berlin theme on the Recent screen (Figure 1–2).

Q&A I do not see the Berlin theme. What should I do?
Your list of available templates may differ from those shown in the figure. You may need to scroll down to locate the Berlin theme or enter "Berlin" in the Search box.

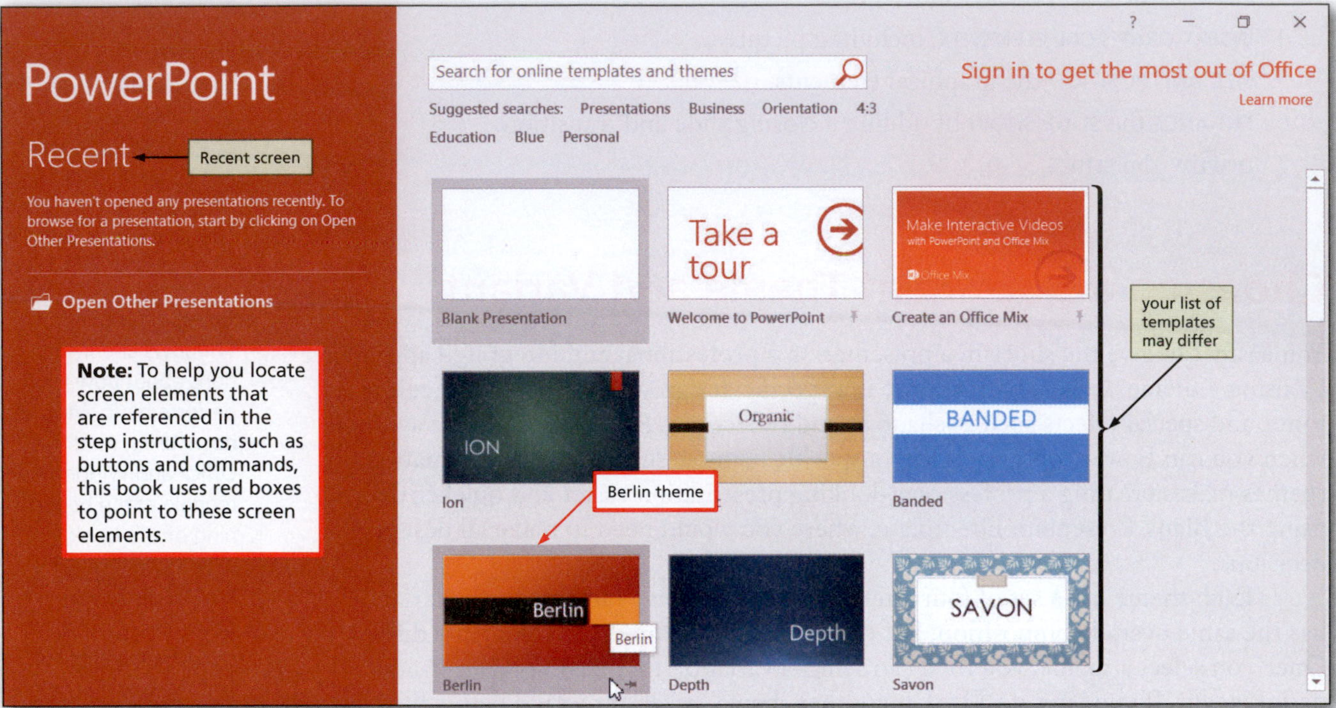

Figure 1–2

2

- Click the Berlin theme to display a theme preview dialog box with a thumbnail view of the theme and its variants (Figure 1–3).

Q&A Can I see previews of other themes?
Yes. Click the right or left arrows on the sides of the theme preview dialog box.

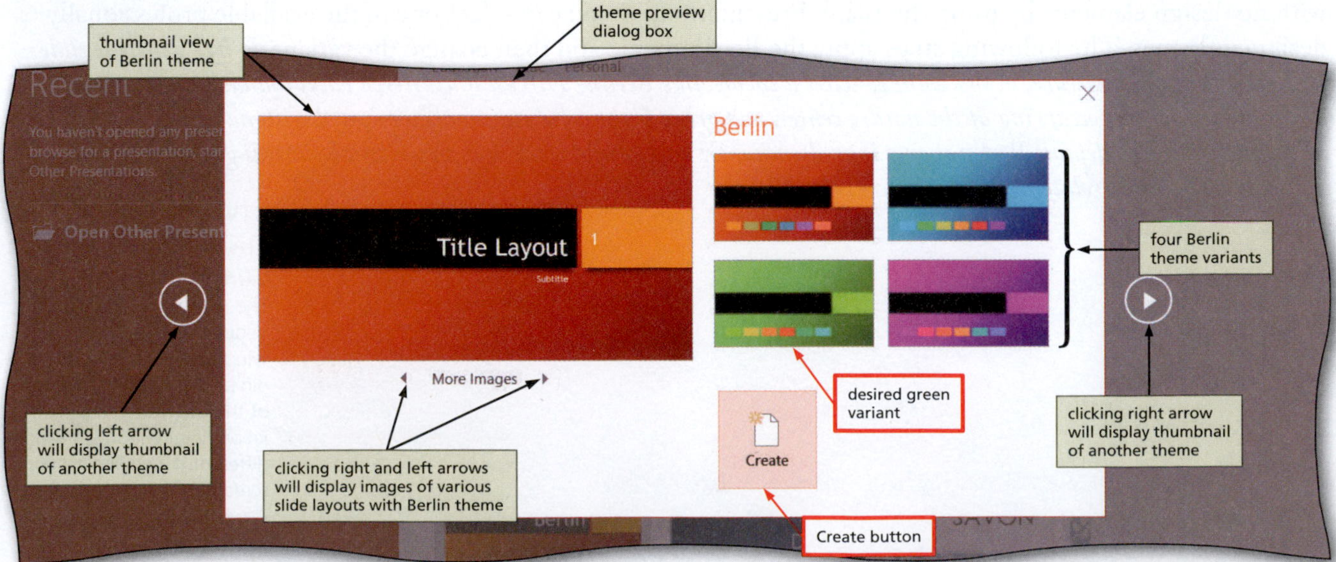

Figure 1–3

3

- Click the lower-left (green) variant to view a preview of that style applied to the thumbnail.

Q&A Can I see previews of the Berlin theme and green variant applied to layouts other than the title slide?
Yes. Click the right or left arrows beside the words, More Images, below the thumbnail. Three other layouts will be displayed: Title and Content, Two Content, and Photo.

- Click the Create button to apply the Berlin theme and green variant to the presentation and to display Slide 1 (Figure 1–4).

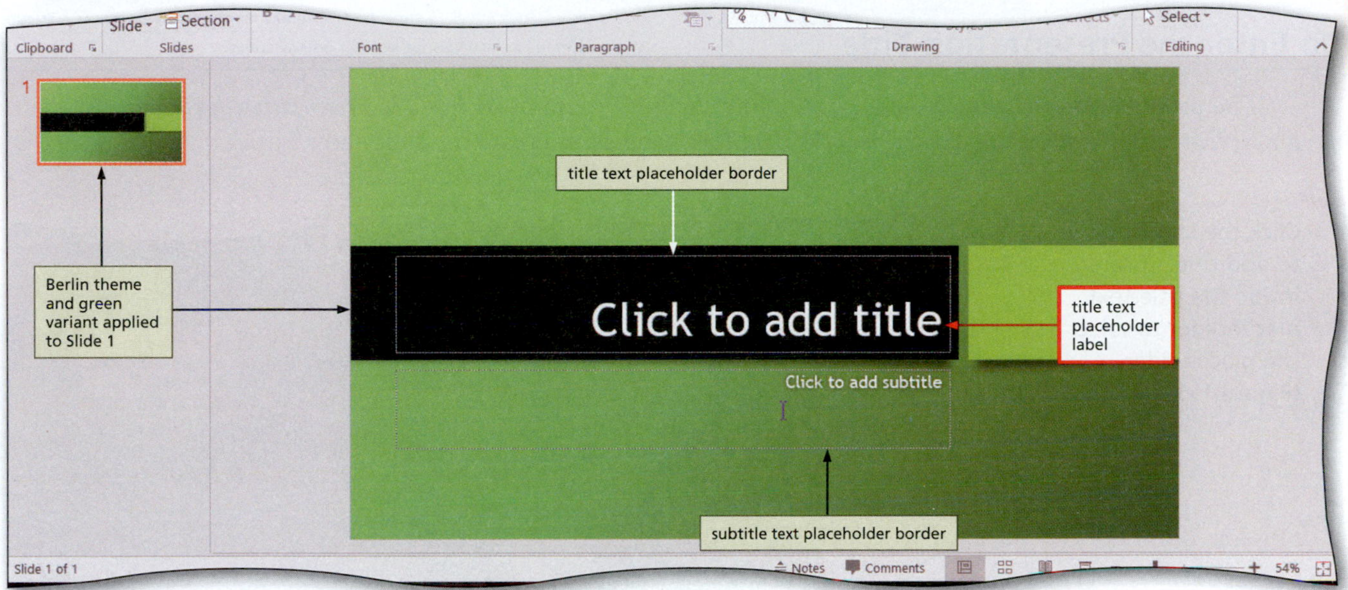

Figure 1–4

Creating a Title Slide

When you open a new presentation, the default **Title Slide** layout appears. The purpose of this layout is to introduce the presentation to the audience. PowerPoint includes other standard layouts for each of the themes. The slide layouts are set up in **landscape orientation**, where the slide width is greater than its height. In landscape orientation, the slide size is preset to 10 inches wide and 7.5 inches high when printed on a standard sheet of paper measuring 11 inches wide and 8.5 inches high.

Placeholders are boxes with dotted or hatch-marked borders that are displayed when you create a new slide. Most layouts have both a title text placeholder and at least one content placeholder. Depending on the particular slide layout selected, title and subtitle placeholders are displayed for the slide title and subtitle; a content text placeholder is displayed for text, art, or a table, chart, picture, graphic, or movie. The title slide has two text placeholders where you can type the main heading, or title, of a new slide and the subtitle.

With the exception of the Blank slide layout, PowerPoint assumes every new slide has a title. To make creating a presentation easier, any text you type after a new slide appears becomes title text in the title text placeholder. The following steps create the title slide for this presentation.

BTW
PowerPoint Screen Resolution
If you are using a computer or mobile device to step through the project in this module and you want your screens to match the figures in this book, you should change your screen's resolution to 1366 x 768. For information about how to change a computer's resolution, refer to the Office and Windows module at the beginning of this book.

CONSIDER THIS

How do I choose the words for the slide?

All presentations should follow the 7 × 7 rule, which states that each slide should have a maximum of seven lines, and each line should have a maximum of seven words. PowerPoint designers must choose their words carefully and, in turn, help viewers read the slides easily.

Avoid line wraps. Your audience's eyes want to stop at the end of a line. Thus, you must plan your words carefully or adjust the font size so that each point displays on only one line.

To Enter the Presentation Title

1 INSERT PRESENTATION SLIDES | 2 ENTER TEXT | 3 FORMAT TEXT | 4 INSERT GRAPHICAL ELEMENTS
5 SIZE & POSITION | 6 ENHANCE SLIDE SHOW | 7 DISPLAY SLIDES

The presentation title for Project 1 is Autumn Family Programs. ***Why?*** *The presentation discusses three programs that will be held during the fall months.* The following steps create the slide show's title.

- Click the label, 'Click to add title', located inside the title text placeholder to select the placeholder (Figure 1–5).

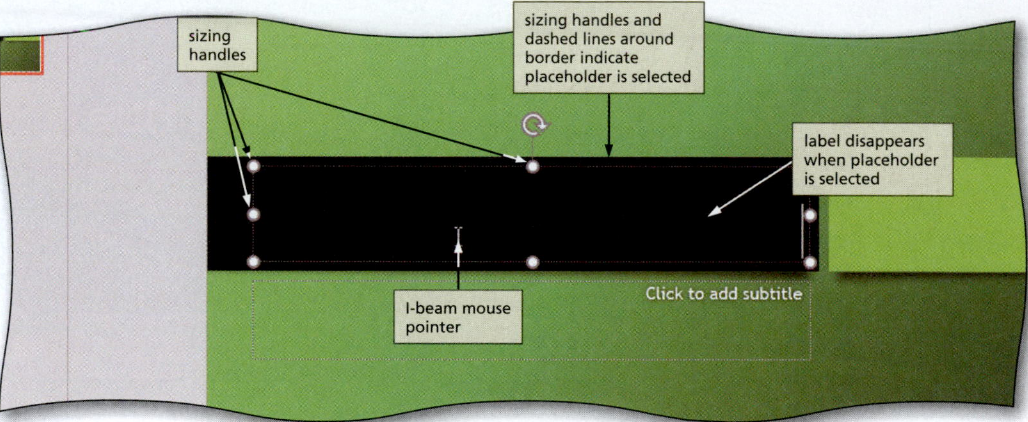

Figure 1–5

- Type **`Autumn Family Programs`** in the title text placeholder. Do not press the ENTER key (Figure 1–6).

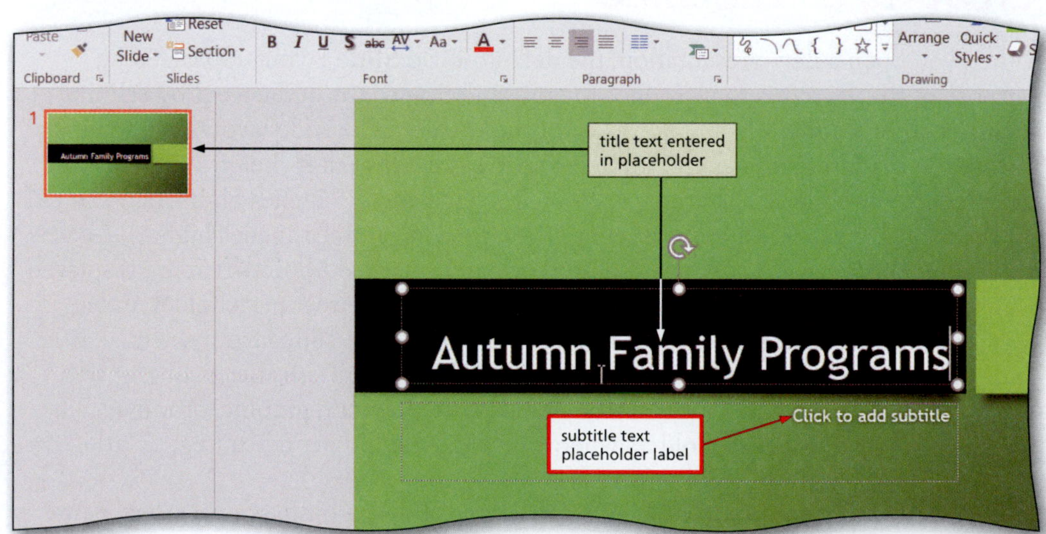

Figure 1–6

Correcting a Mistake When Typing

If you type the wrong letter, press the BACKSPACE key to erase all the characters back to and including the one that is incorrect. If you mistakenly press the ENTER key after typing the title and the insertion point is on the new line, simply press the BACKSPACE key to return the insertion point to the right of the last letter in the word, Programs.

By default, PowerPoint allows you to reverse up to the last 20 changes by clicking the Undo button on the Quick Access Toolbar. The ScreenTip that appears when you point to the Undo button changes to indicate the type of change just made. For example, if you type text in the title text placeholder and then point to the Undo button, the ScreenTip that appears is Undo Typing. For clarity, when referencing the Undo button in this project, the name displaying in the ScreenTip is used. You can reapply a change that you reversed with the Undo button by clicking the Redo button on the Quick Access Toolbar. Clicking the Redo button reverses the last undo action. The ScreenTip name reflects the type of reversal last performed.

BTW

Touch Screen Differences

The Office and Windows interfaces may vary if you are using a touch screen. For this reason, you might notice that the function or appearance of your touch screen differs slightly from this module's presentation.

Paragraphs

Text in the subtitle text placeholder supports the title text. It can appear on one or more lines in the placeholder. To create more than one subtitle line, you press the ENTER key after typing some words. PowerPoint creates a new line, which is the second paragraph in the placeholder. A **paragraph** is a segment of text with the same format that begins when you press the ENTER key and ends when you press the ENTER key again. This new paragraph is the same level as the previous paragraph. A **level** is a position within a structure, such as an outline, that indicates the magnitude of importance. PowerPoint allows for five paragraph levels.

CONSIDER THIS

How do you use the touch keyboard with a touch screen?

To display the on-screen keyboard, tap the Touch Keyboard button on the Windows taskbar. When finished using the touch keyboard, tap the X button on the touch keyboard to close the keyboard.

To Enter the Presentation Subtitle Paragraph

1 INSERT PRESENTATION SLIDES | 2 ENTER TEXT | 3 FORMAT TEXT | 4 INSERT GRAPHICAL ELEMENTS
5 SIZE & POSITION | 6 ENHANCE SLIDE SHOW | 7 DISPLAY SLIDES

The first subtitle paragraph is related to the title. ***Why?*** *The subtitle gives an additional detail, the nature center's name.* The following steps enter the presentation subtitle.

- Click the label, 'Click to add subtitle', located inside the subtitle text placeholder to select the placeholder (Figure 1–7).

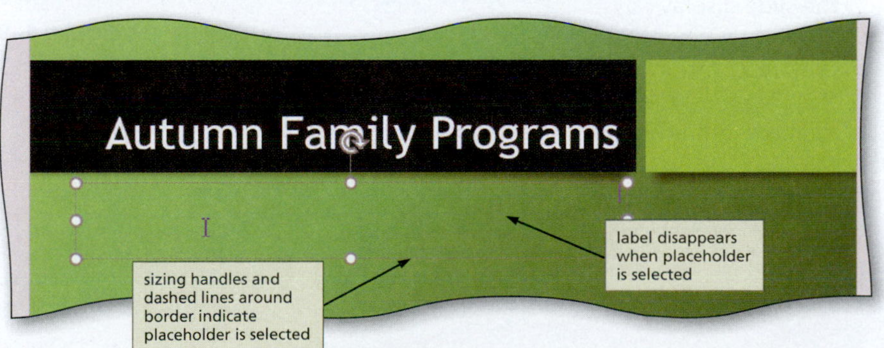

Figure 1–7

- Type **Tall Oaks Nature Center** but do not press the ENTER key (Figure 1–8).

Figure 1–8

To Zoom a Slide

1 INSERT PRESENTATION SLIDES | 2 ENTER TEXT | 3 FORMAT TEXT | 4 INSERT GRAPHICAL ELEMENTS
5 SIZE & POSITION | 6 ENHANCE SLIDE SHOW | 7 DISPLAY SLIDES

You can **zoom** the view of the slide on the screen so that the text or other content is enlarged or shrunk. When you zoom in, you get a close-up view of your slide; when you zoom out, you see more of the slide at a reduced size. You will be modifying the text and other slide components as you create the presentation, so you can enlarge the slide on the screen. ***Why?*** *Zooming the slide can help you see slide elements more clearly so that you can position them precisely where desired.* The following step changes the zoom to 70 percent.

Experiment

- Repeatedly click the Zoom In and Zoom Out buttons on the status bar and watch the size of the slide change in the Slide pane.
- Click the Zoom In or Zoom Out button as many times as necessary until the Zoom button on the status bar displays 70% on its face (Figure 1–9).

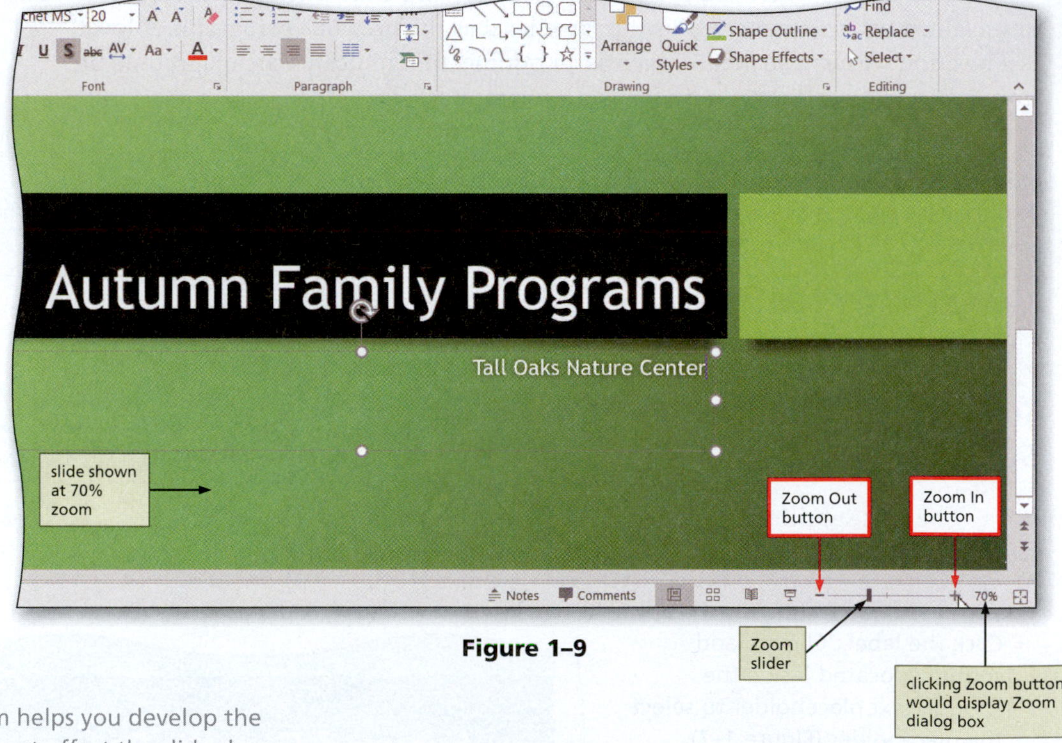

Figure 1–9

Q&A If I change the zoom percentage, will the slide display differently when I run the presentation?

No. Changing the zoom helps you develop the slide content and does not affect the slide show.

Other Ways

1. Drag Zoom slider on status bar
2. Click Zoom level button on status bar, select desired zoom percent or type (Zoom dialog box), click OK button
3. Click Zoom button (View tab | Zoom group), select desired zoom percent or type (Zoom dialog box), click OK button
4. For touch screens: Pinch two fingers together in Slide pane (zoom out) or stretch two fingers apart (zoom in)

Formatting Characters in a Presentation

Recall that each document theme determines the color scheme, font set, and layout of a presentation. You can use a specific document theme and then change the characters' formats any time before, during, or after you type the text.

Fonts and Font Styles

Characters that appear on the screen are a specific shape and size. Examples of how you can modify the appearance, or **format**, of these typed characters on the screen and in print include changing the font, style, size, and color. The **font**, or typeface, defines the appearance and shape of the letters, numbers, punctuation marks, and symbols. **Style** indicates how the characters are formatted. PowerPoint's text font styles include regular, italic, bold, and bold italic. **Size** specifies the height of the characters and is gauged by a measurement system that uses points. A **point** is 1/72 of an inch in height. Thus, a character with a font size of 36 is 36/72 (or 1/2) of an inch in height. **Color** defines the hue of the characters.

This presentation uses the Berlin document theme, which has particular font styles and font sizes. The Berlin document theme default title text font is named Trebuchet MS. It has no special effects, and its size is 54 point. The Berlin default subtitle text font also is Trebuchet MS with a font size of 20 point.

To Select a Paragraph

You can use many techniques to format characters. When you want to apply the same formats to multiple words or paragraphs, it is helpful to select these words. ***Why?*** *It is efficient to select the desired text and then make the desired changes to all the characters simultaneously.* The first formatting change you will make will apply to the title slide subtitle. The following step selects this paragraph.

- Triple-click the paragraph, Tall Oaks Nature Center, in the subtitle text placeholder to select the paragraph (Figure 1–10).

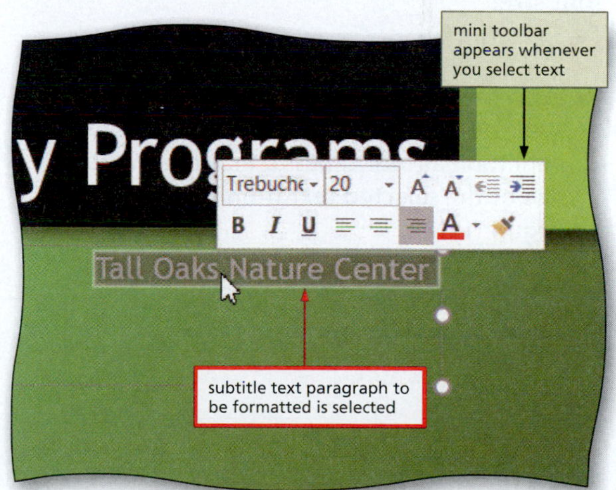

Figure 1–10

Other Ways

1. Position pointer to left of first paragraph and drag to end of line

To Italicize Text

Different font styles often are used on slides. ***Why?*** *These style changes make the words more appealing to the reader and emphasize particular text.* **Italic** text has a slanted appearance. Used sparingly, it draws the readers' eyes to these characters. The following step adds emphasis to the line of the subtitle text by changing regular text to italic text.

- With the subtitle text still selected, click the Italic button on the mini toolbar to italicize that text on the slide (Figure 1–11).

Q&A If I change my mind and decide not to italicize the text, how can I remove this style?
Immediately click the Undo button on the Quick Access Toolbar, click the Italic button a second time, or press CTRL+Z.

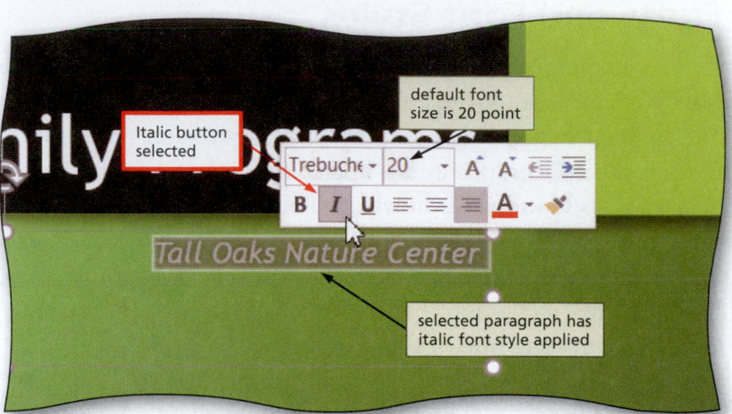

Figure 1–11

Other Ways

1. Right-click selected text, click Italic button in mini toolbar near shortcut menu
2. Select text, click Italic button (Home tab | Font group)
3. Click Font dialog box launcher (Home tab | Font group), click Font tab (Font dialog box), click Italic in Font style list, click OK button
4. Select text, press CTRL+I

To Increase Font Size

Why? *To add emphasis, you increase the font size for the subtitle text.* The 'Increase Font Size' button on the mini toolbar increases the font size in preset increments. The following step uses this button to increase the font size.

- With the text, Tall Oaks Nature Center, selected, click the 'Increase Font Size' button on the mini toolbar four times to increase the font size of the selected text from 20 to 36 point (Figure 1–12).

Figure 1–12

Other Ways

1. Click Font Size arrow on mini toolbar, click desired font size in Font Size gallery
2. Click 'Increase Font Size' button (Home tab | Font group)
3. Click Font Size arrow (Home tab | Font group), click desired font size in Font size gallery
4. Press CTRL+SHIFT+>

1 INSERT PRESENTATION SLIDES | 2 ENTER TEXT | 3 FORMAT TEXT | 4 INSERT GRAPHICAL ELEMENTS
5 SIZE & POSITION | 6 ENHANCE SLIDE SHOW | 7 DISPLAY SLIDES

To Select a Word

PowerPoint designers use many techniques to emphasize words and characters on a slide. To accentuate the word, Autumn, on your slide, you want to increase the font size and change the font color to orange for this word in the title text. To make these changes, you should begin by selecting the word, Autumn. ***Why?*** *You could perform these actions separately, but it is more efficient to select the word and then change the font attributes.* The following step selects a word.

- Position the pointer somewhere in the word to be selected (in this case, in the word, Autumn).
- Double-click the word to select it (Figure 1–13).

Figure 1–13

Other Ways

1. Position pointer before first character, press CTRL+SHIFT+RIGHT ARROW
2. Position pointer before first character, drag right to select word

1 INSERT PRESENTATION SLIDES | 2 ENTER TEXT | 3 FORMAT TEXT | 4 INSERT GRAPHICAL ELEMENTS
5 SIZE & POSITION | 6 ENHANCE SLIDE SHOW | 7 DISPLAY SLIDES

To Change the Text Color

PowerPoint allows you to use one or more text colors in a presentation. You decide to change the color of the word you selected, Autumn. ***Why?*** *The color, orange, is associated with that season, and you want to add more emphasis, subtly, to this word in your title slide text.* The following steps add emphasis to this word by changing the font color from white to orange.

- With the word, Autumn, selected, click the Font Color arrow on the mini toolbar to display the Font Color gallery, which includes Theme Colors and Standard Colors (Figure 1–14).

Q&A If the mini toolbar disappears from the screen, how can I display it once again?
Right-click the text, and the mini toolbar should appear.

Experiment

- Point to various colors in the gallery and watch the word's font color change.

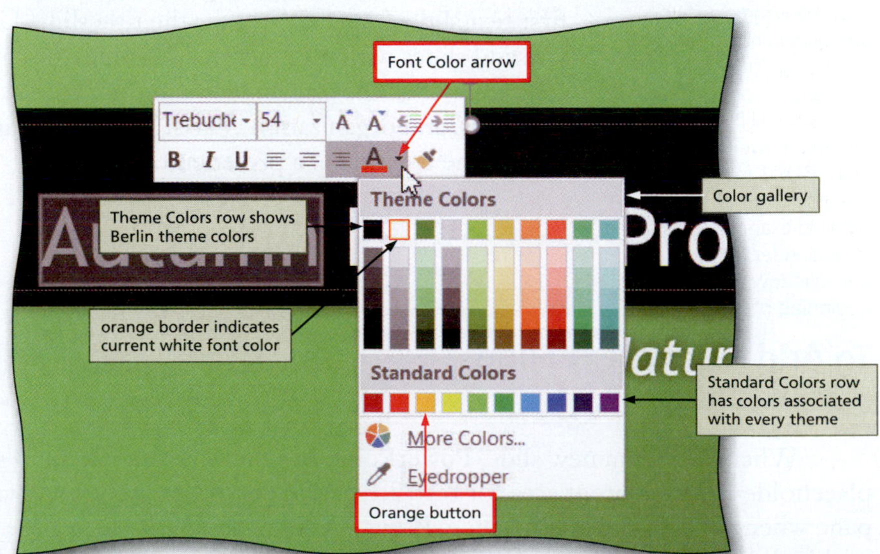

Figure 1–14

2

- Click Orange in the Standard Colors row on the mini toolbar (third color from left) to change the font color to Orange (Figure 1–15).

Figure 1–15

Q&A Why did I select the color Orange?
Orange is one of the 10 standard colors associated with every document theme, and it is a universal color representing the fall colors. The new color will emphasize the fact that the presentation focuses on programs suited for this time of year.

What is the difference between the colors shown in the Theme Colors area and the Standard Colors?
The 10 colors in the top row of the Theme Colors area are two text, two background, and six accent colors in the Berlin theme; the five colors in each column under the top row display different transparencies. The Standard Colors are available in every document theme.

3

- Click outside the selected area to deselect the word.

4

- Save the presentation on your hard disk, OneDrive, or other storage location using Tall Oaks as the file name.

Q&A Why should I save the presentation at this time?
You have performed many tasks while creating this presentation and do not want to risk losing work completed thus far.

Other Ways

1. Right-click selected text, click Font on shortcut menu, click Font Color button, click desired color
2. Click Font Color arrow (Home tab | Font group), click desired color

BTW
Organizing Files and Folders
You should organize and store files in folders so that you easily can find the files later. For example, if you are taking an introductory technology class called CIS 101, a good practice would be to save all PowerPoint files in a PowerPoint folder in a CIS 101 folder. For a discussion of folders and detailed examples of creating folders, refer to the Office and Windows module at the beginning of this book.

Adding a New Slide to a Presentation

With the text for the title slide for the presentation created, the next step is to add the first text slide immediately after the title slide. Usually, when you create a presentation, you add slides with text, pictures, graphics, or charts. Some placeholders allow you to double-click the placeholder and then access other objects, such as videos, charts, diagrams, and organization charts. You can change the layout for a slide at any time during the creation of a presentation.

To Add a New Text Slide with a Bulleted List

1 INSERT PRESENTATION SLIDES | 2 ENTER TEXT | 3 FORMAT TEXT | 4 INSERT GRAPHICAL ELEMENTS
5 SIZE & POSITION | 6 ENHANCE SLIDE SHOW | 7 DISPLAY SLIDES

When you add a new slide, PowerPoint uses the Title and Content slide layout. This layout provides a title placeholder and a content area for text, art, charts, and other graphics. A vertical scroll bar appears in the Slide pane when you add the second slide. ***Why?*** *The scroll bar allows you to move from slide to slide easily.* A small image of this slide also appears in the Slides tab. The following step adds a new slide with the Title and Content slide layout.

1

- Click the New Slide button (Home tab | Slides group) to insert a new slide with the Title and Content layout (Figure 1–16).

Q&A

Why does the bullet character display a white dot?
The Berlin document theme determines the bullet characters. Each paragraph level has an associated bullet character.

I clicked the New Slide arrow instead of the New Slide button. What should I do?
Click the Title and Content slide thumbnail in the Berlin layout gallery.

How do I know which slide number I am viewing?
The left edge of the status bar shows the current slide number followed by the total number of slides in the document. In addition, the slide number is displayed to the left of the slide thumbnail.

What are those six icons grouped in the middle of the Slide pane?
You can click one of the icons to insert a specific type of content: table, chart, SmartArt graphic, pictures, online pictures, or video.

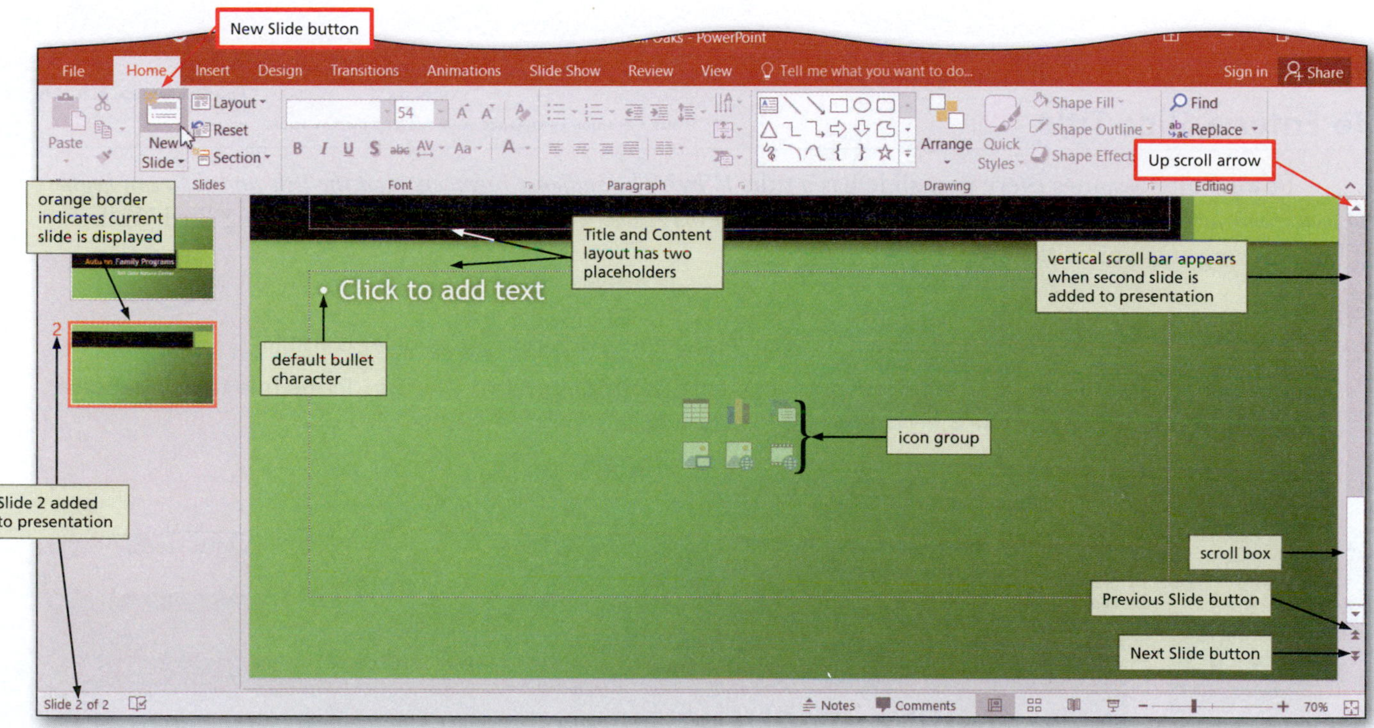

Figure 1–16

Other Ways

1. Click New Slide button (Insert tab | Slides group)
2. Press CTRL+M

BTW
The Ribbon and Screen Resolution
PowerPoint may change how the groups and buttons within the groups appear on the ribbon, depending on the computer or mobile device's screen resolution. Thus, your ribbon may look different from the ones in this book if you are using a screen resolution other than 1366 x 768.

Creating a Text Slide with a Multilevel Bulleted List

The information in the Slide 2 text placeholder is presented in a bulleted list with three levels. A **bulleted list** is a list of paragraphs, each of which may be preceded by a bullet character, such as a dot, arrow, or checkmark. Most themes display a bullet character at the start of a paragraph by default. A slide that consists of more than one level of bulleted text is called a **multilevel bulleted list slide**. In a multilevel bulleted list, a lower-level paragraph is a subset of a higher-level paragraph. It usually contains information that supports the topic in the paragraph immediately above it.

As you can see in Figure 1–1b, two of the Slide 2 paragraphs appear at the same level, called the first level: Enjoy a hike on natural surface trails, and 9 a.m. every Saturday. Beginning with the second level, each paragraph indents to the right of the preceding level and is pushed down to a lower level. For example, if you increase the indent of a first-level paragraph, it becomes a second-level paragraph. The second and fourth paragraphs on Slide 2 are second-level paragraphs. The last paragraph, Extra supplies will be available, is a third-level paragraph.

Creating a text slide with a multilevel bulleted list requires several steps. Initially, you enter a slide title in the title text placeholder. Next, you select the content text placeholder. Then, you type the text for the multilevel bulleted list, increasing and decreasing the indents as needed. The next several sections add a slide with a multilevel bulleted list.

BTW

File Type

Depending on your Windows settings, the file type .pptx may be displayed on the title bar immediately to the right of the file name after you save the file. The file type .pptx identifies a PowerPoint document.

To Enter a Slide Title

1 INSERT PRESENTATION SLIDES | 2 ENTER TEXT | 3 FORMAT TEXT | 4 INSERT GRAPHICAL ELEMENTS
5 SIZE & POSITION | 6 ENHANCE SLIDE SHOW | 7 DISPLAY SLIDES

PowerPoint assumes every new slide has a title. ***Why?*** *The audience members read the title and then can begin to focus their attention on the information being presented on that slide.* The title for Slide 2 is Morning Bird Walks. The following step enters this title.

- If necessary, click the Up scroll arrow several times until the entire title text placeholder is visible.
- Click the label 'Click to add title', to select it and then type **`Morning Bird Walks`** in the title text placeholder. Do not press the ENTER key (Figure 1–17).

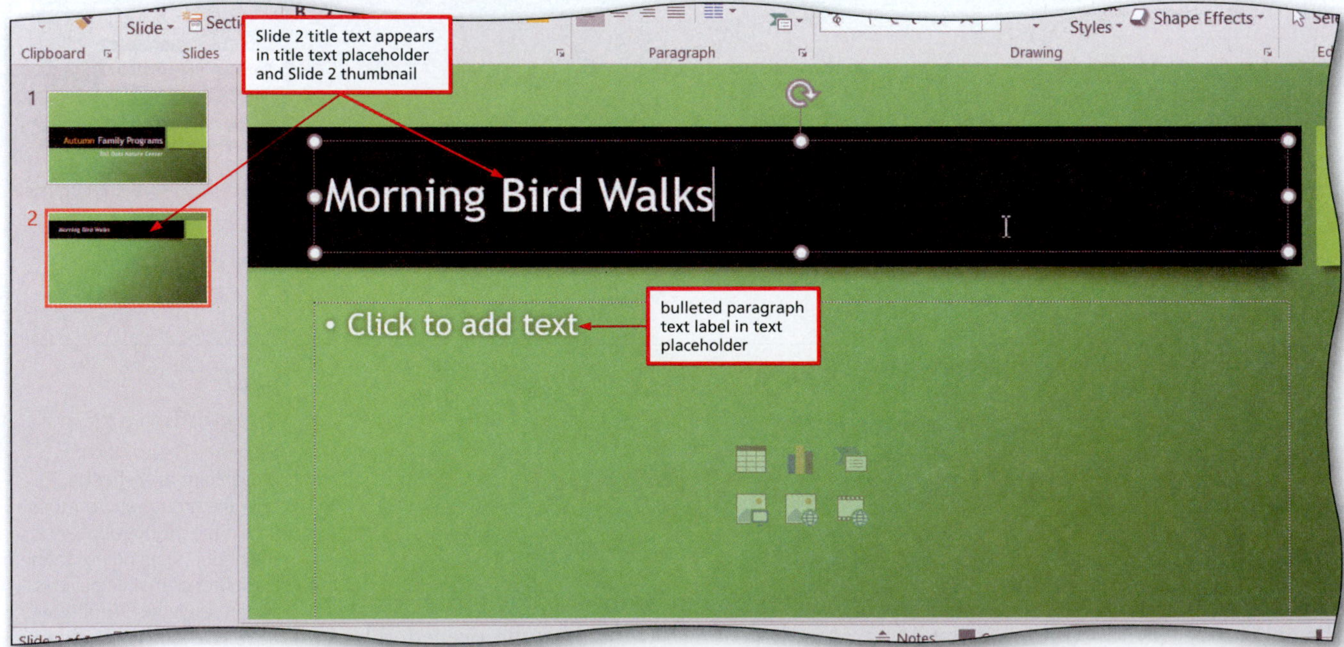

Figure 1–17

To Select a Text Placeholder

Why? *Before you can type text into a content placeholder, you first must select it.* The following step selects the text placeholder on Slide 2.

- Click the label, 'Click to add text', to select the content placeholder (Figure 1–18).

Q&A Why does my pointer have a different shape?
If you move the pointer away from the bullet, it will change shape.

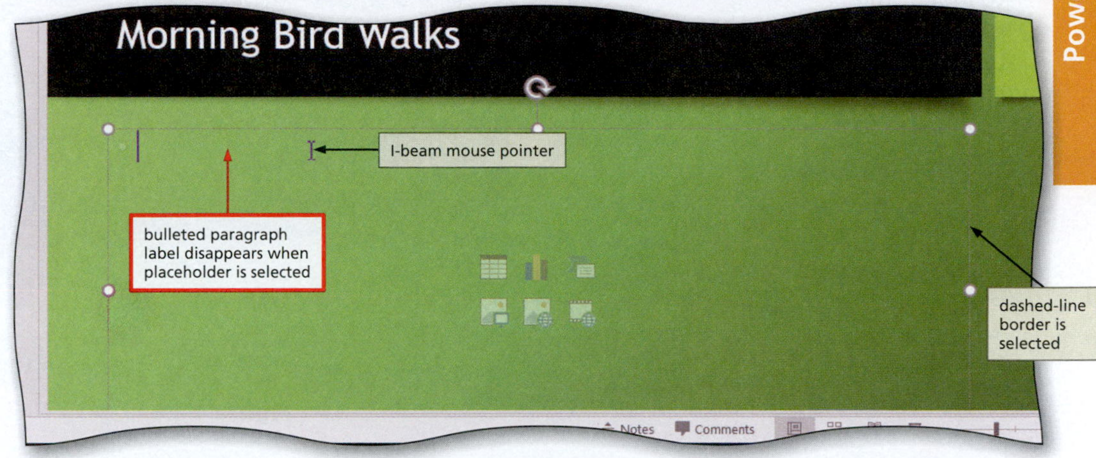

Figure 1–18

Other Ways

1. Press CTRL+ENTER

To Type a Multilevel Bulleted List

The content placeholder provides an area for the text characters. When you click inside a placeholder, you then can type or paste text. As discussed previously, a bulleted list is a list of paragraphs, each of which is preceded by a bullet. A paragraph is a segment of text ended by pressing the ENTER key. The theme determines the bullets for each level. ***Why?*** *The bullet variations are determined by the specific paragraph levels, and they generally vary in size, shape, and color.*

The content text placeholder is selected, so the next step is to type the multilevel bulleted list that consists of six paragraphs, as shown in Figure 1–1b. Creating a lower-level paragraph is called **demoting** text; creating a higher-level paragraph is called **promoting** text. The following steps create a multilevel bulleted list consisting of three levels.

- Type `Enjoy a hike on natural surface trails` and then press the ENTER key (Figure 1–19).

Figure 1–19

2

- Click the 'Increase List Level' button (Home tab | Paragraph group) to indent the second paragraph below the first and create a second-level paragraph (Figure 1–20).

Figure 1–20

Why does the bullet for this paragraph have a different size?
A different bullet is assigned to each paragraph level.

3

- Type **Approximately 1.5 miles** and then press the ENTER key (Figure 1–21).

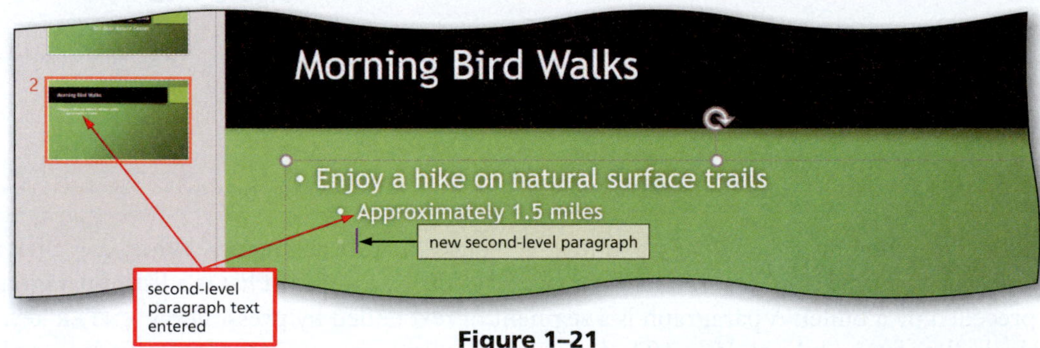

Figure 1–21

4

- Click the 'Decrease List Level' button (Home tab | Paragraph group) so that the second-level paragraph becomes a first-level paragraph (Figure 1–22).

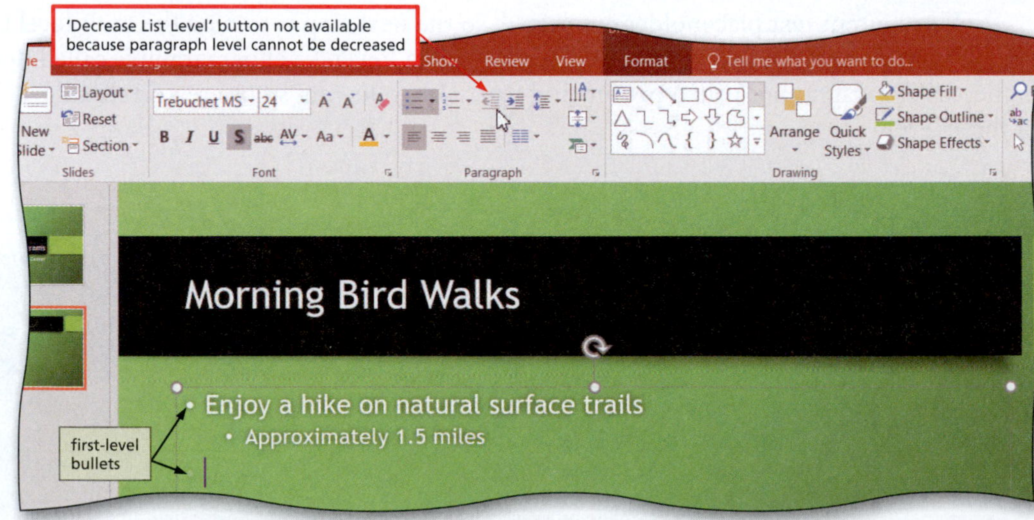

Figure 1–22

Can I delete bullets on a slide?
Yes. If you do not want bullets to display in a particular paragraph, click the Bullets button (Home tab | Paragraph group) or right-click the paragraph and then click the Bullets button on the shortcut menu.

Other Ways

1. Press TAB to promote paragraph; press SHIFT+TAB to demote paragraph

To Type the Remaining Text for Slide 2

The following steps complete the text for Slide 2.

1. Type **`9 a.m. every Saturday`** and then press the ENTER key.
2. Click the 'Increase List Level' button (Home tab | Paragraph group) to demote the paragraph to the second level.
3. Type **`Bring binoculars and a field guide`** and then press the ENTER key to add a new paragraph at the same level as the previous paragraph.
4. Click the 'Increase List Level' button (Home tab | Paragraph group) to demote the paragraph to the third level.
5. Type **`Extra supplies will be available`** but do not press the ENTER key (Figure 1–23).

Q&A I pressed the ENTER key in error, and now a new bullet appears after the last entry on this slide. How can I remove this extra bullet?
Press the BACKSPACE key twice.

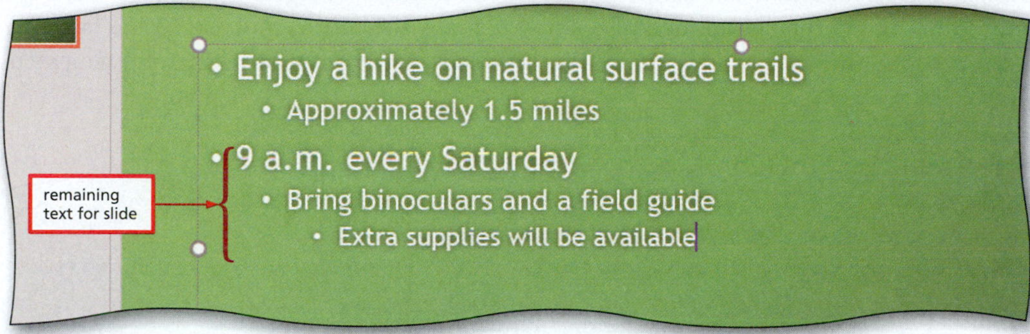

Figure 1–23

BTW

Automatic Spelling Correction

As you type, PowerPoint automatically corrects some misspelled words. For example, if you type availalbe, PowerPoint automatically corrects the misspelling and displays the word, available, when you press the SPACEBAR or type a punctuation mark. To see a complete list of automatically corrected words, click File on the ribbon to open the Backstage view, click the Options tab in the Backstage view, click Proofing in the left pane (PowerPoint Options dialog box), click the AutoCorrect Options button, and then scroll through the list near the bottom of the dialog box.

To Select a Group of Words

1 INSERT PRESENTATION SLIDES | 2 ENTER TEXT | 3 FORMAT TEXT | 4 INSERT GRAPHICAL ELEMENTS
5 SIZE & POSITION | 6 ENHANCE SLIDE SHOW | 7 DISPLAY SLIDES

PowerPoint designers use many techniques to emphasize words and characters on a slide. To highlight the day of the week when the walks are held, you want to bold and increase the font size of the words, every Saturday, in the body text. The following steps select two words. ***Why?*** *You could perform these actions separately, but it is more efficient to select the words and then change the font attributes.*

1

- Position the pointer immediately to the left of the first character of the text to be selected (in this case, the e in the word, every) (Figure 1–24).

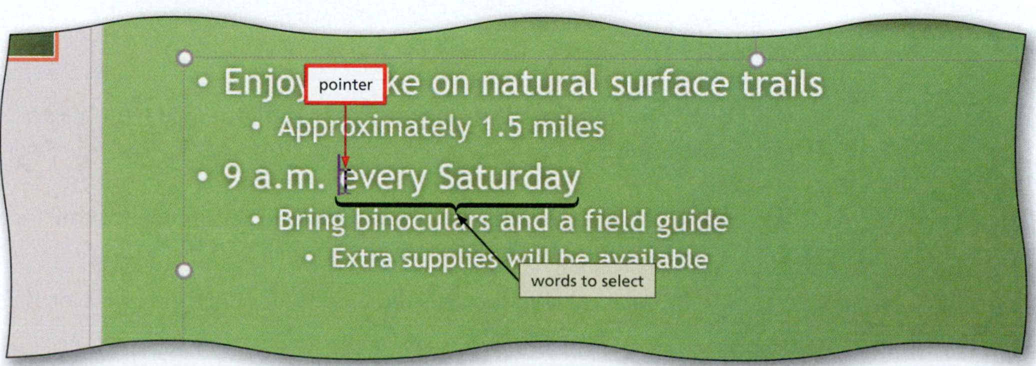

Figure 1–24

- Drag the pointer through the last character of the text to be selected (in this case, the y in the word, Saturday) (Figure 1–25).

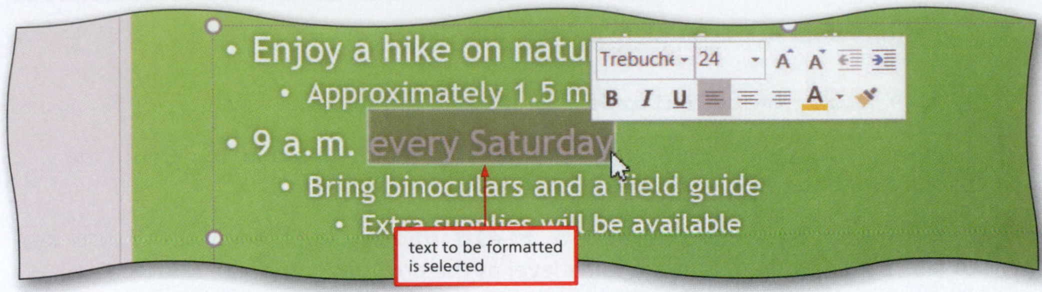

Figure 1–25

Other Ways

1. Press CTRL+SHIFT+RIGHT ARROW repeatedly until desired words are selected

To Bold Text

Why? Bold characters display somewhat thicker and darker than those that display in a regular font style. Clicking the Bold button on the mini toolbar is an efficient method of bolding text. To add more emphasis to the fact that the body needs nature for cooling purposes, you want to bold the words, every Saturday. The following step bolds this text.

- With the words, every Saturday, selected, click the Bold button on the mini toolbar to bold the two words (Figure 1–26).

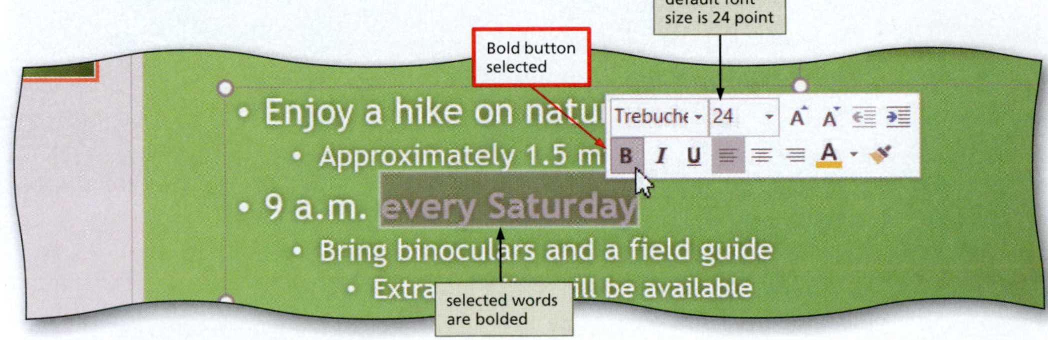

Figure 1–26

Other Ways

1. Right-click selected text, click Font on shortcut menu, click Font tab (Font dialog box), click Bold in Font style list, click OK button
2. Select text, click Bold button (Home tab | Font group)
3. Click Font dialog box launcher (Home tab | Font group), click Font tab (Font dialog box), click Bold in Font style list, click OK button
4. Select text, press CTRL+B

To Increase Font Size

The following steps increase the font size from 24 to 28 point. ***Why?** To add emphasis, you increase the font size for the words, every Saturday.*

1. With the words, every Saturday, still selected, click the 'Increase Font Size' button on the mini toolbar once (Figure 1–27).
2. Click outside the selected area to deselect the two words.

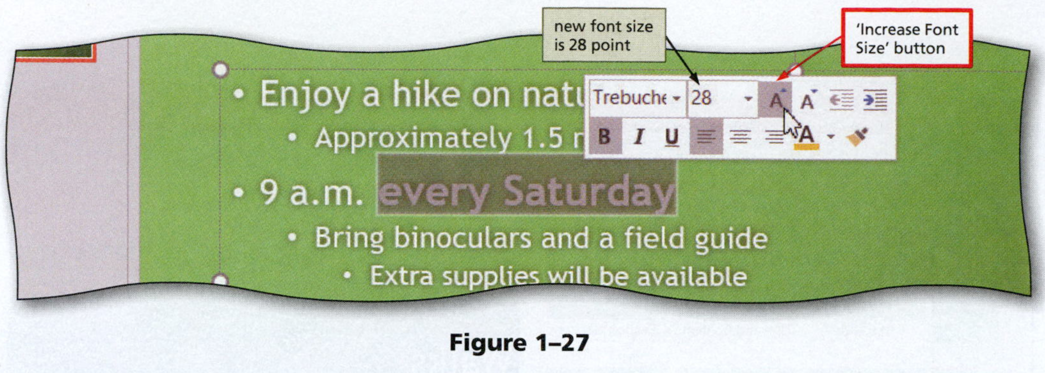

Figure 1–27

Adding New Slides, Changing Slide Layouts, and Changing the Theme

Slide 3 in Figure 1–1c contains two pictures: a grasshopper and a dragonfly. Slide 4 in Figure 1–1d contains an illustration of a firefly and does not contain a bulleted list. When you add a new slide, PowerPoint applies the Title and Content layout. This layout and the Title Slide layout for Slide 1 are the default styles. A **layout** specifies the arrangement of placeholders on a slide. These placeholders are arranged in various configurations and can contain text, such as the slide title or a bulleted list, or they can contain content, such as SmartArt graphics, pictures, charts, tables, and shapes. The placement of the text, in relationship to content, depends on the slide layout. You can specify a particular slide layout when you add a new slide to a presentation or after you have created the slide.

Using the **layout gallery**, you can choose a slide layout. The nine layouts in this gallery have a variety of placeholders to define text and content positioning and formatting. Three layouts are for text: Title Slide, Section Header, and Title Only. Five are for text and content: Title and Content, Two Content, Comparison, Content with Caption, and Picture with Caption. The Blank layout has no placeholders. If none of these standard layouts meets your design needs, you can create a **custom layout**. A custom layout specifies the number, size, and location of placeholders, background content, and optional slide and placeholder-level properties.

When you change the layout of a slide, PowerPoint retains the text and objects and repositions them into the appropriate placeholders. Using slide layouts eliminates the need to resize objects and the font size because PowerPoint automatically sizes the objects and text to fit the placeholders. At any time when creating the slide content, you can change the theme and variant to give the presentation a different look and feel.

BTW

Customizing a Slide Layout

PowerPoint provides a wide variety of slide layouts for each theme, but you can customize the layouts to make your deck unique. Display the View tab, click Slide Master (View tab | Master Views group), select the thumbnail below the slide master in the left pane that you would like to customize, and then make the desired modifications.

To Add a New Slide and Enter a Slide Title and Headings

1 INSERT PRESENTATION SLIDES | 2 ENTER TEXT | 3 FORMAT TEXT | 4 INSERT GRAPHICAL ELEMENTS
5 SIZE & POSITION | 6 ENHANCE SLIDE SHOW | 7 DISPLAY SLIDES

The text on Slide 3 in Figure 1–1c consists of a title and two headings. The appropriate layout for this slide is named Comparison. ***Why?*** *The Comparison layout has two headings and two text placeholders adjacent to each other, so an audience member easily can compare and contrast the items shown side by side.* The following steps add Slide 3 to the presentation with the Comparison layout and then enter the title and heading text for this slide.

1

- Click the New Slide arrow in the Slides group to display the Berlin layout gallery (Figure 1–28).

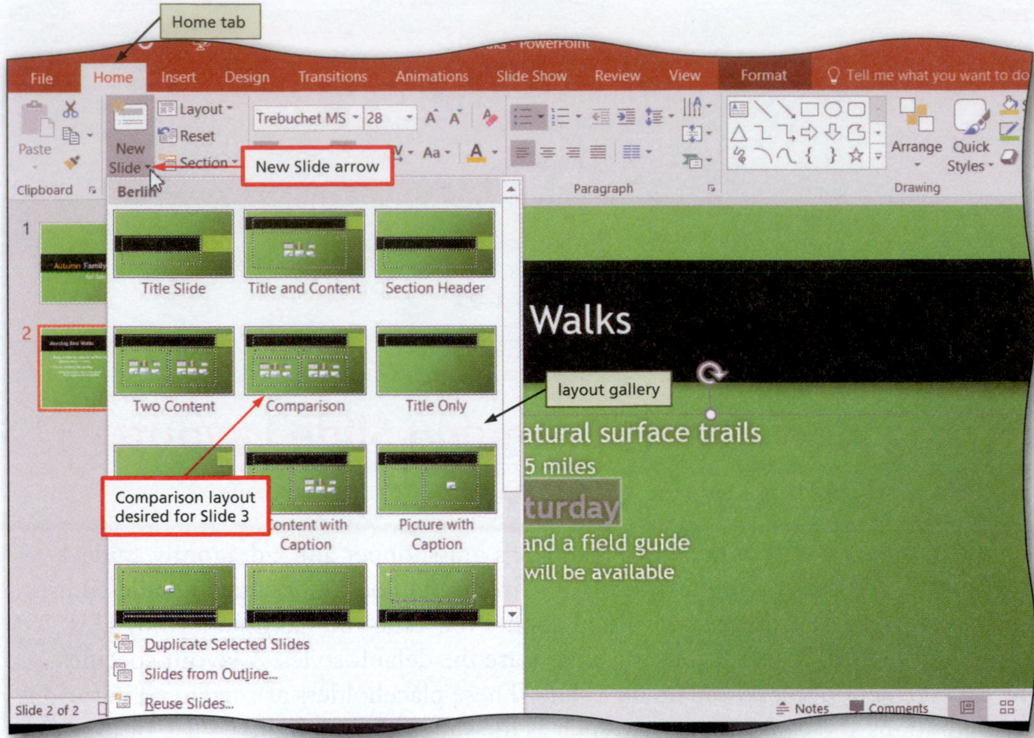

Figure 1–28

2

- Click Comparison to add Slide 3 and apply that layout (Figure 1–29).

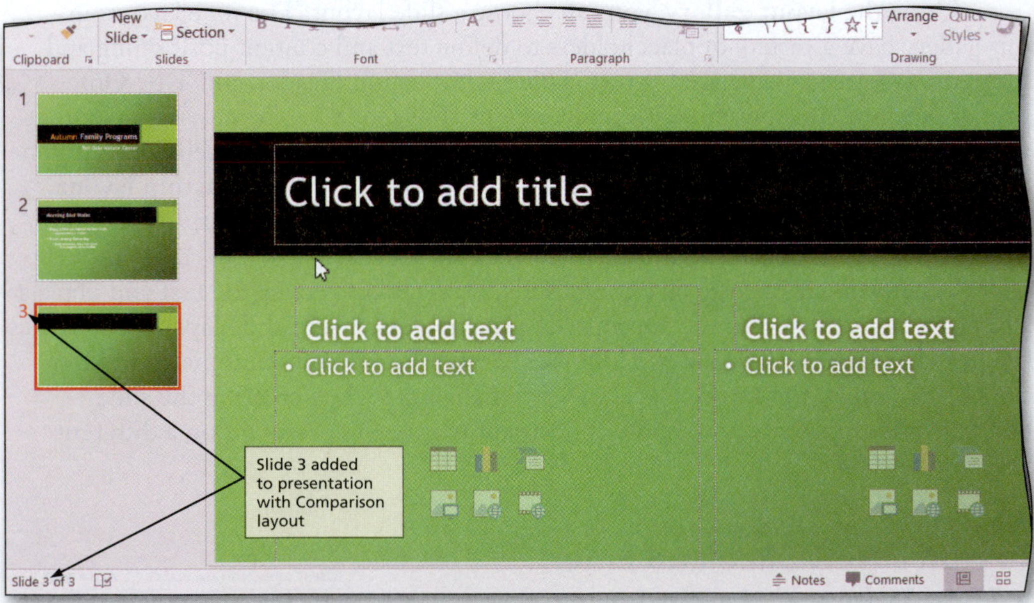

Figure 1–29

- Type **Afternoon Insect Identification** in the title text placeholder.
- Click the left heading placeholder with the label, 'Click to add text', to select this placeholder (Figure 1–30).

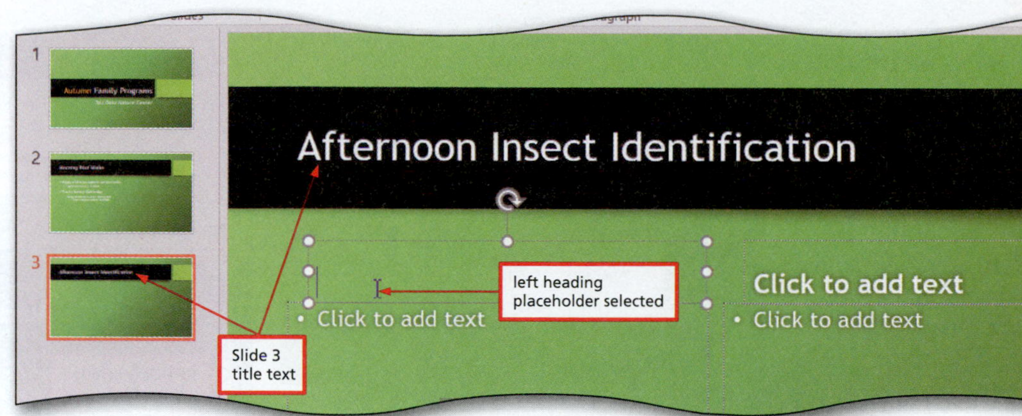

Figure 1–30

- Type **Grasshoppers** and then press the ENTER key.
- Type **(also known as locusts)** but do not press the ENTER key.
- Select the right heading placeholder and then type **Dragonflies** and press the ENTER key.
- Type **(often mistaken for damselflies)** but do not press the ENTER key (Figure 1–31).

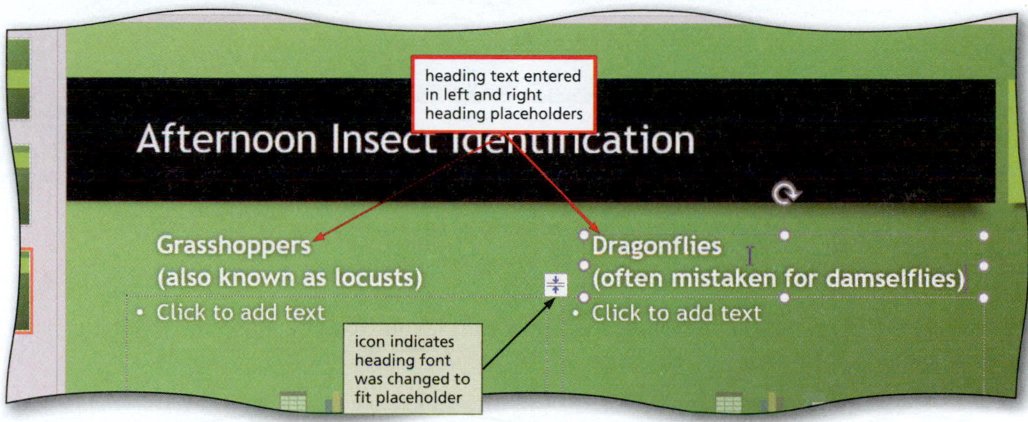

Figure 1–31

Q&A What is the white box with the arrow between the placeholders?
The text is too large to fit in the placeholder using the default font and paragraph attributes, so PowerPoint adjusts the text so it displays properly. That icon informs you that the font was altered.

To Add a Slide with the Title Only Layout

1 INSERT PRESENTATION SLIDES | 2 ENTER TEXT | 3 FORMAT TEXT | 4 INSERT GRAPHICAL ELEMENTS
5 SIZE & POSITION | 6 ENHANCE SLIDE SHOW | 7 DISPLAY SLIDES

The following steps add Slide 4 to the presentation with the Title Only slide layout style. ***Why?*** *The only text on the slide is the title, and the majority of the slide content is the illustration.*

1

- If necessary, click Home on the ribbon to display the Home tab.
- Click the New Slide arrow (Home tab | Slides group) to display the Berlin layout gallery (Figure 1–32).

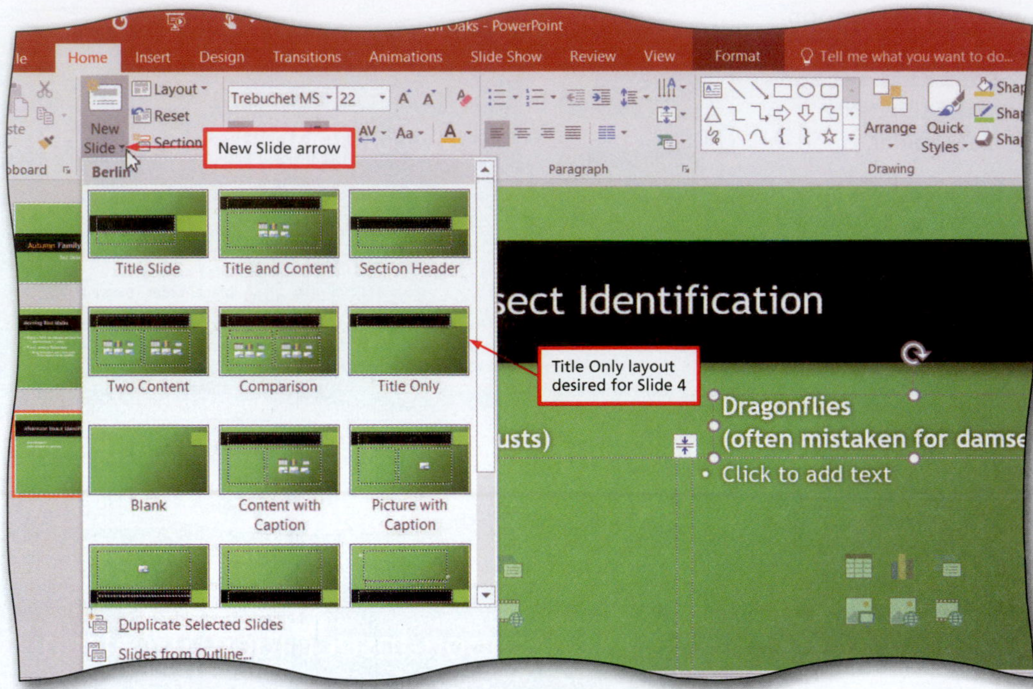

Figure 1–32

2

- Click Title Only to add a new slide and apply that layout to Slide 4 (Figure 1–33).

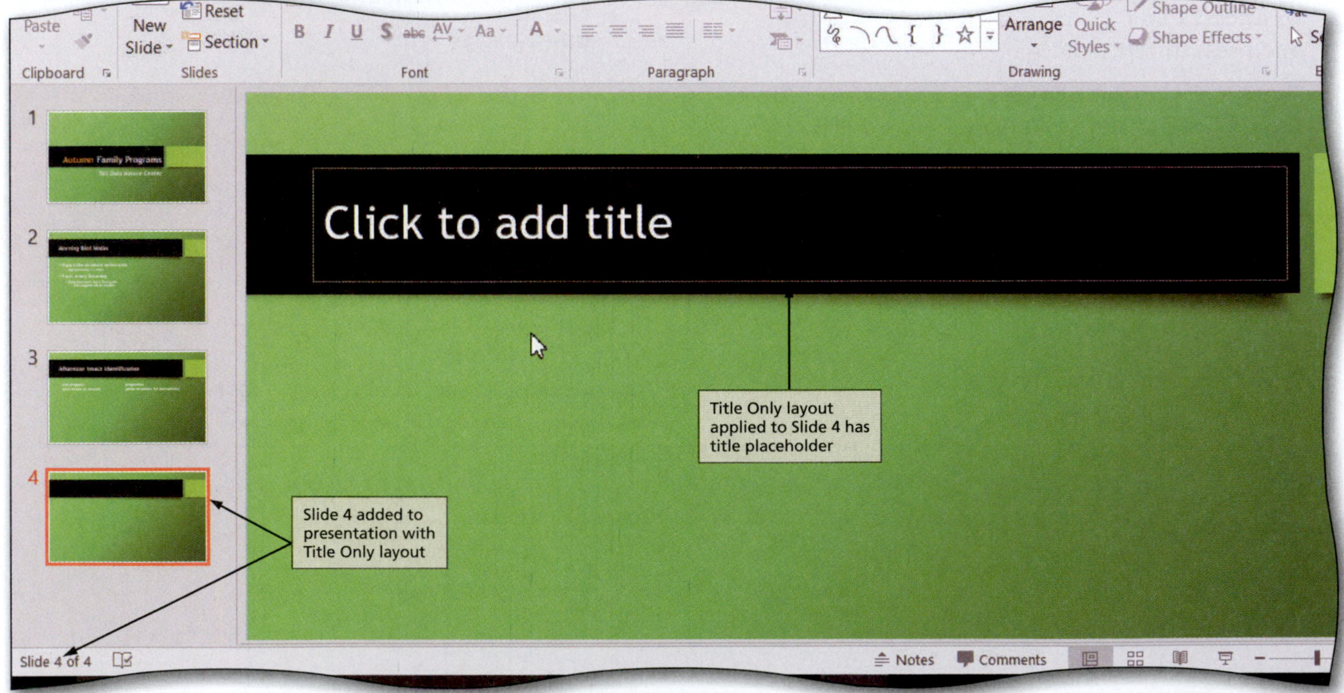

Figure 1–33

To Enter a Slide Title

The only text on Slide 4 is the title. The following step enters the title text for this slide.

1 Type `Twilight Firefly Hikes` as the title text but do not press the ENTER key (Figure 1–34).

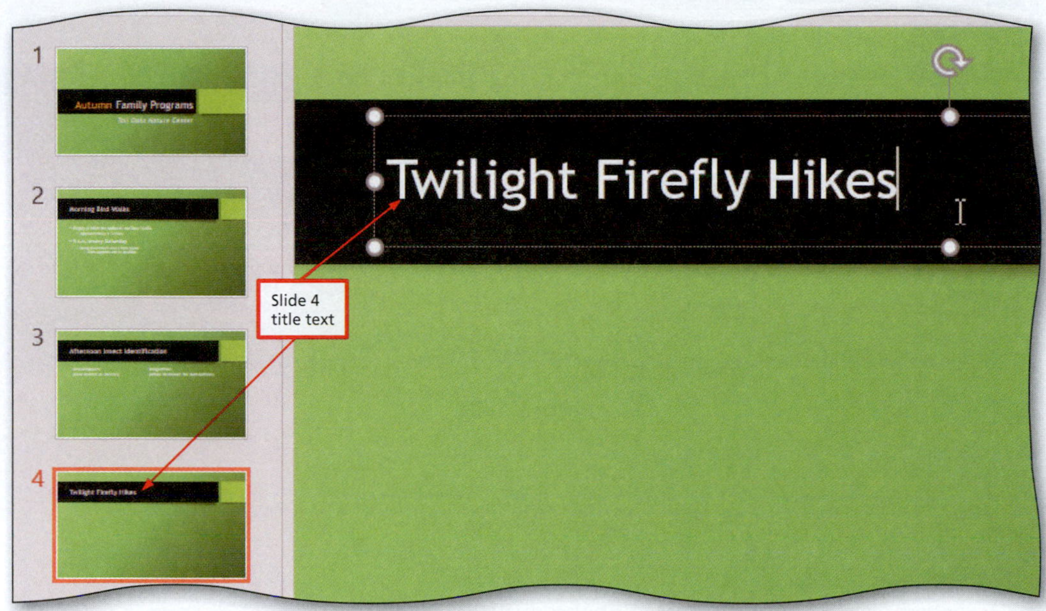

Figure 1–34

To Change the Theme

1 INSERT PRESENTATION SLIDES | 2 ENTER TEXT | 3 FORMAT TEXT | 4 INSERT GRAPHICAL ELEMENTS
5 SIZE & POSITION | 6 ENHANCE SLIDE SHOW | 7 DISPLAY SLIDES

A theme provides consistency in design and color throughout the entire presentation by setting the color scheme, font set, and layout of a presentation. This collection of formatting choices includes a set of colors (the Theme Colors group), a set of heading and content text fonts (the Theme Fonts group), and a set of lines and fill effects (the Theme Effects group). These groups allow you to choose and change the appearance of all the slides or individual slides in your presentation. ***Why?*** *At any time while creating the slide deck, you may decide to switch the theme so that the slides have a totally different appearance.* The following steps change the theme for this presentation from Berlin to Main Event.

- Click Design on the ribbon to display the Design tab (Figure 1–35).

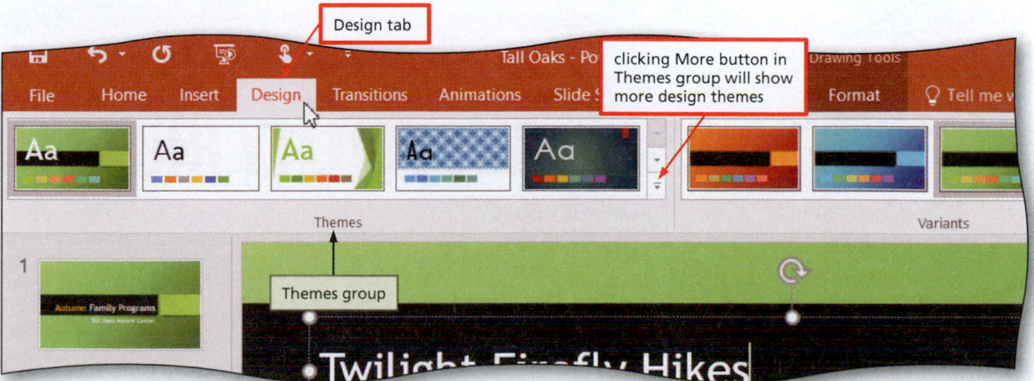

Figure 1–35

2

- Click the More button (Design tab | Themes group) to expand the gallery, which shows more theme gallery options. If necessary, scroll down to the bottom of the gallery to view the Main Event thumbnail (Figure 1–36).

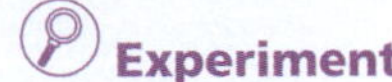

Experiment

- Point to various document themes in the Themes gallery and watch the colors and fonts change on the title slide.

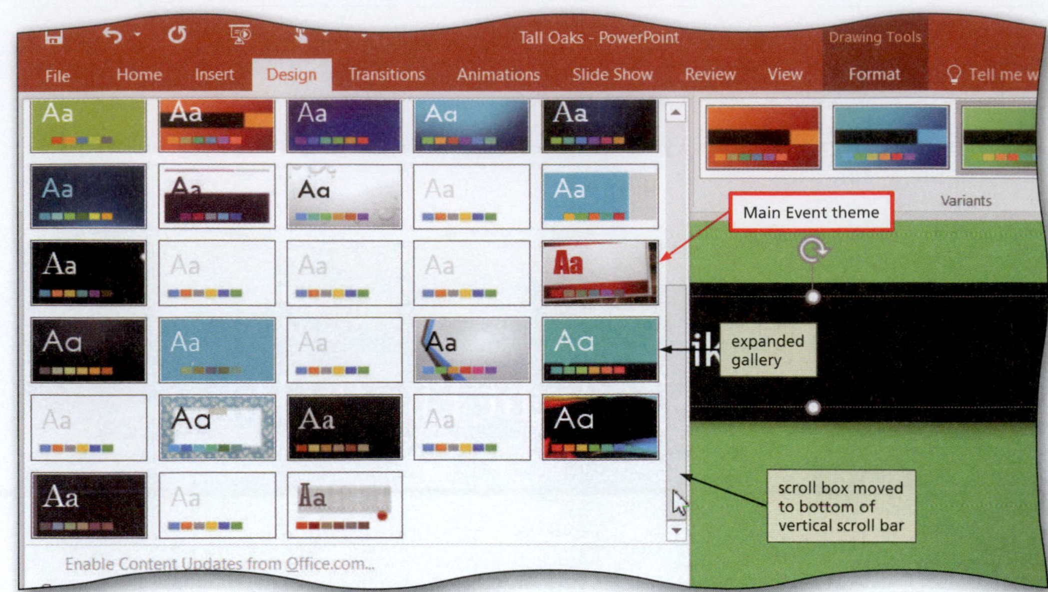

Figure 1–36

Q&A Are the themes displayed in a specific order?
No. Your themes might be in a different order than shown here.

How can I determine the theme names?
If you point to a theme, a ScreenTip with the theme's name appears on the screen.

3

- Click the Main Event theme to apply this theme to all four slides (Figure 1–37).

Q&A If I decide at some future time that this design does not fit the theme of my presentation, can I apply a different design?
Yes. You can repeat these steps at any time while creating your presentation.

Figure 1–37

To Change the Variant

When you began creating this presentation, you selected the Berlin theme and then chose a green variant. You can change the color variation at any time for any theme. ***Why?*** *The new Main Event theme has a default red color, but you want to emphasize the green color associated with nature, just like you initially did when you chose the green variant for the Berlin theme.* The following steps change the variant from red to green.

- Point to the green variant (Design tab | Variants group) to see a preview of the green variant on Slide 4 (Figure 1–38).

Experiment

- Point to the orange, green, and blue variants and watch the colors change on the slide.

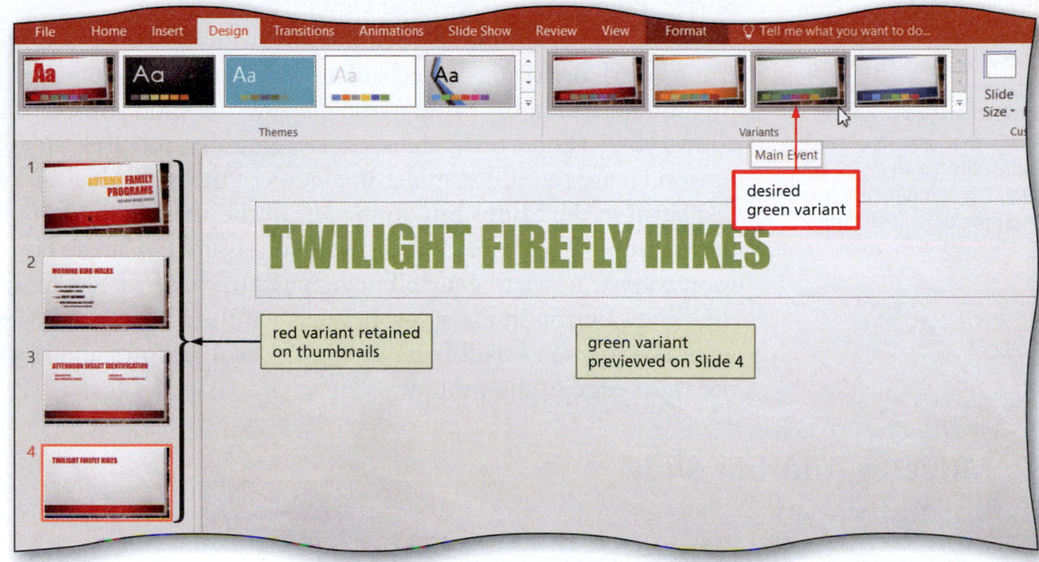

Figure 1–38

- Click the green variant to apply this color to all four slides (Figure 1–39).

Q&A If I decide at some future time that this color variation does not fit the theme of my presentation, can I apply a different variant?
Yes. You can repeat these steps at any time.

Figure 1–39

- Save the presentation again on the same storage location with the same file name.

Q&A Why should I save the presentation again?
You have made several modifications to the presentation since you last saved it. Thus, you should save it again.

Break Point: If you wish to take a break, this is a good place to do so. You can exit PowerPoint now. To resume at a later time, run PowerPoint, open the file called Tall Oaks, and continue following the steps from this location forward. For a detailed example of exiting PowerPoint, running PowerPoint, and opening a file, refer to the Office and Windows module at the beginning of the book.

PowerPoint Views

BTW
Welcome Back!
If you are designing a slide in your deck other than Slide 1 and then save and close the document, PowerPoint's Welcome back! feature allows you to continue where you left off at the last save when you open the document. You may need to adjust the zoom if you are working at a different level than the default setting.

The PowerPoint window display varies depending on the view. A **view** is the mode in which the presentation appears on the screen. You will use some views when you are developing slides and others when you are delivering your presentation. When creating a presentation, you most likely will use Normal, Slide Sorter, Notes Pane, and Outline views. When presenting your slides to an audience, you most likely will use Slide Sorter, Presenter, and Reading views.

The default view is **Normal view**, which is composed of three areas that allow you to work on various aspects of a presentation simultaneously. The large area in the middle, called the **Slide pane**, displays the slide you currently are developing and allows you to enter text, tables, charts, graphics, pictures, video, and other elements. As you create the slides, miniature views of the individual slides, called thumbnails, are displayed in the **Slides tab** on the left of the screen. You can rearrange the thumbnails in this pane. The **Notes pane**, by default, is hidden at the bottom of the window. If you want to type notes to yourself or remarks to share with your audience, you can click the Notes button in the status bar to open the Notes pane. After you have created at least two slides, a **scroll bar** containing **scroll arrows** and **scroll boxes** will appear on the right edge of the window.

To Move to Another Slide in Normal View

1 INSERT PRESENTATION SLIDES | 2 ENTER TEXT | 3 FORMAT TEXT | 4 INSERT GRAPHICAL ELEMENTS
5 SIZE & POSITION | 6 ENHANCE SLIDE SHOW | 7 DISPLAY SLIDES

Why? *When creating or editing a presentation in Normal view (the view you are currently using), you often want to display a slide other than the current one.* Before continuing with developing this project, you want to display the title slide. You can click the desired slide in the Slides tab or drag the scroll box on the vertical scroll bar; if you are using a touch screen, you can tap the desired slide in the Slides tab. When you drag the scroll box, the **slide indicator** shows the number and title of the slide you are about to display. Releasing shows the slide. The following steps move from Slide 4 to Slide 1 using the scroll box in the Slide pane.

- Position the pointer on the scroll box.
- Press and hold down the mouse button so that Slide: 4 of 4 Twilight Firefly Hikes appears in the slide indicator (Figure 1–40).

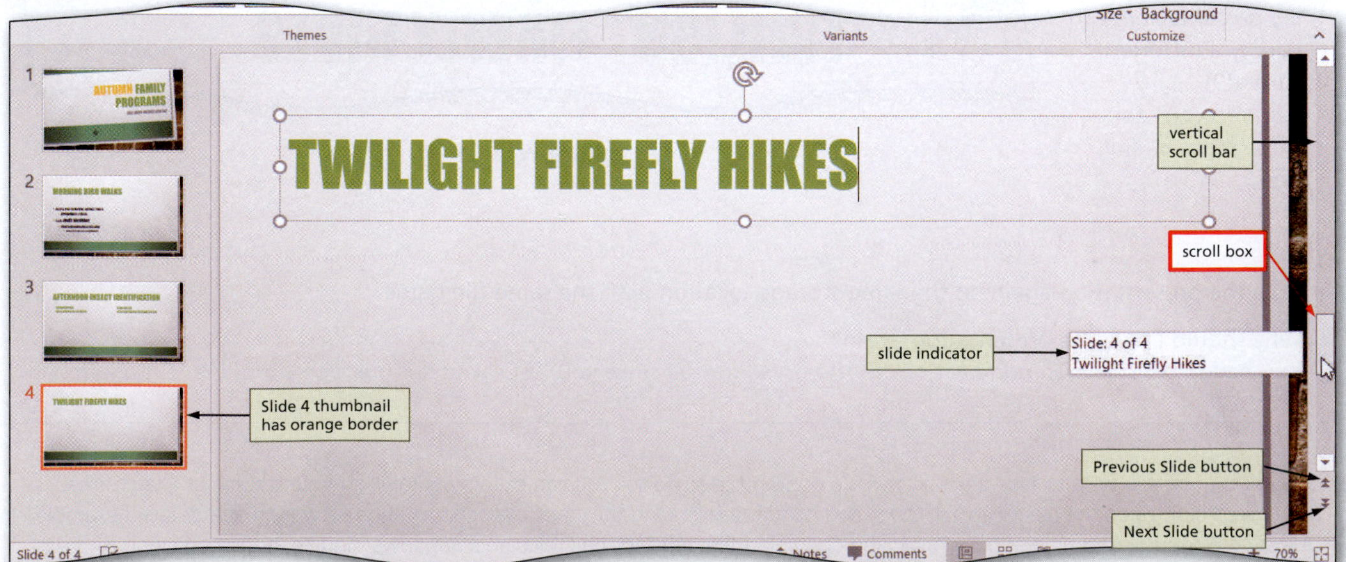

Figure 1–40

2

- Drag the scroll box up the vertical scroll bar until Slide: 1 of 4 Autumn Family Programs appears in the slide indicator (Figure 1–41).

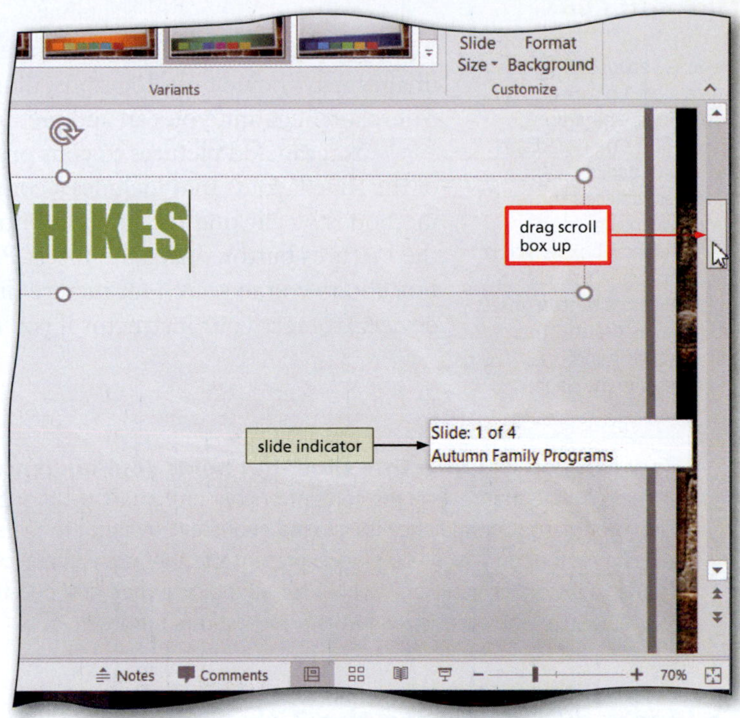

Figure 1–41

3

- Release so that Slide 1 appears in the Slide pane and the Slide 1 thumbnail has an orange border in the Slides tab (Figure 1–42).

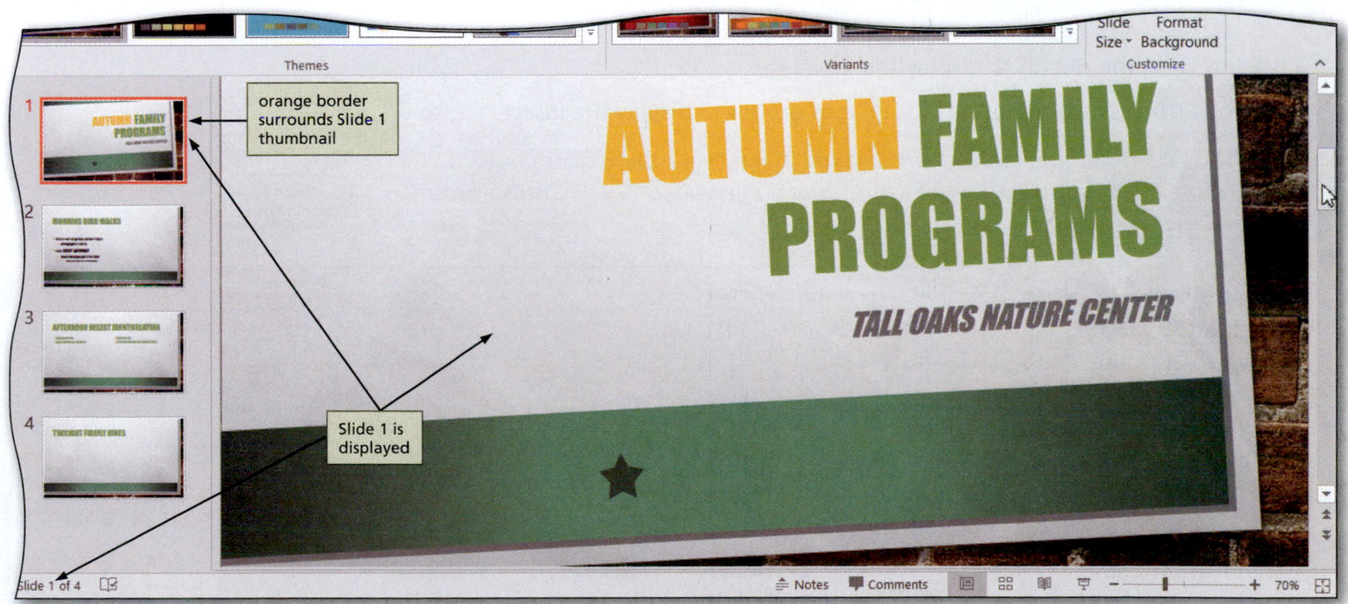

Figure 1–42

Other Ways

1. Click Next Slide button or Previous Slide button to move forward or back one slide
2. Click slide in Slides tab
3. Press PAGE DOWN or PAGE UP to move forward or back one slide

BTW
Microsoft Clip Organizer
Previous versions of Microsoft Office stored photos, illustrations, animations, videos, and other media in the Clip Organizer. Office 2016 has replaced this feature with the Insert Pictures dialog box, which is displayed when you click the Online Pictures button (Insert tab | Images group). You then can search for and insert files using Bing Image Search.

Inserting Pictures into Slides

Adding pictures can help increase the visual and audio appeal of many slides. These images may include photographs, illustrations, and other artwork. If you have a Microsoft account, you can add pictures from websites, including Flickr and OneDrive.

You can add pictures to your presentation in two ways. One way is by selecting one of the slide layouts that includes a content placeholder with a Pictures button. A second method is by clicking the Pictures button in the Images area on the Insert tab. Clicking the Pictures button opens the Insert Picture dialog box. The **Insert Picture dialog box** allows you to search for picture files that are stored on your computer or a storage device. Contact your instructor if you need the pictures used in the following steps.

CONSIDER THIS

How can you design a title slide that holds your audience's attention?
Develop a slide that reflects the content of your presentation but does so in a thought-provoking way. A title, at the very least, should prepare your audience for the material they are about to see and hear. Look for ways to focus attention on your theme and the method in which you plan to present this theme. A unique photograph or graphic can help generate interest. You may decide to introduce your topic with a startling fact, a rhetorical question, or a quotation. The device you choose depends upon your audience, the occasion, and the presentation's purpose.

To Insert a Picture into the Title Slide

1 INSERT PRESENTATION SLIDES | 2 ENTER TEXT | 3 FORMAT TEXT | **4 INSERT GRAPHICAL ELEMENTS**
5 SIZE & POSITION | 6 ENHANCE SLIDE SHOW | 7 DISPLAY SLIDES

Slide 1 uses the Title Slide layout, which has two placeholders for text but none for graphical content. You desire to place a graphic on Slide 1. ***Why?*** *It is likely that your viewers will see an image on this slide before they read any text, so you want to include a picture to create interest in the presentation and introduce your audience to the topic.* For this presentation, you will insert a photograph of several leaves that have changed colors. Later in this module, you will resize and position the picture in an appropriate location. The following steps add a picture to Slide 1.

1

- Click Insert on the ribbon to display the Insert tab.
- Click the Pictures button (Insert tab | Images group) to display the Insert Picture dialog box.

Q&A What should I do if no pictures are displayed when I click the Pictures button?
You may need to click the Online Pictures button instead of the Pictures button.

2

- Navigate to the Data Files and the Module 01 folder. Click the Autumn Leaves picture to select that file (Figure 1–43).

Q&A Why do I see only a list of file names and not thumbnails of the pictures in my folder?
Your view is different from the view shown in Figure 1–43.

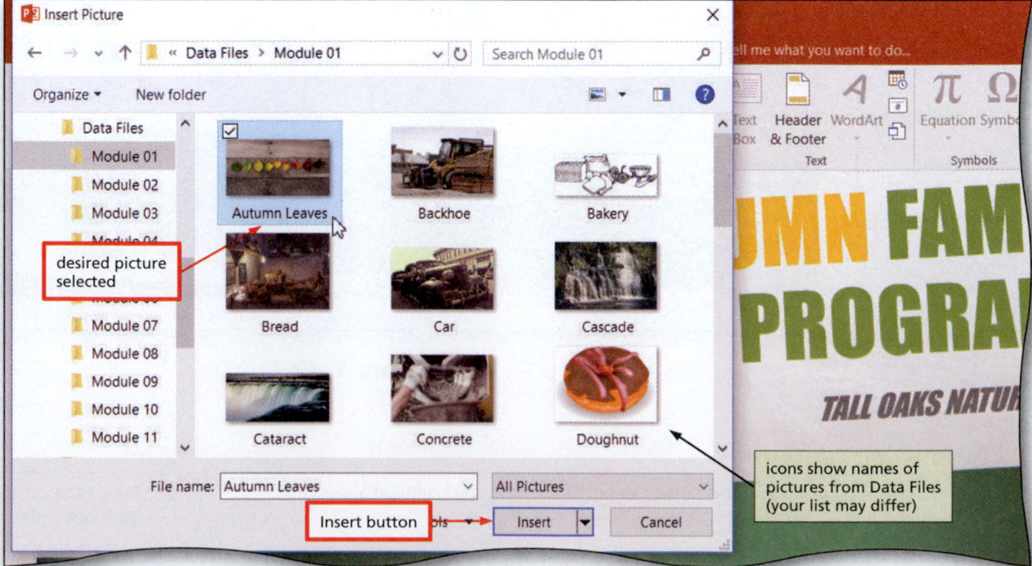

Figure 1–43

3

- Click the Insert button (Insert Picture dialog box) to insert the picture into Slide 1 (Figure 1–44).

Q&A Can I double-click the picture or file name instead of selecting it and clicking the Insert button?
Yes. Either method inserts the picture.

Why is this picture displayed in this location on the slide?
The slide layout does not have a content placeholder, so PowerPoint inserts the file in an area of the slide. You will move and resize the picture later in this module.

Figure 1–44

To Insert a Picture into a Slide without a Content Placeholder

The next step is to add an owl picture to Slide 2. This slide has a bulleted list in the text placeholder, so the icon group does not display in the center of the placeholder. Later in this module, you will resize the inserted picture. The following steps add one picture to Slide 2.

1 Click the Slide 2 thumbnail in the Slides tab to display Slide 2.

2 Click Insert on the ribbon to display the Insert tab and then click the Pictures button (Insert tab | Images group) to display the Insert Picture dialog box.

3 If necessary, scroll down the list of files, click Owl to select the file, and then click the Insert button to insert the picture into Slide 2 (Figure 1–45).

Q&A Why is my picture a different size from the one shown in Figure1-1b?
The clip was inserted into the slide and not into a content placeholder. You will resize the picture later in this module.

desired picture inserted into Slide 2

Figure 1–45

BTW

Wrapping Text around a Photo
PowerPoint does not allow you to wrap text around a picture or other graphics, such as tables, shapes, and charts. This feature, however, is available in Word.

To Insert a Picture into a Content Placeholder

1 INSERT PRESENTATION SLIDES | 2 ENTER TEXT | 3 FORMAT TEXT | 4 INSERT GRAPHICAL ELEMENTS
5 SIZE & POSITION | 6 ENHANCE SLIDE SHOW | 7 DISPLAY SLIDES

Slide 3 uses the Comparison layout, which has a content placeholder below each of the two headings. You desire to insert pictures into both content placeholders. ***Why?*** *You want to display two insects that participants likely will identify during the program at the nature center.* The following steps insert a picture of a grasshopper into the left content placeholder and a dragonfly into the right content placeholder on Slide 3.

- Click the Slide 3 thumbnail in the Slides tab to display Slide 3 (Figure 1–46).

Figure 1–46

- Click the Pictures icon in the left content placeholder to select that placeholder and to open the Insert Picture dialog box.
- If necessary, scroll down the list of files, click Grasshopper to select the file, and then double-click to insert the picture into the left content placeholder (Figure 1–47).

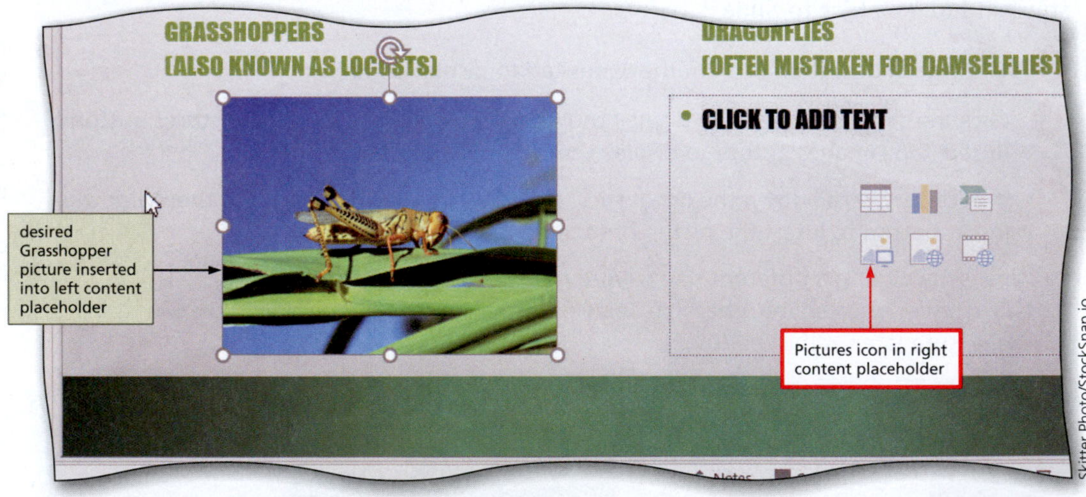

Figure 1–47

Q&A Do I need to select the file name before double-clicking to insert the picture?
No. You just can double-click the file name.

3
- Click the Pictures icon in the right content placeholder to select that placeholder and to open the Insert Picture dialog box.
- If necessary, scroll down the list to display the Dragonfly file name and then insert this picture into the right content placeholder (Figure 1–48).

Figure 1–48

To Insert a Picture into a Slide without a Content Placeholder

Next, you will add a picture to Slide 4. This picture is an illustration, not an actual photograph, of a firefly. You will not insert this file into a content placeholder, so it will display in the center of the slide. Later in this module, you will resize this picture. You locate and insert illustrations in the same manner you used to insert photos. The following steps add an illustration picture to Slide 4.

1. Click the Slide 4 thumbnail in the Slides tab.
2. Display the Insert tab, click the Pictures button, and then insert the Firefly file into Slide 4 (Figure 1–49).

Figure 1–49

Break Point: If you wish to take a break, this is a good place to do so. You can save your presentation and then exit PowerPoint now. To resume at a later time, run PowerPoint, open the file called Tall Oaks, and continue following the steps from this location forward.

Resizing Photos and Illustrations

Sometimes it is necessary to change the size of pictures and illustrations. **Resizing** includes enlarging or reducing the size of a graphic. You can resize these images using a variety of techniques. One method involves changing the size of a picture by specifying exact dimensions in a dialog box. Another method involves sliding or dragging one of the graphic's sizing handles to the desired location. A selected graphic appears surrounded by a **selection rectangle**, which has small circles, called **sizing handles** or move handles, at each corner and middle location.

To Proportionally Resize Pictures

1 INSERT PRESENTATION SLIDES | 2 ENTER TEXT | 3 FORMAT TEXT | 4 INSERT GRAPHICAL ELEMENTS
5 SIZE & POSITION | 6 ENHANCE SLIDE SHOW | 7 DISPLAY SLIDES

Why? On Slides 1, 2, and 4, the picture and illustration sizes are too large to display aesthetically on the slides. At times it is important to maintain the proportions of a picture, such as when a person is featured prominently. To change the size of a picture and keep the width and height in proportion to each other, drag the corner sizing handles to view how the image will look on the slide. Using these corner handles maintains the graphic's original proportions. If, however, the proportions do not need to be maintained precisely, as with the owl picture on Slide 2, drag the side sizing handles to alter the proportions so that the graphic's height and width become larger or smaller. The following steps proportionally decrease the size of the Slide 1 picture using a corner sizing handle.

- Click the Slide 1 thumbnail in the Slides tab to display Slide 1.
- Click the leaves picture to select it and display the selection rectangle.
- Point to the lower-right corner sizing handle on the picture so that the pointer changes to a two-headed arrow (Figure 1–50).

Q&A I am using a touch screen and do not see a two-headed arrow when I press and hold the lower-right sizing handle. Why?
Touch screens may not display pointers; you can just press and slide sizing handles to resize.

Figure 1–50

2

- Drag the sizing handle diagonally toward the upper-left corner of the slide until the lower-right sizing handle or the crosshair is positioned approximately as shown in Figure 1–51.

Q&A What if the picture is not the same size as the one shown in Figure 1–51?
Repeat Steps 1 and 2.

Can I drag any corner sizing handle diagonally inward toward the opposite corner to resize the picture?
Yes.

3

- Release to resize the picture.

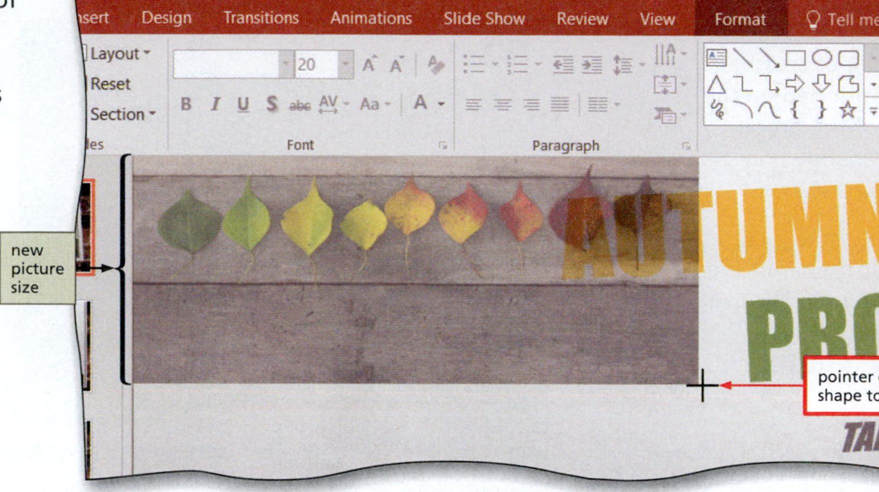

Figure 1–51

To Nonproportionally Resize the Photograph on Slide 2

1 INSERT PRESENTATION SLIDES | 2 ENTER TEXT | 3 FORMAT TEXT | 4 INSERT GRAPHICAL ELEMENTS
5 SIZE & POSITION | 6 ENHANCE SLIDE SHOW | 7 DISPLAY SLIDES

***Why?** The height of the owl picture in Slide 2 extends from the top to the bottom of the slide. The width, however, will cover some of the text when the picture is positioned on the right side of the slide.* The width of this picture can be decreased slightly without negatively distorting the original image. You can decrease the width of a picture by sliding or dragging one of the sizing handles on the sides of the image. The following steps resize the width of the nature bottle picture using a sizing handle along the side of the image.

1

- Display Slide 2 and then click the owl picture to select it and display the selection rectangle.
- Click the Zoom Out button as many times as necessary until the Zoom level is 50%.
- Point to the middle sizing handle on the bottom edge of the picture so that the pointer changes to a two-headed arrow (Figure 1–52).

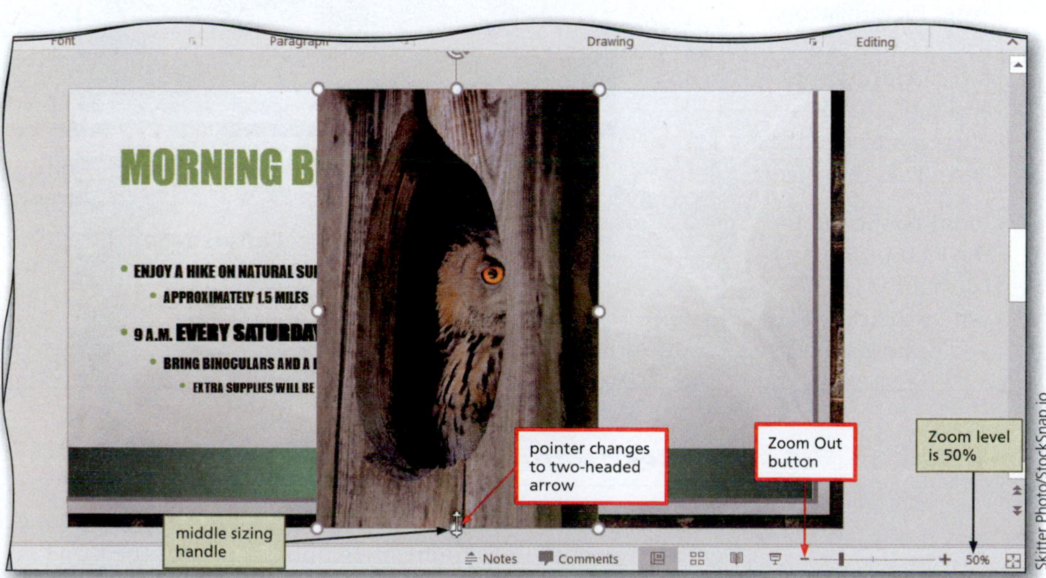

Figure 1–52

2

- Drag the sizing handle upward until the sizing handle or crosshair is positioned on the top of the green bar, as shown in Figure 1–53.

Q&A What if the picture is not the same size as the one shown in Figure 1–53?
Repeat Steps 1 and 2.

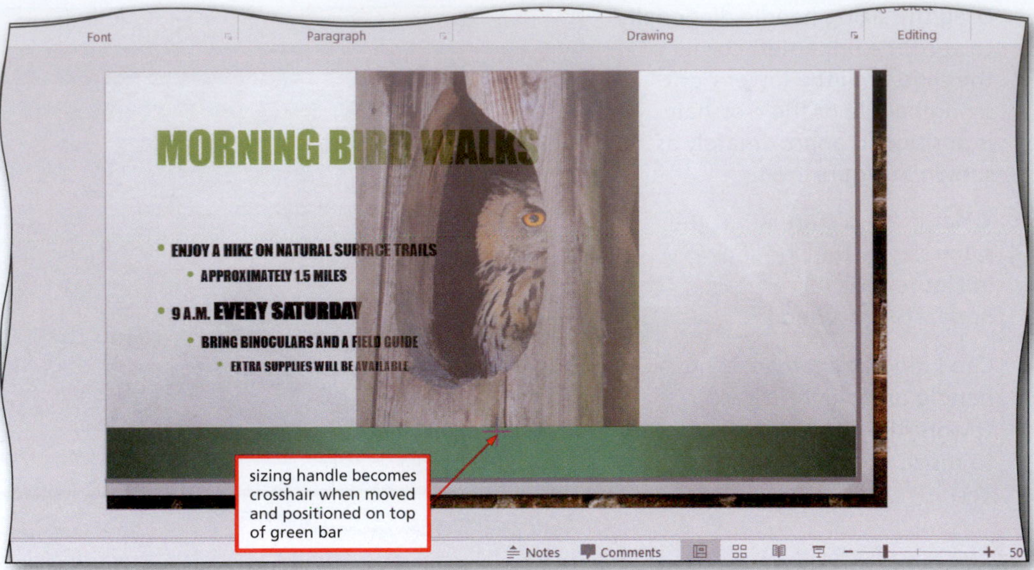

Figure 1–53

3

- Release to resize the picture.
- Click outside the picture to deselect it (Figure 1–54).

Q&A What if I want to return the picture to its original size and start again?
With the picture selected, click the Reset Picture arrow (Picture Tools Format tab | Adjust group) and then click Reset Picture & Size in the Reset Picture gallery.

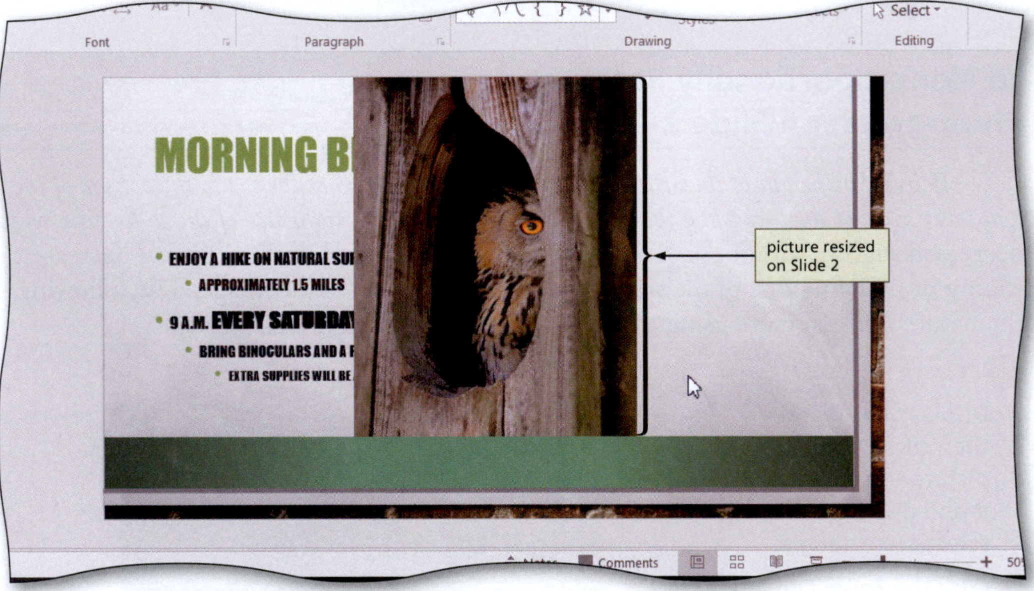

Figure 1–54

What happened to the Picture Tools Format tab?
When you click outside the picture, PowerPoint deselects the object and removes the Picture Tools Format tab from the screen.

To Resize the Illustration on Slide 4

The firefly picture illustration on Slide 4 can be reduced slightly to fit entirely on the slide. You resize an illustration in the same manner that you resize a photograph. You want to maintain the proportions of the character and nature in this illustration, so you will drag one of the corner sizing handles. The following steps resize this illustration using a corner sizing handle.

1. Display Slide 4 and then click the firefly illustration to select it.
2. Drag any corner sizing handle on the illustration diagonally inward until the illustration is positioned and resized approximately as shown in Figure 1–55.

Figure 1–55

To Move Pictures

1 INSERT PRESENTATION SLIDES | 2 ENTER TEXT | 3 FORMAT TEXT | 4 INSERT GRAPHICAL ELEMENTS
5 SIZE & POSITION | 6 ENHANCE SLIDE SHOW | 7 DISPLAY SLIDES

***Why?** After you insert a photo or an illustration on a slide, you might want to reposition it. The leaves picture on Slide 1 could be moved to the lower-left side of the slide, the owl on Slide 2 could be moved to the right side of the slide, and the illustration on Slide 4 could be positioned in the center of the slide.* PowerPoint displays **Smart Guides** automatically when a picture, shape, or other object is moved and is close to lining up with another slide element. These layout guides, which display as dashed lines, help you align slide elements vertically and horizontally. They display when aligning to the left, right, top, bottom, and middle of placeholders and other objects on a slide. For example, a Smart Guide will display to help you align the right or left edge of a picture in relation to a text placeholder or to another picture. The following steps center the illustration on Slide 4 and move the pictures on Slides 2 and 1.

1.
- If necessary, click the firefly illustration on Slide 4 to select it.
- With the four-headed arrow displaying, drag the illustration downward and toward the left until the horizontal Smart Guide is displayed under the title text placeholder and the vertical Smart Guide is displayed through the center of the slide, as shown in Figure 1–56, and then release.
- If necessary, select the illustration and then use the ARROW keys to position it precisely as shown in Figure 1–56.

Q&A The firefly still is not located exactly where I want it to display. What can I do to align the image?
Press the CTRL key while you press the ARROW keys. This key combination moves the illustration in smaller increments than when you press only an ARROW key.

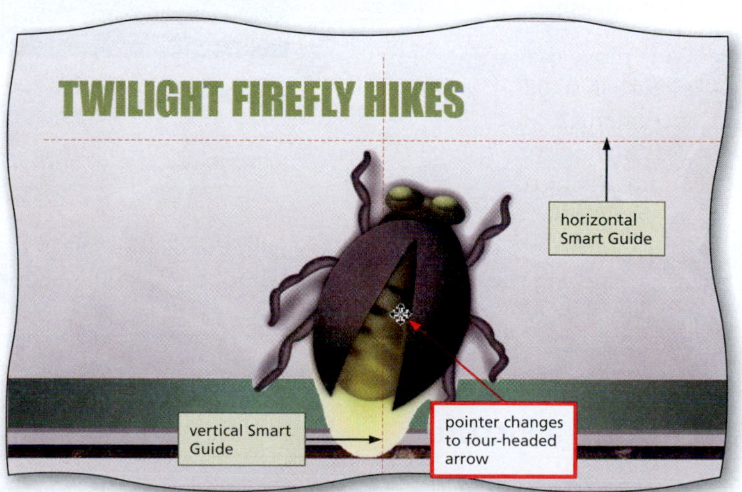

Figure 1–56

2

- Display Slide 2 and then click the owl picture to select it.
- Drag the picture downward and to the right until the horizontal Smart Guide is displayed above the title text placeholder and the right edge is aligned with the vertical gray bar on the right side of the slide (Figure 1–57).

Figure 1–57

3

- Display Slide 1 and then click the leaves picture to select it.
- Drag the picture downward until the horizontal Smart Guide is displayed under the title text placeholder and the vertical Smart Guide is displayed near the left side of the slide, as shown in Figure 1–58, and then release.

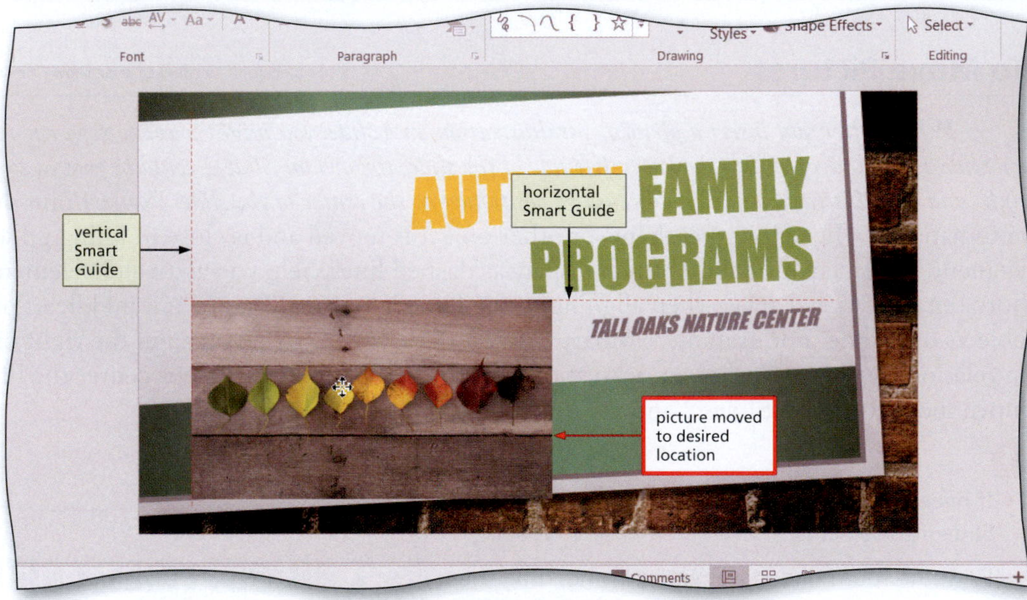

Figure 1–58

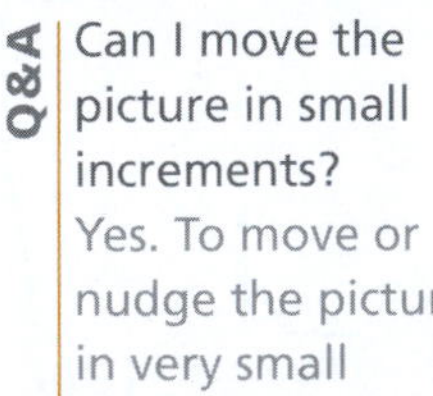

Q&A Can I move the picture in small increments?

Yes. To move or nudge the picture in very small increments, hold down the CTRL key with the picture selected while pressing the ARROW keys. You cannot perform this action using a touch screen.

To Rotate a Picture

1 INSERT PRESENTATION SLIDES | 2 ENTER TEXT | 3 FORMAT TEXT | 4 INSERT GRAPHICAL ELEMENTS
5 SIZE & POSITION | 6 ENHANCE SLIDE SHOW | 7 DISPLAY SLIDES

***Why?** The Main Event Title Slide layout is angled, so the picture would complement the design by being angled, too.* Dragging the **rotation handle** above a selected object allows you to rotate an object in any direction. The following steps rotate the leaves picture.

- With the leaves picture selected, position the mouse pointer over the rotation handle so that it changes to a Free Rotate pointer (Figure 1–59).

Figure 1–59

- Drag the rotation handle counterclockwise and then move the picture so that it is displayed as shown in Figure 1–60.

Figure 1–60

Ending a Slide Show with a Closing Slide

All the text for the slides in the Tall Oaks slide show has been entered. This presentation thus far consists of a title slide, one text slide with a multilevel bulleted list, a third slide with a Comparison layout, and a fourth slide for an illustration. A closing slide that resembles the title slide is the final slide to create.

CONSIDER THIS

What factors should you consider when developing a closing slide for the presentation?

After the last slide appears during a slide show, the default PowerPoint setting is to end the presentation with a **black slide**. This black slide appears only when the slide show is running and concludes the slide show, so your audience never sees the PowerPoint window. It is a good idea, however, to end your presentation with a final closing slide to display at the end of the presentation. This slide ends the presentation gracefully and should be an exact copy, or a very similar copy, of your title slide. The audience will recognize that the presentation is drawing to a close when this slide appears. It can remain on the screen when the audience asks questions, approaches the speaker for further information, or exits the room.

To Duplicate a Slide

Why? When two slides contain similar information and have the same format, duplicating one slide and then making minor modifications to the new slide saves time and increases consistency. Slide 5 will have the same layout and design as Slide 1. The most expedient method of creating this slide is to copy Slide 1 and then make minor modifications to the new slide. The following steps duplicate the title slide.

1

- With Slide 1 selected, click the New Slide arrow (Home tab | Slides group) to display the Main Event layout gallery (Figure 1–61).

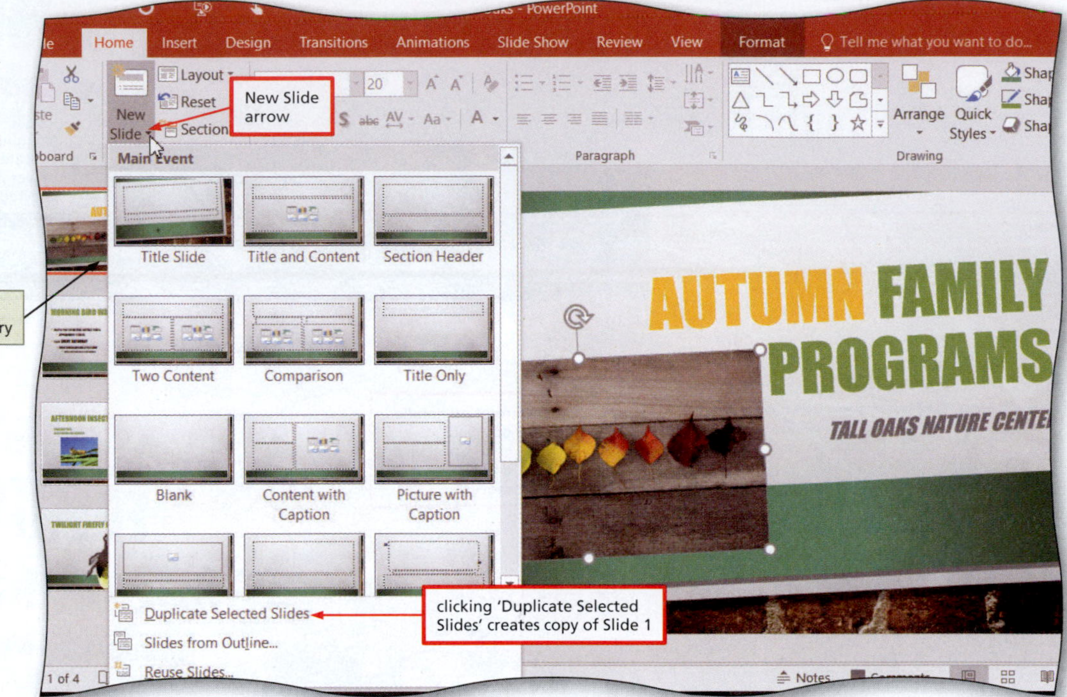

Figure 1–61

2

- Click 'Duplicate Selected Slides' in the Main Event layout gallery to create a new Slide 2, which is a duplicate of Slide 1 (Figure 1–62).

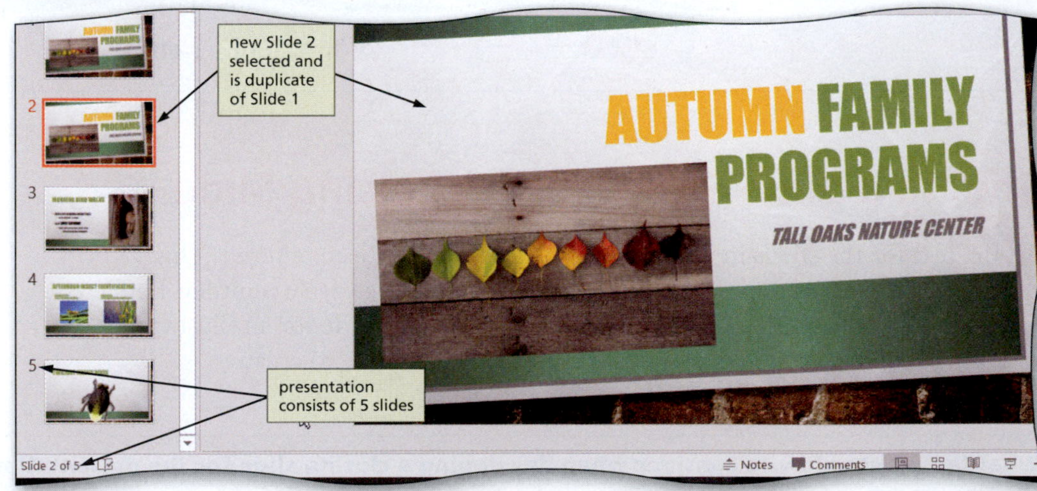

Figure 1–62

To Arrange a Slide

The new Slide 2 was inserted directly below Slide 1 because Slide 1 was the selected slide. This duplicate slide needs to display at the end of the presentation directly after the final title and content slide. ***Why?*** *It is a closing slide that reinforces the concept presented in Slide 1 and indicates to your audiences that your presentation is ending.*

Changing slide order is an easy process and is best performed in the Slides tab. When you click the thumbnail and begin to drag it to a new location, the remaining thumbnails realign to show the new sequence. When you release, the slide drops into the desired location. Hence, this process of sliding or dragging and then dropping the thumbnail in a new location is called **drag and drop**. You can use the drag-and-drop method to move any selected item, including text and graphics. The following step moves the new Slide 2 to the end of the presentation so that it becomes a closing slide.

- With Slide 2 selected, drag the Slide 2 slide thumbnail below the last slide in the Slides tab so that it becomes the new Slide 5 (Figure 1–63).

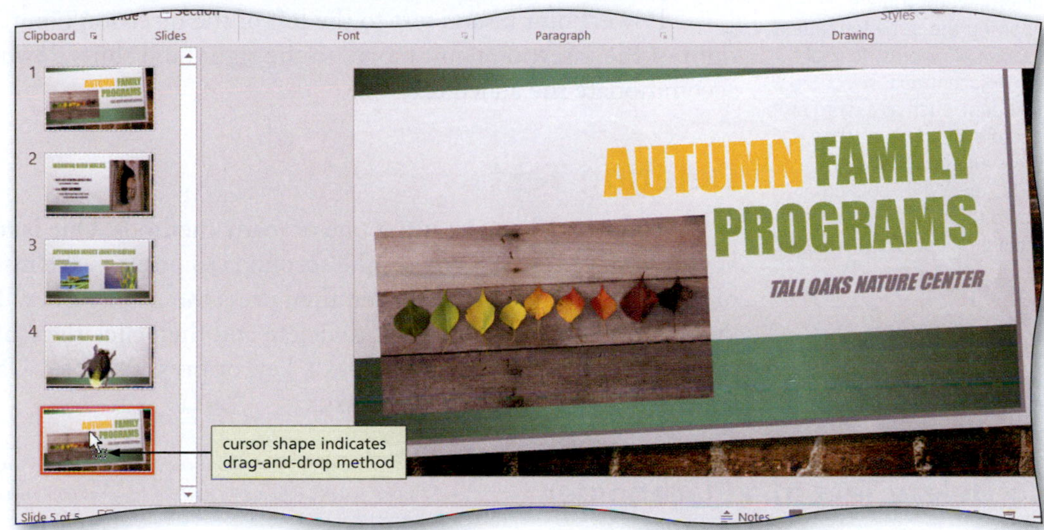

Figure 1–63

Other Ways

1. Click Slide Sorter button on status bar, drag thumbnail to new location
2. Click Slide Sorter button (View tab | Presentation Views group), click slide thumbnail, drag thumbnail to new location

Break Point: If you wish to take a break, this is a good place to do so. Be sure to save the Tall Oaks file again and then you can exit PowerPoint. To resume at a later time, run PowerPoint, open the file called Tall Oaks, and continue following the steps from this location forward.

Making Changes to Slide Text Content

After creating slides in a presentation, you may find that you want to make changes to the text. Changes may be required because a slide contains an error, the scope of the presentation shifts, or the style is inconsistent. This section explains the types of changes that commonly occur when creating a presentation.

You generally make three types of changes to text in a presentation: additions, replacements, and deletions.

- Additions are necessary when you omit text from a slide and need to add it later. You may need to insert text in the form of a sentence, word, or single character. For example, you may want to add the presenter's middle name on the title slide.
- Replacements are needed when you want to revise the text in a presentation. For example, you may want to substitute the word, *their*, for the word, *there*.

- Deletions are required when text on a slide is incorrect or no longer is relevant to the presentation. For example, a slide may look cluttered. Therefore, you may want to remove one of the bulleted paragraphs to add more space.

Editing text in PowerPoint basically is the same as editing text in a word processing program. The following sections illustrate the most common changes made to text in a presentation.

BTW
Selecting Nonadjacent Text
In PowerPoint, you can use keyboard keys to select letters, numbers, or special characters not next to each other. This is especially helpful when you are applying the same formatting to multiple words. To select nonadjacent text, select the first item, such as a word or paragraph, as usual; then, press and hold down the CTRL key. While holding down the CTRL key, select additional items.

Replacing Text in an Existing Slide

When you need to correct a word or phrase, you can replace the text by selecting the text to be replaced and then typing the new text. As soon as you press any key on the keyboard, the selected text is deleted and the new text is displayed.

PowerPoint inserts text to the left of the insertion point. The text to the right of the insertion point moves to the right (and shifts downward if necessary) to accommodate the added text.

Deleting Text

You can delete text using one of many methods. One is to use the BACKSPACE key to remove text just typed. The second is to position the insertion point to the left of the text you want to delete and then press the DELETE key. The third method is to drag through the text you want to delete and then click the Cut button on the mini toolbar, press DELETE or BACKSPACE key, or press CTRL+X. Use the third method when deleting large sections of text.

To Delete Text in a Placeholder

1 INSERT PRESENTATION SLIDES | 2 ENTER TEXT | **3 FORMAT TEXT** | 4 INSERT GRAPHICAL ELEMENTS
5 SIZE & POSITION | 6 ENHANCE SLIDE SHOW | **7 DISPLAY SLIDES**

Why? *To keep the ending slide clean and simple, you want to edit a few words in the slide title and subtitle text.* The following steps change Autumn to Register For and then change Tall Oaks Nature Center to Call 555-8928 today! in the placeholders.

- With Slide 5 selected, position the pointer immediately to the left of the first character of the text to be selected in the title text placeholder (in this case, the A in the word, Autumn).
- Drag the pointer through the last character of the text to be selected (in this case, the n in the word, Autumn) (Figure 1–64).

Q&A
Can I drag from left to right or right to left?
Yes. Either direction will select the letters.

Could I also have selected the word, Autumn, by double-clicking it?
Yes. Either method works to select a word.

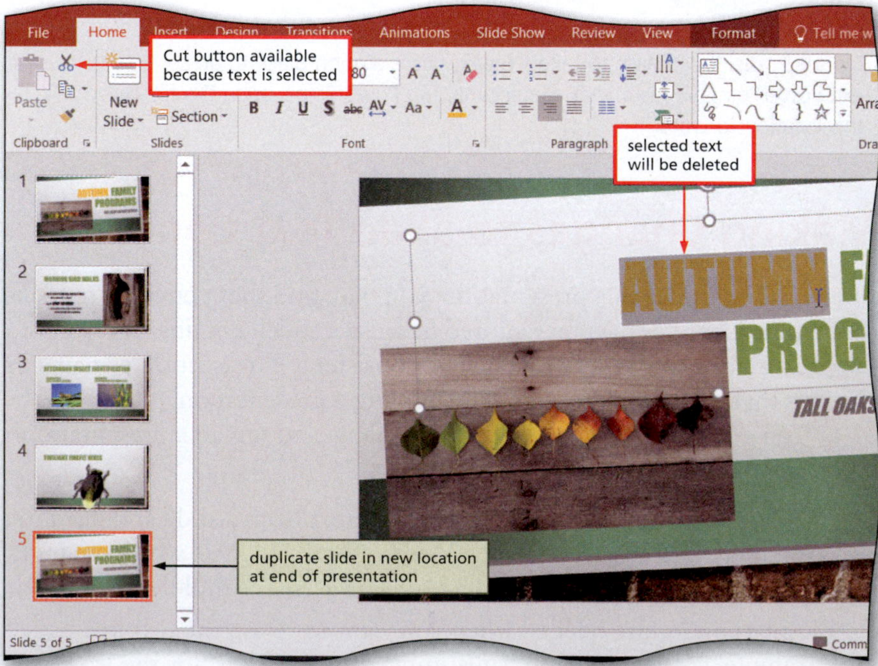

Figure 1–64

2

- Press the DELETE key to delete the selected text.
- Type `Register for` as the first words in the title text placeholder (Figure 1–65).

Q&A Could I have typed these words while the word, Autumn, was selected without cutting the text first?

Yes. Either method works to replace words. You will use this alternate method in the next step.

Why does the text display with all capital letters despite the fact that I am typing uppercase and lowercase letters?

The Main Event theme uses the All Caps effect for the title and subtitle text. This effect converts lowercase letters to uppercase letters.

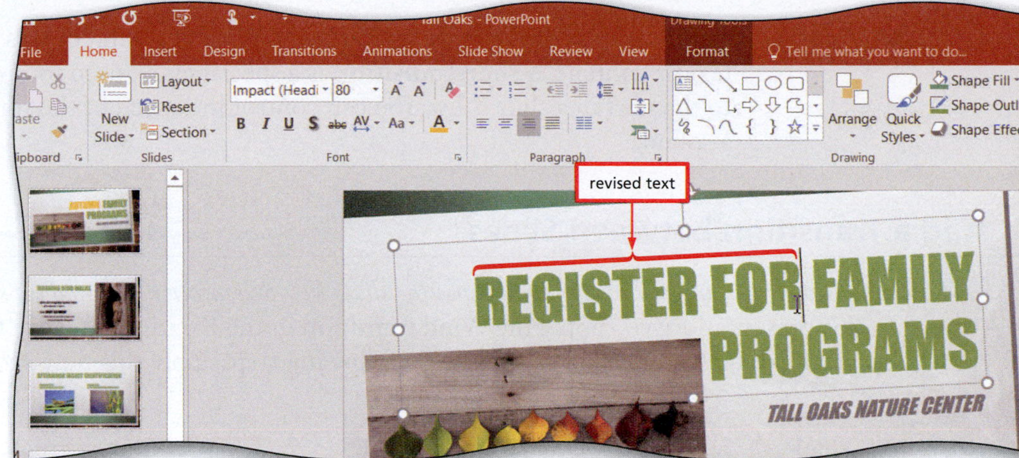

Figure 1–65

3

- Position the pointer anywhere in the subtitle text placeholder other than on the picture and then triple-click to select all the text, Tall Oaks Nature Center (Figure 1–66).

Figure 1–66

- Type `Call 816-555-8928 today!` as the new subtitle text (Figure 1-67).
- If requested by your instructor, change the last four digits of the phone number in the subtitle text placeholder, 8928, to the last four digits of your phone number.

Figure 1–67

Other Ways

1. Right-click selected text, click Cut on shortcut menu
2. Select text, press DELETE or BACKSPACE key
3. Select text, press CTRL+X

Adding a Transition

PowerPoint includes a wide variety of visual and sound effects that can be applied to text or content. A **slide transition** is a special effect used to progress from one slide to the next in a slide show. You can control the speed of the transition effect and add a sound.

To Add a Transition between Slides

1 INSERT PRESENTATION SLIDES | 2 ENTER TEXT | 3 FORMAT TEXT | 4 INSERT GRAPHICAL ELEMENTS
5 SIZE & POSITION | 6 ENHANCE SLIDE SHOW | 7 DISPLAY SLIDES

Why? Transitions add interest when you advance the slides in a presentation and make a slide show presentation look professional. In this presentation, you apply the Wind transition in the Exciting category to all slides and change the transition speed from 2 seconds to 3 seconds. The following steps apply this transition to the presentation.

- Click the Transitions tab on the ribbon and then point to the More button (Transitions tab | Transition to This Slide group) in the Transition to This Slide gallery (Figure 1–68).

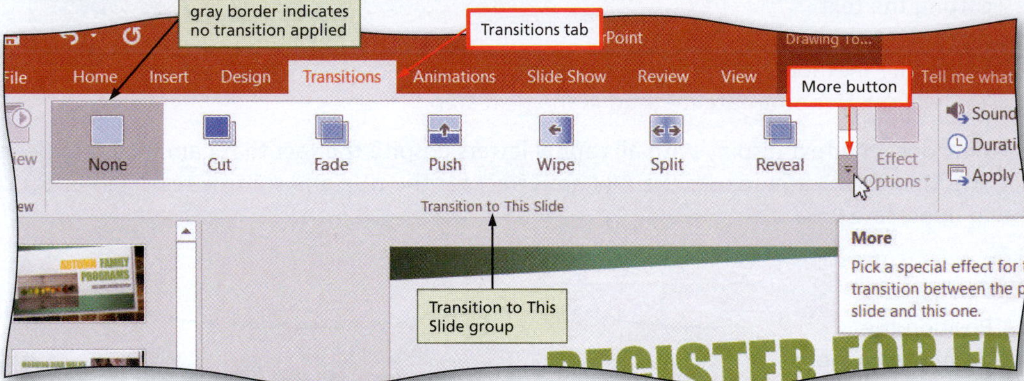

Figure 1–68

Q&A Is a transition applied now?
No. None, the first slide icon in the Transition to This Slide group, is selected, which indicates no transition has been applied.

- Click the More button to expand the Transitions gallery.
- Point to the Wind transition in the Exciting category in the Transitions gallery (Figure 1–69).

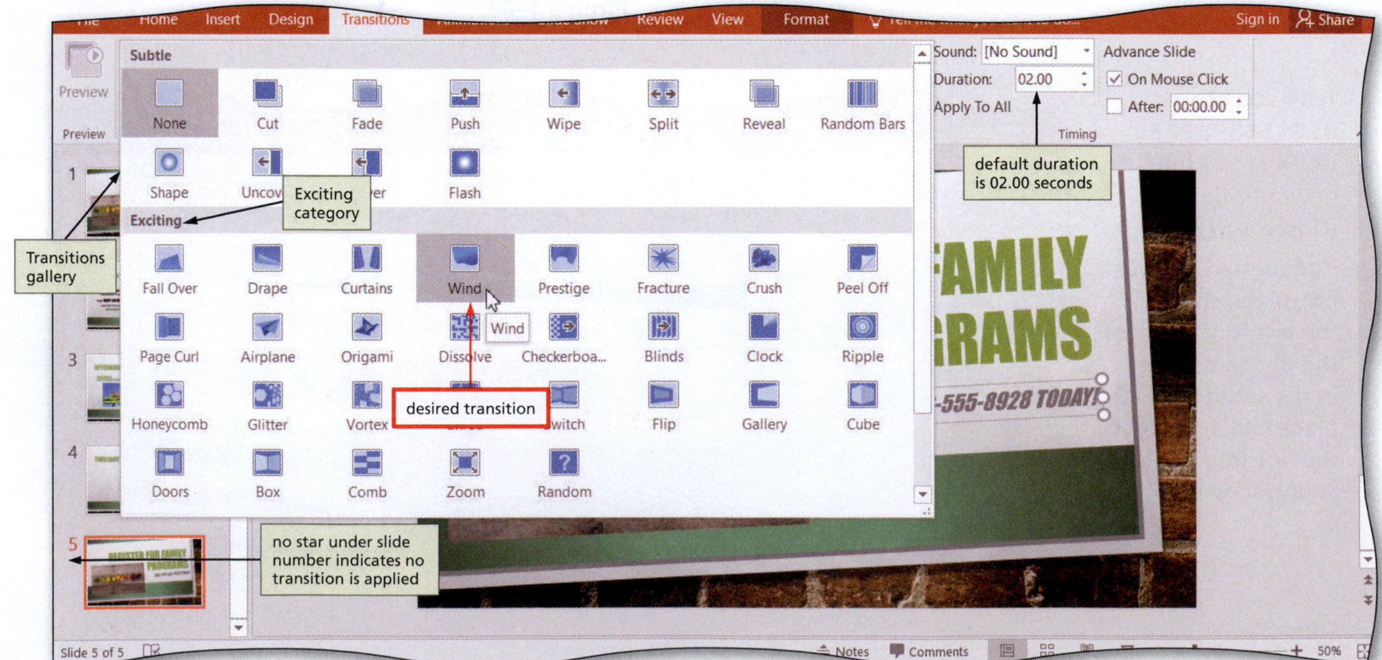

Figure 1–69

3

- Click Wind in the Exciting category in the Transitions gallery to view a preview of this transition and to apply this transition to the closing slide.

Q&A Why does a star appear next to Slide 5 in the Slides tab?
The star indicates that a transition animation effect is applied to that slide.

- Click the Duration up arrow (Transitions tab | Timing group) four times to change the transition speed from 02.00 seconds to 03.00 seconds (Figure 1–70).

Figure 1–70

Q&A Why did the time change from the default 02.00 to 03.00?
Each transition has a default duration time. The default Wind transition time is 02.00 seconds.

4

- Click the Preview Transitions button (Transitions tab | Preview area) to view the transition and the new transition time (Figure 1–71).

Q&A Can I adjust the duration time I just set?
Yes. Click the Duration up or down arrows or type a speed in the Duration box and preview the transition until you find the time that best fits your presentation.

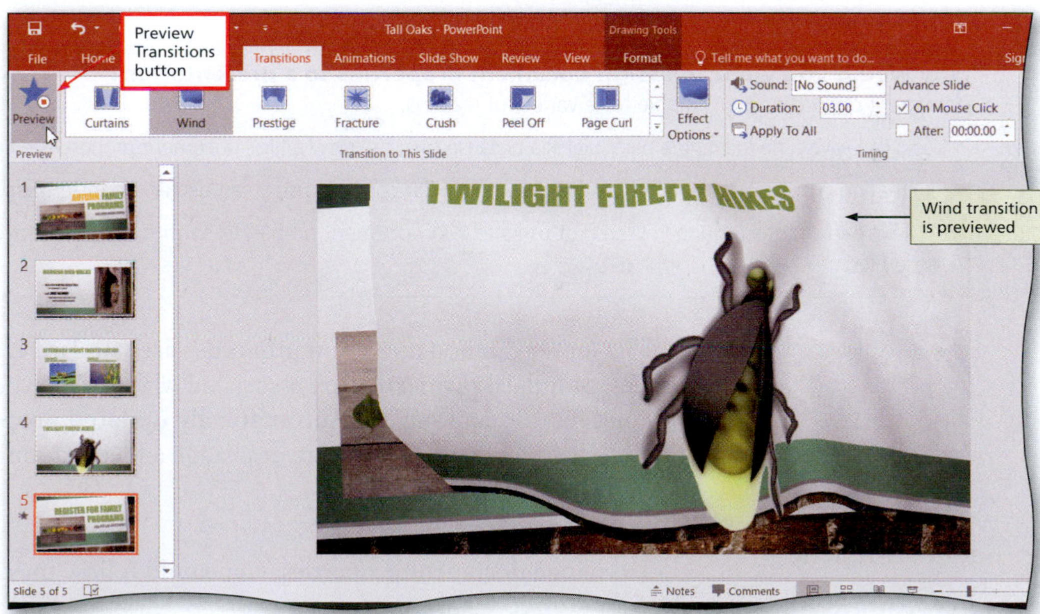

Figure 1–71

5

- Click the 'Apply To All' button (Transitions tab | Timing group) to apply the Wind transition and the increased transition time to Slides 1 through 4 in the presentation (Figure 1–72).

Q&A What if I want to apply a different transition and duration to each slide in the presentation?
Repeat Steps 2 and 3 for each slide individually.

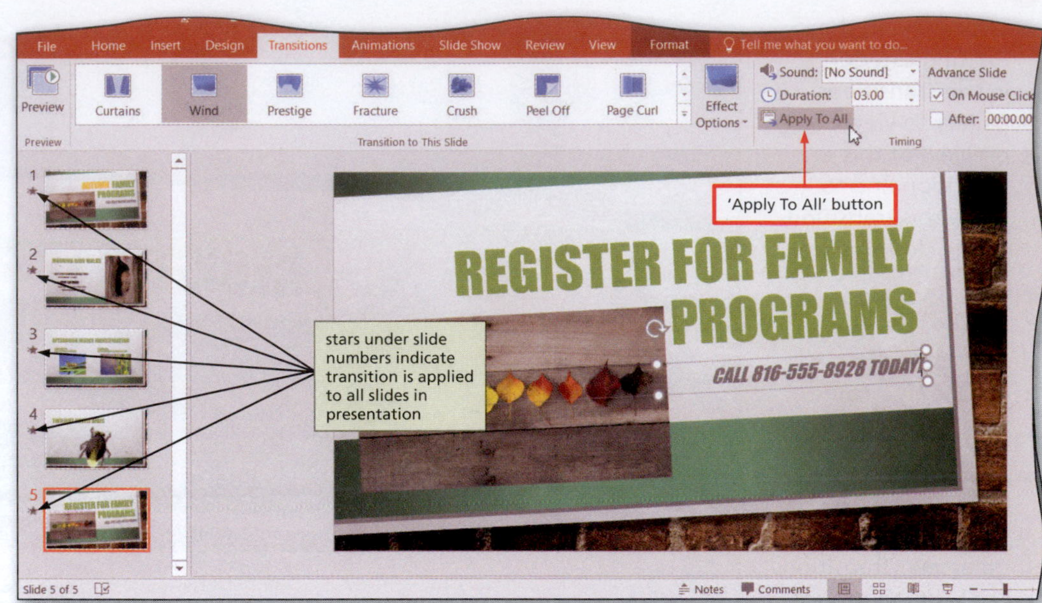
'Apply To All' button
stars under slide numbers indicate transition is applied to all slides in presentation
REGISTER FOR FAMILY PROGRAMS
CALL 816-555-8928 TODAY!

Figure 1–72

Document Properties

PowerPoint helps you organize and identify your files by using **document properties**, which are the details about a file such as the project author, title, and subject. For example, a class name or presentation topic can describe the file's purpose or content.

CONSIDER THIS

Why would you want to assign document properties to a presentation?

Document properties are valuable for a variety of reasons:

- Users can save time locating a particular file because they can view a file's document properties without opening the presentation.
- By creating consistent properties for files having similar content, users can better organize their presentations.
- Some organizations require PowerPoint users to add document properties so that other employees can view details about these files.

The more common document properties are standard and automatically updated properties. **Standard properties** are associated with all Microsoft Office files and include author, title, and subject. **Automatically updated properties** include file system properties, such as the date you create or change a file, and statistics, such as the file size.

BTW
Printing Document Properties
PowerPoint 2016 does not allow you to print document properties. This feature, however, is available in other Office 2016 apps, including Word and Excel.

To Change Document Properties

To change document properties, you would follow these steps.

1. Click File on the ribbon to open the Backstage view and then, if necessary, click the Info tab in the Backstage view to display the Info gallery.
2. If the property you wish to change is displayed in the Properties list in the right pane of the Info gallery, try to click that property. If a text box with that property is displayed, type the text for the property in the box, and then click the Back button in the upper-left corner of the Backstage view to return to the PowerPoint window. Skip the remaining steps.

3. If the property you wish to change is not displayed in the Properties list in the right pane of the Info gallery or you cannot change it in the Info gallery, click the Properties button in the right pane to display the Properties menu, and then click Advanced Properties on the Properties menu to display the Summary tab in the Properties dialog box.

Q&A Why are some of the document properties in my Document Information Panel already filled in?
The person who installed Office 2016 on your computer or network may have set or customized the properties.

4. Type the desired text in the appropriate property boxes.
5. Click the OK button (Properties dialog box) to close the dialog box
6. Click the Back button in the upper-left corner of the Backstage view to return to the PowerPoint presentation window.

BTW
PowerPoint Help
At any time while using PowerPoint, you can find answers to questions and display information about various topics through PowerPoint Help. Used properly, this form of assistance can increase your productivity and reduce your frustrations by minimizing the time you spend learning how to use PowerPoint. For instructions about PowerPoint Help and exercises that will help you gain confidence in using it, read the Office and Windows module at the beginning of this book.

Viewing the Presentation in Slide Show View

The 'Start From Beginning' button, located in the Quick Access Toolbar, allows you to show a presentation using a computer. As the name implies, the first slide to be displayed always will be Slide 1. You also can run a presentation starting with the slide currently displaying when you click the Slide Show button on the status bar. In either case, PowerPoint displays the slides on the full screen without any of the PowerPoint window objects, such as the ribbon. The full-screen slide hides the toolbars, menus, and other PowerPoint window elements.

To Start Slide Show View

1 INSERT PRESENTATION SLIDES | 2 ENTER TEXT | 3 FORMAT TEXT | 4 INSERT GRAPHICAL ELEMENTS
5 SIZE & POSITION | 6 ENHANCE SLIDE SHOW | 7 DISPLAY SLIDES

Why? You run a presentation for your audience so they can see the slides in their entirety and view any transitions or other effects added to the slides. When making a presentation, you use **Slide Show view**. You can start Slide Show view from Normal view or Slide Sorter view. Slide Show view begins when you click the 'Start From Beginning' button or the Slide Show button. The following steps start Slide Show view starting with Slide 1.

1

- Point to the 'Start From Beginning' button (Figure 1–73).

Q&A What would have displayed if I had clicked the Slide Show button instead of the 'Start From Beginning' button?
When you click the Slide Show button to start the presentation, PowerPoint begins the show with the currently displayed slide, which in this case is Slide 5. Only Slide 5 would display during the slide show.

Figure 1–73

- Click the 'Start From Beginning' button to display the transition and the title slide (Figure 1–74).

Q&A Where is the PowerPoint window?
When you run a slide show, the PowerPoint window is hidden. It will reappear once you end your slide show.

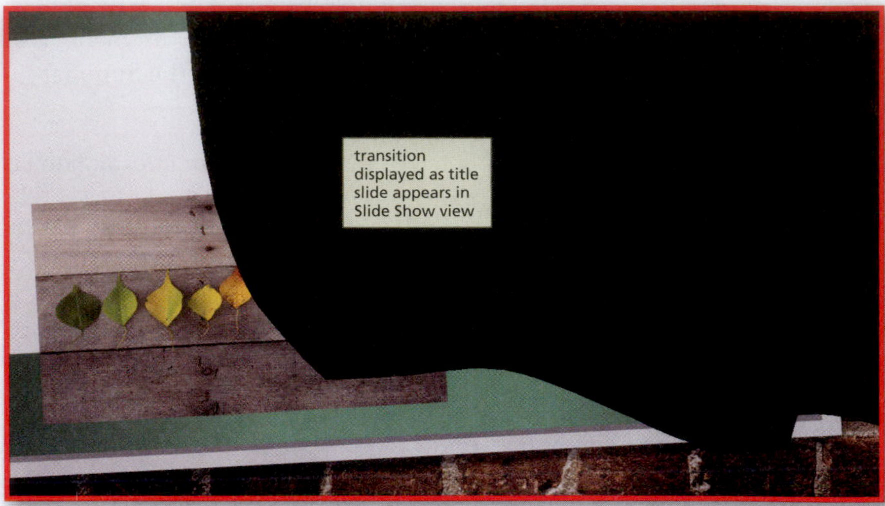

Figure 1–74

Other Ways

1. Display Slide 1, click Slide Show button on status bar
2. Click 'Start From Beginning' button (Slide Show tab | Start Slide Show group)
3. Press F5

To Move Manually through Slides in a Slide Show

1 INSERT PRESENTATION SLIDES | 2 ENTER TEXT | 3 FORMAT TEXT | 4 INSERT GRAPHICAL ELEMENTS
5 SIZE & POSITION | 6 ENHANCE SLIDE SHOW | 7 DISPLAY SLIDES

After you begin Slide Show view, you can move forward or backward through the slides. PowerPoint allows you to advance through the slides manually or automatically. During a slide show, each slide in the presentation shows on the screen, one slide at a time. Each time you click, the next slide appears. The following steps move manually through the slides. ***Why?*** *You can control the length of time each slide is displayed and change the preset order if you need to review a slide already shown or jump ahead to another slide designed to display later in the presentation.*

- Click each slide until Slide 5 (Register for Family Programs) is displayed (Figure 1–75).

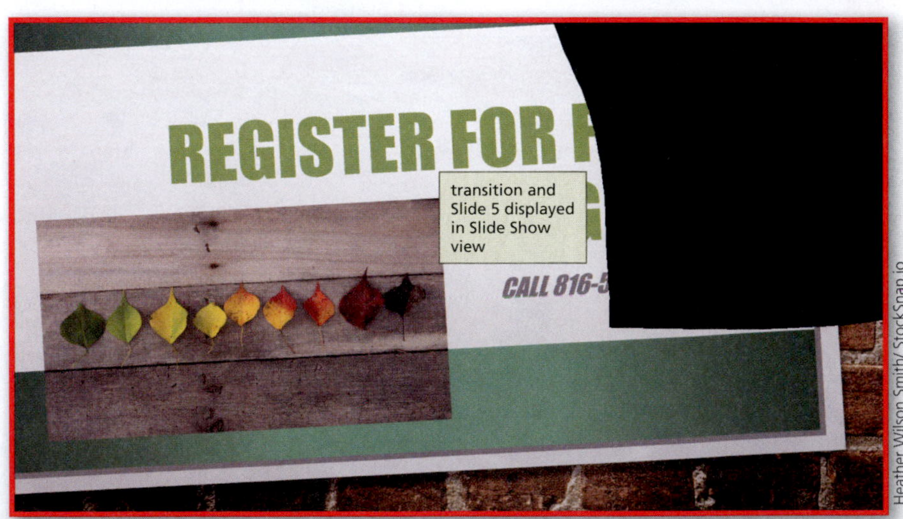

Heather Wilson Smith/ StockSnap.io

Figure 1–75

2

- Click Slide 5 so that the black slide appears with a message announcing the end of the slide show (Figure 1–76).

I see a small toolbar in the lower-left corner of my slide. What is this toolbar?
You may see the Slide Show toolbar when you begin running a slide show and then click a slide or move the pointer. The buttons on this toolbar allow you to navigate to the next slide or the previous slide, to mark up the current slide, or to change the current display. If you do not see the toolbar, hover the mouse near the lower-left corner of the screen.

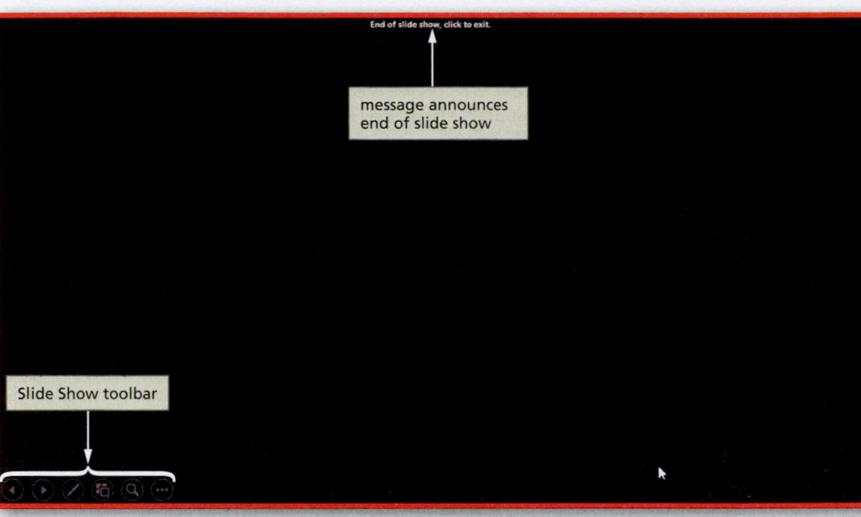

Figure 1–76

3

- Click the black slide to return to Normal view in the PowerPoint window.

Other Ways

1. Press PAGE DOWN to advance one slide at a time, or press PAGE UP to go back one slide at a time
2. Press RIGHT ARROW or DOWN ARROW to advance one slide at a time, or press LEFT ARROW or UP ARROW to go back one slide at a time
3. If Slide Show toolbar is displayed, click Next Slide or Previous Slide button on toolbar

To Save and Print the Presentation

It is a good practice to save a presentation before printing it, in the event you experience difficulties printing. For a detailed example of the procedure summarized below for saving and printing a presentation, refer to the Office and Windows module at the beginning of this book.

1 Save the presentation again on the same storage location with the same file name.

2 Print the presentation.

Q&A Do I have to wait until my presentation is complete to print it?
No, you can print a presentation at any time while you are creating it.

3 Because the project now is complete, you can exit PowerPoint.

BTW

Conserving Ink and Toner

If you want to conserve ink or toner, you can instruct PowerPoint to print draft quality documents by clicking File on the ribbon to open the Backstage view, clicking the Options tab in the Backstage view to display the PowerPoint Options dialog box, clicking Advanced in the left pane (PowerPoint Options dialog box), scrolling to the Print area in the right pane, not placing a check mark in the High quality check box, and then clicking the OK button. Then, use the Backstage view to print the document as usual.

BTW

Distributing a Document

Instead of printing and distributing a hard copy of a document, you can distribute the document electronically. Options include sending the document via email; posting it on cloud storage (such as OneDrive) and sharing the file with others; posting it on social media, a blog, or other website; and sharing a link associated with an online location of the document. You also can create and share a PDF or XPS image of the document, so that users can view the file in Acrobat Reader or XPS Viewer instead of in PowerPoint.

Summary

In this module, you learned how to use PowerPoint to create and enhance a presentation. Topics covered included applying and changing a document theme and variant, creating a title slide and text slides with a bulleted list, inserting pictures and then resizing and moving them on a slide, formatting and editing text, adding a slide transition, and viewing the presentation in Slide Show view.

CONSIDER THIS: PLAN AHEAD

What decisions will you need to make when creating your next presentation?

Use these guidelines as you complete the assignments in this module and create your own slide show decks outside of this class.

1. Determine the content you want to include on your slides.
2. Determine which theme and variant are appropriate.
3. Identify the slide layouts that best communicate your message.
4. Format various text elements to emphasize important points.
   a) Select appropriate font sizes.
   b) Emphasize important words with bold or italic type and color.
5. Locate graphical elements, such as pictures, that reinforce your message.
   a) Size and position them aesthetically on slides.
6. Determine a storage location for the presentation.
7. Determine the best method for distributing the presentation.

Apply Your Knowledge

Reinforce the skills and apply the concepts you learned in this module.

Modifying Character Formats and Paragraph Levels and Moving an Illustration

Note: To complete this assignment, you will be required to use the Data Files. Please contact your instructor for information about accessing the Data Files.

Instructions: Run PowerPoint. Open the presentation called Apply 1-1 Email Fraud, which is located in the Data Files.

The two slides in the presentation discuss phishing, which is a scam in which a perpetrator attempts to obtain an individual's personal and/or financial information. The document you open is an unformatted presentation. You are to modify the document theme, indent the paragraphs, resize and move the image, and format the text so the slides look like Figure 1–77.

Perform the following tasks:

1. Change the document theme to Droplet. Select the blue (third) variant.
2. On the title slide, use your name in place of Student Name and bold and italicize your name.
3. If requested by your instructor, change your first name to your grandmother's first name on the title slide.
4. Increase the title text font size to 60 point and then bold this text. Resize and position the illustration using the Smart Guides to align the image with the bottom of the subtitle placeholder and the right edge of the placeholders, as shown in Figure 1–77a.
5. On Slide 2, increase the indent of the second, third, and fourth paragraphs to second-level paragraphs. Then combine paragraphs six and seven (Work related and Personal) to read, `Work and personal messages can contain threats`, as shown in Figure 1–77b. Increase the indent of this paragraph to second level.

(a) Slide 1 (Title Slide with a Picture)

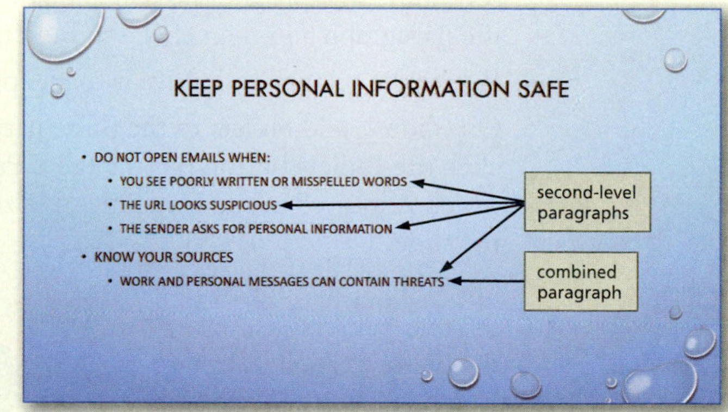

(b) Slide 2 (Multilevel Bulleted List)

Figure 1–77

6. Apply the Ripple transition in the Exciting category to both slides. Change the duration to 3.00 seconds. Click the 'Start From Beginning' button to start the show from the first slide. Then click to display each slide and again to end the presentation.

Continued >

Apply Your Knowledge *continued*

7. Save the presentation using the file name, Apply 1-1 Phishing.
8. Submit the revised document in the format specified by your instructor.
9. In Step 5 you combined two paragraphs and added text. How did this action improve the slide content?

Extend Your Knowledge

Extend the skills you learned in this module and experiment with new skills. You may need to use Help to complete the assignment.

Changing Slide Theme, Layout, and Text

Note: To complete this assignment, you will be required to use the Data Files. Please contact your instructor for information about accessing the Data Files.

Instructions: Run PowerPoint. Open the presentation called Extend 1-1 Waterfalls, which is located in the Data Files. Slide 1 is shown in Figure 1-78. You are aware that geologists have classified many types of waterfalls, including cascade and cataract, and the three slides in this file are part of a presentation you are developing for your geology class on this topic. Choose a theme, format the slides, and create a closing slide.

Perform the following tasks:

1. Change the document theme to Slice and the variant to green.
2. On Slide 1, format the text using techniques you learned in this module, such as changing the font size and color and bolding and italicizing words.
3. Replace the text, Student Name, with your name. In addition, delete the bullet preceding your name because, in most cases, a bullet is displayed as the first character in a list consisting of several paragraphs, not just one line of text. To delete the bullet, position the insertion point in the paragraph and then click the Bullets button (Home tab | Paragraph group).
4. Resize the picture and move it to an appropriate area on the slide.
5. On Slide 2, add bullets to the three paragraphs. To add bullets, select the paragraphs and then click the Bullets button (Home tab | Paragraph group). Insert the picture called Cascade, which is located in the Data Files, resize it, and then move it to an appropriate area on the slide.
6. On Slide 3, add bullets to the two paragraphs. Insert the picture called Cataract, which is located in the Data Files, resize it, and then move it to an appropriate area on the slide.
7. Create a closing slide using the title slide as a guide. Change the subtitle text to Natural Wonders and then underline this text. Insert the two waterfall pictures, Cascade and Cataract, and then size and move all three pictures to appropriate places on the slide.

Figure 1–78

8. Apply the Drape transition in the Exciting category to all slides and then change the duration for Slide 1 to 3.50 seconds. Click the 'Start From Beginning' button to start the show from the first slide. Then click to display each slide and again to end the presentation.
9. Save the presentation using the file name, Extend 1-1 Natural Wonders.
10. Submit the revised document in the format specified by your instructor.
11. If requested by your instructor, replace your last name on Slide 1 with the name of your hometown.
12. How did you determine the appropriate size and location of the three pictures on the closing slide?

Expand Your World

Create a solution that uses cloud and web technologies by learning and investigating on your own from general guidance.

Modifying and Exporting a Presentation

Note: To complete this assignment, you will be required to use the Data Files. Please contact your instructor for information about accessing the Data Files.

Instructions: Run PowerPoint. Open the presentation called Expand 1-1 Youth Group, which is located in the Data Files. The local youth group in your community is sponsoring a talent show, and you are part of a committee to publicize the event. You want to share the one slide you developed with some of the participants, so you have decided to store the file on OneDrive. You are going to modify the slide you have created, shown in Figure 1–79, and save it to OneDrive.

Perform the following tasks:

1. Insert the pictures called Musician and Singers, which are located in the Data Files. Size and then move them to the areas indicated in Figure 1–79. Use the guides to help you position the pictures.
2. If requested to do so by your instructor, change the words, Phoenix, AZ, to the town and state where you were born.
3. Save the presentation using the file name, Expand 1-1 Talent Show.
4. Export the file to your OneDrive account.
5. Submit the assignment in the format specified by your instructor.
6. When would you save one of your files for school or your job to OneDrive? Do you think using OneDrive enhances collaboration efforts? Why?

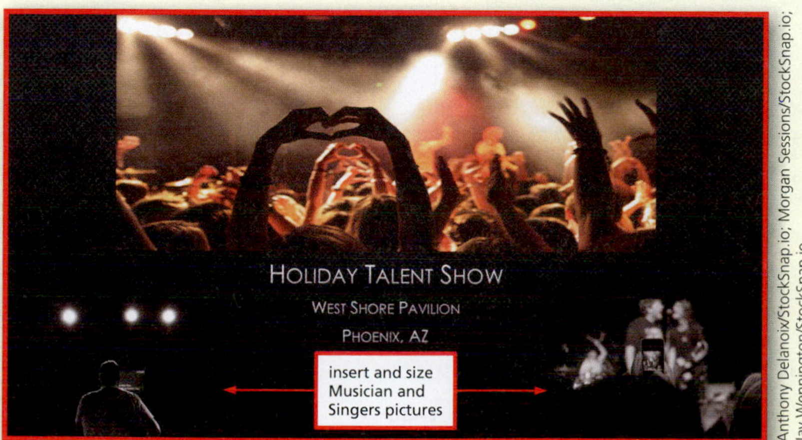

Anthony Delanoix/StockSnap.io; Morgan Sessions/StockSnap.io; Jay Wennington/StockSnap.io

Figure 1–79

In the Labs

Design, create, modify, and/or use a presentation following the guidelines, concepts, and skills presented in this module. Labs 1 and 2, which increase in difficulty, require you to create solutions based on what you learned in the module; Lab 3 requires you to apply your creative thinking and problem-solving skills to design and implement a solution.

Lab 1: Creating a Presentation with Pictures

Note: To complete this assignment, you will be required to use the Data Files. Please contact your instructor for information about accessing the Data Files.

Problem: Your friend, Bobby, has expanded her Bake Shoppe and wants to publicize new offerings. She has asked you to help her create a presentation that showcases pastries and breads. You prepare the PowerPoint presentation shown in Figure 1–80.

Perform the following tasks:

1. Run PowerPoint. Create a new presentation using the Retrospect document theme. Do not change the variant.
2. Using Figure 1–80a, create the title slide. Type the title text and subtitle text shown in the figure. Decrease the font size of the title text to 60 point and bold this text. Change the font color to Orange, Accent 1 (in Theme Colors row).

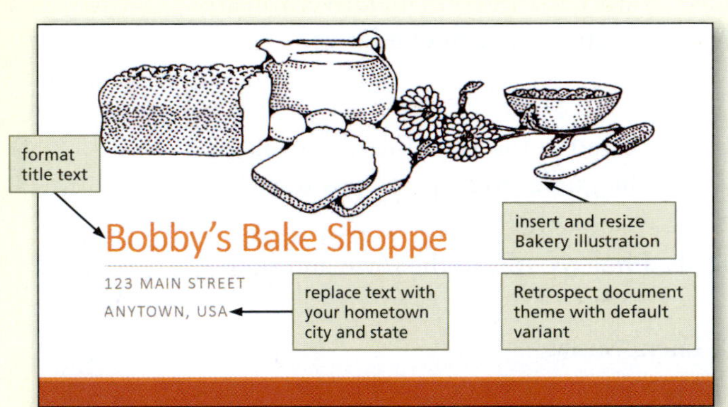

(a) Slide 1 (Title Slide)

(b) Slide 2

Drew Coffman/StockSnap.io

(c) Slide 3

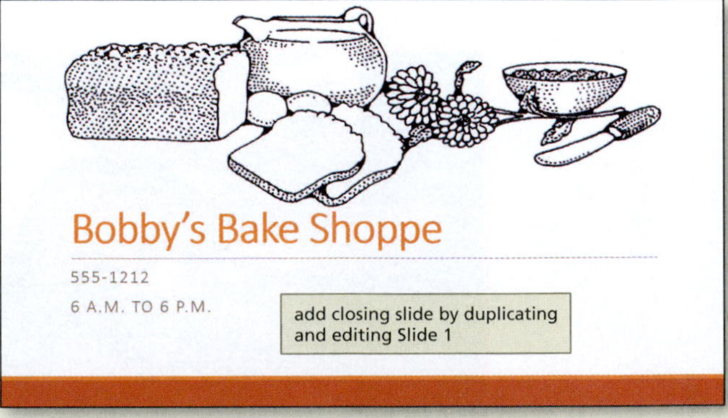

(d) Slide 4 (Closing Slide)

Figure 1–80

3. On Slide 1, insert the illustration called Bakery, which is located in the Data Files. Move the illustration up to the top of the slide and then use the Smart Guides to align its left and right edges with the sides of the text placeholders. Use the lower-center sizing handle to resize this illustration so that it fits above the title text.
4. Replace the words, Anytown, USA, with your hometown city and state.
5. Create Slide 2 using the Title Only layout. Type the title text, Fresh Daily, bold this text, and then change the font color to Orange, Accent 1 (in Theme Colors row). Insert the picture called Doughnut, which is located in the Data Files, resize it as shown in Figure 1–80b, and then move it to the left side of the slide. Insert the picture called Muffin, which is located in the Data Files, and then resize and move it to the right side of the slide, as shown in the figure.
6. Using Figure 1–80c as a guide, create Slide 3 using the Picture with Caption layout. Insert the picture called Bread, which is located in the Data Files. Type the title text, Artisan Breads, increase the font size to 48 point, and then bold this text. Type `All natural ingredients` as the subtitle text, press the Tab key four times, and then type `No preservatives` in the placeholder. Increase this subtitle text size to 28 point.
7. Create a closing slide by duplicating Slide 1. Change the subtitle text using Figure 1–80d as a guide.
8. Apply the Clock transition in the Exciting category to all slides. Change the duration to 2.00 seconds.
9. Click the 'Start From Beginning' button to start the show from the first slide. Then click to display each slide and again to end the presentation.
10. Save the presentation using the file name, Lab 1-1 Bake. Submit the document in the format specified by your instructor.
11. What is the significance of changing the font color on Slides 1 and 2 but not Slide 3?

Lab 2: Creating a Presentation with Bulleted Lists and Pictures

Note: To complete this assignment, you will be required to use the Data Files. Please contact your instructor for information about accessing the Data Files.

Problem: The history museum in your town is a popular destination for residents, tourists, and researchers. Among the more popular exhibits are the dinosaurs, mummies, and antiques. You want to highlight these three attractions, so you create the presentation shown in Figure 1–81.

Perform the following tasks:

1. Run PowerPoint. Create a new presentation using the Quotable document theme.
2. Using Figure 1–81, create the title slide. Use your name in place of Student Name.
3. If requested by your instructor, substitute the name of your hometown in place of your last name.
4. On Slide 1 (Figure 1–81a), italicize the text, History Museum. Increase the font size of the subtitle text, Popular Exhibits, to 32 point and the font size of your name to 24 point. Change the font color of the title text to Dark Blue (in Standard Colors row).
5. Create the three slides shown in Figures 1-81b, 1-81c, and 1-81d. Use the Comparison layout for Slide 2, the Section Header layout for Slide 3, and the Two Content layout for Slide 4. Change the color of the title text on these three text slides to Dark Blue. Increase the font size of the subtitle text on Slides 2 and 3 to 24 point.

Continued >

In the Labs *continued*

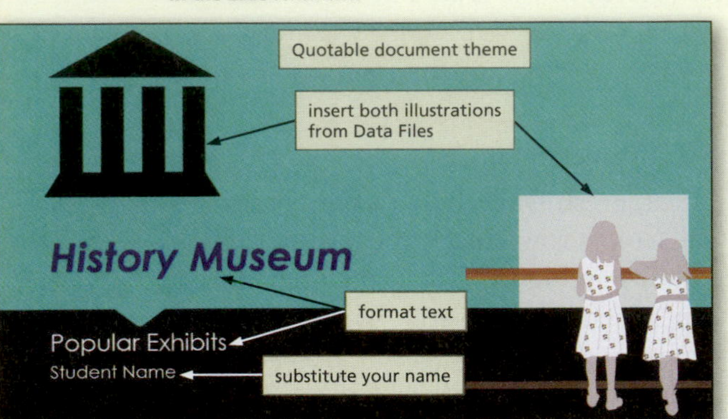

(a) Slide 1 (Title Slide)

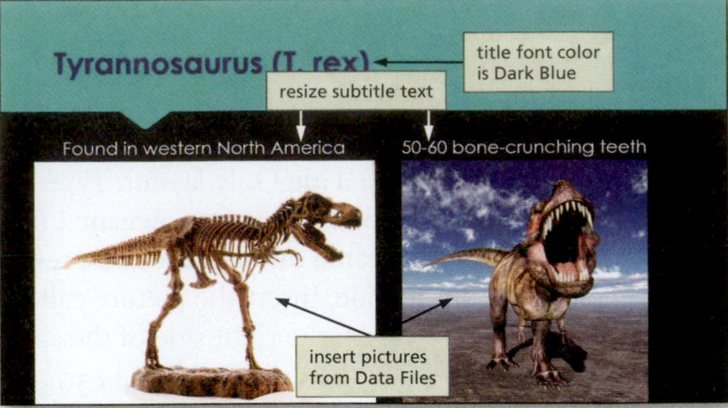

(b) Slide 2

insert picture from Data Files
title font color is Dark Blue
Ancient Egyptian Sarcophagus
Stone-carved burial container contains mummified body

(c) Slide 3

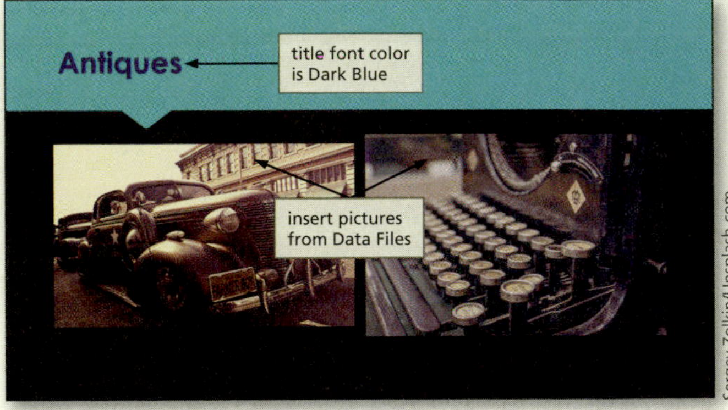

(d) Slide 4

Sergey Zolkin/Unsplash.com, Gabe Rodriguez/Unsplash.com

Figure 1–81

6. Add the pictures shown in Figures 1-81a through 1-81d using the guides on Slides 1 and 3 to help align them. The pictures to be inserted are called Museum Icon, Girls in Museum, T-rex Skeleton, T-rex 3D, Pharaoh, Car, and Typewriter, and they are located in the Data Files. Zoom the slides and then resize the pictures when necessary.
7. Apply the Gallery transition in the Exciting category to all slides. Change the duration to 2.25 seconds.
8. Click the 'Start From Beginning' button to start the show from the first slide. Then click to display each slide and again to end the presentation.
9. Save the presentation using the file name, Lab 1-2 History Museum.
10. Submit the revised document in the format specified by your instructor.
11. How does changing the title text font color to Dark Blue complement the theme color?

Lab 3: Consider This: Your Turn

Design and Create a Presentation about the Building Construction Technology Program

Note: To complete this assignment, you will be required to use the Data Files. Please contact your instructor for information about accessing the Data Files.

Part 1: Your school is expanding the courses offered in the Building Construction Technology Program, and the department chair has asked you to help promote the program. He informs you that students obtain hands-on experience using the latest methods of construction, and they receive instruction in the classroom and in the lab. The capstone courses are held in the field, where students build an actual energy-efficient home from the ground up. The skills learned and experience gained prepare students for careers in carpentry, masonry, plumbing, electrical, project supervision, cost estimating, and drafting. Use the concepts and techniques presented in this module to prepare a presentation with a minimum of four slides that showcase the Building Construction Technology program. Select a suitable theme, and include a title slide, bulleted list, closing slide, and transition. The presentation should contain pictures and illustrations resized appropriately. Several pictures are available in the Data Files: Backhoe, Concrete, Hammer, Hard Hat, Measuring Tape, Nail, and Tool Belt. Review and revise your presentation as needed. Submit your assignment in the format specified by your instructor.

Part 2: You made several decisions while creating the presentation in this assignment: what theme to use, where to place text, how to format the text (font, font size, paragraph alignment, bulleted paragraphs, italics, bold, color). You decided which images to use and where to position them. You also chose a transition. What was the rationale behind each of these decisions? When you reviewed the slides, what further revisions did you make and why? Where would you recommend showing this slide show?

2 Enhancing a Presentation with Pictures, Shapes, and WordArt

Objectives

You will have mastered the material in this module when you can:

- Search for and download an online theme
- Insert and format pictures
- Insert and size a shape
- Apply effects to a shape
- Add text to a shape
- Change the text font
- Insert a picture to create a background
- Insert and format WordArt
- Format slide backgrounds
- Find and replace text and check spelling
- Add and print speaker notes

Introduction

In our visually oriented culture, audience members enjoy viewing effective graphics. Whether reading a document or viewing a PowerPoint presentation, people increasingly want to see photographs, artwork, graphics, and a variety of typefaces. Researchers have known for decades that documents with visual elements are more effective than those that consist of only text because the illustrations motivate audiences to study the material. People remember at least one-third more information when the document they are seeing or reading contains visual elements. These graphics help clarify and emphasize details, so they appeal to audience members with differing backgrounds, reading levels, attention spans, and motivations.

Project — Presentation with Pictures, Shapes, and WordArt

The project in this module focuses on publicizing a basketball camp held each summer for children living in the park district. Professionals teach boys and girls a variety of offensive and defensive skills during this fun and educational event. The presentation shown in Figure 2–1 follows graphical guidelines and has a variety of illustrations and visual elements that are colorful and appealing to child athletes and their parents. For example, the pictures have particular shapes and effects. The enhanced type has a style that blends well with the formatted background and illustrations. Pictures and type are formatted using picture styles and WordArt, which give the presentation a professional look. You plan to present the material during winter and spring sports tournaments, so you want to add notes explaining concepts you will be discussing during these events.

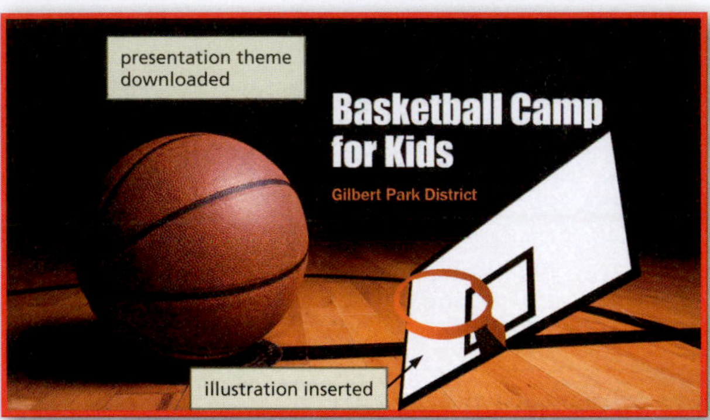

(a) Slide 1 (Title Slide)

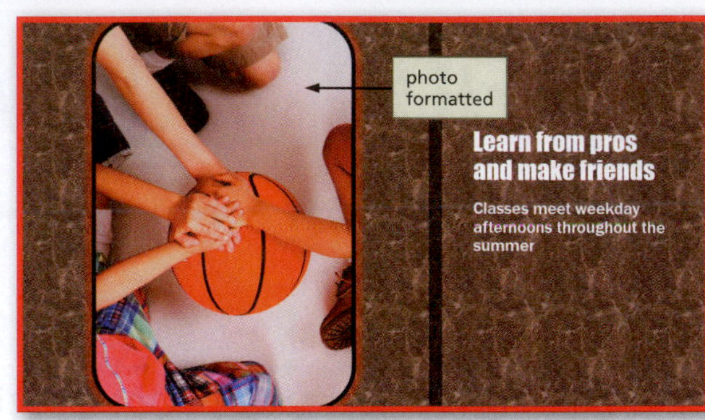

(b) Slide 2 (Formatted Picture)

(c) Slide 3 (Shapes Inserted and Formatted)

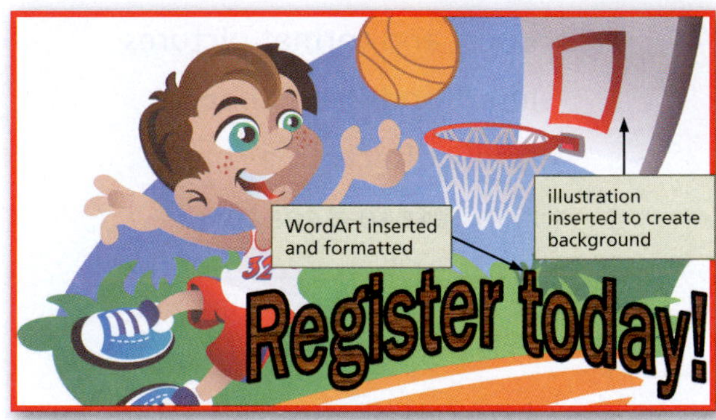

(d) Slide 4 (Picture Background)

Figure 2–1

For an introduction to Windows and instructions about how to perform basic Windows tasks, read the Office and Windows module at the beginning of this book, where you can learn how to resize windows, change screen resolution, create folders, move and rename files, use Windows Help, and much more.

In this module, you will learn how to create the slides shown in Figure 2–1. The following roadmap identifies general activities you will perform as you progress through this module:

1. **DOWNLOAD** a theme and **SELECT SLIDES** for the presentation.
2. **INSERT** and **FORMAT PICTURES** for the slides.
3. **INSERT** and **FORMAT SHAPES** on one slide.
4. **FORMAT SLIDE BACKGROUNDS** with a gradient, texture, and picture fill.
5. **INSERT** and **FORMAT WORDART** by changing the shape, fill, and outline.
6. **REVIEW, REVISE,** and **PRINT SLIDES** by finding a synonym, checking spelling, and adding speaker notes.

Downloading a Theme and Editing Slides

In Module 1, you selected a theme and then typed the content for the title and text slides. In this module, you will type the slide content for the title and text slides, select a background, insert and format pictures and shapes, and then insert and format WordArt. To begin creating the four slides in this presentation, you will download a theme, delete unneeded slides in this downloaded presentation, and then enter text in three of the four slides.

To Search for and Download an Online Theme

1 DOWNLOAD & SELECT SLIDES | 2 INSERT & FORMAT PICTURES | 3 INSERT & FORMAT SHAPES
4 FORMAT SLIDE BACKGROUNDS | 5 INSERT & FORMAT WORDART | 6 REVIEW, REVISE, & PRINT SLIDES

PowerPoint displays many themes that are varied and appealing and give you an excellent start at designing a presentation. At times, however, you may have a specific topic and design concept and could use some assistance in starting to develop the presentation. Microsoft offers hundreds of predesigned themes and templates that could provide you with an excellent starting point. ***Why?*** *You can search for one of these ready-made presentations, or you can browse one of the predefined categories, such as business and education. The themes and templates can save you time and help you develop content.* The following steps search for a theme with a basketball concept.

- Run PowerPoint and then type **`basketball`** in the 'Search for online templates and themes' box (Figure 2–2).

Q&A

Why are my theme thumbnails displaying in a different order?
The order changes as you choose themes for presentations. In addition, Microsoft occasionally adds and modifies the themes, so the order may change.

Can I choose one of the keywords listed below the 'Search for online templates and themes' box?
Yes. Click one of the terms in the Suggested searches list to display a variety of templates and themes relating to those topics.

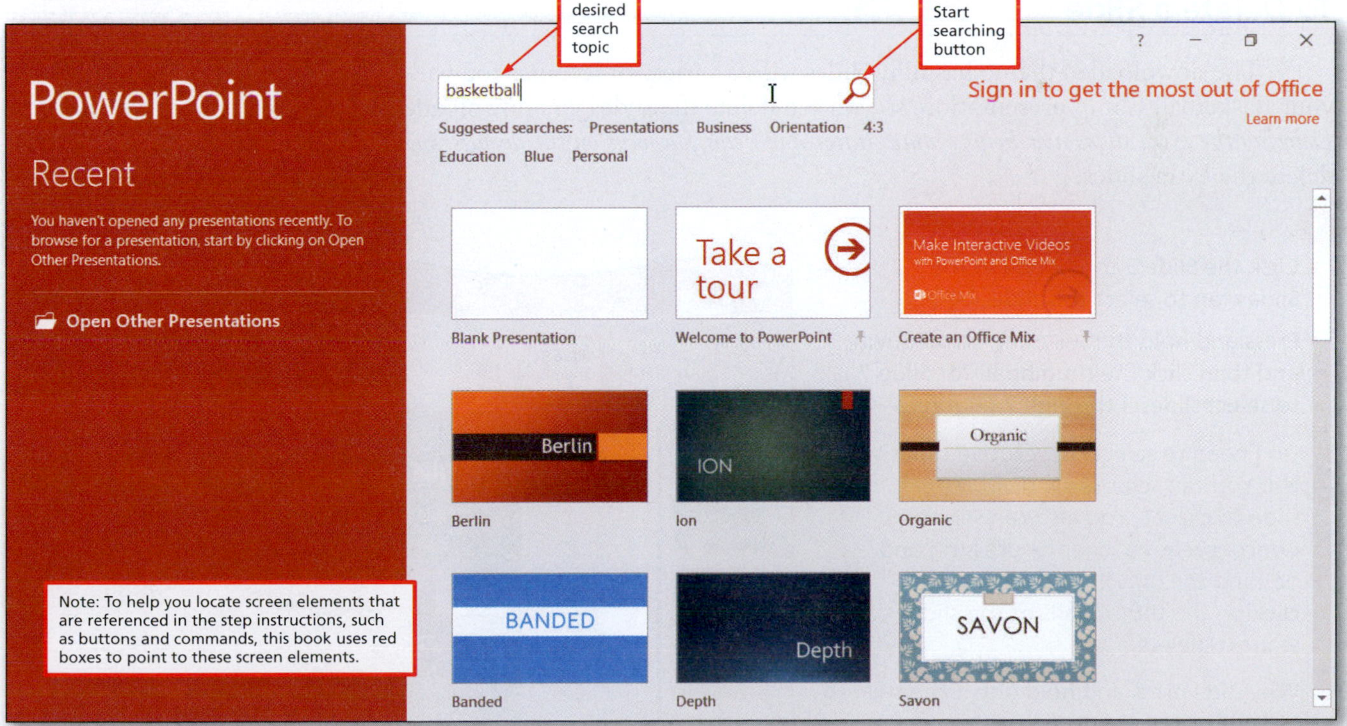

Figure 2–2

- Click the Start searching button (the magnifying glass) or press the ENTER key to search for and display all themes with the keyword, basketball.
- Click the 'Basketball presentation (widescreen)' theme to display a theme preview dialog box with a thumbnail view of the theme (Figure 2–3).

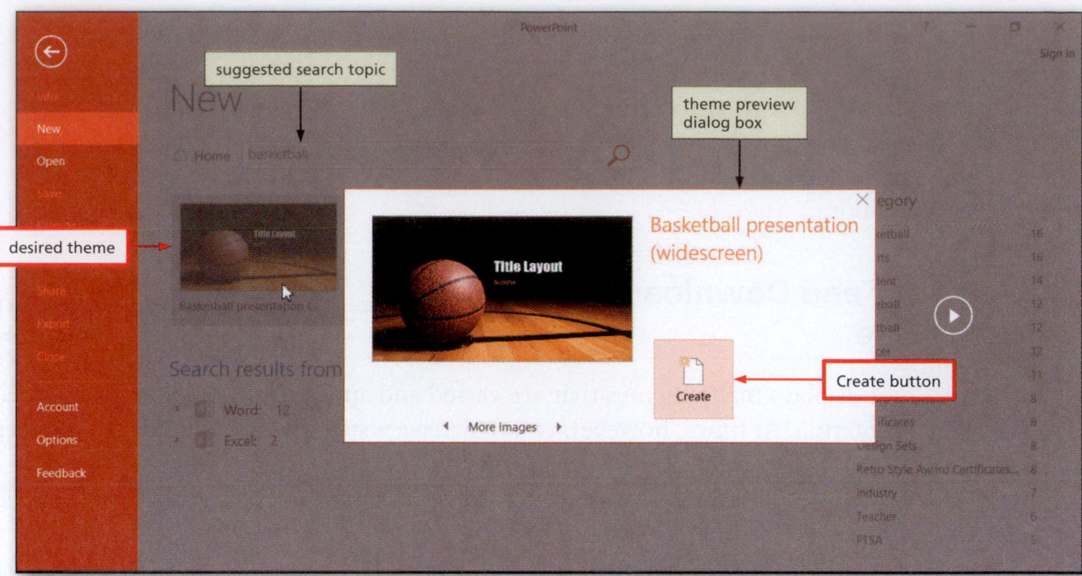

Figure 2–3

Q&A Can I see previews of the slides in this theme?
Yes. Click the right or left arrows beside the words, More Images, below the thumbnail. On some devices, a preview of all slides starts automatically after you tap the theme.

- Click the Create button to download the theme and open a presentation with that theme in PowerPoint.

To Delete a Slide

1 DOWNLOAD & SELECT SLIDES | 2 INSERT & FORMAT PICTURES | 3 INSERT & FORMAT SHAPES
4 FORMAT SLIDE BACKGROUNDS | 5 INSERT & FORMAT WORDART | 6 REVIEW, REVISE, & PRINT SLIDES

The downloaded theme has nine slides with a variety of layouts. You will use four different layouts in your Basketball Camp presentation, so you can delete the slides you downloaded that you will not need. ***Why?*** *Deleting the extra slides now helps reduce clutter and helps you focus on the layouts you will use.* The following steps delete the extra slides.

- Click the Slide 3 thumbnail in the Slides tab to select this slide.
- Press and hold the SHIFT key, scroll down, and then click the thumbnail for Slide 7 to select slides 3 through 7 (Figure 2–4).

Q&A Do I need to select consecutive slides?
No. You can select an individual slide to delete. You also can select nonconsecutive slides by pressing and holding the CTRL key down and then clicking the thumbnails of the slides you want to delete.

Why did I press and hold down the SHIFT key instead of the CTRL key?
Holding down the SHIFT key selects consecutive slides between the first and last selected slides, whereas holding the CTRL key selects only the slides you click.

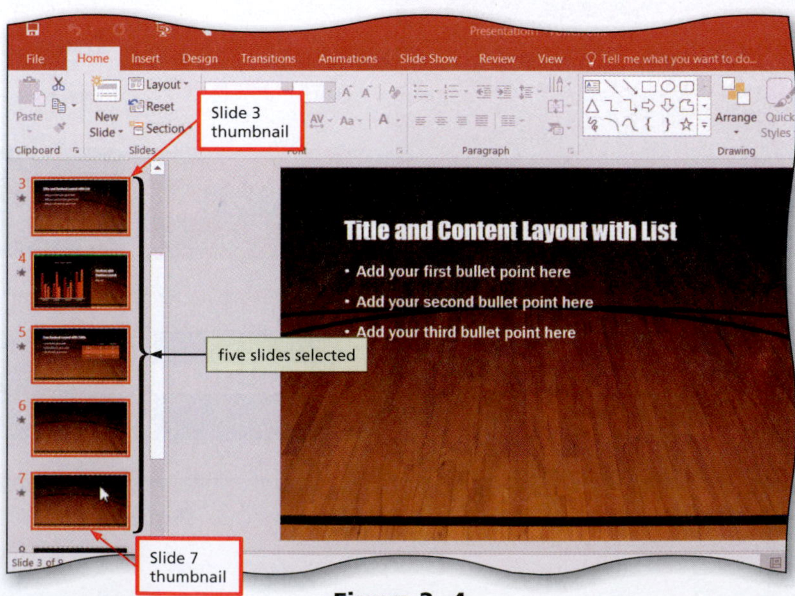

Figure 2–4

- Right-click any selected slide to display the shortcut menu (Figure 2–5).

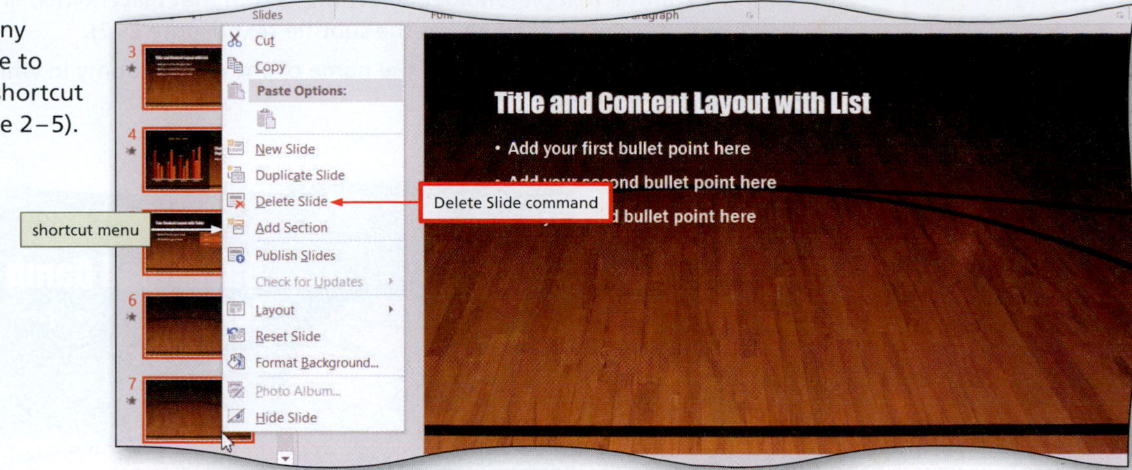

Figure 2–5

3

- Click Delete Slide to delete the selected slides from the presentation (Figure 2–6).

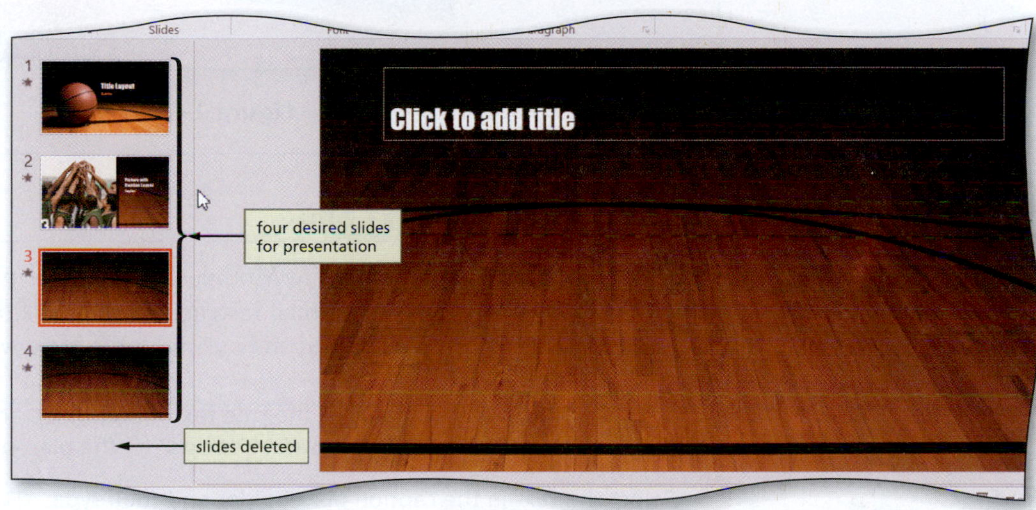

Figure 2–6

Other Ways

1. Select slide(s), press DELETE
2. Select slide(s), press BACKSPACE

To Create a Title Slide

Recall from Module 1 that the title slide introduces the presentation to the audience. In addition to introducing the presentation, this project uses the title slide to capture the audience's attention by using title text and an illustration. ***Why?*** *The presentation focuses on basketball, so the picture of a ball and court on the title slide can be supplemented with a backboard illustration that you will insert later on this slide.* The following steps create the slide show's title slide.

For an introduction to Office and instructions about how to perform basic tasks in Office apps, read the Office and Windows module at the beginning of this book, where you can learn how to run an application, use the ribbon, save a file, open a file, print a file, exit an application, use Help, and much more.

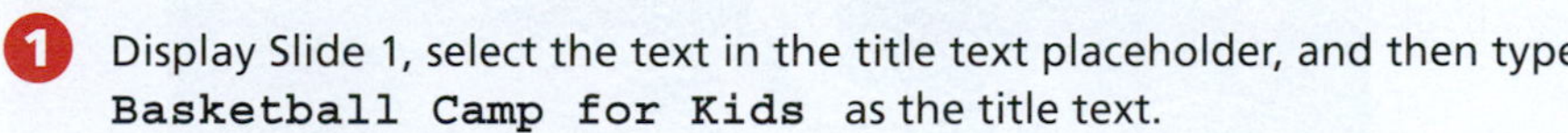

1 Display Slide 1, select the text in the title text placeholder, and then type `Basketball Camp for Kids` as the title text.

Q&A Why do I have to select the text in the placeholder before typing?
This downloaded template includes text in some of the placeholders that must be replaced with your own text.

BTW
PowerPoint Screen Resolution
If you are using a computer or mobile device to step through the project in this module and you want your screens to match the figures in this book, you should change your screen's resolution to 1366 x 768. For information about how to change a computer's resolution, refer to the Office and Windows module at the beginning of this book.

2 Click the subtitle text placeholder, select the text in that placeholder, and then type `Gilbert Park District` as the subtitle text (Figure 2–7).

- If requested by your instructor, type the name of the city or county in which you were born instead of the word, Gilbert.

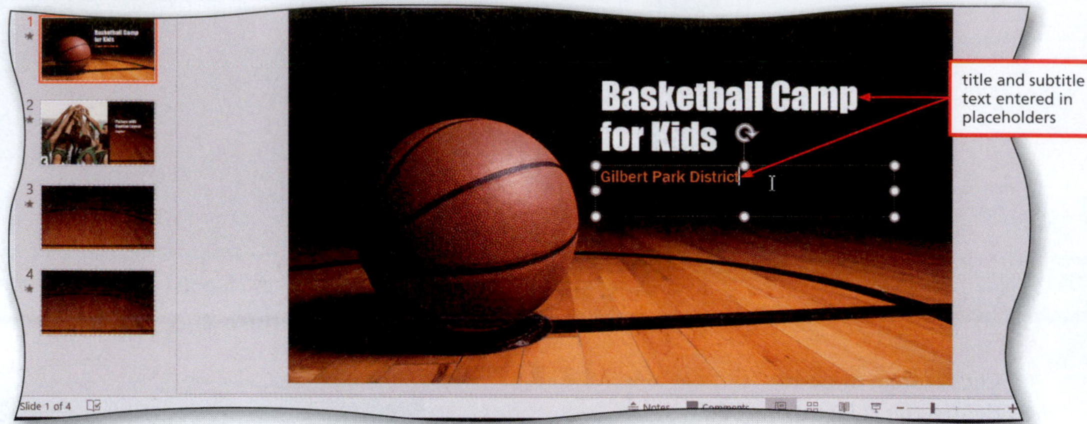

Figure 2–7

BTW
Touch Screen Differences
The Office and Windows interfaces may vary if you are using a touch screen. For this reason, you might notice that the function or appearance of your touch screen differs slightly from this module's presentation.

To Create the First Text Slide

The first text slide you create in Module 2 emphasizes two benefits of attending the weekly camp: receiving professional instruction and developing friendships. The following steps create the Slide 2 text slide using the Picture with Caption layout.

1 Display Slide 2, select the text in the title text placeholder, and then type `Learn from pros and make acquaintances` in the placeholder.

2 Select the text in the caption placeholder and then type `Classes meet weekday mornings throughout the summer` in this placeholder (Figure 2–8).

BTW
The Ribbon and Screen Resolution
PowerPoint may change how the groups and buttons within the groups appear on the ribbon, depending on the computer or mobile device's screen resolution. Thus, your ribbon may look different from the ones in this book if you are using a screen resolution other than 1366 × 768.

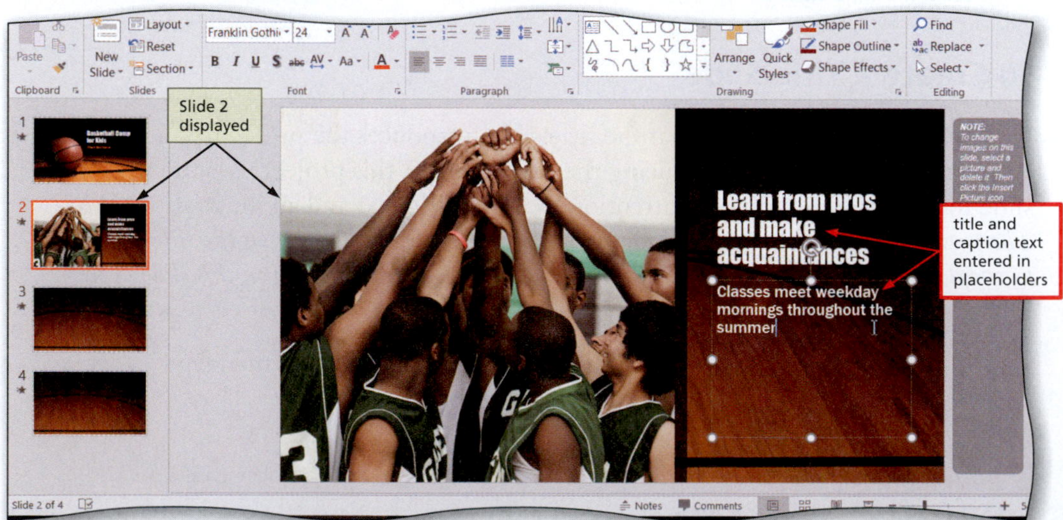

Figure 2–8

To Create the Second Text Slide

The second text slide you create shows three skills that will be taught: ball handling, offensive moves, and defensive strategies. The following steps add a title to Slide 3, which uses the Title Only layout, and save the presentation.

1. Display Slide 3 and then type `You will lern...` in the title text placeholder. The word, lern, is misspelled intentionally; the red wavy line indicates the misspelling (Figure 2-9).
2. Save the presentation using `Basketball Camp` as the file name.

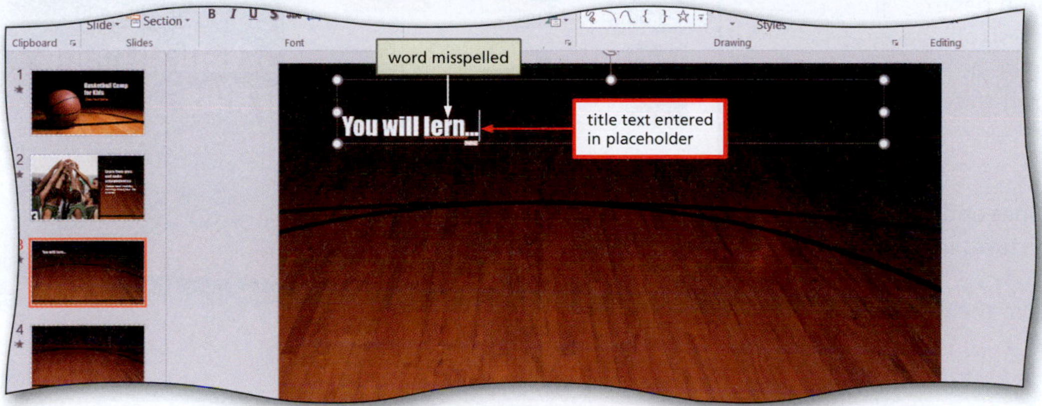

Figure 2–9

Inserting and Formatting Pictures in a Presentation

With the text entered in three of the four slides, the next step is to insert pictures into Slides 1 and 2 and then format the pictures. These graphical images draw the viewers' eyes to the slides and help them retain the information presented.

In the following pages, you will perform these tasks:

1. Insert an illustration into Slide 1.
2. Resize the illustration.
3. Change the Slide 2 photo.
4. Change the photo's brightness and contrast.
5. Change the photo's style and effect.
6. Add and modify the photo's border.

BTW

Organizing Files and Folders

You should organize and store files in folders so that you easily can find the files later. For example, if you are taking an introductory technology class called CIS 101, a good practice would be to save all PowerPoint files in a PowerPoint folder in a CIS 101 folder. For a discussion of folders and detailed examples of creating folders, refer to the Office and Windows module at the beginning of this book.

To Insert a Picture into a Slide without a Content Placeholder

1 DOWNLOAD & SELECT SLIDES | **2 INSERT & FORMAT PICTURES** | 3 INSERT & FORMAT SHAPES
4 FORMAT SLIDE BACKGROUNDS | 5 INSERT & FORMAT WORDART | 6 REVIEW, REVISE, & PRINT SLIDES

In Module 1, you inserted photos and an illustration into slides without a content placeholder. ***Why?*** *Some slide layouts do not have a content placeholder, so you must insert and move the pictures to appropriate locations on the slide.* The illustration for Slide 1 is available in the Data Files. Contact your instructor if you need the pictures used in the following steps. The instructions in this module show the required files in the Module 02 folder in the Data Files folder. The following steps insert an illustration into the title slide.

1

- Display Slide 1 and then click Insert on the ribbon to display the Insert tab.
- Click the Pictures button (Insert tab | Images group) to display the Insert Picture dialog box.

2

- If necessary, navigate to the PowerPoint Module 02 folder and then click Backboard to select the file name (Figure 2–10).

Q&A

What if Backboard is not displayed in the navigation pane?
Drag the navigation pane scroll bar (Insert Picture dialog box) until Backboard appears. If this file is not in the list, see your instructor.

Why do I see just file names and not thumbnails of the pictures in my folder?
Your view is different from the view shown in Figure 2–10.

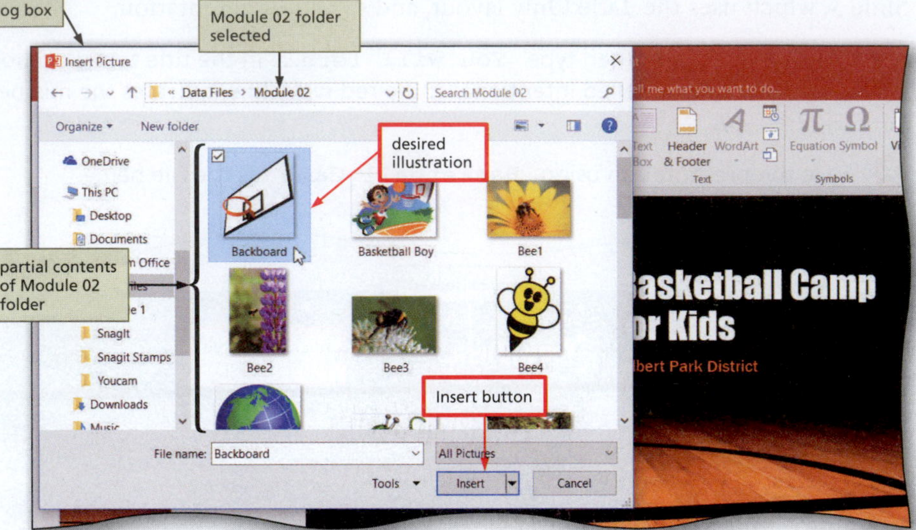

Figure 2–10

- Click the Insert button (Insert Picture dialog box) to insert the illustration into Slide 1.
- Drag the upper-left sizing handle diagonally toward the lower-right corner of the slide until the crosshair is positioned approximately as shown in Figure 2–11.

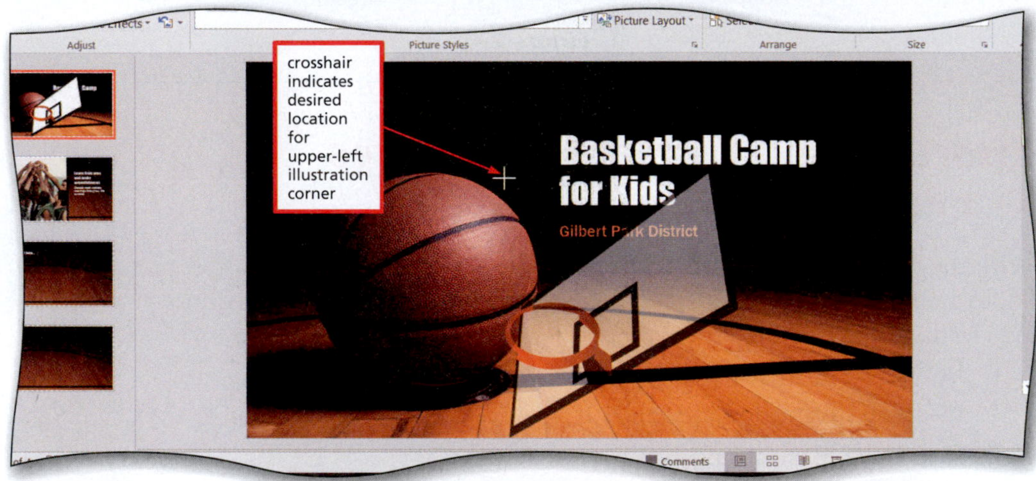

Figure 2–11

- Release to resize the illustration.
- Drag the illustration to the right until the vertical Smart Guide is displayed near the right side of the slide, as shown in Figure 2–12, and then release.

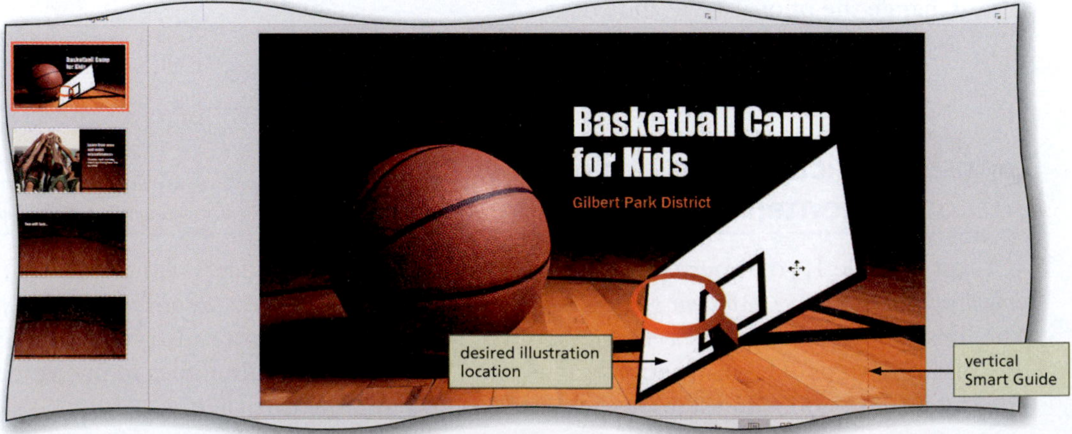

Figure 2–12

To Change a Picture

Why? The downloaded theme included the photo of several team members on Slide 2. You need to change the photo because those players are wearing green uniforms, which are not the clothes your camp participants will wear. The next task in the presentation is to change the default picture on Slide 2 to one of the pictures in the Data Files. The following steps change the Slide 2 photo to the Teamwork photo, which, in this example, is located in the Module 02 folder in the Data Files folder.

1

- Display Slide 2 and then right-click the picture to display the shortcut menu (Figure 2–13).

Q&A Why are the Style and Crop buttons displayed near the shortcut menu on my screen?
These two buttons display either above or below the shortcut menu depending upon where you right-click on the screen.

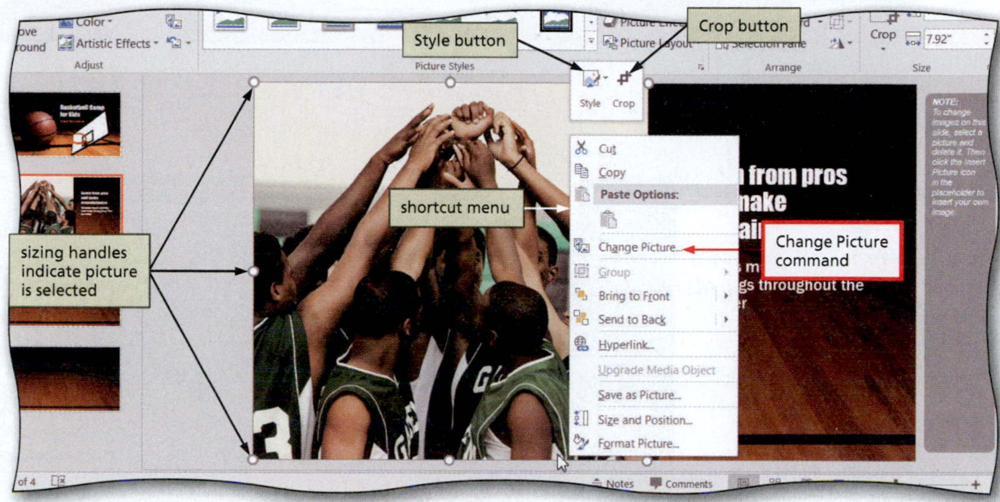

Figure 2–13

2

- Click Change Picture to display the Insert Pictures dialog box (Figure 2–14).

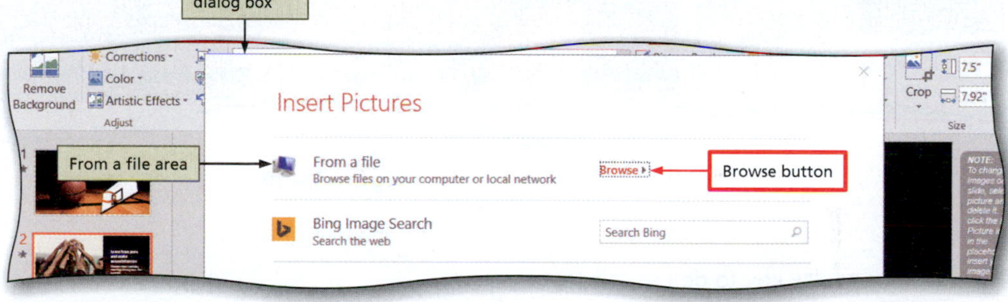

Figure 2–14

3

- Click the Browse button in the 'From a file' area to display the Insert Picture dialog box.
- If necessary, navigate to the PowerPoint Module 02 folder, scroll down, and then click Teamwork to select the file (Figure 2–15).

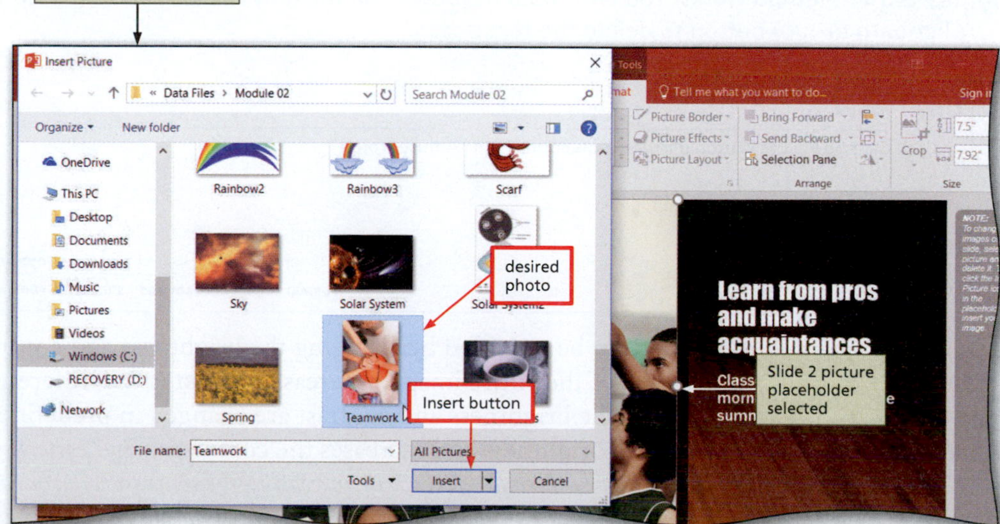

Figure 2–15

4

- Click the Insert button (Insert Picture dialog box) to insert the photo into the Slide 2 picture placeholder.
- Click the gray text box on the right side of the slide to select this object (Figure 2–16).

Q&A Why should I select and then delete this gray text box?
When you delete the box, the slide will expand to the right to fill that space and you will be able to view a larger slide image.

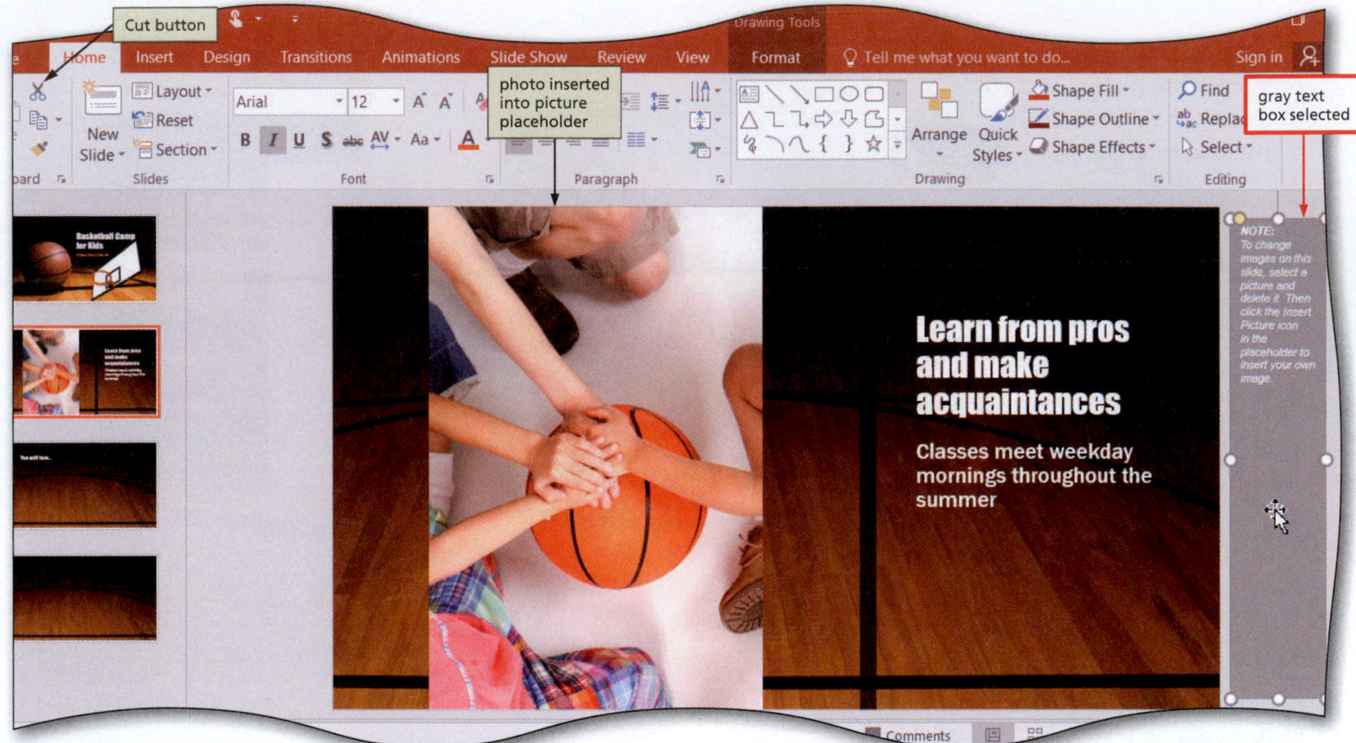

Figure 2–16

5

- Press the DELETE key to delete this text box.

Q&A Could I have followed the directions in the gray box on the right to change the image?
Yes, either method works. You also could have selected the gray box and then clicked the Cut button (Home tab | Clipboard group) button to delete the text box.

Other Ways

1. Click Change Picture button (Picture Tools Format tab | Adjust group)

To Correct a Picture

1 DOWNLOAD & SELECT SLIDES | 2 INSERT & FORMAT PICTURES | 3 INSERT & FORMAT SHAPES
4 FORMAT SLIDE BACKGROUNDS | 5 INSERT & FORMAT WORDART | 6 REVIEW, REVISE, & PRINT SLIDES

A photo's color intensity can be modified by changing the brightness and contrast. **Brightness** determines the overall lightness or darkness of the entire image, whereas **contrast** is the difference between the darkest and lightest areas of the image. The brightness and contrast are changed in predefined percentage increments. The following step decreases the brightness and increases the contrast. ***Why?*** *Altering the photo's brightness will coordinate with the dark colors on the basketball court while increasing the contrast will sharpen the image. It is important for the audience to recognize the basketball and the players' overlapping hands but not focus on each aspect of this photo.*

1

- Select the Teamwork photo on Slide 2 and then click Format on the ribbon to display the Picture Tools Format tab.
- Click the Corrections button (Picture Tools Format tab | Adjust group) to display the Corrections gallery.
- Scroll down to display the last row of images in the Corrections gallery and then point to Brightness: –20% Contrast: +40% (second picture in last Brightness/Contrast row) to display a live preview of these corrections on the picture (Figure 2–17).

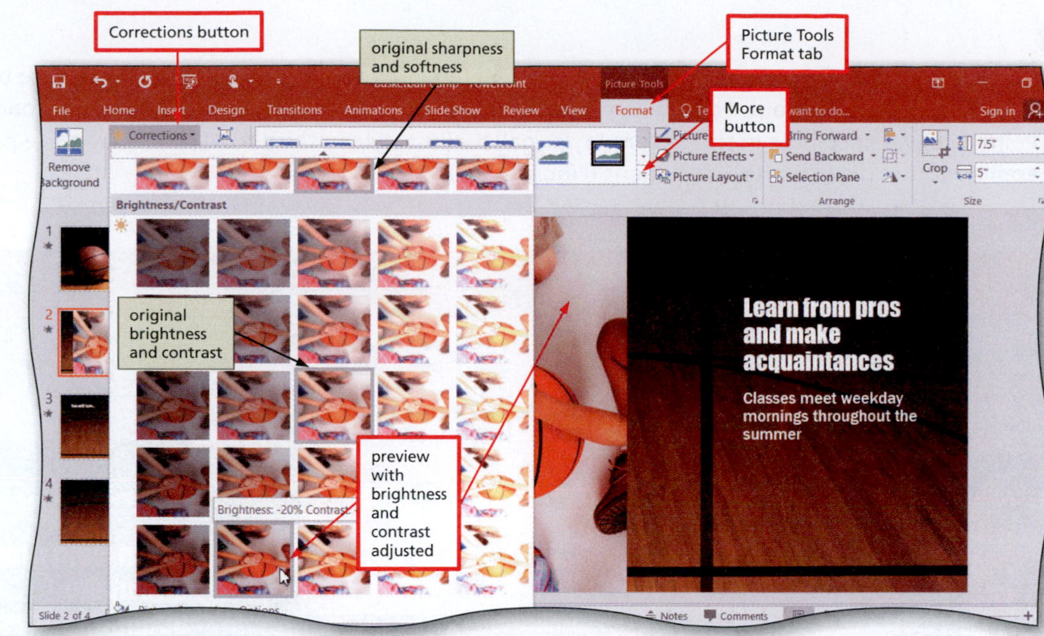

Figure 2–17

Q&A Can I use live preview on a touch screen?
Live preview is not available on a touch screen.

Why is a gray border surrounding the pictures in the center of the Sharpen/Soften and Brightness/Contrast areas of the gallery?
The image on Slide 2 currently has normal sharpness, brightness, and contrast (0%), which is represented by these center images in the gallery.

Experiment

- Point to various pictures in the Brightness/Contrast area and watch the brightness and contrast change on the picture in Slide 2.
- Click Brightness: –20% Contrast: +40% to apply this correction to the Teamwork photo.

Q&A How can I remove all effects from the picture?
Click the Reset Picture button (Picture Tools Format tab | Adjust group).

Other Ways

1. Click Picture Corrections Options (Corrections gallery), move Brightness or Contrast sliders or enter number in box next to slider (Format Picture pane)

To Apply a Picture Style

1 DOWNLOAD & SELECT SLIDES | 2 INSERT & FORMAT PICTURES | 3 INSERT & FORMAT SHAPES
4 FORMAT SLIDE BACKGROUNDS | 5 INSERT & FORMAT WORDART | 6 REVIEW, REVISE, & PRINT SLIDES

A **style** is a named group of formatting characteristics. The picture on Slide 2 emphasizes the concept of teamwork in this sport, and you can increase its visual appeal by applying a style. ***Why?*** *PowerPoint provides more than 25 picture styles that enable you easily to change a picture's look to a more visually appealing style, including a variety of shapes, angles, borders, and reflections.* You want to use a style that applies a shadow to the Teamwork photo. The following steps apply a picture style to the Slide 2 photo.

1

- With the Slide 2 picture selected and the Picture Tools Format tab displaying, click the More button in the Picture Styles gallery (Picture Tools Format tab | Picture Styles group) (shown in Figure 2–17) to expand the gallery.
- Point to Bevel Rectangle in the Picture Styles gallery (last style in third row) to display a live preview of that style applied to the picture in the document (Figure 2–18).

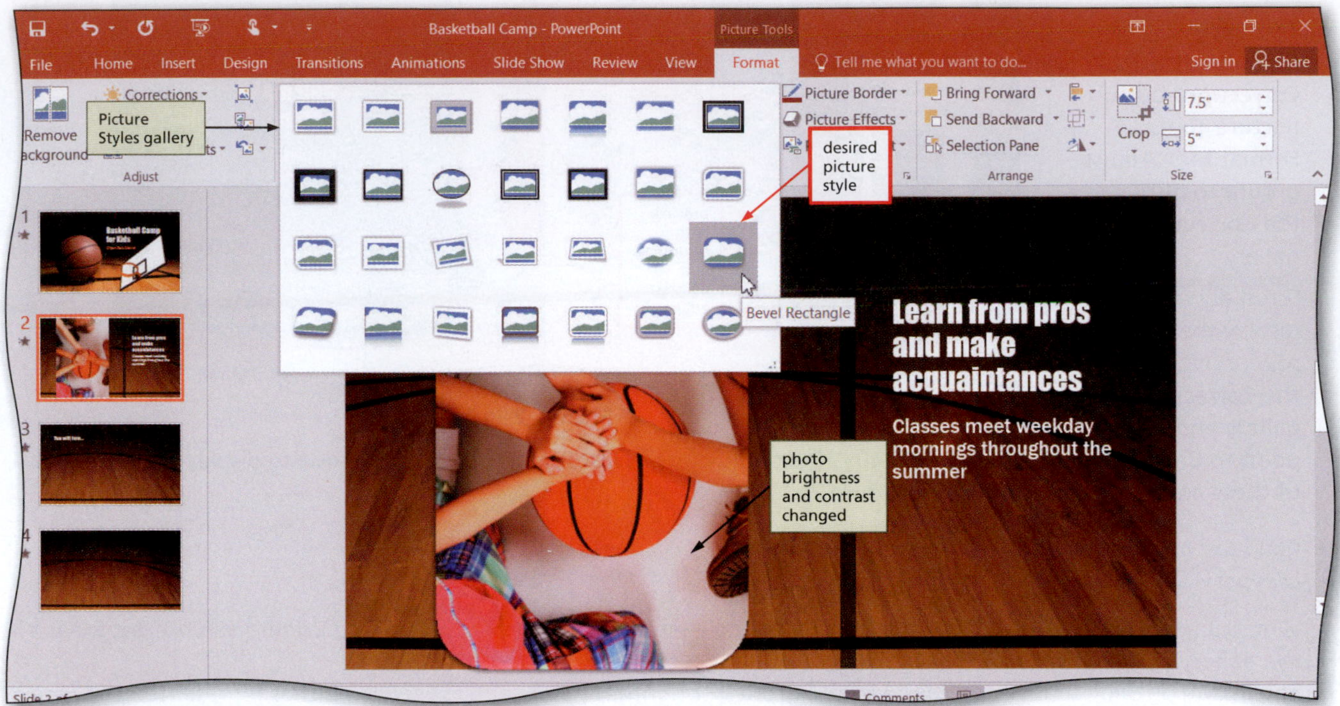

Figure 2–18

Experiment

- Point to various picture styles in the Picture Styles gallery and watch the style of the picture change in the document window.

2

- Click Bevel Rectangle in the Picture Styles gallery to apply the style to the selected picture.

To Add a Picture Border

The next step is to add a border to the Slide 2 picture. ***Why?*** *Some picture styles do not have a border; others, such as the Bevel Rectangle style you applied to this picture, do have this edging. This border is small, and you want a larger edge around the photo to draw attention to the graphic.* The following steps add a border to the Teamwork picture.

1

- With the Slide 2 picture still selected, click the Picture Border arrow (Picture Tools Format tab | Picture Styles group) to display the Picture Border gallery.

Q&A What if the Picture Tools Format tab no longer is displayed on my ribbon?
Click the picture to display the Picture Tools Format tab.

2

- Point to Weight on the Picture Border gallery to display the Weight gallery.
- Point to 6 pt to display a live preview of this line weight on the picture (Figure 2–19).

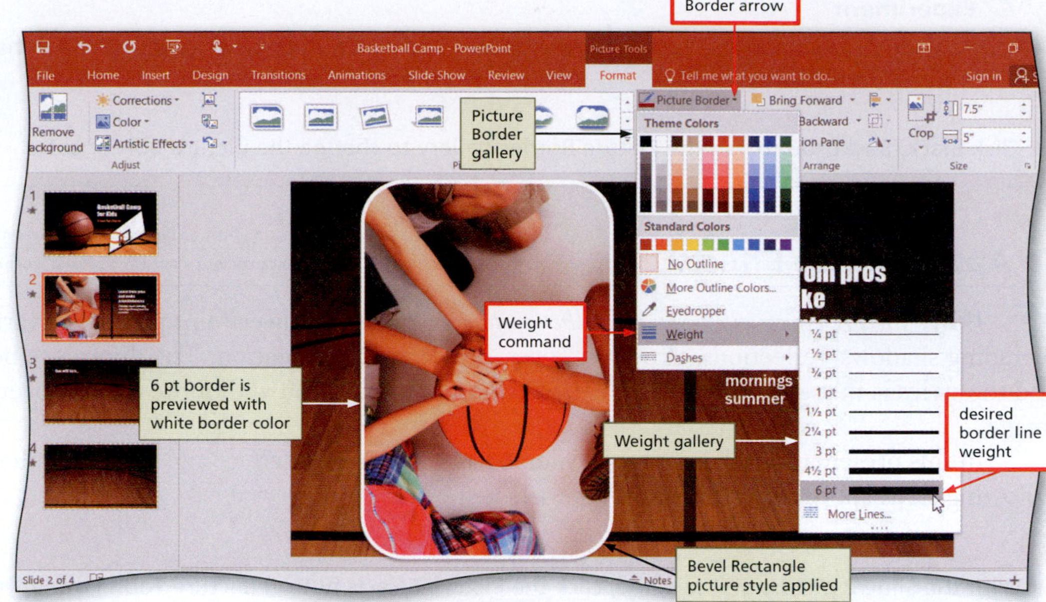

Figure 2–19

Q&A Can I make the line width more than 6 pt?
Yes. Click More Lines, Click Solid line in the Line section of the Format Picture pane, and then increase the amount in the Width box.

Experiment

- Point to various line weights in the Weight gallery and watch the line thickness change.

3

- Click 6 pt to add this line weight to the picture.

To Change a Picture Border Color

1 DOWNLOAD & SELECT SLIDES | 2 INSERT & FORMAT PICTURES | 3 INSERT & FORMAT SHAPES
4 FORMAT SLIDE BACKGROUNDS | 5 INSERT & FORMAT WORDART | 6 REVIEW, REVISE, & PRINT SLIDES

The default color for the border you added to the Slide 2 picture is white, but you will change the border color to black. ***Why?*** *The black color coordinates with other elements on the slide, especially the lines on the basketball and the court.* The following steps change the Slide 2 picture border color.

1

- With the Slide 2 photo still selected, click the Picture Border arrow (Picture Tools Format tab | Picture Styles group) to display the Picture Border gallery again.

2

- Point to Black, Background 1 (first color in first row) in the Picture Border gallery to display a live preview of that border color on the picture (Figure 2–20).

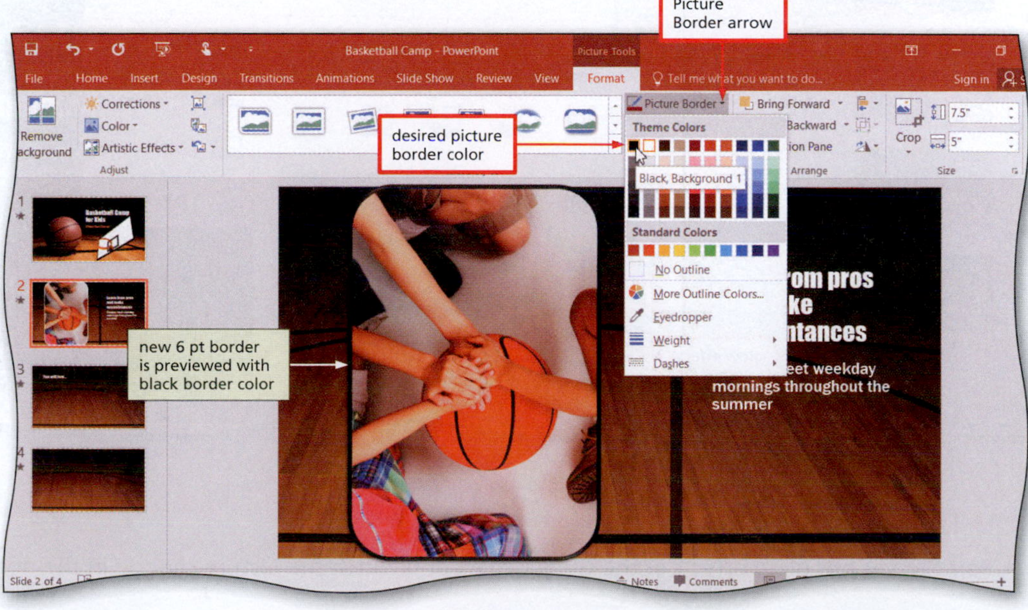

Figure 2–20

 **Experiment**

- Point to various colors in the Picture Border gallery and watch the border on the picture change in the slide.

3

- Click Black, Background 1 in the Picture Border gallery to change the picture border color.

To Apply Picture Effects

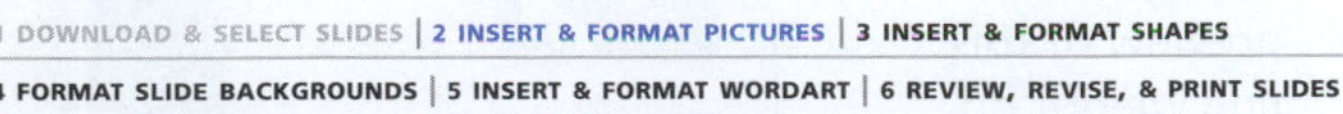

Why? Picture effects allow you to further customize a picture. PowerPoint provides a variety of picture effects, including shadows, reflections, glow, soft edges, bevel, and 3-D rotation. The difference between the effects and the styles is that each effect has several options, providing you with more control over the exact look of the image.

In this presentation, the photo on Slide 2 has a brown glow effect and a bevel applied to its edges. The following steps apply picture effects to the selected picture.

- With the Slide 2 picture still selected, click the Picture Effects button (Picture Tools Format tab | Picture Styles group) to display the Picture Effects menu.

Q&A What if the Picture Tools Format tab no longer is displayed on my ribbon?

Click the picture to display the Picture Tools Format tab.

- Point to Glow on the Picture Effects menu to display the Glow gallery.
- Point to Brown, 18 pt glow, Accent color 3 in the Glow Variations area (third glow in last row) to display a live preview of the selected glow effect applied to the picture in the document window (Figure 2–21).

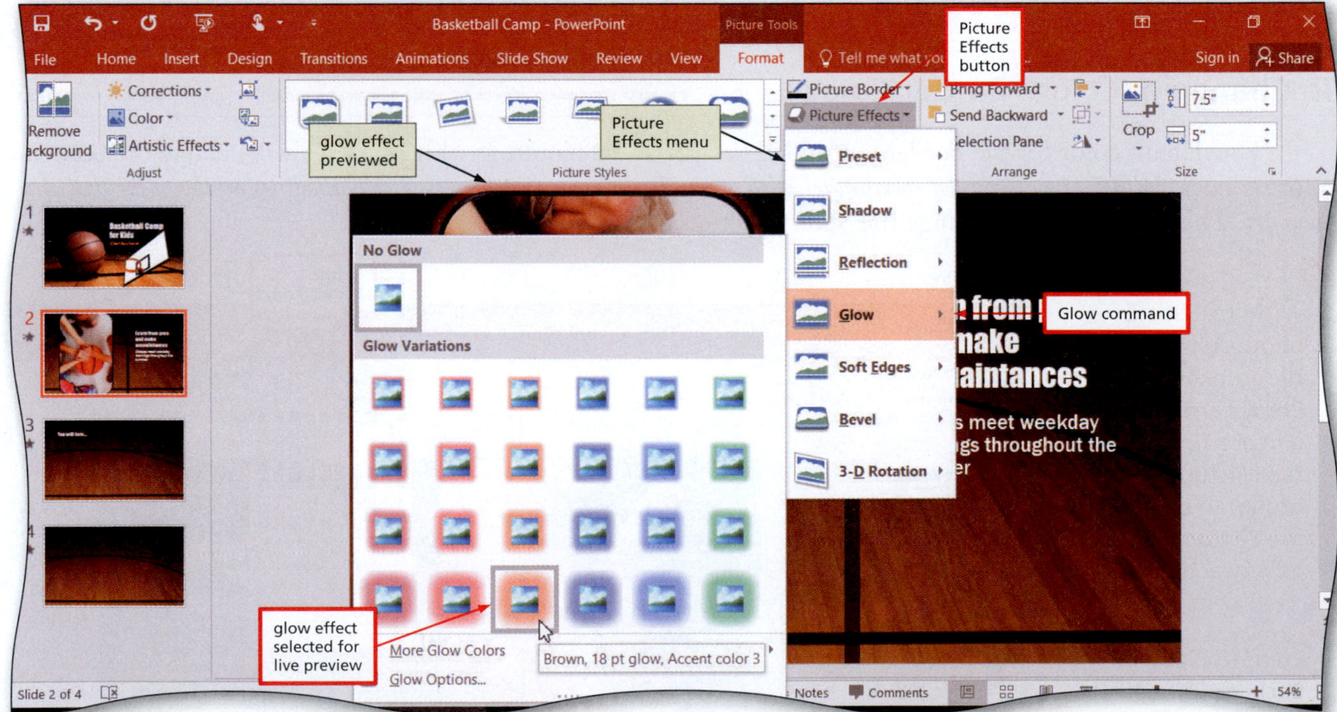

Figure 2–21

Experiment

- Point to various glow effects in the Glow gallery and watch the picture change in the document window.

2

- Click Brown, 18 pt glow, Accent color 3 in the Glow gallery to apply the selected picture effect.

3

- Click the Picture Effects button (Picture Tools Format tab | Picture Styles group) to display the Picture Effects menu again.
- Point to Bevel on the Picture Effects menu to display the Bevel gallery.
- Point to Angle (first bevel in second Bevel row) to display a live preview of the selected bevel effect applied to the Slide 2 picture (Figure 2–22).

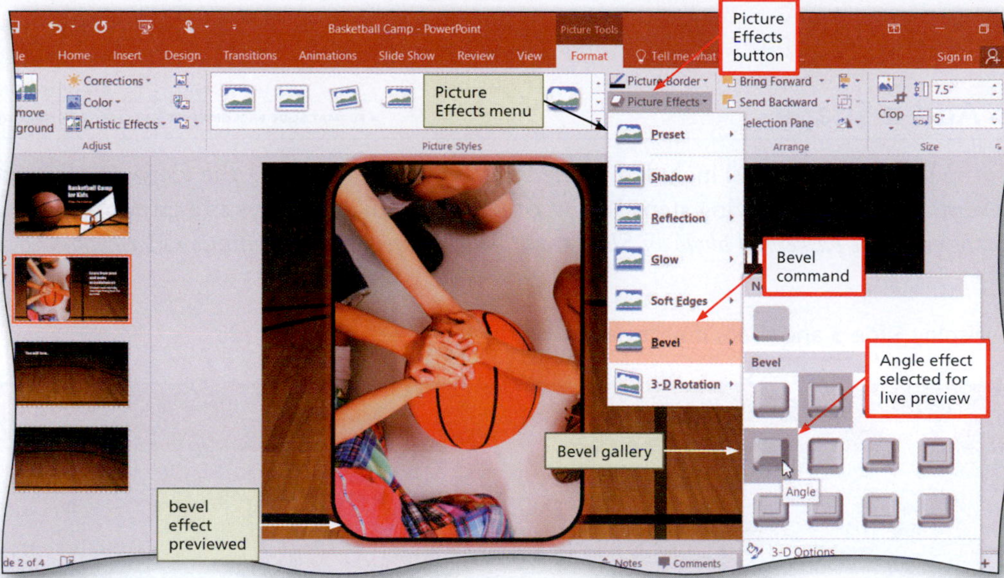

Figure 2–22

- Point to various bevel effects in the Bevel gallery and watch the picture change in the slide.

4

- Click Angle in the Bevel gallery to apply the selected picture effect.

Other Ways

1. Right-click picture, click Format Picture on shortcut menu, select desired options (Format Picture pane), click Close button
2. Click Format Shape pane launcher (Picture Tools Format tab | Picture Styles group), select desired options (Format Picture pane), click Close button

Break Point: If you wish to take a break, this is a good place to do so. Be sure to save the Basketball Camp file again and then you can exit PowerPoint. To resume at a later time, run PowerPoint, open the file called Basketball Camp, and continue following the steps from this location forward.

Inserting and Formatting a Shape

One method of getting the audience's attention and reinforcing the major concepts being presented is to have graphical elements on the slide. PowerPoint provides a wide variety of predefined shapes that can add visual interest to a slide. Shape elements include lines, basic geometrical shapes, arrows, equation shapes, flowchart symbols, stars, banners, and callouts. After adding a shape to a slide, you can change its default characteristics by adding text, bullets, numbers, and styles. You also can combine multiple shapes to create a more complex graphic.

The predefined shapes are found in the Shapes gallery. This collection is found on the Home tab | Drawing group and the Insert tab | Illustrations group. Once you have inserted and selected a shape, the Drawing Tools Format tab is displayed, and the Shapes gallery also is displayed in the Insert Shapes group.

BTW

Inserting Special Characters

Along with adding shapes to a slide, you can insert characters not found on your keyboard, such as the section sign (§), the copyright sign (©), and Greek capital letters (e.g., Δ, Ω, and ß). To insert these characters, click the Insert tab and then click the Symbol button (Insert tab | Symbols group). When the Symbol dialog box is displayed, you can use the same font you currently are using in your presentation, or you can select another font. The Webdings, Wingdings, Wingdings 2, and Wingdings 3 fonts have a variety of symbols.

Slide 3 in this presentation is enhanced in a variety of ways. First, an oval, an arrow, and a pentagon shape are inserted on the slide and formatted. Then, text is added to the oval and pentagon and formatted. The pentagon is copied, and the text is modified in this new shape. Finally, the arrow shape is duplicated twice and moved into position.

To Add a Shape

1 DOWNLOAD & SELECT SLIDES | 2 INSERT & FORMAT PICTURES | **3 INSERT & FORMAT SHAPES**
4 FORMAT SLIDE BACKGROUNDS | 5 INSERT & FORMAT WORDART | 6 REVIEW, REVISE, & PRINT SLIDES

Many of the shapes included in the Shapes gallery can direct the viewer to important aspects of the presentation. The following steps add an oval shape, which displays as a circle, to Slide 3. ***Why?*** *A circle shape complements the basketball photo on Slide 1 and helps reinforce the presentation's basketball theme.*

- Display Slide 3 and then, if necessary, click the Home tab (Figure 2–23).

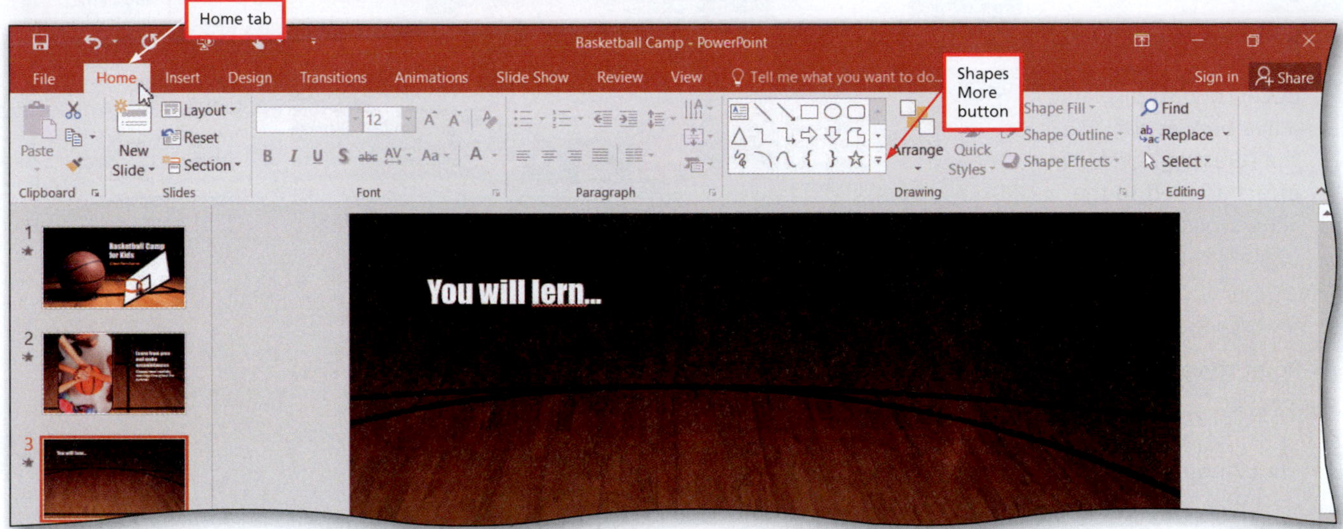

Figure 2–23

- Click the Shapes More button (Home tab | Drawing group) shown in Figure 2–23 to display the Shapes gallery (Figure 2–24).

Q&A I do not see a Shapes More button and the three rows of the shapes shown in Figure 2–24. Instead, I have a Shapes button. Why?
Monitor dimensions and resolution affect how buttons display on the ribbon. Click the Shapes button to display the entire Shapes gallery.

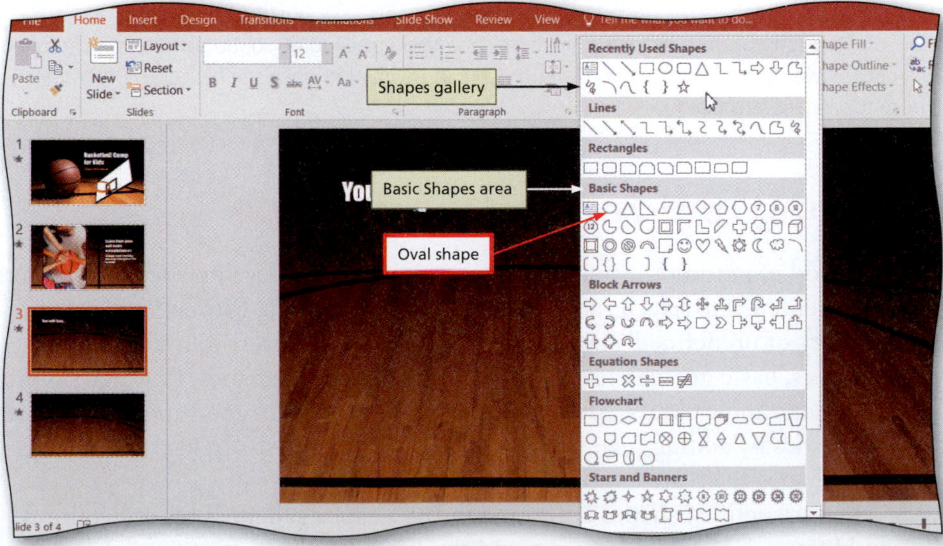

Figure 2–24

3

- Click the Oval shape in the Basic Shapes area of the Shapes gallery.

Why did my pointer change shape?
The pointer changed to a plus shape to indicate the Oval shape has been added to the Clipboard.

- Position the pointer (a crosshair) near the center of the slide, as shown in Figure 2–25.

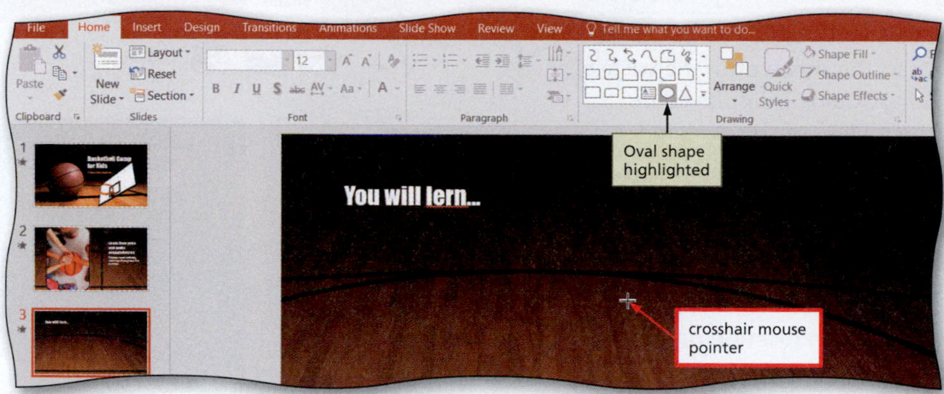

Figure 2–25

4

- Click Slide 3 to insert the Oval shape.

Other Ways

1. Click Shapes button (Insert tab | Illustrations group)

To Resize a Shape

1 DOWNLOAD & SELECT SLIDES | 2 INSERT & FORMAT PICTURES | **3 INSERT & FORMAT SHAPES**
4 FORMAT SLIDE BACKGROUNDS | 5 INSERT & FORMAT WORDART | 6 REVIEW, REVISE, & PRINT SLIDES

The next step is to resize the Oval shape. ***Why?*** *The oval should be enlarged so that it is a focal point in the middle area of the slide.* The following steps resize the selected shape.

1

- Press and hold down the SHIFT key and then drag the upper-left corner sizing handle until the shape is resized approximately as shown in Figure 2–26 and the top is aligned with a horizontal Smart Guide.

Why did I need to press the SHIFT key while enlarging the shape?
Holding down the SHIFT key while dragging keeps the proportions of the original shape.

What if my shape is not selected?
To select a shape, click it.

If I am using a touch screen, how can I maintain the shape's original proportion?
If you drag one of the corner sizing handles, the object should stay in proportion.

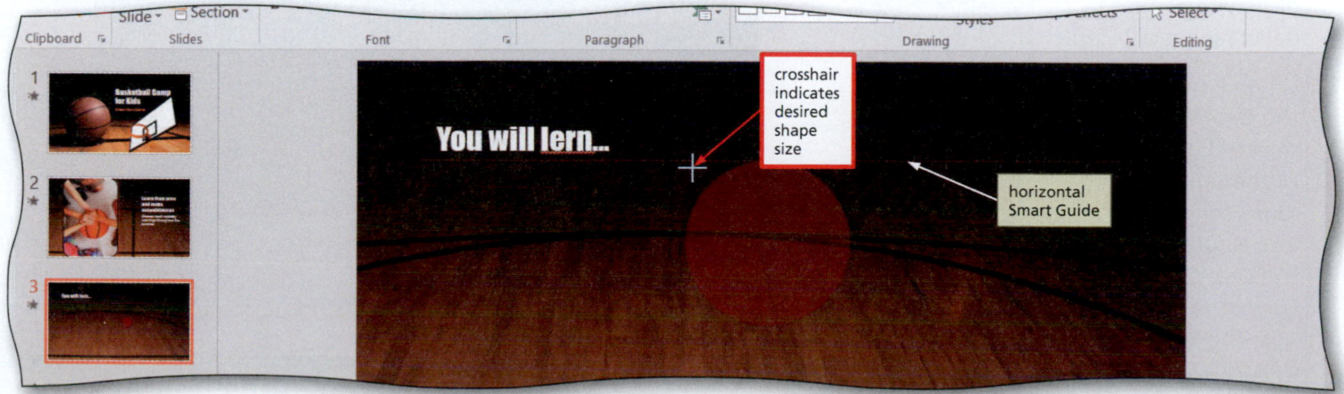

Figure 2–26

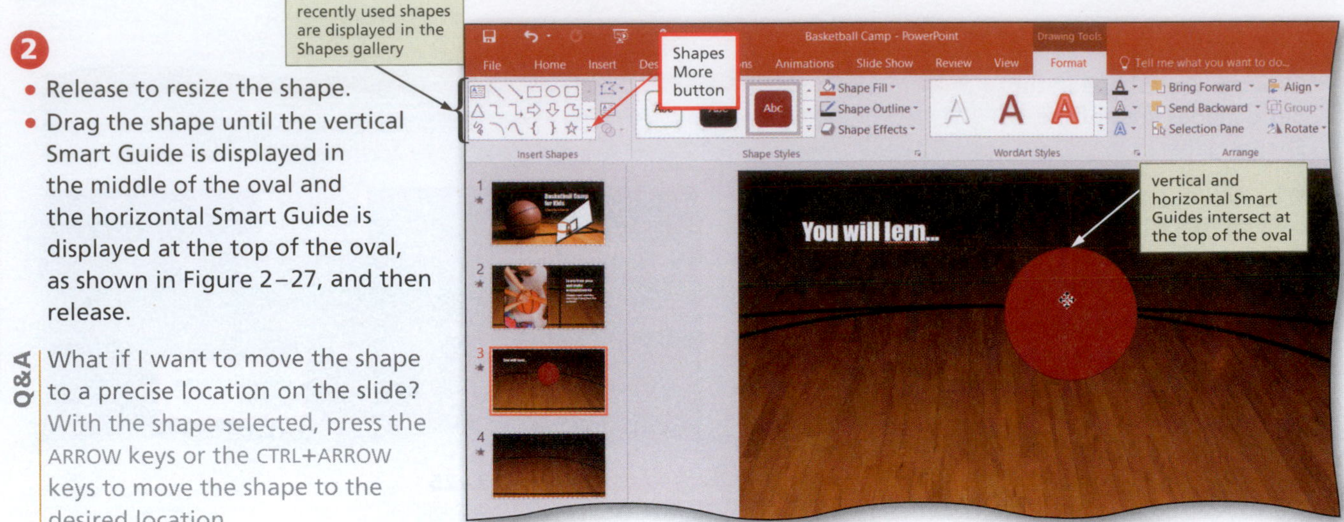

2

- Release to resize the shape.
- Drag the shape until the vertical Smart Guide is displayed in the middle of the oval and the horizontal Smart Guide is displayed at the top of the oval, as shown in Figure 2–27, and then release.

Q&A What if I want to move the shape to a precise location on the slide?
With the shape selected, press the ARROW keys or the CTRL+ARROW keys to move the shape to the desired location.

Figure 2–27

Other Ways

1. Enter shape height and width in Height and Width boxes (Drawing Tools Format tab | Size group)
2. Click Size and Position pane launcher (Drawing Tools Format tab | Size group), click Size tab, enter desired height and width values in boxes, click Close button

To Add Other Shapes

1 DOWNLOAD & SELECT SLIDES | 2 INSERT & FORMAT PICTURES | **3 INSERT & FORMAT SHAPES**
4 FORMAT SLIDE BACKGROUNDS | 5 INSERT & FORMAT WORDART | 6 REVIEW, REVISE, & PRINT SLIDES

Ovals, squares, arrows, stars, and equation shapes are among the items included in the Shapes gallery. These shapes can be combined to show relationships among the elements, and they can help illustrate the basic concepts presented in your slide show. ***Why?*** *Arrows are especially useful in showing the relationship among slide elements and guiding the viewer's eyes to move from one shape to the next.* More than two dozen arrow shapes are displayed in the Block Arrows section of the Shapes gallery. The following steps add one of these arrows and the pentagon shapes to Slide 3.

1

- Click the Shapes More button (Drawing Tools Format tab | Insert Shapes group) shown in Figure 2–27 to display the Shapes gallery (Figure 2–28).

Q&A When I inserted the Oval shape, I selected it on the Home tab. Is the same Shapes gallery also displayed on the Drawing Tools Format tab?
Yes. The Shapes gallery is displayed on this tab once an object is inserted and selected on the slide.

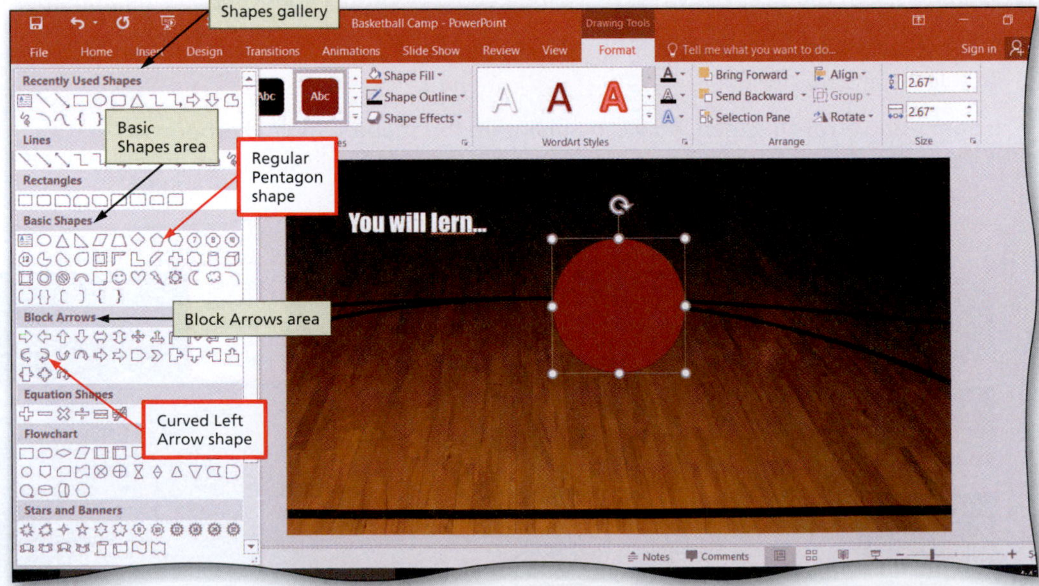

Figure 2–28

2

- Click the Curved Left Arrow shape in the Block Arrows area of the Shapes gallery.
- Position the pointer to the right of the oval shape in Slide 3 and then click to insert the Curved Left Arrow shape.

3

- Press and hold down the SHIFT key and then drag a corner sizing handle until the arrow shape is approximately the size shown in Figure 2–29.

Q&A If I am using a touch screen, how can I maintain the Oval shape's original proportion?
The object should stay in proportion when you drag one of the corner sizing handles.

- If necessary, drag the Curved Left Arrow shape to the right side of the oval, as shown in Figure 2–29, and then release.

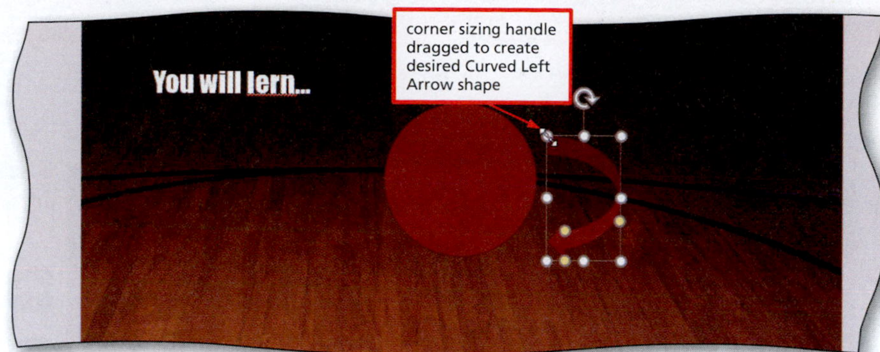

Figure 2–29

4

- Display the Shapes gallery and then click the Regular Pentagon shape in the Basic Shapes area of the gallery (shown in Figure 2–28).
- Position the pointer toward the lower-left side of the Curved Left Arrow shape and then click to insert the Regular Pentagon shape.

5

- Press and hold down the SHIFT key and then drag a corner sizing handle to resize the pentagon shape so that it is the size shown in Figure 2–30.
- Drag the pentagon shape so that its tip is placed at the intersection of the horizontal Smart Guide above the pentagon and the vertical Smart Guide in the middle of the shape, as shown in Figure 2–30, and then release.

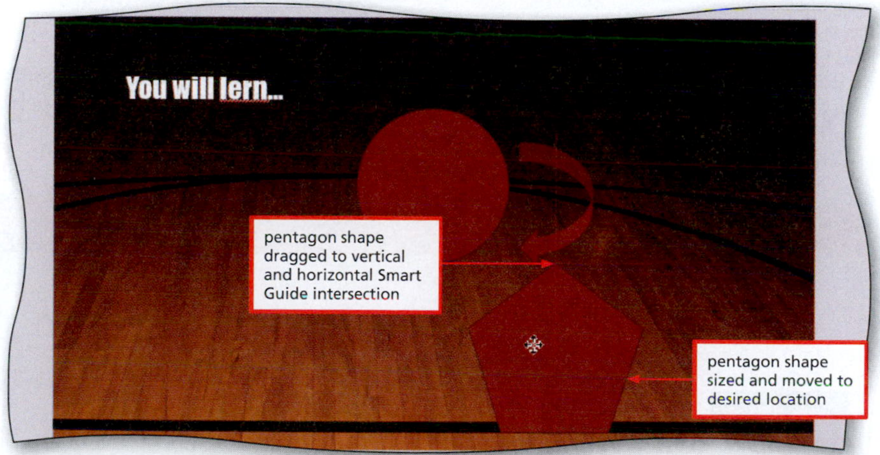

Figure 2–30

To Apply a Shape Style

1 DOWNLOAD & SELECT SLIDES | 2 INSERT & FORMAT PICTURES | 3 INSERT & FORMAT SHAPES
4 FORMAT SLIDE BACKGROUNDS | 5 INSERT & FORMAT WORDART | 6 REVIEW, REVISE, & PRINT SLIDES

Formatting text in a shape follows the same techniques as formatting text in a placeholder. You can change font, font color and size, and alignment. You later will add information about a skill to the Oval shape, but first you want to apply a shape style. ***Why?*** *The style will give depth and dimension to the object.* The Quick Styles gallery has a variety of styles that change depending upon the theme applied to the presentation. The following steps apply a style to the oval.

1

- Display the Home tab, click the oval to select it, and then click the Quick Styles button (Home tab | Drawing group) (Figure 2–31).

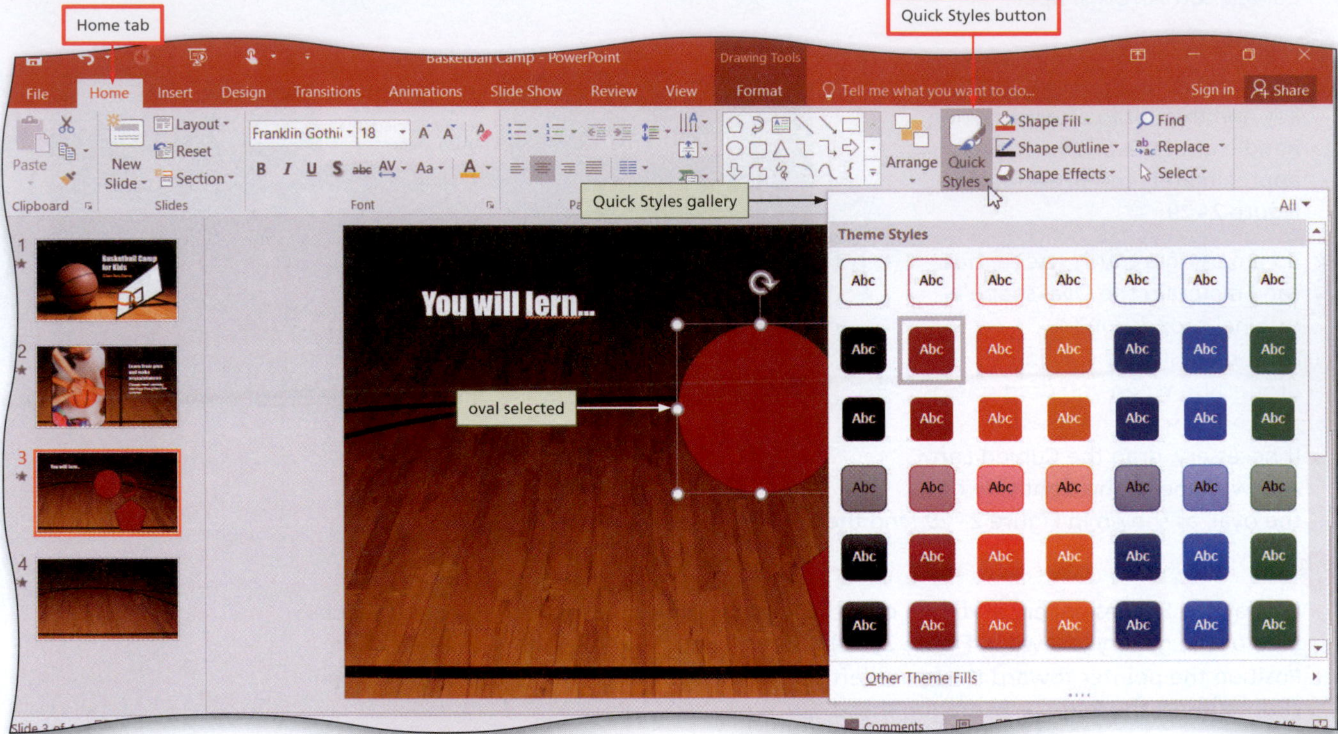

Figure 2–31

2

- Point to Light 1 Outline, Colored Fill – Black, Dark 1 in the Quick Styles gallery (first shape in third Theme Styles row) to display a live preview of that style applied to the oval in the slide (Figure 2–32).

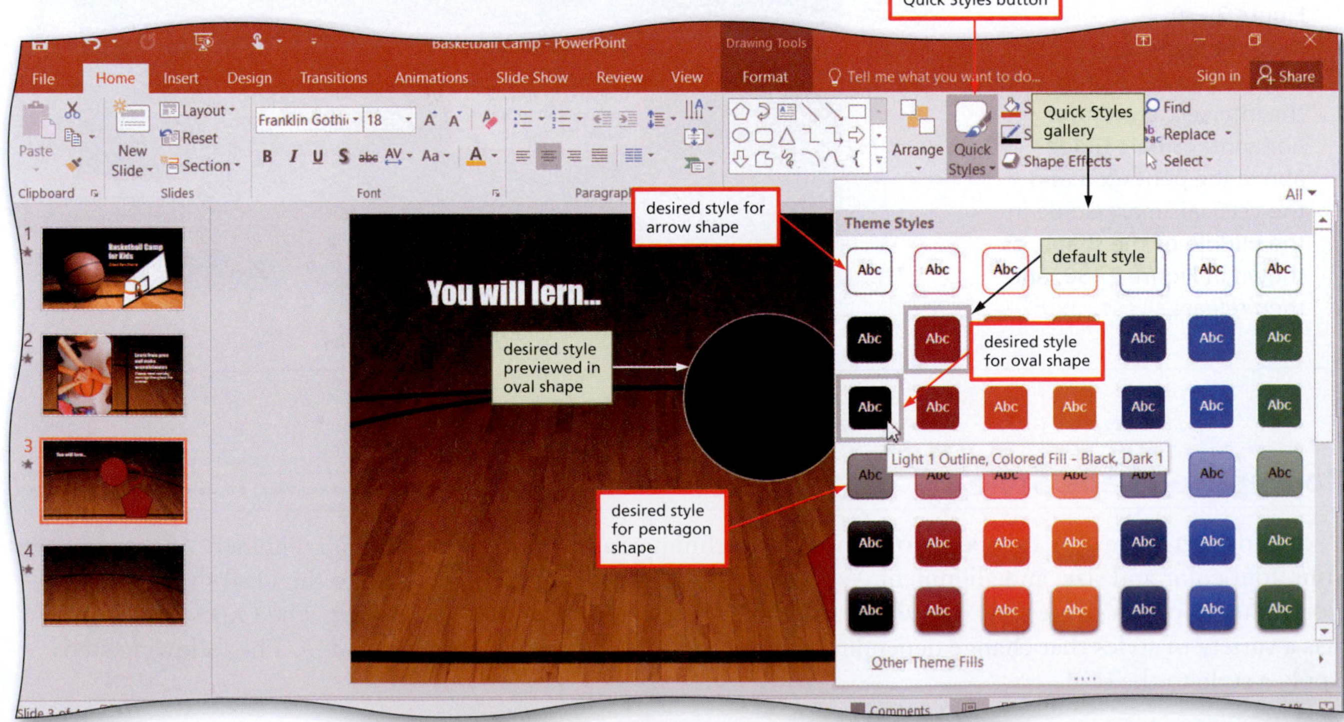

Figure 2–32

Experiment

- Point to various styles in the Quick Styles gallery and watch the style of the shape change.

3

- Click Light 1 Outline, Colored Fill – Black, Dark 1 in the Quick Styles gallery to apply the selected style to the oval.

Other Ways

1. Click Shape Styles More button (Drawing Tools Format tab | Shape Styles group), select style
2. Right-click shape, click Style button on mini toolbar, select desired style

To Apply Another Style

You later will add text to the oval and pentagon about particular skills taught at the camp, but now you want to format the arrow and pentagon shapes. ***Why?*** *You can apply shape styles to the arrow and pentagon that will coordinate with the oval's style. A light style color in the arrow shape will help join darker style colors of the oval and rectangle. This formatting will add interest and emphasize the relationship between basketball playing skills.* The following steps apply styles to the arrow and pentagon shapes.

BTW

Deleting a Shape

If you want to delete a shape you have added to a slide, click that shape to select it and then press the delete key. If you want to DELETE multiple shapes, press the CTRL key while clicking the undesired shapes and then press the DELETE key.

1. Click the arrow shape to select it.
2. Click the Quick Styles button (Home tab | Drawing group) to display the Quick Styles gallery and then apply the Colored Outline – Black, Dark 1 style (first style in first Theme Styles row) to the arrow shape.
3. Click the pentagon shape to select it and then click the Quick Styles button.
4. Click Subtle Effect – Black, Dark 1 (first style in fourth Theme Styles row) to apply that style to the pentagon shape (Figure 2–33).

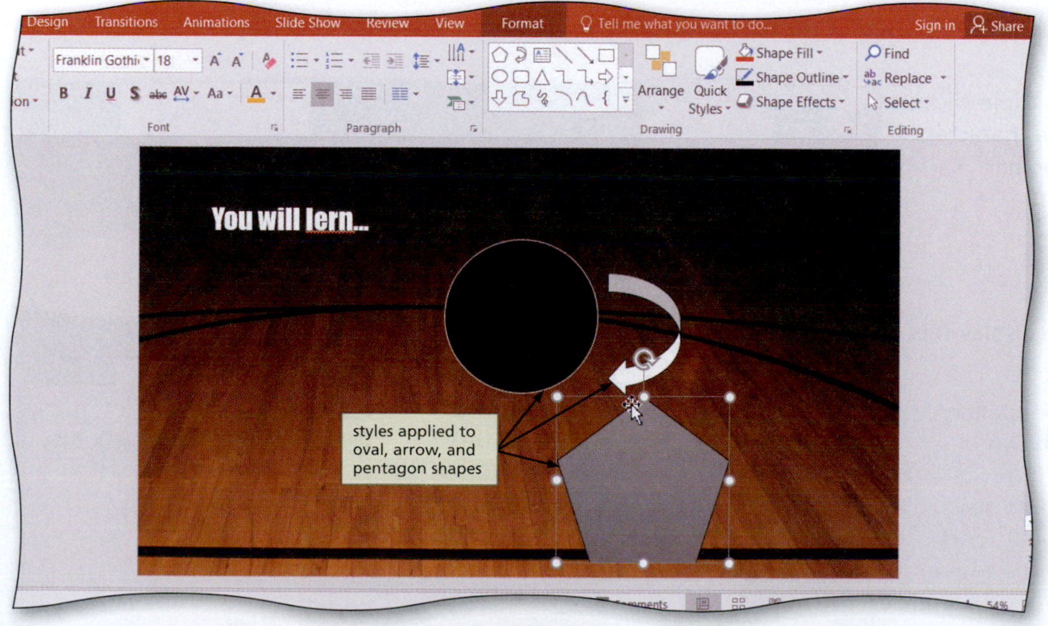

Figure 2–33

To Add Text to a Shape

The three shapes on Slide 3 help call attention to the key aspects of your presentation. ***Why?** Your goal is to emphasize key skills the campers will learn.* The next step is to add this information to Slide 3. The following steps add text to the oval and pentagon shapes.

1

- With the pentagon selected, type `Offensive moves` to add the text in the shape.

2

- Click the oval to select it and then type **`Ball handling skills`** to add the text in the shape (Figure 2–34).

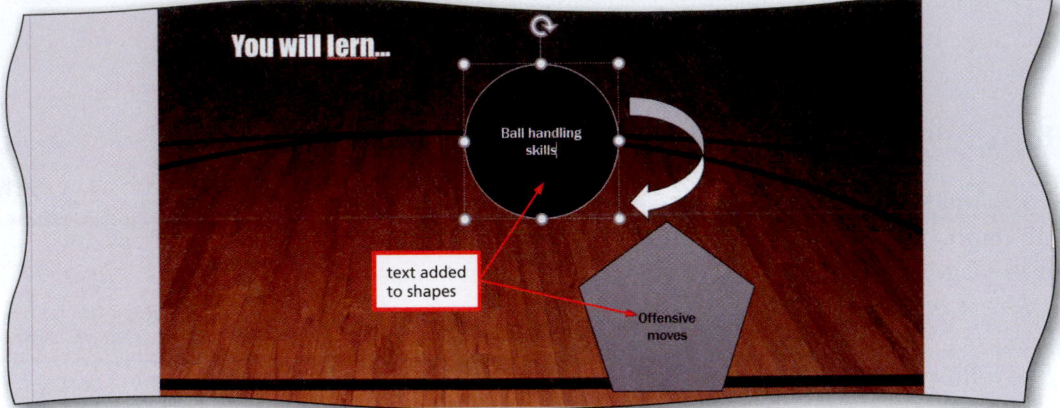

Figure 2–34

To Change the Font

The default theme font is Franklin Gothic Medium. To draw more attention to text in the shapes and to help differentiate these slide elements from the title text, you want to change the font to Century Schoolbook. ***Why?** Century Schoolbook is a serif typeface, meaning the ends of some of the letter are adorned with small decorations, called serifs. These adornments slow down the viewer's reading speed, which might help them retain the information they saw.* To change the font, you must select the letters you want to format. In Module 1, you selected a paragraph and then formatted the characters, and you follow the same procedure to change the font. The following steps change the text font in the shape.

1

- With the oval selected, triple-click the text to select all the characters and display the mini toolbar (Figure 2–35).

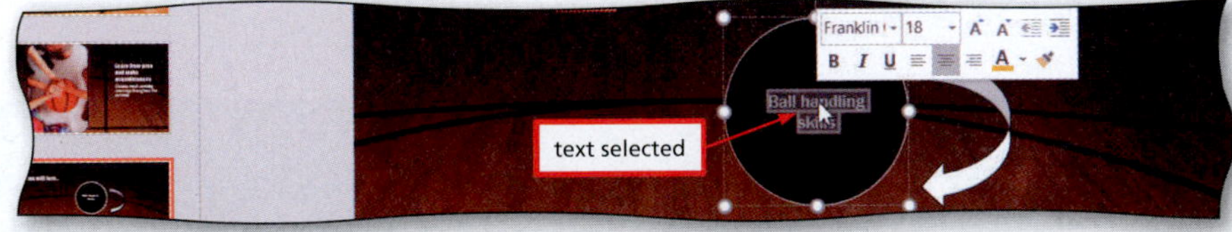

Figure 2–35

2

- Click the Font arrow to display the Font gallery (Figure 2–36).

Q&A Will the fonts in my Font gallery be the same as those shown in Figure 2–36?
Your list of available fonts may differ, depending on what fonts you have installed and the type of printer you are using.

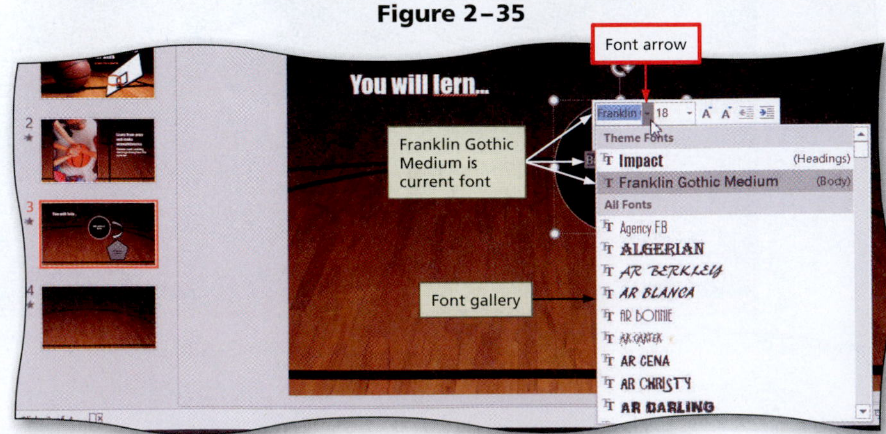

Figure 2–36

3

- Drag or scroll through the Font gallery and then point to Century Schoolbook (or a similar font) to display a live preview of the title text in the Century Schoolbook font (Figure 2–37).

Experiment

- Point to various fonts in the Font gallery and watch the subtitle text font change in the slide.
- Click Century Schoolbook (or a similar font) to change the font of the selected text to Century Schoolbook.

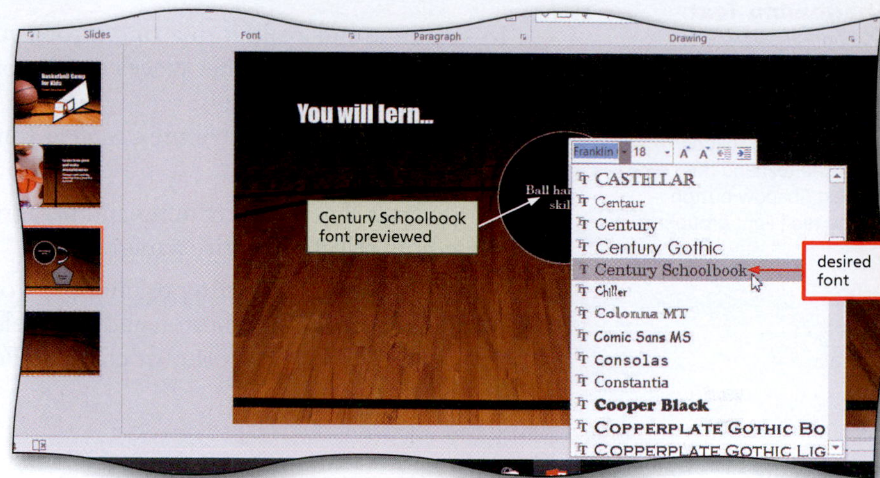

Figure 2–37

Other Ways

1. Click Font arrow (Home tab | Font group), click desired font in Font gallery
2. Right-click selected text, click Font on shortcut menu (Font dialog box), click Font tab, select desired font in Font list, click OK button
3. Click Font dialog box launcher (Home tab | Font group), click Font tab (Font dialog box), select desired font in Font list, click OK button
4. Press CTRL+SHIFT+F, click Font tab (Font dialog box), select desired font in the Font list, click OK button
5. Right-click selected text, click Font arrow on mini toolbar, select desired font

To Format the Text

To increase readability, you can format the oval text by increasing the font size, bolding the characters, and changing the font color to orange. The following steps format the oval text.

BTW

Text in a Shape

When you add text to a shape, it becomes part of the shape. If you rotate or flip the shape, the text also rotates or flips.

1. With the oval text selected, click the Increase Font Size button (Home tab | Font group) two times to increase the font size to 24 pt.
2. Click the Bold button (Home tab | Font group) to bold the text.
3. Click the Font Color arrow and change the color to Orange (third color in Standard Colors row) (Figure 2–38).

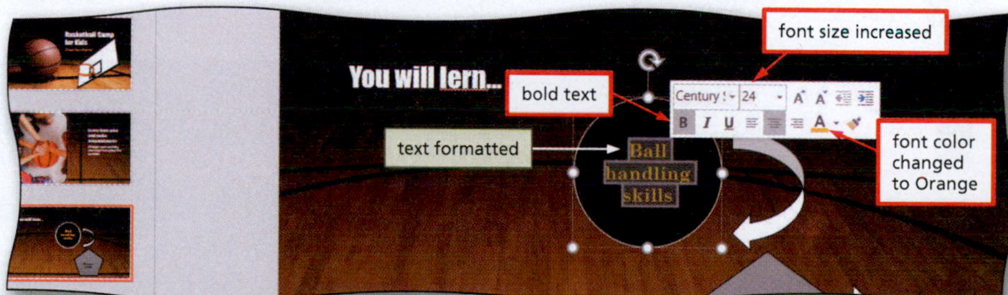

Figure 2–38

Q&A

What should I do if one or more letters of the word, handling, wrap to the third line in the shape?

Press and hold down the SHIFT key and then drag a corner sizing handle outward slightly to resize the oval shape.

Could I also add a shadow behind the text to add depth and help the letters display prominently?

Yes. Select the text and then click the Text Shadow button (Home tab | Font group).

Other Ways

1. Right-click selected text, click desired text format button on mini toolbar

BTW
Shadowing Text
Adding a shadow to text gives depth and helps the letters display prominently by adding a shadow behind them. To add a shadow, select the text and then click the Text Shadow button (Home tab | Font group).

Format Painter

To save time and avoid formatting errors, you can use the Format Painter to apply custom formatting to other places in your presentation quickly and easily. You can use this feature in three ways:

- To copy only character attributes, such as font and font effects, select text that has these qualities.
- To copy both character attributes and paragraph attributes, such as alignment and indentation, select the entire paragraph.
- To apply the same formatting to multiple words, phrases, or paragraphs, double-click the Format Painter button and then select each item you want to format. You then can press the ESC key or click the Format Painter button to turn off this feature.

To Format Text Using the Format Painter

1 DOWNLOAD & SELECT SLIDES | 2 INSERT & FORMAT PICTURES | **3 INSERT & FORMAT SHAPES**
4 FORMAT SLIDE BACKGROUNDS | 5 INSERT & FORMAT WORDART | 6 REVIEW, REVISE, & PRINT SLIDES

Why? *To save time and duplicated effort, you quickly can use the Format Painter to copy formatting attributes from the oval shape text and apply them to pentagon shape text.* The following steps use the Format Painter to copy formatting features.

- With the oval text still selected, double-click the Format Painter button (Home tab | Clipboard group).
- Move the pointer off the ribbon (Figure 2–39).

Q&A
Why does the Format Painter button on my screen display only a paint brush and not the words, Format Painter?
Monitor dimensions and resolution affect how buttons display on the ribbon.

Why did my pointer change shape?
The pointer changed shape by adding a paintbrush to indicate that the Format Painter function is active.

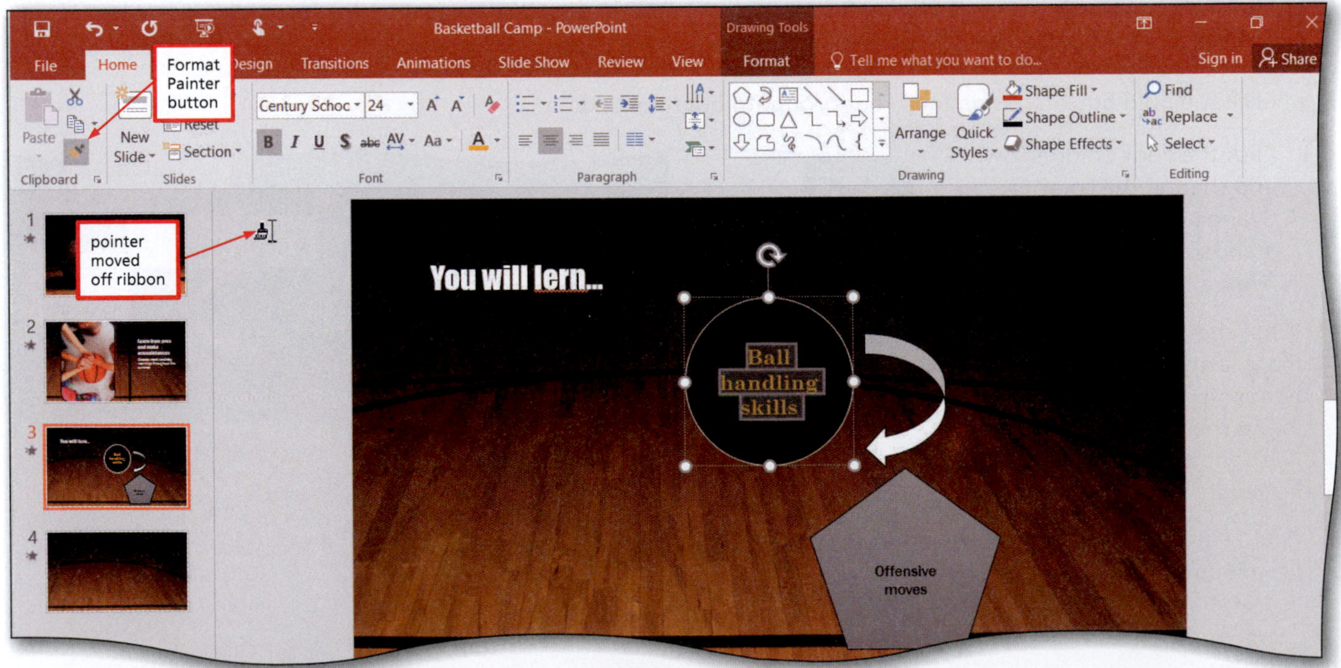

Figure 2–39

2

- Triple-click the pentagon text to apply the format to all characters (Figure 2–40).
- Click the Format Painter button or press the ESC key to turn off the Format Painter feature.

Q&A What should I do if one or more letters of the word, Offensive, wrap to a second line in the shape?
Press and hold down the SHIFT key and then drag a corner sizing handle outward slightly to resize the pentagon shape.

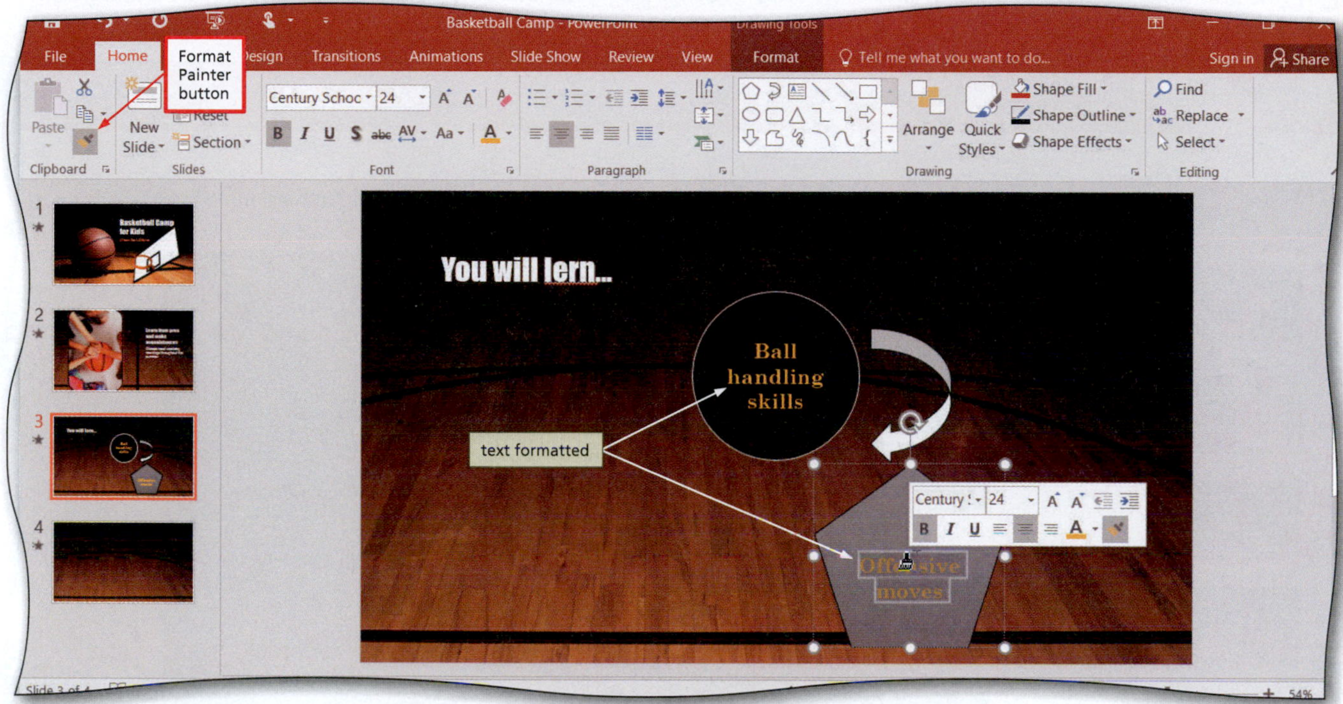

Figure 2–40

Other Ways

1. Select text, double-click Format Painter button on mini toolbar

To Copy and Paste a Shape

1 DOWNLOAD & SELECT SLIDES | 2 INSERT & FORMAT PICTURES | 3 INSERT & FORMAT SHAPES
4 FORMAT SLIDE BACKGROUNDS | 5 INSERT & FORMAT WORDART | 6 REVIEW, REVISE, & PRINT SLIDES

Good basketball players have both offensive and defensive skills. You already have created the shape stating the campers will work on refining their offensive talents. You now need to create a second shape with information about defensive instruction that will be provided at the camp. The following steps copy the pentagon shape and then change the text. *Why? You could repeat all the steps you performed to create the first pentagon, but it is much more efficient to duplicate the shape and then edit the text.*

- With the pentagon shape selected, click the Copy button (Home tab | Clipboard group) (Figure 2–41).

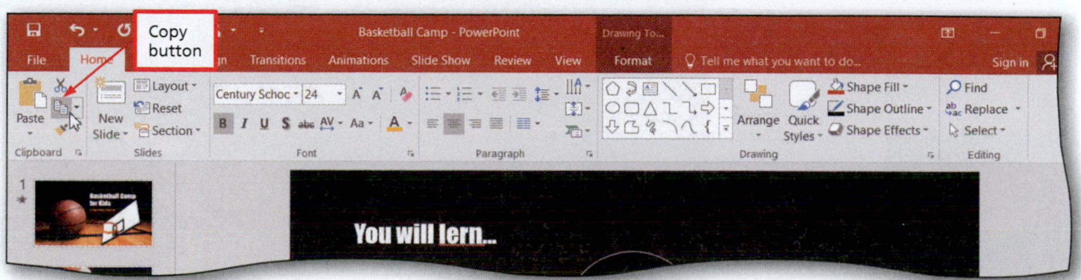

Figure 2–41

2

- Click the Paste button (Home tab | Clipboard group) to insert a duplicate Regular Pentagon shape on Slide 3.
- Drag the new pentagon shape to the left of the original pentagon shape, as shown in Figure 2–42.
- In the left pentagon shape, select the text, Offensive moves, and then type `Defensive mindset` as the replacement text (Figure 2–42).

Q&A What should I do if one or more letters of the word, Defensive, wrap to a second line in the shape?
Press and hold down the SHIFT key and then drag a corner sizing handle outward slightly to resize the pentagon shape.

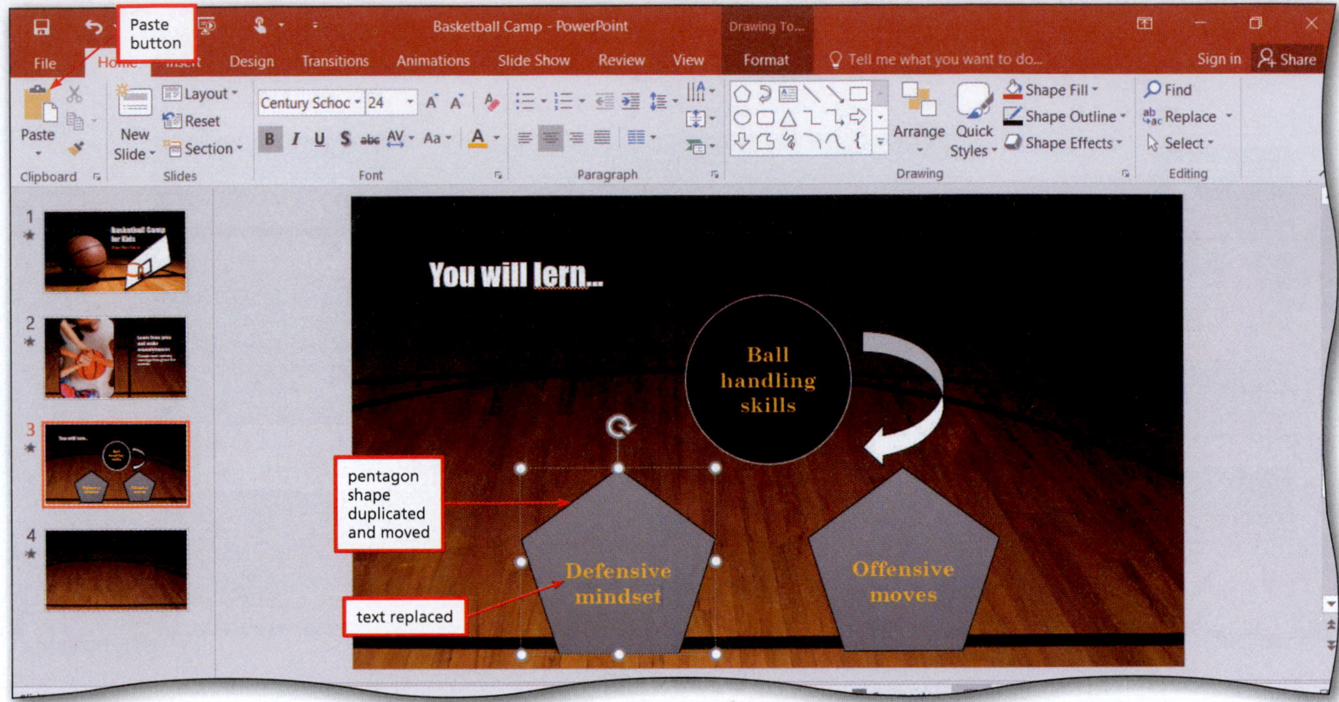

Figure 2–42

3

- Select the arrow shape and then click the Copy button (Home tab | Clipboard group) (Figure 2–43).

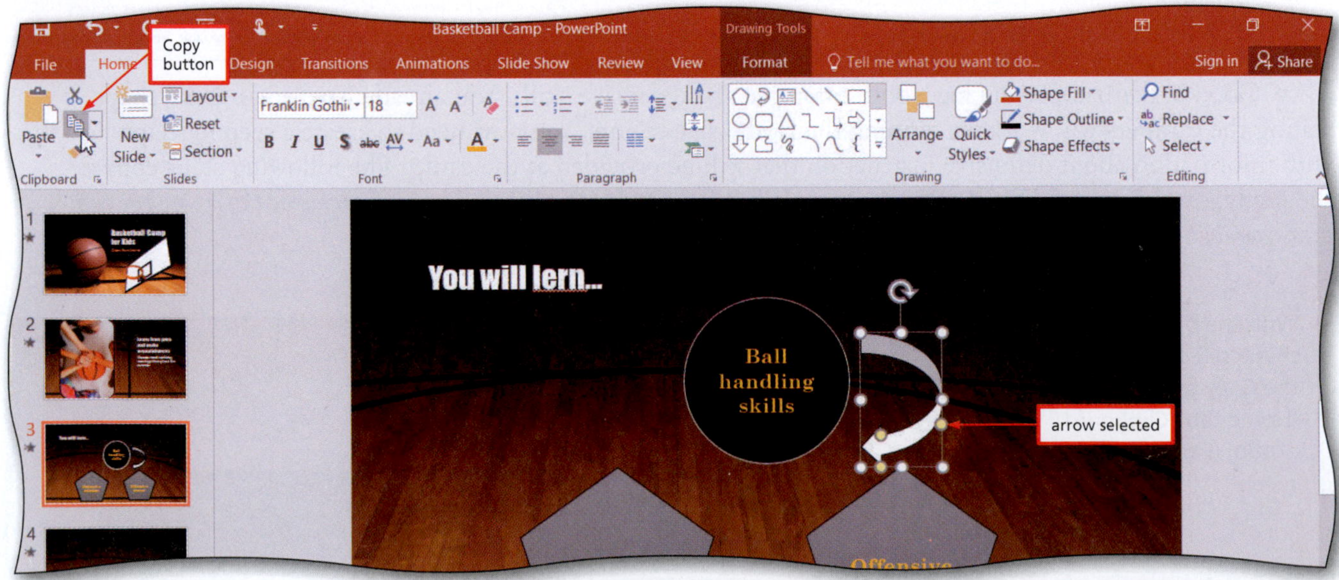

Figure 2–43

- Click the Paste button (Home tab | Clipboard group) two times to insert two duplicate arrow shapes on Slide 3.
- Drag one of the duplicate arrow shapes between the two pentagon shapes and then drag the other duplicate arrow shape between the left pentagon shape and the oval shape (Figure 2–44).

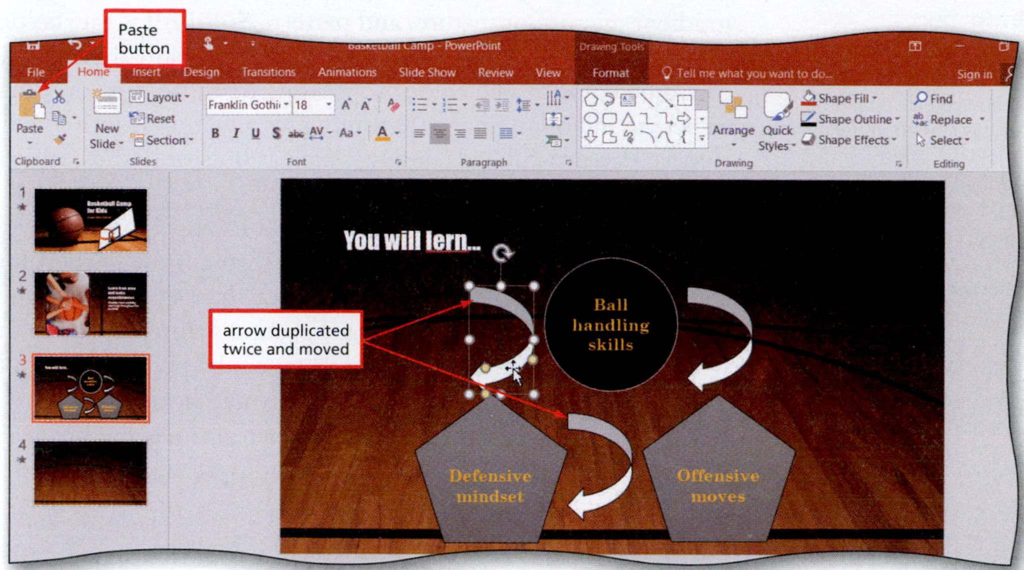

Figure 2–44

- With the left arrow selected, drag its rotation handle clockwise or counterclockwise so that it is displayed as shown in Figure 2–45. Repeat this procedure for the other two arrows, and then adjust the shapes' locations on Slide 3 so that the arrows touch their adjacent shapes (Figure 2–45).

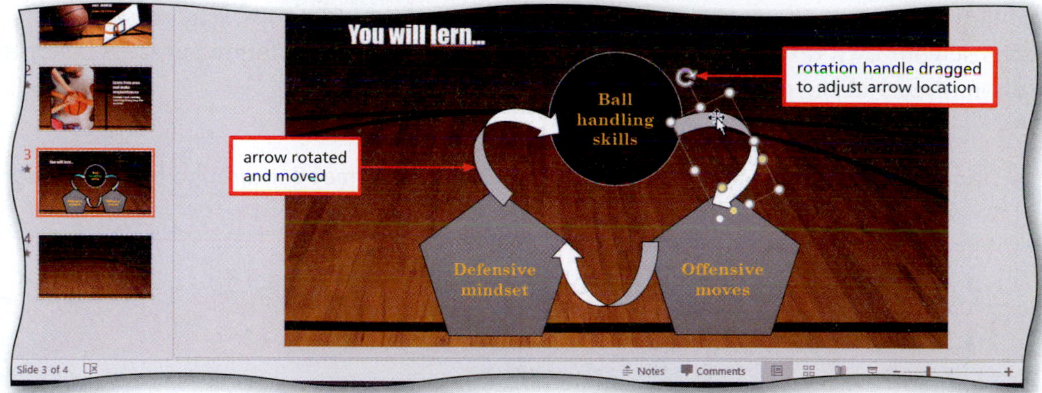

Figure 2–45

- If the end of an arrow is underneath an oval or a pentagon shape, select the arrow, click the Drawing Tools Format tab, and then click the Bring Forward button (Drawing Tools Format tab | Arrange group) to bring the arrow on top of the shape.

Other Ways

1. Right-click selected shape, click Copy on shortcut menu, right-click blank area, click Paste on shortcut menu
2. Select shape, press CTRL+C, press CTRL+V

Break Point: If you wish to take a break, this is a good place to do so. Be sure to save the Basketball Camp file again and then you can exit PowerPoint. To resume at a later time, run PowerPoint, open the file called Basketball Camp, and continue following the steps from this location forward.

Formatting Slide Backgrounds

A slide's background is an integral part of a presentation because it can generate audience interest. Every slide can have the same background, or different backgrounds can be used in a presentation. This background is considered **fill**, which is the content

BTW
Undo Text Formatting Changes
To remove a formatting change you have made to text, such as an underline or bolding, select the text and then click the button that originally applied the format. For example, to undo bolding, select the text and then click the Bold button. If you apply a format and then immediately decide to remove this effect, click the Undo button on the Quick Access Toolbar.

that makes up the interior of a shape, line, or character. Four fills are available: solid, gradient, picture or texture, and pattern. **Solid fill** is one color used throughout the entire slide. **Gradient fill** is one color shade gradually progressing to another shade of the same color or one color progressing to another color. **Picture or texture fill** uses a specific file or an image that simulates a material, such as cork, granite, marble, or canvas. **Pattern fill** adds designs, such as dots or dashes, which repeat in rows across the slide.

Once you add a fill, you can adjust its appearance. For example, you can adjust its **transparency**, which allows you to see through the background, so that any text on the slide is visible. You also can select a color that is part of the theme or a custom color. You can use an **offset**, another background feature, to move the background away from the slide borders in varying distances by percentage. A **tiling option** repeats the background image many times vertically and horizontally on the slide; the smaller the tiling percentage, the greater the number of times the image is repeated.

To Insert a Texture Fill

1 DOWNLOAD & SELECT SLIDES | 2 INSERT & FORMAT PICTURES | 3 INSERT & FORMAT SHAPES
4 FORMAT SLIDE BACKGROUNDS | 5 INSERT & FORMAT WORDART | 6 REVIEW, REVISE, & PRINT SLIDES

***Why?** Various texture fills are available to give your background a unique look.* The 24 pictures in the Texture gallery give the appearance of a physical object, such as water drops, sand, tissue paper, and a paper bag. You also can use your own texture pictures for custom backgrounds. The following steps insert the Brown marble texture fill on Slide 2 in the presentation.

- Display Slide 2. Click the Design tab and then click the Format Background button (Design tab | Customize group) to display the Format Background pane (Figure 2–46).

Figure 2–46

2

- With the Fill section displaying (Format Background pane), if necessary, click 'Picture or texture fill' and then click the Texture button to display the Texture gallery (Figure 2–47).

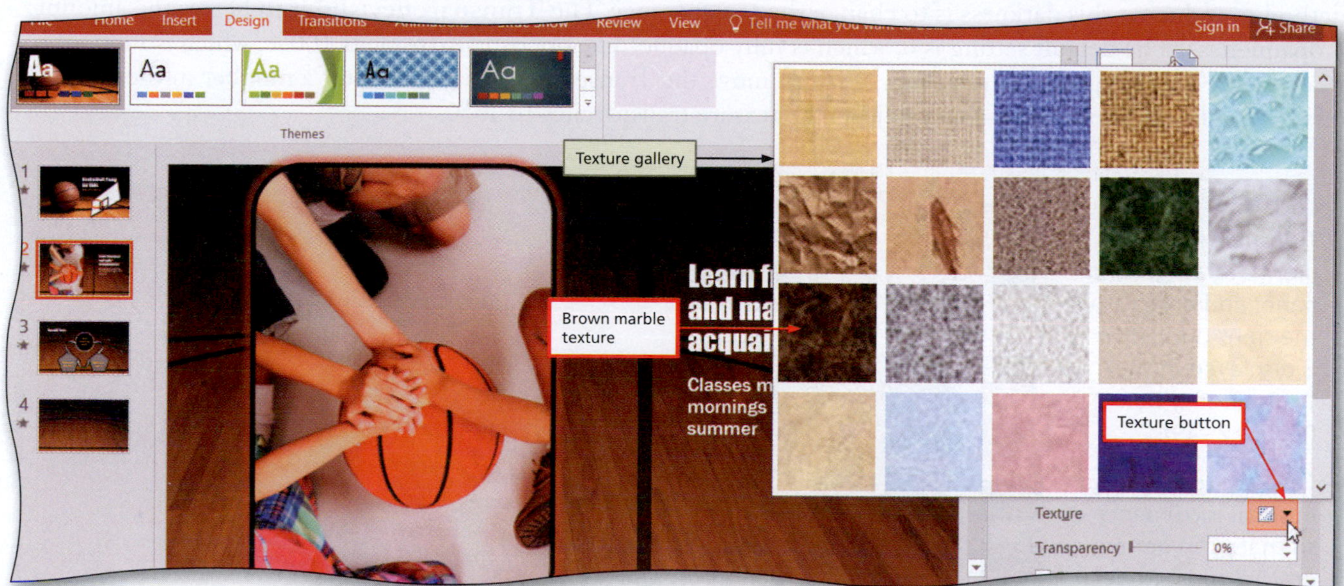

Figure 2–47

3

- Click the Brown marble texture (first texture in third row) to insert this texture fill as the background on Slide 2 (Figure 2–48).

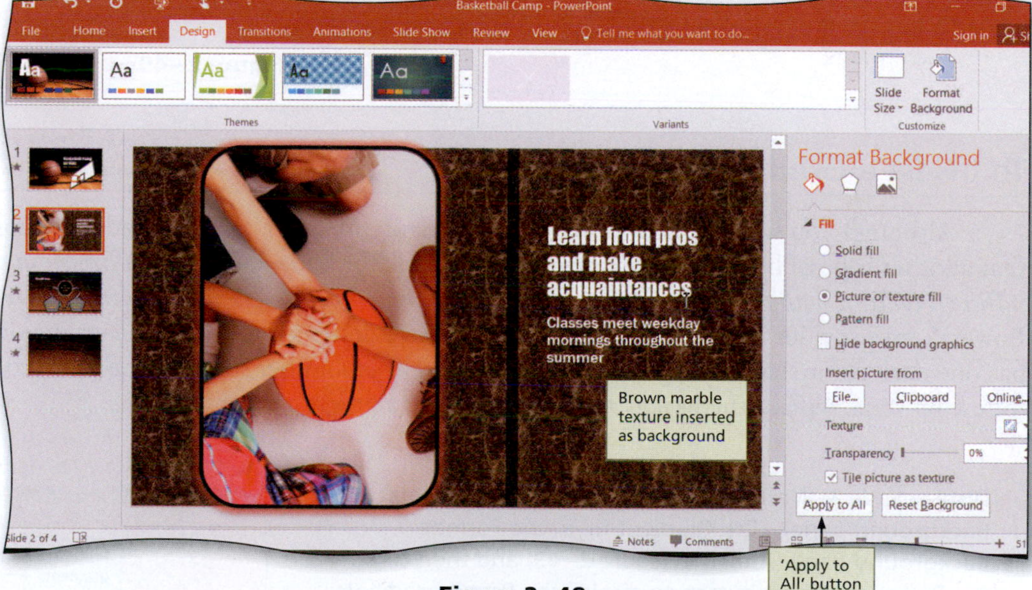

Figure 2–48

Q&A Is a live preview available to see the various textures on this slide?

No. Live preview is not an option with the background textures and fills.

Could I insert this background on all four slides simultaneously?

Yes. You would click the 'Apply to All' button to insert the Brown marble background on all slides.

Other Ways

1. Right-click background, click Format Background on shortcut menu, select desired options (Format Background pane)

To Format the Background Texture Fill Transparency

1 DOWNLOAD & SELECT SLIDES | 2 INSERT & FORMAT PICTURES | 3 INSERT & FORMAT SHAPES
4 FORMAT SLIDE BACKGROUNDS | 5 INSERT & FORMAT WORDART | 6 REVIEW, REVISE, & PRINT SLIDES

Why? *The Brown marble texture on Slide 2 is dark, and its pattern may detract from the photo and text.* One method of reducing this darkness is to change the transparency. The **Transparency slider** indicates the amount of opaqueness. The default setting is 0, which is fully opaque. The opposite extreme is 100%, which is fully transparent. To change the transparency, you can move the Transparency slider or enter a number in the box next to the slider. The following step adjusts the texture transparency to 15%.

1

- Click the Transparency slider (Format Background pane) and drag it to the right until 15% is displayed in the Transparency box (Figure 2–49).

Q&A Can I move the slider in small increments so that I can get a precise percentage easily?
Yes. Click the up or down arrows in the Transparency box to move the slider in 1% increments.

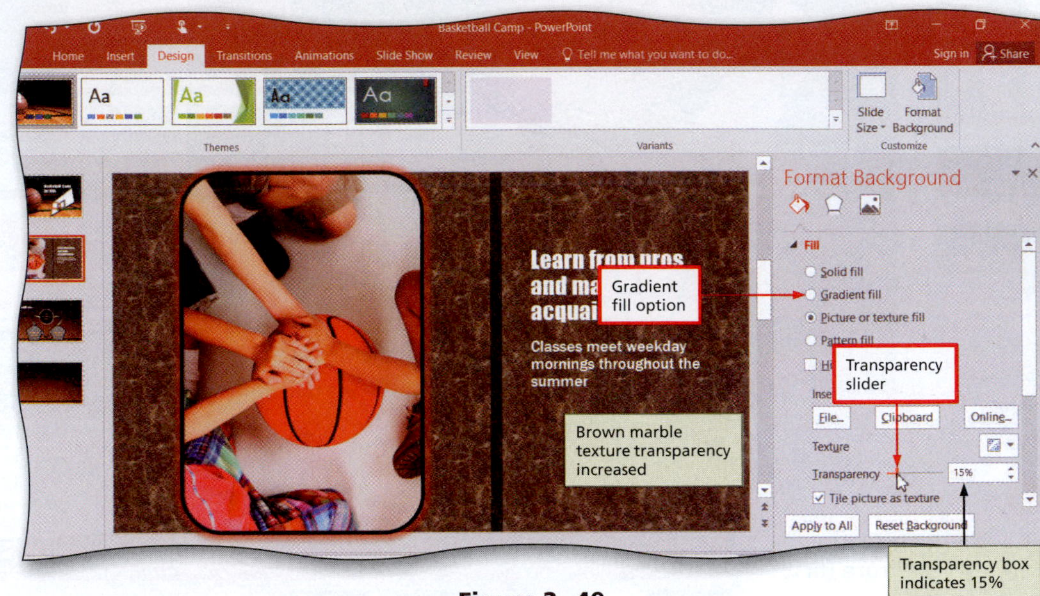

Figure 2–49

To Insert a Gradient Fill

1 DOWNLOAD & SELECT SLIDES | 2 INSERT & FORMAT PICTURES | 3 INSERT & FORMAT SHAPES
4 FORMAT SLIDE BACKGROUNDS | 5 INSERT & FORMAT WORDART | 6 REVIEW, REVISE, & PRINT SLIDES

Although you selected Brown marble texture fill on Slide 2 and changed the transparency, you decide that another type of background may be more suitable for Slide 3. ***Why?*** *The Brown marble texture does not offer sufficient contrast with the oval symbol and may detract from the messages presented in the three symbols.* For each theme, PowerPoint provides 30 preset **gradient fills** with five designs for each of the six major theme colors. Each fill has one dark color shade that gradually lightens to either another shade of the same color or another color. The following steps replace the background on Slide 3 to a preset gradient fill.

1

- Display Slide 3. With the Fill section displaying (Format Background pane), click Gradient fill in the Format Background pane (shown in Figure 2–49) and then click the Preset gradients button to display the Preset gradients gallery (Figure 2–50).

Q&A Are the backgrounds displayed in a specific order?
Yes. The first row has light colors at the top of the background; the middle rows have darker fills at the bottom; the bottom row has overall dark fills on all edges.

Is a live preview available to see the various gradients on this slide?
No. Live preview is not an option with the background textures and fills.

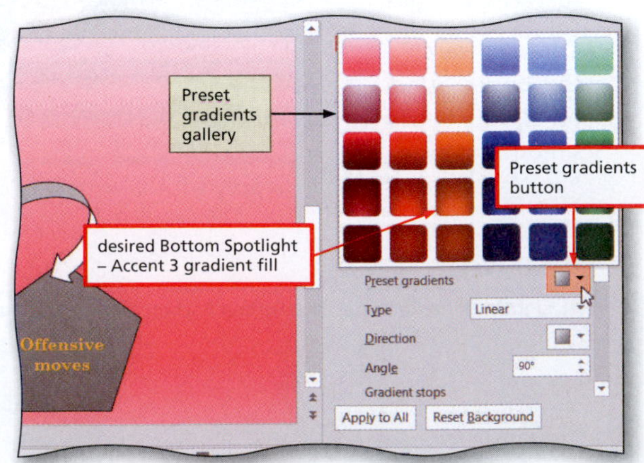

Figure 2–50

2

- Click Bottom Spotlight – Accent 3 (third fill in fourth row) to apply that style to Slide 3 (Figure 2–51).

Q&A If I decide later that this background gradient does not fit the theme of my presentation, can I apply a different background?
Yes. You can repeat these steps at any time while creating your presentation.

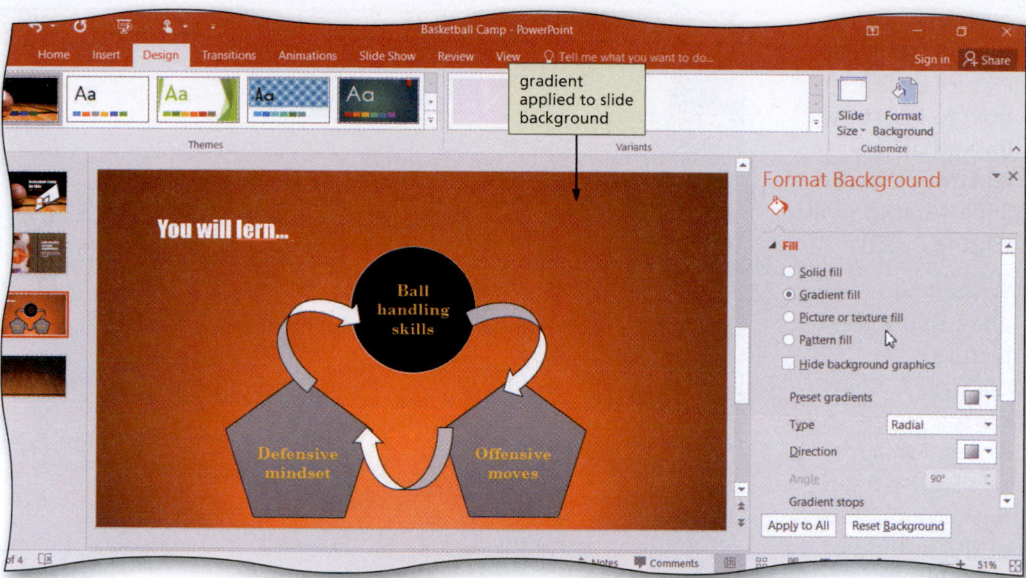

Figure 2–51

Other Ways

1. Click Design tab on ribbon, click Format Background button (Customize group), select desired options (Format Background pane)
2. Right-click background, click Format Background on shortcut menu, select desired options (Format Background pane)

To Insert a Picture to Create a Background

Why? For variety and interest, you want to use an illustration as the Slide 4 background. This picture is stored in the Data Files folder. PowerPoint will stretch the height and width of this picture to fill the slide area. The following steps insert the illustration, Basketball Boy, on Slide 4 only.

- Display Slide 4. With the Fill section displaying (Format Background pane), if necessary, click 'Picture or texture fill' and then click the File button (Format Background pane) to display the Insert Picture dialog box. If necessary, navigate to the Module 02 folder in the Data Files folder or the location where your data files are located.

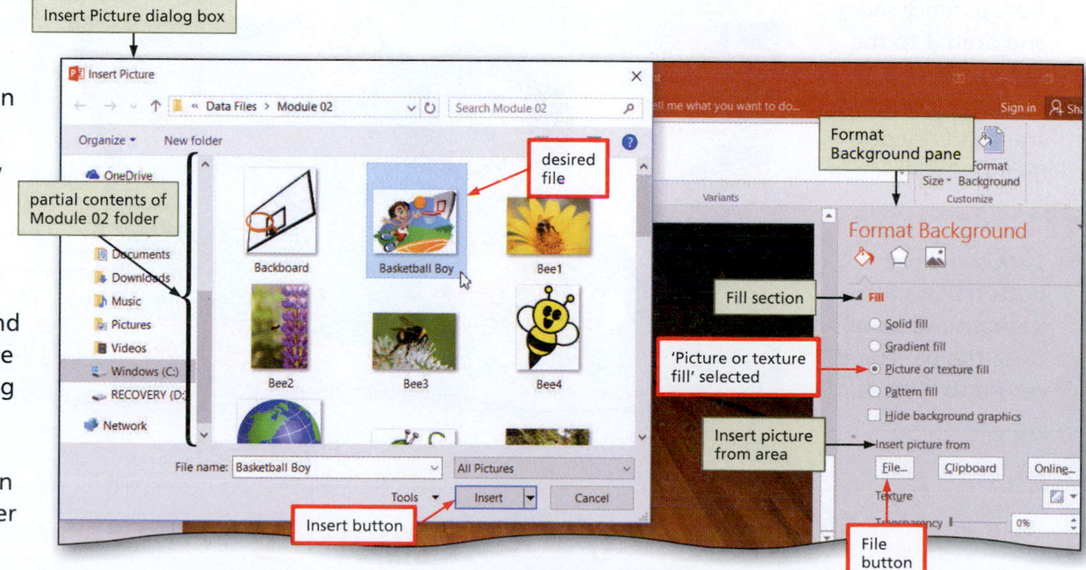

Figure 2–52

- Click Basketball Boy to select the file name (Figure 2–52).

2

- Click the Insert button (Insert Picture dialog box) to insert the Basketball Boy illustration as the Slide 4 background (Figure 2–53).

Q&A What if I do not want to use this picture?
Click the Undo button on the Quick Access Toolbar or click the Reset Background button at the bottom of the Format Background pane.

Figure 2–53

To Format the Background Picture Fill Transparency

1 DOWNLOAD & SELECT SLIDES | 2 INSERT & FORMAT PICTURES | 3 INSERT & FORMAT SHAPES
4 FORMAT SLIDE BACKGROUNDS | 5 INSERT & FORMAT WORDART | 6 REVIEW, REVISE, & PRINT SLIDES

***Why?** The Basketball Boy illustration on Slide 4 has vibrant colors that will conflict with the WordArt you will add later in this project.* You can adjust the transparency of picture in the same manner that you change the transparency of a slide texture. The following steps adjust the transparency of the background picture to 30% and then close the Format Background pane.

- Click the Transparency slider and drag it to the right until 30% is displayed in the Transparency box (Figure 2–54).

- Click the Close button (Format Background pane) to close the pane and return to Slide 4.

Figure 2–54

Inserting and Formatting WordArt

One method of adding appealing visual elements to a presentation is by using **WordArt** styles. This feature is found in other Microsoft Office applications, including Word and Excel. This gallery of decorative effects allows you to type new text or convert existing text to WordArt. You then can add elements such as fills, outlines, and effects.

WordArt **fill** in the interior of a letter can consist of a solid color, texture, picture, or gradient. The WordArt **outline** is the exterior border surrounding each letter or symbol. PowerPoint allows you to change the outline color, weight, and style. You also can add an **effect**, which helps add emphasis or depth to the characters. Some effects are shadows, reflections, glows, bevels, and 3-D rotations.

To Insert WordArt

1 DOWNLOAD & SELECT SLIDES | 2 INSERT & FORMAT PICTURES | 3 INSERT & FORMAT SHAPES
4 FORMAT SLIDE BACKGROUNDS | 5 INSERT & FORMAT WORDART | 6 REVIEW, REVISE, & PRINT SLIDES

The basketball camp is a very popular event among boys and girls in the community, and the sessions fill every year. Parents need to register their student early to reserve a place. You want to emphasize this concept, and the last slide in the presentation is an excellent location to urge your audience to take action. ***Why?** Audience members remember the first and last things they see and hear.* You quickly can add a visual element to the slide by selecting a WordArt style from the WordArt Styles gallery and then applying it to some text. The following steps insert WordArt.

- Display the Insert tab and then click the WordArt button (Insert tab | Text group) to display the WordArt gallery (Figure 2–55).

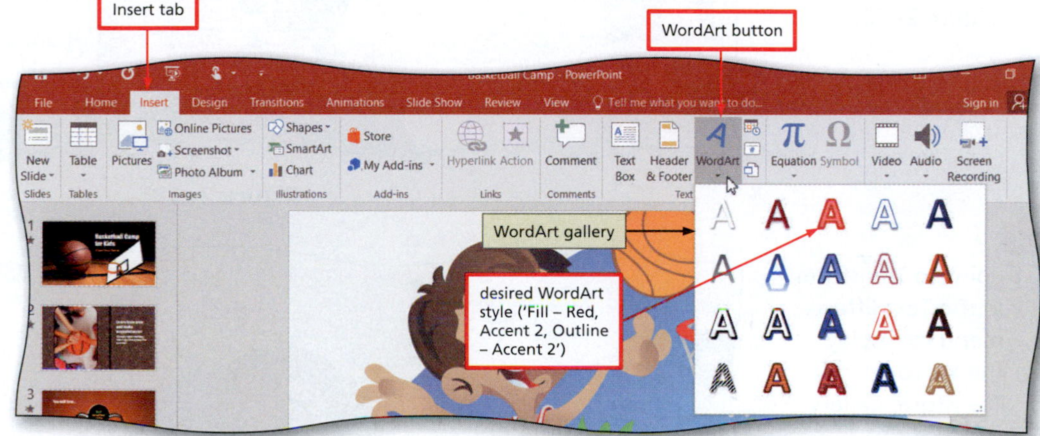

Figure 2–55

- Click 'Fill – Red, Accent 2, Outline – Accent 2' (third style in first row) to insert the WordArt object (Figure 2–56).

Figure 2–56

- Type **Register today!** in the object as the WordArt text (Figure 2–57).

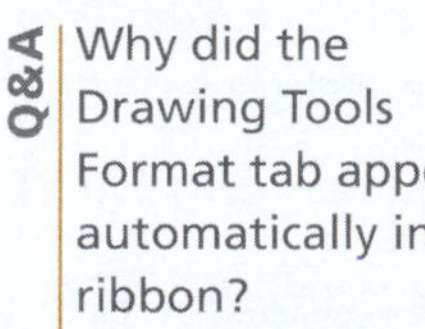

Q&A Why did the Drawing Tools Format tab appear automatically in the ribbon?
It appears when you select text to which you could add a WordArt style or other effect.

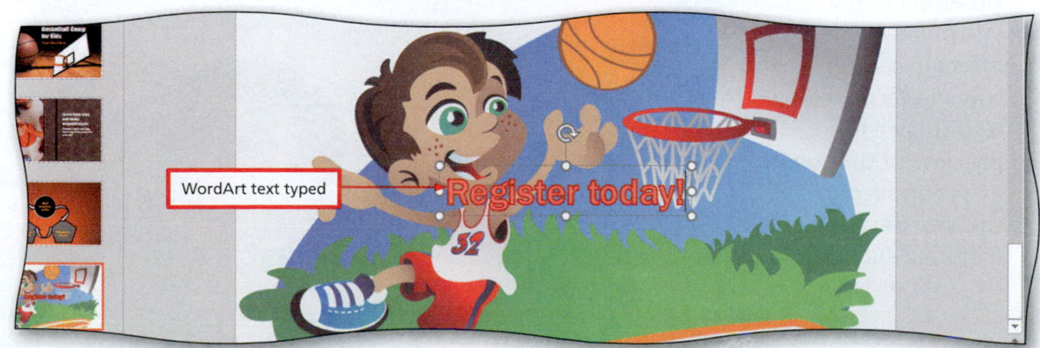

Figure 2–57

To Change the WordArt Shape

Why? *The WordArt text is useful to emphasize the need to register children early for camp. You further can emphasize this text by changing its shape.* PowerPoint provides a variety of graphical shapes that add interest to WordArt text. The following steps change the WordArt shape to Chevron Up.

1

- With the WordArt object still selected, click the Text Effects button (Drawing Tools Format tab | WordArt Styles group) to display the Text Effects menu (Figure 2–58).

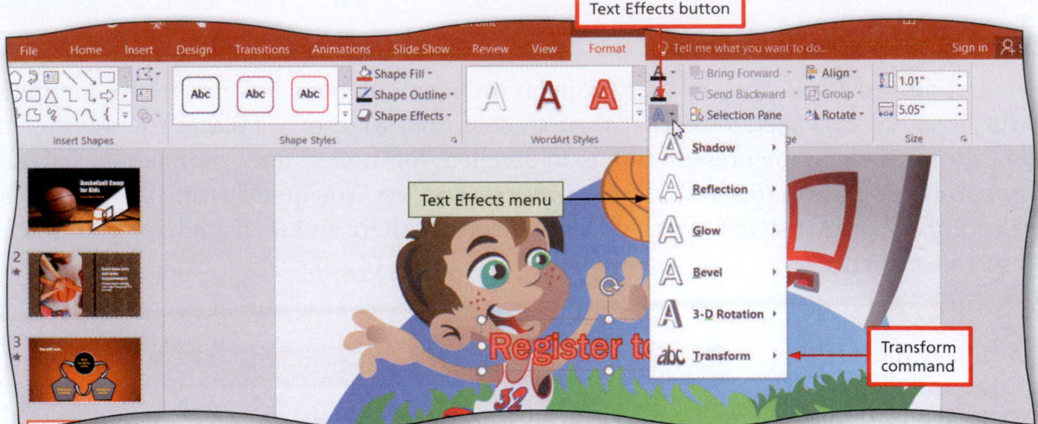

Figure 2–58

2

- Point to Transform in the Text Effects menu to display the WordArt Transform gallery (Figure 2–59).

Figure 2–59

- Point to the Chevron Up effect in the Warp area (first effect in second row in Warp area) to display a live preview of that text effect applied to the WordArt object (Figure 2–60).

Figure 2–60

Experiment

- Point to various effects in the Transform gallery and watch the format of the text and borders change.

Q&A How can I see the preview of a Transform effect if the gallery overlays the WordArt letters?
Move the WordArt box to the left or right side of the slide and then repeat Steps 1 and 2.

4

- Click the Chevron Up shape to apply this text effect to the WordArt object.

Q&A Can I change the shape I applied to the WordArt?
Yes. Position the insertion point in the box and then repeat Steps 1 and 2.

5

- Drag the lower-right sizing handle diagonally toward the lower-right corner of the slide until the crosshair is positioned approximately as shown in Figure 2–61.

Figure 2–61

6

- Release to resize the WordArt object.
- Drag the WordArt object toward the right side of the slide until it is positioned approximately as shown in Figure 2–62.

Figure 2–62

To Apply a WordArt Text Fill

1 DOWNLOAD & SELECT SLIDES | 2 INSERT & FORMAT PICTURES | 3 INSERT & FORMAT SHAPES
4 FORMAT SLIDE BACKGROUNDS | 5 INSERT & FORMAT WORDART | 6 REVIEW, REVISE, & PRINT SLIDES

Various texture fills are available to give your WordArt characters a unique look. You used a texture fill to add interest to the Slide 3 background. The following steps add the Medium wood texture as a fill for the WordArt characters. ***Why?*** *The brown fill coordinates well with the red WordArt outline and is similar to the color of the basketball court in the Slide 1 and Slide 2 backgrounds.*

1

- With the WordArt object selected, click the Text Fill arrow (Drawing Tools Format tab | WordArt Styles group) to display the Text Fill gallery.
- Point to Texture in the Text Fill gallery to display the Texture gallery.

2

- If necessary, scroll down and then point to the Medium wood texture (last texture in last row) to display a live preview of that texture applied to the WordArt object (Figure 2–63).

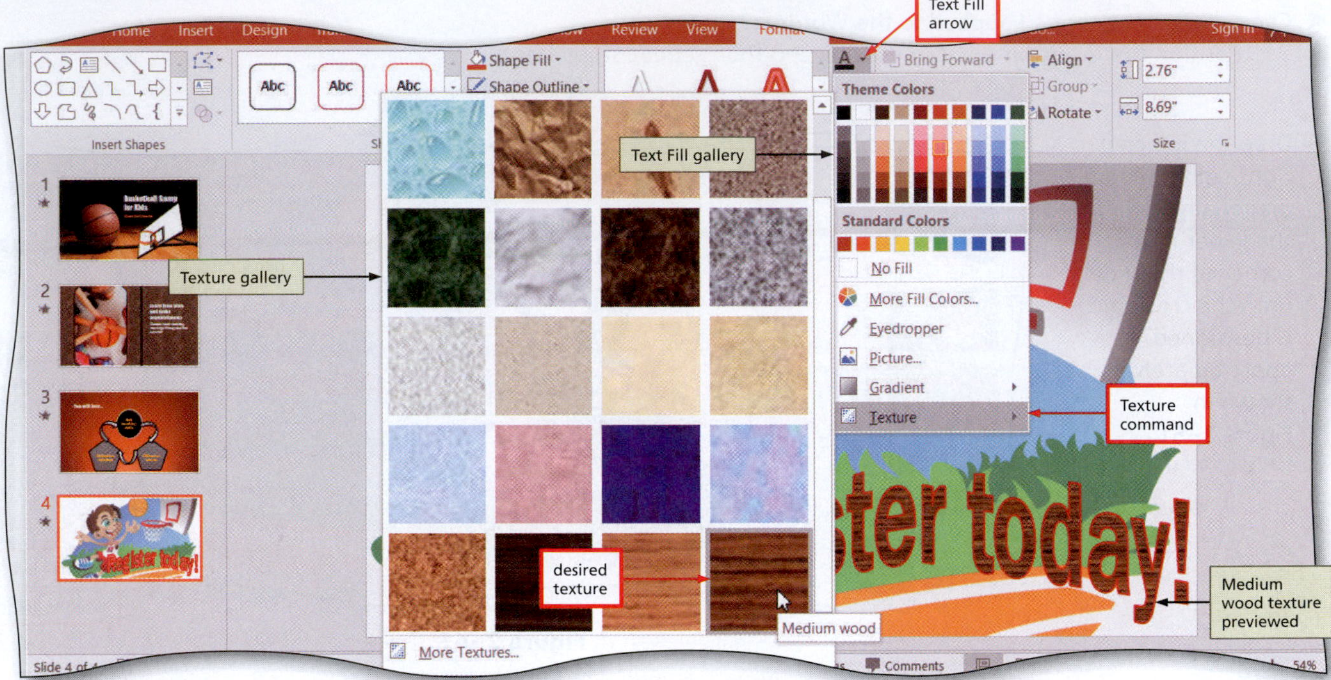

Figure 2–63

Experiment

- Point to various styles in the Texture gallery and watch the fill change.

3

- Click the Medium wood texture to apply this texture as the fill for the WordArt object.

Q&A Can I apply this texture simultaneously to text that appears in more than one place on my slide?
Yes. You can select one area of text, press and then hold the CTRL key while you select the other text, and then apply the texture.

To Change the Weight of the WordArt Outline

1 DOWNLOAD & SELECT SLIDES | 2 INSERT & FORMAT PICTURES | 3 INSERT & FORMAT SHAPES
4 FORMAT SLIDE BACKGROUNDS | 5 INSERT & FORMAT WORDART | 6 REVIEW, REVISE, & PRINT SLIDES

The letters in the WordArt style applied have an outline around the edges. You can increase the width of the outlines. ***Why?*** *The thicker line will emphasize this characteristic and add another visual element.* As with fonts, lines also are measured in points, and PowerPoint gives you the option to change the line **weight**, or thickness, starting with ¼ point (pt) and increasing in ¼-point increments. Other outline options include modifying the color and the line style, such as changing to dots or dashes or a combination of dots and dashes. The following steps change the WordArt outline weight to 6 pt.

1

- With the WordArt object still selected, click the Text Outline arrow (Drawing Tools Format tab | WordArt Styles group) to display the Text Outline gallery.
- Point to Weight in the gallery to display the Weight list.
- Point to 6 pt to display a live preview of this line weight on the WordArt text outline (Figure 2–64).

Figure 2–64

Can I make the line width more than 6 pt?
Yes. Click More Lines and increase the amount in the Width box.

Experiment

- Point to various line weights in the Weight list and watch the line thickness change.

2

- Click 6 pt to apply this line weight to the WordArt text outline.

Must my text have an outline?
No. To delete the outline, click No Outline in the Text Outline gallery.

To Change the Color of the WordArt Outline

1 DOWNLOAD & SELECT SLIDES | 2 INSERT & FORMAT PICTURES | 3 INSERT & FORMAT SHAPES
4 FORMAT SLIDE BACKGROUNDS | 5 INSERT & FORMAT WORDART | 6 REVIEW, REVISE, & PRINT SLIDES

Why? The WordArt outline color and the boy's shorts are similar, so you can add contrast by changing one of these slide elements. The following steps change the WordArt outline color.

1

- With the WordArt object still selected, display the Text Outline gallery.
- Point to Black, Background 1 (first color in Theme Colors row) to display a live preview of this outline color (Figure 2–65).

Figure 2–65

 **Experiment**

- Point to various colors in the gallery and watch the outline colors change.

2

- Click Black, Background 1 to apply this color to the WordArt outline.
- Click outside of the WordArt box to deselect this slide element (Figure 2–66).

Figure 2–66

Reviewing and Revising Individual Slides

The text, pictures, and shapes for all slides in the Basketball Camp presentation have been entered. Once you complete a slide show, you might decide to change elements. PowerPoint provides several tools to assist you with making changes. They include finding and replacing text, inserting a synonym, checking spelling, and printing speaker notes. The following pages discuss these tools.

BTW
Finding and Replacing Text
When finding and replacing text, you do not need to display the slide that contains the word for which you are searching. You can perform this action when any slide is displayed. To see the results of the search and replace action, however, you need to display the slide where the change occurred.

Replace Dialog Box

At times, you might want to change all occurrences of a word or phrase to another word or phrase. For example, an instructor may have one slide show to accompany a lecture for several introductory classes, and he wants to update slides with the particular class name and section that appear on several slides. He manually could change the characters, but PowerPoint includes an efficient method of replacing one word with another. The Find and Replace feature automatically locates specific text and then replaces it with desired text.

In some cases, you may want to replace only certain occurrences of a word or phrase, not all of them. To instruct PowerPoint to confirm each change, click the Find Next button in the Replace dialog box instead of the Replace All button. When PowerPoint locates an occurrence of the text, it pauses and waits for you to click either the Replace button or the Find Next button. Clicking the Replace button changes the text; clicking the Find Next button instructs PowerPoint to disregard that particular instance and look for the next occurrence of the Find what text.

To Find and Insert a Synonym

1 DOWNLOAD & SELECT SLIDES | 2 INSERT & FORMAT PICTURES | 3 INSERT & FORMAT SHAPES
4 FORMAT SLIDE BACKGROUNDS | 5 INSERT & FORMAT WORDART | **6 REVIEW, REVISE, & PRINT SLIDES**

Why? When reviewing your slide show, you may decide that a particular word does not express the exact usage you intended or that you used the same word on multiple slides. In these cases, you could find a **synonym**, or word similar in meaning, to replace the inappropriate or duplicate word. PowerPoint provides a **thesaurus**, which is a list of synonyms and antonyms, to help you find a replacement word.

In this project, you want to find a synonym to replace the word, acquaintances, on Slide 2. The following steps locate an appropriate synonym and replace the word.

1

- Display Slide 2 and then place the insertion point in the word, acquaintances.
- Right-click to display a shortcut menu related to the word, acquaintances. Then, point to Synonyms on the shortcut menu to display a list of synonyms for this word (Figure 2–67).

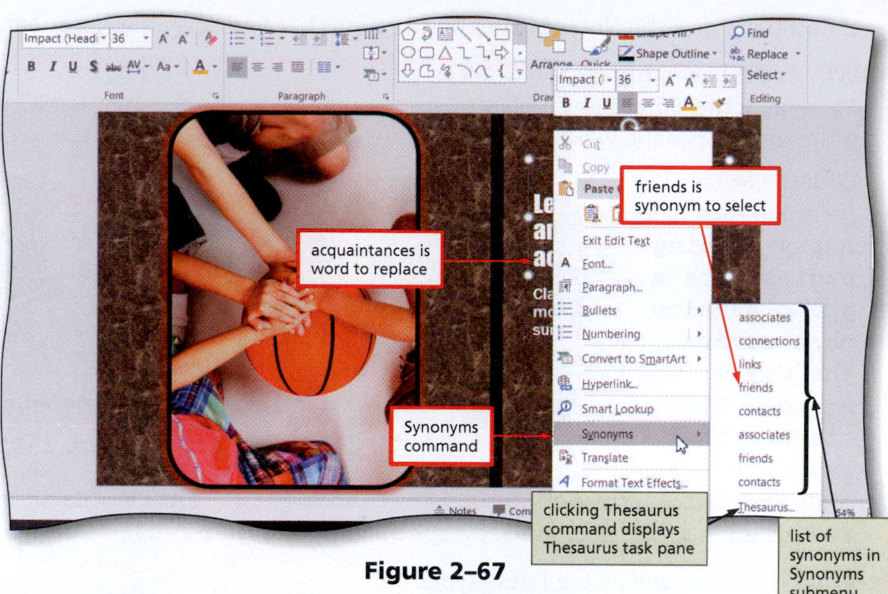

Figure 2–67

Q&A How do I locate a synonym for multiple words?
You need to select all the words and then right-click to display the shortcut menu.

If I am using a touch screen, how do I find a synonym?
Tap the Thesaurus button (Review tab | Proofing group) to display the Thesaurus pane for the selected word. Then, in the pane, tap the arrow next to the word to display a shortcut menu.

2

- Click the synonym you want (friends) on the Synonyms submenu to replace the word, acquaintances, in the presentation with the word, friends (Figure 2–68).

Figure 2–68

Q&A What if a suitable word does not display in the Synonyms submenu?
You can display the Thesaurus pane by clicking Thesaurus on the Synonyms submenu. A complete thesaurus with synonyms displays in the pane along with an antonym, which is a word with an opposite meaning.

Other Ways

1. Click Thesaurus (Review tab | Proofing group)
2. Press SHIFT+F7

To Add Notes

1 DOWNLOAD & SELECT SLIDES | 2 INSERT & FORMAT PICTURES | 3 INSERT & FORMAT SHAPES
4 FORMAT SLIDE BACKGROUNDS | 5 INSERT & FORMAT WORDART | **6 REVIEW, REVISE, & PRINT SLIDES**

Why? As you create slides, you may find material you want to state verbally and do not want to include on the slide. After adding these comments, you can print a set of speaker notes that will print below a small image of the slide. You can type and format comments in the **Notes pane** as you work in Normal view and then print this information as **notes pages**. The Notes pane is hidden until you click the Notes button on the status bar to open the pane. If you want to close the Notes pane, click the Notes button again. Charts, tables, and pictures added to the Notes pane also print on these pages. The following steps add text to the Notes pane on Slides 2, 3, and 4.

Note: In the following step, the word, skills, has been misspelled intentionally as skils to illustrate the use of PowerPoint's spell check feature. Your slides may contain different misspelled words, depending upon the accuracy of your typing.

1

- If necessary, click the Notes button on the status bar to display the Notes pane for Slide 2.

Q&A Why might I need to click the Notes button?
By default, the Notes pane is closed when you begin a new presentation. Once you display the Notes pane for any slide, the Notes pane will remain open unless you click the Notes button to close it.

- Click the Notes pane and then type **Every morning begins with a group session that covers the day's agenda. The coaches then separate the campers into groups to cover fundamental skils. Each morning ends with a contest designed to be fun and competitive.** (Figure 2–69).

Figure 2–69

Q&A What if I cannot see all the lines I typed?
You can drag the splitter bar up to enlarge the Notes pane. Clicking the Notes pane scroll arrows or swiping up or down on the Notes pane allows you to view the entire text.

2

- Display Slide 3, click the Notes pane, and then type **Campers will gain confidence while learning sportsmanship and strategies.** (Figure 2–70).

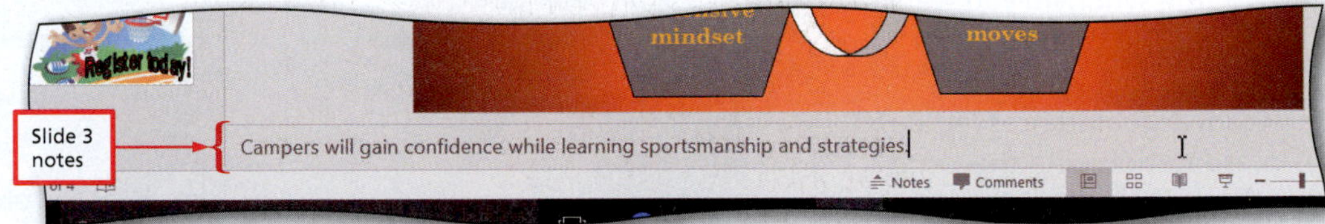

Figure 2–70

3

- Display Slide 4 and then type **Space is limited. Every camper will receive a t-shirt, snacks, and water. Parents are encouraged to attend the awards ceremony at the end of the camp session.** in the Notes pane (Figure 2–71).

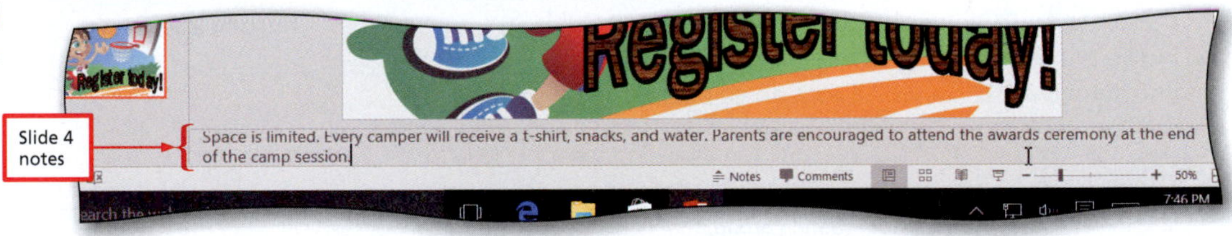

Figure 2–71

To Find and Replace Text

1 DOWNLOAD & SELECT SLIDES | 2 INSERT & FORMAT PICTURES | 3 INSERT & FORMAT SHAPES
4 FORMAT SLIDE BACKGROUNDS | 5 INSERT & FORMAT WORDART | 6 REVIEW, REVISE, & PRINT SLIDES

While reviewing your slides, you realize that the camp will be held in the afternoon, not in the morning. To change this word throughout a presentation, you could view each slide, look for the word, morning, delete the word, and then type the replacement word, afternoon. A more efficient and effective method of performing this action is to use PowerPoint's Find and Replace feature. ***Why?*** *This method locates each occurrence of a word or phrase automatically and then replaces it with specified text.* The word, morning, displays three times in the slides and notes. The following steps use Find and Replace to replace all occurrences of the word, morning, with the word, afternoon.

1

- If necessary, display the Home tab and then click the Replace button (Home tab | Editing group) to display the Replace dialog box.
- Type **morning** in the Find what box (Replace dialog box).
- Click the Replace with box and then type **afternoon** in the box (Figure 2–72).

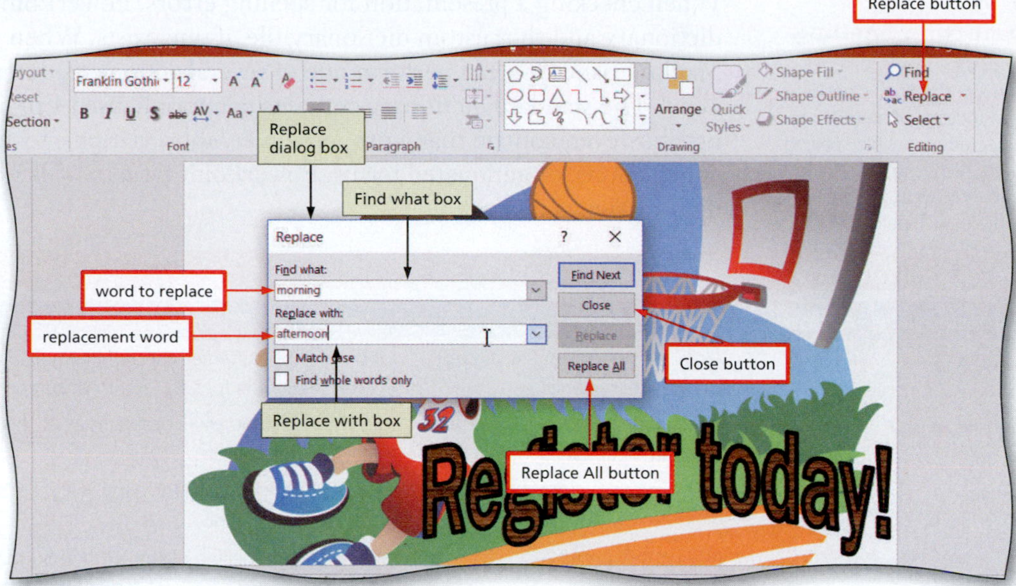

Figure 2–72

- Click the Replace All button (Replace dialog box) to instruct PowerPoint to replace all occurrences of the Find what word, morning, with the Replace with word, afternoon (Figure 2–73).

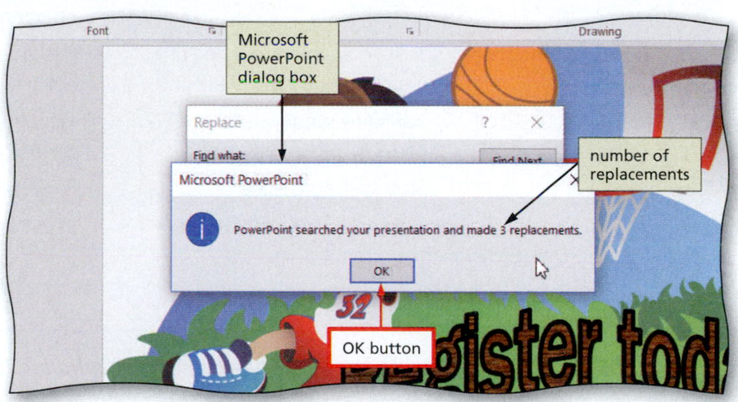

Figure 2–73

Q&A If I accidentally replaced the wrong text, can I undo this replacement?
Yes. Press CTRL+Z or click the Undo button on the Quick Access Toolbar to undo all replacements. If you had clicked the Replace button instead of the Replace All button, PowerPoint would undo only the most recent replacement.

- Click the OK button (Microsoft PowerPoint dialog box).
- Click the Close button (Replace dialog box).

Other Ways

1. Press CTRL+H

Checking Spelling

After you create a presentation, you should check it visually for spelling errors and style consistency. In addition, you can use PowerPoint's Spelling tool to identify possible misspellings on the slides and in the notes. You should proofread your presentation carefully by pointing to each word and saying it aloud as you point to it. Be mindful of commonly misused words such as its and it's, through and though, and to and too.

PowerPoint checks the entire presentation for spelling mistakes using a standard dictionary contained in the Microsoft Office group. This dictionary is shared with the other Microsoft Office applications such as Word and Excel. A custom dictionary is available if you want to add special words such as proper names, cities, and acronyms.

BTW
Formatting Notes Pane Text
You can format text in the Notes pane in the same manner you format text on a slide. To add emphasis, for example, you can italicize key words or change the font color and size.

BTW
Detecting Spelling Errors
The x in the Spell Check icon indicates PowerPoint detected a possible spelling error. A check mark in the icon indicates the entered text contains no spelling errors.

When checking a presentation for spelling errors, PowerPoint opens the standard dictionary and the custom dictionary file, if one exists. When a word appears in the Spelling pane, you can perform one of several actions, as described in Table 2–1.

The standard dictionary contains commonly used English words. It does not, however, contain many proper names, abbreviations, technical terms, poetic contractions, or antiquated terms. PowerPoint treats words not found in the dictionaries as misspellings.

Table 2–1 Spelling Pane Buttons and Actions

Button Name/Action	When to Use	Action
Ignore	Word is spelled correctly but not found in dictionaries	PowerPoint continues checking rest of the presentation but will flag that word again if it appears later in document.
Ignore All	Word is spelled correctly but not found in dictionaries	PowerPoint ignores all occurrences of the word and continues checking rest of presentation.
Add	Add word to custom dictionary	PowerPoint opens custom dictionary, adds word, and continues checking rest of presentation.
Change	Word is misspelled	Click proper spelling of the word in Suggestions list. PowerPoint corrects word, continues checking rest of presentation, but will flag that word again if it appears later in document.
Change All	Word is misspelled	Click proper spelling of word in Suggestions list. PowerPoint changes all occurrences of misspelled word and continues checking rest of presentation.
Listen to the pronunciation	To hear the pronunciation of a word	Click the audio speaker icon next to the properly spelled word near the bottom of the Spelling pane.
View synonyms	See some synonyms for the correctly spelled word	View the bullet list of synonyms below the correctly spelled word near the bottom of the Spelling pane.
Close	Stop spelling checker	PowerPoint closes spelling checker and returns to PowerPoint window.

To Check Spelling

1 DOWNLOAD & SELECT SLIDES | 2 INSERT & FORMAT PICTURES | 3 INSERT & FORMAT SHAPES
4 FORMAT SLIDE BACKGROUNDS | 5 INSERT & FORMAT WORDART | **6 REVIEW, REVISE, & PRINT SLIDES**

***Why?** Although PowerPoint's spelling checker is a valuable tool, it is not infallible. You should not rely on the spelling checker to catch all your mistakes.* The following steps check the spelling on all slides in the Basketball Camp presentation.

1

- Click Review on the ribbon to display the Review tab.
- Click the Spelling button (Review Tab | Proofing group) to start the spelling checker and display the Spelling pane (Figure 2–74).

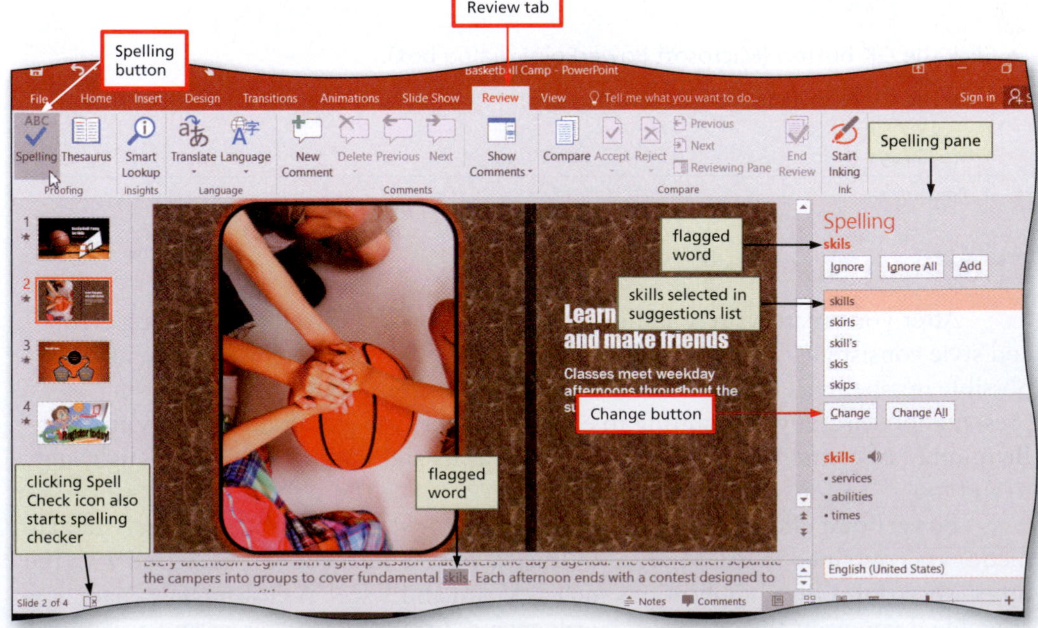

Figure 2–74

2

- With the word, skils, selected in the list and in the Notes pane, click the Change button (Spelling pane) to replace the misspelled flagged word, skils, with the selected correctly spelled word, skills, and then continue the spelling check (Figure 2–75).

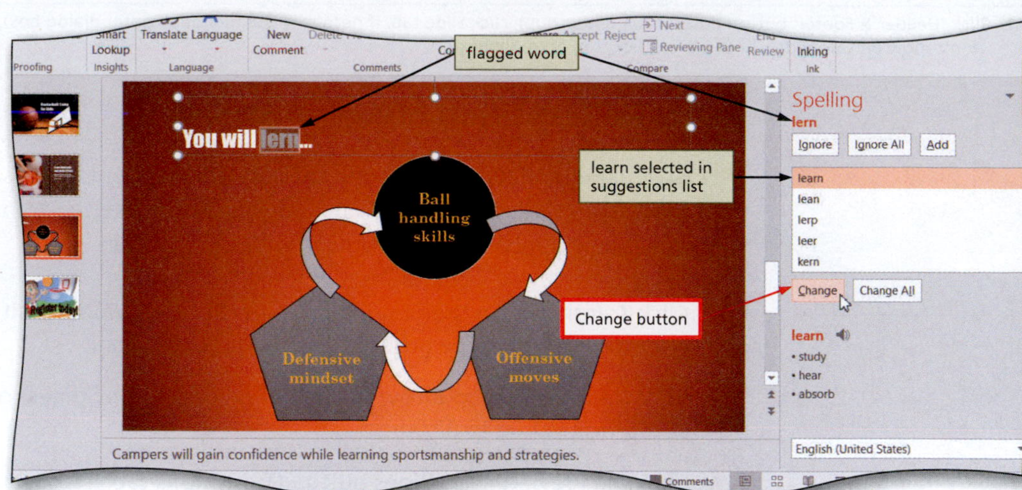

Figure 2–75

Q&A Could I have clicked the Change All button instead of the Change button?

Yes. When you click the Change All button, you change the current and future occurrences of the misspelled word. The misspelled word, skils, appears only once in the presentation, so clicking the Change or the Change All button in this instance produces identical results.

Occasionally a correctly spelled word is flagged as a possible misspelled word. Why?

Your custom dictionary does not contain the word, so it is seen as spelled incorrectly. You can add this word to a custom dictionary to prevent the spelling checker from flagging it as a mistake.

3

- Replace the misspelled word, lern, with the word, learn.
- Continue checking all flagged words in the presentation. When the Microsoft PowerPoint dialog box appears, click the OK button (Microsoft PowerPoint dialog box) to close the spelling checker and return to the slide where a possible misspelled word appeared.

Other Ways

1. Click Spell Check icon on status bar
2. Right-click flagged word, click correct word
3. Press F7

To Insert a Slide Number

PowerPoint can insert the slide number on your slides automatically to indicate where the slide is positioned within the presentation. The number location on the slide is determined by the presentation theme. You have the option to not display this slide number on the title slide. To insert a slide number on all slides except the title slide, you would follow these steps.

1. Display the Insert tab and then click the Slide Number button (Insert tab | Text group) to display the Header and Footer dialog box.
2. Click the Slide number check box (Header and Footer dialog box) to place a check mark in it.

Q&A Can I prevent the slide number from being displayed on the title slide?

Yes. Click the 'Don't show on title slide' check box (Header and Footer dialog box) to place a check mark in it.

3. Click the 'Apply to All' button (Header and Footer dialog box) to close the dialog box and insert the slide number.

Q&A How does clicking the 'Apply to All' button differ from clicking the Apply button?

The Apply button inserts the slide number only on the currently displayed slide, whereas the 'Apply to All' button inserts the slide number on every slide.

BTW

PowerPoint Help

At any time while using PowerPoint, you can find answers to questions and display information about various topics through PowerPoint Help. Used properly, this form of assistance can increase your productivity and reduce your frustrations by minimizing the time you spend learning how to use PowerPoint. For instructions about PowerPoint Help and exercises that will help you gain confidence in using it, read the Office and Windows module at the beginning of this book.

Other Ways

1. Click 'Header & Footer' button (Insert tab | Text group), click Slide tab, if necessary (Header and Footer dialog box), click Slide number and 'Don't show on title slide' check boxes, click 'Apply to All' button

To Add a Transition between Slides

A final enhancement you will make in this presentation is to change the transition from Fade to Wipe for all slides and increase the transition duration. The following steps apply this transition to the presentation.

1. Click Transitions on the ribbon and then click the Wipe transition (Transitions tab | Transition to This Slide group) to apply this transition.
2. Click the Duration up arrow in the Timing group four times to change the transition speed from 01.00 to 02.00.
3. Click the Preview Transitions button (Transitions tab | Preview area) to view the new transition and time.
4. Click the 'Apply To All' button (Transitions tab | Timing group) to apply this transition and speed to all four slides in the presentation (Figure 2–76).

Q&A Can I apply a particular transition or duration to one slide and then change the transition or timing for a different slide in the presentation?

Yes. Select a slide and then select a transition and duration. Do not click the 'Apply To All' button. Repeat this process to apply the transition and duration to individual slides.

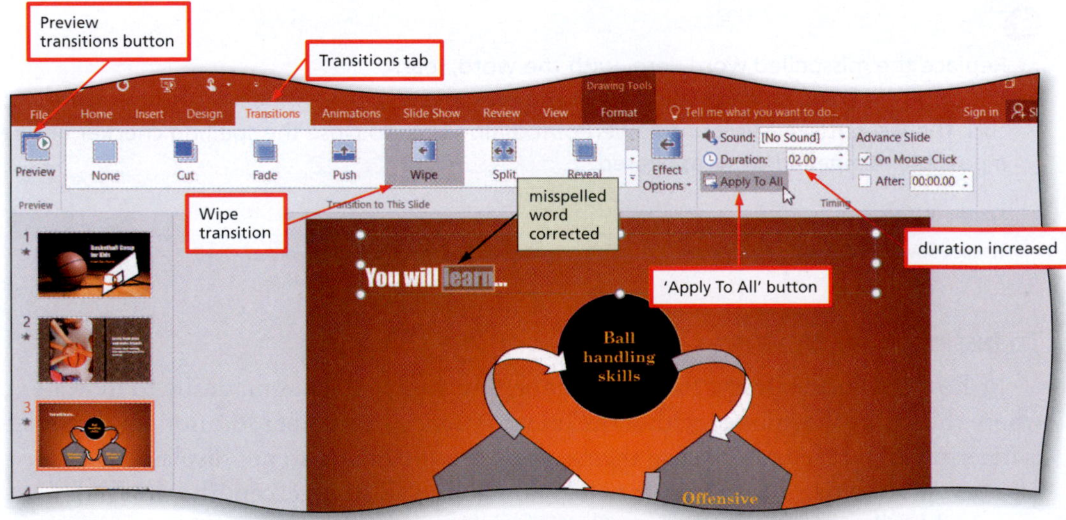

Figure 2–76

CONSIDER THIS

How can I use handouts to organize my speech?

As you develop a lengthy presentation with many visuals, handouts can help you organize your material. Print handouts with the maximum number of slides per page. Use scissors to cut each thumbnail and then place these miniature slide images adjacent to each other on a flat surface. Any type on the thumbnails will be too small to read, so the images will need to work with only the support of the verbal message you provide. You can rearrange these thumbnails as you organize your speech. When you return to your computer, you can rearrange the slides on your screen to match the order of your thumbnail printouts. Begin speaking the actual words you want to incorporate in the body of the talk. This process of glancing at the thumbnails and hearing yourself say the key ideas of the speech is one of the best methods of organizing and preparing for the actual presentation. Ultimately, when you deliver your speech in front of an audience, the images on the slides or on your note cards should be sufficient to remind you of the accompanying verbal message.

To Print Speaker Notes

Why? Comments added to slides in the Notes pane give the speaker information that supplements the text on the slide. They will print with a small image of the slide at the top and the comments below the slide. The following steps print the speaker notes.

1

- Display Slide 1, click File on the ribbon to open the Backstage view, and then click the Print tab in the Backstage view to display Slide 1 in the Print gallery.
- Click 'Full Page Slides' in the Settings area to display the Print gallery (Figure 2–77).

Q&A Why does the preview of my slide appear in black and white?

Your printer determines how the preview appears. If your printer is not capable of printing color images, the preview will not appear in color.

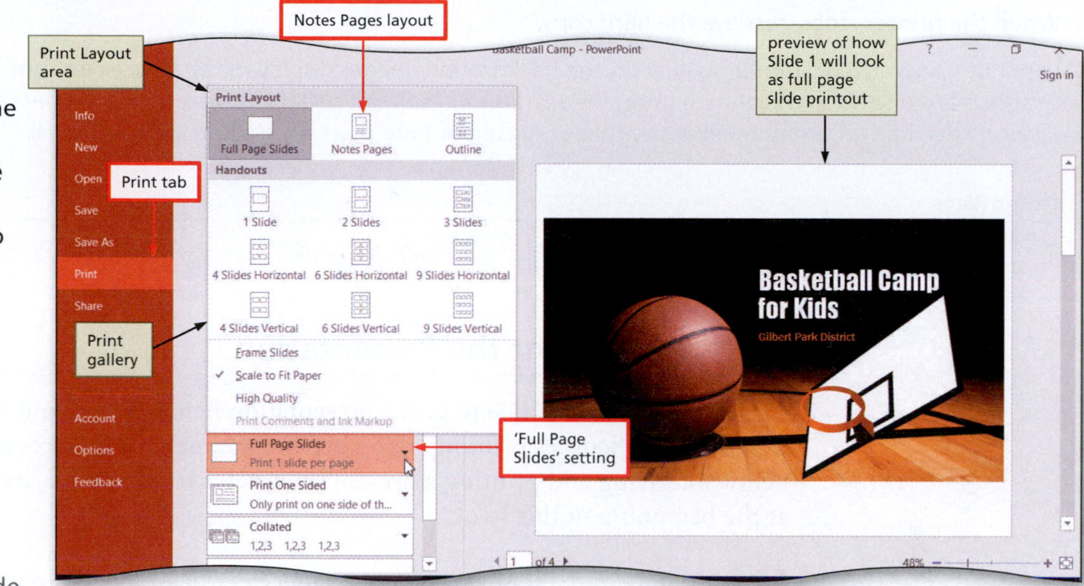

Figure 2–77

2

- Click Notes Pages in the Print Layout area to select this option and then click the Next Page button three times to display a preview of Slide 4 (Figure 2–78).

Q&A Can I preview Slides 1, 2, or 3 now?

Yes. Click the Previous Page button to preview the other slides.

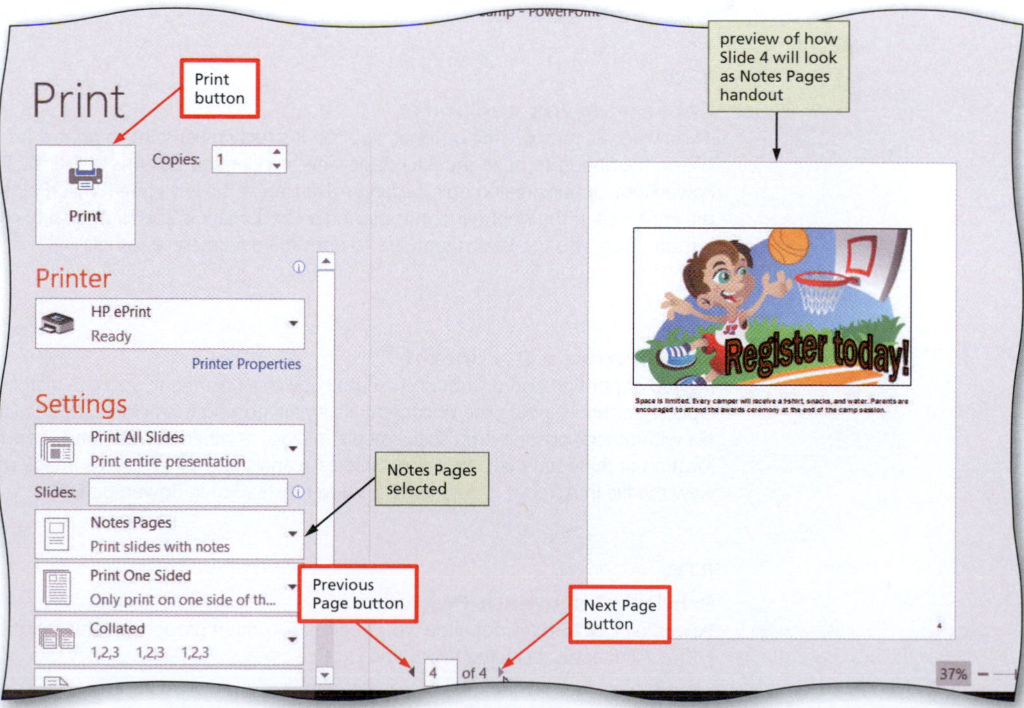

Figure 2–78

- Verify that the printer listed on the Printer Status button will print a hard copy of the presentation. If necessary, click the Printer Status button to display a list of available printer options and then click the desired printer to change the currently selected printer.
- Click the Print button in the Print gallery to print the notes pages on the currently selected printer.
- When the printer stops, retrieve the hard copy.

Q&A I am not using a color printer, so why do the background images display in the figures but not in my printout?
Graphics are displayed depending upon the settings in the Print gallery. For example, the background will print if Color is specified whereas it will not with a Grayscale or Pure Black and White setting.

Other Ways

1. Press CTRL+P, select desired options

To Save and Print the Presentation

It is a good practice to save a presentation before printing it, in the event you experience difficulties printing. For a detailed example of the procedure summarized below for saving and printing a presentation, refer to the Office and Windows module at the beginning of this book.

1. Save the presentation again on the same storage location with the same file name.
2. Print the presentation.

Q&A Do I have to wait until my presentation is complete to print it?
No, you can follow these steps to print a presentation at any time while you are creating it.

3. Because the project now is complete, you can exit PowerPoint.

BTW

Conserving Ink and Toner

If you want to conserve ink or toner, you can instruct PowerPoint to print draft quality documents by clicking File on the ribbon to open the Backstage view, clicking the Options tab in the Backstage view to display the PowerPoint Options dialog box, clicking Advanced in the left pane (PowerPoint Options dialog box), scrolling to the Print area in the right pane, not placing a check mark in the High quality check box, and then clicking the OK button. Then, use the Backstage view to print the document as usual.

BTW

Distributing a Document

Instead of printing and distributing a hard copy of a document, you can distribute the document electronically. Options include sending the document via email; posting it on cloud storage (such as OneDrive) and sharing the file with others; posting it on social media, a blog, or other website; and sharing a link associated with an online location of the document. You also can create and share a PDF or XPS image of the document, so that users can view the file in Acrobat Reader or XPS Viewer instead of in PowerPoint.

BTW

Printing Document Properties

PowerPoint 2016 does not allow you to print document properties. This feature, however, is available in other Office 2016 apps, including Word and Excel.

Summary

In this module, you have learned how to insert and format pictures, add and format shapes, insert and format WordArt, add and format slide backgrounds, find and replace text, check spelling, add notes, and print speaker notes.

CONSIDER THIS: PLAN AHEAD

What decisions will you need to make when creating your next presentation?

Use these guidelines as you complete the assignments in this module and create your own slide show decks outside of this class.

1. Determine if an online theme can help you design and develop the presentation efficiently and effectively.
2. Identify personal pictures that would create interest and promote the message being presented.
3. Consider modifying pictures.
   a) Add corrections.
   b) Add styles.
   c) Add effects.
   d) Add and format borders.
4. Locate shapes that supplement the verbal and written message.
   a) Size and position them aesthetically on slides.
   b) Add styles.
5. Develop WordArt that emphasizes major presentation messages.
   a) Modify the shape.
   b) Change the weight and color to coordinate with slide elements.
6. Format individual slide backgrounds.
   a) Add and modify fills.
   b) Insert a picture background.
7. Change fonts to emphasize particular slide components.
8. Search for synonyms that help express your thoughts.
9. Create speaker notes.
10. Check spelling.

Apply Your Knowledge

Reinforce the skills and apply the concepts you learned in this module.

Changing the Background and Adding Photos and WordArt

Note: To complete this assignment, you will be required to use the Data Files. Please contact your instructor for information about accessing the Data Files.

Instructions: Run PowerPoint. Open the presentation called Apply 2–1 Bees, which is located in the Data Files. The four slides in the presentation discuss bee stings. The document you open is an unformatted presentation. You are to add pictures, apply picture styles, add WordArt, change slide layouts, and apply a transition so the slides look like Figure 2–79.

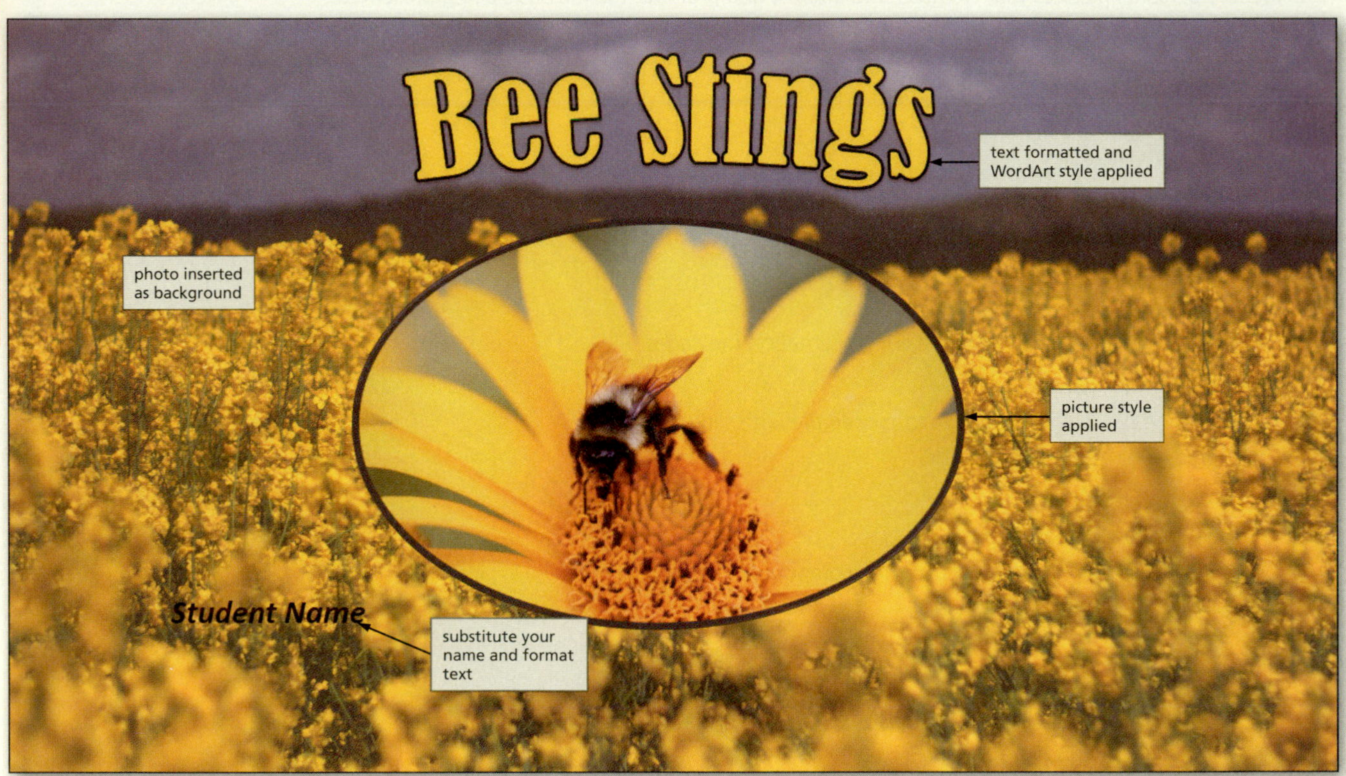

(a) Slide 1

Figure 2–79

Perform the following tasks:

1. On the title slide, use your name in place of Student Name and then bold and italicize this text (Figure 2–79a).
2. If requested to do so by your instructor, change your first name to your mother's first name on the title slide.
3. Increase the title text font size to 96 point and change the font to Bernard MT Condensed. Apply the WordArt style, Fill – White, Outline – Accent 1, Shadow (in first row). Change text fill color to Yellow (in Standard Colors row). Change text outline to Black, Text 1 (in first Theme Colors row) and then change the outline weight to 2¼ pt. Apply the Transform text effect, Arch Up (in Follow Path row) to this text.
4. Apply the Beveled Oval, Black picture style to the picture on Slide 1 and then move the picture to the center of the slide as shown in Figure 2–79a. Use the vertical Smart Guide to align the picture in this location.
5. Create a background on Slide 1 by inserting the photo, Spring, which is located in the Data Files.

6. On Slide 2, change the layout to Title and Content. Increase the title text font to 54 point, change the font color to Green (in Standard Colors row), and then bold this text. Increase the list font size to 32 point, as shown in Figure 2–79b.
7. Create a background on Slides 2 and 3 by inserting the Light Gradient – Accent 4 gradient fill (in first Preset gradients row).
8. On Slide 2, insert the picture, Bee2, move it to the right side of the slide, and then apply the Soft Edge Rectangle picture style to the picture.

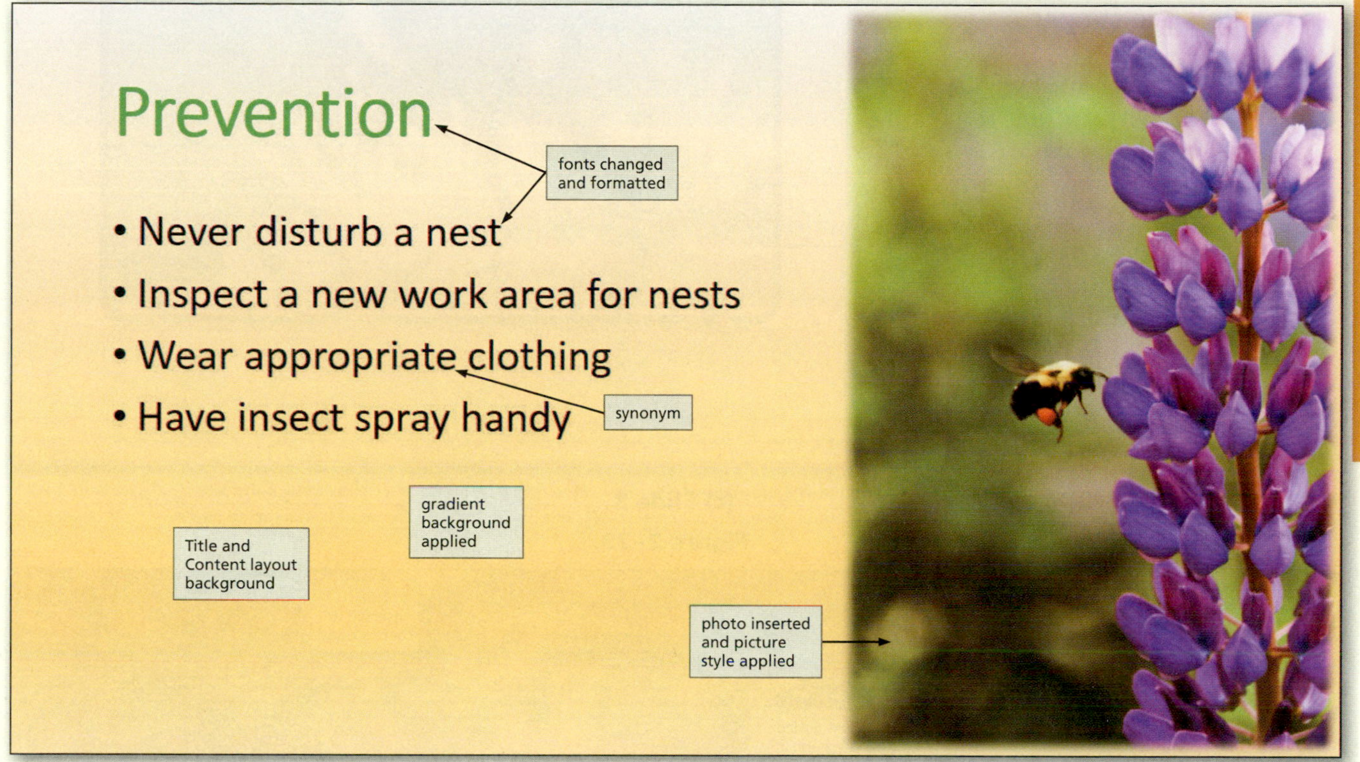

(b) Slide 2

Figure 2–79

9. On Slide 2, type `Wear long pants and a long-sleeved shirt when hiking or working outside.` in the Notes pane.
10. Replace the word, proper, with the synonym, appropriate.
11. On Slide 3 (Figure 2–79c), increase the title text font to 54 point, change the font color to Green (in Standard Colors row), and then bold this text. Increase the list font size to 24 point. Insert the photo, Bee3, and then apply the Reflected Bevel, Black picture style and change the picture brightness to Brightness: +20% Contrast: 0% (Normal) (in Brightness/Contrast area).
12. Type `Apply ice to control swelling.` in the Notes pane.
13. Create a new Slide 4 with the blank layout. Create a background on Slide 4 by inserting the photo, Hiking. Insert the illustration, Bee4. Resize this illustration and move it to the woman's right arm, as shown in Figure 2–79d.
14. On Slide 4, insert the Oval Callout shape (in first row in Callouts area) and then move it to the right side of the woman's head. Apply the Subtle Effect – Gold, Accent 4 (in fourth row) shape style to the callout. Size the shape as shown in the figure. Type `I am glad I have insect repellent in my backpack` in the shape. Bold and italicize this text and then change the font size to 20 point, as shown in Figure 2–79d.
15. Apply the Wind transition in the Exciting category to all slides. Change the duration to 2.50 seconds.

Continued >

Apply Your Knowledge *continued*

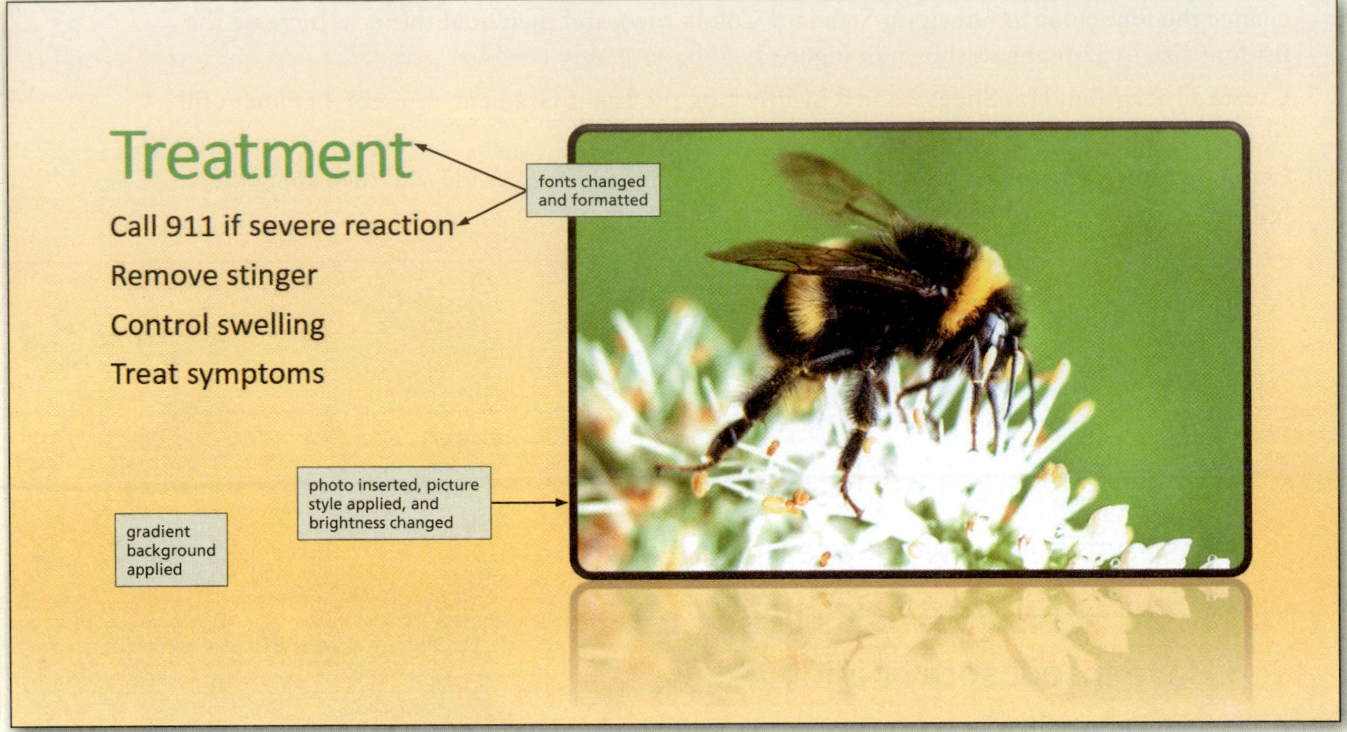

(c) Slide 3

Figure 2–79

(d) Slide 4

Figure 2–79

16. Save the presentation using the file name, Apply 2–1 Bee Stings.
17. Submit the revised document in the format specified by your instructor.
18. In Step 4 you applied the Beveled Oval, Black picture style to the photo on Slide 1. How did this style enhance the photo and the slide?

Extend Your Knowledge

Extend the skills you learned in this module and experiment with new skills. You may need to use Help to complete the assignment.

Changing Slide Backgrounds, Inserting Shapes and WordArt, and Finding and Replacing Text

Note: To complete this assignment, you will be required to use the Data Files. Please contact your instructor for information about accessing the Data Files.

Instructions: Run PowerPoint. Open the presentation, Extend 2–1 Monarch, which is located in the Data Files. You will create backgrounds including inserting a photo to create a background, apply a WordArt Style and effect, add shapes, and find and replace text to create the presentation.

Perform the following tasks:

1. Change the document theme to Basis and choose the orange variant (third variant).
2. Find and replace the words, stay alive, with the word, survive, on all slides.
3. On all slides, create a background by inserting the photo, Sky. Change the transparency to 25%.
4. On the title slide (Figure 2–80a), apply the WordArt style, Fill - Black, Text 1, Outline – Background 1, Hard Shadow – Accent 1 (second style in third row), to the title text, and then increase the font size to 72 point. Apply the WordArt Glow text effect, Red, 18 pt glow, Accent color 3 (in Glow Variations area), and then italicize this text. Also, align the text in the middle of the text box by clicking the Align Text button (Home tab | Paragraph group) and then selecting Middle in the Align Text gallery. You may need to use Help for assistance in aligning this text.

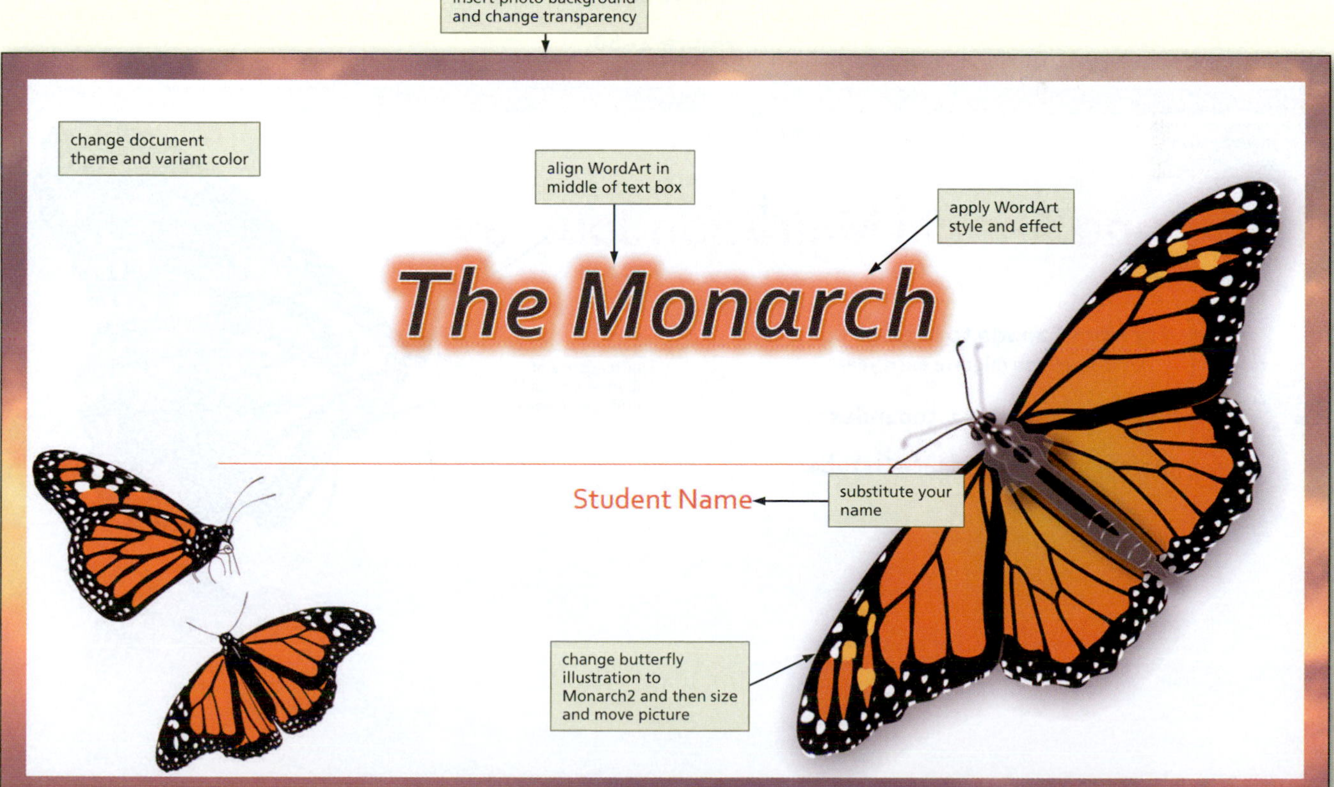

(a) Slide 1

Figure 2–80

Continued >

Extend Your Knowledge *continued*

5. If requested to do so by your instructor, add your current or previous pet's name as the Slide 1 subtitle text in place of Student Name.

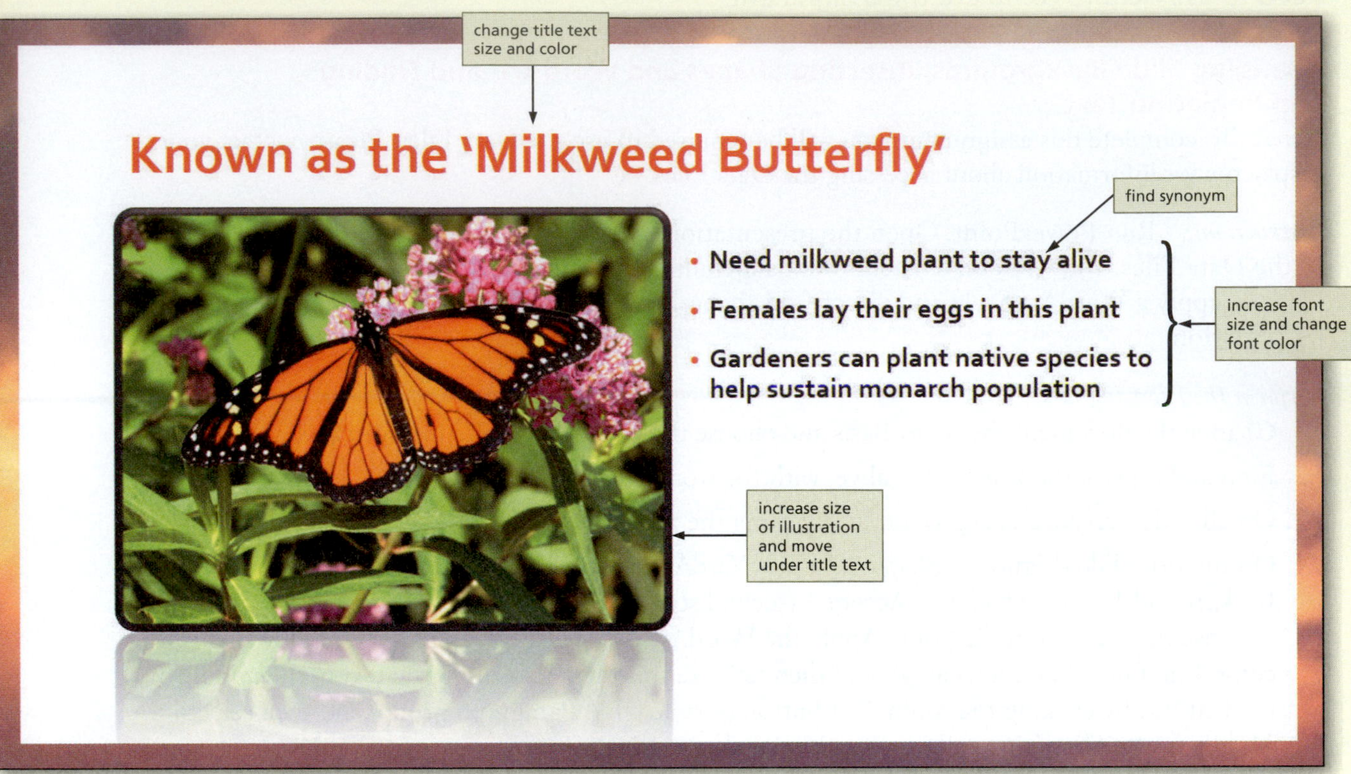

(b) Slide 2

Figure 2–80

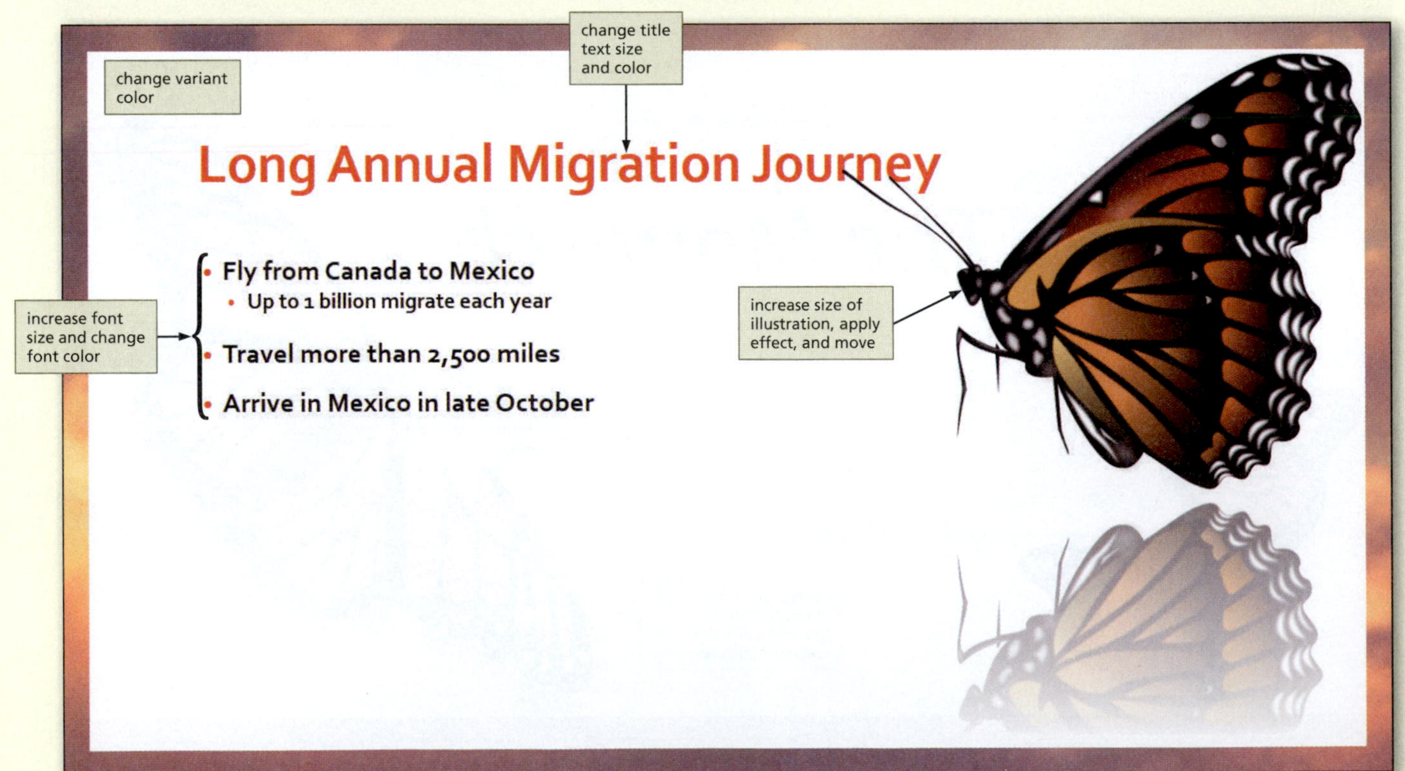

(c) Slide 3

Figure 2–80

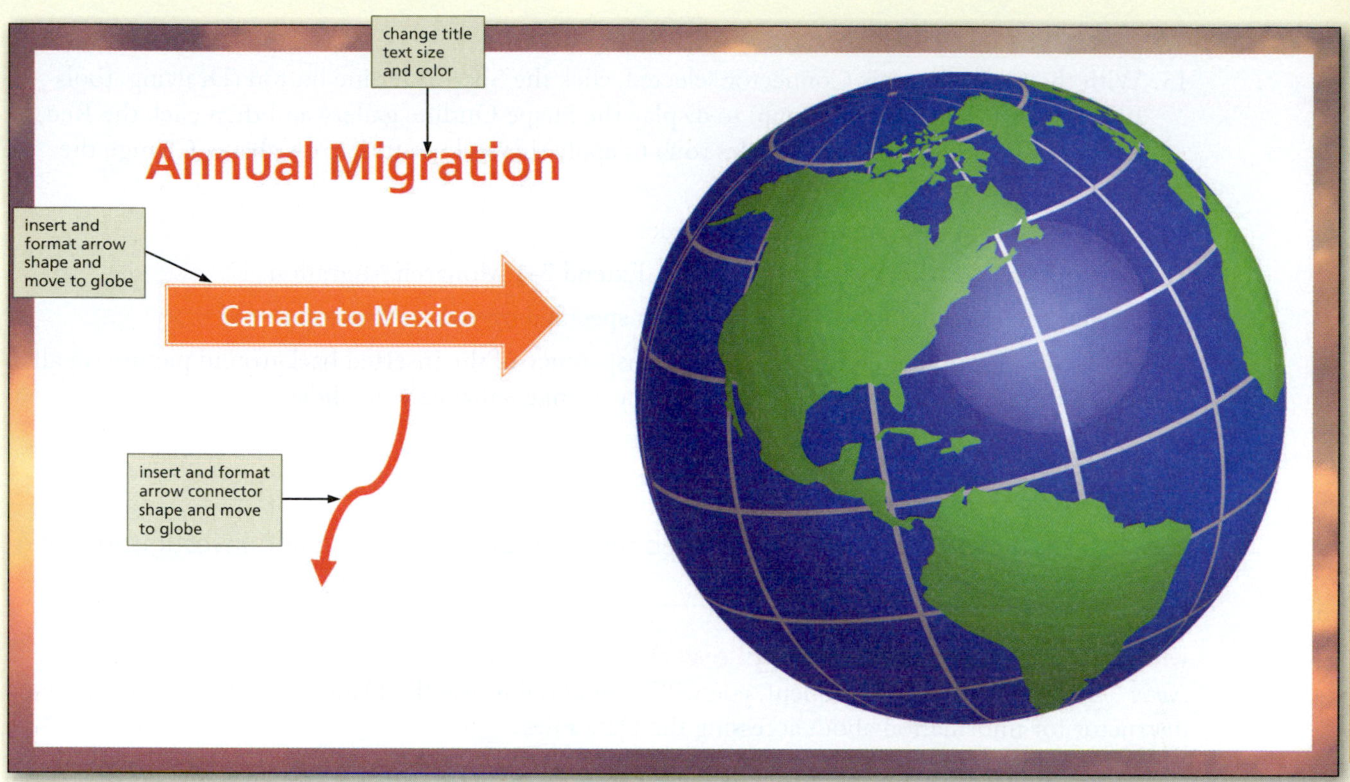

(d) Slide 4

Figure 2–80

6. On Slide 1, move the butterfly illustration in the upper-left corner to the lower-left corner of the slide. Change the butterfly illustration in the upper-right corner of the slide to the illustration, Monarch2. Increase the size of this illustration to approximately 6.26" × 5.44" and move it to the lower-right side of the slide as shown in Figure 2–80a. *Hint*: Use the Size group on the Picture Tools Format tab to enter these measurements for the illustration.
7. On Slides 2 and 3, increase the font size of the first-level paragraphs to 20 point and the one second-level paragraph on Slide 3 to 16 point. Also, change the color of this text to Black, Text 1 (in first Theme Colors row) and then bold this text.
8. On Slide 2 (Figure 2–80b), increase the size of the illustration to approximately 4.14" × 5.53", apply the Reflected Bevel, Black picture style, and then move it under the title text.
9. On Slide 3 (Figure 2–80c), increase the size of the illustration to approximately 4.35" × 5.2", apply the Half Reflection, 8 pt offset reflection picture effect (Reflection Variations area), and then move this illustration to the upper-right corner of the slide.
10. On Slides 2, 3, and 4, decrease the size of the title text to 40 point and then bold this text.
11. On Slide 4 (Figure 2–80d), insert the Right Arrow shape (in Block Arrows area) and position it on the globe illustration near the Canada–United States border. Size the shape as shown in the figure. Type **`Canada to Mexico`** in the shape. Bold this text and then change the font size to 24 point. Apply the Light 1 Outline, Colored Fill – Orange, Accent 4 shape style (in third Theme Styles row) to the shape.
12. On Slide 4, insert a Curved Arrow Connector shape by displaying the Shapes gallery, clicking this shape (in Lines area), and then positioning the pointer over central Canada in the globe illustration. Then, click and drag the pointer to central Mexico. Size this arrow so it is approximately 0.84" × 1.91". Hint: You can size a shape in the same manner as you size a picture or illustration.

Continued >

Extend Your Knowledge *continued*

13. With the Curved Arrow Connector selected, click the Shape Outline button (Drawing Tools Format tab | Shape Styles group) to display the Shape Outline gallery and then click the Red, Accent 1 style (in first Theme Styles row) to apply this style to this arrow shape. Change the shape outline weight to 6 pt.
14. Apply an appropriate transition to all slides.
15. Save the presentation using the file name, Extend 2–1 Monarch Migration.
16. Submit the revised document in the format specified by your instructor.
17. In this assignment, you changed the transparency of the inserted background picture on all the slides to 25%. How did this transparency change enhance your slides?

Expand Your World

Create a solution that uses cloud and web technologies by learning and investigating on your own from general guidance.

Modifying a Presentation Using PowerPoint Online

Note: To complete this assignment, you will be required to use the Data Files. Please contact your instructor for information about accessing the Data Files.

Instructions: The park district director in your community is planning a basketball camp for next summer. He has asked you to help him promote this event, and he wants to focus on the skills boys and girls will learn and develop. You inform him that you have created a Basketball Camp presentation for your computer class, and he would like you to customize the content of these slides slightly to promote the summer camp.

Perform the following tasks:

1. Run a browser. Search for the text, PowerPoint Online, using a search engine. Visit several websites to learn about PowerPoint Online. Navigate to the Office Online website. You will need to sign in to your Microsoft account. Run PowerPoint Online.
2. Locate the Basketball Camp presentation in the Recent list and then click the file name to open the file. Click the Edit Presentation button and then click 'Edit in PowerPoint Online' and display the ribbon. Modify the presentation you created for the Basketball Camp presentation by adding the name and address of the nearest park district headquarters on the title slide. In addition, add the date that is the first Saturday in June next year and a starting time of 1 p.m.
3. If requested by your instructor, add the name of one of your high school teachers as the park district director's name on the title slide.
4. Save the presentation using the file name, Expand 2–1 Basketball Camp.
5. Submit the assignment in the format specified by your instructor.
6. Other than the content the director asked you to include on the title slide, how does the presentation you created using PowerPoint Online differ from the presentation you created in the Module 2 project? Which tabs are not available in PowerPoint Online? View the Home, Design, and Transitions tabs. Do you think the formatting functions, themes, and transitions are adequate to develop effective presentations? Why or why not?

In the Labs

Design, create, modify, and/or use a presentation following the guidelines, concepts, and skills presented in this module. Labs 1 and 2, which increase in difficulty, require you to create solutions based on what you learned in the module; Lab 3 requires you to apply your creative thinking and problem-solving skills to design and implement a solution.

Lab 1: Creating a Presentation, Inserting Photos, Applying Picture Styles, and Inserting Shapes

Note: To complete this assignment, you will be required to use the Data Files. Please contact your instructor for information about accessing the Data Files.

Problem: Your astronomy class is studying the dwarf planet, Pluto, and the New Horizon probe that has been taking photographs of this planet. Prepare the PowerPoint presentation shown in Figure 2–81.

Perform the following tasks:

1. Run PowerPoint. Create a new presentation using the Celestial theme.
2. On Slide 1, insert the photo, Pluto1, as shown in Figure 2–81a. Apply the Metal Oval picture style to the picture, decrease the size of the picture slightly, and then move it to the left side of the slide as shown in the figure.
3. Type **`Pluto Up Close`** as the Slide 1 title text. Press the ENTER key after the words, PLUTO and UP, so the text is displayed on three lines. Change the font to Britannic Bold and increase the font size to 88 point. Apply the WordArt style Gradient Fill – Gray (first style in

(a) Slide 1

Figure 2–81

Continued >

In the Labs *continued*

second row). Change the text outline color to Black, Background 1 (in Theme Colors row) and the text outline weight to 3 pt. Also, apply the Perspective Heroic Extreme Left 3-D Rotation (in Perspective area) to this text. Type **`New Horizons Probe`** as the subtitle text. Change the font to Arial, decrease the font size to 16 point, and then bold this text.

4. Insert four new slides. Create Slides 2 and 5 with the Two Content layout, Slide 3 with the Panoramic Picture with Caption layout, and Slide 4 with the Title Only layout.
5. Using Figures 2–81b through 2–81e as a guide, type the title and content text. On Slide 2, change the title font to Arial, increase the font size to 44 point, and then change the font color to Red (in Standard Colors row). Use the Format Painter to apply these formatting changes to the title text on Slides 4 and 5.
6. On Slide 3, change the font size of the two paragraphs to 24 point and then bold this text.
7. On Slide 5, change the bulleted list font size to 28 point and then bold this text.
8. Using Figures 2–81b through 2–81e as a guide, insert all illustrations on Slides 2 through 5. The pictures and illustration to be inserted, which are available in the Data Files, are called Pluto2 (for Slide 2), Solar System (for Slide 3), Pluto3 (for Slide 4), and Solar System2 (for Slide 5).
9. Size the pictures and then use the Smart Guides to position these images. You may want to zoom the slides to help you align these graphic elements.
10. On Slide 2, apply the Bevel Perspective picture style to the picture, change the picture border color to Red, and then change the border weight to 3 pt, as shown in Figure 2–81b.

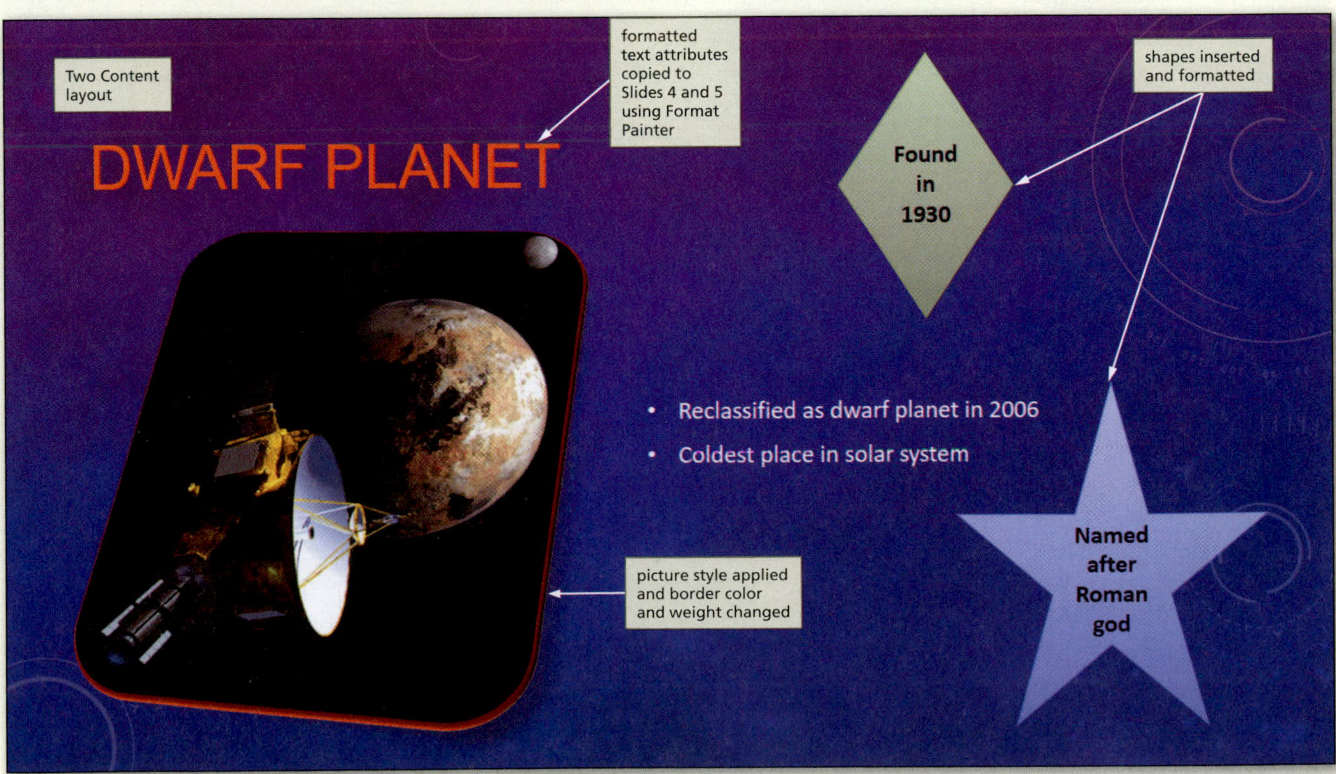

(b) Slide 2

Figure 2–81

11. On Slide 2, insert the Diamond shape located in the Basic Shapes area to the right of the title text. Apply the Subtle Effect – Olive Green, Accent 4 shape style (in Theme Styles area) to the shape, type **`Found in 1930`** in the shape, and then bold this text. Insert the 5-Point Star shape located in the Stars and Banners area in the lower-right corner of the slide. Apply the Subtle Effect – Blue, Accent 2 shape style (in Theme Styles area) to the shape, type **`Named after Roman god`** in the shape, and then bold this text. Adjust the size and position of these two shapes, as shown in the figure.
12. On Slide 3, insert the Sun shape located in the Basic Shapes area on the lower-right corner of the slide. Apply the Intense Effect – Gold, Accent 5 shape style (in Theme Styles area) to the shape. Size the shape as shown in the figure. Type the text, **`Pluto takes 248 earth years to orbit the sun`** in the shape and then bold this text, as shown in Figure 2–81c.

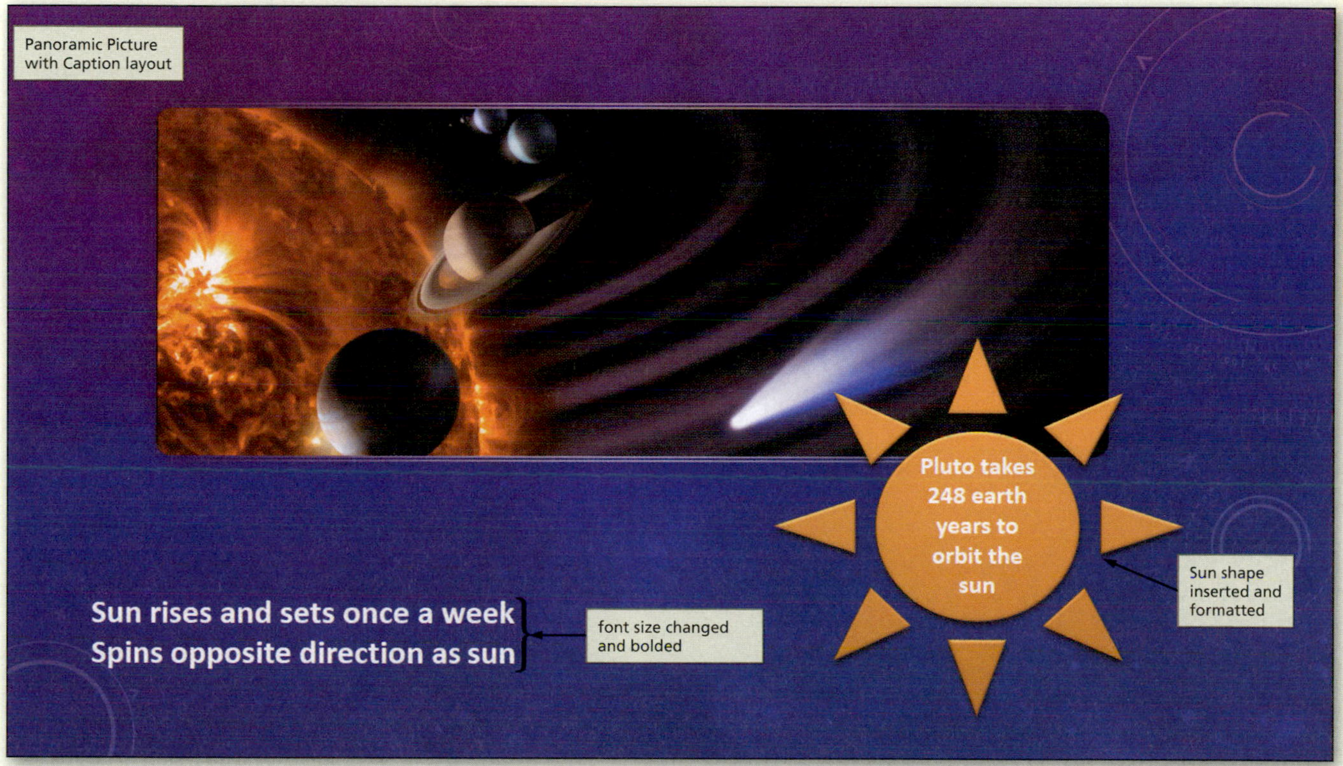

(c) Slide 3

Figure 2–81

13. On Slide 4, insert the Oval shape. Select this shape, hold down the SHIFT key, and then draw a circle .75" × .75", as shown in Figure 2–81d. *Hint*: Use the Size group in the Drawing Tools Format tab to enter the exact measurement of the shape. Change the shape fill gradient to Linear Down (in first Light Variations area). Then copy and paste this shape four times. Move the five shapes around the Pluto illustration, as shown in the figure.
14. On Slide 5, apply the Simple Frame, White picture style to the illustration. Insert the Left Arrow shape located in the Block Arrows area to the right of the illustration. Change the shape fill to Red. Size the shape as shown in the figure. Type **`Pluto`** in the shape and then bold this text, as shown in Figure 2–81e.
15. On Slide 2, type **`Pluto was discovered on February 18, 1930, by Clyde Tombaugh of the Lowell Observatory.`** in the Notes pane.
16. On Slide 3, type **`It takes five hours for the sun's rays to reach Pluto. It takes only eight minutes for the sun's rays to reach Earth.`** in the Notes pane.

Continued >

In the Labs *continued*

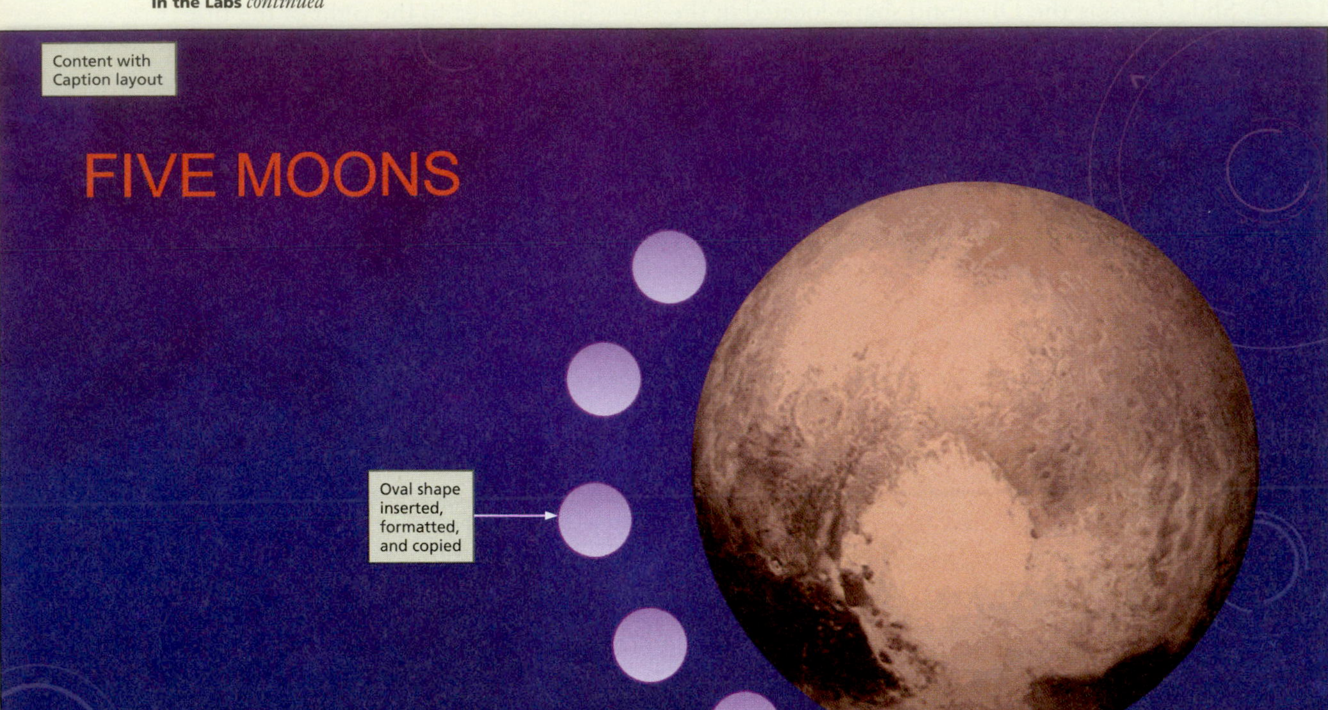

(d) Slide 4

Figure 2–81

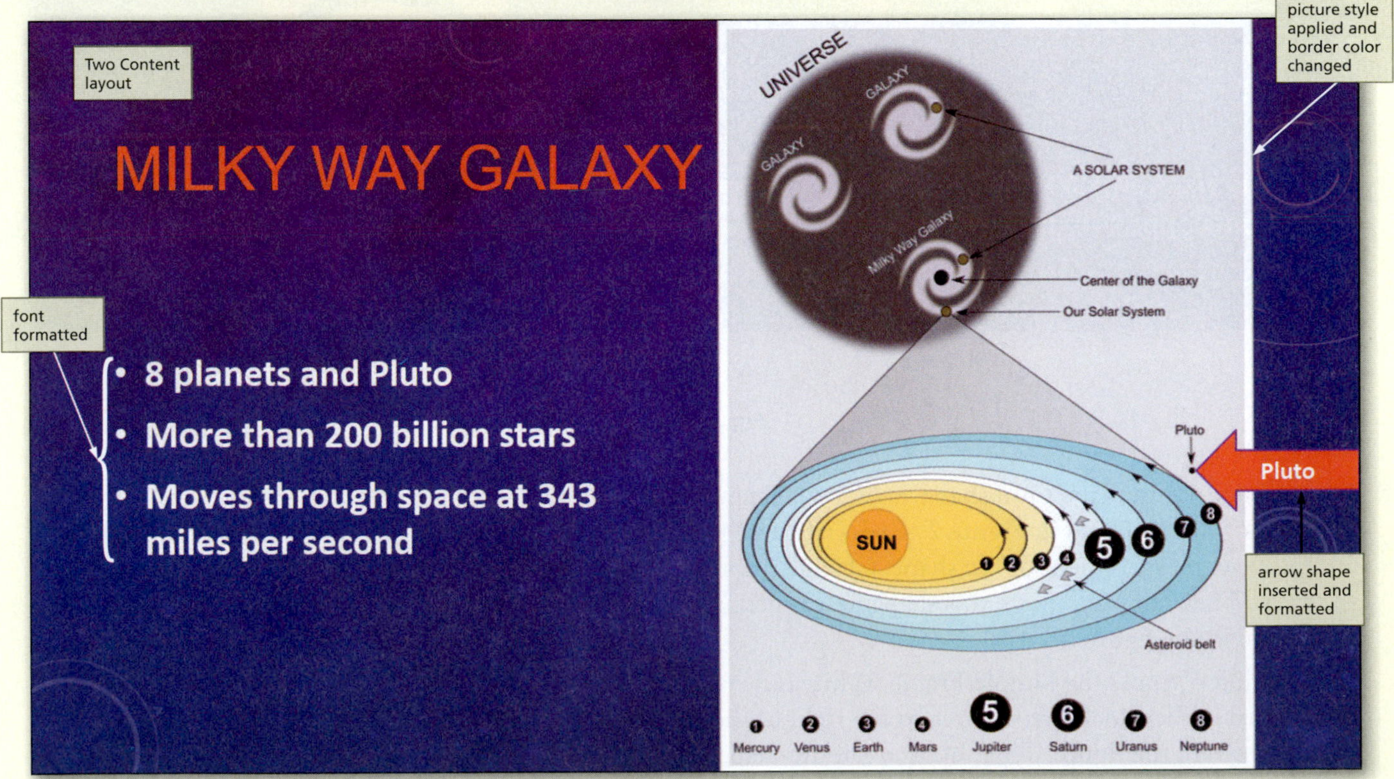

(e) Slide 5

Figure 2–81

17. If requested by your instructor, type the name of the city or county in which you were born into the title placeholder on Slide 3.
18. Apply the Vortex transition in the Exciting category to all slides. Change the duration to 3.0 seconds.

19. Check the spelling and correct any errors. Save the presentation using the file name, Lab 2–1 Pluto Up Close.
20. Print the notes pages.
21. Submit the document in the format specified by your instructor.
22. In Step 2, you applied the Metal Oval picture style to the picture. How did this improve the design of the slide? Why did you put a 3 pt red border on the picture on Slide 2?

Lab 2: Creating a Presentation Using an Online Theme Template, Shapes, and WordArt

Note: To complete this assignment, you will be required to use the Data Files. Please contact your instructor for information about accessing the Data Files.

Problem: Your local library has hired a singer for the summer reading program. Her weekly show is centered around music and art, and one of her songs is about the colors of the rainbow. In addition to her backdrop of rainbow colors, you decide to develop a presentation to teach the children more about rainbows. You create the presentation shown in Figure 2–82.

Perform the following tasks:

1. Run PowerPoint and then search for an online template by typing **nature** in the 'Search for online templates and themes' box. Choose the template called Nature presentation, illustrated landscape design (widescreen).
2. Delete Slides 12 and 13, delete Slides 6 through 10, and then delete Slides 3 and 4. Duplicate Slide 2 and then move Slide 4 to the end of the presentation.
3. Type the title and text content for all slides, as shown in Figures 2–82a through 2–82e.

(a) Slide 1

Figure 2–82

Continued >

In the Labs *continued*

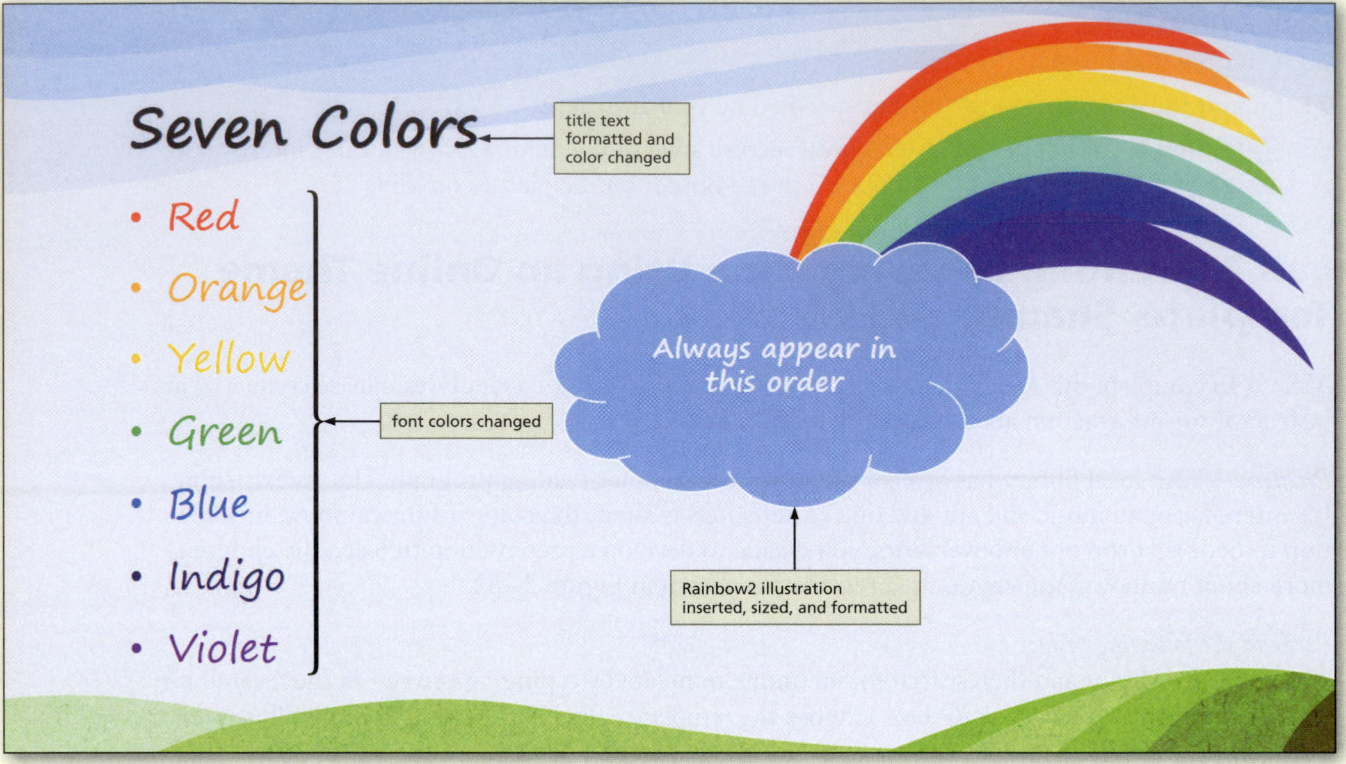

(b) Slide 2

Figure 2–82

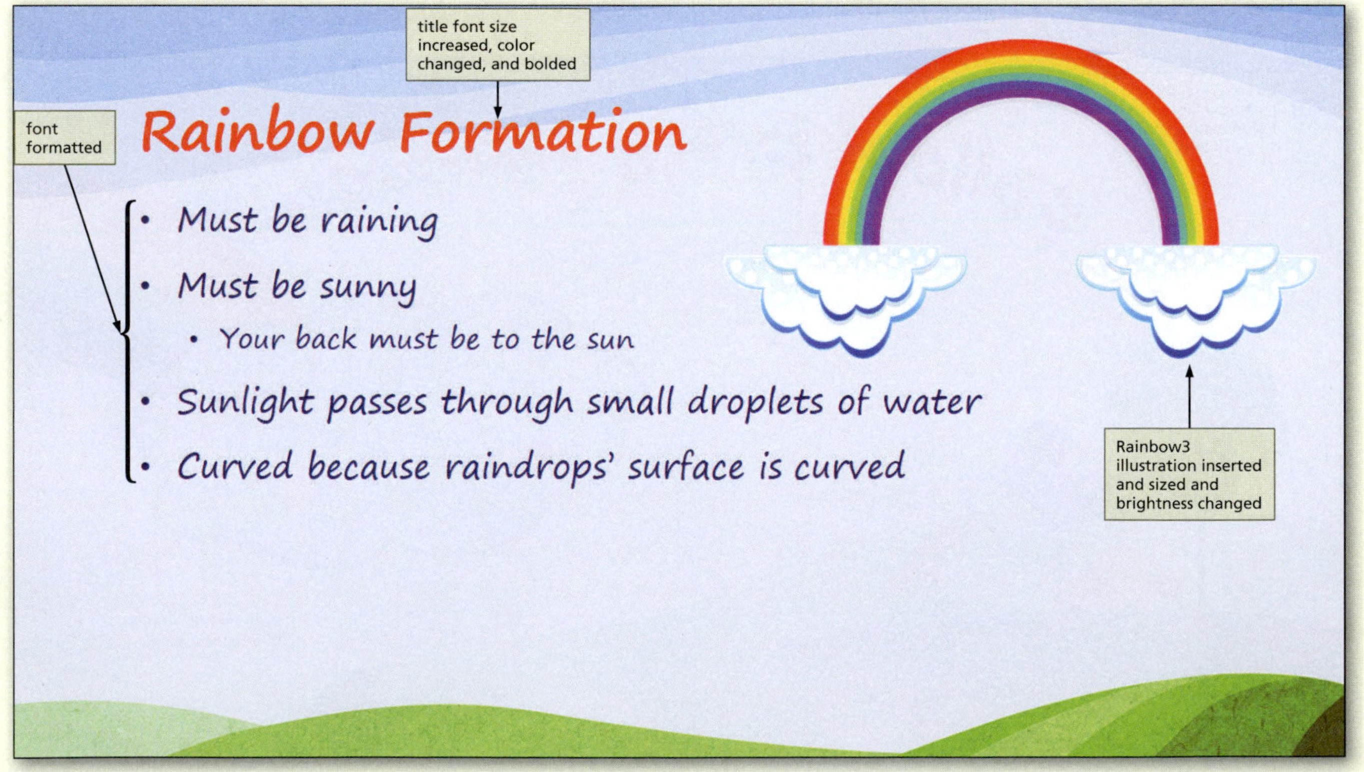

(c) Slide 3

Figure 2–82

4. Insert the illustrations shown in Figures 2–82b through 2–82d from the Data Files. The illustrations are called Rainbow1 (for Slide 1), Rainbow2 (for Slide 2), Rainbow3 (for Slide 3), and People (for Slide 4). Size the illustrations using Figure 2–82 as a guide.

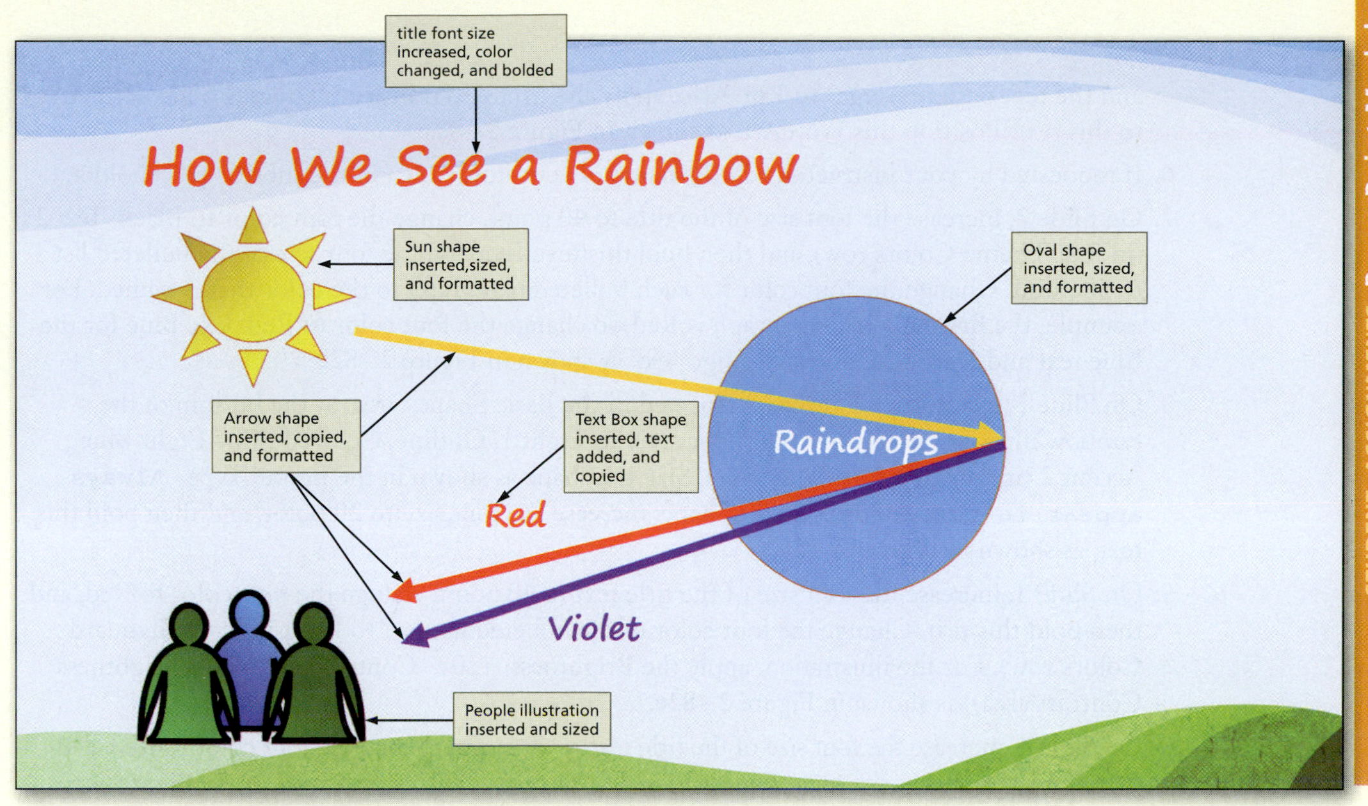

(d) Slide 4

Figure 2–82

(e) Slide 5

Figure 2–82

5. On the title slide, select the title text and then apply the WordArt style Fill – White, Outline – Accent 1, Shadow (fourth style in first row). Increase the font size to 72 point. Change the text fill to Red (in Standard Colors row), the text outline color to Purple (in Standard Colors row),

Continued >

In the Labs *continued*

and the text outline weight to 3 pt. Also, apply the Arch Up transform effect (Follow Path area), to this text. Position this WordArt, as shown in Figure 2–82a.

6. If requested by your instructor, add the name of your hometown in the subtitle placeholder.
7. On Slide 2, increase the font size of the title to 40 point, change the font color to Black, Text 2 (in first Theme Colors row), and then bold this text. Increase the font size of the bulleted list to 28 point. Change the font color for each bulleted paragraph to the color that is named. For example, the first bulleted paragraph is Red, so change the font color to Red. Use Blue for the Blue text and Dark Blue for the Indigo text, as shown in Figure 2–82b.
8. On Slide 2, insert the Cloud shape, located in the Basic Shapes area, at the bottom of the rainbow illustration. Change the shape style to Light 1, Outline, Colored Fill – Light Blue, Accent 2 (in third Theme Styles row). Size the shape as shown in the figure. Type `Always appear in this order` in the shape, increase the font size to 20 point, and then bold this text, as shown in Figure 2–82b.
9. On Slide 3, increase the font size of the title text to 40 point, change the font color to Red, and then bold this text. Change the font color of the bulleted list text to Dark Blue (in Standard Colors row). For the illustration, apply the Brightness: +20% Contrast: +40% (in Brightness/Contrast area), as shown in Figure 2–82c.
10. On Slide 4, increase the font size of the title text to 40 point, change the font color to Red, and then bold this text, as shown in Figure 2–82d. Insert the Sun shape, located in the Basic Shapes area, in the upper left area of the slide below the title text. Change the shape fill color to Yellow (in Standard Colors row) and then apply the From Top Left Corner gradient (in Dark Variations area) to the shape. Size and position the shape as shown in the figure.
11. On Slide 4, insert the Oval shape located in the Basic Shapes area, resize the shape so that it is approximately 3" × 3", and then change the Shape Fill color to Light Blue, Accent 2 (in Theme Colors row). Move this shape to the area shown in the figure. Type `Raindrops` in the shape, increase the font size to 24 point, and then bold this text.
12. On Slide 4, insert the Arrow shape, located in the Lines area, from the edge of the sun shape to the right side of the blue shape, as shown in Figure 2–82d. Change the weight to 6 pt. Copy and paste this arrow two times and use the sizing handles to position the arrows, as shown in the figure. Change the upper Arrow shape outline color to Yellow, the middle Arrow shape to Red, and the lower Arrow shape to Purple.
13. On Slide 4, insert the Text Box shape, located in the Basic Shapes area, type `Red` in the shape, change the font color to Red, increase the font size to 24 point, and then bold this text. Copy and paste this shape one time, change the text to `Violet,` and then change the font color to Purple. Move these two text box shapes to the areas shown in the figure.
14. On Slide 5, change the title text font color to Red and then bold this text, as shown in Figure 2–82e. Change the font color of the text to Purple and then bold this text. Apply the Simple Frame, White picture style to the picture. Add a 3 pt Purple border and then apply the Offset Left shadow (in Outer area) picture effect.
15. Change the transition to Origami in the Exciting category to all slides. Change the duration to 2.5 seconds.
16. Check spelling and correct all errors. Save the presentation using the file name, Lab 2–2 About Rainbows.

17. Submit the revised document in the format specified by your instructor.
18. You searched for an online rainbow theme. Do you think any of the other themes would have worked well for your presentation? Does choosing specific slide layouts while beginning the exercise help save time creating the presentation?

Lab 3: Consider This: Your Turn

Design and Create a Presentation about Learning to Knit and Crochet

Note: To complete this assignment, you will be required to use the Data Files. Please contact your instructor for information about accessing the Data Files.

Part 1: More than 50 million people knit or crochet to create fun and useful items, to relax, or to exchange ideas with fellow hobbyists at a regional guild or group. The local craft store in your community is offering a series of classes on knitting and crocheting techniques, and the manager has asked you to help promote the event. The introductory course includes instruction on selecting yarn, hooks, and needles; reading patterns; and making basic stitches. The intermediate and advanced courses include knitting in the round; making sleeves, button holes, and cables; and bead and filet crocheting. Classes are scheduled for four weeks on consecutive Saturdays beginning the first week of every month. All students will learn new skills and complete a fashionable project, which could include creating afghans, hats, and scarves for community residents in need. Use the concepts and techniques presented in this module to prepare a presentation to promote the classes. Select a suitable theme, and include a title slide, bulleted lists, shapes, and WordArt. The presentation should contain photos and illustrations appropriately resized. Six photos and illustrations are available in the Data Files: Green Yarn, Mitten, Two Mittens, Penguin, Quilt, and Scarf. Apply picture styles and effects. Add a title slide and closing slide to complete your presentation. Format the title slide with a shape. Format the background with at least one picture and apply a background texture to at least one slide. Review and revise your presentation as needed. Submit your assignment in the format specified by your instructor.

Part 2: You made several decisions while creating the presentation in this assignment: where to place text, how to format the text (such as font, font size, and where to use WordArt), which graphical image(s) to use, what styles and effects to apply, where to position the graphical images, how to format the graphical images, and which shapes to use to add interest to the presentation. What was the rationale behind each of these decisions? When you reviewed the document, what further revisions did you make and why? Where would you recommend showing this slide show?

3 Reusing a Presentation and Adding Media and Animation

Objectives

You will have mastered the material in this module when you can:

- Color a photo
- Add an artistic effect to a photo
- Align paragraph text
- Change views
- Ungroup, change the color of, and regroup an illustration
- Copy a slide element from one slide to another
- Insert and edit a video clip
- Insert an audio clip
- Control audio and video clips
- Insert entrance, emphasis, and exit effects
- Control animation timing
- Change theme colors
- Change a theme and variant on one slide
- Print handouts

BTW

Media in Presentations

Well-produced video and audio clips add value to a presentation when they help explain a concept that cannot be captured in a photo or illustration. Before you insert these files on a slide, however, consider whether they really add any value to your overall slide show. Audiences quickly tire of extraneous movement and sounds on slides, and they will find such media clips annoying. The audience's attention should focus primarily on the presenter; extraneous or inappropriate media files may divert their attention and, in turn, decrease the quality of the presentation.

Introduction

At times, you will need to revise a PowerPoint presentation. Changes may include inserting and adding effects to photos, altering the colors of photos and illustrations, and updating visual elements displayed on a slide. Applying a different theme, changing fonts, and substituting graphical elements can give a slide show an entirely new look. Adding media, including sounds, video, and music, can enhance a presentation and help audience members retain the information being presented. Adding animation can reinforce important points and enliven a presentation.

Project — Presentation with Video, Audio, Animation, and Photos with Effects

The project in this module follows graphical guidelines and uses PowerPoint to create the presentation shown in Figure 3–1. The slides in this revised presentation, which discusses the Spokes Bike Club, have a variety of audio and visual elements. For example, the photos in the slides' backgrounds have artistic effects applied that soften the images and help the audience focus on other elements on the slides. The bicycle wheel photo has colors that blend well with the background. The bullet list is animated with entrance, emphasis, and exit effects. The video has been edited to play only one portion and has effects to add audience interest. Bicycle riding sounds integrate with the visual elements.

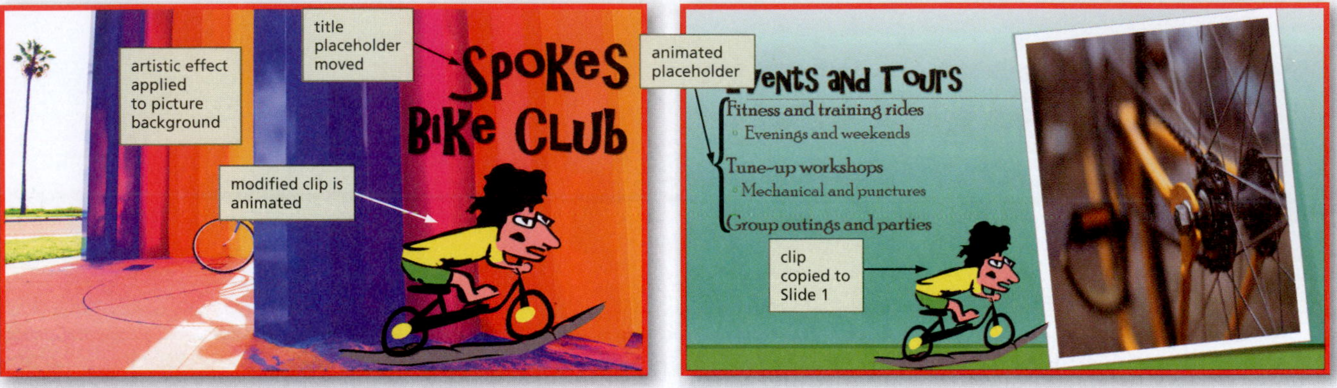

(a) Slide 1 (Title Slide with Picture Background, Modified Clip, and Animated Clip)

(b) Slide 2 (Bulleted List)

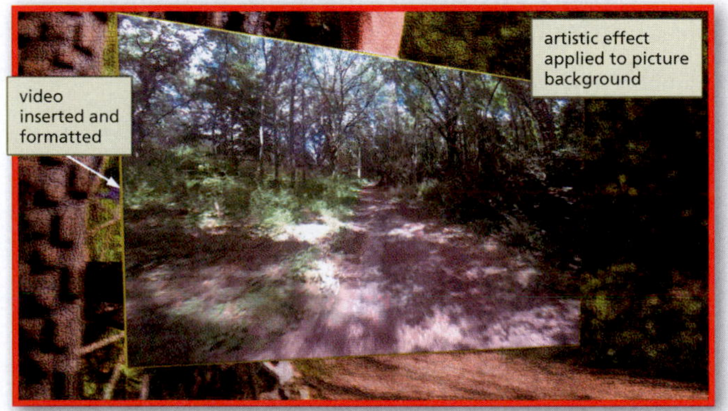

(c) Slide 3 (Picture Background and Video Clip)

(d) Slide 4 (Video Playing Full Screen)

Figure 3–1

For an introduction to Windows and instructions about how to perform basic Windows tasks, read the Office and Windows module at the beginning of this book, where you can learn how to resize windows, change screen resolution, create folders, move and rename files, use Windows Help, and much more.

Overall, the slides have myriad media elements and effects that are exciting for your audience to watch and hear.

In this module, you will learn how to create the slides shown in Figure 3–1. The following roadmap identifies general activities you will perform as you progress through this module:

1. **INSERT** and **ADD EFFECTS** to photos, including changing colors and styles.
2. **MODIFY PLACEHOLDERS** on the slides by moving and changing sizes.

3. **MODIFY** and **COPY** an **ILLUSTRATION** to customize its appearance.
4. **ADD MEDIA** files to slides.
5. **ANIMATE SLIDE CONTENT** with entrance, emphasis, and exit effects.
6. **CUSTOMIZE SLIDE ELEMENTS** by changing a theme and variant on one slide and changing the theme colors.

Inserting Photos and Adding Effects

The Spokes Bike Club presentation consists of three slides that have some text, a clip art image, a formatted background, and a transition applied to all slides. You will insert a photo into one slide and then modify it and another photo by adding artistic effects and recoloring. You also will copy the clip art from Slide 2 to Slide 1 and modify the objects in this clip. In Module 2, you inserted photos, made corrections, and added styles and effects; the new effects you apply in this module will add to your repertoire of photo enhancements that increase interest in your presentation.

In the following pages, you will perform these tasks:

1. Insert the first photo into Slide 1.
2. Recolor the Slide 1 photo.
3. Add an artistic effect to the Slide 3 photo.
4. Send the Slide 1 photo back behind all other slide objects.

BTW

PowerPoint Screen Resolution

If you are using a computer or mobile device to step through the project in this module and you want your screens to match the figures in this book, you should change your screen's resolution to 1366 x 768. For information about how to change a computer's resolution, refer to the Office and Windows module at the beginning of this book.

BTW

Organizing Files and Folders

You should organize and store files in folders so that you easily can find the files later. For example, if you are taking an introductory technology class called CIS 101, a good practice would be to save all PowerPoint files in a PowerPoint folder in a CIS 101 folder. For a discussion of folders and detailed examples of creating folders, refer to the Office and Windows module at the beginning of this book.

To Insert and Resize a Photo into a Slide without Content Placeholders

The first step is to insert a photo into Slide 1. This photo is available in the Data Files. Please contact your instructor for information about accessing the required file. The following steps insert a photo into Slide 1.

1. Run PowerPoint and then open the presentation, Spokes, from the Data Files.
2. Save the presentation using the file name, Spokes Bike Club.
3. With Slide 1 displaying, click Insert on the ribbon to display the Insert tab and then click the Pictures button (Insert tab | Images group) to display the Insert Picture dialog box.
4. If necessary, navigate to the photo location (in this case, the Module 03 folder in the Data Files folder).
5. Click Hidden Bike to select the file.
6. Click the Insert button (Insert Picture dialog box) to insert the photo into Slide 1.
7. Drag the sizing handles to resize the photo so that it covers the entire slide. You can click the Height and Width arrows (Picture Tools Format tab | Size group) to adjust the picture size so that it is approximately 7.5" x 13.33" (Figure 3–2).

For an introduction to Office and instructions about how to perform basic tasks in Office apps, read the Office and Windows module at the beginning of this book, where you can learn how to run an application, use the ribbon, save a file, open a file, print a file, exit an application, use Help, and much more.

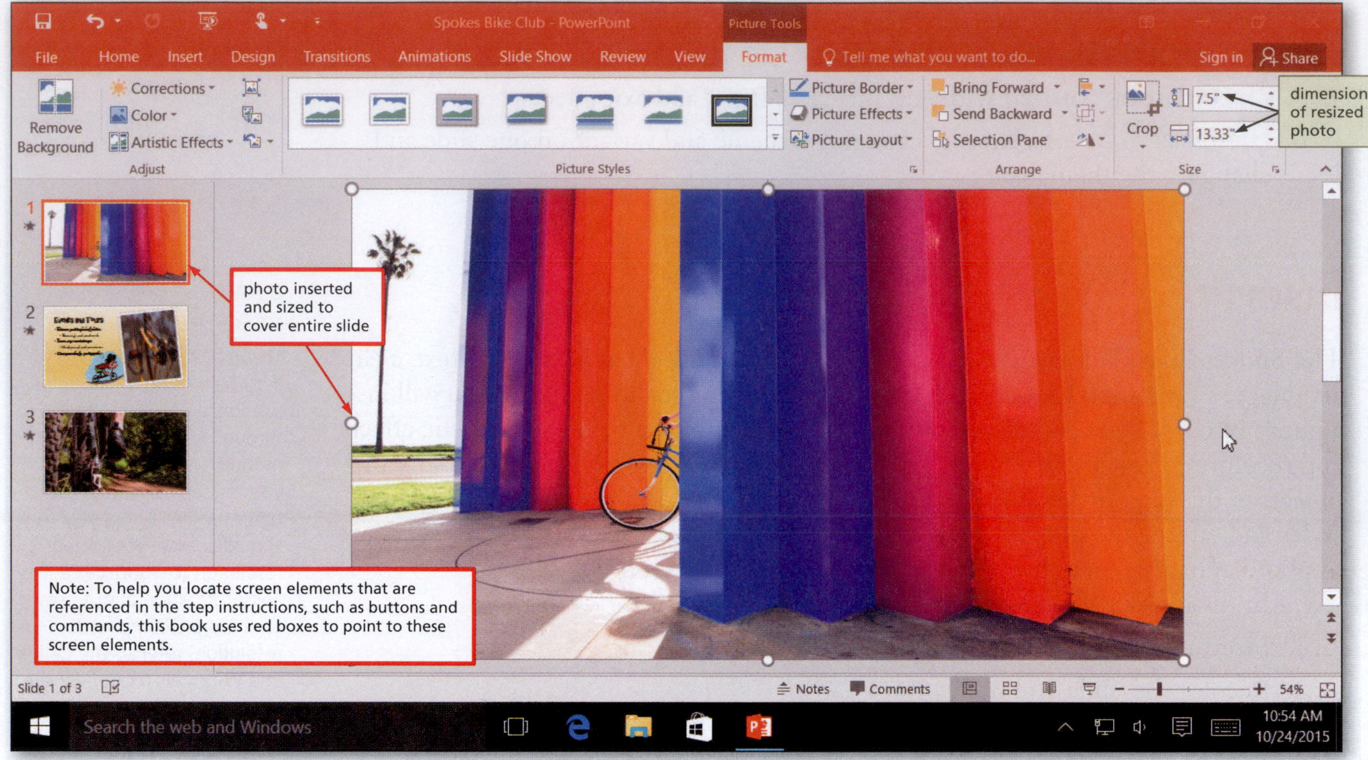

Figure 3–2

BTW

Touch Screen Differences

The Office and Windows interfaces may vary if you are using a touch screen. For this reason, you might notice that the function or appearance of your touch screen differs slightly from this module's presentation.

Adjusting Photo Colors

PowerPoint allows you to adjust colors to match or add contrast to slide elements by coloring photos. The Color gallery has a wide variety of preset formatting combinations. The thumbnails in the gallery display the more common color saturation, color tone, and recolor adjustments. **Color saturation** changes the intensity of colors. High saturation produces vivid colors; low saturation produces gray tones. **Color tone** affects the coolness, called blue, or the warmness, called orange, of photos. When a digital camera does not measure the tone correctly, a **color cast** occurs, and, as a result, one color dominates the photo. **Recolor** effects convert the photo into a wide variety of hues. The more common are **grayscale**, which changes the color photo into black, white, and shades of gray, and **sepia**, which changes the photo colors into brown, gold, and yellow, reminiscent of a faded photo. You also can fine-tune the color adjustments by clicking the Picture Color Options and More Variations commands in the Color gallery.

To Color a Photo

1 INSERT & ADD EFFECTS | 2 MODIFY PLACEHOLDERS | 3 MODIFY & COPY ILLUSTRATIONS
4 ADD MEDIA | 5 ANIMATE SLIDE CONTENT | 6 CUSTOMIZE SLIDE ELEMENTS

The Office theme and text on Slides 1 and 2 are simple and fulfill the need to communicate the presentation's bicycling message. The photos on Slides 1 and 3 help set the tone of riding on an open road and enjoying the freedom that biking brings. You may want to add an effect to photos. ***Why?** An effect adds variety to the presentation and helps enhance ordinary photos.* The following steps recolor the Slide 1 photo to intensify the bright colors.

1

- With Slide 1 displaying and the Hidden Bike photo selected, click the Color button (Picture Tools Format tab | Adjust group) to display the Color gallery (Figure 3–3).

Q&A Why does the Adjust group look different on my screen?
Your monitor is set to a different resolution. See the Office 2016 and Windows 10 module for an explanation of screen resolution and the appearance of the ribbon.

Why are gray borders surrounding the thumbnails in the Color Saturation, Color Tone, and Recolor areas in the gallery?
The gray borders show the color saturation, tone, and recolor settings currently in effect for the image on Slide 1.

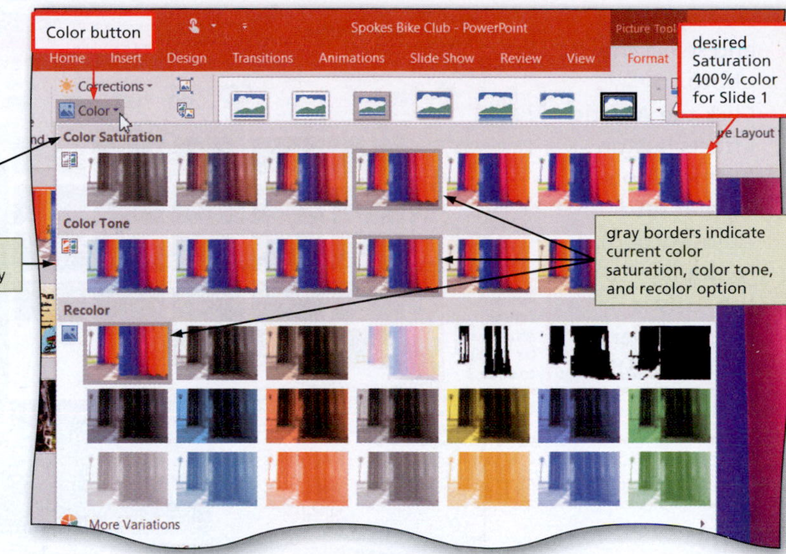

Figure 3–3

2

- Point to Saturation: 400% (last thumbnail in Color Saturation row) to display a live preview of this adjustment on the photo.

 **Experiment**

- Point to various thumbnails in the Color Saturation area and watch the saturation change on the photo in Slide 1.
- Click Saturation: 400% to apply this saturation to the Hidden Bike photo (Figure 3–4).

Q&A Could I have applied this recoloring to the photo if it had been a background instead of a file inserted into the slide?
No. Artistic effects and recoloring cannot be applied to backgrounds.

Figure 3–4

Other Ways

1. Click Format Picture on shortcut menu, click Picture icon, click Picture Color, use Saturation slider (Format Picture pane)

To Add an Artistic Effect to a Photo

1 INSERT & ADD EFFECTS | 2 MODIFY PLACEHOLDERS | 3 MODIFY & COPY ILLUSTRATIONS
4 ADD MEDIA | 5 ANIMATE SLIDE CONTENT | 6 CUSTOMIZE SLIDE ELEMENTS

Artists use a variety of techniques to create effects in their paintings. They can vary the amount of paint on their brushstroke, use fine bristles to add details, mix colors to increase or decrease intensity, and smooth their paints together to blend the colors. You, likewise, can add similar effects to your photos using PowerPoint's built-in artistic effects. ***Why?*** *The completed Slide 3 will have both a photo and a video, so applying an artistic effect to the photo will provide a contrast between the two images.* The following steps add an artistic effect to the Slide 3 photo.

- Display Slide 3 and select the photo.
- Click the Artistic Effects button (Picture Tools Format tab | Adjust group) to display the Artistic Effects gallery (Figure 3–5).

Figure 3–5

- Point to Cement (first thumbnail in fourth row) to display a live preview of this effect on the photo.

Experiment

- Point to various artistic effects and watch the hues change on the photo in Slide 3.
- Click Cement to apply this artistic effect to the photo (Figure 3–6).

Figure 3–6

Q&A Can I adjust a photo by recoloring and applying an artistic effect?

Yes. You can apply both a color and an effect. You may prefer at times to mix these adjustments to create a unique image.

Other Ways

1. Click Format Picture on shortcut menu, click Effects icon, click Artistic Effects

To Change the Stacking Order

1 INSERT & ADD EFFECTS | 2 MODIFY PLACEHOLDERS | 3 MODIFY & COPY ILLUSTRATIONS
4 ADD MEDIA | 5 ANIMATE SLIDE CONTENT | 6 CUSTOMIZE SLIDE ELEMENTS

The objects on a slide stack on top of each other, much like individual cards in a deck. To change the order of these objects, you use the Bring Forward and Send Backward commands. **Bring Forward** moves an object toward the top of the stack, and **Send Backward** moves an object underneath another object. When you click the Bring Forward arrow, PowerPoint displays a menu with an additional command, **Bring to Front**, which moves a selected object to the top of the stack. Likewise, when you click the Send Backward arrow, the **Send to Back** command moves the selected object underneath all objects on the slide. The following steps arrange the Slide 1 photo. ***Why?*** *On this slide, the photo is on top of the placeholders, so you no longer can see the text. If you send the photo to the bottom of the stack on the slide, the letters will become visible.*

1

- Display Slide 1 and then select the Hidden Bike photo.
- Click the Picture Tools Format tab and then click the Send Backward arrow (Picture Tools Format tab | Arrange group) to display the Send Backward menu (Figure 3–7).

Q&A How can I see objects that are not on the top of the stack?
Press TAB or SHIFT+TAB to display each slide object.

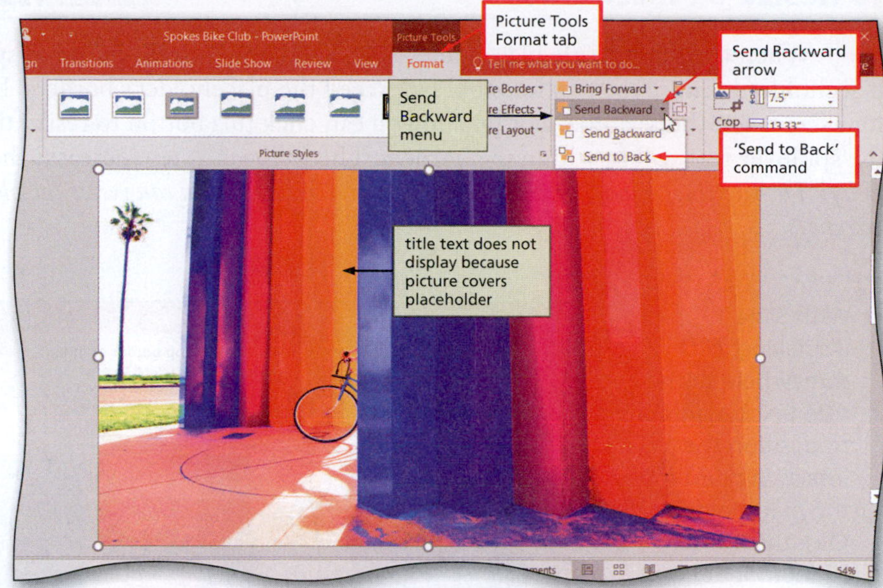

Figure 3–7

2

- Click 'Send to Back' to move the photo underneath all slide objects (Figure 3–8).

Figure 3–8

Other Ways

1. Click Send Backward arrow (Picture Tools Format tab | Arrange group), press K
2. Right-click photo, point to 'Send to Back' on shortcut menu, click 'Send to Back'

Modifying Placeholders

You have become familiar with inserting text and graphical content in the three types of placeholders: title, subtitle, and content. These placeholders can be moved, resized, and deleted to meet desired design requirements. In addition, placeholders can be added to a slide when needed. After you have modified the placeholder locations, you can view thumbnails of all your slides simultaneously by changing views.

In the following pages, you will perform these tasks:

1. Resize the Slide 1 title text placeholder.
2. Align the Slide 1 title text.
3. Move the Slide 1 title text placeholder.
4. Delete the Slide 1 subtitle text placeholder.
5. Change views.

BTW
The Ribbon and Screen Resolution
PowerPoint may change how the groups and buttons within the groups appear on the ribbon, depending on the computer or mobile device's screen resolution. Thus, your ribbon may look different from the ones in this book if you are using a screen resolution other than 1366 x 768.

To Resize a Placeholder

1 INSERT & ADD EFFECTS | 2 MODIFY PLACEHOLDERS | 3 MODIFY & COPY ILLUSTRATIONS
4 ADD MEDIA | 5 ANIMATE SLIDE CONTENT | 6 CUSTOMIZE SLIDE ELEMENTS

When the Slide 1 title placeholder is selected, the AutoFit button displays on the left side of the placeholder because the two lines of text exceed the placeholder's borders. PowerPoint attempts to reduce the font size when the text does not fit, and you can click this button to resize the existing text in the placeholder so the spillover text will fit within the borders. The following step increases the Slide 1 title text placeholder size. ***Why?*** *The two lines of text exceed the placeholder's borders, so you can resize the placeholder and fit the letters within the rectangle.*

- With Slide 1 displaying, click somewhere in the title text paragraphs to position the insertion point in the placeholder. Click the border of the title text placeholder to select it and then point to the top-middle sizing handle.
- Drag the top title text placeholder border upward to enlarge the placeholder (Figure 3–9).

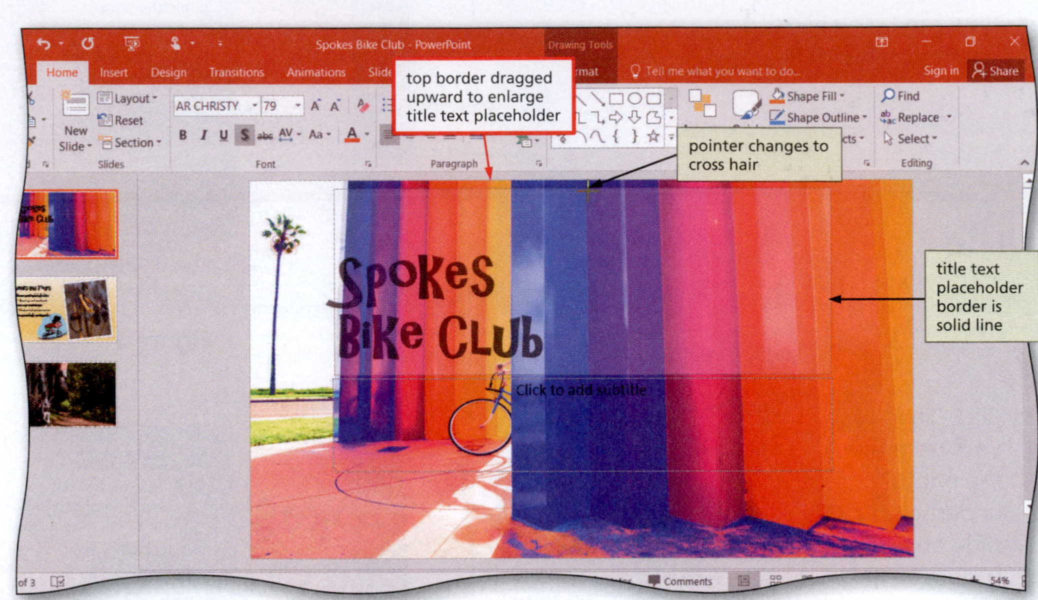

Figure 3–9

Q&A Can I drag other sizing handles to enlarge or shrink the placeholder?
Yes, you also can drag the left, right, top, and corner sizing handles to resize a placeholder. When you drag a corner sizing handle, the box keeps the same proportion and simply enlarges or shrinks the overall shape.

To Align Paragraph Text

1 INSERT & ADD EFFECTS | 2 MODIFY PLACEHOLDERS | 3 MODIFY & COPY ILLUSTRATIONS
4 ADD MEDIA | 5 ANIMATE SLIDE CONTENT | 6 CUSTOMIZE SLIDE ELEMENTS

The presentation theme determines the formatting characteristics of fonts and colors. It also establishes paragraph formatting, including the alignment of text. Some themes **center** the text paragraphs between the left and right placeholder borders, while others **left-align** the paragraph so that the first character of a text line is near the left border or **right-align** the paragraph so that the last character of a text line is near the right border. The paragraph also can be **justified** so that the text is aligned to both the left and right borders. When PowerPoint justifies text, it adds extras spaces between the words to fill the entire line.

The words, Spokes Bike Club, are left-aligned in the Slide 1 title text placeholder. Later, you will add an illustration on the right side of the slide below this text, so you desire to right-align the paragraph. ***Why?*** *Both the text and the picture will be located on the right side of the slide, so the alignments complement each other.* The following steps change the alignment of the Slide 1 title text placeholder.

1

- With the Home tab displayed, click somewhere in the title text paragraph of Slide 1 to position the insertion point in the text to be formatted (Figure 3–10).

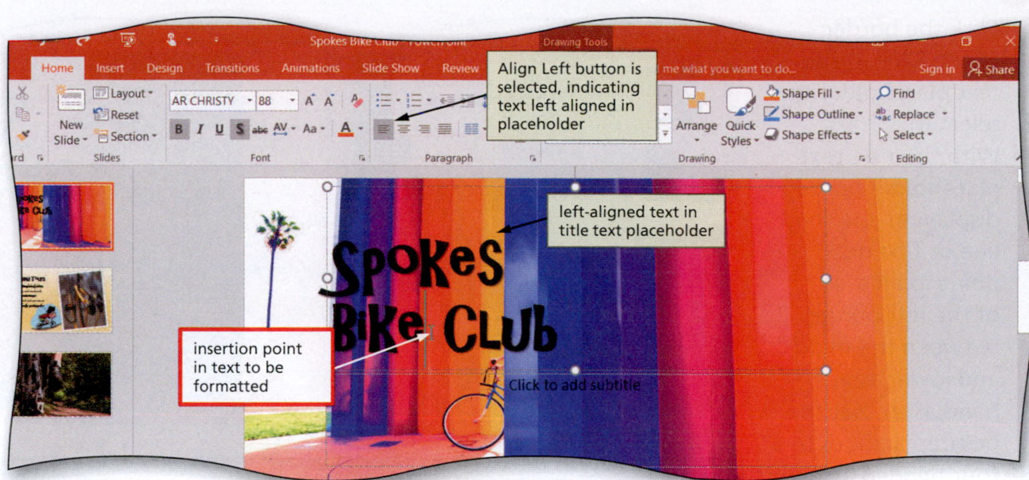

Figure 3–10

2

- Click the Align Right button (Home tab | Paragraph group) to move the text to the right side of the title text placeholder (Figure 3–11).

What if I want to return the paragraph to left-alignment?
Click the Align Left button (Home tab | Paragraph group).

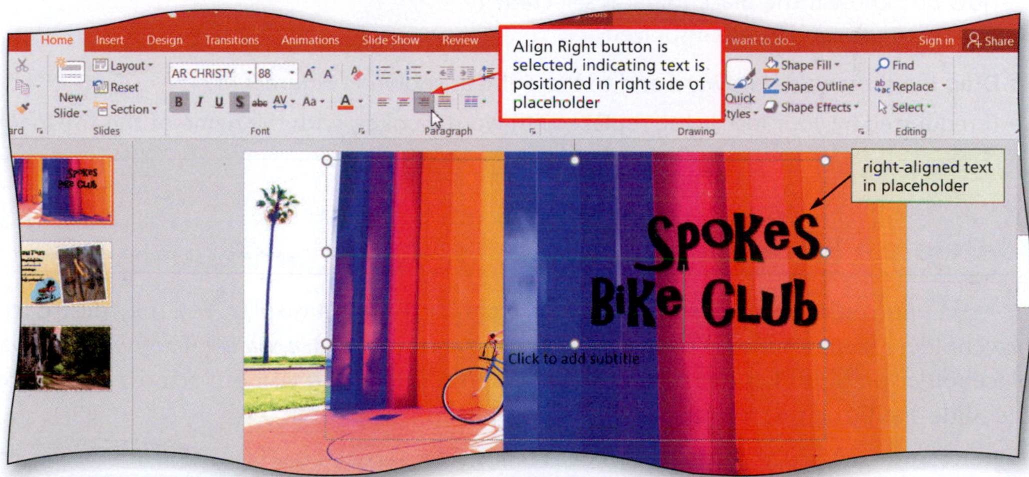

Figure 3–11

Other Ways

1. Right-click paragraph, click Align Right button on mini toolbar
2. Right-click paragraph, click Paragraph on shortcut menu, click Alignment arrow (Paragraph dialog box), click Right, click OK button
3. Click Paragraph dialog box launcher (Home tab | Paragraph group), click Alignment arrow (Paragraph dialog box), click Right, click OK button
4. Press CTRL+R

To Move a Placeholder

1 INSERT & ADD EFFECTS | 2 MODIFY PLACEHOLDERS | 3 MODIFY & COPY ILLUSTRATIONS
4 ADD MEDIA | 5 ANIMATE SLIDE CONTENT | 6 CUSTOMIZE SLIDE ELEMENTS

Why? If you desire to have a placeholder appear in a different area of the slide, you can move it to a new location. The theme layouts determine where the text and content placeholders display on the slide. The Slide 1 title text placeholder currently displays in the middle third of the slide, but the text in this placeholder would be more aesthetically pleasing if it were moved to the upper-right corner of the slide. The following step moves the Slide 1 title text placeholder.

- Click the border of the Slide 1 title text placeholder to select it.
- With the title text placeholder border displaying as a solid line or fine dots, point to an area of the left border between the middle and lower sizing handles so that the pointer changes to a four-headed arrow.

Figure 3–12

Q&A Can I click any part of the border to select it?
Yes. You can click any of the four border lines.

How do I know if the placeholder is selected?
The selection handles are displayed.

- Drag the placeholder upward and to the right, as shown in Figure 3–12.
- If requested by your instructor, replace with word, Spokes, with the name of the city in which you were born.

To Delete a Placeholder

1 INSERT & ADD EFFECTS | 2 MODIFY PLACEHOLDERS | 3 MODIFY & COPY ILLUSTRATIONS
4 ADD MEDIA | 5 ANIMATE SLIDE CONTENT | 6 CUSTOMIZE SLIDE ELEMENTS

When you run a slide show, empty placeholders do not display. You may desire to delete unused placeholders from a slide. ***Why?*** *So they are not a distraction when you are designing slide content.* The subtitle text placeholder on Slide 1 is not required for this presentation, so you can remove it. The following steps remove the Slide 1 subtitle text placeholder.

- Click a border of the subtitle text placeholder so that it displays as a solid or finely dotted line (Figure 3–13).

- Press the DELETE key to remove the subtitle text placeholder.

Figure 3–13

Q&A Can I also click the Cut button to delete the placeholder?
Yes. Generally, however, the Cut button is used when you desire to remove a selected slide element, place it on the Clipboard, and then paste it in another area. The DELETE key is used when you do not want to reuse that particular slide element.

Other Ways

1. Select placeholder, press BACKSPACE
2. Right-click placeholder border, click Cut on shortcut menu

To Add a Text Box

You occasionally may need to insert a small amount of text in an area of a slide where no content placeholder is located. A text box allows you to emphasize or set off text that you consider important for your audience to read. To add a text box to a slide, you would perform the following steps.

1. Click the Text Box button (Insert tab | Text group), click the slide, and then drag the object to the desired location on the slide.
2. Click inside the text box to add or paste text.
3. If necessary, change the look and style of the text box characters by using formatting features (Home tab | Font group).

Changing Views

You have been using **Normal view** to create and edit your slides. Once you completed your slides in projects for previous modules, you reviewed the final products by displaying each slide in **Slide Show view**, which occupies the full computer screen. You were able to view how the transitions, graphics, and effects will display in an actual presentation before an audience.

PowerPoint has other views to help review a presentation for content, organization, and overall appearance. **Slide Sorter view** allows you to look at several slides at one time. **Reading view** is similar to Slide Show view because each slide displays individually, but the slides do not fill the entire screen. Using this view, you easily can progress through the slides forward or backward with simple controls at the bottom of the window. Switching between Slide Sorter, Reading, and Normal views helps you review your presentation, assess whether the slides have an attractive design and adequate content, and make sure they are organized for the most impact. After reviewing the slides, you can change the view to Normal so that you may continue working on the presentation.

To Change Views

1 INSERT & ADD EFFECTS | 2 MODIFY PLACEHOLDERS | 3 MODIFY & COPY ILLUSTRATIONS
4 ADD MEDIA | 5 ANIMATE SLIDE CONTENT | 6 CUSTOMIZE SLIDE ELEMENTS

Why? You have made several modifications to the slides, so you should check for balance and consistency. The following steps change the view from Normal view to Slide Sorter view, then Reading view, and back to Normal view.

- Click the Slide Sorter view button on the right side of the status bar to display the presentation in Slide Sorter view (Figure 3–14).

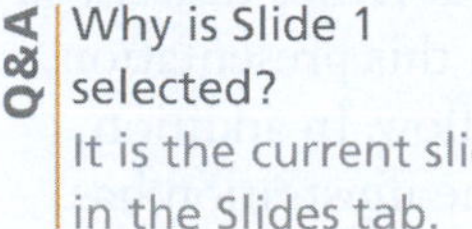

Q&A Why is Slide 1 selected?
It is the current slide in the Slides tab.

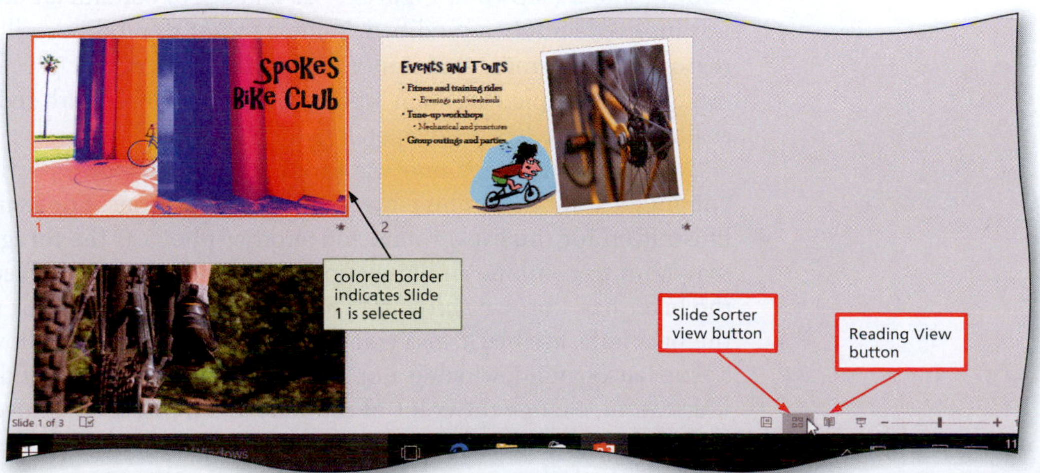

Figure 3–14

- Click the Reading View button on the right side of the status bar to display Slide 1 of the presentation in Reading view (Figure 3–15).

Figure 3–15

- Click the Next button two times to advance through the presentation.
- Click the Previous button two times to display Slide 2 and then Slide 1.
- Click the Menu button to display commonly used commands (Figure 3–16).

- Click End Show to return to Slide Sorter view, which is the view you were using before Reading view.
- Click the Normal view button to display the presentation in Normal view.

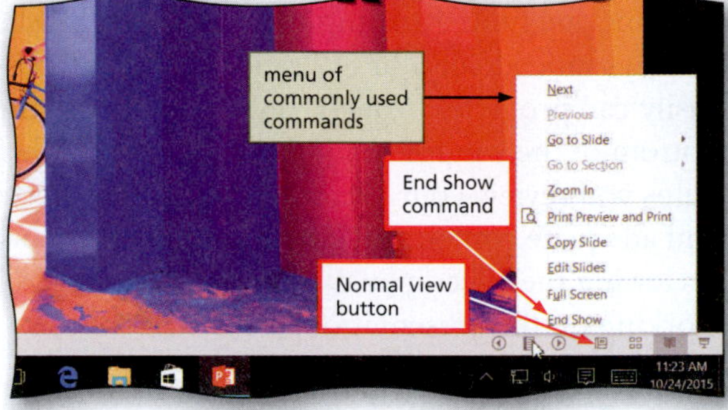

Figure 3–16

Modifying and Copying an Illustration

Slides 1 and 2 (shown in Figures 3–1a and 3–1b) contain an illustration of a biker that was inserted and then modified. You may want to modify an illustration for various reasons. Many times, you cannot find an illustration that precisely represents your topic. For example, you want a picture of a red flower with red petals, but the only available picture has yellow petals.

Occasionally, you may want to remove or change a portion of an illustration or you might want to combine two or more illustrations. For example, you can use one illustration for the background and another photo as the foreground. Other times, you may want to combine an illustration with another type of object. In this presentation, the biker has a brown shirt, and you want to change the color to yellow. In addition, the bike hubs are black, and you want to change them to yellow. The illustration has a blue background, which is not required to display on the slide. You will ungroup the illustration, change the color of the shirt and hubs, and remove the blue background.

Modifying the clip on Slide 2 and then copying it to Slide 1 requires several steps. In the following pages, you will perform these tasks:

1. Zoom Slide 2 to examine the illustration.
2. Ungroup the illustration.

3. Change objects' color.
4. Delete objects.
5. Regroup the illustration.
6. Copy the illustration from Slide 2 to Slide 1.

To Zoom a Slide

You will be modifying small areas of the illustration, so it will help you select the relevant pieces if the graphic is enlarged. The following step changes the zoom to 90 percent.

1 Display Slide 2 and then drag the Zoom slider or click the Zoom level button or the Zoom In button to change the zoom level to 90%. If necessary, click the Down scroll arrow several times so that the entire graphic is visible (Figure 3–17).

Figure 3–17

To Ungroup an Illustration

1 INSERT & ADD EFFECTS | 2 MODIFY PLACEHOLDERS | **3 MODIFY & COPY ILLUSTRATIONS**
4 ADD MEDIA | 5 ANIMATE SLIDE CONTENT | 6 CUSTOMIZE SLIDE ELEMENTS

The next step is to ungroup the biker illustration, also called a clip, on Slide 2. When you **ungroup** an illustration, PowerPoint breaks it into its component objects. A clip may be composed of a few individual objects or several complex groups of objects. These groups can be ungrouped repeatedly until they decompose into individual objects. ***Why?*** *Because an illustration is a collection of complex groups of objects, you may need to ungroup a complex object into less complex objects before being able to modify a specific object.* When you ungroup a clip and click the Yes button in the Microsoft PowerPoint dialog box, PowerPoint converts the clip to a PowerPoint object. The following steps ungroup an illustration.

- Click the biker clip to select it and then click Format on the ribbon to display the Picture Tools Format tab.
- Click the Group Objects button (Picture Tools Format tab | Arrange group) to display the Group Objects menu (Figure 3–18).

Q&A Why does the Group Objects button look different on my screen?
Your monitor is set to a different resolution. See the Office 2016 and Windows 10 module for an explanation of screen resolution and the appearance of the ribbon.

Figure 3–18

- Click Ungroup on the Group Objects menu to display the Microsoft PowerPoint dialog box (Figure 3–19).

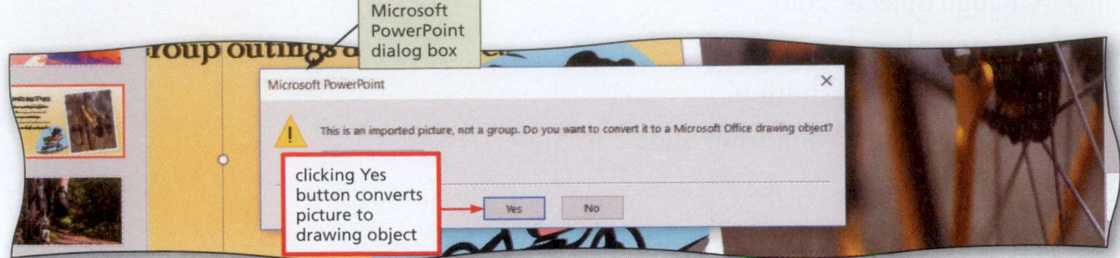

Figure 3–19

3

- Click the Yes button (Microsoft PowerPoint dialog box) to convert the clip to a Microsoft Office drawing.

Q&A What happens if I click the No button?
The clip will remain displayed on the slide as an illustration and will not ungroup.

- Click Format on the ribbon to display the Drawing Tools Format tab. Click the Group Objects button (Drawing Tools Format tab | Arrange group) and then click Ungroup again to display the objects that form the biker clip (Figure 3–20).

Q&A Why does the ribbon change from the Picture Tools Drawing tab to the Drawing Tools Format tab and show different options this time?
The illustration has become a drawing object, so tools related to drawing now display.

Why do all those circles display in the clip?
The circles are sizing handles for each of the clip's objects, which resemble pieces of a jigsaw puzzle.

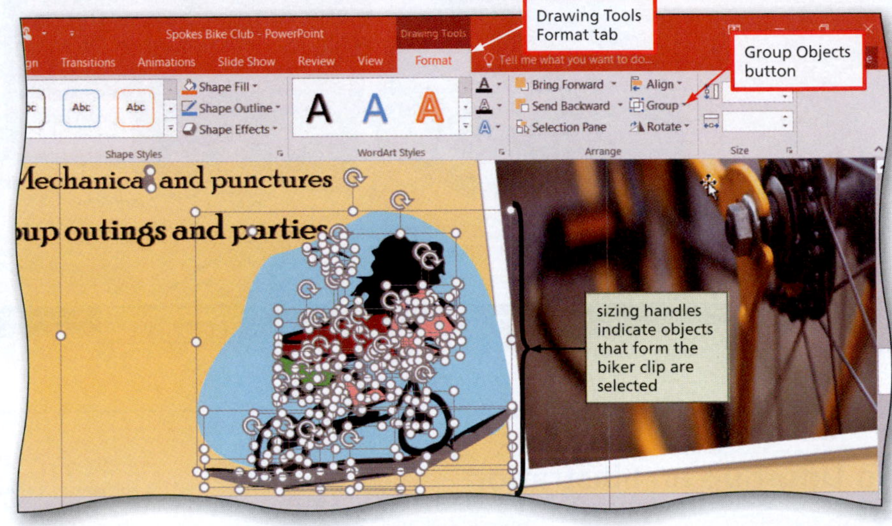

Figure 3–20

Other Ways

1. Right-click clip, point to Group on shortcut menu, click Ungroup
2. Press CTRL+SHIFT+G

To Change the Color of a Clip Object

1 INSERT & ADD EFFECTS | 2 MODIFY PLACEHOLDERS | 3 MODIFY & COPY ILLUSTRATIONS
4 ADD MEDIA | 5 ANIMATE SLIDE CONTENT | 6 CUSTOMIZE SLIDE ELEMENTS

Now that the biker illustration is ungrouped, you can change the color of the objects. You must exercise care when selecting the correct object to modify. ***Why?*** *A clip might be composed of hundreds of objects.* The following steps change the color of the biker's shirt from brown to yellow.

- Click an area of the slide that is not part of the clip to deselect all the clip pieces.
- Click the biker's shirt to display sizing handles around the brown colored area (Figure 3–21).

Q&A What if I selected a different area by mistake?
Click outside the clip and retry.

Figure 3–21

- Click the Shape Fill arrow (Drawing Tools Format tab | Shape Styles group) to display the Shape Fill gallery.
- Point to Yellow (fourth color in Standard Colors row) to display a live preview of the shirt color (Figure 3–22).

Experiment

- Point to various colors and watch the biker's shirt color change.

Figure 3–22

- Click the color Yellow to change the biker's shirt color (Figure 3–23).

Q&A Why is the bar under the Shape Fill button now yellow?
The button displays the last fill color selected.

Figure 3–23

- Click the rear wheel hub to select it.
- Click the Shape Fill button (Drawing Tools Format tab | Shape Styles group) to change the wheel hub color to Yellow (Figure 3–24).

Q&A Why did I not need to click the Shape Fill arrow to select this color?
PowerPoint uses the last fill color selected. This color displays in the bar under the bucket icon on the button.

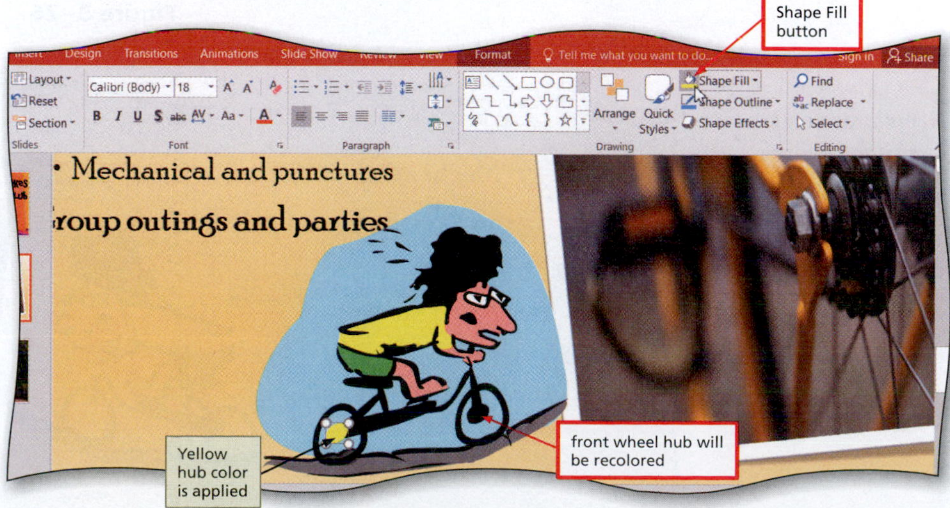

Figure 3–24

5

- Change the front wheel hub color to Yellow (Figure 3–25).

Q&A Can I select multiple objects so I can color them simultaneously?
Yes. While pressing the SHIFT key, click the desired elements to select them.

Figure 3–25

Other Ways

1. Click Shape Fill arrow (Home tab | Drawing group)
2. Right-click object, click Fill button below shortcut menu
3. Right-click object, click Format Shape on shortcut menu, click 'Fill & Line' icon

To Delete a Clip Object

With the biker's shirt and hub colors changed, you want to delete the blue background object. ***Why?*** *This object clutters the slide and is not a necessary element of the clip.* The following steps delete this object.

1

- Click the background in any area where the blue color displays to select this object (Figure 3–26).

Q&A Can I select multiple objects so I can delete them simultaneously?
Yes. While pressing the SHIFT key, click the unwanted elements to select them.

Figure 3–26

2

- Press the DELETE key to delete this object (Figure 3–27).

Figure 3–27

3

- Click one black sweat droplet, press the SHIFT key, and then click the other five sweat droplets to select all six objects (Figure 3–28).

Q&A What can I do if I am having difficulty selecting just these six objects?

Try increasing the zoom, or select a few objects at a time and then delete them.

- Press the DELETE key to delete these objects.

Figure 3–28

To Regroup Objects

1 INSERT & ADD EFFECTS | 2 MODIFY PLACEHOLDERS | **3 MODIFY & COPY ILLUSTRATIONS**
4 ADD MEDIA | 5 ANIMATE SLIDE CONTENT | 6 CUSTOMIZE SLIDE ELEMENTS

When you ungrouped the biker clip, you eliminated the embedding data or linking information that tied all the individual pieces together. If you attempt to move or size this clip now, you might encounter difficulties because it consists of multiple objects and is no longer one unified piece. Dragging or sizing affects only a selected object, not the entire collection of objects, so you must use caution when objects are not completely regrouped. You can **regroup** all of the ungrouped objects so they are reassembled into a single unit. The individual pieces of the biker clip now will be regrouped. ***Why?*** *When they are regrouped, they cannot be accidentally moved or manipulated.* The following steps regroup these objects into one object.

1

- Position the selection pointer (the left-pointing arrow) in the lower-left corner of the biker illustration and then drag diagonally to the upper-right corner of the illustration so that the entire illustration is covered with a gray box (Figure 3–29).

Q&A Must I drag diagonally from left to right?

No. You can drag in any direction as long as the gray box covers all the clip.

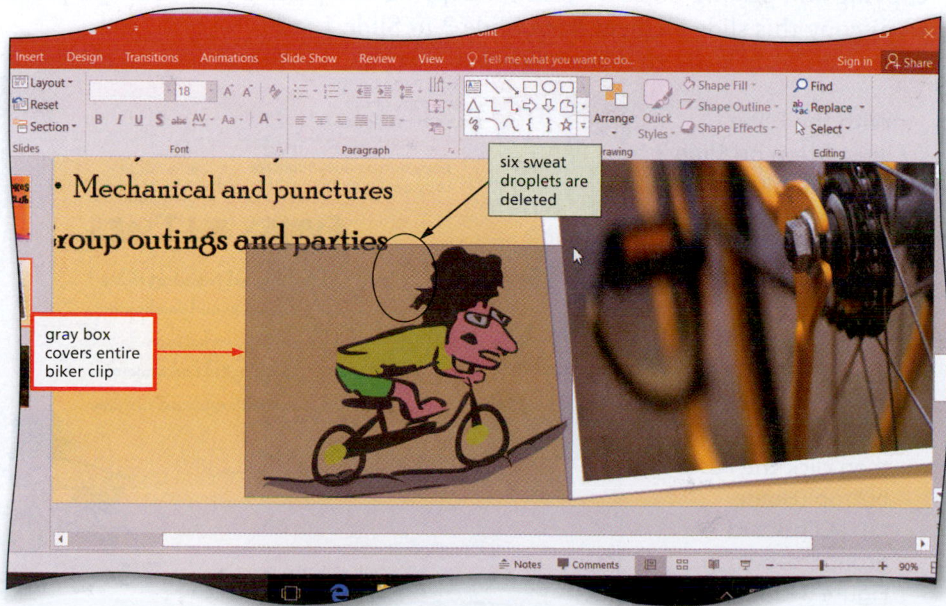

Figure 3–29

- Release the mouse to display all the selected pieces of the illustration.
- Click the Drawing Tools Format tab, and then click the Group Objects button (Drawing Tools Format tab | Arrange group) to display the Group Objects menu (Figure 3–30).

- Click Regroup to recombine all the clip objects.

Figure 3–30

- Use the Zoom slider to change the zoom level to 60%.

Other Ways

1. Right-click selected clip, point to Group on shortcut menu, click Regroup

To Copy a Clip from One Slide to Another

1 INSERT & ADD EFFECTS | 2 MODIFY PLACEHOLDERS | **3 MODIFY & COPY ILLUSTRATIONS** | 4 ADD MEDIA | 5 ANIMATE SLIDE CONTENT | 6 CUSTOMIZE SLIDE ELEMENTS

The biker clip on Slide 2 also can display in its modified form on the title slide. You first must copy it using the Office Clipboard and then paste it in the desired location. The **Office Clipboard** is a temporary storage location that can hold a maximum of 24 text or graphics items copied from any Office program. ***Why?*** *You have made modifications to the illustration that you would like to duplicate on the title slide.* The same procedure of copying and pasting objects works for copying and pasting text from one placeholder to another. The following steps copy this slide element from Slide 2 to Slide 1.

- With the biker illustration on Slide 2 selected, display the Home tab and then click the Copy button (Home tab | Clipboard group) (Figure 3–31).

- Display Slide 1 and then click the Paste button (Home tab | Clipboard group), shown in Figure 3–31, to insert the biker illustration into the title slide.

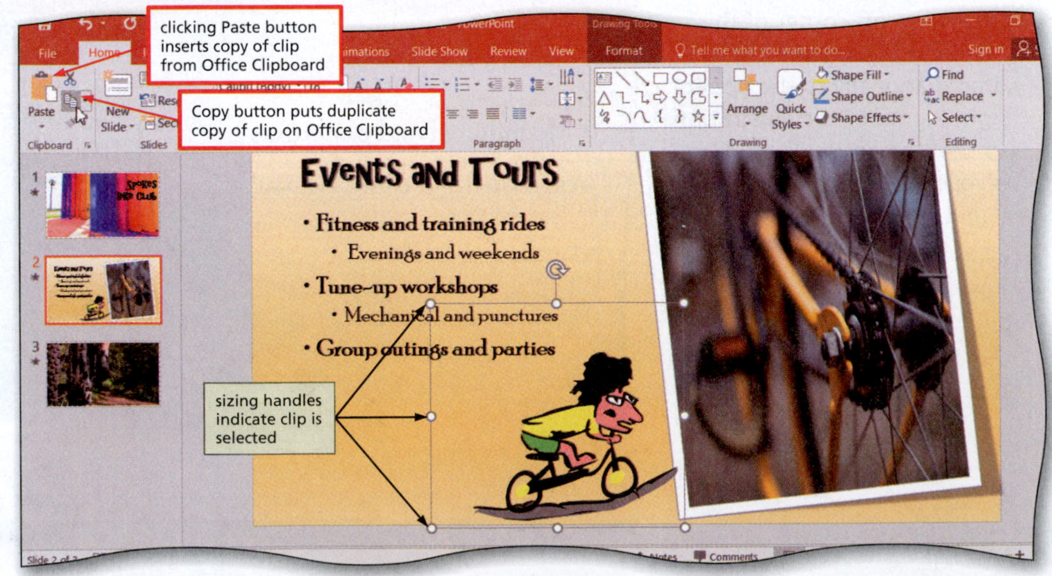

Figure 3–31

Q&A Is the clip deleted from the Office Clipboard when I paste it into the slide?

No.

- Increase the biker illustration size by dragging one of the corner sizing handles outward until the biker is the size shown in Figure 3–32 (approximately 5.24" x 6.55" as indicated on the Drawing Tools Format tab). Drag the biker to the location shown in this figure.

Figure 3–32

Break Point: If you wish to take a break, this is a good place to do so. Be sure to save the Spokes Bike Club file again and then you can quit PowerPoint. To resume at a later time, start PowerPoint, open the file called Spokes Bike Club, and continue following the steps from this location forward.

Adding Media to Slides

Media files can enrich a presentation if they are used correctly. Video files can be produced with a camera and editing software, and sound files can come from the Internet, files stored on your computer, or an audio track on a CD. To hear the sounds, you need a sound card and speakers or headphones on your system.

Once an audio or video clip is inserted into a slide, you can specify options that affect how the file is displayed and played. For example, you can have the video play automatically when the slide is displayed, or you can click the video frame when you are ready to start the playback. You also can have the video fill the entire slide, which is referred to as **full screen**. If you decide to play the slide show automatically and have it display full screen, you can drag the video frame to the gray area off the slide so that it does not display briefly before going to full screen. You can select the 'Loop until Stopped' option to have the video repeat until you click the next slide, or you can choose to not have the video frame display on the slide until you click the slide.

If your video clip has recorded sounds, the volume controls give you the option to set how loudly this audio will play. They also allow you to mute the sound so that your audience will hear no background noise or music.

In the following pages, you will perform these tasks:

1. Insert a video file into Slide 3.
2. Trim the video file to shorten the play time.
3. Add video options that determine the clip's appearance and playback.
4. Insert an audio file into Slide 1.
5. Add audio options that determine the clip's appearance and playback.
6. Resize the Slide 3 video clip.
7. Add a video style to the Slide 3 clip.
8. Add a border to the Slide 3 clip and then change the border weight and color.

BTW

Using Codecs

Video and audio content developers use a codec (**co**mpressor/**dec**ompressor) to reduce the file size of digital media. The reduced file size helps transfer files across the Internet quickly and smoothly and helps save space on storage media. Your computer can play any compressed file if the specific codec used to compress the file is available on your computer. If the codec is not installed or is not recognized, your computer attempts to download this file from the Internet. Many codec files are available to download from the Internet at no cost.

To Insert a Video File

Slide 3 has another photo of a biker, and you have a video clip of a person riding a bike through a wooded area. You want to use a majority of the clip and eliminate a few seconds from the beginning and end. PowerPoint allows you to insert this clip into your slide and then trim the file. ***Why?*** *You want to play just a portion of the video when you preview the clip or run the slide show.* This clip is available in the Data Files. The following steps insert this video clip into Slide 3.

1

- Display Slide 3 and then display the Insert tab. Click the Insert Video button (Insert tab | Media group) to display the Insert Video menu (Figure 3–33).

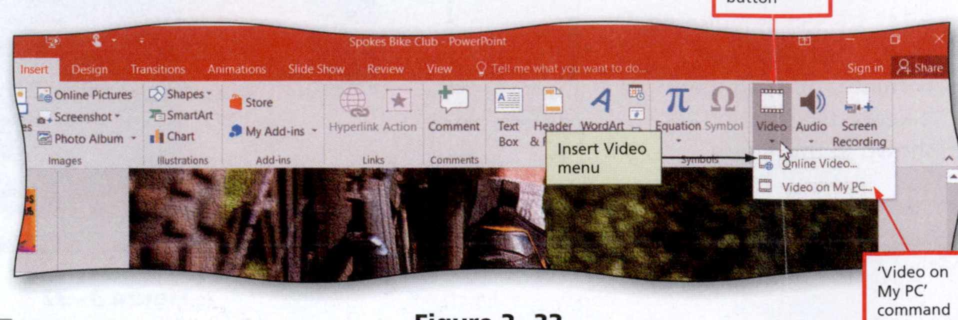

Figure 3–33

2

- Click 'Video on My PC' on the Insert Video menu to display the Insert Video dialog box.
- If the list of files for Module 03 is not displayed in the Insert Video dialog box, navigate to the location where the files are located.
- Click Mountain Bike Video to select the file (Figure 3–34).

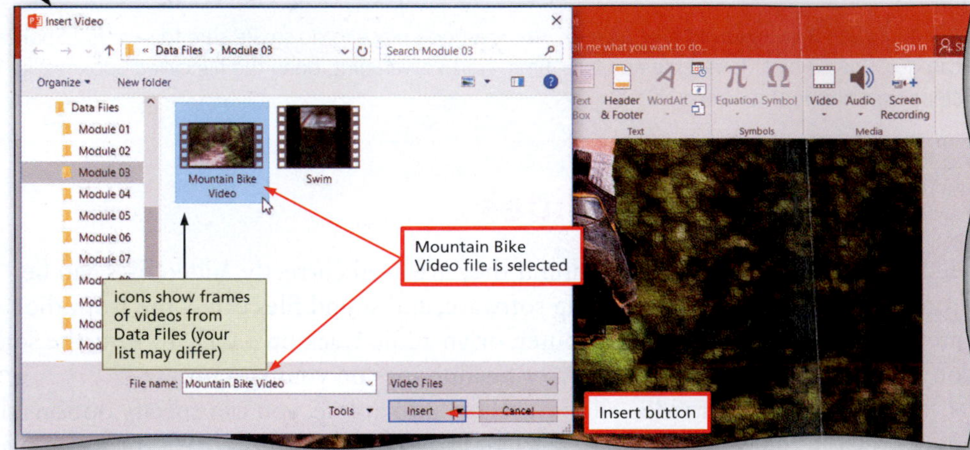

Figure 3–34

3

- Click the Insert button (Insert Video dialog box) to insert the video clip into Slide 3 (Figure 3–35).

Q&A Can I adjust the color of a video clip?
Yes. You can correct the brightness and contrast, and you also can recolor a video clip using the same methods you learned in this module to color a photo.

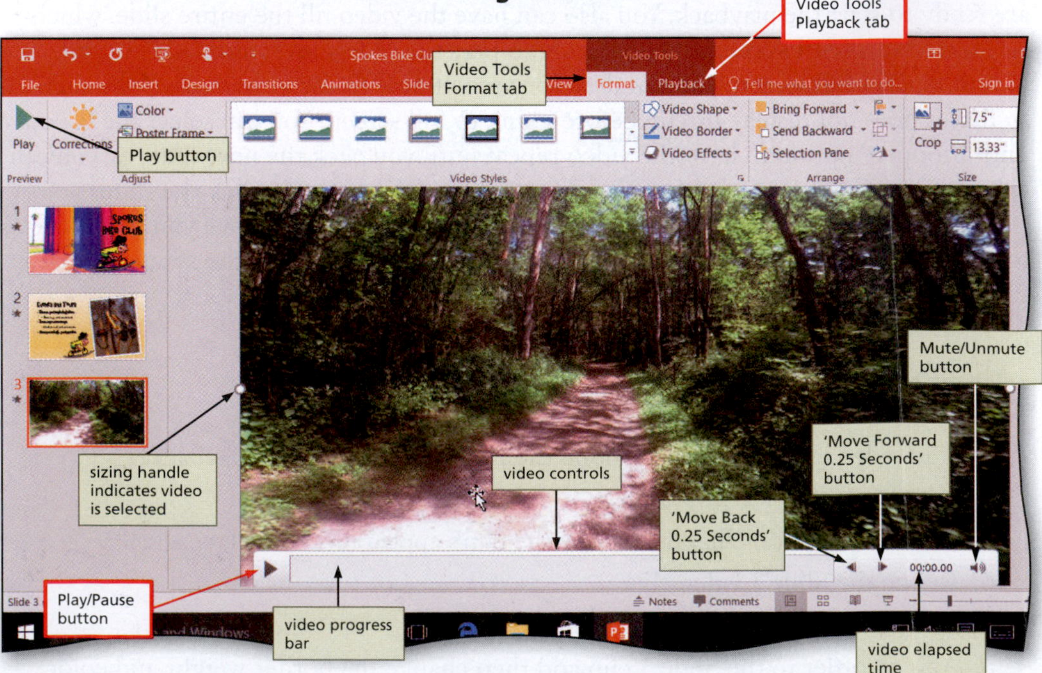

Figure 3–35

To Trim a Video File

Why? *The Mountain Bike Video file has a running time of slightly more than 32 seconds. Much of the video is the same view of the bike path through the woods, so you decide to delete a few seconds from the beginning and the end to shorten the duration.* PowerPoint's **Trim Video** feature allows you to trim the beginning and end of your clip by designating your desired Start Time and End Time. These precise time measurements are accurate to one-thousandth of a second. The start point is indicated by a green marker, and the end point is indicated by a red marker. The following steps trim the Mountain Bike Video clip.

1

- With the video clip selected on Slide 3, click the Play/Pause button in the video controls underneath the video to play the entire video.

Q&A Can I play the video by clicking the Play button in the Preview group?
Yes. This Play button plays the entire clip. You may prefer to click the Play/Pause button displayed in the video controls to stop the video and examine one of the frames.

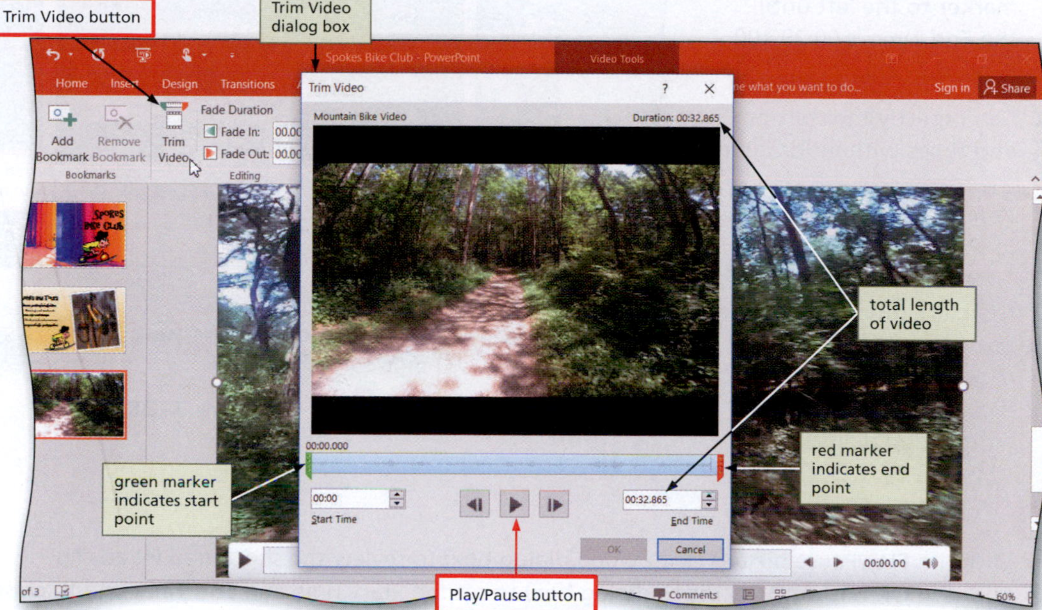

Figure 3–36

- Click Playback on the ribbon to display the Video Tools Playback tab.
- Click the Trim Video button (Video Tools Playback tab | Editing group) to display the Trim Video dialog box (Figure 3–36).

2

- Point to the start point, which is indicated by the green marker on the right side, so that the pointer changes to a two-headed arrow.
- Slide or drag the green marker to the right until the Start Time is approximately 00:05.991 (Figure 3–37).

Figure 3–37

- Point to the end point, which is indicated by the red marker on the right side, so that the pointer changes to a two-headed arrow.
- Slide or drag the red marker to the left until the End Time is 00:29.100 (Figure 3–38).

Q&A Can I specify the start or end times without dragging the markers?
Yes. You can enter the time in the Start Time or End Time boxes, or you can click the Start Time or End Time box arrows. You also can click the Next Frame and Previous Frame buttons (Trim Video dialog box).

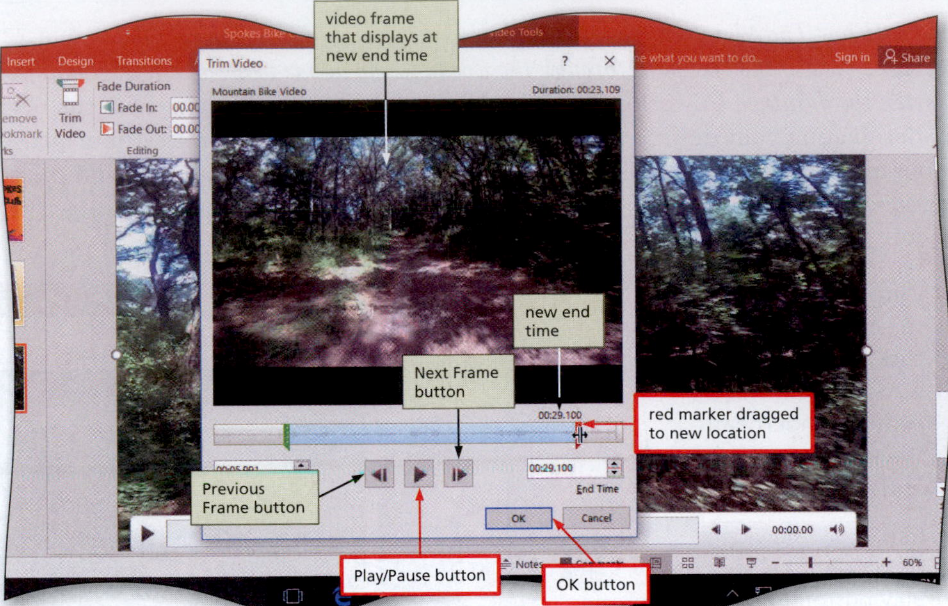

Figure 3–38

- Click the Play/Pause button (Trim Video dialog box) to review the shortened video clip.
- Click the OK button (Trim Video dialog box) to set the Start Time and End Time and to close the Trim Video dialog box.

Other Ways

1. Right-click clip, click Trim on shortcut menu

1 INSERT & ADD EFFECTS | 2 MODIFY PLACEHOLDERS | 3 MODIFY & COPY ILLUSTRATIONS
4 ADD MEDIA | 5 ANIMATE SLIDE CONTENT | 6 CUSTOMIZE SLIDE ELEMENTS

To Add Video Options

Once the video clip is inserted into Slide 3, you can specify that the video plays automatically when the slide is displayed. ***Why?*** *When you are giving your presentation, you do not want to click the mouse to start the video.* You also can adjust the volume of the sound recorded on the file. The following steps add the option of playing the video full screen automatically and also decrease the volume of the clip.

- With the Video Tools Playback tab displaying, click the Start arrow (Video Tools Playback tab | Video Options group) to display the Start menu (Figure 3–39).

Q&A What does the On Click option do?
The video clip would begin playing when a presenter clicks the frame during the slide show.

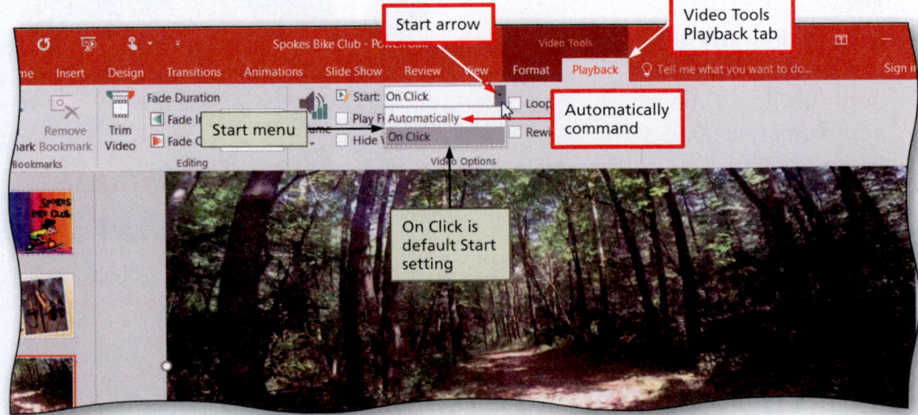

Figure 3–39

2

- Click Automatically in the Start menu to run the video clip automatically when the slide is displayed.

3

- Click the 'Play Full Screen' check box (Video Tools Playback tab | Video Options group) to place a check mark in it.
- Click the Volume button (Video Tools Playback tab | Video Options group) to display the Volume menu (Figure 3–40).

- Click Medium on the Volume menu to set the audio volume.

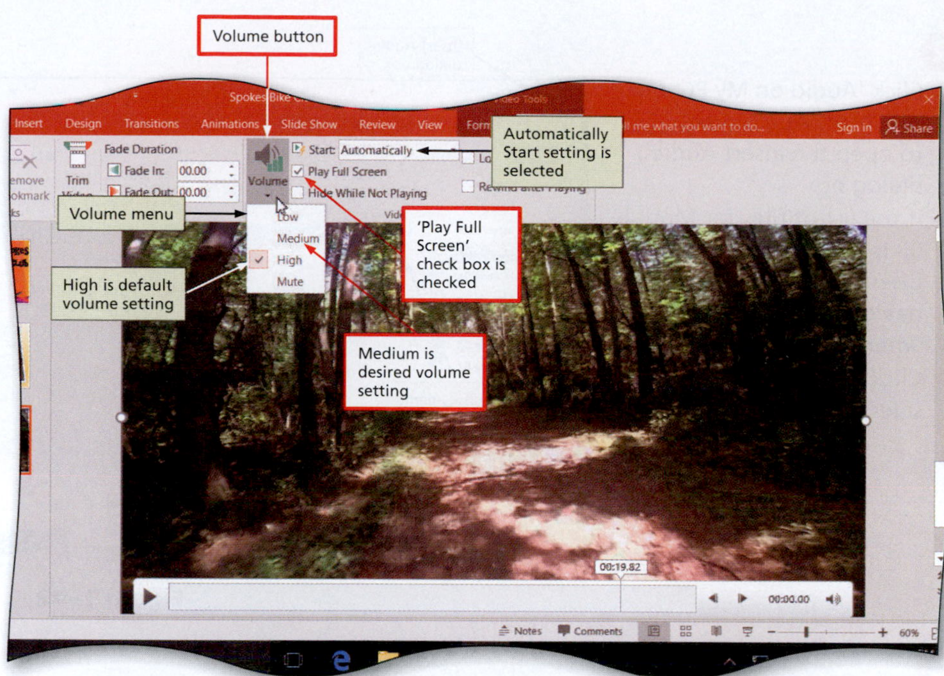

Figure 3–40

Q&A | Will the Mute option silence the video's background sounds?
Yes. Click Mute if you do not want your audience to hear any recorded sounds.

To Insert an Audio File

If you have a digital audio recorder or an app on your smartphone or mobile device, you can record sounds to insert into your presentation. The following steps insert an audio clip into Slide 1. ***Why?*** *An audio clip of pedaling sounds adds interest to the start of your presentation when Slide 1 is displayed.*

- Display Slide 1 and then click Insert on the ribbon to display the Insert tab.
- Click the Insert Audio button (Insert tab | Media group) to display the Insert Audio menu (Figure 3–41).

Figure 3–41

- Click 'Audio on My PC' on the Insert Audio menu to open the Insert Audio dialog box.
- If the list of files for Module 03 is not displayed in the Insert Audio dialog box, navigate to the location where the files are located.
- Click Pedaling Sounds to select the file (Figure 3–42).

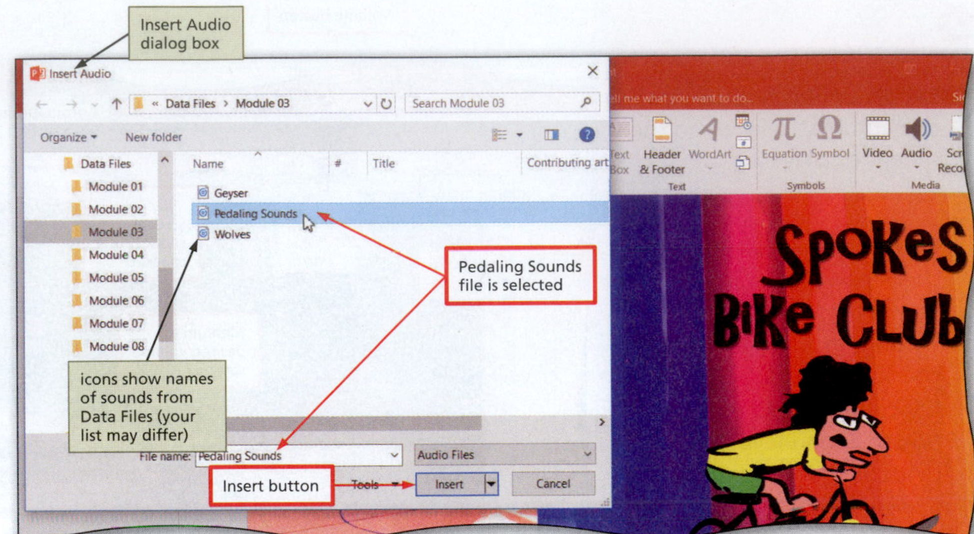

Figure 3–42

- Click the Insert button (Insert Audio dialog box) to insert the audio clip into Slide 1 (Figure 3–43).

Q&A Why does a sound icon display on the slide?

The icon indicates an audio file is inserted.

Do the audio control buttons have the same functions as the video control buttons that displayed when I inserted the Mountain Bike Video clip?

Yes. The controls include playing and pausing the sound, moving back or forward 0.25 seconds, audio progress, elapsed time, and muting or unmuting the sound.

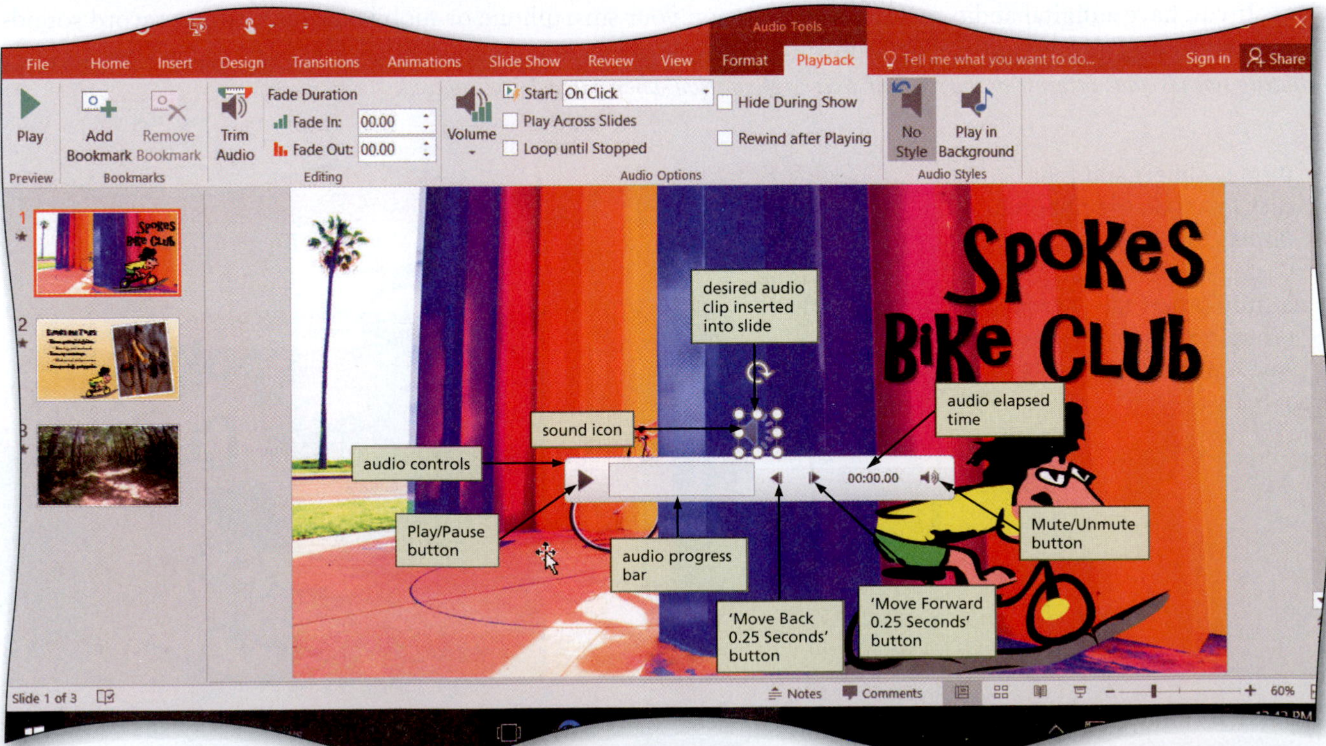

Figure 3–43

4

- Drag the sound icon to the lower-left corner of the slide (Figure 3–44).

Q&A Must I move the icon on the slide?
No. Although your audience will not see the icon when you run the slide show, it is easier for you to see the audio controls in this area of this slide.

Figure 3–44

To Add Audio Options

1 INSERT & ADD EFFECTS | 2 MODIFY PLACEHOLDERS | 3 MODIFY & COPY ILLUSTRATIONS
4 ADD MEDIA | 5 ANIMATE SLIDE CONTENT | 6 CUSTOMIZE SLIDE ELEMENTS

Once an audio clip is inserted into a slide, you can specify options that control playback and appearance. As with the video options you applied to the Mountain Bike Video clip, the audio clip can play either automatically or when clicked, it can repeat the clip while a particular slide is displayed, and you can drag the sound icon off the slide and set the volume. The following steps add the options of starting automatically, playing until the slide no longer is displayed, and hiding the sound icon on the slide. ***Why?*** *You do not want to click the screen to start the sound, so you do not need to see the icon. In addition, you want the pedaling sound to repeat while the slide is displayed to coordinate with the bicycle picture prominently shown and to keep the audience's attention focused on the topic of riding a bike.*

1

- If necessary, click Playback on the ribbon to display the Audio Tools Playback tab. Click the Start arrow (Audio Tools Playback tab | Audio Options group) to display the Start menu (Figure 3–45).

2

- Click Automatically in the Start menu.

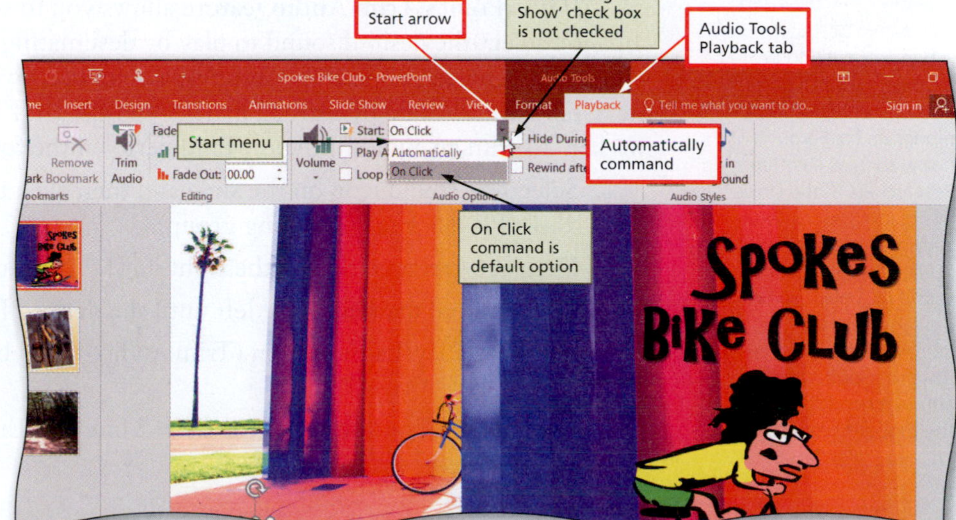

Figure 3–45

Q&A Does the On Click option function the same way for an audio clip as On Click does for a video clip?
Yes. If you were to select On Click, the sound would begin playing only after the presenter clicks Slide 1 during a presentation.

- Click the 'Loop until Stopped' check box (Audio Tools Playback tab | Audio Options group) to place a check mark in it.

Q&A What is the difference between the 'Loop until Stopped' option and the 'Play Across Slides' option?
The audio clip in the 'Loop until Stopped' option repeats for as long as one slide is displayed. In contrast, the 'Play Across Slides' option would play the clip only once, but it would continue to play while other slides in the presentation are displayed. Once the end of the clip is reached, the sound would end and not repeat.

- Click the 'Hide During Show' check box (Audio Tools Playback tab | Audio Options group) to place a check mark in it (Figure 3–46).

Figure 3–46

Q&A Why would I want the icon to display during the show?
If you had selected the On Click option, you would need to find this icon on the slide and click it to start playing the clip.

Can I adjust the sound's volume?
Yes. You can adjust the volume or mute the sound by clicking the Volume button (Audio Tools Playback tab | Audio Options group) or by clicking the Mute/Unmute button on the Media Controls bar and using the volume slider.

BTW
Ideal Decibels for Creativity
When you need to be creative, move to an environment filled with moderate background noise, such as a coffee shop. Researchers at the University of British Columbia state that a noise level of approximately 70 decibels, which is the sound of a quiet conversation or highway noise from afar, fosters original ideas. Anything louder than this ambient noise level decreases the thought process.

To Trim an Audio File

PowerPoint's **Trim Audio** feature allows you to set the beginning and end of a clip. You select the desired sound to play by designating a Start Time and End Time, which are accurate to one-thousandth of a second. As with the video file markers, the Start Time is indicated by a green marker and the End Time is indicated by a red marker. To trim an audio file, you would perform the following steps.

1. Select the sound icon on the slide and then click the Trim Audio button (Audio Tools Playback tab | Editing group).
2. Drag the green marker to the right until the desired Start Time is displayed.
3. Drag the red marker to the left until the desired End Time is displayed.
4. Click the Play/Pause button (Trim Audio dialog box) to review the shortened audio clip.
5. Click the OK button to set the Start Time and End Time and to close the Trim Audio dialog box.

To Resize a Video

The default Mountain Bike Video frame size can be changed. You resize a video clip in the same manner that you resize photos and illustrations. The following steps will decrease the Mountain Bike Video frame using a sizing handle. ***Why?*** *You want to fit the video near the center of the slide.*

1

- Display Slide 3 and select the video frame. Click Format on the ribbon to display the Video Tools Format tab (Figure 3–47).

Figure 3–47

2

- With the video selected, drag any corner sizing handle diagonally inward until the frame is resized to approximately 5.5″ x 9.78″.
- Drag the clip to the location shown in Figure 3–48.

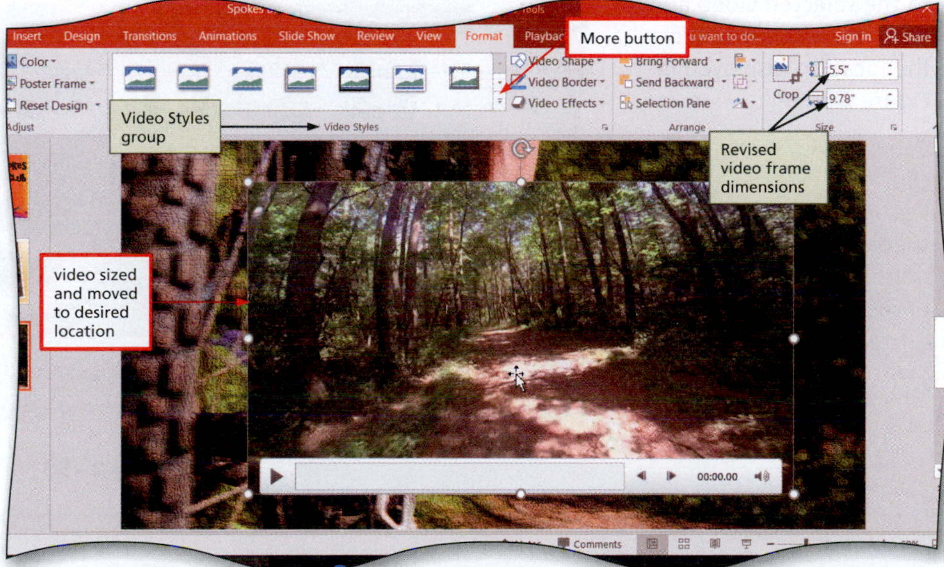

Figure 3–48

To Add a Video Style

The video styles are similar to the photo styles you applied in Module 2 and include various shapes, angles, borders, and reflections. The following steps apply a video style to the Mountain Bike Video clip on Slide 3. ***Why?*** *The Mountain Bike Video clip on Slide 3 displays full screen when it is playing, but you decide to increase the visual appeal of the clip when it is not playing by applying a video style.*

- With the video selected and the Video Tools Format tab displaying, click the More button in the Video Styles gallery (Video Tools Format tab | Video Styles group) (shown in Figure 3–48) to expand the gallery.
- Point to Reflected Perspective Right in the Intense area of the Video Styles gallery (sixth style in first row) to display a live preview of that style applied to the video frame on the slide (Figure 3–49).

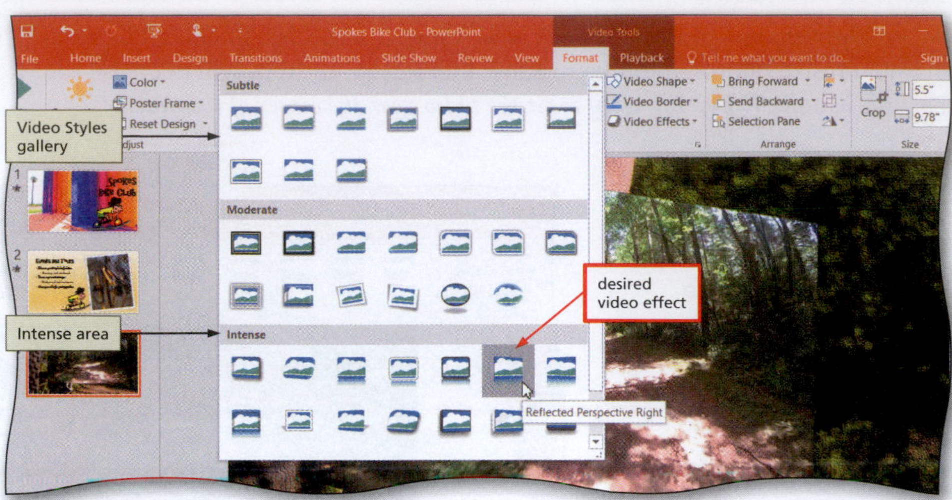

Figure 3–49

Experiment

- Point to various photo styles in the Video Styles gallery and watch the style of the video frame change in the document window.

- Click Reflected Perspective Right in the Video Styles gallery to apply the style to the selected video and then move the video to the location displayed in Figure 3–50.

Q&A Can I preview the movie clip?

Yes. Point to the clip and then click the Play button on the ribbon (Preview group) or the Play/Pause button on the video controls below the video.

Figure 3–50

To Add a Video Border

You have added borders to photos, and this design element can be added to video frames. The following steps apply a border to the Mountain Bike Video clip. ***Why?*** *A border adds visual interest and distinguishes the video frame from the photo background.*

- With the video clip selected, click the Video Border button (Video Tools Format tab | Video Styles group) and then point to Weight on the Video Border gallery to display the Weight gallery.

- Point to 2¼ pt to display a live preview of this line weight on the video frame (Figure 3–51).

Experiment

- Point to various line weights in the Weight gallery and watch the line thickness change.

- Click 2¼ pt to add this line weight to the video.

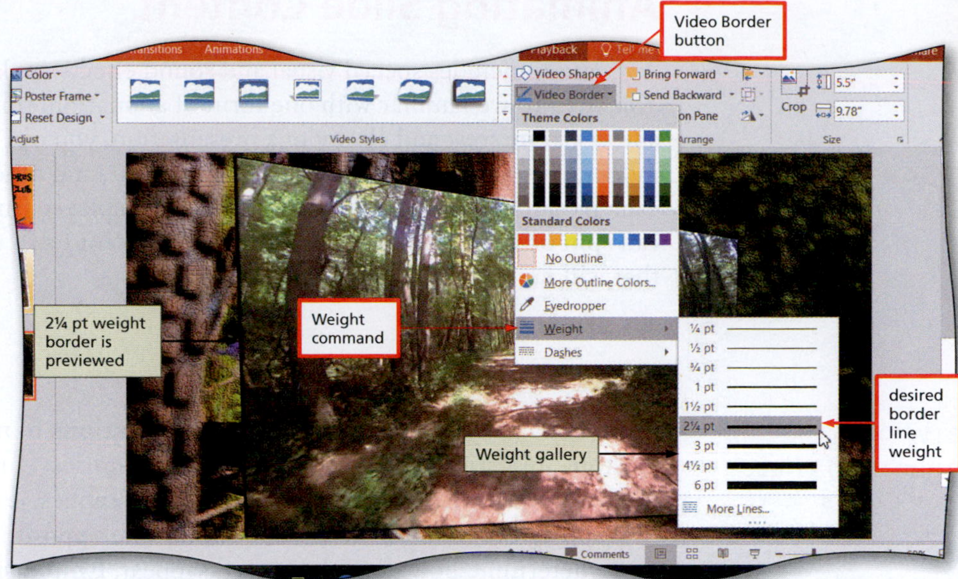

Figure 3–51

1 INSERT & ADD EFFECTS | 2 MODIFY PLACEHOLDERS | 3 MODIFY & COPY ILLUSTRATIONS
4 ADD MEDIA | 5 ANIMATE SLIDE CONTENT | 6 CUSTOMIZE SLIDE ELEMENTS

To Change a Video Border Color

Once you have added a border to a video, you can modify the default color. The following steps change the video border color to yellow. ***Why?*** *Yellow is used as an accent color in many components of the Spokes Bike Club slides.*

1
- With the video clip selected, click the Video Border button (Video Tools Format tab | Video Styles group) and then point to Yellow (fourth color in Standard Colors row) to display a live preview of this border color on the video frame (Figure 3–52).

Experiment

- Point to various colors in the gallery and watch the line colors change.

- Click Yellow to change the video border color.

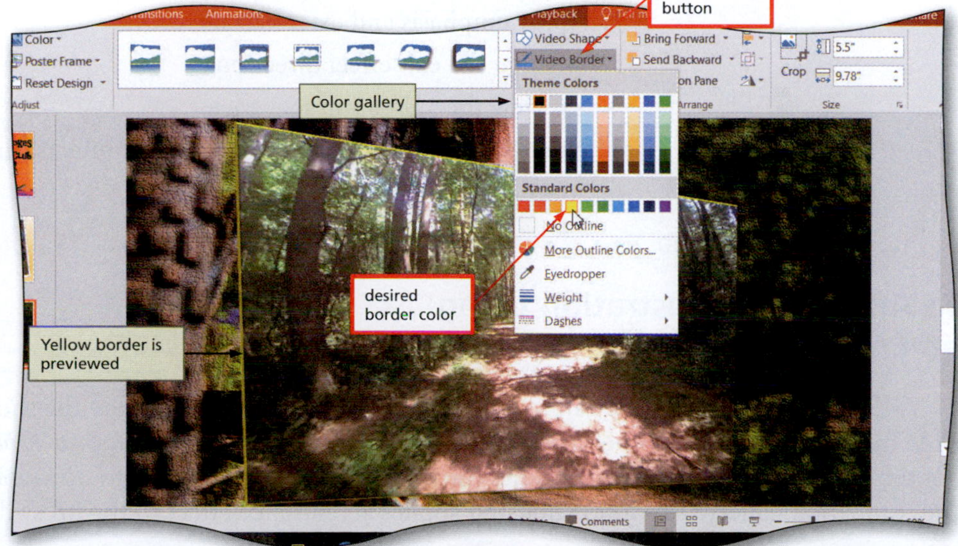

Figure 3–52

Other Ways

1. Click Format Video on shortcut menu, click Fill & Line icon, click Color button

Break Point: If you wish to take a break, this is a good place to do so. Be sure to save the Spokes Bike Club file again and then you can quit PowerPoint. To resume at a later time, start PowerPoint, open the file called Spokes Bike Club, and continue following the steps from this location forward.

Animating Slide Content

Animation includes special visual and sound effects applied to text or other content. You already are familiar with one form of animation: transitions between slides. To add visual interest and clarity to a presentation, you can animate various parts of an individual slide, including pictures, shapes, text, and other slide elements. For example, each paragraph on the slide can spin as it is displayed. Individual letters and shapes also can spin or move in various motions. PowerPoint has a variety of built-in animations that will fade, wipe, or fly-in text and graphics.

Custom Animations

BTW
Animation Effect Icon Colors
Animation effects allow you to control how objects enter, move on, and exit slides. Using a traffic signal analogy may help you remember the sequence of events. Green icons indicate when the animation effect starts on the slide. Yellow icons represent the object's motion; use them with caution so they do not distract from the message you are conveying to your audience. Red icons indicate when the object stops appearing on a slide.

You can create your own **custom animations** to meet your unique needs. Custom animation effects are grouped in categories: entrance, exit, emphasis, and motion paths. **Entrance effects**, as the name implies, determine how slide elements first appear on a slide. **Exit effects** work in the opposite manner as entrance effects: They determine how slide elements disappear. **Emphasis effects** modify text and objects displayed on the screen. For example, letters may darken or increase in font size. The entrance, exit, and emphasis animations are grouped into categories: Basic, Subtle, Moderate, and Exciting. You can set the animation speed to Very Fast, Fast, Medium, Slow, or Very Slow.

The Slide 2 illustration shows a person riding a bike. When the slide is displayed, the audience will see this biker enter from the lower-left corner, move across the slide, stop beside the bicycle picture, rock slightly, and then continue across the slide toward the right corner.

In the following pages, you will perform these tasks:

1. Apply an entrance effect to the biker illustration and then change the direction.
2. Apply emphasis and exit effects.
3. Change the exit effect direction.
4. Preview the animation sequence.
5. Modify the entrance, emphasis, and exit effects' timing.
6. Animate text paragraphs.

To Animate an Illustration Using an Entrance Effect

1 INSERT & ADD EFFECTS | 2 MODIFY PLACEHOLDERS | 3 MODIFY & COPY ILLUSTRATIONS
4 ADD MEDIA | 5 ANIMATE SLIDE CONTENT | 6 CUSTOMIZE SLIDE ELEMENTS

The biker you modified will not appear on Slide 2 when you display the slide. Instead, it will enter the slide from the lower-left corner. ***Why?*** *The biker is facing right, so he will appear to be pedaling forward.* It will then continue across the slide until it reaches the lower-right side of the photo. Entrance effects are colored green in the Animation gallery. The following step applies an entrance effect to the biker illustration in Slide 2.

- Display Slide 2, select the biker clip, and then click Animations on the ribbon to display the Animations tab.
- Click the Fly In animation in the Animation gallery (Animations tab | Animation group) to display a live preview of this animation and to apply this entrance animation to the biker illustration (Figure 3–53).

Q&A
Are more entrance animations available?
Yes. Click the More button in the Animation gallery to see additional animations. You can select one of the 13 entrance animations that are displayed, or you can click the 'More Entrance Effects' command to expand the selection. You can click any animation to see a preview of the effect.

Q&A Why does the number 1 appear in a box on the left side of the clip?
The 1 is a sequence number and indicates Fly In is the first animation that will appear on the slide when you click the slide.

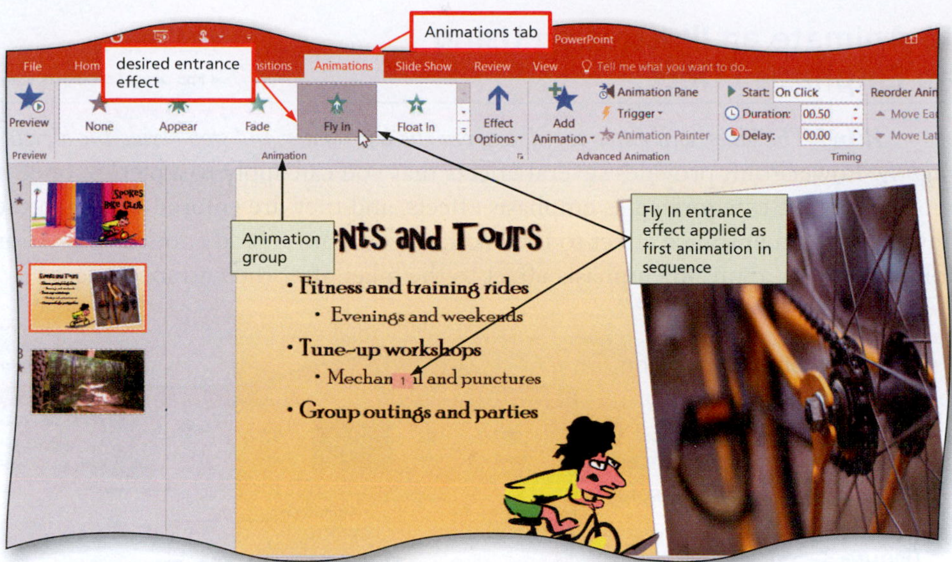

Figure 3–53

To Change Animation Direction

1 INSERT & ADD EFFECTS | 2 MODIFY PLACEHOLDERS | 3 MODIFY & COPY ILLUSTRATIONS
4 ADD MEDIA | 5 ANIMATE SLIDE CONTENT | 6 CUSTOMIZE SLIDE ELEMENTS

Why? By default, the illustration appears on the slide by entering from the bottom edge, and you want it to enter from the left. You can modify this direction and specify that it enters from another side or from a corner. The following steps change the biker entrance animation to enter from the left.

1

- Click the Effect Options button (Animations tab | Animation group) to display the Direction gallery (Figure 3–54).

Q&A Why does a pink box appear around the From Bottom arrow?
From Bottom is the default entrance direction applied to the animation.

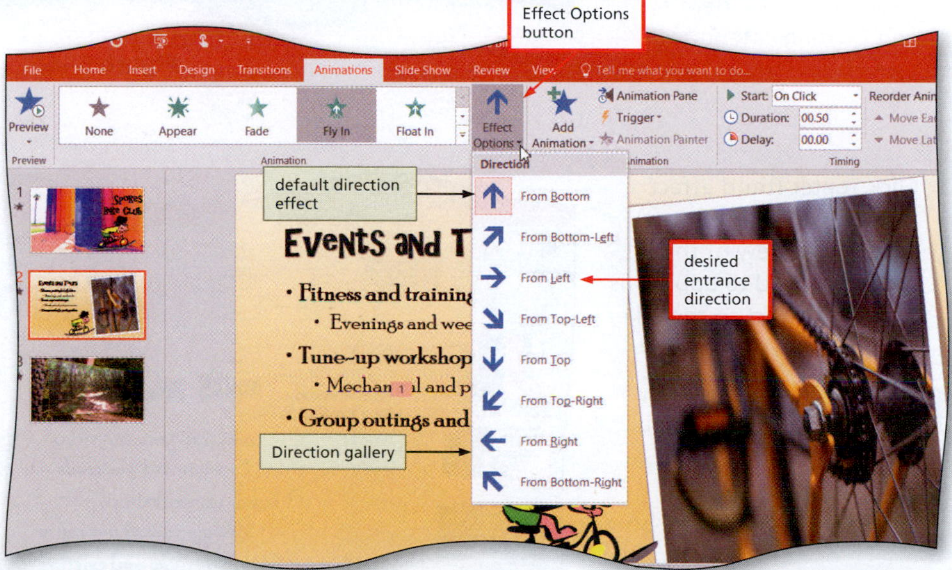

Figure 3–54

2

- Click the From Left arrow to see a preview of this animation and apply this direction to the entrance animation.

Q&A Can I change this entrance effect?
Yes. Repeat Step 1 to select another direction.

To Animate an Illustration Using an Emphasis Effect

Why? The biker will enter the slide from the left corner and stop beside the bicycle photo. You then want it to rock slightly. PowerPoint provides several effects that you can apply to a picture once it appears on a slide. These movements are categorized as emphasis effects, and they are colored yellow in the Animation gallery. You already have applied an entrance effect to the biker, so you want to add another animation to this illustration. The following steps apply an emphasis effect to the biker after the entrance effect.

1

- Select the biker illustration and then click the Add Animation button (Animations tab | Advanced Animation group) to display the Animation gallery (Figure 3–55).

Q&A Are more emphasis effects available in addition to those shown in the Animation gallery?
Yes. To see additional emphasis effects, click 'More Emphasis Effects' in the lower portion of the Animation gallery. The effects are arranged in the Basic, Subtle, Moderate, and Exciting categories.

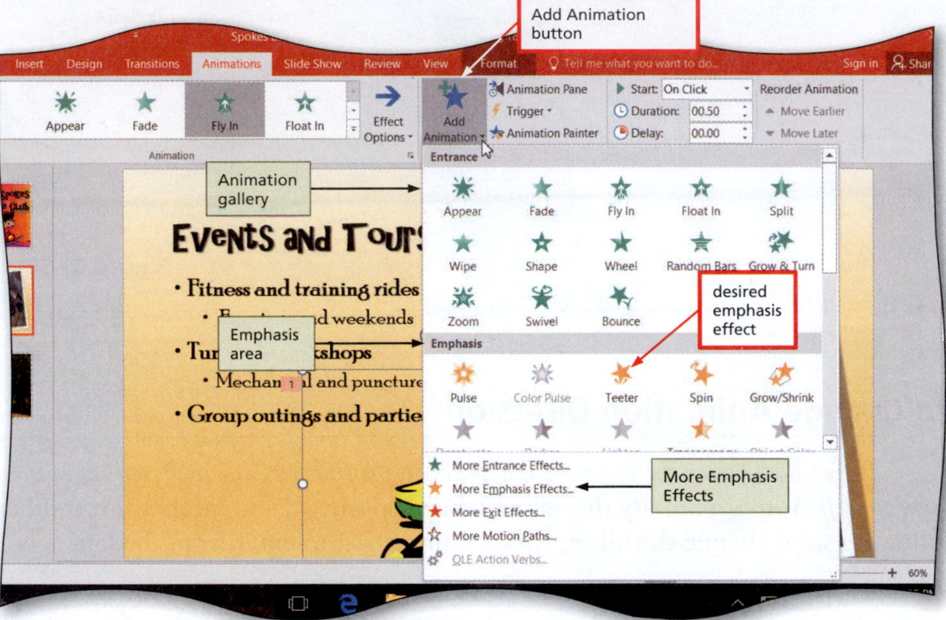

Figure 3–55

2

- Click Teeter (third effect in the first Emphasis row) to see a preview of this animation and to apply this emphasis effect to the biker illustration (Figure 3–56).

Q&A Do I need to use both an entrance and an emphasis effect, or can I use only an emphasis effect?
You can use one or the other effect, or both effects.

Why does the number 2 appear in a box below the number 1 on the left side of the illustration?
The 2 in the numbered tag indicates a second animation is applied in the animation sequence.

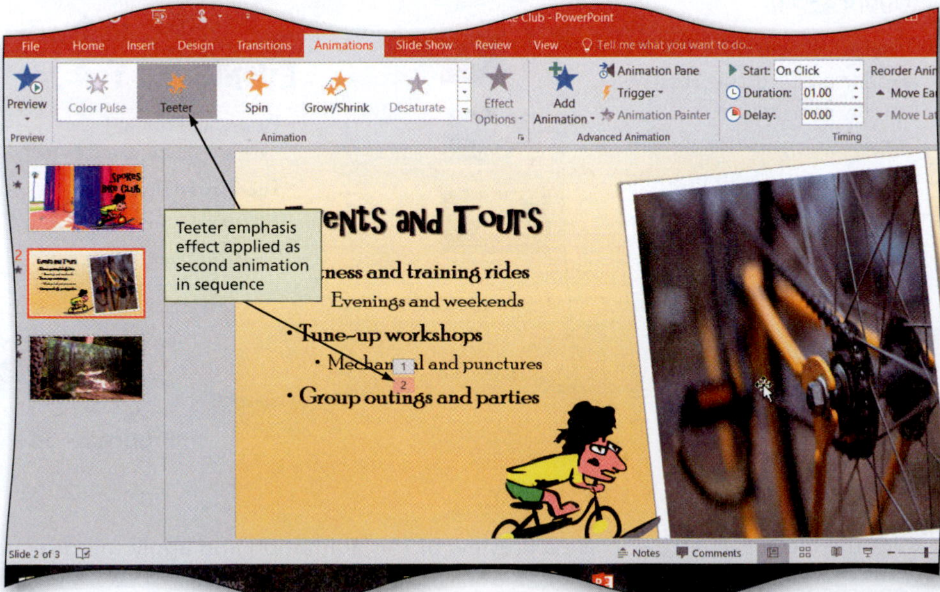

Figure 3–56

To Animate an Illustration Using an Exit Effect

The animated biker will enter the slide from the lower-left corner, stop beside the bicycle photo, and then teeter. It then will continue across the slide and exit in the lower-right corner. To continue this animation sequence, you first need to apply an exit effect. As with the entrance and emphasis effects, PowerPoint provides a wide variety of effects that you can apply to remove an illustration from a slide. These exit effects are colored red in the Animation gallery. You already have applied the Fly In entrance effect, so you will apply the Fly Out exit effect. ***Why?** It would give continuity to the animation sequence.* The following steps add this exit effect to the biker illustration after the emphasis effect.

1

- Select the biker illustration and then click the Add Animation button (Animations tab | Advanced Animation group) again to display the Animation gallery.
- Scroll down to display all the exit effects in the gallery (Figure 3–57).

Q&A Are more exit effects available in addition to those shown in the Animation gallery?
Yes. To see additional exit effects, click 'More Exit Effects' in the lower portion of the Animation gallery. The effects are arranged in the Basic, Subtle, Moderate, and Exciting categories.

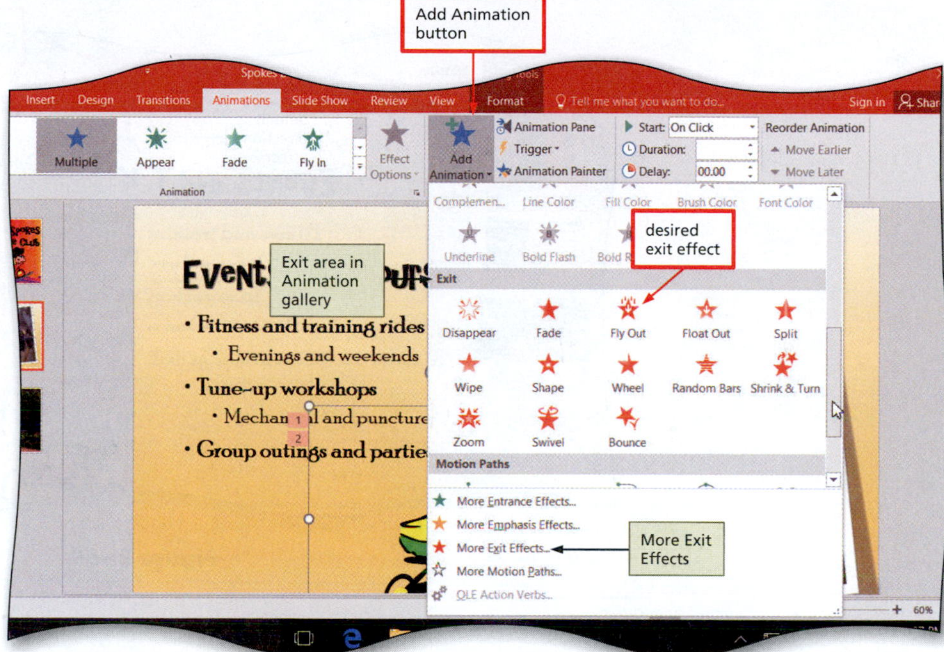

Figure 3–57

2

- Click Fly Out to see a preview of this animation and to add this exit effect to the sequence of biker illustration animations (Figure 3–58).

Q&A How can I tell that this exit effect has been applied?
The Fly Out effect is displayed in the Animation gallery (Animations tab | Animation group), and the number 3 is displayed to the left of the biker illustration.

How can I delete an animation effect?
Click the number associated with the animation you wish to delete and then press the DELETE key.

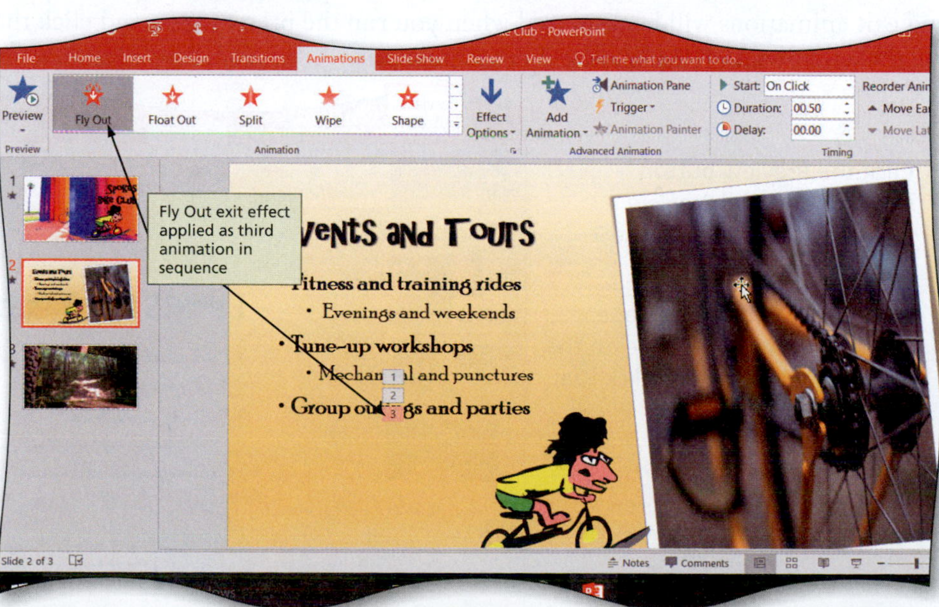

Figure 3–58

To Change Exit Animation Direction

The default direction for a picture to exit a slide is To Bottom. In this presentation, you want the biker to exit in the lower-right corner. ***Why?*** *To give the impression it is continuing down a bike path across the slide.* The following steps change the exit animation direction from To Bottom to To Right.

1. Click the Effect Options button (Animations tab | Animation group) to display the Direction gallery (Figure 3–59).

2. Click the To Right arrow to apply this direction to the exit animation effect.

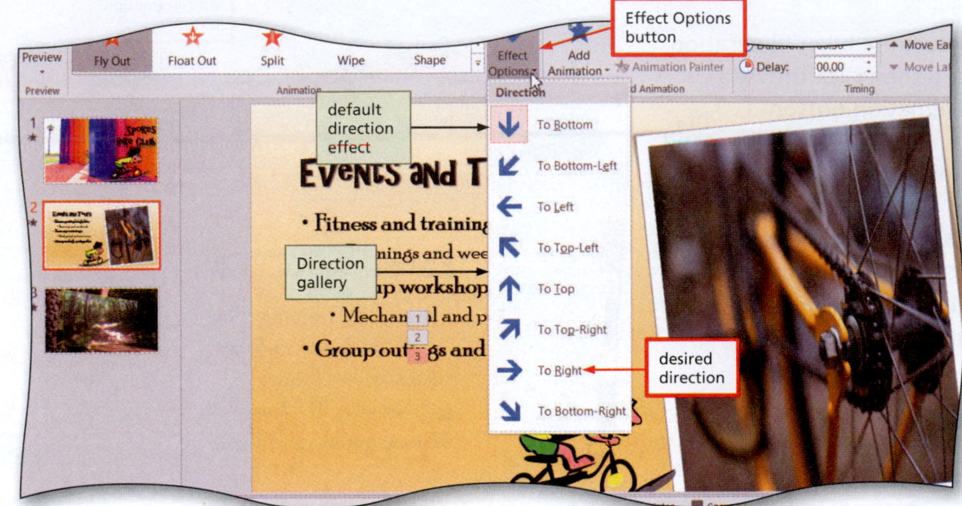

Figure 3–59

To Preview an Animation Sequence

1 INSERT & ADD EFFECTS | 2 MODIFY PLACEHOLDERS | 3 MODIFY & COPY ILLUSTRATIONS
4 ADD MEDIA | 5 ANIMATE SLIDE CONTENT | 6 CUSTOMIZE SLIDE ELEMENTS

Why? *Although you have not completed developing the presentation, you should view the animation you have added to check for continuity and verify that the animation is displaying as you expected.* By default, the entrance, emphasis, and exit animations will be displayed when you run the presentation and click the slide. The following step runs the presentation and displays the three animations.

1
- Click the Preview button (Animations tab | Preview group) to view all the Slide 2 animations (Figure 3–60).

Q&A Why does a red square appear in the middle of the circle on the Preview button when I click that button?

The red square indicates the animation sequence is in progress. Ordinarily, a green arrow is displayed in the circle.

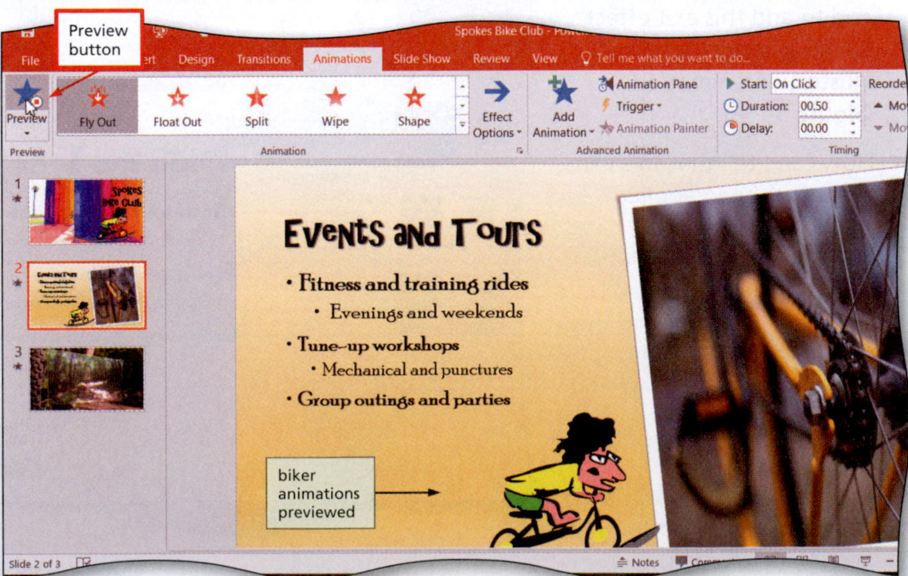

Figure 3–60

To Modify Entrance Animation Timing

The three animation effects are displayed quickly. To create a dramatic effect, you can change the timing. The default setting is to start each animation with a click, but you can change this setting so that the entrance effect is delayed until a specified number of seconds has passed. The following steps modify the start, delay, and duration settings for the entrance animation. ***Why?*** *You want the slide title text to display and then, a few seconds later, the biker to start to move across the slide slowly.*

- Click the tag numbered 1 on the left side of the biker illustration and then click the Start arrow (Animations tab | Timing group) to display the Start menu (Figure 3–61).

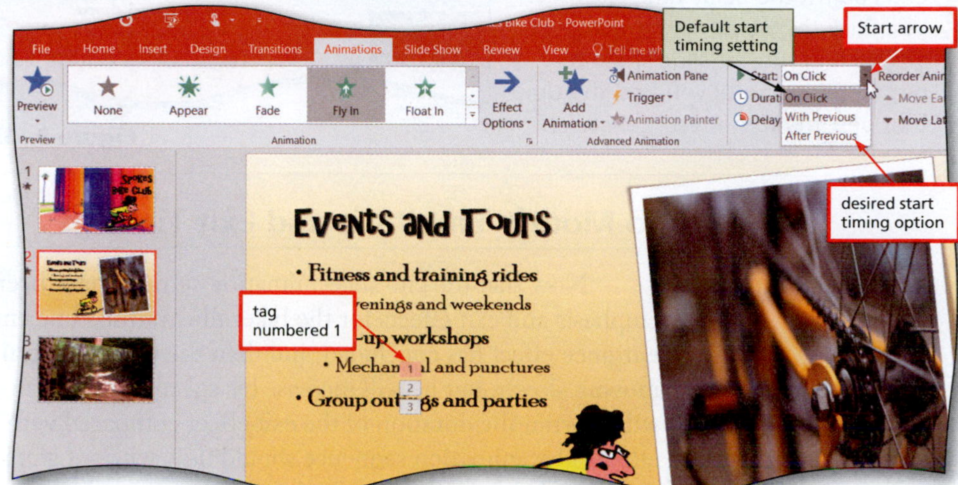

Figure 3–61

- Click After Previous to change the start option.

Q&A Why did the numbered tags change from 1, 2, 3 to 0, 1, 2?
The first animation now occurs automatically without a click. The first and second clicks now will apply the emphasis and exit animations.

What is the difference between the With Previous and After Previous settings?
The With Previous setting starts the effect simultaneously with any prior animation; the After Previous setting starts the animation after a prior animation has ended. If the prior animation is fast or a short duration, it may be difficult for a viewer to discern the difference between these two settings.

- Click the Duration up arrow (Animations tab | Timing group) several times to increase the time from 00.50 second to 02.00 seconds (Figure 3–62).
- Click the Preview button to view the animations.

Q&A What is the difference between the duration time and the delay time?
The duration time is the length of time in which the animation occurs; the delay time is the length of time that passes before the animation begins.

Can I type the speed in the Duration box instead of clicking the arrow to adjust the speed?
Yes. Typing the numbers allows you to set a precise timing.

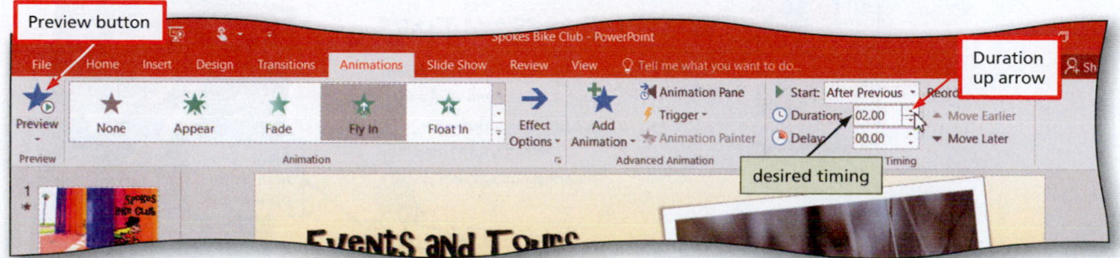

Figure 3–62

4

- Click the Delay up arrow (Animations tab | Timing group) several times to increase the delay time from 00.00 seconds to 03.00 seconds (Figure 3–63).
- Click the Preview button to view the animations.

Q&A Can I adjust the delay time I just set?
Yes. Click the Delay up or down arrows and run the slide show to display Slide 2 until you find the time that best fits your presentation.

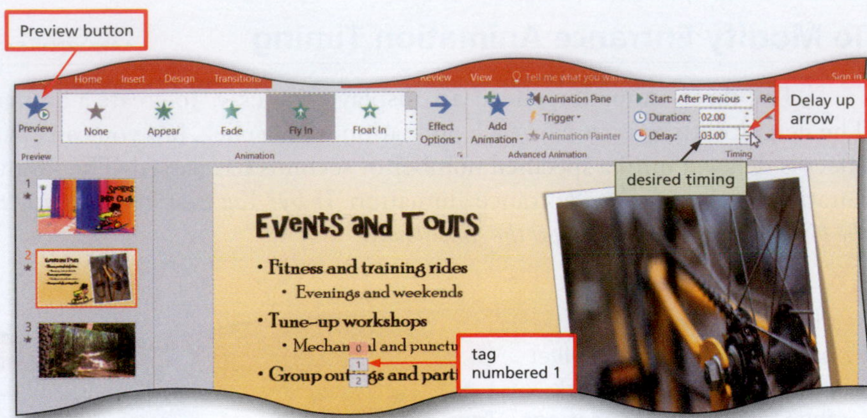

Figure 3–63

To Modify Emphasis and Exit Timings

Now that the entrance animation settings have been modified, you can change the emphasis and exit effects for the biker illustration. The emphasis effect can occur once the entrance effect has concluded, and then the exit effect can commence. The biker will start moving slowly, but he will increase his speed after he pauses briefly. You, consequently, will shorten the duration of the exit effect compared with the duration of the entrance effect. The animation sequence should flow without stopping, so you will not change the default delay timing of 00.00 seconds for the emphasis and exit effects. The following steps modify the start and duration settings for the emphasis and exit animations.

1. Click the tag numbered 1, which represents the emphasis effect, on the left side of the biker illustration.
2. Click the Start arrow (Animations tab | Timing group) to display the Start menu and then click After Previous to change the start option.
3. Click the Duration up arrow (Animations tab | Timing group) several times to increase the time to 02.00 seconds.
4. Click the tag numbered 1, which now represents the exit effect, click the Start arrow, and then click After Previous.
5. Click the Duration up arrow twice to increase the time to 01.00 seconds.
6. Preview the Slide 2 animation (Figure 3–64).

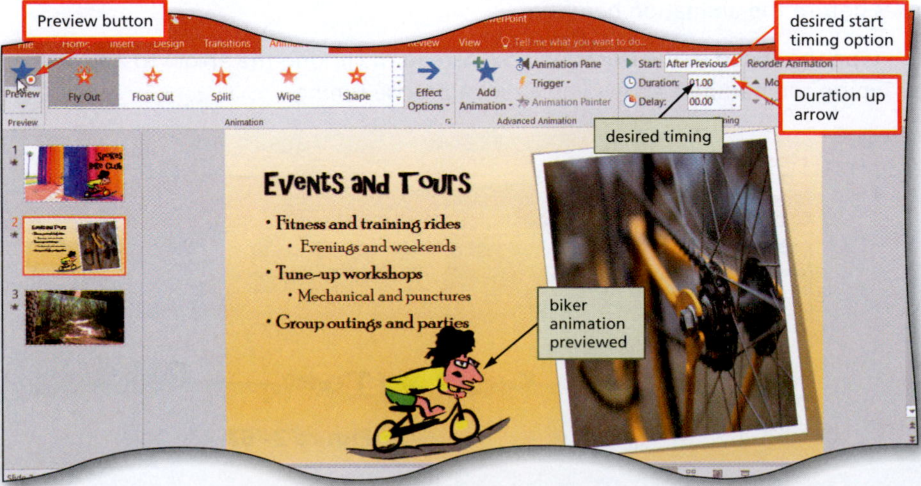

Figure 3–64

To Animate Content Placeholder Paragraphs

The biker illustration on Slide 2 has one entrance, one emphasis, and one exit animation. You decide to add similar animations to the five bulleted paragraphs in the Slide 2 content placeholder. ***Why?*** *For a special effect, you can add several emphasis animations to one slide element.* The following steps add one entrance and two emphasis animations to the bulleted list paragraphs.

- Double-click the Slide 2 content placeholder border so that it displays as a solid line (Figure 3–65).

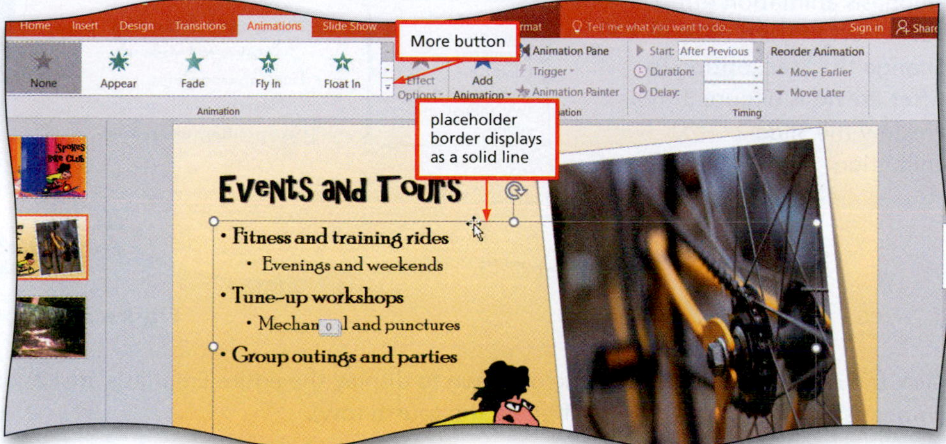

Figure 3–65

- Click the More button (shown in Figure 3–65) in the Animation group (Animations tab | Animation group) to expand the Animation gallery (Figure 3–66).

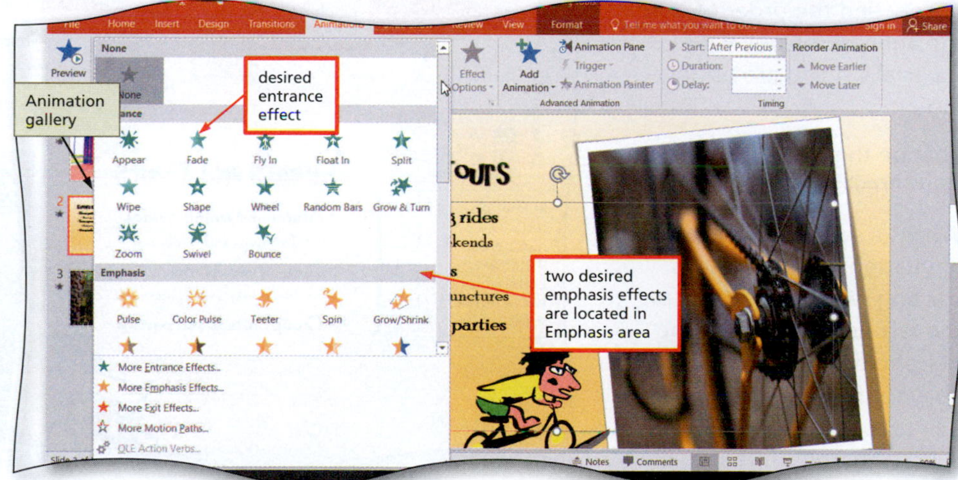

Figure 3–66

- Click the Fade entrance effect in the Animation gallery (second effect in first row) to add and preview this animation.
- Change the Start option to With Previous.
- Change the Duration time to 02.00 seconds (Figure 3–67).

Q&A Do I need to change the delay time?

No. The paragraphs can start appearing on the slide when the biker exit effect is beginning.

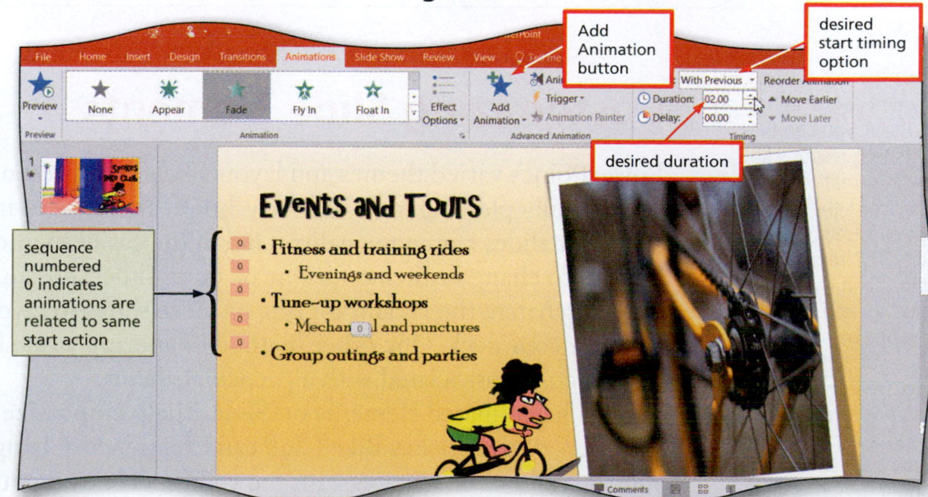

Figure 3–67

- Click the Add Animation button (Animations tab | Advanced Animation group), scroll down to display the entire Emphasis area, and then click the Font Color emphasis animation effect (last effect in third row).
- Change the Start option to After Previous (Figure 3–68).
- Preview the Slide 2 animation.

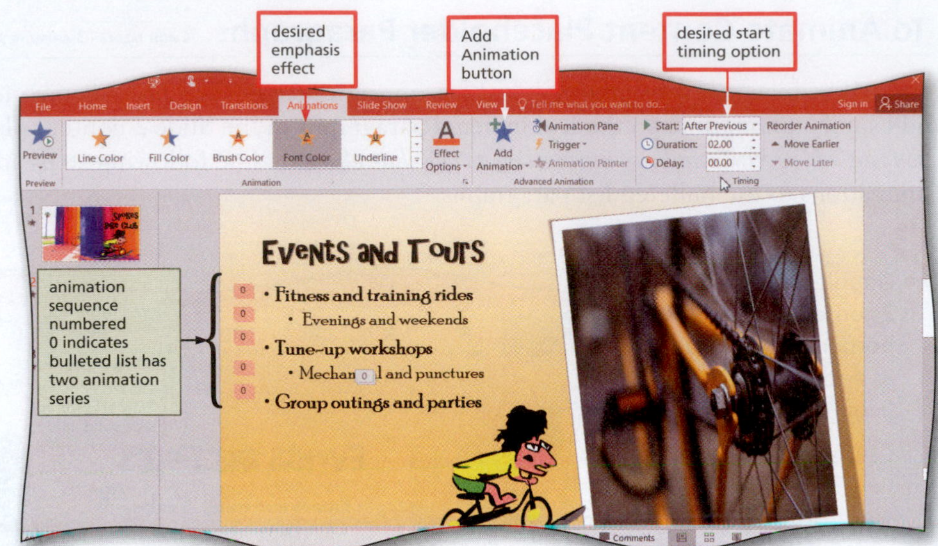

Figure 3–68

5

- Click the Add Animation button, scroll down to display the entire Emphasis area again, and then click the Underline emphasis animation effect (first effect in the fourth row).

Q&A Why do the animation effects display differently in the Animation gallery on my screen?
The width of the Animation gallery and the order of the animations may vary, especially if you are using a tablet.

- Change the Start option to With Previous (Figure 3–69).

Q&A Why is a second set of animation numbered tags starting with 0 displaying on the left side of the content placeholder?
They represent the three animations associated with the paragraphs in that placeholder.

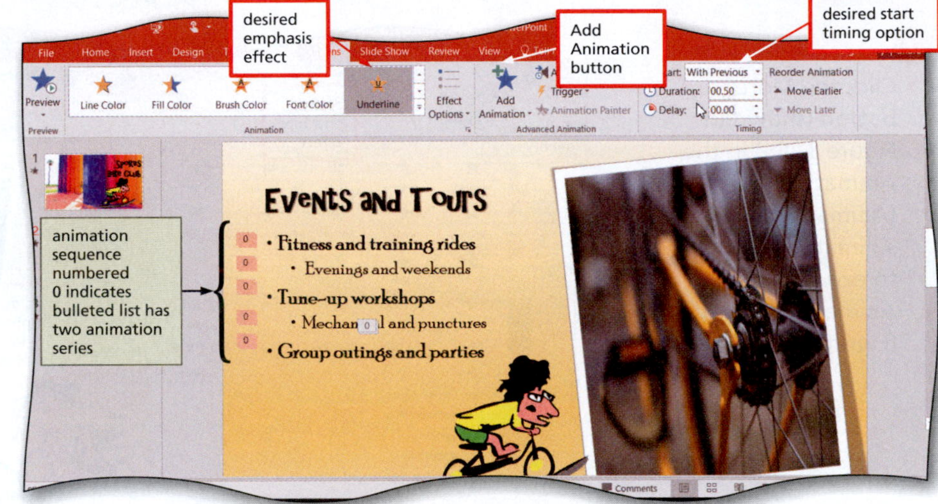

Figure 3–69

BTW
PowerPoint Help
At any time while using PowerPoint, you can find answers to questions and display information about various topics through PowerPoint Help. Used properly, this form of assistance can increase your productivity and reduce your frustrations by minimizing the time you spend learning how to use PowerPoint. For instructions about PowerPoint Help and exercises that will help you gain confidence in using it, read the Office and Windows module at the beginning of this book.

Customizing Slide Elements

PowerPoint's varied themes and layouts help give presentations a unified and aesthetically pleasing look. You may, however, desire to modify the default settings to give your slides a unique quality. One of the easier methods of developing a custom show is to change a theme for one or more slides, not an entire presentation. Similarly, you can change the variant for one or more slides to give a coordinating look to the slides in your deck. One other method of altering your slides slightly is to change the default colors associated with a particular theme.

The animated elements on Slide 2 help emphasize the events and tours that members of the Spokes Bike Club can experience. Changing the theme colors for that slide to yellow coordinates with the yellow slide elements.

To Change the Theme and Variant on One Slide

The Office theme applied to the presentation is appropriate for this topic. The font and placeholder locations are simple and add variety without calling attention to the design elements. The following steps change the theme and variant for Slide 2. ***Why?*** *To call attention to the material in the bulleted list on Slide 2, you can apply an equally effective theme that has a design element on the bottom that resembles a bike path. You then can modify this new theme by changing the variant on one slide.*

1

- With Slide 2 displaying, display the Design tab and then click the More button (Design tab | Themes group) to expand the Theme gallery.
- Point to the Retrospect theme to see a preview of that theme on Slide 2 (Figure 3–70).

Experiment

- Point to various document themes in the Themes gallery and watch the colors and fonts change on Slide 2.

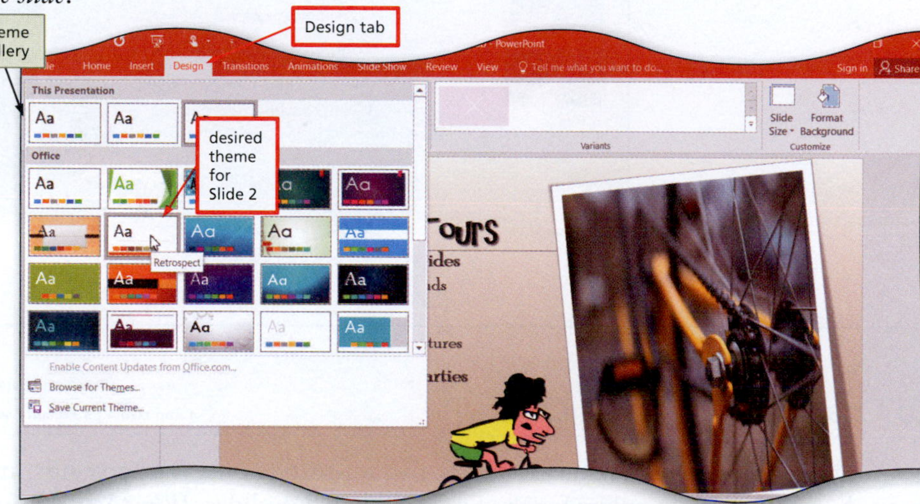

Figure 3–70

2

- Right-click the Retrospect theme to display a shortcut menu (Figure 3–71).

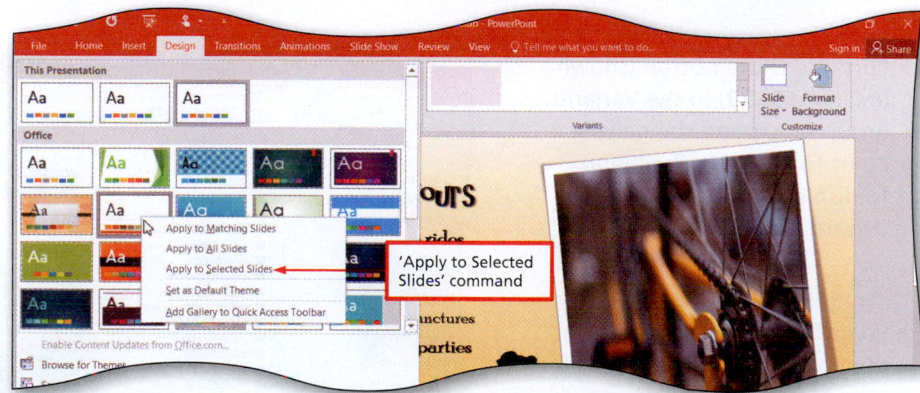

Figure 3–71

3

- Click 'Apply to Selected Slides' to apply the Retrospect theme to Slide 2.
- Right-click the green variant (second variant in row) to display a shortcut menu (Figure 3–72).

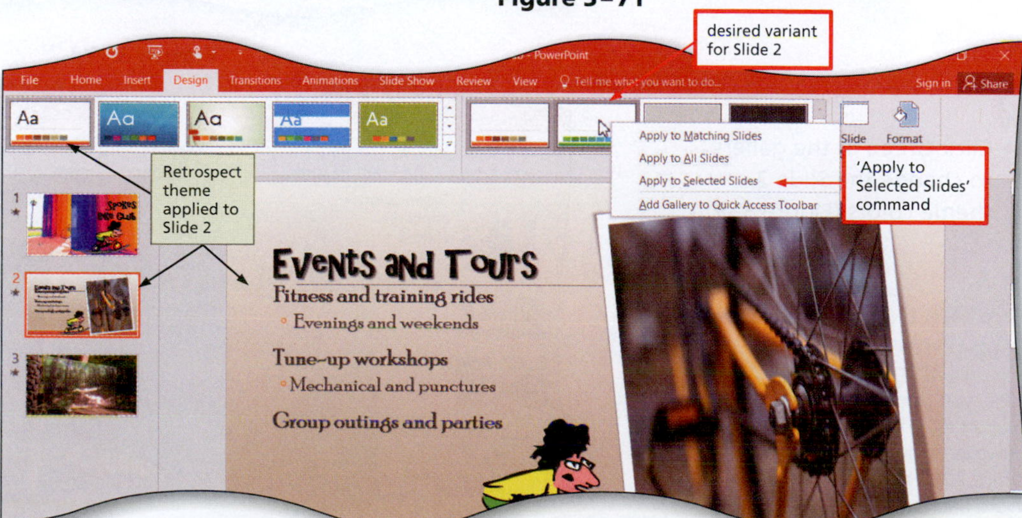

Figure 3–72

- Click 'Apply to Selected Slides' to apply the green variant to Slide 2 (Figure 3–73).

Figure 3–73

To Change the Theme Colors

1 INSERT & ADD EFFECTS | 2 MODIFY PLACEHOLDERS | 3 MODIFY & COPY ILLUSTRATIONS
4 ADD MEDIA | 5 ANIMATE SLIDE CONTENT | 6 CUSTOMIZE SLIDE ELEMENTS

Every theme has 10 standard colors: two for text, two for backgrounds, and six for accents. The following steps change the theme colors for the Spokes Bike Club slides. ***Why?*** *You can change the look of your presentation and add variety by applying the colors from one theme to another theme.*

- Click the More button (shown in Figure 3–73) in the Variants group to expand the gallery.
- Point to Colors in the menu to display the Colors gallery (Figure 3–74).

Experiment

- Point to various color rows in the gallery and watch the colors change on Slide 2.

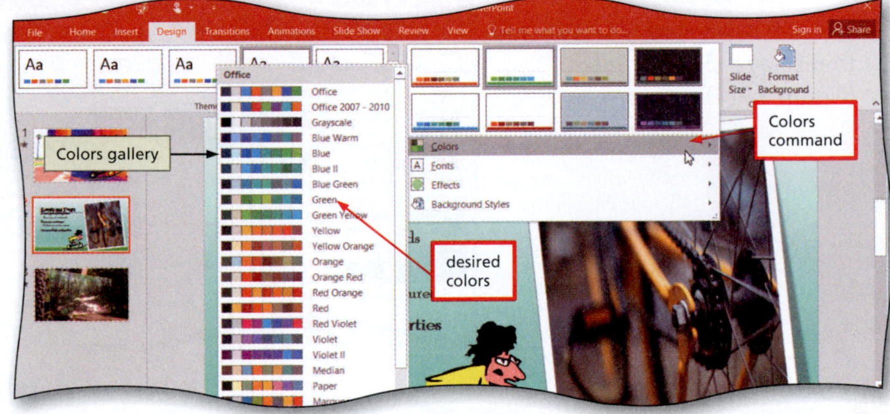

Figure 3–74

- Click Green in the gallery to change the Slide 2 theme colors (Figure 3–75).

BTW
Printing Document Properties
PowerPoint 2016 does not allow you to print document properties. This feature, however, is available in other Office 2016 apps, including Word and Excel.

Figure 3–75

To Run a Slide Show with Media

All changes are complete, so you now can view the Spokes Bike Club presentation. The following steps start Slide Show view.

1. Click the 'Start From Beginning' button on the Show tab to display the title slide and listen to the bicycle engine sound. Allow the audio clip to repeat several times.
2. Press the SPACEBAR to display Slide 2. Watch the biker and bulleted list animations.
3. Press the SPACEBAR to display Slide 3. Watch the video clip.
4. Press the SPACEBAR to end the slide show and then press the SPACEBAR again to exit the slide show.

To Preview and Print a Handout

1 INSERT & ADD EFFECTS | 2 MODIFY PLACEHOLDERS | 3 MODIFY & COPY ILLUSTRATIONS
4 ADD MEDIA | 5 ANIMATE SLIDE CONTENT | 6 CUSTOMIZE SLIDE ELEMENTS

Printing handouts is useful for reviewing a presentation. You can analyze several slides displayed simultaneously on one page. Additionally, many businesses distribute handouts of the slide show before or after a presentation so attendees can refer to a copy. Each page of the handout can contain reduced images of one, two, three, four, six, or nine slides. The three-slides-per-page handout includes lines beside each slide so that your audience can write notes conveniently. The following steps preview and print a presentation handout with two slides per page. ***Why?*** *Two of the slides are predominantly pictures, so your audience does not need full pages of those images. The five bulleted paragraphs on Slide 2 can be read easily on one-half of a sheet of paper.*

1
- Click File on the ribbon to open the Backstage view and then click the Print tab.
- Click the Previous Page button to display Slide 1 in the Print gallery.
- Click 'Full Page Slides' in the Settings area to display the Full Page Slides gallery (Figure 3–76).

Q&A Why does the preview of my slide appear in black and white?
Your printer determines how the preview appears. If your printer is not capable of printing color images, the preview will appear in black and white.

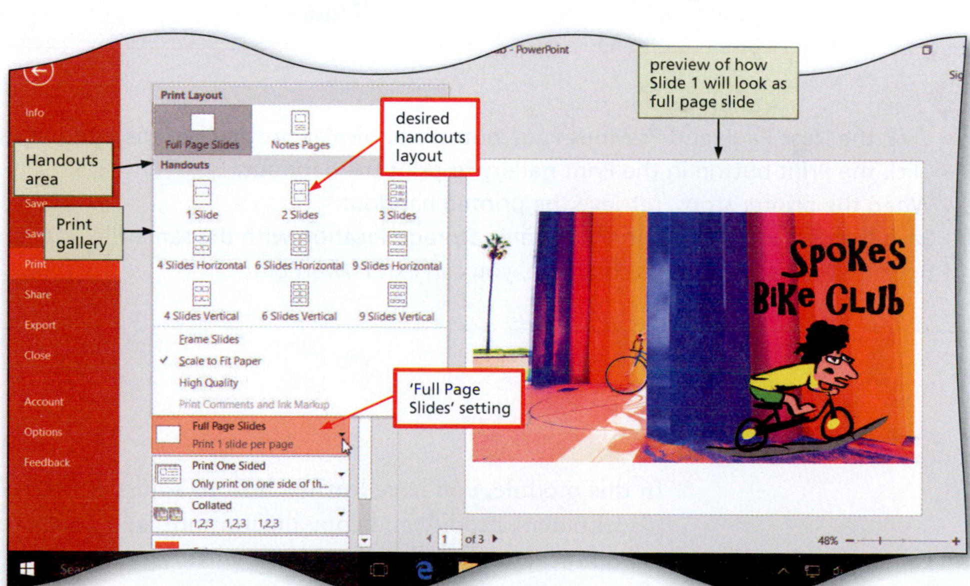

Figure 3–76

BTW
Conserving Ink and Toner
If you want to conserve ink or toner, you can instruct PowerPoint to print draft quality documents by clicking File on the ribbon to open the Backstage view, clicking the Options tab in the Backstage view to display the PowerPoint Options dialog box, clicking Advanced in the left pane (PowerPoint Options dialog box), scrolling to the Print area in the right pane, not placing a check mark in the High quality check box, and then clicking the OK button. Then, use the Backstage view to print the document as usual.

2

- Click 2 Slides in the Handouts area to select this option and display a preview of the handout (Figure 3–77).

Q&A The current date displays in the upper-right corner of the handout, and the page number displays in the lower-right corner of the footer. Can I change their location or add other information to the header and footer?

Yes. Click the 'Edit Header & Footer' link at the bottom of the Print gallery, click the Notes and Handouts tab (Header and Footer dialog box), and then decide what content to include on the handout page.

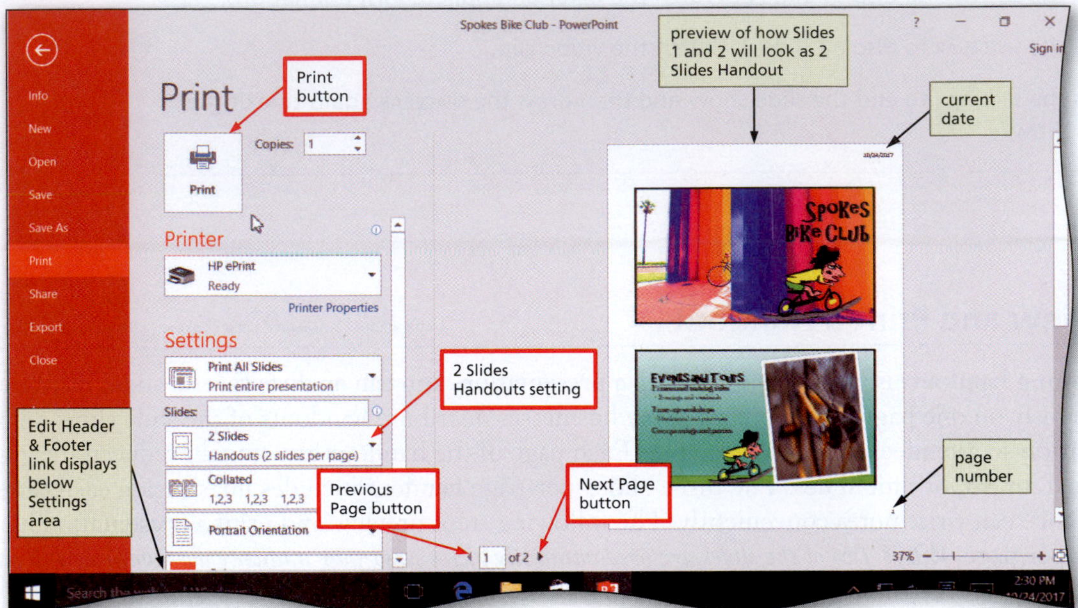

Figure 3–77

3

- Click the Next Page and Previous Page buttons to display previews of the two pages in the handout.
- Click the Print button in the Print gallery to print the handout.
- When the printer stops, retrieve the printed handout.
- Save the presentation again in the same storage location with the same file name.
- Because the project now is complete, you can exit PowerPoint.

Summary

In this module, you have learned how to adjust photo colors and effects, modify placeholders, modify and copy illustrations, add and format media, animate slide content, customize slides, and print a handout.

BTW

Distributing a Document

Instead of printing and distributing a hard copy of a document, you can distribute the document electronically. Options include sending the document via email; posting it on cloud storage (such as OneDrive) and sharing the file with others; posting it on social media, a blog, or other website; and sharing a link associated with an online location of the document. You also can create and share a PDF or XPS image of the document, so that users can view the file in Acrobat Reader or XPS Viewer instead of in PowerPoint.

CONSIDER THIS: PLAN AHEAD

What decisions will you need to make when creating your next presentation?

Use these guidelines as you complete the assignments in this module and create your own slide show decks outside of this class.

1. Determine if adjusting photo colors and effects can increase visual appeal.
   a) Change color saturation.
   b) Change tones.
   c) Recolor the image.
2. Vary paragraph alignment.
   a) Themes dictate whether paragraph text is aligned left, center, or right in a placeholder, but you can modify these design decisions when necessary. Moving placeholders and changing paragraph alignment can help create a unique slide.
   b) Different effects are achieved when text alignment shifts in a presentation.
3. Use multimedia selectively.
   a) Locate video, music, and sound files that are appropriate for your audience and that you have permission to use.
   b) Use media files only when necessary, however, because they draw the audience's attention away from the presenter and toward the slides.
   c) Using too many multimedia files can be overwhelming.
4. Use animation sparingly.
   a) PowerPoint audience members usually take notice the first time an animation is displayed on the screen, so be certain the animation will help focus on the precise points being presented during a particular time of the presentation.
   b) Avoid using animation for the sake of using animation. Use animation only when necessary to add emphasis.
   c) Animation overuse annoys and desensitizes audience members.
   d) Carefully decide how text or a slide element enters and exits a slide and how it is displayed once it is present on the slide.
5. Use handouts to organize your speech and to distribute to audiences.
   a) Determine if a handout with two slides per page will help unify your message when you distribute copies to an audience.

Apply Your Knowledge

Reinforce the skills and apply the concepts you learned in this module.

Resizing a Photo by Entering Exact Measurements, Formatting a Video Border, Trimming a Video File, Resizing and Moving a Placeholder, and Animating a Photo and Title

Note: To complete this assignment, you will be required to use the Data Files. Please contact your instructor for information about accessing the Data Files.

Instructions: Run PowerPoint. Open the presentation called Apply 3-1 Cats, which is located in the Data Files. The four slides in the presentation, shown in Figure 3–78, discuss the factors you should consider when adopting a cat. The local pet store is holding a special event for cat adoptions. The document you open is composed of slides containing pictures and a video. You will apply artistic effects or modify some of these graphic elements. You also will move placeholders. In addition, you will animate photos and a title using an entrance effect.

Continued >

Apply Your Knowledge *continued*

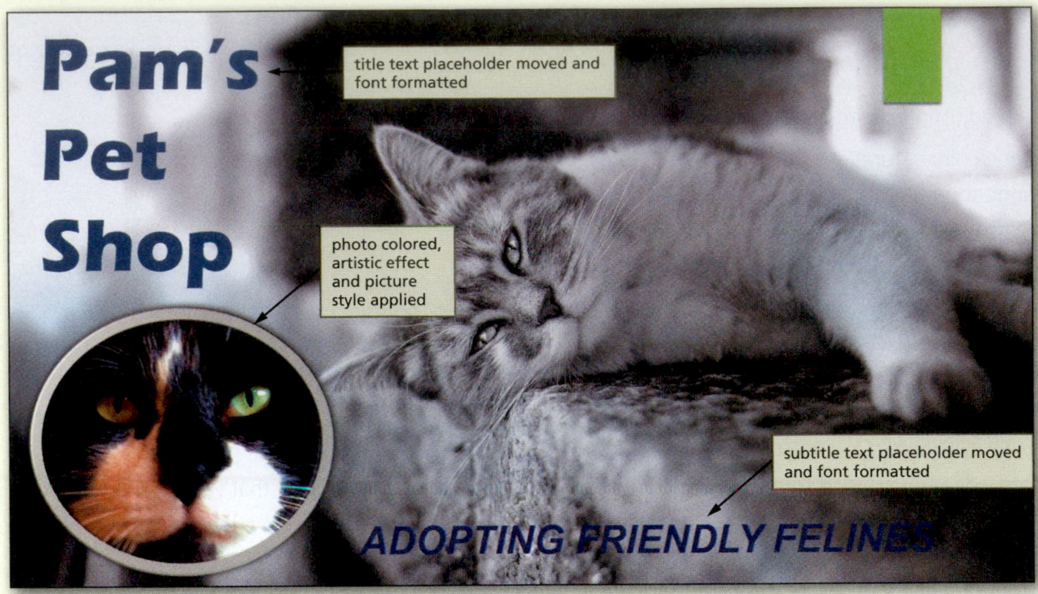

(a) Slide 1

Figure 3–78a

Perform the following tasks:

1. On Slide 1 (Figure 3–78a), move the title text placeholder to the upper area of the slide, the subtitle text placeholder to the lower area of the slide, and the green-eyed cat picture to the bottom left corner of the slide, as shown in the figure. Color the green-eyed cat picture by selecting Saturation: 200% from the Color Saturation area, and apply the Paint Brush artistic effect to the picture, as shown in figure. Decrease the picture size to 3.35"×3.88" and apply the Metal Oval picture style to the picture. Apply the Float In animation entrance effect, change the duration to 2.50, and then change the Start timing setting to With Previous.
2. On Slide 1, change the title font to Eras Bold ITC, increase the font size to 72 point, and then change the font color to Dark Blue, Background 2 (in Theme Colors row). Change the size of the title text placeholder to 3.73"×3.75" and then move it to the left area of the slide using the Smart Guides to line it up with the left edge of the picture, as shown in the figure. Apply the Fly In animation and then change the direction to From Right to the title text font and change the duration to 2.00. Change the Start timing setting to After Previous.
3. On Slide 1, change the subtitle font to Arial, increase the font size to 36 point, change the font color to Dark Blue (in Standard Colors row), and then bold and italicize this text.
4. On Slide 2 (Figure 3–78b), change the title text font to Arial, increase the font size to 44 point, bold this text, and then change the font color to Light Green (in Standard Colors row). Align this text left. Use the Format Painter to format the title text font on Slides 3 and 4 with the same features as the title text font on Slide 2.
5. Increase the size of the bulleted list font on Slide 2 to 24 point and then bold this text. Apply the Grow & Turn entrance effect to the bulleted list and then change the duration to 1.75. Change the Start timing setting to After Previous.
6. On Slide 2, increase the size of the right cat picture to approximately 4.12"×4.29" and then apply the Bevel Rectangle picture style to the cat picture. Decrease the size of the kitten picture in the center of the slide to approximately 4.24"×4.98" and then apply the Soft Edge Oval picture style to the kitten picture. Move the cat and kitten pictures to the locations shown in the figure.
7. On Slide 3 (Figure 3–78c), increase the size of the video to 5"×8.88". Apply the Rotated, Gradient video style in the Moderate area to the video, change the border weight to 6 pt, and

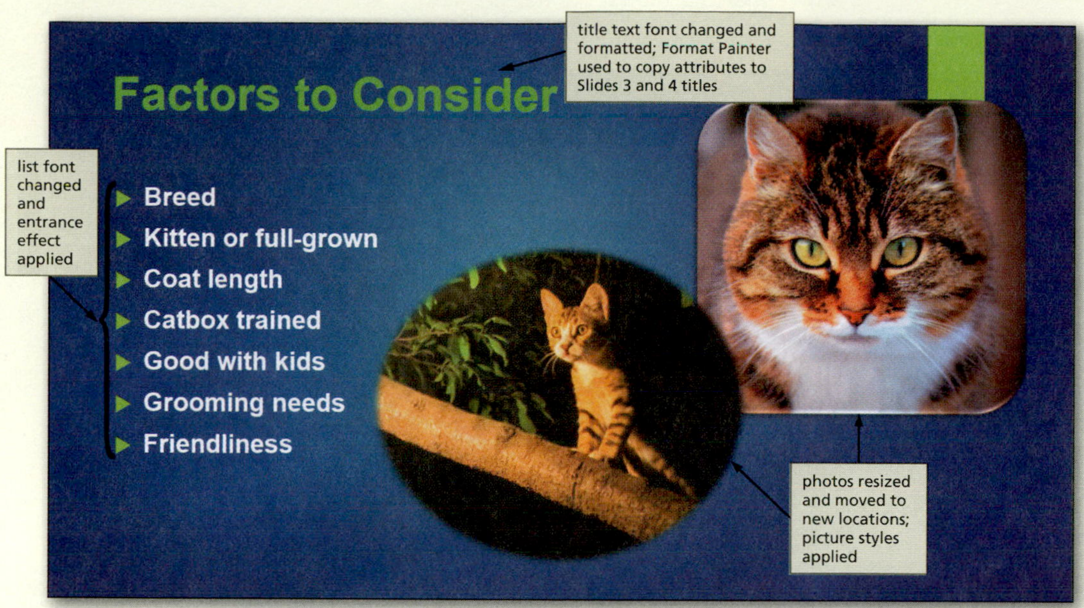

(b) Slide 2

Figure 3–78b

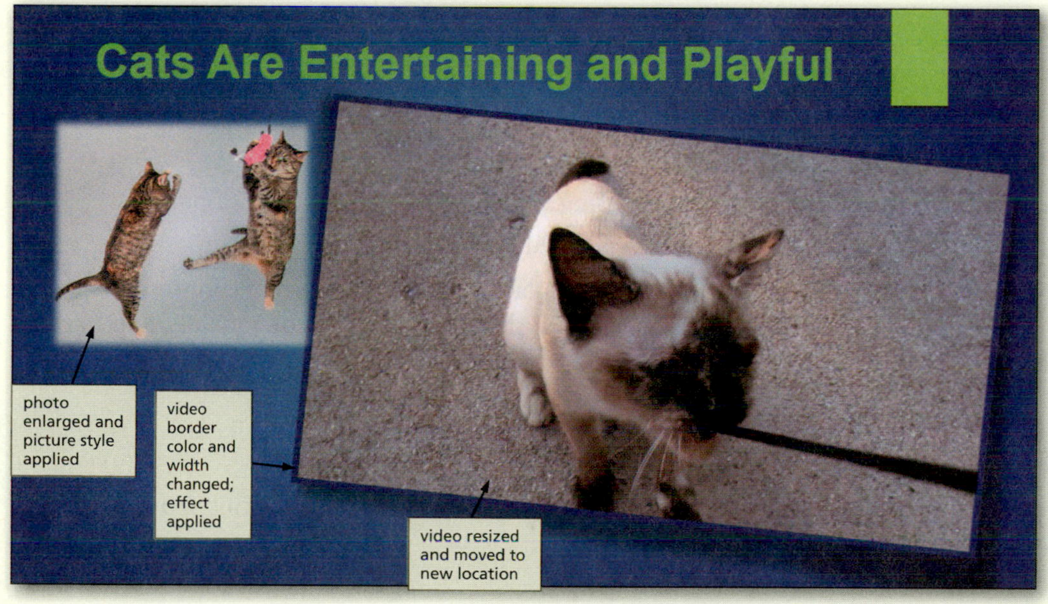

(c) Slide 3

Figure 3–78c

then change the border color to Dark Blue (in Standard Colors row). Move the video to the location shown in the figure. Trim the video so that the Start Time is 00:15.073. Start this video automatically.

8. Increase the size of the picture to approximately 3.1" × 3.51" on Slide 3. Apply the Soft Edge Rectangle picture style to the picture.
9. On Slide 4 (Figure 3–78d), reset the picture to its original color and style by clicking the Reset Picture button (Picture Tools Format tab | Adjust group). Increase the size of the picture to approximately 5.75" × 10.21", apply the Beveled Oval, Black picture style, and then move the picture to the location shown in the figure.

Continued >

Apply Your Knowledge *continued*

(d) Slide 4

Figure 3–78d

10. If requested by your instructor, add your mother's first name as a second line under the subtitle on Slide 1.
11. Apply the Clock transition in the Exciting category to all the slides. Change the duration to 3.00 seconds.
12. View the presentation and then save the file using the file name, Apply 3–1 Adopt a Cat.
13. Submit the revised document in the format specified by your instructor.
14. In Step 2, you changed the size of the title text placeholder and then moved it to the upper left area of the slide. How did this style improve the slide? On Slide 3, you trimmed the start time of the video. Why?

Extend Your Knowledge

Extend the skills you learned in this module and experiment with new skills. You may need to use Help to complete the assignment.

Changing Theme Colors, Coloring a Picture, Inserting and Trimming a Video File, Adding a Text Box, and Animating an Illustration

Note: To complete this assignment, you will be required to use the Data Files. Please contact your instructor for information about accessing the Data Files.

Instructions: Run PowerPoint. Open the presentation called Extend 3-1 Swimming, which is located in the Data Files. You will change theme colors, insert a video file, trim a video file, and insert a text box to create the presentation shown in Figure 3–79.

Perform the following tasks:

1. Change the theme variant to Black on Slide 1 only. Change the theme color to Blue II on Slide 3 only.
2. On Slide 1 (Figure 3–79a), change the title text font to Britannic Bold, increase the font size to 48 point, change the font color to Yellow (in Standard Colors row), and then center the text.

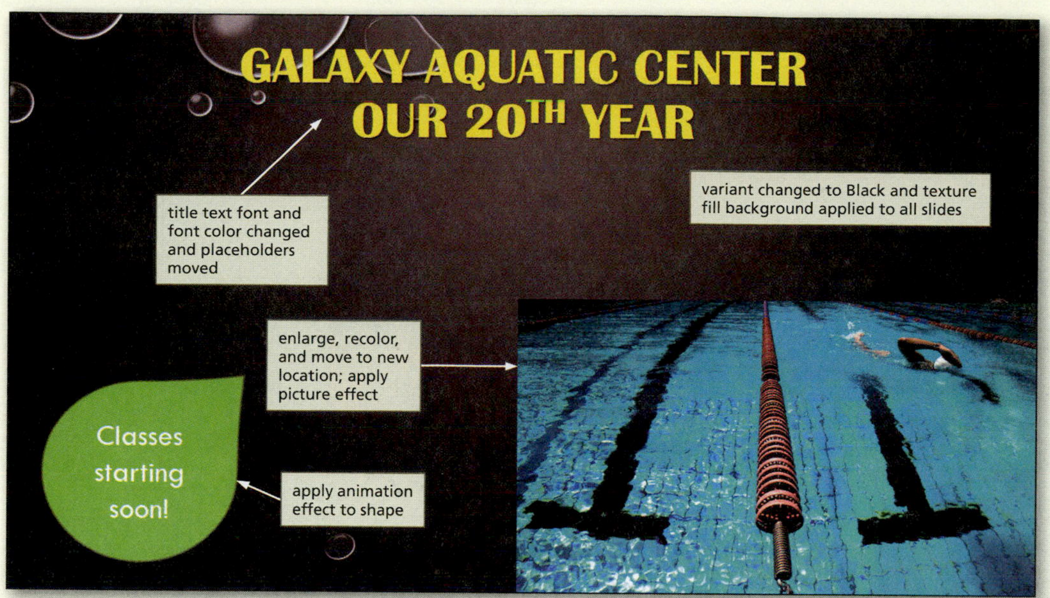

(a) Slide 1

Figure 3–79a

Change the font case to UPPERCASE. (*Hint*: The Change Case button is located in the Font group (Home tab | Font group).) Move the title text placeholder to the top of the slide, as shown in the figure. Delete the subtitle text placeholder.

3. Increase the size of the picture on Slide 1 to approximately 6.19" × 11", apply the Moderate Frame, White picture style, and then move the picture to the center of the slide, using the vertical Smart Guide to help you align this picture. Recolor the picture using the Blue, Accent color 3 Dark color (in Recolor area). Adjust the title text placeholder so that the text is below the picture border.
4. On Slide 1, apply the Grow/Shrink Emphasis effect to the Teardrop shape and then change the duration to 3.00. Change the Start timing setting to After Previous.
5. On Slide 2 (Figure 3–79b), change the title text font to Franklin Gothic Heavy, increase the font size to 40 point, change the font color to Dark Blue (in Standard Colors row), and then center the text. Use the Format Painter to apply these attributes to the title text font on Slide 4.
6. Apply the Bevel Perspective picture style to the picture. Increase the size of the picture to approximately 5.01" × 7.63" and then position it on the right side of the slide.
7. On Slide 2, apply the Zoom Entrance effect to the bulleted list, change the duration to 2:00, and then change the Start timing setting to After Previous.
8. On Slide 3 (Figure 3–79c), insert the video file called Swim, which is located in the Data Files. Increase the size of the video to approximately 6.41" × 8.74" and move the video to the location shown in the figure. Apply the Simple Frame, White video style and then change the Video Border color to Yellow (in Standard Colors row). Trim the video so that the End Time is 00:14.151. Start this video automatically.
9. Insert a text box on the left side of Slide 3 and type `Video highlights from one of our swim meets` in the text box, change the font to Arial, change font size to 24 point, and then bold and italicize this text. Adjust the size of the text box so that it measures approximately 2.52" × 2.01", and then use the horizontal Smart Guide to center the text box between the left end of the slide and the left edge of the video file.

Continued >

Extend Your Knowledge *continued*

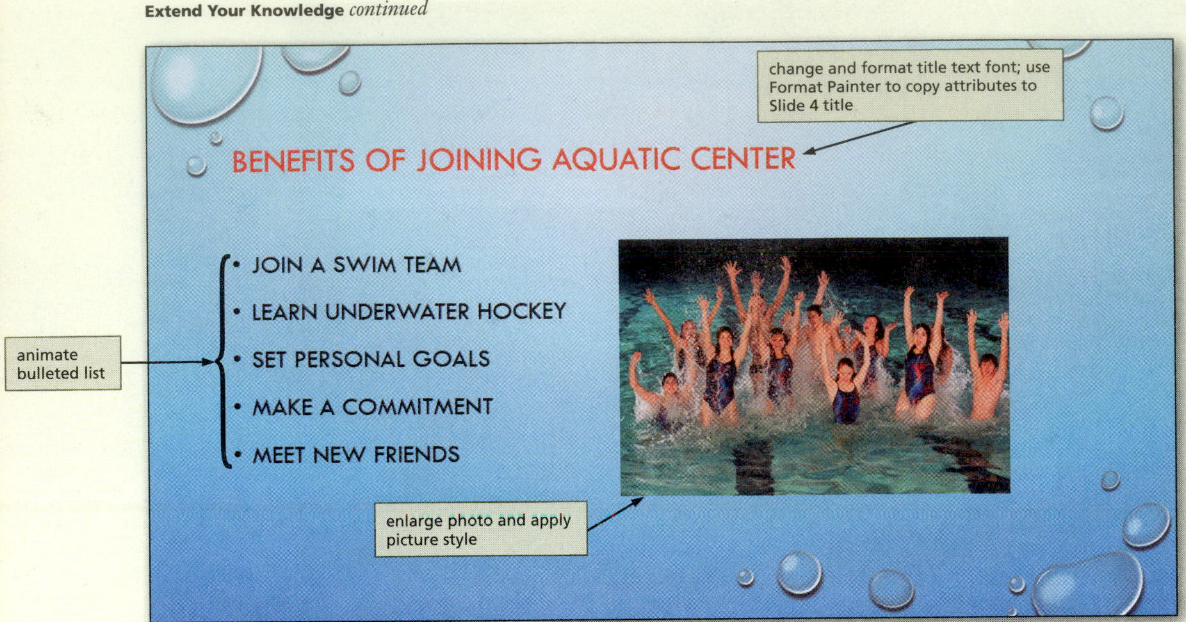

(b) Slide 2

Figure 3–79b

(c) Slide 3

Figure 3–79c

10. On Slide 4 (Figure 3–79d), increase the size of the swimmer picture to approximately 3.88" × 6.29" and apply the Beveled Oval, Black picture style to the picture. Change the border color to Light Green (in Standard Colors row) and then change the border weight to 6 pt. Position this picture on the left side of the slide under the title using the Smart Guides to align the picture with the left, right, and bottom edges of the placeholder.
11. On Slide 4, apply the Float Out exit effect to the flippers illustration and then change the duration to 5.00. Change the Start timing setting to After Previous.
12. If requested by your instructor, insert a text box on Slide 3 under the text box and add the time of day you were born.

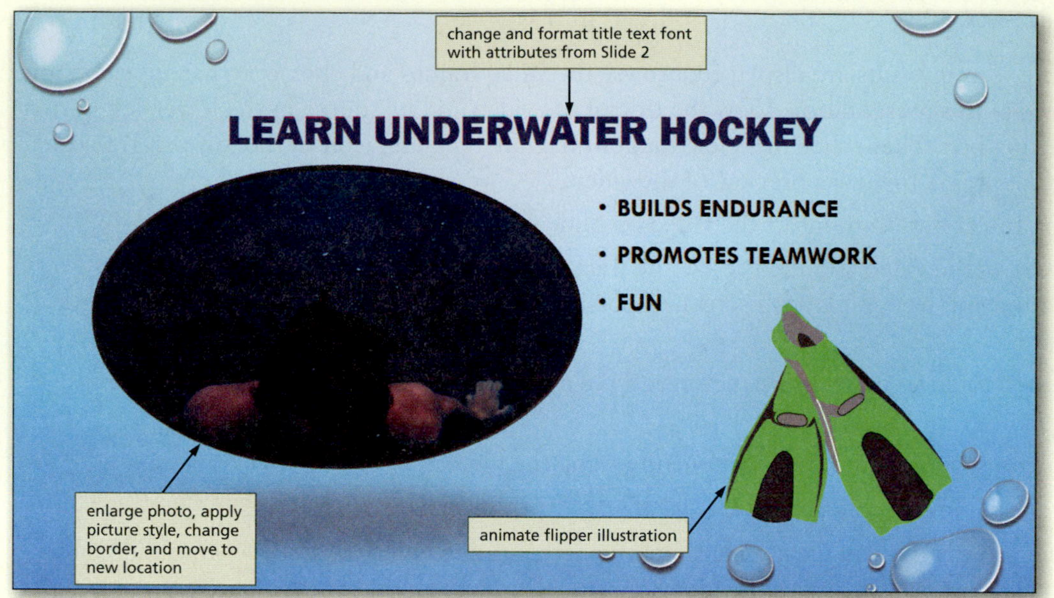

(d) Slide 4

Figure 3–79d

13. Apply an appropriate transition to all slides.
14. View the presentation and then save the file using the file name, Extend 3-1 Galaxy Aquatic Center.
15. Submit the revised document in the format specified by your instructor.
16. In this assignment, you inserted a video file and trimmed it. How did this enhance the presentation?

Expand Your World

Create a solution that uses cloud or web technologies by learning and investigating on your own from general guidance.

Inserting Video Files from the Web

Instructions: The Spokes Bike Club presentation you created in the module has a video you inserted from the Data Files. The bicyclist in this video mounted a camera on his helmet and recorded his ride through the forest. Using a helmet can help reduce head and brain injury risk and increase rider visibility to motorists and other cyclists. Many organizations promoting bicycling safety have created videos describing how to select and fit a bicycle helmet, and these videos are posted to online websites. PowerPoint allows you to insert online videos easily in a manner similar to how you inserted the Mountain Bike Video clip. You are going to search for and then insert one of these online videos into the Spokes Bike Club presentation.

Perform the following tasks:

1. In PowerPoint, open the Spokes Bike Club file, insert a new Slide 4 with the Title and Content layout, and then type `Helmet Safety Tips` as the title text. Use the Format Painter to copy the title text font formatting from Slide 2 to the new Slide 4 title. Center this title text.
2. Format the Slide 4 background with a gradient or texture fill.
3. Click the Insert Video icon in the content placeholder to display the Insert Video dialog box. Click the YouTube button in the dialog box and then type `bicycling helmet safety` as the search text in the Search YouTube search box.

Continued >

Expand Your World *continued*

4. When the search results are displayed, browse the video frames and click one that appears to fit the theme of this presentation. View the title of the video and its source in the lower-left corner of the dialog box. Then, click the View Larger (magnifying glass) icon in the lower-right corner of the video frame to view a preview of the video.
5. Click the Insert button to insert the video on Slide 4.
6. Add a style to the video and then resize the frame. Start this file automatically during the presentation and have it play full screen, if possible. If necessary, trim the video to the length you desire.
7. If requested to do so by your instructor, add the city where you were born to the Slide 4 title text.
8. View the presentation and then save the file using the file name, Expand 3-1 Spokes.
9. Submit the assignment in the format specified by your instructor.
10. What criteria did you use to select a particular YouTube video? What decisions did you make to choose a background and video style?

In the Labs

Design, create, modify, and/or use a presentation following the guidelines, concepts, and skills presented in this module. Labs 1 and 2, which increase in difficulty, require you to create solutions based on what you learned in the module; Lab 3 requires you to apply your creative thinking and problem-solving skills to design and implement a solution.

Lab 1: Changing the Stacking Order, Inserting an Audio File, and Animating a Photo, Illustration, and Title

Note: To complete this assignment, you will be required to use the Data Files. Please contact your instructor for information about accessing the Data Files.

Problem: Your local library is featuring information about national parks. Your travel club is planning to visit Yellowstone National Park next year, and you decide to gather some general information to present to the club. You create the slides shown in Figure 3–80.

Perform the following tasks:

1. Run PowerPoint. Open the presentation called Lab 3-1 Yellowstone, which is located in the Data Files. On Slide 1, increase the size of the waterfall picture to 7.5" × 11.54" and then move the picture to the left side of the slide, as shown in Figure 3–80a.
2. On Slide 1, select the title text placeholder. Display the Animation gallery, click 'More Entrance Effects,' and then apply the Expand entrance effect (in Subtle area) to the title text. Change the Start timing option to With Previous and the duration to 03.00 seconds. Bring the title text Forward so that the eagle's wings do not block the title.
3. On Slide 1, decrease the size of the eagle illustration to approximately 4.43" × 5.3" and then move it to the position shown in the figure. Apply the Fly In entrance effect with the From Bottom-Right direction to the illustration and then change the start timing option to After Previous and the duration to 02.50 seconds. Add the Fly Out exit animation with the To Left direction to the eagle illustration and then change the Start timing option to After Previous and the duration to 3.00 seconds.

(a) Slide 1

Figure 3–80a

4. On Slide 2 (Figure 3–80b), change the size of the video so that it measures approximately 5.93" × 8.9". Change the video style to the Canvas, White style (in Intense area) and then change the border weight to 6 pt. Have the video start Automatically. Trim the video by changing the Start Time to 00:28.008 and changing the End Time to 00:50.55. Move the video to the location shown in the figure.
5. On Slide 3 (Figure 3–80c), increase the size of the picture to approximately 6.26" × 8.23" and then apply the Moderate Frame, Black picture style to the picture. Move the picture to the location shown in the figure. Start the audio file Automatically and hide this file during the show. Trim the audio file so that the Start Time is at 01:00 and the End Time is at 02:00.

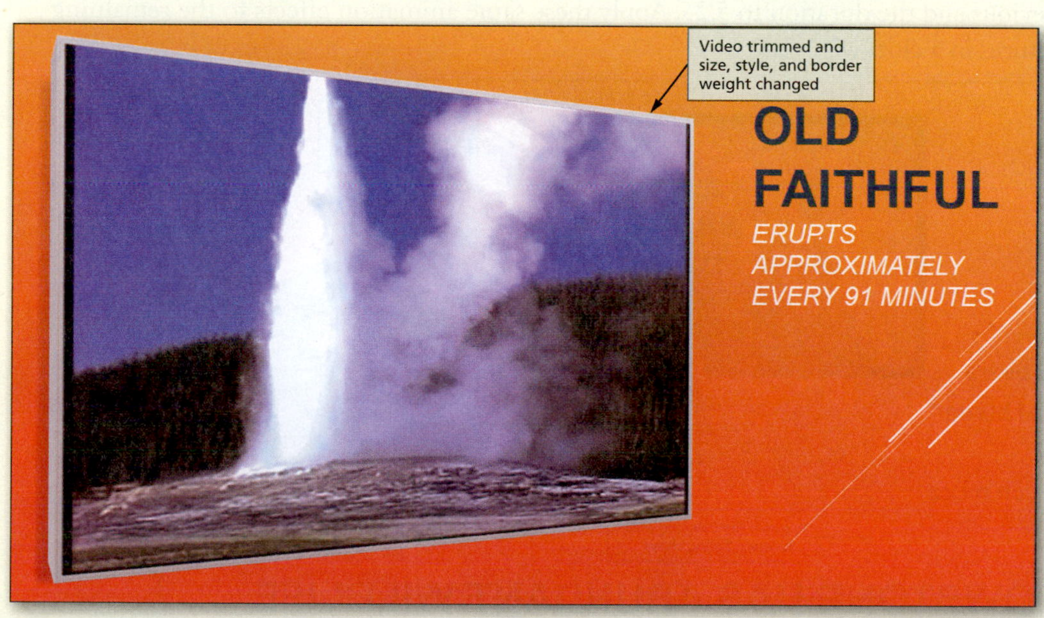

(b) Slide 2

Figure 3–80b

Continued >

In the Labs *continued*

(c) Slide 3

Figure 3–80c

6. On Slide 4 (Figure 3–80d), apply the Moderate Frame, Black picture style to the bear picture. Apply the Metal Oval picture style to the wolf picture. Move the two pictures to the locations shown, and bring the wolf picture forward, as shown in the figure.
7. Apply the Fade entrance effect to the two pictures. Change the Start timing option to After Previous and the duration to 02.50.
8. Insert the audio file called Wolves, which is located in the Data Files. Change the volume to Medium, start Automatically, and hide the audio file during the show.
9. On Slide 5 (Figure 3–80e) apply the Metal Oval picture style to the four fish pictures. Apply the Bounce entrance effect to the upper left picture and then change the Start timing option to After Previous and the duration to 5.25. Apply these same animation effects to the remaining three pictures in a clockwise order.

(d) Slide 4

Figure 3–80d

(e) Slide 5

Figure 3–80e

10. Apply the Wind transition in the Exciting category to all the slides. Change the duration to 2.50 seconds.
11. If requested by your instructor, insert a text box on Slide 2 and add the name of the street where you lived as a child.
12. View the presentation and then save the file using the file name, Lab 3–1 Visiting Yellowstone.
13. Submit the document in the format specified by your instructor.
14. On Slide 1, why did you bring the title text to the front of the eagle illustration? Why did you choose the Bounce entrance effect with a 05.25 duration on the four fish pictures on Slide 5?

Lab 2: Adding Audio Options, Ungrouping a Clip, Changing the Color of a Clip Object, Deleting a Clip Object, and Regrouping Objects

Note: To complete this assignment, you will be required to use the Data Files. Please contact your instructor for information about accessing the Data Files.

Problem: You work at a nature center and are asked to do a PowerPoint presentation on how to attract hummingbirds to your yard. You create the presentation shown in Figure 3–81.

Perform the following tasks:

1. Run PowerPoint. Open the presentation called Lab 3-2 Hummingbirds, which is located in the Data Files. On Slide 1 (Figure 3–81a), change the volume of the audio file to High and then select Start Automatically, 'Play Across Slides', 'Loop until Stopped', 'Rewind after Playing', and 'Hide During Show'.
2. Copy the hummingbird illustration from Slide 2 (Figure 3–81b) to Slide 1 and then delete it from Slide 2. Decrease the size of this illustration so that it measures approximately

Continued >

In the Labs *continued*

1.71" × 1.87" and then move it to the location shown in Figure 3–81a. Apply the Fly In 'From Top–Right' entrance effect to the illustration, change the Start timing setting to After Previous, and then change the duration to 02.50.

3. Increase the title text font on Slide 1 to 72 point, bold the text, and then change the color of the title text font to Red (in Standard Colors). Decrease the size of the title text placeholder to approximately 1.65" × 7.62" and then position the title on top of the red rectangle. Apply the Fly In entrance effect with the From Top direction to the title, change the Start timing option to After Previous, and then change the duration to 02.50.
4. On Slide 1, change the shape fill color of the red rectangle to Lime, Accent 1 (in first Theme Colors row). Decrease the size of the rectangle shape to approximately 1.7" × 6.96", as shown in the figure. Increase the font size of the three paragraphs in the rectangle shape to 28 point and then bold this text.
5. On Slide 1, apply the Appear entrance effect to the first paragraph in the list and then change the start timing option to After Previous and the duration to 02.50. Apply the same animation settings for the second and third paragraphs in the list.
6. On Slide 2 (Figure 3–81b), move the video to the right side of the slide, increase the size to approximately 5.84" × 8.2", apply the Beveled Oval, Black video style (in Moderate area) to the video, change the video border color to Red (in Standard Colors), and then change the border weight to 3 pt. Trim the video so that the End Time is 00:17.88. Change the volume to High and then start the video automatically.
7. On Slide 2 (Figure 3–81b), apply the Float In entrance effect to the title text and then change the direction to Float Down. Change the start timing option to With Previous and the duration to 03.00.
8. On Slide 3 (Figure 3–81c), apply the Shape entrance effect to the title text and then change the Start timing option to With Previous and the duration to 3.00.
9. On Slide 3, select the hummingbird and flowers illustration and zoom in to view the three pink flowers. Ungroup this illustration. Select the three pink flowers and change their fill color to Red (in Standard Colors). Delete the three green leaves in the middle of the dark green stem.

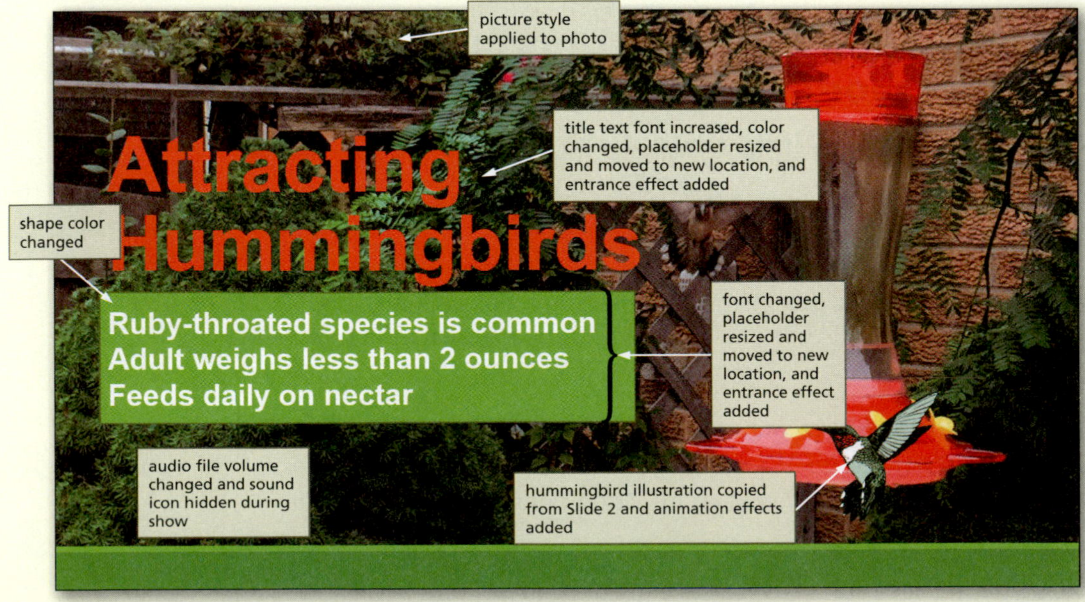

(a) Slide 1

Figure 3–81a

(b) Slide 2

Figure 3–81b

(c) Slide 3

Figure 3–81c

Regroup the illustration, increase the size to approximately 3.14" × 4.85", and then zoom out and move it to the area shown in the figure.

10. On Slide 3, apply the Reflected Bevel, White picture style to the flower picture. Resize the picture to approximately 3.1" × 4.17" and then move it to the right side of the slide, as shown in the figure. Apply the Zoom entrance effect to this picture. Change the Start timing option to On Click and the duration to 2.00.
11. If requested by your instructor, insert a text box at the lower-right corner of Slide 2 and type the color of your eyes in the text box.
12. Change the transition to None for all slides.

Continued >

In the Labs *continued*

13. View the presentation and then save the file using the file name, Lab 3–2 Attracting Hummingbirds.
14. Submit the revised document in the format specified by your instructor.
15. In Step 9, you changed the color of the three flowers from pink to red. Why? Why did you change the volume of the audio file to High?

Lab 3: Consider This: Your Turn

Design and Create a Presentation about Winter Bird Feeding

Note: To complete this assignment, you will be required to use the Data Files. Please contact your instructor for information about accessing the Data Files.

Part 1: Winter storms in cold climates can affect wild birds. Ice and deep snow reduce the natural food supply, and birds, consequently, have a difficult time surviving and thriving. People can help the birds by buying or making feeders, hanging them in the backyard, and keeping them clean and full. Nutritious winter seed foods include mixes of black oil sunflowers, hulled peanuts, and white millet. Suet and peanut butter are high-energy foods that help the birds stay warm. Providing water also helps the birds from becoming dehydrated. Place the feeders at least 10 feet from shrubs and compact the snow beneath them. Use the concepts and techniques presented in this module to create a presentation with this information to show at your local garden center. Select a suitable theme, change the theme colors, and then include a title slide, photos, and illustration. The Data Files contain a video called Birds in Winter and photos and illustrations called Bird Feeder, Red Jay, and Birds in Tree. Trim the video file and add a style. The illustration can be ungrouped, and you can change the color of it and the photos to add some visual interest to the presentation. Add animation to the slide content using effects and timing. Review and revise your presentation as needed and then save the file using the file name, Lab 3-3 Winter Bird Feeding. Submit your assignment in the format specified by your instructor.

Part 2: You made several decisions while creating the presentation in this assignment: selecting a theme and changing the theme colors, coloring and adding effects to the illustration and photos, trimming the video and adding a style, and adding animation. What was the rationale behind each of these decisions? When you reviewed the document, what further revisions did you make and why? Where would you recommend showing this slide show?

1 Creating a Worksheet and a Chart

Objectives

You will have mastered the material in this module when you can:

- Describe the Excel worksheet
- Enter text and numbers
- Use the Sum button to sum a range of cells
- Enter a simple function
- Copy the contents of a cell to a range of cells using the fill handle
- Apply cell styles
- Format cells in a worksheet
- Create a 3-D pie chart
- Change a worksheet name and sheet tab color
- Change document properties
- Preview and print a worksheet
- Use the AutoCalculate area to display statistics
- Correct errors on a worksheet

Introduction

Almost every organization collects vast amounts of data. Often, data is consolidated into a summary so that people in the organization better understand the meaning of the data. An Excel worksheet allows data to be summarized and charted easily. A **chart** conveys a visual representation of data. In this module, you will create a worksheet that includes a chart. The data in the worksheet and chart comprise a personal budget that contains monthly estimates for each income and expense category.

Project — Personal Budget Worksheet and Chart

The project in this module follows proper design guidelines and uses Excel to create the worksheet and chart shown in Figure 1–1a and Figure 1–1b. The worksheet contains budget data for Linda Fox. She has compiled a list of her expenses and sources of income and wants to use this information to create an easy-to-read worksheet to see how much she will be ahead or behind each month. In addition, she would like a 3-D pie chart to show her estimated expenses by category for each of the 12 months.

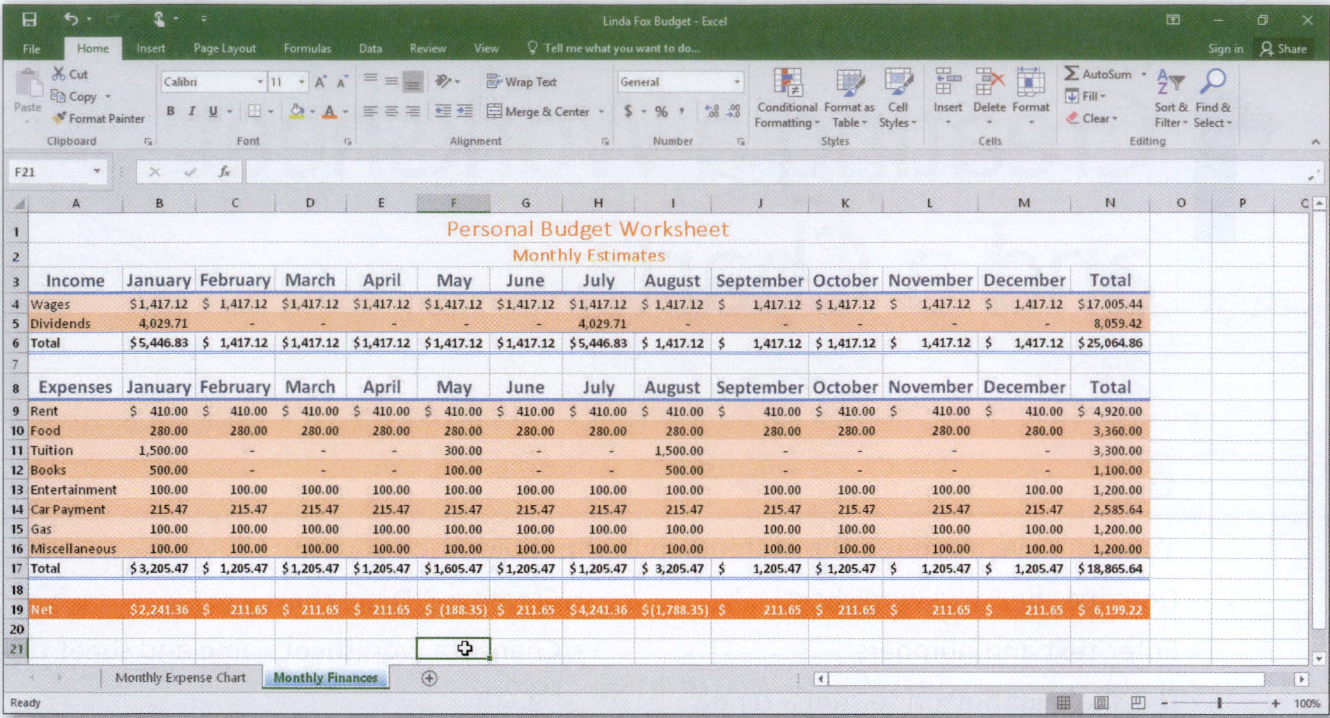

Personal Budget Worksheet													
Monthly Estimates													
Income	January	February	March	April	May	June	July	August	September	October	November	December	Total
Wages	$1,417.12	$ 1,417.12	$1,417.12	$1,417.12	$1,417.12	$1,417.12	$1,417.12	$ 1,417.12	$ 1,417.12	$ 1,417.12	$ 1,417.12	$ 1,417.12	$17,005.44
Dividends	4,029.71	-	-	-	-	-	4,029.71	-	-	-	-	-	8,059.42
Total	$5,446.83	$ 1,417.12	$1,417.12	$1,417.12	$1,417.12	$1,417.12	$5,446.83	$ 1,417.12	$ 1,417.12	$ 1,417.12	$ 1,417.12	$ 1,417.12	$25,064.86
Expenses	January	February	March	April	May	June	July	August	September	October	November	December	Total
Rent	$ 410.00	$ 410.00	$ 410.00	$ 410.00	$ 410.00	$ 410.00	$ 410.00	$ 410.00	$ 410.00	$ 410.00	$ 410.00	$ 410.00	$ 4,920.00
Food	280.00	280.00	280.00	280.00	280.00	280.00	280.00	280.00	280.00	280.00	280.00	280.00	3,360.00
Tuition	1,500.00	-	-	-	300.00	-	-	1,500.00	-	-	-	-	3,300.00
Books	500.00	-	-	-	100.00	-	-	500.00	-	-	-	-	1,100.00
Entertainment	100.00	100.00	100.00	100.00	100.00	100.00	100.00	100.00	100.00	100.00	100.00	100.00	1,200.00
Car Payment	215.47	215.47	215.47	215.47	215.47	215.47	215.47	215.47	215.47	215.47	215.47	215.47	2,585.64
Gas	100.00	100.00	100.00	100.00	100.00	100.00	100.00	100.00	100.00	100.00	100.00	100.00	1,200.00
Miscellaneous	100.00	100.00	100.00	100.00	100.00	100.00	100.00	100.00	100.00	100.00	100.00	100.00	1,200.00
Total	$3,205.47	$ 1,205.47	$1,205.47	$1,205.47	$1,605.47	$1,205.47	$1,205.47	$ 3,205.47	$ 1,205.47	$ 1,205.47	$ 1,205.47	$ 1,205.47	$18,865.64
Net	$2,241.36	$ 211.65	$ 211.65	$ 211.65	$ (188.35)	$ 211.65	$4,241.36	$(1,788.35)	$ 211.65	$ 211.65	$ 211.65	$ 211.65	$ 6,199.22

Figure 1–1(a) Personal Budget Worksheet

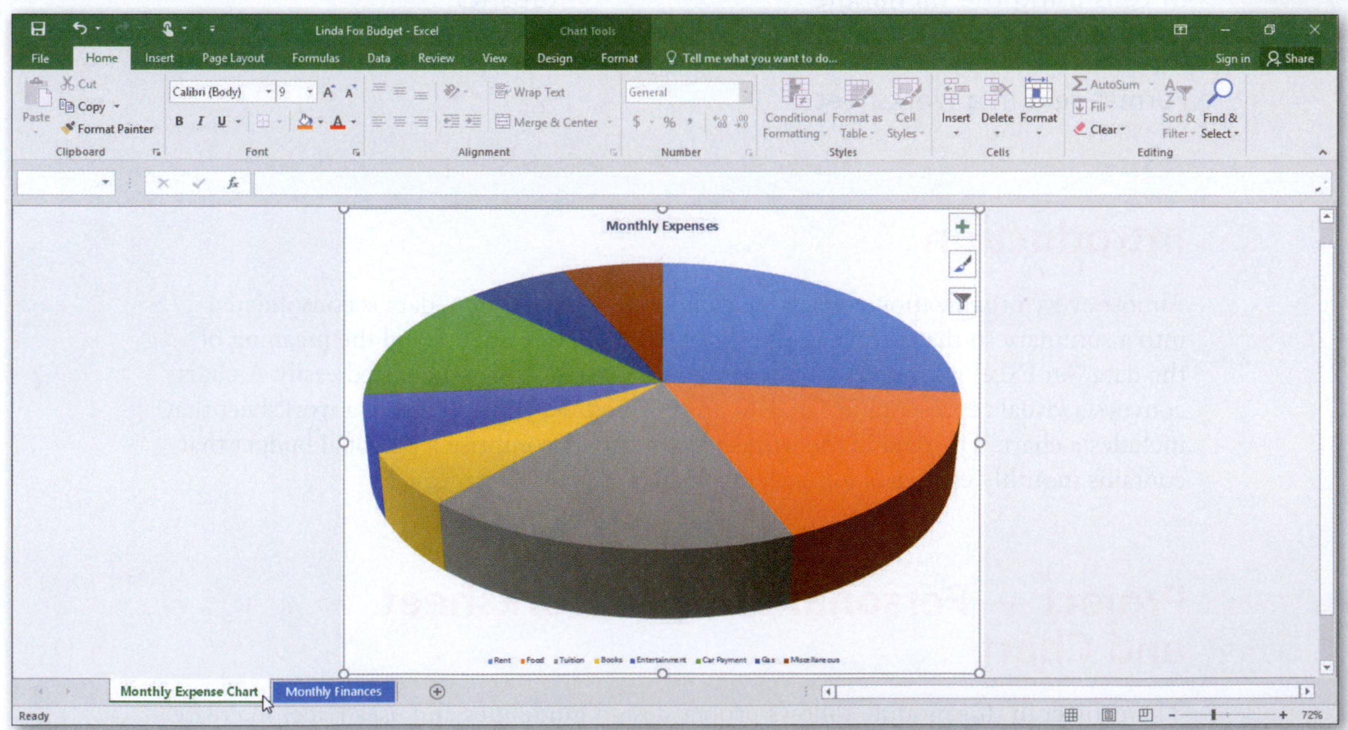

Figure 1–1(b) Pie Chart Showing Monthly Expenses by Category

The first step in creating an effective worksheet is to make sure you understand what is required. The person or persons requesting the worksheet may supply their requirements in a requirements document, or you can create one. A requirements document includes a needs statement, a source of data, a summary of calculations, and any other special requirements for the worksheet, such as charting and web support. Figure 1–2 shows the requirements document for the new workbook to be created in this module.

Worksheet Title	Personal Budget Worksheet
Word	A yearly projection of Linda Fox's personal budget
Source of data	Data supplied by Linda Fox includes monthly estimates for income and expenses
Calculations	The following calculations must be made: 1. For each month, a total for income and expenses 2. For each budget item, a total for the item 3. For the year, total all income and expenses 4. Net = income – expenses

Figure 1–2

For an introduction to Windows and instructions about how to perform basic Windows tasks, read the Office and Windows module at the beginning of this book, where you can learn how to resize windows, change screen resolution, create folders, move and rename files, use Windows Help, and much more.

In this module, you will learn how to perform basic workbook tasks using Excel. The following roadmap identifies general activities you will perform as you progress through this module:

1. ENTER TEXT in a blank worksheet.
2. CALCULATE SUMS AND USE FORMULAS in the worksheet.
3. FORMAT TEXT in the worksheet.
4. INSERT a pie CHART into the worksheet.
5. Assign a NAME to the sheet TAB.
6. PREVIEW AND PRINT the WORKSHEET.

CONSIDER THIS

Why is it important to plan a worksheet?

The key to developing a useful worksheet is careful planning. Careful planning can reduce your effort significantly and result in a worksheet that is accurate, easy to read, flexible, and useful. When analyzing a problem and designing a worksheet solution, what steps should you follow?

- Define the problem, including need, source of data, calculations, charting, and web or special requirements.
- Design the worksheet.
- Enter the data and formulas.
- Test the worksheet.

After carefully reviewing the requirements document (Figure 1–2) and making the necessary decisions, the next step is to design a solution or draw a sketch of the worksheet based on the requirements, including titles, column and row headings, the location of data values, and the 3-D pie chart, as shown in Figure 1–3. The dollar signs and commas that you see in the sketch of the worksheet indicate formatted numeric values.

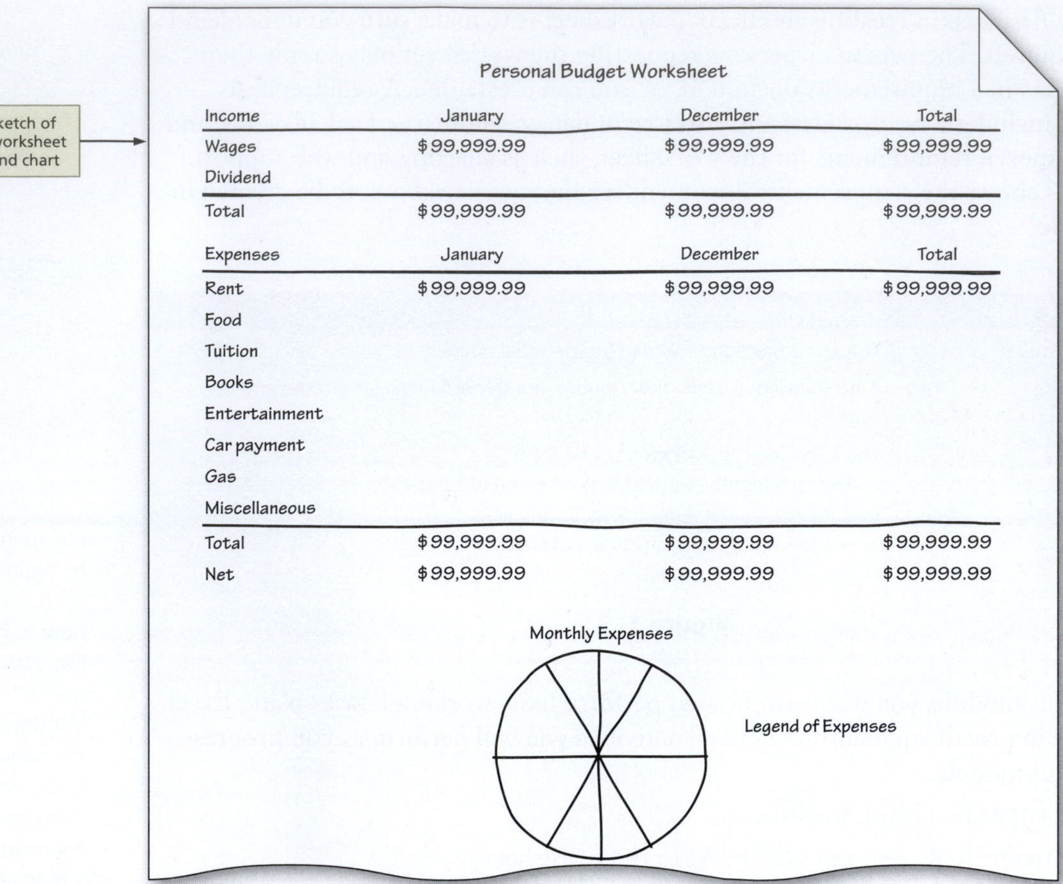

Figure 1–3

For an introduction to Office and instructions about how to perform basic tasks in Office apps, read the Office and Windows module at the beginning of this book, where you can learn how to run an application, use the ribbon, save a file, open a file, print a file, exit an application, use Help, and much more.

With a good understanding of the requirements document, an understanding of the necessary decisions, and a sketch of the worksheet, the next step is to use Excel to create the worksheet and chart.

Selecting a Cell

To enter data into a cell, you first must select it. The easiest way to **select** a cell (make it active) is to use the mouse to move the block plus sign pointer to the cell and then click.

An alternative method is to use the arrow keys that are located just to the right of the alphanumeric keys on a standard keyboard. An arrow key selects the cell adjacent to the active cell in the direction of the arrow on the key.

You know a cell is selected, or active, when a heavy border surrounds the cell and the active cell reference appears in the Name box on the left side of the formula bar. Excel also changes the color of the active cell's column and row headings to a darker shade.

BTW
Touch Screen Differences
The Office and Windows interfaces may vary if you are using a touch screen. For this reason, you might notice that the function or appearance of your touch screen differs slightly from this module's presentation.

Entering Text

In Excel, any set of characters containing a letter, hyphen (as in a telephone number), or space is considered **text**. Text is used for titles, such as column and row titles, on the worksheet.

Worksheet titles and subtitles should be as brief and meaningful as possible. A worksheet title could include the name of the organization, department, or a description of the content of the worksheet. A worksheet subtitle, if included, could include a more detailed description of the content of the worksheet. Examples of worksheet titles are January 2018 Payroll and Year 2018 Projected Budget, and examples of subtitles are Finance Department and Monthly Projections, respectively.

As shown in Figure 1–4, data in a worksheet is identified by row and column titles so that the meaning of each entry is clear. Rows typically contain information such as categories of data. Columns typically describe how data is grouped in the worksheet, such as by month or by department.

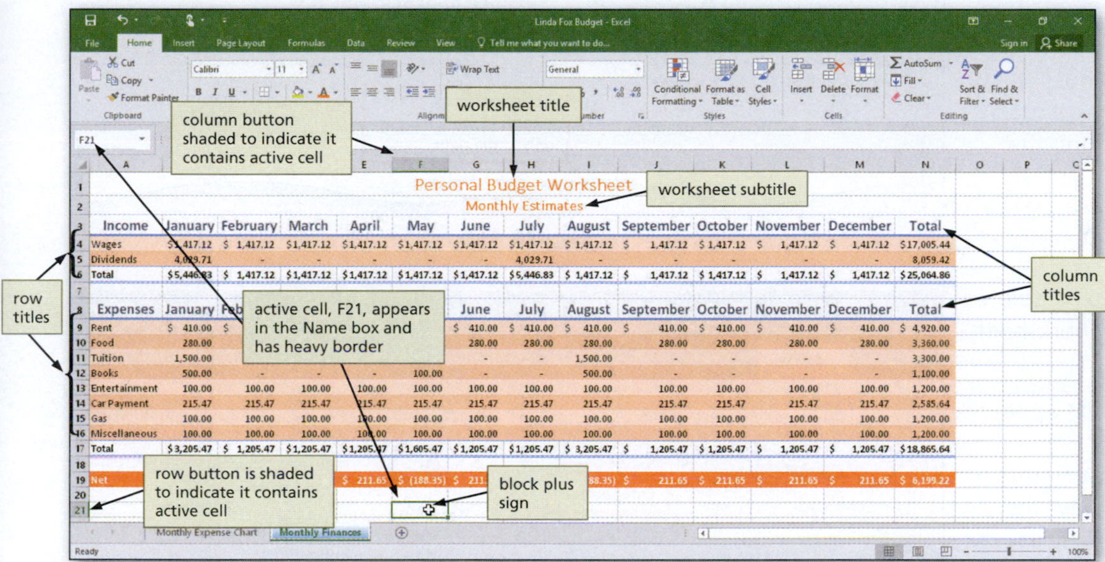

Figure 1–4

BTW

Excel Screen Resolution

If you are using a computer to step through the project in this module and you want your screens to match the figures in this book, you should change your screen's resolution to 1366 x 768. For information about how to change a computer's resolution, refer to the Office and Windows module at the beginning of this book.

To Enter the Worksheet Titles

1 ENTER TEXT | 2 CALCULATE SUMS & USE FORMULAS | 3 FORMAT TEXT
4 INSERT CHART | 5 NAME TAB | 6 PREVIEW & PRINT WORKSHEET

As shown in Figure 1–4, the worksheet title, Personal Budget Worksheet, identifies the purpose of the worksheet. The worksheet subtitle, Monthly Estimates, identifies the type of data contained in the worksheet. ***Why?*** *A title and subtitle help the reader to understand clearly what the worksheet contains.* The following steps enter the worksheet titles in cells A1 and A2. Later in this module, the worksheet titles will be formatted so that they appear as shown in Figure 1–4.

1

- Run Excel and create a blank workbook in the Excel window.
- If necessary, click cell A1 to make cell A1 the active cell (Figure 1–5).

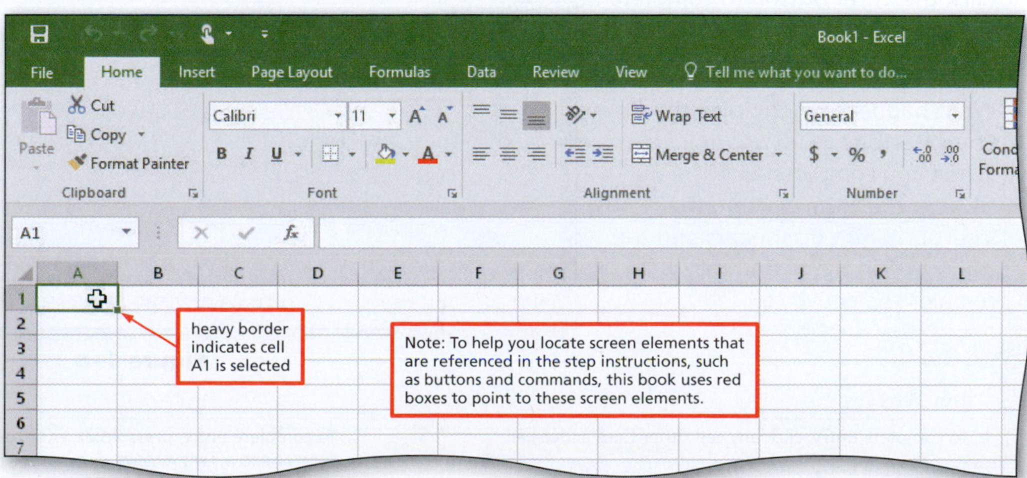

Figure 1–5

2

- Type **Personal Budget Worksheet** in cell A1 (Figure 1–6).

Q&A Why did the appearance of the formula bar change?
Excel displays the title in the formula bar and in cell A1. When you begin typing a cell entry, Excel enables two additional boxes in the formula bar: the Cancel button and the Enter button. Clicking the Enter button completes an entry. Clicking the Cancel button cancels an entry.

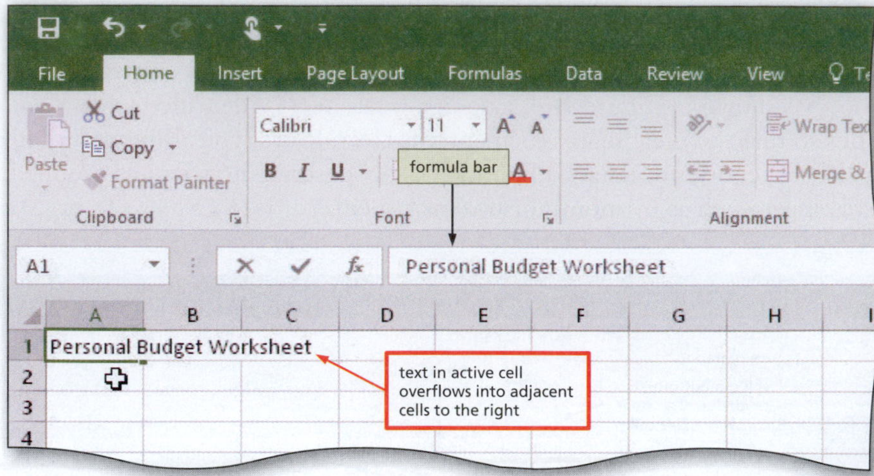

Figure 1–6

- Click the Enter button to complete the entry and enter the worksheet title (Figure 1–7).

Q&A Why does the entered text appear in three cells?
When the text is longer than the width of a cell, Excel displays the overflow characters in adjacent cells to the right as long as those adjacent cells contain no data. If the adjacent cells contain data, Excel hides the overflow characters. The overflow characters are visible in the formula bar whenever that cell is active.

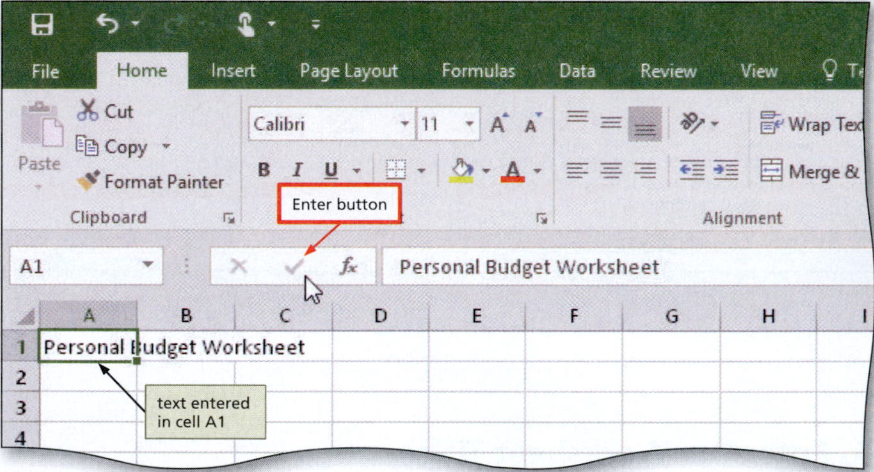

Figure 1–7

- Click cell A2 to select it.
- Type **Monthly Estimates** as the cell entry.
- Click the Enter button to complete the entry and enter the worksheet subtitle (Figure 1–8).

Q&A What happens when I click the Enter button?
When you complete an entry by clicking the Enter button, the insertion point disappears and the cell in which the text is entered remains the active cell.

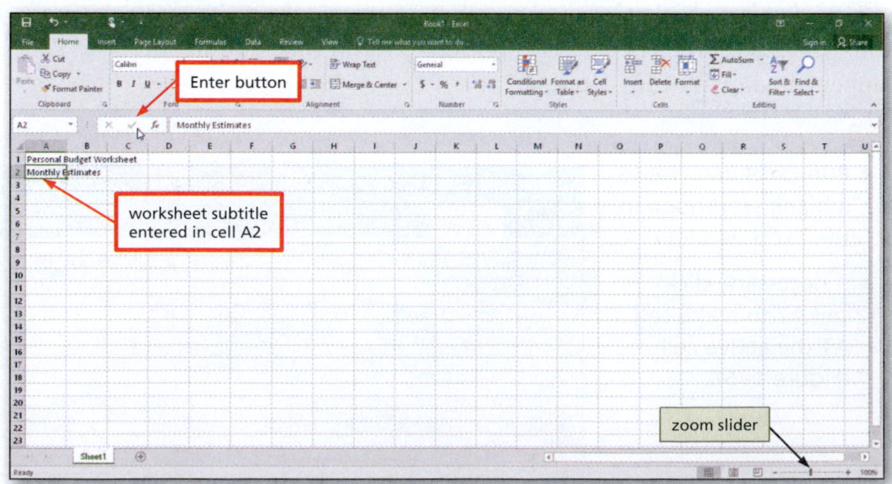

Figure 1–8

Other Ways

1. To complete entry, click any cell other than active cell
2. To complete entry, press ENTER
3. To complete entry, press HOME, PAGE UP, PAGE DOWN, END, UP ARROW, DOWN ARROW, LEFT ARROW, or RIGHT ARROW

CONSIDER THIS

Why is it difficult to read the text on my screen?
If you are having trouble reading the cell values in your spreadsheet, you can zoom in to make the cells larger. When you zoom in, fewer columns and rows display on your screen, and you might have to scroll more often. To zoom in, drag the zoom slider on the right of the status bar, or click the plus button on the zoom slider, until you reach your desired zoom level. In addition to the zoom slider, you also can zoom by clicking the Zoom button (View tab | Zoom group), selecting a desired zoom percentage (Zoom dialog box), and then clicking the OK button (Zoom dialog box).

AutoCorrect

The **AutoCorrect** feature of Excel works behind the scenes, correcting common mistakes when you complete a text entry in a cell. AutoCorrect makes three types of corrections for you:

1. Corrects two initial uppercase letters by changing the second letter to lowercase.
2. Capitalizes the first letter in the names of days.
3. Replaces commonly misspelled words with their correct spelling. For example, it will change the misspelled word *recieve* to *receive* when you complete the entry. AutoCorrect will correct the spelling of hundreds of commonly misspelled words automatically.

BTW
The Ribbon and Screen Resolution
Excel may change how the groups and buttons within the groups appear on the ribbon, depending on the computer's screen resolution. Thus, your ribbon may look different from the ones in this book if you are using a screen resolution other than 1366 x 768.

To Enter Column Titles

1 ENTER TEXT | 2 CALCULATE SUMS & USE FORMULAS | 3 FORMAT TEXT
4 INSERT CHART | 5 NAME TAB | 6 PREVIEW & PRINT WORKSHEET

The worksheet is divided into two parts, income and expense, as shown in Figure 1–4. Grouping income and expense data by month is a common method for organizing budget data. The column titles shown in row 3 identify the income section of the worksheet and indicate that the income values will be grouped by month. Likewise, row 8 is clearly identified as the expense section and similarly indicates that the expense values will be estimated on a per month basis. The following steps enter the column titles in row 3. ***Why?*** *Data entered in columns should be identified using column titles to identify what the column contains.*

- Click cell A3 to make it the active cell.
- Type **Income** to begin entry of a column title in the active cell (Figure 1–9).

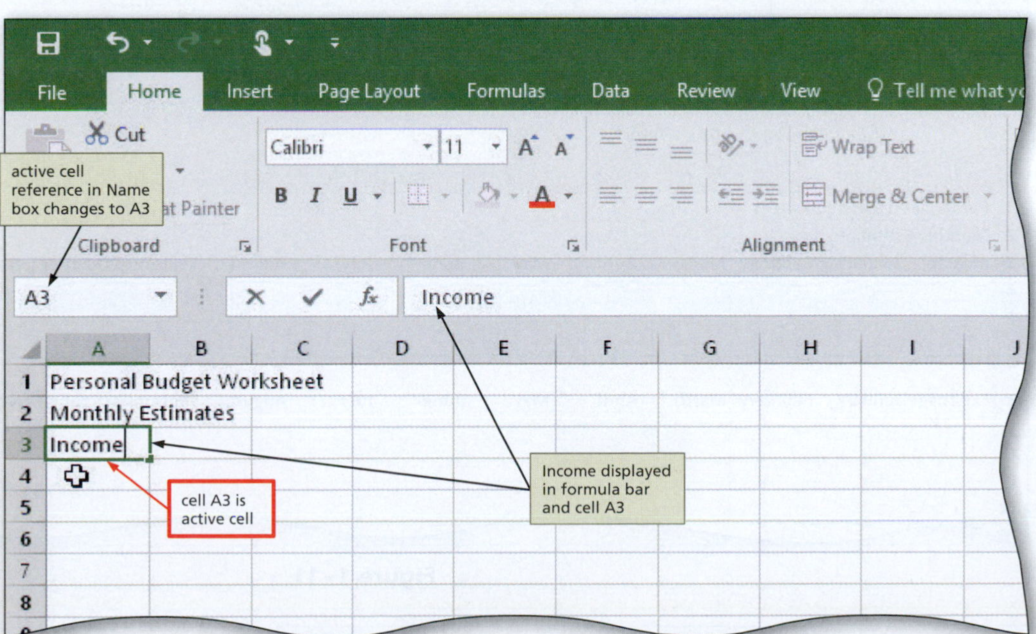

Figure 1–9

2

- Press the RIGHT ARROW key to enter the column title and make the cell to the right the active cell (Figure 1–10).

Q&A Why is the RIGHT ARROW key used to complete the entry in the cell?
Pressing an arrow key to complete an entry makes the adjacent cell in the direction of the arrow (up, down, left, or right) the next active cell. However, if your next entry is in a nonadjacent cell, you can complete your current entry by clicking the next cell in which you plan to enter data. You also can press the ENTER key and then click the appropriate cell for the next entry.

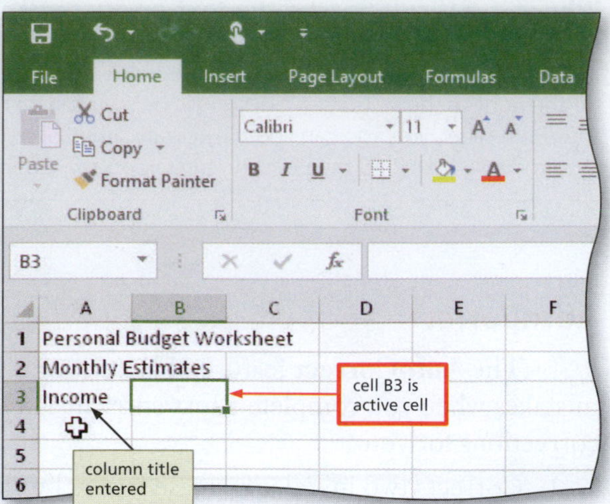

Figure 1–10

3

- Repeat Steps 1 and 2 to enter the remaining column titles; that is, enter `January` in cell B3, `February` in cell C3, `March` in cell D3, `April` in cell E3, `May` in cell F3, `June` in cell G3, `July` in cell H3, `August` in cell I3, `September` in cell J3, `October` in cell K3, `November` in cell L3, `December` in cell M3, and `Total` in cell N3 (complete the last entry in cell N3 by clicking the Enter button in the formula bar).
- Click cell A8 to select it.
- Repeat Steps 1 and 2 to enter the remaining column titles; that is, enter `Expenses` in cell A8, `January` in cell B8, `February` in cell C8, `March` in cell D8, `April` in cell E8, `May` in cell F8, `June` in cell G8, `July` in cell H8, `August` in cell I8, `September` in cell J8, `October` in cell K8, `November` in cell L8, `December` in cell M8, and `Total` in cell N8 (complete the last entry in cell N8 by clicking the Enter button in the formula bar) (Figure 1–11).

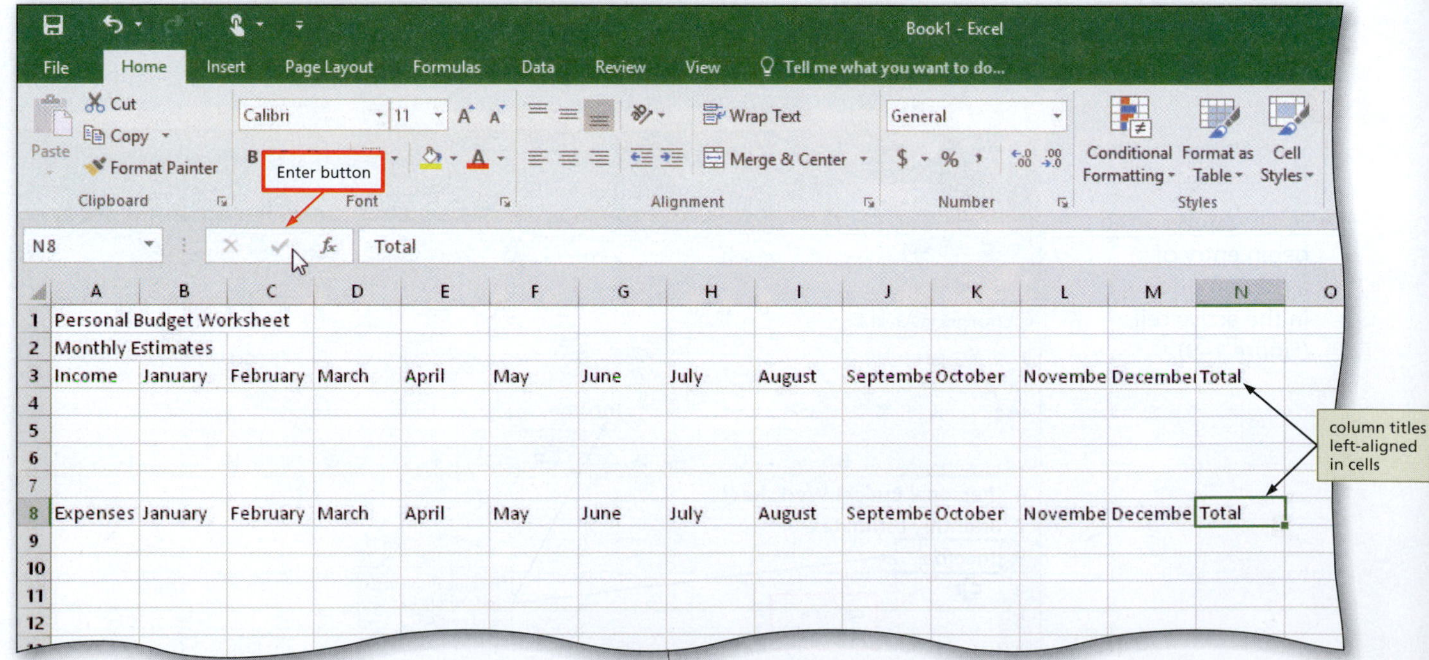

Figure 1–11

To Enter Row Titles

The next step in developing the worksheet for this project is to enter the row titles in column A. For the Personal Budget Worksheet data, the row titles contain a list of income types and expense types. Each income or expense item should be placed in its own row. ***Why?*** *Entering one item per row allows for maximum flexibility, in case more income or expense items are added in the future.* The following steps enter the row titles in the worksheet.

1

- Click cell A4 to select it.
- Type `Wages` and then click cell A5 or press the DOWN ARROW key to enter a row title (Figure 1–12).

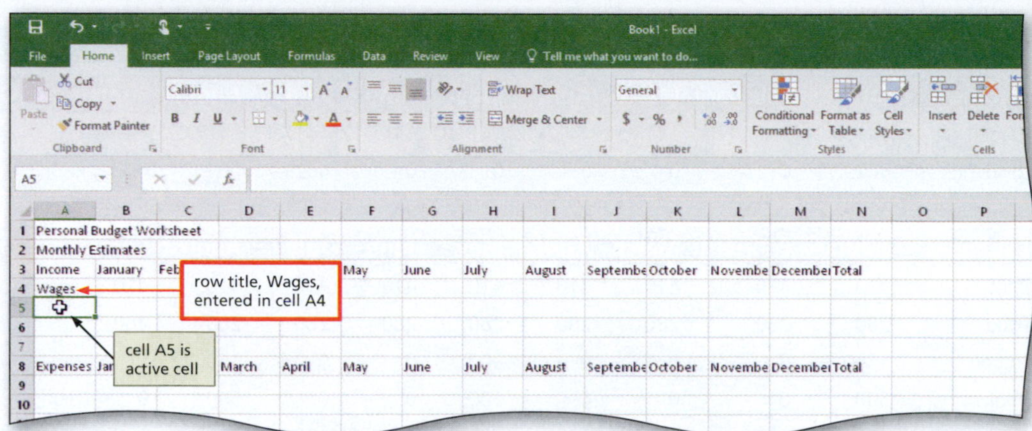

Figure 1–12

2

- Repeat Step 1 to enter the remaining row titles in column A; that is, enter `Dividends` in cell A5, `Total` in cell A6, `Rent` in cell A9, `Food` in cell A10, `Tuition` in cell A11, `Books` in cell A12, `Entertainment` in cell A13, `Car Payment` in cell A14, `Gas` in cell A15, `Miscellaneous` in cell A16, `Total` in cell A17, and `Net` in cell A19 (Figure 1–13).

Q&A Why is the text left-aligned in the cells?
Excel automatically left-aligns the text in the cell. Excel treats any combination of numbers, spaces, and nonnumeric characters as text. For example, Excel would recognize the following entries as text: 401AX21, 921–231, 619 321, 883XTY. How to change the text alignment in a cell is discussed later in this module.

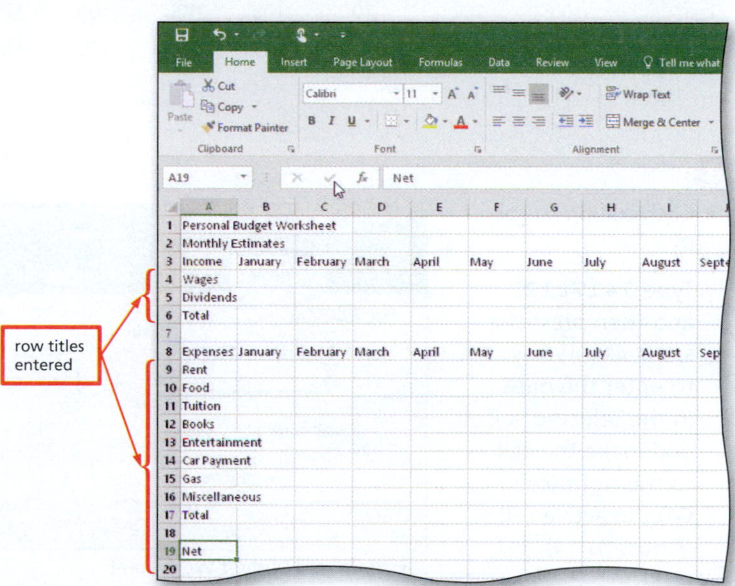

Figure 1–13

Entering Numbers

In Excel, you enter a **number** into a cell to represent an amount or value. A number can contain only the following characters:

0 1 2 3 4 5 6 7 8 9 + – ( ) , / . $ % E e

If a cell entry contains any other keyboard character (including spaces), Excel interprets the entry as text and treats it accordingly. The use of special characters is explained when they are used in this book.

To Enter Numbers

The Personal Budget Worksheet numbers used in Module 1 are summarized in Table 1–1. These numbers, which represent yearly income and expense amounts, are entered in rows 4–5 and 9–16. ***Why?*** *One of the most powerful features of Excel is the ability to perform calculations on numeric data. Before you can perform calculations, you first must enter the data.* The following steps enter the numbers in Table 1–1 one row at a time.

Table 1–1 Personal Budget Worksheet

Income	January	February	March	April	May	June	July	August	September	October	November	December
Wages	1417.12	1417.12	1417.12	1417.12	1417.12	1417.12	1417.12	1417.12	1417.12	1417.12	1417.12	1417.12
Dividends	4029.71	0	0	0	0	0	4029.71	0	0	0	0	0

Expenses	January	February	March	April	May	June	July	August	September	October	November	December
Rent	410	410	410	410	410	410	410	410	410	410	410	410
Food	280	280	280	280	280	280	280	280	280	280	280	280
Tuition	1500	0	0	0	300	0	0	1500	0	0	0	0
Books	500	0	0	0	100	0	0	500	0	0	0	0
Entertainment	100	100	100	100	100	100	100	100	100	100	100	100
Car Payment	215.47	215.47	215.47	215.47	215.47	215.47	215.47	215.47	215.47	215.47	215.47	215.47
Gas	100	100	100	100	100	100	100	100	100	100	100	100
Miscellaneous	100	100	100	100	100	100	100	100	100	100	100	100

1

- Click cell B4 to select it.
- Type `1417.12` and then press the RIGHT ARROW key to enter the data in the selected cell and make the cell to the right (cell C4) the active cell (Figure 1–14).

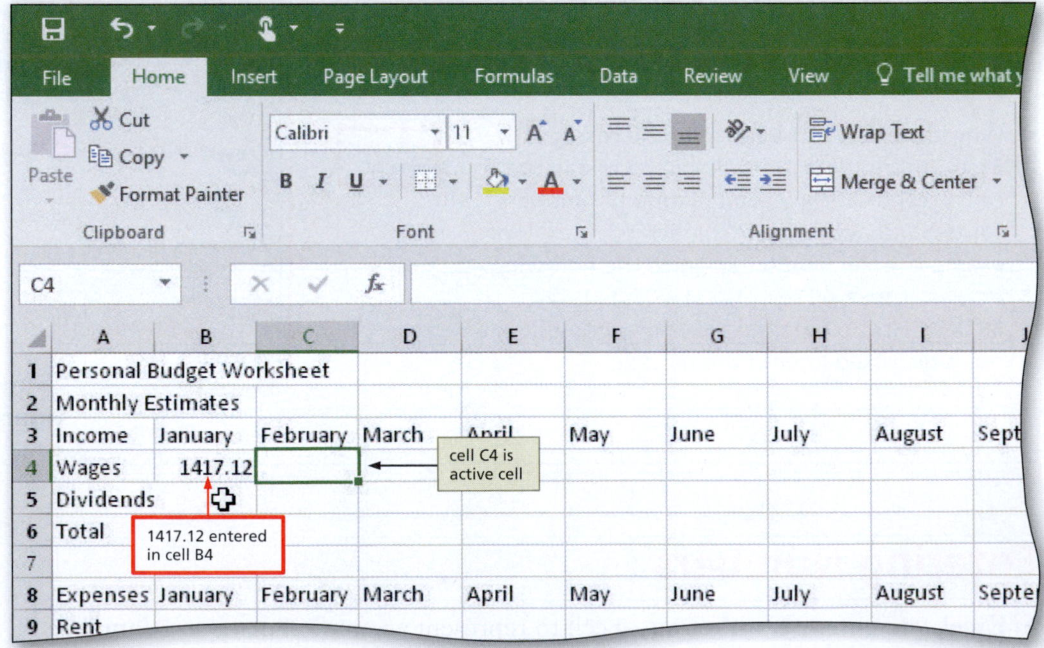

Figure 1–14

Q&A Do I need to enter dollar signs, commas, or trailing zeros for the amounts?
You are not required to type dollar signs, commas, or trailing zeros. When you enter a dollar value that has cents, however, you must add the decimal point and the numbers representing the cents. Later in this module, you will learn how to format numbers with dollar signs, commas, and trailing zeros to improve their appearance and readability.

2

- Enter `1417.12` in cells C4, D4, E4, F4, G4, H4, I4, J4, K4, L4, and M4 to complete the first row of numbers in the worksheet (Figure 1–15).

Q&A Why are the numbers right-aligned?
When you enter numeric data in a cell, Excel recognizes the values as numbers and automatically right-aligns the values in order to vertically align decimal and integer values.

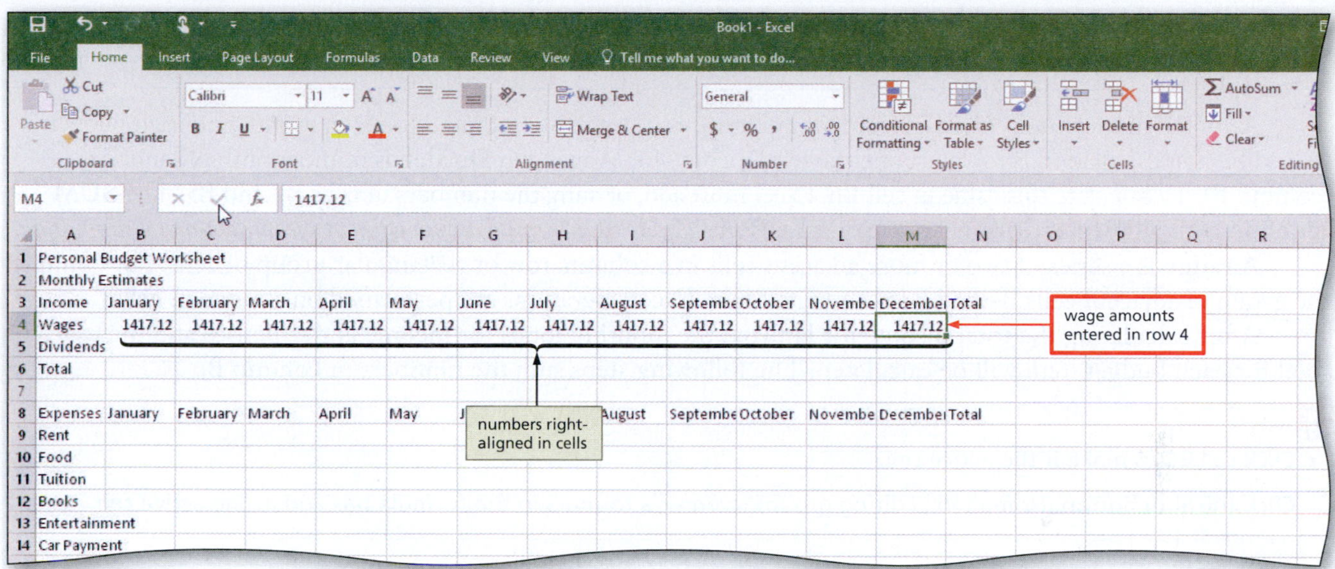

Figure 1–15

3

- Click cell B5 to select it and complete the entry in the previously selected cell.
- Enter the remaining numbers provided in Table 1–1 for each of the nine remaining budget items in row 5 and rows 9–16 (Figure 1–16).

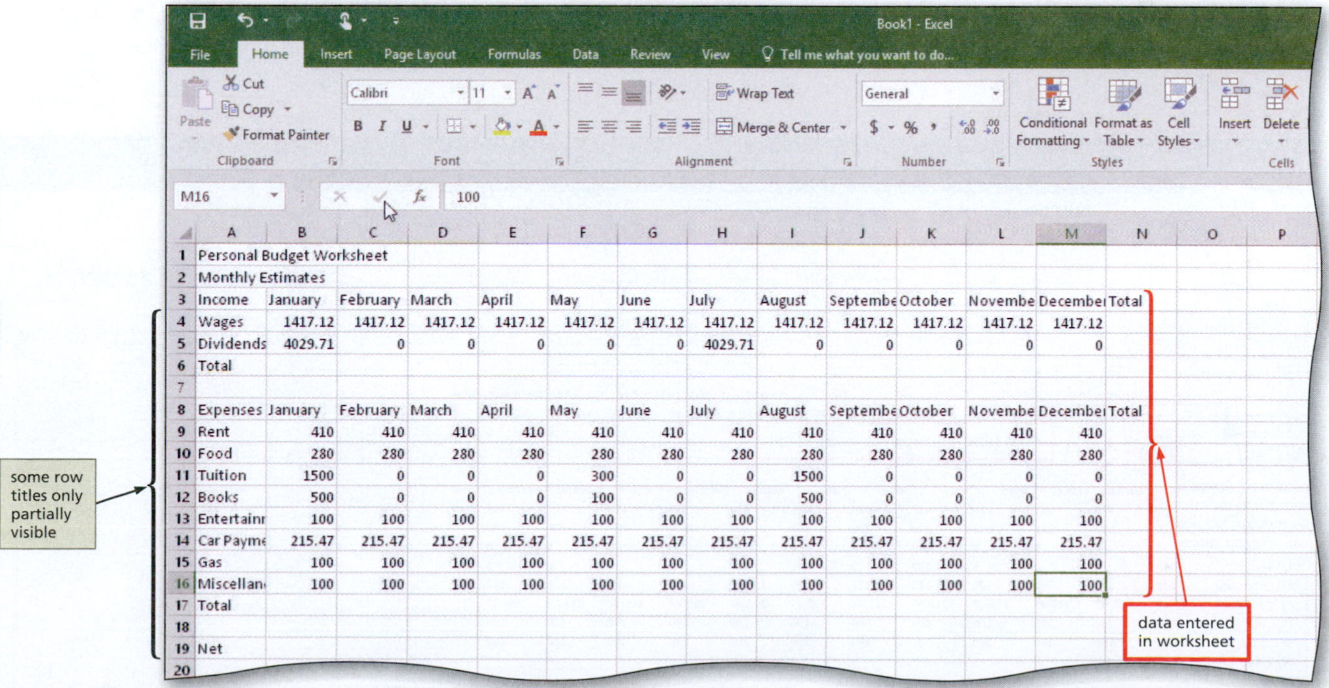

Figure 1–16

Calculating a Sum

The next step in creating the worksheet is to perform any necessary calculations, such as calculating the column and row totals. In Excel, you easily can perform calculations using a **function**, or a predefined formula. When you use functions, Excel performs the calculations for you, which helps to prevent errors and allows you to work more efficiently.

1 ENTER TEXT | **2 CALCULATE SUMS & USE FORMULAS** | 3 FORMAT TEXT
4 INSERT CHART | 5 NAME TAB | 6 PREVIEW & PRINT WORKSHEET

To Sum a Column of Numbers

As stated in the requirements document in Figure 1–2, totals are required for each month and each budget item. The first calculation is to determine the total income for Wages and Dividends in the month of January (column B). To calculate this value in cell B6, Excel must add, or sum, the numbers in cells B4 and B5. The **SUM function** adds all the numbers in a range of cells. ***Why?*** *Excel's SUM function is an efficient means to accomplish this task.*

A **range** is a series of two or more adjacent cells in a column, row or rectangular group of cells. For example, the group of adjacent cells B4 and B5 is a range. Many Excel operations are performed on a range of cells.

After calculating the total income for January, the monthly totals for income and expenses and the yearly total for each budget item will be calculated. The following steps sum the numbers in column B.

- Click cell B6 to make it the active cell.
- Click the Sum button (Home tab | Editing group) to enter a formula in the formula bar and in the active cell (Figure 1–17).

Q&A

What if my screen displays the Sum menu?
If you are using a touch screen, you may not have a separate Sum button and Sum arrow. In this case, select the desired option (Sum) on the Sum menu.

How does Excel know which cells to sum?
Excel automatically selects what it considers to be your choice of the range to sum. When proposing the range, Excel first looks for a range of cells with numbers above the active cell and then to the left. If Excel proposes the wrong range, you can correct it by dragging through the correct range before pressing the ENTER key. You also can enter the correct range by typing the beginning cell reference, a colon (:), and the ending cell reference.

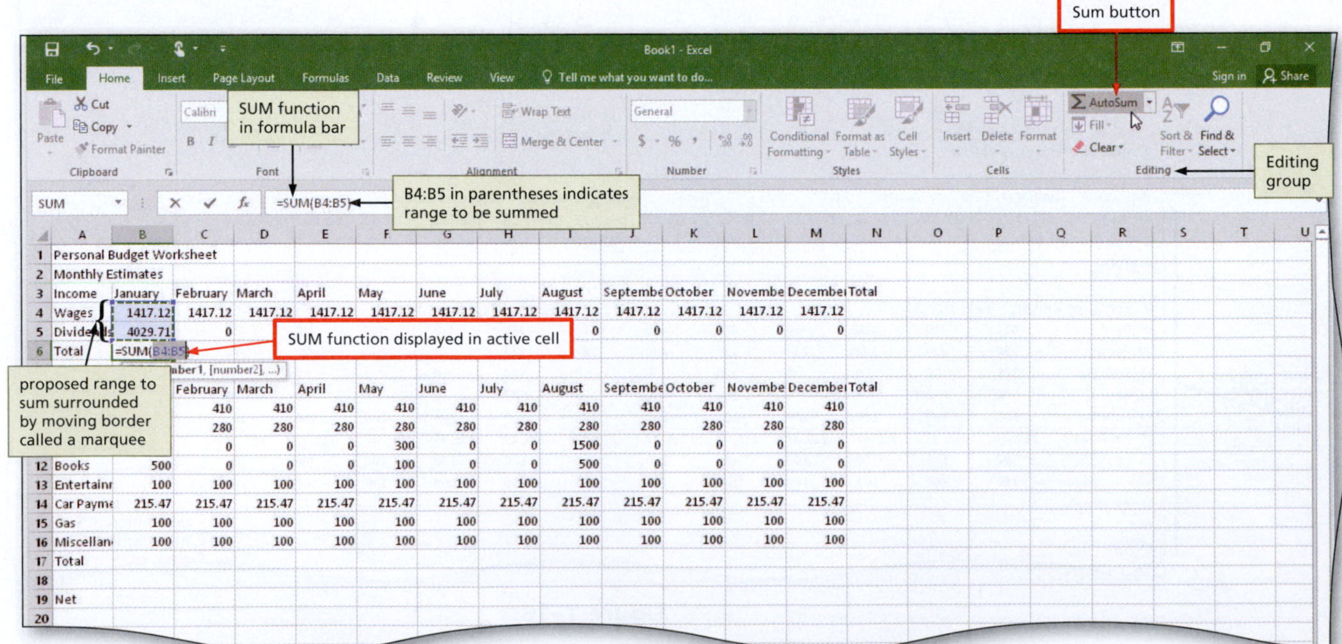

Figure 1–17

2

- Click the Enter button in the formula bar to enter the sum in the active cell.

Q&A What is the purpose of the arrow next to the Sum button on the ribbon?
The Sum arrow (shown in Figure 1–17) displays a list of functions that allow you to easily determine the average of a range of numbers, the number of items in a selected range, or the maximum or minimum value of a range.

3

- Repeat Steps 1 and 2 to enter the SUM function in cell B17 (Figure 1–18).

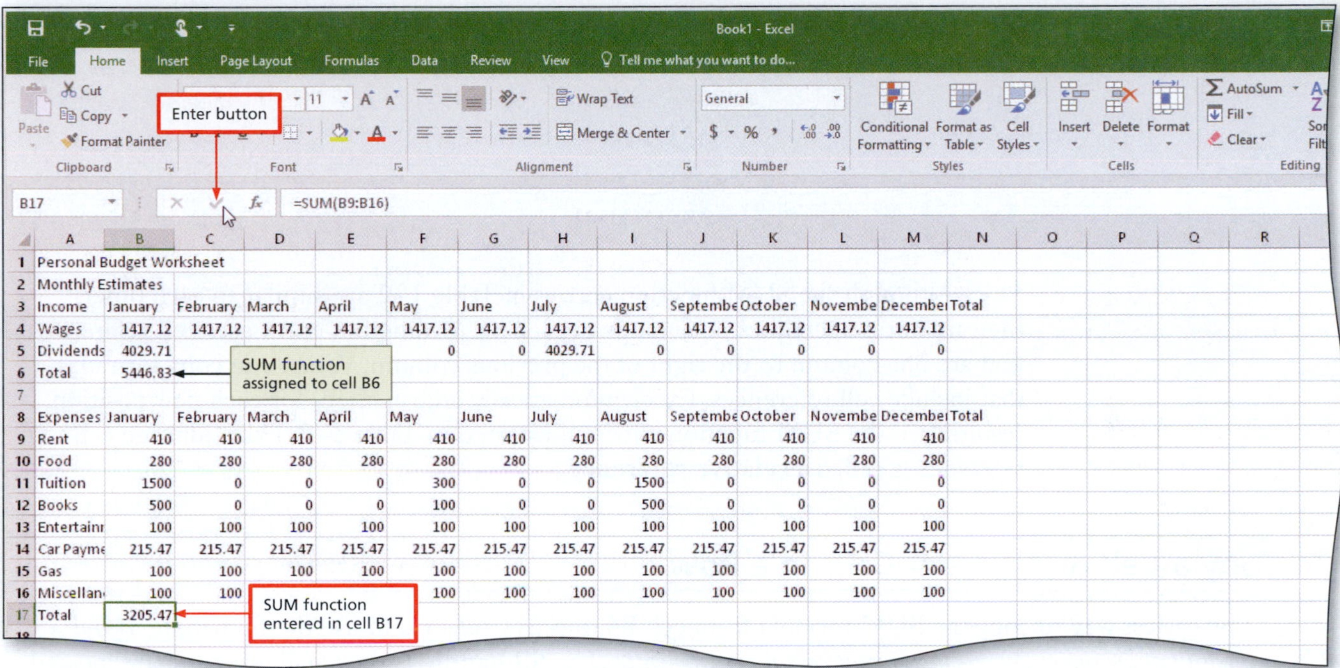

Figure 1–18

Other Ways

1. Click Insert Function button in formula bar, select SUM in Select a function list, click OK button (Insert Function dialog box), click OK button (Function Arguments dialog box)
2. Click Sum arrow (Home tab | Editing group), click More Functions in list, scroll to and then click SUM (Insert Function dialog box), click OK button, select range (Function Arguments dialog box), click OK button
3. Type **=S** in cell, select SUM in list, select range, click Enter button
4. Press ALT+EQUAL SIGN (=) twice

Using the Fill Handle to Copy a Cell to Adjacent Cells

You want to calculate the totals for income during each month in cells C6:M6. Table 1–2 illustrates the similarities between the function and range used in cell B6 and the function and ranges required to sum the totals in cells C6, D6, E6, F6, G6, H6, I6, J6, K6, L6, and M6.

To calculate each total for each range across the worksheet, you could follow the same steps shown previously in Figure 1–17 and Figure 1–18. A more efficient method, however, would be to copy the SUM function from cell B6 to the range C6:M6. The cell being copied is called the **source area** or **copy area**. The range of cells receiving the copy is called the **destination area** or **paste area**.

Table 1–2 Sum Function Entries in Row 6

Cell	SUM Function Entries	Result
B6	=SUM(B4:B5)	Sums cells B4 and B5
C6	=SUM(C4:C5)	Sums cells C4 and C5
D6	=SUM(D4:D5)	Sums cells D4 and D5
E6	=SUM(E4:E5)	Sums cells E4 and E5
F6	=SUM(F4:F5)	Sums cells F4 and F5
G6	=SUM(G4:G5)	Sums cells G4 and G5
H6	=SUM(H4:H5)	Sums cells H4 and H5
I6	=SUM(I4:I5)	Sums cells I4 and I5
J6	=SUM(J4:J5)	Sums cells J4 and J5
K6	=SUM(K4:K5)	Sums cells K4 and K5
L6	=SUM(L4:L5)	Sums cells L4 and L5
M6	=SUM(M4:M5)	Sums cells M4 and M5

Although the SUM function entries in Table 1–2 are similar to each other, they are not exact copies. The range in each SUM function entry uses cell references that are one column to the right of the previous column. When you copy formulas that include cell references, Excel automatically adjusts them for each new position, resulting in the SUM function entries illustrated in Table 1–2. Each adjusted cell reference is called a **relative reference**.

To Copy a Cell to Adjacent Cells in a Row

1 ENTER TEXT | **2 CALCULATE SUMS & USE FORMULAS** | 3 FORMAT TEXT
4 INSERT CHART | 5 NAME TAB | 6 PREVIEW & PRINT WORKSHEET

The easiest way to copy the SUM formula from cell B6 to cells C6:M6 is to use the fill handle. ***Why?*** *Using the fill handle copies content to adjacent cells more efficiently.* The **fill handle** is the small green square located in the lower-right corner of the heavy border around the active cell. The following steps use the fill handle to copy cell B6 to the adjacent cells C6:M6.

1

- With cell B6 active, point to the fill handle to activate it. Your pointer changes to a crosshair (Figure 1–19).

Q&A Why is my fill handle not a green square?
If you are using a touch screen, the fill handle appears as a black and white rectangle with a blue down arrow in it.

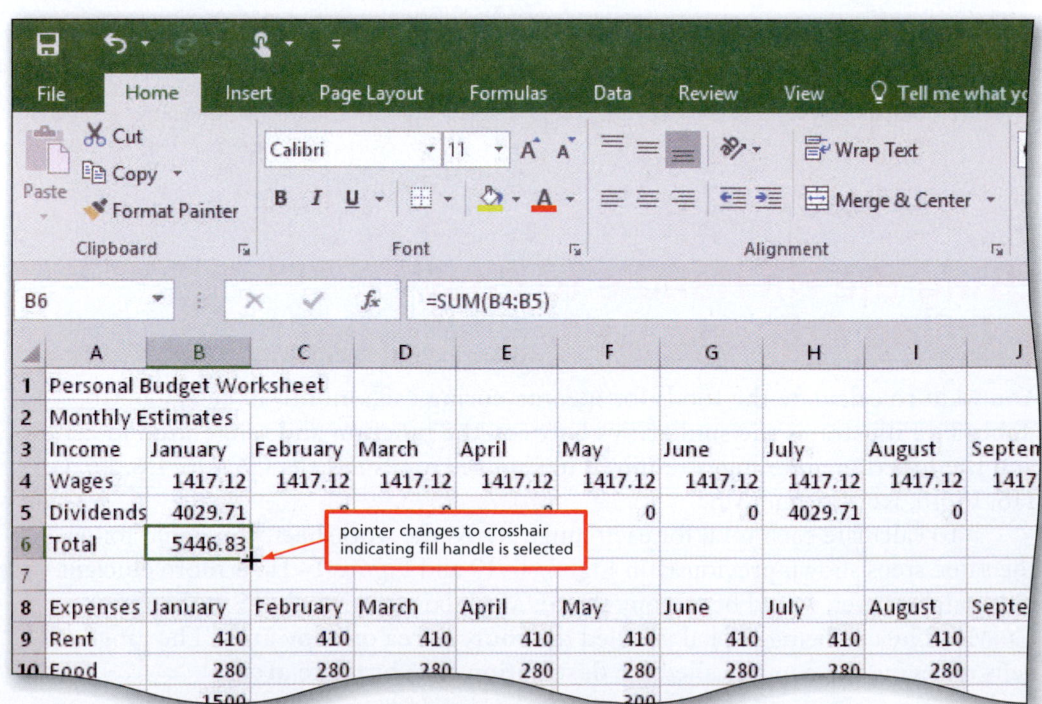

Figure 1–19

2

- Drag the fill handle to select the destination area, range C6:M6, which will draw a heavy green border around the source area and the destination area (Figure 1–20). Do not release the mouse button.

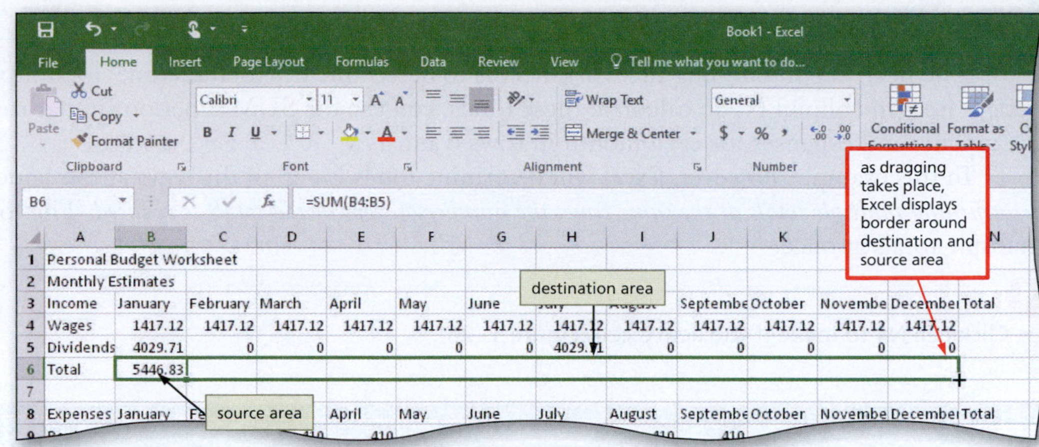

Figure 1–20

3

- Release the mouse button to copy the SUM function from the active cell to the destination area and calculate the sums (Figure 1–21).

Q&A What is the purpose of the 'Auto Fill Options' button?

The 'Auto Fill Options' button allows you to choose whether you want to copy the values from the source area to the destination area with the existing formatting, without the formatting, or with the formatting but without the functions.

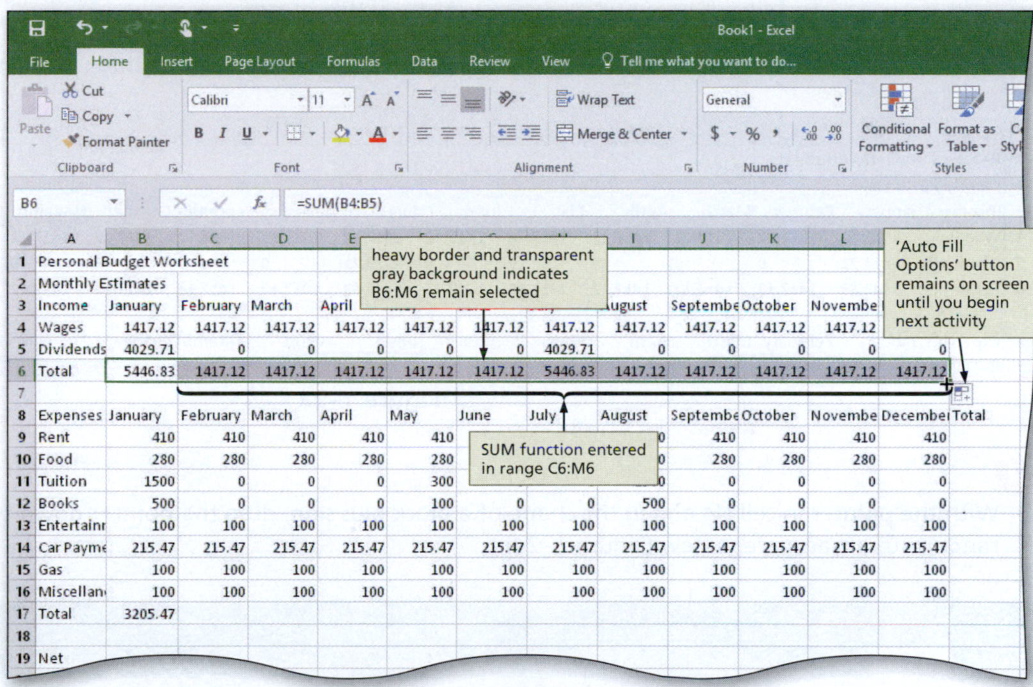

Figure 1–21

4

- Repeat Steps 1–3 to copy the SUM function from cell B17 to the range C17:M17 (Figure 1–22).

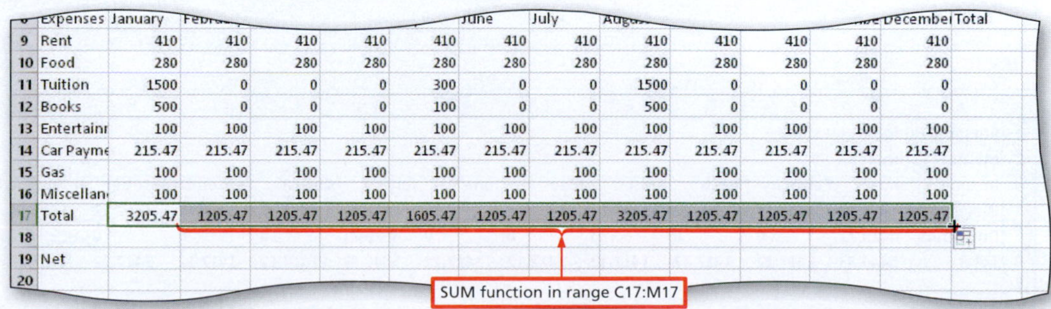

Figure 1–22

Other Ways

1. Select source area, click Copy button (Home tab | Clipboard group), select destination area, click Paste button (Home tab | Clipboard group)
2. Right-click source area, click Copy on shortcut menu, select and right-click destination area, click Paste on shortcut menu

To Calculate Multiple Totals at the Same Time

The next step in building the worksheet is to determine the total income, total expenses, and total for each budget item in column N. To calculate these totals, you use the SUM function similar to how you used it to total the income and expenses for each month in rows 6 and 17.

In this example, however, Excel will determine totals for all of the rows at the same time. ***Why?*** *By determining multiple totals at the same time, the number of steps to add totals is reduced.* The following steps sum multiple totals at once.

1

- Click cell N4 to make it the active cell (Figure 1–23).

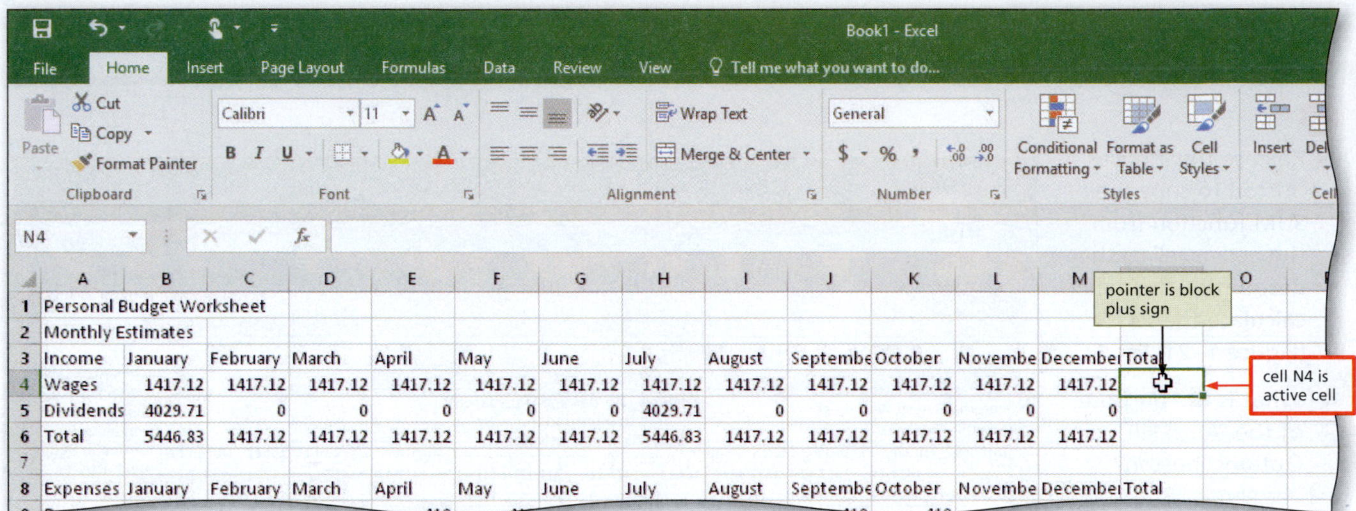

Figure 1–23

2

- With the pointer in cell N4 and in the shape of a block plus sign, drag the pointer down to cell N6 to highlight the range with a transparent view (Figure 1–24).

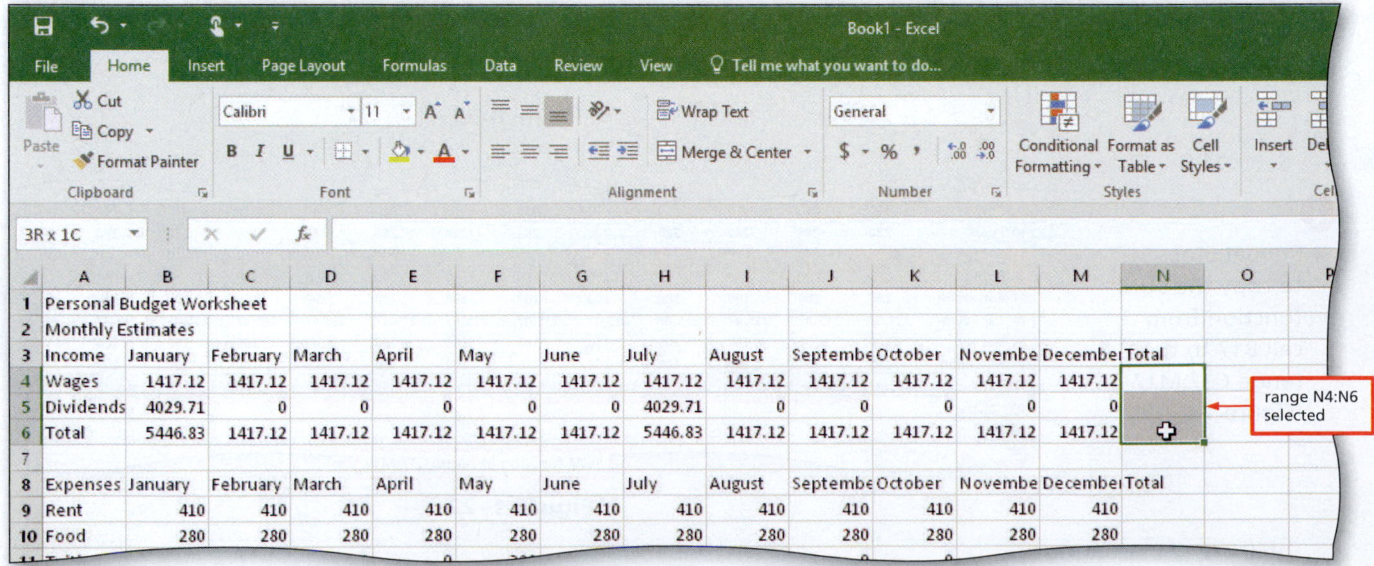

Figure 1–24

3

- Click the Sum button (Home tab | Editing group) to calculate the sums of the corresponding rows (Figure 1–25).

Q&A How does Excel create unique totals for each row?
If each cell in a selected range is adjacent to a row of numbers, Excel assigns the SUM function to each cell when you click the Sum button.

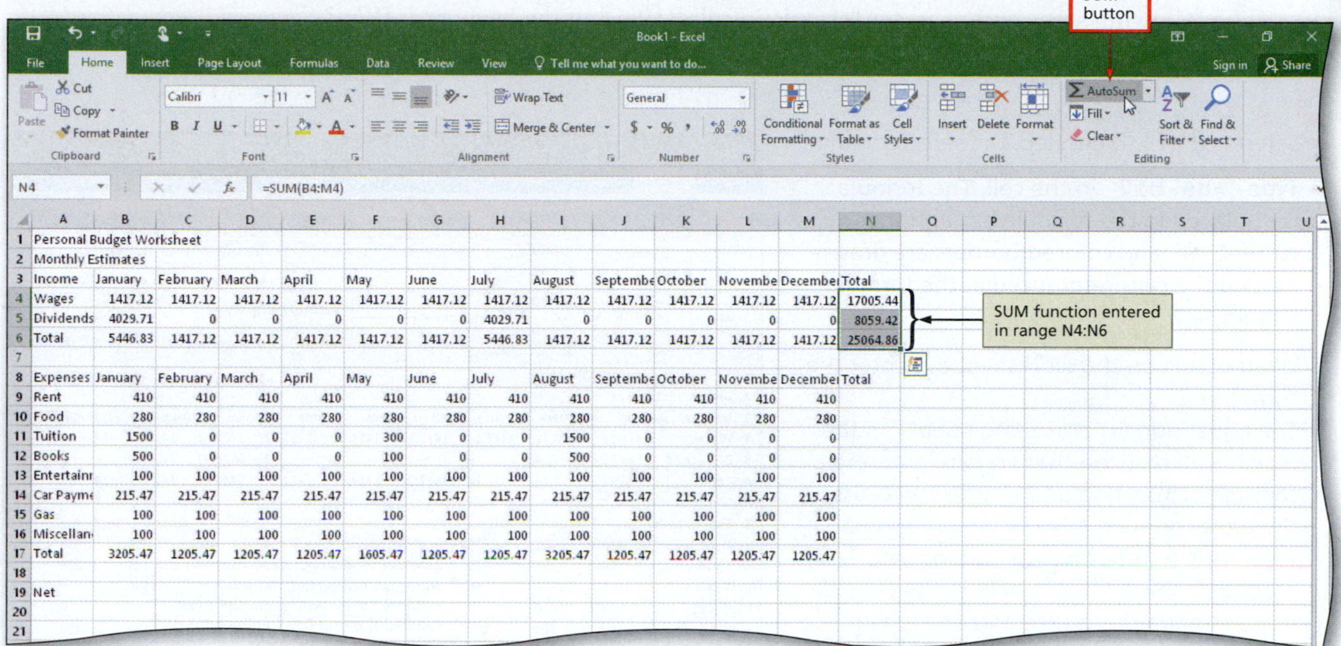

Figure 1–25

4

- Repeat Steps 1–3 to select cells N9 to N17 and calculate the sums of the corresponding rows (Figure 1–26).

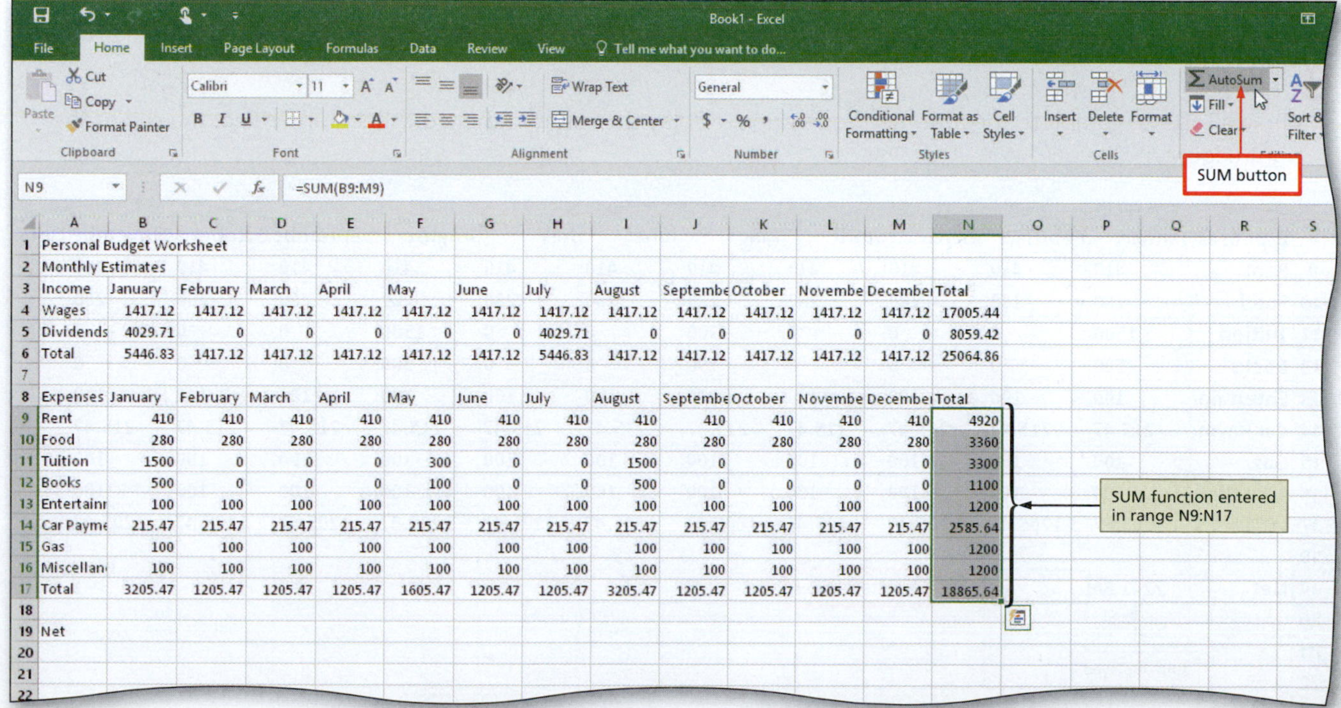

Figure 1–26

To Enter a Formula Using the Keyboard

The net for each month, which will appear in row 19, is equal to the income total in row 6 minus the expense total in row 17. The formula needed in the worksheet is noted in the requirements document as follows:

Net (row 19) = Income (row 6) – Expenses (row 17)

The following steps enter the net formula in cell B19 using the keyboard. ***Why?*** *Sometimes a predefined function does not fit your needs; therefore, you enter a formula of your own.*

1

- Select cell B19 to deselect the selected range.
- Type `=b6-b17` in the cell. The formula is displayed in the formula bar and the current cell, and colored borders are drawn around the cells referenced in the formula (Figure 1–27).

Q&A What occurs on the worksheet as I enter the formula?

The equal sign (=) preceding b6–b17 in the formula alerts Excel that you are entering a formula or function and not text. Because the most common error when entering a formula is to reference the wrong cell, Excel highlights the cell references in the formula in color, and uses same colors to highlight the borders of the cells to help you ensure that your cell references are correct. The minus sign (–) following b6 in the formula is the arithmetic operator that directs Excel to perform the subtraction operation.

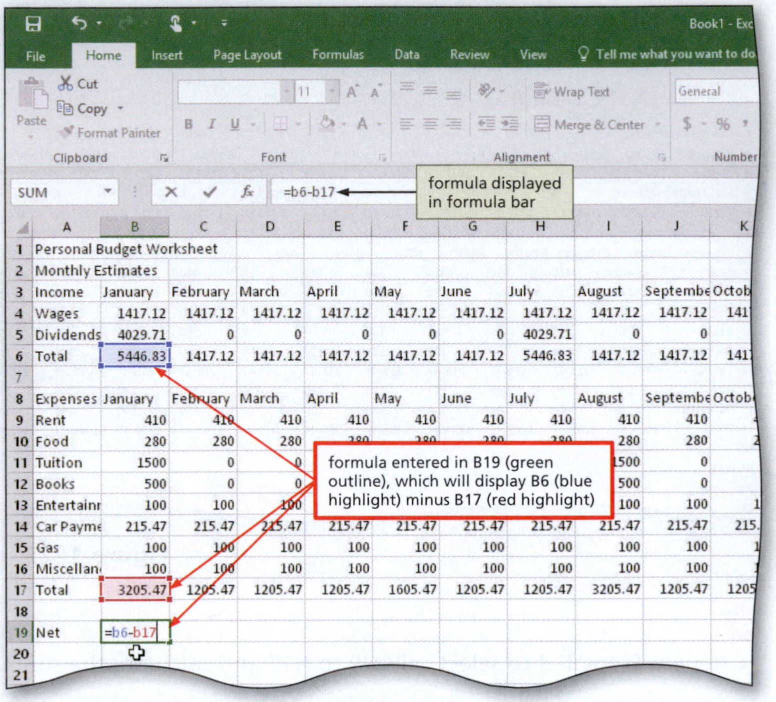

SUM | =b6-b17 ← formula displayed in formula bar

	A	B	C	D	E	F	G	H	I	J	K
1	Personal Budget Worksheet										
2	Monthly Estimates										
3	Income	January	February	March	April	May	June	July	August	Septembe	Octob
4	Wages	1417.12	1417.12	1417.12	1417.12	1417.12	1417.12	1417.12	1417.12	1417.12	141
5	Dividends	4029.71	0	0	0	0	0	4029.71	0	0	
6	Total	5446.83	1417.12	1417.12	1417.12	1417.12	1417.12	5446.83	1417.12	1417.12	141
7											
8	Expenses	January	February	March	April	May	June	July	August	Septembe	Octob
9	Rent	410	410	410	410	410	410	410	410	410	
10	Food	280	280	280					280	280	
11	Tuition	1500	0	0					1500	0	
12	Books	500	0	0					500	0	
13	Entertainr	100	100	100					100	100	1
14	Car Payme	215.47	215.47	215.47	215.47	215.47	215.47	215.47	215.47	215.47	215.
15	Gas	100	100	100	100	100	100	100	100	100	
16	Miscellan	100	100	100	100	100	100	100	100	100	
17	Total	3205.47	1205.47	1205.47	1205.47	1605.47	1205.47	1205.47	3205.47	1205.47	1205
18											
19	Net	=b6-b17									

formula entered in B19 (green outline), which will display B6 (blue highlight) minus B17 (red highlight)

Figure 1–27

2

- Click cell C19 to complete the arithmetic operation, display the result in the worksheet, and select the cell to the right (Figure 1–28).

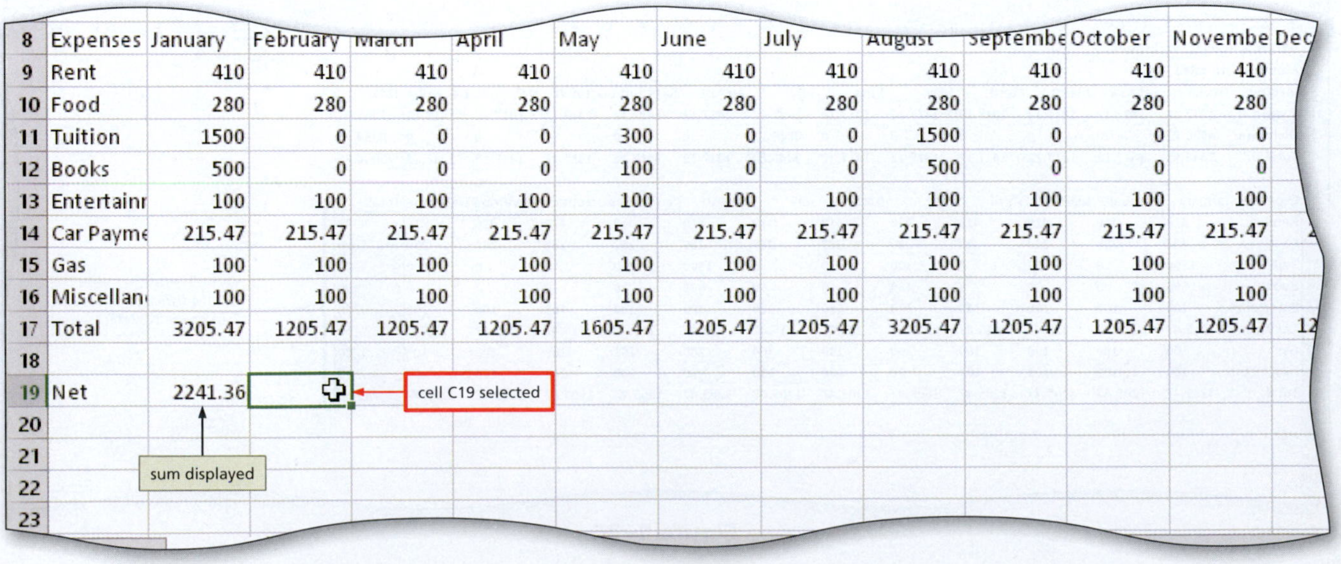

8	Expenses	January	February	March	April	May	June	July	August	Septembe	October	Novembe	Dec
9	Rent	410	410	410	410	410	410	410	410	410	410	410	
10	Food	280	280	280	280	280	280	280	280	280	280	280	
11	Tuition	1500	0	0	0	300	0	0	1500	0	0	0	
12	Books	500	0	0	0	100	0	0	500	0	0	0	
13	Entertainr	100	100	100	100	100	100	100	100	100	100	100	
14	Car Payme	215.47	215.47	215.47	215.47	215.47	215.47	215.47	215.47	215.47	215.47	215.47	2
15	Gas	100	100	100	100	100	100	100	100	100	100	100	
16	Miscellan	100	100	100	100	100	100	100	100	100	100	100	
17	Total	3205.47	1205.47	1205.47	1205.47	1605.47	1205.47	1205.47	3205.47	1205.47	1205.47	1205.47	12
18													
19	Net	2241.36											
20													
21													
22													
23													

cell C19 selected

sum displayed

Figure 1–28

To Copy a Cell to Adjacent Cells in a Row

The easiest way to copy the SUM formula from cell B19 to cells C19, D19, E19, F19, G19, H19, I19, J19, K19, L19, M19, and N19 is to use the fill handle. The following steps use the fill handle to copy the formula in cell B19 to the adjacent cells C19:N19.

1. Select cell B19.
2. Drag the fill handle to select the destination area, range C19:N19, which draws a shaded border around the source area and the destination area. Release the mouse button to copy the simple formula function from the active cell to the destination area and calculate the results.
3. Save the worksheet on your hard drive, OneDrive, or other storage location using Linda Fox Budget as the file name.

Q&A Why should I save the workbook at this time?
You have performed many tasks while creating this workbook and do not want to risk losing work completed thus far.

Break Point: If you wish to take a break, this is a good place to do so. You can exit Excel. To resume at a later time, run Excel, open the file called Linda Fox Budget, and continue following the steps from this location forward.

Formatting the Worksheet

The text, numeric entries, and functions for the worksheet now are complete. The next step is to format the worksheet. You **format** a worksheet to emphasize certain entries and make the worksheet easier to read and understand.

Figure 1–29a shows the worksheet before formatting. Figure 1–29b shows the worksheet after formatting. As you can see from the two figures, a worksheet that is formatted not only is easier to read but also looks more professional.

To change the unformatted worksheet in Figure 1–29a so that it looks like the formatted worksheet in Figure 1–29b, the following tasks must be completed:

BTW
Organizing Files and Folders
You should organize and store files in folders so that you easily can find the files later. For example, if you are taking an introductory technology class called CIS 101, a good practice would be to save all Excel files in an Excel folder in a CIS 101 folder. For a discussion of folders and detailed examples of creating folders, refer to the Office and Windows module at the beginning of this book.

What steps should I consider when formatting a worksheet?
The key to formatting a worksheet is to consider the ways you can enhance the worksheet so that it appears professional. When formatting a worksheet, consider the following steps:

- Identify in what ways you want to emphasize various elements of the worksheet.
- Increase the font size of cells.
- Change the font color of cells.
- Center the worksheet titles, subtitles, and column headings.
- Modify column widths to best fit text in cells.
- Change the font style of cells.

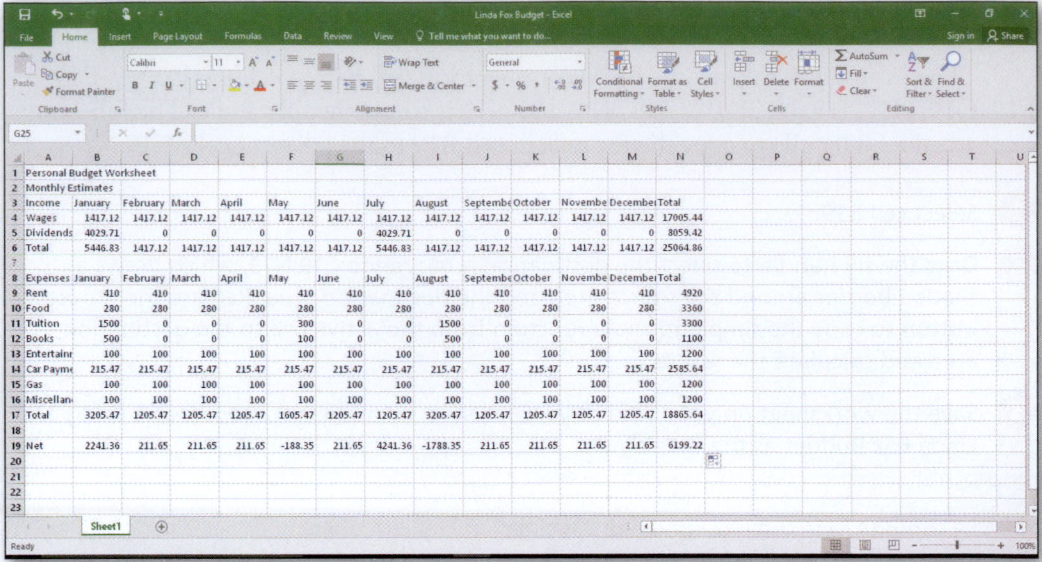

(a) Unformatted Worksheet

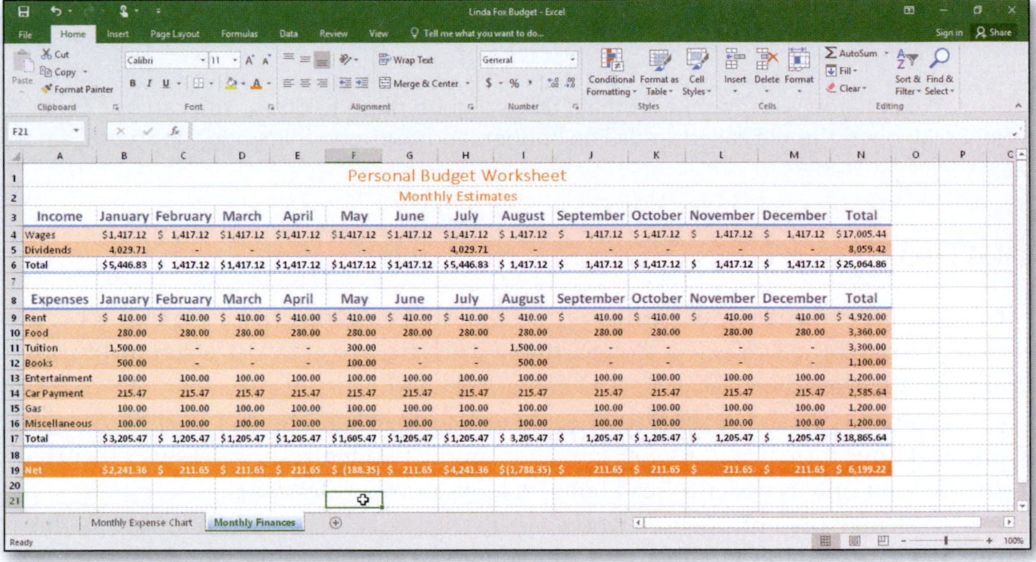

(b) Formatted Worksheet

Figure 1–29

1. Change the font, change the font style, increase the font size, and change the font color of the worksheet titles in cells A1 and A2.
2. Center the worksheet titles in cells A1 and A2 across columns A through N.
3. Format the body of the worksheet. The body of the worksheet, range A3:N19, includes the column titles, row titles, and numbers. Formatting the body of the worksheet changes the numbers to use a dollars-and-cents format, with dollar signs in rows 4 and 9 and in the total rows (row 6 and 17); changes the styles of some rows; adds underlining that emphasizes portions of the worksheet; and modifies the column widths to fit the text in the columns and make the text and numbers readable.

Although the formatting procedures are explained in the order described above, you could make these format changes in any order. Modifying the column widths, however, usually is done last because other formatting changes may affect the size of data in the cells in the column.

Font Style, Size, and Color

The characters that Excel displays on the screen are a specific font, style, size, and color. The **font**, or font face, defines the appearance and shape of the letters, numbers, and special characters. Examples of fonts include Calibri, Cambria, Times New Roman, Arial, and Courier. **Font style** indicates how the characters are emphasized. Common font styles include regular, bold, underline, and italic. The **font size** specifies the size of the characters. Font size is gauged by a measurement system called points. A single point is 1/72 of one inch in height. Thus, a character with a **point size** of 10 is 10/72 of one inch in height. Finally, Excel has a wide variety of **font colors** from which to choose to define the color of the characters.

When Excel first runs, the default font for the entire workbook is Calibri, with a font size, font style, and font color of 11-point regular black. You can change the font characteristics in a single cell, a range of cells, the entire worksheet, or the entire workbook.

To Change a Cell Style

1 ENTER TEXT | 2 CALCULATE SUMS & USE FORMULAS | **3 FORMAT TEXT**
4 INSERT CHART | 5 NAME TAB | 6 PREVIEW & PRINT WORKSHEET

You can change several characteristics of a cell, such as the font, font size, and font color, all at once by assigning a predefined cell style to a cell. A **cell style** is a predefined font, font size, and font color that you can apply to a cell. ***Why?*** *Using the predefined styles provides a consistent appearance to common portions of your worksheets, such as worksheet titles, worksheet subtitles, column headings, and total rows.* The following steps assign the Title cell style to the worksheet title in cell A1.

- Click cell A1 to make cell A1 the active cell.
- Click the Cell Styles button (Home tab | Styles group) to display the Cell Styles gallery (Figure 1–30).

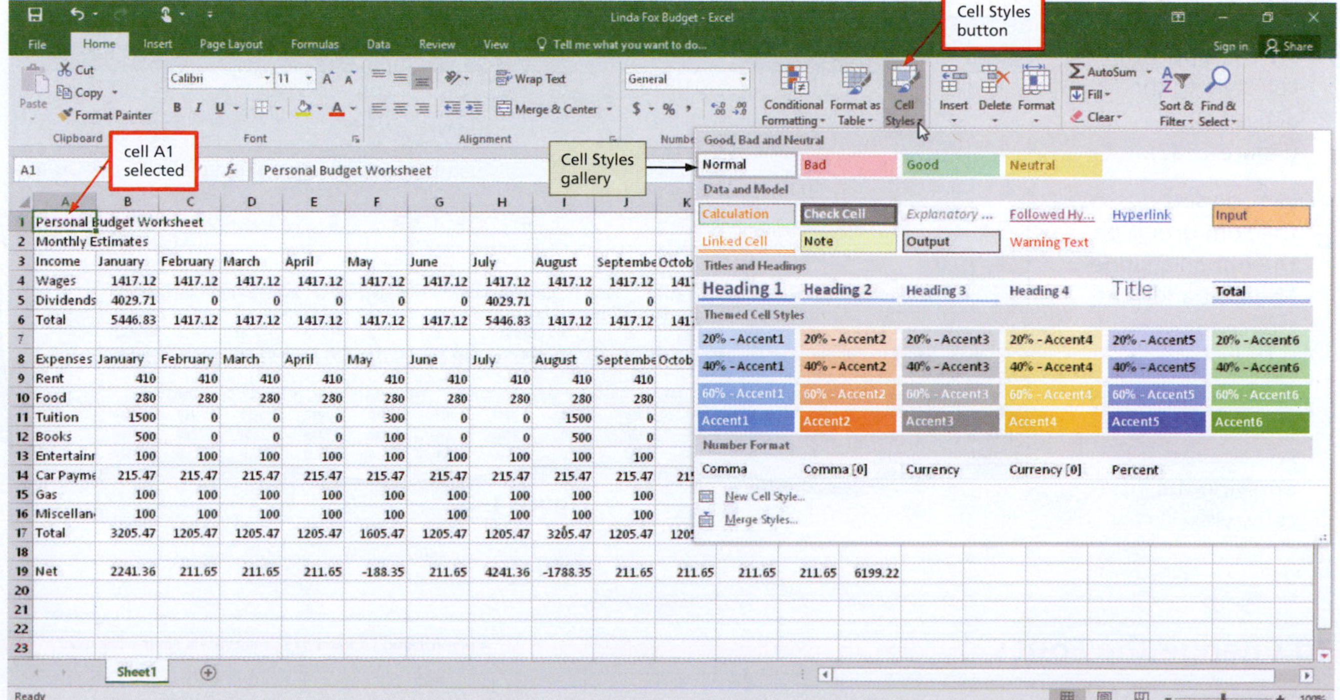

Figure 1–30

2

- Point to the Title cell style in the Titles and Headings area of the Cell Styles gallery to see a live preview of the cell style in the active cell (Figure 1–31).

Q&A Can I use live preview on a touch screen?
Live preview is not available on a touch screen.

Experiment

- Point to other cell styles in the Cell Styles gallery to see a live preview of those cell styles in cell A1.

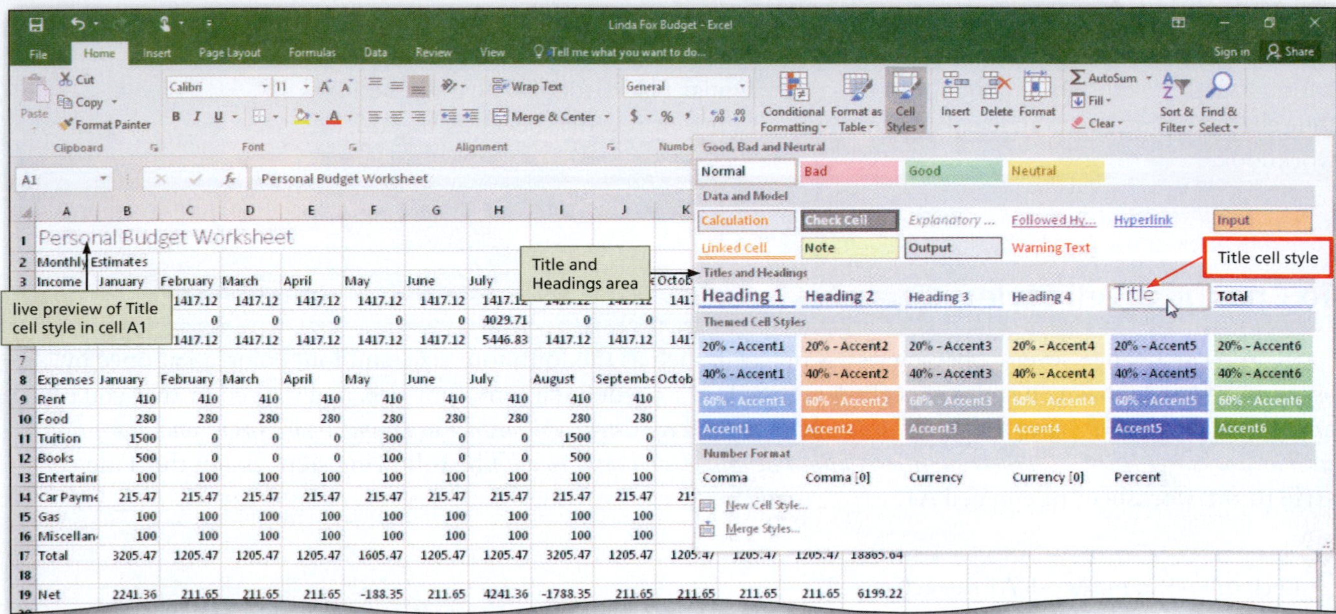

Figure 1–31

3

- Click the Title cell style to apply the cell style to the active cell (Figure 1–32).

Q&A Why do settings in the Font group on the ribbon change?
The font and font size change to reflect the font changes applied to the active cell, cell A1, as a result of applying the Title cell style.

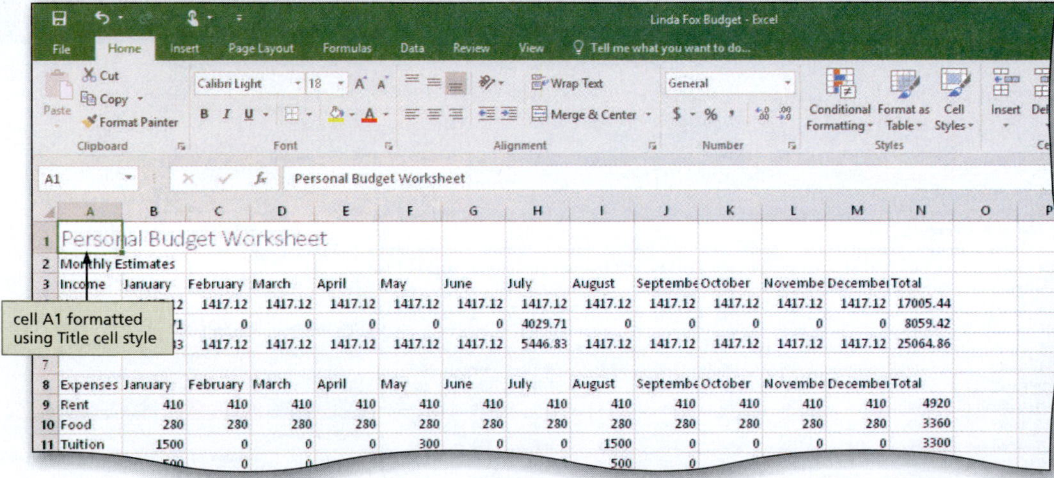

Figure 1–32

1 ENTER TEXT | 2 CALCULATE SUMS & USE FORMULAS | 3 FORMAT TEXT
4 INSERT CHART | 5 NAME TAB | 6 PREVIEW & PRINT WORKSHEET

To Change the Font

Why? *Different fonts often are used in a worksheet to make it more appealing to the reader and to relate or distinguish data in the worksheet.* The following steps change the worksheet subtitle's font to Calibri Light.

1

- Click cell A2 to make it the active cell.
- Click the Font arrow (Home tab | Font group) to display the Font gallery. If necessary, scroll to Calibri Light.
- Point to Calibri Light in the Font gallery to see a live preview of the selected font in the active cell (Figure 1–33).

Experiment

- Point to several other fonts in the Font gallery to see a live preview of the other fonts in the selected cell.

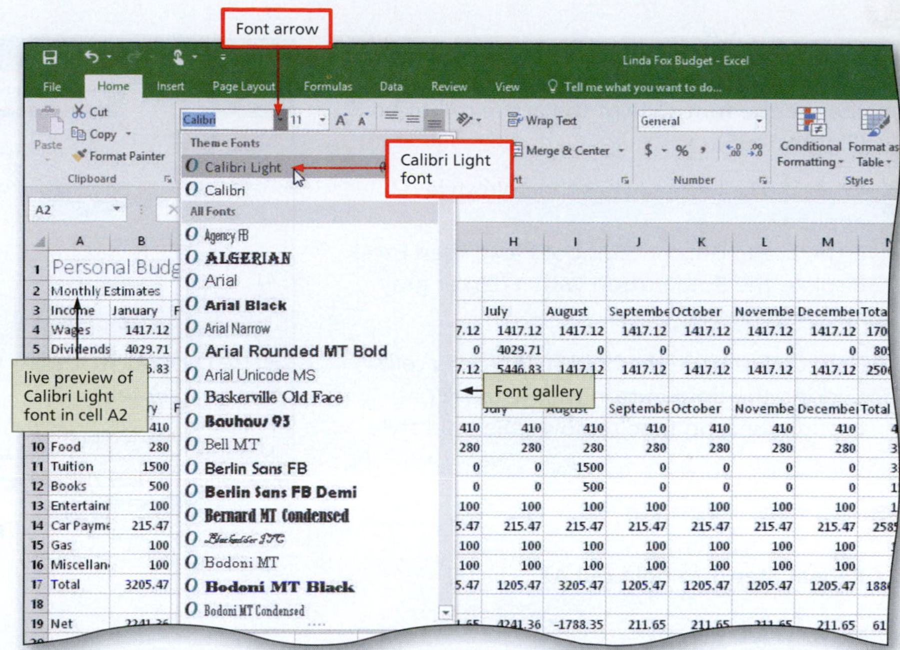

Figure 1–33

2

- Click Calibri Light in the Font gallery to change the font of the worksheet subtitle to Calibri Light (Figure 1–34).

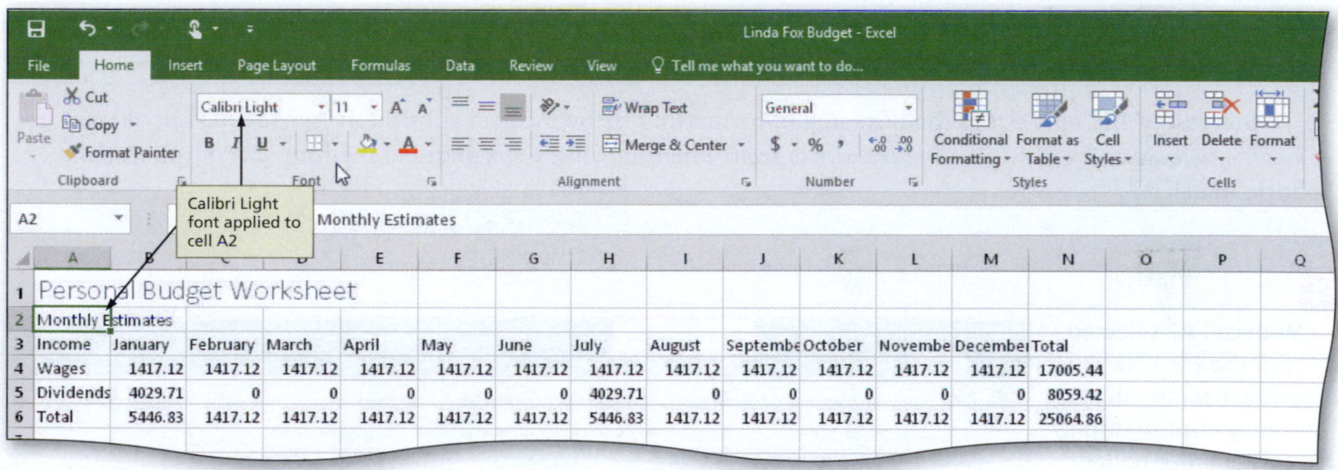

Figure 1–34

Other Ways

1. Click Font Settings Dialog Box Launcher, click Font tab (Format Cells dialog box), click desired font in Font list, click OK button
2. Right-click cell to display mini toolbar, click Font box arrow on mini toolbar, click desired font in Font gallery
3. Right-click selected cell, click Format Cells on shortcut menu, click Font tab (Format Cells dialog box), click desired font, click OK button

To Apply Bold Style to a Cell

Bold, or boldface, text has a darker appearance than normal text. ***Why?** You apply bold style to a cell to emphasize it or make it stand out from the rest of the worksheet.* The following steps apply bold style to the worksheet title and subtitle.

1

- Click cell A1 to make it active and then click the Bold button (Home tab | Font group) to change the font style of the active cell to bold (Figure 1–35).

Q&A What if a cell already has the bold style applied?
If the active cell contains bold text, then Excel displays the Bold button with a darker gray background.

How do I remove the bold style from a cell?
Clicking the Bold button (Home tab | Font group) a second time removes the bold style.

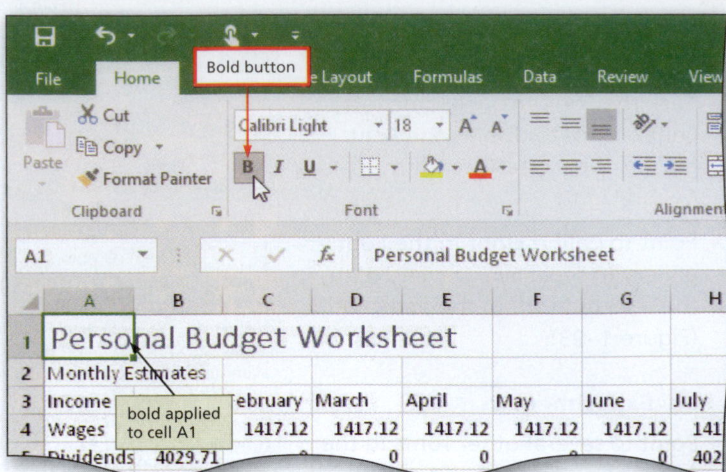

Figure 1–35

2

- Repeat Step 1 to bold cell A2.

Other Ways

1. Click Font Settings Dialog Box Launcher, click Font tab (Format Cells dialog box), click Bold in Font style list, click OK button
2. Right-click selected cell, click Bold button on mini toolbar
3. Right-click selected cell, click Format Cells on shortcut menu, click Font tab (Format Cells dialog box), click Bold, click OK button
4. Press CTRL+B

To Increase the Font Size of a Cell Entry

1 ENTER TEXT | 2 CALCULATE SUMS & USE FORMULAS | **3 FORMAT TEXT**
4 INSERT CHART | 5 NAME TAB | 6 PREVIEW & PRINT WORKSHEET

Increasing the font size is the next step in formatting the worksheet subtitle. ***Why?*** *You increase the font size of a cell so that the entry stands out and is easier to read.* The following steps increase the font size of the worksheet subtitle in cell A2.

1

- With cell A2 selected, click the Font Size arrow (Home tab | Font group) to display the Font Size gallery.
- Point to 14 in the Font Size gallery to see a live preview of the active cell with the selected font size (Figure 1–36).

Experiment

- If you are using a mouse, point to several other font sizes in the Font Size list to see a live preview of those font sizes in the selected cell.

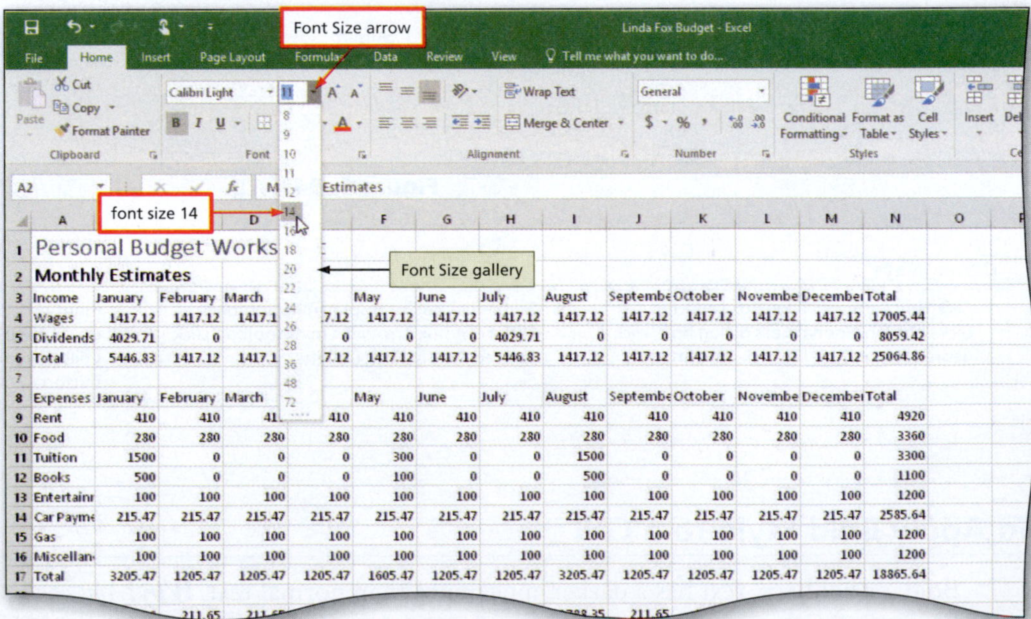

Figure 1–36

1

- Click 14 in the Font Size gallery to change the font size in the active cell (Figure 1–37).

Q&A Can I choose a font size that is not in the Font Size gallery?
Yes. An alternative to selecting a font size in the Font Size gallery is to click the Font Size box (Home tab | Font group), type the font size you want, and then press the ENTER key.

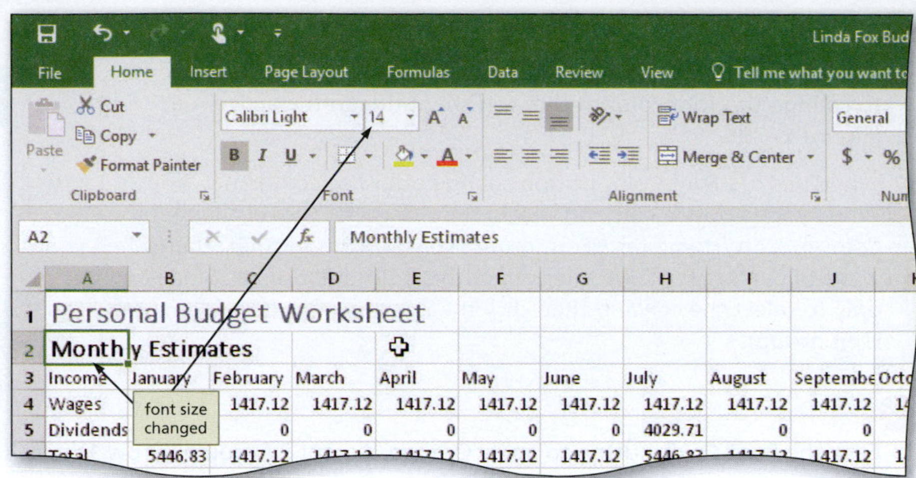

Figure 1–37

Other Ways

1. Click 'Increase Font Size' button (Home tab | Font group) or 'Decrease Font Size' button (Home tab | Font group)
2. Click Font Settings Dialog box Launcher, click Font tab (Format Cells dialog box), click desired size in Size list, click OK button
3. Right-click cell to display mini toolbar, click Font Size arrow on mini toolbar, click desired font size in Font Size gallery
4. Right-click selected cell, click Format Cells on shortcut menu, click Font tab (Format Cells dialog box), select font size in Size box, click OK button

To Change the Font Color of a Cell Entry

1 ENTER TEXT | 2 CALCULATE SUMS & USE FORMULAS | 3 FORMAT TEXT
4 INSERT CHART | 5 NAME TAB | 6 PREVIEW & PRINT WORKSHEET

The next step is to change the color of the font in cells A1 and A2 to orange. ***Why?*** *Changing the font color of cell entries can help the text stand out more. You also can change the font colors to match the company or product's brand colors.* The following steps change the font color of a cell entry.

1

- Click cell A1 and then click the Font Color arrow (Home tab | Font group) to display the Font Color gallery.
- Point to 'Orange, Accent 2' (column 6, row 1) in the Theme Colors area of the Font Color gallery to see a live preview of the font color in the active cell (Figure 1–38).

Experiment

- Point to several other colors in the Font Color gallery to see a live preview of other font colors in the active cell.

Q&A How many colors are in the Font Color gallery?
You can choose from approximately 70 different font colors in the Font Color gallery. Your Font Color gallery may have more or fewer colors, depending on the color settings of your operating system. The Theme Colors area contains colors that are included in the current workbook's theme.

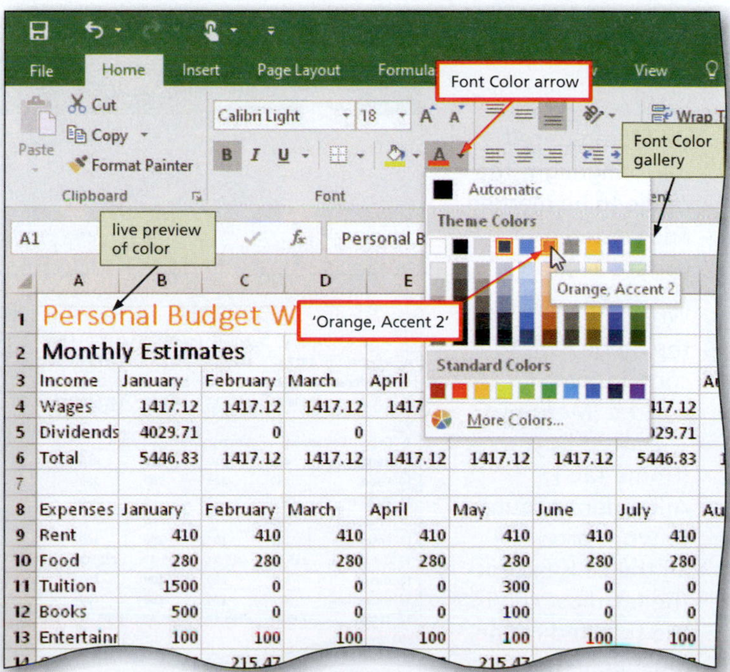

Figure 1–38

2

- Click 'Orange, Accent 2' (column 6, row 1) in the Font Color gallery to change the font color of the worksheet title in the active cell (Figure 1–39).

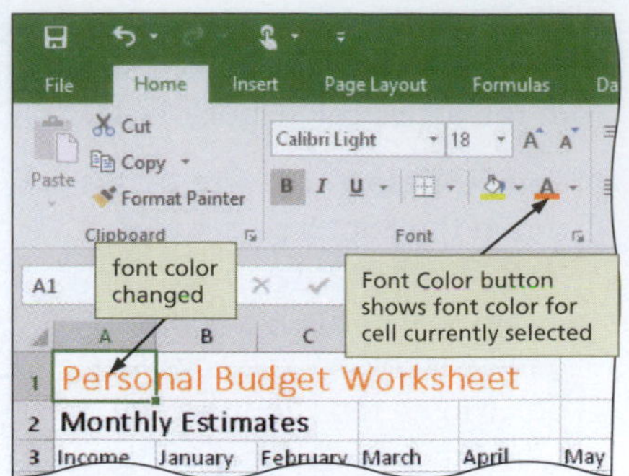

Figure 1–39

Q&A Why does the Font Color button change after I select the new font color?
When you choose a color on the Font Color gallery, Excel changes the Font Color button (Home tab | Font group) to your chosen color. Then when you want to change the font color of another cell to the same color, you need only to select the cell and then click the Font Color button (Home tab | Font group).

3

- Click the Font Color button to apply Orange, Accent 2 (column 6, row 1) to cell A2.

Other Ways

1. Click Font Settings Dialog Box Launcher, click Font tab (Format Cells dialog box), click desired color in Color list, click OK button
2. Right-click the cell to display mini toolbar, click Font Color arrow on mini toolbar, click desired font color in Font Color gallery
3. Right-click selected cell, click Format Cells on shortcut menu, click Font tab (Format Cells dialog box), select color in Font Color gallery, click OK button

To Center Cell Entries across Columns by Merging Cells

1 ENTER TEXT | 2 CALCULATE SUMS & USE FORMULAS | **3 FORMAT TEXT**
4 INSERT CHART | 5 NAME TAB | 6 PREVIEW & PRINT WORKSHEET

The final step in formatting the worksheet title and subtitle is to center them across columns A through N. ***Why?*** *Centering a title across the columns used in the body of the worksheet improves the worksheet's appearance.* To do this, the 14 cells in the range A1:N1 are combined, or merged, into a single cell that is the width of the columns in the body of the worksheet. The 14 cells in the range A2:N2 are merged in a similar manner. **Merging cells** involves creating a single cell by combining two or more selected cells. The following steps center the worksheet title and subtitle across columns by merging cells.

1

- Select cell A1 and then drag to cell N1 to highlight the range to be merged and centered (Figure 1–40).

Q&A What if a cell in the range B1:N1 contains data?
For the 'Merge & Center' button (Home tab | Alignment group) to work properly, all the cells except the leftmost cell in the selected range must be empty.

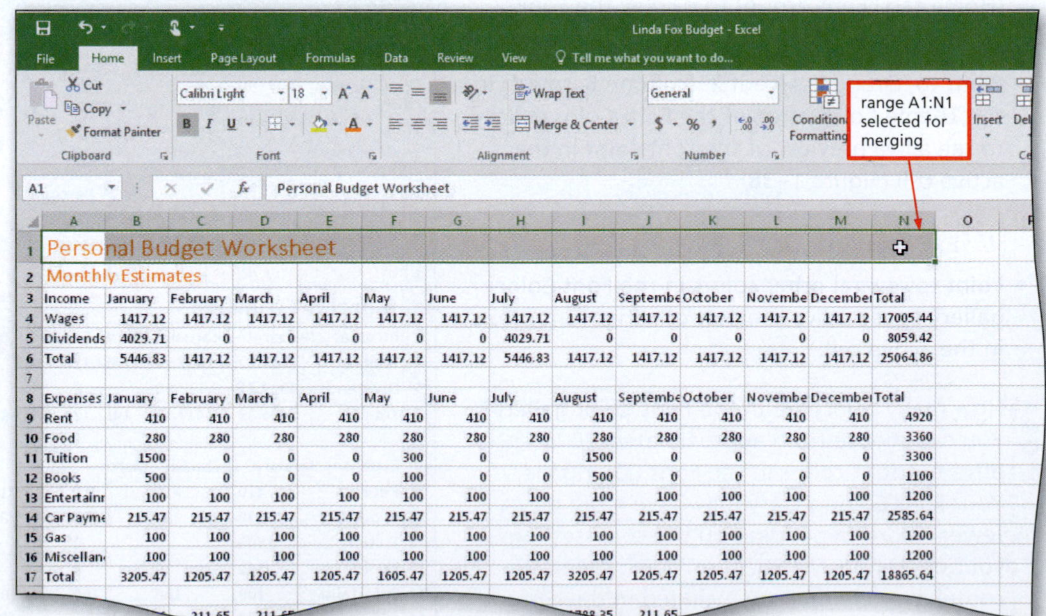

Figure 1–40

2

- Click the 'Merge & Center' button (Home tab | Alignment group) to merge cells A1 through N1 and center the contents of the leftmost cell across the selected columns (Figure 1–41).

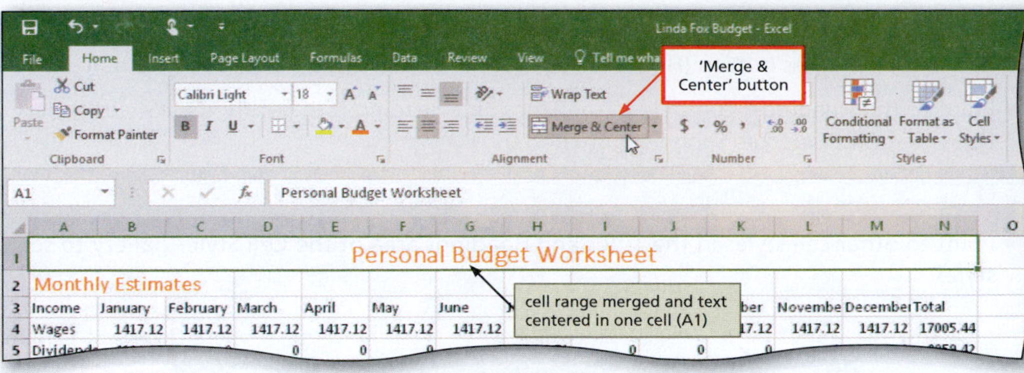

Figure 1–41

Q&A

What if my screen displays a Merge & Center menu?

Select the desired option on the Merge & Center menu if you do not have a separate 'Merge & Center' button and 'Merge & Center' arrow.

What happened to cells B1 through N1?

After the merge, cells B1 through N1 no longer exist. The new cell A1 now extends across columns A through N.

3

- Repeat Steps 1 and 2 to merge and center the worksheet subtitle across cells A2 through N2 (Figure 1–42).

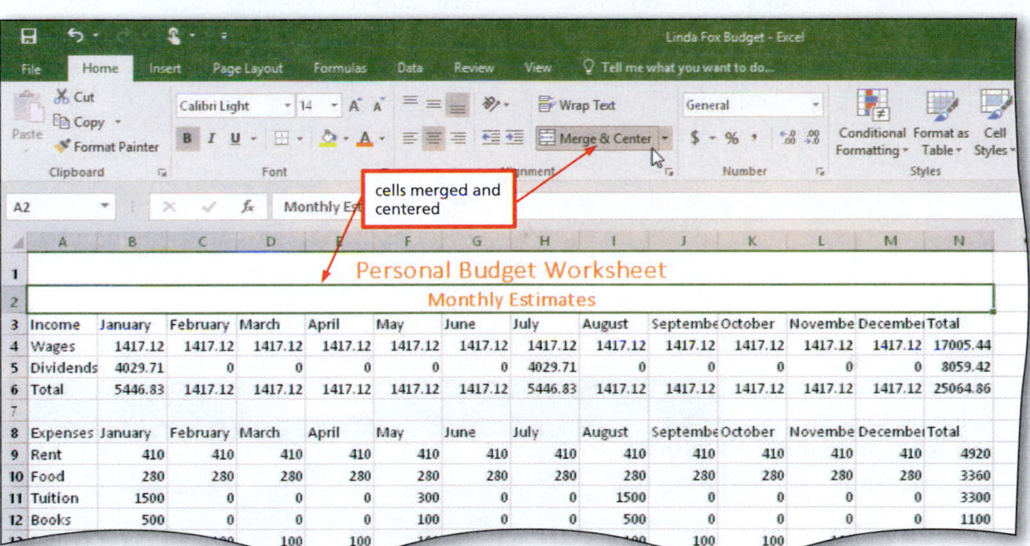

Figure 1–42

Q&A

Are cells B1 through N1 and B2 through N2 lost forever?

No. The opposite of merging cells is **splitting** a merged cell. After you have merged multiple cells into one cell, you can unmerge, or split, the cell to display the original range of cells. You split a merged cell by selecting it and clicking the 'Merge & Center' button. For example, if you click the 'Merge & Center' button a second time in Step 2, it will split the merged cell A1 into cells A1, B1, C1, D1, E1, F1, G1, H1, I1, J1, K1, L1, M1, and N1, and move the title to it's original location in cell A1.

Other Ways

1. Right-click selection, click 'Merge & Center' button on mini toolbar
2. Right-click selected cell, click Format Cells on shortcut menu, click Alignment tab (Format Cells dialog box), select 'Center Across Selection' in Horizontal list, click OK button

1 ENTER TEXT | 2 CALCULATE SUMS & USE FORMULAS | **3 FORMAT TEXT**
4 INSERT CHART | 5 NAME TAB | 6 PREVIEW & PRINT WORKSHEET

To Format Rows Using Cell Styles

The next step to format the worksheet is to format the rows. ***Why?*** *Row titles and the total row should be formatted so that the column titles and total row can be distinguished from the data in the body of the worksheet. Data rows can be formatted to make them easier to read as well.* The following steps format the column titles and total row using cell styles in the default worksheet theme.

- Click cell A3 and then drag to cell N3 to select the range.
- Click the Cell Styles button (Home tab | Styles group) to display the Cell Styles gallery.
- Point to the Heading 1 cell style in the Titles and Headings area of the Cell Styles gallery to see a live preview of the cell style in the selected range (Figure 1–43).

Experiment

- Point to other cell styles in the Titles and Headings area of the Cell Styles gallery to see a live preview of other styles.

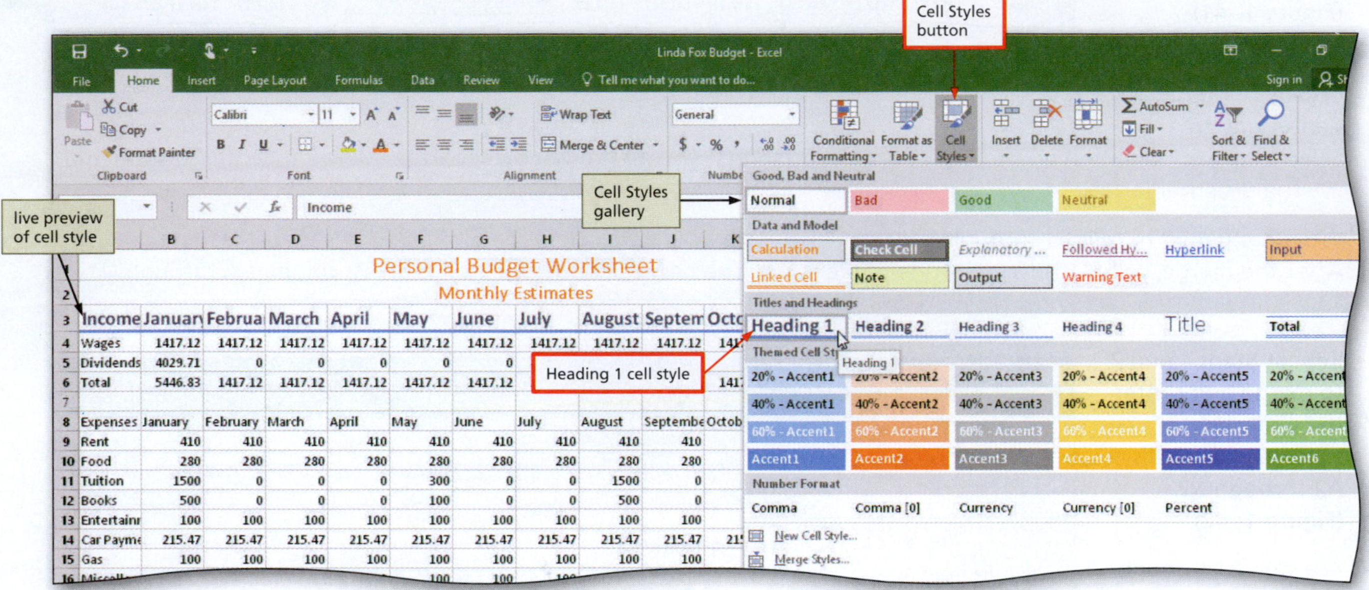

Figure 1–43

- Click the Heading 1 cell style to apply the cell style to the selected range.
- Click the Center button (Home tab | Alignment group) to center the column headings in the selected range.
- Select the range A8 to N8 (Figure 1–44).

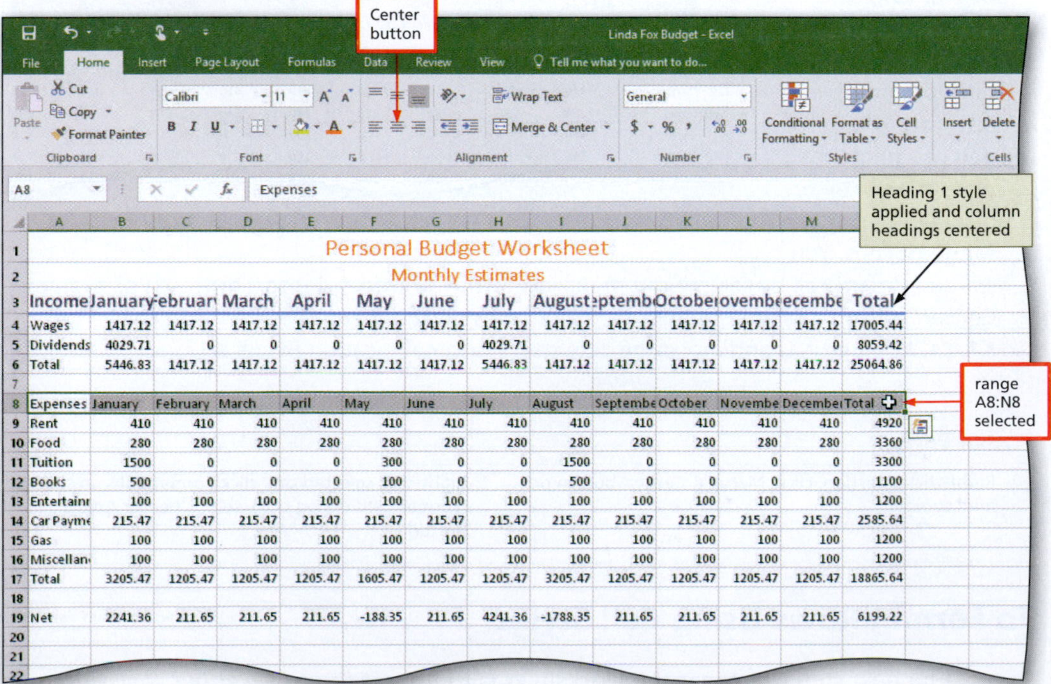

Figure 1–44

3

- Apply the Heading 1 cell style format and then center the headings (Figure 1–45).

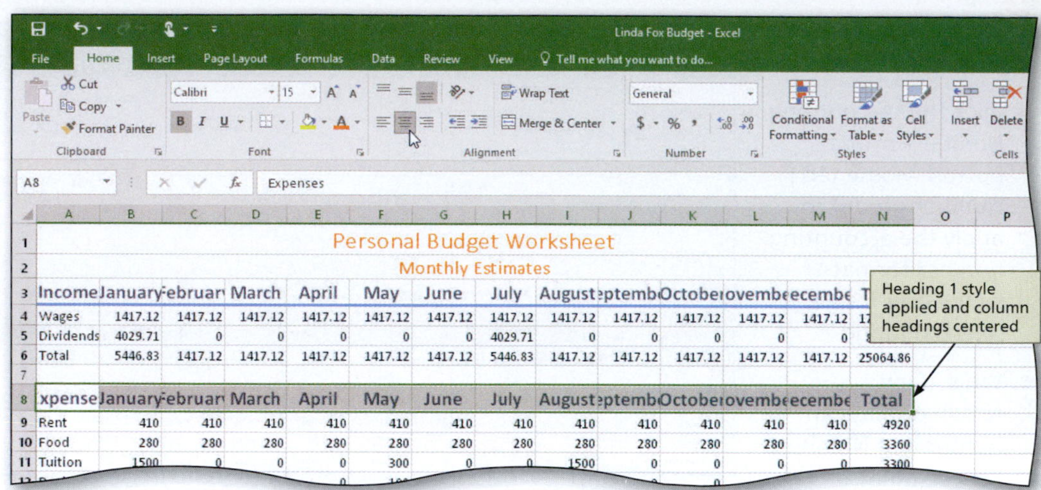

Figure 1–45

4

- Format the range A6:N6 and A17:N17 with the Total cell style format.
- Format the range A19:N19 with the Accent2 cell style format.
- Format the range A4:N4, A9:N9, A11:N11, A13:N13, A15:N15 with the 20% - Accent2 cell style format.
- Format the range A5:N5, A10:N10, A12:N12, A14:N14, A16:N16 with the 40% - Accent2 cell style format. Deselect the selected ranges

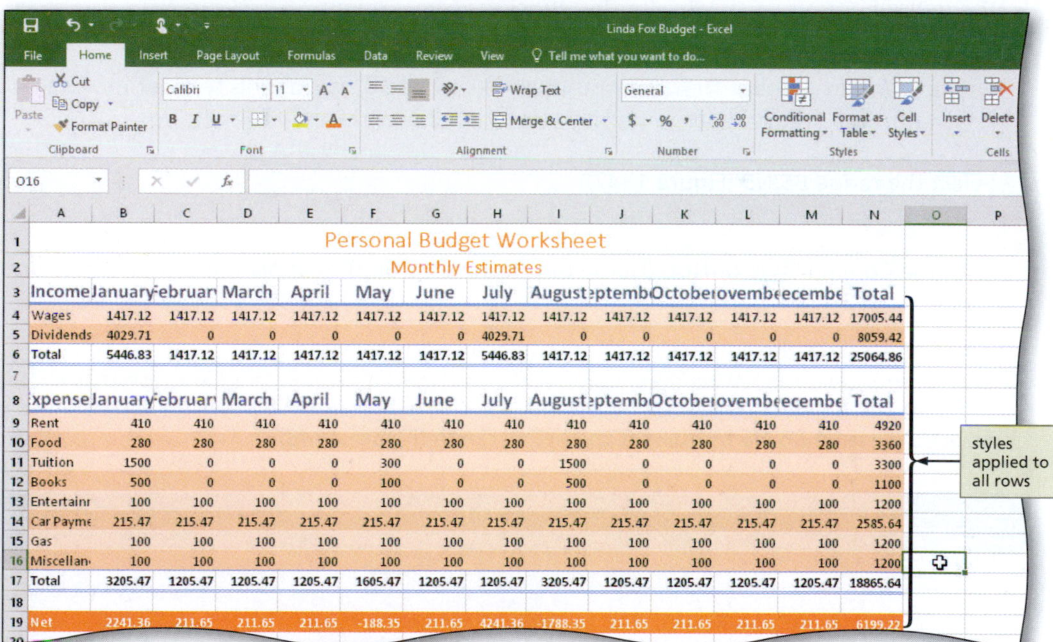

Figure 1–46

To Format Numbers in the Worksheet

1 ENTER TEXT | 2 CALCULATE SUMS & USE FORMULAS | **3 FORMAT TEXT**
4 INSERT CHART | 5 NAME TAB | 6 PREVIEW & PRINT WORKSHEET

The requirements document requested that numbers in the first row and last row of each section should be formatted to use a dollar-and-cents format, while other numbers receive a comma format. ***Why?*** *Using a dollar-and-cents format for selected cells makes it clear to users of the worksheet that the numbers represent dollar values without cluttering the entire worksheet with dollar signs, and applying the comma format makes larger numbers easier to read.* Excel allows you to apply various number formats, many of which are discussed in later modules. The following steps use buttons on the ribbon to format the numbers in the worksheet.

- Select the range B4:N4.
- Click the 'Accounting Number Format' button (Home tab | Number group) to apply the accounting number format to the cells in the selected range.

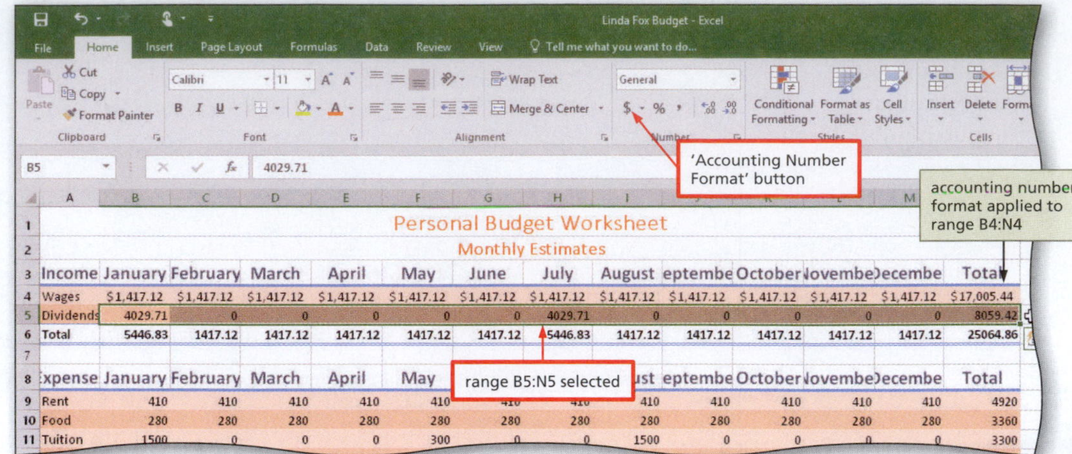

Figure 1–47

Q&A What if my screen displays an Accounting Number Format menu?
If you are using a touch screen, you may not have a separate 'Accounting Number Format' button and 'Accounting Number Format' arrow. In this case, select the desired option on the Accounting Number Format menu.

What effect does the accounting number format have on the selected cells?
The accounting number format causes numbers to be displayed with two decimal places and to align vertically. Cell widths are adjusted automatically to accommodate the new formatting.

- Select the range B5:N5 (Figure 1–47).

- Click the Comma Style button (Home tab | Number group) to apply the comma style format to the selected range.

Q&A What effect does the comma style format have on the selected cells?
The comma style format formats numbers to have two decimal places and commas as thousands separators.

- Select the range B6:N6 to make it the active range (Figure 1–48).

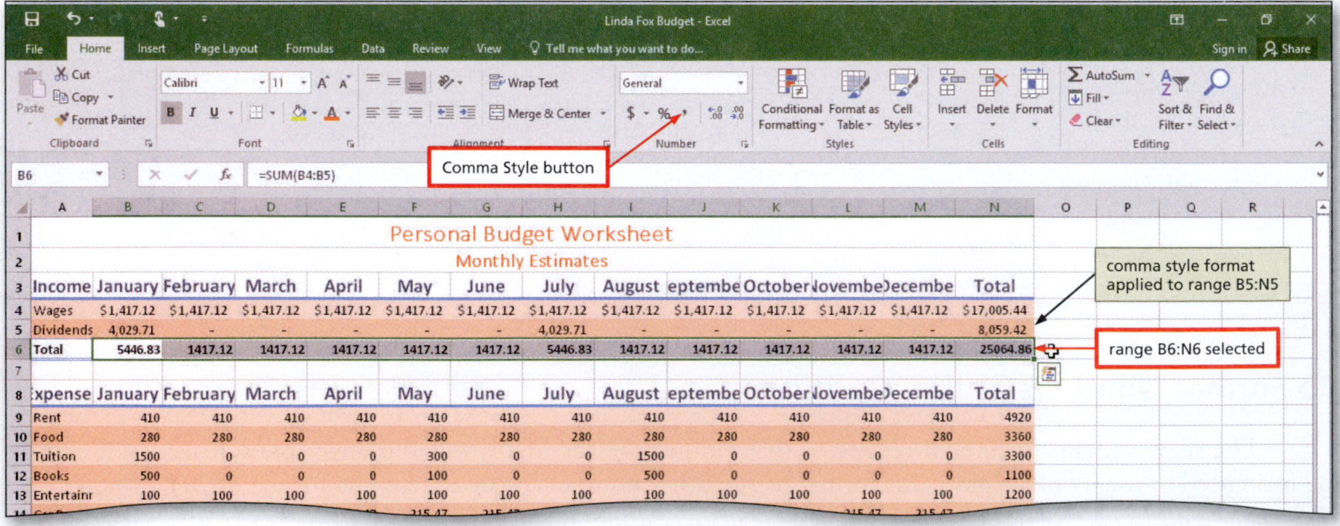

Figure 1–48

3

- Click the 'Accounting Number Format' button (Home tab | Number group) to apply the accounting number format to the cells in the selected range.

4

- Format the ranges B9:N9, B17:N17, and B19:N19 with the accounting number format.
- Format the range B10:N16 with the comma style format. Click cell A1 to deselect the selected ranges (Figure 1–49).

Q&A How do I select the range B10:N16?
Select this range the same way as you select a range of cells in a column or row; that is, click the first cell in the range (B10, in this case) and drag to the last cell in the range (N16, in this case).

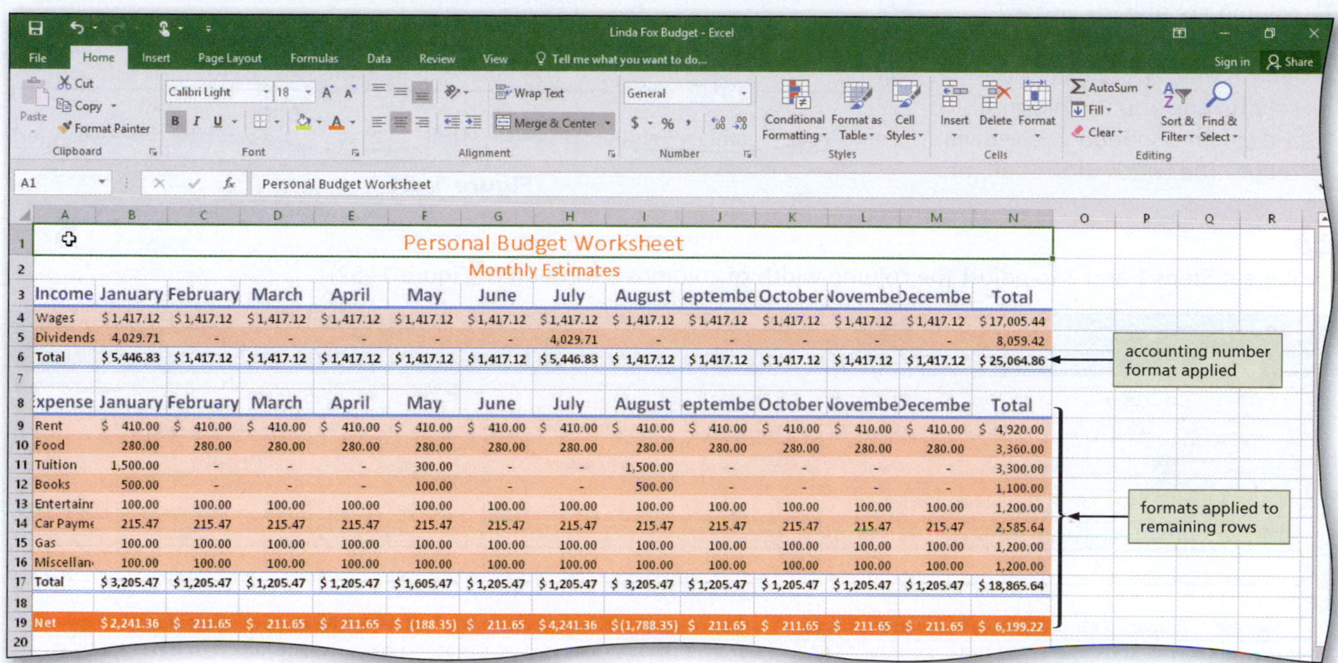

Figure 1–49

Other Ways

1. Click 'Accounting Number Format' or Comma Style button on mini toolbar
2. Right-click selected cell, click Format Cells on shortcut menu, click Number tab (Format Cells dialog box), select Accounting in Category list or select Number and click 'Use 1000 Separator', click OK button

To Adjust the Column Width

1 ENTER TEXT | 2 CALCULATE SUMS & USE FORMULAS | 3 FORMAT TEXT
4 INSERT CHART | 5 NAME TAB | 6 PREVIEW & PRINT WORKSHEET

The last step in formatting the worksheet is to adjust the width of the columns so that each title is visible. ***Why?*** *To make a worksheet easy to read, the column widths should be adjusted appropriately.* Excel offers other methods for adjusting cell widths and row heights, which are discussed later in this book. The following steps adjust the width of columns A through N so that the contents of the columns are visible.

- Point to the boundary on the right side of the column A heading above row 1 to change the pointer to a split double arrow (Figure 1–50).

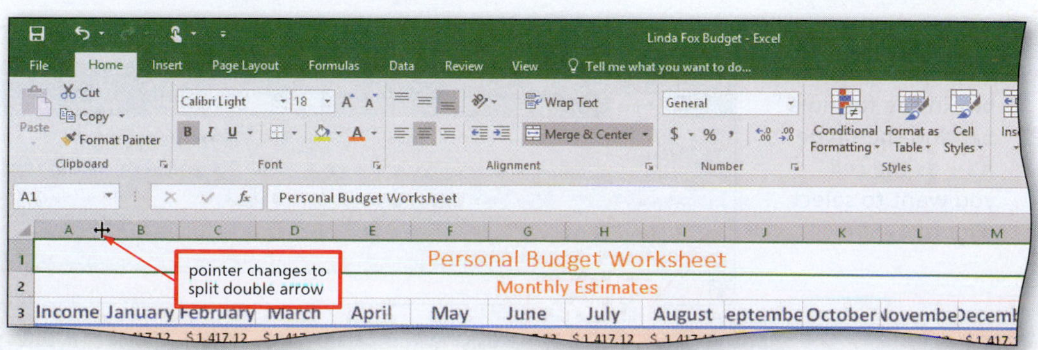

Figure 1–50

2

- Double-click the boundary to adjust the width of the column to accommodate the width of the longest item in the column (Figure 1–51).

Q&A What if all of the items in the column are already visible?
If all of the items are shorter in length than the width of the column and you double-click the column boundary, Excel will reduce the width of the column.

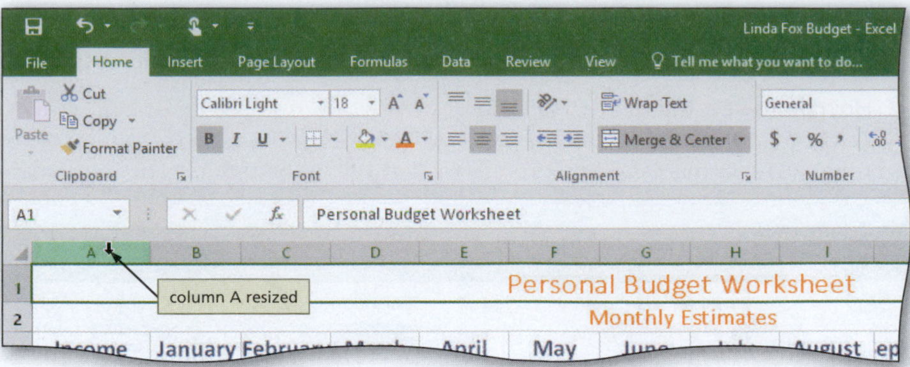

Figure 1–51

3

- Repeat Steps 1 and 2 to adjust the column width of columns B through N (Figure 1–52).

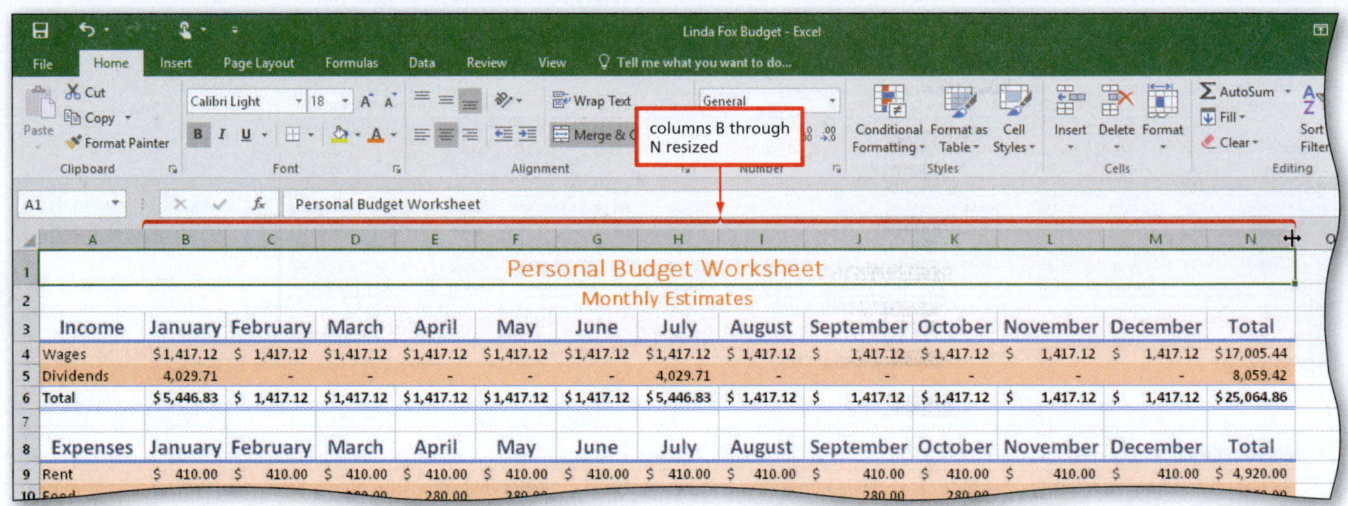

Figure 1–52

To Use the Name Box to Select a Cell

1 ENTER TEXT | 2 CALCULATE SUMS & USE FORMULAS | **3 FORMAT TEXT**
4 INSERT CHART | 5 NAME TAB | 6 PREVIEW & PRINT WORKSHEET

The next step is to chart the monthly expenses. To create the chart, you need to identify the range of the data you want to feature on the chart and then select it. In this case you want to start with cell A3. Rather than clicking cell A3 to select it, you will select the cell by using the Name box, which is located to the left of the formula bar. ***Why?*** *You might want to use the Name box to select a cell if you are working with a large worksheet and it is faster to type the cell name rather than scrolling to and clicking it.* The following steps select cell A3 using the Name box.

- Click the Name box in the formula bar and then type **a3** as the cell you want to select (Figure 1–53).

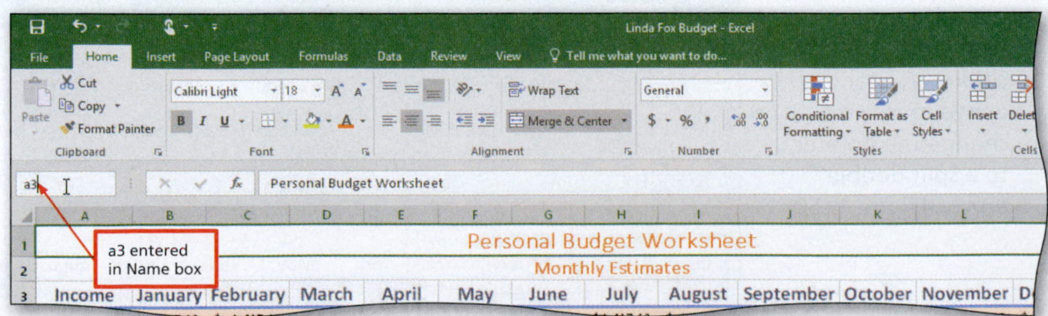

Figure 1–53

2

- Press the ENTER key to change the active cell in the Name box and make cell A3 the active cell (Figure 1–54).

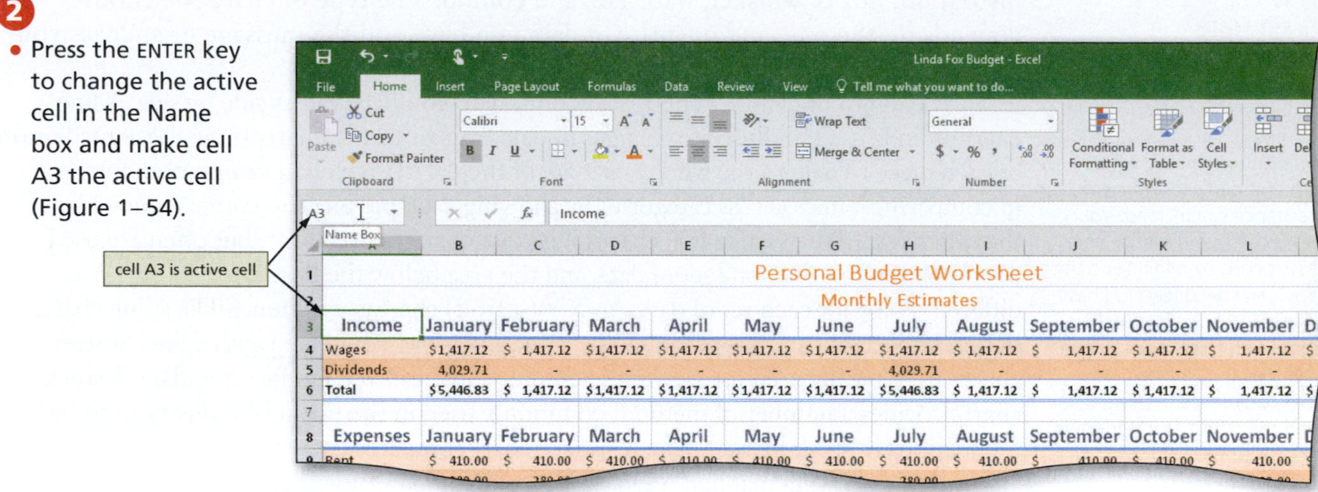

Figure 1–54

Other Ways to Select Cells

As you will see in later modules, in addition to using the Name box to select any cell in a worksheet, you also can use it to assign names to a cell or range of cells. Excel supports several additional ways to select a cell, as summarized in Table 1–3.

Table 1–3 Selecting Cells in Excel

Key, Box, or Command	Function
ALT+PAGE DOWN	Selects the cell one worksheet window to the right and moves the worksheet window accordingly.
ALT+PAGE UP	Selects the cell one worksheet window to the left and moves the worksheet window accordingly.
ARROW	Selects the adjacent cell in the direction of the arrow on the key.
CTRL+ARROW	Selects the border cell of the worksheet in combination with the arrow keys and moves the worksheet window accordingly. For example, to select the rightmost cell in the row that contains the active cell, press CTRL+RIGHT ARROW. You also can press the END key, release it, and then press the appropriate arrow key to accomplish the same task.
CTRL+HOME	Selects cell A1 or the cell one column and one row below and to the right of frozen titles and moves the worksheet window accordingly.
Find command on Find & Select menu (Home tab | Editing group) or SHIFT+F5	Finds and selects a cell that contains specific contents that you enter in the Find and Replace dialog box. If necessary, Excel moves the worksheet window to display the cell. You also can press CTRL+F to display the Find and Replace dialog box.
Go To command on Find & Select menu (Home tab | Editing group) or F5	Selects the cell that corresponds to the cell reference you enter in the Go To dialog box and moves the worksheet window accordingly. You also can press CTRL+G to display the Go To dialog box.
HOME	Selects the cell at the beginning of the row that contains the active cell and moves the worksheet window accordingly.
Name box	Selects the cell in the workbook that corresponds to the cell reference you enter in the Name box.
PAGE DOWN	Selects the cell down one worksheet window from the active cell and moves the worksheet window accordingly.
PAGE UP	Selects the cell up one worksheet window from the active cell and moves the worksheet window accordingly.

Break Point: If you wish to take a break, this is a good place to do so. Be sure to save the Linda Fox Budget file again and then you can exit Excel. To resume at a later time, run Excel, open the file called Linda Fox Budget, and continue following the steps from this location forward.

Adding a Pie Chart to the Worksheet

Excel includes 15 chart types from which you can choose, including column, line, pie, bar, area, X Y (scatter), stock, surface, radar, treemap, sunburst,

BTW

Excel Help

At any time while using Excel, you can find answers to questions and display information about various topics through Excel Help. Used properly, this form of assistance can increase your productivity and reduce your frustrations by minimizing the time you spend learning how to use Excel. For instructions about Excel Help and exercises that will help you gain confidence in using it, read the Office and Windows module at the beginning of this book.

histogram, box & whisker, waterfall, and combo. The type of chart you choose depends on the type and quantity of data you have and the message or analysis you want to convey.

A column or cylinder chart is a good way to compare values side by side. A line chart often is used to illustrate changes in data over time. Pie charts show the contribution of each piece of data to the whole, or total, of the data. A pie chart can go even further in comparing values across categories by showing each pie piece in comparison with the others. Area charts, like line charts, illustrate changes over time, but often are used to compare more than one set of data, and the area below the lines is filled in with a different color for each set of data. An X Y (scatter) chart is used much like a line chart, but each piece of data is represented by a dot and is not connected with a line. Scatter charts are typically used for viewing scientific, statistical, and engineering data. A stock chart provides a number of methods commonly used in the financial industry to show fluctuations in stock market data. A surface chart compares data from three columns and/or rows in a 3-D manner. A radar chart can compare aggregate values of several sets of data in a manner that resembles a radar screen, with each set of data represented by a different color. A combo chart allows you to combine multiple types of charts.

Excel 2016 includes five new charts. Treemap and sunburst charts are hierarchy charts, used to compare parts to a whole. A treemap chart uses nested rectangles to show data in a hierarchy. A sunburst chart stacks multiple pie charts on one another to illustrate related data. New statistical charts include histogram and box & whisker charts. A histogram chart shows the distribution of data. A box & whisker chart, or box plot, is used to display variation within a set of data. The new waterfall chart is used to visualize increases and decreases within a set of data and is grouped with stock charts.

As outlined in the requirements document in Figure 1–2, the budget worksheet should include a pie chart to graphically represent the yearly expense totals for each item in Linda Fox's budget. The pie chart shown in Figure 1–55 is on its own sheet in the workbook. The pie chart resides on a separate sheet, called a **chart sheet**, which contains only the chart.

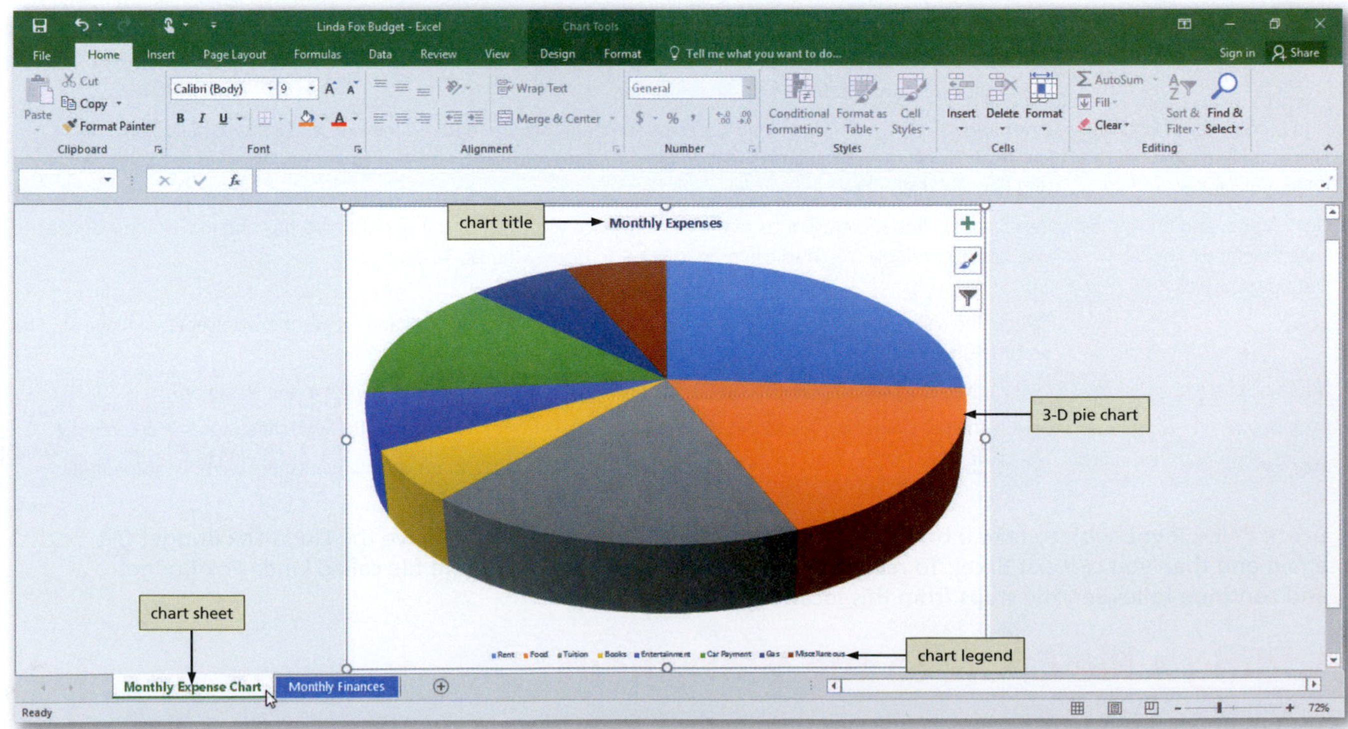

Figure 1–55

In this worksheet, the ranges you want to chart are the nonadjacent ranges A9:A16 (expense titles) and N9:N16 (yearly expense totals). The expense titles in the range A9:A16 will identify the slices of the pie chart; these entries are called category names. The range N9:N16 contains the data that determines the size of the slices in the pie; these entries are called the **data series**. Because eight budget items are being charted, the 3-D pie chart contains eight slices.

To Add a 3-D Pie Chart

Why? *When you want to see how each part relates to the whole, you use a pie chart.* The following steps draw the 3-D pie chart.

- Select the range A9:A16 to identify the range of the category names for the 3-D pie chart.
- While holding down the CTRL key, select the nonadjacent range N9:N16.
- Click Insert on the ribbon to display the Insert tab.
- Click the 'Insert Pie or Doughnut Chart' button (Insert tab | Charts group) to display the Insert Pie or Doughnut Chart gallery (Figure 1–56).

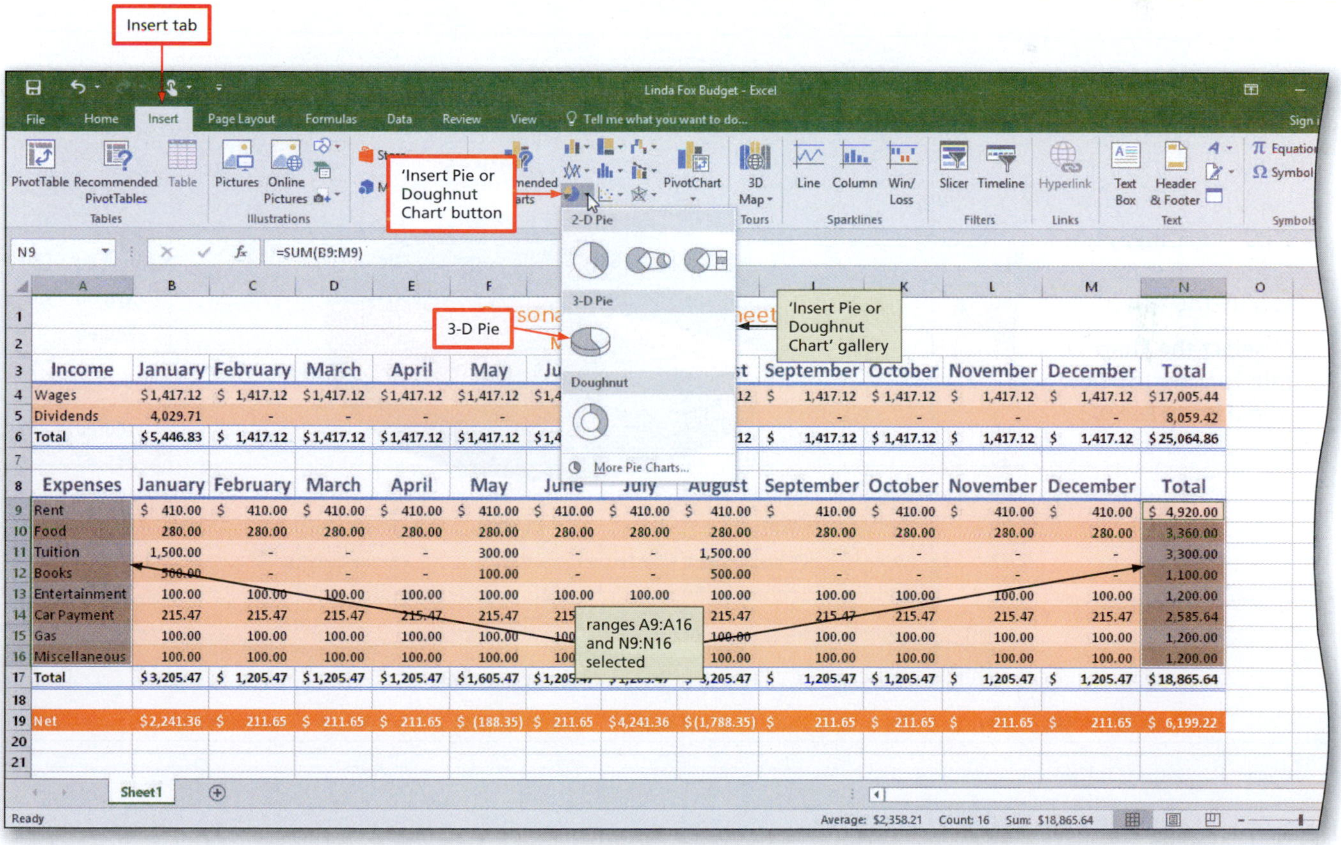

Insert tab

'Insert Pie or Doughnut Chart' button

3-D Pie

'Insert Pie or Doughnut Chart' gallery

ranges A9:A16 and N9:N16 selected

Figure 1–56

2

- Click 3-D Pie in the Insert Pie or Doughnut Chart gallery to insert the chart in the worksheet (Figure 1–57).

Q&A Why have new tabs appeared on the ribbon?
The new tabs provide additional options and functionality when you are working with certain objects, such as charts, and only display when you are working with those objects.

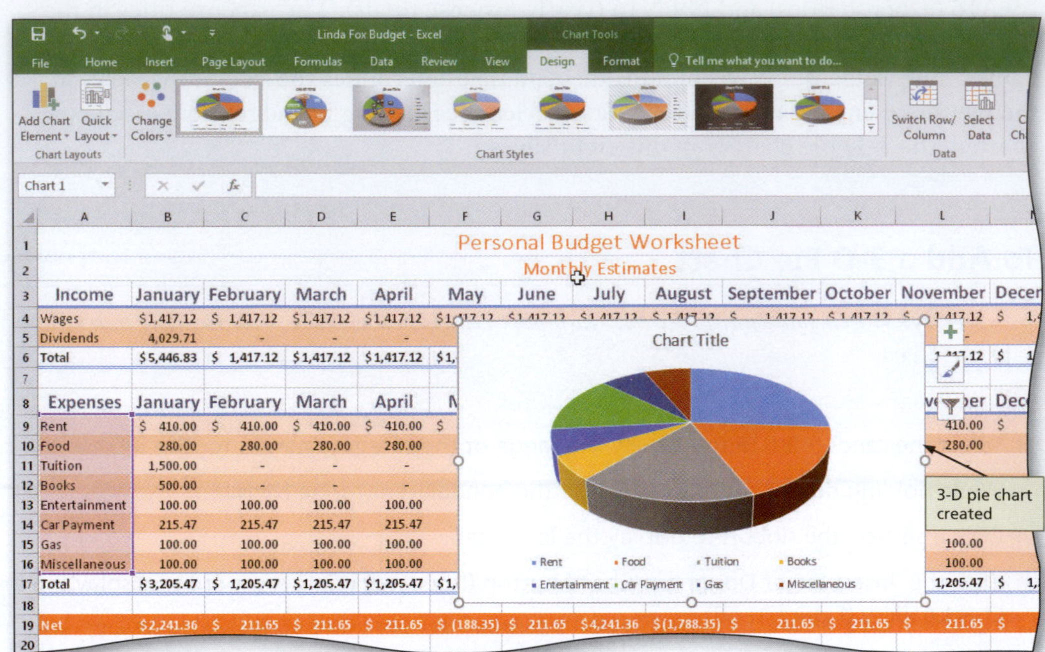

Figure 1–57

3

- Click and drag to select all the text in the chart title.
- Type `Monthly Expenses` to specify the title.
- Deselect the chart title to view the new title (Figure 1–58).

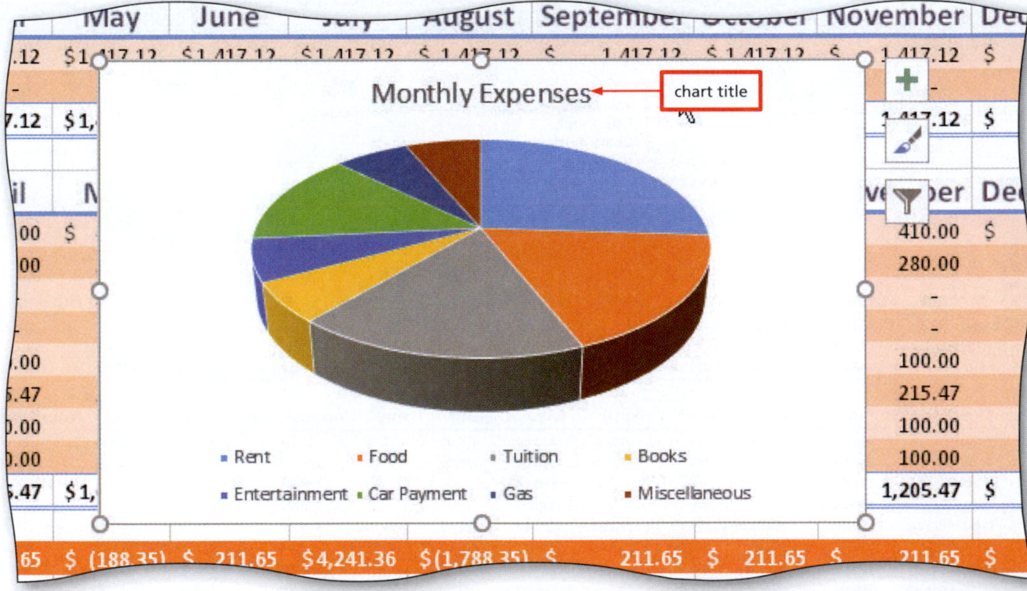

Figure 1–58

To Apply a Style to a Chart

1 ENTER TEXT | 2 CALCULATE SUMS & USE FORMULAS | 3 FORMAT TEXT
4 INSERT CHART | 5 NAME TAB | 6 PREVIEW & PRINT WORKSHEET

***Why?** If you want to enhance the appearance of a chart, you can apply a chart style.* The following steps apply Style 5 to the 3-D pie chart.

1

- Click the Chart Styles button to display the Chart Styles gallery.
- Scroll in the Chart Style gallery to display the Style 5 chart style (Figure 1–59).

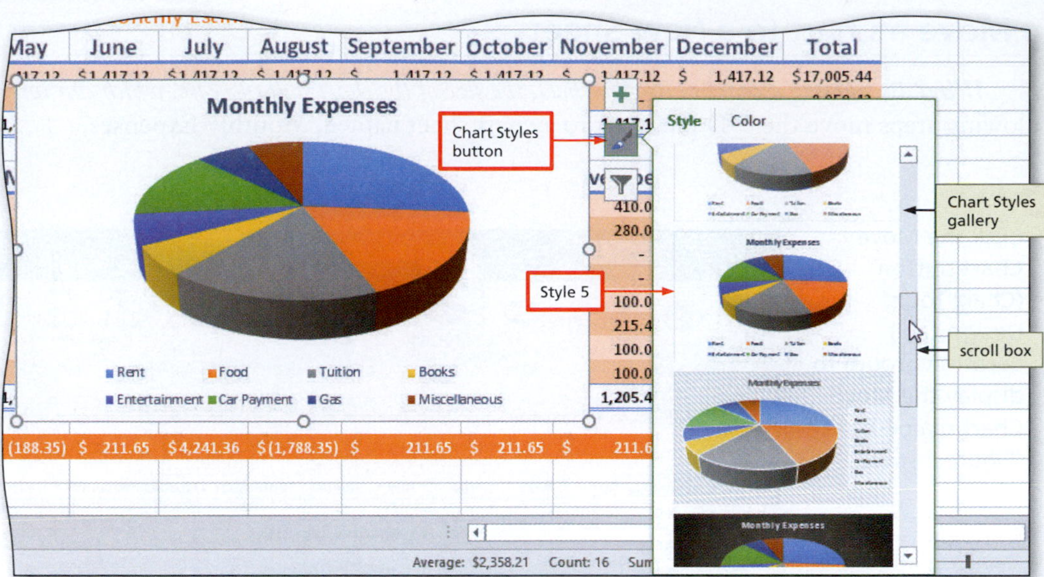

Figure 1–59

2

- Click Style 5 in the Chart Styles gallery to change the chart style to Style 5 (Figure 1–60).

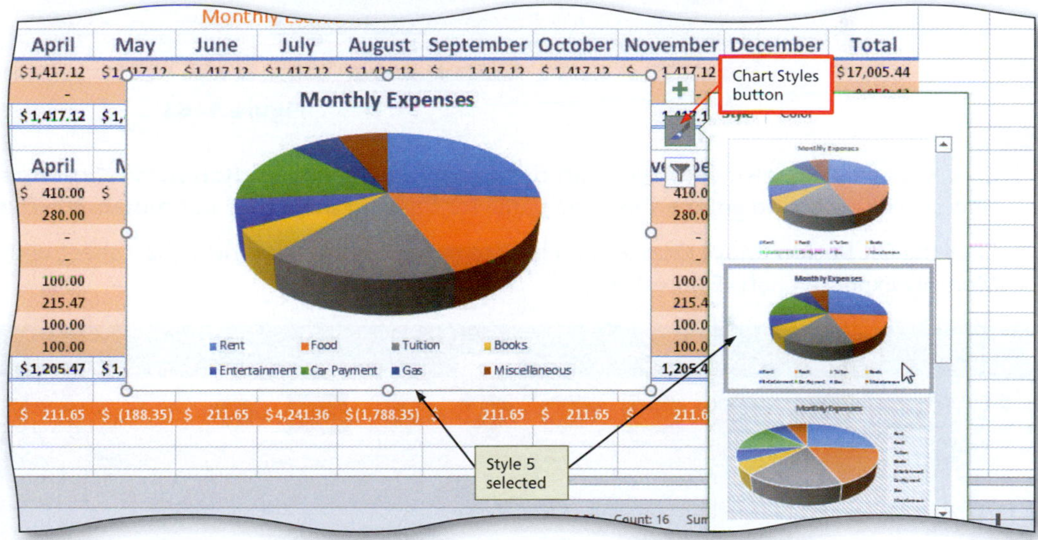

Figure 1–60

3

- Click the Chart Styles button to close the Chart Styles gallery.

Changing the Sheet Tab Names

The sheet tabs at the bottom of the window allow you to navigate between any worksheet in the workbook. You click the sheet tab of the worksheet you want to view in the Excel window. By default, the worksheets are named Sheet1, Sheet2, and so on. The worksheet names become increasingly important as you move toward more sophisticated workbooks, especially workbooks in which you reference cells between worksheets.

BTW

Exploding a Pie Chart

If you want to draw attention to a particular slice in a pie chart, you can offset the slice so that it stands out from the rest. A pie chart with one or more slices offset is referred to as an exploded pie chart. To offset a slice, click the slice two times to select it (do not double-click) and then drag the slice outward.

To Move a Chart to a New Sheet

***Why?** By moving a chart to its own sheet, the size of the chart will increase, which can improve readability.* The following steps move the 3-D pie chart to a chart sheet named, Monthly Expenses.

1

- Click the Move Chart button (Chart Tools Design tab | Location group) to display the Move Chart dialog box (Figure 1–61).

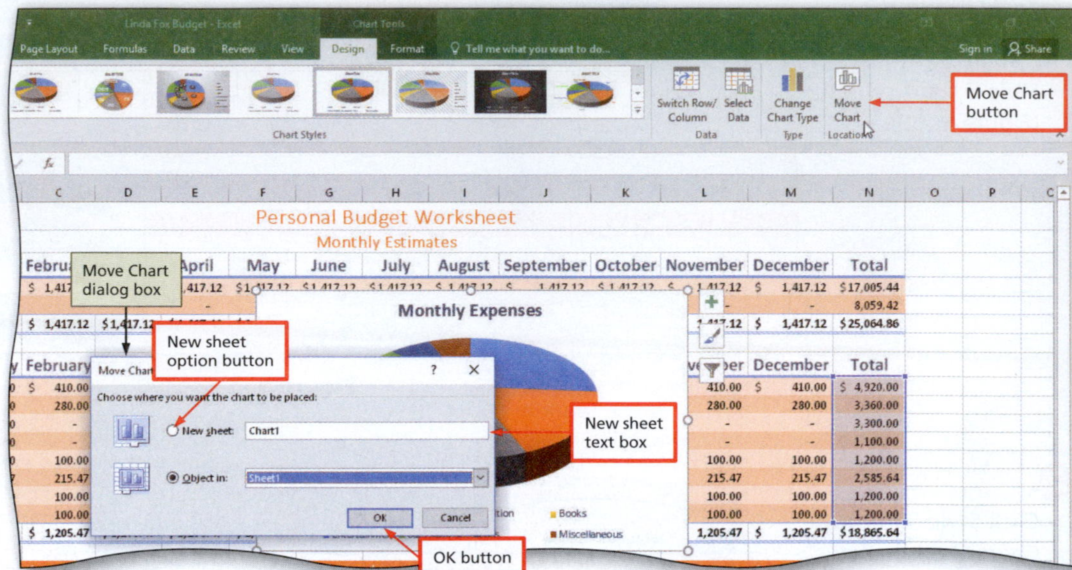

Figure 1–61

2

- Click New sheet to select it (Move Chart dialog box) and then type **Monthly Expense Chart** in the New sheet text box to enter a sheet tab name for the worksheet that will contain the chart.
- Click the OK button (Move Chart dialog box) to move the chart to a new chart sheet with the sheet tab name, Monthly Expense Chart (Figure 1–62).

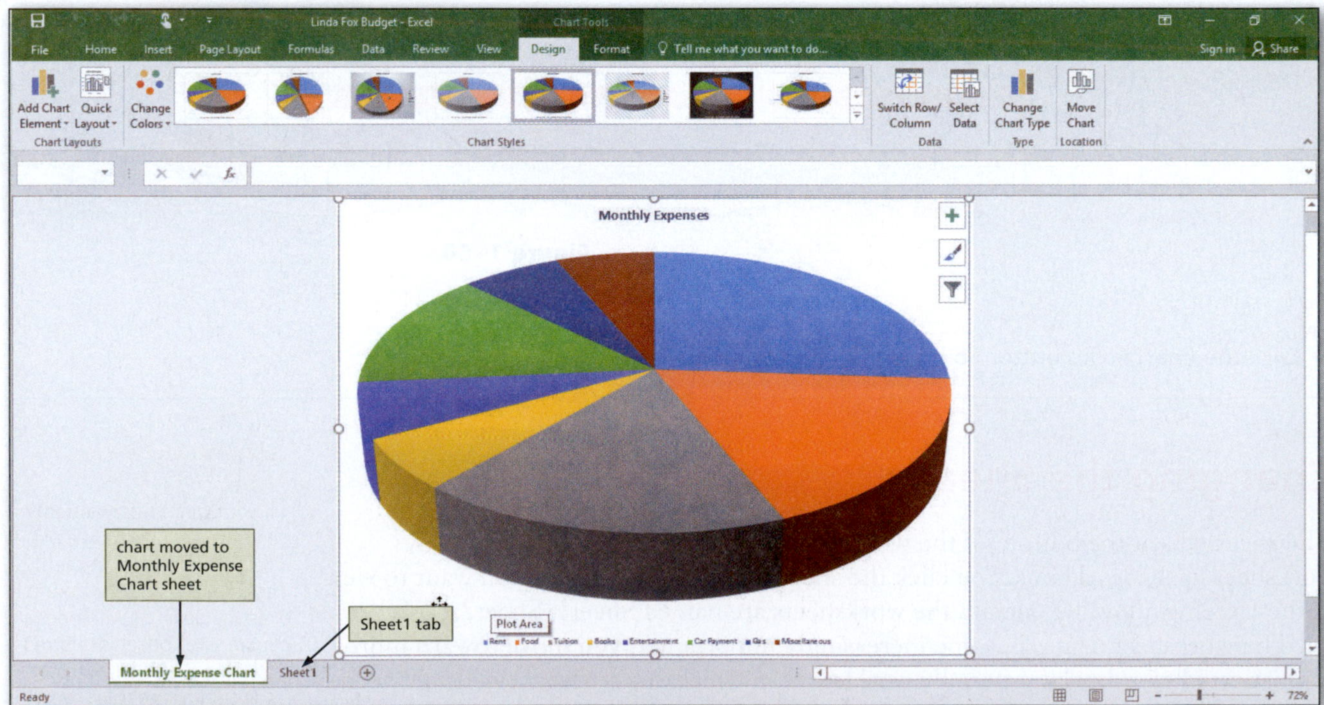

Figure 1–62

To Change the Sheet Tab Name

You decide to change the name of the Sheet1 tab to Monthly Finances. ***Why?*** *Use simple, meaningful names for each sheet tab. Sheet tab names often match the worksheet title. If a worksheet includes multiple titles in multiple sections of the worksheet, use a sheet tab name that encompasses the meaning of all of the sections.* The following steps rename the sheet tab.

1

- Double-click the sheet tab labeled Sheet1 in the lower-left corner of the window.
- Type **`Monthly Finances`** as the sheet tab name and then press the ENTER key to assign the new name to the sheet tab (Figure 1–63).

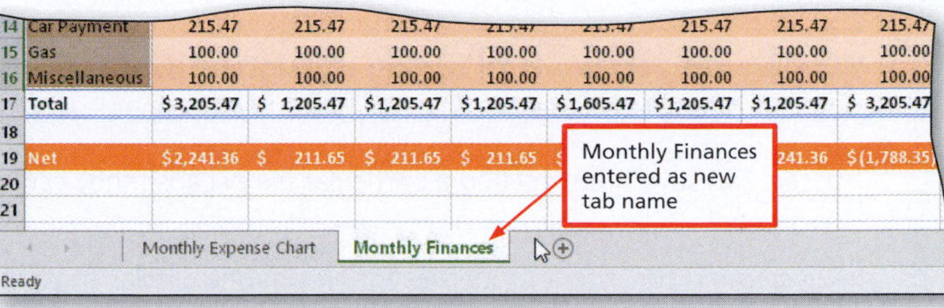

Figure 1–63

Q&A What is the maximum length for a sheet tab name?
Sheet tab names can be up to 31 characters (including spaces) in length. Longer worksheet names, however, mean that fewer sheet tabs will display on your screen. If you have multiple worksheets with long sheet tab names, you may have to scroll through sheet tabs.

2

- Right-click the sheet tab labeled, Monthly Finances, in the lower-left corner of the window to display a shortcut menu.
- Point to Tab Color on the shortcut menu to display the Tab Color gallery (Figure 1–64).

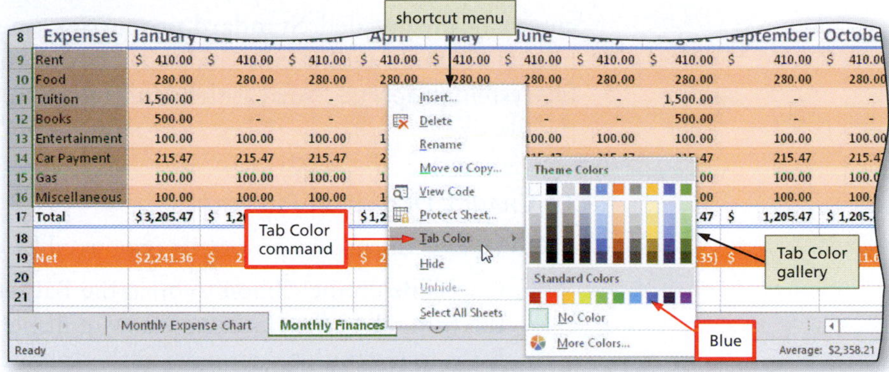

Figure 1–64

3

- Click a color that matches your shirt in the Theme Colors area to change the color of the tab (Figure 1–65).
- If necessary, click Home on the ribbon to display the Home tab.
- Save the workbook again on the same storage location with the same file name.

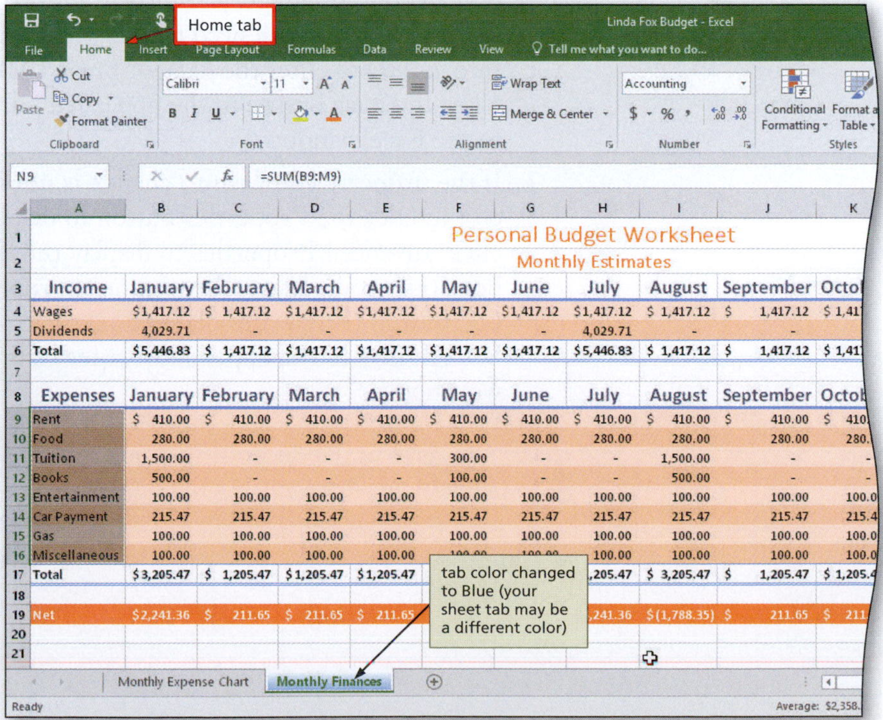

Figure 1–65

Q&A Why should I save the workbook again?
You have made several modifications to the workbook since you last saved it. Thus, you should save it again.

Document Properties

Excel helps you organize and identify your files by using **document properties**, which are the details about a file such as the project author, title, and subject. For example, you could use the class name or topic to describe the workbook's purpose or content in the document properties.

CONSIDER THIS

Why would you want to assign document properties to a workbook?
Document properties are valuable for a variety of reasons:

- Users can save time locating a particular file because they can view a file's document properties without opening the workbook.
- By creating consistent properties for files having similar content, users can better organize their workbooks.
- Some organizations require Excel users to add document properties so that other employees can view details about these files.

Common document properties include standard properties and those that are automatically updated. **Standard properties** are associated with all Microsoft Office files and include author, title, and subject. **Automatically updated properties** include file system properties, such as the date you create or change a file, and statistics, such as the file size.

To Change Document Properties

To change document properties, you would follow these steps.

1. Click File on the ribbon to open the Backstage view and then, if necessary, click the Info tab in the Backstage view to display the Info gallery. The Properties list is found in the right pane of the Info gallery.
2. If the property you wish to change is in the Properties list, click to the right of the property category to display a text box. (Note that not all properties are editable.) Type the desired text for the property and then click anywhere in the Info gallery to enter the data, or press TAB to navigate to the next property. Click the Back button in the upper-left corner of the Backstage view to return to the Excel window.
3. If the property you wish to change is not in the Properties list or you cannot edit it, click the Properties button to display the Properties menu, and then click Advanced Properties to display the Summary tab in the Properties dialog box. Type your desired text in the appropriate property text boxes. Click the OK button (Properties dialog box) to close the dialog box and then click the Back button in the upper-left corner of the Backstage view to return to the workbook.

Q&A

Why do some of the document properties in my Properties dialog box contain data?
Depending on where you are using Office 2016, your school, university, or place of employment may have customized the properties.

Printing a Worksheet

After creating a worksheet, you may want to print it. Printing a worksheet enables you to distribute the worksheet to others in a form that can be read or viewed but not edited. It is a good practice to save a workbook before printing a worksheet, in the event you experience difficulties printing.

CONSIDER THIS

What is the best method for distributing a workbook?

The traditional method of distributing a workbook uses a printer to produce a hard copy. A **hard copy** or **printout** is information that exists on paper. Hard copies can be useful for the following reasons:

- Some people prefer proofreading a hard copy of a workbook rather than viewing it on the screen to check for errors and readability.
- Hard copies can serve as a backup reference if your storage medium is lost or becomes corrupted and you need to recreate the workbook.

Instead of distributing a hard copy of a workbook, users can distribute the workbook as an electronic image that mirrors the original workbook's appearance. An electronic image of a workbook is not an editable file; it simply displays a picture of the workbook. The electronic image of the workbook can be sent as an email attachment, posted on a website, or copied to a portable storage medium such as a USB flash drive. Two popular electronic image formats, sometimes called fixed formats, are PDF by Adobe Systems and XPS by Microsoft. In Excel, you can create electronic image files through the Save As dialog box and the Export, Share, and Print tabs in the Backstage view. Electronic images of workbooks, such as PDF and XPS, can be useful for the following reasons:

- Users can view electronic images of workbooks without the software that created the original workbook (e.g., Excel). Specifically, to view a PDF file, you use a program called Adobe Reader, which can be downloaded free from Adobe's website. Similarly, to view an XPS file, you use a program called XPS Viewer, which is included in the latest version of Windows.
- Sending electronic workbooks saves paper and printer supplies. Society encourages users to contribute to **green computing**, which involves reducing the electricity consumed and environmental waste generated when using computers, mobile devices, and related technologies.

To Preview and Print a Worksheet in Landscape Orientation

1 ENTER TEXT | 2 CALCULATE SUMS & USE FORMULAS | 3 FORMAT TEXT
4 INSERT CHART | 5 NAME TAB | **6 PREVIEW & PRINT WORKSHEET**

Pages printed in **portrait orientation** have the short (8½") edge at the top of the printout; the printed page is taller than it is wide. **Landscape orientation** prints the long (11") edge at the top of the paper; the printed page is wider than it is tall. With the completed workbook saved, you may want to print it. ***Why?*** *Because the worksheet is included in a report delivered in person, you will print a hard copy on a printer.* The following steps print a hard copy of the contents of the worksheet.

- Click File on the ribbon to open the Backstage view.
- Click the Print tab in the Backstage view to display the Print gallery (Figure 1–66).

Q&A

How can I print multiple copies of my worksheet?
Increase the number in the Copies box in the Print gallery.

What if I decide not to print the worksheet at this time?
Click the Back button in the upper-left corner of the Backstage view to return to the workbook window.

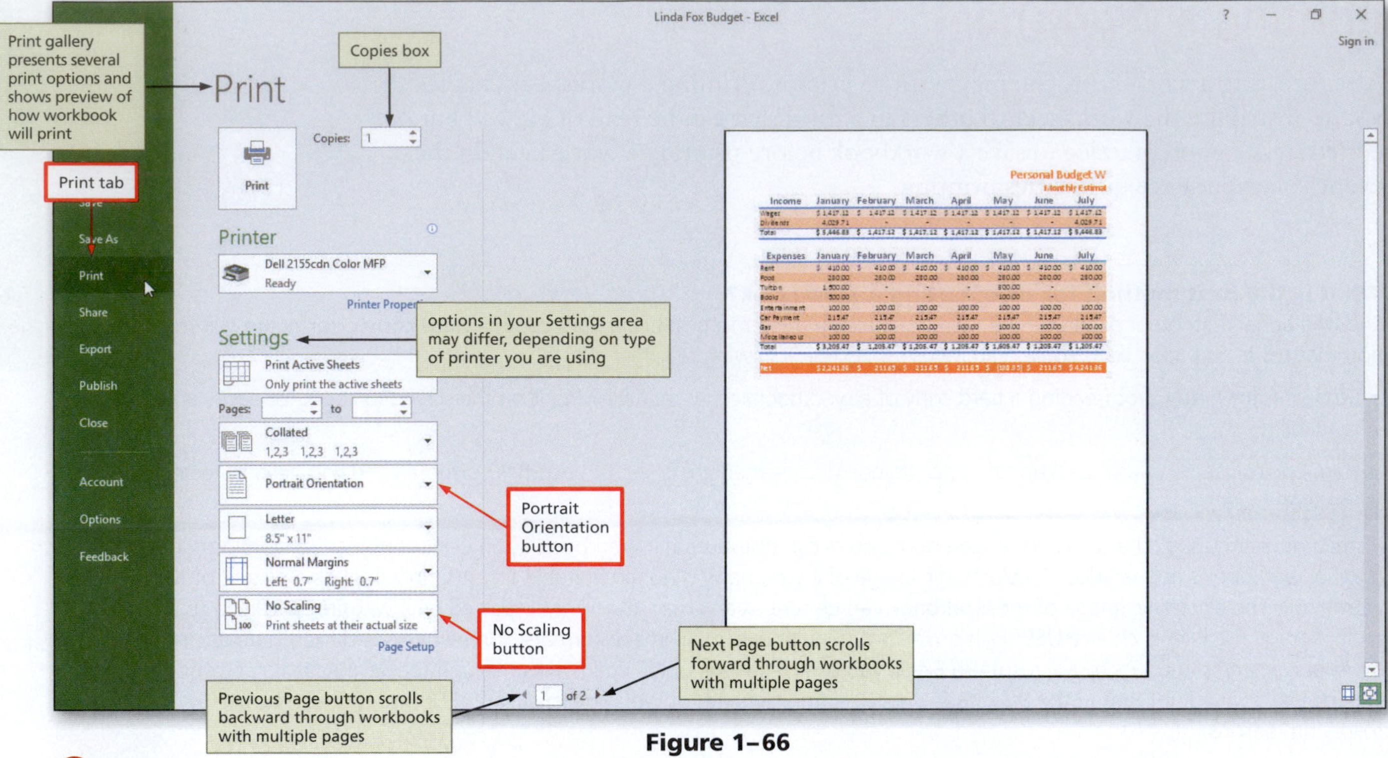

Figure 1–66

2

- Verify that the printer listed on the Printer Status button will print a hard copy of the workbook. If necessary, click the Printer Status button to display a list of available printer options and then click the desired printer to change the currently selected printer.

3

- Click the Portrait Orientation button in the Settings area and then select Landscape Orientation to change the orientation of the page to landscape.
- Click the No Scaling button and then select 'Fit Sheet on One Page' to print the entire worksheet on one page (Figure 1–67).

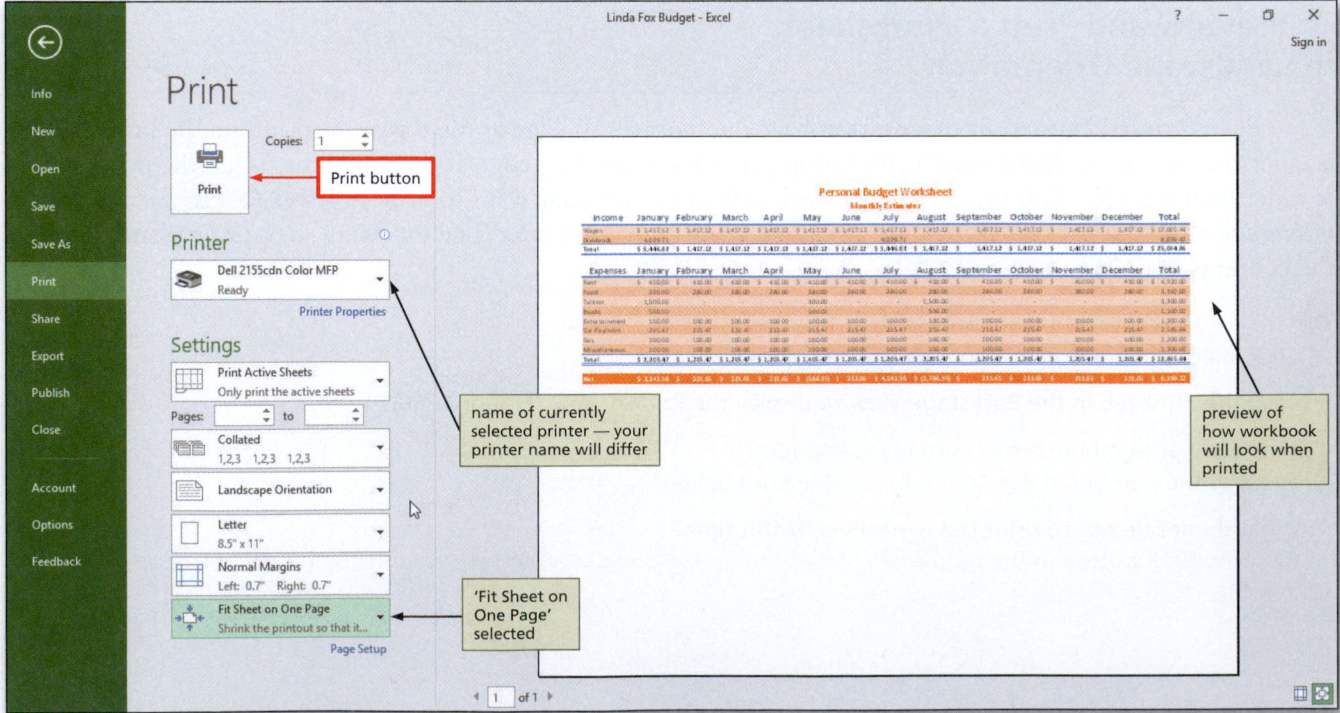

Figure 1–67

4

- Click the Print button in the Print gallery to print the worksheet in landscape orientation on the currently selected printer.
- When the printer stops, retrieve the hard copy (Figure 1–68).

Q&A Do I have to wait until my worksheet is complete to print it?
No, you can print a document at any time while you are creating it.

Personal Budget Worksheet
Monthly Estimates

Income	January	February	March	April	May	June	July	August	September	October	November	December	Total
Wages	$ 1,417.12	$ 1,417.12	$ 1,417.12	$ 1,417.12	$ 1,417.12	$ 1,417.12	$ 1,417.12	$ 1,417.12	$ 1,417.12	$ 1,417.12	$ 1,417.12	$ 1,417.12	$ 17,005.44
Dividends	4,029.71	-	-	-	-	-	4,029.71	-	-	-	-	-	8,059.42
Total	**$ 5,446.83**	**$ 1,417.12**	**$ 1,417.12**	**$ 1,417.12**	**$ 1,417.12**	**$ 1,417.12**	**$ 5,446.83**	**$ 1,417.12**	**$ 1,417.12**	**$ 1,417.12**	**$ 1,417.12**	**$ 1,417.12**	**$ 25,064.86**

Expenses	January	February	March	April	May	June	July	August	September	October	November	December	Total
Rent	$ 410.00	$ 410.00	$ 410.00	$ 410.00	$ 410.00	$ 410.00	$ 410.00	$ 410.00	$ 410.00	$ 410.00	$ 410.00	$ 410.00	$ 4,920.00
Food	280.00	280.00	280.00	280.00	280.00	280.00	280.00	280.00	280.00	280.00	280.00	280.00	3,360.00
Tuition	1,500.00	-	-	-	300.00	-	-	1,500.00	-	-	-	-	3,300.00
Books	500.00	-	-	-	100.00	-	-	500.00	-	-	-	-	1,100.00
Entertainment	100.00	100.00	100.00	100.00	100.00	100.00	100.00	100.00	100.00	100.00	100.00	100.00	1,200.00
Car Payment	215.47	215.47	215.47	215.47	215.47	215.47	215.47	215.47	215.47	215.47	215.47	215.47	2,585.64
Gas	100.00	100.00	100.00	100.00	100.00	100.00	100.00	100.00	100.00	100.00	100.00	100.00	1,200.00
Miscellaneous	100.00	100.00	100.00	100.00	100.00	100.00	100.00	100.00	100.00	100.00	100.00	100.00	1,200.00
Total	**$ 3,205.47**	**$ 1,205.47**	**$ 1,205.47**	**$ 1,205.47**	**$ 1,605.47**	**$ 1,205.47**	**$ 1,205.47**	**$ 3,205.47**	**$ 1,205.47**	**$ 1,205.47**	**$ 1,205.47**	**$ 1,205.47**	**$ 18,865.64**
Net	$ 2,241.36	$ 211.65	$ 211.65	$ 211.65	$ (188.35)	$ 211.65	$ 4,241.36	$ (1,788.35)	$ 211.65	$ 211.65	$ 211.65	$ 211.65	$ 6,199.22

Figure 1–68

Other Ways

1. Press CTRL+P to open Print Gallery, press ENTER

Autocalculate

You easily can obtain a total, an average, or other information about the numbers in a range by using the **AutoCalculate area** on the status bar. First, select the range of cells containing the numbers you want to check. Next, right-click the AutoCalculate area to display the Customize Status Bar shortcut menu (Figure 1–69). The check marks indicate that the calculations are displayed in the status bar; more than one may be selected. The functions of the AutoCalculate commands on the Customize Status Bar shortcut menu are described in Table 1–4.

BTW

Distributing a Workbook

Instead of printing and distributing a hard copy of a workbook, you can distribute the workbook electronically. Options include sending the workbook via email; posting it on cloud storage (such as OneDrive) and sharing the file with others; posting it on social media, a blog, or other website; and sharing a link associated with an online location of the workbook. You also can create and share a PDF or XPS image of the workbook, so that users can view the file in Acrobat Reader or XPS Viewer instead of in Excel.

Table 1–4 Commonly Used Status Bar Commands

Command	Function
Average	AutoCalculate area displays the average of the numbers in the selected range
Count	AutoCalculate area displays the number of non-empty cells in the selected range
Numerical Count	AutoCalculate area displays the number of cells containing numbers in the selected range
Minimum	AutoCalculate area displays the lowest value in the selected range
Maximum	AutoCalculate area displays the highest value in the selected range
Sum	AutoCalculate area displays the sum of the numbers in the selected range

To Use the AutoCalculate Area to Determine a Maximum

The following steps determine the largest monthly total in the budget. ***Why?** Sometimes, you want a quick analysis, which can be especially helpful when your worksheet contains a lot of data.*

1

- Select the range B19:M19. Right-click the status bar to display the Customize Status Bar shortcut menu (Figure 1–69).

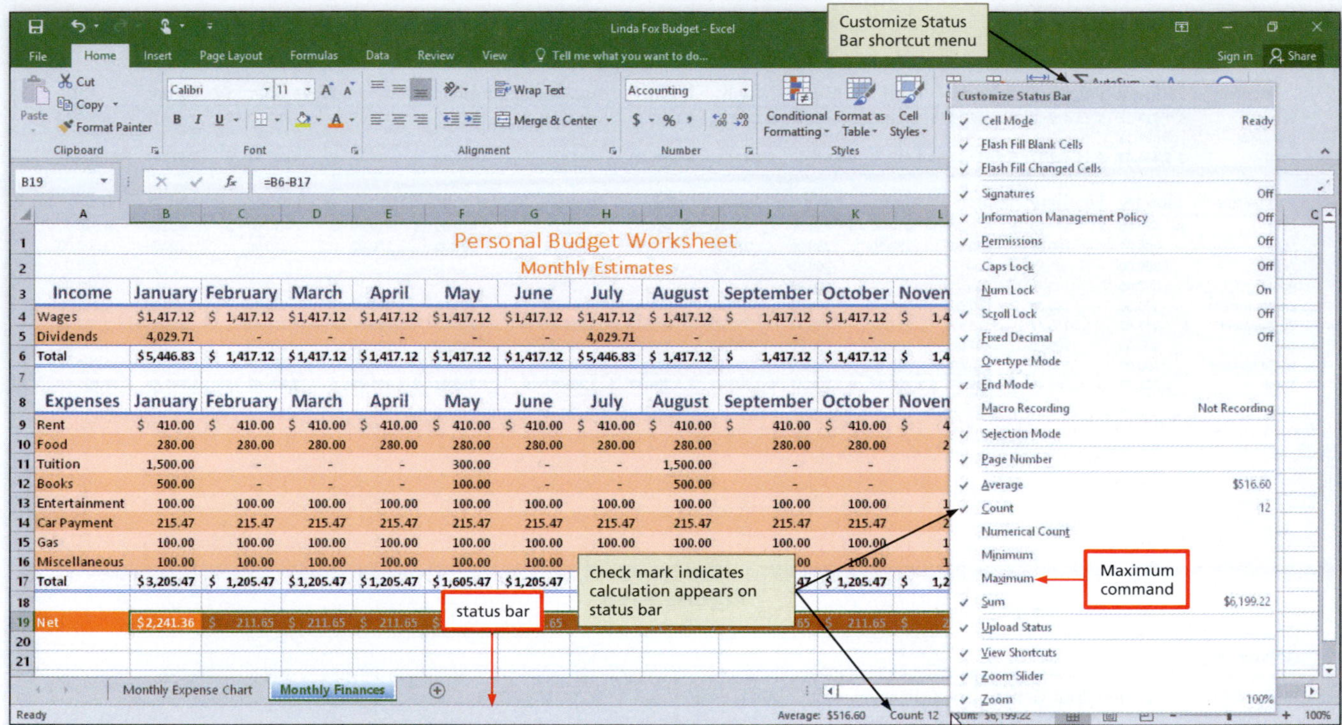

Figure 1–69

2

- Click Maximum on the shortcut menu to display the Maximum value in the range B19:M19 in the AutoCalculate area of the status bar.
- Click anywhere on the worksheet to close the shortcut menu (Figure 1–70).

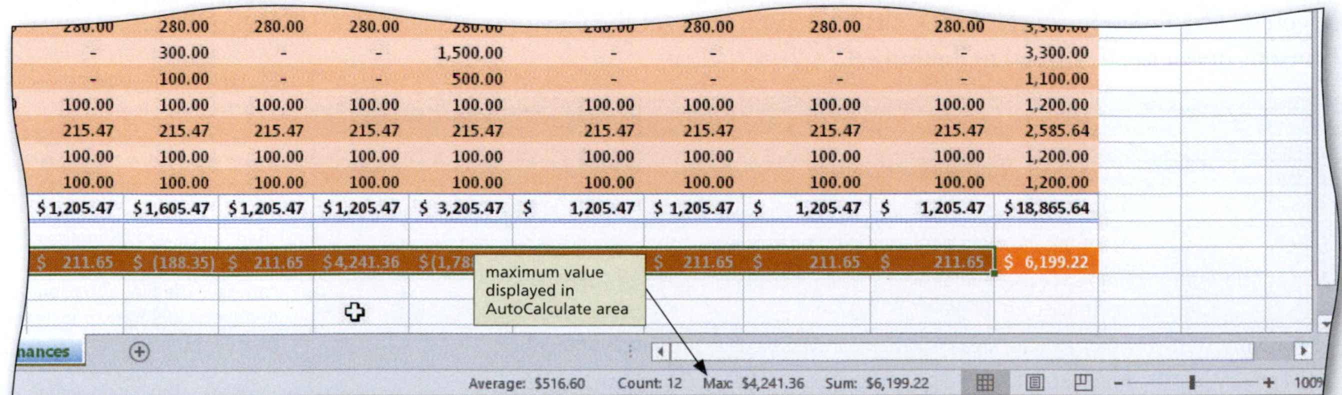

Figure 1–70

- Right-click the AutoCalculate area and then click Maximum on the shortcut menu to deselect it. The Maximum value will no longer appear on the status bar.
- Close the shortcut menu.

- Save the workbook using the same file name in the same storage location.
- If desired, sign out of your Microsoft account.
- Exit Excel.

Correcting Errors

You can correct data entry errors on a worksheet using one of several methods. The method you choose will depend on the extent of the error and whether you notice it while entering the data or after you have entered the incorrect data into the cell.

Correcting Errors while Entering Data into a Cell

If you notice an error while you are entering data into a cell, press the BACKSPACE key to erase the incorrect character(s) and then enter the correct character(s). If the error is a major one, click the Cancel box in the formula bar or press the ESC key to erase the entire entry and then reenter the data.

Correcting Errors after Entering Data into a Cell

If you find an error in the worksheet after entering the data, you can correct the error in one of two ways:

1. If the entry is short, select the cell, retype the entry correctly, and then click the Enter button or press the ENTER key. The new entry will replace the old entry.
2. If the entry in the cell is long and the errors are minor, using Edit mode may be a better choice than retyping the cell entry. In **Edit mode**, Excel displays the active cell entry in the formula bar and a flashing insertion point in the active cell, and you can edit the contents directly in the cell — a procedure called **in-cell editing.**
   a. Double-click the cell containing the error to switch Excel to Edit mode (Figure 1–71).
   b. Make corrections using the following in-cell editing methods.
      (1) To insert new characters between two characters, place the insertion point between the two characters and begin typing. Excel inserts the new characters to the left of the insertion point.

11	Tuition	1,500.00	-	-	-	300.00	-	-	1,500.00	-	-	
12	Books	500.00	-	-	-	100.00	-	-	500.00	-	-	
13	Entertainment	100.00	100.00	100.00	100.00	100.00	100.00	100.00	100.00	100.00	100.00	
14	Car Payment	215.47	215.47	215.47	215.47	215.47	215.47	215.47	215.47	215.47	215.47	
15	Gas	100.00	100.00	100.00	100.00	100.00	100.00	100.00	100.00	100.00	100.00	
16	Miscellaneous	100.00		00.00	100.00	100.00	100.00	100.00	100.00	100.00	100.00	
17	Total	$3,205.47		05.47	$1,205.47	$1,605.47	$1,205.47	$1,205.47	$ 3,205.47	$ 1,205.47	$ 1,205.47	$
18												
19	Net	$2,241.36	$ 211.65	$ 211.65	$ 211.65	$ (188.35)	$ 211.65	$4,241.36	$(1,788.35)	$ 211.65	$ 211.65	$
20												
21												

in-cell editing

Monthly Expense Chart | Monthly Finances

Edit

Figure 1–71

(2) To delete a character in the cell, move the insertion point to the left of the character you want to delete and then press the DELETE key, or place the insertion point to the right of the character you want to delete and then press the BACKSPACE key. You also can drag to select the character or adjacent characters you want to delete and then press the DELETE key or CTRL+X, or click the Cut button (Home tab | Clipboard group).

(3) When you are finished editing an entry, click the Enter button or press the ENTER key.

There are two ways for entering data in Edit mode: Insert mode and Overtype mode. In the default **Insert mode**, as you type a character, Excel inserts the character and moves all characters to the right of the typed character one position to the right. You can change to Overtype mode by pressing the INSERT key. In **Overtype mode**, Excel replaces, or overtypes, the character to the right of the insertion point. The INSERT key toggles the keyboard between Insert mode and Overtype mode.

While in Edit mode, you may have reason to move the insertion point to various points in the cell, select portions of the data in the cell, or switch from inserting characters to overtyping characters. Table 1–5 summarizes the more common tasks performed during in-cell editing.

Table 1–5 Summary of In-Cell Editing Tasks

	Task	Mouse Operation	Keyboard
1.	Move the insertion point to the beginning of data in a cell.	Point to the left of the first character and click.	Press HOME
2.	Move the insertion point to the end of data in a cell.	Point to the right of the last character and click.	Press END
3.	Move the insertion point anywhere in a cell.	Point to the appropriate position and click the character.	Press RIGHT ARROW or LEFT ARROW
4.	Highlight one or more adjacent characters.	Drag through adjacent characters.	Press SHIFT+RIGHT ARROW or SHIFT+LEFT ARROW
5.	Select all data in a cell.	Double-click the cell with the insertion point in the cell if the data in the cell contains no spaces.	
6.	Delete selected characters.	Click the Cut button (Home tab | Clipboard group).	Press DELETE
7.	Delete characters to the left of the insertion point.		Press BACKSPACE
8.	Delete characters to the right of the insertion point.		Press DELETE
9.	Toggle between Insert and Overtype modes.		Press INSERT

Undoing the Last Cell Entry

The Undo button on the Quick Access Toolbar (Figure 1–72) allows you to erase recent cell entries. Thus, if you enter incorrect data in a cell and notice it immediately, click the Undo button and Excel changes the cell entry to what it was prior to the incorrect data entry.

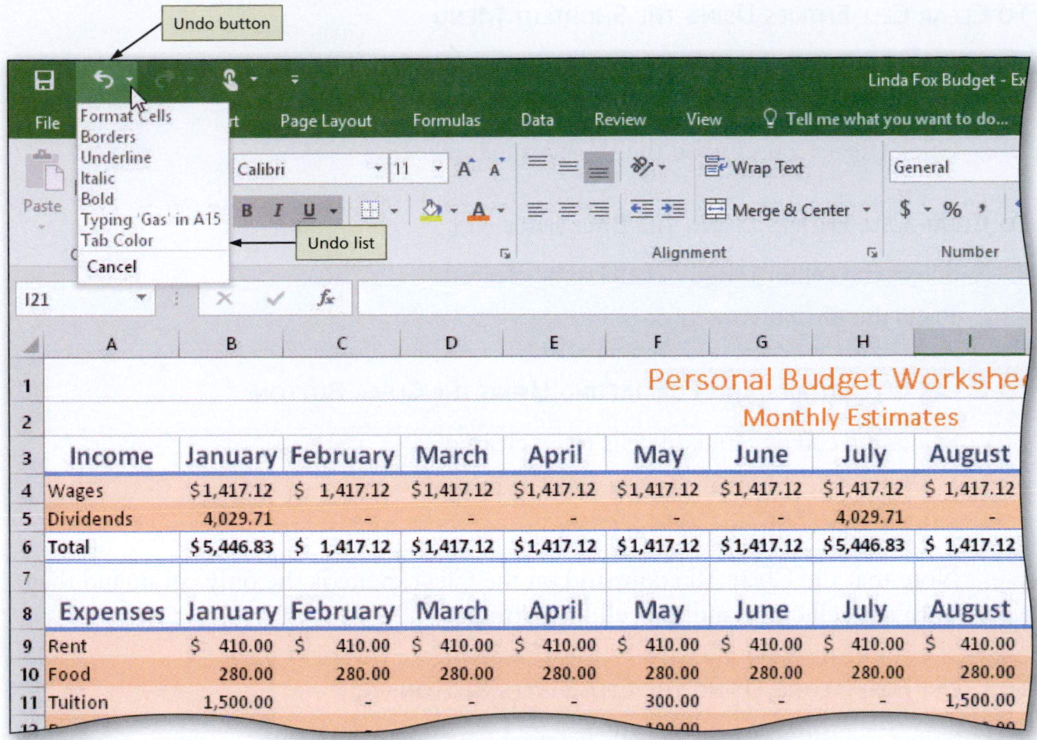

Figure 1–72

Excel remembers the last 100 actions you have completed. Thus, you can undo up to 100 previous actions by clicking the Undo arrow to display the Undo list and then clicking the action to be undone (Figure 1–72). You can drag through several actions in the Undo list to undo all of them at once. If no actions are available for Excel to undo, then the dimmed appearance of the Undo button indicates that it is unavailable.

The Redo button, next to the Undo button on the Quick Access Toolbar, allows you to repeat previous actions; that is, if you accidentally undo an action, you can use the Redo button to perform the action again.

Clearing a Cell or Range of Cells

If you enter data into the wrong cell or range of cells, you can erase, or clear, the data using one of the first four methods listed below. The fifth method clears the formatting from the selected cells. To clear a cell or range of cells, you would perform the following steps:

To Clear Cell Entries Using the Fill Handle

1. Select the cell or range of cells and then point to the fill handle so that the pointer changes to a crosshair.
2. Drag the fill handle back into the selected cell or range until a shadow covers the cell or cells you want to erase.

To Clear Cell Entries Using the Shortcut Menu

1. Select the cell or range of cells to be cleared.
2. Right-click the selection.
3. Click Clear Contents on the shortcut menu.

To Clear Cell Entries Using the Backspace Key

1. Select the cell or range of cells to be cleared.
2. Press the BACKSPACE key.

To Clear Cell Entries and Formatting Using the Clear Button

1. Select the cell or range of cells to be cleared.
2. Click the Clear button (Home tab | Editing group).
3. Click Clear Contents on the Clear menu.

Note that the Clear All command on the Clear menu is the only command that clears both the cell entry and the cell formatting.

To Clear Formatting Using the Cell Styles Button

1. Select the cell or range of cells from which you want to remove the formatting.
2. Click the Cell Styles button (Home tab | Styles group) and then click Normal in the Cell Styles gallery.

As you are clearing cell entries, always remember that you should *never press the SPACEBAR to clear a cell.* Pressing the SPACEBAR enters a blank character. A blank character is interpreted by Excel as text and is different from an empty cell, even though the cell may appear empty.

Clearing the Entire Worksheet

If the required worksheet edits are extremely extensive or if the requirements drastically change, you may want to clear the entire worksheet and start over. To clear the worksheet or delete an embedded chart, you would use the following steps.

To Clear the Entire Worksheet

1. Click the Select All button on the worksheet. The Select All button is located above the row 1 identifier and to the left of the column A heading.
2. Click the Clear button (Home tab | Editing group) and then click Clear All on the menu to delete both the entries and formats.

The Select All button selects the entire worksheet. Instead of clicking the Select All button, you can press CTRL+A. To clear an unsaved workbook, click the Close Window button on the workbook's title bar or click the Close button in the Backstage view. Click the No button if the Microsoft Excel dialog box asks if you want to save changes. To start a new, blank workbook, click the New button in the Backstage view.

Summary

In this module you have learned how to create a personal budget worksheet and chart. Topics covered included selecting a cell, entering text, entering numbers, calculating a sum, using the fill handle, formatting a worksheet, adding a pie chart, changing sheet tab names, printing a worksheet, AutoCalculate, and correcting errors.

CONSIDER THIS: PLAN AHEAD

What decisions will you need to make when creating workbooks and charts in the future?

1. Determine the workbook structure.
   a) Determine the data you will need for your workbook.
   b) Sketch a layout of your data and your chart.
2. Create the worksheet.
   a) Enter titles, subtitles, and headings.
   b) Enter data, functions, and formulas.
3. Format the worksheet.
   a) Format the titles, subtitles, and headings using styles.
   b) Format the totals.
   c) Format the numbers.
   d) Format the text.
   e) Adjust column widths.
4. Create the chart.
   a) Determine the type of chart to use.
   b) Determine the chart title and data.
   c) Format the chart.

Apply Your Knowledge

Reinforce the skills and apply the concepts you learned in this module.

Changing the Values in a Worksheet

Note: To complete this assignment, you will be required to use the Data Files. Please contact your instructor for information about accessing the required files.

Instructions: Run Excel. Open the workbook Apply 1–1 Lima Wholesale (Figure 1–73a). The workbook you open contains sales data for Lima Wholesale. You are to apply formatting to the worksheet and move the chart to a new sheet tab.

Table 1–6 New Worksheet Data

Cell	Change Cell Contents To
A2	Monthly Departmental Sales
B5	15242.36
C7	114538.23
D5	25747.85
E6	39851.44
F7	29663.77
G6	19885.41

Perform the following tasks:

1. Make the changes to the worksheet described in Table 1–6 so that the worksheet appears as shown in Figure 1–73b. As you edit the values in the cells containing numeric data, watch the totals in row 8, the totals in column H, and the chart change.
2. Change the worksheet title in cell A1 to the Title cell style and then merge and center it across columns A through H.
3. Use buttons in the Font group on the Home tab on the ribbon to change the worksheet subtitle in cell A2 to 16-point font and then center it across columns A through H. Change the font color of cell A2 to Dark Blue, Text 2, Darker 25%.
4. Apply the worksheet name, Monthly Sales, and the Dark Blue, Text 2, Darker 25% color to the sheet tab.
5. Move the chart to a new sheet called Sales Analysis Chart (Figure 1–73c). Change the chart title to SALES TOTALS.
6. If requested by your instructor, replace Lima in cell A1 with your last name.
7. Save the workbook using the file name, Apply 1–1 Lima Wholesale Sales Analysis.
8. Submit the revised workbook as specified by your instructor and exit Excel.
9. Besides the styles used in the worksheet, what other changes could you make to enhance the worksheet?

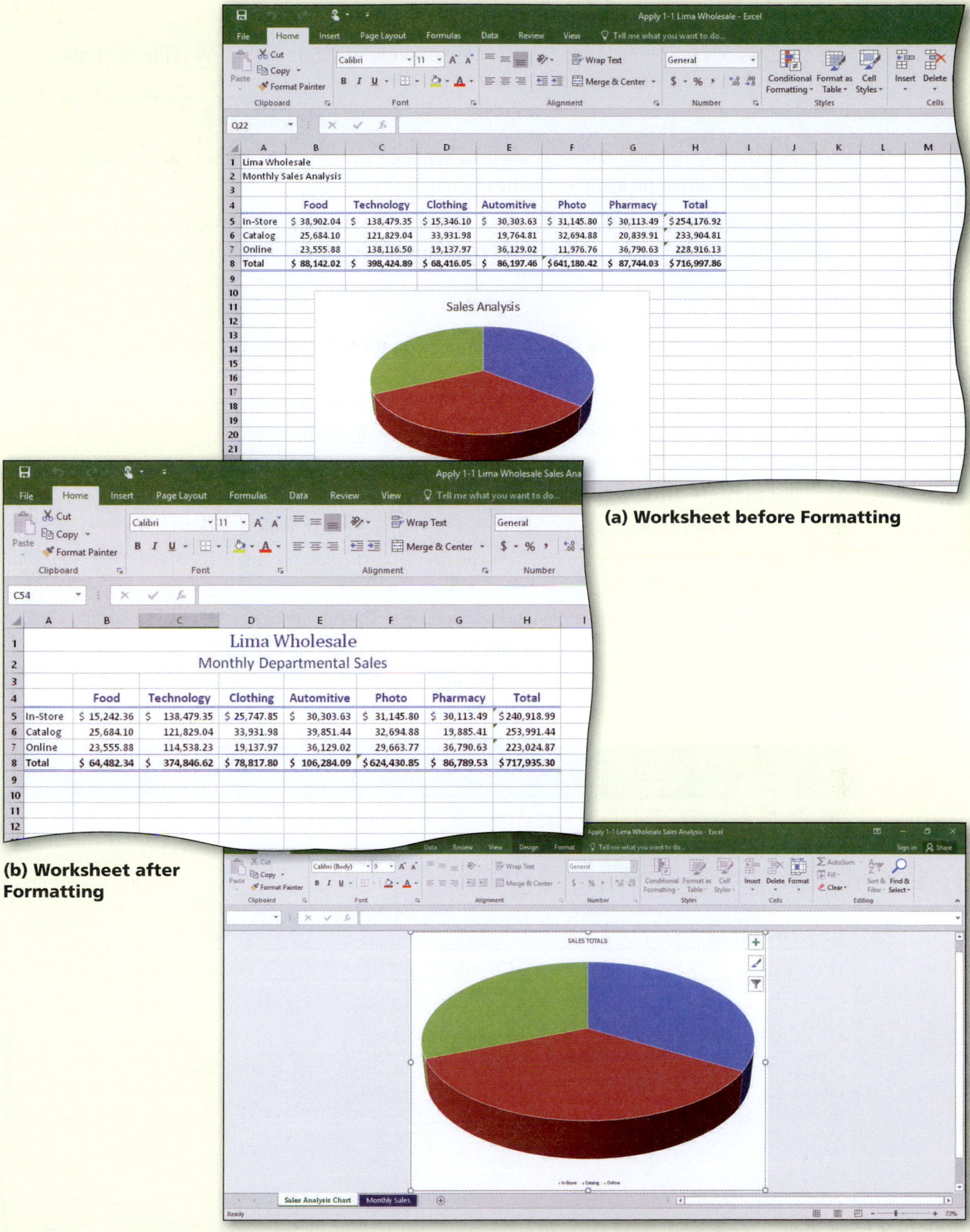

	A	B	C	D	E	F	G	H
1	Lima Wholesale							
2	Monthly Sales Analysis							
3								
4		Food	Technology	Clothing	Automitive	Photo	Pharmacy	Total
5	In-Store	$ 38,902.04	$ 138,479.35	$ 15,346.10	$ 30,303.63	$ 31,145.80	$ 30,113.49	$254,176.92
6	Catalog	25,684.10	121,829.04	33,931.98	19,764.81	32,694.88	20,839.91	233,904.81
7	Online	23,555.88	138,116.50	19,137.97	36,129.02	11,976.76	36,790.63	228,916.13
8	Total	$ 88,142.02	$ 398,424.89	$ 68,416.05	$ 86,197.46	$641,180.42	$ 87,744.03	$716,997.86

Sales Analysis

(a) Worksheet before Formatting

	A	B	C	D	E	F	G	H
1	Lima Wholesale							
2	Monthly Departmental Sales							
3								
4		Food	Technology	Clothing	Automitive	Photo	Pharmacy	Total
5	In-Store	$ 15,242.36	$ 138,479.35	$ 25,747.85	$ 30,303.63	$ 31,145.80	$ 30,113.49	$240,918.99
6	Catalog	25,684.10	121,829.04	33,931.98	39,851.44	32,694.88	19,885.41	253,991.44
7	Online	23,555.88	114,538.23	19,137.97	36,129.02	29,663.77	36,790.63	223,024.87
8	Total	$ 64,482.34	$ 374,846.62	$ 78,817.80	$ 106,284.09	$624,430.85	$ 86,789.53	$717,935.30

(b) Worksheet after Formatting

(c) 3-D Pie Chart on Separate Sheet

Figure 1–73

Extend Your Knowledge

Extend the skills you learned in this module and experiment with new skills. You may need to use Help to complete the assignment.

Creating Styles and Formatting a Worksheet

Note: To complete this assignment, you will be required to use the Data Files. Please contact your instructor for information about accessing the required files.

Instructions: Run Excel. Open the workbook Extend 1–1 Dasminne Grocery (Figure 1–74). The workbook you open contains sales data for Dasminne Grocery. You are to create styles and format a worksheet using them.

Perform the following tasks:

1. Select cell A4. Use the New Cell Style command in the Cell Styles gallery to create a style that uses the Blue, Accent 1, Darker 50% font color (row 6, column 5). Name the style, MyHeadings.
2. Select cell A5. Use the New Cell style dialog box to create a style that uses the Blue, Accent 1, Darker 25% (row 5, column 5) font color. Name the style, MyRows.
3. Select cell ranges B4:G4 and A5:A8. Apply the MyHeadings style to the cell ranges.
4. Select the cell range B5:G7. Apply the MyRows style to the cell range.
5. Apply a worksheet name to the sheet tab and apply a color of your choice to the sheet tab.
6. If requested by your instructor, change the font color for the text in cells A1 and A2 to the color of your eyes, if available.
7. Save the workbook using the file name, Extend 1–1 Dasminne Grocery Third Quarter.
8. Submit the revised workbook as specified by your instructor and exit Excel.
9. What other styles would you create to improve the worksheet's appearance?

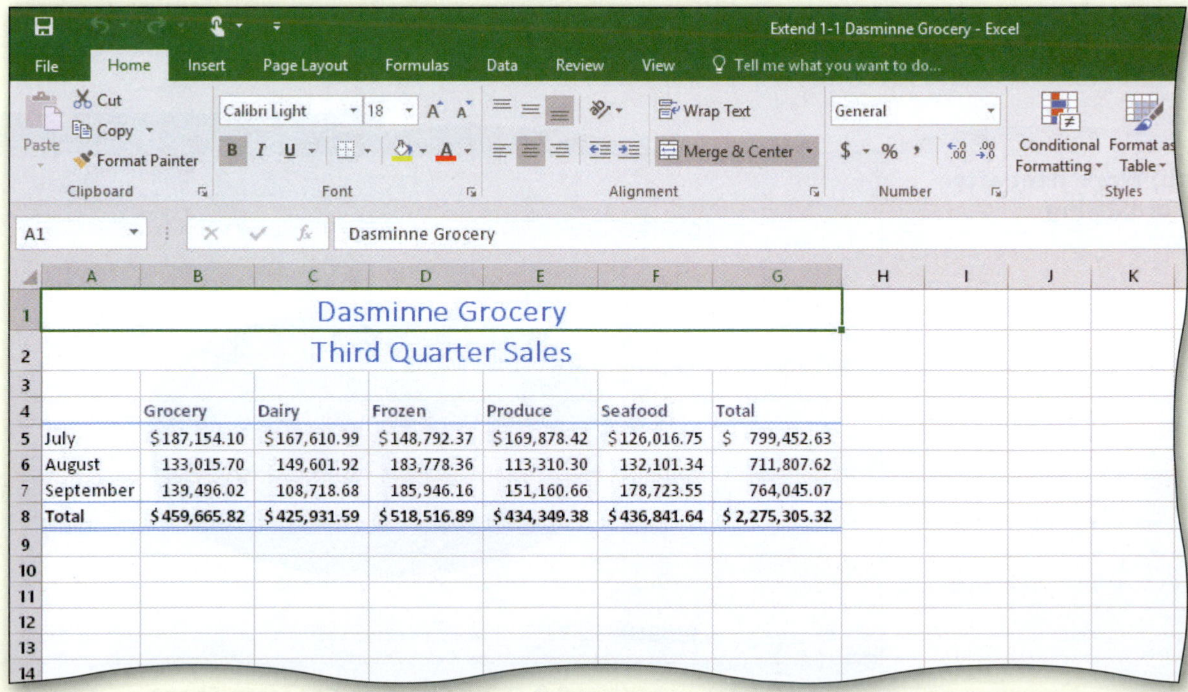

Figure 1–74

Expand Your World

Create a solution that uses cloud or web technologies by learning and investigating on your own from general guidance.

College Loan Calculator

Instructions: You are tasked with determining how long it will take you to pay back your college loans. You decide to download and use one of Excel's templates to create your worksheet.

Perform the following tasks:

1. Click the New tab in the Backstage view and then search for and click the College loan calculator template to download it.
2. Enter data for your estimated salary after graduation, the date you will begin paying back loans, as well as fictitious (but realistic) information for four loans, including loan number, lender, loan amount, annual interest rate, beginning date, and length (in years).
3. Save the file as Expand 1-1: College Loans. Print the worksheet.
4. Submit the assignment as specified by your instructor.
5. Which template would you use if you wanted to plan and keep track of a budget for a wedding?

In the Labs

Design, create, modify, and/or use a workbook following the guidelines, concepts, and skills presented in this module. Labs 1 and 2, which increase in difficulty, require you to create solutions based on what you learned in the module; Lab 3 requires you to apply your creative thinking and problem-solving skills to design and implement a solution.

Lab 1: First Quarter Revenue Analysis Worksheet

Problem: You work as a spreadsheet specialist for Katie's Kicks, which has four regional shops in the state of Florida. Your manager has asked you to develop a first quarter revenue analysis similar to the one shown in Figure 1–75.

Perform the following tasks:

1. Run Excel and create a new blank workbook. Enter the worksheet title, Katie's Kicks, in cell A1 and the worksheet subtitle, First Quarter Revenue Analysis, in cell A2. Beginning in row 4, enter the region data shown in Table 1–7.

Table 1–7 Katie's Kicks

	North	South	East	West
Sneakers	72714.58	77627.29	76607.31	49008.32
Shoes	45052.23	69165.66	76243.41	84844.01
Sandals	77630.94	78684.24	56601.25	72716.68
Accessories	65423.73	77690.69	58383.67	54433.07
Miscellaneous	55666.92	78618.97	47317.09	68594.40

2. Create totals for each region, product, and company grand total.
3. Format the worksheet title with the Title cell style. Center the title across columns A through F.

Continued >

STUDENT ASSIGNMENTS

In the Labs *continued*

4. Format the worksheet subtitle to 16-point Calibri Light, and change the font color to Blue-Gray, Text 2. Center the subtitle across columns A through F.
5. Use Cell Styles to format the range A4:F4 with the Heading 3 cell style, the range B4:F4 with the Accent1 cell style, and the range A10:F10 with the Total cell style.
6. Center the column titles in row 4. Apply the accounting number format to the ranges B5:F5 and B10:F10. Apply the comma style format to the range B6:F9. Adjust any column widths to the widest text entry in each column.
7. Select the ranges B4:E4 and B10:E10 and then insert a 3-D pie chart. Apply the Style 3 chart style to the chart. Move the chart to a new worksheet named Revenue Analysis Chart. Change the chart title to First Quarter Revenue Analysis.
8. Rename the Sheet1 tab, First Quarter, and apply the Green color to the sheet tab.
9. If requested by your instructor, change the font color of the text in cells A1 and A2 to the color of the shirt you currently are wearing.
10. Save the workbook using the file name, Lab 1-1 Katie's Kicks.
11. Preview and print the worksheet in landscape orientation.
12. If you wanted to chart the item totals instead of the regions, which ranges would you use to create the chart?
13. Submit the assignment as specified by your instructor.

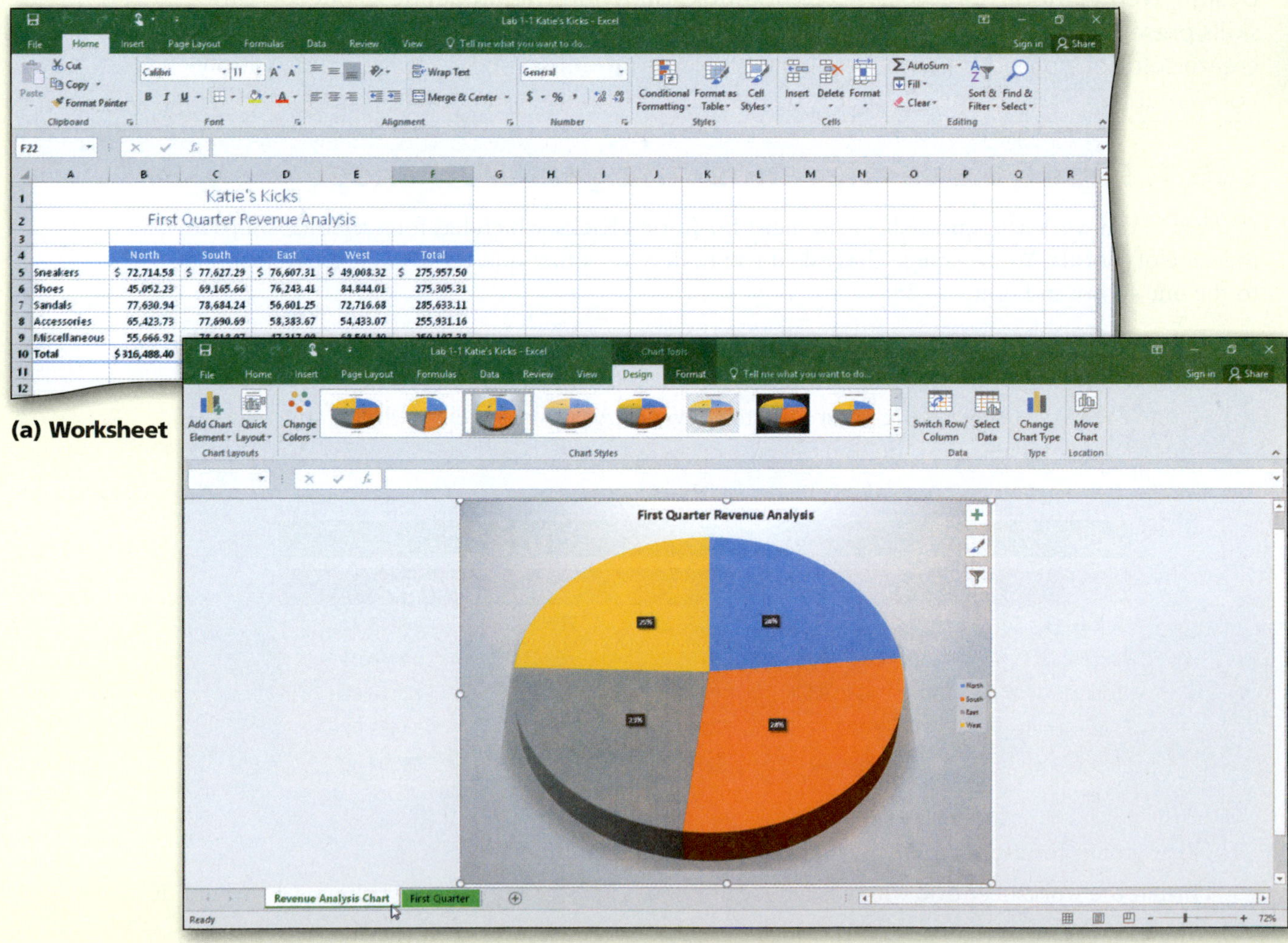

(a) Worksheet

(b) Pie Chart

Figure 1–75

Lab 2: Sales Analysis Worksheet

Problem: As the chief accountant for Davis Mobile Concepts, a leading car audio dealer serving four states, you have been asked by the vice president to create a worksheet to analyze the yearly sales for each state (Figure 1–76). The packages and corresponding sales by state for the year are shown in Table 1–8.

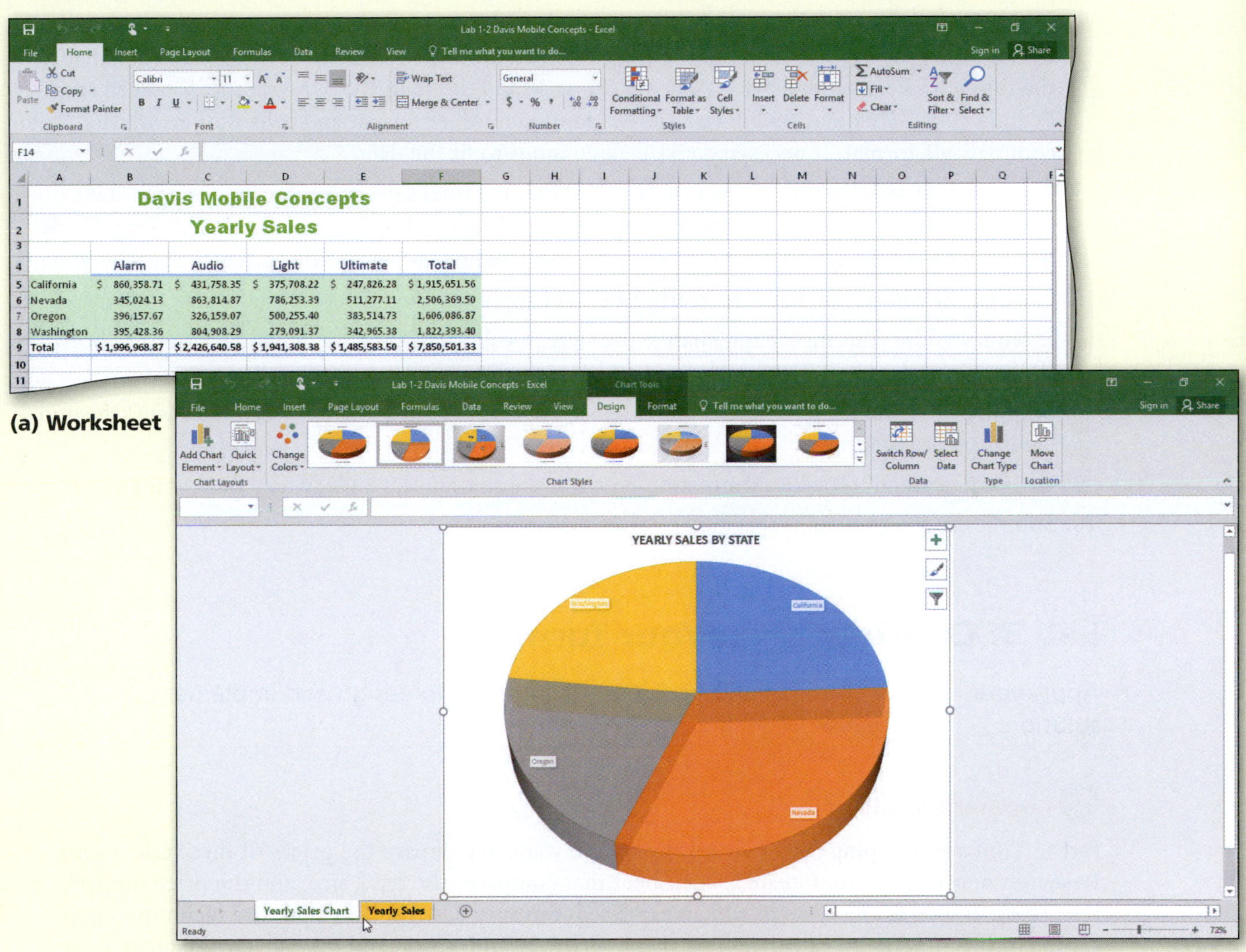

(a) Worksheet

(b) Pie Chart

Figure 1–76

Perform the following tasks:

1. Create the worksheet shown in Figure 1–76a using the data in Table 1–8.

Table 1–8 Davis Mobile Concepts

	Alarm	Audio	Light	Ultimate
California	860358.71	431758.35	375708.22	247826.28
Nevada	345024.13	863814.87	786253.39	511277.11
Oregon	396157.67	326159.07	500255.40	383514.73
Washington	395428.36	804908.29	279091.37	342965.38

Continued >

In the Labs *continued*

2. Use the SUM function to determine total revenue for each of the four packages, the totals for each state, and the company total. Add column and row headings for the totals row and totals column, as appropriate.
3. Format the worksheet title and subtitle with the Title cell style and center them across columns A through F. Use the Font group on the ribbon to format the worksheet title and subtitle as 18-point Arial Black. Format the title and subtitle with Green, Accent 6 font color. Center the titles across columns A through F.
4. Format the range B4:F4 with the Heading 2 cell style and center the text in the cells. Format the range A5:F8 with the 20% - Accent6 cell style and the range A9:F9 with the Total cell style. Format cells B5:F5 and B9:F9 with the accounting number format and cells B6:F8 with the comma style format. If necessary, resize all columns to fit the data.
5. Create a 3-D pie chart on its own sheet that shows the total sales contributions of each state. Chart the state names (A5:A8) and corresponding totals (F5:F8). Use the sheet tab name, Yearly Sales Chart. Apply a chart style of your choosing. Change the chart title to Yearly Sales by State.
6. Change the Sheet1 tab name to Yearly Sales and apply the Orange color to the sheet tab.
7. If requested by your instructor, change the state in cell A8 to the state in which you were born. If your state already is listed in the spreadsheet, choose a different state.
8. Save the workbook using the file name, Lab 1-2 Davis Mobile Concepts. Print the worksheet in landscape orientation.
9. If you wanted to make a distinction between the rows in the table, what could you do?
10. Submit the assignment as specified by your instructor.

Lab 3: Consider This: Your Turn

Apply your creative thinking and problem-solving skills to design and implement a solution.

Comparing Televisions

Part 1: You are shopping for a new television and want to compare the prices of three televisions. Research new televisions. Create a worksheet that compares the type, size, and the price for each television, as well as the costs to add an extended warranty. Use the concepts and techniques presented in this module to calculate the average price of a television and average cost of an extended warranty and to format the worksheet. Submit your assignment in the format specified by your instructor.

Part 2: Based upon the data you found, how could you chart the information to show the comparisons? Which chart would be the best to use? Include a chart to compare the different television costs.

2 Formulas, Functions, and Formatting

Objectives

You will have mastered the material in this module when you can:

- Use Flash Fill
- Enter formulas using the keyboard
- Enter formulas using Point mode
- Apply the MAX, MIN, and AVERAGE functions
- Verify a formula using Range Finder
- Apply a theme to a workbook
- Apply a date format to a cell or range
- Add conditional formatting to cells
- Change column width and row height
- Check the spelling on a worksheet
- Change margins and headers in Page Layout view
- Preview and print versions and sections of a worksheet

Introduction

In Module 1, you learned how to enter data, sum values, format a worksheet to make it easier to read, and draw a chart. This module continues to illustrate these topics and presents some new ones.

The new topics covered in this module include using formulas and functions to create a worksheet. Recall from Module 1 that a function is a prewritten formula that is built into Excel. Other new topics include using option buttons, verifying formulas, applying a theme to a worksheet, adding borders, formatting numbers and text, using conditional formatting, changing the widths of columns and heights of rows, checking spelling, generating alternative worksheet displays and printouts, and adding page headers and footers to a worksheet. One alternative worksheet display and printout shows the formulas in the worksheet instead of the values. When you display the formulas in the worksheet, you see exactly what text, data, formulas, and functions you have entered into it.

Project — Worksheet with Formulas and Functions

The project in this module follows proper design guidelines and uses Excel to create the worksheet shown in Figure 2–1. Every two weeks, the owners of Olivia's Art Supply create a salary report by hand, where they keep track of employee payroll data. Before paying employees, the owners must summarize the hours worked, pay rate, and tax information for each employee to ensure that the business properly compensates its employees. This report also includes the following information for each employee: name, email address, number of dependents, hours worked, hourly pay rate, tax information, net pay, and hire date. As the complexity of creating the salary report increases, the owners want to use Excel to make the process easier.

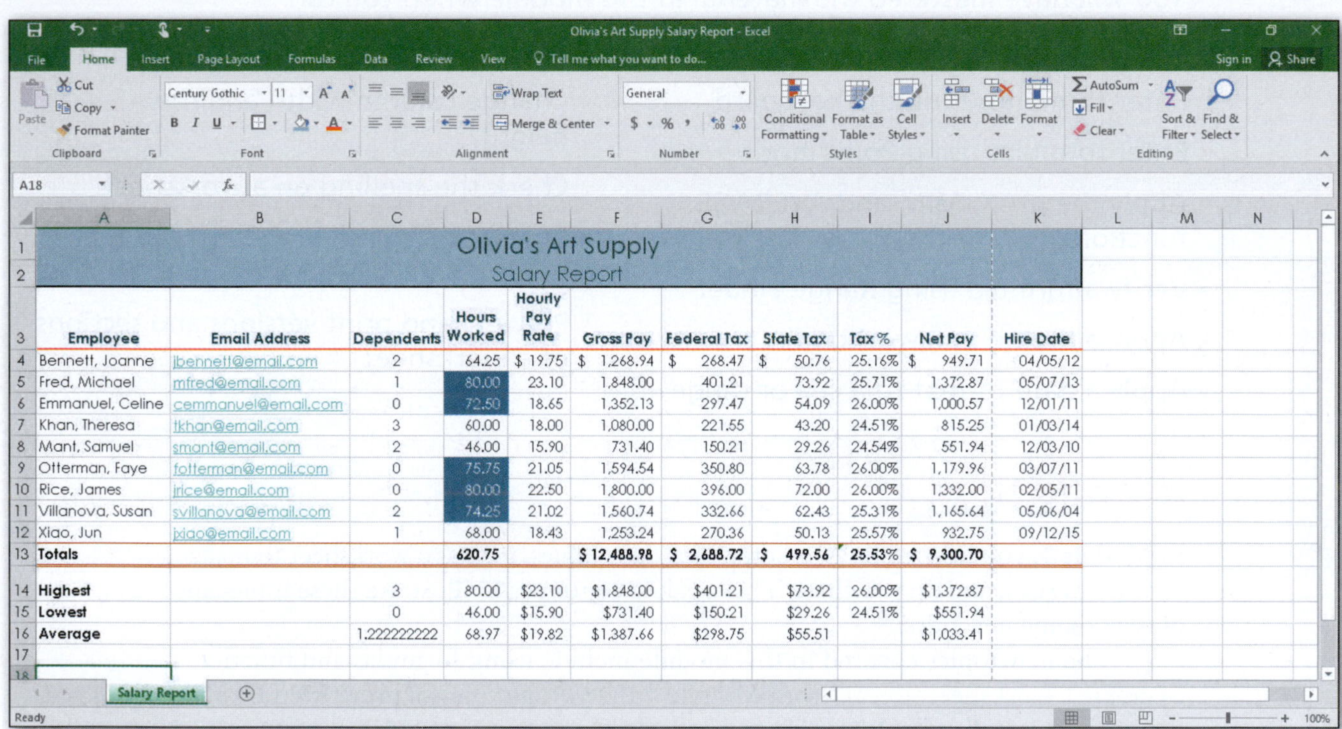

Figure 2–1

Recall that the first step in creating an effective worksheet is to make sure you understand what is required. The people who request the worksheet usually provide the requirements. The requirements document for the Olivia's Art Supply Salary Report worksheet includes the following needs: source of data, summary of calculations, and other facts about its development (Figure 2–2).

Worksheet Title	Olivia's Art Supply Salary Report
Needs	An easy-to-read worksheet that summarizes the company's salary report (Figure 2–3). For each employee, the worksheet is to include the employee's name, email address, number of dependents, hours worked, hourly pay rate, gross pay, federal tax, state tax, total tax percent, net pay, and hire date. The worksheet also should include the total pay for all employees, as well as the highest value, lowest value, and average for each category of data.
Source of Data	Supplied data includes employee names, number of dependents, hours worked, hourly pay rate, and hire dates.
Calculations	The following calculations must be made for each of the employees: 1. Gross Pay = Hours Worked * Hourly Pay Rate 2. Federal Tax = 0.22 * (Gross Pay * Number of Dependents * 24.32) 3. State Tax = 0.04 * Gross Pay 4. Tax % = (Federal Tax + State Tax) / Gross Pay 5. Net Pay = Gross Pay * (Federal Tax + State Tax) 6. Compute the totals for hours worked, gross pay, federal tax, state tax, and net pay 7. Compute the total tax percent 8. Use the MAX and MIN functions to determine the highest and lowest values for number of dependents, hours worked, hourly pay rate, gross pay, federal tax, state tax, total tax percent, and net pay 9. Use the AVERAGE function to determine the average for hours worked, number of dependents, hourly pay rate, gross pay, federal tax, state tax, and net pay

Figure 2–2

In addition, using a sketch of the worksheet can help you visualize its design. The sketch for the Olivia's Art Supply Salary Report worksheet includes a title, a subtitle, column and row headings, and the location of data values (Figure 2–3). It also uses specific characters to define the desired formatting for the worksheet, as follows:

1. The row of Xs below the leftmost column heading defines the cell entries as text, such as employee names.

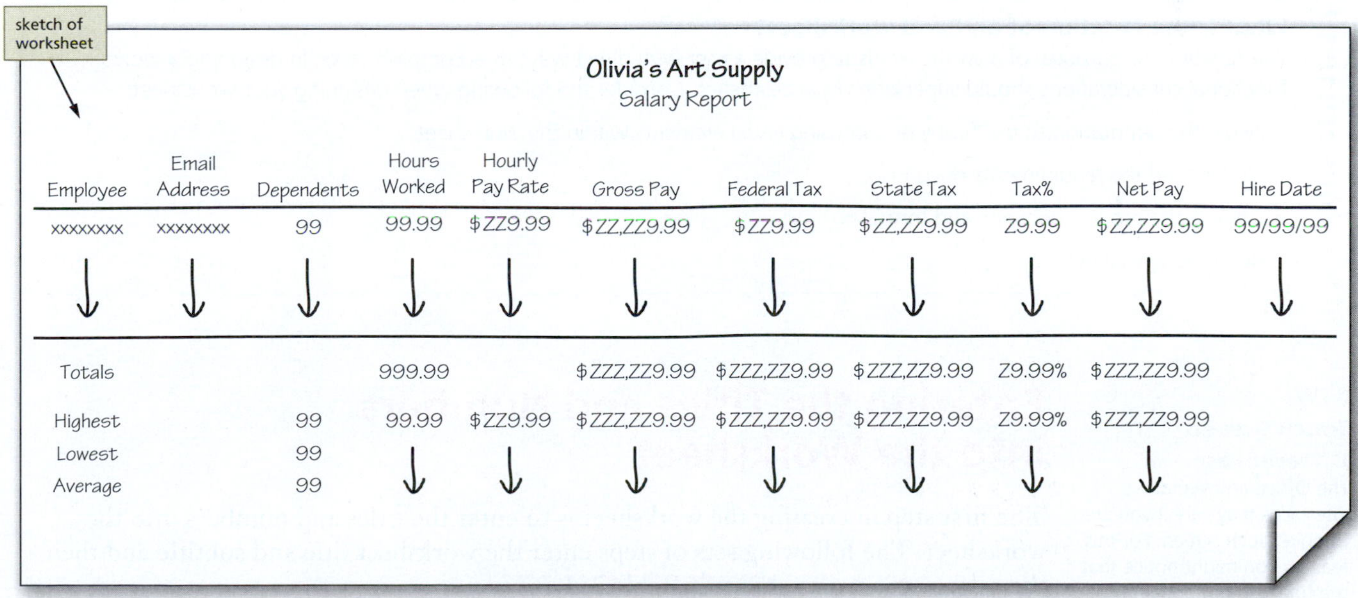

Figure 2–3

For an introduction to Windows and instructions about how to perform basic Windows tasks, read the Office and Windows module at the beginning of this book, where you can learn how to resize windows, change screen resolution, create folders, move and rename files, use Windows Help, and much more.

For an introduction to Office and instructions about how to perform basic tasks in Office apps, read the Office and Windows module at the beginning of this book, where you can learn how to run an application, use the ribbon, save a file, open a file, print a file, exit an application, use Help, and much more.

2. The rows of Zs and 9s with slashes, dollar signs, decimal points, commas, and percent signs in the remaining columns define the cell entries as numbers. The Zs indicate that the selected format should instruct Excel to suppress leading 0s. The 9s indicate that the selected format should instruct Excel to display any digits, including 0s.
3. The decimal point means that a decimal point should appear in the cell entry and indicates the number of decimal places to use.
4. The slashes in the last column identify the cell entry as a date.
5. The dollar signs that are adjacent to the Zs below the totals row signify a floating dollar sign, or one that appears next to the first significant digit.
6. The commas indicate that the selected format should instruct Excel to display a comma separator only if the number has sufficient digits (values in the thousandths) to the left of the decimal point.
7. The percent sign (%) in the Tax % column indicates a percent sign should appear after the number.

In this module, you will learn how to use functions and create formulas. The following roadmap identifies general activities you will perform as you progress through this module:

1. ENTER FORMULAS in the worksheet.
2. ENTER FUNCTIONS in the worksheet.
3. VERIFY FORMULAS in the worksheet.
4. FORMAT the WORKSHEET.
5. CHECK SPELLING.
6. PRINT the WORKSHEET.

CONSIDER THIS

What is the function of an Excel worksheet?

The function, or purpose, of a worksheet is to provide a user with direct ways to accomplish tasks. In designing a worksheet, functional considerations should supersede visual aesthetics. Consider the following when designing your worksheet:

- Avoid the temptation to use flashy or confusing visual elements within the worksheet.
- Understand the requirements document.
- Choose the proper functions and formulas.
- Build the worksheet.

BTW
Touch Screen Differences
The Office and Windows interfaces may vary if you are using a touch screen. For this reason, you might notice that the function or appearance of your touch screen differs slightly from this module's presentation.

Entering the Titles and Numbers into the Worksheet

The first step in creating the worksheet is to enter the titles and numbers into the worksheet. The following sets of steps enter the worksheet title and subtitle and then the salary report data shown in Table 2–1.

To Enter the Worksheet Title and Subtitle

With a good comprehension of the requirements document, an understanding of the necessary decisions, and a sketch of the worksheet, the next step is to use Excel to create the worksheet. The following steps enter the worksheet title and subtitle into cells A1 and A2.

1. Run Excel and create a blank workbook in the Excel window.
2. If necessary, select cell A1. Type `Olivia's Art Supply` in the selected cell and then press the DOWN ARROW key to enter the worksheet title.
3. Type `Salary Report` in cell A2 and then press the DOWN ARROW key to enter the worksheet subtitle.

BTW

Screen Resolution

If you are using a computer or mobile device to step through the project in this module and you want your screens to match the figures in this book, you should change your screen's resolution to 1366 x 768. For information about how to change a computer's resolution, refer to the Office and Windows module at the beginning of this book.

To Enter the Column Titles

The column titles in row 3 begin in cell A3 and extend through cell K3. The employee names and the row titles begin in cell A4 and continue down to cell A16. The employee data is entered into rows 4 through 12 of the worksheet. The remainder of this section explains the steps required to enter the column titles, payroll data, and row titles, as shown in Figure 2–4, and then to save the workbook. The following steps enter the column titles.

1. With cell A3 selected, type `Employee` and then press the RIGHT ARROW key to enter the column heading.
2. Type `Email Address` in cell B3 and then press the RIGHT ARROW key.
3. In cell C3, type `Dependents` and then press the RIGHT ARROW key.
4. In cell D3, type `Hours` and then press the ALT+ENTER keys to enter the first line of the column heading. Type `Worked` and then press the RIGHT ARROW key to enter the column heading.

Q&A Why do I use the ALT+ENTER keys?

You press ALT+ENTER in order to start a new line in a cell. The final line can be completed by clicking the Enter button, pressing the ENTER key, or pressing one of the arrow keys. When you see ALT+ENTER in a step, press the ENTER key while holding down the ALT key and then release both keys.

5. Type `Hourly` in cell E3, press the ALT+ENTER keys, type `Pay Rate,` and then press the RIGHT ARROW key.
6. Type `Gross Pay` in cell F3 and then press the RIGHT ARROW key.
7. Type `Federal Tax` in cell G3 and then press the RIGHT ARROW key.
8. Type `State Tax` in cell H3 and then press the RIGHT ARROW key.
9. Type `Tax %` in cell I3 and then press the RIGHT ARROW key.
10. Type `Net Pay` in cell J3 and then press the RIGHT ARROW key.
11. Type `Hire Date` in cell K3 and then press the RIGHT ARROW key.

BTW

Wrapping Text

If you have a long text entry, such as a paragraph, you can instruct Excel to wrap the text in a cell. This method is easier than your pressing ALT+ENTER to end each line of text within the paragraph. To wrap text, right-click in the cell, click Format Cells on a shortcut menu, click the Alignment tab, and then click Wrap text. Excel will increase the height of the cell automatically so that the additional lines will fit. If you want to control where each line ends in the cell, rather than letting Excel wrap the text based on the cell width, you must end each line with ALT+ENTER.

To Enter the Salary Data

The salary data in Table 2-1 includes a hire date for each employee. Excel considers a date to be a number and, therefore, it displays the date right-aligned in the cell. The following steps enter the data for each employee, except their email addresses, which will be entered later in this module.

BTW

Two-Digit Years

When you enter a two-digit year value (xx) that is less than 30, Excel changes that value to 20xx; when you enter a value that is 30 or greater (zz), Excel changes the value to 19zz. Use four-digit years, if necessary, to ensure that Excel interprets year values the way you intend.

1. Select cell A4. Type `Bennett, Joanne` and then press the RIGHT ARROW key two times to enter the employee name and make cell C4 the active cell.
2. Type `2` in cell C4 and then press the RIGHT ARROW key.
3. Type `64.25` in cell D4 and then press the RIGHT ARROW key.
4. Type `19.75` in cell E4.
5. Click cell K4 and then type `4/5/12`.
6. Enter the payroll data in Table 2–1 for the eight remaining employees in rows 5 through 12.

Q&A

In Step 5, why did the date change from 4/5/12 to 4/5/2012?
When Excel recognizes a date in mm/dd/yy format, it formats the date as mm/dd/yyyy. Most professionals prefer to view dates in mm/dd/yyyy format as opposed to mm/dd/yy format to avoid confusion regarding the intended year. For example, a date displayed as 3/3/50 could imply a date of 3/3/1950 or 3/3/2050.

Table 2–1 Olivia's Art Supply Salary Report Data

Employee	Email Address	Dependents	Hours Worked	Hourly Pay Rate	Hire Date
Bennett, Joanne		2	64.25	19.75	4/5/12
Fred, Michael		1	80.00	23.10	5/7/13
Emmanuel, Celine		0	72.50	18.65	12/1/11
Khan, Theresa		3	60.00	18.00	1/3/14
Mant, Samuel		2	46.00	15.90	12/3/10
Otterman, Faye		0	75.75	21.05	3/7/11
Rice, James		0	80.00	22.50	2/5/11
Villanova, Susan		2	74.25	21.02	5/6/04
Xiao, Jun		1	68.00	18.43	9/12/15

BTW

The Ribbon and Screen Resolution

Excel may change how the groups and buttons within the groups appear on the ribbon, depending on the computer or mobile device's screen resolution. Thus, your ribbon may look different from the ones in this book if you are using a screen resolution other than 1366 x 768.

Flash Fill

When you are entering data in a spreadsheet, occasionally Excel will recognize a pattern in the data you are entering. **Flash Fill** is an Excel feature that looks for patterns in the data and automatically fills or formats data in remaining cells. For example if column A contains a list of 10 phone numbers without parentheses around the area code or dashes after the prefix, Flash Fill can help create formatted phone numbers with relative ease. To use Flash Fill, simply start entering formatted phone numbers in cells next to the unformatted numbers. After entering a few formatted phone numbers, Flash Fill will suggest similarly formatted phone numbers for the remaining cells in the column. If you do not want to wait for Excel to offer suggestions, type one or two examples and then click the Flash Fill button (Data tab | Data Tools group). Flash fill will autocomplete the remaining cells. If Flash Fill makes a mistake, simply click the Undo button, enter a few more examples, and try again. In addition to formatting data, Flash Fill can perform tasks such as concatenating data from multiple cells and separating data from one cell into multiple cells.

To Use Flash Fill

In the Olivia's Art Supply Salary Report worksheet, you can use Flash Fill to generate email addresses using first and last names from another column in the worksheet. ***Why?*** *The Flash Fill feature is a convenient way to avoid entering a lot of data manually.* The following steps use Flash Fill to generate employee email addresses using the names entered in column A.

1

- Click cell B4 to select it.
- Type **jbennett@email.com** and then press the DOWN ARROW key to select cell B5.
- Type **mfred@email.com** and then click the Enter button to enter Michael Fred's email address in cell B5 (Figure 2–4).

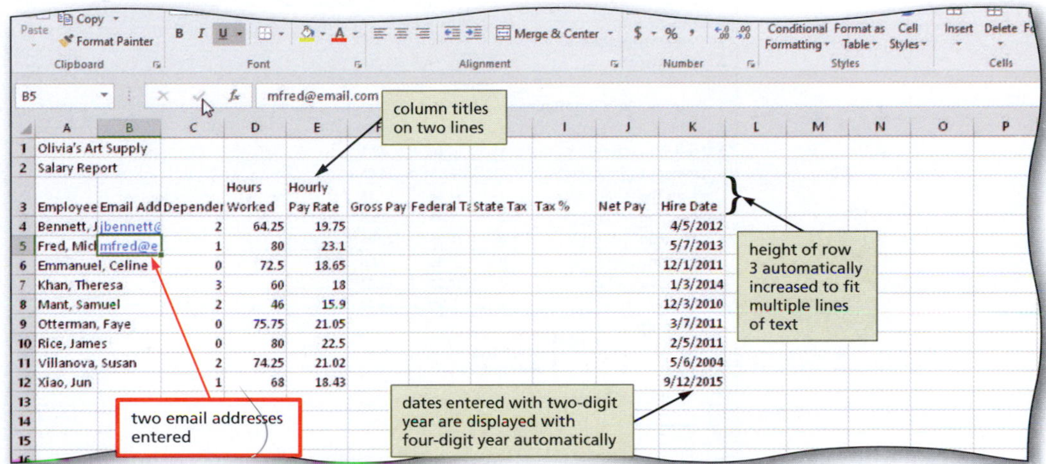

Figure 2–4

2

- Click Data on the ribbon to select the Data tab.
- Click Flash Fill (Data tab | Data Tools group) to enter similarly formatted email addresses in the range B6:B12.
- Remove the entries from cells B1 and B2 (Figure 2–5).

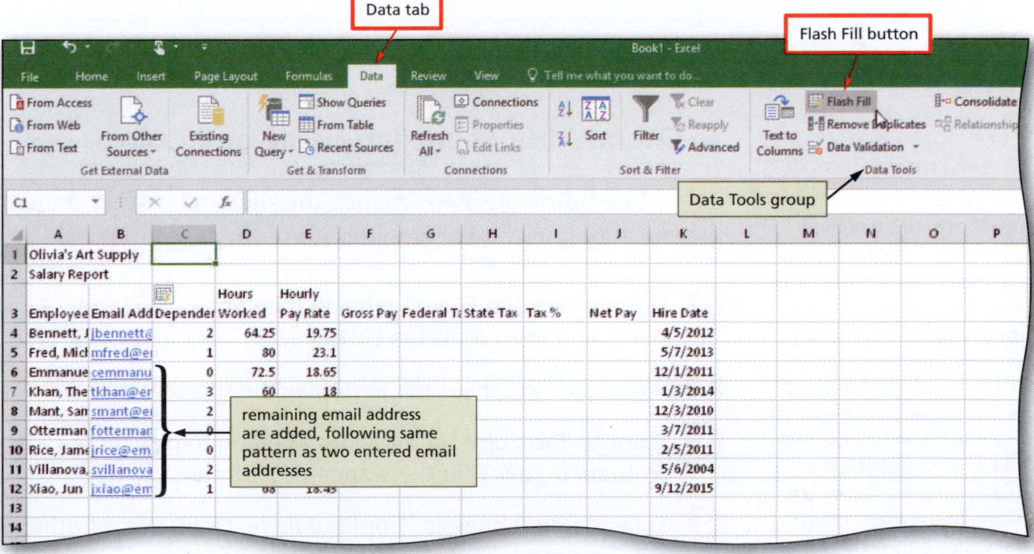

Figure 2–5

Q&A

Why was I unable to click the Flash Fill button after entering the first email address?
One entry might not have been enough for Excel to recognize a pattern. For instance, Flash Fill might have used the letter *j* before each last name in the email address, instead of using the first initial and last name.

What would have happened if I kept typing examples without clicking the Flash Fill button?
As soon as Excel recognized a pattern, it would have displayed suggestions for the remaining cells. Pressing the ENTER key when the suggestions appear will populate the remaining cells.

BTW
Formatting Worksheets
With early worksheet programs, users often skipped rows to improve the appearance of the worksheet. With Excel it is not necessary to skip rows because you can increase row heights to add white space between information.

To Enter the Row Titles

The following steps add row titles for the rows that will contain the totals, highest, lowest, and average amounts.

1. Select cell A13. Type `Totals` and then press the DOWN ARROW key to enter a row header.
2. Type `Highest` in cell A14 and then press the DOWN ARROW key.
3. Type `Lowest` in cell A15 and then press the DOWN ARROW key.
4. Type `Average` in cell A16 and then press the DOWN ARROW key (Figure 2–6).

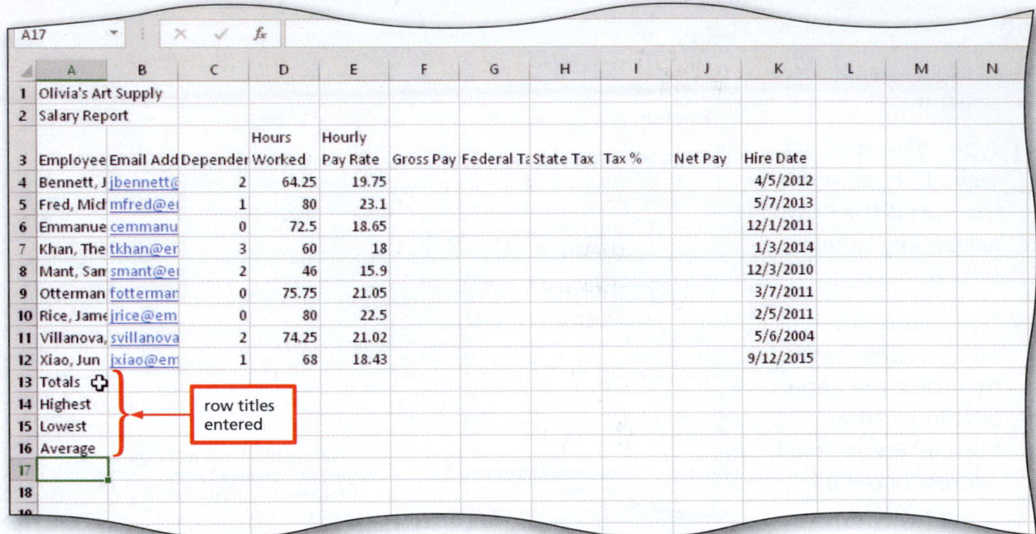

A17

	A	B	C	D	E	F	G	H	I	J	K	L	M	N
1	Olivia's Art Supply													
2	Salary Report													
3	Employee	Email Add	Depender	Hours Worked	Hourly Pay Rate	Gross Pay	Federal Ta	State Tax	Tax %	Net Pay	Hire Date			
4	Bennett, J	jbennett@	2	64.25	19.75						4/5/2012			
5	Fred, Mid	mfred@e	1	80	23.1						5/7/2013			
6	Emmanue	cemmanu	0	72.5	18.65						12/1/2011			
7	Khan, The	tkhan@er	3	60	18						1/3/2014			
8	Mant, Sam	smant@e	2	46	15.9						12/3/2010			
9	Otterman	fotterman	0	75.75	21.05						3/7/2011			
10	Rice, Jame	jrice@em	0	80	22.5						2/5/2011			
11	Villanova,	svillanova	2	74.25	21.02						5/6/2004			
12	Xiao, Jun	jxiao@em	1	68	18.43						9/12/2015			
13	Totals													
14	Highest													
15	Lowest													
16	Average													
17														
18														

Figure 2–6

BTW
Organizing Files and Folders
You should organize and store files in folders so that you easily can find the files later. For example, if you are taking an introductory technology class called CIS 101, a good practice would be to save all Excel files in an Excel folder in a CIS 101 folder. For a discussion of folders and detailed examples of creating folders, refer to the Office and Windows module at the beginning of this book.

To Change the Sheet Tab Name and Color

The following steps change the sheet tab name, change the tab color, and save the workbook in the Excel folder (for your assignments).

1. Double-click the Sheet1 tab and then enter `Salary Report` as the sheet tab name and then press the ENTER key.
2. Right-click the sheet tab to display the shortcut menu.
3. Point to Tab Color on the shortcut menu to display the Tab Color gallery. Click Green (column 6, row 7) in the Standard Colors area to apply the color to the sheet tab.
4. Save the workbook in your hard drive, OneDrive, or other storage location using Olivia's Art Supply Salary Report as the file name.

Q&A
Why should I save the workbook at this time?
You have performed many tasks while creating this workbook and do not want to risk losing work completed thus far.

Entering Formulas

One of the reasons Excel is such a valuable tool is that you can assign a formula to a cell, and Excel will calculate the result. A **formula** consists of cell references, numbers, and arithmetic operators that instruct Excel to perform a calculation. Consider, for example, what would happen if you had to multiply 64.25 by 19.75 and then manually enter the product for Gross Pay, 1,268.94, in cell F4. Every time the values in cells D4 or E4 changed, you would have to recalculate the product and enter the new value in cell F4. By contrast, if you enter a formula in cell F4 to multiply the values in cells D4 and E4, Excel recalculates the product whenever new values are entered into those cells and displays the result in cell F4.

A formula in a cell that contains a reference back to itself is called a **circular reference**. Excel warns you when you create circular references. In almost all cases, circular references are the result of an incorrect formula. A circular reference can be direct or indirect. For example, placing the formula =A1 in cell A1 results in a direct circular reference. A **direct circular reference** occurs when a formula refers to the same cell in which it is entered. An **indirect circular reference** occurs when a formula in a cell refers to another cell or cells that include a formula that refers back to the original cell.

BTW

Entering Numbers in a Range

An efficient way to enter data into a range of cells is to select a range and then enter the first number in the upper-left cell of the range. Excel responds by accepting the value and moving the active cell selection down one cell. When you enter the last value in the first column, Excel moves the active cell selection to the top of the next column.

To Enter a Formula Using the Keyboard

1 ENTER FORMULAS | 2 ENTER FUNCTIONS | 3 VERIFY FORMULAS
4 FORMAT WORKSHEET | 5 CHECK SPELLING | 6 PRINT WORKSHEET

The formulas needed in the worksheet are noted in the requirements document as follows:

1. Gross Pay (column F) = Hours Worked × Hourly Pay Rate
2. Federal Tax (column G) = 0.22 × (Gross Pay − Dependents × 24.32)
3. State Tax (column H) = 0.04 × Gross Pay
4. Tax % (column I) = (Federal Tax + State Tax) / Gross Pay
5. Net Pay (column J) = Gross Pay − (Federal Tax + State Tax)

The gross pay for each employee, which appears in column F, is equal to hours worked in column D times hourly pay rate in column E. Thus, the gross pay for Joanne Bennett in cell F4 is obtained by multiplying 64.25 (cell D4) by 19.75 (cell E4) or = C4 × D4. The following steps enter the initial gross pay formula in cell F4 using the keyboard. ***Why?*** *In order for Excel to perform the calculations, you must first enter the formulas.*

1

- **With cell F4 selected, type =d4*e4 in the cell to display the formula in the formula bar and the current cell and to display colored borders around the cells referenced in the formula (Figure 2–7).**

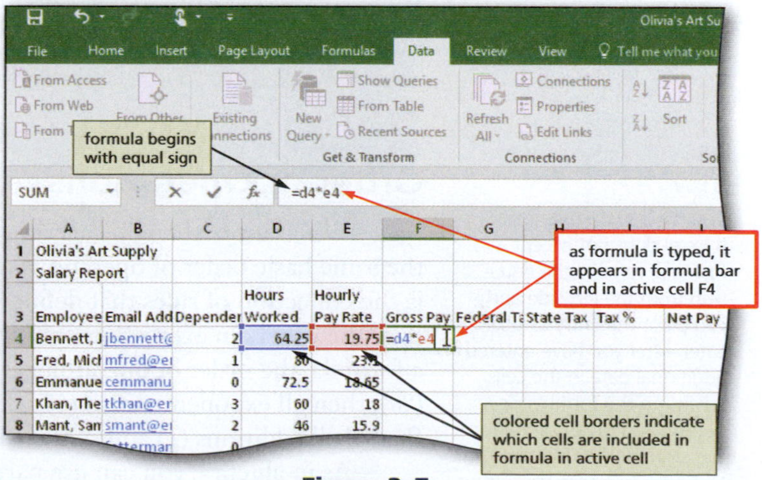

formula begins with equal sign

as formula is typed, it appears in formula bar and in active cell F4

colored cell borders indicate which cells are included in formula in active cell

Figure 2–7

Q&A

What happens when I enter the formula?

The **equal sign** (=) preceding d4*e4 alerts Excel that you are entering a formula or function — not text. Because the most common error when entering a formula is to reference the wrong cell, Excel colors the cells referenced in the formula. The colored cells help you determine whether the cell references are correct. The asterisk (*) following d4 is the arithmetic operator for multiplication.

Is there a function, similar to the SUM function, that calculates the product of two or more numbers?

Yes. The **PRODUCT function** calculates the product of two or more numbers. For example, the function, =PRODUCT(D4,E4) will calculate the product of cells D4 and E4.

2

- Press the RIGHT ARROW key to complete the arithmetic operation indicated by the formula, display the result in the worksheet, and select the cell to the right (Figure 2–8). The number of decimal places on your screen may be different than shown in Figure 2–8, but these values will be adjusted later in this module.

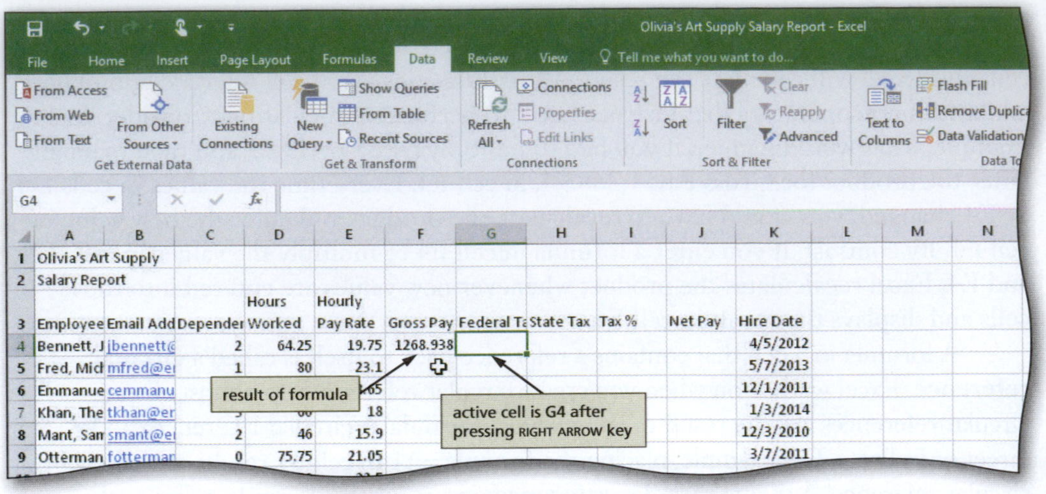

Figure 2–8

BTW
Automatic Recalculation
Every time you enter a value into a cell in the worksheet, Excel automatically recalculates all formulas. You can change to manual recalculation by clicking the Calculation Options button (Formulas tab | Calculation group) and then clicking Manual. In manual calculation mode, pressing the F9 key instructs Excel to recalculate all formulas.

Arithmetic Operations

Excel provides powerful functions and capabilities that allow you to perform arithmetic operations easily and efficiently. Table 2–2 describes multiplication and other valid Excel arithmetic operators.

Table 2–2 Arithmetic Operations Listed in Order of Operations

Arithmetic Operator	Meaning	Example of Usage	Result
–	Negation	–78	Negative 78
%	Percentage	=23%	Multiplies 23 by 0.01
^	Exponentiation	=3 ^ 4	Raises 3 to the fourth power
*	Multiplication	=61.5 * C5	Multiplies the contents of cell C5 by 61.5
/	Division	=H3 / H11	Divides the contents of cell H3 by the contents of cell H11
+	Addition	=11 + 9	Adds 11 and 9
–	Subtraction	=22 – F15	Subtracts the contents of cell F15 from 22

BTW
Troubling Formulas
If Excel does not accept a formula, remove the equal sign from the left side and complete the entry as text. Later, after you have entered additional data in the cells reliant on the formula or determined the error, reinsert the equal sign to change the text back to a formula and edit the formula as needed.

Order of Operations

When more than one arithmetic operator is involved in a formula, Excel follows the same basic order of operations that you use in algebra. The **order of operations** is the collection of rules that define which mathematical operations take precedence over the others in expressions with multiple operations. Moving from left to right in a formula, the order of operations is as follows: first negation (–), then all percentages (%), then all exponentiations (^), then all multiplications (*) and divisions (/), and, finally, all additions (+) and subtractions (–).

As in algebra, you can use parentheses to override the order of operations. For example, if Excel follows the order of operations, 8 * 3 + 2 equals 26. If you use parentheses, however, to change the formula to 8 * (3 + 2), the result is 40, because the parentheses instruct Excel to add 3 and 2 before multiplying by 8. Table 2–3 illustrates several examples of valid Excel formulas and explains the order of operations.

Table 2–3 Examples of Excel Formulas

Formula	Result
=G15	Assigns the value in cell G15 to the active cell.
=2^4 + 7	Assigns the sum of 16 + 7 (or 23) to the active cell.
=100 + D2 or =D2 +100 or =(100 + D2)	Assigns 100 plus the contents of cell D2 to the active cell.
=25% * 40	Assigns the product of 0.25 times 40 (or 10) to the active cell.
– (K15 * X45)	Assigns the negative value of the product of the values contained in cells K15 and X45 to the active cell. *Tip:* You do not need to type an equal sign before an expression that begins with a minus sign, which indicates a negation.
=(U8 – B8) * 6	Assigns the difference between the values contained in cells U8 and B8 times 6 to the active cell.
=J7 / A5 + G9 * M6 – Z2 ^ L7	Completes the following operations, from left to right: exponentiation (Z2 ^ L7), then division (J7 / A5), then multiplication (G9 * M6), then addition (J7 / A5) + (G9 * M6), and finally subtraction (J7 / A5 + G9 * M6) – (Z2 ^ L7). If cells A5 = 6, G9 = 2, J7 = 6, L7 = 4, M6 = 5, and Z2 = 2, then Excel assigns the active cell the value –5; that is, 6 / 6 + 2 * 5 – 2 ^ 4 = –5.

BTW

Parentheses

Remember that you can use parentheses to override the order of operations. You cannot use brackets or braces in place of parentheses in arithmetic operations.

To Enter Formulas Using Point Mode

1 ENTER FORMULAS | 2 ENTER FUNCTIONS | 3 VERIFY FORMULAS
4 FORMAT WORKSHEET | 5 CHECK SPELLING | 6 PRINT WORKSHEET

The sketch of the worksheet in Figure 2–3 calls for the federal tax, state tax, tax percentage, and net pay for each employee to appear in columns G, H, I, and J, respectively. All four of these values are calculated using formulas in row 4:

Federal Tax (cell G4) = 0.22 × (Gross Pay − Dependents × 24.32) or = 0.22 * (F4 − C4 * 24.32)
State Tax (cell H4) = 0.04 × Gross Pay or = 0.04 * F4
Tax % (cell I4) = (Federal Tax + State Tax) / Gross Pay or = (G4 + H4) / F4
Net Pay (cell J4) = Gross Pay − (Federal Tax + State Tax) or = F4 − (G4 + H4)

An alternative to entering the formulas in cells G4, H4, I4, and J4 using the keyboard is to enter the formulas using the pointer and Point mode. **Point mode** allows you to select cells for use in a formula by using the pointer. The following steps enter formulas using Point mode. ***Why?*** *Using Point mode makes it easier to create formulas without worrying about typographical errors when entering cell references.*

1

- With cell G4 selected, type **=0.22*(** to begin the formula and then click cell F4 to add a cell reference in the formula (Figure 2–9).

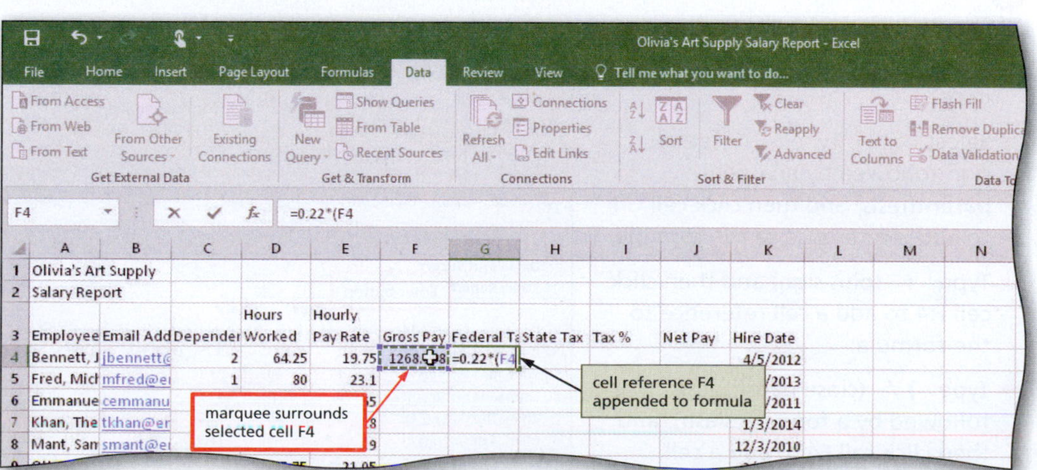

Figure 2–9

- Type – (minus sign) and then click cell C4 to add a subtraction operator and a reference to another cell to the formula.
- Type `*24.32)` to complete the formula (Figure 2–10).

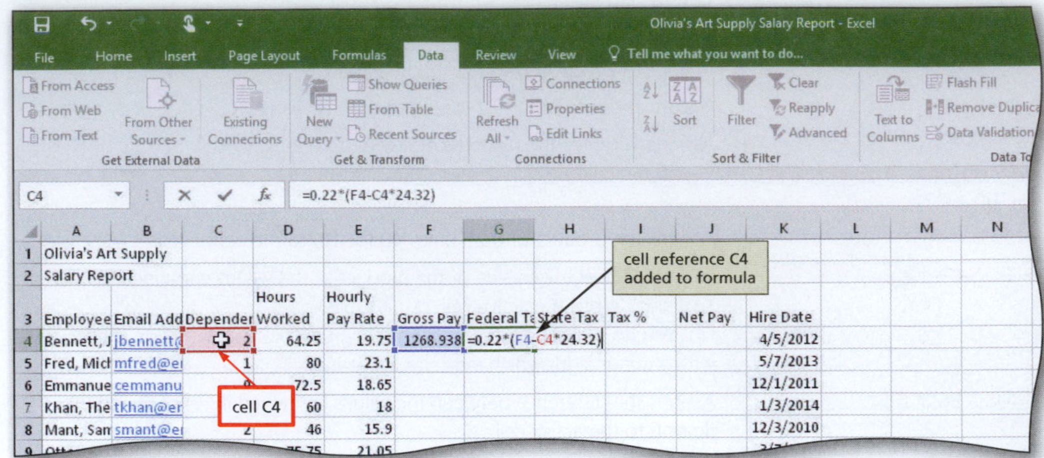

Figure 2–10

- Click the Enter button in the formula bar and then select cell H4 to prepare to enter the next formula.
- Type `=0.04*` and then click cell F4 to add a cell reference to the formula (Figure 2–11).

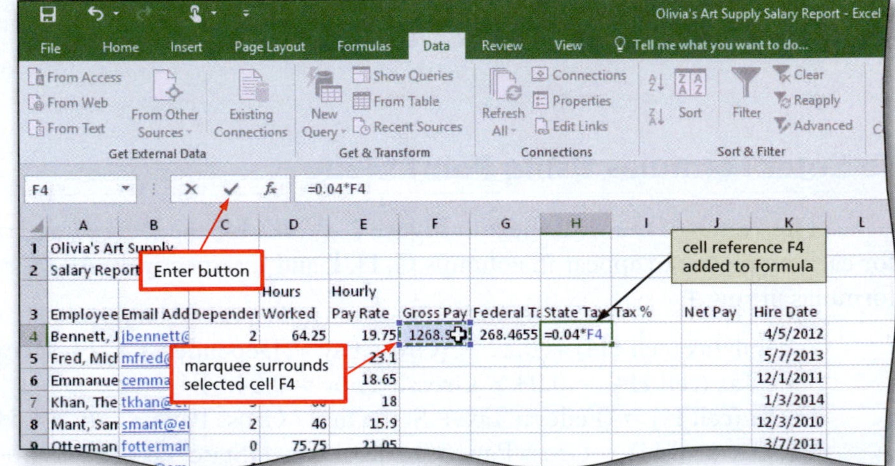

Figure 2–11

Q&A Why should I use Point mode to enter formulas?

Using Point mode to enter formulas often is faster and more accurate than using the keyboard, but only when the cell you want to select does not require you to scroll. In many instances, as in these steps, you may want to use both the keyboard and pointer when entering a formula in a cell. You can use the keyboard to begin the formula, for example, and then use the pointer to select a range of cells.

4

- Click the Enter button in the formula bar to enter the formula in cell H4.
- Select cell I4. Type `=(` (equal sign followed by an open parenthesis) and then click cell G4 to add a reference to the formula.
- Type `+` (plus sign) and then click cell H4 to add a cell reference to the formula.
- Type `)/` (close parenthesis followed by a forward slash), and then click cell F4 to add a cell reference to the formula.
- Click the Enter button in the formula bar to enter the formula in cell I4 (Figure 2–12).

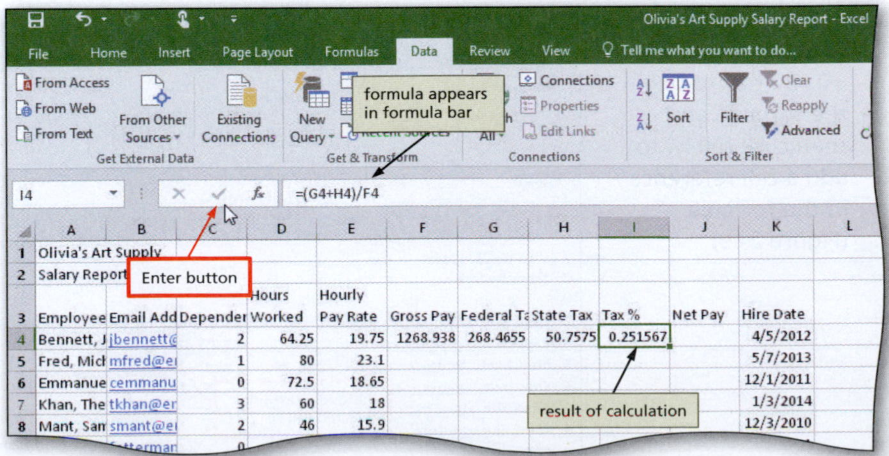

Figure 2–12

5

- Click cell J4, type = (equal sign) and then click cell F4.
- Type –((minus sign followed by an open parenthesis) and then click cell G4.
- Type + (plus sign), click cell H4, and then type) (close parenthesis) to complete the formula (Figure 2–13).
- Click the Enter button.

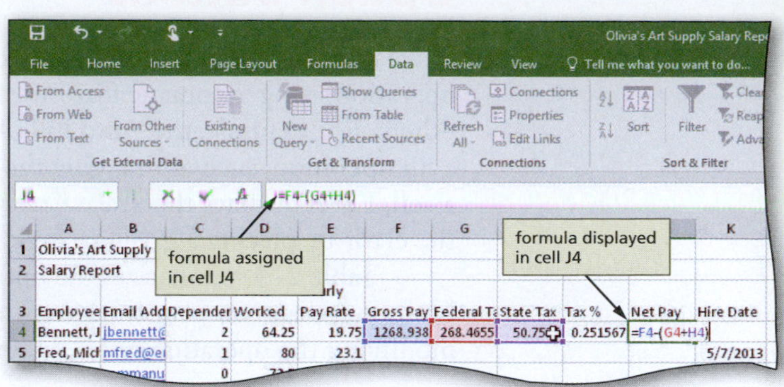

Figure 2–13

To Copy Formulas Using the Fill Handle

The five formulas for Joanne Bennett in cells F4, G4, H4, I4, and J4 now are complete. The next step is to copy them to the range F5:J12. When copying formulas in Excel, the source area is the cell, or range, from which data or formulas are being copied. When a range is used as a source, it sometimes is called the **source range**. The destination area is the cell, or range, to which data or formulas are being copied. When a range is used as a destination, it sometimes is called the **destination range**. Recall from Module 1 that the fill handle is a small square in the lower-right corner of the active cell or active range. The following steps copy the formulas using the fill handle.

1. Select the source range, F4:J4 in this case, activate the fill handle, drag the fill handle down through cell J12, and then continue to hold the mouse button to select the destination range.

2. Release the mouse button to copy the formulas to the destination range (Figure 2–14).

Q&A How does Excel adjust the cell references in the formulas in the destination area?
Recall that when you copy a formula, Excel adjusts the cell references so that the new formulas contain new cell references corresponding to the new locations and perform calculations using the appropriate values. Thus, if you copy downward, Excel adjusts the row portion of cell references relative to the source cell. If you copy across, then Excel adjusts the column portion of cell references relative to the source cell. Cell references that adjust relative to the location of the source cell are called **relative cell references**.

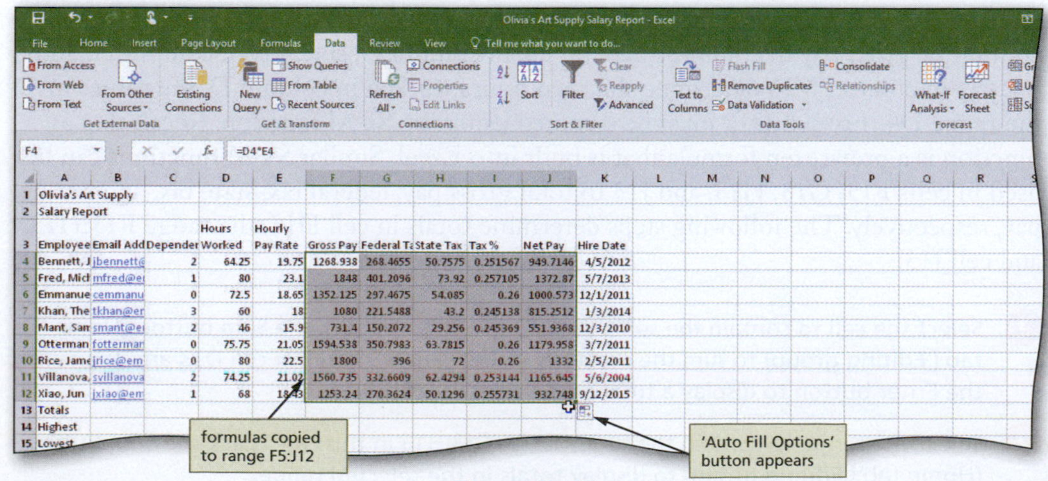

Figure 2–14

Option Buttons

Excel displays option buttons in a worksheet to indicate that you can complete an operation using automatic features such as AutoCorrect, Auto Fill, error checking, and others. For example, the 'Auto Fill Options' button shown in Figure 2 – 14 appears after a fill operation, such as dragging the fill handle. When an error occurs in a formula in a cell, Excel displays the Trace Error button next to the cell and identifies the cell with the error by placing a green triangle in the upper left of the cell.

Table 2–4 summarizes the option buttons available in Excel. When one of these buttons appears on your worksheet, click its arrow to produce the list of options for modifying the operation or to obtain additional information.

Table 2–4 Option Buttons in Excel

Name	Menu Function
Auto Fill Options	Provides options for how to fill cells following a fill operation, such as dragging the fill handle
AutoCorrect Options	Undoes an automatic correction, stops future automatic corrections of this type, or causes Excel to display the AutoCorrect Options dialog box
Insert Options	Lists formatting options following an insertion of cells, rows, or columns
Paste Options	Specifies how moved or pasted items should appear (for example, with original formatting, without formatting, or with different formatting)
Trace Error	Lists error-checking options following the assignment of an invalid formula to a cell

CONSIDER THIS

Why is the Paste Options button important?

The Paste Options button provides powerful functionality. When performing copy and paste operations, the button allows you great freedom in specifying what it is you want to paste. You can choose from the following options:

- Paste an exact copy of what you copied, including the cell contents and formatting.
- Copy only formulas.
- Copy only formatting.
- Copy only values.
- Copy a combination of these options.
- Copy a picture of what you copied.

BTW

Selecting a Range

You can select a range using the keyboard. Press the F8 key and then use the arrow keys to select the desired range. After you are finished, make sure to press the F8 key to turn off the selection process or you will continue to select ranges.

To Determine Totals Using the Sum Button

The next step is to determine the totals in row 13 for the hours worked in column D, gross pay in column F, federal tax in column G, state tax in column H, and net pay in column J. To determine the total hours worked in column D, the values in the range D4 through D12 must be summed using the SUM function. Recall that a function is a prewritten formula that is built into Excel. Similar SUM functions can be used in cells F13, G13, H13, and J13 to total gross pay, federal tax, state tax, and net pay, respectively. The following steps determine totals in cell D13, the range F13:H13, and cell J13.

1. Select the cell to contain the sum, cell D13 in this case. Click the Sum button (Home tab | Editing group) to sum the contents of the range D4:D12 in cell D13 and then click the Enter button to display a total in the selected cell.

2. Select the range to contain the sums, range F13:H13 in this case. Click the Sum button (Home tab | Editing group) to display totals in the selected range.

3 Select the cell to contain the sum, cell J13 in this case. Click the Sum button (Home tab | Editing group) to sum the contents of the range J4:J12 in cell J13 and then click the Enter button to display a total in the selected cell (Figure 2–15).

Q&A Why did I have to click the Enter button?
When calculating a sum for a single column, you click the Enter button. If you are calculating the sum for multiple ranges, you click the Sum button.

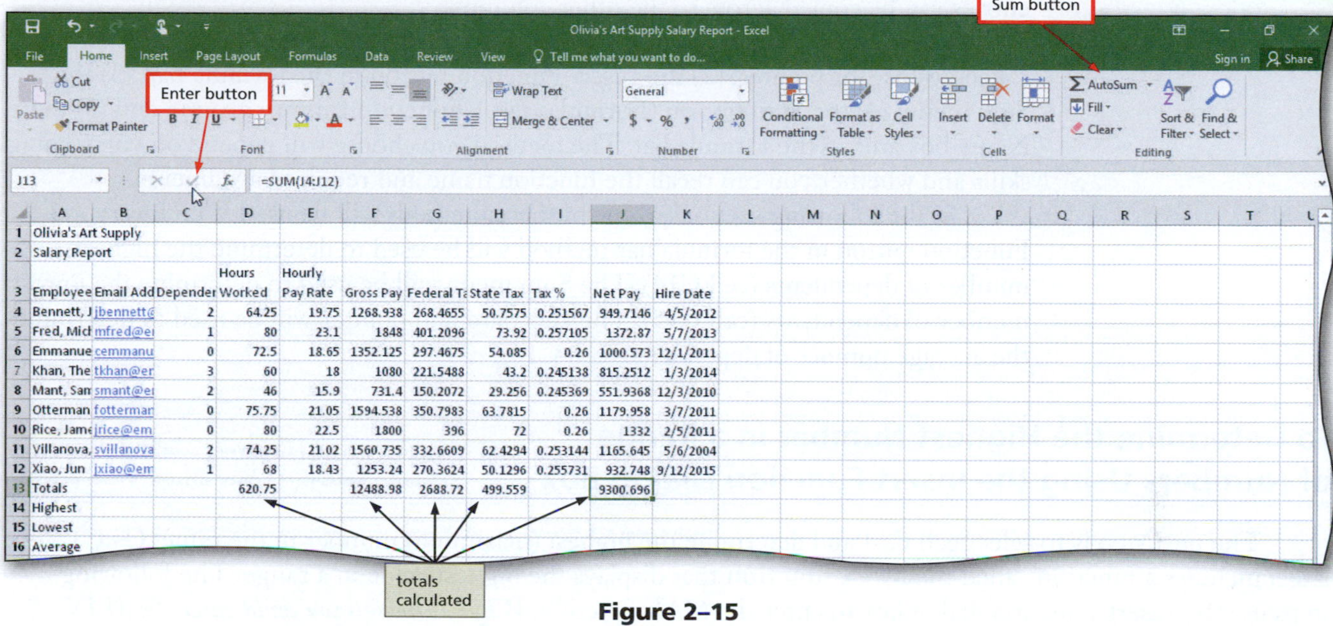

Figure 2–15

To Determine the Total Tax Percentage

With the totals in row 13 determined, the next step is to copy the tax percentage formula in cell I12 to cell I13. The following step copies the tax percentage formula.

1 Select the cell to be copied, I12 in this case, and then drag the fill handle down through cell I13 to copy the formula (Figure 2–16).

Q&A Why was the SUM function not used for tax percentage in I13?
The total tax percentage is calculated using the totals of the Gross Pay, Federal Tax and State Tax columns, not by summing the tax percentage column.

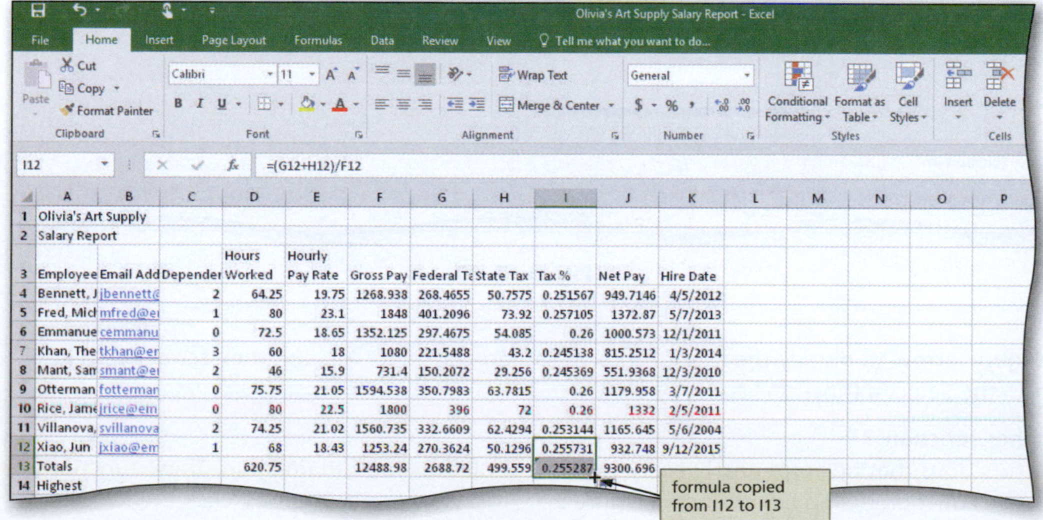

Figure 2–16

Using the AVERAGE, MAX, and MIN Functions

BTW
Statistical Functions
Excel usually considers a blank cell to be equal to 0. The statistical functions, however, ignore blank cells. Excel thus calculates the average of three cells with values of 10, blank, and 8 to be 9 [(10 + 8) / 2] and not 6 [(10 + 0 + 8) / 3].

The next step in creating the Olivia's Art Supply Salary Report worksheet is to compute the highest value, lowest value, and average value for the number of dependents listed in the range C4:C12 using the MAX, MIN, and AVERAGE functions in the range C14:C16. Once the values are determined for column C, the entries can be copied across to the other columns.

With Excel, you can enter functions using one of five methods: (1) keyboard, touch gesture, or pointer; (2) the Insert Function button in the formula bar; (3) the Sum menu; (4) the Sum button (Formulas tab | Function Library group); and (5) the Name box area in the formula bar. The method you choose will depend on your typing skills and whether you can recall the function name and required arguments.

In the following sections, three of these methods will be used. The Insert Function button in the formula bar method will be used to determine the highest number of dependents (cell C14). The Sum menu will be used to determine the lowest number of dependents (cell C15). The keyboard and pointer will be used to determine the average number of dependents (cell C16).

To Determine the Highest Number in a Range of Numbers Using the Insert Function Dialog Box

1 ENTER FORMULAS | 2 ENTER FUNCTIONS | 3 VERIFY FORMULAS
4 FORMAT WORKSHEET | 5 CHECK SPELLING | 6 PRINT WORKSHEET

The next step is to select cell C14 and determine the highest (maximum) number in the range C4:C12. Excel includes a function called the **MAX function** that displays the highest value in a range. The following steps use the Insert Function dialog box to enter the MAX function. ***Why?*** *Although you could enter the MAX function using the keyboard and Point mode as described previously, an alternative method to entering the function is to use the Insert Function button in the formula bar to open the Insert Function dialog box. The Insert Function dialog box is helpful if you do not remember the name of a function or need to search for a particular function by what it does.*

- Select the cell to contain the maximum number, cell C14 in this case.
- Click the Insert Function button in the formula bar to display the Insert Function dialog box.
- Click MAX in the Select a function list (Insert Function dialog box; Figure 2–17). You may need to scroll.

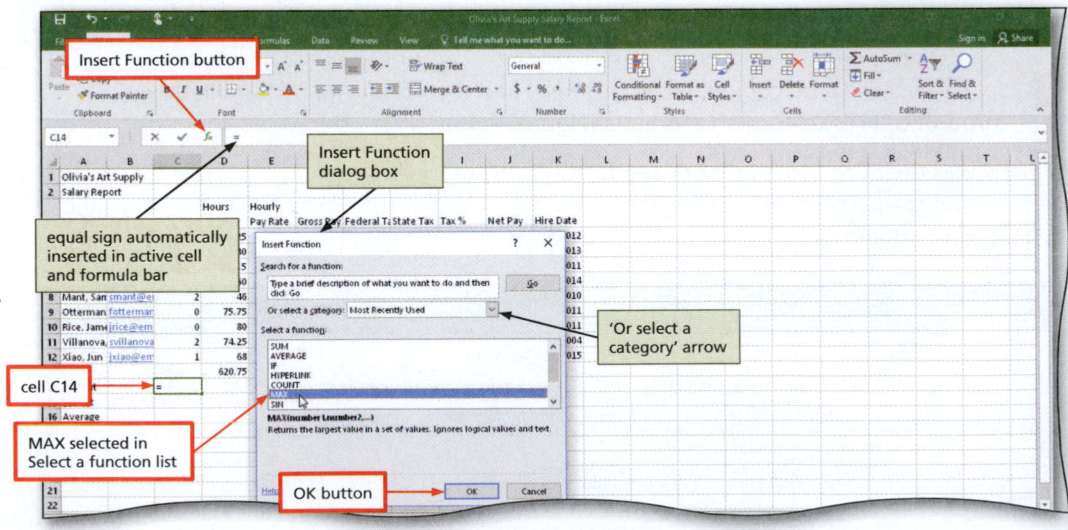

Figure 2–17

Q&A
What if the MAX function is not in the Select a function list?
Click the 'Or select a category' arrow to display the list of function categories, select All, and then scroll down and select the MAX function in the Select a function list.

How can I learn about other functions?
Excel has more than 400 functions that perform nearly every type of calculation you can imagine. These functions are categorized in the Insert Function dialog box shown in Figure 2–17. To view the categories, click the 'Or select a category' arrow. Click the name of a function in the Select a function list to display a description of the function.

2

- Click the OK button (Insert Function dialog box) to display the Function Arguments dialog box.
- Replace the text in the Number1 box with the text, `c4:c12` (Function Arguments dialog box) to enter the first argument of the function (Figure 2–18).

Q&A What are the numbers that appear to the right of the Number1 box in the Function Arguments dialog box?
The numbers shown to the right of the Number1 box are the values in the selected range (or if the range is large, the first few numbers only). Excel also displays the value the MAX function will return to cell C14 in the Function Arguments dialog box, shown in Figure 2–18.

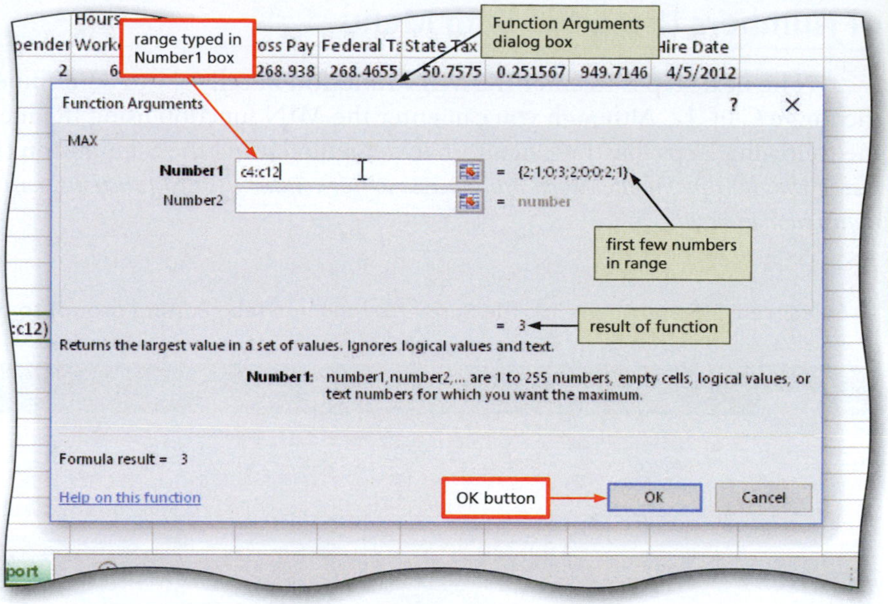

Figure 2–18

3

- Click the OK button (Function Arguments dialog box) to display the highest value in the chosen range in cell C14 (Figure 2–19).

Q&A Why should I not just enter the highest value that I see in the range C4:C12 in cell C14?
In this example, rather than entering the MAX function, you could examine the range C4:C12, determine that the highest number of dependents is 3, and manually enter the number 3 as a constant in cell C14. Excel would display the number similar to how it appears in Figure 2–19. However, because C14 would then contain a constant, Excel would continue to display 3 in cell C14 even if the values in the range change. If you use the MAX function, Excel will recalculate the highest value in the range each time a new value is entered.

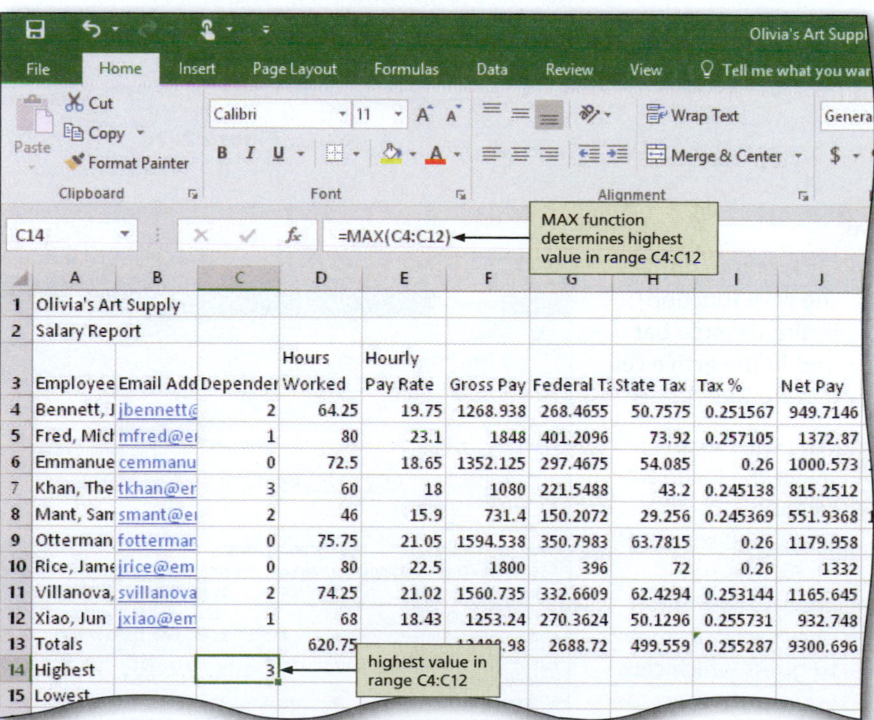

Figure 2–19

Other Ways

1. Click Sum arrow (Home tab | Editing group), click Max
2. Click Sum arrow (Formulas tab | Function Library group), click Max
3. Type **=MAX(** in cell, specify range, type **)**

To Determine the Lowest Number in a Range of Numbers Using the Sum Menu

The next step is to enter the **MIN function** in cell C15 to determine the lowest (minimum) number in the range C4:C12. Although you can enter the MIN function using the method used to enter the MAX function, the following steps illustrate an alternative method using the Sum button (Home tab | Editing group). ***Why?*** *Using the Sum menu allows you quick access to five commonly used functions, without having to memorize their names or required arguments.*

1

- Select cell C15 and then click the Sum arrow (Home tab | Editing group) to display the Sum menu (Figure 2–20).

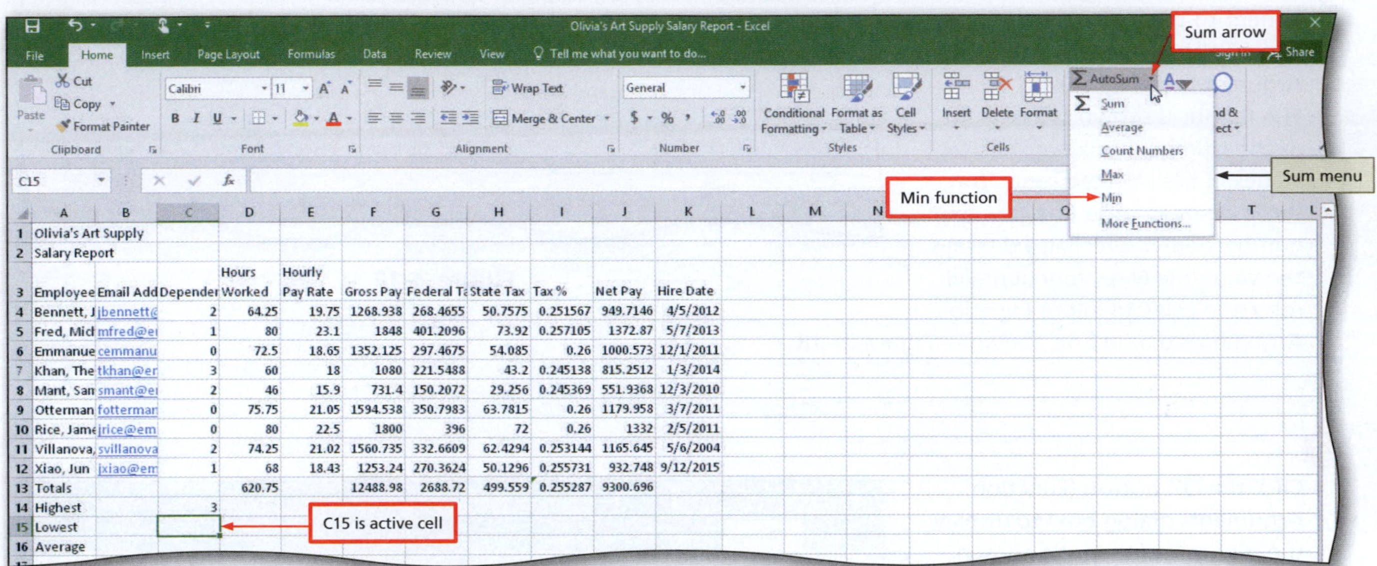

Figure 2–20

2

- Click Min to display the MIN function in the formula bar and in the active cell (Figure 2–21).

Q&A Why does Excel select the incorrect range?
The range selected by Excel is not always the right one. Excel attempts to guess which cells you want to include in the function by looking for ranges containing numeric data that are adjacent to the selected cell.

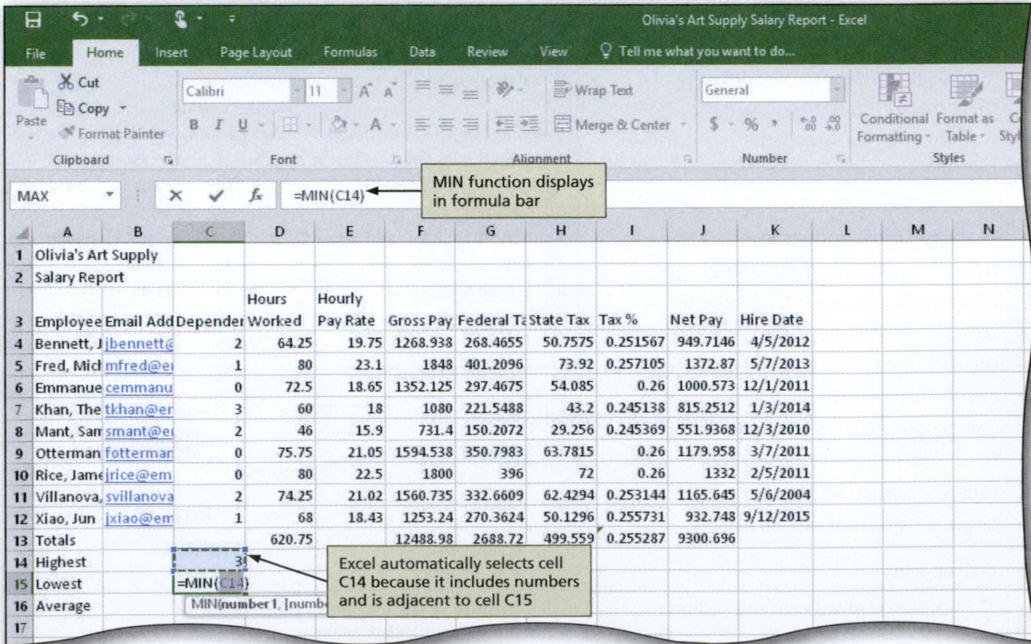

Figure 2–21

3

- Click cell C4 and then drag through cell C12 to update the function with the new range (Figure 2–22).

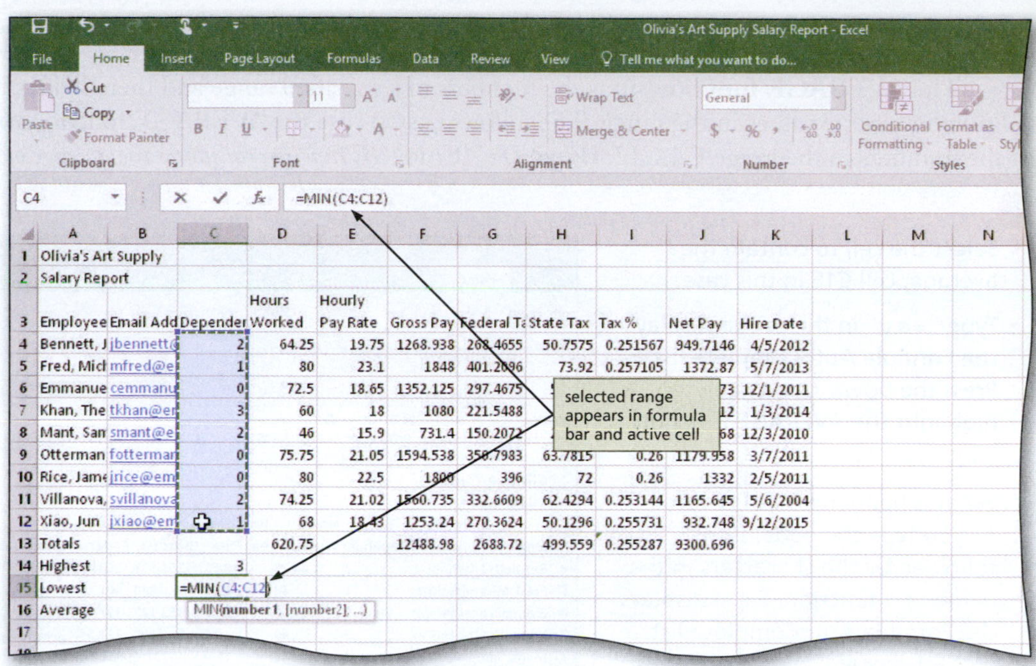

Figure 2–22

4

- Click the Enter button to determine the lowest value in the range C4:C12 and display the result in cell C15 (Figure 2–23).

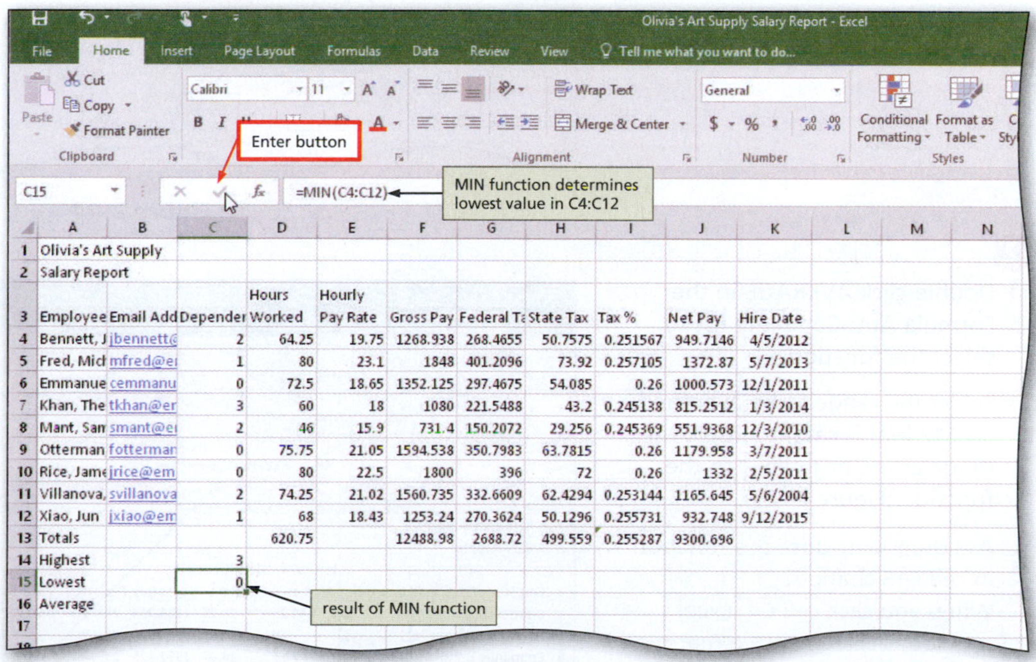

Figure 2–23

Other Ways

1. Click Insert Function button in formula bar, select Statistical category if necessary, click MIN, specify arguments
2. Click Sum arrow (Formulas tab | Function Library group), click Min
3. Type `=MIN(` in cell, fill in arguments, type)

To Determine the Average of a Range of Numbers Using the Keyboard

The **AVERAGE function** sums the numbers in a specified range and then divides the sum by the number of cells with numeric values in the range. The following steps use the AVERAGE function to determine the average of the numbers in the range C4:C12. ***Why?*** *The AVERAGE function calculates the average of a range of numbers.*

1

- Select the cell to contain the average, cell C16 in this case.
- Type **=av** in the cell to display the Formula AutoComplete list. Press the DOWN ARROW key to highlight the AVERAGE function (Figure 2–24).

Q&A What is happening as I type?
As you type the equal sign followed by the characters in the name of a function, Excel displays the Formula AutoComplete list. This list contains those functions whose names match the letters you have typed.

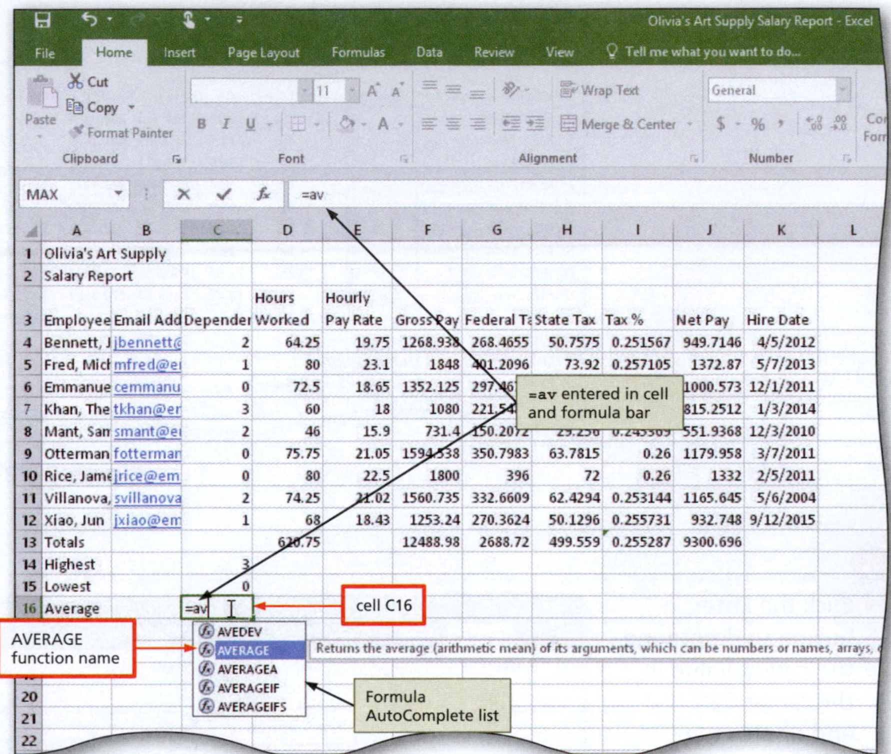

Figure 2–24

2

- Double-click AVERAGE in the Formula AutoComplete list to select the function.
- Select the range to be averaged, C4:C12 in this case, to insert the range as the argument to the function (Figure 2–25).

Q&A As I drag, why does the function in cell C16 change?
When you click cell C4, Excel surrounds cell C4 with a marquee and appends C4 to the left parenthesis in the formula bar. When you begin dragging, Excel appends to the argument a colon (:) and the cell reference of the cell where the pointer is located.

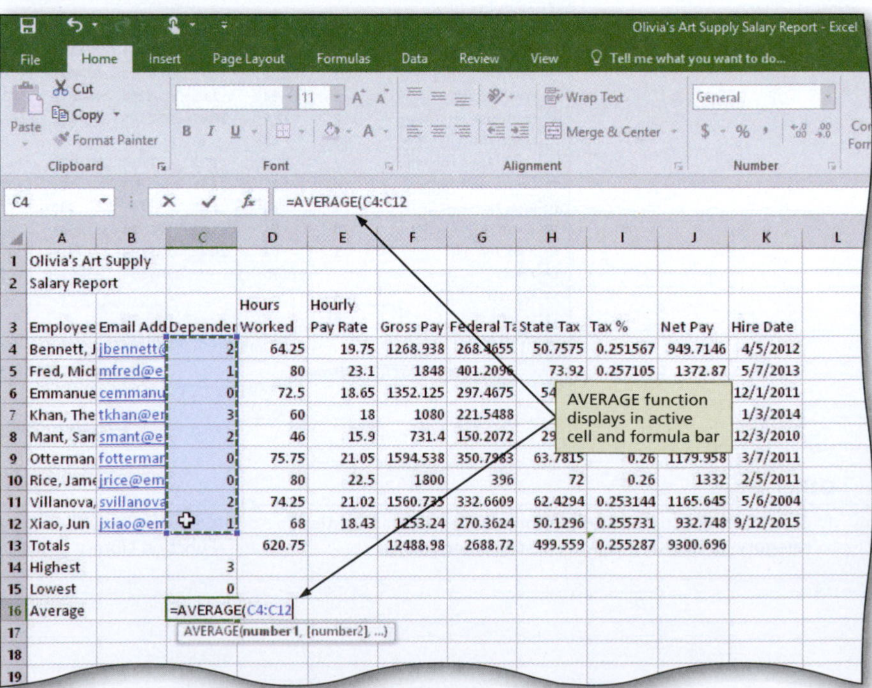

Figure 2–25

3
- Click the Enter button to compute the average of the numbers in the selected range and display the result in the selected cell (Figure 2–26).

Q&A

Can I use the arrow keys to complete the entry instead?

No. While in Point mode, the arrow keys change the selected cell reference in the range you are selecting instead of completing the entry.

What is the purpose of the parentheses in the function?

Most Excel functions require that the argument (in this case, the range C4:C12) be included within parentheses following the function name. In this case, Excel appended the right parenthesis to complete the AVERAGE function when you clicked the Enter button.

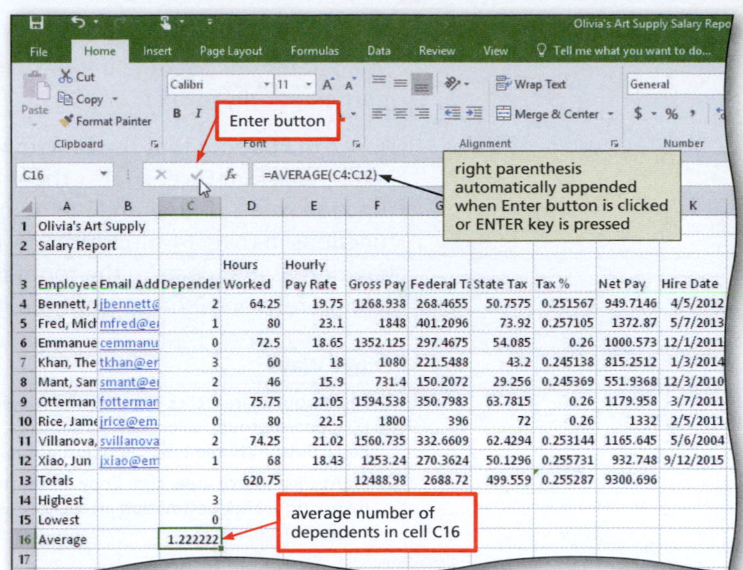

Figure 2–26

To Copy a Range of Cells across Columns to an Adjacent Range Using the Fill Handle

The next step is to copy the AVERAGE, MAX, and MIN functions in the range C14:C16 to the adjacent range D14:J16. The following steps use the fill handle to copy the functions.

1. Select the source range from which to copy the functions, in this case C14:C16.
2. Drag the fill handle in the lower-right corner of the selected range through cell J16 to copy the three functions to the selected range.
3. Select cell I16 and then press the DELETE key to delete the average of the Tax % (Figure 2–27).

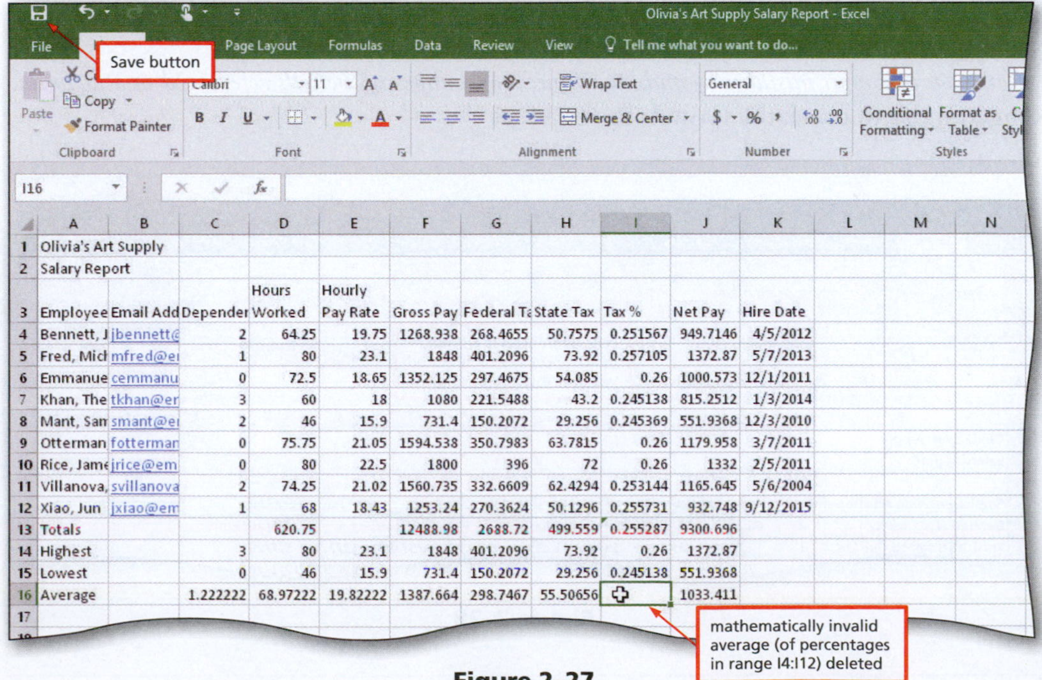

Figure 2–27

4 Save the workbook again on the same storage location with the same file name.

Q&A

Why delete the formula in cell I16?
You deleted the average in cell I16 because averaging this type of percentage is mathematically invalid.

How can I be sure that the function arguments are correct for the cells in range D14:J16?
Remember that Excel adjusts the cell references in the copied functions so that each function refers to the range of numbers above it in the same column. Review the functions in rows 14 through 16 by clicking on individual cells and examining the function as it appears in the formula bar. You should see that the functions in each column reference the appropriate ranges.

Other Ways

1. Select source area, click Copy button (Home tab | Clipboard group), select destination area, click Paste button (Home tab | Clipboard group)
2. Right-click source area, click Copy on shortcut menu; right-click destination area, click Paste icon on shortcut menu
3. Select source area and then point to border of range; while holding down CTRL, drag source area to destination area
4. Select source area, press CTRL+C, select destination area, press CTRL+V

Break Point: If you wish to take a break, this is a good place to do so. You can exit Excel now. To resume at a later time, run Excel, open the file called Olivia's Art Supply Salary Report, and continue following the steps from this location forward.

Verifying Formulas Using Range Finder

One of the more common mistakes made with Excel is to include an incorrect cell reference in a formula. An easy way to verify that a formula references the cells you want it to reference is to use Range Finder. **Range Finder** checks which cells are referenced in the formula assigned to the active cell.

To use Range Finder to verify that a formula contains the intended cell references, double-click the cell with the formula you want to check. Excel responds by highlighting the cells referenced in the formula so that you can verify that the cell references are correct.

To Verify a Formula Using Range Finder

1 ENTER FORMULAS | 2 ENTER FUNCTIONS | 3 VERIFY FORMULAS
4 FORMAT WORKSHEET | 5 CHECK SPELLING | 6 PRINT WORKSHEET

Why? *Range Finder allows you to correct mistakes by making immediate changes to the cells referenced in a formula.* The following steps use Range Finder to check the formula in cell I4.

1
- Double-click cell I4 to activate Range Finder (Figure 2–28).

2
- Press the ESC key to quit Range Finder and then click anywhere in the worksheet, such as cell A18, to deselect the current cell.

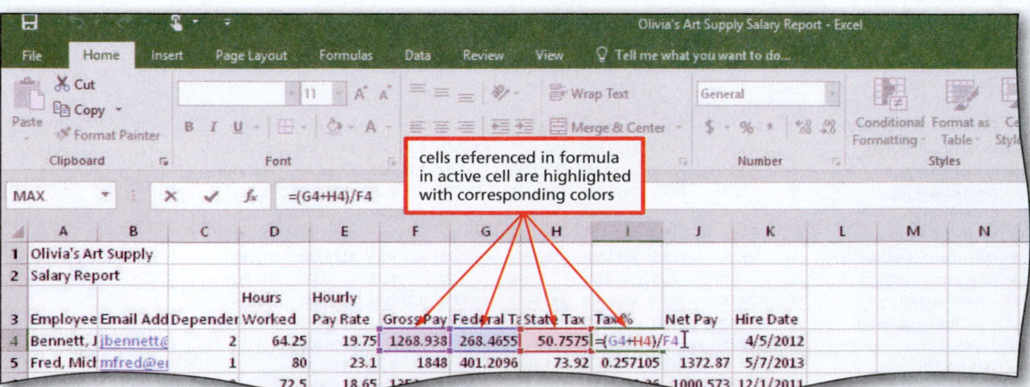

Figure 2–28

Formatting the Worksheet

Although the worksheet contains the appropriate data, formulas, and functions, the text and numbers need to be formatted to improve their appearance and readability.

In Module 1, cell styles were used to format much of the worksheet. This section describes how to change the unformatted worksheet in Figure 2–29a to the formatted worksheet in Figure 2–29b using a theme and other commands on the ribbon. A **theme** formats a worksheet by applying a collection of fonts, font styles, colors, and effects to give it a consistent appearance.

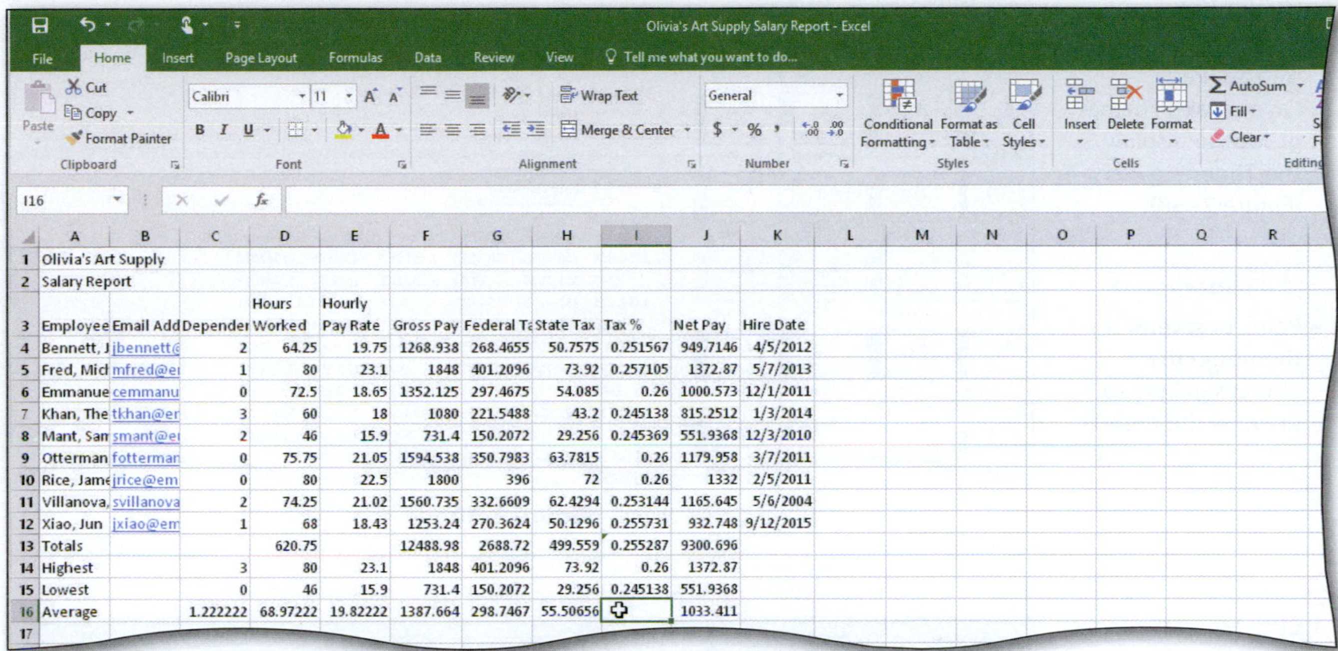

	A	B	C	D	E	F	G	H	I	J	K
1	Olivia's Art Supply										
2	Salary Report										
3	Employee	Email Add	Depender	Hours Worked	Hourly Pay Rate	Gross Pay	Federal Ta	State Tax	Tax %	Net Pay	Hire Date
4	Bennett, J	jbennett@	2	64.25	19.75	1268.938	268.4655	50.7575	0.251567	949.7146	4/5/2012
5	Fred, Mic	mfred@e	1	80	23.1	1848	401.2096	73.92	0.257105	1372.87	5/7/2013
6	Emmanue	cemmanu	0	72.5	18.65	1352.125	297.4675	54.085	0.26	1000.573	12/1/2011
7	Khan, The	tkhan@er	3	60	18	1080	221.5488	43.2	0.245138	815.2512	1/3/2014
8	Mant, Sam	smant@e	2	46	15.9	731.4	150.2072	29.256	0.245369	551.9368	12/3/2010
9	Otterman	fotterman	0	75.75	21.05	1594.538	350.7983	63.7815	0.26	1179.958	3/7/2011
10	Rice, Jame	jrice@em	0	80	22.5	1800	396	72	0.26	1332	2/5/2011
11	Villanova,	svillanova	2	74.25	21.02	1560.735	332.6609	62.4294	0.253144	1165.645	5/6/2004
12	Xiao, Jun	jxiao@em	1	68	18.43	1253.24	270.3624	50.1296	0.255731	932.748	9/12/2015
13	Totals			620.75		12488.98	2688.72	499.559	0.255287	9300.696	
14	Highest		3	80	23.1	1848	401.2096	73.92	0.26	1372.87	
15	Lowest		0	46	15.9	731.4	150.2072	29.256	0.245138	551.9368	
16	Average		1.222222	68.97222	19.82222	1387.664	298.7467	55.50656		1033.411	

(a) Unformatted Worksheet

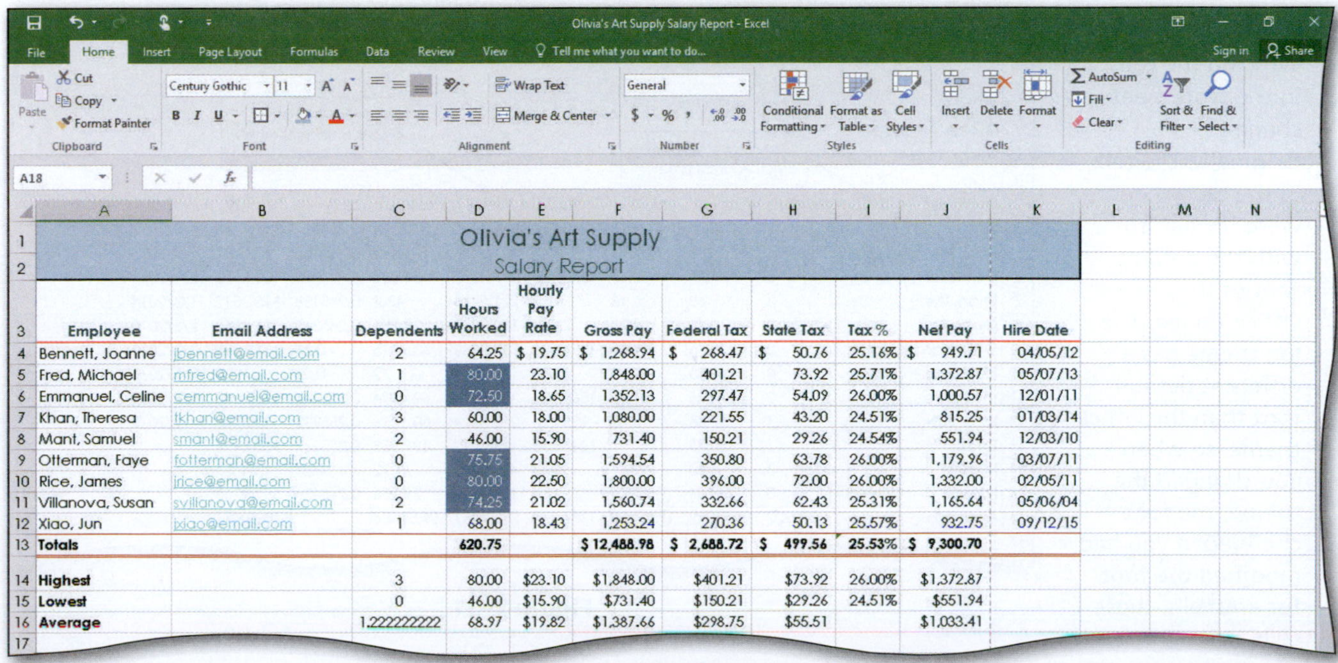

	A	B	C	D	E	F	G	H	I	J	K
1	Olivia's Art Supply										
2	Salary Report										
3	Employee	Email Address	Dependents	Hours Worked	Hourly Pay Rate	Gross Pay	Federal Tax	State Tax	Tax %	Net Pay	Hire Date
4	Bennett, Joanne	jbennett@email.com	2	64.25	$ 19.75	$ 1,268.94	$ 268.47	$ 50.76	25.16%	$ 949.71	04/05/12
5	Fred, Michael	mfred@email.com	1	80.00	23.10	1,848.00	401.21	73.92	25.71%	1,372.87	05/07/13
6	Emmanuel, Celine	cemmanuel@email.com	0	72.50	18.65	1,352.13	297.47	54.09	26.00%	1,000.57	12/01/11
7	Khan, Theresa	tkhan@email.com	3	60.00	18.00	1,080.00	221.55	43.20	24.51%	815.25	01/03/14
8	Mant, Samuel	smant@email.com	2	46.00	15.90	731.40	150.21	29.26	24.54%	551.94	12/03/10
9	Otterman, Faye	fotterman@email.com	0	75.75	21.05	1,594.54	350.80	63.78	26.00%	1,179.96	03/07/11
10	Rice, James	jrice@email.com	0	80.00	22.50	1,800.00	396.00	72.00	26.00%	1,332.00	02/05/11
11	Villanova, Susan	svillanova@email.com	2	74.25	21.02	1,560.74	332.66	62.43	25.31%	1,165.64	05/06/04
12	Xiao, Jun	jxiao@email.com	1	68.00	18.43	1,253.24	270.36	50.13	25.57%	932.75	09/12/15
13	**Totals**			**620.75**		**$ 12,488.98**	**$ 2,688.72**	**$ 499.56**	**25.53%**	**$ 9,300.70**	
14	**Highest**		3	80.00	$23.10	$1,848.00	$401.21	$73.92	26.00%	$1,372.87	
15	**Lowest**		0	46.00	$15.90	$731.40	$150.21	$29.26	24.51%	$551.94	
16	**Average**		1.222222222	68.97	$19.82	$1,387.66	$298.75	$55.51		$1,033.41	

(b) Formatted Worksheet

Figure 2–29

To Change the Workbook Theme

Why? *A company or department may choose a specific theme as their standard theme so that all of their documents have a similar appearance. Similarly, you may want to have a theme that sets your work apart from the work of others. Other Office programs, such as Word and PowerPoint, include the same themes so that all of your Microsoft Office documents can share a common look.* The following steps change the workbook theme to the Ion theme.

1

- Click Page Layout to display the Page Layout tab.
- Click the Themes button (Page Layout tab | Themes group) to display the Themes gallery (Figure 2–30).

Experiment

- Point to several themes in the Themes gallery to preview the themes.

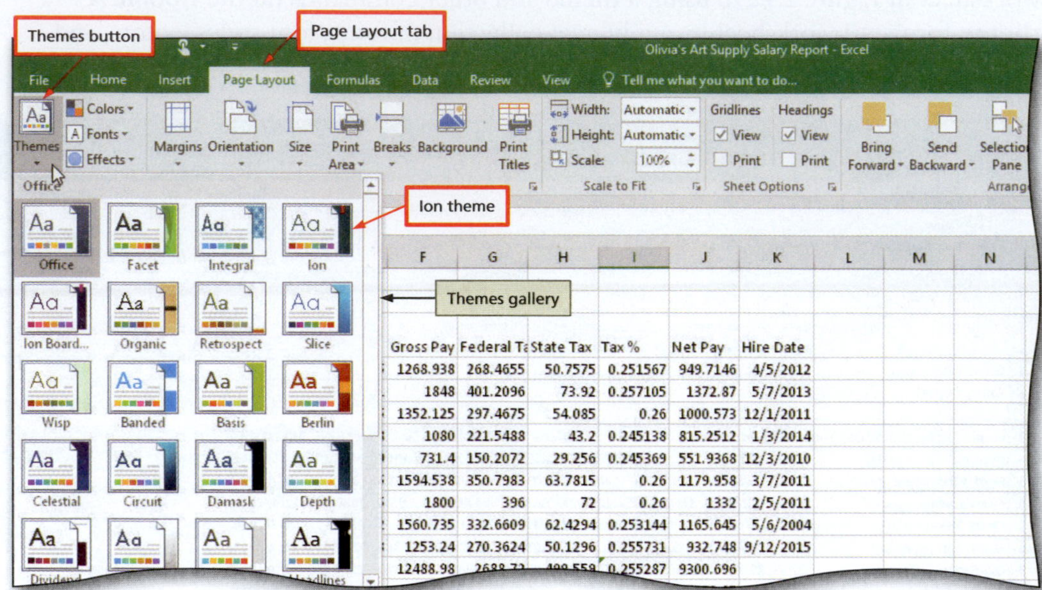

Figure 2–30

2

- Click Ion in the Themes gallery to change the workbook theme (Figure 2–31).

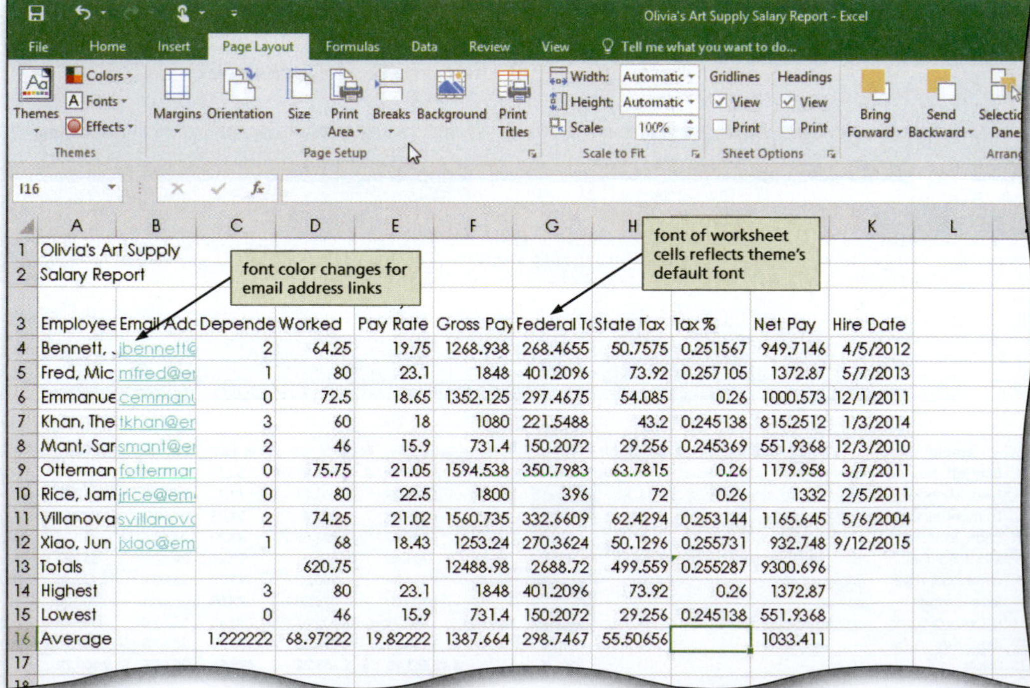

Figure 2–31

Q&A Why did the cells in the worksheet change?
Originally, the cells in the worksheet were formatted with the default font of the default Office theme. The Ion theme has a different default font than the Office theme, so when you changed the theme, the font changed. If you had modified the font for any cells, those cells would not have changed to the default font of the Ion theme.

To Format the Worksheet Titles

The following steps merge and center the worksheet titles, apply the Title cells style to the worksheet titles, and decrease the font of the worksheet subtitle.

1. Display the Home tab.

2. Select the range to be merged, A1:K1 in this case, and then click the 'Merge & Center' button (Home tab | Alignment group) to merge and center the text in the selected range.

3. Select the range A2:K2 and then click the 'Merge & Center' button (Home tab | Alignment group) to merge and center the text.

4. Select the range to contain the Title cell style, in this case A1:A2, click the Cell Styles button (Home tab | Styles group) to display the Cell Styles gallery, and then click the Title cell style in the Cell Styles gallery to apply the Title cell style to the selected range.

5. Select cell A2 and then click the 'Decrease Font Size' button (Home tab | Font group) to decrease the font size of the selected cell to the next lower font size (Figure 2–32).

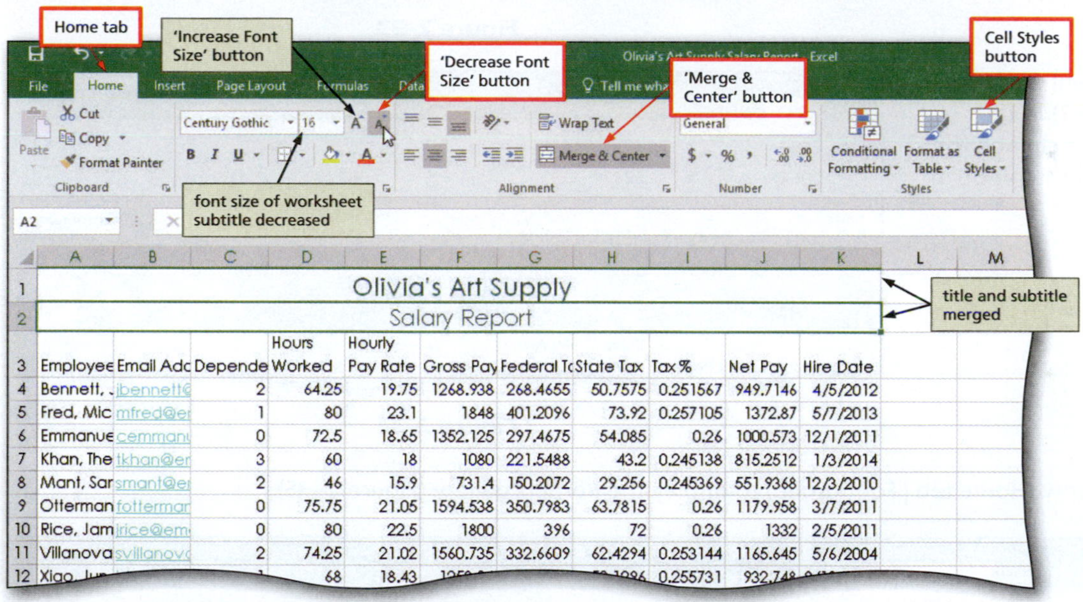

Figure 2–32

Q&A
What happens when I click the 'Decrease Font Size' button?
When you click the 'Decrease Font Size' button, Excel assigns the next smaller font size in the Font Size gallery to the selected range. The 'Increase Font Size' button works in a similar manner, assigning the next larger font size in the Font Size gallery to the selected range.

CONSIDER THIS

Which colors work best when formatting your worksheet?
Knowing how people perceive colors can help you focus attention on parts of your worksheet. Warmer colors (red and orange) tend to reach toward the reader. Cooler colors (blue, green, and violet) tend to pull away from the reader.

To Change the Background Color and Apply a Box Border to the Worksheet Title and Subtitle

1 ENTER FORMULAS | 2 ENTER FUNCTIONS | 3 VERIFY FORMULAS
4 FORMAT WORKSHEET | 5 CHECK SPELLING | 6 PRINT WORKSHEET

Why? A background color and border can draw attention to the title of a worksheet. The final formats assigned to the worksheet title and subtitle are the blue-gray background color and thick outside border. The following steps complete the formatting of the worksheet titles.

1

- Select the range A1:A2 and then click the Fill Color arrow (Home tab | Font group) to display the Fill Color gallery (Figure 2–33).

Experiment

- Point to a variety of colors in the Fill Color gallery to preview the selected colors in the range A1:A2.

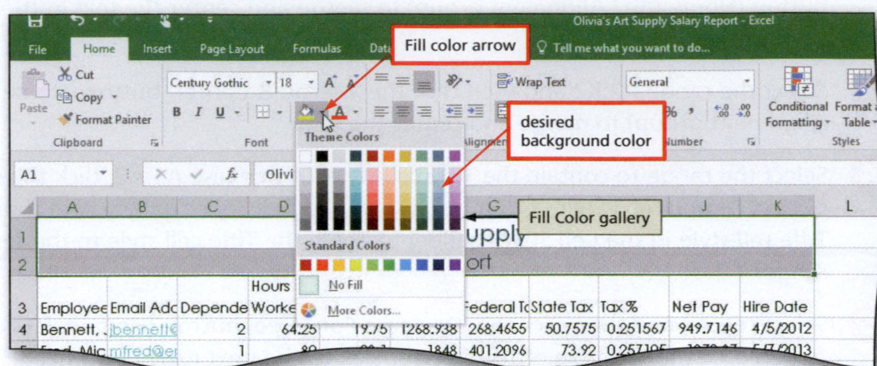

Figure 2–33

2

- Click Blue-Gray, Accent 5, Lighter 60% (column 9, row 3) in the Theme Colors area to change the background color of the range of cells (Figure 2–34).

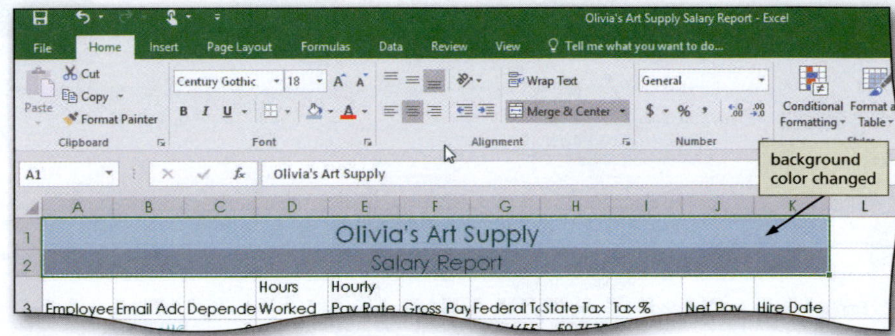

Figure 2–34

3

- Click the Borders arrow (Home tab | Font group) to display the Borders gallery (Figure 2–35).

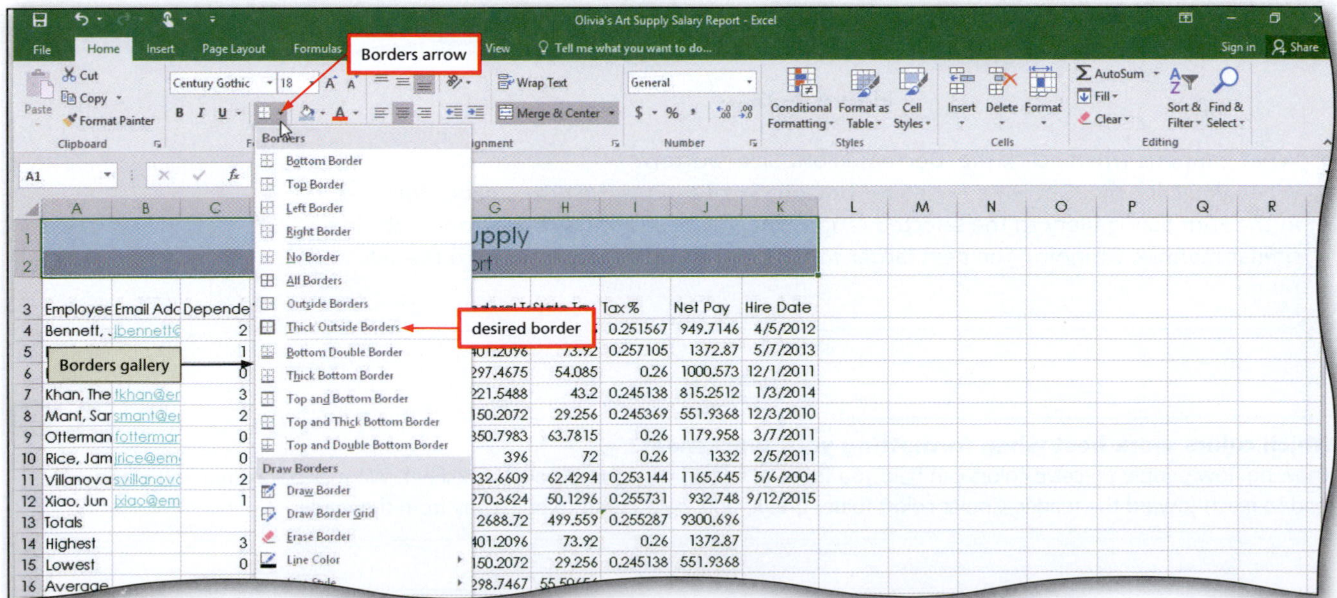

Figure 2–35

4
- Click 'Thick Outside Borders' in the Borders gallery to create a thick outside border around the selected range.
- Click anywhere in the worksheet, such as cell A18, to deselect the current range (Figure 2–36).

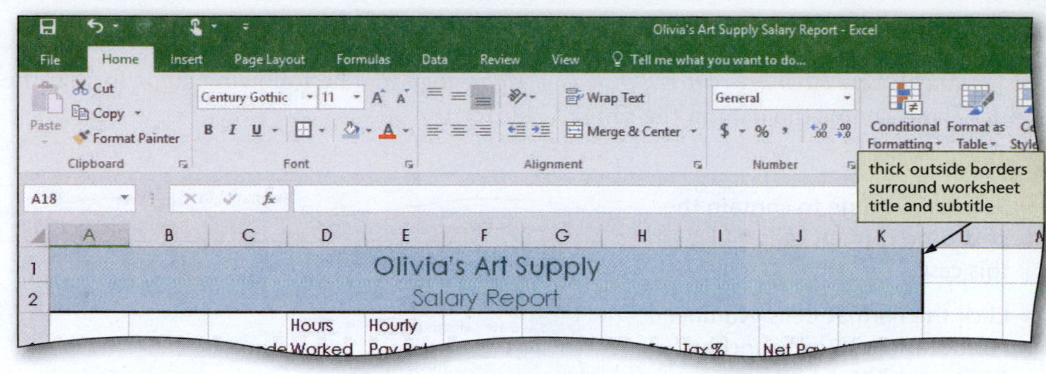

Figure 2–36

Other Ways

1. Click Font Settings Dialog Box Launcher (Home tab | Font group), click Fill tab (Format Cells dialog box), click desired fill, click OK button
2. Right-click range, click Format Cells on shortcut menu, click Fill tab (Format Cells dialog box), click desired fill, click OK button
3. Press CTRL+1, click Fill tab (Format Cells dialog box), click desired fill, click OK button

To Apply a Cell Style to the Column Headings and Format the Total Rows

As shown in Figure 2–29b, the column titles (row 3) should have the Heading 3 cell style and the totals row (row 13) should have the Total cell style. The headings in the range A14:A16 should be bold. The following steps assign these styles and formats to row 3, row 13, and the range A14:A16.

BTW

Color Selection

Bright colors jump out of a dark background and are easiest to see. White or yellow text on a dark blue, green, purple, or black background is ideal for highlighting.

1. Select the range to be formatted, cells A3:K3 in this case.
2. Use the Cell Styles gallery to apply the Heading 3 cell style to the range A3:K3.
3. Click the Center button (Home tab | Alignment group) to center the column headings.
4. Apply the Total cell style to the range A13:K13.
5. Bold the range A14:A16 (Figure 2–37).

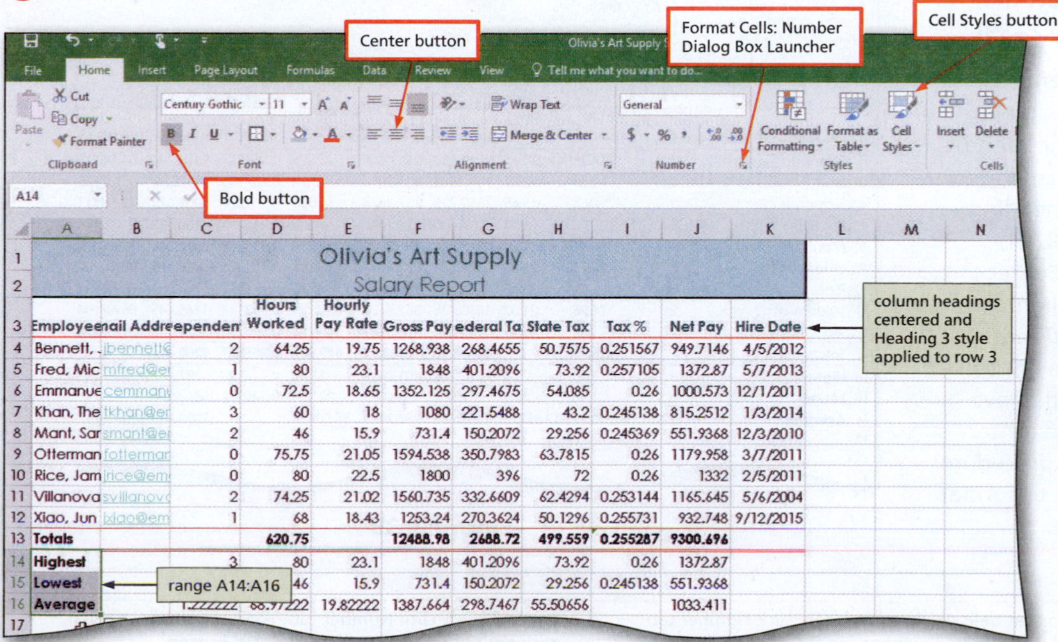

Figure 2–37

BTW

Background Colors

The most popular background color is blue. Research shows that the color blue is used most often because this color connotes serenity, reflection, and proficiency. Use color in spreadsheets to highlight data or to format worksheet elements such as titles. In most cases, colors should not be used for data presentation.

To Format Dates and Center Data in Cells

Why? *You may want to change the format of the dates to better suit your needs. In addition, numbers that are not used in calculations often are centered instead of right-aligned.* The following steps format the dates in the range K4:K12 and center the data in the range C4:C16.

- Select the range to contain the new date format, cells K4:K12 in this case.
- Click the Format Cells: Number Format Dialog Box Launcher (Home tab | Number group) (shown in Figure 2–37) to display the Format Cells dialog box.
- If necessary, click the Number tab (Format Cells dialog box), click Date in the Category list, and then click 03/14/12 in the Type list to choose the format for the selected range (Figure 2–38).

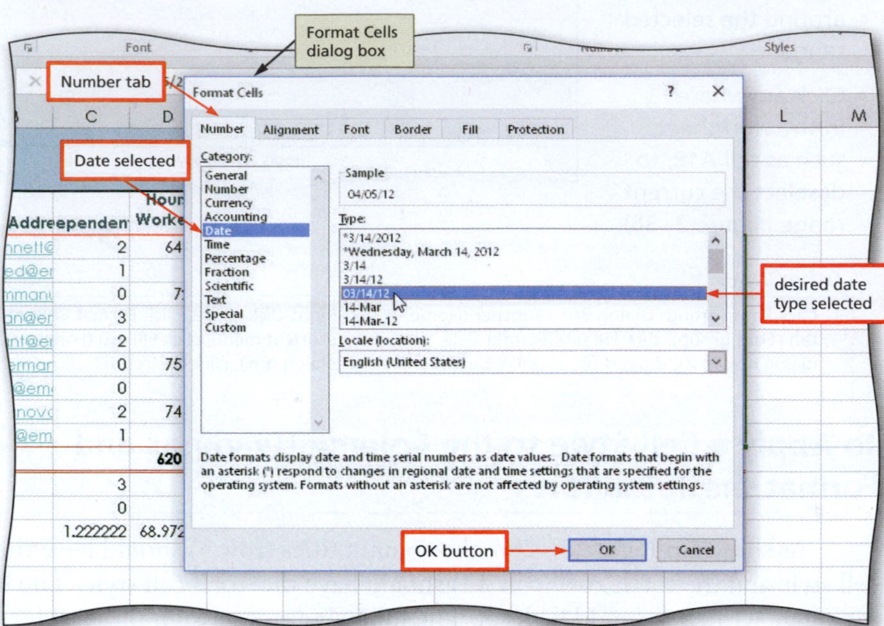

Figure 2–38

- Click the OK button (Format Cells dialog box) to format the dates in the current column using the selected date format style.

3

- Select the range C4:C16 and then click the Center button (Home tab | Alignment group) to center the data in the selected range.
- Select cell E4 to deselect the selected range (Figure 2–39).

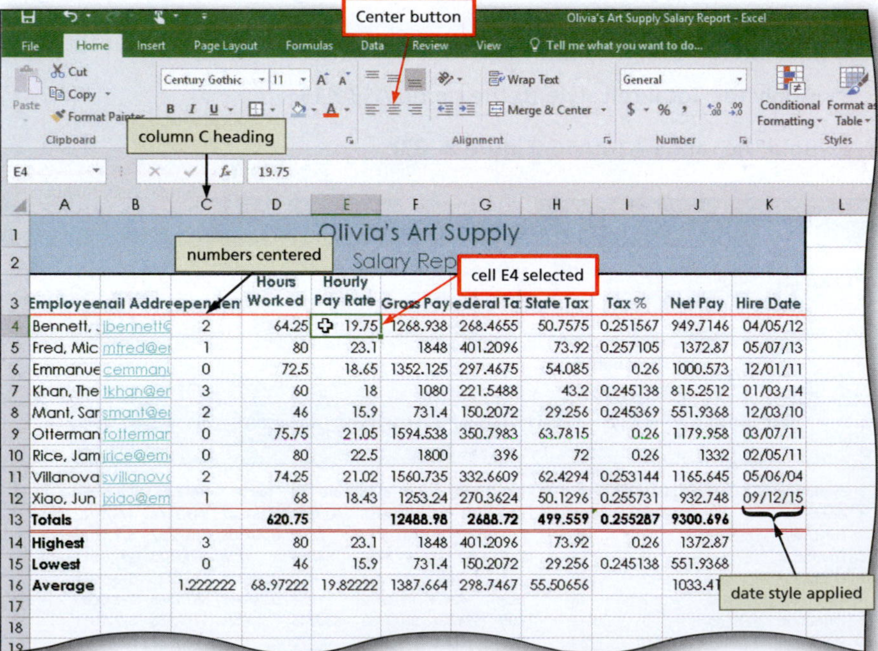

Figure 2–39

Q&A How can I format an entire column at once?

Instead of selecting the range C4:C16 in Step 3, you could have clicked the column C heading immediately above cell C1, and then clicked the Center button (Home tab | Alignment group). In this case, all cells in column C down to the last cell in the worksheet would have been formatted to use center alignment. This same procedure could have been used to format the dates in column K.

Other Ways

1. Right-click range, click Format Cells on shortcut menu, click Number tab (Format Cells dialog box), click desired number format, click OK button
2. Press CTRL+1, click Number tab (Format Cells dialog box), click desired number format, click OK button

To Apply an Accounting Number Format and Comma Style Format Using the Ribbon

As shown in Figure 2–29b, the worksheet is formatted to resemble an accounting report. In columns E through H and J, the numbers in the first row (row 4), the totals row (row 13), and the rows below the totals (rows 14 through 16) have dollar signs, while the remaining numbers (rows 5 through 12) in columns E through H and column J do not. The following steps assign formats using the 'Accounting Number Format' button and the Comma Style button. ***Why?*** *This gives the worksheet a more professional look.*

1. Select the range to contain the accounting number format, cells E4:H4 in this case.

2. While holding down the CTRL key, select cell J4, the range F13:H13, and cell J13 to select the nonadjacent ranges and cells.

3. Click the 'Accounting Number Format' button (Home tab | Number group) to apply the accounting number format with fixed dollar signs to the selected nonadjacent ranges.

Q&A What is the effect of applying the accounting number format?
The 'Accounting Number Format' button assigns a fixed dollar sign to the numbers in the ranges and rounds the figure to the nearest 100th. A fixed dollar sign is one that appears to the far left of the cell, with multiple spaces between it and the first digit in the cell.

4. Select the ranges to contain the comma style format, cells E5:H12 and J5:J12 in this case.

5. Click the Comma Style button (Home tab | Number group) to assign the comma style format to the selected ranges.

6. Select the range D4:D16 and then click the Comma Style button (Home tab | Number group) to assign the comma style format to the selected range (Figure 2–40).

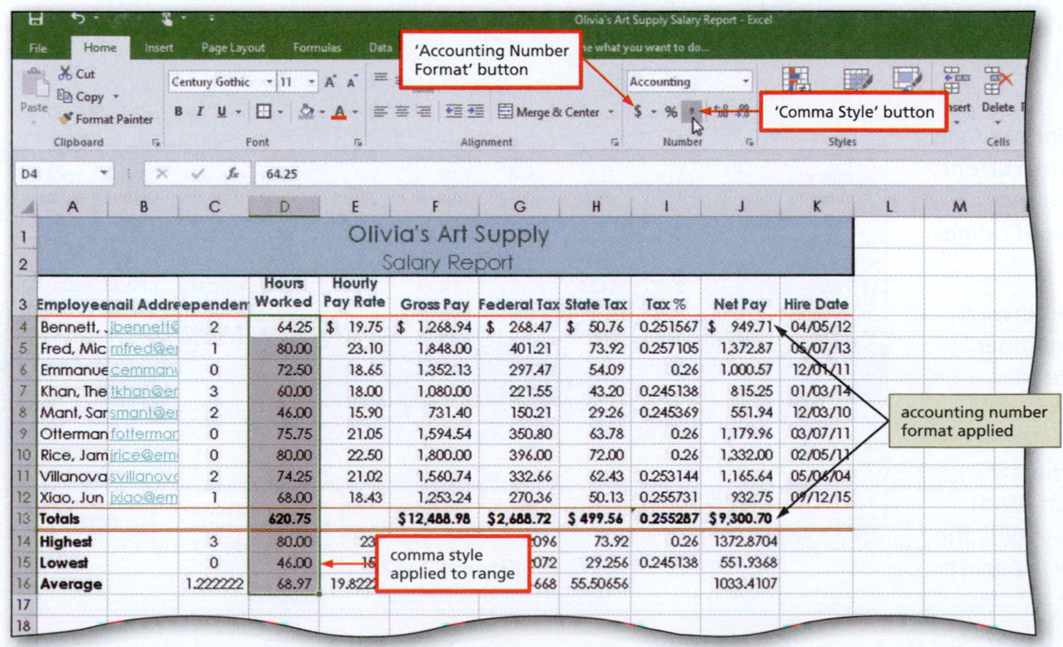

Figure 2–40

To Apply a Currency Style Format with a Floating Dollar Sign Using the Format Cells Dialog Box

Why? *The Currency format places dollar signs immediately to the left of the number (known as floating dollar signs, as they change position depending on the number of digits in the cell) and displays a zero for cells that have a value of zero.* The following steps use the Format Cells dialog box to apply the currency style format with a floating dollar sign to the numbers in the ranges E14:H16 and J14:J16.

- Select the ranges (E14:H16 and J14:J16) and then click the Number Format Dialog Box Launcher (Home tab | Number group) to display the Format Cells dialog box.
- If necessary, click the Number tab to display the Number sheet (Format Cells dialog box).
- Click Currency in the Category list to select the necessary number format category and then click the third style ($1,234.10) in the Negative numbers list to select the desired currency format for negative numbers (Figure 2–41).

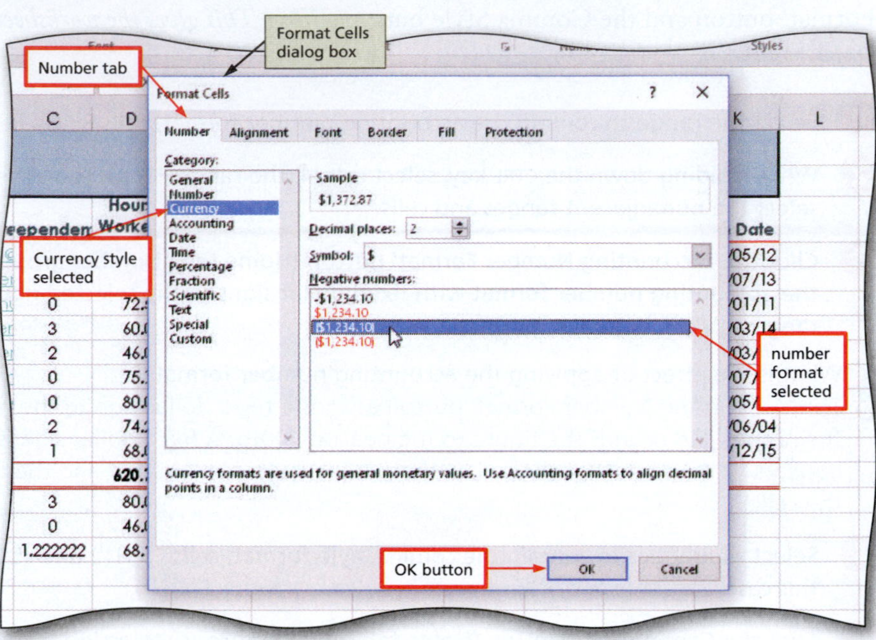

Figure 2–41

Q&A How do I decide which number format to use?
Excel offers many ways to format numbers. Once you select a number category, you can select the number of decimal places, whether to include a dollar sign (or a symbol of another currency), and how negative numbers should appear. Selecting the appropriate negative numbers format is important, because some formats add a space to the right of the number in order to align numbers in the worksheet on the decimal points and some do not.

- Click the OK button (Format Cells dialog box) to assign the currency style format with a floating dollar sign to the selected ranges (Figure 2–42).

5	Fred, Mic	mfred@er	1	80.00	23.10	1,848.00	401.21	73.92	0.257105	1,372.87	05/07/13
6	Emmanue	cemman	0	72.50	18.65	1,352.13	297.47	54.09	0.26	1,000.57	12/01/11
7	Khan, The	tkhan@er	3	60.00	18.00	1,080.00	221.55	43.20	0.245138	815.25	01/03/14
8	Mant, Sar	smant@er	2	46.00	15.90	731.40	150.21	29.26	0.245369	551.94	12/03/10
9	Otterman	fotterman	0	75.75	21.05	1,594.54	350.80	63.78	0.26	1,179.96	03/07/11
10	Rice, Jam	jrice@em	0	80.00	22.50	1,800.00	396.00	72.00	0.26	1,332.00	02/05/11
11	Villanova	svillanov	2	74.25	21.02	1,560.74	332.66	62.43	0.253144	1,165.64	05/06/04
12	Xiao, Jun	jxiao@em	1	68.00	18.43	1,253.24	270.36	50.13	0.255731	932.75	09/12/15
13	**Totals**			**620.75**		**$12,488.98**	**$2,688.72**	**$ 499.56**	**0.255287**	**$9,300.70**	
14	**Highest**		3	80.00	$23.10	$1,848.00	$401.21	$73.92	0.26	$1,372.87	
15	**Lowest**		0	46.00	$15.90	$731.40	$150.21	$29.26	0.245138	$551.94	
16	**Average**		1.222222	68.97	$19.82	$1,387.66	$298.75	$55.51		$1,033.41	

currency style applied to selected ranges

Figure 2–42

Q&A What is the difference between using the accounting number style and currency style?
When using the currency style, recall that a floating dollar sign always appears immediately to the left of the first digit. With the accounting number style, the fixed dollar sign always appears on the left side of the cell.

Other Ways

1. Press CTRL+1, click Number tab (Format Cells dialog box), click Currency in Category list, select format, click OK button
2. Press CTRL+SHIFT+DOLLAR SIGN ($)

To Apply a Percent Style Format and Use the Increase Decimal Button

The next step is to format the tax percentage in column I. ***Why?*** *Currently, Excel displays the numbers as decimal fractions when they should appear as percentages.* The following steps format the range I4:I15 to the percent style format with two decimal places.

1

- Select the range to format, cells I4:I15 in this case.
- Click the Percent Style button (Home tab | Number group) to display the numbers in the selected range as a rounded whole percent.

Q&A What is the result of clicking the Percent Style button?
The Percent Style button instructs Excel to display a value as a percentage, which is determined by multiplying the cell entry by 100, rounding the result to the nearest percentage, and adding a percent sign. For example, when cell I4 is formatted using the Percent Style buttons, Excel displays the actual value 0.251567 as 25%.

2

- Click the Increase Decimal button (Home tab | Number group) two times to display the numbers in the selected range with two decimal places (Figure 2–43).

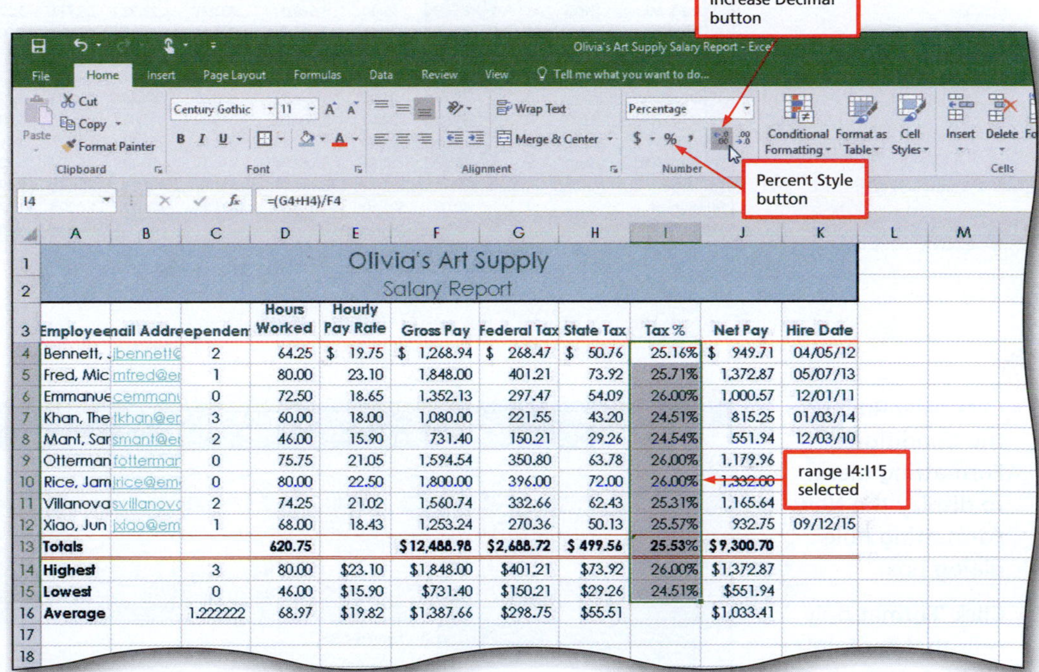

Figure 2–43

Other Ways

1. Right-click selected range, click Format Cells on shortcut menu, click Number tab (Format Cells dialog box), click Percentage in Category list, select format, click OK button
2. Press CTRL+1, click Number tab (Format Cells dialog box), click Percentage in Category list, select format, click OK button
3. Press CTRL+SHIFT+PERCENT SIGN (%)

Conditional Formatting

Conditional formatting offers you the ability to automatically change how a cell appears — the font, font color, background fill, and other options — based on the value in the cell. Excel offers a variety of commonly used conditional formatting rules, along with the ability to create your own custom rules and formatting. The next step is to emphasize the values greater than 72 in column D by formatting them to appear with a blue background and white font color (Figure 2–44).

BTW
Conditional Formatting
You can assign any format to a cell, a range of cells, a worksheet, or an entire workbook conditionally. If the value of the cell changes and no longer meets the specified condition, Excel suppresses the conditional formatting.

To Apply Conditional Formatting

The following steps assign conditional formatting to the range D4:D12. ***Why?*** *After formatting, any cell with a value greater than 72 in column D will appear with a blue background and a white font.*

1

- Select the range D4:D12.
- Click the Conditional Formatting button (Home tab | Styles group) to display the Conditional Formatting menu (Figure 2–44).

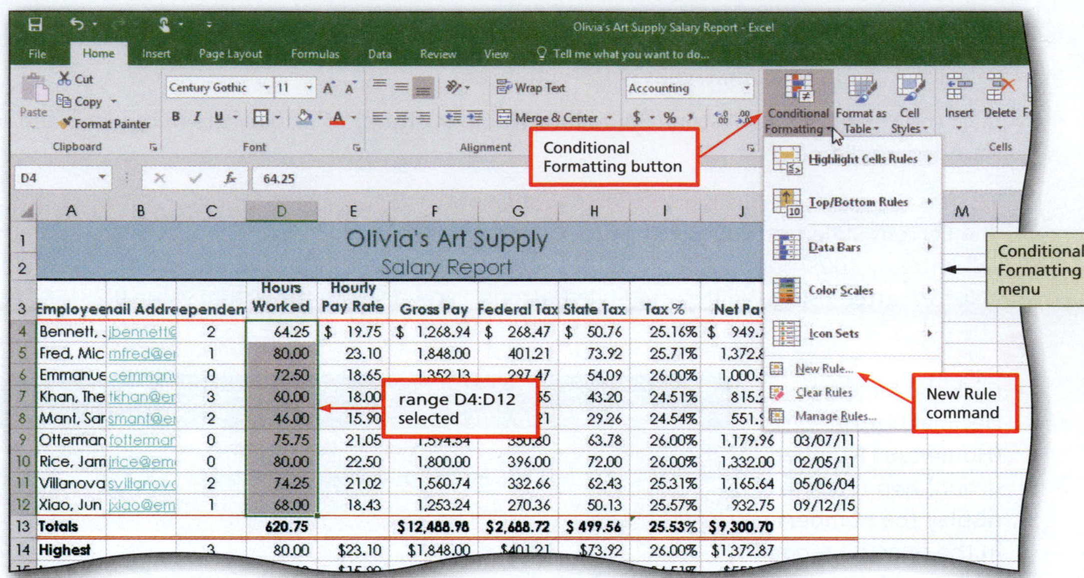

Figure 2–44

2

- Click New Rule on the Conditional Formatting menu to display the New Formatting Rule dialog box.
- Click 'Format only cells that contain' in the Select a Rule Type area (New Formatting Rule dialog box) to change the Edit the Rule Description area.
- In the Edit the Rule Description area, click the arrow in the relational operator box (second box) to display a list of relational operators, and then select greater than to select the desired operator.

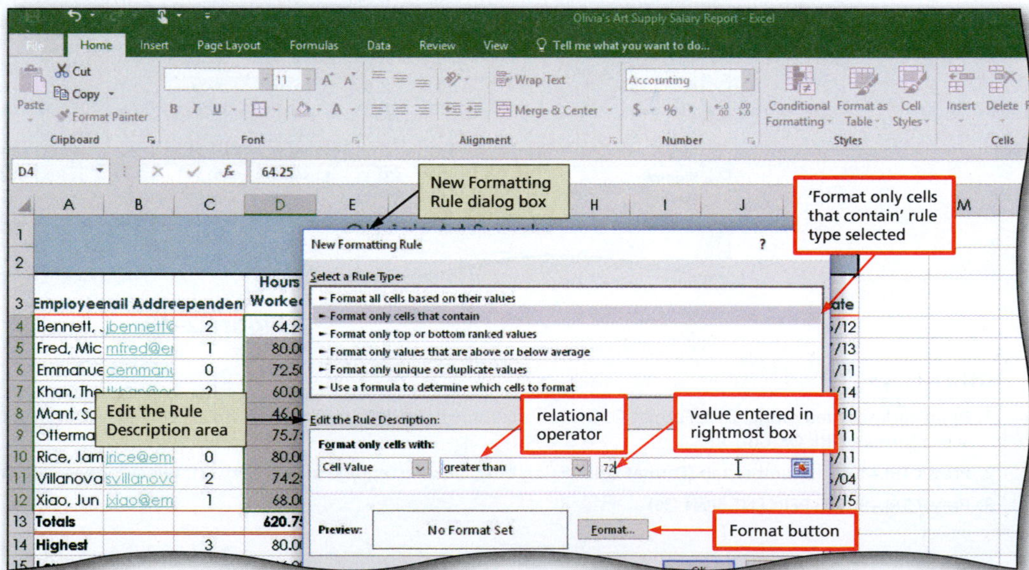

Figure 2–45

- Select the rightmost box, and then type 72 to enter the value of the rule description (Figure 2–45).

Q&A What do the changes in the Edit the Rule Description area indicate?
The Edit the Rule Description area allows you to view and edit the rules for the conditional format. In this case, the rule indicates that Excel should format only those cells with cell values greater than 72.

3

- Click the Format button (New Formatting Rule dialog box) to display the Format Cells dialog box.
- If necessary, click the Font tab (Format Cells dialog box) to display the Font sheet. Click the Color arrow to display the Color gallery and then click White, Background 1 (column 1, row 1) in the Color gallery to select the font color (Figure 2–46).

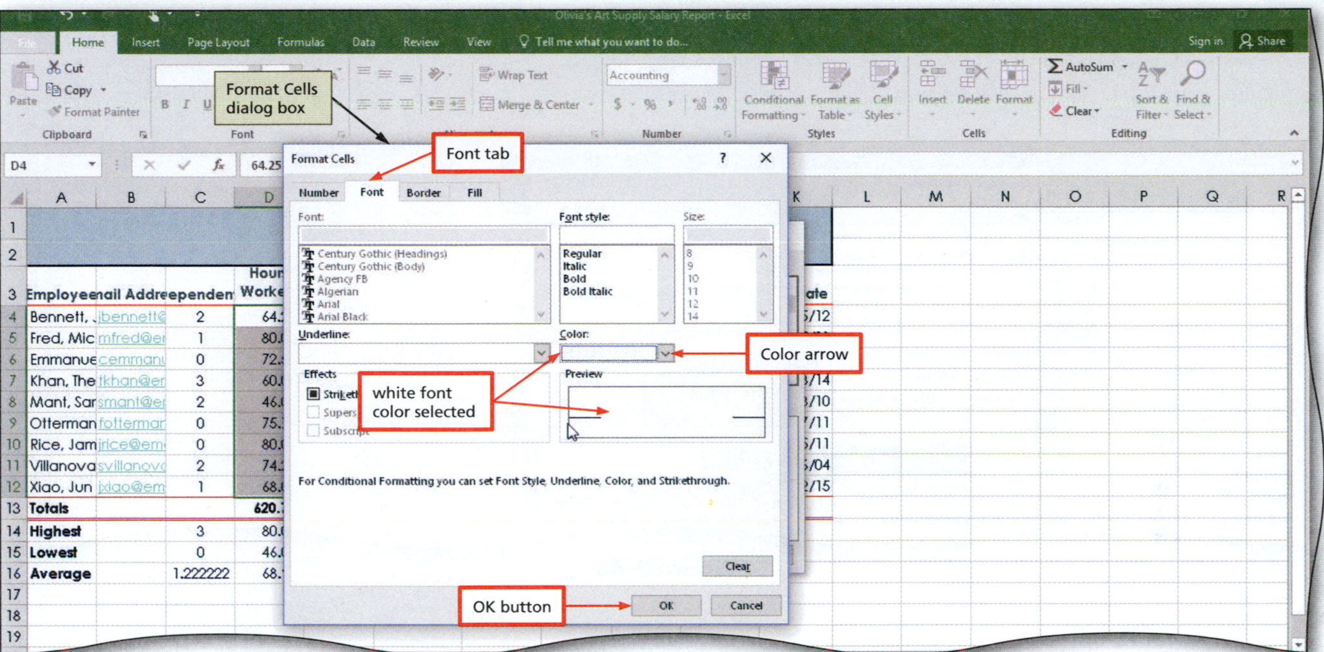

Figure 2–46

4

- Click the Fill tab (Format Cells dialog box) to display the Fill sheet and then click the blue color in column 9, row 1 to select the background color (Figure 2–47).

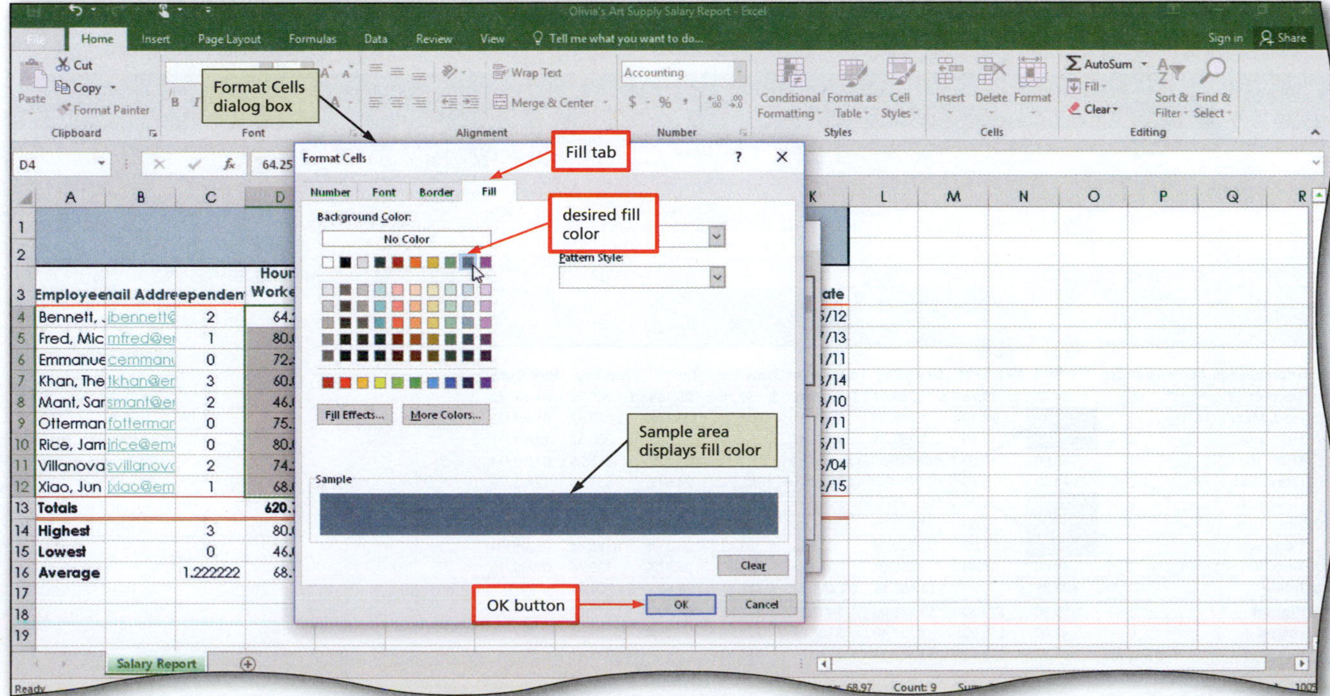

Figure 2–47

- Click the OK button (Format Cells dialog box) to close the Format Cells dialog box and display the New Formatting Rule dialog box with the desired font and background colors displayed in the Preview area (Figure 2–48).

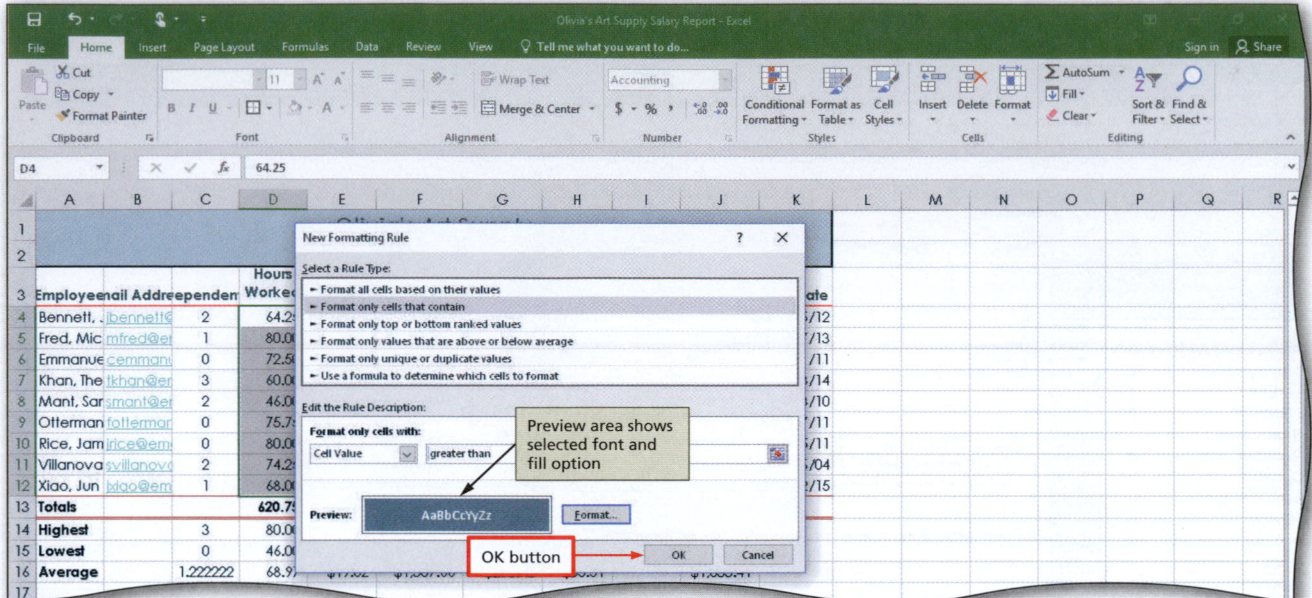

Figure 2–48

6

- Click the OK button (New Formatting Rule dialog box) to assign the conditional format to the selected range.
- Click anywhere in the worksheet, such as cell A18, to deselect the current range (Figure 2–49).

Q&A What should I do if I make a mistake setting up a rule?

If after you have applied the conditional formatting you realize you made a mistake when creating a rule, select the cell(s) with the rule you want to edit, click the Conditional Formatting button (Home tab | Styles group), select the rule you want to edit, and then click either the Edit Rule button (to edit the selected rule) or the Delete Rule button (to delete the selected rule).

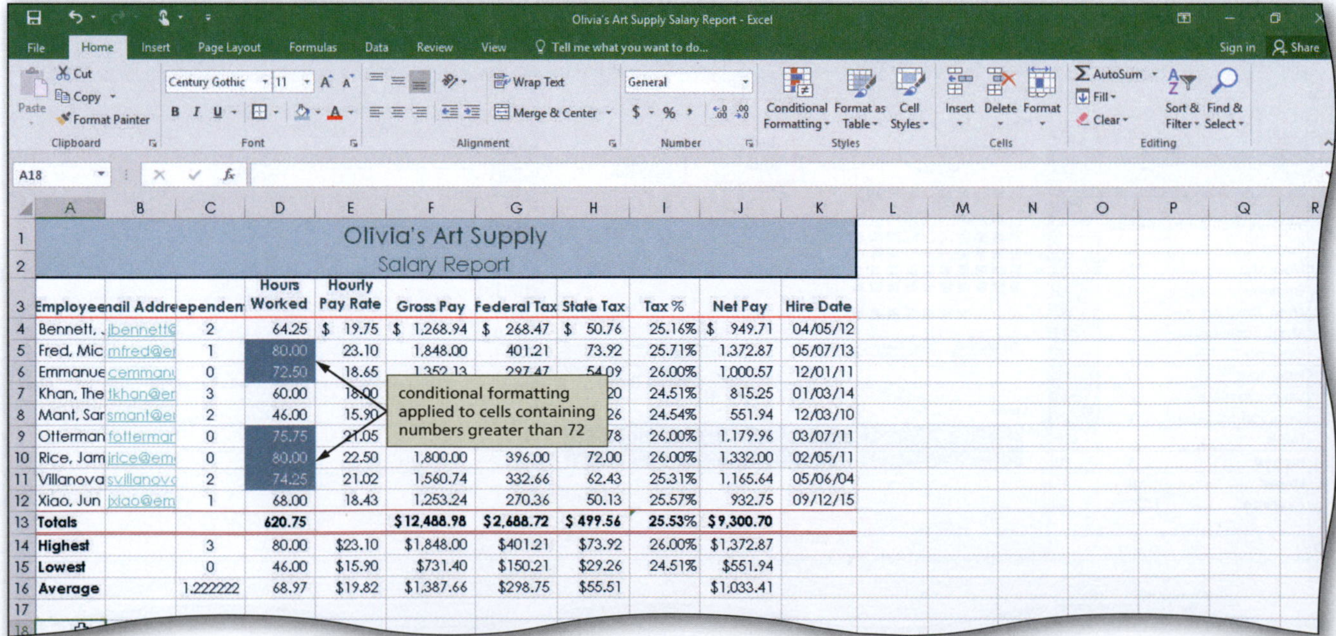

Figure 2–49

Conditional Formatting Operators

As shown in the New Formatting Rule dialog box, when the selected rule type is "Format only the cells that contain," the second text box in the Edit the Rule Description area allows you to select a relational operator, such as greater than, to use in the condition. The eight different relational operators from which you can choose for conditional formatting are summarized in Table 2–5.

Table 2–5 Summary of Conditional Formatting Relational Operators

Relational Operator	Formatting will be applied if...
between	cell value is between two numbers
not between	cell value is not between two numbers
equal to	cell value is equal to a number
not equal to	cell value is not equal to a number
greater than	cell value is greater than a number
less than	cell value is less than a number
greater than or equal to	cell value is greater than or equal to a number
less than or equal to	cell value is less than or equal to a number

BTW

Excel Help

At any time while using Excel, you can find answers to questions and display information about various topics through Excel Help. Used properly, this form of assistance can increase your productivity and reduce your frustrations by minimizing the time you spend learning how to use Excel. For instructions about Excel Help and exercises that will help you gain confidence in using it, read the Office and Windows module at the beginning of this book.

Changing Column Width and Row Height

You can change the width of the columns or height of the rows at any time to make the worksheet easier to read or to ensure that an entry fits properly in a cell. By default, all of the columns in a blank worksheet have a width of 8.43 characters, or 64 pixels. This value may change depending on the theme applied to the workbook. For example, when the Ion theme was applied to the workbook in this module, the default width of the columns changed to 8.38 characters. A **character** is defined as a letter, number, symbol, or punctuation mark. An average of 8.43 characters in 11-point Calibri font (the default font used by Excel) will fit in a cell.

The default row height in a blank worksheet is 15 points (or 20 pixels), which easily fits the 11-point default font. Recall from Module 1 that a point is equal to 1/72 of an inch. Thus, 15 points is equal to about 1/5 of an inch.

Another measure of the height and width of cells is pixels. A **pixel**, which is short for picture element, is a dot on the screen that contains a color. The size of the dot is based on your screen's resolution. At the resolution of 1366 × 768 used in this book, 1366 pixels appear across the screen and 768 pixels appear down the screen for a total of 1,049,088 pixels. It is these 1,049,088 pixels that form the font and other items you see on the screen.

BTW

Hidden Rows and Columns

For some people, trying to unhide a range of columns using the mouse can be frustrating. An alternative is to use the keyboard: select the columns to the right and left of the hidden columns and then press CTRL+SHIFT+) (RIGHT PARENTHESIS). To use the keyboard to hide a range of columns, press CTRL+0 (zero). You also can use the keyboard to unhide a range of rows by selecting the rows immediately above and below the hidden rows and then pressing CTRL+SHIFT+((LEFT PARENTHESIS). To use the keyboard to hide a range of rows, press CTRL+9.

To Change Column Width

When changing the column width, you can set the width manually or you can instruct Excel to size the column to best fit. **Best fit** means that the width of the column will be increased or decreased so that the widest entry will fit in the column. ***Why?*** *Sometimes, you may prefer more or less white space in a column than best fit provides. To change the white space, Excel allows you to change column widths manually.*

When the format you assign to a cell causes the entry to exceed the width of a column, Excel changes the column width to best fit. If you do not assign a format to a cell or cells in a column, the column width will remain 8.43 characters. Recall from Module 1 that to set a column width to best fit, double-click the right boundary of the column heading above row 1. The following steps change the column widths.

1

- Drag through column headings A, B, and C above row 1 to select the columns.
- Point to the boundary on the right side of column heading C to cause the pointer to become a split double arrow (Figure 2–50).

Q&A What if I want to make a large change to the column width?
If you want to increase or decrease column width significantly, you can right-click a column heading and then use the Column Width command on the shortcut menu to change the column's width. To use this command, however, you must select one or more entire columns.

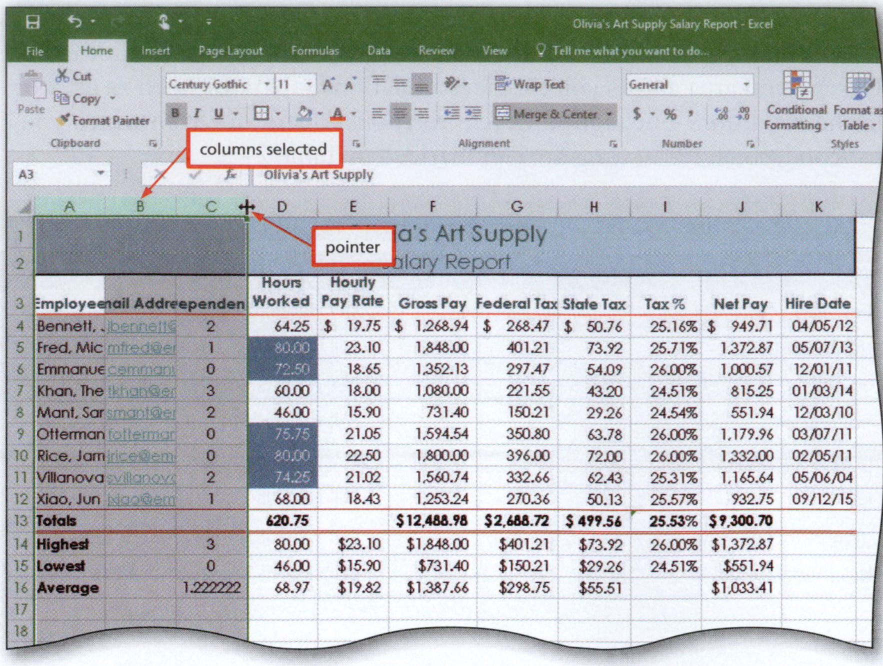

Figure 2–50

2

- Double-click the right boundary of column heading C to change the width of the selected columns to best fit.
- Point to the right boundary of the column H heading above row 1.
- When the pointer changes to a split double arrow, drag until the ScreenTip indicates Width: 10.25 (87 pixels). Do not release the mouse button (Figure 2–51).

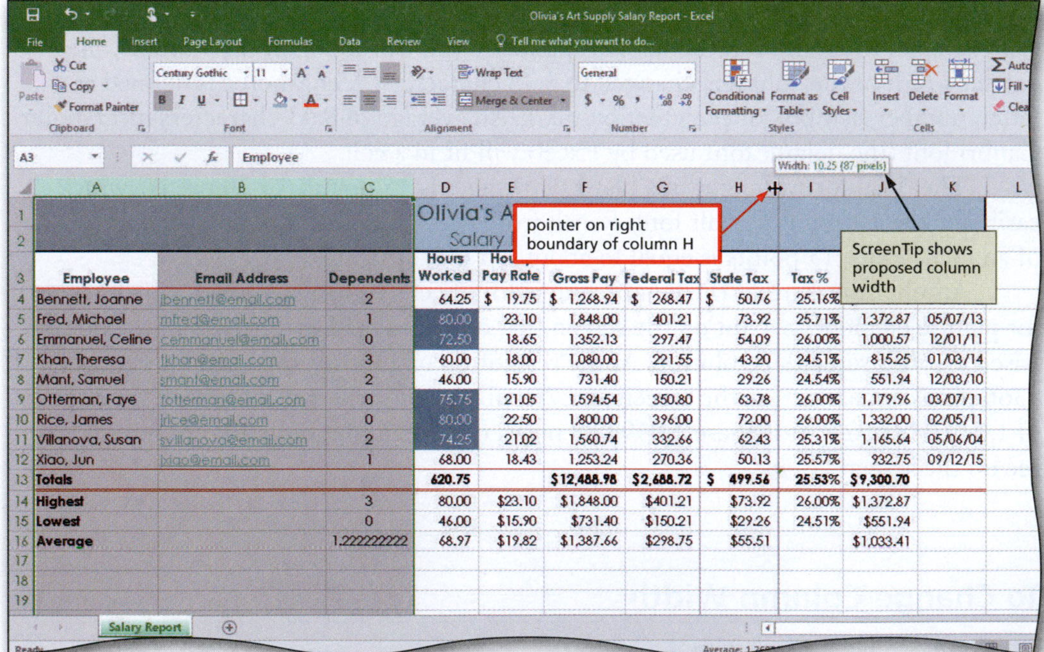

Figure 2–51

Q&A What happens if I change the column width to zero (0)?
If you decrease the column width to 0, the column is hidden. Hiding cells is a technique you can use to hide data that might not be relevant to a particular report. To instruct Excel to display a hidden column, position the mouse pointer to the right of the column heading boundary where the hidden column is located and then drag to the right.

3

- Release the mouse button to change the column width.
- Click the column D heading above row 1 to select the column.
- While holding down the CTRL key, click the column E heading and then the column I heading above row 1 so that nonadjacent columns are selected.
- Point to the boundary on the right side of the column I heading above row 1.
- Drag until the ScreenTip indicates Width: 7.50 (65 pixels). Do not release the mouse button (Figure 2–52).

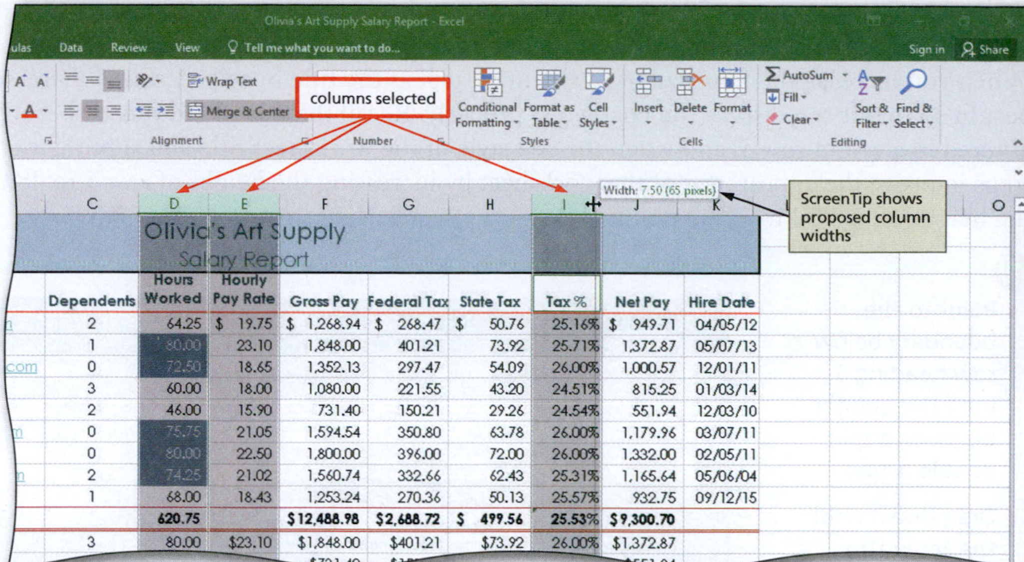

Figure 2–52

4

- Release the mouse button to change the column widths.
- Click the column F heading and drag to select the column G heading.
- While holding down the CTRL key, click the column J heading and drag to select the column K heading above row 1 so that nonadjacent columns are selected.
- Drag the right boundary of column G until the ScreenTip indicates Width: 11.00 (93 pixels). Release the mouse button to change the column widths.
- Click anywhere in the worksheet, such as cell A18, to deselect the columns (Figure 2–53).

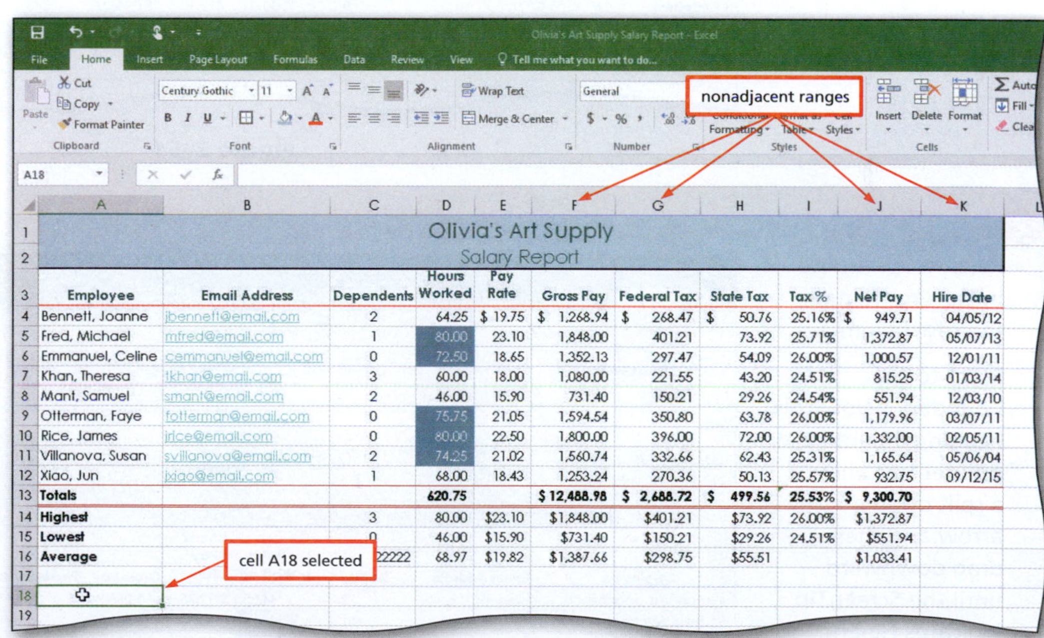

Figure 2–53

Other Ways

1. Click column heading or drag through multiple column headings, right-click selected column, click Column Width on shortcut menu, enter desired column width, click OK button

To Change Row Height

Why? *You also can increase or decrease the height of a row manually to improve the appearance of the worksheet.* When you increase the font size of a cell entry, such as the title in cell A1, Excel increases the row height to best fit so that it can display the characters properly. Recall that Excel did this earlier when multiple lines were entered in a cell in row 3, and when the cell style of the worksheet title and subtitle was changed. The following steps improve the appearance of the worksheet by increasing the height of row 3 to 48.00 points and increasing the height of row 14 to 27.00 points.

- Point to the boundary below row heading 3 until the pointer becomes a split double arrow.
- Drag down until the ScreenTip indicates Height: 48.00 (64 pixels). Do not release the mouse button (Figure 2–54).

Figure 2–54

- Release the mouse button to change the row height.
- Point to the boundary below row heading 14 until the pointer becomes a split double arrow and then drag downward until the ScreenTip indicates Height: 27.00 (36 pixels). Do not release the mouse button (Figure 2–55).

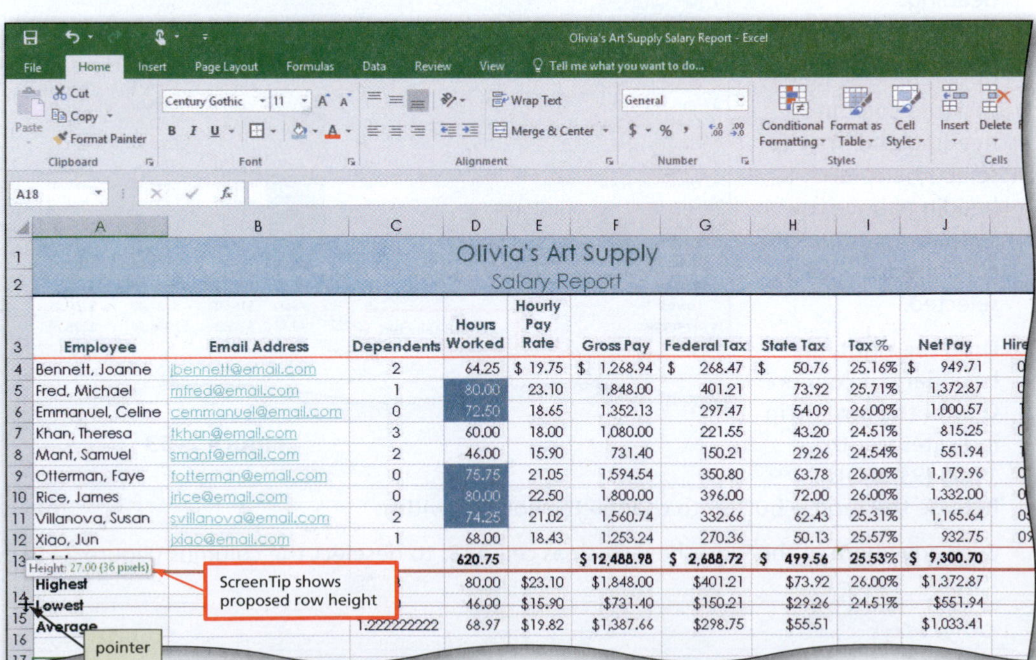

Figure 2–55

- **Release the mouse button to change the row height.**
- **Click anywhere in the worksheet, such as cell A18, to deselect the current cell (Figure 2–56).**

Q&A Can I hide a row?

Yes. As with column widths, when you decrease the row height to 0, the row is hidden. To instruct Excel to display a hidden row, position the pointer just below the row heading boundary where the row is hidden and then drag downward. To set a row height to best fit, double-click the bottom boundary of the row heading. You also can hide and unhide rows by right-clicking the row or column heading and selecting the option to hide or unhide the cells.

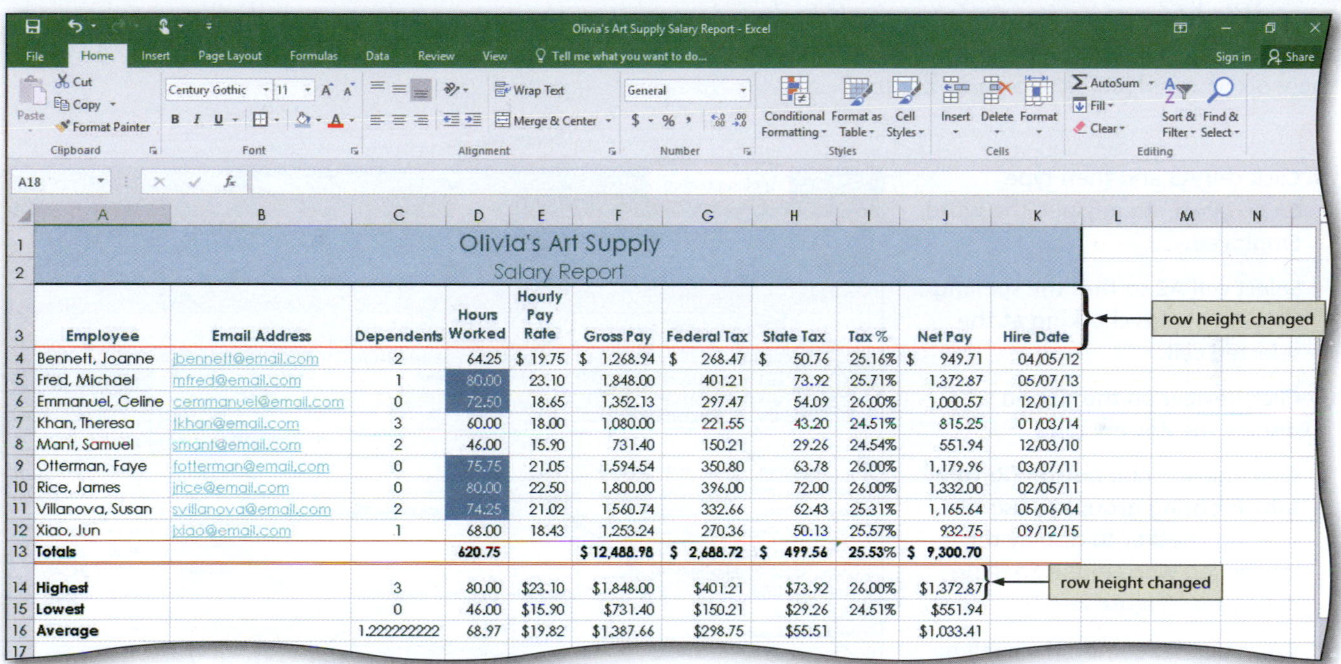

Figure 2–56

Other Ways

1. Right-click row heading or drag through multiple row headings, right-click selected heading, click Row Height on shortcut menu, enter desired row height, click OK button

Break Point: If you wish to take a break, this is a good place to do so. Be sure to save the Olivia's Art Supply Salary Report file again and then you can exit Excel. To resume at a later time, run Excel, open the file called Olivia's Art Supply Salary Report, and continue following the steps from this location forward.

Checking Spelling

Excel includes a **spelling checker** you can use to check a worksheet for spelling errors. The spelling checker looks for spelling errors by comparing words on the worksheet against words contained in its standard dictionary. If you often use specialized terms that are not in the standard dictionary, you may want to add them to a custom dictionary using the Spelling dialog box. When the spelling checker finds a word that is not in either dictionary, it displays the word in the Spelling dialog box. You then can correct it if it is misspelled.

BTW

Spell Checking

While Excel's spell checker is a valuable tool, it is not infallible. You should proofread your workbook carefully by pointing to each word and saying it aloud as you point to it. Be mindful of misused words such as its and it's, through and though, and to and too. Nothing undermines a good impression more than a professional looking report with misspelled words.

CONSIDER THIS

Does the spelling checker catch all spelling mistakes?

While Excel's spelling checker is a valuable tool, it is not infallible. You should proofread your workbook carefully by pointing to each word and saying it aloud as you point to it. Be mindful of misused words such as its and it's, through and though, your and you're, and to and too. Nothing undermines a good impression more than a professional report with misspelled words.

To Check Spelling on the Worksheet

1 ENTER FORMULAS | 2 ENTER FUNCTIONS | 3 VERIFY FORMULAS
4 FORMAT WORKSHEET | 5 CHECK SPELLING | 6 PRINT WORKSHEET

***Why?** Everything in a worksheet should be checked to make sure there are no spelling errors.* To illustrate how Excel responds to a misspelled word, the following steps purposely misspell the word, Employee, in cell A3 as the word, Empolyee, as shown in Figure 2–57.

1

- Click cell A3 and then type `Empolyee` to misspell the word, Employee.
- Select cell A2 so that the spelling checker begins checking at the selected cell.
- Click Review on the ribbon to display the Review tab.
- Click the Spelling button (Review tab | Proofing group) to use the spelling checker to display the misspelled word in the Spelling dialog box (Figure 2–57).

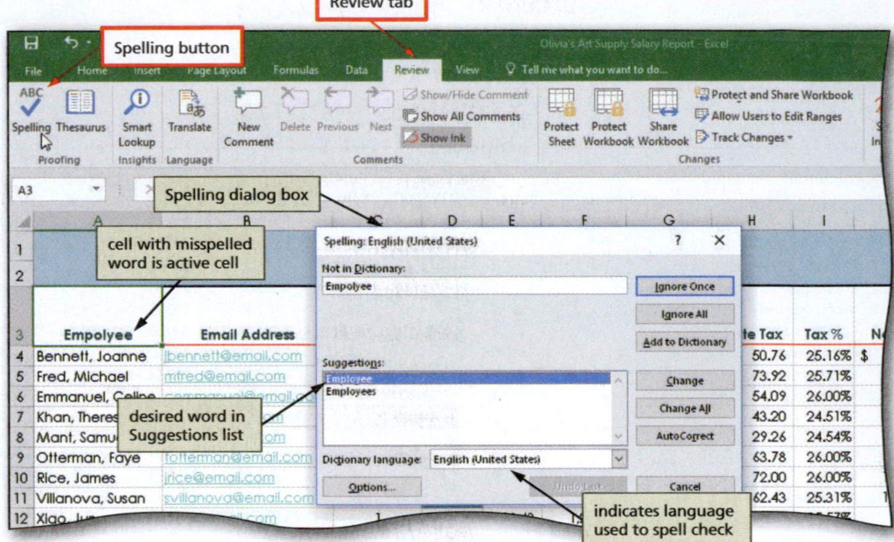

Figure 2–57

Q&A What happens when the spelling checker finds a misspelled word?

When the spelling checker identifies that a cell contains a word not in its standard or custom dictionary, it selects that cell as the active cell and displays the Spelling dialog box. The Spelling dialog box displays the word that was not found in the dictionary and offers a list of suggested corrections (Figure 2–58).

2

- Verify that the word highlighted in the Suggestion area is correct.
- Click the Change button (Spelling dialog box) to change the misspelled word to the correct word (Figure 2–58).
- Click the Close button to close the Spelling dialog box.
- If a Microsoft Excel dialog box is displayed, click the OK button.

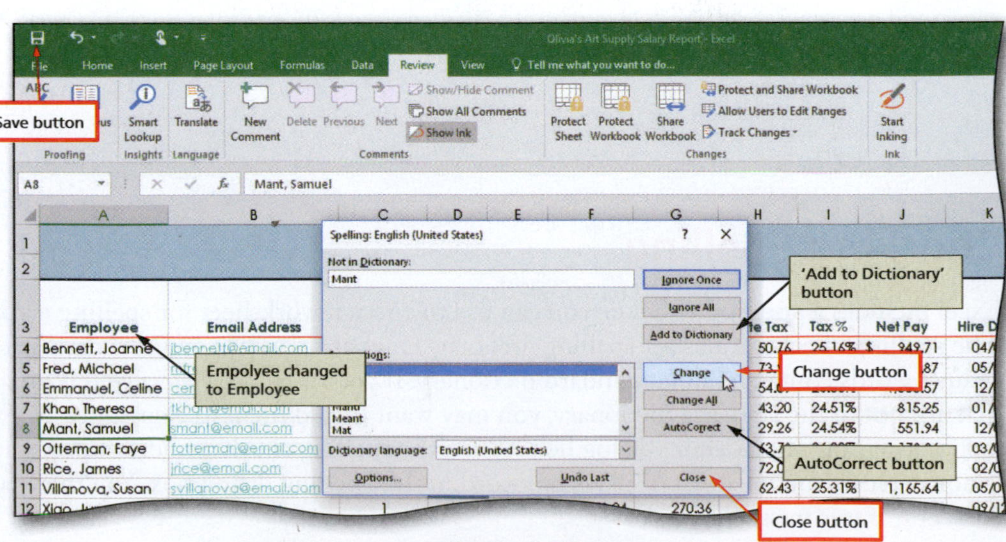

Figure 2–58

3

- Click anywhere in the worksheet, such as cell A18, to deselect the current cell.
- Display the Home tab.
- Save the workbook again on the same storage location with the same file name.

Q&A What other actions can I take in the Spelling dialog box?
If one of the words in the Suggestions list is correct, select it and then click the Change button. If none of the suggested words are correct, type the correct word in the 'Not in Dictionary' text box and then click the Change button. To change the word throughout the worksheet, click the Change All button instead of the Change button. To skip correcting the word, click the Ignore Once button. To have Excel ignore the word for the remainder of the worksheet, click the Ignore All button.

Other Ways

1. Press F7

Additional Spelling Checker Considerations

Consider these additional guidelines when using the spelling checker:

- To check the spelling of the text in a single cell, double-click the cell to make the formula bar active and then click the Spelling button (Review tab | Proofing group).
- If you select a single cell so that the formula bar is not active and then start the spelling checker, Excel checks the remainder of the worksheet, including notes and embedded charts.
- If you select a cell other than cell A1 before you start the spelling checker, Excel will display a dialog box when the spelling checker reaches the end of the worksheet, asking if you want to continue checking at the beginning.
- If you select a range of cells before starting the spelling checker, Excel checks the spelling of the words only in the selected range.
- To check the spelling of all the sheets in a workbook, right-click any sheet tab, click 'Select All Sheets' on the sheet tab shortcut menu, and then start the spelling checker.
- To add words to the dictionary, such as your last name, click the 'Add to Dictionary' button in the Spelling dialog box (shown in Figure 2–58) when Excel flags the word as not being in the dictionary.
- Click the AutoCorrect button (shown in Figure 2–58) to add the misspelled word and the correct version of the word to the AutoCorrect list. For example, suppose that you misspell the word, do, as the word, dox. When the spelling checker displays the Spelling dialog box with the correct word, do, in the Suggestions list, click the AutoCorrect button. Then, anytime in the future that you type the word, dox, Excel will change it to the word, do.

BTW

Error Checking

Always take the time to check the formulas of a worksheet before submitting it to your supervisor. You can check formulas by clicking the Error Checking button (Formulas tab | Formula Auditing group). You also should test the formulas by employing data that tests the limits of formulas. Experienced spreadsheet specialists spend as much time testing a workbook as they do creating it, and they do so before placing the workbook into production.

BTW

Distributing a Workbook

Instead of printing and distributing a hard copy of a workbook, you can distribute the workbook electronically. Options include sending the workbook via email; posting it on cloud storage (such as OneDrive) and sharing the file with others; posting it on social media, a blog, or other website; and sharing a link associated with an online location of the workbook. You also can create and share a PDF or XPS image of the workbook, so that users can view the file in Acrobat Reader or XPS Viewer instead of in Excel.

Printing the Worksheet

Excel allows for a great deal of customization in how a worksheet appears when printed. For example, the margins on the page can be adjusted. A header or footer can be added to each printed page as well. A **header** is text and graphics that print at the top of each page. Similarly, a **footer** is text and graphics that print at the bottom of each page. Excel also has the capability to alter the worksheet in Page Layout view. Page Layout view allows you to create or modify a worksheet while viewing how it will look in printed format. The default view that you have worked in up until this point in the book is called Normal view.

To Change the Worksheet's Margins, Header, and Orientation in Page Layout View

1 ENTER FORMULAS | 2 ENTER FUNCTIONS | 3 VERIFY FORMULAS
4 FORMAT WORKSHEET | 5 CHECK SPELLING | **6 PRINT WORKSHEET**

The following steps change to Page Layout view, narrow the margins of the worksheet, change the header of the worksheet, and set the orientation of the worksheet to landscape. ***Why?*** *You may want the printed worksheet to fit on one page. You can do that by reducing the page margins and changing the page orientation to fit wider printouts across a sheet of paper. You can use the header to identify the content on each page.* **Margins** are those portions of a printed page outside the main body of the printed document and always are blank when printed. The current worksheet is too wide for a single page and requires landscape orientation to fit on one page in a readable manner.

1

- Click the Page Layout button on the status bar to view the worksheet in Page Layout view (Figure 2–59).

Q&A What are the features of Page Layout view?
Page Layout view shows the worksheet divided into pages. A gray background separates each page. The white areas surrounding each page indicate the print margins. The top of each page includes a Header area, and the bottom of each page includes a Footer area. Page Layout view also includes rulers at the top and left margin of the page that assists you in placing objects on the page, such as charts and pictures.

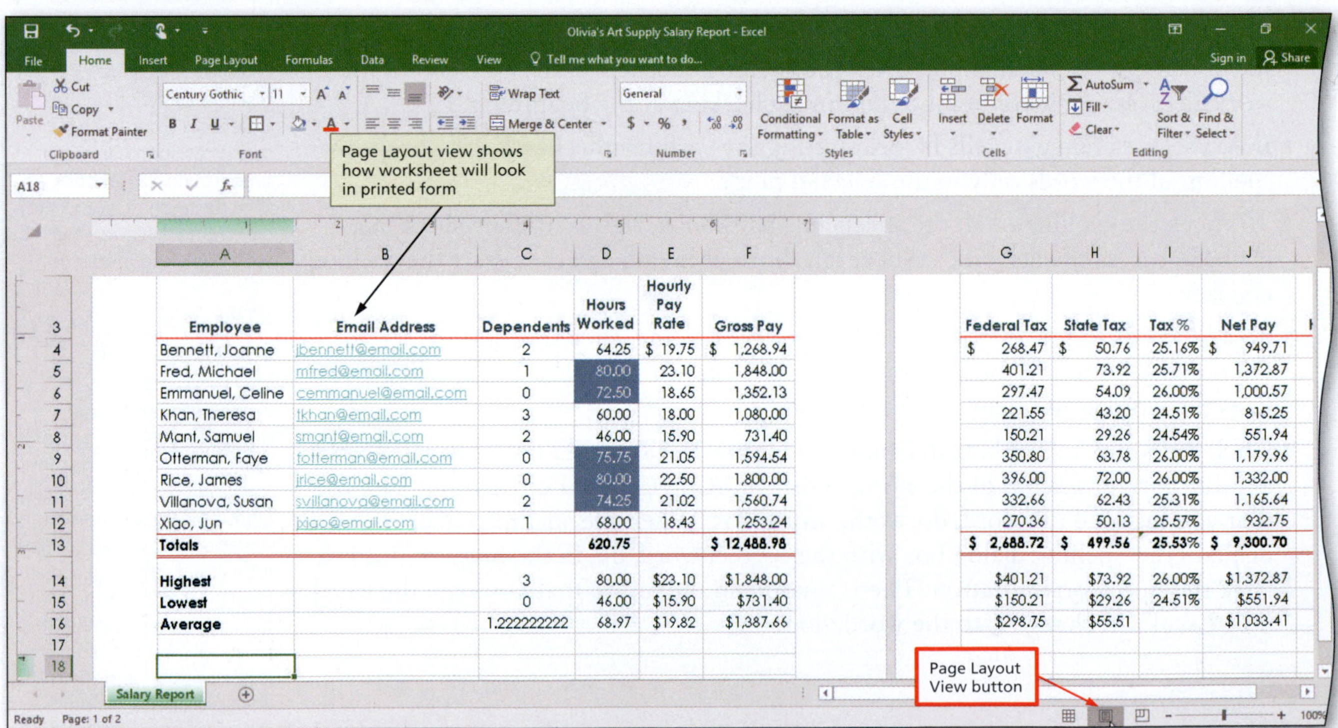

Figure 2–59

2

- Display the Page Layout tab.
- Click the Adjust Margins button (Page Layout tab | Page Setup group) to display the Margins gallery (Figure 2–60).

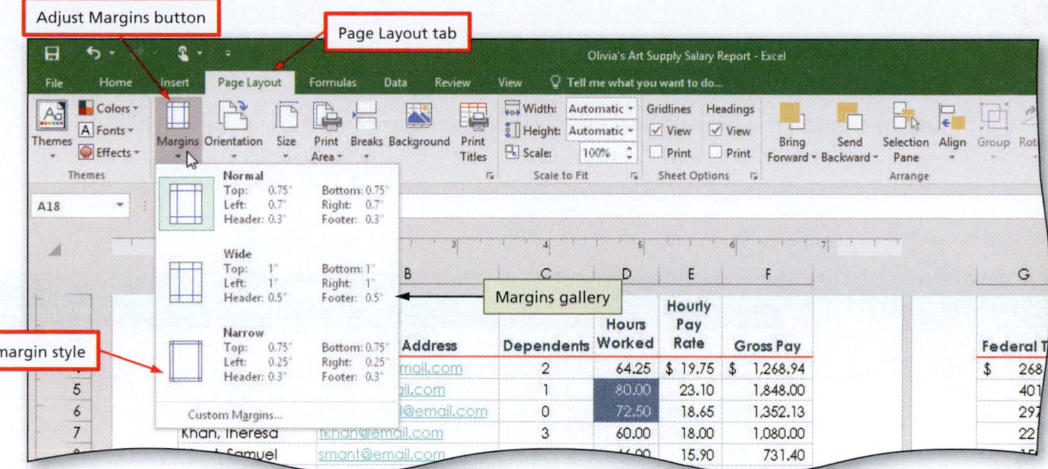

Figure 2–60

3

- Click Narrow in the Margins gallery to change the worksheet margins to the Narrow margin style.
- Click the center of the Header area above the worksheet title.
- Type `Jayne Smith` and then press the ENTER key. Type `Chief Financial Officer` to complete the worksheet header (Figure 2–61).
- If requested by your instructor, type your name instead of Jayne Smith.
- Select cell A6 to deselect the header.

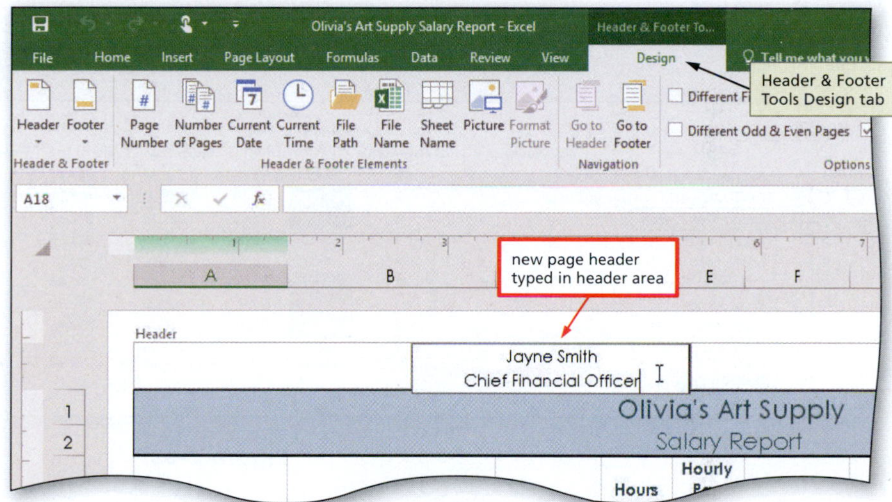

Figure 2–61

Q&A What else can I place in a header?

You can add additional text, page number information, date and time information, the file path of the workbook, the file name of the workbook, the sheet name of the workbook, and pictures to a header.

4

- Display the Page Layout tab.
- Click the 'Change Page Orientation' button (Page Layout tab | Page Setup group) to display the Change Page Orientation gallery (Figure 2–62).

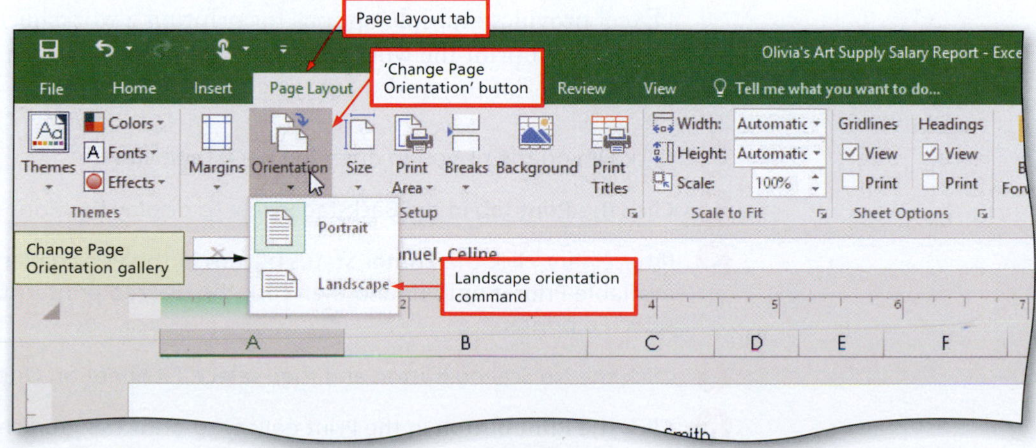

Figure 2–62

5

- Click Landscape in the Change Page Orientation gallery to change the worksheet's orientation to landscape (Figure 2–63).

Q&A Do I need to change the orientation every time I want to print the worksheet?
No. Once you change the orientation and save the workbook, Excel will save the orientation setting for that workbook until you change it. When you open a new workbook, Excel sets the orientation to portrait.

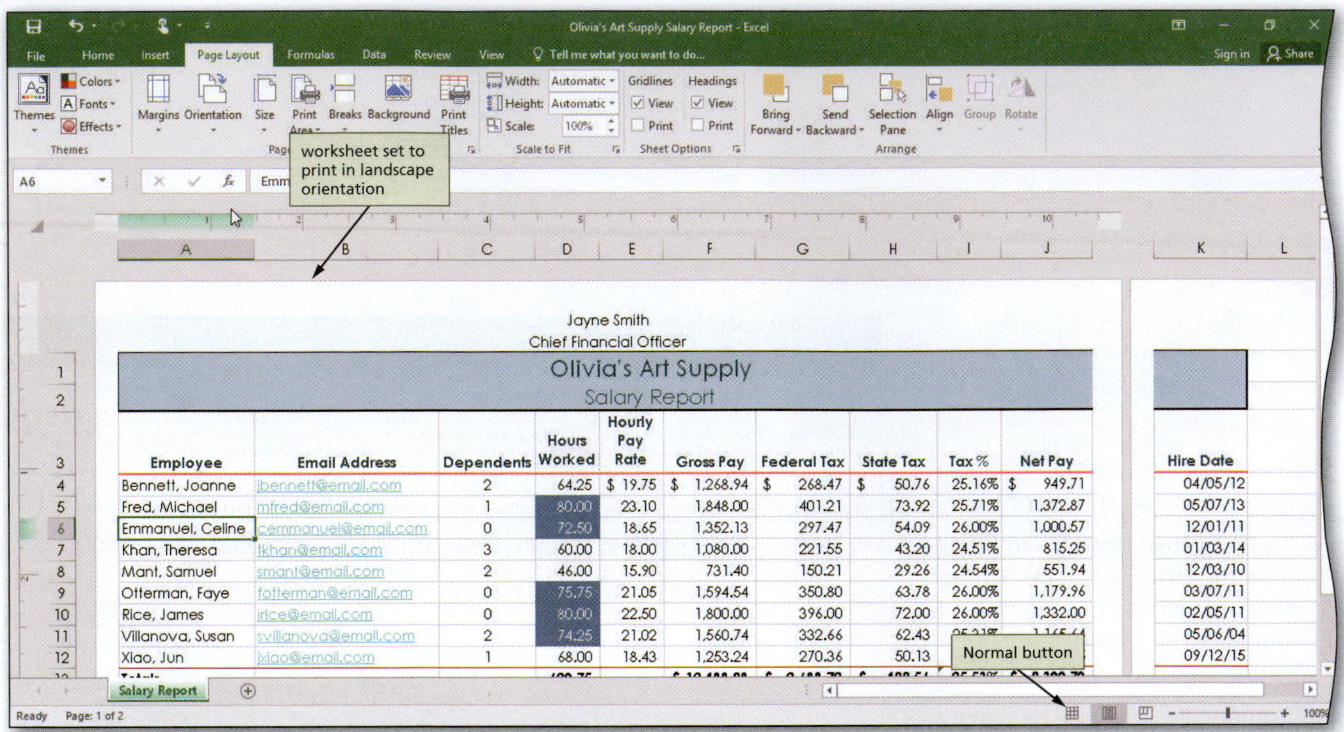

Figure 2–63

Other Ways

1. Click Page Setup Dialog Box Launcher (Page Layout tab | Page Setup group), click Page tab (Page Setup dialog box), click Portrait or Landscape, click OK button

To Print a Worksheet

Excel provides multiple options for printing a worksheet. In the following sections, you first print the worksheet and then print a section of the worksheet. The following steps print the worksheet.

1. Click File on the ribbon to open the Backstage view.
2. Click the Print tab in the Backstage view to display the Print gallery.
3. If necessary, click the Printer Status button in the Print gallery to display a list of available Printer options and then click the desired printer to change the currently selected printer.
4. Click the No Scaling button and then select 'Fit Sheet on One Page' to select it.
5. Click the Print button in the Print gallery to print the worksheet in landscape orientation on the currently selected printer.

6 When the printer stops, retrieve the hard copy (Figure 2–64).

Jayne Smith
Chief Financial Officer

Olivia's Art Supply
Salary Report

Employee	Email Address	Dependents	Hours Worked	Hourly Pay Rate	Gross Pay	Federal Tax	State Tax	Tax %	Net Pay	Hire Date
Bennett, Joanne	jbennett@email.com	2	64.25	$ 19.75	$ 1,268.94	$ 268.47	$ 50.76	25.16%	$ 949.71	04/05/12
Fred, Michael	mfred@email.com	1	80.00	23.10	1,848.00	401.21	73.92	25.71%	1,372.87	05/07/13
Emmanuel, Celine	cemmanuel@email.com	0	72.50	18.65	1,352.13	297.47	54.09	26.00%	1,000.57	12/01/11
Khan, Theresa	tkhan@email.com	3	60.00	18.00	1,080.00	221.55	43.20	24.51%	815.25	01/03/14
Mant, Samuel	smant@email.com	2	46.00	15.90	731.40	150.21	29.26	24.54%	551.94	12/03/10
Otterman, Faye	fotterman@email.com	0	75.75	21.05	1,594.54	350.80	63.78	26.00%	1,179.96	03/07/11
Rice, James	jrice@email.com	0	80.00	22.50	1,800.00	396.00	72.00	26.00%	1,332.00	02/05/11
Villanova, Susan	svillanova@email.com	2	74.25	21.02	1,560.74	332.66	62.43	25.31%	1,165.64	05/06/04
Xiao, Jun	jxiao@email.com	1	68.00	18.43	1,253.24	270.36	50.13	25.57%	932.75	09/12/15
Totals			**620.75**		**$ 12,488.98**	**$ 2,688.72**	**$ 499.56**	**25.53%**	**$ 9,300.70**	
Highest		3	80.00	$23.10	$1,848.00	$401.21	$73.92	26.00%	$1,372.87	
Lowest		0	46.00	$15.90	$731.40	$150.21	$29.26	24.51%	$551.94	
Average		1.222222222	68.97	$19.82	$1,387.66	$298.75	$55.51		$1,033.41	

Figure 2–64

To Print a Section of the Worksheet

1 ENTER FORMULAS | 2 ENTER FUNCTIONS | 3 VERIFY FORMULAS
4 FORMAT WORKSHEET | 5 CHECK SPELLING | **6 PRINT WORKSHEET**

You can print portions of the worksheet by selecting the range of cells to print and then clicking the Selection option button in the Print what area in the Print dialog box. ***Why?*** *To save paper, you only want to print the portion of the worksheet you need, instead of printing the entire worksheet.* The following steps print the range A3:F16.

- Select the range to print, cells A3:F16 in this case.
- Click File on the ribbon to open the Backstage view.
- Click the Print tab to display the Print gallery.
- Click 'Print Active Sheets' in the Settings area (Print tab | Print gallery) to display a list of options that determine what Excel should print (Figure 2–65).

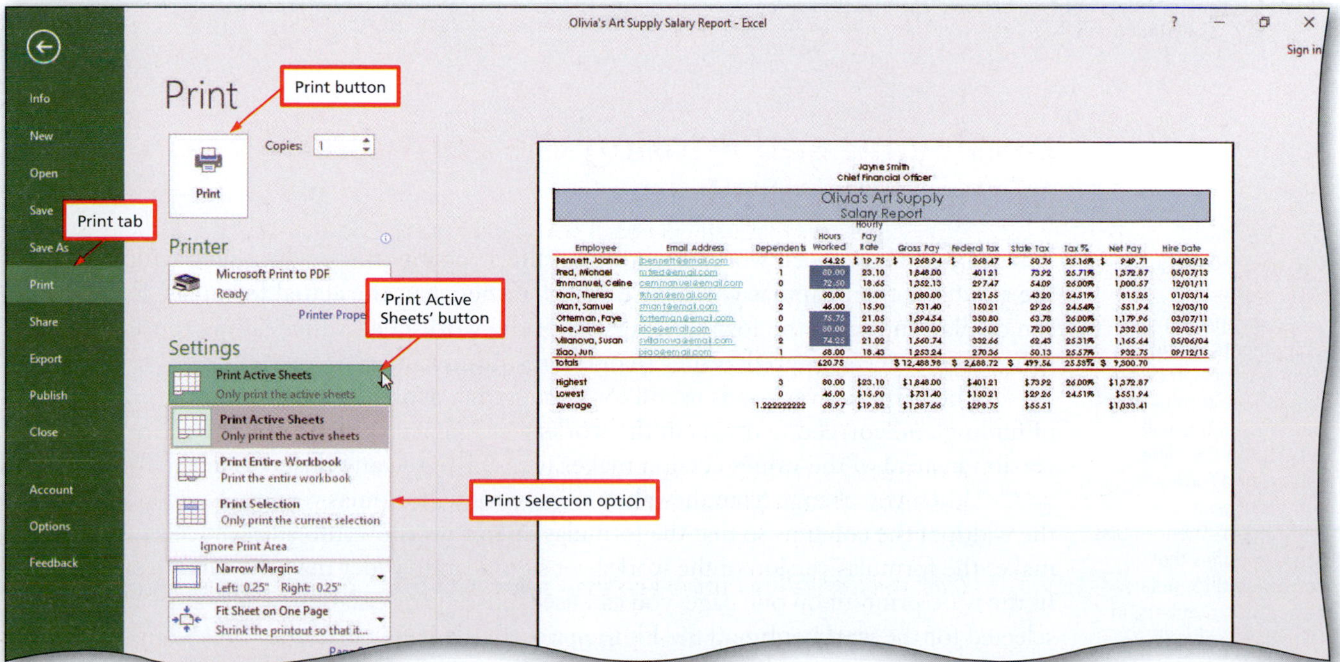

Figure 2–65

- Click Print Selection to instruct Excel to print only the selected range.
- Click the Print button in the Print gallery to print the selected range of the worksheet on the currently selected printer (Figure 2–66).
- Click the Normal button on the status bar to return to Normal view.
- Click anywhere in the worksheet, such as cell A18, to deselect the range A3:F16.

Q&A

What can I print?

Excel includes three options for selecting what to print (Figure 2–65). As shown in the previous steps, the Print Selection option instructs Excel to print the selected range. The 'Print Active Sheets' option instructs Excel to print the active worksheet (the worksheet currently on the screen) or selected worksheets. Finally, the 'Print Entire Workbook' option instructs Excel to print all of the worksheets in the workbook.

Jayne Smith
Chief Financial Officer

Employee	Email Address	Dependents	Hours Worked	Hourly Pay Rate	Gross Pay
Bennett, Joanne	jbennett@email.com	2	64.25	$ 19.75	$ 1,268.94
Fred, Michael	mfred@email.com	1	80.00	23.10	1,848.00
Emmanuel, Celine	cemmanuel@email.com	0	72.50	18.65	1,352.13
Khan, Theresa	tkhan@email.com	3	60.00	18.00	1,080.00
Mant, Samuel	smant@email.com	2	46.00	15.90	731.40
Otterman, Faye	fotterman@email.com	0	75.75	21.05	1,594.54
Rice, James	jrice@email.com	0	80.00	22.50	1,800.00
Villanova, Susan	svillanova@email.com	2	74.25	21.02	1,560.74
Xiao, Jun	jxiao@email.com	1	68.00	18.43	1,253.24
Totals			**620.75**		**$ 12,488.98**
Highest		3	80.00	$23.10	$1,848.00
Lowest		0	46.00	$15.90	$731.40
Average		1.222222222	68.97	$19.82	$1,387.66

Figure 2–66

Other Ways

1. Select range, click Print Area button (Page Layout tab | Page Setup group), click 'Set Print Area', click File tab to open Backstage view, click Print tab, click Print button

Displaying and Printing the Formulas Version of the Worksheet

BTW

Values versus Formulas

When completing class assignments, do not enter numbers in cells that require formulas. Most instructors will check both the values version and formulas version of your worksheets. The formulas version verifies that you entered formulas, rather than numbers, in formula-based cells.

Thus far, you have been working with the values version of the worksheet, which shows the results of the formulas you have entered, rather than the actual formulas. Excel also can display and print the formulas version of the worksheet, which shows the actual formulas you have entered, rather than the resulting values.

The formulas version is useful for debugging a worksheet. **Debugging** is the process of finding and correcting errors in the worksheet. Viewing and printing the formulas version instead of the values version makes it easier to see any mistakes in the formulas.

When you change from the values version to the formulas version, Excel increases the width of the columns so that the formulas do not overflow into adjacent cells, which makes the formulas version of the worksheet significantly wider than the values version. To fit the wide printout on one page, you can use landscape orientation, which already has been selected for the workbook, and the Fit to option in the Page tab in the Page Setup dialog box.

To Display the Formulas in the Worksheet and Fit the Printout on One Page

The following steps change the view of the worksheet from the values version to the formulas version of the worksheet and then print the formulas version on one page. ***Why?*** *Printing the formulas in the worksheet can help you verify that your formulas are correct and that the worksheet displays the correct calculations.*

1

- Press CTRL+ACCENT MARK (`) to display the worksheet with formulas.
- Click the right horizontal scroll arrow until column K appears (Figure 2–67).

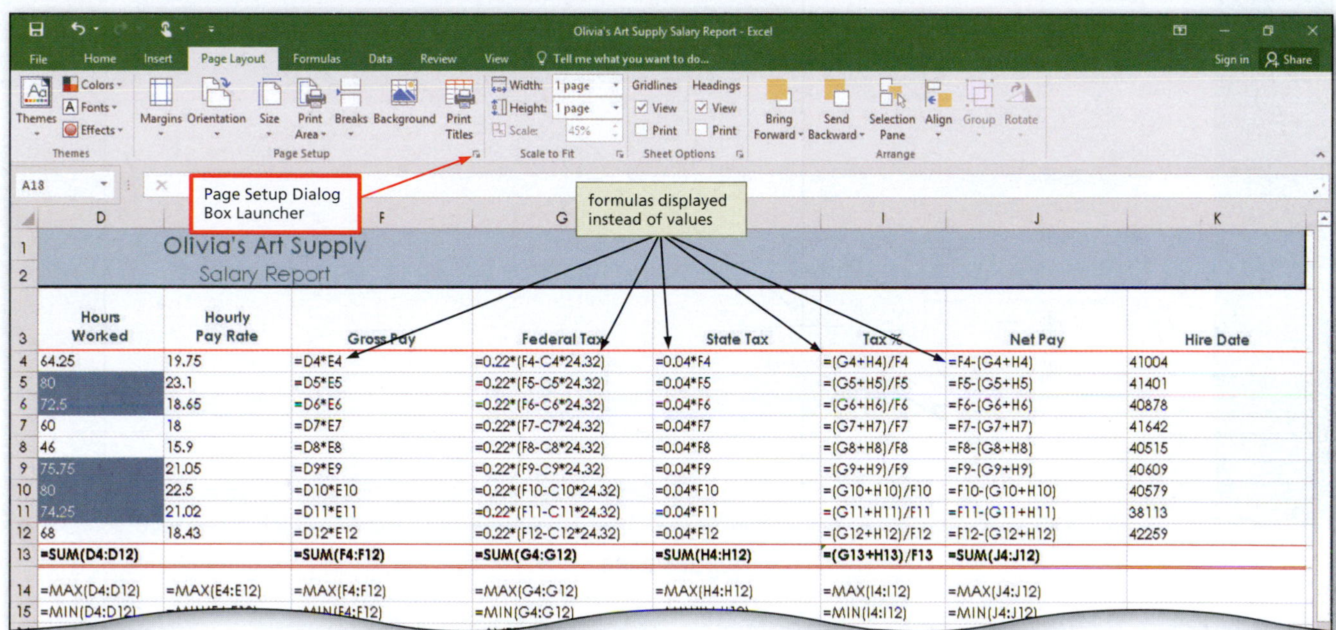

Figure 2–67

2

- Click the Page Setup Dialog Box Launcher (Page Layout tab | Page Setup group) to display the Page Setup dialog box (Figure 2–68).
- If necessary, click Landscape in the Orientation area in the Page tab to select it.
- If necessary, click the Fit to option button in the Scaling area to select it.

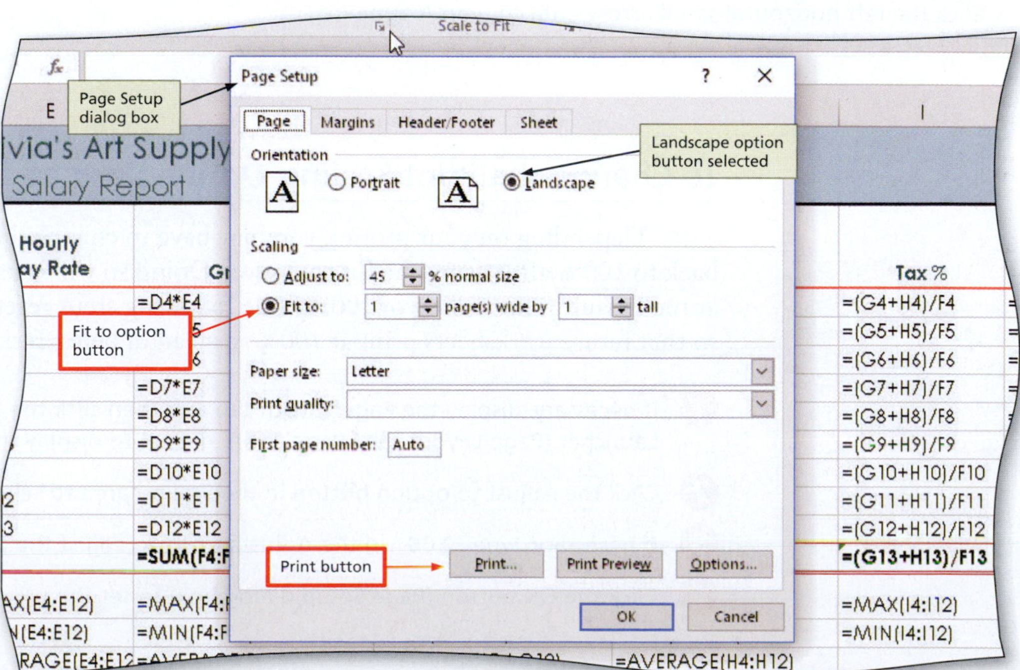

Figure 2–68

3

- Click the Print button (Page Setup dialog box) to open the Print tab in the Backstage view. In the Backstage view, select the Print Active Sheets option in the Settings area of the Print gallery (Figure 2–69).
- Click the Print button to print the worksheet.

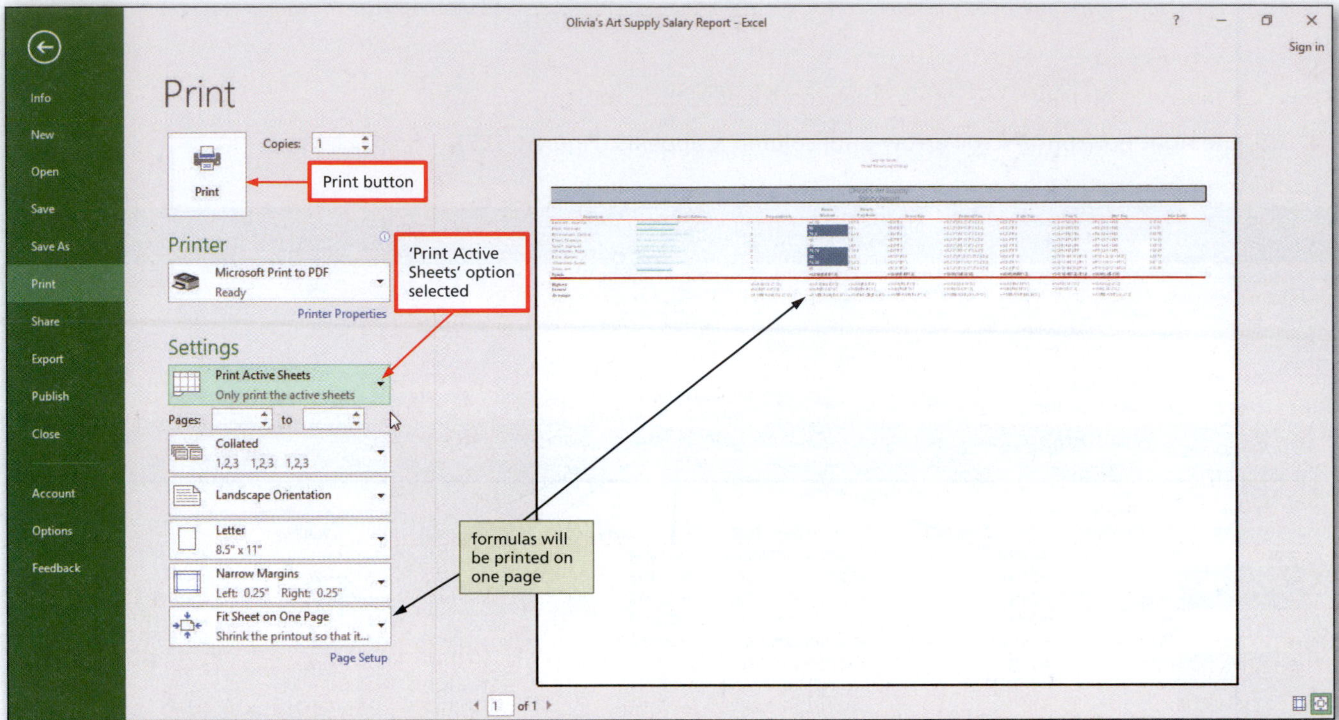

Figure 2–69

4

- After viewing and printing the formulas version, press CTRL+ACCENT MARK (`) to instruct Excel to display the values version.
- Click the left horizontal scroll arrow until column A appears.

To Change the Print Scaling Option Back to 100%

Depending on your printer, you may have to change the Print Scaling option back to 100% after using the Fit to option. Doing so will cause the worksheet to print at the default print scaling of 100%. The following steps reset the Print Scaling option so that future worksheets print at 100%, instead of being resized to print on one page.

1. If necessary, display the Page Layout tab and then click the Page Setup Dialog Box Launcher (Page Layout tab | Page Setup group) to display the Page Setup dialog box.
2. Click the Adjust to option button in the Scaling area to select the Adjust to setting.
3. If necessary, type `100` in the Adjust to box to adjust the print scaling to 100%.
4. Click the OK button (Page Setup dialog box) to set the print scaling to normal.

5. Display the Home tab.
6. Save the workbook again on the same storage location with the same file name.
7. If desired, sign out of your Microsoft account.
8. Exit Excel.

Q&A What is the purpose of the Adjust to box in the Page Setup dialog box?
The Adjust to box allows you to specify the percentage of reduction or enlargement in the printout of a worksheet. The default percentage is 100%. When you click the Fit to option button, this percentage changes to the percentage required to fit the printout on one page.

Summary

In this module you have learned how to enter formulas, calculate an average, find the highest and lowest numbers in a range, verify formulas using Range Finder, add borders, align text, format numbers, change column widths and row heights, and add conditional formatting to a range of numbers. In addition, you learned how to use the spelling checker to identify misspelled words in a worksheet, print a section of a worksheet, and display and print the formulas version of the worksheet using the Fit to option.

CONSIDER THIS: PLAN AHEAD

What decisions will you need to make when creating workbooks in the future?

1. Determine the workbook structure.
   a) Determine the formulas and functions you will need for your workbook.
   b) Sketch a layout of your data and functions.
2. Create the worksheet.
   a) Enter the titles, subtitles, and headings.
   b) Enter the data, desired functions, and formulas.
3. Format the worksheet.
   a) Determine the theme for the worksheet.
   b) Format the titles, subtitles, and headings using styles.
   c) Format the totals, minimums, maximums, and averages.
   d) Format the numbers and text.
   e) Resize columns and rows.

Apply Your Knowledge

Reinforce the skills and apply the concepts you learned in this module.

Cost Analysis Worksheet

Note: To complete this assignment, you will be required to use the Data Files. Please contact your instructor for information about accessing the required files.

Instructions: Run Excel. Open the workbook Apply 2-1 Proximity Bus. You will enter and copy formulas and functions and apply formatting to the worksheet in order to analyze the costs associated with a bus company's fleet of vehicles, as shown in Figure 2–70.

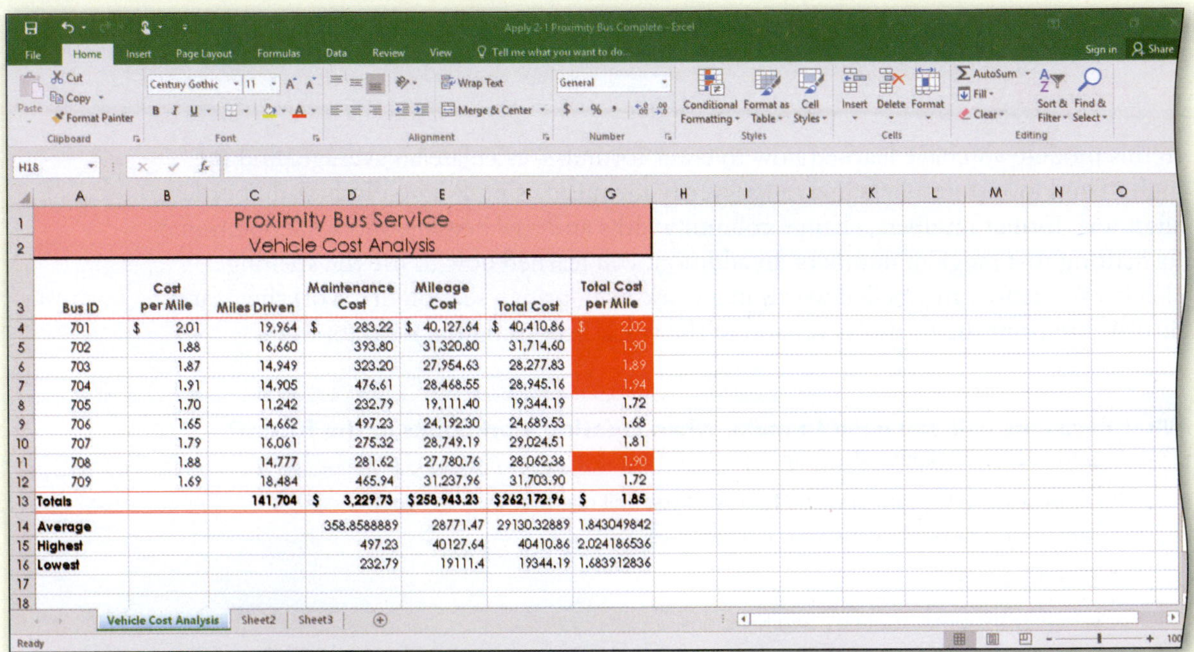

Figure 2–70

Perform the following tasks:

1. Use the following formulas in cells E4, F4, and G4:
   Mileage Cost (cell E4) = Cost per Mile * Miles Driven or = B4 * C4
   Total Cost (cell F4) = Maintenance Cost + Mileage Cost or = D4 + E4
   Total Cost per Mile (cell G4) = Total Cost / Miles Driven or = F4 / C4
   Use the fill handle to copy the three formulas in the range E4:G4 to the range E5:G12.
2. Determine totals for the miles driven, maintenance cost, mileage cost, and total cost in row 13. Copy the formula in cell G12 to G13 to assign the formula in cell G12 to G13 in the total line. If necessary, reapply the Total cell style to cell G13.
3. In the range D14:D16, determine the average value, highest value, and lowest value, respectively, for the values in the range D4:D12. Use the fill handle to copy the three functions to the range E14:G16.
4. Format the worksheet as follows:
   a. Change the workbook theme to Vapor Trail by using the Themes button (Page Layout tab | Themes group)
   b. Cell A1 — change to Title cell style
   c. Cell A2 — change to a font size of 16
   d. Cells A1:A2 — Red, Accent 1, Lighter 60% fill color and a thick outside borders
   e. Cells B4, D4:G4, and D13:G13 — accounting number format with two decimal places and fixed dollar signs by using the 'Accounting Number Format' button (Home tab | Number group)

f. Cells B5:B12, and D5:G12 — comma style format with two decimal places by using the Comma Style button (Home tab | Number group)
g. Cells C4:C13 — comma style format with no decimal places.
h. Cells G4:G12 — apply conditional formatting so that cells with a value greater than 1.85 appear with a red background color and white font

5. If necessary increase the size of any columns that do not properly display data.
6. Switch to Page Layout view. Enter your name, course, laboratory assignment number, and any other information, as specified by your instructor, in the Header area.
7. Preview and print the worksheet in landscape orientation. Save the workbook using the file name, Apply 2-1 Proximity Bus Complete.
8. Use Range Finder to verify the formula in cell G13.
9. Print the range A3:D16. Press CTRL+ACCENT MARK (`) to change the display from the values version of the worksheet to the formulas version. Print the formulas version in landscape orientation on one page by using the Fit to option in the Page tab in the Page Setup dialog box. Press CTRL+ACCENT MARK (`) to change the display of the worksheet back to the values version. Close the workbook without saving it.
10. Besides adding a header to your document, can you think of anything else that could be added when printing the worksheet?
11. Submit the workbook as specified by your instructor.

Extend Your Knowledge

Extend the skills you learned in this module and experiment with new skills. You may need to use Help to complete the assignment.

Creating a Customer Tracking Worksheet for Jonee's Animal Supply

Note: To complete this assignment, you will be required to use the Data Files. Please contact your instructor for information about accessing the required files.

Instructions: Run Excel. Open the workbook Extend 2–1 Jonee's Animal Supply. You are to apply Flash Fill and four types of conditional formatting to cells in a worksheet (Figure 2–71).

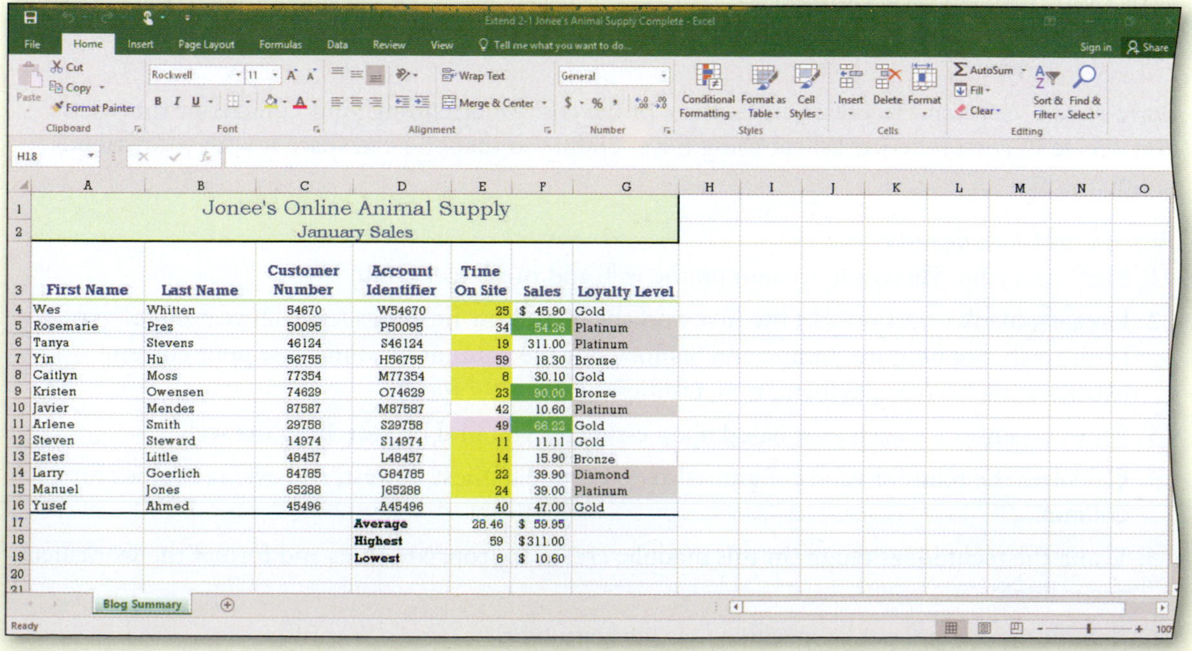

Jonee's Online Animal Supply
January Sales

First Name	Last Name	Customer Number	Account Identifier	Time On Site	Sales	Loyalty Level
Wes	Whitten	54670	W54670	25	$ 45.90	Gold
Rosemarie	Prez	50095	P50095	34	54.26	Platinum
Tanya	Stevens	46124	S46124	19	311.00	Platinum
Yin	Hu	56755	H56755	59	18.30	Bronze
Caitlyn	Moss	77354	M77354	8	30.10	Gold
Kristen	Owensen	74629	O74629	23	90.00	Bronze
Javier	Mendez	87587	M87587	42	10.60	Platinum
Arlene	Smith	29758	S29758	49	66.22	Gold
Steven	Steward	14974	S14974	11	11.11	Gold
Estes	Little	48457	L48457	14	15.90	Bronze
Larry	Goerlich	84785	G84785	22	39.90	Diamond
Manuel	Jones	65288	J65288	24	39.00	Platinum
Yusef	Ahmed	45496	A45496	40	47.00	Gold
			Average	28.46	$ 59.95	
			Highest	59	$311.00	
			Lowest	8	$ 10.60	

Figure 2–71

Continued >

Extend Your Knowledge *continued*

Perform the following tasks:

1. Add the account identifiers to the cells in the range D4:D16. The account identifier is determined by taking the first initial of the customer's last name followed by the entire customer number. For example, the account identifier for Wes Whitten is W54670. Continue entering two or three account identifiers, then use Flash Fill to complete the remaining cells. If necessary, add the thick bottom border back to cell D16.
2. Select the range E4:E16. Click the Conditional Formatting button (Home tab | Styles group) and then click New Rule on the Conditional Formatting menu. Select 'Format only top or bottom ranked values' in the Select a Rule Type area (New Formatting Rule dialog box).
3. If requested by your instructor, enter any value between 10 and 30 in the text box, (otherwise enter 20) in the Edit the Rule Description (New Formatting Rule dialog box) area, and then click the '% of the selected range' check box to select it.
4. Click the Format button, and choose a light purple background in the Fill sheet to assign this conditional format. Click the OK button in each dialog box and view the worksheet.
5. With range E4:E16 selected, apply a conditional format to the range that uses a yellow background color to highlight cells with scores that are below average. *Hint:* Explore some of the preset conditional rules to assist with formatting this range of cells.
6. With range F4:F16 selected, apply a conditional format to the range that uses a white font and green background to highlight cells that contain a value between 50 and 150.
7. With range G4:G16 selected, apply a conditional format to the range that uses a light gray background color to highlight cells that contain Platinum or Diamond. (*Hint:* You need to apply two separate formats, one for Platinum and one for Diamond.)
8. When might you want to look for values above the average in a worksheet?
9. Save the workbook using the file name, Extend 2–1 Jonee's Animal Supply Complete. Submit the revised workbook as specified by your instructor.

Expand Your World

Create a solution that uses cloud or web technologies by learning and investigating on your own from general guidance.

Four-Year College Cost Calculator

Instructions: You want to create an estimate of the cost for attending your college for four years. You decide to create the worksheet using Excel Online so that you can share it with your friends online.

Perform the following tasks:

1. Sign in to your Microsoft account on the web and run Excel Online.
2. Create a blank workbook. In the first worksheet, use row headings for each year of college (Freshman, Sophomore, Junior, and Senior). For the column headings, use your current expenses (such as car payment, rent, utilities, tuition, and food).
3. Enter expenses for each year based upon estimates you find by searching the web.
4. Calculate the total for each column. Also determine highest, lowest, and average values for each column.
5. Using the techniques taught in this module, create appropriate titles and format the worksheet accordingly.
6. Submit the assignment as specified by your instructor.

In the Labs

Design, create, modify, and/or use a workbook following the guidelines, concepts, and skills presented in this module. Labs 1 and 2, which increase in difficulty, require you to create solutions based on what you learned in the module; Lab 3 requires you to apply your creative thinking and problem-solving skills to design and implement a solution.

Lab 1: Insurance Premium Worksheet

Problem: You are a part-time assistant in the accounting department at Aylin Insurance, an Orlando-based insurance company. You have been asked to use Excel to generate a report that summarizes the existing balances on annual premiums, similar to the one shown in Figure 2–72. Include the three columns of customer data in Table 2-6 in the report, plus two additional columns to compute a monthly fee and a current balance for each customer. Assume no negative unpaid monthly balances.

Perform the following tasks:

1. Enter and format the worksheet title `Aylin Insurance` and worksheet subtitle `Premium Analysis` in cells A1 and A2. Change the theme of the worksheet to the Berlin theme. Apply the Title cell style to cells A1 and A2. Change the font size in cell A1 to 26 points, and change the font size in cell A2 to 18 points. Merge and center the worksheet title and subtitle across columns A through E. Draw a thick outside border around the range A1:A2.
2. Change the width of column A to 20.00 points. Change the widths of columns B through E to 14.00 points. Change the heights of row 3 to 36.00 points and row 14 to 25.50 points.

Table 2–6 Aylin Insurance Premium Data

Customer	Previous Balance	Payments
Albasco, Robin	1600.72	72.15
Deon, Jade	1518.62	382.3
Goodman, Brad	679.29	80.69
Hill, Raine	1060.42	107.6
Klonde, Albert	1178.83	125.63
Lang, Rose	1280.2	79.85
Moore, Jeffrey	1253.88	389.79
Piper, Taylor	477.11	278.52
Sothens, Mary	821.31	153.14

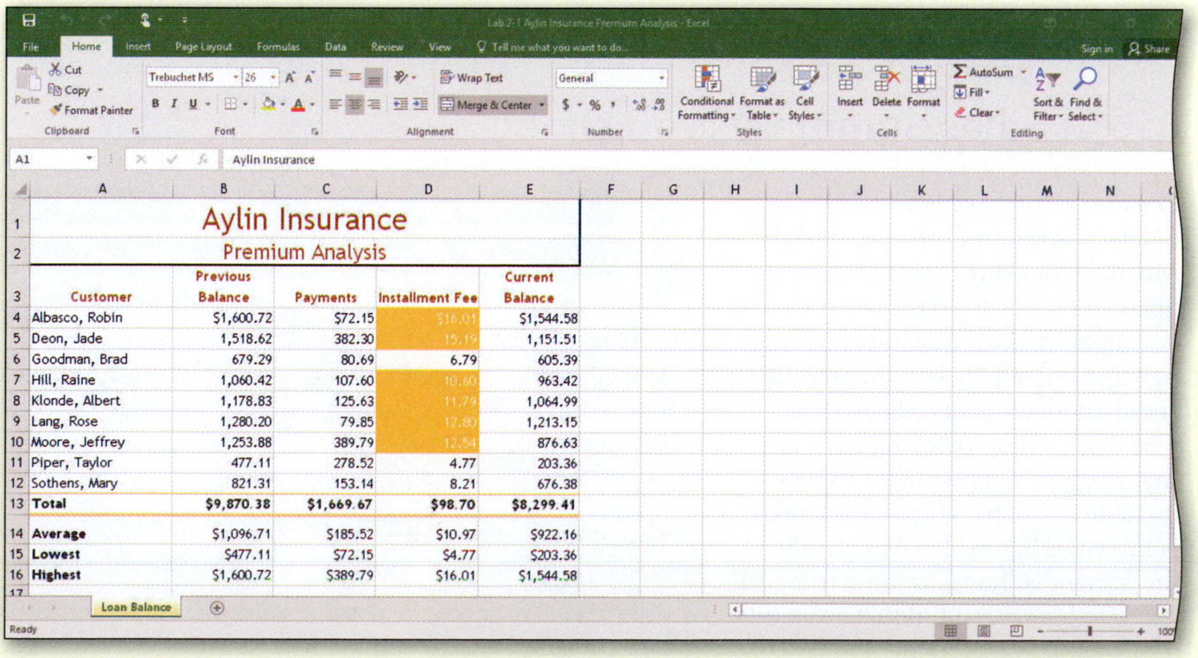

Figure 2–72

Continued >

In the Labs *continued*

3. Enter the column titles in row 3 and row titles in the range A13:A16, as shown in Figure 2–72. Center the column titles in the range A3:E3. Apply the Heading 4 cell style to the range A3:E3. Apply the Total cell style to the range A13:E13. Bold the titles in the range A13:A16. Change the font size in the range A3:E16 to 12 points.
4. Enter the data in Table 2-6 in the range A4:C12.
5. Use the following formulas to determine the installment fee in column D and the current balance in column E for the first customer. Copy the two formulas down through the remaining customers.
   a. Installment Fee (cell D4) = 1% * Previous Balance
   b. Current Balance (E4) = Previous Balance – Payments + Installment Fee
6. Determine the totals in row 13.
7. Determine the average, minimum, and maximum values in cells B14:B16 for the range B4:B12, and then copy the range B14:B16 to C14:E16.
8. Format the numbers as follows: (a) assign the currency style with a floating dollar sign to the cells containing numeric data in the ranges B4:E4 and B13:E16, and (b) assign a number style with two decimal places and a thousand's separator (currency with no dollar sign) to the range B5:E12.
9. Use conditional formatting to change the formatting to white font on an orange background in any cell in the range D4:D12 that contains a value greater than 10.
10. Change the worksheet name from Sheet1 to Loan Balance and the sheet tab color to the Orange standard color.
11. Change the worksheet header with your name, course number, and other information as specified by your instructor.
12. Use the spelling checker to check the spelling in the worksheet. Preview and then print the worksheet in landscape orientation. Save the workbook using the file name, Lab 2-1 Aylin Insurance Premium Analysis.
13. When you created the formula for the installment fee, you used 1%. What would you have to do if the rate changed today to 2% to update the formulas?

Lab 2: Sales Summary Worksheet

Problem: You have been asked to build a worksheet for International Moving Company that analyzes the financing needs for the company's first year in business. The company plans to begin operations in January with an initial investment of $750,000.00. The expected revenue and costs for the company's first year are shown in Table 2–7. The desired worksheet is shown in Figure 2–73. The initial investment is shown as the starting balance for January (cell B4). The amount of financing required by the company is shown as the lowest ending balance (cell F18).

Table 2–7 International Moving Company Financing Needs Data

Month	Incomes	Expenses
January	1209081	1262911
February	1163811	1381881
March	1300660	1250143
April	1229207	1209498
May	1248369	1355232
June	1196118	1260888
July	1162970	1242599
August	1195824	1368955
September	1305669	1235604
October	1224741	1383254
November	1159644	1411768
December	1210000	1540000

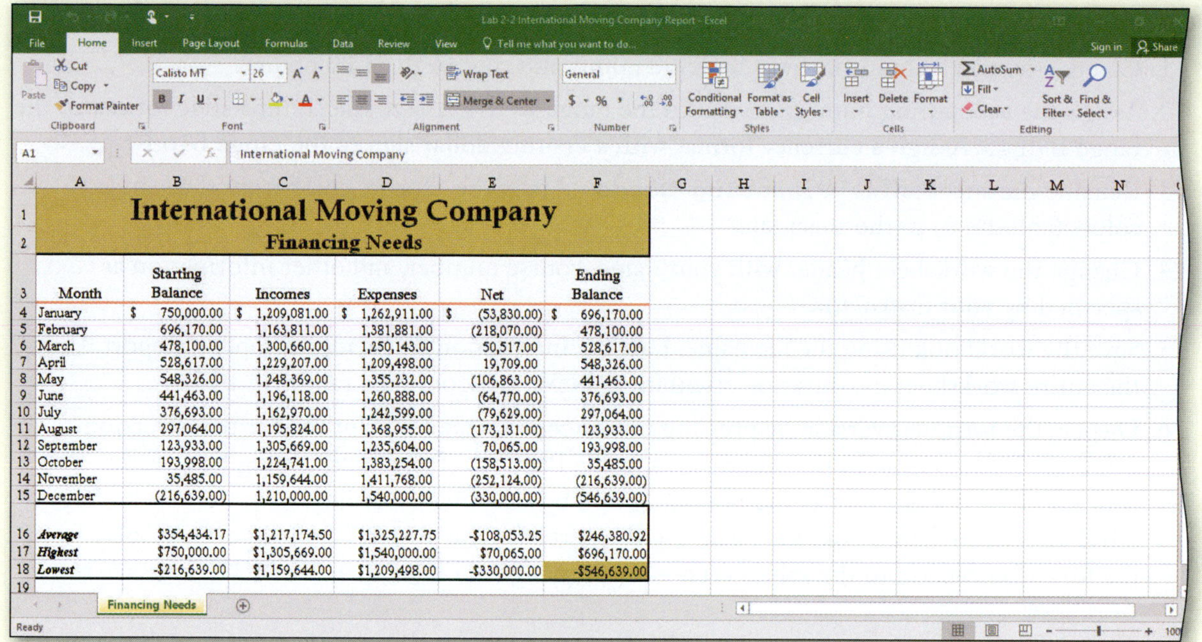

	A	B	C	D	E	F
1	International Moving Company					
2	Financing Needs					
3	Month	Starting Balance	Incomes	Expenses	Net	Ending Balance
4	January	$ 750,000.00	$ 1,209,081.00	$ 1,262,911.00	$ (53,830.00)	$ 696,170.00
5	February	696,170.00	1,163,811.00	1,381,881.00	(218,070.00)	478,100.00
6	March	478,100.00	1,300,660.00	1,250,143.00	50,517.00	528,617.00
7	April	528,617.00	1,229,207.00	1,209,498.00	19,709.00	548,326.00
8	May	548,326.00	1,248,369.00	1,355,232.00	(106,863.00)	441,463.00
9	June	441,463.00	1,196,118.00	1,260,888.00	(64,770.00)	376,693.00
10	July	376,693.00	1,162,970.00	1,242,599.00	(79,629.00)	297,064.00
11	August	297,064.00	1,195,824.00	1,368,955.00	(173,131.00)	123,933.00
12	September	123,933.00	1,305,669.00	1,235,604.00	70,065.00	193,998.00
13	October	193,998.00	1,224,741.00	1,383,254.00	(158,513.00)	35,485.00
14	November	35,485.00	1,159,644.00	1,411,768.00	(252,124.00)	(216,639.00)
15	December	(216,639.00)	1,210,000.00	1,540,000.00	(330,000.00)	(546,639.00)
16	*Average*	$354,434.17	$1,217,174.50	$1,325,227.75	-$108,053.25	$246,380.92
17	*Highest*	$750,000.00	$1,305,669.00	$1,540,000.00	$70,065.00	$696,170.00
18	*Lowest*	-$216,639.00	$1,159,644.00	$1,209,498.00	-$330,000.00	-$546,639.00

Figure 2–73

Perform the following tasks:

1. Apply the Slate theme to a new workbook.
2. Increase the width of column A to 12.00 and the width of columns B through F to 14.50.
3. Enter the worksheet title `International Moving Company` in cell A1 and the worksheet subtitle `Financing Needs` in cell A2. Enter the column titles in row 3, as shown in Figure 2–74. In row 3, use ALT+ENTER to start a new line in a cell.
4. Enter the financing needs data described in Table 2-7 in columns A, C, and D in rows 4 through 15. Enter the initial starting balance (cell B4) of 750000.00. Enter the row titles in the range A16:A18, as shown in Figure 2–73.
5. For the months of February through December, the starting balance is equal to the previous month's ending balance. Obtain the starting balance for February by setting the starting balance of February to the ending balance of January. Use a cell reference rather than typing in the data. Copy the formula for February to the remaining months.
6. Obtain the net amounts in column E by subtracting the expenses in column D from the incomes in column C. Enter the formula in cell E4 and copy it to the range E5:E15. Obtain the ending balance amounts in column F by adding the starting balance in column B to the net in column E. Enter the formula in cell F4 and copy it to the range F5:F15.
7. In the range B16:B18, use the AVERAGE, MAX, and MIN functions to determine the average value, highest value, and lowest value in the range B4:B15. Copy the range B16:B18 to the range C16:F18.
8. One at a time, merge and center the worksheet title and subtitle across columns A through F. Select cells A1 and A2 and change the background color to Tan, Accent 2 from the theme colors (column 6, row 1). Apply the Title cell style to cells A1 and A2. Change the worksheet title in cell A1 to 26-point. Bold both the title and subtitle. Draw a thick outside border around the range A1:A2.
9. Center the titles in row 3, columns A through F. Apply the Heading 2 cell style to the range A3:F3. Italicize and bold the row titles in the range A16:A18.
10. Draw a thick outside border around the range A16:F18. Change the background color for cell F18 to the same colors applied to the worksheet title in Step 8.

Continued >

In the Labs *continued*

11. Change the row heights of row 3 to 42.00 points and row 16 to 33.00 points.
12. Assign the accounting number format to the range B4:F4. Assign the comma style format to the range B5:F15. Assign a currency format with a floating dollar sign to the range B16:F18.
13. Rename the sheet tab as `Financing Needs`. Apply the Orange color from the standard colors (column 3) to the sheet tab.
14. Change the worksheet header with your name, course number, and other information as specified by your instructor.
15. Save the workbook using the file name, Lab 2-2 International Moving Company Report. Print the entire worksheet in landscape orientation. Next, print only the range A3:B15.
16. Display the formulas version by pressing CTRL+ACCENT MARK (`). Print the formulas version using the Fit to option in the Scaling area in the Page tab (Page Setup dialog box). After printing the worksheet, reset the Scaling option by selecting the Adjust to option in the Page tab (Page Setup dialog box) and changing the percent value to 100%. Change the display from the formulas version to the values version by pressing CTRL+ACCENT MARK (`). Do not save the workbook.
17. Submit the revised workbook as requested by your instructor.
18. In reviewing the worksheet you created, how do you think the company could obtain a positive result without increasing income or decreasing expenses?

Lab 3: Consider This: Your Turn

Apply your creative thinking and problem-solving skills to design and implement a solution.

Internet Service Summary

Instructions Part 1: You and your friends have decided to subscribe to a new Internet service provider. You would like to maximize services while keeping costs low. Research and find three Internet service providers in your area. If you cannot find three service providers in your area, you can research three service providers in another area of your choosing. For each company, find the best service package as well as the basic service package. Using the cost figures you find, calculate the cost per month for each service for a year. Include totals, minimum, maximum, and average values. Use the concepts and techniques presented in this module to create and format the worksheet.

Instructions Part 2: Which companies did you choose for your report? Which services offered the best deals that you would be willing to use?

3 Working with Large Worksheets, Charting, and What-If Analysis

Objectives

You will have mastered the material in this module when you can:

- Rotate text in a cell
- Create a series of month names
- Copy, paste, insert, and delete cells
- Format numbers using format symbols
- Enter and format the system date
- Use absolute and mixed cell references in a formula
- Use the IF function to perform a logical test
- Create and format sparkline charts
- Change sparkline chart types and styles
- Use the Format Painter button to format cells
- Create a clustered column chart on a separate chart sheet
- Use chart filters to display a subset of data in a chart
- Change the chart type and style
- Reorder sheet tabs
- Change the worksheet view
- Freeze and unfreeze rows and columns
- Answer what-if questions
- Goal seek to answer what-if questions
- Use the Smart Lookup Insight
- Understand accessibility features

Introduction

This module introduces you to techniques that will enhance your ability to create worksheets and draw charts. This module also covers other methods for entering values in cells, such as allowing Excel to automatically enter and format values based on a perceived pattern in the existing values. In addition, you will learn how to use absolute cell references and how to use the IF function to assign a value to a cell based on a logical test.

When you set up a worksheet, you should use cell references in formulas whenever possible, rather than constant values. The use of a cell reference allows you to change a value in multiple formulas by changing the value in a single cell. The cell references in a formula are called assumptions. **Assumptions** are values in cells that you can change to determine new values for formulas. This module emphasizes the use of assumptions and shows how to use assumptions to answer what-if questions, such as what happens to the six-month operating income if you decrease the Equipment

For an introduction to Windows and instructions about how to perform basic Windows tasks, read the Office and Windows module at the beginning of this book, where you can learn how to resize windows, change screen resolution, create folders, move and rename files, use Windows Help, and much more.

For an introduction to Office and instructions about how to perform basic tasks in Office apps, read the Office and Windows module at the beginning of this book, where you can learn how to run an application, use the ribbon, save a file, open a file, print a file, exit an application, use Help, and much more.

BTW

Excel Screen Resolution

If you are using a computer or mobile device to step through the project in this module and you want your screens to match the figures in this book, you should change your screen's resolution to 1366 x 768. For information about how to change a computer's resolution, refer to the Office and Windows module at the beginning of this book.

Repair and Maintenance expenses assumption by 1%. Being able to analyze the effect of changing values in a worksheet is an important skill in making business decisions.

Worksheets are normally much larger than those you created in the previous modules, often extending beyond the size of the Excel window. When you cannot view the entire worksheet on the screen at once, working with a large worksheet can be frustrating. This module introduces several Excel commands that allow you to control what is displayed on the screen so that you can focus on critical parts of a large worksheet. One command allows you to freeze rows and columns so that they remain visible, even when you scroll. Another command splits the worksheet into separate panes so that you can view different parts of a worksheet on the screen at once. Another changes the magnification to allow you to see more content, albeit at a smaller size. This is useful for reviewing the general layout of content on the worksheet.

From your work in Module 1, you know how easily you can create charts in Excel. This module covers additional charting techniques that allow you to convey meaning visually, such as by using sparkline charts or clustered column charts. This module also introduces the Accessibility checker.

Project — Financial Projection Worksheet with What-If Analysis and Chart

The project in this module uses Excel to create the worksheet and clustered column chart shown in Figures 3-1a and 3-1b. Kaitlyn's Ice Cream Shoppe operates kiosks at colleges and universities and serves both hard and soft serve ice cream. Each December and June, the chief executive officer projects monthly sales revenues, costs of goods sold, gross margin, expenses, and operating income for the upcoming six-month period, based on figures from the previous six months. The CEO requires an easy-to-read worksheet that shows financial projections for the upcoming six months to use for procuring partial financing and for determining staffing needs. The worksheet should allow for quick analysis, if projections for certain numbers change, such as the percentage of expenses

Kaitlyn's Ice Cream Shoppe 9/29/2017

Six-Month Financial Projection

	January	February	March	April	May	June	Total
Revenue	$55,000.00	$62,500.00	$67,000.00	$90,250.00	$77,500.00	$74,750.00	$427,000.00
Cost of Goods Sold	11,687.50	13,281.25	14,237.50	19,178.13	16,468.75	15,884.38	90,737.50
Gross Margin	$43,312.50	$49,218.75	$52,762.50	$71,071.88	$61,031.25	$58,865.63	$336,262.50
Expenses							
Bonus	$0.00	$0.00	$5,000.00	$5,000.00	$5,000.00	$5,000.00	$20,000.00
Commission	12,375.00	14,062.50	15,075.00	20,306.25	17,437.50	16,818.75	96,075.00
Site Rental	5,500.00	6,250.00	6,700.00	9,025.00	7,750.00	7,475.00	42,700.00
Marketing	2,750.00	3,125.00	3,350.00	4,512.50	3,875.00	3,737.50	21,350.00
Equipment Repair and Maintenance	2,200.00	2,500.00	2,680.00	3,610.00	3,100.00	2,990.00	17,080.00
Total Expenses	$22,825.00	$25,937.50	$32,805.00	$42,453.75	$37,162.50	$36,021.25	$197,205.00
Operating Income	$20,487.50	$23,281.25	$19,957.50	$28,618.13	$23,868.75	$22,844.38	$139,057.50

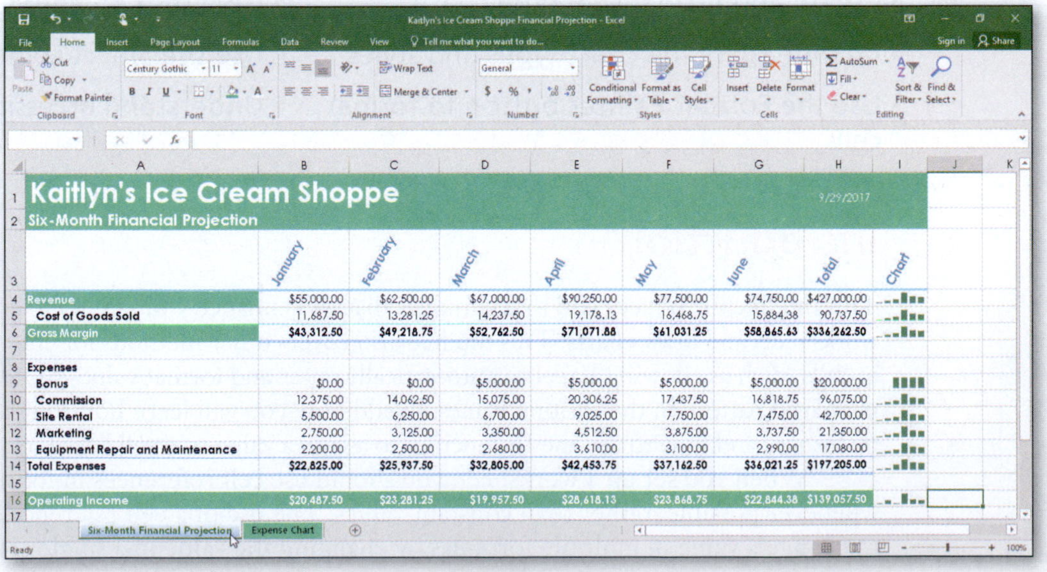

(a) Worksheet

Figure 3–1

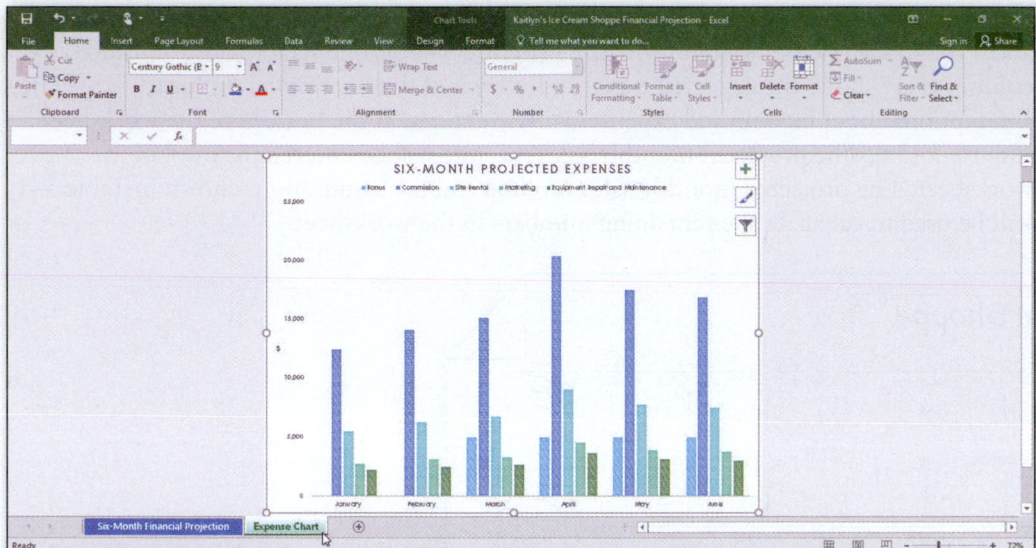

(b) Clustered Column Chart

Figure 3–1 (Continued)

allocated to commission or the cost of the kiosk rentals. In addition, you need to create a column chart that shows the breakdown of expenses for each month in the period.

The requirements document for the Kaitlyn's Ice Cream Shoppe Six-Month Financial Projection worksheet is shown in Figure 3–2. It includes the needs, source of data, summary of calculations, and chart requirements.

BTW

Touch Screen Differences

The Office and Windows interfaces may vary if you are using a touch screen. For this reason, you might notice that the function or appearance of your touch screen differs slightly from this module's presentation.

Worksheet Title	Kaitlyn's Ice Cream Shoppe Six-Month Financial Projection
Needs	• A woksheet that shows Kaitlyn's Ice Cream Shoppe projected monthly sales revenue, cost of goods sold, gross margin, expenses, and operating income for a six-month period. • A clustered column chart that shows the expected contribution of each expense category to total expenses.
Source of Data	Data supplied by the business owner includes projections of the monthly sales and expenses based on prior year figures (see Table 3–1). Remaining numbers in the worksheet are based on formulas.
Calculations	The following calculations are needed for each month: • Cost of Goods Sold = Revenue * (1 – Margin) • Gross Margin = Revenue – Cost of Goods Sold • Bonus expense = Predetermined bonus amount if Revenue exceeds the Revenue for Bonus, otherwise Bonus = 0 • Commission expense = Commission percentage × Revenue • Site Rental expense = Kiosk Rental Percentage × Revenue • Marketing expense = Marketing percentage × Revenue • Equipment Repair and Maintenance expense = Equipment Repair and Maintenance percentage × Revenue • Total expenses = sum of all expenses • Operating Income = Gross Margin – Total expenses
Chart Requirements	• Show sparkline charts for revenue and each of the items noted in the calculations area above. • Show a clustered column chart that shows the contributions of each month's expense categories to the total monthly expense figure.

Figure 3–2

Using a sketch of the worksheet can help you visualize its design. The sketch of the worksheet consists of titles, column and row headings, location of data values, calculations, and a rough idea of the desired formatting (Figure 3–3a). The sketch of the clustered column chart shows the expected expenses for each of the six months (Figure 3–3b). The assumptions about income and expenses will be entered at the bottom of the worksheet (Figure 3–3a). The projected monthly sales revenue will be entered in row 4 of the worksheet. The projected monthly sales revenue and the assumptions shown in Table 3–1 will be used to calculate the remaining numbers in the worksheet.

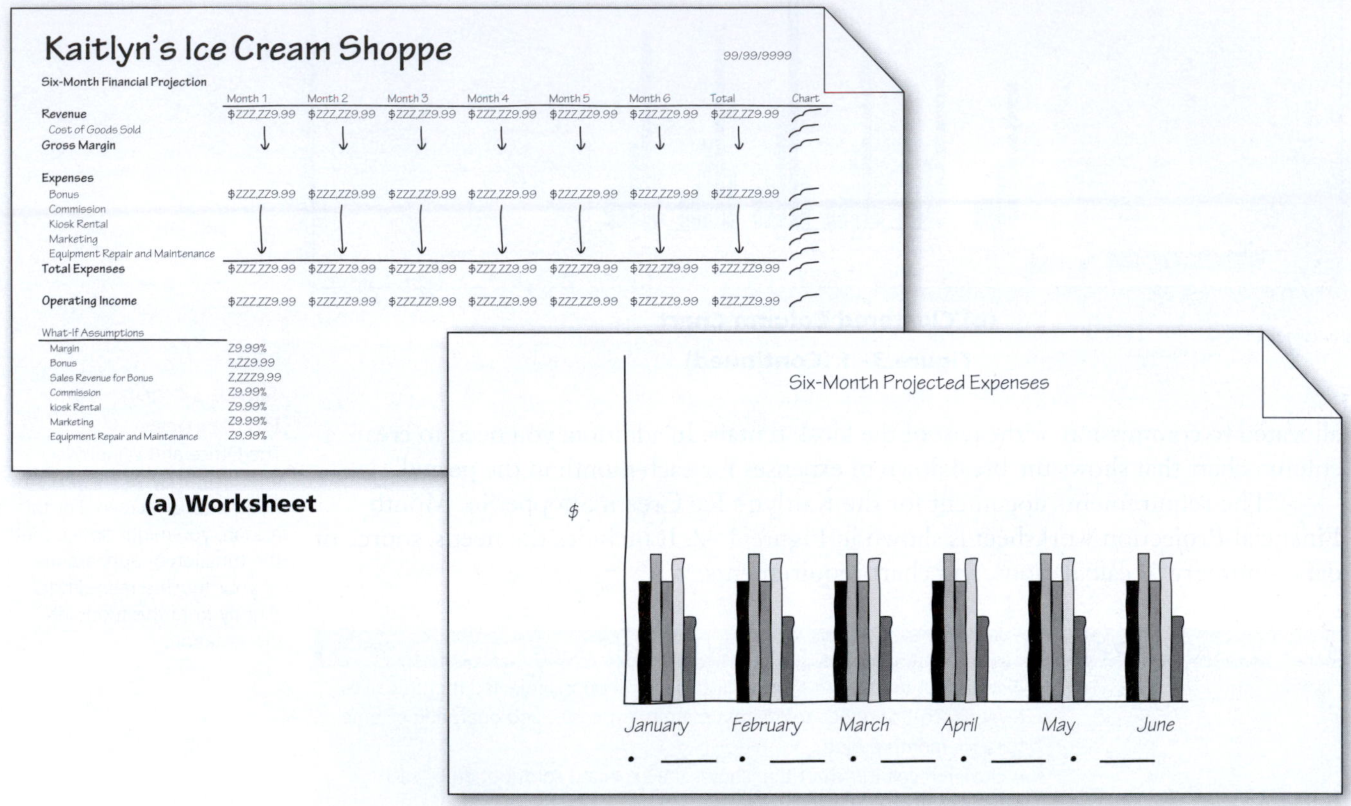

(a) Worksheet

(b) Clustered Column Chart

Figure 3–3

Table 3–1 Kaitlyn's Ice Cream Shoppe Six-Month Financial Projections Data and What-If Assumptions

Projected Monthly Total Sales Revenues	
January	55,000.00
February	62,500.00
March	67,000.00
April	90,250.00
May	77,500.00
June	74,750.00
What-If Assumptions	
Margin	78.75%
Bonus	$3,500.00
Sales Revenue for Bonus	65,000.00
Commission	25.00%
Site Rental	10.00%
Marketing	5.00%
Equipment Repair and Maintenance	3.50%

With a solid understanding of the requirements document, an understanding of the necessary decisions, and a sketch of the worksheet, the next step is to use Excel to create the worksheet.

In this module, you will learn how to create and use the workbook shown in Figure 3–1. The following roadmap identifies general activities you will perform as you progress through this module:

1. ENTER the HEADINGS and DATA in the worksheet.
2. ENTER FORMULAS and FUNCTIONS in the worksheet.
3. CREATE SPARKLINE CHARTS in a range of cells.
4. FORMAT the WORKSHEET.
5. CREATE a COLUMN CHART on a separate chart sheet.
6. CHANGE VIEWS of the worksheet.
7. ASK WHAT-IF QUESTIONS.

BTW

Excel Help

At any time while using Excel, you can find answers to questions and display information about various topics through Excel Help. Used properly, this form of assistance can increase your productivity and reduce your frustrations by minimizing the time you spend learning how to use Excel. For instructions about Excel Help and exercises that will help you gain confidence in using it, read the Office and Windows module at the beginning of this book.

To Enter the Worksheet Titles and Apply a Theme

The worksheet contains two titles in cells A1 and A2. In the previous modules, titles were centered across the worksheet. With large worksheets that extend beyond the size of a window, it is best to leave titles left-aligned, as shown in the sketch of the worksheet in Figure 3–3a, so that the worksheet will print the title on the first page if the worksheet requires multiple pages. This allows the user to easily find the worksheet title when necessary. The following steps enter the worksheet titles and change the workbook theme to Savon.

1. Run Excel and create a blank workbook in the Excel window.
2. Select cell A1 and then type `Kaitlyn's Ice Cream Shoppe` as the worksheet title.
3. Select cell A2, type `Six-Month Financial Projection` as the worksheet subtitle, and then press the ENTER key to enter the worksheet subtitle.
4. Apply the Savon theme to the workbook.

BTW

The Ribbon and Screen Resolution

Excel may change how the groups and buttons within the groups appear on the ribbon, depending on the computer or mobile device's screen resolution. Thus, your ribbon may look different from the ones in this book if you are using a screen resolution other than 1366 x 768.

BTW

Rotating Text in a Cell

In Excel, you use the Alignment sheet in the Format Cells dialog box (shown in Figure 3–5) to position data in a cell by centering, left-aligning, or right-aligning; indenting; aligning at the top, bottom, or center; and rotating. If you enter 90 in the Degrees box in the Orientation area, the text will appear vertically and read from bottom to top in the cell.

Rotating Text and Using the Fill Handle to Create a Series

The data on the worksheet, including month names and the What-If Assumptions section, now can be added to the worksheet.

CONSIDER THIS

What should you take into account when planning a worksheet layout?

Using Excel, you can change text and number formatting in many ways, which affects the visual impact of the worksheet. Rotated text often provides a strong visual appeal. Rotated text also allows you to fit more text into a smaller column width. When laying out a worksheet, keep in mind the content you want to emphasize and the length of the cell titles relative to the numbers.

To Rotate Text in a Cell

The design of the worksheet calls specifically for data for the six months of the selling season. Because there always will be only six months of data in the worksheet, place the months across the top of the worksheet as column headings rather than as row headings. Place the income and expense categories in rows, as they are more numerous than the number of months. This layout allows you to easily navigate the worksheet. Ideally, a proper layout will create a worksheet that is longer than it is wide.

When you first enter text, its angle is zero degrees (0°), and it reads from left to right in a cell. Excel allows you to rotate text in a cell counterclockwise by entering a number between 1° and 90°. ***Why?*** *Rotating text is one method of making column headings visually distinct.* The following steps enter the month name, January, in cell B3 and format cell B3 by rotating the text.

1

- If necessary, click the Home tab and then select cell B3 because this cell will include the first month name in the series of month names.
- Type **January** as the cell entry and then click the Enter button.
- Click the Alignment Settings Dialog Box Launcher (Home tab | Alignment group) to display the Format Cells dialog box (Figure 3–4).

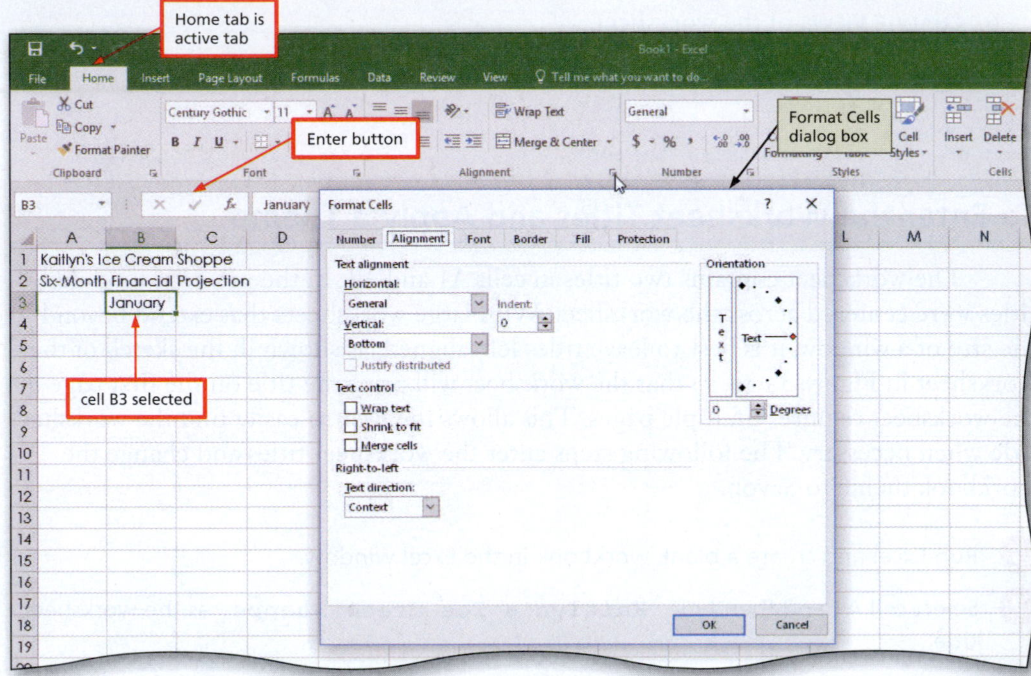

Figure 3–4

2

- Click the 60° point in the Orientation area (Format Cells dialog box) to move the indicator in the Orientation area to the 60° point and display a new orientation in the Degrees box (Figure 3–5).

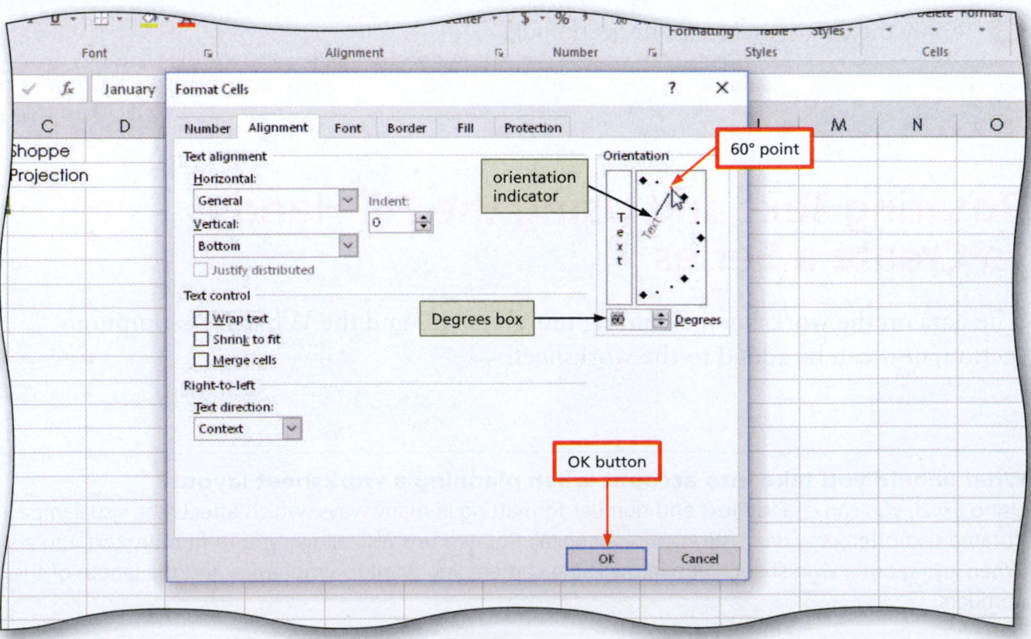

Figure 3–5

- Click the OK button (Format Cells dialog box) to rotate the text in the active cell and increase the height of the current row to best fit the rotated text (Figure 3–6).

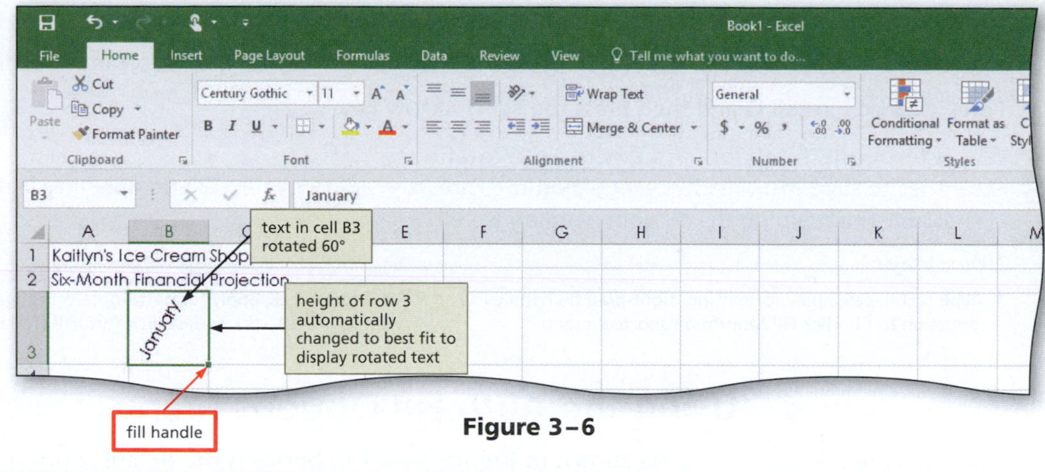

Figure 3–6

Other Ways

1. Right-click selected cell, click Format Cells on shortcut menu, click Alignment tab (Format Cells dialog box), click 60° point, click OK button

To Use the Fill Handle to Create a Series of Month Names

1 ENTER HEADINGS & DATA | 2 ENTER FORMULAS & FUNCTIONS | 3 CREATE SPARKLINE CHARTS
4 FORMAT WORKSHEET | 5 CREATE COLUMN CHART | 6 CHANGE VIEWS | 7 ASK WHAT-IF QUESTIONS

***Why?** Once the first month in the series has been entered and formatted, you can complete the data series using the fill handle rather than typing and formatting all the entries.* The following steps use the fill handle and the entry in cell B3 to create a series of month names in cells C3:G3.

- Drag the fill handle on the lower-right corner of cell B3 to the right to select the range to fill, C3:G3 in this case. Do not release the mouse button (Figure 3–7).

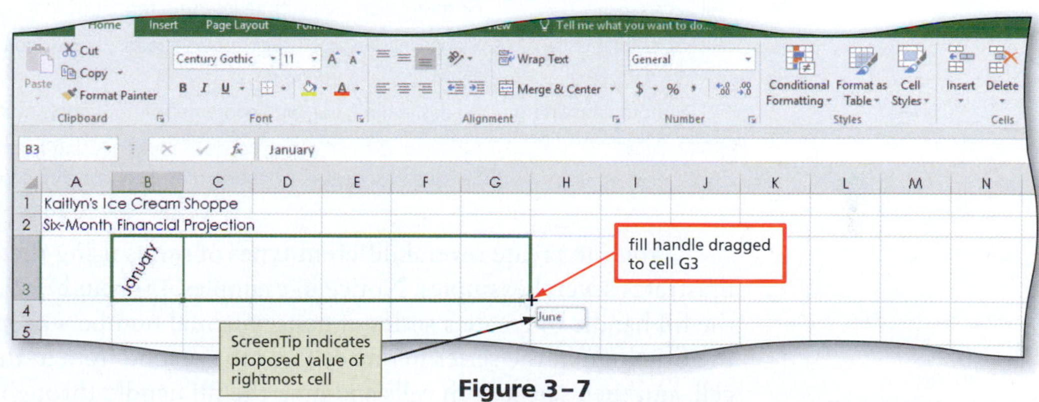

Figure 3–7

2

- Release the mouse button to create a month name series in the selected range and copy the format of the selected cell to the selected range.
- Click the 'Auto Fill Options' button below the lower-right corner of the fill area to display the Auto Fill Options menu (Figure 3–8).

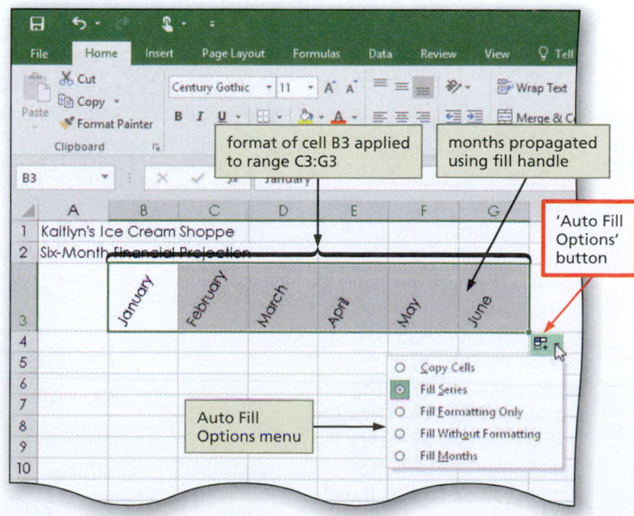

Figure 3–8

Q&A What if I do not want to copy the format of cell B3 during the auto fill operation?

In addition to creating a series of values, dragging the fill handle instructs Excel to copy the format of cell B3 to the range C3:G3. With some fill operations, you may not want to copy the formats of the source cell or range to the destination cell or range. If this is the case, click the 'Auto Fill Options' button after the range fills and then select the desired option on the Auto Fill Options menu (Figure 3–8).

- Click the 'Auto Fill Options' button to hide the Auto Fill Options menu.
- Select cell H3, type `Total`, and then press the RIGHT ARROW key to enter a column heading.
- Type `Chart` in cell I3 and then press the RIGHT ARROW key.

Q&A

Why is the word, Total, formatted with a 60° rotation?

Excel tries to save you time by recognizing the format in adjacent cell G3 and applying it to cell H3. Such behavior also occurs when typing the column heading in cell I3.

Other Ways

1. Type text in cell, apply formatting, right-drag fill handle in direction to fill, click Fill Months on shortcut menu
2. Type text in cell, apply formatting, select range, click Fill button (Home tab | Editing group), click Series, click AutoFill (Series dialog box), click OK button

BTW

The Fill Handle

If you drag the fill handle up or to the left, Excel will decrement the series rather than increment the series. To copy a word, such as January or Monday, which Excel might interpret as the start of a series, hold down the CTRL key while you drag the fill handle to a destination area. If you drag the fill handle back into the middle of a cell, Excel erases the contents of the cell.

Using the Auto Fill Options Menu

As shown in Figure 3–8, Fill Series is the default option that Excel uses to fill an area, which means it fills the destination area with a series, using the same formatting as the source area. If you choose another option on the Auto Fill Options menu, Excel changes the contents of the destination range. Following the use of the fill handle, the 'Auto Fill Options' button remains active until you begin the next Excel operation. Table 3–2 summarizes the options on the Auto Fill Options menu.

Table 3–2 Options Available on the Auto Fill Options Menu

Auto Fill Option	Description
Copy Cells	Fill destination area with contents using format of source area. Do not create a series.
Fill Series	Fill destination area with series using format of source area. This option is the default.
Fill Formatting Only	Fill destination area using format of source area. No content is copied unless fill is series.
Fill Without Formatting	Fill destination area with contents, without applying the formatting of source area.
Fill Months	Fill destination area with series of months using format of source area. Same as Fill Series and shows as an option only if source area contains the name of a month.

BTW

Custom Fill Sequences

You can create your own custom fill sequences for use with the fill handle. For example, if you often type the same list of products or names in Excel, you can create a custom fill sequence. You then can type the first product or name and then use the fill handle automatically to fill in the remaining products or names. To create a custom fill sequence, display the Excel Options dialog box by clicking Options in the Backstage view. Click the Advanced tab (Excel Options dialog box) and then click the 'Edit Custom Lists' button in the General section (Excel Options dialog box).

You can create several different types of series using the fill handle. Table 3–3 illustrates several examples. Notice in examples 4 through 7, 9, and 11 that, if you use the fill handle to create a series of nonsequential numbers or months, you must enter the first item in the series in one cell and the second item in the series in an adjacent cell, and then select both cells and drag the fill handle through the destination area.

Table 3–3 Examples of Series Using the Fill Handle

Example	Contents of Cell(s) Copied Using the Fill Handle	Next Three Values of Extended Series
1	4:00	5:00, 6:00, 7:00
2	Qtr2	Qtr3, Qtr4, Qtr1
3	Quarter 1	Quarter 2, Quarter 3, Quarter 4
4	22-Jul, 22-Sep	22-Nov, 22-Jan, 22-Mar
5	2017, 2018	2019, 2020, 2021
6	1, 2	3, 4, 5
7	625, 575	525, 475, 425
8	Mon	Tue, Wed, Thu
9	Sunday, Tuesday	Thursday, Saturday, Monday
10	4th Section	5th Section, 6th Section, 7th Section
11	2205, 2208	2211, 2214, 2217

To Increase Column Widths

Why? *In Module 2, you increased column widths after the values were entered into the worksheet. Sometimes, you may want to increase the column widths before you enter values and, if necessary, adjust them later.* The following steps increase the column widths.

- Move the pointer to the boundary between column heading A and column heading B so that the pointer changes to a split double arrow in preparation of adjusting the column widths.
- Drag the pointer to the right until the ScreenTip displays the desired column width, Width: 38.00 (309 pixels) in this case. Do not release the mouse button (Figure 3–9).

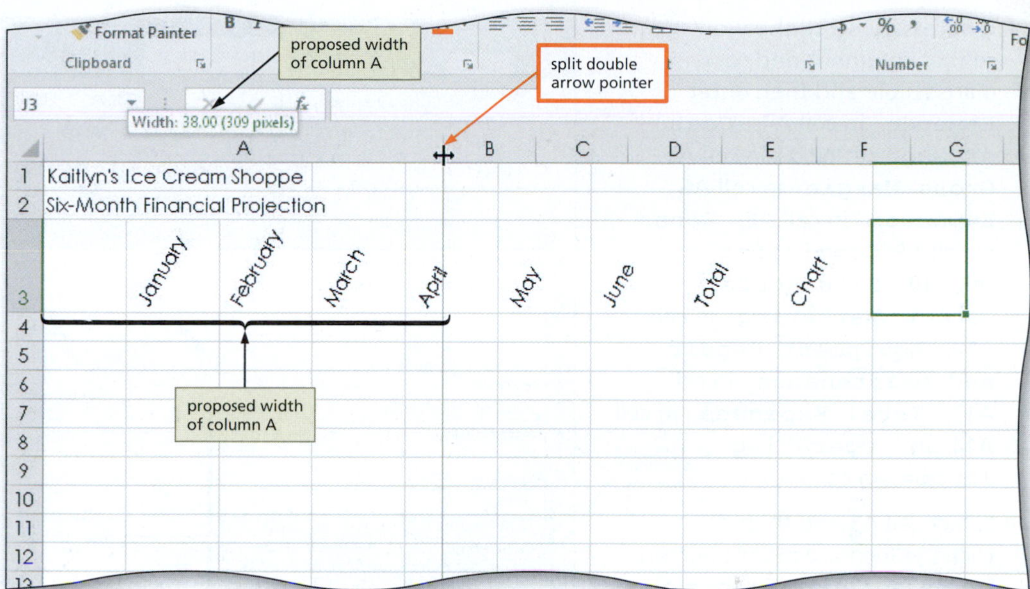

Figure 3–9

- Release the mouse button to change the width of the column.
- Click column heading B to select the column and then drag through column heading G to select the range in which to change the widths.
- Move the pointer to the boundary between column headings B and C in preparation of resizing column B and then drag the pointer to the right until the ScreenTip displays the desired width, Width: 14.50 (121 pixels) in this case. Do not lift your finger or release the mouse button (Figure 3–10).

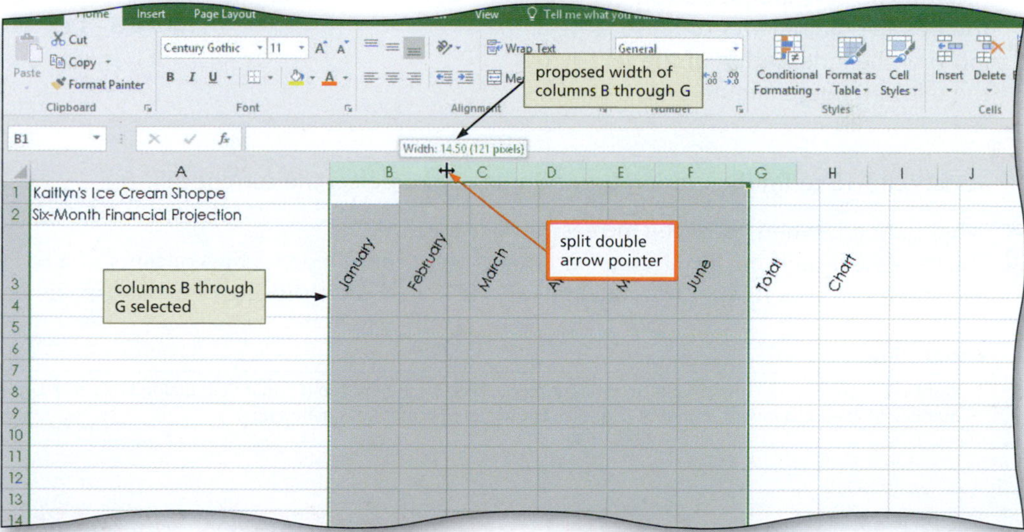

Figure 3–10

- Release the mouse button to change the width of the selected columns.
- If necessary, scroll the worksheet so that column H is visible and then use the technique described in Step 1 to increase the width of column H to 18.00 (149 pixels).

To Enter and Indent Row Titles

1 ENTER HEADINGS & DATA | 2 ENTER FORMULAS & FUNCTIONS | 3 CREATE SPARKLINE CHARTS
4 FORMAT WORKSHEET | 5 CREATE COLUMN CHART | 6 CHANGE VIEWS | 7 ASK WHAT-IF QUESTIONS

Excel allows you to indent text in cells. The following steps enter the row titles in column A and indent several of the row titles to create a visual hierarchy. ***Why?*** *You can create a hierarchy by indenting some of the row titles, like in an outline or table of contents.*

- If necessary, scroll the worksheet so that column A and row 4 are visible and then enter `Revenue` in cell A4, `Cost of Goods Sold` in cell A5, `Gross Margin` in cell A6, `Expenses` in cell A8, `Bonus` in cell A9, `Commission` in cell A10, `Site Rental` in cell A11, `Marketing` in cell A12, `Equipment Repair and Maintenance` in cell A13, `Total Expenses` in cell A14, and `Operating Income` in cell A16.
- Select cell A5 and then click the Increase Indent button (Home tab | Alignment group) to increase the indentation of the text in the selected cell.
- Select the range A9:A13 and then click the Increase Indent button (Home tab | Alignment group) to increase the indentation of the text in the selected range (Figure 3–11).

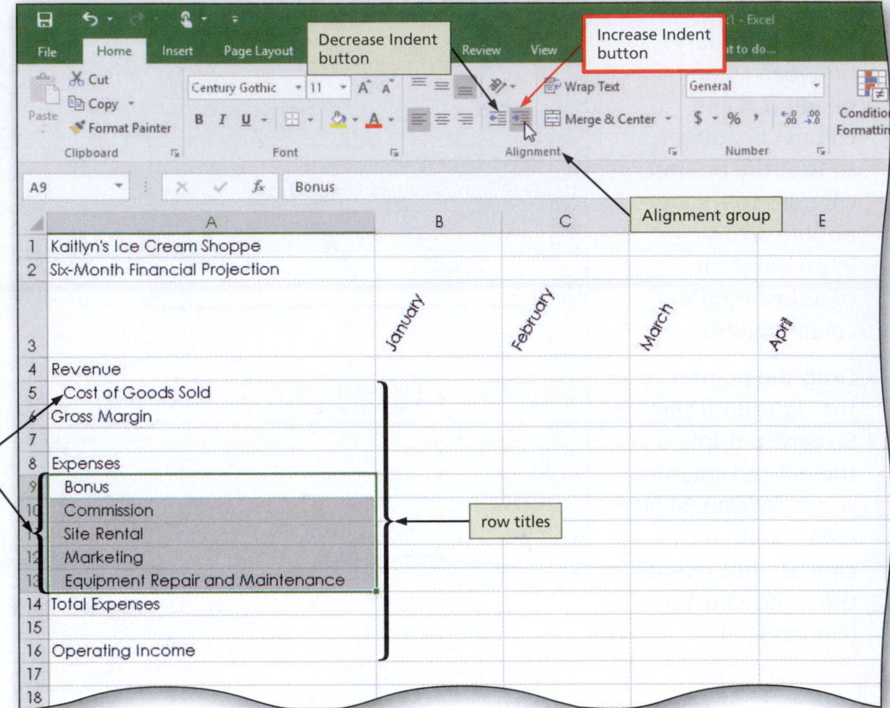

Figure 3–11

- Select cell A18 to finish entering the row titles and deselect the current cell.

Q&A What happens when I click the Increase Indent button?
The Increase Indent button (Home tab | Alignment group) indents the contents of a cell two spaces to the right each time you click it. The Decrease Indent button decreases the indent by two spaces each time you click it.

Other Ways

1. Right-click range, click Format Cells on shortcut menu, click Alignment tab (Format Cells dialog box), click Left (Indent) in Horizontal list, type number of spaces to indent in Indent box, click OK button (Format Cells dialog box)

Copying a Range of Cells to a Nonadjacent Destination Area

The What-If Assumptions section should be placed in an area of the worksheet that is accessible yet does not impair the view of the main section of the worksheet. As shown in Figure 3–3a, the What-If Assumptions will be placed below the calculations in the worksheet. This will allow the reader to see the main section of the worksheet when first opening the workbook. Additionally, the row titles in the Expenses area are the same as the row titles in the What-If Assumptions table, with the exception of the two additional entries in cells A19 (Margin) and A21 (Sales Revenue for Bonus). Hence, the row titles in the What-If Assumptions table can be created by copying the range A9:A13 to the range A19:A23 and then inserting two rows for the additional entries in cells A19 and A21. You cannot use the fill handle to copy the range because the source area (range A9:A13) is not adjacent to the destination area (range A19:A23).

A more versatile method of copying a source area is to use the Copy button and Paste button (Home tab | Clipboard group). You can use these two buttons to copy a source area to an adjacent or nonadjacent destination area.

BTW

Fitting Entries in a Cell

An alternative to increasing column widths or row heights is to shrink the characters in a cell to fit the current width of the column. To shrink to fit, click Format Cells Alignment Dialog Box Button Launcher (Home tab | Alignment group) and then place a check mark in the 'Shrink to fit' check box in the Text control area (Format Cells dialog box).

To Copy a Range of Cells to a Nonadjacent Destination Area

1 ENTER HEADINGS & DATA | 2 ENTER FORMULAS & FUNCTIONS | 3 CREATE SPARKLINE CHARTS
4 FORMAT WORKSHEET | 5 CREATE COLUMN CHART | 6 CHANGE VIEWS | 7 ASK WHAT-IF QUESTIONS

The Copy button copies the contents and format of the source area to the **Office Clipboard**, a temporary storage area in the computer's memory that allows you to collect text and graphics from any Office document and then paste them into almost any other type of document. The Paste button pastes a copy of the contents of the Office Clipboard in the destination area. ***Why?*** *Copying the range of cells rather than reentering the content assures consistency within the worksheet.* The following steps enter the What-If Assumptions row heading and then use the Copy and Paste buttons to copy the range A9:A13 to the nonadjacent range A19:A23.

1

- With cell A18 selected, type **What-If Assumptions** as the new row title and then click the Enter button.
- Select the range A9:A13 and then click the Copy button (Home tab | Clipboard group) to copy the values and formats of the selected range, A9:A13 in this case, to the Office Clipboard.
- Select cell A19, the top cell in the destination area (Figure 3–12).

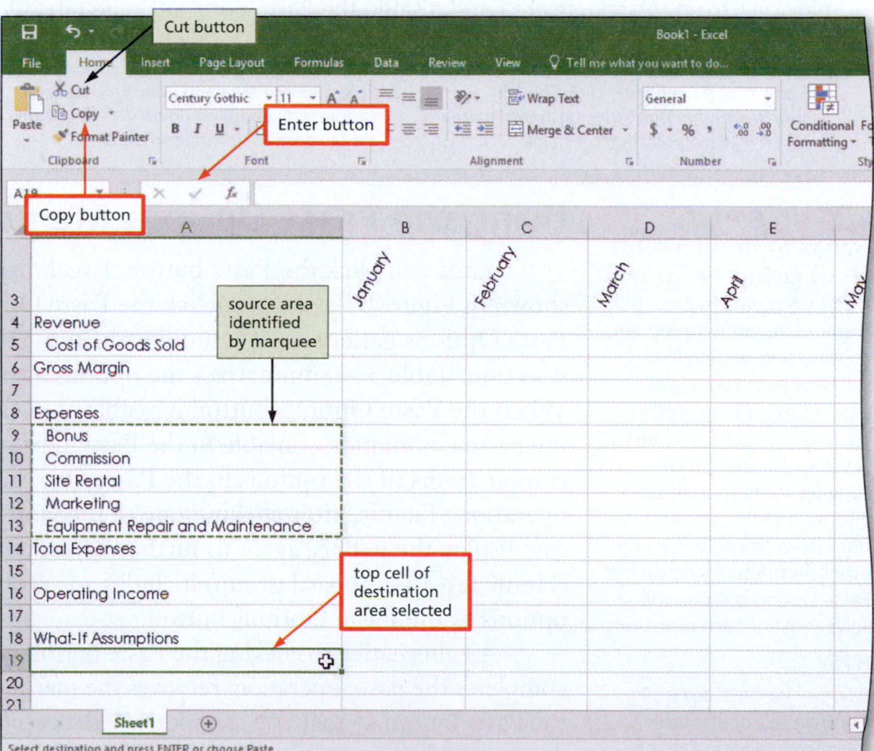

Figure 3–12

Q&A Why do I not select the entire destination area?
You are not required to select the entire destination area (A19:A23) because Excel only needs to know the upper-left cell of the destination area. In the case of a single column range, such as A19:A23, the top cell of the destination area (cell A19) also is the upper-left cell of the destination area.

- Click the Paste button (Home tab | Clipboard group) to copy the values and formats of the last item placed on the Office Clipboard, range A9:A13, to the destination area, A19:A23. If necessary, scroll down to see the complete destination area (Figure 3–13).

Q&A What if there was data in the destination area before I clicked the Paste button?
Any data contained in the destination area prior to the copy and paste is lost. When you complete a copy, the values and formats in the destination area are replaced with the values and formats of the source area. If you accidentally delete valuable data, click the Undo button on the Quick Access Toolbar or press CTRL+Z.

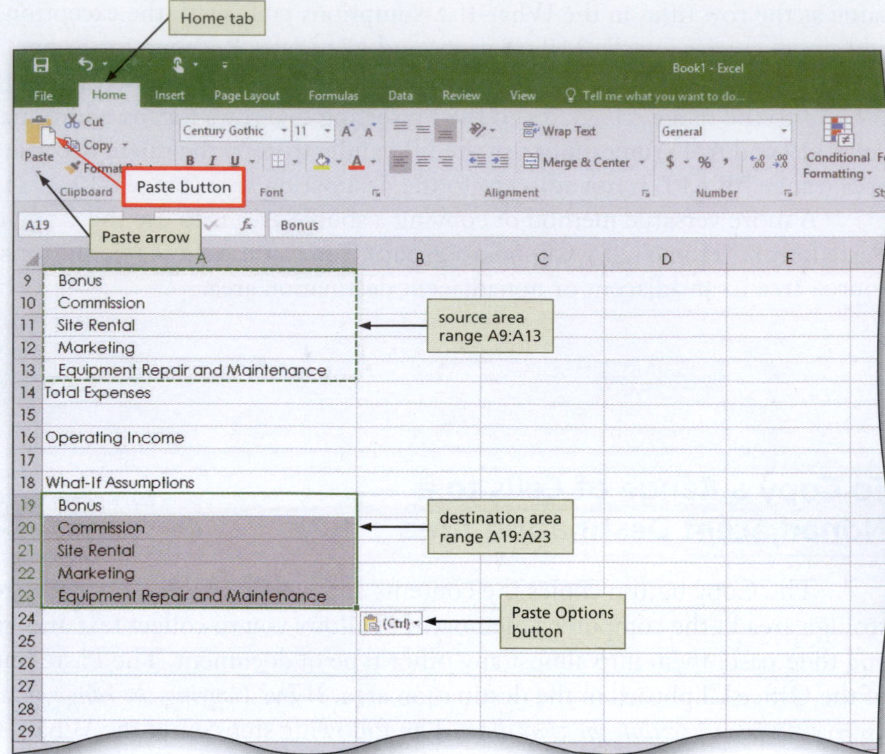

Figure 3–13

3

- Press the ESC key to remove the marquee from the source area and disable the Paste button (Home tab | Clipboard group).

Other Ways

1. Right-click source area, click Copy on shortcut menu, right-click destination area, click Paste icon on shortcut menu
2. Select source area and point to border of range; while holding down CTRL key, drag source area to destination area
3. Select source area, press CTRL+C, select destination area, press CTRL+V

BTW

Copying and Pasting from Other Programs

If you need data in Excel that is stored in another program, copying and pasting likely will help you. You might need to experiment before you are successful, because Excel might attempt to copy formatting or other information that you did not intend to paste from the other program. Trying various Paste Option buttons will solve most of such problems.

BTW

Move It or Copy It

Contrary to popular belief, move and copy operations are not the same. When you move a cell, the data in the original location is cleared and the format of the cell is reset to the default. When you copy a cell, the data and format of the copy area remains intact. In short, you should copy cells to duplicate entries and move cells to rearrange entries.

Using the Paste Options Menu

After you click the Paste button, Excel displays the Paste Options button, as shown in Figure 3–13. If you click the Paste Options arrow and select an option in the Paste Options gallery, Excel modifies the most recent paste operation based on your selection. Table 3–4 summarizes the options available in the Paste Options gallery. When the Paste Options button is visible, you can use keyboard shortcuts to access the paste commands available in the Paste Options gallery. Additionally, you can use combinations of the options in the Paste Options gallery to customize your paste operation. That is, after clicking one of the icons in the Paste Options gallery, you can display the gallery again to further adjust your paste operation. The Paste button (Home tab | Clipboard group) includes an arrow that, when clicked, displays the same options as the Paste Options button.

An alternative to clicking the Paste button is to press the ENTER key. The ENTER key completes the paste operation, removes the marquee from the source area, and disables the Paste button so that you cannot paste the copied source area to other destination areas. The ENTER key was not used in the previous set of steps so that the capabilities of the Paste Options button could be discussed. The Paste Options button does not appear on the screen when you use the ENTER key to complete the paste operation.

Using Drag and Drop to Move or Copy Cells

You also can use the mouse to move or copy cells. First, you select the source area and point to the border of the cell or range. You know you are pointing to the

Table 3–4 Paste Gallery Commands

Paste Option Icon	Paste Option	Description
	Paste	Copy contents and format of source area. This option is the default.
	Formulas	Copy formulas from the source area, but not the contents and format.
	Formulas & Number Formatting	Copy formulas and format for numbers and formulas of source area, but not the contents.
	Keep Source Formatting	Copy contents, format, and styles of source area.
	No Borders	Copy contents and format of source area, but not any borders.
	Keep Source Column Widths	Copy contents and format of source area. Change destination column widths to source column widths.
	Transpose	Copy the contents and format of the source area, but transpose, or swap, the rows and columns.
	Values	Copy contents of source area but not the formatting for formulas.
	Values & Number Formatting	Copy contents and format of source area for numbers or formulas, but use format of destination area for text.
	Values & Source Formatting	Copy contents and formatting of source area but not the formula.
	Formatting	Copy format of source area but not the contents.
	Paste Link	Copy contents and format and link cells so that a change to the cells in source area updates the corresponding cells in destination area.
	Picture	Copy an image of the source area as a picture.
	Linked Picture	Copy an image of the source area as a picture so that a change to the cells in source area updates the picture in destination area.

border of the cell or range when the pointer changes to a four-headed arrow. To move the selected cell or cells, drag the selection to the destination area. To copy a selection, hold down the CTRL key while dragging the selection to the destination area. You know Excel is in Copy mode when a small plus sign appears next to the pointer. Be sure to release the mouse button before you release the CTRL key. Using the mouse to move or copy cells is called **drag and drop**.

Using Cut and Paste to Move Cells

Another way to move cells is to select them, click the Cut button (Home tab | Clipboard group) (Figure 3–12) to remove the cells from the worksheet and copy them to the Office Clipboard, select the destination area, and then click the Paste button (Home tab | Clipboard group) or press the ENTER key. You also can use the Cut command on the shortcut menu, instead of the Cut button on the ribbon.

BTW

Cutting

When you cut a cell or range of cells using the Cut command on a shortcut menu or Cut button (Home tab | Clipboard group), Excel copies the cells to the Office Clipboard; it does not remove the cells from the source area until you paste the cells in the destination area by either clicking the Paste button (Home tab | Clipboard group) or pressing the ENTER key. When you complete the paste, Excel clears the cell's or range of cell's entries and their formats from the source area.

Inserting and Deleting Cells in a Worksheet

At any time while the worksheet is on the screen, you can insert cells to enter new data or delete cells to remove unwanted data. You can insert or delete individual cells; a range of cells, rows, or columns; or entire worksheets.

To Insert a Row

Why? According to the sketch of the worksheet in Figure 3–3a, two rows must be inserted in the What-If Assumptions table, one above Bonus for the Margin assumption and another between Bonus and Commission for the Sales Revenue for Bonus assumption. The following steps insert the new rows into the worksheet.

- Right-click row heading 20, the row below where you want to insert a row, to display the shortcut menu and the mini toolbar (Figure 3–14).

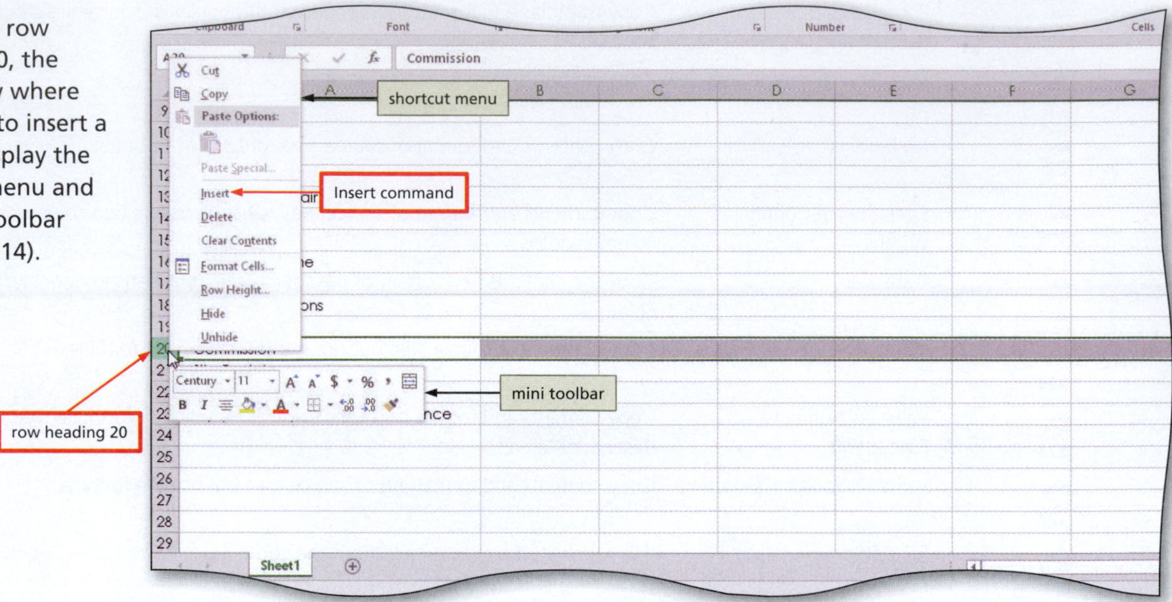

Figure 3–14

- Click Insert on the shortcut menu to insert a new row in the worksheet by shifting the selected row and all rows below it down one row.
- Select cell A20 in the new row and then type `Sales Revenue for Bonus` to enter a new row title (Figure 3–15).

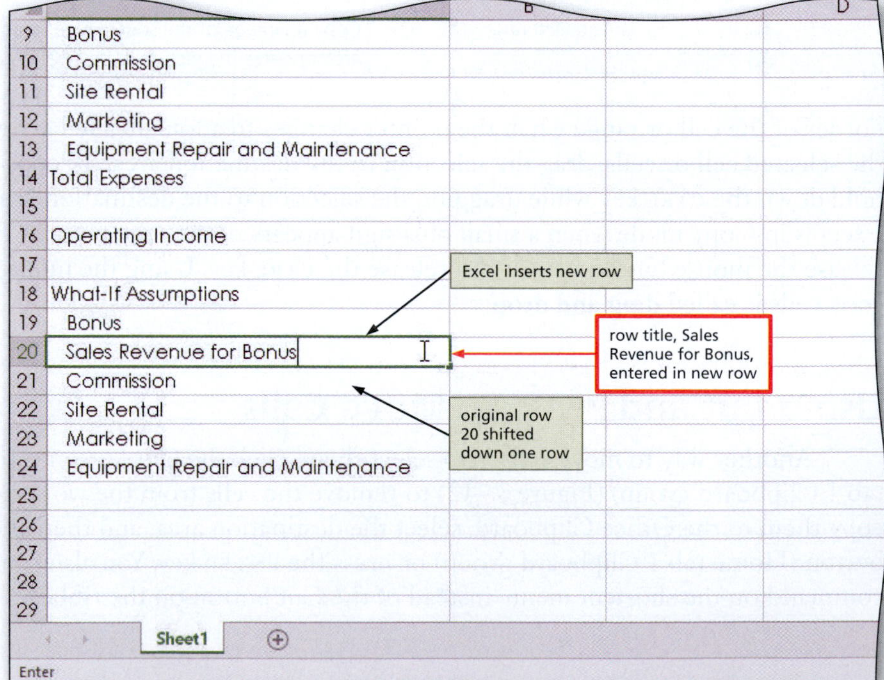

Figure 3–15

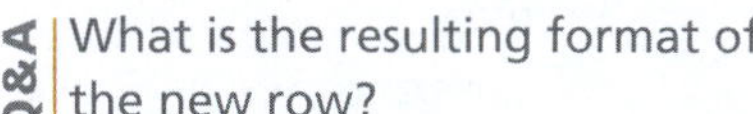

Q&A What is the resulting format of the new row?

The cells in the new row inherit the formats of the cells in the row above them. You can change this behavior by clicking the Insert Options button that appears below the inserted row. Following the insertion of a row, the Insert Options button allows you to select from the following options: (1) 'Format Same As Above', (2) 'Format Same As Below', and (3) Clear Formatting. The 'Format Same as Above' option is the default. The Insert Options button remains active until you begin the next Excel operation. Excel does not display the Insert Options button if the initial row does not contain any formatted data.

- Right-click row heading 19, the row below where you want to insert a row, to display the shortcut menu and the mini toolbar.
- Click Insert on the shortcut menu to insert a new row in the worksheet.
- Click the Insert Options button below row 19 (Figure 3–16).
- Click 'Format Same As Below' on the menu.
- Select cell A19 in the new row and then type **Margin** to enter a new row title.

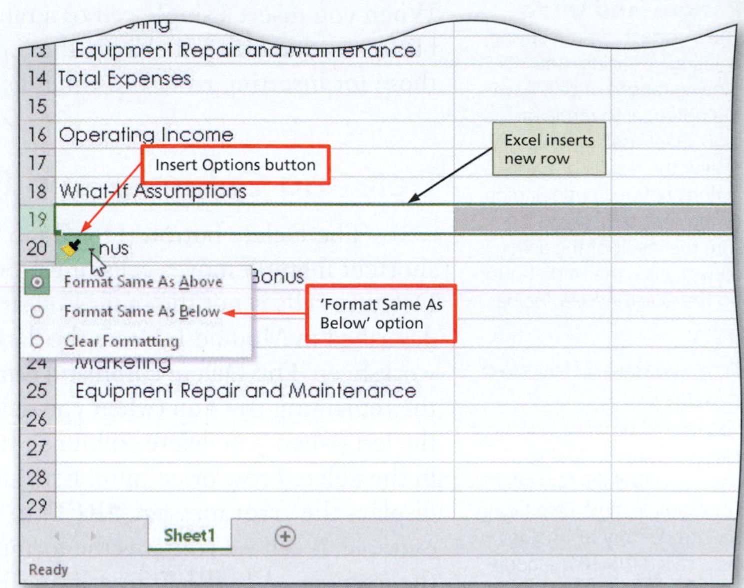

Figure 3–16

Q&A What would happen if cells in the shifted rows were included in formulas?

If the rows that shift down included cell references in formulas located in the worksheet, Excel would automatically adjust the cell references in the formulas to their new locations. Thus, in Step 2, if a formula in the worksheet referenced a cell in row 19 before the insert, then Excel would adjust the cell reference in the formula to row 20 after the insert.

- Save the workbook on your hard drive, OneDrive, or other storage location using **Kaitlyn's Ice Cream Shoppe Financial Projection** as the file name.

Other Ways

1. Click Insert Cells arrow (Home tab | Cells group), click 'Insert Sheet Rows'
2. Press CTRL+SHIFT+PLUS SIGN, click Entire row (Insert dialog box), click OK button

BTW

Inserting Multiple Rows

If you want to insert multiple rows, you have two choices. You can insert a single row by using the Insert command on the shortcut menu and then repeatedly press the F4 key to continue inserting rows. Alternatively, you can select a number of existing rows equal to the number of rows that you want to insert. For instance, if you want to insert five rows, select five existing rows in the worksheet, right-click the selected rows, and then click Insert on the shortcut menu.

Inserting Columns

You insert columns into a worksheet in the same way you insert rows. To insert columns, select one or more columns immediately to the right of where you want Excel to insert the new column or columns. Select the number of columns you want to insert, click the Insert arrow (Home tab | Cells group), and then click 'Insert Sheet Columns' in the Insert list; or right-click the selected column(s) and then click Insert on the shortcut menu. The Insert command on the shortcut menu requires that you select an entire column (or columns) to insert a column (or columns). Following the insertion of a column, Excel displays the Insert Options button, which allows you to modify the insertion in a fashion similar to that discussed earlier when inserting rows.

BTW

Dragging Ranges

You can move and insert a selected cell or range between existing cells by holding down the SHIFT key while you drag the selection to the gridline where you want to insert the selected cell or range. You also can copy and insert by holding down the CTRL+SHIFT keys while you drag the selection to the desired gridline.

Inserting Single Cells or a Range of Cells

You can use the Insert command on the shortcut menu or the Insert Cells command on the Insert menu — produced by clicking the Insert button (Home tab | Cells group) — to insert a single cell or a range of cells. You should be aware that if you shift a single cell or a range of cells, however, it no longer lines up with its associated cells. To ensure that the values in the worksheet do not get out of order,

BTW
Ranges and Undo
The incorrect use of copying, deleting, inserting, and moving ranges of cells have the potential to render a worksheet useless. Carefully review the results of these actions before continuing on to the next task. If you are not sure the result of the action is correct, click the Undo button on the Quick Access Toolbar.

BTW
Organizing Files and Folders
You should organize and store files in folders so that you easily can find the files later. For example, if you are taking an introductory technology class called CIS 101, a good practice would be to save all Excel files in an Excel folder in a CIS 101 folder. For a discussion of folders and detailed examples of creating folders, refer to the Office and Windows module at the beginning of this book.

spreadsheet experts recommend that you insert only entire rows or entire columns. When you insert a single cell or a range of cells, Excel displays the Insert Options button so that you can change the format of the inserted cell, using options similar to those for inserting rows and columns.

Deleting Columns and Rows

The Delete button (Home tab | Cells group) or the Delete command on the shortcut menu removes cells (including the data and format) from the worksheet. Deleting cells is not the same as clearing cells. The Clear Contents command, described in Module 1, clears the data from the cells, but the cells remain in the worksheet. The Delete command removes the cells from the worksheet and shifts the remaining rows up (when you delete rows) or shifts the remaining columns to the left (when you delete columns). If formulas located in other cells reference cells in the deleted row or column, Excel does not adjust these cell references. Excel displays the error message **#REF!** in those cells to indicate a cell reference error. For example, if cell A7 contains the formula =A4+A5 and you delete row 5, Excel assigns the formula =A4+#REF! to cell A6 (originally cell A7) and displays the error message, #REF!, in cell A6. Excel also displays an Error Options button when you select the cell containing the error message, #REF!, which allows you to select options to determine the nature of the problem.

To Enter Numbers with Format Symbols

1 ENTER HEADINGS & DATA | 2 ENTER FORMULAS & FUNCTIONS | 3 CREATE SPARKLINE CHARTS
4 FORMAT WORKSHEET | 5 CREATE COLUMN CHART | 6 CHANGE VIEWS | 7 ASK WHAT-IF QUESTIONS

The next step in creating the Financial Projection worksheet is to enter the what-if assumptions values in the range B19:B25. The numbers in the table can be entered and then formatted using techniques from Modules 1 and 2, or each number can be entered with **format symbols**, which assign a format to numbers as they are entered. When a number is entered with a format symbol, Excel displays it with the assigned format. Valid format symbols include the dollar sign ($), comma (,), and percent sign (%).

If you enter a whole number, it appears without any decimal places. If you enter a number with one or more decimal places and a format symbol, Excel displays the number with two decimal places. Table 3–5 illustrates several examples of numbers entered with format symbols. The number in parentheses in column 4 indicates the number of decimal places.

Table 3–5 Numbers Entered with Format Symbols

Format Symbol	Typed in Formula Bar	Displays in Cell	Comparable Format
,	374,149	374,149	Comma(0)
	5,833.6	5,833.60	Comma(2)
$	$58917	$58,917	Currency(0)
	$842.51	$842.51	Currency(2)
	$63,574.9	$63,574.90	Currency(2)
%	85%	85%	Percent(0)
	12.80%	12.80%	Percent(2)
	68.2242%	68.2242%	Percent(4)

Why? *In some cases, using a format symbol is the most efficient method for entering and formatting data.* The following step enters the numbers in the What-If Assumptions table with format symbols.

1

- Enter the following values, using format symbols to apply number formatting: `78.75%` in cell B19, `3,500.00` in cell B20, `65,000.00` in cell B21, `25.00%` in cell B22, `10.00%` in cell B23, `5.00%` in cell B24, and `3.50%` in cell B25 (Figure 3–17).

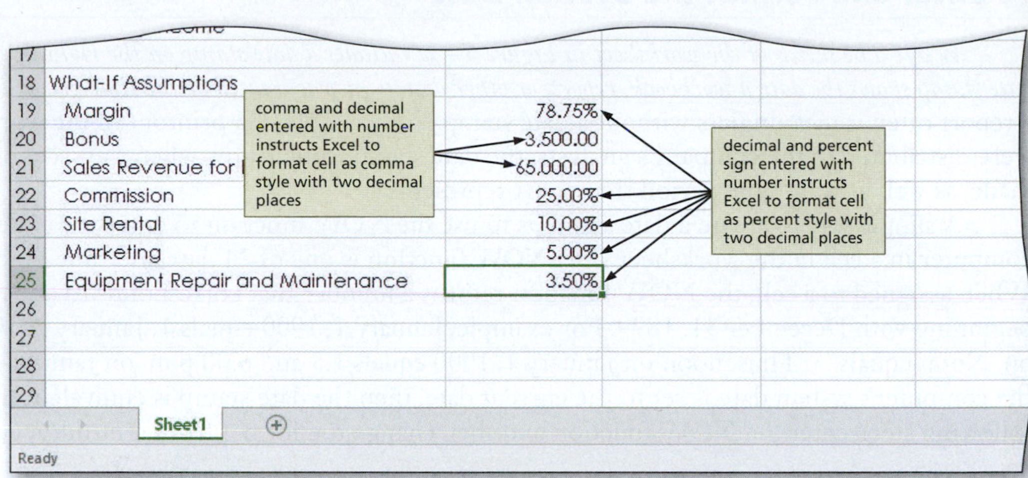

Figure 3–17

Other Ways

1. Right-click range, click Format Cells on shortcut menu, click Number tab (Format Cells dialog box), click category in Category list, select desired format, click OK button
2. Press CTRL+1, click Number tab (Format Cells dialog box), click category in Category list, select desired format, click OK button

To Enter the Projected Monthly Sales

The following steps enter the projected revenue, listed previously in Table 3–1, in row 4 and compute the projected six-month revenue in cell H4.

1. If necessary, display the Home tab.
2. Enter `55,000.00` in cell B4, `62,500.00` in cell C4, `67,000.00` in cell D4, `90,250.00` in cell E4, `77,500.00` in cell F4, and `74,750.00` in cell G4.
3. Select cell H4 and then click the Sum button (Home tab | Editing group) twice to create a sum in the selected cell (Figure 3–18).

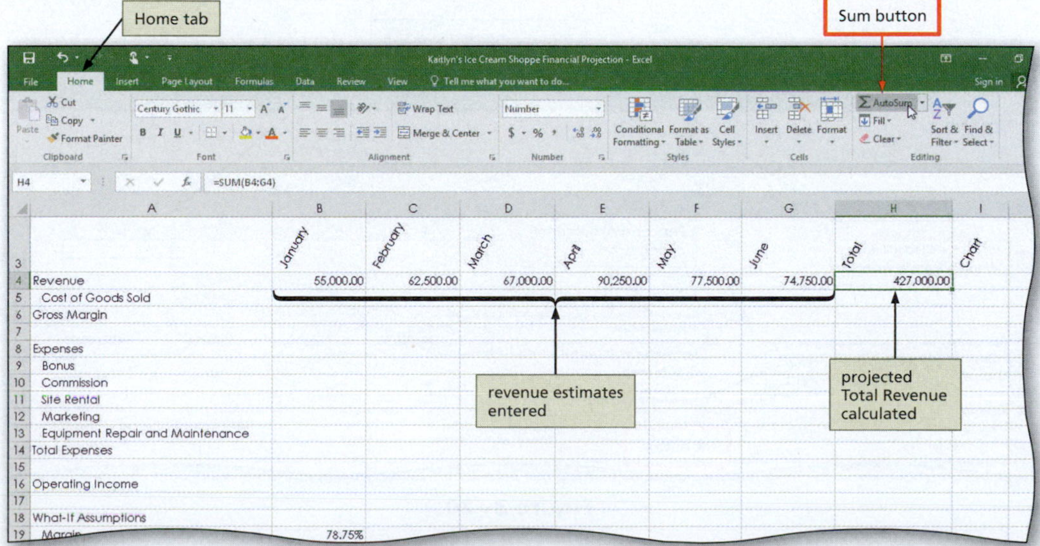

Figure 3–18

To Enter and Format the System Date

Why? The sketch of the worksheet in Figure 3–3a includes a date stamp on the right side of the heading section. A date stamp shows the date a workbook, report, or other document was created or the time period it represents. In business, a report often is meaningless without a date stamp. For example, if a printout of the worksheet in this module were distributed to the company's analysts, the date stamp would show when the six-month projections were made, as well as what time period the report represents.

A simple way to create a date stamp is to use the NOW function to enter the system date tracked by your computer in a cell in the worksheet. The **NOW function** is one of 24 date and time functions available in Excel. When assigned to a cell, the NOW function returns a number that corresponds to the system date and time beginning with December 31, 1899. For example, January 1, 1900 equals 1, January 2, 1900 equals 2, and so on. Noon equals .5. Thus, noon on January 1, 1900 equals 1.5 and 6:00 p.m. on January 1, 1900 equals 1.75. If the computer's system date is set to the current date, then the date stamp is equivalent to the current date. The following steps enter the NOW function and then change the format from mm/dd/yyyy hh:mm to mm/dd/yyyy.

1

- Select cell H1 and then click the Insert Function button in the formula bar to display the Insert Function dialog box.
- Click the 'Or select a category' arrow (Insert Function dialog box) and then select 'Date & Time' to populate the 'Select a function' list with data and time functions.
- Scroll down in the 'Select a function' list and then click NOW to select the required function (Figure 3–19).

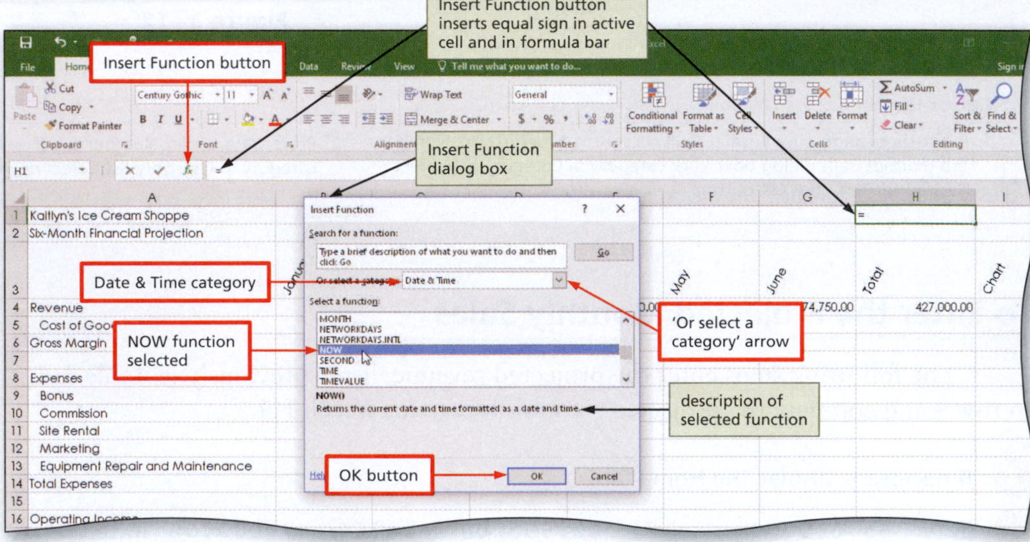

Figure 3–19

2

- Click the OK button (Insert Function dialog box) to close the Insert Function dialog box and display the Function Arguments dialog box (Figure 3–20).

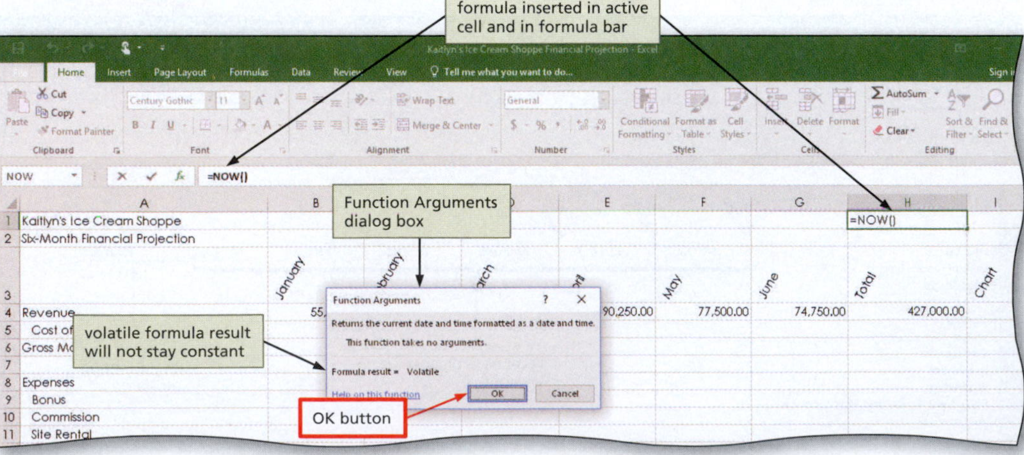

Figure 3–20

Q&A What is meant by 'Formula result = Volatile' in the Function Arguments dialog box?

The NOW function is an example of a volatile function. A **volatile function** is one where the number that the function returns is not constant but changes each time the worksheet is opened. As a result, any formula using the NOW function will have a variable result.

- Click the OK button (Function Arguments dialog box) to display the system date and time in the selected cell, using the default date and time format, which is mm/dd/yyyy hh:mm.

Q&A What does the mm/dd/yyyy hh:mm format represent?
The mm/dd/yyyy hh:mm format can be explained as follows: the first mm is the month, dd is the day of the month, yyyy is the year, hh is the hour of the day, and the second mm is the minutes past the hour. Excel applies this date and time format to the result of the NOW function.

- Right-click cell H1 to display a shortcut menu and mini toolbar.
- Click Format Cells on the shortcut menu to display the Format Cells dialog box.
- If necessary, click the Number tab (Format Cells dialog box) to display the Number sheet.
- Click Date in the Category list (Format Cells dialog box) to display the date format options in the Type list. Scroll down in the Type list and then click 3/14/2012 to display a sample of the data in the Sample area in the dialog box (Figure 3–21).

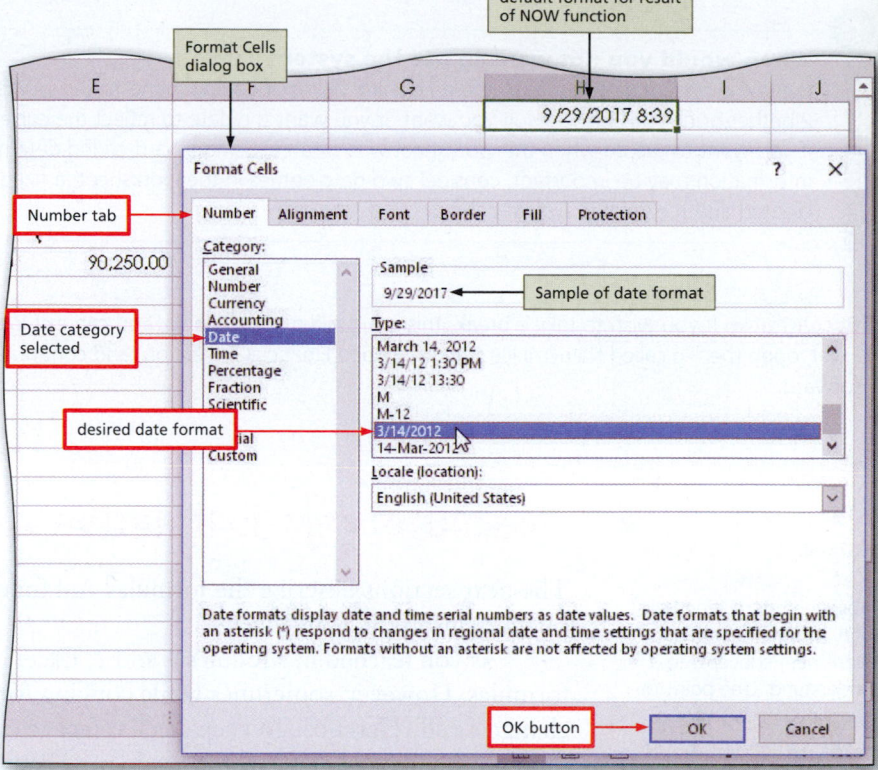

Figure 3–21

Q&A Why do the dates in the Type box show March 14, 2012 instead of the current date?
March 14, 2012 is just used as a sample date in this version of Office.

- Click the OK button (Format Cells dialog box) to display the system date (the result of the NOW function) in the format mm/dd/yyyy.
- Double-click the border between columns H and I to change the width of the column to best fit (Figure 3–22).

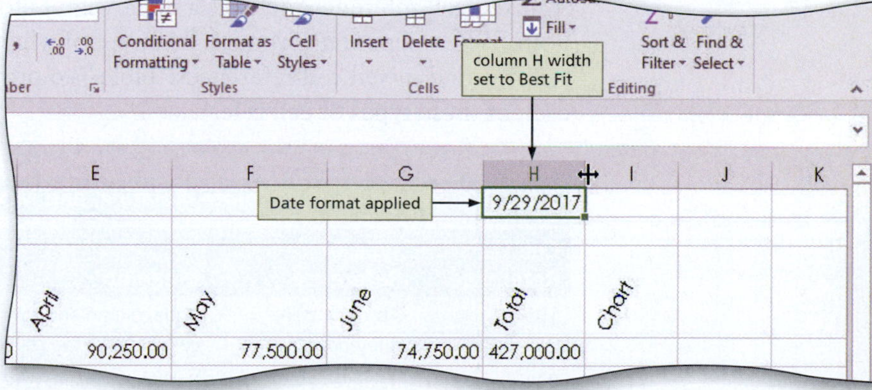

Figure 3–22

Experiment

- If instructed by your professor, select cell H2 and enter the place of your birth.
- Save the workbook again on the same storage location with the same file name.

Q&A Why should I save the workbook again?
You have made several modifications to the workbook since you last saved it. Thus, you should save it again.

Other Ways

1. Click 'Date & Time' button (Formulas tab | Function Library group), click NOW
2. Press CTRL+SEMICOLON (this enters the date as a static value, meaning the date will not change when the workbook is opened at a later date)
3. Press CTRL+SHIFT+# to format date as day-month-year

CONSIDER THIS

When would you not want to use the system date?

Using the system date results in the date value being updated whenever the worksheet is opened. Think carefully about whether or not this is the result you want. If you want the date to reflect the current date, using the system date is appropriate. If you want to record when the worksheet was created, using a hard-coded date makes more sense. If both pieces of information may be important, consider two date entries in the worksheet: a fixed entry identifying the date the worksheet was created and the volatile system date.

Break Point: If you wish to take a break, this is a good place to do so. You can exit Excel now. To resume at a later time, run Excel, open the file called Kaitlyn's Ice Cream Shoppe Financial Projection, and continue following the steps from this location forward.

BTW

Absolute Referencing

Absolute referencing is one of the more difficult worksheet concepts to understand. One point to keep in mind is that the paste operation is the only operation affected by an absolute cell reference. An absolute cell reference instructs the paste operation to use the same cell reference as it copies a formula from one cell to another.

Absolute Versus Relative Addressing

The next sections describe the formulas and functions needed to complete the calculations in the worksheet.

As you learned in Modules 1 and 2, Excel modifies cell references when copying formulas. However, sometimes while copying formulas you do not want Excel to change a cell reference. To keep a cell reference constant when copying a formula or function (that is, the cell references do not change relative to where you are copying the formula), Excel uses a technique called **absolute cell referencing**. To specify an absolute cell reference in a formula, enter a dollar sign ($) before any column letters or row numbers you want to keep constant in formulas you plan to copy. For example, B4 is an absolute cell reference, whereas B4 is a relative cell reference. Both reference the same cell. The difference becomes apparent when they are copied to a destination area. A formula using the absolute cell reference B4 instructs Excel to keep the cell reference B4 constant (absolute) in the formula as it is copied to the destination area. A formula using the **relative cell reference** B4 instructs Excel to adjust the cell reference as it is copied to the destination area. A cell reference where one factor remains constant and the other one varies is called a **mixed cell reference**. A mixed cell reference includes a dollar sign before the column or the row, not before both. When planning formulas, be aware of when you might need to use absolute, relative, and mixed cell references. Table 3–6 provides some additional examples of each of these types of cell references.

Table 3–6 Examples of Absolute, Relative, and Mixed Cell References

Cell Reference	Type of Reference	Meaning
B4	Absolute cell reference	Both column and row references remain the same when you copy this cell, because the cell references are absolute.
B4	Relative cell reference	Both column and row references are relative. When copied to another cell, both the column and row in the cell reference are adjusted to reflect the new location.
B$4	Mixed reference	This cell reference is mixed. The column reference changes when you copy this cell to another column because it is relative. The row reference does not change because it is absolute.
$B4	Mixed reference	This cell reference is mixed. The column reference does not change because it is absolute. The row reference changes when you copy this cell reference to another row because it is relative.

Figure 3–23 illustrates how the type of cell reference used affects the results of copying a formula to a new place in a worksheet. In Figure 3–23a, cells D6:D9 contain formulas. Each formula multiplies the content of cell A2 by 2; the difference between formulas lies in how cell A2 is referenced. Cells C6:C9 identify the type of reference: absolute, relative, or mixed.

Figure 3–23b shows the values that result from copying the formulas in cells D6:D9 to ranges E6:E9, F7:F10, and G11:G14. Figure 3–23c shows the formulas that result from copying the formulas. While all formulas initially multiplied the content of cell A2 by 2, the values and formulas in the destination ranges illustrate how Excel adjusts cell references according to how you reference those cells in original formulas.

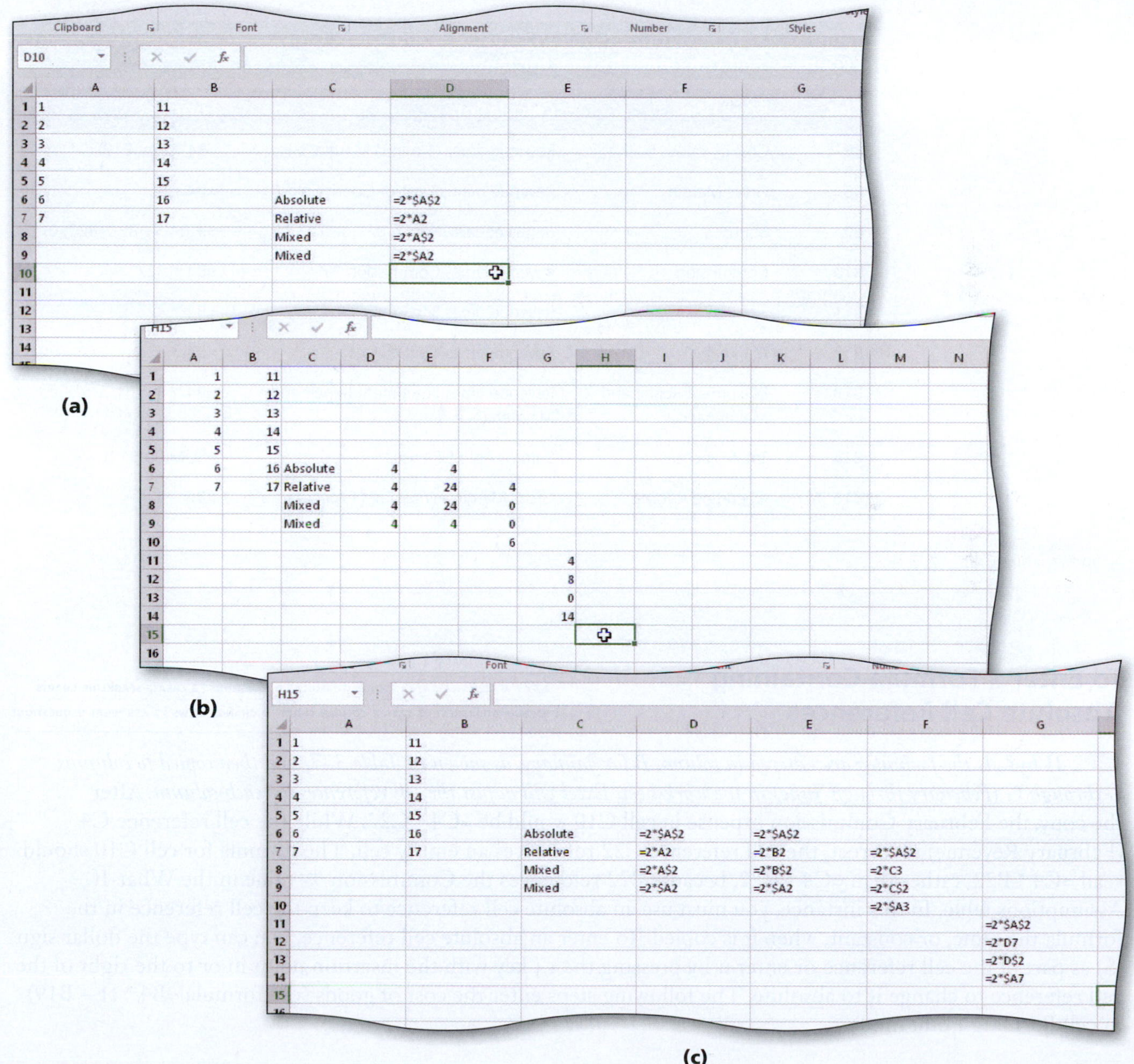

Figure 3–23

In the worksheet, you need to enter formulas that calculate the following values for January: cost of goods sold (cell B5), gross margin (cell B6), expenses (range B9:B13), total expenses (cell B14), and operating income (cell B16). The formulas are based on the projected monthly revenue in cell B4 and the assumptions in the range B19:B25.

The calculations for each column (month) are the same, except for the reference to the projected monthly revenue in row 4, which varies according to the month (B4 for January, C4 for February, and so on). Thus, the formulas for January can be entered in column B and then copied to columns C through G. Table 3–7 shows the formulas for determining the January cost of goods sold, gross margin, expenses, total expenses, and operating income in column B.

Table 3–7 Formulas for Determining Cost of Goods Sold, Gross Margin, Expenses, Total Expenses, and Operating Income for January

Cell	Row Title	Calculation	Formula
B5	Cost of Goods Sold	Revenue times (1 minus Margin %)	=B4 * (1 – B19)
B6	Gross Margin	Revenue minus Cost of Goods Sold	=B4 – B5
B9	Bonus	Bonus equals value in B20 or 0	=IF(B4 >= B21, B20, 0)
B10	Commission	Revenue times Commission %	=B4 * B22
B11	Site Rental	Revenue times Site Rental %	=B4 * B23
B12	Marketing	Revenue times Marketing %	=B4 * B24
B13	Equipment Repair and Maintenance	Revenue times Equipment Repair and Maintenance %	=B4 * B25
B14	Total Expenses	Sum of April Expenses	=SUM(B9:B13)
B16	Operating Income	Gross Margin minus Total Expenses	=B6 – B14

To Enter a Formula Containing Absolute Cell References

Why? *As the formulas are entered in column B for January, as shown in Table 3–7, and then copied to columns C through G (February through June) in the worksheet, Excel will adjust the cell references for each column.* After the copy, the February Commission expense in cell C10 would be =C4 * C22. While the cell reference C4 (February Revenue) is correct, the cell reference C22 references an empty cell. The formula for cell C10 should read =C4 * B22, rather than =C4 * C22, because B22 references the Commission % value in the What-If Assumptions table. In this instance, you must use an absolute cell reference to keep the cell reference in the formula the same, or constant, when it is copied. To enter an absolute cell reference, you can type the dollar sign ($) as part of the cell reference or enter it by pressing the F4 key with the insertion point in or to the right of the cell reference to change it to absolute. The following steps enter the cost of goods sold formula =B4 * (1 – B19) in cell B5 using Point mode.

1

- Click cell B5 to select the cell in which to enter the first formula.
- Type = (equal sign), select cell B4, type `*(1-B19` to continue entering the formula, and then press the F4 key to change the cell reference from a relative cell reference to an absolute cell reference. Type) (closing parenthesis) to complete the formula (Figure 3–24).

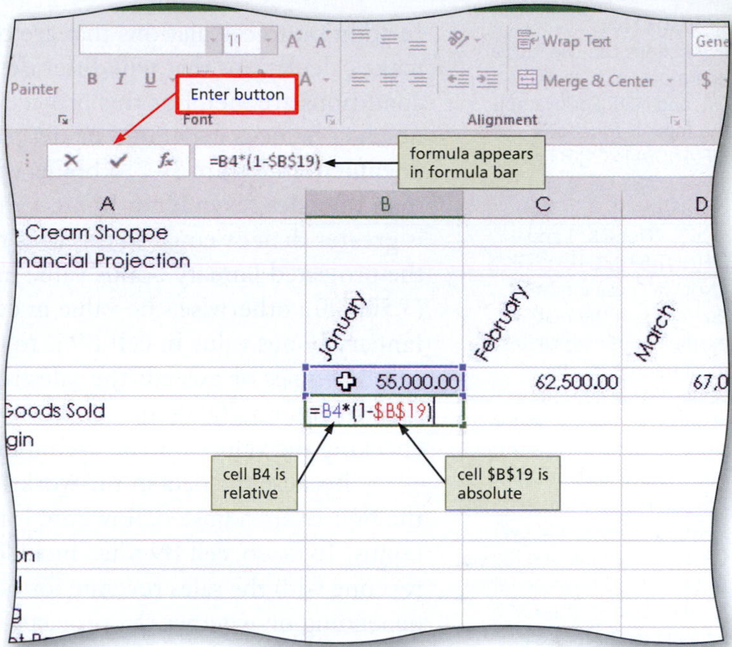

Figure 3–24

Q&A Is an absolute reference required in this formula?

No, a mixed cell reference also could have been used. The formula in cell B5 will be copied across columns, rather than down rows. So, the formula entered in cell B5 in Step 1 could have been entered as =B4*(1–$B19) using a mixed cell reference, rather than =B4*(1–B19), because when you copy a formula across columns, the row does not change. The key is to ensure that column B remains constant as you copy the formula across columns. To change the absolute cell reference to a mixed cell reference, continue to press the F4 key until you achieve the desired cell reference.

2

- Click the Enter button in the formula bar to display the result, 11687.5, instead of the formula in cell B5 (Figure 3–25).

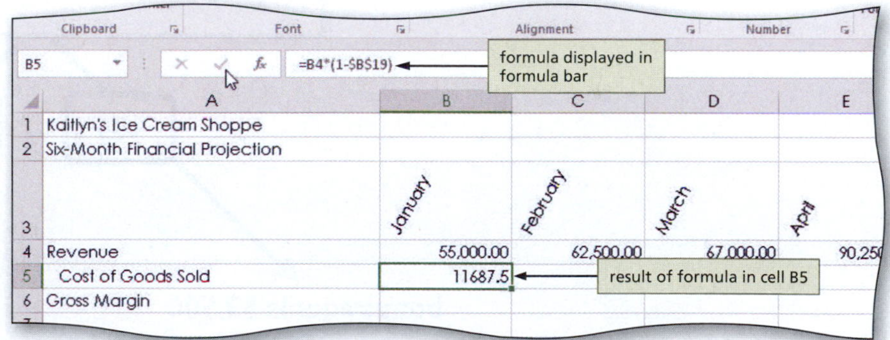

Figure 3–25

3

- Click cell B6 to select the cell in which to enter the next formula, type = (equal sign), click cell B4, type – (minus sign), and then click cell B5 to add a reference to the cell to the formula.
- Click the Enter button in the formula bar to display the result in the selected cell, in this case gross margin for January, 43,312.50, in cell B6 (Figure 3–26).

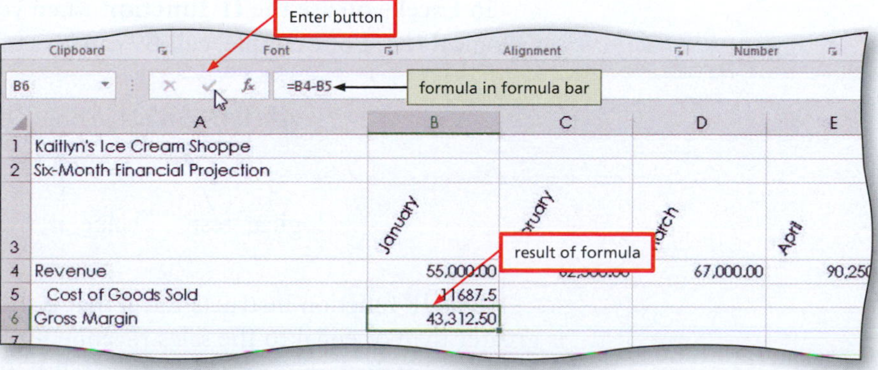

Figure 3–26

BTW

Logical Operators in IF Functions

IF functions can use logical operators, such as AND, OR, and NOT. For example, the three IF functions =IF(AND(A1>C1, B1<C2), "OK", "Not OK") and =IF(OR(K5>J5, C3<K6), "OK", "Not OK") and =IF(NOT(B10<C10), "OK", "Not OK") use logical operators. In the first example, both logical tests must be true for the value_if_true OK to be assigned to the cell. In the second example, one or the other logical tests must be true for the value_if_ true OK to be assigned to the cell. In the third example, the logical test B10<C10 must be false for the value_if_true OK to be assigned to the cell.

Making Decisions — The IF Function

In addition to calculations that are constant across all categories, you may need to make calculations that will differ depending on whether a particular condition or set of conditions are met. For this project, you need to vary compensation according to how much revenue is generated in any particular month. According to the requirements document in Figure 3–2, a bonus will be paid in any month where revenue is greater than the sales revenue for bonus value. If the projected January revenue in cell B4 is greater than or equal to the sales revenue for bonus in cell B21 (65,000.00), then the projected January bonus value in cell B9 is equal to the bonus value in cell B20 (3,500.00); otherwise, the value in cell B9 is equal to 0. One way to assign the projected January bonus value in cell B9 is to manually check to see if the projected revenue in cell B4 equals or exceeds the sales revenue for the bonus amount in cell B21 and, if so, then to enter 3,500.00 in cell B9. You can use this manual process for all six months by checking the values for the each month.

Because the data in the worksheet changes each time a report is prepared or the figures are adjusted, however, it is preferable to have Excel calculate the monthly bonus. To do so, cell B9 must include a formula or function that compares the projected revenue with the sales revenue for bonus value, and displays 3,500.00 or 0.00 (zero), depending on whether the projected January revenue in cell B4 is greater than, equal to, or less than the sales revenue for bonus value in cell B21. This decision-making process is a **logical test**. It can be represented in diagram form, as shown in Figure 3–27.

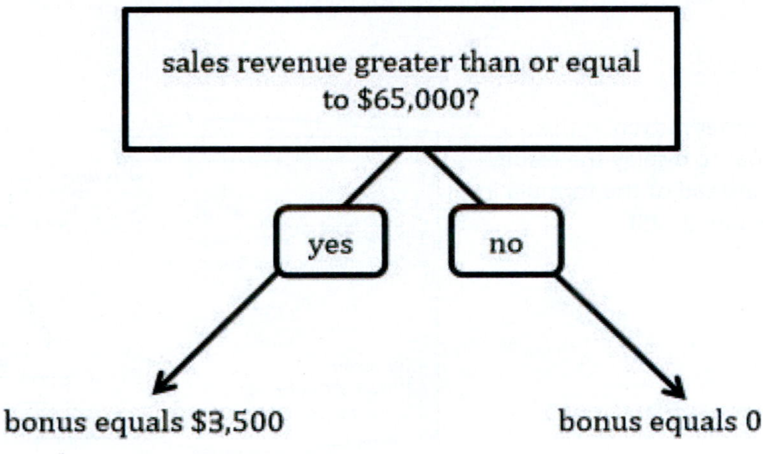

Figure 3–27

In Excel, you use the **IF function** when you want to assign a value to a cell based on a logical test. For example, cell B9 can be assigned the following IF function:

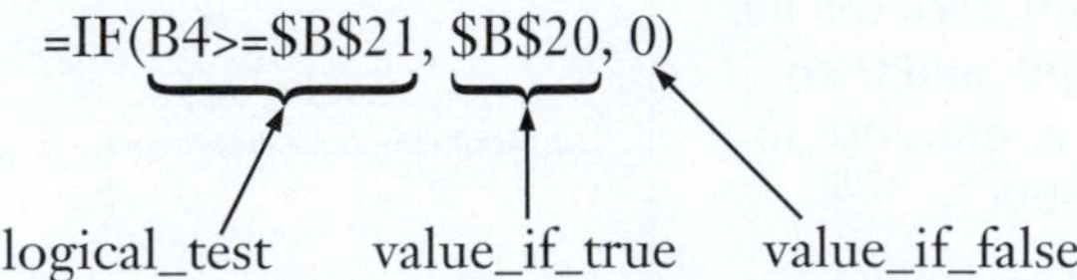

This IF function instructs Excel that if the projected January revenue in cell B4 is greater than or equal to the sales revenue for bonus value in cell B21, then Excel should display the bonus value found in cell B20 in cell B9. If the projected January revenue in cell B4 is not greater than or equal to the sales revenue for bonus value in cell B21, then Excel should display a 0 (zero) in cell B9.

The general form of the IF function is:

=IF(logical_test, value_if_true, value_if_false)

The argument, logical_test, is made up of two expressions and a comparison operator. Each expression can be a cell reference, a number, text, a function, or a formula. In this example, the logical test compares the projected revenue with the sales revenue for bonus, using the comparison operator greater than or equal to. Valid comparison operators, their meanings, and examples of their use in IF functions are shown in Table 3–8. The argument, value_if_true, is the value you want Excel to display in the cell when the logical test is true. The argument, value_if_false, is the value you want Excel to display in the cell when the logical test is false.

Table 3–8 Comparison Operators

Comparison Operator	Meaning	Example
=	Equal to	=IF(A1=A2, "True", "False")
<	Less than	=IF(A1<A2, "True", "False")
>	Greater than	=IF(A1>A2, "True", "False")
>=	Greater than or equal to	=IF(A1>=A2, "True", "False")
<=	Less than or equal to	=IF(A1<=A2, "True", "False")
<>	Not equal to	=IF(A1<>A2, "True", "False")

To Enter an IF Function

1 ENTER HEADINGS & DATA | 2 ENTER FORMULAS & FUNCTIONS | 3 CREATE SPARKLINE CHARTS
4 FORMAT WORKSHEET | 5 CREATE COLUMN CHART | 6 CHANGE VIEWS | 7 ASK WHAT-IF QUESTIONS

Why? *Use an IF function to determine the value for a cell based on a logical test.* The following steps assign the IF function =IF(B4>=B21,B20,0) to cell B9. This IF function determines whether or not the worksheet assigns a bonus for January.

- Click cell B9 to select the cell for the next formula.
- Click the Insert Function button in the formula bar to display the Insert Function dialog box.
- Click the 'Or select a category' arrow (Insert Function dialog box) and then select Logical in the list to populate the 'Select a function' list with logic functions.
- Click IF in the 'Select a function' list to select the required function (Figure 3–28).

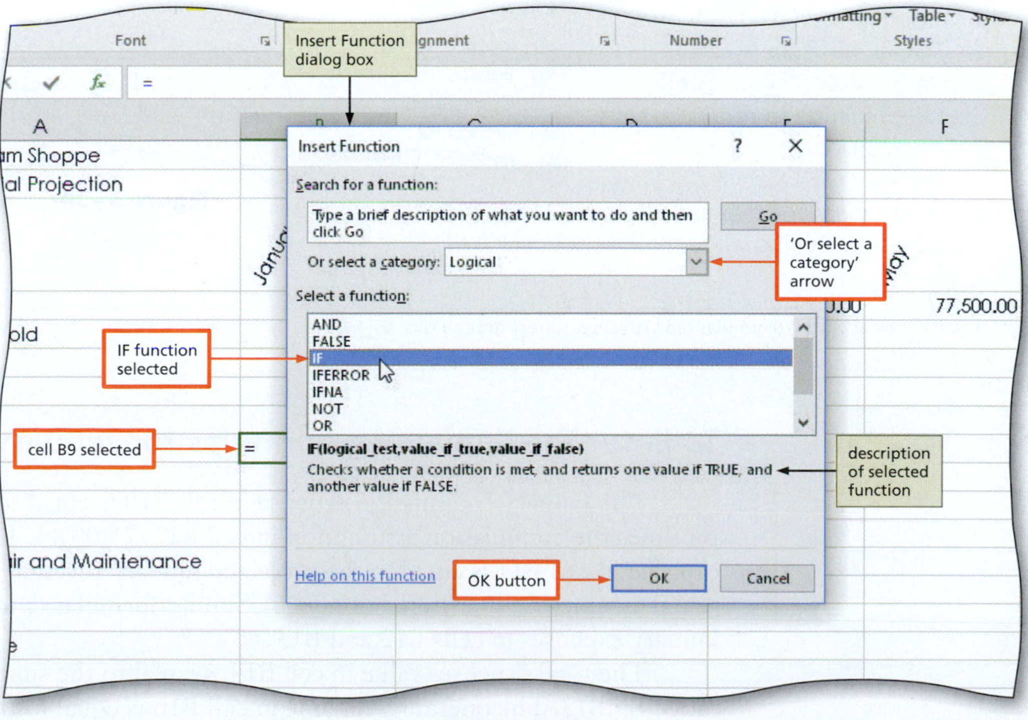

Figure 3–28

- Click the OK button (Insert Function dialog box) to display the Function Arguments dialog box.
- Type **b4>=b21** in the Logical_test box to enter a logical test for the IF function.
- Type **b20** in the Value_if_true box to enter the result of the IF function if the logical test is true.
- Type **0** (zero) in the Value_if_false box to enter the result of the IF function if the logical test is false (Figure 3–29).

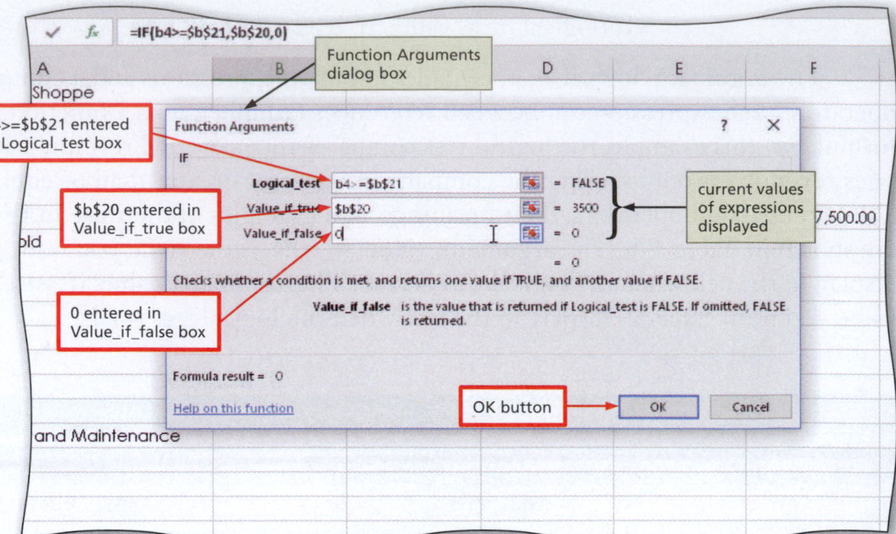

Figure 3–29

- Click the OK button (Function Arguments dialog box) to insert the IF function in the selected cell (Figure 3–30).

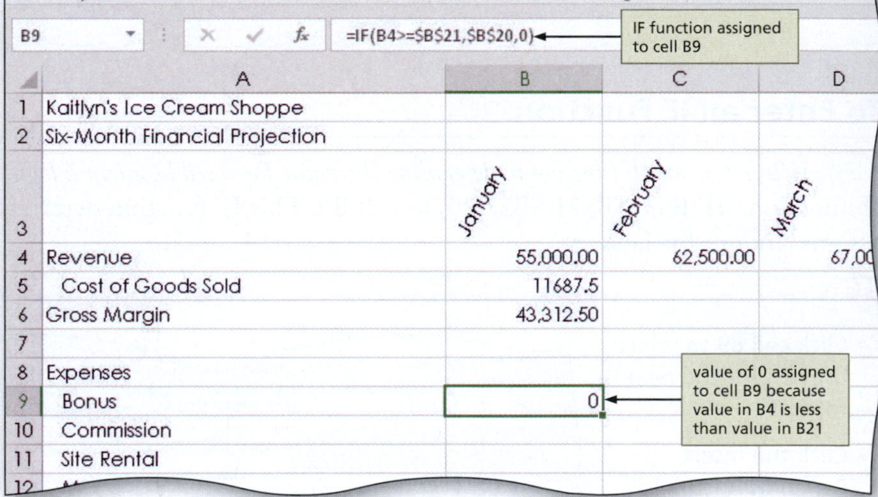

Figure 3–30

Q&A Why does cell B9 contain the value 0 (zero)?

The value that Excel displays in cell B9 depends on the values assigned to cells B4, B20, and B21. For example, if the value for January revenue in cell B4 is increased to 65,000.00 or higher, then the IF function in cell B9 will display 3,500.00. If you change the sales revenue for bonus in cell B21 from 65,000.00 to another number and the value in cell B4 is greater than or equal to the value in cell B21, it also will change the results in cell B9.

Other Ways

1. Click Logical button (Formulas tab | Function Library group), click IF

To Enter the Remaining Formulas for January

The January commission expense in cell B10 is equal to the revenue in cell B4 times the commission assumption in cell B22 (25.00%). The January site rental expense in cell B11 is equal to the projected January revenue in cell B4 times the site rental assumption in cell B23 (10.00%). Similar formulas determine the remaining January expenses in cells B12 and B13.

The total expenses value in cell B14 is equal to the sum of the expenses in the range B9:B13. The operating income in cell B16 is equal to the gross margin in cell B6 minus the total expenses in cell B14. Because the formulas are short, they are typed in the following steps, rather than entered using Point mode.

1. Select cell B10. Type **=b4*b22** and then press the DOWN ARROW key to enter the formula in the selected cell. Type **=b4*b23** and then press the DOWN ARROW key to enter the formula in cell B11. Type **=b4*b24,** press the DOWN ARROW key, type **=b4*b25,** and then press the DOWN ARROW key again.

2. With cell B14 selected, click the Sum button (Home tab | Editing group) twice to insert a SUM function in the selected cell. Select cell B16 to prepare to enter the next formula. Type **=b6-b14** and then press the ENTER key to enter the formula in the selected cell.

3. Press CTRL+ACCENT MARK (`) to display the formulas version of the worksheet (Figure 3–31).

4. When you are finished viewing the formulas version, press CTRL+ACCENT MARK (`) again to return to the values version of the worksheet.

Q&A Why should I view the formulas version of the worksheet?
Viewing the formulas version (Figure 3–31) of the worksheet allows you to check the formulas you entered in the range B5:B16. Recall that formulas were entered in lowercase. You can see that Excel converts all the formulas from lowercase to uppercase.

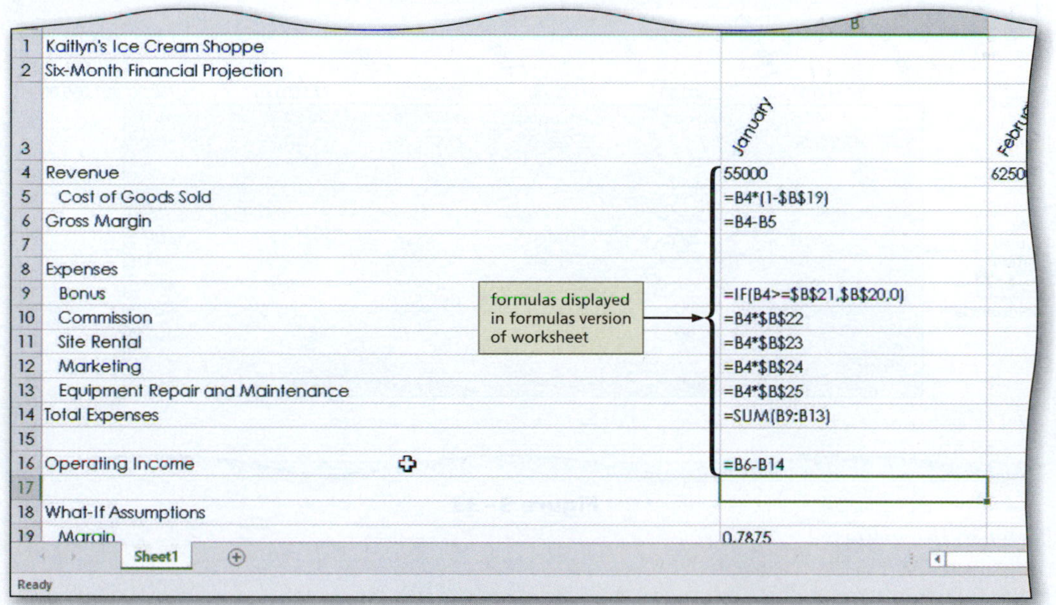

Figure 3–31

BTW
Replacing a Formula with a Constant
Using the following steps, you can replace a formula with its result so that the cell value remains constant: (1) click the cell with the formula; (2) press the F2 key or click in the formula bar; (3) press the F9 key to display the value in the formula bar; and (4) press the ENTER key.

BTW
Error Messages
When Excel cannot calculate a formula, it displays an error message in a cell. These error messages always begin with a number sign (#). The more commonly occurring error messages are as follows: #DIV/0! (tries to divide by zero); #NAME? (uses a name Excel does not recognize); #N/A (refers to a value not available); #NULL! (specifies an invalid intersection of two areas); #NUM! (uses a number incorrectly); #REF (refers to a cell that is not valid); #VALUE! (uses an incorrect argument or operand); and ##### (refers to cells not wide enough to display entire entry).

To Copy Formulas with Absolute Cell References Using the Fill Handle

1 ENTER HEADINGS & DATA | 2 ENTER FORMULAS & FUNCTIONS | 3 CREATE SPARKLINE CHARTS
4 FORMAT WORKSHEET | 5 CREATE COLUMN CHART | 6 CHANGE VIEWS | 7 ASK WHAT-IF QUESTIONS

Why? Using the fill handle ensures a quick, accurate copy of the formulas. The following steps use the fill handle to copy the January formulas in column B to the other five months in columns C through G.

- Select the range B5:B16 and then point to the fill handle in the lower-right corner of the selected cell, B16 in this case, to display the crosshair pointer (Figure 3–32).

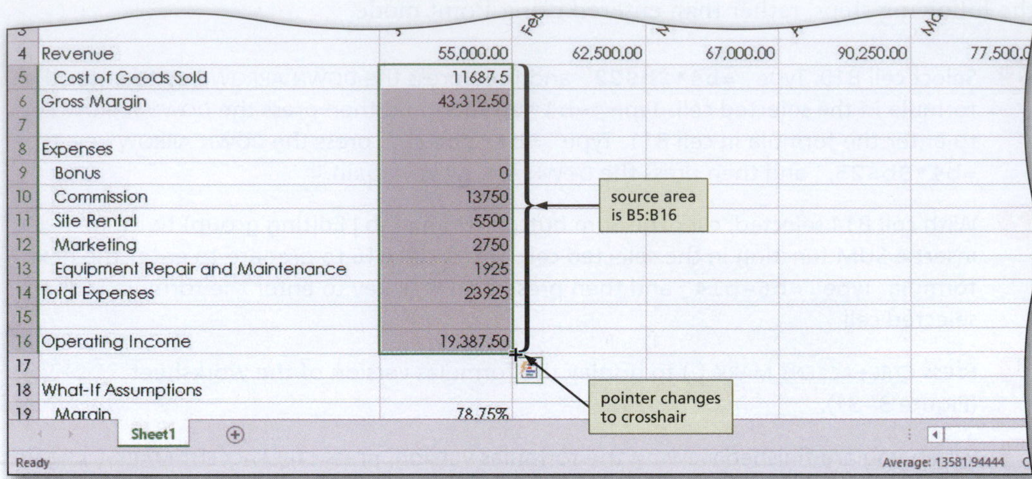

Figure 3–32

2

- Drag the fill handle to the right to copy the formulas from the source area, B5:B16 in this case, to the destination area, C5:G16 in this case, and display the calculated amounts (Figure 3–33).

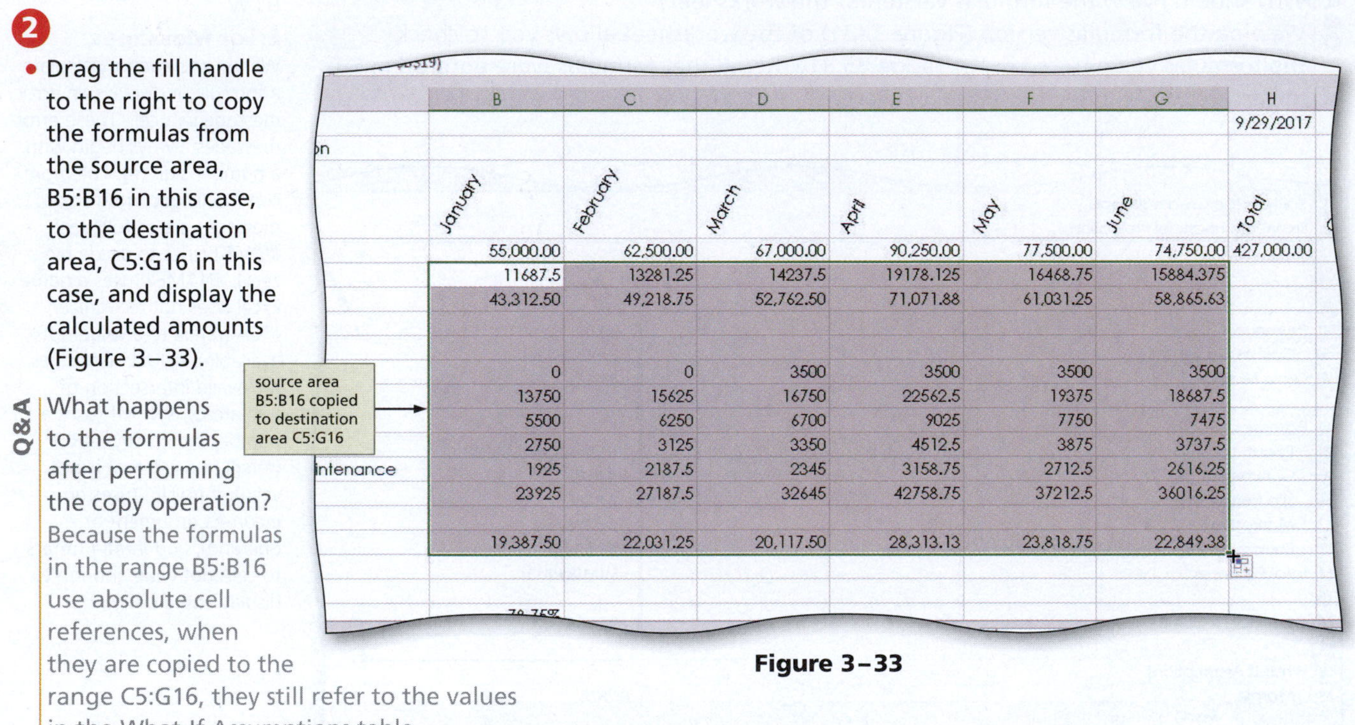

Figure 3–33

Q&A What happens to the formulas after performing the copy operation?
Because the formulas in the range B5:B16 use absolute cell references, when they are copied to the range C5:G16, they still refer to the values in the What-If Assumptions table.

To Determine Row Totals in Nonadjacent Cells

The following steps determine the row totals in column H. To determine the row totals using the Sum button, select only the cells in column H containing numbers in adjacent cells to the left. If, for example, you select the range H5:H16, Excel will display 0s as the sum of empty rows in cells H7, H8, and H15.

1. Select the range H5:H6. While holding down the CTRL key, select the range H9:H14 and cell H16, as shown in Figure 3–34.

2. Click the Sum button (Home tab | Editing group) to display the row totals in the selected ranges (Figure 3–34).

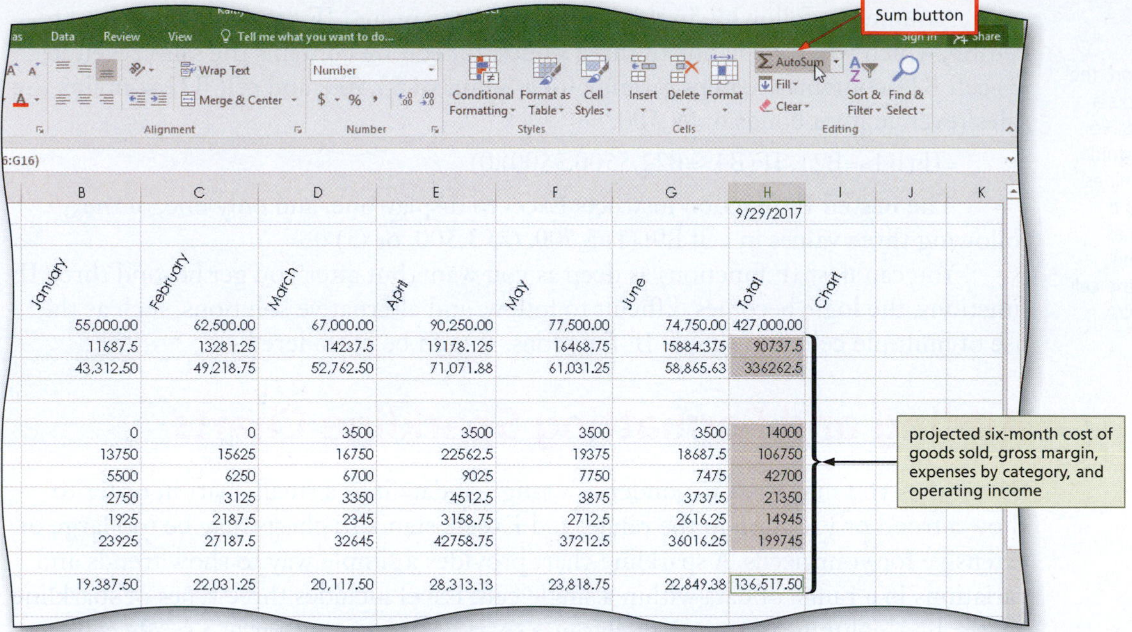

Figure 3–34

3 Save the workbook again on the same storage location with the same file name.

Nested Forms of the IF Function

A **nested IF function** is one in which the action to be taken for the true or false case includes yet another IF function. The second IF function is considered to be nested, or layered, within the first. You can use a nested IF function to add another condition to the decision-making process. Study the nested IF function below, which would add another level of bonus to the compensation at Kaitlyn's Ice Cream Shoppe. In this case, Kaitlyn's Ice Cream Shoppe assigns a bonus for sales of $65,000 and above. For months where sales make that level, additional bonus money is available for sales of $80,000 and above. In this case, three outcomes are possible, two of which involve paying a bonus. Figure 3–35 depicts a decision tree for this logical test.

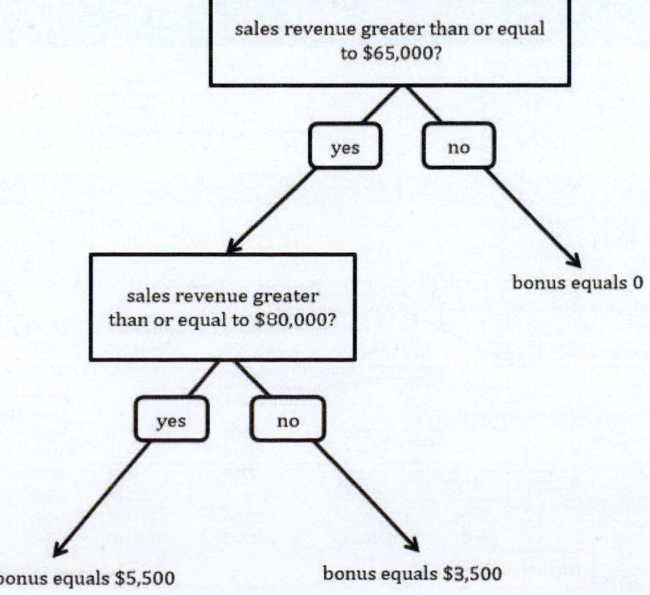

Figure 3–35

BTW
Using IFERROR
Similar to the IF function, the IFERROR function checks a formula for correctness. For example, =IFERROR(formula, "Error Message") examines the formula argument. If an error appears (such as #N/A), Excel displays the Error Message text in the cell instead of the Excel #N/A error.

Assume the following in this example: (1) the nested IF function is assigned to cell B9, which will display one of three values; (2) cell B4 contains the sales revenue; (3) cell B21 contains the sales revenue for a bonus of $3,500; and cell B22 contains the sales revenue for a bonus of $5,500.

=IF(B4>=B21, IF(B4>=B22,5500,3500),0)

The nested IF function instructs Excel to display one, and only one, of the following three values in cell B9: (1) 5,500, (2) 3,500, or (3) 0.

You can nest IF functions as deep as you want, but after you get beyond three IF functions, the logic becomes difficult to follow, and alternative solutions, such as the use of multiple cells and simple IF functions, should be considered.

Adding and Formatting Sparkline Charts

Sometimes you may want to condense a range of data into a small chart in order to show a trend or variation in the range, and Excel's standard charts may be too large or extensive for your needs. A sparkline chart provides a simple way to show trends and variations in a range of data within a single cell. Excel includes three types of sparkline charts: line, column, and win/loss. Because sparkline charts appear in a single cell, you can use them to convey succinct, eye-catching summaries of the data they represent.

To Add a Sparkline Chart to the Worksheet

1 ENTER HEADINGS & DATA | 2 ENTER FORMULAS & FUNCTIONS | **3 CREATE SPARKLINE CHARTS**
4 FORMAT WORKSHEET | 5 CREATE COLUMN CHART | 6 CHANGE VIEWS | 7 ASK WHAT-IF QUESTIONS

Each row of monthly data, including those containing formulas, provides useful information that can be summarized by a line sparkline chart. ***Why?*** *A line sparkline chart is a good choice because it shows trends over the six-month period for each row of data.* The following steps add a line sparkline chart to cell I4 and then use the fill handle to create line sparkline charts in the range I5:I16 to represent the monthly data shown in rows 4 through 16.

- If necessary, scroll the worksheet so that both columns B and I and row 3 are visible on the screen.
- Select cell I4 to prepare to insert a sparkline chart in the cell.
- Display the Insert tab and then click the Line Sparkline button (Insert tab | Sparklines group) to display the Create Sparklines dialog box (Figure 3–36).

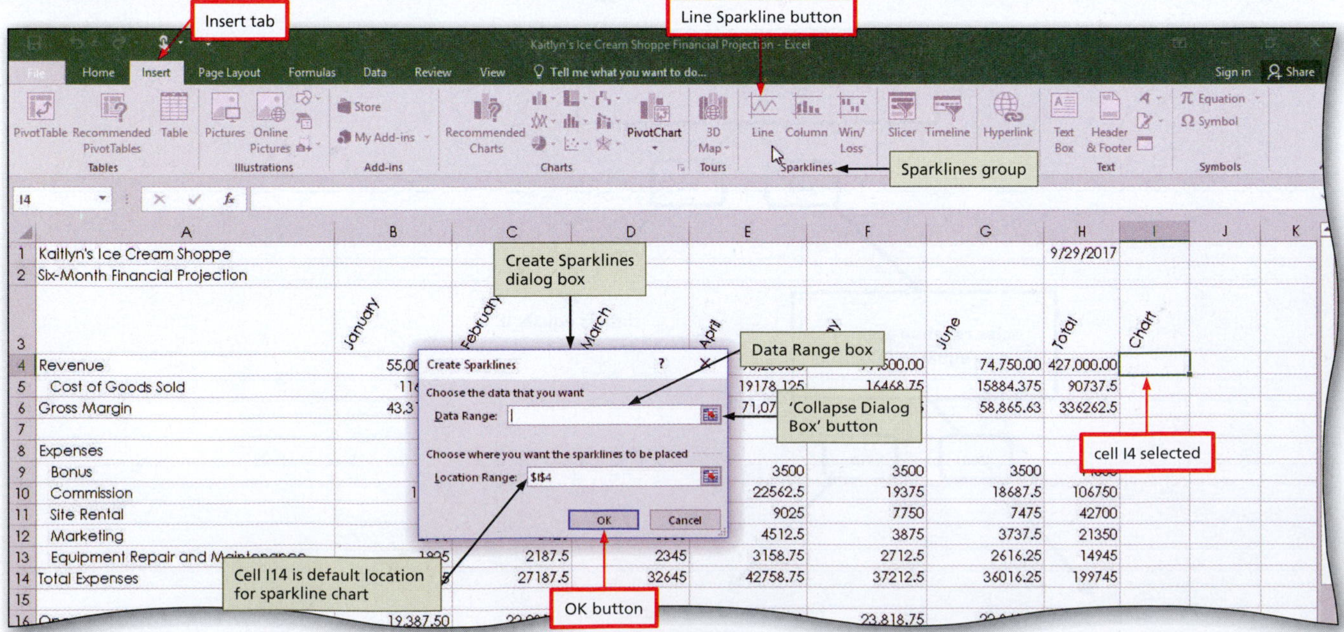

Figure 3–36

2

- Drag through the range B4:G4 to select the range. Do not release the mouse button (Figure 3–37).

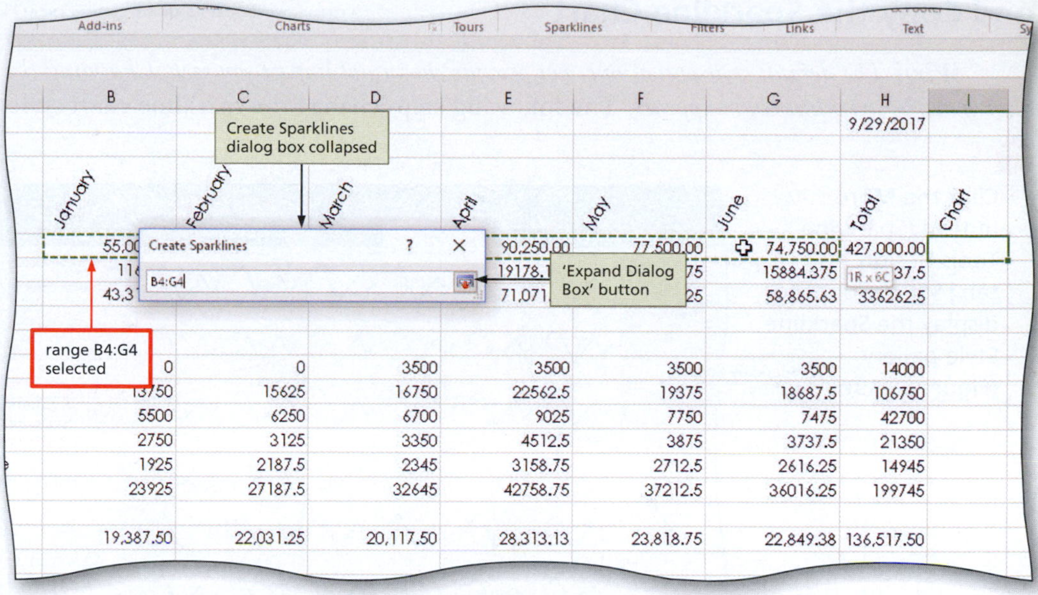

Q&A What happened to the Create Sparklines dialog box?

When a dialog box includes a 'Collapse Dialog Box' button (Figure 3–36), selecting cells or a range collapses the dialog box so that only the current text box is visible. This allows you to select your desired range without the dialog box getting in the way. Once the selection is made, the dialog box expands back to its original size. You also can click the 'Collapse Dialog Box' button to make your selection and then click the 'Expand Dialog Box' button (Figure 3–37) to expand the dialog box.

Create Sparklines dialog box collapsed
'Expand Dialog Box' button
range B4:G4 selected

Figure 3–37

3

- Release the mouse button to insert the selected range, B4:G4 in this case, in the Data Range box.
- Click the OK button shown in Figure 3–36 (Create Sparklines dialog box) to insert a line sparkline chart in the selected cell and display the Sparkline Tools Design tab (Figure 3–38).

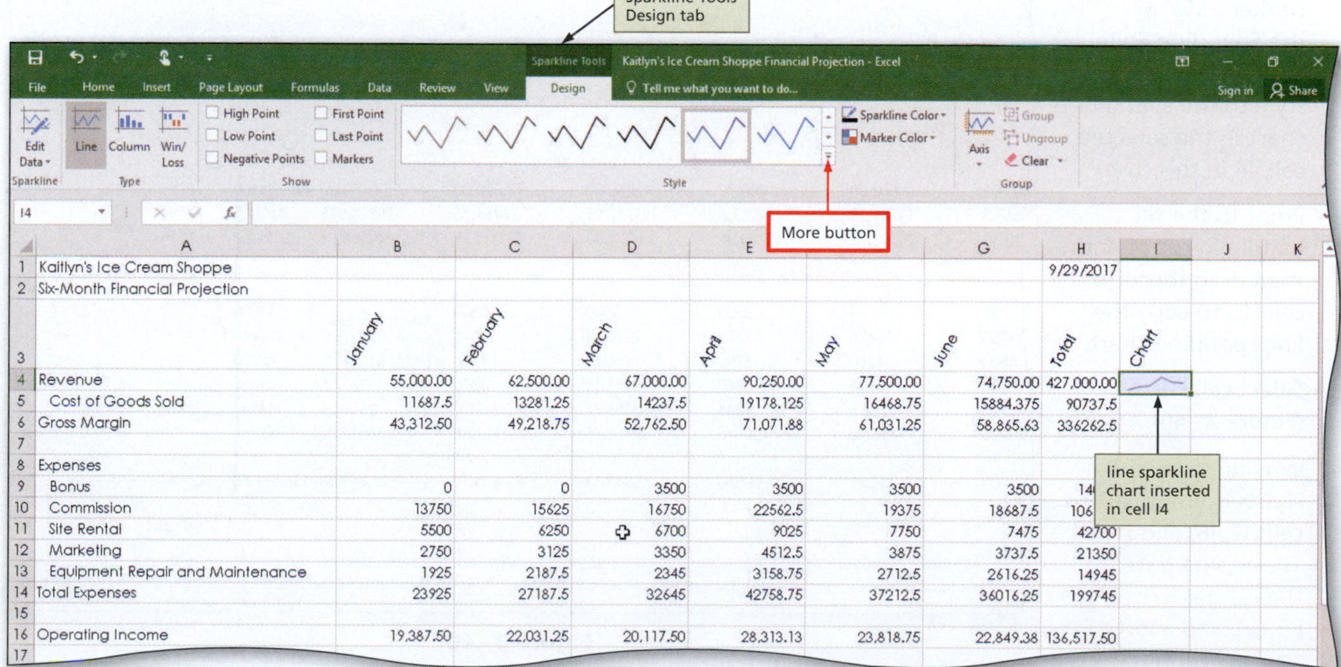

Figure 3–38

To Change the Sparkline Style and Copy the Sparkline Chart

1 ENTER HEADINGS & DATA | 2 ENTER FORMULAS & FUNCTIONS | 3 CREATE SPARKLINE CHARTS
4 FORMAT WORKSHEET | 5 CREATE COLUMN CHART | 6 CHANGE VIEWS | 7 ASK WHAT-IF QUESTIONS

Why? The default style option may not provide the visual impact you seek. Changing the sparkline style allows you to alter how the sparkline chart appears. The following steps change the sparkline chart style.

1

- Click the More button (Sparkline Tools Design tab | Style group) to display the Sparkline Style gallery (Figure 3–39).

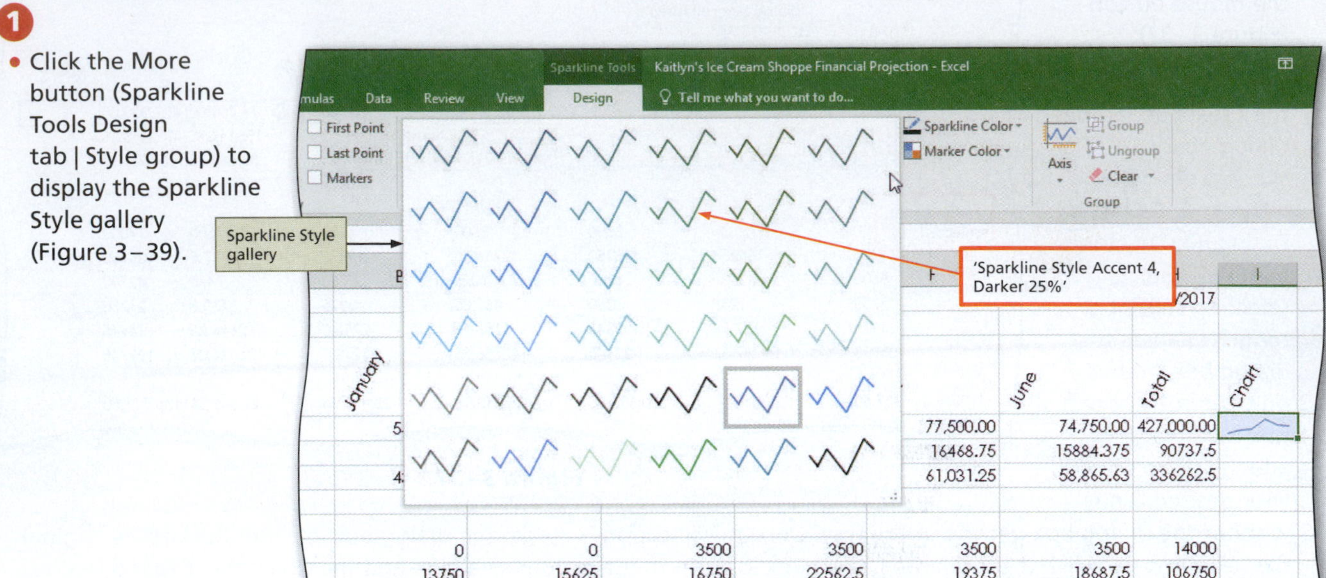

Figure 3–39

2

- Click 'Sparkline Style Accent 4, Darker 25%' in the Sparkline Style gallery to apply the style to the sparkline chart in the selected cell, I4 in this case.
- Point to the fill handle in cell I4 and then drag through cell I16 to copy the line sparkline chart.
- Select cell I18 (Figure 3–40).

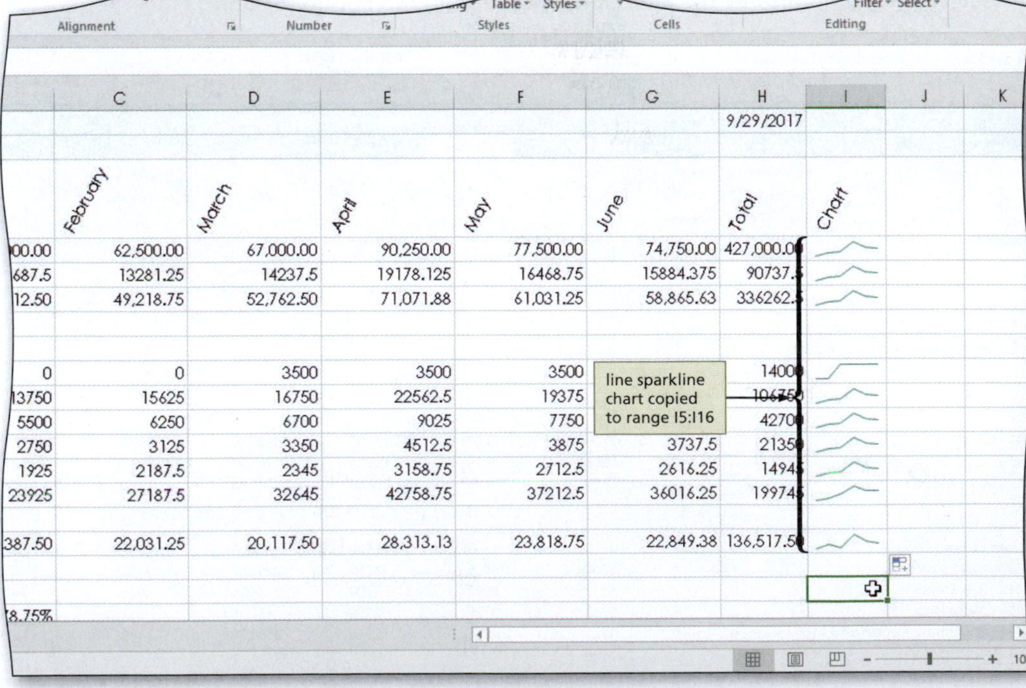

Figure 3–40

Q&A Why do sparkline charts not appear in cells I7, I8, and I15?
There is no data in the ranges B7:G7, B8:G8, and B15:G15, so Excel cannot draw sparkline charts. If you added data to cells in those ranges, Excel would then generate line sparkline charts for those rows, because the drag operation defined sparkline charts for cells I7, I8, and I15.

To Change the Sparkline Type

In addition to changing the sparkline chart style, you also can change the sparkline chart type. ***Why?*** *You may decide that a different chart type will better illustrate the characteristics of your data.* As shown in Figure 3–40, most of the sparkline charts look similar. Changing the sparkline chart type allows you to decide if a different chart type will better present your data to the reader. The following steps change the line sparkline charts to column sparkline charts.

1

- Select the range I4:I16 to select the sparkline charts.
- Click the Sparkline Tools Design tab to make it the active tab.
- Click the 'Convert to Column Sparkline' button (Sparkline Tools Design tab | Type group) to change the sparkline charts in the selected range to the column type (Figure 3–41).

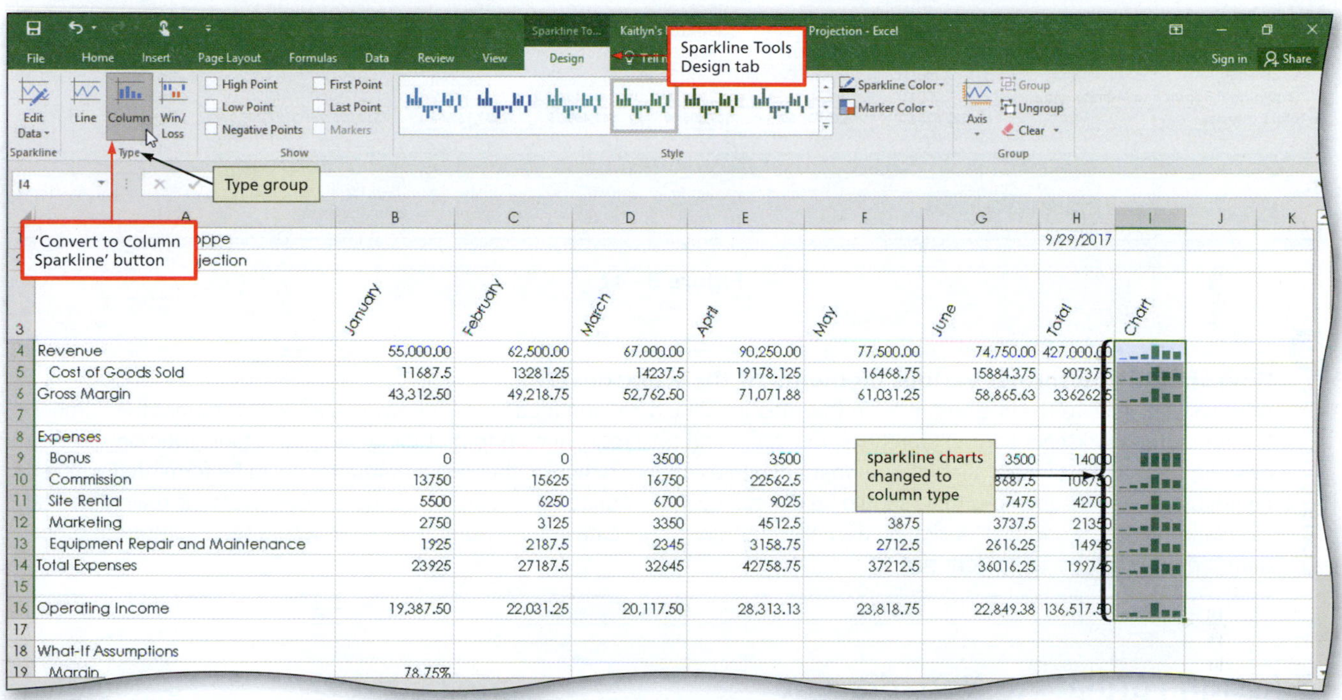

Figure 3–41

- Select cell I18.
- Save the workbook again on the same storage location with the same file name.

Formatting the Worksheet

The worksheet created thus far shows the financial projections for the six-month period, from January to June. Its appearance is uninteresting, however, even though some minimal formatting (formatting assumptions numbers, changing the column widths, formatting the date, and formatting the sparkline chart) was performed earlier. This section completes the formatting of the worksheet by making the numbers easier to read and emphasizing the titles, assumptions, categories, and totals, as shown in Figure 3–42.

BTW

Customizing Sparkline Charts

You can customize sparkline charts in a number of ways on the Sparkline Tools Design tab. In the Show group (Sparkline Tools Design tab), you can specify values to show as markers on the chart, such as the highest value, lowest value, any negative numbers, the first point, and the last point. You can change the color of the sparkline and markers in the Style group (Sparkline Tools Design tab).

Kaitlyn's Ice Cream Shoppe

Six-Month Financial Projection

9/29/2017

	January	February	March	April	May	June	Total	Chart
Revenue	$55,000.00	$62,500.00	$67,000.00	$90,250.00	$77,500.00	$74,750.00	$427,000.00	
Cost of Goods Sold	11,687.50	13,281.25	14,237.50	19,178.13	16,468.75	15,884.38	90,737.50	
Gross Margin	$43,312.50	$49,218.75	$52,762.50	$71,071.88	$61,031.25	$58,865.63	$336,262.50	
Expenses								
Bonus	$0.00	$0.00	$5,000.00	$5,000.00	$5,000.00	$5,000.00	$20,000.00	
Commission	12,375.00	14,062.50	15,075.00	20,306.25	17,437.50	16,818.75	96,075.00	
Site Rental	5,500.00	6,250.00	6,700.00	9,025.00	7,750.00	7,475.00	42,700.00	
Marketing	2,750.00	3,125.00	3,350.00	4,512.50	3,875.00	3,737.50	21,350.00	
Equipment Repair and Maintenance	2,200.00	2,500.00	2,680.00	3,610.00	3,100.00	2,990.00	17,080.00	
Total Expenses	$22,825.00	$25,937.50	$32,805.00	$42,453.75	$37,162.50	$36,021.25	$197,205.00	
Operating Income	$20,487.50	$23,281.25	$19,957.50	$28,618.13	$23,868.75	$22,844.38	$139,057.50	

title and subtitle formatted

range A1:I2 formatted

currency style with floating dollar sign

Figure 3–42

CONSIDER THIS

How should you format various elements of the worksheet?

A worksheet, such as the one presented in this module, should be formatted in the following manner: (1) format the numbers; (2) format the worksheet title, column titles, row titles, and total rows; and (3) format the assumptions table. Numbers in heading rows and total rows should be formatted with a currency symbol. Other dollar amounts should be formatted with a comma style. The assumptions table should be diminished in its formatting so that it does not distract from the main data and calculations in the worksheet. Assigning a smaller font size to the data in the assumptions table would set it apart from other data formatted with a larger font size.

To Assign Formats to Nonadjacent Ranges

1 ENTER HEADINGS & DATA | 2 ENTER FORMULAS & FUNCTIONS | 3 CREATE SPARKLINE CHARTS
4 FORMAT WORKSHEET | 5 CREATE COLUMN CHART | 6 CHANGE VIEWS | 7 ASK WHAT-IF QUESTIONS

The following steps assign formats to the numbers in rows 4 through 16. ***Why?*** *These formats increase the readability of the data.*

- Select the range B4:H4 as the first range to format.
- While holding down the CTRL key, select the nonadjacent ranges B6:H6, B9:H9, B14:H14, and B16:H16, and then release the CTRL key to select nonadjacent ranges.
- Click the Number Format Dialog Box Launcher (Home tab | Number group) to display the Format Cells dialog box.
- Click Currency in the Category list (Format Cells dialog box), if necessary select 2 in the Decimal places box and then select $ in the Symbol list to ensure a dollar sign shows in the cells to be formatted, and select the black font color ($1,234.10) in the Negative numbers list to specify the desired currency style for the selected ranges (Figure 3–43).

Q&A Why was this particular style chosen for the negative numbers?

In accounting, negative numbers often are shown with parentheses surrounding the value rather than with a negative sign preceding the value. Although the data being used in this module contains no negative numbers, you still must select a negative number format. It is important to be consistent when selecting negative number formats if you are applying different formats in a column; otherwise, the decimal points may not line up.

Q&A Why is the Format Cells dialog box used to create the format for the ranges in this step?
The requirements for this worksheet call for a floating dollar sign. You can use the Format Cells dialog box to assign a currency style with a floating dollar sign, instead of using the 'Accounting Number Format' button (Home tab | Number group), which assigns a fixed dollar sign.

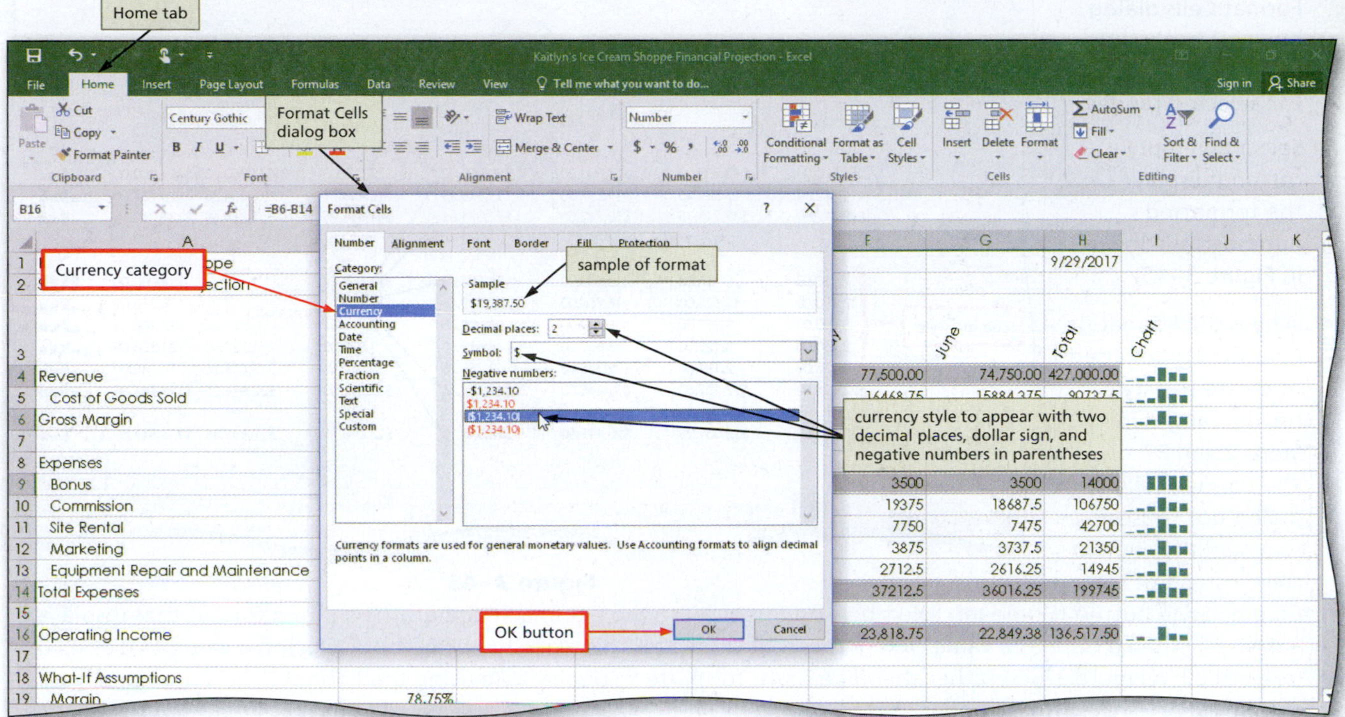

Figure 3–43

2

- Click the OK button (Format Cells dialog box) to close the Format Cells dialog box and apply the desired format to the selected ranges.
- Select the range B5:H5 as the next range to format.
- While holding down the CTRL key, select the range B10:H13, and then release the CTRL key to select nonadjacent ranges.
- Click the Number Format Dialog Box Launcher (Home tab | Number group) to display the Format Cells dialog box.
- Click Currency in the Category list (Format Cells dialog box), if necessary select 2 in the Decimal places box, select None in the Symbol list so that a dollar sign does not show in the cells to be formatted, and select the black font color (1,234.10) in the Negative numbers list (Figure 3–44).

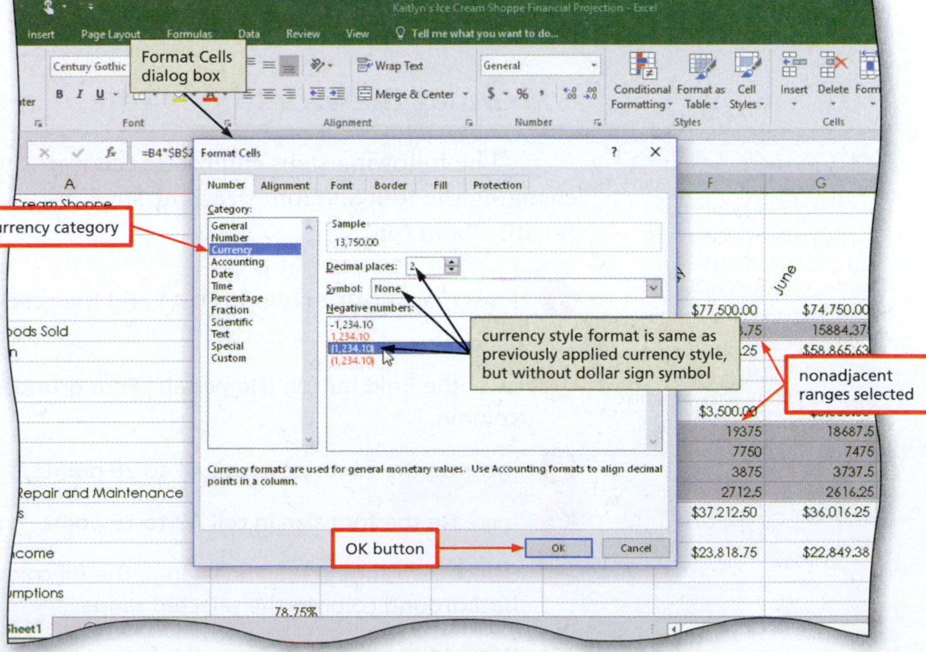

Figure 3–44

- Click the OK button (Format Cells dialog box) to close the Format Cells dialog box and apply the desired format to the selected ranges.
- Select an empty cell and display the formatted numbers, as shown in Figure 3–45.

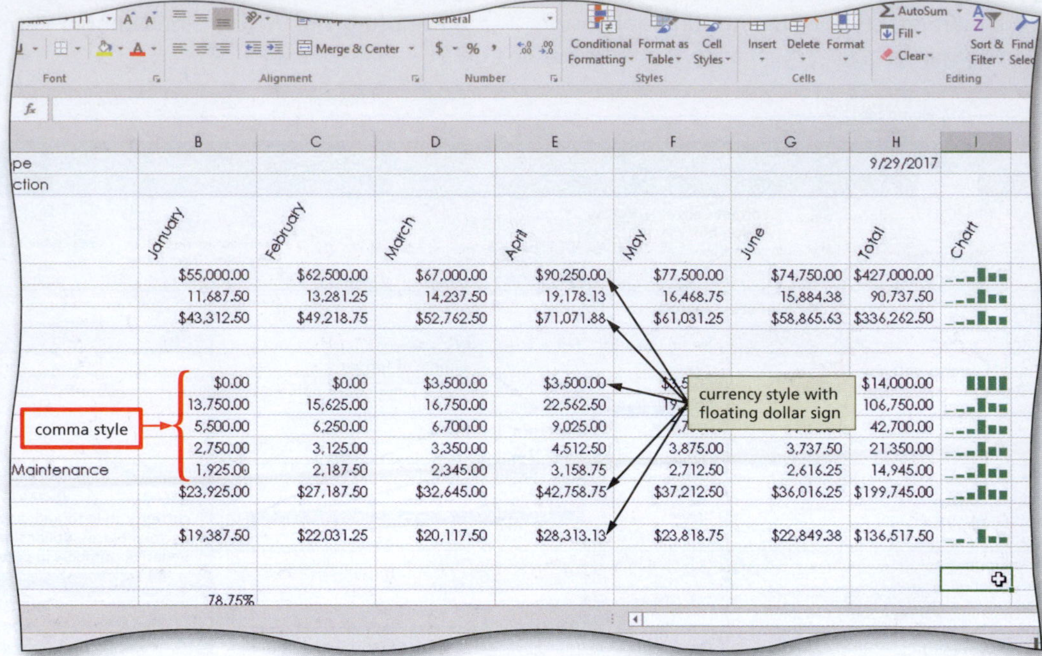

Figure 3–45

Q&A Why is the Format Cells dialog box used to create the style for the ranges in Steps 2 and 3?
The Format Cells dialog box is used to assign the comma style instead of the Comma Style button (Home tab | Number group), because the Comma Style button assigns a format that displays a dash (–) when a cell has a value of 0. The specifications for this worksheet call for displaying a value of 0 as 0.00 (see cell B9 in Figure 3–45) rather than as a dash. To create a comma style using the Format Cells dialog box, you use a currency style with no dollar sign.

Other Ways

1. Right-click range, click Format Cells on shortcut menu, click Number tab (Format Cells dialog box), click category in Category list, select format, click OK button (Format Cells dialog box)
2. Press CTRL+1, click Number tab (Format Cells dialog box), click category in Category list, select format, click OK button (Format Cells dialog box)

BTW

Toggle Commands

Many of the commands on the ribbon, in galleries, and as shortcut keys function as toggles. For example, if you click Freeze Panes in the Freeze Panes gallery, the command changes to Unfreeze Panes the next time you view the gallery. These types of commands work like on-off switches, or toggles.

To Format the Worksheet Titles

The following steps emphasize the worksheet titles in cells A1 and A2 by changing the font and font size. The steps also format all of the row headers in column A with a bold font style.

1. Press CTRL+HOME to select cell A1 and then click the column A heading to select the column.
2. Click the Bold button (Home tab | Font group) to bold all of the data in the selected column.
3. Increase the font size in cell A1 to 28 point.
4. Increase the font size in cell A2 to 16 point.
5. Select the range A1:I2 and change the fill color to Green, Accent 4 to add a background color to the selected range.
6. With A1:I2 selected, change the font color to White, Background 1.
7. Click an empty cell to deselect the range (Figure 3–46).

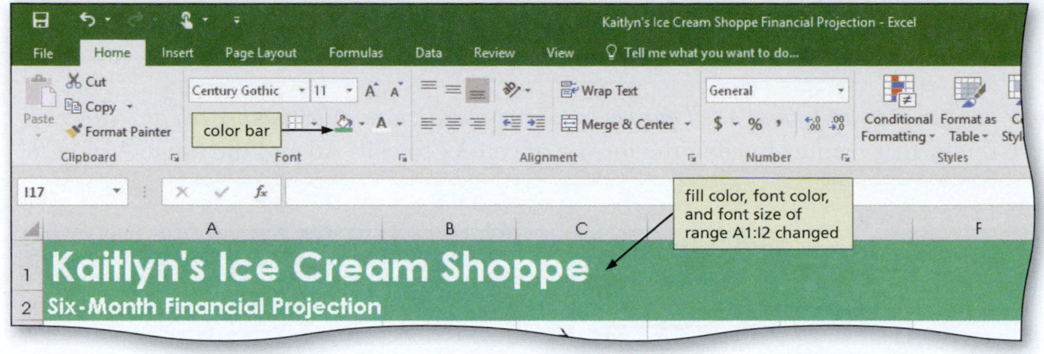

Figure 3–46

Other Ways

1. Right-click range, click Format Cells on shortcut menu, click Fill tab (Format Cells dialog box) to color background (or click Font tab to color font), click OK button
2. Press CTRL+1, click Fill tab (Format Cells dialog box) to color background (or click Font tab to color font), click OK button

To Assign Cell Styles to Nonadjacent Rows and Colors to a Cell

The following steps improve the appearance of the worksheet by formatting the headings in row 3 and the totals in rows 6, 14, and 16. Cell A4 also is formatted with a background color and font color.

1. Select the range A3:I3 and apply the Heading 2 cell style.
2. Select the range A6:H6 and while holding down the CTRL key, select the ranges A14:H14 and A16:H16.
3. Apply the Total cell style to the selected nonadjacent ranges.
4. Select cell A4 and click the Fill Color button (Home tab | Font group) to apply the last fill color used (Green, Accent 4) to the cell contents.
5. Click the Font Color button (Home tab | Font group) to apply the last font color used (White, Background 1) to the cell contents (Figure 3–47).

BTW

The Fill and Font Color Buttons

You may have noticed that the color bar at the bottom of the Fill Color and Font Color buttons (Home tab | Font group) (Figure 3–46) changes to the most recently selected color. To apply this same color to a cell background or text, select a cell and then click the Fill Color button to use the color as a background or click the Font Color button to use the color as a font color.

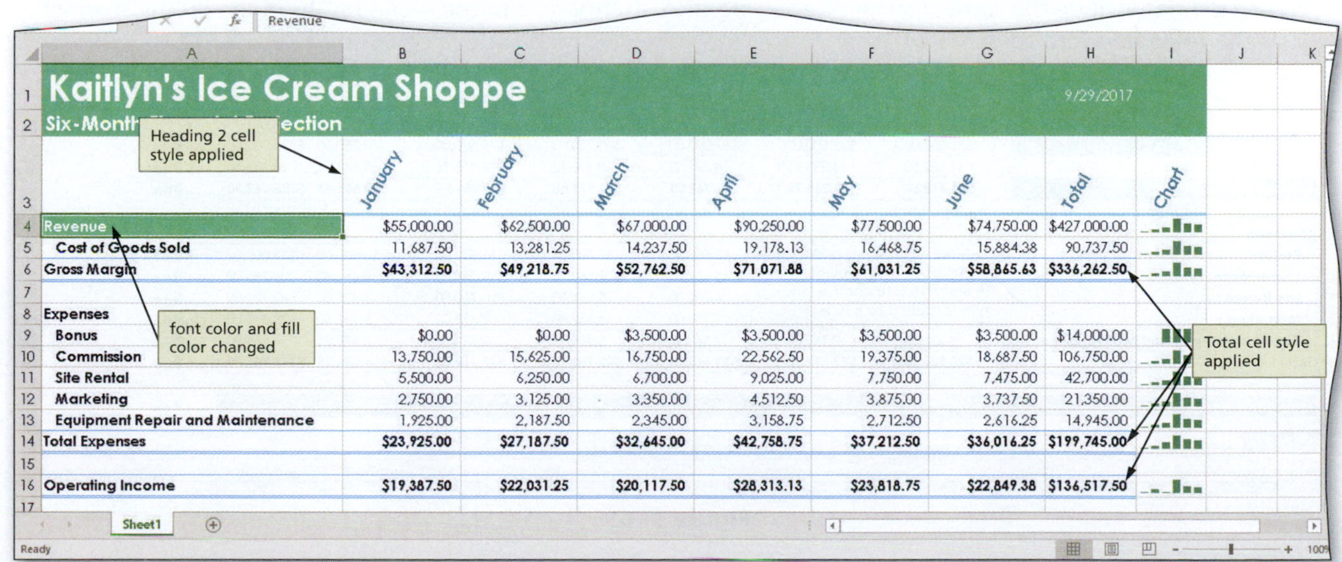

Figure 3–47

To Copy a Cell's Format Using the Format Painter Button

1 ENTER HEADINGS & DATA | 2 ENTER FORMULAS & FUNCTIONS | 3 CREATE SPARKLINE CHARTS
4 FORMAT WORKSHEET | 5 CREATE COLUMN CHART | 6 CHANGE VIEWS | 7 ASK WHAT-IF QUESTIONS

***Why?** Using the format painter, you can format a cell quickly by copying a cell's format to another cell or a range of cells.* The following steps use the format painter to copy the format of cell A4 to cells A6 and the range A16:H16.

1

- If necessary, click cell A4 to select a source cell for the format to paint.
- Double-click the Format Painter button (Home tab | Clipboard group) and then move the pointer onto the worksheet to cause the pointer to change to a block plus sign with a paintbrush (Figure 3–48).

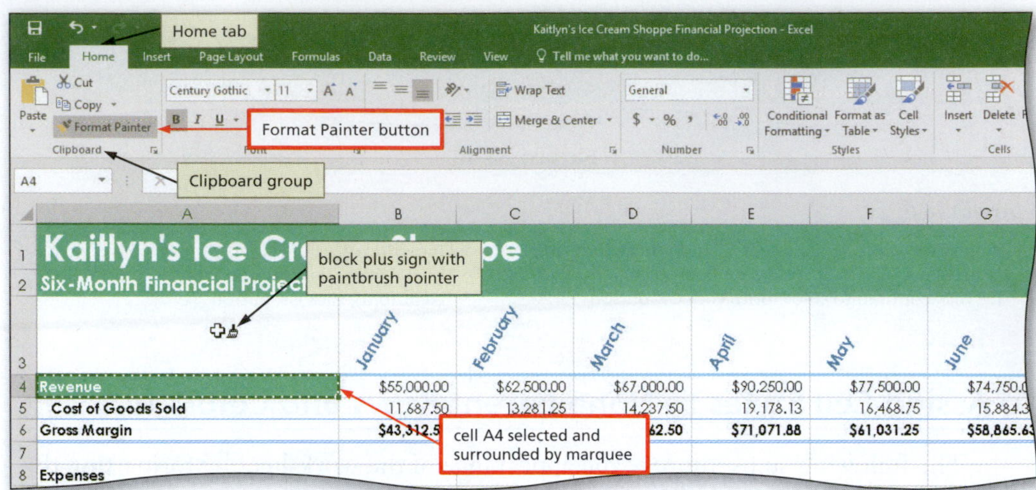

Figure 3–48

2

- Click cell A6 to assign the format of the source cell, A4 in this case, to the destination cell, A6 in this case.
- With the pointer still a block plus sign with a paintbrush, drag through the range A16:H16 to assign the format of the source cell, A4 in this case, to the destination range, A16:H16 in this case.
- Click the Format Painter button or press the ESC key to turn off the format painter.
- Apply the currency style to the range B16:H16 to cause the cells in the range to appear with a floating dollar sign and two decimal places (Figure 3–49).

Q&A Why does the currency style need to be reapplied to the range B16:H16?

Sometimes, the use of the format painter results in unintended outcomes. In this case, changing the background fill color and font color for the range B16:H16 resulted in the loss of the currency style because the format being copied did not include the currency style. Reapplying the currency style to the range results in the proper number style, fill color, and font color.

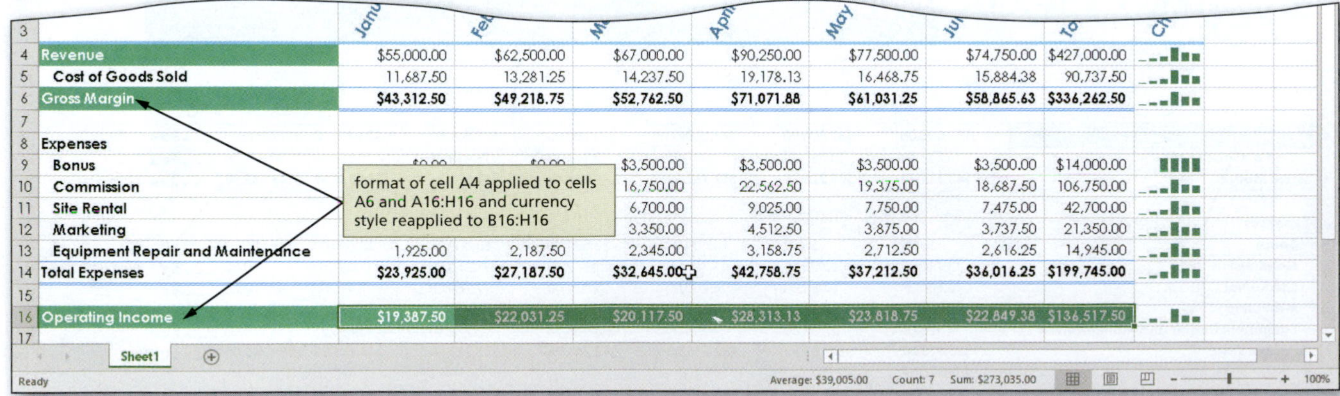

Figure 3–49

Other Ways

1. Click Copy button (Home tab | Clipboard group), select cell, click Paste arrow (Home tab | Clipboard group), click Formatting button in Paste gallery
2. Right-click cell, click Copy on shortcut menu, right-click cell, click Formatting icon on shortcut menu

To Format the What-If Assumptions Table

The following steps format the What-If Assumptions table, the final step in improving the appearance of the worksheet.

1. Select cell A18.
2. Change the font size to 8 pt.
3. Italicize and underline the text in cell A18.
4. Select the range A19:B25, and change the font size to 8 pt.
5. Select the range A18:B25 and then click the Fill Color button (Home tab | Font group) to apply the most recently used background color to the selected range.
6. Click the Font Color button (Home tab | Font group) to apply the most recently used font color to the selected range.
7. Deselect the range A18:B25 and display the What-If Assumptions table, as shown in Figure 3–50.
8. Save the workbook on the same storage location with the same file name.

Q&A What happens when I click the Italic and Underline buttons?

When you assign the italic font style to a cell, Excel slants the characters slightly to the right, as shown in cell A18 in Figure 3–50. The underline format underlines only the characters in the cell, rather than the entire cell, as is the case when you assign a cell a bottom border.

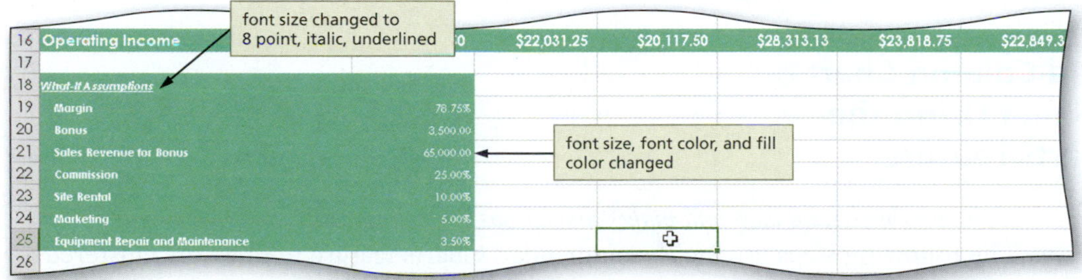

Figure 3–50

BTW
Painting a Format to Nonadjacent Ranges
Double-click the Format Painter button (Home tab | Clipboard group) and then drag through the nonadjacent ranges to paint the formats to the ranges. Click the Format Painter button again to deactivate it.

BTW
Selecting Nonadjacent Ranges
One of the more difficult tasks to learn is selecting nonadjacent ranges. To complete this task, do not hold down the CTRL key when you select the first range because Excel will consider the current active cell to be the first selection, and you may not want the current active cell in the selection. Once the first range is selected, hold down the CTRL key and drag through the nonadjacent ranges. If a desired range is not visible in the window, use the scroll arrows to view the range. You need not hold down the CTRL key while you scroll.

Break Point: If you wish to take a break, this is a good place to do so. You can exit Excel now. To resume at a later time, run Excel, open the file called Kaitlyn's Ice Cream Shoppe Financial Projection, and continue following the steps from this location forward.

Adding a Clustered Column Chart to the Workbook

The next step in the module is to create a clustered column chart on a separate sheet in the workbook, as shown in Figure 3–51. Use a clustered column chart to compare values side by side, broken down by category. Each column shows the value for a particular category, by month in this case.

The clustered column chart in Figure 3–51 shows the projected expense amounts, by category, for each of the six months. The clustered column chart allows the user to see how the various expense categories compare with each other each month, and across months.

Recall that charts can either be embedded in a worksheet or placed on a separate chart sheet. The clustered column chart will reside on its own sheet, because if placed on the worksheet, it would not be visible when the worksheet first opens and could be missed.

BTW
Charts
When you change a value on which a chart is dependent, Excel immediately redraws the chart based on the new value. With bar charts, you can drag the bar in the chart in one direction or another to change the corresponding value in the worksheet.

BTW
Chart Items
When you rest the pointer over a chart item, such as a legend, bar, or axis, Excel displays a chart tip containing the name of the item.

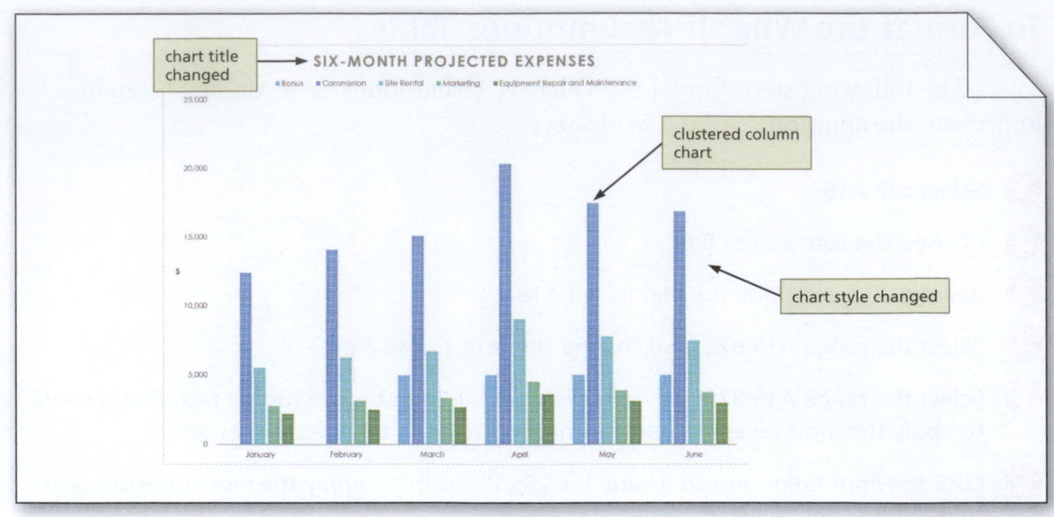

Figure 3–51

In this worksheet, the ranges to chart are the nonadjacent ranges B3:G3 (month names) and A9:G13 (monthly projected expenses, by category). The month names in the range B3:G3 will identify the major groups for the chart; these entries are called **category names**. The range A9:G13 contains the data that determines the individual columns in each month cluster, along with the names that identify each column; these entries are called the **data series**. Because six months of five expense categories are being charted, the chart will contain six clusters of five columns each, unless a category has the value of zero for a given month.

To Draw a Clustered Column Chart on a Separate Chart Sheet Using the Recommended Charts Feature

1 ENTER HEADINGS & DATA | 2 ENTER FORMULAS & FUNCTIONS | 3 CREATE SPARKLINE CHARTS
4 FORMAT WORKSHEET | **5 CREATE COLUMN CHART** | 6 CHANGE VIEWS | 7 ASK WHAT-IF QUESTIONS

Why? This Excel feature evaluates the selected data and makes suggestions regarding which chart types will provide the most suitable representation. The following steps use the Recommended Charts feature to draw the clustered column chart on a separate chart sheet.

1

- Select the range A3:G3 to identify the range of the categories.
- Hold down the CTRL key and select the data range A9:G13.
- Display the Insert tab.
- Click the Recommended Charts button (Insert tab | Charts group) to display the Insert Chart dialog box with the Recommended Charts tab active (Figure 3–52).

Experiment

- Click the various recommended chart types, reading the description for each of its best use and examining the chart preview.

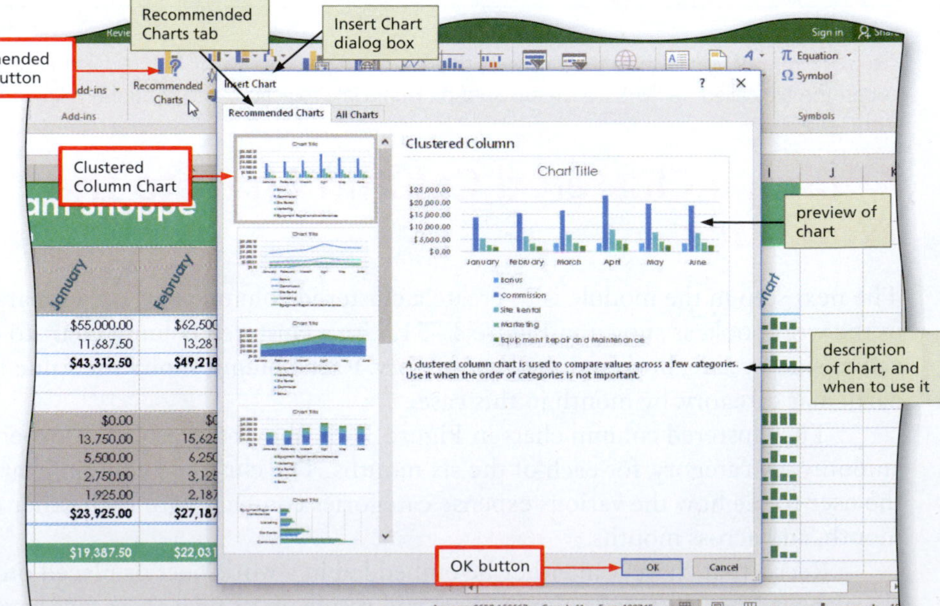

Figure 3–52

2

- Click the first Clustered Column recommended chart to select it and then click the OK button (Insert Chart dialog box).
- When Excel draws the chart, click the Move Chart button (Chart Tools Design tab | Location group) to display the Move Chart dialog box.
- Click New sheet (Move Chart dialog box) and then type **Expense Chart** in the New sheet text box to enter a sheet tab name for the chart sheet (Figure 3–53).

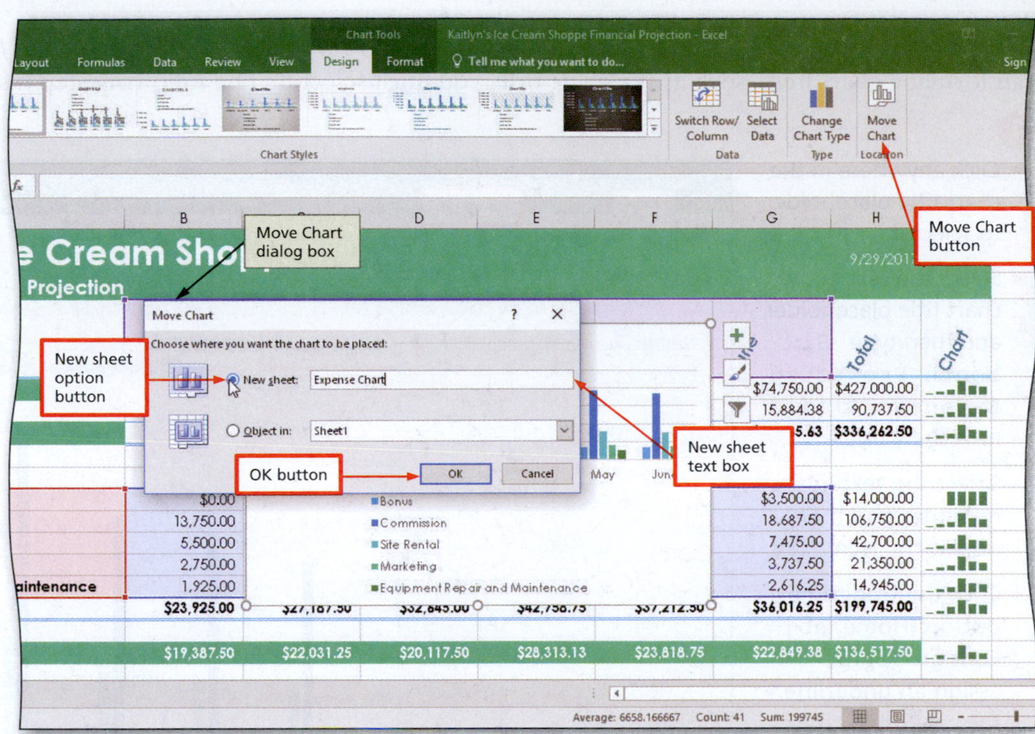

Figure 3–53

3

- Click the OK button (Move Chart dialog box) to move the chart to a new chart sheet with a new sheet tab name, Expense Chart (Figure 3–54).

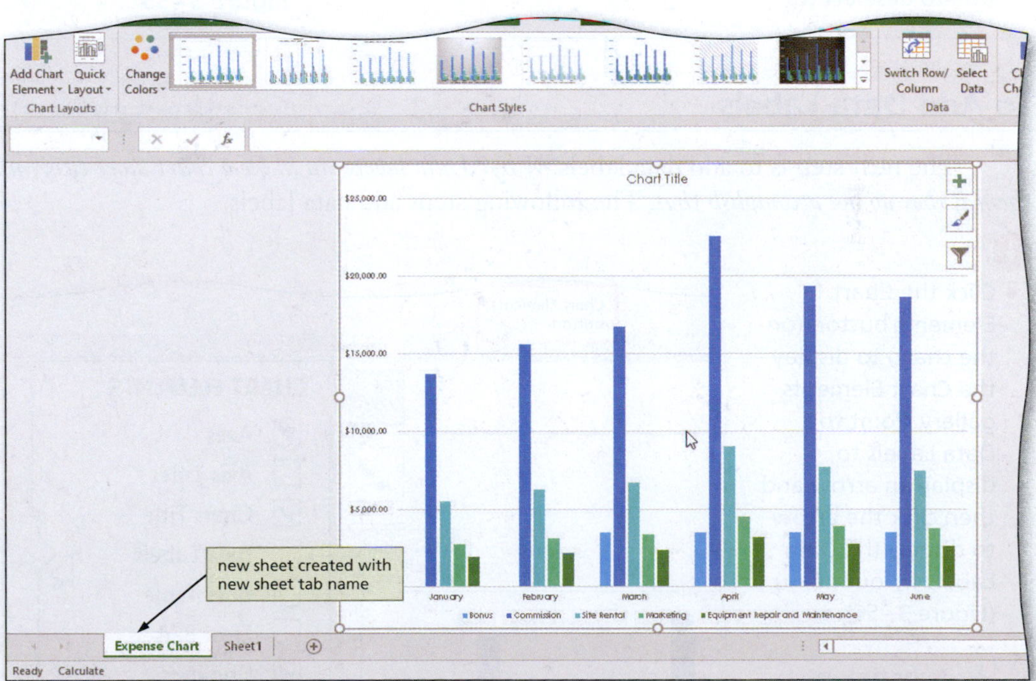

Figure 3–54

Q&A Why do January and February have only four columns charted?
Both January and February have a value of $0 for the Bonus category. Values of zero are not charted in a column chart, so these two months have one fewer column than the other months.

Other Ways

1. Select range to chart, PRESS F11

To Insert a Chart Title

The next step is to insert a chart title. ***Why?*** *A chart title identifies the chart content for the viewer.* Before you can format a chart item, such as the chart title, you must select it. The following step inserts a chart title.

- Click anywhere in the chart title placeholder to select it.
- Select the text in the chart title placeholder and then type `Six-Month Projected Expenses` to add a new chart title.
- Select the text in the new title and then display the Home tab.
- Click the Underline button (Home tab | Font group) to assign an underline format to the chart title (Figure 3–55).
- Click anywhere outside of the chart title to deselect it.

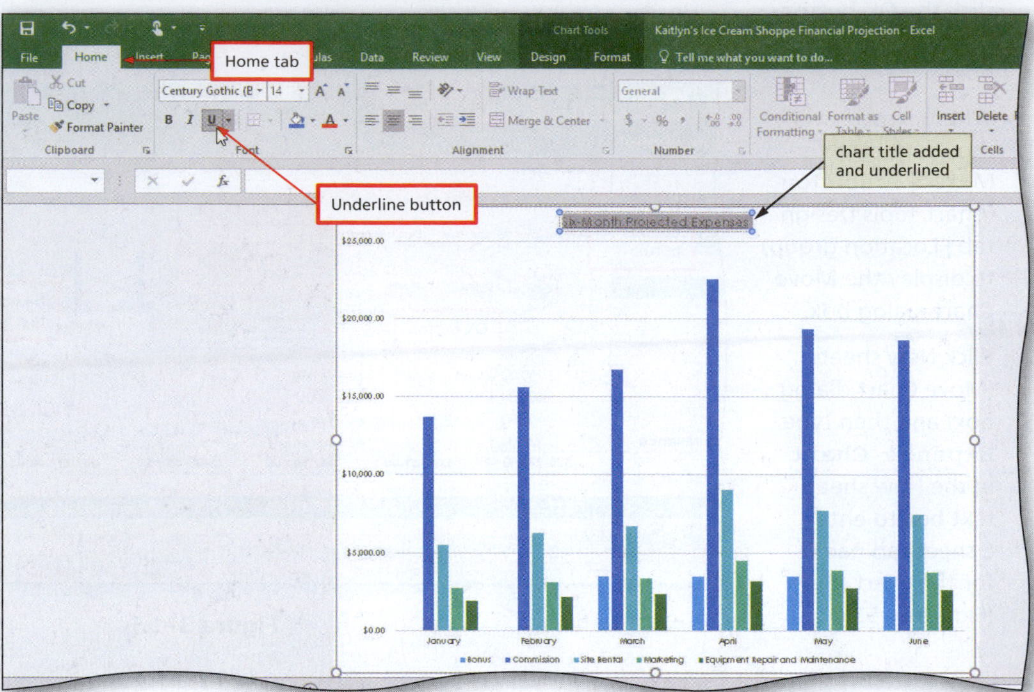

Figure 3–55

To Add Data Labels

The next step is to add data labels. ***Why?*** *Data labels can make a chart more easily understood. You can remove them if they do not accomplish that.* The following steps add data labels.

- Click the Chart Elements button (on the chart) to display the Chart Elements gallery. Point to Data Labels to display an arrow and then click the arrow to display the Data Labels fly-out menu (Figure 3–56).

Experiment

- If you are using a mouse, point to each option on the Data Labels fly-out menu to see a live preview of the data labels.

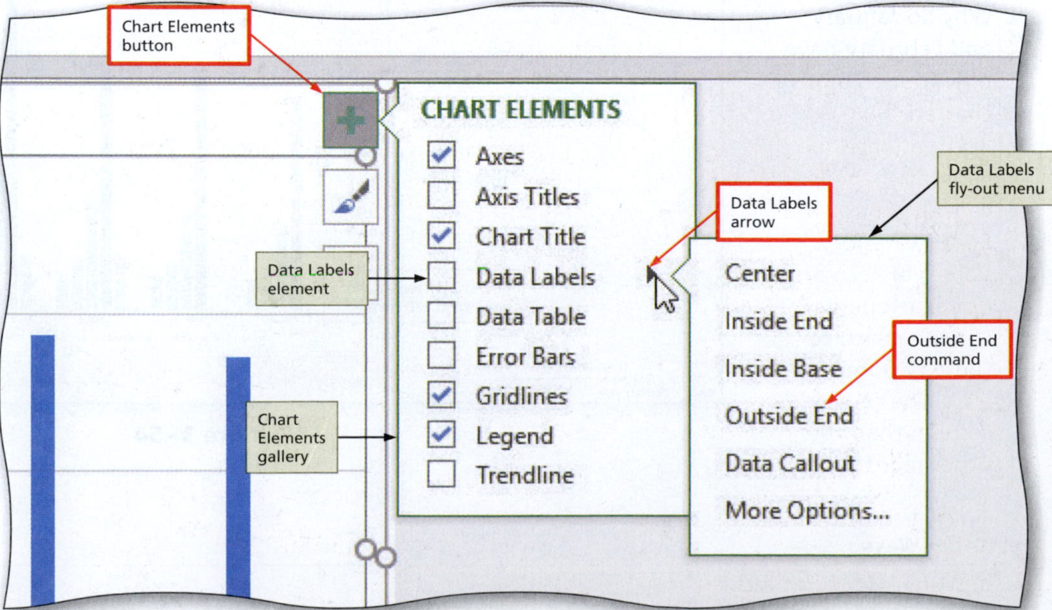

Figure 3–56

2

- Click Outside End on the Data Labels fly-out menu so that data labels are displayed outside the chart at the end of each column.
- Click the Chart Elements button to close the gallery (Figure 3–57).

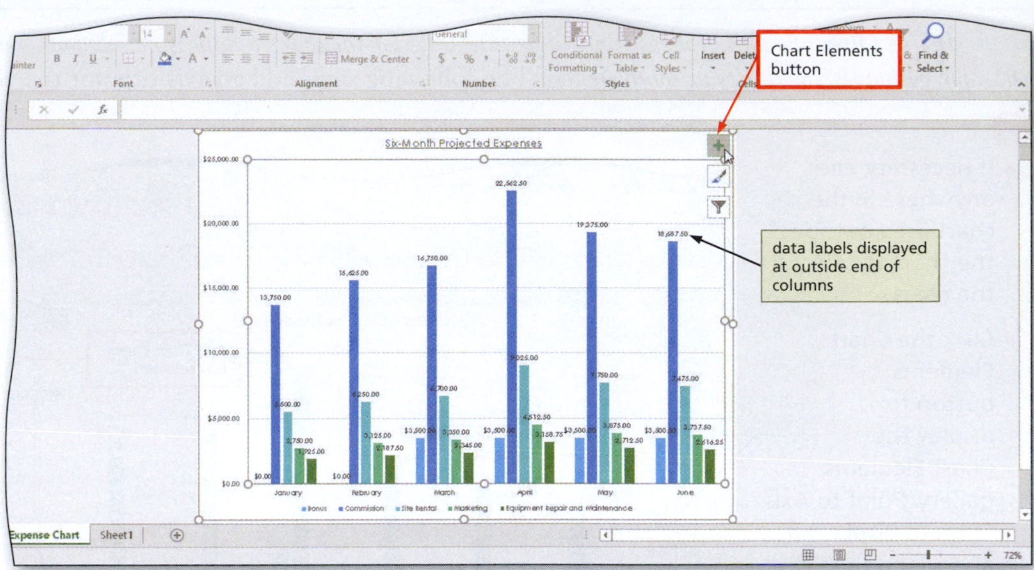

Figure 3–57

To Apply Chart Filters

1 ENTER HEADINGS & DATA | 2 ENTER FORMULAS & FUNCTIONS | 3 CREATE SPARKLINE CHARTS
4 FORMAT WORKSHEET | 5 CREATE COLUMN CHART | 6 CHANGE VIEWS | 7 ASK WHAT-IF QUESTIONS

Why? *With some data, you may find that certain data series or categories make it difficult to examine differences and patterns between other series or categories. Excel allows you to easily filter data series and categories to allow more in-depth examinations of subsets of data.* In this case, filters can be used to temporarily remove the compensation categories Bonus and Commission from the chart, to allow a comparison across the non-compensation expenses. The following steps apply filters to the clustered column chart.

1

- Click the Chart Filters button (on the chart) to display the Chart Filters gallery.
- In the Series section, click the Bonus and Commission check boxes to remove their check marks and then click the Apply button to filter these series from the chart (Figure 3–58).

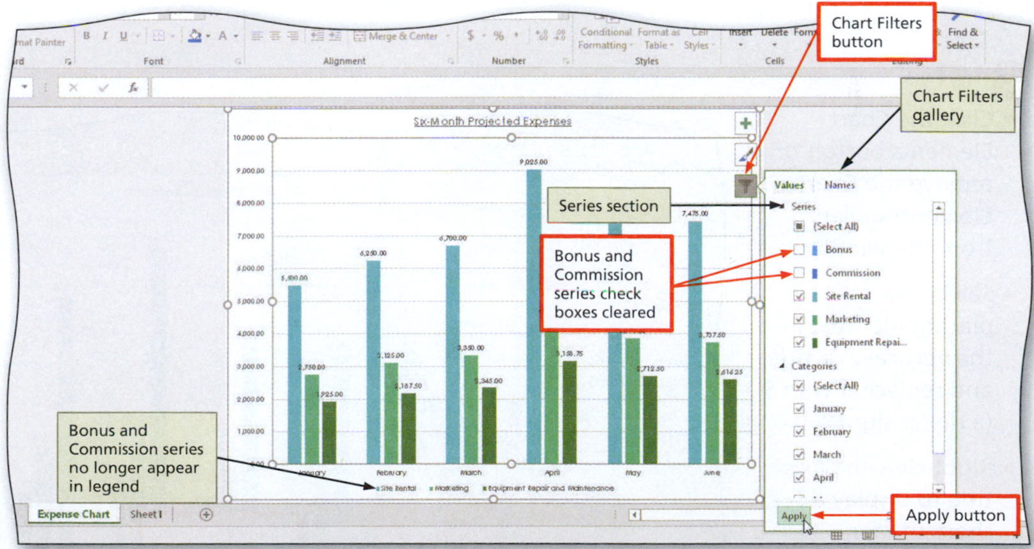

Figure 3–58

Q&A What happens when I remove the check marks from Bonus and Commission?

When you remove the check marks from Bonus and Commission, Excel filters the Bonus and Commission series out and redraws the chart without them.

2

- Click the Chart Filters button to close the gallery.

To Add an Axis Title to the Chart

***Why?** Often the unit of measurement or categories for the charted data is not obvious. You can add an axis title, or titles for both axes, for clarity or completeness.* The following steps add an axis title for the vertical axis.

1

- If necessary, click anywhere in the chart area outside the chart to select the chart.
- Click the Chart Elements button to display the Chart Elements gallery. Point to Axis Titles to display an arrow and then click the arrow to display the Axis Titles fly-out menu.

Experiment

- Point to each option on the fly-out menu to see a live preview of the axes' titles.

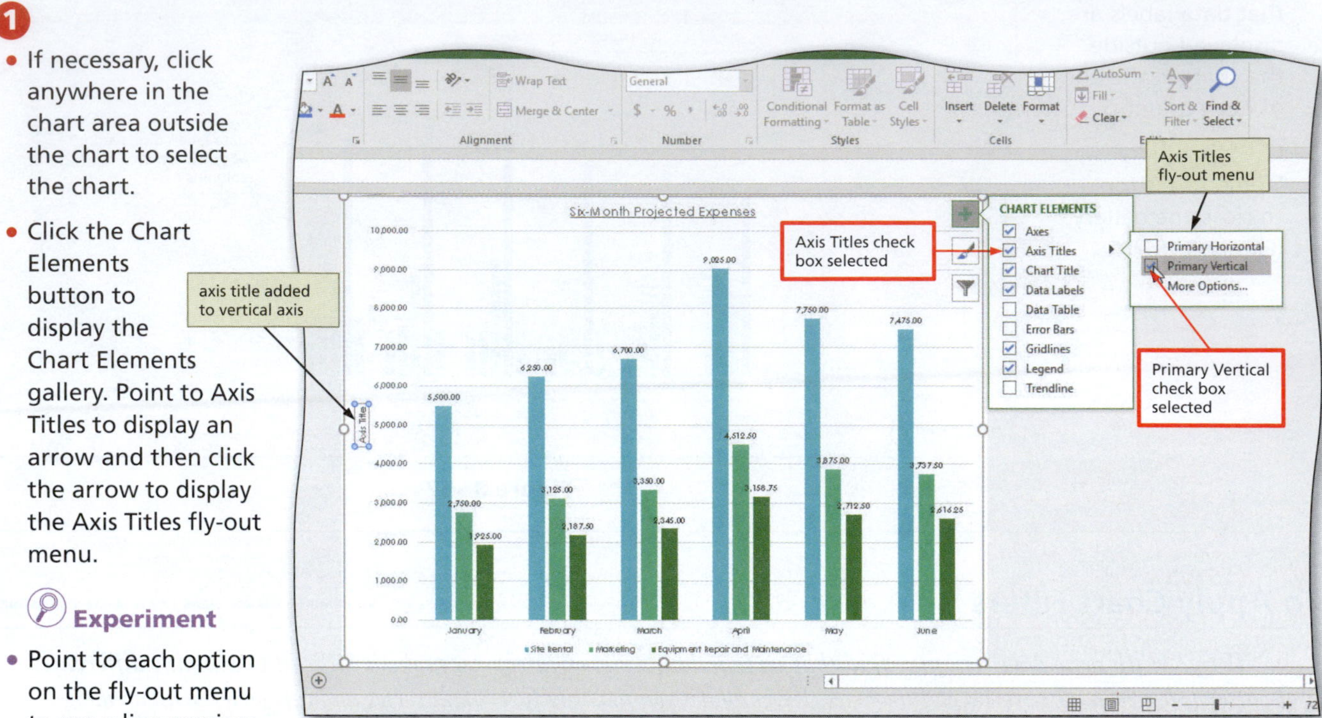

Figure 3–59

- Click Primary Vertical on the Axis Titles fly-out menu to add an axis title to the vertical axis (Figure 3–59).

2

- Click the Chart Elements button to remove the Chart Elements gallery from the window.
- Select the placeholder text in the vertical axis title and replace it with $ (a dollar sign).
- Right-click the axis title to display a shortcut menu (Figure 3–60).

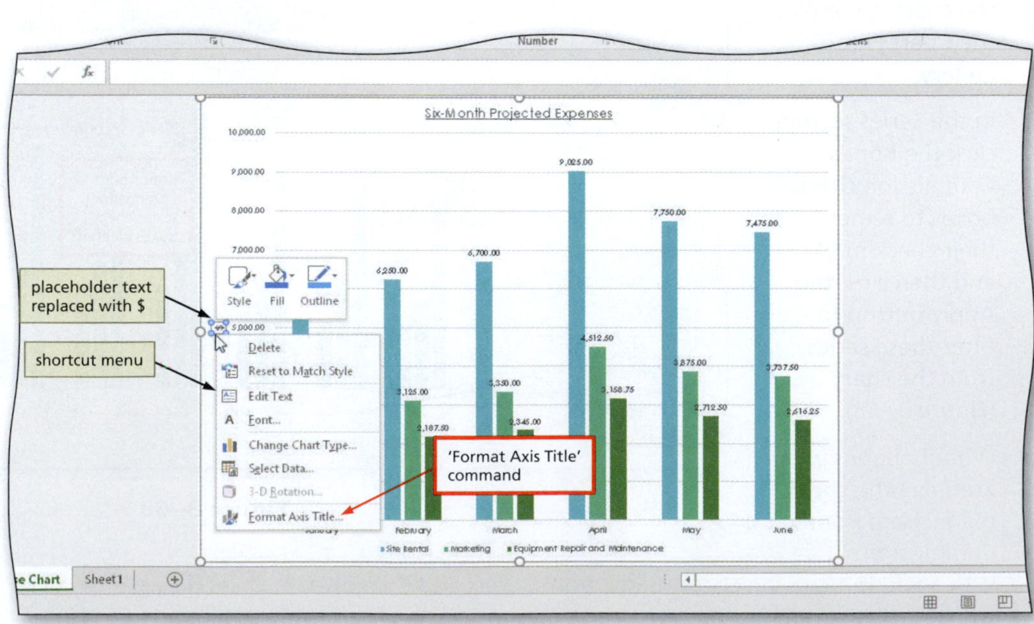

Figure 3–60

- Click 'Format Axis Title' on the shortcut menu to open the Format Axis Title task pane.
- If necessary, click the Title Options tab, click the 'Size & Properties' button, and then, if necessary, click the Alignment arrow to expand the Alignment section.
- Click the Text direction arrow to display the Text direction list (Figure 3–61).

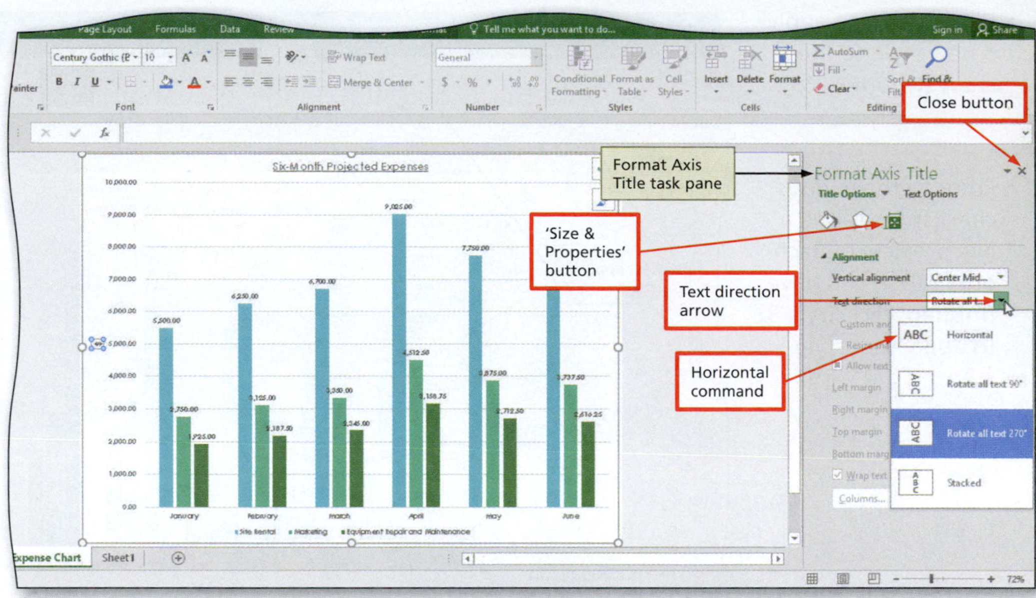

Figure 3–61

- Click Horizontal in the Text direction list to change the orientation of the vertical axis title.
- Click the Close button (shown in Figure 3–61) on the task pane to close the Format Axis Title task pane.

To Change the Chart Style

1 ENTER HEADINGS & DATA | 2 ENTER FORMULAS & FUNCTIONS | 3 CREATE SPARKLINE CHARTS
4 FORMAT WORKSHEET | 5 CREATE COLUMN CHART | 6 CHANGE VIEWS | 7 ASK WHAT-IF QUESTIONS

***Why?** You decide that a chart with a different look would better convey meaning to viewers.* The following steps change the chart style.

- Click the More button (Chart Tools Design tab | Chart Styles group) (shown in Figure 3–61) to display the Chart Styles gallery (Figure 3–62).

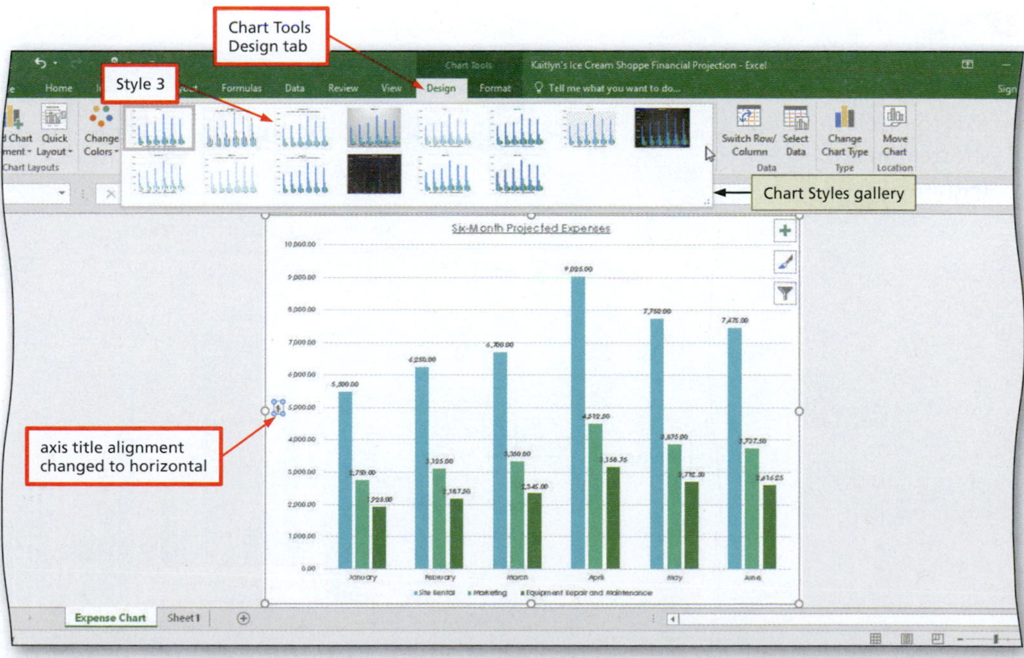

Figure 3–62

- Click Style 3 to apply a new style to the chart (Figure 3–63).

Experiment

- Point to the various chart styles to see a live preview of each one. When you have finished, click Style 3 to apply that style.

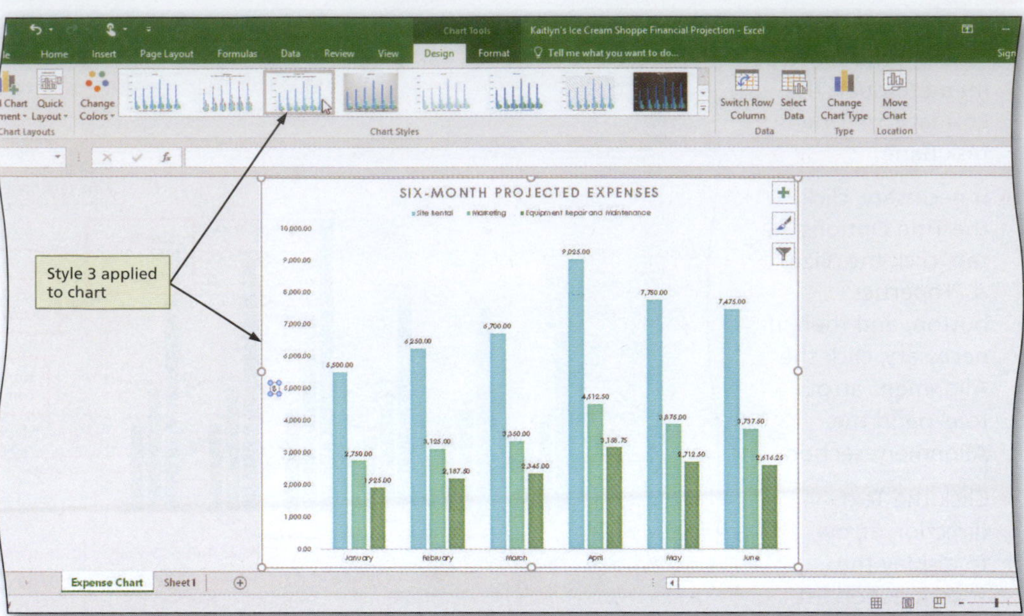

Figure 3–63

To Modify the Chart Axis Number Format

1 ENTER HEADINGS & DATA | 2 ENTER FORMULAS & FUNCTIONS | 3 CREATE SPARKLINE CHARTS
4 FORMAT WORKSHEET | 5 CREATE COLUMN CHART | 6 CHANGE VIEWS | 7 ASK WHAT-IF QUESTIONS

Why? *The two decimal places in the vertical chart axis numbers are not necessary and make the axis appear cluttered.* The following steps format the numbers in the chart axis to contain no decimal places.

- Right-click any value on the vertical axis to display the shortcut menu (Figure 3–64).

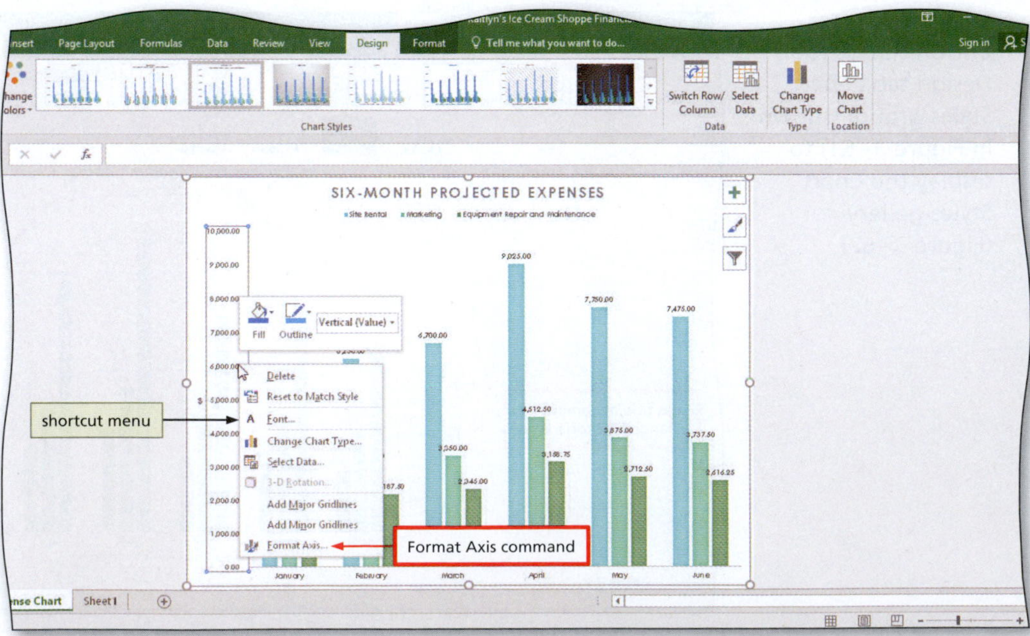

Figure 3–64

2

- Click Format Axis on the shortcut menu to open the Format Axis task pane.
- If necessary, click the Axis Options tab in the Format Axis task pane and then scroll until Number is visible. Click the Number arrow to expand the Number section and then scroll to review options related to formatting numbers.
- Change the number in the Decimal places text box to 0 (Figure 3–65).

3

- Close the Format Axis task pane.

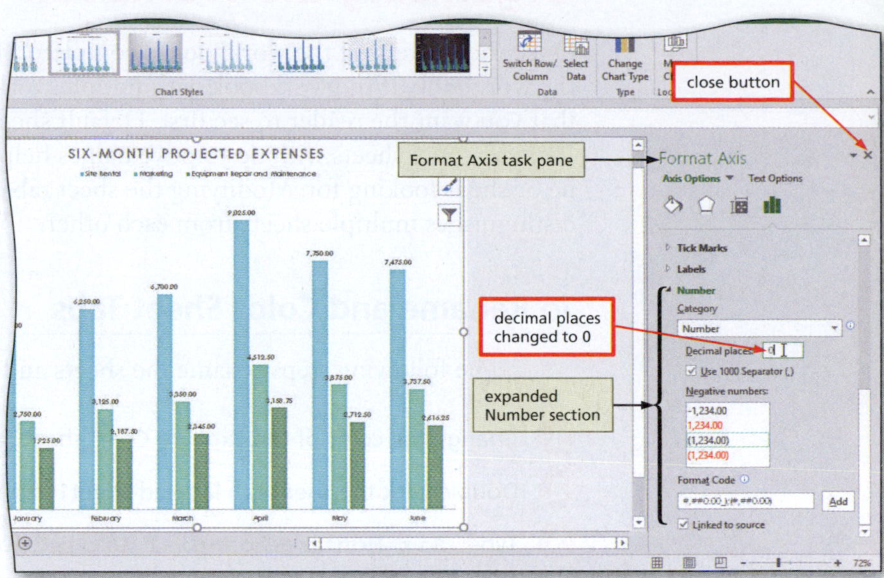

Figure 3–65

To Remove Filters and Data Labels

You decide that the data labels on the bars are distracting and add no value to the chart. You decide to remove the data labels and filters so that all expense data is once again visible. The following steps remove the data labels and the filters.

1. Click the Chart Elements button to display the Chart Elements gallery.
2. Click the Data Labels check box to remove the check mark for the data labels.
3. Click the Chart Elements button again to close the gallery.
4. Click the Chart Filters button to display the Chart Filters fly-out menu.
5. In the Series section, click Bonus and then Commission, click the Apply button to add the compensation data back into the chart, and then click the Chart Filters button again to close the menu (Figure 3–66).

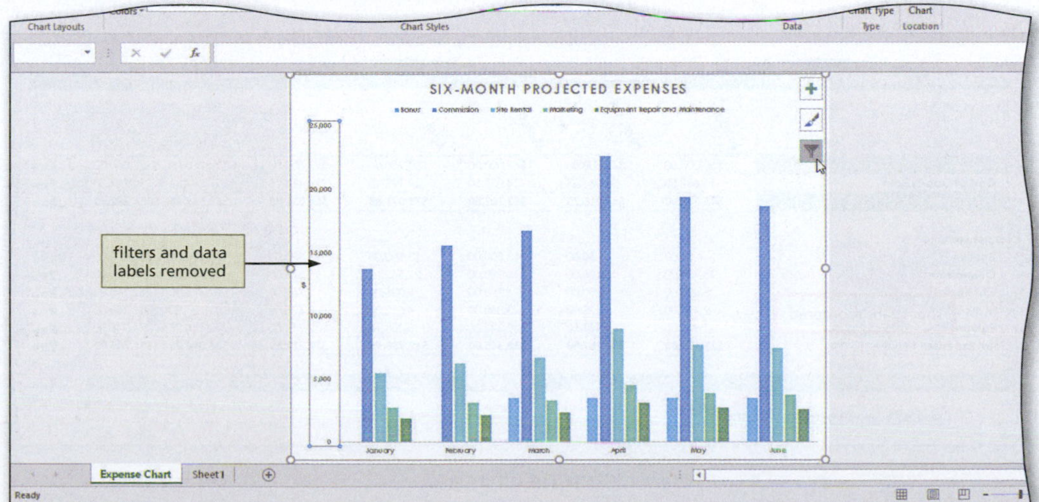

Figure 3–66

BTW

Chart Templates

Once you create and format a chart to your liking, consider saving the chart as a template so that you can use it to format additional charts. Save your chart as a chart template by accessing the chart shortcut menu and then selecting 'Save as Template' from that shortcut menu. The chart template will appear in the Templates folder for Charts. When you want to use the template, click the Templates folder in the All Charts sheet (Insert Chart dialog box) and then select your template.

Organizing the Workbook

Once the content of the workbook is complete, you can address the organization of the workbook. If the workbook has multiple worksheets, place the worksheet on top that you want the reader to see first. Default sheet names in Excel are not descriptive. Renaming the sheets with descriptive names helps the reader find information that he or she is looking for. Modifying the sheet tabs through the use of color further distinguishes multiple sheets from each other.

To Rename and Color Sheet Tabs

The following steps rename the sheets and color the sheet tabs.

1. Change the color of the Expense Chart sheet tab to Green, Accent 4 (column 8, row 1).
2. Double-click the sheet tab labeled Sheet1 at the bottom of the screen.
3. Type `Six-Month Financial Projection` as the new sheet tab name and then press the ENTER key.
4. Change the sheet tab color of the Six-Month Financial Projection sheet to Blue, Accent 2 (column 6, row 1) and then select an empty cell (Figure 3–67).

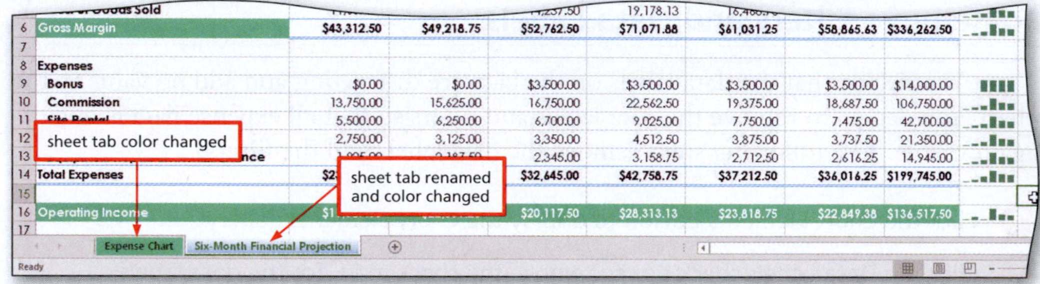

Figure 3–67

1 ENTER HEADINGS & DATA | 2 ENTER FORMULAS & FUNCTIONS | 3 CREATE SPARKLINE CHARTS
4 FORMAT WORKSHEET | 5 CREATE COLUMN CHART | 6 CHANGE VIEWS | 7 ASK WHAT-IF QUESTIONS

To Reorder the Sheet Tabs

Why? *You want the most important worksheets to appear first in a workbook, so you need to change the order of sheets.* The following step reorders the sheets so that the worksheet precedes the chart sheet in the workbook.

- Drag the Six-Month Financial Projection tab to the left so that it precedes the Expense Chart sheet tab to rearrange the sequence of the sheets (Figure 3–68).

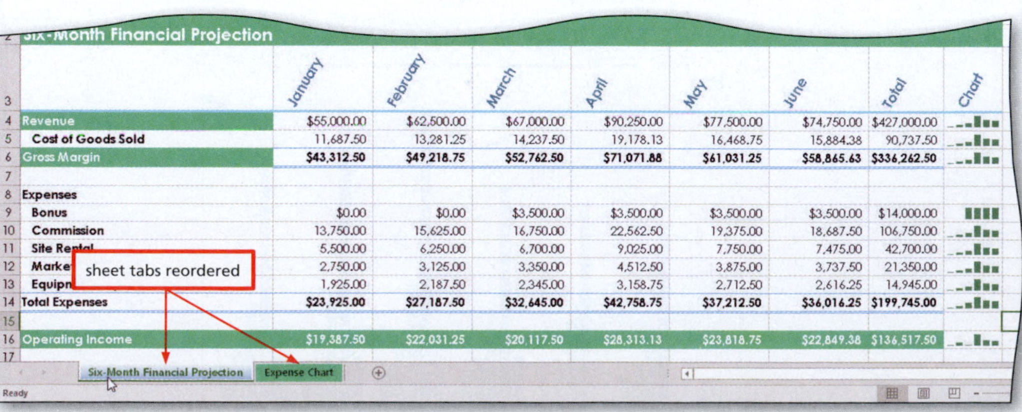

Figure 3–68

Other Ways

1. To move sheet, right-click sheet tab, click Move or Copy on shortcut menu, click OK button

To Check Spelling in Multiple Sheets

By default, the spelling checker reviews spelling only in the selected sheets. It will check all the cells in the selected sheets, unless you select a range of two or more cells. Before checking the spelling, the following steps select both worksheets in the workbook so that both are checked for any spelling errors.

1. With the Six-Month Financial Projection sheet active, press CTRL+HOME to select cell A1. Hold down the CTRL key and then click the Expense Chart tab to select both sheets.
2. Display the Review tab and then click the Spelling button (Review tab | Proofing group) to check spelling in the selected sheets.
3. Correct any errors and then click the OK button (Spelling dialog box or Microsoft Excel dialog box) when the spelling checker is finished.

BTW

Checking Spelling

Unless you first select a range of cells or an object before starting the spelling checker, Excel checks the entire selected worksheet, including all cell values, cell comments, embedded charts, text boxes, buttons, and headers and footers.

To Preview and Print the Worksheet

After checking the spelling, the next step is to preview and print the worksheets. As with spelling, Excel previews and prints only the selected sheets. In addition, because the worksheet is too wide to print in portrait orientation, the orientation must be changed to landscape. The following steps adjust the orientation and scale, preview the worksheets, and then print the worksheets.

1. If both sheets are not selected, hold down the CTRL key and then click the tab of the inactive sheet.
2. Click File on the ribbon to open the Backstage view.
3. Click the Print tab in the Backstage view to display the Print gallery.
4. Click the Portrait Orientation button in the Settings area and then select Landscape Orientation to select the desired orientation.
5. Click the No Scaling button in the Settings area and then select 'Fit Sheet on One Page' to cause the worksheets to print on one page.
6. Verify that the selected printer will print a hard copy of the document. If necessary, click the printer button to display a list of available printer options and then click the desired printer to change the currently selected printer.
7. Click the Print button in the Print gallery to print the worksheet in landscape orientation on the currently selected printer.
8. When the printer stops, retrieve the printed worksheets (shown in Figure 3–69a and Figure 3–69b).
9. Right-click the Six-Month Financial Projection tab, and then click Ungroup Sheets on the shortcut menu to deselect the Expense Chart tab.
10. Save the workbook again on the same storage location with the same file name.

BTW

Distributing a Workbook

Instead of printing and distributing a hard copy of a workbook, you can distribute the workbook electronically. Options include sending the workbook via email; posting it on cloud storage (such as OneDrive) and sharing the file with others; posting it on social media, a blog, or other website; and sharing a link associated with an online location of the workbook. You also can create and share a PDF or XPS image of the workbook, so that users can view the file in Acrobat Reader or XPS Viewer instead of in Excel.

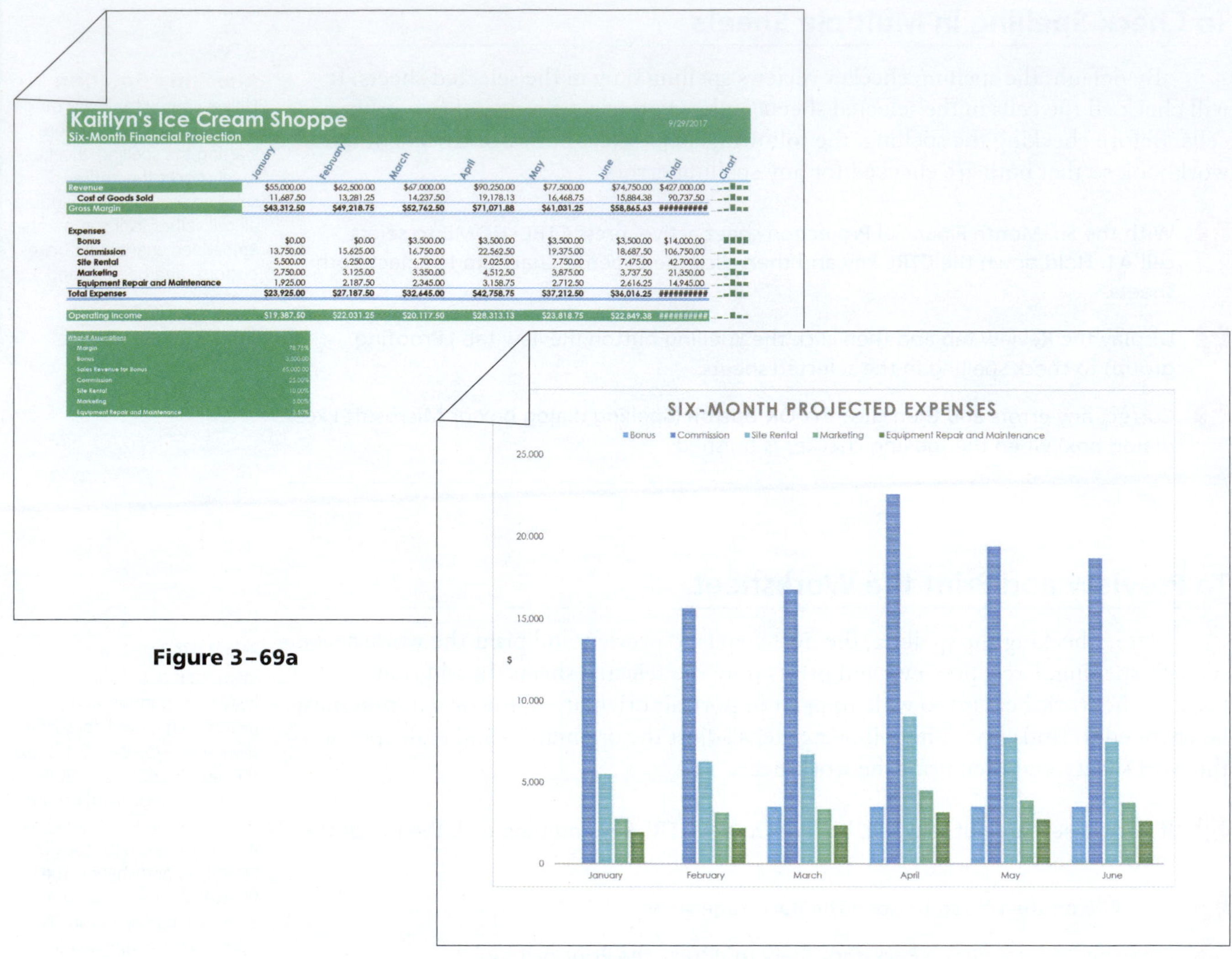

Kaitlyn's Ice Cream Shoppe
Six-Month Financial Projection
9/29/2017

	January	February	March	April	May	June	Total	Chart
Revenue	$55,000.00	$62,500.00	$67,000.00	$90,250.00	$77,500.00	$74,750.00	$427,000.00	
Cost of Goods Sold	11,687.50	13,281.25	14,237.50	19,178.13	16,468.75	15,884.38	90,737.50	
Gross Margin	$43,312.50	$49,218.75	$52,762.50	$71,071.88	$61,031.25	$58,865.63	##########	
Expenses								
Bonus	$0.00	$0.00	$3,500.00	$3,500.00	$3,500.00	$3,500.00	$14,000.00	
Commission	13,750.00	15,625.00	16,750.00	22,562.50	19,375.00	18,687.50	106,750.00	
Site Rental	5,500.00	6,250.00	6,700.00	9,025.00	7,750.00	7,475.00	42,700.00	
Marketing	2,750.00	3,125.00	3,350.00	4,512.50	3,875.00	3,737.50	21,350.00	
Equipment Repair and Maintenance	1,925.00	2,187.50	2,345.00	3,158.75	2,712.50	2,616.25	14,945.00	
Total Expenses	$23,925.00	$27,187.50	$32,645.00	$42,758.75	$37,212.50	$36,016.25	##########	
Operating Income	$19,387.50	$22,031.25	$20,117.50	$28,313.13	$23,818.75	$22,849.38	##########	

What-If Assumptions	
Margin	78.75%
Bonus	3,500.00
Sales Revenue for Bonus	65,000.00
Commission	25.00%
Site Rental	10.00%
Marketing	5.00%
Equipment Repair and Maintenance	3.50%

Figure 3–69a

Figure 3–69b

Changing the View of the Worksheet

With Excel, you easily can change the view of the worksheet. For example, you can magnify or shrink the worksheet on the screen. You also can view different parts of the worksheet at the same time by using panes.

To Shrink and Magnify the View of a Worksheet or Chart

1 ENTER HEADINGS & DATA | 2 ENTER FORMULAS & FUNCTIONS | 3 CREATE SPARKLINE CHARTS
4 FORMAT WORKSHEET | 5 CREATE COLUMN CHART | **6 CHANGE VIEWS** | 7 ASK WHAT-IF QUESTIONS

You can magnify (zoom in) or shrink (zoom out) the appearance of a worksheet or chart by using the Zoom button (View tab | Zoom group). ***Why?*** *When you magnify a worksheet, Excel enlarges the view of the characters on the screen, but shows fewer columns and rows. Alternatively, when you shrink a worksheet, Excel is able to display more columns and rows.* Magnifying or shrinking a worksheet affects only the view; it does not change the window size or the size of the printout of the worksheet or chart. The following steps shrink and magnify the view of the worksheet.

1

- If cell A1 is not active, press CTRL+HOME.
- Display the View tab and then click the Zoom button (View tab | Zoom group) to display a list of magnifications in the Zoom dialog box (Figure 3–70).

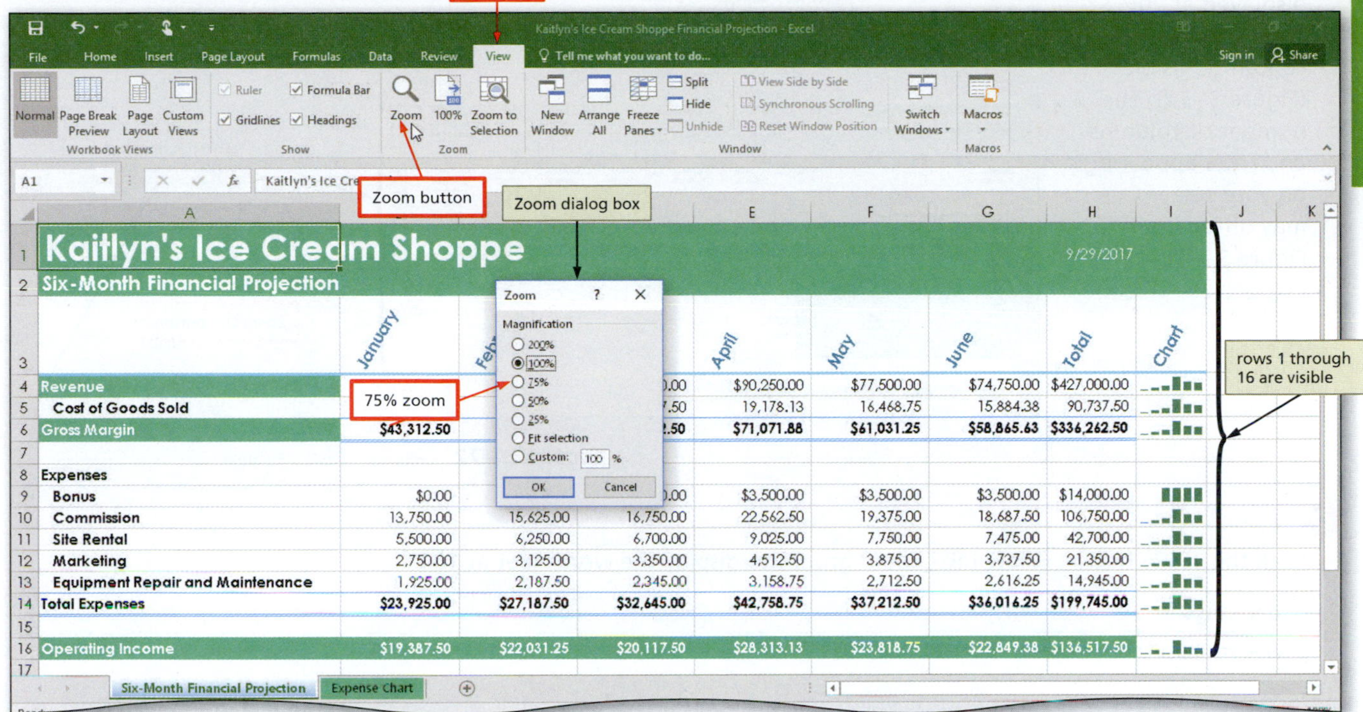

Figure 3–70

2

- Click 75% and then click the OK button (Zoom dialog box) to shrink the display of the worksheet (Figure 3–71). The number of columns and rows appearing on your screen may differ from Figure 3–71.

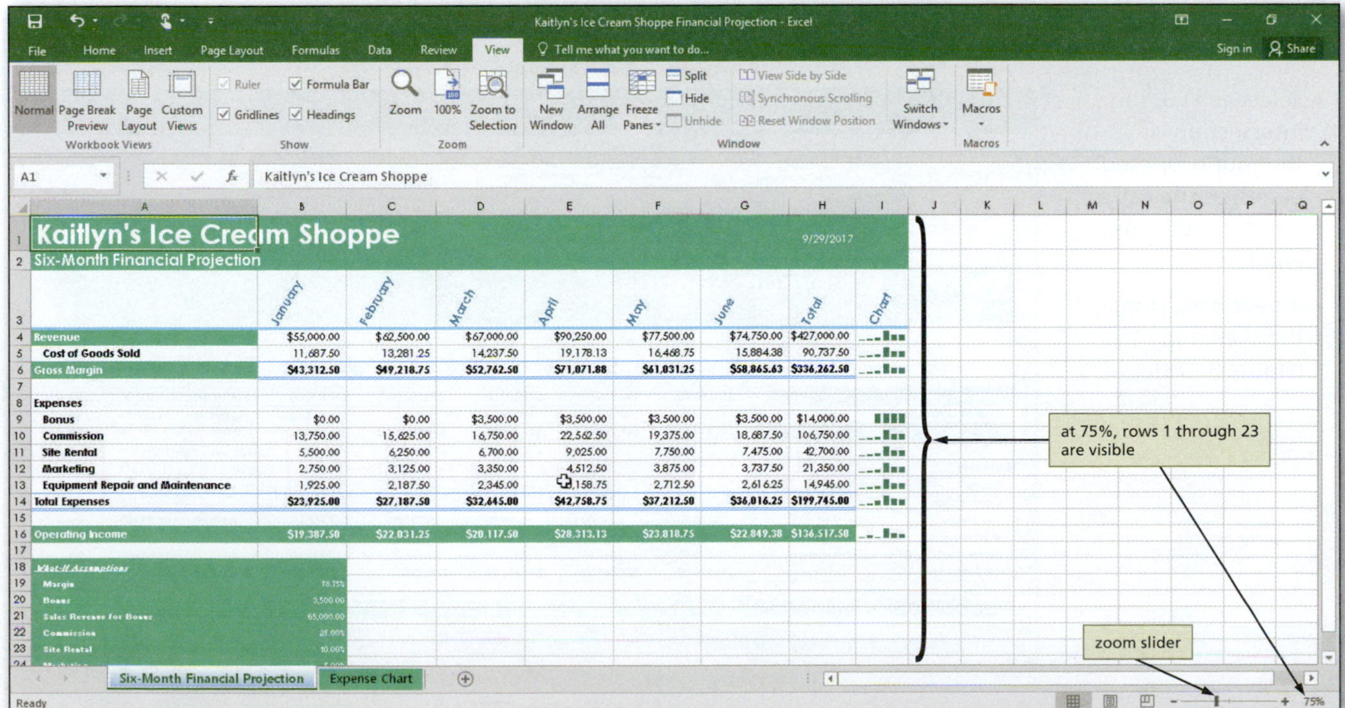

Figure 3–71

- Click the Zoom Out button on the status bar until the worksheet is displayed at 70% and all worksheet content is visible (Figure 3–72). The number of columns and rows appearing on your screen may differ from Figure 3–72.

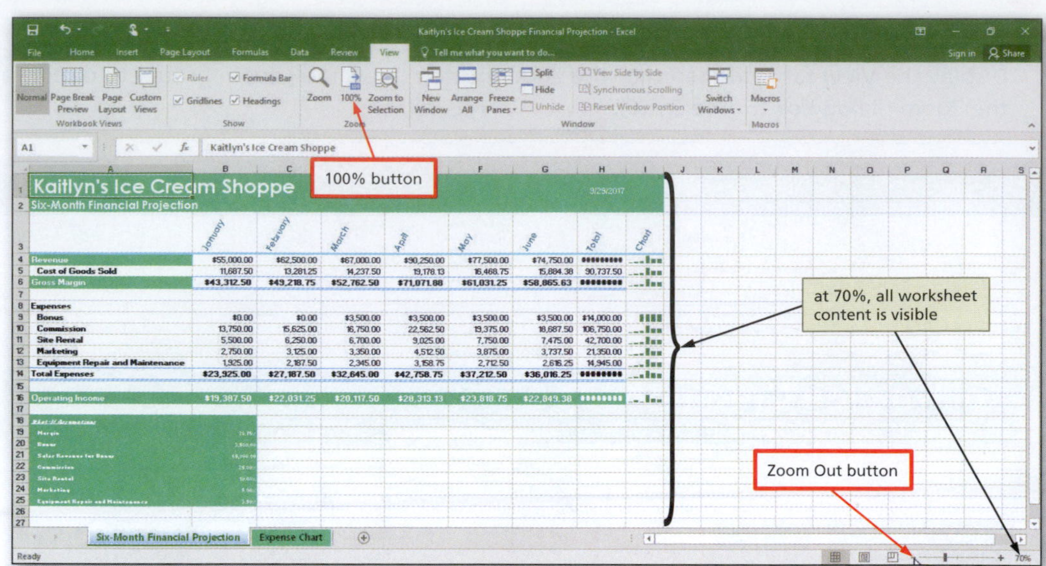

Figure 3–72

- Click the 100% button (View tab | Zoom group) to display the worksheet at 100%.

Other Ways

1. Drag zoom slider to increase or decrease zoom level

To Split a Window into Panes

1 ENTER HEADINGS & DATA | 2 ENTER FORMULAS & FUNCTIONS | 3 CREATE SPARKLINE CHARTS
4 FORMAT WORKSHEET | 5 CREATE COLUMN CHART | **6 CHANGE VIEWS** | **7 ASK WHAT-IF QUESTIONS**

When working with a large worksheet, you can split the window into two or four panes to view different parts of the worksheet at the same time. ***Why?*** *Splitting the Excel window into four panes at cell E8 allows you to view all four corners of the worksheet simultaneously.* The following steps split the Excel window into four panes.

1

- Select cell E8, the intersection of the four proposed panes, as the cell at which to split the window.
- If necessary, display the View tab (Figure 3–73).

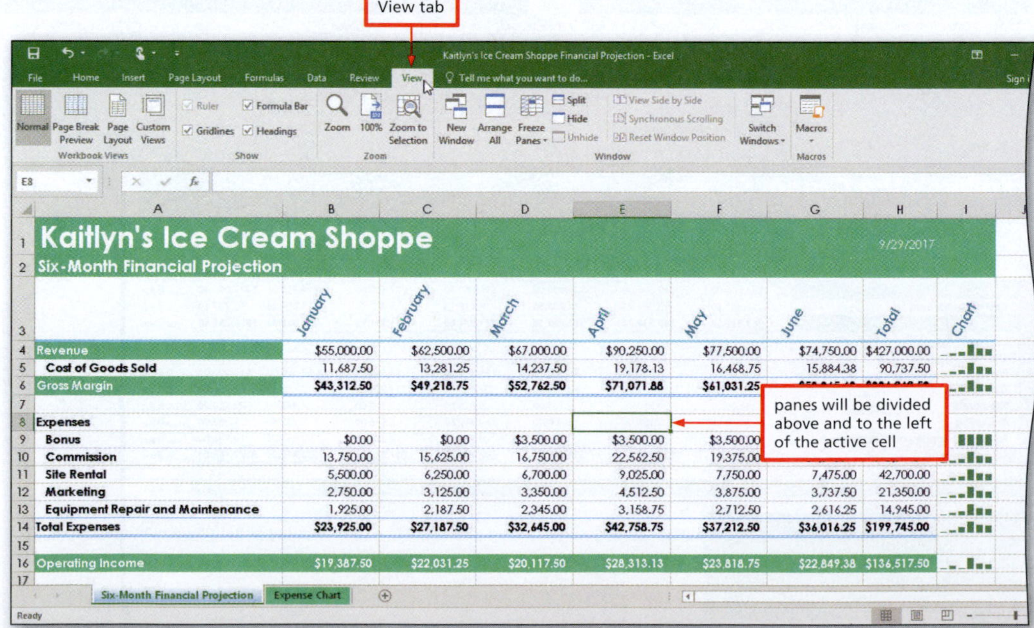

Figure 3–73

2

- Click the Split button (View tab | Window group) to divide the window into four panes.
- Use the scroll arrows to show the four corners of the worksheet at the same time (Figure 3–74).

Q&A What is shown in the four panes?
The four panes in Figure 3–74 show the following: (1) range A1:D7 in the upper-left pane; (2) range E1:J7 in the upper-right pane; (3) range A17:D25 in the lower-left pane; and (4) range E17:J25 in the lower-right pane. The vertical split bar is the vertical bar running up and down the middle of the window. The horizontal split bar is the horizontal bar running across the middle of the window. If you use the scroll bars below the window, you will see that the panes split by the horizontal split bar scroll together horizontally. The panes split by the vertical split bar scroll together vertically when using the scroll bars to the right of the window. To resize the panes, drag either split bar to the desired location.

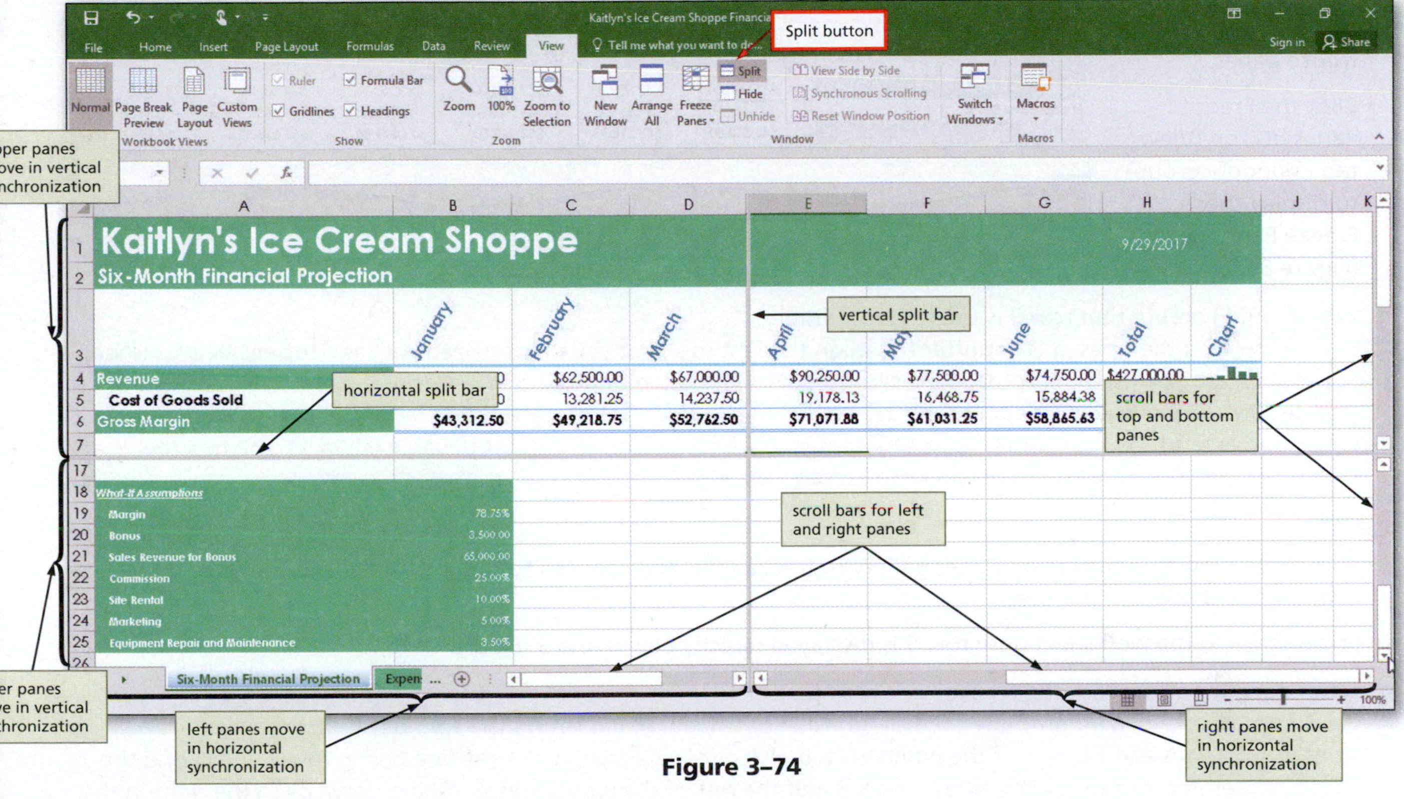

Figure 3–74

To Remove the Panes from the Window

The following step removes the panes from the window.

1 Click the Split button (View tab | Window group) to remove the four panes from the window.

Other Ways

1. Double-click intersection of horizontal and vertical split bars

1 ENTER HEADINGS & DATA | 2 ENTER FORMULAS & FUNCTIONS | 3 CREATE SPARKLINE CHARTS
4 FORMAT WORKSHEET | 5 CREATE COLUMN CHART | 6 CHANGE VIEWS | 7 ASK WHAT-IF QUESTIONS

To Freeze Worksheet Columns and Rows

Why? Freezing worksheet columns and rows is a useful technique for viewing large worksheets that extend beyond the window. Normally, when you scroll down or to the right, the column content in the top rows and the row content in the leftmost columns no longer appear on the screen. When the content of these rows and/or columns helps to identify or define other content still visible on the worksheet, it can make it difficult to remember what the numbers in the visible cells represent. To alleviate this problem, Excel allows you to freeze columns and rows, so that their content, typically column or row titles, remains on the screen, no matter how far down or to the right you scroll. You also may wish to keep numbers visible that you need to see when making changes to content in another part of the worksheet, such as the revenue, cost of goods sold, and gross margin information in rows 4 through 6. The following steps use the Freeze Panes button (View tab | Window group) to freeze the worksheet title and column titles in row 3, and the row titles in column A.

1

- Scroll the worksheet until Excel displays row 3 as the first row and column A as the first column on the screen.
- Select cell B4 as the cell on which to freeze panes.
- Click the Freeze Panes button (View tab | Window group) to display the Freeze Panes gallery (Figure 3–75).

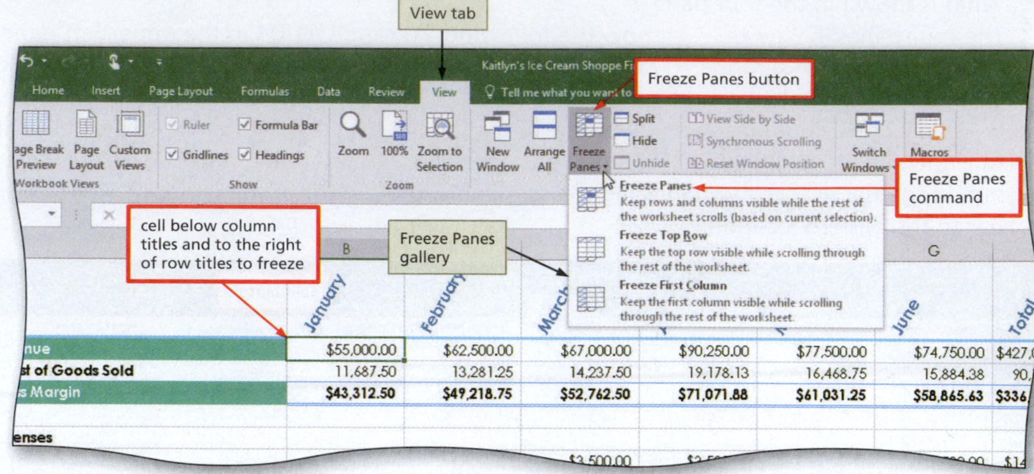

Figure 3–75

Q&A Why should I ensure that row 3 is the first row visible?
Before freezing the titles, it is important to align the first row that you want frozen with the top of the worksheet. For example, if you used the Freeze Panes button in cell B4 while displaying row 1, then Excel would freeze and display the worksheet title and subtitle, leaving only a few rows of data visible in the Six-Month Financial Projection area of the worksheet. To ensure that you can view as much data as possible, always scroll to a row that maximizes the view of your important data before freezing panes.

2

- Click Freeze Panes in the Freeze Panes gallery to freeze rows and columns to the left and above the selected cell, column A and row 3 in this case.
- Scroll down in the worksheet until row 9 is displayed directly below row 3 (Figure 3–76).

Q&A What happens after I click the Freeze Panes command?
Excel displays a thin, dark gray line on the right side of column A, indicating the split between the frozen row titles in column A and the rest of the worksheet. It also displays a thin, dark gray line below row 3, indicating the split between the frozen column titles in row 3 and the rest of the worksheet. Scrolling down or to the right in the worksheet will not scroll the content of row 3 or column A off the screen (Figure 3–76).

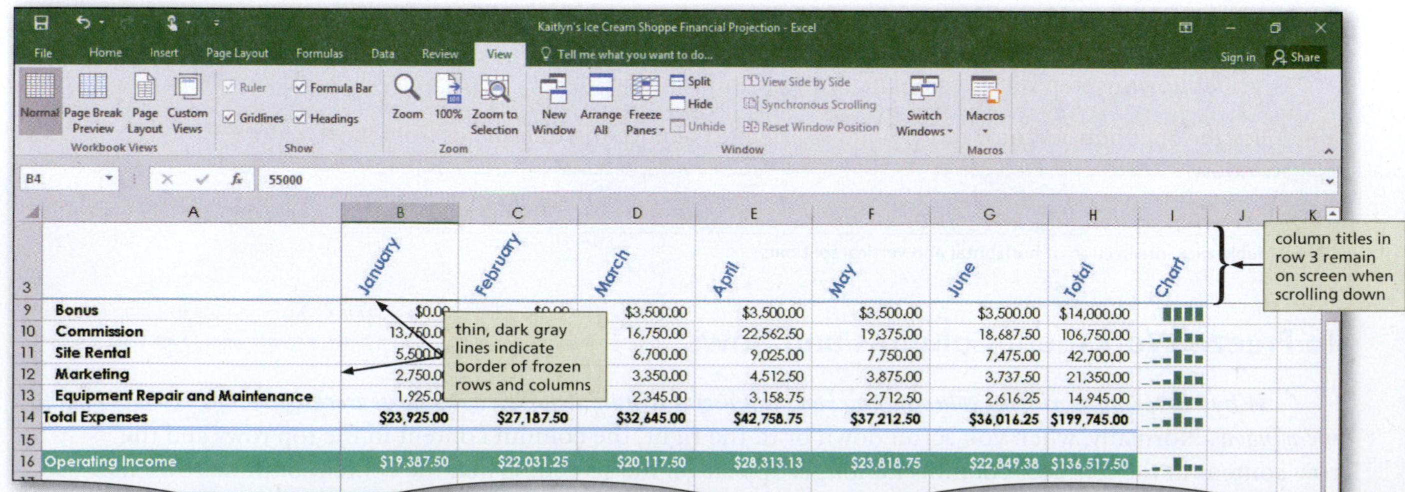

Figure 3–76

To Unfreeze the Worksheet Columns and Rows

Why? *Keep columns and rows frozen only as long as you need to view the worksheet in that configuration.* The following steps unfreeze the titles in column A and row 3 to allow you to work with the worksheet without frozen rows and columns, or to freeze the worksheet at a different location.

1. Press CTRL+HOME to select cell B4 and view the upper-left corner of the screen.
2. Click the Freeze Panes button (View tab | Window group) to display the Freeze Panes gallery.
3. Click Unfreeze Panes in the Freeze Panes gallery to unfreeze the frozen columns and rows.
4. Display the Home tab.
5. Save the workbook again on the same storage location with the same file name.

Q&A

Why does pressing CTRL+HOME select cell B4?

When the titles are frozen and you press CTRL+HOME, Excel selects the upper-leftmost cell of the unfrozen section of the worksheet. For example, in Step 1 of the previous steps, Excel selected cell B4. When the titles are unfrozen, pressing CTRL+HOME selects cell A1.

BTW

Freezing Titles

If you want to freeze only column headings, select the appropriate cell in column A before you click the Freeze Panes button (View tab | Window group). If you want to freeze only row titles, select the appropriate cell in row 1 before you click the Freeze Panes button. To freeze both column headings and row titles, select the cell that is the intersection of the column and row titles before you click the Freeze Panes button.

What-If Analysis

The automatic recalculation feature of Excel is a powerful tool that can be used to analyze worksheet data. Using Excel to scrutinize the impact of changing values in cells that are referenced by formulas in other cells is called **what-if analysis** or sensitivity analysis. When new data is entered, Excel not only recalculates all formulas in a worksheet but also redraws any associated charts.

In the workbook created in this module, many of the formulas are dependent on the assumptions in the range B19:B25. Thus, if you change any of the assumption values, Excel recalculates all formulas. Excel redraws the clustered column chart as well, because it is based on these numbers.

To Analyze Data in a Worksheet by Changing Values

1 ENTER HEADINGS & DATA | 2 ENTER FORMULAS & FUNCTIONS | 3 CREATE SPARKLINE CHARTS
4 FORMAT WORKSHEET | 5 CREATE COLUMN CHART | 6 CHANGE VIEWS | **7 ASK WHAT-IF QUESTIONS**

Why? *The effect of changing one or more values in the What-If Assumptions table — essentially posing what-if questions — allows you to review the results of different scenarios.* In this case, you are going to examine what would happen to the six-month operating income (cell H16) if the following changes were made in the What-If Assumptions table: Bonus \$3,500.00 to \$5,000.00; Commission 25.00% to 22.50%; Equipment Repair and Maintenance 3.50% to 4.00%. To answer a question like this, you need to change only the second, fourth, and seventh values in the What-If Assumptions table. The following step splits the screen, which allows you to view income and expense figures simultaneously, and then changes values in the worksheet to answer a what-if question. When a new value is entered, Excel recalculates the formulas in the worksheet and redraws the clustered column chart to reflect the new data.

- Scroll the worksheet so that row 4 is the first row visible on the worksheet.
- Click in cell A7 to select the row above which to split the window.
- Click the Split button (View tab | Window group) to split the window after row 6.
- Use the scroll arrows in the lower-right pane to scroll the window content until row 9 is the first row visible in the lower part of the screen, as shown in Figure 3–77.
- Enter `5,000` in cell B20, `22.50%` in cell B22, and `4.00%` in cell B25 (Figure 3–77), which causes the six-month operating income in cell H16 to increase from $136,517.50 to $139,057.50.
- Save the workbook again on the same storage location with the same file name.

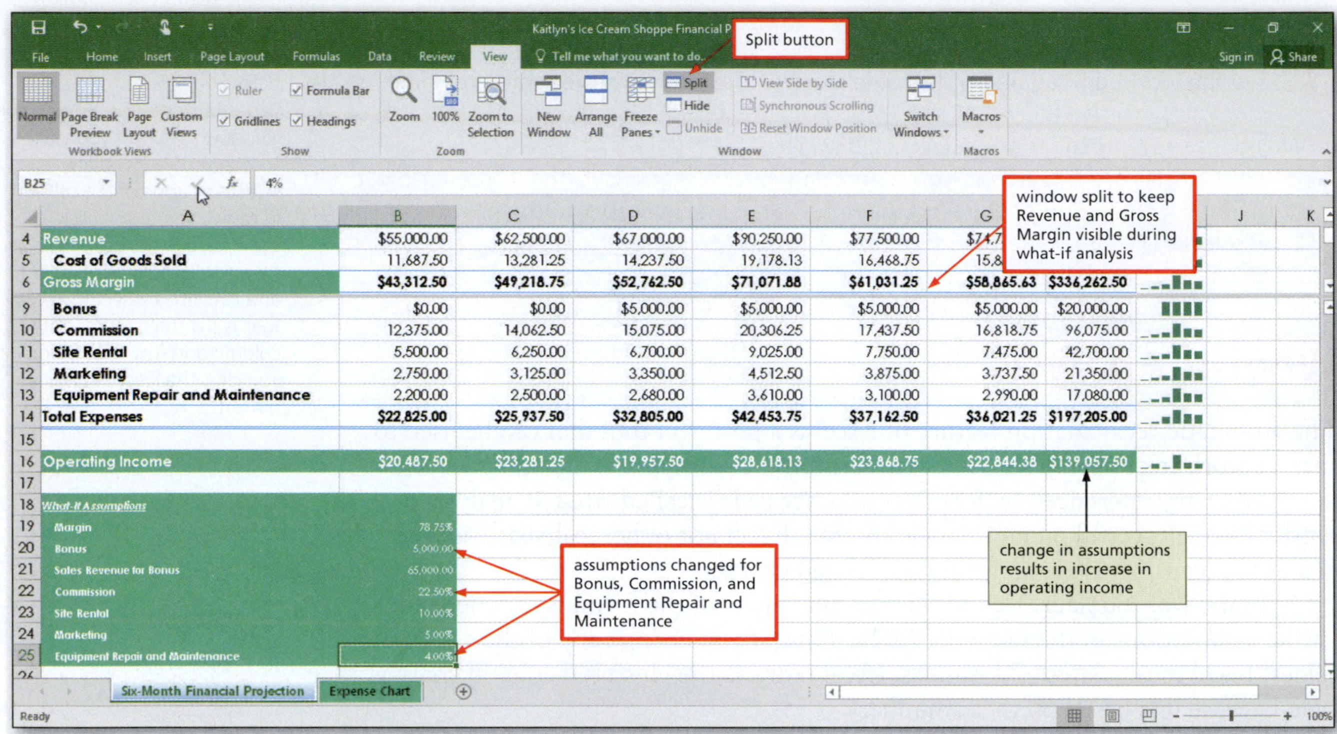

Figure 3–77

To Goal Seek

Why? If you know the result you want a formula to produce, you can use goal seeking to determine the value of a cell on which the formula depends. The previous step, which made changes to the What-If Assumptions table, resulted in an operating income that approaches but does not reach $145,000.00. The following steps use the Goal Seek command (Data tab | Forecast group) to determine what Site Rental percentage (cell B23), in conjunction with the earlier changes in assumptions, will yield a six-month operating income of $145,000 in cell H16, rather than the $139,057.50 calculated in the previous set of steps.

1

- If necessary, use the scroll arrows in the lower pane to ensure that you can view all of the What-If Assumptions table and the Operating Income figures.
- Select cell H16, the cell that contains the six-month operating income.
- Display the Data tab and then click the 'What-If Analysis' button (Data tab | Forecast group) to display the What-If Analysis menu (Figure 3–78).

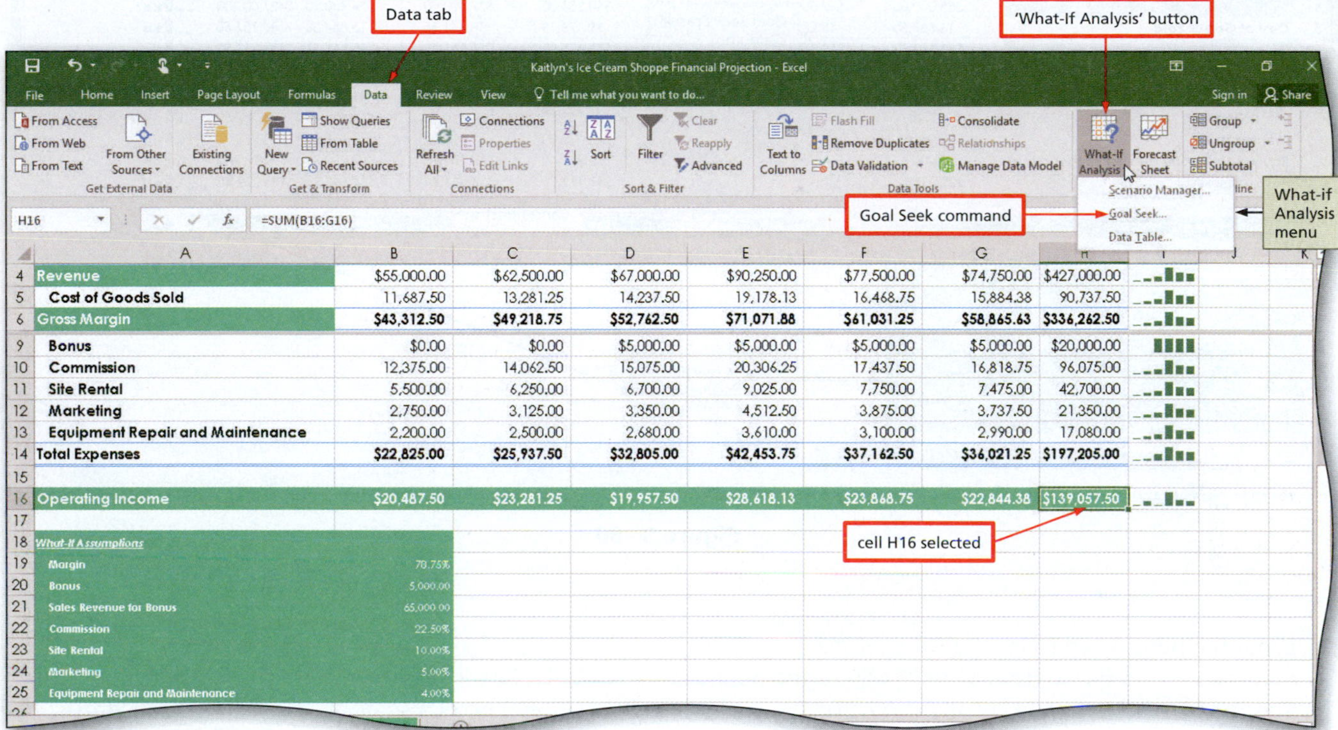

Figure 3–78

2

- Click Goal Seek to display the Goal Seek dialog box with the Set cell box set to the selected cell, H16 in this case.
- Click the To value text box, type **145,000** and then click the 'By changing cell' box to select the 'By changing cell' box.
- Click cell B23 on the worksheet to assign the current cell, B23 in this case, to the 'By changing cell' box (Figure 3–79).

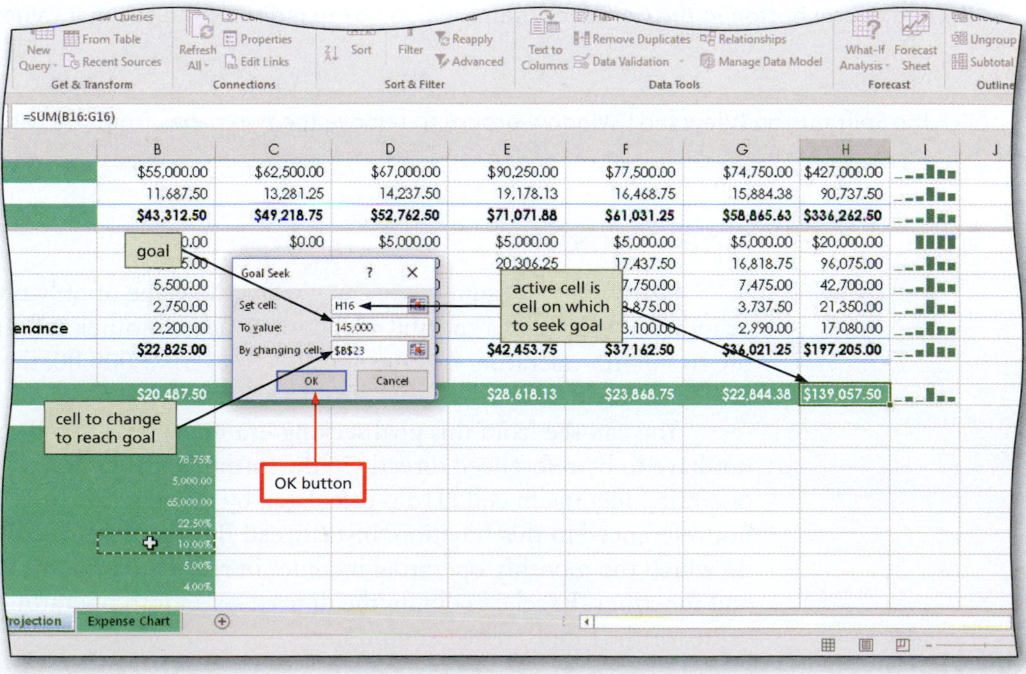

Figure 3–79

- Click the OK button (Goal Seek dialog box) to goal seek for the sought-after value in the To value text box, $145,000.00 in cell H16 in this case (Figure 3–80).

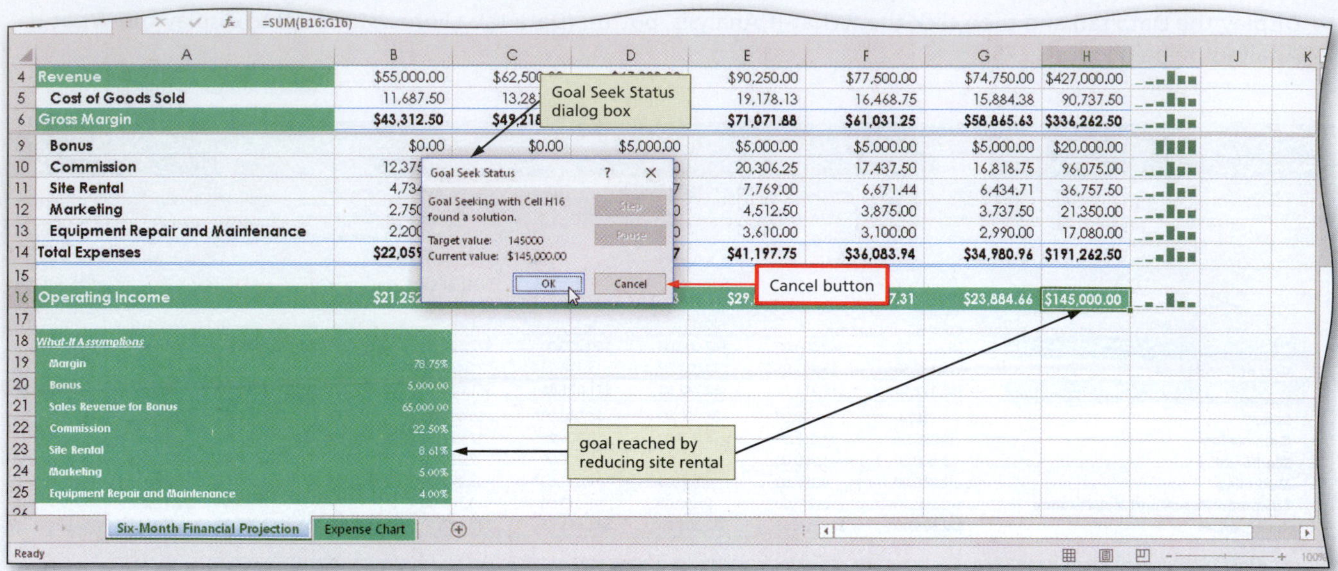

Figure 3–80

Q&A
What happens when I click the OK button?
Excel changes cell H16 from $139,057.50 to the desired value of $145,000.00. More importantly, Excel changes the Site Rental assumption in cell B23 from 10.00% to 8.61% (Figure 3–80). Excel also displays the Goal Seek Status dialog box. If you click the OK button, Excel keeps the new values in the worksheet. If you click the Cancel button, Excel redisplays the original values.

- Click the Cancel button in the Goal Seek Status dialog box to redisplay the original values in the worksheet.

- Click the Split button (View tab | Window group) to remove the two panes from the window.

Goal Seeking

Goal seeking assumes you can change the value of only one cell referenced directly or indirectly to reach a specific goal for a value in another cell. In this example, to change the six-month operating income in cell H16 to $145,000.00, the Site Rental percentage in cell B23 must decrease by 1.39% from 10.00% to 8.61%.

You can see from this goal seeking example that the cell to change (cell B23) does not have to be referenced directly in the formula or function. For example, the six-month operating income in cell H16 is calculated by the function =SUM(B16:G16). Cell B23 is not referenced in this function. Instead, cell B23 is referenced in the formulas in row 11, on which the monthly operating incomes in row 16 are based. By tracing the formulas and functions, Excel can obtain the desired six-month operating income by varying the value for the Site Rental assumption.

Insights

The Insights feature in Excel uses the Bing search engine and other Internet resources to help you locate more information about the content in your workbooks. One common use of this feature is to look up the definition of a word. When looking up a definition, Excel uses contextual data so that it can return the most relevant information.

To Use the Smart Lookup Insight

Smart Lookup uses Bing and other Internet resources to find useful information about text in your spreadsheet and then displays that information in the Insights task pane. ***Why?*** *If you need additional information about some terminology in a workbook you are creating or viewing, Smart Lookup can provide that information.* The following steps use Smart Lookup to look up information about the text in cell A6.

- Select cell A6.
- Display the Review tab and then click Smart Lookup (Review tab | Insights group) to display the Insights task pane containing information about the text in the selected cell (Figure 3–81).

Q&A Why did I see a 'We value your privacy' message?
This message appears the first time you use the Smart Lookup insight. If you agree to the terms, click the Got it button to continue.

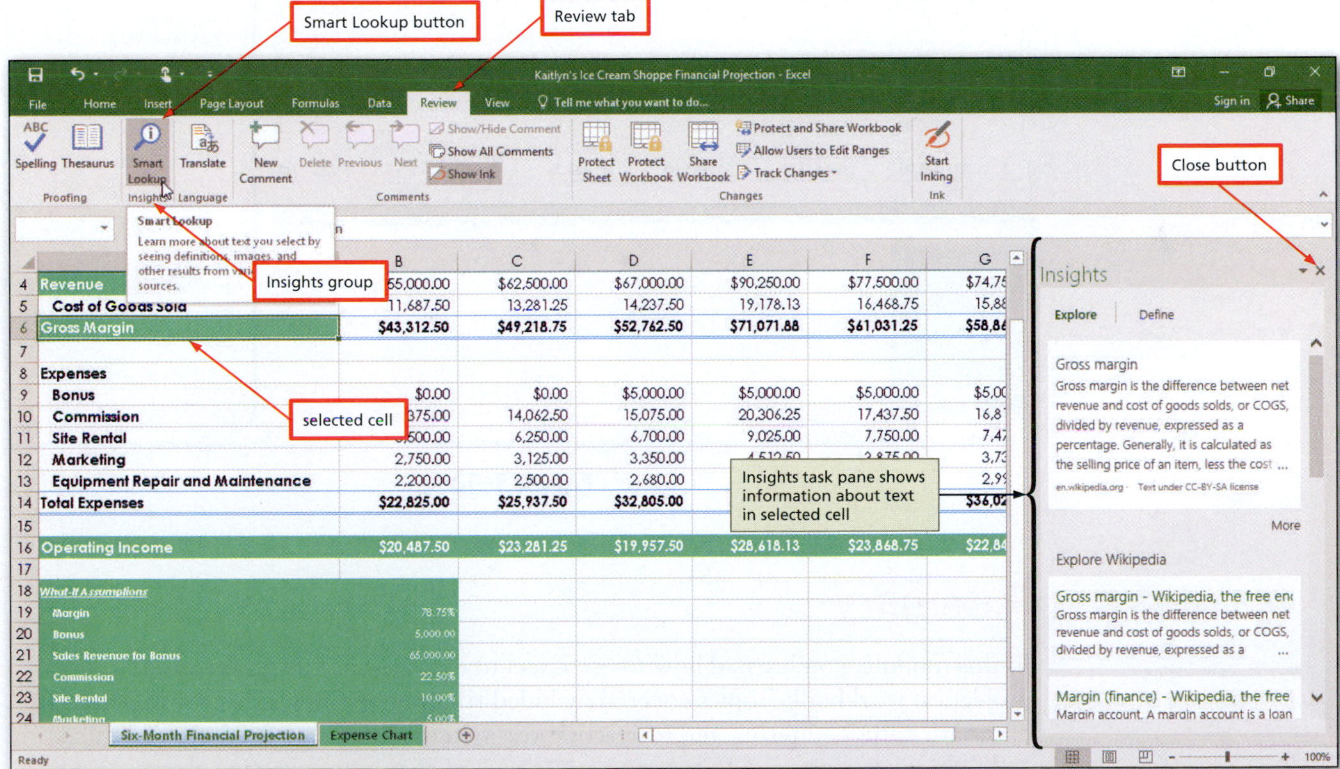

Figure 3–81

2

- Click the Close button on the Insights task pane to close the task pane.
- If desired, sign out of your Microsoft account.
- Exit Excel.

Accessibility Features

Excel provides a utility that can be used to check a workbook for potential issues related to **accessibility**. Accessibility refers to the practice of removing barriers that may prevent individuals with disabilities from interacting with your data or the app. To use the Check Accessibility command, click File on the ribbon to open the Backstage view, click the Info tab, click the 'Check for Issues' button, and then click Check Accessibility. Excel will check your workbook for content that could prove difficult for people with disabilities to read, either alone or with adaptive tools. The resulting report (Figure 3–82 shows an example) will identify issues and offer suggestions for addressing the reported issues.

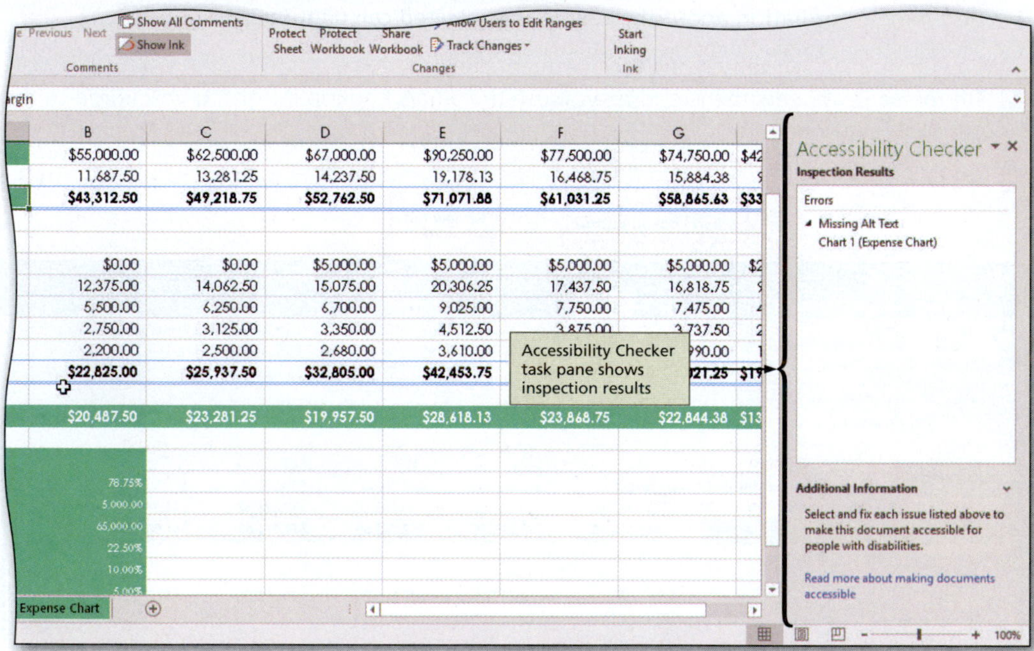

Figure 3–82

Summary

In this module, you learned how to use Excel to create a six-month financial projection workbook. Topics covered included rotating text in a cell, creating a series of month names, entering and formatting the system date, using absolute and mixed cell references, using the IF function, creating and changing sparkline charts, using the format painter, creating a clustered column chart, using chart filters, reordering sheet tabs, changing the worksheet view, freezing and unfreezing rows and columns, answering what-if questions, goal seeking, using Smart Lookup, and understanding accessibility features.

CONSIDER THIS: PLAN AHEAD

What decisions will you need to make when creating your next worksheet to evaluate and analyze data using what-if analysis?

Use these guidelines as you complete the assignments in this module and create your own worksheets for evaluating and analyzing data outside of this class.

1. Determine the workbook structure.
   a) Determine the data you will need for your worksheet.
   b) Determine the layout of your data on the worksheet.
   c) Determine the layout of the assumptions table on the worksheet.
   d) Determine the location and features of any charts.
2. Create the worksheet.
   a) Enter titles, subtitles, and headings.
   b) Enter data, functions, and formulas.
3. Format the worksheet.
   a) Format the titles, subtitles, and headings.
   b) Format the numbers as necessary.
   c) Format the text.
4. Create and use charts.
   a) Select data to chart.
   b) Select a chart type for selected data.
   c) Format the chart elements.
   d) Filter charts if necessary to view subsets of data.
5. Perform what-if analyses.
   a) Adjust values in the assumptions table to review scenarios of interest.
   b) Use Goal Seek to determine how to adjust a variable value to reach a particular goal or outcome.

Apply Your Knowledge

Reinforce the skills and apply the concepts you learned in this module.

Understanding Logical Tests and Absolute Cell Referencing

Note: To complete this assignment, you will be required to use the Data Files. Please contact your instructor for information about accessing the required files.

Instructions Part 1: For each of the following logical tests, indicate whether an IF function in Excel would return a value of True or False; given the following cell values: C2 = 88; H12 = 15; L3 = 24; M14 = 150; and G4 = 5.

1. C2 > H12 — Returned value: ____________________
2. L3 = G4 — Returned value: ____________________
3. M14 + 15 * H12 / 10 <= L3 — Returned value: ____________________
4. M14 – G4 < H12 / C2 — Returned value: ____________________
5. (C2 + H12) * 2 >= L3 – (C2 / 4) * 2 — Returned value: ____________________
6. L3 + 300 > H12 * G4 + 10 — Returned value: ____________________
7. G4 * M14 >= 2 * (H12 + 25) — Returned value: ____________________
8. H12 = 10 * (C2 / 8) — Returned value: ____________________

Instructions Part 2: Write cell L23 as a relative reference, absolute reference, mixed reference with the column varying, and mixed reference with the row varying.

____________ ____________ ____________ ____________

Instructions Part 3: Run Excel. Open the workbook Apply 3-1 Absolute Cell References. You will re-create the numerical grid pictured in Figure 3–83.

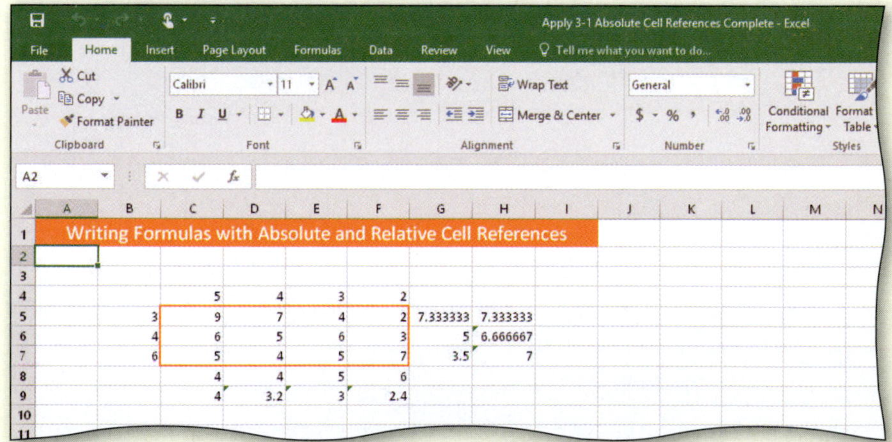

Figure 3–83

Perform the following tasks:

1. Enter a formula in cell C8 that divides the sum of cells C5 through C7 by cell C4. Write the formula so that when you copy it to cells D8:F8, Excel adjusts all the cell references according to the destination cells. Verify your formula by checking it against the values found in cells C8, D8, E8, and F8 in Figure 3–83.

2. Enter a formula in cell G5 that divides the sum of cells C5 through F5 by cell B5. Write the formula so that when you copy the formula to cells G6 and G7, Excel adjusts all the cell references according to the destination cells. Verify your formula by checking it against the values found in cells G5, G6, and G7 in Figure 3–83.
3. Enter a formula in cell C9 that divides the sum of cells C5 through C7 by cell C4. Write the formula using an absolute cell reference so that when you copy the formula to cells D9:F9, cell C4 remains absolute. Verify your formula by checking it against the values found in cells C9, D9, E9, and F9 in Figure 3–83.
4. Enter a formula in cell H5 that divides the sum of cells C5:F5 by cell B5. Write the formula using an absolute cell reference so that when you copy the formula to cells H6 and H7, cell B5 remains absolute. Verify your formula by checking it with the values found in cells H5, H6, and H7 in Figure 3–83.
5. Apply the worksheet name, Cell References, to the sheet tab and apply the Orange, Accent 2 Theme color to the sheet tab.
6. If requested by your instructor, add a dash followed by your name to the worksheet title in cell A1.
7. Save the workbook using the file name, Apply 3-1 Absolute Cell References Complete. Submit the revised workbook as specified by your instructor.
8. How would you rewrite the formula in cell H5 using relative and mixed cell references only, to come up with the same result as showing in Figure 3–83, and to produce the results currently showing in cells G6 and G7 in cells H6 and H7 when the formula in cell H5 is copied to those cells?

Extend Your Knowledge

Extend the skills you learned in this module and experiment with new skills. You may need to use Help to complete the assignment.

The Fill Handle and Nested IF Functions

Note: To complete this assignment, you will be required to use the Data Files. Please contact your instructor for information about accessing the required files.

Perform the following tasks:

Instructions Part 1: Run Excel. Open the workbook Extend 3-1 Fill and IF. If necessary, make Fill the active sheet.

1. Use the fill handle on one column at a time to propagate the 12 series through row 14, as shown in Figure 3–84. (*Hint*: Search in Help to learn more about the fill handle and Auto Fill.) In cells O2:O13, indicate the actions used with the fill handle to propagate the series. For instance, in cell O2, enter **Drag**. For instances where you need to select something other than the cell in row 2 prior to using the fill handle, enter the selection and then the drag action, **A2:A3 Drag** for example.
2. Select cell D20. While holding down the CTRL key, one at a time drag the fill handle three cells to the right, to the left, up, and down to generate four series of numbers beginning with zero and incremented by one.
3. Select cell H20. Point to the cell border so that the pointer changes to a plus sign with four arrows. Drag the pointer down to cell H22 to move the contents of cell H20 to cell H22.
4. If necessary, select cell H22. Point to the cell border so that the pointer changes to a plus sign with four arrows. While holding down the CTRL key, drag the pointer to cell K22 to copy the contents of cell H22 to cell K22.

Continued >

Extend Your Knowledge *continued*

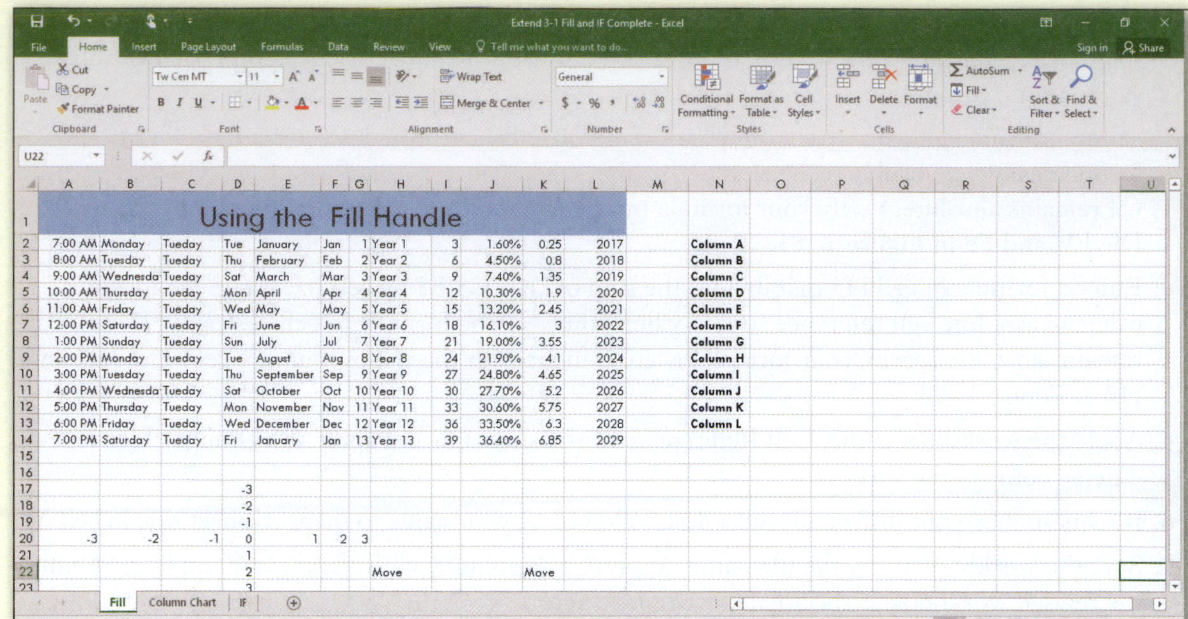

Figure 3–84

5. Select cell K20. Drag the fill handle in to the center of cell K20 until that the cell is shaded and the cell contents are deleted.
6. Select cell range H2:I14, and insert a 3-D column chart on a new sheet.
7. Change the chart title to Annual Breakdown.
8. Add a data table with no legend keys to the chart.
9. Apply the chart sheet name, Column Chart, to the sheet and move the sheet to follow the Fill sheet.
10. Save the workbook using the file name, Extend 3-1 Fill and IF Complete.

Instructions Part 2: Switch to the IF sheet in the Extend 3-1 Fill and IF Complete workbook.

1. Write an IF function in cell C2 that assigns a grade of 'Pass' if the score in cell B2 is 50 or above, and a grade of 'Fail' if the score in cell B2 is below 50. Copy this function to cells C3:C18.
2. Write a nested IF function in cell D2 that assigns a grade of A for scores between 80 and 100, a grade of B for scores between 65 and 79, a grade of C for scores between 50 and 64, and a grade of F for scores below 50. (*Hint*: Search in Help for nested IF when constructing your function.) Copy this function to cells D3:D18.
3. If requested by your instructor, change the student number in cell A3 on the IF sheet to your student number.
4. Save the workbook and submit the revised workbook as specified by your instructor.
5. Students who do not take a test receive a score of NS. How would you include a score of NS as a grade in each of Steps 1 and 2?

Expand Your World

Create a solution that uses cloud or web technologies by learning and investigating on your own from general guidance.

Analyzing and Graphing Development Indicators

Note: To complete this assignment, you will be required to use the Data Files. Please contact your instructor for information about accessing the required files.

Instructions: You are working as part of a group creating a report on historical education trends in the developing nation of Mali, comparing three related development indicators concerning school enrollment over time. Your task is to format the worksheet containing the historical data, chart the historical education indicators, and make the chart available to your group using OneDrive. Run Excel and then open the workbook, Expand 3-1 Education Indicators.

Perform the following tasks:

1. Save the workbook using the file name, Expand 3-1 Education Indicators Charted.
2. Format the worksheet using techniques you have learned to present the data in a visually appealing form.
3. Create charts that present the data for each of the three indicators. Think about what interested you in these indicators in the first place, and decide which chart types will best present the data. (*Hint:* If you are not sure which types to use, consider selecting the data and using the Recommended Chart button to narrow down and preview suitable choices.) Format the charts to best present the data in a clear, attractive format.
4. Give each worksheet a descriptive name and color the tabs using theme colors. Reorder the sheets so that the data table appears first, followed by the charts.
5. If requested by your instructor, export the file to OneDrive.
6. Submit the revised workbook as specified by your instructor.
7. Justify your choice of chart types in Step 3. Explain why you selected these types over other suitable choices.

In the Labs

Design, create, modify and/or use a workbook following the guidelines, concepts, and skills presented in this module. Labs 1 and 2, which increase in difficulty, require you to create solutions based on what you learned in the module; Lab 3 requires you to apply your creative thinking and problem-solving skills to design and implement a solution.

Lab 1: Eight-Year Financial Projection

Problem: Your supervisor in the finance department at August Online Technology has asked you to create a worksheet for the flagship product that will project the annual gross margin, total expenses, operating income, income taxes, and net income for the next eight years based on the assumptions in Table 3–9. The desired worksheet is shown in Figure 3–85.

Table 3–9 August Online Technology Financial Projection Assumptions	
Units Sold in Prior Year	235,411
Unit Cost	$150.00
Annual Sales Growth	3.25%
Annual Price Increase	3.00%
Margin	29.90%

Continued >

STUDENT ASSIGNMENTS

In the Labs *continued*

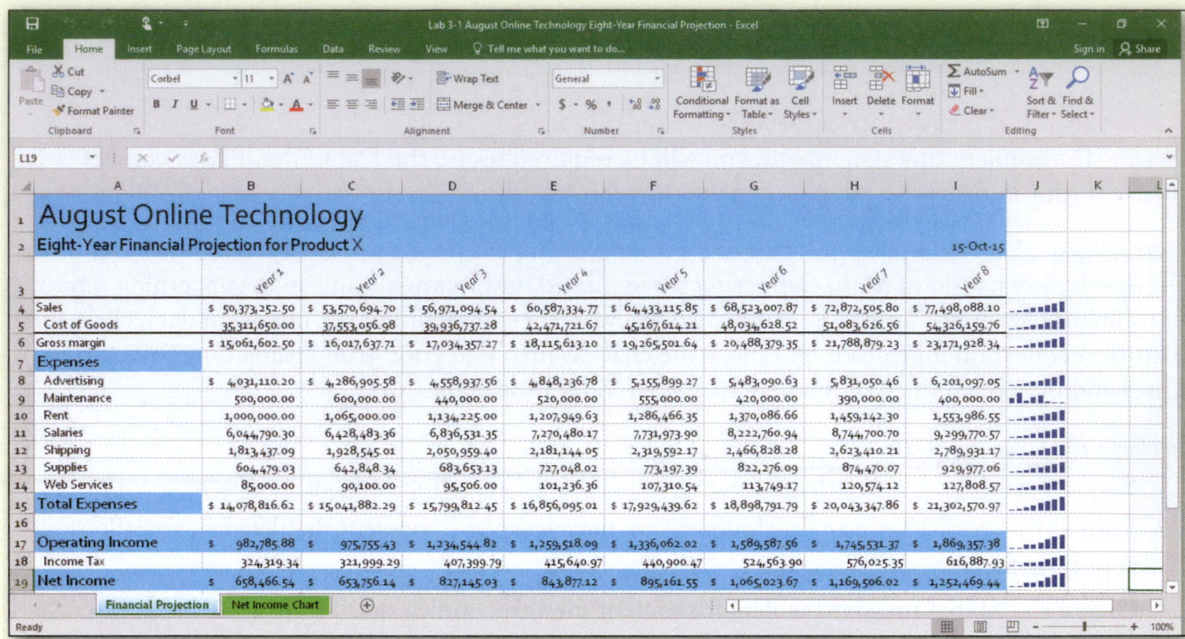

Figure 3–85

Perform the following tasks:

Instructions Part 1: Run Excel, open a blank workbook, and then create the worksheet.

1. Apply the Parallax theme to the worksheet.
2. Enter the worksheet title **`August Online Technology`** in cell A1 and the subtitle **`Eight-Year Financial Projection for Product X`** in cell A2. Format the worksheet title in cell A1 to 26-point and the worksheet subtitle in cell A2 to 16-point. Enter the system date in cell I2 using the NOW function. Format the date to the 14-Mar-12 style.
3. Change the following column widths: A = 24.00 characters; B through I = 14.00 characters. Change the heights of rows 7, 15, 17, 19, and 22 to 18.00 points.
4. Enter the eight column titles Year 1 through Year 8 in the range B3:I3 by entering Year 1 in cell B3 and then dragging cell B3's fill handle through the range C3:I3. Format cell B3 as follows:
   a. Increase the font size to 12.
   b. Center and italicize it.
   c. Angle its contents 45 degrees.
5. Use the Format Painter button to copy the format assigned to cell B3 to the range C3:I3.
6. Enter the row titles, as shown in Figure 3-85, in the range A4:A19. Change the font size in cells A7, A15, A17, and A19 to 14-point. Add thick bottom borders to the ranges A3:I3 and A5:I5. Use the Increase Indent button (Home tab | Alignment group) to increase the indent of the row titles in cell A5, the range A8:A14, and cell A18.
7. If requested by your instructor, change the entry in row 14 by inserting your surname prior to the text, Web Services.
8. Enter the table title **`Assumptions`** in cell A22. Enter the assumptions in Table 3–9 in the range A23:B27. Use format symbols when entering the numbers. Change the font size of the table title in cell A22 to 14-point and underline it.

9. Select the range B4:I19 and then click the Number Format Dialog Box Launcher (Home tab | Number group) to display the Format Cells dialog box. Use the Number category (Format Cells dialog box) to assign the appropriate style that displays numbers with two decimal places and negative numbers in black font and enclosed in parentheses to the range B4:I19.
10. Complete the following entries:
    a. Year 1 Sales (cell B4) = Units Sold in Prior Year * (Unit Cost / (1 – Margin))
    b. Year 2 Sales (cell C4) = Year 1 Sales * (1 + Annual Sales Growth) * (1 + Annual Price Increase). Copy cell C4 to the range D4:I4.
    c. Year 1 Cost of Goods (cell B5) = Year 1 Sales * (1 – Margin). Copy cell B5 to the range C5:I5.
    d. Gross Margin (cell B6) = Year 1 Sales – Year 1 Cost of Goods. Copy cell B6 to the range C6:I6.
    e. Year 1 Advertising (cell B8) = 1250 + 8% * Year 1 Sales. Copy cell B8 to the range C8:I8.
    f. Maintenance (row 9): Year 1 = 500,000; Year 2 = 600,000; Year 3 = 440,000; Year 4 = 520,000; Year 5 = 555,000; Year 6 = 420,000; Year 7 = 390,000; Year 8 = 400,000.
    g. Year 1 Rent (cell B10) = 1,000,000
    h. Year 2 Rent (cell C10) = Year 1 Rent + (6.5% * Year 1 Rent). Copy cell C10 to the range D10:I10.
    i. Year 1 Salaries (cell B11) = 12% * Year 1 Sales. Copy cell B11 to the range C11:I11.
    j. Year 1 Shipping (cell B12) = 3.6% * Year 1 Sales. Copy cell B12 to the range C12:I12.
    k. Year 1 Supplies (cell B13) = 1.2% * Year 1 Sales. Copy cell B13 to the range C13:I13.
    l. Year 1 Web Services (cell B14) = 85,000
    m. Year 2 Web Services (cell C14) = Year 1 Web Services + (6% * Year 1 Web Services). Copy cell C14 to the range D14:I14.
    n. Year 1 Total Expenses (cell B15) = SUM(B8:B14). Copy cell B15 to the range C15:I15.
    o. Year 1 Operating Income (cell B17) = Year 1 Gross Margin – Year 1 Total Expenses. Copy cell B17 to the range C17:I17.
    p. Year 1 Income Tax (cell B18): If Year 1 Operating Income is less than 0, then Year 1 Income Tax equals 0; otherwise Year 1 Income Tax equals 33% * Year 1 Operating Income. Copy cell B18 to the range C18:I18.
    q. Year 1 Net Income (cell B19) = Year 1 Operating Income – Year 1 Income Tax. Copy cell B19 to the range C19:I19.
    r. In cell J4, insert a column sparkline chart (Insert tab | Sparklines group) for cell range B4:I4.
    s. Insert column sparkline charts in cells J5, J6, J8:J15, and J17:J19 using ranges B5:I5, B6:I6, B8:I8 – B15:I15, and B17:I17 – B19:I19 respectively.
11. Apply the Currency number format with a dollar sign, two decimal places, and negative numbers in black with parentheses to the following ranges: B4:I4, B6:I6, B8:I8, B15:I15, B17:I17, and B19:I19. Apply the comma style format to the following ranges: B5:I5 and B9:I14. Apply the Number format with two decimal places and the 1000 separator to the range B18:I18.
12. Change the background colors, as shown in Figure 3–85. Use Blue, Accent 1, Lighter 40% for the background colors.
13. Save the workbook using the file name, Lab 3-1 August Online Technology Eight-Year Financial Projection.
14. Preview the worksheet. Use the Orientation button (Page Layout tab | Page Setup group) to fit the printout on one page in landscape orientation. Preview the formulas version (CTRL+`) of the worksheet in landscape orientation using the Fit to option. Press CTRL+` to instruct Excel to display the values version of the worksheet. Save the workbook again.

Continued >

In the Labs *continued*

Instructions Part 2: Create a chart to present the data, shown in Figure 3–86. If necessary, run Excel and open the workbook Lab 3-1 August Online Technology Eight-Year Financial Projection.

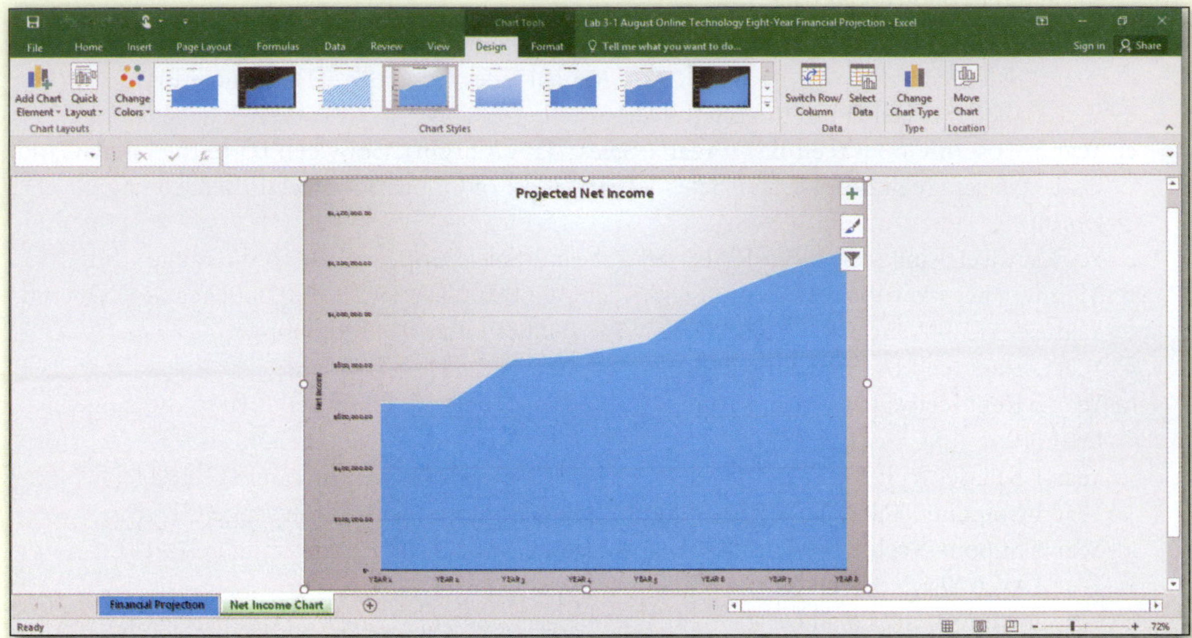

Figure 3–86

1. Use the nonadjacent ranges B3:I3 and B19:I19 to create a Stacked Area chart (*Hint:* use the Recommended Charts button). When the chart appears, click the Move Chart button to move the chart to a new sheet.
2. Change the chart title to `Projected Net Income`.
3. Use the Chart Elements button to add a vertical axis title. Edit the axis title text to read `Net Income`. Bold the axis title.
4. Change the Chart Style to Style 4 in the Chart Styles Gallery (Chart Tools Design tab | Chart Styles group). Use the 'Chart Quick Colors' button (Chart Tools Design tab | Chart Styles group) to change the color scheme to Monochromatic, Color 5.
5. Rename the sheet tabs Financial Projection and Net Income Chart. Rearrange the sheets so that the worksheet is leftmost and change the tab colors to those of your choosing.
6. Click the Financial Projection tab to return to the worksheet. Save the workbook using the same file name (Lab 3-1 August Online Technology Eight-Year Financial Projection) as defined in Part 1.

Instructions Part 3: Use Goal Seek to analyze three different sales scenarios. If necessary, open the workbook Lab 3-1 August Online Technology Eight-Year Financial Projection.

1. Divide the window into two panes between rows 6 and 7. Use the scroll bars to show both the top and bottom of the worksheet. Using the numbers in columns 2 and 3 of Table 3–10, analyze the effect of changing the annual sales growth (cell B25) and annual price increase (cell B26) on the net incomes in row 19. Record the answers for each case and submit the results in a form as requested by your instructor.

Table 3–10 August Online Technology Alternative Projections

Case	Annual Sales Growth	Annual Price Increase
1	4.25%	2.00%
2	2.25%	3.00%
3	1.25%	4.00%

2. Close the workbook without saving it and then reopen it. Use the 'What-If Analysis' button (Data tab | Forecast group) to goal seek. Determine a margin that would result in a Year 8 net income of $1,500,000. Save the workbook with your needed changes as Lab 3-1 August Online Technology Eight-Year Financial Projection GS. Submit the workbook with the new values or the results of the goal seek as requested by your instructor.
3. How would you use what-if analysis tools to determine what Annual Sales Growth you would need to achieve in order to keep prices steady over the eight-year projection period?

Lab 2: Updating a Weekly Payroll Worksheet

Note: To complete this assignment, you will be required to use the Data Files. Please contact your instructor for information about accessing the required files.

Problem: PHM Reliable Catering is a company that provides catering services to both small and large businesses. You have been asked to update the weekly payroll report to reflect changes in personnel, to update certain mandatory deductions, and to add overtime computations. The final worksheet is shown in Figure 3–87. Run Excel. Open the workbook, Lab 3-2 PHM Reliable Catering Weekly Payroll Report.

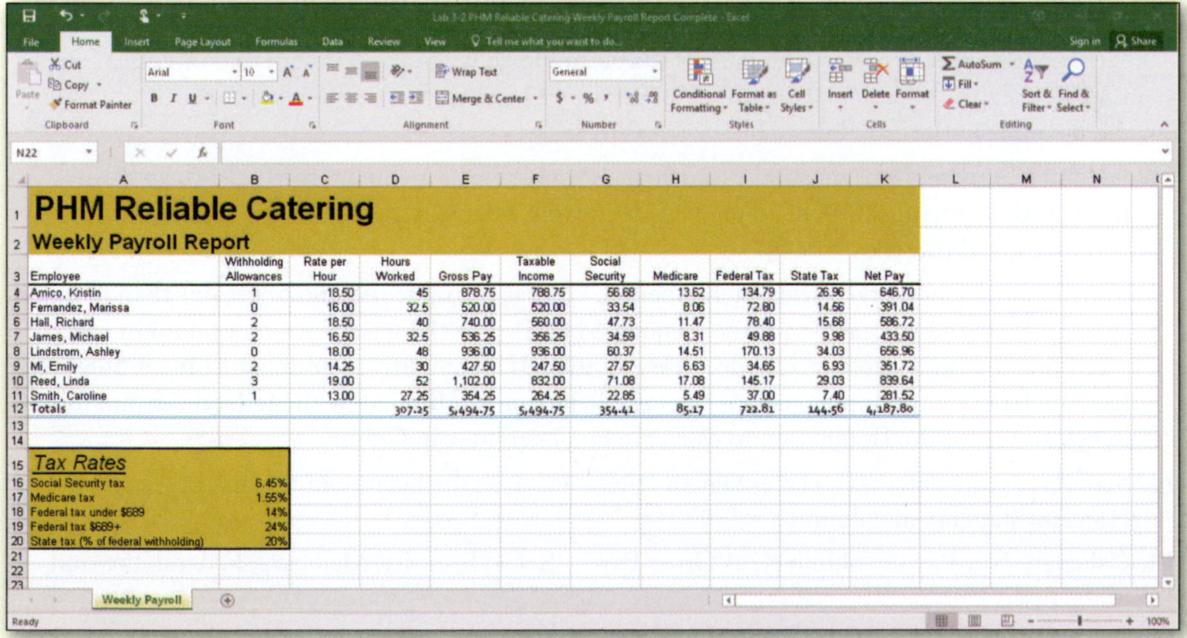

Figure 3–87

Continued >

In the Labs *continued*

Perform the following tasks:

1. Save the workbook using the file name, Lab 3-2 PHM Reliable Catering Weekly Payroll Report Complete.
2. Apply the Depth theme to the worksheet.
3. Delete rows 12 through 14 to remove the statistics below the Totals row.
4. Delete column B. Set column A width to 31.00 and columns B through K to 11.00. Select row 3 and set text to wrap in this row using the Wrap Text button (Home tab | Alignment group), and then set the row height to best fit.
5. Delete the record for the employee Evans, Timothy. Add two blank lines directly above the row for Mi, Emily, and add the information for the two new employees listed in Table 3–11.

Table 3–11 PHM Reliable Catering New Employee Data

Employee	Withholding Allowances	Rate Per Hour	Hours Worked
James, Michael	2	16.50	32.5
Lindstrom, Ashley	0	18.00	48

6. If requested by your instructor, replace one of the employee's names with your name.
7. If necessary, use the fill handle in cell E6 to copy the gross pay formula to the rows of the two new employees.
8. Add the Tax Rates information shown in Figure 3–87 in cells A15:B20 to your worksheet.
9. Change the font size in cell A1 to 28-point. Change the font size in cell A2 to 18-point. Change the font in cell A15 to 18-point italic and underlined. Change the row height for rows 1, 2, and 15 to best fit.
10. Insert three columns to the right of the Gross Pay column. Add the column titles `Taxable Income`, `Social Security`, and `Medicare` in cells F3:H3. Center the contents of cells B3:K3. Calculate the Social Security and Medicare taxes in columns G and H by multiplying the tax rates in the Tax Rates table by the Gross Pay.
11. Federal tax calculations must take into account two tiers of income tax, which are applied to the taxable income. Calculate the taxable income, which is the Gross Pay — (number of withholding allowances × $90).
12. Calculate the federal tax withheld. If an employee has a taxable income of greater than or equal to $689, then the federal tax withheld equals $110.85 plus the federal tax rate found in cell B19 multiplied by the taxable income in excess of $689. If an employees taxable income is $689 or less, the federal tax withheld equals the taxable income multiplied by the federal tax rate found in cell B18. Use the IF function to calculate the federal tax in Column I.
13. State tax is calculated as a percentage of federal tax. Use the tax rate in the Tax Rates table to calculate state tax in column J.
14. Calculate Net Pay in column K, as Gross Pay — Social Security, Medicare, Federal Tax, and State Tax.
15. Use the background color Gold, Accent 5, Darker 25% for the ranges A1:K2 and A15:B20.
16. Center the range B4:B11. Apply the currency style with two decimal places, no dollar signs, and negative numbers in black and parentheses to the range C4:C11 and E4:K12.
17. Apply a Thick Bottom Border to the range A3:K3. Apply the Total cell style to the range A12:K12. Apply a Thick Outside Border to the range A15:B20.

18. Change the sheet tab name to Weekly Payroll and the tab color to match the color used as background color in cell A1.
19. Preview the worksheet. Fit the printout of the worksheet on one page in landscape orientation. Save the workbook again.
20. Submit the workbook as specified by your instructor.

Lab 3: Consider This: Your Turn

Apply your creative thinking and problem-solving skills to design and implement a solution.

Transportation Costs

Instructions Part 1: You are thinking about buying a new vehicle, and you want to make sure that you buy one that offers the highest fuel savings. You decide to research hybrid cars as well as gas-only cars. Your friends are also interested in your results. Together, you decide to research the fuel costs associated with various types of vehicles. Research the gas mileage for six vehicles: three should run only on gas, and the others should be hybrid vehicles, combining gas and battery power. After you find the gas mileage for each vehicle, you will use formulas to calculate the fuel cost for one month, one year, and three years. Assume that in a typical month, you will drive 500 miles. Develop a worksheet following the general layout in Table 3–12 that shows the fuel cost analysis. Use the formulas listed in Table 3–13 and the concepts and techniques presented in this module to create the worksheet. You will need to find the average price of gas for your market. Add a chart showing the cost comparisons as an embedded chart.

Table 3–12 Fuel Cost Analysis

Vehicle	Miles Per Gallon	Fuel Cost 1 Month	Fuel Cost 1 Year	Fuel Cost 3 Years
Gas 1		Formula A	Formula B	Formula C
Gas 2		—	—	—
Gas 3		—	—	—
Hybrid 1		—	—	—
Hybrid 2		—	—	—
Hybrid 3		—	—	—
Assumptions				
Distance per Month	500			
Price of Gas				

Table 3–13 Fuel Cost Analysis Formulas

Formula A = (Distance per Month / Miles per Gallon)*Price of Gas
Formula B = ((Distance per Month / Miles per Gallon)*Price of Gas)*12
Formula C = ((Distance Per Month / Miles per Gallon)*Price of Gas)*36

Instructions Part 2: You made several decisions while creating the workbook for this assignment. Why did you select the chart type used to compare fuel costs? What other costs might you want to consider when making your purchase decision?

1 Databases and Database Objects: An Introduction

Objectives

You will have mastered the material in this module when you can:

- Describe the features of the Access window
- Create a database
- Create tables in Datasheet and Design views
- Add records to a table
- Close a database
- Open a database
- Print the contents of a table
- Import data
- Create and use a query
- Create and use a form
- Create and print custom reports
- Modify a report in Layout view
- Perform special database operations
- Design a database to satisfy a collection of requirements

Introduction

The term **database** describes a collection of data organized in a manner that allows access, retrieval, and use of that data. Microsoft Access 2016, usually referred to as simply Access, is a database management system. A **database management system** is software that allows you to use a computer to create a database; add, change, and delete data in the database; ask and answer questions concerning the data; and create forms and reports using the data.

Project — Database Creation

PrattLast Associates is a human resources outsourcing company that provides HR services, such as payroll, hiring, training, and employee benefits management to small and medium-size businesses in the Midwest. Organizations might outsource only one function, such as payroll, or might outsource several functions. While there are many different ways to charge customers, PrattLast charges a set amount per employee per month. The amount varies based on number and type of functions outsourced.

Account managers serve their respective client companies by providing HR solutions and understanding the businesses for which they are responsible. The PrattLast account managers can earn bonuses if their client companies elect to outsource additional HR functions. For example, if the business currently outsources only payroll but is convinced by the account manager to add hiring to the outsourced functions, the account manager receives a bonus.

To ensure that operations run smoothly, PrattLast organizes data on its accounts and account managers in a database managed by Access. In this way, PrattLast keeps its data current and accurate and can analyze it for trends; PrattLast can also create a variety of useful reports.

In a **relational database** such as those maintained by Access, a database consists of a collection of tables, each of which contains information on a specific subject. Figure 1–1 shows the database for PrattLast Associates. It consists of two tables: the Account table (Figure 1–1a) contains information about PrattLast accounts, and the Account Manager table (Figure 1–1b) contains information about the account managers to whom these accounts are assigned.

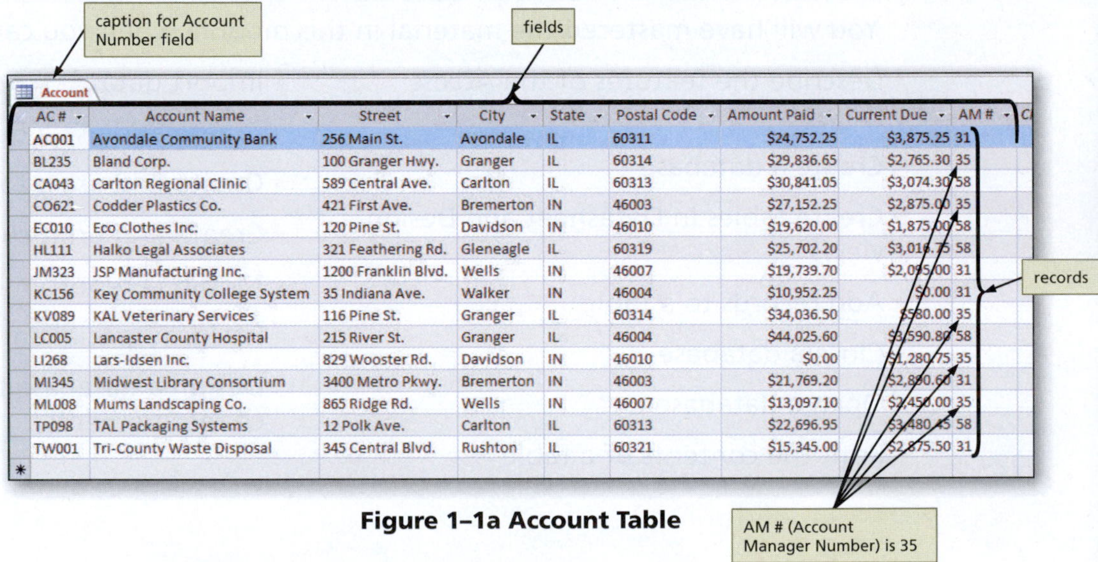

AC #	Account Name	Street	City	State	Postal Code	Amount Paid	Current Due	AM #
AC001	Avondale Community Bank	256 Main St.	Avondale	IL	60311	$24,752.25	$3,875.25	31
BL235	Bland Corp.	100 Granger Hwy.	Granger	IL	60314	$29,836.65	$2,765.30	35
CA043	Carlton Regional Clinic	589 Central Ave.	Carlton	IL	60313	$30,841.05	$3,074.30	58
CO621	Codder Plastics Co.	421 First Ave.	Bremerton	IN	46003	$27,152.25	$2,875.00	35
EC010	Eco Clothes Inc.	120 Pine St.	Davidson	IN	46010	$19,620.00	$1,875.00	58
HL111	Halko Legal Associates	321 Feathering Rd.	Gleneagle	IL	60319	$25,702.20	$3,016.75	58
JM323	JSP Manufacturing Inc.	1200 Franklin Blvd.	Wells	IN	46007	$19,739.70	$2,095.00	31
KC156	Key Community College System	35 Indiana Ave.	Walker	IN	46004	$10,952.25	$0.00	31
KV089	KAL Veterinary Services	116 Pine St.	Granger	IL	60314	$34,036.50	$580.00	35
LC005	Lancaster County Hospital	215 River St.	Granger	IL	46004	$44,025.60	$3,590.80	58
LI268	Lars-Idsen Inc.	829 Wooster Rd.	Davidson	IN	46010	$0.00	$1,280.75	35
MI345	Midwest Library Consortium	3400 Metro Pkwy.	Bremerton	IN	46003	$21,769.20	$2,890.60	31
ML008	Mums Landscaping Co.	865 Ridge Rd.	Wells	IN	46007	$13,097.10	$2,450.00	35
TP098	TAL Packaging Systems	12 Polk Ave.	Carlton	IL	60313	$22,696.95	$3,480.45	58
TW001	Tri-County Waste Disposal	345 Central Blvd.	Rushton	IL	60321	$15,345.00	$2,875.50	31

Figure 1–1a Account Table

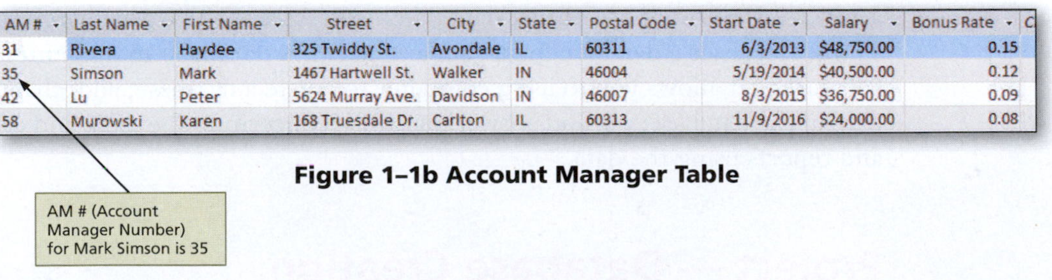

AM #	Last Name	First Name	Street	City	State	Postal Code	Start Date	Salary	Bonus Rate
31	Rivera	Haydee	325 Twiddy St.	Avondale	IL	60311	6/3/2013	$48,750.00	0.15
35	Simson	Mark	1467 Hartwell St.	Walker	IN	46004	5/19/2014	$40,500.00	0.12
42	Lu	Peter	5624 Murray Ave.	Davidson	IN	46007	8/3/2015	$36,750.00	0.09
58	Murowski	Karen	168 Truesdale Dr.	Carlton	IL	60313	11/9/2016	$24,000.00	0.08

Figure 1–1b Account Manager Table

The rows in the tables are called **records**. A record contains information about a given person, product, or event. A row in the Account table, for example, contains information about a specific account, such as the account's name, address information, and other data.

The columns in the tables are called fields. A **field** contains a specific piece of information within a record. In the Account table, for example, the fourth field, City, contains the name of the city where the account is located.

The first field in the Account table is AC #, which is an abbreviation for Account Number. PrattLast Associates assigns each account a number; the PrattLast account numbers consist of two uppercase letters followed by a three-digit number.

The account numbers are unique; that is, no two accounts have the same number. Such a field is a **unique identifier**. A unique identifier, as its name suggests, is a way of uniquely identifying each record in the database. A given account number will appear only in a single record in the table. Only one record exists, for example, in which the account number is JM323. A unique identifier is also called a **primary key**. Thus, the Account Number field is the primary key for the Account table. This means the Account Number field can be used to uniquely identify a record in the table. No two records can have the same value in the Account Number field.

The next seven fields in the Account table are Account Name, Street, City, State, Postal Code, Amount Paid, and Current Due. The Amount Paid column contains the amount that the account has paid PrattLast Associates year to date (YTD) prior to the current period. The Current Due column contains the amount due to PrattLast for the current period. For example, account JM323 is JSP Manufacturing Inc. The address is 1200 Franklin Blvd., in Wells, Indiana. The postal code is 46007. The amount paid is $19,739.70 and the current due amount is $2,095.00.

PrattLast assigns a single account manager to work with each account. The last column in the Account table, AM # (an abbreviation for Account Manager Number) gives the number of the account's account manager. The account manager number for JSP Manufacturing is 31.

The first field in the Account Manager table is also AM #, for Account Manager Number. The account manager numbers are unique, so the Account Manager Number field is the primary key of the Account Manager table.

The other fields in the Account Manager table are Last Name, First Name, Street, City, State, Postal Code, Start Date, Salary, and Bonus Rate. The Start Date field gives the date the account manager began working for PrattLast. The Salary field gives the salary paid to the account manager thus far this year. The Bonus Rate gives the potential bonus percentage based on personal performance. The bonus rate applies when the account manager either brings in new business or recommends productivity improvements. For example, account manager 31 is Haydee Rivera. Her address is 325 Twiddy St., in Avondale, Illinois. Her postal code is 60311. Haydee started working for PrattLast on June 3, 2013. So far this year, she has been paid $48,750.00 in salary. Her bonus rate is 0.15 (15%).

The account manager number appears in both the Account table and the Account Manager table, and relates accounts and account managers. Account manager 42, Peter Lu, was recently promoted to account manager and has not yet been assigned any accounts. His account manager number, therefore, does not appear on any row in the Account table.

BTW

Naming Fields

Access 2016 has a number of reserved words, words that have a special meaning to Access. You cannot use these reserved words as field names. For example, Name is a reserved word and could not be used in the Account table to describe an account's name. For a complete list of reserved words in Access 2016, consult Access Help.

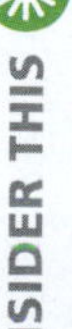

How would you find the name of the account manager for Midwest Library Consortium?

In the Account table, you see that the account manager number for account Midwest Library Consortium is 31. To find the name of this account manager, look for the row in the Account Manager table that contains 31 in the AM # column. After you have found it, you know that the account manager for Midwest Library Consortium is Haydee Rivera.

CONSIDER THIS

How would you find all the accounts assigned to Haydee Rivera?

First, look in the Account Manager table to find that her number is 31. You would then look through the Account table for all the accounts that contain 31 in the AM # column. Haydee's accounts are AC001 (Avondale Community Bank), JM323 (JSP Manufacturing Inc.), KC156 (Key Community College System), MI345 (Midwest Library Consortium), and TW001 (Tri-County Waste Disposal).

For an introduction to Windows and instructions about how to perform basic Windows tasks, read the Office and Windows module at the beginning of this book, where you can learn how to resize windows, change screen resolution, create folders, move and rename files, use Windows Help, and much more.

In this module, you will learn how to create and use the database shown in Figure 1–1. The following roadmap identifies general activities you will perform as you progress through this module:

1. CREATE the FIRST TABLE, Account Manager, using Datasheet view.
2. ADD RECORDS to the Account Manager table.
3. PRINT the CONTENTS of the Account Manager table.
4. IMPORT RECORDS into the second table, Account.
5. MODIFY the SECOND TABLE using Design view.
6. CREATE a QUERY for the Account table.
7. CREATE a FORM for the Account table.
8. CREATE a REPORT for the Account table.

Creating a Database

For an introduction to Office and instructions about how to perform basic tasks in Office apps, read the Office and Windows module at the beginning of this book, where you can learn how to run an application, use the ribbon, save a file, open a file, print a file, exit an application, use Help, and much more.

In Access, all the tables, reports, forms, and queries that you create are stored in a single file called a database. A database is a structure that can store information about multiple types of objects, the properties of those objects, and the relationships among the objects. The first step is to create the database that will hold your tables, reports, forms, and queries. You can use either the Blank desktop database option or a template to create a new database. If you already know the tables and fields you want in your database, you would use the Blank desktop database option. If not, you can use a template. Templates can guide you by suggesting some commonly used databases.

To Create a Database

Because you already know the tables and fields you want in the PrattLast Associates database, you would use the Blank desktop database option rather than using a template. The following steps create the database.

1. Run Access.
2. Using the steps in the "To Create an Access Database" section in the Office and Windows module, create the database on your hard disk, OneDrive, or other storage location using PrattLast Associates as the file name (Figure 1–2).

Q&A

The title bar for my Navigation Pane contains All Tables rather than All Access Objects, as in the figure. Is that a problem?

It is not a problem. The title bar indicates how the Navigation Pane is organized. You can carry out the steps in the text with either organization. To make your screens match the ones in the text, click the Navigation Pane arrow and then click Object Type.

I do not have the Search bar that appears in the figure. Is that a problem?

It is not a problem. If your Navigation Pane does not display a Search bar and you want your screens to match the ones in the text, right-click the Navigation Pane title bar arrow to display a shortcut menu, and then click Search Bar.

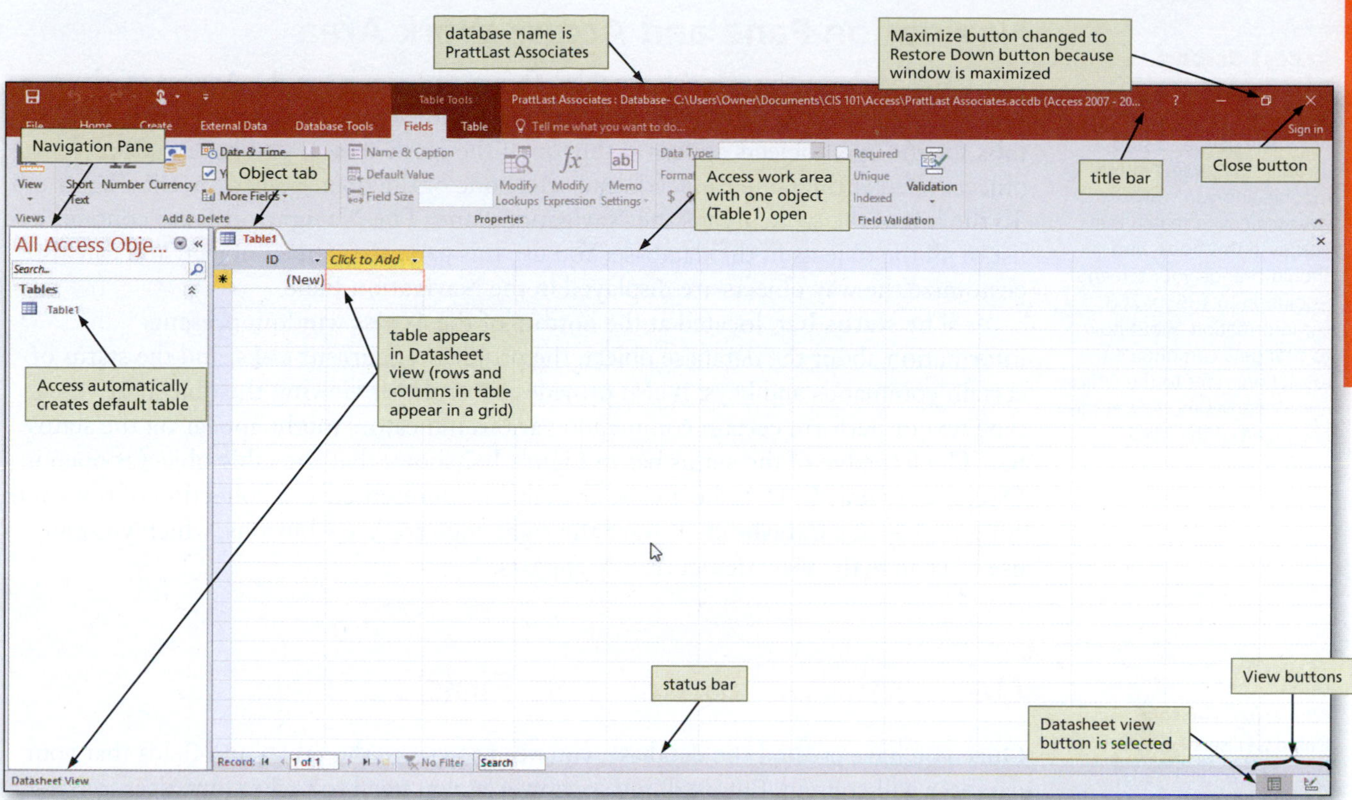

Figure 1–2

To Create a Database Using a Template

Ideally, you will design your own database, create a blank database, and then create the tables you have determined that your database should contain. If you are not sure what database design you will need, you could use a template. Templates can guide you by suggesting some commonly used databases. To create a database using a template, you would use the following steps.

1. If you have another database open, close it without exiting Access by clicking File on the ribbon to open the Backstage view and then clicking Close.
2. If you do not see a template that you want, you can search Microsoft Office online for additional templates.
3. Click the template you want to use. Be sure you have selected one that indicates it is for a desktop database.
4. Enter a file name and select a location for the database.
5. Click the Create button to create the database.

BTW

Available Templates

The templates gallery includes both desktop and web-based templates. If you are creating an Access database for your own use, select a desktop template. Web-based templates allow you to create databases that you can publish to a SharePoint server.

BTW

Organizing Files and Folders

You should organize and store files in folders so that you easily can find the files later. For example, if you are taking an introductory computer class called CIS 101, a good practice would be to save all Access files in an Access folder in a CIS 101 folder. For a discussion of folders and detailed examples of creating folders, refer to the Office and Windows module at the beginning of this book.

The Access Window

The Access window consists of a variety of components to make your work more efficient. These include the Navigation Pane, Access work area, ribbon, shortcut menus, and Quick Access Toolbar. Some of these components are common to other Microsoft Office apps; others are unique to Access.

BTW
Access Screen Resolution
If you are using a computer or mobile device to step through the project in this module and you want your screens to match the figures in this book, you should change your screen's resolution to 1366 x 768. For information about how to change a computer's resolution, refer to the Office and Windows module at the beginning of this book.

Navigation Pane and Access Work Area

You work on objects such as tables, forms, and reports in the **Access work area**. In the work area in Figure 1–2, a single table, Table1, is open in the work area. **Object tabs** for the open objects appear at the top of the work area. If you have multiple objects open at the same time, you can select one of the open objects by clicking its tab. To the left of the work area is the Navigation Pane. The **Navigation Pane** contains a list of all the objects in the database. You use this pane to open an object. You can also customize the way objects are displayed in the Navigation Pane.

The **status bar**, located at the bottom of the Access window, presents information about the database object, the progress of current tasks, and the status of certain commands and keys; it also provides controls for viewing the object. As you type text or perform certain commands, various indicators might appear on the status bar. The left edge of the status bar in Figure 1–2 shows that the table object is open in **Datasheet view**. In Datasheet view, the table is represented as a collection of rows and columns called a **datasheet**. Toward the right edge are View buttons, which you can use to change the view that currently appears.

BTW
Naming Tables
Database users typically have their own guidelines for naming tables. Some use the singular version of the object being described while others use the prefix tbl with a table name. This book uses the singular version of the object (Account, Account Manager).

Determining Tables and Fields

Once you have created the database, you need to create the tables and fields that your database will contain. Before doing so, however, you need to make some decisions regarding the tables and fields.

BTW
Multiple-Word Names
There are several ways to handle multiple word names. You can omit the space (AccountNumber) or use an underscore in place of the space (Account_Number). Another option is to use an underscore in place of a space, but use the same case for all letters (ACCOUNT_NUMBER or account_number).

Naming Tables and Fields

In creating your database, you must name tables, fields, and other objects. Before beginning the design process, you must understand the rules Access applies to table and field names. These rules are:

1. Names can be up to 64 characters in length.
2. Names can contain letters, digits, and spaces, as well as most of the punctuation symbols.
3. Names cannot contain periods (.), exclamation points (!), accent graves (`), or square brackets ([ ]).
4. Each field in a table must have a unique name.

The approach to naming tables and fields used in this text is to begin the names with an uppercase letter and to use lowercase for the other letters. In multiple-word names, each word begins with an uppercase letter, and there is a space between words (for example, Account Number).

Determining the Primary Key

For each table, you need to determine the primary key, the unique identifier. In many cases, you will have obvious choices, such as Account Number or Account Manager Number. If you do not have an obvious choice, you can use the primary key that Access creates automatically. It is a field called ID. It is an **autonumber field**, which means that Access will assign the value 1 to the first record, 2 to the second record, and so on.

Determining Data Types for the Fields

For each field in your database, you must determine the field's **data type**, that is, the type of data that can be stored in the field. Four of the most commonly used data types in Access are:

1. **Short Text** — The field can contain any characters. A maximum number of 255 characters is allowed in a field whose data type is Short Text.
2. **Number** — The field can contain only numbers. The numbers can be either positive or negative. Fields assigned this type can be used in arithmetic operations. You usually assign fields that contain numbers but will not be used for arithmetic operations (such as postal codes) a data type of Short Text.
3. **Currency** — The field can contain only monetary data. The values will appear with currency symbols, such as dollar signs, commas, and decimal points, and with two digits following the decimal point. Like numeric fields, you can use currency fields in arithmetic operations. Access assigns a size to currency fields automatically.
4. **Date & Time** — The field can contain dates and/or times.

Table 1–1 shows the other data types that are available in Access.

BTW
Data Types
Different database management systems have different available data types. Even data types that are essentially the same can have different names. The Currency data type in Access, for example, is referred to as Money in SQL Server.

BTW
AutoNumber Fields
AutoNumber fields also are called AutoIncrement fields. In Design view, the New Values field property allows you to increment the field sequentially (Sequential) or randomly (Random). The default is sequential.

Table 1-1 Additional Data Types

Data Type	Description
Long Text	Field can store a variable amount of text or combinations of text and numbers where the total number of characters may exceed 255.
AutoNumber	Field can store a unique sequential number that Access assigns to a record. Access will increment the number by 1 as each new record is added.
Yes/No	Field can store only one of two values. The choices are Yes/No, True/False, or On/Off.
OLE Object	Field can store an OLE object, which is an object linked to or embedded in the table.
Hyperlink	Field can store text that can be used as a hyperlink address.
Attachment	Field can contain an attached file. Images, spreadsheets, documents, charts, and other elements can be attached to this field in a record in the database. You can view and edit the attached file.
Calculated	Field specified as a calculation based on other fields. The value is not actually stored.

In the Account table, because the Account Number, Account Name, Street, City, and State can all contain letters, their data types should be Short Text. The data type for Postal Code is Short Text instead of Number because you typically do not use postal codes in arithmetic operations; you do not add postal codes or find an average postal code, for example. The Amount Paid and Current Due fields contain monetary data, so their data types should be Currency. The Account Manager Number field contains numbers, but you will not use these numbers in arithmetic operations, so its data type should be Short Text.

Similarly, in the Account Manager table, the data type for the Account Manager Number, Last Name, First Name, Street, City, State, and Postal Code fields should all be Short Text. The Start Date field should have a data type of Date & Time. The Salary field contains monetary amounts, so its data type should be Currency. The Bonus Rate field contains numbers that are not dollar amounts, so its data type should be Number.

For fields whose data type is Short Text, you can change the field size, that is, the maximum number of characters that can be entered in the field. If you set the field size

BTW
Currency Symbols
To show the symbol for the Euro (€) instead of the dollar sign, change the Format property for the field whose data type is currency. To change the default symbols for currency, change the settings in Windows.

for the State field to 2, for example, Access will not allow the user to enter more than two characters in the field. On the other hand, fields whose data type is Number often require you to change the field size, which is the storage space assigned to the field by Access. Table 1–2 shows the possible field sizes for Number fields.

Table 1-2 Field Sizes for Number Fields

Field Size	Description
Byte	Integer value in the range of 0 to 255
Integer	Integer value in the range of -32,768 to 32,767
Long Integer	Integer value in the range of -2,147,483,648 to 2,147,483,647
Single	Numeric values with decimal places to seven significant digits—requires 4 bytes of storage
Double	Numeric values with decimal places to more accuracy than Single—requires 8 bytes of storage
Replication ID	Special identifier required for replication
Decimal	Numeric values with decimal places to more accuracy than Single or Double—requires 12 bytes of storage.

CONSIDER THIS

What is the appropriate size for the Bonus Rate field?

If the size were Byte, Integer, or Long Integer, only integers could be stored. If you try to store a value that has decimal places, such as 0.18, in fields of these sizes, the portion to the right of the decimal point would be removed, giving a result of 0. To address this problem, the bonus rate should have a size of Single, Double, or Decimal. With such small numbers involved, Single, which requires the least storage of the three, is the appropriate choice.

BTW

Naming Files

The following characters cannot be used in a file name: question mark (?), quotation mark ("), slash (/), backslash (\ ), colon (:), asterisk (*), vertical bar (|), greater than symbol (>), and less than symbol (<).

Creating a Table

To create a table in Access, you must define its structure. That is, you must define all the fields that make up the table and their characteristics. You must also indicate the primary key.

In Access, you can use two different views to create a table: Datasheet view and Design view. In **Datasheet view**, the data in the table is presented in rows and columns, similar to a spreadsheet. Although the main reason to use Datasheet view is to add or update records in a table, you can also use it to create a table or to later modify its structure. The other view, **Design view**, is only used to create a table or to modify the structure of a table.

As you might expect, Design view has more functionality for creating a table than Datasheet view. That is, there are certain actions that can only be performed in Design view. One such action is assigning Single as the field size for the Bonus Rate field. In this module, you will create the first table, the Account Manager table, in Datasheet view. Once you have created the table in Datasheet view, you will use Design view to change the field size.

Whichever view you choose to use, before creating the table, you need to know the names and data types of the fields that will make up the table. You can also decide to enter a description for a particular field to explain important details about the field. When you select this field, this description will appear on the status bar. You might also choose to assign a **caption** to a particular field. If you assign a caption, Access will display the value you assign, rather than the field name, in datasheets and in forms. If you do not assign a caption, Access will display the field name.

CONSIDER THIS

When would you want to use a caption?

You would use a caption whenever you want something other than the field name displayed. One common example is when the field name is relatively long and the data in the field is relatively short. In the Account Manager table, the name of the first field is Account Manager Number, but the field contains data that is only two characters long. You will change the caption for this field to AM #, which is much shorter than Account Manager Number yet still describes the field. Doing so will enable you to greatly reduce the width of the column.

The results of these decisions for the fields in the Account Manager table are shown in Table 1–3. The table also shows the data types and field sizes of the fields as well as any special properties that need to be changed. The Account Manager Number field has a caption of AM #, enabling the width of the Account Manager Number column to be reduced in the datasheet.

Table 1-3 Structure of Account Manager Table

Field Name	Data Type	Field Size	Description
Account Manager Number	Short Text	2	Primary Key **Description:** Unique identifier of account manager **Caption:** AM #
Last Name	Short Text	15	
First Name	Short Text	15	
Street	Short Text	20	
City	Short Text	20	
State	Short Text	2	
Postal Code	Short Text	5	
Start Date	Date/Time	(This appears as Date & Time on the menu of available data types)	
Salary	Currency		
Bonus Rate	Number	Single	Format: Fixed Decimal Places: 2

CONSIDER THIS

How do you determine the field size?

You need to determine the maximum number of characters that can be entered in the field. In some cases, it is obvious. Field sizes of 2 for the State field and 5 for the Postal Code field are certainly the appropriate choices. In other cases, you need to determine how many characters you want to allow. In the list shown in Table 1–3, PrattLast decided allowing 15 characters was sufficient for last names. This field size can be changed later if it proves to be insufficient.

CONSIDER THIS

What is the purpose of the Format and Decimal Places properties?

The format guarantees that bonus rates will be displayed with a fixed number of decimal places. Setting the decimal places property to 2 guarantees that the rates will be displayed with precisely two decimal places. Thus, a bonus rate of 0.2 will be displayed as 0.20.

1 CREATE FIRST TABLE | 2 ADD RECORDS | 3 PRINT CONTENTS | 4 IMPORT RECORDS
5 MODIFY SECOND TABLE | 6 CREATE QUERY | 7 CREATE FORM | 8 CREATE REPORT

To Modify the Primary Key

When you first create your database, Access automatically creates a table for you. You can immediately begin defining the fields. If, for any reason, you do not have this table or inadvertently delete it, you can create the table by clicking Create on the ribbon and then clicking the Table button (Create tab | Tables group). In either case, you are ready to define the fields.

The following steps change the name, data type, and other properties of the first field to match the Account Manager Number field in Table 1–3, which is the primary key. ***Why?*** *Access has already created the first field as the primary key field, which it has named ID. Account Manager Number is a more appropriate choice.*

1

- Right-click the column heading for the ID field to display a shortcut menu (Figure 1–3).

Q&A Why does my shortcut menu look different?
You displayed a shortcut menu for the column instead of the column heading. Be sure you right-click the column heading.

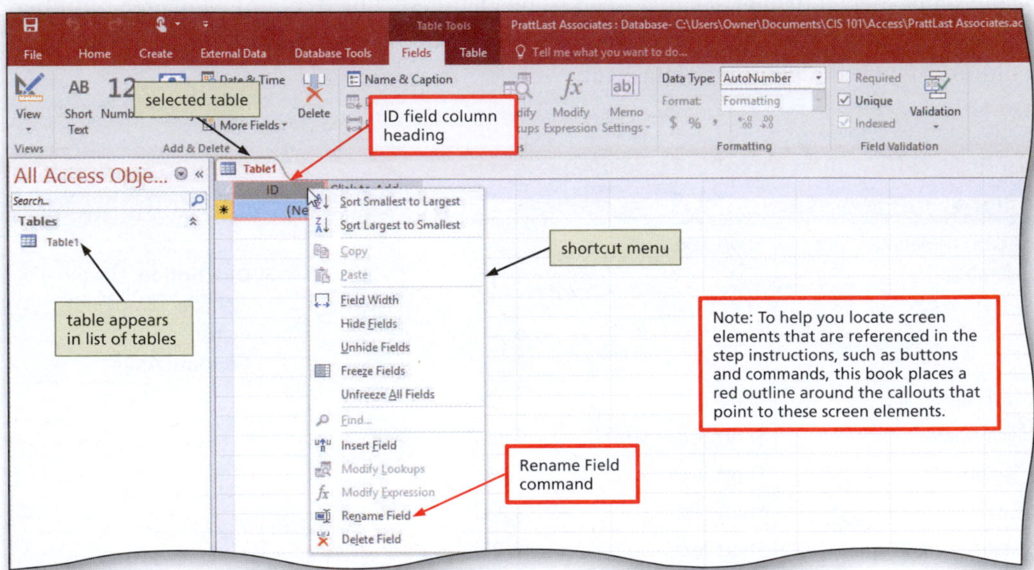

Figure 1–3

- Click Rename Field on the shortcut menu to highlight the current name.
- Type `Account Manager Number` to assign a name to the new field.
- Click the white space immediately below the field name to complete the addition of the field (Figure 1–4).

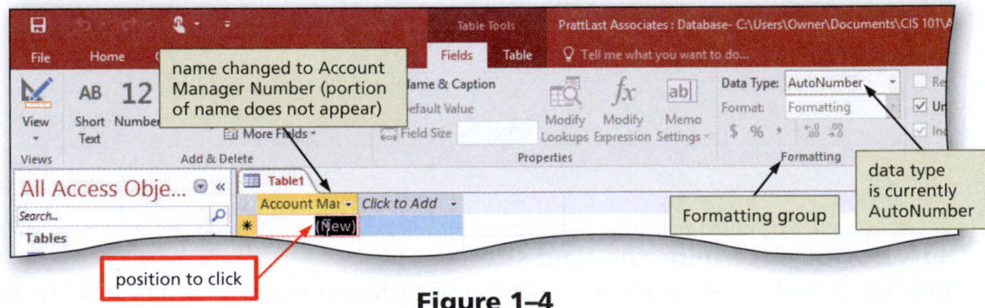

Figure 1–4

Q&A Why does the full name of the field not appear?
The default column size is not large enough for Account Manager Number to be displayed in its entirety. You will address this issue in later steps.

3

- Because the data type needs to be changed from AutoNumber to Short Text, click the Data Type arrow (Table Tools Fields tab | Formatting group) to display a menu of available data types (Figure 1–5).

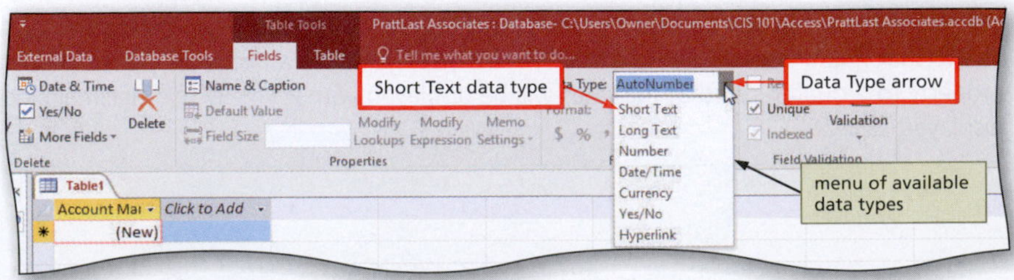

Figure 1–5

- Click Short Text to select the data type for the field (Figure 1–6).

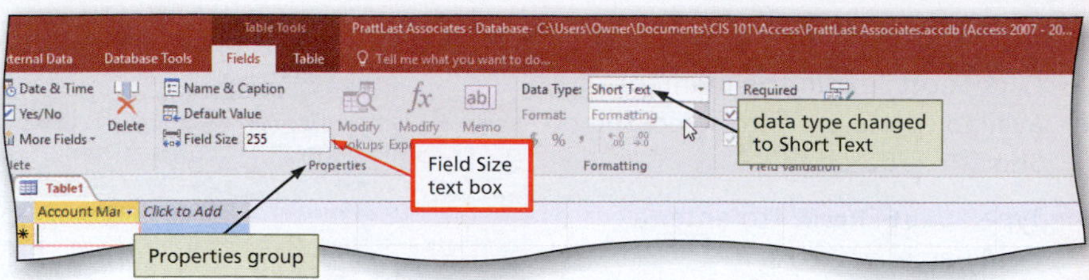

Figure 1–6

- Click the Field Size text box (Table Tools Fields tab | Properties group) to select the current field size, use either the DELETE or BACKSPACE keys to erase the current field size, if necessary, and then type `2` as the new field size.
- Click the Name & Caption button (Table Tools Fields tab | Properties group) to display the Enter Field Properties dialog box.
- Click the Caption text box (Enter Field Properties dialog box), and then type **AM #** as the caption.
- Click the Description text box, and then type **Unique identifier of account manager** as the description (Figure 1–7).

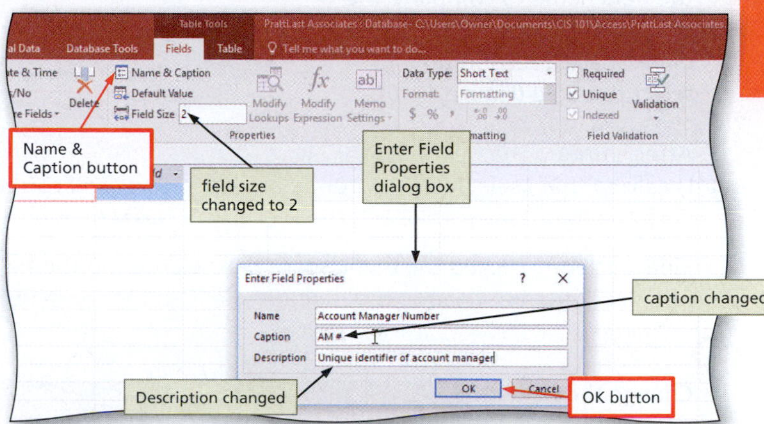

Figure 1–7

- Click the OK button (Enter Field Properties dialog box) to change the caption and description (Figure 1–8).

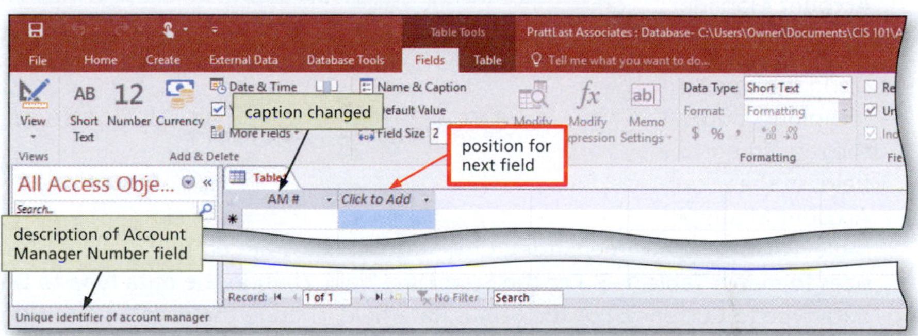

Figure 1–8

To Define the Remaining Fields in a Table

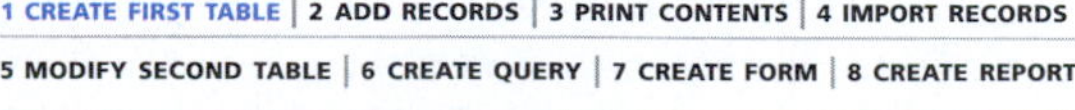

To define an additional field, you click the 'Click to Add' column heading, select the data type, and then type the field name. This is different from the process you used to modify the ID field. The following steps define the remaining fields shown in Table 1–3. These steps do not change the field size of the Bonus Rate field, however. ***Why?*** *You can only change the field size of a Number field in Design view. Later, you will use Design view to change this field size and change the format and number of decimal places.*

- Click the 'Click to Add' column heading to display a menu of available data types (Figure 1–9).

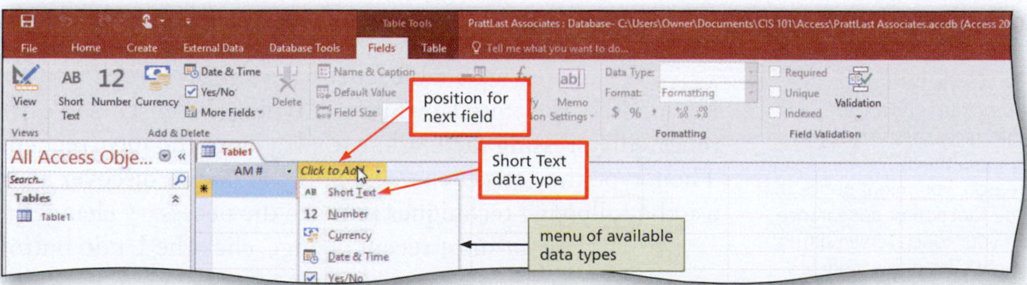

Figure 1–9

- Click Short Text in the menu of available data types to select the Short Text data type.
- Type `Last Name` to enter a field name.
- Click the blank space below the field name to complete the change of the name. Click the blank space a second time to select the field (Figure 1–10).

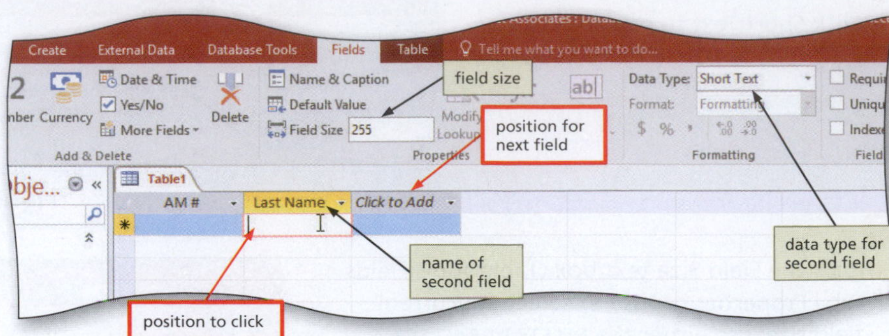

Figure 1–10

Q&A After entering the field name, I realized that I selected the wrong data type. How can I correct it?
Click the Data Type arrow, and then select the correct type.

I inadvertently clicked the blank space before entering the field name. How can I correct the name?
Right-click the field name, click Rename Field on the shortcut menu, and then type the new name.

- Change the field size to 15 just as you changed the field size of the Account Manager Number field.
- Using the same technique, add the remaining fields in the Account Manager table. For the First Name, Street, City, State, and Postal Code fields, use the Short Text data type, but change the field sizes to match Table 1–3. For the Start Date field, change the data type to Date/Time. For the Salary field, change the data type to Currency. For the Bonus Rate field, change the data type to Number (Figure 1–11).

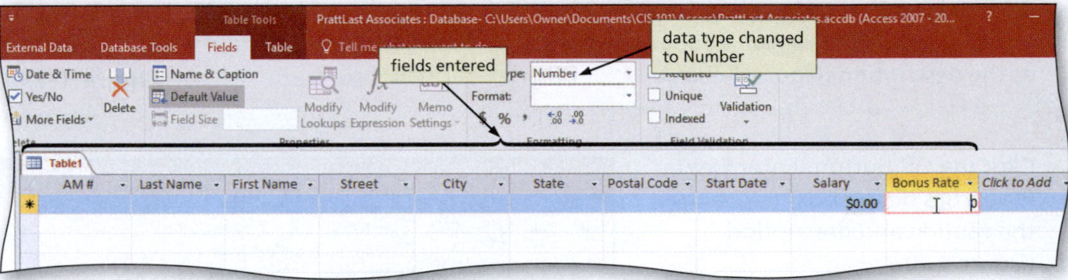

Figure 1–11

Q&A I have an extra row between the row containing the field names and the row that begins with the asterisk. What happened? Is this a problem? If so, how do I fix it?
You inadvertently added a record to the table by pressing a key. Even pressing the SPACEBAR would add a record. You now have an unwanted record. To fix it, press the ESC key or click the Undo button to undo the action. You may need to do this more than once.

When I try to move on to specify another field, I get an error message indicating that the primary key cannot contain a null value. How do I correct this?
First, click the OK button to remove the error message. Next, press the ESC key or click the Undo button to undo the action. You may need to do this more than once.

BTW
Touch Screen Differences
The Office and Windows interfaces may vary if you are using a touch screen. For this reason, you might notice that the function or appearance of your touch screen differs slightly from this module's presentation.

Making Changes to the Structure

When creating a table, check the entries carefully to ensure they are correct. If you discover a mistake while still typing the entry, you can correct the error by repeatedly pressing the BACKSPACE key until the incorrect characters are removed. Then, type the correct characters. If you do not discover a mistake until later, you can use the following techniques to make the necessary changes to the structure:

- To undo your most recent change, click the Undo button on the Quick Access Toolbar. If there is nothing that Access can undo, this button will be dim, and clicking it will have no effect.

- To delete a field, right-click the column heading for the field (the position containing the field name), and then click Delete Field on the shortcut menu.
- To change the name of a field, right-click the column heading for the field, click Rename Field on the shortcut menu, and then type the desired field name.
- To insert a field as the last field, click the 'Click to Add' column heading, click the appropriate data type on the menu of available data types, type the desired field name, and, if necessary, change the field size.
- To insert a field between existing fields, right-click the column heading for the field that will follow the new field, and then click Insert Field on the shortcut menu. Right-click the column heading for the field, click Rename Field on the shortcut menu, and then type the desired field name.
- To move a field, click the column heading for the field to be moved to select the field, and then drag the field to the desired position.

As an alternative to these steps, you might want to start over. To do so, click the Close button for the table, and then click the No button in the Microsoft Access dialog box. Click Create on the ribbon, and then click the Table button to create a table. You then can repeat the process you used earlier to define the fields in the table.

To Save a Table

1 CREATE FIRST TABLE | 2 ADD RECORDS | 3 PRINT CONTENTS | 4 IMPORT RECORDS
5 MODIFY SECOND TABLE | 6 CREATE QUERY | 7 CREATE FORM | 8 CREATE REPORT

The Account Manager table structure is complete. The final step is to save the table within the database. As part of the process, you will give the table a name. The following steps save the table, giving it the name Account Manager. ***Why?*** *PrattLast has decided that Account Manager is an appropriate name for the table.*

- Click the Save button on the Quick Access Toolbar to display the Save As dialog box (Figure 1–12).

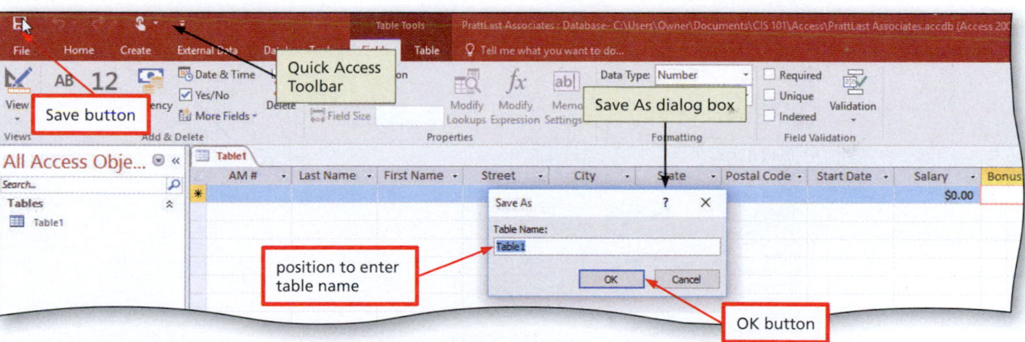

Figure 1–12

- Type `Account Manager` to change the name assigned to the table.
- Click the OK button (Save As dialog box) to save the table (Figure 1–13).

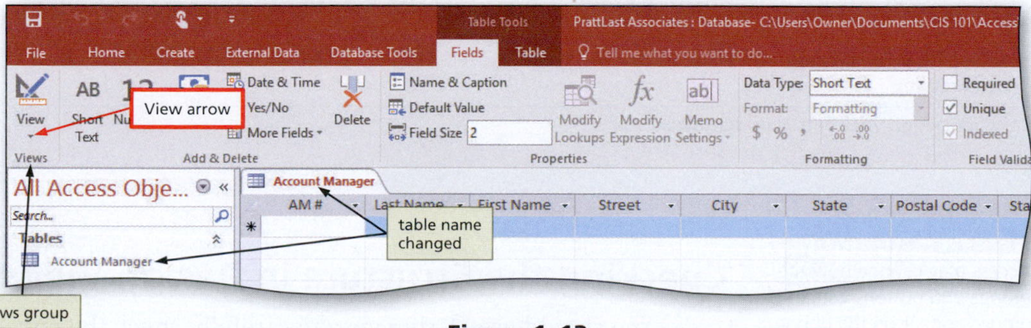

Figure 1–13

Other Ways

1. Click File on the ribbon, click Save in the Backstage view
2. Right-click tab for table, click Save on shortcut menu
3. Press CTRL+S

1 CREATE FIRST TABLE | 2 ADD RECORDS | 3 PRINT CONTENTS | 4 IMPORT RECORDS
5 MODIFY SECOND TABLE | 6 CREATE QUERY | 7 CREATE FORM | 8 CREATE REPORT

To View the Table in Design View

Even when creating a table in Datasheet view, Design view can be helpful. ***Why?*** *You easily can view the fields, data types, and properties to ensure you have entered them correctly. It is also easier to determine the primary key in Design view.* The following steps display the structure of the Account Manager table in Design view so that you can verify the design is correct.

- Click the View arrow (Table Tools Fields tab | Views group) to display the View menu (Figure 1–14).

Q&A Could I just click the View button rather than the arrow?
Yes. Clicking the button is equivalent to clicking the command represented by the icon currently appearing on the button. Because the icon on the button in Figure 1–14 is for Design view, clicking the button would display the table in Design view. If you are uncertain, you can always click the arrow and select from the menu.

Figure 1–14

- Click Design View on the View menu to view the table in Design view (Figure 1–15).

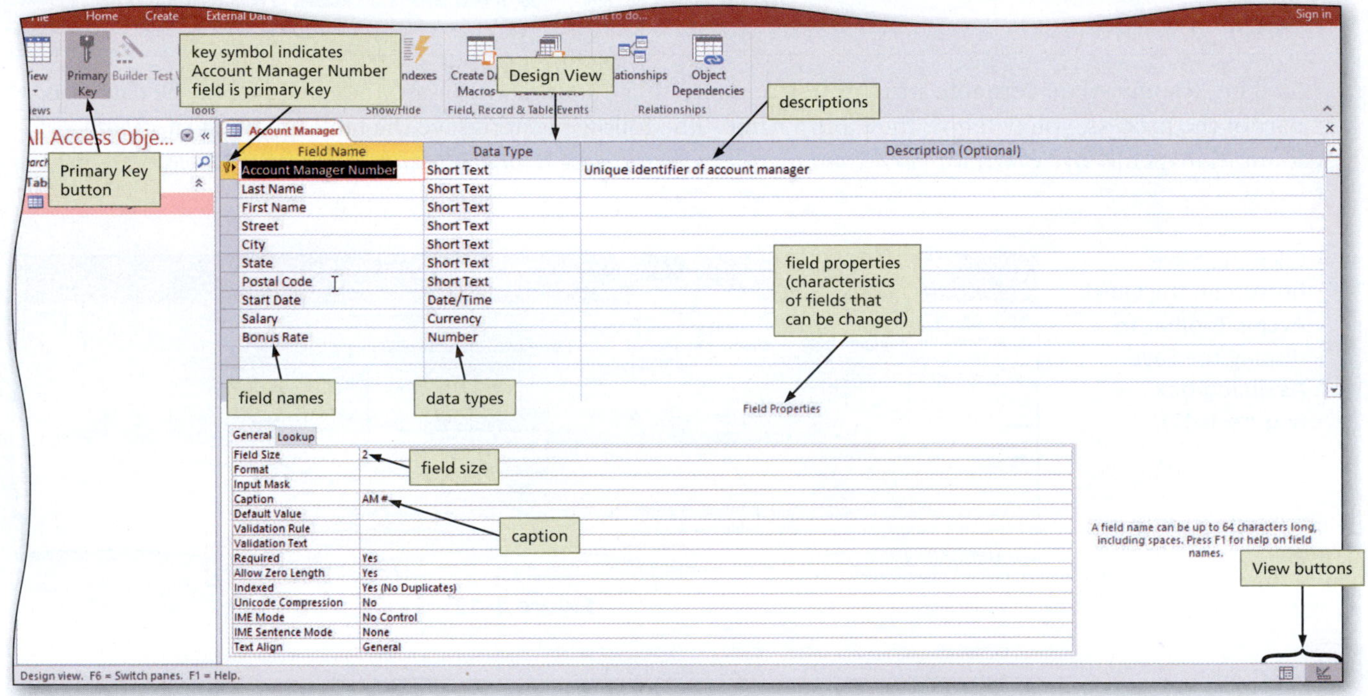

Figure 1–15

Other Ways

1. Click Design View button on status bar

BTW
The Ribbon and Screen Resolution
Access may change how the groups and buttons within the groups appear on the ribbon, depending on the computer or mobile device's screen resolution. Thus, your ribbon may look different from the ones in this book if you are using a screen resolution other than 1366 x 768.

Checking the Structure in Design View

You should use Design view to carefully check the entries you have made. In Figure 1–15, for example, you can see that the Account Manager Number field is the primary key of the Account Manager table by the key symbol in front of the field name. If your table does not have a key symbol, you can click the Primary Key button (Table Tools Design tab | Tools group) to designate a field as the primary key. You can also check that the data type, description, field size, and caption are all correct.

For the other fields, you can see the field name, data type, and description without taking any special action. To see the field size and/or caption for a field, click the field's **row selector**, the small box to the left of the field. Clicking the row selector for the Last Name field, for example, displays the properties for that field. You then can check to see that the field size is correct. In addition, if the field has a caption, you can check to see if that is correct. If you find any mistakes, you can make the necessary corrections on this screen. When you have finished, click the Save button to save your changes.

To Change a Field Size in Design View

1 CREATE FIRST TABLE | 2 ADD RECORDS | 3 PRINT CONTENTS | 4 IMPORT RECORDS
5 MODIFY SECOND TABLE | 6 CREATE QUERY | 7 CREATE FORM | 8 CREATE REPORT

Most field size changes can be made in either Datasheet view or Design view. However, changing the field size for Number fields, such as the Bonus Rate field, can only be done in Design view. Because the values in the Bonus Rate field have decimal places, only Single, Double, or Decimal are possible choices for the field size. The difference between these choices concerns the amount of accuracy, that is, the number of decimal places to which the number is accurate. Double is more accurate than Single, for example, but requires more storage space. Because the rates are only two decimal places, Single is an acceptable choice.

The following steps change the field size of the Bonus Rate field to Single, the format to Fixed, and the number of decimal places to 2. ***Why change the format and number of decimal places?*** *Changing the format and number ensures that each value will appear with precisely two decimal places.*

- If necessary, click the vertical scroll bar to display the Bonus Rate field. Click the row selector for the Bonus Rate field to select the field (Figure 1–16).

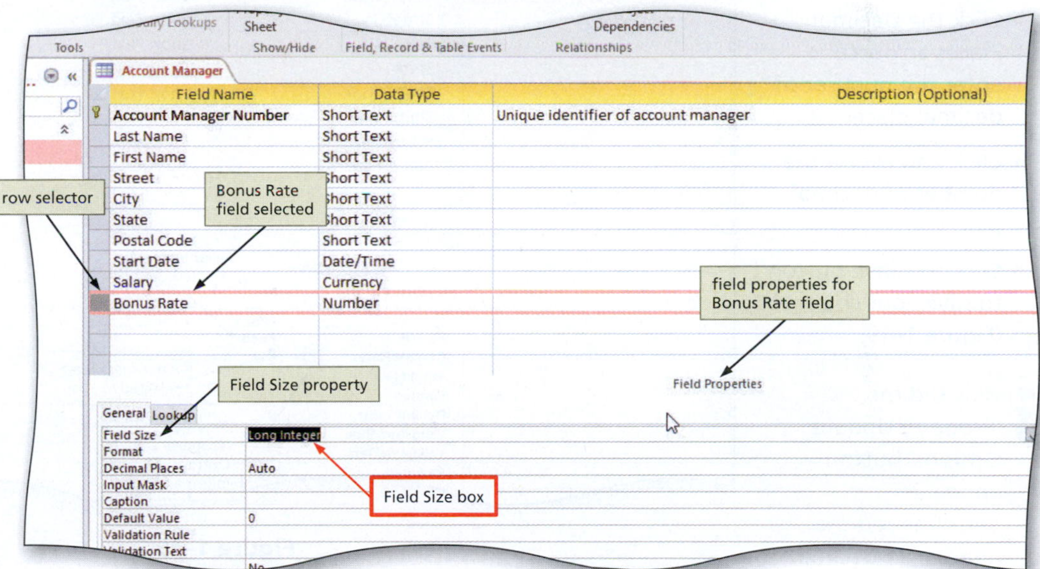

Figure 1–16

- Click the Field Size box to display the Field Size arrow.
- Click the Field Size arrow to display the Field Size menu (Figure 1–17).

Field Size arrow

Single field size

Field Size menu

Figure 1–17

Q&A What would happen if I left the field size set to Long Integer?

If the field size is Long Integer, Integer, or Byte, no decimal places can be stored. For example, a value of .10 would be stored as 0. If you enter rates and the values all appear as 0, chances are you did not change the field size property.

3

- Click Single to select single precision as the field size.
- Click the Format box to display the Format arrow (Figure 1-18).

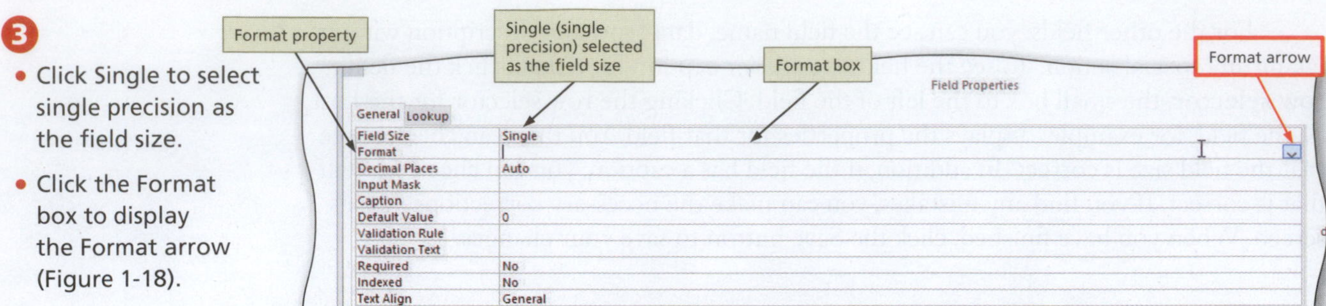

Figure 1–18

4

- Click the Format arrow to display the Format menu.
- Click Fixed to select fixed as the format.
- Click the Decimal Places box to display the Decimal Places arrow.
- Click the Decimal Places arrow to enter the number of decimal places.
- Click 2 to assign the number of decimal places.
- Click the Save button to save your changes (Figure 1–19).

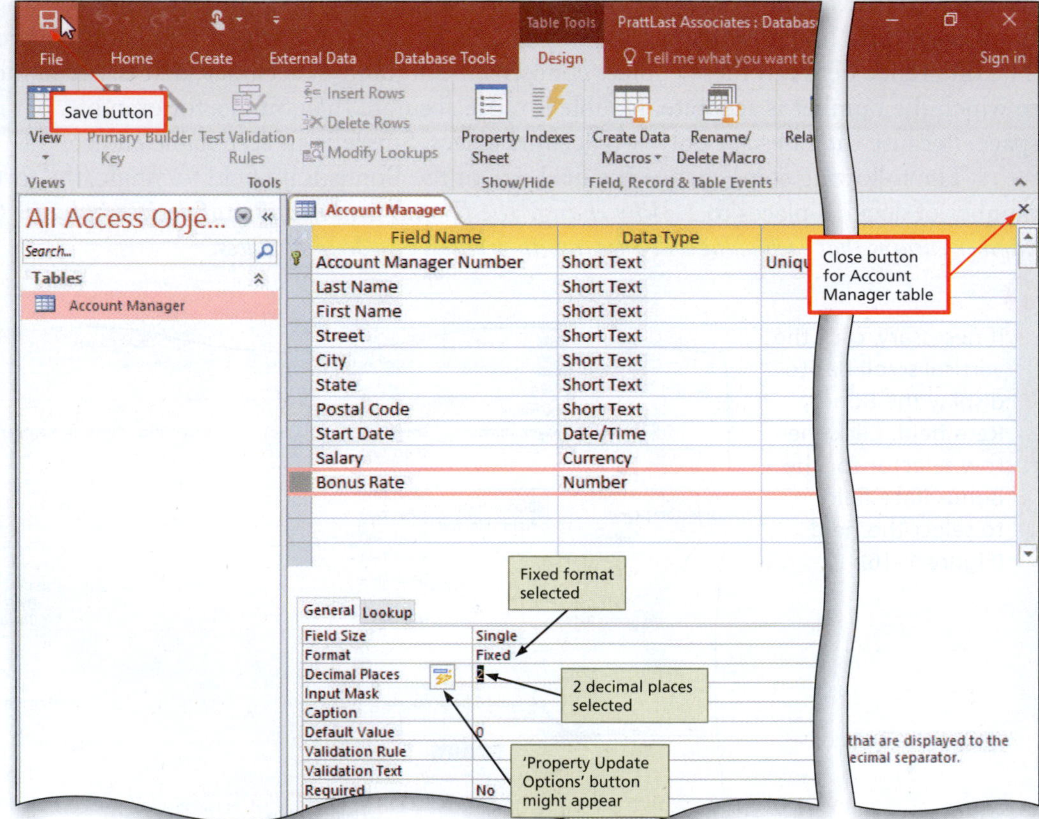

Figure 1–19

Q&A Why did the 'Property Update Options' button appear?

You changed the number of decimal places. The 'Property Update Options' button offers a quick way of making the same change everywhere Bonus Rate appears. So far, you have not added any data or created any forms or reports that use the Bonus Rate field, so no such changes are necessary.

To Close the Table

Once you are sure that your entries are correct and you have saved your changes, you can close the table. The following step closes the table.

1. Click the Close button for the Account Manager table to close the table.

Other Ways

1. Right-click tab for table, click Close on shortcut menu

To Add Records to a Table

Creating a table by building the structure and saving the table is the first step in the two-step process of using a table in a database. The second step is to add records to the table. To add records to a table, the table must be open. When making changes to tables, you work in Datasheet view.

You often add records in phases. ***Why?*** *You might not have enough time to add all the records in one session, or you might not have all the records currently available.* The following steps open the Account Manager table in Datasheet view and then add the first two records in the Account Manager table (Figure 1–20).

AM #	Last Name	First Name	Street	City	State	Postal Code	Start Date	Salary	Bonus Rate
42	Lu	Peter	5624 Murray Ave.	Davidson	IN	46007	8/3/2015	$36,750.00	0.09
31	Rivera	Haydee	325 Twiddy St.	Avondale	IL	60311	6/3/2013	$48,750.00	0.15

Figure 1–20

1

- Right-click the Account Manager table in the Navigation Pane to display the shortcut menu (Figure 1–21).

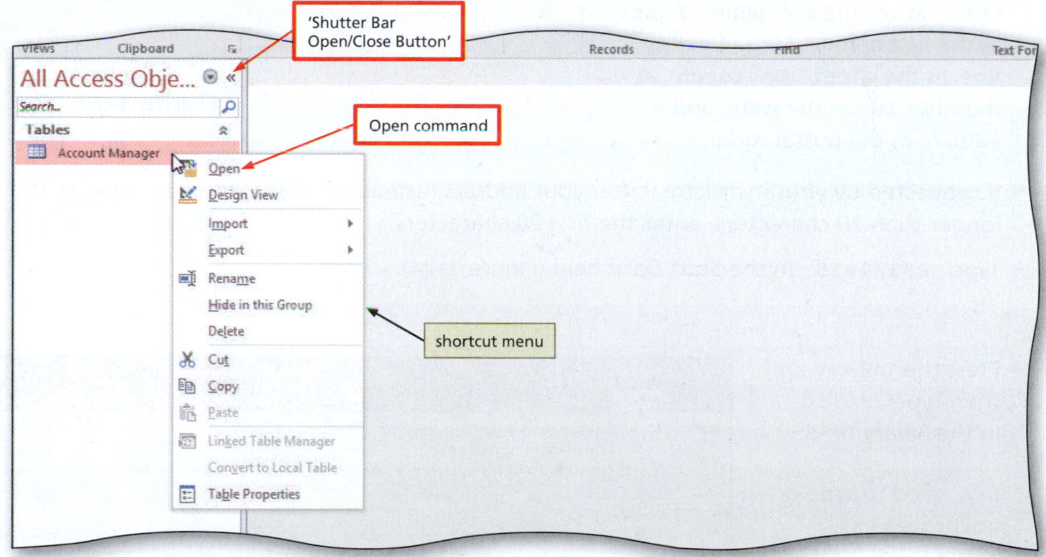

Figure 1–21

2

- Click Open on the shortcut menu to open the table in Datasheet view.
- Click the 'Shutter Bar Open/Close Button' to close the Navigation Pane (Figure 1–22).

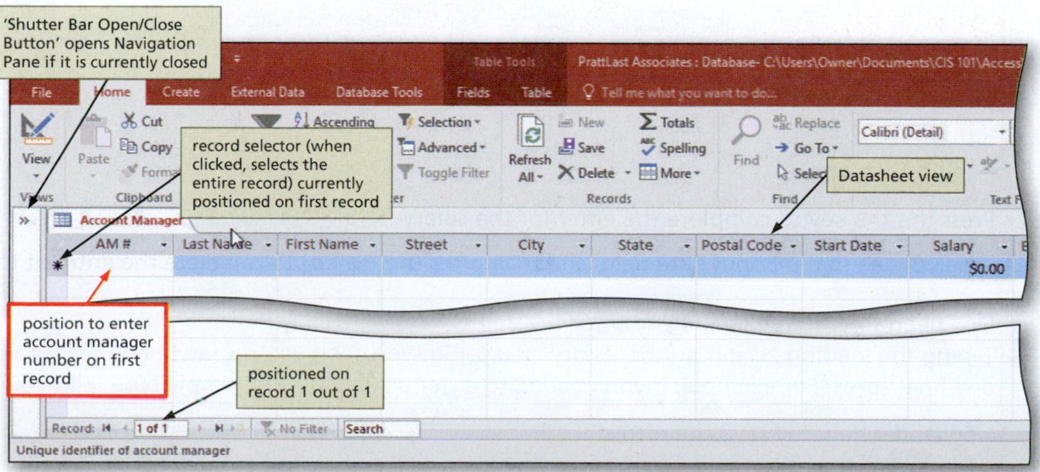

Figure 1–22

3

- Click the first row in the AM # field if necessary to display an insertion point, and type `42` to enter the first account manager number (Figure 1–23).

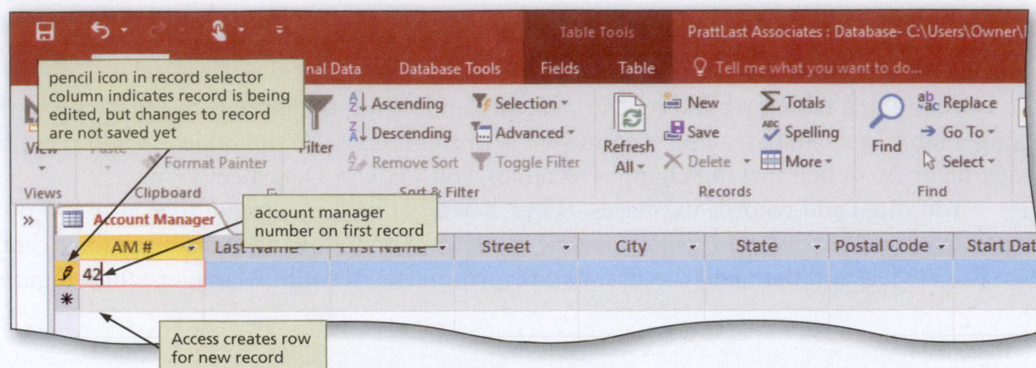

pencil icon in record selector column indicates record is being edited, but changes to record are not saved yet
account manager number on first record
Access creates row for new record

Figure 1–23

4

- Press the TAB key to move to the next field.
- Enter the last name, first name, street, city, state, and postal code by typing the following entries, pressing the TAB key after each one: `Lu` as the last name, `Peter` as the first name, `5624 Murray Ave.` as the street, `Davidson` as the city, `IN` as the state, and `46007` as the postal code.

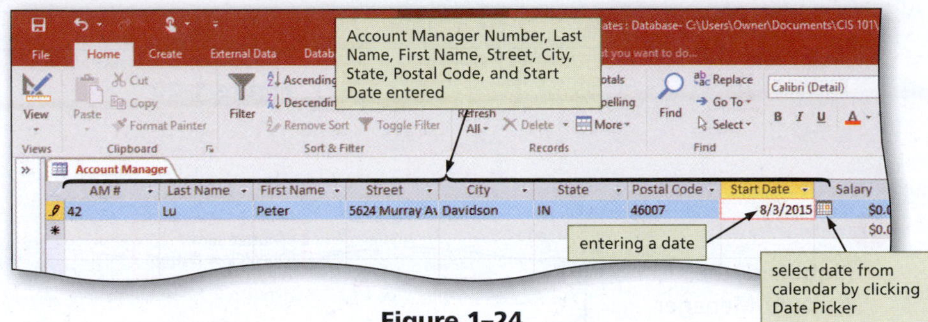

Account Manager Number, Last Name, First Name, Street, City, State, Postal Code, and Start Date entered
entering a date
select date from calendar by clicking Date Picker

Figure 1–24

- If requested by your instructor, enter your address instead of `5624 Murray Ave.` as the street. If your address is longer than 20 characters, enter the first 20 characters.
- Type `8/3/2015` in the Start Date field (Figure 1–24).

5

- Press the TAB key and then type `36750` in the Salary field.

Q&A Do I need to type a dollar sign?

You do not need to type dollar signs or commas. In addition, because the digits to the right of the decimal point are both zeros, you do not need to type either the decimal point or the zeros.

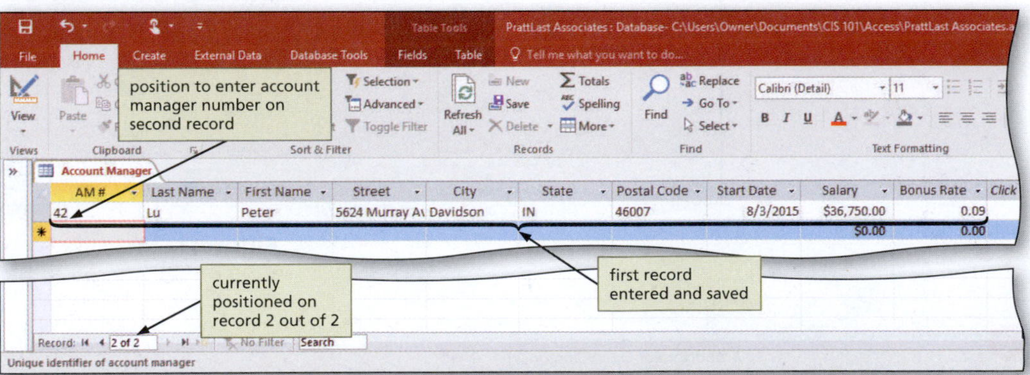

position to enter account manager number on second record
first record entered and saved
currently positioned on record 2 out of 2

Figure 1–25

- Press the TAB key to complete the entry for the Salary field.
- Type `0.09` in the Bonus Rate field, and then press the TAB key to complete the entry of the first record (Figure 1–25).

Q&A Do I need to type the leading zero for the Bonus Rate?

Typing the leading zero is not necessary. You could type .09 if you prefer. In addition, you would not have to type any final zeros. For example, if you needed to enter 0.20, you could simply type .2 as your entry.

How and when do I save the record?

As soon as you have entered or modified a record and moved to another record, Access saves the original record. This is different from other applications. The rows entered in an Excel worksheet, for example, are not saved until the entire worksheet is saved.

6

- Use the techniques shown in Steps 3 through 5 to enter the data for the second record (Figure 1–26).

Q&A Does it matter that I entered account manager 31 after I entered account manager 42? Should the account manager numbers be in order?
The order in which you enter the records is not important. When you close and later reopen the table, the records will be in account manager number order, because the Account Manager Number field is the primary key.

Experiment

- Click the Salary field on either of the records. Be sure the Table Tools Fields tab is selected. Click the Format arrow, and then click each of the formats in the Format box menu to see the effect on the values in the Salary field. When finished, click Currency in the Format box menu.

Q&A I made a mistake in entering the data. When should I fix it?
It is a good idea to fix it now, although you can fix it later as well. In any case, the following section gives you the techniques you can use to make any necessary corrections. If you want to fix it now, read that section and make your corrections before proceeding to the next step.

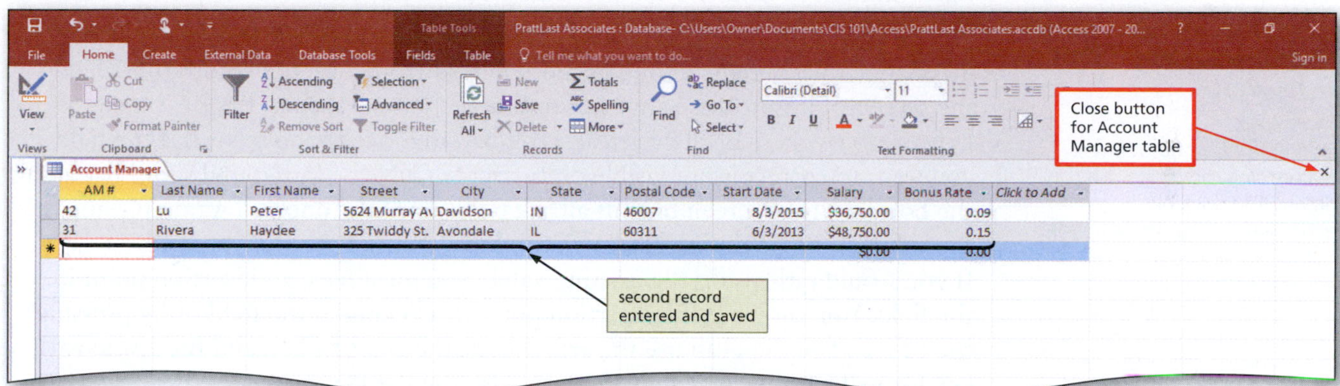

Figure 1–26

7

- Click the Close button for the Account Manager table, shown in Figure 1–26, to close the table (Figure 1–27).
- Exit Access.

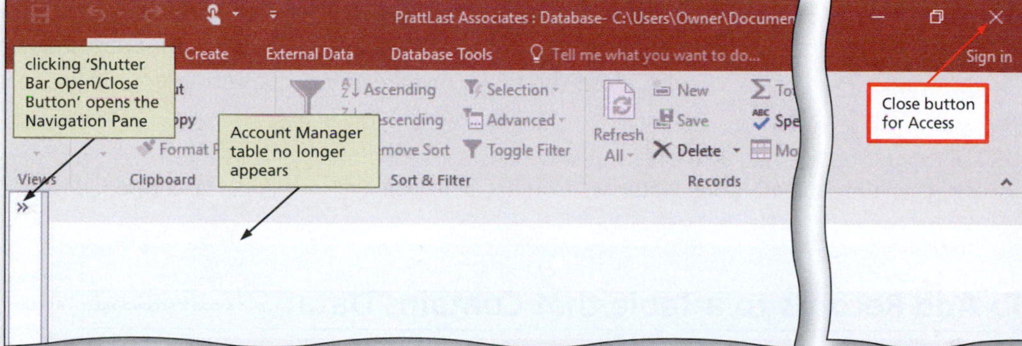

Figure 1–27

Q&A Is it necessary for me to exit Access at this point?
No. The step is here for two reasons. First, you will often not be able to add all the records you need to add in one sitting. In such a case, you will add some records, and then exit Access. When you are ready to resume adding the records, you will run Access, open the table, and then continue the addition process. Second, there is a break point coming up in the module. If you want to take advantage of that break, you need to first exit Access.

Making Changes to the Data

As you enter data, check your entries carefully to ensure they are correct. If you make a mistake and discover it before you press the TAB key, correct it by pressing the BACKSPACE key until the incorrect characters are removed, and then type the correct characters. If you do not discover a mistake until later, you can use the following techniques to make the necessary corrections to the data:

- To undo your most recent change, click the Undo button on the Quick Access Toolbar. If there is nothing that Access can undo, this button will be dimmed, and clicking it will have no effect.
- To add a record, click the 'New (blank) record' button, click the position for the Account Manager Number field on the first open record, and then add the record. Do not worry about it being in the correct position in the table. Access will reposition the record based on the primary key, in this case, the Account Manager Number.
- To delete a record, click the record selector, shown in Figure 1–22, for the record that you want to delete. Then press the DELETE key to delete the record, and click the Yes button when Access asks you to verify that you want to delete the record.
- To change the contents of one or more fields in a record, the record must be on the screen. If it is not, use any appropriate technique, such as the UP ARROW and DOWN ARROW keys or the vertical scroll bar, to move to the record. If the field you want to correct is not visible on the screen, use the horizontal scroll bar along the bottom of the screen to shift all the fields until the one you want appears. If the value in the field is currently highlighted, you can simply type the new value. If you would rather edit the existing value, you must have an insertion point in the field. You can place the insertion point by clicking in the field or by pressing the F2 key. You then can use the arrow keys, the DELETE key, and the BACKSPACE key for making the correction. You can also use the INSERT key to switch between Insert and Overtype mode. When you have made the change, press the TAB key to move to the next field.

If you cannot determine how to correct the data, you may find that you are "stuck" on the record, in which case Access neither allows you to move to another record nor allows you to close the table until you have made the correction. If you encounter this situation, simply press the ESC key. Pressing the ESC key will remove from the screen the record you are trying to add. You then can move to any other record, close the table, or take any other action you desire.

BTW
AutoCorrect Feature
The AutoCorrect feature of Access corrects common data entry errors. AutoCorrect corrects two capital letters by changing the second letter to lowercase and capitalizes the first letter in the names of days. It also corrects more than 400 commonly misspelled words.

BTW
Other AutoCorrect Options
Using the Office AutoCorrect feature, you can create entries that will replace abbreviations with spelled-out names and phrases automatically. To specify AutoCorrect rules, click File on the ribbon to open the Backstage view, click Options, and then click Proofing in the Access Options dialog box.

Break Point: If you wish to take a break, this is a good place to do so. You can exit Access now. To resume at a later time, run Access, open the database called PrattLast Associates, and continue following the steps from this location forward.

To Add Records to a Table that Contains Data

1 CREATE FIRST TABLE | 2 ADD RECORDS | 3 PRINT CONTENTS | 4 IMPORT RECORDS
5 MODIFY SECOND TABLE | 6 CREATE QUERY | 7 CREATE FORM | 8 CREATE REPORT

You can add records to a table that already contains data using a process almost identical to that used to add records to an empty table. The only difference is that you place the insertion point after the last record before you enter the additional data. To position the insertion point after the last record, you can use the **Navigation buttons**, which are buttons used to move within a table, found near the lower-left corner of the screen when a table is open. ***Why not just click the Account Manager Number (AM #) on the first open record?*** *You could click the first open record, but it is a good habit to use the 'New (blank) record' button. Once a table contains more records than will fit on the screen, it is easier to click the 'New (blank) record' button.* The purpose of each Navigation button is described in Table 1–4.

Table 1–4 Navigation Buttons in Datasheet View

Button	Purpose
First record	Moves to the first record in the table
Previous record	Moves to the previous record
Next record	Moves to the next record
Last record	Moves to the last record in the table
New (blank) record	Moves to the end of the table to a position for entering a new record

BTW

Enabling Content

If the database is one that you created, or if it comes from a trusted source, you can enable the content. You should disable the content of a database if you suspect that your database might contain harmful content or damaging macros.

The following steps add the remaining records (Figure 1–28) to the Account Manager table.

AM #	Last Name	First Name	Street	City	State	Postal Code	Start Date	Salary	Bonus Rate
58	Murowski	Karen	168 Truesdale Dr.	Carlton	IL	60313	11/9/2016	$24,000.00	0.08
35	Simson	Mark	1467 Hartwell St.	Walker	IN	46004	5/19/2014	$40,500.00	0.12

Figure 1–28

- Run Access, unless it is already running.
- Open the PrattLast Associates database from your hard disk, OneDrive, or other storage location (Figure 1-29).
- If a Security Warning appears, click the Enable Content button.

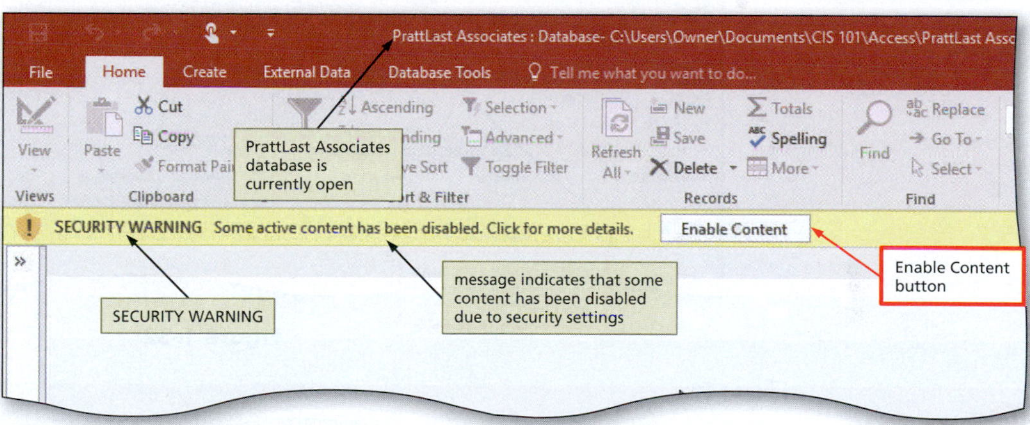

Figure 1–29

2

- If the Navigation Pane is closed, click the 'Shutter Bar Open/Close Button', shown in Figure 1–27, to open the Navigation Pane (Figure 1–30).

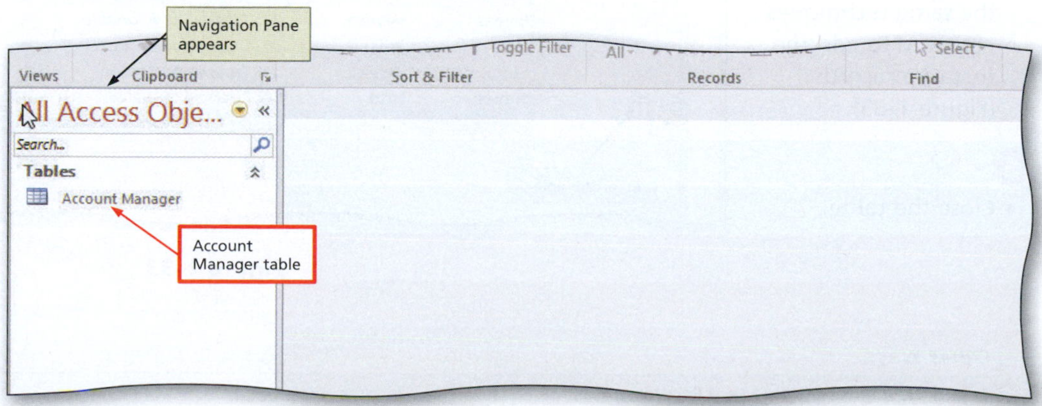

Figure 1–30

3

- Right-click the Account Manager table in the Navigation Pane to display a shortcut menu.
- Click Open on the shortcut menu to open the table in Datasheet view.

Q&A Why do the records appear in a different order than the order in which I entered them?
When you open the table, they are sorted in the order of the primary key. In this case, that means they will appear in Account Manager Number order.

- Close the Navigation Pane by clicking the 'Shutter Bar Open/Close Button' (Figure 1–31).

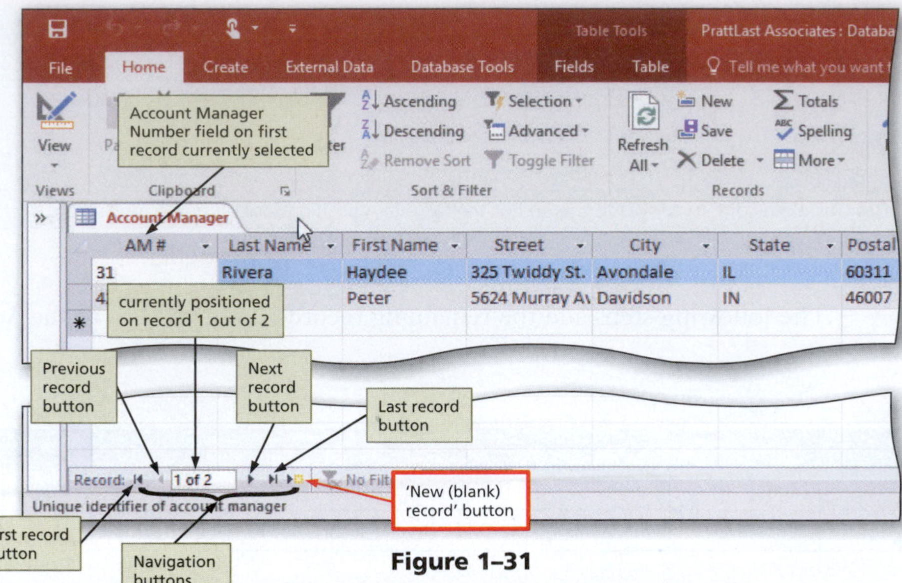

Figure 1–31

4

- Click the 'New (blank) record' button to move to a position to enter a new record (Figure 1–32).

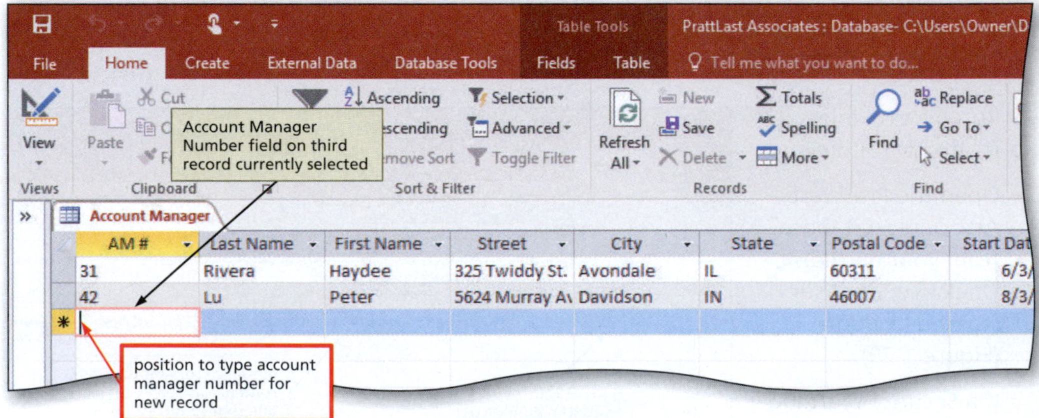

Figure 1–32

5

- Add the records shown in Figure 1–28 using the same techniques you used to add the first two records (Figure 1–33).

6

- Close the table.

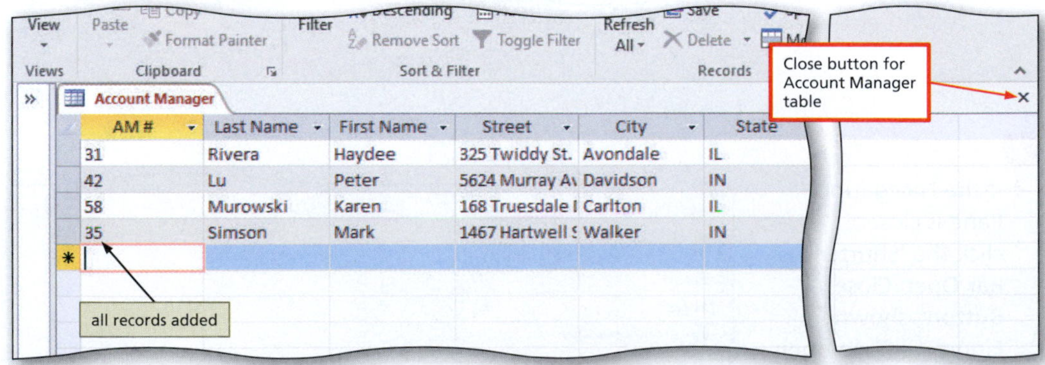

Figure 1–33

Other Ways

1. Click New button (Home tab | Records group)
2. Press CTRL+PLUS SIGN (+)

1 CREATE FIRST TABLE | 2 ADD RECORDS | 3 PRINT CONTENTS | 4 IMPORT RECORDS
5 MODIFY SECOND TABLE | 6 CREATE QUERY | 7 CREATE FORM | 8 CREATE REPORT

To Resize Columns in a Datasheet

Access assigns default column sizes, which do not always provide space to display all the data in the field. In some cases, the data might appear but the entire field name will not. You can correct this problem by resizing the column (changing its size) in the datasheet. In some instances, you may want to reduce the size of a column. ***Why?*** *Some fields, such as the State field, are short enough that they do not require all the space on the screen that is allotted to them.* Changing a column width changes the layout, or design, of a table. The following steps resize the columns in the Account Manager table and save the changes to the layout.

1

- Open the Navigation Pane if it is not already open.
- Open the Account Manager table and then close the Navigation Pane.
- Point to the right boundary of the field selector for the Account Manager Number (AM #) field (Figure 1–34) so that the pointer becomes a two-headed arrow.

Q&A I am using touch and I cannot see the pointer. Is this a problem?

It is not a problem. Remember that if you are using your finger on a touch screen, you will not see the pointer.

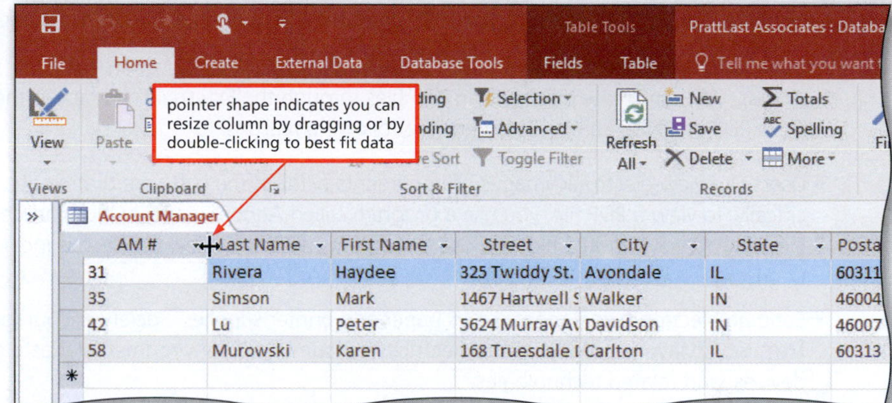

Figure 1–34

2

- Double-click the right boundary of the field selector to resize the field so that it best fits the data.
- Use the same technique to resize all the other fields to best fit the data.
- Save the changes to the layout by clicking the Save button on the Quick Access Toolbar (Figure 1–35).

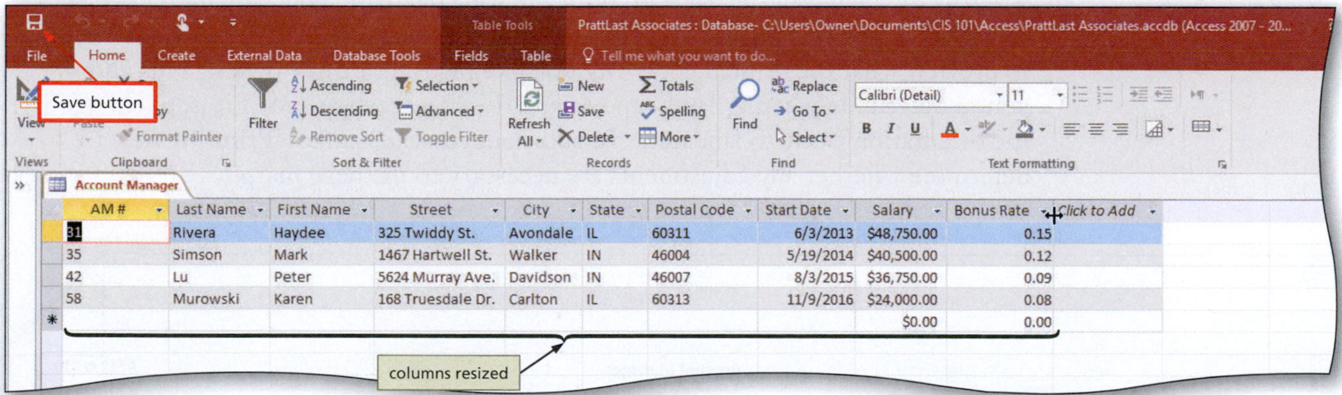

Figure 1–35

3

- Click the table's Close button (shown in Figure 1–33) to close the table.

Q&A What if I closed the table without saving the layout changes?

You would be asked if you want to save the changes.

Other Ways

1. Right-click field name, click Field Width

CONSIDER THIS

What is the best method for distributing database objects?

The traditional method of distributing database objects such as tables, reports, and forms uses a printer to produce a hard copy. A hard copy or printout is information that exists on a physical medium such as paper. Hard copies can be useful for the following reasons:

- Some people prefer proofreading a hard copy of a document rather than viewing it on the screen to check for errors and readability.
- Hard copies can serve as a backup reference if your storage medium is lost or becomes corrupted and you need to recreate the document. Instead of distributing a hard copy, users can distribute the document as an electronic image that mirrors the original document's appearance. The electronic image of the document can be emailed, posted on a website, or copied to a portable storage medium such as a USB flash drive. Two popular electronic image formats, sometimes called fixed formats, are PDF by Adobe Systems and XPS by Microsoft.

In Access, you can create electronic image files through the External Data tab on the ribbon. Electronic images of documents, such as PDF and XPS, can be useful for the following reasons:

- Users can view electronic images of documents without the software that created the original document (e.g., Access). Specifically, to view a PDF file, you use a program called Adobe Reader, which can be downloaded free from Adobe's website. Similarly, to view an XPS file, you use a program called XPS Viewer, which is included in the latest versions of Windows and Edge.
- Sending electronic documents saves paper and printer supplies. Society encourages users to contribute to **green computing**, which involves reducing the electricity consumed and environmental waste generated when using computers, mobile devices, and related technologies.

BTW
Changing Printers
To change the default printer that appears in the Print dialog box, click File on the ribbon, click the Print tab in the Backstage view, click Print in the Print gallery, then click the Name arrow and select the desired printer.

Previewing and Printing the Contents of a Table

When working with a database, you will often need to print a copy of the table contents. Figure 1–36 shows a printed copy of the contents of the Account Manager table. (Yours might look slightly different, depending on your printer.) Because the Account Manager table is substantially wider than the screen, it will also be wider than the normal printed page in portrait orientation. **Portrait orientation** means the printout is across the width of the page. **Landscape orientation** means the printout is across the height of the page. To print the wide database table, you might prefer to use landscape orientation. A convenient way to change to landscape orientation is to preview what the printed copy will look like by using Print Preview. This allows you to determine whether landscape orientation is necessary and, if it is, to change the orientation easily to landscape. In addition, you can also use Print Preview to determine whether any adjustments are necessary to the page margins.

Account Manager 9/12/2017

AM #	Last Name	First Name	Street	City	State	Postal Code	Start Date	Salary	Bonus Rate
31	Rivera	Haydee	325 Twiddy St.	Avondale	IL	60311	6/3/2013	$48,750.00	0.15
35	Simson	Mark	1467 Hartwell St.	Walker	IN	46004	5/19/2014	$40,500.00	0.12
42	Lu	Peter	5624 Murray Ave.	Davidson	IN	46007	8/3/2015	$36,750.00	0.09
58	Murowski	Karen	168 Truesdale Dr.	Carlton	IL	60313	11/9/2016	$24,000.00	0.08

Figure 1–36

To Preview and Print the Contents of a Table

1 CREATE FIRST TABLE | 2 ADD RECORDS | 3 PRINT CONTENTS | 4 IMPORT RECORDS
5 MODIFY SECOND TABLE | 6 CREATE QUERY | 7 CREATE FORM | 8 CREATE REPORT

The following steps use Print Preview to preview and then print the contents of the Account Manager table. ***Why?*** *By previewing the contents of the table in Print Preview, you can make any necessary adjustments to the orientation or to the margins before printing the contents.*

1

- If the Navigation Pane is closed, open the Navigation Pane by clicking the 'Shutter Bar Open/Close Button'.
- Be sure the Account Manager table is selected.

Q&A Why do I have to be sure the Account Manager table is selected? It is the only object in the database.
When the database contains only one object, you do not have to worry about selecting the object. Ensuring that the correct object is selected is a good habit to form, however, to make sure that the object you print is the one you want.

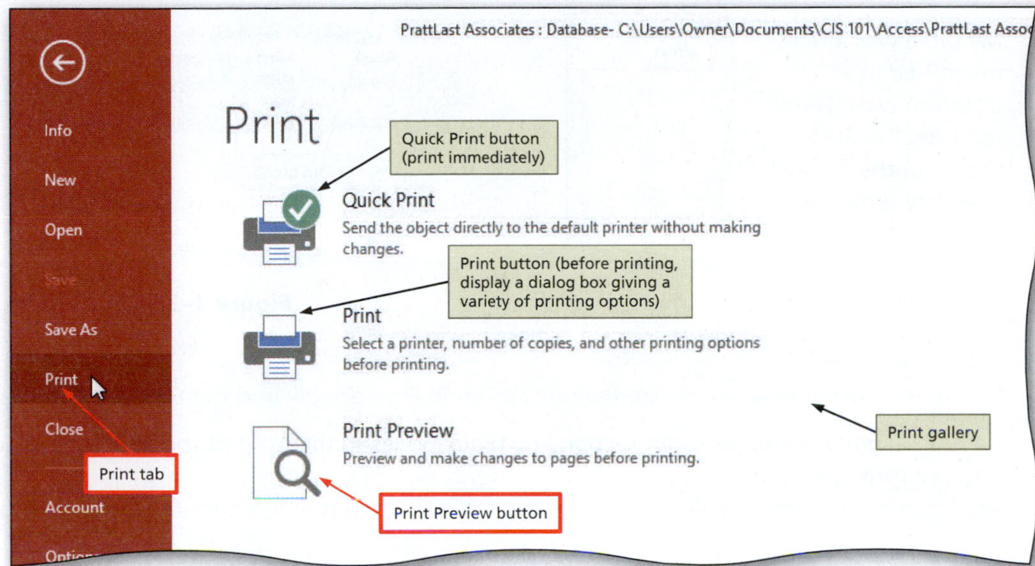

Figure 1–37

- Click File on the ribbon to open the Backstage view.
- Click the Print tab in the Backstage view to display the Print gallery (Figure 1–37).

2

- Click the Print Preview button in the Print gallery to display a preview of what the table will look like when printed (Figure 1–38).

Q&A I cannot read the table. Can I magnify a portion of the table?
Yes. Point the pointer, whose shape will change to a magnifying glass, at the portion of the table that you want to magnify, and then click. You can return to the original view of the table by clicking a second time.

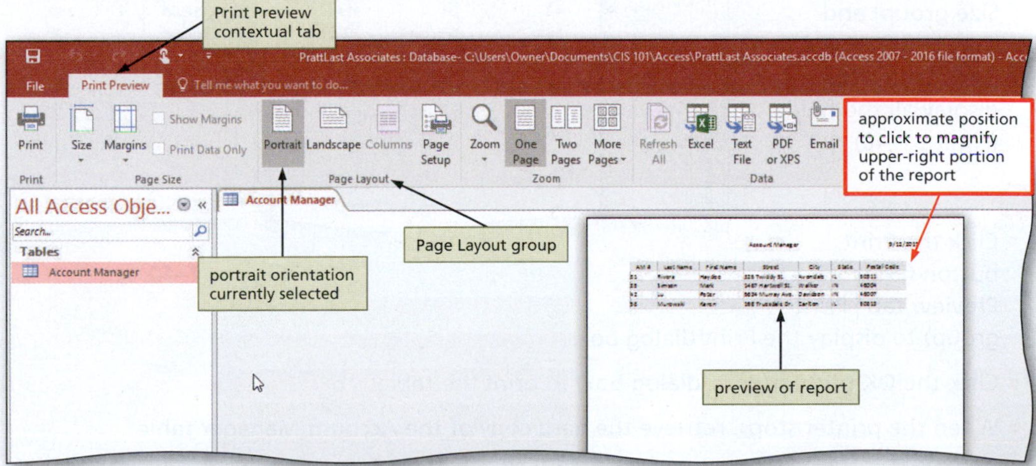

Figure 1–38

- Click the pointer in the position shown in Figure 1–38 to magnify the upper-right section of the table (Figure 1–39).

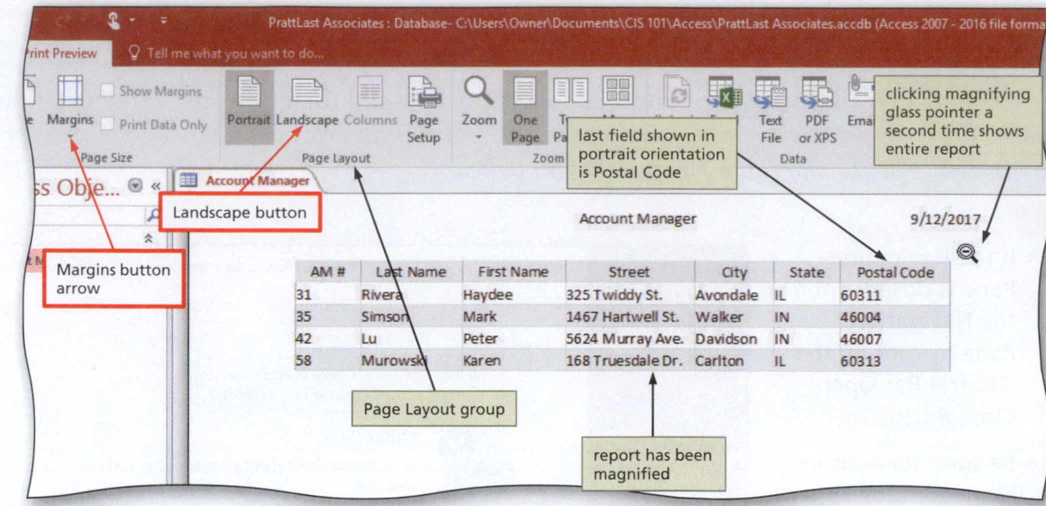

Figure 1–39

Q&A My table was already magnified in a different area. How can I see the area shown in the figure?
One way is to use the scroll bars to move to the desired portion of the table. You can also click the pointer anywhere in the table to produce a screen like the one shown in Figure 1–38, and then click in the location shown in the figure.

When I magnify the upper-right section, my table moves to the right of the screen and there is a lot of white space. Is that a problem?
No, use the horizontal scroll bar to move the table to the left and reduce the size of the white space.

4

- Click the Landscape button (Print Preview tab | Page Layout group) to change to landscape orientation.
- Click the Margins button arrow (Print Preview tab | Page Size group) and then click Normal, if necessary, to display all the fields (Figure 1–40).

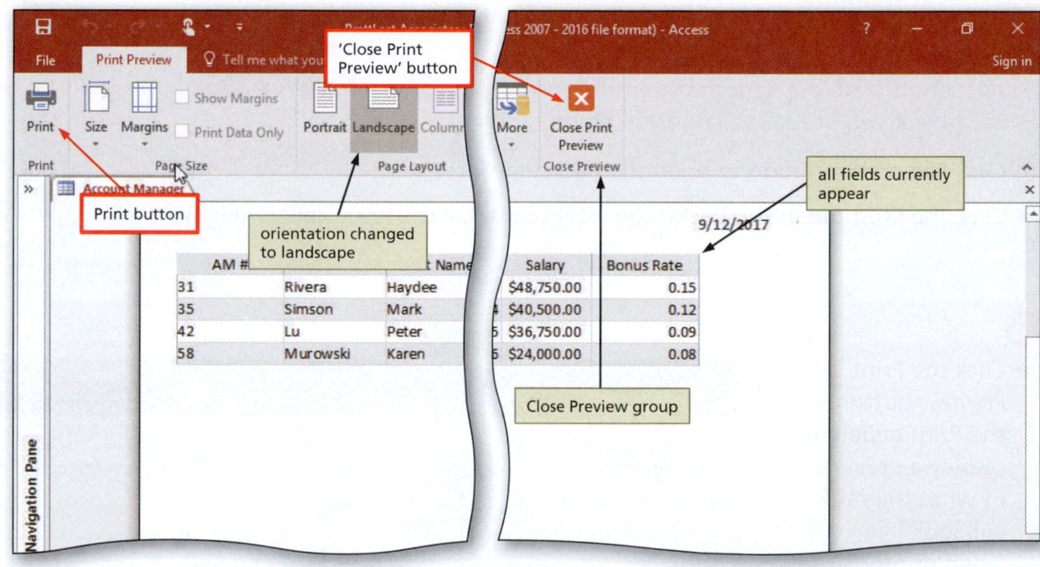

Figure 1–40

- Click the Print button (Print Preview tab | Print group) to display the Print dialog box.
- Click the OK button (Print dialog box) to print the table.
- When the printer stops, retrieve the hard copy of the Account Manager table.
- Click the 'Close Print Preview' button (Print Preview tab | Close Preview group) to close the Print Preview window.

Q&A Do I have to select Print Preview before printing the table?
No. If you want to print without previewing, you would select either Print or Quick Print rather than Print Preview.

Other Ways

1. Press CTRL+P, click OK button in Print dialog box

Importing or Linking Data From Other Applications to Access

If your data for a table is stored in an Excel worksheet, you can **import** the data, which means to make a copy of the data as a table in the Access database. In this case, any changes to the data made in Access would not be reflected in the Excel worksheet.

Figure 1–41, which contains the Account data, is an example of the type of worksheet that can be imported. In this type of worksheet, the data is stored as a **list**, that is, a collection of rows and columns in which all the entries in a column represent the same type of data. In this type of list, the first row contains **column headings**, that is, descriptions of the contents of the column, rather than data. In the worksheet in Figure 1–41, for example, the entry in the first column of the first row is Account Number. This indicates that all the other values in this column are account numbers. The fact that the entry in the second column of the first row is Account Name indicates that all the other values in the second column are account names.

BTW

Linking Versus Importing

When you link to the data in the worksheet, the data appears as a table in the Access database but it is maintained in its original form in Excel. Any changes to the Excel data are reflected when the linked table is viewed in Access. In this arrangement, Access would typically be used as a vehicle for querying and presenting the data, with actual updates being made in Excel.

BTW

Importing Data in Other Formats

You can import data into a table from Excel workbooks, Access databases, XML files, ODBC databases such as SQL Server, text files, HTML documents, Outlook folders, and SharePoint lists.

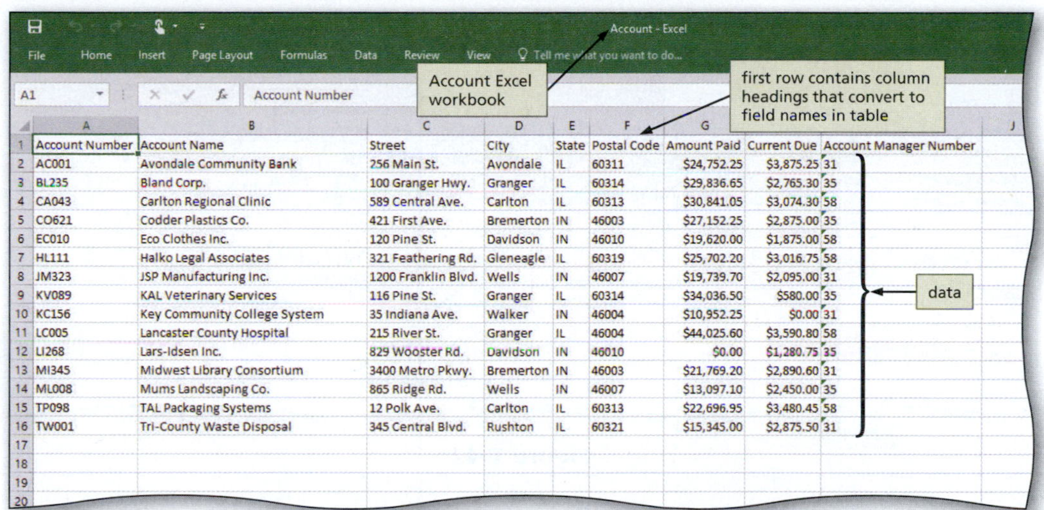

	A	B	C	D	E	F	G		
1	Account Number	Account Name	Street	City	State	Postal Code	Amount Paid	Current Due	Account Manager Number
2	AC001	Avondale Community Bank	256 Main St.	Avondale	IL	60311	$24,752.25	$3,875.25	31
3	BL235	Bland Corp.	100 Granger Hwy.	Granger	IL	60314	$29,836.65	$2,765.30	35
4	CA043	Carlton Regional Clinic	589 Central Ave.	Carlton	IL	60313	$30,841.05	$3,074.30	58
5	CO621	Codder Plastics Co.	421 First Ave.	Bremerton	IN	46003	$27,152.25	$2,875.00	35
6	EC010	Eco Clothes Inc.	120 Pine St.	Davidson	IN	46010	$19,620.00	$1,875.00	58
7	HL111	Halko Legal Associates	321 Feathering Rd.	Gleneagle	IL	60319	$25,702.20	$3,016.75	58
8	JM323	JSP Manufacturing Inc.	1200 Franklin Blvd.	Wells	IN	46007	$19,739.70	$2,095.00	31
9	KV089	KAL Veterinary Services	116 Pine St.	Granger	IL	60314	$34,036.50	$580.00	35
10	KC156	Key Community College System	35 Indiana Ave.	Walker	IN	46004	$10,952.25	$0.00	31
11	LC005	Lancaster County Hospital	215 River St.	Granger	IL	46004	$44,025.60	$3,590.80	58
12	LI268	Lars-Idsen Inc.	829 Wooster Rd.	Davidson	IN	46010	$0.00	$1,280.75	35
13	MI345	Midwest Library Consortium	3400 Metro Pkwy.	Bremerton	IN	46003	$21,769.20	$2,890.60	31
14	ML008	Mums Landscaping Co.	865 Ridge Rd.	Wells	IN	46007	$13,097.10	$2,450.00	35
15	TP098	TAL Packaging Systems	12 Polk Ave.	Carlton	IL	60313	$22,696.95	$3,480.45	58
16	TW001	Tri-County Waste Disposal	345 Central Blvd.	Rushton	IL	60321	$15,345.00	$2,875.50	31
17									
18									
19									
20									

Figure 1–41

CONSIDER THIS

Does it matter how the data in the Excel workbook is formatted? If so, how can you be sure the Excel data is formatted in such a way that you can import it?

The format of data in an Excel workbook is important when you want to import it into Access. To ensure the data is in an appropriate format:

1. Make sure the data is in the form of a list; a collection of rows and columns in which all the entries in a column represent the same type of data.
2. Make sure there are no blank rows within the list. If there are, remove them prior to importing or linking.
3. Make sure there are no blank columns within the list. If there are, remove them prior to importing or linking.
4. Determine whether the first row contains column headings that will make appropriate field names in the resulting table. If not, you should consider adding such a row. In general, the process is simpler if the first row in the worksheet contains appropriate column headings.

The Import process will create a table. In this table, the column headings in the first row of the worksheet become the field names. The rows of the worksheet, other than the first row, become the records in the table. In the process, each field will be assigned the data type that seems the most reasonable, given the data currently in the worksheet. When the Import process is finished, you can use Datasheet view or Design view to modify these data types or to make any other changes to the structure you feel are necessary.

To Import an Excel Worksheet

1 CREATE FIRST TABLE | 2 ADD RECORDS | 3 PRINT CONTENTS | 4 IMPORT RECORDS
5 MODIFY SECOND TABLE | 6 CREATE QUERY | 7 CREATE FORM | 8 CREATE REPORT

You import a worksheet by using the Import Spreadsheet Wizard. In the process, you will indicate that the first row in the worksheet contains the column headings. ***Why?*** *You are indicating that Access is to use those column headings as the field names in the Access table.* In addition, you will indicate the primary key for the table. As part of the process, you could, if appropriate, choose not to include all the fields from the worksheet in the resulting table.

The following steps import the Account worksheet.

- Click External Data on the ribbon to display the External Data tab (Figure 1–42).

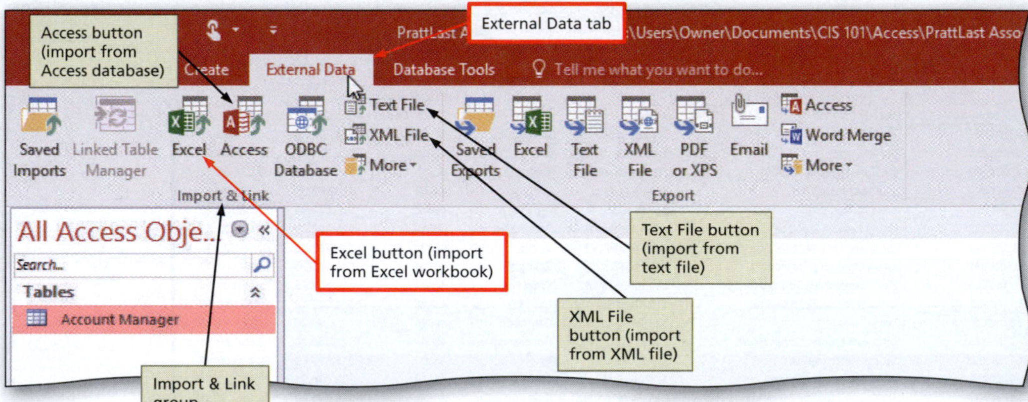

Figure 1–42

- Click the Excel button (External Data tab | Import & Link group) to display the Get External Data - Excel Spreadsheet dialog box.
- Click the Browse button in the Get External Data - Excel Spreadsheet dialog box.
- Navigate to the location containing the workbook (for example, the Access folder in the CIS 101 folder). For a detailed example of this procedure, refer to the Office and Windows module at the beginning of this book.
- Click the Account workbook, and then click the Open button to select the workbook (Figure 1–43).

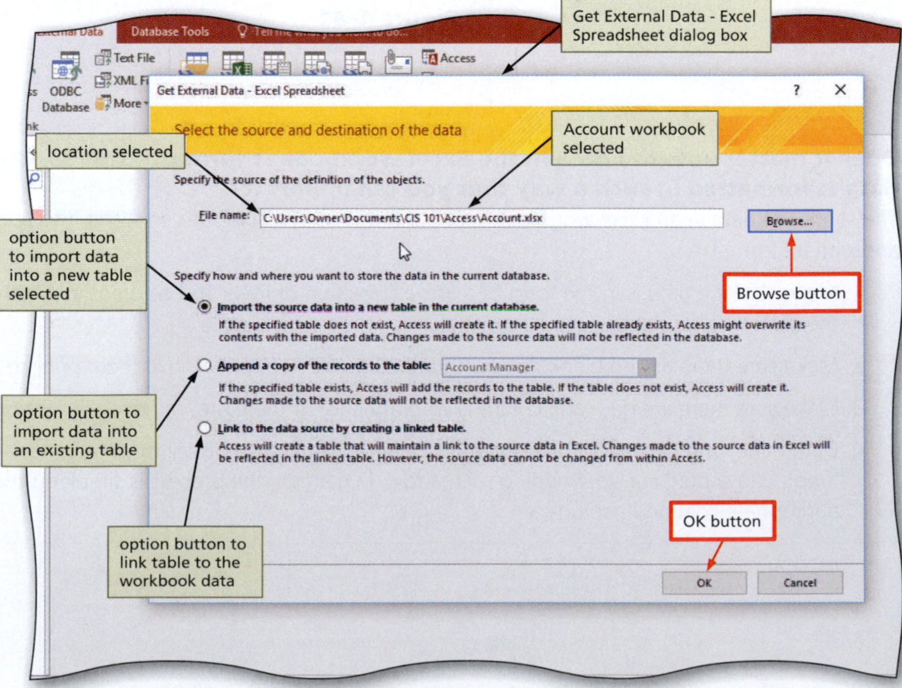

Figure 1–43

3

- With the option button to import the source data to a new table selected, click the OK button to display the Import Spreadsheet Wizard dialog box (Figure 1–44).

What happens if I select the option button to append records to an existing table?
Instead of the records being placed in a new table, they will be added to an existing table that you specify, provided the value in the primary key field does not duplicate that of an existing record.

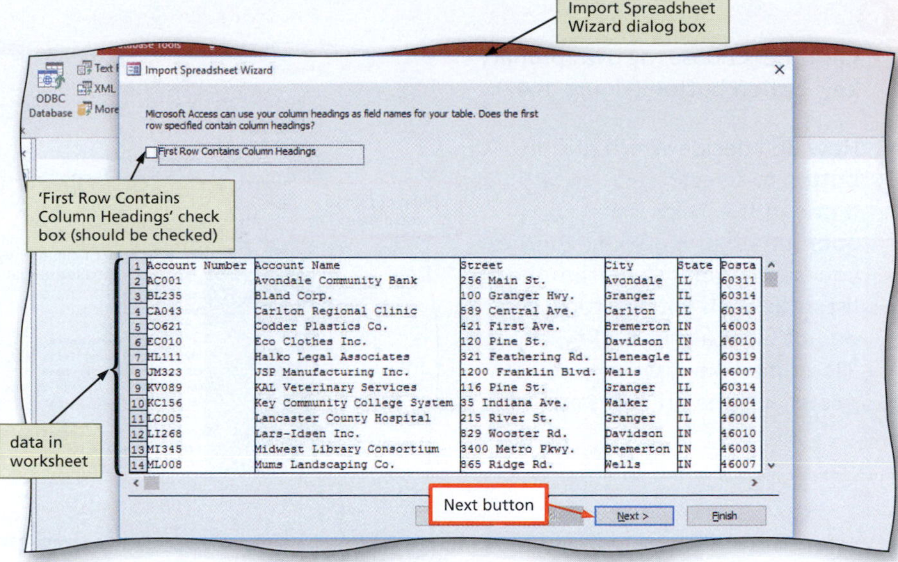

Figure 1–44

4

- Be sure the 'First Row Contains Column Headings' check box is selected. If it is not, click the 'First Row Contains Column Headings' check box to select it.
- Click the Next button (Figure 1–45).

When would I use the Field Options on the Import Spreadsheet Wizard?
You would use these options if you wanted to change properties for one or more fields. You can change the name, the data type, and whether the field is indexed. You can also indicate that some fields should not be imported.

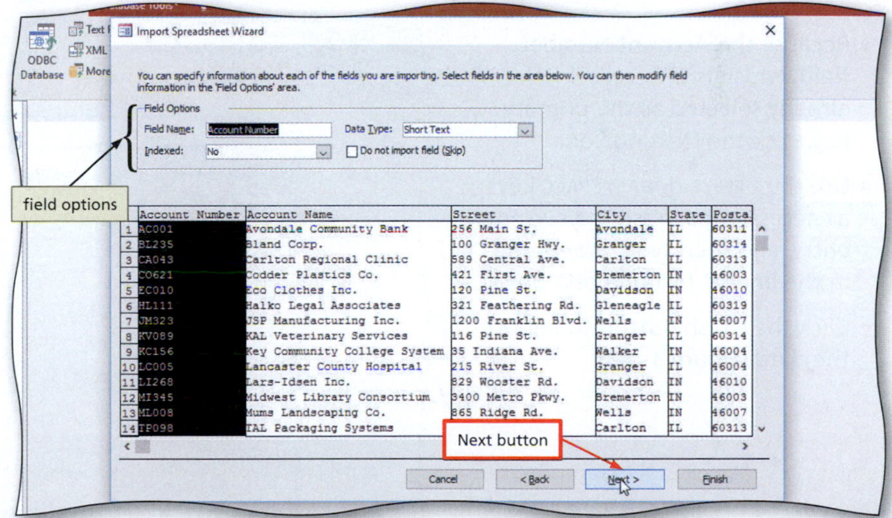

Figure 1–45

5

- Because the Field Options need not be specified, click the Next button (Figure 1–46).

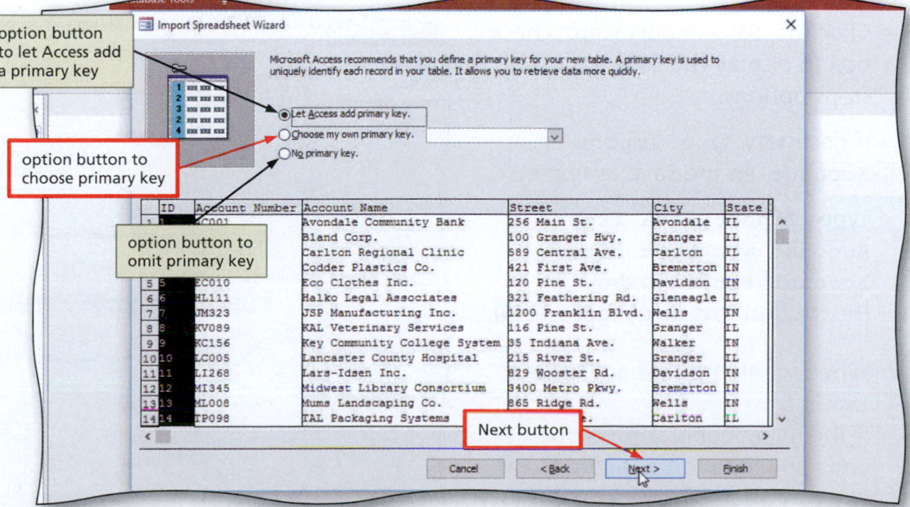

Figure 1–46

6

- Click the 'Choose my own primary key' option button (Figure 1–47).

Q&A How do I decide which option button to select?

If one of the fields is an appropriate primary key, choose your own primary key from the list of fields. If you are sure you do not want a primary key, choose 'No primary key'. Otherwise, let Access add the primary key.

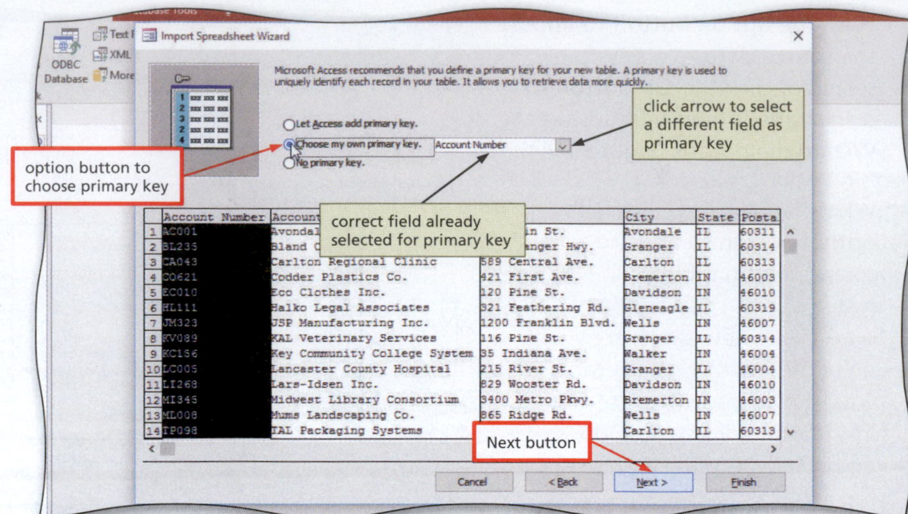

Figure 1–47

7

- Because the Account Number field, which is the correct field, is already selected as the primary key, click the Next button.
- Use the DELETE or BACKSPACE keys as necessary to erase the current entry, and then type `Account` in the Import to Table text box.
- Click the Finish button to import the data (Figure 1–48).

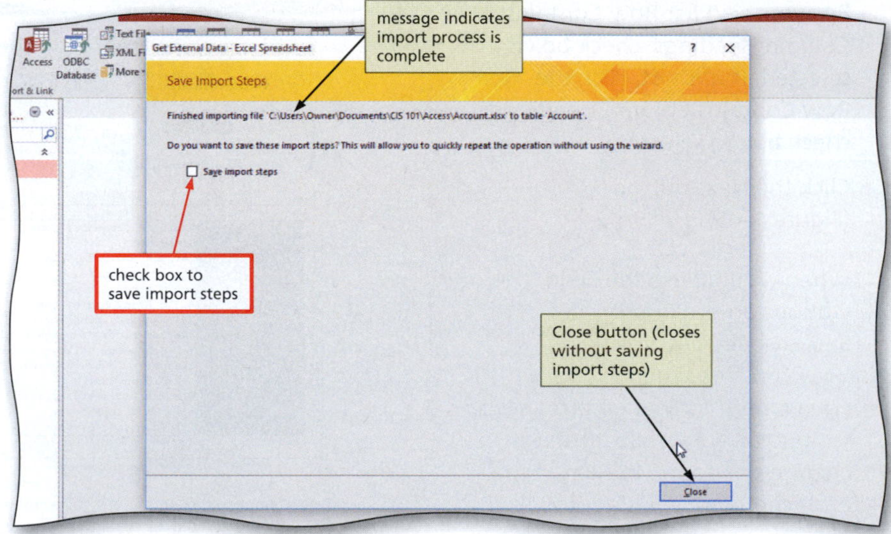

Figure 1–48

8

- Click the 'Save import steps' check box to display the Save import steps options.
- If necessary, type `Import-Account` in the Save as text box.
- Type `Import data from Account workbook into Account table` in the Description text box (Figure 1–49).

Q&A When would I create an Outlook task?

If the import operation is one you will repeat on a regular basis, you can create and schedule the import process just as you can schedule any other Outlook task.

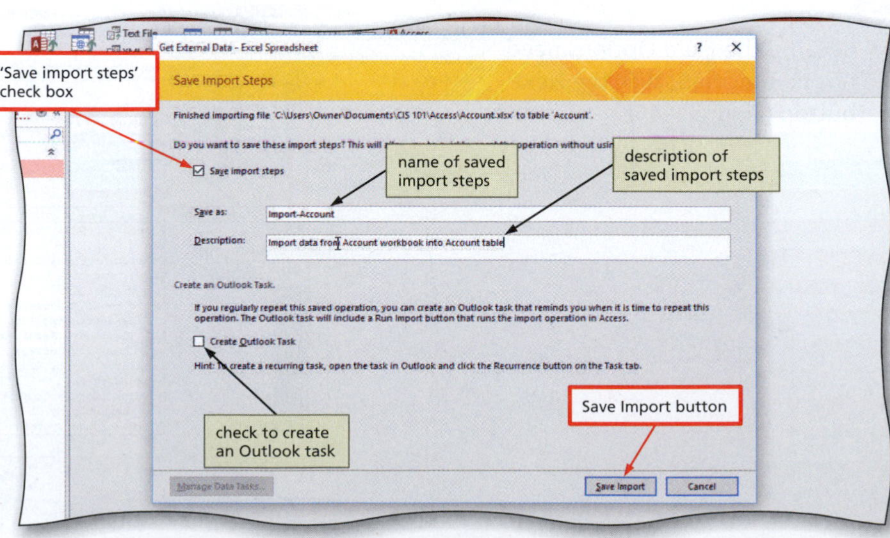

Figure 1–49

9

- Click the Save Import button to save the import steps (Figure 1–50).

Q&A I saved the table as Account Data. How can I change the name?
Right-click the table name in the Navigation Pane. Click Rename on the shortcut menu and change the table name to Account.

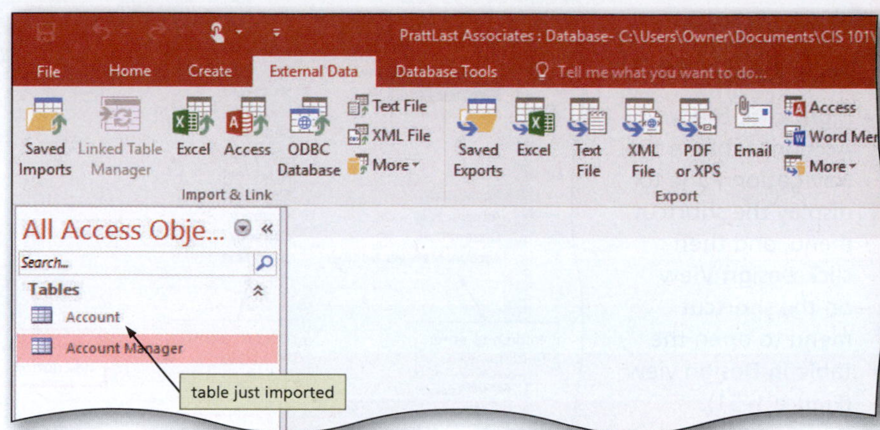

Figure 1–50

Modifying the Table

The import process has created the Account table. The table has the correct fields and records. There are some details the process cannot handle, however. These include field sizes, descriptions, and captions. You will use Design view to make the necessary changes. The information you need is shown in Table 1–5.

BTW
Creating a Table in Design View
To create a table in Design view, display the Create tab, and then click the Table Design button (Create tab | Tables group). You will then see the same screen as in Figure 1–51, except that there will be no entries. Make all the necessary entries for the fields in your table, save the table, and assign the table a name.

Table 1–5 Structure of Account Table

Field Name	Data Type	Field Size	Notes
Account Number	Short Text	5	Primary Key **Description:** Account Number (two uppercase letters followed by 3-digit number) **Caption:** AC #
Account Name	Short Text	30	
Street	Short Text	20	
City	Short Text	20	
State	Short Text	2	
Postal Code	Short Text	5	
Amount Paid	Currency		
Current Due	Currency		
Account Manager Number	Short Text	2	**Description:** Account Manager Number (number of account manager for account) **Caption:** AM #

To Modify a Table in Design View

1 CREATE FIRST TABLE | 2 ADD RECORDS | 3 PRINT CONTENTS | 4 IMPORT RECORDS
5 MODIFY SECOND TABLE | 6 CREATE QUERY | 7 CREATE FORM | 8 CREATE REPORT

You will usually need to modify the design of a table created during the import process. ***Why?*** *Some properties of a table are not specified during the import process, such as descriptions, captions, and field sizes. You might also need to change a data type.* The following steps make the necessary modifications to the design of the Account table.

- Open the Navigation Pane, if necessary.
- Right-click the Account table in the Navigation Pane to display the shortcut menu, and then click Design View on the shortcut menu to open the table in Design view (Figure 1–51).

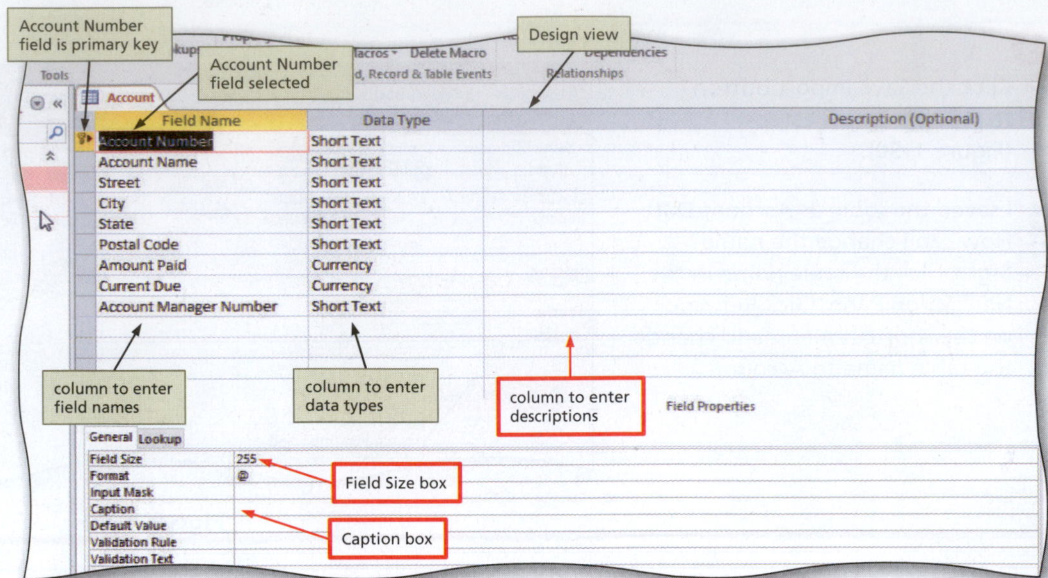

Figure 1–51

- Click the Description (Optional) box for the Account Number field, and then type `Account Number (two uppercase letters followed by a 3-digit number)` as the description.
- With the Account Number field selected, click the Field Size box, erase the current field size, and type `5` as the new field size.
- Click the Caption box, and type `AC #` as the caption (Figure 1–52).

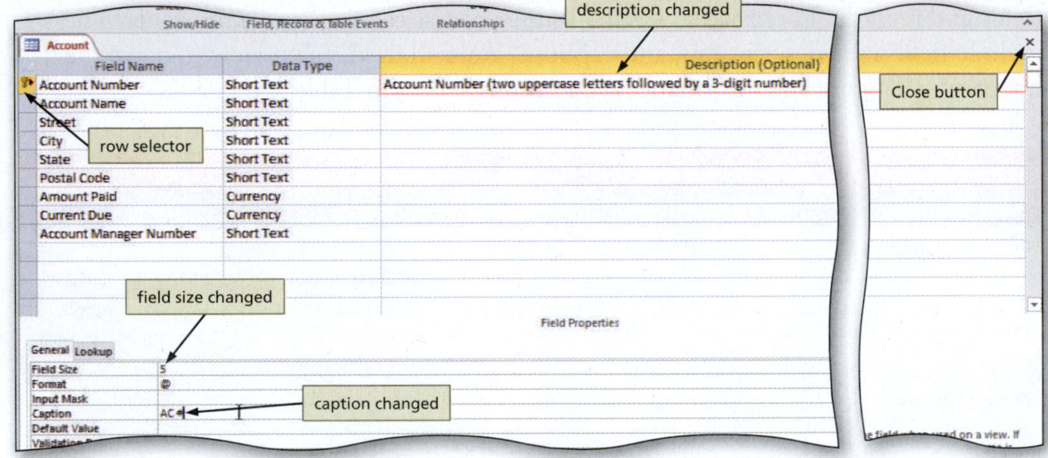

Figure 1–52

Q&A What does the @ symbol represent in the Format box?

The @ symbol is a default format added by Access when the table was imported from Excel.

3

- Make the other changes shown in Table 1–5. To select a field to be changed, click the field's row selector. For most fields, you only need to change the field size. For the Account Manager Number field, you also need to change the description and caption.
- Click the Save button on the Quick Access Toolbar to save your changes.
- Because you know the data will satisfy the new field sizes, click the Yes button when given a message about the possibility of data loss.

Other Ways

1. Press F6 to move between upper and lower panes in Table Design window

Correcting Errors in the Structure

Whenever you create or modify a table in Design view, you should check the entries carefully to ensure they are correct. If you make a mistake and discover it before you press the TAB key, you can correct the error by repeatedly pressing the BACKSPACE key until the incorrect characters are removed. Then, type the correct characters. If you do not discover a mistake until later, you can click the entry, type the correct value, and then press the ENTER key. You can use the following techniques to make changes to the structure:

- If you accidentally add an extra field to the structure, select the field by clicking the row selector (the leftmost column on the row that contains the field to be deleted). Once you have selected the field, press the DELETE key. This will remove the field from the structure.
- If you forget to include a field, select the field that will follow the one you want to add by clicking the row selector, and then press the INSERT key. The remaining fields move down one row, making room for the missing field. Make the entries for the new field in the usual manner.
- If you made the wrong field a primary key field, click the correct primary key entry for the field and then click the Primary Key button (Table Tools Design tab | Tools group).
- To move a field, click the row selector for the field to be moved to select the field, and then drag the field to the desired position.

As an alternative to these steps, you might want to start over. To do so, click the Close button for the window containing the table, and then click the No button in the Microsoft Access dialog box. You then can repeat the process you used earlier to define the fields in the table.

BTW
Importing Data to an Existing Table
When you create a new table in Design view, you can import data from other sources into the table using the External Data tab.

To Close the Table

Now that you have completed and saved the Account table, you can close it. The following step closes the table.

1. Click the Close button for the Account table (see Figure 1–52) to close the table.

To Resize Columns in a Datasheet

You can resize the columns in the datasheet for the Account table just as you resized the columns in the datasheet for the Account Manager table. The following steps resize the columns in the Account table to best fit the data.

1. Open the Account table in Datasheet view.
2. Double-click the right boundary of the field selectors of each of the fields to resize the columns so that they best fit the data.
3. Save the changes to the layout by clicking the Save button on the Quick Access Toolbar.
4. Close the table.

BTW
Resizing Columns
To resize all columns in a datasheet to best fit simultaneously, select the column heading for the first column, hold down the SHIFT key and select the last column in the datasheet. Then, double-click the right boundary of any field selector.

Break Point: If you wish to take a break, this is a good place to do so. You can exit Access now. To resume at a later time, run Access, open the database called PrattLast Associates, and continue following the steps from this location forward.

Additional Database Objects

A database contains many types of objects. Tables are the objects you use to store and manipulate data. Access supports other important types of objects as well; each object has a specific purpose that helps maximize the benefits of a database. Through queries (questions), Access makes it possible to ask complex questions concerning the data in the database and then receive instant answers. Access also allows the user to produce attractive and useful forms for viewing and updating data. Additionally, Access includes report creation tools that make it easy to produce sophisticated reports for presenting data.

BTW

Creating Queries

Although the Simple Query Wizard is a convenient way to create straightforward queries, you will find that many of the queries you create require more control than the wizard provides. In Module 2, you will use Design view to create customized queries.

Creating Queries

Queries are simply questions, the answers to which are in the database. Access contains a powerful query feature that helps you find the answers to a wide variety of questions. Once you have examined the question you want to ask to determine the fields involved in the question, you can begin creating the query. If the query involves no special sort order, restrictions, or calculations, you can use the Simple Query Wizard.

To Use the Simple Query Wizard to Create a Query

1 CREATE FIRST TABLE | 2 ADD RECORDS | 3 PRINT CONTENTS | 4 IMPORT RECORDS
5 MODIFY SECOND TABLE | 6 CREATE QUERY | 7 CREATE FORM | 8 CREATE REPORT

The following steps use the Simple Query Wizard to create a query that PrattLast Associates might use to obtain financial information on its accounts. ***Why?*** *The Simple Query Wizard is the quickest and easiest way to create a query.* This query displays the number, name, amount paid, current due, and account manager number of all accounts.

- If the Navigation Pane is closed, click the 'Shutter Bar Open/Close Button' to open the Navigation Pane.
- Be sure the Account table is selected.
- Click Create on the ribbon to display the Create tab.
- Click the Query Wizard button (Create tab | Queries group) to display the New Query dialog box (Figure 1–53).

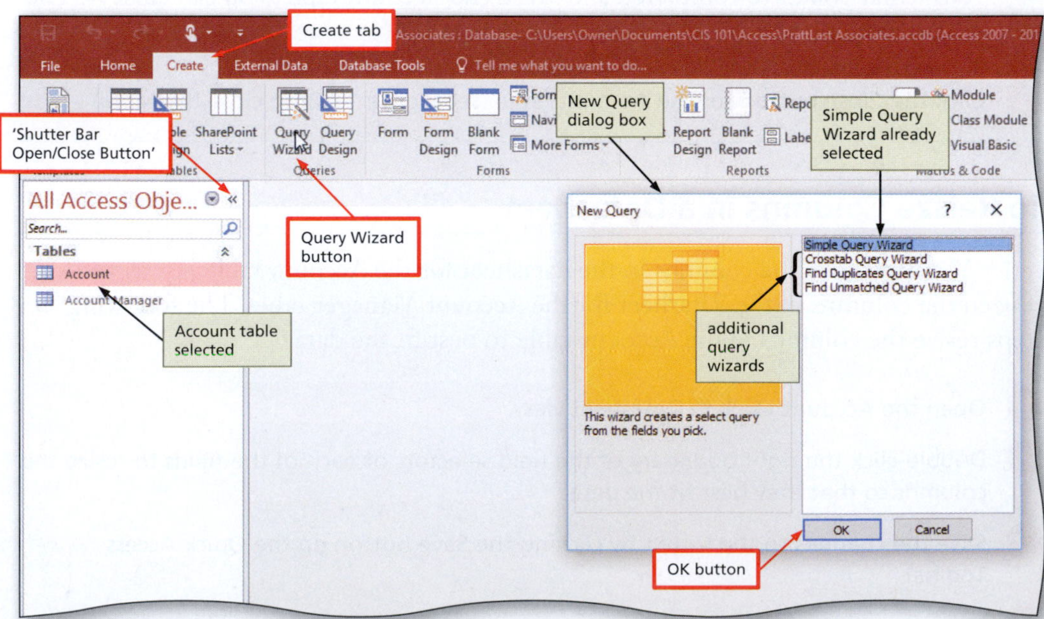

Figure 1–53

2

- Be sure Simple Query Wizard is selected, and then click the OK button (New Query dialog box) to display the Simple Query Wizard dialog box (Figure 1–54).

Q&A What would happen if the Account Manager table were selected instead of the Account table?
The list of available fields would contain fields from the Account Manager table rather than the Account table.

If the list contained Account Manager table fields, how could I make it contain Account table fields?
Click the arrow in the Tables/Queries box, and then click the Account table in the list that appears.

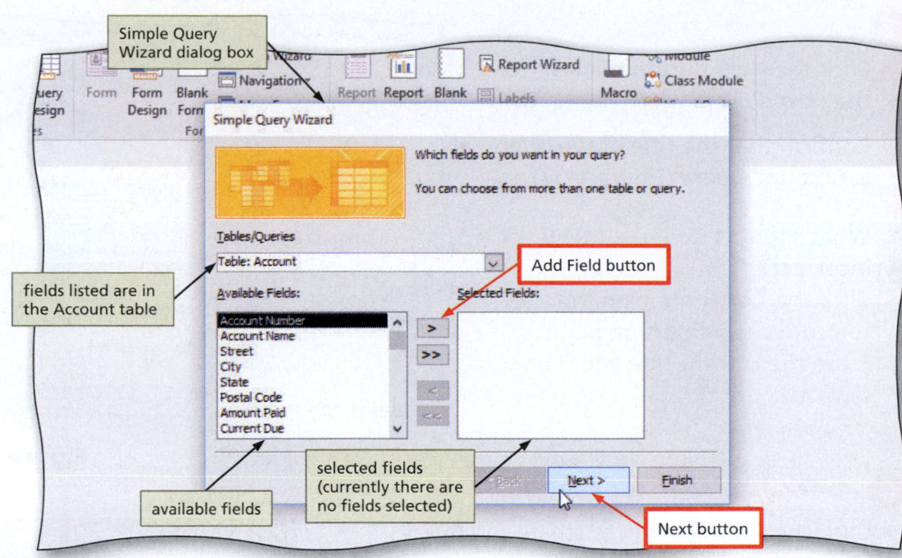

Figure 1–54

3

- With the Account Number field selected, click the Add Field button to add the field to the query.
- With the Account Name field selected, click the Add Field button a second time to add the field.
- Click the Amount Paid field, and then click the Add Field button to add the field.
- In a similar fashion, add the Current Due and Account Manager Number fields (Figure 1–55).

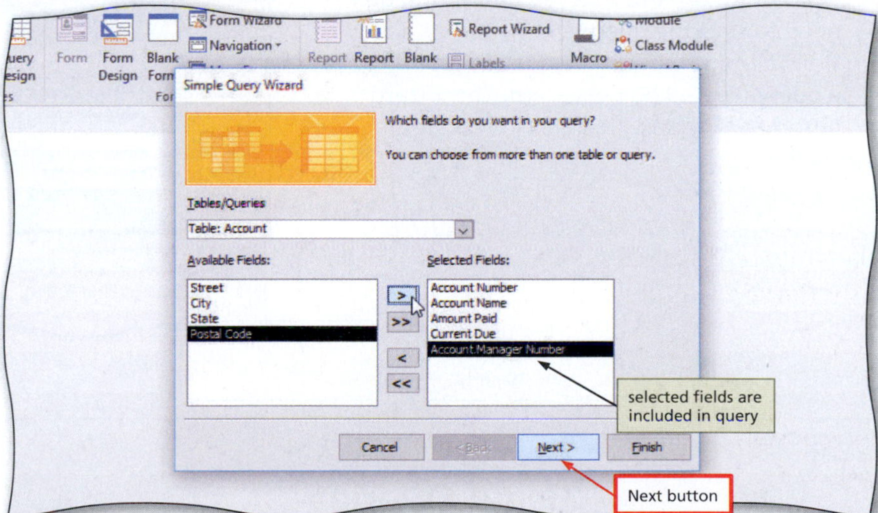

Figure 1–55

4

- Click the Next button to move to the next screen.
- Ensure that the 'Detail (shows every field of every record)' option button is selected (Figure 1–56).

Q&A What is the difference between Detail and Summary?
Detail shows all the records and fields. Summary only shows computations (for example, the total amount paid).

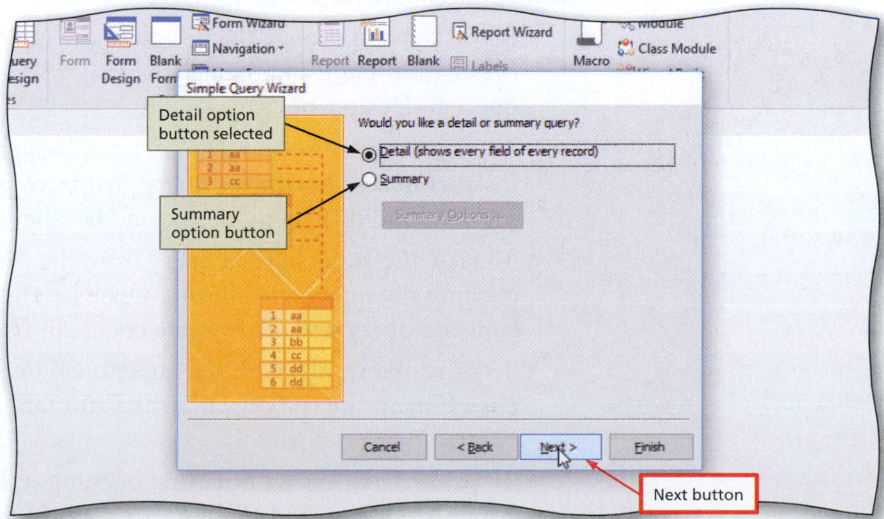

Figure 1–56

- Click the Next button to move to the next screen.
- Confirm that the title of the query is Account Query (Figure 1–57).

Q&A What should I do if the title is incorrect?
Click the box containing the title to produce an insertion point. Erase the current title and then type Account Query.

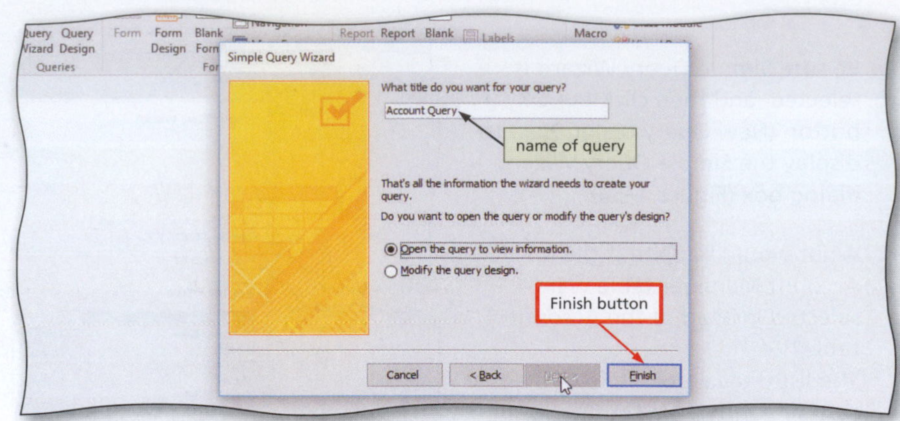

Figure 1–57

- Click the Finish button to create the query (Figure 1–58).
- Click the Close button for the Account Query to remove the query results from the screen.

Q&A If I want to use this query in the future, do I need to save the query?
Normally you would. The one exception is a query created by the wizard. The wizard automatically saves the query it creates.

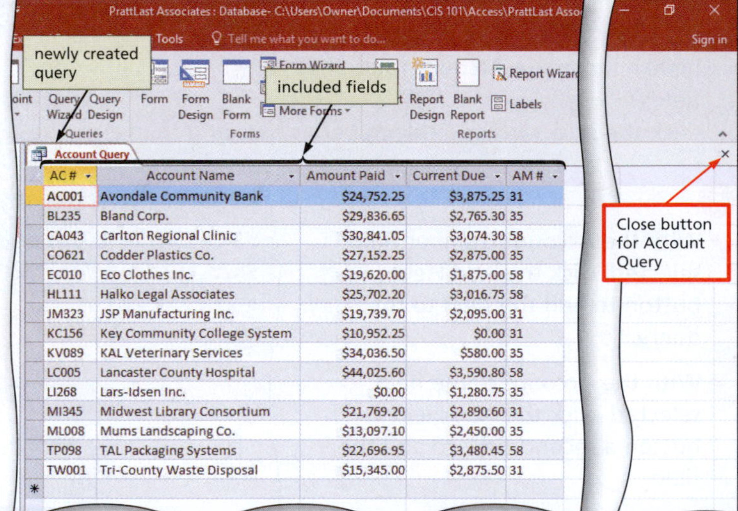

AC #	Account Name	Amount Paid	Current Due	AM #
AC001	Avondale Community Bank	$24,752.25	$3,875.25	31
BL235	Bland Corp.	$29,836.65	$2,765.30	35
CA043	Carlton Regional Clinic	$30,841.05	$3,074.30	58
CO621	Codder Plastics Co.	$27,152.25	$2,875.00	35
EC010	Eco Clothes Inc.	$19,620.00	$1,875.00	58
HL111	Halko Legal Associates	$25,702.20	$3,016.75	58
JM323	JSP Manufacturing Inc.	$19,739.70	$2,095.00	31
KC156	Key Community College System	$10,952.25	$0.00	31
KV089	KAL Veterinary Services	$34,036.50	$580.00	35
LC005	Lancaster County Hospital	$44,025.60	$3,590.80	58
LI268	Lars-Idsen Inc.	$0.00	$1,280.75	35
MI345	Midwest Library Consortium	$21,769.20	$2,890.60	31
ML008	Mums Landscaping Co.	$13,097.10	$2,450.00	35
TP098	TAL Packaging Systems	$22,696.95	$3,480.45	58
TW001	Tri-County Waste Disposal	$15,345.00	$2,875.50	31

Figure 1–58

Using Queries

After you have created and saved a query, Access stores it as a database object and makes it available for use in a variety of ways:

- If you want to change the design of the query, right-click the query in the Navigation Pane and then click Design View on the shortcut menu to open the query in Design view.
- To view the results of the query from Design view, click the Run button to instruct Access to **run** the query, that is, to perform the necessary actions to produce and display the results in Datasheet view.
- To view the results of the query from the Navigation Pane, open it by right-clicking the query and clicking Open on the shortcut menu. Access automatically runs the query and displays the results in Datasheet view.
- To print the results with the query open in either Design view or Datasheet view, click File on the ribbon, click the Print tab, and then click either Print or Quick Print.
- To print the query without first opening it, be sure the query is selected in the Navigation Pane and click File on the ribbon, click the Print tab, and then click either Print or Quick Print.

You can switch between views of a query using the View button (Home tab | Views group). Clicking the arrow in the bottom of the button produces the View button menu. You then click the desired view in the menu. The two query views you will use in this module are Datasheet view (which displays the query results) and Design view (for changing the query design). You can also click the top part of the View button, in which case you will switch to the view identified by the icon on the button. For the most part, the icon on the button represents the view you want, so you can usually simply click the button.

To Use a Criterion in a Query

1 CREATE FIRST TABLE | 2 ADD RECORDS | 3 PRINT CONTENTS | 4 IMPORT RECORDS
5 MODIFY SECOND TABLE | 6 CREATE QUERY | 7 CREATE FORM | 8 CREATE REPORT

After you have determined the fields to be included in a query, you will determine whether you need to further restrict the results of the query. For example, you might want to include only those accounts managed by account manager 35, Mark Simson. In such a case, you need to enter the number 35 as a criterion for the account manager field. ***Why?*** *A criterion is a condition that the records must satisfy in order to be included in the query results.* To do so, you will open the query in Design view, enter the criterion below the appropriate field, and then view the results of the query. The following steps enter a criterion to include only the accounts of account manager 35 and then view the query results.

- Right-click the Account Query in the Navigation Pane to produce a shortcut menu (Figure 1–59).

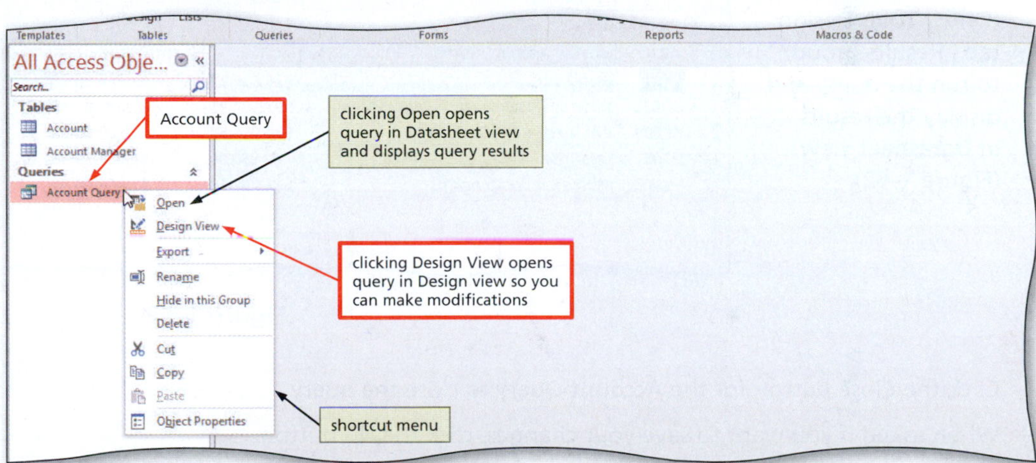

Figure 1–59

- Click Design View on the shortcut menu to open the query in Design view (Figure 1–60).

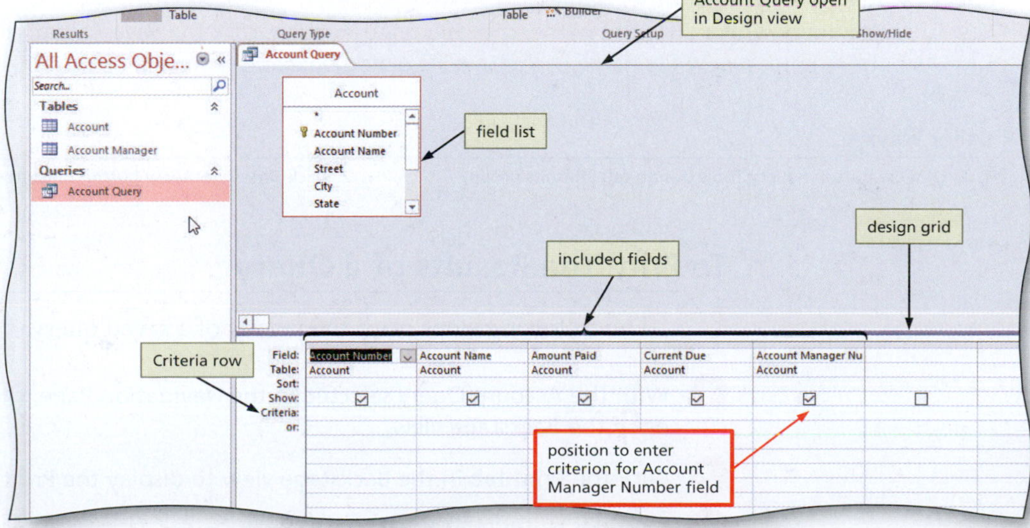

Figure 1–60

3

- Click the Criteria row in the Account Manager Number column of the grid, and then type 35 as the criterion (Figure 1–61).

Q&A The Account Manager Number field is a text field. Do I need to enclose the value for a text field in quotation marks?
You could, but it is not necessary because Access inserts the quotation marks for you automatically.

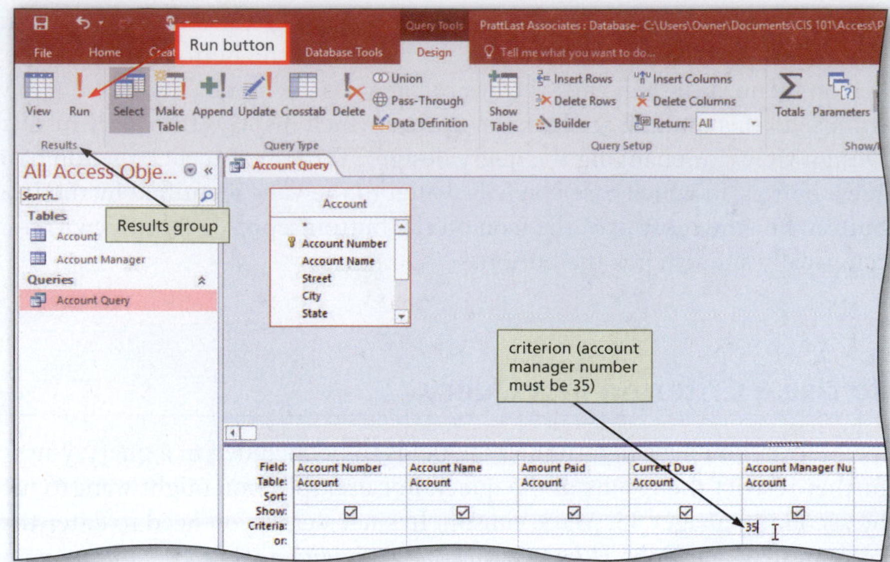

Figure 1–61

4

- Click the Run button (Query Tools Design tab | Results group) to run the query and display the results in Datasheet view (Figure 1–62).

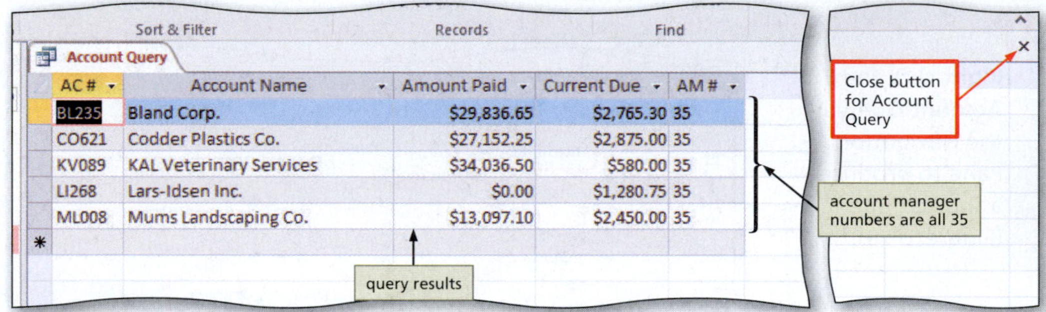

Figure 1–62

5

- Click the Close button for the Account Query to close the query.
- When asked if you want to save your changes, click the No button.

Q&A If I saved the query, what would happen the next time I ran the query?
You would see only accounts of account manager 35.

Could I save a query with another name?
Yes. To save a query with a different name, click File on the ribbon, click the Save As tab, click Save Object As, click the Save As button, enter a new file name in the Save As dialog box, and then click the OK button (Save As dialog box).

Other Ways

1. Click View button (Query Tools Design tab | Results group)
2. Click Datasheet View button on status bar

To Print the Results of a Query

The following steps print the results of a saved query.

1. With the Account Query selected in the Navigation Pane, click File on the ribbon to open the Backstage view.
2. Click the Print tab in the Backstage view to display the Print gallery.
3. Click the Quick Print button to print the query.

Creating Forms

In Datasheet view, you can view many records at once. If there are many fields, however, only some of the fields in each record might be visible at a time. In **Form view**, where data is displayed in a form on the screen, you can usually see all the fields, but only for one record.

1 CREATE FIRST TABLE | 2 ADD RECORDS | 3 PRINT CONTENTS | 4 IMPORT RECORDS
5 MODIFY SECOND TABLE | 6 CREATE QUERY | 7 CREATE FORM | 8 CREATE REPORT

To Create a Form

Like a paper form, a **form** in a database is a formatted document with fields that contain data. Forms allow you to view and maintain data. Forms can also be used to print data, but reports are more commonly used for that purpose. The simplest type of form in Access is one that includes all the fields in a table stacked one above the other. The following steps use the Form button to create a form. ***Why?*** *Using the Form button is the simplest way to create this type of form. The steps use the form to view records and then save the form.*

- Select the Account table in the Navigation Pane.
- If necessary, click Create on the ribbon to display the Create tab (Figure 1–63).

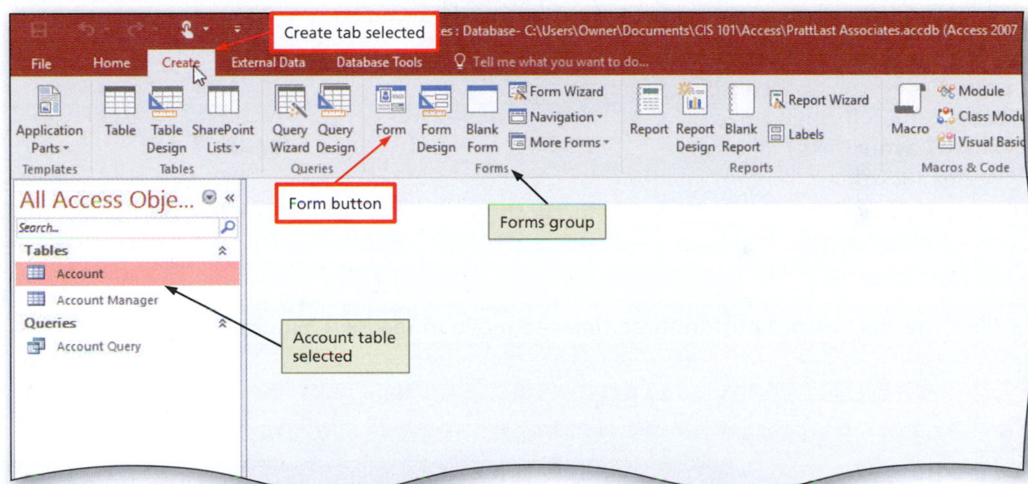

Figure 1–63

- Click the Form button (Create tab | Forms group) to create a simple form (Figure 1–64).

Q&A A Field list appeared on my screen. What should I do?
Click the 'Add Existing Fields' button (Form Layout Tools Design tab | Tools group) to remove the Field list from the screen.

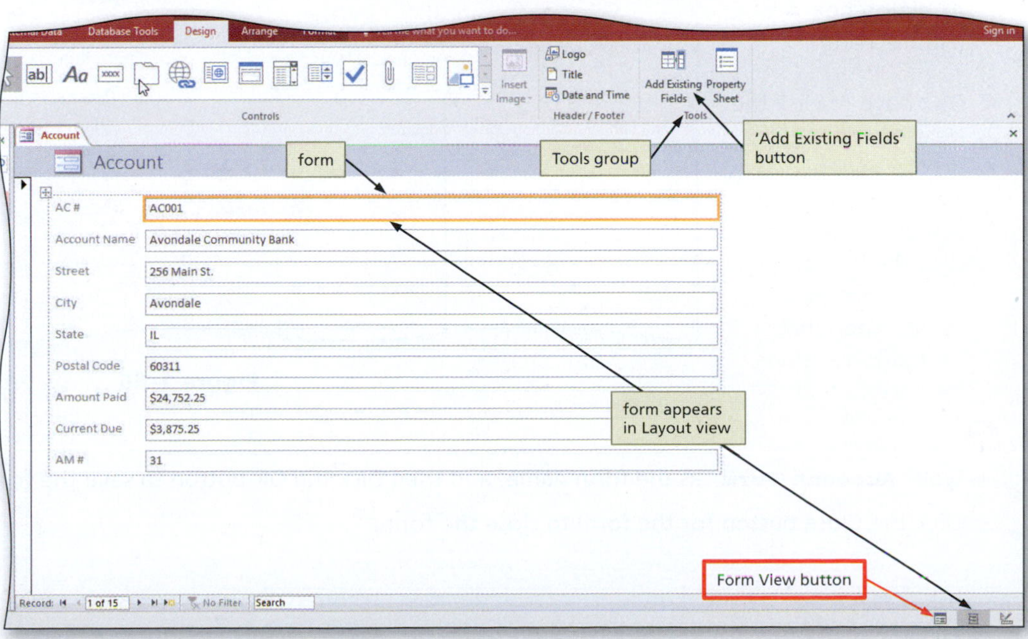

Figure 1–64

- Click the Form View button on the Access status bar to display the form in Form view rather than Layout view.

Q&A What is the difference between Layout view and Form view?
Layout view allows you to make changes to the look of the form. Form view is the view you use to examine or make changes to the data.

How can I tell when I am in Layout view?
Access identifies Layout view in three ways. The left side of the status bar will contain the words, Layout View; shading will appear around the outside of the selected field in the form; and the Layout View button will be selected on the right side of the status bar.

- Click the Next record button three times to move to record 4 (Figure 1–65).

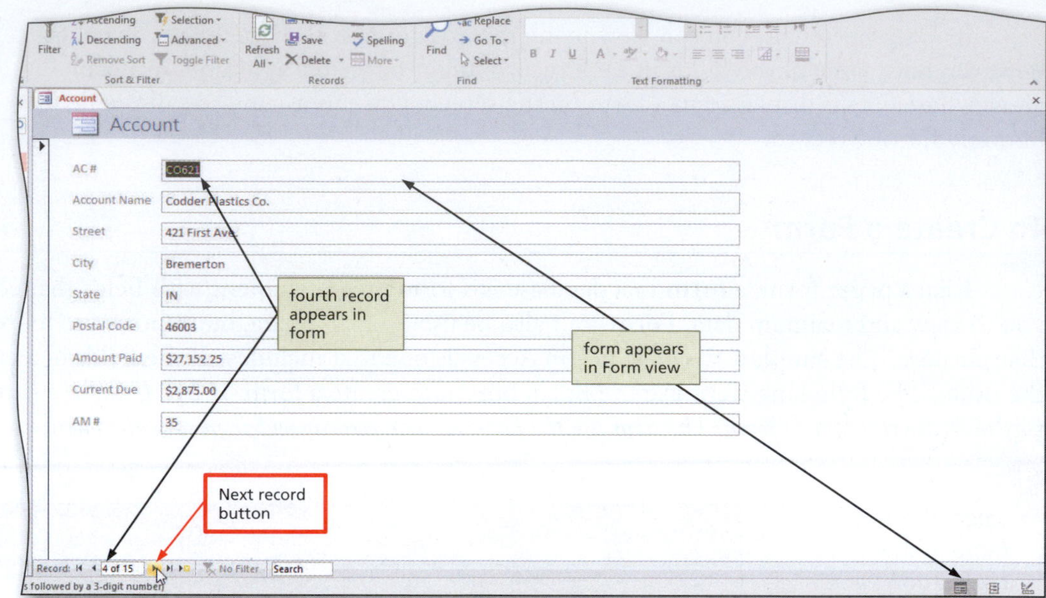

Figure 1–65

- Click the Save button on the Quick Access Toolbar to display the Save As dialog box (Figure 1–66).

Q&A Do I have to click the Next record button before saving?
No. The only reason you were asked to click the button was so that you could experience navigation within the form.

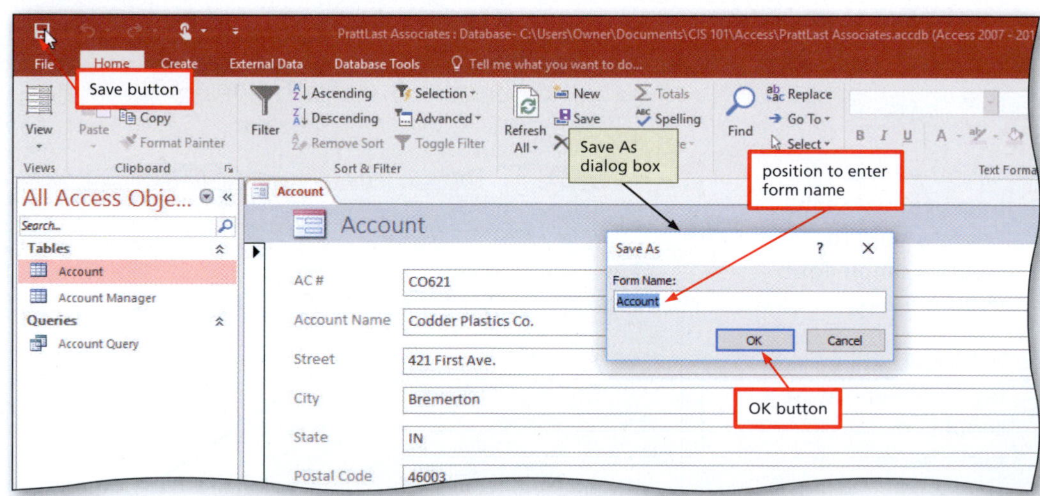

Figure 1–66

- Type `Account Form` as the form name, and then click the OK button to save the form.
- Click the Close button for the form to close the form.

Other Ways

1. Click View button (Form Layout Tools Design tab | Views group)

Using a Form

After you have saved a form, you can use it at any time by right-clicking the form in the Navigation Pane and then clicking Open on the shortcut menu. In addition to viewing data in the form, you can also use it to enter or update data, a process that is very similar to updating data using a datasheet. If you plan to use the form to enter or revise data, you must ensure you are viewing the form in Form view.

Break Point: If you wish to take a break, this is a good place to do so. You can exit Access now. To resume at a later time, run Access, open the database called PrattLast Associates, and continue following the steps from this location forward.

Creating and Printing Reports

PrattLast Associates wants to be able to present account financial data in a useful format. To do so, they will create the Account Financial Report shown in Figure 1–67. To create this report, you will first create a simple report containing all records. Then, you will modify the report to match the one shown in Figure 1–67.

Account Financial Report

Tuesday, September 12, 2017
7:54:24 PM

Account Number	Account Name	Amount Paid	Current Due	Account Manager Number
AC001	Avondale Community Bank	$24,752.25	$3,875.25	31
BL235	Bland Corp.	$29,836.65	$2,765.30	35
CA043	Carlton Regional Clinic	$30,841.05	$3,074.30	58
CO621	Codder Plastics Co.	$27,152.25	$2,875.00	35
EC010	Eco Clothes Inc.	$19,620.00	$1,875.00	58
HL111	Halko Legal Associates	$25,702.20	$3,016.75	58
JM323	JSP Manufacturing Inc.	$19,739.70	$2,095.00	31
KV089	KAL Veterinary Services	$34,036.50	$580.00	35
KC156	Key Community College System	$10,952.25	$0.00	31
LC005	Lancaster County Hospital	$44,025.60	$3,590.80	58
LI268	Lars-Idsen Inc.	$0.00	$1,280.75	35
MI345	Midwest Library Consortium	$21,769.20	$2,890.60	31
ML008	Mums Landscaping Co.	$13,097.10	$2,450.00	35
TP098	TAL Packaging Systems	$22,696.95	$3,480.45	58
TW001	Tri-County Waste Disposal	$15,345.00	$2,875.50	31
		$339,566.70	$36,724.70	

Figure 1–67

To Create a Report

1 CREATE FIRST TABLE | 2 ADD RECORDS | 3 PRINT CONTENTS | 4 IMPORT RECORDS
5 MODIFY SECOND TABLE | 6 CREATE QUERY | 7 CREATE FORM | 8 CREATE REPORT

You will first create a report containing all fields. ***Why?*** *It is easiest to create a report with all the fields and then delete the fields you do not want.* The following steps create and save the initial report. They also modify the report title.

1

- Be sure the Account table is selected in the Navigation Pane.
- Click Create on the ribbon to display the Create tab (Figure 1–68).

Q&A Do I need to select the Account table prior to clicking Create on the ribbon?
You do not need to select the table at that point. You do need to select a table prior to clicking the Report button, because Access will include all the fields in whichever table or query is currently selected.

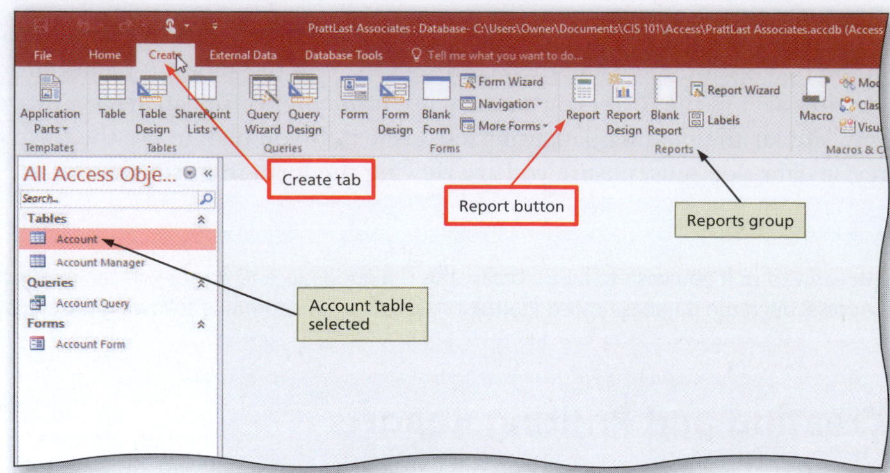

Figure 1–68

2

- Click the Report button (Create tab | Reports group) to create the report (Figure 1–69).

Q&A Why is the report title Account?
Access automatically assigns the name of the table or query as the title of the report. It also automatically includes the date and time. You can change either of these later.

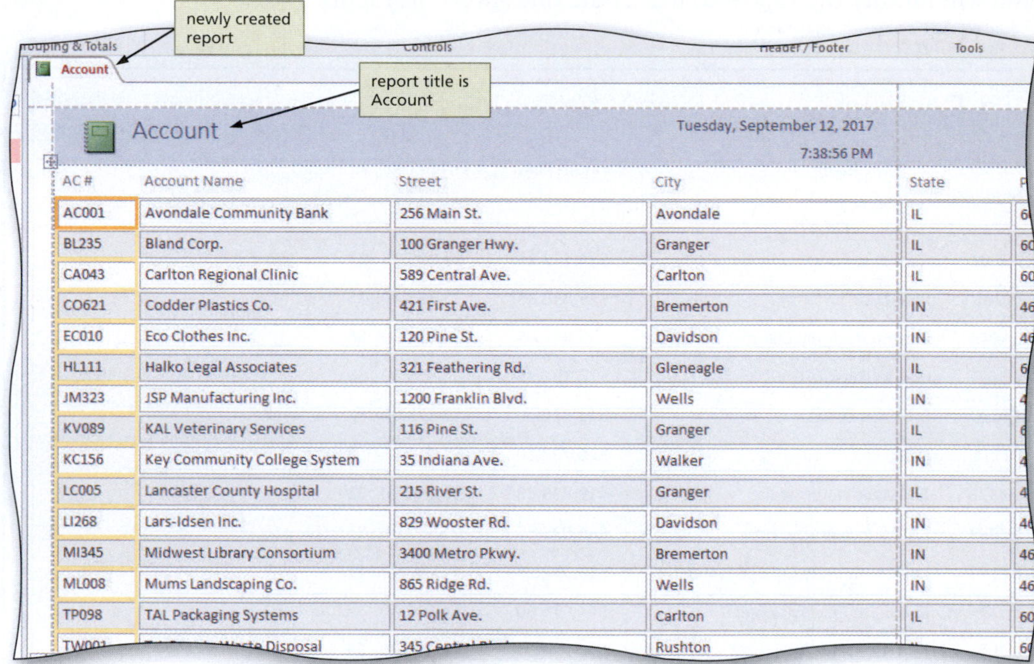

Figure 1–69

3

- Click the Save button on the Quick Access Toolbar to display the Save As dialog box, and then type Account Financial Report as the name of the report (Figure 1–70).

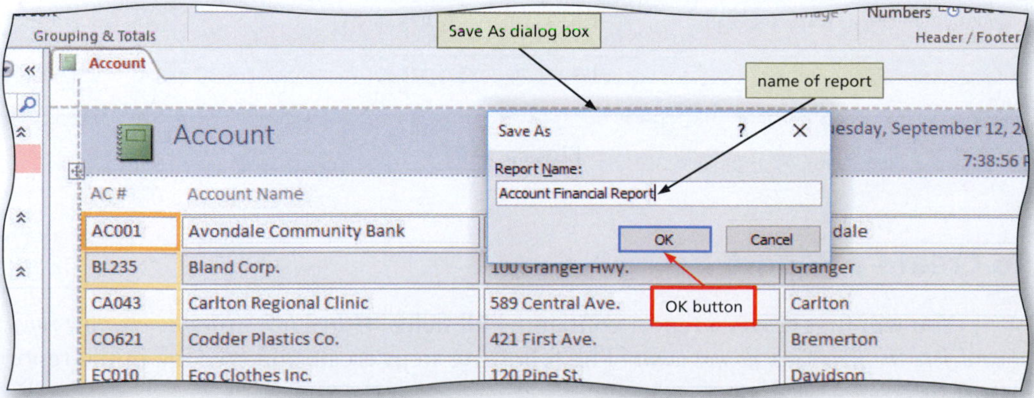

Figure 1–70

- Click the OK button (Save As dialog box) to save the report (Figure 1–71).

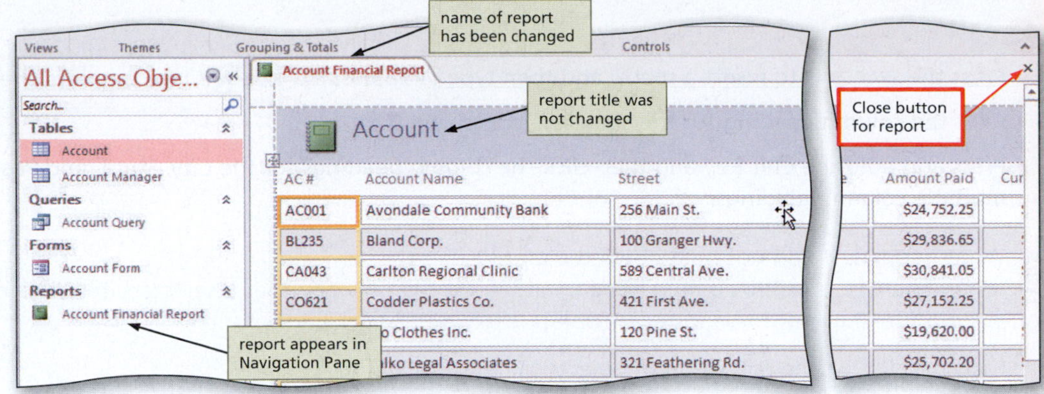

Figure 1–71

Q&A The name of the report changed. Why did the report title not change?
The report title is assigned the same name as the report by default. Changing the name of the report does not change the report title. You can change the title at any time to anything you like.

- Close the report by clicking its Close button.

Using Layout View in a Report

Access has four different ways to view reports: Report view, Print Preview, Layout view, and Design view. Report view shows the report on the screen. Print Preview shows the report as it will appear when printed. Layout view is similar to Report view in that it shows the report on the screen, but it also allows you to make changes to the report. Layout view is usually the easiest way to make such changes. Design view also allows you to make changes, but does not show you the actual report. Design view is most useful when the changes you need to make are especially complex. In this module, you will use Layout view to modify the report.

BTW
Report Navigation
When previewing a report, you can use the Navigation buttons on the status bar to move from one page to another.

To Modify Report Column Headings and Resize Columns

1 CREATE FIRST TABLE | 2 ADD RECORDS | 3 PRINT CONTENTS | 4 IMPORT RECORDS
5 MODIFY SECOND TABLE | 6 CREATE QUERY | 7 CREATE FORM | **8 CREATE REPORT**

To make the report match the one shown in Figure 1–67, you need to change the title, remove some columns, modify the column headings, and also resize the columns. The following steps use Layout view to make the necessary modifications to the report. ***Why?*** *Working in Layout view gives you all the tools you need to make the desired modifications. You can view the results of the modifications immediately.*

- Right-click Account Financial Report in the Navigation Pane, and then click Layout View on the shortcut menu to open the report in Layout view.
- If a Field list appears, click the 'Add Existing Fields' button (Report Layout Tools Design tab | Tools group) to remove the Field list from the screen.
- Close the Navigation Pane.
- Click the report title once to select it.
- Click the report title a second time to produce an insertion point (Figure 1–72).

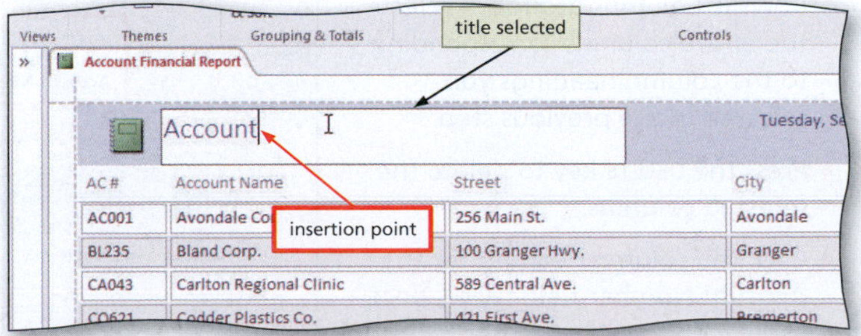

Figure 1–72

Q&A My insertion point is in the middle of Account. How do I produce an insertion point at the position shown in the figure?
You can use the RIGHT ARROW key to move the insertion point to the position in the figure, or you can click the desired position.

2

- Press the SPACEBAR to insert a space, and then type `Financial Report` to complete the title.
- Click the column heading for the Street field to select it.
- Press and hold the CTRL key and then click the column headings for the City, State, and Postal Code fields to select multiple column headings.

Q&A What happens if I do not hold down the CTRL key?
When you click another column heading, it will be the only one that is selected. To select multiple objects, you need to hold the CTRL key down for every object after the first selection.

I selected the wrong collection of objects. What should I do?
You can click somewhere else on the report so that the objects you want are not selected, and then begin the process again. Alternatively, you can repeatedly click the Undo button on the Quick Access Toolbar to undo your selections. Once you have done so, you can select the objects you want.

- Click Arrange on the ribbon to display the Report Layout Tools Arrange tab (Figure 1–73).

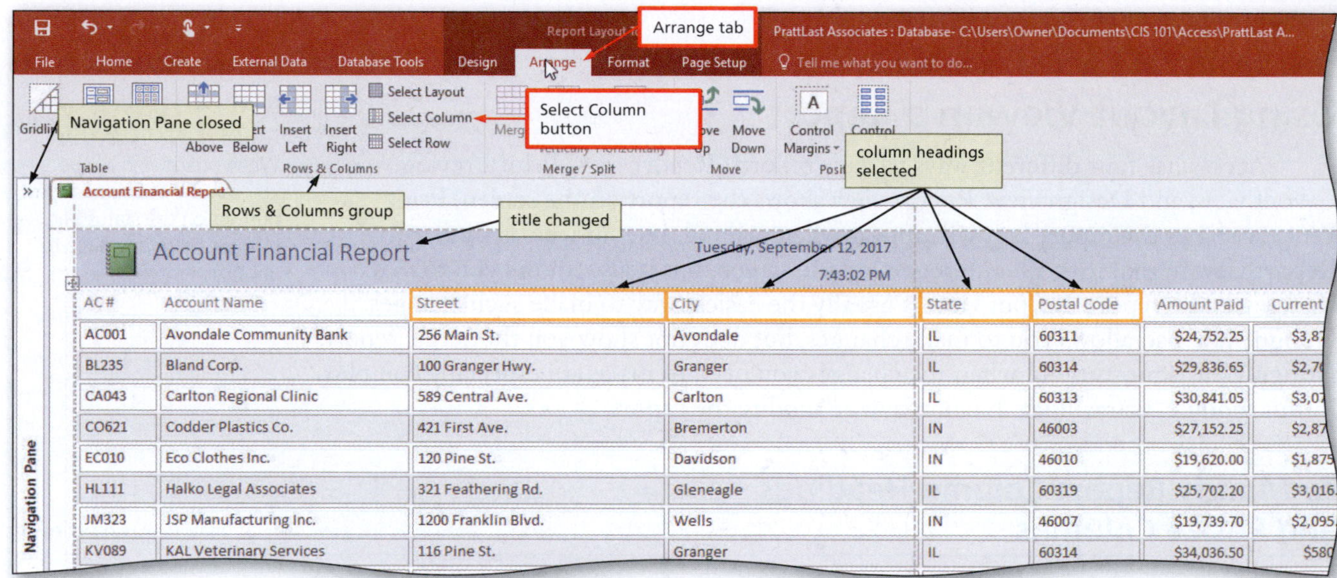

Figure 1–73

- Click the Select Column button (Report Layout Tools Arrange tab | Rows & Columns group) to select the entire columns corresponding to the column headings you selected in the previous step.
- Press the DELETE key to delete the selected columns.
- Click the column heading for the Account Number field twice, once to select it and the second time to produce an insertion point (Figure 1–74).

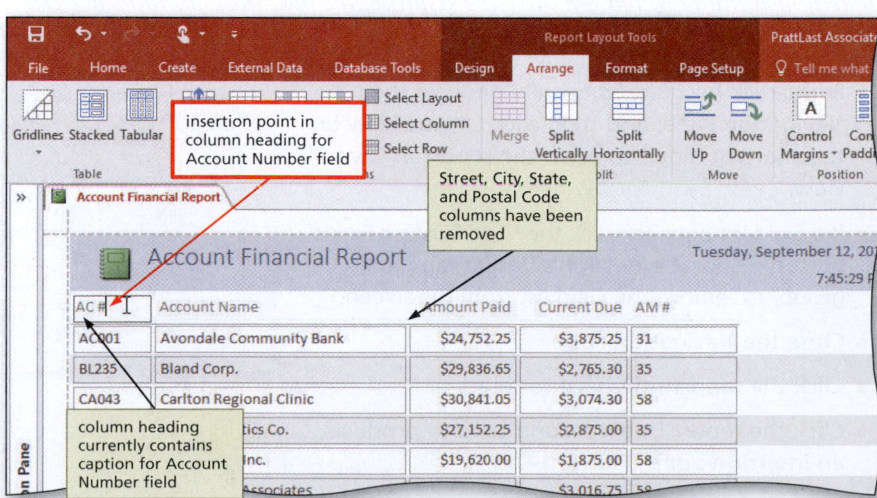

Figure 1–74

Q&A I selected the wrong field. What should I do?
Click somewhere outside the various fields to deselect the one you have selected. Then, click the Account Number field twice.

4

- Use the DELETE or BACKSPACE keys as necessary to erase the current entry, and then type `Account Number` as the new entry.
- Click the heading for the Account Manager Number field twice, erase the current entry, and then type `Account Manager Number` as the new entry.
- Click the Account Number field heading to select it, point to the lower boundary of the heading for the Account Number field so that the pointer changes to a two-headed arrow, and then drag the lower boundary to the approximate position shown in Figure 1–75 to expand the column headings.

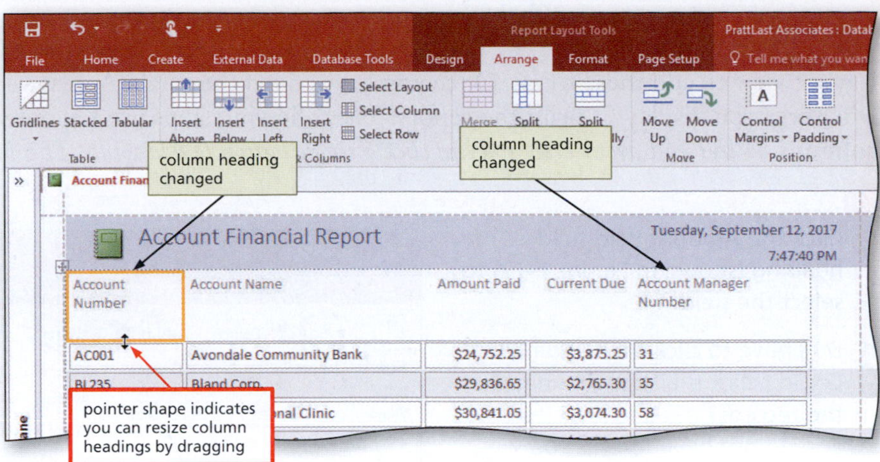

Figure 1–75

Q&A I did something wrong when I dragged and now my report looks strange. What should I do?
Click the Undo button on the Quick Access Toolbar to undo the change. Depending on the specific action you took, you might need to click it more than once.

My screen displays Account Manager Number on one line, not two. Is this a problem?
No. You will adjust the column heading in a later step.

5

- Point to the right boundary of the heading for the Account Number field so that the pointer changes to a two-headed arrow, and then drag the right boundary to the approximate position shown in Figure 1–76 to reduce the width of the column.

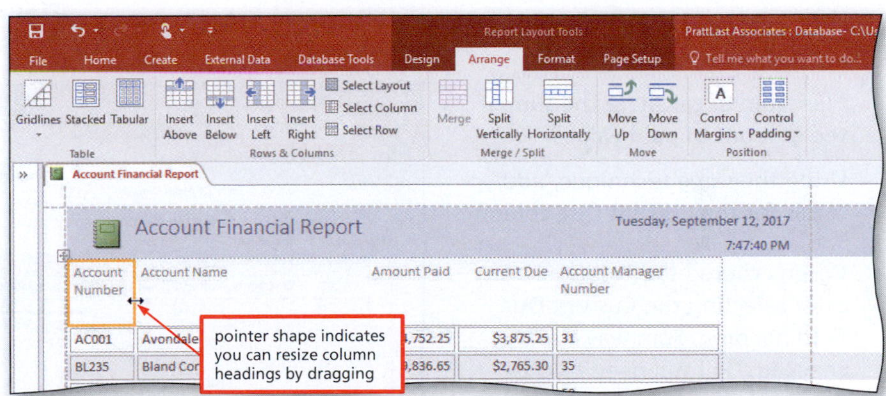

Figure 1–76

6

- Using the same technique, resize the other columns to the sizes shown in Figure 1–77.

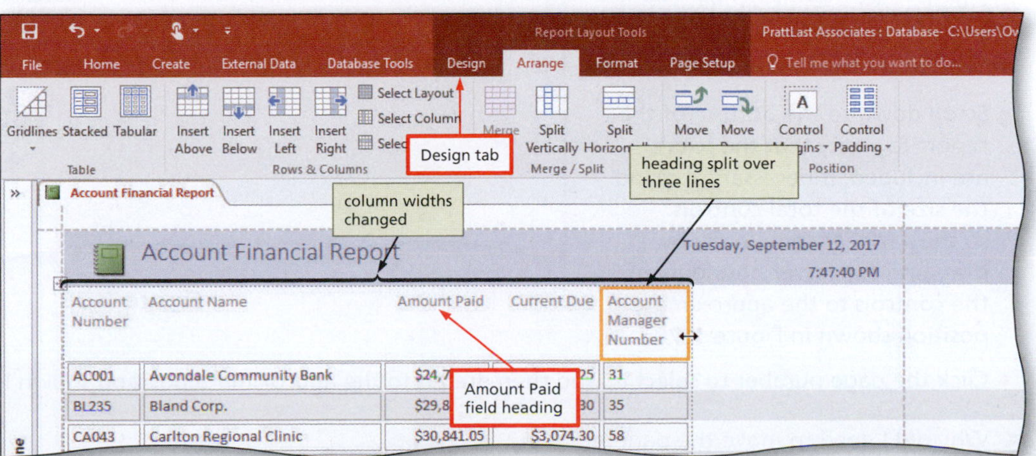

Figure 1–77

To Add Totals to a Report

The report in Figure 1–67 contains totals for the Amount Paid and Current Due columns. You can use Layout view to add these totals. Once you have added the totals, Access will calculate the appropriate values whenever you display or print the report. The following steps use Layout view to include totals for these three columns. ***Why?*** *In Layout view you can click a single button to add totals. This button sums all the values in the field.*

1

- Click the Amount Paid field heading (shown in Figure 1–77) to select the field.

Q&A Do I have to click the heading? Could I click the field on one of the records?
You do not have to click the heading. You also could click the Amount Paid field on any record.

- Click Design on the ribbon to display the Design tab.
- Click the Totals button (Report Layout Tools Design tab | Grouping & Totals group) to display the Totals menu containing a list of available calculations (Figure 1–78).

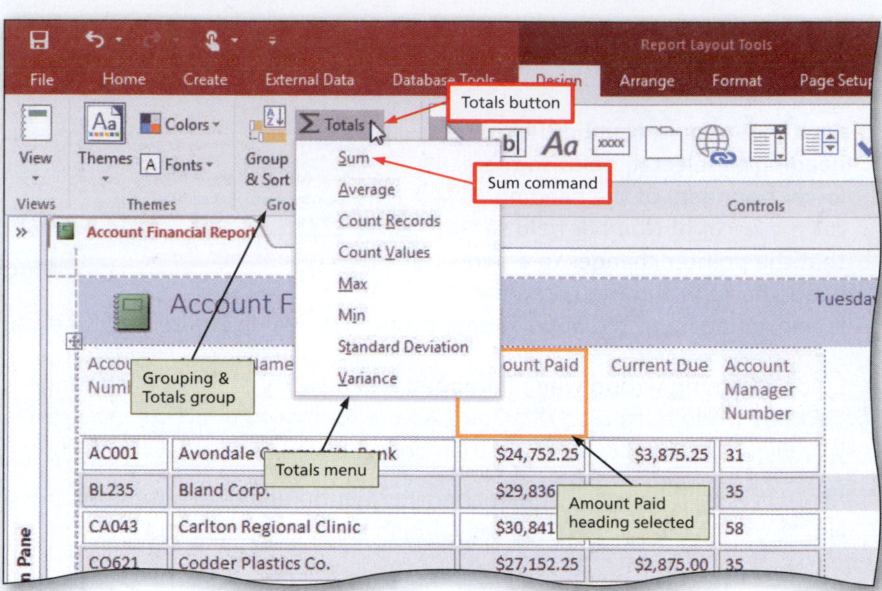

Figure 1–78

2

- Click Sum to calculate the sum of the amount of paid values.
- Using the same technique, add totals for the Current Due column.

Q&A When I clicked the Totals button after selecting the Current Due field heading, Sum was already checked. Do I still need to click Sum?
No. In fact, if you do click it, you will remove the check mark, which will remove the total from the column.

- Scroll down to the bottom of the report to verify that the totals are included. If necessary, expand the size of the total controls so they appear completely by dragging the lower boundary of the controls to the approximate position shown in Figure 1–79.

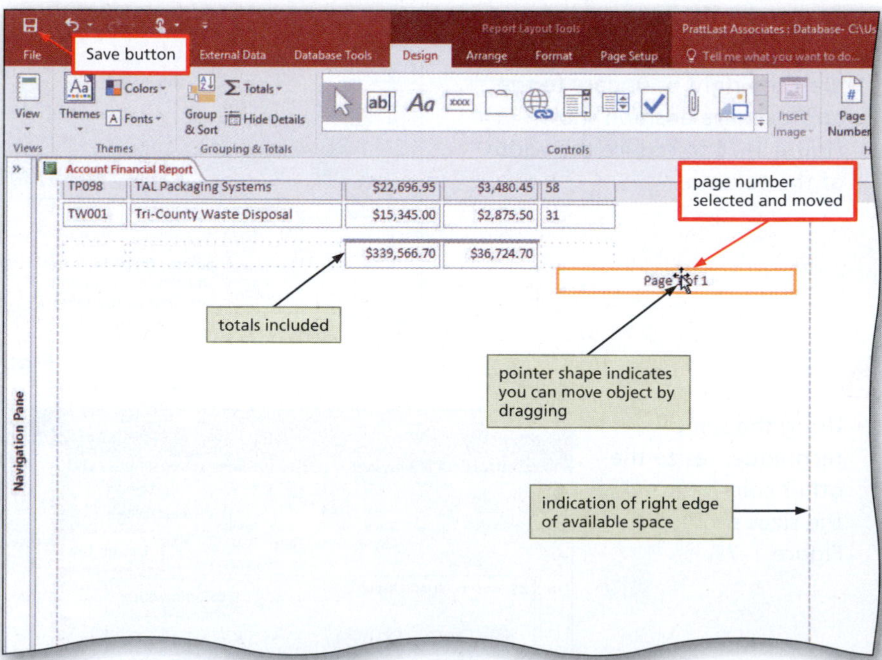

Figure 1–79

- Click the page number to select it, and then drag it to the approximate position shown in Figure 1–79.

Q&A Why did I need to move the page number?
The dotted line near the right-hand edge of the screen indicates the right-hand border of the available space on the printed page, based on whatever margins and orientation are currently selected. A portion of the page number extends beyond this border. By moving the page number, it no longer extends beyond the border.

3
- Click the Save button on the Quick Access Toolbar to save your changes to the report layout.
- Close the report.

To Print a Report

The following steps print the report.

1 Open the Navigation Pane, if necessary, confirm that the Account Financial Report is selected, and then click File on the ribbon to open the Backstage view.

2 Click the Print tab in the Backstage view to display the Print gallery.

3 Click the Quick Print button to print the report.

Q&A

When I print the report, I have pound signs (####) rather than numbers where the totals should be for the Amount Paid and Current Due columns. The report looked fine on the screen. How can I correct it?
The columns are not wide enough to display the complete number. Open the report in Layout view and slightly increase the width of the Amount Paid and Current Due columns by dragging the right boundary of the column headings.

How can I print multiple copies of my report?
Click File on the ribbon to open the Backstage view. Click the Print tab, click Print in the Print gallery to display the Print dialog box, increase the number in the Number of Copies box, and then click the OK button .

How can I print a range of pages rather than printing the whole report?
Click File on the ribbon to open the Backstage view. Click the Print tab, click Print in the Print gallery to display the Print dialog box, click the Pages option button in the Print Range area, enter the desired page range, and then click the OK button (Print dialog box).

BTW

Distributing a Document

Instead of printing and distributing a hard copy of a document, you can distribute the document electronically. Options include sending the document via email; posting it on cloud storage (such as OneDrive) and sharing the file with others; posting it on social media, a blog, or other website; and sharing a link associated with an online location of the document. You also can create and share a PDF or XPS image of the document, so that users can view the file in Acrobat Reader or XPS Viewer instead of in Access.

Database Properties

Access helps you organize and identify your databases by using **database properties,** which are the details about a file. Database properties, also known as **metadata**, can include such information as the project author, title, or subject. **Keywords** are words or phrases that further describe the database. For example, a class name or database topic can describe the file's purpose or content.

Five different types of database properties exist, but the more common ones used in this book are standard and automatically updated properties. **Standard properties** are associated with all Microsoft Office documents and include author, title, and subject. **Automatically updated properties** include file system properties, such as the date you create or change a file, and statistics, such as the file size.

BTW

Exporting a Report as a PDF or XPS File

To export a report as a PDF or XPS file, display the External Data tab, and then click the PDF or XPS button (External Data tab | Export group). Enter the appropriate information in the Publish to PDF or XPS dialog box and click the Publish button.

CONSIDER THIS

Why would you want to assign database properties to a database?
Database properties are valuable for a variety of reasons:

- Users can save time locating a particular file because they can view a file's database properties without opening the database.
- By creating consistent properties for files having similar content, users can better organize their databases.
- Some organizations require Access users to add database properties so that other employees can view details about these files.

To Change Database Properties

To change database properties, you would follow these steps.

1. Click File on the ribbon to open the Backstage view and then, if necessary, click the Info tab in the Backstage view to display the Info gallery.

2. Click the 'View and edit database properties' link in the right pane of the Info gallery to display the PrattLast Associates Properties dialog box.

Q&A Why are some of the database properties already filled in?
The person who installed Office 2016 on your computer or network might have set or customized the properties.

3. If the property you want to change is displayed in the Properties dialog box, click the text box for the property and make the desired change. Skip the remaining steps.

4. If the property you want to change is not displayed in the Properties dialog box, click the appropriate tab so the property is displayed and then make the desired change.

5. Click the OK button in the Properties dialog box to save your changes and remove the dialog box from the screen.

BTW
Tabbed Documents Versus Overlapping Windows
By default, Access 2016 displays database objects in tabbed documents instead of in overlapping windows. If your database is in overlapping windows mode, click File on the ribbon, click Options in the Backstage view, click Current Database in the Access Options dialog box, and select the 'Display Document Tabs' check box and the Tabbed Documents option button.

Special Database Operations

Additional operations involved in maintaining a database are backup, recovery, compacting, and repairing.

Backup and Recovery

It is possible to damage or destroy a database. Users can enter data that is incorrect; programs that are updating the database can end abnormally during an update; a hardware problem can occur; and so on. After any such event has occurred, the database may contain invalid data or it might be totally destroyed.

Obviously, you cannot allow a situation in which data has been damaged or destroyed to go uncorrected. You must somehow return the database to a correct state. This process is called recovery; that is, you **recover** the database.

The simplest approach to recovery involves periodically making a copy of the database (called a **backup copy** or a **save copy**). This is referred to as **backing up** the database. If a problem occurs, you correct the problem by overwriting the actual database — often referred to as the **live database** — with the backup copy.

To back up the database that is currently open, you use the Back Up Database command on the Save As tab in the Backstage view. In the process, Access suggests a name that is a combination of the database name and the current date. For example, if you back up the PrattLast Associates database on October 20, 2017, Access will suggest the name, PrattLast Associates_2017-10-20. You can change this name if you desire, although it is a good idea to use this name. By doing so, it will be easy to distinguish between all the backup copies you have made to determine which is the most recent. In addition, if you discover that a critical problem occurred on October 18, 2017, you may want to go back to the most recent backup before October 18. If, for example, the database was not backed up on October 17 but was backed up on October 16, you would use PrattLast Associates_2017-10-16.

To Back Up a Database

You would use the following steps to back up a database to a file on a hard disk, high-capacity removable disk, or other storage location.

1. Open the database to be backed up.
2. Click File on the ribbon to open the Backstage view, and then click the Save As tab.
3. With Save Database As selected in the File Types area, click 'Back Up Database' in the Save Database As area, and then click the Save As button.
4. Navigate to the desired location in the Save As box. If you do not want the name Access has suggested, enter the desired name in the File name text box.
5. Click the Save button to back up the database.

Access creates a backup copy with the desired name in the desired location. Should you ever need to recover the database using this backup copy, you can simply copy it over the live version.

Compacting and Repairing a Database

As you add more data to a database, it naturally grows larger. When you delete an object (records, tables, forms, or queries), the space previously occupied by the object does not become available for additional objects. Instead, the additional objects are given new space; that is, space that was not already allocated. To remove this empty space from the database, you must **compact** the database. The same option that compacts the database also repairs problems that might have occurred in the database.

To Compact and Repair a Database

You would use the following steps to compact and repair a database.

1. Open the database to be compacted.
2. Click File on the ribbon to open the Backstage view, and then, if necessary, select the Info tab.
3. Click the 'Compact & Repair Database' button in the Info gallery to compact and repair the database.

The database now is the compacted form of the original.

Additional Operations

Additional special operations include opening another database, closing a database without exiting Access, and saving a database with another name. They also include deleting a table (or other object) as well as renaming an object.

When you are working in a database and you open another database, Access will automatically close the database that was previously open. Before deleting or renaming an object, you should ensure that the object has no dependent objects; that is, other objects that depend on the object you want to delete.

To Close a Database without Exiting Access

You would use the following steps to close a database without exiting Access.

1. Click File on the ribbon to open the Backstage view.
2. Click Close.

To Save a Database with Another Name

To save a database with another name, you would use the following steps.

1. Click File on the ribbon to open the Backstage view, and then select the Save As tab.
2. With Save Database As selected in the File Types area and Access Database selected in the Save Database As area, click the Save As button.
3. Enter a name and select a location for the new version.
4. Click the Save button.

CONSIDER THIS

If you want to make a backup, could you just save the database with another name?

You could certainly do that. Using the backup procedure discussed earlier is useful because doing so automatically includes the current database name and the date in the name of the file it creates.

To Delete a Table or Other Object in the Database

You would use the following steps to delete a database object.

1. Right-click the object in the Navigation Pane.
2. Click Delete on the shortcut menu.
3. Click the Yes button in the Microsoft Access dialog box.

To Rename an Object in the Database

You would use the following steps to rename a database object.

1. Right-click the object in the Navigation Pane.
2. Click Rename on the shortcut menu.
3. Type the new name and press the ENTER key.

BTW

Access Help

At any time while using Access, you can find answers to questions and display information about various topics through Access Help. Used properly, this form of assistance can increase your productivity and reduce your frustrations by minimizing the time you spend learning how to use Access. For instructions about Access Help and exercises that will help you gain confidence in using it, read the Office and Windows module at the beginning of this book.

To Exit Access

All the steps in this module are now complete.

1. If desired, sign out of your Microsoft account.
2. Exit Access.

Database Design

BTW

Determining Database Requirements

The determination of database requirements is part of a process known as systems analysis. A systems analyst examines existing and proposed documents, and examines organizational policies to determine exactly the type of data needs the database must support.

This section illustrates the **database design** process, that is, the process of determining the tables and fields that make up the database. It does so by showing how you would design the database for PrattLast Associates from a set of requirements. In this section, you will use commonly accepted shorthand to represent the tables and fields that make up the database as well as the primary keys for the tables. For each table, you give the name of the table followed by a set of parentheses. Within the parentheses is a list of the fields in the table separated by commas. You underline the primary key. For example,

Product (<u>Product Code</u>, Description, On Hand, Price)

represents a table called Product. The Product table contains four fields: Product Code, Description, On Hand, and Price. The Product Code field is the primary key.

Database Requirements

The PrattLast Associates database must maintain information on both accounts and account managers. The business currently keeps this data in two Word tables and two Excel workbooks, as shown in Figure 1–80. They use Word tables for address information and Excel workbooks for financial information.

- For accounts, PrattLast needs to maintain address data. It currently keeps this data in a Word table (Figure 1–80a).
- PrattLast also maintains financial data for each account. This includes the amount paid and current amount due for the account. It keeps these amounts, along with the account name and number, in the Excel worksheet shown in Figure 1–80b.
- PrattLast keeps account manager address data in a Word table, as shown in Figure 1–80c.
- Just as with accounts, it keeps financial data for account managers, including their start date, salary, and bonus rate, in a separate Excel worksheet, as shown in Figure 1–80d.

Finally, PrattLast keeps track of which accounts are assigned to which account managers. Each account is assigned to a single account manager, but each account manager might be assigned many accounts. Currently, for example, accounts AC001 (Avondale Community Bank), JM323 (JSP Manufacturing Inc.), KC156 (Key Community College System), MI345 (Midwest Library Consortium), and TW001 (Tri-County Waste Disposal) are assigned to account manager 31 (Haydee Rivera). Accounts BL235 (Bland Corp.), CO621 (Codder Plastics Co.), KV089 (KAL Veterinary Services), LI268 (Lars-Idsen Inc.), and ML008 (Mums Landscaping Co.) are assigned to account manager 35 (Mark Simson). Accounts CA043 (Carlton Regional Clinic), EC010 (Eco Clothes Inc.), HL111 (Halko Legal Associates), LC005 (Lancaster County Hospital), and TP098 (TAL Packaging Systems) are assigned to account manager 58 (Karen Murowski). PrattLast has an additional account manager, Peter Lu, whose number has been assigned as 42, but who has not yet been assigned any accounts.

BTW

Additional Data for PrattLast Associates

PrattLast could include other types of data in the database. The Account table could include data on a contact person at each organization, such as name, telephone number, and email address. The Account Manager table could include the mobile telephone number, email address, and emergency contact information for the account manager.

Account Number	Account Name	Street	City	State	Postal Code
AC001	Avondale Community Bank	256 Main St.	Avondale	IL	60311
BL235	Bland Corp.	100 Granger Hwy.	Granger	IL	60314
CA043	Carlton Regional Clinic	589 Central Ave.	Carlton	IL	60313
CO621	Codder Plastics Co.	421 First Ave.	Bremerton	IN	46003
EC010	Eco Clothes Inc.	120 Pine St.	Davidson	IN	46010
HL111	Halko Legal Associates	321 Feathering Rd.	Gleneagle	IL	60319
JM323	JSP Manufacturing Inc.	1200 Franklin Blvd.	Wells	IN	46007
KC156	Key Community College System	35 Indiana Ave.	Walker	IN	46004
KV089	KAL Veterinary Services	116 Pine St.	Granger	IL	60314
LC005	Lancaster County Hospital	215 River St.	Granger	IL	46004
LI268	Lars-Idsen Inc.	829 Wooster Rd.	Davidson	IN	46010
MI345	Midwest Library Consortium	3400 Metro Pkwy.	Bremerton	IN	46003
ML008	Mums Landscaping Co.	865 Ridge Rd.	Wells	IN	46007
TP098	TAL Packaging Systems	12 Polk Ave.	Carlton	IL	60313
TW001	Tri-County Waste Disposal	345 Central Blvd.	Rushton	IL	60321

Figure 1–80a Account Addresses

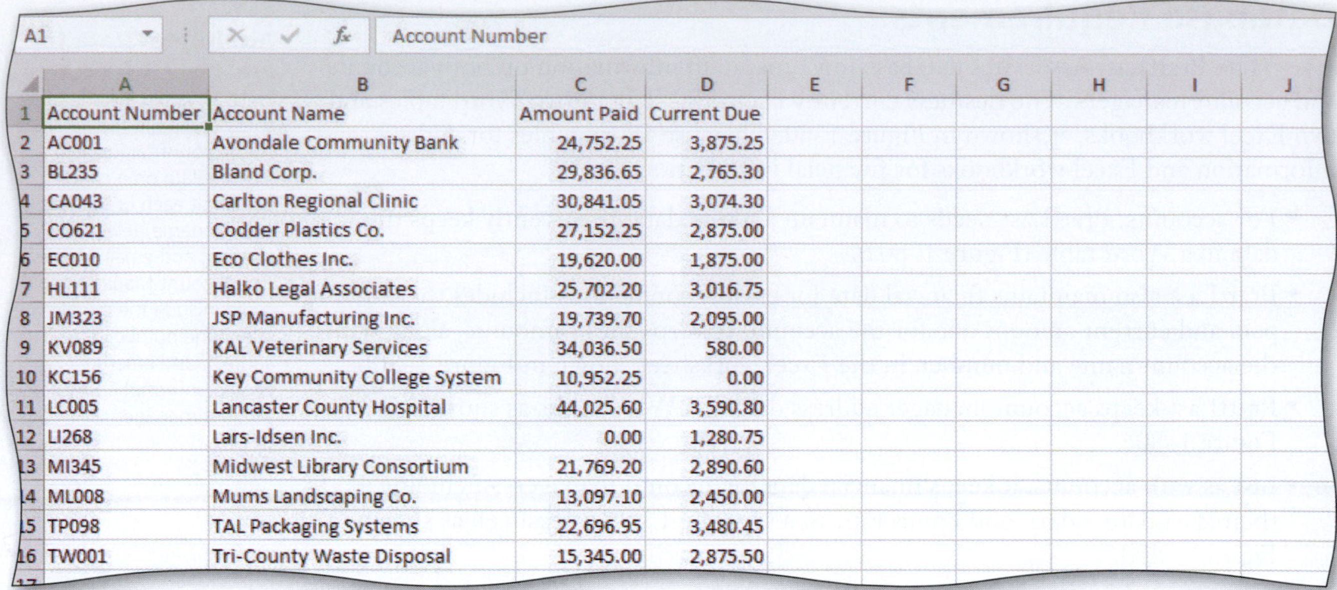

Account Number	Account Name	Amount Paid	Current Due
AC001	Avondale Community Bank	24,752.25	3,875.25
BL235	Bland Corp.	29,836.65	2,765.30
CA043	Carlton Regional Clinic	30,841.05	3,074.30
CO621	Codder Plastics Co.	27,152.25	2,875.00
EC010	Eco Clothes Inc.	19,620.00	1,875.00
HL111	Halko Legal Associates	25,702.20	3,016.75
JM323	JSP Manufacturing Inc.	19,739.70	2,095.00
KV089	KAL Veterinary Services	34,036.50	580.00
KC156	Key Community College System	10,952.25	0.00
LC005	Lancaster County Hospital	44,025.60	3,590.80
LI268	Lars-Idsen Inc.	0.00	1,280.75
MI345	Midwest Library Consortium	21,769.20	2,890.60
ML008	Mums Landscaping Co.	13,097.10	2,450.00
TP098	TAL Packaging Systems	22,696.95	3,480.45
TW001	Tri-County Waste Disposal	15,345.00	2,875.50

Figure 1–80b Account Financial Data

Account Manager Number	Last Name	First Name	Street	City	State	Postal Code
31	Rivera	Haydee	325 Twiddy St.	Avondale	IL	60311
35	Simson	Mark	1467 Hartwell St.	Walker	IN	46004
42	Lu	Peter	5624 Murray Ave.	Davidson	IN	46007
58	Murowski	Karen	168 Truesdale Dr.	Carlton	IL	60313

Figure 1–80c Account Manager Addresses

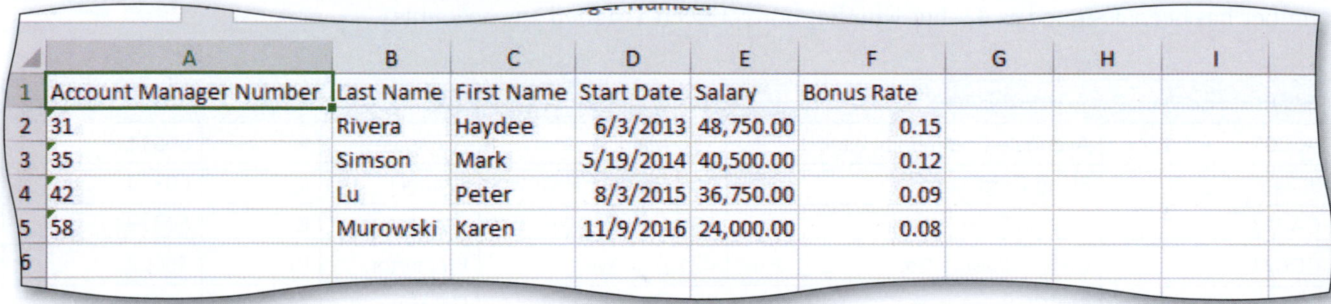

Account Manager Number	Last Name	First Name	Start Date	Salary	Bonus Rate
31	Rivera	Haydee	6/3/2013	48,750.00	0.15
35	Simson	Mark	5/19/2014	40,500.00	0.12
42	Lu	Peter	8/3/2015	36,750.00	0.09
58	Murowski	Karen	11/9/2016	24,000.00	0.08

Figure 1–80d Account Manager Financial Data

Database Design Process

The database design process involves several steps.

CONSIDER THIS

What is the first step in the process?

Identify the tables. Examine the requirements for the database to identify the main objects that are involved. There will be a table for each object you identify.

In a database for one organization, for example, the main objects might be departments and employees. This would require two tables: one for departments and the other for employees. In the database for another organization, the main objects might be accounts and account managers. In this case, there also would be two tables: one for accounts and the other for account managers. In still another organization's database, the main objects might be books, publishers, and authors. This database would require three tables: one for books, a second for publishers, and a third for authors.

Identifying the Tables

For the PrattLast Associates database, the main objects are accounts and account managers. This leads to two tables, which you must name. Reasonable names for these two tables are:

Account
Account Manager

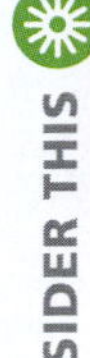

CONSIDER THIS

After identifying the tables, what is the second step in the database design process?
Determine the primary keys. Recall that the primary key is the unique identifier for records in the table. For each table, determine the unique identifier. In a Department table, for example, the unique identifier might be the Department Code. For a Book table, the unique identifier might be the ISBN (International Standard Book Number).

Determining the Primary Keys

The next step is to identify the fields that will be the unique identifiers, or primary keys. Account numbers uniquely identify accounts, and account manager numbers uniquely identify account managers. Thus, the primary key for the Account table is the account number, and the primary key for the Account Manager table is the account manager number. Reasonable names for these fields would be Account Number and Account Manager Number, respectively. Adding these primary keys to the tables gives:

Account (Account Number)

Account Manager (Account Manager Number)

CONSIDER THIS

What is the third step in the database design process after determining the primary keys?
Determine the additional fields. The primary key will be a field or combination of fields in a table. A table will typically contain many additional fields, each of which contains a type of data. Examine the project requirements to determine these additional fields. For example, in an Employee table, additional fields might include Employee Name, Street Address, City, State, Postal Code, Date Hired, and Salary.

Determining Additional Fields

After identifying the primary keys, you need to determine and name the additional fields. In addition to the account number, the Account Address Information shown in Figure 1–80a contains the account name, street, city, state, and postal code. These would be fields in the Account table. The Account Financial Information shown in Figure 1–80b also contains the account number and account name, which are already included in the Account table. The financial information also contains the amount paid and current due. Adding the amount paid and current due fields to those already identified in the Account table and assigning reasonable names gives:

Account (Account Number, Account Name, Street, City, State, Postal Code, Amount Paid, Current Due)

Similarly, examining the Account Manager Address Information in Figure 1–80c adds the last name, first name, street, city, state, and postal code fields to the Account Manager table. In addition to the account manager number, last name, and first name, the Account Manager Financial Information in Figure 1–80d would add the start date, salary, and bonus rate. Adding these fields to the Account Manager table and assigning reasonable names gives:

Account Manager (Account Manager Number, Last Name, First Name, Street, City, State, Postal Code, Start Date, Salary, Bonus Rate)

BTW

Database Design Language (DBDL)
Database Design Language (DBDL) is a commonly accepted shorthand representation for showing the structure of a relational database. You write the name of the table and then within parentheses you list all the columns in the table. If the columns continue beyond one line, indent the subsequent lines.

CONSIDER THIS

What happens as the fourth step, after determining additional fields?
Determine relationships between the tables. A relationship is an association between objects. In a database containing information about departments and employees, there is an association between the departments and the employees. A department is associated with all the employees in the department, and an employee is associated with the department to which he or she is assigned. Technically, you say that a department is related to all the employees in the department, and an employee is related to his or her department.

The relationship between department and employees is an example of a **one-to-many relationship** because one employee is associated with one department, but each department can be associated with many employees. The Department table would be the "one" table in the relationship. The Employee table would be the "many" table in the relationship.

When you have determined that two tables are related, follow these general guidelines:

- Identify the "one" table.
- Identify the "many" table.
- Include the primary key from the "one" table as a field in the "many" table.

Determining and Implementing Relationships between the Tables

According to the requirements, each account has one account manager, but each account manager can have many accounts. Thus, the Account Manager table is the "one" table, and the Account table is the "many" table. To implement this one-to-many relationship between account managers and accounts, add the Account Manager Number field (the primary key of the Account Manager table) to the Account table. This produces:

Account (<u>Account Number</u>, Account Name, Street, City, State, Postal Code, Amount Paid, Current Due, Account Manager Number)

Account Manager (<u>Account Manager Number</u>, Last Name, First Name, Street, City, State, Postal Code, Start Date, Salary, Bonus Rate)

CONSIDER THIS

After creating relationships between tables, what is the fifth step in the database design process?
Determine data types for the fields, that is, the type of data that can be stored in the field.

Assigning Data Types to the Fields

See the earlier section Determing Data Types for the Fields for a discussion of the available data types and their use in the PrattLast Associates database. That section also discusses other properties that can be assigned, such as captions, field size, and the number of decimal places.

BTW
Postal Codes
Some organizations with accounts throughout the country have a separate table of postal codes, cities, and states. When placing an order, you typically are asked for your postal code (or ZIP code), rather than city, state, and postal code. You then are asked to confirm that the city and state correspond to that postal code.

Identifying and Removing Redundancy

Redundancy means storing the same fact in more than one place. It usually results from placing too many fields in a table — fields that really belong in separate tables — and often causes serious problems. If you had not realized there were two objects, such as accounts and account managers, you might have placed all the data in a single Account table. Figure 1–81 shows an example of a table that includes both account and account manager information. Notice that the data for a given account manager (number, name, address, and so on) occurs on more than one record. The data for rep 35, Mark Simson, is repeated in the figure. Storing this data on multiple records is an example of redundancy.

Account table

Account Number	Account Name	Street	...	Account Manager Number	Last Name	First Name
AC001	Avondale Community Bank	256 Main St.	...	31	Rivera	Haydee
BL235	Bland Corp.	100 Granger Hwy.	...	35	Simson	Mark
CA043	Carlton Regional Clinic	589 Central Ave.	...	58	Murowski	Karen
CO621	Codder Plastics Co.	421 First Ave.	...	35	Simson	Mark
EC010	Eco Clothes Inc.	120 Pine St.	...	58	Murowski	Karen
...	...	...	...	...	...	...
...	...	...	...	...	...	...

Figure 1–81

CONSIDER THIS

What problems does this redundancy cause?

Redundancy results in several problems, including:

1. Wasted storage space. The name of account manager 35, Mark Simson, for example, should be stored only once. Storing this information several times is wasteful.
2. More complex database updates. If, for example, Mark Simson's name is spelled incorrectly and needs to be changed in the database, his name would need to be changed in several different places.
3. Possible inconsistent data. Nothing prohibits the account manager's last name from being Simson on account BL235's record and Stimson on account CO621's record. The data would be inconsistent. In both cases, the account manager number is 35, but the last names are different.

CONSIDER THIS

How do you eliminate redundancy?

The solution to the problem is to place the redundant data in a separate table, one in which the data will no longer be redundant. If, for example, you place the data for account managers in a separate table (Figure 1–82), the data for each account manager will appear only once.

Account table

Account Number	Account Name	Street	...	Account Manager Number
AC001	Avondale Community Bank	256 Main St.	...	31
BL235	Bland Corp.	100 Granger Hwy.	...	35
CA043	Carlton Regional Clinic	589 Central Ave.	...	58
CO621	Codder Plastics Co.	421 First Ave.	...	35
EC010	Eco Clothes Inc.	120 Pine St.	...	58
...	...	...	...	...
...	...	...	...	...

Account Manager Table

Account Manager Number	Last Name	First Name	...
31	Rivera	Haydee	...
35	Simson	Mark	...
42	Lu	Peter	...
58	Murowski	Karen	...

Figure 1–82

Notice that you need to have the account manager number in both tables. Without it, there would be no way to tell which account manager is associated with which account. The remaining account manager data, however, was removed from the Account table and placed in the Account Manager table. This new arrangement corrects the problems of redundancy in the following ways:

- Because the data for each account manager is stored only once, space is not wasted.
- Changing the name of an account manager is easy. You need to change only one row in the Account Manager table.
- Because the data for an account manager is stored only once, inconsistent data cannot occur.

Designing to omit redundancy will help you to produce good and valid database designs. You should always examine your design to see if it contains redundancy. If it does, you should decide whether you need to remove the redundancy by creating a separate table.

If you examine your design, you will see that there is one area of redundancy (see the data in Figure 1–1). Cities and states are both repeated. Every account whose postal code is 60314, for example, has Granger as the city and IL as the state. To remove this redundancy, you would create a table with the primary key Postal Code and City and State as additional fields. City and State would be removed from the Account table. Having City, State, and Postal Code in a table is very common, however, and usually you would not take such action. No other redundancy exists in your tables.

Summary

In this module you have learned to create an Access database, create tables and add records to a database, print the contents of tables, import data, create queries, create forms, create reports, and change database properties. You have also learned how to design a database.

CONSIDER THIS

What decisions will you need to make when creating your next database?

Use these guidelines as you complete the assignments in this module and create your own databases outside of this class.

1. Identify the tables that will be included in the database.
2. Determine the primary keys for each of the tables.
3. Determine the additional fields that should be included in each of the tables.
4. Determine relationships between the tables.
   a) Identify the "one" table.
   b) Identify the "many" table.
   c) Include the primary key of the "one" table as a field in the "many" table.
5. Determine data types for the fields in the tables.
6. Determine additional properties for fields.
   a) Determine if a caption is warranted.
   b) Determine if a description of the field is warranted.
   c) Determine field sizes.
   d) Determine formats.
7. Identify and remove any unwanted redundancy.
8. Determine a storage location for the database.
9. Determine the best method for distributing the database objects.

CONSIDER THIS

How should you submit solutions to questions in the assignments identified with a symbol?
Every assignment in this book contains one or more questions identified with a symbol. These questions require you to think beyond the assigned database. Present your solutions to the questions in the format required by your instructor. Possible formats may include one or more of these options: write the answer; create a document that contains the answer; present your answer to the class; discuss your answer in a group; record the answer as audio or video using a webcam, smartphone, or portable media player; or post answers on a blog, wiki, or website.

Apply Your Knowledge

Reinforce the skills and apply the concepts you learned in this module.

Adding a Caption, Changing a Data Type, and Creating a Query, Form, and Report

Note: To complete this assignment, you will be required to use the Data Files. Please contact your instructor for information about accessing the Data Files.

Instructions: Friendly Janitorial Services provides janitorial services to local businesses. The company uses a team-based approach and each team has a team leader or supervisor. Friendly Janitorial Services has a database that keeps track of its supervisors and its clients. Each client is assigned to a single supervisor; each supervisor may be assigned many clients. The database has two tables. The Client table contains data on the clients who use Friendly Janitorial Services. The Supervisor table contains data on the supervisors. You will add a caption, change a data type, and create a query, a form, and a report, as shown in Figure 1–83.

Perform the following tasks:

1. Run Access, open the Apply Friendly Janitorial Services database from the Data Files, and enable the content.
2. Open the Supervisor table in Datasheet view, add SU # as the caption for the Supervisor Number field, and resize all columns to best fit the data. Save the changes to the layout of the table and close the table.
3. Open the Client table in Design view and change the data type for the Supervisor Number field to Short Text. Change the field size for the field to 3 and add SU # as the caption for the Supervisor Number field. Save the changes to the table and close the table. Then, open the Client table in Datasheet view and resize all columns to best fit the data. Save the changes to the layout of the table and close the table.
4. Use the Simple Query Wizard to create a query for the Client table that contains the Client Number, Client Name, Amount Paid, Current Due, and Supervisor Number. The query is a detail query. Use the name Client Query for the query and close the query.
5. Create a simple form for the Supervisor table. Save the form and use the name Supervisor for the form. Close the form.
6. Create the report shown in Figure 1–83 for the Client table. The report includes totals for both the Amount Paid and Current Due fields. Be sure the totals appear completely. You might need to expand the size of the total controls. Move the page number so that it is within the margins. Save the report as Client Financial Report.
7. If requested by your instructor, add your last name to the title of the report, that is, change the title to Client Financial Report LastName where LastName is your actual last name.
8. Compact and repair the database.
9. Submit the revised database in the format specified by your instructor.
10. How would you change the field name of the Street field in the Client table to Address?

Continued >

Apply Your Knowledge *continued*

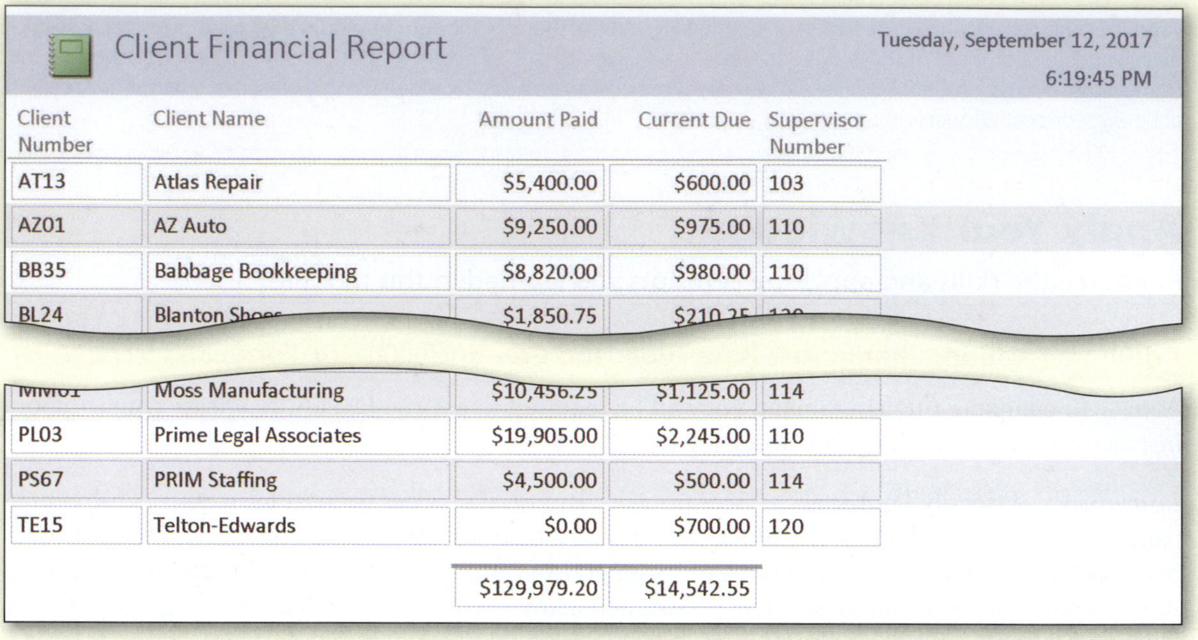

Client Financial Report

Tuesday, September 12, 2017
6:19:45 PM

Client Number	Client Name	Amount Paid	Current Due	Supervisor Number
AT13	Atlas Repair	$5,400.00	$600.00	103
AZ01	AZ Auto	$9,250.00	$975.00	110
BB35	Babbage Bookkeeping	$8,820.00	$980.00	110
BL24	Blanton Shoes	$1,850.75	$210.25	1…
MM01	Moss Manufacturing	$10,456.25	$1,125.00	114
PL03	Prime Legal Associates	$19,905.00	$2,245.00	110
PS67	PRIM Staffing	$4,500.00	$500.00	114
TE15	Telton-Edwards	$0.00	$700.00	120
		$129,979.20	$14,542.55	

Figure 1–83

Extend Your Knowledge

Extend the skills you learned in this module and experiment with new skills. You may need to use Help to complete the assignment.

Using a Database Template to Create an Events Database

Instructions: Access includes both desktop database templates and web-based templates. You can use a template to create a beginning database that can be modified to meet your specific needs. You will use a template to create an Events database. The database template includes sample tables, queries, forms, and reports. You will modify the database and create the Events Query shown in Figure 1–84.

Perform the following tasks:

1. Run Access.
2. Select the Desktop event management template in the template gallery and create a new database with the file name Extend Events.
3. Enable the content and close the Event List form.
4. Open the Navigation Pane and change the organization to Object Type.
5. Open the Events table in Datasheet view and delete the Attachments field in the table. The Attachments field has a paperclip as the column heading.
6. Add the Event Type field to the end of the table. Assign the Short Text data type with a field size of 15.
7. Save the changes to the Events table and close the table.
8. Use the Simple Query Wizard to create the Events Query shown in Figure 1–84. Close the query.

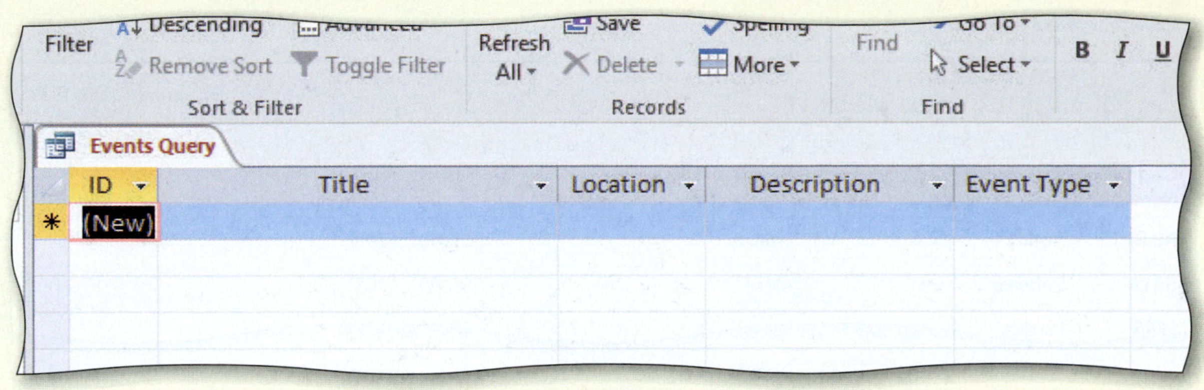

Figure 1–84

9. Open the Current Events report in Layout view. Delete the controls containing the current date and current time in the upper-right corner of the report. Change the title of the report to Current Events List.
10. Save the changes to the report.
11. If requested to do so by your instructor, add your first and last names to the end of the title and save the changes to the report.
12. Submit the revised database in the format specified by your instructor.
13. a. Why would you use a template instead of creating a database from scratch with just the fields you need?

    b. The Attachment data type allows you to attach files to a database record. If you were using this database to keep track of events for a 4th of July celebration in a small town, what specific documents might you attach to an Events record?

Expand Your World

Create a solution, which uses cloud and web technologies, by learning and investigating on your own from general guidance.

Problem: You and two friends recently started a business that provides temporary non-medical help to individuals and families in need of assistance. You want to be able to share query results and reports, so you have decided to store the items in the cloud. You are still learning Access, so you are going to create a sample query and the report shown in Figure 1–85, export the results, and save to a cloud storage location, such as Microsoft OneDrive, Dropbox, or Google Drive.

Note: To complete this assignment, you will be required to use the Data Files. Please contact your instructor for information about accessing the Data Files.

Instructions:

1. Open the Expand Temporary Help database from the Data Files and enable the content.
2. Use the Simple Query Wizard to create a query that includes the Client Number, First Name, Last Name, Balance, and Helper Number. Save the query as Client Query.
3. Export the Client Query as an XPS document to a cloud-based storage location of your choice.
4. Create the report shown in Figure 1–85. Save the report as Client Status Report.

Continued >

Expand Your World *continued*

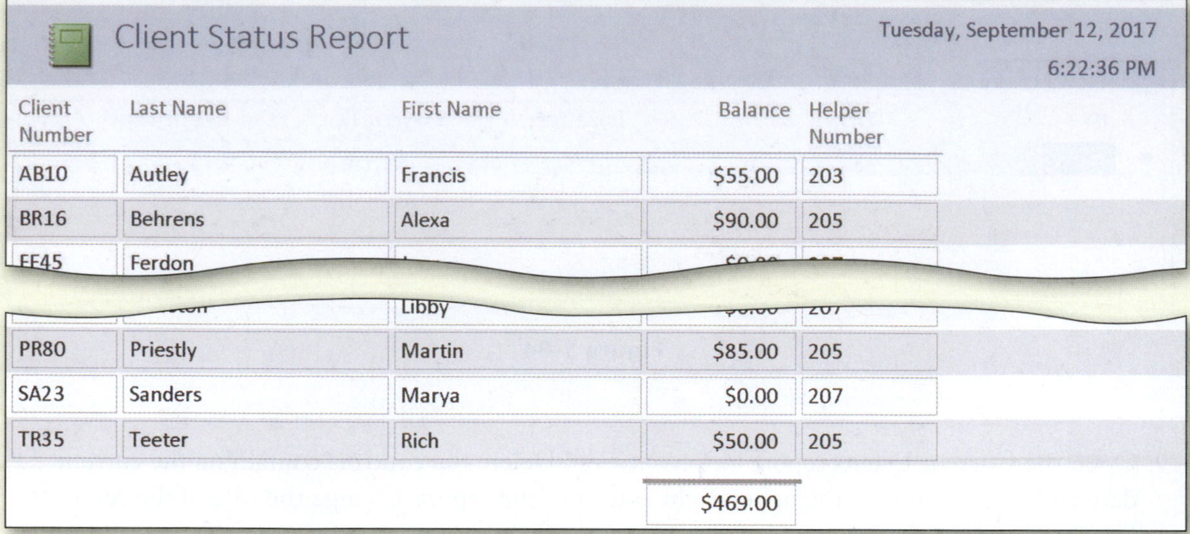

Figure 1–85

5. Export the Client Status Report as a PDF document to a cloud-based storage location of your choice. You do not need to change any optimization or export settings. Do not save the export steps.
6. If requested to do so by your instructor, open the Helper table and change the last name and first name for helper 203 to your last name and your first name.
7. Submit the assignment in the format specified by your instructor.
8. Which cloud-based storage location did you use for this assignment? Why?

In the Labs

Design, create, modify, and/or use a database following the guidelines, concepts, and skills presented in this module. Labs are listed in order of increasing difficulty. Labs 1 and 2, which increase in difficulty, require you to create solutions based on what you learned in the module; Lab 3 requires you to apply your creative thinking and problem-solving skills to design and implement a solution.

Lab 1: Creating Objects for the Garden Naturally Database

Problem: Garden Naturally is a company that provides products for the organic gardening community. Sales representatives are responsible for selling to distributors, nurseries, and retail stores. The company recently decided to store its customer and sales rep data in a database. Each customer is assigned to a single sales rep, but each sales rep may be assigned many customers. The database and the Sales Rep table have been created, but the Salary YTD field needs to be added to the table. The records shown in Table 1–6 must be added to the Sales Rep table. The company plans to import the Customer table from the Excel worksheet shown in Figure 1–86. Garden Naturally would like to finish storing this data in a database and has asked you to help.

Note: To complete this assignment, you will be required to use the Data Files. Please contact your instructor for information about accessing the Data Files.

Instructions: Perform the following tasks:

1. Run Access, open the Lab 1 Garden Naturally database from the Data Files, and enable the content.
2. Open the Sales Rep table in Datasheet view and add the Salary YTD field to the end of the table. The field has the Currency data type. Assign the caption SR # to the Sales Rep Number field.
3. Add the records shown in Table 1–6.

Table 1–6 Data for Sales Rep Table

Sales Rep Number	Last Name	First Name	Street	City	State	Postal Code	Start Date	Commission Rate	Salary YTD
32	Ortiz	Gloria	982 Victoria Ln.	Chesnee	NJ	07053	9/12/2015	.05	$32,555.65
35	Sinson	Mike	45 Elm St.	Quaker	DE	19719	8/28/2017	.04	$1,500.00
29	Gupta	Rufus	678 Hillcrest Rd.	Gossett	PA	19157	6/1/2015	.06	$35,075.30
26	Jones	Pat	43 Third St.	Greer	PA	19158	5/16/2016	.05	$33,100.50

4. Resize the columns to best fit the data. Save the changes to the layout of the table.
5. Import the Lab 1–1 Customer workbook shown in Figure 1–86 into the database. The first row of the workbook contains the column headings. Customer Number is the primary key for the new table. Assign the name Customer to the table. Save the Import steps, and assign the name Import-Customer Workbook to the steps. Assign Import Customer Workbook as the description.

	A	B	C	D	E	F	G	H	I
1	Customer Number	Customer Name	Address	City	State	Postal Code	Amount Paid	Balance Due	Sales Rep Number
2	AA30	All About Gardens	47 Berton St.	Greer	PA	19158	$1,190.00	$365.00	26
3	CT02	Christmas Tree Farm	483 Cantor Rd.	Pleasantburg	NJ	07025	$2,285.50	$825.35	29
4	GG01	Garden Gnome	10 Main St.	Gossett	PA	19157	$1,300.00	$297.50	29
5	GT34	Green Thumb Growers	26 Jefferson Hwy.	Pleasantburg	NJ	07025	$3,325.45	$865.50	32
6	LH15	Lawn & Home Store	33 Maple St.	Chambers	NJ	07037	$895.00	$515.00	26
7	ML25	Mum's Landscaping	196 Lincoln Ave.	Quaker	DE	19719	$0.00	$1,805.00	29
8	OA45	Outside Architects	234 Magnolia Rd.	Gaston	DE	19723	$4,205.50	$945.00	32
9	PL10	Pat's Landscaping	22 Main St.	Chesnee	NJ	07053	$1,165.00	$180.00	26
10	PN18	Pyke Nurseries	10 Grant Blvd.	Adelphia	PA	19159	$2,465.00	$530.00	32
11	SL25	Summit Lawn Service	345 Oaktree Rd.	Chesnee	NJ	07053	$3,225.45	$675.50	26
12	TG38	TriState Growers	24 Main St.	Gaston	DE	19723	$1,075.00	$0.00	29
13	TW34	TAL Wholesalers	234 Cantor Rd.	Pleasantburg	NJ	07025	$4,125.00	$350.00	26
14	TY03	TLC Yard Care	24 Berton St.	Greer	PA	19158	$1,845.00	$689.45	29
15	YS04	Yard Shoppe	124 Elm St.	Quaker	DE	19719	$445.00	$575.00	32
16	YW01	Young's Wholesalers	5239 Lancaster Hwy.	Adelphia	PA	19156	$1,785.50	$345.60	32
17									
18									
19									
20									
21									

Figure 1–86

Continued >

In the Labs *continued*

6. Open the Customer table in Design view and make the following changes:
   a. Change the field size for the Customer Number field to 4. Change the field size for the Customer Name field to 30. Change the field size for the Address field to 25 and the field size for the City field to 20. Change the field size for the State field to 2 and the field size for the Postal Code field to 5. Change the field size for the Sales Rep Number field to 2.
   b. Add the caption CU # to the Customer Number field.
   c. Add the caption SR # to the Sales Rep Number field.
7. Save the changes to the Customer table. If a Microsoft Access dialog box appears with the 'Some data may be lost' message, click the Yes button.
8. Open the Customer table in Datasheet view and resize all columns to best fit the data. Save the changes to the layout of the table.
9. Create a query using the Simple Query Wizard for the Customer table that displays the Customer Number, Customer Name, Amount Paid, Balance Due, and Sales Rep Number. Save the query as Customer Query.

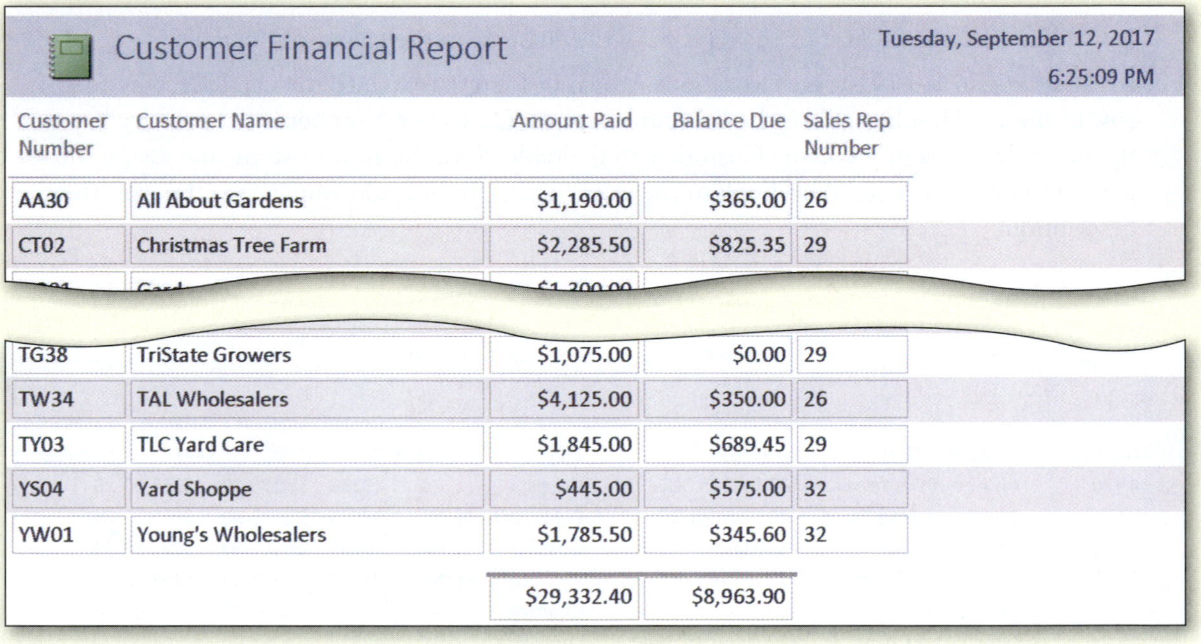

Customer Financial Report — Tuesday, September 12, 2017 6:25:09 PM

Customer Number	Customer Name	Amount Paid	Balance Due	Sales Rep Number
AA30	All About Gardens	$1,190.00	$365.00	26
CT02	Christmas Tree Farm	$2,285.50	$825.35	29
TG38	TriState Growers	$1,075.00	$0.00	29
TW34	TAL Wholesalers	$4,125.00	$350.00	26
TY03	TLC Yard Care	$1,845.00	$689.45	29
YS04	Yard Shoppe	$445.00	$575.00	32
YW01	Young's Wholesalers	$1,785.50	$345.60	32
		$29,332.40	$8,963.90	

Figure 1–87

10. Create the report shown in Figure 1–87 for the Customer table. The report should include the Customer Number, Customer Name, Amount Paid, Balance Due, and Sales Rep Number fields. Include totals for the Amount Paid and Balance Due fields. Be sure to change the column headings to those shown in Figure 1–87. Save the report as Customer Financial Report.
11. If requested to do so by your instructor, change the address for Pat Jones in the Sales Rep table to your address. If your address is longer than 20 characters, simply enter as much as you can.
12. Submit the revised database in the format specified by your instructor.
13. The Commission Rate field has a field size of Single. If you changed the field size to Integer, what values would appear in the Commission Rate column? Why?

Lab 2: Creating the Museum Gift Shop Database

Problem: The local science museum operates a gift shop that sells science-related items. The gift shop purchases the items from vendors that deal in science-related games, toys, and other merchandise. Currently, the information about the items and the vendors is stored in two Excel workbooks. Each item is assigned to a single vendor, but each vendor may be assigned many items. You are to create a database that will store the item and vendor information. You have already determined that you need two tables, a Vendor table and an Item table, in which to store the information.

Note: To complete this assignment, you will be required to use the Data Files. Please contact your instructor for information about accessing the Data Files.

Instructions: Perform the following tasks:

1. Use the Blank desktop database option to create a new database in which to store all objects related to the items for sale. Call the database Lab 2 Museum Gift Shop.
2. Import the Lab 1–2 Vendor Data Excel workbook into the database. The first row of the workbook contains the column headings. Vendor Code is the primary key for the new table. Assign the name Vendor to the table. Do not save the Import steps.
3. Open the Vendor table in Datasheet view. Change the field size for the Vendor Code field to 2; the field size for the Vendor Name field to 25; and the field size for the Telephone Number field to 12. Assign the caption VC to the Vendor Code field.
4. Import the Lab 1–2 Item Data Excel workbook into the database. The first row of the workbook contains the column headings. Item Number is the primary key for this table. Assign the name Item to the table. Do not save the Import steps.
5. Open the Item table in Design view. Change the field size for the Item Number field to 4. Change the field size for the Description field to 28. Add the caption Wholesale for the Wholesale Cost field, the caption Retail for the Retail Price field, and the caption VC for the vendor code. The On Hand field should be an Integer field. Be sure that the field size for the Vendor Code in the Item table is identical to the field size for the Vendor Code in the Vendor table. Save the changes to the table and close the table.
6. Open the Item table in Datasheet view and resize the columns to best fit the data. Save the changes to the layout of the table and close the table.
7. Create a query for the Item table. Include the Item Number, Description, Wholesale Cost, Retail Price, and Vendor Code. Save the query as Item Query.
8. Create a simple form for the Item table. Use the name Item for the form.
9. Create the report shown in Figure 1–88 for the Item table. Do not add any totals. Save the report as Item Status Report.

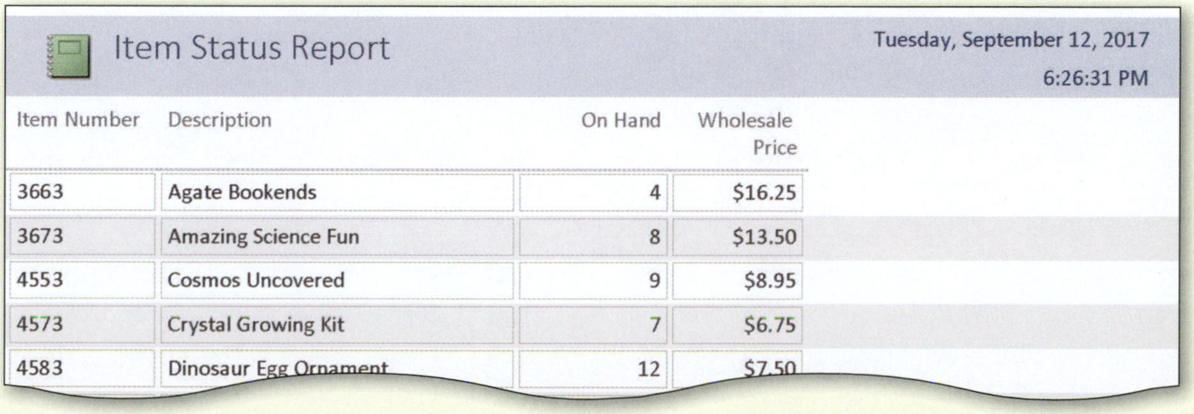

Item Status Report — Tuesday, September 12, 2017 6:26:31 PM

Item Number	Description	On Hand	Wholesale Price
3663	Agate Bookends	4	$16.25
3673	Amazing Science Fun	8	$13.50
4553	Cosmos Uncovered	9	$8.95
4573	Crystal Growing Kit	7	$6.75
4583	Dinosaur Egg Ornament	12	$7.50

Figure 1–88

Continued >

In the Labs *continued*

10. If requested to do so by your instructor, change the telephone number for Atherton Wholesalers to your telephone number.
11. Submit the database in the format specified by your instructor.
12. If you had designed this database, could you have used the field name, Name, for the Vendor Name field name? If not, why not?

Lab 3: Consider This: Your Turn

Apply your creative thinking and problem solving skills to design and implement a solution.

Creating the Camshay Marketing Database

Note: To complete this assignment, you will be required to use the Data Files. Please contact your instructor for information about accessing the Data Files.

Part 1: Camshay Marketing Associates is a small company that specializes in data mining for marketing research and analysis. The company focuses on the service, nonprofit, and retail sectors. Camshay uses marketing analysts to work collaboratively with clients. Marketing analysts are paid a base salary and can earn incentive pay for maintaining and expanding client relationships. Based on the information in the Lab 1–3 Camshay Marketing workbook, use the concepts and techniques presented in this module to design and create a database to store the Camshay Marketing data. Change data types and field sizes as necessary. Add captions where appropriate. Create a form for the Client table and a report for the Client table similar to the Account Financial Report shown in Figure 1-67. Use the simple query wizard to create a query for the Client table that includes the Client Number, Client Name, Current Due and Marketing Analyst Number. Open the query and add a criterion to the query results to find only those clients whose amount due is $0.00 and save this modified query with a different name. Submit your assignment in the format specified by your instructor.

Part 2: You made several decisions while determining the table structures and adding data to the tables in this assignment. What method did you use to add the data to each table? Are there any other methods that would also have worked?

2 Querying a Database

Objectives

You will have mastered the material in this module when you can:

- Create queries using Design view
- Include fields in the design grid
- Use text and numeric data in criteria
- Save a query and use the saved query
- Create and use parameter queries
- Use compound criteria in queries
- Sort data in queries
- Join tables in queries
- Create a report and a form from a query
- Export data from a query to another application
- Perform calculations and calculate statistics in queries
- Create crosstab queries
- Customize the Navigation Pane

Introduction

One of the primary benefits of using a database management system such as Access is having the ability to find answers to questions related to data stored in the database. When you pose a question to Access, or any other database management system, the question is called a query. A **query** is simply a question presented in a way that Access can process.

To find the answer to a question, you first create a corresponding query using the techniques illustrated in this module. After you have created the query, you instruct Access to run the query, that is, to perform the steps necessary to obtain the answer. Access then displays the answer in Datasheet view.

For an introduction to Windows and instructions about how to perform basic Windows tasks, read the Office and Windows module at the beginning of this book, where you can learn how to resize windows, change screen resolution, create folders, move and rename files, use Windows Help, and much more

Project — Querying a Database

Examples of questions related to the data in the PrattLast Associates database are shown in Figure 2–1.

In addition to these questions, PrattLast managers need to find information about accounts located in a specific city, but they want to enter a different city each time they ask the question. The company can use a parameter query to accomplish this task. PrattLast managers also want to summarize data in a specific way, which might involve performing calculations, and they can use a crosstab query to present the data in the desired form.

Give me the number, name, amount paid, and current due for all accounts whose name starts with K.

AC #	Account Name	Amount Paid	Current Due
KV089	KAL Veterinary Services	$34,036.50	$580.00
KC156	Key Community College System	$10,952.25	$0.00

Give me the account number, account name, amount paid, current due, and account manager number for all accounts whose current due amounts are greater than $2,500.00 and whose account manager number is 31.

AC #	Account Name	Amount Paid	Current Due	AM #
AC001	Avondale Community Bank	$24,752.25	$3,875.25	31
MI345	Midwest Library Consortium	$21,769.20	$2,890.60	31
TW001	Tri-County Waste Disposal	$15,345.00	$2,875.50	31

Give me the account number, account name, amount paid, and current due for account JM323.

AC #	Account Name	Amount Paid	Current Due
JM323	JSP Manufacturing Inc.	$19,739.70	$2,095.00

Summarize the total current due amounts by state and by account manager.

State	Total Of Curr	31	35	58
IL	$23,258.35	$6,750.75	$3,345.30	$13,162.30
IN	$13,466.35	$4,985.60	$6,605.75	$1,875.00

Database

List the account number, account name, account manager number, and amount paid for all accounts. Sort the results by account manager number. For accounts with the same account manager number, further sort the results by amount paid.

AC #	Account Name	AM #	Amount Paid
KC156	Key Community College System	31	$10,952.25
TW001	Tri-County Waste Disposal	31	$15,345.00
JM323	JSP Manufacturing Inc.	31	$19,739.70
MI345	Midwest Library Consortium	31	$21,769.20
AC001	Avondale Community Bank	31	$24,752.25
LI268	Lars-Idsen Inc.	35	$0.00
ML008	Mums Landscaping Co.	35	$13,097.10
CO621	Codder Plastics Co.	35	$27,152.25
BL235	Bland Corp.	35	$29,836.65
KV089	KAL Veterinary Services	35	$34,036.50
EC010	Eco Clothes Inc.	58	$19,620.00
TP098	TAL Packaging Systems	58	$22,696.95
HL111	Halko Legal Associates	58	$25,702.20
CA043	Carlton Regional Clinic	58	$30,841.05
LC005	Lancaster County Hospital	58	$44,025.60

Give me the average amount paid by accounts of each account manager.

AM #	AvgOfAmou
31	$18,511.68
35	$20,824.50
58	$28,577.16

For each account manager, list the account manager number, last name, and first name. Also, list the account number and account name for each of the account manager's accounts.

AM #	Last Name	First Name	AC #	Account Name
31	Rivera	Haydee	AC001	Avondale Community Bank
31	Rivera	Haydee	JM323	JSP Manufacturing Inc.
31	Rivera	Haydee	KC156	Key Community College System
31	Rivera	Haydee	MI345	Midwest Library Consortium
31	Rivera	Haydee	TW001	Tri-County Waste Disposal
35	Simson	Mark	BL235	Bland Corp.
35	Simson	Mark	CO621	Codder Plastics Co.
35	Simson	Mark	KV089	KAL Veterinary Services
35	Simson	Mark	LI268	Lars-Idsen Inc.
35	Simson	Mark	ML008	Mums Landscaping Co.
42	Lu	Peter		
58	Murowski	Karen	CA043	Carlton Regional Clinic
58	Murowski	Karen	EC010	Eco Clothes Inc.
58	Murowski	Karen	HL111	Halko Legal Associates
58	Murowski	Karen	LC005	Lancaster County Hospital
58	Murowski	Karen	TP098	TAL Packaging Systems

List the account number, account name, amount paid, current due, and the total amount (amount paid plus current due) for each account.

AC #	Account Name	Amount Paid	Current Due	Total Amour
AC001	Avondale Community Bank	$24,752.25	$3,875.25	$28,627.50
BL235	Bland Corp.	$29,836.65	$2,765.30	$32,601.95
CA043	Carlton Regional Clinic	$30,841.05	$3,074.30	$33,915.35
CO621	Codder Plastics Co.	$27,152.25	$2,875.00	$30,027.25
EC010	Eco Clothes Inc.	$19,620.00	$1,875.00	$21,495.00
HL111	Halko Legal Associates	$25,702.20	$3,016.75	$28,718.95
JM323	JSP Manufacturing Inc.	$19,739.70	$2,095.00	$21,834.70
KC156	Key Community College System	$10,952.25	$0.00	$10,952.25
KV089	KAL Veterinary Services	$34,036.50	$580.00	$34,616.50
LC005	Lancaster County Hospital	$44,025.60	$3,590.80	$47,616.40
LI268	Lars-Idsen Inc.	$0.00	$1,280.75	$1,280.75
MI345	Midwest Library Consortium	$21,769.20	$2,890.60	$24,659.80
ML008	Mums Landscaping Co.	$13,097.10	$2,450.00	$15,547.10
TP098	TAL Packaging Systems	$22,696.95	$3,480.45	$26,177.40
TW001	Tri-County Waste Disposal	$15,345.00	$2,875.50	$18,220.50

Figure 2–1

In this module, you will learn how to create and use the queries shown in Figure 2–1. The following roadmap identifies general activities you will perform as you progress through this module:

1. **CREATE QUERIES** in Design view.
2. **USE CRITERIA** in queries.
3. **SORT DATA** in queries.
4. **JOIN TABLES** in queries.
5. **EXPORT** query **RESULTS.**
6. **PERFORM CALCULATIONS** in queries.
7. **CREATE** a **CROSSTAB** query.
8. **CUSTOMIZE** the **NAVIGATION PANE**.

For an introduction to Office and instructions about how to perform basic tasks in Office apps, read the Office and Windows module at the beginning of this book, where you can learn how to run an application, use the ribbon, save a file, open a file, print a file, exit an application, use Help, and much more.

Creating Queries

As you learned in Module 1, you can use queries in Access to find answers to questions about the data contained in the database. *Note:* In this module, you will save each query example. When you use a query for another task, such as to create a form or report, you will assign a specific name to a query, for example, Manager-Account Query. In situations in which you will not use the query again, you will assign a name using a convention that includes the module number and a query number, for example, m02q01. Queries are numbered consecutively.

BTW
Select Queries
The queries you create in this module are select queries. In a select query, you retrieve data from one or more tables using criteria that you specify and display the data in a datasheet.

To Create a Query in Design View

In Module 1, you used the Simple Query Wizard to create a query. Most of the time, however, you will use Design view, which is the primary option for creating queries. ***Why?*** *Once you have created a new query in Design view, you have more options than with the wizard and can specify fields, criteria, sorting, calculations, and so on.* The following steps create a new query in Design view.

1

- Run Access and open the database named PrattLast Associates from your hard disk, OneDrive, or other storage location.
- Click the 'Shutter Bar Open/Close Button' to close the Navigation Pane.
- Click Create on the ribbon to display the Create tab (Figure 2–2).

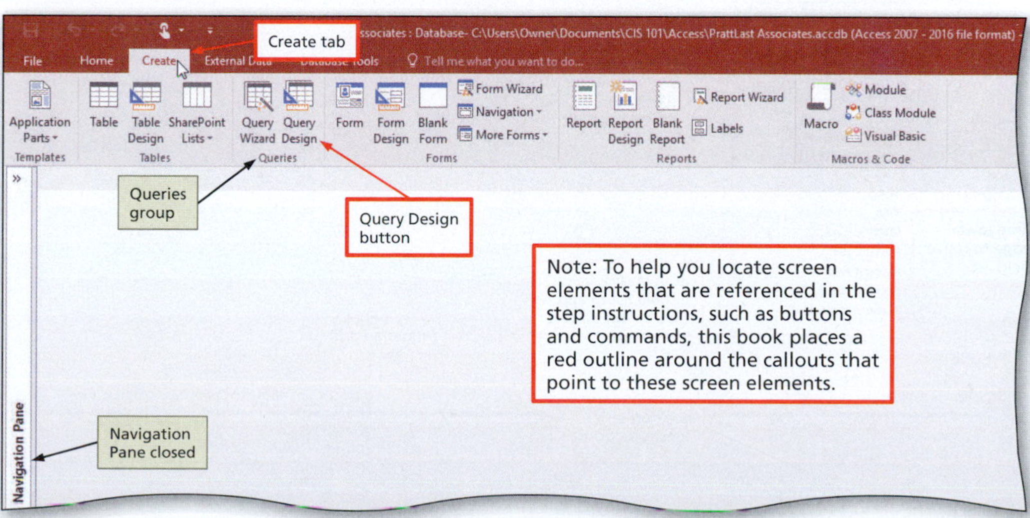

Figure 2–2

2

- Click the Query Design button (Create tab | Queries group) to create a new query (Figure 2–3).

Q&A Is it necessary to close the Navigation Pane?
No. Closing the pane gives you more room for the query, however, so it is usually a good practice.

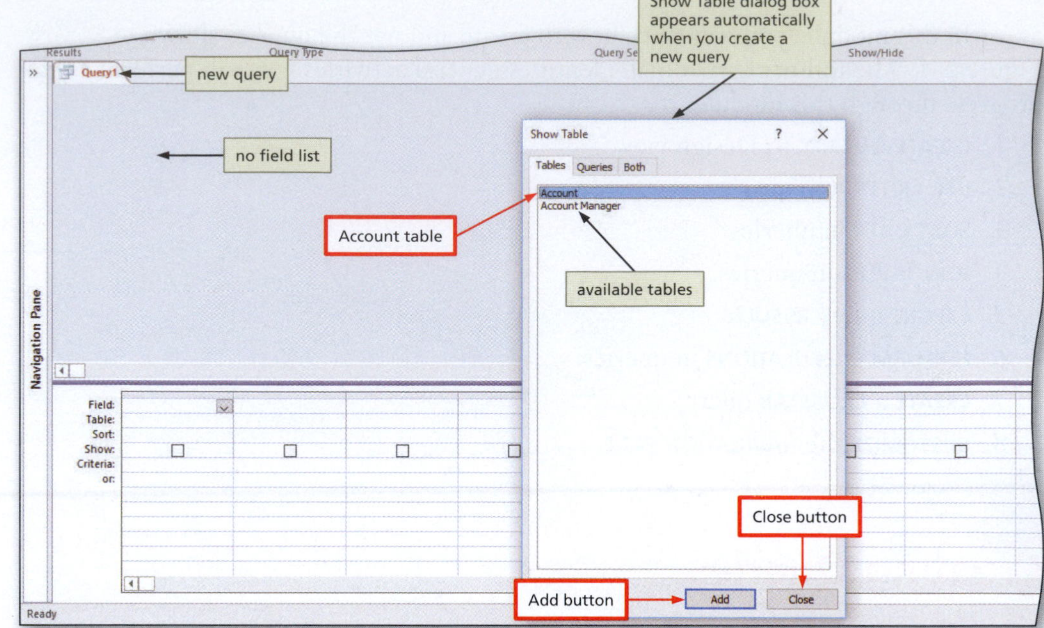

Figure 2–3

3

- Ensure the Account table (Show Table dialog box) is selected. If it is not, click the Account table to select it.
- Click the Add button to add the selected table to the query.
- Click the Close button to remove the dialog box from the screen.

Q&A What if I inadvertently add the wrong table?
Right-click the table that you added in error and click Remove Table on the shortcut menu. You also can just close the query, indicate that you do not want to save it, and then start over.

- Drag the lower edge of the field list down far enough so all fields in the table appear (Figure 2–4).

Q&A Is it essential that I resize the field list?
No. You can always scroll through the list of fields using the scroll bar. Resizing the field list so that all fields appear is usually more convenient.

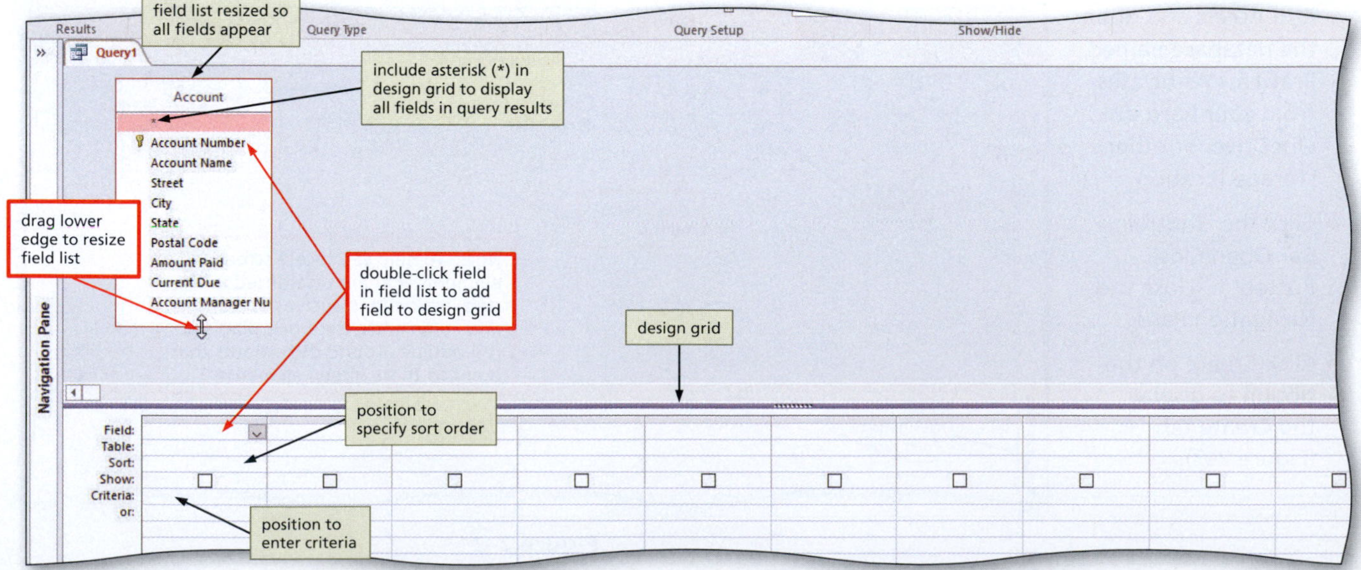

Figure 2–4

To Add Fields to the Design Grid

Once you have a new query displayed in Design view, you are ready to make entries in the **design grid**, the portion of the window where you specify fields and criteria for the query. The design grid is located in the lower pane of the window. You add the fields you want included in the query to the Field row in the grid. ***Why add fields to the grid?*** *Only the fields that appear in the design grid are included in the query results.* The following step begins creating a query that PrattLast Associates might use to obtain the account number, account name, amount paid, and current due for a particular account.

1

- Double-click the Account Number field in the field list to add the field to the query.

Q&A What if I add the wrong field?
Click just above the field name in the design grid to select the column and then press the DELETE key to remove the field.

- Double-click the Account Name field in the field list to add the field to the query.
- Add the Amount Paid field to the query.
- Add the Current Due field to the query (Figure 2–5).

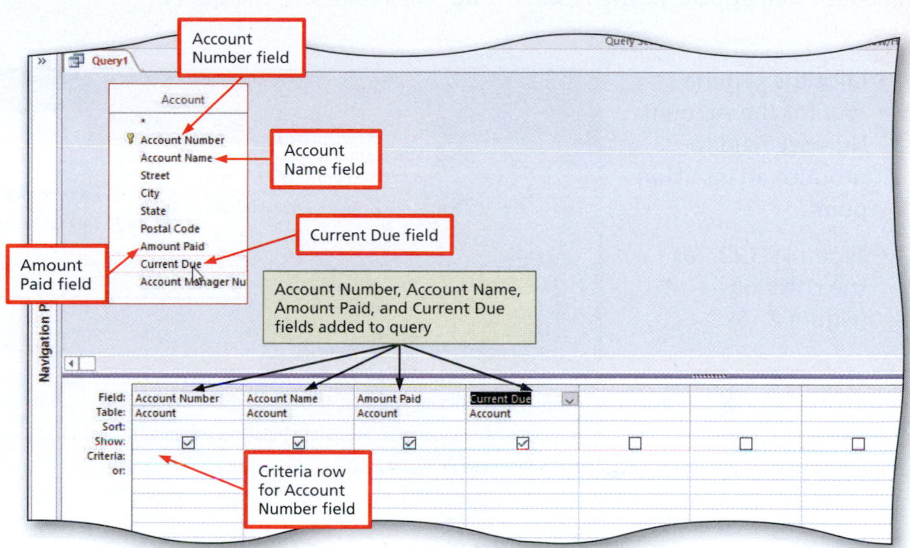

Figure 2–5

Q&A What if I want to include all fields? Do I have to add each field individually?
No. Instead of adding individual fields, you can double-click the asterisk (*) to add the asterisk to the design grid. The asterisk is a shortcut indicating all fields are to be included.

Determining Criteria

When you use queries, usually you are looking for those records that satisfy some criterion. In the simple query you created in the previous module, for example, you entered a criterion to restrict the records to those with the account manager number 35. In another query, you might want the name, amount paid, and current due amounts for the account whose number is JM323, for example, or for those accounts whose names start with the letters, La. You enter criteria in the Criteria row in the design grid below the field name to which the criterion applies. For example, to indicate that the account number must be JM323, you first must add the Account Number field to the design grid. You then would type JM323 in the Criteria row below the Account Number field.

Running the Query

After adding the appropriate fields and defining the query's criteria, you must run the query to get the results. To view the results of the query from Design view, click the Run button to instruct Access to run the query, that is, to perform the necessary actions to produce and display the results in Datasheet view.

BTW
Touch Screen Differences
The Office and Windows interfaces may vary if you are using a touch screen. For this reason, you might notice that the function or appearance of your touch screen differs slightly from this module's presentation.

BTW
Access Screen Resolution
If you are using a computer or mobile device to step through the project in this module and you want your screens to match the figures in this book, you should change your screen's resolution to 1366 x 768. For information about how to change a computer's resolution, refer to the Office and Windows module at the beginning of this book.

To Use Text Data in a Criterion

To use **text data** (data in a field whose data type is Short Text) in criteria, simply type the text in the Criteria row below the corresponding field name, just as you did in Module 1. In Access, you do not need to enclose text data in quotation marks as you do in many other database management systems. ***Why?*** *Access will enter the quotation marks automatically, so you can simply type the desired text.* The following steps finish creating a query that PrattLast Associates might use to obtain the account number, account name, amount paid, and current due amount of account JM323. These steps add the appropriate criterion so that only the desired account will appear in the results. The steps also save the query.

1

- Click the Criteria row for the Account Number field to produce an insertion point.
- Type **JM323** as the criterion (Figure 2–6).

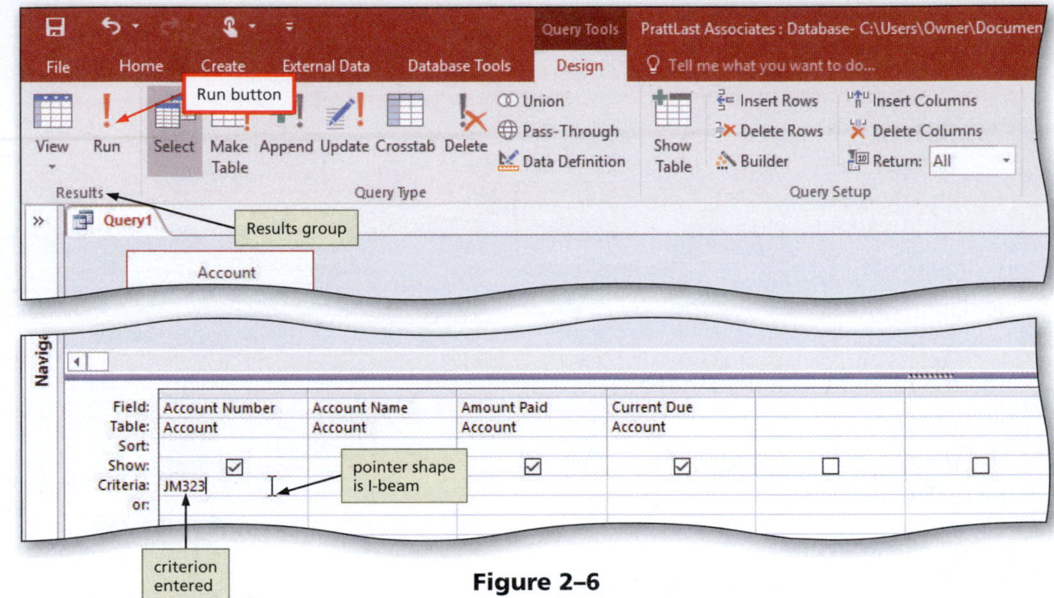

Figure 2–6

2

- Click the Run button (Query Tools Design tab | Results group) to run the query (Figure 2–7).

Q&A Can I also use the View button in the Results group to run the query?
Yes. You can click the View button to view the query results in Datasheet view.

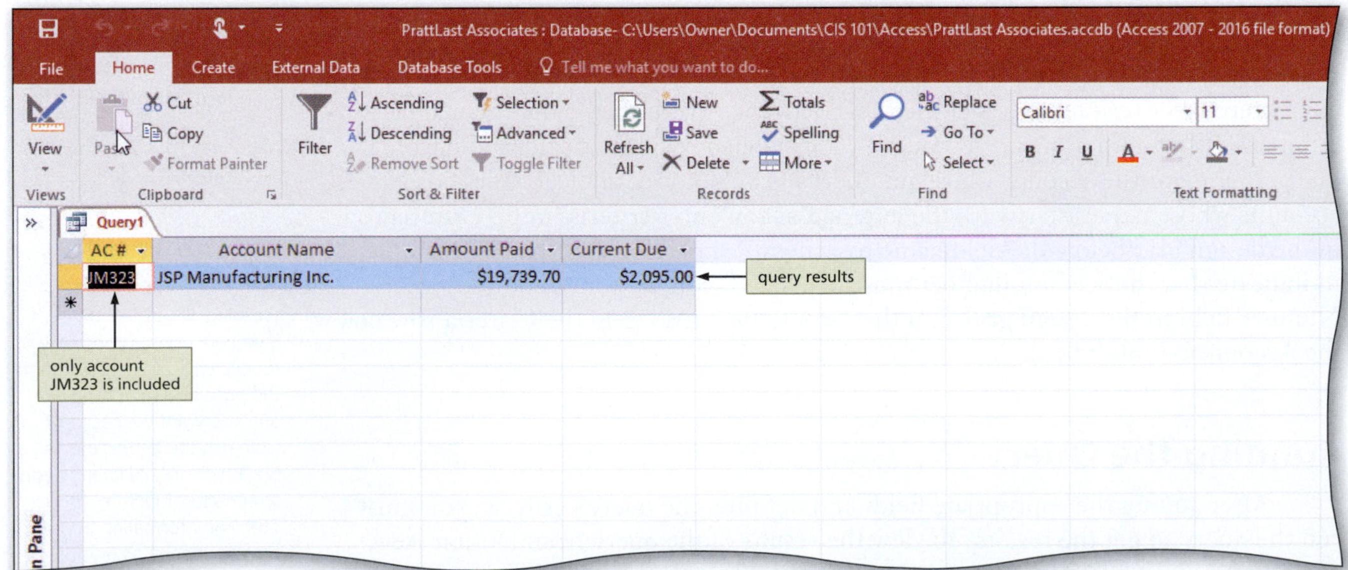

Figure 2–7

3

- Click the Save button on the Quick Access Toolbar to display the Save As dialog box.
- Type `m02q01` as the name of the query (Figure 2–8).

Q&A Can I also save from Design view?
Yes. You can save the query when you view it in Design view just as you can save it when you view query results in Datasheet view.

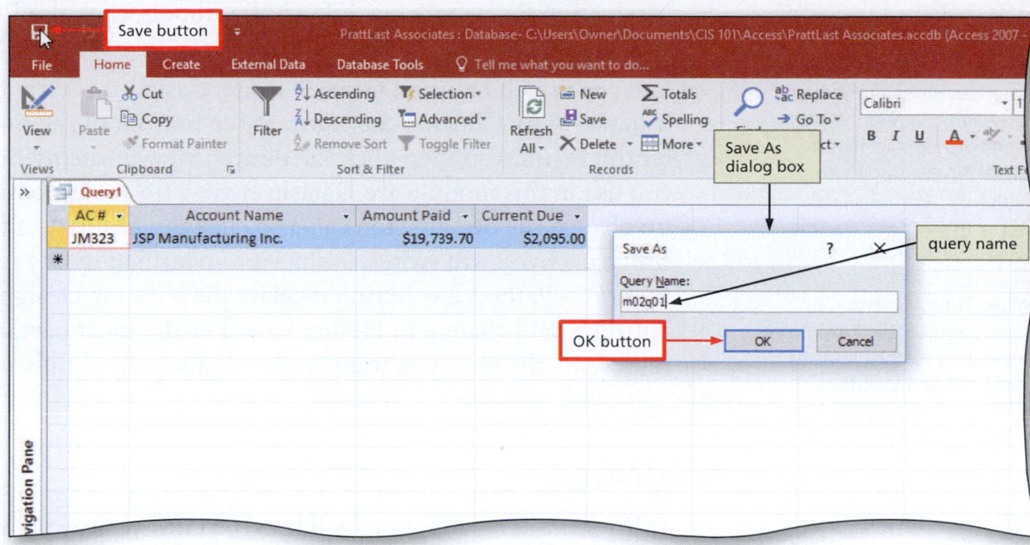

Figure 2–8

4

- Click the OK button (Save As dialog box) to save the query (Figure 2–9).

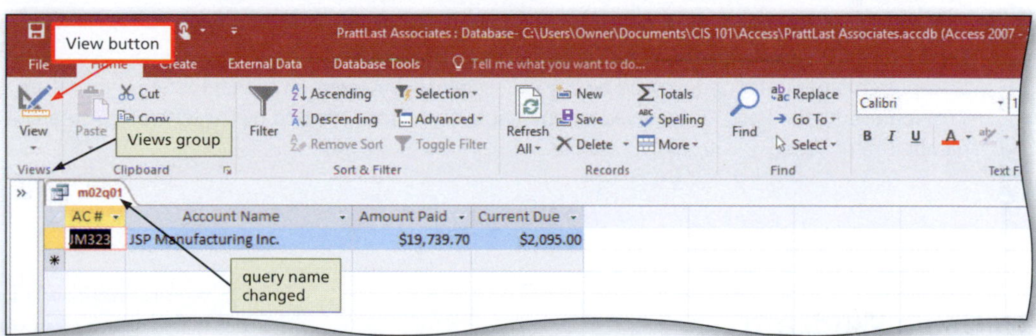

Figure 2–9

Other Ways

1. Right-click query tab, click Save on shortcut menu
2. Press CTRL+S

Using Saved Queries

After you have created and saved a query, you can use it in a variety of ways:

- To view the results of a query that is not currently open, open it by right-clicking the query in the Navigation Pane and clicking Open on the shortcut menu.
- If you want to change the design of a query that is already open, return to Design view and make the changes.
- If you want to change the design of a query that is not currently open, right-click the query in the Navigation Pane and then click Design View on the shortcut menu to open the query in Design view.
- To print the results with a query open, click File on the ribbon, click the Print tab in the Backstage view, and then click Quick Print.

BTW

The Ribbon and Screen Resolution

Access may change how the groups and buttons within the groups appear on the ribbon, depending on the computer or mobile device's screen resolution. Thus, your ribbon may look different from the ones in this book if you are using a screen resolution other than 1366 x 768.

BTW
Organizing Files and Folders
You should organize and store files in folders so that you easily can find the files later. For example, if you are taking an introductory computer class called CIS 101, a good practice would be to save all Access files in an Access folder in a CIS 101 folder. For a discussion of folders and detailed examples of creating folders, refer to the Office and Windows module at the beginning of this book.

- To print a query without first opening it, be sure the query is selected in the Navigation Pane and click File on the ribbon, click the Print tab in the Backstage view, and then click Quick Print.
- You can switch between views of a query using the View button (Home tab | Views group). Clicking the arrow at the bottom of the button produces the View button menu. You then click the desired view in the menu. The two query views you use in this module are Datasheet view (to see the results) and Design view (to change the design). You can also click the top part of the View button, in which case you will switch to the view identified by the icon on the button. In Figure 2–9, the View button displays the icon for Design view, so clicking the button would change to Design view. For the most part, the icon on the button represents the view you want, so you can usually simply click the button.

Wildcards

Microsoft Access supports wildcards. **Wildcards** are symbols that represent any character or combination of characters. One common wildcard, the **asterisk** (*), represents any collection of characters. Another wildcard symbol is the **question mark (?)**, which represents any individual character.

CONSIDER THIS

What does S* represent? What does T?m represent?
S* represents the letter, S, followed by any collection of characters. A search for S* might return System, So, or Superlative. T?m represents the letter, T, followed by any single character, followed by the letter, m. A search for T?m might return the names Tim or Tom.

To Use a Wildcard

1 CREATE QUERIES | 2 USE CRITERIA | 3 SORT DATA | 4 JOIN TABLES | 5 EXPORT RESULTS
6 PERFORM CALCULATIONS | 7 CREATE CROSSTAB | 8 CUSTOMIZE NAVIGATION PANE

The following steps modify the previous query to use the asterisk wildcard so that PrattLast Associates can select only those accounts whose names begin with K. ***Why?*** *Because you do not know how many characters will follow the K, the asterisk wildcard symbol is appropriate.* The steps also save the query with a new name using the Save As command.

1

- Click the View button (Home tab | Views group), shown in Figure 2–9, to return to Design view.
- If necessary, click the Criteria row below the Account Number field to produce an insertion point.

Q&A The text I entered now has quotation marks surrounding it. What happened?
Criteria for text data needs to be enclosed in quotation marks. You do not have to type the quotation marks; Access adds them automatically.

- Use the DELETE or BACKSPACE key as necessary to delete the current entry.
- Click the Criteria row below the Account Name field to produce an insertion point.
- Type `K*` as the criterion (Figure 2–10).

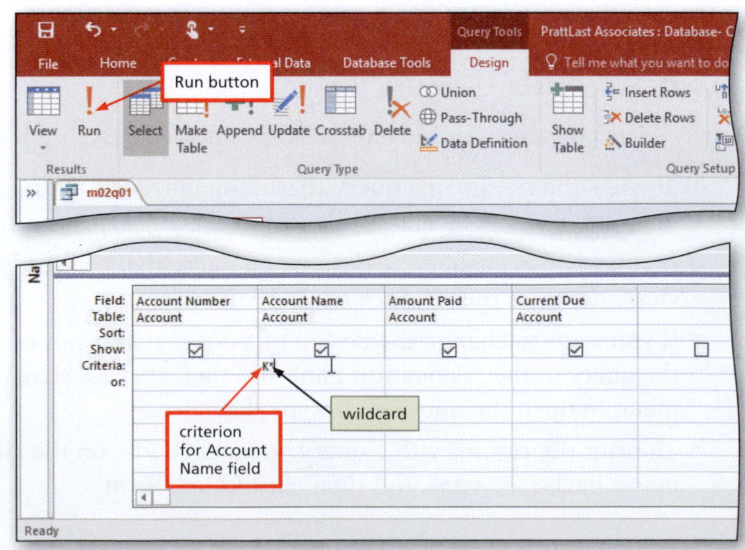

Figure 2–10

2

- Run the query by clicking the Run button (Query Tools Design tab | Results group) (Figure 2–11).

Experiment

- Change the letter K to lowercase in the criterion and run the query to determine whether case makes a difference when entering a wildcard.

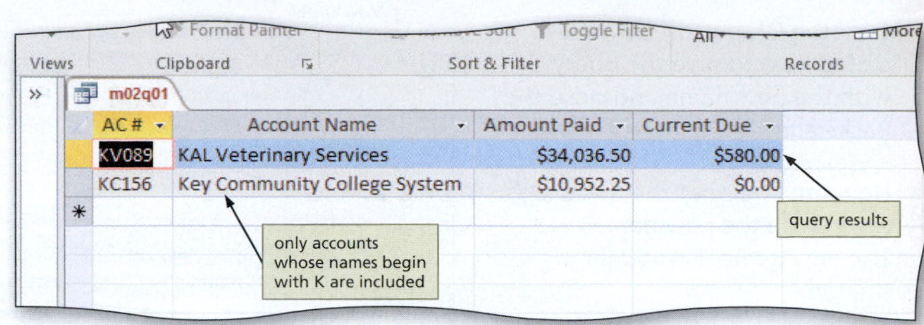

Figure 2–11

3

- Click File on the ribbon to open the Backstage view.
- Click the Save As tab in the Backstage view to display the Save As gallery.
- Click 'Save Object As' in the File Types area (Figure 2–12).

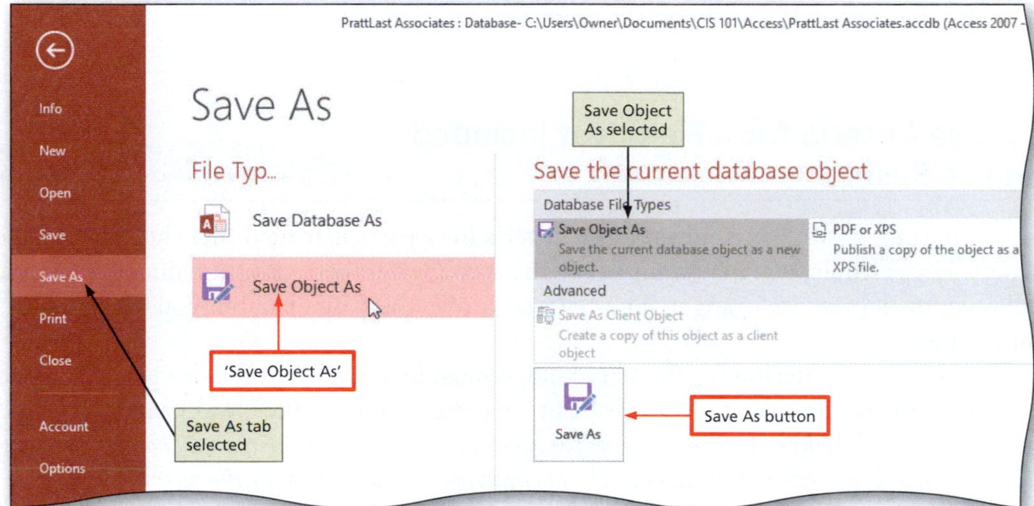

Figure 2–12

Q&A Can I just click the Save button on the Quick Access Toolbar as I did when saving the previous query?

If you clicked the Save button, you would replace the previous query with the version you just created. Because you want to save both the previous query and the new one, you need to save the new version with a different name. To do so, you must use Save Object As, which is available through the Backstage view.

4

- With Save Object As selected in the File Types gallery, click the Save As button to display the Save As dialog box.
- Erase the name of the current query and type **m02q02** as the name for the saved query (Figure 2–13).

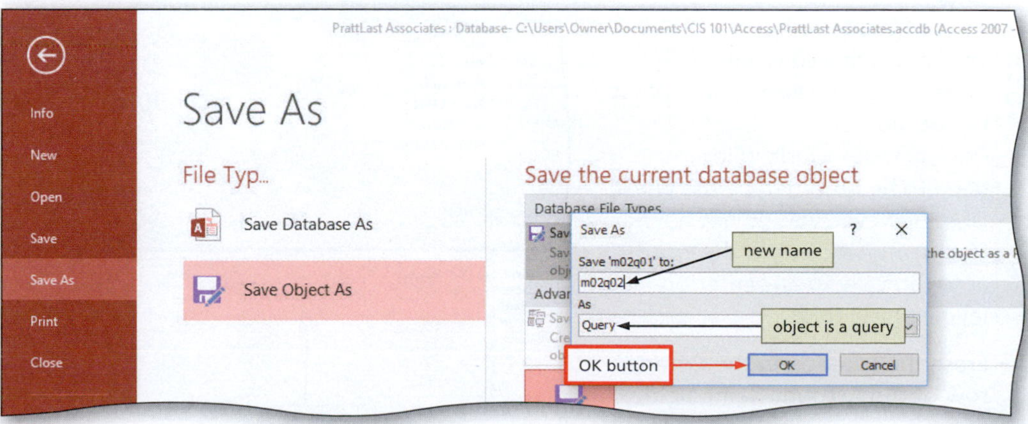

Figure 2–13

Q&A The current entry in the As text box is Query. Could I save the query as some other type of object?

Although you usually would want to save the query as another query, you can also save it as a form or report by changing the entry in the As text box. If you do, Access would create either a simple form or a simple report for the query.

- Click the OK button (Save As dialog box) to save the query with the new name and close the Backstage view (Figure 2–14).

Q&A How can I tell that the query was saved with the new name?
The new name will appear on the tab.

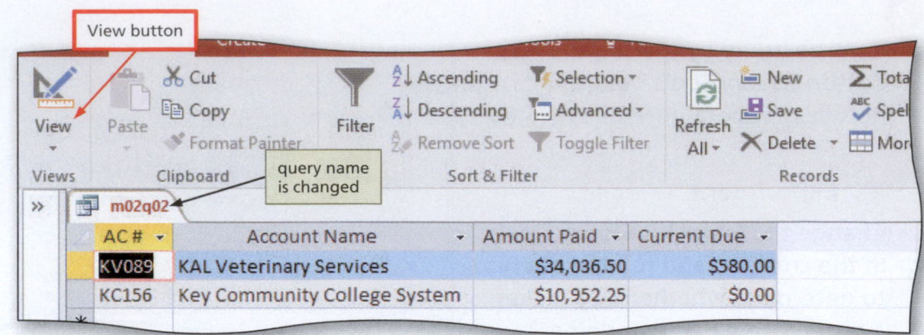

Figure 2–14

Other Ways

1. Click Design View button on status bar

To Use Criteria for a Field Not Included in the Results

1 CREATE QUERIES | 2 USE CRITERIA | 3 SORT DATA | 4 JOIN TABLES | 5 EXPORT RESULTS
6 PERFORM CALCULATIONS | 7 CREATE CROSSTAB | 8 CUSTOMIZE NAVIGATION PANE

In some cases, you might require criteria for a particular field that should not appear in the results of the query. For example, you may want to see the account number, account name, amount paid, and current due for all accounts located in Granger. The criteria involve the City field, but you do not want to include the City field in the results.

To enter a criterion for the City field, it must be included in the design grid. Normally, it would then appear in the results. To prevent this from happening, remove the check mark from its check box in the Show row of the grid. ***Why?*** *A check mark in the Show check box instructs Access to show the field in the result. If you remove the check mark, you can use the field in the query without displaying it in the query results.*

The following steps modify the previous query so that PrattLast Associates can select only those accounts located in Granger. PrattLast does not want the city to appear in the results, however. The steps also save the query with a new name.

- Click the View button (Home tab | Views group), shown in Figure 2–14, to return to Design view.

Q&A The text I entered is now preceded by the word, Like. What happened?
Criteria that include wildcards need to be preceded by the word, Like. However, you do not have to type it; Access adds the word automatically to any criterion involving a wildcard.

- Erase the criterion in the Criteria row of the Account Name field.
- Add the City field to the query.
- Type `Granger` as the criterion for the City field (Figure 2–15).

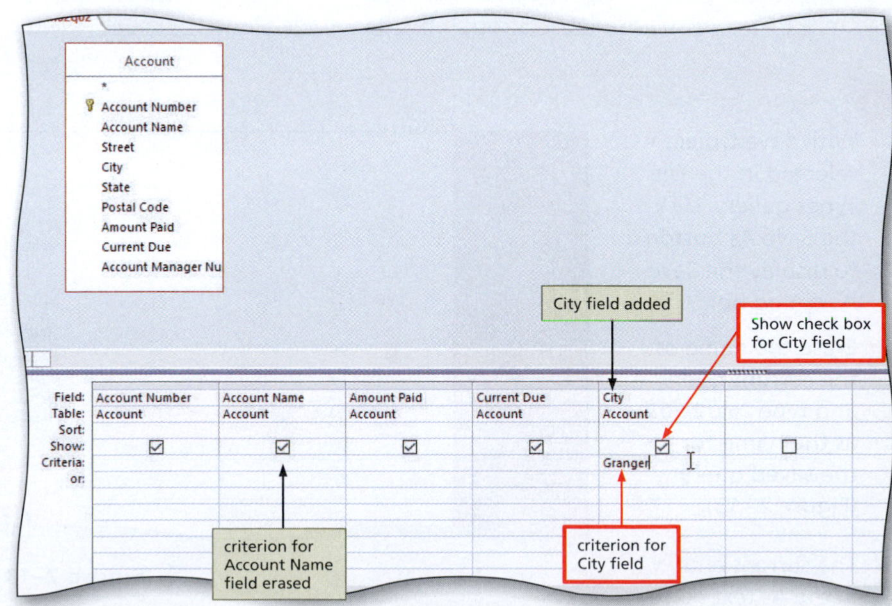

Figure 2–15

2

- Click the Show check box for the City field to remove the check mark (Figure 2–16).

Q&A Could I have removed the check mark before entering the criterion?

Yes. The order in which you perform the two operations does not matter.

check mark removed from Show check box, indicating that City field will not appear in query results

Access automatically adds quotation marks

Figure 2–16

- Run the query (Figure 2–17).

Experiment

- Click the View button to return to Design view, enter a different city name as the criterion, and run the query. Repeat this process with additional city names, including at least one city name that is not in the database. When finished, change the criterion back to Granger.

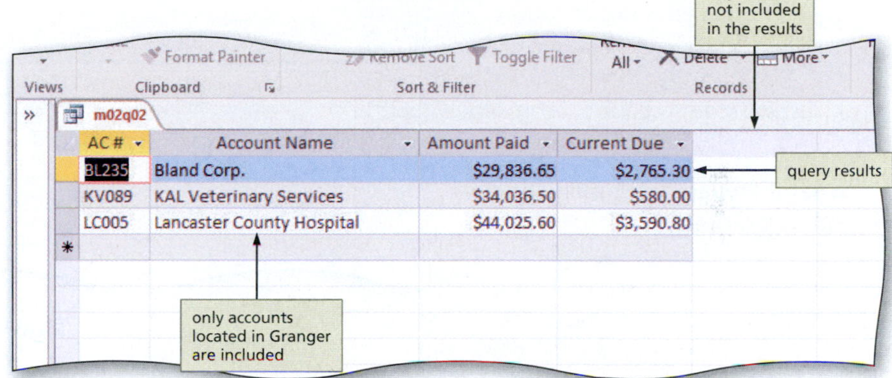

Figure 2–17

Creating a Parameter Query

If you wanted to find accounts located in Wells instead of Granger, you would either have to create a new query or modify the existing query by replacing Granger with Wells as the criterion. Rather than giving a specific criterion when you first create the query, occasionally you may want to be able to enter part of the criterion when you run the query and then have the appropriate results appear. For example, you might want a query to return the account number, account name, amount paid, and current due for all accounts in a specific city, specifying a different city each time you run the query. A user could run the query, enter Wells as the city, and then see all the accounts in Wells. Later, the user could use the same query but enter Granger as the city, and then see all the accounts in Granger.

To enable this flexibility, you create a **parameter query**, which is a query that prompts for input whenever it is used. You enter a parameter (the prompt for the user) rather than a specific value as the criterion. You create the parameter by enclosing the criterion value in square brackets. It is important that the value in the brackets does not match the name of any field. If you enter a field name in square brackets, Access assumes you want that particular field and does not prompt the user for input. To prompt the user to enter the city name as the input, you could place [Enter City] as the criterion in the City field.

BTW

Designing Queries

Before creating queries, examine the contents of the tables involved. You need to know the data type for each field and how the data for the field is stored. If a query includes a state, for example, you need to know whether state is stored as the two-character abbreviation or as the full state name.

To Create and View a Parameter Query

The following steps create a parameter query. ***Why?*** *The parameter query will give users at PrattLast the ability to enter a different city each time they run the query rather than having a specific city as part of the criterion in the query.* The steps also save the query with a new name.

- Return to Design view.
- Erase the current criterion in the City column, and then type **[Enter City]** as the new criterion (Figure 2–18).

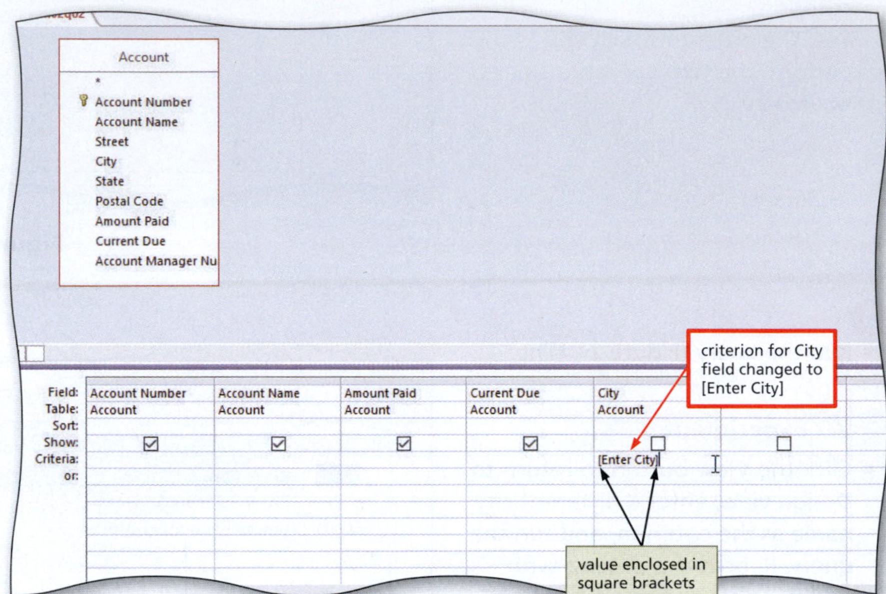

Figure 2–18

Q&A What is the purpose of the square brackets?
The square brackets indicate that the text entered is not text that the value in the column must match. Without the brackets, Access would search for records in which the city is Enter City.

What if I typed a field name in the square brackets?
Access would simply use the value in that field. To create a parameter query, you must not use a field name in the square brackets.

- Click the Run button (Query Tools Design tab | Results group) to display the Enter Parameter Value dialog box (Figure 2–19).

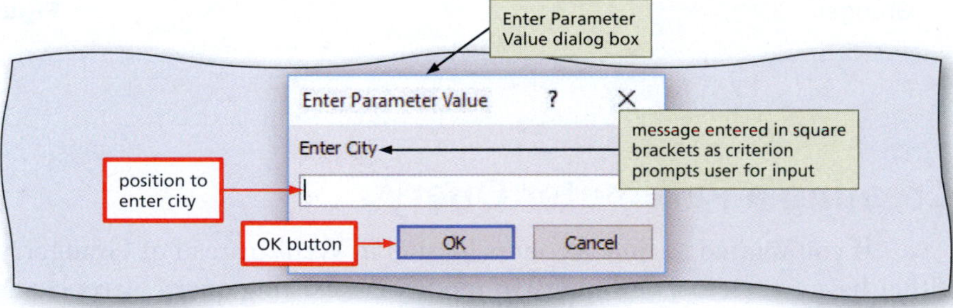

Figure 2–19

- Type **Wells** as the parameter value in the Enter City text box, and then click the OK button (Enter Parameter Value dialog box) to close the dialog box and view the query (Figure 2–20).

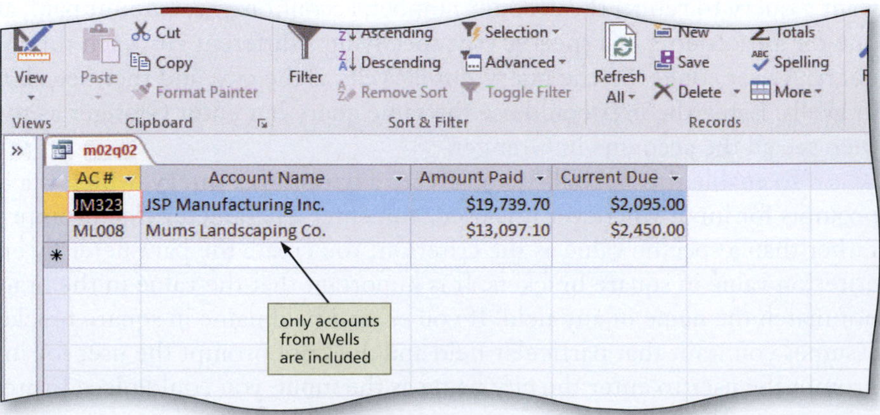

Figure 2–20

Experiment

- Try using other characters between the square brackets. In each case, run the query. When finished, change the characters between the square brackets back to Enter City.

4

- Click File on the ribbon to open the Backstage view.
- Click the Save As tab in the Backstage view to display the Save As gallery.
- Click 'Save Object As' in the File Types area.
- With Save Object As selected in the File Types area, click the Save As button to display the Save As dialog box.

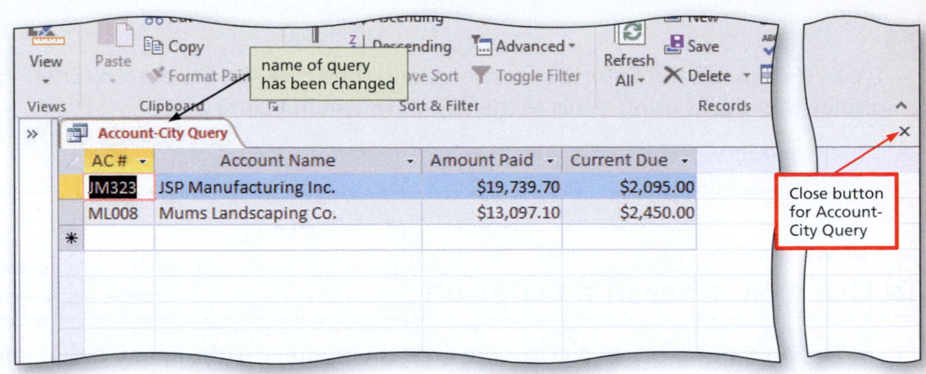

Figure 2–21

- Type `Account-City Query` as the name for the saved query.
- Click the OK button (Save As dialog box) to save the query with the new name and close the Backstage view (Figure 2–21).

- Click the Close button for the Account-City Query to close the query.

Break Point: If you wish to take a break, this is a good place to do so. You can exit Access now. To resume later, run Access, open the database called PrattLast Associates, and continue following the steps from this location forward.

To Use a Parameter Query

You use a parameter query like any other saved query. You can open it or you can print the query results. In either case, Access prompts you to supply a value for the parameter each time you use the query. If changes have been made to the data since the last time you ran the query, the results of the query may be different, even if you enter the same value for the parameter. ***Why?*** *In addition to the ability to enter different field values each time the parameter query is run, the query always uses the data that is currently in the table.* The following steps use the parameter query named Account-City Query.

- Open the Navigation Pane.
- Right-click the Account-City Query to produce a shortcut menu.
- Click Open on the shortcut menu to open the query and display the Enter Parameter Value dialog box (Figure 2–22).

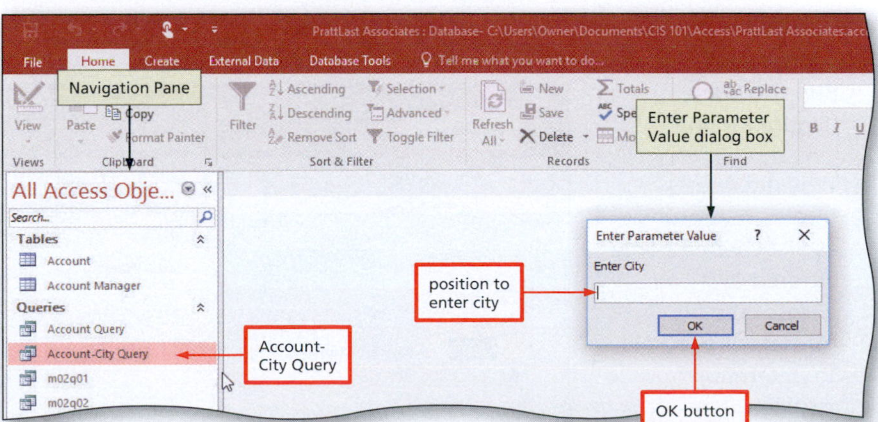

Figure 2–22

Q&A The title bar for my Navigation Pane contains Tables and Related Views rather than All Access Objects as it did in Module 1. What should I do?
Click the Navigation Pane arrow and then click 'All Access Objects'.

I do not have the Search bar at the top of the Navigation Pane that I had in Module 1. What should I do?
Right-click the Navigation Pane title bar arrow to display a shortcut menu, and then click Search Bar.

2

- Type **Wells** in the Enter City text box, and then click the OK button (Enter Parameter Value dialog box) to display the results using Wells as the city, as shown in Figure 2–21.
- Close the query.

To Use a Number in a Criterion

1 CREATE QUERIES | 2 USE CRITERIA | 3 SORT DATA | 4 JOIN TABLES | 5 EXPORT RESULTS
6 PERFORM CALCULATIONS | 7 CREATE CROSSTAB | 8 CUSTOMIZE NAVIGATION PANE

To enter a number in a criterion, type the number without any dollar signs or commas. ***Why?*** *If you enter a dollar sign, Access assumes you are entering text. If you enter a comma, Access considers the criterion invalid.* The following steps create a query that PrattLast Associates might use to display all accounts whose current due amount is $0. The steps also save the query with a new name.

1

- Close the Navigation Pane.
- Click Create on the ribbon to display the Create tab.
- Click the Query Design button (Create tab | Queries group) to create a new query.
- If necessary, click the Account table (Show Table dialog box) to select the table.
- Click the Add button to add the selected table to the query.

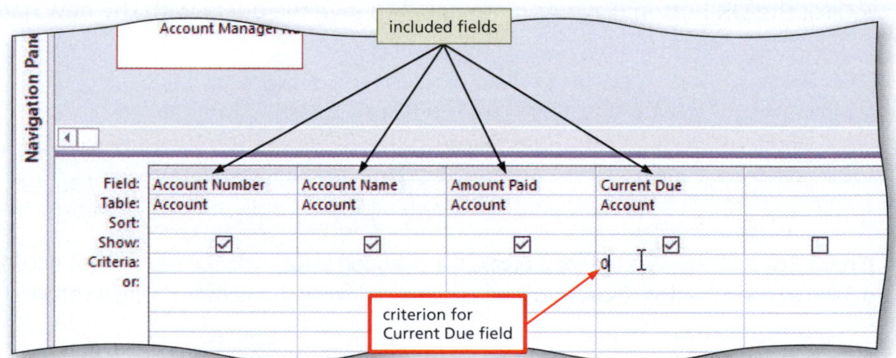

Figure 2–23

- Click the Close button to remove the dialog box from the screen.
- Drag the lower edge of the field list down far enough so all fields in the list are displayed.
- Include the Account Number, Account Name, Amount Paid, and Current Due fields in the query.
- Type 0 as the criterion for the Current Due field (Figure 2–23).

Q&A Do I need to enter a dollar sign and decimal point?
No. Access will interpret 0 as $0 because the data type for the Current Due field is currency.

2

- Run the query (Figure 2–24).

Q&A Why did Access display the results as $0.00 when I only entered 0?
Access uses the format for the field to determine how to display the result. In this case, the format indicated that Access should include the dollar sign, decimal point, and two decimal places.

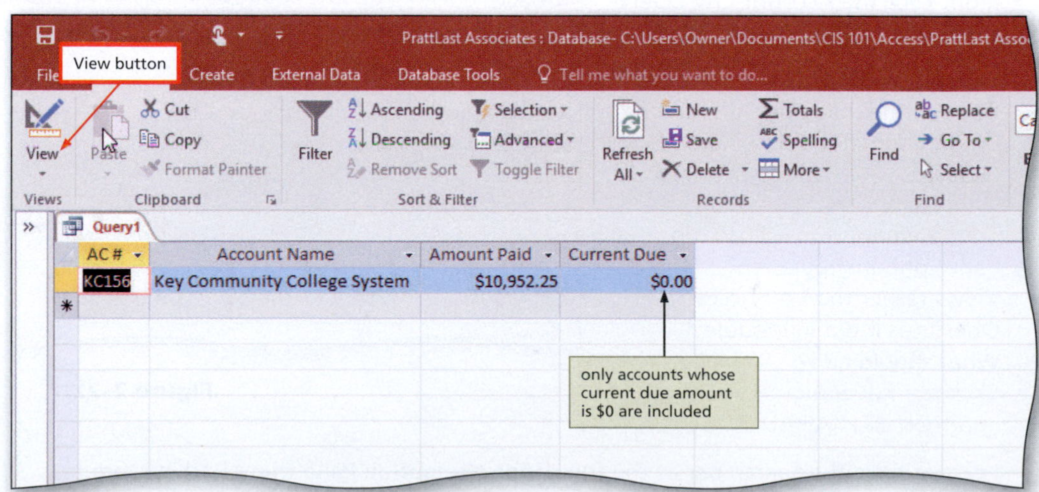

Figure 2–24

3

- Save the query as m02q03.

Q&A How do I know when to use the Save button to save a query or use the Backstage view to perform a Save As?
If you are saving a new query, the simplest way is to use the Save button on the Quick Access Toolbar. If you are saving changes to a previously saved query but do not want to change the name, use the Save button. If you want to save a previously saved query with a new name, you must use the Backstage view and perform a Save Object As.

- Close the query.

Comparison Operators

Unless you specify otherwise, Access assumes that the criteria you enter involve equality (exact matches). In the last query, for example, you were requesting those accounts whose current due amount is equal to 0 (zero). In other situations, you might want to find a range of results; for example, you could request accounts whose current due is greater than $1,000.00. If you want a query to return something other than an exact match, you must enter the appropriate **comparison operator**. The comparison operators are > (greater than), < (less than), >= (greater than or equal to), <= (less than or equal to), and NOT (not equal to).

To Use a Comparison Operator in a Criterion

1 CREATE QUERIES | 2 USE CRITERIA | 3 SORT DATA | 4 JOIN TABLES | 5 EXPORT RESULTS
6 PERFORM CALCULATIONS | 7 CREATE CROSSTAB | 8 CUSTOMIZE NAVIGATION PANE

The following steps use the > operator to create a query that PrattLast Associates might use to find all account managers whose start date is after 1/1/2015. ***Why?** A date greater than 1/1/2015 means the date comes after 1/1/2015.* The steps also save the query with a new name.

1

- Start a new query using the Account Manager table.
- Include the Account Manager Number, Last Name, First Name, and Start Date fields.
- Type **>1/01/2015** as the criterion for the Start Date field (Figure 2–25).

Q&A Why did I not have to type the leading zero in the Month portion of the date?
It is fine as you typed it. You also could have typed 01/1/2015. Some people often type the day using two digits, such as 1/01/2015. You also could have typed a leading zero for both the month and the day: 01/01/2015.

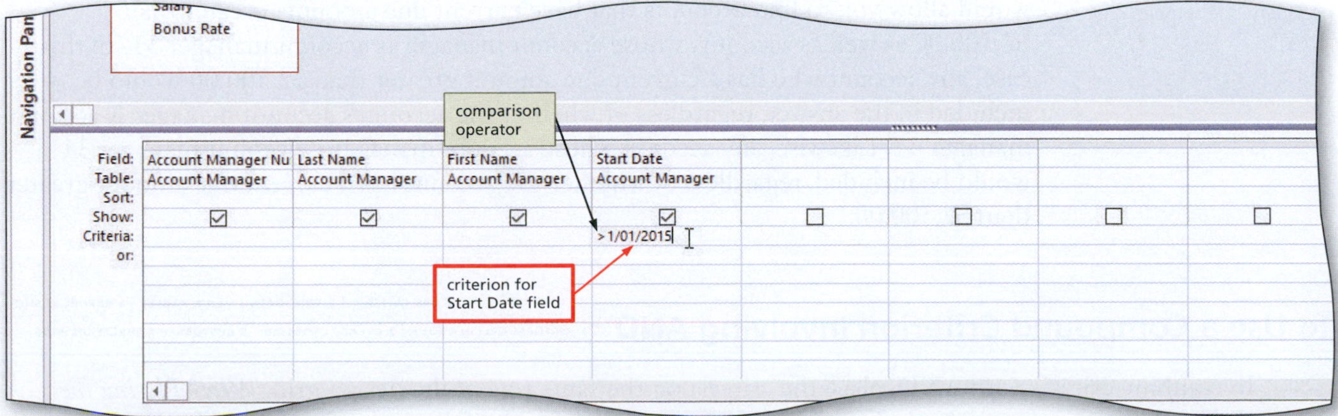

Figure 2–25

- Run the query (Figure 2–26).

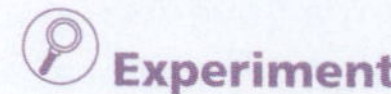

- Return to Design view. Try a different criterion involving a comparison operator in the Start Date field and run the query. When finished, return to Design view, enter the original criterion (>1/01/2015) in the Start Date field, and run the query.

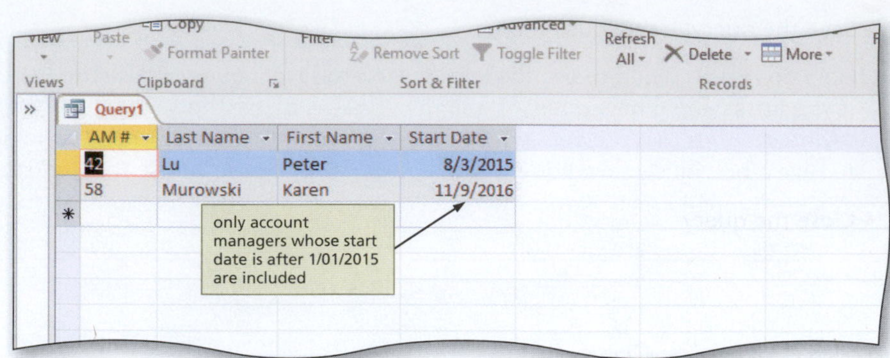

Figure 2–26

Q&A I returned to Design view and noticed that Access changed 1/01/2015 to #1/01/2015#. Why does the date now have number signs around it?
This is the date format in Access. You usually do not have to enter the number signs because in most cases Access will insert them automatically.

My records are in a different order. Is this a problem?
No. The important thing is which records are included in the results. You will see later in this module how you can specify the specific order you want for cases when the order is important.

Can I use the same comparison operators with text data?
Yes. Comparison operators function the same whether you use them with number fields, currency fields, date fields, or text fields. With a text field, comparison operators use alphabetical order in making the determination.

- Save the query as m02q04.
- Close the query.

BTW
Queries: Query-by-Example
Query-By-Example, often referred to as QBE, was a query language first proposed in the mid-1970s. In this approach, users asked questions by filling in a table on the screen. The Access approach to queries is based on Query-By-Example.

Using Compound Criteria

Often your search data must satisfy more than one criterion. This type of criterion is called a **compound criterion** and is created using the words AND or OR.

In an **AND criterion**, each individual criterion must be true in order for the compound criterion to be true. For example, an AND criterion would allow you to find accounts that have current due amounts greater than $2,500.00 and whose account manager is manager 31.

An **OR criterion** is true if either individual criterion is true. An OR criterion would allow you to find accounts that have current due amounts greater than $2,500.00 as well as accounts whose account manager is account manager 31. In this case, any account who has a current due amount greater than $2,500.00 would be included in the answer, regardless of whether the account's account manager is account manager 31. Likewise, any account whose account manager is account manager 31 would be included, regardless of whether the account has a current due amount greater than $2,500.00.

To Use a Compound Criterion Involving AND

1 CREATE QUERIES | 2 USE CRITERIA | 3 SORT DATA | 4 JOIN TABLES | 5 EXPORT RESULTS
6 PERFORM CALCULATIONS | 7 CREATE CROSSTAB | 8 CUSTOMIZE NAVIGATION PANE

To combine criteria with AND, place the criteria on the same row of the design grid. ***Why?*** *Placing the criteria in the same row indicates that both criteria must be true in Access.* The following steps use an AND criterion to enable PrattLast to find those accounts who have a current due amount greater than $2,500.00 and whose account manager is manager 31. The steps also save the query.

1

- Start a new query using the Account table.
- Include the Account Number, Account Name, Amount Paid, Current Due, and Account Manager Number fields.
- Type `>2500` as the criterion for the Current Due field.
- Type `31` as the criterion for the Account Manager Number field (Figure 2–27).

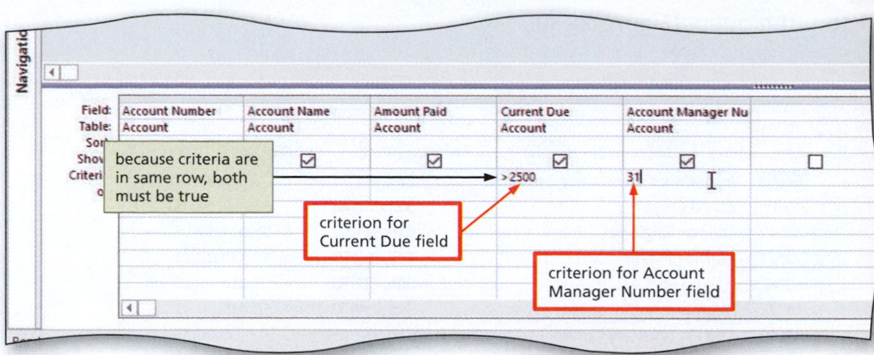

Figure 2–27

- Run the query (Figure 2–28).

- Save the query as m02q05.

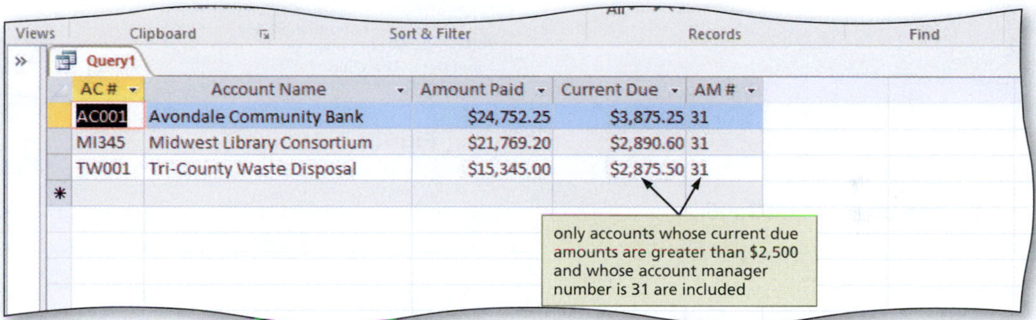

Figure 2–28

To Use a Compound Criterion Involving OR

1 CREATE QUERIES | 2 USE CRITERIA | 3 SORT DATA | 4 JOIN TABLES | 5 EXPORT RESULTS
6 PERFORM CALCULATIONS | 7 CREATE CROSSTAB | 8 CUSTOMIZE NAVIGATION PANE

To combine criteria with OR, each criterion must go on separate rows in the Criteria area of the grid. ***Why?*** *Placing criteria on separate rows indicates at least one criterion must be true in Access.* The following steps use an OR criterion to enable PrattLast to find those accounts who have a current due amount greater than $2,500.00 or whose account manager is manager 31 (or both). The steps also save the query with a new name.

- Return to Design view.
- If necessary, click the Criteria entry for the Account Manager Number field and then use the BACKSPACE key or the DELETE key to erase the entry ("31").
- Click the or row (the row below the Criteria row) for the Account Manager Number field, and then type `31` as the entry (Figure 2–29).

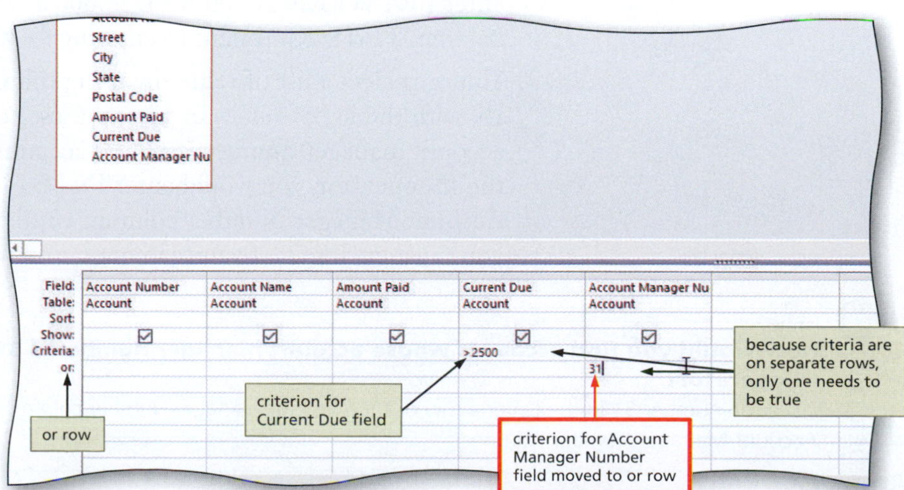

Figure 2–29

2

- Run the query (Figure 2–30).

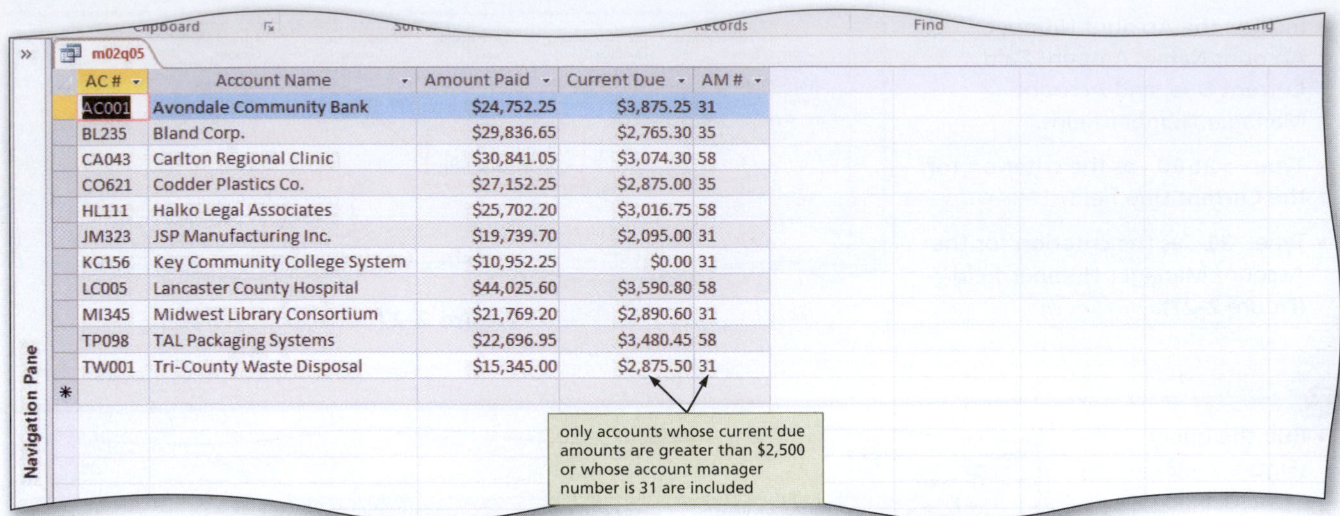

AC #	Account Name	Amount Paid	Current Due	AM #
AC001	Avondale Community Bank	$24,752.25	$3,875.25	31
BL235	Bland Corp.	$29,836.65	$2,765.30	35
CA043	Carlton Regional Clinic	$30,841.05	$3,074.30	58
CO621	Codder Plastics Co.	$27,152.25	$2,875.00	35
HL111	Halko Legal Associates	$25,702.20	$3,016.75	58
JM323	JSP Manufacturing Inc.	$19,739.70	$2,095.00	31
KC156	Key Community College System	$10,952.25	$0.00	31
LC005	Lancaster County Hospital	$44,025.60	$3,590.80	58
MI345	Midwest Library Consortium	$21,769.20	$2,890.60	31
TP098	TAL Packaging Systems	$22,696.95	$3,480.45	58
TW001	Tri-County Waste Disposal	$15,345.00	$2,875.50	31

Clipboard
Records
Find
m02q05
Navigation Pane
only accounts whose current due amounts are greater than $2,500 or whose account manager number is 31 are included

Figure 2–30

- Save the query as m02q06.

Special Criteria

You can use three special criteria in queries:

1. If you want to create a criterion involving a range of values in a single field, you can use the **AND operator**. You place the word AND between the individual conditions. For example, if you wanted to find all accounts whose amount paid is greater than or equal to $20,000.00 and less than or equal to $40,000.00, you would enter >= 20000 AND <= 40000 as the criterion in the Amount Paid column.
2. You can select values in a given range by using the **BETWEEN operator**. This is often an alternative to the AND operator. For example, to find all accounts whose amount paid is between $20,000.00 and $40,000.00, inclusive, you would enter BETWEEN 20000 AND 40000 as the criterion in the Amount Paid column. This is equivalent to entering >=20000 and <=40000.
3. You can select a list of values by using the **IN operator**. You follow the word IN with the list of values in parentheses. For example, to find accounts whose account manager number is 31 and accounts whose account manager is 35 using the IN operator, you would enter IN ("31","35") on the Criteria row in the Account Manager Number column. Unlike when you enter a simple criterion, you must enclose text values in quotation marks.

BTW

Rearranging Fields in a Query

To move a field in the design grid, click the column selector for the field to select the field and drag it to the appropriate location.

CONSIDER THIS

How would you find accounts whose account manager number is 31 or 35 without using the IN operator?

Place the number 31 in the Criteria row of the Account Manager Number column. Place the number 35 in the or row of the Account Manager Number column.

Sorting

In some queries, the order in which the records appear is irrelevant. All you need to be concerned about are the records that appear in the results. It does not matter which one is first or which one is last.

In other queries, however, the order can be very important. You may want to see the cities in which accounts are located and would like them arranged alphabetically. Perhaps you want to see the accounts listed by account manager number. Further, within all the accounts of any given account manager, you might want them to be listed by amount paid from largest amount to smallest.

To order the records in a query result in a particular way, you **sort** the records. The field or fields on which the records are sorted is called the **sort key**. If you are sorting on more than one field (such as sorting by amount paid within account manager number), the more important field (Account Manager Number) is called the **major key** (also called the **primary sort key**) and the less important field (Amount Paid) is called the **minor key** (also called the **secondary sort key**).

To sort in Microsoft Access, specify the sort order in the Sort row of the design grid below the field that is the sort key. If you specify more than one sort key, the sort key on the left will be the major sort key, and the one on the right will be the minor key.

BTW
Sorting Data in a Query
When sorting data in a query, the records in the underlying tables (the tables on which the query is based) are not actually rearranged. Instead, the DBMS determines the most efficient method of simply displaying the records in the requested order. The records in the underlying tables remain in their original order.

BTW
Clearing the Design Grid
You can also clear the design grid using the ribbon. To do so, click the Home tab, click the Advanced button to display the Advanced menu, and then click Clear Grid on the Advanced menu.

To Clear the Design Grid

1 CREATE QUERIES | 2 USE CRITERIA | 3 SORT DATA | 4 JOIN TABLES | 5 EXPORT RESULTS
6 PERFORM CALCULATIONS | 7 CREATE CROSSTAB | 8 CUSTOMIZE NAVIGATION PANE

Why? *If the fields you want to include in the next query are different from those in the previous query, it is usually simpler to start with a clear grid, that is, one with no fields already in the design grid.* You always can clear the entries in the design grid by closing the query and then starting over. A simpler approach to clearing the entries is to select all the entries and then press the DELETE key. The following steps return to Design view and clear the design grid.

1

- Return to Design view.
- Click just above the Account Number column heading in the grid to select the column.

Q&A I clicked above the column heading, but the column is not selected. What should I do?
You did not point to the correct location. Be sure the pointer changes into a down-pointing arrow and then click again.

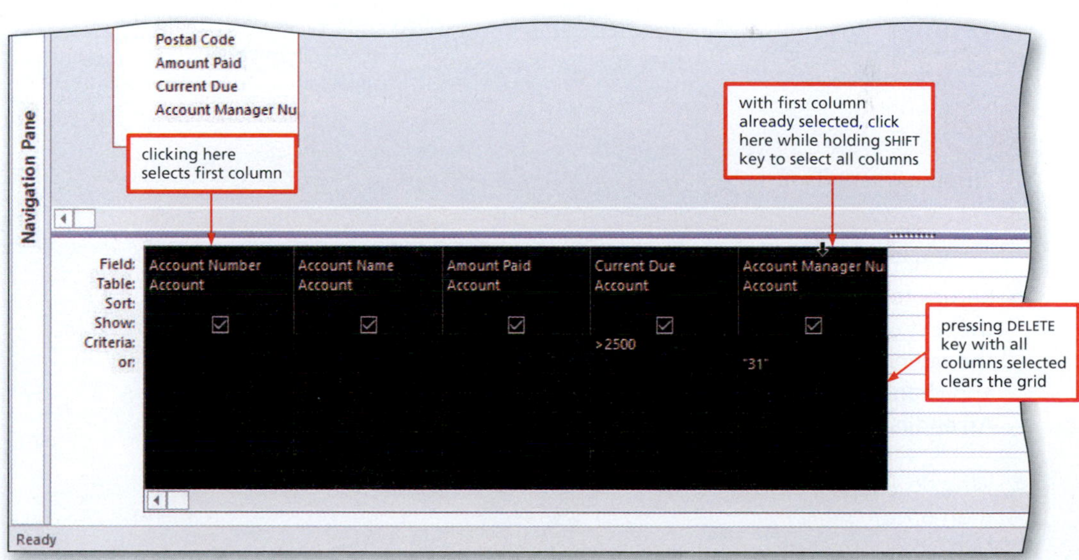

Figure 2–31

- Hold the SHIFT key down and click just above the Account Manager Number column heading to select all the columns (Figure 2–31).

- Press the DELETE key to clear the design grid.

To Sort Data in a Query

If you determine that the query results should be sorted, you will need to specify the sort key. The following steps sort the cities in the Account table by indicating that the City field is to be sorted. The steps specify Ascending sort order. ***Why?*** *When sorting text data, Ascending sort order arranges the results in alphabetical order.*

1

- Include the City field in the design grid.
- Click the Sort row in the City field column, and then click the Sort arrow to display a menu of possible sort orders (Figure 2–32).

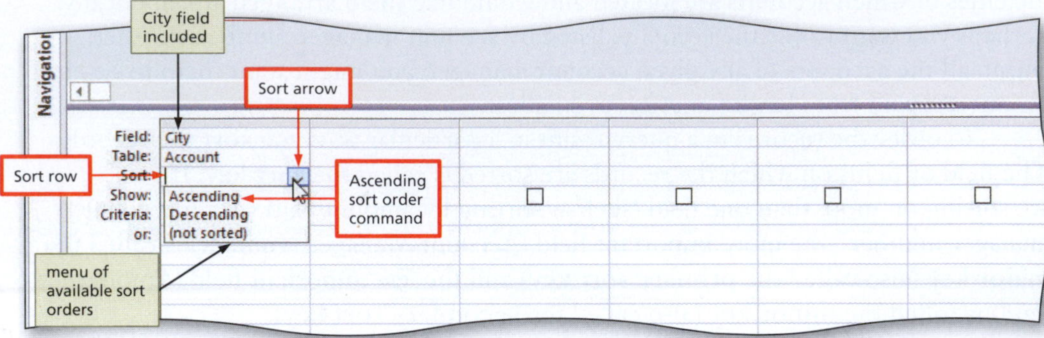

Figure 2–32

2

- Click Ascending to select the sort order (Figure 2–33).

Figure 2–33

3

- Run the query (Figure 2–34).

Experiment

- Return to Design view and change the sort order to Descending. Run the query. Return to Design view and change the sort order back to Ascending. Run the query.

Q&A Why do some cities appear more than once?

More than one account is located in those cities.

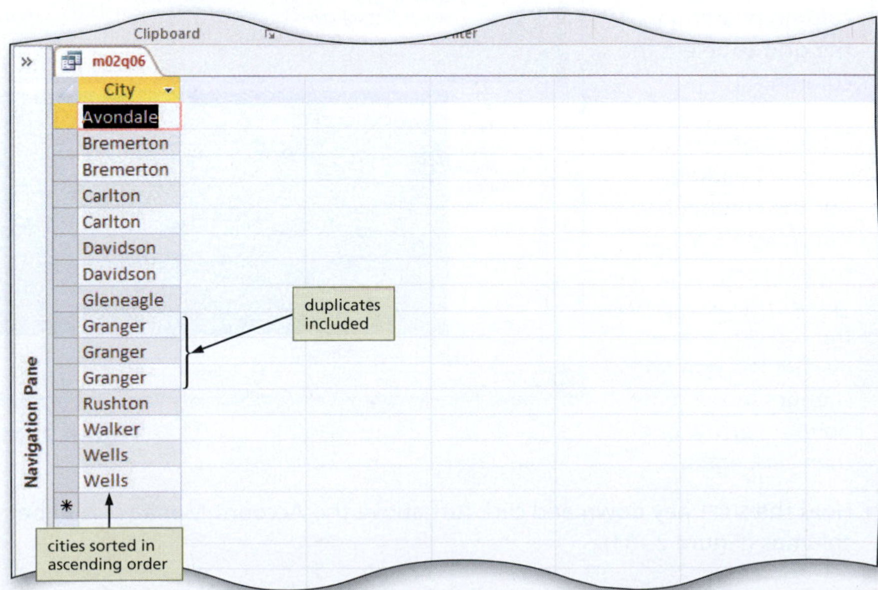

Figure 2–34

To Omit Duplicates

When you sort data, duplicates normally are included. In the query shown in Figure 2–34, for example, Bremerton appears twice. Several other cities appear multiple times as well. You eliminate duplicates using the query's property sheet. A **property sheet** is a window containing the various properties of the object. To omit duplicates, you will use the property sheet to change the Unique Values property from No to Yes.

The following steps create a query that PrattLast Associates might use to obtain a sorted list of the cities in the Account table in which each city is listed only once. ***Why?*** *Unless you wanted to know how many accounts were located in each city, the duplicates typically do not add any value.* The steps also save the query with a new name.

1

- Return to Design view.
- Click the second field (the empty field to the right of City) in the design grid to produce an insertion point.
- If necessary, click Design on the ribbon to display the Design tab.
- Click the Property Sheet button (Query Tools Design tab | Show/Hide group) to display the property sheet (Figure 2–35).

Q&A My property sheet looks different. What should I do?
If your sheet looks different, close the property sheet and repeat this step.

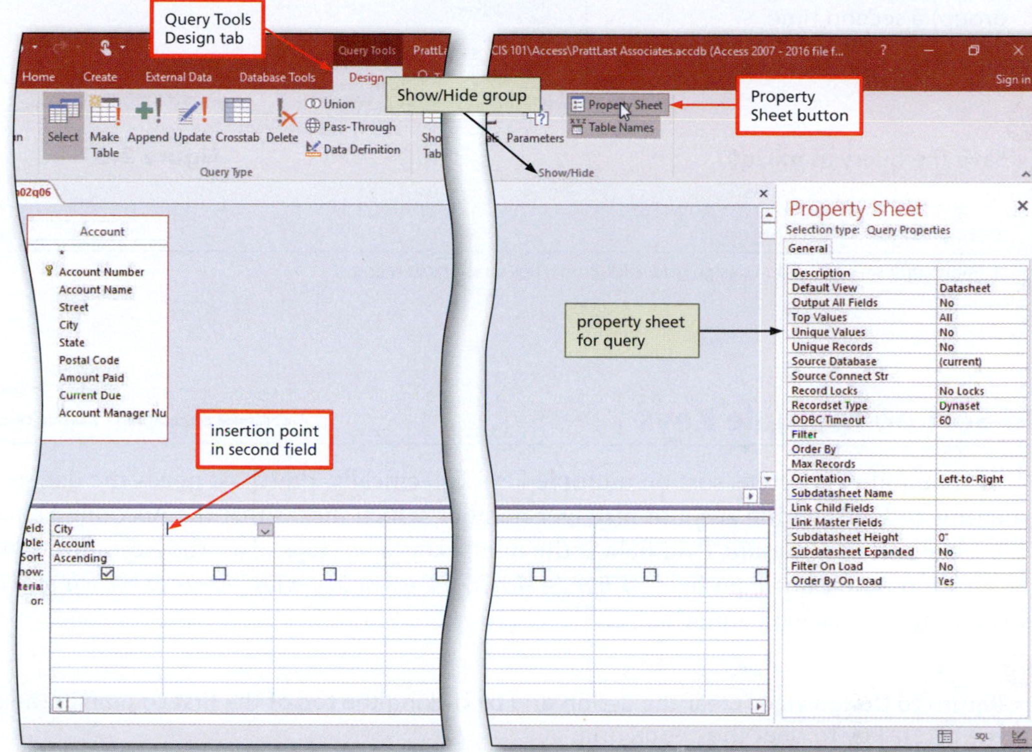

Figure 2–35

2

- Click the Unique Values property box, and then click the arrow that appears to display a list of available choices (Figure 2–36).

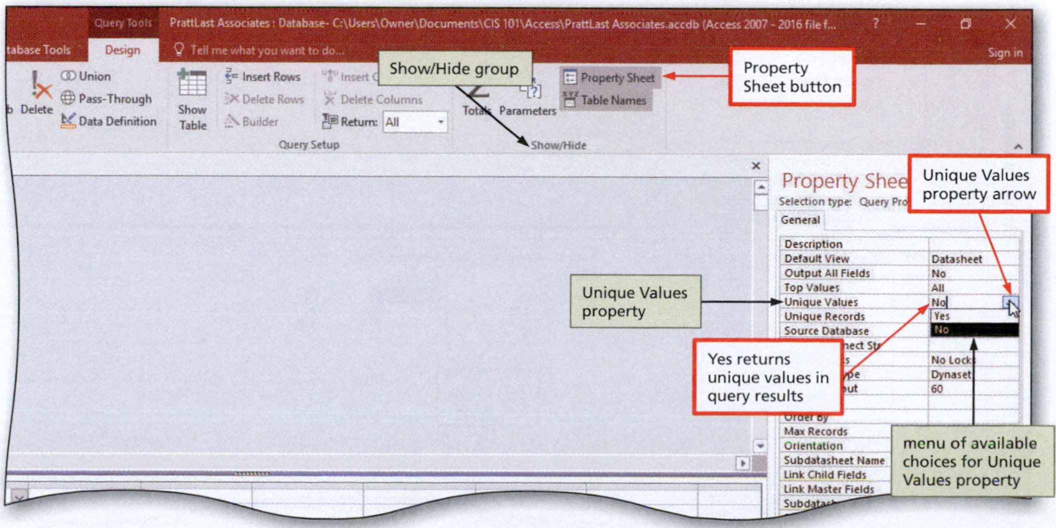

Figure 2–36

- Click Yes to indicate that the query will return unique values, which means that each value will appear only once in the query results.
- Close the Query Properties property sheet by clicking the Property Sheet button (Query Tools Design tab | Show/Hide group) a second time.
- Run the query (Figure 2–37).

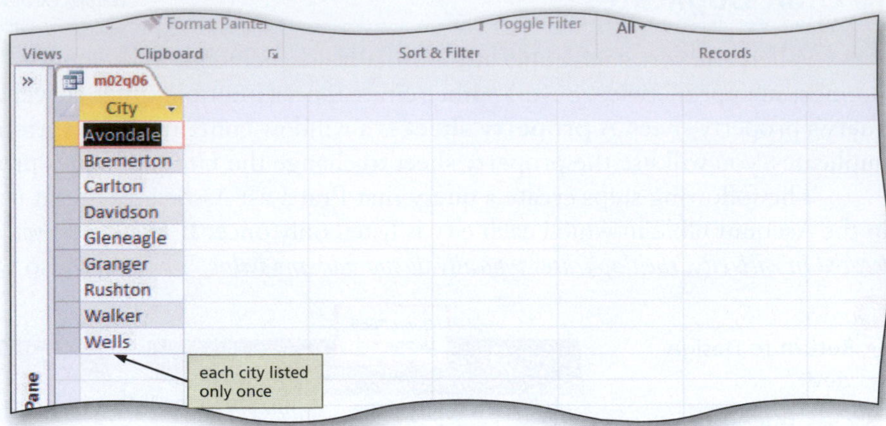

Figure 2–37

- Save the query as m02q07.

Other Ways

1. Right-click second field in design grid, click Properties on shortcut menu

To Sort on Multiple Keys

1 CREATE QUERIES | 2 USE CRITERIA | 3 SORT DATA | 4 JOIN TABLES | 5 EXPORT RESULTS
6 PERFORM CALCULATIONS | 7 CREATE CROSSTAB | 8 CUSTOMIZE NAVIGATION PANE

The following steps sort on multiple keys. Specifically, PrattLast needs the data to be sorted by amount paid (low to high) within account manager number, which means that the Account Manager Number field is the major key and the Amount Paid field is the minor key. The steps place the Account Manager Number field to the left of the Amount Paid field. ***Why?*** *In Access, the major key must appear to the left of the minor key.* The steps also save the query with a new name.

- Return to Design view. Clear the design grid by clicking the top of the first column in the grid, and then pressing the DELETE key to clear the design grid.
- In the following order, include the Account Number, Account Name, Account Manager Number, and Amount Paid fields in the query.
- Select Ascending as the sort order for both the Account Manager Number field and the Amount Paid field (Figure 2–38).

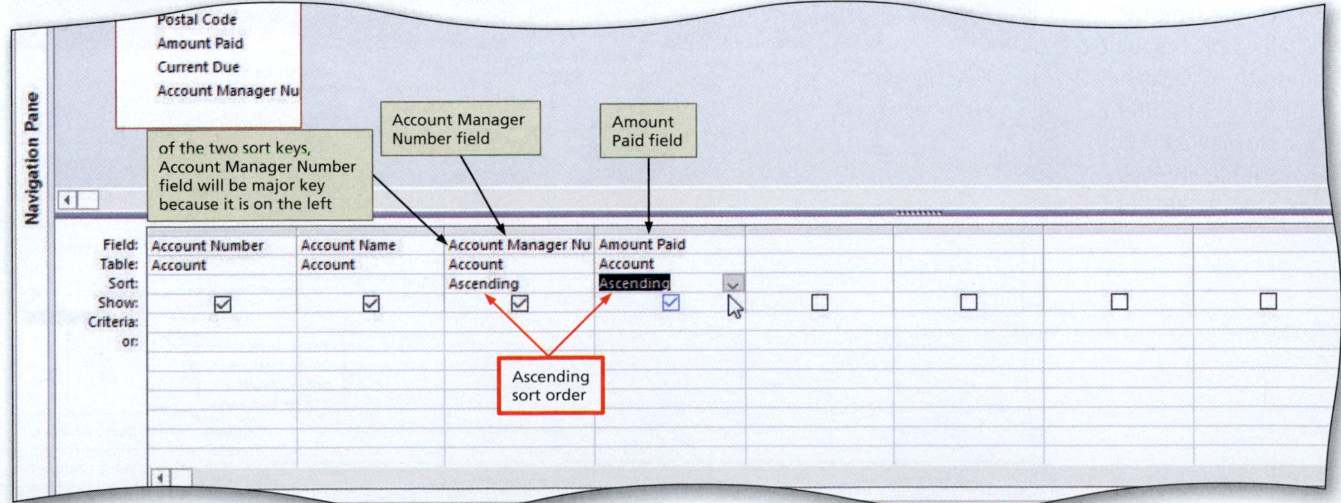

Figure 2–38

2

- Run the query (Figure 2–39).

Experiment

- Return to Design view and try other sort combinations for the Account Manager Number and Amount Paid fields, such as Ascending for Account Manager Number and Descending for Amount Paid. In each case, run the query to see the effect of the changes. When finished, select Ascending as the sort order for both fields.

Q&A What if the Amount Paid field is to the left of the Account Manager Number field?

It is important to remember that the major sort key must appear to the left of the minor sort key in the design grid. If you attempted to sort by amount paid within account manager number, but placed the Amount Paid field to the left of the Account Manager Number field, your results would not accurately represent the intended sort.

Format Painter
Toggle Filter
All
Views
Clipboard
Sort & Filter
Records
m02q07
Navigation Pane

AC #	Account Name	AM #	Amount Paid
KC156	Key Community College System	31	$10,952.25
TW001	Tri-County Waste Disposal	31	$15,345.00
JM323	JSP Manufacturing Inc.	31	$19,739.70
MI345	Midwest Library Consortium	31	$21,769.20
AC001	Avondale Community Bank	31	$24,752.25
LI268	Lars-Idsen Inc.	35	$0.00
ML008	Mums Landscaping Co.	35	$13,097.10
CO621	Codder Plastics Co.	35	$27,152.25
BL235	Bland Corp.	35	$29,836.65
KV089	KAL Veterinary Services	35	$34,036.50
EC010	Eco Clothes Inc.	58	$19,620.00
TP098	TAL Packaging Systems	58	$22,696.95
HL111	Halko Legal Associates	58	$25,702.20
CA043	Carlton Regional Clinic	58	$30,841.05
LC005	Lancaster County Hospital	58	$44,025.60

within group of accounts with the same account manager number, rows are sorted by amount paid in ascending order
overall order is by account manager number in ascending order

Figure 2–39

- Save the query as m02q08.

CONSIDER THIS

Is there any way to sort the records in this same order, but have the Amount Paid field appear to the left of the Account Manager Number field in the query results?

Yes. Remove the check mark from the Account Manager Number field, and then add an additional Account Manager Number field at the end of the query. The first Account Manager Number field will be used for sorting but will not appear in the results. The second will appear in the results, but will not be involved in the sorting process.

CONSIDER THIS

How do you approach the creation of a query that might involve sorting?

Examine the query or request to see if it contains words such as *order* or *sort*. Such words imply that the order of the query results is important. If so, you need to sort the query.

- If sorting is required, identify the field or fields on which the results are to be sorted. In the request, look for language such as *ordered by* or *sort the results by*, both of which would indicate that the specified field is a sort key.
- If using multiple sort keys, determine the major and minor keys. If you are using two sort keys, determine which one is the more important, or the major key. Look for language such as *sort by amount paid within account manager number*, which implies that the overall order is by account manager number. In this case, the Account Manager Number field would be the major sort key and the Amount Paid field would be the minor sort key.
- Determine sort order. Words such as *increasing*, *ascending*, or *low-to-high* imply Ascending order. Words such as *decreasing*, *descending*, or *high-to-low* imply Descending order. Sorting in *alphabetical order* implies Ascending order. If there were no words to imply a particular order, you would typically use Ascending.
- Examine the query or request to see if there are any special restrictions. One common restriction is to exclude duplicates. Another common restriction is to list only a certain number of records, such as the first five records.

To Create a Top-Values Query

Rather than show all the results of a query, you may want to show only a specified number of records or a percentage of records. ***Why?*** *You might not need to see all the records, just enough to get a general idea of the results.* Creating a **top-values query** allows you to restrict the number of records that appear. When you sort records, you can limit results to those records having the highest (descending sort) or lowest (ascending sort) values. To do so, first create a query that sorts the data in the desired order. Next, use the Return box on the Design tab to change the number of records to be included from All to the desired number or percentage.

The following steps create a query for PrattLast Associates that shows only the first five records that were included in the results of the previous query. The steps also save the resulting query with a new name.

1

- Return to Design view.
- If necessary, click Design on the ribbon to display the Design tab.
- Click the Return arrow (Query Tools Design tab | Query Setup group) to display the Return menu (Figure 2–40).

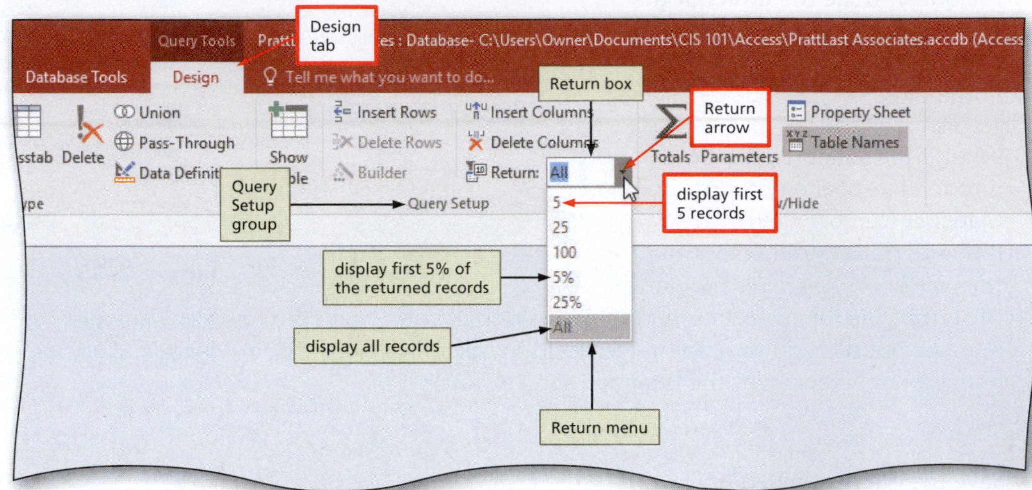

Figure 2–40

2

- Click 5 in the Return menu to specify that the query results should contain the first five rows.

Q&A Could I have typed the 5? What about other numbers that do not appear in the list?
Yes, you could have typed the 5. For numbers not appearing in the list, you must type the number.

- Run the query (Figure 2–41).

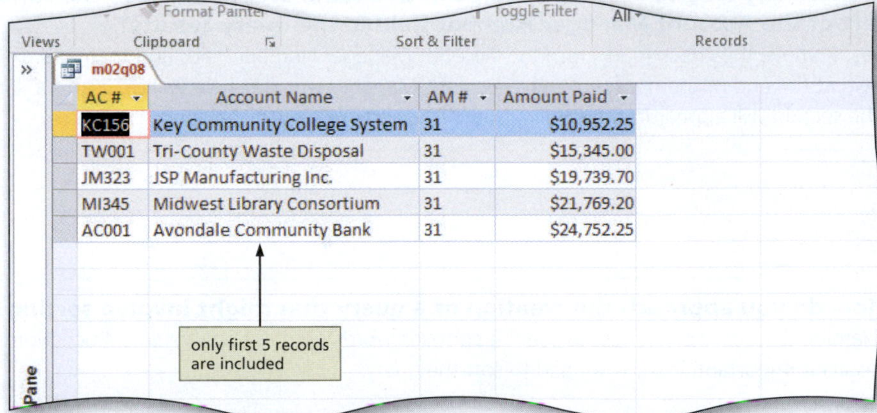

Figure 2–41

3

- Save the query as m02q09.
- Close the query.

Q&A Do I need to close the query before creating my next query?
Not necessarily. When you use a top-values query, however, it is important to change the value in the Return box back to All. If you do not change the Return value back to All, the previous value will remain in effect. Consequently, you might not get all the records you should in the next query. A good practice whenever you use a top-values query is to close the query as soon as you are done. That way, you will begin your next query from scratch, which ensures that the value is reset to All.

Joining Tables

In designing a query, you need to determine whether more than one table is required. For example, if the question being asked involves data from both the Account and Account Manager tables, then both tables are required for the query. For example, you might want a query that gives the number and name of each account (from the Account table) along with the number and name of the account's account manager (from the Account Manager table). Both the Account and Account Manager tables are required for this query. You need to **join** the tables to find records in the two tables that have identical values in matching fields (Figure 2–42). In this example, you need to find records in the Account table and the Account Manager table that have the same value in the Account Manager Number fields.

BTW

Ad Hoc Relationships

When you join tables in a query, you are creating an ad hoc relationship, that is, a relationship between tables created for a specific purpose. In Module 3, you will create general-purpose relationships using the Relationships window.

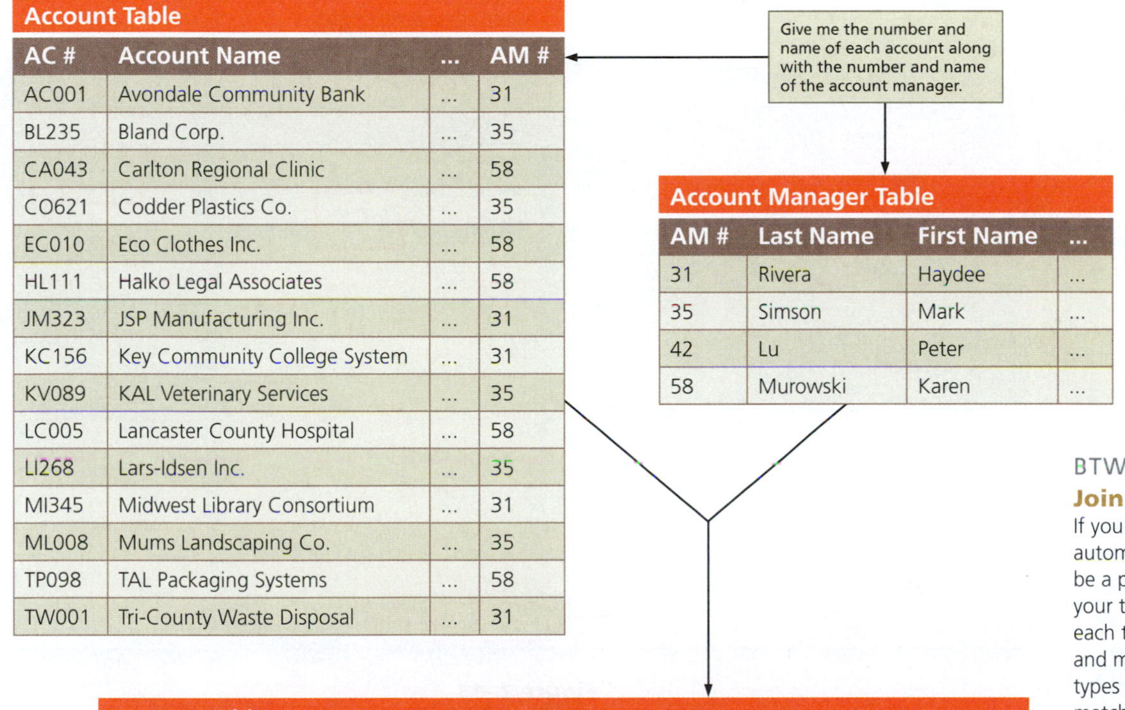

Account Table

AC #	Account Name	...	AM #
AC001	Avondale Community Bank	...	31
BL235	Bland Corp.	...	35
CA043	Carlton Regional Clinic	...	58
CO621	Codder Plastics Co.	...	35
EC010	Eco Clothes Inc.	...	58
HL111	Halko Legal Associates	...	58
JM323	JSP Manufacturing Inc.	...	31
KC156	Key Community College System	...	31
KV089	KAL Veterinary Services	...	35
LC005	Lancaster County Hospital	...	58
LI268	Lars-Idsen Inc.	...	35
MI345	Midwest Library Consortium	...	31
ML008	Mums Landscaping Co.	...	35
TP098	TAL Packaging Systems	...	58
TW001	Tri-County Waste Disposal	...	31

Account Manager Table

AM #	Last Name	First Name	...
31	Rivera	Haydee	...
35	Simson	Mark	...
42	Lu	Peter	...
58	Murowski	Karen	...

Account Table

AC #	Account Name	...	AM #	Last Name	First Name	...
AC001	Avondale Community Bank	...	31	Rivera	Haydee	...
BL235	Bland Corp.	...	35	Simson	Mark	...
CA043	Carlton Regional Clinic	...	58	Murowski	Karen	...
CO621	Codder Plastics Co.	...	35	Simson	Mark	...
EC010	Eco Clothes Inc.	...	58	Murowski	Karen	...
HL111	Halko Legal Associates	...	58	Murowski	Karen	...
JM323	JSP Manufacturing Inc.	...	31	Rivera	Haydee	...
KV089	KAL Veterinary Services	...	35	Simson	Mark	...
KC156	Key Community College System	...	31	Rivera	Haydee	...
LC005	Lancaster County Hospital	...	58	Murowski	Karen	...
LI268	Lars-Idsen Inc.	...	35	Simson	Mark	...
MI345	Midwest Library Consortium	...	31	Rivera	Haydee	...
ML008	Mums Landscaping Co.	...	35	Simson	Mark	...
TP098	TAL Packaging Systems	...	58	Murowski	Karen	...
TW001	Tri-County Waste Disposal	...	31	Rivera	Haydee	...

Figure 2–42

BTW

Join Line

If you do not get a join line automatically, there may be a problem with one of your table designs. Open each table in Design view and make sure that the data types are the same for the matching field in both tables and that one of the matching fields is the primary key in a table. Correct these errors and create the query again.

BTW

Join Types

The type of join that finds records from both tables that have identical values in matching fields is called an inner join. An inner join is the default join in Access. Outer joins are used to show all the records in one table as well as the common records; that is, the records that share the same value in the join field. In a left outer join, all rows from the table on the left are included. In a right outer join, all rows from the table on the right are included.

To Join Tables

If you have determined that you need to join tables, you first will bring field lists for both tables to the upper pane of the Query window while working in Design view. Access will draw a line, called a **join line**, between matching fields in the two tables, indicating that the tables are related. You then can select fields from either table. Access joins the tables automatically.

The first step is to create a new query and add the Account Manager table to the query. Then, add the Account table to the query. A join line should appear, connecting the Account Manager Number fields in the two field lists. ***Why might the join line not appear?*** *If the names of the matching fields differ from one table to the other, Access will not insert the line. You can insert it manually, however, by clicking one of the two matching fields and dragging the pointer to the other matching field.*

The following steps create a query to display information from both the Account table and the Account Manager table.

1

- Click Create on the ribbon to display the Create tab.
- Click the Query Design button (Create tab | Queries group) to create a new query.
- If necessary, click the Account Manager table (Show Table dialog box) to select the table.
- Click the Add button (Show Table dialog box) to add a field list for the Account Manager Table to the query (Figure 2–43).

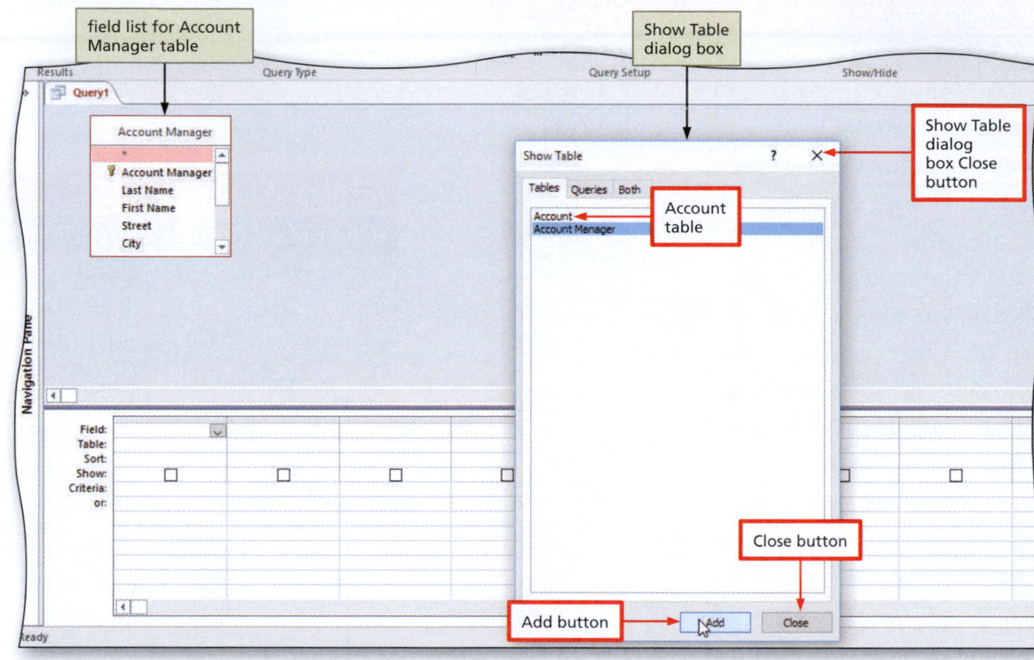

Figure 2–43

2

- Click the Account table (Show Table dialog box).
- Click the Add button (Show Table dialog box) to add a field list for the Account table.
- Close the Show Table dialog box by clicking the Close button.
- Expand the size of the two field lists so all the fields in the Account Manager and Account tables appear (Figure 2–44).

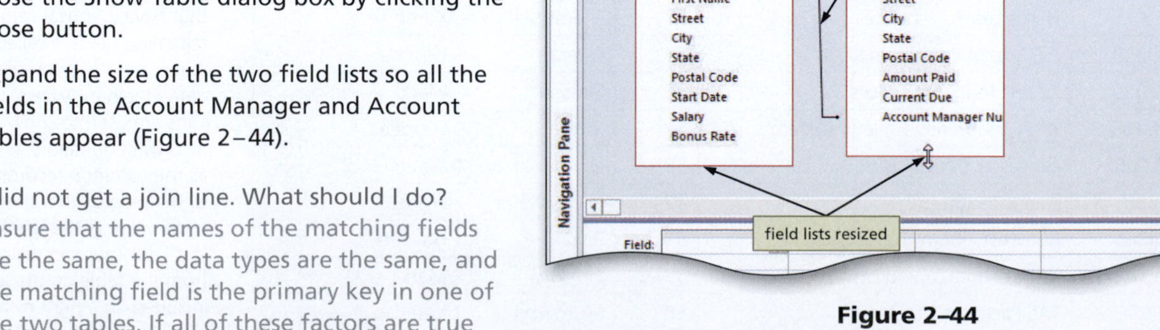

Figure 2–44

Q&A I did not get a join line. What should I do?
Ensure that the names of the matching fields are the same, the data types are the same, and the matching field is the primary key in one of the two tables. If all of these factors are true and you still do not have a join line, you can produce one by pointing to a matching field and dragging to the other matching field.

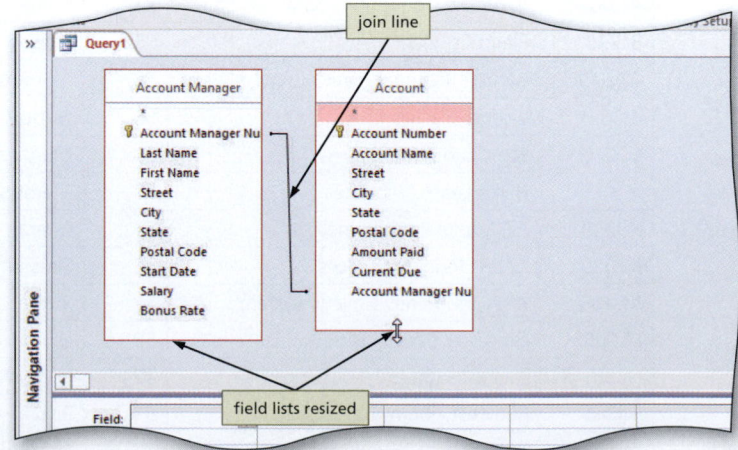

3

- In the design grid, include the Account Manager Number, Last Name, and First Name fields from the Account Manager Table as well as the Account Number and Account Name fields from the Account table.
- Select Ascending as the sort order for both the Account Manager Number field and the Account Number field (Figure 2–45).

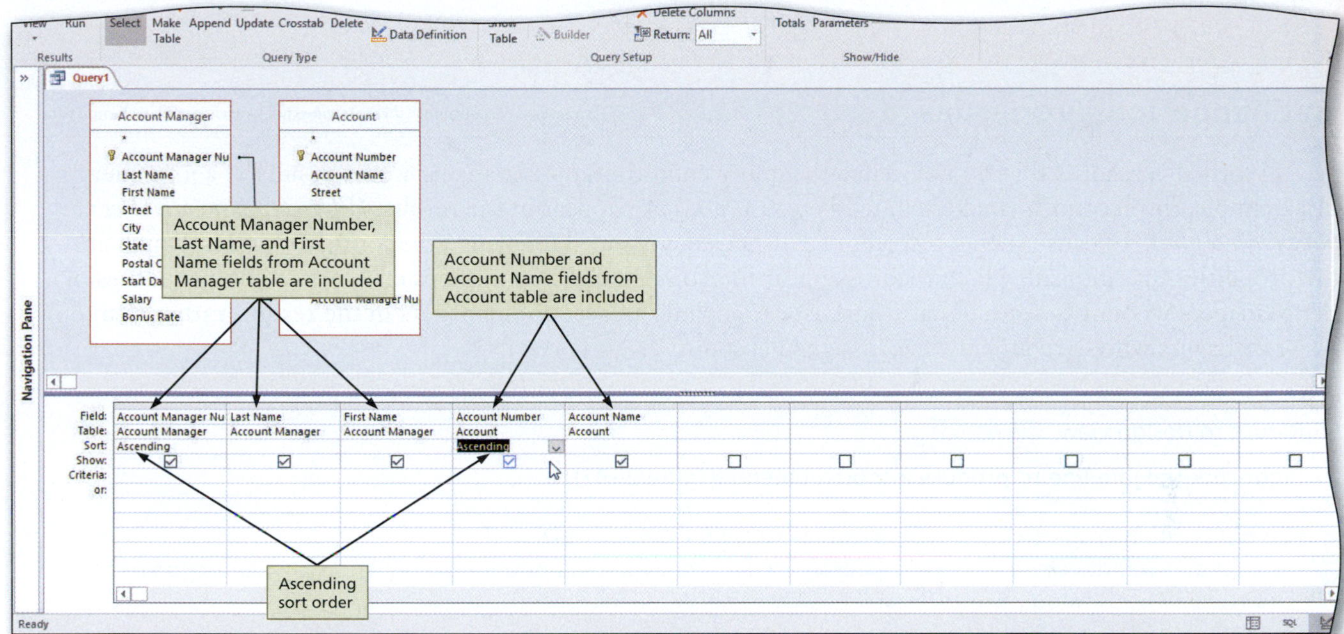

Figure 2–45

4

- Run the query (Figure 2–46).

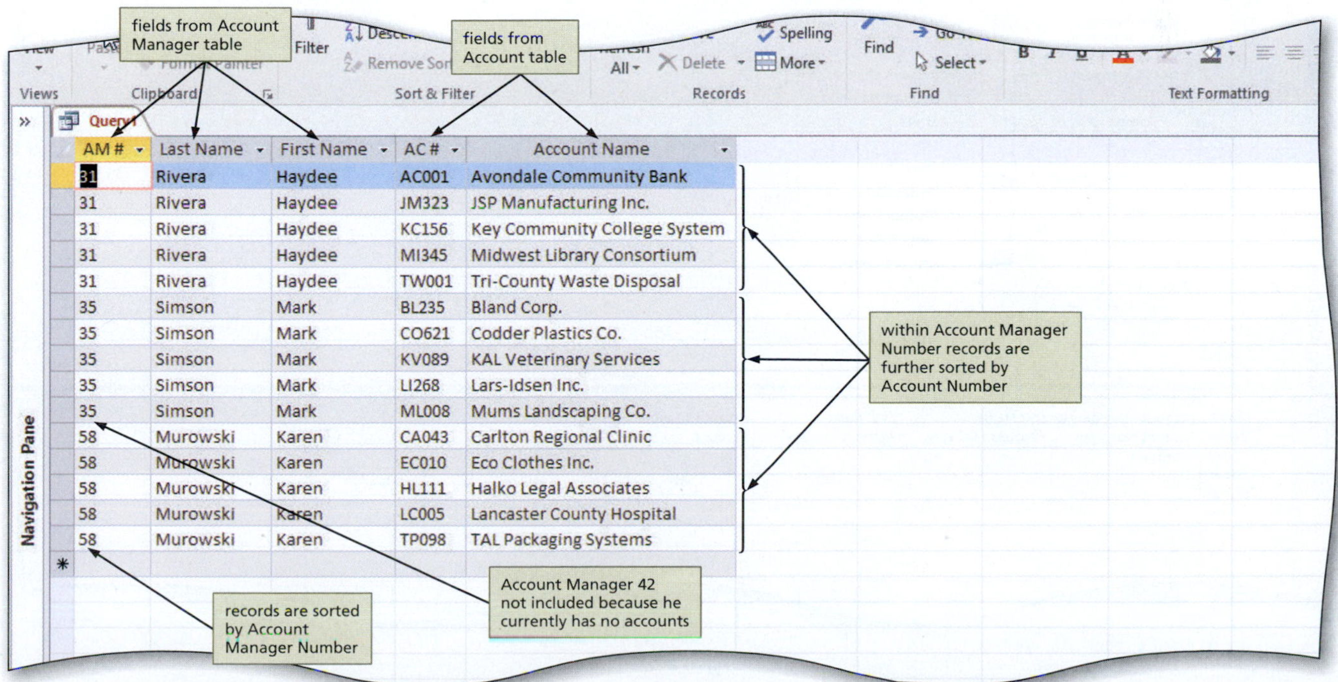

Figure 2–46

- Click the Save button on the Quick Access Toolbar to display the Save As dialog box.
- Type **`Manager-Account Query`** as the query name.
- Click the OK button (Save As dialog box) to save the query.

To Change Join Properties

1 CREATE QUERIES | 2 USE CRITERIA | 3 SORT DATA | 4 JOIN TABLES | 5 EXPORT RESULTS
6 PERFORM CALCULATIONS | 7 CREATE CROSSTAB | 8 CUSTOMIZE NAVIGATION PANE

Normally, records that do not match the query conditions do not appear in the results of a join query. For example, the account manager named Peter Lu does not appear in the results. ***Why?*** *He currently does not have any accounts.* To cause such a record to be displayed, you need to change the **join properties**, which are the properties that indicate which records appear in a join. The following steps change the join properties of the Manager-Account Query so that PrattLast can include all account managers in the results, rather than only those managers who have already been assigned accounts.

- Return to Design view.
- Right-click the join line to produce a shortcut menu (Figure 2–47).

Q&A

I do not see Join Properties on my shortcut menu. What should I do?

If Join Properties does not appear on your shortcut menu, you did not point to the appropriate portion of the join line. You will need to point to the correct (middle) portion and right-click again.

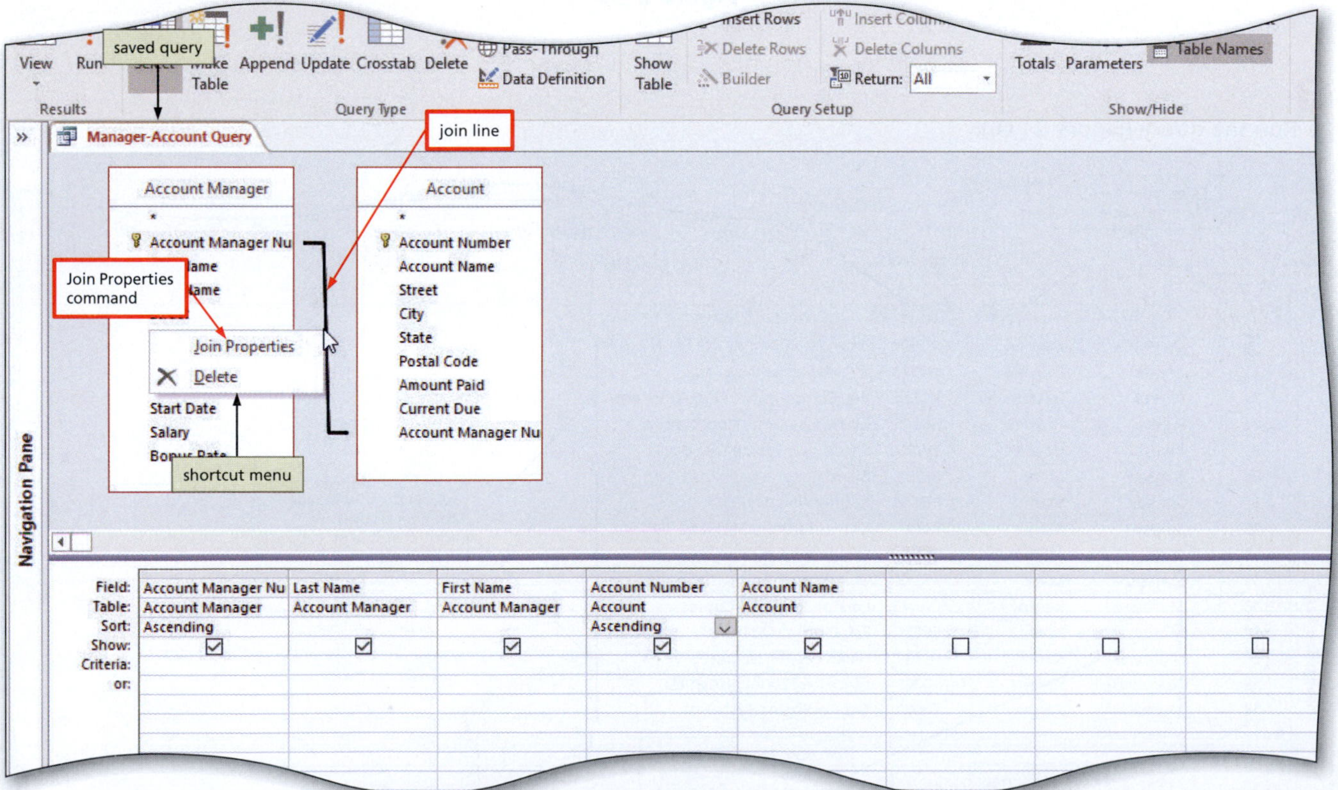

Figure 2–47

2

- Click Join Properties on the shortcut menu to display the Join Properties dialog box (Figure 2–48).

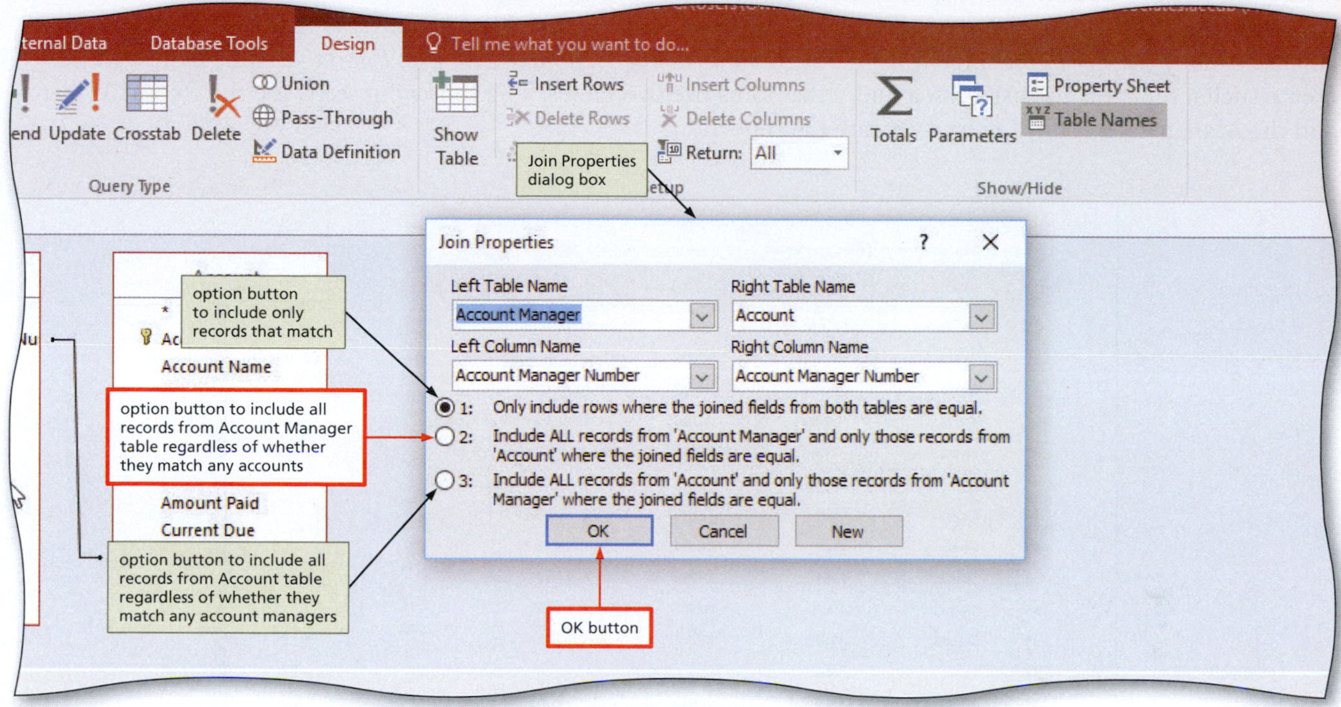

Figure 2–48

3

- Click option button 2 (Join Properties dialog box) to include all records from the Account Manager Table regardless of whether they match any accounts.
- Click the OK button (Join Properties dialog box) to modify the join properties.
- Run the query (Figure 2–49).

Experiment

- Return to Design view, change the Join properties, and select option button 3. Run the query to see the effect of this option. When done, return to Design view, change the join properties, and once again select option button 2.

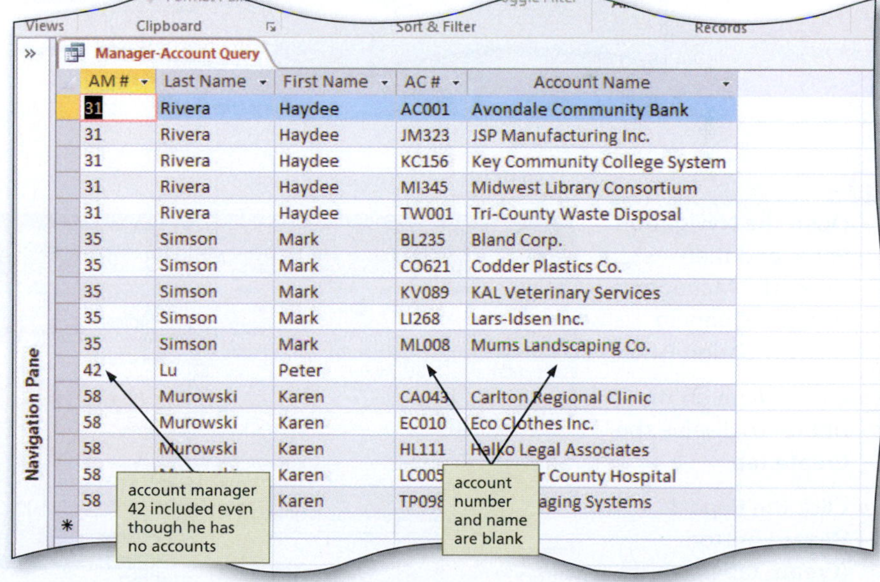

AM #	Last Name	First Name	AC #	Account Name
31	Rivera	Haydee	AC001	Avondale Community Bank
31	Rivera	Haydee	JM323	JSP Manufacturing Inc.
31	Rivera	Haydee	KC156	Key Community College System
31	Rivera	Haydee	MI345	Midwest Library Consortium
31	Rivera	Haydee	TW001	Tri-County Waste Disposal
35	Simson	Mark	BL235	Bland Corp.
35	Simson	Mark	CO621	Codder Plastics Co.
35	Simson	Mark	KV089	KAL Veterinary Services
35	Simson	Mark	LI268	Lars-Idsen Inc.
35	Simson	Mark	ML008	Mums Landscaping Co.
42	Lu	Peter		
58	Murowski	Karen	CA043	Carlton Regional Clinic
58	Murowski	Karen	EC010	Eco Clothes Inc.
58	Murowski	Karen	HL111	Halko Legal Associates
58		Karen	LC005	County Hospital
58		Karen	TP098	aging Systems

Figure 2–49

4

- Click the Save button on the Quick Access Toolbar to save the changes to the query.
- Close the Manager-Account Query.

Q&A I see a dialog box that asks if I want to save the query. What should I do?
Click the OK button to save the query.

To Create a Report from a Query

You can use queries in the creation of reports. The report in Figure 2–50 involves data from more than one table. ***Why?*** *The Last Name and First Name fields are in the Account Manager table. The Account Number and Account Name fields are in the Account table. The Account Manager Number field is in both tables.* The easiest way to create such a report is to base it on a query that joins the two tables. The following steps use the Report Wizard and the Manager-Account Query to create the report.

Manager-Account Report

AM #	Last Name	First Name	AC #	Account Name
31	Rivera	Haydee	AC001	Avondale Community Bank
31	Rivera	Haydee	JM323	JSP Manufacturing Inc.
31	Rivera	Haydee	KC156	Key Community College System
31	Rivera	Haydee	MI345	Midwest Library Consortium
31	Rivera	Haydee	TW001	Tri-County Waste Disposal
35	Simson	Mark	BL235	Bland Corp.
35	Simson	Mark	CO621	Codder Plastics Co.
35	Simson	Mark	KV089	KAL Veterinary Services
35	Simson	Mark	LI268	Lars-Idsen Inc.
35	Simson	Mark	ML008	Mums Landscaping Co.
42	Lu	Peter		
58	Murowski	Karen	CA043	Carlton Regional Clinic
58	Murowski	Karen	EC010	Eco Clothes Inc.
58	Murowski	Karen	HL111	Halko Legal Associates
58	Murowski	Karen	LC005	Lancaster County Hospital
58	Murowski	Karen	TP098	TAL Packaging Systems

Figure 2–50

1

- Open the Navigation Pane, and then select the Manager-Account Query in the Navigation Pane.
- Click Create on the ribbon to display the Create tab.
- Click the Report Wizard button (Create tab | Reports group) to display the Report Wizard dialog box (Figure 2–51).

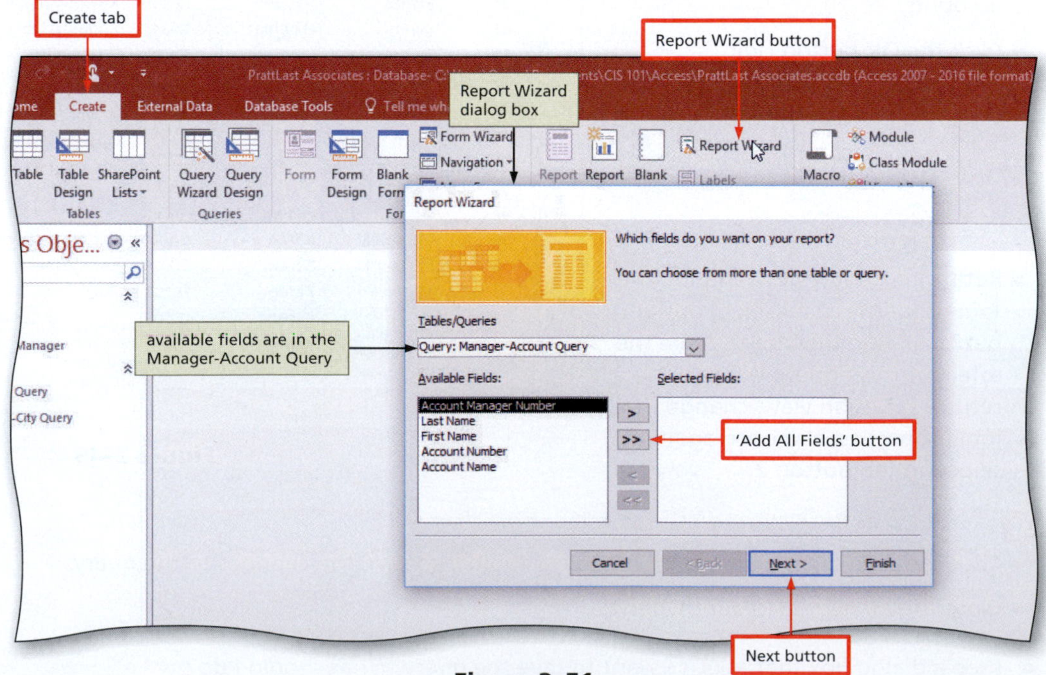

Figure 2–51

2

- Click the 'Add All Fields' button (Report Wizard dialog box) to add all the fields in the Manager-Account Query.
- Click the Next button to display the next Report Wizard screen (Figure 2–52).

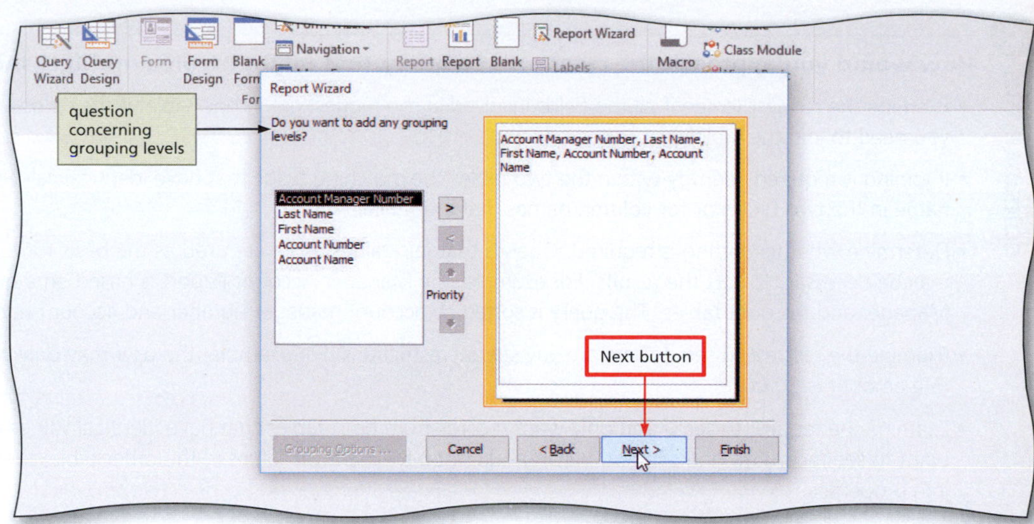

Figure 2–52

3

- Because you will not specify any grouping, click the Next button in the Report Wizard dialog box to display the next Report Wizard screen.
- Because you already specified the sort order in the query, click the Next button again to display the next Report Wizard screen.
- Make sure that Tabular is selected as the Layout and Portrait is selected as the Orientation.
- Click the Next button to display the next Report Wizard screen.
- Erase the current title, and then type **Manager-Account Report** as the new title.
- Click the Finish button to produce the report (Figure 2–53).

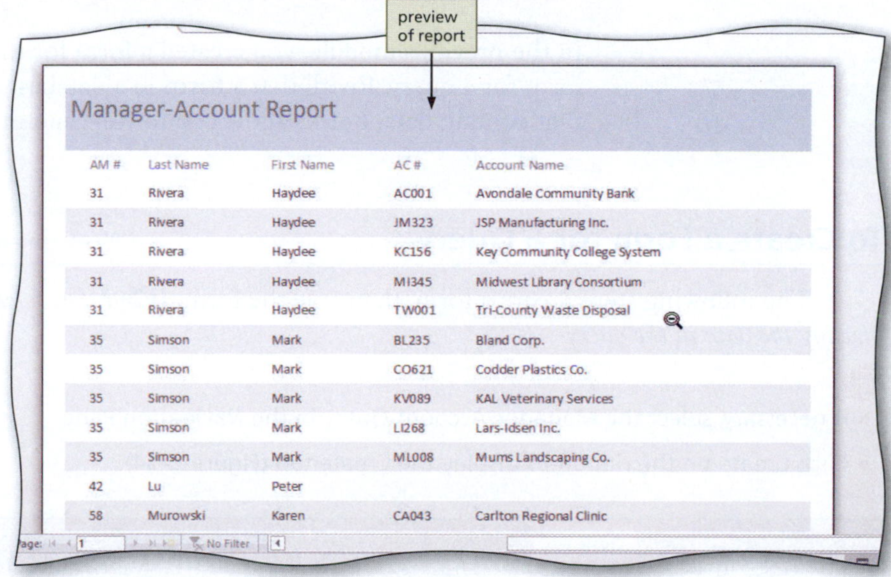

Figure 2–53

Q&A My report is very small and does not look like the one in the figure. What should I do?
Click the pointer, which should look like a magnifying glass, anywhere in the report to magnify the report.

- Close the Manager-Account Report.

To Print a Report

The following steps print a hard copy of the report.

1. With the Manager-Account Report selected in the Navigation Pane, click File on the ribbon to open the Backstage view.
2. Click the Print tab in the Backstage view to display the Print gallery.
3. Click the Quick Print button to print the report.

CONSIDER THIS

How would you approach the creation of a query that might involve multiple tables?

- Examine the request to see if all the fields involved in the request are in one table. If the fields are in two (or more) tables, you need to join the tables.
- If joining is required, identify within the two tables the matching fields that have identical values. Look for the same column name in the two tables or for column names that are similar.
- Determine whether sorting is required. Queries that join tables often are used as the basis for a report. If this is the case, it may be necessary to sort the results. For example, the Manager-Account Report is based on a query that joins the Account Manager and Account tables. The query is sorted by account manager number and account number.
- Examine the request to see if there are any special restrictions. For example, the user may only want accounts whose current due amount is $0.00.
- Examine the request to see if you only want records from both tables that have identical values in matching fields. If you want to see records in one of the tables that do not have identical values in the other table, then you need to change the join properties.

Creating a Form for a Query

In the previous module, you created a form for the Account table. You can also create a form for a query. Recall that a **form** in a database is a formatted document with fields that contain data. Forms allow you to view and maintain data.

To Create a Form for a Query

The following steps create a form, then save the form. ***Why?*** *The form will be available for future use in viewing the data in the query.*

- If necessary, select the Manager-Account Query in the Navigation Pane.
- Click Create on the ribbon to display the Create tab (Figure 2–54).

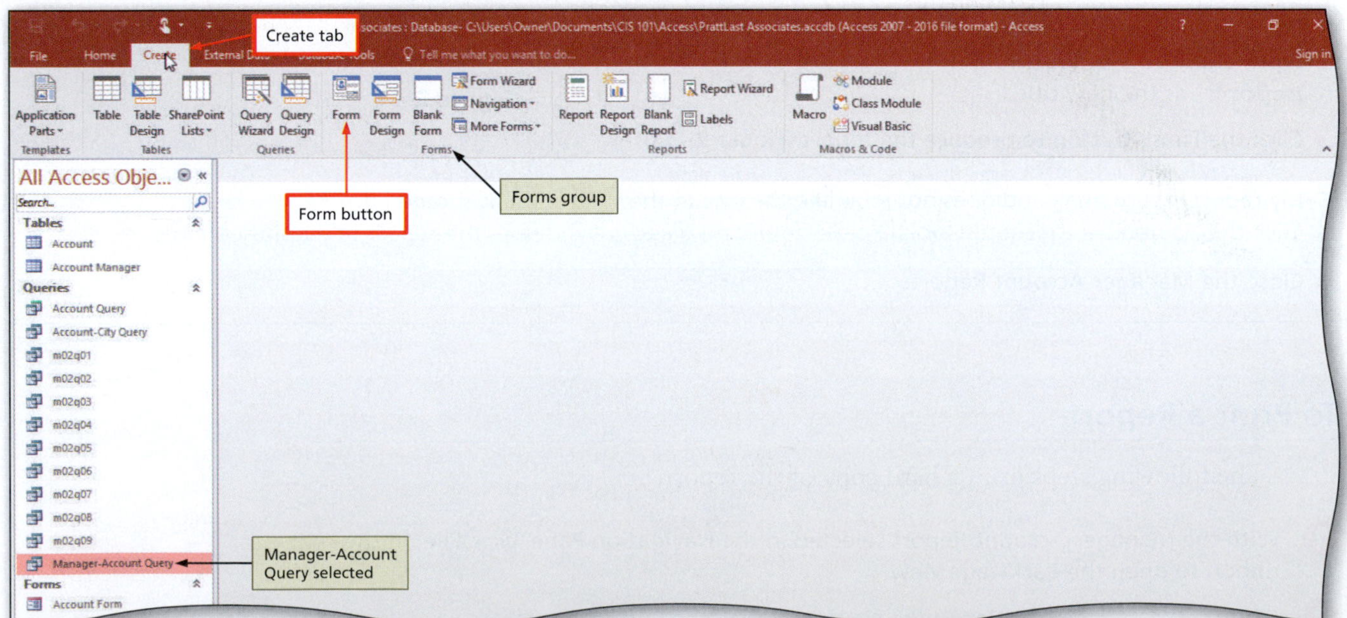

Figure 2–54

2

- Click the Form button (Create tab | Forms group) to create a simple form (Figure 2–55).

Q&A I see a field list also. What should I do?
Click the Close button for the Field List.

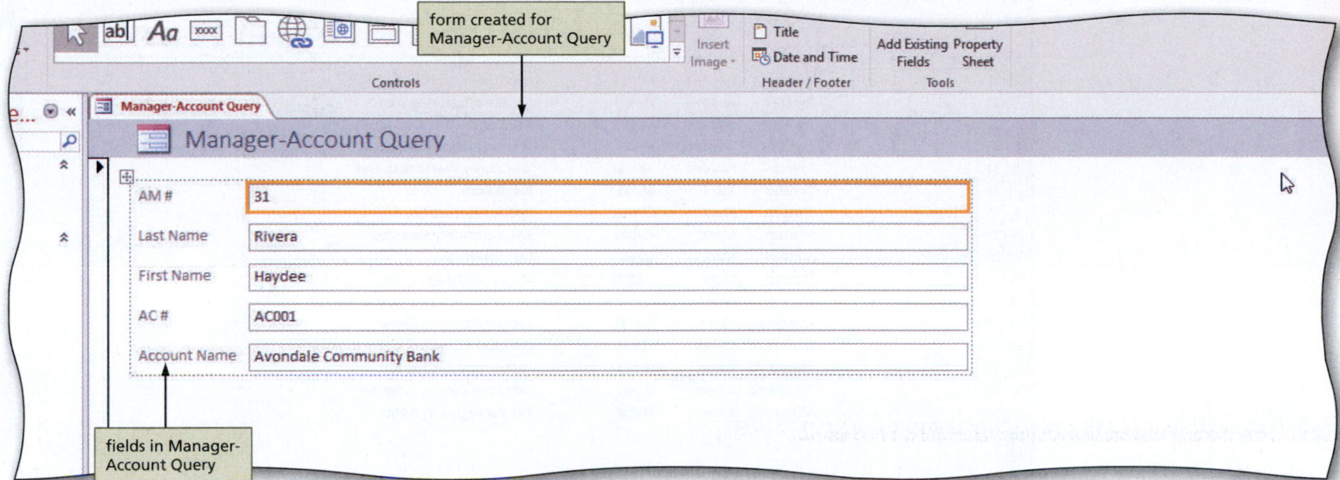

Figure 2–55

3

- Click the Save button on the Quick Access Toolbar to display the Save As dialog box.
- Type `Manager-Account Form` as the form name.
- Click the OK button to save the form.
- Click the Close button for the form to close the form.

Using a Form

After you have saved a form, you can use it at any time by right-clicking the form in the Navigation Pane and then clicking Open on the shortcut menu. If you plan to use the form to enter data, you must ensure you are viewing the form in Form view.

Break Point: If you wish to take a break, this is a good place to do so. You can exit Access now. To resume later, run Access, open the database called PrattLast Associates, and continue following the steps from this location forward.

Exporting Data From Access to Other Applications

You can **export**, or copy, tables or queries from an Access database so that another application (for example, Excel or Word) can use the data. The application that will receive the data determines the export process to be used. You can export to text files in a variety of formats. For applications to which you cannot directly export data, you often can export an appropriately formatted text file that the other application can import. Figure 2–56 shows the workbook produced by exporting the Manager-Account Query to Excel. The columns in the workbook have been resized to best fit the data.

BTW
Exporting Data
You frequently need to export data so that it can be used in other applications and by other users in an organization. For example, the Accounting department might require financial data in an Excel format to perform certain financial functions. Marketing might require a list of account names and addresses in Word or RTF format for marketing campaigns.

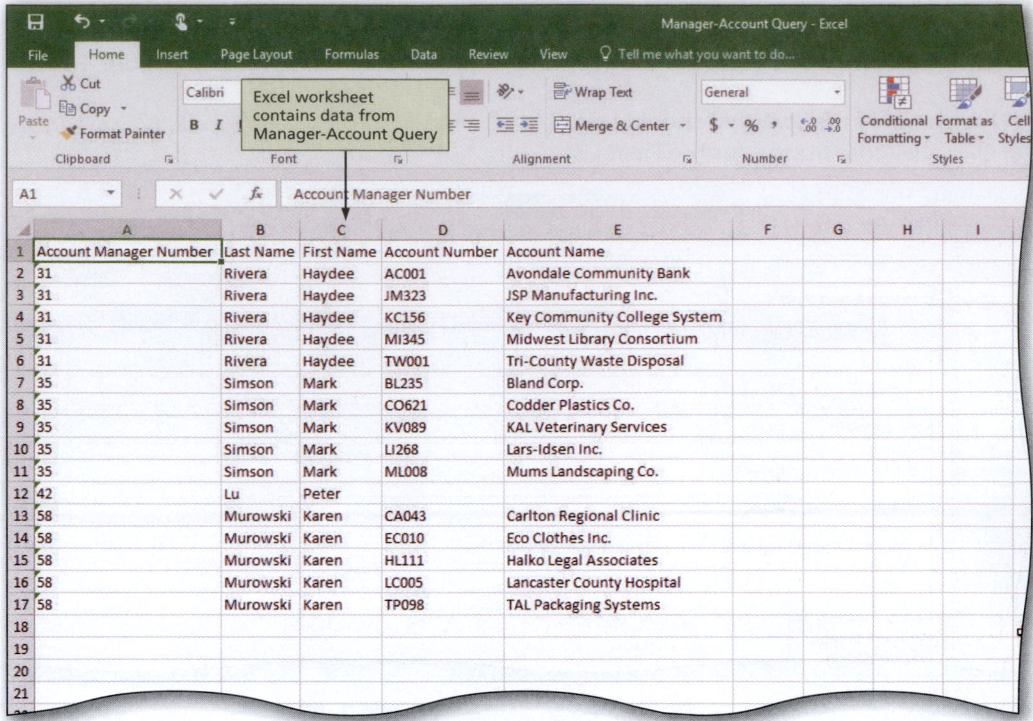

	A	B	C	D	E
1	Account Manager Number	Last Name	First Name	Account Number	Account Name
2	31	Rivera	Haydee	AC001	Avondale Community Bank
3	31	Rivera	Haydee	JM323	JSP Manufacturing Inc.
4	31	Rivera	Haydee	KC156	Key Community College System
5	31	Rivera	Haydee	MI345	Midwest Library Consortium
6	31	Rivera	Haydee	TW001	Tri-County Waste Disposal
7	35	Simson	Mark	BL235	Bland Corp.
8	35	Simson	Mark	CO621	Codder Plastics Co.
9	35	Simson	Mark	KV089	KAL Veterinary Services
10	35	Simson	Mark	LI268	Lars-Idsen Inc.
11	35	Simson	Mark	ML008	Mums Landscaping Co.
12	42	Lu	Peter		
13	58	Murowski	Karen	CA043	Carlton Regional Clinic
14	58	Murowski	Karen	EC010	Eco Clothes Inc.
15	58	Murowski	Karen	HL111	Halko Legal Associates
16	58	Murowski	Karen	LC005	Lancaster County Hospital
17	58	Murowski	Karen	TP098	TAL Packaging Systems

Figure 2–56

To Export Data to Excel

1 CREATE QUERIES | 2 USE CRITERIA | 3 SORT DATA | 4 JOIN TABLES | 5 EXPORT RESULTS
6 PERFORM CALCULATIONS | 7 CREATE CROSSTAB | 8 CUSTOMIZE NAVIGATION PANE

For PrattLast Associates to make the Manager-Account Query available to Excel users, it needs to export the data. To export data to Excel, select the table or query to be exported and then click the Excel button in the Export group on the External Data tab. The following steps export the Manager-Account Query to Excel and save the export steps. ***Why save the export steps?*** *By saving the export steps, you could easily repeat the export process whenever you like without going through all the steps.* You would use the saved steps to export data in the future by clicking the Saved Exports button (External Data tab | Export group) and then selecting the steps you saved.

1

- If necessary, click the Manager-Account Query in the Navigation Pane to select it.
- Click External Data on the ribbon to display the External Data tab (Figure 2–57).

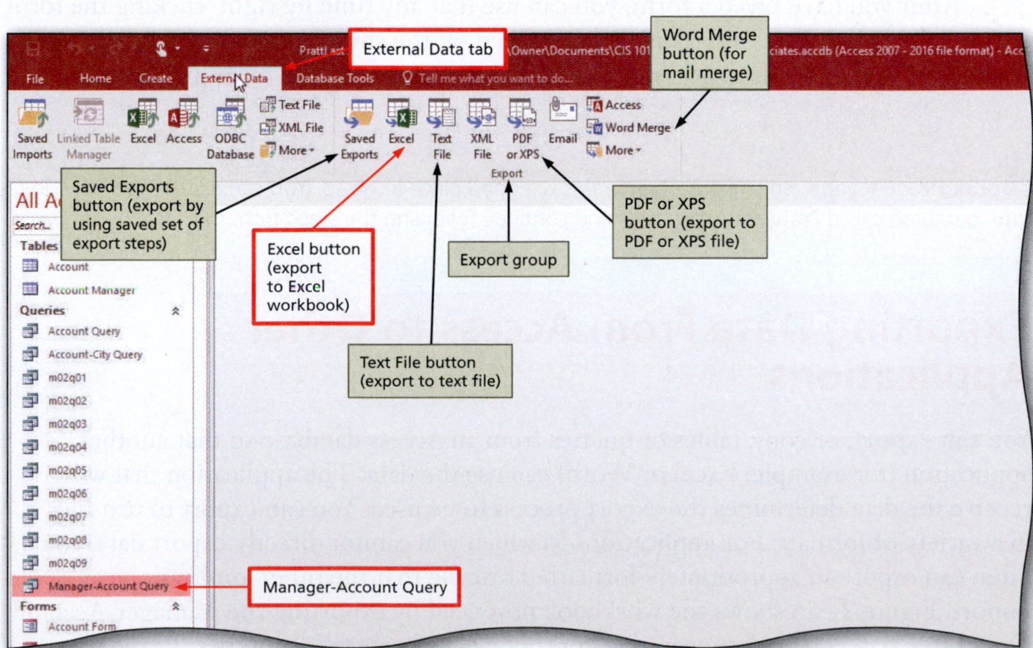

Figure 2–57

2

- Click the Excel button (External Data tab | Export group) to display the Export-Excel Spreadsheet dialog box.
- Click the Browse button (Export-Excel Spreadsheet dialog box), and then navigate to the location where you want to export the query (your hard disk, OneDrive, or other storage location).
- Confirm that the file format is Excel Workbook (*.xlsx), and the file name is Manager-Account Query, and then click the Save button (File Save dialog box) to select the file name and location (Figure 2–58).

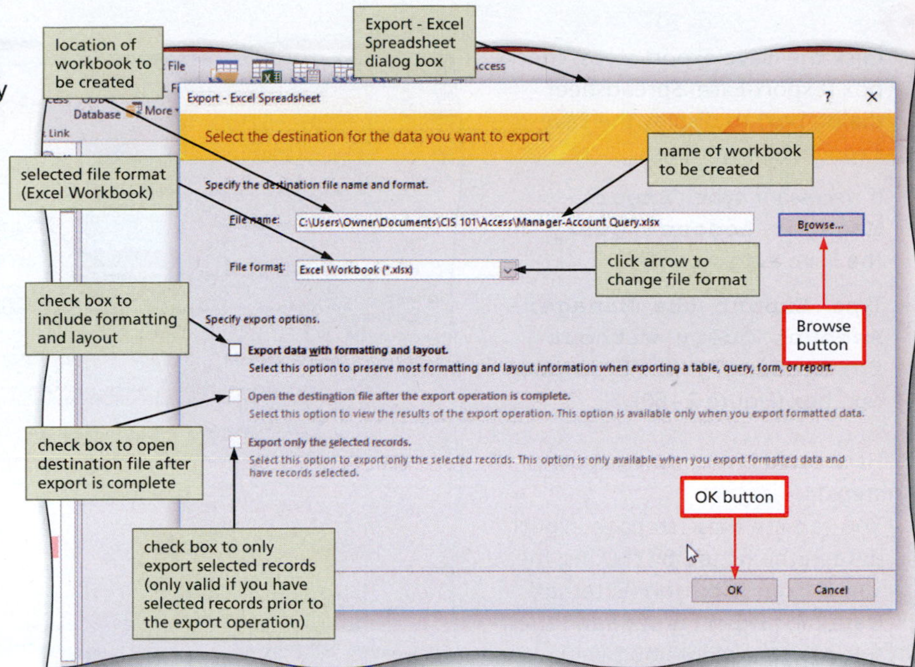

Figure 2–58

Q&A

Did I need to browse?
No. You could type the appropriate file location.

Could I change the name of the file?
You could change it. Simply replace the current file name with the one you want.

What if the file I want to export already exists?
Access will indicate that the file already exists and ask if you want to replace it. If you click the Yes button, the file you export will replace the old file. If you click the No button, you must either change the name of the export file or cancel the process.

- Click the OK button (Export-Excel Spreadsheet dialog box) to export the data (Figure 2–59).

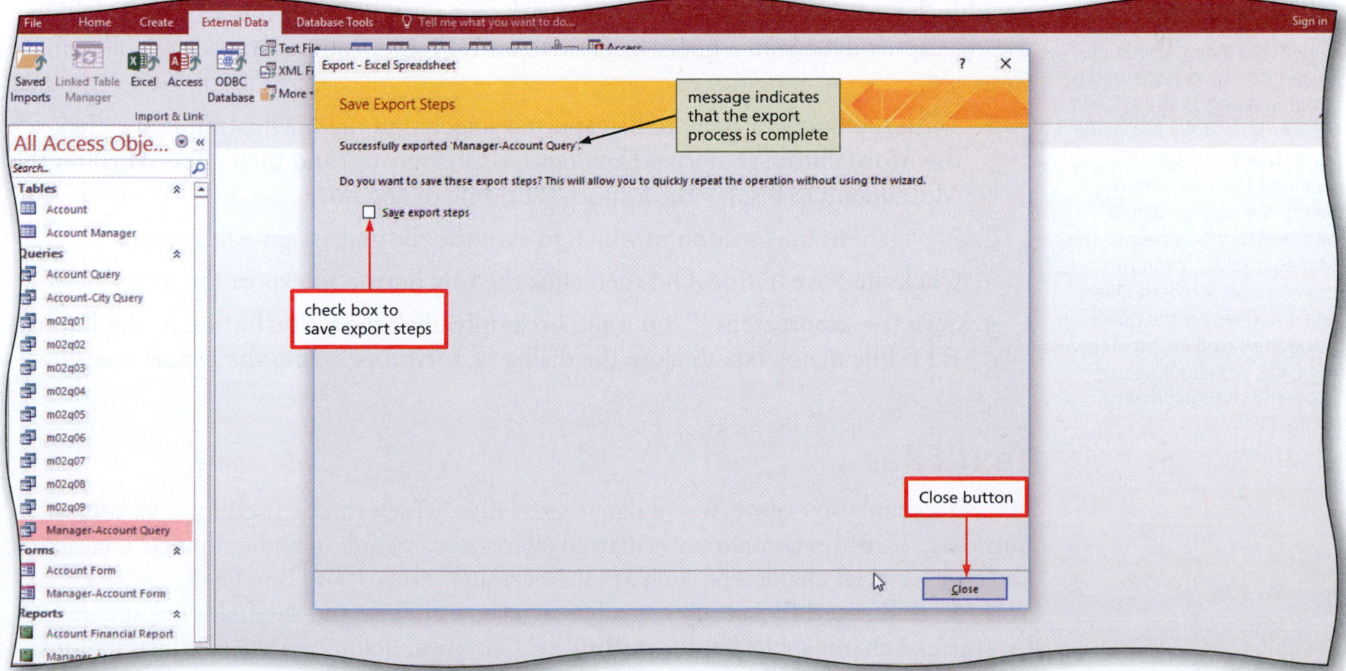

Figure 2–59

3

- Click the 'Save export steps' check box (Export-Excel Spreadsheet dialog box) to display the Save Export Steps options.
- If necessary, type `Export-Manager-Account Query` in the Save as text box.
- Type `Export the Manager-Account Query without formatting` in the Description text box (Figure 2–60).

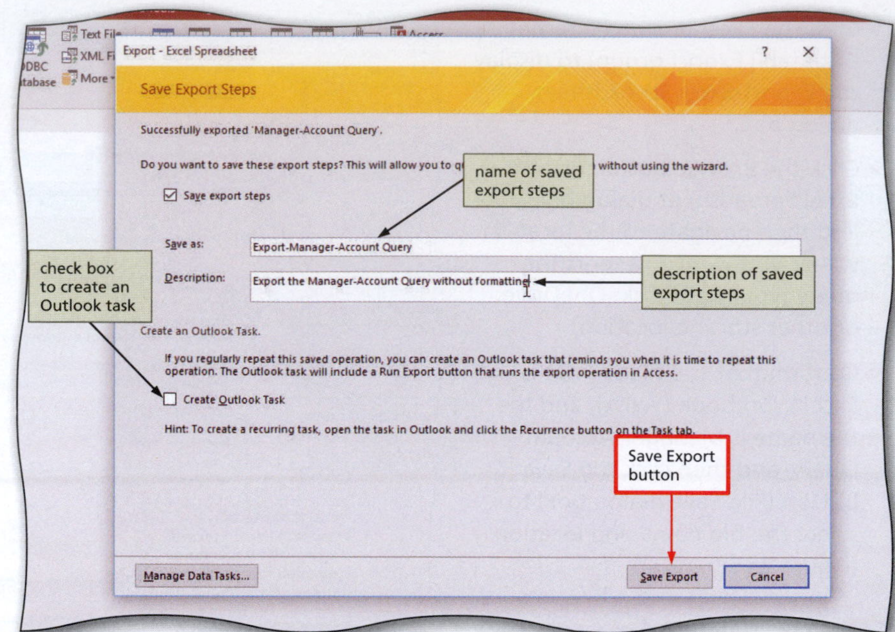

Figure 2–60

Q&A How could I re-use the export steps?

You can use these steps to export data in the future by clicking the Saved Exports button (External Data tab | Export group) and then selecting the steps you saved.

4

- Click the Save Export button (Export-Excel Spreadsheet dialog box) to save the export steps.

Other Ways

1. Right-click database object in Navigation Pane, click Export.

BTW

Saving Export Steps

Because query results are based on the data in the underlying tables, a change to an underlying table would result in a new query answer. For example, if the last name for account manager 35 changed from Simson to Smith, the change would be made in the Account Manager table. If you run the Manager-Account Query again and export the query using the saved export steps, the Excel workbook would show the changed name.

To Export Data to Word

It is not possible to export data from Access to the standard Word format. It is possible, however, to export the data as a rich text format (RTF) file, which Word can use. To export data from a query or table to an RTF file, you would use the following steps.

1. With the query or table to be exported selected in the Navigation Pane, click the More button (External Data tab | Export group) and then click Word on the More menu to display the Export-RTF File dialog box.
2. Navigate to the location in which to save the file and assign a file name.
3. Click the Save button, and then click the OK button to export the data.
4. Save the export steps if you want, or simply click the Close button in the Export-RTF File dialog box to close the dialog box without saving the export steps.

Text Files

You can also export Access data to text files, which can be used for a variety of purposes. Text files contain unformatted characters, including alphanumeric characters, and some special characters, such as tabs, carriage returns, and line feeds.

In **delimited files**, each record is on a separate line and the fields are separated by a special character, called the **delimiter**. Common delimiters are tabs, semicolons, commas, and spaces. You can also choose any other value that does not appear within the field contents as the delimiter. The comma-separated values (CSV) file often used in Excel is an example of a delimited file.

In **fixed-width files**, the width of any field is the same on every record. For example, if the width of the first field on the first record is 12 characters, the width of the first field on every other record must also be 12 characters.

To Export Data to a Text File

When exporting data to a text file, you can choose to export the data with formatting and layout. This option preserves much of the formatting and layout in tables, queries, forms, and reports. For forms and reports, this is the only option for exporting to a text file.

If you do not need to preserve the formatting, you can choose either delimited or fixed-width as the format for the exported file. The most common option, especially if formatting is not an issue, is delimited. You can choose the delimiter. You can also choose whether to include field names on the first row. In many cases, delimiting with a comma and including the field names is a good choice.

To export data from a table or query to a comma-delimited file in which the first row contains the column headings, you would use the following steps.

1. With the query or table to be exported selected in the Navigation Pane, click the Text File button (External Data tab | Export group) to display the Export-Text File dialog box.
2. Select the name and location for the file to be created.
3. If you need to preserve formatting and layout, be sure the 'Export data with formatting and layout' check box is checked. If you do not need to preserve formatting and layout, make sure the check box is not checked. Once you have made your selection, click the OK button in the Export-Text File dialog box.
4. To create a delimited file, be sure the Delimited option button is selected in the Export Text Wizard dialog box. To create a fixed-width file, be sure the Fixed Width option button is selected. Once you have made your selection, click the Next button.
5. a. If you are exporting to a delimited file, choose the delimiter that you want to separate your fields, such as a comma. Decide whether to include field names on the first row and, if so, click the 'Include Field Names on First Row' check box. If you want to select a text qualifier, select it in the Text Qualifier list. When you have made your selections, click the Next button.
   b. If you are exporting to a fixed-width file, review the position of the vertical lines that separate your fields. If any lines are not positioned correctly, follow the directions on the screen to reposition them. When you have finished, click the Next button.
6. Click the Finish button to export the data.
7. Save the export steps if you want, or simply click the Close button in the Export-Text File dialog box to close the dialog box without saving the export steps.

BTW

Distributing a Document

Instead of printing and distributing a hard copy of a document, you can distribute the document electronically. Options include sending the document via email; posting it on cloud storage (such as OneDrive) and sharing the file with others; posting it on social media, a blog, or other website; and sharing a link associated with an online location of the document. You also can create and share a PDF or XPS image of the document, so that users can view the file in Acrobat Reader or XPS Viewer instead of in Access.

Adding Criteria to a Join Query

Sometimes you will want to join tables, but you will not want to include all possible records. For example, you would like to create a report showing only those accounts whose amount paid is greater than $20,000.00. In this case, you would relate the tables and include fields just as you did before. You will also include criteria. To include only those accounts whose amount paid is more than $20,000.00, you will include >20000 as a criterion for the Amount Paid field.

To Restrict the Records in a Join

The following steps modify the Manager-Account Query so that the results for PrattLast Associates include a criterion. ***Why?*** *PrattLast wants to include only those accounts whose amount paid is more than $20,000.00.*

1

- Open the Navigation Pane, if necessary, and then right-click the Manager-Account Query to produce a shortcut menu.
- Click Design View on the shortcut menu to open the Manager-Account Query in Design view.
- Close the Navigation Pane.
- Add the Amount Paid field to the query.
- Type `>20000` as the criterion for the Amount Paid field (Figure 2–61).

Field:	Account Manager Nu	Last Name	First Name	Account Number	Account Name	Amount Paid
Table:	Account Manager	Account Manager	Account Manager	Account	Account	Account
Sort:	Ascending			Ascending		
Show:	☑	☑	☑	☑	☑	☑
Criteria:						>20000
or:						

criterion for Amount Paid field

amount paid must be greater than $20,000

Figure 2–61

2

- Run the query (Figure 2–62).

3

- Close the query.
- When asked if you want to save your changes, click the No button.

Q&A What would happen if I saved the changes?
The next time you used this query, you would only see accounts whose amount paid is more than $20,000.00.

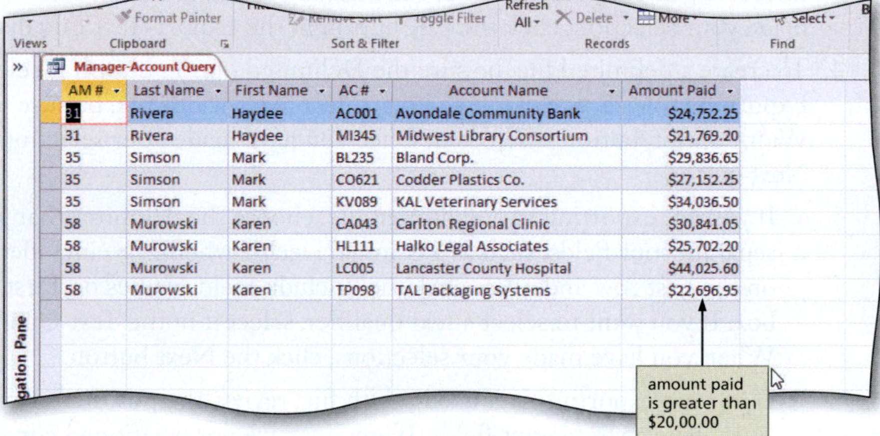

AM #	Last Name	First Name	AC #	Account Name	Amount Paid
31	Rivera	Haydee	AC001	Avondale Community Bank	$24,752.25
31	Rivera	Haydee	MI345	Midwest Library Consortium	$21,769.20
35	Simson	Mark	BL235	Bland Corp.	$29,836.65
35	Simson	Mark	CO621	Codder Plastics Co.	$27,152.25
35	Simson	Mark	KV089	KAL Veterinary Services	$34,036.50
58	Murowski	Karen	CA043	Carlton Regional Clinic	$30,841.05
58	Murowski	Karen	HL111	Halko Legal Associates	$25,702.20
58	Murowski	Karen	LC005	Lancaster County Hospital	$44,025.60
58	Murowski	Karen	TP098	TAL Packaging Systems	$22,696.95

Figure 2–62

BTW
Expression Builder
Access includes a tool to help you create complex expressions. If you click Build on the shortcut menu (see Figure 2–63), Access displays the Expression Builder dialog box, which includes an expression box, operator buttons, and expression elements. You can type parts of the expression directly and paste operator buttons and expression elements into the box. You also can use functions in expressions.

Calculations

If a special calculation is required for a query, you need to determine whether the calculation is an **individual record calculation** (for example, adding the values in two fields for one record) or a **group calculation** (for example, finding the total of the values in a particular field on all the records).

PrattLast Associates might want to know the total amount (amount paid and current due) for each account. This would seem to pose a problem because the Account table does not include a field for total amount. You can calculate it, however, because the total amount is equal to the amount paid plus the current due. A field that can be computed from other fields is called a **calculated field** or a **computed field** and is not usually included in the table. Including it introduces the possibility for errors in the table. If the value in the field does not happen to match the results of the calculation, the data is inconsistent. A calculated field is an individual record calculation because each calculation only involves fields in a single record.

PrattLast might also want to calculate the average amount paid for the accounts of each account manager. That is, they may want the average for accounts of account manager 31, the average for accounts of account manager 35, and so on. This type of calculation is called a **group calculation** because each calculation involves groups of records. In this example, the accounts of account manager 31 would form one group, the accounts of account manager 35 would be a second group, and the accounts of account manager 58 would form a third group.

1 CREATE QUERIES | 2 USE CRITERIA | 3 SORT DATA | 4 JOIN TABLES | 5 EXPORT RESULTS
6 PERFORM CALCULATIONS | 7 CREATE CROSSTAB | 8 CUSTOMIZE NAVIGATION PANE

To Use a Calculated Field in a Query

If you need a calculated field in a query, you enter a name, or alias, for the calculated field, a colon, and then the calculation in one of the columns in the Field row of the design grid for the query. Any fields included in the expression must be enclosed in square brackets ([ ]). For example, for the total amount, you will type Total Amount:[Amount Paid]+[Current Due] as the expression.

You can type the expression directly into the Field row in Design view. The preferred method, however, is to select the column in the Field row and then use the Zoom command on its shortcut menu. When Access displays the Zoom dialog box, you can enter the expression. ***Why use the Zoom command?*** *You will not be able to see the entire entry in the Field row, because the space available is not large enough.*

You can use addition (+), subtraction (-), multiplication (*), or division (/) in calculations. If you have multiple calculations in an expression, you can include parentheses to indicate which calculations should be done first.

The following steps create a query that PrattLast Associates might use to obtain financial information on its accounts, including the total amount (amount paid + current due), which is a calculated field.

1

- Create a query with a field list for the Account table.
- Add the Account Number, Account Name, Amount Paid, and Current Due fields to the query.
- Right-click the Field row in the first open column in the design grid to display a shortcut menu (Figure 2–63).

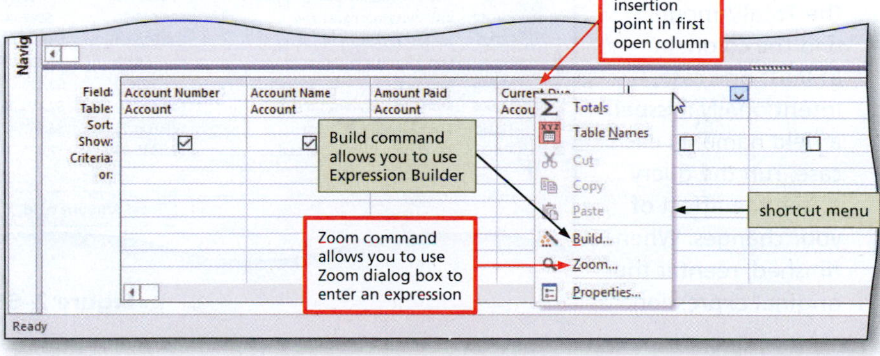

Figure 2–63

2

- Click Zoom on the shortcut menu to display the Zoom dialog box.
- Type **`Total Amount:[Amount Paid]+[Current Due]`** in the Zoom dialog box (Figure 2–64).

Q&A Do I always need to put square brackets around field names?

If the field name does not contain spaces, square brackets are technically not required. It is a good practice, however, to get in the habit of using the brackets in field calculations.

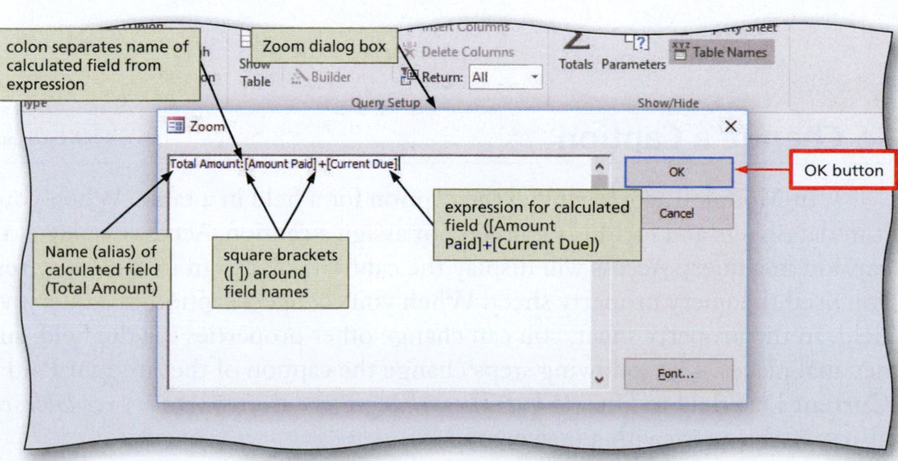

Figure 2–64

- Click the OK button (Zoom dialog box) to enter the expression (Figure 2–65).

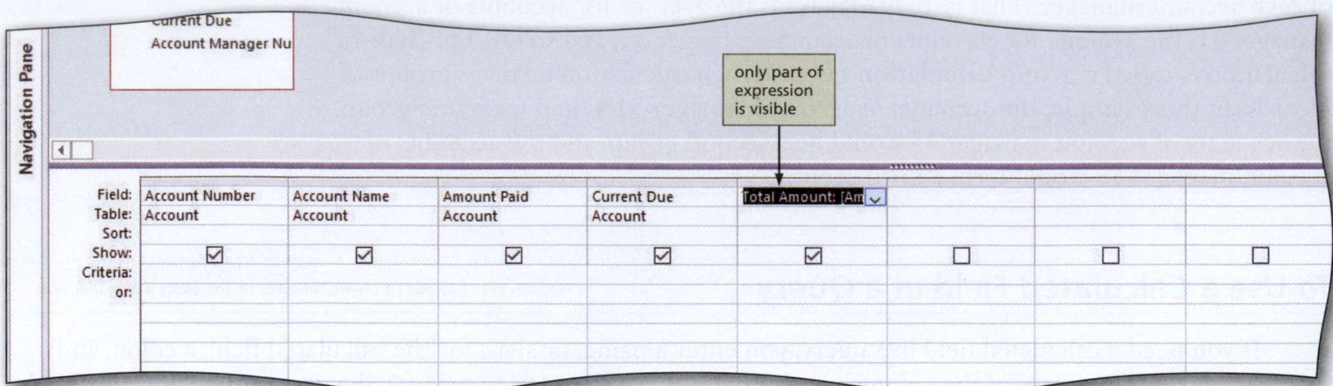

Figure 2–65

- Run the query (Figure 2–66).

Experiment

- Return to Design view and try other expressions. In at least one case, omit the Total Amount and the colon. In at least one case, intentionally misspell a field name. In each case, run the query to see the effect of your changes. When finished, reenter the original expression.

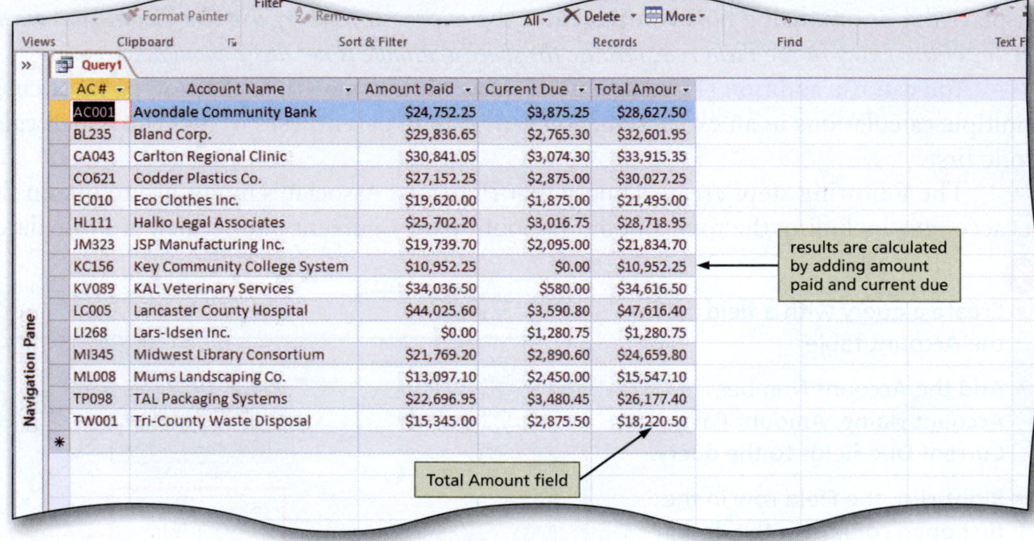

Figure 2–66

Other Ways

1. Press SHIFT+F2

1 CREATE QUERIES | 2 USE CRITERIA | 3 SORT DATA | 4 JOIN TABLES | 5 EXPORT RESULTS
6 PERFORM CALCULATIONS | 7 CREATE CROSSTAB | 8 CUSTOMIZE NAVIGATION PANE

To Change a Caption

In Module 1, you changed the caption for a field in a table. When you assigned a caption, Access displayed it in datasheets and forms. If you did not assign a caption, Access displayed the field name. You can also change a caption in a query. Access will display the caption you assign in the query results. When you omitted duplicates, you used the query property sheet. When you change a caption in a query, you use the property sheet for the field. In the property sheet, you can change other properties for the field, such as the format and number of decimal places. The following steps change the caption of the Amount Paid field to Paid and the caption of the Current Due field to Due. ***Why?** These changes give shorter, yet very readable, column headings for the fields.* The steps also save the query with a new name.

1

- Return to Design view.
- If necessary, click Design on the ribbon to display the Query Tools Design tab.
- Click the Amount Paid field in the design grid, and then click the Property Sheet button (Query Tools Design tab | Show/Hide group) to display the properties for the Amount Paid field.
- Click the Caption box, and then type **Paid** as the caption (Figure 2–67).

Q&A My property sheet looks different. What should I do?
Close the property sheet and repeat this step.

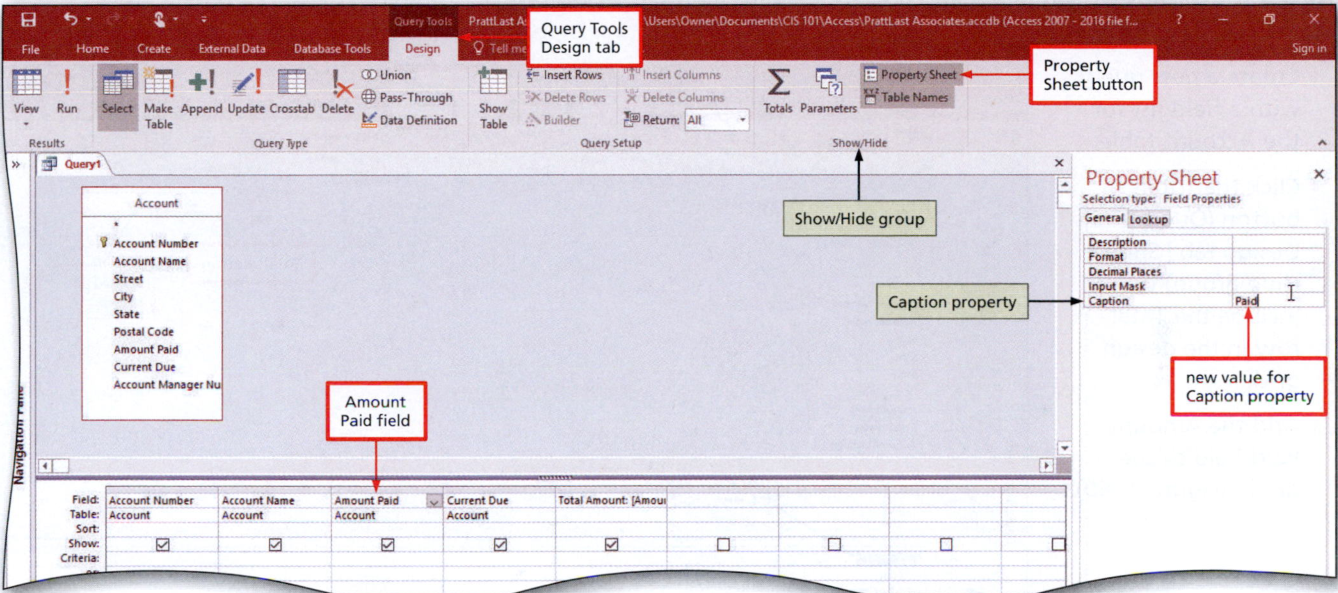

Figure 2–67

2

- Click the Current Due field in the design grid to view its properties in the Property Sheet.
- Click the Caption box, and then type **Due** as the caption.
- Close the Property Sheet by clicking the Property Sheet button a second time.
- Run the query (Figure 2–68).

3

- Save the query as m02q10.
- Close the query.

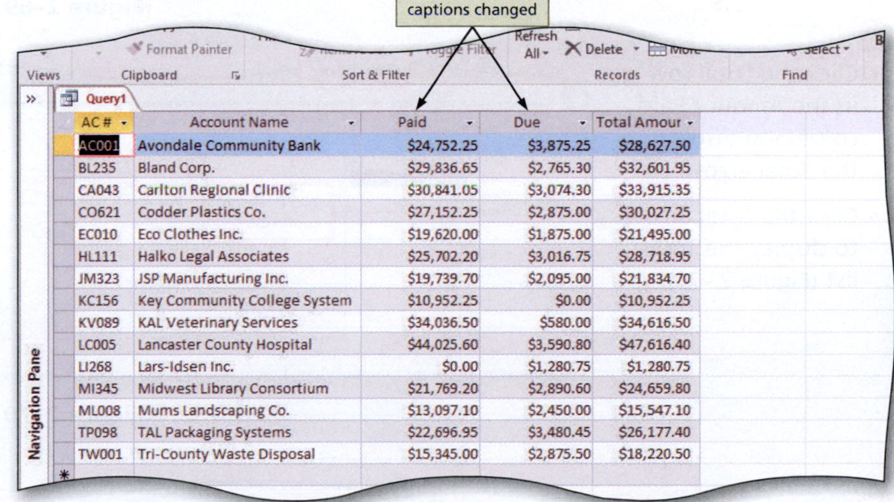

AC #	Account Name	Paid	Due	Total Amour
AC001	Avondale Community Bank	$24,752.25	$3,875.25	$28,627.50
BL235	Bland Corp.	$29,836.65	$2,765.30	$32,601.95
CA043	Carlton Regional Clinic	$30,841.05	$3,074.30	$33,915.35
CO621	Codder Plastics Co.	$27,152.25	$2,875.00	$30,027.25
EC010	Eco Clothes Inc.	$19,620.00	$1,875.00	$21,495.00
HL111	Halko Legal Associates	$25,702.20	$3,016.75	$28,718.95
JM323	JSP Manufacturing Inc.	$19,739.70	$2,095.00	$21,834.70
KC156	Key Community College System	$10,952.25	$0.00	$10,952.25
KV089	KAL Veterinary Services	$34,036.50	$580.00	$34,616.50
LC005	Lancaster County Hospital	$44,025.60	$3,590.80	$47,616.40
LI268	Lars-Idsen Inc.	$0.00	$1,280.75	$1,280.75
MI345	Midwest Library Consortium	$21,769.20	$2,890.60	$24,659.80
ML008	Mums Landscaping Co.	$13,097.10	$2,450.00	$15,547.10
TP098	TAL Packaging Systems	$22,696.95	$3,480.45	$26,177.40
TW001	Tri-County Waste Disposal	$15,345.00	$2,875.50	$18,220.50

Figure 2–68

Other Ways

1. Right-click field in design grid, click Properties on shortcut menu

To Calculate Statistics

For group calculations, Microsoft Access supports several built-in statistics: COUNT (count of the number of records), SUM (total), AVG (average), MAX (largest value), MIN (smallest value), STDEV (standard deviation), VAR (variance), FIRST (first value), and LAST (last value). These statistics are called aggregate functions. An **aggregate function** is a function that performs some mathematical function against a group of records. To use an aggregate function in a query, you include it in the Total row in the design grid. In order to do so, you must first include the Total row by clicking the Totals button on the Design tab. ***Why?*** *The Total row usually does not appear in the grid.*

The following steps create a new query for the Account table. The steps include the Total row in the design grid, and then calculate the average amount paid for all accounts.

1

- Create a new query with a field list for the Account table.
- Click the Totals button (Query Tools Design tab | Show/Hide group) to include the Total row in the design grid.
- Add the Amount Paid field to the query (Figure 2–69).

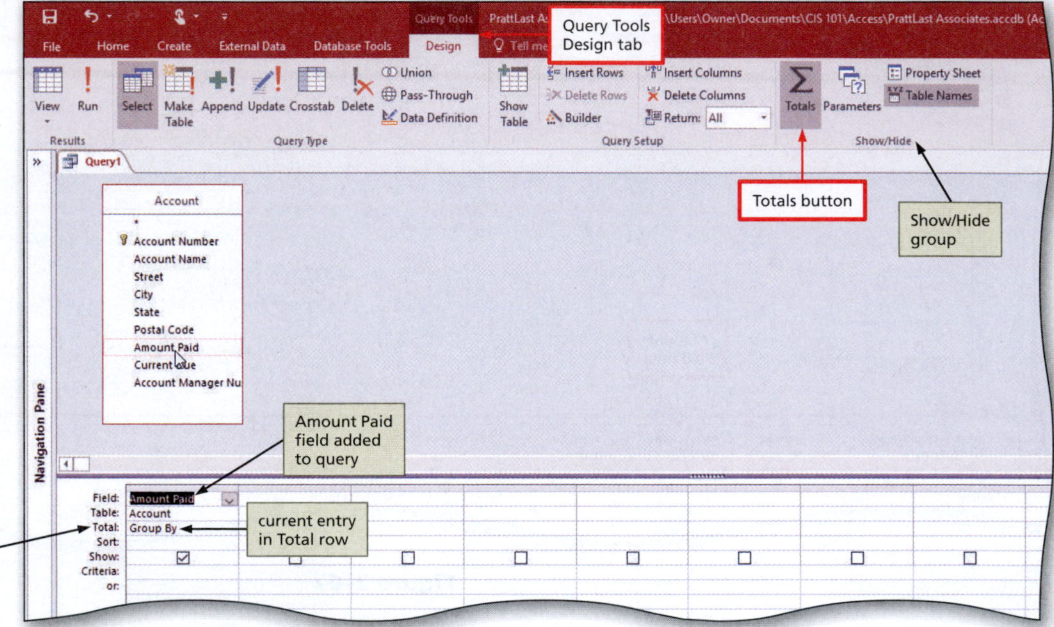

Figure 2–69

2

- Click the Total row in the Amount Paid column to display the Total arrow.
- Click the Total arrow to display the Total list (Figure 2–70).

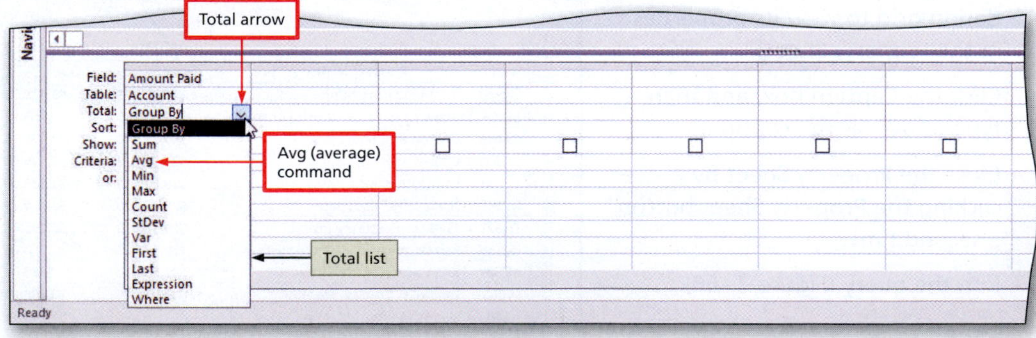

Figure 2–70

3

- Click Avg to select the calculation that Access is to perform (Figure 2–71).

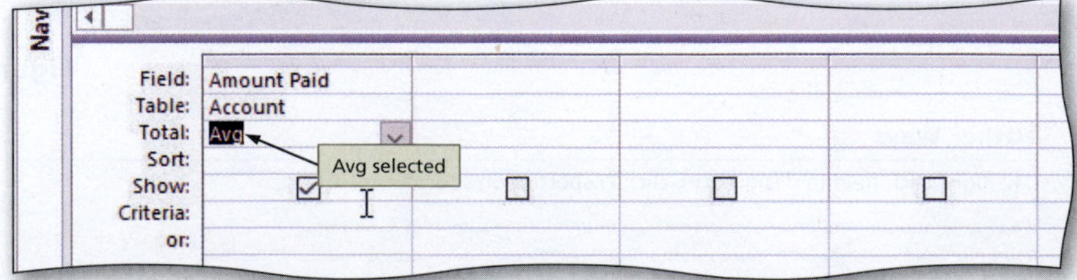

Figure 2–71

4

- Run the query (Figure 2–72).

Experiment

- Return to Design view and try other aggregate functions. In each case, run the query to see the effect of your selection. When finished, select Avg once again.

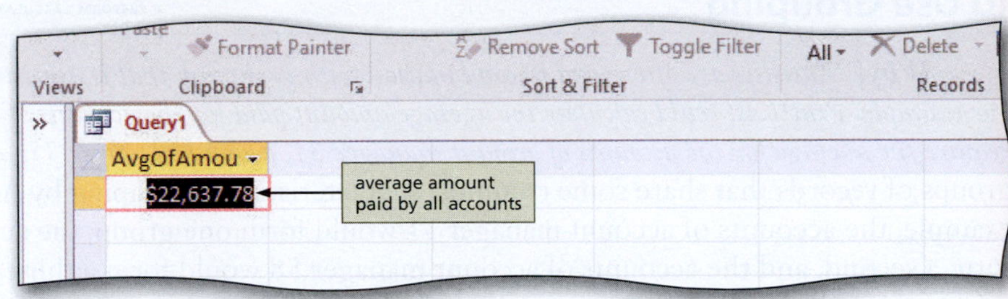

Figure 2–72

To Use Criteria in Calculating Statistics

Why? Sometimes calculating statistics for all the records in the table is appropriate. In other cases, however, you will need to calculate the statistics for only those records that satisfy certain criteria. To enter a criterion in a field, first you select Where as the entry in the Total row for the field, and then enter the criterion in the Criteria row. Access uses the word, Where, to indicate that you will enter a criterion. The following steps use this technique to calculate the average amount paid for accounts of account manager 31. The steps also save the query with a new name.

1

- Return to Design view.
- Include the Account Manager Number field in the design grid.
- Click the Total row in the Account Manager Number column.
- Click the Total arrow in the Account Manager Number column to produce a Total list (Figure 2–73).

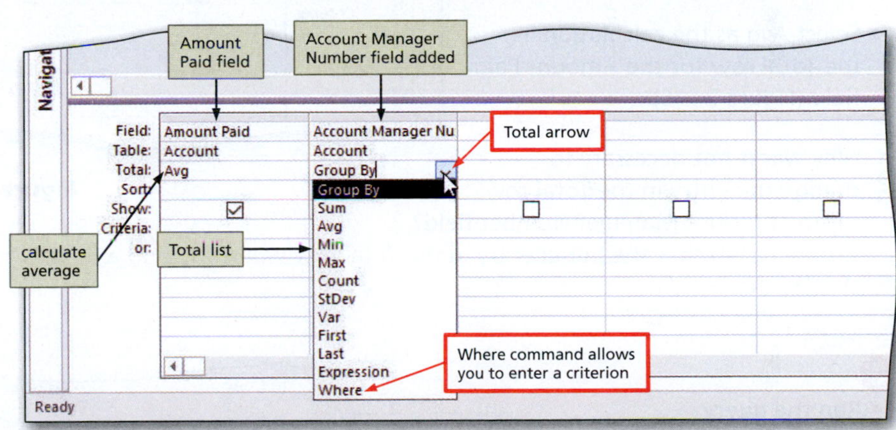

Figure 2–73

2

- Click Where to be able to enter a criterion.
- Type 31 as the criterion for the Account Manager Number field (Figure 2–74).

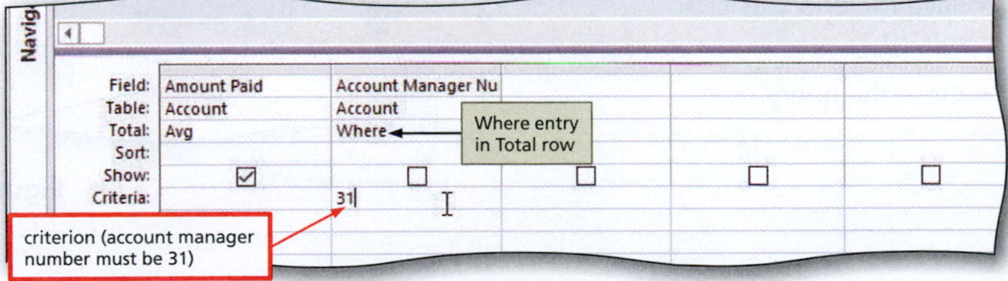

Figure 2–74

3

- Run the query (Figure 2–75).

4

- Save the query as m02q11.

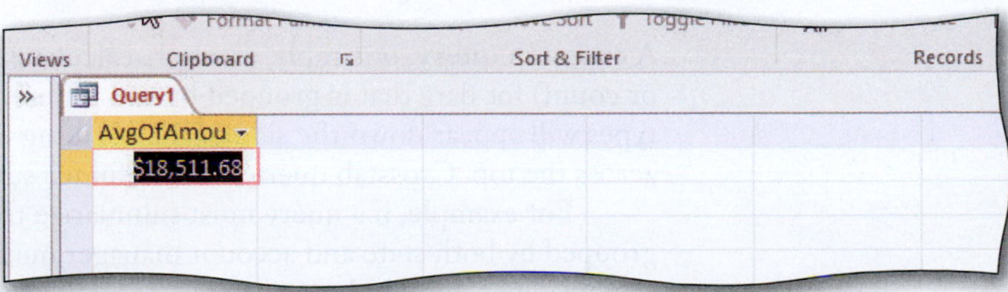

Figure 2–75

To Use Grouping

Why? Statistics are often used in combination with grouping; that is, statistics are calculated for groups of records. For example, PrattLast could calculate the average amount paid for the accounts of each account manager, which would require the average for the accounts of account manager 31, account manager 35, and so on. **Grouping** means creating groups of records that share some common characteristic. In grouping by Account Manager Number, for example, the accounts of account manager 31 would form one group, the accounts of account manager 35 would form a second, and the accounts of account manager 58 would form a third group. The calculations are then made for each group. To indicate grouping in Access, select Group By as the entry in the Total row for the field to be used for grouping.

The following steps create a query that calculates the average amount paid for the accounts of each account manager at PrattLast Associates. The steps also save the query with a new name.

1

- Return to Design view and clear the design grid.
- Include the Account Manager Number field in the query.
- Include the Amount Paid field in the query.
- Select Avg as the calculation in the Total row for the Amount Paid field (Figure 2–76).

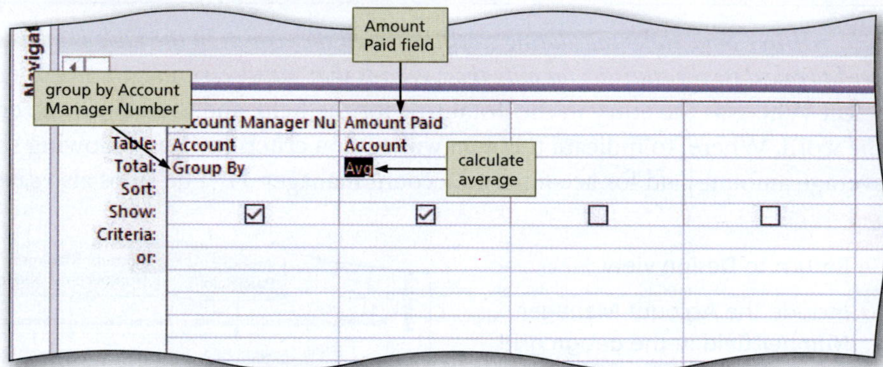

Figure 2–76

Q&A Why was it not necessary to change the entry in the Total row for the Account Manager Number field?
Group By, which is the initial entry in the Total row when you add a field, is correct. Thus, you did not need to change the entry.

2

- Run the query (Figure 2–77).

3

- Save the query as m02q12.
- Close the query.

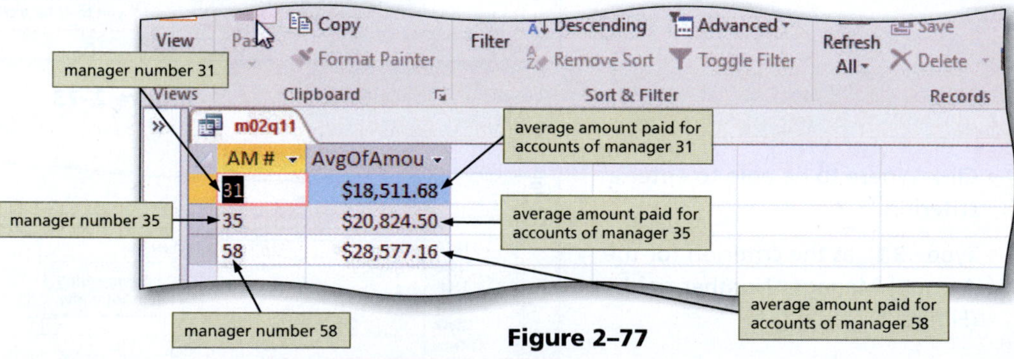

Figure 2–77

Crosstab Queries

A **crosstab query**, or simply, crosstab, calculates a statistic (for example, sum, average, or count) for data that is grouped by two different types of information. One of the types will appear down the side of the resulting datasheet, and the other will appear across the top. Crosstab queries are useful for summarizing data by category or group.

For example, if a query must summarize the sum of the current due amounts grouped by both state and account manager number, you could have states as the row headings, that is, down the side. You could have account manager numbers as the column headings, that is, across the top. The entries within the datasheet represent the total of the current due amounts. Figure 2–78 shows a crosstab in which the total of current due amounts is grouped by both state and account manager number, with states down the left side and account manager numbers across the top. For example, the entry in the row labeled IL and in the column labeled 31 represents the total of the current due amounts by all accounts of account manager 31 who are located in Illinois.

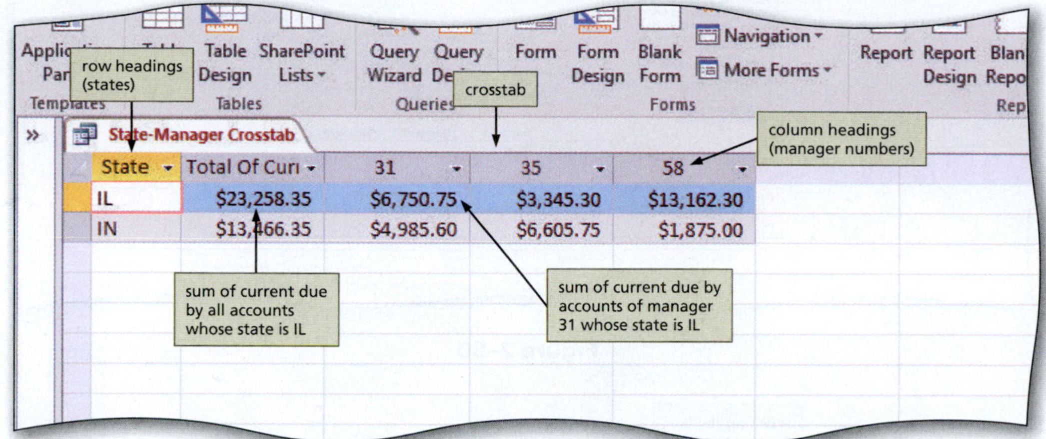

Figure 2–78

How do you know when to use a crosstab query?

If data is to be grouped by two different types of information, you can use a crosstab query. You will need to identify the two types of information. One of the types will form the row headings and the other will form the column headings in the query results.

CONSIDER THIS

To Create a Crosstab Query

1 CREATE QUERIES | 2 USE CRITERIA | 3 SORT DATA | 4 JOIN TABLES | 5 EXPORT RESULTS
6 PERFORM CALCULATIONS | 7 CREATE CROSSTAB | 8 CUSTOMIZE NAVIGATION PANE

The following steps use the Crosstab Query Wizard to create a crosstab query. ***Why?*** *PrattLast Associates wants to group data on current due amounts by two types of information: state and account manager.*

- Click Create on the ribbon to display the Create tab.
- Click the Query Wizard button (Create tab | Queries group) to display the New Query dialog box (Figure 2–79).

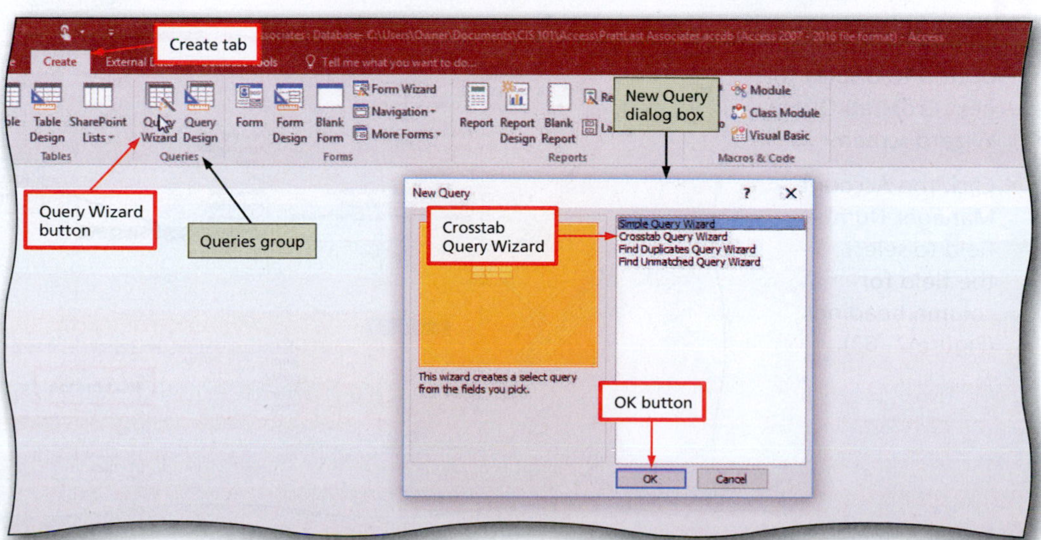

Figure 2–79

2

- Click Crosstab Query Wizard (New Query dialog box).
- Click the OK button to display the Crosstab Query Wizard dialog box (Figure 2–80).

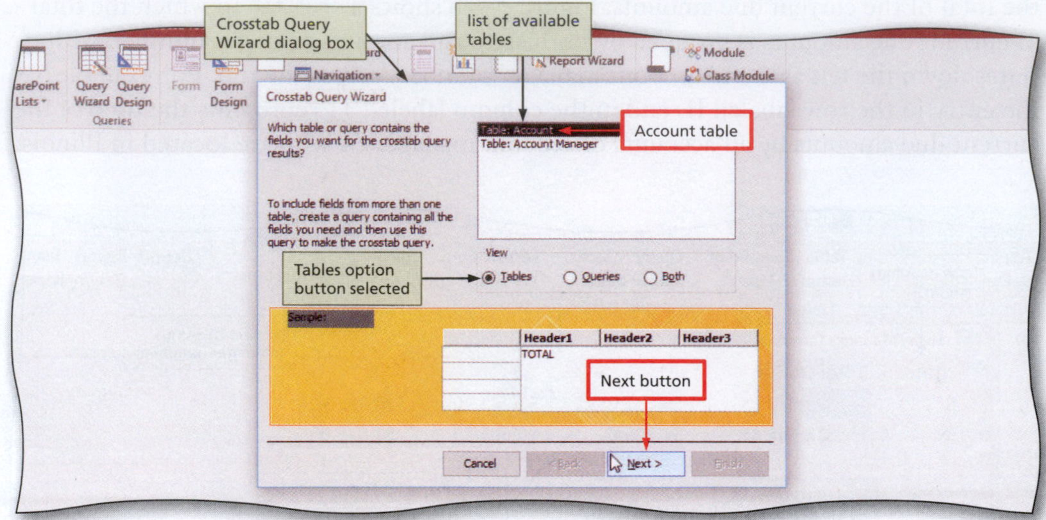

Figure 2–80

- With the Tables option button selected, click Table: Account to select the Account table, and then click the Next button to display the next Crosstab Query Wizard screen.
- Click the State field, and then click the Add Field button to select the State field for row headings (Figure 2–81).

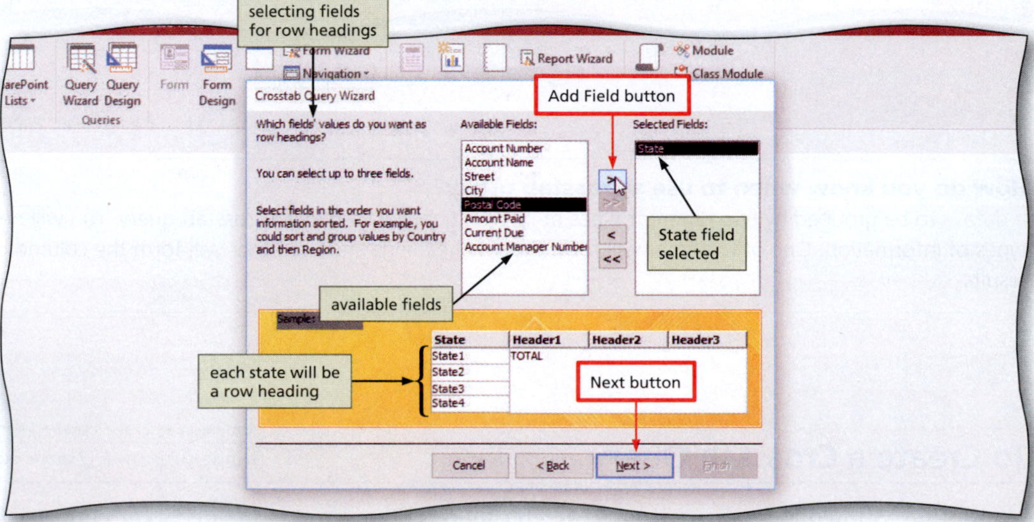

Figure 2–81

- Click the Next button to display the next Crosstab Query Wizard screen.
- Click the Account Manager Number field to select the field for column headings (Figure 2–82).

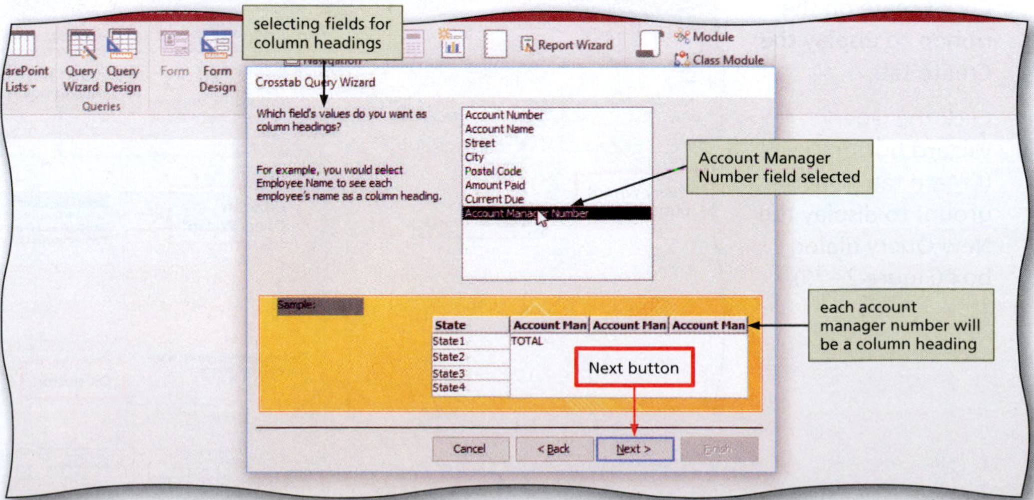

Figure 2–82

- Click the Next button to display the next Crosstab Query Wizard screen.
- Click the Current Due field to select the field for calculations.

Experiment

- Click other fields. For each field, examine the list of calculations that are available. When finished, click the Current Due field again.
- Click Sum to select the calculation to be performed (Figure 2–83).

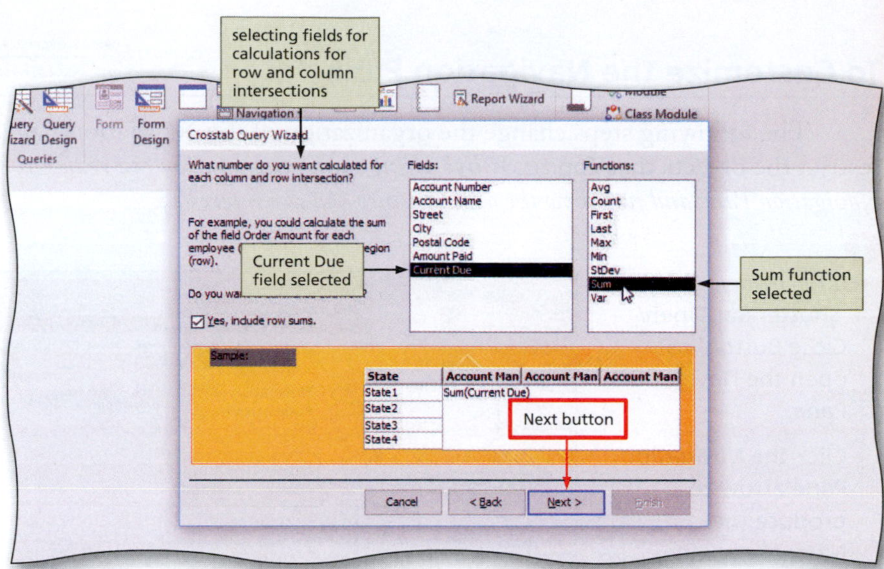

Figure 2–83

Q&A My list of functions is different. What did I do wrong?
Either you clicked the wrong field, or the Current Due field has the wrong data type. For example, if you mistakenly assigned it the Short Text data type, you would not see Sum in the list of available calculations.

6

- Click the Next button to display the next Crosstab Query Wizard screen.
- Erase the text in the name text box and type `State-Manager Crosstab` as the name of the query (Figure 2–84).

- If requested to do so by your instructor, name the crosstab query as FirstName LastName Crosstab where FirstName and LastName are your first and last names.
- Click the Finish button to produce the crosstab shown in Figure 2–78.
- Close the query.

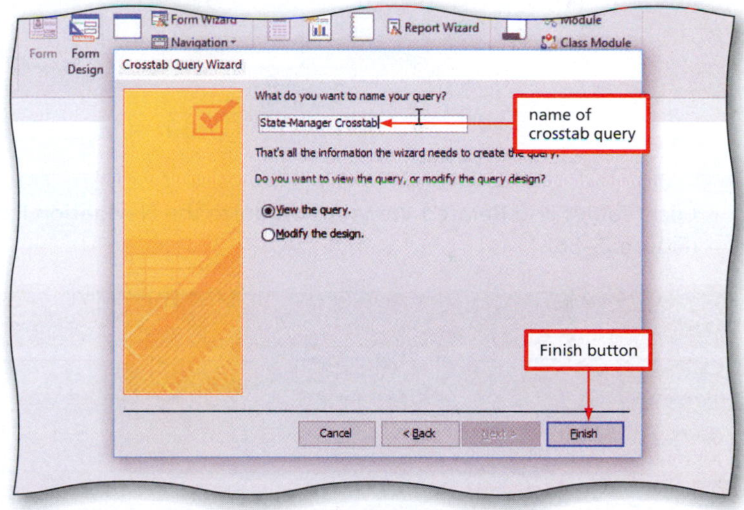

Figure 2–84

Customizing the Navigation Pane

Currently, the entries in the Navigation Pane are organized by object type. That is, all the tables are together, all the queries are together, and so on. You might want to change the way the information is organized. For example, you might want to have the Navigation Pane organized by table, with all the queries, forms, and reports associated with a particular table appearing after the name of the table. You can also use the Search bar to restrict the objects that appear to only those that have a certain collection of characters in their name. For example, if you entered the letters, Ma, only those objects containing Ma somewhere within the name will be included.

BTW
Access Help
At any time while using Access, you can find answers to questions and display information about various topics through Access Help. Used properly, this form of assistance can increase your productivity and reduce your frustrations by minimizing the time you spend learning how to use Access. For instructions about Access Help and exercises that will help you gain confidence in using it, read the Office and Windows module at the beginning of this book.

To Customize the Navigation Pane

The following steps change the organization of the Navigation Pane. They also use the Search bar to restrict the objects that appear. ***Why?*** *Using the Search bar, you can reduce the number of objects that appear in the Navigation Pane and just show the ones in which you are interested.*

1

- If necessary, click the 'Shutter Bar Open/Close Button' to open the Navigation Pane.
- Click the Navigation Pane arrow to produce the Navigation Pane menu (Figure 2–85).

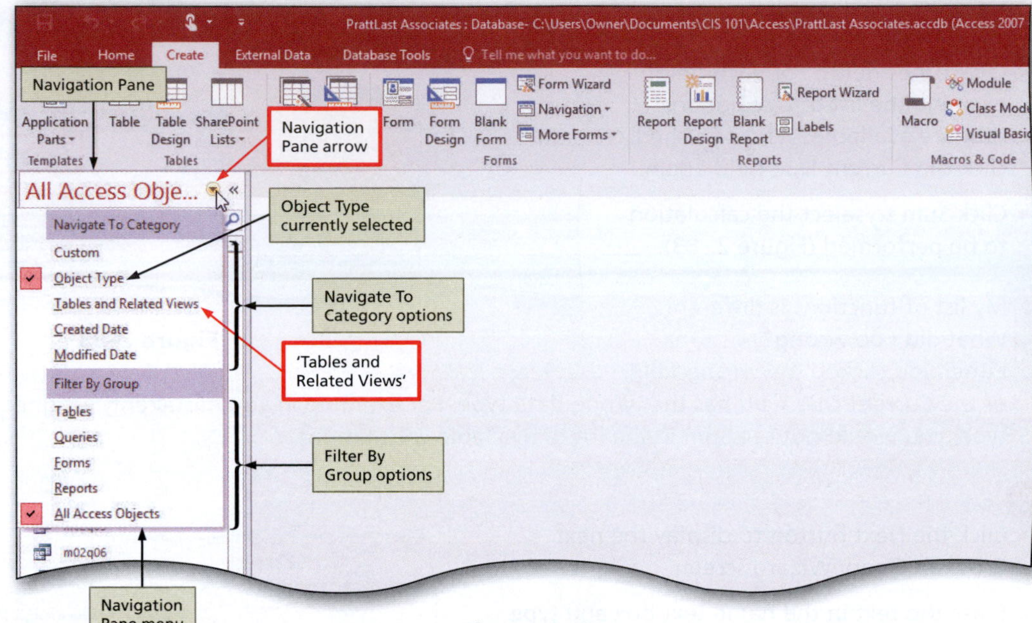

Figure 2–85

2

- Click 'Tables and Related Views' to organize the Navigation Pane by table rather than by the type of object (Figure 2–86).

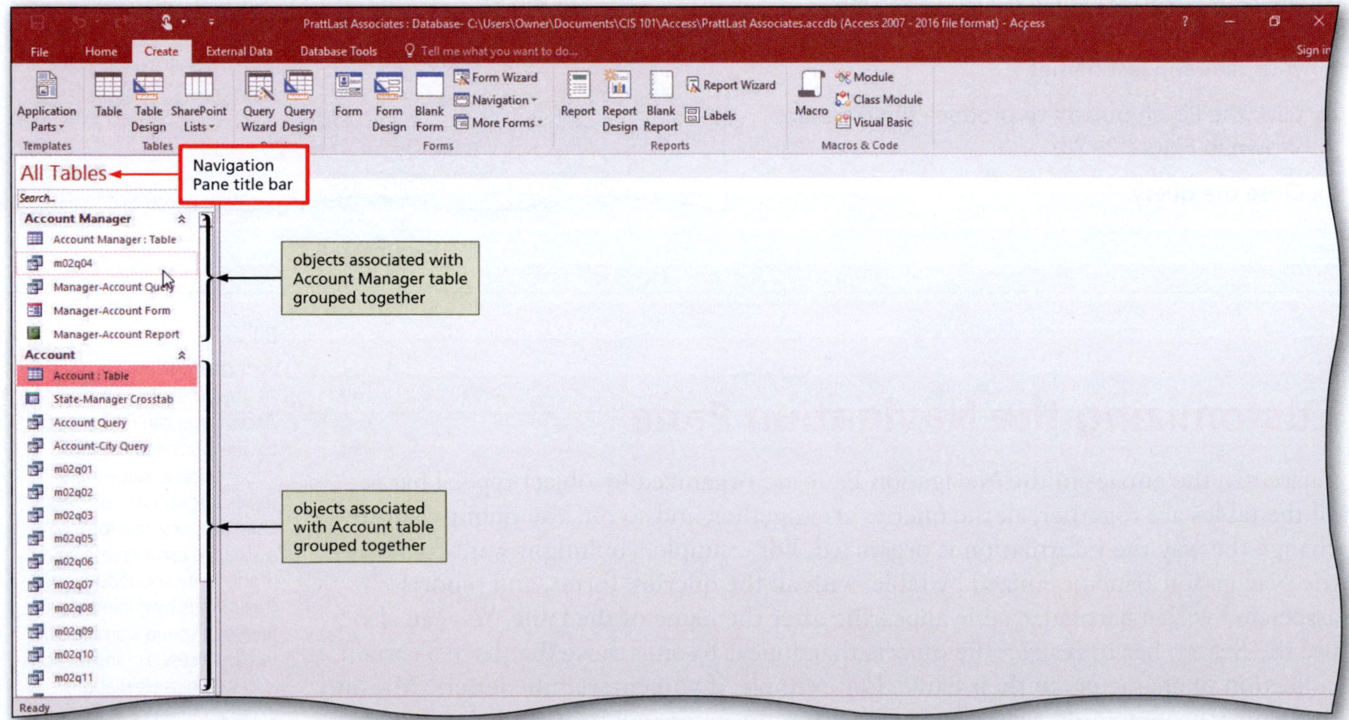

Figure 2–86

3

- Click the Navigation Pane arrow to produce the Navigation Pane menu.
- Click Object Type to once again organize the Navigation Pane by object type.

Experiment

- Select different Navigate To Category options to see the effect of the option. With each option you select, select different Filter By Group options to see the effect of the filtering. When you have finished experimenting, select the 'Object Type Navigate To Category' option and the 'All Access Objects Filter By Group' option.

- If the Search bar does not appear, right-click the Navigation Pane and click Search Bar on the shortcut menu.
- Click in the Search box to produce an insertion point.
- Type **Ma** as the search string to restrict the objects displayed to only those containing the desired string (Figure 2–87).

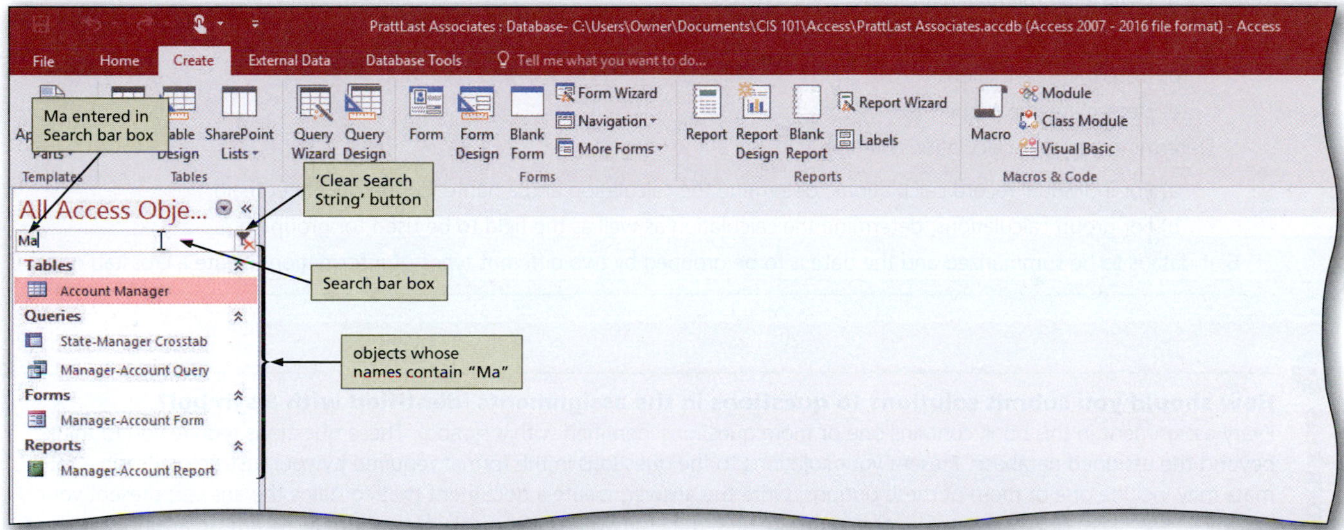

Figure 2–87

4

- Click the 'Clear Search String' button to remove the search string and redisplay all objects.

Q&A Did I have to click the button to redisplay all objects? Could I simply have erased the current string to achieve the same result?

You did not have to click the button. You could have used the DELETE or BACKSPACE keys to erase the current search string.

- If desired, sign out of your Microsoft account.
- Exit Access.

Summary

In this module you have learned to create queries, enter fields, enter criteria, use text and numeric data in queries, use wildcards, use compound criteria, create parameter queries, sort data in queries, join tables in queries, perform calculations in queries, and create crosstab queries. You also learned to create a report and a form that used a query, to export a query, and to customize the Navigation Pane.

What decisions will you need to make when creating queries?

Use these guidelines as you complete the assignments in this module and create your own queries outside of this class.

1. Identify the fields by examining the question or request to determine which fields from the tables in the database are involved.
2. Identify restrictions or the conditions that records must satisfy to be included in the results.
3. Determine whether special order is required.
   a) Determine the sort key(s).
   b) If using two sort keys, determine the major and minor key.
   c) Determine sort order. If there are no words to imply a particular order, you would typically use Ascending.
   d) Determine restrictions, such as excluding duplicates.
4. Determine whether more than one table is required.
   a) Determine which tables to include.
   b) Determine the matching fields.
   c) Determine whether sorting is required.
   d) Determine restrictions.
   e) Determine join properties.
5. Determine whether calculations are required.
   a) For individual record calculations, determine the calculation and a name for the calculated field.
   b) For group calculations, determine the calculation as well as the field to be used for grouping.
6. If data is to be summarized and the data is to be grouped by two different types of information, create a crosstab query.

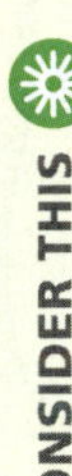

How should you submit solutions to questions in the assignments identified with a symbol?

Every assignment in this book contains one or more questions identified with a symbol. These questions require you to think beyond the assigned database. Present your solutions to the questions in the format required by your instructor. Possible formats may include one or more of these options: write the answer; create a document that contains the answer; present your answer to the class; discuss your answer in a group; record the answer as audio or video using a webcam, smartphone, or portable media player; or post answers on a blog, wiki, or website.

Apply Your Knowledge

Reinforce the skills and apply the concepts you learned in this module.

Using Wildcards in a Query, Creating a Parameter Query, Joining Tables, and Creating a Report

Instructions: Run Access. Open the Apply Friendly Janitorial Services database that you modified in Apply Your Knowledge in Module 1. (If you did not complete the exercise, see your instructor for a copy of the modified database.)

Perform the following tasks:

1. Create a query for the Client table and add the Client Number, Client Name, Amount Paid, and Current Due fields to the design grid. Add a criterion to find all clients whose names start with the letter B. Run the query and then save it as Apply 2 Step 1 Query.
2. Create a query for the Client table and add the Client Number, Client Name, Amount Paid, and Supervisor Number fields to the design grid. Sort the records in descending order by Amount Paid. Add a criterion for the Supervisor Number field that allows the user to enter a different supervisor each time the query is run. Run the query and enter 114 as the supervisor number to test the query. Save the query as Apply 2 Step 2 Query.

3. Create a query for the Client table and add the Client Number, Client Name, and Current Due fields to the design grid. Add a criterion to find all clients whose current due amount is less than $500.00. Run the query and then save it as Apply 2 Step 3 Query.
4. Create a query that joins the Supervisor and Client tables. Add the Supervisor Number, Last Name, and First Name fields from the Supervisor table and the Client Number and Client Name fields from the Client table to the design grid. Sort the records in ascending order by Client Number within Supervisor Number. Run the query and save it as Supervisor-Client Query.
5. Create the report shown in Figure 2–88. The report uses the Supervisor-Client Query.

Supervisor-Client Report

SU #	Last Name	First Name	CL #	Client Name
103	Estevez	Enrique	AT13	Atlas Repair
103	Estevez	Enrique	CP03	Calder Plastics
103	Estevez	Enrique	HC17	Hill Crafts
103	Estevez	Enrique	KD15	Klean n Dri
110	Hillsdale	Rachel	AZ01	AZ Auto
110	Hillsdale	Rachel	BB35	Babbage Bookkeeping
110	Hillsdale	Rachel	CJ45	C Joe Diner
110	Hillsdale	Rachel	HN23	Hurley National Bank
110	Hillsdale	Rachel	PL03	Prime Legal Associates
114	Liu	Chou	CC25	Cramden Co.
114	Liu	Chou	MM01	Moss Manufacturing
114	Liu	Chou	PS67	PRIM Staffing
120	Short	Chris	BL24	Blanton Shoes
120	Short	Chris	KC12	Kady Regional Clinic
120	Short	Chris	TE15	Telton-Edwards

Figure 2–88

6. If requested to do so by your instructor, rename the Supervisor-Client Report in the Navigation Pane as LastName-Client Report where LastName is your last name.
7. Submit the revised database in the format specified by your instructor.
8. What criteria would you enter in the Street field if you wanted to find all clients whose businesses were on Beard?

Extend Your Knowledge

Extend the skills you learned in this module and experiment with new skills. You may need to use Help to complete the assignment.

Creating Crosstab Queries Using Criteria and Exporting a Query

Note: To complete this assignment, you will be required to use the Data Files. Please contact your instructor for information about accessing the Data Files.

Continued >

Extend Your Knowledge *continued*

Instructions: Run Access. Open the Extend TAL Maintenance database, which is located in the Data Files. TAL Maintenance is a small business that provides various outdoor maintenance services, such as painting, lawn maintenance, and parking lot re-paving, to commercial customers. The owner has created an Access database in which to store information about the customers the company serves and team leaders working for the company. You will create the crosstab query shown in Figure 2–89. You will also query the database using specified criteria and export a query.

Perform the following tasks:

1. Create the crosstab query shown in Figure 2–89. The crosstab groups the total of customers' balance by city and team leader number.

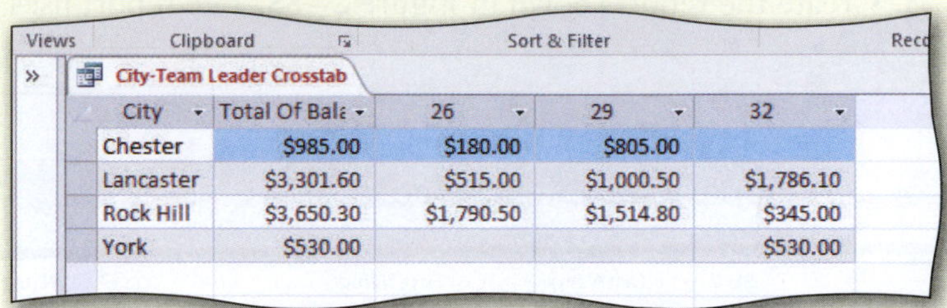

City	Total Of Bal:	26	29	32
Chester	$985.00	$180.00	$805.00	
Lancaster	$3,301.60	$515.00	$1,000.50	$1,786.10
Rock Hill	$3,650.30	$1,790.50	$1,514.80	$345.00
York	$530.00			$530.00

Figure 2–89

2. Create a query to find all customers who are not located in Rock Hill. Include the Customer Number, Customer Name, and Balance fields in the query results. Save the query as Extend 2 Step 2 Query.
3. Create a query to find all team leaders whose first name is either Alex or Alix. Include the Team Leader Number, First Name, and Last Name in the query results. Save the query as Extend 2 Step 3 Query.
4. Create a query to find all customers where the team leader number is either 29 or 32 and the balance is greater than $550.00. Include the Customer Number, Customer Name, Balance, and Team Leader Number fields in the design grid in that order. Use the IN operator in your query design. Sort the results by customer number within team leader number. Save the query as Extend 2 Step 4 Query.
5. Export the City-Team Leader Crosstab as a Word file with the name City-Team Leader Crosstab.rtf and save the export steps.
6. Open the Customer table and change the balance for account C04 to $1,000.50.
7. If requested to do so by your instructor, change the customer name of customer K10 from Kathy's Books to Last Name Books where Last Name is your last name.
8. Use the saved export steps to export the City-Team Leader Crosstab again. When asked if you want to replace the existing file, click Yes.
9. Submit the revised database and the exported RTF file in the format specified by your instructor.
10. How would you create the query in Step 4 without using the IN operator?

Expand Your World

Create a solution, which uses cloud and web technologies, by learning and investigating on your own from general guidance.

Problem: You are taking a general science course and the instructor would like you to gather some weather statistics and query the statistics as part of the unit on climate change.

Instructions:

1. Examine a website that contains historical weather data, such as accuweather.com or weatherunderground.com. Select weather data for the city in which you were born for the month of January, 2014. If you cannot find your city, then select a large city near your current location.
2. Create a database that contains one table and has the following fields: Day of the month (1 through 31), Day of the week, high temperature for the day, and low temperature for the day. (*Hint:* Use the autonumber data type to record the day of the month.)
3. Create queries that do the following:
   a. Display the five days with the highest high temperature.
   b. Display the five days with lowest low temperature.
   c. Display the average high and low temperature for the entire month.
   d. Calculate the difference between the high and low temperatures for each day.
   e. Display the high and low temperatures for each day in both Fahrenheit and Celsius. (*Hint:* Use the Internet to find the conversion formula.)
4. Submit the revised database in the format specified by your instructor.
5. Use an Internet search engine to find the historical average high and low temperatures in January for your city.
6. Which websites did you use to gather data and search for the historical averages? How does the query result in Step 3c differ from the historical average?

In the Labs

Design, create, modify, and/or use a database following the guidelines, concepts, and skills presented in this module. Labs are listed in order of increasing difficulty. Labs 1 and 2, which increase in difficulty, require you to create solutions based on what you learned in the module; Lab 3 requires you to apply your creative thinking and problem solving skills to design and implement a solution.

Lab 1: Querying the Garden Naturally Database

Problem: The management of Garden Naturally has determined a number of questions it wants the database management system to answer. You must obtain the answers to these questions.

Note: Use the database modified in Lab 1 of Module 1 for this assignment, or see your instructor for information on accessing the required files.

Instructions: Perform the following tasks:

1. Run Access. Open the Lab 1 Garden Naturally database you modified in Module 1 and create a new query for the Customer table. Add the Customer Number, Customer Name, Amount Paid, Balance Due, and Sales Rep Number fields to the design grid, and restrict the query results to only those customers where the sales rep number is 29. Save the query as Lab 2-1 Step 1 Query.
2. Create a query for the Customer table that includes the Customer Number, Customer Name, and Balance Due fields for all customers located in Delaware (DE) with a balance due greater than $1,000.00. Save the query as Lab 2-1 Step 2 Query.
3. Create a query for the Customer table that includes the Customer Number, Customer Name, Address, City, and State fields for all customers located in cities that begin with Ch. Save the query as Lab 2-1 Step 3 Query.

Continued >

In the Labs *continued*

4. Create a query for the Customer table that lists all states in ascending order. Each state should appear only once. Save the query as Lab 2-1 Step 4 Query.
5. Create a query for the Customer table that allows the user to type the name of the desired city when the query is run. The query results should display the Customer Number, Customer Name, Balance Due, and Amount Paid fields in that order. Test the query by searching for those records where the customer is located in Quaker. Save the query as Lab 2-1 Step 5 Query.
6. Create a query for the Sales Rep table that includes the First Name, Last Name, and Start Date for all sales reps who started after June 1, 2015. Save the query as Lab 2-1 Step 6 Query.
7. Create a query that joins the Sales Rep and Customer tables. Include the Sales Rep Number, Last Name, and First Name from the Sales Rep table. Include the Customer Number, Customer Name, and Amount Paid from the Customer table. Sort the records in ascending order by sales rep's last name and then by customer name. All sales reps should appear in the result even if they currently have no customers. Save the query as Lab 2-1 Step 7 Query.
8. Open the Lab 2-1 Step 7 Query in Design view and remove the Sales Rep table from the query. Add the Balance Due field to the design grid. Calculate the total of the balance and amount paid amounts. Assign the alias Total Amount to the calculated field. Change the caption for the Amount Paid field to Paid and the caption for the Balance Due field to Owed. Save the query as Lab 2-1 Step 8 Query.
9. Create a query for the Customer table to display the total amount paid for sales rep 26. Save the query as Lab 2-1 Step 9 Query.
10. Create a query for the Customer table to display the average balance due for each sales rep. Save the query as Lab 2-1 Step 10 Query.
11. Create the crosstab query shown in Figure 2–90. The crosstab groups the average of customers' amount paid by state and sales rep number. Save the crosstab as State-Sales Rep Crosstab.

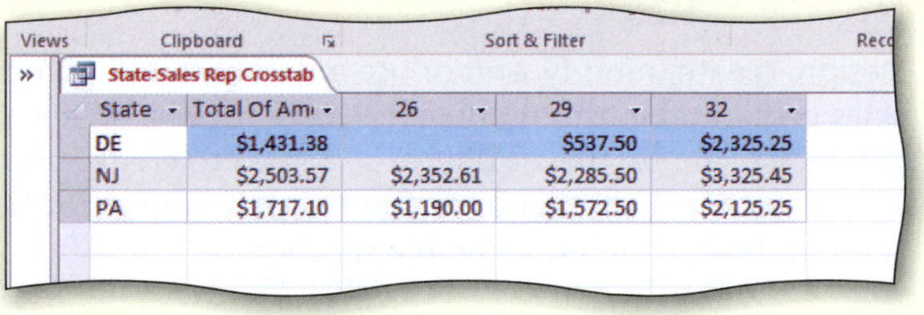

State	Total Of Am	26	29	32
DE	$1,431.38		$537.50	$2,325.25
NJ	$2,503.57	$2,352.61	$2,285.50	$3,325.45
PA	$1,717.10	$1,190.00	$1,572.50	$2,125.25

Figure 2–90

12. If requested to do so by your instructor, open the Lab 2-1 Step 1 query and change the caption for the Sales Rep Number field to your last name.
13. Submit the revised database in the format specified by your instructor.
14. How would you modify the query in Step 7 to include only sales reps that currently have customers?

Lab 2: Querying the Museum Gift Shop Database

Problem: The manager of the Museum gift shop has determined a number of questions she wants the database management system to answer. You must obtain answers to these questions.

Note: Use the database created in Lab 2 of Module 1 for this assignment or see your instructor for information on accessing the required files.

Instructions: Perform the following tasks:

1. Run Access. Open the Lab 2 Museum Gift Shop database and create a query for the Item table that includes all fields and all records in the Item table. Name the query Lab 2-2 Step 1 Query.

2. Create a query for the Item table that includes the Item Number, Description, Wholesale Cost, and Vendor Code fields for all records where the vendor code is AW. Save the query as Lab 2-2 Step 2 Query.
3. Create a query for the Item table that includes the Item Number and Description fields for all items where the description starts with G. Save the query as Lab 2-2 Step 3 Query.
4. Create a query for the Item table that includes the Item Number and Description for all items with a Wholesale Cost greater than $15.00. Save the query as Lab 2-2 Step 4 Query.
5. Create a query for the Item table that includes the Item Number, Description, and Wholesale Cost fields for all items with a Wholesale Cost between $5.00 and $10.00. Save the query as Lab 2-2 Step 5 Query.
6. Create a query for the Item table that includes the Item Number, Description, On Hand, and Wholesale Cost fields for all items where the number on hand is less than 5 and the wholesale cost is less than $15.00. Save the query as Lab 2-2 Step 6 Query.
7. Create a query for the Item table that includes the Item Number, Description, Wholesale Cost, and Vendor Code for all items that have a Wholesale Cost greater than $20.00 or a Supplier Code of SD. Save the query as Lab 2-2 Step 7 Query.
8. Create a query that joins the Vendor and the Item tables. Include the Vendor Code and Vendor Name from the Vendor table and the Item Number, Description, Wholesale Cost, and Retail Price fields from the Item table. Sort the query in ascending order by Description within Vendor Code. Save the query as Vendor-Item Query.
9. Create a form for the Vendor-Item Query. Save the form as Vendor-Item Form.
10. If requested to do so by your instructor, rename the form in the Navigation Pane as LastName-Item Form where LastName is your last name.
11. Create the report shown in Figure 2–91. The report uses the Vendor-Item Query but does not use all the fields in the query.

Vendor-Item Report

Vendor Name	Description	Wholesale	Retail
Atherton Wholesalers	Amazing Science Fun	$13.50	$24.99
Atherton Wholesalers	Crystal Growing Kit	$6.75	$12.97
Atherton Wholesalers	Discovery Dinosaurs	$12.35	$19.95
Atherton Wholesalers	Gem Nature Guide	$9.50	$14.95
Atherton Wholesalers	Onyx Jar	$7.50	$13.97
Gift Specialties	Agate Bookends	$16.25	$27.97
Gift Specialties	Dinosaur Egg Ornament	$7.50	$14.99
Gift Specialties	Fibonacci Necklace	$16.75	$29.99
Gift Specialties	Gyrobot	$27.99	$49.99
Gift Specialties	Molecule Necklace	$16.25	$29.95
Smith Distributors	Cosmos Uncovered	$8.95	$15.00
Smith Distributors	Fun with Math	$12.95	$24.95
Smith Distributors	Geek Toys Guide	$5.10	$9.99
Smith Distributors	Paper Planes	$7.10	$13.99
Smith Distributors	Slime Time	$15.35	$24.99

Figure 2–91

Continued >

In the Labs *continued*

12. Create a query for the Item table that includes the Item Number, Description, Wholesale Cost, and Retail Price. Calculate the difference between Retail Price and Wholesale Cost (Retail Price – Wholesale Cost). Assign the alias Mark Up to the calculated field. Save the query as Lab 2-2 Step 12 Query.
13. Create a query for the Item table that displays the average Wholesale Cost and the average Retail Price of all items. Save the query as Lab 2-2 Step 13 Query.
14. Create a query for the Item table that displays the Item Number, Description, On Hand, and Retail Price for the 5 items with the lowest retail price. Save the query as Lab 2-2 Step 14 Query.
15. Submit the revised database in the format specified by your instructor.
16. How could you modify the query in step 2 to find all vendors where the vendor code is AW or GS? If there is more than one way to perform this query, list all ways.

Lab 3: Consider This: Your Turn

Querying the Camshay Marketing Database

Instructions: Open the Lab 3 Camshay Marketing database you created in Module 1. If you did not create this database, contact your instructor for information about accessing the required files.

Part 1: Use the concepts and techniques presented in this module to create queries for the following. Save each query.

a. Find all marketing analysts who started between June 1, 2015 and September 30, 2015. Show the marketing analyst's first name, last name, salary YTD, and incentive YTD.
b. Find the client name and street address of all clients located in a city that starts with Bu.
c. Find the client number, client name, amount paid and current due of all clients whose amount paid is $0.00 or whose current due is $0.00.
d. Find the client number, client name, amount paid, current due, and total amount for all clients located in North Carolina (NC).
e. Create a parameter query for the Client table that will allow the user to enter a different city each time the query is run. The user should see all fields in the query result.
f. Create a crosstab query that groups the amount paid total by city and marketing analyst.
g. Find the marketing analyst for each client. List the marketing analyst number, first name, last name, client number, client name, and current due. Sort the results by client number within marketing analyst number.
h. Open the query you created in Step g above and restrict retrieval to only those clients whose current due amount is greater than $5,000.00.
i. Change the organization of the Navigation Pane so that all objects associated with the Client table are grouped together and all objects associated with the Marketing Analyst are grouped together.

Submit your assignment in the format specified by your instructor.

Part 2: You made several decisions while creating the queries in this assignment, including the parameter query in Step e. What was the rationale behind your decisions? There are two ways to create the query in step e. What are they? Which one did you use?

3 Maintaining a Database

Objectives

You will have mastered the material in this module when you can:

- Add, change, and delete records
- Search for records
- Filter records
- Update a table design
- Use action queries to update records
- Use delete queries to delete records
- Specify validation rules, default values, and formats
- Create and use single-value lookup fields
- Create and use multivalued lookup fields
- Add new fields to an existing report
- Format a datasheet
- Specify referential integrity
- Use a subdatasheet
- Sort records

Introduction

Once you have created a database and loaded it with data, you must maintain it. **Maintaining the database** means modifying the data to keep it up to date by adding new records, changing the data for existing records, and deleting records. Updating can include mass updates or mass deletions (i.e., updates to, or deletions of, many records at the same time).

Maintenance of a database can also involve the need to **restructure the database** periodically. Restructuring can include adding new fields to a table, changing the characteristics of existing fields, and removing existing fields. Restructuring also includes the creation of validation rules and referential integrity. Validation rules ensure the validity of the data in the database, whereas referential integrity ensures the validity of the relationships between entities. Maintaining a database can also include filtering records, a process that ensures that only the records that satisfy some criterion appear when viewing and updating the data in a table. Changing the appearance of a datasheet is also a maintenance activity.

BTW

Organizing Files and Folders

You should organize and store files in folders so that you easily can find the files later. For example, if you are taking an introductory computer class called CIS 101, a good practice would be to save all Access files in an Access folder in a CIS 101 folder. For a discussion of folders and detailed examples of creating folders, refer to the Office and Windows module at the beginning of this book.

Project — Maintaining a Database

PrattLast Associates faces the task of keeping its database up to date. As the company takes on new accounts and account managers, it will need to add new records, make changes to existing records, and delete records. PrattLast believes that it can serve its

For an introduction to Windows and instructions about how to perform basic Windows tasks, read the Office and Windows module at the beginning of this book, where you can learn how to resize windows, change screen resolution, create folders, move and rename files, use Windows Help, and much more.

accounts better by changing the structure of the database to categorize the accounts by type. The company will do this by adding an Account Type field to the Account table. Account managers also believe they can provide better customer service if the database includes the list of human resource services that are of interest to each account. The company will do so by adding a Services Needed field to the Account table. Because accounts may need more than one service, this field will be a multivalued field, which is a field that can store multiple values or entries. Along with these changes, PrattLast staff wants to change the appearance of a datasheet when displaying data.

PrattLast would like the ability to make mass updates, that is, to update or delete many records in a single operation. It wants rules that make sure users can enter only valid, or appropriate, data into the database. PrattLast also wants to ensure that the database cannot contain the name of an account that is not associated with a specific account manager.

Figure 3 – 1 summarizes some of the various types of activities involved in maintaining the PrattLast Associates database.

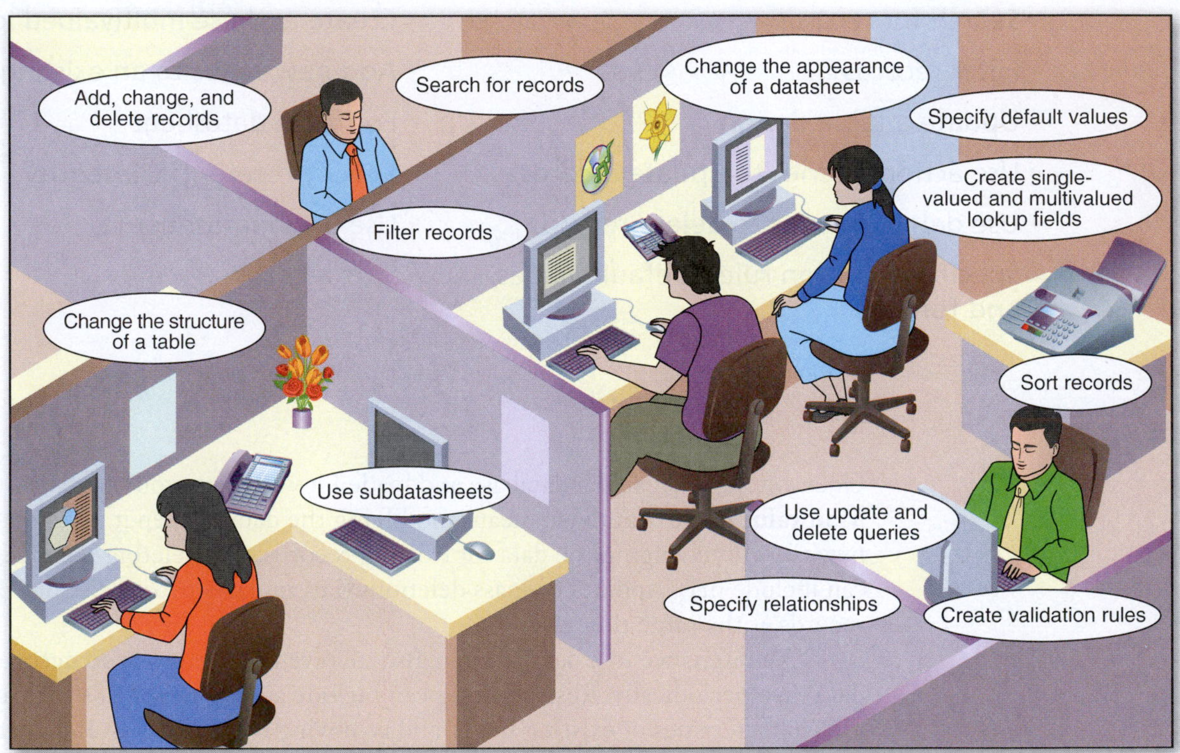

Figure 3 – 1

For an introduction to Office and instructions about how to perform basic tasks in Office apps, read the Office and Windows module at the beginning of this book, where you can learn how to run an application, use the ribbon, save a file, open a file, print a file, exit an application, use Help, and much more.

In this module, you will learn how to maintain a database by performing the tasks shown in Figure 3 – 1. The following roadmap identifies general activities you will perform as you progress through this module:

1. **UPDATE RECORDS** using a form.
2. **FILTER RECORDS** using various filtering options.
3. **CHANGE** the **STRUCTURE** of a table.
4. Make **MASS CHANGES** to a table.

5. Create VALIDATION RULES.
6. CHANGE the APPEARANCE of a datasheet.
7. Specify REFERENTIAL INTEGRITY.
8. ORDER RECORDS in a datasheet.

Updating Records

Keeping the data in a database current requires updating records in three ways: adding new records, changing the data in existing records, and deleting existing records. In Module 1, you added records to a database using Datasheet view; that is, as you added records, the records appeared on the screen in a datasheet. The data looked like a table. When you need to add additional records, you can use the same techniques.

In Module 1, you used a simple form to view records. You can also use a **split form**, a form that allows you to simultaneously view both simple form and datasheet views of the data. You can use either portion of a split form to add or update records. To add new records, change existing records, or delete records, you use the same techniques you used in Datasheet view.

BTW

The Ribbon and Screen Resolution

Access may change how the groups and buttons within the groups appear on the ribbon, depending on the computer or mobile device's screen resolution. Thus, your ribbon may look different from the ones in this book if you are using a screen resolution other than 1366 x 768.

To Create a Split Form

1 UPDATE RECORDS | 2 FILTER RECORDS | 3 CHANGE STRUCTURE | 4 MASS CHANGES | 5 VALIDATION RULES
6 CHANGE APPEARANCE | 7 REFERENTIAL INTEGRITY | 8 ORDER RECORDS

The following steps create a split form. ***Why?*** *With a split form, you have the advantage of seeing a single record in a form, while simultaneously viewing several records in a datasheet.*

1

- Run Access and open the database named PrattLast Associates from your hard disk, OneDrive, or other storage location.
- Open the Navigation Pane if it is currently closed.
- If necessary, click the Account table in the Navigation Pane to select it.
- Click Create on the ribbon to display the Create tab.
- Click the More Forms button (Create tab | Forms group) to display the More Forms menu (Figure 3–2).

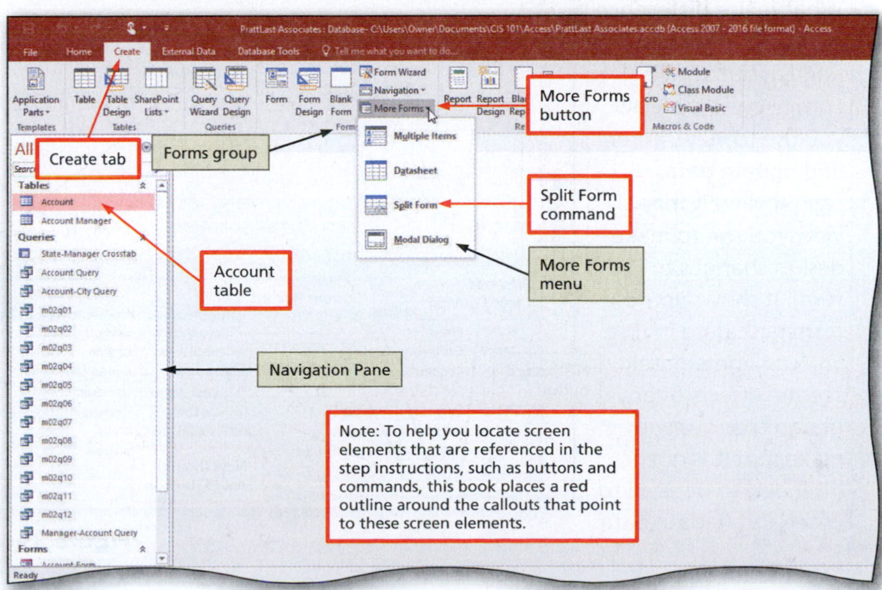

Figure 3–2

2

- Click Split Form to create a split form based on the Account table.
- Close the Navigation Pane (Figure 3–3).

Q&A Is the form automatically saved?
No. You will take specific actions later to save the form.

Q&A A field list appeared when I created the form. What should I do?
Click the 'Add Existing Fields' button (Design tab | Tools group) to remove the field list.

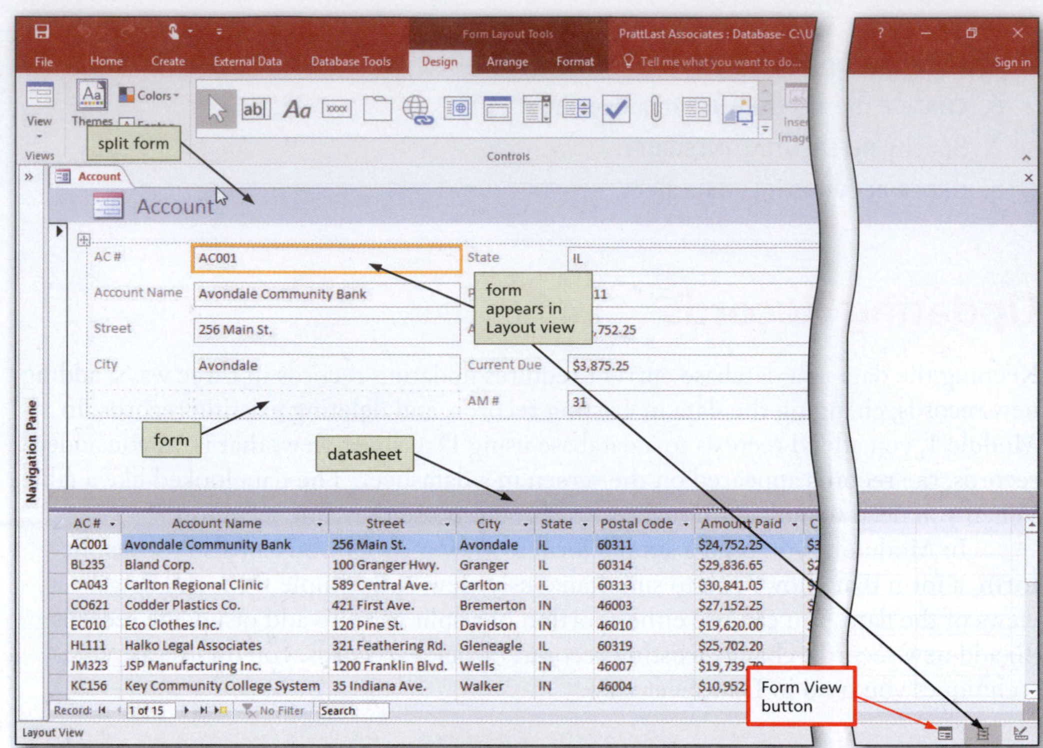

Figure 3–3

3

- Click the Form View button on the Access status bar to display the form in Form view rather than Layout view (Figure 3–4).

Q&A What is the difference between Form view and Layout view?
Form view is the view you use to view, enter, and update data. Layout view is the view you use to make design changes to the form. It shows you the form with data in it so you can immediately see the effects of any design changes you make, but it is not intended to be used to enter and update data.

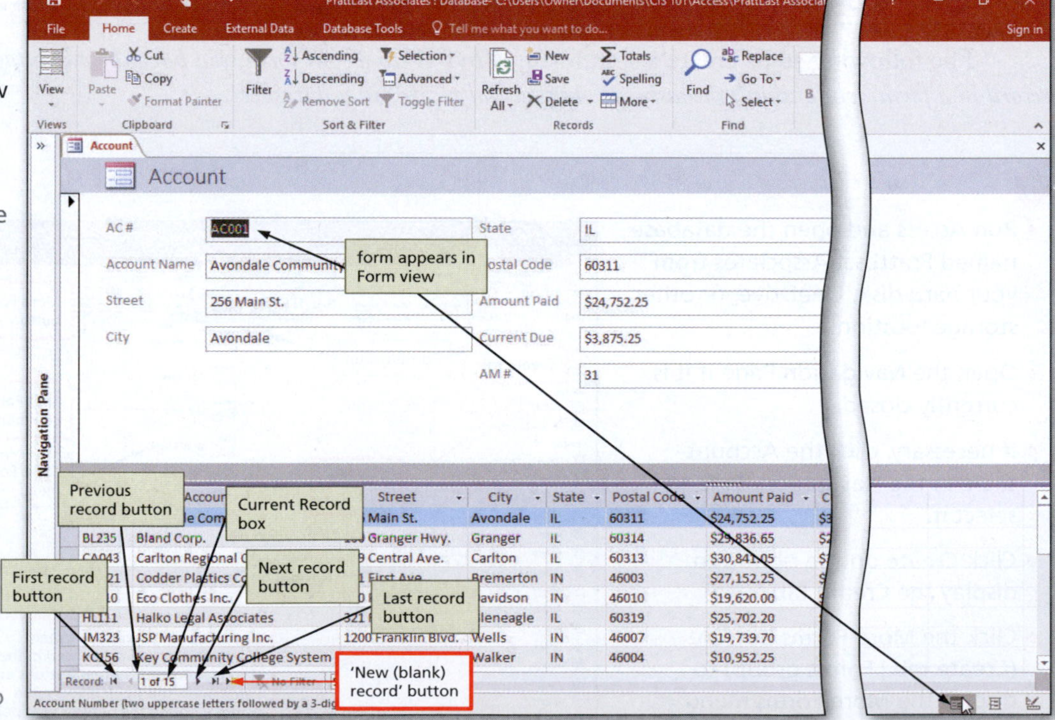

Figure 3–4

Experiment

- Click the various Navigation buttons (First record, Next record, Previous record, Last record, and 'New (blank) record') to see each button's effect. Click the Current Record box, change the record number, and press the ENTER key to see how to move to a specific record.

4

- Click the Save button on the Quick Access Toolbar to display the Save As dialog box.
- Type `Account Split Form` as the form name (Figure 3–5).

5

- Click the OK button (Save As dialog box) to save the form.

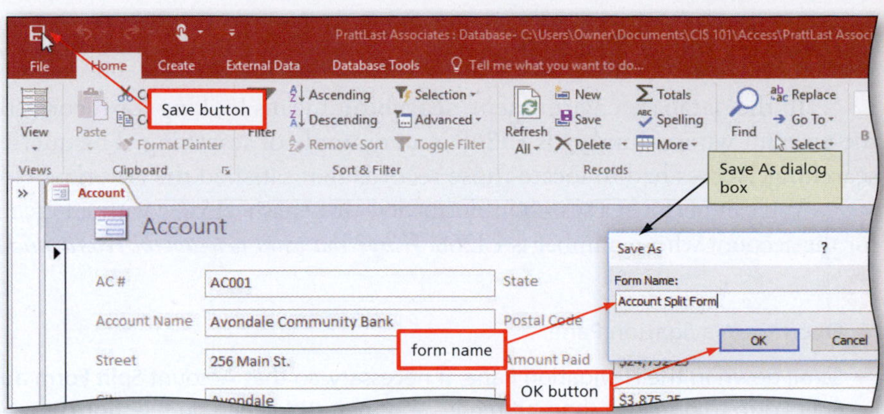

Figure 3–5

Other Ways

1. Right-click tab for form, click Form View on shortcut menu

To Use a Form to Add Records

1 UPDATE RECORDS | **2 FILTER RECORDS** | **3 CHANGE STRUCTURE** | **4 MASS CHANGES** | **5 VALIDATION RULES**
6 CHANGE APPEARANCE | **7 REFERENTIAL INTEGRITY** | **8 ORDER RECORDS**

Once a form or split form is open in Form view, you can add records using the same techniques you used to add records in Datasheet view. In a split form, the changes you make on the form are automatically made on the datasheet. You do not need to take any special action. The following steps use the split form that you just created to add records. ***Why?*** *With a split form, as you add a record, you can immediately see the effect of the addition on the datasheet.*

- Click the 'New (blank) record' button on the Navigation bar to enter a new record, and then type the data for the new record, as shown in Figure 3–6. Press the TAB key after typing the data in each field, except after typing the data for the final field (Account Manager Number).

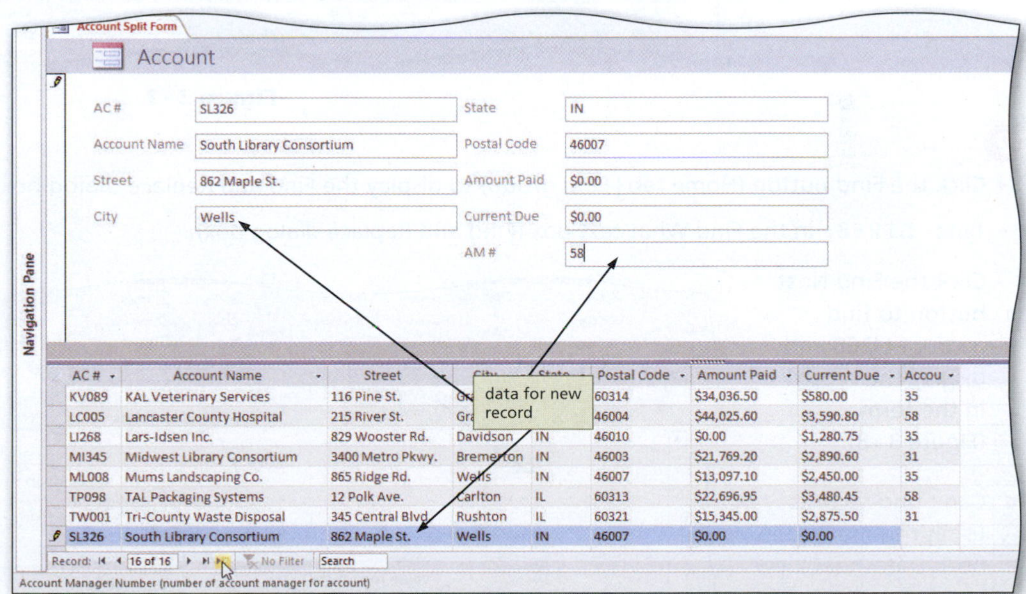

Figure 3–6

2

- Press the TAB key to complete the entry of the record.
- Close the form.

Other Ways

1. Click New button (Home tab | Records group)
2. Press CTRL+PLUS SIGN (+)

To Search for a Record

1 UPDATE RECORDS | 2 FILTER RECORDS | 3 CHANGE STRUCTURE | 4 MASS CHANGES | 5 VALIDATION RULES
6 CHANGE APPEARANCE | 7 REFERENTIAL INTEGRITY | 8 ORDER RECORDS

In the database environment, **searching** means looking for records that satisfy some criteria. Looking for the account whose number is LI268 is an example of searching. The queries in Module 2 were also examples of searching. Access had to locate those records that satisfied the criteria.

You can perform a search in Form view or Datasheet view without creating a query. The following steps search for the account whose number is LI268. ***Why?*** *You want to locate the record quickly so you can update this account's record.*

- Open the Navigation Pane.
- Scroll down in the Navigation Pane, if necessary, so that Account Split Form appears on your screen, right-click Account Split Form to display a shortcut menu, and then click Open on the shortcut menu to open the form in Form view.

Q&A Which command on the shortcut menu gives me Form view? I see both Layout View and Design View, but no option for Form View.
The Open command opens the form in Form view.

- Close the Navigation Pane (Figure 3–7).

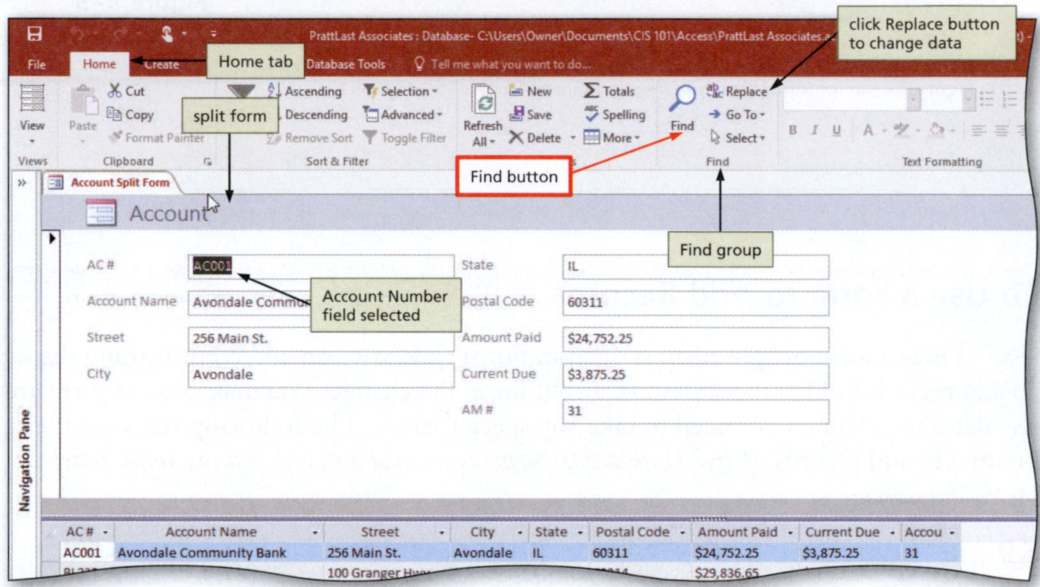

Figure 3–7

- Click the Find button (Home tab | Find group) to display the Find and Replace dialog box.
- Type `LI268` in the Find What text box (Find and Replace dialog box).
- Click the Find Next button to find account LI268 and display the record in the form (Figure 3–8).

Q&A Can I find records using this method in both Datasheet view and Form view?
Yes. You use the same process to find records whether you are viewing the data with a split form, in Datasheet view, or in Form view.

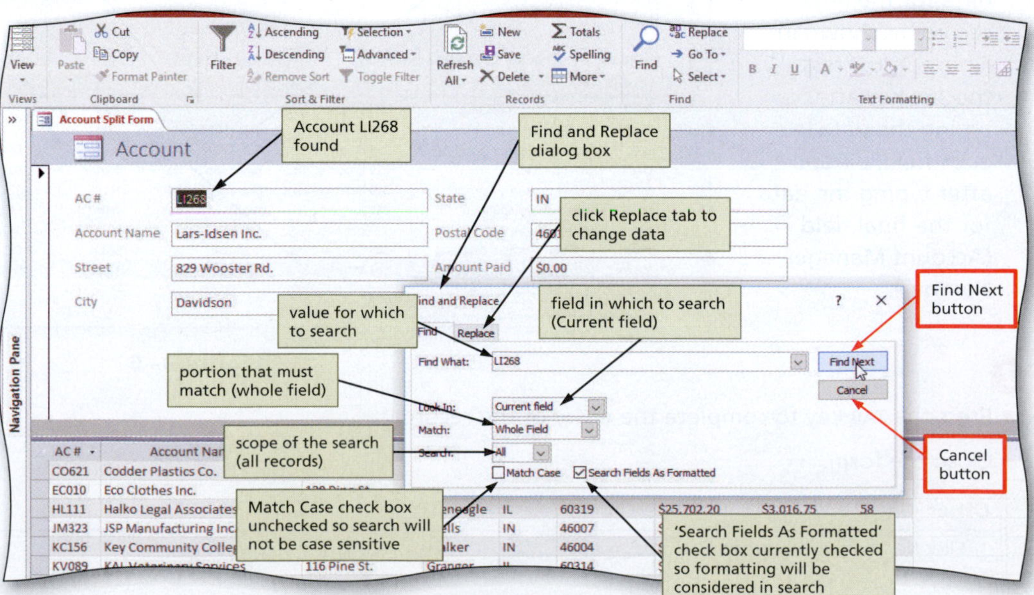

Figure 3–8

3

- Click the Cancel button (Find and Replace dialog box) to remove the dialog box from the screen.

Q&A Why does the button in the dialog box read, Find Next, rather than simply Find?
In some cases, after locating a record that satisfies a criterion, you might need to find the next record that satisfies the same criterion. For example, if you just found the first account whose account manager number is 31, you might then want to find the second such account, then the third, and so on. To do so, click the Find Next button. You will not need to retype the value each time.

Other Ways

1. Press CTRL+F

Can you replace one value with another using the Find and Replace dialog box?
Yes. Either click the Replace button (Home tab | Find group) or click the Replace tab in the Find and Replace dialog box. You can then enter both the value to find and the new value.

CONSIDER THIS

To Update the Contents of a Record

1 UPDATE RECORDS | 2 FILTER RECORDS | 3 CHANGE STRUCTURE | 4 MASS CHANGES | 5 VALIDATION RULES
6 CHANGE APPEARANCE | 7 REFERENTIAL INTEGRITY | 8 ORDER RECORDS

The following step uses Form view to change the name of account LI268 from Lars-Idsen Inc. to Lars-Idsen-Fleming Inc. ***Why?*** *PrattLast determined that this account's name was incorrect and must be changed.* After locating the record to be changed, select the field to be changed by clicking the field. You can also press the TAB key repeatedly until the desired field is selected. Then make the appropriate changes. (Clicking the field automatically produces an insertion point. If you use the TAB key, you will need to press the F2 key to produce an insertion point.)

- Click in the Account Name field in the form for account LI268 immediately to the right of the n in Idsen.
- Type a hyphen (-) and then type `Fleming` after Idsen.
- Press the TAB key to complete the change and move to the next field (Figure 3–9).

Q&A Could I have changed the contents of the field in the datasheet portion of the split form?
Yes. You first need to ensure the record to be changed appears in the datasheet. You then can change the value just as in the form.

Q&A Do I need to save my change?
No. Once you move to another record or close this form, the change to the name will become permanent.

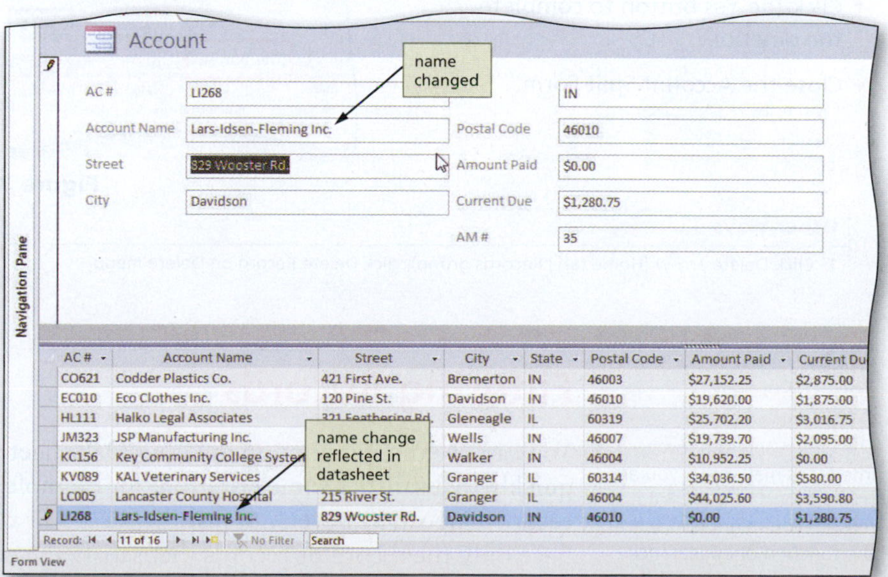

Figure 3–9

To Delete a Record

1 UPDATE RECORDS | 2 FILTER RECORDS | 3 CHANGE STRUCTURE | 4 MASS CHANGES | 5 VALIDATION RULES
6 CHANGE APPEARANCE | 7 REFERENTIAL INTEGRITY | 8 ORDER RECORDS

When records are no longer needed, you should delete the records (remove them) from the table. The following steps delete account JM323. ***Why?*** *Account JM323 is no longer served by PrattLast Associates and its final payment has been received, so the record can be deleted.*

1

- With the Account Split Form open, click the record selector in the datasheet for account JM323 to select the record (Figure 3–10).

Q&A That technique works in the datasheet portion. How do I select the record in the form portion?
With the desired record appearing in the form, click the record selector (the triangle in front of the record) to select the entire record.

Q&A What do I do if the record I want to delete does not appear on the screen?
First search for the record you want to delete using the Find and Replace dialog box.

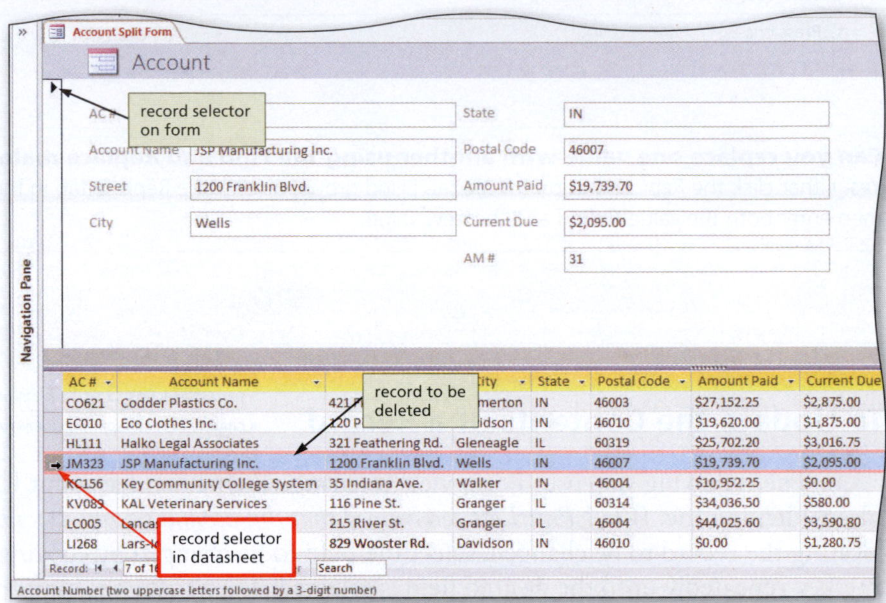

Figure 3–10

2

- Press the DELETE key to delete the record (Figure 3–11).

3

- Click the Yes button to complete the deletion.
- Close the Account Split Form.

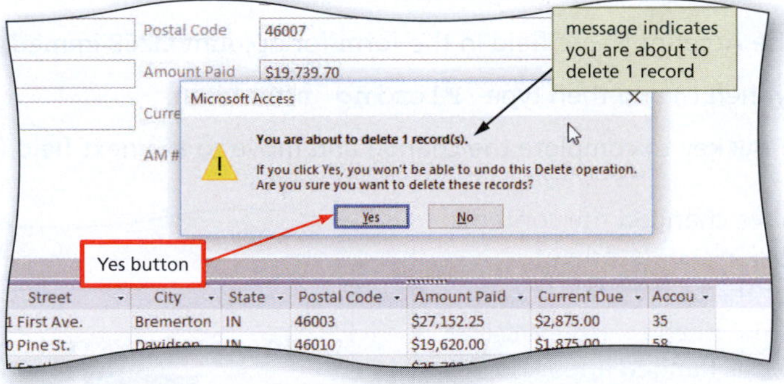

Figure 3–11

Other Ways

1. Click Delete arrow (Home tab | Records group), click Delete Record on Delete menu

BTW
Touch Screen Differences
The Office and Windows interfaces may vary if you are using a touch screen. For this reason, you might notice that the function or appearance of your touch screen differs slightly from this module's presentation.

Filtering Records

You can use the Find button in either Datasheet view or Form view to locate a record quickly that satisfies some criterion (for example, the account number is LI268). All records appear, however, not just the record or records that satisfy the criterion. To have only the record or records that satisfy the criterion appear, use a **filter**. Four types of filters are available: Filter By Selection, Common Filters, Filter By Form, and Advanced Filter/Sort. You can use a filter in either Datasheet view or Form view.

To Use Filter By Selection

To use Filter By Selection, you give Access an example of the data you want by selecting the data within the table. You then choose the option you want on the Selection menu. The following steps use Filter By Selection in Datasheet view to display only the records for accounts in Granger. *Why? Filter by Selection is appropriate for displaying these records and is the simplest type of filter.*

1

- Open the Navigation Pane.
- Open the Account table, and close the Navigation Pane.
- Click the City field on the second record to specify Granger as the city (Figure 3–12).

Q&A Could I have selected the City field on another record where the city is also Granger to select the same city?
Yes. It does not matter which record you select as long as the city is Granger.

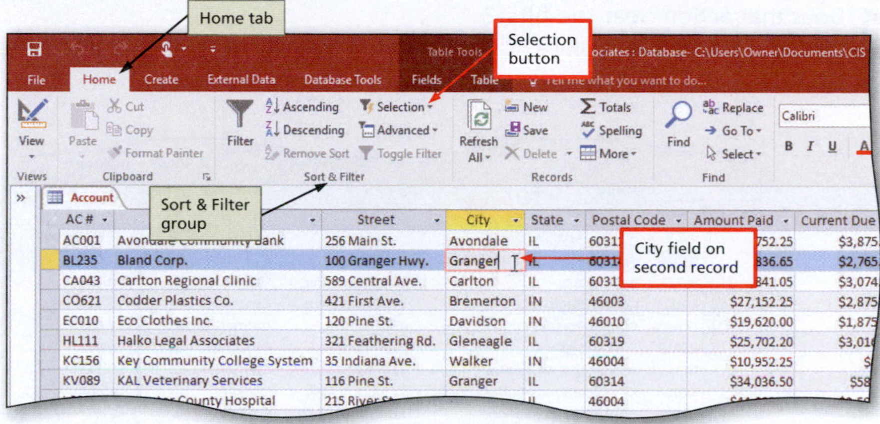

Figure 3–12

2

- Click the Selection button (Home tab | Sort & Filter group) to display the Selection menu (Figure 3–13).

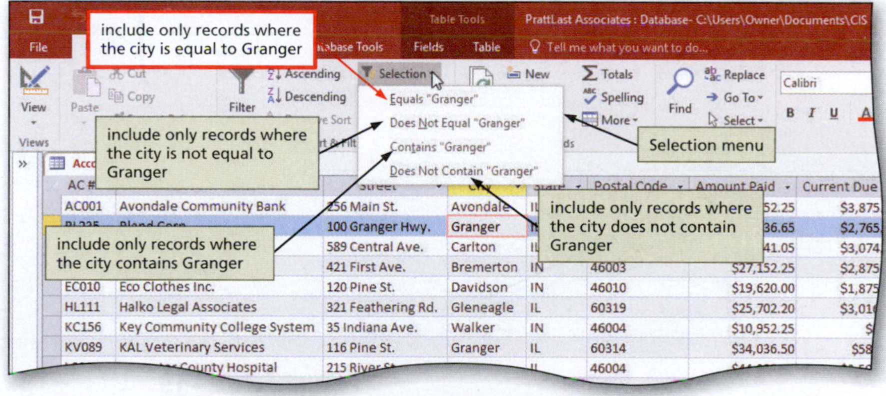

Figure 3–13

3

- Click Equals "Granger" to select only those accounts whose city is Granger (Figure 3–14).

Q&A Can I also filter in Form view?
Yes. Filtering works the same whether you are viewing the data with a split form, in Datasheet view, or in Form view.

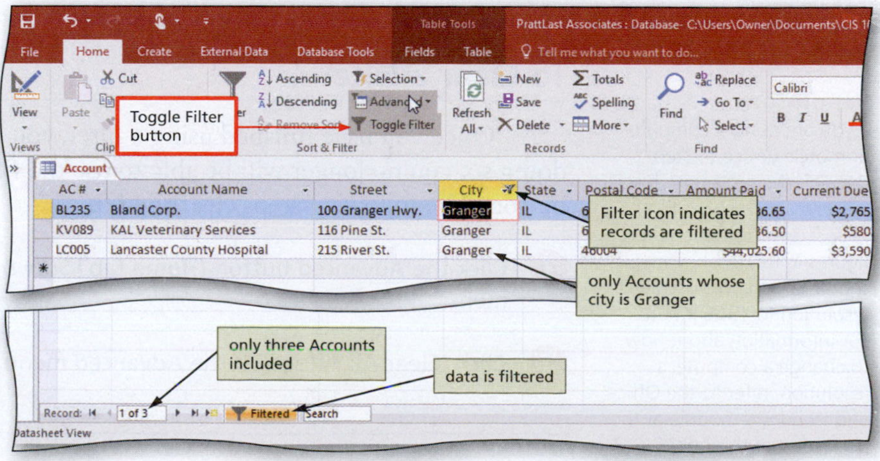

Figure 3–14

To Toggle a Filter

The Toggle Filter button toggles between filtered and unfiltered displays of the records in the table. That is, if only filtered records currently appear, clicking the Toggle Filter button will redisplay all records. If all records are currently displayed and there is a filter that is in effect, clicking the Toggle Filter button will display only the filtered records. If no filter is active, the Toggle Filter button will be dimmed, so clicking it would have no effect.

The following step toggles the filter. ***Why?** PrattLast wants to once again view all the records.*

1

- Click the Toggle Filter button (Home tab | Sort & Filter group) to toggle the filter and redisplay all records (Figure 3–15).

Q&A Does that action clear the filter?
No. The filter is still in place. If you click the Toggle Filter button a second time, you will again see only the filtered records.

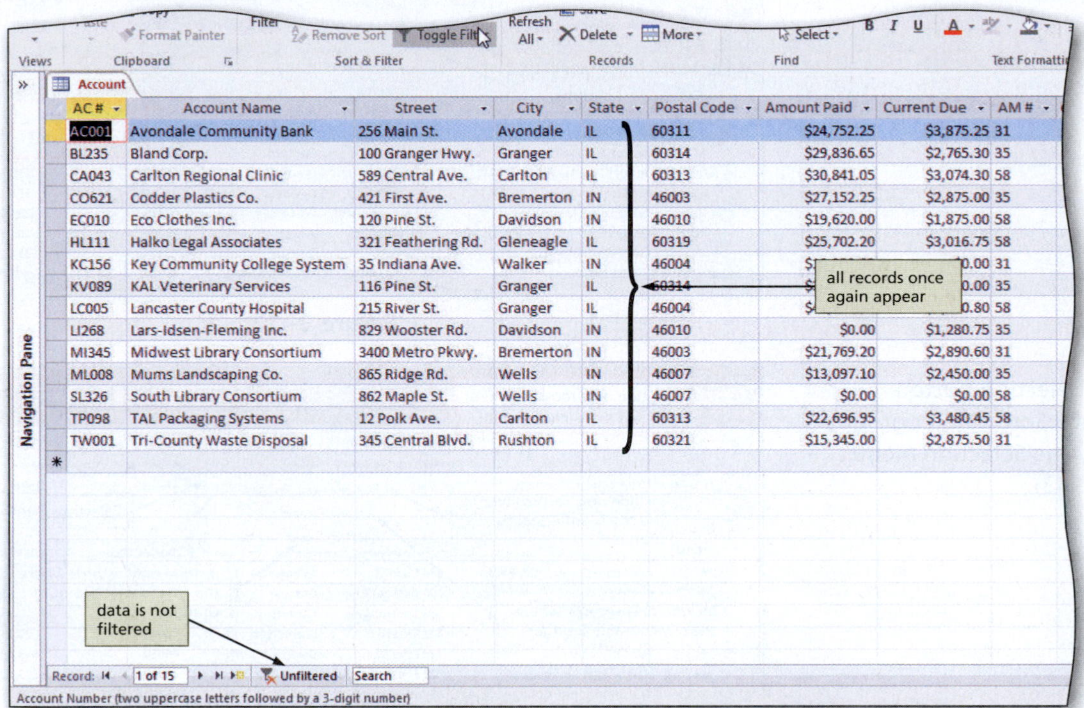

Figure 3–15

BTW
Access Screen Resolution
If you are using a computer or mobile device to step through the project in this module and you want your screens to match the figures in this book, you should change your screen's resolution to 1366 x 768. For information about how to change a computer's resolution, refer to the Office and Windows module at the beginning of this book.

To Clear a Filter

Once you have finished using a filter, you can clear (remove) the filter. After doing so, you no longer will be able to use the filter by clicking the Toggle Filter button. The following steps clear the filter.

1 Click the Advanced button (Home tab | Sort & Filter group) to display the Advanced menu.

2 Click 'Clear All Filters' on the Advanced menu.

To Use a Common Filter

If you have determined you want to include those accounts whose city begins with G, Filter By Selection would not be appropriate. ***Why?*** *None of the options within Filter by Selection would support this type of criterion.* You can filter individual fields by clicking the arrow to the right of the field name and using one of the **common filters** that are available for the field. Access includes a collection of filters that perform common filtering tasks; you can modify a common filter by customizing it for the specific field. The following steps customize a common filter to include only those accounts whose city begins with G.

1

- Click the City arrow to display the common filter menu.
- Point to the Text Filters command to display the custom text filters (Figure 3–16).

Q&A I selected the City field and then clicked the Filter button on the Home tab | Sort & Filter group. My screen looks the same. Is this right?
Yes. That is another way to display the common filter menu.

Q&A If I wanted certain cities included, could I use the check boxes?
Yes. Be sure the cities you want are the only ones checked.

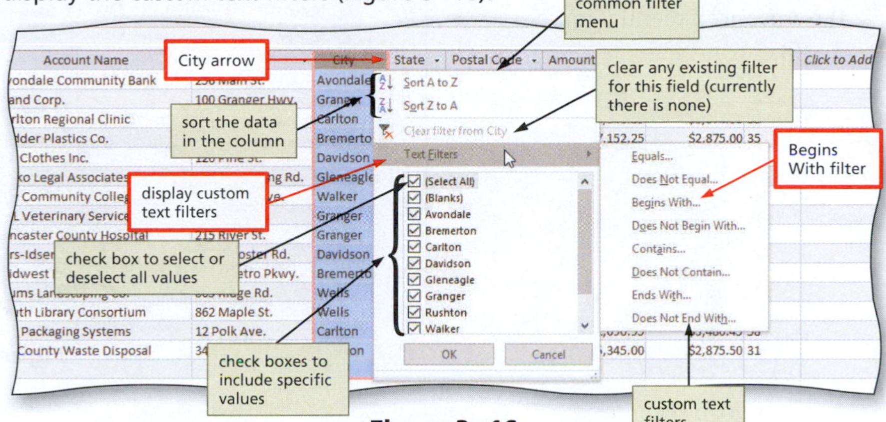

Figure 3–16

2

- Click Begins With to display the Custom Filter dialog box.
- Type G as the 'City begins with' value (Figure 3–17).

Experiment

- Try other options in the common filter menu to see their effects. When done, once again select those accounts whose city begins with G.

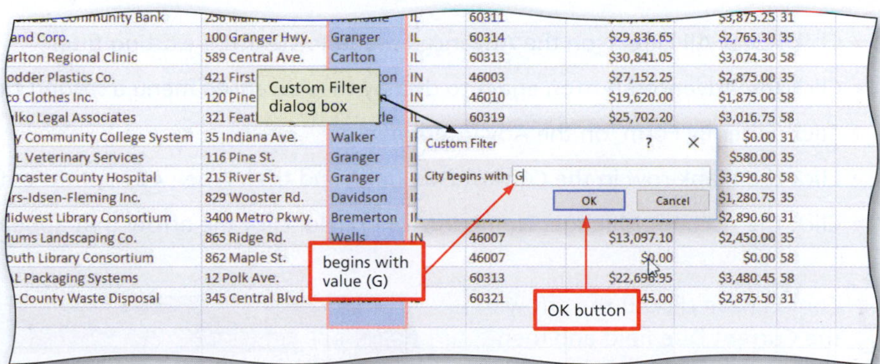

Figure 3–17

3

- Click the OK button to filter the records (Figure 3–18).

Q&A Can I use the same technique in Form view?
In Form view, you would need to click the field and then click the Filter button to display the Common Filter menu. The rest of the process would be the same.

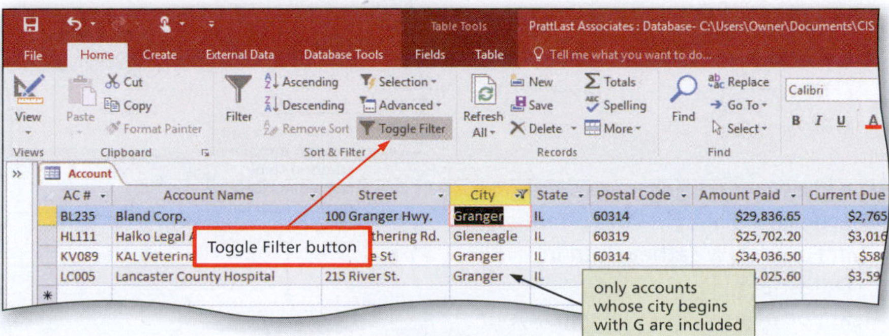

Figure 3–18

4

- Click the Toggle Filter button (Home tab | Sort & Filter group) to toggle the filter and redisplay all records.

Other Ways

1. Right-click field, click Text Filters on shortcut menu

To Use Filter By Form

Filter By Selection and the common filters method you just used are quick and easy ways to filter by the value in a single field. For filters that involve multiple fields, however, these methods are not appropriate, so you would use Filter By Form. ***Why?*** *Filter By Form allows you to filter based on multiple fields and criteria.* For example, Filter By Form would allow you to find only those accounts whose current due amounts are less than $2,000.00 and whose account manager number is 35. The following steps use Filter By Form to restrict the records that appear.

1

- Click the Advanced button (Home tab | Sort & Filter group) to display the Advanced menu (Figure 3–19).

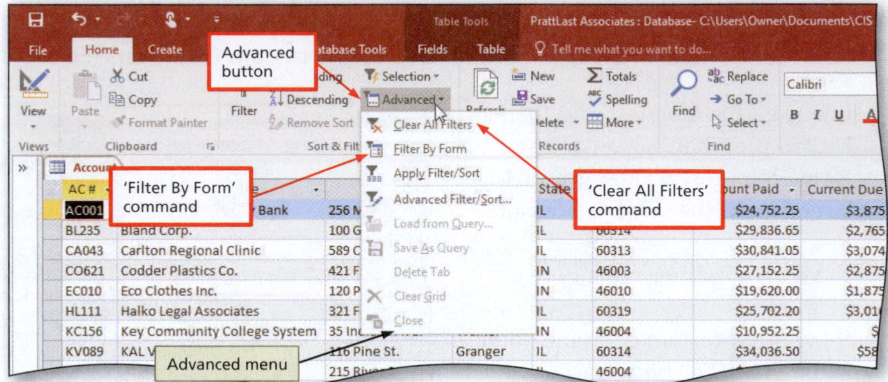

Figure 3–19

2

- Click 'Clear All Filters' on the Advanced menu to clear the existing filter.
- Click the Advanced button again to display the Advanced menu a second time.
- Click 'Filter By Form' on the Advanced menu.
- Click the blank row in the Current Due field, and then type `<2000` to enter a criterion for the Current Due field.
- Click the Account Manager Number (AM #) field, click the arrow that appears, and then click 35 (Figure 3–20).

Q&A Could I have clicked the arrow in the Current Due field and then made a selection rather than typing a criterion?
No. Because your criterion involves something other than equality, you need to type the criterion rather than selecting from a list.

Q&A Is there any difference in the process if I am viewing a table in Form view rather than in Datasheet view?
In Form view, you will make your entries in a form rather than a datasheet. Otherwise, the process is the same.

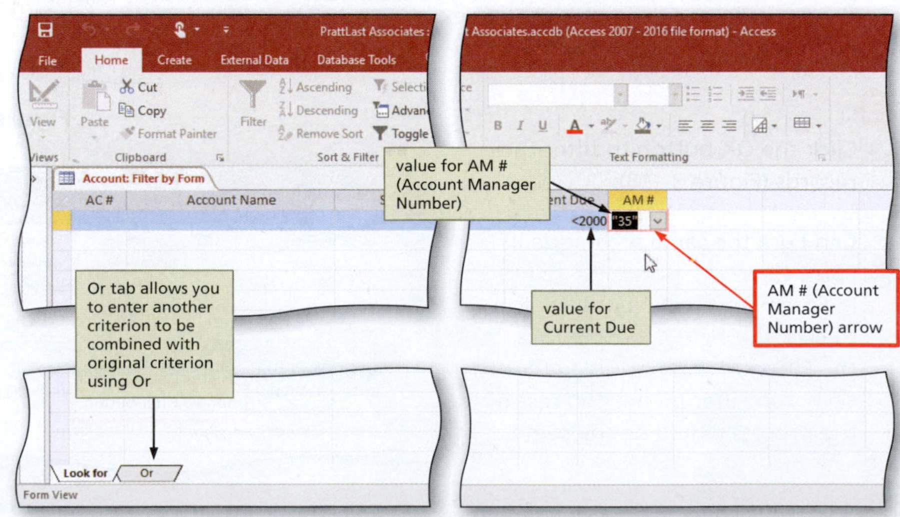

Figure 3–20

3

- Click the Toggle Filter button (Home tab | Sort & Filter group) to apply the filter (Figure 3–21).

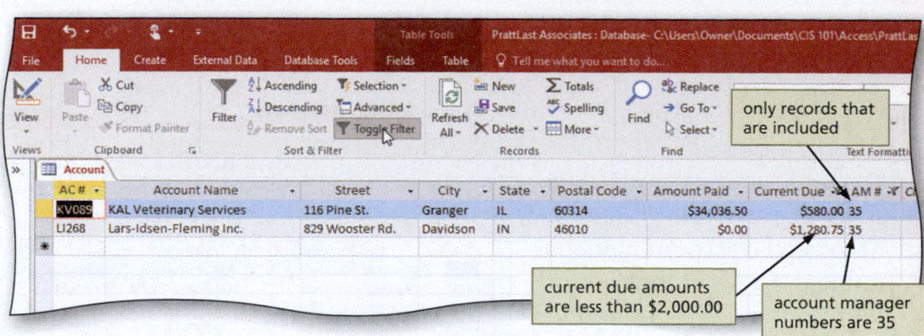

Figure 3–21

Experiment

- Select 'Filter by Form' again and enter different criteria. In each case, toggle the filter to see the effect of your selection. When done, once again select those accounts whose Current Due amounts are less than (<) 2000 and whose account manager number is 35.

Other Ways

1. Click the Advanced button (Home tab | Sort & Filter group), click Apply Filter/Sort on Advanced menu

To Use Advanced Filter/Sort

1 UPDATE RECORDS | 2 FILTER RECORDS | 3 CHANGE STRUCTURE | 4 MASS CHANGES | 5 VALIDATION RULES
6 CHANGE APPEARANCE | 7 REFERENTIAL INTEGRITY | 8 ORDER RECORDS

In some cases, your criteria will be too complex even for Filter By Form. You might decide you want to include any account whose current due amounts are greater than $3,000 and whose account manager number is 58. Additionally, you might want to include any account whose current due amount is $0, no matter who the account's manager is. Further, you might want to have the results sorted by account name. The following steps use Advanced Filter/Sort to accomplish this task. ***Why?*** *Advanced Filter/Sort supports complex criteria as well as the ability to sort the results.*

1

- Click the Advanced button (Home tab | Sort & Filter group) to display the Advanced menu, and then click 'Clear All Filters' on the Advanced menu to clear the existing filter.
- Click the Advanced button to display the Advanced menu a second time.
- Click 'Advanced Filter/Sort' on the Advanced menu.
- Expand the size of the field list so all the fields in the Account table appear.
- Add the Account Name field and select Ascending as the sort order to specify the order in which the filtered records will appear.
- Include the Account Manager Number field and enter 58 as the criterion.
- Include the Current Due field and enter >3000 as the criterion in the Criteria row and 0 as the criterion in the or row (Figure 3–22).

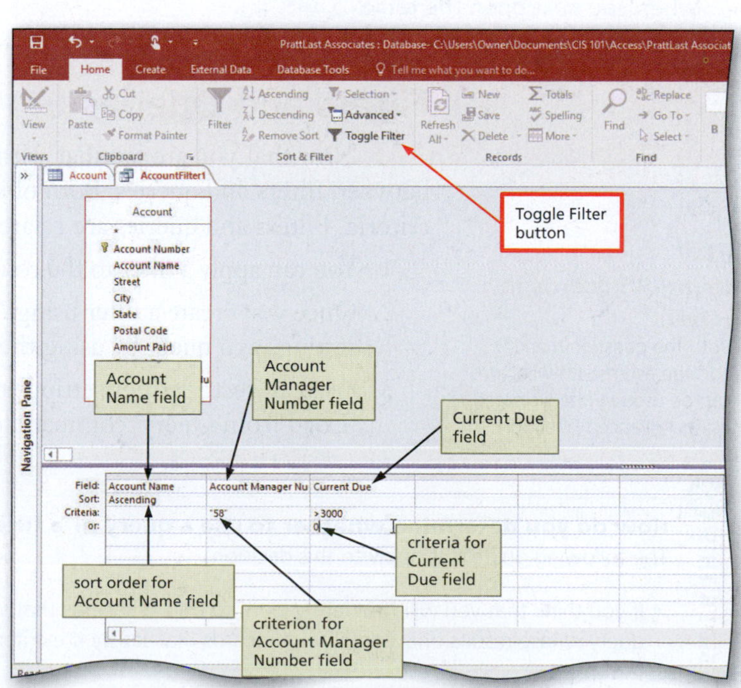

Figure 3–22

2

- Click the Toggle Filter button (Home tab | Sort & Filter group) to toggle the filter so that only records that satisfy the criteria will appear (Figure 3–23).

Q&A Why are those particular records included?
The first, second, fourth, and sixth records are included because the account manager number is 58 and the current due amount is greater than $3,000. The other records are included because the current due amount is $0.00.

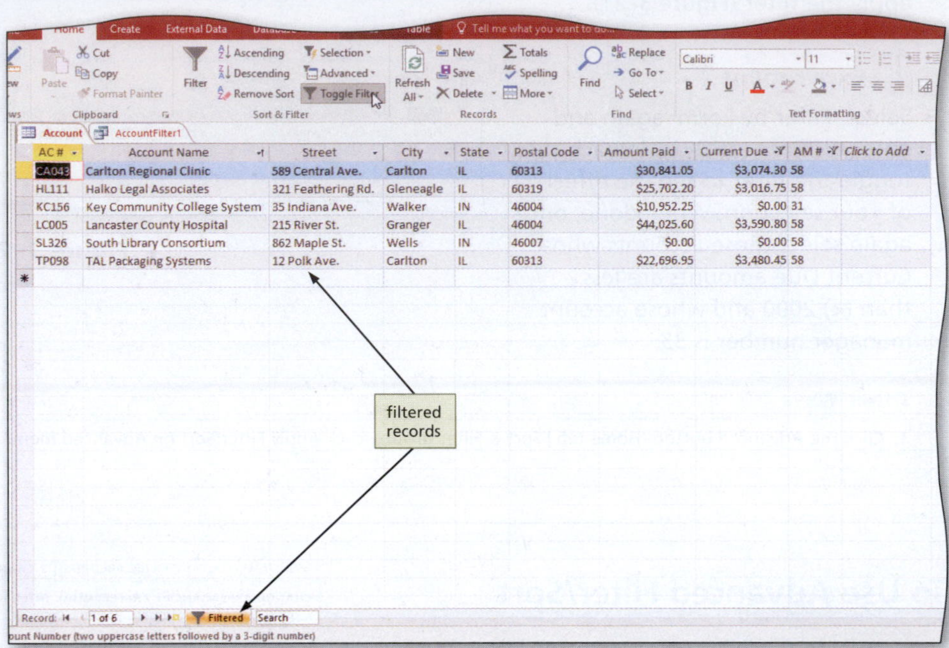

Figure 3–23

Experiment

- Select 'Advanced Filter/Sort' again and enter different sorting options and criteria. In each case, toggle the filter to see the effect of your selection. When done, change back to the sorting options and criteria you entered in Step 1.

3

- Close the Account table. When asked if you want to save your changes, click the No button.

Q&A Should I not have cleared all filters before closing the table?
If you are closing a table and not saving the changes, it is not necessary to clear the filter. No filter will be active when you next open the table.

Filters and Queries

Now that you are familiar with how filters work, you might notice similarities between filters and queries. Both objects are used to locate data that meets specific criteria. Filters and queries are related in three ways.

1. You can apply a filter to the results of a query just as you can apply a filter to a table.
2. Once you create a filter using Advanced Filter/Sort, you can save the filter settings as a query by using the 'Save as Query' command on the Advanced menu.
3. You can restore filter settings that you previously saved in a query by using the 'Load from Query' command on the Advanced menu.

BTW
Using Wildcards in Filters
Both the question mark(?) and the asterisk (*) wildcards can be used in filters created using Advanced Filter/Sort.

CONSIDER THIS

How do you determine whether to use a query or a filter?

The following guidelines apply to this decision.

- If you think that you will frequently want to display records that satisfy this exact criterion, you should consider creating a query whose results only contain the records that satisfy the criterion. To display those records in the future, simply open the query.
- If you are viewing data in a datasheet or form and decide you want to restrict the records to be included, it is easier to create a filter than a query. You can create and use the filter while you are viewing the data.
- If you have created a filter that you would like to be able to use again, you can save the filter as a query.

CONSIDER THIS

Once you have decided to use a filter, how do you determine which type of filter to use?

- If your criterion for filtering is that the value in a particular field matches or does not match a certain specific value, you can use Filter By Selection.
- If your criterion only involves a single field but is more complex (for example, the criterion specifies that the value in the field begins with a certain collection of letters) you can use a common filter.
- If your criterion involves more than one field, use Filter By Form.
- If your criterion involves more than a single And or Or, or if it involves sorting, you will probably find it simpler to use Advanced Filter/Sort.

Break Point: If you wish to take a break, this is a good place to do so. You can quit Access now. To resume at a later time, run Access, open the database called PrattLast Associates, and continue following the steps from this location forward.

Changing the Database Structure

When you initially create a database, you define its **structure**; that is, you assign names and types to all the fields. In many cases, the structure you first define will not continue to be appropriate as you use the database.

Perhaps a field currently in the table is no longer necessary. If no one ever uses a particular field, it is not needed in the table. Because it is occupying space and serving no useful purpose, you should remove it from the table. You would also need to delete the field from any forms, reports, or queries that include it.

More commonly, an organization will find that it needs to add data that was not anticipated at the time the database was first designed. The organization's own requirements may have changed. In addition, outside regulations that the organization must satisfy may change as well. Either case requires the addition of fields to an existing table.

Although you can make some changes to the database structure in Datasheet view, it is usually easier and better to make these changes in Design view.

BTW
Using the Find Button
You can use the Find button (Home tab | Find group) to search for records in datasheets, forms, query results, and reports.

BTW
Changing Data Types
It is possible to change the data type for a field that already contains data. Before doing so, you should consider the effect on other database objects, such as forms, queries, and reports. For example, you could convert a Short Text field to a Long Text field if you find that you do not have enough space to store the data that you need. You also could convert a Number field to a Currency field or vice versa.

To Delete a Field

If a field in one of your tables is no longer needed, you should delete the field; for example, it may serve no useful purpose, or it may have been included by mistake. To delete a field, you would use the following steps.

1. Open the table in Design view.
2. Click the row selector for the field to be deleted.
3. Press the DELETE key.
4. When Access displays the dialog box requesting confirmation that you want to delete the field, click the Yes button.

To Move a Field

If you decide you would rather have a field in one of your tables in a different position in the table, you can move it. To move a field, you would use the following steps.

1. Open the table in Design view.
2. Click the row selector for the field to be deleted.
3. Drag the field to the desired position.
4. Release the mouse button to place the field in the new position.

To Add a New Field

1 UPDATE RECORDS | 2 FILTER RECORDS | 3 CHANGE STRUCTURE | 4 MASS CHANGES | 5 VALIDATION RULES
6 CHANGE APPEARANCE | 7 REFERENTIAL INTEGRITY | 8 ORDER RECORDS

You can add fields to a table in a database. The following steps add the Account Type field to the Account table immediately after the Postal Code field. ***Why?*** *PrattLast Associates has decided that it needs to categorize its accounts by adding an additional field, Account Type. The possible values for Account Type are SER (which indicates the account is a service organization), NON (which indicates the account is a nonprofit), or IND (which indicates the account is an industrial/manufacturing company).*

- If necessary, open the Navigation Pane, open the Account table in Design view, and then close the Navigation Pane.
- Right-click the row selector for the Amount Paid field, and then click Insert Rows on the shortcut menu to insert a blank row above the selected field (Figure 3–24).

- Click the Field Name column for the new field to produce an insertion point.
- Type `Account Type` as the field name and then press the TAB key.

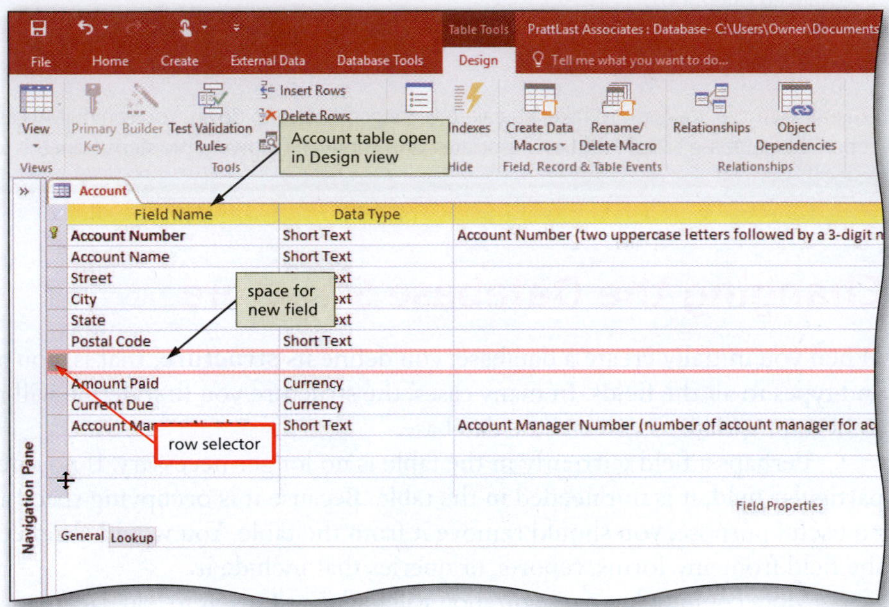

Figure 3–24

Other Ways

1. Click Insert Rows button (Table Tools Design tab | Tools group)

To Create a Lookup Field

1 UPDATE RECORDS | 2 FILTER RECORDS | 3 CHANGE STRUCTURE | 4 MASS CHANGES | 5 VALIDATION RULES
6 CHANGE APPEARANCE | 7 REFERENTIAL INTEGRITY | 8 ORDER RECORDS

A **lookup field** allows the user to select from a list of values when updating the contents of the field. The following steps make the Account Type field a lookup field. ***Why?*** *The Account Type field has only three possible values, making it an appropriate lookup field.*

- If necessary, click the Data Type column for the Account Type field, and then click the Data Type arrow to display the menu of available data types (Figure 3–25).

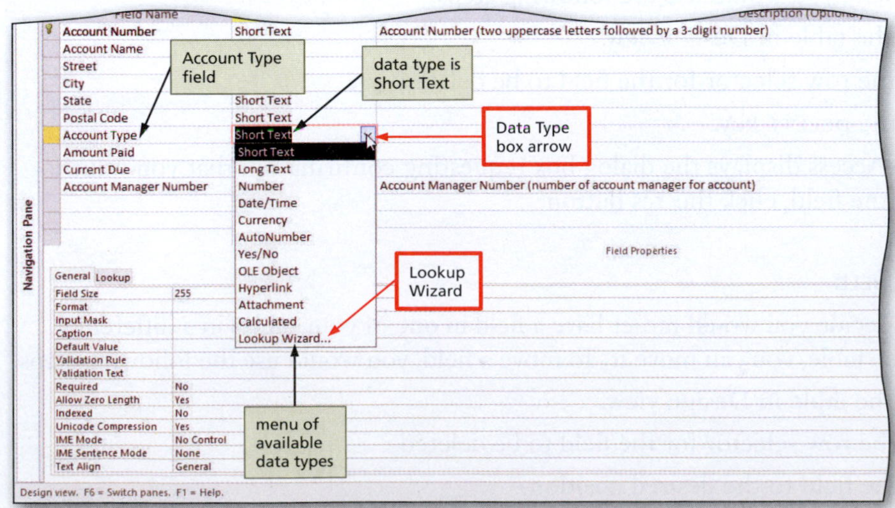

Figure 3–25

2

- Click Lookup Wizard, and then click the 'I will type in the values that I want.' option button (Lookup Wizard dialog box) to indicate that you will type in the values (Figure 3–26).

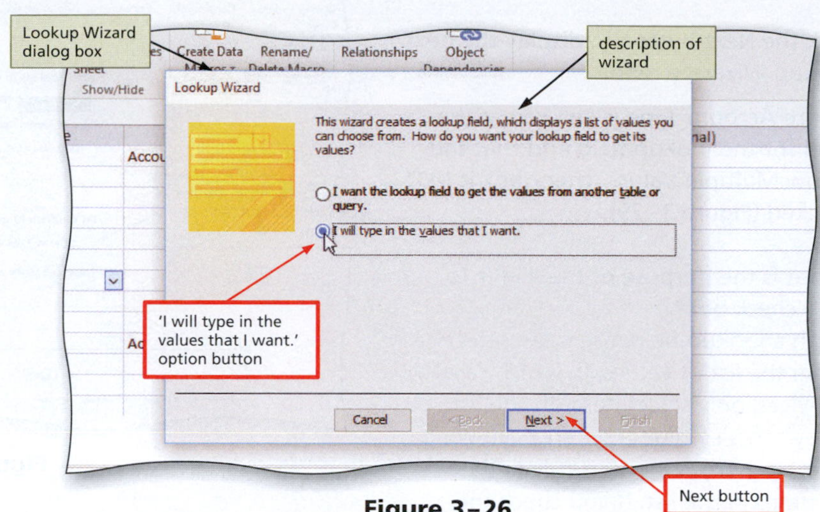

Figure 3–26

Q&A When would I use the other option button?
You would use the other option button if the data to be entered in this field were found in another table or query.

3

- Click the Next button to display the next Lookup Wizard screen (Figure 3–27).

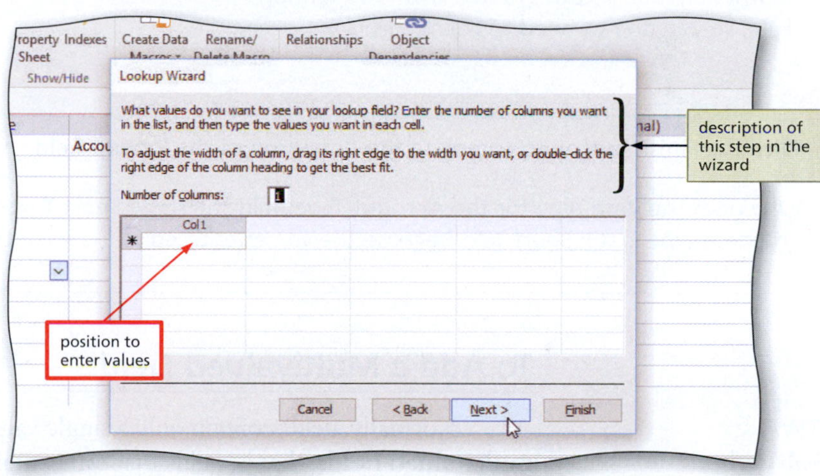

Figure 3–27

Q&A Why did I not change the field size for the Account Type field?
You could have changed the field size to 3, but it is not necessary. When you create a lookup field and indicate specific values for the field, you automatically restrict the field size.

4

- Click the first row of the table (below Col1), and then type **SER** as the value in the first row.
- Press the DOWN ARROW key, and then type **NON** as the value in the second row.
- Press the DOWN ARROW key, and then type **IND** as the value in the third row (Figure 3–28).

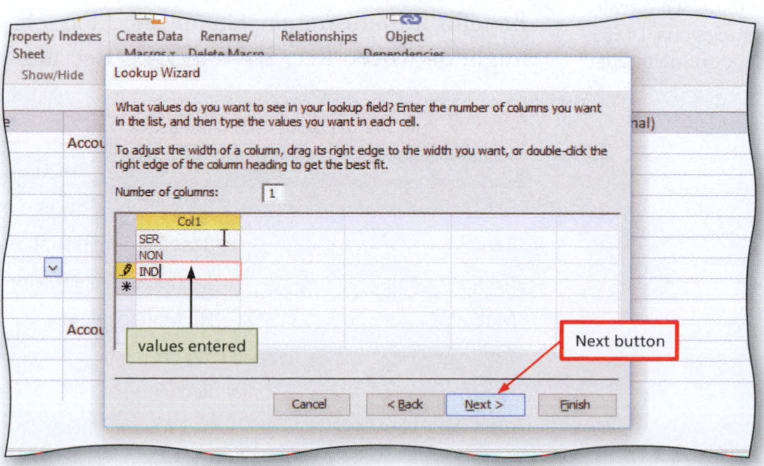

Figure 3–28

5

- Click the Next button to display the next Lookup Wizard screen.
- Ensure Account Type is entered as the label for the lookup field and that the 'Allow Multiple Values' check box is NOT checked (Figure 3–29).

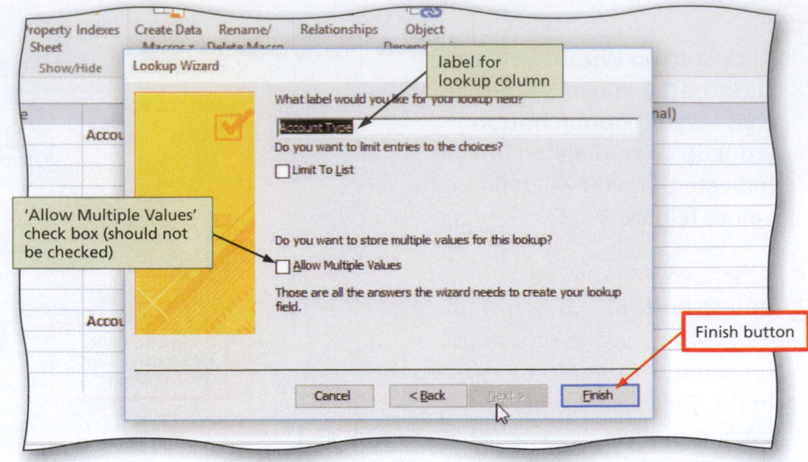

Figure 3–29

Q&A What is the purpose of the 'Limit To List' check box?
With a lookup field, users can select from the list of values, in which case they can only select items in the list. They can also type their entry, in which case they are not necessarily limited to items in the list. If you check the 'Limit To List' check box, users would be limited to items in the list, even if they type their entry. You will accomplish this same restriction later in this module with a validation rule, so you do not need to check this box.

6

- Click the Finish button to complete the definition of the lookup field.

Q&A Why does the data type for the Account Type field still show Short Text?
The data type is still Short Text because the values entered in the wizard were entered as text.

To Add a Multivalued Field

BTW
Multivalued Fields
Do not use multivalued fields if you plan to move your data to another relational database management system, such as SQL Server at a later date. SQL Server and other relational DMBSs do not support multivalued fields.

Normally, fields contain only a single value. In Access, it is possible to have **multivalued fields**, that is, fields that can contain more than one value. PrattLast Associates wants to use such a field to store the abbreviations of the various services its accounts need (see Table 3–1 for the service abbreviations and descriptions). Unlike the Account Type, where each account had only one type, accounts can require multiple services. One account might need Bck, Ben, Com, Pay, and Rsk (Background Checks, Benefits Administration, Compliance, Payroll, and Risk Management). Another account might only need Rec, Trn, and Wrk (Recruiting, Training, and Workman's Compensation).

Table 3–1 Service Abbreviations and Descriptions

Service Abbreviation	Description
Bck	Background Checks
Ben	Benefits Administration
Com	Compliance (Regulatory)
Mgt	HR Management
Pay	Payroll
Rec	Recruiting
Rsk	Risk Management
Tch	HR Technology
Trn	Training
Wrk	Workman's Compensation

Creating a multivalued field uses the same process as creating a lookup field, with the exception that you check the 'Allow Multiple Values' check box. The following steps create a multivalued field.

1. Right-click the row selector for the Amount Paid field, and then click Insert Rows on the shortcut menu to insert a blank row.
2. Click the Field Name column for the new field, type `Services Needed` as the field name, and then press the TAB key.
3. Click the Data Type arrow to display the menu of available data types for the Services Needed field, and then click Lookup Wizard in the menu of available data types to start the Lookup Wizard.
4. Click the 'I will type in the values that I want.' option button to indicate that you will type in the values.
5. Click the Next button to display the next Lookup Wizard screen.
6. Click the first row of the table (below Col1), and then type `Bck` as the value in the first row.
7. Enter the remaining values from the first column in Table 3–1. Before typing each value, press the DOWN ARROW key to move to a new row.
8. Click the Next button to display the next Lookup Wizard screen.
9. Ensure that Services Needed is entered as the label for the lookup field.
10. Click the 'Allow Multiple Values' check box to allow the user to enter multiple values.
11. Click the Finish button to complete the definition of the Lookup Wizard field.

BTW

Modifying Table Properties

You can change the properties of a table by opening the table in Design view and then clicking the Property Sheet button. To display the records in a table in an order other than primary key (the default sort order), use the Order By property. For example, to display the Account table automatically in Account Name order, change the Order By property setting to Account.Account Name in the property box, close the property sheet, and save the change to the table design. When you open the Account table in Datasheet view, the records will be sorted in Account Name order.

BTW

Calculated Fields

You can use the Result Type field property to format the calculated field values.

To Modify Single Valued or Multivalued Lookup Fields

At some point you might want to change the list of choices in a lookup field. If you need to modify a single value or multivalued lookup field, you would use the following steps.

1. Open the table in Design view and select the field to be modified.
2. Click the Lookup tab in the Field Properties pane.
3. Change the list in the Row Source property to the desired list of values.

To Add a Calculated Field

1 UPDATE RECORDS | 2 FILTER RECORDS | **3 CHANGE STRUCTURE** | 4 MASS CHANGES | 5 VALIDATION RULES
6 CHANGE APPEARANCE | 7 REFERENTIAL INTEGRITY | 8 ORDER RECORDS

A field that can be computed from other fields is called a **calculated field** or a **computed field.** In Module 2, you created a calculated field in a query that provided total amount data. In Access 2016, it is also possible to include a calculated field in a table. Users will not be able to update this field. ***Why?*** *Access will automatically perform the necessary calculation and display the correct value whenever you display or use this field in any way.* The following steps add to the Account table a field that calculates the sum of the Amount Paid and Current Due fields.

1

- Right-click the row selector for the Account Manager Number field, and then click Insert Rows on the shortcut menu to insert a blank row above the selected field.
- Click the Field Name column for the new field.
- Type `Total Amount` as the field name, and then press the TAB key.

- Click the Data Type arrow to display the menu of available data types (Figure 3–30).

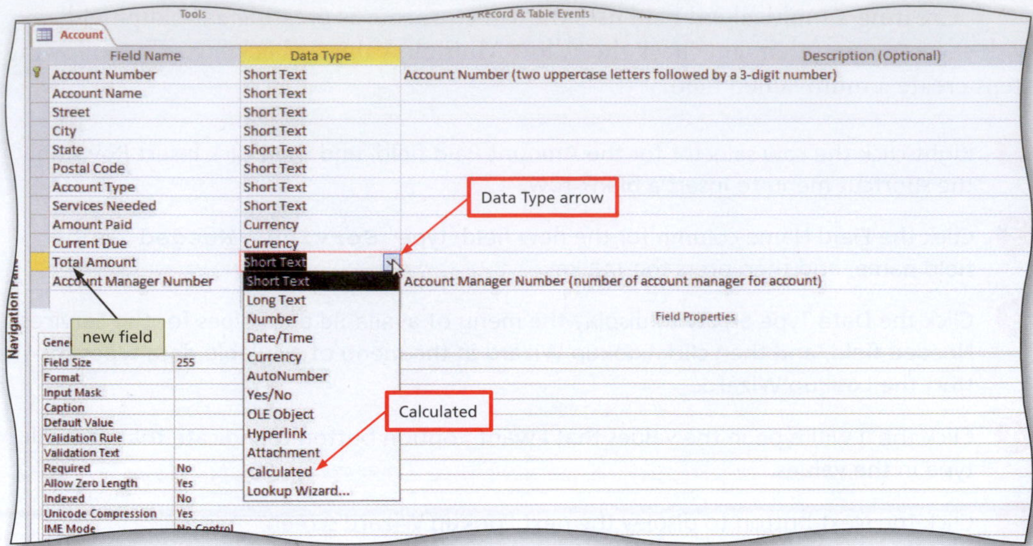

Figure 3–30

2

- Click Calculated to select the Calculated data type and display the Expression Builder dialog box (Figure 3–31).

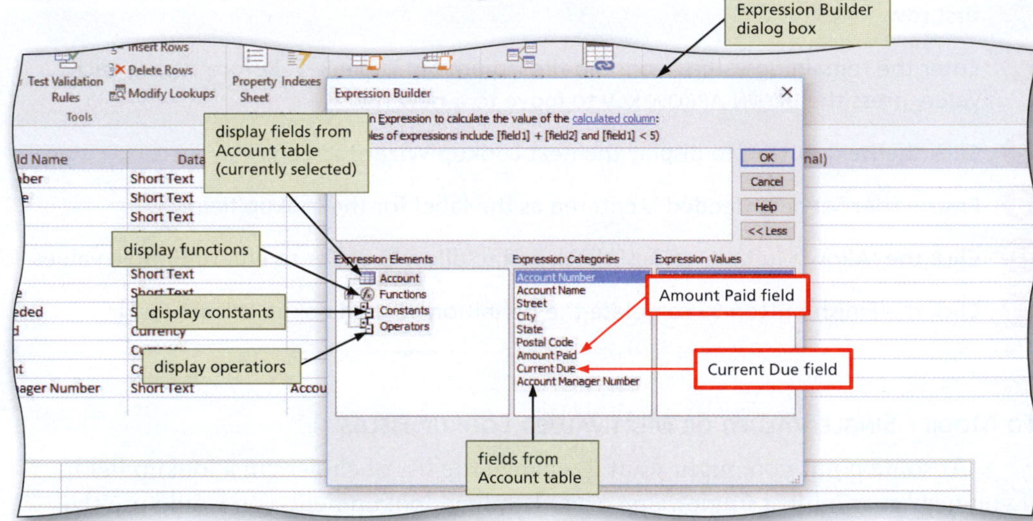

Figure 3–31

Q&A I do not have the list of fields in the Expression Categories area. What should I do?
Click Account in the Expression Elements area.

3

- Double-click the Amount Paid field in the Expression Categories area (Expression Builder dialog box) to add the field to the expression.
- Type a plus sign (+).

Q&A Could I select the plus sign from a list rather than typing it?
Yes. Click Operators in the Expression Elements area to display available operators, and then double-click the plus sign.

- Double-click the Current Due field in the Expression Categories area (Expression Builder dialog box) to add the field to the expression (Figure 3–32).

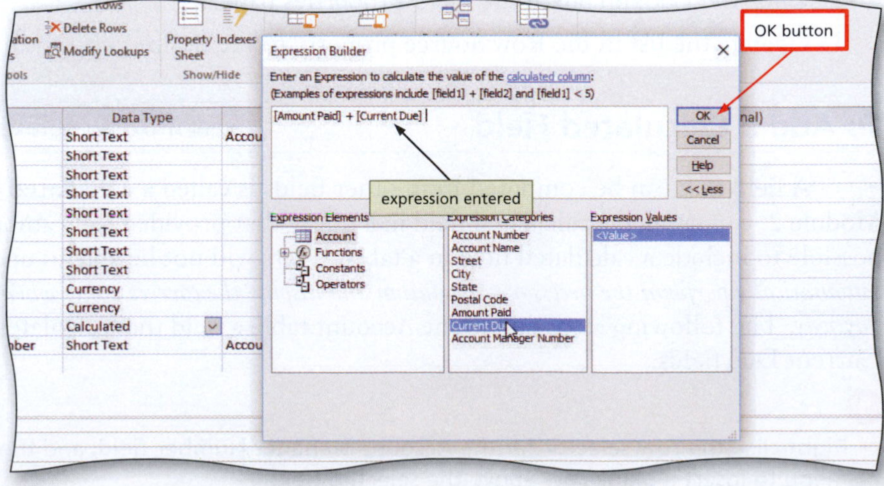

Figure 3–32

4

- Click the OK button (Expression Builder dialog box) to enter the expression in the Expression property of the Total Amount (Figure 3–33).

Q&A Could I have typed the expression in the Expression Builder dialog box rather than selecting the fields from a list?
Yes. You can use whichever technique you find more convenient.

Q&A When I entered a calculated field in a query, I typed the expression in the Zoom dialog box. Could I have used the Expression Builder instead?
Yes. To do so, you would click Build rather than Zoom on the shortcut menu.

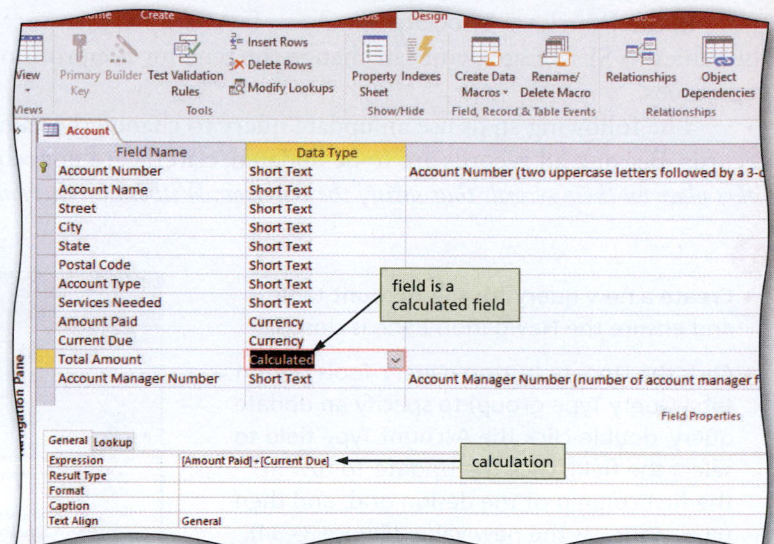

Figure 3–33

To Save the Changes and Close the Table

The following steps save the changes; that is, they save the addition of the new fields and close the table.

1. Click the Save button on the Quick Access Toolbar to save the changes.
2. Close the Account table.

Mass Changes

In some cases, rather than making individual changes to records, you will want to make mass changes. That is, you will want to add, change, or delete many records in a single operation. You can do this with action queries. Unlike the select queries that you created in Module 2, which simply presented data in specific ways, an **action query** adds, deletes, or changes data in a table. An **update query** allows you to make the same change to all records satisfying some criterion. If you omit the criterion, you will make the same changes to all records in the table. A **delete query** allows you to delete all the records satisfying some criterion. You can add the results of a query to an existing table by using an **append query**. You also can add the query results to a new table by using a **make-table query**.

BTW
Database Backup
If you are doing mass changes to a database, be sure to back up the database prior to doing the updates.

To Use an Update Query

1 UPDATE RECORDS | 2 FILTER RECORDS | 3 CHANGE STRUCTURE | 4 MASS CHANGES | 5 VALIDATION RULES
6 CHANGE APPEARANCE | 7 REFERENTIAL INTEGRITY | 8 ORDER RECORDS

The new Account Type field is blank on every record in the Account table. One approach to entering the information for the field would be to step through the entire table, assigning each record its appropriate value. If most of the accounts have the same type, it would be more convenient to use an update query to assign a single value to all accounts and then update the Account Type for those accounts whose type differs. An update query makes the same change to all records satisfying a criterion.

In the PrattLast Associates database, for example, many accounts are type SER. Initially, you can set all the values to SER. Later, you can change the type for nonprofit organizations and industrial/manufacturing companies.

The following steps use an update query to change the value in the Account Type field to SER for all the records. Because all records are to be updated, criteria are not required. ***Why?*** *If there is a criterion, the update only takes place on those records that satisfy the criterion. Without a criterion, the update applies to all records.*

1

- Create a new query for the Account table, and ensure the Navigation Pane is closed.
- Click the Update button (Query Tools Design tab | Query Type group) to specify an update query, double-click the Account Type field to select the field, click the Update To row in the first column of the design grid, and then type **SER** as the new value (Figure 3–34).

Q&A If I change my mind and do not want an update query, how can I change the query back to a select query?
Click the Select button (Query Tools Design tab | Query Type group).

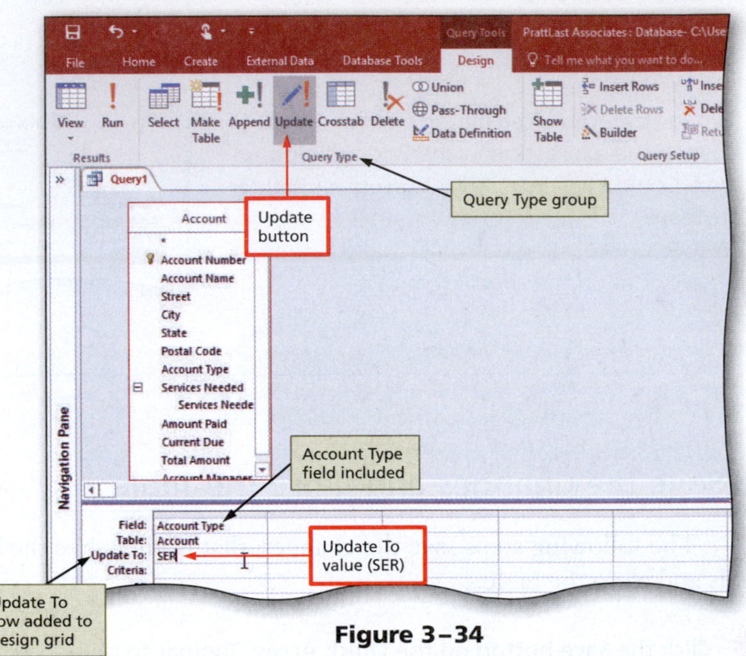

Figure 3–34

2

- Click the Run button (Query Tools Design tab | Results group) to run the query and update the records (Figure 3–35).

Q&A The dialog box did not appear on my screen when I ran the query. What happened?
If the dialog box did not appear, it means that you did not click the Enable Content button when you first opened the database. Close the database, open it again, and enable the content. Then, create and run the query again.

3

- Click the Yes button to make the changes.

Experiment

- Create an update query to change the account type to COM. Enter a criterion to restrict the records to be updated, and then run the query. Open the table to view your changes. When finished, create and run an update query to change the account type to SER on all records.

- Close the query. Because you do not need to use this update query again, do not save the query.

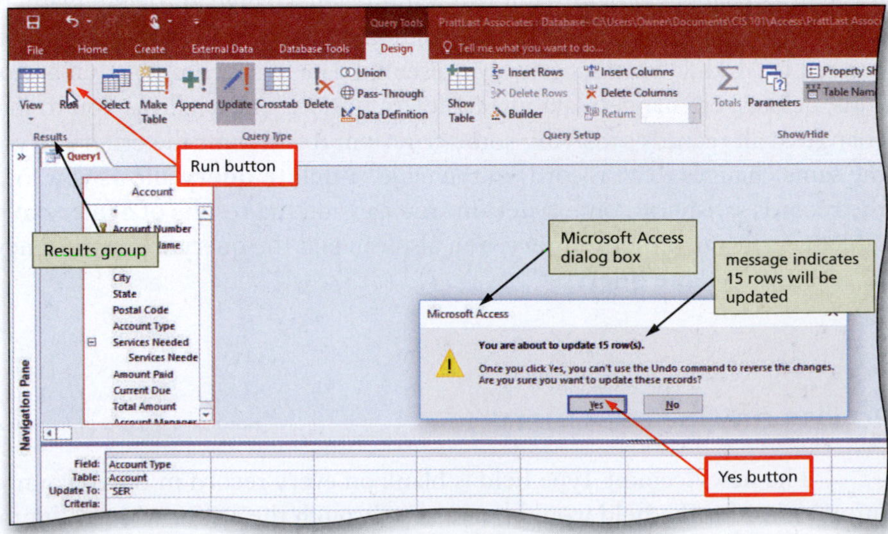

Figure 3–35

Other Ways

1. Right-click any open area in upper pane, point to Query Type on shortcut menu, click Update Query on Query Type submenu

To Use a Delete Query

In some cases, you might need to delete several records at a time. If, for example, PrattLast no longer services accounts in Indiana (IN), the accounts with this value in the State field can be deleted from the PrattLast Associates database. Instead of deleting these accounts individually, which could be very time-consuming in a large database, you can delete them in one operation by using a delete query, which is a query that deletes all the records satisfying the criteria entered in the query. To create a delete query, you would use the following steps.

1. Create a query for the table containing the records to be deleted.
2. In Design view, indicate the fields and criteria that will specify the records to delete.
3. Click the Delete button (Query Tools Design tab | Query Type group).
4. Run the query by clicking the Run button (Query Tools Design tab | Results group).
5. When Access indicates the number of records to be deleted, click the Yes button.

BTW
Viewing Records Before Updating
You can view records affected by an update query before running the query. To do so, use the Select button to convert the query to a select query, add any additional fields that would help you identify the records, and then view the results. Make any necessary corrections to the query in Design view. When you are satisfied, use the Update button to once again convert the query to an update query.

To Use an Append Query

An append query adds a group of records from one table, called the Source table, to the end of another table, called the Destination table. For example, suppose that PrattLast Associates acquires some new accounts; these new accounts are accompanied by a related database. To avoid entering all this information manually, you can append it to the Account table in the PrattLast Associates database using the append query. To create an append query, you would use the following steps.

1. Create a query for the Source table.
2. In Design view, indicate the fields to include, and then enter any necessary criteria.
3. View the query results to be sure you have specified the correct data, and then return to Design view.
4. Click the Append button (Query Tools Design tab | Query Type group).
5. When Access displays the Append dialog box, specify the name of the Destination table and its location. Run the query by clicking the Run button (Query Tools Design tab | Results group).
6. When Access indicates the number of records to be appended, click the OK button.

BTW
Delete Queries
If you do not specify any criteria in a delete query, Access will delete all the records in the table.

To Use a Make-Table Query

In some cases, you might want to create a new table that contains only records from an existing table. If so, use a make-table query to add the records to a new table. To create a make-table query, you would use the following steps.

1. Create a query for the Source table.
2. In Design view, indicate the fields to include, and then enter any necessary criteria.
3. View the query results to be sure you have specified the correct data, and then return to Design view.
4. Click the Make Table button (Query Tools Design tab | Query Type group).
5. When Access displays the Make Table dialog box, specify the name of the Destination table and its location. Run the query by clicking the Run button (Query Tools Design tab | Results group).
6. When Access indicates the number of records to be inserted, click the OK button.

BTW
Archive Tables
You can use a make table query to create an archive table. An archive table is a table that contains data that is no longer used in operations but that might still be needed by the organization.

Break Point: If you wish to take a break, this is a good place to do so. You can quit Access now. To resume at a later time, run Access, open the database called PrattLast Associates, and continue following the steps from this location forward.

Validation Rules

BTW
Using Wildcards in Validation Rules
You can include wildcards in validation rules. For example, if you enter the expression, like T?, in the validation rule for the State field, the only valid entries for the field will be TN or TX.

You now have created, loaded, queried, and updated a database. Nothing you have done so far, however, restricts users to entering only valid data, that is, data that follows the rules established for data in the database. An example of such a rule would be that account types can only be SER, NON, or IND. To ensure the entry of valid data, you create **validation rules**, or rules that a user must follow when entering the data. When the database contains validation rules, Access prevents users from entering data that does not follow the rules. You can also specify **validation text**, which is the message that appears if a user attempts to violate the validation rule.

Validation rules can indicate a **required field**, a field in which the user *must* enter data; failing to enter data into a required field generates an error. Validation rules can also restrict a user's entry to a certain **range of values**; for example, the values in the Current Due field must be between $0 and $10,000. Alternatively, rules can specify a **default value**, that is, a value that Access will display on the screen in a particular field before the user begins adding a record. To make data entry of account numbers more convenient, you can also have lowercase letters appear automatically as uppercase letters. Finally, validation rules can specify a collection of acceptable values.

To Change a Field Size

BTW
Using the Between Operator in Validation Rules
You can use the BETWEEN operator to specify a range of values. For example, to specify that entries in the Current Due field must be between $0 and $10,000, type BETWEEN 0 and 10000 as the rule.

The Field Size property for text fields represents the maximum number of characters a user can enter in the field. Because the field size for the Account Number field is five, for example, a user would not be able to enter a sixth character in the field. Occasionally, you will find that the field size that seemed appropriate when you first created a table is no longer appropriate. In the Account table, there is a street name that needs to be longer than 20 characters. To allow this name in the table, you need to change the field size for the Street field to a number that is large enough to accommodate the new name. The following step changes the field size for the Street field from 20 to 25.

1. Open the Account table in Design view and close the Navigation Pane.
2. Select the Street field by clicking its row selector.
3. Click the Field Size property to select it, delete the current entry (20), and then type 25 as the new field size.

To Specify a Required Field

1 UPDATE RECORDS | 2 FILTER RECORDS | 3 CHANGE STRUCTURE | 4 MASS CHANGES | 5 VALIDATION RULES
6 CHANGE APPEARANCE | 7 REFERENTIAL INTEGRITY | 8 ORDER RECORDS

To specify that a field is to be required, change the value for the Required property from No to Yes. The following step specifies that the Account Name field is a required field. ***Why?*** *Users will not be able to leave the Account Name field blank when entering or editing records.*

- Select the Account Name field by clicking its row selector.
- Click the Required property box in the Field Properties pane, and then click the down arrow that appears.
- Click Yes in the list to make Account Name a required field (Figure 3–36).

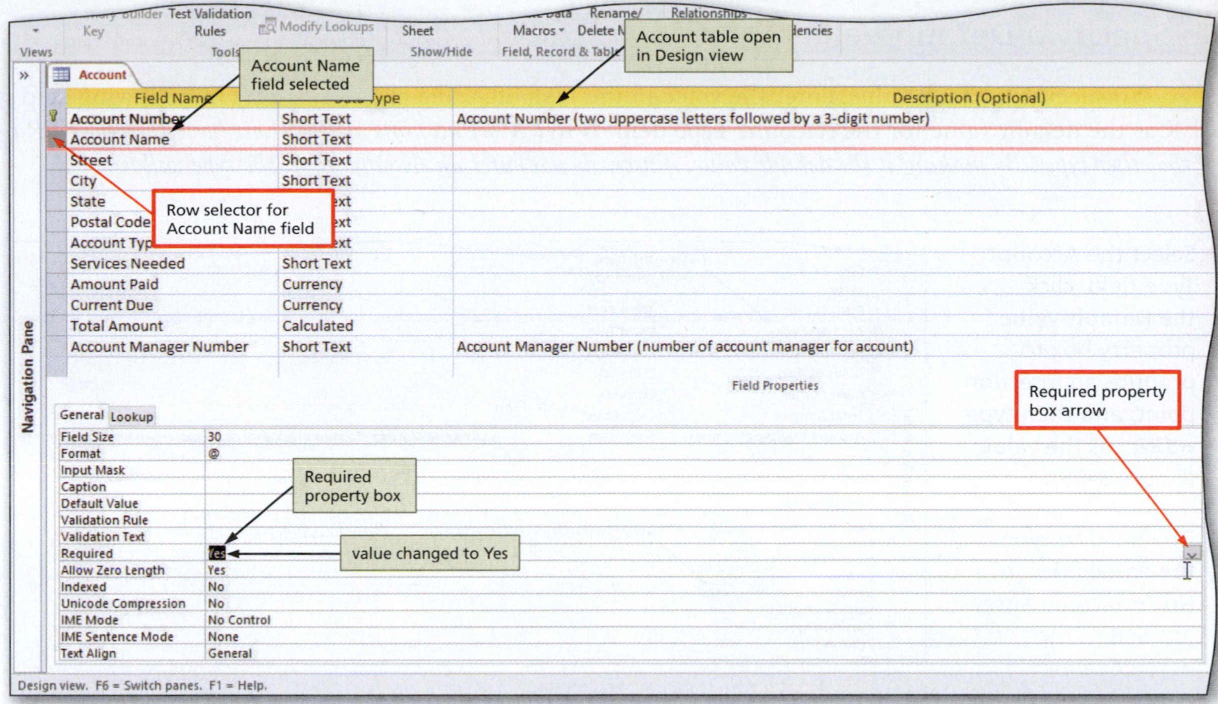

Figure 3–36

To Specify a Range

The following step specifies that entries in the Current Due field must be between $0 and $10,000. To indicate this range, the criterion specifies that the Current Due amount must be both >= 0 (greater than or equal to 0) and <= 10000 (less than or equal to 10,000). ***Why?*** *Combining these two criteria with the word, and, is logically equivalent to being between $0.00 and $10,000.00.*

1

- Select the Current Due field by clicking its row selector, click the Validation Rule property box to produce an insertion point, and then type `>=0 and <=10000` as the rule.
- Click the Validation Text property box to produce an insertion point, and then type `Must be at least $0.00 and at most $10,000.00` as the text (Figure 3–37).

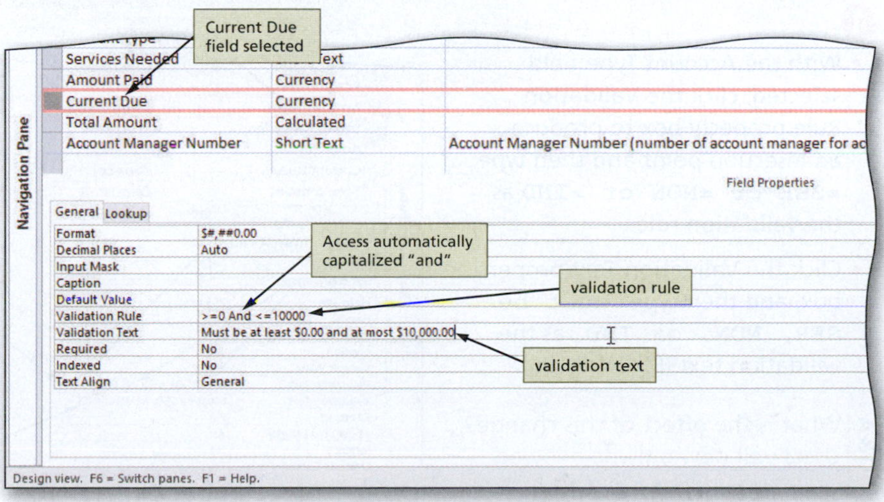

Figure 3–37

Q&A What is the effect of this change?
Users will now be prohibited from entering a Current Due amount that is either less than $0.00 or greater than $10,000.00 when they add records or change the value in the Current Due field.

To Specify a Default Value

To specify a default value, enter the value in the Default Value property box. The following step specifies SER as the default value for the Account Type field. ***Why?*** *More accounts at PrattLast have the type SER than either of the other types. By making it the default value, if users do not enter an Account Type, the type will be SER.*

1

- Select the Account Type field, click the Default Value property box to produce an insertion point, and then type **=SER** as the value (Figure 3–38).

Q&A Do I need to type the equal (=) sign?
No. You could enter just SER as the default value.

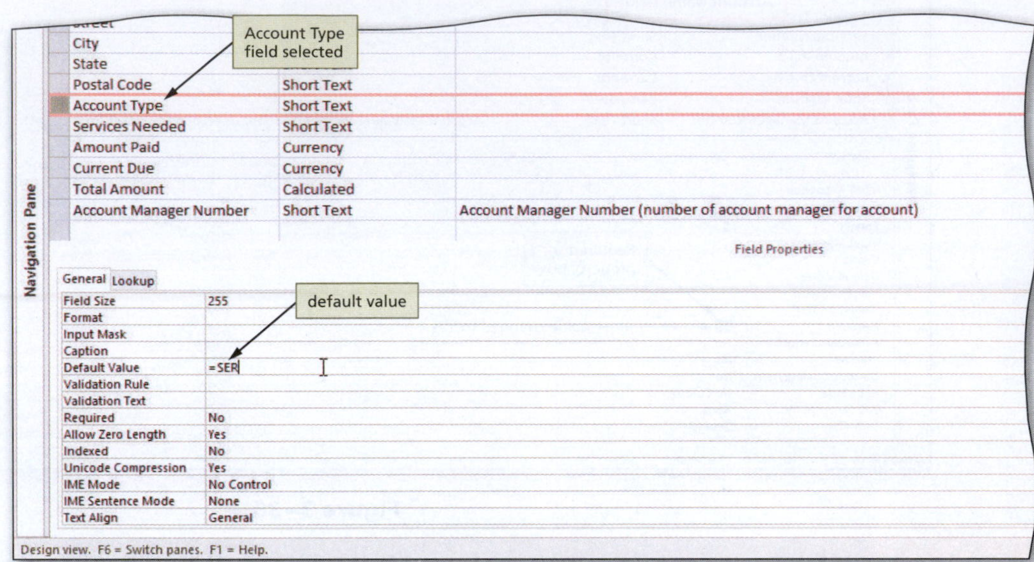

Figure 3–38

To Specify a Collection of Legal Values

The only **legal values**, or **allowable values**, for the Account Type field are SER, NON, and IND. The following step creates a validation rule to specify these as the only legal values for the Account Type field. ***Why?*** *The validation rule prohibits users from entering any other value in the Account Type field.*

1

- With the Account Type field selected, click the Validation Rule property box to produce an insertion point and then type **=SER or =NON or =IND** as the validation rule.
- Click the Validation Text property box, and then type **Must be SER, NON, or IND** as the validation text (Figure 3–39).

Q&A What is the effect of this change?
Users will now only be allowed to enter SER, NON, or IND in the Account Type field when they add records or make changes to this field.

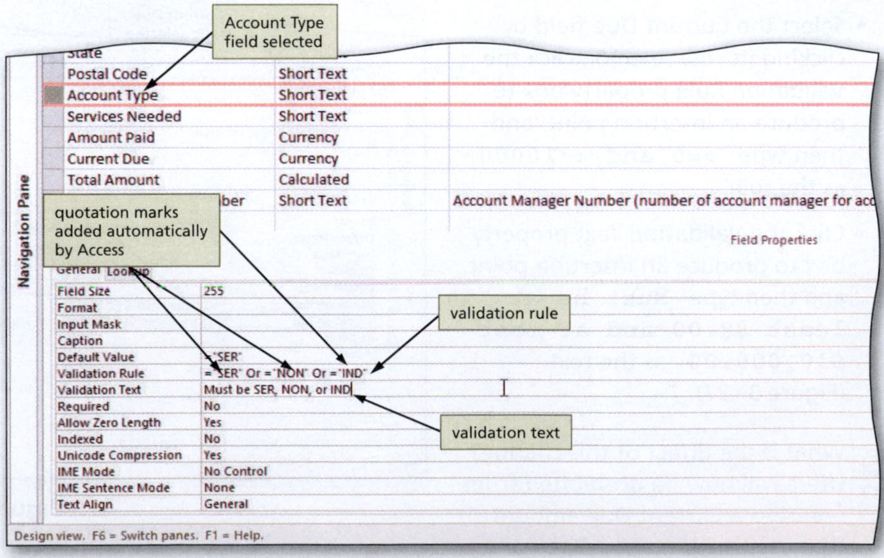

Figure 3–39

To Specify a Format

To affect the way data appears in a field, you can use a **format**. To use a format with a Short Text field, you enter a special symbol, called a **format symbol**, in the field's Format property box. The Format property uses different settings for different data types. The following step specifies a format for the Account Number field using the > symbol. ***Why?*** *The > format symbol causes Access to display lowercase letters automatically as uppercase letters, which is appropriate for the Account Number field.* There is another symbol, the < symbol, which causes Access to display uppercase letters automatically as lowercase letters.

1

- Select the Account Number field.
- Click the Format property box, erase the current format (@), if it appears on your screen, and then type > (Figure 3–40).

Q&A Where did the current format (@) come from and what does it mean?
Access added this format when you created the table by importing data from an Excel workbook. It simply means any character or a space. It is not needed here.

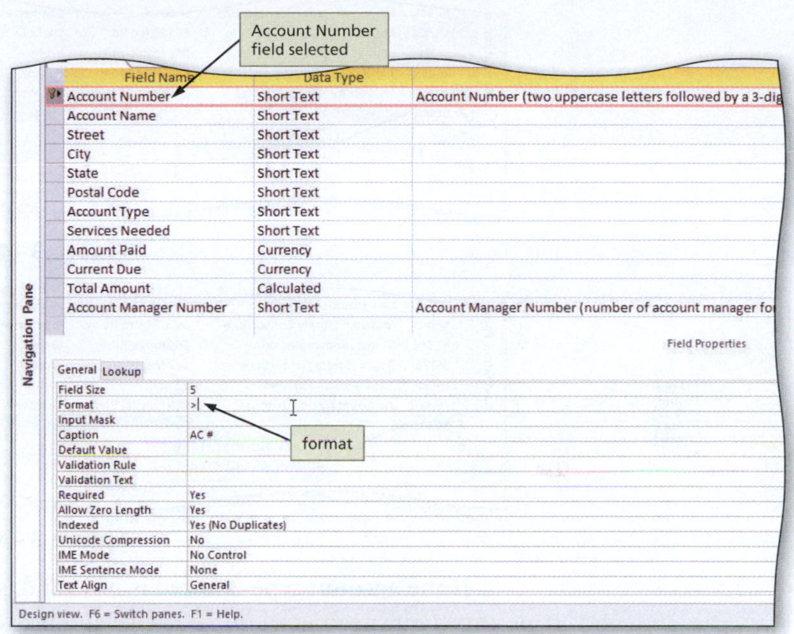

Figure 3–40

To Save the Validation Rules, Default Values, and Formats

The following steps save the validation rules, default values, and formats.

1 Click the Save button on the Quick Access Toolbar to save the changes (Figure 3–41).

2 If a Microsoft Access dialog box appears, click the No button to save the changes without testing current data.

Q&A When would you want to test current data?
If you have any doubts about the validity of the current data, you should be sure to test the current data.

3 Close the Account table.

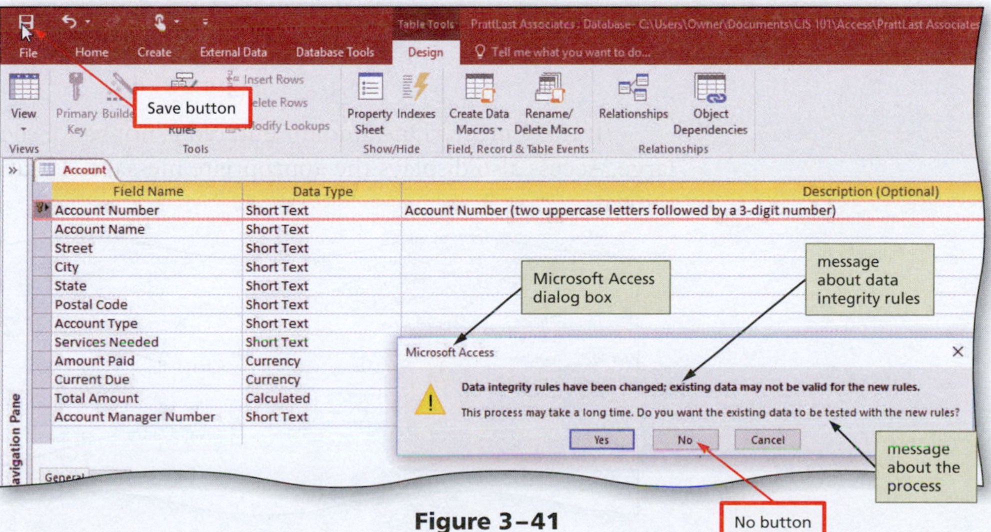

Figure 3–41

Updating a Table that Contains Validation Rules

Now that the PrattLast database contains validation rules, Access restricts the user to entering data that is valid and is formatted correctly. If a user enters a number that is out of the required range, for example, or enters a value that is not one of the possible choices, Access displays an error message in the form of a dialog box. The user cannot update the database until the error is corrected.

If the account number entered contains lowercase letters, such as bc486 (Figure 3–42), Access will display the data automatically as BC486 (Figure 3–43).

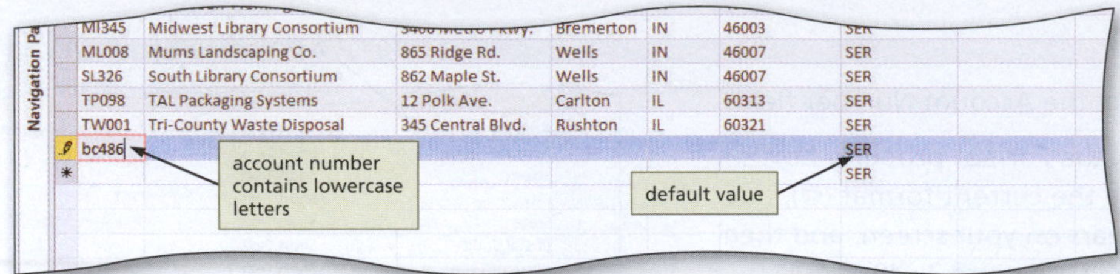

Figure 3–42

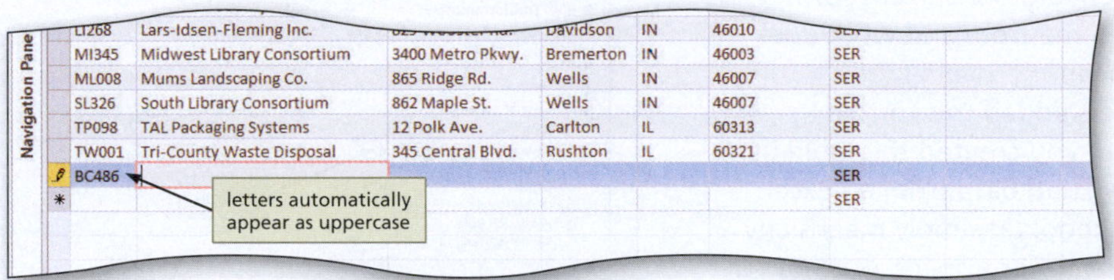

Figure 3–43

If the account type entered is not valid, such as xxx, Access will display the text message you specified (Figure 3–44) and prevent the data from being entering into the database.

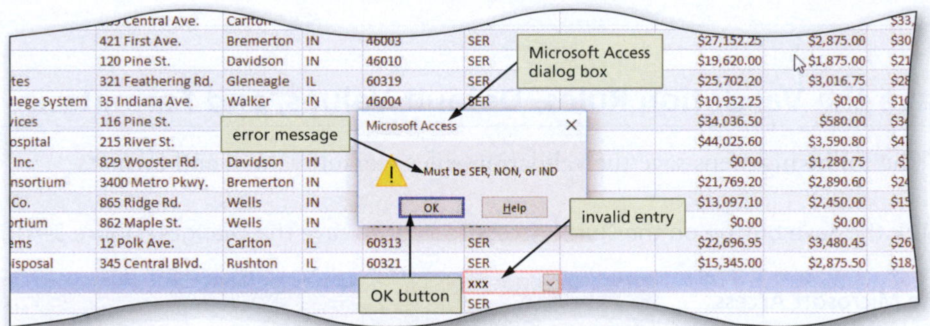

Figure 3–44

If the Current Due amount entered is not valid, such as 50000, which is too large, Access also displays the appropriate message (Figure 3–45) and refuses to accept the data.

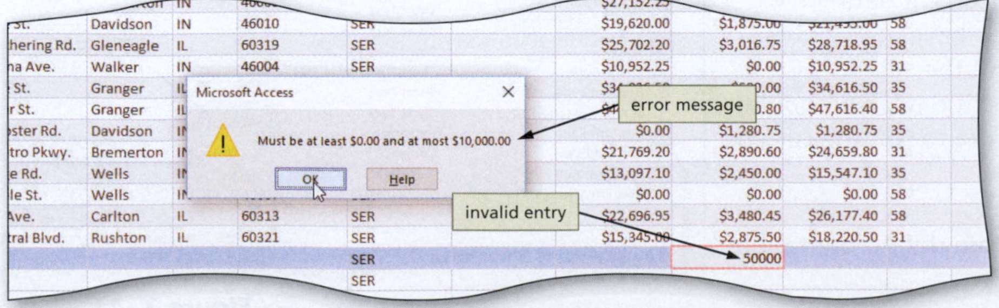

Figure 3–45

If a required field contains no data, Access indicates this by displaying an error message as soon as you attempt to leave the record (Figure 3–46). The field must contain a valid entry before Access will move to a different record.

Figure 3–46

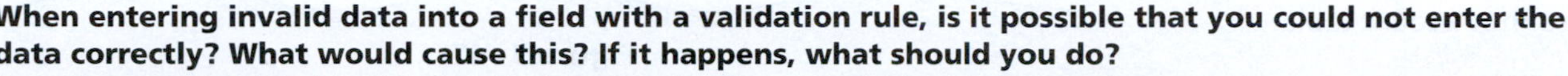

CONSIDER THIS

When entering invalid data into a field with a validation rule, is it possible that you could not enter the data correctly? What would cause this? If it happens, what should you do?

If you cannot remember the validation rule you created or if you created the rule incorrectly, you might not be able to enter the data. In such a case, you will be unable to leave the field or close the table because you have entered data into a field that violates the validation rule.

If this happens, first try again to type an acceptable entry. If this does not work, repeatedly press the BACKSPACE key to erase the contents of the field and then try to leave the field. If you are unsuccessful using this procedure, press the ESC key until the record is removed from the screen. The record will not be added to the database.

Should the need arise to take this drastic action, you probably have a faulty validation rule. Use the techniques of the previous sections to correct the existing validation rules for the field.

Making Additional Changes to the Database

Now that you have changed the structure and created validation rules, there are additional changes to be made to the database. You will use both the lookup and multivalued lookup fields to change the contents of the fields. You will also update both the form and the report to reflect the changes in the table.

To Change the Contents of a Field

1 UPDATE RECORDS | 2 FILTER RECORDS | 3 CHANGE STRUCTURE | 4 MASS CHANGES | **5 VALIDATION RULES**
6 CHANGE APPEARANCE | 7 REFERENTIAL INTEGRITY | 8 ORDER RECORDS

Now that the size for the Street field has been increased, you can change the Street name for account BL235 from 100 Granger Hwy. to 100 South Granger Hwy. and then resize the column, just as you resized columns in Module 1. ***Why?*** *Changing the field size for the field does not automatically increase the width of the corresponding column in the datasheet.* The following steps change the Street name and resize the column in the datasheet to accommodate the new name.

- Open the Account table in Datasheet view and ensure the Navigation Pane is closed.
- Click in the Street field for account BL235 immediately to the left of the letter, G, of Granger to produce an insertion point.
- Change the name of the street from 100 Granger Hwy. to 100 South Granger Hwy. by typing `South` and a space, and then pressing the TAB key.

Q&A I cannot add the extra characters. Whatever I type replaces what is currently in the cell. What happened and what should I do?
You are typing in Overtype mode, not Insert mode. Press the INSERT key and correct the entry.

- Resize the Street column to best fit the new data by double-clicking the right boundary of the field selector for the Street field, that is, the column heading (Figure 3–47).
- Save the changes to the layout by clicking the Save button on the Quick Access Toolbar.
- Close the Account table.

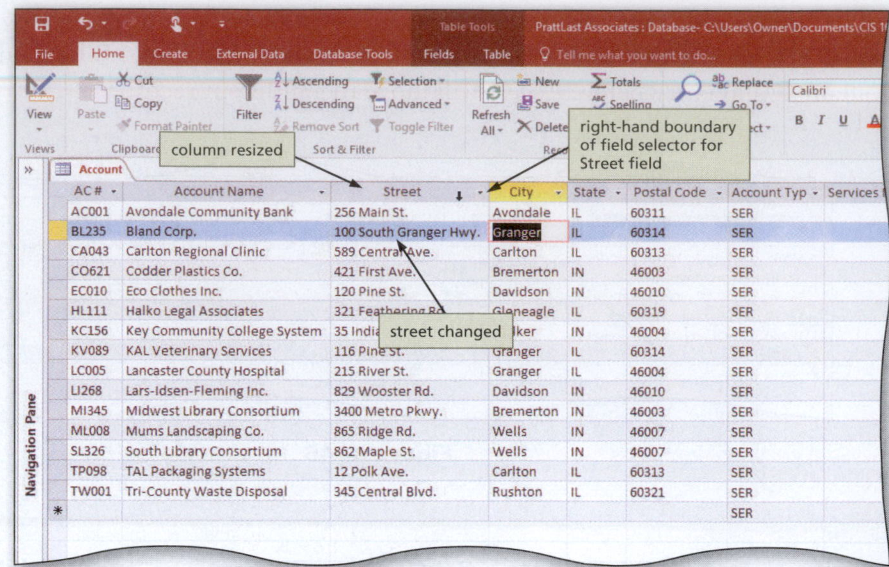

Figure 3–47

To Use a Lookup Field

1 UPDATE RECORDS | 2 FILTER RECORDS | 3 CHANGE STRUCTURE | 4 MASS CHANGES | 5 VALIDATION RULES
6 CHANGE APPEARANCE | 7 REFERENTIAL INTEGRITY | 8 ORDER RECORDS

Earlier, you changed all the entries in the Account Type field to SER. You have created a rule that will ensure that only legitimate values (SER, NON, or IND) can be entered in the field. You also made Account Type a lookup field. ***Why?*** *You can make changes to a lookup field for individual records by simply clicking the field to be changed, clicking the arrow that appears in the field, and then selecting the desired value from the list.* The following steps change the incorrect Account Type values to the correct values.

- Open the Account table in Datasheet view and ensure the Navigation Pane is closed.
- Click in the Account Type field on the second record (BL235) to display an arrow.
- Click the arrow to display the drop-down list of available choices for the Account Type field (Figure 3–48).

Q&A I got the drop-down list as soon as I clicked. I did not need to click the arrow. What happened?
If you click in the position where the arrow would appear, you will get the drop-down list. If you click anywhere else, you would need to click the arrow.

Q&A Could I type the value instead of selecting it from the list?
Yes. Once you have either deleted the previous value or selected the entire previous value, you can begin typing. You do not have to type the full entry. When you begin with the letter, I, for example, Access will automatically add the ND.

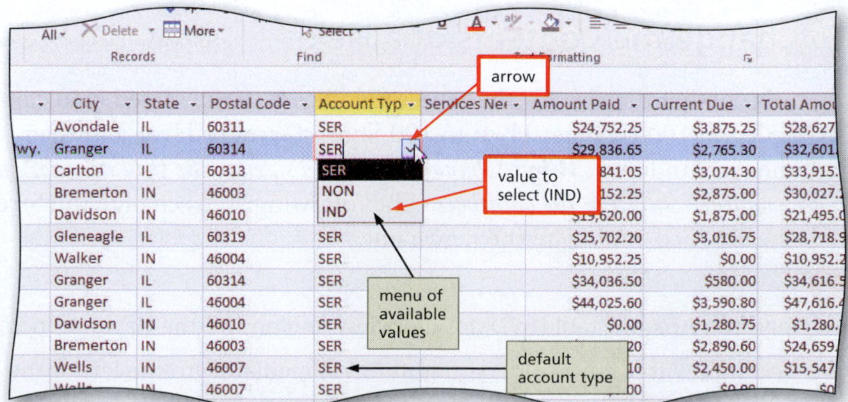

Figure 3–48

2

- Click IND to change the value.
- In a similar fashion, change the values on the other records to match those shown in Figure 3–49.

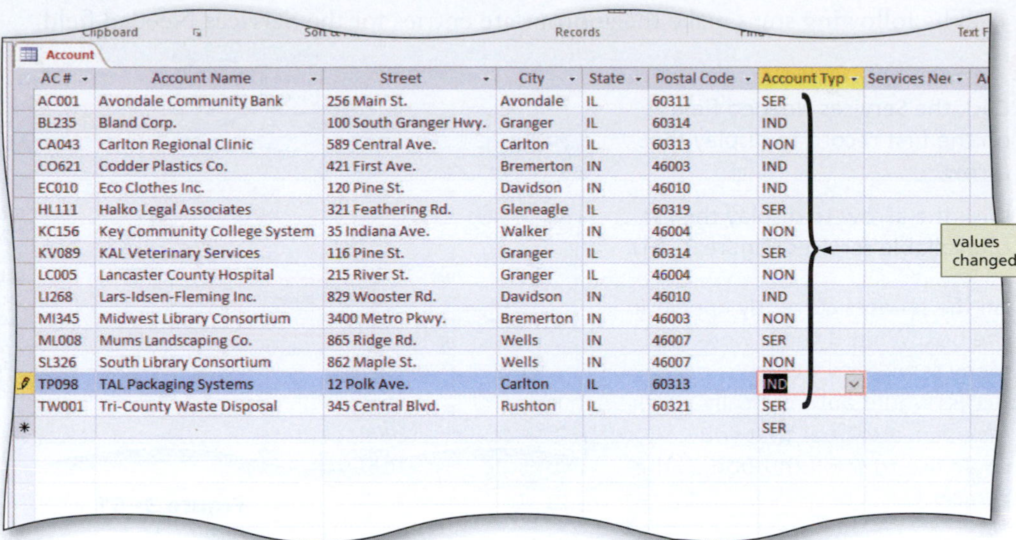

Figure 3–49

To Use a Multivalued Lookup Field

1 UPDATE RECORDS | 2 FILTER RECORDS | 3 CHANGE STRUCTURE | 4 MASS CHANGES | **5 VALIDATION RULES**
6 CHANGE APPEARANCE | 7 REFERENTIAL INTEGRITY | 8 ORDER RECORDS

Using a multivalued lookup field is similar to using a regular lookup field. The difference is that when you display the drop down list, the entries will all be preceded by check boxes. ***Why?*** *Having the check boxes allows you to make multiple selections. You check all the entries that you want.* The appropriate entries are shown in Figure 3–50. As indicated in the figure, the services needed for account AC001 are Bck, Ben, Com, Pay, and Rsk.

Account Number	Account Name	Services Needed
AC001	Avondale Community Bank	Bck, Ben, Com, Pay, Rsk
BL235	Bland Corp.	Bck, Mgt, Rsk, Tch, Wrk
CA043	Carlton Regional Clinic	Mgt, Pay, Rsk, Tch
CO621	Codder Plastics Co.	Ben, Pay, Rsk, Trn, Wrk
EC010	Eco Clothes Inc.	Rec, Trn, Wrk
HL111	Halko Legal Associates	Ben, Com, Pay, Rsk, Tch, Trn
KC156	Key Community College System	Ben, Com, Mgt, Rsk, Wrk
KV089	KAL Veterinary Services	Ben, Com, Tch, Trn
LC005	Lancaster County Hospital	Ben, Mgt, Pay, Rsk, Tch, Wrk
LI268	Lars-Idsen-Fleming Inc.	Ben, Pay, Wrk
MI345	Midwest Library Consortium	Bck, Ben, Com, Pay, Tch, Trn
ML008	Mums Landscaping Co.	Bck, Pay, Wrk
SL126	South Library Consortium	Bck, Ben, Com, Pay, Tch, Trn
TP098	TAL Packaging Systems	Ben, Com, Pay, Trn, Wrk
TW001	Tri-County Waste Disposal	Bck, Pay, Rec, Wrk

Figure 3–50

The following steps make the appropriate entries for the Services Needed field.

1

- Click the Services Needed field on the first record to display the arrow.
- Click the arrow to display the list of available services (Figure 3–51).

Q&A All the services currently appear in the box. What if there were too many services to fit?
Access would automatically include a scroll bar that you could use to scroll through all the choices.

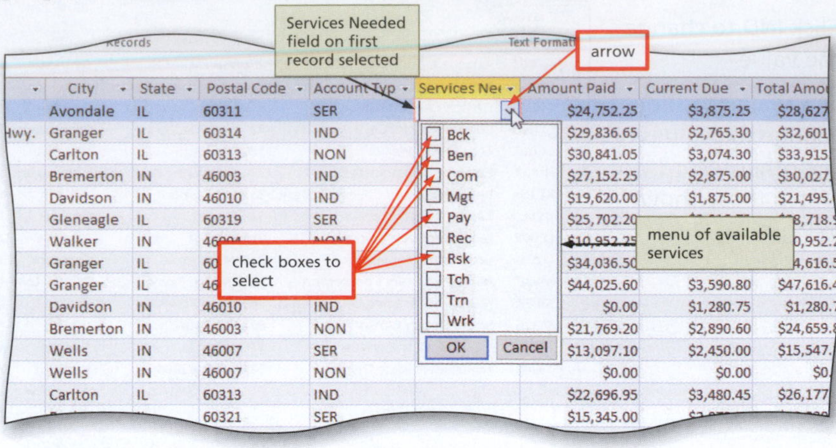

Figure 3–51

2

- Click the Bck, Ben, Com, Pay, and Rsk check boxes to select the services for the first account (Figure 3–52).

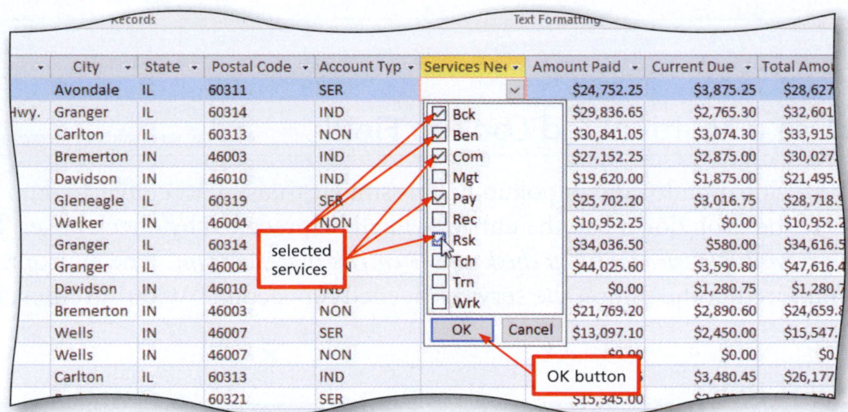

Figure 3–52

3

- Click the OK button to complete the selection.
- Using the same technique, enter the services given in Figure 3–50 for the remaining accounts.
- Double-click the right boundary of the field selector for the Services Needed field to resize the field so that it best fits the data (Figure 3–53).

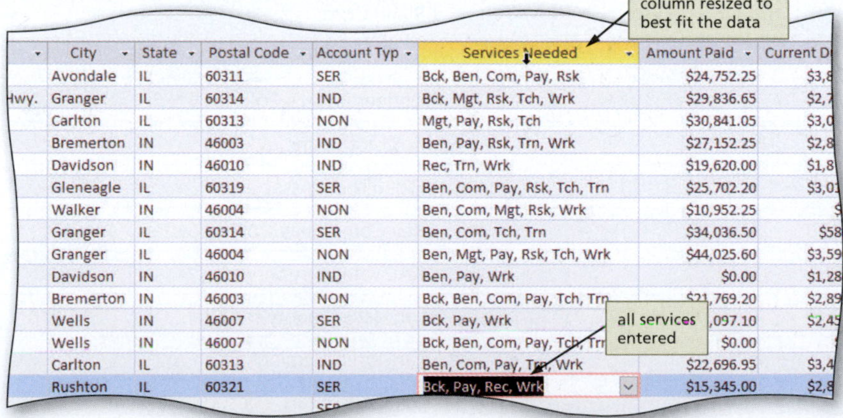

Figure 3–53

4

- Save the changes to the layout by clicking the Save button on the Quick Access Toolbar.
- Close the Account table.

Q&A What if I closed the table without saving the layout changes?
You would be asked if you want to save the changes.

To Update a Form to Reflect Changes in the Table

Earlier, you clicked the Form button (Create tab | Forms group) to create a simple form that contained all the fields in the Account table. Now that you have added fields, the form you created, Account Form, no longer contains all the fields in the table. The following steps delete the Account Form and then create it a second time.

1. Open the Navigation Pane, and then right-click the Account Form in the Navigation Pane to display a shortcut menu.
2. Click Delete on the shortcut menu to delete the selected form, and then click the Yes button in the Microsoft Access dialog box to confirm the deletion.
3. Click the Account table in the Navigation Pane to select the table.
4. If necessary, click Create on the ribbon to display the Create tab.
5. Click the Form button (Create tab | Forms group) to create a simple form (Figure 3–54).
6. Click the Save button on the Quick Access Toolbar to save the form.
7. Type `Account Form` as the form name, and then click the OK button to save the form.
8. Close the form.

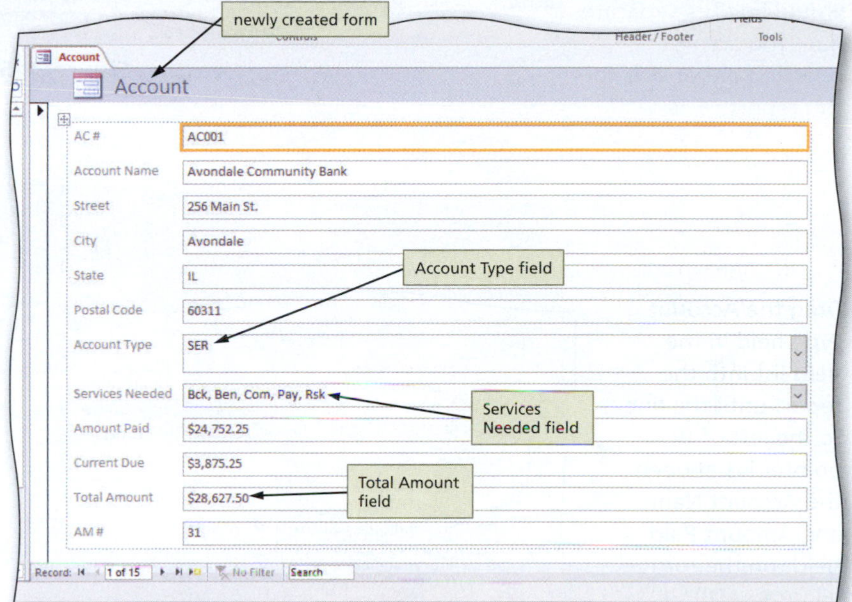

Figure 3–54

To Update a Report to Reflect Changes in the Table

1 UPDATE RECORDS | 2 FILTER RECORDS | 3 CHANGE STRUCTURE | 4 MASS CHANGES | **5 VALIDATION RULES**
6 CHANGE APPEARANCE | 7 REFERENTIAL INTEGRITY | 8 ORDER RECORDS

You also might want to include the new fields in the Account Financial Report you created earlier. Just as you did with the form, you could delete the current version of the report and then create it all over again. It would be better, however, to modify the report in Layout view. ***Why?*** *There are several steps involved in creating the Account Financial report, so it is more complicated than the process of re-creating the form.* In Layout view, you easily can add new fields. The following steps modify the Account Financial Report by adding the Account Type and Total Amount fields. To accommodate the extra fields, the steps also change the orientation of the report from Portrait to Landscape.

1

- Open the Navigation Pane, if necessary, and then right-click the Account Financial Report in the Navigation Pane to display a shortcut menu.
- Click Layout View on the shortcut menu to open the report in Layout view.
- Close the Navigation Pane.
- Click the 'Add Existing Fields' button (Report Layout Tools Design tab | Tools group) to display a field list (Figure 3–55).

Q&A Why are there two Services Needed fields in the list?
They serve different purposes. If you were to select Services Needed, you would get all the services for a given account on one line. If you were to select Services Needed. Value, each resource would be on a separate line. You are not selecting either one for this report.

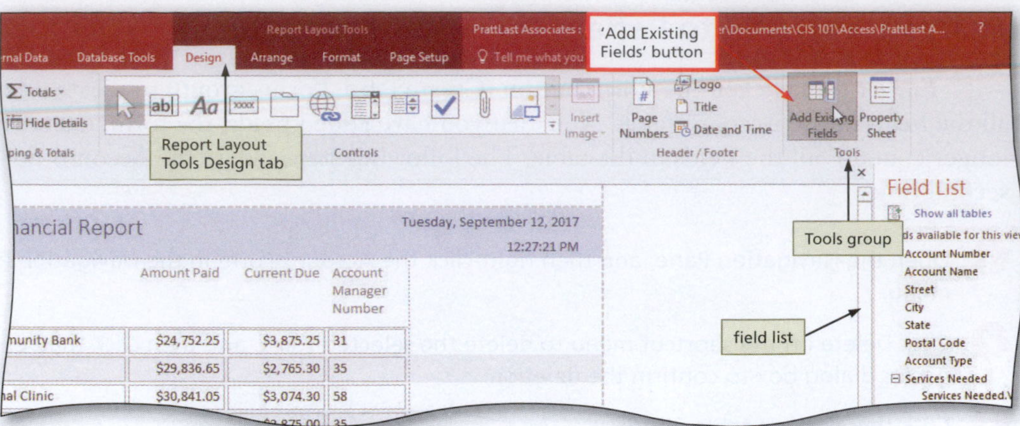

Figure 3–55

2

- Drag the Account Type field in the field list into the report until the line to the left of the pointer is between the Account Name and Amount Paid fields on the form (Figure 3–56).

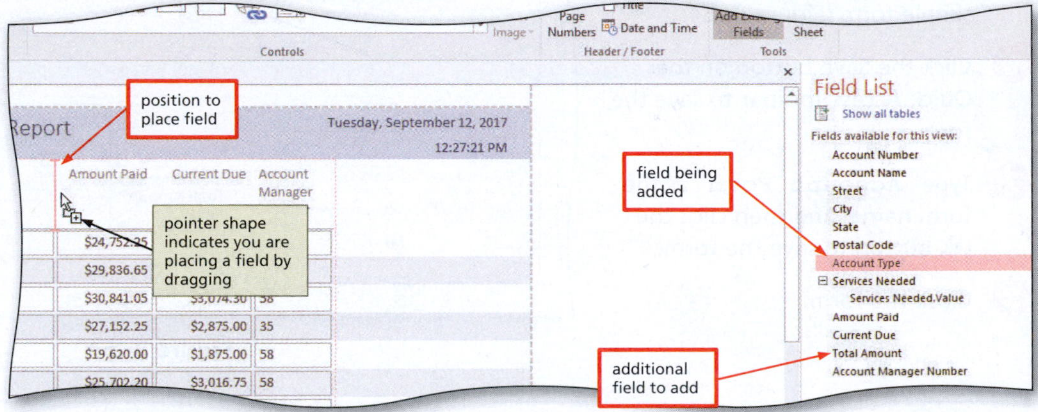

Figure 3–56

- Release the mouse button to place the field.

Q&A What if I make a mistake?
You can delete the field by clicking the column heading for the field, clicking the Select Column command (Report Layout Tools Arrange tab | Rows & Columns group), and then pressing the DELETE key. You can move the field by dragging it to the correct position. As an alternative, you can close the report without saving it and then open it again in Layout view.

- Using the same technique, add the Total Amount field between the Current Due and Account Manager Number fields.
- Click the 'Add Existing Fields' button (Report Layout Tools Design tab | Tools group) to remove the field list from the screen.

Q&A What would I do if the field list covered the portion of the report where I wanted to insert a new field?
You can move the field list to a different position on the screen by dragging its title bar.

- Click Page Setup on the ribbon to display the Report Layout Tools Page Setup tab.

- Click the Landscape button (Report Layout Tools Page Setup tab | Page Layout group) to change the orientation of the report to Landscape (Figure 3–57).

- Click the Save button on the Quick Access Toolbar to save your changes.
- Close the report.

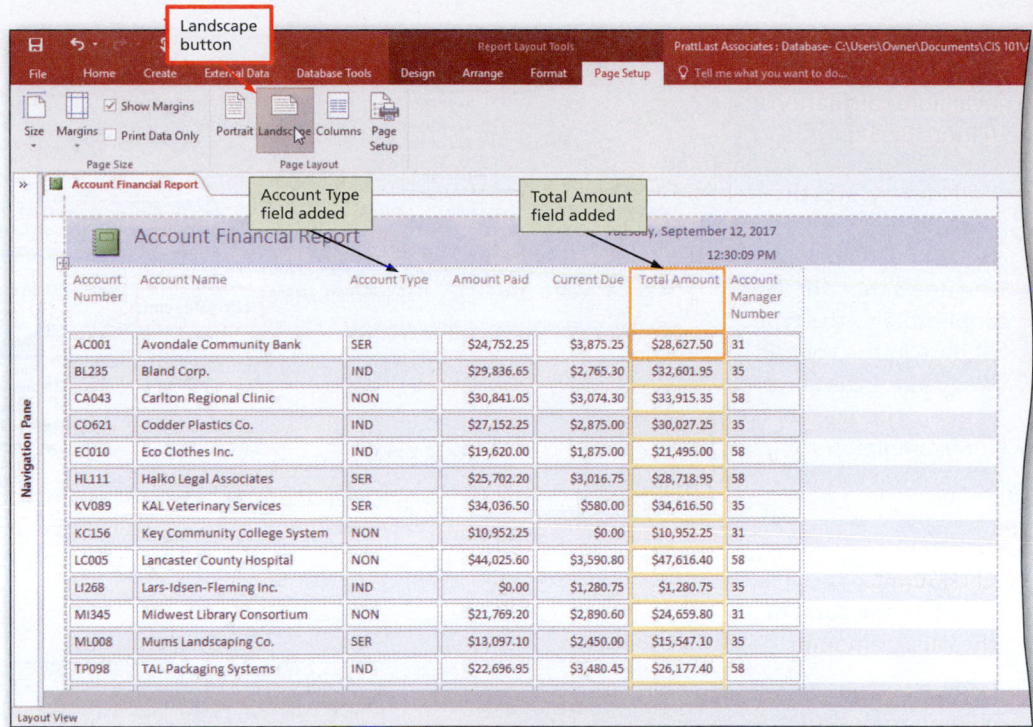

Landscape button

Account Type field added

Total Amount field added

Account Financial Report

Account Number	Account Name	Account Type	Amount Paid	Current Due	Total Amount	Account Manager Number
AC001	Avondale Community Bank	SER	$24,752.25	$3,875.25	$28,627.50	31
BL235	Bland Corp.	IND	$29,836.65	$2,765.30	$32,601.95	35
CA043	Carlton Regional Clinic	NON	$30,841.05	$3,074.30	$33,915.35	58
CO621	Codder Plastics Co.	IND	$27,152.25	$2,875.00	$30,027.25	35
EC010	Eco Clothes Inc.	IND	$19,620.00	$1,875.00	$21,495.00	58
HL111	Halko Legal Associates	SER	$25,702.20	$3,016.75	$28,718.95	58
KV089	KAL Veterinary Services	SER	$34,036.50	$580.00	$34,616.50	35
KC156	Key Community College System	NON	$10,952.25	$0.00	$10,952.25	31
LC005	Lancaster County Hospital	NON	$44,025.60	$3,590.80	$47,616.40	58
LI268	Lars-Idsen-Fleming Inc.	IND	$0.00	$1,280.75	$1,280.75	35
MI345	Midwest Library Consortium	NON	$21,769.20	$2,890.60	$24,659.80	31
ML008	Mums Landscaping Co.	SER	$13,097.10	$2,450.00	$15,547.10	35
TP098	TAL Packaging Systems	IND	$22,696.95	$3,480.45	$26,177.40	58

Figure 3–57

To Print a Report

The following steps print the report.

1. With the Account Financial Report selected in the Navigation Pane, click File on the ribbon to open the Backstage view.
2. Click the Print tab in the Backstage view to display the Print gallery.
3. Click the Quick Print button to print the report.

BTW

Distributing a Document

Instead of printing and distributing a hard copy of a document, you can distribute the document electronically. Options include sending the document via email; posting it on cloud storage (such as OneDrive) and sharing the file with others; posting it on social media, a blog, or other website; and sharing a link associated with an online location of the document. You also can create and share a PDF or XPS image of the document, so that users can view the file in Acrobat Reader or XPS Viewer instead of in Access.

Changing the Appearance of a Datasheet

You can change the appearance of a datasheet in a variety of ways. You can include totals in the datasheet. You can also change the appearance of gridlines or the text colors and font.

To Include Totals in a Datasheet

1 UPDATE RECORDS | 2 FILTER RECORDS | 3 CHANGE STRUCTURE | 4 MASS CHANGES | 5 VALIDATION RULES
6 CHANGE APPEARANCE | 7 REFERENTIAL INTEGRITY | 8 ORDER RECORDS

The following steps first include an extra row, called the Total row, in the datasheet for the Account Manager table. *Why? It is possible to include totals and other statistics at the bottom of a datasheet in the Total row.* The steps then display the total of the salaries for all the account managers.

1

- Open the Account Manager table in Datasheet view and close the Navigation Pane.
- Click the Totals button (Home tab | Records group) to include the Total row in the datasheet.
- Click the Total row in the Salary column to display an arrow.

- Click the arrow to display a menu of available calculations (Figure 3–58).

Will I always get the same list?
No. You will only get the items that are applicable to the type of data in the column. You cannot calculate the sum of text data, for example.

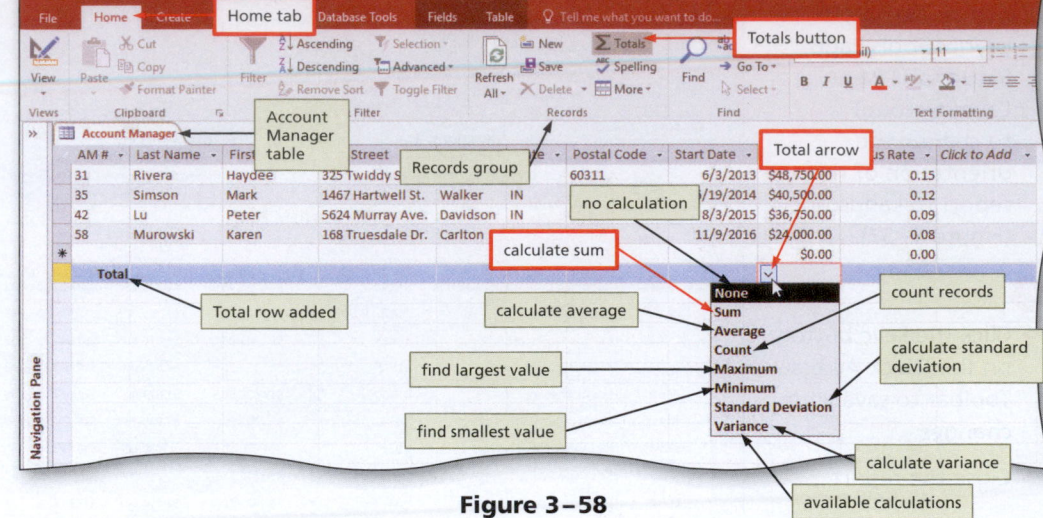

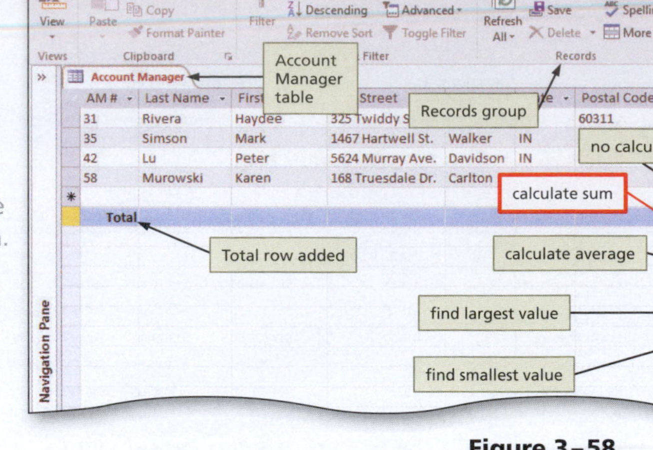

Figure 3–58

2

- Click Sum to calculate the total of the salary amounts.
- Resize the Salary column to best fit the total amount (Figure 3–59).

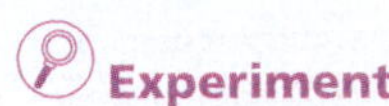

- Experiment with other statistics. When finished, once again select the sum.

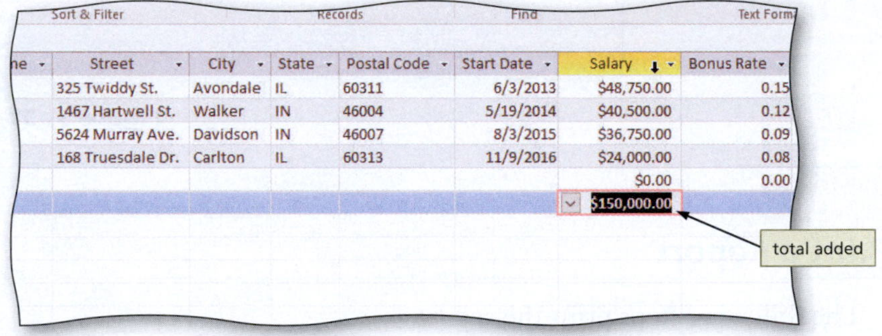

Figure 3–59

To Remove Totals from a Datasheet

If you no longer want the totals to appear as part of the datasheet, you can remove the Total row. The following step removes the Total row.

1 Click the Totals button (Home tab | Records group), which is shown in Figure 3–58, to remove the Total row from the datasheet.

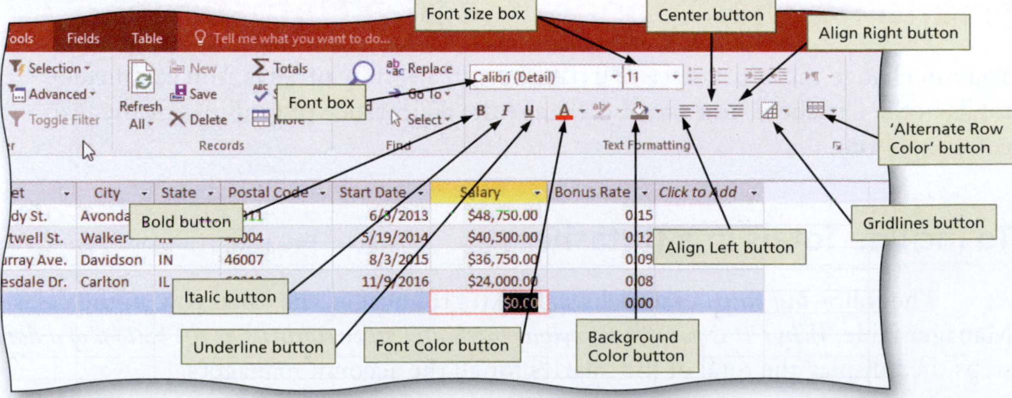

Figure 3–60

Figure 3–60 shows the various buttons, found in the Text Formatting group on the Home tab, that are available to change the datasheet appearance. The changes to the datasheet will be reflected not only on the screen, but also when you print or preview the datasheet.

To Change Gridlines in a Datasheet

1 UPDATE RECORDS | 2 FILTER RECORDS | 3 CHANGE STRUCTURE | 4 MASS CHANGES | 5 VALIDATION RULES
6 CHANGE APPEARANCE | 7 REFERENTIAL INTEGRITY | 8 ORDER RECORDS

The following steps change the datasheet so that only horizontal gridlines are included. ***Why?** You might prefer the appearance of the datasheet with only horizontal gridlines.*

- Open the Account Manager table in Datasheet view, if it is not already open.
- If necessary, close the Navigation Pane.
- Click the datasheet selector, the box in the upper-left corner of the datasheet, to select the entire datasheet (Figure 3–61).

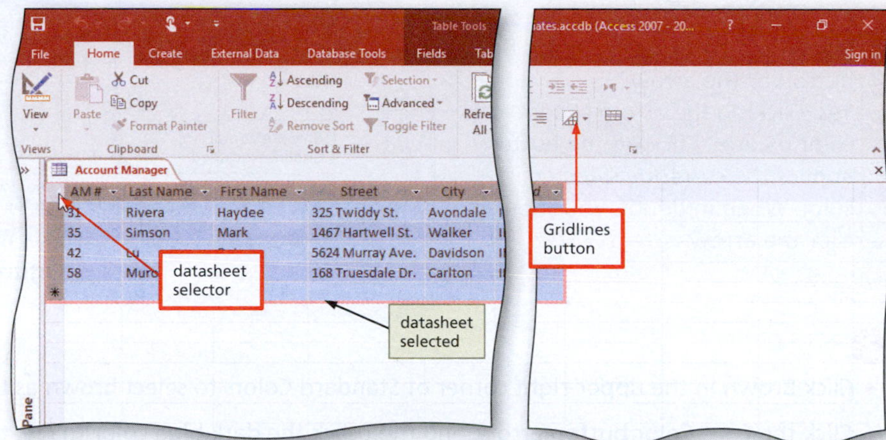

Figure 3–61

- Click the Gridlines button (Home tab | Text Formatting group) to display the Gridlines gallery (Figure 3–62).

Q&A Does it matter whether I click the button or the arrow?
In this case, it does not matter. Either action will display the gallery.

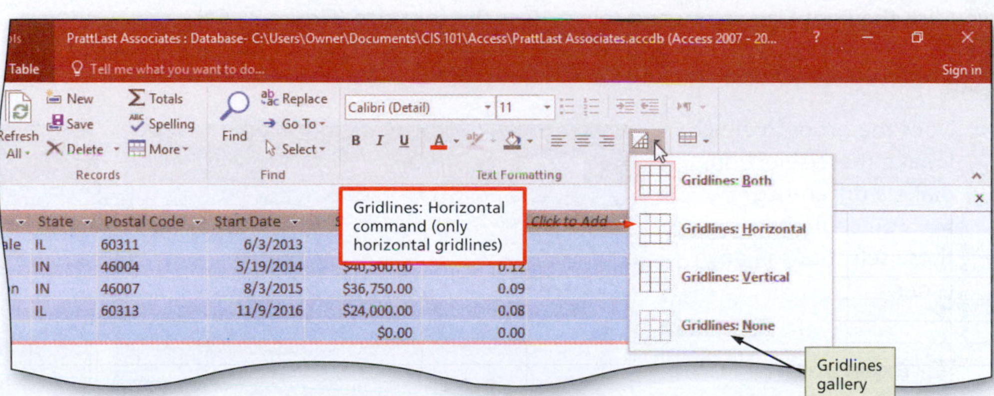

Figure 3–62

- Click Gridlines: Horizontal in the Gridlines gallery to include only horizontal gridlines.

Experiment

- Experiment with other gridline options. When finished, once again select horizontal gridlines.

To Change the Colors and Font in a Datasheet

1 UPDATE RECORDS | 2 FILTER RECORDS | 3 CHANGE STRUCTURE | 4 MASS CHANGES | 5 VALIDATION RULES
6 CHANGE APPEARANCE | 7 REFERENTIAL INTEGRITY | 8 ORDER RECORDS

You can also modify the appearance of the datasheet by changing the colors and the font. The following steps change the Alternate Fill color, a color that appears on every other row in the datasheet. ***Why?** Having rows appear in alternate colors is an attractive way to visually separate the rows.* The steps also change the font color, the font, and the font size.

1

- With the datasheet for the Account Manager table selected, click the 'Alternate Row Color' button arrow (Home tab | Text Formatting group) to display the color palette (Figure 3–63).

Q&A Does it matter whether I click the button or the arrow?
Yes. Clicking the arrow produces a color palette. Clicking the button applies the currently selected color. When in doubt, you should click the arrow.

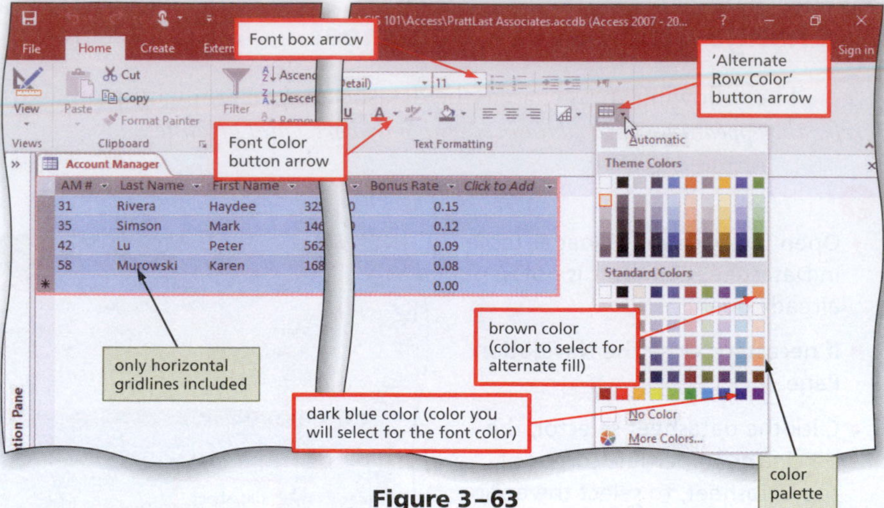

Figure 3–63

2

- Click Brown in the upper-right corner of Standard Colors to select brown as the alternate color.
- Click the Font Color button arrow, and then click the dark blue color that is the second color from the right in the bottom row in the Standard Colors to select the font color.
- Click the Font arrow, scroll down in the list until Bodoni MT appears, and then select Bodoni MT as the font. (If it is not available, select any font of your choice.)
- Click the Font Size arrow and select 10 as the font size (Figure 3–64).

Q&A Does the order in which I make these selections make a difference?
No. You could have made these selections in any order.

Experiment

- Experiment with other colors, fonts, and font sizes. When finished, return to the options selected in this step.

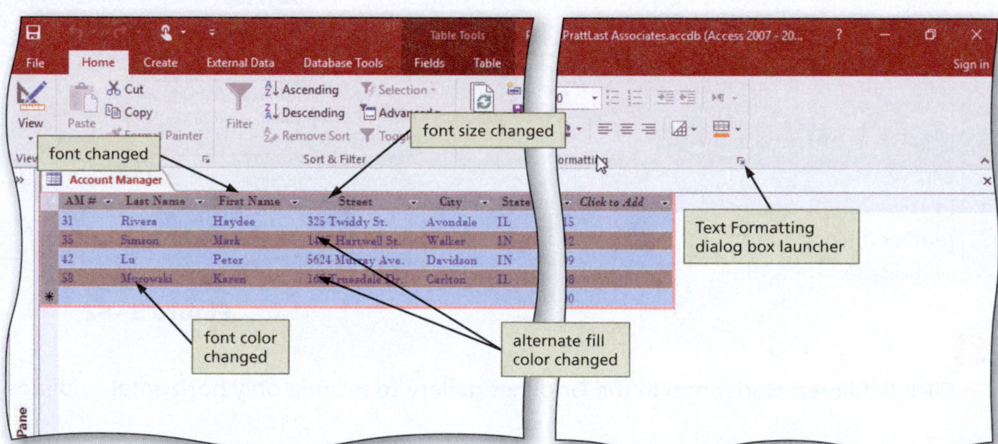

Figure 3–64

Using the Datasheet Formatting Dialog Box

As an alternative to using the individual buttons, you can click the Datasheet Formatting dialog box launcher, which is the arrow at the lower-right of the Text Formatting group, to display the Datasheet Formatting dialog box (Figure 3–65). You can use the various options within the dialog box to make changes to the datasheet format. Once you are finished, click the OK button to apply your changes.

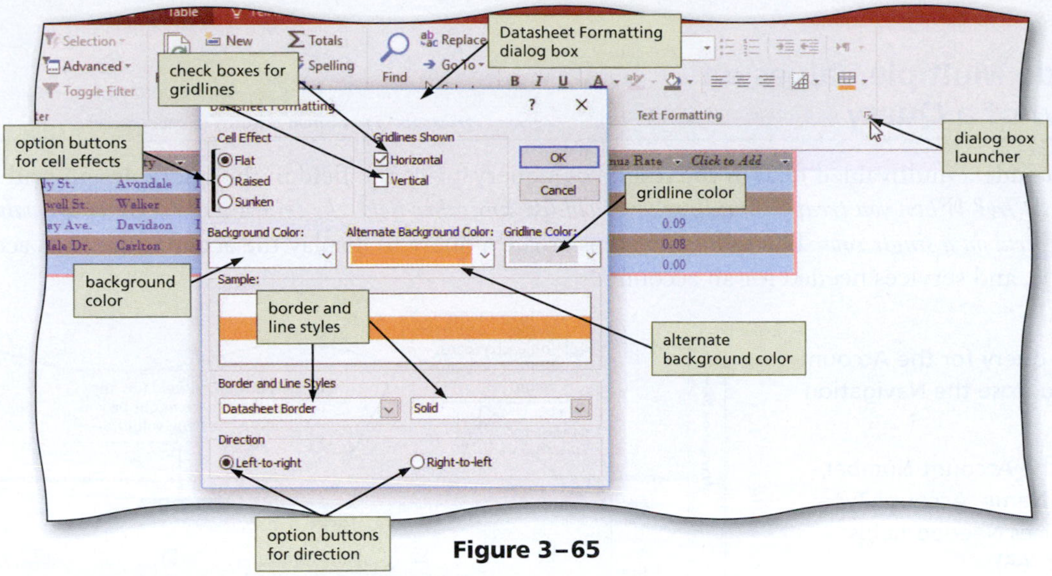

Datasheet Formatting dialog box
check boxes for gridlines
option buttons for cell effects
dialog box launcher
gridline color
background color
border and line styles
alternate background color
option buttons for direction

Figure 3–65

To Close the Datasheet without Saving the Format Changes

The following steps close the datasheet without saving the changes to the format. Because the changes are not saved, the next time you open the Account Manager table in Datasheet view it will appear in the original format. If you had saved the changes, the changes would be reflected in its appearance.

1. Close the Account Manager table.
2. Click the No button in the Microsoft Access dialog box when asked if you want to save your changes.

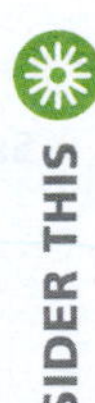

What kind of decisions should I make in determining whether to change the format of a datasheet?

- Would totals or other calculations be useful in the datasheet? If so, include the Total row and select the appropriate computations.
- Would another gridline style make the datasheet more useful? If so, change to the desired gridlines.
- Would alternating colors in the rows make them easier to read? If so, change the alternate fill color.
- Would a different font and/or font color make the text stand out better? If so, change the font color and/or the font.
- Is the font size appropriate? Can you see enough data at one time on the screen and yet have the data be readable? If not, change the font size to an appropriate value.
- Is the column spacing appropriate? Are some columns wider than they need to be? Do some columns not display all the data? Change the column sizes as necessary.

As a general guideline, once you have decided on a particular look for a datasheet, all datasheets in the database should have the same look, unless there is a compelling reason for a datasheet to differ.

Multivalued Fields in Queries

You can use multivalued fields in queries in the same way you use other fields in queries. You can choose to display the multiple values either on a single row or on multiple rows in the query results.

To Include Multiple Values on One Row of a Query

1 UPDATE RECORDS | 2 FILTER RECORDS | 3 CHANGE STRUCTURE | 4 MASS CHANGES | 5 VALIDATION RULES
6 CHANGE APPEARANCE | 7 REFERENTIAL INTEGRITY | 8 ORDER RECORDS

To include a multivalued field in the results of a query, place the field in the query design grid just like any other field. ***Why?*** *When you treat the multivalued field like any other field, the results will list all of the values for the multivalued field on a single row.* The following steps create a query to display the account number, account name, account type, and services needed for all accounts.

- Create a query for the Account table and close the Navigation Pane.
- Include the Account Number, Account Name, Account Type, and Services Needed fields (Figure 3–66).

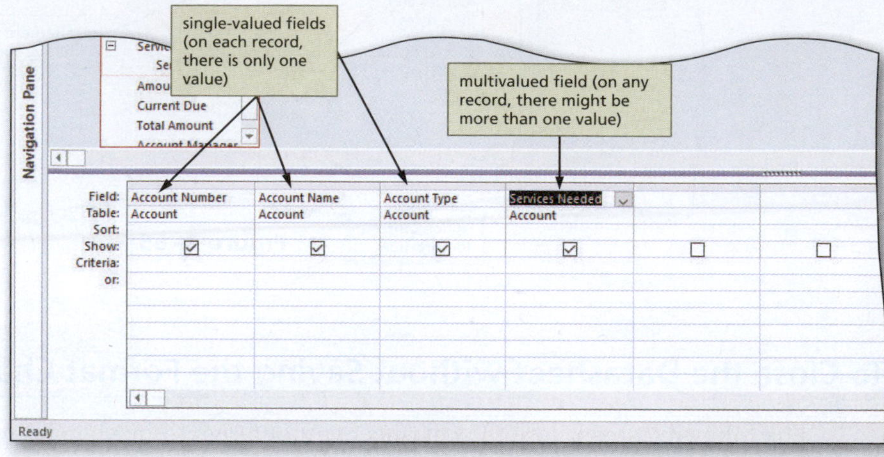

Figure 3–66

- Run the query and view the results (Figure 3–67).

Q&A Can I include criteria for the multivalued field?
Yes. You can include criteria for the multivalued field.

- Save the query as m03q01.

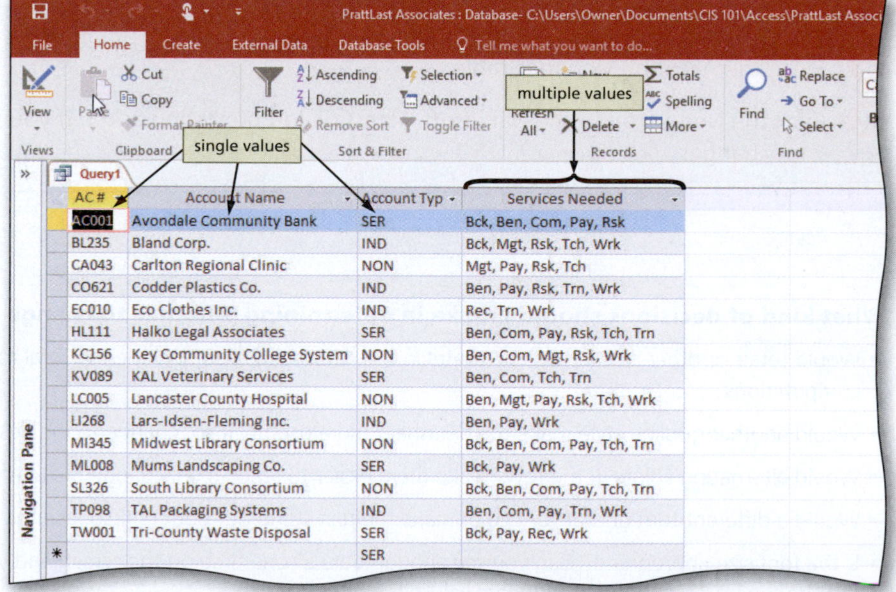

AC #	Account Name	Account Typ	Services Needed
AC001	Avondale Community Bank	SER	Bck, Ben, Com, Pay, Rsk
BL235	Bland Corp.	IND	Bck, Mgt, Rsk, Tch, Wrk
CA043	Carlton Regional Clinic	NON	Mgt, Pay, Rsk, Tch
CO621	Codder Plastics Co.	IND	Ben, Pay, Rsk, Trn, Wrk
EC010	Eco Clothes Inc.	IND	Rec, Trn, Wrk
HL111	Halko Legal Associates	SER	Ben, Com, Pay, Rsk, Tch, Trn
KC156	Key Community College System	NON	Ben, Com, Mgt, Rsk, Wrk
KV089	KAL Veterinary Services	SER	Ben, Com, Tch, Trn
LC005	Lancaster County Hospital	NON	Ben, Mgt, Pay, Rsk, Tch, Wrk
LI268	Lars-Idsen-Fleming Inc.	IND	Ben, Pay, Wrk
MI345	Midwest Library Consortium	NON	Bck, Ben, Com, Pay, Tch, Trn
ML008	Mums Landscaping Co.	SER	Bck, Pay, Wrk
SL326	South Library Consortium	NON	Bck, Ben, Com, Pay, Tch, Trn
TP098	TAL Packaging Systems	IND	Ben, Com, Pay, Trn, Wrk
TW001	Tri-County Waste Disposal	SER	Bck, Pay, Rec, Wrk
*		SER	

Figure 3–67

To Include Multiple Values on Multiple Rows of a Query

1 UPDATE RECORDS | 2 FILTER RECORDS | 3 CHANGE STRUCTURE | 4 MASS CHANGES | 5 VALIDATION RULES
6 CHANGE APPEARANCE | 7 REFERENTIAL INTEGRITY | 8 ORDER RECORDS

You might want to see the multiple services needed for an account on separate rows rather than a single row. ***Why?*** *Each row in the results will focus on one specific service that is needed.* To do so, you need to use the Value property of the Services Needed field by following the name of the field with a period and then the word, Value. The following steps use the Value property to display each service on a separate row.

1

- Return to Design view and ensure that the Account Number, Account Name, Account Type, and Services Needed fields are included in the design grid.
- Click the Services Needed field to produce an insertion point, press the RIGHT ARROW key as necessary to move the insertion point to the end of the field name, and then type a period.
- If the word, Value, did not automatically appear after the period, type the word `Value` after the period following the word, Needed, to use the Value property (Figure 3–68).

Q&A I do not see the word, Services. Did I do something wrong?
No. There is not enough room to display the entire name. If you wanted to see it, you could point to the right boundary of the column selector and then either drag or double-click.

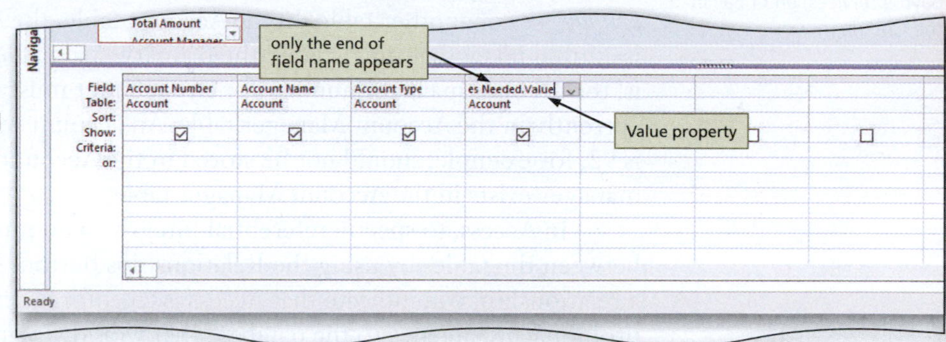

Figure 3–68

Q&A I see Services Needed.Value as a field in the field list. Could I have deleted the Services Needed field and added the Services Needed.Value field?
Yes. Either approach is fine.

2

- Run the query and view the results (Figure 3–69).

Q&A Can I now include criteria for the multivalued field?
Yes. You could enter a criterion just like in any other query.

Q&A Could I sort the rows by account number?
Yes. Select Ascending as the sort order just as you have done in other queries.

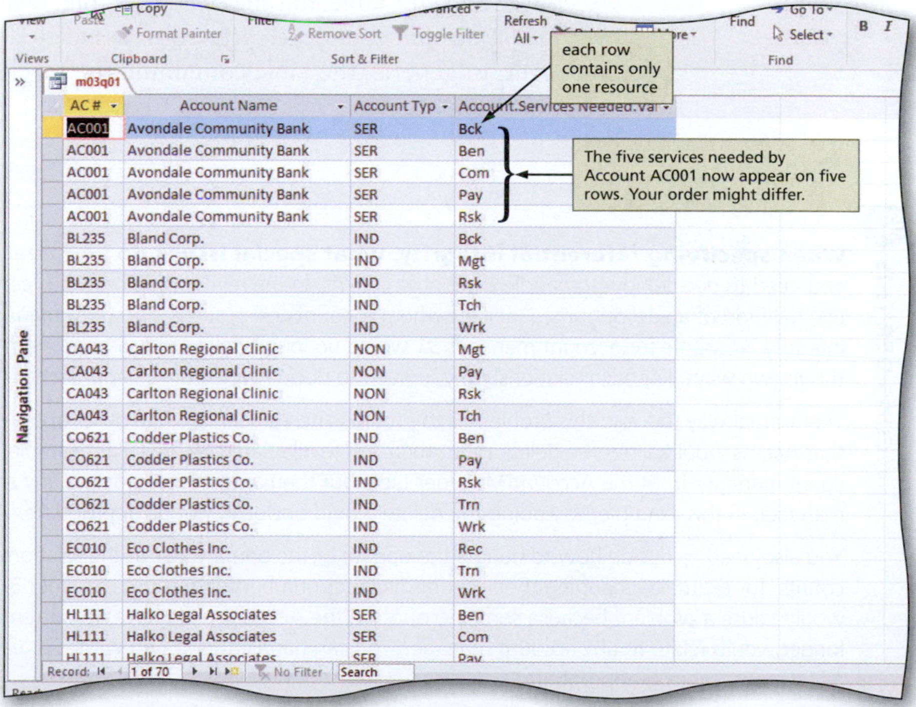

AC #	Account Name	Account Typ	Account.Services Needed.Val
AC001	Avondale Community Bank	SER	Bck
AC001	Avondale Community Bank	SER	Ben
AC001	Avondale Community Bank	SER	Com
AC001	Avondale Community Bank	SER	Pay
AC001	Avondale Community Bank	SER	Rsk
BL235	Bland Corp.	IND	Bck
BL235	Bland Corp.	IND	Mgt
BL235	Bland Corp.	IND	Rsk
BL235	Bland Corp.	IND	Tch
BL235	Bland Corp.	IND	Wrk
CA043	Carlton Regional Clinic	NON	Mgt
CA043	Carlton Regional Clinic	NON	Pay
CA043	Carlton Regional Clinic	NON	Rsk
CA043	Carlton Regional Clinic	NON	Tch
CO621	Codder Plastics Co.	IND	Ben
CO621	Codder Plastics Co.	IND	Pay
CO621	Codder Plastics Co.	IND	Rsk
CO621	Codder Plastics Co.	IND	Trn
CO621	Codder Plastics Co.	IND	Wrk
EC010	Eco Clothes Inc.	IND	Rec
EC010	Eco Clothes Inc.	IND	Trn
EC010	Eco Clothes Inc.	IND	Wrk
HL111	Halko Legal Associates	SER	Ben
HL111	Halko Legal Associates	SER	Com
HL111	Halko Legal Associates	SER	Pay

Record: 1 of 70 No Filter Search

Figure 3–69

3

- Save the query as a new object in the database named m03q02.
- Close the query.

Break Point: If you wish to take a break, this is a good place to do so. You can quit Access now. To resume at a later time, run Access, open the database called PrattLast Associates, and continue following the steps from this location forward.

Referential Integrity

BTW
Using Criteria with Multivalued Fields
To enter criteria in a multivalued field, simply enter the criteria in the Criteria row. For example, to find all accounts who need payroll services, enter Pay in the Criteria row.

When you have two related tables in a database, it is essential that the data in the common fields match. There should not be an account in the Account table whose account manager number is 31, for example, unless there is a record in the Account Manager table whose number is 31. This restriction is enforced through **referential integrity**, which is the property that ensures that the value in a foreign key must match that of another table's primary key.

A **foreign key** is a field in one table whose values are required to match the *primary key* of another table. In the Account table, the Account Manager Number field is a foreign key that must match the primary key of the Account Manager table; that is, the account manager number for any account must exist as an account manager currently in the Account Manager table. An account whose account manager number is 92, for example, should not be stored in the Account table because no such account manager exists in the Account Manager table.

In Access, to specify referential integrity, you must explicitly define a relationship between the tables by using the Relationships button. As part of the process of defining a relationship, you indicate that Access is to enforce referential integrity. Access then prohibits any updates to the database that would violate the referential integrity.

The type of relationship between two tables specified by the Relationships command is referred to as a **one-to-many relationship**. This means that *one* record in the first table is related to, or matches, *many* records in the second table, but each record in the second table is related to only *one* record in the first. In the PrattLast Associates database, for example, a one-to-many relationship exists between the Account Manager table and the Account table. *One* account manager is associated with *many* accounts, but each account is associated with only a single account manager. In general, the table containing the foreign key will be the *many* part of the relationship.

CONSIDER THIS

When specifying referential integrity, what special issues do you need to address?

You need to decide how to handle deletions of fields. In the relationship between accounts and account managers, for example, deletion of an account manager for whom accounts exist, such as account manager number 31, would violate referential integrity. Accounts for account manager 31 would no longer relate to any account manager in the database. You can handle this in two ways. For each relationship, you need to decide which of the approaches is appropriate.

The normal way to avoid this problem is to prohibit such a deletion. The other option is to **cascade the delete.** This means that Access would allow the deletion but then delete all related records. For example, it would allow the deletion of the account manager from the Account Manager table but then automatically delete any accounts related to the deleted account manager. In this example, cascading the delete would obviously not be appropriate.

You also need to decide how to handle the update of the primary key. In the relationship between account managers and accounts, for example, changing the account manager number for account manager 31 to 32 in the Account Manager table would cause a problem because some accounts in the Account table have account manager number 31. These accounts no longer would relate to any account manager. You can handle this in two ways. For each relationship, you need to decide which of the approaches is appropriate.

The normal way to avoid this problem is to prohibit this type of update. The other option is to **cascade the update.** This means to allow the change, but make the corresponding change in the foreign key on all related records. In the relationship between accounts and account managers, for example, Access would allow the update but then automatically make the corresponding change for any account whose account manager number was 31. It will now be 32.

To Specify Referential Integrity

The following steps use the Relationships button on the Database Tools tab to specify referential integrity by explicitly indicating a relationship between the Account Manager and Account tables. The steps also ensure that updates will cascade, but that deletes will not. ***Why?*** *By indicating a relationship between tables, and specifying that updates will cascade, it will be possible to change the Account Manager Number for an account manager, and the same change will automatically be made for all accounts of that account manager. By not specifying that deletes will cascade, it will not be possible to delete an account manager who has related accounts.*

- Click Database Tools on the ribbon to display the Database Tools tab. (Figure 3–70).

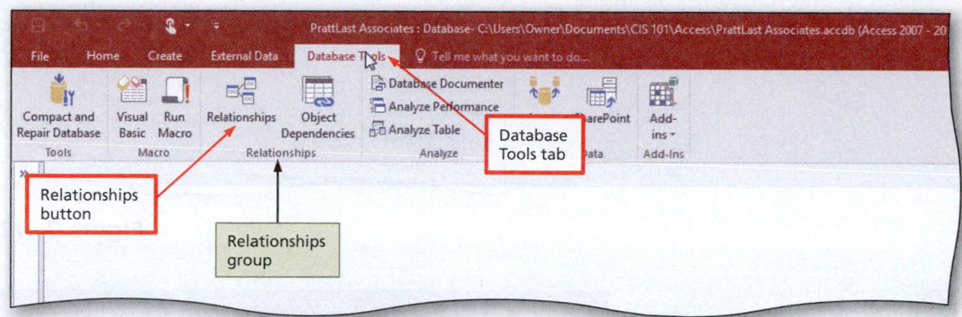

Figure 3–70

- Click the Relationships button (Database Tools tab | Relationships group) to open the Relationships window and display the Show Table dialog box (Figure 3–71).

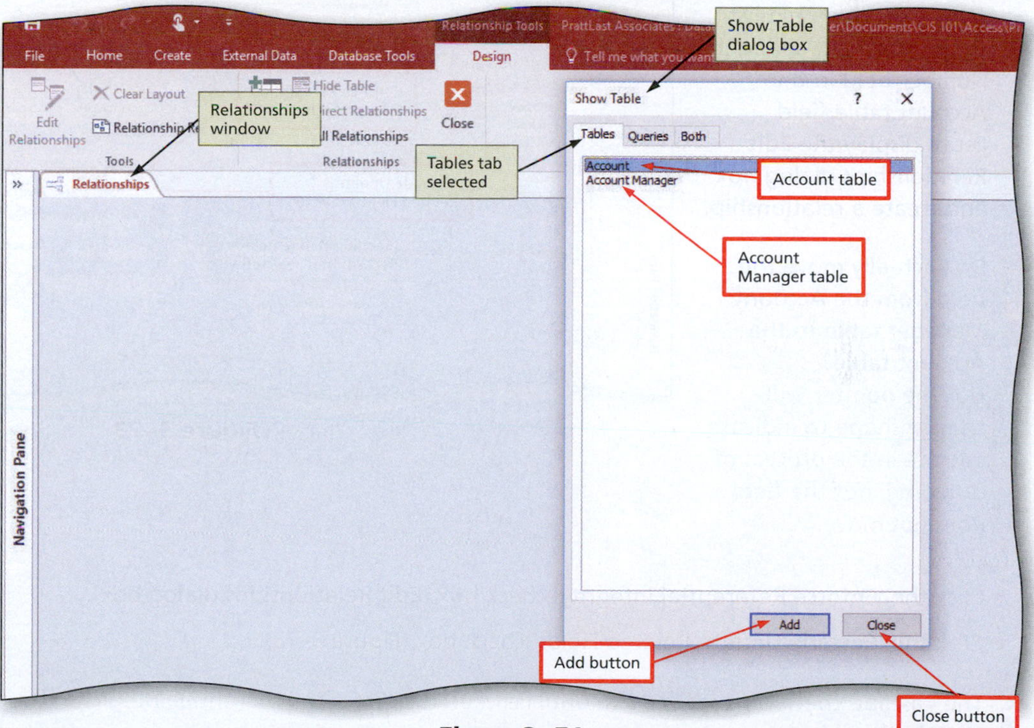

Figure 3–71

- Click the Account Manager table (Show Table dialog box), and then click the Add button to add a field list for the Account Manager table to the Relationships window.
- Click the Account table (Show Table dialog box), and then click the Add button to add a field list for the Account table to the Relationships window.

- Click the Close button (Show Table dialog box) to close the dialog box.
- Resize the field lists that appear so all fields are visible (Figure 3–72).

Q&A Do I need to resize the field lists?
No. You can use the scroll bars to view the fields. Before completing the next step, however, you would need to make sure the Account Manager Number fields in both tables appear on the screen.

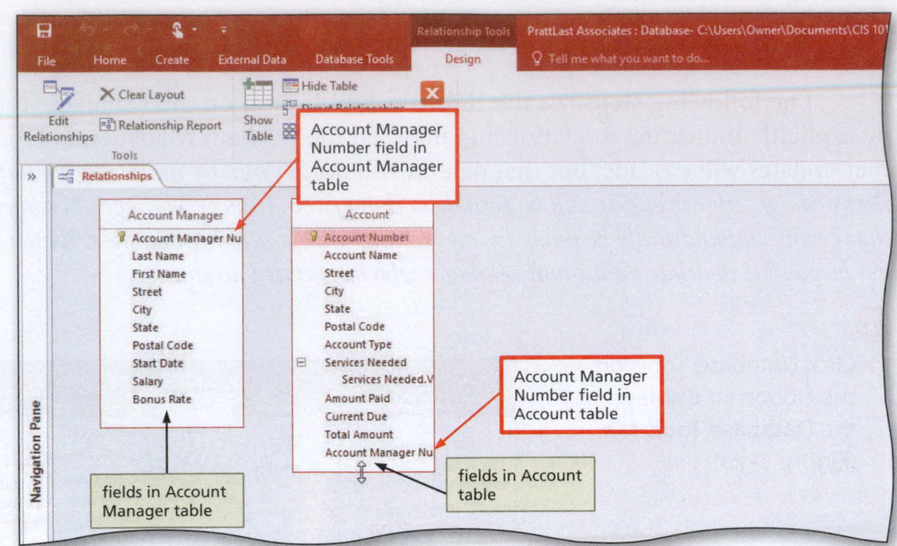

Figure 3–72

4

- Drag the Account Manager Number field in the Account Manager table field list to the Account Manager Number field in the Account table field list to display the Edit Relationships dialog box and create a relationship.

Q&A Do I actually move the field from the Account Manager table to the Account table?
No. The pointer will change shape to indicate you are in the process of dragging, but the field does not move.

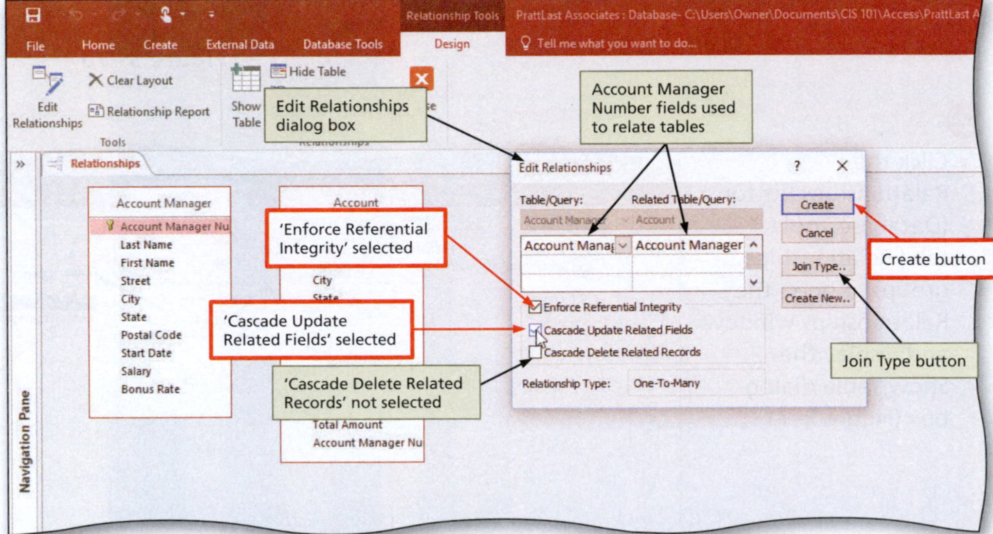

Figure 3–73

- Click the 'Enforce Referential Integrity' check box (Edit Relationships dialog box).
- Click the 'Cascade Update Related Fields' check box (Figure 3–73).

Q&A The Cascade check boxes were dim until I clicked the 'Enforce Referential Integrity' check box. Is that correct?
Yes. Until you have chosen to enforce referential integrity, the cascade options are not applicable.

5

- Click the Create button (Edit Relationships dialog box) to complete the creation of the relationship (Figure 3–74).

Q&A What is the symbol at the lower end of the join line?
It is the mathematical symbol for infinity. It is used here to denote the "many" end of the relationship.

Q&A Can I print a copy of the relationship?
Yes. Click the Relationship Report button (Relationship Tools Design tab | Tools group) to produce a report of the relationship. You can print the report. You can also save it as a report in the database for future use. If you do not want to save it, close the report after you have printed it and do not save the changes.

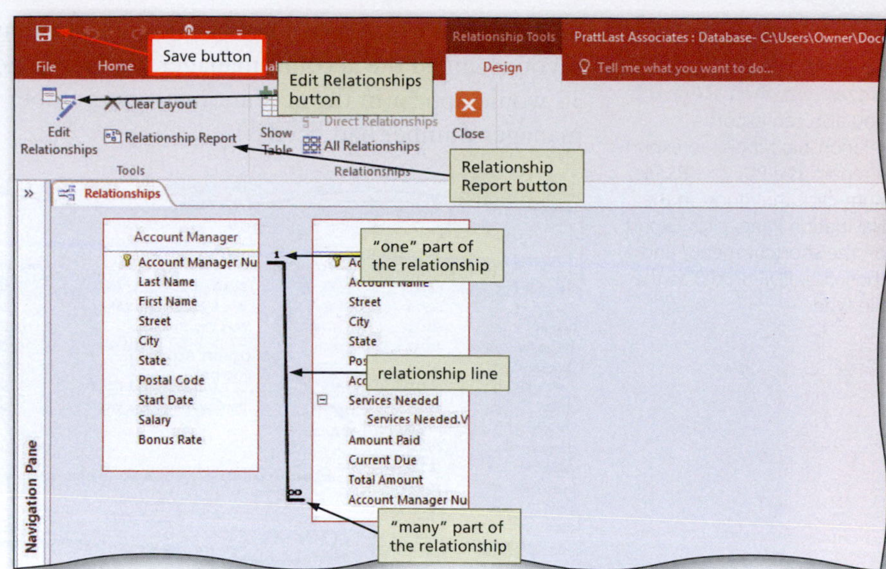

Figure 3–74

6

- Click the Save button on the Quick Access Toolbar to save the relationship you created.
- Close the Relationships window.

Q&A Can I later modify the relationship if I want to change it in some way?
Yes. Click Database Tools on the ribbon to display the Database Tools tab, and then click the Relationships button (Database Tools tab | Relationships group) to open the Relationships window. To add another table, click the Show Table button on the Design tab. To remove a table, click the Hide Table button. To edit a relationship, select the relationship and click the Edit Relationships button.

CONSIDER THIS

Can I change the join type as I can in queries?

Yes. Click the Join Type button in the Edit Relationships dialog box. Click option button 1 to create an INNER join, that is, a join in which only records with matching values in the join fields appear in the result. Click option button 2 to create a LEFT join, that is, a join that includes all records from the left-hand table, but only records from the right-hand table that have matching values in the join fields. Click option button 3 to create a RIGHT join, that is, a join that includes all records from the right-hand table, but only records from the left-hand table that have matching values in the join fields.

Effect of Referential Integrity

Referential integrity now exists between the Account Manager and Account tables. Access now will reject any number in the Account Manager Number field in the Account table that does not match an account manager number in the Account Manager table. Attempting to change the account manager number for an account to one that does not match any account manager in the Account Manager table would result in the error message shown in Figure 3–75. Similarly, attempting to add an account whose account manager number does not match would produce the same error message.

Access also will reject the deletion of an account manager for whom related accounts exist. Attempting to delete account manager 31 from the Account Manager table, for example, would result in the message shown in Figure 3–76.

Access would, however, allow the change of an account manager number in the Account Manager table. It would then automatically make the corresponding change

BTW
Relationships
You also can use the Relationships window to specify a one-to-one relationship. In a one-to-one relationship, the matching fields are both primary keys. If PrattLast Associates maintained a company car for each account manager, the data concerning the cars might be kept in a Car table, in which the primary key is Account Manager Number — the same primary key as the Account Manager table. Thus, there would be a one-to-one relationship between account managers and cars.

BTW
Exporting a Relationship Report
You also can export a relationship report. To export a report as a PDF or XPS file, right-click the report in the Navigation Pane, click Export on the shortcut menu, and then click PDF or XPS as the file type.

to the account manager number for all the account manager's accounts. For example, if you changed the account manager number of account manager 31 to 32, the number 32 would appear in the account manager number field for accounts whose account manager number had been 31.

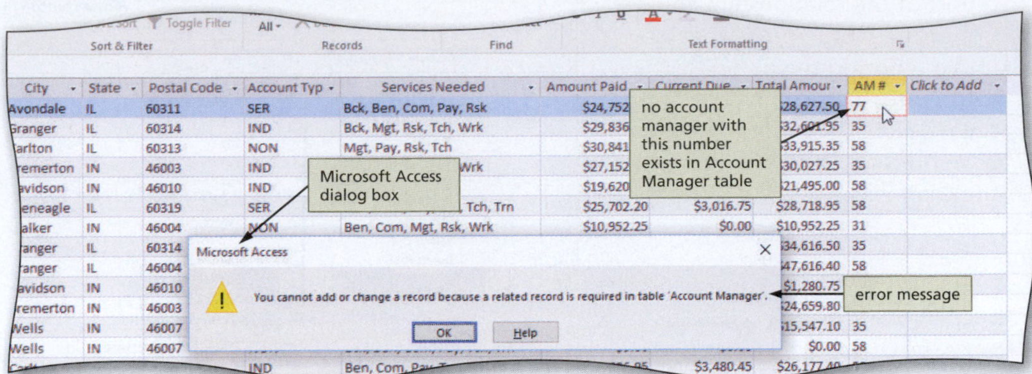

Figure 3–75

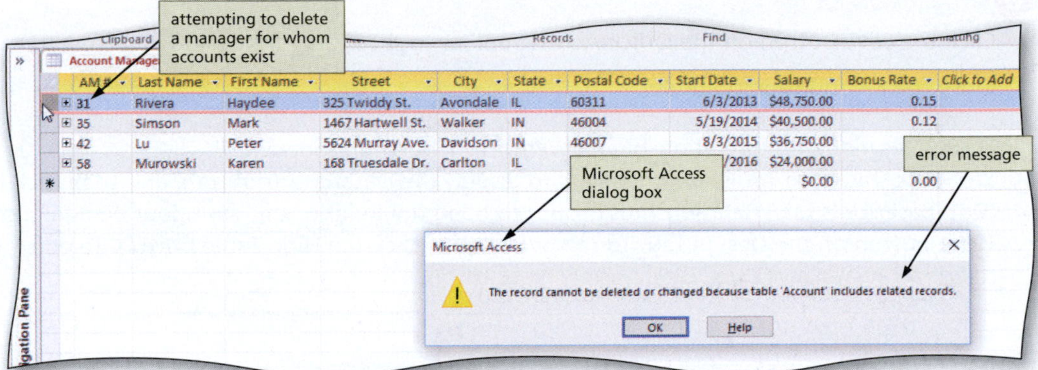

Figure 3–76

To Use a Subdatasheet

1 UPDATE RECORDS | 2 FILTER RECORDS | 3 CHANGE STRUCTURE | 4 MASS CHANGES | 5 VALIDATION RULES
6 CHANGE APPEARANCE | **7 REFERENTIAL INTEGRITY** | **8 ORDER RECORDS**

One consequence of the tables being explicitly related is that the accounts for an account manager can appear below the account manager in a **subdatasheet**. ***Why is a subdatasheet useful?*** *A subdatasheet is useful when you want to review or edit data in joined or related tables.* The availability of such a subdatasheet is indicated by a plus sign that appears in front of the rows in the Account Manager table. The following steps display the subdatasheet for account manager 35.

- Open the Account Manager table in Datasheet view and close the Navigation Pane (Figure 3–77).

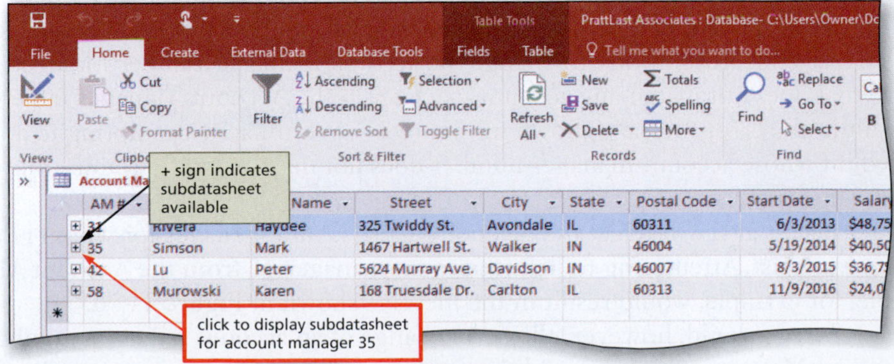

Figure 3–77

2

- Click the plus sign in front of the row for account manager 35 to display the subdatasheet (Figure 3–78).

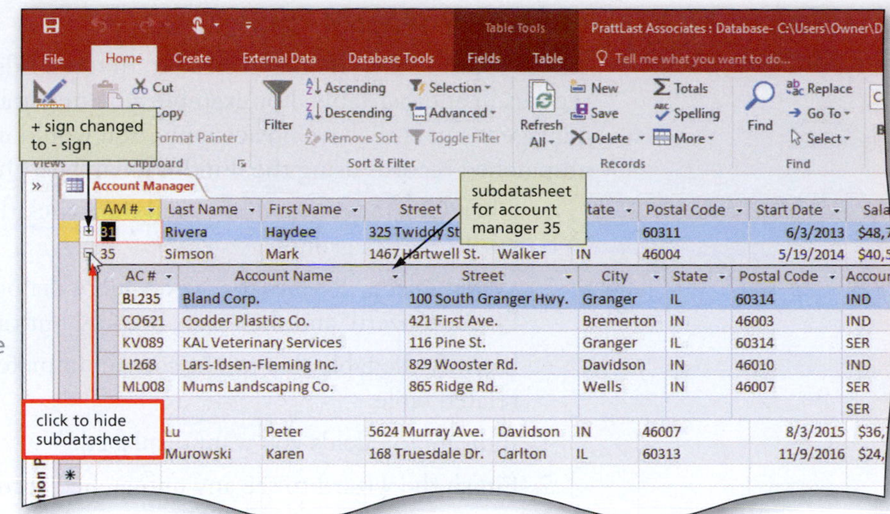

Figure 3–78

How do I hide the subdatasheet when I no longer want it to appear?

When you clicked the plus sign, it changed to a minus sign. Click the minus sign.

Experiment

- Display subdatasheets for other account managers. Display more than one subdatasheet at a time. Remove the subdatasheets from the screen.

3

- If requested by your instructor, replace the city and state for account manager 35 with your city and state.
- Close the Account Manager table.

Handling Data Inconsistency

In many organizations, databases evolve and change over time. One department might create a database for its own internal use. Employees in another department may decide they need their own database containing much of the same information. For example, the Purchasing department of an organization might create a database of products that it buys and the Receiving department may create a database of products that it receives. Each department is keeping track of the same products. When the organization eventually merges the databases, they might discover inconsistencies and duplication. The Find Duplicates Query Wizard and the Find Unmatched Query Wizard can assist in clearing the resulting database of duplication and errors.

BTW

Database Design: Validation

In most organizations, decisions about what is valid and what is invalid data are made during the requirements gathering process and the database design process.

To Find Duplicate Records

One reason to include a primary key for a table is to eliminate duplicate records. A possibility still exists, however, that duplicate records can get into your database. You would use the following steps to find duplicate records using the 'Find Duplicates Query Wizard'.

1. Click Create on the ribbon, and then click the Query Wizard button (Create tab | Queries group).
2. When Access displays the New Query dialog box, click the 'Find Duplicates Query Wizard' and then click the OK button.
3. Identify the table and field or fields that might contain duplicate information.
4. Indicate any other fields you want displayed.
5. Finish the wizard to see any duplicate records.

To Find Unmatched Records

Occasionally, you might need to find records in one table that have no matching records in another table. For example, you may want to determine which account managers currently have no accounts. You would use the following steps to find unmatched records using the 'Find Unmatched Query Wizard'.

1. Click Create on the ribbon, and then click the Query Wizard button (Create tab | Queries group).
2. When Access displays the New Query dialog box, click the 'Find Unmatched Query Wizard' and then click the OK button.
3. Identify the table that might contain unmatched records, and then identify the related table.
4. Indicate the fields you want displayed.
5. Finish the wizard to see any unmatched records.

Ordering Records

Normally, Access sequences the records in the Account table by account number whenever listing them because the Account Number field is the primary key. You can change this order, if desired.

To Use the Ascending Button to Order Records

1 UPDATE RECORDS | 2 FILTER RECORDS | 3 CHANGE STRUCTURE | 4 MASS CHANGES | 5 VALIDATION RULES
6 CHANGE APPEARANCE | 7 REFERENTIAL INTEGRITY | 8 ORDER RECORDS

To change the order in which records appear, use the Ascending or Descending buttons. Either button reorders the records based on the field in which the insertion point is located. The following steps order the records by city using the Ascending button. ***Why?*** *Using the Ascending button is the quickest and easiest way to order records.*

1

- Open the Account table in Datasheet view.
- Click the City field on the first record to select the field (Figure 3–79).

Q&A Did I have to click the field on the first record?
No. Any other record would have worked as well.

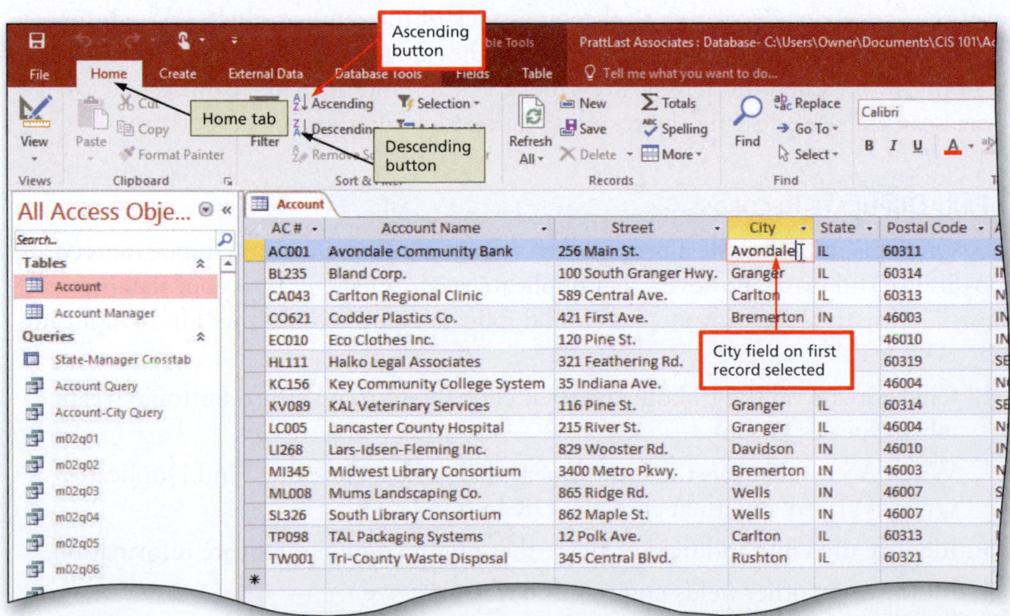

Figure 3–79

- Click the Ascending button (Home tab | Sort & Filter group) to sort the records by City (Figure 3–80).

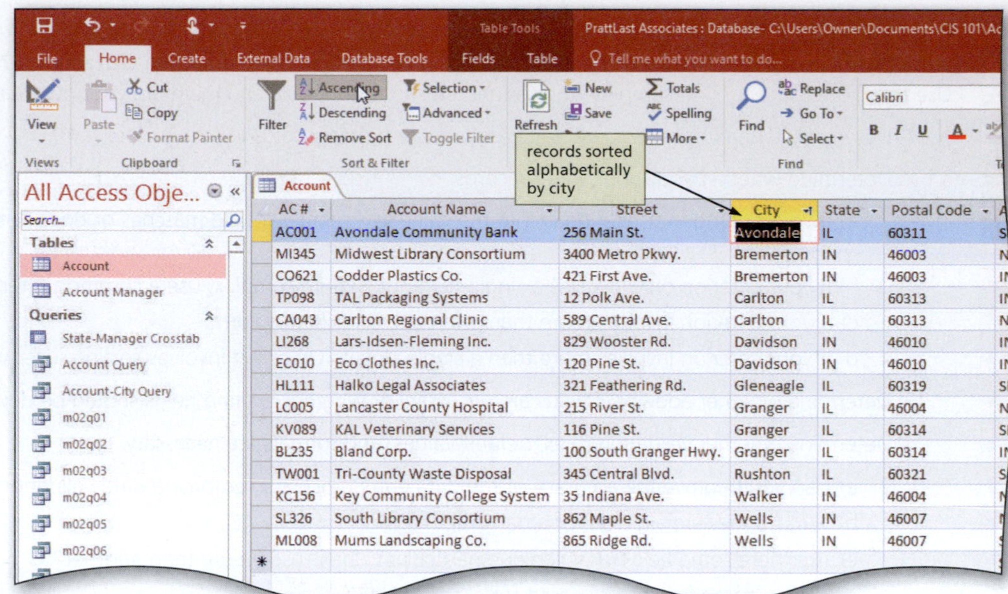

Figure 3–80

- Close the Account table.
- Click the No button (Microsoft Access dialog box) when asked if you want to save your changes.

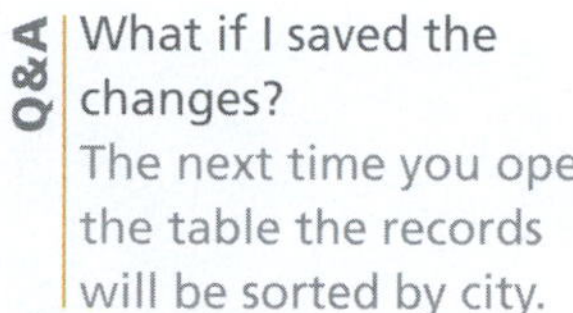

What if I saved the changes?
The next time you open the table the records will be sorted by city.

- If desired, sign out of your Microsoft account.
- Exit Access.

Other Ways

1. Right-click field name, click Sort A to Z (for ascending) or Sort Z to A (for descending)
2. Click the field selector arrow and click Sort A to Z or Sort Z to A

To Use the Ascending Button to Order Records on Multiple Fields

Just as you are able to sort the answer to a query on multiple fields, you can also sort the data that appears in a datasheet on multiple fields. To do so, the major and minor keys must be next to each other in the datasheet with the major key on the left. If this is not the case, you can drag the columns into the correct position. Instead of dragging, however, usually it will be easier to use a query that has the data sorted in the desired order.

To sort on a combination of fields where the major key is just to the left of the minor key, you would use the following steps.

1. Click the field selector at the top of the major key column to select the entire column.
2. Hold down the SHIFT key and then click the field selector for the minor key column to select both columns.
3. Click the Ascending button to sort the records.

BTW

Access Help

At any time while using Access, you can find answers to questions and display information about various topics through Access Help. Used properly, this form of assistance can increase your productivity and reduce your frustrations by minimizing the time you spend learning how to use Access. For instructions about Access Help and exercises that will help you gain confidence in using it, read the Office and Windows module at the beginning of this book.

Summary

In this module you have learned how to use a form to add records to a table, search for records, delete records, filter records, change the database structure, create and use lookup fields, create calculated fields, create and use multivalued fields, make mass changes, create validation rules, change the appearance of a datasheet, specify referential integrity, and use subdatasheets.

STUDENT ASSIGNMENTS

CONSIDER THIS

What decisions will you need to make when maintaining your own databases?

Use these guidelines as you complete the assignments in this module and maintain your own databases outside of this class.

1. Determine when it is necessary to add, change, or delete records in a database.
2. Determine whether you should filter records.
    a) If your criterion for filtering is that the value in a particular field matches or does not match a certain specific value, use Filter By Selection.
    b) If your criterion only involves a single field but is more complex, use a common filter.
    c) If your criterion involves more than one field, use Filter By Form.
    d) If your criterion involves more than a single And or Or, or if it involves sorting, use Advanced Filter/Sort.
3. Determine whether additional fields are necessary or whether existing fields should be deleted.
4. Determine whether validation rules, default values, and formats are necessary.
    a) Can you improve the accuracy of the data entry process by enforcing data validation?
    b) What values are allowed for a particular field?
    c) Are there some fields in which one particular value is used more than another?
    d) Should some fields be required for each record?
    e) Are there some fields for which special formats would be appropriate?
5. Determine whether changes to the format of a datasheet are desirable.
    a) Would totals or other calculations be useful in the datasheet?
    b) Would different gridlines make the datasheet easier to read?
    c) Would alternating colors in the rows make them easier to read?
    d) Would a different font and/or font color make the text stand out better?
    e) Is the font size appropriate?
    f) Is the column spacing appropriate?
6. Identify related tables in order to implement relationships between the tables.
    a) Is there a one-to-many relationship between the tables?
    b) If so, which table is the one table?
    c) Which table is the many table?
7. When specifying referential integrity, address deletion and update policies.
    a) Decide how to handle deletions. Should deletion be prohibited or should the delete cascade?
    b) Decide how to handle the update of the primary key. Should the update be prohibited or should the update cascade?

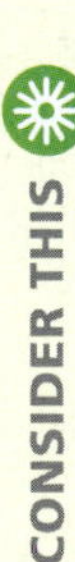

CONSIDER THIS

How should you submit solutions to questions in the assignments identified with a symbol?

Every assignment in this book contains one or more questions identified with a symbol. These questions require you to think beyond the assigned database. Present your solutions to the questions in the format required by your instructor. Possible formats may include one or more of these options: write the answer; create a document that contains the answer; present your answer to the class; discuss your answer in a group; record the answer as audio or video using a webcam, smartphone, or portable media player; or post answers on a blog, wiki, or website.

Apply Your Knowledge

Reinforce the skills and apply the concepts you learned in this module.

Adding Lookup Fields, Specifying Validation Rules, Updating Records, Updating Reports, and Creating Relationships

Instructions: Run Access. Open the Apply Friendly Janitorial Services database that you modified in Apply Your Knowledge in Module 2. (If you did not complete the exercise, see your instructor for a copy of the modified database.)

Perform the following tasks:

1. Open the Client table in Design view.
2. Add a Lookup field called Client Type to the Client table. The field should appear after the Postal Code field. The field will contain data on the type of client. The client types are IND (industrial, manufacturing), RET (retail stores), and SER (service, nonprofit). Save the changes to the Client table.
3. Create the following validation rules for the Client table.
   a. Specify the legal values IND, RET, and SER for the Client Type field. Enter `Must be IND, RET, or SER` as the validation text.
   b. Format the Client Number field to ensure that any letters entered in the field appear as uppercase.
   c. Make the Client Name field a required field.
4. Save the changes and close the table. You do not need to test the current data.
5. Create an update query for the Client table. Change all the entries in the Client Type field to SER. Run the query and save it as Client Type Update Query.
6. Open the Client table in Datasheet view, update the following records, and then close the table:
   a. Change the client type for clients CC25, CP03, MM01, and TE15 to IND.
   b. Change the client type for clients AZ01, BL24, and HC17 to RET.
7. Create a split form for the Client table. Save the form as Client Split Form.
8. Open the Client Split Form in Form view, find client HC17, and change the client name to Hilltop Crafters. Close the form.
9. Open the Client Financial Report in Layout view and add the Client Type field to the report as shown in Figure 3–81. Save the report.

Client Number	Client Name	Client Type	Amount Paid	Current Due	Supervisor Number
AT13	Atlas Repair	SER	$5,400.00	$600.00	103
AZ01	AZ Auto	RET	$9,250.00	$975.00	110
BB35	Babbage Bookkeeping	SER	$8,820.00	$980.00	110

Figure 3–81

10. Establish referential integrity between the Supervisor table (the one table) and the Client table (the many table). Cascade the update but not the delete. Save the relationship.
11. If requested to do so by your instructor, rename the Client Split Form as Split Form for First Name Last Name where First Name Last Name is your name.
12. Submit the revised database in the format specified by your instructor.
13. The values in the Client Type field are currently in the order IND, RET, SER. How would you reorder the values to SER, IND, RET in the Client Type list?

Extend Your Knowledge

Extend the skills you learned in this module and experiment with new skills. You may need to use Help to complete the assignment.

Creating Action Queries, Changing Table Properties, and Adding Totals to a Datasheet

Note: To complete this assignment, you will be required to use the Data Files. Please contact your instructor for information about accessing the Data Files.

Continued >

Extend Your Knowledge *continued*

Instructions: Babbage Bookkeeping is a small company that provides bookkeeping services to small businesses. PrattLast Associates has been approached about buying Babbage Bookkeeping. PrattLast is interested in knowing how many clients the companies have in common. Babbage also needs to do some database maintenance by finding duplicate records and finding unmatched records.

Perform the following tasks:

1. Run Access and open the Extend Babbage Bookkeeping database. Create a make-table query to create the Potential Accounts table in the Babbage Bookkeeping database shown in Figure 3–82. Run the query and save it as Make Table Query.

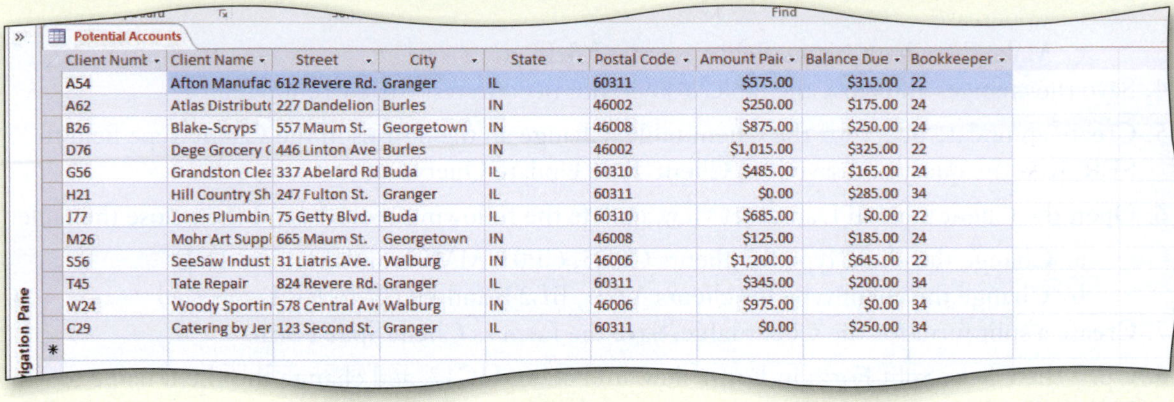

Potential Accounts

Client Numb	Client Name	Street	City	State	Postal Code	Amount Paid	Balance Due	Bookkeeper
A54	Afton Manufac	612 Revere Rd.	Granger	IL	60311	$575.00	$315.00	22
A62	Atlas Distribut	227 Dandelion	Burles	IN	46002	$250.00	$175.00	24
B26	Blake-Scryps	557 Maum St.	Georgetown	IN	46008	$875.00	$250.00	24
D76	Dege Grocery (	446 Linton Ave	Burles	IN	46002	$1,015.00	$325.00	22
G56	Grandston Clea	337 Abelard Rd	Buda	IL	60310	$485.00	$165.00	24
H21	Hill Country Sh	247 Fulton St.	Granger	IL	60311	$0.00	$285.00	34
J77	Jones Plumbin	75 Getty Blvd.	Buda	IL	60310	$685.00	$0.00	22
M26	Mohr Art Suppl	665 Maum St.	Georgetown	IN	46008	$125.00	$185.00	24
S56	SeeSaw Indust	31 Liatris Ave.	Walburg	IN	46006	$1,200.00	$645.00	22
T45	Tate Repair	824 Revere Rd.	Granger	IL	60311	$345.00	$200.00	34
W24	Woody Sportin	578 Central Ave	Walburg	IN	46006	$975.00	$0.00	34
C29	Catering by Jer	123 Second St.	Granger	IL	60311	$0.00	$250.00	34

Figure 3–82

2. Open the Potential Accounts table and change the font to Arial with a font size of 10. Resize the columns to best fit the data. Save the changes to the table and close the table.
3. Open the Bookkeeper table and add the Totals row to the table. Calculate the average hourly rate and the total Earnings YTD. Save the changes to the table layout and close the table.
4. Use the Find Duplicates Query Wizard to find duplicate information in the City field of the Client table. Include the Client Name in the query. Save the query as City Duplicates Query and close the query.
5. Use the Find Unmatched Query Wizard to find all records in the Bookkeeper table that do not match records in the Client table. Bookkeeper Number is the common field in both tables. Include the Bookkeeper Number, Last Name, and First Name in the query. Save the query as Bookkeeper Unmatched Query and close the query.
6. If requested to do so by your instructor, change the client name in the Client table for client number B26 to First Name Last Name where First Name Last Name is your name. If your name is longer than the space allowed, simply enter as much as you can.
7. Submit the revised database in the format specified by your instructor.
8. What differences, if any, are there between the Client table and the Potential Accounts table you created with the make-table query?

Expand Your World

Create a solution, which uses cloud and web technologies, by learning and investigating on your own from general guidance.

Problem: You own a small business that employs college students to do odd jobs for homeowners in the college town where you live. You created an Access database to keep track of your customers and workers and have been teaching yourself more about database design and how best to use Access to promote and manage your business.

Perform the following tasks:

1. Run Access and open the Expand Odd Jobs database. Edit the relationship between the Worker table and the Customer table to cascade the updates. Save the change to the relationship.
2. Create a relationship report for the relationship and save the report as First Name Last Name Relationship Report where First Name Last Name is your name.
3. Export the relationship as an RTF/Word document to a cloud-based storage location of your choice. Do not save the export steps.
4. Research the web to find a graphic that depicts a one-to-many relationship for a relational database. (*Hint:* Use your favorite search engine and enter keywords such as ERD diagram, entity-relationship diagram, or one to many relationship.)
5. Insert the graphic into the relationship report using an app of your choice, such as Word Online, and save the modified report.
6. Share the modified report with your instructor.
7. Submit the revised database in the format specified by your instructor.
8. Which cloud-based storage location did you use? How did you locate your graphic? Which app did you use to modify the report?

In the Labs

Design, create, modify, and/or use a database following the guidelines, concepts, and skills presented in this module. Labs are listed in order of increasing difficulty. Labs 1 and 2, which increase in difficulty, require you to create solutions based on what you learned in the module. Lab 3 requires you to apply your creative thinking and problem-solving skills to design and implement a solution.

Lab 1: Maintaining the Garden Naturally Database

Problem: Garden Naturally is expanding rapidly and needs to make some database changes to handle the expansion. The company needs to know more about its customers, such as general types of products needed. It also needs to add validation rules and update records in the database.

Note: Use the database modified in Lab 1 of Module 2 for this assignment, or see your instructor for information on accessing the files required for this book.

Instructions: Perform the following tasks:

1. Open the Lab 1 Garden Naturally database and open the Customer table in Design view.
2. Add a multivalued lookup field, Product Types Needed, to the Customer table. The field should appear after the Postal Code field. Table 3–2 lists the product type abbreviations that management would like in the multivalued field as well as a description. Save the change to the table.

Table 3–2 Product Type Abbreviations and Descriptions

Product Type Abbreviations	Product Type Descriptions
Comp	Composting Needs
Frtl	Fertilizers
Grdn	Garden Supplies
Grnh	Greenhouse Supplies
Lawn	Lawn and Landscaping
Seed	Seeds
Soil	Soils and Nutrients
Watr	Watering Equipment

Continued >

In the Labs *continued*

3. Add a calculated field named Total Amount (Amount Paid + Balance Due) to the Customer table. The field should follow the Balance Due field. Save the change to the table.
4. Create the following rules for the Customer table and save the changes:
   a. Ensure that any letters entered in the Customer Number field appear as uppercase.
   b. Make Customer Name a required field.
   c. Ensure that only the values DE, NJ, and PA can be entered in the State field. Include validation text.
   d. Assign a default value of NJ to the State field.
5. Use Filter By Form to find all records where the city is Gaston and the balance due is $0.00. Delete the record(s). Do not save the filter.
6. Open the Customer table in Datasheet view and add the data shown in Figure 3–83 to the Product Types Needed field. Resize the field to best fit and save the changes to the layout of the table.

Customer Table

Customer Number	Customer Name	Product Types Needed
AA30	All About Gardens	Grdn, Seed, Soil, Watr
CT02	Christmas Tree Farm	Comp, Frtl, Seed, Soil, Watr
GG01	Garden Gnome	Frtl, Grdn, Lawn
GT34	Green Thumb Growers	Frtl, Grnh, Seed
LH15	Lawn & Home Store	Comp, Frtl, Grdn, Lawn
ML25	Mum's Landscaping	Frtl, Soil, Watr
OA45	Outside Architects	Grdn, Watr
PL10	Pat's Landscaping	Frtl, Grdn, Watr
PN18	Pyke Nurseries	Comp, Frtl, Grnh, Seed, Soil
SL25	Summit Lawn Service	Grdn, Lawn, Watr
TW34	TAL Wholesalers	Comp, Frtl, Seed, Soil
TY03	TLC Yard Care	Lawn, Watr
YS04	Yard Shoppe	Grdn, Lawn, Watr
YW01	Young's Wholesalers	Comp, Frtl, Grdn, Lawn, Seed, Soil

Figure 3–83

7. Open the Sales Rep table in Design view and change the field size for the Address field to 25. Save the changes and close the table.
8. Open the Sales Rep table in Datasheet view, find the record for sales rep 32, and change the address to 982 Victoria Station Rd. Resize the column to best fit.
9. If requested to do so by your instructor, change the last name for sales rep 35 to your last name. If your last name is longer than 15 characters, simply enter as much as you can.
10. Save the changes to the layout of the table and close the Sales Rep table.
11. Establish referential integrity between the Sales Rep table (the one table) and the Customer table (the many table). Cascade the update but not the delete.
12. Submit the revised database in the format specified by your instructor.
13. The State field currently has three possible values. How would you add MD to the State field list?

Lab 2: Maintaining the Museum Gift Shop Database

Problem: The manager of the Science Museum gift shop needs to change the database structure, add validation rules, and update records. Also, a volunteer at the gift shop was asked to add some items to the database. By mistake, the volunteer created a new database in which to store the items. These items need to be added to the Museum Gift Shop database.

Note: To complete this assignment, you will be required to use the Data Files. Please contact your instructor for information about accessing the Data Files. Use the database modified in Lab 2 of Module 2 for this assignment or see your instructor for information on accessing the files required for this book.

Instructions: Perform the following tasks:

1. Open the Lab 2 Museum Gift Shop database, and then open the Item table in Design view.
2. Add a lookup field, Item Type, to the Item table. The field should appear after the Description field. The field will contain data on the type of item for sale. The item types are ACT (activity, game), BKS (book), and NOV (novelty, gift).
3. Add the following validation rules to the Item table and save the changes:
   a. Make Description a required field.
   b. Specify the legal values ACT, BKS, and NOV for the Item Type field. Include validation text.
   c. Assign ACT as the default value for the Item Type field.
   d. Specify that the number on hand must be between 0 and 50, inclusive. Include validation text.
4. Using a query, assign the value ACT to the Item Type field for all records. Save the query as Update Query.
5. Create a split form for the Item table and save it as Item Split Form.
6. Use the split form to change the item type for items 6234, 6345, and 7123 to BKS. Change the item type for items 3663, 4583, 6185, 8196, and 8344 to NOV.
7. Open the Lab 2 Additional Items database from the Data Files.
8. Create and run a query to append the data in the Additional Items table to the Item table in the Lab 2 Museum Gift Shop database. Save the query as Append Query and close the Lab 2 Additional Items database.
9. Open the Lab 2 Museum Gift Shop database and then open the Item table. The result of the append query will be the table shown in Figure 3–84.

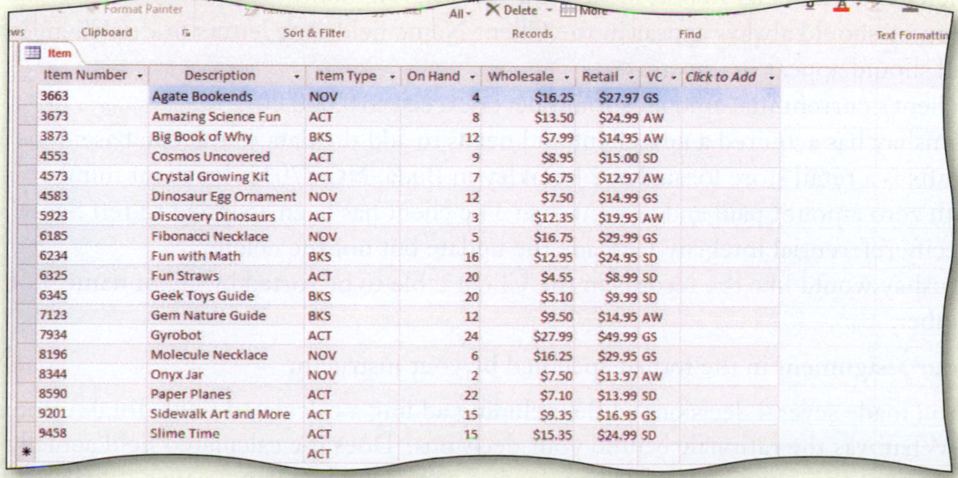

Item Number	Description	Item Type	On Hand	Wholesale	Retail	VC	Click to Add
3663	Agate Bookends	NOV	4	$16.25	$27.97	GS	
3673	Amazing Science Fun	ACT	8	$13.50	$24.99	AW	
3873	Big Book of Why	BKS	12	$7.99	$14.95	AW	
4553	Cosmos Uncovered	ACT	9	$8.95	$15.00	SD	
4573	Crystal Growing Kit	ACT	7	$6.75	$12.97	AW	
4583	Dinosaur Egg Ornament	NOV	12	$7.50	$14.99	GS	
5923	Discovery Dinosaurs	ACT	3	$12.35	$19.95	AW	
6185	Fibonacci Necklace	NOV	5	$16.75	$29.99	GS	
6234	Fun with Math	BKS	16	$12.95	$24.95	SD	
6325	Fun Straws	ACT	20	$4.55	$8.99	SD	
6345	Geek Toys Guide	BKS	20	$5.10	$9.99	SD	
7123	Gem Nature Guide	BKS	12	$9.50	$14.95	AW	
7934	Gyrobot	ACT	24	$27.99	$49.99	GS	
8196	Molecule Necklace	NOV	6	$16.25	$29.95	GS	
8344	Onyx Jar	NOV	2	$7.50	$13.97	AW	
8590	Paper Planes	ACT	22	$7.10	$13.99	SD	
9201	Sidewalk Art and More	ACT	15	$9.35	$16.95	GS	
9458	Slime Time	ACT	15	$15.35	$24.99	SD	
*		ACT					

Figure 3–84

Continued >

10. Create an advanced filter for the Item table. Filter the table to find all items with fewer than 10 items on hand. Sort the filter by Item Type and Description. Save the filter settings as a query and name the filter Reorder Filter. Clear the filter from the Item table.
11. Using a query, delete all records in the Item table where the description starts with the letter M. Run the query and save it as Delete Query.
12. If requested to do so by your instructor, right-click the Item table in the Navigation Pane, click Table Properties, and add a description for the Item table that includes your first and last name and the date you completed this assignment. Save the change to the table property.
13. Specify referential integrity between the Vendor table (the one table) and the Item table (the many table). Cascade the update but not the delete.
14. Add the Item Type field to the Item Status Report. It should follow the Description field.
15. Submit the revised database in the format specified by your instructor.
16. There are two ways to enter the validation rule in Step 3d. What are they? Which one did you use?

Lab 3: Consider This: Your Turn

Maintaining the Camshay Marketing Database

Instructions: Open the Lab 3 Camshay Marketing database you used in Module 2. If you did not use this database, contact your instructor for information about accessing the required files.

Part 1: Use the concepts and techniques presented in this module to modify the database according to the following requirements:

a. Grant Auction House is no longer a client of Camshay. Use Find or Filter By Selection to delete this record.
b. A Total Amount field that summed the Amount Paid and Current Due fields would be beneficial for the reports that Camshay needs.
c. Camshay could better serve its clients by adding a field that would list each client's type of business or organizations. Businesses are nonprofit (NON), service (SER), or retail (RET).
d. Most businesses are service organizations. Buda Community Clinic, Hendley County Hospital, and Granger Foundation are nonprofit organizations. The Bikeshop and Woody Sporting Goods are retail stores.
e. The Client Financial Report must show the Total Amount.
f. An entry should always appear in the Client Name field. Any letters in the Client Number field should appear in uppercase.
g. A client's current due amount should never exceed $10,000.00.
h. Camshay has acquired a new client and needs to add the data to the database. Fine Wooden Crafts is a retail store located at 24 Oakley in Buda, NC 27032. Its client number is FW01 with zero amount paid and current due. The client has been assigned to Jeff Scott.
i. Specify referential integrity. Cascade the update but not the delete.
j. Camshay would like the records in the Client table to be sorted by client name, not client number.

Submit your assignment in the format specified by your instructor.

Part 2: You made several decisions while including adding a calculated field, Total Amount, to the database. What was the rationale behind your decisions? Does the calculated field actually exist in the database? Are there any issues that you need to consider when you create a calculated field?

1 Managing Email Messages with Outlook

Objectives

You will have mastered the material in this module when you can:

- Add a Microsoft account to Outlook
- Set language preferences and sensitivity levels
- Apply a theme
- Compose, address, and send an email message
- Open, read, print, and close an email message
- Preview and save a file attachment
- Display the People Pane
- Reply to an email message
- Check spelling as you type an email message
- Attach a file to an outgoing email message
- Forward an email message
- Copy another person when sending an email message
- Create and move messages into a folder
- Delete an email message
- View the mailbox size

This introductory module covers features and functions common to managing email messages in Outlook 2016.

Roadmap

In this module, you will learn how to perform basic email messaging tasks. The following roadmap identifies general activities you will perform as you progress through this module:

1. CONFIGURE the ACCOUNT OPTIONS
2. COMPOSE AND SEND an email message
3. VIEW AND PRINT an email message
4. REPLY to an email message
5. ATTACH a FILE to an email message
6. ORGANIZE email MESSAGES in folders

At the beginning of the step instructions throughout each module, you will see an abbreviated form of this roadmap. The abbreviated roadmap uses colors to indicate module progress: gray means the module is beyond that activity, blue means the task being shown is covered in that activity, and black means that activity is yet to be covered. For example, the following abbreviated roadmap indicates the module would be showing a task in the View and Print activity.

1 CONFIGURE ACCOUNT OPTIONS | 2 COMPOSE & SEND | 3 VIEW & PRINT | 4 REPLY
5 ATTACH FILE | 6 ORGANIZE MESSAGES

Use the abbreviated roadmap as a progress guide while you read or step through the instructions in this module.

Introduction to Outlook

Outlook 2016 helps you organize and manage your communications, contacts, schedules, and tasks. **Email** (short for **electronic mail**) is the transmission of messages and files between computers or smart devices over a network. An **email client**, such as Microsoft Outlook 2016, is an app that allows you to compose, send, receive, store, and delete email messages. Outlook can access mail servers in a local network, such as your school's network, or on a remote network, such as the Internet. Finally, you can use Outlook to streamline your messages so that you easily can find and respond to them later.

To use Outlook, you must have an email account. An **email account** is an electronic mailbox you receive from an **email service provider**, which is an organization that provides servers for routing and storing email messages. Your employer or school could set up an email account for you, or you can do so yourself through your Internet service provider (ISP) or using a web application such as a Microsoft account, Google Gmail, Yahoo! Mail, or iCloud Mail. Outlook does not create or issue email accounts; it merely provides you with access to them. When you have an email account, you also have an **email address**, which identifies your email account on a network so you can send and receive email messages.

Project — Composing and Sending Email Messages

The project in this module follows the general guidelines for using Outlook to compose, open, and reply to email messages, as shown in Figure 1–1. To communicate with individuals and groups, you typically send or receive some kind of message. Phone calls, letters, texting, and email are examples of ways to communicate a message. Email is a convenient way to send information to multiple people at once.

A work study student in the Pathways Internship Office at Langford College, Sophia Garza, uses Outlook to communicate with faculty and fellow students. This module uses Microsoft Outlook 2016 to compose, send, read, reply to, and forward email messages regarding an upcoming Internship Fair. Sophia has been asked by Ms. Ella Pauley, the director of the internship program, to coordinate the marketing of the Pathways Internship Fair this October. Using Outlook, Sophia reads email messages from her director and students regarding internship opportunities. She replies to email messages and includes a document containing a flyer about the Internship Fair. To organize messages, she also creates folders and then stores the messages in the folders.

BTW
The Outlook Window
The modules in this book begin with the Outlook window appearing as it did at the initial installation of the software. Your Outlook window may look different depending on your screen resolution and other Outlook settings.

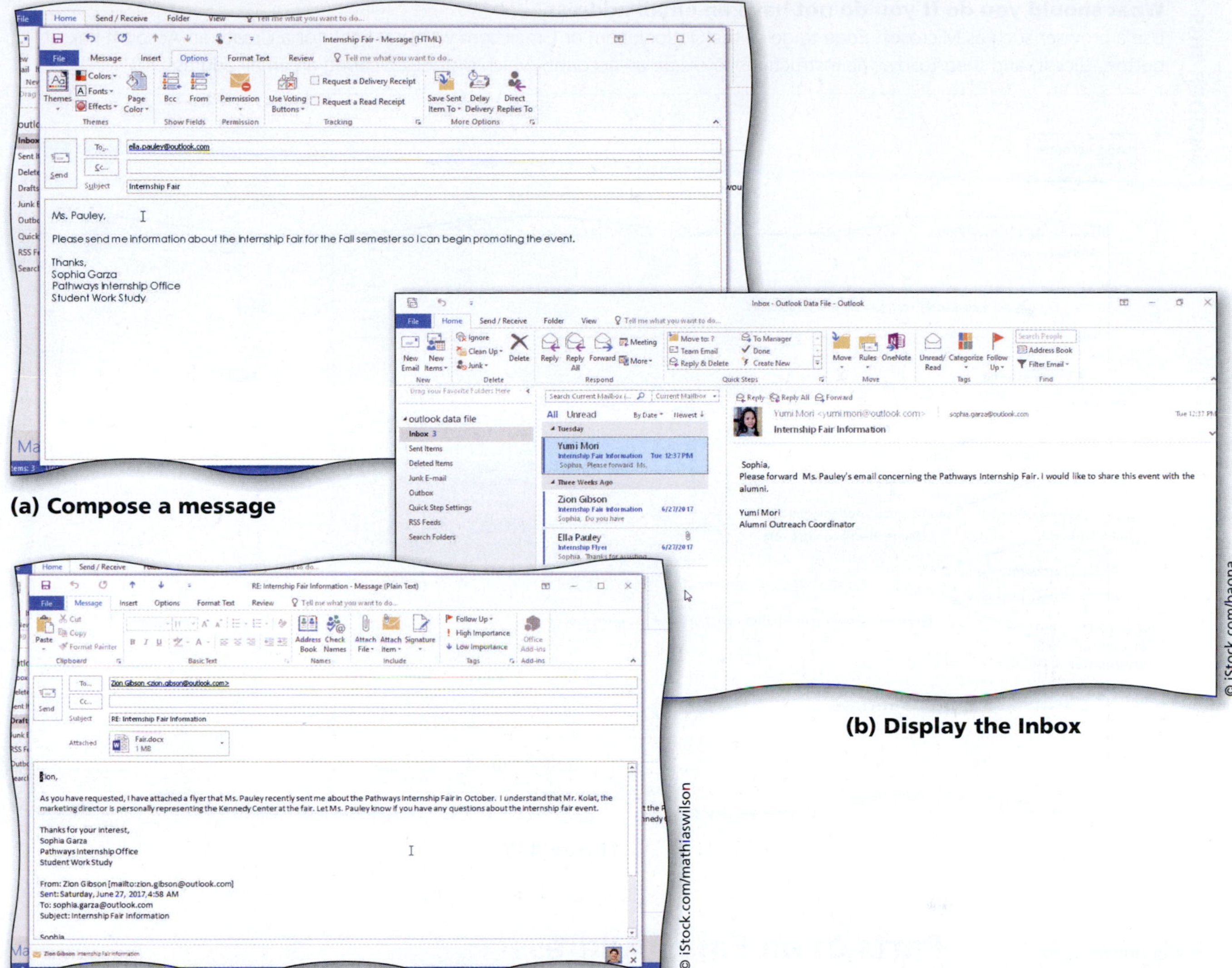

(a) Compose a message

(b) Display the Inbox

(c) Reply and attach a file to a message

© iStock.com/baona

© iStock.com/mathiaswilson

Figure 1–1

Setting Up Outlook

Many computer users have an email account from an online email service provider such as Outlook.com or Gmail.com and another email account at work or school. Instead of using a web app for your online email account and another app for your school account, you can use Outlook 2016 to access all of your email messages in a single location. When you access your email in Outlook 2016, you can take advantage of a full set of features that include social networking, translation services, and file management. You can read your downloaded messages offline and set options to organize your messages in a way that is logical and convenient for you.

The first time you start Outlook on a personal computer, the Auto Account Setup feature guides you to provide information that Outlook needs to send and receive email messages (Figure 1–2). First, the setup feature prompts you to provide your name, which will appear in email messages that you send to other people. Next, the setup feature requests your email address and a password.

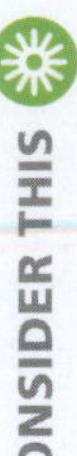

What should you do if you do not have an email address?
Use a browser such as Microsoft Edge to go to the Outlook.com or Gmail.com website. Look for a Create an Account link or button, click it, and then follow the instructions to create an account, which includes creating an email address.

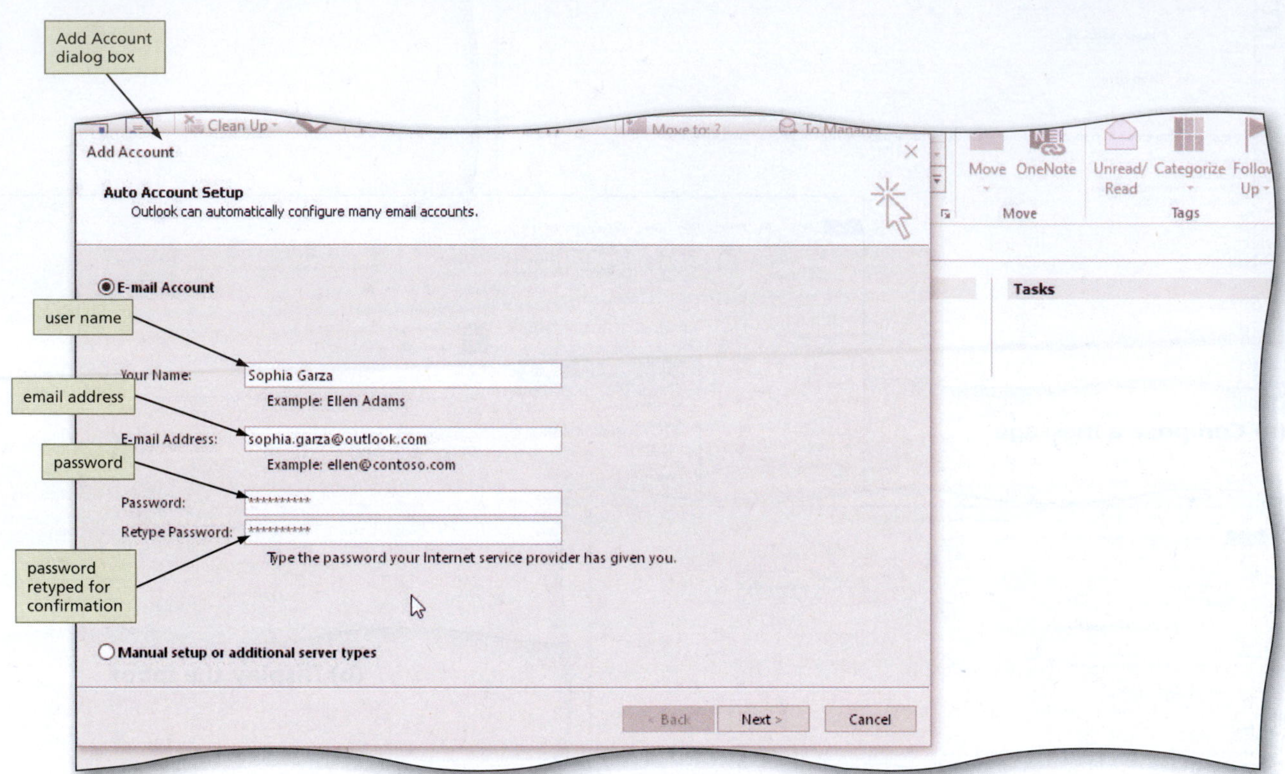

Figure 1–2

For an introduction to Windows and instructions about how to perform basic Windows tasks, read the Office and Windows module at the beginning of this book, where you can learn how to resize windows, change screen resolution, create folders, move and rename files, use Windows Help, and much more.

Parts of an Email Address

An email address is divided into two parts. The first part contains a **user name**, which is a combination of characters, such as letters of the alphabet and numbers, that identifies a specific user. The last part is a **domain name**, which is the name associated with a specific Internet address and is assigned by your email service provider. A user name must be different from other user names in the same domain. For example, the outlook.com domain can have only one user named Sophia.Garza. An email address contains an @ (pronounced *at*) symbol to separate the user name from the domain name. Figure 1–3 shows an email address for Sophia Garza, which would be read as sophia dot garza at outlook dot com.

Figure 1–3

To Run Outlook

If you are using a computer or mobile device to step through the project in this module and you want your screens to match the figures in this book, you should change your screen's resolution to 1366 × 768. For information about how to change a computer's resolution, refer to the Office and Windows module at the beginning of this book.

The following steps, which assume Windows 10 is running, use the Start menu to run Outlook based on a typical installation. You may need to ask your instructor how to run Outlook on your computer. For a detailed example of the procedure summarized below, refer to the Office and Windows module.

1. Click the Start button on the Windows 10 taskbar to display the Start menu.
2. Click All apps at the bottom of the left pane of the Start menu to display a list of apps installed on the computer or mobile device.
3. Scroll to and then click Outlook 2016 in the All apps list to run Outlook.
4. If the Outlook window is not maximized, click the Maximize button on its title bar to maximize the window.

One of the few differences between Windows 8 and Windows 10 occur in the steps to run Outlook. If you are using Windows 8, scroll the Start screen and then click the Outlook 2016 tile.

To Add an Email Account

You can add one or more of your personal email accounts to Outlook. For most accounts, Outlook automatically detects and configures the account after you type your name, email address, and password. Add an email account to Outlook when you are working on your personal or home computer only. You do not want your personal information or email messages on a public computer. Although most people add an email account the first time Outlook runs, you can add email accounts at any time. This module assumes you already set up an email account in Outlook. If you choose to add an email account to Outlook, you would use the following steps.

1. If you started Outlook for the first time, click the Next button to set up an email account. Otherwise, click the File tab, and then click Add Account.
2. If necessary, click the Yes button to add an email account, and then click the Next button to display the Add Account window.
3. Click the Your Name text box, and then type your first and last name to associate your name with the account.
4. Click the E-mail Address text box, and then type your full email address to associate your email address with the account.
5. Click the Password text box, and then type your password to verify the password to your email account.
6. Click the Retype Password text box, and then type your password again to confirm your password.
7. Click the Next button to configure your account settings and sign in to your mail server.
8. Click the Finish button to add your email account.

BTW

The Ribbon and Screen Resolution

Outlook may change how the groups and buttons within the groups appear on the ribbon, depending on the computer or mobile device's screen resolution. Thus, your ribbon may look different from the ones in this book if you are using a screen resolution other than 1366 × 768.

CONSIDER THIS

Will your screen look different if you are using a touch screen?

The Office and Windows interfaces may vary if you are using a touch screen. For this reason, you might notice that the function or appearance of your touch screen differs slightly from this module's presentation.

CONSIDER THIS

How do you remove an email account?

- To remove an email account in Outlook, click the File tab on the ribbon.
- If necessary, click the Info tab in the Backstage view.
- Click the Account Settings button, and then click Account Settings to display the Account Settings dialog box.
- Click the account you want to remove, and then click Remove.
- In the Account Settings dialog box, click the Yes button.

To Change the Navigation Bar Options

1 CONFIGURE ACCOUNT OPTIONS | 2 COMPOSE & SEND | 3 VIEW & PRINT
4 REPLY | 5 ATTACH FILE | 6 ORGANIZE MESSAGES

The first time you start Outlook, the lower-left corner of the screen provides compact navigation by default. To change the Navigation bar from displaying small icons representing Mail, Calendar, Contacts, and Task to a text view, you can disable the compact navigation setting on the Navigation bar. The following steps change the Navigation bar options. ***Why?*** *Instead of small icons, you can display the Mail, Calendar, Contacts, and Task text labels.*

1

- Click the Navigation Options button (three dots) on the Navigation bar to display a list of Navigation bar options (Figure 1–4).

Q&A The left pane in my Outlook window is not expanded as it is in Figure 1–4. What should I do?

Click the Expand the Folder Pane button, which is a small arrow button to the left of today's date in the Outlook window.

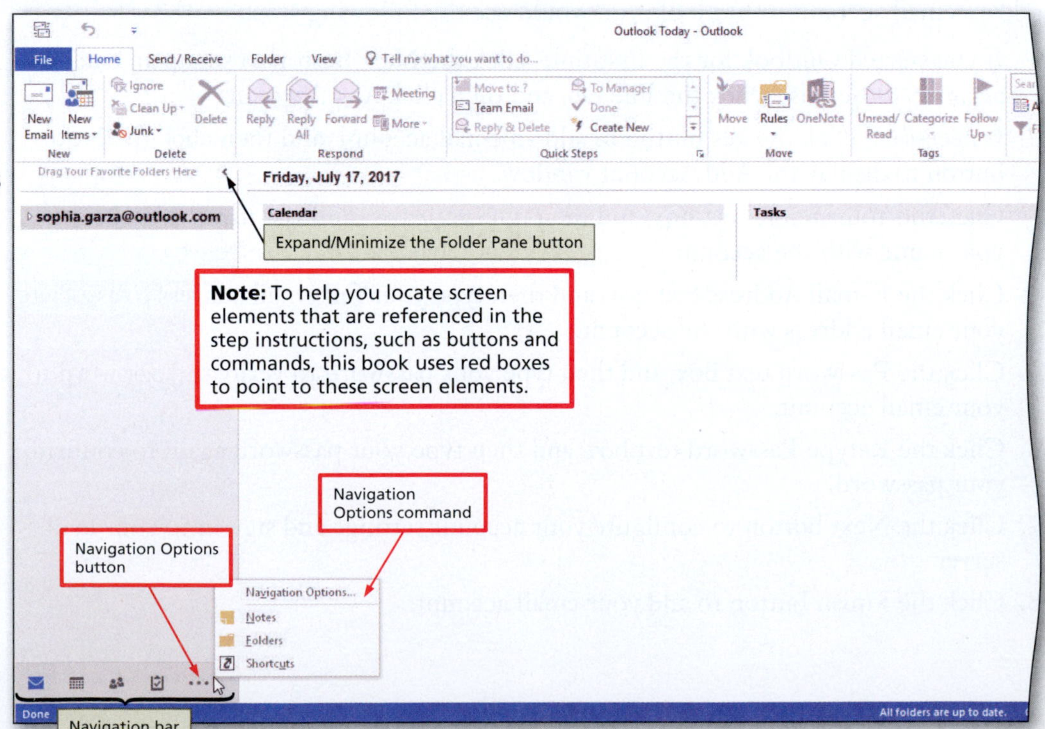

Figure 1–4

- Click Navigations Options to display the Navigation Options dialog box.
- If necessary, click the Compact Navigation check box (Navigation Options dialog box) to remove the check mark and disable the compact navigation setting on the Navigation bar (Figure 1–5).

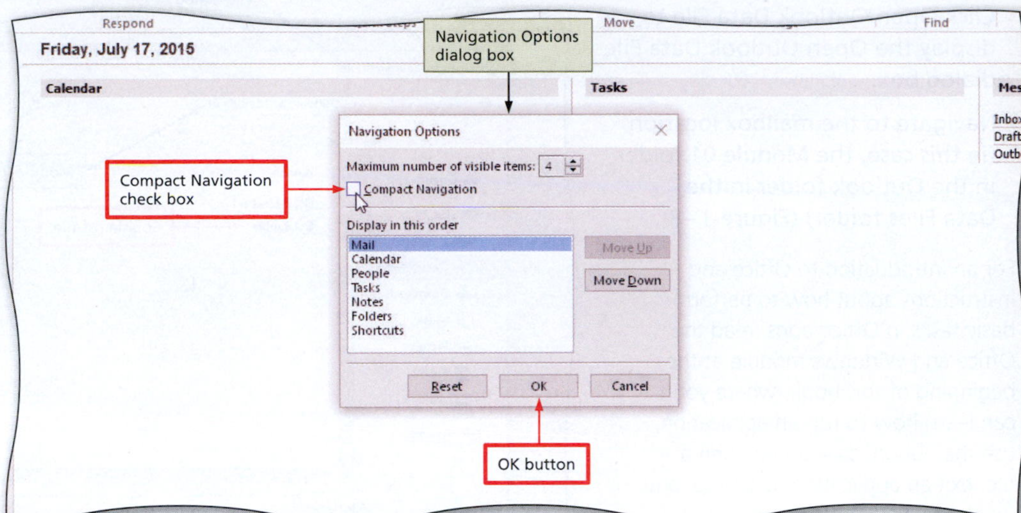

Figure 1–5

- Click the OK button to change the Navigation bar so it displays text labels instead of icons (Figure 1–6).

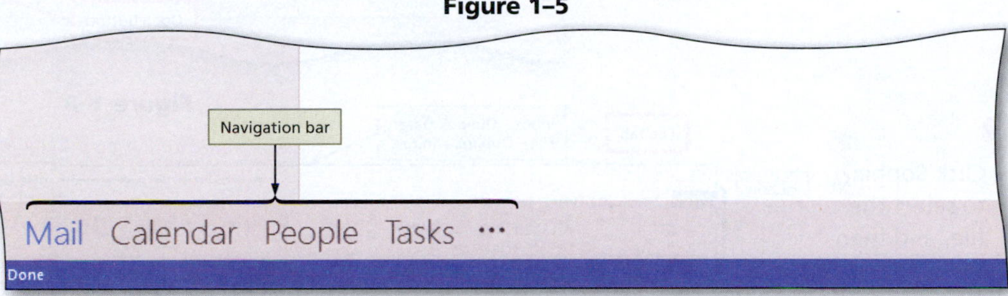

Figure 1–6

To Open an Outlook Data File

Microsoft Outlook uses a special file format called a **personal storage table (.pst file)** to save your email files, calendar entries, and contacts. The email messages with which you work in this module are stored in a personal storage table file named Sophia.pst, which is an Outlook mailbox located with the Data Files. To complete this assignment, you will be required to use the Data Files. Please contact your instructor for information about accessing the Data Files. In this example, the Sophia mailbox is located in the Module 01 folder in the Outlook folder in the Data Files folder. The following steps open the Sophia.pst file in Outlook, display the Inbox for the Sophia file, and then make your Sophia mailbox match the figures in this module. *Why? Opening or importing a .pst file allows you to move your email and other Outlook information to another computer.*

1

- Click File on the ribbon to open the Backstage view.
- Click the Open & Export tab in the Backstage view to display the Open gallery (Figure 1–7).

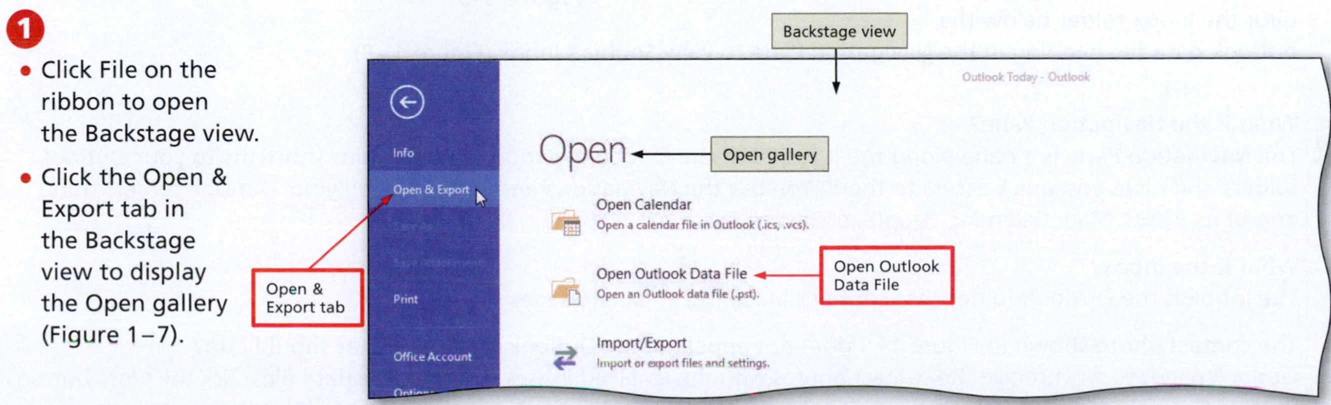

Figure 1–7

- Click Open Outlook Data File to display the Open Outlook Data File dialog box.
- Navigate to the mailbox location (in this case, the Module 01 folder in the Outlook folder in the Data Files folder) (Figure 1–8).

For an introduction to Office and instructions about how to perform basic tasks in Office apps, read the Office and Windows module at the beginning of this book, where you can learn how to run an application, use the ribbon, save a file, open a file, exit an application, use Help, and much more.

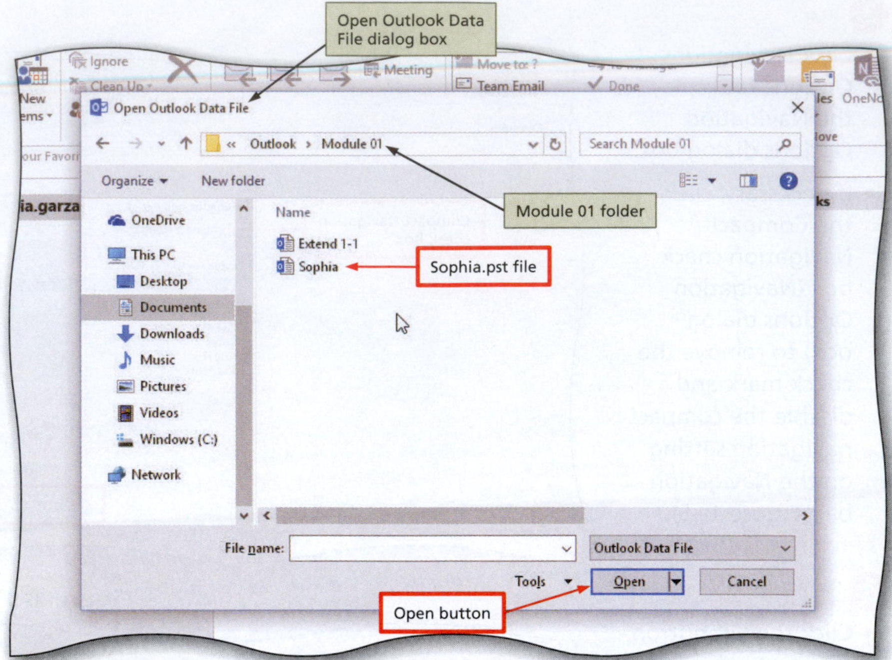

Figure 1–8

3

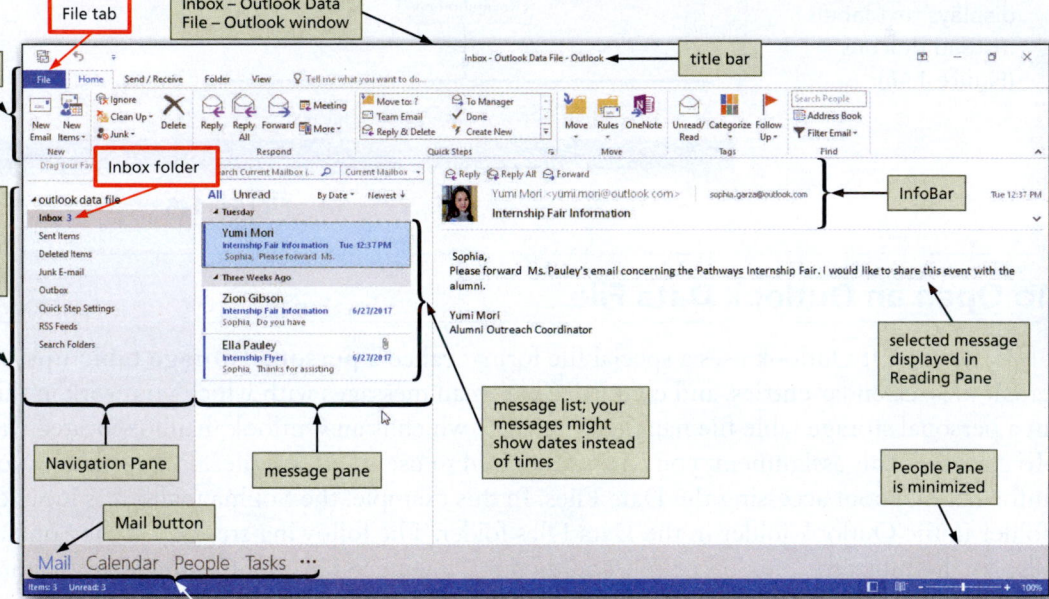

- Click Sophia to select the file, and then click the OK button (Open Outlook Data File dialog box) to open the Sophia mailbox in your Outlook window.
- If necessary, click the white triangle next to the outlook data file mailbox in the Navigation Pane to expand the folders.
- Click the Inbox folder below the outlook data file heading in the Navigation Pane to view Sophia's Inbox (Figure 1–9).

File tab
Inbox – Outlook Data File – Outlook window
title bar
ribbon
Inbox folder
InfoBar
Mail folder pane; the order of your folders may differ
selected message displayed in Reading Pane
message list; your messages might show dates instead of times
Navigation Pane
message pane
People Pane is minimized
Mail button
Navigation bar

Figure 1–9

Q&A

What is the Navigation Pane?
The **Navigation Pane** is a pane along the left side of the Outlook window that contains shortcuts to your Outlook folders and gives you quick access to them. You use the Navigation Pane to browse all your Outlook folders using one of its views: Mail, Calendar, People, or Tasks.

What is the Inbox?
The **Inbox** is the Outlook folder that contains incoming email messages.

The contact photo shown in Figure 1–9 does not appear in my Outlook window. What should I do?
Outlook needs to synchronize the contact photos with the email addresses in the Sophia data file. Click the Close button to close Outlook, restart it, and then expand the outlook data file in the Navigation Pane to have the photos appear. You also might need to import the data file rather than opening it. In Step 2 on this page, click Import/Export instead of Open Outlook Data File.

To Set Language Preferences

You can use the Outlook Options dialog box to set the Office Language Preferences. ***Why?*** *You can specify the editing and display languages, such as the languages used in the dictionaries, grammar checking, and sorting.* Usually, Outlook configures the language settings to match your operating system; however, if you want to change those settings, you can adjust the Language preferences. The following steps set the Language preferences.

1

- Click File on the ribbon to open the Backstage view (Figure 1–10).

Q&A Why does my account information appear in the Backstage view? If you have already set up an email account in Outlook, it appears on the Info tab in the Backstage view. Other options, such as Rules and Alerts, might also appear.

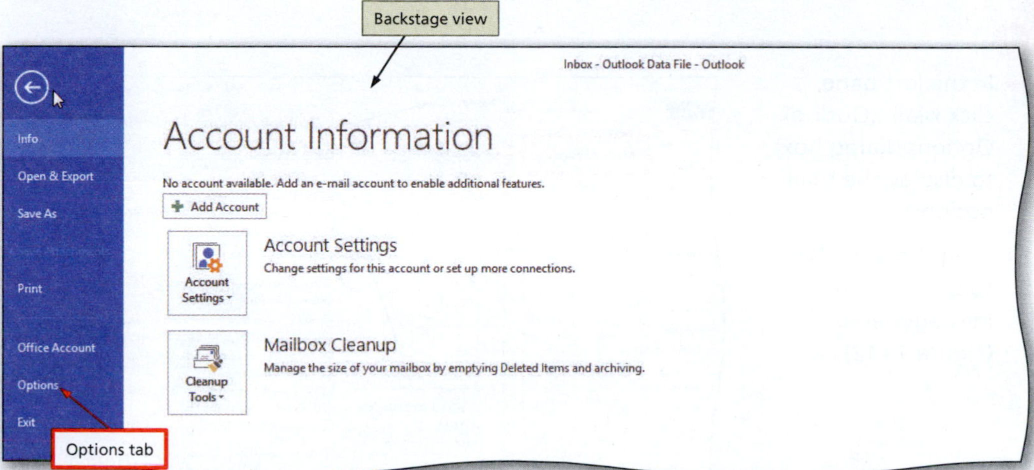

Figure 1–10

2

- Click the Options tab in the Backstage view to display the Outlook Options dialog box.
- In the left pane, click Language (Outlook Options dialog box) to display the Language options.
- Click the '[Add additional editing languages]' arrow to display a list of editing languages that can be added to Outlook (Figure 1–11).

Q&A How do I set a default language? After selecting an editing language that you want to use, click the name of the language and then click the 'Set as Default' button.

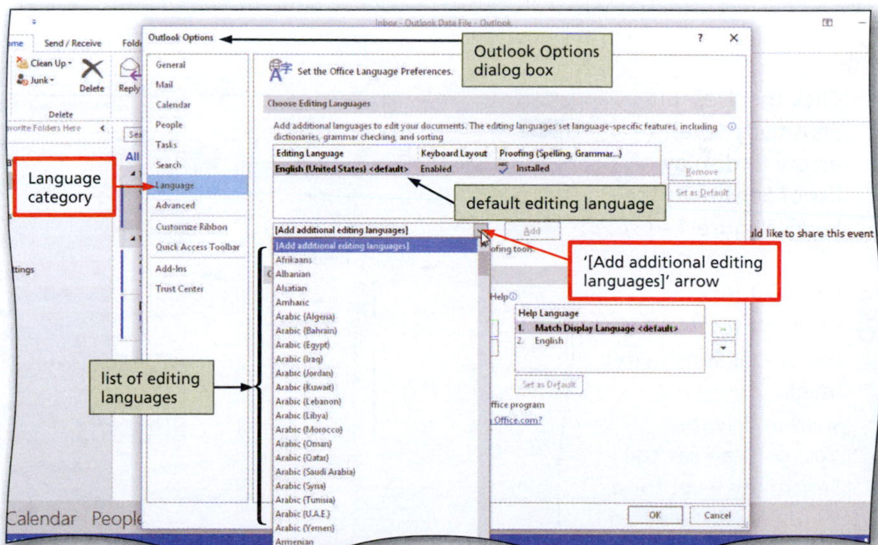

Figure 1–11

3

- If necessary, scroll the list and then click English (United States) to set the default editing language. Otherwise, click the '[Add additional editing languages]' arrow again to close the list.

To Set the Sensitivity Level for All New Messages

The **Sensitivity level** of a message advises the recipient on how to treat the contents of the message. Sensitivity levels are Normal, Personal, Private, and Confidential. Changing the Sensitivity setting in the Outlook Options dialog box changes the default Sensitivity level of all messages created afterward. ***Why?*** *For example, if you set the Sensitivity level of a message to Confidential, the information should not be disclosed to anyone except the recipient.* The following steps set the default Sensitivity level.

1

- In the left pane, click Mail (Outlook Options dialog box) to display the Mail options.
- Drag the scroll bar to display the Send messages area (Figure 1–12).

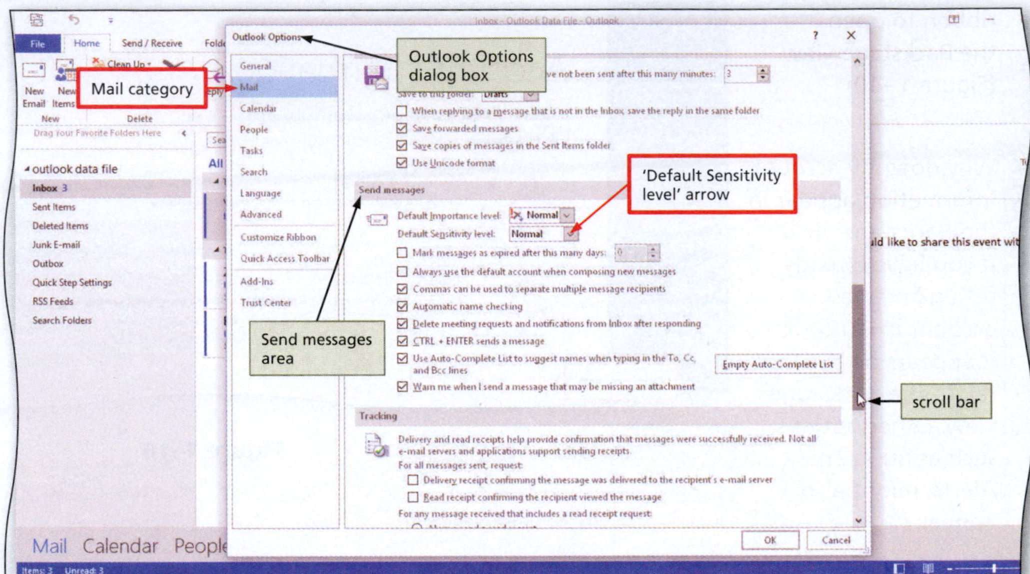

Figure 1–12

2

- Click the 'Default Sensitivity level' arrow to display a list of Sensitivity levels (Figure 1–13).

Q&A Can I set one message to an individual Sensitivity level such as private?

Yes, you can set the Sensitivity level for a single message using the More Options Dialog Box Launcher (Options tab | More Options group) to open the Properties dialog box. Click the Sensitivity button and then click Private to change the sensitivity of a single message to private.

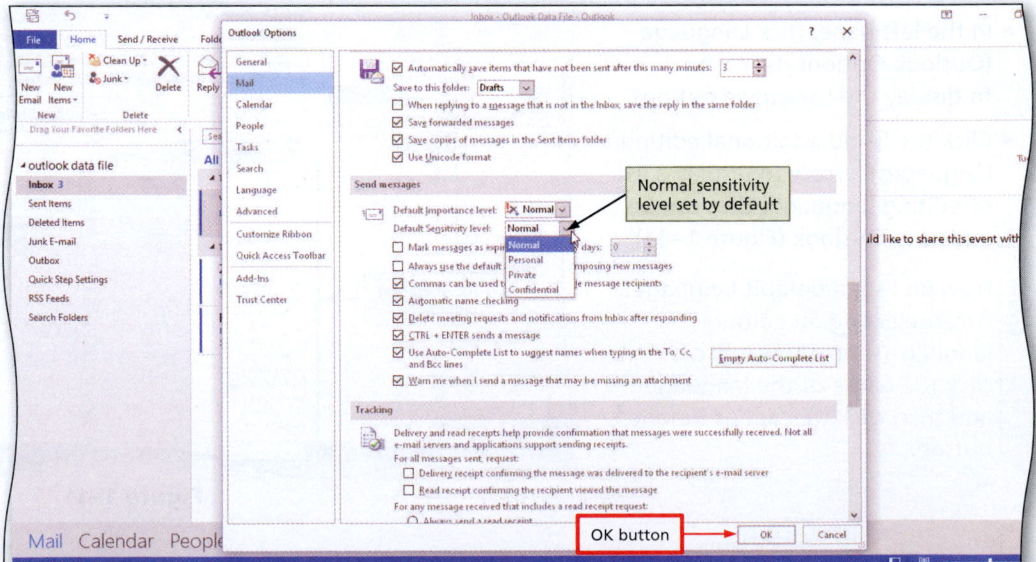

Figure 1–13

- If necessary, click Normal to set the default Sensitivity level of all new messages.
- Click the OK button to close the Outlook Options dialog box.

Q&A What should I do if the ribbon does not stay open?
Click any tab on the ribbon, and then click the 'Pin the ribbon' button (thumbtack icon) in the lower-right corner of the ribbon to keep the ribbon open.

Composing and Sending Email messages

Composing an email message is the most frequent personal and business task you perform in Microsoft Outlook. Composing an email message consists of four basic steps: open a new message window, enter message header information, enter the message text, and add a signature. When composing an email message, it is best to keep your message text concise and to the point. If you must write a longer, detailed message, break up your message into bullet points or into separate emails each with a clear summary of action.

An email message is organized into two areas: the message header and the message area. The information in the **message header** routes the message to its recipients and identifies the subject of the message. The message header identifies the primary recipient(s) in the To box. If you have multiple recipients in the To box, you can separate each email address with a semicolon. Recipients in the Cc (courtesy copy or carbon copy) and Bcc (blind courtesy copy) boxes, if displayed, also receive the message; however, the names of the recipients in the Bcc box are not visible to other recipients. The **subject line** states the purpose of the message.

The **message area**, where you type an email message, consists of a greeting line or salutation, the message text, an optional closing, and one or more signature lines as shown in Table 1–1.

BTW

Inserting Hyperlinks

To insert a web address in an email message, click where you want to insert the hyperlink, and then click the Hyperlink button (Insert tab | Links group) to display the Insert Hyperlink dialog box. In the Address text box, type the web address you want to insert as a hyperlink, and then click the OK button to insert the hyperlink into the message body.

Table 1–1 Message Area Parts

Part	Description
Greeting line or salutation	Sets the tone of the message and can be formal or informal, depending on the nature of the message. You can use a colon (:) or comma (,) at the end of the greeting line.
Message text	Informs the recipient or requests information.
Closing	Informs the recipient or requests information. A closing signals an end to the message using courtesy words such as *Thank you* or *Regards*. Because the closing is most appropriate for formal email messages, it is optional.
Signature line(s)	Identifies the sender and may contain additional information, such as a job title, business name, and phone number(s). In a signature, the name usually is provided on one line followed by other information listed on separate lines.

To Compose an Email Message

1 CONFIGURE ACCOUNT OPTIONS | 2 COMPOSE & SEND | 3 VIEW & PRINT
4 REPLY | 5 ATTACH FILE | 6 ORGANIZE MESSAGES

An email message from Sophia Garza, the work study student in the Pathways Internship Office, requests information about the Internship Fair from the director named Ella Pauley. The following steps compose a new email message. ***Why?*** *Composing email messages is a direct and efficient method to connect with personal and professional contacts.*

- Click the New Email button (Home tab | New group) to open the Untitled – Message (HTML) window (Figure 1–14).

Q&A What does HTML mean in the title bar?

HTML is the format for the new email message. Outlook messages can use two other formats: Rich Text Format (RTF) and Plain Text. All of these formats are discussed later in this module.

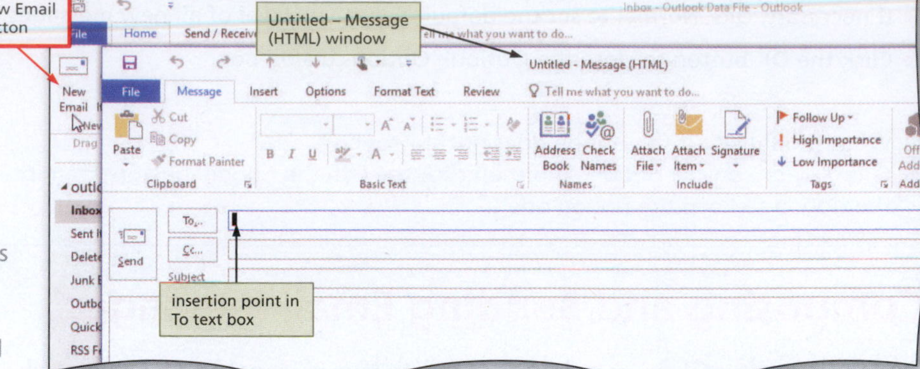

Figure 1–14

- Type **ella.pauley@outlook.com** (with no spaces) in the To text box to enter the email address of the recipient.
- Click the Subject text box, and then type **Internship Fair** to enter the subject line.
- Press the TAB key to move the insertion point into the message area (Figure 1–15).

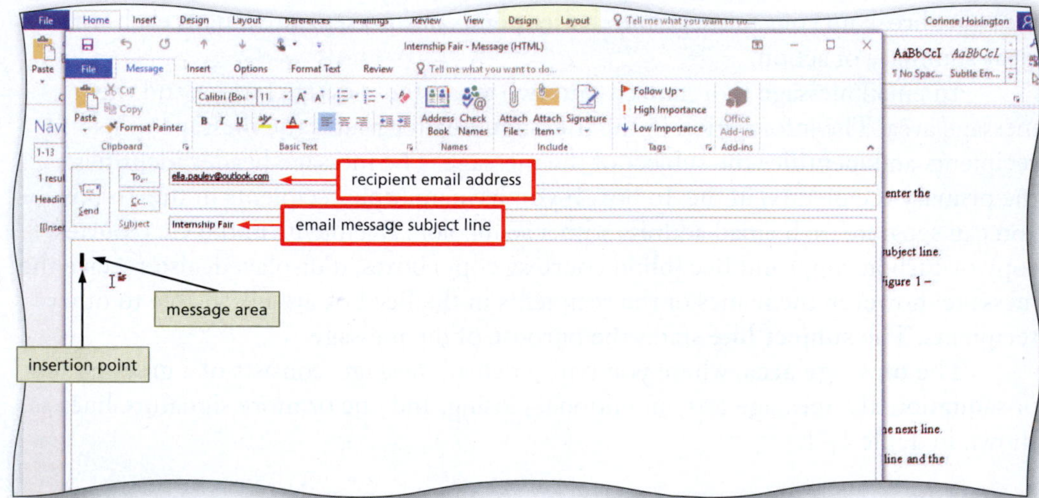

Figure 1–15

3

- Type **Ms. Pauley,** as the greeting line.
- Press the ENTER key to move the insertion point to the beginning of the next line.
- Press the ENTER key again to insert a blank line between the greeting line and the message text (Figure 1–16).

Q&A What does it mean if I use all capital letters in my email message?

Writing in all capital letters is considered the same as shouting. Use proper capitalization as you compose your email.

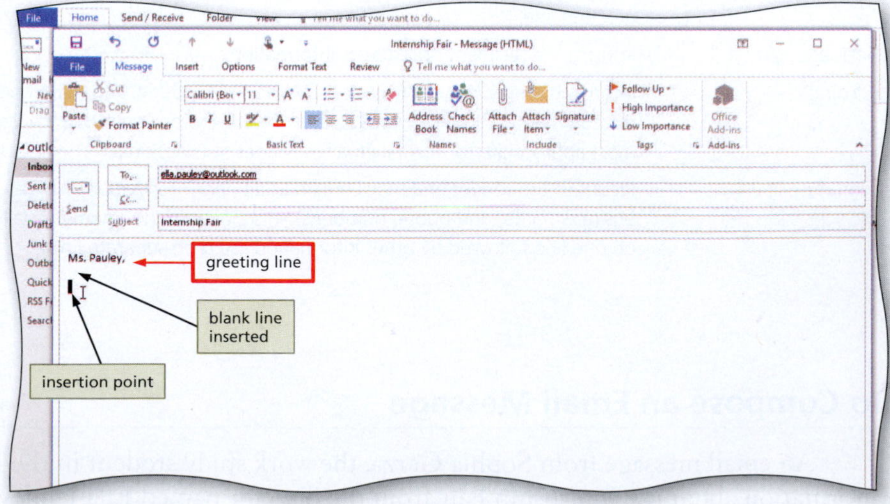

Figure 1–16

- Type `Please send me information about the Internship Fair for the Fall semester so I can begin promoting the event.` to enter the message text.
- Press the ENTER key two times to insert a blank line below the message text (Figure 1–17).

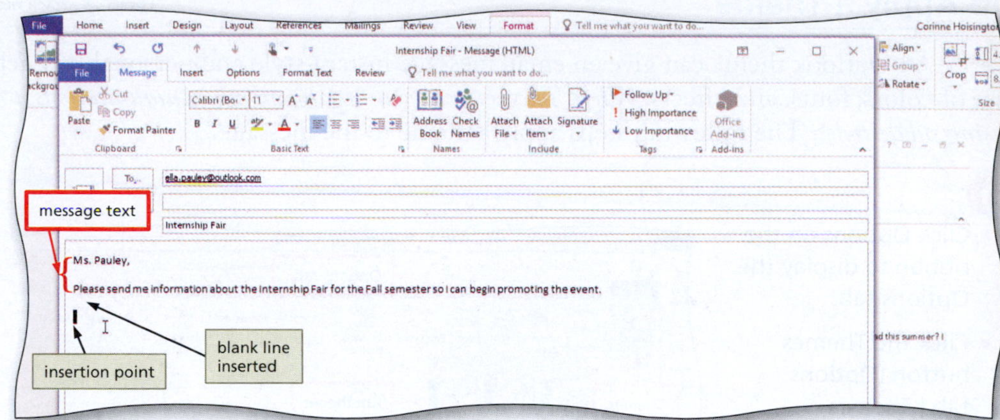

Figure 1–17

- Type `Thanks,` to enter the closing for the message.
- Press the ENTER key to move the insertion point to the next line.
- Type `Sophia Garza` as the first line of the signature.
- Press the ENTER key to move the insertion point to the next line.
- Type `Pathways Internship Office` as the second line of the signature.
- Press the ENTER key to move the insertion point to the next line.
- Type `Student Work Study` as the third line of the signature (Figure 1–18).

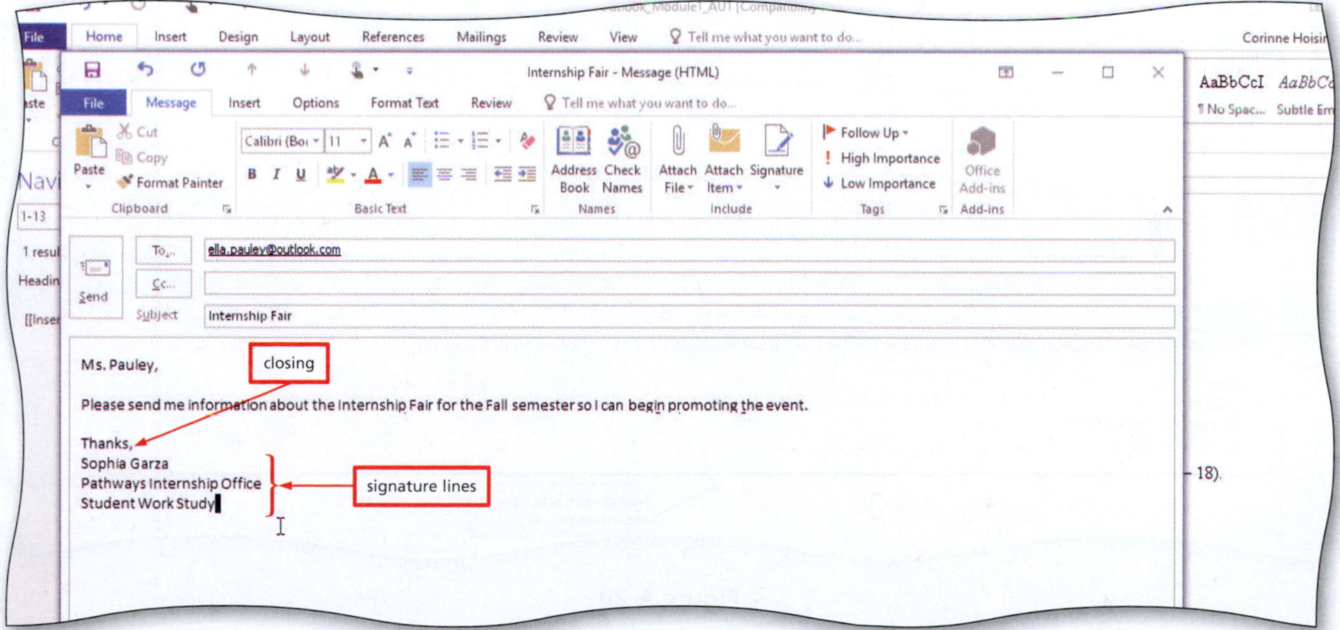

Figure 1–18

Q&A

What if I make an error while typing an email message?

Press the BACKSPACE key until you have deleted the error and then retype the text correctly. You also can click the Undo button on the Quick Access Toolbar to undo your most recent action.

Do I always need to type my last name in the signature of an email message?

No. If you and your recipient know each other, you can type only your first name as the signature.

Other Ways

1. Click Inbox folder, press CTRL+N

To Apply a Theme

An Outlook theme can give an email message instant style and personality. Each theme provides a unique set of colors, fonts, and effects. ***Why?** Themes give your organization's communications a modern, professional look using subtle styles.* The following steps apply a theme to the message.

- Click Options on the ribbon to display the Options tab.
- Click the Themes button (Options tab | Themes group) to display the Themes gallery (Figure 1–19).

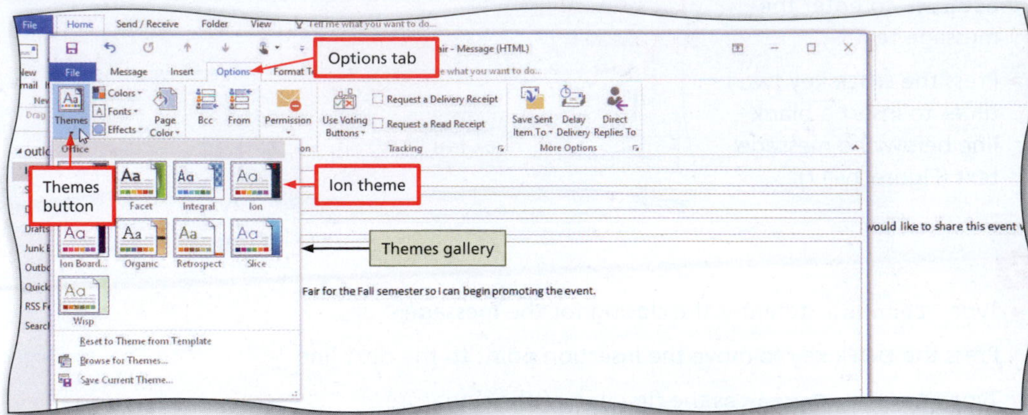

Figure 1–19

- Click Ion in the Themes gallery to change the theme of the message (Figure 1–20).

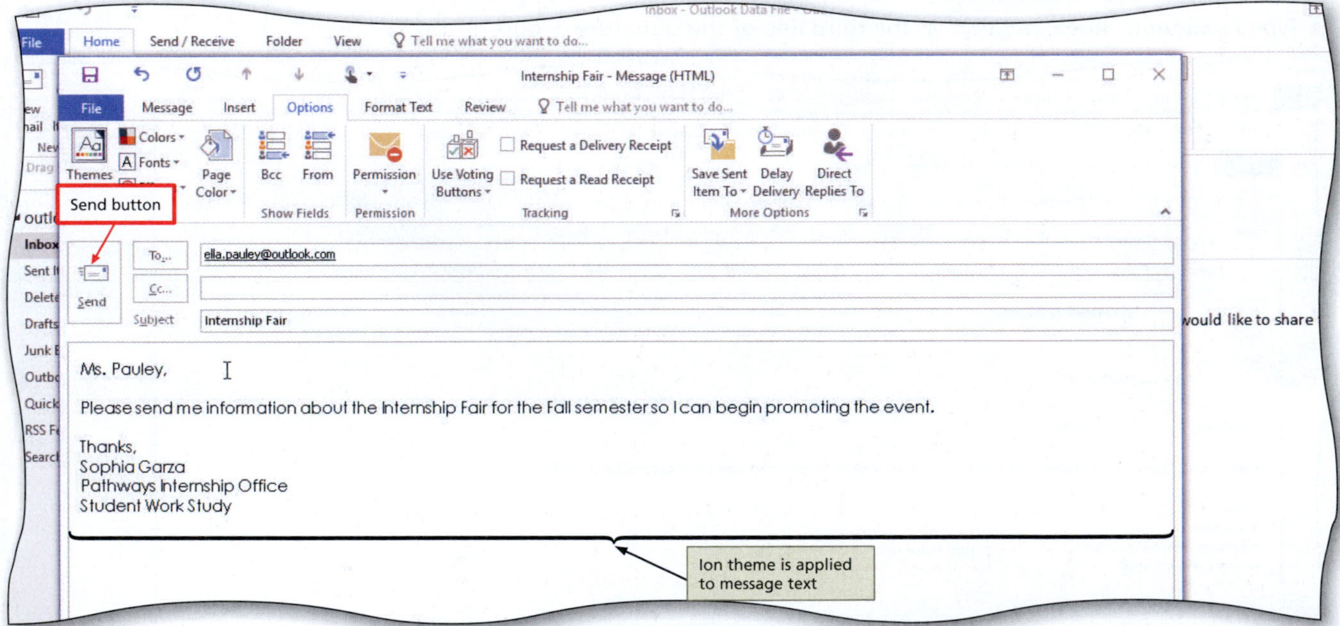

Figure 1–20

CONSIDER THIS

How can you create your own theme for your messages to strengthen your company's brand?

- Format a message with a customized font, colors, and background.
- Click the Themes button (Options tab | Themes group) to display the Themes gallery.
- Click Save Current Theme to display the Save Current Theme dialog box.
- Type a name in the File name text box to name your new theme.
- Click the Save button to save your new theme.

To Send an Email Message

Why? *After you complete a message, send it to the recipient, who typically receives the message in seconds.* The following step sends the completed email message to the recipient.

- Click the Send button in the message header to send the email message and close the message window.

Q&A

What happened to the email message?
Outlook automatically sends email messages to their recipient(s) when you click Send in a new message window if you have your own email account set up.

Why did I get an error message that stated that 'No valid email accounts are configured. Add an account to send email'?
If you do not have an email account set up in Outlook, you cannot connect to the Internet to send the email. Click Cancel to close the error message.

Other Ways

1. Press ALT+S

How Email Messages Travel from Sender to Receiver

When you send someone an email message, it travels across the Internet to the computer at your email service provider that handles outgoing email messages. This computer, called the **outgoing email server**, examines the email address on your message, selects the best route for sending the message across the Internet, and then sends the email message. Many outgoing email servers use **SMTP (Simple Mail Transfer Protocol)**, which is a communications protocol, or set of rules for communicating with other computers. An email program such as Outlook contacts the outgoing email server and then transfers the email message(s) in its Outbox to that server. If the email program cannot contact the outgoing email server, the email message(s) remains in the Outbox until the program can connect to the server.

As an email message travels across the Internet, routers direct the email message to a computer at your recipient's email service provider that handles incoming email messages. A **router** is a device that forwards data on a network. The computer handling incoming email messages, called the incoming email server, stores the email message(s) until your recipient uses an email program such as Outlook to retrieve the email message(s). Some email servers use **POP3**, the latest version of **Post Office Protocol (POP)**, a communications protocol for incoming email. Figure 1–21 shows how an email message may travel from a sender to a receiver.

In most cases, the Auto Account Setup feature does not require you to enter the name of your POP or SMTP server, but many businesses require that you manually enter these server settings. You can verify these Internet email settings in the Change Account dialog box, which is displayed by tapping or clicking the File tab on the ribbon to open the Backstage view, tapping or clicking the Account Settings button in the Backstage view, tapping or clicking Account Settings to display the Account Settings dialog box, selecting your email address, and then tapping or clicking the Change button. Figure 1–22 shows the Change Account dialog box for Sophia Garza. Notice that this account uses a mail server named m.hotmail.com.

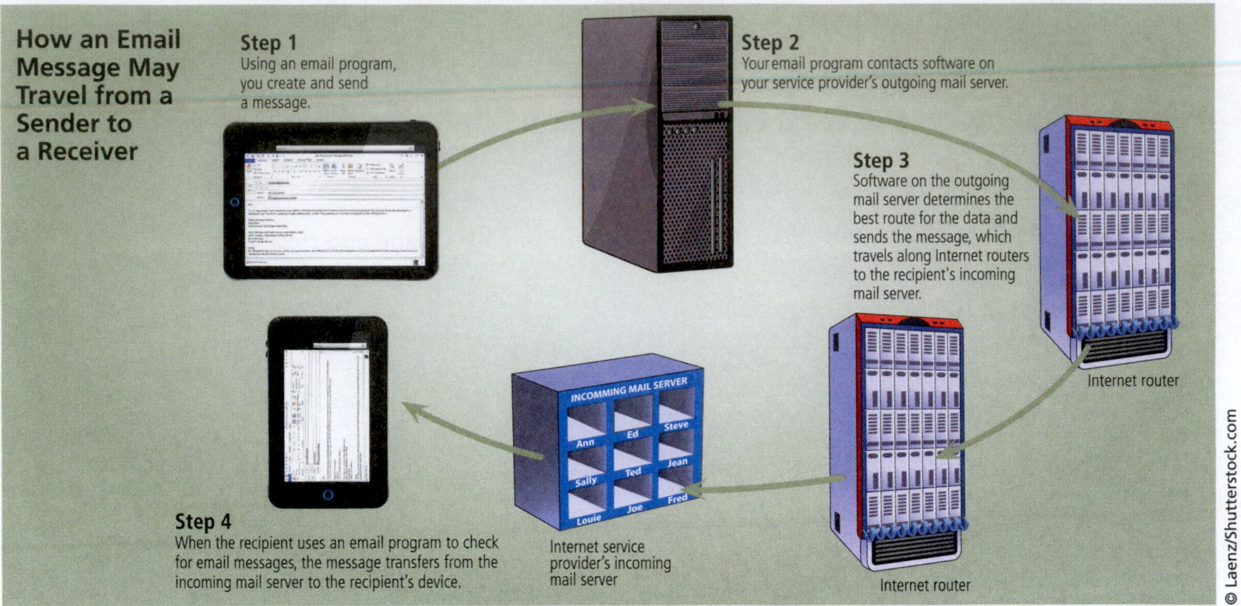

Figure 1–21

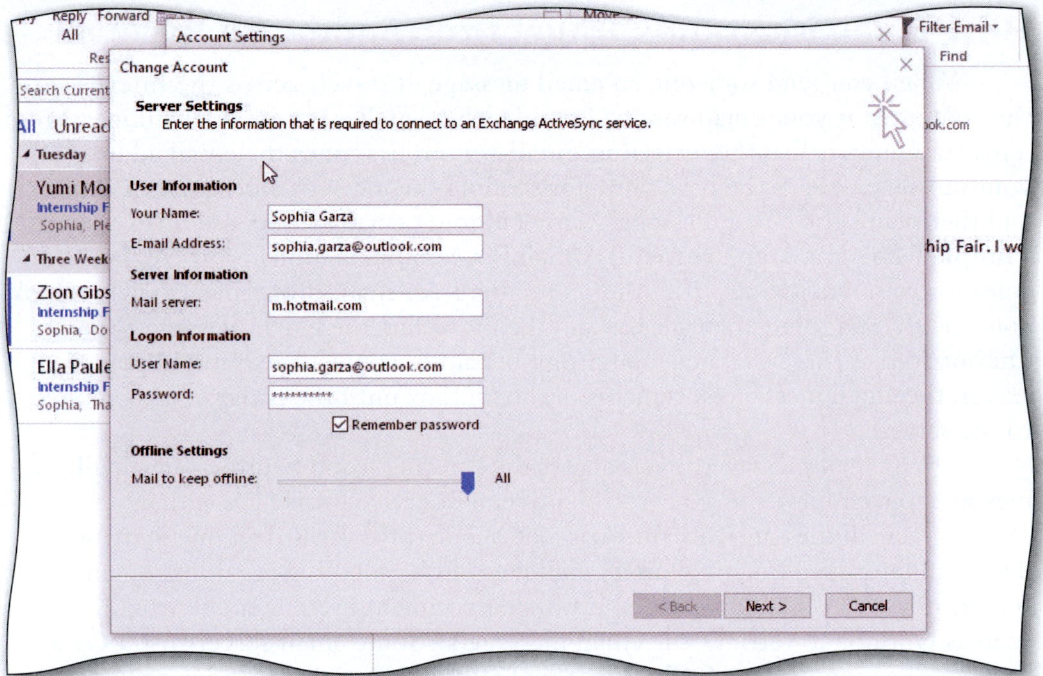

Figure 1–22

Working with Incoming Messages

When you receive email messages, Outlook directs them to your Inbox and displays them in the **message pane**, which lists the contents of the selected folder (Figure 1–23). The list of messages displayed in the message pane is called the **message list**. An unread (unopened) email message in the message list includes a blue vertical bar in front of the message and displays the subject text and time of arrival in a blue bold font. An open envelope icon indicates a previously read (opened) message.

The blue number next to the Inbox folder shows how many unread messages are stored in the Inbox. The email messages on your computer may be different.

You can read incoming messages in three ways: in an open window, in the Reading Pane, or as a hard copy. A **hard copy (printout)** is information presented on a physical medium such as paper.

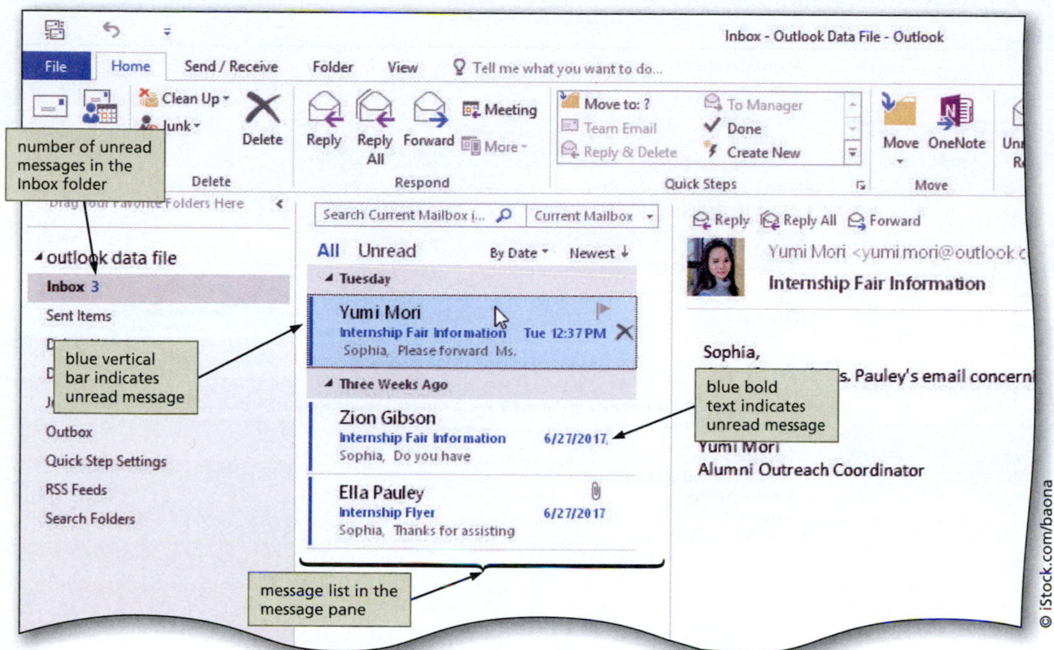

Figure 1–23

BTW

Know the Sender

If you receive an email message from someone you do not know, you should not open it because it might trigger a virus. Unsolicited email messages, known as **spam** or **junk email**, are email messages sent from an unknown sender to many email accounts, usually advertising a product or service such as low-cost medication, low-interest loans, or free credit reports. Do not click a hyperlink in an email message from an unknown sender. A **hyperlink** is a word, phrase, symbol, or picture in an email message or on a webpage that, when tapped or clicked, directs you to another document or website.

To View an Email Message in the Reading Pane

1 CONFIGURE ACCOUNT OPTIONS | 2 COMPOSE & SEND | 3 VIEW & PRINT
4 REPLY | 5 ATTACH FILE | 6 ORGANIZE MESSAGES

Why? *You can preview messages in your Inbox without opening them by using the Reading Pane.* The **Reading Pane** appears on the right side of the Outlook window by default and displays the contents of a message without requiring you to open the message. An advantage of viewing messages in the Reading Pane is that if a message includes content that could be harmful to your computer, such as a malicious script or an attachment containing a virus, the Reading Pane does not activate the harmful content. An **attachment** is a file such as a document or picture you send along with an email message. The attached document can be a file saved to your local computer or from OneDrive, as long as you have Microsoft's cloud service account connected. The instructor Ella Pauley has sent a response to Sophia concerning the Internship Fair. The following step displays an email message from a sender.

- Click the message header from Ella Pauley in the Inbox message list to select the email message and display its contents in the Reading Pane (Figure 1–24).

Q&A What happens to the message header when I select another message?
Outlook automatically marks messages as read after you preview the message in the Reading Pane and select another message to view. A read message is displayed in the message list without a vertical blue line or bold text.

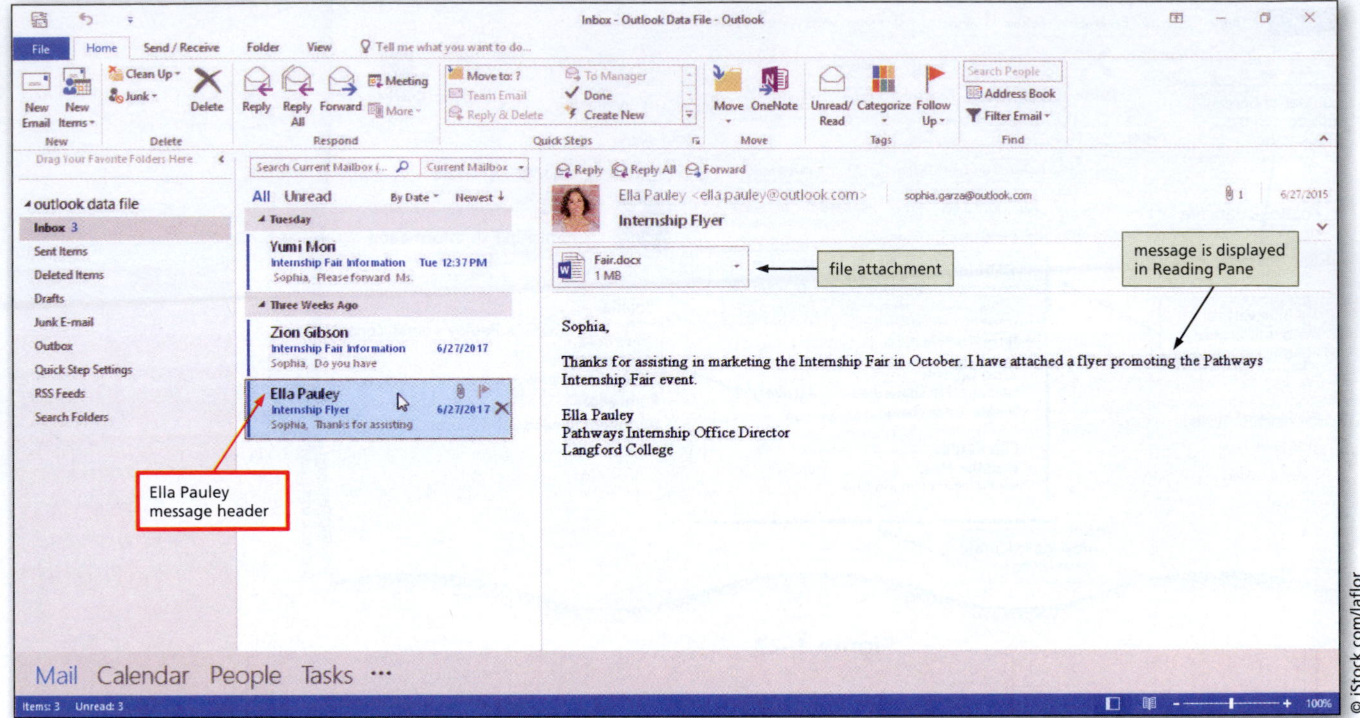

© iStock.com/laflor

Figure 1–24

To Open an Email Message in a Window

1 CONFIGURE ACCOUNT OPTIONS | 2 COMPOSE & SEND | 3 VIEW & PRINT
4 REPLY | 5 ATTACH FILE | 6 ORGANIZE MESSAGES

Why? To fully evaluate an email message and use additional Outlook tools for working with messages, you display the email message in a window. The following step displays an email message from a sender in a window.

- Double-click the Ella Pauley message in the message list to display the selected email message in its own window (Figure 1–25).

Q&A Can I change the status of a message from unread to read without opening the message or displaying its contents in the Reading Pane?
Yes. Right-click the message you want to change, and then click Mark as Read on the shortcut menu.

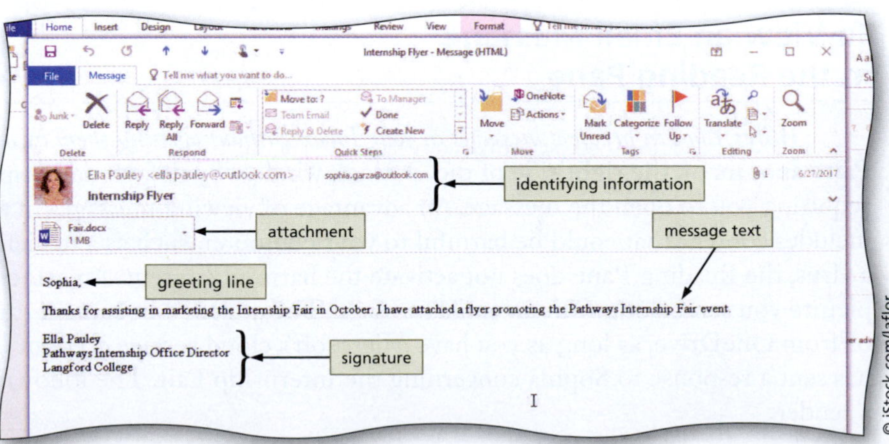

© iStock.com/laflor

Figure 1–25

Other Ways

1. Click message header, press CTRL+O

Opening Attachments

Email messages that include attachments are identified by a paper clip icon in the message list. Users typically attach a file to an email message to provide additional information to the recipient. An attachment in a message can appear in a line below the subject line or in the message body. To help protect your computer, Outlook does not allow you to receive files as attachments if they are a certain file type, such as .exe (executable) or .js (JavaScript), because of their potential for introducing a virus into your computer. When Outlook blocks a suspicious attachment in a message, the blocked file appears in the InfoBar at the top of your message. An **InfoBar** is a banner displayed at the top of an email message that indicates whether an email message has been replied to or forwarded.

The **Attachment Preview** feature in Outlook allows you to preview an attachment you receive in an email message from either the Reading Pane in an unopened message or the message area of an opened message. Outlook has built-in previewers for several file types, such as other Office programs, pictures, text, and webpages. Outlook includes attachment previewers that work with other Microsoft Office programs so that users can preview an attachment without opening it. These attachment previewers are turned on by default. To preview an attached file created in an Office application, you must have Office installed on your computer. For example, to preview an Excel attachment in Outlook, you must have Excel installed. If an attachment cannot be previewed, you can double-click the attachment to open the file.

BTW

Organizing Files and Folders

You should organize and store files in folders so that you easily can find the files later. For example, if you are taking an introductory technology class called CIS 101, a good practice would be to save all Outlook files in an Outlook folder in a CIS 101 folder. For a discussion of folders and detailed examples of creating folders, refer to the Office and Windows module at the beginning of this book.

To Preview and Save an Attachment

1 CONFIGURE ACCOUNT OPTIONS | 2 COMPOSE & SEND | **3 VIEW & PRINT**
4 REPLY | 5 ATTACH FILE | 6 ORGANIZE MESSAGES

Why? *When you receive a message with an attachment, you can preview the attached file without opening it if you are not sure of the contents.* A common transmission method of viruses is by email attachments, so be sure that you trust the sender before opening an attached file. The following steps preview and save an attachment without opening the file. You should save the attachment on your hard disk, OneDrive, or a location that is most appropriate to your situation. These steps assume you already have created folders for storing your files, for example, a CIS 101 folder (for your class) that contains an Outlook folder with a Module 01 folder (for your assignments). Thus, these steps save the attachment in the Module 01 folder in your desired save location. For a detailed example of the procedure for saving a file in a folder or saving a file on OneDrive, refer to the Office and Windows module at the beginning of this book.

1

- Click the Fair.docx file attachment in the message header of the opened email from Ella Pauley to preview the attachment within Outlook (Figure 1–26).

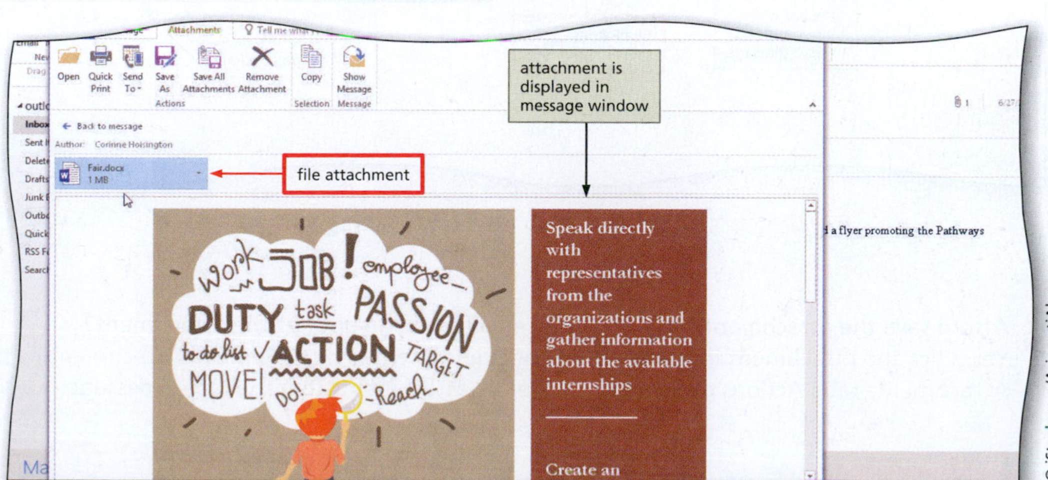

© iStock.com/ArimurtiAlan

Figure 1–26

- Click the Save As button (Attachment Tools Attachments tab | Actions group) to display the Save Attachment dialog box.
- Navigate to the desired save location (in this case, the Module 01 folder in your Outlook folder or your class folder on your computer or OneDrive).
- If requested by your instructor, add your last name to the end of the file name (Figure 1–27).

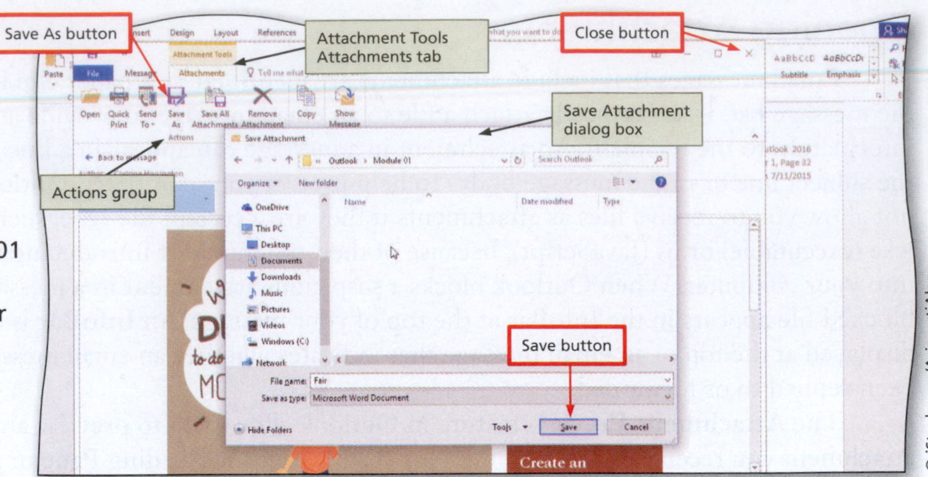

Figure 1–27

- Click the Save button (Save Attachment dialog box) to save the document in the selected folder in the selected location with the entered file name.
- Click the Close button to close the attachment preview window and email message (Figure 1–28).

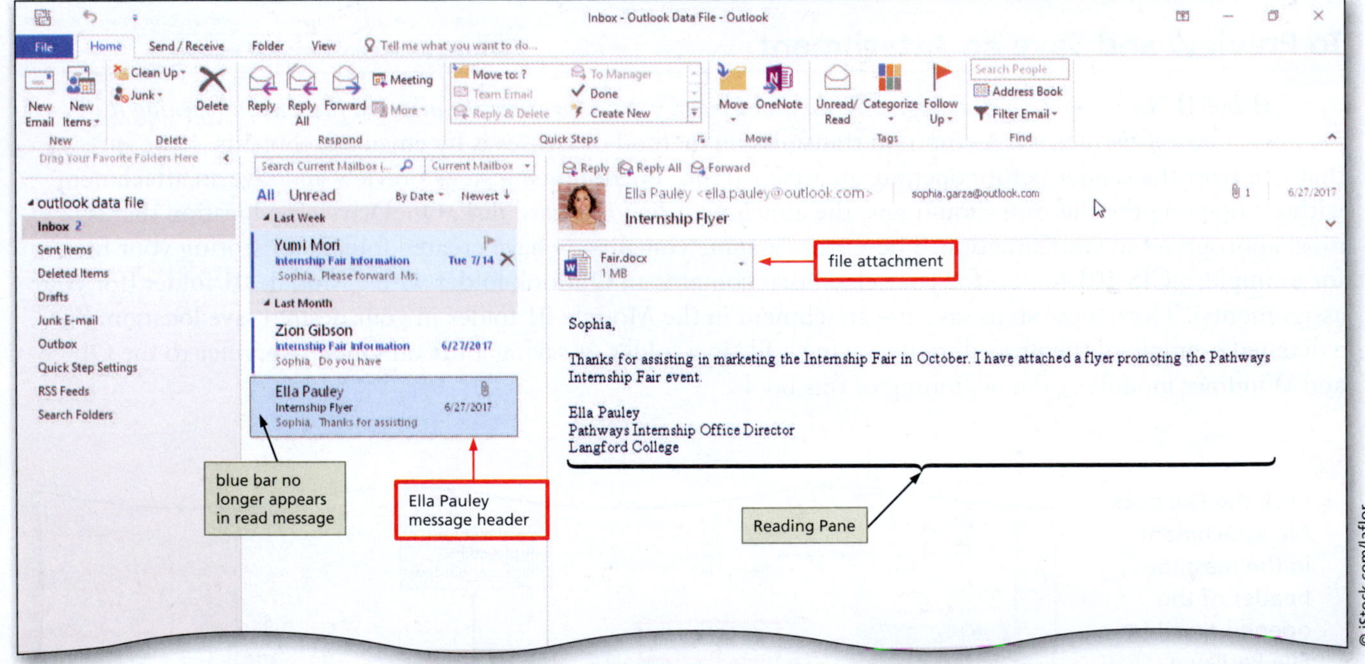

Figure 1–28

Q&A

After I save the attachment, can I keep the email message but not the attachment?

Yes. Click the attachment in the Reading Pane, and then click the Remove Attachment button (Attachment Tools Attachments tab | Actions group) to remove the attachment from the email message.

Other Ways

1. Right-click attachment, click Save As

To Open an Attachment

If you know the sender and you know the attachment is safe, you can open the attached file. The following steps open an attachment. ***Why?*** *By opening a Word attachment in Microsoft Word, you can edit the document with the full features of Word.*

- If necessary, click the message header from Ella Pauley in the Inbox message list to select the email message and display its contents in the Reading Pane.
- Double-click the attachment in the Reading Pane to open the file attachment in Microsoft Word in Protected View (Figure 1–29).

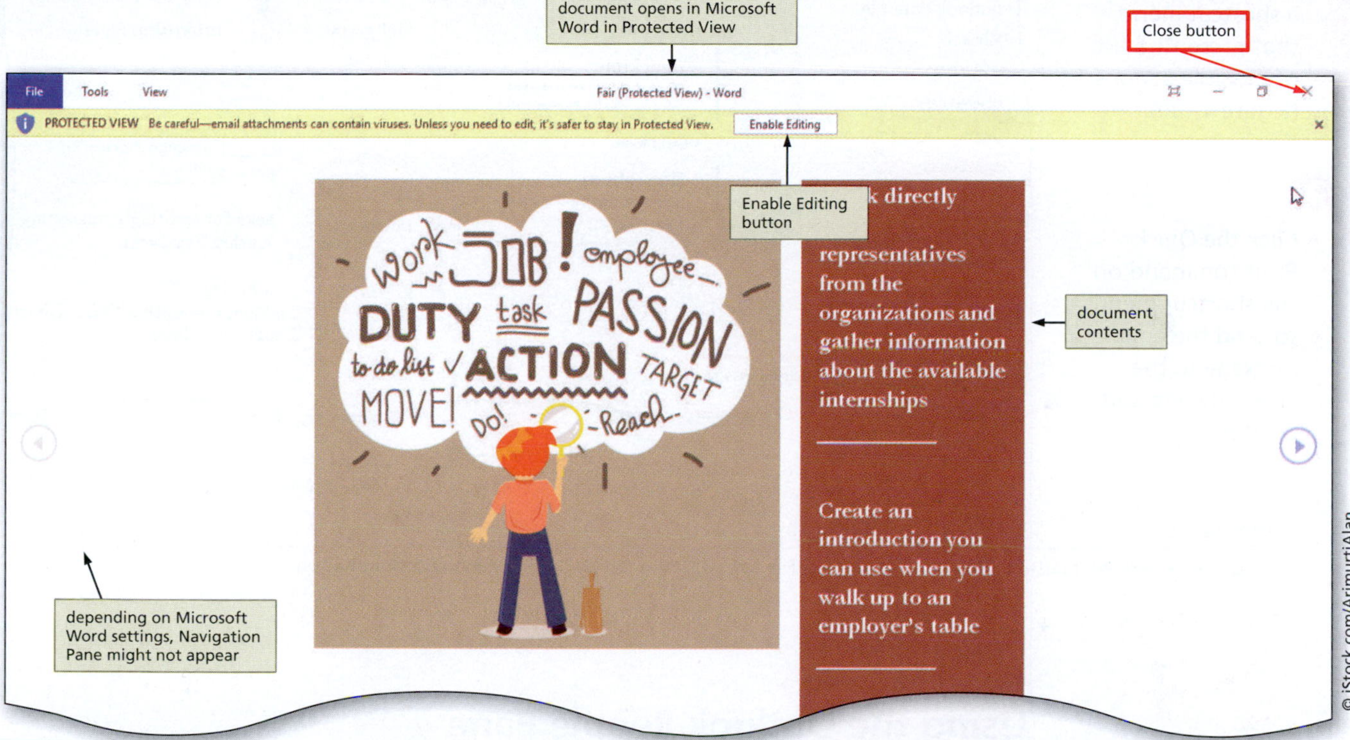

Figure 1–29

Q&A Why does the attachment open in Protected View in Microsoft Word?
File attachments can contain viruses, worms, or other kinds of malware, which can harm your computer. To help protect your computer, Microsoft Office apps open files from these potentially unsafe locations in Protected View. Click the Enable Editing button if you trust the sender to edit the document.

- Click the Close button to close the Word file.

To Print an Email Message

Occasionally, you may want to print the contents of an email message. ***Why?*** *A hard copy of an email message can serve as reference material if your storage medium becomes corrupted and you need to view the message when your computer is not readily available.* A printed copy of an email message also serves as a **backup**, which is an additional copy of a file or message that you store for safekeeping. You can print the contents of an email message from an open message window or directly from the Inbox window.

You would like to have a hard copy of Ella Pauley's email message for reference about the upcoming internship fair. The following steps print an email message.

1

- If necessary, click Home on the ribbon to display the Home tab.
- In the message list, right-click the Ella Pauley message header to display a shortcut menu that presents a list of possible actions (Figure 1–30).

2

- Click the Quick Print command on the shortcut menu to send the email message to the currently selected printer.

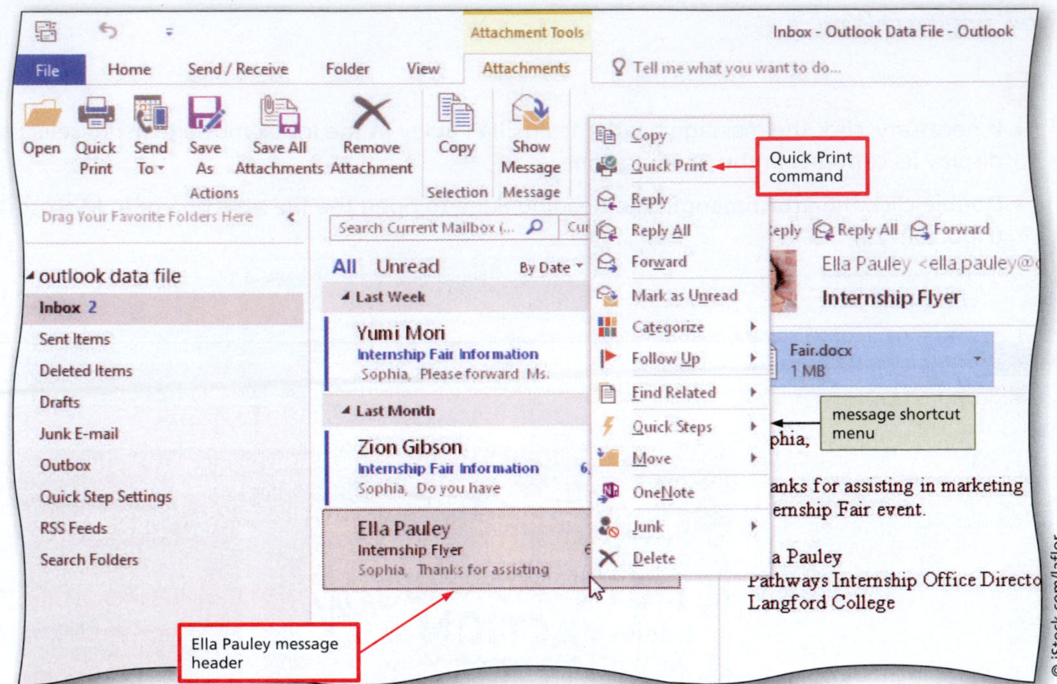

Figure 1–30

Other Ways

1. Press CTRL+P, click Print button
2. Click File tab, click Print tab (Backstage view), click Print button

Using the Outlook People Pane

Outlook provides a means of viewing email history, attachments, and meetings associated with each sender in the Reading pane. The **People Pane** accesses information about each of your contacts. The People Pane can display the photos and contact information of the email sender and recipient at the bottom of the Reading Pane in one location.

To Change the View of the People Pane

By default, the People Pane is not displayed in the Reading Pane. By changing the People Pane to the Minimized setting, the contact information is displayed as a one-line bar below an open email message and does not take up a lot of room in the Reading Pane or open message window. To view more details, you can change the People Pane view to Normal. ***Why?*** *When you are reading a message in Outlook, you can use the People Pane to view more information about the contacts associated with the message, such as the senders and receivers of the message.* The following steps change the view of the People Pane.

- Click View on the ribbon to display the View tab.
- Click the People Pane button (View tab | People Pane group) to display the People Pane gallery (Figure 1–31).

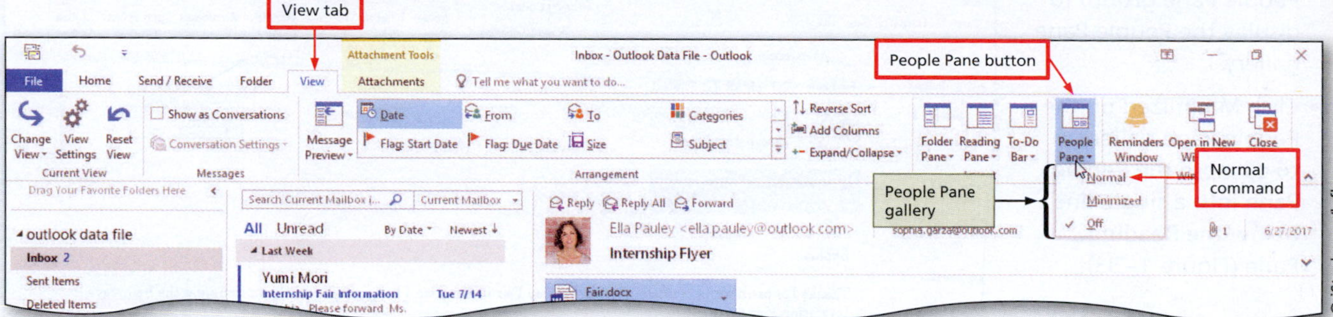

© iStock.com/laflor

Figure 1–31

- Click Normal in the People Pane gallery to display the People Pane in Normal view below the email message in the Reading Pane (Figure 1–32).

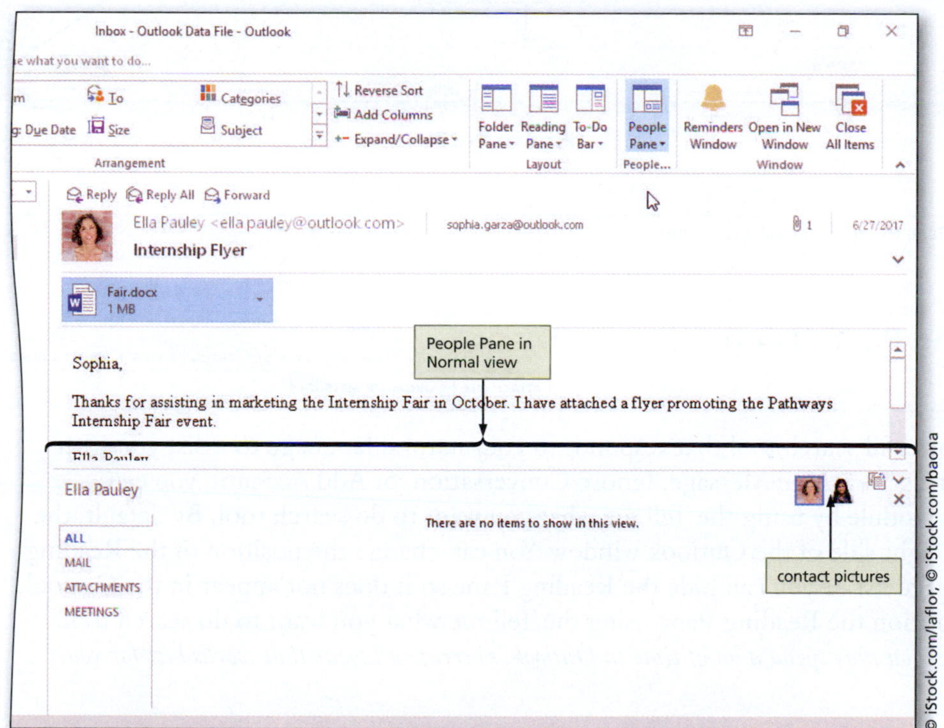

© iStock.com/laflor, © iStock.com/baona

Figure 1–32

If you are using your finger on a touch screen and are having difficulty completing the steps in this module, consider using a stylus. Many people find it easier to be precise with a stylus than with a finger. In addition, with a stylus you see the pointer. If you still are having trouble completing the steps with a stylus, try using a mouse.

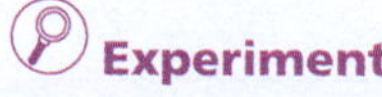

Experiment

- Double-click the first contact picture in the People Pane. A contact card opens that displays the contact information. When you are finished, click the Close button to close the contact card.

Q&A

When the People Pane expands to Normal view, should messages from this sender be listed below the sender's name?

Yes. Email messages appear in the People Pane if you have previously corresponded with the sender.

A yellow message appears below Ella Pauley's name in the People Pane. How should I respond to the message?

Close the message by clicking its Close button.

- Click the People Pane button (View tab | People Pane group) to display the People Pane gallery.
- Click Minimized on the People Pane gallery to collapse the People Pane into a single line below the Reading Pane (Figure 1–33).

Q&A Does the People Pane update contact information automatically?
The People Pane automatically updates information about your professional and social network contacts while Outlook is running.

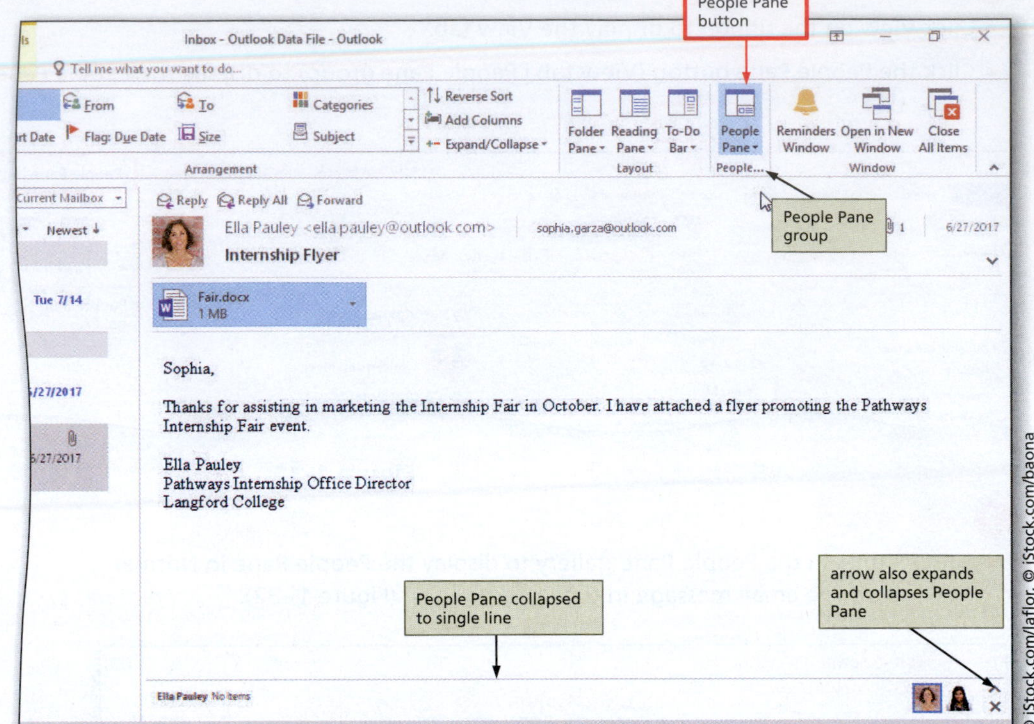

Figure 1–33

Other Ways

1. Click arrow to the right of the People Pane to expand or collapse pane

To Reposition the Reading Pane Using the Tell Me Search Tool

1 CONFIGURE ACCOUNT OPTIONS | 2 COMPOSE & SEND | 3 VIEW & PRINT | 4 REPLY
5 ATTACH FILE | 6 ORGANIZE MESSAGES

Outlook 2016 includes a powerful search tool that responds to your natural language to assist you with most tasks. By typing phrases such as New Mail Message, Ignore Conversation, or Add Account, you can perform the previous tasks in this module by using the Tell me what you want to do search tool. By default, the Reading Pane is displayed on the right side of the Outlook window. You can change the position of the Reading Pane so it appears below the message list or you can hide the Reading Pane so it does not appear in the Outlook window. The following steps reposition the Reading Pane using the Tell me what you want to do search tool. ***Why?*** *In your work and personal life, you may spend a lot of time in Outlook, so create a layout that works best for your own needs.*

- Click the 'Tell me what you want to do' text box, and then type `Reading Pane` (Figure 1–34).

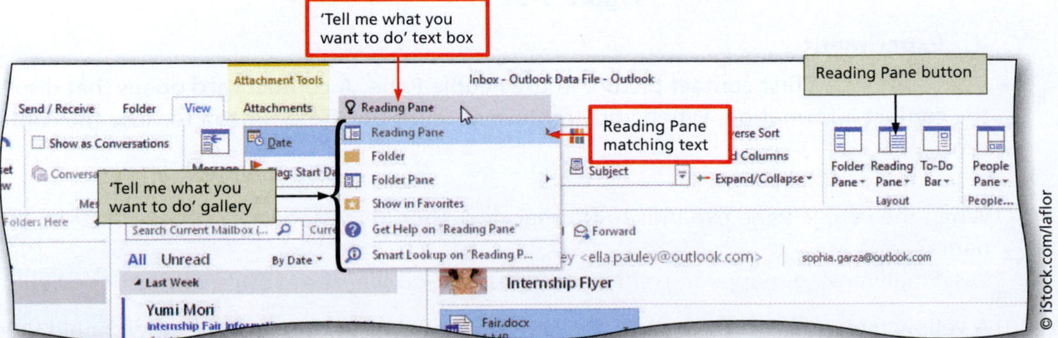

Figure 1–34

2

- Click the Reading Pane matching text option to display the Reading Pane options (Figure 1–35).

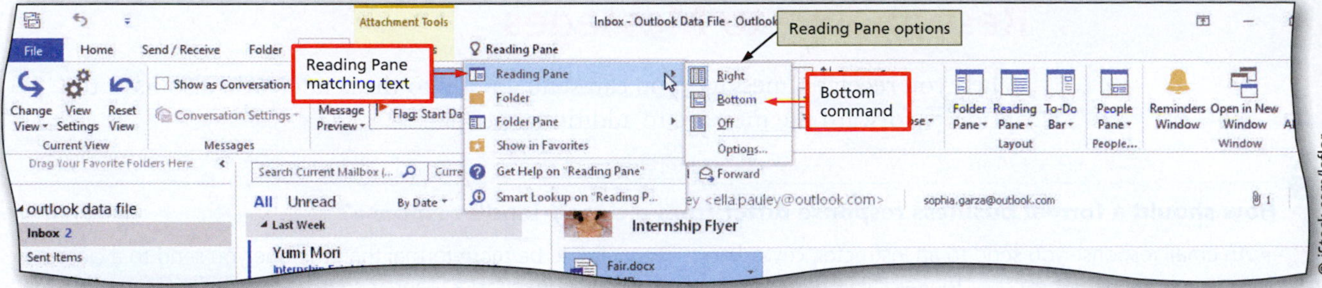

Figure 1–35

- Click Bottom in the Reading Pane options to place the Reading Pane for all mail folders at the bottom of the window (Figure 1–36).

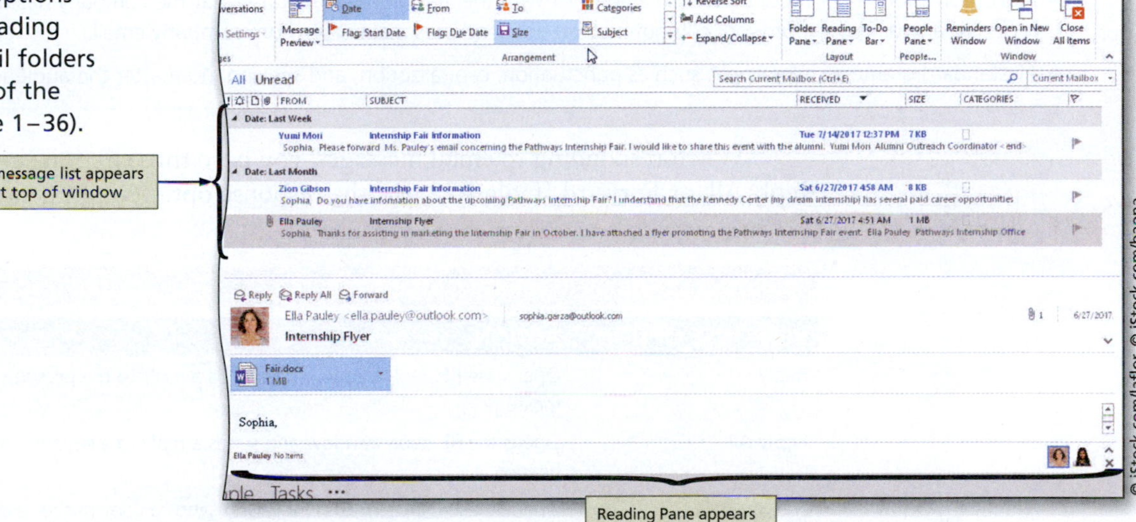

Figure 1–36

- Using the ribbon, click the Reading Pane button (View tab | Layout group) to display the Reading Pane gallery.
- Click Right on the Reading Pane gallery to return the Reading Pane to the right side of the Outlook window for all mail folders (Figure 1–37).

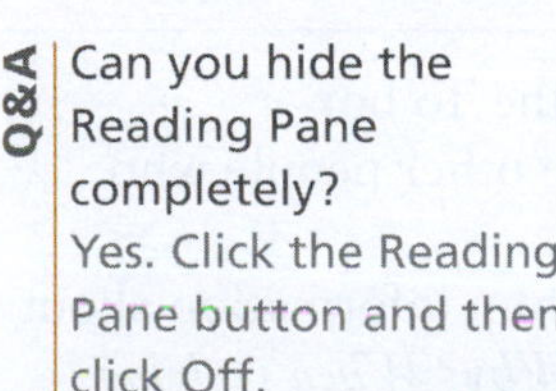

Q&A Can you hide the Reading Pane completely?

Yes. Click the Reading Pane button and then click Off.

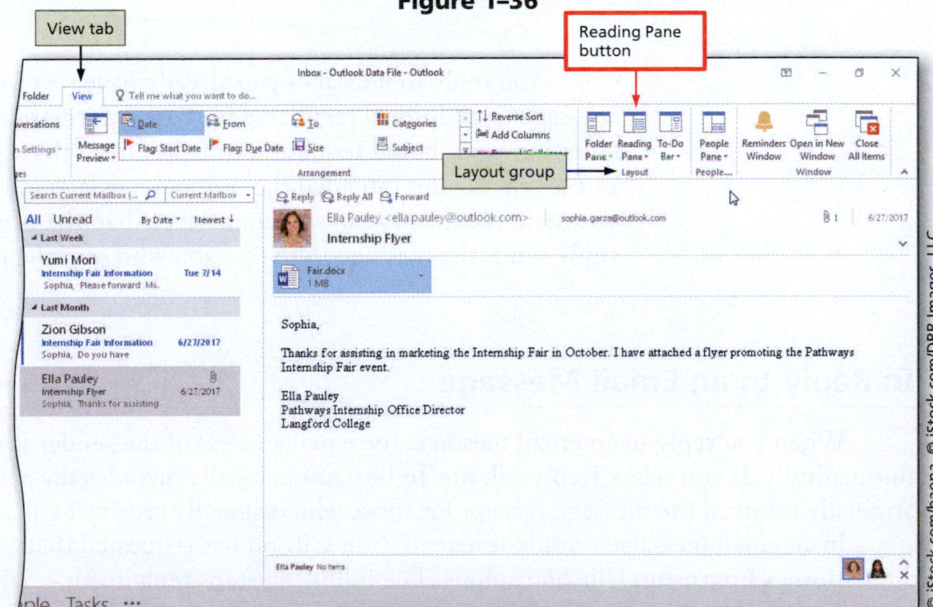

Figure 1–37

Break Point: If you wish to take a break, this is a good place to do so. To resume at a later time, continue to follow the steps from this location forward.

Responding to Messages

When you receive a message, you can send a reply to the sender. You also have the option to forward the message to additional people.

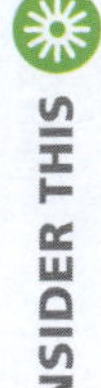

How should a formal business response differ from a close friend's response?

- An email response you send to an instructor, coworker, or client should be more formal than the one you send to a close friend placing your best foot forward. For example, conversational language to a friend, such as "Can't wait to go out!" is not appropriate in professional email messages.
- A formal email message should be business-like and get to the point quickly. An informal email is more conversational and friendly.
- Most professionals are required to sign a contract with their employer that states that the company has the right to have access to anything on your work computer so do not send personal emails from company email.
- All standard grammar rules apply, such as punctuation, capitalization, and spelling, no matter the audience.

When responding to email messages, you have three options in Outlook: Reply, Reply All, or Forward. Table 1–2 lists the response options and their actions.

Table 1–2 Outlook Response Options

RESPONSE OPTION	ACTION
Reply	Opens the RE: reply window and sends a reply to the person who sent the message.
Reply All	Opens the RE: reply window and sends a reply to everyone listed in the message header.
Forward	Opens the FW: message window and sends a copy of the selected message to additional people, if you want to share information with others. The original message text is included in the message window.

You reply to messages you already have received. You can forward an email message to additional recipients to share information with others. Based on the situation, you should request permission from the sender before forwarding a message, in case the sender intended the original message to remain private. When forwarding, you send the message to someone other than the original sender of the message. A reply sends the message to the person who sent the message.

To Reply to an Email Message

When you reply to an email message, the email address of the sender is inserted in the To box automatically. If you select Reply All, the To box automatically includes the sender and the other people who originally received the message (except for those who originally received a BCC message).

In an email message, a student named Zion Gibson has requested that Sophia send him information about the Pathways Internship Fair on campus. The following steps reply to an email message. ***Why?*** *When replying to a colleague, responding in a professional manner in an email message indicates how serious you are about your role and enhances your reputation within the organization.*

1

- Click Home on the ribbon to display the Home tab.
- Click the Zion Gibson message header in the message list to select it and display its contents in the Reading Pane (Figure 1–38).

Figure 1–38

2

- Click the Reply button (Home tab | Respond group) to reply to the message in the Reading Pane (Figure 1–39).

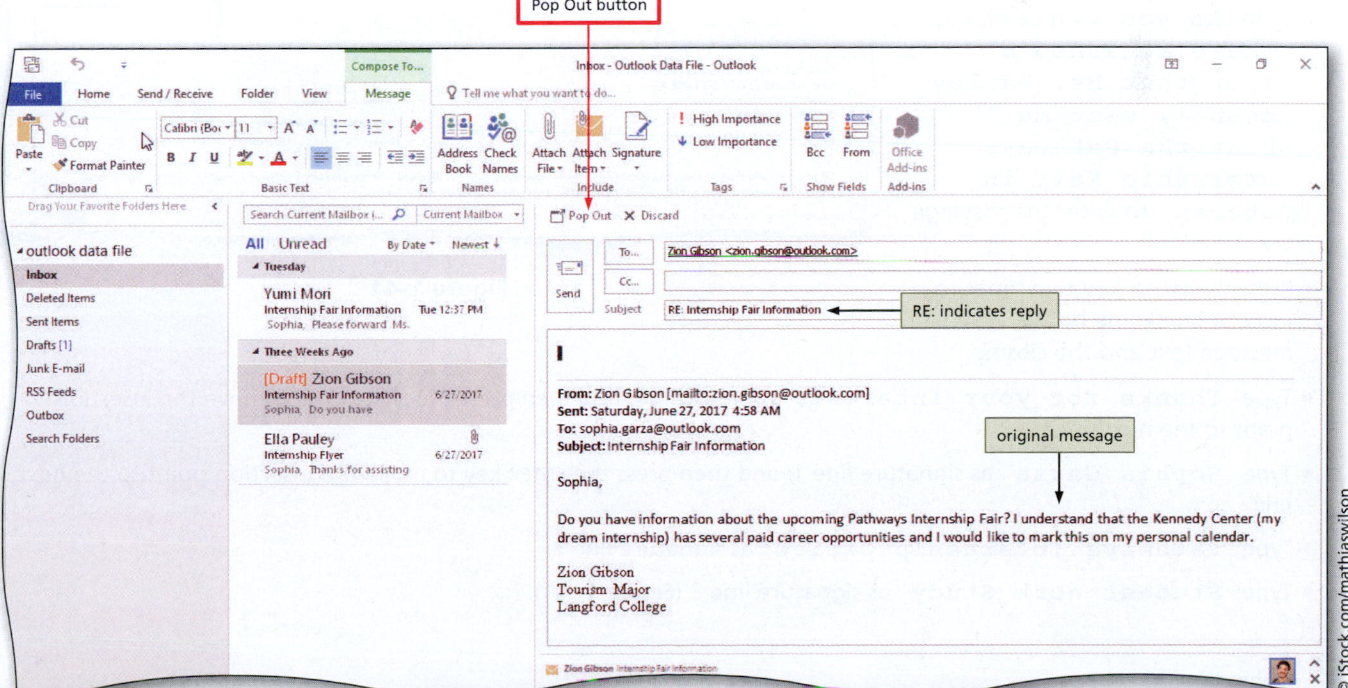

Figure 1–39

- Click the Pop Out button to display the RE: Internship Fair Information – Message (HTML) window (Figure 1–40).

Q&A Why does RE: appear at the beginning of the subject line and in the title bar?

The RE: indicates this message is a reply to another message. The subject of the original message appears after the RE:.

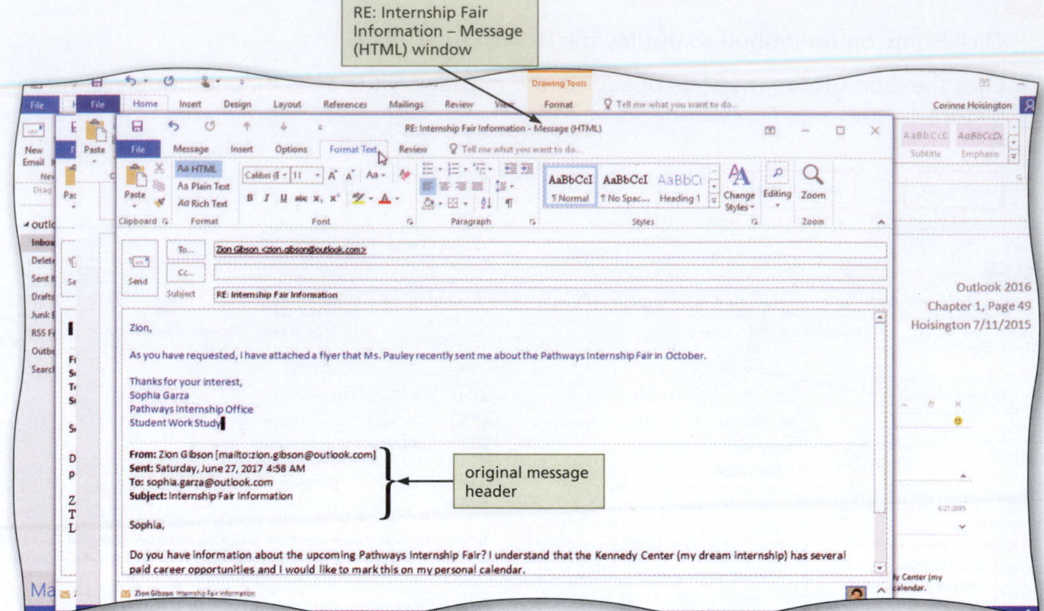

Figure 1–40

4

- If necessary, click the message area below the message header to position the insertion point at the top of the message area.
- Type **`Zion,`** as the greeting line.
- Press the ENTER key two times to insert a blank line between the greeting line and the message text.
- Type **`As you requested, I have attached a flyer that Ms. Pauley recently sent me about the Pathways Internship Fair in October.`** to enter the message text.
- Press the ENTER key two times to insert a blank line between the message text and the closing.
- Type **`Thanks for your interest,`** as the closing, and then press the ENTER key to move the insertion point to the next line.
- Type **`Sophia Garza`** as signature line 1, and then press the ENTER key to move the insertion point to the next line.
- Type **`Pathways Internship Office`** as signature line 2.
- Type **`Student Work Study`** as signature line 3 (Figure 1–41).

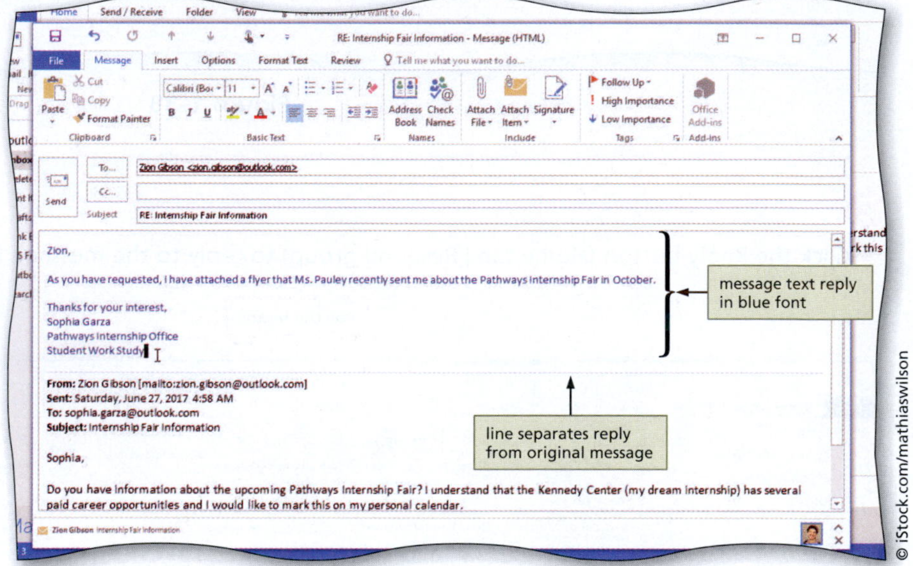

Figure 1–41

Other Ways

1. Click Reply or Reply All in Reading Pane
2. Right-click message header, click Reply
3. With message selected, press CTRL+R

Message Formats

As shown in Figure 1–42, Outlook's default (preset) message format is **HTML (Hypertext Markup Language)**, which is a format that allows you to view pictures and text formatted with color and various fonts and font sizes. **Formatting** refers to changing the appearance of text in a document such as the font (typeface), font size, color, and alignment of the text in a document.

Before you send an email message, reply to an email message, or forward an email message, consider which message format you want to use. A **message format** determines whether an email message can include pictures or formatted text, such as bold, italic, and colored fonts. Select a message format that is appropriate for your message and your recipient. Outlook offers three message formats: HTML, Plain Text, and Rich Text, as summarized in Table 1–3. If you select the HTML format, for example, the email program your recipient uses must be able to display formatted messages or pictures. If your recipient does not have high speed connectivity, a Plain Text format is displayed quickly, especially on a device such as a smartphone. Reading email in plain text offers important security benefits, reducing the possibility of a virus within the email.

Table 1–3 Message Formats

MESSAGE FORMAT	DESCRIPTION
HTML	HTML is the default format for new messages in Outlook. HTML lets you include pictures and basic formatting, such as text formatting, numbering, bullets, and alignment. HTML is the recommended format for Internet mail because the more popular email programs use it.
Plain Text	Plain Text format is recognized by all email programs and is the most likely format to be allowed through a company's virus-filtering program. Plain Text does not support basic formatting, such as bold, italic, colored fonts, or other text formatting. It also does not support pictures displayed directly in the message.
Rich Text	Rich Text Format (RTF) is a Microsoft format that only the latest versions of **Microsoft Exchange** (a Microsoft message system that includes an email program and a mail server) and Outlook recognize. RTF supports more formats than HTML or Plain Text; it also supports hyperlinks. A hyperlink can be text, a picture, or other object that is displayed in an email message.

CONSIDER THIS

Can I use plain text formatting to guard against email viruses?
HTML-formatted messages can contain viruses. To minimize the risk of receiving a virus infected email message, change the format of messages you read. You can configure Outlook to format all opened messages in Plain Text. Click File on the ribbon to open the Backstage view. Click the Options tab. Click the Trust Center option in the Outlook Options dialog box, and then click the Trust Center Settings button to display the Trust Center dialog box. Click Email Security (Trust Center dialog box), and in the Read as Plain Text section, click the 'Read all standard mail in plain text' check box.

To Change the Message Format

1 CONFIGURE ACCOUNT OPTIONS | 2 COMPOSE & SEND | 3 VIEW & PRINT | **4 REPLY**
5 ATTACH FILE | **6 ORGANIZE MESSAGES**

Why? You want to make sure that your reply message is not blocked by an antivirus program, so you will change the message format to Plain Text. The following steps change the message format to Plain Text.

- Click Format Text on the ribbon in the message window to display the Format Text tab (Figure 1–42).

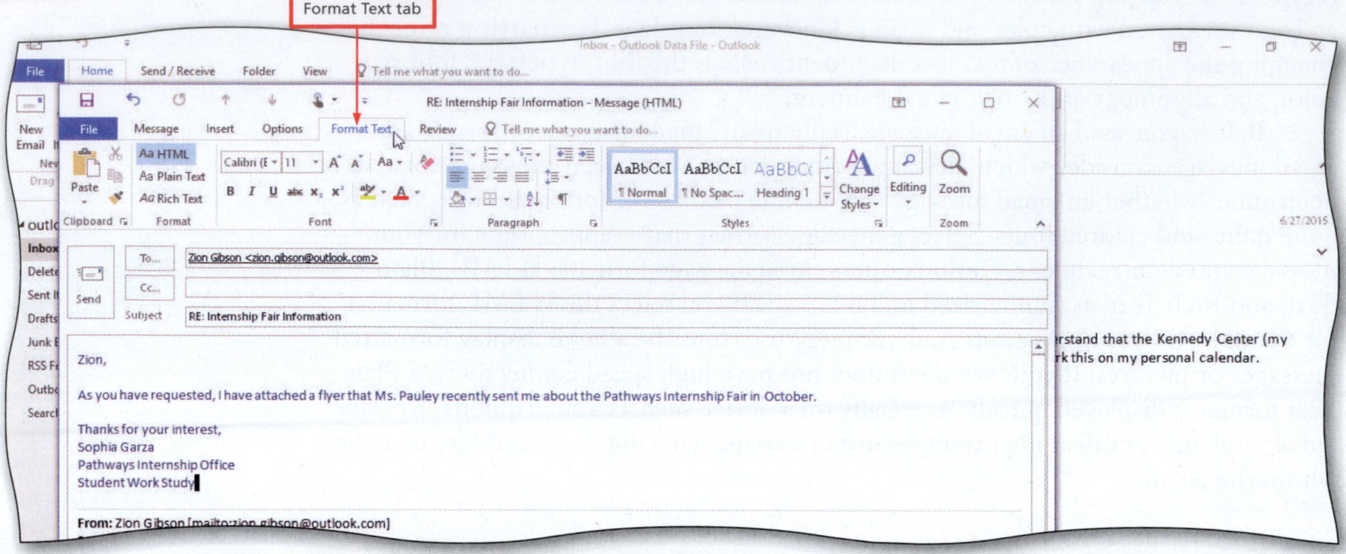

Figure 1–42

- Click the Plain Text button (Format Text tab | Format group) to select the Plain Text message format, which removes all formatting in the message.
- When the Microsoft Outlook Compatibility Checker dialog box is displayed, click the Continue button to change the formatted text to plain text (Figure 1–43).

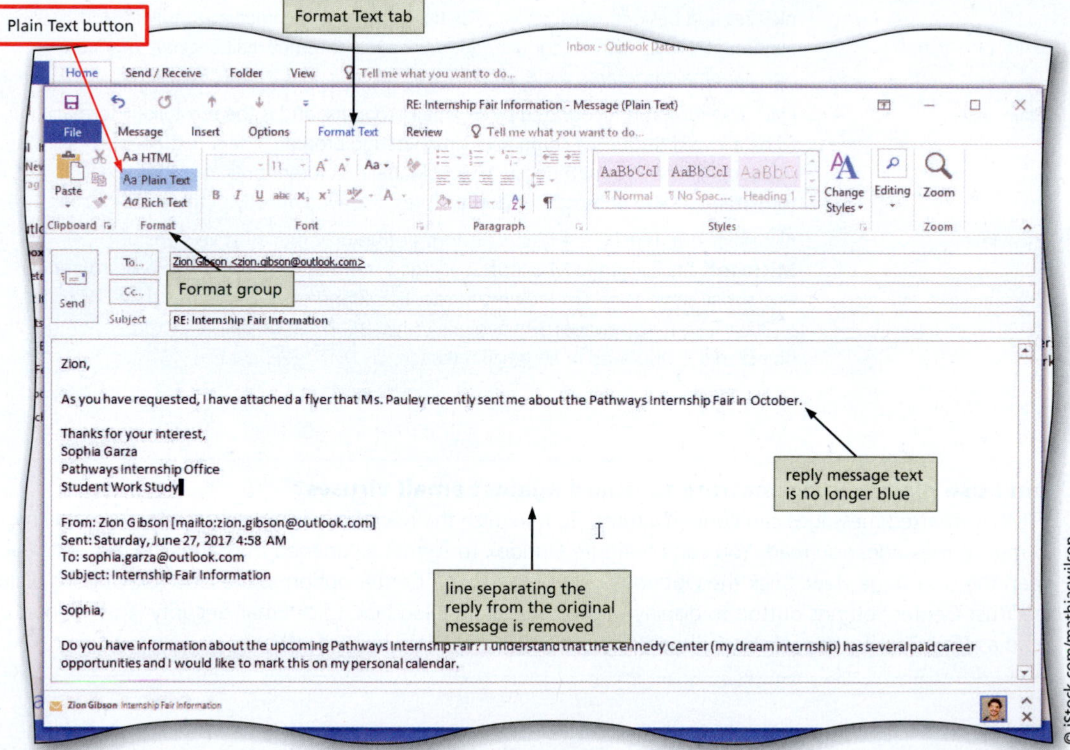

Figure 1–43

© iStock.com/mathiaswilson

Q&A What happened to the line separating the existing message and the new message?
When Plain Text is selected as the message format, all formatting such as text color, font type, lines, themes, and size is removed.

Checking Spelling and Grammar

Outlook checks your message for possible spelling and grammar errors as you type and flags any potential errors in the message text with a red, green, or blue wavy underline. A red wavy underline means the flagged text is not in Outlook's main dictionary because it is a proper name or misspelled. A green wavy underline indicates the text may be incorrect grammatically. A blue wavy underline indicates the text may contain a contextual spelling error such as the misuse of homophones (words that are pronounced the same but have different spellings or meanings, such as one and won). Although you can check the entire message for spelling and grammar errors at once, you also can check these flagged errors as they appear on the screen.

A flagged word is not necessarily misspelled. For example, many names, abbreviations, and specialized terms are not in Outlook's main dictionary. In these cases, you instruct Outlook to ignore the flagged word. As you type, Outlook also detects duplicate words while checking for spelling errors. For example, if your email message contains the phrase *to the the store*, Outlook places a red wavy underline below the second occurrence of the word, *the*.

BTW

Misspelled Words in an Email Message

When you misspell words in a professional email message, your clients may think you are just sending a quick message and not giving the email your full attention when responding.

CONSIDER THIS

Should I remove the original message when replying?

Many email users prefer to reply to a message without including the original email message along with their response. To remove the original message from all email replies, click File to open the Backstage view, and then click the Options tab. Click Mail to display the Mail options. In the Replies and forwards section, click the 'When replying to a message box' arrow, select the 'Do not include original message' option, and then click OK.

1 CONFIGURE ACCOUNT OPTIONS | 2 COMPOSE & SEND | 3 VIEW & PRINT | **4 REPLY**
5 ATTACH FILE | 6 ORGANIZE MESSAGES

To Check the Spelling of a Correctly Typed Word

Sophia adds one more sentence to her email message, recalling that Zion is interested in an internship at the Kennedy Center. In the message, the Kennedy Center employer with the last name of Kolat has a red wavy line below it even though it is spelled correctly, indicating the word is not in Outlook's main dictionary. The following steps ignore the error and remove the red wavy line. ***Why?*** *The main dictionary contains most common words, but does not include most proper names, technical terms, or acronyms.*

1

- Click after the first sentence in the email message to Zion to place the insertion point, and then press the SPACEBAR to insert a space.
- Type `I understand that Mr. Kolat, the marketing director, is personally representing the Kennedy Center at the fair.` to enter a second sentence in the message text, and then click a blank spot in the window to have Outlook mark a spelling error (Figure 1–44).

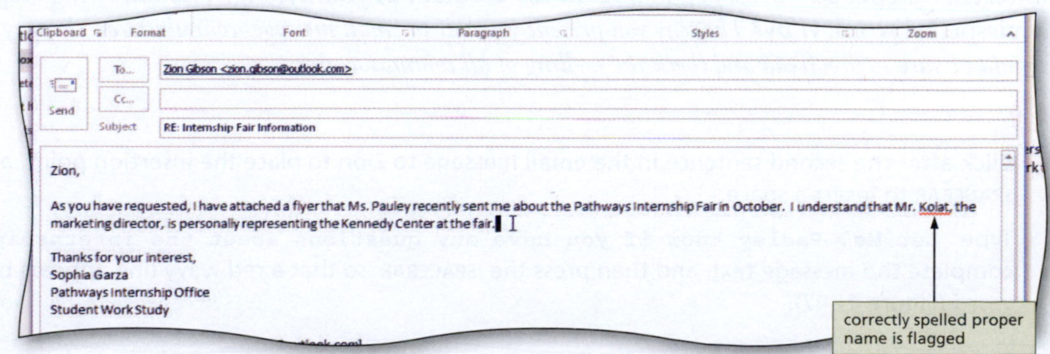

Figure 1–44

Q&A

Why does a red wavy line appear below Kolat even though the last name is spelled correctly?
Outlook places a red wavy line below any word that is not in its main dictionary.

- Right-click the red wavy line below the proper name to display a shortcut menu that presents a list of suggested spelling corrections for the flagged word (in this case, the last name) (Figure 1–45).

Q&A What if Outlook does not flag my spelling and grammar errors with wavy underlines?

To verify that the check spelling and grammar as you type features are enabled, click the File tab on the ribbon to open the Backstage view and then click Options to display the Outlook Options dialog box. Click Mail (Outlook Options dialog box) and click the Editor Options button to display the Editor Options dialog box. In the 'When correcting spelling in Outlook' section, ensure the 'Check spelling as you type' check box contains a check mark. Click the OK button two times to close each open dialog box.

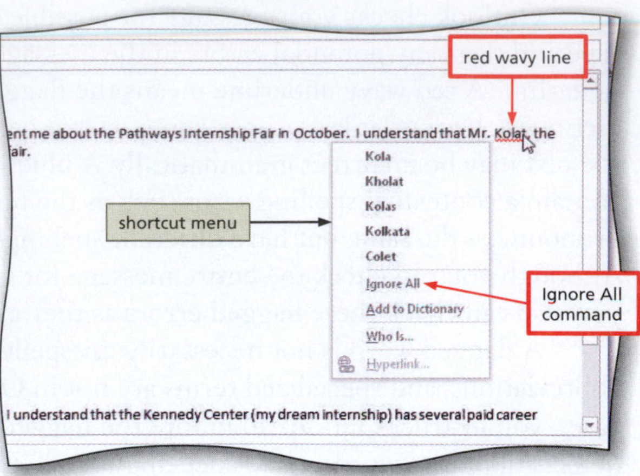

Figure 1–45

- Click Ignore All on the shortcut menu to ignore this flagged error, close the shortcut menu, and remove the red wavy line beneath the proper name (Figure 1–46).

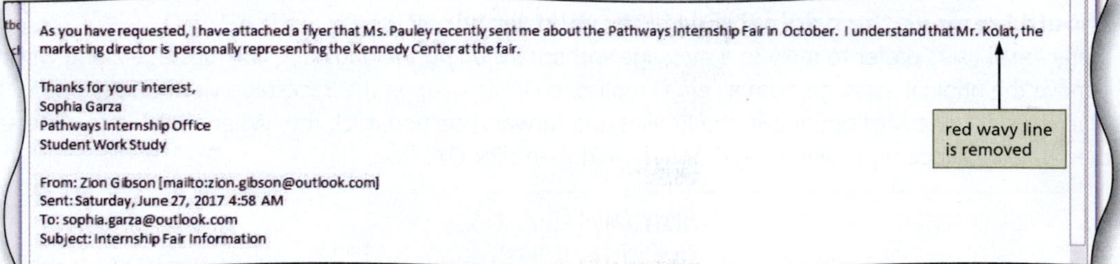

Figure 1–46

To Check the Spelling of Misspelled Text

1 CONFIGURE ACCOUNT OPTIONS | 2 COMPOSE & SEND | 3 VIEW & PRINT | 4 REPLY
5 ATTACH FILE | 6 ORGANIZE MESSAGES

In the following steps, the word *event* is misspelled intentionally as *evnt* to illustrate Outlook's check spelling as you type feature. If you are performing the steps in this project, your email message may contain different misspelled words, depending on the accuracy of your typing. The following steps check the spelling of a misspelled word. ***Why?*** *The way you present yourself in email messages contributes to the way you are perceived, so you should be sure to proofread and check the spelling of all communications.*

- Click after the second sentence in the email message to Zion to place the insertion point, and then press the SPACEBAR to insert a space.
- Type `Let Ms. Pauley know if you have any questions about the internship fair evnt.` to complete the message text, and then press the SPACEBAR so that a red wavy line appears below the misspelled word (Figure 1–47).

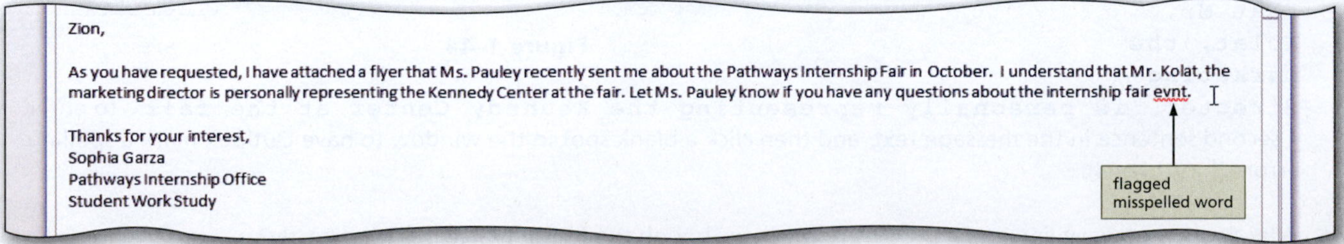

Figure 1–47

- Right-click the flagged word (evnt, in this case) to display a shortcut menu that presents a list of suggested spelling corrections for the flagged word (Figure 1–48).

Q&A What should I do if the correction I want to use is not listed on the shortcut menu?
You can click outside the shortcut menu to close it and then retype the correct word.

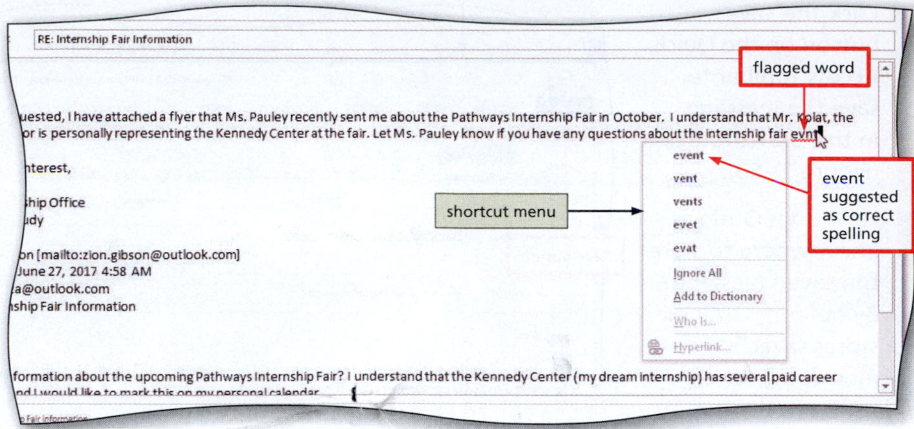

Figure 1–48

- Click the correct spelling on the shortcut menu (in this case, event) to replace the misspelled word in the email message with the correctly spelled word (Figure 1–49).

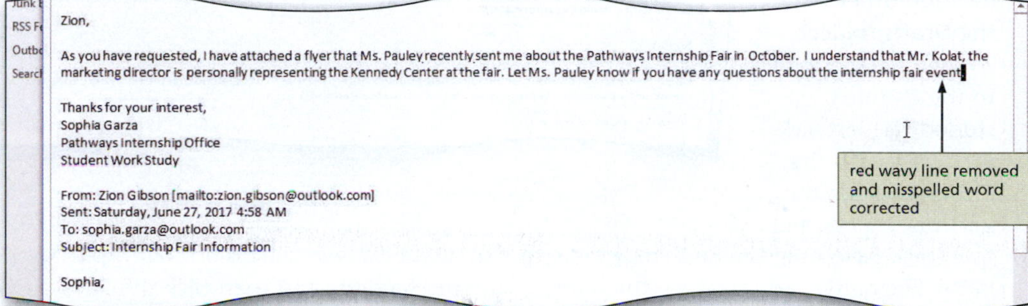

Figure 1–49

Other Ways

1. Click Review tab (message window), click Spelling & Grammar button (Review tab | Proofing group)
2. Press F7

Saving and Closing an Email Message

Occasionally, you begin composing a message but cannot complete it. You may be waiting for information from someone else to include in the message, or you might prefer to rewrite the message later after you have time to evaluate its content. One option is to save the message, which stores the message in the Drafts folder for your email account until you are ready to send it. The Drafts folder is the default location for all saved messages. Later, you can reopen the message, finish writing it, and then send it.

To Save and Close an Email Message without Sending It

1 CONFIGURE ACCOUNT OPTIONS | 2 COMPOSE & SEND | 3 VIEW & PRINT | 4 REPLY
5 ATTACH FILE | 6 ORGANIZE MESSAGES

The Internship Fair information that Zion Gibson requested has been drafted, but Sophia is not ready to send it yet. The following steps save a message in the Drafts folder for completion at a later time. ***Why?*** *If you are in the middle of composing a lengthy or important email and get called away, you can save your work so you can resume it later.*

- Click the Save button on the Quick Access Toolbar to save the message in the Drafts folder (Figure 1–50).

Q&A How does Outlook know where to store the saved message?
By default, Outlook stores saved messages in the Drafts folder for your email account.

Can I save the message to a location other than the Drafts folder?
To save the message to the Outlook student folder, click the File tab on the ribbon to open the Backstage view, and then click Save As in the Backstage view to display the Save As dialog box. Navigate to the Outlook student folder. In the File name text box, type the name of the message file and then click the Save button. The message is saved with the extension .msg, which represents an Outlook message.

What should I do if Outlook did not save the message in the Drafts folder?
Click the Home tab, click the Move button, click Other Folder, select the Drafts folder for Sophia Garza's Outlook Data File, and then click the OK button.

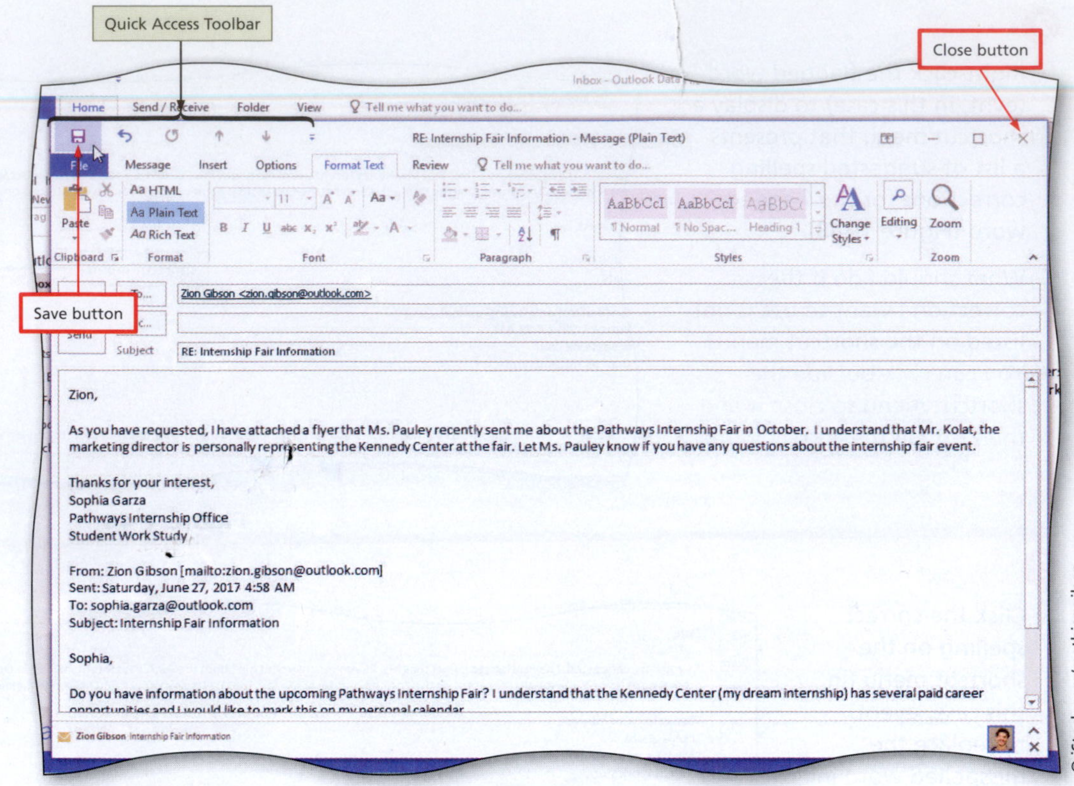

Figure 1–50

2

- Click the Close button on the title bar to close the RE: Internship Fair Information – Message (HTML) window (Figure 1–51).

Q&A How do I know when a message is a draft rather than an incoming message?
The message appears in the message list with [Draft] displayed in red.

What happens if I click the Close button without saving the message?
If you create a message and then click the Close button, Outlook displays a dialog box asking if you want to save the changes. If you click Yes, Outlook saves the file to the Drafts folder and closes the message window. If you click No, Outlook discards the email message and closes the message window.

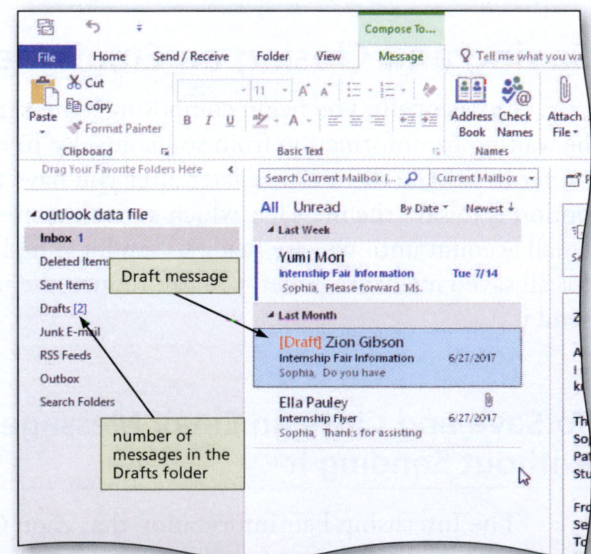

Figure 1–51

Other Ways

1. Click Close button and click Yes to keep saved draft of message
2. Press F12

To Open a Saved Email Message

The following steps open the message saved in the Drafts folder. ***Why?** By default, Outlook saves any email message in the Drafts folder every three minutes.* You can also save a message and reopen it later.

1

- Click the Drafts folder in the Navigation Pane to display the message header for the Zion Gibson email message in the message list (Figure 1–52).

Q&A What should I do if the message does not appear in my Drafts folder?

If the message does not appear in the Drafts folder, return to the Inbox, and then click the message header in the message pane.

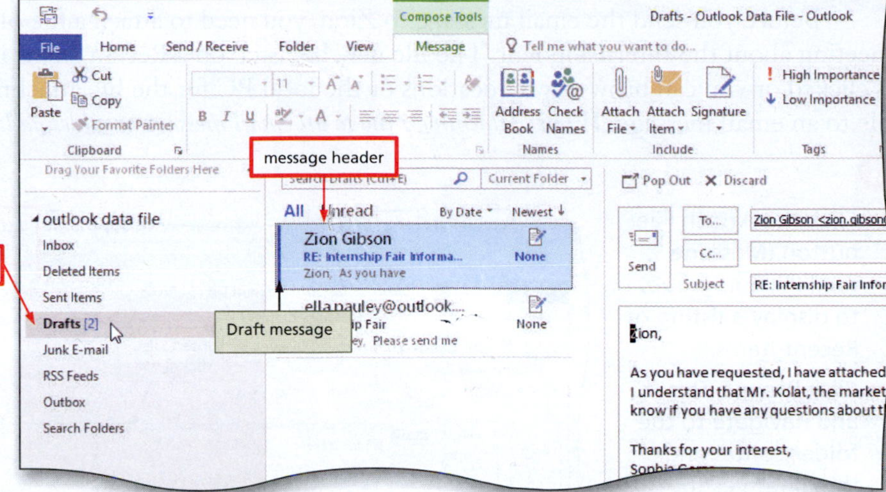

Figure 1–52

2

- Double-click the Zion Gibson message header in the Drafts folder to open the email message (Figure 1–53).

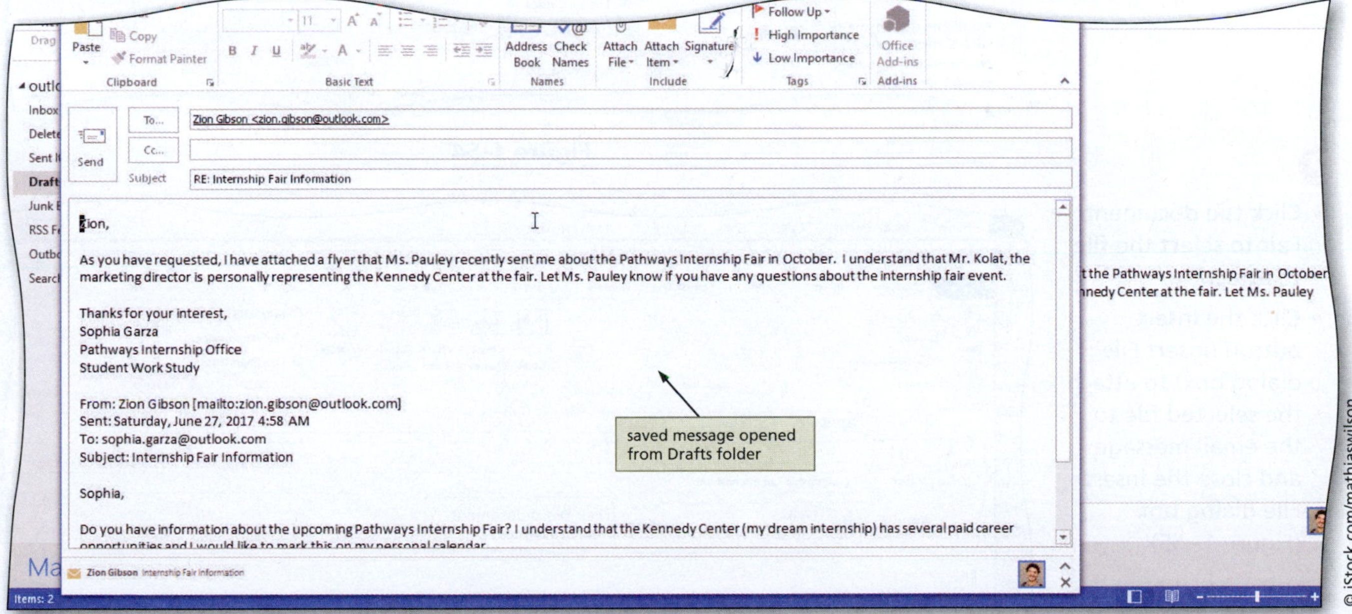

Figure 1–53

Other Ways

1. Right-click message, and click Open
2. With message selected, press CTRL+O

To Attach a File to an Email Message

To share a file such as a photo, flyer, or business document through email, you attach the file to an email message. Outlook does not have a predefined file size limit for attachments, but an email service provider may restrict the size of incoming attachments or the size of the email mailbox. Very large email attachments may be rejected by the recipient's email service provider and returned to the sender as undeliverable. Consider storing large files in OneDrive and sharing a link to the file within an email.

Before you send the email message to Zion, you need to attach a file of a flyer describing the informational meeting about the Internship Fair. The file may be listed on a Recent Items listing when the Attach File button is clicked or you can browse web locations or the local PC for the file attachment(s). The following steps attach a file to an email message. ***Why?*** *Attaching a file to an email message provides additional information to a recipient.*

1

- Click the Attach File button (Message tab | Include group) to display a listing of Recent Items.
- Click Browse This PC and navigate to the folder containing the data files for this module (in this case, the Module 01 folder in the Outlook folder in the Data Files folder) (Figure 1–54).

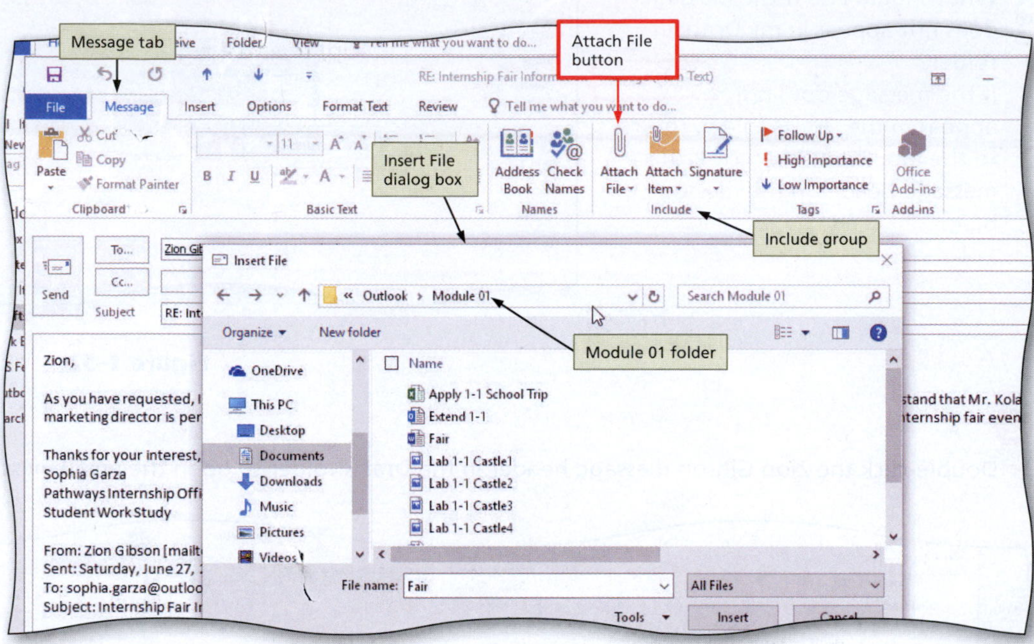

Figure 1–54

2

- Click the document Fair to select the file to attach.
- Click the Insert button (Insert File dialog box) to attach the selected file to the email message and close the Insert File dialog box (Figure 1–55).

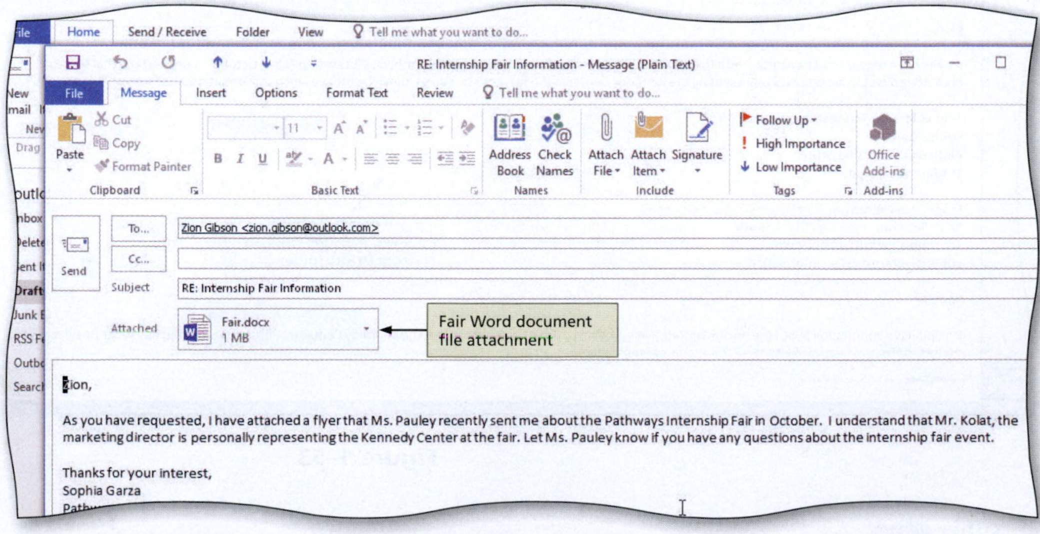

Figure 1–55

Q&A What should I do if I saved the Fair document to include my last name in the filename?

Select that document and then click the Insert button.

Other Ways

1. Click Insert tab, click Attach File button (Insert tab | Include group)
2. Drag file to message area
3. Right-click file attachment, click Copy, right-click message area, click Paste

To Set Message Importance and Send the Message

Why? *When you have a message that requires urgent attention, you can send the message with a high importance level.* Outlook provides the option to assign an **importance level** to a message, which indicates to the recipient the priority level of an email message. The default importance level for all new messages is normal importance, but you can change the importance level to high or low, depending on the priority level of the email message. A message sent with **high importance** displays a red exclamation point in the message header and indicates to the recipient that the message requires a higher priority than other messages he or she might have received. The **low importance** option displays a blue arrow and indicates to the recipient a low priority for the message. The following steps set the high importance option for a single email message and to send the message.

- Click the High Importance button (Message tab | Tags group) to add a high importance level (a red exclamation point) to the email message (Figure 1–56).

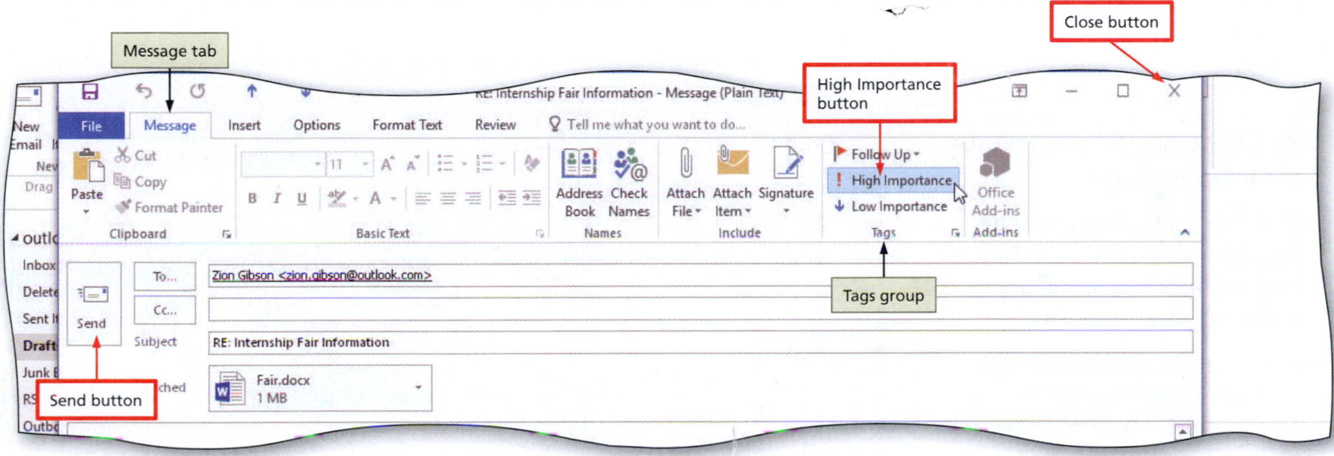

Figure 1–56

Q&A When does a red exclamation point appear in a message with high importance?
The red exclamation point appears in the message header when the message is received.

How would I set a low importance to an email message?
Click the Low Importance button (Message tab | Tags group).

- Click the Send button in the message header to send the email message.
- If necessary, click the Cancel button to close the Microsoft Outlook dialog box and then click the Close button to close the message window.

Q&A A message appeared that states 'No valid email accounts are configured. Add an account to send email'. What does this mean?
The Sophia.pst data file is an Outlook Data File, which cannot send an email message. If you are using the Sophia.pst data file, the sent message remains in the Drafts folder unless you configure an email account. You can set up and configure your own email address in Outlook to send an email message.

What happens to the actual email message after I send it?
After Outlook closes the message window, it stores the email message reply in the Outbox folder while it sends the message to the recipient. You might not see the message in the Outbox because Outlook usually stores it there only briefly. Next, Outlook moves the message to the Sent Items folder. The original message in the message list now shows an envelope icon with a purple arrow to indicate a reply was sent.

CONSIDER THIS

Can you place a tag in an email message that requests the recipient to respond within a certain time period?

- If you are sending an email message that requires a timely response, you can click the Follow Up button (Message tab | Tags group) to insert a flag icon indicating that the recipient should respond within a specified period of time.
- Based on your expected response time, you can select the Follow Up flag for Today, Tomorrow, This Week, Next Week, No Date, or Custom.

To Forward an Email Message

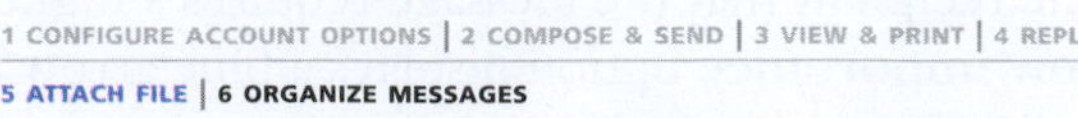

When you forward an email message, you resend a received or sent email message to another recipient. Yumi Mori, the Alumni Outreach coordinator, sent Sophia an email message requesting that she forward Ms. Pauley's email message about the Internship Fair to advertise on their website. Sophia adds Ms. Pauley as a courtesy copy (cc) recipient to make her aware that Yumi is receiving a copy of her email message. The following steps forward a previously received email message. ***Why?*** *Forwarding sends an email to someone who was not on the original recipient list.*

- Click the Inbox folder to display the Inbox messages.
- Click the Yumi Mori message header and read her message requesting information about the Pathways Internship Fair.
- Click the Ella Pauley message header in the message list to select the email message (Figure 1–57).

Q&A

Why do my message headers show times instead of dates?

Outlook shows today's messages with times in the headers and messages prior to today with dates in the headers.

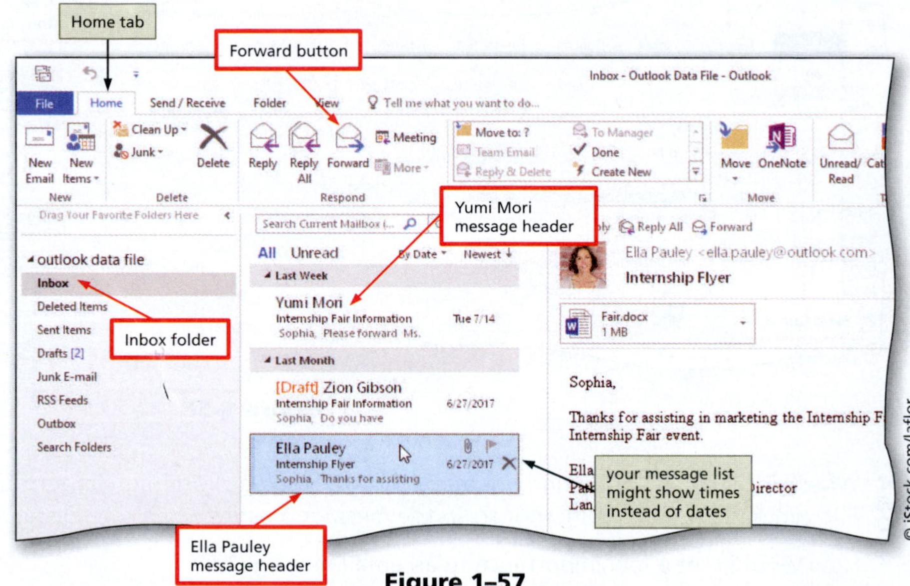

Figure 1–57

- Click the Forward button (Home tab | Respond group) to display the message in the Reading Pane (Figure 1–58).

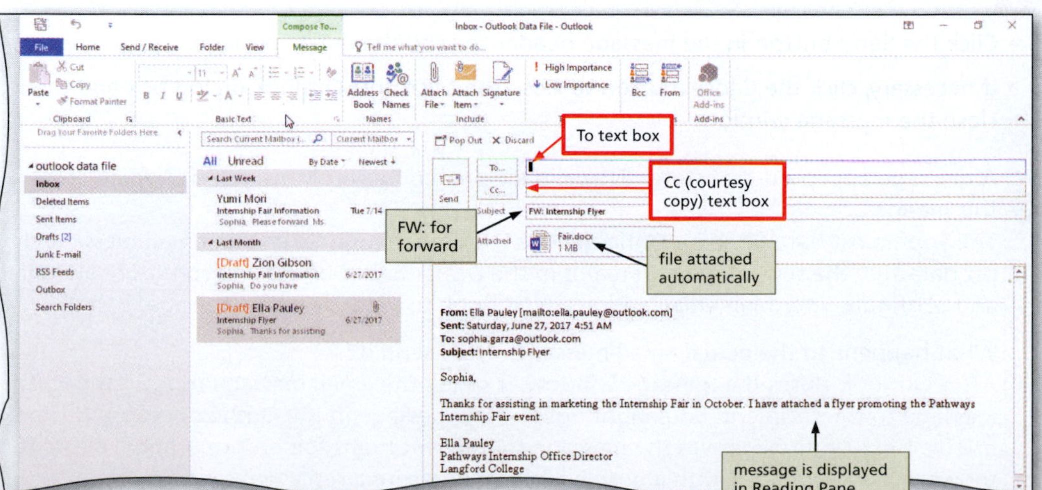

Figure 1–58

3

- Click the To text box, and then type `yumi.mori@outlook.com` (with no spaces) as the recipient's email address.
- Click the Cc text box, and then type `ella.pauley@outlook.com` (with no spaces) to send a courtesy copy to inform the original sender that you are forwarding her email message (Figure 1–59).

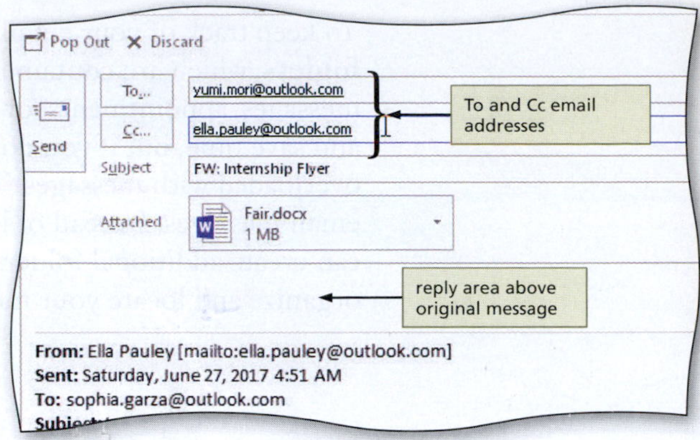

Figure 1–59

Experiment

- Click the Bcc button (Message tab | Show Fields group) to display the Bcc (blind carbon copy) text box. When you are finished, click the Bcc button (Message tab | Show Fields group) again to hide the Bcc text box.

Q&A Why does the original message appear in the message area of the window?
By default, Outlook displays the original message below the new message area for all message replies and forwards.

4

- Click the message area above the original message text, type **Yumi,** as the greeting line and then press the SPACEBAR.
- Right-click Yumi and then click Ignore All to remove the red wavy line.
- Press the ENTER key two times to enter a blank line before the message text.
- Type `Per your request, I am forwarding the email and internship fair flyer from Ms. Pauley about the Pathways Internship event.` to enter the message text.

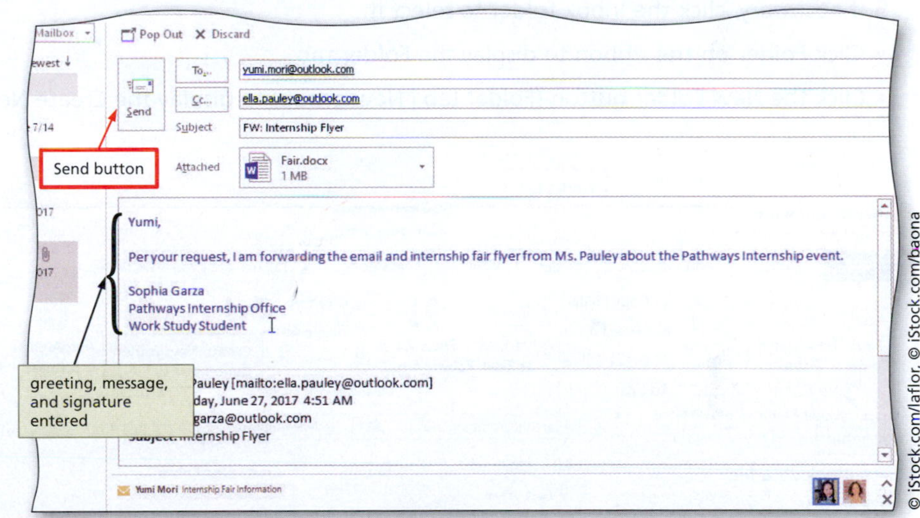

Figure 1–60

- Press the ENTER key two times to place a blank line between the message text and the signature lines.
- Type `Sophia Garza` as signature line 1, and then press the ENTER key to move the insertion point to the next line.
- Type `Pathways Internship Office,` and then press the ENTER key.
- Type `Work Study Student` as the third line of the signature to represent her title (Figure 1–60).

Q&A Does Outlook automatically forward the attachment to the recipient?
Yes. Outlook automatically adds the attachment to the forwarded message unless you choose to remove it.

5

- Click the Send button in the message header to forward the message.
- If necessary, click the Cancel button to close the Microsoft Outlook dialog box.

Other Ways

1. Right-click message header, click Forward
2. Click message header, press CTRL+F

Organizing Messages with Outlook Folders

To keep track of your email messages effectively, Outlook provides a basic set of **folders**, which are containers for storing Outlook items of a specific type, such as messages, appointments, or contacts. Email is supposed to help you be more efficient and save time, but if you do not manage it effectively, you can quickly become overloaded with messages. The Inbox is an email folder that stores your incoming email messages. Instead of leaving all of your incoming messages in the Inbox, you can create additional folders and then move messages to these new folders so you can organize and locate your messages easily.

1 CONFIGURE ACCOUNT OPTIONS | 2 COMPOSE & SEND | 3 VIEW & PRINT | 4 REPLY
5 ATTACH FILE | **6 ORGANIZE MESSAGES**

To Create a New Folder in the Inbox Folder

By creating multiple folders within the Inbox folder, and then organizing messages in the new folders, you can find a specific email message easily. The following steps create a folder within the Inbox folder. ***Why?*** *Folders provide an efficient method for managing your email.*

- If necessary, click the Inbox folder to select it.
- Click Folder on the ribbon to display the Folder tab.
- Click the New Folder button (Folder tab | New group) to display the Create New Folder dialog box (Figure 1–61).

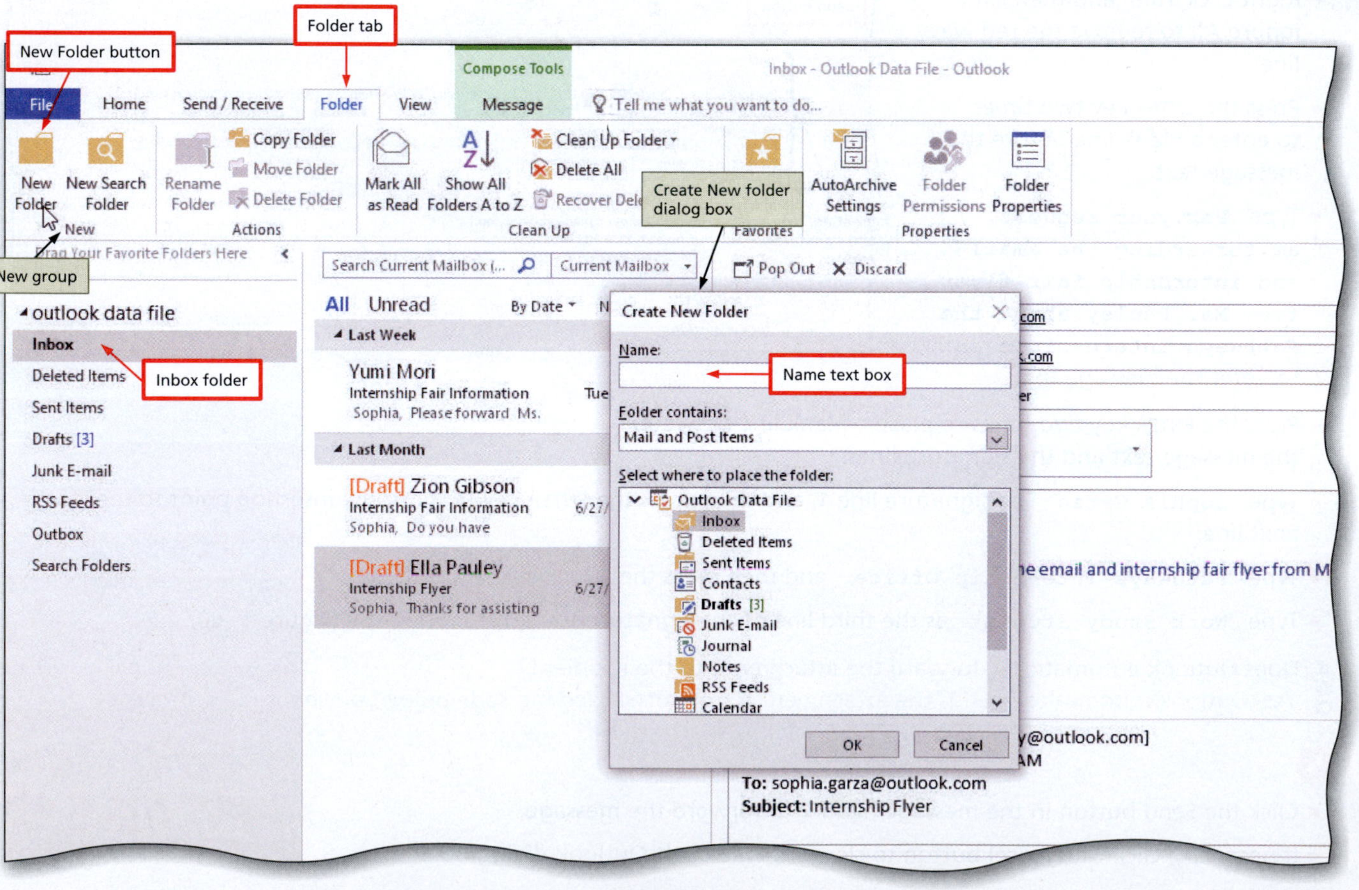

Figure 1–61

2

- Click the Name text box, and then type **Internship Fair** to name the folder within the Inbox folder.
- If necessary, click the Folder contains arrow, and then click 'Mail and Post Items' in the list to place only email messages in the new folder.
- If necessary, click Inbox in the 'Select where to place the folder' list to place the new folder within the Inbox folder (Figure 1–62).

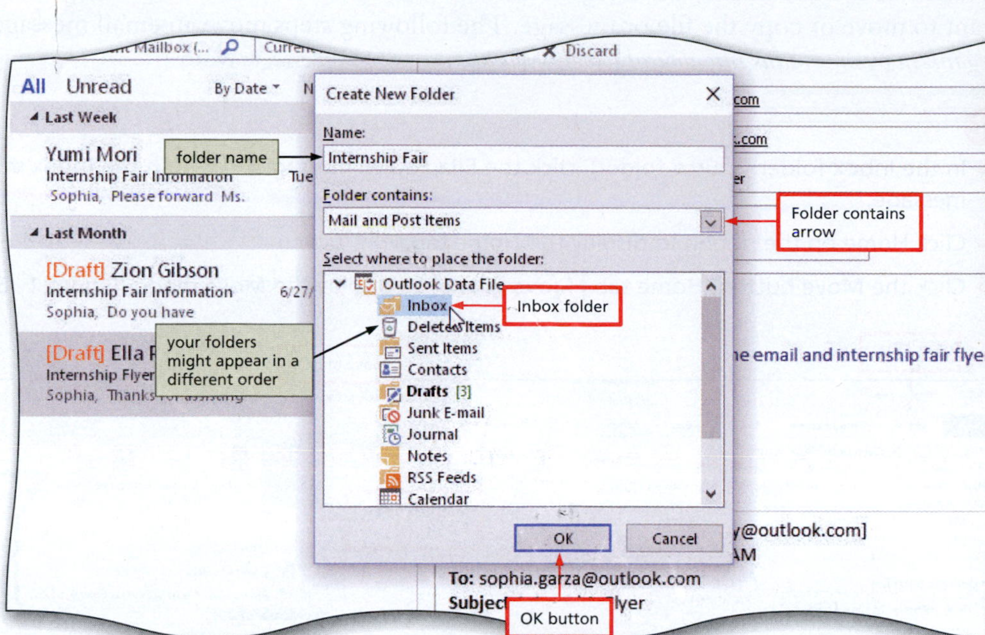

Figure 1–62

3

- Click the OK button to create the Internship Fair folder within the Inbox and close the Create New Folder dialog box (Figure 1–63).

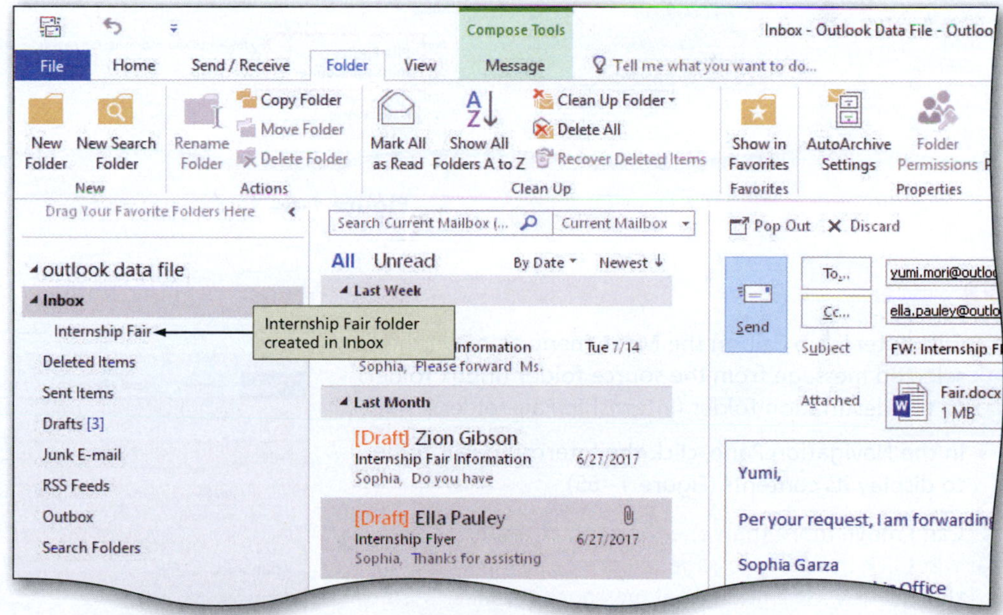

Figure 1–63

Q&A Why is the Internship Fair folder indented below the Inbox folder?
The Internship Fair folder is stored within the Inbox folder. Outlook indents the folder in the list to indicate that it is within the main folder.

Other Ways

1. Right-click folder in Folder pane, click New Folder

To Move an Email Message to a Folder

1 CONFIGURE ACCOUNT OPTIONS | 2 COMPOSE & SEND | 3 VIEW & PRINT | 4 REPLY
5 ATTACH FILE | **6 ORGANIZE MESSAGES**

Organizing important email messages about the Internship Fair event into the Internship Fair folder saves time when you search through hundreds or thousands of email messages later. Specifically, you will move the message from Ella Pauley from the Inbox folder to the Internship Fair folder. In this case, the Inbox folder is called the source folder, and the Internship Fair folder is called the destination folder. A **source folder** is the location of the document or message to be moved or copied. A **destination folder** is the location where you want to move or copy the file or message. The following steps move an email message into a folder. ***Why?** By organizing your emails into topical folders, you can access your messages easily.*

- In the Inbox folder (source folder), click the Ella Pauley message header in the Inbox message list to select the email message.
- Click Home on the ribbon to display the Home tab.
- Click the Move button (Home tab | Move group) to display the Move menu (Figure 1–64).

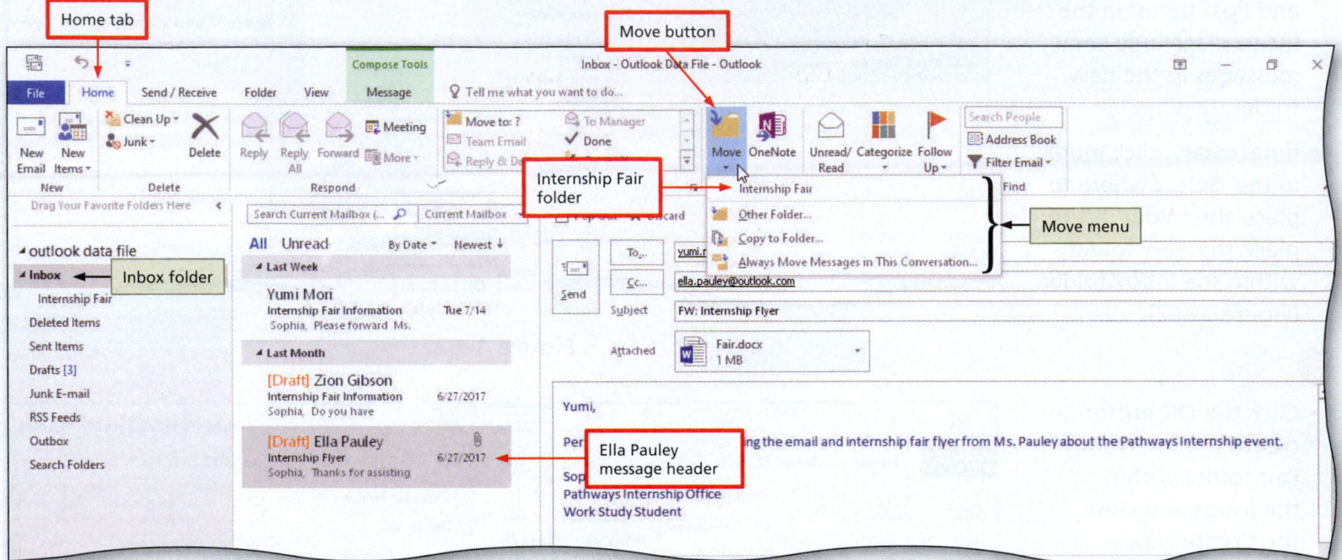

Figure 1–64

- Click Internship Fair on the Move menu to move the selected message from the source folder (Inbox folder) to the destination folder (Internship Fair folder).
- In the Navigation Pane, click the Internship Fair folder to display its contents (Figure 1–65).

Q&A Can I move more than one message at a time?
Yes. Click the first message to select it. While holding the CTRL key, click additional messages to select them. Click the Move button (Home tab | Move group) and then click the destination folder to select it.

Can I copy the email messages instead of moving them?
Yes. Select the message(s) to copy, and then click the Move button (Home tab | Move group). Click Copy to Folder on the menu to display the Copy Items dialog box. Select the destination folder, and then click the OK button to copy the selected message to the destination folder.

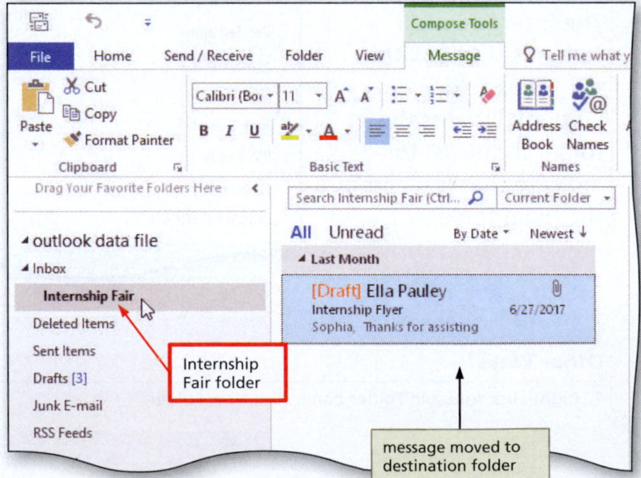

Figure 1–65

Other Ways

1. Right-click selected message, point to Move, click folder
2. Click selected message, drag message into destination folder

Outlook Quick Steps

An Outlook feature called **Quick Steps** provides shortcuts to perform redundant tasks with a single keystroke. For example, you can move an email message to a folder using a one-click Quick Step. You can use the built-in Quick Steps to move a file to a folder, send email to your entire team, or reply and then delete an email message.

To Move an Email Message Using Quick Steps

If you frequently move messages to a specific folder, you can use a Quick Step to move a message in one click. The following steps create a Quick Step to move an email message into a specific folder. ***Why?*** *Quick Steps allow you to customize email actions that you use most often.*

1

- Click the Inbox folder in the Navigation Pane to select the Inbox folder.
- If necessary, click Home to display the Home tab.
- Click Move to: ? in the Quick Steps gallery (Home tab | Quick Steps group) to display the First Time Setup dialog box (Figure 1–66).

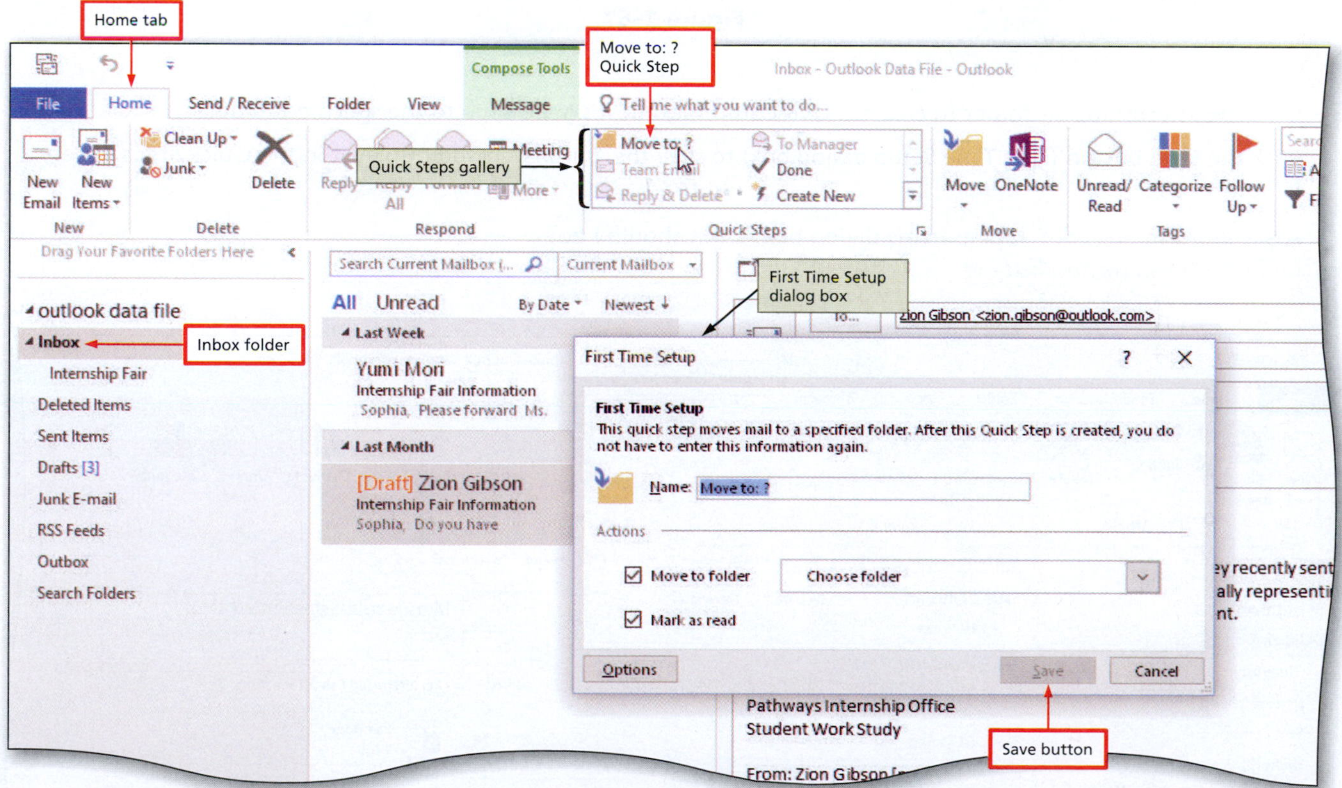

Figure 1–66

Q&A What should I do if Move to: ? does not appear on the Home tab?
Click the More button (Home tab | Quick Steps group), point to New Quick Step, and then click Move to Folder.

- Click the Move to folder arrow (First Time Setup dialog box) to display the list of available folders (Figure 1–67).

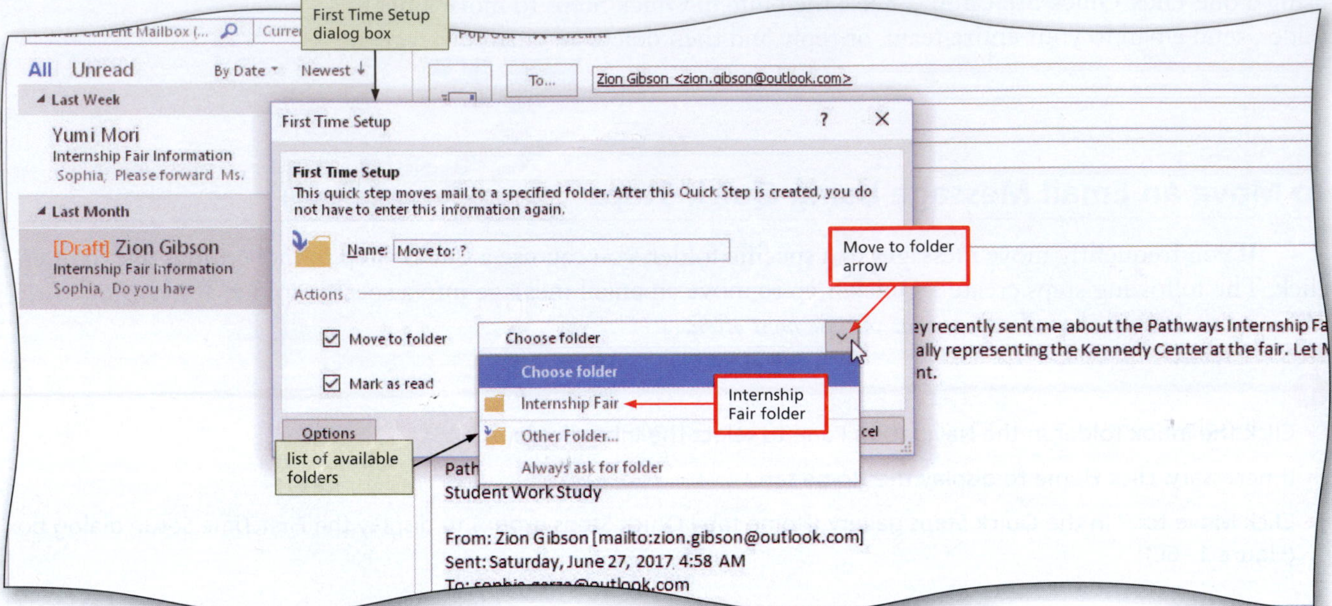

Figure 1–67

- Click the Internship Fair folder to create a Quick Step that moves a message to the specified folder.
- Click the Save button (First Time Setup dialog box) to save the Quick Step and display it in the Quick Steps gallery (Figure 1–68).

Q&A A Save button does not appear in my dialog box. What should I do?
Click the Finish button instead.

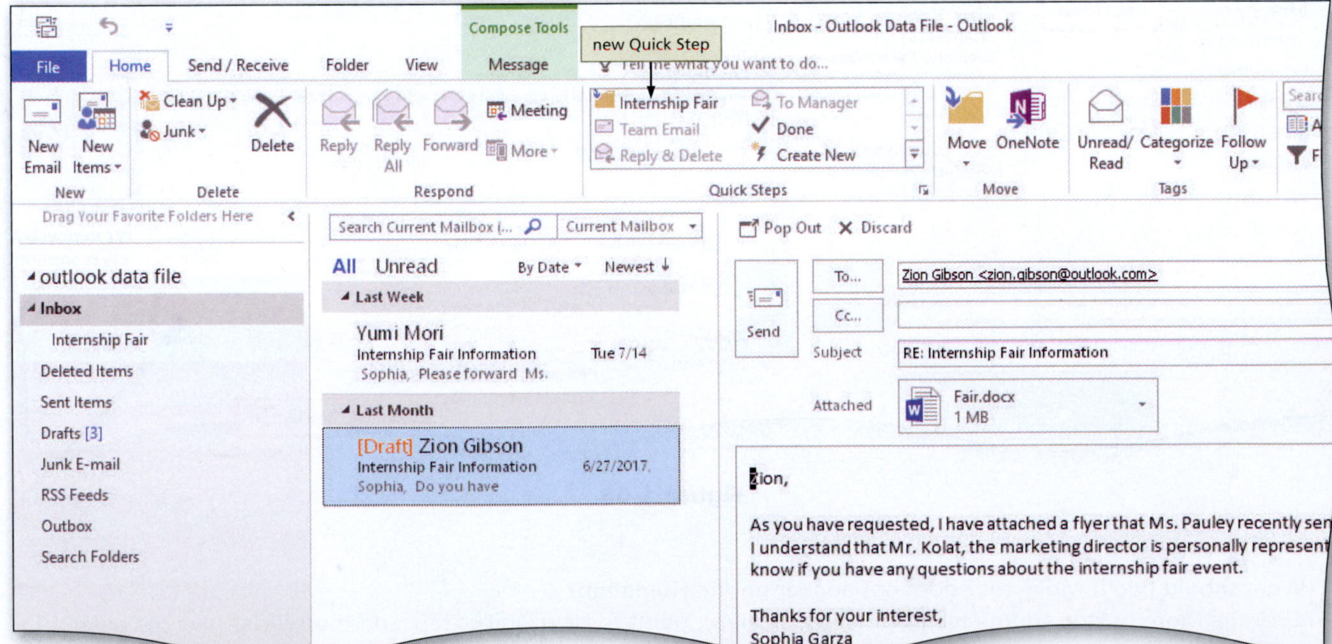

Figure 1–68

4

- In the Inbox folder, click the Yumi Mori message header in the Inbox message list to select the email message.
- Click Internship Fair in the Quick Steps gallery (Home tab | Quick Steps group) to move the message to the Internship Fair folder.
- In the Navigation Pane, click the Internship Fair folder to display its contents (Figure 1–69).

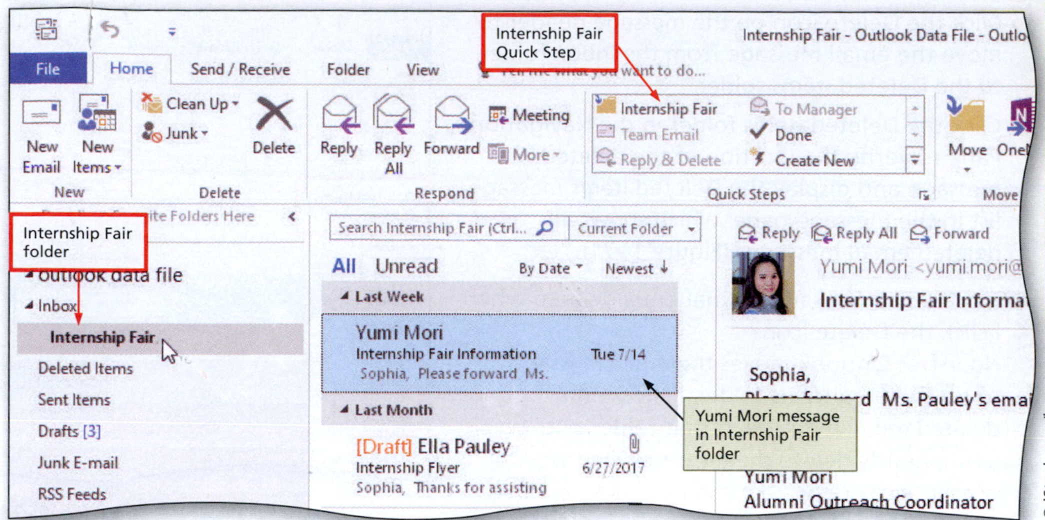

Figure 1–69

To Delete an Email Message

1 CONFIGURE ACCOUNT OPTIONS | 2 COMPOSE & SEND | 3 VIEW & PRINT | 4 REPLY
5 ATTACH FILE | 6 ORGANIZE MESSAGES

When you delete a message from a folder, Outlook moves the message from the folder to the Deleted Items folder. For example, Sophia no longer needs to keep the email message from Zion Gibson in the Inbox and has decided to delete it. The following steps delete an email message. ***Why?*** *Delete messages you no longer need so you do not exceed the limits of your mailbox.*

- Click the Inbox folder in the Navigation Pane to select the Inbox folder.
- Point to the Zion Gibson message header in the message list to display the Delete icon (Figure 1–70).

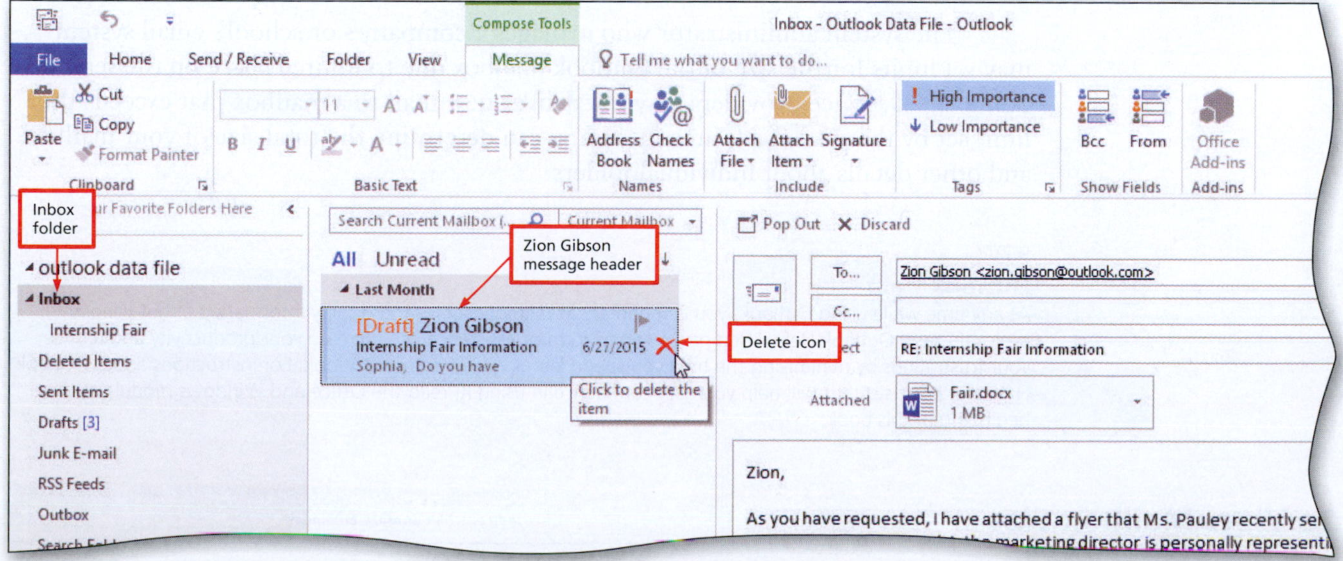

Figure 1–70

2

- Click the Delete icon on the message header to move the email message from the Inbox folder to the Deleted Items folder.
- Click the Deleted Items folder in the Navigation Pane to verify the location of the deleted message and display the Deleted Items message list in the message pane, which shows all deleted email messages (Figure 1–71).

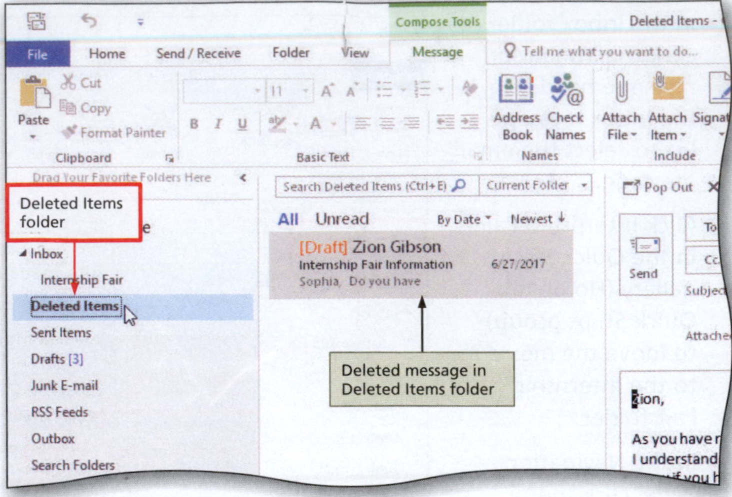

Figure 1–71

Q&A

Is the email message permanently deleted when I click the Delete icon?

No. After Outlook moves the email message to the Deleted Items folder, it stores the deleted email message in that folder until you permanently delete the message. One way to permanently delete a message is to select the Deleted Items folder to view its contents in the message pane and then select the item to be deleted. Click the Delete icon on the message header and then click the Yes button in the Microsoft Outlook dialog box to permanently delete the selected item from Outlook.

Other Ways

1. Drag email message to Deleted Items folder
2. Click email message, press DELETE
3. Click email message, press CTRL+D

CONSIDER THIS

How can you ignore future messages in an email thread?

- You can ignore future messages in an email thread through the Ignore Conversation feature. An **email thread** is a message that includes a running list of all the follow-up replies starting with the original email.
- Select an email message header that you no longer wish to view future messages and click the Ignore Conversation button (Home tab | Delete group) to delete this message as well as future messages within the email thread.

Working with the Mailbox

The system administrator who manages a company's or school's email system may set limits for the size of the Outlook mailbox due to limited space on the server. Some email service providers may not deliver new mail to a mailbox that exceeds the limit set by the system administrator. You can determine the total size of your mailbox and other details about individual folders.

BTW

Outlook Help

At any time while using Outlook, you can find answers to questions and display information about various topics through Outlook Help. Used properly, this form of assistance can increase your productivity and reduce your frustrations by minimizing the time you spend learning how to use Outlook. For instructions about Outlook Help and exercises that will help you gain confidence in using it, read the Office and Windows module at the beginning of this book.

1 CONFIGURE ACCOUNT OPTIONS | 2 COMPOSE & SEND | 3 VIEW & PRINT | 4 REPLY
5 ATTACH FILE | 6 ORGANIZE MESSAGES

To View Mailbox Size

The following steps view the amount of space available in the mailbox. ***Why?*** *You can determine if you are close to your mailbox size limit.*

1

- Click outlook data file in the Navigation Pane to select the mailbox.
- Click Folder on the ribbon to display the Folder tab (Figure 1–72).

Q&A What is the outlook data file in the Navigation Pane?
In this case, the outlook data file is the mailbox of Sophia Garza.

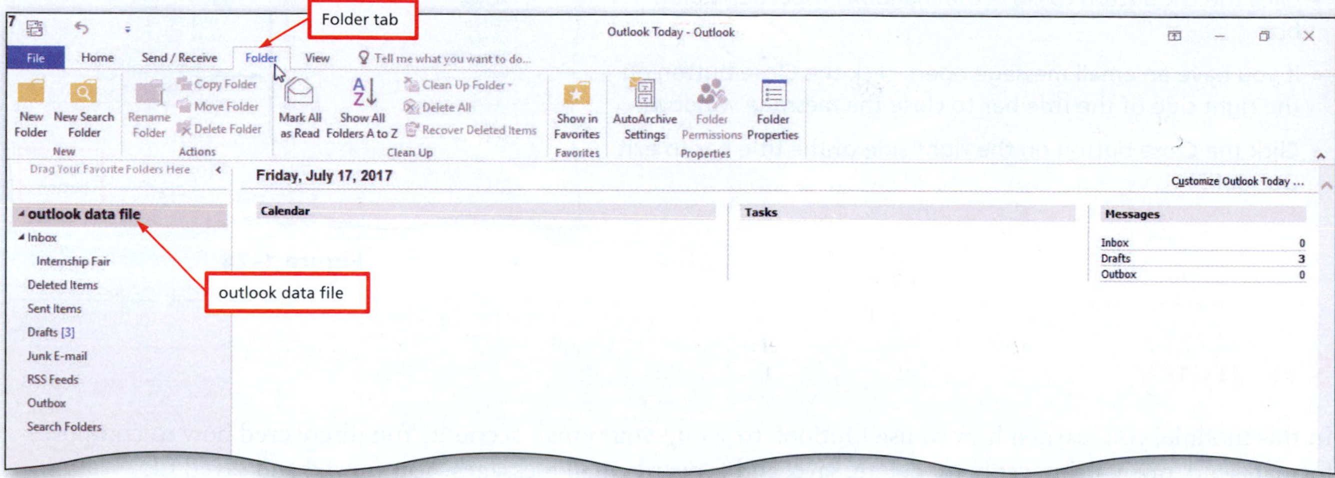

Figure 1–72

2

- Click the Folder Properties button (Folder tab | Properties group) to display the Properties dialog box for the mailbox (Figure 1–73).

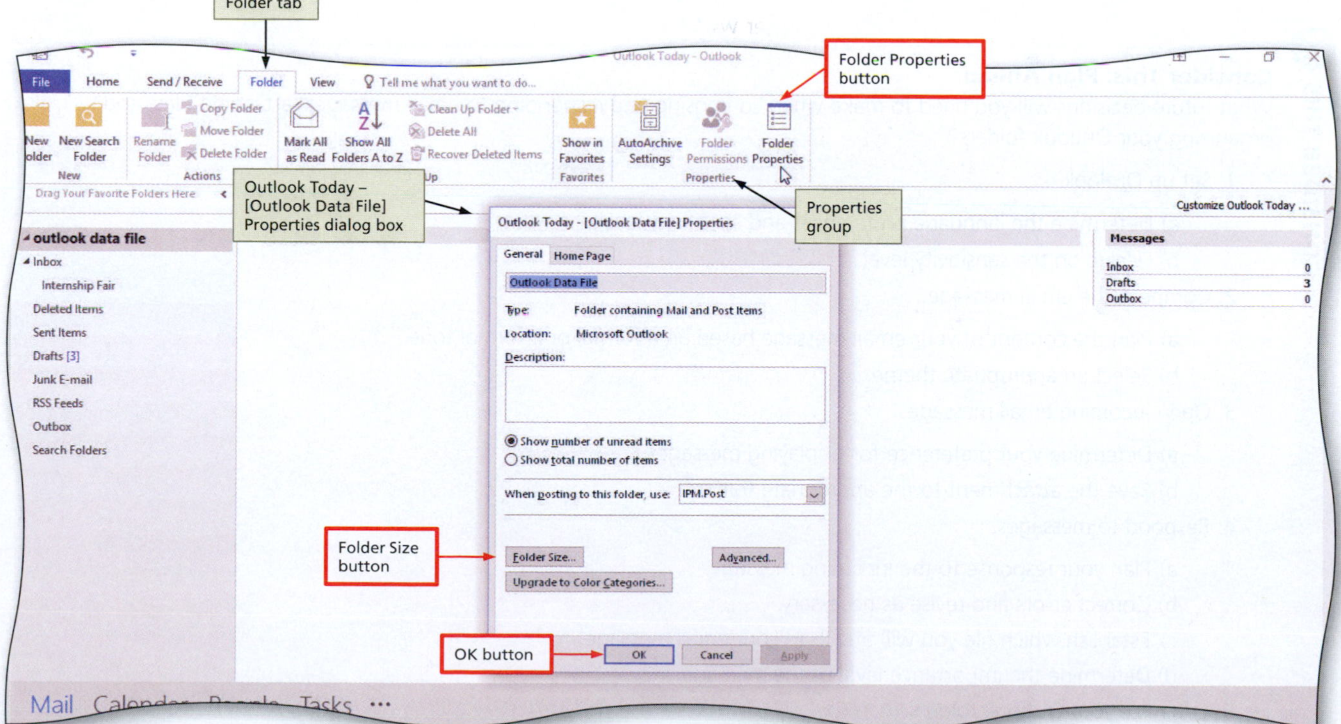

Figure 1–73

3

- Click the Folder Size button (mailbox Properties dialog box) to display the Folder Size dialog box (Figure 1–74).

4

- After viewing the folder sizes, click the Close button to close the Folder Size dialog box.
- Click the OK button to close the mailbox Properties dialog box.
- If you have an email message open, click the Close button on the right side of the title bar to close the message window.
- Click the Close button on the right side of the title bar to exit Outlook.

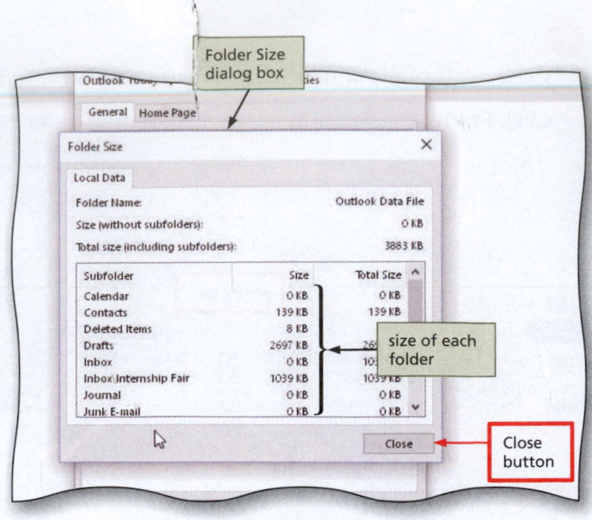

Figure 1–74

Summary

In this module, you learned how to use Outlook to set up your email account. You discovered how to compose, format, send, open, print, reply to, delete, save, and forward email messages. You viewed and saved file attachments and attached a file to an email message. You learned how to add a courtesy copy to an email message and set the sensitivity and importance of email messages. Finally, you created a folder in the Inbox and moved an email message to the new folder.

CONSIDER THIS

Consider This: Plan Ahead

What future decisions will you need to make when composing and responding to email messages, attaching files, and organizing your Outlook folders?

1. Set up Outlook.
   a) Determine the language preferences and sensitivity level.
   b) Decide on the sensitivity level.
2. Compose the email message.
   a) Plan the content of your email message based on a formal or informal tone.
   b) Select an appropriate theme.
3. Open incoming email messages.
   a) Determine your preference for displaying messages.
   b) Save the attachment to the appropriate folder.
4. Respond to messages.
   a) Plan your response to the incoming message.
   b) Correct errors and revise as necessary.
   c) Establish which file you will attach to your email message.
   d) Determine the importance level of the message.
5. Organize your Outlook folders.
   a) Establish your folder names.
   b) Plan where each email message should be stored.

CONSIDER THIS

How should you submit solutions to questions in the assignments identified with a ❋ symbol?

Every assignment in this book contains one or more questions with a ❋ symbol. These questions require you to think beyond the assigned file. Present your solutions to the question in the format required by your instructor. Possible formats may include one or more of these options: write the answer; create a document that contains the answer; present your answer to the class; discuss your answer in a group; record the answer as audio or video using a webcam, smartphone, or portable media player; or post answers on a blog, wiki, or website.

Apply Your Knowledge

Reinforce the skills and apply the concepts you learned in this module.

Note: To complete this assignment, you will be required to use the Data Files. Please contact your instructor for information about accessing the Data Files.

Creating an Email with an Attachment

Instructions: Run Outlook. You are to send an email message addressed to your instructor with information about the French Club's Spring Break trip to Saint Martin. You also attach an Excel workbook called Apply 1-1 School Trip, which is located in the Data Files.

Perform the following tasks:

1. Compose a new email message addressed to your instructor and add your own email address as a courtesy copy address.
2. Type `French Club Spring Break` as the subject of the email message.
3. Type `Greetings,` as the greeting line. Check spelling as you type.
4. Enter the text shown in Figure 1–75 for the message text.
5. Type `Thanks,` as the closing line.
6. Enter your name as the first signature line.
7. Type `French Club Publicity Manager` as the second signature line.
8. If requested by your instructor, type your personal cell phone number as the third signature line.
9. Attach the Excel workbook called Apply 1-1 School Trip, which is located in the Data Files, to the email message.
10. Click the File tab, and then click Save As. Save the message on your hard drive, OneDrive, or a location that is most appropriate to your situation using the file name Apply 1-1 French Club Trip.
11. Submit the email message in the format specified by your instructor.
12. Exit Outlook.
13. ❋ The attachment in the email message contained an Excel workbook. What file types are typically not allowed as a file attachment? Name at least two file types and explain why they are not allowed.

Continued >

Apply Your Knowledge *continued*

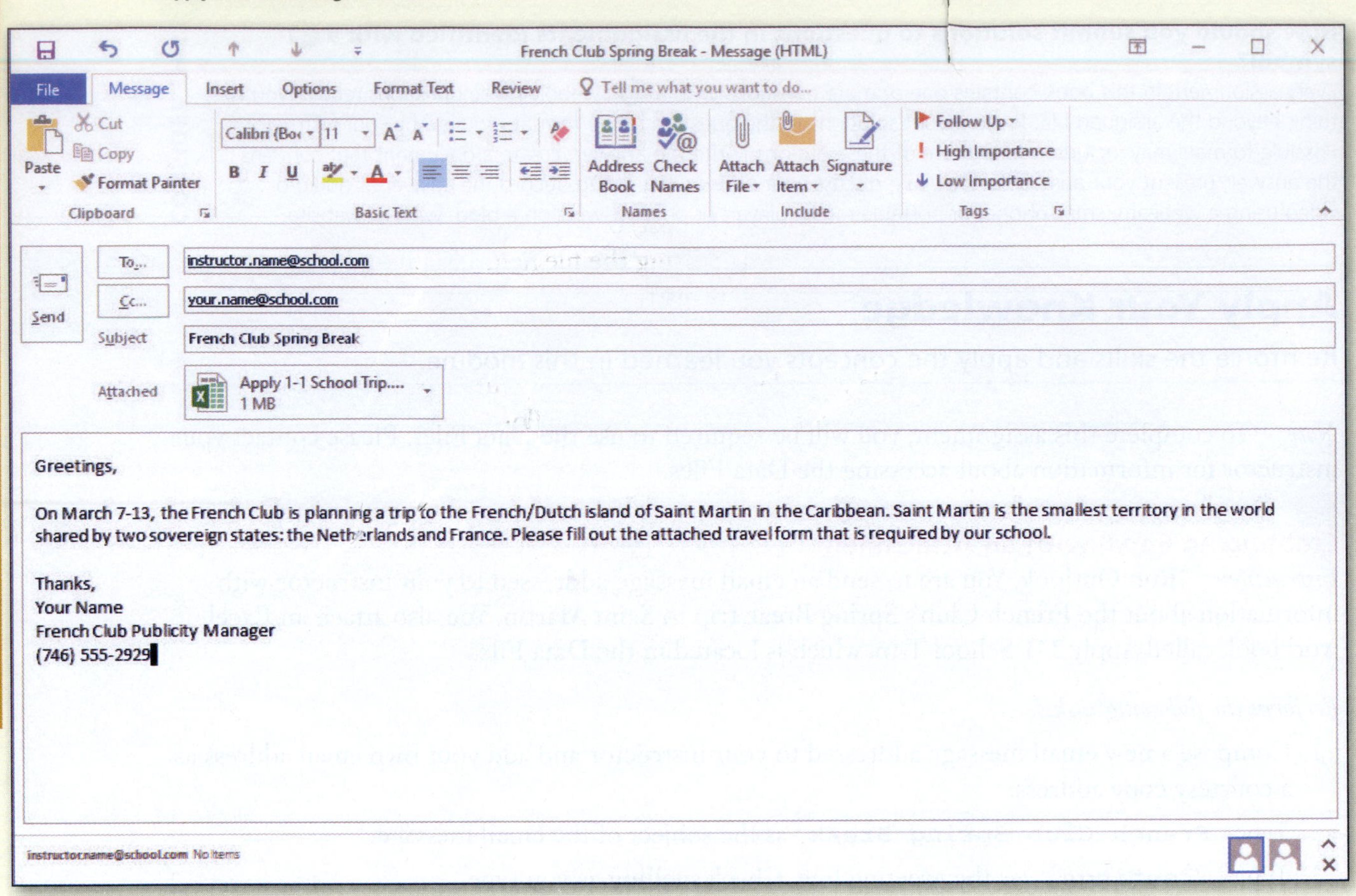

Figure 1–75

Extend Your Knowledge

Extend the skills you learned in this module and experiment with new skills. You may need to use Help to complete the assignment.

Organizing Email Messages

Note: To complete this assignment, you will be required to use the Data Files. Please contact your instructor for information about accessing the Data Files.

Instructions: Run Outlook. You are organizing a trip to Boston for you and your friends where you will participate as a group in an Escape Room activity and stay at a hostel. In the Extend 1-1.pst mailbox file, you will create two folders, add a folder in the Favorites section, and then move messages into the appropriate folders. You also will apply a follow-up flag for the messages in one of the folders. Use Outlook Help to learn how to duplicate a folder in the Favorites section, how to add a flag to a message for follow-up, and how to create an Outlook Data File (.pst file).

Perform the following tasks:

1. Open the Outlook mailbox file called Extend 1-1.pst, which is located in the Data Files.
2. Create two new folders within the Inbox folder. Name the first folder Escape Room and the second folder Hostels. Move the messages into the appropriate folders. Make sure that only mail items are contained in the new folders.
3. The Favorites section is at the top of the Folder Pane on the left. Display a duplicate of the Escape Room folder in the Favorites section.

4. Reply to the Boston Bay Hostel message indicating that you would like to book the hostel for the night of May 11. Sign your name to the email message. Assign high importance to the message.
5. Based on the message headers and content of the email messages in the Extend 1-1 mailbox, move each message to the appropriate folders you created. Figure 1–76 shows the mailbox with the messages moved to the new folders.
6. Export the Inbox mailbox to an Outlook Data File (.pst) on your hard drive, OneDrive, or a location that is most appropriate to your situation using the file name Extend 1-1 Boston.pst, and then submit it in the format specified by your instructor.
7. Exit Outlook.
8. Saving your mailbox as a .pst file provides a backup copy of your email messages to submit to your instructor. What are other reasons for saving your mailbox as a .pst file?

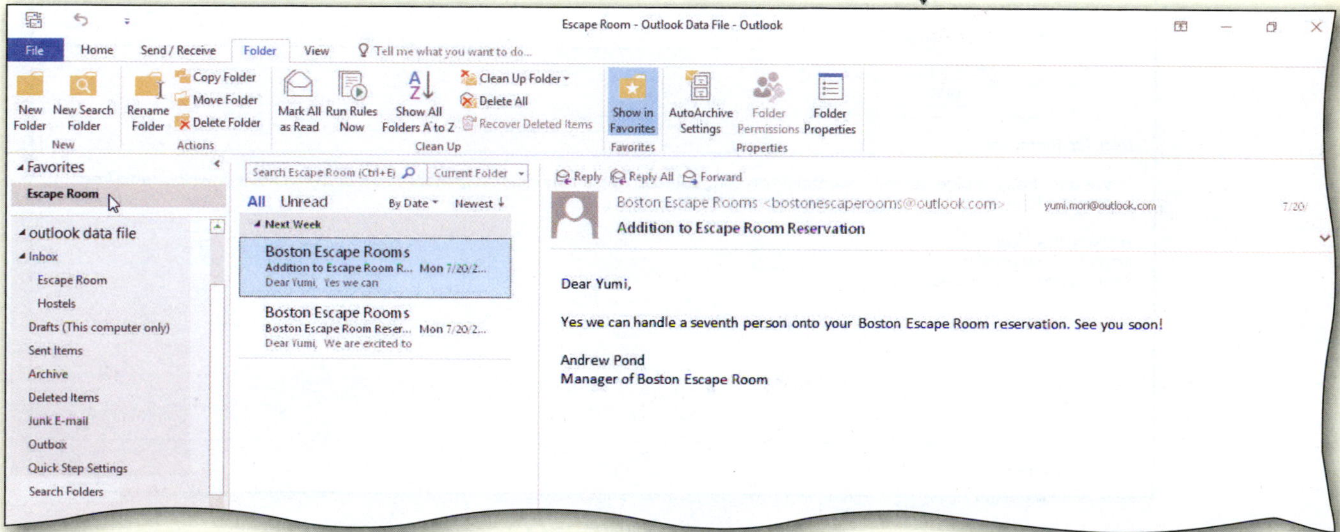

Figure 1–76

Expand Your World: Cloud and Web Technologies

Opening an Outlook.com Web-Based Email Message in the Outlook Client

Create a solution that uses cloud or web technologies by learning and investigating on your own from general guidance.

Note: To complete this assignment, you will be required to use the Data Files. Please contact your instructor for information about accessing the Data Files.

Instructions: In your Health class, you are presenting the topic, *Using a Health App to Track Your Workout*. Using Outlook, you compose an email message shown in Figure 1–77 and include a PowerPoint file attachment. Save the attachment from your outlook.com account to your OneDrive and edit the PowerPoint slides as a web app. Share the PowerPoint slides by providing a link to your OneDrive. Sharing files in the cloud as links can eliminate large attachments and saves email storage space.

Continued >

Expand Your World *continued*

Perform the following tasks:

1. If necessary, create a Microsoft account at outlook.com.
2. Compose a new email message from the client program, Outlook (not outlook.com). Address the email message to your Microsoft account with the message text shown in Figure 1–77. Select a theme of your choice. Replace the signature with your name and school name.

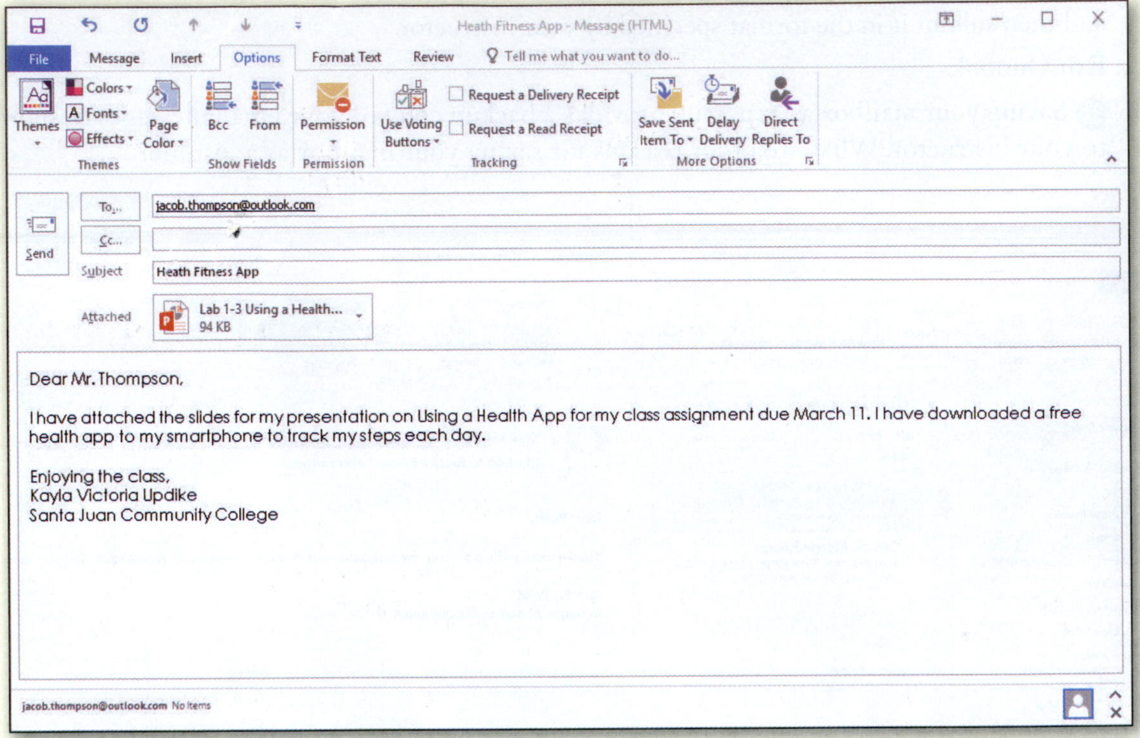

Figure 1–77

3. Attach the PowerPoint presentation called Lab 1-3 Using a Health App, which is located in the Data Files, to the email message.
4. Send the email message with high importance.
5. Open your Microsoft account at outlook.com. Open the email message that you sent from Outlook, click the attachment, and then click View online to view the PowerPoint file attachment.
6. Click Edit and Reply to edit the PowerPoint presentation in Microsoft PowerPoint Online.
7. If requested by your instructor, change the name on the first slide to your name on the first line and the name of your hometown on the second line.
8. Add a fourth slide to the PowerPoint presentation showing how far you have to walk to burn the calories in a typical slice of pizza. (*Hint:* Research this statistic on the web.)
9. Click the Insert tab, and then add a clip art image about walking to the fourth slide.
10. Click the File tab, and then click Share to share the PowerPoint file.
11. Click 'Share with people', and then type your instructor's email address and a short message describing how sharing a file by sending a link to your OneDrive can be easier than sending an attachment. Include your name at the end of the message.

12. Click the Share button to send the shared link of the completed PowerPoint file to your instructor.
13. Exit PowerPoint Online, and then exit Outlook.
14. In this exercise, you sent an email message from the Outlook client to your web-based email service provider at outlook.com. What are the advantages of using a Microsoft account with Outlook on your personal computer and checking the same email address at outlook.com when you are on a public computer?

In the Labs

Design, create, modify, and/or use files following the guidelines, concepts, and skills presented in this module. Labs 1 and 2, which increase in difficulty, require you to create solutions based on what you learned in the module; Lab 3 requires you to apply your creative thinking and problem-solving skills to design and implement a solution.

Lab 1: Composing an Email Message with Attachments

Note: To complete this assignment, you will be required to use the Data Files. Please contact your instructor for information about accessing the Data Files.

Problem: On a recent trip to Europe, your aunt took photos of castles using a digital camera. Because your aunt is new to technology, she asks you to extract the castle photos (provided in the Data Files) from her camera's memory card. She would like you to send them to her using email, because she is not on Facebook. Compose an email message to your aunt as shown in Figure 1–78 with the four picture attachments of castles.

Perform the following tasks:

1. Compose a new email message. Address the message to yourself with a courtesy copy to your instructor.
2. Enter the subject, message text, and signature shown in Figure 1–78. Insert blank lines where they are shown in the figure. If Outlook flags any misspelled words as you type, check their spelling and correct them.
3. Change the theme of the email message to the Integral theme.
4. If requested by your instructor, change the city and state from Zagreb, MN, to the city and state of your birth. Also change the signature to your name.
5. Attach the four image files called Lab 1-1 Castle1, Lab 1-1 Castle2, Lab 1-1 Castle3, and Lab 1-1 Castle4, which are located in the Data Files, to the email message.
6. Send the email message.
7. When you receive the message, open it, and then save the message on your hard drive, OneDrive, or a location that is most appropriate to your situation using the file name Lab 1-1 Castles. Submit the file in the format specified by your instructor.
8. Using one of your own email service providers, determine the maximum allowed mailbox size. Report the name of your email service provider, the maximum size, and whether you feel that is enough storage space.

Continued >

In the Labs *continued*

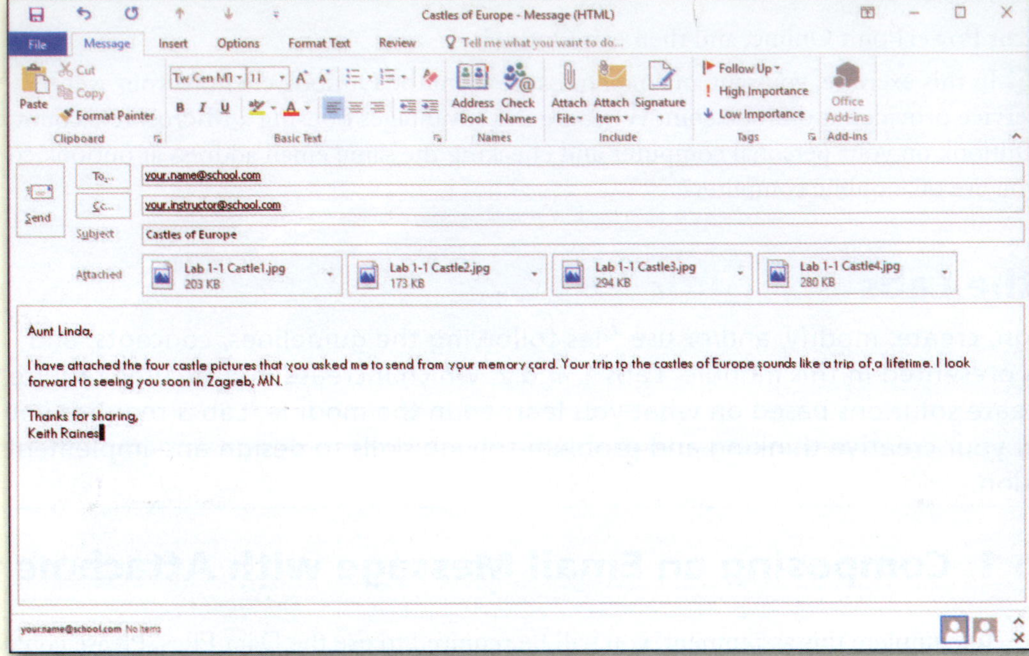

Figure 1–78

Lab 2: Composing and Replying to an Email Message

Problem: You recently moved into a new apartment. To turn on the electricity in your new apartment and place the bill in your name, you must fill out the request for electricity form. You need to send your completed form to the Compton Electric Company. First, you compose the email message shown in Figure 1–79a, and then you attach a file. Compton Electric Company responds to your email as shown in Figure 1–79b.

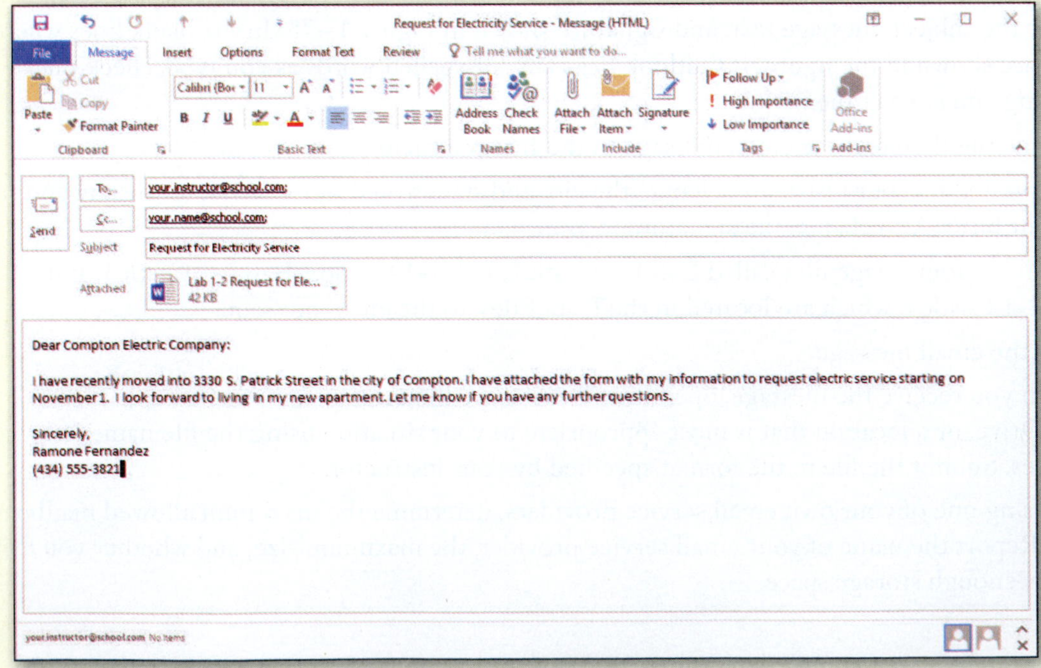

(a) Composed Email Message

Figure 1–79 (Continues)

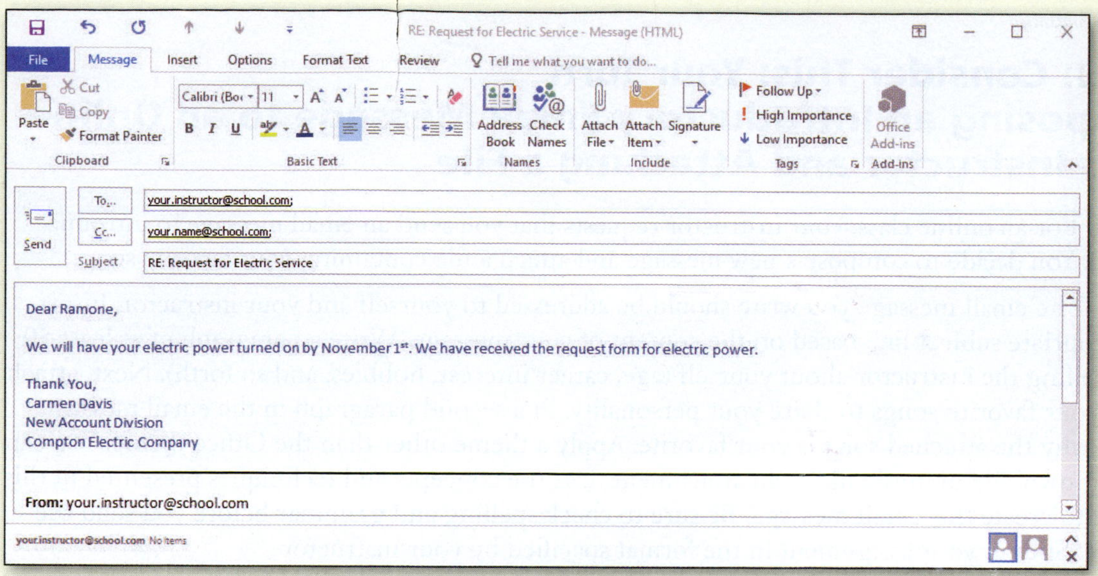

(b) Response to Email Message

Figure 1–79

Perform the following tasks:

1. Create a new email message. Address the message to your instructor with a courtesy copy to yourself.
2. Enter the subject, message text, and signature shown in Figure 1–79a. Check spelling and grammar.
3. If requested by your instructor, change the address in the email message to your own address.
4. Change the theme of the email message to the Slice theme.
5. Change the importance of this email to high importance because you would like to move in immediately.
6. Attach the document called Lab 1-2 Request for Electricity, which is located in the Data Files, to the email message. You do not need to fill out this form.
7. Send the email message and use the HTML format for the message.
8. When you receive the email message, move it to a new folder in your Inbox named Apartment.
9. Open the message in the Apartment folder, and then compose the reply. Figure 1–79b shows the reply from Compton Electric Company. Reply using the text in the email message shown in Figure 1–79b. If Outlook flags any misspelled words as you type, check their spelling and correct them.
10. If necessary, change the format of the email message to Plain Text, and then send the message to yourself.
11. When you receive the RE: Request for Electric Service message, move it to the Apartment folder in your Inbox folder.
12. Select the original Request for Electricity message in the Sent Items folder. Save the message on your hard drive, OneDrive, or a location that is most appropriate to your situation using the file name Lab 1-2 Electric. Submit the file in the format specified by your instructor.
13. Some company and utility websites do not include a phone number or a physical address. Why do you think that these business and utility sites only include an email address for correspondence?

Continued >

In the Labs *continued*

Lab 3: Consider This: Your Turn
Composing an Introductory Email Message to an Online Class Instructor and Attaching a File

Problem: For an online class, your instructor requests that you send an email message to introduce yourself. You decide to compose a new message and attach a file containing your favorite song.

Part 1: The email message you write should be addressed to yourself and your instructor. Insert an appropriate subject line based on the content of your message. Write a paragraph of at least 50 words telling the instructor about yourself (age, career interest, hobbies, and so forth). Next, attach one of your favorite songs to share your personality. In a second paragraph in the email message, explain why the attached song is your favorite. Apply a theme other than the Office theme. You can use your own digital music file as an attachment. Use the concepts and techniques presented in this module to create this email message. Be sure to check spelling and grammar before you send the message. Submit your assignment in the format specified by your instructor.

Part 2: You made several decisions while creating the email message in this assignment. When you decide on the subject of an email message, what considerations should you make? Why is it important that the email subject be eye-catching and informative? Why should you not use the following subject lines: FYI, Hey You, or Open This?

File Home Send / Receive Folder View Tell me what you want to do

2 Managing Calendars with Outlook

Objectives

You will have mastered the material in this module when you can:

- Describe the components of the Outlook Calendar
- Add a personal calendar to Outlook
- Add a city to the calendar Weather Bar list
- Navigate the calendar using the Date Navigator
- Display the calendar in various views
- Add national holidays to the default calendar
- Enter, save, move, edit, and delete appointments and events
- Organize your calendar with color categories
- Set the status of and a reminder for an appointment
- Import an iCalendar and view it in overlay mode
- Schedule and modify events
- Schedule meetings
- Respond to meeting requests
- Peek at a calendar
- Print a calendar
- Save and share a calendar

Managing Calendars with Outlook

This introductory module covers features and functions common to managing calendars in Outlook 2016.

Roadmap

In this module, you will learn how to perform basic calendar tasks. The following roadmap identifies general activities you will perform as you progress through this module:

1. CONFIGURE the CALENDAR OPTIONS
2. CREATE AND MANIPULATE APPOINTMENTS
3. SCHEDULE EVENTS
4. SCHEDULE MEETINGS
5. PRINT a CALENDAR
6. SAVE AND SHARE a CALENDAR

At the beginning of step instructions throughout the module, you will see an abbreviated form of this roadmap. The abbreviated roadmap uses colors to indicate module progress: gray means the module is beyond that activity, blue means the task being shown is covered in that activity, and black means that activity is yet to be covered. For example, the following abbreviated roadmap indicates the module would be showing a task in the Schedule Events activity.

1 CONFIGURE CALENDAR OPTIONS | 2 CREATE & MANIPULATE APPOINTMENTS | 3 SCHEDULE EVENTS
4 SCHEDULE MEETINGS | 5 PRINT CALENDAR | 6 SAVE & SHARE CALENDAR

Use the abbreviated roadmap as a progress guide while you read or step through the instructions in this module.

Introduction to the Outlook Calendar

Plan your day, keep track of your deadlines, and increase your daily productivity. Whether you are a student, club organizer, or business professional, you can take advantage of the Outlook Calendar to schedule and manage appointments, events, and meetings. In particular, you can use Calendar to keep track of your class schedule and appointments and to schedule meetings. If you are traveling and do not have electronic access to your calendar, you can print a copy to keep with you. You can use Outlook to view a daily, weekly, or monthly calendar.

In addition to using Calendar in your academic or professional life, you will find it helpful for scheduling personal time. Most people have multiple appointments to keep each day, week, or month. Calendar can organize activity-related information in a structured, readable manner. You can create a calendar folder for a specific project and share it with your friends and professional colleagues.

BTW
Using Calendars
You can share your calendar with others online using OneDrive to make appointments, check free times, schedule meetings, and refer to contact information. This is especially useful when you are arranging and syncing events that depend on other people's schedules.

Project — Appointments, Events, and Meetings in Calendar

By creating a daily time management schedule, you can stay organized and reduce your stress level. Managing your schedule using a calendar can increase productivity while maximizing free time. Outlook is the perfect tool to maintain both a professional and a personal schedule. The **Calendar** is the Outlook folder that contains your personal schedule of appointments, events, and meetings. In this project, Sophia Garza, the student work study employee for the Pathways Internship Office, sets up the basic features of Calendar to create her calendar for her appointments, classes, work schedules, and meetings (Figure 2–1).

People use a calendar to keep track of their schedules and to organize and manage their time. For students, a class list with room numbers and class times would be a good start toward managing their school schedule. For business professionals, the calendar is a dynamic tool that requires frequent updating to keep track of appointments and meetings. You also may want to keep track of personal items, such as doctor appointments, birthdays, and family gatherings.

BTW
Deleting Items Permanently
Items you delete, including events and email messages, are stored in the Deleted Items folder in Mail view until you empty the folder by right-clicking the Deleted Items folder and then clicking Empty Folder on the shortcut menu.

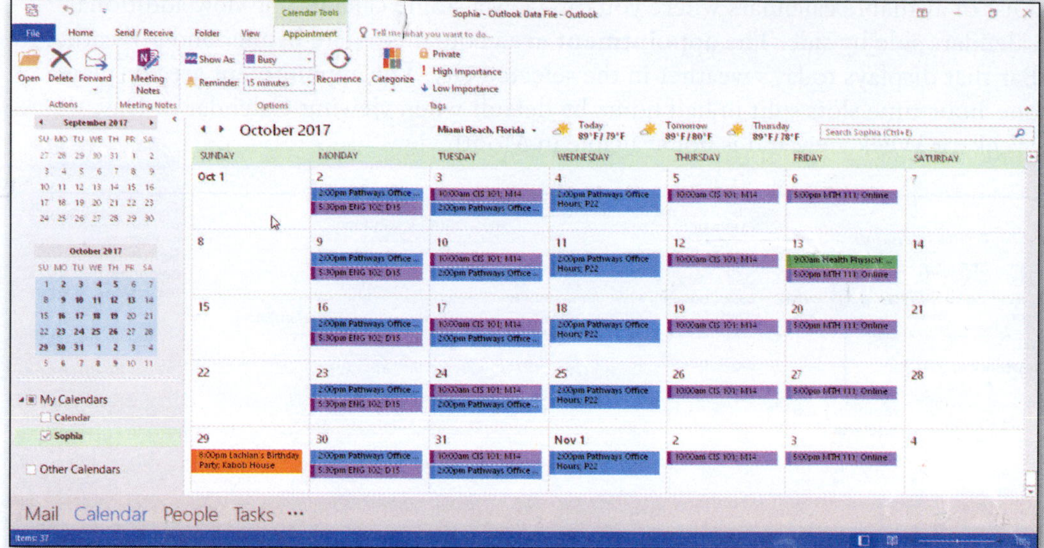

Figure 2–1

Configuring the Outlook Calendar

When you start Outlook, the Mail view appears. The Navigation bar displays four views — Mail, Calendar, People, and Tasks. You changed the Navigation bar icons to text in Module 1. By selecting Calendar, you can create a customized calendar to assist in scheduling your day, week, and month. Before scheduling your first calendar appointment, you can add a personal calendar and customize your settings to fit the way you work. Each day as you check your calendar for the day's events, the Weather Bar displays your local weather so you can plan whether you need an umbrella or take other weather precautions. By adding national holidays to your Outlook calendar, you can make sure these dates are prominent in your calendar.

BTW

The Ribbon and Screen Resolution

Outlook may change how the groups and buttons within the groups appear on the ribbon, depending on the computer's screen resolution. Thus, your ribbon may look different from the ones in this book if you are using a screen resolution other than 1366 × 768.

CONSIDER THIS

What advantages does a digital calendar like Outlook provide compared to a paper planner or wall calendar?

A digital calendar provides access from any location by synching your computer or smartphone with the cloud to view your appointments and meetings. You can view your schedule within an email meeting invitation. You can view more than one calendar at a time, share others' calendars, and overlay calendars to plan a meeting date with colleagues.

Calendar Window

The Calendar - Outlook Data File - Microsoft Outlook window shown in Figure 2–2 includes a variety of features to help you work efficiently. It contains many elements similar to the windows in other Office programs, as well as some that are unique to Outlook. The main elements of the Calendar window are the Navigation Pane and the appointment area.

The Navigation Pane includes two panes: the Date Navigator and the My Calendars pane. The **Date Navigator** includes the present month's calendar and the future month's calendar in Figure 2–2. The calendar displays the current month with a blue box around the current date, scroll arrows to advance from one month to another, and any date on which an item is scheduled in bold. The **My Calendars pane** includes a list of available calendars where you can view a single calendar or view additional calendars side by side. The **appointment area** contains a date banner and a Weather Bar that displays today's weather in the selected city. The appointment area displays one-hour time slots split in half hours by default when viewing Calendar in Day, Work Week, or Week view and is not available in Month view.

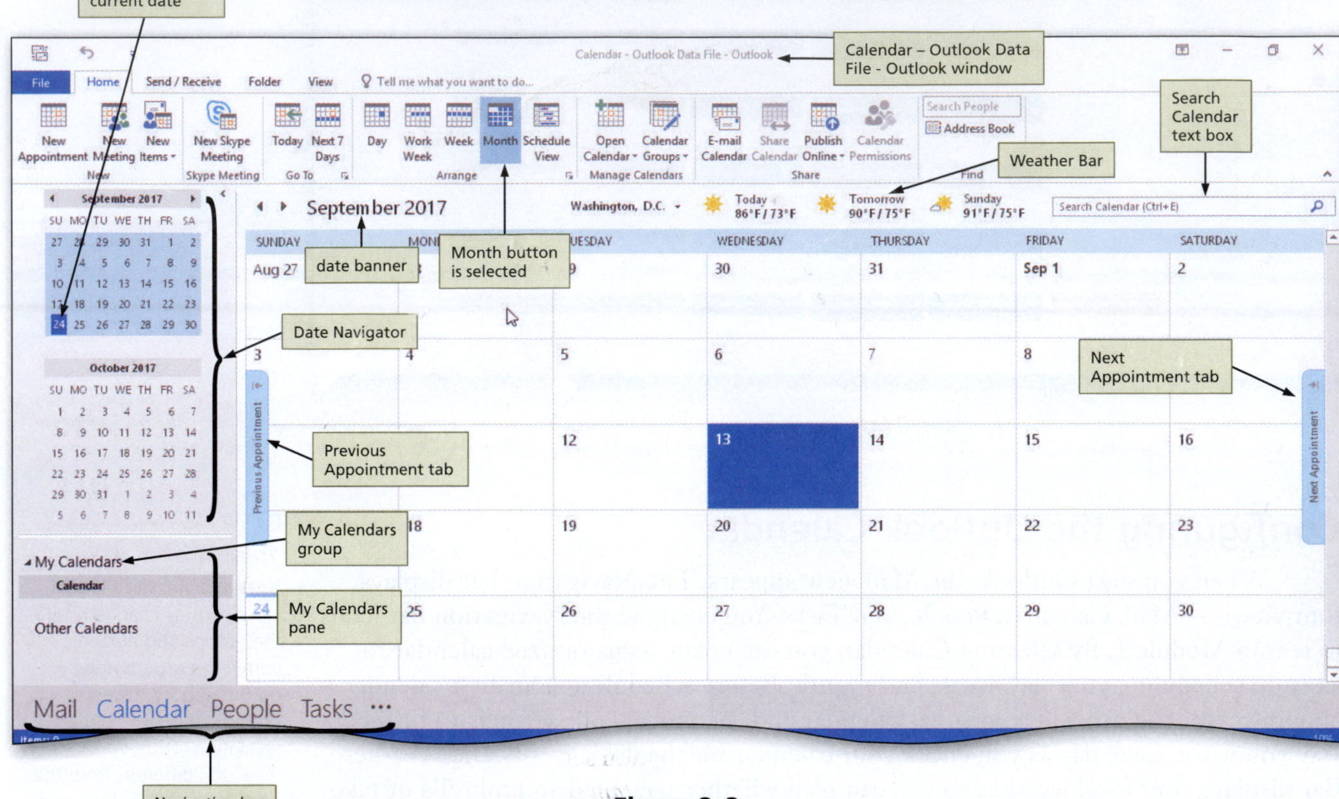

Figure 2–2

Calendar Items

An **item** is any element in Outlook that contains information. Examples of calendar items include appointments, events, and meetings. All calendar items start as an appointment. Outlook defines an **appointment**, such as a doctor's appointment, as an activity that does not involve other people or resources, such as conference rooms. Outlook defines an **event**, such as a seminar or vacation, as an activity that occurs at least once and lasts 24 hours or longer. An appointment becomes an event when you schedule it for the entire day. An annual event, such as a birthday, anniversary, or holiday, occurs yearly on a specific date. Events do not occupy time slots in the appointment area and, instead, are displayed in a banner below the day heading when viewing the calendar in Day, Work Week, or Week view. An appointment becomes a **meeting** when people and other resources, such as meeting rooms, are invited.

When you create items on your calendar, it is helpful to show your time using the appointment status information. You set the appointment status for a calendar item using the Show As button, which provides four options for showing your time on the calendar: Free, Tentative, Busy, and Out of Office. For example, if you are studying or working on a project, you might show your time as busy because you are unable to perform other tasks at the same time. On the other hand, a dental appointment or a class would show your time as Out of Office because you need to leave your home or office to attend. Table 2 – 1 describes the items you can schedule on your calendar and the appointment status option associated with each item. Each calendar item also can be one-time or recurring.

BTW

Searching for Calendar Items

To find a calendar item, click the Search *Calendar Name* text box, and then type a word or phrase in the calendar item you are seeking. Items that contain the text you typed are listed with the search text highlighted. When you are finished, click the Close Search button (Search Tools Search tab | Close group).

Table 2–1 Calendar Items

Calendar Item	Description	Show as Default
One-time appointment	Default calendar item, involves only your schedule and does not invite other attendees or require resources such as a conference room	Busy
Recurring appointment	Occurs at regular intervals, such as weekly, biweekly, monthly, or bimonthly	Busy
One-time event	Occurs at least once and lasts 24 hours or longer, such as a vacation or conference	Free
Recurring event	Occurs at regular intervals, such as weekly, biweekly, monthly, or bimonthly, such as holidays	Free
One-time meeting	Includes people and other resources, such as meeting rooms	Busy
Recurring meeting	Occurs at regular intervals, such as weekly, biweekly, monthly, or bimonthly, such as staff meetings or department meetings	Busy

To Create a Calendar Folder

1 CONFIGURE CALENDAR OPTIONS | 2 CREATE & MANIPULATE APPOINTMENTS | 3 SCHEDULE EVENTS | 4 SCHEDULE MEETINGS | 5 PRINT CALENDAR | 6 SAVE & SHARE CALENDAR

When you schedule an appointment, Outlook adds the appointment to the Calendar folder by default. Sophia Garza plans to keep track of her work study business tasks at the job at the Pathways Internship Office as well as her personal and academic items instead of creating separate calendars for every aspect of her life. Users often create multiple calendars to keep personal items separate from academic or business items. As in other Outlook folders, such as the Inbox, you can create multiple folders within the Calendar folder that each contains one or more calendars. The following steps create a calendar to store your personal and school-related information separate from your default Calendar within the same calendar group. ***Why?*** *In certain situations, you may need to keep more than one calendar, such as one for business items and another for personal items.*

- Run Outlook 2016.
- Click Calendar on the Navigation bar to display the Outlook Calendar.
- Click Folder on the ribbon to display the Folder tab (Figure 2–3).

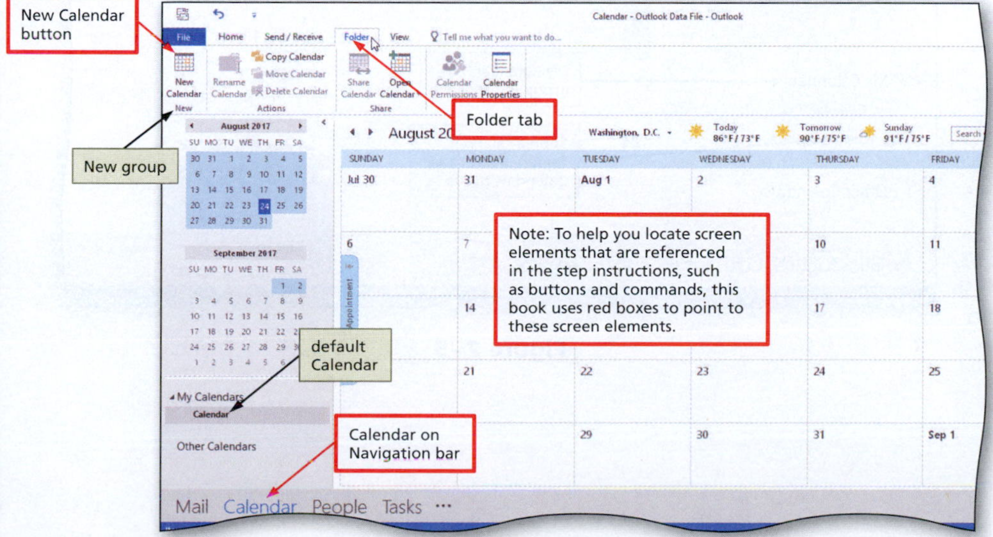

Figure 2–3

For an introduction to Office and instructions about how to perform basic tasks in Office apps, read the Office and Windows module at the beginning of this book, where you can learn how to run an app, use the ribbon, save a file, open a file, exit an app, use Help, and much more.

One of the few differences between Windows 8 and Windows 10 occur in the steps to run Outlook. If you are using Windows 8, scroll the Start screen and then click the Outlook 2016 tile.

BTW

Outlook and Screen Resolution

If you are using a computer or mobile device to step through the project in this module and you want your screens to match the figures in this book, you should change your screen's resolution to 1366 x 768. For information about how to change a computer's resolution, refer to the Office and Windows module at the beginning of this book.

2

- Click the New Calendar button (Folder tab | New group) to display the Create New Folder dialog box.
- Type `Sophia` in the Name text box (Create New Folder dialog box) to enter a name for the new folder.
- Click the Folder contains arrow button to display a list of items the folder will contain.
- If necessary, click Calendar Items to specify what the folder will contain.
- If necessary, click Calendar in the 'Select where to place the folder' list to specify where the folder will be stored (Figure 2–4).

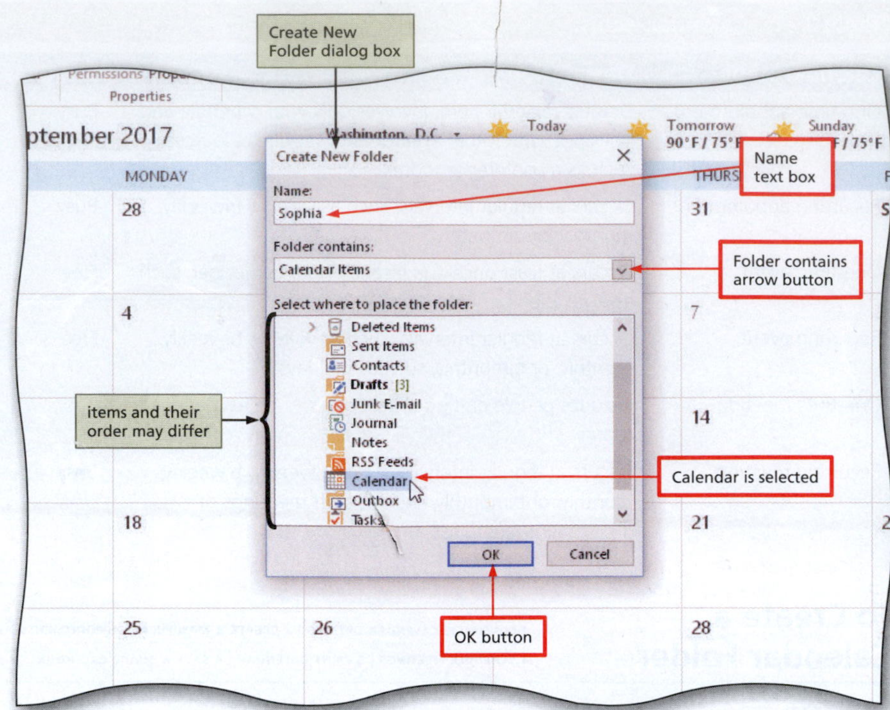

Figure 2–4

3

- Click the OK button to close the Create New Folder dialog box and add the new folder to the My Calendars group (Figure 2–5).

Q&A

Why is the named Sophia calendar not displayed in the Outlook window?
Outlook does not automatically display the newly created calendar until you select it.

I received an error message indicating that calendars cannot be created in Exchange ActiveSync accounts. What should I do?
Use a browser to sign into your email account at outlook.com. Use the Calendar feature at outlook.com to create a calendar. Restart Outlook 2016. After syncing, the new calendar should appear in Outlook 2016.

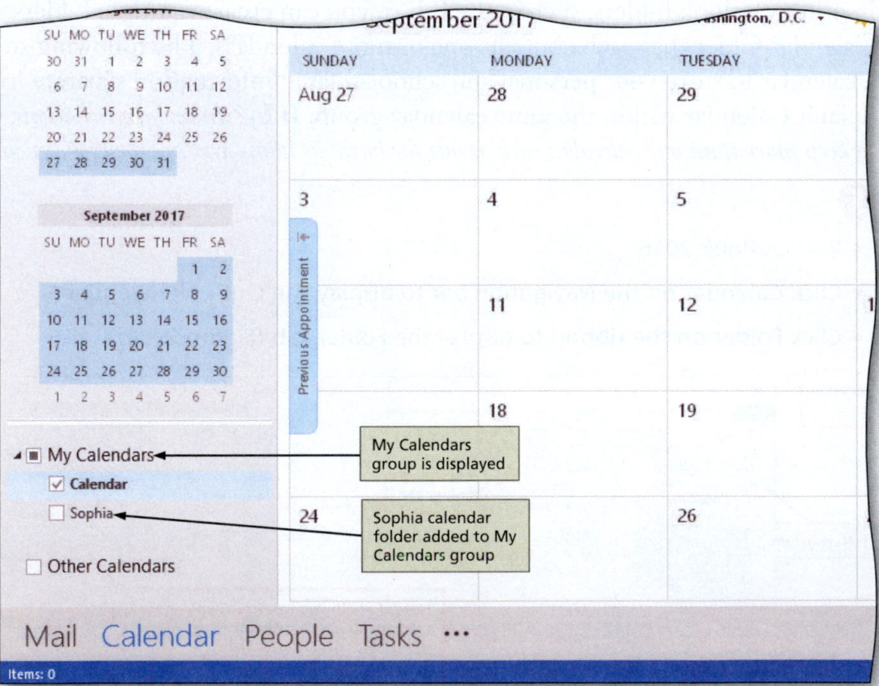

Figure 2–5

4

- In the My Calendars pane, click Sophia to insert a check mark in the check box, so that both the default Calendar and the Sophia calendars are selected and displayed in the appointment area of the Outlook window (Figure 2–6).

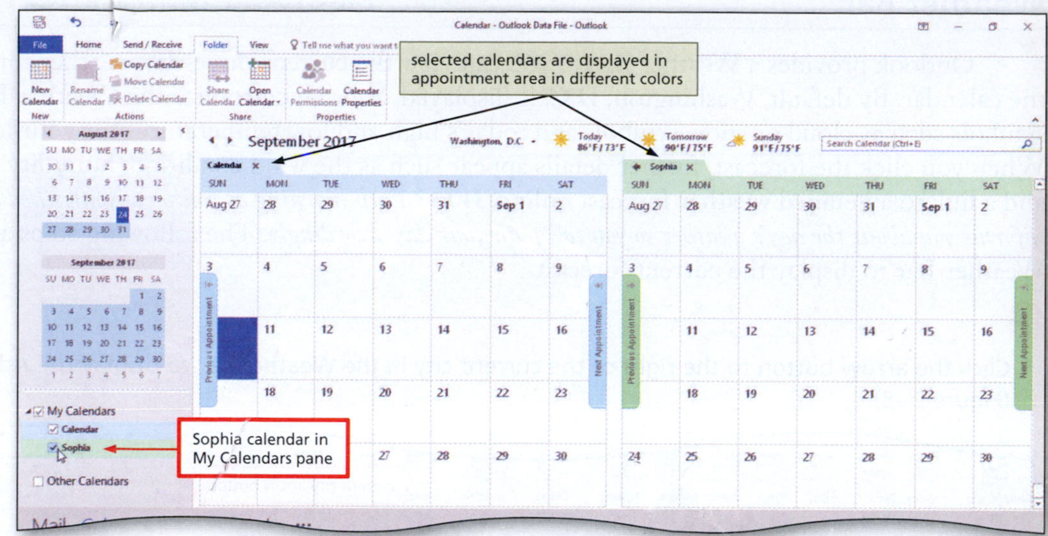

Figure 2–6

Q&A Why is the default calendar displayed in a different color from Sophia's calendar?
Outlook automatically assigns a different color to each new calendar you create to make it easier to distinguish one calendar from the other. Your calendar colors might be different from those shown in Figure 2–6.

Can I select a color for the calendar?
Yes. Click the View tab, click the Color button (View tab | Color group), and then select a color from the Color gallery.

5

- Click Calendar in the My Calendars pane to remove the check mark from the Calendar check box so that the default calendar no longer is displayed in the appointment area (Figure 2–7).

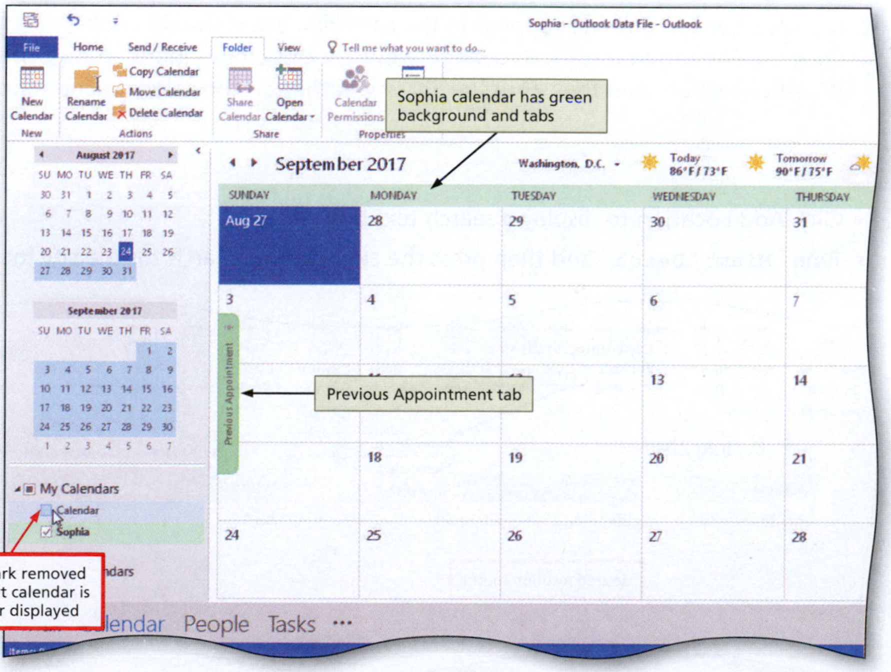

Q&A Why does my view look different from what is shown?
Figure 2–7 shows Month view, which is the default view for Calendar. If this is not the current view, click the Month button (Home tab | Arrange group).

What is the purpose of the colored tabs on each side of the appointment area?
The tabs are for navigating to the previous and next appointments.

Sophia calendar has green background and tabs
Previous Appointment tab
check mark removed so default calendar is no longer displayed

Figure 2–7

Other Ways

1. Press CTRL+SHIFT+E

To Add a City to the Calendar Weather Bar

Outlook provides a Weather Bar so you can view the current three-day weather forecast when you open the calendar. By default, Washington, D.C. is displayed. You can customize the Weather Bar to display weather symbols such as cloud or snow symbols and today's high and low temperatures for your local weather conditions. When you click the forecast, further details appear such as the wind condition, humidity level, precipitation, and a link to a detailed weather forecast online. ***Why?*** *Each morning as you view your schedule, the Weather Bar informs you about the day's weather so you can plan your day accordingly.* The following steps add a city to the calendar Weather Bar to display the current forecast.

- Click the arrow button to the right of the current city in the Weather Bar to display the Add Location command (Figure 2–8).

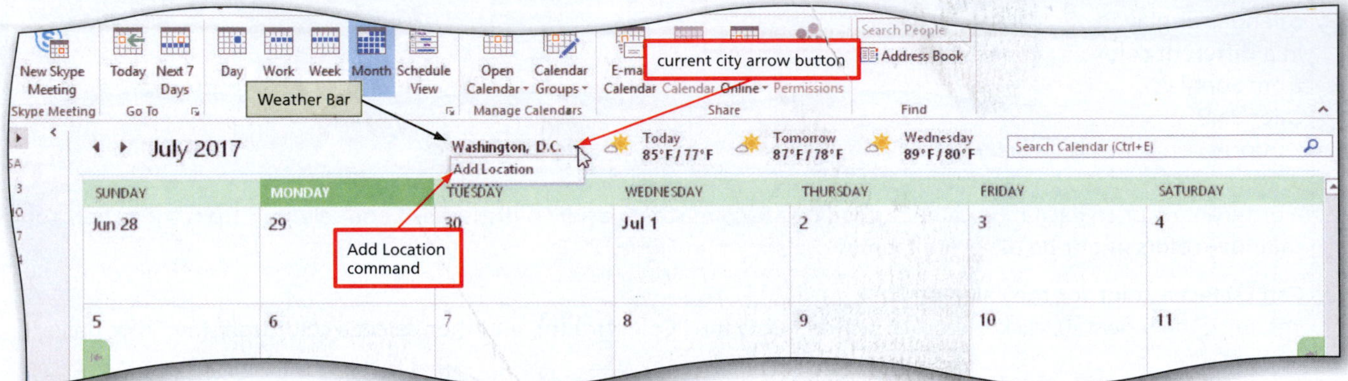

Figure 2–8

Q&A My Weather Bar does not appear in the calendar. What should I do?
Click the File tab to display Backstage View, click Options, and then click the Calendar category. Scroll down to the Weather section, and then click the Show weather on the calendar check box to insert a check mark.

- Click Add Location to display a search text box.
- Type **Miami Beach** and then press the ENTER key to search for the city location (Figure 2–9).

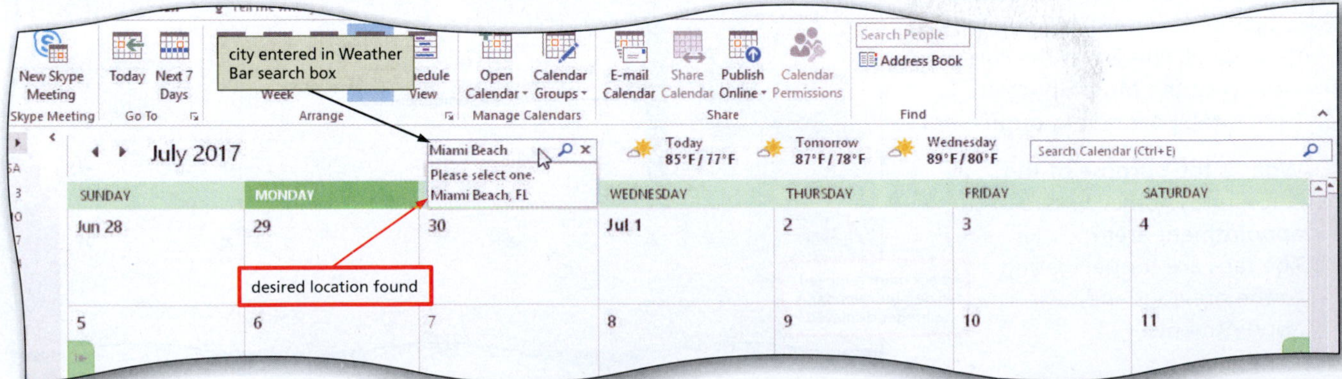

Figure 2–9

Q&A Can I search for a city using a postal code?
Yes. Type the postal code to search for the location in the Weather Bar search text box.

3

- Click Miami Beach, FL to select the location and display its three-day forecast in the Weather Bar.
- If requested by your instructor, replace Miami Beach, FL with your hometown in the Weather Bar (Figure 2–10).

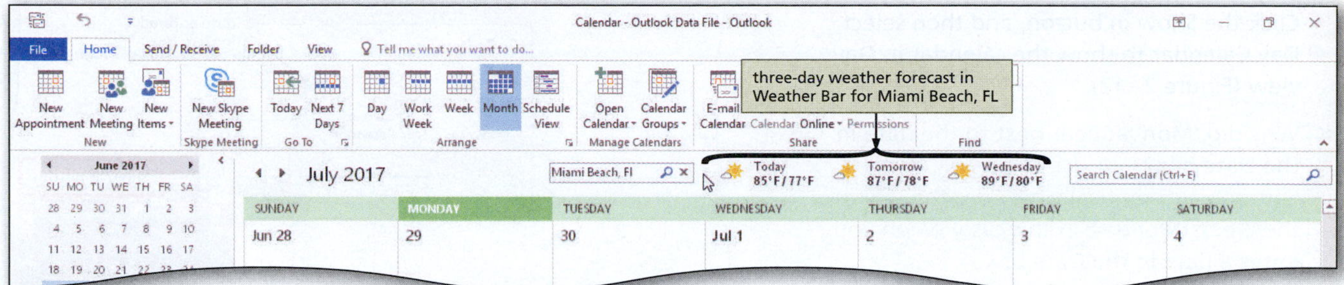

Figure 2–10

Q&A

Why does my Weather Bar display the message 'Weather service is not available'?

Most likely, you are not connected to the Internet. You must have Internet connectivity to display the weather forecast.

For an introduction to Windows and instructions about how to perform basic Windows tasks, read the Office and Windows module at the beginning of this book, where you can learn how to resize windows, change screen resolution, create folders, move and rename files, use Windows Help, and much more.

Navigating the Calendar

Each Microsoft Outlook folder displays the items it contains in a layout called a view. The **calendar view** is the arrangement and format of the folder contents by day, work week, week, month, or schedule, which is a horizontal layout. Recall that the default view of the Calendar folder is Month view. Some people prefer a different view of their calendar, such as weekly or daily. For instance, you might want to view all the items for a day at one time, in which case Day view would work best. Although the Outlook window looks different in each view, you can accomplish the same tasks in each view: you can add, edit, or delete appointments, events, and meetings.

To Go to a Specific Date

1 CONFIGURE CALENDAR OPTIONS | 2 CREATE & MANIPULATE APPOINTMENTS | 3 SCHEDULE EVENTS
4 SCHEDULE MEETINGS | 5 PRINT CALENDAR | 6 SAVE & SHARE CALENDAR

To display a date that is not visible in the current view so that you can view that date in the appointment area, one option is to use the Go to Date Dialog Box Launcher. The following steps display a specific date in the appointment area in a calendar. ***Why?** Rather than scrolling through your calendars in Outlook to find a specific date, you can quickly find a date in Outlook by using the Go To Date dialog box.*

1

- Click Home on the ribbon to display the Home tab.
- Click the Go to Date Dialog Box Launcher (Home tab | Go To group) to display the Go To Date dialog box (Figure 2–11).

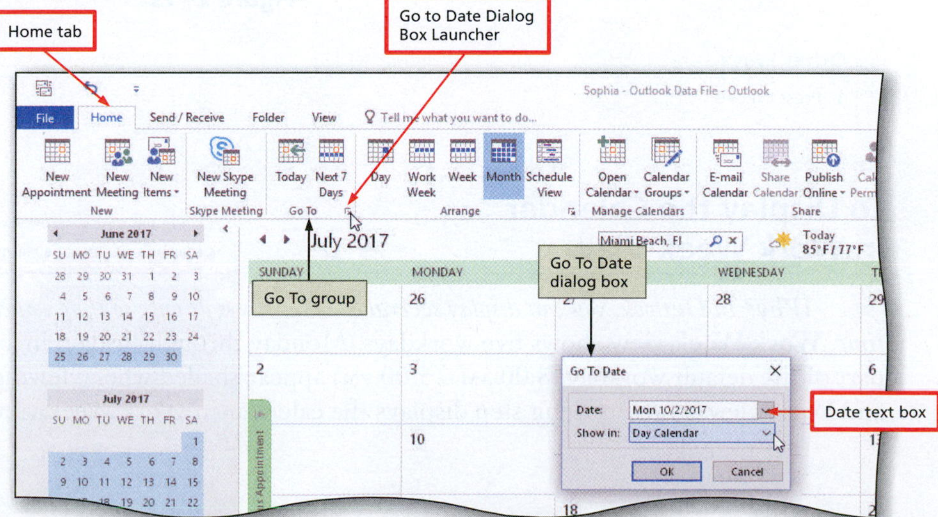

Figure 2–11

- Type `10/2/2017` in the Date text box to enter the date you want to display in the current calendar.
- Click the Show in button, and then select Day Calendar to show the calendar in Day view (Figure 2–12).

Q&A Why did 'Mon' appear next to the date in the Date box?
Outlook automatically includes the day of the week (Monday, in this case) when you enter a date in the Date box.

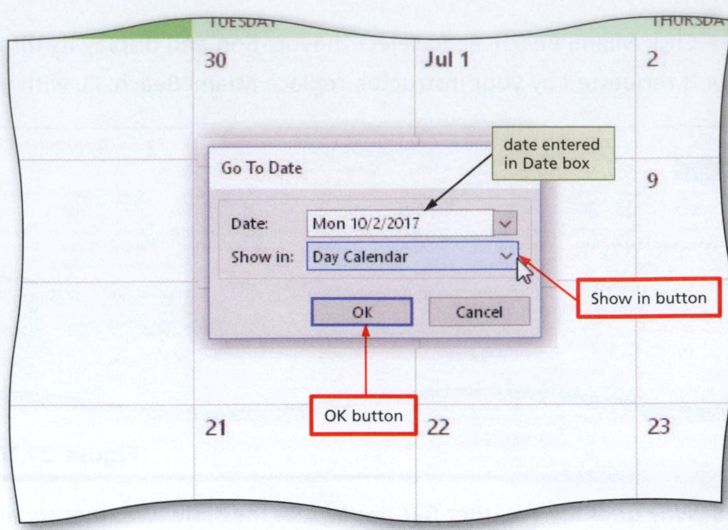

Figure 2–12

- Click the OK button to close the Go To Date dialog box and display the selected date in Day view (Figure 2–13).

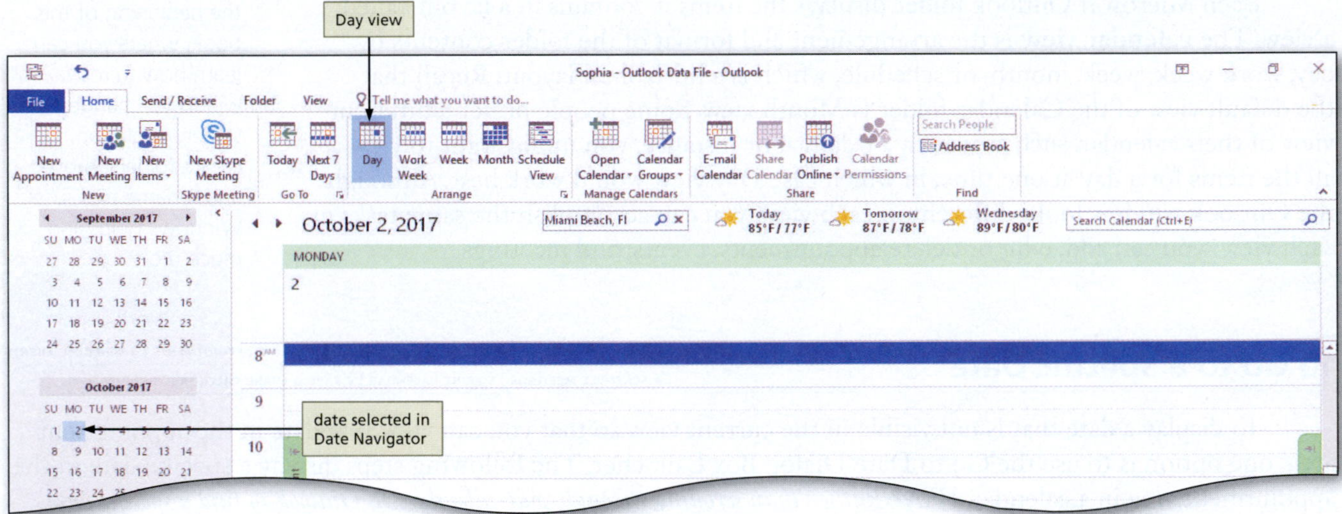

Figure 2–13

Other Ways

1. Press CTRL+G

To Display the Calendar in Work Week View

1 CONFIGURE CALENDAR OPTIONS | 2 CREATE & MANIPULATE APPOINTMENTS | 3 SCHEDULE EVENTS
4 SCHEDULE MEETINGS | 5 PRINT CALENDAR | 6 SAVE & SHARE CALENDAR

Why? In Outlook, you can display several calendar days at once so that you can see multiple appointments at the same time. **Work Week view** shows five workdays (Monday through Friday) in a columnar style. Hours that are not part of the default workday (8:00 AM – 5:00 PM) appear shaded when viewing the calendar in Day, Work Week, and Week view. The following step displays the calendar in Work Week view.

- Click the Work Week button (Home tab | Arrange group) to display the work week in the appointment area for the selected date (Figure 2–14).

Experiment

- Scroll up and down in Work Week view to see how the color changes to reflect hours outside the default workday.

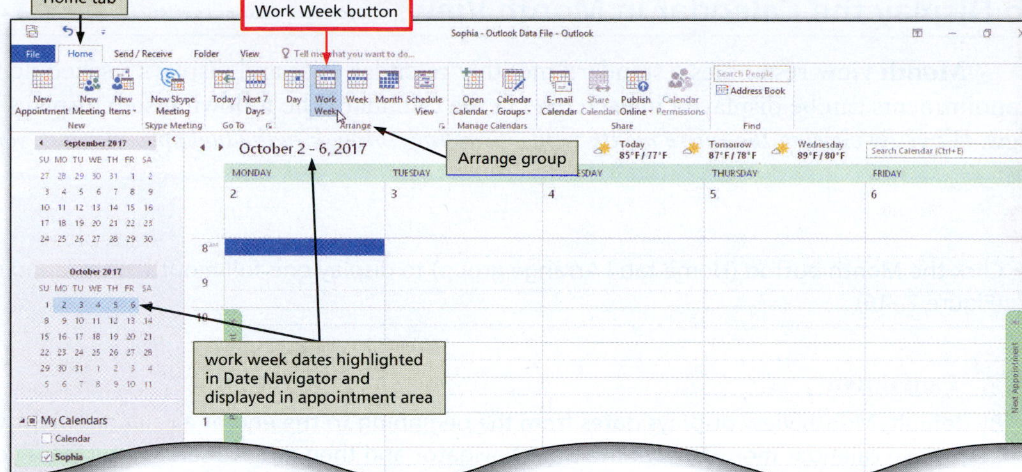

Figure 2–14

Q&A Why is Monday through Friday highlighted on the Date Navigator?

The calendar days displayed in the appointment area are highlighted on the Date Navigator.

Other Ways

1. Press CTRL+ALT+2

To Display the Calendar in Week View

1 CONFIGURE CALENDAR OPTIONS | 2 CREATE & MANIPULATE APPOINTMENTS | 3 SCHEDULE EVENTS
4 SCHEDULE MEETINGS | 5 PRINT CALENDAR | 6 SAVE & SHARE CALENDAR

***Why?** The advantage of displaying a calendar in Week view is to see how many appointments are scheduled for any given week, including weekends.* In **Week view**, the seven days of the selected week appear in the appointment area. The following step displays the calendar in Week view.

- Click the Week button (Home tab | Arrange group) to display the full week, including weekends, in the appointment area (Figure 2–15).

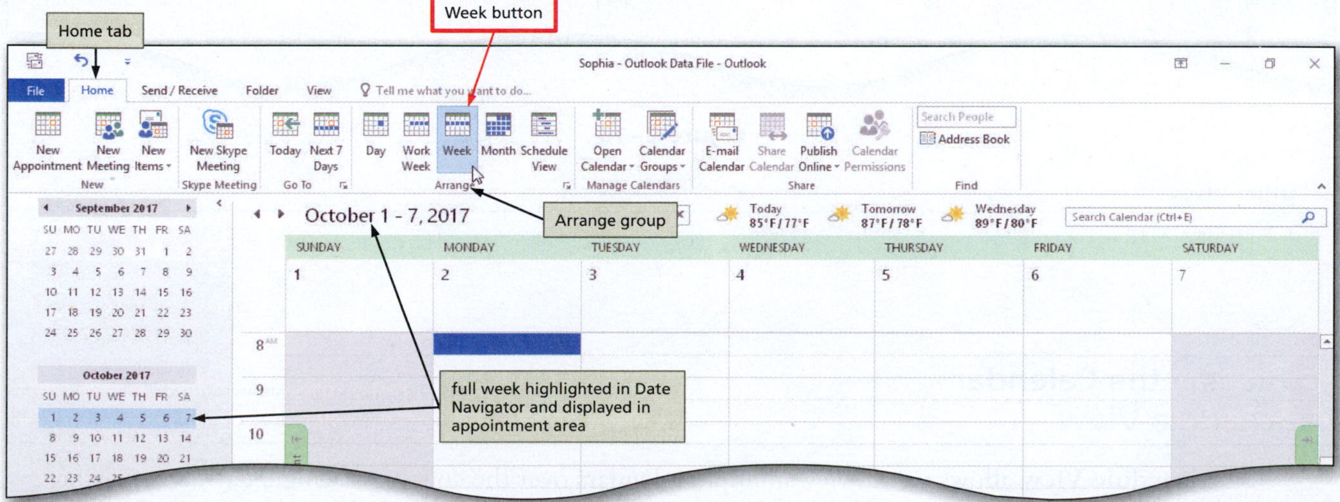

Figure 2–15

Other Ways

1. Press CTRL+ALT+3

To Display the Calendar in Month View

1 CONFIGURE CALENDAR OPTIONS | 2 CREATE & MANIPULATE APPOINTMENTS | 3 SCHEDULE EVENTS
4 SCHEDULE MEETINGS | 5 PRINT CALENDAR | 6 SAVE & SHARE CALENDAR

Month view resembles a standard monthly calendar page and displays a schedule for an entire month. Appointments can be displayed in each date in the calendar. The following step displays the calendar in Month view. ***Why?*** *By viewing the entire month without scrolling through individual appointments, you can see when you have an open day.*

- Click the Month button (Home tab | Arrange group) to display one full month in the appointment area (Figure 2–16).

Experiment

- By default, Month view displays dates from the beginning to the end of a calendar month. To select several weeks across two calendar months, click the Date Navigator and then drag to select the weeks you want to view.

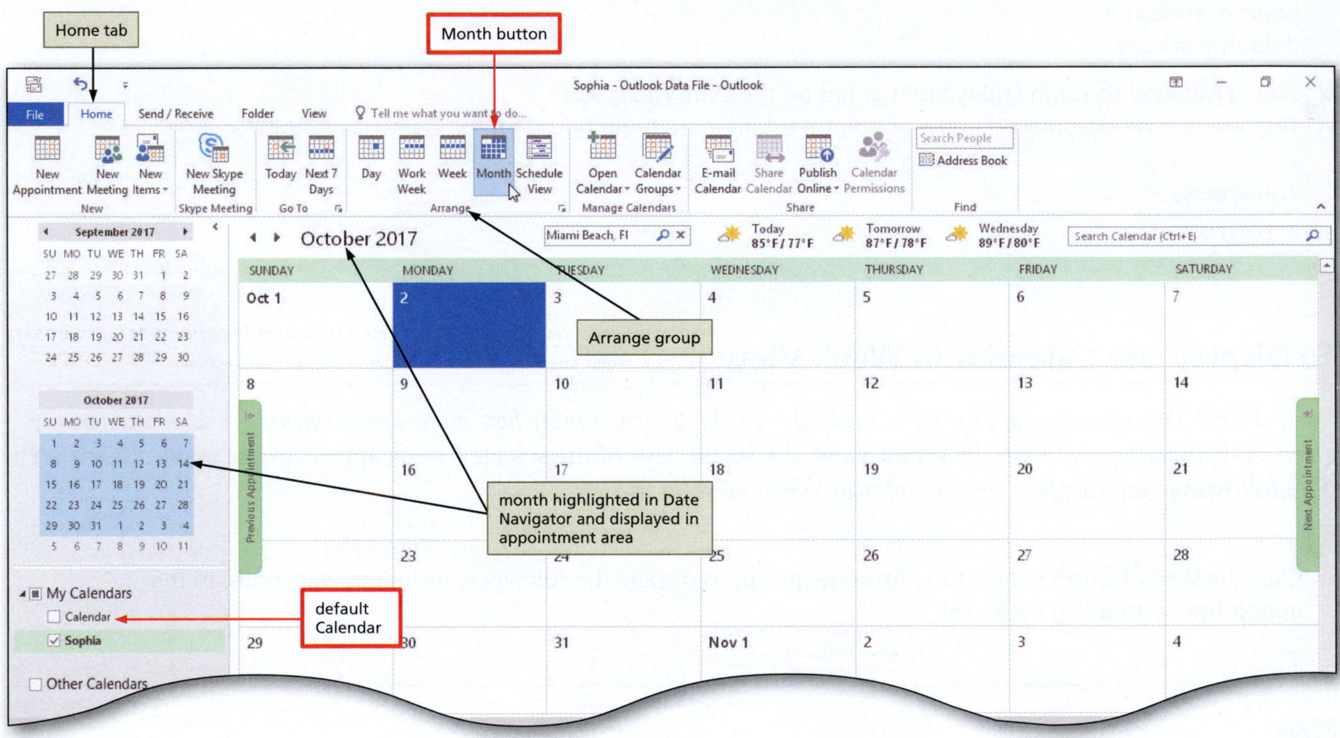

Figure 2–16

Other Ways

1. Press CTRL+ALT+4

To Display the Calendar in Schedule View

1 CONFIGURE CALENDAR OPTIONS | 2 CREATE & MANIPULATE APPOINTMENTS | 3 SCHEDULE EVENTS
4 SCHEDULE MEETINGS | 5 PRINT CALENDAR | 6 SAVE & SHARE CALENDAR

The **Schedule View** allows you to view multiple calendars over the course of a single day in a horizontal layout to make scheduling meetings easier. The following steps display the default Calendar and the Sophia calendar in Schedule View. ***Why?*** *Schedule View is useful when trying to see multiple calendars so that you can check for overlapping items.*

1

- Click Calendar (default Calendar) in the My Calendars pane to insert a check mark in the check box and to display both the default Calendar and Sophia's calendar in the appointment area (Figure 2–17).

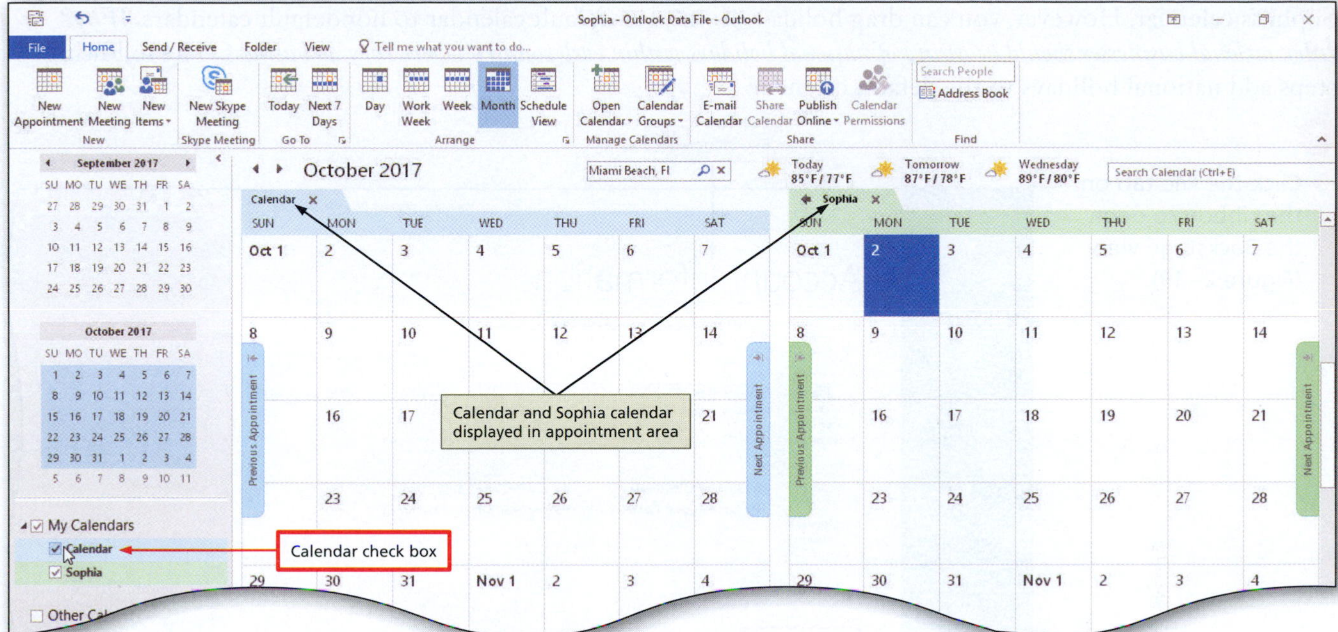

Figure 2–17

Q&A Why are both calendars displayed in Month view?
Outlook uses the view of the existing calendar for a newly displayed calendar. In this case, Sophia's calendar was displayed in Month view, so the default Calendar also is displayed in Month view.

2

- Click the Schedule View button (Home tab | Arrange group) to display both calendars in Schedule View (Figure 2–18).

Q&A Why does Schedule View show a single day instead of multiple days?
Schedule View displays one day at a time.

What does the dark blue shaded area in the calendar represent?
The dark blue shaded area represents the time slot selected in Day view.

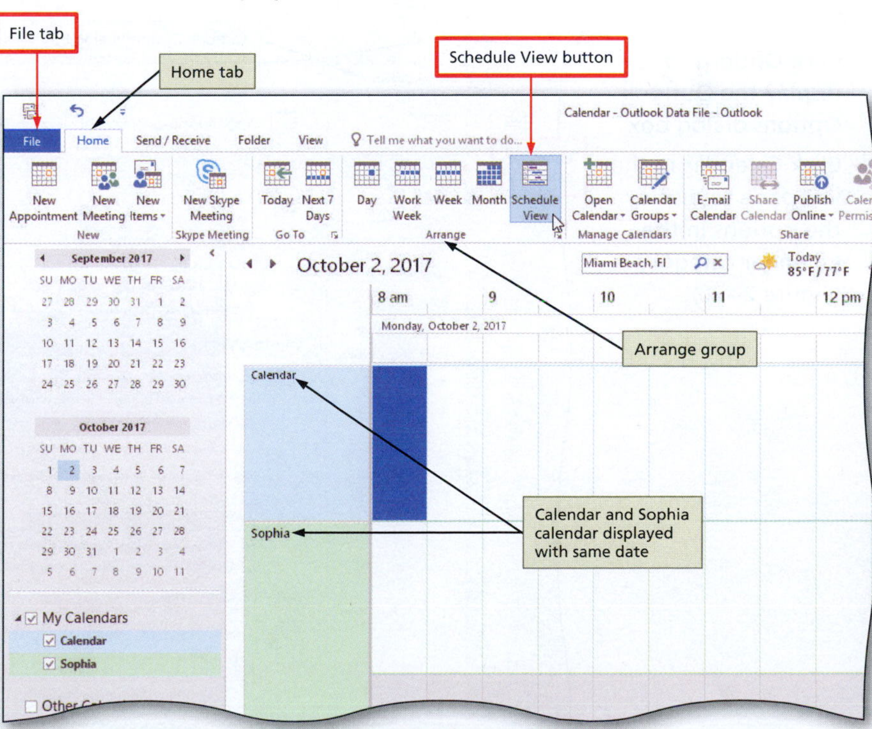

Figure 2–18

Other Ways

1. Press CTRL+ALT+5

To Add Holidays to the Default Calendar

Before you add appointments to a calendar, you can mark the standard holidays for one or more countries. You can add holidays to your default calendar folder only, not to a public folder or nondefault calendar such as Sophia's calendar. However, you can drag holidays from your default calendar to nondefault calendars. ***Why?*** *International businesses should be aware of national holidays within each country where they do business.* The following steps add national holidays to the default calendar.

- Click the File tab on the ribbon to open the Backstage view (Figure 2–19).

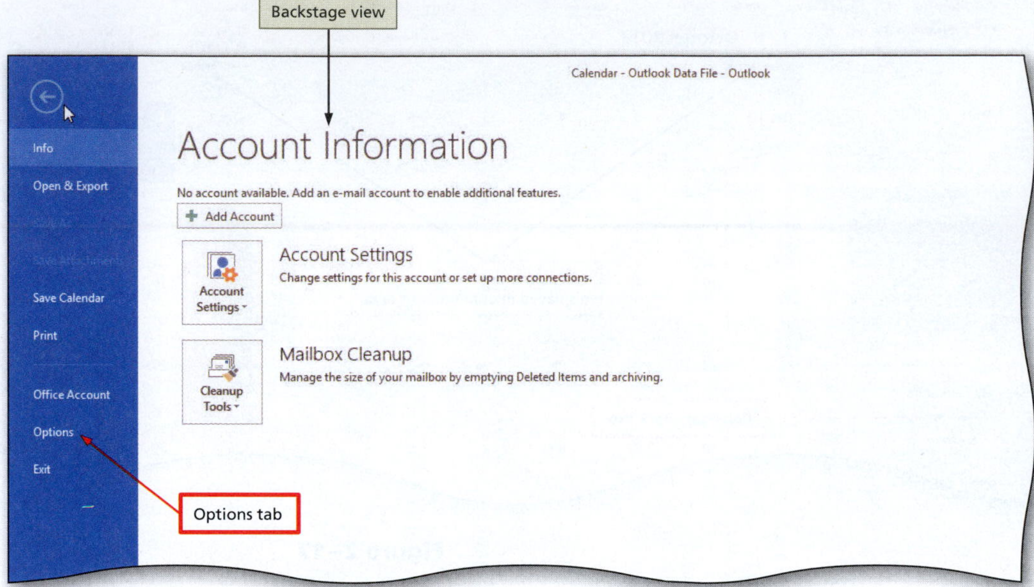

Figure 2–19

- Click Options to display the Outlook Options dialog box.
- Click Calendar in the left pane to display the options in the Calendar category (Figure 2–20).

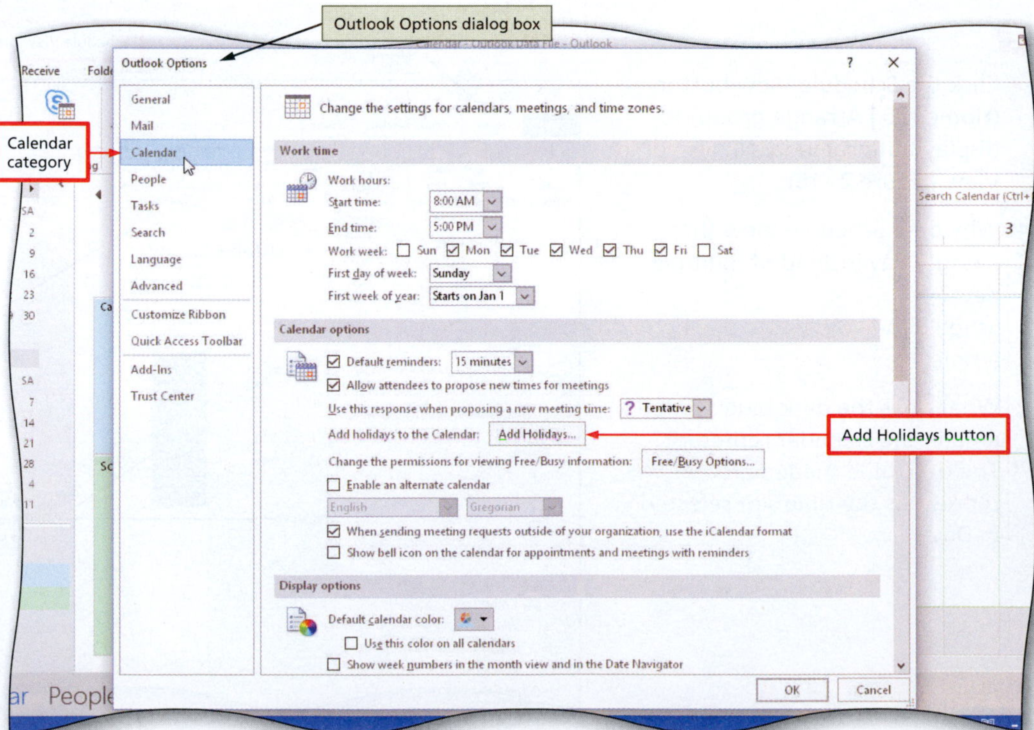

Figure 2–20

3

- Click the Add Holidays button to display the Add Holidays to Calendar dialog box (Figure 2–21).

Q&A Can I select multiple countries to display more than one set of national holidays?
Yes. You can select the holidays of multiple countries to display in the default calendar.

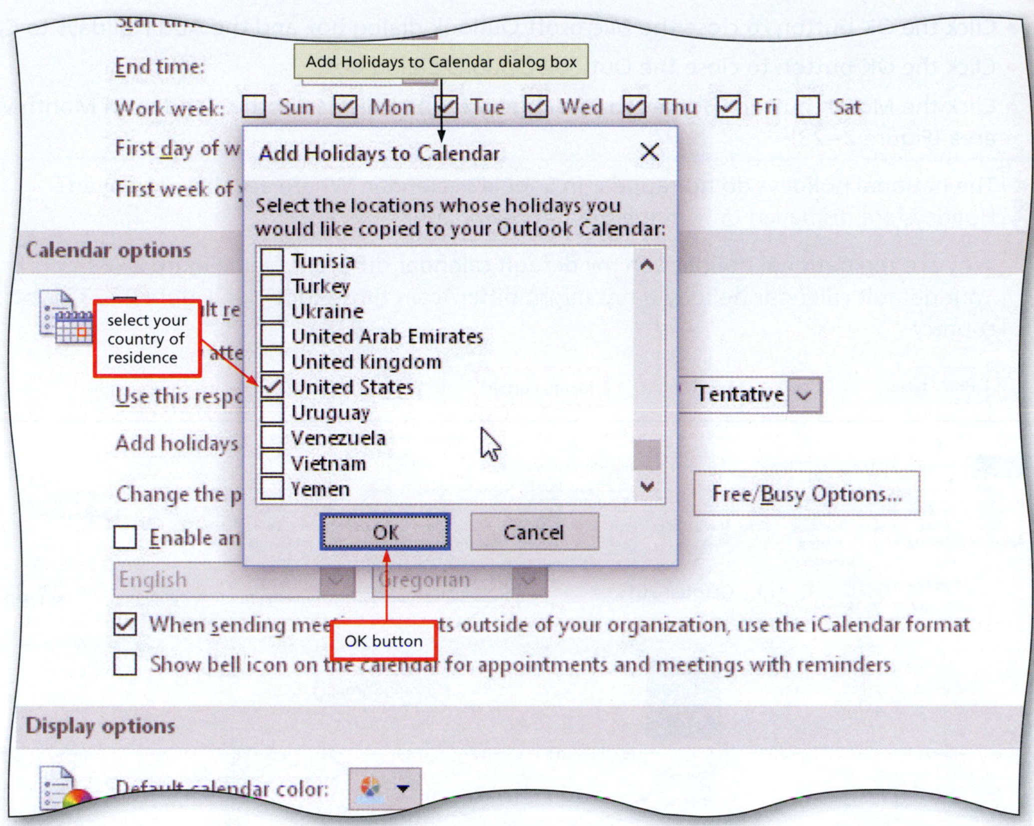

Figure 2–21

4

- If necessary, click the check box for your country of residence to add that country's national holidays to the default calendar.
- Click the OK button to close the dialog box, import the holidays, and display the confirmation message that the holidays were added to your calendar (Figure 2–22).

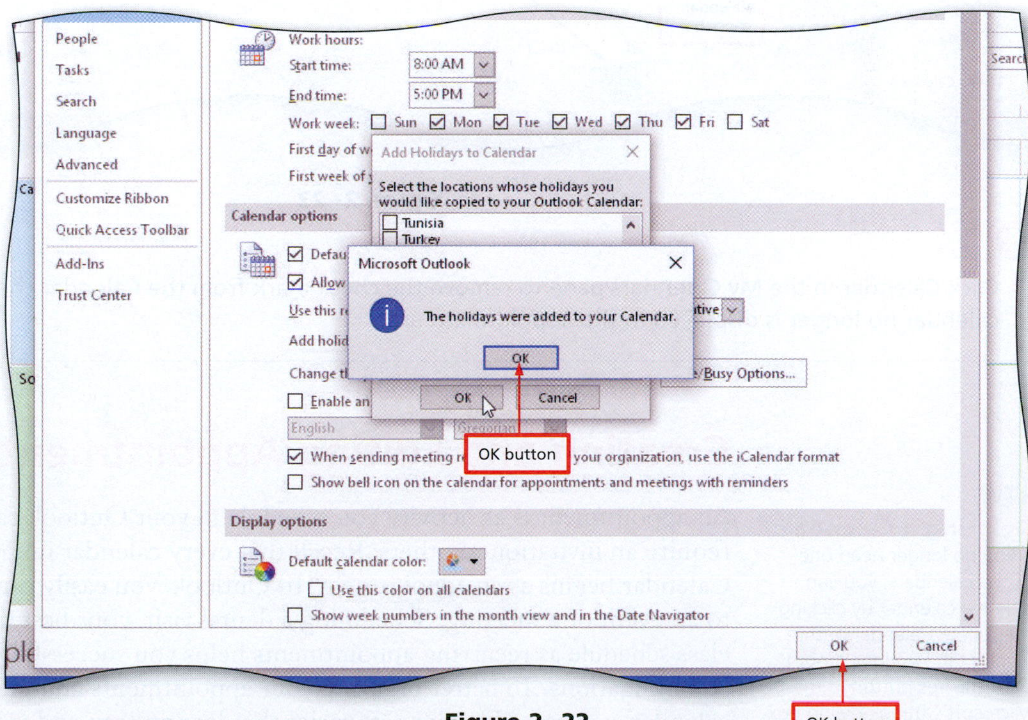

Figure 2–22

- Click the OK button to close the Microsoft Outlook dialog box and the Add Holidays to Calendar dialog box.
- Click the OK button to close the Outlook Options dialog box.
- Click the Month button (Home tab | Arrange group) to display both calendars in Month view in the appointment area (Figure 2–23).

Q&A The national holidays do not appear in Sophia's calendar. Where are they displayed?
Holidays are displayed only in the default calendar.

Why are the national holidays on my default calendar different from Figure 2–23?
Your default calendar holiday dates might differ from those shown in Figure 2–23 if you selected a different country.

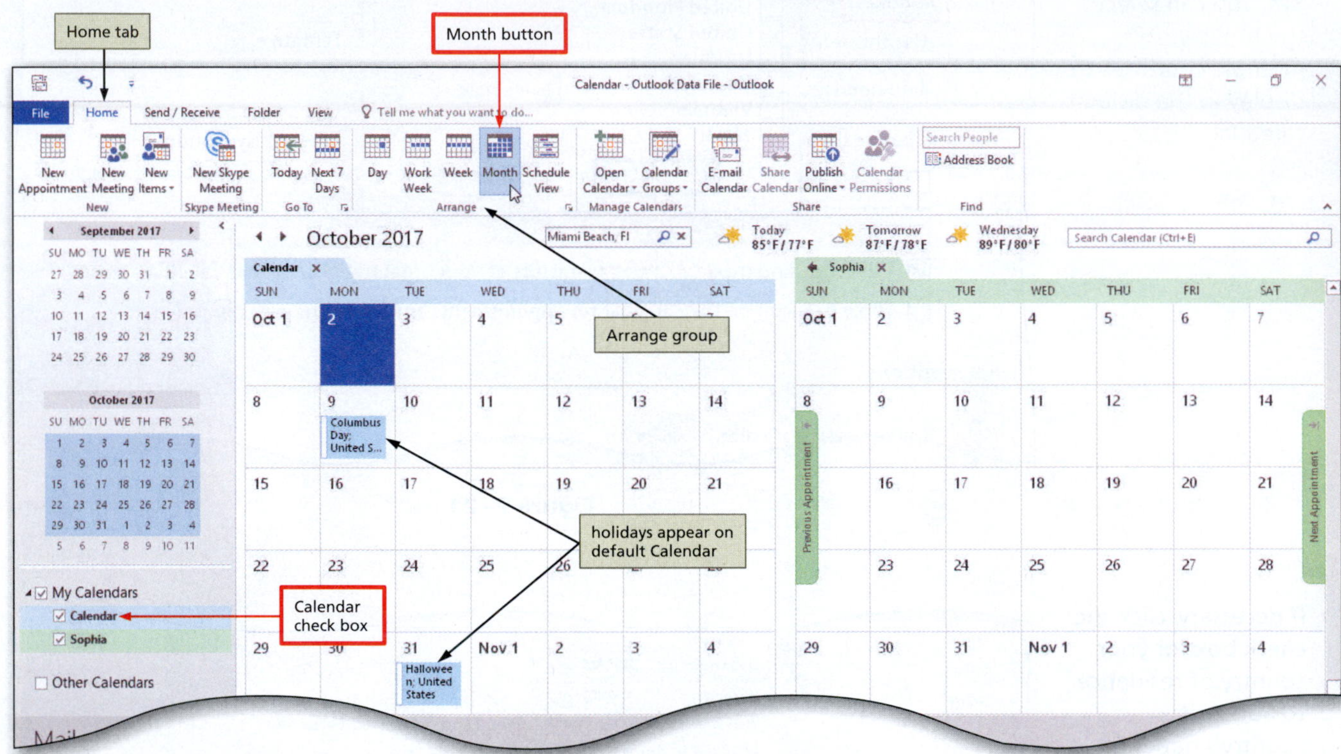

Figure 2–23

- Click Calendar in the My Calendars pane to remove the check mark from the Calendar check box so that the default calendar no longer is displayed in the appointment area.

BTW
Deleting a Calendar
If you no longer need one of the calendars, you can delete a calendar by clicking the Delete Calendar button (Folder tab | Actions group). Click the Yes button in the Microsoft Outlook dialog box to delete the folder. Outlook sends the deleted folder to the Deleted Items folder.

Creating and Editing Appointments

An appointment is an activity you schedule in your Outlook calendar that does not require an invitation to others. Recall that every calendar item you schedule in Outlook Calendar begins as an appointment. In Outlook, you easily can change an appointment to an event or a meeting. Scheduling a dental visit, your best friend's birthday, or a class schedule as recurring appointments helps you successfully manage your activities and obligations. To better organize your appointments and meetings in your Outlook calendar, you can add color categories that let you scan and visually associate similar items. For example, you can set the color blue to represent your academic classes and the color green for doctor's appointments.

Creating Appointments in the Appointment Area

A **one-time appointment**, such as a concert event, conference call, or course exam date, is an appointment that occurs only once on a calendar. A **recurring appointment**, such as a class throughout an academic course, repeats on the calendar at regular intervals. Appointments can be created in two ways: using the appointment area, where you enter the appointment directly in the appropriate time slot, or using the Untitled – Appointment window, where you can enter more specific details about the appointment such as the location or address of the activity.

BTWs

Touch Screen Differences

The Office and Windows interfaces may vary if you are using a touch screen. For this reason, you might notice that the function or appearance of your touch screen differs slightly from this module's presentation.

To Create a One-Time Appointment Using the Appointment Area

1 CONFIGURE CALENDAR OPTIONS | **2 CREATE & MANIPULATE APPOINTMENTS** | 3 SCHEDULE EVENTS
4 SCHEDULE MEETINGS | 5 PRINT CALENDAR | 6 SAVE & SHARE CALENDAR

When you click a day on the calendar in the Navigation Pane, Outlook displays the calendar for the date selected in Day view in the appointment area. Day view shows a daily view of a specific date in half-hour increments. The following steps use the appointment area to create a one-time appointment for Sophia's yearly health physical. ***Why?*** *If you are scheduling a one-time activity such as a doctor's appointment, you can type directly in the appointment area because you do not need a detailed description.*

- Click the month name October on the Date Navigator to display a list of months with the associated year (Figure 2–24).

Experiment

- View several dates that are not consecutive by clicking a date in the Date Navigator, holding down the CTRL key, and then clicking additional days.

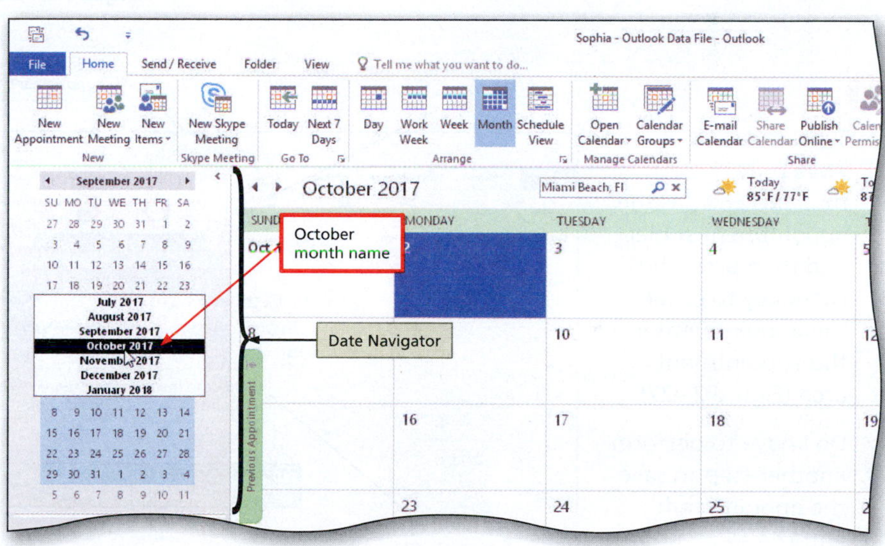

Figure 2–24

- If necessary, click October 2017 on the Date Navigator to display the selected month in the appointment area.
- Click 13 in the October 2017 calendar on the Date Navigator to display the selected date in the appointment area in Day view (Figure 2–25).

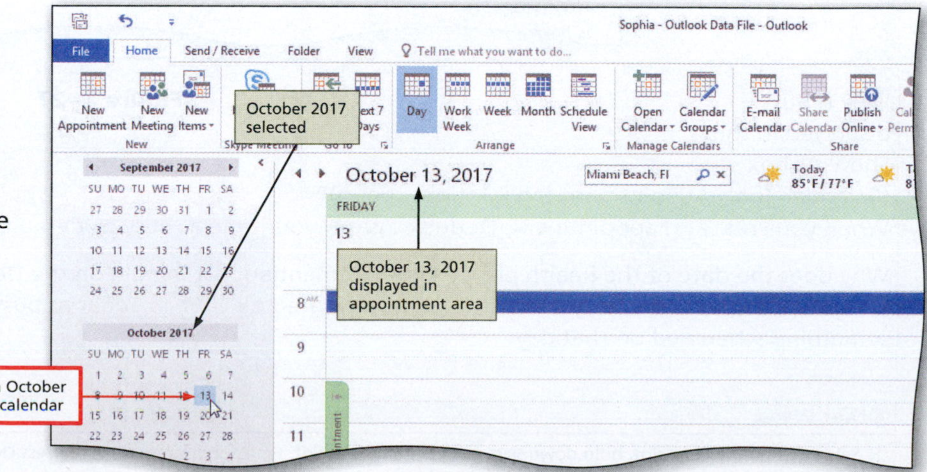

Figure 2–25

- Drag to select two half-hour increments from the 9:00 AM to the 10:00 AM time slot in the appointment area (Figure 2–26).

Q&A What if I select more or less than two half-hour increments?
If you incorrectly select the appointment time, repeat this step to try again.

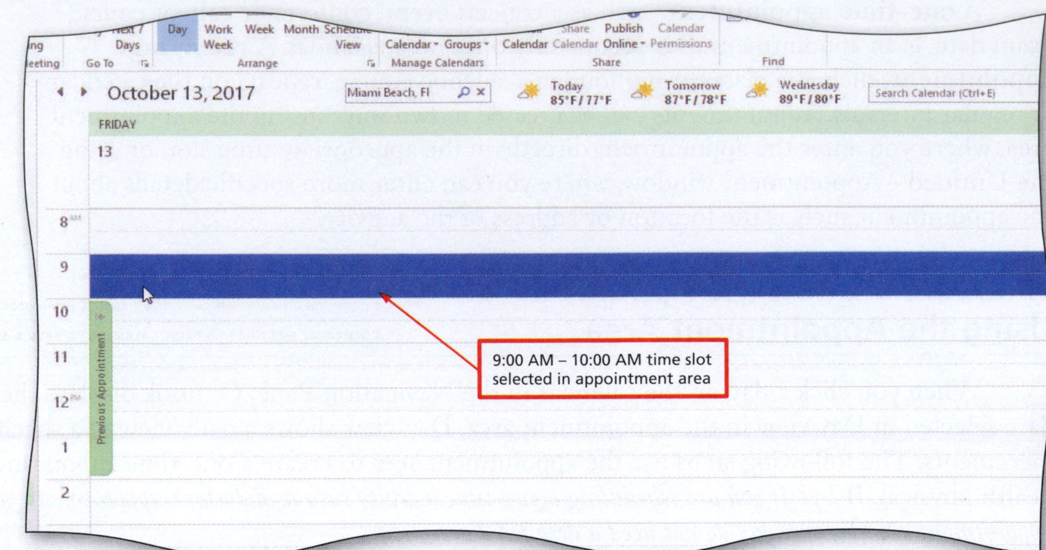

Figure 2–26

- Type **Health Physical: Dr. Bolton** as the appointment subject and then press the ENTER key to enter the appointment in the appointment area (Figure 2–27).

appointment status shown as Busy
Calendar Tools Appointment tab
bold date means one or more appointments are scheduled on that day
white dots indicate appointment is selected
appointment entered

Figure 2–27

Q&A Do I have to perform another step to save the appointment entry?
No, the appointment entry is saved automatically when you press the ENTER key.

Why is Busy displayed in the Show As box (Calendar Tools Appointment tab | Options group)?
When you create an appointment, Outlook assigns your time as busy by default.

Why does the date of the health physical appointment appear in bold on the Date Navigator?
Outlook displays in bold any date with a time allocated on your calendar as busy to indicate that you have something scheduled on that day.

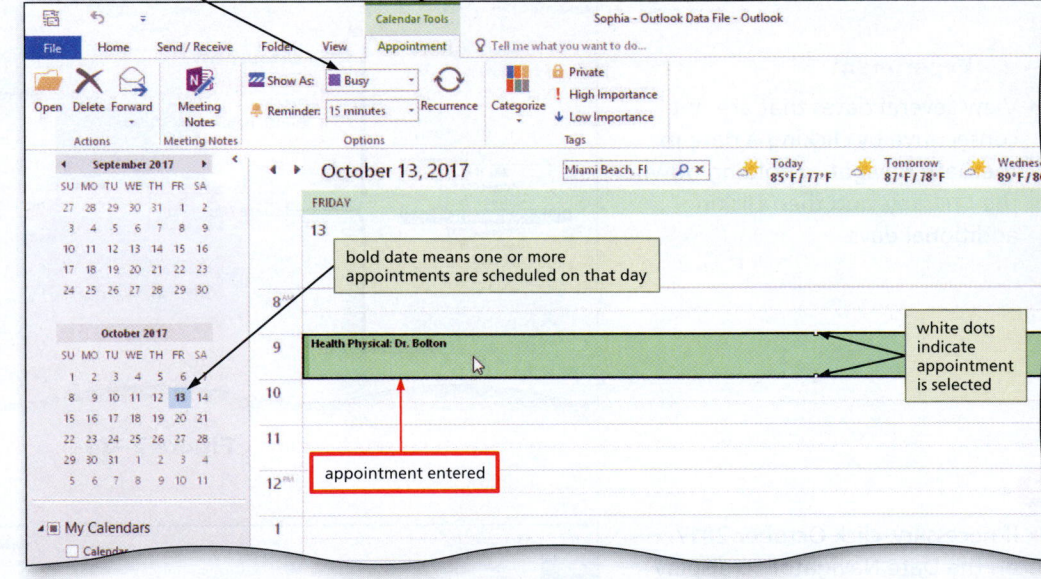

Other Ways

1. Select beginning time slot, hold down SHIFT, click ending time slot, type appointment name, press ENTER

Organize the Calendar with Color Categories

As you add appointments to the Outlook Calendar, you can use categories to color-code the appointments by type. Adding color categories allows you to quickly scan and visually group similar items such as classes or work-related appointments. For example, Sophia can assign her work tasks to a blue category, doctor's appointments to green, classes to orange, and all friends- and family-related activities to purple. After you associate each category with a color, she can categorize each appointment. The associated color is used as the item's background color on the calendar in the appointment area.

BTW

Adding a Calendar Group

To organize multiple calendars, you can create calendar groups. Click the Calendar Groups button (Home tab | Manage Calendars group) and then click Create New Calendar Group. Type a name for the new calendar group, and then click the OK button.

To Add Color Categories

Why? *Color categories enable you to easily identify and group associated items in the Outlook Calendar.* The following steps add color categories in the calendar.

- Click the Categorize button (Calendar Tools Appointment tab | Tags group) to display the Categorize list of color categories (Figure 2–28).

Q&A Can you use color categories for any type of email account?

You should use a Microsoft account as your Outlook email account to take advantage of categories and other special features.

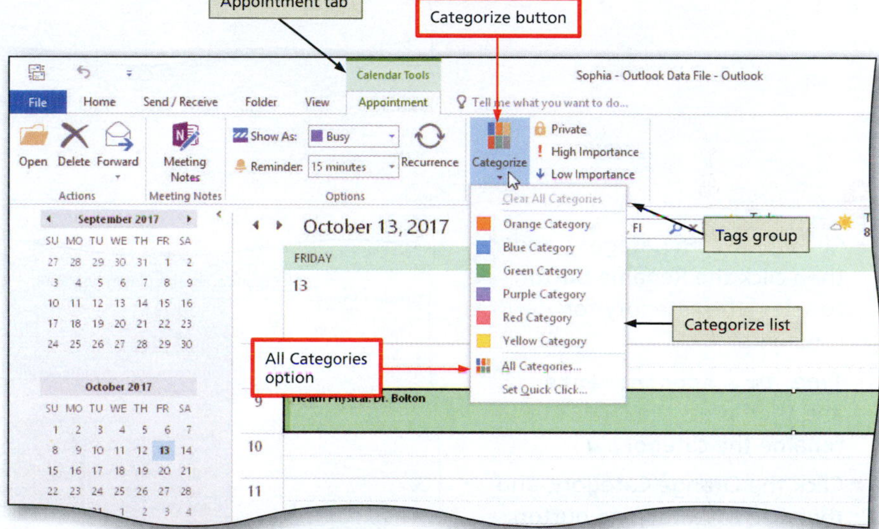

Figure 2–28

- Click All Categories to display the Color Categories dialog box (Figure 2–29).

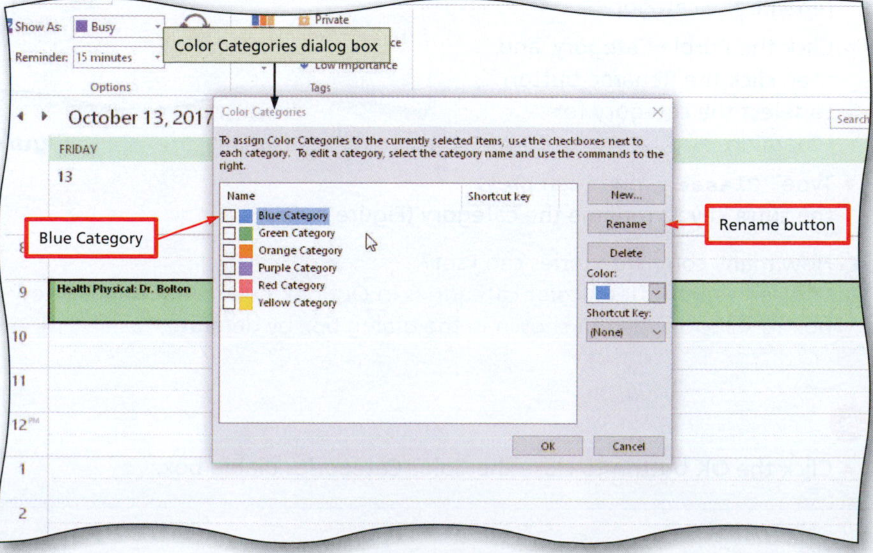

Figure 2–29

- Click the Blue Category to select the category.
- Click the Rename button to select the category for renaming.
- Type `Work` and then press the ENTER key to rename the category (Figure 2–30).

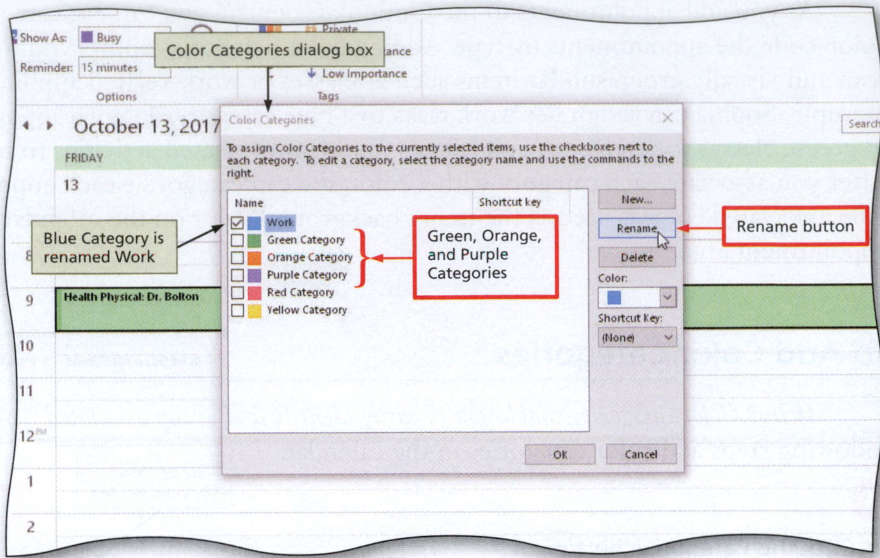

Figure 2–30

- Click the Green Category, and then click the Rename button to select the category for renaming.
- Type `Dr. Appointments` and then press the ENTER key to rename the category.
- Click the Orange Category, and then click the Rename button to select the category for renaming.
- Type `Friends & Family` and then press the ENTER key to rename the category.
- Click the Purple Category, and then click the Rename button to select the category for renaming.
- Type `Classes` and then press the ENTER key to rename the category (Figure 2–31).

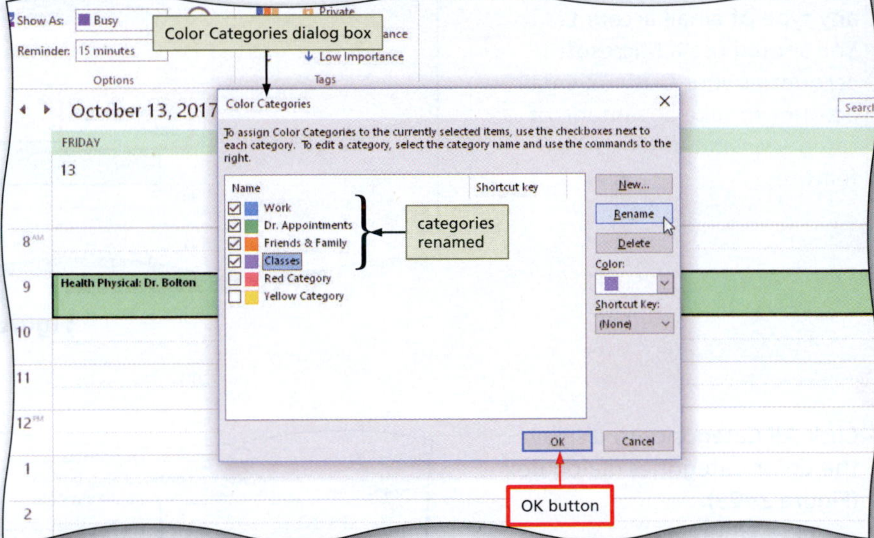

Figure 2–31

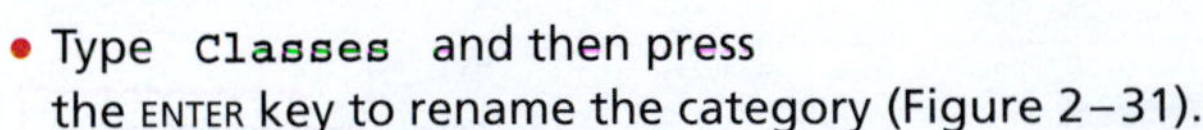

Q&A How many color categories can I set?

You can assign fifteen color categories in Outlook Calendar. Click the New button in the Color Categories dialog box to select colors not shown in the dialog box by default.

- Click the OK button to close the Color Categories dialog box.

To Assign a Color Category to an Appointment

1 CONFIGURE CALENDAR OPTIONS | 2 CREATE & MANIPULATE APPOINTMENTS | 3 SCHEDULE EVENTS
4 SCHEDULE MEETINGS | 5 PRINT CALENDAR | 6 SAVE & SHARE CALENDAR

The following steps assign a color category to a calendar appointment. ***Why?*** *By color coding your Outlook calendar appointments, you can quickly distinguish among your assigned categories such as class, work, or birthdays.*

1

- If necessary, click the Health Physical appointment at 9:00 AM to select the appointment.
- Click the Categorize button (Calendar Tools Appointment tab | Tags group) to display the Categorize list of color categories (Figure 2–32).

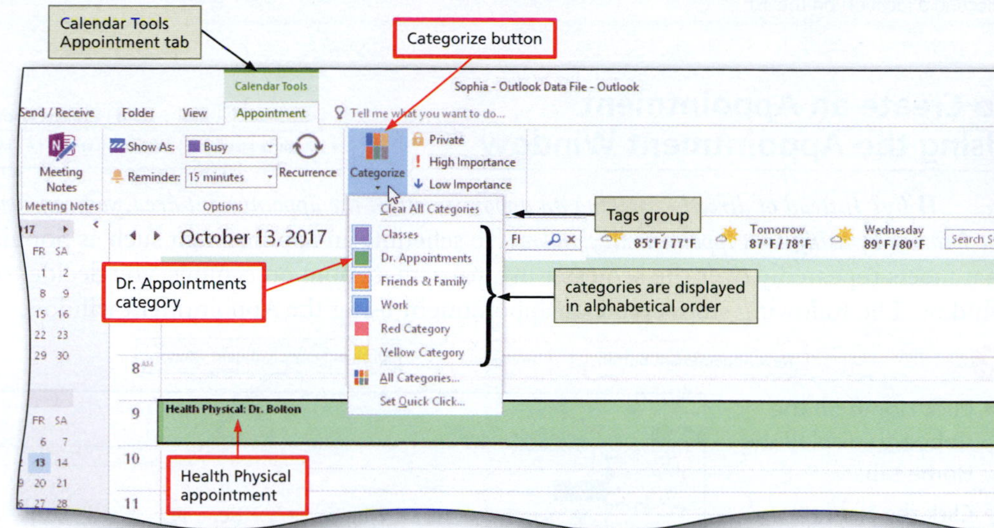

Figure 2–32

2

- Click the green Dr. Appointments category to display the selected appointment with a medium-green background (Figure 2–33).

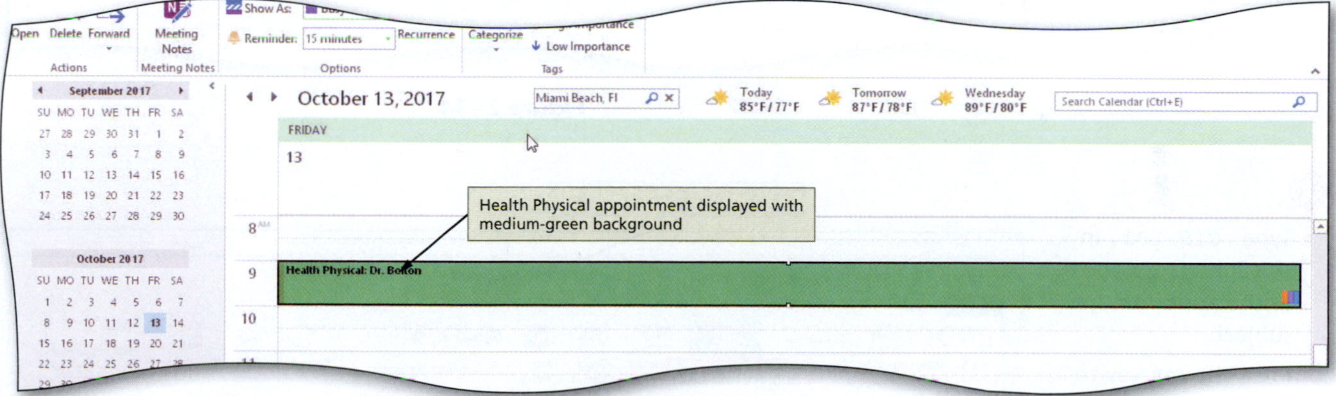

Figure 2–33

Creating Appointments Using the Appointment Window

Another way to create an appointment is by using the Appointment window, which provides additional options for entering an appointment, such as the location of the appointment and a recurrence pattern. When you set a **recurrence pattern**, Outlook schedules the appointment on the calendar at regular intervals for a designated period of time, such as a class that Sophia takes for an entire semester on Tuesdays and Thursdays.

Outlook also allows you to configure a **reminder**, similar to an alarm clock reminder, which is an alert window that briefly appears on your screen to remind you of an upcoming appointment. You also can set a chime or other sound to play as part of the reminder.

BTW
Entering Locations
As you enter calendar items, you can include location information by clicking the Location box arrow and selecting a location on the list.

Another option when creating an appointment is to set the **appointment status,** which is how the time for a calendar item is marked on your calendar. The default appointment status setting is Busy, as indicated in the previous steps, but you can change the status to reflect your availability as appropriate.

To Create an Appointment Using the Appointment Window

1 CONFIGURE CALENDAR OPTIONS | 2 CREATE & MANIPULATE APPOINTMENTS | 3 SCHEDULE EVENTS
4 SCHEDULE MEETINGS | 5 PRINT CALENDAR | 6 SAVE & SHARE CALENDAR

***Why?** Instead of directly entering an appointment in the appointment area, you can specify various details such as the location by using the Appointment window.* To schedule an appointment such as Sophia's CIS 101 computer class that meets repeatedly over the semester in a particular room on campus, you decide to use the Appointment window. The following steps create an appointment using the Appointment window.

1

- Click Home on the ribbon to display the Home tab.
- Click the New Appointment button (Home tab | New group) to open the Untitled – Appointment window (Figure 2–34).

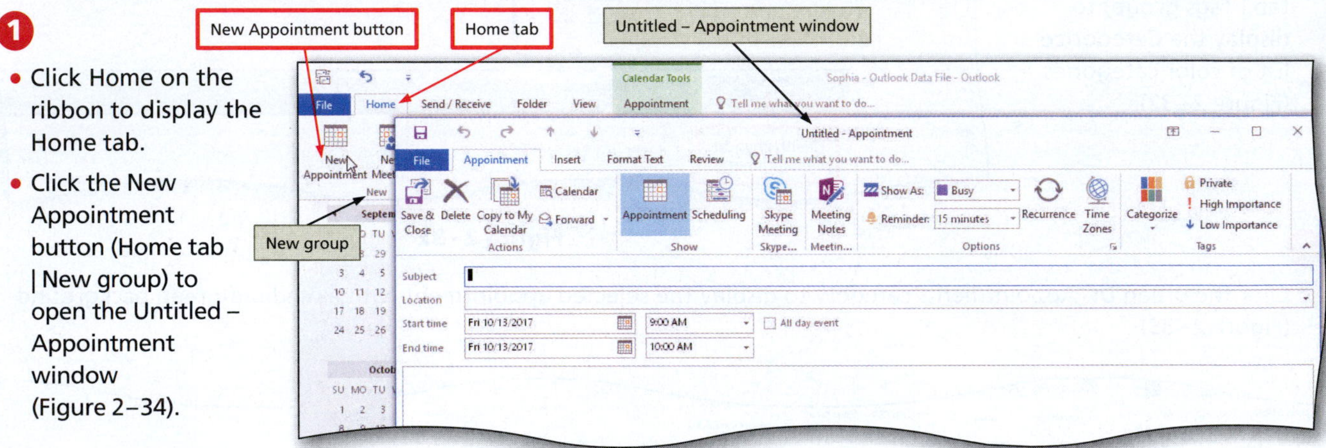

Figure 2–34

- Type `CIS 101` in the Subject text box as the appointment subject.
- Press the TAB key to move the insertion point to the Location box.
- Type `M14` as the room number of the class (Figure 2–35).

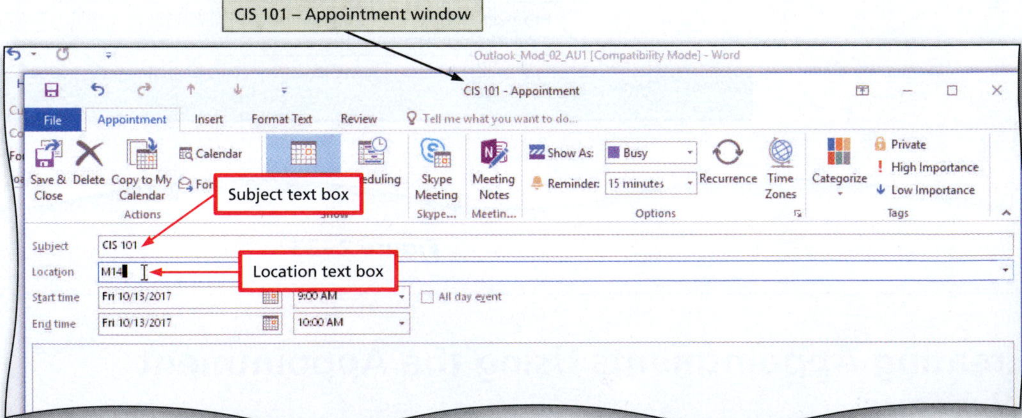

Figure 2–35

Q&A

Why did the title of the window change from Untitled – Appointment to CIS 101 – Appointment?

The title bar displays the name of the appointment. Because the name of the appointment has changed, the name on the title bar also changes.

Why are the date and time already specified?

When you start to create a new appointment, Outlook sets the start and end times using the time selected in the appointment area.

- Click the Start time calendar button to display a calendar for the current month (Figure 2–36).

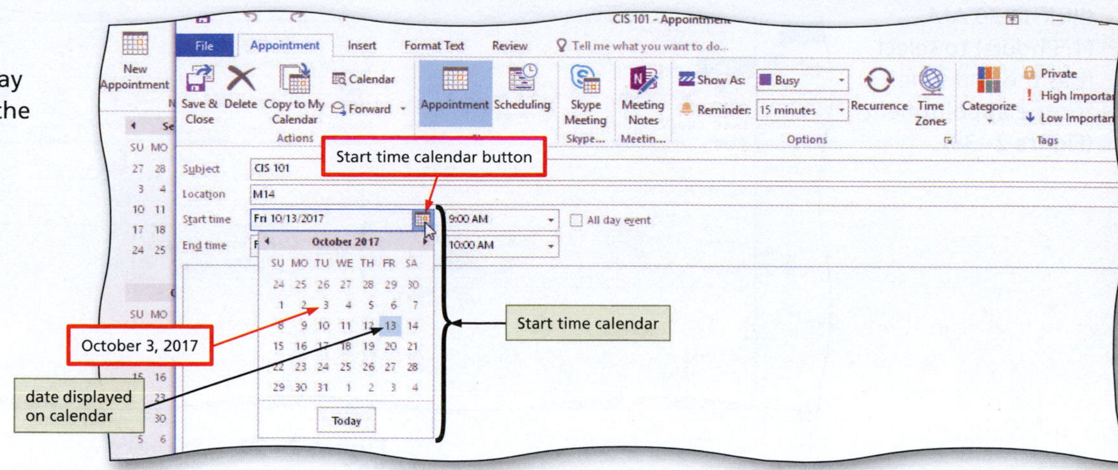

Figure 2–36

- Click 3 on the calendar to select the next CIS 101 class as October 3, 2017.
- Click the Start time box arrow to display a list of time slots (Figure 2–37).

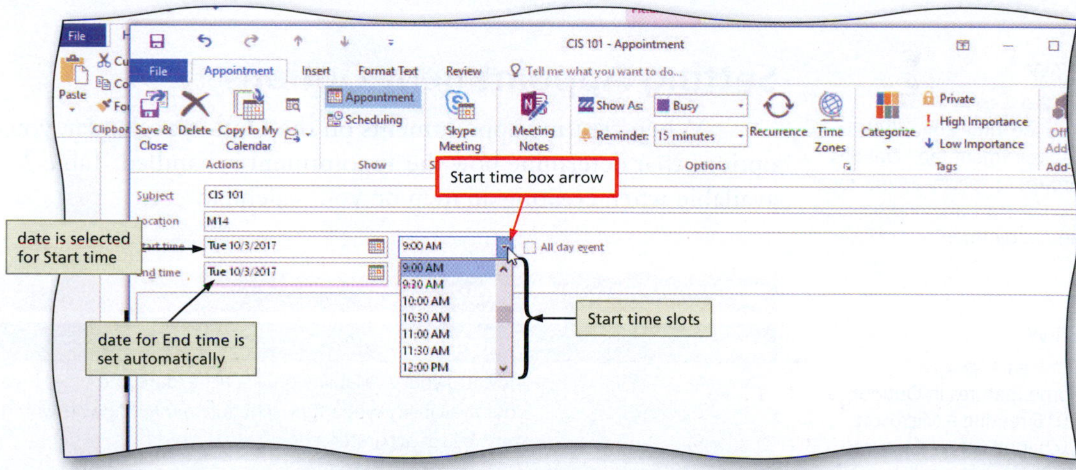

Figure 2–37

- Click 10:00 AM to select it as the Start time for the appointment.
- Click the End time box arrow to display a list of time slots (Figure 2–38).

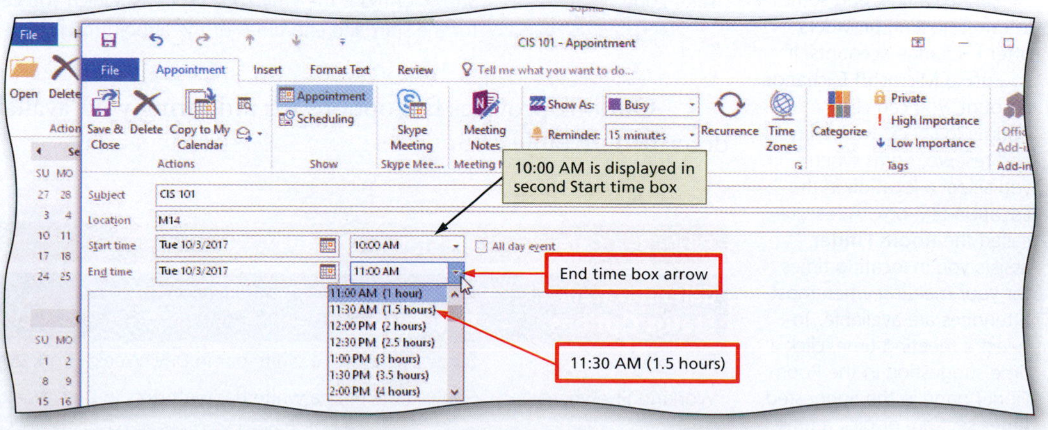

Figure 2–38

Q&A

Why did the End time change to the same date as the Start time?

Outlook automatically sets appointments to occur during a single day.

Why does the second end time list have a duration for each time?

Outlook automatically displays the duration next to the end time to help you set the length of the appointment.

- Click 11:30 AM (1.5 hours) to select it as the End time for the appointment (Figure 2–39).

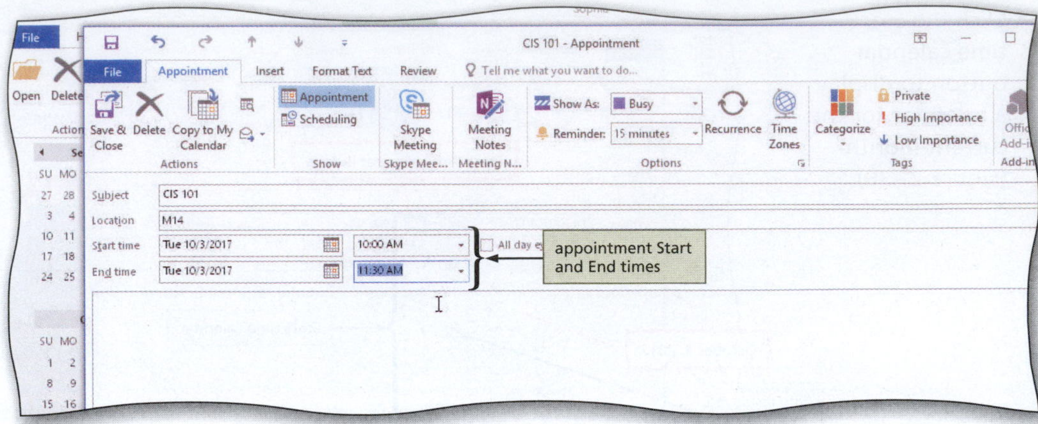

Figure 2–39

Other Ways

1. Press CTRL+SHIFT+A

BTW
Time Zones
Use the Time Zones button (Appointment tab | Options group) to specify a time zone for the start and end times of an appointment.

BTW
Room Finder
Some features in Outlook 2016 require a Microsoft Exchange Server account. **Exchange** is a collaborative communications server that many organizations use. Microsoft Office 365 includes Exchange Online, and some Internet hosting providers offer Exchange accounts. If you use a Microsoft Exchange account, you can click Rooms to check availability and reserve rooms when you select a location in the Location text box. A feature called the **Room Finder** assists you in locating times for your meeting when most attendees are available. To select a meeting time, click a time suggestion in the Room Finder pane in the Suggested times section, or pick a time on the free/busy calendar.

Setting Appointment Options

When creating appointments on the Outlook calendar, you can set a number of options that determine how the appointment is handled. Table 2–2 lists the options available when creating an item on your calendar.

Table 2–2 Calendar Window Options

Option	Description
Show As	Indicates your availability on a specific date and time; if you want to show others your availability when they schedule a meeting with you during a specific time, this must be set accurately
Reminder	Alerts you at a specific time prior to the item's occurrence
Recurrence	If an item on your calendar repeats at regularly scheduled intervals, sets the recurring options so that you only have to enter the item once on your calendar
Time Zone	Shows or hides the time zone controls, which you can use to specify the time zones for the start and end times of the appointment

Outlook provides five options for indicating your availability on the Calendar, as described in Table 2–3.

Table 2–3 Calendar Item Status Options

Calendar Item Status Options	Description
Free	Shows time with a white bar in Day, Week, Work Week, or Month view
Working Elsewhere	Shows time with a white bar with dots in Day, Week, Work Week, or Month view
Tentative	Shows time with a slashed bar in Day, Week, Work Week, or Month view
Busy	Shows time with a solid bar in Day, Week, Work Week, or Month view
Out of Office	Shows time with a purple bar in Day, Week, Work Week, or Month view

To Change the Status of an Appointment

1 CONFIGURE CALENDAR OPTIONS | 2 CREATE & MANIPULATE APPOINTMENTS | 3 SCHEDULE EVENTS
4 SCHEDULE MEETINGS | 5 PRINT CALENDAR | 6 SAVE & SHARE CALENDAR

To make sure your time is displayed accurately on the calendar, you can change the appointment status from the default of Busy to Out of Office, meaning Sophia is not in the internship office during class time while attending CIS 101. The following steps change the status of an appointment. ***Why?*** *You can display time indicators such as Busy or Out of Office to show calendar entries that reflect your availability. If you share your calendar, others can see at a glance if you are available.*

1

- Click the Show As box arrow (Appointment tab | Options group) in the CIS 101 appointment to display the Show As list of appointment status options (Figure 2–40).

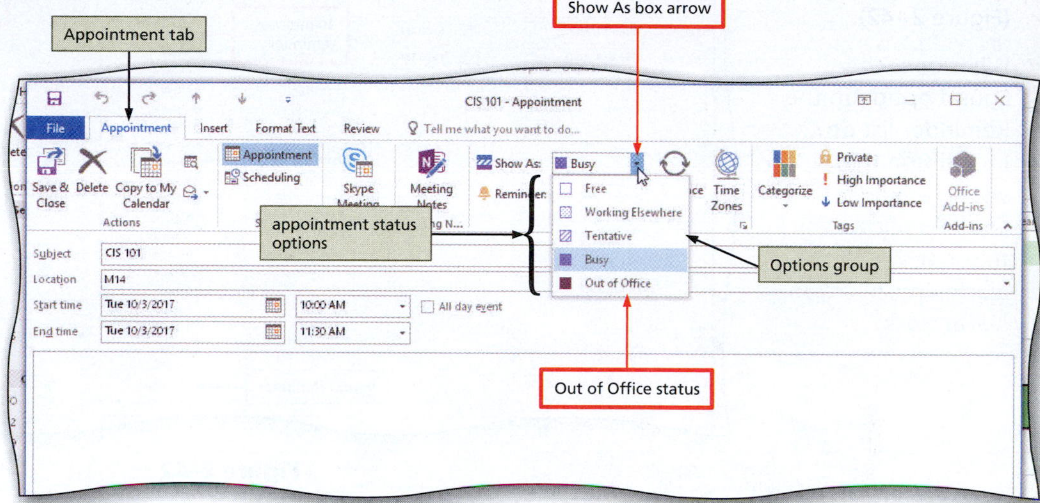

Figure 2–40

2

- Click Out of Office to change the appointment status (Figure 2–41).

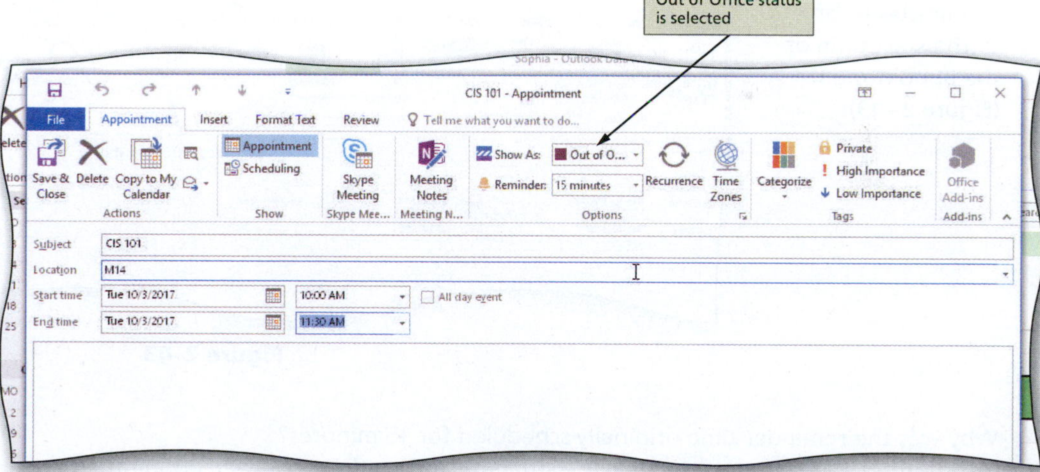

Figure 2–41

To Set a Reminder for an Appointment

1 CONFIGURE CALENDAR OPTIONS | 2 CREATE & MANIPULATE APPOINTMENTS | 3 SCHEDULE EVENTS
4 SCHEDULE MEETINGS | 5 PRINT CALENDAR | 6 SAVE & SHARE CALENDAR

With the start and end dates and times for the class set and the appointment status selected, Sophia wants to schedule a reminder so that she does not forget class. ***Why?*** *Your Outlook Calendar can be your personal alarm clock by displaying reminders of your appointments with options such as snooze and dismiss.* When the reminder is displayed, you can open the appointment for further review. The following steps set a 30-minute reminder for an appointment.

- Click the Reminder box arrow (Appointment tab | Options group) to display the Reminder list of available reminder intervals (Figure 2–42).

Q&A What does the Sound option in the Reminder list do?
In addition to a visual reminder, Outlook allows you to set an auditory alarm, much like an alarm clock.

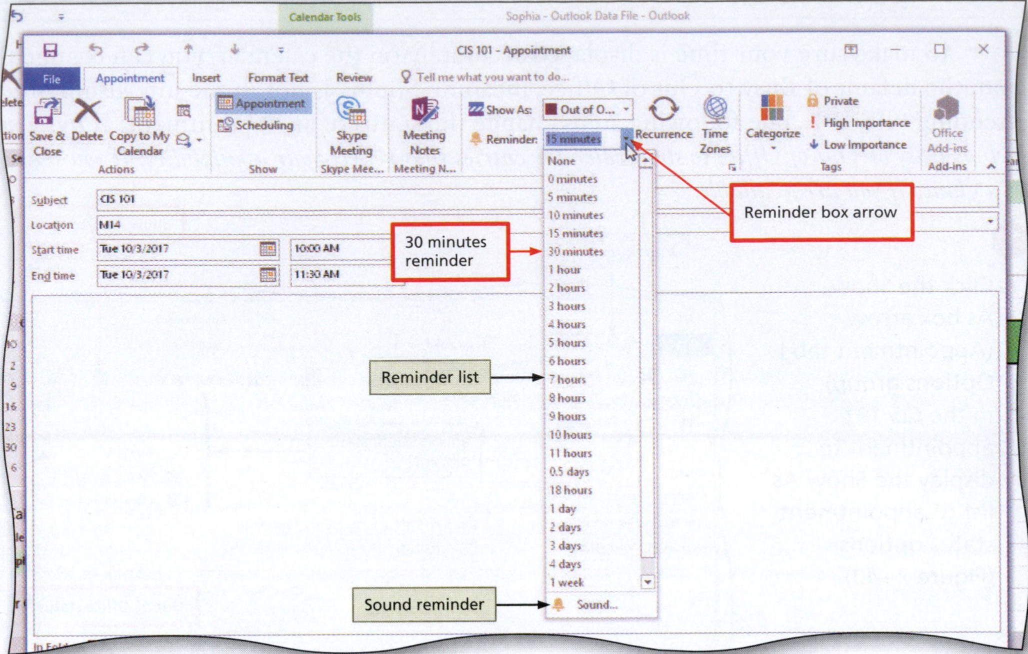

Figure 2–42

- Click 30 minutes to set a reminder for 30 minutes prior to the start time of the appointment (Figure 2–43).

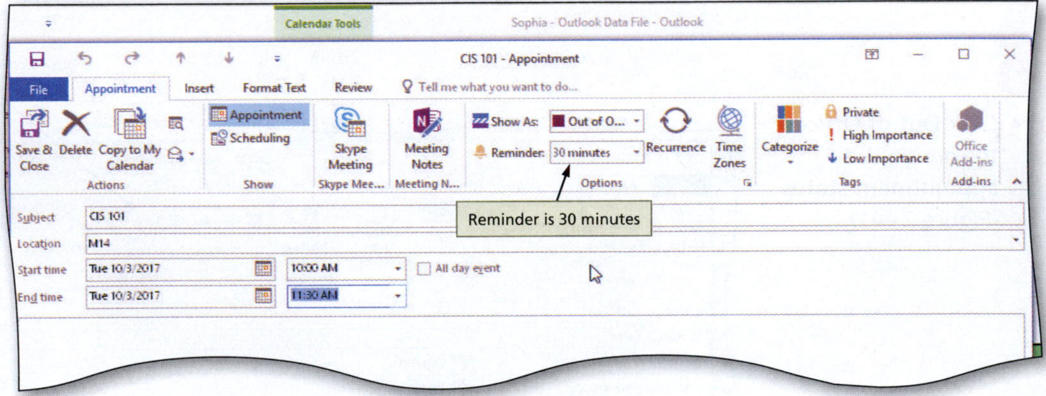

Figure 2–43

Q&A Why was the reminder time originally scheduled for 15 minutes?
By default, a Reminder is set to occur 15 minutes before the start of an appointment. However, you can increase or decrease the default reminder time.

CONSIDER THIS

Can you customize the sound that is played when a reminder is displayed?

- When you click the Reminder box arrow (Calendar Tools Appointment tab | Options group), click Sound to open the Reminder Sound dialog box.
- Click the Browse button, and then select the sound .wav file that you want played.
- Click the Open button. Click the OK button to select the custom reminder sound.
- A reminder time must be selected before the Sound command appears.

Creating Recurring Appointments

Many appointments are recurring appointments, meaning they happen at regular intervals for a designated period of time. The recurring appointment is configured with a recurrence pattern designating the rate of recurrence, for example, weekly, and on what day(s) of the week the appointment occurs.

To Set Recurrence Options for an Appointment

1 CONFIGURE CALENDAR OPTIONS | 2 CREATE & MANIPULATE APPOINTMENTS | 3 SCHEDULE EVENTS
4 SCHEDULE MEETINGS | 5 PRINT CALENDAR | 6 SAVE & SHARE CALENDAR

The next CIS 101 class is on October 3 and is held every Tuesday and Thursday from 10:00 AM to 11:30 AM at regular intervals for the rest of the semester, making it a recurring appointment. The following steps configure a recurrence pattern for an appointment. ***Why?*** *By establishing a recurrence pattern, you do not have to enter each class into the schedule for the entire semester.*

- Click the Recurrence button (Appointment tab | Options group) to display the Appointment Recurrence dialog box (Figure 2–44).

Q&A Why are the start and end times and the duration already set in the Appointment time area of the Appointment Recurrence dialog box?

Outlook uses the settings you already selected for the appointment.

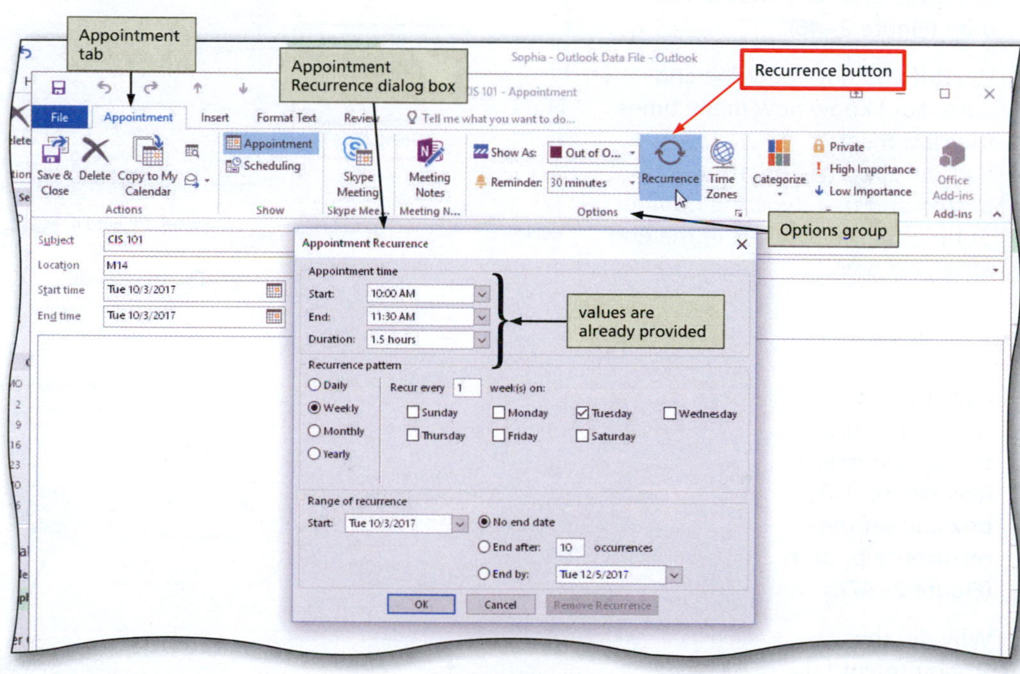

Figure 2–44

- If necessary, in the Recurrence pattern area, click the Weekly option button (Appointment Recurrence dialog box) to set the recurrence pattern.
- If necessary, in the Recur every text box (Appointment Recurrence dialog box), type `1` to schedule the frequency of the recurrence pattern.
- Click Thursday to insert a check mark in the check box and to schedule the class two times per week (in this case, Tuesday and Thursday) (Figure 2–45).

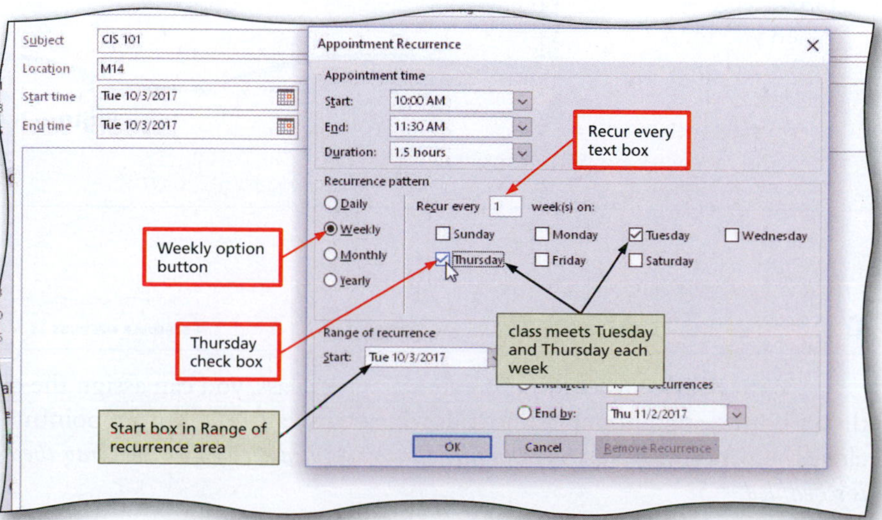

Figure 2–45

Q&A Why is the Tuesday check box already selected in the Recurrence pattern area?
Tuesday is already selected because the class starts on that day of the week.

Why does the Start box in the 'Range of recurrence' area contain a date?
When you display the Appointment Recurrence dialog box, Outlook automatically sets the range of recurrence with the date the appointment starts.

3

- In the Range of recurrence area, click the End by option button (Appointment Recurrence dialog box), and then press the TAB key two times to select the End by box.
- Type `12/14/2017` as the day the class ends to replace the displayed end date with a new date (Figure 2–46).

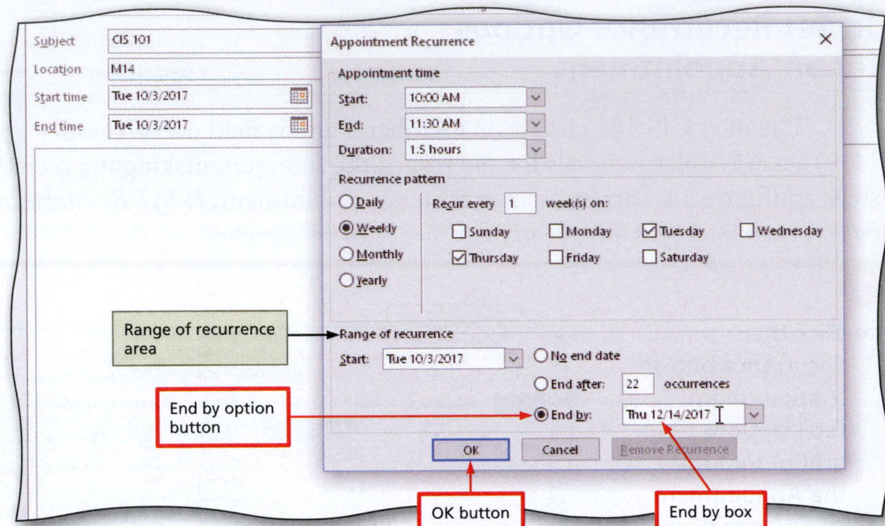

Figure 2–46

Q&A What if I do not know the end date, but I know how many times the class meets?
You can click the End after option button and then type the number of times the class meets in the End after text box.

4

- Click the OK button to close the Appointment Recurrence dialog box and set the recurrence pattern (Figure 2–47).

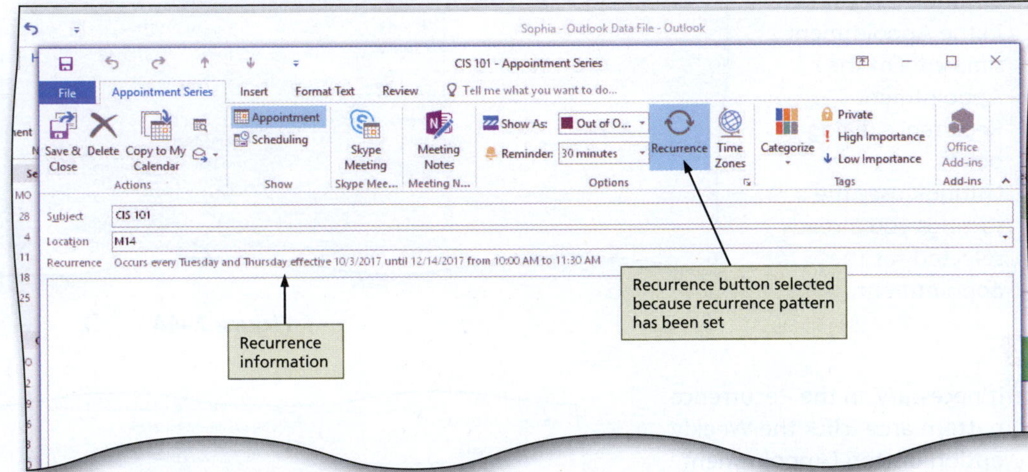

Figure 2–47

Q&A Why did the Appointment tab change to the Appointment Series tab?
When you set a recurrence pattern, the tab name changes to reflect that you are working with a series.

To Save an Appointment

1 CONFIGURE CALENDAR OPTIONS | 2 CREATE & MANIPULATE APPOINTMENTS | 3 SCHEDULE EVENTS
4 SCHEDULE MEETINGS | 5 PRINT CALENDAR | 6 SAVE & SHARE CALENDAR

With the details entered for the CIS 101 class, you can assign the appointment to a color category and then save the appointment. The following steps categorize the appointment, save the appointment series, and close the window. ***Why?*** *By changing the color-coded category and saving the appointment, your recurring appointment is scheduled.*

1

- Click the Categorize button (Appointment Series tab | Tags group) to display a list of color-coded categories (Figure 2–48).

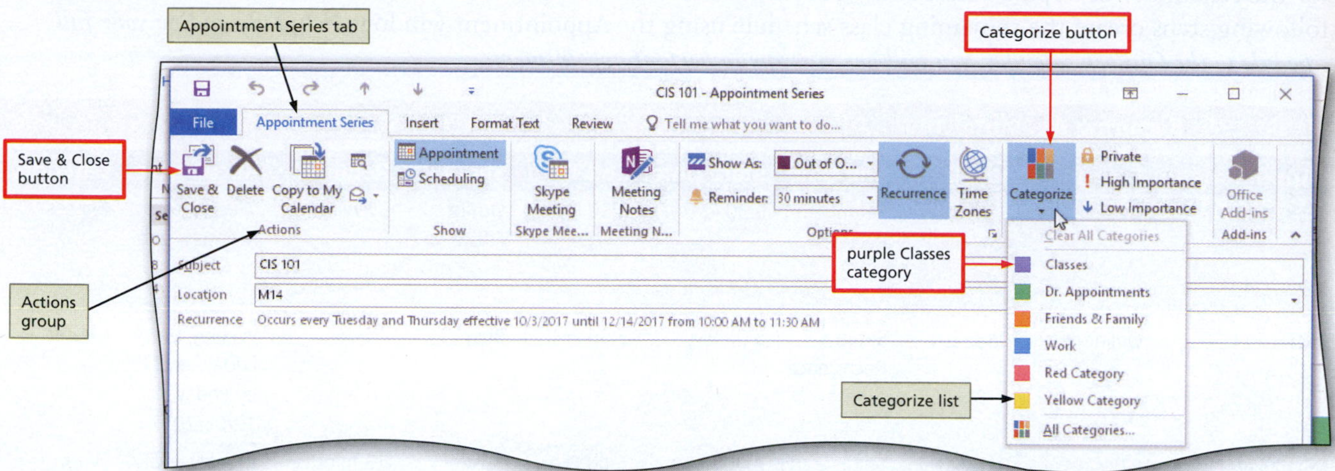

Figure 2–48

BTW

Organizing Files and Folders

You should organize and store files in folders so that you easily can find the files later. For example, if Sophia is taking an introductory computer class called CIS 101, a good practice would be to save all Outlook files in an Outlook folder in a CIS 101 folder. For a discussion of folders and detailed examples of creating folders, refer to the Office and Windows module at the beginning of this book.

2

- Click the purple Classes category to assign this appointment to a category.
- Click the Save & Close button (Appointment Series tab | Actions group) to save the recurring appointment on the calendar and close the window.
- Click Home on the ribbon to display the Home tab.
- Click the Month button (Home tab | Arrange group) to display the calendar in Month view (Figure 2–49).

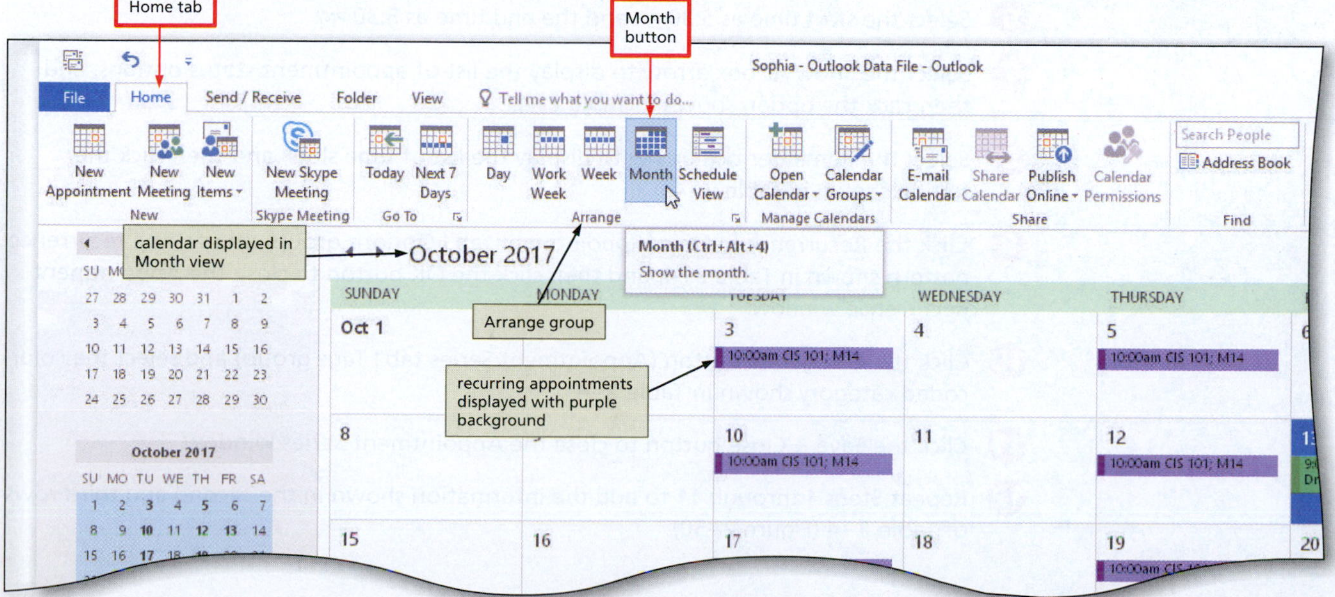

Figure 2–49

To Add More Recurring Appointments

With the CIS 101 class appointment series created, the next step is to create recurring appointments for the remainder of Sophia's class and work schedule using the appointment information in Table 2–4. The following steps create the remaining class schedule using the Appointment window. ***Why?*** *By adding your full schedule to the Outlook calendar, you will not miss any important appointments.*

Table 2–4 Recurring Appointments

Appointment	Location	Start Date	End Date	Start Time	End Time	Show As	Reminder	Recurrence	Category
ENG 102	D15	10/02/2017	Set in Recurrence	5:30 PM	8:30 PM	Out of Office	30 minutes	Weekly, every Monday; end by Monday, 12/11/2017	Classes
MTH 111	Online	10/06/2017	Set in Recurrence	5:00 PM	5:00 PM	Busy	1 hour	Weekly, every Friday; end by Friday, 12/08/2017	Classes
Pathways Office Hours	P22	10/02/2017	Set in Recurrence	2:00 PM	5:00 PM	Busy	15 minutes	Weekly, every Monday, Tuesday, & Wednesday; end by Wednesday 12/13/2017	Work

1. If necessary, click Home to display the Home tab.
2. Click the New Appointment button (Home tab | New group) to open the Appointment window.
3. Type `ENG 102` as the appointment subject.
4. Type `D15` as the location.
5. Select October 2, 2017 to set the start date.
6. Select the start time as 5:30 PM and the end time as 8:30 PM.
7. Select the Show As box arrow to display the list of appointment status options, and then click the option shown in Table 2–4.
8. Select the Reminder box arrow to display the list of time slots, and then click the option shown in Table 2–4.
9. Click the Recurrence button (Appointment tab | Options group) and set the recurrence pattern shown in Table 2–4, and then click the OK button to close the Appointment Recurrence window.
10. Click the Categorize button (Appointment Series tab | Tags group) and select the color-coded category shown in Table 2–4.
11. Click the Save & Close button to close the Appointment Series window.
12. Repeat Steps 1 through 11 to add the information shown in the second and third rows of Table 2–4 (Figure 2–50).

Q&A Why is the Calendar Tools Appointment Series tab displayed instead of the Calendar Tools Appointment tab?
The Calendar Tools Appointment Series tab is displayed when you select an appointment that is part of a series. This tab provides tools for working with recurring appointments.

What if I have appointments that recur other than weekly?
You can set daily, weekly, monthly, or yearly recurrence patterns in the Appointment Recurrence dialog box. A recurring appointment can be set to have no end date, to end after a certain number of occurrences, or to end by a certain date.

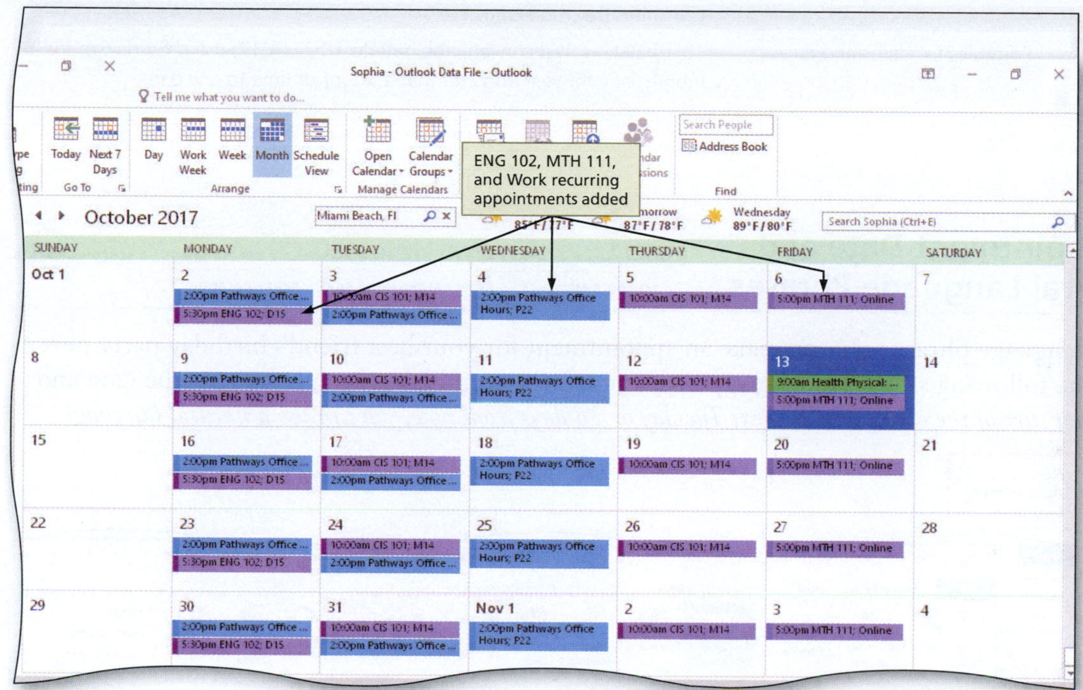

Figure 2–50

Using Natural Language Phrasing

In the previous steps, you entered dates and times in the Appointment window using standard numeric entries, such as 10/08/2017. You also can specify appointment dates and times using natural language. A **natural language phrase** is a phrase closely resembling how people speak during normal conversation. For example, you can type a phrase, such as "next Thursday" or "two weeks from yesterday," or you can type a single word, such as "midnight," and Outlook will calculate the correct date and time relative to the current date and time on the computer's system clock.

Outlook also can convert abbreviations and ordinal numbers into complete words and dates. For example, you can type "Feb" instead of "February" or "the first of May" instead of "5/1." Outlook's Calendar also can convert words such as "yesterday" and "tomorrow" and the names of holidays that occur on the same date each year, such as Valentine's Day. Table 2 – 5 lists various natural language options.

BTW
Outlook Help
At any time while using Outlook, you can find answers to questions and display information about various topics through Outlook Help. Used properly, this form of assistance can increase your productivity and reduce your frustrations by minimizing the time you spend learning how to use Outlook. For instructions about Outlook Help and exercises that will help you gain confidence in using it, read the Office and Windows module at the beginning of this book.

Table 2–5 Natural Language Options

Category	Examples
Dates Spelled Out	July twenty-third, March 17th, first of May This Fri, next Sat, two days from now
Times Spelled Out	Noon, midnight Nine o'clock AM, five-twenty
Descriptions of Times and Dates	Now Yesterday, today, tomorrow
Holidays	Cinco de Mayo Christmas Day, Christmas Eve
Formulas for dates and times	10/15/2017 + 12d converts the date to 10/27/2017; use *d* for day, *m* for month, or *y* for year and add that amount of time to any date

To Create an Appointment Date and Time Using Natural Language Phrases

1 CONFIGURE CALENDAR OPTIONS | 2 CREATE & MANIPULATE APPOINTMENTS | 3 SCHEDULE EVENTS
4 SCHEDULE MEETINGS | 5 PRINT CALENDAR | 6 SAVE & SHARE CALENDAR

Using a natural language phrase, you can make an appointment for your best friend's birthday party next Monday at 8:00 PM. The following steps create an appointment using natural language phrases for the date and time. ***Why?*** *If you are not sure of the exact date for next Tuesday or 36 days from now, you can use a natural language phrase.*

- Click the New Appointment button (Home tab | New group) to open the Untitled – Appointment window.
- Type **`Lachlan's Birthday Party`** in the Subject text box, and then press the TAB key to move the insertion point to the Location text box.
- Type **`Kabob House`** to add the location (Figure 2–51).

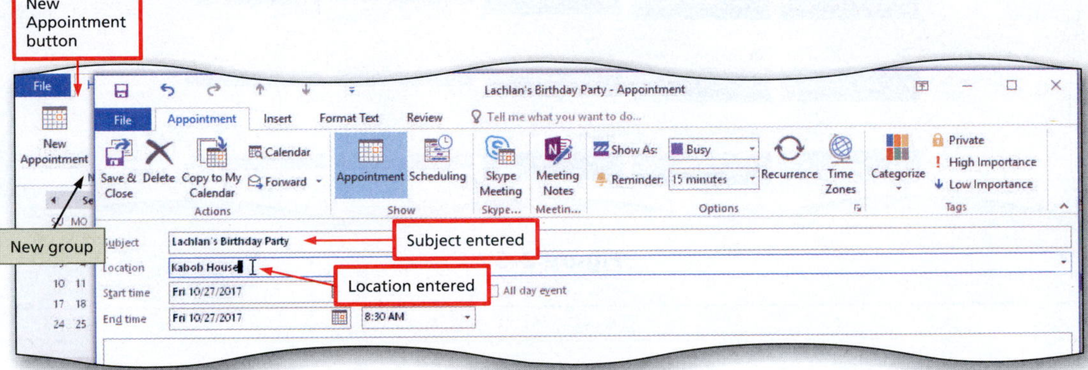

Figure 2–51

- Press the TAB key to select the first Start time text box, and then type **`next sunday`** to enter the start date.

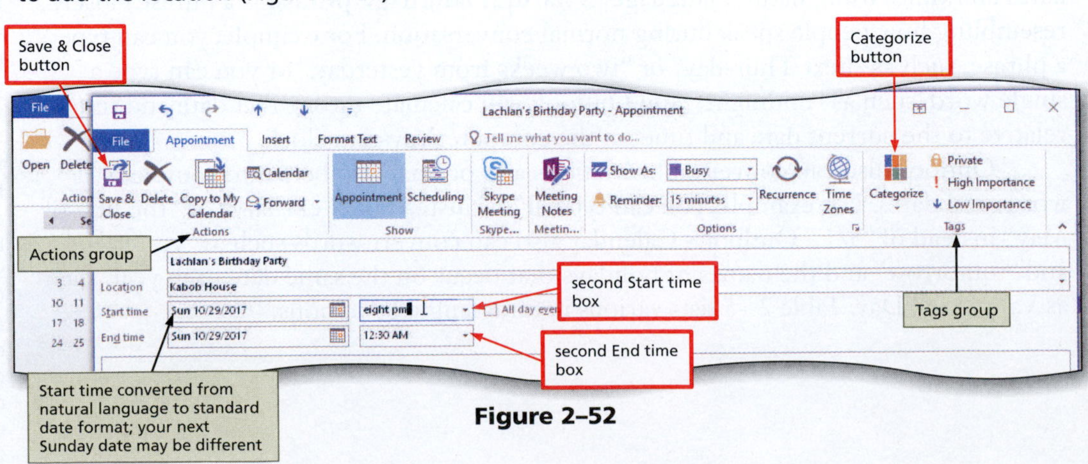

Figure 2–52

- Press the TAB key to convert the phrase to a start date and to select the second Start time text box.
- Type `eight pm` as the time in the second Start time text box to enter the start time (Figure 2–52).

Q&A

Do I need to use proper capitalization when entering natural language phrases?
No. Outlook converts the text to the proper date or time, regardless of the capitalization.

Why did the text change to a numeric date when I pressed the TAB key?
If you enter the date using natural language phrasing, Outlook converts typed text to the correct date format when you click to move the insertion point to a different box.

3

- Press the TAB key two times to convert the Start time entry to 8:00 pm.
- Type `eleven pm` as the time in the second End time box.
- Press the ENTER key to convert the end time text to 11:00 pm.
- Click the Categorize button (Appointment tab | Tags group) to display the Categorize list.
- Click the orange Friends & Family category to assign this appointment to a category.
- Click the Save & Close button (Appointment tab | Actions group) to save the appointment and close the window.
- If necessary, scroll to next Sunday's date (Figure 2–53).

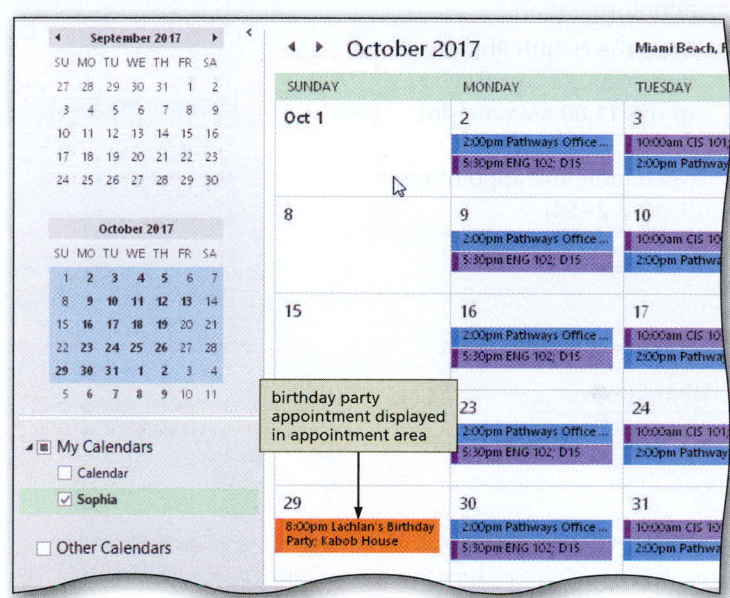

Figure 2–53

Editing Appointments

Schedules often need to be rearranged, so Outlook provides several ways to edit appointments. You can change the subject or location by clicking the appointment and editing the information directly in the appointment area. You can change the subject, location, date, or time by double-clicking the appointment and making corrections using the Appointment window. You can specify whether all occurrences in a series of recurring appointments need to be changed, or only a single occurrence should be altered.

BTW
Emailing Calendar Items
To send a calendar item to someone else, click the item, such as an appointment, and then click the Forward button (Calendar Tools Appointment tab | Actions group). Enter the email address of the recipient and send the message.

To Move an Appointment to a Different Time on the Same Day

1 CONFIGURE CALENDAR OPTIONS | 2 CREATE & MANIPULATE APPOINTMENTS | 3 SCHEDULE EVENTS
4 SCHEDULE MEETINGS | 5 PRINT CALENDAR | 6 SAVE & SHARE CALENDAR

Suppose that you cannot attend the Health Physical appointment at 9:00 AM on October 13, 2017. The appointment needs to be rescheduled to 11:00 AM for the same amount of time. ***Why?*** *Instead of deleting and then retyping the appointment, you can drag it to a new time slot.* The following step moves an appointment to a new time slot.

- If necessary, click a scroll arrow on the Calendar in the Navigation Pane until October 2017 is displayed in the calendar on the Date Navigator.
- Click 13 in the October 2017 calendar on the Date Navigator to display the selected date in the appointment area.
- Drag the Health Physical appointment from 9:00 AM to the 11:00 AM time slot on the same day to reschedule the appointment (Figure 2–54).

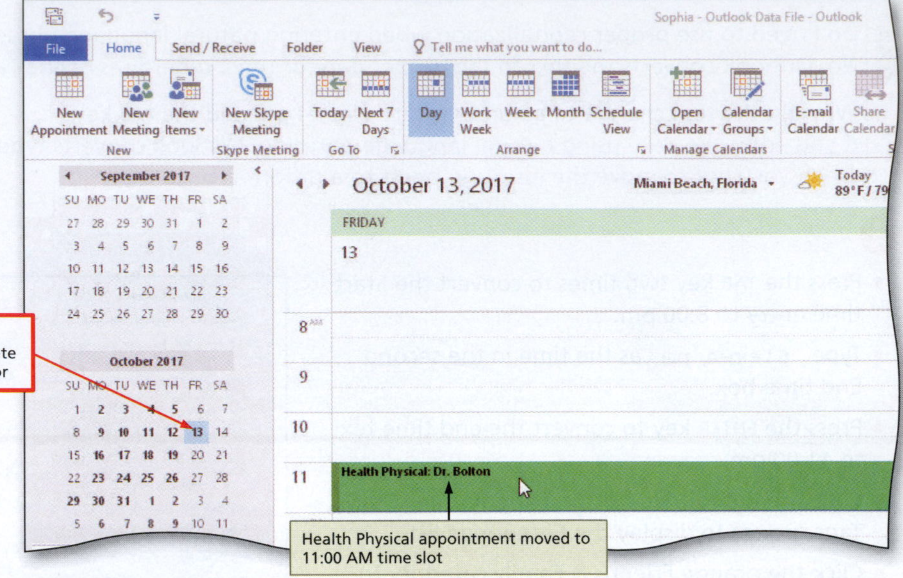

Figure 2–54

Other Ways

1. Double-click appointment, change time
2. Press CTRL+O, change time

BTW
Moving a Recurring Appointment
If you move a recurring appointment, you move only the selected instance of the appointment. To move all instances of a recurring appointment, open the appointment, click the Recurrence button (Appointment Series tab | Options group), and then change the recurrence pattern.

To Move an Appointment to a Different Date

1 CONFIGURE CALENDAR OPTIONS | **2 CREATE & MANIPULATE APPOINTMENTS** | 3 SCHEDULE EVENTS
4 SCHEDULE MEETINGS | 5 PRINT CALENDAR | 6 SAVE & SHARE CALENDAR

Why? If you are moving an appointment to a new date at the same time, you can drag the appointment to the new date on the Date Navigator instead of retyping it. The following step moves an appointment to a new date in the same time slot.

- Drag the Health Physical appointment on October 13, 2017 to October 20, 2017 on the Date Navigator to move the appointment to a new date (Figure 2–55).

Figure 2–55

To Delete a Single Occurrence of a Recurring Appointment

Because your school is closed for a Fall Break holiday on November 6, 2017, no classes will meet during that day. The following steps delete a single occurrence of a recurring appointment. ***Why?*** *Occasionally, appointments are canceled and must be deleted from the schedule.*

1

- Click the forward navigation arrow in the Date Navigator until November 2017 is displayed.
- Click 6 in the November 2017 calendar on the Date Navigator to display the selected date in the appointment area.
- If necessary, scroll down and click the class, ENG 102, scheduled for November 6, 2017, to select the appointment and display the Calendar Tools Appointment Series tab (Figure 2–56).

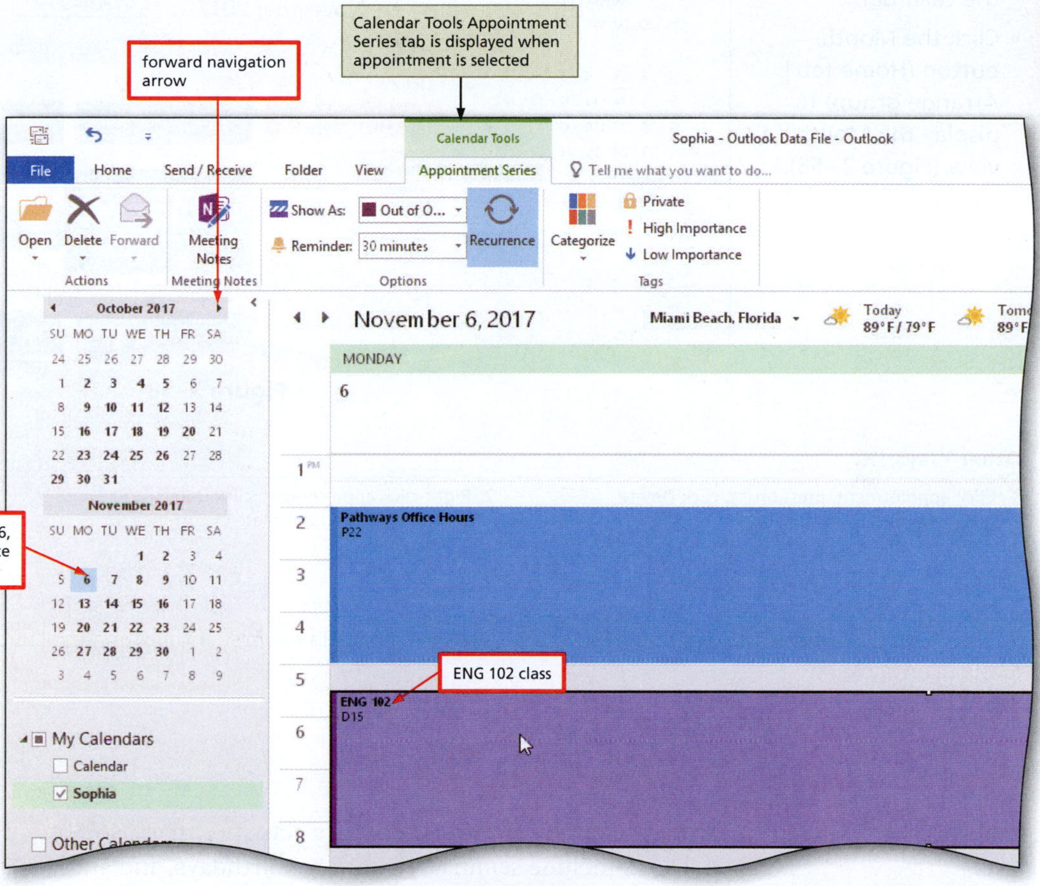

Figure 2–56

2

- Click the Delete button (Calendar Tools Appointment Series tab | Actions group) to display the Delete list (Figure 2–57).

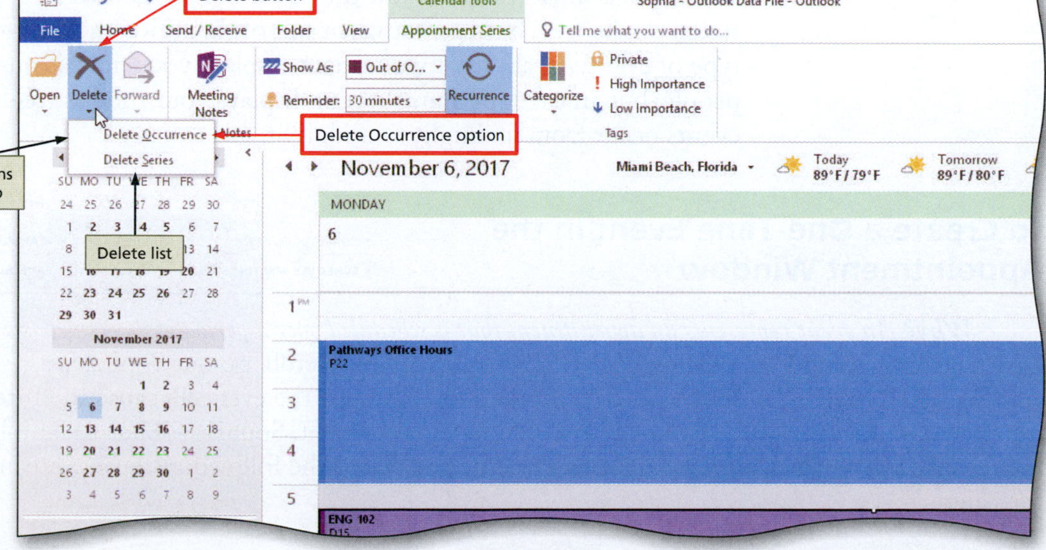

Figure 2–57

- Click Delete Occurrence on the Delete list to delete only the selected occurrence (single appointment) from the calendar.
- Click the Month button (Home tab | Arrange group) to display the Month view (Figure 2–58).

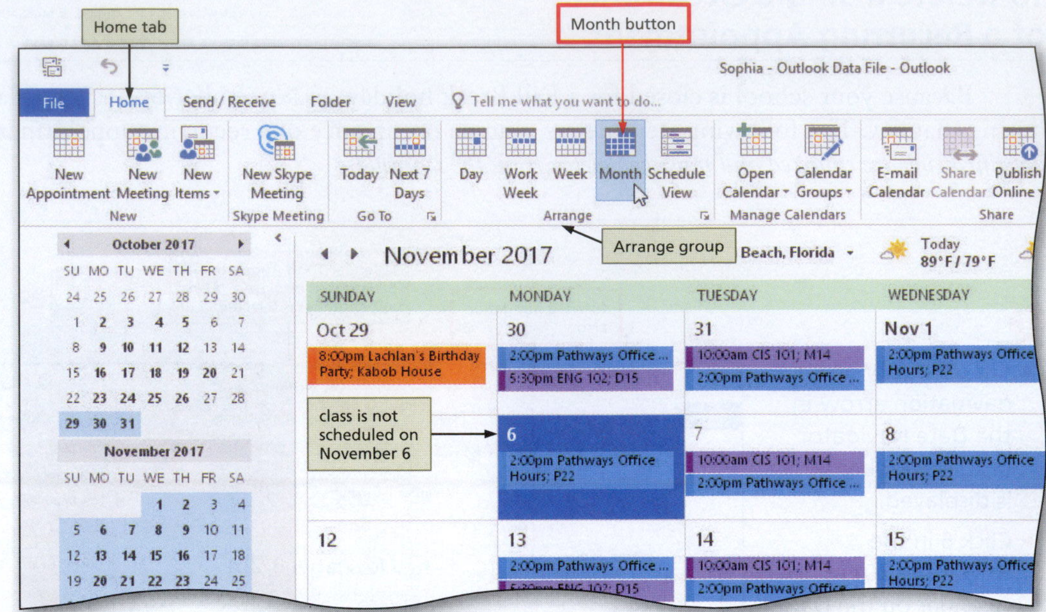

Figure 2–58

Other Ways

1. Click appointment, press DELETE, click Delete this occurrence, click OK
2. Right-click appointment, click Delete on shortcut menu, click Delete Occurrence

Break Point: If you wish to take a break, this is a good place to do so. To resume at a later time, continue to follow the steps from this location forward.

Scheduling Events

Similar to appointments, events are activities that last 24 hours or longer. Examples of events include seminars, vacations, birthdays, and anniversaries. Events can be one-time or recurring and differ from appointments in one primary way — they do not appear in individual time slots in the appointment area. Instead, the event description appears in a small banner below the day heading. As with an appointment, the event status can be free, busy, tentative, or out of the office and categorized according to the type of event. An all-day appointment displays your time as busy when viewed by other people, but an event or annual event displays your time as free. By default, all-day events occur from midnight to midnight.

To Create a One-Time Event in the Appointment Window

1 CONFIGURE CALENDAR OPTIONS | 2 CREATE & MANIPULATE APPOINTMENTS | 3 SCHEDULE EVENTS
4 SCHEDULE MEETINGS | 5 PRINT CALENDAR | 6 SAVE & SHARE CALENDAR

Why? An event represents an appointment that is scheduled over a period of days such as a conference. The Pathways Internship Fair is being held at Hamblen Hall on October 6 but Sophia is assisting with the setup starting on October 5, so she wants to block out both days for the event. Because the Internship Fair will last for a couple days, Outlook will schedule the conference as an event. Sophia will be at Hamblen Hall both days, so she decides to show her time for the event as Out of Office. The following steps create an event on the calendar.

1

- Click the New Items button (Home tab | New group) to display the New Items list (Figure 2–59).

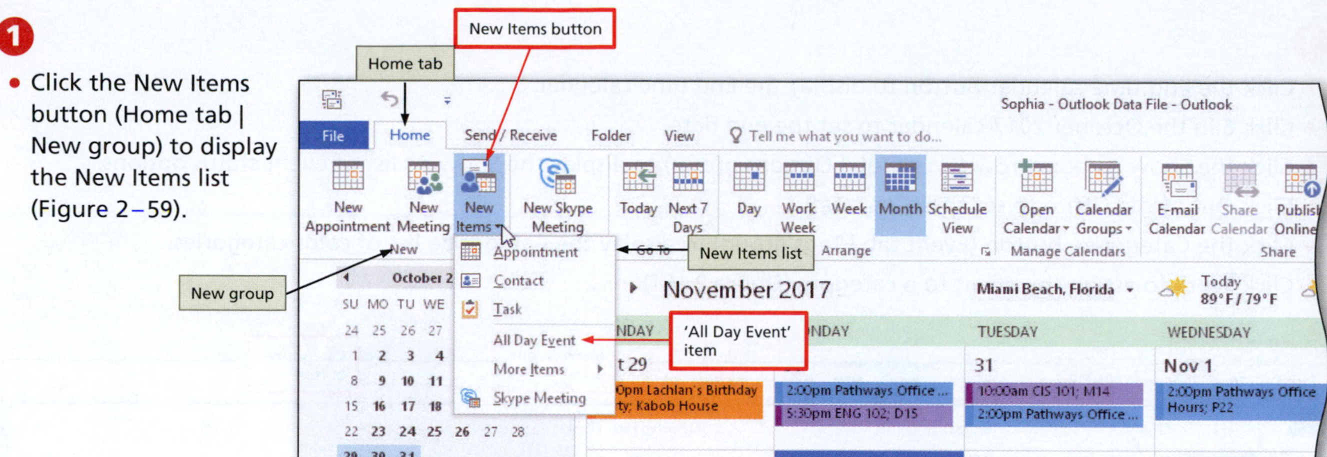

Figure 2–59

2

- Click 'All Day Event' to open the Untitled – Event window.
- Type **Internship Fair** in the Subject text box, and then press the TAB key to move the insertion point to the Location text box.
- Type **Hamblen Hall** as the location of the event.
- Click the Start time calendar button to display the Start time calendar.
- If necessary, display the October 2017 calendar.
- Click 5 in the October 2017 calendar to display Thu 10/5/2017 as the day the Internship Fair setup begins (Figure 2–60).

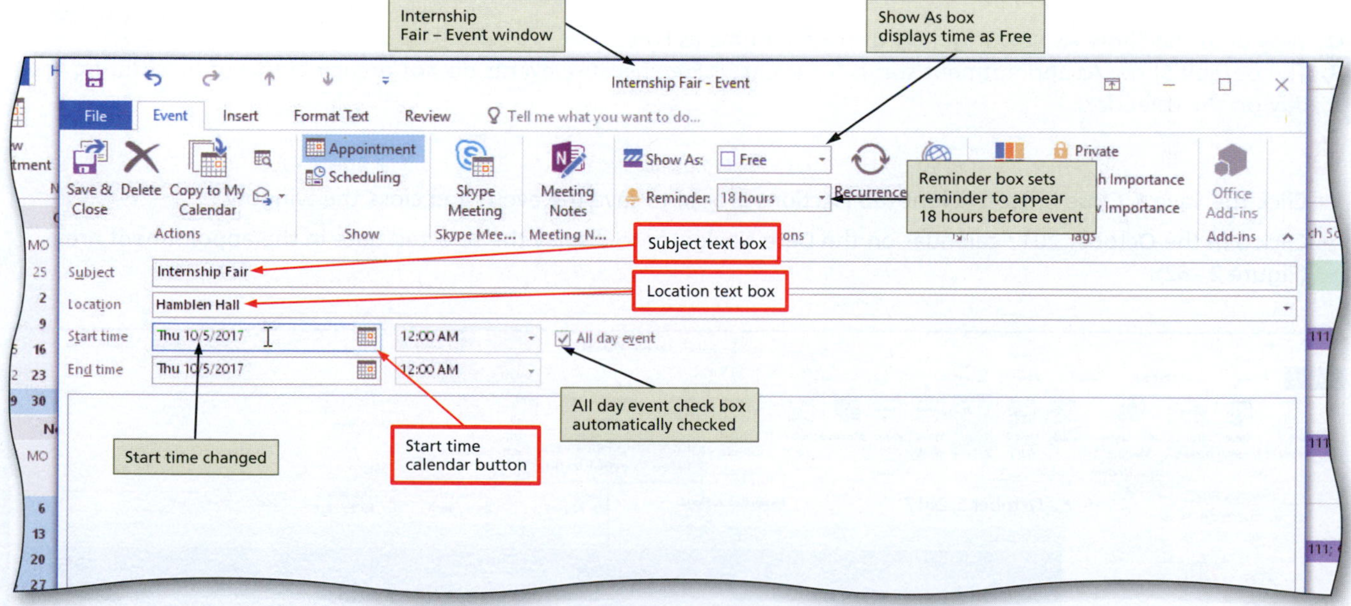

Figure 2–60

Q&A Can I create an event by checking the 'All day event' check box in an appointment?
Yes. Click the New Appointment button (Home tab | New group) and then click 'All day event' to create an event.

- Click the End time calendar button to display the End time calendar.
- Click 6 in the October 2017 calendar to set the end date.
- Click the Show As box arrow (Event tab | Options group) to display the Show As list of event status options.
- Click Out of the Office to set the event status.
- Click the Categorize button (Event tab | Tags group) to display the Categorize list of color categories.
- Click Work to assign the event to a category (Figure 2–61).

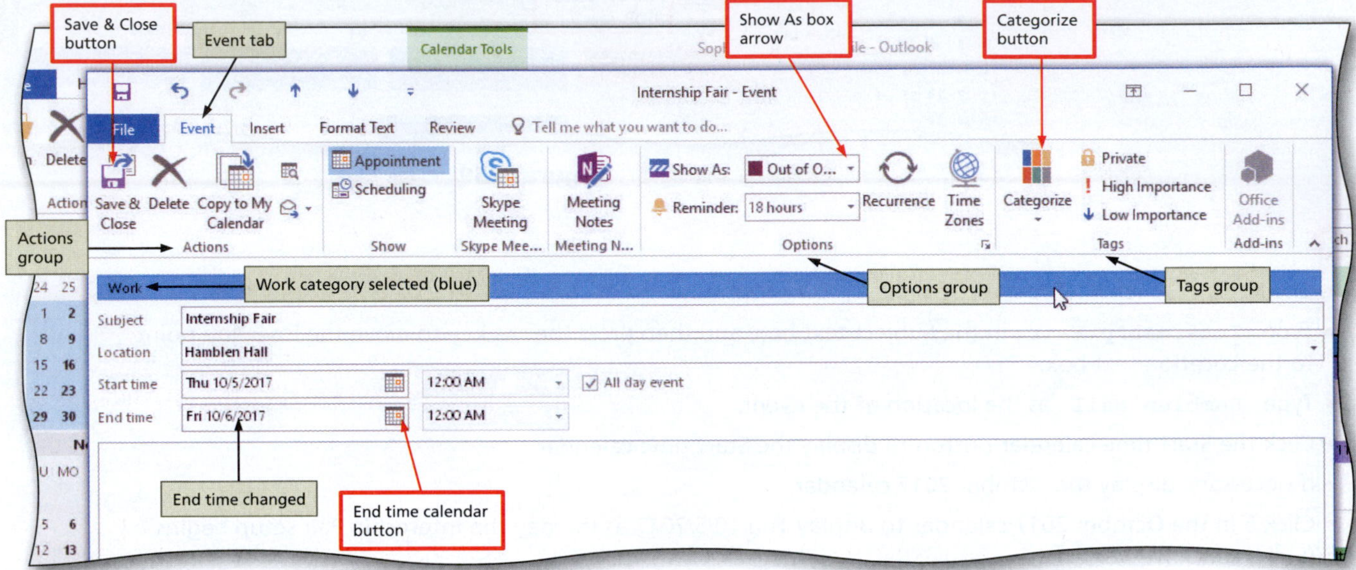

Figure 2–61

Q&A Why does the Show As box originally display the time as Free?
The default Show As appointment status for events is Free because events do not occupy blocks of time during the day on the calendar.

- Click the Save & Close button (Event tab | Actions group) to save the event and close the window.
- Click 5 in the October 2017 calendar on the Date Navigator to display the selected date in the appointment area (Figure 2–62).

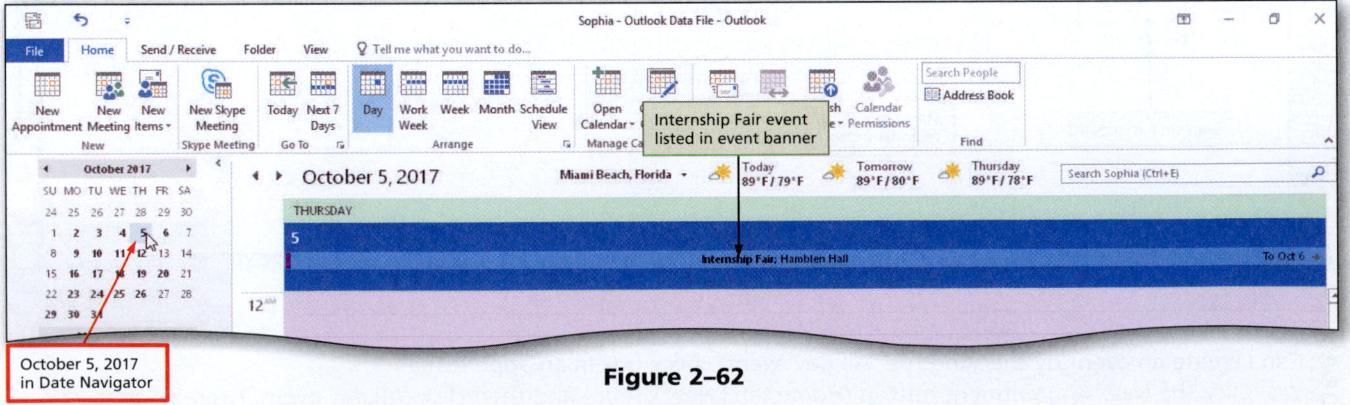

Figure 2–62

Q&A Why is the Internship Fair event displayed at the top of the Day view of the calendar?
Events do not occupy time slots on the Day view of the calendar, so they appear as banners at the top of the calendar on the day they occur.

To Delete a One-Time Event

Ms. Pauley, the Internship Office director, decides that the Internship Fair must be cancelled due to a conflict with another event in the local area. ***Why?*** *Because the schedule has changed, the Internship Fair event is cancelled but will be rescheduled later in the semester.* The following step deletes an event from your calendar.

- Click the Internship Fair event banner in the appointment area of the calendar to select it and to display the Calendar Tools Appointment tab on the ribbon.
- Click the Delete button (Calendar Tools Appointment tab | Actions group) to delete the Internship Fair event from the calendar (Figure 2–63).

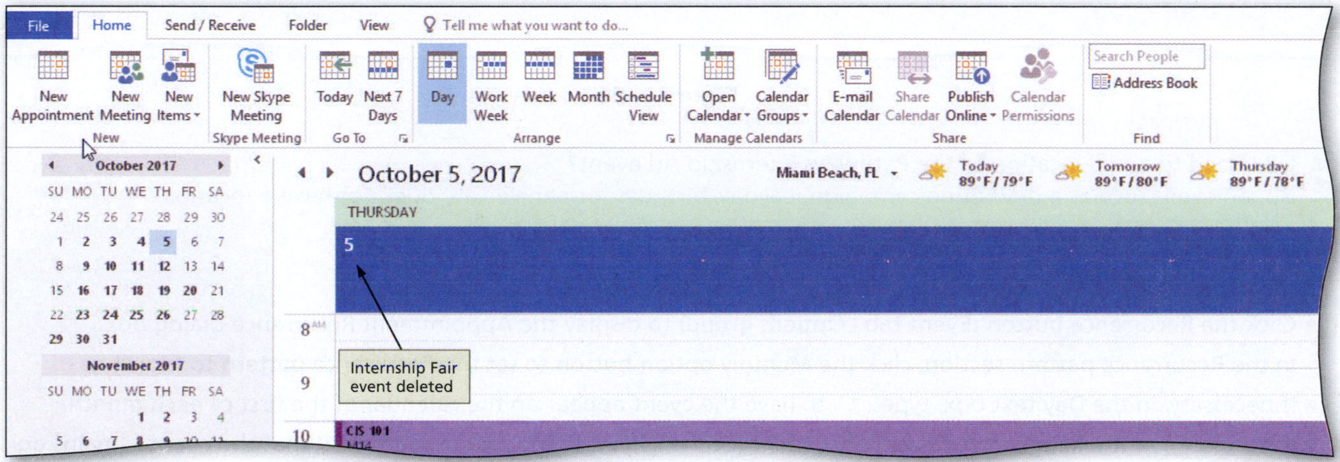

Figure 2–63

Other Ways

1. Select event, press DELETE

To Create a Recurring Event Using the Appointment Window

A recurring event is similar to a recurring appointment in that it occurs at regular intervals on your calendar. However, editing a recurring event is slightly different from editing one-time events. You can specify whether all occurrences in a series of recurring events need to be changed or if a single occurrence should be altered.

On the first day of each month, the college highlights an internship opportunity that Sophia wants to add to the calendar to keep track of when to prepare the marketing campaign for the internship. The following steps create a recurring event for the internship opportunity. ***Why?*** *To keep up with a periodic event such as your monthly or weekly occasion, the recurring event feature gives you a way to remind yourself of important dates.*

- Click the New Items button (Home tab | New group) to display the New Items list.
- Click 'All Day Event' to open the Untitled – Event window.
- In the Subject text box, type `Pathways Internship Ad` as the subject.
- In the first Start time text box, type `10/01/2017` as the date, and then press the ENTER key (Figure 2–64).

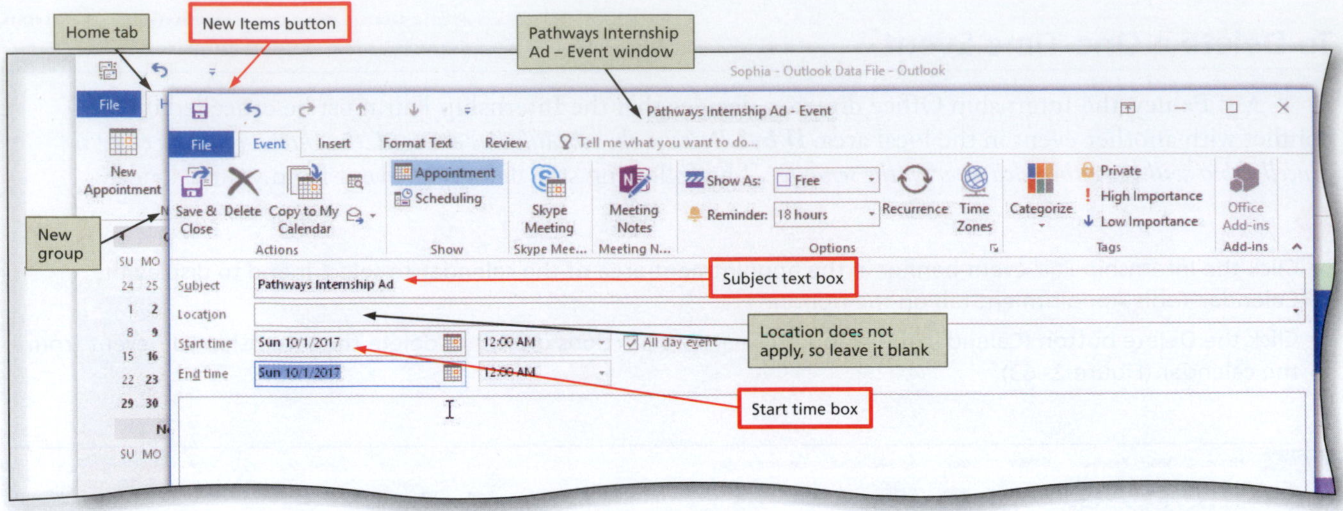

Figure 2–64

Q&A Do I need to add a location to the Pathways Internship Ad event?
No, an event such as a marketing campaign, payday, birthday, or anniversary does not have a location.

2

- Click the Recurrence button (Event tab | Options group) to display the Appointment Recurrence dialog box.
- In the Recurrence pattern section, click the Monthly option button to set the Recurrence pattern to Monthly.
- If necessary, in the Day text box, type `1` to have the event appear on the calendar at the first of each month.
- If necessary, in the Range of recurrence section, click the 'No end date' option button so that the event remains on the calendar indefinitely (Figure 2–65).

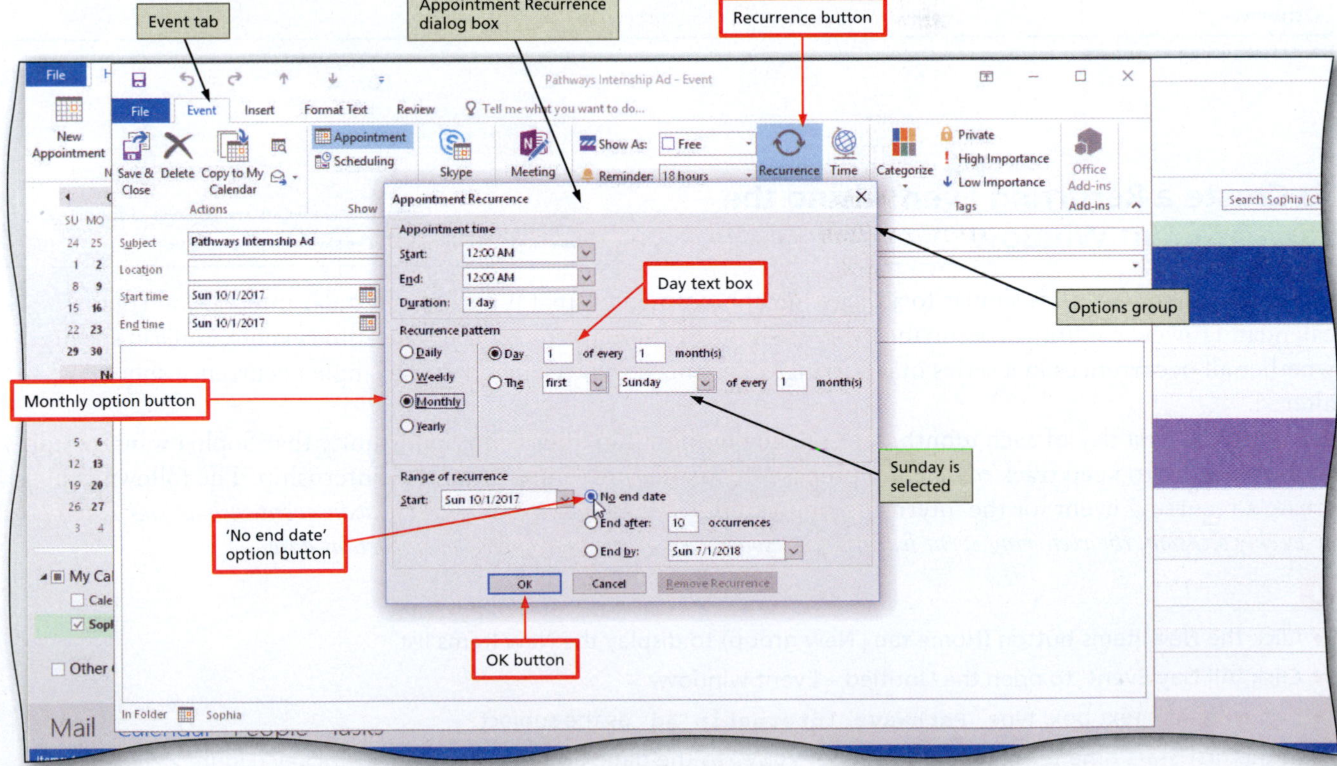

Figure 2–65

3

- Click the OK button to accept the recurrence settings and close the Appointment Recurrence dialog box.
- Click the Reminder box arrow (Recurring Event tab | Options group) to display the Reminder list of reminder time slots.
- Click None to remove the reminder from the event.
- Click the Categorize button (Recurring Event tab | Tags group) to display the Categorize list of color categories.
- Click the blue Work category to assign the event to a category (Figure 2–66).

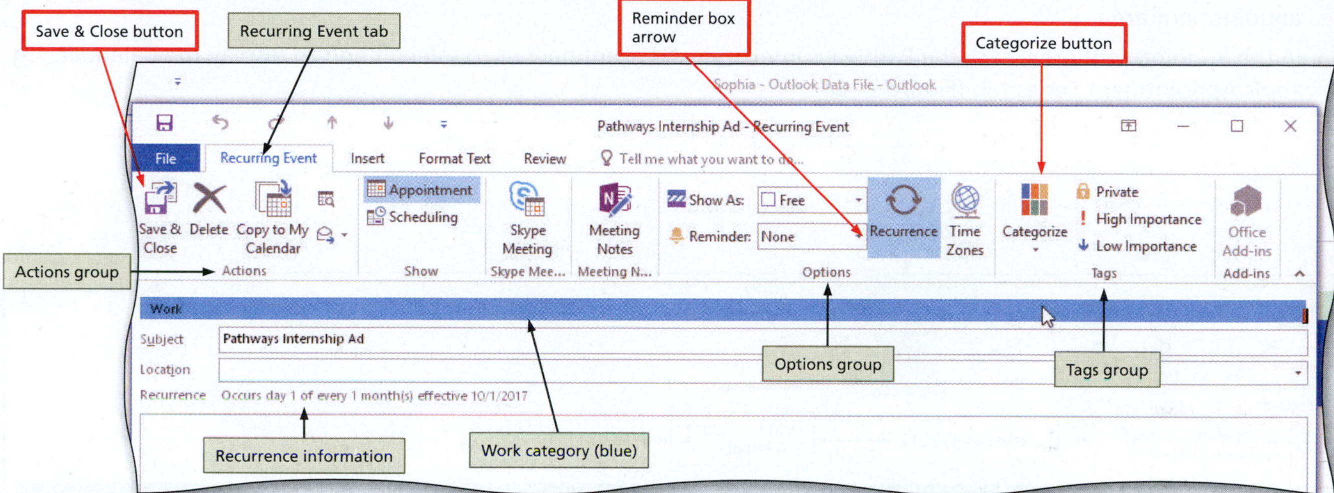

Figure 2–66

4

- Click the Save & Close button (Recurring Event tab | Actions group) to save the event and close the window.
- Click the Month button (Home tab | Arrange group) to view the Pathways Internship Ad event on the calendar (Figure 2–67).

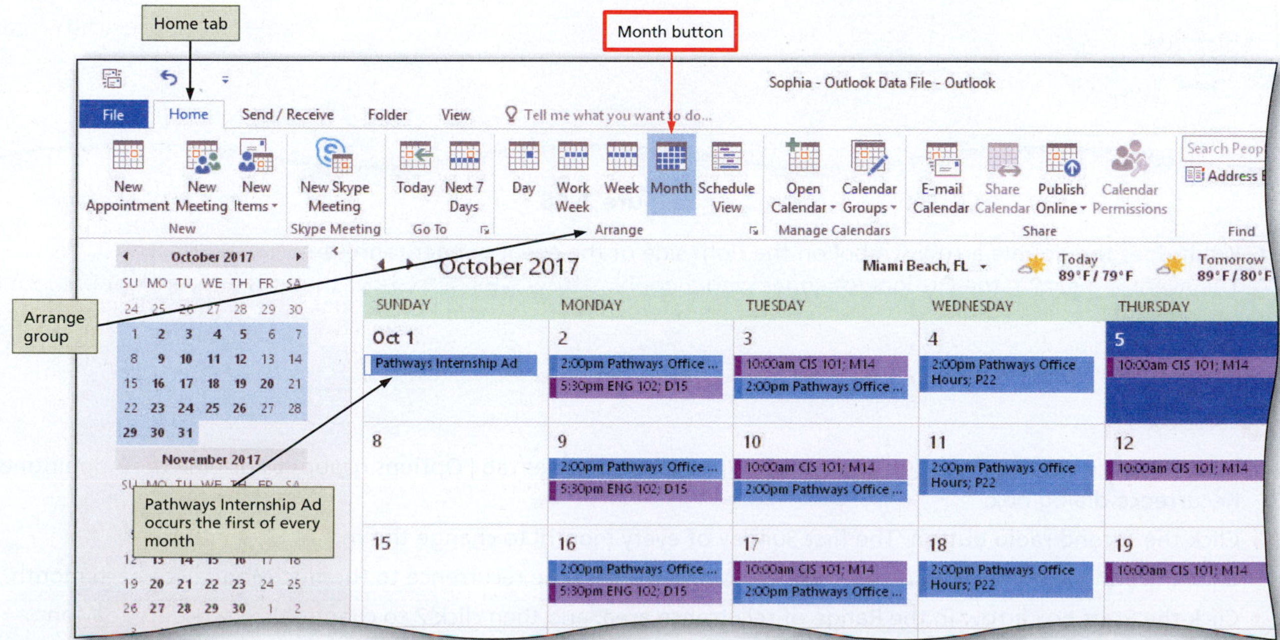

Figure 2–67

To Move a Recurring Event to a Different Day

Why? A recurring date may change to a different day or duration. The Internship Office Sophia works for is changing the internship ad rollout to the first Monday of each month. The recurring Pathways Internship Ad event must be changed for the entire series. The following steps change the date for all occurrences in a series.

- Click the Day button (Home tab | Arrange group) to display the Day view.
- Click 1 in the Date Navigator to display October 1, 2017 and the Pathways Internship Ad event banner in the appointment area.
- In the appointment area, click the Pathways Internship Ad event banner to select it and to display the Calendar Tools Appointment Series tab (Figure 2–68).

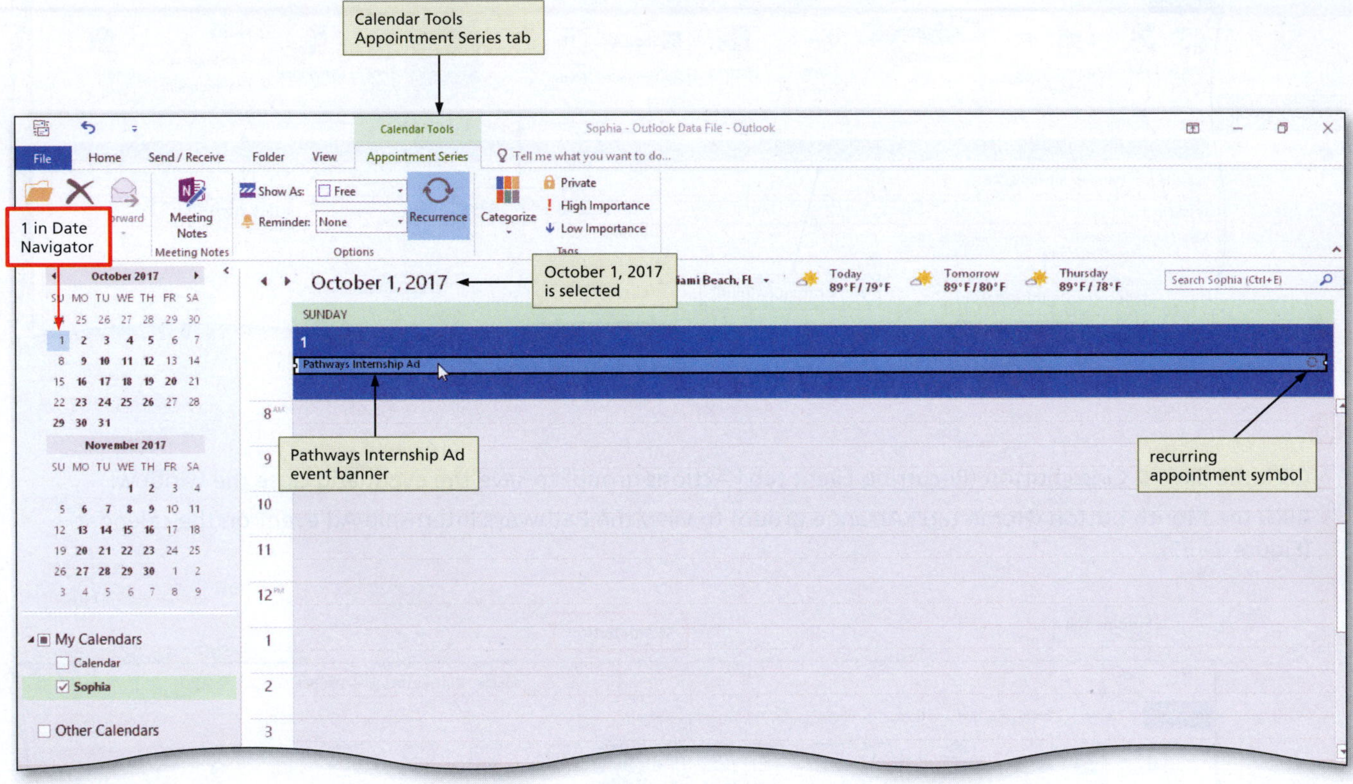

Figure 2–68

Q&A What does the double arrow symbol on the right side of the event banner represent?
The event appears in the Outlook calendar with a double arrow symbol to show that it is a recurring appointment.

2

- Click the Recurrence button (Calendar Tools Appointment Series tab | Options group) to display the Appointment Recurrence dialog box.
- Click the second radio button 'The first Sunday of every month' to change the recurrence pattern.
- Click the Sunday box arrow and then click to Monday to set the recurrence to the first Monday of each month.
- Click the Start box arrow in the Range of recurrence area, and then click 2 to change the start date to Mon 10/2/2017 (Figure 2–69).

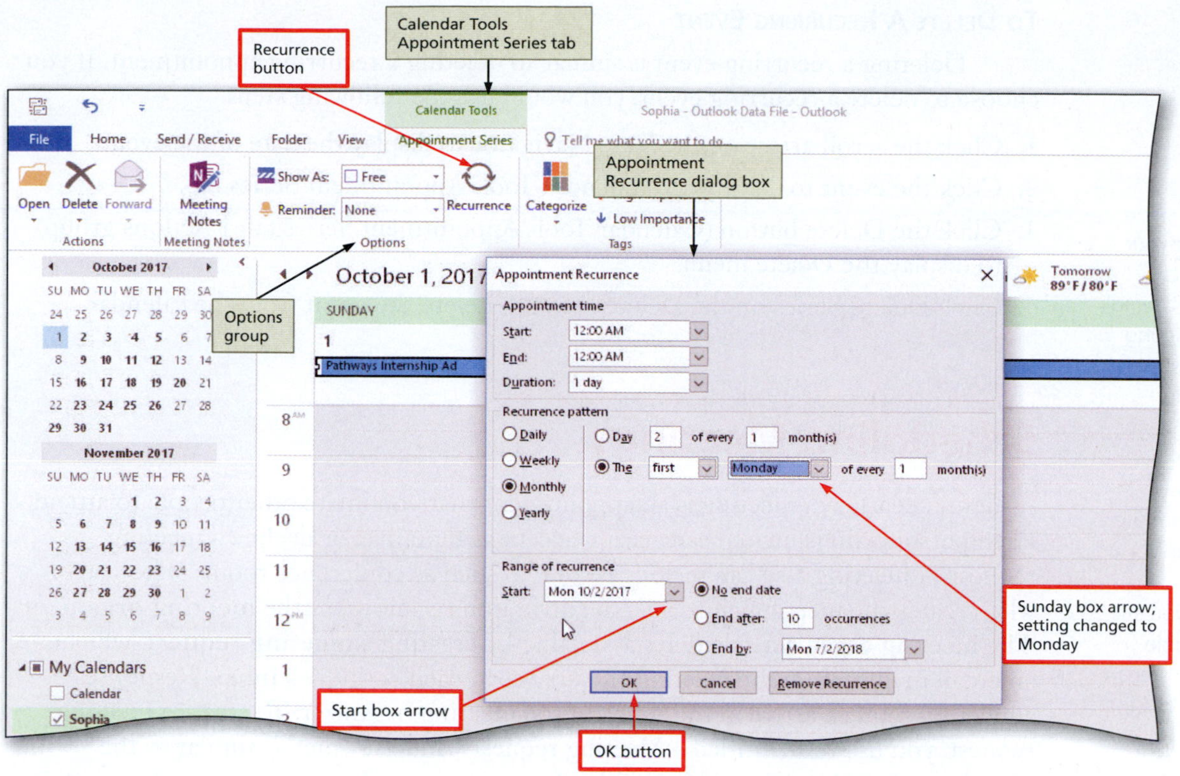

Figure 2–69

3

- Click the OK button to close the Appointment Recurrence dialog box and change the event day.
- Click the Month button (Home tab | Arrange group) to view the full month calendar (Figure 2–70).

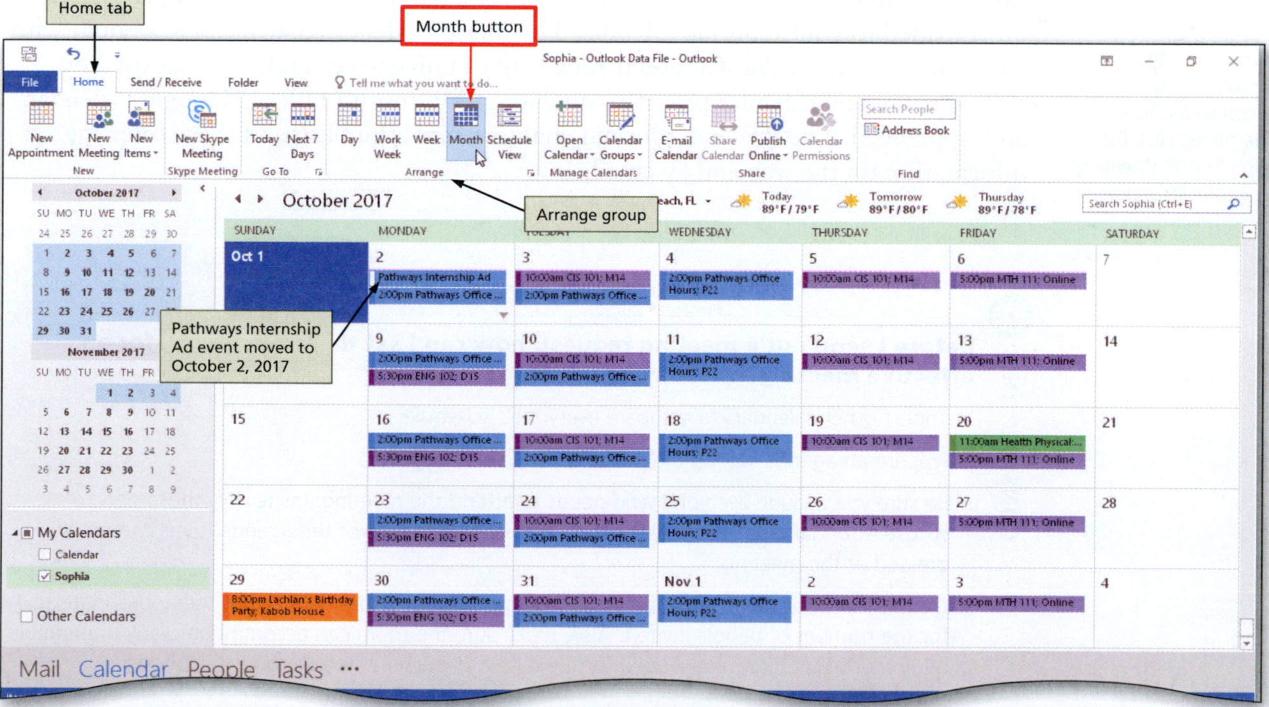

Figure 2–70

Other Ways

1. Double-click event, click entire series option button, click Recurrence button
2. Click event, press CTRL+O, click entire series option button, click Recurrence button

To Delete a Recurring Event

Deleting a recurring event is similar to deleting a recurring appointment. If you choose to delete a recurring event, you would use the following steps.

1. Click the scroll arrow on the Date Navigator to display the date of the event.
2. Click the event to display the Calendar Tools Appointment Series tab.
3. Click the Delete button (Calendar Tools Appointment Series tab | Actions group) to display the Delete menu.
4. Click Delete Series on the Delete menu to delete the event from the calendar.

If you are using your finger on a touch screen and are having difficulty completing the steps in this module, consider using a stylus. Many people find it easier to be precise with a stylus than with a finger. In addition, with a stylus you see the pointer. If you still are having trouble completing the steps with a stylus, try using a mouse.

Scheduling Meetings

As defined earlier, a meeting is an appointment that you invite other people to attend. Each person who is invited can accept, accept as tentative, or decline a meeting request. A meeting also can include resources such as conference rooms. The person who creates the meeting and sends the invitations is known as the **meeting organizer**. The meeting organizer schedules a meeting by creating a **meeting request**, which is an email invitation to the meeting and arrives in each attendee's Inbox. Responses to a meeting request arrive in the Inbox of the meeting organizer. To create a meeting request, you use the Untitled – Meeting request window, which is similar to the Untitled – Appointment window with a few exceptions. The meeting request window includes the To text box, where you enter an email address for **attendees**, who are people invited to the meeting, and the Send button, which sends the invitation for the meeting to the attendees. When a meeting request arrives in the attendee's Inbox, it displays an icon different from an email message icon.

Before you invite others to a meeting, confirm that the meeting date and time are available. Your school or business may have shared calendars that can be downloaded to your Outlook calendar. This shared calendar may be an iCalendar with an .ics file extension. An **iCalendar** represents a universal calendar format used by several email and calendar programs, including Microsoft Outlook, Google Calendar, and Apple iCal. The iCalendar format enables users to publish and share calendar information on the web and by email.

BTW

Scheduling Assistant

If you have an Exchange account, you can use the **Scheduling Assistant** to find a meeting time when attendees and resources, such as rooms, are available. When you set up a meeting and are connected to an Exchange server, click the Scheduling button (Meeting tab | Show group) and add attendees to view their schedules.

CONSIDER THIS

Before I send out a meeting request, how can I set the groundwork for an effective meeting?

- Import other calendars to compare everyone's schedule.
- Prepare an agenda stating the purpose of the meeting.
- Be sure you include everyone who needs to attend the meeting. Invite only those people whose attendance is absolutely necessary to ensure that all of the agenda items can be addressed at the meeting.
- Confirm that the location of the meeting is available and that the room is the appropriate size for the number of people invited. Also, make sure the room can accommodate any multimedia equipment that might be needed for the meeting, such as a projector or telephone.

To Import an iCalendar File

Before scheduling a meeting, you can open your school's calendar to view your availability. Your school has a shared calendar in the iCalendar format that contains the school's master schedule. The following steps import an iCalendar file into Outlook. ***Why?*** *By importing another calendar, you can compare available dates for a meeting.*

- Click the File tab on the ribbon to open the Backstage view.
- Click Open & Export to display the Open gallery (Figure 2–71).

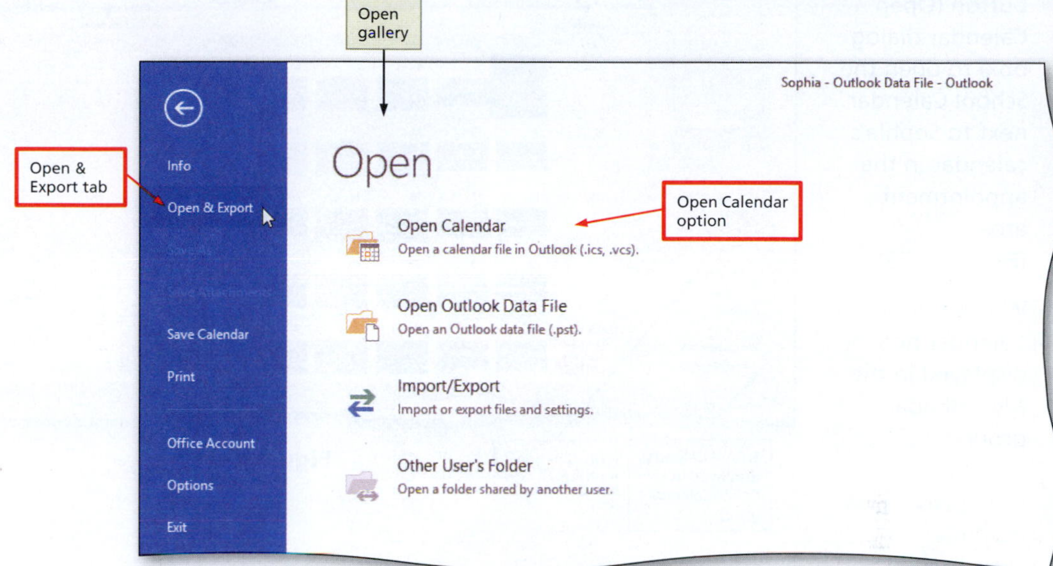

Figure 2–71

- Click Open Calendar in the Open gallery to display the Open Calendar dialog box.
- Navigate to the mailbox location (in this case, the Module 02 folder in the Outlook folder) (Figure 2–72).

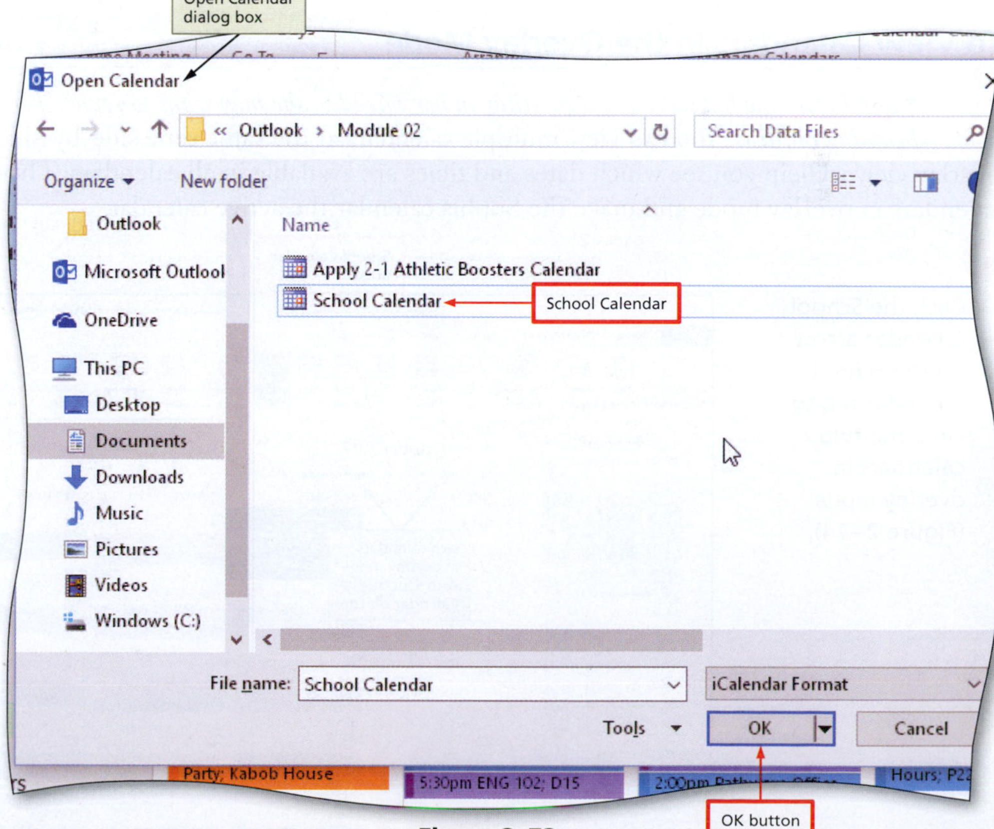

Figure 2–72

3

- Click School Calendar to select the file, and then click the OK button (Open Calendar dialog box) to open the School Calendar next to Sophia's calendar in the appointment area (Figure 2–73).

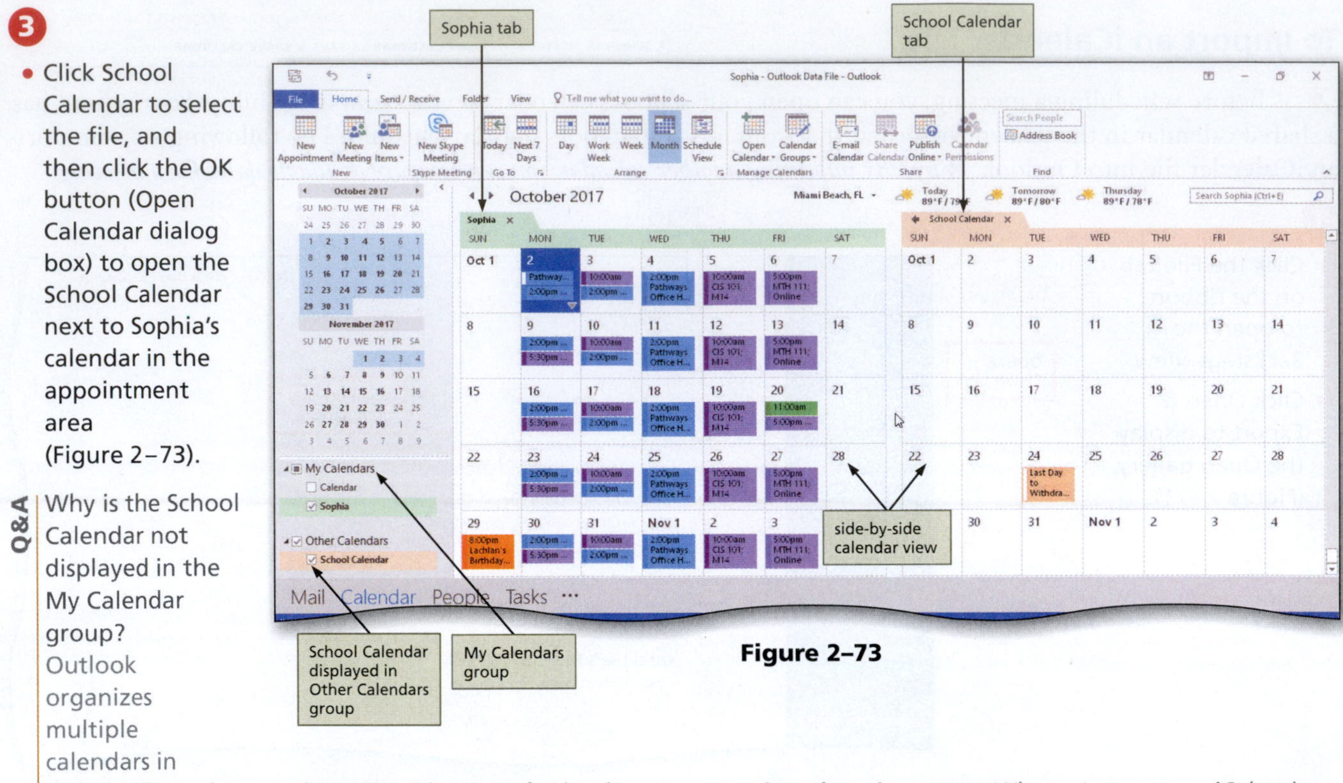

Figure 2–73

Q&A

Why is the School Calendar not displayed in the My Calendar group?

Outlook organizes multiple calendars in groups. If you frequently work with a set of calendars, you can view them in groups. When you open an iCalendar, it initially might appear in an Other Calendars group.

To View Calendars in the Overlay Mode

1 CONFIGURE CALENDAR OPTIONS | 2 CREATE & MANIPULATE APPOINTMENTS | 3 SCHEDULE EVENTS
4 SCHEDULE MEETINGS | 5 PRINT CALENDAR | 6 SAVE & SHARE CALENDAR

Why? Before Sophia schedules a meeting on her calendar, she may want to review her school's official calendar to avoid scheduling conflicts. You can view multiple calendars at the same time side-by-side or combined into an overlay view to help you see which dates and times are available in all calendars. The following steps display both calendars in overlay mode and make the Sophia calendar the active calendar.

1

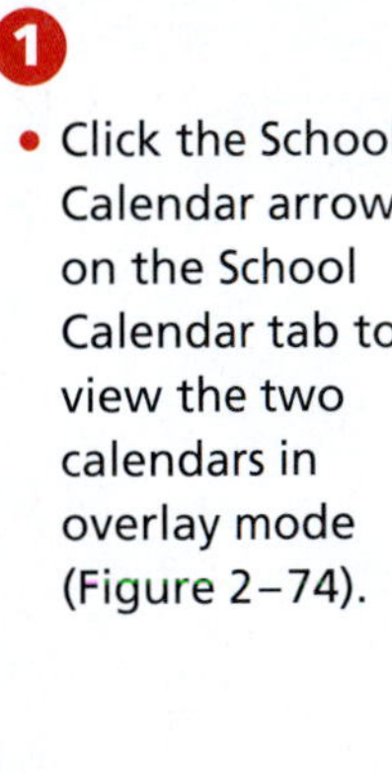

- Click the School Calendar arrow on the School Calendar tab to view the two calendars in overlay mode (Figure 2–74).

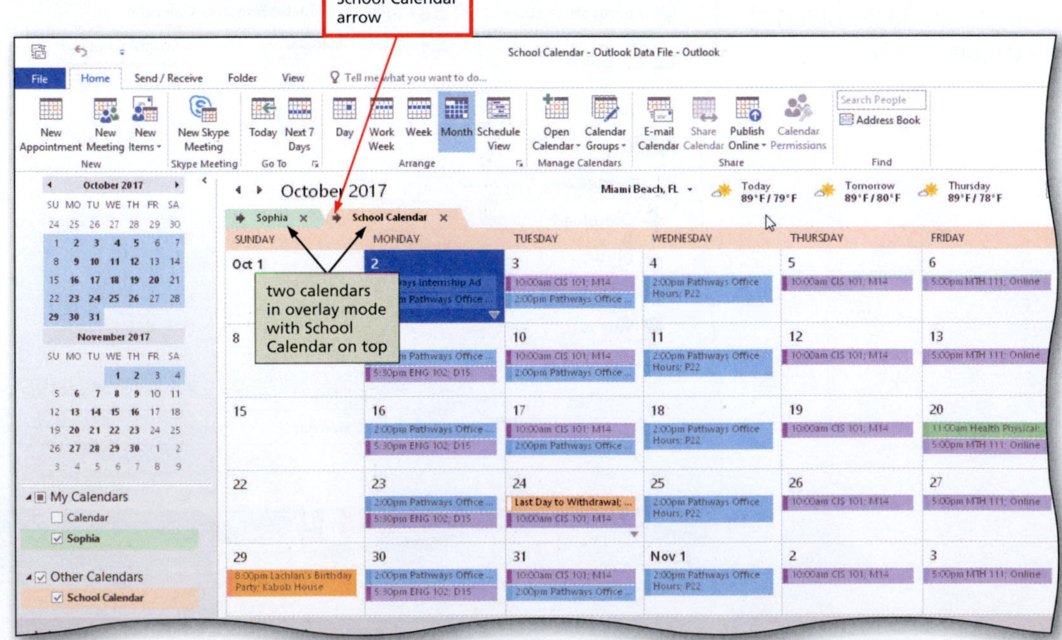

Figure 2–74

2

- Click the Sophia tab to display the Sophia calendar in front of the School Calendar (Figure 2–75).

Q&A What happens if I click the arrow on Sophia's calendar at this point?
Outlook again displays the calendars side by side.

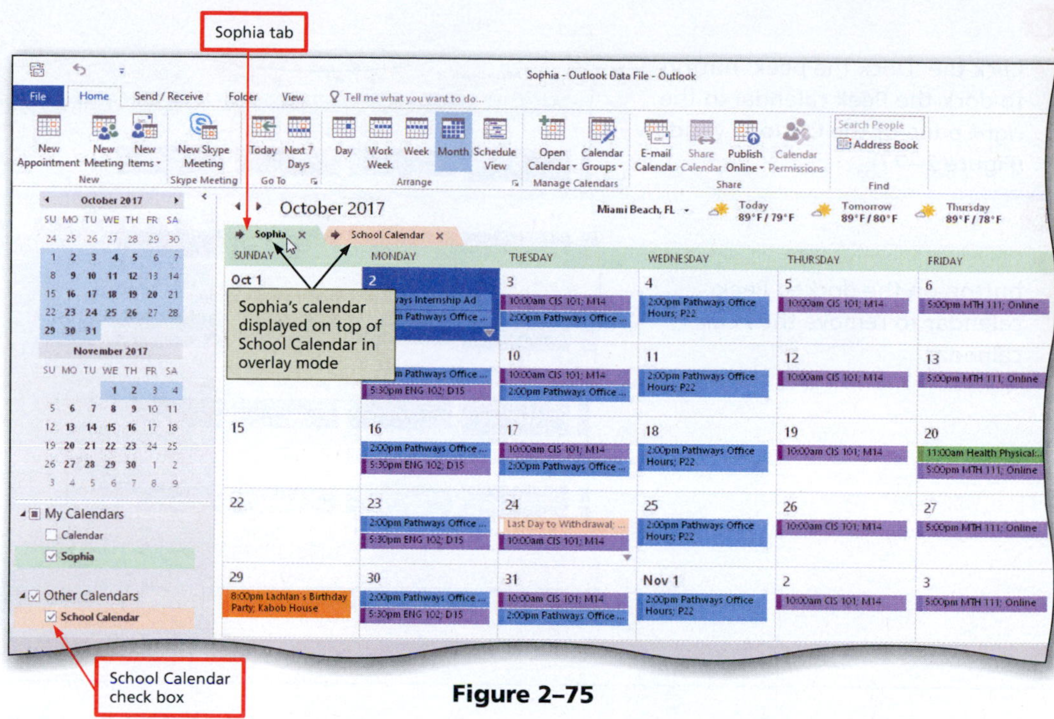

Figure 2–75

To View and Dock the Peek Calendar

1 CONFIGURE CALENDAR OPTIONS | 2 CREATE & MANIPULATE APPOINTMENTS | 3 SCHEDULE EVENTS
4 SCHEDULE MEETINGS | 5 PRINT CALENDAR | 6 SAVE & SHARE CALENDAR

The Outlook Navigation bar provides a **Peek** feature, a pop-up window that provides access to email, calendar, people, and tasks. ***Why?*** *Using the Peek feature, you can take a quick glance at your schedule without having to rearrange windows or lose your train of thought.* When you hover over Calendar in the Navigation Pane, a Peek calendar of the current month opens and the current date is highlighted with a blue background. The Peek calendar can be docked in the right pane of the calendar. Appointments and meetings scheduled for today appear below the calendar. The following steps view, dock, and remove the Peek calendar.

1

- Click the School Calendar check box in the Navigation Pane to remove the School Calendar from the Outlook window.
- Point to Calendar on the Navigation bar to display the Peek calendar with today's appointments or meetings (Figure 2–76).

Q&A Why do I not see any appointments or meetings in the Peek calendar?
If you do not have any appointments or meetings today in the default Calendar, the Peek calendar does not display any calendar items.

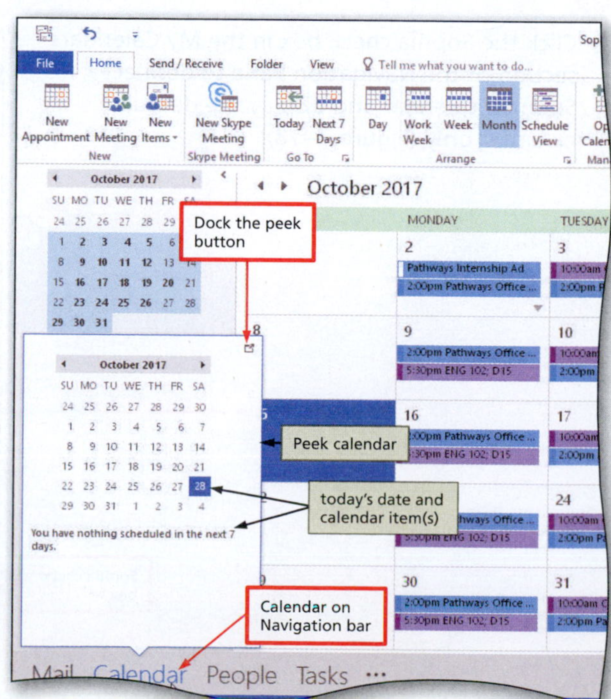

Figure 2–76

2

- Click the 'Dock the peek' button to dock the Peek calendar in the right pane of the Outlook window (Figure 2–77).

3

- Click the 'Remove the peek' button on the docked Peek calendar to remove the Peek calendar.

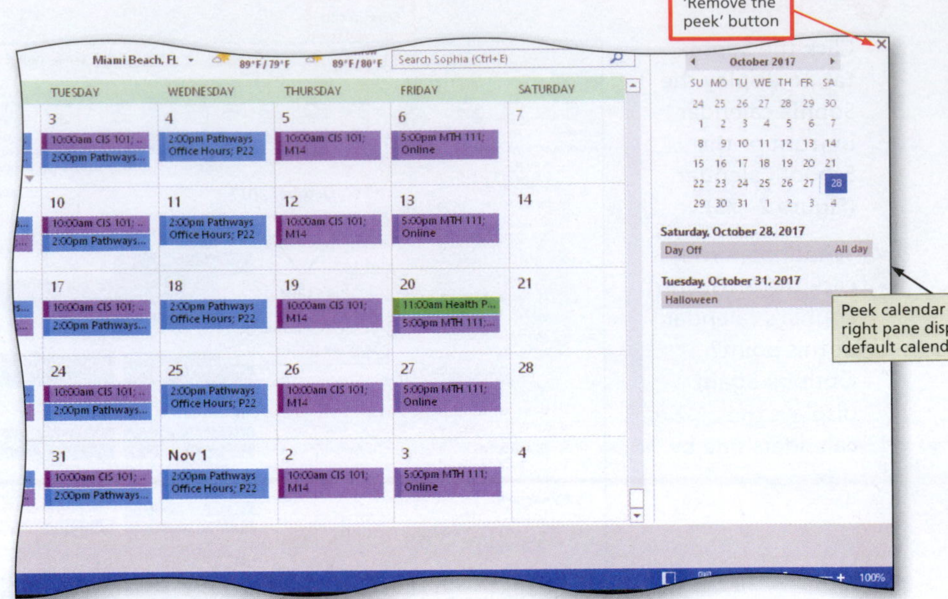

Figure 2–77

To Create and Send a Meeting Request

1 CONFIGURE CALENDAR OPTIONS | 2 CREATE & MANIPULATE APPOINTMENTS | 3 SCHEDULE EVENTS
4 SCHEDULE MEETINGS | 5 PRINT CALENDAR | 6 SAVE & SHARE CALENDAR

***Why?** To find the best time to meet with other people, request a meeting, and keep track of the meeting date in your Inbox, you can send a meeting request in Outlook.* Sophia needs to meet with Ms. Pauley to discuss rescheduling the Pathways Internship Fair. Rather than send an email message requesting the meeting, she decides to use Outlook Calendar to create this meeting. Meetings can be scheduled on your default calendar or supplemental calendars. The following steps display the default calendar, create a meeting request, and send an invitation to the financial aid office. If you are completing this project on a personal computer, your email address must be set up in Outlook (see Module 1) so you can send an email meeting invitation. Use the email address of your instructor instead of the Ms. Pauley's email address.

- Click the Sophia check box in the My Calendars section of the Navigation Pane to deselect Sophia's calendar and display the default calendar only (Figure 2–78).

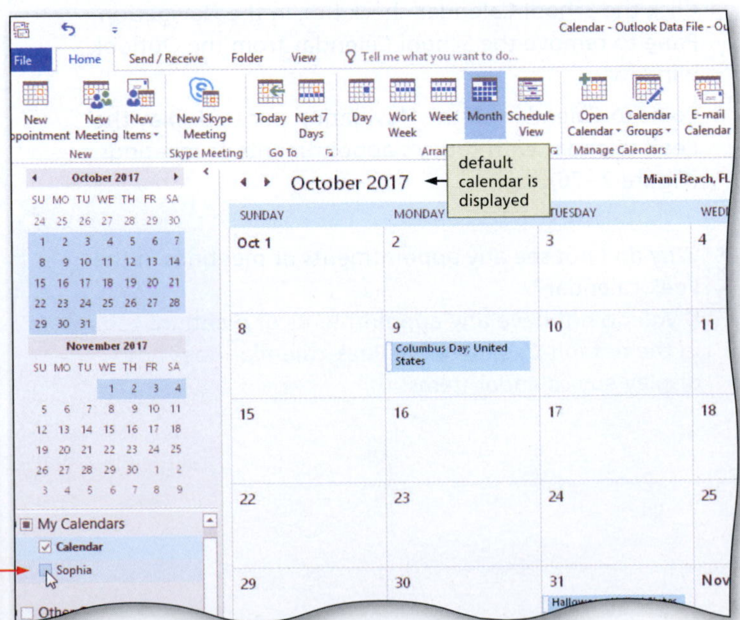

Figure 2–78

2

- Click the New Meeting button (Home tab | New group) to open the Untitled – Meeting window.
- Click the To text box and then type `ella.pauley@outlook.com` (substitute your instructor's email address for the email address) as the invitee to this meeting.
- Press the TAB key to move the insertion point to the Subject text box.
- Type `New Date for Pathways Internship Fair` as the subject of the meeting.
- Press the TAB key to move the insertion point to the Location text box.
- Type `P22` as the location of the meeting (Figure 2–79).

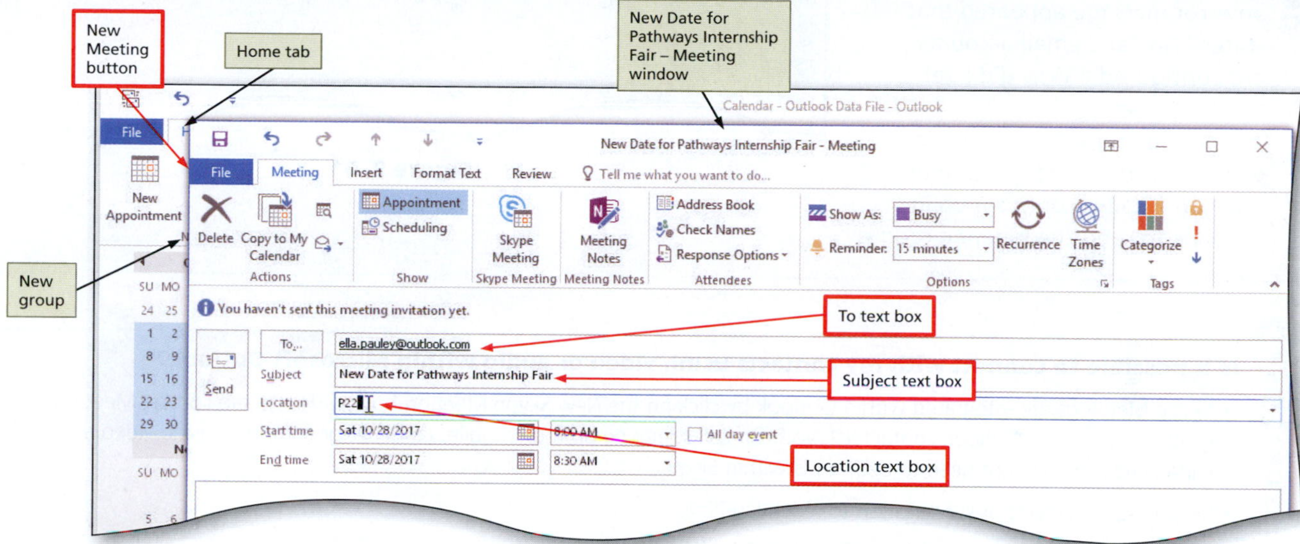

Figure 2–79

Q&A Why does the message header include the text, "You haven't sent this meeting invitation yet"?

This notice reminds you that you have not yet sent the invitation to the meeting. If you review this invitation after sending it, the notice no longer appears.

3

- Press the TAB key to select the date in the first Start time box.
- Type `10/2/2017` as the start date of the meeting, and then press the TAB key to select the time in the second Start time box.
- Type `1:30 PM` as the start time for the meeting, and then press the TAB key two times to select the time in the second End time box.
- Type `2:30 PM` as the end time for the meeting (Figure 2–80).

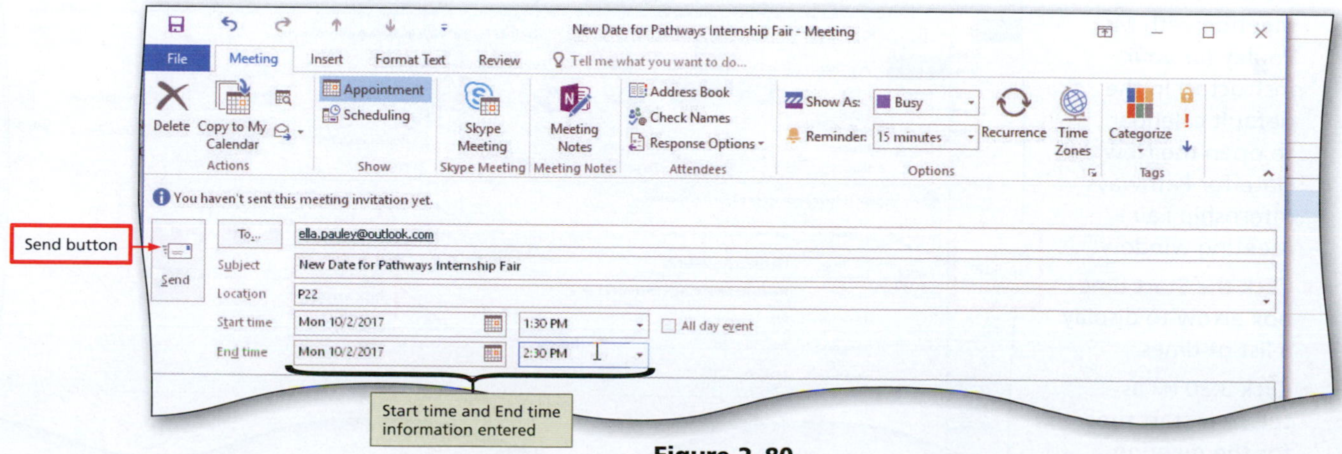

Figure 2–80

- Click the Send button to send the invitation and add the meeting to the calendar.
- If necessary, add an email account to Outlook to send the invitation to view the meeting on the calendar (Figure 2–81).

Figure 2–81

Q&A When I sent the meeting request, an error message appeared that states "No valid email accounts are configured." Why did I get this error message?

A meeting request sends an email to each of the invitees. You must have an email account set up in Outlook to send the meeting request.

CONSIDER THIS

Is it possible to connect with my contacts using video or audio within Microsoft Outlook?

- Skype Meetings are integrated within Outlook by clicking the New Skype Meeting button (Home tab | Skype Meeting group). Using your Outlook contact list, you can call someone on their mobile, landline, or computer using video and audio capabilities. You do not need to be friends within Skype.
- Skype requires credit or subscription to reach landlines.

To Change the Time of a Meeting and Send an Update

1 CONFIGURE CALENDAR OPTIONS | 2 CREATE & MANIPULATE APPOINTMENTS | 3 SCHEDULE EVENTS
4 SCHEDULE MEETINGS | 5 PRINT CALENDAR | 6 SAVE & SHARE CALENDAR

Your schedule has changed, which means you need to change the time of the meeting about the Pathways Internship Fair and send an update about the change. Though the invitee can propose a new time, only the originator can change or delete the meeting. ***Why?*** *You can update any meeting request to add or remove attendees or resources, change the meeting to a recurring series, or move the meeting to a different date or time.* The following steps change the time of the meeting and send an update to the attendee. If you are completing this project on a personal computer, your email account must be set up in Outlook (see Module 1) to be able to view the meeting request.

- Double-click the meeting with Ms. Pauley (or your instructor) in the default calendar to open the New Date for Pathways Internship Fair – Meeting window.
- Click the Start time box arrow to display a list of times.
- Click 3:30 PM as the new start time for the meeting (Figure 2–82).

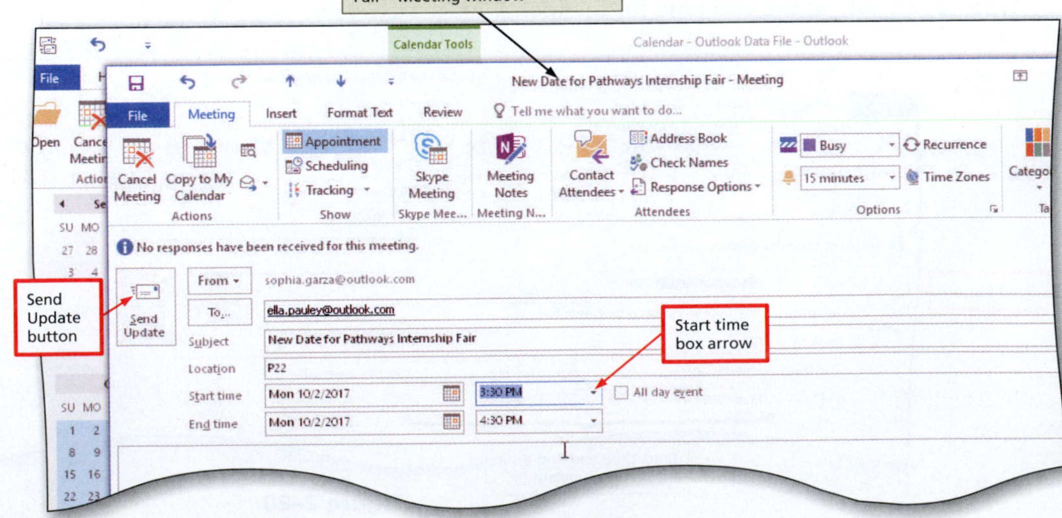

Figure 2–82

2

- Click the Send Update button in the message header to send the new information, close the meeting request, and view the updated meeting in the appointment area (Figure 2–83).

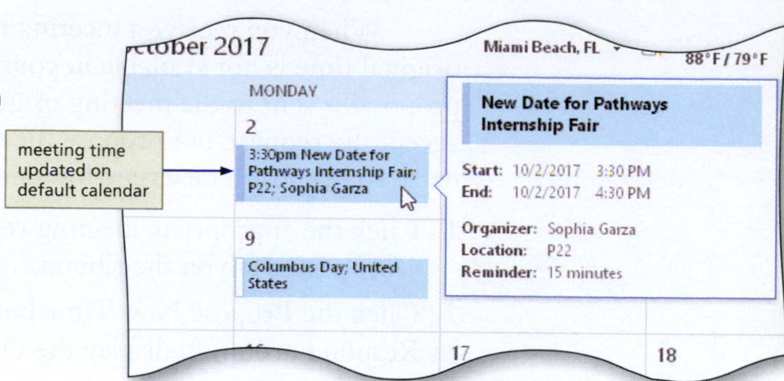

Figure 2–83

Q&A What if I need to cancel the meeting?
To remove a meeting, click the meeting in the appointment area to display the Calendar Tools Meeting tab, click the Cancel Meeting button (Calendar Tools Meeting tab | Actions group), and then click the Send Cancellation button to send the cancellation notice to the attendee and remove the meeting from the calendar.

Other Ways

1. Drag meeting to new time, click 'Save changes and send update', click OK, click Send Update

To Reply to a Meeting Request

1 CONFIGURE CALENDAR OPTIONS | 2 CREATE & MANIPULATE APPOINTMENTS | 3 SCHEDULE EVENTS
4 SCHEDULE MEETINGS | 5 PRINT CALENDAR | 6 SAVE & SHARE CALENDAR

Ms. Pauley has received Sophia's meeting request in an email message and wants to respond. ***Why?*** *Outlook allows invitees to choose from four response options: Accept, Tentative, Decline, or Propose New Time.* The following steps accept the meeting request. If you have a meeting request in your personal email that is set up using Outlook, substitute your meeting request in the following steps. If you do not have any meeting requests, read these steps without performing them.

1

- Click Mail on the Navigation bar to display the Inbox folder.
- Double-click the email message header to open the meeting invitation (Figure 2–84).

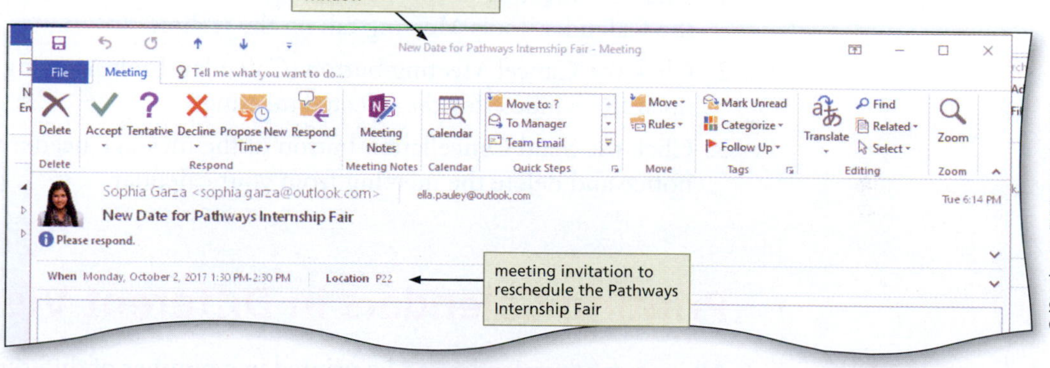

Figure 2–84

2

- Click the Accept button (Meeting tab | Respond group) to display the options for accepting the meeting (Figure 2–85).

3

- Click Send the Response Now to send the accept response and add the meeting to the calendar.

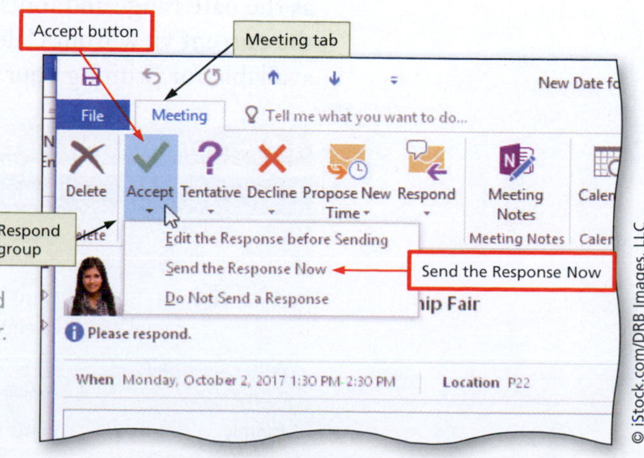

Figure 2–85

Q&A What happened to the meeting invitation in the Inbox?
When you accept or tentatively accept a meeting request, the invitation is deleted from the Inbox and the meeting is added to your calendar. The meeting response is in the Sent Items folder.

What happens when I decline a meeting request?
When a meeting request is declined, it is removed from your Inbox and the meeting is not added to your calendar. The reply is placed in the Sent Items folder.

To Propose A New Meeting Time

When you receive a meeting invitation, you can propose a new time if the original time is not available in your calendar. When you propose a new time, a proposal is sent to the meeting originator via email, indicating that you tentatively accept the request, but propose the meeting be held at a different time or on a different date. To propose a new time for a meeting, you would perform the following steps.

1. Click the appropriate meeting request to display the Calendar Tools Meeting Occurrence tab on the ribbon.
2. Click the Propose New Time button (Calendar Tools Meeting Occurrence tab | Respond group) to display the Occurrence menu.
3. Click the Tentative and Propose New Time option to display the Propose New Time dialog box for the selected meeting.
4. Drag through the time slot that you want to propose, or enter the appropriate information in the Meeting start and Meeting end boxes (Propose New Time dialog box).
5. Click the Propose time button to open the New Time Proposed – Meeting Response window.
6. Click the Send button.

To Cancel A Meeting

To cancel a meeting, you would perform the following steps.

1. Click the meeting request in the appointment area to select the meeting and display the Calendar Tools Meeting tab on the ribbon.
2. Click the Cancel Meeting button (Calendar Tools Meeting tab | Actions group) to open the window for the selected meeting.
3. Click the Send Cancellation button in the message header to send the cancellation notice and delete the meeting from your calendar.

Printing Calendars in Different Views

All or part of a calendar can be printed in a number of different views, or **print styles**. You can print a monthly, daily, or weekly view of your calendar and select options such as the date range and fonts to use. You also can view your calendar in a list by changing the current view from Calendar view to List view. Table 2–6 lists the print styles available for printing your calendar from Calendar view.

Table 2–6 Print Styles for Calendar View

Print Style	Description
Daily	Prints a daily appointment schedule for a specific date including one day per page, a daily task list, an area for notes, and a two-month calendar
Weekly Agenda	Prints a seven-day weekly calendar with one week per page and a two-month calendar
Weekly Calendar	Prints a seven-day weekly calendar with one week per page and an hourly schedule, similar to the Daily style
Monthly	Prints five weeks per page of a particular month or date range
Tri-fold	Prints a page for each day, including a daily task list and a weekly schedule
Calendar Details	Prints a list of calendar items and supporting details

To Print the Calendar in Weekly Calendar Style

Why? *Printing a calendar enables you to distribute the calendar to others in a form that can be read or viewed, but cannot be edited.* Sophia can print her calendar to create a hard copy of her first week of classes. The following steps print a calendar in a weekly calendar style.

1

- Click Calendar on the Navigation bar to display the Outlook calendar.
- If necessary, click the Sophia check box to display Sophia's calendar.
- If necessary, click the other check boxes to close the other calendars.
- Click the Go to Date Dialog Box Launcher (Home tab | Go To group) to display the Go To Date dialog box.
- Type `10/1/2017` in the Date text box to select that date.
- If necessary, click the Show in button, and then click Month Calendar to show the month view in the appointment area.
- Click the OK button to close the Go To Date dialog box (Figure 2–86).

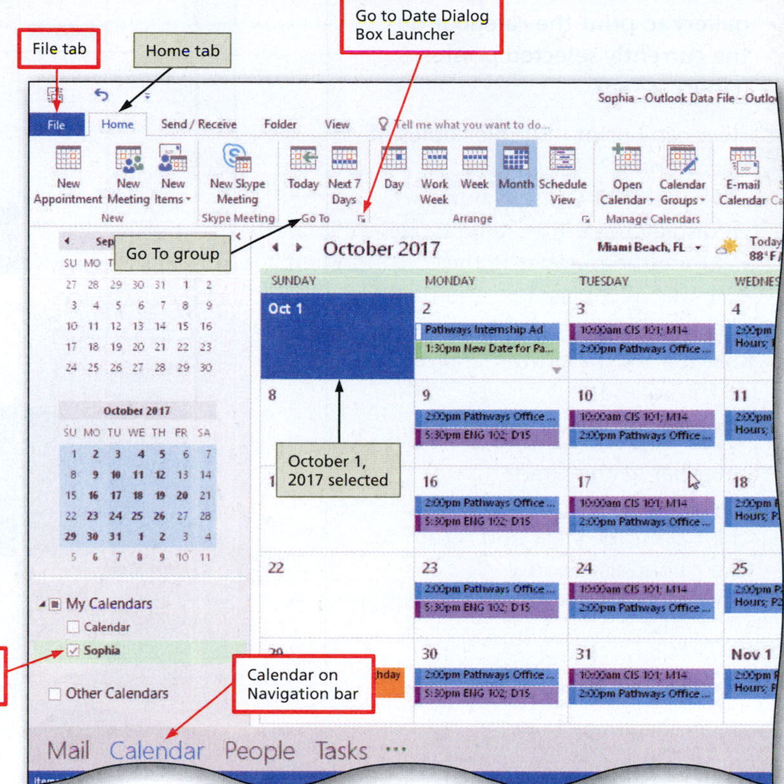

Figure 2–86

2

- Click File on the ribbon to open the Backstage view.
- Click the Print tab in the Backstage view to display the Print gallery.
- Click Weekly Calendar Style in the Settings list to preview how the printed calendar will look in Weekly Calendar Style (Figure 2–87).

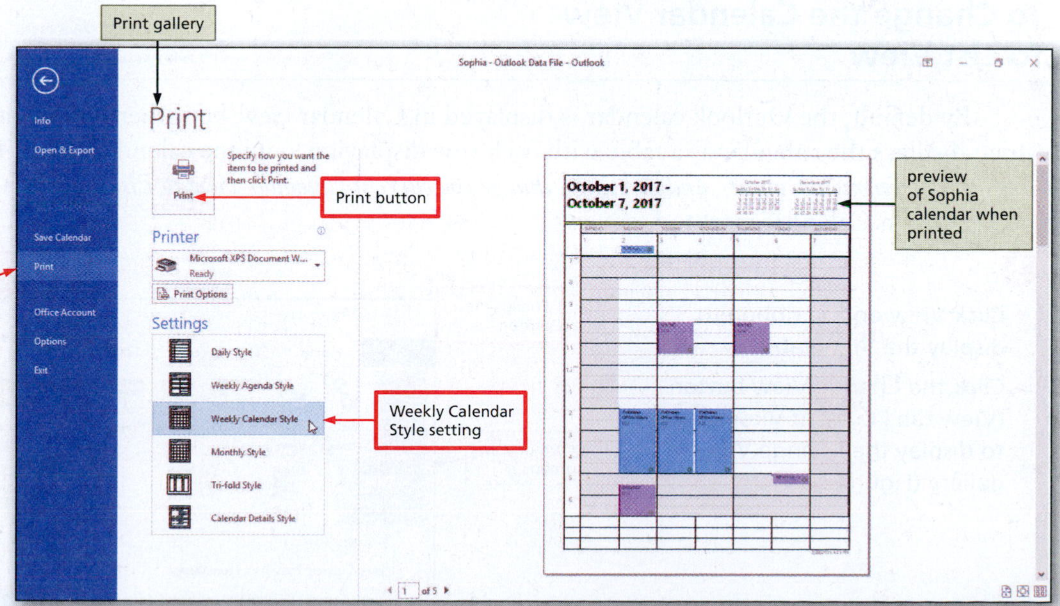

Figure 2–87

Experiment

- Click the other settings to preview the different print styles. When finished, select Weekly Calendar Style.

- If necessary, click the desired printer to change the currently selected printer.
- Click the Print button in the Print gallery to print the calendar on the currently selected printer (Figure 2–88).

Q&A How can I print multiple copies of my calendar?
Click the Print Options button to display the Print dialog box, increase the number in the Number of copies box, and then click the Print button to send the calendar to the printer and return to the calendar.

What if I decide not to print the calendar at this time?
Click File on the ribbon to close the Backstage view and return to the calendar window.

October 1, 2017 - October 7, 2017

Figure 2–88

Other Ways

1. Press CTRL+P, press ENTER

To Change the Calendar View to List View

1 CONFIGURE CALENDAR OPTIONS | 2 CREATE & MANIPULATE APPOINTMENTS | 3 SCHEDULE EVENTS
4 SCHEDULE MEETINGS | **5 PRINT CALENDAR** | 6 SAVE & SHARE CALENDAR

By default, the Outlook calendar is displayed in Calendar view, but other options include a List view, which displays the calendar as a table with each row displaying a unique calendar item. ***Why?*** *To display all of your calendar appointments, events, and meetings, change the current Calendar view to List view.* The following steps change the view from Calendar view to List view.

- Click View on the ribbon to display the View tab.
- Click the Change View button (View tab | Current View group) to display the Change View gallery (Figure 2–89).

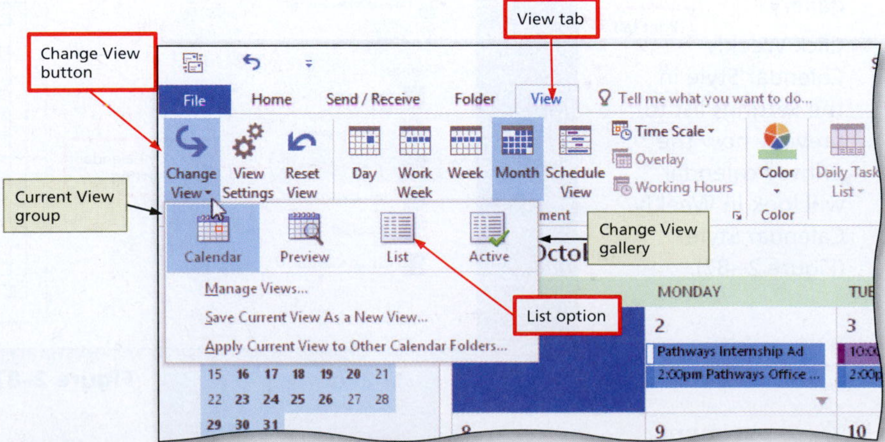

Figure 2–89

- Click List in the Change View gallery to display a list of calendar items in the appointment area (Figure 2–90).

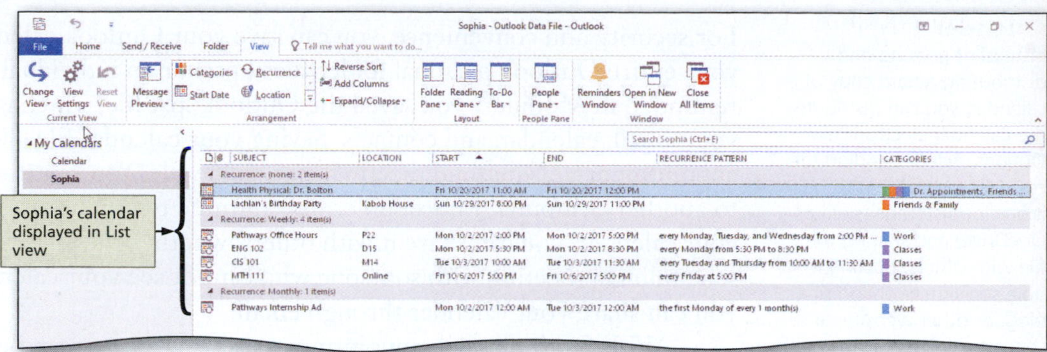

Figure 2–90

To Print the Calendar in List View

To print a list of your calendar items in a table, print the List view display. The following steps print the calendar in Table style.

BTW

Changing Settings before Printing

To change the margins, page orientation, or paper size before printing, click the Print Options button in the Print gallery and then click the Page Setup button to display the Page Setup: Table Style dialog box.

1. Click File on the ribbon to open the Backstage view.
2. Click the Print tab in the Backstage view to display the Print gallery.
3. Click the Table Style option in the Settings list to preview the calendar in Table Style.
4. If necessary, click the Printer box to display a list of available printer options, and then click the desired printer to change the selected printer.
5. Click the Print button to send the list of appointments to the selected printer (Figure 2–91).

Q&A When I changed the view from List view to Calendar view, why did the Calendar display the current date and not the date I printed?

The calendar always displays the current date when you change from List view to Calendar view.

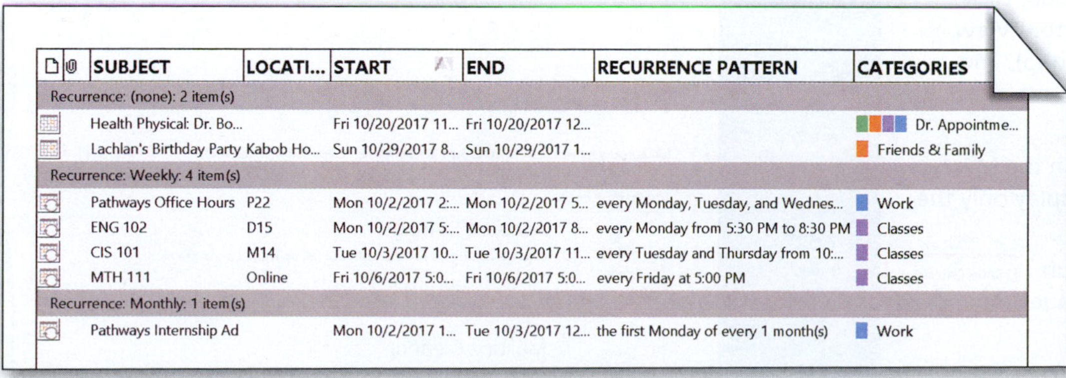

SUBJECT	LOCATI...	START	END	RECURRENCE PATTERN	CATEGORIES
Recurrence: (none): 2 item(s)					
Health Physical: Dr. Bo...		Fri 10/20/2017 11...	Fri 10/20/2017 12...		Dr. Appointme...
Lachlan's Birthday Party	Kabob Ho...	Sun 10/29/2017 8...	Sun 10/29/2017 1...		Friends & Family
Recurrence: Weekly: 4 item(s)					
Pathways Office Hours	P22	Mon 10/2/2017 2:...	Mon 10/2/2017 5...	every Monday, Tuesday, and Wednes...	Work
ENG 102	D15	Mon 10/2/2017 5:...	Mon 10/2/2017 8...	every Monday from 5:30 PM to 8:30 PM	Classes
CIS 101	M14	Tue 10/3/2017 10...	Tue 10/3/2017 11...	every Tuesday and Thursday from 10:...	Classes
MTH 111	Online	Fri 10/6/2017 5:0...	Fri 10/6/2017 5:0...	every Friday at 5:00 PM	Classes
Recurrence: Monthly: 1 item(s)					
Pathways Internship Ad		Mon 10/2/2017 1...	Tue 10/3/2017 12...	the first Monday of every 1 month(s)	Work

Figure 2–91

Other Ways

1. Press CTRL+P, click Print

BTW
Distributing a Calendar
Instead of printing and distributing a hard copy of a calendar, you can distribute the calendar electronically. Options include sending the calendar via email; posting it on cloud storage (such as OneDrive) and sharing the file with others; posting it on a social networking site, blog, or other website; and sharing a link associated with an online location of the calendar. You also can create and share a PDF or XPS image of the calendar, so that users can view the file in Acrobat Reader or XPS Viewer instead of in Outlook.

Saving and Sharing the Calendar

For security and convenience, you can save your Outlook calendar by backing up your entire Outlook personal folder files (.pst) or an individual calendar (.ics). As a reminder, in Module 1 you saved the Outlook .pst file, which contained a backup of your email, calendar, and contacts. Saving your calendar file allows you to back up your appointments, events, and meetings in a single file. You can then move your calendar to another computer, for example, and continue to schedule items there. Besides saving your calendar, you can share it with others, whether they use Outlook or not. Finally, scheduling a meeting with someone who cannot see your calendar can be difficult, so you can share your calendar through email.

With Outlook, each appointment, task, or contact can be saved as a separate iCalendar file or you can save the whole calendar to your local computer or external storage device. An iCalendar file with the .ics file extension can be imported by other programs such as Google Calendar. Instead of emailing an iCalendar file as an attachment to share your calendar, you can share portions of your entire calendar through a built-in function in Outlook.

To Save a Calendar as an iCalendar File

1 CONFIGURE CALENDAR OPTIONS | 2 CREATE & MANIPULATE APPOINTMENTS | 3 SCHEDULE EVENTS
4 SCHEDULE MEETINGS | 5 PRINT CALENDAR | **6 SAVE & SHARE CALENDAR**

You have performed many tasks while creating this calendar and do not want to risk losing work completed thus far. Accordingly, you should save the calendar on your hard disk, OneDrive, or a location that is most appropriate to your situation.

The following steps assume you already have created folders for storing your files, for example, an Outlook folder (for your class) that contains a Module 02 folder (for your assignments). Thus, these steps save the calendar in the Module 02 folder in the Outlook folder in your desired save location. For a detailed example of the procedure for saving a file in a folder or saving a file on OneDrive, refer to the Office and Windows module at the beginning of this book.

Why? *By saving a copy of your calendar to an iCalendar format, you can back up or share your calendar with your business colleagues or friends.* The following steps save a calendar. They assume you already have created folders for storing your files, for example, an Outlook folder (for your class) that contains a Module 02 folder (for your assignments).

- Click View on the ribbon, click the Change View button (View tab | Current View group), and then click Calendar to return to Calendar view.
- Use the check boxes in the My Calendars pane to display only the Sophia calendar.
- Click File on the ribbon to display the Backstage view (Figure 2–92).

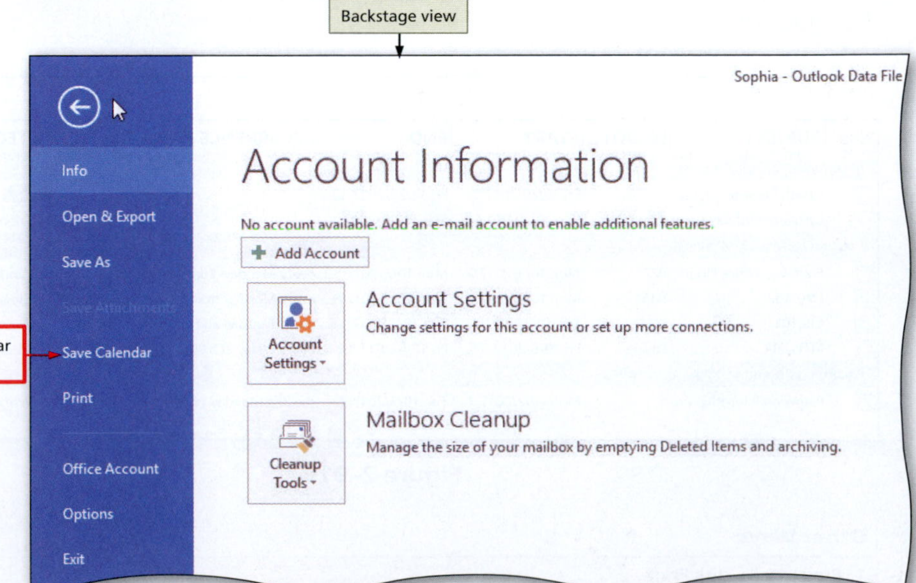

Figure 2–92

2

- Click the Save Calendar tab to display the Save As dialog box.
- Navigate to the desired save location (in this case, the Module 02 folder in the Outlook folder or your class folder) (Figure 2–93).

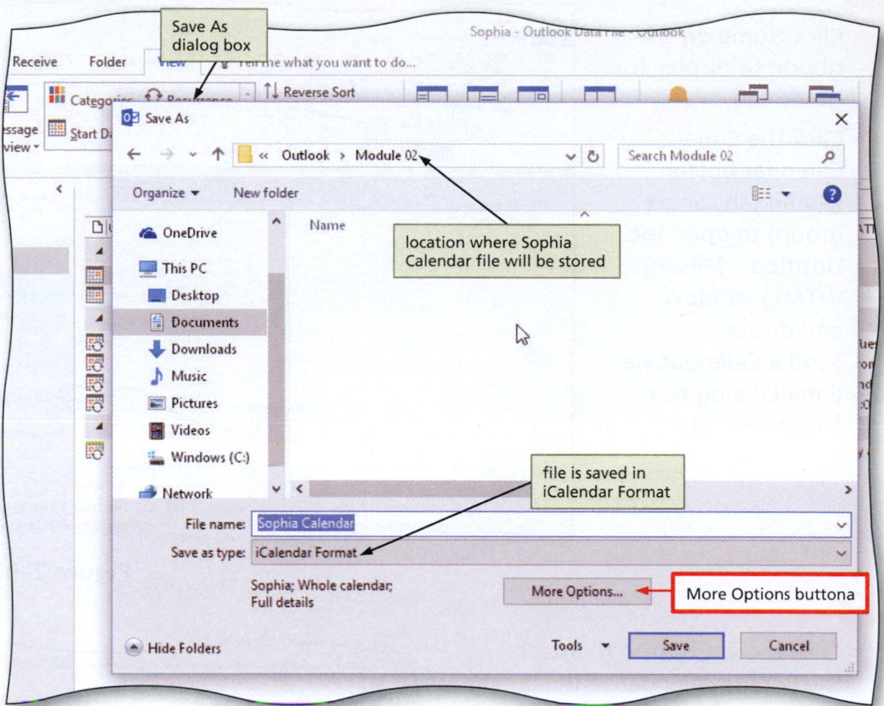

Figure 2–93

- Click the More Options button to display the Save As dialog box.
- Click the Date Range arrow to display the Date Range list (Figure 2–94).

- If necessary, click Whole calendar on the Date Range list to save the calendar's full details.
- Click the OK button (Save As dialog box) to specify the whole calendar date range.
- Click the Save button to save the calendar as an iCalendar file in the selected location.

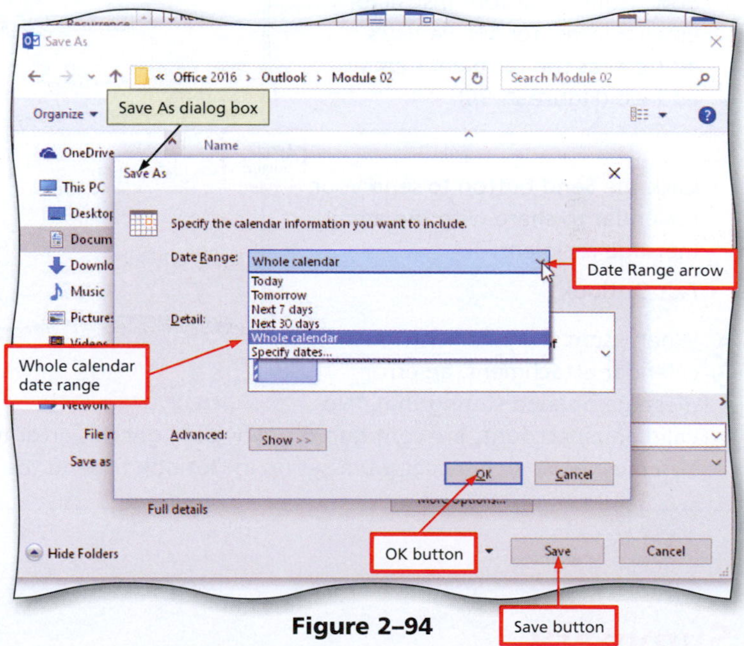

Figure 2–94

To Share a Calendar

1 CONFIGURE CALENDAR OPTIONS | 2 CREATE & MANIPULATE APPOINTMENTS | 3 SCHEDULE EVENTS
4 SCHEDULE MEETINGS | 5 PRINT CALENDAR | **6 SAVE & SHARE CALENDAR**

Ms. Pauley, the director of the Pathways Internship Office, needs to meet with Sophia to reschedule the fair. She requests a copy of Sophia's calendar. ***Why?*** *Sophia can send a copy of her calendar in an email message directly from Outlook to inform Ms. Pauley when she is available for a meeting.* The following steps share a calendar by forwarding the selected calendar. These steps assume you have an email account set up in Outlook.

- Click Home on the ribbon to display the Home tab.
- Click the E-mail Calendar button (Home tab | Share group) to open the Untitled – Message (HTML) window and display the Send a Calendar via E-mail dialog box (Figure 2–95).

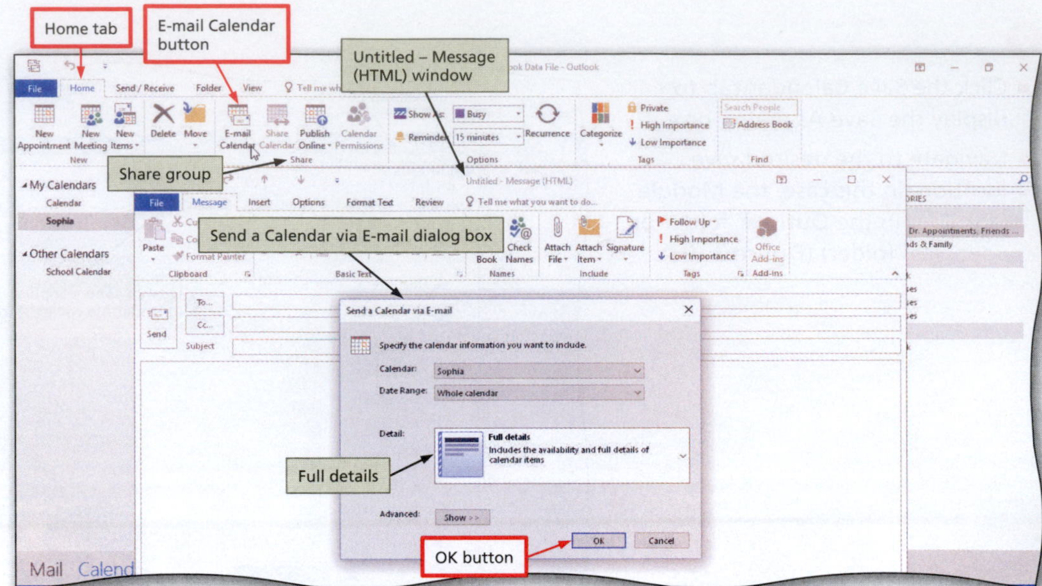

Figure 2–95

- Click the OK button to attach the Sophia calendar to the email message.
- Click the To text box, and then type **ella.pauley@outlook.com** (substitute your instructor's email address for Ms. Pauley's address) as the recipient's email address (Figure 2–96).

- Click the Send button to send your iCalendar to share with the email message recipient.
- Exit Outlook.

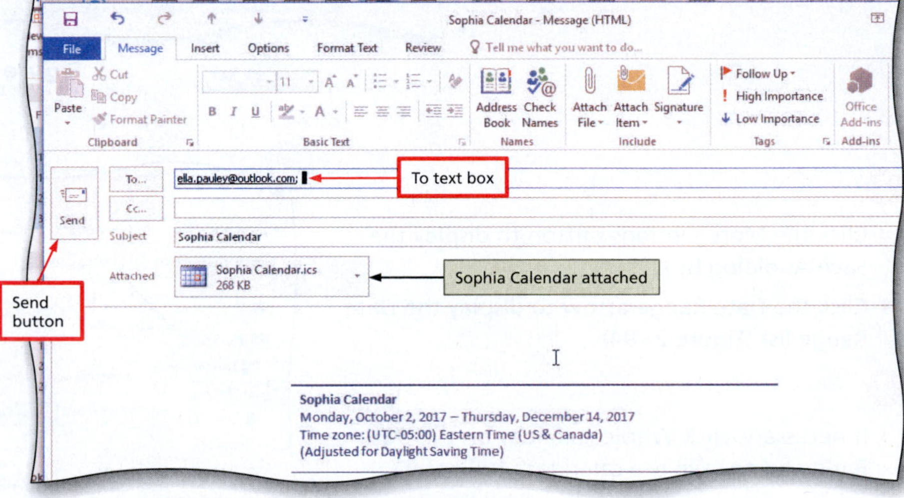

Figure 2–96

Q&A When I sent the email with the calendar attachment, an error message opened stating that "No valid email accounts are configured." Why did I get this error message?

You must have an email account set up in Outlook to send the calendar.

Summary

In this module, you have learned how to use Outlook to create a personal schedule by entering appointments, creating recurring appointments, moving appointments to new dates, and scheduling events. You also learned how to invite attendees to a meeting, accept a meeting request, and change the time of a meeting. To review your schedule, you learned to view and print your calendar in different views and print styles. Finally, you learned how to save your calendar and share your schedule with others.

CONSIDER THIS

What decisions will you need to make when configuring the Outlook calendar; scheduling appointments, events, and meetings; printing calendars; and saving and sharing your calendar in the future?

1. Configure the Outlook Calendar:
   a. Determine the purpose of your calendar — personal, professional, or for a group.
   b. Determine the city displayed on the Weather Bar and if you prefer holidays in your default calendar.
2. Schedule appointments, events, and meetings:
   a. Determine if each calendar item is an appointment, event, or a meeting.
   b. Determine which appointments and events are one-time or recurring.
   c. Plan which color-coded categories would best organize your calendar items.
3. Edit appointments, events, and meetings:
   a. Update the details of your calendar items as your schedule changes.
   b. Respond to meeting requests.
4. Print your calendar:
   a. Plan which calendar style would best fit your needs.
5. Save and share your calendar:
   a. Plan where your calendar should be stored.
   b. Determine how you will share your calendar with friends and colleagues.

CONSIDER THIS

How should you submit solutions to questions in the assignments identified with a symbol?

Every assignment in this book contains one or more questions identified with a symbol. These questions require you to think beyond the assigned file. Present your solutions to the questions in the format required by your instructor. Possible formats may include one or more of these options: write the answer; create a document that contains the answer; present your answer to the class; discuss your answer in a group; record the answer as audio or video using a webcam, smartphone, or portable media player; or post answers on a blog, wiki, or website.

Apply Your Knowledge

Reinforce the skills and apply the concepts you learned in this module.

Note: To complete this assignment, you will be required to use the Data Files. Please contact your instructor for information about accessing the Data Files.

Updating a Calendar

Instructions: Run Outlook. You are updating the Athletic Boosters iCalendar named Apply 2-1 Athletic Boosters Calendar, which is located in the Data Files, by revising the scheduled activities.

Perform the following tasks:

1. Open the Apply 2-1 Athletic Boosters Calendar.ics file from the Data Files.
2. Display only this iCalendar in the Outlook Calendar window. Use Month view to display the calendar for March 2017.
3. Add a monthly Athletic Boosters Meeting appointment for the first Wednesday of each month starting at 2 PM and lasting for one hour from March through December 2017.
4. Change the color category of the monthly Athletic Boosters Meeting to orange.
5. Change the Senior Night appointment from March 10 to March 17. Move the appointment to one hour later with the same duration.
6. Change the location of the Ladies Basketball Awards appointment on March 18 to Hanel Hall.

Continued >

Apply Your Knowledge *continued*

7. Reschedule the Fundraising Meeting appointment from Thursdays starting on February 23 until April 13 to meet at the same time on Mondays starting on March 6 until April 17.
8. Change the starting and ending time of the Athletic Booster Picnic on May 6 to two hours later.

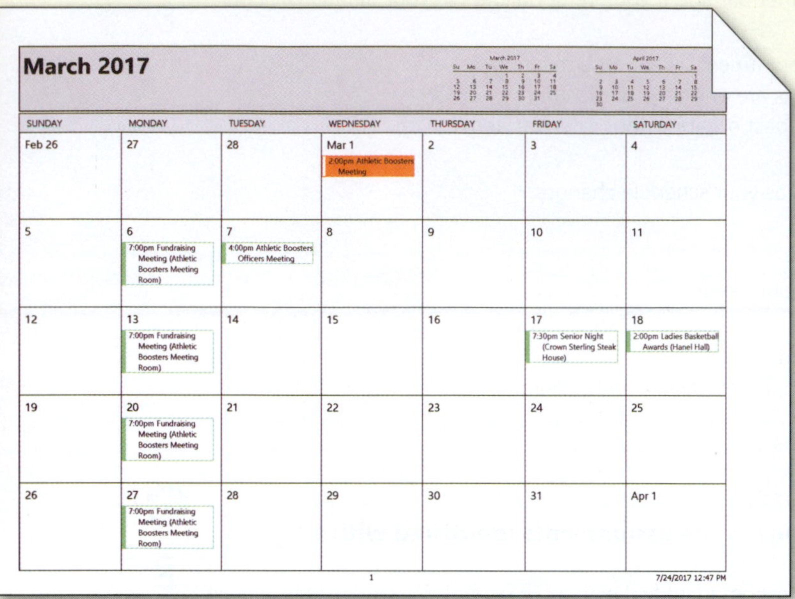

Figure 2–97

9. If requested by your instructor, change the location of the picnic from Morristown Park to a park named after your birth city.
10. Save the Calendar as Apply 2-1 Athletic Boosters Updated and submit the iCalendar in the format specified by your instructor.
11. Print the final calendar in Month view, shown in Figure 2–97, and then submit the printout to your instructor.
12. Delete this calendar from Outlook and exit Outlook.
13. Most calendar programs save files with the .ics format. Why is it convenient that most calendar programs use the same format?

Extend Your Knowledge

Extend the skills you learned in this module and experiment with new skills. You may need to use Help to complete the assignment.

Creating and Sharing a Calendar

Instructions: Run Outlook. You are volunteering at a local animal shelter a couple days a week. Create a new calendar to share your availability to help at the shelter. Use Outlook Help to learn how to create a calendar group, change the color of the calendar, and create a private appointment.

Perform the following tasks:

1. Create a new calendar group called Pet Shelter.
2. Create a blank calendar named Volunteers and then move it to the Pet Shelter calendar group.
3. Change the color of the entire calendar to brown.
4. Add a recurring Feed Animals appointment from 5:00 PM to 6:30 PM on Monday and Wednesday beginning on June 5, 2017 and continuing for 20 occurrences at the Laredo Animal Shelter.
5. Create an event named Adoption Week starting on June 26, 2017 at the Laredo Animal Shelter lasting 7 days from this Monday to next Monday.
6. Add a recurring Post Animal of the Week Online as an All Day event starting on June 2 and lasting for 12 months on the first Friday of each month.
7. If requested by your instructor, change the Weather Bar to display weather information for your hometown. The completed calendar is shown in Figure 2–98.
8. Save the Calendar file as Extend Your Knowledge 2-1 Pet Shelter and submit the iCalendar in the format specified by your instructor.

9. Exit Outlook.
10. Think about the reason you might share your Outlook Calendar. In the case of sharing your schedule and other volunteer's calendars with the animal shelter, why would a digital calendar be more helpful to the director of the shelter instead of a paper schedule?

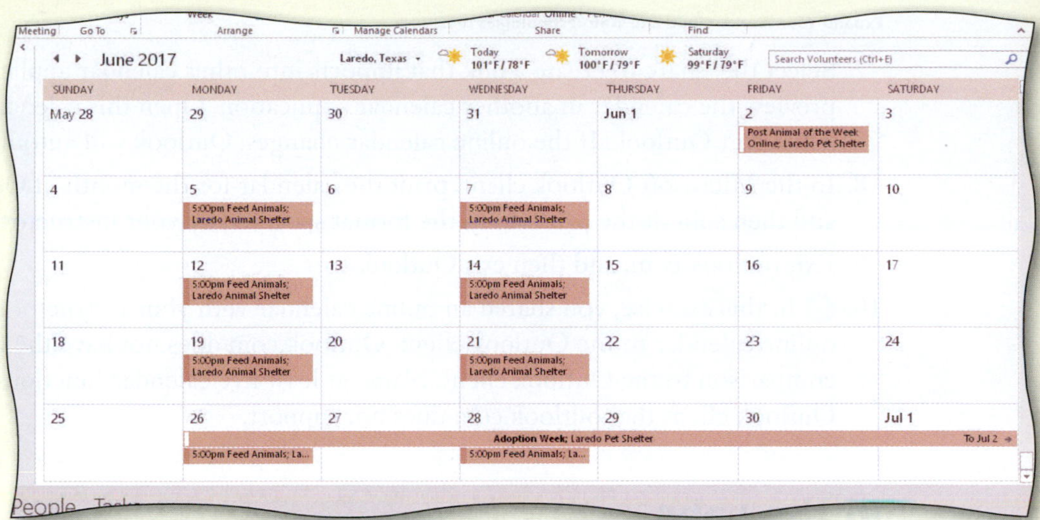

Figure 2–98

Expand Your World: Cloud and Web Technologies

Opening a Web-Based Calendar in the Outlook Client

Instructions: In your role as a barista at a new local coffee shop, you have been asked by the manager to assist with marketing the café on social media by posting to Facebook and Twitter. Use the calendar dates shown in Table 2–7 to create an online calendar at Outlook.com using your Microsoft account. Share the online calendar with your instructor. Using Outlook, open the online calendar and print the calendar in the Outlook client. Sharing your calendar in the cloud as a link allows anyone to see your calendar such as the café's manager, even if they do not have their own calendar established.

Perform the following tasks:

1. If necessary, create a Microsoft account at outlook.com.
2. Open the calendar option at outlook.com and add a calendar named Social Media for Coffee Shop Calendar with the description, `Online Marketing`.
3. Open the Social Media for Coffee Shop Calendar only and add the items shown in Table 2–7 to the online calendar.
4. If requested by your instructor, add a promotional calendar item on your birthday in 2017 titled Barista's Birthday — 1 Free Scone per Coffee Order.
5. Click the Share button to view the sharing options for this calendar. Select the option to send people a view-only link to access this calendar online. Select the ICS option to import into another calendar application to show event details.
6. Submit the outlook.com calendar link to view in a web browser in a format specified by your instructor.

Table 2–7 Social Media for Coffee Shop Calendar Items

Description	Recurrence	Due Date	Availability
Pumpkin Latte Promotion	None	First Sunday in October 2017 at 5 AM	Free
Join the Jolt Frequent Customer Program	Monthly	First day of each month starting in October 2017 at midnight, never ends	Free
Happy Caffeine Hours	Mondays	Every Monday in October 2017 from 4:00 PM for 2 hours	Busy
Halloween Coffee Roasters 20% Off	None	October 31, 2017 All Day Event	Busy

Continued >

Expand Your World: Cloud and Web Technologies *continued*

7. Select the 'share to create a link that imports into other calendar applications (ICS)' option to preview the calendar in another calendar application. Open this calendar link in the calendar in Microsoft Outlook. If the online calendar changes, Outlook will automatically update.
8. In the Microsoft Outlook client, print the calendar for the month of October in Monthly style, and then submit the printout in the format specified by your instructor.
9. Exit outlook.com, and then exit Outlook.
10. In this exercise, you shared an online calendar with your instructor and also imported the online calendar to the Outlook client. Outlook.com does not have the full functionality in comparison to the Outlook client. Name at least five calendar functions that are part of the Outlook client that outlook.com does not support.

In the Labs

Design, create, modify, and/or use files following the guidelines, concepts, and skills presented in this module. Labs 1 and 2, which increase in difficulty, require you to create solutions based on what you learned in the module; Lab 3 requires you to apply your creative thinking and problem-solving skills to design and implement a solution.

Lab 1: Creating Recurring Events

Problem: You would like to set up a calendar to remember to take care of your car scheduled maintenance, loan, cleaning, and, inspection as shown in Figure 2–99.

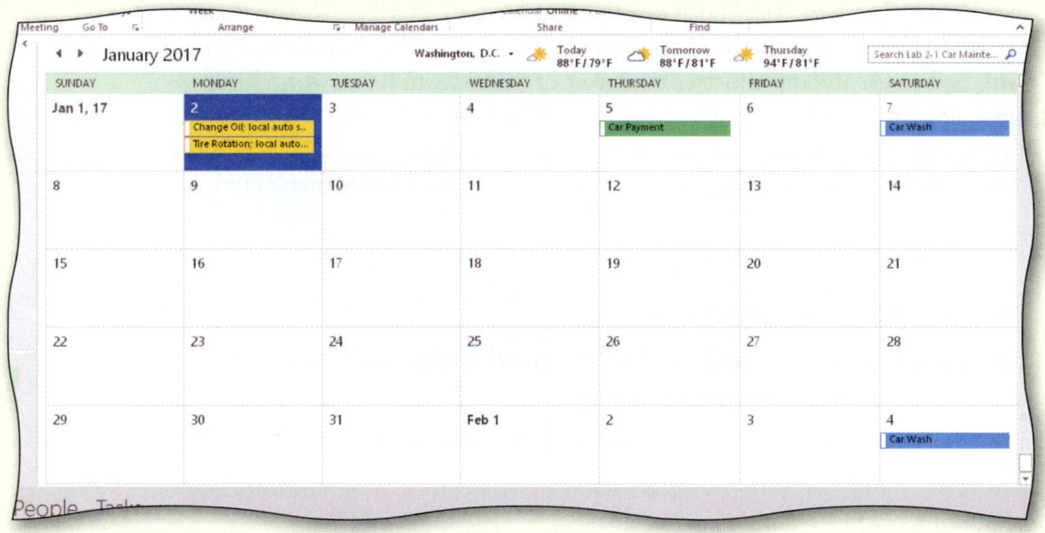

Figure 2–99

Perform the following tasks:

1. Create a Calendar named Lab 2-1 Car Maintenance Calendar in Outlook.
2. Create the events in the calendar in the year 2017, using the information listed in Table 2–8.
3. For each event, enter the location as local auto shop for the category Schedule Maintenance, otherwise leave the location blank.
4. For each event, show the time as Free.
5. For each event, set the reminder to one day.
6. For each monthly event, set the event to recur every month during 2017.
7. Each event should be an All Day event.

8. If requested by your instructor, add your favorite car model as a car show (for example, Mustang Car Show) on your birthday as an event in your 2017 Calendar.
9. Save the calendar as an .ics file and submit it in a format specified by your instructor.
10. Print the month of May using the Monthly Style and submit it in a format specified by your instructor.
11. A calendar can keep you organized. In the case of scheduling your car payment, how can a digital calendar assist in increasing your credit score?

Table 2–8 Car Maintenance Schedule

Calendar Item	Due Date	Category	Color Code
Car Wash	First Saturday of each month	Cleaning	blue
Change Oil	Starting on January 2 and occurring every 120 days	Scheduled Maintenance	yellow
Car payment	5th day of the month	Payment	green
Add Antifreeze	October 15th	Scheduled Maintenance	yellow
Tire Rotation	January 2 and July 2	Scheduled Maintenance	yellow
New Tires	August 1	Scheduled Maintenance	yellow
Car inspection	May 30th	Tax and Scheduled Maintenance	red, yellow

Lab 2: Creating a Calendar

Problem: You were recently hired part-time by your local news station as a restaurant and events reviewer. By taking the time to develop a plan for your restaurant and event visits, as shown in Figure 2–100, you will remember to produce regular reviews for the news station.

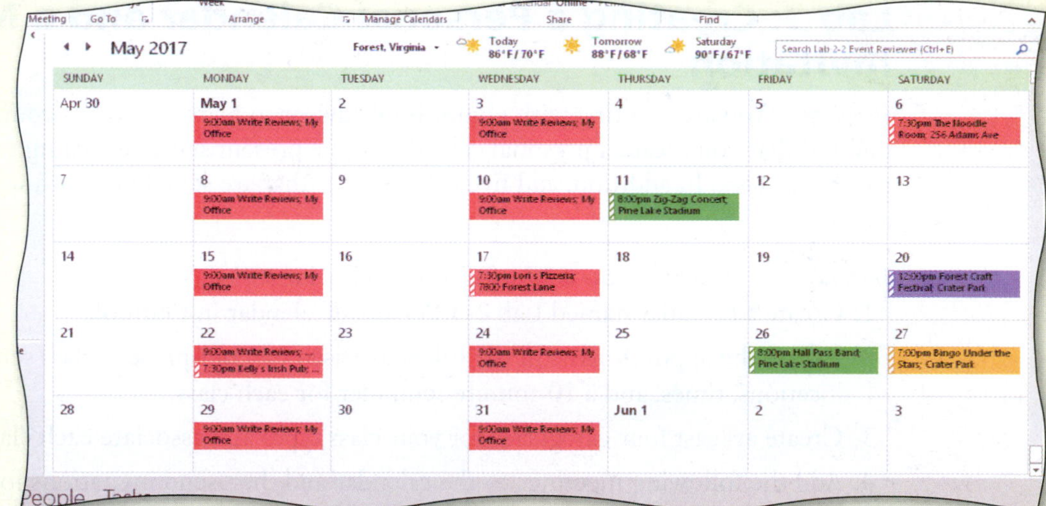

Figure 2–100

Instructions: Open Outlook. Perform the following tasks:

1. Create a calendar named Lab 2-2 Event Reviewer Calendar in Outlook.
2. Create the appointments in the calendar, using the information listed in Table 2–9.

Table 2–9 Local Restaurant and Events Table

Restaurant or Event	Location	Event Date	Category	Color Code
The Noodle Room	256 Adams Ave	May 6, 2017	Restaurant	red
Zig-Zag Concert	Pine Lake Stadium	May 11, 2017	Concert	green
Lori's Pizzeria	7800 Forest Lane	May 17, 2017	Restaurant	red
Forest Craft Festival	Crater Park	May 20, 2017	Festival	purple
Kelly's Irish Pub	129 45th St	May 22, 2017	Restaurant	red
Hall Pass Band	Pine Lake Stadium	May 26, 2017	Concert	green
Bingo Under the Stars	Crater Park	May 27, 2017	Other	yellow

Continued >

In the Labs *continued*

3. For each event in the table, set the reminder as 2 hours.
4. For each event, show the time as Tentative.
5. Set each restaurant dinner for 7:30 PM for one hour, concerts at 8 PM for two hours, festivals at noon for two hours, and other events at 7 PM for 2.5 hours.
6. For each Monday and Wednesday throughout the month of May 2017, add a recurring appointment. Enter `Write Reviews` as the subject. For location, enter `My Office`. Show the time as Busy. The appointment should start at 9:00 AM and end two hours later. Add all four color-coded categories and set a 10-minute reminder.
7. Delete the one occurrence of the recurring appointment on May 17.
8. If requested by your instructor, change your Weather Bar to show the weather for your hometown.
9. Save the calendar as an .ics file and submit it in a format specified by your instructor.
10. Print the calendar for the month of May in Monthly style, and then submit the printout in the format specified by your instructor.
11. What are the advantages of syncing your Outlook Calendar to a mobile phone?

Lab 3: Creating a Personal Calendar and a Meeting Invitation

Problem: You are meeting with your school advisor to plan next year's course schedule. She has requested that you create a personal calendar of the present semester listing your present classes, time, room numbers. In addition, add five other events that are scheduled with work, hobbies, or other activities.

Instructions: Open Outlook. Perform the following tasks:

1. Create a calendar named Lab 2-3 Personal Calendar in Outlook.
2. Create the appointments in the calendar based on your present class schedule with class names, locations, times, and a 10-minute reminder for each class.
3. Create at least four categories for your class types and associate each class type to the category.
4. Add the following meetings to the calendar and then send invitations for upcoming meetings to your instructor, as shown in Table 2–10. All the meetings are held in the Advisor's Office. Send a meeting invitation to yourself.

Table 2–10 Advisor Calendar Meetings

Description	Date	Time	Show As	Reminder
Discuss Career Interest	June 3	1:00 PM – 2:00 PM	Out of Office	30 minutes
Class Schedule Selection	June 8	12:00 PM – 2:00 PM	Tentative	30 minutes

5. If requested by your instructor, add a third meeting titled `Class Performance` on June 2nd at 9:00 AM for one to meet with your instructor; include a one-day reminder and show as working elsewhere.
6. Save your calendar as an iCalendar named Lab 3-3 Personal Calendar. Submit your assignment in the format specified by your instructor.

Part 2: If you receive a meeting request, you can respond in several ways. What are the four ways to respond to a meeting request? You can add comments with each of these responses. Provide comments to each of the four meeting requests responses explaining why you can or cannot attend the meeting with your advisor.

Index

D

E

F

Index

S

T

X

Z